McDougal Littell

CLASSZONE

Visit classzone.com and get connected.

ClassZone resources provide instruction, planning and assessment support for teachers.

State-Specific Resources

- Select your state and access state-specific resources

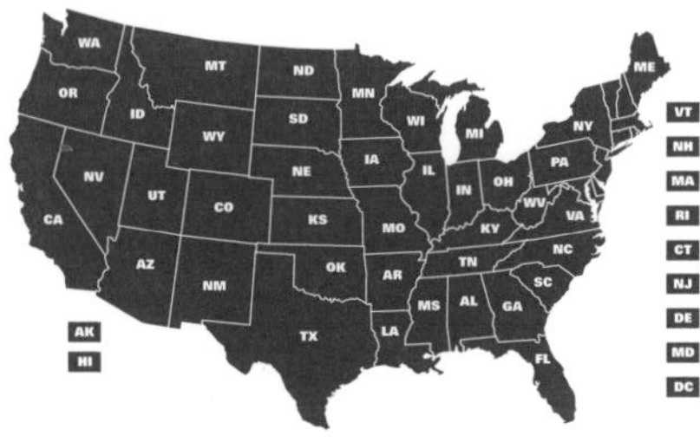

Literature and Reading Center

- Selection-specific content includes vocabulary practice, research links, and extension activities for writing and critical thinking
- Author Online provides information about each author, as well as in-depth author studies on selected writers
- English Learner support for a variety of languages includes audio summaries of selections and a Multi-Language Academic Glossary

Vocabulary and Spelling Center

- Vocabulary practice and games
- Spelling lessons
- Multi-Language Academic Glossary

Writing and Grammar Center

- Quick-Fix Editing Machine provides grammar help in a student-friendly format
- Writing Templates and graphic organizers promote clear, orderly communication

Media Center

- Media Analysis Guides encourage critical thinking skills
- Project Ideas, Storyboards, and Production Templates inspire creative media projects

You have immediate access to the the online version of the textbook and *ClassZone* resources at **www.classzone.com**

MCDKLMLHLPIHU

Use this code to create your own user name and password.

McDougal Littell

Where Great Lessons Begin

McDougal Littell

LITERATURE

Essential Course of Study

Table of Contents

Student Guide

Embedded Standards Support

Full Standards Correlation

McDougal Littell
EVANSTON, ILLINOIS • BOSTON • DALLAS

ART CREDITS

COVER

Untitled (1990), Jerry N. Uelsmann. © Jerry N. Uelsmann.

T1 © Image 100/PunchStock; **T3** *left-1* Photo © Duane McCubrey; *left-2* Photo © Mark Schmidt; *left-3* Photo © Bruce Forrester; *left-4* © McDougal Littell; *left-5* Photo © Howard Gollub; *left-6* Photo © Tamra Stallings; *right-1* Photo © Mark Schmidt; *right-2* © Robert J. Marzano; *right-3* © McDougal Littell; *right-4* Photo © Dawson & Associates Photography; *right-5* Photo © Gitchell's Studio; **T4** *left-1* © Michael Romeo; *left-2* Photo © Monica Ani; *left-3* Photo © William McBride; *right-1* Photo © Bill Caldwell; *right-2* Photo © Gabriel Pauluzzi; *right-3* Photo © Steven Scheffler; **T5** © Carolina K. Smith/ShutterStock; **T6-T7** © Photo by Ed-Imaging, Chicago; **T7** *top left,* Untitled (1990), Jerry N. Uelsmann. © Jerry N. Uelsmann; *top right, Cool Hand* (2005), Gil Mayers. Mixed media. © Gilbert Mayers/SuperStock; *bottom* © Robert J. Marzano; **T8** Will and Deni McIntyre/Corbis; **T8- T9** Photo by Ed-Imaging, Chicago; **T9** *top left,* Illustration by Micahel McCurdy. © 1991 by Michael McCurdy, from *American Tall Tales* by Mary Pope Osborne. Used by permission of Alfred A. Knopf, an imprint of Random House Children's Books, a division of Random House, Inc.; *top right* Photo © Duane McCubrey; *bottom right* Photo © Gitchell's Studio.

BACK COVER

© Image 100/PunchStock.

ISBN 13: 978-0-618-56869-7 ISBN 10: 0-618-56869-7

Printed in China.

1 2 3 4 5 6 7 8 9—DSC—12 11 10 09 08 07

SENIOR PROGRAM CONSULTANTS

JANET ALLEN
Reading and Literacy Specialist, Lecturer, Consultant, and Author. Creator of the "It's Never Too Late for Literacy" institutes

ARTHUR N. APPLEBEE
Leading Professor, School of Education at the University at Albany, State University of New York; Director of the Center on English Learning and Achievement

JIM BURKE
Lecturer and Author; Teacher of English at Burlingame High School, Burlingame, California

DOUGLAS CARNINE
Professor of Education at the University of Oregon; Director of the Western Region Reading First Technical Assistance Center

YVETTE JACKSON
Executive Director of the National Urban Alliance for Effective Education

ROBERT T. JIMÉNEZ
Professor of Language, Literacy, and Culture at Vanderbilt University

JUDITH A. LANGER
Distinguished Professor at the University at Albany, State University of New York; Director of the Center on English Learning and Achievement; Director of the Albany Institute for Research in Education

ROBERT J. MARZANO
Senior Scholar at Mid-Continent Research for Education and Learning (McREL); Associate Professor at Cardinal Stritch University in Milwaukee, Wisconsin; President of Marzano & Associates

DONNA M. OGLE
Professor of Reading and Language at National-Louis University in Chicago, Illinois

CAROL BOOTH OLSON
Senior Lecturer in the Department of Education at the University of California, Irvine; Director of the UCI site of the National Writing Project

CAROL ANN TOMLINSON
Professor of Educational Research, Foundations, and Policy at the University of Virginia; Co-Director of the University's Institutes on Academic Diversity

ENGLISH LEARNER SPECIALISTS

MARY LOU MCCLOSKEY
Director of Teacher Development and Curriculum Design for Educo in Atlanta, Georgia

LYDIA STACK
International ESL consultant

CURRICULUM SPECIALIST

WILLIAM L. MCBRIDE
Curriculum Specialist, Lecturer and Author

MEDIA SPECIALISTS

DAVID M. CONSIDINE
Professor of Instructional Technology and Media Studies at Appalachian State University in North Carolina

LARKIN PAULUZZI
Teacher and Media Specialist; trainer for the New Jersey Writing Project

LISA K. SCHEFFLER
Teacher and Media Specialist

McDougal Littell

LITERATURE

Where Great Lessons Begin

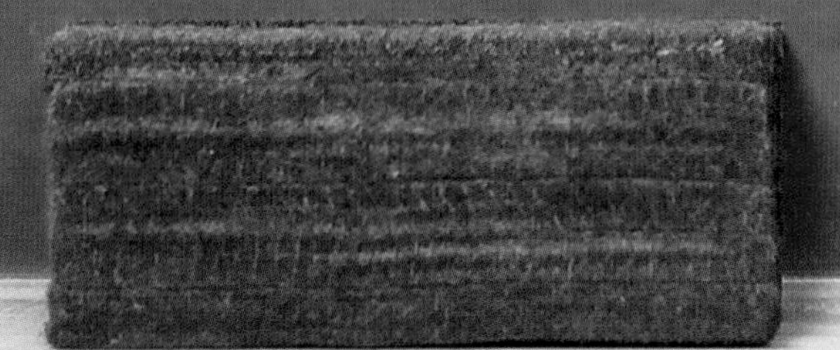

Great Lessons Begin with **You.**

You teach. You inspire. We help.

We help you with support for every standard, every selection, and every student.

Resource Manager
Provides all-in-one support for true differentiation.

WriteSmart CD-ROM
An interactive writing instruction tool, resource bank, and rubric generator.

Standards Lessons File
Gives you a fast, organized approach to teaching every standard.

CONSULTANT'S CORNER

Bob Marzano

McDougal Littell provides maximum support to teachers in terms of instructional strategies and addressing national and state standards. Used well, this literature series can dramatically enhance student achievement while maximizing teacher creativity.

Great Lessons Begin with
Your Students.

They wonder. They question. We help.

We help your students become active readers, writers, and thinkers.

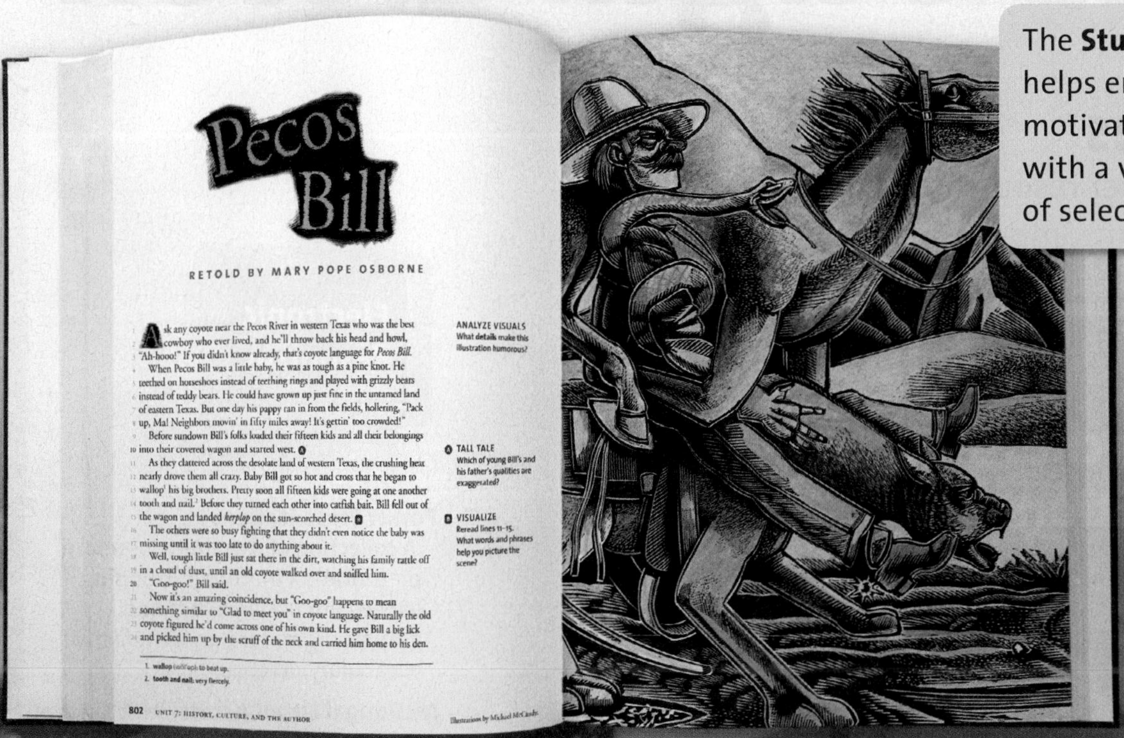

The **Student's Edition** helps engage and motivate students with a vibrant mix of selections.

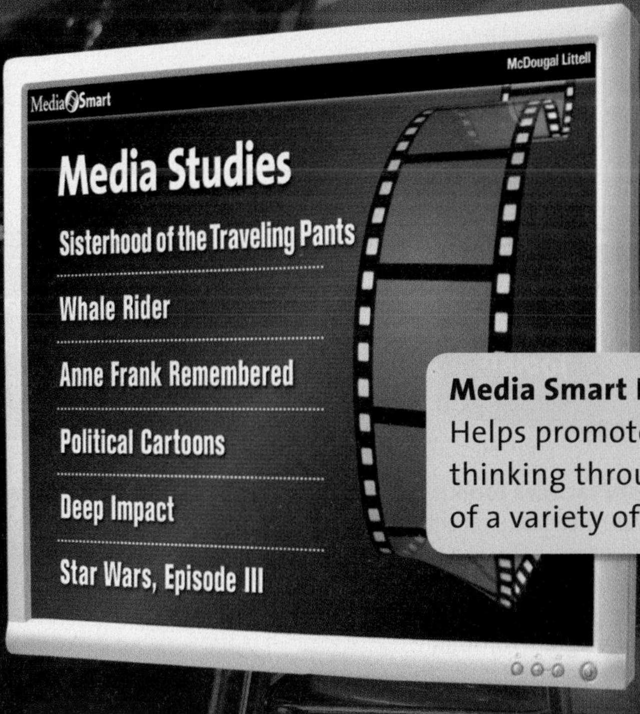

Media Smart DVD-ROM
Helps promote critical thinking through analysis of a variety of media.

Media Smart — McDougal Littell

Media Studies
- Sisterhood of the Traveling Pants
- Whale Rider
- Anne Frank Remembered
- Political Cartoons
- Deep Impact
- Star Wars, Episode III

CONSULTANT'S CORNER

Janet Allen
In choosing to work on writing a literature program, I found a home with McDougal Littell because all our decisions could be based on students' needs and teachers' expertise. It was a perfect match for my interests and experience.

Carol Ann Tomlinson
Students come to us as a mixed set. They don't learn in the same ways, aren't motivated by the same things, and don't function at the same pace or depth. What I've always cared about is how teachers can help diverse learners succeed by teaching flexibly......that flexibility is built into this program.

Great Lessons Begin with

McDougal Littell

Teacher Resources

Time-saving, easy-to-use teacher resources make lesson planning and preparation simple.

Core Teacher Resources include:

Teacher's Edition

Easy Planner CD-Rom

Resource Manager

MediaSmart
Helps promote critical thinking through analysis of a variety of media.

WriteSmart
An interactive writing instruction tool, resource bank, and rubric generator.

Power Presentations
A collection of dynamic classroom presentation materials including leveled discussion questions, graphic organizers, and interactive vocabulary practice.

McDougal Littell Assessment System
Test Generator

Assessment File
Provides comprehensive opportunities to assess student progress with an array of tests including placement, selection, unit, and benchmark.

Best Practices Toolkit
Motivate students with engaging activities, over 200 graphic organizer transparencies, and research-based strategies from our program consultants.

Standards Lesson File
Stand-alone lessons ensure standards mastery.

Literature.

Student Resources

A complete program of technology and print resources provides support for differentiated student learning.

Core Student Resources include:

Pupil Edition

eEdition online and CD-ROM

Interactive Reader & Writer

- **Strategic Reading Support**
- **Critical Analysis**

Both versions of the Interactive Reader & Writer include leveled readings, additional nonfiction, and test preparation.

Audio Anthology
Enables students to hear pronunciation, phrasing, and interpretations as they follow along in their textbook.

Multi-Language Academic Glossary Online
Facilitates comprehension of academic vocabulary with key terms and definitions in 10 languages.

Classzone.com
Provides a wealth of interactive resources for literature, reading, writing, grammar, vocabulary, spelling, and assessment.

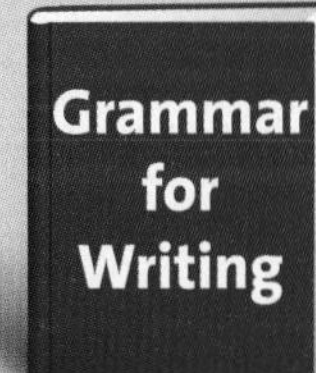

Grammar for Writing Workbook

Novels
Over 700 novels, works of nonfiction, and plays promote independent learning and reading.

Grammar for Writing

Grammar for Writing Workbook
Supports systematic, student-friendly instruction in all aspects of grammar, usage, and mechanics.

Great Lessons Begin with

Assessment that Informs Your Daily Instruction

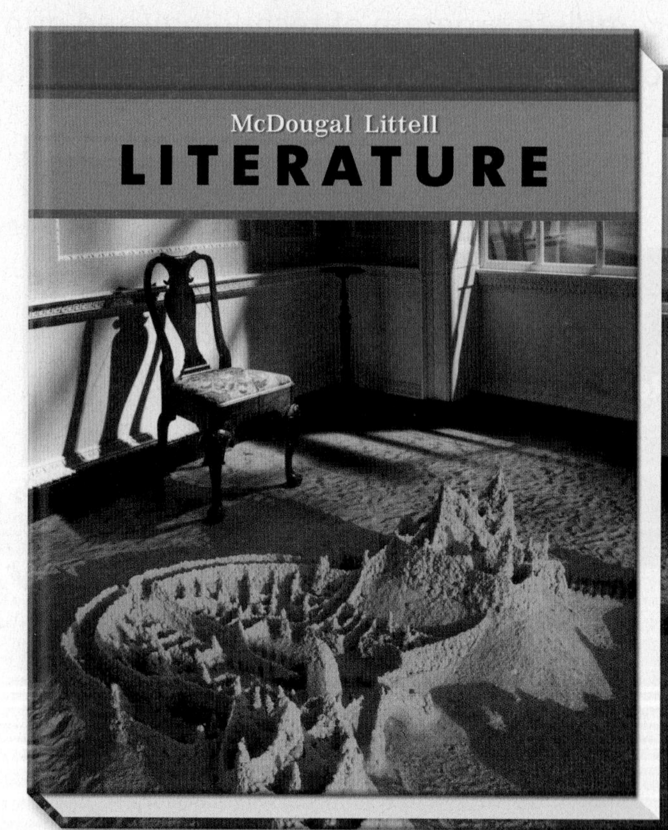

Ongoing, integrated test practice and assessment give you the power, flexibility and feedback to prepare all your students for success. McDougal Littell also provides tools for reteaching and remediation that ensure skills mastery for all students.

- **Assessment File** Everything you need to structure an assessment plan that both evaluates student success and informs instruction. In addition to Selection Tests, Quizzes, and Daily Skills Practice, you will also have Benchmark Tests to track your students' accomplishments.
- **Grammar for Writing** A comprehensive handbook that provides instruction and practice for all aspects of grammar, usage, and mechanics and facilitates preparation for standardized tests.

- **WriteSmart** A rich presentation tool for writing instruction that includes Ideas for Writing, InterActive Student Models for guided and independent analysis, InterActive Graphic Organizers, InterActive Revision Lessons, and a Rubric Generator.
- **Test Generator** This CD-ROM helps you assess both skills and comprehension with leveled, customizable test questions.

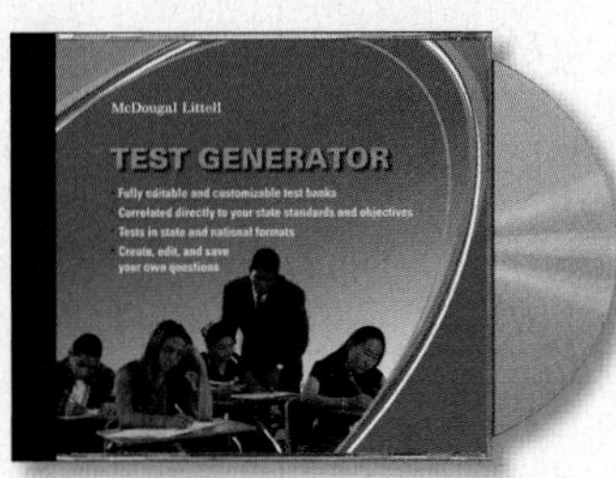

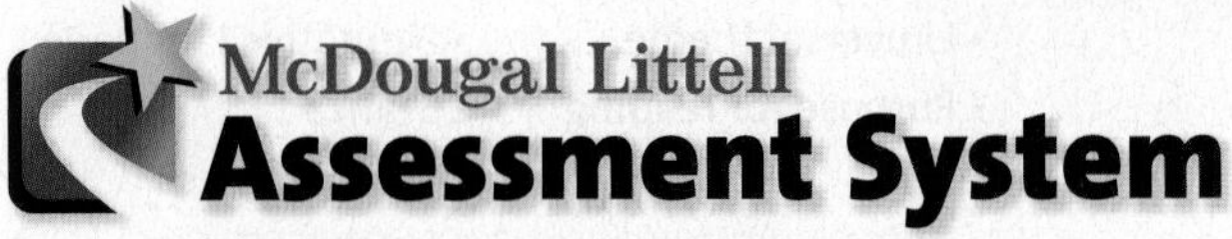

Available at **CLASSZONE.COM.**

The **McDougal Littell Assessment System (MLAS)** is a flexible, web-based program that allows you to use assessment as a teaching tool. This seamless testing and remediation system gives you a fast and easy way to:

TEST Unique testing is custom-built to your standards.

SCORE Automatic scoring gives you results in minutes.

REPORT Diagnostic reports show you what standards were missed.

RETEACH Personalized remediation helps you target reteaching.

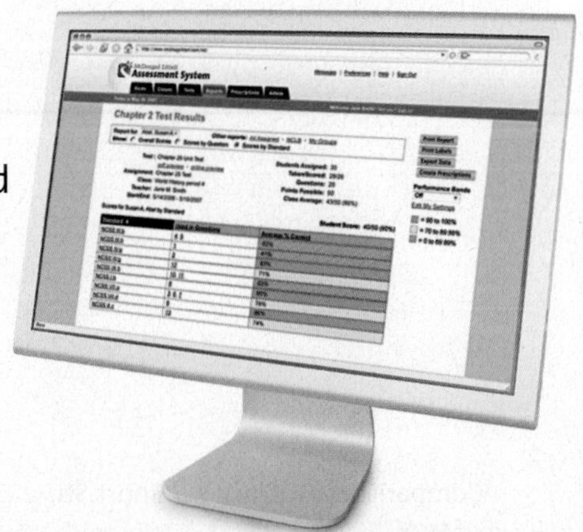

Introducing

The Essential Course of Study

So much to read and test with so little time! McDougal Littell helps you choose the lessons your students need to master critical skills that appear on all types of assessments.

The Essential Course of Study on the pages that follow indicates which selections and workshops you should teach in order to cover the main skills needed in the language arts curriculum. ▶

Essential Course of Study

For a full listing of state standards see page S1.

	UNIT 1 Plot and Conflict	UNIT 2 Character and Point of View	UNIT 3 Setting and Mood	UNIT 4 Theme and Symbol	UNIT 5 Poetry
LITERATURE	Reader's Workshop: Plot and Conflict *Raymond's Run* *The Ransom of Red Chief* *The Clean Sweep* *The Hitchhiker* • Plot • Inferences • Conflict • Predict • Sequence • Foreshadowing	Reader's Workshop: Character and Point of View *The Treasure of Lemon Brown* *Rules of the Game* *Flowers for Algernon* • Point of view • Inferences • Conclusions • Character traits	Reader's Workshop: Setting and Mood *The Drummer Boy of Shiloh* *The Monkey's Paw* *Mi Madre/ Canyon de Chelly* • Setting • Inferences • Mood • Predict • Imagery • Speaker	Reader's Workshop: Theme and Symbol *Gil's Furniture Bought and Sold* *Pandora's Box* *The Old Grandfather and His Little Grandson/ The Wise Old Woman* *The Diary of Anne Frank* • Symbol • Inferences • Theme • Universal theme • Purpose for reading	Reader's Workshop: Appreciating Poetry *Simile: Willow and Ginko* *Macavity: The Mystery Cat/ Vermin* *Speech to the Young: Speech to the.../ Mother to Son* *On the Grasshopper and.../ Ode to Solitude* *Boots of Spanish.../ The Song of Hiawatha* • Poetic form • Figurative language • Stanza • Sound devices • Rhyme scheme • Rhythm/Meter
NONFICTION AND INFORMATIONAL MATERIAL	*My First Free Summer* • Memoir • Cause-effect	*Harriet Tubman: Conductor on the Underground Railroad* *The Mysterious Mr. Lincoln* • Characterization • Monitor • Main idea and details • Biography	*The Story of an Eyewitness/ Letter from New Orleans: Leaving Desire* • Scope • Purpose for reading	*A Diary from Another World/ The Last Seven Months of Anne Frank* • Synthesize • Generalizations	
WRITING	Personal Narrative		Comparison-contrast Essay	Short Story	
SPEAKING, LISTENING, AND MEDIA	Staging a Scene				

UNIT 6 Style, Voice, and Tone	UNIT 7 History, Culture, and the Author	UNIT 8 Facts and Information	UNIT 9 Argument and Persuasion	UNIT 10 The Power of Research	Student Resources Handbook
Reader's Workshop: Style, Voice, and Tone *New York Day Women* *The Lady, or the Tiger?* *Roughing It* • Style • Sequence • Tone • Paraphrase • Voice • Monitor	Reader's Workshop: History, Culture, and the Author *The Snapping Turtle* *Out of Bounds* • Author's background • Compare and contrast • Cultural conflict • Inferences				
Us and Them • Irony • Evaluate	*One Last Time* *Dreams from My Father* *Out of Many, One* • Author's perspective • Autobiography • Cause-effect • Treatment • Compare and contrast	Reader's Workshop: Reading Informational Text *The Spider Man Behind Spider-Man* *Interview with a Songcatcher Kabul's Singing Sensation* • Text features • Summarize • Fact and opinion • Main ideas and details	Reader's Workshop: Argument and Persuasion *Zoos: Myth.../ Zoos Connect Us ...* *Position on Dodge Ball.../ The Weak Shall Inherit ...* *The Sanctuary of the School* *Educating Sons/ The First Americans* • Argument • Fact and opinion • Persuasion • Author's purpose • Compare/ contrast • Historical context	Research Strategies Workshop	Reading Handbook • Reading informational texts • Reading persuasive texts
Literary Analysis	Cause-Effect Essay		Persuasive Essay	Research Report	Writing Handbook
Online Database	Multimedia Presentation		Persuasive Speech	Web Site	

McDougal Littell

LITERATURE

ACKNOWLEDGMENTS

INTRODUCTORY UNIT

Scholastic: Excerpt from *Slam!* by Walter Dean Myers. Copyright © 1996 by Walter Dean Myers. Used by permission of Scholastic Inc./Scholastic Press.

Arte Público Press: "Teenagers," from *Communion* by Pat Mora. Copyright © 1991 by Pat Mora. Reprinted with permission from the publisher Arte Público Press.

Gary DaSilva: Excerpt from *Brighton Beach Memoirs* by Neil Simon. Copyright © 1984 by Neil Simon. Reprinted by permission of Gary DaSilva, agent for Neil Simon.

Lerner Books: Excerpt from *Steve Jobs: Thinks Different* by Ann Brashares. Copyright © 2001 by The Millbrook Press. Used by permission of Lerner Books.

McIntosh & Otis: Excerpt from "The Winter Hibiscus" by Minfong Ho, from *Join In: Multiethnic Short Stories by Outstanding Writers for Young Adults* edited by Donald R. Gallo. Copyright © 1993 by Minfong Ho. Reprinted by permission of McIntosh & Otis.

Continued on page R147

ART CREDITS

COVER, TITLE PAGE

Untitled (1990), Jerry N. Uelsmann. © Jerry N. Uelsmann.

Continued on page R151

ISBN 13: 978-0-618-56865-9 ISBN 10: 0-618-56865-4

Printed in the United States of America.

1 2 3 4 5 6 7 8 9—DWO—12 11 10 09 08 07

ii

McDougal Littell

LITERATURE

Janet Allen

Arthur N. Applebee

Jim Burke

Douglas Carnine

Yvette Jackson

Robert T. Jiménez

Judith A. Langer

Robert J. Marzano

Mary Lou McCloskey

Donna M. Ogle

Carol Booth Olson

Lydia Stack

Carol Ann Tomlinson

McDougal Littell

EVANSTON, ILLINOIS • BOSTON • DALLAS

SENIOR PROGRAM CONSULTANTS

JANET ALLEN Reading and Literacy Specialist; creator of the popular "It's Never Too Late"/"Reading for Life" Institutes. Dr. Allen is an internationally known consultant who specializes in literacy work with at-risk students. Her publications include *Tools for Content Literacy; It's Never Too Late: Leading Adolescents to Lifelong Learning; Yellow Brick Roads: Shared and Guided Paths to Independent Reading; Words, Words, Words: Teaching Vocabulary in Grades 4–12;* and *Testing 1, 2, 3 . . . Bridging Best Practice and High-Stakes Assessments.* Dr. Allen was a high school reading and English teacher for more than 20 years and has taught courses in both subjects at the University of Central Florida. She directed the Central Florida Writing Project and received the Milken Foundation National Educator Award.

ARTHUR N. APPLEBEE Leading Professor, School of Education at the University at Albany, State University of New York; Director of the Center on English Learning and Achievement. During his varied career, Dr. Applebee has been both a researcher and a teacher, working in institutional settings with children with severe learning problems, in public schools, as a staff member of the National Council of Teachers of English, and in professional education. Among his many books are *Curriculum as Conversation: Transforming Traditions of Teaching and Learning; Literature in the Secondary School: Studies of Curriculum and Instruction in the United States;* and *Tradition and Reform in the Teaching of English: A History.* He was elected to the International Reading Hall of Fame and has received, among other honors, the David H. Russell Award for Distinguished Research in the Teaching of English.

JIM BURKE Lecturer and Author; Teacher of English at Burlingame High School, Burlingame, California. Mr. Burke is a popular presenter at educational conferences across the country and is the author of numerous books for teachers, including *School Smarts: The Four Cs of Academic Success; The English Teacher's Companion; Reading Reminders; Writing Reminders;* and *ACCESSing School: Teaching Struggling Readers to Achieve Academic and Personal Success.* He is the recipient of NCTE's Exemplary English Leadership Award and was inducted into the California Reading Association's Hall of Fame.

DOUGLAS CARNINE Professor of Education at the University of Oregon; Director of the Western Region Reading First Technical Assistance Center. Dr. Carnine is nationally known for his focus on research-based practices in education, especially curriculum designs that prepare instructors of K–12 students. He has received the Lifetime Achievement Award from the Council for Exceptional Children and the Ersted Award for outstanding teaching at the University of Oregon. Dr. Carnine frequently consults on educational policy with government groups, businesses, communities, and teacher unions.

YVETTE JACKSON Executive Director of the National Urban Alliance for Effective Education. Nationally recognized for her work in assessing the learning potential of underachieving urban students, Dr. Jackson is also a presenter for the Harvard Principal Center and is a member of the Differentiation Faculty of the Association for Supervision and Curriculum Development. Dr. Jackson's research focuses on literacy, gifted education, and cognitive mediation theory. She designed the Comprehensive Education Plan for the New York City Public Schools and has served as their Director of Gifted Programs and Executive Director of Instruction and Professional Development.

ROBERT T. JIMÉNEZ Professor of Language, Literacy, and Culture at Vanderbilt University. Dr. Jiménez's research focuses on the language and literacy practices of Latino students. A former bilingual education teacher, he is now conducting research on how written language is thought about and used in contemporary Mexico. Dr. Jiménez has received several research and teaching honors, including two Fulbright awards from the Council for the International Exchange of Scholars and the Albert J. Harris Award from the International Reading Association. His published work has appeared in the *American Educational Research Journal, Reading Research Quarterly, The Reading Teacher, Journal of Adolescent and Adult Literacy,* and *Lectura y Vida.*

iv

JUDITH A. LANGER Distinguished Professor at the University at Albany, State University of New York; Director of the Center on English Learning and Achievement; Director of the Albany Institute for Research in Education. An internationally known scholar in English language arts education, Dr. Langer specializes in developing teaching approaches that can enrich and improve what gets done on a daily basis in classrooms. Her publications include *Getting to Excellent: How to Create Better Schools* and *Effective Literacy Instruction: Building Successful Reading and Writing Programs.* She was inducted into the International Reading Hall of Fame and has received many other notable awards, including an honorary doctorate from the University of Uppsala, Sweden, for her research on literacy education.

ROBERT J. MARZANO Senior Scholar at Mid-Continent Research for Education and Learning (McREL); Associate Professor at Cardinal Stritch University in Milwaukee, Wisconsin; President of Marzano & Associates. An internationally known researcher, trainer, and speaker, Dr. Marzano has developed programs that translate research and theory into practical tools for K–12 teachers and administrators. He has written extensively on such topics as reading and writing instruction, thinking skills, school effectiveness, assessment, and standards implementation. His books include *Building Background Knowledge for Academic Achievement; Classroom Management That Works: Research-Based Strategies for Every Teacher;* and *What Works in Schools: Translating Research Into Action.*

DONNA M. OGLE Professor of Reading and Language at National-Louis University in Chicago, Illinois; Past President of the International Reading Association. Creator of the well-known KWL strategy, Dr. Ogle has directed many staff development projects translating theory and research into school practice in middle and secondary schools throughout the United States and has served as a consultant on literacy projects worldwide. Her extensive international experience includes coordinating the Reading and Writing for Critical Thinking Project in Eastern Europe, developing integrated curriculum for a USAID Afghan Education Project, and speaking and consulting on projects in several Latin American countries and in Asia. Her books include *Coming Together as Readers; Reading Comprehension: Strategies for Independent Learners; All Children Read;* and *Literacy for a Democratic Society.*

CAROL BOOTH OLSON Senior Lecturer in the Department of Education at the University of California, Irvine; Director of the UCI site of the National Writing Project. Dr. Olson writes and lectures extensively on the reading/writing connection, critical thinking through writing, interactive strategies for teaching writing, and the use of multicultural literature with students of culturally diverse backgrounds. She has received many awards, including the California Association of Teachers of English Award of Merit, the Outstanding California Education Research Award, and the UC Irvine Excellence in Teaching Award. Dr. Olson's books include *Reading, Thinking, and Writing About Multicultural Literature* and *The Reading/Writing Connection: Strategies for Teaching and Learning in the Secondary Classroom.*

CAROL ANN TOMLINSON Professor of Educational Research, Foundations, and Policy at the University of Virginia; Co-Director of the University's Institutes on Academic Diversity. An internationally known expert on differentiated instruction, Dr. Tomlinson helps teachers and administrators develop effective methods of teaching academically diverse learners. She was a teacher of middle and high school English for 22 years prior to teaching at the University of Virginia. Her books on differentiated instruction have been translated into eight languages. Among her many publications are *How to Differentiate Instruction in Mixed-Ability Classrooms* and *The Differentiated Classroom: Responding to the Needs of All Learners.*

v

ENGLISH LEARNER SPECIALISTS

MARY LOU MCCLOSKEY Past President of Teachers of English to Speakers of Other Languages (TESOL); Director of Teacher Development and Curriculum Design for Educo in Atlanta, Georgia. Dr. McCloskey is a former teacher in multilingual and multicultural classrooms. She has worked with teachers, teacher educators, and departments of education around the world on teaching English as a second and foreign language. She is author of *On Our Way to English, Voices in Literature, Integrating English,* and *Visions: Language, Literature, Content.* Her awards include the Le Moyne College Ignatian Award for Professional Achievement and the TESOL D. Scott Enright Service Award.

LYDIA STACK International ESL consultant. Her areas of expertise are English language teaching strategies, ESL standards for students and teachers, and curriculum writing. Her teaching experience includes 25 years as an elementary and high school ESL teacher. She is a past president of TESOL. Her awards include the James E. Alatis Award for Service to TESOL (2003) and the San Francisco STAR Teacher Award (1989). Her publications include *On Our Way to English; Wordways: Games for Language Learning;* and *Visions: Language, Literature, Content.*

CURRICULUM SPECIALIST

WILLIAM L. MCBRIDE Curriculum Specialist. Dr. McBride is a nationally known speaker, educator, and author who now trains teachers in instructional methodologies. A former reading specialist, English teacher, and social studies teacher, he holds a Masters in Reading and a Ph.D. in Curriculum and Instruction from the University of North Carolina at Chapel Hill. Dr. McBride has contributed to the development of textbook series in language arts, social studies, science, and vocabulary. He is also known for his novel *Entertaining an Elephant,* which tells the story of a burned-out teacher who becomes re-inspired with both his profession and his life.

MEDIA SPECIALISTS

DAVID M. CONSIDINE Professor of Instructional Technology and Media Studies at Appalachian State University in North Carolina. Dr. Considine has served as a media literacy consultant to the U.S. government and to the media industry, including Discovery Communications and Cable in the Classroom. He has also conducted media literacy workshops and training for county and state health departments across the United States. Among his many publications are *Visual Messages: Integrating Imagery into Instruction,* and *Imagine That: Developing Critical Viewing and Thinking Through Children's Literature.*

LARKIN PAULUZZI Teacher and Media Specialist; trainer for the New Jersey Writing Project. Ms. Pauluzzi puts her extensive classroom experience to use in developing teacher-friendly curriculum materials and workshops in many different areas, including media literacy. She has led media literacy training workshops in several districts throughout Texas, guiding teachers in the meaningful and practical uses of media in the classroom. Ms. Pauluzzi has taught students at all levels, from Title I Reading to AP English IV. She also spearheads a technology club at her school, working with students to produce media and technology to serve both the school and the community.

LISA K. SCHEFFLER Teacher and Media Specialist. Ms. Scheffler has designed and taught media literacy and video production curriculum, in addition to teaching language arts and speech. Using her knowledge of mass communication theory, coupled with real classroom experience, she has developed ready-to-use materials that help teachers incorporate media literacy into their curricula. She has taught film and television studies at the University of North Texas and has served as a contributing writer for the Texas Education Agency's statewide viewing and representing curriculum.

vi

TEACHER ADVISORS

These are some of the many educators from across the country who played a crucial role in the development of the tables of contents, the lesson design, and other key components of this program:

Virginia L. Alford, MacArthur High School, San Antonio, Texas

Yvonne L. Allen, Shaker Heights High School, Shaker Heights, Ohio

Dave T. Anderson, Hinsdale South High School, Darien, Illinois

Kacy Colleen Anglim, Portland Public Schools District, Portland, Oregon

Beverly Scott Bass, Arlington Heights High School, Fort Worth, Texas

Jordana Benone, North High School, Torrance, California

Patricia Blood, Howell High School, Farmingdale, New Jersey

Marjorie Bloom, Eau Gallie High School, Melbourne, Florida

Edward J. Blotzer, Wilkinsburg Junior/Senior High School, Wilkinsburg, Pennsylvania

Stephen D. Bournes, Evanston Township High School, Evanston, Illinois

Barbara M. Bowling, Mt. Tabor High School, Winston-Salem, North Carolina

Kiala Boykin-Givehand, Duval County Public Schools, Jacksonville, Florida

Laura L. Brown, Adlai Stevenson High School, Lincolnshire, Illinois

Cynthia Burke, Yavneh Academy, Dallas, Texas

Hoppy Chandler, San Diego City Schools, San Diego, California

Gary Chmielewski, St. Benedict High School, Chicago, Illinois

Delorse Cole-Stewart, Milwaukee Public Schools, Milwaukee, Wisconsin

Kathy Dahlgren, Skokie, Illinois

Diana Dilger, Rosa Parks Middle School, Dixmoor, Illinois

L. Calvin Dillon, Gaither High School, Tampa, Florida

Dori Dolata, Rufus King High School, Milwaukee, Wisconsin

Jon Epstein, Marietta High School, Marietta, Georgia

Helen Ervin, Fort Bend Independent School District, Sugarland, Texas

Sue Friedman, Buffalo Grove High School, Buffalo Grove, Illinois

Chris Gee, Bel Air High School, El Paso, Texas

Paula Grasel, The Horizon Center, Gainesville, Georgia

Christopher Guarraia, Centreville High School, Clifton, Virginia

Rochelle L. Greene-Brady, Kenwood Academy, Chicago, Illinois

Michele M. Hettinger, Niles West High School, Skokie, Illinois

Elizabeth Holcomb, Forest Hill High School, Jackson, Mississippi

Jim Horan, Hinsdale Central High School, Hinsdale, Illinois

James Paul Hunter, Oak Park-River Forest High School, Oak Park, Illinois

Susan P. Kelly, Director of Curriculum, Island Trees School District, Levittown, New York

Beverley A. Lanier, Varina High School, Richmond, Virginia

Pat Laws, Charlotte-Mecklenburg Schools, Charlotte, North Carolina

Diana R. Martinez, Treviño School of Communications & Fine Arts, Laredo, Texas

Natalie Martinez, Stephen F. Austin High School, Houston, Texas

Elizabeth Matarazzo, Ysleta High School, El Paso, Texas

Carol M. McDonald, J. Frank Dobie High School, Houston, Texas

Amy Millikan, Consultant, Chicago, Illinois

Terri Morgan, Caprock High School, Amarillo, Texas

Eileen Murphy, Walter Payton Preparatory High School, Chicago, Illinois

Lisa Omark, New Haven Public Schools, New Haven, Connecticut

Kaine Osburn, Wheeling High School, Wheeling, Illinois

Andrea J. Phillips, Terry Sanford High School, Fayetteville, North Carolina

Cathy Reilly, Sayreville Public Schools, Sayreville, New Jersey

Mark D. Simon, Neuqua Valley High School, Naperville, Illinois

Scott Snow, Sequin High School, Arlington, Texas

Jane W. Speidel, Brevard County Schools, Viera, Florida

Cheryl E. Sullivan, Lisle Community School District, Lisle, Illinois

Anita Usmiani, Hamilton Township Public Schools, Hamilton Square, New Jersey

Linda Valdez, Oxnard Union High School District, Oxnard, California

Nancy Walker, Longview High School, Longview, Texas

Kurt Weiler, New Trier High School, Winnetka, Illinois

Elizabeth Whittaker, Larkin High School, Elgin, Illinois

Linda S. Williams, Woodlawn High School, Baltimore, Maryland

John R. Williamson, Fort Thomas Independent Schools, Fort Thomas, Kentucky

Anna N. Winters, Simeon High School, Chicago, Illinois

Tonora D. Wyckoff, North Shore Senior High School, Houston, Texas

Karen Zajac, Glenbard South High School, Glen Ellyn, Illinois

Cynthia Zimmerman, Mose Vines Preparatory High School, Chicago, Illinois

Lynda Zimmerman, El Camino High School, South San Francisco, California

Ruth E. Zurich, Brown Deer High School, Brown Deer, Wisconsin

MCDOUGAL LITTELL LITERATURE

CONTENTS IN BRIEF

viii

PART 3: FACTS AND OPINIONS

STUDENT RESOURCE BANK

LITERATURE AND READING CENTER
- Author Biographies
- Additional Selection Background
- Literary Analysis Frames
- Power Thinking Activities

WRITING AND GRAMMAR CENTER
- Writing Templates and Graphic Organizers
- Publishing Options
- Quick-Fix Editing Machine

VOCABULARY AND SPELLING CENTER
- Vocabulary Strategies and Practice
- Multi-Language Glossary of Academic Vocabulary
- Vocabulary Flash Cards
- Spelling Lessons

MEDIA CENTER
- Production Templates
- Analysis Guides

RESEARCH CENTER
- Web Research Guide
- Citation Guide

ASSESSMENT CENTER
- Assessment Practice and Test-Taking Tips
- SAT/ACT Practice and Tips

MORE TECHNOLOGY

eEdition
- Interactive Selections
- Audio Summaries

WriteSmart
- Writing Prompts and Templates
- Interactive Student Models
- Interactive Graphic Organizers
- Interactive Revision Lessons
- Rubric Generator

MediaSmart DVD
- Media Lessons
- Interactive Media Studies

ix

UNIT 1

The Main Events
PLOT AND CONFLICT

• IN FICTION • IN DRAMA • IN MEDIA • IN NONFICTION • IN POETRY

x

xi

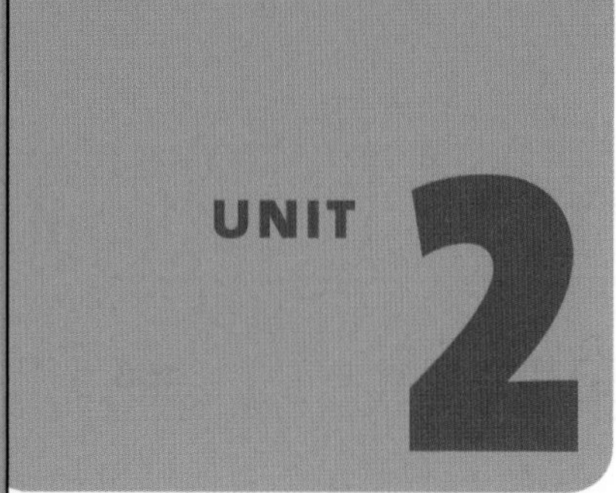

UNIT 2

Through Different Eyes

CHARACTER AND POINT OF VIEW

• IN FICTION • IN MEDIA • IN NONFICTION • IN POETRY

xii

xiii

UNIT 3

The Place to Be
SETTING AND MOOD

• IN FICTION • IN NONFICTION • IN POETRY

xiv

xv

UNIT 4

A World of Meaning
THEME AND SYMBOL

• IN FICTION • IN POETRY • IN DRAMA • IN MEDIA

Skills and Standards

FICTION

COMPARING THEME

POETRY

xvi

Skills and Standards

DRAMA

MEDIA

VOCABULARY STRATEGIES

xvii

UNIT 5

Painting with Words
POETRY

UNIT 6

A Unique Imprint
STYLE, VOICE, AND TONE

• IN FICTION • IN NONFICTION • IN POETRY

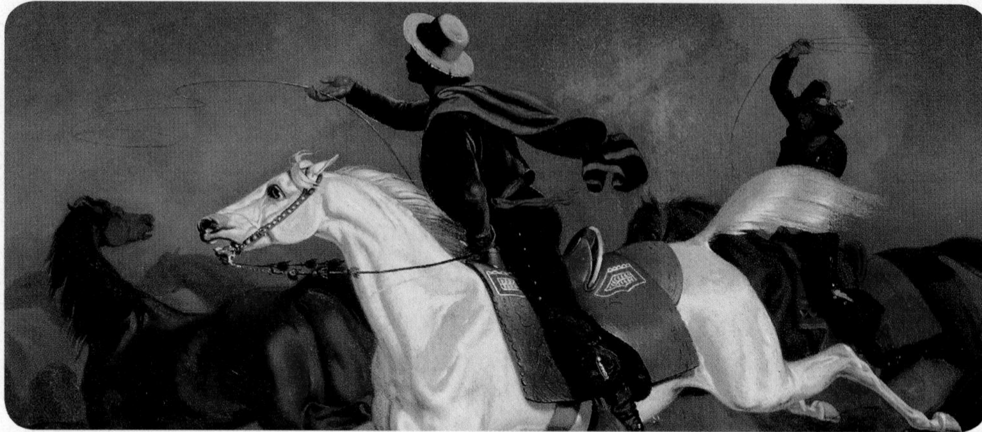

Skills and Standards

FICTION

NONFICTION

xx

UNIT 7

Our Place in the World
HISTORY, CULTURE, AND THE AUTHOR

• IN FICTION • IN NONFICTION • IN MEDIA • IN POETRY

xxii

VOCABULARY STRATEGIES

xxiii

UNIT 8

Believe It or Not

FACTS AND INFORMATION

• IN NONFICTION • IN MEDIA

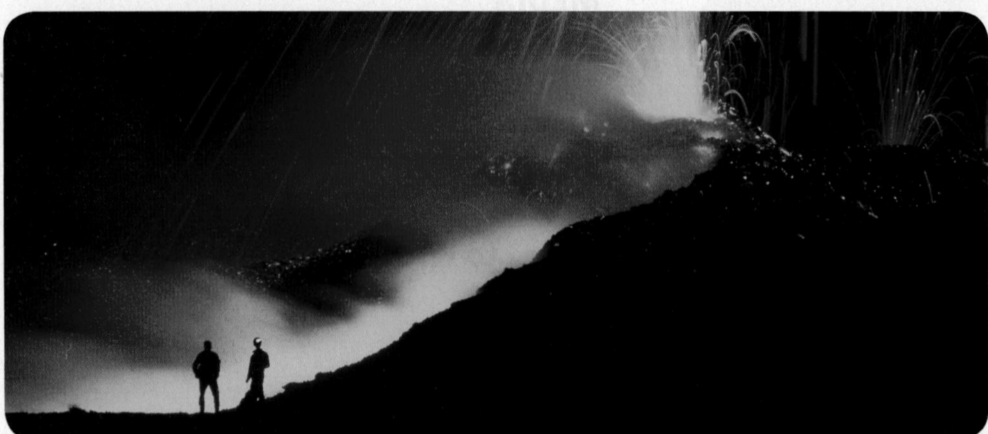

xxiv

UNIT 9

State Your Case
ARGUMENT AND PERSUASION

• IN NONFICTION • IN MEDIA • IN LITERATURE

xxvi

VOCABULARY STRATEGIES

xxvii

UNIT 10

Investigation and Discovery
THE POWER OF RESEARCH

Skills and Standards
Use Reference Materials and Technology, Evaluate Sources

Research, Synthesis

xxviii

Student Resource Bank

Selections by Genre

FICTION

SHORT STORIES

NOVEL EXCERPT

NOVELLA EXCERPT

ORAL TRADITION

NONFICTION

AUTOBIOGRAPHY/MEMOIR

BIOGRAPHY

ESSAYS

INFORMATIONAL NONFICTION

LETTERS, DIARIES, JOURNALS

NARRATIVE NONFICTION

SPEECHES/INTERVIEWS

POETRY

DRAMA

xxxi

Features

READER'S WORKSHOPS

LITERATURE CENTER at ClassZone.com

WRITING WORKSHOPS

WriteSmart

VOCABULARY STRATEGIES

SPEAKING, LISTENING, AND VIEWING

MEDIA CENTER at ClassZone.com

MEDIA STUDY

MediaSmart DVD

GRAMMAR AND WRITING

xxxii

The Power of Ideas

INTRODUCING THE ESSENTIALS

- Literary Genres Workshop
- Reading Strategies Workshop
- Writing Process Workshop

1

For help using this Introductory Unit, see

RESOURCE MANAGER—Introductory Unit p. 1

About the Art The images on this page are (clockwise from top right) a photograph that illustrates Isaac Asimov's science-fiction story "Hallucination" (see page 335), a detail of William H. Johnson's oil painting *Harriet Tubman* (see page 260), and a detail of *The Promenade, Fifth Avenue* by Bill Jacklin, which appears with Edwidge Danticat's story "New York Day Women" on page 674.

What Are Life's Big Questions?

These pages will help you introduce students to the concept of **key ideas** and how they can be explored in literature. Remind students of the title of this unit, **The Power of Ideas.** Draw a cluster diagram on the board. Have students volunteer ideas that have had an impact on society, history, and their own lives, and the effects of those ideas.

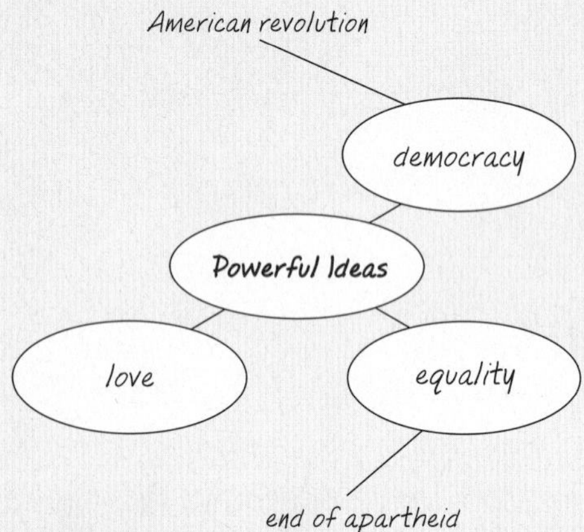

Then have students read the introductory paragraph on this page. Ask them to identify some of the big questions they have thought about at various times in their lives. Write these questions on the board and discuss some of the themes that emerge. For example, their questions might probe the meaning of life, the definition of happiness, or an individual's role in a family or in society. Tell students that answers to these big questions —expressed through philosophy, religion, art, music, politics, or literature—become powerful ideas like those that they identified in the cluster diagram.

Have a volunteer read the first **Big Question** on page 3. Ask students what ideas are stimulated by it. For example, *Are people basically good?* might lead to speculation about the nature of good and evil, punishment for bad deeds, or ways in which individuals can become better people.

The Power of Ideas

What Are Life's Big Questions?

We never stop searching for answers to life's big questions. Asking questions such as the ones shown here is our way of making sense of who we are, where we're going, and how we fit into the world. While our own experiences can guide us toward answers, good literature can also help. Through reading, writing, and talking about literature, we can explore the big questions in life and gain meaningful insights into our own lives and the world.

What does it mean to BELONG?

Humans are naturally social beings. We create groups—families, friends, communities—that bind us together. But what happens when you're on the outside of a group and can't find a way in? Explore the meaning of belonging through the writing of Naomi Shihab Nye, Daniel Keyes, David Sedaris, and others. Then ask yourself: Is it always good to belong?

Why does the PAST *matter?*

There's an old saying: "History repeats itself"—in other words, everything that happens in the world is bound to happen again. If that's the case, then we can look to the past to help us understand conflicts and issues that challenge us in the present. In this book, you'll read about the Civil War, Paul Revere, and Harriet Tubman. Find out what we can still learn from them all these years later.

Introductory Unit Resources

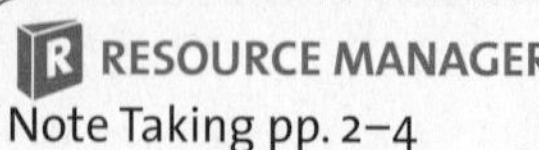

RESOURCE MANAGER
Note Taking pp. 2–4

BEST PRACTICES TOOLKIT

Graphic Organizers/Strategies
Story Map • Venn Diagram • Drawing Conclusions • Read Aloud/Think Aloud • Reciprocal Teaching • Invisible Writing • Writing Templates • Spider Map

Reading Support
Audio Anthology CD*

Technology
ClassZone.com

* Resources for Differentiation

Are people basically GOOD?

In her diary, Anne Frank wrote: "... I still believe, in spite of everything, that people are truly good at heart." This sentiment is surprising, given that Anne was one of the millions of Jews who lost their lives in Nazi concentration camps during World War II. Today, we might find ourselves asking this same question. After all, war and crime are still facts of life. What do you think? Are people really good?

What's really IMPORTANT?

Some objects, such as flashy cars and diamonds, are worth a lot of money. But then there are other things—a photograph or a beautiful sunset, for instance—that are priceless. Authors such as Sandra Cisneros, Walter Dean Myers, and Joseph Bruchac all write about the things people treasure most. Reading about what others value can help you decide for yourself what's really important to *you*.

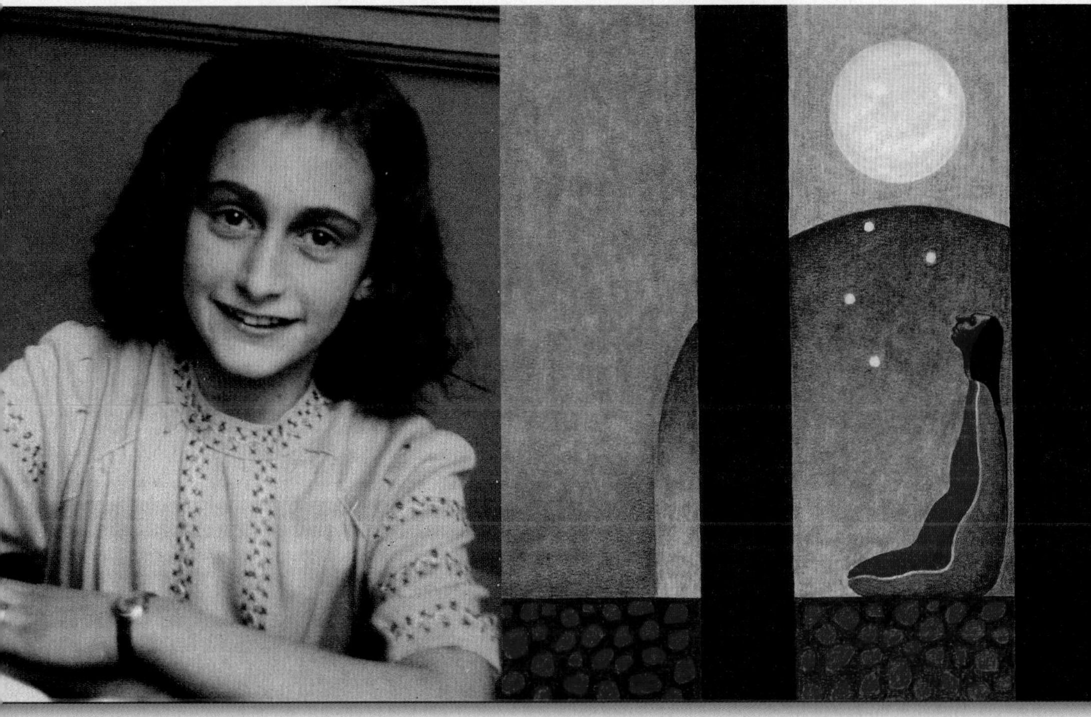

Explain that the literature students will read throughout the anthology will offer ways to think about various **Big Questions** and will help them explore important ideas in new ways. The literature will also help them connect these ideas to their own lives and experiences.

Read through the remaining **Big Questions** on pages 2–3. Discuss with students their thoughts and reactions to each one. Explain that every lesson in this anthology will begin with a **Big Question** to guide their analysis of the literature and to help them make important connections.

OBJECTIVES

- understand the types and characteristics of different literary genres
- become familiar with the academic vocabulary used to write about and discuss literature

The Genres

Determine Readiness Have volunteers read the introductory text and the description of each genre aloud. Then distribute copies of the previous year's textbook or other anthologies and ask students to find examples of the types of fiction, poetry, drama, and nonfiction listed on page 4. Display a chart such as this one and record students' responses:

Genre	Examples
Fiction	
short story	
novel	
novella	

Discuss and Review Have students think about the selections in the chart and make some generalizations about the characteristics of each genre. Then have them compare and contrast genres. Ask them how a poet would describe an important historical event, such as a battle, compared to the way a historian, a short-story writer, or a playwright would describe it. Discuss why a reader might choose the poetic account instead of the nonfiction article, or vice versa. Lead students to understand that both writers and readers use different genres to help them explore ideas from a variety of approaches and perspectives.

If students need help . . . Have them use the note-taking frame for this unit to help them focus on important ideas.

RESOURCE MANAGER—Copy Master
Note Taking pp. 2–4

Literary Genres Workshop

Exploring Ideas in Literature

How do you answer important questions in life? For most people, the answers don't come easily. Throughout history, people have turned to everything from ancient cave walls, fragile paper manuscripts, and up-to-the-minute blogs in search of answers to life's big questions. Exploring literature of all types can help you think about these questions—and answers—in new and exciting ways.

The Genres

What draws you to the books you read or the movies you see? Most likely, their ideas appeal to you. Family relationships, competition between friends, impossible decisions—powerful ideas such as these are at the heart of all good literature, not just the novels and movies you encounter today. Believe it or not, centuries-old poetry, classic dramas, and inspiring biographies can also help you grapple with ideas that are thought-provoking and relevant in today's world.

In this book, you'll explore ideas in a variety of **genres,** or forms, of literature. You'll even consider the ideas in popular media forms, such as ads and movies. First, though, familiarize yourself with the characteristics of each genre.

GENRES AT A GLANCE

FICTION
Fiction refers to stories about made-up events and characters.
- short stories
- novels
- novellas

POETRY
Poetry is a type of literature in which words are chosen and arranged in a precise way to create certain sounds and meanings.
- odes
- sonnets
- narrative poems
- lyric poems

DRAMA
Drama is meant to be performed. Characters and conflicts are developed through dialogue and action.
- comedies
- radio plays
- historical dramas

NONFICTION
Nonfiction is writing that tells about real people, events, and places.
- autobiographies
- essays
- news articles
- biographies
- speeches
- feature articles

TYPES OF MEDIA

***Media* refers to forms of communication that reach large numbers of people.**
- TV shows
- advertising
- Web sites

DIFFERENTIATED INSTRUCTION

FOR LESS–PROFICIENT READERS

Comprehension Support [paired option] Have students work in pairs to quiz each other on literary genres and types of media. Students should take turns asking each other questions based on the definitions on page 4, such as *Which genre has made-up events and characters?* and *Which genre includes news articles?* Encourage students to reread to clarify any incorrect answers. Allow pairs to continue this activity until they feel they have mastered the content.

FOR ENGLISH LEARNERS

Vocabulary Support Make sure students understand that *genre* (*género* for Spanish-speaking students) means "type or category of literature." Each genre has its own set of characteristics. Writing that shows these characteristics belongs to that genre.

FICTION

Does fiction mean "fake"? Some authors dream up every element of a story, from the setting to the plot and the characters. Others may be inspired by real events and people, and build a story around them. Whether it's an original product of an author's imagination or an idea "ripped straight from the headlines," all good fiction guarantees a stirring **plot,** a vivid **setting,** and compelling **characters.** Most works of fiction also have **themes,** or larger messages about life. Fiction usually takes one of three forms.

- A **short story** often focuses on a single event or incident. Most stories are short enough to be read without taking a break.
- A **novel** is a longer work of fiction that weaves together many different events, storylines, and characters.
- A **novella** is generally longer than a short story but shorter than a novel. Novellas usually feature a limited number of characters.

ACADEMIC VOCABULARY FOR FICTION

- plot
- conflict
- character
- setting
- theme
- narrator
- point of view

Read the Model In the novel *Slam!*, Greg Harris has just transferred from a high school in Harlem to a more academically challenging school for the arts. At his old school, Greg was the star of his basketball team. Will he still shine on the court now that he's on unfamiliar ground? As you read this excerpt, notice how Greg describes his athletic abilities. In what ways does his attitude help you to understand the **key idea** of self-confidence?

from

SLAM!

Novel by **Walter Dean Myers**

Basketball is my thing. I can hoop. Case closed. I'm six four and I got the moves, the eye, and the heart. You can take my game to the bank and wait around for the interest. With me it's not like playing a game, it's like the only time I'm being for real. Bringing the ball down the court makes me feel like a bird that just learned to fly. I see my guys moving down in front of me and everything feels and looks right. Patterns come up and a small buzz comes into my head that starts to build up and I know it won't end until the ball swishes through the net. If somebody starts messing with my game it's like they're getting into my head. But if I've got the ball it's okay, because I can take care of the situation. That's the word and I know it the same way I know my tag, Slam. Yeah, that's it. Slam. But without the ball, without the floorboards under my feet, without the mid-court line that takes me halfway home, you can get to me.

So when Mr. Tate, the principal at my new school, started talking about me laying low for the season until I got my grades together I was like seriously turned out. The night after he talked to my moms I couldn't sleep. It wasn't the hissing of the radiator or my little brother talking in his sleep in the other bed, it was the idea of not playing ball that was bouncing crazylike through my head.

Close Read

1. Characters and conflicts are two key elements of good fiction. Which characters are introduced in this excerpt? What is Greg's conflict?
2. **Key Idea: Self-Confidence** Greg's confidence springs from his "game." Other than athletic ability, what else can be a source of **self-confidence?**

FICTION

Record the **Academic Vocabulary for Fiction** on the board. Have students read the introductory paragraph on page 5 independently and define each term, based on their prior knowledge and the ideas in the text. Review their definitions together.

- *plot:* the action of a story
- *conflict:* a struggle between opposing forces
- *character:* a person involved in the action
- *setting:* where and when the action takes place
- *theme:* a message or lesson brought out by the action of the story and the characters
- *narrator:* the character or voice that tells a story
- *point of view:* the perspective from which a story is told

Have students complete a Story Map for a familiar folk tale or fairy tale. Then use a three-way Venn diagram to compare and contrast the forms of fiction described on this page. Make sure students understand that all of the forms include the elements of fiction identified in the **Academic Vocabulary.**

BEST PRACTICES TOOLKIT—Transparency
Story Map p. D16

Read the Model Read the introductory paragraph and the model aloud as students follow along silently. Then have students answer the **Close Read** questions.

Close Read
Possible answers:

1. *The narrator, Greg; Mr. Tate, the principal; Greg's mom; and Greg's little brother are introduced. The conflict is that Mr. Tate does not want Greg to play basketball until his grades improve, an idea that horrifies Greg.*

If students need help . . . Provide examples of internal and external conflict to help students identify Greg's.

2. *Students may say that being good at music, art, school, or any activity, or having supportive family and friends can be sources of self-confidence.*

CHECK UNDERSTANDING Have students summarize a story they know, using the **Academic Vocabulary for Fiction.**

DIFFERENTIATED INSTRUCTION

FOR LESS–PROFICIENT READERS

Concept Support Review points of view:

- *first-person:* narrator is a character in the story; uses the pronouns *I* and *we*
- *third-person limited:* narrator is outside the story and knows the thoughts and feelings of only one character; uses the pronouns *he, she,* and *they*
- *third-person omniscient:* narrator is outside the story and knows the thoughts and feelings of all the characters; uses the pronouns *he, she,* and *they*

Have students identify the point of view of *Slam!* Discuss why the author chose it.

FOR ENGLISH LEARNERS

Vocabulary Support: Cognates Point out these cognates to Spanish-speaking students. Remind them to look for others.

- *fiction/ficción*
- *character/carácter*
- *conflict/conflicto*
- *theme/tema*
- *narrator/narrador*

POETRY

Record the **Academic Vocabulary for Poetry** on the board. Have students use their prior knowledge to define each term. Ask volunteers to read aloud the first three paragraphs on page 6. Revise definitions, if necessary.

Display this diagram of the three major components of poetry:

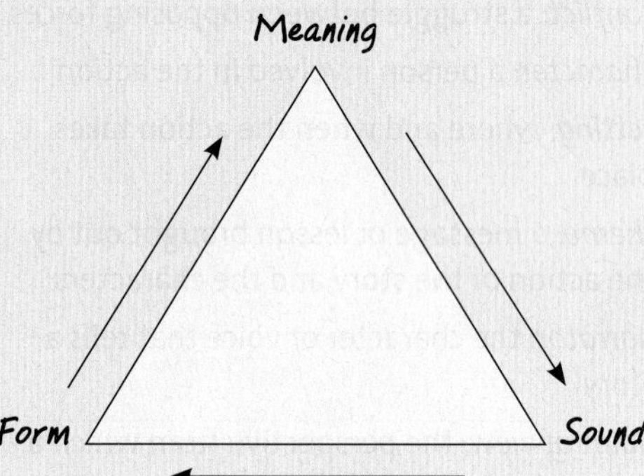

Tell students that form, meaning, and sound all contribute to each other and to the total effectiveness of a poem. For example, the lines of poem might break in a way that helps show the pattern of rhyme. The rhyme creates mood and emphasizes certain words, helping to reinforce the meaning.

Read the Model Read "Teenagers" aloud or play the reading from the *Audio Anthology CD.* Then have students read the poem silently and answer the **Close Read** questions.

Close Read

Possible answers:

1. *The poem is organized into lines and stanzas. The language is compressed.*
2. *According to the speaker, teenagers are puzzling. Instead of knowing everything about their children, parents of teens are suddenly confronted by "strangers" whose language they cannot speak. Teens might feel that they are the same as they always were and that their parents are the ones who have changed.*

If students need help . . . Work with them to identify words and phrases that show the speaker's changed relationship with his or her children.

CHECK UNDERSTANDING Have students summarize the ways in which a poem is different from a short story.

POETRY

"Poetry: the best words in the best order." This is how British poet Samuel Taylor Coleridge summed up the goal and the struggle of writing poetry. Poets search for the perfect words and then arrange them in precise ways to achieve specific effects. The result can be both ear-catching and unforgettable.

As you know, poetry looks different on the page than fiction or nonfiction. Poems are made up of **lines,** which are often arranged into groups called **stanzas.** In some poems, the lines and stanzas reflect the rules of a particular form, such as a haiku or a sonnet. In others, there is no recognizable form; instead, the poet lets the ideas drive what the poem looks like on the page.

In poetry, sounds and language are just as important as form. Does the poem have a brisk **rhythm** or singsong **rhymes?** What sensory details help readers clearly picture what's being described? Every choice a poet makes can affect the overall meaning and sound of the poem.

Read the Model You already know what it's like to be a teenager—but how about the parent of one? As you read this poem, think about the **key idea** of relationships, especially between parents and teenagers.

ACADEMIC VOCABULARY FOR POETRY

- form
- line
- stanza
- speaker
- rhyme
- rhythm
- sound devices
- imagery

Teenagers

Poem by **Pat Mora**

One day they disappear
into their rooms.
Doors and lips shut
and we become strangers
in our own home.

I pace the hall, hear whispers,
a code I knew but can't remember,
mouthed by mouths I taught to speak.

Years later the door opens.
I see faces I once held,
open as sunflowers in my hands. I see
familiar skin now stretched on long bodies
that move past me
glowing almost like pearls.

Close Read

1. What specific characteristics tell you that "Teenagers" is a poem, rather than a work of fiction?
2. **Key Idea: Relationships** According to this poem, how do parents view their **relationships** with their teenaged children? How might teenagers' views differ?

DIFFERENTIATED INSTRUCTION

FOR LESS–PROFICIENT READERS

Comprehension Support [small-group option]

1. Display a three-column chart. In the first column, write the major components of poetry. In the second, list related terms and devices. (***form:*** *line, stanza;* ***meaning:*** *speaker, imagery, metaphor, simile, symbol, personification;* ***sound:*** *rhyme, rhythm, alliteration, onomatopoeia)*
2. Have students then work in small groups to define each term. Suggest they consult the Glossary of Literary Terms (page R102).
3. Record their definitions in the third column and suggest that students copy the chart into their notebooks.

Concept Support Ask students to label the lines, stanzas, sound devices (including rhyme), and imagery in "Teenagers." Discuss their analyses.

DRAMA

You may use the term *drama* in everyday speech to mean something or somebody acting in a dramatic way (as in, "What a drama queen!"). In literature, though, a **drama** is any work that is written to be performed on a stage. A drama has all the elements of good fiction—plot, characters, setting, and theme. Unlike a work of fiction, however, a drama is usually divided into **scenes,** with several scenes grouped into **acts.**

A drama is primarily written as **dialogue** between characters. The playwright, or author, describes the setting, characters' movements, and props as **stage directions,** written in *italics* throughout the play. These notes represent the playwright's vision of the performance. However, a great deal is left to the imagination of the director, the actors, and readers.

ACADEMIC VOCABULARY FOR DRAMA

- plot
- character
- act
- scene
- stage directions
- dialogue

Read the Model This drama takes place in Brooklyn in 1937. Fourteen-year-old Eugene has just discovered that his oldest brother, Stanley, is leaving home. Stanley is ashamed because he gambled away his paycheck, which the family relies on to make ends meet. In this excerpt, Eugene offers Stanley "his life savings" for train fare. As you read, consider the **key idea** of admiration.

from *Brighton Beach Memoirs*

Drama by **Neil Simon**

Eugene. You're leaving home?

Stanley. When I'm gone, you tell Aunt Blanche what happened to my salary. Then she'll know why Mom was so angry. Tell her please not to leave, because it was all my fault, not Mom's. Will you do that?

(He takes the coins out of the cigar box)

Eugene. I have eight cents' worth of stamps, if you want that too.

Stanley. Thanks. *(He picks up a small medal)* What's this?

Eugene. The medal you won for the hundred-yard dash two years ago.

Stanley. From the Police Athletic League. I didn't know you still had this.

Eugene. You gave it to me. You can have it back if you want it.

Stanley. It's not worth anything.

Eugene. It is to me.

Close Read

1. How does Eugene feel about Stanley? Cite details from the dialogue and the stage directions to support your answer.
2. **Key Idea: Admiration** Think of a person you look up to or **admire.** If that person made a mistake, would your opinion of him or her change? Why or why not?

DRAMA

Write the **Academic Vocabulary for Drama** on the board as students read the first two paragraphs independently. Together, define each term, making sure that students understand *act* (major unit of action in a drama or play), *scene* (a section of a play presenting events that occur in one place at one time), *stage directions* (instructions to the actors, director, and stage crew), and *dialogue* (words that characters speak aloud). Have students point out examples of each in the excerpt from the play on this page.

Read the Model Read the introductory paragraph aloud. Then have students read the model silently, before asking for volunteers to take parts and read it aloud. Have students answer the **Close Read** questions independently.

Close Read

Possible answers:

1. *Eugene looks up to Stanley. This admiration is shown by his having kept the medal that Stanley won for the hundred-yard dash and his desire to give Stanley all his money to help him out.*
2. *Students might say that whether their opinion would change would depend on what the person did and why. Admiration is based upon the qualities that are perceived in someone. Therefore, if that person acts counter to those qualities, admiration may be diminished.*

CHECK UNDERSTANDING Have students summarize what they learn about character and conflict from the dialogue in the excerpt.

DIFFERENTIATED INSTRUCTION

FOR LESS–PROFICIENT READERS

Comprehension Support [small-group option] Display this passage of dialogue:

Lola. What's that noise? I think there's someone else in the house!

Tia. Ssssh! I hear footsteps coming up the stairs. Hide in the closet!

Have students work in small groups to insert stage directions that indicate setting, props, and characters' gestures and movements. Have groups act out what they've written.

FOR ENGLISH LEARNERS

Concept Support Use a Venn Diagram to compare and contrast drama and fiction. The diagram might include these details:

Both

- may be based on made-up events and characters or real events and people
- have plots, conflicts, and settings
- reveal characters through what they say and do
- convey themes

Fiction

- may be divided into chapters

Drama

- is organized into acts and scenes
- has stage directions
- is written to be performed on stage

BEST PRACTICES TOOLKIT—Transparency Venn Diagram p. A26

NONFICTION AND INFORMATIONAL TEXT

Have students read the first paragraph independently. Make sure they understand the distinction between nonfiction, which communicates ideas related to real events and real people, and informational nonfiction, which shares knowledge or information for practical purposes. Identify examples of each type of writing from students' previous reading.

Then have volunteers take turns reading the description of each type of nonfiction. Point out that literary nonfiction, such as biographies, autobiographies, essays, and speeches, may be subjective and include the author's own views and opinions in addition to the facts. In contrast, news articles and functional documents are usually more objective.

Work with students to define each of the terms under **Academic Vocabulary for Nonfiction.** Explain that all works of nonfiction have a purpose, but the words *argument* and *persuasion* are related to writing done for the purpose of convincing others to take a certain action or think a particular way.

CHECK UNDERSTANDING Have students give examples of nonfiction texts and explain what they could gain from reading each one.

NONFICTION AND INFORMATIONAL TEXT

Some works of nonfiction, such as biographies and true-life adventures, read like gripping novels. There's a key difference, though. In nonfiction, the events actually happened, and the characters are real people. Informational nonfiction, however, is nothing like fiction. It includes texts such as news articles, manuals, and directions to a friend's house—sources you consult for information. Since you read all kinds of nonfiction texts daily, you should know what to expect from them.

ACADEMIC VOCABULARY FOR NONFICTION

- purpose
- text features
- argument
- persuasion

TYPE OF NONFICTION	CHARACTERISTICS
AUTOBIOGRAPHY/ BIOGRAPHY The true story of a person's life, told by that person (autobiography) or by another person (biography)	• Provides details about a person's life • Written from the first-person point of view (autobiography) or from the third-person point of view (biography) • Presents the writer's own version of his or her life (autobiography) or an outside writer's research (biography)
ESSAY A short work of nonfiction that focuses on a single subject. Common types include reflective, persuasive, and descriptive essays.	• Is intended to share a personal experience, to express feelings, to inform, to entertain, or to persuade • May be written in a **formal** style, with an academic tone • May be written in an **informal** style, with a conversational tone
SPEECH An oral presentation of the ideas, beliefs, or proposals of a speaker	• May be intended to share a personal experience, to express feelings, to inform, to entertain, or to persuade • Relies on powerful language, as well as the speaker's voice and gestures
NEWS/FEATURE ARTICLES Informative writing in newspapers and magazines. News articles report on recent events. Feature articles offer in-depth coverage of human-interest topics.	• Are primarily intended to inform or entertain • Use headlines, subheadings, photographs, and graphic aids to present information • Strive to be objective and fair
FUNCTIONAL DOCUMENTS Writing that serves a practical purpose. Types include consumer documents, such as user manuals, and workplace documents, such as résumés.	• Are written to inform a specific audience (for example, employees or consumers) • Often include charts, diagrams, or other helpful graphic aids

DIFFERENTIATED INSTRUCTION

FOR LESS-PROFICIENT READERS

Comprehension Support [small-group option] Provide small groups of students with brief examples of different types of nonfiction, including biography, autobiography, news articles, feature articles, and functional documents. Have students label each selection, identify its topic and its purpose, and describe how it organizes or presents information. Have groups summarize their ideas in a chart.

FOR ENGLISH LEARNERS

Vocabulary Support: Cognates Many of the terms on this page may look familiar to Spanish speakers. Point out these cognates to students and encourage them to look for others:

- *autobiography/autobiografía*
- *biography/biografía*
- *article/articulo*
- *document/documento*
- *résumé/resumen*

MODEL 1: BIOGRAPHY

As the cofounder and CEO of a major technology corporation, Steve Jobs helped develop some of the first user-friendly personal computers. As you read this excerpt from a biography of Jobs, keep in mind the **key idea** of initiative—the ability to take action.

from

Steve Jobs: [Thinks Different]

Biography by **Ann Brashares**

At thirteen, Jobs's interest in electronics was blossoming. One day he was building an electronic counting machine, and he needed some parts. He knew he could get them from Hewlett-Packard, a giant electronics company not far from his house. Jobs looked up the phone number of Bill Hewlett, the cofounder of Hewlett-Packard. Some kids would have been afraid to dial up one of the richest and most important men in California. Not Steve Jobs.

He boldly chatted with Bill Hewlett for twenty minutes, and Hewlett was so impressed and surprised by the young man that he not only gave him the parts he needed but offered him a summer job, too. That phone call taught an early lesson: If you ask for what you want, you often get it.

Close Read

1. How can you tell that this excerpt is from a biography rather than an autobiography?
2. **Key Idea: Initiative** Jobs was a "go-getter" even at the age of 13. What qualities do you think people must have in order to take **initiative?**

MODEL 2: FEATURE ARTICLE

Did you know that the first computer weighed *30 tons?* As you read this excerpt from a feature article on computer history, look for other mind-boggling facts. Also, consider the **key idea** of progress.

WIRELESS EVOLUTION: THANK YOU ENIAC

WAY BACK WHEN, ONE COMPUTER COULD FILL AN ENTIRE MIDDLE SCHOOL CAFETERIA. TODAY, YOU CAN WEAR ONE ON YOUR BELT LOOP.

by David Santos

Far from a Handheld The first computerized "counting machine" was called ENIAC—Electronic Numerical Integrator and Computer. Completed in 1946, covering three walls, standing eight feet high, and weighing 30 tons, ENIAC required 7,468 vacuum tubes and 6,000 manual switches just to get warmed up!

ENIAC could execute thousands of calculations in seconds. However, reprogramming it took a team of people, three days, and lots of patience.

ENIAC's advanced technology, even with its massive shortcomings, was critical in spurring on the decades of computer evolution that followed.

Close Read

1. What characteristics make this article different from the biography you just read?
2. **Key Idea: Progress** Think about the role technology plays in our society. What are the dangers of technological **progress,** or is it all positive?

DIFFERENTIATED INSTRUCTION

FOR LESS–PROFICIENT READERS

Concept Support [small-group option] Have small groups compare a brief autobiographical excerpt with the sample biography on page 9, examining these aspects:

- point of view
- purpose
- main idea
- writer's style
- types of supporting details

Discuss students' comparisons and draw some conclusions about the two types of nonfiction.

FOR ENGLISH LEARNERS

Vocabulary Support [mixed-readiness pairs] Have pairs work together to define these terms and phrases from **Model 2:**

- *Far from a Handheld* (line 1), "very different from a modern computer than can fit in a person's hand"
- *warmed up* (line 9), "ready to work"

MODEL 1: BIOGRAPHY

Read the introductory paragraph aloud, drawing students' attention to the **key idea.** Then have volunteers read the model before students work on the **Close Read** questions independently.

Close Read

Possible answers:

1. *The details about Steve Jobs are narrated from a third-person point of view, not first-person.*
2. *Students may say that people with initiative have a specific goal or idea of what they want. They possess determination and a willingness to work to overcome obstacles. They have an ability to translate their desires into an action plan. They have confidence in themselves.*

MODEL 2: FEATURE ARTICLE

Have students read the introductory paragraph and model silently before answering the **Close Read** questions.

Close Read

Possible answers:

1. *This article gives in-depth information about a topic. It presents facts and statistics.*
2. *Some students may believe that progress is entirely positive. Others might feel that the drive to perfect technology causes people to lose sight of the reasons they are doing it in the first place.*

If students need help . . . Use a Drawing Conclusions chart to help them use the information in each article to arrive at an understanding of the key idea.

Stated Fact	*Inferred Fact*
Jobs was not afraid to call up Bill Hewlett.	Jobs knew what he wanted and went after it.
Conclusion: Go-getters do what it takes to meet their goals.	

BEST PRACTICES TOOLKIT—Transparency
Drawing Conclusions p. A28

CHECK UNDERSTANDING What is the purpose of each selection on this page?

MEDIA

Record the **Academic Vocabulary for Media** on the board. Draw from students' prior knowledge to help them define each term and give examples.

- *medium:* a format in which ideas are conveyed. The plural of *medium* is *media*.
- *message:* the main idea conveyed through a medium
- *purpose:* the reason for the creation of a media message
- *target audience:* the group for whom a message is intended

Then read the introductory paragraph aloud. Display this diagram to illustrate how the **Academic Vocabulary** relates to the idea of being media literate.

Someone who is media literate can . . .
- detect bias
- evaluate message
- recognize persuasive techniques
- identify purpose and target audience

Have volunteers read different rows in the chart on page 10. Ask students to identify movies, specific advertisements, and Web sites with which they are familiar. As a class, analyze the purpose, message, and target audience of each example.

CHECK UNDERSTANDING Ask students how different target audiences might affect the way in which a message is delivered.

MEDIA

The World Wide Web alerts you to breaking news. A blockbuster movie keeps you on the edge of your seat for two action-packed hours. A clever ad campaign convinces you to buy a product you probably don't need. Media messages are all around you, and they influence your beliefs and actions more than you might realize. That's why it's important to become **media literate**—to learn how to "read" all types of media messages, including the ones shown here.

ACADEMIC VOCABULARY FOR MEDIA
- medium
- message
- purpose
- target audience

TYPE OF MEDIA	CHARACTERISTICS	
FEATURE FILMS Motion pictures that use narrative elements to tell stories	• Created for entertainment and to make money • Rely on music, cinematography, sets, and actors to tell interesting stories • Are at least one hour in length	
NEWS MEDIA Accounts of current events in newspapers and magazines, as well as on television, the radio, and the Web	• Designed to inform and entertain viewers • Present information differently in each medium (TV, Web, print) • Can include bias and inaccuracies, so must be closely examined	
TV SHOWS Programs broadcast on television, including dramas, sitcoms, talk shows, documentaries, and reality shows	• Are usually created to entertain or inform • Are sponsored by advertisers who pay to market their products during commercial breaks • Use camera techniques and dramatic music to make stories more compelling • Typically last for a half hour or an hour	
ADVERTISING Paid promotion of products, services, candidates, or public service messages using print, electronic, and broadcast media	• Is designed to persuade a target audience to buy a product, use a service, or agree with an idea • Uses visuals, sound effects, and actors to persuade viewers • Is presented when and where the target audience is likely to see it	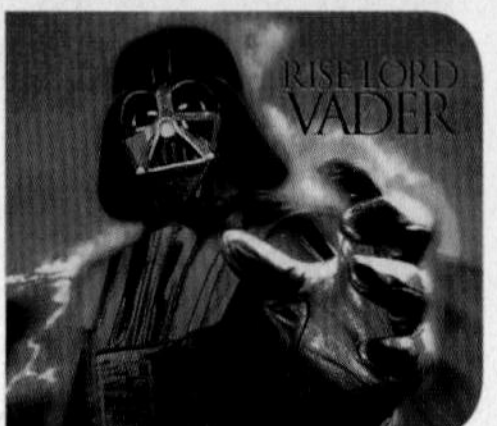
WEB SITES Collections of "pages" on the World Wide Web. Users navigate to pages by clicking menus or hyperlinks.	• Present information through text, graphics, audio, video, animation, and interactive features • Require careful evaluation, as most Web sites are not checked for credibility	

DIFFERENTIATED INSTRUCTION

FOR LESS–PROFICIENT READERS

Concept Support [small-group option] Provide small groups with two or three print ads. Have them identify the purpose, message, and target audience of each ad. Discuss how knowing this information contributes to their media literacy.

FOR ENGLISH LEARNERS

Concept Support Show students examples of each type of media described on this page, or have them locate examples on the Internet. Discuss the major characteristics of each. Invite students to find or identify additional examples.

Strategies That Work: Literature

❶ Ask the Right Questions

It's one thing to "get through" a work of literature but another to really enjoy and participate in the story. To get the most from what you read, make sure you ask the right questions.

Stage of Reading	Kinds of Questions
Before Reading Preview the selection and get your bearings.	• Based on the title, the subheadings, and the first paragraph, what do I think this text is about? • What is my purpose for reading?
During Reading Pause occasionally to monitor understanding.	• What just happened? • What details help me to visualize the characters or events? • What do I predict might happen next?
After Reading Analyze the selection and explore its key ideas.	• How would I summarize the main idea or the basic plot? • What are the key ideas in the story? Did I gain any new insights?

❷ Make Connections

The conflicts and themes in literature can help you make sense of your own life. Use these tips to make connections.

- **Key Ideas** Take time to think about how the key ideas and big questions in this book are relevant to your life. For example, where do you think confidence comes from? Has someone you admire ever disappointed you?
- **Discussion/Journaling** Jot down your thoughts and opinions as you read, or share them with others. You might want to record
  - conflicts or events that you can relate to
  - characters who remind you of people you know
  - ideas you strongly agree or disagree with

❸ Record Your Reactions

Keeping a **Reader's Notebook** can help you organize your questions, thoughts, and analysis. Experiment with different formats to find out which works best for you.

JOURNAL

Pause as you read to record your impressions, predictions, or questions.

Brighton Beach Memoirs

I wonder how Stanley's family will react when he leaves home.

I predict that Eugene will have a hard time dealing with his brother's absence.

GRAPHIC ORGANIZER

After reading, create a graphic organizer to help you analyze characters and events.

Eugene's Character Traits

Eager to Please — *Wants to help out his brother*

Selfless — *Offers life savings*

Honest — *Lets Stanley know the medal is important to him*

Strategies That Work: Literature

Tell students that the strategies on this page will help them get the most from what they read or view, whether in class or outside of school.

1. **Ask the Right Questions** Explain to students that throughout the anthology, they will be guided in asking questions that will help them understand the most important ideas of the selections. Turn to a selection in the first unit, such as "Raymond's Run" on page 32, to point out the **Before Reading** feature, the questions throughout the selection text, and the **After Reading** pages.
2. **Make Connections** Tell students that the selections in the anthology have been chosen for their relevance to the lives of eighth graders. The **Big Question** at the beginning of each selection indicates the value that the work of fiction or nonfiction might have to readers. The question also helps prepare students to make connections to **key ideas** and to their own lives. Tell students that keeping a journal on these connections will enable them to answer some of their own big questions.
3. **Record Your Reactions** Students might find it helpful to designate various sections of their notebooks or parts of each page for different functions. They might wish to have a section for questions, connections, and reactions; another section for their analysis of each work, including a short summary; and a vocabulary section, in which they record the definitions of vocabulary words associated with each selection.

DIFFERENTIATED INSTRUCTION

FOR LESS–PROFICIENT READERS

Concept Support Provide students with a template for their **Reader's Notebook** pages. Discuss the function of each page and encourage students to add other elements as necessary.

Title___ Author___ Genre___ Date___ Pages___ BEFORE READING Questions and predictions: My purpose:	DURING READING Questions: Connections: Predictions: Details that seem important:

AFTER READING Summary:	Notes (and answers):
Overall reaction:	Vocabulary:

OBJECTIVES

- become familiar with the skills and strategies for active reading
- practice reading skills and strategies, such as **preview, use prior knowledge, predict,** and **make inferences**

Tell students that readers might be classified into two categories—passive and active. Passive readers flip the pages and appear to be reading the words, but, in many cases, they cannot remember what they have read a minute after finishing the text. Active readers, on the other hand, employ the skills and strategies described on this page. They take part in the reading process, and, as a result, they are able to remember important ideas and benefit from their reading experience.

Model for students some of the skills and strategies they might use to actively read this page. For example, they can **preview** the text to learn about its organization and content. They can **set a purpose** of reading to find out more about each skill and strategy. They can **monitor** their understanding of what they have read by asking questions and rereading parts of the page.

Then read the text aloud as students follow along silently.

CHECK UNDERSTANDING In what way does prior knowledge help readers make connections?

Reading Strategies Workshop

Becoming an Active Reader

Are you sometimes tempted to race through your reading just to get it done? Have you ever skipped ahead a few scenes or chapters to find out what happens? While you might save time, you probably won't enjoy the experience as much. Reading actively means taking the time to ask questions, clarify, and connect to what you're reading, whether it's a message-board posting, a novel, or even a TV drama. Use these skills and strategies to stay engaged in the process.

SKILLS AND STRATEGIES FOR ACTIVE READING

Preview
Become familiar with the text before you start to read.
- Look at the title, the graphics, and subheadings.
- Skim the first paragraph to get a feel for what the text is about.

Set a Purpose
Know why you are reading.
- Ask: Am I reading for pure entertainment, information, or another reason?
- Think about how your purpose affects your approach. Should you take notes or sit back and enjoy?

Connect
Find something you can personally relate to.
- Consider whether any characters remind you of people in your life.
- Ask: If I were in this situation, would I react differently?

Use Prior Knowledge
Recall what you already know about a topic.
- Before reading, jot down what you already know.
- As you read, connect what you know to what you are learning.

Predict
Guess what's going to happen next.
- Pay attention to certain clues, such as important statements made by characters or repeated details.
- Resist the urge to read ahead.
- Ask: Was my prediction on target, or did I miss the mark?

Visualize
Get a clear mental picture of what is being described.
- Notice the author's description of characters, settings, and events.
- Use these descriptions to help you "see" what's happening like a movie in your mind.

Monitor
Check your own understanding.
- Ask **questions** like, What just happened? Why did the character do that?
- **Clarify** your understanding by rereading confusing parts.
- **Evaluate** yourself as a reader. Ask: How well am I understanding this?

Make Inferences
Make logical guesses by considering the text and your own experiences.
- Record specific details in the text about characters and events.
- Use common sense and your own experiences to help you "read between the lines."

Details in "The Winter Hibiscus"	What I Know	My Inference
Saeng is nervous about passing the driver's test.	It's easy to make mistakes when you're nervous.	Saeng's nerves probably interfered with her judgment during the test.

DIFFERENTIATED INSTRUCTION

FOR LESS-PROFICIENT READERS

Concept Support [paired option]

1. Distribute a nonfiction or fiction excerpt to students. Ask them to make notes that identify where in the text they would use various skills and strategies and how they would apply them. For example, the first note would most likely be a preview note that explains what can be learned from the title, other text features, and the first paragraph.
2. Discuss where students place their notes. Using their ideas, perform a Read Aloud/Think Aloud modeling exercise for one or two paragraphs.
3. Then have pairs complete the Read Aloud. Circulate around the room to check their comprehension of the skills and strategies.

BEST PRACTICES TOOLKIT—Transparency
Read Aloud/Think Aloud p. A34

MODEL: SHORT STORY

This story is about a 16-year-old girl named Saeng, who has moved with her family from Laos to the United States. The time has come for Saeng to take her driver's test. The stakes are high because Saeng's family is counting on her to be their sole driver. In this excerpt, David, a fellow classmate, is letting Saeng borrow his car to take the exam. As you read, use the **Close Read** questions to practice the skills and strategies you just learned.

from The Winter Hibiscus

Short story by **Minfong Ho**

"Ready?" David asked, eyebrow arched quizzically as he handed her his car keys.

Saeng nodded. Her mouth suddenly felt dry, and she licked her lips.

"Don't forget: Step on the gas real gently. You don't want to jerk the car forward the way you did last time," David said with a grin.

"I won't," Saeng said, and managed a smile.

Another car drove up, and the test instructor stepped out of it and onto the curb in front of them. He was a pale, overweight man whose thick lips jutted out from behind a bushy moustache. On his paunch[1] was balanced a clipboard, which he was busy marking.

Finally he looked up and saw Saeng. "Miss Saeng Panouvong?" he asked, slurring the name so much that Saeng did not recognize it as her own until she felt David nudge her slightly.

"Y—yes, sir," Saeng answered.

"Your turn. Get in."

Then Saeng was behind the wheel, the paunchy man seated next to her, clipboard on his lap.

"Drive to the end of the street and take a right," the test instructor said. He spoke in a low, bored staccato[2] that Saeng had to strain to understand.

Obediently, she started up the car, careful to step on the accelerator very slowly, and eased the car out into the middle of the street. *Check the rearview mirror, make the hand gestures, take a deep breath,* Saeng told herself.

Close Read

1. **Make Inferences** Given David's comments in lines 4–5, what can you infer about Saeng and David's relationship?

2. **Monitor** How can you tell that Saeng is nervous? Cite details from lines 1–22 to support your answer.

1. **paunch:** a protruding belly.
2. **staccato:** short, crisp sounds, or way of speaking.

MODEL: SHORT STORY

Tell students that reading this model will enable them to practice the **Skills and Strategies for Active Reading** described on page 12. Each skill and strategy provides different information about and insight into the text. Then read the introduction to the story aloud and discuss important aspects of character, plot, and setting that are revealed.

Have students silently read the excerpt from "The Winter Hibiscus" and answer the **Close Read** questions. The complete story can be found on the *Audio Anthology CD.*

Close Read

Possible answers:

1. *They are good friends. David can be honest with Saeng, and she accepts his criticism. He also wants her to succeed.*
2. *Students might identify these details:*
   - *"Her mouth suddenly felt dry, and she licked her lips." (line 3)*
   - *"managed a smile" (line 6)*
   - *"Check the rearview mirror, make the hand gestures, take a deep breath, Saeng told herself." (lines 21–22)*

If students need help . . . Remind them that if they are not sure of the answer to a question, they should reread that part of the text.

DIFFERENTIATED INSTRUCTION

FOR LESS–PROFICIENT READERS

Comprehension Support [paired option]
Have students read the story in pairs and work together to fill out the second page of their **Reader's Notebook** with questions that they have, connections that they make, and details that they think are important. Discuss what students choose to include in their notebooks and why.

FOR ENGLISH LEARNERS

Options for Reading

- Read the story aloud as students follow along silently. Pause frequently to clarify ideas, answer questions (including the **Close Read** questions), or model strategies.
- Or, have students work in small groups to read the story aloud to each other. Have them use Reciprocal Teaching to increase their comprehension.

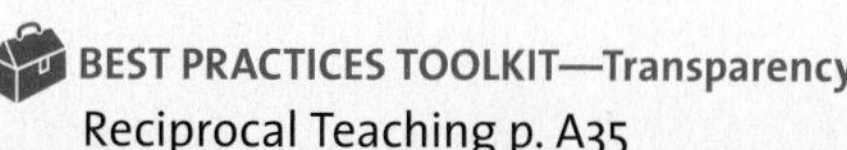

BEST PRACTICES TOOLKIT—Transparency
Reciprocal Teaching p. A35

Close Read

Possible answers:

3. *Students' sketches should show three cars stopped at an intersection, one proceeding in one direction and the other two on a cross street. Students should explain that after all three cars stopped and waited for a moment, the two cars on the cross street finally moved through the intersection, and then Saeng continued forward.*
4. *Students will likely predict that she has failed. She is confused about what to do at the first intersection, and then she runs a stop sign at another street, which is a serious mistake.*
5. *Students' responses will vary, but many will say that being under pressure often leads people to make mistakes because they are trying too hard. Students may support their opinions with references to the story or to personal experiences.*
6. *Saeng is feeling nervous and disappointed. In her heart, she probably knows that she has failed the test.*

If students need help . . . Model the strategies of visualizing, predicting, connecting, and making inferences one at a time, calling upon students to supply the details from the text that will help answer the **Close Read** questions.

So far, so good. At the intersection at the end of the street, she slowed down. Two cars were coming down the cross street toward her at quite a high speed. Instinctively, she stopped and waited for them both to drive past. Instead, they both stopped, as if waiting for her to proceed.

Saeng hesitated. Should she go ahead and take the turn before them or wait until they went past?

Better to be cautious, she decided, and waited, switching gears over to neutral.

For what seemed an interminable[3] moment, nobody moved. Then the other cars went through the intersection, one after the other. Carefully, Saeng then took her turn (*turn signal, hand signal, look both ways*).

As she continued to drive down the street, out of the corner of her eye she saw the instructor mark down something on his clipboard.

A mistake, she thought. *He's writing down a mistake I just made. But what did I do wrong?* She stole a quick look at his face. It was stern but impassive. *Maybe I should ask him right now, what I did wrong,* Saeng wondered.

"Watch out!" he suddenly exclaimed. "That's a stop sign!"

Startled, Saeng jerked the car to a stop—but not soon enough. They were right in the middle of the crossroads.

The instructor shook his head. An almost imperceptible[4] gesture, but Saeng noted it with a sinking feeling in her stomach.

"Back up," he snapped.

Her heart beating hard, Saeng managed to reverse the car and back up to the stop sign that she had just gone through.

"You might as well go back to where we started out," the instructor said. "Take a right here, and another right at the next intersection."

It's over, Saeng thought. *He doesn't even want to see me go up the hill or parallel park or anything. I've failed.*

Swallowing hard, she managed to drive the rest of the way back. In the distance she could see the big M archway outside the McDonald's restaurant, and as she approached, she noticed David standing on the opposite curb, hands on his hips, watching their approach.

With gratitude she noticed that he had somehow managed to stake out two parking spaces in a row so that she could have plenty of space to swerve into place.

She breathed a deep sigh of relief when the car was safely parked. Only after she had turned off the ignition did she dare look the instructor in the face.

"How—how did I do, sir?" she asked him, hating the quaver in her own voice.

"You'll get your results in the mail next week," he said in that bored monotone again, as if he had parroted the same sentence countless times. Then he must have seen the anxious, pleading look on Saeng's face, for he seemed to soften somewhat. "You stopped when you didn't need to—you had right of way[5] at that first intersection," he said. "Then at the second intersection, when you should have stopped at the stop sign, you went right through it." He shrugged. "Too bad," he mumbled. . . .

3. **interminable:** seeming to be without end.
4. **imperceptible:** extremely subtle; hard to notice.
5. **right of way:** customary or legal right of one car to pass in front of another.

Close Read

3. **Visualize** Reread the boxed text, picturing where each car stops. Then give a short summary of what happened at the intersection. (Hint: Sketch the scene in your notebook.)
4. **Predict** Given what's happened so far, do you think Saeng will pass the test? Give a reason for your prediction.
5. **Connect** Do most people perform well under pressure, or are they more likely to make mistakes? Support your opinion.
6. **Make Inferences** What do you think Saeng might be thinking or feeling as the instructor is evaluating her performance on the test?

DIFFERENTIATED INSTRUCTION

FOR LESS-PROFICIENT READERS

Comprehension Support Show students how using a chart such as this one can help them make predictions or inferences. Then have them work together to show how they would answer question 6 using the chart.

Text Details	Prior Knowledge	Prediction or Inference
Saeng goes through a stop sign (lines 38–40).	Going through a stop sign is a serious mistake.	Saeng probably realizes that she failed the test and feels disappointed.

Strategies That Work: Reading

❶ Know Your Purpose

Determining ahead of time *why* you are reading will help focus your effort. Make sure you're using the best strategy for your purpose.

Purpose	Strategy
For Enjoyment	Don't feel you have to hurry. Read at a comfortable pace for you.
To Learn	Take notes on the main ideas and supporting details as you read.
For Research	Remember that you don't have to read every word. Use subheadings, captions, and graphic aids to help you quickly locate information.
To Follow Directions	Closely follow each step. Use illustrations or photographs as guides.

❷ Use Graphic Organizers

Recording your ideas in a graphic organizer can help you analyze and make sense of characters, relationships, and events. Depending on your purpose, you might use a cluster diagram, a Y-chart, or a time line.

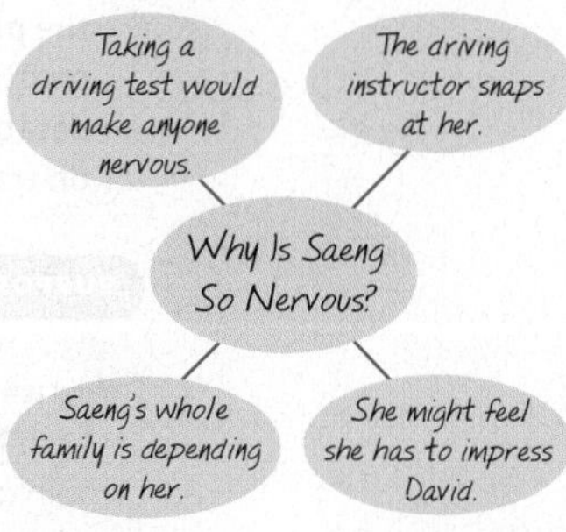

❸ Create a Personal Word List

Tracking down the meanings of words can enrich your understanding of any story—and expand your vocabulary. Start a personal word list and keep adding to it.

- **Choose new words.** The words you include are up to you. As a starting point, you might list the vocabulary words for the selections in this book.
- **Meaning goes beyond the definition.** You have to be able to do more than remember dictionary definitions. Make sure you know synonyms and antonyms for the word and can use it in a sentence.
- **Get some practice.** Visit the **Vocabulary Center** at **ClassZone.com** for interactive practice.
- **Add a word a day.** Find new words in magazines and on Web sites, or be listening for them in conversation. Find their meanings, and make them yours!

Word	*Meaning*
quizzically *adv.* *"The Winter Hibiscus," line 1*	***Definition:*** *expressing doubt, curiosity, or confusion* ***Synonyms:*** *curiously, questioningly* ***Antonyms:*** *knowingly, seriously* ***Sentence:*** *"So, you finished all your homework?" my mother asked quizzically when she saw me watching TV.*

DIFFERENTIATED INSTRUCTION

FOR LESS–PROFICIENT READERS

Concept Support [paired option] Have students work in pairs to complete their **Reader's Notebook** entries, including their vocabulary lists. Discuss the ideas that they include and ways that they might record their information in a graphic organizer or other format.

FOR ENGLISH LEARNERS

Vocabulary Support [mixed-readiness groups] Have students volunteer unknown words from "The Winter Hibiscus." Record them on the board and then assign several to different small groups. Have the groups use context clues and a dictionary to define them. Have groups share their definitions.

Strategies That Work: Reading

Tell students that the strategies described on this page complement the active reading skills and strategies that they employed during their reading of "The Winter Hibiscus."

1. **Know Your Purpose** Tell students that no matter what their purpose, they should read actively. However, their purpose does determine their reading rate and whether or not they take notes during reading. Have volunteers read the strategy for each purpose aloud. Discuss when students have used these strategies in the past and the ways in which they have been effective.
2. **Use Graphic Organizers** Explain that graphic organizers help clarify and show relationships among the details in a selection. For example, a cluster diagram like the one on page 15 shows the development of one main idea. A Y chart shows the ways in which two items are similar or different. A timeline clarifies chronological or sequential order.

   Distribute copies of a brief work of nonfiction. Have students explain their reading strategy and then choose a graphic organizer that they might use to record the important ideas. Discuss their choices.
3. **Create a Personal Word List** Remind students that their **Reader's Notebook** is a good place to keep their list of words and definitions. Help students access the **Vocabulary Center** at **ClassZone.com.**

CHECK UNDERSTANDING Have students complete a graphic organizer that summarizes what happens during Saeng's driving test (pages 13–14).

OBJECTIVES

- understand the relationship between **purpose, audience,** and **format**
- become familiar with the stages of the writing process
- become familiar with the key traits of effective writing
- understand how rubrics can be used to evaluate writing

Consider Your Options

Read aloud the introductory paragraph and the ideas under **Purpose, Audience,** and **Format.** Then draw this diagram on the board to emphasize that the elements are closely related and interdependent.

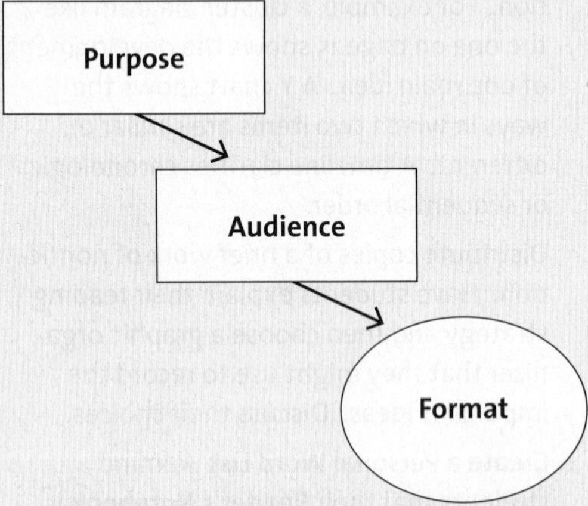

Explain to students that writers most often think about the purpose of their writing first. Once they make a decision about why they are writing, then they can choose the format that will help them fulfill their purpose and best meet the needs of their intended audience. For example, if they want to entertain a friend with an account of their trip to the Grand Canyon, they might choose to write an e-mail or a friendly letter. If they want to draw attention to the need to preserve natural resources in the United States, including sites such as the Grand Canyon, they might write an editorial or article for the school newspaper. If they want to describe the grandeur of the setting, they might write a poem or a descriptive essay. Invite students to think of other reasons that they might want to write about the Grand Canyon. Have them identify an audience and a format for each.

Writing Process Workshop

Expressing Ideas in Writing

Writing is a way to let others know who you are and how your mind works. Through the right words, you can express laugh-out-loud humor, inspiring thoughts, or strong opinions and then share those ideas with the world. You might be writing to your favorite musician, a teacher, an e-mail buddy, or the entire blogosphere. In each case, your words can carry an important message.

Consider Your Options

Any work of writing starts with careful planning. Long before your polished ideas hit the page or screen, take the time to ask some basic questions about the **purpose** and **format** of your writing, and your intended **audience**. Are you crafting a research paper for class or posting a short movie review to an online database? Questions like these can help you get off to a good start—and stay on track later on.

PURPOSE

Why am I writing?
- to entertain
- to inform or explain
- to persuade
- to describe
- to express thoughts and feelings
- to inspire

AUDIENCE

Who are my readers?
- classmates
- teachers
- friends
- community members
- customer service at a company
- Web users

FORMAT

Which format will best suit my purpose and audience?
- essay
- speech
- letter
- research paper
- poem
- short story
- review
- journal entry
- script
- Web site
- power presentation

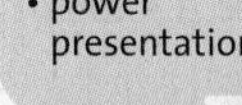

DIFFERENTIATED INSTRUCTION

FOR LESS–PROFICIENT READERS

Concept Support [small-group option] Distribute various examples of writing to students, including editorials, humorous essays, movie reviews, and home pages of Web sites. Have them work in groups to chart the purpose, audience, and format of each. Discuss students' responses and their reasoning.

FOR ENGLISH LEARNERS

Vocabulary Support Make sure students understand that *audience* as it is used on this page refers to readers as well as to those listening to or watching a production.

Continue with the Process

The more you write, the more you'll understand your own process of writing. It takes practice, but eventually you will find what works best for you. As you tackle the **Writing Workshops** in this book, begin by following this basic process.

THE WRITING PROCESS

What Should I Do?	*What Does It Look Like?*
PREWRITING Explore your ideas and decide what you want to write about. To get your ideas flowing, try **freewriting, listing,** or using one of the other prewriting strategies described on page 19.	**LISTING** *Ideas from Slam!* • *passion for an activity* • *what activities am I good at?* • *what if I had to give up doing something I love? (possible short story idea?)*
DRAFTING Transform your prewriting efforts into a rough draft. For a formal essay, it might be helpful to **draft from an outline.** For an informal essay, **draft to discover**—in other words, let your ideas take shape as you write. If you're writing a short story, create a **story map.**	**STORY MAP** ***Setting:*** *High school; Midwestern town.* ***Characters:*** *Judy Brack (student); Mr. Brack (Judy's dad); Mr. Valdez (basketball coach)* ***Conflict:*** *Judy joins boys' basketball team without parents' approval. They want her to quit the team. Should she?*
REVISING AND EDITING Review your draft. Look for ways to clarify the ideas, style, and structure of your writing. • Review the **rubric** (page 18). • Ask a classmate to review your work. • **Proofread** for errors in spelling and grammar.	**PEER SUGGESTIONS** *Judy scored a basket as the buzzer sounded. Her teammates cheered, but she didn't feel like celebrating.* ***Suggestion:*** *Add details to convey the excitement of the game. Try: "Swoosh. From the three-point line, Judy heard the familiar sound of the ball gliding through the net."*
PUBLISHING Share your finished piece with others. Your purpose, audience, and format will determine your publishing choices. Visit the **Writing Center** at **ClassZone.com** for options.	**PUBLISHING OPTIONS**  

Continue with the Process

Read the introductory paragraph aloud. Before continuing, ask students to discuss with a partner the way in which they approach a writing assignment. Tell students that even if they haven't formally followed the four stages of the writing process, they have probably already used some or all of the steps that are outlined on page 17.

Prewriting Read the paragraph aloud. Then discuss other methods that students might use, including the Invisible Writing strategy, as well as graphic organizers, such as webs and cluster diagrams.

 **BEST PRACTICES TOOLKIT**
Invisible Writing p. C2

Drafting Discuss the methods of drafting identified in this paragraph. Then present students with some of the writing templates that might help them organize their ideas for a first draft.

 **BEST PRACTICES TOOLKIT**
Writing Templates p. C16

Revising and Editing Review each approach to revising and editing. Make sure students understand these terms:

- *rubric:* a list of qualities that a strong paper should have
- *proofread:* to read something carefully to look for specific errors

Publishing Tell students that any time they share their work, they are publishing, even if they are just showing it to a friend.

DIFFERENTIATED INSTRUCTION

FOR LESS–PROFICIENT READERS

Concept Support Guide students through the prewriting step by using this script to model the process:

There are several topics I am interested in, but I know a lot about bad habits so I'll start with that one. I'll use a Spider Map to help me decide which bad habit I'll write about.

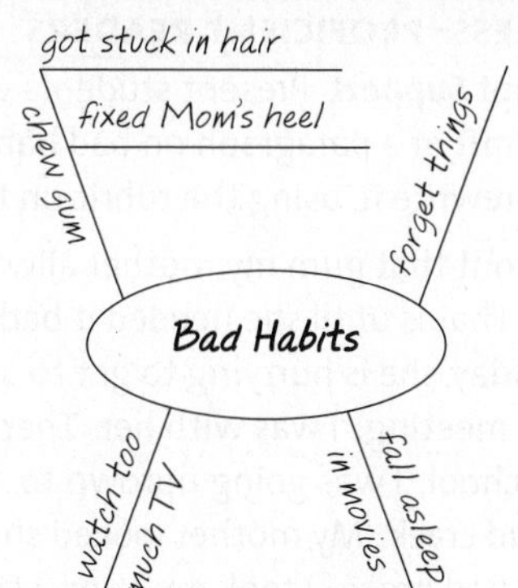

I think I will write about the day my mother's heel broke. I should list the details I want to include in my paragraph:

1. *My mom was hurrying to a big meeting.*
2. *I was with her because there was no school.*
3. *The heel of her shoe broke.*
4. *I used my gum to stick it back on.*

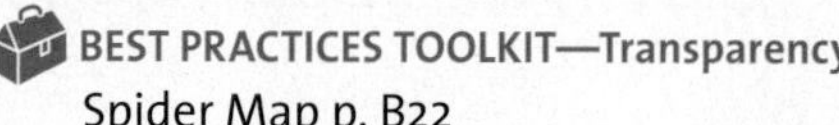
BEST PRACTICES TOOLKIT—Transparency
Spider Map p. B22

Do a Self-Check

Tell students that using a rubric helps them focus on specific areas of their writing. Review each of the **Key Traits** in the rubric to make sure students understand its meaning and purpose.

- **Ideas** Tell students that depending on the purpose connected to their main idea, they will use various supporting details. For example, a narrative paragraph or essay will be developed through incidents. Ask students what kinds of details they would use to persuade, to explain, and to describe.
- **Organization** Remind students of the various methods that might be used to organize their ideas, such as chronological order, spatial order (order of location), problem-solution, cause and effect, or comparison-contrast. Explain that they need to choose the one that is best suited for their topic.
- **Voice** Make sure students understand the meaning of *tone*. Tone is a writer's attitude toward his or her subject. Tell students that tone must be appropriate for the purpose, audience, and format of their writing. For example, if they are writing a business letter, their tone should be formal and serious. This is achieved by their choice of words and their phrasing.
- **Word Choice** Remind students to choose words that say exactly what they want to convey to their readers.
- **Sentence Fluency** Explain that varying sentence structure and length helps keep the reader's attention. Students should check their writing to make sure that their sentences do not always follow a simple subject-verb-object pattern. They should include some questions as well as a mixture of simple, compound, and complex sentences.
- **Conventions** Tell students that spelling and grammar errors confuse and tire readers, who are less likely to continue reading if they have to work too hard to understand what the writer is saying.

CHECK UNDERSTANDING Have students identify at what stage of the writing process they would focus on conventions.

Do a Self-Check

Professional writers know they can never check their work too often or too thoroughly. Use this **key traits rubric** to evaluate any rough draft.

KEY TRAITS RUBRIC

	Strong	*Average*	*Weak*
Ideas 1	• centers around a clear, focused topic • is supported by vivid, well-chosen details	• has a topic, but it could use more development • contains general statements with some details	• has no clear topic • lacks details or has unclear details
Organization 2	• opens in an engaging way and wraps up with a satisfying conclusion • flows in a logical manner	• has both an introduction and a conclusion, but they are uninteresting • lacks some transitions	• has no real introduction or conclusion • contains a confusing jumble of ideas
Voice 3	• conveys a strong sense of individual style • uses a tone that is well suited to the purpose and audience	• sounds "flat" in some places • lapses into an inappropriate tone at times	• has little or no "life" • employs a completely inappropriate tone for the intended purpose and audience
Word Choice 4	• uses words that are precise and colorful • conveys meaning in a powerful yet natural-sounding manner	• uses words that are correct, but ordinary • gets meaning across, but is not memorable	• uses words that are vague or incorrect • fails to convey meaning clearly
Sentence Fluency 5	• includes sentences of varied lengths and structures • creates a pleasing flow from one idea to the next	• has some sentence variety but not enough • lacks flow in some places	• includes mostly short or rambling sentences • is awkward or repetitious
Conventions 6	• shows a strong grasp of grammar and usage • has few problems with mechanics (spelling, capitalization, and punctuation)	• has minor grammar and usage problems • contains some mechanical errors	• has such poor grammar and usage that meaning is unclear • contains so many mechanical errors that the writing is hard to read

DIFFERENTIATED INSTRUCTION

FOR LESS—PROFICIENT READERS

Concept Support Present students with this first draft of a paragraph on bad habits. Have them rewrite it, using the rubric on this page:

Spit out that gum my mother allways tells me. That is until she needed it bad. Last Monday, she is hurrying to get to an important meeting. I was with her. There was no school. I was going uptown to. I heard a loud crack. My mother looked short. Her heel had broke. I took my gum. I stuck her heel on with it. Off she went.

Possible answer: *"Spit out that gum," was my mother's constant refrain, at least until last Monday. On that day, my bad habit came to her rescue! She was hurrying to get to an important meeting at work. I had no school, so I was going uptown with her. Suddenly, we both heard a loud crack, and my mother's right leg shrunk three inches. Her heel had broken off! Quick as a wink, I removed my huge wad of nicely softened gum, stuck her heel on with it, and off she went—balanced once again!*

Strategies That Work: Writing

❶ Use Prewriting Strategies

Anyone who has ever faced a blank page or screen knows how difficult the first steps can be. Try these strategies.

- **Freewrite.** Write for ten minutes, letting whatever comes to you flow without interruption.
- **Get visual.** Use a graphic organizer, such as a cluster diagram or a chart, to flesh out your ideas.
- **Brainstorm with others.** Bounce ideas off other writers for their feedback.
- **Ask big questions.** "Who was the most courageous person in history?" Ask fun or serious questions in search of a topic.

❷ Get Feedback from Peers

Often, it is easier to see trouble spots when the writing is not your own. When you exchange feedback with classmates, keep these guidelines in mind.

When You're the Writer	When You're the Reader
• Ask for specific feedback. Should readers comment on your ideas, look for errors, or both? • Invite your readers to offer honest feedback. Respect their opinions, even if you don't agree. • Clarify their suggestions. Review them on your own, and use the suggestions most helpful to your piece.	• Be respectful of the writer; offer positive feedback first. • Give reasons for your opinions, as well as specific suggestions for improvement. • Offer your feedback, and then let the writer decide on his or her own which changes to make.

❸ Read, Read, Read

Reading will help your writing. Take advantage of reading both peer and professional work. Consider these sources.

LITERATURE
See what worked for the classic and contemporary authors featured in this book. Seek other sources as well, including novels, magazines, and newspapers.

WRITING COMMUNITY
Form a writing group with other students to share your process, works in progress, and finished products.

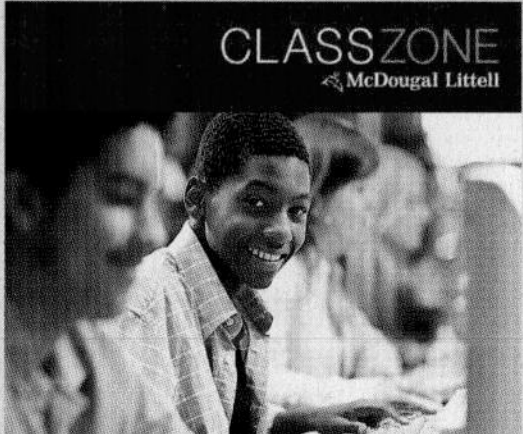

ONLINE RESOURCES
Check out online sources, including the **Writing Center** at **ClassZone.com** for links to blogs and student publications.

Strategies That Work: Writing

Tell students that the strategies on this page will help them with any of their writing, whether in or out of school.

1. **Use Prewriting Strategies** Have volunteers read each strategy aloud. Make sure students understand that freewriting means expressing their thoughts freely, without worrying about relationships among ideas or any sort of order. Explain that brainstorming with others often helps writers make associations that they would not otherwise make. Discuss the other strategies and ask students if and when they have used them in the past.
2. **Get Feedback from Peers** To illustrate the importance of giving feedback in a constructive way, model how not to give it. Model some feedback that is vague or that shows disrespect for the writer. Ask students to critique the content and method of delivery and discuss the possible effect of receiving feedback in this way. Then read the tasks for both writers and readers in the chart and model a constructive way to give feedback, based on these guidelines. Tell students that the rubric on page 18 will help them be more efficient peer readers as they look for those key traits in each other's writing.
3. **Read, Read, Read** Ask students to identify works that they have read recently and found inspiring. Why? Did they like the subject of the writing or admire the style of the author? Explain that, as writers, they can learn a great deal from others' works about what makes good writing and how to produce it. Encourage students to start their own writing groups. If possible, offer to help students access online resources, particularly the **Writing Center** at **ClassZone.com.**

DIFFERENTIATED INSTRUCTION

FOR LESS–PROFICIENT READERS

Concept Support [small-group option]
Provide students with an example of weak writing and discuss ways in which it might be improved. Then have pairs of students practice giving feedback to each other in small groups. Have group members evaluate each pair's efforts.

UNIT 1

The Main Events

PLOT AND CONFLICT

- In Fiction
- In Drama
- In Media
- In Nonfiction
- In Poetry

21

About the Art The photograph on the right illustrates "Raymond's Run" by Toni Cade Bambara, and the image on the left illustrates "The Ransom of Red Chief" by O. Henry. See pages 42 and 52.

For help in planning this unit, see

 RESOURCE MANAGER UNIT 1 pp. 1–11

INTRODUCE THE UNIT

One thing that distinguishes humans from most other living things is our curiosity. Whenever we come across interesting events or situations—on a news program, for example, or in real life—we are brimming over with questions. What is going on here? What problem are these people trying to solve? What will happen next, and how will everyone react? Ask students to share examples of exciting events they recently witnessed or heard about and discuss what made each event exciting. Have them keep these ideas in mind as they think about the images on this page. To spark a discussion, ask these questions:

- Look closely at the pictures. What is happening in each one? What might each person be feeling or thinking? What is revealed about each person, and what is hidden?
- What events might have brought these people together? What might happen next?

Discuss how each image is a doorway into another world. In this unit, students will explore how authors use **plot** and **conflict** to create stories that take readers to these interesting places.

UNIT 1

Skills Trace

SKILLS STRAND	Reader's Workshop: Plot and Conflict pp. 24–31	Raymond's Run pp. 32–45 Short Story *Level: Average*	The Ransom of Red Chief pp. 46–61 Short Story *Level: Challenging*	Clean Sweep pp. 62–75 Short Story *Level: Average*	The Tell-Tale Heart pp. 76–85 Short Story *Level: Challenging*	The Hitchhiker pp. 86–99 Radio Play *Level: Average*	Great Reads: *from* Hoot pp. 100–105 Mystery Novel *Level: Average*
Literary Analysis	Conflict pp. 24–31 Stages of Plot pp. 26–31	Plot pp. 33, 34, 37, 38, 40, 41, 42, 43	Conflict and Resolution pp. 47, 50, 51, 53, 55, 57, 59	Internal and External Conflict pp. 63, 64, 66, 68, 69, 71, 73	Suspense pp. 77, 80, 81, 83, 84	Foreshadowing pp. 87, T88, T90, T91, T92, T93, T94, T96, T97, 98	Form (Mystery Novel) p. 100
Reading and Informational Texts	Analyze the Literature pp. 25, 27–31	Make Inferences pp. 33, 36, 38, 41, 43	Predict pp. 47, 48, 50, 51, 53, 54, 55, 57, 59 Review: Make Inferences pp. 53, 57 Read an Anecdote p. 58	Understand Sequence pp. 63, 66, 67, 69, 72, 73 Review: Predict p. 70	Evaluate Narrator pp. 77, 78, 81, 84	Strategies for Reading a Radio Play pp. 87, T90, T91, T92, T95, T96, 98	
Vocabulary	Academic Vocabulary pp. 24, 26	Word Acquisition pp. 33, T33, 44 Context Clues p. T33 Compound Words p. 44	Word Acquisition pp. 47, T47, 60 Word Maps p. T47 Prefixes (*com-*) p. 60	Word Acquisition pp. 63, T63, 74 Context Clues p. T63 Suffixes That Form Nouns p. 74	Word Acquisition pp. 77, T77, 85 Context Clues p. T77 Reference Aids (Dictionary and Thesaurus) p. 85	Word Acquisition pp. 87, T87 Context Clues p. T87	
Writing, Grammar, and Style		Sentence Fragments p. 45	Methods to Correct Run-On Sentences p. 61	Punctuation of Possessives p. 75		Pronoun-Antecedent Agreement p. 99	
Speaking, Listening, Viewing, and Media	Discuss pp. 24–26	Discuss pp. 32, T34–T42, 43 Analyze Visuals pp. 34, 39, 42	Discuss pp. 46, T48–T58, 59 Analyze Visuals pp. 48, 52	Discuss pp. 62, T64–T72, 73 Analyze Visuals pp. 64, 68	Discuss pp. 76, T78–T83, 84 Analyze Visuals pp. 78, 82	Discuss pp. 86, T88–T97, 98 Analyze Visuals pp. T88, T93, T96	Discuss pp. 100, T105

Assessment-Based Planning: Skills in red are assessed on the Unit 1 Test. **T** = Teacher's Edition page

Media Study: *from* **The Sisterhood of the Traveling Pants** pp. 106–109 Film Clip	**My First Free Summer** pp. 110–117 Memoir *Level: Easy*	**The Great Rat Hunt** pp. 118–131 Memoir *Level: Easy*	*Linked selections* **Paul Revere's Ride** pp. 132–139 Narrative Poem *Level: Average*	*Linked selections* **The Other Riders** pp. 140–143 History Article	**Writing Workshop: Personal Narrative** pp. 144–151
	Memoir pp. 111, 113, 114, 115, 116	Conflict in Nonfiction pp. 119, 120, 122, 123, 124, 126, 128, 129	Narrative Poetry pp. 133, 134, 135, 137, 138, 139 Review: Suspense pp. 136, 139	Form (History Article) pp. 141, 142, 143	
	Identify Cause and Effect pp. 111, 112, 114, 115, 116	Track Chronological Order pp. 119, 122, 124, 127, 129	Paraphrase pp. 133, 136, 137, 139	Take Notes pp. 140, 141, 142, 143 Compare and Contrast p. 143	Analyze a Personal Narrative pp. 145–146, 150
Academic Vocabulary (Film) p. 107	Word Acquisition pp. 111, T111, 117 Context Clues p. T111 Latin Roots (*dict*) p. 117	Word Acquisition pp. 119, T119, 130 Context Clues p. T119 Onomatopoeia p. 130			
		Pronoun Case p. 131			Write a Personal Narrative pp. 144–150 Punctuation of Dialogue p. 150
Discuss pp. 106, 109 Analyze Elements Used to Develop Character and Plot in Film pp. 107–109 Create a Storyboard p. 109	Discuss pp. 110, T112–T115, 116 Analyze Visuals p. 112	Discuss pp. 118, T120–T128, 129 Analyze Visuals pp. 120, 125, T128	Discuss pp. 132, T134–T138, 139 Analyze Visuals p. 134	Discuss pp. 140, T141–T142, 143	Discuss pp. 144–146 Stage a Scene p. 151

Skills Assessed on the Unit 1 Test:

Literary Analysis
- Identify and analyze plot, including stages of plot and suspense
- Identify and analyze conflicts

Reading and Informational Texts
- Understand chronological order in nonfiction
- Understand sequence relationships, including order of events and flashback
- Identify cause-and-effect relationships
- Predict with foreshadowing
- Compare and contrast

Vocabulary
- Determine meanings of derivatives by applying knowledge of Latin words and roots
- Use a dictionary

Writing, Grammar, and Style
- Write a personal narrative
- Avoid sentence fragments
- Understand and use pronouns and their antecedents correctly
- Punctuate possessives correctly
- Additional writing and grammar skills

For additional lesson planning help, see **Easy Planner DVD.**

OBJECTIVES

- establish prior knowledge about **stories**
- discuss the qualities that make a good story

What makes a STORY *worth telling?*

Ask students to think about the variety of settings, characters, and situations that different stories can have. In spite of this diversity, what do they think all good stories have in common?

ACTIVITY Suggest that students jot down their answers to the first two questions before they meet in groups. As they discuss their favorite stories, ask them to think about the following questions: Do they prefer stories set in the past, in the present, or in the future? Do they like characters who are similar to themselves or very different? Are they hooked by exciting events or by quiet ones that show how characters feel? After the discussion, ask them which of the stories mentioned by their classmates they would most like to read, and why.

CHECK UNDERSTANDING Have students summarize the qualities they have decided a good **story** must have.

UNIT 1 Share What You Know

What makes a STORY *worth telling?*

A great **story** can make you laugh, cry, or gasp in surprise, but one thing is for sure: you'll give it your full attention. You might even forget your own troubles as the story unfolds or gain an insight that will change the way you view your life. Something about the fabulous setting, the compelling characters, or the unusual situations presented will stay with you long after you close the book or turn away from the screen.

ACTIVITY Think about the last time you thought to yourself, "That's a great story!" With a group of classmates, discuss the following:

- What story did you think was special?
- Why did you like that story so much?
- How do your reasons for liking it compare with others' reasons for liking what they did?

Based on your discussion, come up with a list of qualities that make a story worth telling.

22

Unit Resources

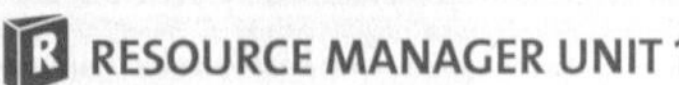

- **RESOURCE MANAGER UNIT 1**
- **BEST PRACTICES TOOLKIT**
- **STANDARDS LESSON FILE**
- Easy Planner DVD
- Write*Smart* CD
- ClassZone.com
- Audio Anthology CD
- Multi-Language Academic Vocabulary Online
- eEdition CD & Online
- McDougal Littell Assessment System
- Test Generator CD
- Media*Smart* DVD

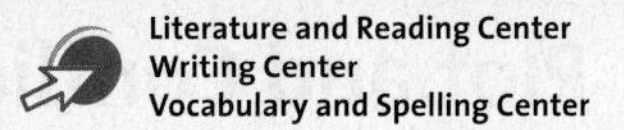
Literature and Reading Center
Writing Center
Vocabulary and Spelling Center

Preview Unit Goals

LITERARY ANALYSIS	• Identify and analyze stages of plot, including exposition, rising action, climax, falling action, and resolution • Identify and analyze types of conflicts • Analyze suspense • Identify and analyze foreshadowing and flashback
READING	• Identify and analyze sequence and cause-effect relationships • Use study skills, including taking notes and skimming
WRITING AND GRAMMAR	• Write a personal narrative • Use apostrophes to punctuate possessive nouns correctly • Maintain pronoun-antecedent agreement • Use subject and object pronouns correctly
SPEAKING, LISTENING, AND VIEWING	• Identify and analyze film elements; analyze plot in a film • Stage a scene
VOCABULARY	• Use knowledge of word roots, base words, and affixes to understand word meaning • Use reference aids, including a dictionary and a thesaurus
ACADEMIC VOCABULARY	• stages of plot • flashback • personal narrative • conflict • foreshadowing

DIFFERENTIATED INSTRUCTION

FOR ENGLISH LEARNERS

Academic Vocabulary [paired option] Use the Academic Vocabulary copy master to teach these terms: *stages of plot, conflict, flashback, foreshadowing, personal narrative.*

1. Read each example. Ask students if they have heard any of these terms before and, if so, in what context.
2. Have students work with a partner to write definitions for the words.
3. Allow students to work individually or in pairs to complete Part B.

Additional Academic Vocabulary [small-group option] Use the second copy master to introduce the terms *cause-effect relationship, pronoun-antecedent agreement, possessive noun, subject pronoun, object pronoun,* and *affix.*

1. Have students work in small groups to complete the sentences.
2. Have students complete Part B individually or with their groups.

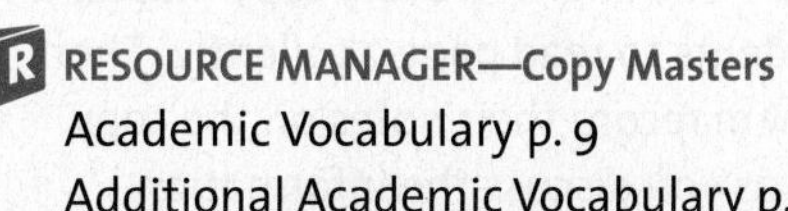
RESOURCE MANAGER—Copy Masters
Academic Vocabulary p. 9
Additional Academic Vocabulary p. 10

Preview Unit Goals

This page gives students an overview of the skills and strategies covered in Unit 1. Point out the different colors of each skill strand and explain that throughout the unit each skill within a strand matches that color. As they read this page, have students consider their ability to use each skill and strategy.

Encourage students to copy the Academic Vocabulary terms in their journals and define them in their own words as they read the unit. Encourage students to use these terms as they discuss and write about the selections.

ADDITIONAL UNIT GOALS

These skills will be taught in this unit but are not the major focus of the unit:

Literary Analysis

- Identify and analyze subplot
- Identify and evaluate narrator
- Identify and analyze irony
- Study a variety of genres: short story, memoir, narrative poetry, mystery novel, radio play, history article

Reading

- Make predictions
- Make inferences and support them
- Trace chronological order
- Compare and contrast legend with true account
- Use graphic organizers to organize ideas

Writing and Grammar

- Insert subjects and predicates to correct sentence fragments
- Correct run-on sentences by using end marks, coordinating conjunctions, and semicolons

Speaking, Listening, and Viewing

- Create a storyboard

Vocabulary

- Use context to determine meanings of compound words
- Use structural analysis to identify word roots, base words, and affixes

Focus and Motivate

OBJECTIVES

- identify and analyze types of conflict (internal, external)
- identify and analyze the stages of plot (exposition, rising action, climax, falling action, resolution)

Teach

Part 1: Conflict—The Fuel of a Story

External Conflict Point out that the external conflicts found in literature and in movies also exist in real life. On the board, begin a web diagram. Ask the class to identify external conflicts that an eighth-grade student might face, and record their ideas in the diagram. Discuss whether any of the external conflicts listed are more difficult to deal with than others. Note that characters, like real people, may face several external conflicts at the same time.

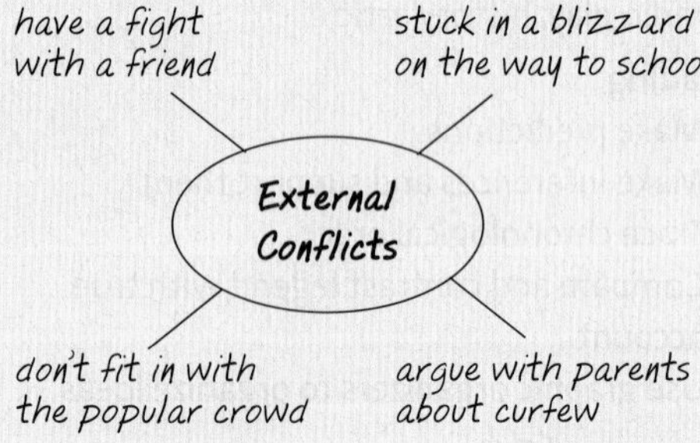

Internal Conflict Point out that an internal conflict is often a choice between two alternatives that are both appealing in some way. Create another web diagram and have students suggest kinds of internal conflicts a student might face. Note that the way a character deals with an internal conflict may lead to other internal and external conflicts.

BEST PRACTICES TOOLKIT—Copy Masters
Analysis Frame: Plot pp. D23, D30, D31

UNIT 1
Reader's Workshop

Plot and Conflict

Will the hero save the world *and* win the girl? Can the young soldier survive the war? How will the family stay alive on the deserted island? Good stories are all around you—in novels and short stories, on television, and in movies. How do they capture your imagination and keep you riveted? Read on to find out.

Part 1: Conflict—The Fuel of a Story

A knight must slay a fierce dragon. A girl faces the consequences of betraying her friend. No matter what they're about, all good stories are fueled by conflict. A **conflict,** or a struggle between opposing forces, can be external or internal.

- An **external conflict** involves a struggle between a character and an outside force, such as another character, a force of nature, or society.
- An **internal conflict** is a struggle that takes place within a character's own mind, as he or she wrestles with difficult thoughts, feelings, or choices.

Whether it is external or internal, a conflict is what drives a story forward, from its beginning to its end. How will the characters handle the conflict? What obstacles will they face? Such questions prompt you to keep turning the pages.

Examine the different types of conflicts described in this graphic.

TYPES OF CONFLICTS

External

Character vs. Character
Ling overhears Julian bragging about his malicious plan to ridicule her best friend. Angered, she confronts Julian and becomes even more incensed when he denies every word. (*Ling vs. Julian*)

External

Character vs. Force of Nature
A blinding snowstorm hits while Yoni is hiking in unfamiliar territory. Suddenly, he loses his bearings and has no idea how to find his way home. (*Yoni vs. snowstorm*)

External

Character vs. Society
The year is 1961. Sarah works in a factory at a time when workers must put in long hours and deal with dismal, even dangerous, conditions on the job. (*Sarah vs. poor working conditions*)

Internal

Character vs. Self
Hannah accepted Raj's marriage proposal against the strong wishes of her family. If she marries him, they will never speak to her again. It's one day before the wedding, and Hannah is doubting her decision. (*marry Raj and alienate her family vs. call off the wedding and lose her true love*)

DIFFERENTIATED INSTRUCTION

FOR ALL STUDENTS
For general guidelines on differentiating instruction, see

BEST PRACTICES TOOLKIT
Differentiated Instruction pp. 31–38

FOR LESS-PROFICIENT READERS
Note Taking Hand out the Note Taking: Conflict—The Fuel of a Story copy master and ask students to read page 24 silently. Then have them record their notes on the copy master as you discuss the information.

RESOURCE MANAGER—Copy Master
Note Taking p. 15

Identify Types of Conflict [paired option]
Have students work in pairs. Each student should think of a recent television program and write down three conflicts faced by characters in that program. Students should then switch papers and label each conflict as external or internal. Have each pair share one example of each type of conflict with the class.

MODEL 1: EXTERNAL CONFLICT

Johnny Tremain, a poor orphaned silversmith, believes he is related to the wealthy merchant Mr. Lyte. Johnny has proof—a cup engraved with the Lyte family name. How does Mr. Lyte react to the news?

from Johnny Tremain

Novel by **Esther Forbes**

"I think," said Mr. Lyte quietly, "all of you ladies and gentlemen will agree that this cup our—ah, cousin, is it?—has brought back tonight is one of this set?"

There was a murmur of assent. Johnny could hear the tiny tinkle, seemingly far away, of Miss Lavinia's spinet.[1]

"It is perfectly obvious that this cup now stands where it belongs. The question is how was it ever separated from its fellows?"

Johnny felt that everyone there except himself knew the answer to this question.

"In fact," the merchant's voice was as smooth as oil, "I declare this to be the very cup which was stolen from me by thieves. They broke through yonder window on the twenty-third of last August. Sheriff, I order you to arrest this boy for burglary."

1. **spinet:** a small, compact upright piano.

Close Read

1. In your own words, describe the conflict that Johnny is facing.
2. Johnny's conflict isn't fully revealed until lines 11–12. What details earlier in the excerpt suggest that a problem is brewing?

MODEL 2: INTERNAL CONFLICT

Eva is thrilled when her friend Kenisha moves back to town. Most of the time, Kenisha is too involved with the popular crowd to acknowledge her old friend. In fact, Kenisha is only nice when she wants to copy Eva's homework. How does Eva feel after she lets Kenisha copy her work?

from *Eva* and the **Mayor**

Short story by **Jean Davies Okimoto**

Eva knew it wasn't right to copy other people's work, but it wasn't as bad as cheating on a test, and a lot of people did it. She knew that didn't make it right, but still it didn't seem like such a big sin, and besides, she wasn't the copier. [The whole thing made her feel pretty mixed up.]

She didn't know for sure if she had let Kenisha copy her work because of all that stuff Gramma Evelyn said about being nice to Kenisha or because she wanted to get in with Kenisha and be one of the cool people.

Close Read

1. What details suggest that Eva is conflicted about her decision to let Kenisha copy her homework? One detail is [boxed.]
2. In your opinion, is Eva overcome with guilt? Support your answer.

MODEL 1: EXTERNAL CONFLICT

Close Read

1. ***Possible answer:*** *Johnny's conflict is with Mr. Lyte, who accuses him of burglary and orders him to be arrested (lines 9–12).*
2. ***Possible answer:*** *These details suggest that a problem is brewing:*
   - *Mr. Lyte refers to Johnny as his "cousin, is it?" (line 2), suggesting that he might not believe Johnny is really a cousin.*
   - *The question Mr. Lyte asks about how the cup was "separated" from the others (lines 5–6) suggests that something is amiss.*
   - *Johnny feels "that everyone there except himself knew the answer to this question" (lines 7–8), suggesting that he is being set up for an unpleasant surprise.*

MODEL 2: INTERNAL CONFLICT

Close Read

1. ***Possible answer:*** *These details suggest Eva's internal conflict:*
   - *"it wasn't as bad as cheating on a test" (lines 1–2)*
   - *"it didn't seem like such a big sin" (line 3)*
   - *"besides, she wasn't the copier" (lines 3–4)*
   - *"The whole thing made her feel pretty mixed up" (line 4)*

   All of these details, including the boxed one, reflect the fact that Eva is trying to convince herself that what she did was not so bad, although deep down she knows that what she did was wrong, regardless of why she did it.
2. ***Possible answer:*** *Yes. The way Eva keeps turning the matter over in her mind, looking at it from all different perspectives and trying not to feel so bad about it, suggests that she is overcome with guilt.*

FOR ENGLISH LEARNERS

Concept Support: Internal Conflict Distribute copies of the Open Mind graphic organizer. Ask students to draw a line down the middle and label the two sides "Better" and "Worse." Then have students record thoughts from the passage that make Eva feel better and worse about what she did.

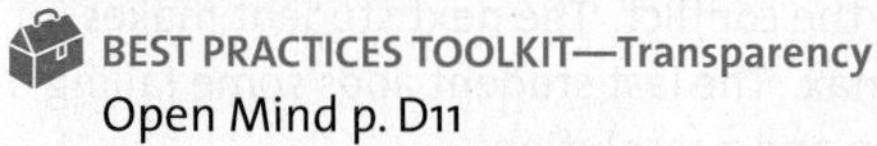
BEST PRACTICES TOOLKIT—Transparency
Open Mind p. D11

FOR ADVANCED LEARNERS/PRE-AP*

Explore a Conflict [small-group option] Have students work in small groups. One group should write about how Kenisha feels after copying Eva's homework. Another should write about how Gramma Evelyn feels when Eva tells her what she did. It is possible that both characters will have conflicting feelings. Ask each group to share their work with the class.

Part 2: Stages of Plot

Plot Explain to students that a successful writer must have a plan or approach for telling a story effectively. Without some exposition, the reader would not understand who the main character is or the basic situation of the story. Without rising action, the plot would go nowhere, and the reader would lose interest. Without a climax, the reader would not experience excitement and suspense as the conflicts reach a crisis point. Without falling action, the reader would not see what happens as a result of the climax. Without a resolution, the reader might still have questions regarding the outcome of the conflict and its effect on the main character.

Display the Plot Diagram transparency and use it to summarize a familiar story. Prompt students with these questions and record their responses on the transparency:

- **Exposition** When and where does the story take place? Who are the characters? What is the main conflict?
- **Rising Action** What events happen as a result of the conflict? What new problems or obstacles do the characters face?
- **Climax** What is the turning point of the story? When is the conflict most intense?
- **Falling Action** How is the conflict finally resolved?
- **Resolution** After the conflict is resolved, what questions still remain? How does the story tie up these loose ends? Does the story have a surprising twist at the end?

BEST PRACTICES TOOLKIT—Transparency
Plot Diagram p. D12

Part 2: Stages of Plot

To draw readers into a story and maintain their interest, a writer must do more than simply introduce an intriguing conflict. He or she has to show how that conflict develops at every twist and turn, at every stage in the story's plot. A **plot,** or the series of events in a story, typically includes five stages. It's important to remember, though, that not every story follows this exact pattern.

Take a look at the following graphic, which shows a traditional plot structure. Notice what happens to the conflict at the different stages.

PLOT AT A GLANCE

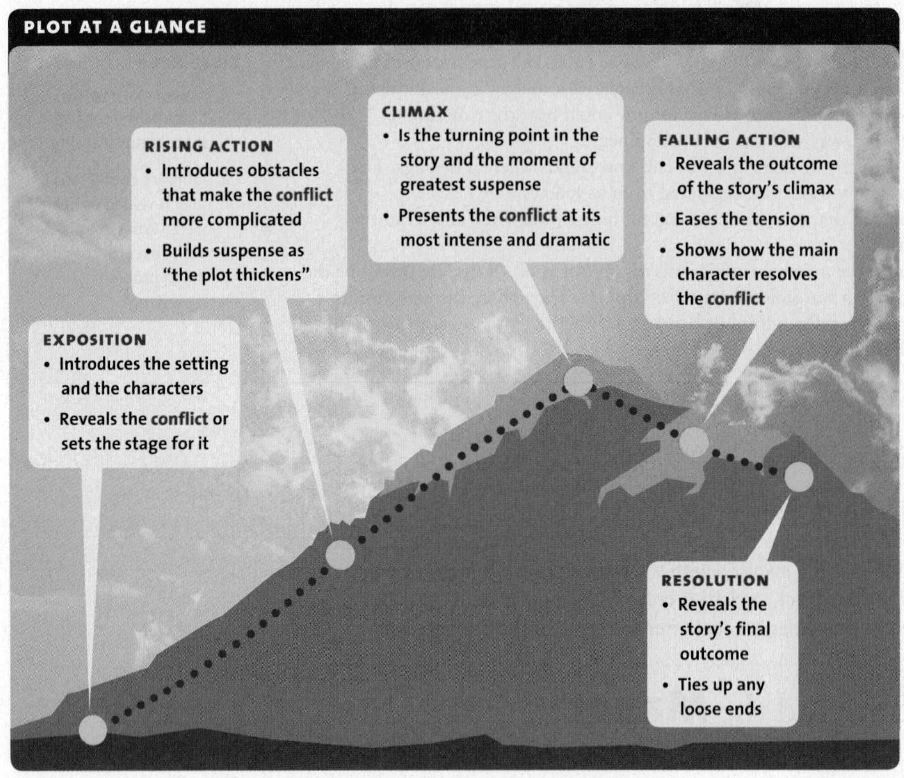

RISING ACTION
• Introduces obstacles that make the conflict more complicated
• Builds suspense as "the plot thickens"
CLIMAX
• Is the turning point in the story and the moment of greatest suspense
• Presents the conflict at its most intense and dramatic
FALLING ACTION
• Reveals the outcome of the story's climax
• Eases the tension
• Shows how the main character resolves the conflict
EXPOSITION
• Introduces the setting and the characters
• Reveals the conflict or sets the stage for it
RESOLUTION
• Reveals the story's final outcome
• Ties up any loose ends

DIFFERENTIATED INSTRUCTION

FOR LESS–PROFICIENT READERS

Note Taking Hand out the Note Taking: Stages of Plot copy master. Read and discuss the information on page 26. Then have students fill in the copy master. Encourage them to define academic terms in their own words so their notes will make sense to them later.

RESOURCE MANAGER—Copy Master
Note Taking p. 16

FOR ADVANCED LEARNERS/PRE–AP

Build Plot Stages Ask four students to help build the stages of plot by making up a simple story. Provide this brief exposition: Juan and Bobby decide to go bowling. Ask the first student to suggest a conflict that these characters must face. The next student should add some rising action that develops from the conflict. The next student makes up a climax. The last student adds some falling action and a resolution.

Part 3: Analyze the Literature

"The Elevator" is about a boy named Martin who recently moved with his father to a new apartment. Living on the seventeenth floor, Martin has no choice but to take the elevator. The idea of the elevator terrifies him. What exactly is Martin so afraid of? Use what you've learned about plot and conflict to analyze this unsettling story.

Short story by **William Sleator**

It was an old building with an old elevator—a very small elevator, with a maximum capacity of three people. Martin, a thin twelve-year-old, felt nervous in it from the first day he and his father moved into the apartment. Of course he was always uncomfortable in elevators, afraid that they would fall, but there was something especially unpleasant about this one. Perhaps its baleful[1] atmosphere was due to the light from the single fluorescent ceiling strip, bleak and dim on the dirty brown walls. Perhaps the problem was the door, which never stayed open quite long enough, and slammed shut with such ominous, clanging finality. Perhaps it was the way the mechanism shuddered in a kind of exhaustion each time it left a floor, as though it might never reach the next one. Maybe it was simply the dimensions of the contraption that bothered him, so small that it felt uncomfortably crowded even when there was only one other person in it.

Coming home from school the day after they moved in, Martin tried the stairs. But they were almost as bad, windowless, shadowy, with several dark landings where the light bulbs had burned out. His footsteps echoed behind him like slaps on the cement, as though there was another person climbing, getting closer. By the time he reached the seventeenth floor, which seemed to take forever, he was winded and gasping.

His father, who worked at home, wanted to know why he was so out of breath. "But why didn't you take the elevator?" he asked, frowning at Martin when he explained about the stairs. Not only are you skinny and weak and bad at sports, his expression seemed to say, but you're also a coward. After that, Martin forced himself to take the elevator. He would have to get used to it, he told himself, just the way he got used to being bullied at school, and always picked last when they chose teams. The elevator was an undeniable fact of life.

Close Read
Exposition (lines 1–40)

1. Reread the boxed details. What do you learn about the main character Martin in the exposition?

1. **baleful:** sinister; ominous.

Practice and Apply

Part 3: Analyze the Literature

Close Read

Exposition (lines 1–40)

1. ***Possible answer:*** *From the boxed details, readers learn that Martin is a twelve-year-old boy who is "uncomfortable in elevators" (line 4), fearing that they might fall. Readers also learn that Martin is not very popular with his classmates, since he is "bullied at school" (line 25) and "always picked last" (line 25) when teams are chosen. Martin feels that his father considers him "bad at sports" (line 22) and "a coward" (line 23). When Martin decides that he will have to "get used to it" (line 24), readers may conclude that Martin will try to deal with his fear of elevators.*

FOR LESS–PROFICIENT READERS

Analysis Support: Plot Lines 1–40 provide the exposition of the story. The setting is an old building. Display a T Chart and label one column "Elevator" and the other "Stairs." Ask students to find specific details that describe these locations and place them on the chart. Ask students how they would feel if they were in either of these places. Which seems more frightening?

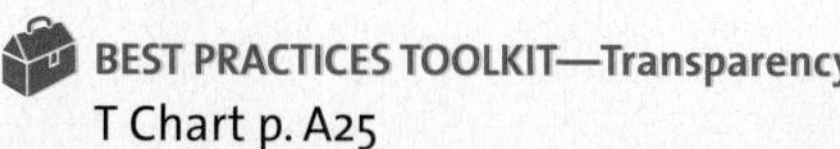

FOR ENGLISH LEARNERS

Concept Support: External and Internal Conflicts Write the following conflicts on the board and ask students to identify each one as external or internal:

- Martin vs. his fear of the elevator *(internal)*
- Martin vs. his father *(external)*
- Martin vs. the stairs *(external)*
- Martin vs. his classmates *(external)*

2. ***Possible answer:*** *The main conflict will probably involve the elevator. Martin is extremely uncomfortable about riding it, but living on the seventeenth floor gives him few options. He has a "fear of being trapped" in the elevator (lines 34–35), and he dislikes being "too close to any other rider" (line 36). The story's conflict will probably involve Martin confronting one or both of these fears.*

Close Read

Rising Action (lines 41–174)

3. ***Possible answer:*** *A large woman gets on the elevator at the fourteenth floor and stares at Martin after the doors close (lines 41–49). This event forces Martin to confront his worst fears and sets the rising action in motion.*
4. *Some students may say that Martin's conflict with this lady is in his head. Evidence includes the following:*
   - *It has been established that Martin would feel uncomfortable with any passenger in the elevator with him (lines 36–40).*
   - *The lady doesn't do anything except watch Martin (lines 67–68).*

   Other students may feel that Martin's conflict is external and cite the following evidence:
   - *Unlike other passengers, the woman "did not stand facing the door" (line 48).*
   - *She stares at him during the entire ride down (lines 56–57).*
   - *She makes it difficult for Martin to leave the elevator (lines 68–70).*

He didn't get used to it. He remained tense in the trembling little box, his eyes fixed on the numbers over the door that blinked on and off so haltingly, as if at any moment they might simply give up. Sometimes he forced himself to look away from them, to the Emergency Stop button, or the red Alarm button. What would happen if he pushed one of them? Would a bell ring? Would the elevator stop between floors? And if it did, how would they get him out?

That was what he hated about being alone on the thing—the fear of being trapped there for hours by himself. But it wasn't much better when there were other passengers. He felt too close to any other rider, too intimate. And he was always very conscious of the effort people made *not* to look at one another, staring fixedly at nothing. Being short, in this one situation, was an advantage, since his face was below the eye level of adults, and after a brief glance they ignored him.

2. Consider what you've read so far about the setting and Martin's feelings about his surroundings. What do you think the main conflict will be about?

Until the morning the elevator stopped at the fourteenth floor, and the fat lady got on. She wore a threadbare green coat that ballooned around her; her ankles bulged above dirty sneakers. As she waddled into the elevator, Martin was sure he felt it sink under her weight. She was so big that she filled the cubicle; her coat brushed against him, and he had to squeeze into the corner to make room for her—there certainly wouldn't have been room for another passenger. The door slammed quickly behind her. And then, unlike everyone else, she did not stand facing the door. She stood with her back to the door, wheezing, staring directly at Martin.

For a moment he met her gaze. Her features seemed very small, squashed together by the loose fleshy mounds of her cheeks. She had no chin, only a great swollen mass of neck, barely contained by the collar of her coat. Her sparse red hair was pinned back by a plastic barrette. And her blue eyes, though tiny, were sharp and penetrating, boring into Martin's face.

Abruptly he looked away from her to the numbers over the door. She didn't turn around. Was she still looking at him? His eyes slipped back to hers, then quickly away. She *was* still watching him. He wanted to close his eyes; he wanted to turn around and stare into the corner, but how could he? The elevator creaked down to twelve, down to eleven. Martin looked at his watch; he looked at the numbers again. They weren't even down to nine yet. And then, against his will, his eyes slipped back to her face. She was still watching him. Her nose tilted up; there was a large space between her nostrils and her upper lip, giving her a piggish look. He looked away again, clenching his teeth, fighting the impulse to squeeze his eyes shut against her.

She had to be crazy. Why else would she stare at him this way? What was she going to do next?

She did nothing. She only watched him, breathing audibly, until the elevator reached the first floor at last. Martin would have rushed past her to get

Close Read
Rising Action begins (lines 41–80)

3. What event sets the rising action in motion?

4. Martin seems to perceive the strange lady as a threat. In your opinion, is this conflict real or in his head? Support your answer.

DIFFERENTIATED INSTRUCTION

FOR LESS–PROFICIENT READERS

Analysis Support: Internal Conflict [paired option] Have students review lines 1–80 of the story, looking for details that help them understand Martin's internal conflict. Ask them to list these details and then meet with partners to compare their lists. Have each pair summarize Martin's internal conflict (*Martin is afraid of elevators and especially of riding with the strange woman*) and share their ideas with the class.

FOR ENGLISH LEARNERS

Concept Support: Conflict [paired option] Have students work in pairs to identify words and phrases that describe the woman's physical appearance, how she acts, and Martin's increasing fear of her. Then have them use the details to draw a picture of what is happening inside the elevator.

out, but there was no room. He could only wait as she turned—reluctantly, it seemed to him—and moved so slowly out into the lobby. And then he ran. He didn't care what she thought. He ran past her, outside into the fresh air, and he ran almost all the way to school. He had never felt such relief in his life.

He thought about her all day. Did she live in the building? He had never seen her before, and the building wasn't very big—only four apartments on each floor. It seemed likely that she didn't live there, and had only been visiting somebody.

But if she were only visiting somebody, why was she leaving the building at seven thirty in the morning? People didn't make visits at that time of day. Did that mean she *did* live in the building? If so, it was likely—it was a certainty—that sometime he would be riding with her on the elevator again.

He was apprehensive as he approached the building after school. In the lobby, he considered the stairs. But that was ridiculous. Why should he be afraid of an old lady? If he *was* afraid of her, if he let it control him, then he was worse than all the names they called him at school. He pressed the button; he stepped into the empty elevator. He stared at the lights, urging the elevator on. It stopped on three.

At least it's not fourteen, he told himself; the person she was visiting lives on fourteen. He watched the door slide open—revealing a green coat, a piggish face, blue eyes already fixed on him as though she knew he'd be there.

It wasn't possible. It was like a nightmare. But there she was, massively real. "Going up!" he said, his voice a humiliating squeak.

She nodded, her flesh quivering, and stepped on. The door slammed. He watched her pudgy hand move toward the buttons. She pressed, not fourteen, but eighteen, the top floor, one floor above his own. The elevator trembled and began its ascent.[2] The fat lady watched him.

He knew she had gotten on at fourteen this morning. So why was she on three, going up to eighteen now? The only floors *he* ever went to were seventeen and one. What was she doing? Had she been waiting for him? Was she riding with him on purpose?

But that was crazy. Maybe she had a lot of friends in the building. Or else she was a cleaning lady who worked in different apartments. That had to be it. He felt her eyes on him as he stared at the numbers slowly blinking on and off—slower than usual, it seemed to him. Maybe the elevator was having trouble because of how heavy she was. It was supposed to carry three adults, but it was old. What if it got stuck between floors? What if it fell?

They were on five now. It occurred to him to press seven, get off there, and walk the rest of the way. And he would have done it, if he could have reached the buttons. But there was no room to get past her without squeezing against her, and he could not bear the thought of any physical contact with her. He concentrated on being in his room. He would be home soon, only another

2. **ascent:** the act of climbing or rising upward.

Close Read
Rising Action continues (lines 81–174)

5. What internal conflict is plaguing Martin in lines 81–84?

6. Tension builds as Martin and the lady meet again. What details in lines 88–105 help to create suspense about what might happen? One detail is boxed.

Close Read

5. ***Possible answer:*** *Martin's internal conflict is deciding whether or not to take the elevator. On the one hand, he is afraid that he might meet the fat lady again. On the other hand, he fears that if he tries to avoid the situation, he will prove himself a coward.*
6. ***Possible answer:*** *Additional details that help build suspense include*
   - *"blue eyes already fixed on him as though she knew he'd be there" (line 89)*
   - *"It was like a nightmare" (line 90)*
   - *"The elevator trembled" (line 94)*
   - *"The fat lady watched him" (line 95)*
   - *"What was she doing? Had she been waiting for him? Was she riding with him on purpose?" (lines 98–99)*
   - *"Maybe the elevator was having trouble because of how heavy she was" (lines 103–104)*
   - *"What if it got stuck between floors? What if it fell?" (line 105)*

FOR LESS–PROFICIENT READERS

Analysis Support: Plot One way that an author can make a plot more suspenseful is by asking questions and not providing the reader with answers. Asking several questions in a row intensifies this effect. Have students find two examples of this technique on page 29 (*lines 98–99, 105*). Read the questions out loud and discuss how they create a feeling of suspense or tension.

FOR ENGLISH LEARNERS

Concept Support: Internal Conflict Martin fears that the elevator will fall. Explain that although his fear is real, elevators in the United States are regularly inspected for safety. Since it is unlikely that the elevator will actually fall, Martin's conflict is with his own fear rather than with the elevator itself. Ask students to share their own experiences of riding in elevators. Can they relate to Martin's concerns about safety and his general discomfort with other passengers?

7. ***Possible answer:***
   - *Martin's father asks, "What are you so worked up about now?" Martin replies, "I'm not worked up" (lines 128–130).*
   - *His father asks, "What am I going to do with you, Martin?" (line 133).*
   - *Martin's father accuses him of being afraid and timid and asks, "When are you going to grow up and act like a man?" (lines 136–137).*
   - *Martin cries when he gets to his room (line 138).*
8. *Students who felt that the conflict was all in Martin's head may decide to change their answers. The lady's behavior has become increasingly strange. For example:*
   - *For no apparent reason, she has gotten on the elevator at the third floor and rides to the eighteenth floor. Previously, she got on at the fourteenth floor and rode to the first.*
   - *She "barely [moves] out of the way" (line 116) when Martin attempts to get off the elevator, and she "quickly [turns] and [watches] him" (lines 118–119) as the door closes.*
   - *The next time Martin tries to use the elevator, "the fat lady [is] waiting for him" (lines 140–141) and actually smiles (line 144) as he backs away in terror.*

minute or so. He could stand anything for a minute, even this crazy lady watching him.

Unless the elevator got stuck between floors. Then what would he do? He tried to push the thought away, but it kept coming back. He looked at her. She was still staring at him, no expression at all on her squashed little features.

When the elevator stopped on his floor, she barely moved out of the way. He had to inch past her, rubbing against her horrible scratchy coat, terrified the door would close before he made it through. She quickly turned and watched him as the door slammed shut. And he thought, *Now she knows I live on seventeen.*

"Did you ever notice a strange fat lady on the elevator?" he asked his father that evening.

"Can't say as I have," he said, not looking away from the television.

He knew he was probably making a mistake, but he had to tell somebody. "Well, she was on the elevator with me twice today. And the funny thing was, she just kept staring at me, she never stopped looking at me for a minute. You think . . . you know of anybody who has a weird cleaning lady or anything?"

"What are you so worked up about now?" his father said, turning impatiently away from the television.

"I'm not worked up. It was just funny the way she kept staring at me. You know how people never look at each other in the elevator. Well, she just kept looking at me."

"What am I going to do with you, Martin?" his father said. He sighed and shook his head. "Honestly, now you're afraid of some poor old lady."

"I'm not afraid."

"You're afraid," said his father, with total assurance. "When are you going to grow up and act like a man? Are you going to be timid all your life?"

He managed not to cry until he got to his room—but his father probably knew he was crying anyway. He slept very little.

And in the morning, when the elevator door opened, the fat lady was waiting for him.

She was expecting him. She knew he lived on seventeen. He stood there, unable to move, and then backed away. And as he did so, her expression changed. She smiled as the door slammed.

He ran for the stairs. Luckily, the unlit flight on which he fell was between sixteen and fifteen. He only had to drag himself up one and a half flights with the terrible pain in his leg. His father was silent on the way to the hospital, disappointed and annoyed at him for being such a coward and a fool.

It was a simple fracture. He didn't need a wheelchair, only a cast and crutches. But he was condemned to the elevator now. Was that why the fat lady had smiled? Had she known it would happen this way?

At least his father was with him on the elevator on the way back from the hospital. There was no room for the fat lady to get on. And even if she did, his

7. What details in lines 121–139 suggest a conflict between father and son?

8. Review your answer to question 4. Then consider the lady's behavior each time Martin sees her on the elevator. Has your answer changed? Explain.

DIFFERENTIATED INSTRUCTION

FOR LESS–PROFICIENT READERS

Analysis Support: Plot Have students act out the scene in which Martin talks to his father (lines 121–137). Ask them to discuss how the father's attitude contributes to the rising action of the plot. How does his reaction to Martin's comments about the strange lady create an external conflict? How else might the father have responded? Discuss how a different response would affect the plot.

FOR ENGLISH LEARNERS

Concept Support: Conflict Draw students' attention to the author's use of italics in lines 119–120: *"Now she knows I live on seventeen."* Italics are often used to show what a character is thinking. Now that the lady knows Martin lives on the seventeenth floor, he fears her even more. This adds to the external and internal conflicts the boy faces. Ask students to read the line aloud with an expression of fear in their voices.

father would see her, he would realize how peculiar she was, and then maybe he would understand. And once they got home, he could stay in the apartment for a few days—the doctor had said he should use the leg as little as possible. A week, maybe—a whole week without going on the elevator. Riding up with his father, leaning on his crutches, he looked around the little cubicle and felt a kind of triumph. He had beaten the elevator, and the fat lady, for the time being. And the end of the week was very far away.

"Oh, I almost forgot," his father reached out his hand and pressed nine.

"What are you doing? You're not getting off, are you?" he asked him, trying not to sound panicky.

"I promised Terry Ullman I'd drop in on her," his father said, looking at his watch as he stepped off.

"Let me go with you. I want to visit her, too," Martin pleaded, struggling forward on his crutches.

But the door was already closing. "Afraid to be on the elevator alone?" his father said, with a look of total scorn. "Grow up, Martin." The door slammed shut.

Martin hobbled to the buttons and pressed nine, but it didn't do any good. The elevator stopped at ten, where the fat lady was waiting for him. She moved in quickly; he was too slow, too unsteady on his crutches to work his way past her in time. The door sealed them in; the elevator started up.

"Hello, Martin," she said, and laughed, and pushed the Stop button.

9. In lines 145–160, the story takes an unexpected turn. How might this development affect Martin's conflict?

Close Read
Climax (line 175)

10. Line 175 is the climax, or turning point, of the story. Do you think Martin is in danger? Explain your opinion.

Close Read
Falling Action and Resolution

11. The author ends this story at the climax and doesn't indicate how the conflict between Martin and the lady is resolved. Why do you think the author made this choice?

9. ***Possible answer:*** *The story takes an unexpected turn when Martin falls on the stairs and breaks his leg. The doctor had advised him to use the leg as little as possible. As a result, he will not have to ride the elevator or see the fat lady for some time.*

Close Read
Climax (line 175)

10. *Students will probably think that Martin is in danger. Details that support this opinion include*

- *The lady gets on the elevator at the tenth floor (line 172) as if she knew that Martin would be alone on the elevator at that moment.*
- *She "[moves] in quickly" (line 173), as if wanting to take advantage of his vulnerability on the crutches.*
- *The phrase* The door sealed them in *(line 174) suggests that he is trapped.*
- *She knows his name, she laughs, and she pushes the Stop button (line 175).*

Close Read
Falling Action and Resolution

11. ***Possible answer:*** *The author probably wanted to keep readers in suspense. Not knowing exactly what happens to Martin allows readers to use their imagination to picture the final outcome.*

Assess and Reteach

Assess

Have students briefly summarize each stage of the plot and identify the conflicts that Martin faces.

Reteach

For students who cannot apply the workshop skills to "The Elevator," try these options:

1. Pair students with classmates who have grasped the lesson. Have each pair fill out a Plot Diagram for the story.

   BEST PRACTICES TOOLKIT—Transparency
   Plot Diagram p. D12

2. Meet with small groups of students and ask them to apply the questions on page 26 of the teacher's edition to "The Elevator." Make sure they understand that the story is unusual because the conflict is not resolved.

DIFFERENTIATED INSTRUCTION

FOR LESS-PROFICIENT READERS

Analysis Support: Plot Some students may feel cheated or tricked because this story has only three of the five stages of a traditional plot. Remind them that a television season finale will often have unresolved conflicts to hook the audience into watching next season. Ask them to think of a television program that ended in a similar way. Which type of ending do they prefer and why?

FOR ADVANCED LEARNERS/PRE-AP

Evaluate Stages of Plot Divide students into two groups. Ask one group to pick up the story at line 175 and write a brief scene of falling action and resolution in which Martin realizes that his fears were misplaced. Ask the other group to write a more sinister and frightening conclusion for Martin. Have both groups present their work. Let the class vote on which version they prefer and have them explain why.

Focus and Motivate

OBJECTIVES

Literary Analysis

- explore the key idea of **motivation**
- identify and analyze stages of plot
- read a short story

Reading

- make and support inferences

Vocabulary

- build vocabulary for reading and writing
- use context to determine meanings of compound words *(also an EL language objective)*

Grammar and Writing

- correct sentence fragments
- use writing to analyze literature

SUMMARY

Squeaky's mentally impaired brother Raymond accompanies her everywhere, even on her training runs. During the big May Day race, as Squeaky dashes toward the finish line, she notices Raymond on the other side of the fence, running as hard as he can. Thrilled that Raymond has found something he can be good at, Squeaky decides to retire and devote herself to training him.

What's worth the EFFORT?

Discuss the question and the ***KEY IDEA.*** Point out that factors influencing **motivation** can be external, such as wanting to impress others; internal, such as hoping to break a personal record; or both. Have students give examples of each kind of motivation before they begin the ***QUICKWRITE*** activity.

Before Reading

Raymond's Run

Short Story by Toni Cade Bambara

What's worth the EFFORT?

KEY IDEA Have you ever wanted something so badly you'd do anything to achieve it? If so, you've felt **motivation**, the drive that causes people to strive toward a goal. In the story you are about to read, a spunky young girl does what it takes to be the fastest runner in her neighborhood.

QUICKWRITE Jot down a list of things you've been willing to work for. Choose a favorite and write a short paragraph telling what motivates you.

1. Hold record for most chin-ups
2. Learn new dance

32

Selection Resources

RESOURCE MANAGER UNIT 1

Plan and Teach pp. 17–24

Literary Analysis

Summary pp. 25†*, 26‡*

Plot pp. 27, 28†*

Question Support p. 35*

Reading

Make Inferences pp. 29, 30†*

Reading Check p. 34

Reading Fluency p. 37

Vocabulary

Study p. 31*

Practice p. 32

Strategy p. 33

Grammar and Writing

Avoid Sentence Fragments p. 36

Assessment

Selection Tests A, B/C pp. 39*, 41*

Test Generator CD

BEST PRACTICES TOOLKIT

Differentiated Instruction pp. 31–38*

Scaffolding Instruction pp. 43–46*

Graphic Organizers/Strategies

New Word Analysis • Read Aloud/Think Aloud • T Chart • Story Map • Character Map • Cluster Diagram • Reporter's Questions

Reading Support

Audio Anthology CD*

Technology

Literature, Vocabulary, and Writing Centers at **ClassZone.com**

Write*Smart* CD

* Resources for Differentiation † Also in Spanish ‡ In Haitian Creole and Vietnamese

LITERARY ANALYSIS: PLOT

A story wouldn't be a story if nothing happened. The series of events that happen in a story make up its **plot.** Most plots include the following parts, or stages:

- **Exposition**—introduces the main characters, the setting, and sometimes the conflict
- **Rising action**—increases tension and builds the conflict
- **Climax**—the point of greatest interest, or the turning point in the story
- **Falling action**—shows the result of the climax and brings the story to a close
- **Resolution**—reveals the final outcome of events and ties up loose ends

As you read "Raymond's Run," notice how each stage of the plot helps build a powerful story.

READING SKILL: MAKE INFERENCES

When you make an **inference** while reading, you use clues from the story and your own knowledge to guess about things the author doesn't say directly. As you read "Raymond's Run," make inferences to better understand the main character's feelings, thoughts, and ideas. Record your inferences in equations.

Squeaky says her dad is the only one faster than she is.	+	Kids like when their parents are talented.	=	Squeaky is proud of her father.

VOCABULARY IN CONTEXT

The boldfaced words help Toni Cade Bambara tell a story about a race that's important in more ways than one. Use context clues to figure out what each word means.

1. Teams of three or four usually compete in **relay** races.
2. The talented young sprinter was considered a track **prodigy.**
3. Mai's teammate is also her good friend, or **sidekick.**
4. Ben is **liable** to get injured if he doesn't warm up before the race.
5. At the start of a race, runners **crouch** close to the ground.
6. The winner might **clutch** the blue ribbon to her chest.

Author Online

Creativity and Concern Raised in urban neighborhoods of New York and New Jersey in the 1940s and 1950s, Toni Cade spent much time daydreaming and exploring her world. Her mother encouraged her to do so. In the dedication of her award-winning novel *The Salt Eaters,* Bambara thanks her "mama . . . who in 1948, having come upon me daydreaming in the middle of the kitchen floor, mopped around me." One day, while looking through an old trunk, Toni found her great-grandmother's sketchbook. The name inscribed there was "Bambara." Impressed with her ancestor's creative drive, she decided to add that name to her own.

Toni Cade Bambara
1939–1995

"A Tremendous Responsibility" Toni Cade Bambara went on to careers as a teacher, community activist, and documentary filmmaker. She continued to write, sharing her personal concern for and understanding of the lives of African-American families and communities. She was always aware of the influence that writers, artists, and cultural workers have on others. "It's a tremendous responsibility," she said. "One's got to see what the factory worker sees, what the prisoner sees, what the welfare children see . . . in order to tell the truth and not get trapped."

MORE ABOUT THE AUTHOR
For more on Toni Cade Bambara, visit the **Literature Center** at **ClassZone.com.**

Teach

STANDARDS FOCUS

LITERARY ANALYSIS

● PLOT

Write this example on the board:

> I saw the other swimmers move ahead of me. Ignoring the pain in my lungs, I made one last effort. My outstretched fingers felt the wall. Yes! I had done it! My parents smiled proudly as I dripped a path to the winners' podium.

Ask students to identify the rising action and the climax. ***Possible answer:*** *The rising action is when the swimmers move ahead. The climax is when the narrator makes one last effort.*

CHECK UNDERSTANDING Ask students to identify the elements of plot in a story they have previously read.

READING SKILL

■ MAKE INFERENCES

Have students make inferences about the narrator's character in the passage above. ***Possible answer:*** *The narrator is strong-willed, motivated, and a good swimmer.*

CHECK UNDERSTANDING Ask pairs to provide each other with a set of clues about their favorite sport or hobby and have partners make inferences, or guess what it is.

RESOURCE MANAGER—Copy Master
Make Inferences p. 29 (for student use while reading the selection)

VOCABULARY SKILL

▲ VOCABULARY IN CONTEXT

DIAGNOSE WORD KNOWLEDGE To determine preteaching needs, have all students complete **Vocabulary in Context.** Have students check their definitions as they read the story: *relay* (p. 34), *prodigy* (p. 36), *sidekick* (p. 37), *liable* (p. 36), *crouch* (p. 40), *clutch* (p. 36).

PRETEACH VOCABULARY Use the Vocabulary Study copy master to help students determine the meaning of each boldfaced word.

1. Read aloud the first sentence, emphasizing the boldfaced word.
2. Ask students to think about how *clutch* is used. Discuss possible meanings, such as "grab."
3. Repeat the procedure for items 2–6.
4. Have students complete the chart in Part B independently.

RESOURCE MANAGER—Copy Master
Vocabulary Study p. 31

For general guidelines on differentiating vocabulary instruction and for alternative vocabulary activities for students not needing vocabulary preteaching, see

BEST PRACTICES TOOLKIT
Scaffolding Vocabulary Instruction pp. 43–46

Vocabulary Center at **ClassZone.com**
Additional Vocabulary Activities

Practice and Apply

ANALYZE VISUALS

Possible answer: *The girl looks proud, self-confident, and rather tough. She probably does not let other people push her around.*

LITERARY ANALYSIS

Ⓐ PLOT: EXPOSITION

Possible answer:

- *Squeaky takes care of her brother Raymond.*
- *She is tough and unafraid of confrontation.*
- *She is skinny and has a squeaky voice, the source of her nickname.*
- *She is a very fast runner.*

If students need help . . . Have them reread lines 4–5 and 10–16. Help them locate details that describe Squeaky's responsibilities, attitude, and physical attributes.

Lines 1–20

ADDITIONAL TEACHING OPPORTUNITY

Dialect The form of language spoken in a specific place by a certain group of people is known as dialect. In this story, Squeaky's use of words and phrases in a way that is different from standard English adds to the realism of her character. Ask students for some examples of dialect in lines 1–20. ***Possible answer:*** *"they have to come by me," "And I don't play the dozens or believe in standing around with somebody in my face," "And tomorrow I'm subject to run the quarter-meter relay"*

RAYMOND'S RUN

TONI CADE BAMBARA

I don't have much work to do around the house like some girls. My mother does that. And I don't have to earn my pocket money by hustling; George runs errands for the big boys and sells Christmas cards. And anything else that's got to get done, my father does. All I have to do in life is mind my brother Raymond, which is enough.

Sometimes I slip and say my little brother Raymond. But as any fool can see he's much bigger and he's older too. But a lot of people call him my little brother cause he needs looking after cause he's not quite right. And a lot of smart mouths got lots to say about that too, especially when George was minding him. But now, if anybody has anything to say to Raymond, anything to say about his big head,[1] they have to come by me. And I don't play the dozens[2] or believe in standing around with somebody in my face doing a lot of talking. I much rather just knock you down and take my chances even if I am a little girl with skinny arms and a squeaky voice, which is how I got the name Squeaky. And if things get too rough, I run. And as anybody can tell you, I'm the fastest thing on two feet. Ⓐ

There is no track meet that I don't win the first place medal. I used to win the twenty-yard dash when I was a little kid in kindergarten. Nowadays, it's the fifty-yard dash. And tomorrow I'm subject to run the quarter-meter **relay** all by myself and come in first, second, and third. The big kids call me Mercury[3] cause I'm the swiftest thing in the neighborhood. Everybody knows that—except two people who know better, my father and me. He can beat me to Amsterdam Avenue with me having a two fire hydrant headstart and him running with his hands in his pockets and whistling. But that's private information. Cause can you imagine some thirty-five-year-old man stuffing himself into PAL shorts to race little kids? So as far as everyone's concerned, I'm

ANALYZE VISUALS
From her posture and her expression, what can you **infer** about the girl in this photograph?

Ⓐ PLOT: EXPOSITION
What have you learned about Squeaky so far?

relay (rē'lā) *n.* a race in which several team members take turns running to complete the race

① **Targeted Passage**

1. **big head:** a result of hydrocephalus, or fluid in parts of the brain, that causes enlargement of the skull.
2. **play the dozens:** exchange rhyming insults.
3. **Mercury:** in Roman mythology, the swift messenger of the gods.

DIFFERENTIATED INSTRUCTION

FOR ALL STUDENTS

Enhance Learning Styles Provide these independent projects for various learning styles:

- **Kinesthetic** Prepare a Readers Theater presentation of the story.
- **Creative** Design a T-shirt for runners.
- **Verbal** Deliver an acceptance speech.

For further details on these projects, see

RESOURCE MANAGER
Ideas for Extension pp. 22–23

FOR LESS–PROFICIENT READERS

In combination with the *Audio Anthology CD,* use one or more Targeted Passages (pp. 34–36, 41, 42) to ensure that students focus on key story events, concepts, and skills.

① **Targeted Passage [Lines 17–30]**

This passage identifies the major conflict in the story: Squeaky wants to win the May Day race.

- How do you know Squeaky is a fast runner?
- How does Squeaky feel about her father beating her in a race?
- How does Squeaky react to Gretchen's claim that she will win the race?

BACKGROUND

Harlem Squeaky's neighborhood is a part of New York City called Harlem, in northern Manhattan. Although it is thought of as a primarily African-American residential district, in fact it is home to people of many different backgrounds. The 1970s and 1980s were difficult decades for Harlem, as it was plagued by many social problems. Although efforts have been made to revive property and improve safety in this part of the city, the people living in Harlem today still suffer considerable unemployment and substandard housing.

CULTURAL CONNECTION

May Day Although Squeaky is eager to run in the May Day races, she wants no part of her community's May Pole dance (lines 115–118). Ancient Greeks and Romans celebrated the return of spring on this day, a rite that was also part of medieval European traditions and included dancing around a decorated pole, crowning a May queen and king, and gathering flowers. May Day is still celebrated in many countries with a variety of festivities.

FOR ENGLISH LEARNERS

Options for Reading Read aloud lines 1–16. Explain that the narrator is a young girl who lives in Harlem. Discuss her dialect and encourage students to use context clues to help them understand the meaning of unfamiliar words and phrases. Then read the rest of the story aloud or have students follow along with the *Audio Anthology CD.*

Key Academic Vocabulary Have students use New Word Analysis to study this academic vocabulary from the selection: *team* (lines 100, 112), *grade* (line 102), *energy* (line 192), *style* (lines 212, 249), *tradition* (line 250).

BEST PRACTICES TOOLKIT—Transparency
New Word Analysis p. E8

Prereading For prereading instruction for English learners, see

BEST PRACTICES TOOLKIT
Scaffolding Reading Instruction pp. 43–46

FOR ADVANCED LEARNERS/PRE–AP

Pre-AP exercises in the bottom channel provide additional challenge for your advanced students. Use them for small groups or individuals.

ADDITIONAL GUIDELINES

For more help with differentiation and tips for classroom management, see

BEST PRACTICES TOOLKIT
Differentiated Instruction pp. 31–38

READING SKILL

B MAKE INFERENCES

Possible answer:

Squeaky keeps Raymond close to the buildings where he is safe. She takes him along when she does her breathing exercises. + *People are protective of their families.*

= *Squeaky really looks out for Raymond and doesn't mind taking care of him, even though it is hard.*

If students need help . . . Use a Read Aloud/Think Aloud strategy to model making inferences about Squeaky's character and her relationship with Raymond based on the details in lines 31–45 and prior knowledge.

BEST PRACTICES TOOLKIT—Transparency
Read Aloud/Think Aloud p. A34

Lines 51–66
REINFORCE *KEY IDEA:* MOTIVATION

Discuss What is Cynthia Procter's **motivation** for practicing piano and studying in secret?
Possible answer: *Cynthia practices secretly so that others will think that skills such as piano-playing and spelling come naturally to her. She wants to impress people with her supposed talent.*

---

the fastest and that goes for Gretchen, too, who has put out the tale that she is going to win the first-place medal this year. Ridiculous. In the second place, she's got short legs. In the third place, she's got freckles. In the first place, no one can beat me and that's all there is to it.

1 Targeted Passage

I'm standing on the corner admiring the weather and about to take a stroll down Broadway so I can practice my breathing exercises, and I've got Raymond walking on the inside close to the buildings, cause he's subject to fits of fantasy and starts thinking he's a circus performer and that the curb is a tightrope strung high in the air. And sometimes after a rain he likes to step down off his tightrope right into the gutter and slosh around getting his shoes and cuffs wet. Then I get hit when I get home. Or sometimes if you don't watch him he'll dash across traffic to the island in the middle of Broadway and give the pigeons a fit. Then I have to go behind him apologizing to all the old people sitting around trying to get some sun and getting all upset with the pigeons fluttering around them, scattering their newspapers and upsetting the waxpaper lunches[4] in their laps. So I keep Raymond on the inside of me, and he plays like he's driving a stage coach which is O.K. by me so long as he doesn't run me over or interrupt my breathing exercises, which I have to do on account of I'm serious about my running, and I don't care who knows it. **B**

Now some people like to act like things come easy to them, won't let on that they practice. Not me. I'll high-prance down 34th Street like a rodeo pony to keep my knees strong even if it does get my mother uptight so that she walks ahead like she's not with me, don't know me, is all by herself on a shopping trip, and I am somebody else's crazy child. Now you take Cynthia Procter for instance. She's just the opposite. If there's a test tomorrow, she'll say something like, "Oh, I guess I'll play handball this afternoon and watch television tonight," just to let you know she ain't thinking about the test. Or like last week when she won the spelling bee for the millionth time, "A good thing you got 'receive,' Squeaky, cause I would have got it wrong. I completely forgot about the spelling bee." And she'll **clutch** the lace on her blouse like it was a narrow escape. Oh, brother. But of course when I pass her house on my early morning trots around the block, she is practicing the scales on the piano over and over and over and over. Then in music class she always lets herself get bumped around so she falls accidentally on purpose onto the piano stool and is so surprised to find herself sitting there that she decides just for fun to try out the ole keys. And what do you know—Chopin's waltzes[5] just spring out of her fingertips and she's the most surprised thing in the world. A regular **prodigy.** I could kill people like that. I stay up all night studying the words for the spelling bee. And you can see me any time of day practicing running. I never walk if I can trot, and shame on Raymond if he can't keep up. But of course he does, cause if he hangs back someone's **liable** to walk up to him and get

B MAKE INFERENCES
Reread lines 31–45. How do you think Squeaky feels about taking care of her brother? Use an equation to note your inference.

clutch (klŭch) *v.* to grasp and hold tightly

prodigy (prŏd'ə-jē) *n.* a person with an exceptional talent

liable (lī'ə-bəl) *adj.* likely to

4. **waxpaper lunches:** sandwiches wrapped in wax paper.
5. **Chopin's** (shō'pănz') **waltzes:** music by composer Frédéric Chopin.

DIFFERENTIATED INSTRUCTION

FOR LESS–PROFICIENT READERS

Reading Skill Follow-Up: Make Inferences [paired option] Remind students that making inferences helps them understand more about the characters, events, and themes in a story. Use three sets of equations similar to the one on page 33 or a chart such as this one. Give students the three text clues and model the process of making inferences with the first one. Then have pairs use prior knowledge to make inferences from the remaining text clues.

Clues from Text	*Prior Knowledge*	*Inference*
Gretchen says she is going to beat Squeaky (lines 27–30).	*I try harder when someone challenges me.*	*Squeaky is going to be especially motivated to win the race.*
Squeaky embarrasses her mother by prancing down the street (lines 46–50).	*I would be too self-conscious to do this.*	*Squeaky is self-possessed and very serious about her running.*
Mary Louise dropped Squeaky for Gretchen (lines 71–76).	*I would be hurt if someone didn't want to be my friend.*	*Squeaky feels betrayed by Mary Louise.*

smart, or take his allowance from him, or ask him where he got that great big pumpkin head. People are so stupid sometimes.

So I'm strolling down Broadway breathing out and breathing in on counts of seven, which is my lucky number, and here comes Gretchen and her **sidekicks:** Mary Louise, who used to be a friend of mine when she first moved to Harlem from Baltimore and got beat up by everybody till I took up for her on account of her mother and my mother used to sing in the same choir when they were young girls, but people ain't grateful, so now she hangs out with the new girl Gretchen and talks about me like a dog; and Rosie, who is as fat as I am skinny and has a big mouth where Raymond is concerned and is too stupid to know that there is not a big deal of difference between herself and Raymond and that she can't afford to throw stones. So they are steady coming up Broadway and I see right away that it's going to be one of those Dodge City[6] scenes cause the street ain't that big and they're close to the buildings just as we are. First I think I'll step into the candy store and look over the new comics and let them pass. But that's chicken and I've got a reputation to consider. So then I think I'll just walk straight on through them or even over them if necessary. But as they get to me, they slow down. I'm ready to fight, cause like I said I don't feature a whole lot of chit-chat, I much prefer to just knock you down right from the jump and save everybody a lotta precious time. **C**

"You signing up for the May Day races?" smiles Mary Louise, only it's not a smile at all. A dumb question like that doesn't deserve an answer. Besides, there's just me and Gretchen standing there really, so no use wasting my breath talking to shadows.

"I don't think you're going to win this time," says Rosie, trying to signify with her hands on her hips all salty, completely forgetting that I have whupped her behind many times for less salt than that.

"I always win cause I'm the best," I say straight at Gretchen who is, as far as I'm concerned, the only one talking in this ventriloquist-dummy routine. Gretchen smiles, but it's not a smile, and I'm thinking that girls never really smile at each other because they don't know how and don't want to know how and there's probably no one to teach us how, cause grown-up girls don't know either. Then they all look at Raymond who has just brought his mule team to a standstill. And they're about to see what trouble they can get into through him.

"What grade you in now, Raymond?"

"You got anything to say to my brother, you say it to me, Mary Louise Williams of Raggedy Town, Baltimore."

"What are you, his mother?" sasses Rosie.

"That's right, Fatso. And the next word out of anybody and I'll be *their* mother too." So they just stand there and Gretchen shifts from one leg to the other and so do they. Then Gretchen puts her hands on her hips and is about to say something with her freckle-face self but doesn't. Then she walks

sidekick (sīd'kĭk') *n.* a close friend

C PLOT: RISING ACTION
Why does Gretchen's approach cause tension for Squeaky?

VISUAL VOCABULARY

ventriloquist-dummy *n.* A ventriloquist controls his or her voice and moves the mouth of a puppet, or dummy, to make it appear to be talking.

6. **Dodge City:** an Old West town, famous for showdowns between outlaws and lawmen.

LITERARY ANALYSIS

C PLOT: RISING ACTION
Possible answer: *Gretchen is Squeaky's main rival in the next day's race. Also, Squeaky is expecting the girls to pick on Raymond.*

FOR ENGLISH LEARNERS

Vocabulary: Idioms and Sayings [mixed-readiness groups] Remind students to use context clues and a dictionary to define unfamiliar words and phrases. Have groups find the meanings of these expressions:

- *uptight* (line 48), "tense"
- *took up for her* (line 73), "defended her"
- *hangs out* (line 75), "spends time with"
- *throw stones* (line 79), "criticize"
- *chicken* (line 83), "cowardly"
- *all salty* (line 93), "bold"
- *whupped her behind* (lines 93–94), "defeated her"
- *sasses* (line 105), "talks rudely"

Visual Vocabulary Explain that *ventriloquist* comes from a word that means "speaking from the belly." A good ventriloquist's lips should show no movement while speaking. Have pairs of students practice saying something without moving their lips. Discuss why this exercise is so difficult.

around me looking me up and down but keeps walking up Broadway, and her sidekicks follow her. So me and Raymond smile at each other and he says, "Gidyap" to his team and I continue with my breathing exercises, strolling down Broadway toward the ice man on 145th with not a care in the world cause I am Miss Quicksilver[7] herself.

I take my time getting to the park on May Day because the track meet is the last thing on the program. The biggest thing on the program is the May Pole dancing, which I can do without, thank you, even if my mother thinks it's a shame I don't take part and act like a girl for a change. You'd think my mother'd be grateful not to have to make me a white organdy dress with a big satin sash and buy me new white baby-doll shoes that can't be taken out of the box till the big day. You'd think she'd be glad her daughter ain't out there prancing around a May Pole getting the new clothes all dirty and sweaty and trying to act like a fairy or a flower or whatever you're supposed to be when you should be trying to be yourself, whatever that is, which is, as far as I am concerned, a poor Black girl who really can't afford to buy shoes and a new dress you only wear once a lifetime cause it won't fit next year. **D**

D MAKE INFERENCES Reread lines 115–126. What do you think Squeaky's relationship with her mother is like?

I was once a strawberry in a Hansel and Gretel pageant when I was in nursery school and didn't have no better sense than to dance on tiptoe with my arms in a circle over my head doing umbrella steps and being a perfect fool just so my mother and father could come dressed up and clap. You'd think they'd know better than to encourage that kind of nonsense. I am not a strawberry. I do not dance on my toes. I run. That is what I am all about. So I always come late to the May Day program, just in time to get my number pinned on and lay in the grass till they announce the fifty-yard dash.

I put Raymond in the little swings, which is a tight squeeze this year and will be impossible next year. Then I look around for Mr. Pearson, who pins the numbers on. I'm really looking for Gretchen, if you want to know the truth, but she's not around. The park is jam-packed. Parents in hats and corsages and breast-pocket handkerchiefs peeking up. Kids in white dresses and light-blue suits. The parkees[8] unfolding chairs and chasing the rowdy kids from Lenox[9] as if they had no right to be there. The big guys with their caps on backwards, leaning against the fence swirling the basketballs on the tips of their fingers, waiting for all these crazy people to clear out the park so they can play. Most of the kids in my class are carrying bass drums and glockenspiels[10] and flutes. You'd think they'd put in a few bongos or something for real like that. **E**

E MAKE INFERENCES Reread lines 135–136. How is Squeaky's life affected by having to take care of Raymond? Think about how she might deal with Raymond next year.

Then here comes Mr. Pearson with his clipboard and his cards and pencils and whistles and safety pins and 50 million other things he's always dropping all over the place with his clumsy self. He sticks out in a crowd because he's

7. **Miss Quicksilver:** a reference to how fast quicksilver (mercury) flows.
8. **parkees:** people who regularly gather in the park.
9. **Lenox:** street in Harlem in New York City.
10. **glockenspiels** (glŏk'ən-spēlz'): musical instruments with tuned metal bars played with light hammers.

READING SKILL

D MAKE INFERENCES

***Possible answer:** Squeaky's relationship with her mother seems tense. Her mother wants her to be more feminine; Squeaky doesn't have the time or patience for activities that are just for show and cost money as well. She is focused on being a great runner.*

If students need help . . . Use a T Chart to contrast Squeaky's feelings about May Day and her mother's attitude. Then guide students to make inferences about the relationship based on the differences between them.

Squeaky's Mother	*Squeaky*
• *wants Squeaky to dress up and dance* • *wants Squeaky to act like a girl*	• *thinks that dancing and new clothes are a waste* • *wants to be herself*

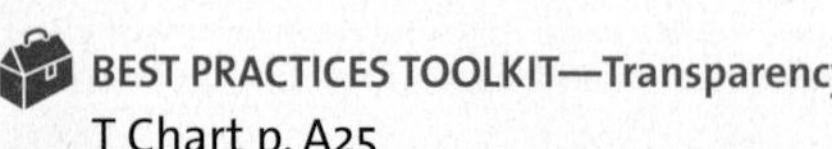
BEST PRACTICES TOOLKIT—Transparency T Chart p. A25

READING SKILL

E MAKE INFERENCES

***Possible answer:** Squeaky always has to think about Raymond and how to keep him safe. As he gets older and bigger, this will become more difficult.*

Extend the Discussion How do you think Squeaky's continued responsibility for Raymond has shaped her personality?

DIFFERENTIATED INSTRUCTION

FOR ENGLISH LEARNERS

Language: Conversational English Patterns [small-group option]

- Explain that Squeaky's dialect or manner of speaking includes slang and nonstandard expressions. For example, Squeaky says *ain't* instead of *isn't* in line 121 and "didn't have no better sense" in line 128 instead of "didn't have any better sense."
- Have students work in small groups to identify other examples in the story. Discuss their findings.

FOR ADVANCED LEARNERS/PRE-AP

Analyze Style Point out that in lines 138–144, the author presents a series of sentence fragments, a departure from the structure in the rest of the story. Ask students to discuss what purpose this style change accomplishes and how it affects their reading and understanding of this part of the story.

on stilts. We used to call him Jack and the Beanstalk to get him mad. But I'm the only one that can outrun him and get away, and I'm too grown for that silliness now.

"Well, Squeaky," he says, checking my name off the list and handing me number seven and two pins. And I'm thinking he's got no right to call me Squeaky, if I can't call him Beanstalk.

"Hazel Elizabeth Deborah Parker," I correct him and tell him to write it down on his board.

"Well, Hazel Elizabeth Deborah Parker, going to give someone else a break this year?" I squint at him real hard to see if he is seriously thinking I should lose the race on purpose just to give someone else a break. "Only six girls running this time," he continues, shaking his head sadly like it's my fault all

ANALYZE VISUALS
How does the boy in this picture **compare** with the way you imagine Raymond?

ANALYZE VISUALS

Possible answer: *The boy in the picture looks smaller and younger than Raymond.*

FOR LESS–PROFICIENT READERS

Concept Support [small-group option]
Distribute copies of the Story Map transparency. Guide students to fill in the title, setting, and characters. Then point out that most stories include more than one problem or conflict, but that there is usually one major conflict that drives the action of the plot. Have groups brainstorm a list of problems in the story and then decide which one is the main conflict. Next, they should work together to fill in several major events that have happened so far. Encourage them to add more events as they continue reading, including the resolution at the end of the story.

Title: *"Raymond's Run"*

Setting: *Harlem*

Characters: *Squeaky, Raymond, Mary Louise, Gretchen, Rosie*

Conflict: *Squeaky wants to win the May Day race, but she faces serious competition from Gretchen.*

Plot

- ***Event 1:*** *Squeaky has a confrontation with Gretchen and her friends.*
- ***Event 2:*** *Squeaky registers for the race.*
- ***Event 3:*** *Mr. Pearson hints that he would like her to give someone else a chance to win this year.*

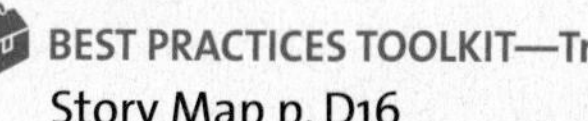
BEST PRACTICES TOOLKIT—Transparency
Story Map p. D16

Lines 165–173
DISCUSSION PROMPTS

Use these prompts to help students understand more about Squeaky's character and outlook on life:

Connect Would you feel the same as Squeaky does about Mr. Pearson's suggestion? Explain. *Students may say that they would feel outraged too at the suggestion that they let someone else win.*

Analyze What does Squeaky's inability to pretend she is in the country reveal about her character? ***Possible answer:*** *She is too honest and realistic to pretend that she is somewhere or someone else.*

Evaluate Do you think Squeaky could ever "throw" a race? Why or why not? ***Possible answer:*** *No. Running is too important to Squeaky. Letting someone else win would destroy her integrity, an important part of who she is. It is also important to her to just be herself.*

LITERARY ANALYSIS

F PLOT: RISING ACTION

Possible answer: *The descriptions of the other races and Squeaky's thoughts about them, Raymond's excitement, and Gretchen's preparation all add to the tension and anticipation.*

of New York didn't turn out in sneakers. "That new girl should give you a run for your money." He looks around the park for Gretchen like a periscope[11] in a submarine movie. "Wouldn't it be a nice gesture if you were . . . to ahhh . . ."

I give him such a look he couldn't finish putting that idea into words. Grownups got a lot of nerve sometimes. I pin number seven to myself and stomp away, I'm so burnt. And I go straight for the track and stretch out on the grass while the band winds up with "Oh, the Monkey Wrapped His Tail Around the Flag Pole," which my teacher calls by some other name. The man on the loudspeaker is calling everyone over to the track and I'm on my back looking at the sky, trying to pretend I'm in the country, but I can't, because even grass in the city feels hard as sidewalk, and there's just no pretending you are anywhere but in a "concrete jungle" as my grandfather says.

The twenty-yard dash takes all of two minutes cause most of the little kids don't know no better than to run off the track or run the wrong way or run smack into the fence and fall down and cry. One little kid, though, has got the good sense to run straight for the white ribbon up ahead so he wins. Then the second-graders line up for the thirty-yard dash and I don't even bother to turn my head to watch cause Raphael Perez always wins. He wins before he even begins by psyching the runners, telling them they're going to trip on their shoelaces and fall on their faces or lose their shorts or something, which he doesn't really have to do since he is very fast, almost as fast as I am. After that is the forty-yard dash which I used to run when I was in first grade. Raymond is hollering from the swings cause he knows I'm about to do my thing cause the man on the loudspeaker has just announced the fifty-yard dash, although he might just as well be giving a recipe for angel food cake cause you can hardly make out what he's sayin for the static. I get up and slip off my sweat pants and then I see Gretchen standing at the starting line, kicking her legs out like a pro. Then as I get into place I see that ole Raymond is on line on the other side of the fence, bending down with his fingers on the ground just like he knew what he was doing. I was going to yell at him but then I didn't. It burns up your energy to holler. (F)

F PLOT: RISING ACTION What details in this paragraph increase the excitement and tension?

Every time, just before I take off in a race, I always feel like I'm in a dream, the kind of dream you have when you're sick with fever and feel all hot and weightless. I dream I'm flying over a sandy beach in the early morning sun, kissing the leaves of the trees as I fly by. And there's always the smell of apples, just like in the country when I was little and used to think I was a choo-choo train, running through the fields of corn and chugging up the hill to the orchard. And all the time I'm dreaming this, I get lighter and lighter until I'm flying over the beach again, getting blown through the sky like a feather that weighs nothing at all. But once I spread my fingers in the dirt and **crouch** over the Get on Your Mark, the dream goes and I am solid again and am telling

crouch *v.* to stoop with bent knees

11. **periscope:** a tube with mirrors or prisms inside through which a person can see the reflection of an object at the other end.

DIFFERENTIATED INSTRUCTION

FOR ADVANCED LEARNERS/PRE–AP

Analyze Character Point out that readers learn about many dimensions of Squeaky's character. Ask students to organize their insights into her character in a Character Map. Have students include details from the text as well as their own inferences. Then have students present their maps to the class.

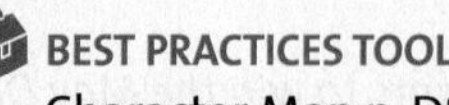
BEST PRACTICES TOOLKIT—Transparency
Character Map p. D8

myself, Squeaky you must win, you must win, you are the fastest thing in the world, you can even beat your father up Amsterdam if you really try. **G** And then I feel my weight coming back just behind my knees then down to my feet then into the earth and the pistol shot explodes in my blood and I am off and weightless again, flying past the other runners, my arms pumping up and down and the whole world is quiet except for the crunch as I zoom over the gravel in the track. I glance to my left and there is no one. To the right, a blurred Gretchen, who's got her chin jutting out as if it would win the race all by itself. And on the other side of the fence is Raymond with his arms down to his side and the palms tucked up behind him, running in his very own style, and it's the first time I ever saw that and I almost stop to watch my brother Raymond on his first run. But the white ribbon is bouncing toward me and I tear past it, racing into the distance till my feet with a mind of their own start digging up footfuls of dirt and brake me short. Then all the kids standing on the side pile on me, banging me on the back and slapping my head with their May Day programs, for I have won again and everybody on 151st Street can walk tall for another year.

"In first place . . ." the man on the loudspeaker is clear as a bell now. But then he pauses and the loudspeaker starts to whine. Then static. And I lean down to catch my breath and here comes Gretchen walking back, for she's overshot the finish line too, huffing and puffing with her hands on her hips taking it slow, breathing in steady time like a real pro and I sort of like her a little for the first time. "In first place . . ." and then three or four voices get all mixed up on the loudspeaker and I dig my sneaker into the grass and stare at Gretchen who's staring back, we both wondering just who did win. I can hear old Beanstalk arguing with the man on the loudspeaker and then a few others running their mouths about what the stopwatches say. Then I hear Raymond yanking at the fence to call me and I wave to shush him, but he keeps rattling the fence like a gorilla in a cage like in them gorilla movies, but then like a dancer or something he starts climbing up nice and easy but very fast. And it occurs to me, watching how smoothly he climbs hand over hand and remembering how he looked running with his arms down to his side and with the wind pulling his mouth back and his teeth showing and all, it occurred to me that Raymond would make a very fine runner. Doesn't he always keep up with me on my trots? And he surely knows how to breathe in counts of seven cause he's always doing it at the dinner table, which drives my brother George up the wall. And I'm smiling to beat the band cause if I've lost this race, or if me and Gretchen tied, or even if I've won, I can always retire as a runner and begin a whole new career as a coach with Raymond as my champion. After all, with a little more study I can beat Cynthia and her phony self at the spelling bee. And if I bugged my mother, I could get piano lessons and become a star. And I have a big rep as the baddest thing around. And I've got a roomful of ribbons and medals and awards. But what has Raymond got to call his own? **H**

G MAKE INFERENCES Why do you think Squeaky always feels this way before a race?

2 Targeted Passage

H PLOT: CLIMAX Why is this a **turning point** in the story?

READING SKILL

G MAKE INFERENCES

Possible answer: *This is Squeaky's way of focusing her energy before the race. Imagining herself flying and her childhood memories make her feel free. She goes through the same ritual each time, freeing her mind and letting her body take over.*

Lines 205–216

DISCUSSION PROMPTS

Use these prompts to help students understand Squeaky's response to running:

Connect How do you feel when you read the description of Squeaky's sensations in this part of the story? *Students may say that they can almost feel the energy surging through them.*

Analyze How does the language in this part of the story create an impression of Squeaky's speed? ***Possible answer:*** *She describes the pistol shot as exploding in her blood and then herself as "flying" past the other runners. She also says that Gretchen is "blurred."*

Synthesize Does Squeaky run with her mind or with her body? Explain. ***Possible answer:*** *Her body seems to take over. She stops thinking and just moves until her feet, "with a mind of their own," bring her to a stop.*

LITERARY ANALYSIS

H PLOT: CLIMAX

Possible answer: *This is a turning point because Squeaky sees beyond her own ambitions to recognize her brother's potential. She realizes that there is more to her life than running and that by helping her brother she could enrich both his life and her own.*

If students need help . . . Explain that the plot threads of Raymond's situation and Squeaky's running come together at this moment: Squeaky finds a new path for both Raymond and herself.

FOR LESS-PROFICIENT READERS

2 Targeted Passage [Lines 205–236]

This passage increases suspense and foreshadows the turning point of the story.

- Why is Squeaky surprised when she sees Raymond running?
- Why aren't the results announced immediately?
- What does Squeaky notice about Raymond when he climbs over the fence? What thought occurs to her?

FOR ENGLISH LEARNERS

Reading: Background Point out the delay in announcing the winner in lines 220–229. Explain that if two runners are close together, it may be difficult to see who actually broke the tape. Therefore, officials also time the runners with stopwatches, which precisely record the moment when someone completes the course. In this situation, Gretchen and Squeaky cross the finish line so closely that the officials have to compare the times in order to determine the winner of the race.

ANALYZE VISUALS

Possible answer: She feels that she is the best runner in the race. One clue is the way she holds up one finger to mean "I'm number one."

Lines 246–257

REINFORCE *KEY IDEA:* MOTIVATION

Discuss In what way has Squeaky's **motivation** for running changed? ***Possible answer:*** *Now her running will be for the sake of helping Raymond reach his potential as an athlete.*

LITERARY ANALYSIS

❶ PLOT: FALLING ACTION AND RESOLUTION

Possible answer: *Squeaky is just as excited about her realization that Raymond is a runner as she is about winning. She has a new respect for Gretchen and a new outlook for the future.*

SELECTION WRAP-UP

REFLECT What would you predict about Squeaky's potential for success in life? Why?

★ CRITIQUE How would your appreciation and enjoyment of the story be affected if Squeaky used standard English? Explain.

READING FLUENCY

Distribute the copy masters and have students practice fluency.

RESOURCE MANAGER—Copy Master
Reading Fluency p. 37

ANALYZE VISUALS
What can you **infer** about how the girl in red feels about herself? Tell what clues you used to make your inference.

So I stand there with my new plans, laughing out loud by this time as Raymond jumps down from the fence and runs over with his teeth showing and his arms down to the side, which no one before him has quite mastered as a running style. And by the time he comes over I'm jumping up and down so glad to see him—my brother Raymond, a great runner in the family tradition. But of course everyone thinks I'm jumping up and down because the men on the loudspeaker have finally gotten themselves together and compared notes and are announcing, "In first place—Miss Hazel Elizabeth Deborah Parker." (Dig that.) "In second place—Miss Gretchen P. Lewis." And I look over at Gretchen wondering what the "P" stands for. And I smile. Cause she's good, no doubt about it. Maybe she'd like to help me coach Raymond; she obviously is serious about running, as any fool can see. And she nods to congratulate me and then she smiles. And I smile. We stand there with this big smile of respect between us. It's about as real a smile as girls can do for each other, considering we don't practice real smiling every day, you know, cause maybe we too busy being flowers or fairies or strawberries instead of something honest and worthy of respect . . . you know . . . like being people. ❶

❸ Targeted Passage

❶ PLOT: FALLING ACTION AND RESOLUTION
How does Squeaky react to the announcement that she won the race?

DIFFERENTIATED INSTRUCTION

FOR LESS-PROFICIENT READERS

❸ Targeted Passage [Lines 246–262]

This passage presents the resolution of the conflicts: Squeaky wins the race and reconciles with Gretchen.

- What is the real reason that Squeaky is jumping up and down?
- How do Squeaky's feelings about Gretchen change after the race?
- What do Squeaky's future plans include?

FOR ADVANCED LEARNERS/PRE-AP

Analyze [small-group option] Squeaky's complete name is announced at the end of the race. In what way might the use of her full name rather than her nickname symbolize how she has changed? Ask students to discuss this idea in small groups.

After Reading

Comprehension

1. **Recall** Tell what nickname the big kids have given Squeaky. Why do they call her that?
2. **Clarify** Why does Squeaky feel the May Pole dance is a waste of time?
3. **Clarify** Describe Squeaky's reaction when she sees Raymond running parallel to her in the race.

Literary Analysis

4. **Make Inferences** Review the inference equations you created as you read the story. Use these **inferences** to answer this question: Why might Squeaky react to other people the way she does? Give details from the story to support your answer.
5. **Compare and Contrast** What are some differences between Squeaky and Gretchen? What are some similarities?
6. **Analyze Plot** The plot of "Raymond's Run" revolves around Squeaky's desire to win the May Day race. Using a diagram like the one shown, note the events that happen at each stage of the **plot**.

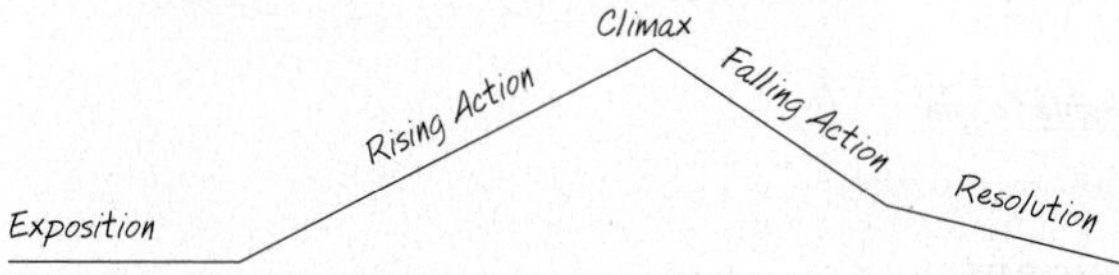

7. **Draw Conclusions** How do the events in the story change the way Squeaky views competition?
8. **Evaluate a Character** Does the character Squeaky seem like a real person? Why or why not?

Extension and Challenge

9. **Big Question Activity** Review the Quickwrite activity on page 32. If Squeaky were in your class, what do you think her response to this activity would be? Complete the activity again, writing about her **motivation** as if you were she.
10. **Inquiry and Research** According to Squeaky, Raymond has a "big head." Find out more about hydrocephalus, the condition he has. With the medical advances of today, is there a treatment or cure for hydrocephalus? What is known about the causes of it? Present your findings to the class.

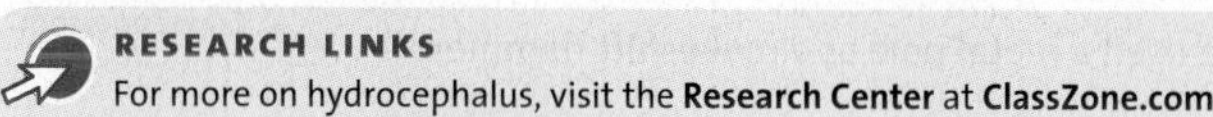

RESEARCH LINKS
For more on hydrocephalus, visit the **Research Center** at **ClassZone.com.**

Practice and Apply

After Reading

For additional support of postreading questions, use these copy masters:

RESOURCE MANAGER—Copy Masters
Reading Check p. 34 (to check understanding of the selection)
Plot p. 27 (for practice of literary analysis standards focus)
Question Support p. 35 (After Reading questions adapted for English learners and less-proficient readers)
Additional selection questions are provided for teachers on page 21.

For additional activities to challenge students, see

Power Thinking at **ClassZone.com**

ANSWERS

Comprehension

1. *The big kids call her Mercury, because she runs so quickly.*
2. *Squeaky would rather spend her time running than dressing up or dancing.*
3. *She is amazed and pleased to see Raymond running beside her.*

Literary Analysis

Possible answers:

4. **STANDARDS FOCUS Make Inferences** *Squeaky is intolerant of anything or anyone that is not real, such as Cynthia Procter's pretense that she does not practice or study. She says that "you should be trying to be yourself" (line 124). She has no time for anyone who makes fun of Raymond, such as Rosie, who "has a big mouth where Raymond is concerned" (line 77).*
5. ***Differences:*** *Gretchen has friends and freckles and does not have a responsibility like Raymond. Squeaky has Raymond rather than friends.* ***Similarities:*** *Both are the same age, are runners, and are competitive.*
6. **STANDARDS FOCUS Plot**
   - ***Exposition:*** *introduces Squeaky, her desire to win the race, Raymond*
   - ***Rising Action:*** *encounter with Gretchen, wait for the race to begin, race against Gretchen, wait for the winner to be announced*
   - ***Climax:*** *Squeaky decides she doesn't care if she wins and realizes Raymond could be a good runner.*
   - ***Falling Action and Resolution:*** *Squeaky wins the race, smiles at Gretchen, and plans to coach Raymond.*
7. *Squeaky has a new respect for her competitors.*
8. *Yes. Squeaky speaks and acts in a way that is consistent with her character as a young girl from Harlem who has to defend herself and her brother.*

Extension and Challenge

9. *Students' responses should identify her goal to be the best runner. To do this, she practices hard, taking Raymond along. They might identify her motivation as both external and internal. She wants to show people like Gretchen that she is the best runner. She also has an inner drive to overcome obstacles and succeed.*
10. *Students' reports should include answers to the questions and should draw information from reliable sources.*

ANSWERS

Vocabulary in Context

VOCABULARY PRACTICE

1. *a friend*
2. *holding it close*
3. *talented*
4. *picking a flower from the garden*
5. *likely*
6. *a team effort*

 RESOURCE MANAGER—Copy Master
Vocabulary Practice p. 32

VOCABULARY IN WRITING

Have students brainstorm possible thoughts and feelings, using a Cluster Diagram. Then have them review the vocabulary list and identify words that could be used to express these ideas.

BEST PRACTICES TOOLKIT—Transparency
Cluster Diagram p. B18

VOCABULARY STRATEGY: COMPOUND WORDS *(also an EL language objective)*

As a class, identify context clues in each sentence. Then break the compound words into their components before students define them.

Possible answers:

1. *"a complete stopping of activity or movement"*
2. *"path marked off to indicate where pedestrians can cross a street"*
3. *"electrical device that amplifies sound"*
4. *"received from the original source"*
5. *"temporary substitute for something else"*

RESOURCE MANAGER—Copy Master
Vocabulary Strategy p. 33

Vocabulary Center at **ClassZone.com**
Additional Vocabulary Activities

Vocabulary in Context

VOCABULARY PRACTICE

Answer each question to show your understanding of the vocabulary words.

1. Is a **sidekick** likely to be a friend or someone you just met?
2. If you were to **clutch** something, would you be tossing it away or holding it close?
3. Which would you expect a sports **prodigy** to be—clumsy or talented?
4. When are you more likely to **crouch**—picking a flower from the garden or reaching for a glass in the cabinet?
5. If a person is **liable** to do something, does that mean it's likely or unlikely to happen?
6. What's more important in a **relay** race—one good runner or a team effort?

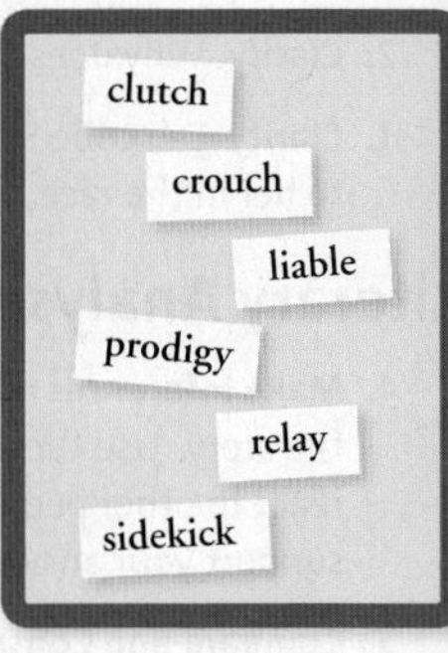

VOCABULARY IN WRITING

Pretend you are going to run in a race with Squeaky. Using at least two vocabulary words, write a paragraph about your thoughts and feelings at the starting line. You could begin like this.

> **EXAMPLE SENTENCE**
>
> *I'm going to run in this race, even if I'm not **liable** to win.*

VOCABULARY STRATEGY: COMPOUND WORDS

Compound words are made up of two or more smaller words. Sometimes the meaning of a compound word can be figured out from the meaning of the two words. Other times, as with the word *sidekick,* you would have to look at context clues or the dictionary to find out the meaning.

PRACTICE Use context clues to figure out the meaning of each boldfaced compound word. Then write the definition. You can consult a dictionary if you need to.

1. Traffic was at a **standstill** after the semitrailer blocked the highway.
2. When the children get to the **crosswalk,** have them look both ways before crossing the street.
3. If the audience is having trouble hearing you, make the announcement over the **loudspeaker.**
4. Since you heard it directly from the source, it's **firsthand** knowledge.
5. We couldn't find the tools, so we used a metal pole as a **makeshift** hammer.

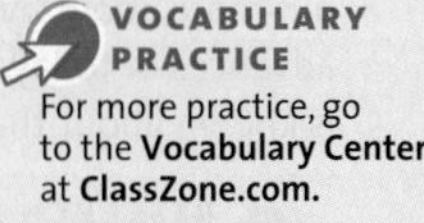
VOCABULARY PRACTICE
For more practice, go to the **Vocabulary Center** at **ClassZone.com.**

DIFFERENTIATED INSTRUCTION

FOR ENGLISH LEARNERS

Vocabulary in Writing Give students some sentence frames to help them express their thoughts and use vocabulary words in their sentences.

If I were racing against Squeaky, I would feel ____.

She is a [vocabulary word].

I would not be [vocabulary word] to win. I would run anyway, though, because it would be ____.

FOR ADVANCED LEARNERS/PRE-AP

Vocabulary in Writing Have students write their paragraphs in a "stream-of-consciousness" style, similar to the technique the author used in the story to express Squeaky's thoughts.

Reading-Writing Connection

Increase your understanding of "Raymond's Run" by responding to these prompts. Then complete the **Grammar and Writing** exercise.

WRITING PROMPTS	SELF-CHECK
A. Short Response: Describe a Character's World Squeaky's personality and experiences are influenced by her environment. Write **one paragraph** describing Squeaky's neighborhood and how it affected her.	***A strong description will . . .*** • provide details about the streets and traffic • show Squeaky's relationship to neighborhood people and places
B. Extended Response: Write an Article Imagine you are a newspaper writer covering the May Day events at the park. You are assigned to interview runners and ask them about their **motivation** for participating. Write a **two- or three-paragraph** article that will appear in the next day's paper.	***A thorough article will . . .*** • answer *who, what, when, where,* and *why* questions • include quotes from characters in the story

GRAMMAR AND WRITING

AVOID SENTENCE FRAGMENTS A **sentence fragment** is an incomplete sentence. It is missing a subject (whom or what the sentence is about), a predicate (what the subject is or does), or both. The missing part(s) must be added in order to fix, or complete, the sentence.

Original: My brother. (*This is a sentence fragment because it is missing a predicate.*) He likes movies with a lot of action.

Revised: My brother likes movies with a lot of action. (*This is now a complete sentence because it contains the subject "My brother" and the predicate "likes movies with a lot of action."*)

PRACTICE Decide whether the following sentence fragments in bold are missing a subject, a predicate, or both. Then combine each fragment with the sentence before it, inserting any additional words as needed.

1. The crowd gathered in the park. **For the May Day festivities.**
2. They gathered, as usual. **The regulars, or parkees.**
3. For many, the May Pole dance is the highlight. **For others, the races.**
4. I'm sure I'll win again. **Always do.**
5. He was the surprise of the day. **Squeaky's brother Raymond.**

*For more help with fragments, see page R64 in the **Grammar Handbook**.*

Reading-Writing Connection

WRITING PROMPTS

- For **Prompt A,** have students skim the story and jot down details about the physical environment and the social setting.
- For **Prompt B,** suggest that students first brainstorm possible motivations for participating in various May Day events, including the track meet and the dancing.

For an extended Reading-Writing Connection activity, see

Writing Center at **ClassZone.com**

GRAMMAR AND WRITING

Remind students that sentence fragments are unacceptable in formal writing, although writers may include them in dialogue.

Possible answers:

1. *(both) The crowd gathered in the park for the May Day festivities.*
2. *(predicate) The regulars, or parkees, gathered as usual.*
3. *(predicate) For many, the May Pole dance is the highlight; for others, the races are the highlight.*
4. *(subject) I'm sure I'll win again, because I always do.*
5. *(predicate) Squeaky's brother Raymond was the surprise of the day.*

RESOURCE MANAGER—Copy Master
Avoid Sentence Fragments p. 36

Assess and Reteach

Assess

RESOURCE MANAGER—Copy Masters
Selection Tests A, B/C pp. 39–40, 41–42

Test Generator CD

Reteach

STANDARDS LESSON FILE
Literature Lesson 5: Elements of Plot
Reading Lesson 8: Making Inferences
Grammar Lesson 1: Avoiding Sentence Fragments

DIFFERENTIATED INSTRUCTION

FOR LESS–PROFICIENT WRITERS

For Prompt A:

1. Help students identify some of Squeaky's characteristics: *tough, opinionated, energetic, street smart, independent.*
2. Then have students find details in the story that tell about Squeaky's family life, her acquaintances, and where she lives.
3. Chart the connection between the circumstances of Squeaky's life and her character traits before students write their paragraphs.

For Prompt B:

1. Distribute copies of the Reporter's Questions.
2. Have students work in groups to answer the questions from the perspective of Squeaky and insert relevant quotations from the story.
3. Then have students use the details and quotations to independently write a one-paragraph article.

BEST PRACTICES TOOLKIT—Transparency
Reporter's Questions p. C9

Focus and Motivate

OBJECTIVES

Literary Analysis
- explore the key idea of **the unexpected**
- identify and analyze conflict and resolution
- read a short story and an anecdote

Reading
- make predictions

Vocabulary
- build vocabulary for reading and writing
- determine meanings of derivatives by applying knowledge of the Latin prefix *com- (also an EL language objective)*

Grammar and Writing
- correct run-on sentences
- use writing to analyze literature

SUMMARY

Bill and Sam are con men who kidnap the son of a prominent citizen in a small town and hold him for a $2,000 ransom. The boy, who insists on being called Red Chief, terrorizes Bill until Bill begs Sam to reduce the ransom. In reply to the ransom note, the boy's father offers to take his son back if the men will pay him $250. The men agree and happily leave the boy, their money, and the town behind.

Is any plan FOOLPROOF?

Discuss the question and the ***KEY IDEA***. Ask if students have ever heard the saying "Expect **the unexpected.**" Have them share anecdotes of times when they followed that advice and times when they did not. Then have students complete the ***LIST IT*** activity.

Before Reading

The Ransom of Red Chief

Short Story by O. Henry

Is any plan FOOLPROOF?

KEY IDEA You can make a list. You can check it twice. You can go over every last detail of a plan in your mind. But even when you think you've thought of everything, **the unexpected** can change the outcome in surprising, terrible, or sometimes hysterically funny ways. In the story you are about to read, the main characters have a plan for making some quick money, but things don't work out the way they had hoped.

LIST IT With a partner, plan a surprise party for a friend by making a list of what you need to do. Then, next to each item, write down something unexpected that could possibly happen to spoil that part of the plan.

Lu's Party!
E-mail our group to invite them.
Forget to take Lu off the list.

46

Selection Resources

RESOURCE MANAGER UNIT 1

Plan and Teach pp. 43–50

Literary Analysis
Summary pp. 51†*, 52‡*
Conflict and Resolution pp. 53, 54†*
Question Support p. 61*

Reading
Predict pp. 55, 56†*
Reading Check p. 60
Reading Fluency p. 63

Vocabulary
Study p. 57*
Practice p. 58
Strategy p. 59

Grammar and Writing
Avoid Run-On Sentences p. 62

Assessment
Selection Tests A, B/C pp. 65*, 67*
Test Generator CD

BEST PRACTICES TOOLKIT

Differentiated Instruction pp. 31–38*
Scaffolding Instruction pp. 43–46*

Graphic Organizers/Strategies
Reciprocal Teaching • Definition Mapping • T Chart • Making Inferences • Sequence Circle

Reading Support
Audio Anthology CD*

Technology
Literature, Vocabulary, and Writing Centers at **ClassZone.com**
Write*Smart* CD

* Resources for Differentiation † Also in Spanish ‡ In Haitian Creole and Vietnamese

LITERARY ANALYSIS: CONFLICT AND RESOLUTION

A story's plot centers on **conflicts,** or struggles between opposing forces. By the end of the story, the conflicts are usually **resolved,** or settled. For example, a fight between two characters might be resolved when one character wins and one character loses. As you read "The Ransom of Red Chief," pay attention to the conflicts and note how they are resolved.

READING STRATEGY: PREDICT

When you watch TV shows or read books, do you ever try to guess what will happen next? If you do, you're making **predictions.** As you read this story, use clues from the text and your own common sense to make predictions. Keep track of whether your predictions were right, or whether you were surprised by the way events unfolded.

My Prediction	Actual Event	Correct or Surprised?
The boy will fight back when kidnapped.	Boy fights back.	correct

Review: Make Inferences

VOCABULARY IN CONTEXT

O. Henry's characters use the words listed, but they aren't as smart as their big vocabulary suggests. See how many words you can match with their numbered definitions.

WORD LIST			
	collaborate	diatribe	provisions
	commend	impudent	ransom
	comply	proposition	

1. payment demanded for the release of a person or property
2. to act according to a command or request
3. verbal attack; harsh criticism
4. bold and disrespectful
5. to work together on a project
6. to praise
7. necessary supplies, especially food
8. a suggested plan

Author Online

Unexpected Twists
The early life of O. Henry, whose real name was William Sydney Porter, was filled with ups, downs, and unexpected turns. As a young man, he held many different jobs. He clerked in his uncle's drugstore, worked as a ranch hand, and became a bank teller. Several years after leaving his position at the bank, he was convicted of having embezzled, or stolen, money from his employer. It certainly wasn't his plan to be put in jail, but that's where he found his next occupation.

O. Henry
1862–1910

A Trailblazing Storyteller While behind bars, Porter began penning stories to help support his young daughter. Upon his release, he changed his name to O. Henry, became a fiction writer, and contributed weekly stories to newspapers. He grew into one of the country's best-loved authors. O. Henry wrote adventure stories, humorous stories, and slice-of-life tales of ordinary people. The stories often had surprise endings. Today, stories that end with an unexpected twist are said to be written in the "O. Henry style."

MORE ABOUT THE AUTHOR
For more on O. Henry, visit the **Literature Center** at **ClassZone.com.**

Teach

STANDARDS FOCUS

LITERARY ANALYSIS

● CONFLICT AND RESOLUTION

Write this example on the board:

The hikers had been on the trail for two hours when the downpour began. Luckily, their guide led them to a cabin where they took shelter from the storm.

Ask students to identify the conflict and its resolution. ***Possible answer:*** *The conflict is that the hikers are caught in a storm. It is resolved when they find shelter.*

CHECK UNDERSTANDING Ask students to identify conflicts and resolutions in stories that they have previously read.

READING STRATEGY

■ PREDICT

Write this example on the board:

Jenna sighed. She had never met a more difficult three-year-old. With relief, she heard the parents' car pull in the driveway. Soon they were asking, "Can you babysit again next week?"

Ask students what they think Jenna's answer will be. ***Possible answer:*** *She will probably say no.*

CHECK UNDERSTANDING Have students explain their predictions.

RESOURCE MANAGER—Copy Master
Predict p. 55 (for student use while reading the selection)

VOCABULARY SKILL

▲ VOCABULARY IN CONTEXT

DIAGNOSE WORD KNOWLEDGE To determine preteaching needs, have all students complete **Vocabulary in Context.** ***Answers:*** 1. *ransom* 2. *comply* 3. *diatribe* 4. *impudent* 5. *collaborate* 6. *commend* 7. *provisions* 8. *proposition*

PRETEACH VOCABULARY Use the Vocabulary Study copy master to help students create a word map for each boldfaced word.

1. Read aloud the first sentence in Part A.
2. Help students create a word map for *collaborate.* Point out that they may not be able to fill in every box for every word.
3. Repeat the procedure for each of the other sentences.
4. Have students complete Part B independently.

RESOURCE MANAGER—Copy Master
Vocabulary Study p. 57

For general guidelines on differentiating vocabulary instruction and for alternative vocabulary activities for students not needing vocabulary preteaching, see

BEST PRACTICES TOOLKIT
Scaffolding Vocabulary Instruction pp. 43–46

Vocabulary Center at **ClassZone.com**
Additional Vocabulary Activities

Practice and Apply

ANALYZE VISUALS

Possible answer: *The boy's expression suggests that he is sly and mischievous. The feathers in his hair suggest that he likes to role-play and may be very imaginative.*

About the Art Esao Andrews is noted for his slightly off-kilter and humorous paintings, such as the one on page 49. He typically uses oil on wood and has been influenced by other artists as well as by his life experiences.

Lines 1–16
DISCUSSION PROMPTS

Use these prompts to help students understand the kidnapping plan:

Connect Do Sam and Bill match your image of kidnappers? Explain. *Students may say that the men seem too friendly or casual to be cold-blooded, ruthless kidnappers.*

Analyze Do Bill and Sam put a lot of thought into their plan? How do you know? ***Possible answers:***

- *No. Sam mentions that they talked it over on the steps of the hotel (line 10), which suggests that they came up with the kidnapping idea on the spur of the moment.*
- *Yes. The phrase* talked it over *(line 10) suggests that Sam and Bill considered all of the logical reasons why "a kidnapping project" (line 12) in Summit, specifically, was the safest way to get the money they needed.*

Evaluate Do you think the reasoning behind their plan is sound? Explain. ***Possible answer:*** *They are probably right about Summit's lack of law enforcement resources, but their idea that rural communities foster greater parental love than other places seems questionable.*

READING STRATEGY

A PREDICT

Possible answer: *No. The narrator's comment suggests that something will go wrong with the plan.*

Extend the Discussion What is the effect of Sam's comment on readers?

O. HENRY

It looked like a good thing; but wait till I tell you. We were down South, in Alabama—Bill Driscoll and myself—when this kidnapping idea struck us. It was, as Bill afterward expressed it, "during a moment of temporary mental apparition";[1] but we didn't find that out till later.

There was a town down there, as flat as a flannel-cake, and called Summit, of course. It contained inhabitants of as undeleterious[2] and self-satisfied a class of peasantry as ever clustered around a Maypole.

Bill and me had a joint capital of about six hundred dollars, and we needed just two thousand dollars more to pull off a fraudulent town-lot scheme in Western Illinois with. We talked it over on the front steps of the hotel. Philoprogenitiveness,[3] says we, is strong in semi-rural communities; therefore, and for other reasons, a kidnapping project ought to do better there than in the radius of newspapers that send reporters out in plain clothes to stir up talk about such things. We knew that Summit couldn't get after us with anything stronger than constables, and, maybe, some lackadaisical bloodhounds and a **diatribe** or two in the *Weekly Farmers' Budget.* So, it looked good.

We selected for our victim the only child of a prominent citizen named Ebenezer Dorset. The father was respectable and tight, a mortgage fancier and a stern, upright collection-plate passer and forecloser. The kid was a boy of ten, with bas-relief[4] freckles, and hair the color of the cover of the magazine you buy at the news-stand when you want to catch a train. Bill and me figured that Ebenezer would melt down for a **ransom** of two thousand dollars to a cent. But wait till I tell you. **A**

ANALYZE VISUALS
What personality **traits** might the boy in the painting possess?

1 Targeted Passage

diatribe (dī'ə-trīb') *n.* bitter, abusive criticism

ransom (răn'səm) *n.* payment demanded for the release of a person or property

A PREDICT
Reread lines 17–23. Based on Sam's final comment, do you think the men's plan will be successful? Add this prediction to your chart.

1. **apparition** (ăp'ə-rĭsh'ən): a sudden or unusual sight.
2. **undeleterious** (ŭn-dĕl'ĭ-tîr'ē-əs): harmless.
3. **philoprogenitiveness** (fĭl'ō-prō-jĕn'ĭ-tĭv-nĕs): love for one's own children.
4. **bas-relief** (bä'rĭ-lēf'): slightly raised.

Illustrations by Esao Andrews.

DIFFERENTIATED INSTRUCTION

FOR ALL STUDENTS

Hands-On Learning [mixed-interest groups] Have students work in small groups to create a storyboard for one or more episodes from "The Ransom of Red Chief." Ask groups to use their storyboards as the basis of a dramatic adaptation of that part of the story.

FOR LESS–PROFICIENT READERS

In combination with the *Audio Anthology CD,* use one or more Targeted Passages (pp. 48, 50, 54, 57) to ensure that students focus on key story events, concepts, and skills.

1 Targeted Passage [Lines 5–23]

This passage explains Sam and Bill's motives for kidnapping and why they choose Summit.

- Why do Sam and Bill feel that Summit is the safest place to carry out their plan?
- How much more money do Sam and Bill need? Why do they need the money?
- What are some possible reasons that Sam and Bill choose the son of Ebenezer Dorset as their "victim"?

BACKGROUND

David and Goliath In lines 142–143, Sam compares the sound the boy is making to one David might have made as he knocked out Goliath. According to the Bible, Goliath was a giant warrior in the Philistine army. He challenged any Israelite to try to overcome him. David, a young boy, accepted. He used his slingshot to bring the giant Goliath down.

Pirates of Penzance In line 312, after reading the reply from the boy's father, Sam exclaims, "Great Pirates of Penzance!" *The Pirates of Penzance* is a Gilbert and Sullivan opera, which opened in 1879 and became an enormous success both in America and in England. The plot revolves around a band of pirates, a group of beautiful women, mistaken identities, and numerous complications.

FOR ENGLISH LEARNERS

Options for Reading Read lines 1–23 aloud. Explain that the kidnappers' wordy language is meant to be humorous because it doesn't seem to suit these characters. Continue reading the story aloud, or have students read along with the *Audio Anthology CD.* Have groups use a Reciprocal Teaching strategy to help their comprehension.

BEST PRACTICES TOOLKIT—Transparency
Reciprocal Teaching p. A35

Key Academic Vocabulary Have students use Definition Mapping to learn this academic vocabulary: *scheme* (lines 10, 219, 281), *project* (line 12), *features* (lines 39, 273), *approach* (line 81), *attitude* (line 117).

BEST PRACTICES TOOLKIT—Transparency
Definition Mapping p. E6

Prereading For prereading instruction for English learners, see

BEST PRACTICES TOOLKIT
Scaffolding Reading Instruction pp. 43–46

FOR ADVANCED LEARNERS/PRE-AP

Pre-AP exercises in the bottom channel provide additional challenge for your advanced students. Use them for small groups or individuals.

ADDITIONAL GUIDELINES

For more help with differentiation and tips for classroom management, see

BEST PRACTICES TOOLKIT
Differentiated Instruction pp. 31–38

About two miles from Summit was a little mountain, covered with a dense cedar brake.[5] On the rear elevation of this mountain was a cave. There we stored **provisions.**

provisions (prə-vĭzh′ənz) *n.* necessary supplies; food

One evening after sundown, we drove in a buggy past old Dorset's house. The kid was in the street, throwing rocks at a kitten on the opposite fence.

"Hey, little boy!" says Bill, "would you like to have a bag of candy and a nice ride?"

Targeted Passage

The boy catches Bill neatly in the eye with a piece of brick.

"That will cost the old man an extra five hundred dollars," says Bill, climbing over the wheel.

That boy put up a fight like a welter-weight cinnamon bear; but, at last, we got him down in the bottom of the buggy and drove away. We took him up to the cave, and I hitched the horse in the cedar brake. After dark I drove the buggy to the little village, three miles away, where we had hired it, and walked back to the mountain. **B**

B CONFLICT Who is in conflict and why?

Bill was pasting court plaster[6] over the scratches and bruises on his features. There was a fire burning behind the big rock at the entrance of the cave, and the boy was watching a pot of boiling coffee, with two buzzard tail feathers stuck in his red hair. He points a stick at me when I come up, and says:

"Ha! cursed paleface, do you dare to enter the camp of Red Chief, the terror of the plains?" **C**

C PREDICT How do you think the boy will respond to being held in captivity?

"He's all right now," says Bill, rolling up his trousers and examining some bruises on his shins. "We're playing Indian. We're making Buffalo Bill's show look like magic-lantern views[7] of Palestine in the town hall. I'm Old Hank, the Trapper, Red Chief's captive, and I'm to be scalped at daybreak. By Geronimo! that kid can kick hard."

SOCIAL STUDIES CONNECTION

In 1883, William F. Cody began producing Buffalo Bill's Wild West Show, a traveling extravaganza celebrating and glorifying the American West.

Yes, sir, that boy seemed to be having the time of his life. The fun of camping out in a cave had made him forget that he was a captive himself. He immediately christened me Snake-eye, the Spy, and announced that, when his braves returned from the warpath, I was to be broiled at the stake at the rising of the sun.

Then we had supper; and he filled his mouth full of bacon and bread and gravy, and began to talk. He made a during-dinner speech something like this:

"I like this fine. I never camped out before; but I had a pet 'possum once, and I was nine last birthday. I hate to go to school. Rats ate up sixteen of Jimmy Talbot's aunt's speckled hen's eggs. Are there any real Indians in these woods? I want some more gravy. Does the trees moving make the wind blow? We had five puppies. What makes your nose so red, Hank? My father has lots of money. Are the stars hot? I whipped Ed Walker twice, Saturday. I don't like girls. You dassent[8] catch toads unless with a string. Do oxen make any noise?

5. **brake:** a thick grouping of trees.
6. **court plaster:** adhesive cloth for covering cuts and scratches.
7. **magic-lantern views:** slides.
8. **dassant:** dare not.

LITERARY ANALYSIS

B CONFLICT

Possible answer: *Bill and Sam are in conflict with their kidnapping victim. When they try to get the boy into the buggy, he puts up a fight.*

If students need help . . . Remind them that conflict is a struggle between two opposing forces. It might be external, such as a fight between characters, or it might be internal, such as a character's anxiety or worry over a problem.

READING STRATEGY

C PREDICT

Remind students to record their predictions in their charts from page 47. ***Possible answer:*** *The boy will not like being held captive and will cause problems for the kidnappers.*

If students need help . . . List these details about the boy on the board: *throws rocks at kittens, fights when the men try to put him in the buggy, shows no fear over being kidnapped.* Guide students to use this information to make a logical guess about his future behavior as a captive.

SOCIAL STUDIES CONNECTION

By the age of 14, William F. Cody had already prospected for gold and secured a position as a rider for the Pony Express. When the Civil War broke out, he fought with the Seventh Kansas Cavalry and continued scouting for the army after the war ended. He won his nickname "Buffalo Bill" at this time, hunting buffalo to help feed the crew building the transcontinental railroad. Meanwhile, he was becoming well known for his exploits through a series of novels written about "Buffalo Bill." The author of these books persuaded Bill to take a role in a play he had written, and Cody's stage career was born. He acted in theaters for several years before organizing his own show, which at times included more than 1,000 performers. They traveled throughout North America and Europe, making "Buffalo Bill" a household name.

DIFFERENTIATED INSTRUCTION

FOR LESS–PROFICIENT READERS

② Targeted Passage [Lines 27–54]

This passage sets up the major conflict of the story: Sam and Bill kidnap the boy.

- Where do the men take the boy?
- What is Bill doing when Sam returns to the cave? Why?
- How would you describe the boy's behavior?

FOR ENGLISH LEARNERS

Culture: Clarify Explain that the boy is pretending to be Red Chief, a Native American warrior, who has captured "Old Hank" (Bill).

- The word *paleface* (line 43) refers to a non–Native American.
- In lines 46–48, Bill says that compared to playing with the boy, Buffalo Bill's show, full of excitement and daring stunts, looks like a boring slide show.
- Geronimo (line 48) was a well-known Native American warrior.

Why are oranges round? Have you got beds to sleep on in this cave? Amos Murray has got six toes. A parrot can talk, but a monkey or a fish can't. How many does it take to make twelve?" **D**

Every few minutes he would remember that he was an Indian, and pick up his stick rifle and tiptoe to the mouth of the cave to search for the scouts of the hated paleface. Now and then he would let out a war whoop that made Old Hank the Trapper shiver. That boy had Bill terrorized from the start.

"Red Chief," says I to the kid, "would you like to go home?"

"Aw, what for?" says he. "I don't have any fun at home. I hate to go to school. I like to camp out. You won't take me back home again, Snake-eye, will you?"

"Not right away," says I. "We'll stay here in the cave awhile."

"All right!" says he. "That'll be fine. I never had such fun in all my life."

We went to bed about eleven o'clock. We spread down some wide blankets and quilts and put Red Chief between us. We weren't afraid he'd run away. He kept us awake for three hours, jumping up and reaching for his rifle and screeching: "Hist! pard," in mine and Bill's ears, as the fancied crackle of a twig or the rustle of a leaf revealed to his young imagination the stealthy approach of the outlaw band. At last, I fell into a troubled sleep, and dreamed that I had been kidnapped and chained to a tree by a ferocious pirate with red hair.

Just at daybreak, I was awakened by a series of awful screams from Bill. They weren't yells, or howls, or shouts, or whoops, or yawps, such as you'd expect from a manly set of vocal organs—they were simply indecent, terrifying, humiliating screams, such as women emit when they see ghosts or caterpillars. It's an awful thing to hear a strong, desperate, fat man scream incontinently in a cave at daybreak.

I jumped up to see what the matter was. Red Chief was sitting on Bill's chest, with one hand twined in Bill's hair. In the other he had the sharp case-knife we used for slicing bacon; and he was industriously and realistically trying to take Bill's scalp, according to the sentence that had been pronounced upon him the evening before.

I got the knife away from the kid and made him lie down again. But, from that moment, Bill's spirit was broken. He laid down on his side of the bed, but he never closed an eye again in sleep as long as that boy was with us. I dozed off for a while, but along toward sun-up I remembered that Red Chief had said I was to be burned at the stake at the rising of the sun. I wasn't nervous or afraid; but I sat up and leaned against a rock. **E**

"What you getting up so soon for, Sam?" asked Bill.

"Me?" says I. "Oh, I got a kind of a pain in my shoulder. I thought sitting up would rest it."

"You're a liar!" says Bill. "You're afraid. You was to be burned at sunrise, and you was afraid he'd do it. And he would, too, if he could find a match. Ain't it awful, Sam? Do you think anybody will pay out money to get a little imp like that back home?"

D PREDICT
On your chart, note whether the boy's response to captivity matches your prediction. Do you think the boy's current attitude about his captivity will make the men's plan go more smoothly?

E CONFLICT
In what way has his interaction with the boy affected Bill?

READING STRATEGY

D PREDICT

Possible answers:

- ***My Prediction:*** *The boy will not like being held captive and will cause problems for the kidnappers.*
- ***Actual Event:*** *He is enjoying himself.*
- ***Correct or Surprised?:*** *surprised*
- ***My Prediction:*** *Because the boy isn't resisting them, it will be easier to keep him until the ransom is paid.*

Lines 84–94

REINFORCE *KEY IDEA:* THE UNEXPECTED

Discuss What is the boy trying to do to Bill? Why is this action **unexpected?** ***Possible answers:*** *The boy is trying to scalp Bill. This is unexpected because it is daybreak, a time when Bill would expect the boy to be sleeping. Also, the boy is the men's captive, yet he is behaving as if he is the one in control.*

LITERARY ANALYSIS

E CONFLICT

Possible answer: *Sam describes Bill as a "broken" man (line 96). Bill is anxious and afraid of the boy.*

If students need help . . . Explain that in this sentence, *broken* means "weakened" or "destroyed."

FOR LESS–PROFICIENT READERS

Comprehension Support [small-group option]

1. Have students list the events from lines 1–107 in the left column of a T Chart.
2. In the right column, have them place a check mark next to the events that Bill and Sam expected.
3. Next to the other events, have students describe what the men thought would happen.
4. Discuss the significance of the discrepancy between reality and expectation. Help students use this information to make predictions.

BEST PRACTICES TOOLKIT—Transparency
T Chart p. A25

FOR ENGLISH LEARNERS

Language: Conversational English Patterns
Point out the use of *ain't* and the lack of subject-verb agreement in lines 104–107. Explain that since Bill and Sam probably haven't had much formal education, this way of speaking is realistic for their characters. Ask students to find and record other examples of nonstandard speech as they read. Have them write the standard English version next to each example. Review their lists as a class.

Lines 111–130
DISCUSSION PROMPTS

Use these prompts to help students understand the irony of this passage:

Connect If you were Bill, what thoughts would you have at this moment? *Students might say that they would be wishing they hadn't thought of this kidnapping scheme. They might be feeling as if they were the ones being held captive, not vice versa.*

Compare and Contrast What does Sam expect to see when he surveys the countryside? What does he actually see? ***Possible answer:*** *Sam expects to see people searching frantically for the lost boy, dragging the creek and riding across the countryside. Instead, what he sees is a peaceful scene with one farmer plowing in the distance.*

Synthesize What does the irony in this passage suggest about the outcome of the scheme? ***Possible answer:*** *It will end much differently from the way Sam and Bill planned.*

ANALYZE VISUALS

Possible answer: *The boy holds a rock above his head as the man cowers, holding his arms in front of himself for protection. The boy seems to be winning the conflict.*

"Sure," said I. "A rowdy kid like that is just the kind that parents dote on. Now, you and the Chief get up and cook breakfast, while I go up on the top of this mountain and reconnoiter."[9]

I went up on the peak of the little mountain and ran my eye over the contiguous vicinity. Over toward Summit I expected to see the sturdy yeomanry of the village armed with scythes and pitchforks beating the countryside for the dastardly kidnappers. But what I saw was a peaceful landscape dotted with one man plowing with a dun mule. Nobody was dragging the creek; no couriers dashed hither and yon, bringing tidings of no news to the distracted parents. There was a sylvan[10] attitude of somnolent sleepiness pervading that section of the external outward surface of Alabama that lay exposed to my view. "Perhaps," says I to myself, "it has not yet been discovered that the wolves have borne away the tender lambkin from the fold. Heaven help the wolves!" says I, and I went down the mountain to breakfast.

When I got to the cave I found Bill backed up against the side of it, breathing hard, and the boy threatening to smash him with a rock half as big as a coconut.

"He put a red-hot boiled potato down my back," explained Bill, "and then mashed it with his foot; and I boxed his ears. Have you got a gun about you, Sam?"

I took the rock away from the boy and kind of patched up the argument. "I'll fix you," says the kid to Bill. "No man ever yet struck the Red Chief but what he got paid for it. You better beware!"

9. **reconnoiter** (rē'kə-noi'tər): to seek information about an enemy's whereabouts.
10. **sylvan** (sĭl'vən): like woods or forests.

ANALYZE VISUALS
Who seems to be winning the **conflict** in the painting? Tell how you know.

DIFFERENTIATED INSTRUCTION

FOR ADVANCED LEARNERS/PRE–AP

Analyze Style [small-group option] Point out the redundant language in lines 111–121, such as *somnolent sleepiness* and *external outward surface*. Explain that this is one technique O. Henry uses to add to the humor and to develop the characters and plot. He also uses many other devices, such as those listed in this chart. Encourage groups to find examples of each and discuss how they affect readers' understanding and appreciation of the story.

Devices	*Examples*
similes	*"a kind of sigh from Bill, like a horse gives out when you take his saddle off" (lines 145–146)*
metaphors	*"two-legged skyrocket of a kid" (line 173)*
allusions	*"war whoop, such as David might have emitted when he knocked out the champion Goliath" (lines 142–143)*
imagery	*"shook him until his freckles rattled" (line 155)*

After breakfast the kid takes a piece of leather with strings wrapped around it out of his pocket and goes outside the cave unwinding it.

"What's he up to now?" says Bill anxiously. "You don't think he'll run away, do you, Sam?" **F**

"No fear of it," says I. "He don't seem to be much of a homebody. But we've got to fix up some plan about the ransom. There don't seem to be much excitement around Summit on account of his disappearance; but maybe they haven't realized yet that he's gone. His folks may think he's spending the night with Aunt Jane or one of the neighbors. Anyhow, he'll be missed today. Tonight we must get a message to his father demanding the two thousand dollars for his return."

Just then we heard a kind of war whoop, such as David might have emitted when he knocked out the champion Goliath. It was a sling that Red Chief had pulled out of his pocket, and he was whirling it around his head.

I dodged, and heard a heavy thud and a kind of a sigh from Bill, like a horse gives out when you take his saddle off. A rock the size of an egg had caught Bill just behind his left ear. He loosened himself all over and fell in the fire across the frying pan of hot water for washing the dishes. I dragged him out and poured cold water on his head for half an hour.

By and by, Bill sits up and feels behind his ear and says: "Sam, do you know who my favorite Biblical character is?"

"Take it easy," says I. "You'll come to your senses presently."

"King Herod,"[11] says he. "You won't go away and leave me here alone, will you, Sam?"

I went out and caught that boy and shook him until his freckles rattled.

"If you don't behave," says I, "I'll take you straight home. Now, are you going to be good, or not?"

"I was only funning," says he, sullenly. "I didn't mean to hurt Old Hank. But what did he hit me for? I'll behave, Snake-eye, if you won't send me home, and if you'll let me play the Scout today." **G**

"I don't know the game," says I. "That's for you and Mr. Bill to decide. He's your playmate for the day. I'm going away for a while, on business. Now, you come in and make friends with him and say you are sorry for hurting him, or home you go, at once." **H**

I made him and Bill shake hands, and then I took Bill aside and told him I was going to Poplar Cove, a little village three miles from the cave, and find out what I could about how the kidnapping had been regarded in Summit. Also, I thought it best to send a peremptory letter to old man Dorset that day, demanding the ransom and dictating how it should be paid.

"You know, Sam," says Bill, "I've stood by you without batting an eye in earthquakes, fire, and flood—in poker games, dynamite outrages, police raids, train robberies, and cyclones. I never lost my nerve yet till we kidnapped that

F MAKE INFERENCES
How do you think Bill is starting to feel about the plan to get two thousand dollars?

G PREDICT
Do you expect that the boy will behave better going forward? Add the prediction to your chart.

H CONFLICT
In what ways has the conflict changed since the beginning of the story?

11. **King Herod:** an ancient king of Judea who once ordered the execution of all Bethlehem boys under the age of two.

READING SKILL: *Review*

F MAKE INFERENCES

Possible answer: *Bill might not be as determined to follow through with the plan, or he might be thinking that $2,000 isn't enough for all the aggravation he has endured.*

READING STRATEGY

G PREDICT

Possible answer: *The boy doesn't want to be sent home, so he will try to behave better.*

LITERARY ANALYSIS

H CONFLICT

Possible answer: *In the beginning, the boy tried to fight off Bill and Sam. Now he doesn't want to go home, but Bill and Sam are not as anxious to keep him.*

If students need help . . . Have them reread lines 34–38 and contrast the boy's attitude then with his attitude now.

FOR LESS–PROFICIENT READERS

Reading Strategy Follow-Up: Predict Remind students that they must use evidence from the text to make logical predictions. Once students have read through line 132, ask what they think the boy will do—will he forget about what Bill did or pay him back? Guide students to use what they know already to make their predictions. For example:

- The boy follows through on his promises. He wakes up at daybreak to scalp Bill (lines 84–94).
- Sam only "kind of patched up" the argument between Bill and the boy (line 128).
- The boy tells Bill to "beware" (line 130).

Record students' predictions in the chart from page 47. Then have them read further to confirm their predictions. Discuss how, even if they turn out to be incorrect, predictions will add to their understanding of character and plot.

Review: Make Inferences Remind students that when they infer, they use clues from the text and their own knowledge to understand something that is not stated directly. Distribute copies of the Making Inferences transparency and discuss how students can use it to organize details from the story, their own knowledge, and their inferences. Encourage students to use this chart to answer question F.

 **BEST PRACTICES TOOLKIT—Transparency**
Making Inferences p. A13

Lines 177–185

REINFORCE *KEY IDEA:* THE UNEXPECTED

Discuss What is **the unexpected** decision that Bill and Sam make? Is there any way they could have anticipated their struggles with the boy? ***Possible answer:*** *Bill and Sam decide to lower their ransom demand from what they originally wanted. Unless they took the time to get to know the boy first, they could not have anticipated how difficult he would be to hold captive.*

READING STRATEGY

1 PREDICT

Possible answer: *The boy's father will most likely pay the ransom, but he may try to catch the kidnappers at the same time.*

Extend the Discussion In what way is the signature "Two Desperate Men" an example of irony?

two-legged skyrocket of a kid. He's got me going. You won't leave me long with him, will you, Sam?"

"I'll be back sometime this afternoon," says I. "You must keep the boy amused and quiet till I return. And now we'll write the letter to old Dorset."

Bill and I got paper and pencil and worked on the letter while Red Chief, with a blanket wrapped around him, strutted up and down, guarding the mouth of the cave. Bill begged me tearfully to make the ransom fifteen hundred dollars instead of two thousand. "I ain't attempting," says he, "to decry[12] the celebrated moral aspect of parental affection, but we're dealing with humans, and it ain't human for anybody to give up two thousand dollars for that forty-pound chunk of freckled wildcat. I'm willing to take a chance at fifteen hundred dollars. You can charge the difference up to me."

So, to relieve Bill, I acceded, and we **collaborated** a letter that ran this way:

collaborate (kə-lăb′ə-rāt′) *v.* to work together on a project

EBENEZER DORSET, ESQ.:

We have your boy concealed in a place far from Summit. It is useless for you or the most skillful detectives to attempt to find him. Absolutely, the only terms on which you can have him restored to you are these: We demand fifteen hundred dollars in large bills for his return: the money to be left at midnight at the same spot and in the same box as your reply—as hereinafter described. If you agree to these terms, send your answer in writing by a solitary messenger tonight at half-past eight o'clock. After crossing Owl Creek on the road to Poplar Cove, there are three large trees about a hundred yards apart, close to the fence of the wheat field on the right-hand side. At the bottom of the fence post, opposite the third tree, will be found a small pasteboard box.

The messenger will place the answer in this box and return immediately to Summit.

If you attempt any treachery or fail to **comply** with our demand as stated, you will never see your boy again.

comply (kəm-plī′) *v.* to act according to a command or request

If you pay the money as demanded, he will be returned to you safe and well within three hours. These terms are final, and if you do not accede to them no further communication will be attempted.

TWO DESPERATE MEN. **1**

3 Targeted Passage

1 PREDICT
How do you think the boy's father will respond to the men's demands? Add the prediction to your chart.

I addressed this letter to Dorset and put it in my pocket. As I was about to start, the kid comes up to me and says:

"Aw, Snake-eye, you said I could play the Scout while you was gone."

"Play it, of course," says I. "Mr. Bill will play with you. What kind of a game is it?"

"I'm the Scout," says Red Chief, "and I have to ride to the stockade to warn the settlers that the Indians are coming. I'm tired of playing Indian myself. I want to be the Scout."

12. **decry:** to criticize.

DIFFERENTIATED INSTRUCTION

FOR LESS–PROFICIENT READERS

3 Targeted Passage [Lines 177–205]

This passage advances the plot: Bill and Sam write the ransom note to the boy's father.

- Why does Bill ask Sam if they can lower the ransom demand?
- What must Mr. Dorset do if he agrees to the ransom demand?
- What will happen if Mr. Dorset does not follow the terms of the letter?

Review: Make Inferences Review how to make inferences (*make logical guesses based on information in the text and prior knowledge*). Ask students which of the two men is the leader (*Sam is the boss; Bill follows his lead and depends on him to make the decisions*). Then have students work backwards to find the evidence in lines 108–210 and use their own knowledge to support this inference.

"All right," says I. "It sounds harmless to me. I guess Mr. Bill will help you foil the enemy."

"What am I to do?" asks Bill, looking at the kid suspiciously.

"You are the hoss," says Scout. "Get down on your hands and knees. How can I ride to the stockade without a hoss?"

"You'd better keep him interested," said I, "till we get the scheme going. Loosen up."

Bill gets down on his all fours, and a look comes in his eye like a rabbit's when you catch it in a trap.

"How far is it to the stockade, kid?" he asks, in a husky manner of voice.

"Ninety miles," says the Scout. "And you have to hurry to get there on time. Whoa, now!"

The Scout jumps on Bill's back and digs his heels in his side.

"For Heaven's sake," says Bill, "hurry back, Sam, as soon as you can. I wish we hadn't made the ransom more than a thousand. Say, you quit kicking me or I'll get up and warm you good." (J)

> **(J) CONFLICT**
> Who seems to be winning the struggle?

I walked over to Poplar Cove and sat around the post office and store, talking with the chawbacons that came in to trade. One whiskerando says that he hears Summit is all upset on account of Elder Ebenezer Dorset's boy having been lost or stolen. That was all I wanted to know. I referred casually to the price of black-eyed peas, posted my letter surreptitiously and came away. The postmaster said the mail carrier would come by in an hour to take the mail on to Summit. (K)

> **(K) PREDICT**
> What do you think will happen now that the letter has been posted?

When I got back to the cave Bill and the boy were not to be found. I explored the vicinity of the cave, and risked a yodel or two, but there was no response.

So I sat down on a mossy bank to await developments.

In about half an hour I heard the bushes rustle, and Bill wabbled out into the little glade in front of the cave. Behind him was the kid, stepping softly like a scout, with a broad grin on his face. Bill stopped, took off his hat and wiped his face with a red handkerchief. The kid stopped about eight feet behind him.

"Sam," says Bill, "I suppose you think I'm a renegade, but I couldn't help it. I'm a grown person with masculine proclivities and habits of self-defense, but there is a time when all systems of egotism and predominance fail. The boy is gone. I have sent him home. All is off. There was martyrs in old times," goes on Bill, "that suffered death rather than give up the particular graft they enjoyed. None of 'em ever was subjugated to such supernatural tortures as I have been. I tried to be faithful to our articles of depredation;[13] but there came a limit." (L)

> **(L) CONFLICT**
> Reread lines 241–253. Bill thinks the conflict has been resolved. What details let the reader know that he is wrong?

"What's the trouble, Bill?" I asks him.

"I was rode," says Bill, "the ninety miles to the stockade, not barring an inch. Then, when the settlers was rescued, I was given oats. Sand ain't a

13. **depredation** (dĕp'rĭ-dā'shən): robbery.

LITERARY ANALYSIS

(J) CONFLICT

Possible answer: *The boy is definitely in control. Bill has become his victim.*

READING STRATEGY

(K) PREDICT

Remind students to record their predictions in their charts from page 47. ***Possible answer:*** *Something else will go wrong.*

LITERARY ANALYSIS

(L) CONFLICT

Possible answer: *In lines 241–245, Sam describes the boy as standing right behind Bill, who doesn't know he is there.*

Lines 241–253

DISCUSSION PROMPTS

Use these prompts to help students appreciate the humor of this passage:

Connect What is your attitude toward Bill at this point in the story? *Most students will probably say that they feel sorry for him.*

Analyze Why is Bill's ignorance of the boy's presence funny? ***Possible answer:*** *Readers can anticipate how unhappy he will be when he discovers that the boy is still there, standing right behind him.*

Evaluate How does Bill's language in lines 246–253 add to the humorous effect? ***Possible answer:*** *His language is dramatic and overblown, more suited to an enormously traumatic event than to the nuisance of a ten-year-old boy. He compares himself to a martyr.*

FOR ADVANCED LEARNERS/PRE–AP

Analyze [small-group option] Discuss these three types of irony with students:

- *situational:* when one thing is expected to happen but something entirely different takes place
- *dramatic:* when a character is unaware of something that audience members or other characters know
- *verbal:* when someone says something but means the opposite

Explain that irony is one of O. Henry's trademarks, or characteristic devices. When reading O. Henry's stories, it is best to expect the unexpected! Have students work in small groups to find examples of each type of irony in lines 1–296. Have them share what they find and then ask them to predict a possible ending for the story based on what they've learned about O. Henry's ironic style.

THE RANSOM OF RED CHIEF 55

Lines 257–285
DISCUSSION PROMPTS

Use these prompts to help students understand Sam's plan for collecting the ransom:

Recall How has the boy tormented Bill, both physically and mentally, while Sam has been away? ***Possible answer:*** *The boy has pestered Bill with unanswerable questions (lines 257–260), kicked Bill's legs until they are covered with bruises (lines 263–264), and bitten Bill's hand (lines 264–265).*

Infer Why does Sam ask Bill if heart disease runs in his family (lines 274–275)? ***Answer:*** *Bill thinks the boy is gone, but Sam knows the boy is standing right behind him. Sam hopes that Bill will not have a heart attack when he learns the truth.*

Speculate Based on what you know about the boy, how do you think Ebenezer Dorset will respond to Bill and Sam's ransom note? ***Possible answer:*** *Since the boy is a terror with Bill and Sam, he might terrorize his family in the same way. Perhaps Dorset will refuse to pay the ransom.*

palatable substitute. And then, for an hour I had to try to explain to him why there was nothin' in holes, how a road can run both ways and what makes the grass green. I tell you, Sam, a human can only stand so much. I takes him by the neck of his clothes and drags him down the mountain. On the way he kicks my legs black and blue from the knees down; and I've got to have two or three bites on my thumb and hand cauterized.[14]

"But he's gone"—continues Bill—"gone home. I showed him the road to Summit and kicked him about eight feet nearer there at one kick. I'm sorry we lose the ransom; but it was either that or Bill Driscoll to the madhouse."

Bill is puffing and blowing, but there is a look of ineffable peace and growing content on his rose-pink features.

"Bill," says I, "there isn't any heart disease in your family, is there?"

"No," says Bill, "nothing chronic except malaria and accidents. Why?"

"Then you might turn around," says I, "and have a look behind you."

Bill turns and sees the boy, and loses his complexion and sits down plump on the ground and begins to pluck aimlessly at grass and little sticks. For an hour I was afraid of his mind. And then I told him that my scheme was to put the whole job through immediately and that we would get the ransom and be off with it by midnight if old Dorset fell in with our **proposition**. So Bill braced up enough to give the kid a weak sort of a smile and a promise to play the Russian in a Japanese war with him as soon as he felt a little better.

proposition (prŏp'ə-zĭsh'ən) *n.* a suggested plan

I had a scheme for collecting that ransom without danger of being caught by counterplots that ought to **commend** itself to professional kidnappers. The tree under which the answer was to be left—and the money later on—was close to the road fence with big, bare fields on all sides. If a gang of constables should be watching for anyone to come for the note they could see him a long way off crossing the fields or in the road. But no, sirree! At half-past eight I was up in that tree as well hidden as a tree toad, waiting for the messenger to arrive.

commend (kə-mĕnd') *v.* to speak highly of; to praise; to recommend

Exactly on time, a half-grown boy rides up the road on a bicycle, locates the pasteboard box at the foot of the fence post, slips a folded piece of paper into it and pedals away again back toward Summit.

I waited an hour and then concluded the thing was square. I slid down the tree, got the note, slipped along the fence till I struck the woods, and was back at the cave in another half an hour. I opened the note, got near the lantern,

14. **cauterized** (kô'tə-rīzd'): burned a wound to stop bleeding.

DIFFERENTIATED INSTRUCTION

FOR LESS-PROFICIENT READERS

Reading Strategy Follow-Up: Predict Have students reread lines 286–299. Ask them what Sam thinks the note will say. Then ask them what they predict it will say and why. List students' predictions on the board and check them after students read the note on the next page.

FOR ENGLISH LEARNERS

Comprehension: Cause and Effect To increase students' comprehension of lines 274–285, explain these cause-and-effect relationships:

- Because Bill thinks the boy is gone, it is a shock to find out he isn't.
- The realization that the boy is still there causes Bill to become pale and act oddly.
- This behavior leads Sam to fear that Bill has lost his mind.

and read it to Bill. It was written with a pen in a crabbed hand, and the sum and substance of it was this:

Two Desperate Men.

Gentlemen: I received your letter today by post, in regard to the ransom you ask for the return of my son. I think you are a little high in your demands, and I hereby make you a counter-proposition, which I am inclined to believe you will accept. You bring Johnny home and pay me two hundred and fifty dollars in cash, and I agree to take him off your hands. You had better come at night, for the neighbors believe he is lost, and I couldn't be responsible for what they would do to anybody they saw bringing him back.

Very respectfully,

Ebenezer Dorset. (M)

(M) MAKE INFERENCES Reread the note from Ebenezer Dorset. From this passage, what can you infer about how well he knows his son?

"Great Pirates of Penzance!" says I; "of all the **impudent**—"

impudent (ĭm'pyə-dənt) *adj.* bold and disrespectful

But I glanced at Bill, and hesitated. He had the most appealing look in his eyes I ever saw on the face of a dumb or a talking brute.

(4) **Targeted Passage**

"Sam," says he, "what's two hundred and fifty dollars, after all? We've got the money. One more night of this kid will send me to bed in Bedlam.[15] Besides being a thorough gentleman, I think Mr. Dorset is a spendthrift for making us such a liberal offer. You ain't going to let the chance go, are you?"

"Tell you the truth, Bill," says I, "this little he ewe lamb has somewhat got on my nerves, too. We'll take him home, pay the ransom, and make our getaway." (N)

(N) CONFLICT AND RESOLUTION Who wins out in the conflict between the kidnappers and the boy's father?

We took him home that night. We got him to go by telling him that his father had bought a silver-mounted rifle and a pair of moccasins for him, and we were going to hunt bears the next day.

It was just twelve o'clock when we knocked at Ebenezer's front door. Just at the moment when I should have been abstracting the fifteen hundred dollars from the box under the tree, according to the original proposition, Bill was counting out two hundred and fifty dollars into Dorset's hand.

When the kid found out we were going to leave him at home he started up a howl like a calliope[16] and fastened himself as tight as a leech to Bill's leg. His father peeled him away gradually, like a porous plaster.

"How long can you hold him?" asks Bill.

"I'm not as strong as I used to be," says old Dorset, "but I think I can promise you ten minutes."

"Enough," says Bill. "In ten minutes I shall cross the Central, Southern, and Middle Western States, and be legging it trippingly for the Canadian border."

And, as dark as it was, and as fat as Bill was, and as good a runner as I am, he was a good mile and a half out of Summit before I could catch up with him. (O)

(O) CONFLICT AND RESOLUTION How is the conflict between the men and the boy finally resolved?

15. **Bedlam:** an insane asylum.

16. **calliope** (kə-lī'ə-pē'): an instrument with steam whistles.

Lines 302–321

REINFORCE *KEY IDEA:* THE UNEXPECTED

Discuss What is **unexpected** about the letter from Mr. Dorset? ***Possible answer:*** *In the letter, instead of pleading for the safe return of his son, Mr. Dorset says that the kidnappers will have to pay him to take the boy back.*

READING SKILL: *Review*

(M) MAKE INFERENCES

Possible answer: *Dorset knows how difficult his son is, and he is quite certain that the boy is driving his captors crazy.*

LITERARY ANALYSIS

(N) CONFLICT AND RESOLUTION

Possible answer: *The boy's father wins the conflict. Bill and Sam are willing to pay him to take the boy back.*

LITERARY ANALYSIS

(O) CONFLICT AND RESOLUTION

Possible answer: *Dorset holds the boy while Bill and Sam run as fast as they can out of Summit. The conflict is resolved when the boy and the men part company.*

SELECTION WRAP-UP

REFLECT Ask students to consider what the point of view adds to this story. How does it affect their perception of character?

CRITIQUE Several elements of this story, including Mr. Dorset's reaction, are not very realistic. Ask students to consider whether this lack of realism affects their appreciation of the story.

READING FLUENCY

Distribute the copy masters and have students practice fluency.

RESOURCE MANAGER—Copy Master
Reading Fluency p. 63

FOR LESS-PROFICIENT READERS

(4) Targeted Passage [Lines 302–328]

This passage presents the ironic climax of the plot: instead of paying the ransom, the boy's father demands $250 to take the boy back.

- What is the plan that Mr. Dorset outlines for the kidnappers?
- How do Bill and Sam react to this proposal?
- What is the boy's reaction to going home? What must Bill and Sam do to gain his cooperation?

FOR ENGLISH LEARNERS

Vocabulary: Prefixes [mixed-readiness groups] Explain that the prefix *counter-* means "opposite" or "opposing." Point out its use in *counterplots* in line 287 and *counter-proposition* in line 305. Have students work in small groups to define each word, keeping in mind the meaning of the prefix and root.

DISCUSSION PROMPTS

Use these prompts to help students understand the connection between the events in this article and the key idea:

Connect Have you ever found something valuable in a place you wouldn't have expected? Explain. *Students might say that they have found money on the sidewalk or in a coat pocket.*

Analyze How did circumstances unexpectedly favor the landlady? ***Possible answer:*** *Her daughter was at the university and in a position to show the manuscript to someone who knew how to get it evaluated and eventually sold.*

Synthesize What is the moral of this story? ***Possible answer:*** *Be very careful about throwing away things you find unexpectedly without looking them over first.*

Reading for Information

ANECDOTE O. Henry was a master of unexpected plot twists. In the following anecdote, which was originally read on the radio, you will learn about a happy coincidence that involves an undiscovered O. Henry story.

Manuscript Found in an Attic

MARCUS ROSENBAUM

O. Henry

When I told my father that I was moving to Des Moines, he told me about the only time he'd been there. It was in the 1930s, he said, when he was the business manager of the literary magazine of Southern Methodist University in Dallas. His friend Lon Tinkle was the magazine's editor. Lon also taught English at SMU, and there was a student in his class who had a severely deformed back. It was the Depression, and the young woman came from a family that was so poor she couldn't afford the operation that would correct the problem.

Her mother, who ran a boardinghouse in Galveston, was cleaning out the attic one day when she came across an old dusty manuscript. Scribbled across the top were the words, "By O. Henry." It was a nice story, and she sent it along to her daughter at SMU, who showed it to Lon. Lon had never seen the story before, but it *sounded* like O. Henry, it had an O. Henry story line, and he knew that William Sydney Porter, aka O. Henry, had lived in Houston at one time. So it was entirely possible that the famous author had gone to the beach and stayed in the Galveston boardinghouse, had written the story while he was there, and had inadvertently left the manuscript behind. Lon showed the manuscript to my father, who contacted an O. Henry expert at Columbia University in New York. The expert said he'd like to see it, so my father got on a train and took it to him.

The expert authenticated the story as O. Henry's, and my father set out to sell it. Eventually, he found himself in Des Moines, meeting with Gardner Cowles, a top editor at the Des Moines *Register.* Cowles loved the story and bought it on the spot. My father took the proceeds to the young woman in Lon Tinkle's class. It was just enough for her to have the operation she so desperately needed—and, as far as we know, to live happily ever after.

My father never told me what the O. Henry story was about. But I doubt that it could have been better than his own story: a story about O. Henry that was an O. Henry story itself.

58 UNIT 1: PLOT AND CONFLICT

DIFFERENTIATED INSTRUCTION

FOR LESS-PROFICIENT READERS

Comprehension Support [paired option] Distribute copies of a Sequence Circle to students. Have them work in pairs to chart the sequence of the events in this article. Fill out the first segment together (*student's mother finds a manuscript in her attic*), pointing out that the first paragraph of the article is background information. Have students complete and share their diagrams.

 **BEST PRACTICES TOOLKIT—Transparency** Sequence Circle pp. B21, B46

FOR ENGLISH LEARNERS

Options for Reading To help students increase their comprehension, read the article aloud, pausing frequently to explain unfamiliar words and clarify the relationships of the people mentioned. Or, give students a brief overview and then have them read along silently with the *Audio Anthology CD.*

After Reading

Comprehension

1. **Recall** Why do Sam and Bill need two thousand dollars?
2. **Clarify** Why does the boy prefer to stay with Sam and Bill rather than go home?
3. **Represent** Reread lines 24–26 on page 50. Use the details in this paragraph to draw a simple map showing Summit, the mountain, and the cave.

Literary Analysis

4. **Predict** Look back at the chart you created as you read. Which outcomes surprised you and which did not? Tell what **unexpected** circumstances affected Bill and Sam's plan to get money.
5. **Analyze Conflict and Resolution** When an outcome is the opposite of what might be expected, it is said to be **ironic.** Which of the resolutions to this story's conflicts are ironic? Show your thinking in two graphics like the ones shown.

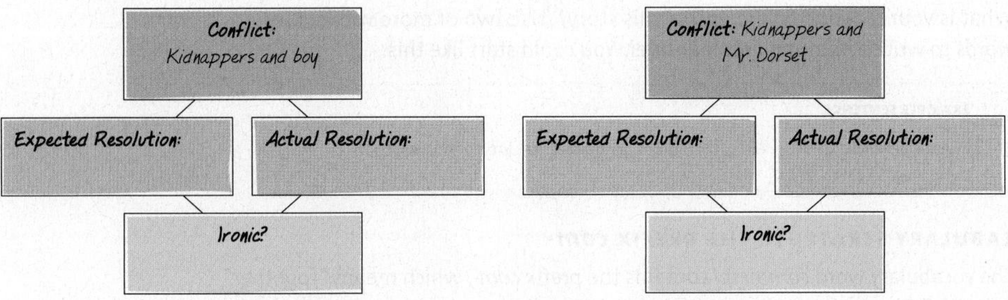

6. **Draw Conclusions** Look back at lines 8–16. From the vocabulary Sam uses, as well as the way he presents himself and Bill to the reader at the beginning of the story, do you think the partners are typically successful in their schemes? Cite evidence to support your conclusion.

Extension and Challenge

7. **Creative Project: Music** Choose a familiar tune and rewrite the words to retell the story of "The Ransom of Red Chief." Include details that bring out the **irony** in the story.
8. **Literary Criticism** O. Henry's short stories remain popular with readers in part because they often have **surprise endings.** Read the article "Manuscript Found in an Attic" on page 58. What do you think the author means when he describes it as "a story about O. Henry that was an O. Henry story itself"?

Practice and Apply

After Reading

For additional support of postreading questions, use these copy masters:

RESOURCE MANAGER—Copy Masters
Reading Check p. 60 (to check understanding of the selection)
Conflict and Resolution p. 53 (for practice of literary analysis standards focus)
Question Support p. 61 (After Reading questions adapted for English learners and less-proficient readers)

Additional selection questions are provided for teachers on page 47.

For additional activities to challenge students, see

Power Thinking at **ClassZone.com**

ANSWERS

Comprehension

1. *They need the money for a land swindle.*
2. *The boy is having fun camping in a cave.*
3. *Students' maps should show the cave as two miles from Summit on the back of a small mountain.*

Literary Analysis

Possible answers:

4. **STANDARDS FOCUS Predict** *Surprises include the boy's behavior and his reaction to being kidnapped, the lack of concern over his disappearance, and his father's indifference about his return. Because Johnny is such a terror, Bill and Sam are willing to pay money to get rid of him rather than hold out for ransom.*
5. **STANDARDS FOCUS Conflict and Resolution**
   - *The expected resolution to the first conflict is that the boy would cooperate so he could go home. Instead, he terrorizes the men into wanting to send him home without getting the ransom. This outcome is ironic.*
   - *The second expected resolution is that Mr. Dorset would be anxious to pay the money to get his son returned. Instead, he demands money from the kidnappers, which they pay. This too is ironic.*
6. *They probably are not successful. First, they have only $600 and need more. Second, their language sounds impressive but they might be compensating for their lack of competence.*

Extension and Challenge

7. *Students' songs should include a summary of the main events in the story and illustrate the irony by explaining what Bill and Sam thought would happen and what actually happens.*
8. *The fact that the money is just enough for the girl to have the surgery makes it an O. Henry kind of story.*

ANSWERS

Vocabulary in Context

VOCABULARY PRACTICE

1. *ransom*
2. *provisions*
3. *collaborate*
4. *diatribe*
5. *impudent*
6. *comply*
7. *proposition*
8. *commend*

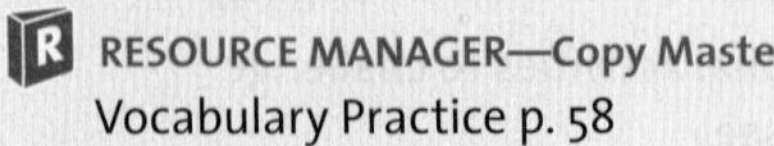

RESOURCE MANAGER—Copy Master
Vocabulary Practice p. 58

VOCABULARY IN WRITING

Have students clarify their feelings about the ending of the story by discussing it with a partner before they begin to write.

VOCABULARY STRATEGY: THE PREFIX *com-* *(also an EL language objective)*

Recommend to students that they review the words and definitions before they begin the activity. Tell them to first match the words that they know for certain in order to narrow down the answer choices for the less familiar words.

Answers:

1. *combine*
2. *confirm*
3. *collect*
4. *concur*

RESOURCE MANAGER—Copy Master
Vocabulary Strategy p. 59

Vocabulary Center at **ClassZone.com**
Additional Vocabulary Activities

Vocabulary in Context

VOCABULARY PRACTICE

Choose the vocabulary word that best completes each the sentence.

collaborate | impudent | commend | proposition | comply | provisions | diatribe | ransom

1. The kidnappers demanded a ____ before they returned the boy.
2. They had enough ____ stashed in a cave to last a week.
3. Since neither of them could complete the scheme alone, the kidnappers had to _____.
4. The worst they expected was a ____ in the local paper.
5. Red Chief was so _____, adults didn't like being around him.
6. The father did not ____ with the terms of the letter.
7. Red Chief's father had a different _____ for the kidnappers.
8. You can't ____ the parents' actions, but you can certainly understand them.

VOCABULARY IN WRITING

What is your reaction to the end of this story? Use two or more vocabulary words to write a one-paragraph answer. You could start like this.

EXAMPLE SENTENCE

*I was surprised at how the kidnappers' **proposition** got turned around.*

VOCABULARY STRATEGY: THE PREFIX *com-*

The vocabulary word *commend* contains the prefix *com-*, which means "together" or "with." The prefix can be spelled *com-*, *col-*, *cor-*, or *con-*, depending on the letter that follows it. Learning to recognize this prefix with its various spellings can help you remember the meanings of many words.

PRACTICE Choose the word from the list that matches each numbered definition. If necessary, consult a dictionary.

collect | combine | concur | confirm

1. to join together
2. to establish that something is true
3. to bring together in a group, gather
4. to be in agreement, or harmony

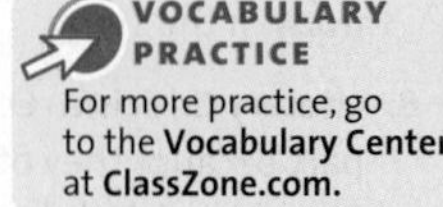

VOCABULARY PRACTICE
For more practice, go to the **Vocabulary Center** at **ClassZone.com.**

DIFFERENTIATED INSTRUCTION

FOR ENGLISH LEARNERS

Vocabulary Practice Encourage Spanish-speaking students to use their knowledge of cognates to help them remember the definitions of several of the vocabulary words, including *collaborate (colaborar), impudent (impudente), proposition (proposición)*, and *provision (provisión).*

FOR ADVANCED LEARNERS/PRE–AP

Vocabulary Strategy Challenge students to list as many words as they can with the prefix *com-* and its forms without using a dictionary. Combine students' lists on the board and have them use their knowledge of the prefix to define the words.

Reading-Writing Connection

Demonstrate your understanding of "The Ransom of Red Chief" by responding to these prompts. Then complete the **Grammar and Writing** exercise.

WRITING PROMPTS	SELF-CHECK
A. Short Response: Write a Postcard For the boy, being with Sam and Bill was like being at camp. Write a **one-paragraph postcard** that he might have sent to his father while he was gone.	***A good postcard will . . .*** • include words and phrases similar to those used by the boy in the story • cite events from the story from the boy's perspective
B. Extended Response: Analyze What Went Wrong Bill and Sam thought they had a brilliant scheme to make money, but they didn't plan for the **unexpected.** In **two or three paragraphs,** tell why they thought their plan would work and what they were mistaken about.	***A successful analysis will . . .*** • include a topic sentence • identify mistakes the men made in their thinking

GRAMMAR AND WRITING

AVOID RUN-ON SENTENCES A **run-on sentence,** sometimes called a run-on, is two or more sentences written as though they were a single sentence. To correct a run-on, you can

- insert an end mark and start a new sentence
- insert a **coordinating conjunction,** such as *and, but,* or *so,* after a comma
- change a comma to a **semicolon**

Original: I thought Randy would win the class elections, Mary believed Ling would be the winner.

Revised: I thought Randy would win the class elections, but Mary believed Ling would be the winner.

PRACTICE Rewrite the following sentences so that they are no longer run-ons.

1. I thought I wouldn't like being away from home, it's actually really fun.
2. I promised to behave, they threatened to send me home.
3. There weren't daily newspapers, nosy reporters wouldn't be coming around.
4. They didn't count on the boy's adventurous spirit they were surprised by it.
5. Parents worry about keeping their children safe, they don't worry about keeping people safe from their children.

For more help with run-on sentences, see page R64 in the ***Grammar Handbook.***

DIFFERENTIATED INSTRUCTION

FOR LESS–PROFICIENT WRITERS

For Prompt A:

1. Direct students to revisit lines 45–75 and 211–226. Help them list words and phrases that identify the boy's activities and feelings in these passages.
2. Then give students an outline of a post-card format. Have them work in pairs to complete their card, using details from the list.

For Prompt B:

1. Have students work in pairs to identify what went wrong with the kidnappers' plan. Discuss students' ideas.
2. Then help students form a strong topic sentence for their paragraph, such as *Everything that could go wrong with the kidnapping plan did go wrong.*
3. Have students write one paragraph using the topic sentence discussed. Suggest that they follow chronological order in their paragraphs.

Reading-Writing Connection

WRITING PROMPTS

- For **Prompt A,** have students skim the story and list the games that the boy plays with Bill and the other activities he enjoys while being kidnapped.
- For **Prompt B,** have students refer back to their prediction charts to help them identify details for their paragraphs.

For an extended Reading-Writing Connection activity, see

Writing Center at **ClassZone.com**

GRAMMAR AND WRITING

Review each method of correcting run-ons. Discuss when to use each. For example, if the ideas are not closely related, then they should be expressed in two separate sentences.

Possible answers:

1. *I thought I wouldn't like being away from home, but it's actually really fun.*
2. *I promised to behave when they threatened to send me home.*
3. *There weren't daily newspapers, so nosy reporters wouldn't be coming around.*
4. *They didn't count on the boy's adventurous spirit, and they were surprised by it.*
5. *People worry about keeping their children safe; they don't worry about keeping people safe from their children.*

RESOURCE MANAGER—Copy Master
Avoid Run-On Sentences p. 62

Assess and Reteach

Assess

RESOURCE MANAGER—Copy Masters
Selection Tests A, B/C pp. 65–66, 67–68

Test Generator CD

Reteach

STANDARDS LESSON FILE
Literature Lesson 6: Conflict
Reading Lesson 1: Predicting
Reading Lesson 8: Making Inferences
Vocabulary Lesson 4: Prefixes
Grammar Lesson 2: Avoiding Run-Ons

Focus and Motivate

OBJECTIVES

Literary Analysis
- explore the key idea of **treasure**
- identify and analyze types of conflict
- read a short story

Reading
- identify sequence relationships
- identify and analyze flashback

Vocabulary
- build vocabulary for reading and writing
- use knowledge of suffixes to determine word meanings *(also an EL language objective)*

Grammar and Writing
- punctuate possessive nouns correctly
- use writing to analyze literature

SUMMARY

Katie works in her mother's cleaning business, which her mother started after Katie's father died. While cleaning out Mrs. Leonardo's attic, she finds an old children's book, the cause of a breach between Mrs. Leonardo and her sister. Through Katie's efforts, Mrs. Leonardo reconciles with her sister, and Katie learns that memories, including her own, are powerful and precious.

When does trash become TREASURE?

Discuss the question and the ***KEY IDEA*** with students. Ask students to share examples of their own **treasures.** Then have students complete the ***WEB IT*** activity.

Before Reading

Clean Sweep

Short Story by Joan Bauer

When does trash become TREASURE?

KEY IDEA There is an old saying, "One man's trash is another man's **treasure.**" A scrap of cloth, a wrinkled photo, or a worn, torn book can have great value to a person if there are special memories attached. In "Clean Sweep," a girl finds out not only that a simple object can hold good memories, but also that those memories can help heal.

WEB IT What do you value that someone else might be tempted to throw away? Create a web to show some memories that are connected to that item. Expand your web by adding details that explain what makes the object special to you.

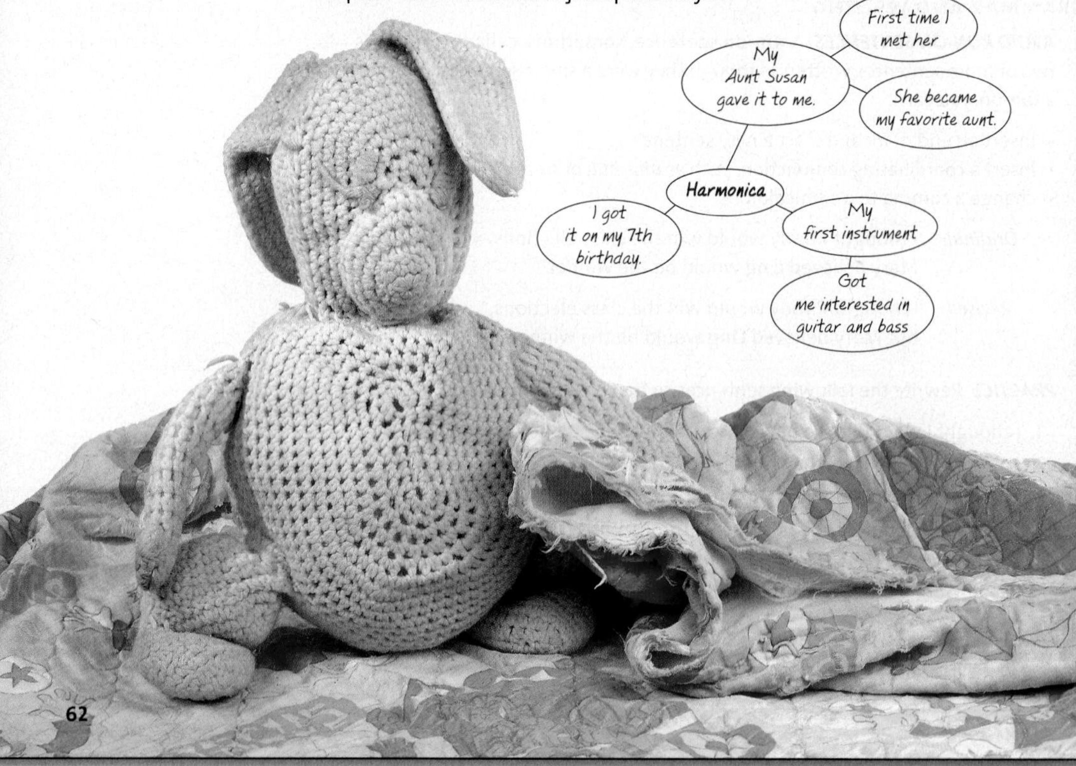

Harmonica
My Aunt Susan gave it to me.
First time I met her
She became my favorite aunt.
I got it on my 7th birthday.
My first instrument
Got me interested in guitar and bass

62

Selection Resources

RESOURCE MANAGER UNIT 1

Plan and Teach pp. 69–76

Literary Analysis
Summary pp. 77†*, 78‡*
Internal and External Conflict pp. 79, 80†*
Question Support p. 87*

Reading
Sequence pp. 81, 82†*
Reading Check p. 86
Reading Fluency p. 89

Vocabulary
Study p. 83*
Practice p. 84
Strategy p. 85

Grammar and Writing
Punctuate Possessives Correctly p. 88

Assessment
Selection Tests A, B/C pp. 91*, 93*
Test Generator CD

BEST PRACTICES TOOLKIT
Differentiated Instruction pp. 31–38*
Scaffolding Instruction pp. 43–46*

Graphic Organizers/Strategies
Read Aloud/Think Aloud • Venn Diagram

Reading Support
Audio Anthology CD*

Technology
Literature, Vocabulary, and Writing Centers at **ClassZone.com**
Write*Smart* CD

* Resources for Differentiation † Also in Spanish ‡ In Haitian Creole and Vietnamese

LITERARY ANALYSIS: INTERNAL AND EXTERNAL CONFLICT

You already know that a **conflict** is a struggle between opposing forces. It creates the tension or suspense in a story or play. Recognizing the types of conflict can help you better understand the actions of the characters.

- **External conflict** is a struggle between a character and an outside force. The outside force could be another character, society, or a force of nature.
- **Internal conflict** is a struggle within a character's mind. This type of conflict may occur when the character has to make a difficult decision or deal with contradictory feelings.

As you read "Clean Sweep," notice how a past event causes internal and external conflict.

READING SKILL: SEQUENCE

To fully understand a story, you must recognize the **sequence,** or order, of the events described. While events are often presented in the order in which they occur, sometimes the action is interrupted to present a scene from an earlier time. This scene, called a **flashback,** can help explain a character's actions. To help you figure out when events occurred, look for signal words and phrases such as these:

four years ago *moments later* *while*

As you read "Clean Sweep," keep track of the sequence by recording important events on a sequence chart.

Review: **Predict**

VOCABULARY IN CONTEXT

The boldfaced words help Joan Bauer tell about one teenager's experience with loss and familial responsibility. To see how many you know, substitute a different word or words for each.

1. The room was dark and **dingy.**
2. A **minuscule** amount of light came through the window.
3. Her sense of **propriety** kept her from interrupting him.
4. She acted calm in front of her class, but she was in **turmoil.**
5. I can't stand the **vileness** of rotten eggs.
6. It was an **aberration,** not what she usually sees.

Author Online

Laughter and Life As a child, Joan Bauer dreamed of becoming a comedian or a comedy writer when she grew up. The funny adults in her life inspired her. Her mother loved to make people laugh, and her grandmother, Nana, was a storyteller whose tales always included humor. But real life wasn't always amusing. When Joan was eight years old, her parents divorced. This and other family troubles proved devastating. However, she continued writing, finding that it helped ease her pain. Now an award-winning author, Joan Bauer admits to often drawing from these difficult life experiences while creating her touching, amusing stories.

Joan Bauer
born 1951

Hope and Humor "I want to create stories that link life's struggles with laughter," Bauer has said. "Laughter is a gift we've been given . . . not just to make us feel good, but to empower us to overcome dark times." Her novels and stories are about how we can help each other by sharing both the struggle and the laughter.

MORE ABOUT THE AUTHOR
For more on Joan Bauer, visit the **Literature Center** at **ClassZone.com.**

Teach

STANDARDS FOCUS

LITERARY ANALYSIS

● INTERNAL AND EXTERNAL CONFLICT

Have students identify an external and an internal conflict in this paragraph:

> Li gripped the rock tightly. Five years ago, she had clung to the same mountain cliff. Unable to hold on, she had fallen and broken her leg. It had taken her months to recover. Now, clearing her head of bad memories, she breathed deeply and began her descent.

Possible answer: *External conflict—the climber's struggle to descend the mountain; internal conflict—her fight to keep her nerve.*

CHECK UNDERSTANDING Have students identify conflicts in stories they know.

READING SKILL

■ SEQUENCE

Have students trace the sequence of events in the passage above, including the flashback. ***Possible answer:*** *Five years ago, the climber fell and broke her leg. She slowly recovered. Now she is once again descending a mountain.*

CHECK UNDERSTANDING Have pairs use signal words and phrases to identify the sequence of events in their day.

RESOURCE MANAGER—Copy Master
Sequence p. 81 (for student use while reading the selection)

VOCABULARY SKILL

▲ VOCABULARY IN CONTEXT

DIAGNOSE WORD KNOWLEDGE To determine preteaching needs, have all students complete **Vocabulary in Context.** *Students' responses will vary.* ***Possible answers:*** 1. *dirty* 2. *tiny* 3. *appropriateness* 4. *chaos* 5. *disgusting* 6. *unusual occurrence*

PRETEACH VOCABULARY Use the Vocabulary Study copy master to help students determine the meaning of each boldfaced word.

1. Read aloud the first sentence, emphasizing the boldfaced word.
2. Ask students to think about possible meanings for *aberration,* such as "unusual action."
3. Repeat the procedure for items 2–6.
4. Have students answer the questions in Part B independently.

RESOURCE MANAGER—Copy Master
Vocabulary Study p. 83

For general guidelines on differentiating vocabulary instruction and for alternative vocabulary activities for students not needing vocabulary preteaching, see

BEST PRACTICES TOOLKIT
Scaffolding Vocabulary Instruction pp. 43–46

Vocabulary Center at **ClassZone.com**
Additional Vocabulary Activities

Practice and Apply

ANALYZE VISUALS

***Possible answer:** The girl seems to enjoy housework, perhaps because she can listen to music while she does it.*

LITERARY ANALYSIS

Ⓐ CONFLICT

Possible answer:

External conflicts:

- *The narrator and her mother are in conflict with dust mites (lines 14–17).*
- *They are also in conflict with customers who don't want to pay a good rate for their services (lines 20–23).*

If students need help . . . Tell them that a conflict occurs whenever someone struggles or makes an effort to do something—to win a game, to get up in the morning, or to do homework, for example. Ask students for further examples of everyday conflicts they experience. Then return to lines 14–17 and 20–23 and have students explain each conflict they find.

Clean Sweep

Joan Bauer

"HAVE YOU EVER SEEN A DUST MITE?"

My mother always lowers her voice when she asks this; it adds to the emotional impact. Never in the four years since she's had the cleaning business has anyone ever said they've seen one. That's because the only people who have seen dust mites are scientists who put dust balls on slides and look at them under microscopes. Personally I have better things to do than look at **minuscule** animals who cause great torture among the allergic, but my mother has a photo of a dust mite blown up to ten gazillion times its size—she is holding it up now, as she always does in this part of her presentation—and the two women who sit on the floral couch before her gasp appropriately and shut their eyes, because dust mites, trust me, are ugly. Think *Invasion of the Body Snatchers* meets *The Hunchback of Notre Dame,* and you're just beginning to enter into the **vileness** of this creature.

"They're everywhere," Mom says to the women. "Under the bed, on the sheets, clinging to the blinds; hiding, waiting. And at Clean Sweep," she offers quietly, but dramatically, "we *kill* them for you. We hate them even more than you do. *This* is why we're in business."

The two women look at each other and say *yes,* they want the cleaning service to start immediately.

Mom tells them our price. One woman, as expected, says, "That sounds a little high." People are so cheap. Everyone wants quality, no one wants to pay for it. Here's the suburban dream—to hire great workers who are such meek morons that they don't have the guts to ask for a living wage. Ⓐ

This is not my mother's problem. She holds up the dust mite enlargement to make the point. "We cost more because we know where he and his army are hiding."

ANALYZE VISUALS
What can you **conclude** about this girl's feelings toward housework?

minuscule (mĭn′ə-skyo͞ol′ *adj.* very small; tiny

vileness (vīl′nəs) *n.* unpleasantness; disgusting quality

Ⓐ CONFLICT
What conflicts do the main character and her family face with each job

DIFFERENTIATED INSTRUCTION

FOR ALL STUDENTS

Interest Stations Post suggested projects for students to work on independently.

- **Ad Campaign** Develop jingles and media ads for the Clean Sweep company.
- **Story Map** Outline the story of another Clean Sweep customer.
- **Consumer Report** Research environmentally safe cleaning products for the home.

For further details on these projects, see

R RESOURCE MANAGER
Ideas for Extension pp. 74–75

FOR LESS–PROFICIENT READERS

In combination with the *Audio Anthology CD,* use one or more Targeted Passages (pp. 66, 69, 70, 72) to ensure that students focus on key story events, concepts, and skills.

FOR ENGLISH LEARNERS

Options for Reading Read aloud lines 1–19 to help students understand the scene. Make sure they understand that the narrator's mother is using pictures of dust mites (like the one on page 66) to sell her cleaning services to two women. Ask students why these pictures might convince the women to use the cleaning service. Then have students read the rest of the story along with the *Audio Anthology CD.*

BACKGROUND

Allergies The narrator's brother, Benjamin, suffers from an allergy to dust. Symptoms of an allergy occur when the body's immune system reacts to substances such as mold, dust, dander, and pollen. These allergens do not pose a threat to the body, but the immune system perceives them as harmful and goes into a defensive mode, releasing histamines and other chemicals from cells. This reaction causes allergy symptoms, including itching, swelling, coughing, rashes, and headaches.

FOR ENGLISH LEARNERS

Culture: Clarify Explain these references, used humorously to describe dust mites:

- *Invasion of the Body Snatchers* (lines 11–12) is a science fiction film in which humans are killed by imposters who look normal but have no feelings and are gradually taking over the world.
- One of the main characters in the novel *The Hunchback of Notre Dame* (line 12) is Quasimodo, a hideously deformed man living in the cathedral.

Key Academic Vocabulary Have students use context clues to help them master this academic vocabulary from the selection: *impact* (lines 3, 68), *eliminating* (lines 28, 38), *contrast* (line 39), *random* (line 62), *widespread* (line 148), *potential* (line 241).

Prereading For prereading instruction for English learners, see

BEST PRACTICES TOOLKIT
Scaffolding Reading Instruction pp. 43–46

FOR ADVANCED LEARNERS/PRE–AP

Pre-AP exercises in the bottom channel provide additional challenge for your advanced students. Use them for small groups or individuals.

ADDITIONAL GUIDELINES

For more help with differentiation and tips for classroom management, see

BEST PRACTICES TOOLKIT
Differentiated Instruction pp. 31–38

SCIENCE CONNECTION

Dust mites live in warm, moist surroundings, such as mattresses, chairs, stuffed toys, and pillows. They travel from room to room on clothing, and they feed on the dead skin of humans and animals. For people allergic to dust mites, several measures can be taken to reduce their population. Washing their potential habitats frequently with hot water can help, as can replacing carpeting with tile or wood flooring.

LITERARY ANALYSIS

B CONFLICT

Possible answer: *The narrator is irritated by her brother's complaining and suspects that he is exaggerating his illness, but she says nothing and does his work for him.*

If students need help . . . Point out the words and phrases that show the narrator's impatience and irritation with her brother: *devoted underachiever, knows how to get out of work, he could give seminars on this, gets the perfect look of abject pain.*

Extend the Discussion Why do you think the narrator lets her brother get away with this behavior?

READING SKILL

C SEQUENCE

Possible answer: *The word* today *in line 49 indicates that the story's plot is underway.*

If students need help . . . Take this opportunity to help students set up their charts. Make sure that they leave boxes to the left of this one for events that occur in the flashback. Remind them that as they read, they should pay attention to word cues that indicate whether the action is moving forward or into the past.

She used to say "we know where he and his friends are hiding," but "army" sounds more fierce, and when you are serious about eliminating dust, you'd better let everyone know it's war.

"Well . . . ," the other woman says, unsure.

Mom presses in. "We suggest two cleanings per week for one month to achieve total elimination. Then weekly cleanings should do, unless you have special needs."

Special needs in the cleaning world range from cleaning out attics to detoxification[1] of teenage bedrooms. I am a specialist in cleaning rooms of kids who have just gone off to college. It takes nerves of steel. And I have them.

My brother Benjamin doesn't. To begin with, he's allergic to dust—bad news when the family business is dedicated to eliminating it. To end with, he's a devoted underachiever, in stark contrast to myself. And Benjamin knows how to get out of work—he could give seminars on this. He gets the perfect look of abject[2] pain over his face, says he's not feeling too well, he's sorry, he doesn't want to be a *burden.* He talks about the pain moving across his back, down his leg, and into his ankle. Then he gets dizzy and has to sit down; lying down comes moments later after his face gets a little pale (I don't know how he does this) and his hand touches his forehead which, I swear, has small drops of sweat on it. Then he'll try to get up and help, but by this time, you feel like such a snake that a sick person is going to get sicker because of your insensitive demands that you say, no, you rest, I'll do it. B

This is what he's done to me today, and I'm not in the mood for the game. He tells me, groaning, he'll *try* to make it to Mrs. Leonardo's today to help her pack up her attic, but he's not sure he can even sit. He's lying on the couch in misery saying if he can sit, he will try to stand, and if he attempts standing, he will attempt actual walking—Mrs. Leonardo's house being four houses down the street. I throw my book bag at him. Suggest he *crawl* to Mrs. Leonardo's house and he says, "Thanks, Katie. Just thanks." To which I reply, "Look, Benny Boy, I'm getting sick of carrying your weight around here. If you think I'm going to do your job and mine until I die, think again." Benjamin groans deep, turns off the light, closes his eyes and says his headache is cosmic and could I please go get him some aspirin. C

I don't get the aspirin. It's a big bad world out there and he needs to find it out now, at fourteen. This is what big sisters are for.

So I'm basically crabby and bitter all day; taking it out on random people. After school I have mounds of homework. You wonder what teachers are thinking—I have three hundred pages of reading in three textbooks plus a paper due on Friday. Have you ever noticed that it takes a textbook dozens of pages to say what normal people can cover fast?

Example:

What was the full impact of World War II?

1. **detoxification** (dē-tŏk'sə-fĭ-kā'shən): the process of removing toxic substances.
2. **abject** (ăb'jĕkt'): of the most miserable kind; wretched.

SCIENCE CONNECTION

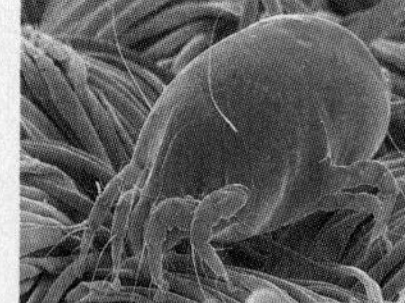

Dust mites are microscopic organisms found in house dust the world over. Some people are allergic to the feces and skin shed by the mites.

1 Targeted Passage

B CONFLICT
How does the narrator feel about her brother's behavior? Tell how she handles it.

C SEQUENCE
Reread lines 49–51. What words or phrases show that the specific events of this story are starting now? Record the event on your chart.

DIFFERENTIATED INSTRUCTION

FOR LESS–PROFICIENT READERS

1 Targeted Passage [Lines 34–63]

This passage helps readers understand the narrator through contrast with her brother.

- Why does the narrator say she has "nerves of steel"?
- Why does Katie end up doing most of her brother's work?
- Do you think Katie has a right to be annoyed? Why?
- How would you describe Katie's life?

Concept Support Point out that an external conflict may lead to internal struggles and vice versa. For example, Katie is in conflict with her brother Benjamin in lines 37–48. He avoids working; she needs him to do his share. This external conflict causes her to feel resentment and anger, an internal conflict. Have students read lines 60–62. Ask them how Katie's internal conflict then leads to other external conflicts (*she refuses to get her brother aspirin; she takes out her anger and bitterness on other people*).

Clear-cut teenage answer: We won.

So I'm close to dying young from excessive homework, and I have to help Mrs. Leonardo clean out her attic. She is paying big bucks for this, and, believe me, my family needs the money.

Mrs. Leonardo wants people there on time and working like ants. Ants carry their weight on their backs and are thrilled as anything to be abused. But that is the insect world; I am not one of them. I'm not in the mood to sit with her in her **dingy** attic and lug tons of garbage down the stairs and listen to her stories of how her family deserted her. I know that sounds mean, but Mrs. Leonardo is a mean person. It's easy to see why she's alone. The big joke is that when her husband died, he had a big smile on his face in the casket that he'd never had in real life. The funeral director said they tried to wipe that grin off his face, but they couldn't do it.

dingy (dĭn′jē) *adj.* dirty or discolored

So I'm on my knees in the dust, putting things in bags, while Mrs. Leonardo tells me about her selfish brother Horace who deserted her, and her uncaring, money-grubbing cousin Cynthia who backed out of the driveway eight years ago and never came back. She tells me how she helped them and loaned them money which they never paid back. She's going on and on about how the world is a dark, dark place. I clear my throat: "Boy, Mrs. Leonardo, you've got a lot of stuff up here. Are you sure you want to keep it all?" **D**

D SEQUENCE
Reread lines 82–88. What words help signal that the narrator is returning to the main story she is telling?

This is the wrong thing to say. Mrs. Leonardo's gray eyes get spitting mad and she says, *well,* she's seventy-six years old and she's had a *very* interesting life and she doesn't want to throw out anything of value. I look in a box with IRS tax forms dating back to 1955.

"Mrs. Leonardo, the IRS says you only need to keep tax records from the last three years. We could dump this whole box . . ." My mother told me this.

She lunges as much as a seventy-six-year-old person can and says she isn't giving her tax records to anyone so they can steal her secrets. Like tons of thieves are out there ready to pounce on this.

But at twenty-five dollars per hour, you learn to be patient. "Think of the money," my mother always says, "and the graciousness will come." So I'm taping the box and writing IMPORTANT PAPERS 1955–1963. Maybe she could turn this attic into a museum and people could walk through and learn all the things you should never hold on to.

Benjamin would have cracked under this pressure. Mrs. Leonardo is kneeling by a huge trunk, saying how the younger generation (mine) doesn't understand about manners, **propriety,** or simple human decency. Her grandniece, Veronica, walks around with her belly button showing. She pulls old clothes out of the trunk and yanks this old lace tablecloth out and just looks at it. Finally, she says she got it when she was married and she's only used it once. She waited for a special occasion and only one came—her twentieth anniversary. No other occasion was special enough, and then her husband died right before

propriety (prə-prī′ĭ-tē) *n.* the quality of being proper; appropriateness

Lines 70–88
DISCUSSION PROMPTS

Use these prompts to help students understand the relationship between Mrs. Leonardo and Katie:

Connect Have you ever done chores for anyone like Mrs. Leonardo? If so, what do you think is the hardest part of the job for Katie? *Students may say that they have done chores for some fussy and demanding people, too. They may say that the hardest part of Katie's job is keeping her patience and being polite.*

Analyze Why does Katie mention the joke about Mr. Leonardo's death? ***Possible answer:*** *It illustrates her point about how mean Mrs. Leonardo is.*

Synthesize Based on what you have learned so far about Katie's life, why do you think she is not in the mood to listen to Mrs. Leonardo complain? ***Possible answer:*** *Katie's life is difficult, too. She has academic pressures, her brother is no help, and she has to work for her mother because her family needs the money.*

READING SKILL

D SEQUENCE

Possible answer: *In line 82, the words* So I'm *indicate that the narrator is returning to the main story.*

FOR ENGLISH LEARNERS

Vocabulary: Idioms and Sayings Explain that some sayings include exaggeration to emphasize an idea. In line 70, for example, the narrator says she's "close to dying young from excessive homework." This exaggeration illustrates the pressure in her life. She also describes her job for Mrs. Leonardo as lugging "tons" of garbage. Ask students to find other examples of sayings that include exaggeration, such as "cracked under this pressure" (line 103). Discuss the meaning of each.

Language: Punctuation and Print Cues Point out the italicized words on page 66: *burden* (line 42), *try* (line 50), *crawl* (line 54). Explain that the use of italics for one or two words within a sentence or paragraph signals readers to emphasize the words. Demonstrate by reading lines 40–42, 50–51, and 54–55 with additional emphasis on each italicized word. Then have students locate the sentences with italicized words on page 67. Have students read the sentences aloud, emphasizing each italicized word.

LITERARY ANALYSIS

E CONFLICT

Possible answer: *Katie gives Mrs. Leonardo advice on what she should do with her tablecloth.*

Extend the Discussion What might be a reason that Mrs. Leonardo reacts as she does to Katie's suggestion?

Lines 103–116

REINFORCE *KEY IDEA:* TREASURE

Discuss Why didn't Mrs. Leonardo use her special tablecloth more than once? What does her experience suggest about preserving treasures? ***Possible answer:*** *She used her tablecloth for her twentieth anniversary because "no other occasion was special enough" (line 110). Before she could use it again, her husband died. Her experience suggests that treasured items should not be locked away in a trunk but should be enjoyed as much as possible before it is too late.*

ANALYZE VISUALS

Possible answer: *The attic has quite a few boxes and other items stacked on either side, suggesting that the person or people who live here like to save things. However, the items are arranged neatly, and the open floor is swept clean, which suggests that the residents are organized and have given some thought to what they should save and what they should throw away.*

their twenty-fifth anniversary and the tablecloth has been in this trunk ever since—only used once, she keeps saying—beautiful Egyptian linen. She looks kind of sad, though stiff. I say, "You could start using it now, Mrs. Leonardo," which is the wrong thing to say. She shuts that trunk and asks me just who do I think she's going to invite to dinner since everyone she's ever done anything for has either deserted her or died. **E**

I don't know how to answer a question like this. My mother didn't cover it during Clean Sweep boot camp training where I learned how to scour a bathtub that a toddler spilled ink in, how to clean pet stains from any carpet known to man, how to wash windows and not leave streaks, how to open a refrigerator with year-old meat and not gag in front of the client. I pledged that the customer was always right and I, the lowly dust eliminator, was always, always wrong.

But I'm not sure what to do. If I agree with her, I'm not helping, and if I listen, I won't get the job done. The truth is, I don't like Mrs. Leonardo—so there's a big part of me that doesn't care—even though I know this is probably inhumane because she's a sad person, really. Kneeling there in the dust, surrounded by the boxes of her so-called interesting life, going on and on

E CONFLICT
What causes Mrs. Leonardo to be upset with Katie?

ANALYZE VISUALS
What do the **details** in the picture tell you about the person or people who live here?

DIFFERENTIATED INSTRUCTION

FOR ADVANCED LEARNERS/PRE–AP

Evaluate [small-group option] Discuss readers' dependence on a first-person narrator. Because this type of narrator is a character in the story, events and other characters are described from his or her perspective, which may not be totally objective. Ask students if they think Katie is a reliable narrator. Why or why not? Have students discuss their ideas in small groups, supporting their opinion with evidence from the story.

about people who are gone. I'm thinking about the next stage of the job—the actual cleaning of the attic which is going to take two people, and I know Benjamin will be hurled into monumental physical **aberrations** up here.

aberration (ăb′ə-rā′shən) *n.* an abnormal alteration

I'm tired, too, and my paper is late on King Lear who, in my opinion, thought too much and couldn't deliver. I'm thinking about my personal life—yes, dust eliminators have them. We have feelings; we have needs, dreams. I'm feeling that I work too much and I wish my mom had another business because what I do all day at school is exhausting enough without having to do heavy lifting after school and on the weekends. I think about when my dad died four years ago, and because of disorganization—that is, getting behind on paying his life insurance premiums—his insurance policy was cancelled and we got no insurance money when he died. He never meant to hurt us, but it was so scary not knowing if we could keep the house mixed with all the pain of losing him. We never got a regular time of mourning because we were fighting to stay afloat. Mom was trying to sort through Dad's huge piles of papers. We loved him so much, but he could never get rid of what Mom called his "clutter demons." F

② Targeted Passage

It took several months, but we got his papers sorted. We learned firsthand how you get organized, clean up, and obliterate dust. We became total aces at it; learned how widespread the problem truly is. We knew then we needed to share what we'd learned with others who were suffering, and felt that twenty-five dollars an hour was reasonable. G

I'm not sure if Mrs. Leonardo wants someone to help or someone to complain to. Between you and me, I feel that listening to complaining *and* busting dust should earn thirty-five dollars per hour. But, I'm remembering being in our attic after my dad died; trying to go through his things. He had a trunk that his grandfather had given him—inside were all his photos and papers from school. I remember reading some of his essays from high school and just crying. I couldn't throw those out. Mom said going through all that was therapeutic[3] for me because it was like being with him, kind of. He was forty-one years old when he died. Had a heart attack at work and was dead by the time the ambulance came. H

Just thinking about the day makes me shaky. Over the years I've dissected every last thing I remember about the last morning I saw him. I should have made him breakfast—I knew how much he liked it when I did. I should have hugged him when he went out the door, but I was on the phone with Roger Rugsby who was my biology partner who needed me to go over my lab notes or he would fail. I missed the bus and Dad missed his train and he took me to school. I was late, so I hurled myself out of the car and he said, "Go get 'em, kiddo." That's the last thing he ever said to me. But I did better than Benjamin who overslept and didn't even see Dad that morning. I

Mrs. Leonardo leans over a trunk like the one my father had. I want to say something encouraging to her, like, "Gee, Mrs. Leonardo, I know how hard it

F CONFLICT
What internal and external conflicts does Katie face as a result of her dad's death?

G SEQUENCE
When did Katie's mother form Clean Sweep?

H CONFLICT
Reread lines 153–158. How does Katie react while looking through her father's things?

I SEQUENCE
Reread lines 161–163. Note the phrase that lets you know a **flashback** is coming. When do the events in this paragraph take place?

3. **therapeutic** (thĕr′ə-pyo͞o′tĭk): having healing powers.

LITERARY ANALYSIS

F CONFLICT

Possible answers:

- ***Internal conflicts:*** *Katie suffered the pain of losing her father and the anxiety of not knowing whether she and her family could keep their house. She is exhausted by the added responsibility of having to work for her mother.*
- ***External conflicts:*** *Katie and her family have to cope with a lack of money as a result of her father's disorganization. She has too much work.*

If students need help . . . Together, list all of the conflicts identified in these lines. Then discuss each one and classify it as internal or external.

READING SKILL

G SEQUENCE

Remind students to record these events at the beginning of their sequence charts from page 63. ***Possible answer:*** *Four years ago, Katie's father died. Several months later, Katie's mother started Clean Sweep.*

LITERARY ANALYSIS

H CONFLICT

Possible answer: *Katie cries when she reads his high-school essays. She is unable to throw them away.*

Extend the Discussion Why does her mother call the experience of sorting through her father's things "therapeutic" for Katie?

READING SKILL

I SEQUENCE

Possible answer: *The flashback is signaled by the words* Just thinking about the day. *This event took place four years ago, on the day Katie's father died.*

FOR LESS–PROFICIENT READERS

② Targeted Passage [Lines 132–169]

This passage develops some of the major conflicts in the story.

- What kinds of pressures does Katie have in her life?
- What event changed her life?
- Why does she have to work so hard for her mother?
- What does Katie wish she had done differently on the day her father died?

Comprehension Support Use Read Aloud/Think Aloud to clarify sequence in lines 132–176. Point out the transition into the past that is signaled with the words *I think about when my dad died four years ago* in lines 137–138. Discuss the key events that occur in the flashback before the action returns to the present in line 170.

BEST PRACTICES TOOLKIT—Transparency
Read Aloud/Think Aloud p. A34

Lines 173–176
REINFORCE *KEY IDEA:* TREASURE

Discuss What does Katie **treasure** more than photographs? Why? ***Possible answer:*** *She treasures memories because they are filled with sights, smells, love, and happiness.*

Lines 177–193
DISCUSSION PROMPTS

Use these prompts to help students understand Mrs. Leonardo's story:

Connect Why is it so difficult for Katie to know what to say to Mrs. Leonardo in this situation? Would you find it equally difficult? *Katie does not know the story behind the book or what happened with Mrs. Leonardo's sister. Most students will say that they would have trouble, too.*

Analyze Based on the details in this passage, what is the reason that Mrs. Leonardo hasn't spoken to her sister in years? ***Possible answer:*** *Mrs. Leonardo and her sister had a fight over the book. Mrs. Leonardo didn't believe that her sister didn't have it.*

Synthesize Why do you think that Mrs. Leonardo is tearful when she finds the book? ***Possible answers:*** *She regrets doubting her sister and not speaking to her as a result. Finding the book brings back memories of her mother and childhood.*

READING SKILL: *Review*

J PREDICT

Possible answer: *She might get in touch with her sister or send her the book with a note of apology.*

---

must be going through all these memories," or, "I hope sorting through all this is helping you the way it helped me." Memories are the only things we have left sometimes. You can hold a photo of a person you loved who's gone, but it isn't alive. Memories—the best ones—are filled with sights, smells, love, and happiness. I try to hold some of those in my heart for my dad each day.

She goes through the trunk, stony-faced. I can't tell what she's found, can't tell if she's going to torch the contents or hold them to her heart. I lug a big bag over and throw old newspapers inside. Mrs. Leonardo stops going through the trunk. She's holding something in her hands, not moving. I look at her stiff face and for a moment in the weird light of the attic, she looks like she's going to cry. But that's impossible. Then I hear a sniff and she says softly, "My mother read this book to my sister and me every night before bed."

I look at the book—a well-worn brown leather cover. Doesn't look like much.

"I thought she had it," Mrs. Leonardo says sadly.

"Who had it?"

"My sister, Helen. I thought she had the book. She always wanted it."

In these situations it's best to say, "Oh."

"I thought . . . I thought I'd sent it to her after Mother died." She looks down.

I say, "It's hard to remember what you've done after someone important dies."

"But, she'd asked me for it. It was the one thing she'd wanted."

"Well . . ."

"I haven't talked to her since Mother died. I thought she . . ."

I'm not sure how to ask this. Is Helen still alive?

I dance around it. "What do you think you should do with the book, Mrs. Leonardo?" She doesn't answer.

I try again. "Why did Helen want it so bad?"

She hands me the book. "She said these stories were her best memories of childhood." I look through it. "The Naughty Little Frog," "The Little Lost Tulip," "Spanky, the Black Sheep." It's amazing what we put up with as children. But then I remember my favorite bedtime story—"Rupert, the Church Mouse"—about this little mouse who lives in a church and polishes all the stained glass windows every night before he goes to sleep so the light can come forth every morning.

"I know she lives in Vermont," Mrs. Leonardo offers. "I heard from a cousin a while ago . . ." Her voice trails off. J

"I think you should call her, Mrs. Leonardo."

She shakes her old head. No—she couldn't possibly.

"I think you should call her and tell her you've got the book."

She glares at me. "I believe we're done for today." She grabs the book from my hands, puts it back in the trunk.

"Sorry, ma'am. I didn't mean . . ."

She heads down the attic stairs.

3 Targeted Passage

J PREDICT
Now that she's found the book, what do you think Mrs. Leonardo might do in regard to her sister?

DIFFERENTIATED INSTRUCTION

FOR LESS-PROFICIENT READERS

Reading Skill Follow-Up: Sequence [paired option]

- Remind students that flashback events from lines 132–169 are placed at the beginning of the sequence chart to indicate that they take place at an earlier time.
- Give pairs time to update their charts and include events from the flashback before reviewing them as a class. As students continue reading, they should complete their charts.

Past

Katie's father dies. → *Her family organizes his things.* → *Her mother starts Clean Sweep.*

Present

Katie cleans the attic. → *Mrs. Leonardo finds tablecloth and book.* →

3 Targeted Passage [Lines 177–213]

This passage introduces a subplot involving Mrs. Leonardo and her sister, Helen.

- What does Mrs. Leonardo find in the trunk? Why is this object important to her?
- How did the book cause a misunderstanding between Mrs. Leonardo and her sister?
- What does Katie suggest that Mrs. Leonardo do? How does Mrs. Leonardo react?

I tell Benjamin that I don't want to hear about his problems, that his back looks strong to me, the shooting pain in his leg will go away eventually, and his headache is just a reflection of his deep, inner **turmoil.** I say this as we're walking to Mrs. Leonardo's house.

turmoil (tûr'moil') *n.* a state of extreme confusion or agitation

"I think my whole left side is going numb," he whispers pitifully as we walk up her steps.

"Deal with it."

Mrs. Leonardo is waiting for us. We're late. I don't mention that having to drag a hypochondriac[4] four doors down the street takes time. Great food smells swirl from her kitchen. K

K CONFLICT
In what ways is Katie responsible for her brother?

Mrs. Leonardo looks Benjamin up and down, not impressed. "You've not been here before," she says. Benjamin half smiles and rubs his tennis elbow,[5] which makes me nuts because he doesn't play tennis.

I introduce them. Tell her Benjamin is here to help with dust elimination and heavy lifting, at which point Benjamin leans painfully against the wall and closes his eyes.

"He's a very dedicated worker once he gets started, Mrs. Leonardo."

I jam my elbow into his side.

Okay, so we're cleaning this cavernous[6] attic like there's no tomorrow. We've got all the trunks and boxes wiped down and pushed to the far side. We're running the turbo-charged Clean Sweep Frankenstein portable vacuum that is so powerful it can suck up pets and small children if they get too close. Benjamin is wearing a dust mask over his nose and mouth—he wrote *The Terminator* over it. This boy is appropriately miserable, pulling down spiders' webs, sucking up dust mites. I can almost hear their little screams of terror. Almost, but not quite. My mother claims she can hear dust mites shrieking for mercy and uses this in her presentation if she thinks potential clients can handle it.

"Get the lace tablecloth from the trunk!" Mrs. Leonardo shouts from downstairs.

What's she want with that?

"And bring the book, too," she hollers impatiently.

I don't mention that we've shoved everything in the corner like she said to, that I'll have to move it all to get to the trunk, and, by the way, I'm going as fast as I can. I get the book and the lace tablecloth that's been folded in very old plastic. I look at the book—reddish brown leather—*Aunt Goody's Good Night Stories,* it's called. Benjamin comes over looking like some kind of cosmic alien with his mask, takes the book, starts laughing.

"The Naughty Little Frog," he says reading. "Once upon a time there was a naughty little frog named Edmond. Edmond was so naughty that

4. **hypochondriac** (hī'pə-kŏn'drē-ăk'): a person who continually thinks he or she is ill or about to become ill.
5. **tennis elbow:** pain around the elbow, often caused from playing tennis or similar activities.
6. **cavernous** (kăv'ər-nəs): filled with caverns; like a cave.

LITERARY ANALYSIS

K CONFLICT

Possible answer: *She has to drag him to work and make excuses for him.*

Extend the Discussion How does the responsibility for her brother affect Katie?

Lines 224–241
DISCUSSION PROMPTS

Use these prompts to help students understand Benjamin's significance in the story:

Connect If you were Katie, how would you handle Benjamin? *Students might say that they would use a mixture of teasing and bullying to get Benjamin to do what they wanted him to, just as Katie does. Others might say that they would leave Benjamin alone and hope he would grow up soon.*

Analyze How does Benjamin emerge as a more fully developed character in these lines? What do you learn about him? ***Possible answers:*** *Benjamin's traits other than his tendency to be constantly ill are revealed in these lines. He has a sense of humor, as shown by the label on his dust mask. He can also work hard when he needs to.*

Synthesize What message about relationships does Benjamin's presence in the story convey? How is Katie's relationship with Benjamin different from Mrs. Leonardo's relationship with her sister? ***Possible answers:*** *Benjamin's character brings out the importance of working at relationships. Katie does not give up on him, unlike Mrs. Leonardo, who ended her relationship with her sister over a relatively petty issue.*

FOR LESS–PROFICIENT READERS

Review: Predict Remind students that when they predict, they use clues from the text to help them make a logical guess about what might happen in the future. Guide students to make an accurate prediction of what Mrs. Leonardo is planning, based on these clues from the text:

- She wants the lace tablecloth, used only for special occasions (lines 242–243).
- She wants the children's book that was important to her sister Helen (line 245).

FOR ENGLISH LEARNERS

Culture: Clarify

- Tell students that using *Frankenstein* as part of the vacuum cleaner's name in line 234 is meant to make people think of the monster from Mary Shelley's book by that name. In other words, this vacuum cleaner is monstrously powerful.
- Explain that *The Terminator* written across Benjamin's mask refers to a movie character who is a humanoid robot programmed to kill certain people.

READING SKILL

L SEQUENCE

***Possible answer:** Mrs. Leonardo sets the table with her special tablecloth and good silverware. She cooks a special meal.*

Lines 270–278

REINFORCE *KEY IDEA:* TREASURE

Discuss What is Mrs. Leonardo's true **treasure?** ***Possible answer:** Mrs. Leonardo's true treasure is her sister's friendship.*

SELECTION WRAP–UP

REFLECT Do you think Katie learns anything from her experience at Mrs. Leonardo's? If so, what?

★ **CRITIQUE** Are the characters in this story realistic? Ask students to support their opinions with logical reasoning and details from the story.

READING FLUENCY

Distribute the copy masters and have students practice fluency.

RESOURCE MANAGER—Copy Master
Reading Fluency p. 89

he never, ever cleaned his lily pad. It got so dirty that his mother had to make him stay on that lily pad several times each day to—"

"You're going to have to wait for the end." I yank the book from his hands and head down the creaky attic stairs with the tablecloth. Mrs. Leonardo is in the kitchen wearing a frilly apron, stirring a pot of something that smells beyond great.

She turns to look at me, puts her wooden spoon down.

"Help me put it on the table," she orders.

I'm smiling a little now because I know this tablecloth's history. I'm wondering who's coming to dinner.

"Looks like you're having a party," I offer as we get the tablecloth squared perfectly on the table.

Mrs. Leonardo says nothing, sets the table for two with what looks like the good silverware, the good napkins. Then she puts the storybook in front of one of the place settings.

"My sister, you see . . ." She pauses emotionally. "Well, she's . . . coming to dinner."

"You mean the one you haven't seen for a long time?"

"I only have *one* sister."

I'm just grinning now and I tell her I hope they have the best dinner in the world.

"Well, I do too." She looks nervously out the window and says whatever work we haven't finished can be done tomorrow. "You were right about . . . calling her, Katie." L

I smile brightly, wondering if she's going to offer me some of her great-smelling food to show her gratitude. She doesn't. I head up the attic stairs and drag Benjamin to safety. He's sneezing like he's going to die. I take off his Terminator dust mask and lean him against a wall. Half of me wants to give Mrs. Leonardo a little hug of encouragement, but the other half warns, *Don't touch clients because they can turn on you.*

"Whatever you're cooking, Mrs. Leonardo, it sure smells good," I shout. "Your sister's going to love it." I'm not sure she hears all of that. Benjamin is into his fifth sneezing attack.

She nods from the kitchen; I push Benjamin out on the street.

"I could have died up there," he shouts, blowing his nose.

"But you didn't."

And I remember the book my dad would read to us when we were little about the baby animals and their parents and how each mother and father animal kissed their babies good night. That book was chewed to death, ripped, stained, and missing the last two pages, but I wouldn't give it up for anything.

We walk back home almost silently, except for Benjamin's sniffs, sneezes, and groans. People just don't understand what important things can be hiding in the dust.

Mom says that all the time in her presentation. ∾

L SEQUENCE
What steps has Mrs. Leonardo taken to prepare for her sister's visit? Add these to your chart.

④ Targeted Passage

DIFFERENTIATED INSTRUCTION

FOR LESS–PROFICIENT READERS

④ Targeted Passage [Lines 269–297]

This passage presents the resolution of the subplot and its impact on Katie.

- Why does Mrs. Leonardo thank Katie?
- How does Katie feel about Mrs. Leonardo's dinner plans?
- How is the book Katie's father used to read to her similar to Mrs. Leonardo's book? How does the memory make Katie feel?

FOR ADVANCED LEARNERS/PRE–AP

Analyze "People just don't understand what important things can be hiding in the dust." Ask students to explore the meanings of this theme statement in a web diagram. Have students share their ideas in a class discussion.

Comprehension

1. **Recall** What job does the Clean Sweep company do?
2. **Clarify** Why does Katie resent her brother?
3. **Summarize** For Katie, what makes working for Mrs. Leonardo so difficult?

Literary Analysis

4. **Identify Sequence** Review the chart you created as you read. Which event or events in the sequence occur as **flashbacks?** What information do you learn about Katie from the flashbacks?
5. **Examine Conflict** Note the internal and external conflicts Katie faces after her dad's death. By the end of the story, which of these conflicts are resolved? Explain.
6. **Identify Subplot** A subplot is a minor plot that involves an additional **conflict** in the story. Use the following graphic to record details of the subplot involving Mrs. Leonardo and her sister. How does this subplot help shed light on Katie's story?

Characters Involved: Mrs. Leonardo and her sister
Conflict:
Resolution:

7. **Analyze Character Motivations** Why do you think Mrs. Leonardo decided to reconnect with her sister?
8. **Make Judgments** Reread lines 221–229 and footnote 4. Would you say that Katie's brother is a hypochondriac? Use examples from the text to support your answer.

Extension and Challenge

9. **Big Question Activity** Look again at the Web It activity on page 62. Imagine you are Katie, and her **treasure** is the book she mentions on page 72, lines 290–293. Complete a new web and include the good memories Katie might connect to the book.
10. **SCIENCE CONNECTION** Katie's family earns a living fighting dust mites. Look back at the information about dust mites on page 66. Research more about them to find out whether they are seriously harmful to people and whether it is possible to get rid of all dust mites in a home. Is Katie's mother being honest in her presentation? Present your findings to the class.

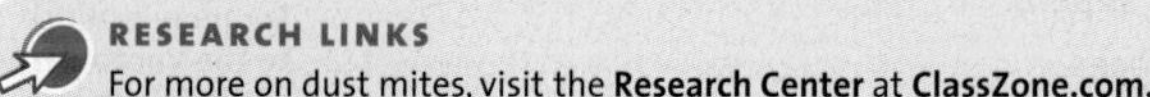

RESEARCH LINKS
For more on dust mites, visit the **Research Center** at **ClassZone.com.**

Practice and Apply

After Reading

For additional support of postreading questions, use these copy masters:

RESOURCE MANAGER—Copy Masters
Reading Check p. 86 (to check understanding of the selection)
Internal and External Conflict p. 79 (for practice of literary analysis standards focus)
Question Support p. 87 (After Reading questions adapted for English learners and less-proficient readers)

Additional selection questions are provided for teachers on page 73.

ANSWERS

Comprehension

1. *The company cleans houses.*
2. *Her brother acts sick and doesn't work as hard as Katie does.*
3. *Mrs. Leonardo is bad-tempered and does not want to throw anything away. She does not want to listen to Katie's suggestions about her sister.*

Literary Analysis

Possible answers:

4. **■ STANDARDS FOCUS Sequence** *Flashbacks include Katie's remembering the day her father died and the aftermath of his death as they sorted through his papers and tried to figure out what to do. The flashbacks reveal that Katie's family relies on the money they make from cleaning houses to survive and that Katie still has difficulty dealing with her father's death.*
5. **● STANDARDS FOCUS Internal and External Conflict** *By the end of the story, Katie has come closer to acceptance of her father's death through her realization that she has some precious memories and reminders of him.*
6. ***Conflict:*** *Mrs. Leonardo thought her sister had the children's book and stopped talking to her.* ***Resolution:*** *Mrs. Leonardo finds the book and calls her sister to invite her to dinner and resolve their argument. This subplot reinforces the importance of Katie's memories of her father.*
7. *Sorting through the boxes brings back memories of the people she once had in her life. The tablecloth reminds her that she has spent her life waiting for a "special occasion." Finally, she realizes that she was wrong and that she lost her sister for a trivial, invalid reason.*
8. *Yes. He does have allergies, but he pretends to have a host of other illnesses such as tennis elbow, even though he doesn't play tennis. Once he starts working, he seems to forget about some of his ailments and even laughs and jokes.*

Extension and Challenge

9. *Students' responses will vary but should include Katie's memory of her father reading the book to her.*
10. **SCIENCE CONNECTION** *Students' responses should include facts about the harmful effects of dust mites and offer an opinion about the honesty of Katie's mother's presentation supported by examples from the text and their research.*

CLEAN SWEEP 73

ANSWERS

Vocabulary in Context

VOCABULARY PRACTICE

1. *antonyms*
2. *antonyms*
3. *synonyms*
4. *antonyms*
5. *antonyms*
6. *synonyms*

RESOURCE MANAGER—Copy Master
Vocabulary Practice p. 84

VOCABULARY IN WRITING

Have students reread lines 75–102 and 232–241, which describe the attic. Suggest that they jot down some of the details and then survey the vocabulary words to see which might help them express their ideas about setting.

VOCABULARY STRATEGY: SUFFIXES THAT FORM NOUNS *(also an EL language objective)*

Together, define the words in the web to demonstrate how to use knowledge of the suffix and the root. For example:

happiness: "the state of being happy or having joy"

argument: "the process of arguing or disagreeing"

Possible answers:

1. *achievement; "state of accomplishing"*
2. *connection; "process of connecting"*
3. *performance; "process of performing"*
4. *sadness; "state of being unhappy"*
5. *shortage; "state of having an insufficient amount"*

RESOURCE MANAGER—Copy Master
Vocabulary Strategy p. 85

Vocabulary Center at **ClassZone.com**
Additional Vocabulary Activities

Vocabulary in Context

VOCABULARY PRACTICE

Decide whether the words in each pair are synonyms (words that mean the same) or antonyms (words that mean the opposite).

1. propriety/rudeness
2. vileness/niceness
3. dingy/shabby
4. minuscule/huge
5. aberration/sameness
6. turmoil/chaos

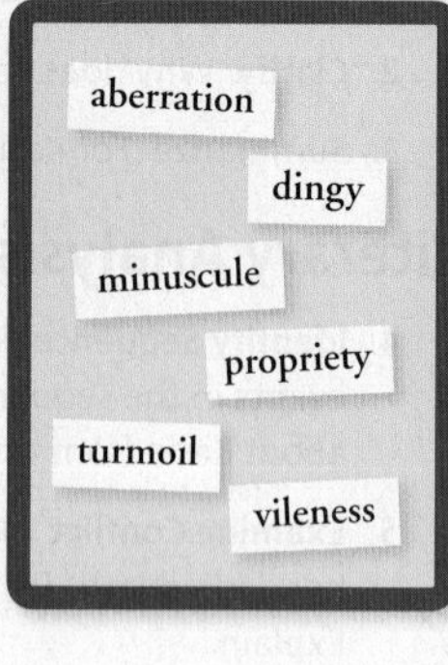

VOCABULARY IN WRITING

What was the state of Mrs. Leonardo's attic when Katie first saw it? Use at least two vocabulary words to write a one-paragraph description. You could start this way.

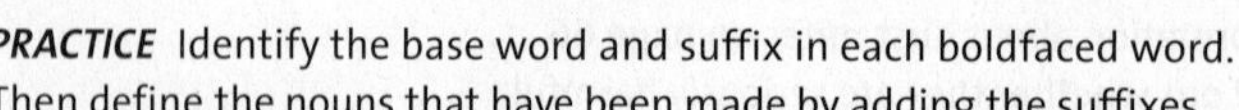
EXAMPLE SENTENCE

The attic was ***dingy*** *and dusty, and it was filled with old clothes and papers.*

VOCABULARY STRATEGY: SUFFIXES THAT FORM NOUNS

A suffix is a word part that appears at the end of a root or base word to form a new word. Some suffixes, such as those in *vileness* and *aberration*, can be added to words to form nouns. The web shown includes other suffixes that have a similar meaning.

If a word seems unfamiliar, see if you can break it into a familiar root and suffix. For example, the word *embellishment* can be broken into *embellish* and *–ment*, which might help you understand that an embellishment is something that is decorated.

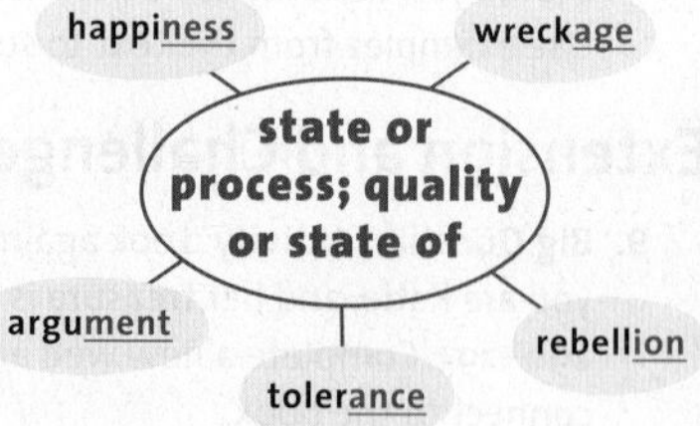

PRACTICE Identify the base word and suffix in each boldfaced word. Then define the nouns that have been made by adding the suffixes.

1. Winning the state championship was quite an **achievement.**
2. To make the **connection,** your flight will have to arrive on time.
3. His **performance** in the concert was superb.
4. One could see the **sadness** in their faces.
5. We have a **shortage** of paper towels in the kitchen.

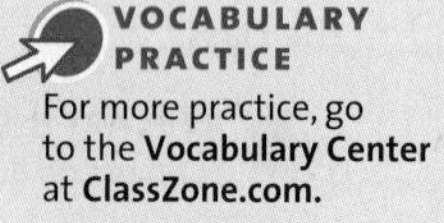
VOCABULARY PRACTICE
For more practice, go to the **Vocabulary Center** at **ClassZone.com.**

DIFFERENTIATED INSTRUCTION

FOR ENGLISH LEARNERS

Vocabulary Strategy [mixed-readiness groups] Have students work in small groups to use their knowledge of suffix meanings and context clues to define these additional words from the story: *specialist* (line 35), *graciousness* (line 99), *insurance* (line 139), *encouragement* (line 283). Have groups share their definitions.

FOR ADVANCED LEARNERS/PRE–AP

Vocabulary Strategy Point out that the spelling of some words changes when the suffix is added. Have students identify the rules governing spelling changes when the suffixes identified in the exercise are used. Have students give another example to illustrate each rule.

Reading-Writing Connection

Increase your understanding of "Clean Sweep" by responding to these prompts. Then complete the **Grammar and Writing** exercise.

WRITING PROMPTS	SELF-CHECK
A. Short Response: Write a Dialogue Reread lines 151–160. Write a **half-page of dialogue** between Katie and her mother that might have occurred while they sorted through her dad's things after his death.	***An effective dialogue will . . .*** • include details about what they found • use words and phrases that show how they feel
B. Extended Response: Compare and Contrast Write **two or three paragraphs** comparing and contrasting Mrs. Leonardo's loss and Katie's loss. How did the losses occur? How did each person react? Explain how forgotten **treasures** helped both characters come to terms with their losses.	***A detailed response will . . .*** • describe each character's loss • show the connection between the treasure and the characters' feelings

GRAMMAR AND WRITING

PUNCTUATE POSSESSIVES CORRECTLY When you're writing about people's possessions, be sure to put the apostrophe in the correct place. To help keep your writing clear, follow these guidelines for punctuating possessive nouns:

- **Singular nouns:** Add an apostrophe and *s*, even if the word ends in *s* (*dog's leash, princess's crown*)
- **Plural nouns ending in *s*:** Add an apostrophe (*hosts' party, employees' benefits*)
- **Plural nouns not ending in *s*:** Add an apostrophe and *s* (*children's toys, mice's footprints*)

Original: When I lifted the trunks' lid, it wobbled and creaked.

Revised: When I lifted the trunk's lid, it wobbled and creaked.

PRACTICE In the following sentences, decide which possessives are used correctly. If incorrect, revise them.

1. We have to categorize the family's papers.
2. I had no idea he could write until I read through Dads' essays.
3. Some of the essays' titles reminded me of how he talked when he helped me with homework.
4. The death of Katies father was out of her control.
5. Childrens' books can hold powerful memories.

For more help with possessives, see page R46 in the **Grammar Handbook.**

Reading-Writing Connection

WRITING PROMPTS

- For **Prompt A,** have students take notes on the items Katie and her mother looked through and their feelings as they did so.
- For **Prompt B,** suggest that students use a Venn Diagram to help them organize differences and similarities between the two characters' losses.

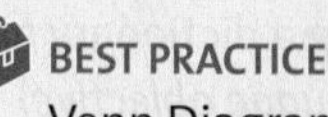

BEST PRACTICES TOOLKIT—Transparency
Venn Diagram p. A26

For writing support, see

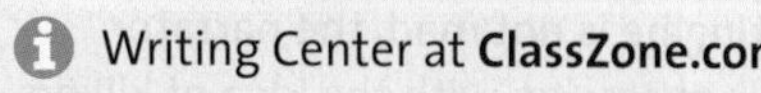

Writing Center at **ClassZone.com**

GRAMMAR AND WRITING

Have volunteers read each rule aloud. Provide additional examples to illustrate each.

Answers:

1. *correct*
2. *Dad's*
3. *correct*
4. *Katie's*
5. *Children's*

RESOURCE MANAGER—Copy Master
Punctuate Possessives Correctly p. 88

Assess and Reteach

Assess

RESOURCE MANAGER—Copy Masters
Selection Tests A, B/C pp. 91–92, 93–94

Test Generator CD

Reteach

STANDARDS LESSON FILE
Literature Lesson 6: Conflict
Literature Lesson 7: Flashbacks
Reading Lesson 6: Recognizing Sequence and Chronological Order
Vocabulary Lesson 5: Noun Suffixes

DIFFERENTIATED INSTRUCTION

FOR LESS–PROFICIENT WRITERS

For Prompt A:

1. Have students reread lines 132–169 in pairs and discuss the feelings that both characters experience.
2. As a class, talk about students' insights, recording significant ideas on the board.
3. Then help students write the first lines of dialogue before pairs complete them independently.

For Prompt B:

1. Help students fill in the Venn Diagrams with details from the story.
2. Identify ways in which the children's books help both Mrs. Leonardo and Katie. For example, the book gives Mrs. Leonardo a reason to call her sister.
3. Suggest that students talk about the similarities between the two characters' losses in one paragraph, the differences in another, and the ways in which both characters are helped in the third paragraph.

Focus and Motivate

OBJECTIVES

Literary Analysis
- explore the key idea of **suspicion**
- identify and analyze suspense
- read a short story

Reading
- identify and evaluate narrator

Vocabulary
- build vocabulary for reading and writing
- use reference aids, including a dictionary and a thesaurus *(also an EL language objective)*

SUMMARY

While insisting he is not mad, the narrator describes his obsession with the idea of killing an old man who lives in his house. When he actually commits the murder, he focuses on a sound that he takes to be the beating of the old man's heart. Then he hides his victim's dismembered body under the floor. When the police arrive to investigate, the narrator begins to hear a pounding sound that grows louder and louder. Convinced that the sound he hears is the old man's heart, the tormented narrator confesses his crime.

What makes you SUSPICIOUS?

Discuss the question with students. To lead into the ***KEY IDEA,*** ask students how they would define ***suspicion.*** How do people behave when they feel suspicious? What causes them to feel this way? Then have small groups work on the ***DISCUSS*** activity.

Before Reading

The Tell-Tale Heart

Short Story by Edgar Allan Poe

What makes you SUSPICIOUS?

KEY IDEA Has something or someone ever seemed dangerous or untrustworthy to you? The feeling you had was **suspicion.** While suspicion might come from a misunderstanding, it can also be a warning that something is very wrong. In this story, you'll meet a man whose own suspicions are his downfall.

DISCUSS With a small group, discuss suspicious characters you've read about or seen on television shows. In what ways did these characters look or act differently from other characters? Continue your discussion by creating a list of warning signs that should make a person suspicious.

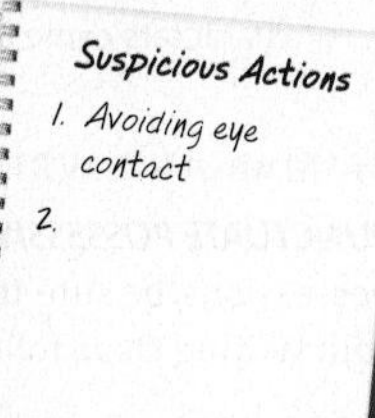

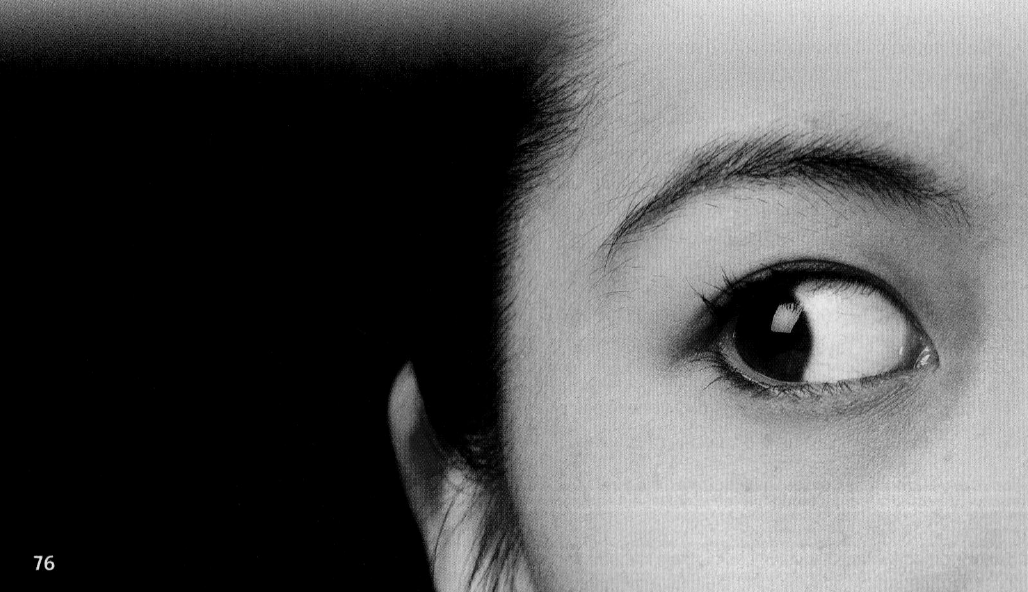

76

Selection Resources

RESOURCE MANAGER UNIT 1

Plan and Teach pp. 95–102

Literary Analysis
Summary pp. 103†*, 104‡*
Suspense pp. 105, 106†*
Question Support p. 113*

Reading
Evaluate Narrator pp. 107, 108†*
Reading Check p. 112
Reading Fluency p. 114

Vocabulary
Study p. 109*
Practice p. 110
Strategy p. 111

Assessment
Selection Tests A, B/C pp. 115*, 117*
Test Generator CD

BEST PRACTICES TOOLKIT
Differentiated Instruction pp. 31–38*
Scaffolding Instruction pp. 43–46*

Graphic Organizers/Strategies
Word Questioning • Two-Column Chart

Reading Support
Audio Anthology CD*

Technology
Literature and Vocabulary Centers at **ClassZone.com**
Write*Smart* CD

* Resources for Differentiation † Also in Spanish ‡ In Haitian Creole and Vietnamese

LITERARY ANALYSIS: SUSPENSE

Writers often "hook" readers by creating a sense of excitement, tension, dread, or fear about what will happen next. This feeling is called **suspense.** Techniques used by Edgar Allan Poe to develop suspense include

- describing a character's anxiety or fear
- relating vivid descriptions of dramatic sights and sounds
- repeating words, phrases, or characters' actions

As you read "The Tell-Tale Heart," notice what causes you to feel suspense.

READING SKILL: EVALUATE NARRATOR

Have you ever suspected someone was not telling you the truth? Just as you can't trust every person you meet, you can't believe all **narrators,** or characters who tell a story. To evaluate a narrator's **reliability,** or trustworthiness, pay attention to his or her actions, attitudes, and statements. Do any raise your suspicions? As you read "The Tell-Tale Heart," record any clues that reveal whether the narrator is reliable or not.

Narrator's Reliability	
Makes Me Suspicious:	*Makes Me Trust Him:*
•	•
•	•
•	•

VOCABULARY IN CONTEXT

Poe uses the following words to reveal how the main character is acting, feeling, and thinking. For each word, choose the numbered word or phrase closest in meaning.

WORD LIST				
	acute	crevice	stealthily	vehemently
	audacity	derision	stifled	vex
	conceive	hypocritical		

1. annoy
2. cautiously
3. intense
4. crack
5. deceptive
6. smothered
7. ridicule
8. think of
9. strongly
10. shameless daring

Author On|ine

Orphan at Two Edgar Allan Poe was born in Boston to parents who made their livings as traveling actors. When Poe was two, his father deserted the family. Less than a year later, his mother died. Edgar was raised in Virginia by family friends, the Allans. After being expelled from both the University of Virginia and the U.S. Military Academy at West Point, Poe began writing for a living.

Edgar Allan Poe
1809–1849

"Madness or Melancholy" Poe got a job as a journalist to support himself and his young wife while he worked on the stories and poems that would earn him the title "father of the modern mystery." A master of suspense, he wrote works that were often dark and full of horrifying images. Poems such as "The Raven" and short stories such as "The Pit and the Pendulum" brought him fame but no fortune. Poverty intensified his despair when his wife, Virginia, fell ill and died. Deeply depressed, Poe died two years later after being found on the streets of Baltimore. Poe's obituary stated he was a man of astonishing skill, a dreamer who walked "in madness or melancholy."

MORE ABOUT THE AUTHOR
For more on Edgar Allan Poe, visit the **Literature Center** at **ClassZone.com.**

Teach

STANDARDS FOCUS

LITERARY ANALYSIS

● SUSPENSE

Read aloud this example:

Thump! Thump! Thump! I woke with a start. Had I dreamed the sounds, or was someone in the house? *Thump! Thump! Thump! Thump!* Footsteps—coming up the stairs!

Ask students what causes the reader to feel suspense while reading this passage. ***Possible answer:*** *Description of the narrator's fear and repetition of the unexplained noise builds tension.*

CHECK UNDERSTANDING Ask students to describe suspenseful moments from films.

READING SKILL

■ EVALUATE NARRATOR

Read aloud this example: *Dogs are disgusting animals! They are loud, dirty, and always biting people.* Ask students if they trust the narrator. Why or why not? ***Possible answer:*** *Since the narrator obviously hates dogs, students may conclude that the narrator is biased and therefore untrustworthy.*

CHECK UNDERSTANDING Ask students to evaluate the narrator of a selection they have recently read.

RESOURCE MANAGER—Copy Master
Evaluate Narrator p. 107 (for student use while reading the selection)

VOCABULARY SKILL

▲ VOCABULARY IN CONTEXT

DIAGNOSE WORD KNOWLEDGE To determine preteaching needs, have all students complete **Vocabulary in Context.** Check students' answers. (**1.** *vex* **2.** *stealthily* **3.** *acute* **4.** *crevice* **5.** *hypocritical* **6.** *stifled* **7.** *derision* **8.** *conceive* **9.** *vehemently* **10.** *audacity*)

PRETEACH VOCABULARY Use the Vocabulary Study copy master to help students determine the meaning of each boldfaced word.

1. Read the first sentence in Part A aloud.
2. Point out the phrase *no one else can hear.* Elicit possible meanings for *acute,* such as "sharp."
3. Have students record their predictions.
4. Repeat for the remaining sentences.
5. Have pairs work together on Part B.

RESOURCE MANAGER—Copy Master
Vocabulary Study p. 109

For general guidelines on differentiating vocabulary instruction and for alternative vocabulary activities for students not needing vocabulary preteaching, see

BEST PRACTICES TOOLKIT
Scaffolding Vocabulary Instruction pp. 43–46

Vocabulary Center at **ClassZone.com**
Additional Vocabulary Activities

Practice and Apply

ANALYZE VISUALS

Possible answer: *In the foreground, the man's anxiety and fear are conveyed by the expression on his face. Dramatic shadows around the room suggest a sense of dread. Jagged lines—such as those in the folds of the men's clothing and the lines on the door—create tension.*

About the Art American illustrator Howard Simpson has contributed to DC Comics' *Green Lantern* and *The Outsiders* and has illustrated Timon and Pumbaa stories for Disney Adventures.

READING SKILL

A EVALUATE NARRATOR

Possible answer: *He is planning to murder an old man because he thinks the man has "the eye of a vulture" (line 11). This plan makes the narrator's opinion that he is not insane seem untrustworthy.*

If students need help . . . Have them reread lines 1–11, paying attention to the narrator's self-description. Ask why the narrator assumes that the reader thinks he's crazy. Do his insights seem accurate? Also, if he really loves the old man (line 9), why would he want to kill him?

The Tell-Tale Heart

Edgar Allan Poe

True!—nervous—very, very dreadfully nervous I had been and am! but why *will* you say that I am mad? The disease had sharpened my senses—not destroyed—not dulled them. Above all was the sense of hearing **acute.** I heard all things in the heaven and in the earth. I heard many things in hell. How, then, am I mad? Hearken! and observe how healthily—how calmly I can tell you the whole story.

It is impossible to say how first the idea entered my brain; but once **conceived,** it haunted me day and night. Object there was none. Passion there was none. I loved the old man. He had never wronged me. He had never given me insult. For his gold I had no desire. I think it was his eye! yes, it was this! He had the eye of a vulture—a pale blue eye, with a film over it. Whenever it fell upon me, my blood ran cold; and so by degrees—very gradually—I made up my mind to take the life of the old man, and thus rid myself of the eye forever.

Now this is the point. You fancy me mad. Madmen know nothing. But you should have seen *me.* You should have seen how wisely I proceeded—with what caution—with what foresight—with what dissimulation[1] I went to work! **A**

I was never kinder to the old man than during the whole week before I killed him. And every night, about midnight, I turned the latch of his door and opened it—oh, so gently! And then, when I had made an opening sufficient for my head, I put in a dark lantern, all closed, closed, so that no light shone out, and then I thrust in my head. Oh, you would have laughed to see how cunningly I thrust it in! I moved it slowly—very, very slowly, so that I might not disturb the old

ANALYZE VISUALS
What details in the picture help create **suspense?**

acute (ə-kyo͞ot′) *adj.* sharp; keen

conceive (kən-sēv) *v.* to think of

① **Targeted Passage**

A EVALUATE NARRATOR
Reread lines 1–16. On the basis of what he plans to do, decide whether the narrator's opinion of himself makes you trust him more or less.

1. **dissimulation** (dĭ-sĭm′yə-lā′shən): a hiding of one's true feelings.

Illustrations by Howard Simpson.

DIFFERENTIATED INSTRUCTION

FOR ALL STUDENTS

Enhance Learning Styles Provide independent projects for various learning styles.

- **Spatial** Create a portrait of the main character.
- **Kinesthetic** Interpret a scene through movement and music.
- **Linguistic** Stage a murder trial.

For further details on these projects, see
RESOURCE MANAGER
Ideas for Extension pp. 100–101

FOR LESS–PROFICIENT READERS

In combination with the *Audio Anthology CD*, use one or more Targeted Passages (pp. 78, 81, 83) to ensure that students focus on key story events, concepts, and skills.

① **Targeted Passage [Lines 1–16]**

This passage introduces the narrator and his strange motivation for committing murder.

- Who is the narrator of this story?
- What does the narrator decide to do?
- Why does the narrator want to kill the old man? What bothers him?
- What evidence does the narrator provide for his claim that he is not mad?

BACKGROUND

The Evil Eye The narrator of "The Tell-Tale Heart" believes that the old man has an "Evil Eye" (line 30). Belief in the Evil Eye crosses many cultures and is rooted in folklore. A person possessed of an Evil Eye is believed to have the ability to harm other people simply by looking at them in a particular way. Belief in the Evil Eye can be found in the ancient Greek and Roman cultures. It spread throughout Europe and persists in some Jewish, Islamic, Buddhist, Hindu, and Christian traditions. Often a beautiful or wealthy person is the victim of a curse cast by someone with an Evil Eye who is jealous of his or her good fortune. The curse may be deliberate or unintentional. A variety of charms or talismans are worn by believers to ward off the Evil Eye.

FOR ENGLISH LEARNERS

Key Academic Vocabulary Have students use Word Questioning to study this academic vocabulary from the selection: *resolve* (line 70), *precise* (line 77), *cease* (line 99), *detect* (line 109), *secure* (line 123), *distinct* (line 131)

BEST PRACTICES TOOLKIT—Transparency
Word Questioning p. E9

Options for Reading Read aloud lines 1–22 and check understanding by asking students to explain what the narrator plans to do. Then have students continue reading along with the *Audio Anthology CD.*

Prereading For prereading instruction for English learners, see

BEST PRACTICES TOOLKIT
Scaffolding Reading Instruction pp. 43–46

FOR ADVANCED LEARNERS/PRE–AP

Pre-AP exercises in the bottom channel provide additional challenge for your advanced students. Use them for small groups or individuals.

ADDITIONAL GUIDELINES

For more help with differentiation and tips for classroom management, see

BEST PRACTICES TOOLKIT
Differentiated Instruction pp. 31–38

man's sleep. It took me an hour to place my whole head within the opening so far that I could see him as he lay upon his bed. Ha!—would a madman have been so wise as this? And then, when my head was well in the room, I undid the lantern cautiously—oh, so cautiously—cautiously (for the hinges creaked)—I undid it just so much that a single thin ray fell upon the vulture eye. And this I did for seven long nights—every night just at midnight—but I found the eye always closed; and so it was impossible to do the work; for it was not the old man who **vexed** me, but his Evil Eye. And every morning, when the day broke, I went boldly into the chamber, and spoke courageously to him, calling him by name in a hearty tone, and inquiring how he had passed the night. So you see he would have been a very profound old man, indeed, to suspect that every night, just at twelve, I looked in upon him while he slept. **B**

Upon the eighth night I was more than usually cautious in opening the door. A watch's minute hand moves more quickly than did mine. Never before that night had I *felt* the extent of my own powers—of my sagacity.[2] I could scarcely contain my feelings of triumph. To think that there I was, opening the door, little by little, and he not even to dream of my secret deeds or thoughts. I fairly chuckled at the idea; and perhaps he heard me; for he moved on the bed suddenly, as if startled. Now you may think that I drew back—but no. His room was as black as pitch with the thick darkness (for the shutters were close fastened, through fear of robbers), and so I knew that he could not see the opening of the door, and I kept pushing it on steadily, steadily.

I had my head in, and was about to open the lantern, when my thumb slipped upon the tin fastening, and the old man sprang up in the bed, crying out—"Who's there?"

I kept quite still and said nothing. For a whole hour I did not move a muscle, and in the meantime I did not hear him lie down. He was still sitting up in the bed listening,—just as I have done, night after night, hearkening to the death watches[3] in the wall. **C**

Presently I heard a slight groan, and I knew it was the groan of mortal terror. It was not a groan of pain or grief—oh, no!—it was the low, **stifled** sound that arises from the bottom of the soul when overcharged with awe. I knew the sound well. Many a night, just at midnight, when all the world slept, it has welled up from my own bosom, deepening, with its dreadful echo, the terrors that distracted me. I say I knew it well. I knew what the old man felt, and pitied him, although I chuckled at heart. I knew that he had been lying awake ever since the first slight noise, when he had turned in the bed. His fears had been ever since growing upon him. He had been trying to fancy them causeless, but could not. He had been saying to himself—"It is nothing but the wind in the chimney—it is only a mouse crossing the floor," or "it is merely a cricket which has made a single chirp." Yes, he has been trying to comfort himself with these suppositions; but he had found all in vain. *All in vain;* because Death,

vex (vĕks) *v.* to disturb; to annoy

B SUSPENSE
Note the actions the narrator repeats. Why does this repetition create a sense of dread?

C SUSPENSE
In what way does the characters' inaction create tension?

stifled (stī'fəld) *adj.* smothered **stifle** *v.*

2. **sagacity** (sə-găs'ĭ-tē): sound judgment.
3. **death watches:** deathwatch beetles—insects that make a tapping sound with their heads.

LITERARY ANALYSIS

B SUSPENSE

Possible answer: *For seven nights in a row, the narrator opens the old man's door at midnight and looks at his eye. Then, each morning, he goes in to ask the old man how he slept. The suspense builds because each time the narrator approaches the old man, he might murder him or be caught.*

LITERARY ANALYSIS

C SUSPENSE

Possible answer: *The longer the characters sit in silence, the more suspenseful the situation becomes. The reader wonders which character will break the silence.*

Lines 45–54
REINFORCE *KEY IDEA:* SUSPICION

Discuss How do the actions of the old man reveal his **suspicion** that something is wrong?
Possible answer: *His question, his groan, and the fact that he stays sitting up in bed, listening, suggest that he suspects he is in danger.*

DIFFERENTIATED INSTRUCTION

FOR LESS–PROFICIENT READERS

Reading Skill Follow-Up: Evaluate Narrator
[paired option] Encourage students to update their charts from page 77 to help them evaluate the narrator. Have students reread lines 21–25. Do they agree with the narrator that his actions are wise? Allow time for students to share their charts with a partner.

FOR ENGLISH LEARNERS

Vocabulary: Multiple-Meaning Words
Remind students to use context clues to figure out the meanings of words used in an unfamiliar way. Make sure they understand how these words are used in the story:

- *mad* (line 2): Though often used to mean "angry," here it means "crazy" or "insane."
- *pitch* (line 42): Often a verb that means "throw," here it is a noun that refers to a thick, dark tarry substance. *Pitch black* means "completely dark."

in approaching him, had stalked with his black shadow before him, and enveloped the victim. And it was the mournful influence of the unperceived shadow that caused him to feel—although he neither saw nor heard—to *feel* the presence of my head within the room.

When I had waited a long time, very patiently, without hearing him lie down, I resolved to open a little—a very, very little **crevice** in the lantern. So I opened it—you cannot imagine how **stealthily**, stealthily—until, at length, a single dim ray, like the thread of the spider, shot from out the crevice and fell full upon the vulture eye.

It was open—wide, wide open—and I grew furious as I gazed upon it. I saw it with perfect distinctness—all a dull blue, with a hideous veil over it that chilled the very marrow in my bones; but I could see nothing else of the old man's face or person: for I had directed the ray as if by instinct, precisely upon the damned spot.

And now have I not told you that what you mistake for madness is but over-acuteness of the senses?—now, I say, there came to my ears a low, dull, quick sound, such as a watch makes when enveloped in cotton. I knew *that* sound well too. It was the beating of the old man's heart. It increased my fury, as the beating of a drum stimulates the soldier into courage. **D**

But even yet I refrained and kept still. I scarcely breathed. I held the lantern motionless. I tried how steadily I could maintain the ray upon the eye. Meantime the hellish tattoo[4] of the heart increased. It grew quicker and quicker, and louder and louder every instant. The old man's terror *must* have been extreme! It grew louder, I say, louder every moment!—do you mark me well? I have told you that I am nervous: so I am. And now at the dead hour of the night, amid the dreadful silence of that old house, so strange a noise as this excited me to uncontrollable terror. Yet, for some minutes longer I refrained and stood still. But the beating grew louder, louder! I thought the heart must burst. And now a new anxiety seized me—the sound would be heard by a neighbor! The old man's hour had come! With a loud yell, I threw open the lantern and leaped into the room. He shrieked once—once only. In an instant I dragged him to the floor, and pulled the heavy bed over him. I then smiled gaily, to find the deed so far done. But, for many minutes, the heart beat on with a muffled sound. This, however, did not vex me; it would not be heard through the wall. At length it ceased. The old man was dead. I removed the bed and examined the corpse. Yes, he was stone, stone dead. I placed my hand upon the heart and held it there many minutes. There was no pulsation. He was stone dead. His eye would trouble me no more. **E**

If still you think me mad, you will think so no longer when I describe the wise precautions I took for the concealment of the body. The night waned,[5] and I worked hastily, but in silence. First of all I dismembered the corpse. I cut off the head and the arms and the legs.

crevice (krĕv'ĭs) *n.* crack

stealthily (stĕl'thə-lē) *adv.* cautiously; secretly

D EVALUATE NARRATOR
What does the narrator claim to be hearing? Decide whether you think he is correct.

(2) Targeted Passage

E SUSPENSE
Reread lines 84–102. What is the scariest or most exciting part of this paragraph? Tell what details contribute to this feeling.

4. **hellish tattoo:** awful drumming.
5. **waned:** approached its end.

READING SKILL

D EVALUATE NARRATOR

Remind students to write their responses in the chart from page 77. ***Possible answer:***

Narrator's Reliability	
Makes Me Suspicious:	*Makes Me Trust Him:*
• *He says he hears the old man's heart, but this seems unlikely.*	•

Lines 69–83
DISCUSSION PROMPTS

Use these prompts to help students understand the narrator's actions and motivation:

Interpret Describe the narrator's mood. What might his mood suggest about him? *Students may say that the narrator seems excited and frantic. His emotional state suggests that he is becoming unbalanced.*

Synthesize Do you think that killing the old man will calm the narrator? Explain. ***Possible answer:*** *The narrator is mentally unbalanced, so killing the old man will not bring him peace.*

LITERARY ANALYSIS

E SUSPENSE

Possible answer: *The most exciting moment is when the narrator leaps into the room with a loud yell and the old man shrieks. The ever-louder heartbeat that the narrator hears, and his increasing anxiety in response to it, builds the suspense leading up to this moment.*

FOR LESS–PROFICIENT READERS

(2) Targeted Passage [Lines 84–102]

This passage presents the climax of the story, as the narrator carries out his plan to kill the old man.

- What finally prompts the narrator to kill the old man?
- How does the narrator commit the murder?
- How does he make sure that the old man is dead?

FOR ADVANCED LEARNERS/PRE–AP

Analyze Tone [small-group option] Ask students to recall that tone is an author's attitude about a subject. Have them reread lines 84–102. Then ask small groups of students to use a Two-Column Chart to record key words and phrases that convey the tone of this passage. Provide time for groups to present their charts to the class.

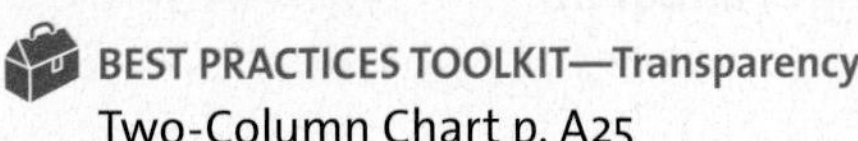
BEST PRACTICES TOOLKIT—Transparency
Two-Column Chart p. A25

Tone of the Passage	*Words and Phrases That Convey Tone*
excited	*"louder every moment!" (line 88)*
dramatic	*"The old man's hour had come!" (line 94)*

ANALYZE VISUALS

Possible answer: *You can infer from the man's smile in the top left panel that he is trying to appear friendly as he welcomes the visitors at the door. In the panel below, he looks nervous. In the panel on the right, the man looks as if he has gone insane.*

ANALYZE VISUALS
What can you **infer** from the character's expression in each of the three panels?

I then took up three planks from the flooring of the chamber, and deposited all between the scantlings.[6] I then replaced the boards so cleverly, so cunningly, that no human eye—not even *his*—could have detected anything wrong. There was nothing to wash out—no stain of any kind—no blood-spot whatever. I had been too wary for that. A tub had caught all—ha! ha!

When I made an end of these labors, it was four o'clock—still dark as midnight. As the bell sounded the hour, there came a knocking at the street door. I went down to open it with a light heart,—for what had I *now* to fear?

6. **scantlings:** small wooden beams supporting the floor.

DIFFERENTIATED INSTRUCTION

FOR ENGLISH LEARNERS

Language: Adverbs [mixed-readiness pairs]

- On pages 82–83, the narrator uses several adverbs to describe his actions. Remind students that adverbs often end in the suffix *-ly,* which means "in a specified way." Explain that knowing the meaning of this suffix can help them figure out the meaning of an adverb.
- Write the word *slow* on the board and review its meaning. Then add the suffix *-ly* to the word and explain that *slowly* means "in a slow way."
- Have students work with a partner to list as many *-ly* adverbs as they can find on pages 82–83. Have them write the definition for each adverb; then have the partners compare and discuss their definitions with the class.

There entered three men, who introduced themselves, with perfect suavity,[7] as officers of the police. A shriek had been heard by a neighbor during the night: suspicion of foul play had been aroused; information had been lodged at the police office, and they (the officers) had been deputed[8] to search the premises.

I smiled,—for *what* had I to fear? I bade the gentlemen welcome. The shriek, I said, was my own in a dream. The old man, I mentioned, was absent in the country. I took my visitors all over the house. I bade them search—search *well.* I led them, at length, to *his* chamber. I showed them his treasures, secure, undisturbed. In the enthusiasm of my confidence, I brought chairs into the room, and desired them *here* to rest from their fatigues, while I myself, in the wild **audacity** of my perfect triumph, placed my own seat upon the very spot beneath which reposed[9] the corpse of the victim.

The officers were satisfied. My *manner* had convinced them. I was singularly at ease. They sat, and while I answered cheerily, they chatted of familiar things. But, ere long, I felt myself getting pale and wished them gone. My head ached, and I fancied a ringing in my ears: but still they sat and still chatted. The ringing became more distinct:—it continued and became more distinct: I talked more freely to get rid of the feeling: but it continued and gained definitiveness—until at length, I found that the noise was *not* within my ears.

No doubt I now grew *very* pale;—but I talked more fluently, and with a heightened voice. Yet the sound increased—and what could I do? It was *a low, dull, quick sound—much such a sound as a watch makes when enveloped in cotton.* I gasped for breath—and yet the officers heard it not. I talked more quickly—more **vehemently;** but the noise steadily increased. I arose and argued about trifles, in a high key and with violent gesticulations,[10] but the noise steadily increased. Why *would* they not be gone? I paced the floor to and fro with heavy strides, as if excited to fury by the observation of the men—but the noise steadily increased. What *could* I do? I foamed—I raved—I swore. I swung the chair upon which I had been sitting, and grated it upon the boards, but the noise arose over all and continually increased. It grew louder—louder—*louder!* And still the men chatted pleasantly, and smiled. Was it possible they heard not?—no, no! They heard!—they suspected!—they *knew!*—they were making a *mockery* of my horror!—this I thought, and this I think. But anything was better than this agony! Anything was more tolerable than this **derision!** I could bear those **hypocritical** smiles no longer! I felt that I must scream or die!—and now—again!—hark! louder! louder! *louder!*— F

"Villains!" I shrieked, "dissemble[11] no more! I admit the deed!—tear up the planks!—here, here!—it is the beating of his hideous heart!"

(3) **Targeted Passage**

audacity (ô-dăs'ĭ-tē) *n.* shameless daring or boldness

vehemently (vē'ə-mənt-lē) *adv.* with intense emotion

derision (dĭ-rĭzh'ən) *n.* ridicule

hypocritical (hĭp'ə-krĭt'ĭ-kəl) *adj.* false or deceptive

F **SUSPENSE**
Think about the emotions that the narrator is feeling. How does Poe help the reader feel the same way?

7. **suavity** (swä'vĭ-tē): graceful politeness.
8. **deputed:** appointed as a representative.
9. **reposed:** rested.
10. **gesticulations** (jĕ-stĭk'yə-lā'shəns): energetic gestures of the hands or arms.
11. **dissemble:** pretend.

FOR LESS–PROFICIENT READERS

(3) **Targeted Passage [Lines 115–152]**

This passage concludes the story: the narrator is driven to confess his crime when he believes he hears the old man's heart beating.

- Why do the police come to investigate?
- How does the narrator initially react to the police?
- What causes a change in the narrator's state of mind?
- Why does the narrator finally confess?

Lines 103–118

DISCUSSION PROMPTS

Use these prompts to help students understand the narrator's behavior after the murder:

Retell Explain what the narrator did and what he was thinking after the murder. *Students should use their own words to tell how the narrator cut up the body and hid it under the floor. He thought he wouldn't be caught because he didn't leave any clues.*

Analyze Consider the narrator's question in line 114: "what had I *now* to fear?" What is implied by the emphasis on the word *now?* ***Possible answer:*** *He thinks that because he has killed the man with the Evil Eye, nothing else can hurt or terrorize him.*

Speculate Based on what has happened so far, what do you think will happen next? *Answers will vary, but students should provide details from the text to support their predictions.*

LITERARY ANALYSIS

F SUSPENSE

Possible answer: *Poe's use of short sentences and phrases—often with words emphasized in italic type or followed by exclamation points—mimics the sound of the dead man's heartbeat and helps the reader feel the narrator's rising panic.*

SELECTION WRAP–UP

REFLECT What part of the story did you find the most suspenseful? Why?

★ **CRITIQUE** Have students consider whether the story should have ended at a different point in time. What would be the effect on the reader if the story ended before the officers arrived?

READING FLUENCY

Distribute the copy masters and have students practice fluency.

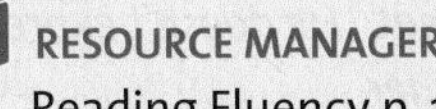

RESOURCE MANAGER—Copy Master
Reading Fluency p. 114

THE TELL–TALE HEART 83

Practice and Apply

After Reading

For additional support of postreading questions, use these copy masters:

RESOURCE MANAGER—Copy Masters
Reading Check p. 112 (to check understanding of the selection)
Suspense p. 105 (for practice of literary analysis standards focus)
Question Support p. 113 (After Reading questions adapted for English learners and less-proficient readers)
Additional selection questions are provided for teachers on page 99.

For additional activities to challenge students, see
Power Thinking at **ClassZone.com**

ANSWERS

Comprehension

1. *The narrator thinks the old man's strange eye is evil.*
2. *He believes he is too clever to be caught, and that he has destroyed all the evidence.*
3. *Students' summaries should include the narrator's actions from entering the old man's room each night to hiding the body.*

Literary Analysis

Possible answers:

4. *The narrator says he loves the old man and does not want his money, so he might be the old man's relative or caretaker.*
5. ● **STANDARDS FOCUS Suspense** *Students' rankings will vary. Techniques include:* ***Lines 1–79:*** *repeated words and actions, vivid description of fear and anxiety.* ***Lines 80–108:*** *repetition of sound of heartbeat, dramatic description of murder.* ***Lines 109–135:*** *narrator's confidence slides into anxiety.* ***Lines 136–162:*** *short sentences with exclamation points signal building of tension about being caught.*
6. ■ **STANDARDS FOCUS Evaluate Narrator** *The narrator is insane; it is difficult to believe what he says. He insists that he is sane, but he murdered someone for an irrational reason. He was obsessed by the look of the man's eye and then by the sound of the man's heartbeat. He doesn't express remorse for the murder.*

After Reading

Comprehension

1. **Recall** Why does the narrator want to kill the old man?
2. **Clarify** Why does the narrator believe he will not be caught after murdering the old man?
3. **Summarize** What actions does the narrator take to prepare for the crime and cover up?

Literary Analysis

4. **Make Inferences** Reread lines 7–13. From this passage, what do you think was the relationship between the narrator and the old man?
5. **Analyze Suspense** Which of Poe's techniques for creating suspense is most effective for you? To find out, review the following story sections. List the techniques used in each section, and then rank the sections from 1–4, with 1 being the most suspenseful.

Rank				
Lines	1–78	79–111	112–133	134–152
Techniques	1. 2.	1. 2.	1. 2.	1. 2.

6. **Evaluate Narrator** How reliable is the narrator of the story? Should you believe what he tells you about himself? Support your answer with details from the chart you created as you read.
7. **Draw Conclusions** Do you think the police knew the narrator was guilty at any point before he confessed? If so, when do you think the police became **suspicious?** Give reasons for your answer.

Extension and Challenge

8. **Readers' Circle** With a group, brainstorm a list of horror stories and movies that most of you are familiar with. Choose at least two of these titles and discuss the techniques the authors or directors used to create suspense. Which of the techniques are similar to the ones Poe uses?
9. **Inquiry and Research** Do research on lie detection to find out what are the most reliable ways of finding out if someone is telling the truth. Present your findings to the class. Does what you learn change your opinion about whether the narrator is reliable?

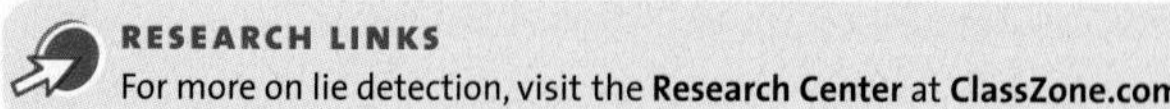

RESEARCH LINKS
For more on lie detection, visit the **Research Center** at **ClassZone.com.**

7. *Yes, the police must have known he was guilty because he behaved so strangely. First, he made a point of smiling at their initial questions about a shriek. Next, he laughed and showed them that the old man's treasures were not disturbed. Also, he showed them the room where the murder took place before they even asked about the old man.*

Extension and Challenge

8. *Responses will vary but should reflect an understanding of the techniques authors use to develop suspense.*
9. *Students should consult at least two reliable sources and present their findings in an organized manner.*

Vocabulary in Context

VOCABULARY PRACTICE

Choose *true* or *false* for each statement.

1. It is difficult to hide a **stifled** yawn.
2. If you have the **audacity** to do something, you are bold and daring.
3. **Derision** is something you feel toward someone you respect.
4. A lion would approach its prey **stealthily.**
5. You could not hear much if you had an **acute** sense of hearing.
6. If someone **conceived** of a plan, he or she heard it from someone else.
7. A person could trip over a **crevice** in the sidewalk.
8. When a person is **hypocritical,** he is honest and true.
9. To **vex** is to delight in something.
10. If you react **vehemently** to something, you don't care much about it.

acute
audacity
conceived
crevice
derision
hypocritical
stealthily
stifled
vehemently
vex

VOCABULARY IN WRITING

Using three or more vocabulary words, write a paragraph about how the narrator felt before the murder. Here is a sample beginning.

EXAMPLE SENTENCE

The man ***conceived*** *an idea that haunted him.*

VOCABULARY STRATEGY: USING REFERENCE AIDS

Choosing the perfect word can make a difference between good and great writing. One reason Poe's writing is still so popular is because of his masterful use of language. When you want to find the most accurate words to express yourself, the following reference aids can help you.

- A **thesaurus** is a reference book of **synonyms,** words with similar meanings. Most word processing software provides an electronic thesaurus tool.

  vex *verb* aggravate, annoy, bother, bug, disturb, provoke

- A **dictionary** lists synonyms after the definitions of some words.

  vex (vĕks) *v.* 1. To annoy. 2. To cause perplexity in. 3. To bring distress or suffering to. **syn** BOTHER, PUZZLE, PLAGUE, AFFLICT

PRACTICE Use a dictionary or thesaurus to find a synonym for each word. Use each synonym in a sentence that matches its distinct meaning.

1. commend 2. dupe 3. impish 4. menace

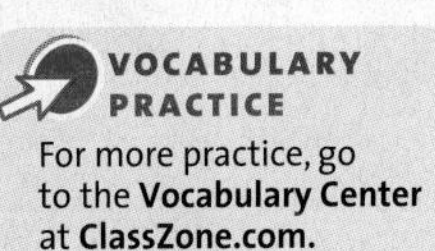

VOCABULARY PRACTICE
For more practice, go to the **Vocabulary Center** at **ClassZone.com.**

DIFFERENTIATED INSTRUCTION

FOR ENGLISH LEARNERS

Vocabulary Practice [paired option] Have students recall how each word was used in the story. Suggest that partners work together to search for each word in the story and use context clues to figure out its meaning.

FOR ADVANCED LEARNERS/PRE–AP

Vocabulary Strategy Challenge students to compose sentences using each of the listed words. Discuss the connotation of each listed word and its synonym.

ANSWERS

Vocabulary in Context

VOCABULARY PRACTICE

1. *true*
2. *true*
3. *false*
4. *true*
5. *false*
6. *false*
7. *true*
8. *false*
9. *false*
10. *false*

RESOURCE MANAGER—Copy Master
Vocabulary Practice p. 110

VOCABULARY IN WRITING

Suggest that students reread the first three paragraphs of the story and then review the vocabulary words to see which ones might best describe the narrator's feelings.

VOCABULARY STRATEGY: USING REFERENCE AIDS *(also an EL language objective)*

Point out that synonyms in a thesaurus do not have exactly the same meaning; each word has its own connotation.

Sample sentences: **1.** *I'd like to praise the actors for their wonderful performance.* **2.** *She was always able to trick her little brother into doing her chores.* **3.** *He was unable to hide his mischievous smile as his teacher sat on a tack.* **4.** *These sharp branches along the trail are a threat to hikers' eyes.*

RESOURCE MANAGER—Copy Master
Vocabulary Strategy p. 111

Vocabulary Center at **ClassZone.com**
Additional Vocabulary Activities

Assess and Reteach

Assess

RESOURCE MANAGER—Copy Masters
Selection Tests A, B/C pp. 115–116, 117–118

Test Generator CD

Reteach

STANDARDS LESSON FILE
Literature Lesson 8: Foreshadowing and Suspense
Literature Lesson 10: Narrator
Vocabulary Lesson 24: Using Dictionaries and Glossaries

Focus and Motivate

OBJECTIVES

Literary Analysis
- explore the key idea of **proof**
- identify and analyze foreshadowing
- read a radio play

Reading
- develop strategies for reading a radio play

Grammar and Writing
- maintain pronoun-antecedent agreement
- use writing to analyze literature

SUMMARY

Ronald Adams leaves his home in New York City to drive to California. While crossing the Brooklyn Bridge, he swerves to avoid hitting a hitchhiker. As he continues westward, he encounters this same man with increasing regularity. His sense of panic increases when he realizes that no one else can see the man. By the time Adams arrives in Gallup, New Mexico, he is beside himself with fear and uncertainty. He calls home. The woman who answers tells him that his mother is in the hospital, prostrate with grief over the death of her son Ronald in a car accident on the Brooklyn Bridge six days before.

Is seeing BELIEVING?

Discuss the question. To lead into the ***KEY IDEA,*** poll students with this question: Does everything have a logical explanation, or do some things happen that cannot be explained or supported by **proof?** Ask students to give reasons for their opinions. Then have groups complete the ***DISCUSS*** activity.

Before Reading

The Hitchhiker

Radio Play by Lucille Fletcher

Is seeing BELIEVING?

KEY IDEA Occasionally, something happens so quickly or unexpectedly, you can't be sure what you've seen. Was that a rabbit racing through the field, or was it just wind in the grass? Did you see a man hiding in the alley, or did you see only a shadow? To be convinced that something is real, you need **proof,** or solid evidence. In *The Hitchhiker,* a man is desperate for proof that what he's seeing can be explained.

DISCUSS Think of something you've seen that you can't explain. Maybe it was oddly shaped footprints in an empty lot, or a bright shape flying through the sky. Share your experience with a small group, and together brainstorm possible explanations. Then tell what proof you'd need to determine which explanation is the right one.

Selection Resources

RESOURCE MANAGER UNIT 1

Plan and Teach pp. 119–126

Literary Analysis
Summary pp. 127†*, 128‡*
Foreshadowing pp. 129, 130†*
Question Support p. 136*

Reading
Reading a Radio Play pp. 131, 132†*
Reading Check p. 135
Reading Fluency p. 138

Vocabulary
Study p. 133*

Grammar and Writing
Maintain Pronoun-Antecedent Agreement p. 137

Assessment
Selection Tests A, B/C pp. 139*, 141*
Test Generator CD

BEST PRACTICES TOOLKIT

Differentiated Instruction pp. 31–38*
Scaffolding Instruction pp. 43–46*

Graphic Organizers/Strategies
Directed Reading-Thinking Activity • New Word Analysis • Two-Column Chart • Sequence Chain • Cause-and-Effect Diagram

Reading Support
Audio Anthology CD*

Technology
Literature, Vocabulary, and Writing Centers at **ClassZone.com**
Write*Smart* CD

* Resources for Differentiation   † Also in Spanish   ‡ In Haitian Creole and Vietnamese

LITERARY ANALYSIS: FORESHADOWING

While reading a story or watching a movie, have you ever gotten a hint about what might happen later on? A device that prepares readers for an event or action occurring later in the plot is called **foreshadowing.** For example, if a character says, "Whatever you do, don't open that door," you might suspect that the door will eventually be opened to create a dramatic effect. Anticipating that event can make you more excited to find out what happens next.

As you read *The Hitchhiker*, make a chart to note events or dialogue that might foreshadow what happens later. You'll complete the chart at the end of the selection.

Foreshadowing	*Events That Were Foreshadowed*

READING STRATEGY: READING A RADIO PLAY

A **radio play** is a play written for radio broadcast, which means that it was originally meant to be heard, not seen. When you're reading a radio play, you'll understand it best if you try to imagine what it would sound like being performed. As you read, look for the following elements, written in italics. Use the information these elements provide to "hear" the radio play in your mind.

- **Stage directions,** or instructions, for the actor will help you know how a line is spoken.
- **Sound effects** are often used to suggest what is happening in the play. They help a listener "see" the action.
- The term *music in* will indicate when and sometimes what kind of music is used to mark a change of scene or show the passing of time.

VOCABULARY IN CONTEXT

The words in Column A help Lucille Fletcher tell about one man's encounter with a mysterious hitchhiker. Match each word with the word or phrase in Column B that is closest in meaning.

Column A	Column B
1. lark	a. guarantee
2. junction	b. carefree adventure
3. sinister	c. evil
4. assurance	d. sameness
5. monotony	e. place of joining

Author Online

Suspenseful Stories As a young adult, Lucille Fletcher wanted to become a novelist. After she took her first job as a script typist and began reading scripts by other writers, she decided she wanted to write plays as well. She was successful at both. Fletcher penned more than 20 radio plays, including the well-known *Sorry, Wrong Number* and *The Hitchhiker.* In addition, she wrote several novels. Her works were suspenseful, full of mystery, and often terrifying.

Lucille Fletcher
1912–2000

MORE ABOUT THE AUTHOR
For more on Lucille Fletcher, visit the **Literature Center** at **ClassZone.com.**

Background

Radio Plays Though the television was invented in the 1920s, most American households did not have television sets until the late 1950s. Before then, families gathered around the radio to listen to their favorite radio plays. These plays took the form of dramas, mysteries, or comedies. Actors at the radio station read their lines into the microphone with dramatic flair. Background music helped set the mood.

Hearing Is Believing Sound effects were an important part of a radio play. They were often produced in the radio studio. Sheet metal, shaken up and down, replicated rolling thunder. A wooden match, broken close to the microphone, sounded like a baseball bat striking a ball. Coconut halves clapped against wood imitated the sound of horses' hooves.

Teach

STANDARDS FOCUS

LITERARY ANALYSIS

● FORESHADOWING

Write this example on the board:

> At last he had what he needed to prove his theory. Overjoyed, he set the valuable document on his desk. He did not notice the slight breeze from the open balcony door behind him.

Ask students what event this passage might foreshadow. ***Possible answer:*** *The papers might be blown out the door.*

CHECK UNDERSTANDING Ask students for examples of foreshadowing from familiar stories or movies.

RESOURCE MANAGER—Copy Master
Foreshadowing p. 129 (for student use while reading the selection)

READING STRATEGY

■ READING A RADIO PLAY

Write this example on the board:

> **Driver.** Where are you going, buddy?
> **Hitchhiker.** I'd love a lift to Amarillo.
> **Driver.** I'm going that way, too. Get in.

Ask students to describe sound effects that would fit the action in this scene. ***Possible answer:*** *the sound of a car stopping, a constant roar of traffic, a car door opening and closing at the end*

CHECK UNDERSTANDING Have students explain what stage directions for the actors might work with the dialogue.

VOCABULARY SKILL

▲ VOCABULARY IN CONTEXT

DIAGNOSE WORD KNOWLEDGE To determine preteaching needs, have all students complete **Vocabulary in Context.** ***Answers:*** **1.** *(b) carefree adventure* **2.** *(e) place of joining* **3.** *(c) evil* **4.** *(a) guarantee* **5.** *(d) sameness*

PRETEACH VOCABULARY As you preteach vocabulary, using the Vocabulary Study copy master, supply these definitions:

lark (lärk) *n.* a carefree or spirited adventure

junction (jŭngk′ shən) *n.* a place where two roads meet

nondescript (nŏn′ dĭ-skrĭpt′) *adj.* having no individual character or form

sinister (sĭn′ĭ-stər) *adj.* suggesting or threatening evil

assurance (ə-shŏŏr′əns) *n.* a guarantee or pledge

monotony (mə-nŏt′n-ē) *n.* tedious sameness

RESOURCE MANAGER—Copy Master
Vocabulary Study p. 133

For alternative vocabulary activities for students not needing vocabulary preteaching, see

Vocabulary Center at **ClassZone.com**
Additional Vocabulary Activities

Practice and Apply

ANALYZE VISUALS

About the Art This print, by photographer Gene Laughter, was prepared using a process called bromoil. This involves several steps that result in the ink's adhering to some parts of the print and not to others.

Activity What mood, or feeling, is established by this photograph? ***Possible answer:*** *The illustration looks foggy and indistinct, creating a ghostly mood.*

Lines 16–26

LITERARY ANALYSIS

● FORESHADOWING

What is the effect of Orson Welles's introduction? ***Possible answer:*** *He helps heighten listeners' anticipation by promising them a spine-tingling presentation. He calls the play a thriller and a shocker. By saying that the company presents the play "proudly and without apologies" (line 19), he makes listeners expect something shocking.*

Extend the Discussion What kind of voice would you expect Welles to use for this introduction?

The Hitchhiker

Lucille Fletcher

CAST OF CHARACTERS

Orson Welles
Ronald Adams
Adams's Mother
Voice of Hitchhiker
Mechanic
Henry, a sleepy man
Woman's Voice, Henry's wife
Girl
Operator
Long-Distance Operator
Albuquerque Operator
New York Operator
Mrs. Whitney

Welles. Good evening, this is Orson Welles . . . (*music in*) Personally I've never met anybody who didn't like a good ghost story, but I know a lot of people who think there are a lot of people who don't like a good ghost story. For the benefit of these, at least, I go on record at the outset of this evening's entertainment with the sober **assurance** that although blood may be curdled on this program none will be spilt. There's no shooting, knifing, throttling, axing or poisoning here. No clanking chains, no cobwebs, no bony and/or hairy hands appearing from secret panels or, better yet, bedroom curtains. If it's any part of that dear old *phosphorescent*[1] foolishness that people who don't like ghost stories don't like, then again I promise you we haven't got it. What we do have is a thriller. If it's half as good as we think it is you can call it a shocker, and we present it proudly and without apologies. After all a story doesn't have to appeal to the heart—it can also appeal to the spine. Sometimes you want your heart to be warmed—sometimes you want your spine to tingle. The tingling, it's to be hoped, will be quite audible as you listen tonight to *The Hitchhiker*—That's the name of our story, *The Hitchhiker*—

1. **phosphorescent** (fŏs′fə-rĕs′ənt): glowing with a cold light.

DIFFERENTIATED INSTRUCTION

FOR ALL STUDENTS

Enhance Learning Styles Provide these independent projects for various learning styles:

- **Spatial** Plot Adams's route on a modern highway map.
- **Musical** Choose music selections to convey the mood throughout the play.
- **Mathematical** Graph the increase in gasoline prices from the 1940s to today.

For further details on these projects, see

RESOURCE MANAGER
Ideas for Extension pp. 124–125

FOR LESS–PROFICIENT READERS

In combination with the *Audio Anthology CD,* use one or more Targeted Passages (pp. 90, 91, 95, 97) to ensure that students focus on key selection events, concepts, and skills.

FOR ENGLISH LEARNERS

Reading: Background Explain the practice of hitchhiking. (See also the **Culture: Connect** note on page 94 of the teacher's edition.) Then provide a brief overview of the plot. Tell students that much of the action takes place in a flashback as Ronald Adams, the main character, narrates what has happened to him over the past six days.

BACKGROUND

Route 66 In lines 30–31, Ronald Adams describes his location as an "auto camp on Route Sixty-six." In the 1940s, Route 66 was the primary highway connecting the Midwest with the West Coast. Its approximately 2,500 miles ran from Chicago, Illinois, to Los Angeles and later Santa Monica, California. It opened in 1926 and was finally rendered obsolete in 1985 when new interstates bypassed the last section in use. Featured in songs, ads, novels, and other elements of popular culture, Route 66 is now considered an important part of the country's history. Efforts are being made to preserve it.

Auto Camps Along with Route 66 and other major highways came a phenomenon known as auto camps. Ronald Adams is stopped in one in Gallup, New Mexico. These were originally sections of land alongside highways that were roped off for the use of travelers. People carried their own tents and gear in their cars. Later, amenities such as toilets and showers, and eventually cabins, were added to these locations.

FOR ENGLISH LEARNERS

Options for Reading Distribute copies of the DRTA transparency. Have students skim the selection and record predictions in the Before Reading row of the chart. Then have small groups read along silently with the *Audio Anthology CD,* pausing at the end of each Targeted Passage to take notes in the During Reading row. When they have finished reading, have them summarize the play.

BEST PRACTICES TOOLKIT—Transparency
Directed Reading-Thinking Activity p. A20

Key Academic Vocabulary Have students use New Word Analysis to study this academic vocabulary: *link* (line 43), *coincidence* (lines 118, 166), *attitude* (lines 181, 464), *tense* (line 283), *residence* (lines 514, 518).

BEST PRACTICES TOOLKIT—Transparency
New Word Analysis p. E8

Prereading For prereading instruction for English learners, see

BEST PRACTICES TOOLKIT
Scaffolding Reading Instruction pp. 43–46

FOR ADVANCED LEARNERS/PRE–AP

Pre-AP exercises in the bottom channel provide additional challenge for your advanced students. Use them for small groups or individuals.

ADDITIONAL GUIDELINES

For more help with differentiation and tips for classroom management, see

BEST PRACTICES TOOLKIT
Differentiated Instruction pp. 31–38

Lines 27–28

READING STRATEGY

READING A RADIO PLAY

What do these first sound effects reveal about the setting of the play? ***Possible answer:*** *This play takes place near a highway or perhaps inside a moving car.*

Lines 30–45

REINFORCE *KEY IDEA:* PROOF

Discuss What **proof** of his sanity does Ronald Adams offer? ***Possible answer:*** *He explains who he is and provides details such as his age, marital status, physical appearance, car, license plate number, and place of birth.*

Lines 61–68

LITERARY ANALYSIS

FORESHADOWING

What potential dangers does Adams's mother warn him about? (Remind students to record their ideas in the chart from page 87.) ***Possible answer:***

Foreshadowing
Adams's mother warns him against falling asleep, speeding, and hitchhikers (lines 61–68).

(*sound: automobile wheels humming over concrete road*)

(*music: something weird and shuddery*)

Adams. I am in an auto camp on Route Sixty-six just west of Gallup, New Mexico. If I tell it perhaps it will help me. It will keep me from going mad. But I must tell this quickly. I am not mad now. I feel perfectly well, except that I am running a slight temperature. My name is Ronald Adams. I am thirty-six years of age, unmarried, tall, dark, with a black mustache. I drive a 1940 Ford V-8, license number 6V-7989. I was born in Brooklyn. All this I know. I know that I am at this moment perfectly sane. That it is not I, who has gone mad—but something else—something utterly beyond my control. But I must speak quickly. At any moment the link with life may break. This may be the last thing I ever tell on earth . . . the last night I ever see the stars. . . .

(*music in*)

Adams. Six days ago I left Brooklyn, to drive to California . . .

Mother. Goodbye, son. Good luck to you, my boy . . .

Adams. Goodbye, mother. Here—give me a kiss, and then I'll go . . .

Mother. I'll come out with you to the car.

Adams. No. It's raining. Stay here at the door. Hey—what is this? Tears? I thought you promised me you wouldn't cry.

Mother. I know dear. I'm sorry. But I—do hate to see you go.

Adams. I'll be back. I'll only be on the coast three months.

Mother. Oh—it isn't that. It's just—the trip. Ronald—I wish you weren't driving.

Adams. Oh—mother. There you go again. People do it every day.

Mother. I know. But you'll be careful, won't you. Promise me you'll be extra careful. Don't fall asleep—or drive fast—or pick up any strangers o the road . . .

Adams. Of course not! You'd think I was still seventeen to hear you talk—

Mother. And wire me as soon as you get to Hollywood, won't you, son?

Adams. Of course I will. Now don't you worry. There isn't anything going to happen. It's just eight days of perfectly simple driving on smooth, decent, civilized roads, with a hotdog or a hamburger stand every ten miles . . . (*fade*)

(*sound: auto hum*)

(*music in*)

Adams. I was in excellent spirits. The drive ahead of me, even the loneliness, seemed like a **lark.** Bu I reckoned without *him.*

(*Music changes to something weird and empty.*)

① Targeted Passage

DIFFERENTIATED INSTRUCTION

FOR LESS–PROFICIENT READERS

① **Targeted Passage [Lines 47–82]**

This passage presents the transition into the flashback and hints at the conflict to come.

- What is Adams's destination? Where and when did he begin his journey?
- Why is Adams's mother crying?
- In what kind of mood does Adams begin his trip? What happens to change how he feels?

Comprehension Support Explain that much of the play's action takes place in the recent past and is told through flashbacks, or episodes that occurred before Adams reached the auto camp in New Mexico. Point out the transition to the first flashback in line 49. The ellipsis and Adams's previous comment cue readers that the action has moved to the past. Music may also indicate a change in the time frame. Have students read to find out where in this play the action moves back to the present. Ask what clues help them figure this out.

FOR ENGLISH LEARNERS

Language: Punctuation and Print Cues Read aloud lines 44–46 to illustrate the effect of an ellipsis in a sentence. Students should hear the trailing off of the speaker's voice. Explain that an ellipsis indicates that the speaker does not complete his or her thought or that there is a longer pause than would be the case with a period. Have small groups practice reading lines 47–53 and 65–77 paying attention to this punctuation cue. Circulate around the room to check on their progress.

② Targeted Passage

Adams. Crossing Brooklyn Bridge that morning in the rain, I saw a man leaning against the cables. He seemed to be waiting for a lift. There were spots of fresh rain on his shoulders. He was carrying a cheap overnight bag in one hand. He was thin, nondescript, with a cap pulled down over his eyes. He stepped off the walk, and if I hadn't swerved, I'd have hit him.

(sound: terrific skidding)

(music in)

Adams. I would have forgotten him completely, except that just an hour later, while crossing the Pulaski Skyway over the Jersey flats, I saw him again. At least, he looked like the same person. He was standing now, with one thumb pointing west. I couldn't figure out how he'd got there, but I thought probably one of those fast trucks had picked him up, beaten me to the Skyway, and let him off. I didn't stop for him. Then—late that night, I saw him again.

(music changing)

Adams. It was on the new Pennsylvania Turnpike between Harrisburg and Pittsburgh. It's 265 miles long, with a very high speed limit. I was just slowing down for one of the tunnels—when I saw him—standing under an arc light by the side of the road. I could see him quite distinctly. The bag, the cap, even the spots of fresh rain spattered over his shoulders. He hailed me this time . . .

Voice *(very spooky and faint)*. Hall-ooo . . . *(echo as through tunnel)* Hall-ooo . . . !

Adams. I stepped on the gas like a shot. That's lonely country through the Alleghenies,[2] and I had no intention of stopping. Besides, the coincidence, or whatever it was, gave me the willies.[3] I stopped at the next gas station.

(sound: auto tires screeching to stop . . . horn honk)

Mechanic. Yes, sir.

Adams. Fill her up.

Mechanic. Certainly, sir. Check your oil, sir?

Adams. No, thanks.

(sound: gas being put into car . . . bell tinkle, et cetera)

Mechanic. Nice night, isn't it?

Adams. Yes. It—hasn't been raining here recently, has it?

Mechanic. Not a drop of rain all week.

Adams. Hm. I suppose that hasn't done your business any harm.

Mechanic. Oh—people drive through here all kinds of weather. Mostly business, you know. There aren't many pleasure cars out on the turnpike this season of the year.

Adams. I suppose not. *(casually)* What about hitchhikers?

Mechanic *(half laughing)*. Hitchhikers *here?*

Adams. What's the matter? Don't you ever see any?

Mechanic. Not much. If we did, it'd be a sight for sore eyes.

Adams. Why?

Mechanic. A guy'd be a fool who started out to hitch rides on this road. Look at it. It's 265 miles long, there's practically no speed limit, and it's a straightaway. Now what car is going to stop to pick up a guy under those conditions? Would you stop?

Adams. No. *(slowly, with puzzled emphasis)* Then you've never seen anybody?

Mechanic. Nope. Mebbe they get the lift before the turnpike starts—I mean, you know—just before the toll house—but then it'd be a mighty long ride. Most cars wouldn't want to pick up a guy for that long a ride. And you know—this is pretty lonesome country here—mountains, and woods . . . You ain't seen anybody like that, have you?

Adams. No. *(quickly)* Oh no, not at all. It was—just a—technical question.

2. **Alleghenies** (ăl′ĭ-gā′nēz): The Allegheny Mountains, a range extending from northern Pennsylvania to western Virginia.

3. **gave me the willies:** made me nervous.

Lines 84–92

LITERARY ANALYSIS

● FORESHADOWING

What happens on the Brooklyn Bridge? (Have students record this event in their charts.) ***Possible answer:*** *A hitchhiker steps off the path, and Adams has to swerve to avoid him. His car skids as a result.*

Extend the Discussion What might this event foreshadow?

Lines 105–114

LITERARY ANALYSIS

● FORESHADOWING

In what ways is Adams's encounter with the hitchhiker both similar to and different from his previous ones? What does seeing him a third time mean? ***Possible answer:*** *The hitchhiker looks exactly the same. On the turnpike, however, he hails Adams. This behavior is different from what he has done before. Seeing him a third time suggests that the hitchhiker will reappear frequently throughout Adams's journey.*

Lines 137–142

READING STRATEGY

■ READING A RADIO PLAY

Why does Adams ask his question casually? ***Possible answer:*** *He doesn't want the mechanic to guess that anything might be wrong.*

FOR LESS-PROFICIENT READERS

② Targeted Passage [Lines 84–119]

This passage presents the major conflict: Adams is becoming unnerved by the reappearance of the same hitchhiker.

- What happens the first time Adams sees the hitchhiker?
- What is Adams's theory about how the hitchhiker beat him to the Skyway?
- Why does Adams start to get nervous when he sees the hitchhiker a third time?

Concept Support [paired option] Display a chart similar to the one on page 87. Discuss the examples of foreshadowing that students have identified already. Then have them reread lines 127–160, Adams's conversation with the mechanic. Point out the kinds of questions that Adams asks, and talk about his reasons for wanting to know this information. Have students work in pairs to add to their charts examples of foreshadowing from this passage.

Foreshadowing	*Events That Were Foreshadowed*
The mechanic says that they have not had "a drop of rain all week" (line 130).	
The mechanic says that a hitchhiker would be a "sight for sore eyes" (lines 141–142).	

Lines 171–176

LITERARY ANALYSIS

● FORESHADOWING

What might the presence of the hitchhiker at a detour indicate for Ronald Adams? ***Possible answer:*** *The hitchhiker might be indicating that Adams's life is about to take an unexpected direction.*

Lines 191–202

READING STRATEGY

■ READING A RADIO PLAY

What do the stage directions in this part of the play help readers visualize? ***Possible answer:*** *The stage directions give readers a mental image of Adams's panicky movements as he starts the car and jams the gears, finally speeding off with a spinning of his wheels.*

If students need help . . . Discuss what action Adams would need to perform to produce each sound effect.

Lines 216–261

DISCUSSION PROMPTS

Use these prompts to help students understand Adams's emotions as his journey progresses:

Connect How would you be feeling after seeing the hitchhiker five times? *Students may say that they would start to feel confused or nervous.*

Analyze Adams says he stops to get a cup of coffee. What is the real reason that he stops at the roadside stand? ***Possible answer:*** *He thinks he sees the hitchhiker there. He is desperate to talk to someone and get reassurance that he is not just seeing things.*

Evaluate How has Adams changed since leaving Brooklyn? ***Possible answer:*** *He is now nervous and uncertain. Traveling this long distance alone no longer seems like the fun adventure he expected it to be.*

Mechanic. I see. Well—that'll be just a dollar forty-nine—with the tax . . . (*fade*)

(*sound: auto hum up*)

(*music changing*)

Adams. The thing gradually passed from my mind, as sheer coincidence. I had a good night's sleep in Pittsburgh. I did not think about the man all next day—until just outside of Zanesville, Ohio, I saw him again.

(*music: dark, ominous note*)

Adams. It was a bright sunshiny afternoon. The peaceful Ohio fields, brown with the autumn stubble, lay dreaming in the golden light. I was driving slowly, drinking it in, when the road suddenly ended in a detour. In front of the barrier, *he* was standing.

(*music in*)

Adams. Let me explain about his appearance before I go on. I repeat. There was nothing **sinister** about him. He was as drab as a mud fence. Nor was his attitude menacing. He merely stood there, waiting, almost drooping a little, the cheap overnight bag in his hand. He looked as though he had been waiting there for hours. Then he looked up. He hailed me. He started to walk forward.

Voice (*far off*). Hall-ooo . . . Hall-ooo . . .

Adams. I had stopped the car, of course, for the detour. And for a few moments, I couldn't seem to find the new road. I knew he must be thinking that I had stopped for him.

Voice (*closer*). Hall-ooo . . . Hallll . . . ooo . . .

(*sound: gears jamming . . . sound of motor turning over hard . . . nervous accelerator*)

Voice (*closer*). Halll . . . oooo . . .

Adams (*panicky*). No. Not just now. Sorry . . .

Voice (*closer*). Going to California?

(*sound: starter starting . . . gears jamming*)

Adams (*as though sweating blood*). No. Not today. The other way. Going to New York. Sorry . . . sorry . . .

(*sound: car starts with squeal of wheels on dirt . . . into auto hum*)

(*music in*)

Adams. After I got the car back onto the road again, I felt like a fool. Yet the thought of picking him up, of having him sit beside me was somehow unbearable. Yet, at the same time, I felt, more than ever, unspeakably alone.

(*sound: auto hum up*)

Adams. Hour after hour went by. The fields, the towns ticked off, one by one. The lights changed. I knew now that I was going to see him again. And though I dreaded the sight, I caught myself searching the side of the road, waiting for him to appear.

(*sound: auto hum up . . . car screeches to a halt . . . impatient honk two or three times . . . door being unbolted*)

Sleepy Man's Voice. Yep? What is it? What do you want?

Adams (*breathless*). You sell sandwiches and pop here, don't you?

Voice (*cranky*). Yep. We do. In the daytime. But we're closed up now for the night.

Adams. I know. But—I was wondering if you could possibly let me have a cup of coffee—black coffee.

Voice. Not at this time of night, mister. My wife's the cook and she's in bed. Mebbe further down the road—at the Honeysuckle Rest . . .

(*sound: door squeaking on hinges as though being closed*)

Adams. No—no. Don't shut the door. (*shakily*) Listen—just a minute ago, there was a man standing here—right beside this stand—a suspicious looking man . . .

Woman's Voice (*from distance*). Hen-ry? Who is it, Hen-ry?

Henry. It's nobuddy, mother. Just a feller thinks he wants a cup of coffee. Go back into bed.

DIFFERENTIATED INSTRUCTION

FOR LESS–PROFICIENT READERS

Reading Strategy Follow-Up: Reading a Radio Play [small-group option] Discuss how some sound effects add to the play's suspenseful mood while others indicate the passage of time or reveal characters' movements. Assign passages from pages 92–93 to small groups. Ask them to record the sound effects they find and explain the function of each.

BEST PRACTICES TOOLKIT—Transparency
Two-Column Chart p. A25

Sound Effect	Function
line 170: dark and ominous music	increases the feeling that something bad is going to happen to Adams
line 209: auto hum up	indicates that Adams's car is moving steadily along the highway and that time is passing

Adams. I don't mean to disturb you. But you see, I was driving along—when I just happened to look—and there he was . . .

Henry. What was he doing?

Adams. Nothing. He ran off—when I stopped the car.

Henry. Then what of it? That's nothing to wake a man in the middle of his sleep about. (*sternly*) Young man, I've got a good mind to turn you over to the sheriff.

Adams. But—I—

Henry. You've been taking a nip, that's what you've been doing. And you haven't got anything better to do than to wake decent folk out of their hard-earned sleep. Get going. Go on.

Adams. But—he looked as though he were going to rob you.

Henry. I ain't got nothin' in this stand to lose. Now—on your way before I call out Sheriff Oakes. (*fades*)

(*sound: auto hum up*)

Adams. I got into the car again and drove on slowly. I was beginning to hate the car. If I could have found a place to stop . . . to rest a little. But I was in the Ozark Mountains of Missouri now. The few resort places there were closed. Only an occasional log cabin, seemingly deserted, broke the **monotony** of the wild wooded landscape. I *had* seen him at that roadside stand; I knew I would see him again—perhaps at the next turn of the road. I knew that when I saw him next, I would run him down . . .

(*sound: auto hum up*)

Adams. But I did not see him again until late next afternoon . . .

(*sound: of railroad warning signal at crossroads*)

Adams. I had stopped the car at a sleepy little **junction** just across the border into Oklahoma—to let a train pass by—when he appeared, across the tracks, leaning against a telephone pole.

(*sound: distant sound of train chugging . . . bell ringing steadily*)

Adams (*very tense*). It was a perfectly airless, dry day. The red clay of Oklahoma was baking under the south-western sun. Yet there were spots of fresh rain on his shoulders. I couldn't stand that. Without thinking, blindly, I started the car across the tracks.

(*sound: train chugging closer*)

Adams. He didn't even look up at me. He was staring at the ground. I stepped on the gas hard, veering the wheel sharply toward him. I could

ANALYZE VISUALS

About the Art French photographer Raymond Depardon (born 1942) has traveled around the world as a photojournalist, often encountering danger while recording events in troubled spots such as Vietnam. He also makes documentary films.

Activity What is disturbing or unusual about this image? ***Possible answer:*** *There are cars visible in the rear-view mirror, but only a sleepy little town appears ahead. The perspective of the photograph is unclear.*

Lines 283–288

REINFORCE *KEY IDEA:* PROOF

Discuss The hitchhiker has spots of rain on his shoulders even though it is a baking hot day in Oklahoma. What might this be **proof** of? ***Possible answers:***

- *The hitchhiker is not real; he is a supernatural creature.*
- *The hitchhiker is a figment of Adams's imagination and stays as Adams first saw him.*

Line 289

LITERARY ANALYSIS

● FORESHADOWING

What situation is this sound effect setting up? ***Possible answer:*** *This sound effect might foreshadow Adams's car being hit by the train.*

FOR LESS–PROFICIENT READERS

Comprehension Support [small-group option]

1. Help students track the passage of time by having them complete a Sequence Chain for the first three days of Adams's trip.
2. Fill in the first box together. *(Day 1: leaves New York, sees the hitchhiker three times, stops in Pittsburgh for the night)*
3. Then have groups organize the events of Day 2 and the start of Day 3 through line 280.
4. Discuss their charts and have them add details to Day 3 as they read further.
5. Tell students that after this point, Adams's days and nights merge as he becomes increasingly disoriented.

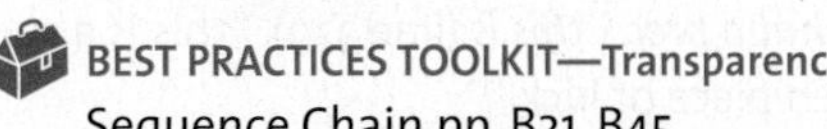

BEST PRACTICES TOOLKIT—Transparency
Sequence Chain pp. B21, B45

FOR ENGLISH LEARNERS

Language: Conversational English Patterns

[mixed-readiness pairs] Direct students' attention to lines 219–260. Explain that the different speech patterns reflect Adams's location in another part of the country. Have students work in pairs to restate these words and phrases in standard English: *Yep* (line 223), *mebbe* (line 229), *nobuddy* (line 239), *feller* (line 239), *ain't got nothin'* (line 258).

Lines 287–308

LITERARY ANALYSIS

● FORESHADOWING

What does this scene suggest about the chances of Adams's arriving in California? ***Possible answer:*** *He will most likely die before reaching California. The hitchhiker seems to be trying to kill him, and Adams is becoming tired and desperate.*

Lines 340–386
DISCUSSION PROMPTS

Use these prompts to help students understand the changes in Adams:

Connect Would you want to be a passenger in Adams's car? Why or why not? *Students might say that they would be nervous, especially after he swerves off the road.*

Compare What is the girl's first impression of Adams? How does it change? ***Possible answer:*** *At first, she thinks she is quite lucky to have been picked up by a good-looking guy who has a nice car. Then he sees a "phantom" and tries to "run him down" (lines 359–374). She no longer feels safe with him.*

Evaluate Is Adams's reason for wanting to run over the hitchhiker rational? Explain. ***Possible answers:***

- *No. He wants to run him over to prove he exists. However, if the hitchhiker is real, Adams could kill him.*
- *Yes. If the car goes right through the hitchhiker, then he is a phantom. If the hitchhiker is run down and injured, then he is a real person. It is a desperate test, but it would give Adams the information he wants.*

hear the train in the distance now, but I didn't care. Then something went wrong with the car. It stalled right on the tracks.

(*sound: Train chugging closer. Above this sound of car stalling.*)

Adams. The train was coming closer. I could hear its bell ringing, and the cry of its whistle. Still he stood there. And now—I knew that he was beckoning—beckoning me to my death.

(*sound: Train chugging close. Whistle blows wildly. Then train rushes up and by with pistons going, et cetera.*)

Adams. Well—I frustrated him that time. The starter had worked at last. I managed to back up. But when the train passed, he was gone. I was all alone in the hot dry afternoon.

(*sound: Train retreating. Crickets begin to sing.*)

(*music in*)

Adams. After that, I knew I had to do something. I didn't know who this man was or what he wanted of me. I only knew that from now on, I must not let myself be alone on the road for one moment.

(*sound: Auto hum up. Slow down. Stop. Door opening.*)

Adams. Hello, there. Like a ride?

Girl. What do you think? How far you going?

Adams. Amarillo . . . I'll take you to Amarillo.

Girl. Amarillo, Texas.

Adams. I'll drive you there.

Girl. Gee!

(*sound: Door closes—car starts.*)

(*music in*)

Girl. Mind if I take off my shoes? My dogs[4] are killing me.

Adams. Go right ahead.

Girl. Gee, what a break this is. A swell car, a decent guy, and driving all the way to Amarillo. All I been getting so far is trucks.

Adams. Hitchhike much?

Girl. Sure. Only it's tough sometimes, in these great open spaces, to get the breaks.

Adams. I should think it would be. Though I'll bet if you get a good pick-up in a fast car, you can get to places faster than—say, another person, in another car?

Girl. I don't get you.

Adams. Well, take me, for instance. Suppose I'm driving across the country, say, at a nice steady clip of about 45 miles an hour. Couldn't a girl like you, just standing beside the road, waiting for lifts, beat me to town after town—provided she got picked up every time in a car doing from 65 to 70 miles an hour?

Girl. I dunno. Maybe she could and maybe she couldn't. What difference does it make?

Adams. Oh—no difference. It's just a—crazy idea I had sitting here in the car.

Girl (*laughing*). Imagine spending your time in a swell car thinking of things like that!

Adams. What would you do instead?

Girl (*admiringly*). What would I do? If I was a good-looking fellow like yourself? Why—I'd just *enjoy* myself—every minute of the time. I'd sit back, and relax, and if I saw a good-looking girl along the side of the road . . . (*sharply*) Hey! Look out!

Adams (*breathlessly*). Did you see him too?

Girl. See who?

Adams. That man. Standing beside the barbed wire fence.

Girl. I didn't see—anybody. There wasn't nothing, but a bunch of steers—and the barbed wire fence. What did you think you was doing? Trying to run into the barbed wire fence?

Adams. There was a man there, I tell you . . . a thin gray man, with an overnight bag in his hand. And I was trying to—run him down.

Girl. Run him down? You mean—kill him?

4. **dogs:** a slang term for feet.

94 UNIT 1: PLOT AND CONFLICT

DIFFERENTIATED INSTRUCTION

FOR ENGLISH LEARNERS

Vocabulary: Idioms and Sayings [mixed-readiness pairs] Have students work in pairs to define these phrases from the play:

- *what a break this is* (line 329), "this is a sudden piece of luck"
- *get you* (line 339), "understand you"
- *keep your eyes peeled* (line 378), "stay alert and watch for something"
- *seeing pink elephants* (line 397), "imagining things that don't really exist"
- *half cracked* (line 405), "crazy"

FOR ENGLISH LEARNERS

Culture: Connect Explain to students that hitchhiking was a fairly common and acceptable way of getting around the United States in the 1970s, especially for young people, such as the girl Adams picks up. The number of hitchhikers has declined since then because of fears that it is no longer safe to accept rides from strangers. In addition, more people can now afford to own cars. Ask students what the attitude toward hitchhiking is in their cultures.

Adams. He's a sort of—phantom. I'm trying to get rid of him—or else prove that he's real. But (*desperately*) you say you didn't see him back there? You're sure?

Girl. I didn't see a soul. And as far as that's concerned, mister . . .

Adams. Watch for him the next time, then. Keep watching. Keep your eyes peeled on the road. He'll turn up again—maybe any minute now. (*excitedly*) There. Look there—

(*sound: Auto sharply veering and skidding.* Girl *screams.*)

(*sound: Crash of car going into barbed wire fence. Frightened lowing*[5] *of steer.*)

Girl. How does this door work? I—I'm gettin' outta here.

Adams. Did you see him that time?

Girl (*sharply*). No. I didn't see him that time. And personally, mister, I don't expect never to see him. All I want to do is to go on living—and I don't see how I will very long driving with you—

Adams. I'm sorry. I—I don't know what came over me. (*frightened*) Please—don't go . . .

Girl. So if you'll excuse me, mister—

Adams. You can't go. Listen, how would you like to go to California? I'll drive you to California.

Girl. Seeing pink elephants all the way? No thanks.

Adams (*desperately*). I could get you a job there. You wouldn't have to be a waitress. I have friends there—my name is Ronald Adams—You can check up.

(*sound: door opening*)

Girl. Uhn-hunh. Thanks just the same.

Adams. Listen. Please. For just one minute. Maybe you think I am half cracked. But this man. You see, I've been seeing this man all the way across the country. He's been following me. And if you could only help me—stay with me—until I reach the coast—

Girl. You know what I think you need, big boy? Not a girl friend. Just a good dose of sleep. . . . There, I got it now.

(*sound: door opens . . . slams*)

Adams. No. You can't go.

Girl (*screams*). Leave your hands offa me, do you hear! Leave your—

Adams. Come back here, please, come back.

(*sound: struggle . . . slap . . . footsteps running away on gravel . . . lowing of steer*)

Adams. She ran from me, as though I were a monster. A few minutes later, I saw a passing truck pick her up. I knew then that I was utterly alone.

(*sound: lowing of steer up*)

Adams. I was in the heart of the great Texas prairies. There wasn't a car on the road after the truck went by. I tried to figure out what to do, how to get hold of myself. If I could find a place to rest. Or even, if I could sleep right here in the car for a few hours, along the side of the road . . . I was getting my winter overcoat out of the back seat to use as a blanket, (Hall-ooo) when I saw him coming toward me, (Hall-ooo), emerging from the herd of moving steer . . .

Voice. Hall-ooo . . . Hall-oooo . . .

(*sound: auto starting violently . . . up to steady hum*)

(*music in*)

Adams. I didn't wait for him to come any closer. Perhaps I should have spoken to him then, fought it out then and there. For now he began to be everywhere. Whenever I stopped, even for a moment—for gas, for oil, for a drink of pop, a cup of coffee, a sandwich—he was there.

(*music faster*)

Adams. I saw him standing outside the auto camp in Amarillo that night, when I dared to slow down. He was sitting near the drinking fountain in a little camping spot just inside the border of New Mexico.

(3) **Targeted Passage**

5. **lowing:** mooing.

Lines 383–391

REINFORCE *KEY IDEA:* PROOF

Discuss Why is Adams so anxious for the girl to see the hitchhiker? What kind of **proof** would that offer him? ***Possible answer:*** *If she can see the hitchhiker, then he will know that he is not crazy. Because she can't, he is frightened that he is losing his mind.*

Lines 410–433

DISCUSSION PROMPTS

Use these prompts to help students understand the literal and metaphorical significance of the sleep references:

Recall When is the last time that Adams had a good night's sleep? ***Answer:*** *In lines 166–167, he mentions having had a good night's sleep in Pittsburgh, but he does not appear to have slept since then.*

Analyze What might sleep symbolize? What does this mean for Adams? ***Possible answer:*** *Sleep can refer to death. Adams's death might be foreshadowed by the mention of sleep in this passage and throughout the play.*

Evaluate Do you agree with the girl's parting advice to Adams (lines 410–411)? Why or why not? ***Possible answers:***

- *Yes. Sleep deprivation can produce very strange symptoms.*
- *No. He wasn't sleep deprived when he first started seeing the hitchhiker.*

Lines 435–437

READING STRATEGY

READING A RADIO PLAY

How does Adams react when he sees the hitchhiker emerging from the herd of steer? ***Answer:*** *He speeds off.*

FOR LESS–PROFICIENT READERS

(3) **Targeted Passage [Lines 371–422]**

This passage presents the rising action: Adams's behavior becomes increasingly odd.

- Why does Adams crash the car into the fence?
- What is the girl's reaction?
- Where does Adams offer to drive her? Why?
- What does he do when she gets out of the car?

FOR ADVANCED LEARNERS/PRE–AP

Analyze Have students track Adams's change in attitude and increasing panic using a Cause-and-Effect Diagram. Fill in the first box together (Cause: Adams leaves for his trip to California. Effect: He is in "excellent spirits" [line 80]). Have students complete the diagram in groups. Ask students: How might Adams's behavior continue to change once the man begins "to be everywhere" (line 440)?

BEST PRACTICES TOOLKIT—Transparency
Cause-and-Effect Diagram pp. B16, B38

ANALYZE VISUALS

About the Art American photographer Andreas Feininger (1906–1999) began his career as an architect before devoting himself entirely to photography. He was a staff photographer for the magazine *Life* and preferred taking pictures of scenes, such as the one here, rather than people.

Activity What elements of this photograph convey desolation or loneliness? ***Possible answer:** The thick clouds, flat landscape, and functional buildings create a desolate air.*

Lines 460–468

LITERARY ANALYSIS

● FORESHADOWING

What do the images in this passage suggest about Adams's future? (Remind students to record their ideas in the chart from page 87.) ***Possible answer:** All of the images in this passage are cold, empty, and lifeless, suggesting a future without hope or even life.*

Line 469

READING STRATEGY

■ READING A RADIO PLAY

What idea does the music communicate? ***Possible answer:** The music seems to indicate that Adams has reached the end of his journey.*

(*music faster*)

Adams. He was waiting for me outside the Navajo Reservation, where I stopped to check my tires. I saw him in Albuquerque[6] where I bought 12 gallons of gas . . . I was afraid now, afraid to stop. I began to drive faster and faster. I was in lunar landscape now—the great arid mesa country of New Mexico. I drove through it with the indifference of a fly crawling over the face of the moon.

(*music faster*)

Adams. But now he didn't even wait for me to stop. Unless I drove at 85 miles an hour over those endless roads—he waited for me at every other mile. I would see his figure, shadowless, flitting before me, still in its same attitude, over the cold and lifeless ground, flitting over dried-up rivers, over broken stones cast up by old glacial upheavals, flitting in the pure and cloudless air . . .

(*music strikes sinister note of finality.*)

Adams. I was beside myself when I finally reached Gallup, New Mexico, this morning. There is an auto camp here—cold, almost deserted at this time of year. I went inside, and asked if there was a telephone. I had the feeling that if only I could speak to someone familiar, someone that I loved, I could pull myself together.

(*sound: nickel put in slot*)

Operator. Number, please?

Adams. Long distance.

Operator. Thank you.

(*sound: return of nickel; buzz*)

Long-Distance Opr. This is long distance.

Adams. I'd like to put in a call to my home in Brooklyn, New York. I'm Ronald Adams. The number is Beechwood 2-0828.

Long-Distance Opr. Thank you. What is your number?

6. **Albuquerque** (ăl'bə-kûr'kē): a city in central New Mexico.

DIFFERENTIATED INSTRUCTION

FOR ENGLISH LEARNERS

Vocabulary: Suffixes [mixed-readiness pairs] Explain that the suffix *-less* means "without" or "lacking." When added to the end of a word, it can change the meaning entirely. Point out the words *endless, shadowless, lifeless,* and *cloudless* in lines 460–468. Have pairs define each word based on their knowledge of the suffix. Compare definitions.

Culture: Clarify Point out how complicated making a long distance phone call was at the time this play is set. As students can see in lines 482 and 486, a long distance operator was involved. Then a connection had to be made to the Albuquerque exchange (line 489) and then to the New York switchboard (line 491) before he finally reached his home number. That is why it was easier to send a telegram. Remind students that in line 71 Adams's mother asks him to send a wire, or telegram, when he arrives in Hollywood.

Adams. 312.

Albuquerque Opr. Albuquerque.

Long-Distance Opr. New York for Gallup. (*pause*)

New York Opr. New York.

Long-Distance Opr. Gallup, New Mexico calling Beechwood 2-0828. (*fade*)

Adams. I had read somewhere that love could banish demons. It was the middle of the morning. I knew Mother would be home. I pictured her, tall, white-haired, in her crisp house-dress, going about her tasks. It would be enough, I thought, merely to hear the even calmness of her voice . . .

Long-Distance Opr. Will you please deposit three dollars and 85 cents for the first three minutes? When you have deposited a dollar and a half, will you wait until I have collected the money?

(*sound: clunk of six coins*)

Long-Distance Opr. All right, deposit another dollar and a half.

(*sound: clunk of six coins*)

Long-Distance Opr. Will you please deposit the remaining 85 cents.

(*sound: clunk of four coins*)

Long-Distance Opr. Ready with Brooklyn—go ahead please.

Adams. Hello.

Mrs. Whitney. Mrs. Adams' residence.

Adams. Hello. Hello—Mother?

Mrs. Whitney (*very flat and rather proper . . . dumb, too, in a frizzy sort of way*). This is Mrs. Adams' residence. Who is it you wished to speak to, please?

Adams. Why—who's this?

Mrs. Whitney. This is Mrs. Whitney.

Adams. Mrs. Whitney? I don't know any Mrs. Whitney. Is this Beechwood 2-0828?

Mrs. Whitney. Yes.

Adams. Where's my mother? Where's Mrs. Adams?

Mrs. Whitney. Mrs. Adams is not at home. She is still in the hospital.

Adams. The hospital!

Mrs. Whitney. Yes. Who is this calling, please? Is it a member of the family?

Adams. What's she in the hospital for?

Mrs. Whitney. She's been prostrated[7] for five days. Nervous breakdown. But who is this calling?

Adams. Nervous breakdown? But—my mother was never nervous . . .

Mrs. Whitney. It's all taken place since the death of her oldest son, Ronald.

Adams. Death of her oldest son, Ronald . . . ? Hey—what is this? What number is this?

Mrs. Whitney. This is Beechwood 2-0828. It's all been very sudden. He was killed just six days ago in an automobile accident on the Brooklyn Bridge.

Long-Distance Opr. (*breaking in*). Your three minutes are up, sir. (*silence*) Your three minutes are up, sir. (*pause*) Your three minutes are up, sir. (*fade*) Sir, your three minutes are up. Your three minutes are up, sir.

Adams (*in a strange voice*). And so, I am sitting here in this deserted auto camp in Gallup, New Mexico. I am trying to think. I am trying to get hold of myself. Otherwise, I shall go mad . . . Outside it is night—the vast, soulless night of New Mexico. A million stars are in the sky. Ahead of me stretch a thousand miles of empty mesa, mountains, prairies—desert. Somewhere among them, he is waiting for me. Somewhere I shall know who he is, and who . . . I . . . am . . .

(*music up*)

(4) **Targeted Passage**

7. **prostrated:** in a state of mental collapse.

Lines 532–542

LITERARY ANALYSIS

● FORESHADOWING

What does Adams learn when he calls home? Was this outcome foreshadowed? (Remind students to record this latest event in the second column of their charts.) ***Possible answer:***

Foreshadowing	*Events That Were Foreshadowed*
Adams swerves to avoid a hitchhiker on the Brooklyn Bridge, and there is a terrible sound of skidding (lines 90–92).	*Adams learns that he died in a car accident on the Brooklyn Bridge (lines 540–542).*

Lines 548–557

REINFORCE *KEY IDEA:* PROOF

Discuss What **proof** does Adams's phone call to his home give him? ***Possible answer:*** *His call home proves that he is no longer living a normal life. He seems to be suspended in a state between life and death.*

SELECTION WRAP-UP

REFLECT What does the play show about the mental and physical effects of isolation on even a healthy psyche?

★ CRITIQUE Are you satisfied with the ending of this play, or should the conflict have been resolved? Explain.

READING FLUENCY

Distribute the copy masters and have students practice fluency.

RESOURCE MANAGER—Copy Master
Reading Fluency p. 138

FOR LESS-PROFICIENT READERS

(4) Targeted Passage [Lines 521–557]

This passage presents the play's climax: Adams finds out he died six days ago.

- Why does Mrs. Whitney answer the phone instead of Adams's mother?
- How does Adams react to the news that he has died?
- What do you think will happen now?

FOR ADVANCED LEARNERS/PRE-AP

Analyze What might Adams's journey represent? Ask students to consider what happens to Adams along the way and the possible significance of the hitchhiker and the conclusion of the play. Have students create a diagram that explores the metaphorical or symbolic significance of his travels and the events that occur. Ask students to share their insights.

Practice and Apply

After Reading

For additional support of postreading questions, use these copy masters:

RESOURCE MANAGER—Copy Masters
Reading Check p. 135 (to check understanding of the selection)
Reading a Radio Play p. 131 (for practice of reading standards focus)
Question Support p. 136 (After Reading questions adapted for English learners and less-proficient readers)

Additional selection questions are provided for teachers on page 123.

ANSWERS

Comprehension

1. *His destination is California.*
2. *He cannot understand how the man is able to travel faster than he is.*
3. *She has been hospitalized with a nervous breakdown after the death of her son in a car accident on the Brooklyn Bridge.*

Literary Analysis

Possible answers:

4. *Adams and his mother seem close. His mother worries about his driving to California and is crying as he says good-bye. He responds kindly to her concern and wants to hear her voice when he is in New Mexico.*
5. ● **STANDARDS FOCUS Foreshadowing** *The comment that Adams's mother made about not picking up hitchhikers should be in the first column. The event that is foreshadowed is the presence of the hitchhiker, possibly Death, throughout Adams's journey. Students might add the terrible skidding noise in line 92 to the first column of their chart, which foreshadowed the car accident that supposedly killed Adams. Students might say the inability of the mechanic and girl to see the hitchhiker as well as the fresh rain splattered on the hitchhiker when it hasn't rained recently foreshadow the idea that he is Death or a figment of Adams's imagination.*
6. ■ **STANDARDS FOCUS Reading a Radio Play** *The sound effects communicate the actions of the car crashing into the fence and the girl slapping Adams and then running off. We know the girl is frightened because of the sound effect of the scream (line 382). Without the sound effects, these events would not be known.*
7. *No one else can see him, and Adams's first sighting of him is where he supposedly met his death on the bridge. Therefore, the hitchhiker may be Death.*
8. ***Similarities:*** *The main characters believe they are sane, but their actions appear insane to others. Both stories have suspenseful plots.* ***Differences:*** The Hitchhiker *is set in several locations in the 1940s. Adams is a victim, and it is not certain what his fate will be. "The Tell-Tale Heart" is set in the narrator's home. The narrator commits a horrible crime, and his fate is clear.*

Extension and Challenge

9. *Students might say that he drives off the road and dies in his attempt to kill the hitchhiker because he says he will find out who the hitchhiker is. Or, he might go home to New York and find out who he is.*
10. *Students' performances should follow the text.*

After Reading

Comprehension

1. **Recall** What is Ronald Adams's original destination?
2. **Clarify** Why does the repeated sight of the hitchhiker give Adams "the willies"?
3. **Clarify** What does Adams learn about his mother at the end of the play?

Literary Analysis

4. **Make Inferences** What kind of relationship did Ronald Adams have with his mother? Cite evidence to support your answer.
5. **Examine Foreshadowing** Now that you've read the play, is there anything you'd like to change or add to the first column of your foreshadowing chart? Make the adjustments and then fill in the second column of the chart. Note which use of foreshadowing was most effective in increasing the suspense you felt as you read.
6. **Analyze the Radio Play** Reread lines 377–384. Tell what actions and emotions are communicated through stage directions and sound effects. Could listeners fully understand what was taking place in this scene if these elements weren't included? Explain.
7. **Draw Conclusions** Who do you think the hitchhiker is? Give **proof** from the play to support your conclusion.
8. **Compare Across Texts** What are some similarities and differences between "The Tell-Tale Heart" and *The Hitchhiker?* Think about the main characters, the settings, and the endings. Present your answers in a Venn diagram like the one shown.

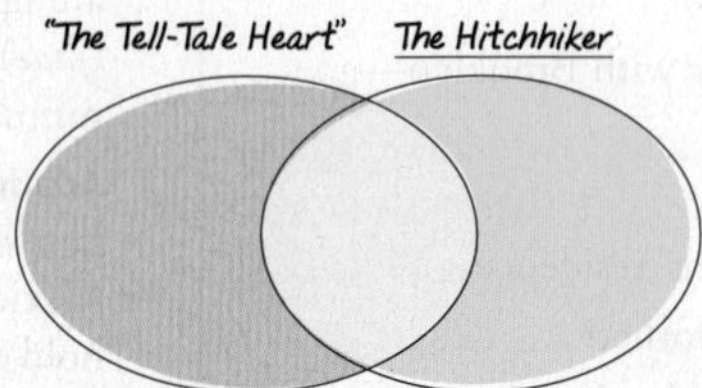

Extension and Challenge

9. **Readers' Circle** Ask one member of your group to reread Adams's last speech aloud. Then discuss what might happen as he continues his journey. Make sure your guesses are based on details from the selection.
10. **Creative Project: Drama** With a small group, choose a scene from *The Hitchhiker* that you think is especially suspenseful. Practice performing the scene, remembering to include sound effects and to follow stage directions. Then perform for the class. Afterward, explain why your group chose the scene you did.

98 UNIT 1: PLOT AND CONFLICT

eading-Writing Connection

Show your understanding of *The Hitchhiker* by responding to these prompts. Then complete the **Grammar and Writing** exercise.

WRITING PROMPTS	SELF-CHECK
A. Short Response: Evaluate Ronald Adams The play opens with Adams telling the listeners, "I am not mad." On the basis of what you learn in the rest of the play, do you agree with his assessment? Write a **one-paragraph evaluation** of Adams's sanity.	***A good evaluation will . . .*** • present an opinion about Adams's mental state • support that opinion with details from the play
B. Extended Response: Write a Scene What if the hitchhiker Adams picked up went to the police to report him? Write a **one- or two-page scene** in which she explains to an officer what happened and what **proof** she has for thinking Adams might be mad or even dangerous.	***An interesting scene will . . .*** • include dialogue about what the girl saw or didn't see while in the car • show whether or not the officers believe her

GRAMMAR AND WRITING

MAINTAIN PRONOUN-ANTECEDENT AGREEMENT An antecedent is the noun or pronoun to which a pronoun refers. For example, in the following sentence, the pronoun *their* refers to the antecedent *they: They took their seats at the café.* Be sure to use singular pronouns with singular antecedents and plural pronouns with plural antecedents. Pair antecedents ending in *one, thing,* or *body* with singular pronouns, such as *he, her, she,* or *his.* In the revised sentence, notice how the pronouns (in yellow) and the antecedent (in green) **agree in number.**

Original: Adams would ask just about anyone whether they had seen the hitchhiker.

Revised: Adams would ask just about anyone whether he or she had seen the hitchhiker.

PRACTICE Correct the pronoun antecedent error in each sentence.

1. Adams first saw someone holding their bag on the bridge.
2. Everyone thought Adams was crazy because they could never see the hitchhiker.
3. Adams's scary story would make anybody fear for their life.
4. Nobody could have suspected that they got a ride from a dead man!

For more help with pronoun-antecedent agreement, see page R52 in the ***Grammar Handbook.***

DIFFERENTIATED INSTRUCTION

FOR LESS–PROFICIENT WRITERS

For Prompt A:

1. As a class, fill in the pros and cons list. Discuss whether the evidence points to Adams's sanity or insanity.
2. Help students form a topic sentence. For example: *Although Adams claims that he is sane, his reactions to events prove otherwise.*
3. Have students finish their paragraphs independently, using details from the relevant list.

For Prompt B:

1. After students have reread lines 318–422, outline the details that the girl might report to the police.
2. Then have students write two passages of dialogue. The girl should be the first speaker, explaining what happened and what she saw. Then the police officer should respond.
3. Have students read their dialogues aloud to a partner and work together to revise them.

Reading-Writing Connection

WRITING PROMPTS

- For **Prompt A,** have students create a pros and cons list and skim the story to find details that illustrate Adams's sanity and others that seem to prove he is insane.
- For **Prompt B,** have students first reread lines 318–422 and take notes on the incidents that occur while the girl is in the car.

For writing support, see

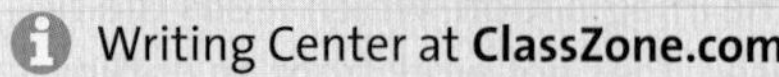

Writing Center at **ClassZone.com**

GRAMMAR AND WRITING

Before students begin the exercise, have them pick out the antecedent with which each pronoun must agree.

Possible answers:

1. *Adams first saw someone holding his bag on the bridge.*
2. *Everyone thought Adams was crazy because he or she could never see the hitchhiker.*
3. *Adams's scary story would make anybody fear for his or her life.*
4. *Nobody could have suspected that he or she got a ride from a dead man!*

RESOURCE MANAGER—Copy Master
Maintain Pronoun-Antecedent Agreement p. 137

Assess and Reteach

Assess

RESOURCE MANAGER—Copy Masters
Selection Tests A, B/C pp. 139–140, 141–142

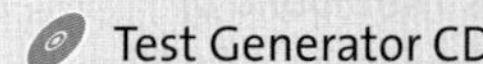

Test Generator CD

Reteach

STANDARDS LESSON FILE
Literature Lesson 8: Foreshadowing and Suspense
Literature Lessons 25 and 26: Elements of Drama
Grammar Lesson 10: Antecedent Agreement with Indefinite Pronouns

Introduce

OBJECTIVE

- read and identify characteristics of a mystery novel excerpt

Meet Carl Hiaasen

Carl Hiaasen describes himself as a "manic reader" as a youngster. His interest in reading led naturally to his interest in writing. He feels that his work as a newspaper reporter contributes to his success as a novelist. "The journalism feeds the imagination, which feeds the fiction." Hiaasen does not work from an outline. With just a main idea and some characters in mind, he leaves open more possibilities for the plot: "I want to be surprised by my characters." He is careful not to "write down" to his young readers, noting that kids "are quite aware when adults are underestimating them."

Try a Mystery Novel

One of the most popular types of fiction is the mystery novel. Writers tap into the human desire to solve a mystery or find out "whodunit." A good reader must pay close attention to details or risk missing an important clue. Evaluating the clues, anticipating what might happen next, and finding out how the story ends are all part of what makes reading a mystery so enjoyable.

One of the best known mystery writers is Agatha Christie. Over two billion of her books have been sold. In *Murder on the Orient Express,* detective Hercule Poirot solves a murder that takes place on a snowbound train. Other mystery novels that students may enjoy include

- Sir Arthur Conan Doyle's *The Hound of the Baskervilles,* about the fate of a family haunted by the legend of a supernatural hound
- Joan Lowery Nixon's *Playing for Keeps,* about a girl who finds love and intrigue while on a cruise with her grandmother
- Avi's *Midnight Magic,* about a servant boy and his master faced with the challenge of defeating a ghost

RESOURCE MANAGER—Copy Master
Identify Genre Features p. 143

Great Reads

Hoot

Novel by Carl Hiaasen

Carl Hiaasen
born 1954

Other Book by Carl Hiaasen

- *Flush*

Meet Carl Hiaasen

Carl Hiaasen (hī′ə-sən) is a Florida native to the core. He began writing about his home state at age six, when his father gave him his first typewriter. Over the years, Hiassen developed the humorous writing style that has made him famous. He is an award-winning reporter and longtime columnist for the *Miami Herald,* as well as being the author of numerous best-selling mystery novels for adults. *Hoot* is his first young adult novel.

Much of Hiaasen's writing reflects his deep love of the outdoors. The heroes in his novels are often fierce protectors of the natural habitats and native species in Florida. The villains represent corporate greed and abuse of the environment. A reviewer once noted that Hiaasen "displays no mercy for anyone perceived as being responsible for defiling his home environment."

Try a Mystery Novel

What makes a book a **mystery novel?** First, you need a crime or unexplained event. There will be various clues left behind and possible motives for what happened. Suspense will build as further clues are revealed. Characters in the story will try to solve the mystery, but you, as the reader, might figure it out before they do. You can never be too sure of the answer, though—there might be a plot twist that changes everything.

100

DIFFERENTIATED INSTRUCTION

FOR LESS–PROFICIENT READERS

Reading Support

- Before students read the excerpt, decide which of the teaching notes on pages 99–103 will be most helpful. Then read the selection aloud, pausing to discuss the relevant notes. Or, have students take turns reading designated passages in small groups, interspersed by discussion.
- Remind students that since this reading is an excerpt from a mystery novel, they should not expect to understand who the barefoot runner is or how he fits into the story of the owls (described under **Read a Great Book** on page 99 of the teacher's edition). They should, however, pay close attention to any details that may be clues.

Read a Great Book

Roy Eberhardt didn't know what he was in for when his family moved from Bozeman, Montana, to Coconut Cove, Florida. He's getting bullied on the bus, but he's used to that. In fact, since his family moves around a lot, he's encountered enough bullies to consider himself "an expert on the breed." It's the stuff that he isn't used to that makes his new home seem strange. For starters, he spies a barefoot boy sprinting alongside the school bus at a speed that would put track stars in state-of-the-art running shoes to shame. Then there's the big, threatening girl who knows too much about him and won't tell him how. Roy needs to find some answers to his questions, but it won't be easy.

from

HOOT

"Are there any other schools around here?" Roy asked Garrett.

"Why? You sick of this one already?" Garrett cackled and plunged a spoon into a lump of clammy apple crisp.

"No way. The reason I asked, I saw this weird kid today at one of the bus stops. Except he didn't get on the bus, and he's not here at school," Roy said, "so I figured he must not go to Trace."

"I don't know *anyone* who doesn't go to Trace," Garrett said. "There's a Catholic school up in Fort Myers, but that's a long ways off. Was he wearing a uniform, this kid? Because the nuns make everybody wear uniforms."

"No, he definitely wasn't in a uniform."

"You're sure he was in middle school? Maybe he goes to Graham," Garrett suggested. Graham was the public high school nearest to Coconut Cove.

101

Read

Read a Great Book

The title, *Hoot,* refers to a species of burrowing owl that faces extinction because of rapid development in the state of Florida. In writing about Roy Eberhardt's attempts to save the habitat of the owls, Carl Hiaasen draws on his own experiences as an adolescent. He also has a stepson who is about Roy's age, which helped him tell the story from the boy's point of view.

Although the story is humorous, it has a serious message. As Hiaasen explains, "The world can be a nasty place, and there's nothing wrong with going after the bad guys in a novel." His writing is often a crusade against injustice. Shortly after the novel was completed, the author read about an incident that took place in Broward County, Florida. The presence of several owls was preventing the development of a piece of property. The owls were soon found dead. Carl Hiaasen comments that it "was creepy how much it resembled the plot of the book."

SHARE AN FYI

Many Catholic and private schools require their students to wear a school uniform (lines 7–10), believing that it results in better behavior and, ultimately, better learning. Some public high schools have adopted a similar policy.

FOR ENGLISH LEARNERS

Read Aloud [paired option] Preread part of the excerpt and have students continue reading in pairs or small groups. Alternatively, read aloud all or part of the excerpt, stopping occasionally for questions, predictions, discussion, or explanation.

Listen to the *Audio Anthology CD* Have students listen to the excerpt as they read along. Lead them in a follow-up discussion.

Reciprocal Questioning [small-group option] After reading lines 62–88 aloud, guide small groups of students through the steps of the Reciprocal Questioning strategy. Then have them use the strategy as they read the last part of the excerpt.

BEST PRACTICES TOOLKIT

Reciprocal Questioning p. A3

SHARE A READING TIP

Writers often use a character to ask questions that the readers would likely want to ask as well. The answers help the writer convey information that the reader needs to know. Notice that Garrett asks many questions in the opening section (lines 2, 8–9, 12, 22, 38).

SHARE AN FYI

Jesse James (line 38) was a notorious outlaw of the American Wild West who robbed banks and trains. He was shot in the back of the head in 1882.

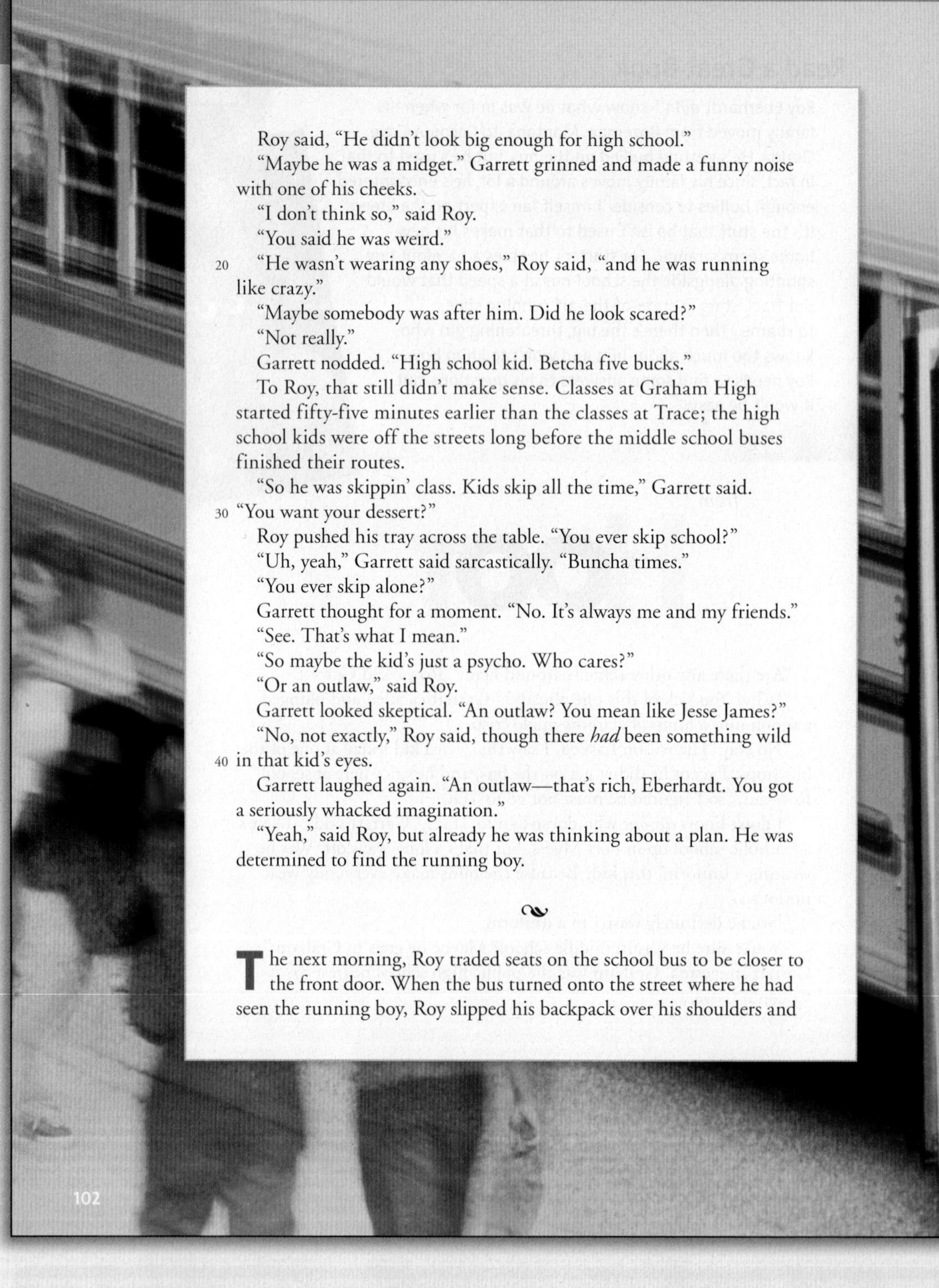

Roy said, "He didn't look big enough for high school."

"Maybe he was a midget." Garrett grinned and made a funny noise with one of his cheeks.

"I don't think so," said Roy.

"You said he was weird."

"He wasn't wearing any shoes," Roy said, "and he was running like crazy."

"Maybe somebody was after him. Did he look scared?"

"Not really."

Garrett nodded. "High school kid. Betcha five bucks."

To Roy, that still didn't make sense. Classes at Graham High started fifty-five minutes earlier than the classes at Trace; the high school kids were off the streets long before the middle school buses finished their routes.

"So he was skippin' class. Kids skip all the time," Garrett said. "You want your dessert?"

Roy pushed his tray across the table. "You ever skip school?"

"Uh, yeah," Garrett said sarcastically. "Buncha times."

"You ever skip alone?"

Garrett thought for a moment. "No. It's always me and my friends."

"See. That's what I mean."

"So maybe the kid's just a psycho. Who cares?"

"Or an outlaw," said Roy.

Garrett looked skeptical. "An outlaw? You mean like Jesse James?"

"No, not exactly," Roy said, though there *had* been something wild in that kid's eyes.

Garrett laughed again. "An outlaw—that's rich, Eberhardt. You got a seriously whacked imagination."

"Yeah," said Roy, but already he was thinking about a plan. He was determined to find the running boy.

The next morning, Roy traded seats on the school bus to be closer to the front door. When the bus turned onto the street where he had seen the running boy, Roy slipped his backpack over his shoulders and

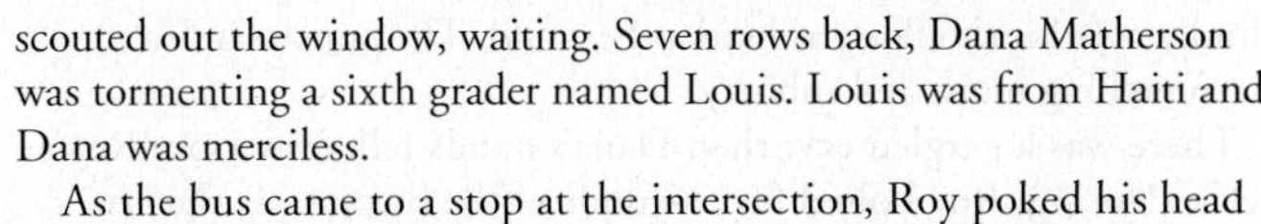

scouted out the window, waiting. Seven rows back, Dana Matherson was tormenting a sixth grader named Louis. Louis was from Haiti and Dana was merciless.

As the bus came to a stop at the intersection, Roy poked his head out the window and checked up and down the street. Nobody was running. Seven kids boarded the bus, but the strange shoeless boy was not among them.

~

It was the same story the next day, and the day after that. By Friday, Roy had pretty much given up. He was sitting ten rows from the door, reading an X-Man comic, as the bus turned the familiar corner and began to slow down. A movement at the corner of his eye made Roy glance up from his comic book—and there he was on the sidewalk, running again! Same basketball jersey, same grimy shorts, same black-soled feet.

As the brakes of the school bus wheezed, Roy grabbed his backpack off the floor and stood up. At that instant, two big sweaty hands closed around his neck.

"Where ya goin', cowgirl?"

"Lemme go," Roy rasped, squirming to break free.

The grip on his throat tightened. He felt Dana's ashtray breath on his right ear: "How come you don't got your boots on today? Who ever heard of a cowgirl wearing Air Jordans?"

"They're Reeboks," Roy squeaked.

The bus had stopped, and the students were starting to board. Roy was furious. He had to get to the door fast, before the driver closed it and the bus began to roll.

But Dana wouldn't let go, digging his fingers into Roy's windpipe. Roy was having trouble getting air, and struggling only made it worse.

"Look at you," Dana chortled from behind, "red as a tomato!"

Roy knew the rules against fighting on the bus, but he couldn't think of anything else to do. He clenched his right fist and brought it up

SHARE WORD MEANINGS

Chortle (line 77) means "to laugh, especially in a satisfying or exultant manner." The word is a blend of *chuckle* and *snort.* Lewis Carroll coined the word *chortle* in his famous poem "Jabberwocky."

SHARE A READING TIP

Hiaasen uses vivid comparisons to help the reader understand what Roy is experiencing. "Roy was gulping like a beached trout" (line 98) and "His legs felt like wet cement, and his lungs were on fire" (lines 113–114) both show in a memorable way how difficult it is for Roy to try to keep up with the barefoot runner.

blindly over his shoulder, as hard as he could. The punch landed on something moist and rubbery.

There was a gargled cry; then Dana's hands fell away from Roy's neck. Panting, Roy bolted for the door of the bus just as the last student, a tall girl with curly blond hair and red-framed eyeglasses, came up the steps. Roy clumsily edged past her and jumped to the ground.

"Where do you think you're going?" the girl demanded.

"Hey, wait!" the bus driver shouted, but Roy was already a blur.

The running boy was way ahead of him, but Roy figured he could stay close enough to keep him in sight. He knew the kid couldn't go at full speed forever.

He followed him for several blocks—over fences, through shrubbery, weaving through yapping dogs and lawn sprinklers and hot tubs. Eventually Roy felt himself tiring. This kid is amazing, he thought. Maybe he's practicing for the track team.

Once Roy thought he saw the boy glance over his shoulder, as if he knew he was being pursued, but Roy couldn't be certain. The boy was still far ahead of him, and Roy was gulping like a beached trout. His shirt was soaked and perspiration poured off his forehead, stinging his eyes.

The last house in the subdivision was still under construction, but the shoeless boy dashed heedlessly through the lumber and loose nails. Three men hanging drywall stopped to holler at him, but the boy never broke stride. One of the same workers made a one-armed lunge at Roy but missed.

Suddenly there was grass under his feet again—the greenest, softest grass that Roy had ever seen. He realized that he was on a golf course, and that the blond kid was tearing down the middle of a long, lush fairway.

On one side was a row of tall Australian pines, and on the other side was a milky man-made lake. Roy could see four brightly dressed figures ahead, gesturing at the barefoot boy as he ran by.

Roy gritted his teeth and kept going. His legs felt like wet cement, and his lungs were on fire. A hundred yards ahead, the boy cut sharply to the right and disappeared into the pine trees. Roy doggedly aimed himself for the woods.

An angry shout echoed, and Roy noticed that the people in the fairway were waving their arms at him, too. He kept right on running. Moments later there was a distant glint of sunlight on metal, followed by a muted *thwack.* Roy didn't actually see the golf ball until it came down six feet in front of him. He had no time to duck or dive out of the way. All he could do was turn his head and brace for the blow.

The bounce caught him squarely above the left ear, and at first it didn't even hurt. Then Roy felt himself swaying and spinning as a brilliant gout of fireworks erupted inside his skull. He felt himself falling for what seemed like a long time, falling as softly as a drop of rain on velvet.

When the golfers ran up and saw Roy facedown in the sand trap, they thought he was dead. Roy heard their frantic cries but he didn't move. The sugar-white sand felt cool against his burning cheeks, and he was very sleepy. ∾

Keep Reading

Roy has gone from reading mysteries to being right in the middle of one. But the barefoot boy is just one of the mysteries in Roy's new hometown, where reptile wranglers are listed in the phone book because you just might find an alligator in your toilet. While Roy is trying to find out who the strange boy is, the Coconut Cove Public Safety Department has another mystery on its hands. Someone is sabotaging the construction of a pancake house, and no one knows why. Keep reading to see how the mystery unfolds.

Discuss

SHARE A READING TIP

A good mystery is full of unexpected turns. Just when the reader believes that Roy will catch up to the barefoot runner, the plot takes a new twist as Roy is hit by a golf ball and falls unconscious to the ground. Hiaasen effectively hooks the reader to continue reading to find out what happens next.

Keep Reading

Share these discussion questions with students after they have finished the excerpt. You might use these questions to lead a class discussion or have students form small groups to discuss them.

- What do you like about Roy? What details from the story make him likable or help you connect with him?
- Why do you think Roy feels so compelled to meet the barefoot boy he sees running next to the bus?
- What do you think of the way that Roy deals with Dana Matherson, the school bully? What might happen to Roy as a result of his actions?
- Roy and Garrett suggest reasons why the barefoot boy might be running. What other reasons can you imagine?
- What do you think will happen next? Do you think that Roy and the barefoot boy will become friends? Why or why not?

Focus and Motivate

OBJECTIVES

Media Literacy

- explore the key idea of making **movie versions** of books
- identify and analyze film elements
- analyze plot in film
- create a storyboard

SUMMARY

In this clip from the feature film *The Sisterhood of the Traveling Pants,* teenager Carmen has just traveled to spend the summer with her father. She looks forward to spending quality time alone with him. However, from the time he picks her up at the train station until their arrival at his home, she is dealt one surprise after another—he has moved, he is living with someone who has teenaged children, and he is getting married at the end of the summer.

How do GREAT *stories begin?*

Discuss the question. Talk about what stories, either in books or in movies, students consider truly great. Spend time analyzing the specific characters and events that make them great. After students read the ***KEY IDEA*** paragraph, invite them to discuss what they have liked or disliked about **movie versions** of their favorite stories. Ask: Why is it sometimes fun and sometimes disappointing to see a movie version of a favorite book?

BACKGROUND

The author of the book version of *The Sisterhood of the Traveling Pants* is Ann Brashares. Brashares believes the popularity of the book and movie springs from the unconditional love and loyalty between the girls in the novel—something many people crave. The story's characters support and challenge each other during what becomes a life-changing summer for each of them. They believe the pants they share might have magical qualities because of all the changes the pants seem to cause in their lives. However, the character Carmen eventually states that the "real magic of the pants" is in the way they hold the girls' friendship together during a time "when it felt like nothing would ever be the same again."

Media Study

from The Sisterhood of the Traveling Pants

Film Clip on *MediaSmart* DVD

How do GREAT *stories begin?*

KEY IDEA Quite often, a popular book is made into a major motion picture. Fans of the book form long lines at theaters, eager to experience big-screen portrayals of gripping moments they know so well. What **movie versions** of books have you enjoyed? What made those movies worthwhile? Prepare to watch a clip from a movie that's based on a well-loved novel. You'll explore what filmmakers do to draw you into the plot of a movie.

Background

A Perfect Fit The novel *The Sisterhood of the Traveling Pants* is about four lifelong best friends who are about to spend their first summer apart. Before their vacations begin, these girls make an amazing discovery. A pair of jeans purchased in a thrift shop fits each one of them perfectly. To stay connected that summer, they agree to mail the jeans to each other. This book's popularity led to sequels to the novel as well as a movie. The scene you'll watch occurs fairly early in the movie and focuses on Carmen, who is about to visit her dad.

106

Media Study Resources

RESOURCE MANAGER UNIT 1

Plan and Teach pp. 145–148

Media Analysis

Summary pp. 149†*, 150‡*

Viewing Guide p. 151

Close Viewing p. 152

Media Activity p. 153

Produce Your Own Media p. 154

STANDARDS LESSON FILE

Media Lesson 1: Active Viewing Strategies

Media Lesson 4: Analyzing Visuals in Film and TV

Media Lesson 7: Evaluating Films and TV Shows

Media Center at **ClassZone.com**

MEDIA VIEWING

Media*Smart* DVD

* Resources for Differentiation † Also in Spanish ‡ In Haitian Creole and Vietnamese

Media Literacy: Plot in Movies

The **exposition** stage of a story is the part that introduces the characters, setting, and conflict. Movies unfold in a similar way, introducing the characters and their struggles. For a movie director, the first steps in developing a plot are to show characters' relationships and predicaments, and to make viewers like you care about these characters. Filmmakers position the characters and the camera in certain ways to help you to follow and react to what's happening.

HOW DIRECTORS TELL THEIR STORIES	STRATEGIES FOR VIEWING
Directors position characters to portray relationships. To show how characters relate to each other in a scene, directors use **blocking,** the arrangement of the characters within a film frame.	Notice how close or how far apart characters stand to one another. Their positions may offer clues about their relationships or their emotions.
Directors position the camera to reveal how what's happening affects the characters. A **close-up shot** is a detailed view of a character or an object. Close-ups can reveal a character's personality and often hint at a character's emotions or thoughts. **Medium shots** show a character from the waist up. This type of shot can capture movements that reveal a character's behavior.	To watch for what might be revealed in close-up or medium shots, ask yourself: • What reactions or thoughts can I infer from a character's facial expressions? • What does a character's body language tell me about how he or she feels about what's happening?
Directors try to stir viewers' emotions. Directors not only want you to understand what's happening in a story but to get you emotionally involved. They want you to follow the plot complications closely and to make you wonder about the outcome.	As you watch a conflict unfold in a scene, ask yourself: • How am I reacting to what's happening? • What does the director do to make me care about what will happen? • What is the mood of the music? Is it upbeat? Sad? How is it affecting me?

MEDIA STUDY: TEACHING OPTIONS

Teaching Option 1: The Basics (1–2 Days)

1. Begin the Media Study using the material provided on pages 106–107.
2. Show the Introduction on Media*Smart*. Then show the First Viewing. As they watch, have students use the Viewing Guide on page 108, along with the corresponding copy master on page 151 of the Resource Manager. Discuss their responses.
3. Return to the pupil edition for the extension activities on page 109.

Teaching Option 2: In-Depth Study (2–3 Days)

1. Begin the Media Study using pages 106–107.
2. Show the Introduction and First Viewing from Media*Smart*.
3. Continue on Media*Smart* with the Media Lessons, using the teacher notes available in the Resources section.
4. Show the Guided Analysis presentation. Have students record their observations on the Student Viewing Guide available in the Resources section from Media*Smart*.
5. Return to the pupil edition, page 109.

Teach

MEDIA LITERACY

Review the terms *plot, character, setting,* and *conflict*. Encourage students to identify these elements in some of their favorite movies. Focusing on one or two of the movies, discuss the ways in which directors introduce viewers to characters and conflicts. At the beginning of a film, what kinds of clues help viewers get to know characters and begin to understand their relationships? Then discuss the chart on page 107.

- **Directors position characters to portray relationships.** Ask students again to recall scenes from their favorite movies, keeping in mind the blocking of key moments. Then have them think about how they would use blocking in other scenarios. How might characters involved in a disagreement be positioned within a room? What about characters who are speaking after being apart for a long period of time?
- **Directors position the camera to reveal how what's happening affects the characters.** Have students take a closer look at the picture from the movie on page 106. What can they say about the relationship between the characters, based on their facial expressions and body language? *(They are close friends and are protective of one another. They enjoy each other's company.)* Have students think about the body language and facial expressions that might accompany these emotions:
  —shock or disbelief *(wide eyes, raising of hand to mouth)*
  —anger *(scowl, fast tapping of foot, slamming objects)*
  —uneasiness or insecurity *(shifting in seat, holding arms close to body)*
  —love or affection *(smile, hand resting on another person's shoulder)*
- **Directors try to stir viewers' emotions.** Encourage students to recall how various movie scenes have affected them. What specific conversations and events have caused them to care about characters? How does background music affect them?

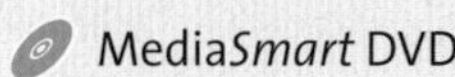
Media*Smart* DVD

Practice and Apply

VIEWING GUIDE

1. As students prepare to view the clip from the movie, explain to them that they will be asked to point out specific techniques the director uses to make them care about the character of Carmen and understand her relationship with her father. Encourage them to observe the following:
   - the use of **blocking** to show how characters relate to each other
   - **close-up shots** and **medium shots** that show the characters' body language and facial expressions and help viewers understand what characters are feeling
   - use of dialogue and music to draw viewers into the scene
2. Suggest to students that they watch the clip more than once, each time making notes about new details. Students might want to watch the clip once without sound so they can focus on body language and facial expressions. After watching it with and without sound, they should note the emotional effect music has on the scene.

RESOURCE MANAGER—Copy Masters
Viewing Guide p. 151
Close Viewing p. 152
Media Activity p. 153

Media*Smart* DVD

ANSWERS

***FIRST VIEWING:* Comprehension**

1. *He reveals that he is getting married.*
2. *Outside the car, Carmen notices a neighborhood with which she is unfamiliar.*

***CLOSE VIEWING:* Media Literacy**

Possible answers:

3. *Carmen is shown hurrying off the train, smiling when she sees her father, and hugging him enthusiastically. The conversation in the car also reveals her excitement: she presents her report card, talks about cooking for him and playing tennis with him, and mentions how long it's been since she's had time alone with him.*
4. *The director is communicating that Carmen feels distant from her father and his new family. She feels like an outsider watching her father interact with his fiancée.*
5. *The song gives the scene continuity, and its effects change as the scene progresses. At the beginning of the scene, the song reflects Carmen's warm feelings for her father and her excitement about visiting him. By the end of the scene, the song feels sad and wistful as it forces viewers to recall her happiness and innocence at the beginning of the scene.*
6. *With this scene, the filmmakers carefully establish the emerging conflict. The conversation in the car reveals that Carmen admires and loves her father, so viewers can understand the hurt and confusion she feels on learning that he has kept secrets from her. Because she lives far from her father and says that she feels she hasn't had enough time with him, viewers can also see why her father's new situation would make her feel threatened. Her facial expressions and body language as she stands in the driveway reveal her shock and her feelings of confusion and betrayal. Viewers can relate to Carmen's feelings because they see her happiness and excitement at the beginning of the scene and watch as it quickly drains away and her father becomes something of a stranger to her.*

- **Film:** *The Sisterhood of the Traveling Pants*
- **Director:** Ken Kwapis
- **Genre:** Drama
- **Running Time:** 2.5 minutes

Viewing Guide for

The Sisterhood of the Traveling Pants

The scene you'll watch focuses on Carmen, who has just arrived to spend the summer with her dad. First, watch the clip to follow what's happening in the scene. Then view the clip a few times to spot techniques that convey the conflict and encourage viewers to connect to the characters. Answer these questions to help you analyze the clip.

NOW VIEW

***FIRST VIEWING:* Comprehension**

1. **Recall** Carmen surprises her dad with her grades. What is the surprise Carmen's dad reveals to her?
2. **Clarify** What is shown from outside of the moving car that gets Carmen's attention?

***CLOSE VIEWING:* Media Literacy**

3. **Analyze Character** How do the filmmakers show Carmen's excitement at spending the summer with her father?
4. **Analyze Blocking** This image of the three characters is an example of how a director can position characters in a film frame to signal character relationships. Through blocking, what is the director communicating to viewers about Carmen's relationship to the others?
5. **Analyze Techniques** One song plays throughout the scene. What effect do you think the song is intended to have on you?
6. **Evaluate Techniques** The scene focuses on two characters having a conversation that leads to a tense moment. How well do the filmmakers set the stage for a conflict that will develop as the movie progresses? Base your opinion on these elements:
   - the details about the characters that are delivered through dialogue
   - the shots the filmmakers use to make the characters' emotions visible
   - your own emotional reactions to what happens in the scene

108

Write or Discuss

Analyze Film You've viewed a clip from *The Sisterhood of the Traveling Pants* to look at how directors portray characters and conflicts. Now put yourself in the shoes of the movie's director. How might the scene be different if it focused less on Carmen and more on her dad and his news? Write a short description of this new version. Think about

- which character would have more close-ups
- how viewers might sympathize more with him
- how the music might differ

Produce Your Own Media

Create a Storyboard A **storyboard** is a device filmmakers use to plan the shooting of a movie. A storyboard can serve as a visual map and is made up of a few images and brief descriptions. Choose an important scene from a novel you've recently read or any of the stories from this unit. With a partner, make a storyboard that portrays a conflict.

HERE'S HOW Use these as tips for creating your storyboard:

- Make your storyboard simple rather than beautiful. Draw or sketch the images, making sure they're easy to understand.
- Within the six separate frames, include close-ups or medium shots that reveal a character's reactions or emotions.
- Show shots that reveal a conflict. Show how at least one character reacts.
- Underneath each frame, write out a specific description or a line of dialogue.

MEDIA TOOLS
For help with creating a storyboard, visit the **Media Center** at **ClassZone.com.**

STUDENT MODEL

"Runners, take your places at the starting line!"
Medium shot of Squeaky getting ready
Close-up shot of Raymond watching
Medium shot of Squeaky running
Medium shot of Raymond running
Medium shot of squeaky winning the race

Tech Tip
Use a word processing program to type the descriptions or dialogue for the storyboard.

Assess and Reteach

Write or Discuss

Analyze Film

- To help students get started, have them free-write about what Carmen's father is likely thinking and feeling throughout this scene. For example, he could be feeling guilty about keeping his new life a secret from Carmen, anxious that she will be angry when she hears the news, and hopeful that Carmen and his fiancée will like each other.
- Once they understand the character of the father, students can figure out how they would use camera shots and music to reveal who he is and what he is feeling. For example, they might opt for more close-up shots of the father to reveal his personality and emotions. The music might sound more ominous or tense at the beginning of the scene as he prepares to tell Carmen his surprise and see her reaction.

Produce Your Own Media

Rubric A strong storyboard should have

- six drawings or sketches that are simple and easy to understand
- close-ups or medium shots that reveal a character's reactions and emotions
- shots that reveal a conflict and how at least one character reacts
- a description or line of dialogue underneath each frame

RESOURCE MANAGER—Copy Master
Produce Your Own Media p. 154

Media*Smart* DVD

MEDIA STUDY WRAP-UP

Summarize Ask students to summarize the techniques directors use to introduce their characters, reveal conflict, and get viewers emotionally involved. Encourage them to refer to specific examples from the clip from *The Sisterhood of the Traveling Pants.* If necessary, guide them to discuss the most important elements of the clip. For example, mention the background music, the use of blocking, and Carmen's facial expressions and body language as she talks to her father and meets her father's new family.

RETEACH

STANDARDS LESSON FILE
Media Lesson 1: Active Viewing Strategies
Media Lesson 4: Analyzing Visuals in Film and TV
Media Lesson 7: Evaluating Films and TV Shows

Focus and Motivate

OBJECTIVES

Literary Analysis
- explore the key idea of **leaving**
- analyze characteristics of a memoir
- read a memoir

Reading
- analyze cause-and-effect relationships

Vocabulary
- build vocabulary for reading and writing
- use structural analysis to identify word roots and affixes *(also an EL language objective)*
- determine meaning of derivatives by applying knowledge of the Latin root *dict (also an EL language objective)*

SUMMARY

Tired of attending summer school, Alvarez works hard in fifth grade and finally gets her "first free summer." She is not able to enjoy it, however, as the political situation in her homeland, the Dominican Republic, is rapidly deteriorating. The safety of Alvarez's family is threatened, and they flee to the United States.

When is it time to
LEAVE?

Discuss the question. To lead into the ***KEY IDEA,*** ask students if they have ever felt torn about **leaving** a particular place. As pairs work on the ***QUICKWRITE*** activity, have them also explore this question: After you left, were your worries confirmed, or did they turn out to be unwarranted?

Before Reading

My First Free Summer

Memoir by Julia Alvarez

When is it time to
LEAVE?

KEY IDEA Even under the best of circumstances, **leaving** someone or something behind can be difficult. Familiar people and places often provide us with a sense of safety and security. In the memoir you are about to read, Julia Alvarez faces the pain of leaving her homeland, even as she realizes the dangers of staying.

QUICKWRITE Reflect on times when you have had to leave a special person or place. Choose one experience and write a journal entry that explores your feelings about leaving. Were you looking forward to moving on? What were you worried about?

110

Selection Resources

RESOURCE MANAGER UNIT 1

Plan and Teach pp. 155–162

Literary Analysis
Summary pp. 163†*, 164‡*
Memoir pp. 165, 166†*
Question Support p. 173*

Reading
Cause and Effect pp. 167, 168†*
Reading Check p. 172
Reading Fluency p. 174

Vocabulary
Study p. 169*
Practice p. 170
Strategy p. 171

Assessment
Selection Tests A, B/C pp. 175*, 177*
Test Generator CD

BEST PRACTICES TOOLKIT
Differentiated Instruction pp. 31–38*
Scaffolding Instruction pp. 43–46*

Graphic Organizers/Strategies
New Word Analysis • Setting Diagram

Reading Support
Audio Anthology CD*

Technology
Literature and Vocabulary Centers at **ClassZone.com**
Write*Smart* CD

* Resources for Differentiation † Also in Spanish ‡ In Haitian Creole and Vietnamese

TERARY ANALYSIS: MEMOIR

A **memoir** is a form of autobiographical writing in which a writer describes important events in his or her life. Most memoirs

- use the first-person point of view
- are true accounts of actual events
- describe conflicts faced by the writer
- include the writer's feelings about historical events or social issues

As you read "My First Free Summer," look for places where Julia Alvarez shares her feelings about the historical events taking place in the Dominican Republic.

EADING SKILL: CAUSE AND EFFECT

Events are often related by **cause and effect,** which means that one event brings about the other. The first event is the **cause,** and what follows is the **effect.** Sometimes, one cause can have many effects. Recognizing cause and effect relationships can help you understand important turning points, because you'll be aware of the consequences of events and actions.

As you read, look for the effects that the political struggle in Alvarez's homeland had on her life. Use a chart like the one shown to help you keep track of these effects.

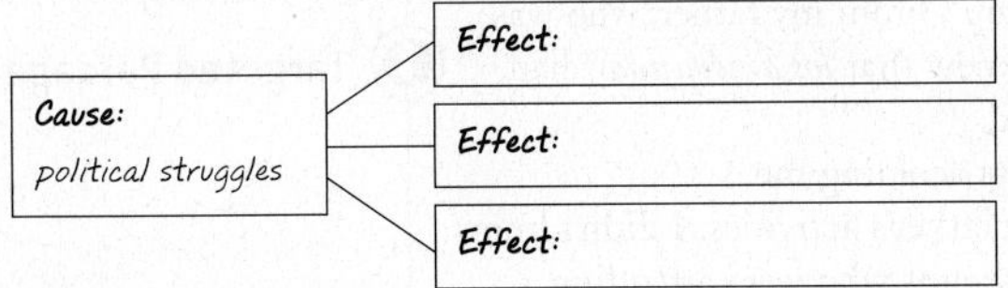

OCABULARY IN CONTEXT

Alvarez uses the vocabulary words to help describe a traumatic childhood experience. See how many you know. Make a chart like the one shown. Put each word in the appropriate column.

WORD LIST			
	contradiction	replete	unravel
	interrogation	summon	

Know Well	Think I Know	Don't Know at All

Author Online

Where Is Home? Julia Alvarez emigrated from the Dominican Republic to the United States when she was ten. Her father had taken part in an underground plot against dictator Rafael Trujillo (rä-fä'yəl' trōō-hē'yō), so the family's safety was in jeopardy. Although Alvarez and her family escaped, she found it difficult being cut off from her homeland and adjusting to a new country. Books offered Alvarez a world where she did not feel alone. Through writing, she could begin to connect her two cultures. She likes to quote another poet in saying, "Language is the only homeland."

Julia Alvarez
born 1950

A Poet First Poetry first drew Alvarez to writing. After receiving degrees in literature and writing, she spent 13 years teaching poetry at several universities. *Homecoming,* a book of her poems, was published in 1984. Since then, Alvarez has gone on to write in a variety of genres, including fiction for both children and adults.

Background

A Brutal Dictator The people of the Dominican Republic suffered under the brutal dictatorship of Rafael Trujillo and his supporters for 31 years (from 1930–1961). Under his rule, masses of people were slaughtered for "crimes" as minor as not hanging his portrait in their homes. Many brave Dominicans, including Alvarez's father, tried to overthrow this government. Those caught faced terrible consequences.

MORE ABOUT THE AUTHOR AND BACKGROUND
To learn more about Julia Alvarez and the Dominican Republic, visit the **Literature Center** at **ClassZone.com.**

Teach

STANDARDS FOCUS

LITERARY ANALYSIS

● MEMOIR

Read the following sentence aloud:

My family was lucky to get out of New Orleans before Hurricane Katrina hit.

What indicates that this sentence is from a memoir? ***Possible answer:*** *It is a first-person account of an actual event.*

CHECK UNDERSTANDING Have students discuss the features of another memoir they have read.

READING SKILL

■ CAUSE AND EFFECT

Have students identify the following as the cause or effect of a cold or flu:

- a sick person infecting you *(cause)*
- missing school *(effect)*
- being tired *(effect)*

CHECK UNDERSTANDING Ask students to make two cause-and-effect statements based on the **Author Online** information.

 RESOURCE MANAGER—Copy Master
Cause and Effect p. 167 (for student use while reading the selection)

VOCABULARY SKILL

▲ VOCABULARY IN CONTEXT

DIAGNOSE WORD KNOWLEDGE To determine preteaching needs, have all students complete **Vocabulary in Context.** As they read, students should check their understanding against the definitions on pages 114–115.

PRETEACH VOCABULARY Use the Vocabulary Study copy master to help students predict meanings for the words.

1. Read item 1 aloud, emphasizing the bold-faced word *contradiction.*
2. Point out the words *opponent's* and *disagree.* Elicit possible meanings for *contradiction,* such as "a different idea or opinion."
3. Have students record their predictions.
4. Repeat the procedure for items 2–5.

 RESOURCE MANAGER—Copy Master
Vocabulary Study p. 169

For general guidelines on differentiating vocabulary instruction and for alternative vocabulary activities for students not needing vocabulary preteaching, see

BEST PRACTICES TOOLKIT
Scaffolding Vocabulary Instruction pp. 43–46

Vocabulary Center at **ClassZone.com**
Additional Vocabulary Activities

Practice and Apply

ANALYZE VISUALS

Possible answer: *The girl is wearing a fancy dress and has elegant posture, but her expression is sad or wistful. Through the nearby window, a beach and ocean are visible. Perhaps the girl wishes she could put on casual clothing and play on the beach.*

About the Art In *The Stillness of an Afternoon*, by artist Bo Bartlett (born 1955), the girl in the painting, like young Alvarez, seems to be waiting for something exciting in a dull, colorless room.

Lines 5–7
DISCUSSION PROMPTS

Use these prompts to help students understand the cause of several events described in the memoir:

Infer In what way might the other students at the school be different from Alvarez? ***Possible answer:*** *They are probably the children of Americans and already know English.*

Evaluate Why will knowing English help Alvarez? ***Possible answer:*** *If the island is liberated, she will be able to take advantage of special educational and work opportunities.*

READING SKILL

A CAUSE AND EFFECT

Have students record their answers in the chart from page 111. ***Possible answer:*** *She has to attend the American school while her friends get many holidays to "honor" the dictator.*

My First Free Summer

JULIA ALVAREZ

I never had summer—I had summer school. First grade, summer school. Second grade, summer school. Thirdgradesummerschoolfourthgradesummerschool. In fifth grade, I vowed I would get interested in fractions, the presidents of the United States, Mesopotamia; I would learn my English.

That was the problem. English. My mother had decided to send her children to the American school so we could learn the language of the nation that would soon be liberating us. For thirty years, the Dominican Republic had endured a bloody and repressive dictatorship.[1] From my father, who was involved in an underground plot, my mother knew that *los américanos*[2] had promised to help bring democracy to the island.

"You have to learn your English!" Mami kept scolding me.

"But why?" I'd ask. I didn't know about my father's activities. I didn't know the dictator was bad. All I knew was that my friends who were attending Dominican schools were often on holiday to honor the dictator's birthday, the dictator's saint day, the day the dictator became the dictator, the day the dictator's oldest son was born, and so on. They marched in parades and visited the palace and had their picture in the paper.

Meanwhile, I had to learn about the pilgrims with their funny witch hats, about the 50 states and where they were on the map, about Dick and Jane[3] and their tame little pets, Puff and Spot, about freedom and liberty and justice for all—while being imprisoned in a hot classroom with a picture of a man wearing a silly wig hanging above the blackboard. And all of this learning I had to do in that impossibly difficult, rocks-in-your-mouth language of English! **A**

ANALYZE VISUALS
Look at the girl's expression, posture, and clothing, as well as the window she leans near. What do these **details** suggest about her situation?

1 Targeted Passage

A CAUSE AND EFFECT
What effect does Mr. Alvarez's political involvement have on Julia's life? Include this in your chart.

1. **dictatorship** (dĭk-tā′tər-shĭp′): a government under an absolute ruler, or dictator.
2. ***los américanos*** (lōs ə-mĕr′ĭ-kä′nōs) *Spanish:* the Americans.
3. **Dick and Jane:** characters in a children's reading textbook.

Detail of *The Stillness of an Afternoon* (2003) Bo Bartlett. Oil on panel, 18½″ × 21″. Courtesy of the artist and P.P.O.W. Gallery, New York

DIFFERENTIATED INSTRUCTION

FOR ALL STUDENTS

Anchor Activity Provide opportunities for independent learning about the nature of dictatorships. Have groups research various leaders of Caribbean nations, describe their rise to power, and evaluate their leadership. For further details on this project, see

RESOURCE MANAGER
Ideas for Extension pp. 160–161

FOR LESS-PROFICIENT READERS

In combination with the *Audio Anthology CD*, use one or more Targeted Passages (pp. 112, 114, 115) to ensure that students focus on key selection events, concepts, and skills.

1 Targeted Passage [Lines 1–17]
This passage introduces Alvarez and describes the conflicts she and her family are facing.

- Where does Alvarez live?
- What kind of school does she attend?
- What does she have trouble learning?
- Who rules the Dominican Republic?
- How is Alvarez's experience different from that of her friends?

BACKGROUND

Trujillo and the Dominican Republic The dictator Rafael Trujillo promoted economic development, but those who most benefited from improvements were members of his family and his supporters. Most Dominicans remained impoverished, even as they watched Trujillo amass a great fortune. The U.S. government did not interfere with his regime, in spite of human rights abuses, because it was concerned about the Castro regime and believed that Trujillo could be a strong anti-Communist force in the Caribbean.

In the late 1950s, both Cuba and Venezuela supported plots against Trujillo. In response, Trujillo was complicit in an assassination attempt on the life of Venezuela's president, Romulo Betancourt. Trujillo was assassinated in 1961, and his family was forced into exile.

In 1965, U.S. President Lyndon Johnson sent military forces to the Dominican Republic to establish order after a military coup. In 1966, the United States organized elections there.

CULTURAL CONNECTION

Dominicans in the United States Although some Dominicans resented American interference, many admired the United States. Today, more than 650,000 Dominicans live in the United States.

FOR ENGLISH LEARNERS

Culture: Clarify Lines 18–22 refer to items found in some American classrooms. Explain that the phrase *pilgrims with their funny witch hats* refers to early settlers in what is now the United States, and that the *man wearing a silly wig* is George Washington, the first president of the United States. Encourage students from other countries to discuss symbols and pictures displayed in those countries' classrooms.

Key Academic Vocabulary Have students use New Word Analysis to study this academic vocabulary: *involve* (line 9), *prospect* (line 24), *principal* (lines 25, 27), *circumstance* (line 33), *attitude* (line 49), *schedule* (line 81).

BEST PRACTICES TOOLKIT—Transparency
New Word Analysis p. E8

Prereading For prereading instruction for English learners, see

BEST PRACTICES TOOLKIT
Scaffolding Reading Instruction pp. 43–46

FOR ADVANCED LEARNERS/PRE-AP

Pre-AP exercises in the bottom channel provide additional challenge for your advanced students. Use them for small groups or individuals.

ADDITIONAL GUIDELINES

For more help with differentiation and tips for classroom management, see

BEST PRACTICES TOOLKIT
Differentiated Instruction pp. 31–38

SOCIAL STUDIES CONNECTION

Trujillo's regime was marked by severe repression of human rights. He often ordered the murder of opponents, and in 1937 he was responsible for the massacre of approximately 20,000 Haitian immigrants in retaliation for the execution of Dominican spies in Haiti. During the 1950s, Trujillo's secret police tortured and jailed many Dominicans. They monitored opponents of the regime, both at home and abroad. To bolster his power, Trujillo also used the secret police to bribe members of the business community, control the press, and create a climate of fear among Dominicans.

LITERARY ANALYSIS

B MEMOIR

Possible answer: *Freedom means not having to go to summer school, as well as running and playing on the beach with her cousins.*

Extend the Discussion What does Alvarez mean when she writes, "Maybe American principles had finally sunk in"?

READING SKILL

C CAUSE AND EFFECT

Have students record their answers in the chart from page 111. ***Possible answer:*** *Because the political situation is tense, most of her friends and cousins have fled to the United States. There is no one to play with.*

Somehow, I managed to scrape by. Every June, when my prospects looked iffy, Mami and I met with the principal. I squirmed in my seat while they arranged for my special summer lessons.

"She is going to work extra hard. Aren't you, young lady?" the principal would quiz me at the end of our session.

My mother's eye on me, I'd murmur, "Yeah."

"Yes, what?" Mami coached.

"Yes." I sighed. "Sir."

It's a wonder that I just wasn't thrown out, which was what I secretly hoped for. But there were extenuating circumstances,[4] the grounds on which the American school stood had been donated by my grandfather. In fact, it had been my grandmother who had encouraged Carol Morgan to start her school. The bulk of the student body was made up of the sons and daughters of American diplomats and business people, but a few Dominicans—most of them friends or members of my family—were allowed to attend.

"You should be grateful!" Mami scolded on the way home from our meeting. "Not every girl is lucky enough to go to the Carol Morgan School!"

In fifth grade, I straightened out. "Yes, ma'am!" I learned to say brightly. "Yes, sir!" To wave my hand in sword-wielding swoops so I could get called on with the right answer. What had changed me? Gratitude? A realization of my luckiness? No, sir! The thought of a fun summer? Yes, ma'am! I wanted to run with the pack of cousins and friends in the common yard that connected all our properties. To play on the trampoline and go off to *la playa*[5] and get brown as a berry. I wanted to be free. Maybe American principles had finally sunk in! B

The summer of 1960 began in bliss: I did not have to go to summer school! *Attitude much improved. Her English progressing nicely. Attentive and cooperative in classroom.* I grinned as Mami read off the note that accompanied my report card of Bs.

But the yard **replete** with cousins and friends that I had dreamed about all year was deserted. Family members were leaving for the United States, using whatever connections they could drum up. The plot had **unraveled.** Every day there were massive arrests. The United States had closed its embassy and was advising Americans to return home.

My own parents were terrified. Every night black Volkswagens blocked our driveway and stayed there until morning. "Secret police," my older sister whispered.

"Why are they secret if they're the police?" I asked.

"Shut up!" my sister hissed. "Do you want to get us all killed?"

Day after day, I kicked a deflated beach ball around the empty yard, feeling as if I'd been tricked into good behavior by whomever God put in charge of the lives of 10-year-olds. I was bored. Even summer school would have been better than this! C

4. **extenuating circumstances** (ĭk-stĕn′yo͞o-ā′tĭng sûr′kəm-stăn′səs): a situation or condition that provides an excuse for an action.
5. ***la playa*** (lä plä′yä) *Spanish:* the beach.

SOCIAL STUDIES CONNECTION

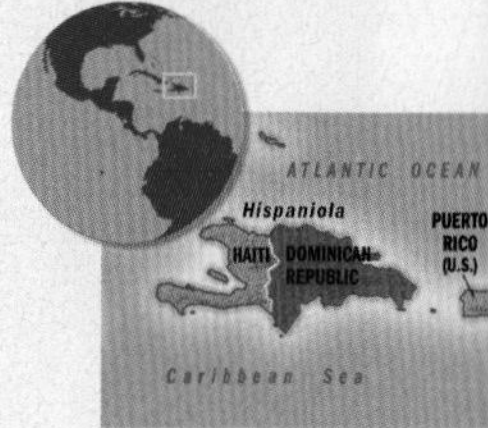

Dictator Trujillo established the SIM (Military Intelligence Service), a secret police force that spied on fellow Dominicans and engaged in torture and murder at Trujillo's request.

2 Targeted Passage

B MEMOIR What does freedom mean to Alvarez at this point in her life?

replete (rĭ-plēt′) *adj.* abundantly supplied

unravel (ŭn-răv′əl) *v.* to undo; come apart

C CAUSE AND EFFECT What's causing Alvarez to have a boring summer?

DIFFERENTIATED INSTRUCTION

FOR LESS–PROFICIENT READERS

2 Targeted Passage [Lines 41–56]

This passage describes a turning point of the memoir: the author works hard in school and avoids summer school, only to find that her playmates have fled the country.

- How does the author change in fifth grade?
- What does she expect will happen in the summer?
- Why have Americans been advised to return home?

FOR ENGLISH LEARNERS

Vocabulary: Cognates [shared-language groups] Have groups scan the selection for cognates and report their findings to the class. Spanish cognates on this page include

- *circumstance/circunstancia* (line 33)
- *school/escuela* (line 36)
- *diplomat/diplomático, -a* (line 37)
- *common/común* (line 45)
- *principle/principio* (line 47)
- *police/policía* (line 58)

One day toward the end of the summer, my mother **summoned** my sisters and me. She wore that too-bright smile she sometimes pasted on her terrified face.

"Good news, girls! Our papers and tickets came! We're leaving for the United States!"

Our mouths dropped. We hadn't been told we were going on a trip anywhere, no less to some place so far away.

I was the first to speak up. "But why?"

My mother flashed me the same look she used to give me when I'd ask why I had to learn English.

I was about to tell her that I didn't want to go to the United States, where summer school had been invented and everyone spoke English. But my mother lifted a hand for silence. "We're leaving in a few hours. I want you all to go get ready! I'll be in to pack soon." The desperate look in her eyes did not allow for **contradiction**. We raced off, wondering how to fit the contents of our Dominican lives into four small suitcases. **D**

Our flight was scheduled for that afternoon, but the airplane did not appear. The terminal filled with soldiers, wielding machine guns, checking papers, escorting passengers into a small **interrogation** room. Not everyone returned.

"It's a trap," I heard my mother whisper to my father.

This had happened before, a cat-and-mouse game[6] the dictator liked to play. Pretend that he was letting someone go, and then at the last minute, their family and friends conveniently gathered together—wham! The secret police would haul the whole clan away.

Of course, I didn't know that this was what my parents were dreading. But as the hours ticked away, and afternoon turned into evening and evening into night and night into midnight with no plane in sight, a light came on in my head. If the light could be translated into words, instead, they would say: Freedom and liberty and justice for all . . . I knew that ours was not a trip, but an escape. We had to get to the United States. **E**

The rest of that night is a blur. It is one, then two the next morning. A plane lands, lights flashing. We are walking on the runway, climbing up the stairs into the cabin. An American lady wearing a cap welcomes us. We sit down, ready to depart. But suddenly, soldiers come on board. They go seat by seat, looking at our faces. Finally, they leave, the door closes, and with a powerful roar, we lift off and I fall asleep.

Next morning, we are standing inside a large, echoing hall as a stern American official reviews our documents. What if he doesn't let us in? What if we have to go back? I am holding my breath. My parents' terror has become mine.

He checks our faces against the passport pictures. When he is done, he asks, "You girls ready for school?" I swear he is looking at me.

"Yes, sir!" I speak up.

The man laughs. He stamps our papers and hands them to my father. Then, wonderfully, a smile spreads across his face. "Welcome to the United States," he says, waving us in. ~

summon (sŭm'ən) *v.* to send for; call

contradiction (kŏn'trə-dĭk'shən) *n.* a denial; an expression that is opposite to

D CAUSE AND EFFECT Why is Alvarez's family leaving for the United States on such short notice? Mark this in your chart.

interrogation (ĭn-tĕr'ə-gā'shən) *n.* an official or formal questioning

3 Targeted Passage

E MEMOIR Reread lines 89–94. What changes have occurred in Alvarez's thinking about the Dominican Republic and the United States?

6. **cat-and-mouse game:** cruel, playful game to torment another.

REINFORCE *KEY IDEA:* LEAVING

Discuss Will Alvarez regret **leaving** the Dominican Republic? Explain. ***Possible answer:*** *She might miss some things, but she will probably be relieved to be safe with her family.*

READING SKILL

D CAUSE AND EFFECT

Have students record answers in their charts. ***Possible answer:*** *The government could arrest them if they stayed.*

LITERARY ANALYSIS

E MEMOIR

Possible answer: *After witnessing the events at the airport and on the plane, Alvarez realizes how dangerous her homeland is. The United States represents safety and freedom.*

SELECTION WRAP-UP

REFLECT Which of Alvarez's thoughts and feelings helped you identify with her most strongly?

★ CRITIQUE Were the cause-and-effect relationships between events in the memoir clear? Explain.

READING FLUENCY

Distribute the copy masters and have students practice fluency.

R RESOURCE MANAGER—Copy Master
Reading Fluency p. 174

FOR LESS-PROFICIENT READERS

3 Targeted Passage [Lines 81–100]

This passage describes the suspense of the Alvarez family's escape from their homeland.

- How long does the family have to wait at the airport?
- What happens to some of the passengers in the terminal?
- What do the soldiers do? What effect do their actions have?

FOR ENGLISH LEARNERS

Comprehension: Idioms and Sayings [mixed-readiness pairs] Have students work in pairs to figure out the meanings of these and other phrases in the selection:

- *scrape by* (line 24), "just barely succeed"
- *I straightened out* (line 41), "I behaved"
- *drum up* (line 54), "find"
- *the hours ticked away* (line 90), "time passed slowly"
- *a light came on* (line 91), "I got an idea"

FOR ADVANCED LEARNERS/PRE-AP

Synthesize [paired option] Have students work with a partner to design sets for a dramatization of the memoir. They can use the Setting Diagram to gather and organize their ideas.

BEST PRACTICES TOOLKIT—Transparency
Setting Diagram p. D14

Practice and Apply

After Reading

For additional support of postreading questions, use these copy masters:

RESOURCE MANAGER—Copy Masters
Reading Check p. 172 (to check understanding of the selection)
Memoir p. 165 (for practice of literary analysis standards focus)
Question Support p. 173 (After Reading questions adapted for English learners and less-proficient readers)

Additional selection questions are provided for teachers on page 159.

After Reading

Comprehension

1. **Recall** Why was Alvarez allowed to attend the American school?
2. **Clarify** What happened at the airport as the Alvarez family waited for the plane?

Literary Analysis

3. **Interpret Memoir** What do you think the title of the memoir means? Consider the possible meanings of the word "free." Cite evidence from the selection to support your interpretation.
4. **Analyze Personality Traits** Choose three words or phrases to describe Alvarez as a child. Include them in a web like the one shown. Expand the web by providing specific examples from the memoir that support each description.

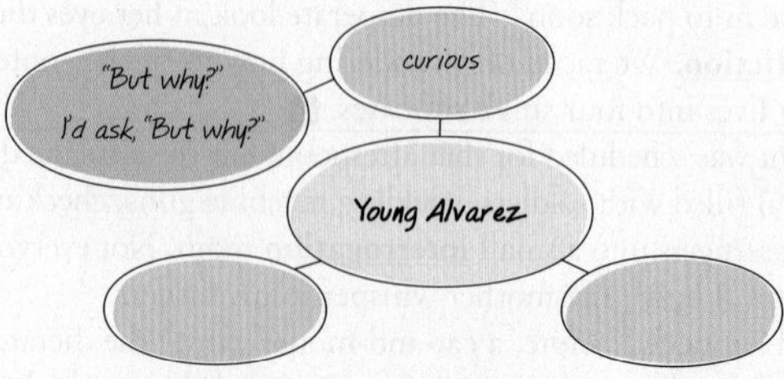

5. **Analyze Perspective** Although the events depicted in the memoir take place when Alvarez was a child, she writes about the experience many years later. Find at least two examples from the selection that show her adult perspective, or view on the topic. What does she know as an adult that she didn't know at the time?
6. **Generalize About Cause and Effect** Review the chart you created as you read. On the basis of the information you collected, make a general statement about how politics can affect one's personal life.
7. **Draw Conclusions** Why do Alvarez's feelings about **leaving** her homeland change by the end of the memoir?

Extension and Challenge

8. **SOCIAL STUDIES CONNECTION** Research one of the following topics to find out more about the Dominican Republic during Trujillo's rule. Present your findings in a poster.
   - The 14th of June Movement
   - "The Butterflies"
   - Trujillo's assassination

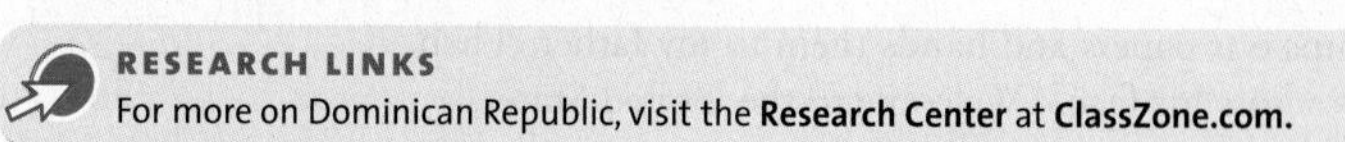
RESEARCH LINKS
For more on Dominican Republic, visit the **Research Center** at **ClassZone.com.**

ANSWERS

Comprehension

1. *Her grandfather donated land for the American school.*
2. *Soldiers took people into an interrogation room. Some returned, but others didn't.*

Literary Analysis

Possible answers:

3. **STANDARDS FOCUS Memoir** *The title has a double meaning. "My First Free Summer" refers both to Alvarez's first summer away from school and to her first summer free from the tyranny of Trujillo.*
4. *Examples of character traits could include the following: funny ("imprisoned in a hot classroom with a picture of a man wearing a silly wig"); curious ("'But why?' I'd ask."); intelligent ("a light came on in my head")*
5. *Alvarez reminds her readers that at the time she did not know about the political struggles taking place. Examples include "I didn't know about my father's activities. I didn't know the dictator was bad" (lines 12–13) and "Of course, I didn't know that this was what my parents were dreading" (line 89).*
6. **STANDARDS FOCUS Cause and Effect** *Students should refer to their charts for ideas about how politics can affect an individual's life.*
7. *Once she realizes how dangerous it would be to stay in the Dominican Republic, she is less scared about leaving and instead worried that she won't be allowed to stay in the United States.*

Extension and Challenge

8. **SOCIAL STUDIES CONNECTION** *Have students display their posters, and then lead a discussion about what life was like in the Dominican Republic during Trujillo's rule. Ask them to imagine what their daily lives would have been like.*

ocabulary in Context

OCABULARY PRACTICE

Choose the word from the list that is the best substitute for each boldfaced word or phrase.

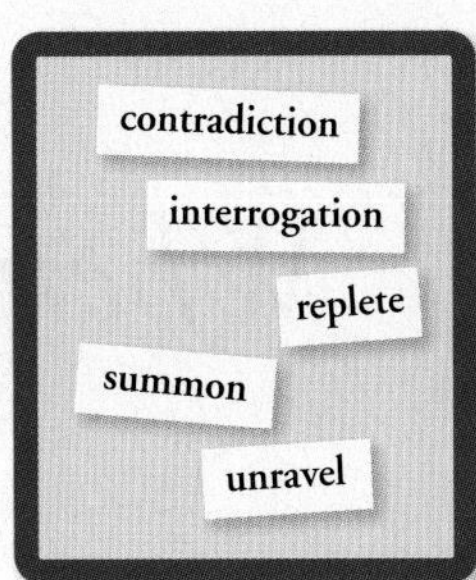

1. Julia had hoped her summer would be **filled** with free time and fun.
2. Her plans for a carefree summer were soon to **come apart.**
3. When Julia's mother spoke, there was no room for **disagreement.**
4. Officials started to **call** the passengers for questioning.
5. The **questioning** took place in a small room.

OCABULARY IN WRITING

Write a paragraph explaining the challenges that Julia and her family faced in the summer of 1960. Use at least two vocabulary words. You might begin this way.

EXAMPLE SENTENCE

*When events started to **unravel**, Julia's family had to leave the country.*

OCABULARY STRATEGY: THE LATIN ROOT *dict*

The vocabulary word *contradiction* contains the Latin root *dict* (also spelled *dic*), which means "say" or "speak." Your understanding of this root can help you to figure out the meaning of other words formed from *dict.*

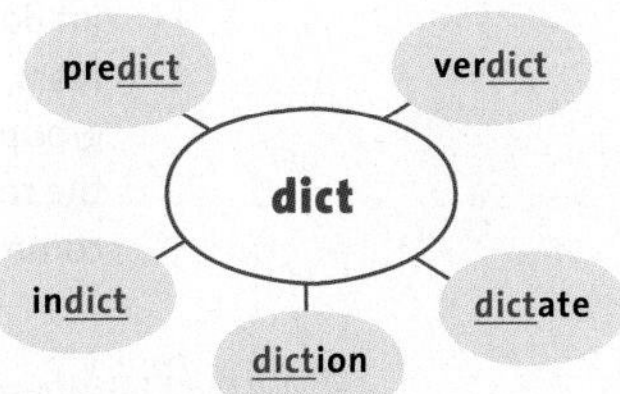

PRACTICE Look up each word that appears in the web. Then decide which word best completes each sentence. Be ready to explain how the meaning of the root is reflected in each word.

1. The jury stated its findings by announcing the ______.
2. To say that someone has done something wrong is to _____ him.
3. The ruler with absolute power will ____ the laws of the land.
4. Were you able to _____, or tell in advance, what would happen?
5. Her precise way of speaking showed that she had wonderful _____.

VOCABULARY PRACTICE
For more practice, go to the **Vocabulary Center** at **ClassZone.com.**

ANSWERS

Vocabulary in Context

VOCABULARY PRACTICE

1. *replete*
2. *unravel*
3. *contradiction*
4. *summon*
5. *interrogation*

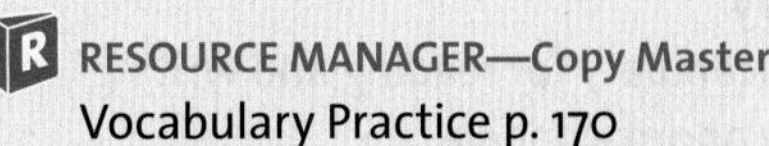

RESOURCE MANAGER—Copy Master
Vocabulary Practice p. 170

VOCABULARY IN WRITING

Have students review the memoir and pay attention to the way the vocabulary words are used. Challenge the students to mention the main events in the memoir and to use all the vocabulary words in their paragraphs.

VOCABULARY STRATEGY: THE LATIN ROOT *dict* *(also an EL language objective)*

Point out that English words with the Latin root *dict* do not all have to do with speaking aloud. The root has a broader meaning that involves communicating ideas, decisions, and commands.

Answers:

1. *verdict*
2. *indict*
3. *dictate*
4. *predict*
5. *diction*

RESOURCE MANAGER—Copy Master
Vocabulary Strategy p. 171

Vocabulary Center at **ClassZone.com**
Additional Vocabulary Activities

DIFFERENTIATED INSTRUCTION

FOR ENGLISH LEARNERS

Vocabulary Practice Make sure students know how to pronounce the vocabulary words in the lesson. Point out that English—unlike some other languages—has few rules for stressing syllables, and that students can find pronunciation information in a dictionary. Review how to interpret stress marks in a dictionary.

FOR ADVANCED LEARNERS/PRE–AP

Vocabulary Strategy Have students brainstorm current events that they find interesting or controversial. Challenge them to use all the words in the web in a paragraph about these events.

Assess and Reteach

Assess

RESOURCE MANAGER—Copy Masters
Selection Tests A, B/C pp. 175–176, 177–178

Test Generator CD

Reteach

STANDARDS LESSON FILE
Reading Lesson 7: Recognizing Cause and Effect
Vocabulary Lesson 10: Latin Roots

Focus and Motivate

OBJECTIVES

Literary Analysis
- explore the key idea of being **scared**
- identify and analyze conflicts and resolutions in nonfiction
- read a memoir

Reading
- trace chronological order

Vocabulary
- build vocabulary for reading and writing
- identify onomatopoeia

Grammar and Writing
- use correct pronoun case
- use writing to analyze literature

SUMMARY

Because of his asthma, the young Laurence Yep isn't able to play sports with his father and brother. Yep believes he is therefore a disappointment to his father. An encounter with a rat in the family's apartment, however, sparks a revealing conversation between Yep and his father. Yep learns that his father had to overcome fear and hardship as a new immigrant from China. He also learns that his value is not determined by his athletic ability.

When is it OK to be SCARED?

Discuss the question. To lead into the ***KEY IDEA,*** ask students to think about some common things that make people **scared.** Why is it difficult to admit being scared? Then have students conduct the ***SURVEY.***

Before Reading

The Great Rat Hunt

Memoir by Laurence Yep

When is it OK to be SCARED?

KEY IDEA A spider. A roller coaster. A hurricane. We're all **scared** of something. Even so, it can be hard to admit to being afraid. If your friends think it's fun to jump off the high dive, you might not want them to know that heights frighten you. In the selection you are about to read, Laurence Yep tells about a time he tried to overcome his fear in order to impress his father.

SURVEY What scares you and your classmates? Find out by conducting an informal survey. On your own, jot down three or four of your fears. Then meet with a small group, combine your lists, and tally the results. Which fears are most common? Which surprised you?

What Scares You?

Fears	*Number of People*
1. Heights	*////*
2. Thunder	*//*
3. The dark	*///*
4.	

118

Selection Resources

RESOURCE MANAGER UNIT 1

Plan and Teach pp. 179–186

Literary Analysis
Summary pp. 187†*, 188‡*
Conflict in Nonfiction pp. 189, 190†*
Question Support p. 197*

Reading
Chronological Order pp. 191, 192†*
Reading Check p. 196
Reading Fluency p. 199

Vocabulary
Study p. 193*
Practice p. 194
Strategy p. 195

Grammar and Writing
Use Correct Pronoun Case p. 198

Assessment
Selection Tests A, B/C pp. 201*, 203*
Test Generator CD

BEST PRACTICES TOOLKIT

Differentiated Instruction pp. 31–38*
Scaffolding Instruction pp. 43–46*

Graphic Organizers/Strategies
Word Questioning • Think-Pair-Share • Monitoring

Reading Support
Audio Anthology CD*

Technology
Literature, Vocabulary, and Writing Centers at **ClassZone.com**
Write*Smart* CD

* Resources for Differentiation † Also in Spanish ‡ In Haitian Creole and Vietnamese

Teach

ERARY ANALYSIS: CONFLICT IN NONFICTION

In the memoir you're about to read, Laurence Yep relates an event from his childhood. To tell this real-life story, he uses some of the same literary elements that appear in his award-winning fiction. For example, the narrative centers around **conflicts,** or struggles between opposing forces. As you read "The Great Rat Hunt," identify the conflicts the young Laurence Yep faces.

ADING SKILL: CHRONOLOGICAL ORDER

Memoirs are often organized in **chronological order,** which means that events are presented in the order in which they happened. To make sure you know when each event occurs, follow these steps:

- Identify individual events taking place.
- Look for words and phrases that signal order, such as *before, after, first, next, then, while, the next day,* or *an hour and a half later.*

As you read "The Great Rat Hunt," keep track of the chronology. In a chart like the one shown, record key events in order, using parallel boxes when two actions occur at the same time.

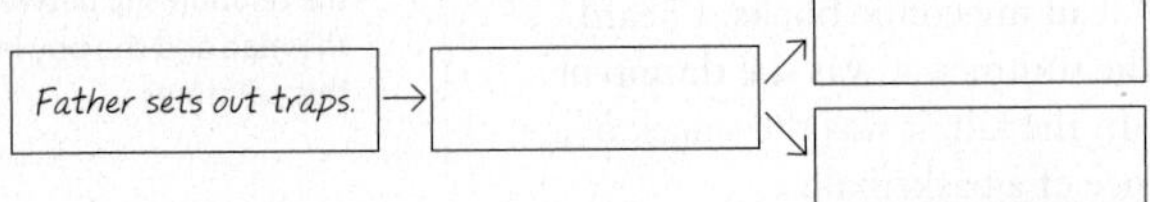

OCABULARY IN CONTEXT

The boldfaced words help Laurence Yep relate a story from his childhood. To see how many you know, substitute a different word or phrase for each one.

1. **barricade** the doorway
2. **rationalize** a bad habit
3. **wince** in pain
4. **perpetual** motion
5. an **improvised** comedy skit
6. known for his quiet **reserve**
7. **vigilant** watchdog
8. the **ravage** caused by the flood
9. embarrassed by my **ineptitude**
10. spoken to me **brusquely**

Author Online

A Man of Accomplishment

Laurence Yep
born 1948

Laurence Yep has said that he approaches American culture as "somewhat of a stranger." Born in San Francisco, California, Yep was always surrounded by people of various backgrounds, none quite like his own. He was raised in an African-American community and commuted to a bilingual school in Chinatown. There, his classmates teased him for not knowing Chinese. Yep began submitting his work to magazines when a high school English teacher made publishing a story a requirement for getting an A in the class. He became a published author at 18 and went on to publish dozens of stories, as well as earning a college degree and a PhD. Many of the main conflicts in his works involve feeling like an outsider.

A Father's Pride Yep's writing has gained him numerous awards, including more than ten for his book *Dragonwings*—a book that, like many of his more recent works, explores Chinese mythology. Yep's success as a writer greatly pleased his father, who displayed his son's writing medals and plaques "in lieu of athletic accomplishments."

MORE ABOUT THE AUTHOR
For more on Laurence Yep, visit the **Literature Center** at **ClassZone.com.**

STANDARDS FOCUS

LITERARY ANALYSIS

● CONFLICT IN NONFICTION

Ask students to read **A Man of Accomplishment** on page 119. Then ask them to identify some of the conflicts Yep faced while growing up. ***Possible answer:*** *Yep felt like a stranger among people with different backgrounds; classmates teased him for not knowing Chinese.*

CHECK UNDERSTANDING Ask students to identify examples of conflict in their community or in the world.

READING SKILL

■ CHRONOLOGICAL ORDER

Write this example on the board:

> Amir came to America when he was ten. While living in Chicago, he learned English and made many new friends. During his senior year, he developed a love for food. He is now a chef in a five-star restaurant.

Ask: What words show chronological order? ***Answer:*** *when, while, during, now*

CHECK UNDERSTANDING Ask students to use chronological order and words such as *later* and *next* to summarize a scene from their favorite TV show or movie.

RESOURCE MANAGER—Copy Master
Chronological Order p. 191 (for student use while reading the memoir)

VOCABULARY SKILL

▲ VOCABULARY IN CONTEXT

DIAGNOSE WORD KNOWLEDGE To determine preteaching needs, have all students complete **Vocabulary in Context.** ***Possible answers:*** **1.** *block* **2.** *make excuses for* **3.** *flinch* **4.** *constant* **5.** *to put together without planning* **6.** *self-restraint* **7.** *alert* **8.** *damage* **9.** *lack of ability* **10.** *abrupt*

PRETEACH VOCABULARY Use the Vocabulary Study copy master to help students use context clues to predict word meanings.

1. Read aloud the first pair of sentences in Part A, emphasizing *barricade.*
2. Point out the context clues *tall* and *couldn't get past.* Elicit possible meanings for *barricade,* such as "wall."
3. Repeat the procedure for items 2–10.
4. Have students do Part B independently.

RESOURCE MANAGER—Copy Master
Vocabulary Study p. 193

For general guidelines on differentiating vocabulary instruction and for alternative vocabulary activities for students not needing vocabulary preteaching, see

BEST PRACTICES TOOLKIT
Scaffolding Vocabulary Instruction pp. 43–46

Vocabulary Center at **ClassZone.com**

ANALYZE VISUALS

Possible answer: *The man has his arm around the boy, which suggests they are close. The boy is pointing something out to the man, and he seems to be listening, which suggests they care about each other.*

About the Art Jan Peng Wang was born in Guangzhou, China, and moved to Canada in 1989. In his oil paintings, he uses classical figures combined with elements of everyday life to explore the conflict that exists between traditional and modern life.

LITERARY ANALYSIS

Ⓐ CONFLICT

Possible answer: *Because of his asthma, Yep can't play sports. Yep's father is athletic and often enjoys practicing with Yep's brother. Since Yep can't play, he feels there's an obstacle to a good relationship with his father and his brother.*

Extend the Discussion What is Yep's attitude toward his father's athletic accomplishments and all of his bumps and scars? How might this attitude affect the way he feels about himself?

The Great Rat Hunt

Laurence Yep

I had asthma[1] when I was young, so I never got to play sports much with my father. While my brother and father practiced, I could only sit in bed, propped up by a stack of pillows. As I read my comic books, I heard them beneath our apartment window. In the summer, it was the thump of my brother's fastball into my father's mitt. In the fall, it was the smack of a football. In the winter, it was the airy bounce of a basketball.

Though my father had come from China when he was eight, he had taken quickly to American games. When he and Mother were young, they had had the same dances and sports leagues as their white schoolmates—but kept separate in Chinatown. (He had met Mother when she tripped him during a co-ed basketball game at the Chinatown Y.)

Father was big as a teenager and good at sports. In fact, a social club in Chinatown had hired him to play football against social clubs in other Chinatowns. There he was, a boy playing against grown men.

During a game in Watsonville, a part-time butcher had broken Father's nose. It never properly healed, leaving a big bump at the bridge. There were other injuries too from baseball, basketball, and tennis. Each bump and scar on his body had its own story, and each story was matched by a trophy or medal.

Though he now ran a grocery store in San Francisco, he tried to pass on his athletic skills to my older brother Eddy and me. During the times I felt well, I tried to keep up with them, but my lungs always failed me. Ⓐ

ANALYZE VISUALS What can you **infer** abou the relationship between the man and the boy in this painting?

① **Targeted Passage**

Ⓐ **CONFLICT** How does Yep's asthma affect his relationship with his father and brother?

1. **asthma** (ăz′mə): a lung disease that at times makes breathing difficult.

Illustrations by Jan Peng Wang

DIFFERENTIATED INSTRUCTION

FOR ALL STUDENTS

Expert Groups [small-group option] Write these topics on the board and allow individuals or groups to select topics to research. Have student experts present what they learned to the class, using visuals as appropriate.

- the history of San Francisco's Chinatown
- the history of Chinese immigrants in California
- similarities and differences among Chinatowns in different U.S. cities

FOR LESS–PROFICIENT READERS

In combination with the *Audio Anthology CD*, use one or more Targeted Passages (pp. 120, 123, 127) to ensure that students focus on key selection events, concepts, and skills.

① **Targeted Passage [Lines 1–22]**

This passage introduces the selection's main conflict: Yep feels inadequate because he is not good at sports like his father and brother.

- Why is Yep in bed reading comic books?
- What details tell you that Yep's father has always been good at sports?
- What does "each story was matched by a trophy or medal" mean?

BACKGROUND

Chinese Immigrants Many Chinese immigrants came to America in the mid-1800s, often heading to California to pursue their fortunes in the Gold Rush. However, the Chinese faced discrimination and were not allowed to own land or file mining claims, making it difficult to make a living. Instead, they often did the most dangerous jobs, including building bridges and roads and constructing the transcontinental railroad. In 1882, the Chinese Exclusion Act stopped much of the Chinese immigration into the United States. Between 1882 and 1943, only diplomats, merchants, students, and their children were allowed to enter the United States.

CULTURAL CONNECTION

Chinatown By 1860, 20 percent of San Francisco's population was Chinese. After the railroads were completed, many of these Chinese immigrants formed the largest Chinese community outside of Asia in the heart of San Francisco. This neighborhood still exists today and is known as Chinatown.

Chinatown provided its residents with everything they needed—work, schools, Chinese newspapers, theater and other entertainment, and food. It gave immigrants a place to feel comfortable and safe in the strange, and often hostile, land of America.

Other U.S. cities have Chinatowns as well, including New York, Boston, Seattle, and Chicago. However, San Francisco's Chinatown is the oldest and largest Chinese-American community in the country.

FOR ENGLISH LEARNERS

Option for Reading Read the first Targeted Passage aloud. Make sure students understand the conflict, the setting, and the characters introduced in this passage. Have students read the rest of the selection silently as they listen to the *Audio Anthology CD*. Pause the CD frequently, allowing students to reflect and make predictions.

Key Academic Vocabulary Have students use Word Questioning to study this academic vocabulary from the selection: *inspect* (line 113), *adjusted* (lines 168, 200), *constructed* (line 181), *aware* (line 226).

BEST PRACTICES TOOLKIT—Transparency
Word Questioning p. E9

Prereading For prereading instruction for English learners, see

BEST PRACTICES TOOLKIT
Scaffolding Reading Instruction pp. 43–46

FOR ADVANCED LEARNERS/PRE–AP

Pre-AP exercises in the bottom channel provide additional challenge for your advanced students. Use them for small groups or individuals.

ADDITIONAL GUIDELINES

For more help with differentiation and tips for classroom management, see

BEST PRACTICES TOOLKIT
Differentiated Instruction pp. 31–38

LITERARY ANALYSIS

B CONFLICT

Possible answer: *Yep recognizes that his father sees playing American sports as a way to fit into American culture. Also, he thinks that since his brother and father share athletic ability, they have a closer relationship.*

LITERARY ANALYSIS

C CONFLICT

Possible answer: *The external conflict the family faces is trying to get rid of a rat living in their store.*

If students need help . . . Remind students that an external conflict is a struggle between a character and an outside force, such as another character or the weather. Ask students what outside force the family is struggling against (*the rat*).

READING SKILL

D CHRONOLOGICAL ORDER

Possible answer:

- *He sets mouse traps.*
- *He puts out poison pellets.*

READING SKILL

E CHRONOLOGICAL ORDER

Possible answer: *Words that show chronological order include* while *(line 53) and* the next day *(line 58). Events to be added to students' charts include*

- *Father calls the exterminator, Pete.*
- *Pete fumigates the store.*
- *Yep and his family stay the night with Aunt Nancy.*
- *The next day, they go home.*

When I had to sit down on the curb, I felt as if I had let my father down. I'd glance up anxiously when I felt his shadow over me; but he looked neither angry nor disgusted—just puzzled, as if he could not understand why my lungs were not like his.

"S-s-sorry." I panted.

"That's okay." He squatted and waved his hat, trying to fan more air at me. In the background, Eddy played catch with himself, waiting impatiently for the lessons to begin again. Ashamed, I would gasp. "Go on . . . and play."

And Father and Eddy would start once more while I watched, doomed to be positively un-American, a weakling, a **perpetual** spectator, an outsider. Worse, I felt as if Eddy were Father's only true son. B

And then came the day when the rat invaded our store. It was Eddy who first noticed it while we were restocking the store shelves. I was stacking packages of pinto beans when Eddy called me. "Hey, do you know what this is?" He waved me over to the cans of soup. On his palm lay some dark drops. "Is it candy?"

Father came out of the storeroom in the rear of our store. Over his back, he carried a huge hundred pound sack of rice. He let it thump to the floor right away. "Throw that away."

"What is it, Father?" I asked.

"Rat droppings," he said. "Go wash your hands."

"Yuck." Eddy flung the droppings down.

While Eddy washed his hands, I helped Father get rid of the evidence. Then he got some wooden traps from a shelf and we set them out.

However, the traps were for mice and not for rats. The rat must have gotten a good laugh while it stole the bait and set off the springs. C

Then Father tried poison pellets, but the rat avoided them all. It even left a souvenir right near the front door.

Father looked grim as he cleaned it up. "I'm through fooling around." D

So he called up his exterminator[2] friend, Pete Wong, the Cockroach King of Chinatown. While Pete fumigated[3] the store, we stayed with my Aunt Nancy over on Mason, where the cable cars kept me up late. They always rang their bells when they rounded the corner. Even when they weren't there, I could hear the cable rattling in its channel beneath the street. It was OK, though, because my cousin Jackie could tell stories all night.

The next day, when we went back home, Father searched around the store, sniffing suspiciously for deadly chemicals. Mother went upstairs to our apartment over the store to get our electric fan. E

She came right back down empty-handed. "I think he's moved up there. I could hear him scratching behind the living room walls."

Father stared at the ceiling as if the rat had gone too far. "Leave it to me," he said. He fished his car keys from his pocket.

perpetual (pər-pĕch'ōō-əl) *adj.* continuing without interruption

B CONFLICT
Reread lines 28–33. Why does Yep feel "un-American" and "as if Eddy were Father's only true son"?

C CONFLICT
What **external conflict** is the Yep family facing?

D CHRONOLOGICAL ORDER
Describe Father's first two attempts to catch the rat. Add them to your chart.

E CHRONOLOGICAL ORDER
Reread lines 52–60. What words make clear the order in which events occurred? Add the events to your chart.

2. **exterminator** (ĭk-stûr'mə-nā'tər): a person whose job it is to get rid of insects or rodents.
3. **fumigated** (fyōō'mĭ-gāt'd): used smoke or fumes to kill rodents or insects.

DIFFERENTIATED INSTRUCTION

FOR LESS–PROFICIENT READERS

Predict [paired option] Remind students that predicting is an effective way to focus their reading. After students have read page 122, have them take part in a Think-Pair-Share activity to predict what Father is going to do next. Have students note their predictions and check them as they read on. Encourage students to stop frequently to predict what will happen next as they read the memoir.

BEST PRACTICES TOOLKIT—Transparency
Think-Pair-Share p. A18

FOR ENGLISH LEARNERS

Culture: Clarify Explain that *cable cars* (line 54) are street cars that are pulled along a track by an underground cable. San Francisco is famous for its cable cars, which are used to climb the city's steep hills.

"Where are you going?" Mother asked.

Father, though, was a man of few words. He preferred to speak by his actions. "I'll be back soon."

An hour and a half later he returned with a rifle. He held it up for the three of us to examine. "Isn't it a beaut? Henry Loo loaned it to me." Henry Loo was a pharmacist and one of Father's fishing buddies.

Mother frowned. "You can't shoot that cannon off in my house."

"It's just a twenty-two." Father tugged a box of cartridges out of his jacket pocket. "Let's go, boys."

Mother sucked in her breath sharply. "Thomas!"

Father was surprised by Mother's objection. "They've got to learn sometime."

Mother turned to us urgently. "It means killing. Like buying Grandpop's chickens. But you'll be the ones who have to make it dead."

"It's not the same," Father argued. "We won't have to twist its neck."

Buying the chicken was a chore that everyone tried to avoid at New Year's when Mother's father insisted on it. To make sure the chicken was fresh, we had to watch the poulterer[4] kill it. And then we had to collect the coppery-smelling blood in a jar for a special dish that only Mother's father would eat. For a moment, I felt queasy.

"You're scaring the boys," Father scolded her.

Mother glanced at him over her shoulder. "They ought to know what they're getting into."

I didn't believe in killing—unless it was a bug like a cockroach. However, I felt different when I saw a real rifle—the shiny barrel, the faint smell of oil, the decorated wooden stock. I **rationalized** the hunt by telling myself I was not murdering rabbits or deer, just a mean old rat—like a furry kind of cockroach.

rationalize (răsh'ə-nə-līz') *v.* to make explanations for one's behavior

"What'll it be, boys?" Father asked.

Taking a deep breath, I nodded my head. "Yes, sir."

Father turned expectantly to Eddy and raised an eyebrow.

From next to me, though, Eddy murmured, "I think I'll help Mother." He wouldn't look at me.

2 Targeted Passage

Father seemed just as shocked as Mother and I. "Are you sure?"

Eddy drew back and mumbled miserably. "Yes, sir."

Mother gave me a quick peck on the cheek. "I expect you to still have ten toes and ten fingers when you finish."

As we left the store, I felt funny. Part of me felt triumphant. For once, it was Eddy who had failed and not me. And yet another part of me wished I were staying with him and Mother. **F**

F CONFLICT
Reread lines 88–103. Why is Yep torn between staying with his mother and going to help his father?

Father said nothing as we left the store and climbed the back stairs. As I trailed him, I thought he was silent because he was disappointed: He would rather have Eddy's help than mine.

4. **poulterer** (pōl'tər-ər): a person who sells domestic fowls, such as chickens, turkeys, ducks, or geese.

Lines 65–87

DISCUSSION PROMPTS

Use these prompts to help students understand the conversation between Yep's mother and father:

Recall What does Yep's father bring back with him? ***Answer:*** *He brings back a gun.*

Infer Why does his mother say, "You can't shoot that cannon off in my house"? ***Possible answer:*** *She doesn't want Yep's father to hurt someone accidentally while he's trying to shoot the rat.*

Analyze Why does Yep's mother mention Grandpop's chickens to her sons? ***Possible answer:*** *She wants to make sure the boys understand that Father means to use the gun to shoot the rat, and that they would be helping to kill it.*

Lines 77–87

REINFORCE *KEY IDEA:* SCARED

Discuss Why is Yep's mother **scaring** her sons? ***Possible answer:*** *Yep's mother wants to make sure the boys understand that they will be killing the rat. The passage shows that she thinks it's better for them to know what they're getting into and be scared, rather than to go into it blindly and regret their actions later.*

LITERARY ANALYSIS

F CONFLICT

Possible answer: *He feels proud of himself for helping his father and being braver than his brother, but he also yearns for the safety of staying with his mother.*

FOR LESS–PROFICIENT READERS

2 Targeted Passage [Lines 88–106]

This passage presents a turning point: Yep swallows his fear and agrees to help his father hunt the rat.

- What does Yep decide to do when his father asks for help in killing the rat?
- What does Eddy decide to do? Why is Eddy's decision significant to Yep?
- How does Yep feel as he leaves the store?
- Why does Yep think Father is disappointed?

FOR ENGLISH LEARNERS

Language: Conversational English Patterns
Point out that Father often uses short words and choppy sentences when he speaks. Explain to students that *beaut* in line 69 is short for *beauty*. When Father says, "It's just a twenty-two," he means that it's a twenty-two caliber rifle, referring to the gun's size. Encourage students to look for more examples of Father's conversational style as they read.

FOR ADVANCED LEARNERS/PRE–AP

Evaluate [small-group option] Yep believes that his father would rather have Eddy's help than his. Ask students to form small groups to discuss whether they agree with Yep's interpretation of his father's silence. Have them explain why or why not.

LITERARY ANALYSIS

G CONFLICT

***Possible answer:** Yep thinks his father is impatient with him because he doesn't catch on quickly enough.*

Extend the Discussion How do you think Yep's father sees him?

Lines 122–148
DISCUSSION PROMPTS

Use these prompts to help students understand the experiences of Yep's father when he first came to the United States:

Recall How did Yep's father learn to hunt? ***Answer:** Some of his friends in Chinatown taught him.*

Analyze What happened when Yep's father first came to America? Why? ***Possible answer:** Yep's father was beaten up by the white kids and the Chinese Americans. He was viewed as an unwelcome outsider.*

Evaluate What does Yep's father do to prove that he belongs in America? Is he successful? ***Possible answer:** He learns how to play American sports. Yes, he is successful because he says he made the boys his friends, and he's proud of his athletic accomplishments.*

READING SKILL

H CHRONOLOGICAL ORDER

***Answer:** Yep's father is loading the gun at the same time that he's talking.*

At the back door of our apartment, he paused and said **brusquely,** "Now for some rules. First, never, never aim the rifle at anyone."

I listened as attentively as I had the disastrous times he'd tried to teach me how to dribble, or catch a football, or handle a pop foul. "I won't." I nodded earnestly.

Father pulled a lever near the middle of the gun. "Next, make sure the rifle is empty." He let me inspect the breech.[5] There was nothing inside.

"Yes, sir," I said and glanced up at him to read his mood. Because Father used so few words, he always sounded a little impatient whenever he taught me a lesson. However, it was hard to tell this time if it was genuine irritation or his normal **reserve.** G

He merely grunted. "Here. Open this." And he handed me the box of cartridges.

I was so nervous that the cartridges clinked inside the box when I took it. As I fumbled at the lid, I almost felt like apologizing for not being Eddy.

Now, when I got edgy, I was the opposite of Father: I got talkier. "How did you learn how to hunt?" I asked. "From your father?"

My father rarely spoke of his father, who had died before I was born. He **winced** now as if the rat had just nipped him. "My old man? Nah. He never had the time. I learned from some of my buddies in Chinatown."[6] He held out his hand.

I passed him a cartridge. "What did you hunt? Bear?"

"We shot quail." Father carefully loaded the rifle.

I was uncomfortable with the idea of shooting the cute little birds I saw in cartoons. "You did?"

He clicked the cartridge into the rifle. "You have to be tough in this world, boy. There are going to be some times when nobody's around to help—like when I first came to America."

That was a long speech for Father. "You had your father." His mother had stayed back in China, because in those days, America would not let her accompany her husband.

"He was too busy working." Father stared back down the stairs as if each step were a year. "When I first came here, I got beaten up by the white kids. And when the white kids weren't around, there were the other Chinese kids."

I furrowed my forehead in puzzlement. I handed him another cartridge. "But they were your own kind."

He loaded the rifle steadily as I gave him the ammunition. "No, they weren't. The boys born here, they like to give a China-born a hard time. They thought I'd be easy pickings. But it was always a clean fight. No knives. No guns. Just our feet and fists. Not like the punks nowadays." He snapped the last cartridge into the rifle. "Then I learned how to play their games, and I made them my friends." He said the last part with pride. H

brusquely (brŭsk'lē) *a*… in an abrupt, sudden manner

reserve (rĭ-zûrv') *n.* sel… restraint in the way one looks or acts

G CONFLICT
How does Yep think his father sees him?

wince (wĭns) *v.* to flinch or shrink in pain or distress

H CHRONOLOGICAL ORDER
What action is taking place at the same time the father is talking abo… his past?

5. **breech:** the part of a gun behind the barrel.
6. **Chinatown:** the name given to some neighborhoods in which there is a large Chinese population with prominent Chinese cultural influence.

DIFFERENTIATED INSTRUCTION

FOR LESS–PROFICIENT READERS

Reading Skill Follow-Up: Chronological Order [paired option] Have students work in pairs to read page 124 and update their charts, introduced on page 119. Remind students to identify the individual events that are taking place and to look for words and phrases that signal order.

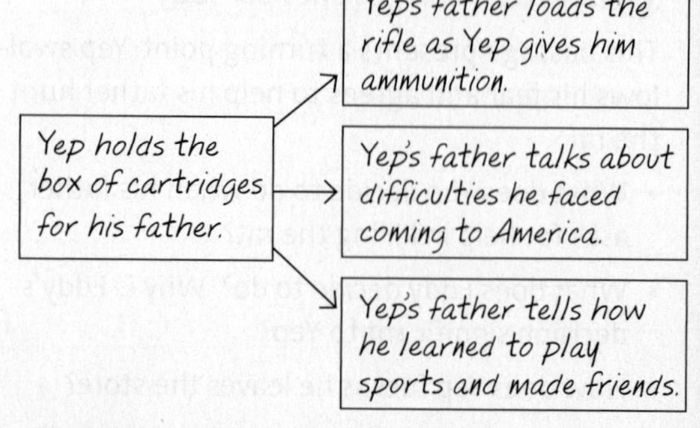
Yep holds the box of cartridges for his father.
Yep's father loads the rifle as Yep gives him ammunition.
Yep's father talks about difficulties he faced coming to America.
Yep's father tells how he learned to play sports and made friends.

And suddenly I began to understand all the trophies and medals in our living room. They were more than awards for sports. Each prize was a sign that my father belonged to America—and at the same time, to Chinatown. And that was why he tried so hard now to teach sports to Eddy and me.

When I finally understood what sports really meant to my father, it only magnified the scale of my **ineptitude.** "I'm not good at fighting." As I closed the lid on the box of ammunition, I thought I ought to prepare him for future disappointments. "I'm not much good at anything."

Careful to keep the rifle pointed away from me, Father unlocked the door. "I said you have to be tough, not stupid. No reason to get a beat-up old mug[7] like mine."

I shook my head, bewildered. "What's wrong with your face?"

Father seemed amused. He stepped away from the door and jerked his head for me to open it. "It's nothing that a steamroller couldn't fix."

"But you have an interesting face," I protested as I grabbed the doorknob.

"Are you blind, boy? This mug isn't ever going to win a beauty contest." He chuckled. "I've been called a lot of names in my time, but never 'interesting.' You've got a way with words."

ANALYZE VISUALS
How would you describe the **mood** of this painting? Tell what elements of the image contribute to the mood.

ineptitude
(ĭn-ĕp'tĭ-tōōd') *n.* clumsiness; lack of competence

7. **mug:** face.

ANALYZE VISUALS

Possible answer: *The mood is somber and sad. The artist has used just a few dark colors to create an image of a boy sitting in a chair with his face hidden behind his hand. The way the boy peeks out from between his fingers suggests that he prefers not to see whatever is in front of him.*

Lines 158–159
REINFORCE *KEY IDEA:* SCARED

Discuss How does Father's statement "I said you have to be tough, not stupid" (line 158) help answer the question "When is it OK to be **scared?**" ***Possible answer:*** *Father means that sometimes it is foolish, or even dangerous, to do things that scare you. So, it is OK to be scared if it prevents you from hurting yourself.*

FOR LESS–PROFICIENT READERS

Concept Support Remind students that a symbol is a person, place, or object that stands for something beyond itself. Discuss what Father's trophies symbolize. Ask students what Yep means when he says, "Each prize was a sign that my father belonged to America—and at the same time, to Chinatown" (lines 150–151). Then have students share objects they are proud of and what these objects symbolize to them.

FOR ENGLISH LEARNERS

Comprehension: Description [mixed-readiness pairs] Display the Monitoring transparency and have students read lines 160–162. Explain that Yep's father is making a joke. Ask students what they think he means. What clues helped them understand? Have student pairs use Monitoring to unlock the meaning of other descriptive phrases in the text, beginning with line 164.

 **BEST PRACTICES TOOLKIT—Transparency** Monitoring p. A12

Lines 168–198
DISCUSSION PROMPTS

Use these prompts to help students understand the closeness developing between Yep and his father:

Connect What does Yep's father say to reassure Yep? Would these words reassure you in this situation? Why or why not? ***Possible answer:*** *Yep's father says, "I'm with you, boy" (line 172). These words would help me because they'd make me feel as though I had support.*

Analyze What does Yep's father trust Yep to do? Why is this important to Yep? ***Possible answer:*** *Yep's father trusts him to take the first watch. This makes Yep feel important and determined to prove himself to his father.*

Synthesize Earlier Yep inferred that his father "was disappointed: He would rather have Eddy's help than mine." After reading this scene, do you agree with Yep? Explain. ***Possible answer:*** *Father's words and actions, such as giving Yep an encouraging grin, reassuring him by saying, "I'm with you boy," and telling him they'd take turns watching, suggest that Yep has made an incorrect inference about his father.*

LITERARY ANALYSIS

❶ CONFLICT

Possible answer: *Yep feels more comfortable during the second silence because he and his father are working together to get the rat. His father has made him feel included and important.*

Lines 203–209
REINFORCE *KEY IDEA:* SCARED

Discuss What happens when the rat appears? How does this scene show what it's like to be **scared?** ***Possible answer:*** *The rat darts forward and heads toward Yep and his father. Yep no longer feels bad about killing the rat and yells, "Shoot it!" (line 209). The passage shows how being scared can make you react without thinking.*

The doorknob was cold in my hand. "I do?"

Father adjusted his grip on the rifle. "I wouldn't buy any real estate from you." And he gave me an encouraging grin. "Now let's kill that rat."

When I opened the door, our home suddenly seemed as foreign to me as Africa. At first, I felt lonely—and a little scared. Then I heard Father reassure me, "I'm with you, boy."

Feeling more confident, I crept through the kitchen and into the living room. Father was right behind me and motioned me to search one half of the room while he explored the other. When I found a hole in the corner away from the fireplace, I caught Father's eye and pointed.

He peered under a chair with me and gave me an approving wink. "Give me a hand," he whispered.

In silent cooperation, we moved the chair aside and then shifted the sofa over until it was between us and the rat hole. Bit by bit, Father and I constructed an upholstered **barricade.** I couldn't have been prouder if we'd built a whole fort together.

Father considerately left the lighter things for me to lift, and I was grateful for his thoughtfulness. The last thing I wanted was to get asthma now from overexertion. When we were done, Father got his rifle from the corner where he had left it temporarily.

As we crouched down behind our **improvised** wall, Father rested the rifle on it. "We'll take turns watching."

"Yes, sir," I said, peering over the barrier. There wasn't so much as a whisker in the hole.

While I scanned the hole with intense radar eyes, Father tried to make himself comfortable by leaning against the sofa. It made me feel important to know Father trusted me; and I was determined to do well. In the center of the living room wall was the fireplace, and on its mantel stood Father's trophies like ranks of soldiers reminding me to be **vigilant.**

We remained in companionable silence for maybe three quarters of an hour. Suddenly, I saw something flicker near the mouth of the hole. "Father," I whispered. ❶

Father popped up alertly and took his rifle. Squeezing one eye shut, he sighted on the rat hole. His crouching body grew tense. "Right." He adjusted his aim minutely. "Right. Take a breath," he recited to himself. "Take up the slack. Squeeze the trigger." Suddenly, he looked up, startled. "Where'd it go?"

As the gray shape darted forward, I could not control my panic. "It's coming straight at us."

The rifle barrel swung back and forth wildly as Father tried to aim. "Where?"

I thought I could see huge teeth and beady, violent eyes. The teeth were the size of daggers and the eyes were the size of baseballs, and they were getting bigger by the moment. It was the rat of all rats. "Shoot it!" I yelled.

barricade (băr'ĭ-kād') n. a structure that blocks passage

improvised (ĭm'prə-vīz... *adj.* to put together wit... little preparation or planning **improvise** *v.*

vigilant (vĭj'ə-lənt) *adj.* watchful; alert

❶ **CONFLICT**
Reread line 196. Compa... the "companionable silence" Yep describes here with an earlier statement, "I thought he was silent because h... was disappointed." Wh... does Yep view the silenc... differently the second time?

DIFFERENTIATED INSTRUCTION

FOR LESS–PROFICIENT READERS

Comprehension Support After students have read lines 153–182, discuss how Father treats Yep after Yep tells him he is "not much good at anything." Note that Father seems to go out of his way to be kind and encouraging to Yep, suggesting that he did not realize Yep felt left out or insecure. Tell students that sometimes conflict can be the result of a misunderstanding between two characters. Have them give another example of how misunderstanding might lead to conflict.

FOR ENGLISH LEARNERS

Comprehension: Comparison Have students read lines 170–171. Explain that when Yep writes that "our home suddenly seemed as foreign to me as Africa," he means it doesn't feel like the same home. Tell students that we all have experiences when a familiar place feels strange. Ask students to write a few sentences about a time when something felt new and foreign to them. When they are finished, ask students to add this to the monitoring chart from page 125.

"Where?" Father shouted desperately.

My courage evaporated. All I could think of was escape. "It's charging." Springing to my feet, I darted from the room.

"Oh, man," Father said, and his footsteps pounded after me.

In a blind panic, I bolted out of the apartment and down the back stairs and into the store. **J**

"Get the SPCA[8]. I think the rat's mad," Father yelled as he slammed the door behind him.

Mother took the rifle from him. "I'd be annoyed too if someone were trying to shoot me."

"No." Father panted. "I mean it's rabid."[9] We could hear the rat scurrying above us in the living room. It sounded as if it were doing a victory dance.

Mother made Father empty the rifle. "You return that to Henry Loo tomorrow," she said. "We'll learn to live with the rat."

As she stowed the rifle in the storeroom, Father tried to regather his dignity. "It may have fleas," he called after her.

Now that my panic was over, I suddenly became aware of the enormity of what I had done. Father had counted on me to help him, and yet I had run, leaving him to the **ravages** of that monster. I was worse than a failure. I was a coward. I had deserted Father right at the time he needed me most. I wouldn't blame him if he kicked me out of his family.

It took what little nerve I had left to look up at my father. At that moment, he seemed to tower over me, as grand and remote as a monument. "I'm sorry," I said miserably.

He drew his eyebrows together as he clinked the shells in his fist. "For what?"

It made me feel even worse to have to explain in front of Eddy. "For running," I said wretchedly.

He chuckled as he dumped the cartridges into his shirt pocket. "Well, I ran too. Sometimes it's smart to be scared."

"When were you ever scared?" I challenged him.

He buttoned his pocket. "Plenty of times. Like when I came to America. They had to pry my fingers from the boat railing."

It was the first time I'd ever heard my father confess to that failing. "But you're the best at everything."

"Nobody's good at everything." He gave his head a little shake as if the very notion puzzled him. "Each of us is good at some things and lousy at others. The trick is to find something that you're good at."

I thought again of the mantel where all of Father's sports trophies stood. Eddy gave every promise of collecting just as many, but I knew I would be lucky to win even one.

"I'm lousy at sports," I confessed.

③ Targeted Passage

J CHRONOLOGICAL ORDER
How much time do you think passes from when Yep and his father begin their rat hunt until they give up? Explain your reasoning.

ravage (răv′ĭj) *n.* serious damage or destruction

8. **SPCA:** Society for the Prevention of Cruelty to Animals.
9. **rabid:** affected by the viral disease rabies.

READING SKILL

J CHRONOLOGICAL ORDER

Possible answer: *Over an hour passes from when Yep and his father begin their rat hunt until they give up. Yep writes that he and his father are silent for about 45 minutes (line 196). Before that, they move furniture, and his father talks about his youth.*

If students need help . . . Encourage students to refer to their charts to see how many events occur between when Yep and his father go into the living room and when they first see the rat.

Lines 240–244
REINFORCE *KEY IDEA:* SCARED

Discuss Why do you think Yep is surprised to learn that his father has been **scared?** ***Possible answer:*** *Yep idealizes his father and thinks he's good at everything, so it is natural he would be surprised to learn his father has been scared. Also, he says that his father has never admitted to fear before.*

FOR LESS–PROFICIENT READERS

③ Targeted Passage [Lines 211–247]

In this passage, Yep learns that he is not the only person in the family who has felt scared.

- How does Yep react when the rat charges?
- Why does Yep apologize to his father? What is Father's reply?
- What surprising story does Father tell about his experience of coming to America?
- What does Father say is "the trick" to success?

FOR ENGLISH LEARNERS

Vocabulary: Multiple-Meaning Words Point out that in lines 216–220, Mother misunderstands Father's use of the multiple-meaning word *mad.* Mother thinks Father is using *mad* to mean "annoyed," but he actually means "crazy." Have students define these other multiple-meaning words as they are used in the story: *fall* (line 5), *funny* (line 101), *dribble* (line 110), *clean* (line 145), *lighter* (line 183).

FOR ADVANCED LEARNERS/PRE–AP

Write a Letter The incident with the rat affects how Yep views both himself and his father. Have students write a letter from the adult Yep to his father, explaining how this seemingly insignificant incident changed his life. Students should address how Yep's self-esteem improved as a result of his interaction with his father and what he learned about fear that day that helps him in his life.

ANALYZE VISUALS

Activity How does this painting reflect the characters and events in Yep's memoir? ***Possible answer:*** *The boy and the man, representing Yep and his father, both seem lost in thought. In the context of the memoir, they could be thinking about the new insights they have gained about each other as a result of the rat hunt.*

LITERARY ANALYSIS

Ⓚ CONFLICT

Possible answer: *Now Yep feels accepted and even liked by his father.*

Extend the Discussion Consider Father's confession that he isn't perfect. How does this help resolve the conflict between Yep and his father?

His eyes flicked back and forth, as if my face were a book open for his inspection. He seemed surprised by what he read there.

Slowly his knees bent until we were looking eye to eye. "Then you'll find something else," he said and put his arm around me. My father never let people touch him. In fact, I hardly ever saw him hug Mother. As his arm tightened, I felt a real love and assurance in that embrace. Ⓚ

Ⓚ CONFLICT How has Yep's relationship with his father changed since the beginning of the story?

Shortly after that, the rat left as mysteriously as it had come. "I must've scared it off," Father announced.

Mother shook her head. "That rat laughed itself to death."

Father disappeared into the storeroom: and for a moment we all thought Mother had gone too far. Then we heard the electric saw that he kept back there. "What are you doing?" Mother called.

He came back out with a block of wood about two inches square. He was carefully sandpapering the splinters from the edges. "Maybe some day we'll find the corpse. Its head ought to look real good over the fireplace."

Mother was trying hard to keep a straight face. "You can't have a trophy head unless you shoot it."

"If it died of laughter like you said, then I killed it," he insisted proudly. "Sure as if I pulled the trigger." He winked at me. "Get the varnish out for our trophy will you?"

I was walking away when I realized he had said "our." I turned and said, "That rat was doomed from the start." I heard my parents both laughing as I hurried away.

SELECTION WRAP–UP

REFLECT How did reading about Yep's father's experiences help you understand his relationship with Yep?

★ CRITIQUE Did you find Yep's feelings of inadequacy believable? Why or why not?

READING FLUENCY

Distribute the copy masters and have students practice fluency.

RESOURCE MANAGER—Copy Master
Reading Fluency p. 199

DIFFERENTIATED INSTRUCTION

FOR ADVANCED LEARNERS/PRE–AP

Analyze a Memoir [small-group option] Have students form small groups to discuss how difficult it might be to reveal one's private thoughts and feelings in writing. Ask why it may have been easier for Yep to write his memoir from a distance as an adult than when it was happening as a child.

Comprehension

1. **Recall** How do Laurence and his brother differ?
2. **Recall** What compliment does Laurence's father give him?
3. **Clarify** What happens to the rat at the end of the selection?

Literary Analysis

4. **Identify Chronological Order** Review the chart you made as you read. Does it contain all the important events of the selection? If not, add them now. Then use your chart to tell what happened right before Father ran out of the apartment. What happened right after?
5. **Examine Conflict** In a conflict map like the one shown, note one of the selection's most important conflicts and the events that lead to its **resolution,** or outcome.

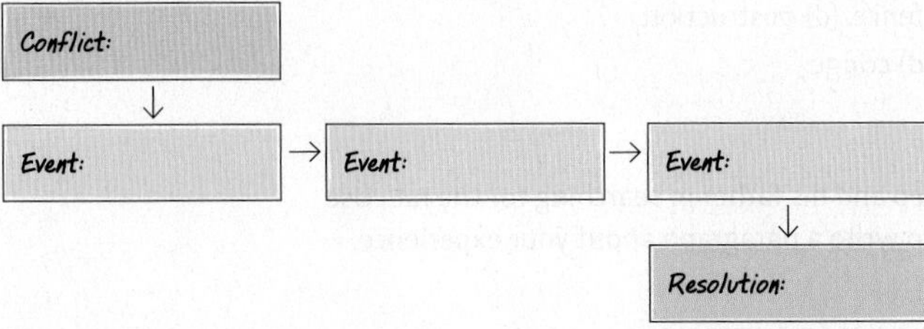

6. **Analyze Characters** Even though Yep was **scared,** he still agreed to help his father capture the rat. What do you learn about Yep from his actions?
7. **Compare and Contrast** Compare Yep's feelings about his role in the family in the beginning of the selection with his feelings at the end. How are they different?
8. **Interpret Meaning** Reread lines 270–271. What do you think it means that Yep's father uses the word "our" to refer to the trophy?

Extension and Challenge

9. **Creative Project: Drama** With two other classmates, rehearse a dramatic reading of the rat-hunt scene. Have one student play the role of Father, one student play the role of Yep, and one student act as the narrator. Perform your reading for the class.
10. **Readers' Circle** Yep's father says, "Sometimes it's smart to be scared." Do you think the encounter with the rat was one of those times, or is Yep's father just trying to make himself and his son feel better? Refer to the selection as you discuss the question.

Practice and Apply

After Reading

For additional support of postreading questions, use these copy masters:

RESOURCE MANAGER—Copy Masters
Reading Check p. 196 (to check understanding of the selection)
Conflict in Nonfiction p. 189 (for practice of literary analysis standards focus)
Question Support p. 197 (After Reading questions adapted for English learners and less-proficient readers)

Additional selection questions are provided for teachers on page 183.

ANSWERS

Comprehension

1. *Eddy, Laurence's brother, is good at sports, while Laurence, who has asthma, can't participate in sports with their father.*
2. *Yep's father tells him he has a way with words.*
3. *The rat disappears on its own.*

Literary Analysis

Possible answers:

4. ■ **STANDARDS FOCUS Chronological Order** *The rat charged, and Yep and his father ran out of the apartment. Afterward, Mother made Father empty the rifle.*
5. ● **STANDARDS FOCUS Conflict in Nonfiction** ***Conflict:*** *Yep feels that his father doesn't like or accept him.* ***Event:*** *The rat appears.* ***Event:*** *They hunt the rat together and fail.* ***Event:*** *Yep learns that his father was scared when he came to America.* ***Resolution:*** *Yep feels accepted by his father and better about himself.*
6. *We learn that Yep is desperate to do something to gain his father's respect.*
7. *At first, Yep feels like an outsider who doesn't belong in the family because he can't play sports like his brother and father. When he learns his father isn't perfect and doesn't expect his sons to be either, Yep feels "love and assurance."*
8. *When Father refers to "our trophy," Yep knows his father values the experience they shared.*

Extension and Challenge

9. *Students should use facial expressions, movement, and tone of voice to help convey the drama of the scene.*
10. *Students should refer not only to their own opinions about the question, but to evidence from the text to support their opinion. They may note that the rat was charging at Yep and his father and may have bitten them if they didn't leave. This indicates that being scared of the rat was indeed smart.*

ANSWERS

Vocabulary in Context

VOCABULARY PRACTICE

1. *(c) multiply*
2. *(d) practice*
3. *(a) openness*
4. *(c) construction*
5. *(b) inattentive*
6. *(d) gracefulness*
7. *(a) finite*
8. *(d) kind*
9. *(a) walkway*
10. *(c) strut*

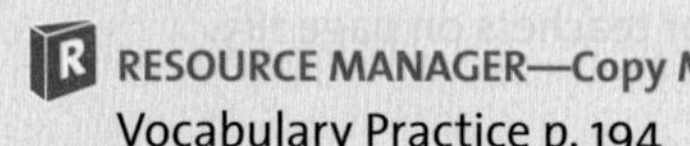

RESOURCE MANAGER—Copy Master
Vocabulary Practice p. 194

VOCABULARY IN WRITING

Ask students to recall the process involved in searching for the rat. Have them think about how they would feel during the search. Then have students choose the best words to describe the experience.

VOCABULARY STRATEGY: ONOMATOPOEIA

Brainstorm with students a list of examples of onomatopoeia, such as *whirr, murmur,* and *meow.* Explain that authors use these words to help bring their writing to life.

Answers:

1. *tick-tock*
2. *crackled*
3. *pop*
4. *buzzing*
5. *plopped*

RESOURCE MANAGER—Copy Master
Vocabulary Strategy p. 195

Vocabulary Center at **ClassZone.com**
Additional Vocabulary Activities

Vocabulary in Context

VOCABULARY PRACTICE

For each item, choose the word that differs most in meaning from the other words.

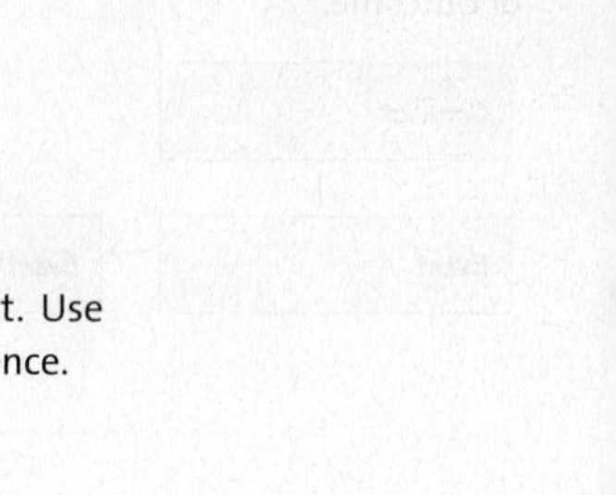

1. (a) justify, (b) rationalize, (c) multiply, (d) explain
2. (a) improvised, (b) ad-libbed, (c) invented, (d) practiced
3. (a) openness, (b) modesty, (c) reserve, (d) coolness
4. (a) destruction, (b) ravage, (c) construction, (d) ruin
5. (a) keen, (b) inattentive, (c) observant, (d) vigilant
6. (a) ineptitude, (b) awkwardness, (c) incompetence, (d) gracefulness
7. (a) finite, (b) infinite, (c) constant, (d) perpetual
8. (a) abruptly, (b) gruffly, (c) brusquely, (d) kindly
9. (a) walkway, (b) barricade, (c) fence, (d) obstruction
10. (a) flinch, (b) wince, (c) strut, (d) cringe

VOCABULARY IN WRITING

Imagine you are trying to assist Yep and his father in searching for the rat. Use three or more vocabulary words to write a paragraph about your experience. You could start like this.

EXAMPLE SENTENCE

The appearance of the rat made me ***wince.***

VOCABULARY STRATEGY: ONOMATOPOEIA

Onomatopoeia is the use of words whose sounds suggest their meaning. Yep uses onomatopoeia in "The Great Rat Hunt" when he writes: "In the fall, it was the smack of a football." *Smack* is a word that sounds like what it means.

PRACTICE In the following sentences, identify the words that are examples of onomatopoeia.

1. You could hear the tick-tock of the clock.
2. The fire crackled as the logs burned.
3. I love to pop popcorn.
4. The crowd was buzzing with excitement.
5. He plopped down in the chair to watch the movie.

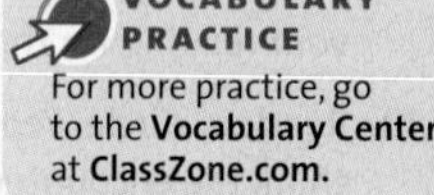

For more practice, go to the **Vocabulary Center** at **ClassZone.com.**

DIFFERENTIATED INSTRUCTION

FOR ENGLISH LEARNERS

Vocabulary in Writing

1. Make sure students understand the meaning of each vocabulary word. Encourage them to review how each word was used in the memoir.
2. Have students choose three or more vocabulary words they think would be useful in writing about searching for a rat.
3. Help students use each word appropriately in the **Vocabulary in Writing** paragraph.

FOR ADVANCED LEARNERS/PRE-AP

Vocabulary Strategy Challenge students to use several examples of onomatopoeia in a short poem about a rat. Invite students to read their poems to a small group.

eading-Writing Connection

Broaden your understanding of "The Great Rat Hunt" by responding to these prompts. Then complete the **Grammar and Writing** exercise.

WRITING PROMPTS	SELF-CHECK
A. Short Response: Write a Description Write a **one-paragraph description** of the rat hunt from the rat's point of view. In the rat's own words (using the pronoun *I*), tell how you outsmarted Mr. Yep and whether you were ever **scared.**	***A strong description will . . .*** • relate the main events of the rat hunt • give a believable account from the rat's point of view
B. Extended Response: Compare and Contrast Both Laurence Yep and his father felt like outsiders. In **two or three paragraphs,** compare their experiences, including the conflicts each person faced and how he dealt with them.	***A detailed response will . . .*** • identify similarities and differences between the son's and father's experiences • cite the conflicts each faced

RAMMAR AND WRITING

USE CORRECT PRONOUN CASE People often misuse the subject and object cases of personal pronouns, especially in sentences containing a compound subject. **Subject pronouns** function as just that—the subject of a sentence. They include the words *I, he, she, we,* and *they.* **Object pronouns** function as the object of a sentence and include the words *me, him, her, us,* and *them.* (*You* and *it* function as both subject and object pronouns.)

Original: Him and his brother have different interests and abilities.

Revised: He and his brother have different interests and abilities. (*The pronoun is functioning as a subject, so it should be* he.)

Original: I outsmarted his father and he.

Revised: I outsmarted his father and him. (*The pronoun is functioning as an object, so it should be* him, *not* he.)

PRACTICE Choose the correct pronoun to complete each sentence.

1. Laurence thinks his father is disappointed in (him, he).
2. One day, (they, them) and the rat confront each other.
3. (Him, He) and his father both have something in common, Laurence discovers.
4. As readers, you and (me, I) learn that even his father isn't perfect.

*For more help with pronoun cases, see page R53 in the **Grammar Handbook.***

Reading-Writing Connection

WRITING PROMPTS

- For **Prompt A,** encourage students to review their chronology charts about events during the rat hunt.
- For **Prompt B,** suggest that students write about the conflicts Yep and his father faced in one paragraph, the similarities between how they faced them in a second paragraph, and the differences in a third paragraph.

For writing support, see

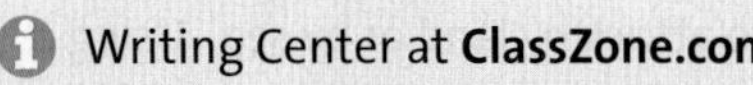

Writing Center at **ClassZone.com**

GRAMMAR AND WRITING

Explain that item 1 contains an object pronoun and items 2, 3, and 4 contain compound subjects. Ask students to identify the pronouns that should be used in each case.

Answers:

1. *him*
2. *they*
3. *He*
4. *I*

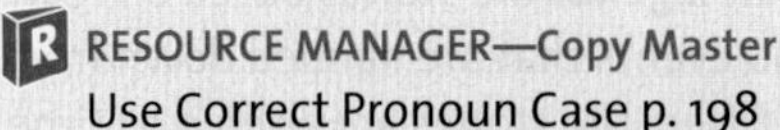

RESOURCE MANAGER—Copy Master
Use Correct Pronoun Case p. 198

Assess and Reteach

Assess

RESOURCE MANAGER—Copy Masters
Selection Tests A, B/C pp. 201–202, 203–204

Test Generator CD

Reteach

STANDARDS LESSON FILE
Literature Lesson 6: Conflict
Literature Lesson 24: Onomatopoeia
Reading Lesson 6: Recognizing Sequence and Chronological Order
Grammar Lesson 13: Pronoun Case with Compound Objects and Subjects

DIFFERENTIATED INSTRUCTION

FOR LESS–PROFICIENT WRITERS

For Prompt A:

1. Have students summarize the specific events of the rat hunt.
2. Then ask students to imagine they are viewing Yep and his father from the rat hole and have them write a descriptive opening sentence about what they see.
3. Have students continue their descriptions with the rest of the events from the hunt.

For Prompt B:

Have students create a Venn diagram comparing and contrasting Yep's and his father's experiences. Students may organize their responses this way:

- **First paragraph:** Focus on Yep and his experiences and conflicts.
- **Second paragraph:** Focus on Yep's father and his experiences and conflicts and how they differ from Yep's.
- **Third paragraph:** Focus on how they each dealt with their conflicts.

Focus and Motivate

OBJECTIVES

Literary Analysis
- explore the key idea of **legends**
- identify and analyze characteristics of narrative poetry
- read poetry

Reading
- paraphrase

SUMMARY

On the evening of April 18, 1775, Paul Revere awaits news about whether British troops are going to attack by land or by sea. Using a lantern signal, Revere's spy tells him the British are arriving by sea. Revere then begins his midnight ride through the towns of Middlesex County, warning of the British troops' impending arrival. He delivers his message in Medford, Lexington, and Concord, warning the American colonists.

When does truth become LEGEND?

Introduce the question to the students and explain that **legends** are stories based on real people and events that are handed down from the past. Often, the stories are altered as time goes on, allowing the facts to become distorted. To lead into the ***KEY IDEA,*** ask students whether these stories can still be considered truth, or have they been too exaggerated? Have small groups work on the ***DISCUSS*** activity. Then ask them to think about why we create legends. How do they enrich our lives?

Before Reading

Paul Revere's Ride

Poem by Henry Wadsworth Longfellow

When does truth become LEGEND?

KEY IDEA George Washington was an amazing leader, but did he really never, ever lie? When highly regarded people are famous for long enough, they sometimes become **legends,** and the stories about them are exaggerated. You're about to read a poem featuring one such person.

DISCUSS In a small group, come up with a list of people you consider legendary. Think about sports heroes, performers, and historical figures. What do these people have in common? Why do you think they became legends? Share your ideas with the class.

132

Selection Resources

RESOURCE MANAGER UNIT 1

Plan and Teach pp. 205–212

Literary Analysis
Narrative Poetry pp. 213, 214†*
Question Support p. 218*

Reading
Paraphrase pp. 215, 216†*
Reading Check p. 217
Reading Fluency p. 219

Assessment
Selection Tests A, B/C pp. 221*, 223*
Test Generator CD

BEST PRACTICES TOOLKIT

Differentiated Instruction pp. 31–38*

Graphic Organizers/Strategies
Reciprocal Teaching • Common Suffixes • Words with Multiple Meanings • Sequence Chain

Reading Support
Audio Anthology CD*

Technology
Literature Center at **ClassZone.com**
Write*Smart* CD

* Resources for Differentiation † Also in Spanish

TERARY ANALYSIS: NARRATIVE POETRY

You've read fictional stories, true stories, and stories presented dramatically. Now you're about to read a **narrative poem,** which is a poem that tells a story. Like a short story, a narrative poem has the following elements:

- a **plot,** or series of events that center on a conflict faced by a main character
- a **setting,** the time and place(s) where the story occurs; setting is usually established in the exposition stage of the plot
- **character(s),** or the individual or individuals who take part in the action

As you read "Paul Revere's Ride," notice how Longfellow uses story elements to describe Paul Revere's adventures.

Review: **Suspense**

EADING SKILL: PARAPHRASE

Have you ever explained a complex idea using easier language, or retold a story in your own words? Restating complete information in simpler terms is called **paraphrasing.** A good paraphrase includes all of the main ideas and supporting details of the original source and is usually just as long, or longer. Paraphrasing challenging passages can help you better understand them. As you read "Paul Revere's Ride," use a chart like the one shown to paraphrase parts of the poem, such as the following lines, that may be difficult to understand:

Original: *Meanwhile, his friend through alley and street*
Wanders and watches, with eager ears . . .

Paraphrase: *At the same time, his friend walks through quiet streets and alleys, looking and listening carefully.*

Line Numbers	Paraphrase

Author Online

An Accomplished Teenager When he was just 14, Henry Wadsworth Longfellow was accepted into Bowdoin College in Maine. He did well in his studies and had nearly 40 poems published before he graduated. He learned French, Italian, and Spanish and translated famous literary works into English.

Henry Wadsworth Longfellow
1807–1882

World Fame After traveling in Europe, Longfellow returned to teach at Harvard University. He continued to write poetry that explored many important American themes. Works such as *The Song of Hiawatha* and *Tales of a Wayside Inn,* which includes "Paul Revere's Ride," brought American history to the attention of readers around the world. Though the death of his wife in 1861 made Longfellow deeply depressed, he remained extraordinarily kind, courteous, and generous. He never refused to give an autograph or welcome visitors who sometimes lingered around his house, hoping for a glimpse of the famous author.

Background

By 1775, many American colonists had begun to rebel against the British government's interference in their affairs. On the night of April 18, British troops left Boston, heading to Concord to arrest the rebel leaders and seize their weapons stockpile. Hoping to warn the rebel leaders of the British advance, Paul Revere, along with William Dawes and Dr. Samuel Prescott, set off on a ride that would make Revere a legend.

MORE ABOUT THE AUTHOR AND BACKGROUND
To learn more about Longfellow and the Revolutionary War, visit the **Literature Center** at **ClassZone.com.**

Teach

STANDARDS FOCUS

LITERARY ANALYSIS

● NARRATIVE POETRY

Read aloud this example:

Many years ago, in Ireland,
A mother, Maggie, now long dead,
Worked long days and all night long
So she could give her children bread.

Ask students: What elements of narrative poetry do these lines contain? ***Possible answer:*** *They contain conflict (hunger), setting (Ireland, long ago), and characters (Maggie, children).*

CHECK UNDERSTANDING Have students choose a subject for a narrative poem. What plot, setting, and character(s) will the poem include?

READING SKILL

■ PARAPHRASE

After students read the description of paraphrasing, discuss how a paraphrase is different from a summary. *(A summary is shorter and leaves out many details from the original text.)* Then have students paraphrase the information in **Author Online.**

CHECK UNDERSTANDING Ask students how paraphrasing can help a reader understand what he or she has read.

RESOURCE MANAGER—Copy Master
Paraphrase p. 215 (for student use while reading the selection)

DIFFERENTIATED INSTRUCTION

FOR ALL STUDENTS

For general guidelines on differentiating instruction, see

BEST PRACTICES TOOLKIT
Differentiated Instruction pp. 31–38

FOR LESS-PROFICIENT READERS

Concept Support Explain that this poem tells the story of a single event of the American Revolution. As they read, have students ask themselves these questions:

- To whom is the poem addressed?
- Who are the main characters in the poem?
- What is the main action in the poem?

FOR ENGLISH LEARNERS

Options for Reading [paired option] Have students listen to the first two or three stanzas of the poem on the *Audio Anthology CD* while they read along. Then have partners use Reciprocal Teaching to summarize, generate questions, clarify, and make predictions about the remainder of the reading.

BEST PRACTICES TOOLKIT—Transparency
Reciprocal Teaching p. A35

Practice and Apply

ANALYZE VISUALS

Possible answer: *The man in the foreground leans into the neck of his horse. His position shows that he is riding at a quick pace. In the background, there are two people on horseback chasing him. This creates a suspenseful mood.*

About the Art Christopher Bing's illustrated edition of Ernest Lawrence Thayer's poem *Casey at the Bat* was named a 2001 Caldecott Honor Book. His second book for children illustrates Longfellow's classic poem *The Midnight Ride of Paul Revere* using scratch-board engravings, maps, and digital images of historical objects. Bing and his family live within minutes of the Freedom Trail, the route Paul Revere rode the night of April 18, 1775.

LITERARY ANALYSIS

Ⓐ NARRATIVE POETRY

Possible answer: *The poem takes place in Middlesex County, in eastern Massachusetts.*

Paul Revere's Ride

HENRY WADSWORTH LONGFELLOW

Listen, my children, and you shall hear
Of the midnight ride of Paul Revere,
On the eighteenth of April, in Seventy-five;
Hardly a man is now alive
Who remembers that famous day and year.

He said to his friend, "If the British march
By land or sea from the town to-night,
Hang a lantern aloft in the belfry arch
Of the North Church tower as a signal light,—
One if by land, and two if by sea;
And I on the opposite shore will be,
Ready to ride and spread the alarm
Through every Middlesex[1] village and farm,
For the country folk to be up and to arm." Ⓐ

ANALYZE VISUALS
What **mood** does this painting convey?

Ⓐ **NARRATIVE POETRY**
According to the first two stanzas, where does the poem take place?

1. **Middlesex:** a county in eastern Massachusetts—the setting of the first battle of the Revolutionary War on April 19, 1775.

DIFFERENTIATED INSTRUCTION

FOR LESS–PROFICIENT READERS

Reading Skill Follow-Up: Paraphrase [paired option] Read the first stanza aloud and then model how to paraphrase it in simpler language. For example: "Gather around, kids, and I'll tell you the story of Paul Revere. He made a famous ride at midnight on April 18, 1775. That was a long time ago, so most of the people who witnessed the event are dead." Then have students work in pairs to paraphrase the next two stanzas in their charts.

Comprehension Support Explain that the poet frequently inverts words and parts of sentences, thus creating a more formal rhythm and serious tone. For example, in line 11 he writes, "I on the opposite shore will be." A more conversational version of this line might place the subject and the verb together: "I will be on the opposite shore." As they read, encourage students to experiment with syntax they find difficult, moving words and parts of sentences around to clarify meaning.

FOR ENGLISH LEARNERS

Vocabulary Support [mixed-readiness pairs] Have students work in pairs to define these words from the poem:

- *hulk* (line 22), "heavy ship"
- *barrack* (line 27), "building that houses soldiers"
- *spurred* (line 58), "wearing spiked wheels attached to riding boots, used to urge the horse on"
- *steed* (line 76), "horse"

Illustration by Christopher Bing.

Then he said "Good-night!" and with muffled oar
Silently rowed to the Charlestown shore,
Just as the moon rose over the bay,
Where swinging wide at her moorings[2] lay
The *Somerset,* British man-of-war;[3]
A phantom ship, with each mast and spar[4]
Across the moon like a prison bar,
And a huge black hulk, that was magnified
By its own reflection in the tide. **B**

Meanwhile, his friend through alley and street
Wanders and watches, with eager ears,
Till in the silence around him he hears
The muster of men at the barrack door,
The sound of arms, and the tramp of feet,
And the measured tread of the grenadiers,[5]
Marching down to their boats on the shore.

B NARRATIVE POETRY
What is the **conflict** being described?

2. **moorings:** the place where the ship is docked.
3. **man-of-war:** a warship, often a large sailing ship, bearing canons and other guns.
4. **spar:** a pole supporting a ship's sail.
5. **grenadiers** (grĕn'ə-dîrz'): British foot soldiers.

BACKGROUND

The Real Midnight Ride Paul Revere was involved with Boston's committee of correspondence, a group that kept track of the movements of British soldiers occupying Boston. In April 1775, members of the committee learned of a British plan to march on Concord, where a large amount of gunpowder was stored. Two couriers—Paul Revere and another Patriot named William Dawes—were sent by the committee to warn Concord. The men took different routes.

The attack was scheduled for April 19. The night before, Revere rowed a boat across Boston harbor to Charlestown. There, he mounted a horse and began his journey. Along the way he encountered a doctor named Samuel Prescott, who offered to help spread the alarm. When the two men were apprehended by a British patrol, Prescott managed to escape. Prescott, Dawes, and others warned Lexington and Concord of the planned British attack, while Revere was held in custody for several hours.

LITERARY ANALYSIS

B NARRATIVE POETRY

Possible answer: *The Revolutionary War between the British and the American colonists is underway. In this poem, the conflict being described is that the British warship, the* Somerset, *rows to the Charlestown shore.*

- *weathercock* (line 95), "device that pivots on a rooftop to indicate wind direction; often in the form of a rooster; also called a weathervane"
- *musket ball* (line 110), "ammunition shot from a shoulder gun used in the 16th through the 18th centuries"
- *redcoats* (line 115), "British soldiers, who wore red uniforms"

Vocabulary: Suffixes Remind students that the suffix *-ion* means "a state or condition." Point out the word *reflection* in line 23. Explain that the word *reflect* is a verb, but that the addition of the suffix *-ion* forms a noun. Display the Common Suffixes transparency. As they read the poem, ask students to find words with these suffixes and to identify the parts of speech.

BEST PRACTICES TOOLKIT—Transparency
Common Suffixes p. E15

FOR ADVANCED LEARNERS/PRE–AP

Analyze Figurative Language Review metaphor, simile, and personification. Then point out the metaphor and the simile in lines 20–21. Ask students what the "phantom ship" and the "mast and spar / Across the moon like a prison bar" reveal about the setting and what mood they create. Challenge students to express the same ideas in language that reflects a modern setting. As they read, encourage them to look for more figurative language.

READING SKILL

C PARAPHRASE

Have students record their answers in the chart from page 133. ***Possible answer:***

Line Numbers	Paraphrase
31–33	He quietly climbed the church bell tower.
34–36	Frightened pigeons flew away.
37–41	He climbed the ladder to the highest window and paused. He looked at the roofs of the moonlit town.

LITERARY ANALYSIS: ***Review***

D SUSPENSE

Possible answer: *Words and phrases include* shadowy something *and* a line of black.

Then he climbed the tower of the Old North Church,
By the wooden stairs, with stealthy tread,[6]
To the belfry chamber overhead,
And startled the pigeons from their perch
On the somber[7] rafters, that round him made
Masses and moving shapes of shade,—
By the trembling ladder, steep and tall,
To the highest window in the wall,
Where he paused to listen and look down
A moment on the roofs of the town
And the moonlight flowing over all. **C**

Beneath, in the churchyard, lay the dead,
In their night encampment on the hill,
Wrapped in silence so deep and still
That he could hear, like a sentinel's[8] tread,
The watchful night-wind, as it went
Creeping along from tent to tent,
And seeming to whisper, "All is well!"
A moment only he feels the spell
Of the place and the hour, and the secret dread
Of the lonely belfry and the dead;
For suddenly all his thoughts are bent
On a shadowy something far away,
Where the river widens to meet the bay,—
A line of black that bends and floats
On the rising tide like a bridge of boats. **D**

Meanwhile, impatient to mount and ride,
Booted and spurred, with a heavy stride
On the opposite shore walked Paul Revere.
Now he patted his horse's side,
Now he gazed at the landscape far and near,
Then, impetuous,[9] stamped the earth,
And turned and tightened his saddle girth;[10]
But mostly he watched with eager search

VISUAL VOCABULARY

belfry *n.* the bell tower in a church.

C PARAPHRASE
Reread lines 31–41. Paraphrase this stanza, remembering to include all details in your own words. Add this to your chart.

D SUSPENSE
Reread lines 52–56. What words or phrases does the writer use in this passage to create a feeling of suspense?

6. **stealthy tread:** quiet footsteps.
7. **somber:** gloomy.
8. **sentinel:** a guard or sentry.
9. **impetuous** (ĭm-pĕch′o͞o-əs): acting suddenly, on impulse.
10. **saddle girth:** the strap attaching a saddle to a horse's body.

DIFFERENTIATED INSTRUCTION

FOR LESS-PROFICIENT READERS

Review: Suspense Remind students that suspense is the excitement or tension readers feel as they wait to find out how a story ends or a conflict is resolved. Review techniques authors use to create suspense, such as foreshadowing, which is the use of hints or clues to suggest events that will occur later in a story. As they read, encourage students to look for examples of foreshadowing as well as other ways the writer creates suspense.

FOR ENGLISH LEARNERS

Vocabulary: Cognates [small-group option] Have small groups scan the selection for cognates and report their findings to the class. Spanish cognates on this page include

- *march/marchar* (line 30)
- *tower/torre* (line 31)
- *pause/hacer una pausa* (line 39)
- *moment/momento* (line 40)
- *floats/flotar* (line 55)

The belfry tower of the Old North Church,
As it rose above the graves on the hill,
Lonely and spectral[11] and somber and still.
And lo! as he looks, on the belfry's height
A glimmer, and then a gleam of light!
He springs to the saddle, the bridle he turns,
But lingers and gazes, till full on his sight
A second lamp in the belfry burns. **E**

A hurry of hoofs in a village street,
A shape in the moonlight, a bulk in the dark,
And beneath, from the pebbles, in passing, a spark
Struck out by a steed flying fearless and fleet;
That was all! And yet, through the gloom and the light,
The fate of a nation was riding that night;
And the spark struck out by that steed, in his flight,
Kindled the land into flame with its heat.
He has left the village and mounted the steep,
And beneath him, tranquil and broad and deep,
Is the Mystic,[12] meeting the ocean tides;
And under the alders[13] that skirt its edge,
Now soft on the sand, now loud on the ledge,
Is heard the tramp of his steed as he rides. **F**

It was twelve by the village clock,
When he crossed the bridge into Medford town.
He heard the crowing of the cock,
And the barking of the farmer's dog,
And felt the damp of the river fog,
That rises after the sun goes down.

It was one by the village clock,
When he galloped into Lexington.
He saw the gilded weathercock
Swim in the moonlight as he passed,
And the meeting-house windows, black and bare,
Gaze at him with a spectral glare,
As if they already stood aghast[14]
At the bloody work they would look upon.

E NARRATIVE POETRY
Who are the **characters** in this narrative poem?

F PARAPHRASE
Reread the lines 73–80. What's happening in this passage? Paraphrase the passage and add it to your chart.

11. **spectral:** ghostly.
12. **Mystic:** a short river flowing into Boston Harbor.
13. **alder:** tree of the birch family.
14. **aghast:** (ə-găst′): terrified.

LITERARY ANALYSIS

E NARRATIVE POETRY

Possible answer: *The characters are Paul Revere and his friend at the Old North Church.*

Lines 73–80
REINFORCE *KEY IDEA:* LEGENDS

Discuss What details in this passage illustrate why Paul Revere has become a **legend?** ***Possible answer:*** *The spark struck by his horse's hoof is compared to the spark of liberty, and Paul Revere is viewed as a man who helped to determine the "fate of a nation."*

READING SKILL

F PARAPHRASE

Have students record their answers in the chart from page 133. ***Possible answer:***

Line Numbers	*Paraphrase*
73–74	*Paul Revere is riding fast and is just a shape seen in the moonlight.*
75–76	*His horse's hooves strike the pebbles and create a spark.*
77–80	*The spark kindled by Revere's ride lights the fire of a nation being born.*

Lines 87–110
DISCUSSION PROMPTS

Use these prompts to help students understand the resolution of the plot:

Recall Where are the three places Revere rides through, and at what time does he arrive in each village? ***Answer:*** *Revere first rides into Medford at midnight; at 1:00 A.M., he arrives in Lexington; at 2:00 A.M., he gets to Concord.*

Infer What are some examples of foreshadowing in this passage? ***Possible answer:*** *The meeting-house windows seem to stare at Revere, "As if they already stood aghast / At the bloody work they would look upon" (lines 99–100).*

FOR LESS–PROFICIENT READERS

Comprehension Support [paired option] Have students work in pairs to read lines 42–51 and 57–67. Help them visualize the places where Paul Revere and his friend are waiting, pointing out that both men see the graveyard, but from different perspectives. Have students discuss how visualizing helps them appreciate the suspense of the passage, and encourage them to practice this strategy as they continue to read the poem.

FOR ENGLISH LEARNERS

Vocabulary: Multiple-Meaning Words Explain that many words in English look and sound the same but have different meanings. Examples include *arms* (line 28), *spell* (line 49), *light* (line 69), and *skirt* (line 84). Have students use Words with Multiple Meanings to find the meanings of these and other words. Challenge them to write sentences using the words—once for each meaning.

 **BEST PRACTICES TOOLKIT—Transparency**
Words with Multiple Meanings p. E31

Lines 111–130

DISCUSSION PROMPTS

Use these prompts to help students understand the resolution of the plot:

Summarize What is the main idea of the final stanza? How does it relate to the rest of the poem? *Students may say that the main idea is that the story will inspire future generations. It explains why Revere's ride is important.*

Analyze How is the next-to-last stanza different from the rest of the poem? ***Possible answer:*** *It flashes forward to the fighting that takes place in the days after Paul Revere's ride.*

Evaluate Why do you think Longfellow did not mention the other men who spread the alarm? ***Possible answer:*** *One possible reason is that a story with a single hero is more dramatic.*

LITERARY ANALYSIS

G NARRATIVE POETRY

Possible answer: *The climax of the plot occurs when Revere arrives in Concord and the British troops and the colonists confront each other.*

SELECTION WRAP-UP

REFLECT What makes the poem exciting to read? Which parts did you like best?

CRITIQUE Have students discuss whether they prefer narrative poetry or other poetic forms, and why.

READING FLUENCY

Distribute the copy masters and have students practice fluency.

RESOURCE MANAGER—Copy Master
Reading Fluency p. 219

It was two by the village clock,
When he came to the bridge in Concord town.
He heard the bleating[15] of the flock,
And the twitter of birds among the trees,
And felt the breath of the morning breeze
Blowing over the meadow brown.
And one was safe and asleep in his bed
Who at the bridge would be first to fall,
Who that day would be lying dead,
Pierced by a British musket ball.

You know the rest. In the books you have read
How the British Regulars[16] fired and fled,—
How the farmers gave them ball for ball,
From behind each fence and farmyard wall,
Chasing the redcoats down the lane,
Then crossing the fields to emerge again
Under the trees at the turn of the road,
And only pausing to fire and load. G

G NARRATIVE POETRY What is the **climax** of the plot? Give reasons for your answer.

So through the night rode Paul Revere;
And so through the night went his cry of alarm
To every Middlesex village and farm,—
A cry of defiance, and not of fear,
A voice in the darkness, a knock at the door,
And a word that shall echo for evermore!
For, borne on the night-wind of the Past,
Through all our history, to the last,
In the hour of darkness and peril[17] and need,
The people will waken and listen to hear
The hurrying hoof-beats of that steed,
And the midnight message of Paul Revere.

15. **bleating:** the cry of sheep.
16. **British Regulars:** members of Great Britain's standing army.
17. **peril:** danger.

DIFFERENTIATED INSTRUCTION

FOR LESS-PROFICIENT READERS

Comprehension Support [paired option] Review the sequence of events on the night of April 18, 1775. Have students place these events in a sequence chain, along with the events of the next day, which are alluded to in lines 107–118.

BEST PRACTICES TOOLKIT—Transparency
Sequence Chain pp. B21, B45

FOR ADVANCED LEARNERS/PRE-AP

Visualize Challenge students to draw a map to help themselves and their classmates better envision Revere's journey. The map doesn't need to be an accurate depiction of where each town is, but it should show the images the poet evokes for each spot (the barking dog, the fog, the moonlit weathercock, and so on). Have students present their maps to the class.

After Reading

Comprehension

1. **Recall** How many lanterns were hung in the belfry of the Old North Church? What do they signify?
2. **Summarize** In your own words, describe what Paul Revere hoped to accomplish with his late-night ride.
3. **Represent** Reread lines 37–56. Draw what you think Revere's friend sees from the bell tower.

Literary Analysis

4. **Analyze Narrative Poetry** In a chart like the one shown, note the story elements in "Paul Revere's Ride." Then tell the main conflict and how it is resolved.

	"Paul Revere's Ride"
Setting	
Characters	
Main Plot Events	• •

5. **Understand Paraphrasing** Now that you've read the whole poem, review the paraphrases you wrote in your chart as you read. Did you capture the correct meaning in each case? If not, revise your paraphrases.
6. **Analyze Suspense** How did Longfellow create tension and excitement in the poem? Consider the way he used **language, rhythm, rhyme,** and **repetition.** Cite specific details to support your answer.
7. **Evaluate Sensory Details** "Paul Revere's Ride" is full of descriptive language that appeals to the senses. List two or three images that you find most striking. Why did you choose these?
8. **Draw Conclusions** Reread lines 119–130. On the basis of this stanza, why do you think Paul Revere became an American **legend?**

Extension and Challenge

9. **SOCIAL STUDIES CONNECTION** Paul Revere did more in his life than ride to warn the colonists that the British army was on its way. Find out where he lived, what he did for a living, and about his involvement in the "Sons of Liberty" before and during the American Revolution. Share your findings with the class.

RESEARCH LINKS
For more on Paul Revere, visit the **Research Center** at **ClassZone.com.**

Practice and Apply

After Reading

For additional support of postreading questions, use these copy masters:

RESOURCE MANAGER—Copy Masters
Reading Check p. 217 (to check understanding of the selection)
Narrative Poetry p. 213 (for practice of literary analysis standards focus)
Question Support p. 218 (After Reading questions adapted for English learners and less-proficient readers)

Additional selection questions are provided for teachers on page 209.

ANSWERS

Comprehension

1. *There were two lanterns. Two meant the British soldiers were coming by sea.*
2. *Paul Revere hoped to warn the people of Middlesex County that the British army was coming so they could be ready to stop the British.*
3. *Drawings will vary but should be based on the details in lines 37–56.*

Literary Analysis

Possible answers:

4. ● **STANDARDS FOCUS Narrative Poetry** ***Setting:*** *April 18, 1775; Middlesex County, Massachusetts.* ***Characters:*** *Paul Revere, his friend, the British, the colonists.* ***Main Plot Events:*** *Paul Revere tells his friend to put up either one or two lanterns in the belfry as a signal; the* Somerset *rows quietly onto the Charlestown shore; his friend hears the British and climbs up the belfry to signal; Revere sees the signal and takes off on his horse to warn the American colonists of the threat; the colonists fight bravely, and the British flee.*
5. ■ **STANDARDS FOCUS Paraphrase** *Students' paraphrases should accurately reflect main ideas and details in the poem.*
6. *Longfellow's early passages are quiet, while Revere waits for the signal. The pace quickens when Revere sets out, and the rhythm sounds like a galloping horse. The repetition of the time on the village clock creates suspense.*
7. *Answers will vary. The image of the pigeons being startled into flight in the quiet night is striking. The sound of the horse is also vividly described.*
8. *Revere is an American legend because he roused the American colonists to fight off the British and made history.*

Extension and Challenge

9. **SOCIAL STUDIES CONNECTION** *As they share their findings, ask students to connect what they have learned about Paul Revere with the impression created in the poem.*

Assess and Reteach

Assess

RESOURCE MANAGER—Copy Masters
Selection Tests A, B/C pp. 221–222, 223–224

Test Generator CD

Reteach

STANDARDS LESSON FILE
Literature Lesson 5: Elements of Plot
Literature Lesson 17: Narrative vs. Lyric Poetry
Reading Lesson 4: Recognizing Main Idea and Details

Focus and Motivate

OBJECTIVES

Reading for Information

- take notes
- skim a text
- use a graphic organizer to organize ideas
- use text features to identify main ideas and details
- compare and contrast a legend with a true account
- read a history article

SUMMARY

This article tells how William Dawes and Samuel Prescott rode with Paul Revere to inform patriots of an anticipated British military operation in Concord. In fact, Samuel Prescott, not Paul Revere, was the rider who delivered the warning to Concord.

What's the Connection?

Distribute copies of the Anticipation Guide to prepare students for reading the selection. Have them respond to these statements before and then after reading the article:

- Without Paul Revere, the town of Concord would have been unprepared for the British.
- Paul Revere encountered no one on his ride.
- William Dawes and Samuel Prescott played roles as important as Paul Revere's on April 18, 1775.

 **BEST PRACTICES TOOLKIT—Transparency**
Anticipation Guide p. A14

Teach

Skill Focus: Take Notes

- Tell students that it is important not to clutter their notes with unimportant details. First, they should read the designated section of the text. Then, they should decide which facts are important enough to record.
- Explain that when a selection is organized sequentially or chronologically, that order should be preserved in the notes.

Possible chart entries appear on page 142.

 **RESOURCE MANAGER—Copy Master**
Take Notes p. 233

Reading for Information

Use with "Paul Revere's Ride," page 134.

The Other Riders

History Article

What's the Connection?

The poem you just read celebrates Paul Revere, but did you know he was not the only brave rider on the eve of the Revolutionary War? The following article tells about two equally important but lesser-known heroes: William Dawes and Samuel Prescott.

Skill Focus: Take Notes

When you read an article for social studies or science class, how do you absorb all the facts? One good way to digest a lot of information is to **take notes.** Writing down important facts and ideas can help you remember them.

Here are some tips for note-taking:

- First, preview the article by looking at its title, subheadings, topic sentences, and graphic aids to determine its topic and main ideas.
- Next, decide how to organize your notes. Can you use the subheadings to create a simple outline or a graphic organizer like the one shown?
- As you take notes, record the main ideas and only the most important facts and details under the appropriate headings. Be sure to include the names, dates, and terms that are necessary for a full understanding of the material.

For help taking notes on the following selection, use a graphic organizer like the one started here.

Subheadings	*Notes*
Rumors of a March on Concord	*Night of April 18, 1775, a rumor reaches William Dawes that the British are planning to take ammunition in Concord.* *Dawes tells Paul Revere; both get orders from Dr. Joseph Warren to ride to inform the leaders of the Provincial Congress of what's going on.*
Sneaking Past Guards	

Selection Resources

 RESOURCE MANAGER UNIT 1

Plan and Teach pp. 225–229

Reading

Summary pp. 231†*, 232‡*

Take Notes pp. 233, 235†*

Reading Check p. 237

Compare and Contrast pp. 234, 236†*

Question Support p. 238*

Assessment

Selection Tests A, B/C pp. 239*, 241*

Test Generator CD

Reading Support

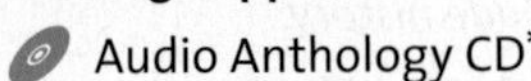

Audio Anthology CD*

BEST PRACTICES TOOLKIT

Anticipation Guide • Jigsaw Reading • Whip Around

* Resources for Differentiation † Also in Spanish ‡ In Haitian Creole and Vietnamese

CK FORWARD STOP REFRESH HOME PRINT

The Other Riders

William Dawes (unknown), attributed to John Johnston. Oil on canvas, 35″ × 29″. © Collection of the Evanston Historical Society, Evanston, Illinois.

Late on the night of April 18, 1775, Boston patriot Joseph Warren learned of a British military operation planned for the next day. To warn John Hancock and Samuel Adams, who were across the Charles River in Lexington, Warren dispatched two riders, Paul Revere and William Dawes. Revere's ride has been celebrated in poems and textbooks, but Dawes's role was at least as important.

Rumors of a March on Concord

On the night of April 18, 1775, rumors of a planned British action to seize ammunition in the town of Concord raced through Boston. Word reached William Dawes, a tanner, who told Paul Revere—who had heard about it from two others already. The two men received orders from Dr. Joseph Warren to ride to inform the leaders of the Provincial Congress of the developments.

Sneaking Past Guards

Dawes's route led him to the British guards at the gate of Boston Neck—the narrowest part of the isthmus—as he rode south out of the city. A naturally witty and friendly man, Dawes had spent numerous afternoons sneaking in and out of the city without being stopped. He would disguise himself as a peddler, smuggling gold coins disguised as buttons that he wore sewn on his coat. Dawes also befriended any British guards who seemed amicable. On the historic night, one of his buddies was on duty. When the guard opened the gate for some British soldiers, Dawes slipped through with them. **A**

Spreading the Word

On his ride west, Dawes alerted more riders, who in turn rallied companies from neighboring towns: Dedham, Needham, Framingham, Newton and Watertown. Avoiding trouble, Dawes made good time and caught up to Revere in Lexington just after midnight. After notifying Hancock and Adams, Dawes and Revere set out for Concord together,

FOCUS ON FORM
You are about to read a **history article,** a nonfiction article about real events and people of historical importance.

A TAKE NOTES
What is the most important information in this section? Make sure to note it under the subheading.

Practice and Apply

FOCUS ON FORM

History Article Have students read **Focus on Form** and identify the significant characteristics of a history article. Explain that, in addition, this type of article

- is written to inform
- presents facts from primary and secondary sources
- may include verified anecdotes, excerpts from historical documents, and direct quotations
- may be organized chronologically
- often includes graphic aids such as maps, timelines, or illustrations

Ask students to list some topics that history articles might explore.

INFORMATIONAL ANALYSIS

A TAKE NOTES

Remind students to write their notes in the chart from page 140. ***Possible answer:***

> ***Sneaking Past Guards:*** *Dawes is friendly with some of the British guards on the gates of Boston. This enables him to get out of the city easily on the night of April 18.*

If students need help . . . Write the article's main idea on the board: *William Dawes played an important part in the historic ride of April 18, 1775.* Then have groups of students consider which of the details in lines 18–26 support that main idea. Explain that those facts belong in their chart.

Lines 11–26

DISCUSSION PROMPTS

Use these prompts to help students understand more about Dawes's role:

Connect Read the description of William Dawes in line 20 and look at his portrait. As a British soldier, would you be suspicious of him? *Students may say that he looks and sounds quite harmless.*

Analyze Why do you think two men receive the orders to ride? ***Possible answer:*** *If one rider does not make it, the other might.*

Synthesize Why was Dawes's mission important? ***Possible answer:*** *The patriots needed to protect their ammunition supplies.*

DIFFERENTIATED INSTRUCTION

FOR LESS–PROFICIENT READERS

Concept Support Remind students to look for words that indicate time order, such as *already* (line 15), *when* (line 25), *in turn* (line 27), and *just after midnight* (line 30).

Comprehension Support To clarify the sequence of events in lines 27–51, have one group summarize Prescott's movements, another Dawes's actions, and the third Revere's, using the map on page 140 and the text. Have each group report their summaries before students take notes.

FOR ENGLISH LEARNERS

Options for Reading One option is for students to read the article silently along with the *Audio Anthology CD.* Or, divide students into small groups. Have each group practice reading a section aloud before reading it to the class. After each group's reading, pause and discuss what important details are included.

BEST PRACTICES TOOLKIT
Jigsaw Reading p. A1

LITERARY ANALYSIS

B HISTORY ARTICLE

Students should note that Revere doesn't make it to Concord, and that Dawes turns back before reaching Concord and retraces his path to Lexington.

If students need help . . . Go over the map key. Then point out where Revere and Dawes meet and where Prescott joins them.

INFORMATIONAL ANALYSIS

C TAKE NOTES

Remind students to record important details in their charts. ***Possible answer:*** *Prescott, not Revere, warns Concord of the British march.*

Extend the Discussion How does this fact change your perception of the historic event?

LITERARY ANALYSIS

D HISTORY ARTICLE

Possible answer: *The last section gives a humorous explanation for why Revere might have been given credit rather than Dawes. It also shows that although Dawes's story is obscure, historians have always been aware of the inaccuracy of the Revere legend.*

Skill Focus: Take Notes

Possible additional entries for the chart on page 140:

Spreading the Word: *Dawes alerts many towns on his ride. He meets Revere in Lexington just after midnight. They are joined by Samuel Prescott.*

A Clever Escape: *The three escape from a British roadblock. Dawes cannot outrun the Redcoats. Instead, he tricks them into leaving him alone.*

Prescott Warns Concord: *Samuel Prescott takes shortcuts to evade capture by the British. He reaches Concord in time to warn them.*

So Forgotten It's Funny: *Over the years, the theory that Dawes's name did not work well in Longfellow's poem has been proposed to explain why Revere was given the credit.*

BACK FORWARD STOP REFRESH HOME PRINT

joined by Dr. Samuel Prescott, a Concord resident who had been visiting a girlfriend.

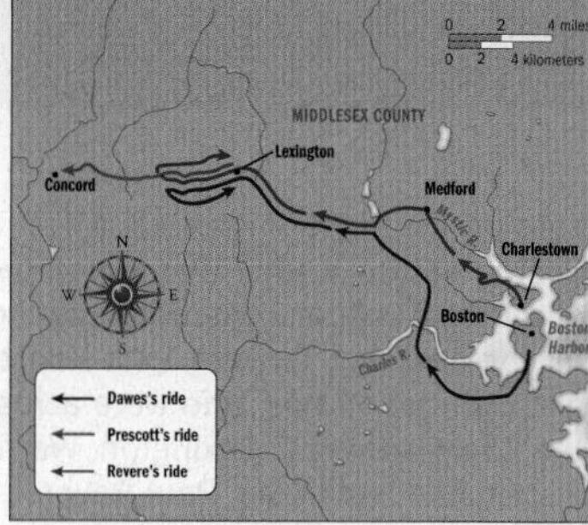

This map of eastern Massachusetts shows the route of each rider. B

B HISTORY ARTICLE
History articles often contain maps, timelines, and other graphic aids to help you track the details presented in the text. As you read this article, follow Revere's, Dawes's, and Prescott's progress on this map.

A Clever Escape

Revere, riding in front, ran into a British roadblock. Dawes and Prescott were captured before they could be warned. As the British tried to lead them into a meadow, Prescott signaled that they should make their escape, and all three rode off. Back on the road towards Lexington, Dawes realized that his horse was too tired to outrun the Redcoats. As he pulled up in the yard of a house, he reared his horse and shouted, "I've got two of them—surround them!" His trick succeeded in scaring off his pursuers, although he fell from his horse and lost his watch.

Prescott Warns Concord

Prescott, the local, rode off toward Concord through fields and creek beds that he knew, quickly outdistancing his would-be captors. It was Prescott who warned the town of Concord of the impending British march. C

C TAKE NOTES
What surprising fact do you learn from this section? Be sure to add this to your notes.

So Forgotten It's Funny

Over the years, Dawes's relative anonymity has become something of a joke. In 1896, Helen F. Moore published a parody of Longfellow's famous poem about the historic night, entitled "The Midnight Ride of William Dawes," one verse of which reads:

'Tis all very well for the children to hear
Of the midnight ride of Paul Revere;
But why should my name be quite forgot,
Who rode as boldly and well, God wot?
Why should I ask? The reason is clear—
My name was Dawes and his Revere.

A cartoon in the early 1960s turned on the same humor, namely that "Dawes" was a name less suited for rhyming than "Revere" (in that comic strip, Longfellow is stuck on "Listen my children while I pause, to tell the ride of William Dawes" when his wife suggests using the name of that other rider). D

D HISTORY ARTICLE
This history article primarily tells about the true story of the people and events of April 18, 1775. What does the additional information in this last section help you understand?

142 UNIT 1: PLOT, CONFLICT, AND SETTING

DIFFERENTIATED INSTRUCTION

FOR LESS—PROFICIENT READERS

Concept Support Adapt a Whip Around strategy to help students check the accuracy of their notes. Call on students in turn to identify important details that they included under each subheading. Add their facts to the class chart. After all students have had a turn, give them time to review and revise their notes.

 BEST PRACTICES TOOLKIT
Whip Around p. B1

FOR ADVANCED LEARNERS/PRE—AP

Evaluate Have groups of students find additional examples of history articles. They might look on the Internet or in periodicals. Ask them to compare elements of the articles they find with this one. They should examine the purpose, the writer's style, kinds of facts included, the use of graphic aids, the tone, and the organization. Have them draw some conclusions about the genre from their comparison.

omprehension

1. **Recall** Who was sent to warn John Hancock and Samuel Adams about a British military operation?
2. **Clarify** What kind of person was William Dawes?
3. **Clarify** What "near miss" did the riders encounter as they rode to Concord?

ritical Analysis

4. **Use Your Notes** Use your notes to create a timeline of the historic events that occurred on the night of April 18, 1775.
5. **Understand a History Article** Now that you've read this history article, what do you think are the main points the author wants to make about the events of April 18, 1775?

ead for Information: Compare and Contrast

WRITING PROMPT

How does the information in "The Other Riders" match up with the story told in "Paul Revere's Ride"? In a paragraph, compare and contrast the legend in the poem with the true account of that night as it is presented in the historical article.

Remember that when you **compare and contrast,** you identify the ways in which two or more things are alike and different. Then follow these steps:

1. In a chart like the one shown, identify the main people and events in the poem. Then identify the main people and events in the article.
2. Note the differences between the two accounts in the last column of the chart.
3. In a sentence, make a general statement about the similarities and differences in the accounts. Support your statement with specific examples.

	from "Paul Revere's Ride"	from "The Other Riders"	Differences
Main Participants			
Main Events			

FOR LESS–PROFICIENT WRITERS

Read for Information Discuss the major differences between the works. Then give students this template for their paragraphs:

Topic sentence: The poem is different from the article in several ways. **Body sentences:** In the poem, [explain what happens and who is responsible]. In contrast, in the article, [explain what happens and who is responsible]. **Conclusion:** Longfellow's poem is entertaining but not entirely factual.

FOR ADVANCED LEARNERS/PRE–AP

Read for Information Have students develop their analysis of the differences and similarities between the two works into an essay. Ask students to conclude by discussing whether or not Longfellow's poem serves a historical purpose, even though it contains inaccuracies.

Practice and Apply

For additional support of postreading questions, use these copy masters:

RESOURCE MANAGER—Copy Masters
Reading Check p. 237
Question Support p. 238
Compare and Contrast p. 234
For additional questions, see page 228.

ANSWERS

Comprehension

1. *Paul Revere and William Dawes were sent to warn Hancock and Adams.*
2. *Dawes was friendly and funny.*
3. *Revere, Dawes, and Prescott were captured by the British at a roadblock.*

Critical Analysis

Possible answers:

4. **STANDARDS FOCUS Take Notes** *Students' timelines should include these events: Dawes meets Revere and Prescott at Lexington just after midnight. They run into a roadblock. They escape. Dawes returns to Lexington after shaking off his pursuers. Prescott reaches Concord.*
5. *The author wants readers to know that Paul Revere was not the only rider to spread the word to other patriots of a British military operation. William Dawes and Samuel Prescott also rode that night and played equally important roles.*

Read for Information: Compare and Contrast

Writing Prompt *Students may note the different number of riders mentioned in each text, the poem's omission of the roadblock story, and the article's crediting of the Concord warning to Prescott instead of Revere.*

Assess and Reteach

Assess

RESOURCE MANAGER—Copy Masters
Selection Tests A, B/C pp. 239–240, 241–242

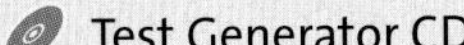

Test Generator CD

Reteach

STANDARDS LESSON FILE
Informational Texts Lesson 1: Text Features

Focus and Motivate

OBJECTIVES

- analyze a student model that reflects the key traits of a personal narrative
- use the writing process to develop a personal narrative
- use dialogue, descriptive detail, chronological order, and sensory language
- revise and edit, using a rubric for a strong personal narrative
- stage a scene from a personal narrative

WRITER'S ROAD MAP

WRITING PROMPTS 1 AND 2

Tell students that sharing a personal experience is a fun way to tell others about themselves. Help them choose a prompt by brainstorming special experiences in their lives or by reviewing the incidents or conflicts in stories in the unit.

ADDITIONAL PROMPTS

Use these prompts for more practice writing personal narratives:

WRITING PROMPT 3

Writing for the Real World Write a personal narrative for a journal, diary, or blog. Focus on a special moment in your life and explain why it was significant.

Moments to Consider

- your 13th birthday
- the day you met your best friend
- a concert you attended

WRITING PROMPT 4

Writing from Media Select an interesting plot from a movie or TV program. Write about a similar situation from your own life.

Ideas to Consider

- a character makes a mistake
- a character makes a new friend
- a neighbor needs help

For additional writing prompts, see

WriteSmart CD

Writing Center at **ClassZone.com**

KEY TRAITS

Review the six ***KEY TRAITS*** with students, focusing primarily on ideas, organization, and voice. Compare the list of traits with the rubric on page 150.

Writing Workshop

Personal Narrative

Like the characters in this unit, you have played a part in many memorable events. Check out the **Writer's Road Map** to get started writing your own personal narrative about something unforgettable that happened to you.

WRITER'S ROAD MAP

Personal Narrative

WRITING PROMPT 1

Writing from Your Life Write a personal narrative telling about a special experience in your life. Include details that will help your reader understand what the experience was like. Be sure to explain why it was important to you.

Experiences to Consider

- your first day in a new place
- a special accomplishment

WRITING PROMPT 2

Writing from Literature Sometimes an incident or a conflict in a literary work can remind you of a similar experience in your own life. Choose an incident or conflict from one of the stories in this unit. Describe the event and tell what similar thing happened to you.

Experiences and Literary Works to Consider

- a time when you learned something new about another person ("Raymond's Run")
- a time when you felt guilty ("The Tell-Tale Heart")

WRITING TOOLS
For prewriting, revision, and editing tools, visit the **Writing Center** at **ClassZone.com.**

KEY TRAITS

1. IDEAS
- Focuses on a single **experience**
- Re-creates the experience with **descriptive details** and **dialogue**

2. ORGANIZATION
- "Hooks" readers with an attention-getting **introduction**
- Uses transitions to make the **order of events** clear
- Has a **conclusion** that summarizes the meaning of the experience

3. VOICE
- Has a **style** that reflects the writer's personality

4. WORD CHOICE
- Brings the experience alive for the reader with **sensory language**

5. SENTENCE FLUENCY
- Includes a variety of **sentence types** (statements, questions, and exclamations)

6. CONVENTIONS
- Uses **correct grammar, spelling, and punctuation**

Writing Workshop Resources

RESOURCE MANAGER UNIT 1
Plan and Teach pp. 243–246
Prewriting–Editing pp. 247–251
Writing Rubric p. 252
Speaking and Listening p. 253
Writing Support p. 254*

STANDARDS LESSON FILE
Writing Lessons 14, 35, 48

BEST PRACTICES TOOLKIT
Scaffolding Writing Instruction pp. 43–46*
Storyboard • Sequence Chain • Writing Template: Autobiographical or Personal Narrative • Two-Column Chart

TECHNOLOGY
 Easy Planner DVD
Writing Center at **ClassZone.com**
 WriteSmart CD

* Resources for Differentiation

Part 1: Analyze a Student Model

Joe Sanders
Humphrey Middle School

Jalapeños, Anyone?

It was an ingenious idea. It was *my* idea. During lunch one day, we loaded up two trays with as many jalapeño peppers as they would hold. Then the fun began.

Let me tell you how it all started. Tom and I were in the cafeteria, eating. It was fourth period in May. I grunted with a mouth full of ham, "I got an idea." Tom was so busy eating his hot dog with everything on it that he didn't hear me.

"Tom!" I yelled, sending bits of ham onto his tray.

"What? Huh?" he replied, looking up from his hot dog momentarily. Tom is my best friend, and he looks exactly like me. If we told you we were twins with different last names, you would probably believe us. We have brown hair and blue eyes. We also wear rimless glasses. We think alike, too.

"So let's hear this great idea of yours," Tom stated, brushing ham from his fries.

"Well, seeing as you like your jalapeños. . . ." I paused for a moment and pointed at his hot dog, which was covered in them. "Maybe you would like to have an eating contest with someone." He didn't hesitate. We decided that Anahi, who is Mexican (and in our heads used to hot stuff), should be the other contestant. She thought it was a good idea, too.

After they each had a tray full of jalapeños in front of them, I started the countdown. "On your mark, get set, go!" Anahi put two in her mouth, then spat them out and ran to the drinking fountain, forfeiting the contest. The rules stated that once you took a drink or ate anything else, you were out of the running.

KEY TRAITS IN ACTION

Intriguing **introduction** makes the reader want to find out about the writer's **experience.**

Includes **dialogue** that matches what people said at the time, even if it contains slang or mistakes in grammar.

Descriptive details and **sensory language** bring the people and action to life.

Transition words make the **order of events** clear.

Teach

Part 1: Analyze a Student Model

Have students read the **Student Model** and **Key Traits in Action.** Then discuss the model with the class, focusing on specific examples of each trait. You may also wish to incorporate these activities:

- **Introduction** Remind students that the opening sentences should make readers want to keep reading. Ask students to analyze how the model's introduction hooks readers. ***Possible answer:*** *The writer says that he had "an ingenious idea" (line 1). Then he tells readers that they "loaded up two trays with as many jalapeño peppers as they would hold" (line 2). Readers will want to know why. The writer further piques readers' interest when he says, "Then the fun began" (line 3).*
- **Dialogue** Tell students that dialogue helps readers feel as though they are witnessing the action of the story. Since people do not usually speak in the same way that they write, realistic dialogue is often more casual and abbreviated than the surrounding sentences. Display these examples and ask students to rewrite them in standard English. Discuss why the dialogue in the essay is more realistic than the rewrites.

  —"I got an idea." *("I have an idea.")*

  —"What? Huh?" *("Excuse me. What did you say?")*

  —"Well, seeing as you like your jalapeños. . . ." *("Since you like eating jalapeño peppers so much. . . .")*

DIFFERENTIATED INSTRUCTION

FOR ALL STUDENTS

Student Portfolios Encourage students to save copies of their writing so they can track their progress throughout the year and also avoid repeating mistakes.

For general guidelines on differentiating writing instruction, see

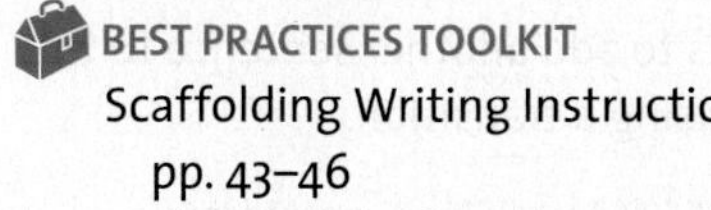

Scaffolding Writing Instruction pp. 43–46

FOR ENGLISH LEARNERS

Language: Skill Words Review these terms:

- *introduction:* the beginning of an essay that introduces main ideas and hooks readers
- *experience:* the event or incident on which a personal narrative is based
- *dialogue:* the exact words spoken by a person or character
- *descriptive details:* words and phrases that help readers form a clear mental image of something that is being described
- *sensory language:* words and phrases that appeal to the senses of sight, hearing, taste, touch, and smell
- *order of events:* the sequence in which things happen in the narrative. In the model, first the writer has an idea. Next, he tells Tom about it. Then, they ask Anahi to be a contestant. After two jalapeños, Anahi gives up and runs to the drinking fountain.

- **Descriptive Details** Remind students that descriptive details help readers visualize what is happening. Ask students to find examples of descriptive details in the model. ***Possible answer:***
  - —"'Tom!' *I yelled, sending bits of ham onto his tray" (line 8).*
  - —*"We have brown hair and blue eyes. We also wear rimless glasses" (lines 11–12).*
  - —*"Anahi put two in her mouth, then spat them out and ran to the drinking fountain . . . " (lines 22–23).*
  - —*"He threw up his hands in triumph even though he looked like he would actually throw up" (lines 32–33).*

  Display these sentences and have students rewrite them, adding descriptive details.
  - —He walked to class.
  - —The tree fell down.
  - —The house was large.
  - —She went shopping.
- **Sentence Types** Remind students that there are four types of sentences: declarative (makes a statement); interrogative (asks a question); imperative (gives a command); and exclamatory (expresses strong emotion). A variety of sentence types makes a narrative more interesting to read.

  Ask students to find an example of each type in this model. ***Possible answer:*** *"Let me tell you how it all started" (line 4) (declarative); "What about you?" (line 44) (interrogative); "Come on, Tom" (line 30) (imperative); "All right, Tom!" (line 34) (exclamatory).* Then ask students to write an original sentence to illustrate each sentence type.

For interactive student models, see

WriteSmart CD

Writing Center at **ClassZone.com**

Meanwhile, Tom was stuffing peppers 37 and 38 in his mouth. He just kept eating, as though he didn't know that his rival had given up. We turned our attention to him and started counting off the jalapeños as he shoveled them in.

"Come on, Tom. You can do it!" I encouraged, pounding the table. "50, 51, 52, 53, 54 . . . Come on . . . 55, 56, 57."

"Yahoo!" Tom shouted. He threw up his hands in triumph even though he looked like he would actually throw up.

The crowd went wild. "All right, Tom!" I yelled. People around us started clapping as he ran frantically to the drinking fountain. When he got back, I handed him his prize—a bag of candy, as promised.

"I am never eating another jalapeño pepper in my life," Tom proclaimed after stuffing his face with chocolate bars. I couldn't do anything but laugh.

It's a little harder to get Tom to partake in my other schemes since I sent him to the drinking fountain for hours! I still have hope that he can pack down 58 peppers if he just works at it, though. I'm sure you can imagine how much luck I'm having convincing him to try.

What about you? Bon appétit!

Includes more **dialogue** to show, rather than tell about, Tom's victory.

This writer's **style** is informal and humorous.

Different **sentence types** (statements, questions, and exclamations) keep the narrative lively. **Conclusion** explains why the writer remembers the experience.

2

DIFFERENTIATED INSTRUCTION

FOR ENGLISH LEARNERS

Comprehension: Transitions Explain that transitional words help clarify the order of events in a narrative. Discuss these examples from the model:

- *During, Then* (lines 1–3)
- *After, then, once* (lines 21–24)
- *Meanwhile* (line 26)
- *as, When* (line 35)
- *after* (line 38)
- *since* (line 40)

Write these sentences on the board: *After the bell rang, I picked up my books and left the room. Then I went to my locker. On the way to my next class, I met a friend. We walked into class just as the bell rang.* Read the sentences aloud and ask students to identify the transitional words and phrases. Then ask students to add another sentence to this paragraph using a transition.

RESOURCE MANAGER—Copy Master
Writing Support p. 254

Part 2: Apply the Writing Process

PREWRITING

What Should I Do?	What Does It Look Like?
1. Choose an experience to share. Take a trip through your memory. List funny, sad, or exciting experiences you have had. Put a star by the one that would be most interesting for you to write about and for your audience to read. **TIP If you are having trouble thinking of experiences, look back at the Writer's Road Map on page 144.**	*Interesting Experiences* / *jalapeño contest ** / *whale-watching trip* / *baby-sitting the Salgado twins* / *kitchen fire at Aunt Erica's* / *breaking my arm during spring vacation*
2. What happened? When? Use a spider map, a cluster diagram, or another graphic organizer to help you gather important facts about the incident. Thinking about the major elements of a story—characters, setting, and action—can help jog your memory. **TIP If this experience is too personal to share with your teacher and classmates, go back to your list and choose a different event.**	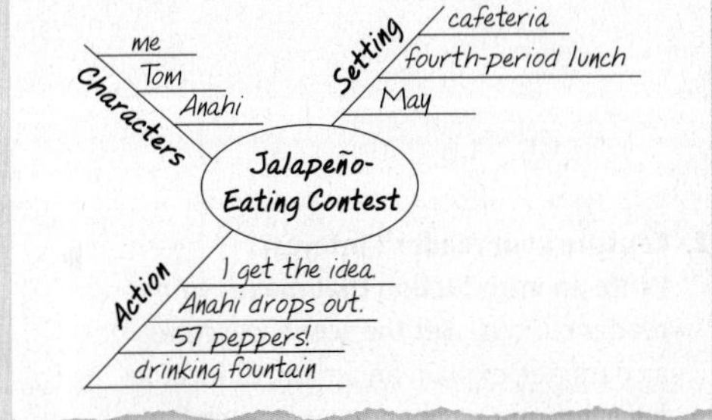
3. Re-create the action for your reader. Think of lively words to describe what happened. Write down the actual words that others said. These descriptions and quotations will help your reader feel like he or she is experiencing the event right alongside you.	***Descriptions:*** *It was my ingenious idea.* / *Tom ran frantically to the water fountain.* / ***Quotations:*** *"So let's hear this great idea of yours."* / *"Come on, Tom. You can do it!"*
4. Think about what the experience meant to you. Write a sentence or two explaining the meaning of your experience. You will probably want to include this statement in your narrative, but thinking about it as you draft can also keep your writing on track.	*Why do I remember the contest? It was a fantastic idea, and it made me laugh. Also, Tom is more cautious about going along with my schemes now.*

FOR LESS–PROFICIENT WRITERS

What Happened? When? Have students use these prompts to generate ideas:

- Where did the experience take place? Was it in school, at home, or somewhere else?
- When did it take place? Was it last summer or last night?
- Who was involved? Who said or did something first to start the action? How did others react?
- What was the most exciting moment? How did the experience end?

FOR ENGLISH LEARNERS

Re-create the Action [mixed-readiness pairs] Provide copies of the Storyboard transparency and have students sketch their narrative events. They may use more than three panels if necessary. When finished, have students work with more fluent partners to discuss the events in their narratives and write sentences that describe each one.

BEST PRACTICES TOOLKIT—Transparency
Storyboard p. C11

Practice and Apply

To support students during the writing process, use these copy masters:

 RESOURCE MANAGER—Copy Masters
Prewriting–Editing pp. 247–251
Writing Rubric p. 252
Writing Support p. 254 *(for English learners)*

Part 2: Apply the Writing Process

PREWRITING

1. **Choose an experience to share.** Encourage students to write down any ideas they have without worrying about other steps in the process. Have them take note of the TIP to generate a list of possible experiences. Once they have a list with a starred item, have them work in pairs to discuss the choices. Which idea does their partner like best? Why?
2. **What happened? When?** Remind students to explore as many of their ideas as possible. On the basis of this step, they may decide to place the star next to a different idea. Point out the TIP so students understand that some topics might not be appropriate for sharing with the group.
3. **Re-create the action for your reader.** Remind students to avoid vague words such as *awesome, great,* or *interesting.* They should explain what made something awesome by using specific descriptions. Ask students to write three descriptive details and three lines of dialogue for each person they plan to include in their narrative. Each line of dialogue should reflect the way the speaker actually talks.
4. **Think about what the experience meant to you.** Have students ask themselves: What made me think of this experience? What made it stand out from other experiences? Did I learn anything from it? Students' responses to these questions may help them write effective introductions and conclusions.

For interactive graphic organizers, see
WriteSmart CD
Writing Center at **ClassZone.com**

DRAFTING

1. **Plan how to tell your narrative.** Point out that most narratives use chronological order to make readers feel as though they are experiencing events as they happen. Distribute copies of the Sequence Chain and have students fill in as many boxes as possible. Remind them to consider whether any event should be described out of sequence, as in a flashback. Have pairs review each other's charts to see whether any events seem out of place.

   BEST PRACTICES TOOLKIT—Transparency
   Sequence Chain pp. B21, B45

2. **Capture your reader's interest.** Have students experiment with different introductions. Even a simple statement can be very powerful and engaging—for example, "It was the scariest moment of my life." Suggest that students review stories from the unit to see how each author hooks the reader. Have students work in small groups. Each student should read two different introductions. Which one does the group prefer? Why?

3. **Make the most of dialogue.** Remind students that the dialogue must fit the speaker. If a small child is speaking, the dialogue should sound like that of a small child. If an adult is speaking, the dialogue should sound like that of an adult. Urge students not to overuse dialogue. A good story will have a balance of description, narration, and dialogue. Suggest that students use dialogue at key moments when knowing someone's exact words will add excitement, interest, or believability. Refer them to page 150 for examples of correctly punctuated dialogue. Also point out the TIP at the end of step 3.

For a personal narrative writing template, see

BEST PRACTICES TOOLKIT—Transparency
Writing Template: Autobiographical or Personal Narrative pp. C16, C18

Write*Smart* CD

Writing Center at **ClassZone.com**

DRAFTING

What Should I Do?	What Does It Look Like?
1. Plan how to tell your narrative. Use a flow chart to get organized. Make sure you haven't left out any important steps. Describing the incident in **chronological order** (also called time order) is usually the clearest way to help readers understand what happened. If you want, you can include a **flashback**. That's an event that took place before the start of your narrative.	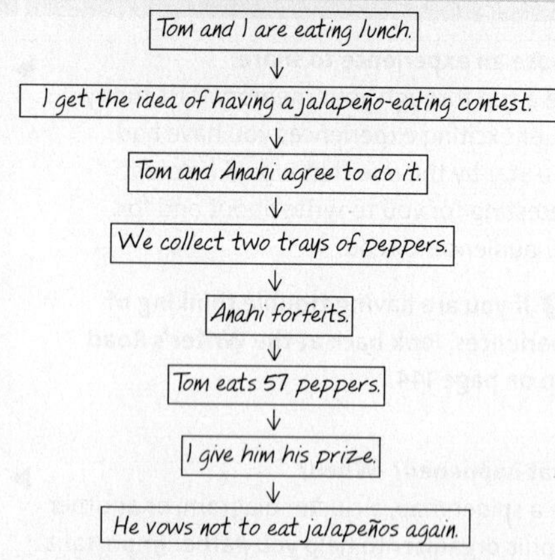
2. Capture your reader's interest. Write an introduction that makes your reader curious. Set the scene, describe a character, explain an action, or include a quotation. Some narratives begin by asking the reader a question.	*It was an ingenious idea. It was my idea. During lunch one day, we loaded up two trays with as many jalapeño peppers as they would hold. Then the fun began.* *Let me tell you how it all started. Tom and I were in the cafeteria, eating. It was fourth period in May. I grunted with a mouth full of ham, "I got an idea." Tom was so busy eating his hot dog with everything on it that he didn't hear me.*
3. Make the most of dialogue. Instead of writing "this happened, and then this happened," try including dialogue that shows your reader what happened. **See page 150:** Check Your Grammar **TIP Before you revise, look back at the key traits on page 144 and the rubric and peer-reader questions on page 150.**	**From prewriting notes . . .** *I got the idea of having a jalapeño-eating contest. Then I told Tom about it.* **. . . to draft** *"Well, seeing as you like your jalapeños. . . ." I paused for a moment and pointed at his hot dog, which was covered in them. "Maybe you would like to have an eating contest with someone."*

DIFFERENTIATED INSTRUCTION

FOR LESS–PROFICIENT WRITERS

Getting Organized Give students this outline to help them organize their narratives:

Introduction
- Hook the reader.
- Tell where and when the experience occurred.
- Identify the people involved.
- Tell why the experience is special.

Body
- Tell what happened first, next, and so on.
- Use transitions to show how events are related to each other.
- Use both description and dialogue.
- Use language that brings the experience to life.

Conclusion
- Explain how the experience ended.
- Tell why it was important to you.

REVISING AND EDITING

What Should I Do?	What Does It Look Like?
1. Check the sequence of events. • Ask a peer reader to underline events that seem confusing or out of order. • Add transitions or move information around to specify what happened when. **See page 150:** Ask a Peer Reader	People around us started clapping. He ran frantically to the drinking fountain. I handed him his prize—a bag of candy, as promised. [as] When he got back,
2. Add sensory language. • (Circle) words that describe how things looked, sounded, tasted, felt, or smelled. • If your narrative doesn't have many circles, add precise sensory details.	Tom is my best friend, and (he looks exactly like me.) If we told you we were twins with different last names, you would probably believe us. We have brown hair and blue eyes. We also wear rimless glasses.
3. Make your narrative stylish. • Reread your narrative. Does it give your reader a sense of your attitude and personality? Do your descriptions of others help readers understand their likes, dislikes, strengths, and weaknesses? • Revise your narrative as needed so that your style shines through. Your narrative might be formal or informal, fast-paced or leisurely, serious or lighthearted.	~~Tom ate all the candy and said he didn't like peppers anymore.~~ "I am never eating another jalapeño pepper in my life," Tom proclaimed after stuffing his face with chocolate bars. I couldn't do anything but laugh.
4. Conclude strongly. • [Bracket] the part of your conclusion that explains why you chose to describe this experience or what you learned from it. • If you have nothing to bracket, add one or more sentences that explain the meaning of the incident.	It's a little harder to get Tom to partake in my other schemes since I sent him to the drinking fountain for hours! I still have hope that he can pack down 58 peppers if he just works at it, though. I'm sure you can imagine how much luck I'm having convincing him to try. What about you? Bon appétit!

FOR ENGLISH LEARNERS

Revising and Editing [paired option] Have students use this checklist and then work in pairs to review the results:

—Have I rearranged events that were out of order?
—Have I added transitions to make the order of events clear?
—Have I added sensory words?
—Does the style reflect my personality?
—Have I concluded with a clear statement of the importance of the experience?

FOR ADVANCED LEARNERS/PRE–AP

Experiment with Style [small-group option] Remind students that, in works of fiction, the author and the narrator are not the same person. Ask students to rewrite all or part of their narratives with a style entirely different from their own. Encourage them to think like the narrator they create. Have them read both the original and the new versions to the group. Which narrator is more effective in telling the story? Why?

REVISING AND EDITING

1. **Check the sequence of events.** Sometimes writers assume that what they have written is clear simply because they are already familiar with the story. Have students work in pairs and read their narratives aloud to each other. What additional information does the reader need? Is there any information that is unnecessary to understanding the narrative? If so, remove it.
2. **Add sensory language.** Distribute copies of a Two-Column Chart. Ask students to list the five senses on the left column. Then have them place descriptive words and phrases from their narratives in the right column across from the appropriate sense. If they have no details for several senses, suggest that they try to add some. Then they can incorporate these details as they revise their narratives.

   BEST PRACTICES TOOLKIT—Transparency
   Two-Column Chart p. A25
3. **Make your narrative stylish.** Have students read the revised text in the right column of their charts. What sense do they get of the writer's personality from phrases such as *stuffing his face with chocolate bars* and *I couldn't do anything but laugh?* As students reread their own work, have them consider whether it reflects their own personality and style. If it does not, how can they insert a little more of themselves into the text?
4. **Conclude strongly.** Remind students that their writing should not just stop; it should conclude. A satisfying ending makes clear why the piece was written. The reader needs to clearly understand why the experience was significant (prompt 1) or how the incident from literature was similar to the writer's own experience (prompt 2). Adding a couple of sentences can make a big difference for the reader.

For interactive revision tools, see
WriteSmart CD
Writing Center at **ClassZone.com**

Preparing to Publish

Support for meeting the goals in the writing rubric is supplied throughout the **Writing Workshop** on pages 144–149.

For Rubric Bank, see

WriteSmart CD

Writing Center at **ClassZone.com**

Assess and Reteach

After reading and assessing students' personal narratives, you might use these lessons to reteach key skills:

STANDARDS LESSON FILE

Writing Lesson 14: Sequence and Chronological Order

Writing Lesson 35: Personal Narrative

Writing Lesson 48: Writing Dialogue

Preparing to Publish

Personal Narrative

Apply the Rubric

A strong personal narrative . . .

☑ describes a single incident

☑ has an intriguing introduction

☑ includes transitions that show the order of events

☑ presents dialogue and specific details to describe exactly what happened

☑ uses sensory language to make the experience come alive

☑ has a distinctive style that reveals the writer's personality

☑ varies sentence types (statements, questions, and exclamations)

☑ concludes by explaining what the experience meant to the writer

Ask a Peer Reader

- Do any events seem out of order or confusing? If so, which ones?
- What else would you like to know about this experience?
- How can I make my introduction more interesting?

Check Your Grammar

- To include dialogue in your narrative, enclose each person's exact words in quotation marks. Begin a new paragraph for each new speaker.

"Come on, Tom. You can do it!" I encouraged, pounding the table. "50, 51, 52, 53, 54 . . . Come on . . . 55, 56, 57."

"Yahoo!!" Tom shouted.

- If the speaker's words are a statement, use a comma to separate them from the rest of the text. If they are a question or an exclamation, use a question mark or an exclamation point instead of a comma.

"So let's hear this great idea of yours," Tom stated, brushing ham from his fries.

"What? Huh?" he replied, looking up from his hot dog.

"All right, Tom!" I yelled.

See page R49: Quick Reference: Punctuation

Writing Online

PUBLISHING OPTIONS

For publishing options, visit the **Writing Center at ClassZone.com.**

ASSESSMENT PREPARATION

For writing and grammar assessment practice, go to the **Assessment Center** at **ClassZone.com.**

150 UNIT 1: PLOT AND CONFLICT

Staging a Scene

Remember how your own heart pounded while you were reading "The Tell-Tale Heart"? You can help give people that exciting "you are there" feeling by staging a scene from your own narrative.

Preparing the Scene

1. **Choose a scene.** Read through your personal narrative. Look for a scene that has exciting action and funny or dramatic dialogue. You may need to rewrite it a little to give explanations or background information.
2. **Pick the actors, props, and scenery.** List the characters involved in the scene. Ask your classmates to volunteer to act the parts. Collect props and scenery. For example, you might look for rimless glasses for the main characters as well as a long table and a few cafeteria trays to suggest a lunchroom. Keep props and scenery simple so they won't distract your audience.
3. **Create a script.** Mark up your scene with directions telling the actors where they should stand or sit and how they should say their lines. Give a copy to each actor.

> *Tom and Anahi sit at a long table in front of trays loaded with jalapeños. Joe and their other classmates gather around.*
>
> ***Joe*** *(sounding serious and official) "On your mark, get set, go!"*
>
> *The contestants begin stuffing peppers into their mouths.*
>
> ***Anahi*** *(with eyes bugging out, runs for the water fountain) "Aarrgghh! Yeecchh! Wwaaaterrr!"*
>
> ***Joe*** *(pounding the table) "Come on, Tom! You can do it! 50, 51, 52 . . ."*

4. **Rehearse.** Set up the scenery and props. Have the actors practice the scene several times until they feel comfortable.

Presenting the Scene

1. **Action!** Have the actors deliver their lines clearly enough to be heard at the back of the room.
2. **Show emotion.** The actors' facial expressions and body language should convey feelings clearly but without exaggeration.
3. **Pay attention to pacing.** Signal the actors to speed up if the audience seems bored or slow down if they seem confused.

See page R82: Evaluate an Oral Interpretation

SPEAKING AND LISTENING

Have students read this page for an overview of how to stage a scene from a personal narrative. Before students begin working, review this rubric with them so that they understand their goals:

Rubric A strong scene presentation

- chooses a scene that contains action, humor, or drama
- uses props and scenery that convey the situation without becoming a distraction
- has a script for each actor with clear directions about where actors should be during the scene and how they should act
- is presented in a way that ensures everyone in the room sees and hears the performance
- is presented with enthusiasm, including appropriate facial expressions and gestures
- maintains an appropriate pace that is neither too hurried or too slow
- has been well rehearsed so that all parts of the presentation go smoothly

RESOURCE MANAGER—Copy Master
Speaking and Listening p. 253

STANDARDS LESSON FILE
Speaking and Listening Lesson 6: Narrative and Original Works

DIFFERENTIATED INSTRUCTION

FOR LESS-PROFICIENT WRITERS

Staging a Scene Have students compare the sample script to the model. Note that

- some dialogue comes directly from the model (lines 22, 30–31). The script indicates how Joe should act or sound as he delivers the lines.
- some dialogue is original. Anahi cries, "Aarrgghh! Yeecchh! Wwaaaterrr!" This line adds realism and excitement to the presentation.
- directions for setting the scene and for what the characters do come from the text (lines 21, 22–23)

Suggest that students do the following:

- Select students to help stage their scenes on the basis of who will do the best job rather than selecting their close friends.
- If some props are impractical, simply pretend or mime the action.
- Offer constructive suggestions to other actors if they need help with pacing or voice projection.

Assessment Practice

CHECK READINESS

Read aloud the paragraph under **ASSESS** and stress to students that this is not the full Unit Test but a way for them to check their readiness for it. Then have students examine the skills listed under **REVIEW** and look back in the unit or in the **Student Resource Bank** for any they need to study.

READ THE SELECTION

Remind students to keep Unit Goals in mind as they read the passage, paying particular attention to

- plot, including stages and suspense
- conflict
- sequence, including order of events and flashback
- cause and effect

To help students focus on **plot** while reading, encourage them to ask questions such as

- What are the key events of the story?
- What details mark each stage of the story, such as the exposition, the rising action, and the resolution?
- How does the author create suspense at each stage of the story?

ANSWER THE QUESTIONS

Direct students to pages R95–R101 of the Test-Taking Handbook to review test-taking strategies. Remind them not to choose the first alternative that seems to fit when answering a multiple-choice question. Instead, students should read through all the choices, eliminate any that are clearly wrong, and then choose the best answer—the one that is most accurate and complete.

Emphasize to students the importance of reading carefully the directions for each section of the test before they begin. A misunderstanding could prevent them from getting credit for what they know. Suggest that they read each set of directions a second time after completing the first item of each section, to be sure they understand the directions in the context of an item.

Assessment Practice

Reading Comprehension

ASSESS

The practice test items on the next few pages match skills listed on the Unit Goals page (page 23) and addressed throughout this unit. Taking this practice test will help you assess your knowledge of these skills and determine your readiness for the Unit Test.

REVIEW

After you take the practice test, your teacher can help you identify any skills you need to review.

- Plot
  - Stages
  - Suspense
- Conflict
- Sequence
  - Order of Events
  - Flashback
- Cause and Effect
- Latin Words and Roots
- Dictionary
- Pronoun-Antecedent Agreement
- Punctuation

ASSESSMENT ONLINE

For more assessment practice and test-taking tips, go to the **Assessment Center** at **ClassZone.com.**

DIRECTIONS *Read this selection and answer the questions that follow.*

The Invaders

Jack Ritchie

None of them left the ship on the first day of its arrival, but I knew that they would be watching carefully for signs of human life.

The skies were dark with scudding clouds, and the cold wind moved high i the trees. Thin snow drifted slowly to the ground.

From the cover of the forest, I now watched as a small, heavily armed group of them left the large craft. When they reached the edge of the woods, they hesitated for a few moments and then moved cautiously forward.

I had seen them before and I knew that in appearance, at least, they were not monsters. They looked very much like us. There were some differences, of course, but all in all, we were really quite similar to them.

I met them first when I was almost a boy and I had been without caution. I approached them and they seemed friendly, but then suddenly they seized me and carried me off in their strange ship.

It was a long journey to their land and when our ship made a landing, I was shown about and exhibited as though I were some kind of animal.

I saw their cities, and I was shown plants and animals completely strange to me. I learned to wear their clothing and even to eat their food.

They taught me to communicate in their strange and difficult tongue until I could, at times, even think in their language.

I had almost given up the hope of ever seeing my home again, but they one day put me back on one of their ships and told me that they were returning m because they wished to establish friendly relations with my people. But by now I knew enough of them to know that this was not true. However, I nodded and smiled and watched for my opportunity to escape.

When the ship landed, I went out with the first search party. It was near evening and as the darkness gathered, I edged away from them and finally I fled into the blackness and safety of the forest.

They came after me, of course, but I was hidden deep in the woods where they could not find me.

Finally they gave up and I watched their ship become smaller and finally disappear, and I hoped fervently that they would never return.

But now they were back again.

DIFFERENTIATED INSTRUCTION

FOR ENGLISH LEARNERS

Assessment Practice: Work Backwards [paired option] Prepare students for the assessment by having them read the questions before reading the text passage. Have pairs follow these steps to learn unfamiliar words in the test directions and questions:

1. Find words you don't recognize and write each one on an index card.
2. Look up the meaning in a dictionary.
3. Write the meaning on the back of the card.
4. Use your word cards to teach and practice the vocabulary with your partner and another pair.

I felt a coldness inside of me as I watched them moving slowly through the trees. They seemed somehow different from the others who had been here before. It was not so much in their appearance as in the air about them—the way they walked, the way they looked about with speculating eyes.

Slowly and instinctively, I realized that this time they were not here on just another raid for a captive or two.

This time they had come to stay.

What could we do now? Could we lure them deeper into the forest and kill them? Could we take their weapons and learn how to use them?

No, I thought despairingly. There were so many more of the invaders on the ship. And more weapons. They would come out and hunt us down like animals. They would hunt us down and kill us all.

I sighed. We must find out what it was that they wanted this time and whatever it might be, we must learn to adjust and to hope for the best.

But I still retreated silently before them, afraid to approach. I watched them search the ground ahead of them and knew they were looking for footprints, for some signs of life. But there was not yet enough snow on the ground to track us down.

Their strangely colored eyes glanced about warily. They were cautious, yes.

They could be a cruel race, I knew. I had seen with my own eyes how they treated their animals and even their own kind.

I sighed again. Yes, we could be cruel, too. In this respect we could not claim to be superior to the invaders.

They paused now in a clearing, their eyes gleaming beneath their helmets.

It was time for me to approach them.

I took a deep breath and stepped into the open.

Their weapons quickly pointed at me.

"Welcome," I said.

They stared at me, and then one of them turned to their bearded leader. "It appears that this savage can speak some English, Captain Standish."

"Welcome," I said again. But I wondered what they would do to my land and my people now

ITEM ANALYSIS

COMPREHENSION	ITEMS	UNIT PAGES
Plot	2, 3, 6, 10, 14, 15	26, 33, 77
Conflict	4, 5, 17	24, 47, 63, 119
Sequence	1, 8, 9, 12, 16	63, 119
Cause and Effect	7, 11, 13	111

VOCABULARY	ITEMS	UNIT PAGES
Latin Words and Roots	1, 2, 3, 4	117
Dictionary	5, 6, 7	85

WRITING AND GRAMMAR	ITEMS	UNIT PAGES
Pronoun-Antecedent Agreement	1, 4, 5, 6	99
Punctuation	2, 3, 7, 8	75

After checking student readiness with this Assessment Practice, you may administer the complete Unit 1 Test in order to more thoroughly evaluate student mastery of unit goals.

FOR LESS–PROFICIENT READERS

Assessment Support Consider these options for completing the **Assessment Practice:**

- Have students "work backwards," reviewing the questions before reading the passage.
- Have students record test words and definitions in their journals for reference.
- Read the passage or parts of it aloud.
- Select random questions in the assessment and have students demonstrate how and where to look for the answers.

FOR ENGLISH LEARNERS

Review Academic Vocabulary Display the following academic vocabulary terms. Then give the definitions in random order and have students match them to the terms.

- *plot:* chain of related events in a story
- *conflict:* struggle between opposing forces
- *exposition:* beginning part of a story that introduces the setting, characters, and major conflict
- *rising action:* middle part of a story in which suspense or tension builds because problems arise that make the conflict more difficult for the main characters
- *climax:* the turning point of a story, when the reader's interest is most intense
- *falling action:* the last part of a story, in which the conflict ends and any remaining questions are answered

ANSWERS

Comprehension

Model a thinking process for answering multiple-choice questions.

1. **B *is correct.*** *The story begins with the invaders leaving the ship and entering the woods (lines 5–7). It is later in the story that the narrator thinks about attacking them (lines 40–41) and then watches them look for footprints (lines 47–48), making* A *and* C *incorrect.* D *is incorrect because the narrator greets the invaders at the end of the story (lines 58–60).*
2. **D *is correct.*** *The exposition of the story describes its cold and snowy setting (lines 3–4).* A, B, *and* C *are incorrect because they all describe details revealed later in the story, not in the exposition.*
3. **B *is correct.*** *The narrator's prediction creates tension because readers wonder who "they" are and why they might be "watching."* A, C, *and* D *are incorrect because they provide details about time, place, and character, but they do not raise questions, hint at events to come, or cause tension.*
4. **B *is correct.*** *The narrator debates whether it is in the best interest of his people to respond with violence or with cooperation (lines 40–46).* A *is incorrect because the narrator shares only bad memories of being in the invaders' country.* C *is incorrect because he never mentions sharing or hiding food.* D *is incorrect because he clearly wants to protect his people, not betray them.*
5. **A *is correct.*** *The story ends with the narrator wondering what the invaders will do to his land and people (lines 63–64).* B *is incorrect because readers know the narrator communicates with the invaders by speaking English to them.* C *is incorrect because the invaders leave the ship and enter the forest at the beginning of the story.* D *is incorrect because the narrator makes the decision not to stay hidden.*
6. **C *is correct.*** *Tension rises as the narrator realizes the seriousness of the fact that the invaders have returned.* A *is part of the exposition, and* B *is part of the flashback, making both incorrect.* D *is incorrect because it comes close to the end of the story.*

Comprehension

DIRECTIONS *Answer these questions about "The Invaders."*

1. Which event happens first in the story?

A The invaders look at the ground for footprints.
B The invaders leave the ship and enter the woods.
C The narrator thinks about attacking the invaders.
D The narrator steps into view and greets the invaders.

2. In the exposition of the story, you learn that

A the narrator speaks English
B the invaders are cruel people
C Captain Standish is a leader
D the weather is cold and snowy

3. Which phrase helps to develop suspense in the story?

A "first day of its arrival" (line 1)
B "I knew that they would be watching" (lines 1–2)
C "thin snow drifted slowly" (line 4)
D "we were really quite similar to them" (line 10)

4. Which conflict does the narrator struggle with in this story?

A choosing whether to return with the invaders to their country
B deciding which response to the invaders will be best for his people
C sharing food with the invaders or hiding it from them
D betraying his people by helping the invaders find what they want

5. Which conflict is not resolved by the end of this story?

A what will happen between the invaders an
the narrator's people
B how the narrator will decide to communicate with the invaders
C whether the invaders can make their way off the ship and into the forest
D if the narrator will choose to stay hidden from the invaders

6. Which line comes at the beginning of the rising action?

A "They looked very much like us." (line 9)
B "I learned to wear their clothing and even to eat their food." (line 17)
C "But now they were back again." (line 32)
D "Yes, we could be cruel, too." (line 54)

7. In line 42, why is the narrator losing hope?

A He fears that his people are outnumbered and will be killed.
B His hiding places in the snowy forest are too visible.
C He thinks that the invaders are looking fo
another captive.
D His footprints might lead the invaders to his people.

8. Which line introduces the flashback within the story?

A "I met them first when I was almost a boy and I had been without caution." (line 11
B "But by now, I knew enough of them to know that this was not true." (lines 22–23
C "There were so many more of the invaders on the ship." (lines 42–43)
D "But I still retreated silently before them, afraid to approach." (line 47)

154

7. **A *is correct.*** *The narrator acknowledges, with despair, how many more invaders and weapons must be on the ship.* B, C, *and* D *are incorrect because line 42 makes no specific mention of hiding places, another captive, or footprints.*
8. **A *is correct.*** *The flashback begins when the narrator recalls meeting the invaders when he was a boy.* B *is incorrect because it comes toward the end of the flashback.* C *and* D *are incorrect because they are in the main part of the story, not the flashback.*
9. **B *is correct.*** *The flashback focuses on the narrator's experience of being captured and taken to the invaders' land.* A *is not part of the flashback.* C *is incorrect because the flashback explains the narrator's growing sense of the invaders' unfriendly intentions.* D *is incorrect because the flashback describes how the narrator became accustomed to his captors' clothing, food, and language, which were strange to him (lines 17–19).*

The flashback reveals that the narrator

A carefully watched the invaders when they left their ship
B was captured as a child by invaders and taken to their land
C grew to believe that the invaders had friendly intentions
D had many habits in common with the invaders

The climax of the story occurs when the narrator

A steps out and speaks to the invaders
B hides from the invaders in the woods
C returns home after being held captive
D hears the invaders talk to their leader

Why does the narrator hide from the new invaders?

A He distrusts the invaders and is trying to decide what to do.
B Other people are coming to help him.
C He wants to surprise the invaders from a well-protected location.
D A search party is looking for him.

Which phrase from the story helps you figure out when an event occurs?

A "There were some differences . . ."
B "It was a long journey . . ."
C "I could, at times, . . ."
D "They paused now . . ."

The narrator rejects the idea of attacking the invaders because

A the strangers have enough people and weapons to harm the local people
B the strangers are peaceful and hope to do good deeds
C neither the strangers nor the local people want to have a fight
D the narrator can speak the strangers' language

14. During the falling action, you discover that the invaders

A arrive on a large ship
B have strangely colored eyes
C are led by an English captain
D mistreat their animals and each other

Written Response

SHORT RESPONSE *Write two or three sentences to answer each question.*

15. Identify one technique the author uses to create suspense. Give an example from the text to support your choice.

16. In the flashback, what steps does the narrator take to escape the invaders?

EXTENDED RESPONSE *Write a paragraph to answer the following question.*

17. Reread lines 37–46. What does the narrator realize about the invaders? Explain how this realization helps him to resolve his conflict.

GO ON

10. A *is correct.* *The narrator's approach of the invaders is the story's highest point of interest and its turning point.* B *is incorrect because it is part of the rising action.* C *is incorrect because it occurs at the end of the story's early flashback.* D *is incorrect because it occurs at the very end of the story.*

11. A *is correct.* *The narrator's thoughts as he hides reveal his distrust and his conflicting thoughts on how to handle the invaders. There is no evidence in the story to support* B, C, *or* D, *making all of them incorrect.*

12. D *is correct.* *The word* now *lets readers know that the action being described is occurring in the present.* A, B, *and* C *do not contain words that indicate when actions and events occurred.*

13. A *is correct.* *The narrator states that the invaders would have ample people and weapons with which to retaliate against an attack (lines 40–44). He describes the strangers as "a cruel race," making* B *incorrect. While* C *may be a factual statement, it is not the reason the narrator rejects the idea of fighting.* D *is incorrect because the narrator does not mention his ability to speak English as a reason not to attack.*

14. C *is correct.* *The falling action follows the story's climax, when the narrator approaches the invaders. It is at this point that readers learn of the English captain (line 62). Readers learn of the large ship, as in* A, *early in the story's exposition. We can eliminate* B *and* D *because these details are revealed in the rising action, prior to the climax.*

Written Response

Possible short responses:

15. *The author varies the length of his sentences, using short, choppy sentences following descriptive passages to create tension. Examples include "But now they were back again" (line 32) and "This time they had come to stay" (line 39).*

16. *The narrator cooperates and watches for an opportunity to escape (lines 23–24). When the ship arrives in his homeland, he goes out with the first search party and flees into the darkness of the forest (lines 25–27). He then stays hidden deep in the woods where the invaders cannot find him (lines 28–29).*

Possible extended response:

17. *The response should describe the narrator's understanding that the invaders' visit this time is different from the raid he remembers as a child. He states, "This time they had come to stay" (line 39). Students should explain that this realization helps him resolve his conflict over how best to respond to the invaders. He realizes that they are determined to settle in the area and that there are probably many of them with a large supply of weapons. These facts lead him to decide it is not in the best interest of his people to become adversaries of the strangers. Instead, he feels strongly that they should attempt to communicate with the strangers and "learn to adjust and to hope for the best" (line 46).*

ANSWERS

Vocabulary

1. **B *is correct.*** *The narrator describes being "shown about" to people in the invaders' land.* A, C, *and* D *do not fit easily into the context of line 15; furthermore,* A *and* D *are unrelated to the word's Latin meaning.*
2. **D *is correct.*** *The invaders wanted to "set up" a friendship with the narrator's people. Also, the definition "make solid" relates to the Latin word* stabilis, *or "firm." Their act would not end or damage a friendship, as in* A *and* B, *because no friendship exists.* C *does not make sense in the context of the paragraph, and "trickery" does not relate to "firm."*
3. **C *is correct.*** *Readers can infer that the narrator has strong emotions in wishing away his captors.* Boil *is often associated with passion or anger. The definitions in* A *and* B *do not fit the context or relate to "boil."* D *makes no sense in the context.*
4. **B *is correct.*** *The context of the sentence suggests that the invaders were thinking about different possibilities as they observed their surroundings. There is no evidence in the story of creating, risk-taking, or "accepting something as true," as in* A, C, *and* D.
5. **A *is correct.*** *Readers are told in the first sentence of the story that the invaders are on a ship.* B *and* C *are incorrect because they do not work in the context of the paragraph.* D *can be eliminated because* craft *is clearly being used as a noun in the sentence.*
6. **C *is correct.*** *In this sentence,* craft *refers to the action of creating bookshelves. In* A, *the pronoun* her *indicates something that belongs to someone, making the word a noun in this context. In* B *and* D, *the article* the *used with* craft *indicates its use as a noun.*
7. **D *is correct.*** Trickery *refers to something intended to trick or outsmart. We can eliminate* A *because it does not make any sense in the context of the sentence. Logically, a fox would not use talent or a profession, as in* B *and* C, *to outsmart hunters.*

Vocabulary

DIRECTIONS *Use context clues and the Latin word and root definitions to answer the following questions.*

1. The Latin prefix *ex-* means "out," and the Latin word *habere* means "to hold" or "to see." What is the most likely meaning of the word *exhibited* as it is used in line 15?
   A made to work hard
   B presented in public
   C held captive in a prison
   D soothed with kind words
2. The word *establish* comes from the Latin word *stabilis,* which means "firm." What is the most likely meaning of the word *establish* as it is used in line 22?
   A to end quickly
   B to damage beyond repair
   C to bring about using trickery
   D to set up and make solid
3. The Latin word *fervere* means "to boil." What is the most likely meaning of the word *fervently* as it is used in line 31?
   A in a dreamy way
   B for a long time
   C with great emotion
   D while cooking
4. The Latin word *speculari* means "to observe." What is the most likely meaning of the word *speculating* as it is used in line 36?
   A creating a new object
   B thinking about or guessing
   C taking a risk in the hope of gain
   D accepting something as true

DIRECTIONS *Use the dictionary entry to answer the following questions.*

craft (krăft) *noun* **1.** A boat, ship, or aircraft. **2.** Skill in doing or making something **3.** An occupation or trade. *verb* **1.** To make by hand. **Synonyms:** *noun:* vehicle, talent, profession, trickery; *verb:* create.

5. Which definition best matches the meanin of the word *craft* as it is used in line 6?
   A noun definition 1
   B noun definition 2
   C noun definition 3
   D verb definition 1
6. In which sentence is the word *craft* used as a verb?
   A She learned her craft from her father, wh was a carpenter.
   B The fine workmanship revealed the sculptor's craft.
   C He tried to craft a set of bookshelves for the library.
   D The small craft was tossed about by the rough waves.
7. Which synonym would best replace the wo *craft* in the following sentence?

   The wily fox used <u>craft</u> to outsmart the hunters.

   A vehicle
   B talent
   C profession
   D trickery

156

DIFFERENTIATED INSTRUCTION

FOR ENGLISH LEARNERS

Assessment Support: Latin Roots Point out that English words derived from Latin roots often have cognates in Spanish and other Romance languages. Help students identify cognates for the base words in items 1–4. Spanish cognates are as follows:

- *exhibit/exhibir*
- *establish/establecer*
- *fervent/ferviente, fervoroso*
- *speculate/especular*

Writing & Grammar

DIRECTIONS *Read this passage and answer the questions that follow.*

(1) When the Pilgrims first landed at Plymouth in 1620, everyone had their dream of a better life. (2) They agreed that they should work together to build a common house for all of the colonists meetings and religious services. (3) Peoples lives were difficult though, especially because there was a shortage of food. (4) Nobody knew whether they would survive. (5) In fact, many settlers died during his first winter in the colony. (6) The Native American Squanto helped everyone who remained find where they could fish and trap animals for food. (7) The Native Americans willingness to share their knowledge of agriculture helped the Pilgrims survive in the new land. (8) Today, the national holiday of Thanksgiving recalls the Pilgrims celebration of their first harvest in Plymouth.

1. To maintain pronoun-antecedent agreement in sentence 1, change *their* to
   - **A** theirs
   - **B** its
   - **C** his or her
   - **D** they
2. Choose the correct way to punctuate the underlined word in sentence 2.
   - **A** colonist's
   - **B** colonists'
   - **C** colonists's
   - **D** colonist's'
3. Choose the correct way to punctuate the underlined word in sentence 3.
   - **A** Peopleses'
   - **B** Peoples'
   - **C** Peoples's
   - **D** People's
4. To maintain pronoun-antecedent agreement in sentence 4, change *they* to
   - **A** he or she
   - **B** them
   - **C** his or her
   - **D** its
5. To maintain pronoun-antecedent agreement in sentence 5, change *his* to
   - **A** their
   - **B** its
   - **C** his or her
   - **D** her
6. To maintain pronoun-antecedent agreement in sentence 6, change *they* to
   - **A** it
   - **B** its
   - **C** their
   - **D** he or she
7. Choose the correct way to punctuate the underlined word in sentence 7.
   - **A** American's
   - **B** Americans's
   - **C** Americanses'
   - **D** Americans'
8. Choose the correct way to punctuate the underlined word in sentence 8.
   - **A** Pilgrims'es
   - **B** Pilgrims'
   - **C** Pilgrims's
   - **D** Pilgrim's

DIFFERENTIATED INSTRUCTION

FOR ENGLISH LEARNERS

Assessment Support: Agreement

- Remind students that pronouns must agree with their antecedents in gender and number. Discuss these examples:
  - —The **man** learned where **it** could go fishing. (incorrect gender)
  - —The **man** learned where **they** could go fishing. (incorrect number)
  - —The **man** learned where **he** could go fishing. (correct gender and number)
- Review indefinite pronouns, which do not refer to a specific person, place, or thing. Some are singular (*everyone, someone*) while others are plural (*all, many*). Illustrate with these examples:
  - —**Everyone** had **their** reasons for coming to Plymouth. (incorrect number)
  - —**Everyone** had **his or her** reasons for coming to Plymouth. (correct number)
  - —**Many** met **his** death. (incorrect number)
  - —**Many** met **their** death. (correct number)

ANSWERS

Writing & Grammar

1. **C *is correct.*** Everyone *is a singular indefinite pronoun that must agree in both number and gender with its pronoun referent. We can eliminate* A *because* theirs *is not a possessive pronoun as the sentence requires.* B *is incorrect because* its *does not refer to people.* D *is incorrect because* they *is a subjective pronoun.*
2. **B *is correct.*** *We add an apostrophe to make a plural noun ending in* s *possessive.* A *is incorrect because it implies a singular noun.* C *and* D *would be incorrect forms in any context.*
3. **D *is correct.*** *We add an apostrophe and an* s *to make the possessive form of a plural noun that does not end in* s. A, B, *and* C *can be eliminated because they are incorrect forms in any context.*
4. **A *is correct.*** He or she *agrees with the singular pronoun* Nobody. B *is incorrect because* them *is an objective pronoun.* C *and* D *are incorrect because* his, her, *and* its *are possessive pronouns, and the clause "they would survive" needs a subject.*
5. **A *is correct.*** Their *agrees in number with* settlers. B *is incorrect because* its *does not correctly refer to* settlers. C *and* D *are incorrect because neither agrees in number with* settlers.
6. **D *is correct.*** He or she *agrees in number with* everyone. A *and* B *can be eliminated because* it *and* its *do not refer to people.* C *is incorrect because* their *is a possessive adjective.*
7. **D *is correct.*** *We add an apostrophe to make the possessive form of a plural noun ending in* s. A *is incorrect because it implies that* Native American *is singular, which does not agree with* their. B *and* C *are incorrect forms in any context.*
8. **B *is correct.*** Pilgrims *is a plural noun.* A *and* C *are incorrect possessive forms.* D *is incorrect because it is the possessive form of the singular noun* Pilgrim.

INTRODUCE *MORE GREAT READS*

In Unit 1, students have discussed a number of big questions. Invite students to tell which question they found most intriguing and why. Then focus attention on the three questions that appear on this page. Discuss the recommended books and their summaries, pointing out how each book connects to the related question. Encourage students to choose one or more of these "great reads" to read independently.

ClassZone.com

To find additional books that match students' interests and ability levels, visit the Literature Center at **ClassZone.com.**

UNIT 1

More Great Reads

Ideas for Independent Reading

Which questions from Unit 1 made an impression on you? Continue exploring them with these books.

What's worth the effort?

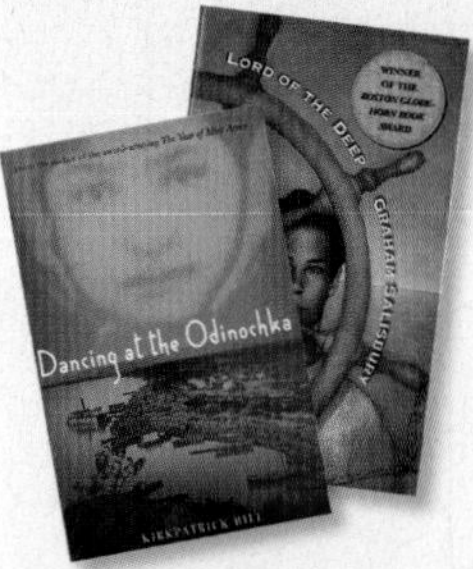

The Circuit: Stories from the Life of a Migrant Child
by Francisco Jiménez

In the 1940s, Francisco and his family crossed the Mexican border. Together they worked picking crops in California, struggling to make a life and a permanent home in a new country.

Dancing at the Odinochka
by Kirkpatrick Hill

Erinia and her family live on a small trading post in Russian America. Life is hard, but Erinia is happy. When America buys the territory, life changes. Will the Pavaloffs be able to survive?

Lord of the Deep
by Graham Salisbury

This summer, 13-year-old Mikey is the youngest deckhand in the marina. He soon realizes that working on his stepdad's boat is complicated. When two customers ask for "special" treatment, Mikey has to decide where his loyalty lies

Is seeing believing?

The Kite Rider
by Geraldine McCaughrean

In thirteenth-century China, Hayou works as a kite rider. It's a terrifying job, but as he soars through the clouds he sometimes sees his father's spirit. Can these sightings give Hayou the wisdom and courage to save his mother and himself?

Sorceress
by Celia Rees

Agnes grew up on a Mohawk reservation in upstate New York. When she starts dreaming of a 17th-century ancestor, she goes home to her Aunt M for help. Is Agnes going crazy, or is someone trying to tell her secrets of her family's past?

The True Confessions of Charlotte Doyle
by Avi

At only 13, Charlotte is a perfect young lady. When she's on a ship traveling to America, she swears she wil never leave her cabin, but by the end of the voyage she's been accused of murder, trie and found guilty.

When is it OK to be scared?

Code Orange
by Caroline B. Cooney

Mitty panics when he remembers his biology paper. He grabs some old medical books from his mother's office and finds an envelope of smallpox scabs from 1912. Has Mitty just unleashed a deadly virus on New York City?

A Girl Named Disaster
by Nancy Farmer

Nhamo isn't even 12 when she's forced to marry a cruel man with three wives. Her grandmother convinces her to run away, and Nhamo must find her way from Mozambique to Zimbabwe on her own.

The Rag and Bone Sho
by Robert Cormier

A little girl has been murdered. Trent, an expert interrogator, is brought to Monument, Massachusetts meet the 12-year-old suspec Jason Dorrant. If Trent can get the boy's confession it'l make his career, but is Jason really guilty?

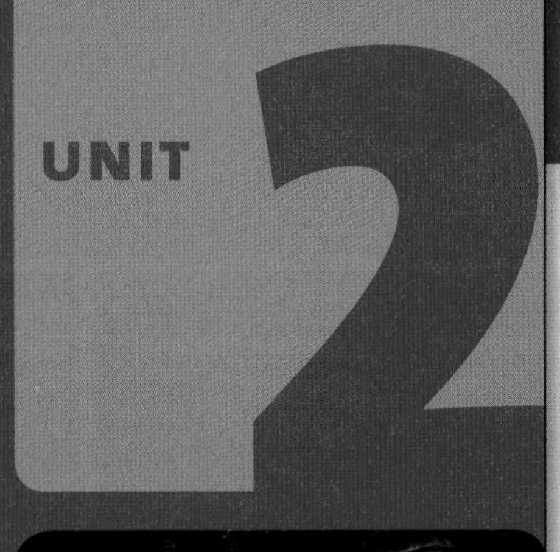

Through Different Eyes

CHARACTER AND POINT OF VIEW

- In Fiction
- In Media
- In Nonfiction
- In Poetry

159

For help in planning this unit, see

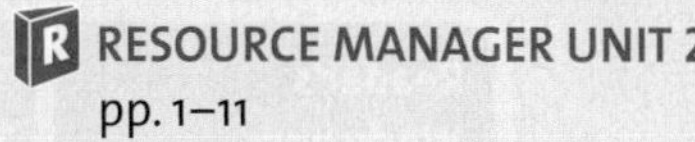
RESOURCE MANAGER UNIT 2
pp. 1–11

INTRODUCE THE UNIT

Each person has a unique point of view—a way of looking at the world that no one else has. One of the reasons we enjoy reading stories is that we like to look at life from the points of view of different characters, to think about the characters and compare them to ourselves and other people we know. We ask ourselves how we would react to similar events and whether we would make the same decisions as the characters do. Invite students to think about these ideas as they discuss the pictures on this page. To spark a discussion, ask these questions:

- Look closely at the pictures. What do these people have in common? In what ways are they different? Does either of them look like anyone you know?
- What might these characters be thinking about? What might they be feeling? In what ways might the world seem different if you looked at it from their point of view?

Remind students that since a writer cannot use pictures to help readers visualize characters, he or she must choose specific details to make the characters vivid and believable. In this unit, students will explore how writers use **point of view** and details to bring their **characters** to life.

About the Art The image of the girl playing chess illustrates "Rules of the Game" by Amy Tan. See page 225. The detail from the oil glazing *They Moved Them* by David Behrens illustrates the Virginia Driving Hawk Sneve story "The Medicine Bag." For more information, see page 240 of the teacher's edition.

UNIT 2

Skills Trace

SKILLS STRAND	Reader's Workshop: Character and Point of View pp. 162–167	*Linked selections* The Treasure of Lemon Brown pp. 168–181 Short Story *Level: Average*	Blues: A National Treasure pp. 182–187 Timeline, History Article, Feature Article	Flowers for Algernon/ *from* Charly pp. 188–221 Short Story/ Screenplay *Level: Challenging*	Rules of the Game pp. 222–237 Short Story *Level: Average*	The Medicine Bag/ Who Are You Today, María? pp. 238–253 Short Story/ Vignette *Level: Easy*
Literary Analysis	Point of View pp. 162–163, 167 Character Traits and Motivation pp. 164–167	Third-Person Limited Point of View pp. 169, 170, 173, 176, 178, 179	Form (Timeline) pp. 183, 187	Character Traits pp. 189, 190, 192, 193, 194, 196, 198, 199, 201, 202, 204, 207, 208, 215, T216, T218, 219 Review: Point of View pp. 193, 197, 201, 212	First-Person Point of View pp. 223, 224, 226, 230, 231, 233, 235	Main Character pp. 239, 240, 242, 243, 244, 245, 246, 247, 248, 250, 251
Reading and Informational Texts	Analyze the Literature pp. 163, 165–167	Make Inferences pp. 169, 172, 174, 175, 177, 178, 179	Identify Scope pp. 182, 183, 185, 186, 187 Evaluate Sources for Usefulness p. 187	Strategies for Reading a Long Story pp. 189, 192, 195, 198, 206, 210, 211, 214, 219	Draw Conclusions pp. 223, 227, 228, 231, 232, 233, 235 Review: Visualize pp. 226, 234, 235	Set a Purpose for Reading p. 239 Compare Characters p. 251
Vocabulary	Academic Vocabulary pp. 162, 164, 166	Word Acquisition pp. 169, T169, 180 Context Clues—General p. T169; Similes p. 180		Word Acquisition pp. 189, T189, 220 Context Clues p. T189 Specialized Vocabulary p. 220	Word Acquisition pp. 223, T223, 236 Context Clues p. T223 Prefixes (*fore-*, *mal-*) p. 236	Word Acquisition pp. 239, T239, 252 Context Clues p. T239 Analogies p. 252
Writing, Grammar, and Style		Verb Tenses p. 181		Comparative and Superlative Forms of Modifiers p. 221	Sentence Combining Using Coordinating Conjunctions p. 237	Write for Assessment p. 253
Speaking, Listening, Viewing, and Media	Discuss pp. 162–166	Discuss pp. 168, T170–T178, 179 Analyze Visuals pp. 170, 174	Discuss pp. 182, T183–T186, 187	Discuss pp. 188, T190–T218, 219 Analyze Visuals pp. 190, 195, 205, 209, 213, T216	Discuss pp. 222, T224–T234, 235 Analyze Visuals pp. 224, 227, 230, 234	Discuss pp. 238, T240–T250, 251 Analyze Visuals pp. 240, 245, 248

Assessment-Based Planning: Skills in red are assessed on the Unit 2 Test. **T** = Teacher's Edition page

Media Study: *from* Whale Rider pp. 254–257 Film Clips	*from* Harriet Tubman: Conductor on the Underground Railroad pp. 258–273 Biography *Level: Average*	The Mysterious Mr. Lincoln pp. 274–281 Biography *Level: Easy*	Barbara Frietchie/ John Henry pp. 282–291 Narrative Poems *Level: Average*	Writing Workshop: Describing a Person pp. 292–299
	Characterization pp. 259, 260, 263, 265, 266, 267, 268, 269, 271	Biography pp. 275, 276, 279, 280	Characterization in Poetry pp. 283, 286, 287, 288, 289, 291	
	Monitor pp. 259, 260, 262, 263, 265, 268, 271 Read a Letter p. 270	Identify Main Idea and Details pp. 275, 276, 278, 280	Recognize Sound Devices pp. 283, 284, 286, 287, 288, 289, 291 Read a Comic Strip p. 290	Analyze a Description of a Person pp. 293–294, 298
Academic Vocabulary (Film) p. 255	Word Acquisition pp. 259, T259, 272 Context Clues—General p. T259; Synonyms p. 272	Word Acquisition pp. 275, T275, 281 Context Clues p. T275 Multiple-Meaning Words p. 281		
	Independent and Dependent Clauses p. 273			Write a Character Description pp. 292–298 Clichés p. 298 Interrogative Pronouns (*Who* and *Whom*) p. 298
Discuss pp. 254, 257 Analyze Visual Elements and Editing in Film pp. 255–256 Plan a Scene p. 257	Discuss pp. 258, T260–T270, 271 Analyze Visuals pp. 260, 262, 267, 269	Discuss pp. 274, T276–T279, 280 Analyze Visuals pp. 276, T279	Discuss pp. 282, T284–T290, 291 Analyze Visuals p. 284	Discuss pp. 292–294 Conduct an Interview p. 299

Skills Assessed on the Unit 2 Test:

Literary Analysis
- Identify and analyze first-person and third-person point of view
- Identify and analyze character traits and motives
- Identify and analyze methods of characterization

Reading and Informational Texts
- Make inferences
- Identify main idea and details

Vocabulary
- Use knowledge of prefixes and base words to determine the meaning of derivatives
- Use context clues to determine the meaning of multiple-meaning words
- Understand and complete analogies

Writing, Grammar, and Style
- Write a description of a person
- Use correct verb tenses
- Use comparative and superlative forms correctly
- Use coordinating conjunctions to combine sentences
- Additional writing and grammar skills

For additional lesson planning help, see **Easy Planner DVD.**

OBJECTIVES

- establish prior knowledge about **character**
- discuss how details can help bring a character to life

What brings a CHARACTER *to life?*

Ask students to think about the last memorable character they encountered in a story. What specific details about that character do they remember?

ACTIVITY Once students have chosen their characters, challenge them to invent details about the characters' appearance, speech, thoughts, and actions, as well as descriptive sensory details associated with the characters. (For example, a character may have a striking laugh or wear strong perfume.) When students present their characters in small groups, ask group members to give each other feedback, identifying the most interesting details and suggesting ways to flesh out the descriptions.

CHECK UNDERSTANDING Have students summarize what they have learned about how details bring **characters** to life.

UNIT 2 Share What You Know

What brings a CHARACTER *to life?*

A great **character** might start out as a few words jotted on a page or as a lump of clay squeezed between an artist's fingers. How can thes[e] humble beginnings result in a person—or a dog, a rabbit, or a robot— who can seem as familiar as your best friend? A skilled creator knows how to add layers of details that make someone who doesn't even ex[ist] in real life seem like someone you've known forever.

ACTIVITY Can you bring a character to life? Follow these steps to give it a try:

- Look through magazines and find a picture of someone or something that looks like he, she, or it could be an interesting character.
- Invent a life for that character. Think about things like where the[y] character lives, what the character cares about most, and how h[e,] she, or it responds to triumphs and challenges.
- Introduce your character to your group. Which of the details you provide most help your classmates feel like they know the perso[n] or creature you've invented?

160

Unit Resources

- **RESOURCE MANAGER UNIT 2**
- **BEST PRACTICES TOOLKIT**
- **STANDARDS LESSON FILE**
- Easy Planner DVD
- Write*Smart* CD
- ClassZone.com
- Audio Anthology CD
- Multi-Language Academic Vocabulary Online
- eEdition CD & Online
- McDougal Littell Assessment System
- Test Generator CD
- Media*Smart* DVD

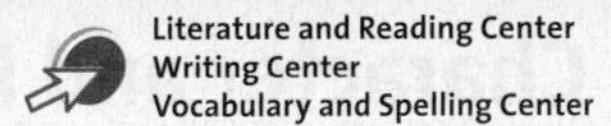

Literature and Reading Center
Writing Center
Vocabulary and Spelling Center

Preview Unit Goals

LITERARY ANALYSIS	• Identify and analyze point of view, including first-person, third-person limited, and third-person omniscient • Identify and analyze character traits and motives • Identify and analyze methods of characterization • Identify, analyze, and evaluate sound devices
READING	• Make inferences and draw conclusions • Identify scope of ideas and information in different texts • Evaluate usefulness of information from different sources
WRITING AND GRAMMAR	• Write a descriptive essay • Identify and use comparative and superlative forms correctly • Combine sentences by using coordinating conjunctions • Identify and use verb tenses correctly.
SPEAKING, LISTENING, AND VIEWING	• Identify and analyze visual elements and editing in film • Conduct an interview
VOCABULARY	• Use context to determine the meaning of multiple-meaning words • Use knowledge of base words and affixes to determine the meaning of words
ACADEMIC VOCABULARY	• point of view • inferences • characterization • traits • scope of ideas • motives

Preview Unit Goals

This page provides an overview of the skills and strategies covered in Unit 2. Each skill strand is a different color. Explain to students that throughout the unit, this color coding lets them know what kinds of skills they are studying. As they read this page, encourage students to think about each skill or strategy and how well they can use it.

Suggest that students copy the Academic Vocabulary terms in their journals and define them in their own words as they read the unit. Encourage them to use the terms as they discuss and write about the unit's selections.

ADDITIONAL UNIT GOALS

These skills will be taught in this unit but are not the major focus of the unit:

Literary Analysis
- Identify, analyze, and evaluate characteristics of a biography
- Identify and analyze narrator, foreshadowing, parallel episodes, anecdotes, and characteristics of a timeline
- Analyze dialect and main character
- Identify static and dynamic characters
- Analyze character change and development
- Interpret symbol
- Study a variety of genres: short story, biography, ballad, play, history article, feature article, timeline

Reading
- Develop strategies for reading a long story
- Set a purpose for reading
- Monitor comprehension
- Identify main ideas and details
- Compare and contrast scope of ideas and information in different texts

Writing and Grammar
- Write a compare-contrast essay
- Describe a person
- Identify and use dependent and independent clauses correctly
- Avoid clauses as fragments by joining dependent and independent clauses

Speaking, Listening, and Viewing
- Analyze characterization in film
- Create a film scene

Vocabulary
- Understand and use specialized vocabulary
- Understand the relationship between words in analogies

DIFFERENTIATED INSTRUCTION

FOR ENGLISH LEARNERS

Academic Vocabulary [paired option] Use the Academic Vocabulary copy master to introduce *point of view, trait, inference, scope of ideas, characterization,* and *motive.*
- Read each word aloud and discuss its definition. Ask students if they have heard any of these words before and, if so, in what context. Then have students work with partners to complete the sentences.
- Allow students to work individually or in pairs to complete Part B.

Additional Academic Vocabulary [small-group option] Use the second copy master to help students study *narrator, foreshadowing, symbol, main idea,* and *analogy.*
- Have small groups discuss the examples and write definitions for the words.
- Have students complete Part B individually or with their groups.

RESOURCE MANAGER—Copy Masters
Academic Vocabulary p. 9
Additional Academic Vocabulary p. 10

Focus and Motivate

OBJECTIVES

- identify and analyze point of view, including first-person, third-person limited, and third-person omniscient
- identify and analyze character traits
- identify and analyze character motivation
- identify and analyze methods of characterization
- identify and analyze narrator

Teach

Part 1: Point of View

Point of View Tell students that each point of view has specific advantages.

- **First-Person** A story told by a first-person narrator helps the reader identify with that character on a more personal level. It is as if the reader is in the story with the narrator as events unfold.
- **Third-Person Limited** In a story told by a third-person limited narrator, readers know how the main character thinks and feels, but the story is not told in the character's own voice. The narrator may comment on the character's ideas, feelings, talents, and flaws in a more objective way than a first-person narrator would.
- **Third-Person Omniscient** When a story is told by a third-person omniscient narrator, it's as if the reader is given supernatural powers and knows everything about everybody. This type of narrator knows the past, present, and future and can also tell about events that are happening at the same time in different places.

Narrator Encourage students to compare and contrast narrators in stories they have read. Ask them to name several stories and answer these questions about each one:

- Who is the narrator? Does the narrator have a personality or just a voice?
- What is the narrator able to tell readers about events and characters?
- Which kind of narrator is this—first-person, third-person limited, or third-person omniscient?

BEST PRACTICES TOOLKIT—Copy Masters
Analysis Frame: Character pp. D23, D28, D29

UNIT 2
Reader's Workshop

Character and Point of View

For a story to really resonate, it must have characters you can care about, relate to, understand, or even love to hate. How do writers create characters that trigger these kinds of reactions? How does *who* tells the story affect your feelings? In this workshop, you'll look closely at characterization and point of view, two techniques that help shape your reactions and opinions.

Part 1: Point of View

Point of view—the vantage point from which a story is told—can affect your understanding of characters and events. Point of view is created by a writer's choice of **narrator,** the voice that tells the story. The narrator may be a charact in the story or an outside observer.

This chart describes three points of view. You'll notice that all the examples focus on two students vying to win a school election. In each example, how does the choice of narrator influence your impressions of the characters?

POINT OF VIEW		EXAMPLE
FIRST-PERSON ***The narrator*** • is a main or minor character in the story • uses the pronouns *I* and *me* to refer to himself or herself • shares his or her thoughts, feelings, and opinions of other characters and events • doesn't know the thoughts, feelings, and opinions of other characters		Nervously, I eyed Gwen, my competition in the election, and flashed her a gracious smile. Believe me—I wasn't feeling very gracious. After Gwen began her speech, I relaxed. What kind of campaign speech is *that?* I thought. There's no way I'll lose now!
THIRD-PERSON LIMITED ***The narrator*** • is not a character in the story but an outside observer • zooms in on the thoughts, feelings, and opinions of one character		Devin had trouble wiping the smile off his face as he listened to Gwen fumble through her speech. For a brief moment, he felt a wave of sympathy for Gwen. Then Devin forgot about his opponent and started planning his acceptance speech in his head.
THIRD-PERSON OMNISCIENT ***The narrator*** • is not a character in the story but an outside observer • is "all knowing"—that is, he or she has access to the thoughts, feelings, and opinions of all the characters	STORY	Feeling confident and superior, Devin gave his opponent, Gwen, a genuine smile as she walked past him. Though Gwen returned Devin's smile, she was suspicious of his kindness. He's probably gloating over my mistakes, Gwen thought angrily.

DIFFERENTIATED INSTRUCTION

FOR ALL STUDENTS

For general guidelines on differentiating instruction, see

BEST PRACTICES TOOLKIT
Differentiated Instruction pp. 31–38

FOR LESS–PROFICIENT READERS

Note Taking Hand out the Note Taking: Point of View copy master and ask students to read page 162 silently. Then have them record their notes on the copy master as you discuss the information.

RESOURCE MANAGER—Copy Master
Note Taking p. 15

Use Point of View [small-group option] Have students work in groups to write a brief narrative of an incident that occurred in school. Be sure to tell each group which point of view they should use. Then ask one student from each group to read the narrative to the class. The class should tell which type of narrator was used and how they knew. If students have difficulty, suggest that they review the examples on page 162.

MODEL 1: FIRST-PERSON

Emily, the young narrator of this novel, is visiting her sick grandmother, Ola. Emily and Ola have spent the entire day together trying on Ola's old hats and scarves. In this excerpt, Emily describes their special relationship.

from **Toning the Sweep**

Novel by **Angela Johnson**

Ola and I lie on our backs in the kitchen, scarves and hats everywhere. I look over at the night-light by the table. It's the only light in the room now. Ola's eyes are closed, but I don't think she's asleep.

I have always loved my grandmother, but I know that she is a strange woman. I know that not too many of my friends would spend an evening trying on hats with their grandmothers. A few years ago they would have. Now most of them don't even admit that they like their grandparents, though they do.

I'm clueless about how to be cool. I've always told my friends that I like my grandmother. Since most of them only get a glimpse of who she is by the books and strange things she sends through the mail, I think secretly they think she's cool. That makes up for me being clueless, I guess.

Close Read

1. One sentence that reflects the first-person point of view has been boxed. Identify another one.
2. Suppose Emily's grandmother was the narrator of this novel. How might that change what you learn about the woman and her granddaughter?

MODEL 2: THIRD-PERSON OMNISCIENT

The narrator of this story shares the thoughts of more than one character. Alfonso is thrilled when Sandra agrees to go on a bike ride with him. Before his date, Alfonso breaks the chain on his bike. Will his brother help him out?

from **Broken Chain**

Short story by **Gary Soto**

"Come on, man, let me use it," Alfonso pleaded. "Please, Ernie, I'll do anything."

Although Ernie could see Alfonso's desperation, he had plans with his friend Raymundo. They were going to catch frogs at the Mayfair canal. He felt sorry for his brother, and gave him a stick of gum to make him feel better, but there was nothing he could do. The canal was three miles away, and the frogs were waiting.

Alfonso took the stick of gum, placed it in his shirt pocket, and left the bedroom with his head down. . . .

At four he decided to get it over with and started walking to Sandra's house, trudging slowly, as if he were waist-deep in water. Shame colored his face. How could he disappoint his first date? She would probably laugh.

Close Read

1. How does Ernie feel about Alfonso's predicament? How does Alfonso himself feel? Cite details to support your answers.
2. Suppose the narrator had not revealed Ernie's thoughts in lines 3–6. How might this affect your impression of Ernie?

MODEL 1: FIRST–PERSON

Close Read

Possible answers:

1. *Another sentence that reflects the first-person point of view is "Ola and I lie on our backs in the kitchen, scarves and hats everywhere" (line 1). The narrator is participating in the story's action and uses the pronouns* I *and* our*.*
2. *If Emily's grandmother were the narrator, readers might still learn about Emily's evening spent trying on hats with her grandmother, but they wouldn't have access to Emily's feelings about her grandmother. Instead, the narrator would probably share her own thoughts and feelings.*

MODEL 2: THIRD–PERSON OMNISCIENT

Close Read

Possible answers:

1. *Ernie understands Alfonso's predicament and feels sympathetic. Details include*
   - *"Ernie could see Alfonso's desperation" (line 3)*
   - *"He felt sorry for his brother, and gave him a stick of gum to make him feel better" (lines 4–5)*

   Alfonso himself feels disappointed, apprehensive, and embarrassed. Supporting details include
   - *"left the bedroom with his head down" (lines 7–8)*
   - *"trudging slowly" (line 10)*
   - *"Shame colored his face." (line 10)*
   - *"She would probably laugh." (line 11)*
2. *If the narrator had not revealed that Ernie feels sorry for his brother, the reader might have concluded that Ernie was unsympathetic or even mean in his refusal to lend Alfonso his bike.*

FOR ENGLISH LEARNERS

Vocabulary Support Help students use context clues to determine the meanings of these words from **Model 1.** Then ask students to use each word in a sentence of their own.

- *clueless* (lines 9, 12), "having no idea about how to do something; feeling uncertain about how to act"
- *cool* (lines 9, 12), "popular, admired, and well-liked"

Concept Support: Point of View Have students review the description of third-person omniscient point of view on page 162. Have them apply each bulleted point to **Model 2.** *(None of the characters—Alfonso, Ernie, Raymundo, or Sandra—tells the story; instead, an outside observer tells the story. The narrator knows the thoughts and feelings of both Ernie and Alfonso.)* Note that the use of the pronoun *I* in line 1 does not indicate a first-person narrator since it is part of a quote reported by the outside observer.

Part 2: Character Traits and Motivation

Character Traits Ask students to think about the process of electing someone to an office, whether it is president of the United States or president of the Student Council. In addition to learning about each candidate's experience and position on issues, a voter needs to learn as much as possible about each candidate as a person. To determine character traits, voters would use techniques similar to those used by readers of fiction. They might judge candidates on how they look, what they say, what they do, and what others say about them.

Be sure students understand that some methods of inferring character traits may be more reliable than others. This is true in fiction as well as in real life. For example, it is more revealing to observe how a person acts than simply to rely on what he or she says. Use these questions to help students discuss and evaluate the effectiveness of each method of characterization:

- **Physical Appearance** What can you learn about a character based on the clothes he or she wears? If the narrator says that a character is gorgeous, what other ideas might you have about the character? What if the character is described as plain?
- **Speech, Thoughts, and Actions** What conclusions can you draw about a character based on the way he or she talks? Based on his or her opinions? Based on how the character treats others?
- **Other Characters** What might you conclude about a character who has many friends, or no friends? What kinds of behavior would indicate that a character is kind or mean? Whose statements about a character would be most reliable—those of a friend, an enemy, or an outside observer?

These questions should lead to a lively discussion of the basis by which we judge others or would like to be judged by others. Be sure to encourage students to keep these factors in mind as they encounter characters in the stories they read.

Part 2: Character Traits and Motivation

As a reader, you can't help but have strong reactions to the people you meet on the page. Did you know that writers use different methods of characterization to create these responses in you? Read on to find out exactly how writers develop lifelike characters with distinct traits and motivations.

CHARACTER TRAITS

Loyal, outgoing, lazy—you might use words like these to describe people in your life. You may not realize it, but you learn about people's qualities, or **traits,** by observing the way they look, talk, and act. For example, a new neighbor probably wouldn't introduce herself by saying, "Hi! I'm outgoing." Instead, you would infer this trait by noticing her big smile and confident voice.

Like people, characters in literature have unique personalities and traits. Sometimes, a narrator will directly tell you what a character is like. More often, you have to infer a character's traits the same way you would a person's—by considering his or her appearance and behavior, for instance.

Writers show you what their characters are like by using the following **indirect methods of characterization.** Look at this graphic, noting the descriptions of the girl Madeleine. What traits can you infer?

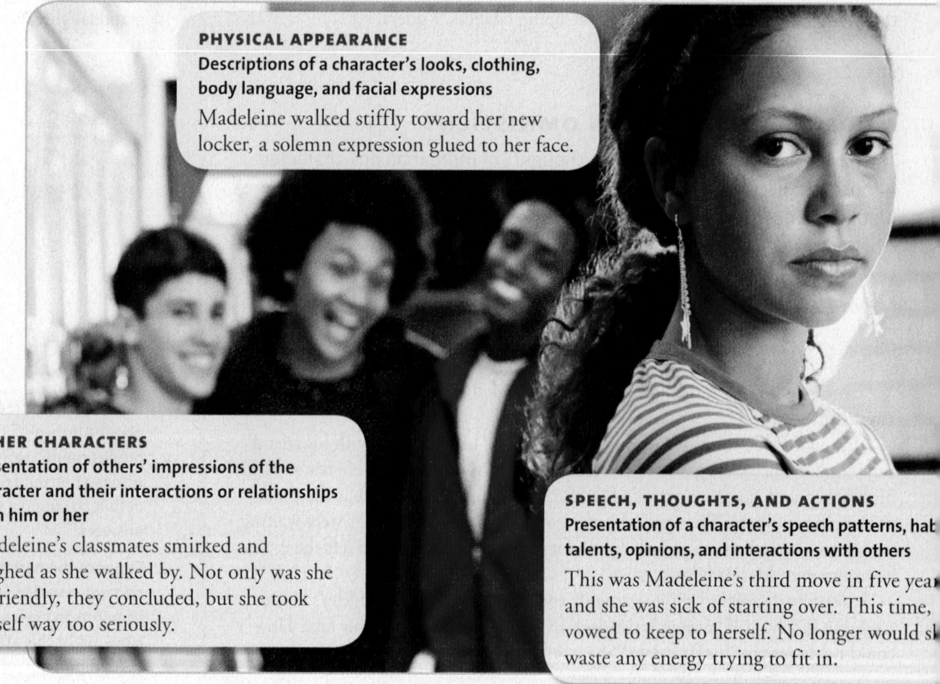

PHYSICAL APPEARANCE
Descriptions of a character's looks, clothing, body language, and facial expressions
Madeleine walked stiffly toward her new locker, a solemn expression glued to her face.
OTHER CHARACTERS
Presentation of others' impressions of the character and their interactions or relationships with him or her
Madeleine's classmates smirked and laughed as she walked by. Not only was she unfriendly, they concluded, but she took herself way too seriously.
SPEECH, THOUGHTS, AND ACTIONS
Presentation of a character's speech patterns, hab
talents, opinions, and interactions with others
This was Madeleine's third move in five yea
and she was sick of starting over. This time,
vowed to keep to herself. No longer would s
waste any energy trying to fit in.

DIFFERENTIATED INSTRUCTION

FOR LESS–PROFICIENT READERS

Note Taking Hand out the Note Taking: Character Traits and Motivation copy master. Read and discuss the information on pages 164 and 166. As a class, complete the first item on the copy master. Then have students continue taking notes on their own. Provide assistance when necessary.

RESOURCE MANAGER—Copy Master
Note Taking p. 16

Concept Support Review with students the various methods of characterization. Ask students to think of a famous person such as an athlete, a movie star, or a musician. Hand out index cards and have students write five details that help to identify the person. On the back of the card, have them write the person's name. Collect the cards and read the details to the class. See how many of the people students can identify correctly.

MODEL 1: CHARACTERIZATION

The narrator of this story takes the 8:12 train to work everyday; he sees the same commuters and sits in the same corner seat. Today, however, he notices a stranger on the platform. What do you learn about the stranger from this brief excerpt?

from **Galloping Foxley**

Short story by **Roald Dahl**

The stranger was standing plumb in the middle of the platform, feet apart and arms folded, looking for all the world as though he owned the whole place. He was a biggish, thickset man, and even from behind he somehow managed to convey a powerful impression of arrogance and oil. Very definitely, he was not one of us. He carried a cane instead of an umbrella, his shoes were brown instead of black, the grey hat was cocked at a ridiculous angle, and in one way and another there seemed to be an excess of silk and polish about his person. More than this I did not care to observe.

Close Read

1. What methods of characterization has the author used to describe the stranger?
2. What kind of person do you think the stranger is? Cite specific details that affected your impression of him.

MODEL 2: CHARACTER TRAITS

Sopeap is a Cambodian teenager whose family recently moved to the United States. One day, a classmate walks into her family's store, lugging a green armchair. How does Sopeap respond to the classmate's request for help?

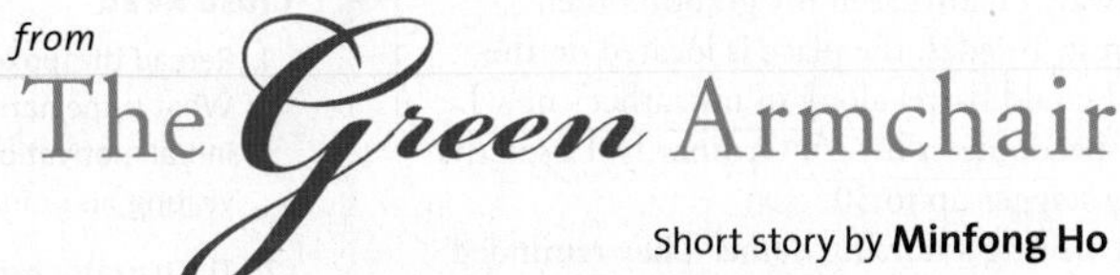

Short story by **Minfong Ho**

Thomas Ramsey. For an awful moment she thought she had said his name out loud, but then realized it had only been in her mind.

Sopeap forced a smile. "Sure," she said, [pleasantly surprised by how casual, how American, she sounded. "Be right with you."]

"Hey, aren't you in my history class?" he asked.

"Algebra," she said quietly. At least he recognized her. She had long since noticed him, intrigued by the aloof, easy banter he carried on with his classmates, as if he were looking at them from the wrong end of a telescope. A bit of a loner, and liking it that way. [*Sort of like me,* she had sometimes thought, clutching onto her solitude as tightly as she held her textbooks. . . .]

Close Read

1. How would you describe Thomas? Identify at least two details in this excerpt that influenced your impression of him.
2. Reread the [boxed] descriptions of Sopeap's thoughts and feelings. What do these descriptions suggest about her traits?

MODEL 1: CHARACTERIZATION

Close Read

Possible answers:

1. *The author primarily uses descriptions of the stranger's physical appearance to introduce readers to the character. However, Dahl also describes the narrator's impressions of and reactions to the stranger ("Very definitely, he was not one of us" [lines 4–5]).*
2. *Students may infer that the stranger is arrogant based on the following details:*
   - *"looking for all the world as though he owned the whole place" (lines 2–3)*
   - *"a powerful impression of arrogance and oil" (line 4)*
   - *"the grey hat was cocked at a ridiculous angle" (lines 6–7)*
   - *"excess of silk and polish" (lines 7–8)*

MODEL 2: CHARACTER TRAITS

Close Read

Possible answers:

1. *Thomas is friendly but not someone who thrives on social interaction. He asks Sopeap, "Hey, aren't you in my history class?" (line 5), and he carries on an "easy banter" (line 7) with other students. At the same time, Sopeap thinks he is "aloof" (line 7) and "A bit of a loner" (line 9).*
2. *These descriptions suggest that Sopeap wants to fit in with her American classmates, but like Thomas, she also is a loner who "clutch[es] onto her solitude" (line 10). Her solitude provides safety and comfort in her new environment.*

FOR LESS-PROFICIENT READERS

Analysis Support: Character Traits [paired option] Ask students to work in pairs. Each student should write down five details that describe a character from either **Model 1** or **Model 2** in the left column of a Two-Column Chart. Students should then switch papers and use the right column to label the character trait for each detail. Students should discuss their responses with their partners.

Description	Trait
stands with "feet apart and arms folded"	confident
"forced a smile"	shy

BEST PRACTICES TOOLKIT—Transparency
Two-Column Chart p. A25

FOR ADVANCED LEARNERS/PRE-AP

Use Character Traits Ask students to list ten character traits that would make them want to get to know someone better. Then have students conduct an informal survey of friends and neighbors in which participants rate the importance of each trait in a potential new friend. For example, what percentage of the survey group rates friendliness as the most desirable trait? Have students present their results in the form of a bar graph.

Character Motivation Point out that in some cases the motivations for people's behavior are very obvious, while in other cases the motivations are very complex. Sometimes a person cannot even explain the reasons for his or her own actions. Give students this situation: Carlos spends two hours cleaning his room on a Saturday morning. Ask students to suggest possible motivations for Carlos's actions as you record their ideas on a Cluster Diagram. Then have students discuss which motivation would make the most interesting starting point for a story in which Carlos was the main character.

 **BEST PRACTICES TOOLKIT—Transparency**
Cluster Diagram p. B18

Close Read
Possible answers:

1. *The narrator's initial motivation is that he will have the chance to drive fast in his father's car (lines 3–4). He has also promised his mother that he will go to the nursing home.*
2. *The narrator is eventually motivated by guilt to go inside. He remembers "all the Christmas and birthday gifts [his] grandmother had given [him]" over the years (lines 13–14). Because she has been so good to him, he feels guilty for not wanting to visit her. Thus, he decides to go in.*
3. *One motivating factor is the chance to drive his father's new car, which goes much faster than the family station wagon. This tells readers that the narrator is interested in cars and likes to drive faster than he should. The second motivating factor is guilt. The narrator admits that he is "loaded with guilt complexes" (lines 10–11). This suggests that the narrator wants to do the right thing and is upset with himself when he doesn't.*

CHARACTER MOTIVATION

Why did the boy decide to volunteer at the animal shelter? What prompted the woman to risk her life for a stranger? A big part of understanding characters is analyzing their **motivations,** or the reasons behind their actions. For instance, did the boy volunteer at the shelter because of his passion for animals or because he has a crush on someone who works there? Think about what each motivation might suggest about the boy's traits.

To uncover a character's motivation, you often have to look for details in the story. As you read, consider the following:

- the narrator's direct comments about a character's motivation
- a character's actions, thoughts, and values
- your own understanding of the emotions—love, greed, ambition, jealousy—that drive human behavior

In this story, 17-year-old Mike finally decides to visit his grandmother in the nursing home. What factors are motivating his actions?

from The Moustache

Short story by **Robert Cormier**

. . . I told my mother I'd go, anyway. I hadn't seen my grandmother since she'd been admitted to Lawnrest. Besides, the place is located on the Southwest Turnpike, which meant I could barrel along in my father's new Le Mans. My ambition was to see the speedometer hit 75. Ordinarily, I used the old station wagon, which can barely stagger up to 50.

Frankly, I wasn't too crazy about visiting a nursing home. They reminded me of hospitals, and hospitals turn me off. I mean, the smell of ether makes me nauseous, and I feel faint at the sight of blood. And as I approached Lawnrest—which is a terrible cemetery kind of name, to begin with—I was sorry I hadn't avoided the trip. Then I felt guilty about it. I'm loaded with guilt complexes. Like driving like a madman after promising my father to be careful. Like sitting in the parking lot, looking at the nursing home with dread and thinking how I'd rather be with Cindy. Then I thought of all the Christmas and birthday gifts my grandmother had given me, and I got out of the car, guilty as usual.

Close Read

1. Reread the boxed text. What is the narrator's initial motivation for visiting his grandmothe
2. The narrator has secon thoughts about his visit once he's in the parking lot. What eventually motivates him to go inside?
3. Consider the two motivating factors that influence the narrator's actions. What do they tell you about him?

DIFFERENTIATED INSTRUCTION

FOR LESS–PROFICIENT READERS

Concept Support Have students review the list of emotions that drive human behavior on page 166. Ask them to think of a character from a story or a movie whose experiences are driven by one of these emotions. Have them make a short report to the class in which they (1) identify the character, (2) explain which emotion drives the character, and (3) explain what the character does as a result of that emotion.

FOR ENGLISH LEARNERS

Concept Support: Character Motivation [mixed-readiness pairs] Give students the following examples and ask them to identify the emotion that motivates each behavior. Then ask student pairs to take turns giving an example of a behavior and naming the emotion that motivates that behavior.

- wanting to win a race *(ambition)*
- refusing to stay alone in a dark room *(fear)*
- stealing someone's lunch money *(greed)*

art 3: Analyze the Literature

Meet Gene, a high school student in Mrs. Tibbetts' second-period class. Gene and his fellow classmates have just found out that Mrs. Tibbetts is taking the advanced English class to a poetry reading. What happens when Mrs. Tibbetts unexpectedly extends the invitation to Gene's class? Read on to find out.

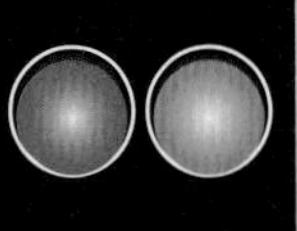

from

I GO ALONG

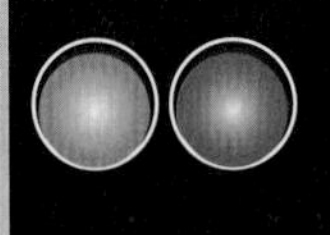

Short story by **Richard Peck**

Since it's only the second period of the day, we're all feeling pretty good. Also it's a Tuesday, a terrible TV night. Everybody in the class puts up their hands. I mean everybody. Even Marty Crawshaw. . . . And Pink Hohenfield, who's in class today for the first time this month. I put up mine. I go along.

Mrs. Tibbetts looks amazed. She's never seen this many hands up in our class. She's never seen anybody's hand except Darla's. . . .

But then she sees we have to be putting her on. So she just says, "Anyone who would like to go, be in the parking lot at five-thirty. And eat first. No eating on the bus."

Mrs. Tibbetts can drive the school bus. Whenever she's taking the advanced class anywhere, she can go to the principal for the keys. She can use the bus anytime she wants to, unless the coach needs it.

Then she opens her attendance book, and we tune out. And at five-thirty that night I'm in the parking lot. I have no idea why. Needless to say, I'm the only one here from second period. Marty Crawshaw and Pink Hohenfield will be out on the access highway about now, at 7-Eleven, sitting on their hoods. Darla couldn't make it either. Right offhand I can't think of anybody who wants to ride a school bus thirty miles to see a poet. Including me.

The advanced-English juniors are milling around behind school. I'm still in my car, and it's almost dark, so nobody sees me.

Then Mrs. Tibbetts wheels the school bus in. She's got the amber fogs flashing, and you can see the black letters along the yellow side: CONSOLIDATED SCHOOL DIST. She swings in and hits the brakes, and the doors fly open. The advanced class starts to climb aboard. They're more orderly than us, but they've got their groups too. . . . I'm settling behind my dashboard. The last kid climbs the bus.

And I seem to be sprinting across the asphalt. I'm on the bus, and the door's hissing shut behind me. When I swing past the driver's seat, I don't look at Mrs. Tibbetts, and she doesn't say anything. I wonder where I'm supposed to sit.

They're still milling around in the aisle, but there are plenty of seats. I find an empty double and settle by the window, pulling my ball cap down in front. It doesn't take us long to get out of town, not in this town. When we go past 7-Eleven, I'm way down in the seat with my hand shielding my face on the window side. Right about then, somebody sits down next to me. I flinch.

Close Read

1. From what point of view is this story told? Explain how you can tell.
2. Reread the boxed sentences. What do they suggest about Gene's character traits?
3. How would this excerpt be different if Mrs. Tibbetts were the narrator?
4. Examine lines 32–34. Why do you think Gene hides when the bus passes the 7-Eleven?
5. Consider Gene's actions and body language in lines 27–34. Based on these details, what can you infer about his personality?

FOR LESS–PROFICIENT READERS

Analysis Support: Character Traits After students read "I Go Along" once, have them reread it and fill in as much information about Gene as possible in a Character Traits Web. When they are finished, ask them to discuss what they think are Gene's positive and negative qualities.

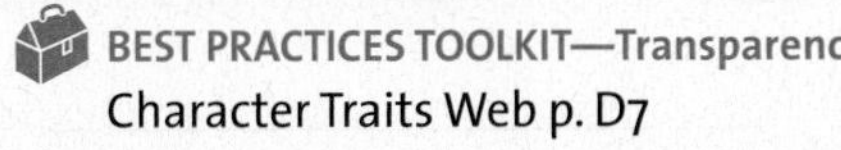

BEST PRACTICES TOOLKIT—Transparency
Character Traits Web p. D7

FOR ADVANCED LEARNERS/PRE–AP

Explore Character Who sat down next to Gene? Why did he decide to go with the advanced class to hear a poet? Did his friends find out? To answer these questions and more, encourage students to locate and read the full text of "I Go Along" by Richard Peck. Have them give a report to the class in which they discuss Gene's character traits and motivations more fully.

Practice and Apply

Part 3: Analyze the Literature

Close Read

Possible answers:

1. *This story uses the first-person point of view. The narrator is a character in the story; uses the pronouns* we, I, mine, our, me, *and* my *to refer to himself and his classmates; and shares his thoughts and feelings.*
2. *The first two lines suggest that Gene is not looking forward to the rest of his classes. He also is a follower and raises his hand when the other students do.*
3. *The reader would have access to Mrs. Tibbetts's thoughts rather than Gene's. We might know what she thinks when all the students raise their hands and when she sees Gene board the bus.*
4. *Gene thinks that some of his classmates are hanging out in the parking lot of the 7-Eleven. As the bus passes the store, Gene shields his face so that his friends will not find out that he has joined the field trip to hear a poet. He probably fears that they will make fun of him.*
5. *Gene is shy and feels uncomfortable doing something that his friends might not approve of. He sits in "an empty double" (line 31), pulls his "ball cap down in front" (line 31), sits "way down in the seat" and shields his face as they pass the 7-Eleven (lines 32–34), and flinches when someone sits next to him (line 34).*

Assess and Reteach

Assess

Have students identify the point of view of "I Go Along," list several of Gene's traits, and suggest a motivation for his actions.

Reteach

For students who cannot apply the workshop skills to "I Go Along," try these options:

1. Have students read the selection aloud, taking notes as they find details that reveal Gene's character traits or motivation.
2. Meet with small groups to review students' Note Taking copy masters. Clarify point of view, character traits, and character motivation, using examples from the selection.

Focus and Motivate

OBJECTIVES

Literary Analysis

- explore the key idea of what people **cherish**
- identify and analyze third-person limited point of view
- read a short story

Reading

- make inferences

Vocabulary

- build vocabulary for reading and writing
- use similes as context clues (comparison and contrast) to determine word meaning *(also an EL language objective)*

Grammar and Writing

- identify and use past, present, and future verb tenses correctly
- use writing to analyze literature

SUMMARY

One night, 14-year-old Greg Ridley meets a homeless man named Lemon Brown who was once a noted blues musician. Lemon Brown shows Greg his treasure: an old harmonica and newspaper reviews of his past performances. Brown is comforted to know that his son, a soldier, was carrying these items when he died. Greg returns home with a new appreciation for his own father.

What do you CHERISH?

To reinforce the question and the ***KEY IDEA,*** have students make a web of words in the first paragraph that relate to **cherishing** (such as *worth, valuable, important, memories, save,* and *treasures*). Then have them do the ***LIST IT*** activity.

The Treasure of Lemon Brown

Short Story by Walter Dean Myers

What do you CHERISH

KEY IDEA Think of what you most **cherish,** or hold dear. Is it worth a lot of money, or is it valuable because of a memory that is important only to you? For example, a photograph of a favorite friend or relative wouldn't bring much money at an auction, but the memories it holds might make it one of the first things you'd save if your home were on fire. In "The Treasure of Lemon Brown," a boy's encounter with an old blues musician helps him discover what he treasures most.

LIST IT Make a list of three to five things that you cherish. They might be tangible (things you can touch, such as a pair of jeans or a pet) or intangible (things you cannot touch, such as a memory or an idea like freedom). Explain why these things are important to you.

168

Selection Resources

RESOURCE MANAGER UNIT 2

Plan and Teach pp. 17–24

Literary Analysis

Summary pp. 25†*, 26‡*

Third-Person Limited Point of View pp. 27, 28†*

Question Support p. 35*

Reading

Make Inferences pp. 29, 30†*

Reading Check p. 34

Reading Fluency p. 37

Vocabulary

Study p. 31*

Practice p. 32

Strategy p. 33

Grammar and Writing

Use Correct Verb Tense p. 36

Assessment

Selection Tests A, B/C pp. 39*, 41*

Test Generator CD

BEST PRACTICES TOOLKIT

Differentiated Instruction pp. 31–38*

Scaffolding Instruction pp. 43–46*

Graphic Organizers/Strategies

Knowledge Rating • Word Sorts • Predicting • Plot Diagram • Character Map

Reading Support

Audio Anthology CD*

Technology

Literature, Vocabulary, and Writing Centers at **ClassZone.com**

Write*Smart* CD

* Resources for Differentiation † Also in Spanish ‡ In Haitian Creole and Vietnamese

LITERARY ANALYSIS: THIRD-PERSON LIMITED POINT OF VIEW

In a story told from the **third-person limited point of view,** the narrator is outside the story and tells what one character sees, thinks, and feels. Look at the following example:

Report cards were due in a week, and Greg had been hoping for the best.

In this sentence, the narrator tells the reader how Greg feels about the report card he's about to receive.

As you read, pay attention to how much the narrator allows you to know about each character's thoughts and feelings and how this affects your understanding of the story.

READING SKILL: MAKE INFERENCES

Writers rarely explain everything to their readers. They provide certain clues and expect readers to use the clues and their own experience to fill in the gaps. This is called **making inferences.**

Often you will need to make inferences to understand the characters in a story. As you read "The Treasure of Lemon Brown," watch for clues that tell you what a character is like and why the character acts a particular way. Use a chart like the one shown to note details about the characters.

Details About Character	*What I Infer*
Greg's father lectures Greg about his poor effort in math.	*Greg's father wants him to succeed in life.*

VOCABULARY IN CONTEXT

Walter Dean Myers uses the boldfaced words to tell about an old man who has a hard and dangerous life, but also a precious treasure. To see how many of the words you know, substitute a different word or phrase for each one.

1. The door was **ajar** and let in a small amount of light.
2. There was a **tremor** in his voice as he told the sad tale.
3. The silence was **ominous** and scary.
4. He would **commence** his trip when the rain stopped.
5. Years of hard work left him with **gnarled** hands.
6. Get his attention and **beckon** him to come closer.
7. The hallway was dark, so he moved **tentatively.**
8. We had an **impromptu** meeting at the street corner.

Author Online

Contest to Career Walter Dean Myers was born to a large family in West Virginia. After his mother died when he was two years old, his father could no longer care for all the children. Myers grew up with foster parents in New York City. A speech impediment made it difficult for him to speak, so he began writing poetry and stories with the encouragement of a teacher who thought writing would help him express himself. Still, he didn't think he could earn a living as an author. After unhappily working as a post-office clerk and a messenger, Myers saw an advertisement for a children's book-writing contest. He had never written for young people before, but he won the contest and began a highly successful writing career.

Walter Dean Myers
born 1937

Writing His Life Myers frequently draws on his own experience in his writing. Many of his characters belong to low-income families and deal with urban problems. He has also written biographies of prominent African Americans, including Malcolm X and Muhammad Ali. Myers has said, "As a black writer, I want to talk about my people." But the characters he creates and the issues he addresses have universal appeal.

MORE ABOUT THE AUTHOR
For more on Walter Dean Myers, visit the **Literature Center** at **ClassZone.com.**

Background

Harlem "The Treasure of Lemon Brown" takes place in Harlem, the neighborhood in which Myers grew up in New York City. Since about 1910, it has been one of the largest African-American communities in the United States.

Teach

STANDARDS FOCUS

LITERARY ANALYSIS

● THIRD–PERSON LIMITED POINT OF VIEW

Write this passage on the board:

> Maria was thrilled to learn that she would spend summer vacation with her grandmother at the beach. She excitedly packed her bags and called her best friend to tell her the news.

Ask students whose point of view they learn about. What do they learn about her? ***Possible answer:*** *Maria's point of view; she is thrilled about spending vacation with her grandmother; she packs her bags and calls her best friend.*

CHECK UNDERSTANDING Ask students how the example on page 169 illustrates third-person point of view.

READING SKILL

■ MAKE INFERENCES

Ask students to look at the photo on page 168. What can they infer about the girl's feelings about the hamster? What clues help them make this inference? ***Possible answer:*** *She treasures the hamster. She holds it gently and smiles at it.*

CHECK UNDERSTANDING Ask students to describe an inference they have made based on a friend's actions or words.

 **RESOURCE MANAGER—Copy Master**
Make Inferences p. 29 (for student use while reading the selection)

VOCABULARY SKILL

▲ VOCABULARY IN CONTEXT

DIAGNOSE WORD KNOWLEDGE To determine preteaching needs, have all students complete **Vocabulary in Context.** ***Possible answers:*** 1. *open slightly* 2. *shake* 3. *alarming* 4. *start* 5. *rough* 6. *signal* 7. *cautiously* 8. *informal*

PRETEACH VOCABULARY Use the Vocabulary Study copy master to help students explore the meaning of each boldfaced word.

1. Read item 1 aloud, emphasizing *ajar.*
2. Point out the context clues *door* and *see a narrow slice.* Elicit predicted meanings for *ajar,* such as "slightly open."
3. Have students record their predictions.
4. Repeat the procedure for items 2–8.
5. Have students complete the third column of the chart as they read the selection.

 **RESOURCE MANAGER—Copy Master**
Vocabulary Study p. 31

For general guidelines on differentiating vocabulary instruction and for alternative vocabulary activities for students not needing vocabulary preteaching, see

BEST PRACTICES TOOLKIT
Scaffolding Vocabulary Instruction pp. 43–46

Vocabulary Center at **ClassZone.com**
Additional Vocabulary Activities

Practice and Apply

ANALYZE VISUALS

Possible answer: *You can infer that Harlem is an urban neighborhood with both older and newer buildings, including plain-looking high-rise apartments.*

About the Art In this collage, Christopher Myers combines cut-up photographs of Harlem storefronts and buildings. He also paints on the collage. In addition to adding color, the painted marks suggest street graffiti and urban decay.

LITERARY ANALYSIS

Ⓐ POINT OF VIEW

Possible answer: *The narrator is describing Greg's thoughts and feelings.*

Extend the Discussion Do you think Greg's father agrees with Greg that playing basketball for the Scorpions is "a chance of a lifetime"? Explain your response.

The Treasure *of* Lemon Brown

Walter Dean Myers

The dark sky, filled with angry, swirling clouds, reflected Greg Ridley's mood as he sat on the stoop[1] of his building. His father's voice came to him again, first reading the letter the principal had sent to the house, then lecturing endlessly about his poor efforts in math.

"I had to leave school when I was 13," his father had said, "that's a year younger than you are now. If I'd had half the chances that you have, I'd . . ."

Greg had sat in the small, pale green kitchen listening, knowing the lecture would end with his father saying he couldn't play ball with the Scorpions. He had asked his father the week before, and his father had said it depended on his next report card. It wasn't often the Scorpions took on new players, especially 14-year-olds, and this was a chance of a lifetime for Greg. He hadn't been allowed to play high school ball, which he had really wanted to do, but playing for the Community Center team was the next best thing. Report cards were due in a week, and Greg had been hoping for the best. But the principal had ended the suspense early when she sent that letter saying Greg would probably fail math if he didn't spend more time studying. Ⓐ

"And you want to play *basketball?*" His father's brows knitted over deep brown eyes. "That must be some kind of a joke. Now you just get into your room and hit those books."

That had been two nights before. His father's words, like the distant thunder that now echoed through the streets of Harlem, still rumbled softly in his ears.

ANALYZE VISUALS
This collage was created by Walter Dean Myers's son. What can you **infer** about Harlem from the details in this image?

① **Targeted Passage**

Ⓐ POINT OF VIEW
Whose thoughts and feelings is the **narrator** describing?

1. **stoop:** a porch or staircase at the entrance of a building.

Illustrations by Christopher Myers

DIFFERENTIATED INSTRUCTION

FOR ALL STUDENTS

Enhance Learning Styles Provide these independent projects for various learning styles:

- **Analytical** Design and fill out an evaluation form for assessing story elements.
- **Musical** Compose and perform a blues song to express Greg's troubles.
- **Kinesthetic** Act out the major scenes in the short story.

For further details on these projects, see

RESOURCE MANAGER
Ideas for Extension pp. 22–23

FOR LESS–PROFICIENT READERS

In combination with the *Audio Anthology CD*, use one or more Targeted Passages (pp. 170, 173, 176, 177) to ensure that students focus on key story events, concepts, and skills.

① Targeted Passage [Lines 1–19]

This passage introduces two of the story's three main characters. It also describes the conflict between Greg and his father: Greg's father will not let him play basketball until his math grades improve.

- On what topic did Greg's father recently lecture him?
- What does Greg really want to do?
- What does Greg's father tell him he must do instead?

BACKGROUND

Harlem The African Americans who swelled the population of Harlem in the early 20th century came from the South. Most were seeking factory jobs and a better life than they could find in rural Southern states, where settled patterns of discrimination—the legacy of slavery—made life difficult. By 1920, half a million African Americans had migrated from the South to New York and other Northern cities.

The migration contributed to a flowering of African-American talent in literature and the arts known as the Harlem Renaissance. In the 1920s, Harlem was home to many talented African-American artists, writers, journalists, and musicians, including noted blues and jazz performers.

While Harlem represented opportunity and cultural achievement at first, social and economic problems gradually overwhelmed the district. Unemployment and crime became widespread. Apartment buildings suffered decay and neglect, and commercial areas became run down. However, recent decades have seen renewal in parts of Harlem. One high-profile project is the revival of the famous Apollo Theater, which had provided a showcase for African-American musicians and entertainers. Today, some residential areas are improving, too, as middle-class African Americans and others move into and renovate Harlem's most historic sections.

CULTURAL CONNECTION

Other Sides of Harlem Before Harlem became an African-American neighborhood, it was home to a large Jewish population. Nearby east Harlem was primarily an Italian neighborhood. After World War II, many Hispanic Americans, particularly immigrants from Puerto Rico, settled in east Harlem. Invite students to share their knowledge of urban neighborhoods in which immigrants from specific cultures have settled.

FOR ENGLISH LEARNERS

Key Academic Vocabulary Have students use Knowledge Rating to study *principal* (lines 3, 14), *team* (line 13), *lecture* (lines 25, 292), *abandoned* (line 28), and *normal* (line 208).

BEST PRACTICES TOOLKIT—Transparency
Knowledge Rating p. E3

Prereading For prereading instruction for English learners, see

BEST PRACTICES TOOLKIT
Scaffolding Reading Instruction pp. 43–46

FOR ADVANCED LEARNERS/PRE–AP

Pre-AP exercises in the bottom channel provide additional challenge for your advanced students. Use them for small groups or individuals.

ADDITIONAL GUIDELINES

For more help with differentiation and tips for classroom management, see

BEST PRACTICES TOOLKIT
Differentiated Instruction pp. 31–38

BACKGROUND

Jobs in the Post Office People who want to apply for a job in the U.S. Postal Service must first take an exam. Different jobs require different tests. For example, at the post office there are separate tests for mail carriers, clerical workers, and motor vehicle operators. The tests are open to anyone who meets the minimum requirements for the job. Scores on the test are ranked, and those with the highest scores are interviewed for the job.

READING SKILL

B MAKE INFERENCES

Possible answer: *You can infer that Greg has a bad attitude about his father and does not respect the things his father feels are important, such as studying and hard work. He is uninterested in his father and the story of how hard he worked to get a good job.*

If students need help . . . Have them reread lines 48–51 to identify what makes Greg's father feel proud. Ask them to guess why this accomplishment might be important to him.

Lines 50–51

REINFORCE *KEY IDEA:* CHERISH

Discuss Do Greg and his father **cherish** the same things? Explain. ***Possible answer:*** *No. Greg cherishes athletic accomplishment, while his father cherishes his achievement of holding a respectable job and passing the test required to get it.*

It was beginning to cool. Gusts of wind made bits of paper dance between the parked cars. There was a flash of nearby lightning, and soon large drops of rain splashed onto his jeans. He stood to go upstairs, thought of the lecture that probably awaited him if he did anything except shut himself in his room with his math book, and started walking down the street instead. Down the block there was an old tenement that had been abandoned for some months. Some of the guys had held an **impromptu** checker tournament there the week before, and Greg had noticed that the door, once boarded over, had been slightly **ajar.**

impromptu (ĭm-prŏmp'to͞o) *adj.* unplanned

ajar (ə-jär') *adj.* partially open

Pulling his collar up as high as he could, he checked for traffic and made a dash across the street. He reached the house just as another flash of lightning changed the night to day for an instant, then returned the graffiti-scarred building to the grim shadows. He vaulted over the outer stairs and pushed **tentatively** on the door. It was open, and he let himself in.

tentatively (tĕn'tə-tĭv-lē) *adv.* uncertainly or hesitantly

The inside of the building was dark except for the dim light that filtered through the dirty windows from the streetlamps. There was a room a few feet from the door, and from where he stood at the entrance, Greg could see a squarish patch of light on the floor. He entered the room, frowning at the musty smell. It was a large room that might have been someone's parlor at one time. Squinting, Greg could see an old table on its side against one wall, what looked like a pile of rags or a torn mattress in the corner, and a couch, with one side broken, in front of the window.

He went to the couch. The side that wasn't broken was comfortable enough, though a little creaky. From this spot he could see the blinking neon sign over the bodega[2] on the corner. He sat a while, watching the sign blink first green then red, allowing his mind to drift to the Scorpions, then to his father. His father had been a postal worker for all Greg's life, and was proud of it, often telling Greg how hard he had worked to pass the test. Greg had heard the story too many times to be interested now. **B**

B MAKE INFERENCES
Reread lines 48–51. What can you infer about Greg's attitude toward his father?

For a moment Greg thought he heard something that sounded like a scraping against the wall. He listened carefully, but it was gone.

Outside the wind had picked up, sending the rain against the window with a force that shook the glass in its frame. A car passed, its tires hissing over the wet street and its red tail lights glowing in the darkness.

Greg thought he heard the noise again. His stomach tightened as he held himself still and listened intently. There weren't any more scraping noises, but he was sure he had heard something in the darkness—something breathing!

He tried to figure out just where the breathing was coming from; he knew it was in the room with him. Slowly he stood, tensing. As he turned, a flash of lightning lit up the room, frightening him with its sudden brilliance. He saw nothing, just the overturned table, the pile of rags and an old newspaper on the floor. Could he have been imagining the sounds? He continued listening,

2. **bodega** (bō-dā'gə): a small grocery store.

DIFFERENTIATED INSTRUCTION

FOR LESS–PROFICIENT READERS

Vocabulary Support Write these words from the story on the board. Have students define the words and sort them into two categories using a Word Sorts worksheet. ***(Possible categories:*** *"bad guys" and "fear")*

- *thugs* (line 138)
- *panic* (line 188)
- *eerie* (line 189)
- *howled* (line 196)
- *scoundrels* (line 218)
- *scalawags* (line 265)

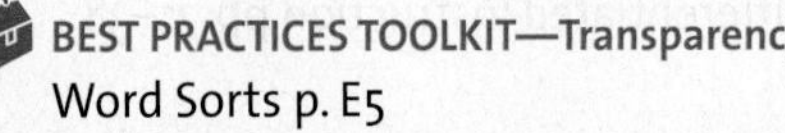
BEST PRACTICES TOOLKIT—Transparency
Word Sorts p. E5

FOR ENGLISH LEARNERS

Culture: Clarify As needed, clarify the following terms used in the text:

- *Community Center* (line 13), "neighborhood building used for sports and other activities that are open to the public"
- *checker(s)* (line 29), "a board game for two players"
- *graffiti* (line 34), "words and drawings painted in a public place where they do not belong"

but heard nothing and thought that it might have just been rats. Still, he thought, as soon as the rain let up he would leave. He went to the window and was about to look out when he heard a voice behind him.

"Don't try nothin' 'cause I got a razor here sharp enough to cut a week into nine days!"

Greg, except for an involuntary **tremor** in his knees, stood stock still. The voice was high and brittle, like dry twigs being broken, surely not one he had ever heard before. There was a shuffling sound as the person who had been speaking moved a step closer. Greg turned, holding his breath, his eyes straining to see in the dark room.

tremor (trĕm′ər) *n.* nervous trembling

The upper part of the figure before him was still in darkness. The lower half was in the dim rectangle of light that fell unevenly from the window. There were two feet, in cracked, dirty shoes from which rose legs that were wrapped in rags.

"Who are you?" Greg hardly recognized his own voice.

"I'm Lemon Brown," came the answer. "Who're you?"

"Greg Ridley."

"What you doing here?" The figure shuffled forward again, and Greg took a small step backward.

"It's raining," Greg said.

"I can see that," the figure said.

The person who called himself Lemon Brown peered forward, and Greg could see him clearly. He was an old man. His black, heavily wrinkled face was surrounded by a halo of crinkly white hair and whiskers that seemed to separate his head from the layers of dirty coats piled on his smallish frame. His pants were bagged to the knee, where they were met with rags that went down to the old shoes. The rags were held on with strings, and there was a rope around his middle. Greg relaxed. He had seen the man before, picking through the trash on the corner and pulling clothes out of a Salvation Army box. There was no sign of the razor that could "cut a week into nine days." C

(2) Targeted Passage

C POINT OF VIEW
How does knowing Greg's thoughts and actions affect your impression of Lemon Brown?

"What are you doing here?" Greg asked.

"This is where I'm staying," Lemon Brown said. "What you here for?"

"Told you it was raining out," Greg said, leaning against the back of the couch until he felt it give slightly.

"Ain't you got no home?"

"I got a home," Greg answered.

"You ain't one of them bad boys looking for my treasure, is you?" Lemon Brown cocked his head to one side and squinted one eye. "Because I told you I got me a razor."

"I'm not looking for your treasure," Greg answered, smiling. "*If* you have one."

"What you mean, *if* I have one," Lemon Brown said. "Every man got a treasure. You don't know that, you must be a fool!"

"Sure," Greg said as he sat on the sofa and put one leg over the back. "What do you have, gold coins?"

"Don't worry none about what I got," Lemon Brown said. "You know who I am?"

LITERARY ANALYSIS

C POINT OF VIEW

Possible answer: *Knowing Greg's thoughts and feelings makes me understand that Lemon Brown is harmless; Greg relaxes when he sees Lemon Brown and says he sees "no sign of the razor."*

If students need help . . . Have students reread lines 91–93 to see what Greg already knows about Lemon Brown.

Extend the Discussion Why do you think Lemon Brown says something threatening to Greg when he first sees him? How might the setting of the story help explain his behavior?

Lines 100–109

REINFORCE *KEY IDEA:* CHERISH

Discuss Why does Greg find it hard to believe that Lemon Brown has a treasure, or something to **cherish?** What kind of treasure is Greg probably thinking about? ***Possible answer:*** *Greg thinks that Lemon Brown could not possess something of great value because he is a poor, homeless man dressed in rags. Greg is thinking of a treasure in the form of money, such as "gold coins" (line 107).*

FOR LESS-PROFICIENT READERS

(2) Targeted Passage [Lines 85–102]

This passage introduces Lemon Brown, the homeless former blues musician.

- Describe Lemon Brown's face.
- How is Lemon Brown dressed? What is tied to his legs?
- Why is Lemon Brown in the abandoned building?
- Why does Lemon Brown ask Greg if he's "one of them bad boys" (line 100)?

Comprehension Support Point out that making logical guesses about what will happen next in a story is part of the fun of reading. Ask students to predict what might happen after Greg hears a voice say, "Don't try nothin' 'cause I got a razor here sharp enough to cut a week into nine days!" (lines 68–69). After students read Lemon's question in line 100, have them predict what Lemon Brown's treasure might be.

BEST PRACTICES TOOLKIT—Transparency
Predicting p. A10

FOR ENGLISH LEARNERS

Culture: Clarify Lemon Brown is too poor to buy clothes and must search through the Salvation Army box (lines 91–93). Explain that the Salvation Army accepts donations of used clothing, furniture, and other practical items. Then it sells the items at very low prices.

ANALYZE VISUALS

Students should cite details from the text as they compare their mental image of Lemon Brown with the picture. In lines 86–90, Lemon is described as having a "wrinkled face," "a halo of crinkly white hair and whiskers," and a "smallish frame." He wears "layers of dirty coats," and over his baggy pants are tied "rags that [go] down to the old shoes." While these details are not reflected in the illustration, the man in the picture is dark-skinned, and his cane suggests that he is old and has difficulty moving, like Lemon Brown (lines 72–73).

READING SKILL

D MAKE INFERENCES

Possible answer: He is proud of who he is.

If students need help . . . Demonstrate the motion that Lemon Brown makes, and read his words in lines 111–112 proudly. Then ask students to use details in lines 114–117 to make other inferences about Lemon Brown and record them in their charts from page 169. Encourage them to continue using their charts to make inferences about Lemon Brown and the other characters as they read.

Details About Character	What I Infer
• Lemon pulls back his shoulders when he says his name.	• Lemon is proud of who he is.
• Lemon sang the blues, traveled in southern states, and was called Sweet Lemon Brown.	• Lemon was a successful blues singer.

ANALYZE VISUALS
How does the man in the picture **compare** with the way you imagine Lemon Brown?

"You told me your name was orange or lemon or something like that."

"Lemon Brown," the old man said, pulling back his shoulders as he did so, "they used to call me Sweet Lemon Brown." **D**

"Sweet Lemon?" Greg asked.

"Yessir. Sweet Lemon Brown. They used to say I sung the blues[3] so sweet that if I sang at a funeral, the dead would **commence** to rocking with the beat. Used to travel all over Mississippi and as far as Monroe, Louisiana, and east on over to Macon, Georgia. You mean you ain't never heard of Sweet Lemon Brown?"

D MAKE INFERENCES
Why does the man pull back his shoulders as he tells Greg his name?

commence (kə-mĕns') *v.* to begin

3. **blues:** a style of music developed from southern African-American songs.

DIFFERENTIATED INSTRUCTION

FOR ENGLISH LEARNERS

Language: Conversational English Patterns Point out that in casual conversation, English speakers may omit certain words but still convey meaning. Have students note instances where Greg and Lemon Brown omit words when they speak. For example, Lemon Brown asks Greg, "What you here for?" (line 95), omitting the word *are,* and Greg responds, "Told you it was raining out" (line 96), omitting *I.* Ask students what words Lemon Brown omits in lines 115, 119, and 123.

FOR ADVANCED LEARNERS/PRE–AP

Analyze Language [paired option] Do fiction writers write like poets? Have partners identify examples of vivid and poetic language that Myers uses to describe the characters, action, and setting. These might include comparisons, exaggerations, and vivid verbs. Have students list and describe their findings and then share them with the class.

"Afraid not," Greg said. "What . . . what happened to you?"

"Hard times, boy. Hard times always after a poor man. One day I got tired, sat down to rest a spell and felt a tap on my shoulder. Hard times caught up with me."

"Sorry about that."

"What you doing here? How come you didn't go on home when the rain come? Rain don't bother you young folks none."

"Just didn't." Greg looked away.

"I used to have a knotty-headed boy just like you." Lemon Brown had half walked, half shuffled back to the corner and sat down against the wall. "Had them big eyes like you got. I used to call them moon eyes. Look into them moon eyes and see anything you want."

"How come you gave up singing the blues?" Greg asked.

"Didn't give it up," Lemon Brown said. "You don't give up the blues; they give you up. After a while you do good for yourself, and it ain't nothing but foolishness singing about how hard you got it. Ain't that right?"

"I guess so."

"What's that noise?" Lemon Brown asked, suddenly sitting upright.

Greg listened, and he heard a noise outside. He looked at Lemon Brown and saw the old man was pointing toward the window.

Greg went to the window and saw three men, neighborhood thugs, on the stoop. One was carrying a length of pipe. Greg looked back toward Lemon Brown, who moved quietly across the room to the window. The old man looked out, then **beckoned** frantically for Greg to follow him. For a moment Greg couldn't move. Then he found himself following Lemon Brown into the hallway and up darkened stairs. Greg followed as closely as he could. They reached the top of the stairs, and Greg felt Lemon Brown's hand first lying on his shoulder, then probing down his arm until he finally took Greg's hand into his own as they crouched in the darkness. **E**

beckon (bĕk'ən) *v.* to signal to come

E MAKE INFERENCES Why does Lemon Brown hold Greg's hand?

"They's bad men," Lemon Brown whispered. His breath was warm against Greg's skin.

"Hey! Rag man!" a voice called. "We know you in here. What you got up under them rags? You got any money?"

Silence.

"We don't want to have to come in and hurt you, old man, but we don't mind if we have to."

Lemon Brown squeezed Greg's hand in his own hard, **gnarled** fist.

gnarled (närld) *adj.* roughened, as from age or work

There was a banging downstairs and a light as the men entered. They banged around noisily, calling for the rag man.

"We heard you talking about your treasure." The voice was slurred. "We just want to see it, that's all."

"You sure he's here?" One voice seemed to come from the room with the sofa.

"Yeah, he stays here every night."

"There's another room over there; I'm going to take a look. You got that flashlight?"

Lines 126–133
REINFORCE *KEY IDEA:* CHERISH

Discuss What clues suggest that Lemon Brown once had a life he could **cherish?**

Possible answer: *He describes his son and how the blues "gave [him] up" because he had such a good life that it was foolish for him to sing the blues. These ideas suggest that Lemon Brown had a life he could cherish.*

READING SKILL

E MAKE INFERENCES

Possible answer: *He holds Greg's hand so that Greg won't be afraid.*

Extend the Discussion What can you infer about Greg's feelings toward Lemon Brown at this point in the story?

FOR LESS–PROFICIENT READERS

Reading Skill Follow-Up: Make Inferences

[paired option] Have students reread page 175 to notice the statements that Lemon Brown makes to Greg about himself and his life. Ask students to work in pairs to note at least three key statements in their charts and then make inferences about what they reveal about Lemon. Afterwards, have pairs compare their charts with other pairs' charts and discuss how making inferences helps them understand the story better.

Details About Character	*What I Infer*
• *Lemon says "hard times" caught up with him. (lines 119–121)*	• *Old age, or maybe personal difficulties, ended Lemon's life as a musician.*
• *Lemon sees similarities between Greg and his son. (lines 126–129)*	• *Lemon is taking a fatherly interest in Greg.*
• *Lemon squeezes Greg's hand when the intruders are about to come in. (line 154)*	• *Lemon feels tense.*

THE TREASURE OF LEMON BROWN 175

LITERARY ANALYSIS

F POINT OF VIEW

Possible answer: *Readers learn more about Greg's feelings. Lines 164–179 mostly describe Greg's fearful response to the intruders.*

If students need help . . . Have students analyze lines 175–179 to see how the narrator reveals Greg's actions, observations, feelings, and thoughts. Point out that there is no similar explanation of what is going on in Lemon Brown's mind.

LITERARY ANALYSIS

G POINT OF VIEW

Possible answer: *Readers would know why Lemon Brown threw himself down the stairs.*

Lines 164–200
DISCUSSION PROMPTS

Use these prompts to help students understand what happens after the thugs enter the building:

Recall Why does Greg hold his breath? ***Possible answer:*** *He doesn't want the thugs to hear him and learn where he and Lemon Brown are hiding.*

Analyze Why is Lemon Brown an "eerie sight" to the thugs? How does Greg help Lemon drive them away? ***Possible answer:*** *Lemon's clothes make him look like a bundle of rags, and he casts a large shadow on the wall. Greg makes a howling sound just before Lemon throws his body down the stairs at the men.*

Infer What can you infer happened after reading the sentence "A rush of warm air came in as the downstairs door opened, then there was only an ominous silence" (lines 198–200)? ***Possible answer:*** *You can infer that the thugs opened the door and left. The silence suggests that only Greg and Lemon Brown are left in the building.*

"Yeah, here, take the pipe too."

Greg opened his mouth to quiet the sound of his breath as he sucked it in uneasily. A beam of light hit the wall a few feet opposite him, then went out.

"Ain't nobody in that room," a voice said. "You think he gone or something?"

"I don't know," came the answer. "All I know is that I heard him talking about some kind of treasure. You know they found that shopping bag lady with that money in her bags."

"Yeah. You think he's upstairs?"

"HEY, OLD MAN, ARE YOU UP THERE?"

Silence.

"Watch my back. I'm going up."

There was a footstep on the stairs, and the beam from the flashlight danced crazily along the peeling wallpaper. Greg held his breath. There was another step and a loud crashing noise as the man banged the pipe against the wooden banister. Greg could feel his temples throb as the man slowly neared them. Greg thought about the pipe, wondering what he would do when the man reached them—what he *could* do. **F**

Then Lemon Brown released his hand and moved toward the top of the stairs. Greg looked around and saw stairs going up to the next floor. He tried waving to Lemon Brown, hoping the old man would see him in the dim light and follow him to the next floor. Maybe, Greg thought, the man wouldn't follow them up there. Suddenly, though, Lemon Brown stood at the top of the stairs, both arms raised high above his head.

"There he is!" a voice cried from below.

"Throw down your money, old man, so I won't have to bash your head in!"

Lemon Brown didn't move. Greg felt himself near panic. The steps came closer, and still Lemon Brown didn't move. He was an eerie sight, a bundle of rags standing at the top of the stairs, his shadow on the wall looming over him. Maybe, the thought came to Greg, the scene could be even eerier.

Greg wet his lips, put his hands to his mouth and tried to make a sound. Nothing came out. He swallowed hard, wet his lips once more and howled as evenly as he could.

"What's that?"

As Greg howled, the light moved away from Lemon Brown, but not before Greg saw him hurl his body down the stairs at the men who had come to take his treasure. There was a crashing noise, and then footsteps. A rush of warm air came in as the downstairs door opened, then there was only an **ominous** silence. **G**

Greg stood on the landing. He listened, and after a while there was another sound on the staircase.

"Mr. Brown?" he called.

"Yeah, it's me," came the answer. "I got their flashlight."

Greg exhaled in relief as Lemon Brown made his way slowly back up the stairs.

"You O.K.?"

"Few bumps and bruises," Lemon Brown said.

F POINT OF VIEW
Whose feelings about the intruders do you lea more about, Greg's or Lemon Brown's?

3 Targeted Passage

ominous (ŏm'ə-nəs) *adj* threatening

G POINT OF VIEW
Reread lines 196–200. How would this passage be different if you knew what Lemon Brown was thinking?

176 UNIT 2: CHARACTER AND POINT OF VIEW

DIFFERENTIATED INSTRUCTION

FOR LESS–PROFICIENT READERS

3 Targeted Passage [Lines 187–200]

This passage illustrates how much Lemon Brown values his treasure and builds suspense about what it might be.

- What do the three thugs think Lemon Brown has?
- What do they do to get his treasure?
- How do Lemon Brown and Greg drive the intruders away?

FOR ADVANCED LEARNERS/PRE–AP

Analyze Plot [small-group option] Have students diagram the plot of the story. Then have small groups discuss the significance of the scene in which Lemon Brown and Greg confront the intruders. They may use these questions as a guide: What does this scene reveal about Lemon Brown? How does the scene develop the relationship between Lemon and Greg? How do the three thugs provide a contrast to Greg's character?

BEST PRACTICES TOOLKIT—Transparency
Plot Diagram p. D12

"I think I'd better be going," Greg said, his breath returning to normal. "You'd better leave, too, before they come back." **H**

"They may hang around outside for a while," Lemon Brown said, "but they ain't getting their nerve up to come in here again. Not with crazy old rag men and howling spooks. Best you stay awhile till the coast is clear. I'm heading out West tomorrow, out to east St. Louis."

"They were talking about treasures," Greg said. "You *really* have a treasure?"

"What I tell you? Didn't I tell you every man got a treasure?" Lemon Brown said. "You want to see mine?"

"If you want to show it to me," Greg shrugged.

"Let's look out the window first, see what them scoundrels be doing," Lemon Brown said.

They followed the oval beam of the flashlight into one of the rooms and looked out the window. They saw the men who had tried to take the treasure sitting on the curb near the corner. One of them had his pants leg up, looking at his knee.

"You sure you're not hurt?" Greg asked Lemon Brown.

"Nothing that ain't been hurt before," Lemon Brown said. "When you get as old as me all you say when something hurts is 'Howdy, Mr. Pain, sees you back again.' Then when Mr. Pain see he can't worry you none, he go on mess with somebody else."

Greg smiled.

"Here, you hold this." Lemon Brown gave Greg the flashlight.

He sat on the floor near Greg and carefully untied the strings that held the rags on his right leg. When he took the rags away, Greg saw a piece of plastic. The old man carefully took off the plastic and unfolded it. He revealed some yellowed newspaper clippings and a battered harmonica.

"There it be," he said, nodding his head. "There it be."

H MAKE INFERENCES
Why does Greg think he should leave?

4 Targeted Passage

Greg looked at the old man, saw the distant look in his eye, then turned to the clippings. They told of Sweet Lemon Brown, a blues singer and harmonica player who was appearing at different theaters in the South. One of the clippings said he had been the hit of the show, although not the headliner. All of the clippings were reviews of shows Lemon Brown had been in more than 50 years ago. Greg looked at the harmonica. It was dented badly on one side, with the reed holes on one end nearly closed.

"I used to travel around and make money for to feed my wife and Jesse—that's my boy's name. Used to feed them good, too. Then his mama died, and he stayed with his mama's sister. He growed up to be a man, and when the war come he saw fit to go off and fight in it. I didn't have nothing to give him except these things that told him who I was, and what he come from. If you know your pappy did something, you know you can do something too. **I**

"Anyway, he went off to war, and I went off still playing and singing. 'Course by then I wasn't as much as I used to be, not without somebody to make it worth the while. You know what I mean?"

I MAKE INFERENCES
Reread lines 247–248. How might Greg apply this idea to his own life?

READING SKILL

H MAKE INFERENCES

Possible answer: *Greg wants to avoid another frightening incident.*

Lines 231–248

REINFORCE *KEY IDEA:* CHERISH

Discuss What two things does Lemon Brown cherish? Why does he value them? ***Possible answer:*** *Lemon cherishes his old harmonica and the newspaper clippings from many years ago about his performances as a blues artist. He values these things because they represent who he was and what he accomplished in life.*

READING SKILL

I MAKE INFERENCES

Possible answer: *Greg might take inspiration from the fact that his father has had a successful career as a postal worker and work harder at school.*

FOR LESS–PROFICIENT READERS

4 Targeted Passage [Lines 231–251]

This passage marks the climax of the story: Lemon Brown reveals his treasure to Greg and explains why he gave the items to his son.

- What treasure does Lemon Brown reveal to Greg?
- Why did Lemon Brown give his treasure to his son?

LITERARY ANALYSIS

J POINT OF VIEW

Possible answer: *His answer, "I guess so," indicates that Greg doesn't really understand why the treasure is so important to Lemon Brown.*

Lines 267–293

DISCUSSION PROMPTS

Use these prompts to help students understand Greg's response to Lemon Brown's treasure:

Connect Apart from material possessions, what might parents pass on to their sons and daughters? *Students may say that they pass on memories, stories, and values.*

Analyze What does Greg not seem to understand about Lemon's treasures? ***Possible answer:*** ***At first, Greg doesn't seem to grasp that Lemon's treasures are valuable because of what they symbolize both to Lemon Brown and to his son.***

Synthesize What do Lemon Brown and Greg's father have in common? ***Possible answer:*** *They both want to pass on to their sons their values and pride in their accomplishments.*

READING SKILL

K MAKE INFERENCES

Possible answer: *Greg now understands that his father lectures him because he loves Greg and wants him to have a good life.*

"Yeah," Greg nodded, not quite really knowing.

"I traveled around, and one time I come home, and there was this letter saying Jesse got killed in the war. Broke my heart, it truly did.

"They sent back what he had with him over there, and what it was is this old mouth fiddle and these clippings. Him carrying it around with him like that told me it meant something to him. That was my treasure, and when I give it to him he treated it just like that, a treasure. Ain't that something?"

"Yeah, I guess so," Greg said. J

"You *guess* so?" Lemon Brown's voice rose an octave as he started to put his treasure back into the plastic. "Well, you got to guess 'cause you sure don't know nothing. Don't know enough to get home when it's raining."

"I guess . . . I mean, you're right."

"You O.K. for a youngster," the old man said as he tied the strings around his leg, "better than those scalawags[4] what come here looking for my treasure. That's for sure."

"You really think that treasure of yours was worth fighting for?" Greg asked. "Against a pipe?"

"What else a man got 'cepting what he can pass on to his son, or his daughter, if she be his oldest?" Lemon Brown said. "For a big-headed boy you sure do ask the foolishest questions."

Lemon Brown got up after patting his rags in place and looked out the window again.

"Looks like they're gone. You get on out of here and get yourself home. I'll be watching from the window so you'll be all right."

Lemon Brown went down the stairs behind Greg. When they reached the front door the old man looked out first, saw the street was clear and told Greg to scoot on home.

"You sure you'll be O.K.?" Greg asked.

"Now didn't I tell you I was going to east St. Louis in the morning?" Lemon Brown asked. "Don't that sound O.K. to you?"

"Sure it does," Greg said. "Sure it does. And you take care of that treasure of yours."

"That I'll do," Lemon said, the wrinkles about his eyes suggesting a smile. "That I'll do."

The night had warmed and the rain had stopped, leaving puddles at the curbs. Greg didn't even want to think how late it was. He thought ahead of what his father would say and wondered if he should tell him about Lemon Brown. He thought about it until he reached his stoop, and decided against it. Lemon Brown would be O.K., Greg thought, with his memories and his treasure.

Greg pushed the button over the bell marked Ridley, thought of the lecture he knew his father would give him, and smiled. K

J POINT OF VIEW What does Greg think about Lemon Brown's treasure?

K MAKE INFERENCES Why does the thought of his father's lecture make Greg smile?

4. **scalawags** (skăl′ə-wăgz′): rascals.

SELECTION WRAP-UP

REFLECT Ask students for their first impressions of Lemon Brown. Ask how they felt about him by the end of the story.

CRITIQUE Ask students whether this story realistically depicts the conflict between a father and his son. Have them explain their responses.

READING FLUENCY

Distribute the copy masters and have students practice fluency.

RESOURCE MANAGER—Copy Master
Reading Fluency p. 37

DIFFERENTIATED INSTRUCTION

FOR ADVANCED LEARNERS/PRE-AP

Analyze Theme [small-group option] Have students form small groups to conduct a more in-depth analysis of the theme of treasure in the story. Pose these questions for discussion:

- Does Lemon Brown make the correct decision by defending his treasure, even though it has no monetary value? Why or why not?
- What might his treasure symbolize to him?
- If it did have monetary value, would you advise him to sell it in order to have a better life?

Ask students to explain their responses.

omprehension

1. **Recall** How does Greg meet Lemon Brown?
2. **Recall** How does Lemon Brown scare off the intruders?
3. **Clarify** Why does Lemon Brown **cherish** his treasure?

terary Analysis

4. **Examine Third-Person Limited Point of View** Whose sights, thoughts, and feelings does the narrator present? Explain how the story might be different if readers knew more about the thoughts of the other characters.
5. **Understand Events** How do Greg's feelings toward Lemon Brown change over time? In a graphic like the one shown, note important events from the story. Under each event, tell how Greg feels about Lemon Brown at that point.

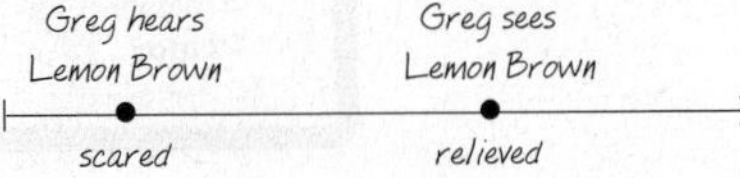

6. **Make Inferences** Review the inferences you noted in your chart. How do you think Lemon Brown's life story helps Greg see his relationship with his father in a new way?
7. **Analyze Dialect** One way writers create realistic characters is to include the characters' **dialect,** the language spoken by people in a particular place or group. Dialect can include unique uses for words and nonstandard grammar. Find three examples of Lemon Brown's dialect. Explain how his language contributes to your understanding of his character.
8. **Draw Conclusions About Characters** In fiction, a character may be either static or dynamic. **Static** characters experience little change over the course of a story. **Dynamic** characters change and grow during a story. Which characters in this story are static? Which are dynamic? Explain.

xtension and Challenge

9. **Readers' Circle** Walter Dean Myers believes it is important for young people to have role models. Discuss with a small group of classmates what makes a good role model and in what ways Lemon Brown is a role model for Greg.
10. **Inquiry and Research** Lemon Brown describes singing the blues as "singing about how hard you got it." Research the blues and find some representative songs. Is Lemon Brown's description of the blues accurate? Play parts of the songs for the class and talk about the kind of life the songs suggest.

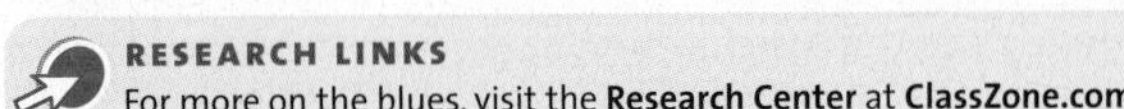

RESEARCH LINKS
For more on the blues, visit the **Research Center** at **ClassZone.com.**

After Reading

For additional support of postreading questions, use these copy masters:

RESOURCE MANAGER—Copy Masters
Reading Check p. 34 (to check understanding of the selection)
Third-Person Limited Point of View p. 27 (for practice of literary analysis standards focus)
Question Support p. 35 (After Reading questions adapted for English learners and less-proficient readers)

Additional selection questions are provided for teachers on page 21.

For additional activities to challenge students, see

Power Thinking at **ClassZone.com**

ANSWERS

Comprehension

1. *Greg seeks shelter from the rain in an abandoned building where Lemon Brown is living.*
2. *Lemon Brown throws himself down the stairs at the intruders.*
3. *Lemon Brown's harmonica and newspaper clippings remind him of his son, who died while carrying this treasure. They also remind him of his life as a blues musician.*

Literary Analysis

Possible answers:

4. ● **STANDARDS FOCUS Third-Person Limited Point of View** *The narrator presents Greg's sights, thoughts, and feelings. If readers knew the thoughts of the other characters, they would have more insight about their motives and attitudes.*
5. *Greg hears Lemon Brown's life story/bored. Thugs enter the building/scared. Lemon Brown confronts the thugs and throws himself down the stairs/terrified, concerned. Greg sees the treasure/doesn't understand. Greg says good-bye to Lemon Brown/respects him and his father.*
6. ■ **STANDARDS FOCUS Make Inferences** *Greg learns that it is important to fathers to pass on their values and an idea of where they "come from." Instead of being annoyed by his father's lectures, Greg now values his father's concern and advice.*
7. *Examples of dialect: "You ain't one of them" (line 100); "There it be" (line 235); "you sure don't know nothing" (lines 261–262). Lemon's dialect suggests that he probably had little formal schooling. This may help to explain why he fell on "hard times" later in life (line 119).*
8. *Greg's father, Lemon Brown, and the thugs are all static because none of them changes or grows during the story. The only dynamic character is Greg, who changes his ideas about his father.*

Extension and Challenge

9. *Students' definitions of a good role model may vary. They may say that Lemon Brown is a role model for Greg in displaying wisdom, courage, and love.*
10. *Students will likely say that Lemon Brown's description of the blues is accurate. Song selections should highlight difficulties people have experienced.*

ANSWERS

Vocabulary in Context

VOCABULARY PRACTICE

1. *synonyms*
2. *synonyms*
3. *synonyms*
4. *antonyms*
5. *synonyms*
6. *antonyms*
7. *antonyms*
8. *antonyms*

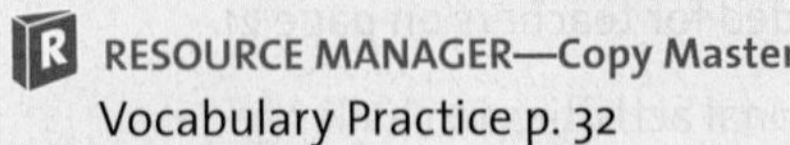

RESOURCE MANAGER—Copy Master
Vocabulary Practice p. 32

VOCABULARY IN WRITING

Ask students to reread lines 138–200 and then scan the list for words that might help them describe Greg's experience. Tell them that not every sentence in the paragraph must include a vocabulary word.

VOCABULARY STRATEGY: SIMILES *(also an EL language objective)*

Have students read the phrase starting with *like* or *as* aloud and visualize what it describes. Then have them use context clues to infer the meaning of the boldfaced word in each sentence.

Definitions may vary but should reflect clue words. ***Possible answers:***

1. *murky—dark*
2. *obstinate—stubborn*
3. *nimble—graceful*
4. *persistent—determined*
5. *tenuous—weak*

RESOURCE MANAGER—Copy Master
Vocabulary Strategy p. 33

Vocabulary Center at **ClassZone.com**
Additional Vocabulary Activities

Vocabulary Practice

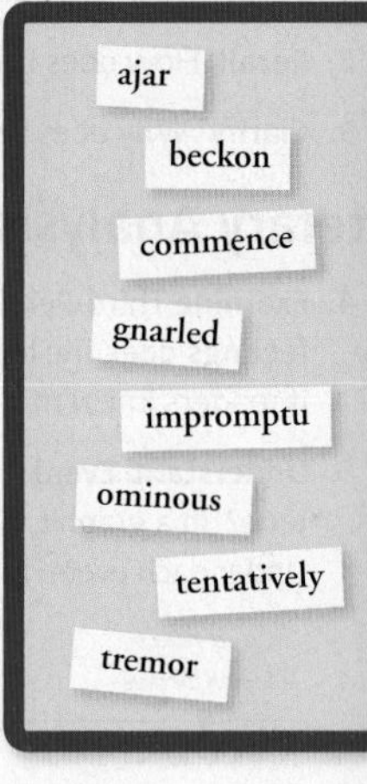

VOCABULARY PRACTICE

Synonyms are words that have the same meaning. **Antonyms** are words that have the opposite meaning. Explain the meaning of the words in each pair and then decide whether they are synonyms or antonyms.

1. beckon/call
2. tentatively/cautiously
3. ominous/haunting
4. gnarled/smooth
5. ajar/open
6. impromptu/planned
7. tremor/stillness
8. commence/stop

VOCABULARY IN WRITING

Use at least three vocabulary words to write a paragraph describing Greg's experience hiding from the neighborhood thugs. You might start like this.

> **EXAMPLE SENTENCE**
>
> *Greg and Lemon Brown climbed the darkened staircase* ***tentatively****.*

VOCABULARY STRATEGY: SIMILES

Similes compare two things that are not alike using the words *like* or *as*. In this selection, Lemon Brown's voice is said to be "high and brittle, **like** dry twigs being broken." This simile helps you hear and understand what the character's voice sounds like.

Similes can also provide a context clue to help you figure out the meaning of an unknown word. If you know the sound of dry twigs being broken, you understand what the word *brittle* means.

PRACTICE Pay attention to the comparison being made by each simile. Use it as a context clue to help you define the boldfaced word.

1. The windows were as **murky** as the muddy waters of the Mississippi.
2. Like a mule unwilling to move, the **obstinate** child held his ground.
3. As she danced across the stage, she looked as **nimble** as a graceful deer.
4. The **persistent** detective looked for clues like a dog sniffing out a bone.
5. Their friendship was becoming as **tenuous** as a fraying rope.

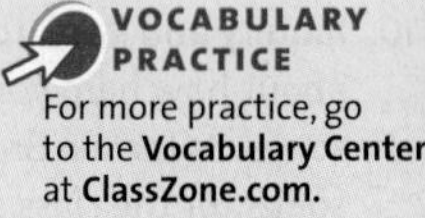

VOCABULARY PRACTICE
For more practice, go to the **Vocabulary Center** at **ClassZone.com.**

DIFFERENTIATED INSTRUCTION

FOR LESS-PROFICIENT READERS

Vocabulary Practice If students are unable to recall the meaning of a vocabulary word, have them reread the sentence in the story to jog their memories. Refer them to these pages for each word as appropriate: *impromptu, ajar, tentatively* (p. 172); *tremor* (p. 173); *commence* (p. 174); *beckon, gnarled* (p. 175); *ominous* (p. 176).

FOR ADVANCED LEARNERS/PRE-AP

Vocabulary Strategy Challenge students by having them write new sentences with different similes for the boldfaced words.

ading-Writing Connection

ncrease your appreciation of "The Treasure of Lemon Brown" by responding to these prompts. Then complete the **Grammar and Writing** exercise.

WRITING PROMPTS	SELF-CHECK
A. Short Response: Describe a Character Imagine that a friend of yours had to find Lemon Brown in a crowd. What would you tell your friend to look for? Write a **one-paragraph description** of Lemon Brown that includes details about his appearance and the treasure he **cherishes.**	***A strong description will . . .*** • include words and phrases that bring Lemon Brown to life • provide details from the story
B. Extended Response: Write a Dialogue What do you think Greg and his father might have said to one another when Greg returned home? Write a **one-page dialogue** between the two of them in which they address the subject of the report card and their feelings about each other.	***A creative dialogue will . . .*** • refer to details from the story • sound like a real teenager and adult are speaking

AMMAR AND WRITING

USE CORRECT VERB TENSE **Verb tense** indicates the time that an action or condition takes place—whether in the **past, present,** or **future.** In your writing, use the same verb tense to describe actions that take place at the same time, and change the verb tense when an action or condition happens at a different time.

Original: I always have a good time when I went to the beach. Last week, I swim and collect seashells. (Have *and* went *are in two different tenses.* Swim *and* collect *are present tense.)*

Revised: I always have a good time when I go to the beach. Last week, I swam and collected seashells. *(In the first sentence, both verbs need to be in the present tense. In the second sentence, the action is happening in the past, so the verbs should be in the past tense.)*

PRACTICE Choose the correct verb tenses in the following paragraph.

I (meet, met, will meet) an old blues musician earlier tonight. He (carries, carried, will carry) a harmonica around in his pocket every day because it reminds him of his son. He (helps, helped, will help) me realize that I should treasure people in my life more. I (work, worked, will work) harder in school to make you proud.

For more help with verb tenses, see page R56 in the ***Grammar Handbook.***

Reading-Writing Connection

WRITING PROMPTS

- For **Prompt A,** distribute a Character Map and have students fill in details about Lemon Brown based on what they recall from the story. Then, suggest they begin their paragraphs with a physical description and next describe what he cherishes.

BEST PRACTICES TOOLKIT—Transparency
Character Map p. D8

- For **Prompt B,** have students review pages 170 and 172 to note details they might include in their dialogue. Suggest that they consider what Greg learned about families and "treasure" from Lemon Brown.

For an extended Reading-Writing Connection activity, see

Writing Center at **ClassZone.com**

GRAMMAR AND WRITING

- Ask students to use the clue words to find the correct verb tense in sentence 1 (*"earlier tonight"*—*past*) and sentence 2 (*"reminds"*—*present*).
- In sentence 3, point out that the action (helping) took place before the present time. In sentence 4, the action (working harder) takes place in the future.

Answers: *met, carries, helped, will work*

RESOURCE MANAGER—Copy Master
Use Correct Verb Tense p. 36

Assess and Reteach

Assess

RESOURCE MANAGER—Copy Masters
Selection Tests A, B/C pp. 39–40, 41–42

Test Generator CD

Reteach

STANDARDS LESSON FILE
Literature Lesson 12: Point of View
Reading Lesson 8: Making Inferences
Vocabulary Lesson 14: Context Clues
Grammar Lesson 16: Basic Verb Tenses

DIFFERENTIATED INSTRUCTION

FOR LESS-PROFICIENT WRITERS

For Prompt A:

1. Have students write sentences summarizing each aspect of their Character Map.
2. After students write an opening sentence that states the main idea, tell them to organize their supporting sentences to present a full description of Lemon Brown. They may need to combine sentences or add transitions to make the text flow logically.

For Prompt B:

1. Have students make notes about what each character might say about (1) the report card and (2) his feelings toward the other.
2. Have them use the notes to write sentences that express that character's thoughts. Remind them to show the characters responding to each other.
3. Ask students to identify each speaker with tags such as *he asked* or *he replied.*

Focus and Motivate

OBJECTIVES

Reading for Information

- identify and compare and contrast **scope** of ideas and information in different texts
- evaluate sources for usefulness
- identify and analyze characteristics of a timeline
- read a timeline, a history article, and a feature article

SUMMARY

The timeline places key events related to blues music in the context of African-American history. "Basic Blues" provides a brief history of the blues from its roots in African-American slave songs to its adoption by rock-and-roll groups in the 1960s. "Musicians Know the Blues Firsthand" focuses on the problem of poverty among elderly blues musicians and describes one man's efforts to help them.

What's the Connection?

Write these statements on an Anticipation Guide. Have students respond to each one before and after reading the selections.

- Blues music has its origins in the songs of enslaved African Americans.
- The blues first appeared in the 1920s.
- Rock and roll was inspired by the blues.
- Blues musicians make a lot of money.

BEST PRACTICES TOOLKIT—Transparency
Anticipation Guide p. A14

Teach

Skill Focus: Identify Scope

To help students understand the concept, compare scope to the field of view that can be seen through a camera. Point out that the lens of the camera can be adjusted for a wide or narrow field of view. Explain that with a small field of view, the picture frames a single, close-up subject such as one flower or a person's face. Contrast this to a wide field of view, which could frame an entire garden or a group of 30 students.

Possible chart entries appear on page 186.

RESOURCE MANAGER—Copy Master
Identify Scope p. 51

Reading for Information

Blues: A National Treasure

- Timeline
- History Article
- Feature Article

Use with "The Treasure of Lemon Brown," page 170.

What's the Connection?

In "The Treasure of Lemon Brown," you met a blues musician, but do you know what blues music is? Where it came from? The other kinds of music it inspired? The selections that follow will tell you about all that and more.

Skill Focus: Identify Scope

Scope refers to a work's range, or breadth, of coverage. In general, the fewer people, places, events, and ideas a work covers, the narrower its scope. For example, the "The Treasure of Lemon Brown" has a narrow scope because it covers just a few key interactions between a couple of characters on a single rainy evening. A story or article with a broad scope might introduce many people or events or cover a long period of time.

To identify how wide or narrow the scope of a selection is, consider how the writer covers the following:

- **People**—How many people are introduced? How well do you get to know them?
- **Places**—How many places, or settings, are described? How much do you get to know about them?
- **Events**—How many events are covered? How much time do these events span? How much do you learn about them?
- **Topic**—What is the topic? How many aspects of it are discussed?

As you read the selections that follow, keep track of your answers to these questions. Then, use your answers to estimate each selection's scope.

	Timeline	*History Article*	*Feature Article*
How many people does it introduce? How well do you get to know them?			
How many places does it describe?			
How many events does it cover? How much time do they span?			
What is the topic? How many aspects of it are discussed?			

182 UNIT 2: CHARACTER AND POINT OF VIEW

Selection Resources

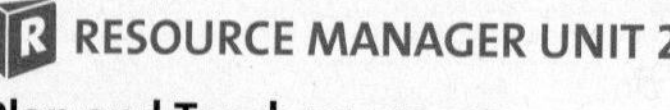

RESOURCE MANAGER UNIT 2

Plan and Teach pp. 43–47

Reading
Summary pp. 49†*, 50‡*
Identify Scope pp. 51, 53†*
Reading Check p. 55
Evaluate Sources for Usefulness pp. 52, 54†*
Question Support p. 56*

Assessment
Selection Tests A, B/C pp. 57*, 59*
Test Generator CD

Reading Support
Audio Anthology CD*

BEST PRACTICES TOOLKIT
Anticipation Guide • Personal Word List

* Resources for Differentiation † Also in Spanish ‡ In Haitian Creole and Vietnamese

Timeline: Evolution of the Blues (A)

The blues emerged as a new form of music in the 20th century, but its roots date back to the music created by enslaved African Americans.

	THE BLUES	AFRICAN-AMERICAN HISTORY
1910s	**1912** W. C. Handy writes the first blues song. He later becomes known as "the father of the blues."	**The Great Migration** Many African Americans leave the South in search of greater opportunity in Northern cities.
1920s	**1923** Ma Rainey, "the mother of the blues," releases her first album.	**The Harlem Renaissance** African-American music, art, and writing thrive in Harlem, New York.
1930s	 **1933** Billie Holiday is discovered; she becomes one of the most famous jazz singers of all time. Her style is characteristic of the blues.	**The Great Depression** African Americans, along with the population as a whole, experience massive unemployment.
1940s	**1943** Blues musician Muddy Waters moves to Chicago, which becomes the center of a new style of blues.	**World War II** More than one million African Americans serve in the military despite widespread segregation and discrimination.
1950s	**1954** Elvis Presley records his first song. Influenced by blues and country music, he becomes known as "the king of rock and roll."	**A Landmark Court Case** In 1954, racial segregation in schools is declared unconstitutional in *Brown v. Board of Education.*
1960s	**1962** The Rolling Stones form. Influenced by the blues, the band creates a new hard-rock style that inspires countless bands to follow.	**The Civil Rights Movement** Congress passes the Civil Rights Act, which makes racial discrimination illegal in public places.
(B) 1970s to present	**1973** Kool Herc begins to DJ in the Bronx. He is seen as the father of hip-hop, a musical style that has blues roots and is known for rapping and instrumental "beats." 	**Struggles and Accomplishments** Though racial tensions still exist, African Americans gain broader economic opportunity than they had in previous decades.

FOCUS ON FORM A timeline is a graphic aid that identifies key events during a certain time period. Labels usually tell the specific time in which notable events occurred.

(A) TIMELINE
Preview the timeline's title and headings. Based on these, what kinds of events will the timeline include?

(B) IDENTIFY SCOPE
What period of time does the entire timeline cover?

Practice and Apply

FOCUS ON FORM

Timeline Discuss with students the purpose and characteristics of a timeline, as described in **Focus on Form.** Additionally, a timeline

- may briefly describe each event
- has a topical focus, such as civil rights
- may include images of people and events
- may appear in a textbook, reference work, magazine article, or newspaper article

Ask students to give examples of timelines they have encountered.

ELEMENTS OF NONFICTION

(A) TIMELINE

Possible answer: *The timeline shows events in the development of the blues in relation to landmarks in African-American history.*

If students need help . . . Point out that the dates in this timeline are arranged vertically—they read from top (oldest) to bottom (most recent). Contrast this to a horizontal timeline by drawing a sketch on the board, using some of the same information from page 183. Point out that a horizontal timeline is read from left to right.

DISCUSSION PROMPTS

Use these prompts to help students understand the information in the timeline:

Recall What important event in the history of the blues took place in 1923? ***Answer:*** *Ma Rainey, "the mother of the blues," released her first album.*

Synthesize How did the blues influence musicians in the 1950s, 1960s, and 1970s? ***Possible answer:*** *Musicians used the blues as a basis for creating new forms of music, such as rock and roll and hip-hop.*

Evaluate What is one benefit of presenting information in a timeline? ***Possible answer:*** *A timeline offers writers a concise way to present information about events that occurred over a long period of time.*

INFORMATIONAL ANALYSIS

(B) IDENTIFY SCOPE

Answer: *It covers the 1910s to the present.*

DIFFERENTIATED INSTRUCTION

FOR LESS–PROFICIENT READERS

Task Support Discuss strategies for reading the timeline based on the reader's purpose.

Purpose	Strategies
Find specific facts about early blues musicians	• Scan second column • Notice dates and names
Learn about the place of blues in African-American history	• Read across first row; then read other rows in order • Read every word

Lines 1–26
DISCUSSION PROMPTS

Use these prompts to help students understand how blues music sounds and how it began as an art form:

Describe What was the first blues music that W. C. Handy ever heard? Describe the performer, the song, the instrument, and how it was being played. ***Answer:*** *A poor man was singing about traveling on the railroad. He played a guitar by sliding a knife against its strings. He repeated the song's refrain.*

Synthesize What makes the blues an American art form? Respond in your own words. ***Possible answer:*** *The blues comes from the songs of enslaved African Americans, such as work songs and spirituals. This kind of music captured their sorrow and pain.*

Evaluate Based on the legend that describes the way W. C. Handy discovered blues music, do you think he deserves to be called the "Father of the Blues"? ***Possible answer:*** *Handy really is not the "Father of the Blues." Blues music is based on music that was being sung long before Handy heard it. However, Handy was one of the first people to write the music down on paper and probably played a large part in making the music accessible to the mainstream public.*

Basic Blues:
An American Art Form

W.C. Handy knew about music. The composer, cornet player, and orchestra leader had traveled a lot, and he had encountered many different types of music along the way. But while waiting for a train late one night, Handy discovered a style of music unlike anything he had ever heard or played: the blues.

The legend goes like this: One night in 1903, Handy arrived at a train station in Tutwiler, Mississippi, to find that his train was about nine hours behind schedule. His companion on the platform was a raggedly dressed fellow with a guitar. The man had an odd style of playing. He slid the back of a knife blade up and down the guitar's strings, creating a warbling sound. As he sang, he repeated an odd refrain—"goin' where the Southern cross the Dog"—which meant nothing to Handy. It turned out that the guitar-playing fellow was a traveling musician headed to a town called Moorhead, which was located at the intersection of two railroads, the Southern and the Yellow Dog. Handy was so intrigued by the musician's unique style and lyrics that he decided to put something similar down on paper. In the years to come, Handy would be known as the "Father of the Blues."

The American blues that Handy heard that night had its roots in the soulful songs of enslaved African Americans, which in turn were influenced by the call-and-response style of singing found in Africa. Field hollers, work songs, and

DIFFERENTIATED INSTRUCTION

FOR LESS–PROFICIENT READERS

Comprehension Support Call students' attention to the photographs and captions on page 184. Prepare them to read the article by asking these questions:

- What musical instruments are shown in the photographs? *(electric guitar, piano)*
- Since Ma Rainey and Bessie Smith are not shown with instruments, what is their likely musical talent? *(They are singers.)*

FOR ENGLISH LEARNERS

Options for Reading Have students read the title and subtitle and tell what information they think they will get from reading the article. Then have students read along as they listen to the *Audio Anthology CD.* Ask students to tell whether their predictions about the content of the article were correct.

pirituals were all sung by enslaved people as a way of expressing both their suffering and their dreams. After the Civil War, some solo musicians in the South adapted these sounds into songs they sang while accompanying themselves on guitar. The term "the blues" goes back to the 18th century, when being sad or depressed meant that you were experiencing the "blue devils." Since many of the songs were about emotional pain and loss, the name fit.

In 1912, Handy became one of the first composers to release sheet music for a blues song, "Memphis Blues." In 1920, Mamie Smith, a vaudeville performer, became the first African American to record a blues record. "Crazy Blues" sold 75,000 copies in its first month. Such "race records," as they were called, were originally marketed to African-American consumers, but by the end of the 1920s, both African-American and white listeners were snapping up copies of blues recordings from such artists as Ma Rainey and Bessie Smith. Blues artists went from doing informal performances in taverns to large-scale stage performances in theaters and nightclubs, and blues musicians were no longer a phenomenon of the South alone. **C**

Throughout the first half of the 20th century, many African Americans began relocating to the North, looking for a better life with more opportunity. When they moved to cities like Chicago and Detroit, they brought blues music with them. Blues musicians at the time invented new ways to play the blues as a means of reflecting the changes they had experienced. One artist, Muddy Waters, traded in his acoustic guitar for an electric one and added new instruments such as an upright bass, drums, and a harmonica. The new blues was livelier, gave folks something to dance to, and paved the way for rhythm and blues and rock and roll.

Waters's style of "electrified blues" was popular until the early 1950s. But then rock and roll took over the American airwaves. This could have been the end of the blues, but starting in the 1960s, a new wave of white musicians from England and the United States revived interest with their own versions of classic blues tunes. Groups like the Rolling Stones, Cream, and Led Zeppelin brought the blues back to the forefront of the American music scene. However, some blues musicians resented the success of these white musicians, who were gaining fortune and fame using the sounds of lesser-known African-American musicians. **D**

In recent years, new artists such as Jonny Lang, Shemekia Copeland, and Susan Tedeschi have contributed their own styles to the evolution of blues music. These new artists have managed to keep the genre fresh, while at the same time paying tribute to generations of past musicians who taught the United States—and the world—how to sing the blues.

C IDENTIFY SCOPE
How many people has the writer mentioned so far? Note how much you learn about each one of them.

D IDENTIFY SCOPE
Over what period of time do the events in this paragraph take place?

INFORMATIONAL ANALYSIS

C IDENTIFY SCOPE

Possible answer: *The writer has mentioned five musicians so far: W. C. Handy; a man at a train depot; Mamie Smith; Ma Rainey; and Bessie Smith. The reader learns just a fact or two about each artist.*

Lines 27–54

DISCUSSION PROMPTS

Use these prompts to help students understand how the blues evolved:

Recall How did traditional blues music begin to reach a wider audience in the 1920s and 1930s? ***Answer:*** *It reached a wider audience through records made by African-American singers such as Mamie Smith, Ma Rainey, and Bessie Smith. Many blues artists also went from performing in taverns to large stages in theaters and nightclubs.*

Analyze How did blues music evolve in Northern cities in the 1940s? ***Possible answer:*** *Electric guitars replaced acoustic ones, and drums, harmonica, and bass were added. The fuller sound that resulted helped turn blues into dance music.*

Speculate Why do you think white musicians in the 1960s were attracted to African-American blues? ***Possible answer:*** *They appreciated its soulful sound and the authentic emotions it expressed.*

INFORMATIONAL ANALYSIS

D IDENTIFY SCOPE

Answer: *The paragraph covers events from the early 1950s to the 1960s.*

Extend the Discussion Why might many African-American blues artists not have achieved as much lasting fame as rock-and-roll bands like the Rolling Stones or Led Zeppelin?

FOR LESS-PROFICIENT READERS

Vocabulary Support Have students create Personal Word Lists of challenging words from the two articles. Suggest that they use context clues, analysis of word parts, and prior knowledge to analyze each word before looking up the definition. Encourage them also to record hard-to-spell words.

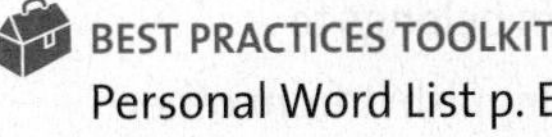
BEST PRACTICES TOOLKIT
Personal Word List p. E2

FOR ENGLISH LEARNERS

Culture: Clarify Explain that *vaudeville* (line 28) was a popular style of entertainment in the United States between the late 19th century and the early 20th century. Its structure included a series of unrelated acts, with performances ranging from musicians and dancers to comedians, magicians, animal acts, acrobats, athletes, one-act plays or scenes from plays, and even short films. The new film industry, radio, and the Great Depression led to the closure of the vaudeville theaters.

INFORMATIONAL ANALYSIS

E IDENTIFY SCOPE

Possible answers: *The article is about one person's efforts to help impoverished blues musicians who never achieved great fame. It focuses on the 1980s.*

If students need help . . . Help them see that most of the paragraphs in the article (lines 24–65) focus on Duffy and the organization he founded.

Skill Focus: Identify Scope

Possible answers for the chart on page 182:

Timeline

- ***People:*** *seven; just one fact about each person*
- ***Places:*** *five (the South, Northern cities, Harlem, Chicago, the Bronx)*
- ***Events:*** *seven events about the blues and seven major events in African-American history; the 20th century*
- ***Topic:*** *the blues; two aspects: how it evolved and how it fits into African-American history*

History Article

- ***People:*** *12; one or two facts about each person*
- ***Places:*** *nine (train depot in Tutwiler, MS; Moorehead; Africa; the South; the North; Chicago; Detroit; England; the United States)*
- ***Events:*** *12 events from the 18th century to recent years*
- ***Topic:*** *the blues; three aspects: how it was discovered, how it began, and how it evolved*

Feature Article

- ***People:*** *five; get to know folklorist Tim Duffy best; brief profile of musician Cootie Stark; less detail about other blues musicians*
- ***Places:*** *eight (New Orleans; Winston-Salem homeless shelter; University of North Carolina; the rural South; Hillsborough, NC; Greenville, SC; Lincoln Center; Newport)*
- ***Events:*** *one main event: Duffy's founding of the Music Maker Foundation; 1980s*
- ***Topic:*** *the problem of many blues musicians not being able to make a living; two aspects: the problem and Duffy's solution*

Musicians Know the Blues Firsthand

Andrew Jacobs

No one ever said the blues was any way to make a living. . . . Broke even in good times, Little Freddie King survived by playing juke joints in New Orleans until old age left his body broken. Deprived of a steady income, he went without dentures or glasses, and one night, a heavy rain brought down the ceiling of his bedroom.

Without an audience for his quirky style of music, Haskel "Whistling Britches" Thompson ended up in a Winston-Salem homeless shelter. . . .

"These people are our culture, our folk musicians, and no one is looking after them," said the bluesman Taj Mahal. "We're always putting our hands over our heart and saying the Pledge of Allegiance and honoring Davy Crockett, yet we're allowing these people and their music to fall through the cracks."

In the 1980s, Tim Duffy came to a similar realization. As a student studying folklore at the University of North Carolina, he grew obsessed with preserving the sounds of these unheralded musicians. But as he traveled the rural South with recording equipment, he grew even more troubled by the poverty that left many artists without instruments and too strapped for heating oil or medicine.

"Their music ended up in archives but the problem is no one gets to hear it," said Mr. Duffy, who lives in Hillsborough, N.C. "And the recordings don't put food on their table, it doesn't get them a gig."

Over the last two decades, Mr. Duffy, 41, has turned his passion into a nonprofit organization, the Music Maker Foundation, which is part recording company, part artist management service, and part social welfare agency. For those able to perform, the foundation promotes roots music and offers artists a touring career; for those too old or sickly, he sends monthly checks that average $100.

When unexpected hardships strike, as in the case of Little Freddie King's collapsing ceiling, Mr. Duffy provides emergency cash. . . .

The foundation also puts CDs into the hands of men like Cootie Stark, a blind guitarist from Greenville, S.C., who had never had his music recorded until he met Mr. Duffy at age 68. Mr. Stark, now 77, has since taken to the stages of Lincoln Center, the Rockport Rhythm and Blues Festival at Newport, and other concert venues. He earns about $8,000 a year selling his CDs.

"It should have happened 45 years ago, but I finally got a break," he said. **E**

E IDENTIFY SCOPE
What is this article about? What time period does it focus on? Jot this information in your chart.

186 UNIT 2: CHARACTER AND POINT OF VIEW

DIFFERENTIATED INSTRUCTION

FOR LESS–PROFICIENT READERS

Comprehension Support Help students understand that the article is organized by problem and solution:

- Paragraph 1 states a problem.
- Paragraphs 2–3 give examples of the problem or comment on it.
- The remaining paragraphs discuss the solution, including an example in the last two paragraphs.

FOR ADVANCED LEARNERS/PRE–AP

Analyze Forms Ask students to write two **Focus on Form** notes: one for a history article and one for a feature article. Have them review the two articles and then use the **Focus on Form** note on page 183 as a model. In each note, suggest that students use a bulleted list to inform readers about

- the genre the form belongs to
- features that distinguish it from other forms of writing
- where each type of article might appear

Comprehension

1. **Recall** Who became known as "the father of the blues" and why?
2. **Summarize** In a few sentences, summarize what gave rise to electrified blues.
3. **Clarify** Reread lines 15–23 in "Musicians Know the Blues Firsthand." What is Taj Mahal pointing out here?

Critical Analysis

4. **Compare Scope** Which of the three selections has the narrowest scope? How do the scopes of the other two selections compare? Use the chart you made as you read to give reasons for your answers.
5. **Draw Conclusions About a Timeline** Why do you suppose a timeline called "Evolution of the Blues" includes key events in African-American history?

Read for Information: Evaluate Sources for Usefulness

WRITING PROMPT

Imagine you have chosen one of the following topics for a report:
- the birth of blues music and how blues has changed over the years
- important events in African-American history
- the life of blues musicians

Explain which selection you would use as a source of information for this topic and why. If more than one selection would be useful to you, be sure to explain what each would provide.

To answer this prompt, first identify the topic you would want to focus on. Then follow these steps:

1. Using the chart you filled in, consider the focus of each selection you just read. What kinds of information does each selection provide?
2. In a paragraph, identify the topic you picked, the selection(s) you would use for a report on that topic, and a brief explanation as to why the selection(s) would be useful to you.

Topic of Report: ______	
Selection I Would Use	**Why I Would Use It**

Practice and Apply

For additional support of postreading questions, use these copy masters:

RESOURCE MANAGER—Copy Masters
Reading Check p. 55
Question Support p. 56
Evaluate Sources for Usefulness p. 52

For additional questions, see page 46.

ANSWERS

Comprehension

1. *W. C. Handy became known as "the father of the blues" because he wrote and published the first blues song.*
2. *After Southern blues artists migrated to Northern cities, they invented new ways to play the blues that reflected their new experiences. They began using electric guitars and added instruments for a livelier sound.*
3. *Taj Mahal is pointing out that blues music is part of our national heritage and therefore should be treasured and preserved.*

Critical Analysis

Possible answers:

4. **■ STANDARDS FOCUS Identify Scope** *"Musicians Know the Blues Firsthand" has the narrowest scope. It focuses on the shortest time period, on one person (Tim Duffy), and on one topic, the problem of poor blues musicians. The other two selections are similar in scope; both cover the development of the blues.*
5. *The key events in African-American history put the musical events in perspective.*

Read for Information: Evaluate Sources for Usefulness

Writing Prompt *Students should explain their choice of sources.*

FOR LESS-PROFICIENT WRITERS

Task Support [paired option] Have pairs work together to complete the chart from page 182.

1. If partners disagree about an answer, have them review or reread the text to come up with an answer both partners can agree on.
2. Ask pairs to make sure they answered all the chart questions for each selection.
3. As a class, discuss which aspects of the selections helped them most in determining the scope.

FOR ADVANCED LEARNERS/PRE-AP

Apply [small-group option] Have students analyze the scope of another history or feature article in this textbook. Then ask them to meet in small groups to summarize and compare the articles in terms of scope.

Assess and Reteach

Assess

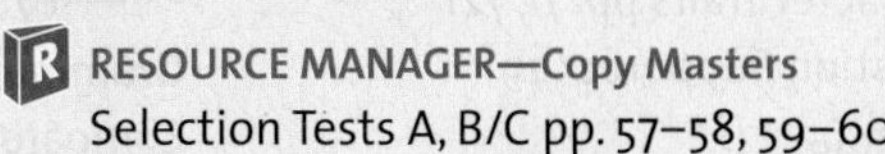
RESOURCE MANAGER—Copy Masters
Selection Tests A, B/C pp. 57–58, 59–60

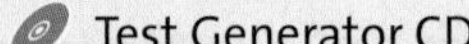
Test Generator CD

Reteach

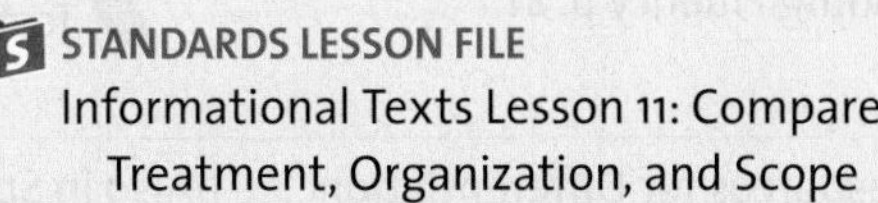
STANDARDS LESSON FILE
Informational Texts Lesson 11: Compare Treatment, Organization, and Scope

Focus and Motivate

OBJECTIVES

Literary Analysis
- explore the key idea of **knowledge**
- identify and analyze character traits
- read a short story and a screenplay

Reading
- develop strategies for reading a long story

Vocabulary
- build vocabulary for reading and writing
- understand and use specialized vocabulary from the field of psychology *(also an EL language objective)*

Grammar and Writing
- identify and use comparative and superlative forms correctly
- use writing to analyze literature

SUMMARY

Charlie Gordon, a man of limited abilities, is chosen to undergo an experimental operation. He becomes a genius. A few weeks later, the mouse upon which the operation was first performed shows signs of deterioration and dies. Charlie soon begins to follow a similar path. In the screenplay, Charlie's pre-operation skill at completing a maze is tested against that of the mouse, Algernon.

When is it better not to KNOW?

Expand on the question and the ***KEY IDEA*** by presenting the saying "Ignorance is bliss." Do students agree that some kinds of **knowledge** make life more difficult? Then have small groups complete the ***DISCUSS*** activity.

Before Reading

Flowers for Algernon

Short Story by Daniel Keyes

from Charly

Screenplay by Stirling Silliphant

When is it better not to KNOW?

KEY IDEA As young children, we want to know everything: why the sky is blue, how computers work, why people can talk but dogs can't. Humans have a natural thirst for **knowledge.** But as we grow up, we sometimes find there are things it's not necessary, or even desirable, to know. In the short story you are about to read, a man learns that knowledge can bring with it some unpleasant truths.

DISCUSS If it were possible, would you want to see what the future holds for you in ten years, even if you couldn't change it? Discuss this question with a small group. Consider the benefits of knowing what your life will be like, as well as the potential negatives.

Selection Resources

RESOURCE MANAGER UNIT 2

Plan and Teach pp. 61–68

Literary Analysis
Summary pp. 69†*, 70‡*
Character Traits pp. 71, 72†*
Question Support p. 79*

Reading
Reading a Long Story pp. 73, 74†*
Reading Check p. 78
Reading Fluency p. 81

Vocabulary
Study p. 75*
Practice p. 76
Strategy p. 77

Grammar and Writing
Compare Correctly p. 80

Assessment
Selection Tests A, B/C pp. 83*, 85*
Test Generator CD

BEST PRACTICES TOOLKIT

Differentiated Instruction pp. 31–38*
Scaffolding Instruction pp. 43–46*

Graphic Organizers/Strategies
Read Aloud/Think Aloud • Reciprocal Teaching • New Word Analysis • Two-Column Chart • Making Inferences • Cause-and-Effect Chain • T Chart • Venn Diagram

Technology

Literature, Vocabulary, and Writing Centers at **ClassZone.com**

Write*Smart* CD

* Resources for Differentiation † Also in Spanish ‡ In Haitian Creole and Vietnamese

LITERARY ANALYSIS: CHARACTER TRAITS

Literary characters are as unique as real people. They have distinct personalities, appearances, and likes and dislikes. These qualities are called **character traits,** and a reader must often infer them based on characters' words and actions.

In "Flowers for Algernon," the main character undergoes a dramatic transformation. As you read, use a Y-chart to note which of his character traits change and which stay the same.

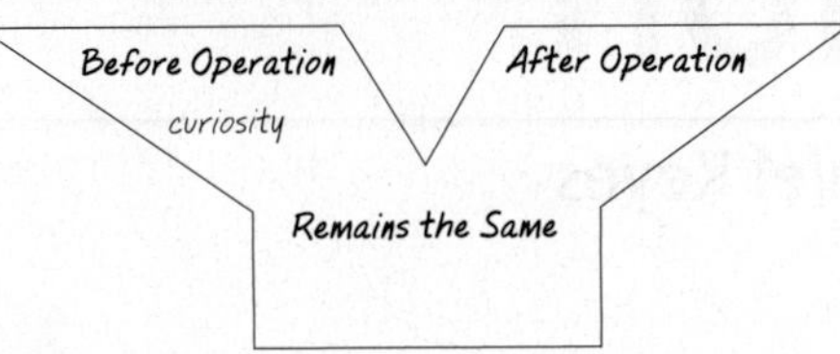

Review: Point of View

READING STRATEGY: READING A LONG STORY

Have you ever felt overwhelmed when reading a long story? The following strategies can help you stay on track:

- Look for ways to break up a long story into smaller parts.
- Pause at the end of these sections and ask yourself questions.
- Think about how later sections relate to earlier ones.

"Flowers for Algernon" is already divided into parts; it is made up of a series of journal entries. As you read, notice the dates, lengths, and language of the journal entries and consider how these things affect your understanding of the selection.

VOCABULARY IN CONTEXT

The boldfaced words help Daniel Keyes tell about a man who is the subject of a medical experiment. Try to figure out what each word means in the context of its sentence.

1. Receiving the medal made his success more **tangible.**
2. He's an **opportunist** because he'll do anything to get ahead.
3. The doctor had a **specialization** in brain development.
4. The research findings created a **sensation** at the conference.
5. Will you **refute** the results, or do you believe them, too?
6. His understanding is **proportional** to his intelligence.
7. His long work hours could **impair** his social life.
8. They laughed at his **absurd** moves when dancing.

Author Online

Daniel Keyes: Wondering, What If? Writing "Flowers for Algernon" brought together two of Daniel Keyes's interests: pyschology and literature. Keyes started his career as an English teacher. A struggling student once approached him and said, "I want to be smart." Keyes wondered what would happen if science discovered a way to increase a person's intelligence, and he explored the idea in "Flowers for Algernon." He later expanded the story into a novel, published in 1966.

Daniel Keyes
born 1927

Stirling Silliphant: Screenwriter Stirling Silliphant's career included winning the Academy Award for best screenplay in 1968. Known for action-filled scripts, he showed the range of his abilities by writing the screenplay for *Charly* (1969), based on the novel *Flowers for Algernon.*

Stirling Silliphant
1918–1996

MORE ABOUT THE AUTHOR
For more on the authors, visit the **Literature Center** at **ClassZone.com.**

Background

IQ In "Flowers for Algernon," the main character takes tests to measure his IQ, or intelligence quotient. IQ is a number that is thought to provide a measurement of a person's intelligence. IQ tests involve memory, reasoning, and numerical ability. Intelligence tests were once considered to be a reliable measure, but today, questions remain about the accuracy of such tests.

Teach

STANDARDS FOCUS

LITERARY ANALYSIS

● CHARACTER TRAITS

Write this example on the board:

After working all day, Charlie goes to night school to improve his reading and writing skills. He always does his home-work and studies for every test.

Ask: What are some of Charlie's character traits, based on his actions in this passage? ***Possible answer:*** *He is motivated to learn. He works hard.*

CHECK UNDERSTANDING Ask students to describe the traits of a character from a story they have recently read.

 **RESOURCE MANAGER—Copy Master**
Character Traits p. 71 (for student use while reading the selection)

READING STRATEGY

■ READING A LONG STORY

Discuss the strategies on page 189. Then generate questions that students might ask at the end of each section, such as *What important events happen in this part of the story? How do these events affect the characters? How does this part relate to what I have already read?* Have students write key questions on a bookmark to use as they read.

CHECK UNDERSTANDING Ask students to identify other strategies they have used to help them follow a long story.

VOCABULARY SKILL

▲ VOCABULARY IN CONTEXT

DIAGNOSE WORD KNOWLEDGE To determine preteaching needs, have all students complete **Vocabulary in Context.** *Students' responses will vary.* ***Possible answers:*** **1.** *real* **2.** *someone who takes advantage* **3.** *area of expertise* **4.** *feeling of excitement* **5.** *disagree with* **6.** *in balance with* **7.** *damage* **8.** *ridiculous*

PRETEACH VOCABULARY Help students determine the meaning of each boldfaced word on the Vocabulary Study copy master.

1. Have students conceal the word definitions. Read aloud the first sentence, emphasizing the boldfaced word.
2. Discuss possible meanings for *absurd,* such as "far-fetched" or "impossible."
3. Repeat for each of the other sentences.
4. Have students do Part B independently.

 **RESOURCE MANAGER—Copy Master**
Vocabulary Study p. 75

For general guidelines on differentiating vocabulary instruction and for alternative vocabulary activities for students not needing vocabulary preteaching, see

 **BEST PRACTICES TOOLKIT**
Scaffolding Vocabulary Instruction pp. 43–46

ⓘ Vocabulary Center at **ClassZone.com**

Practice and Apply

ANALYZE VISUALS

Possible answer: The cool colors with a hint of blue suggest a melancholy mood. The imperfect brushstrokes create an anxious mood.

About the Art Sylvia Chesley Smith used a gestural brushstroke technique in this illustration. The expressive brushstrokes reveal the movements of her body as she applied the paint and encourage the viewer to focus on her as the artist and on the emotion she wants to express.

Lines 1–6

REINFORCE *KEY IDEA:* KNOWLEDGE

Discuss What do the ideas expressed in these lines show about Charlie's self-**knowledge?** ***Possible answer:*** *He knows he is not very smart. That is why he wants to be smarter.*

LITERARY ANALYSIS

Ⓐ CHARACTER TRAITS

Remind students to write their inferences in the "Before Operation" section of the chart from page 189. ***Possible answer:*** *He is an adult, but he thinks and writes like a child. He seems trusting of others.*

If students need help . . . Use a Read Aloud/Think Aloud strategy for lines 1–11 to help students understand how to make inferences from details in the text.

BEST PRACTICES TOOLKIT—Transparency
Read Aloud/Think Aloud p. A34

Flowers *for* Algernon

Daniel Keyes

progris riport 1—martch 5 1965

Dr. Strauss says I shud rite down what I think and evrey thing that happins to me from now on. I dont know why but he says its importint so they will see if they will use me. I hope they use me. Miss Kinnian says maybe they can make me smart. I want to be smart. My name is Charlie Gordon. I am 37 years old and 2 weeks ago was my brithday. I have nuthing more to rite now so I will close for today.

progris riport 2—martch 6

I had a test today. I think I faled it. and I think that maybe now they wont use me. What happind is a nice young man was in the room and he had some white cards with ink spilled all over them. He sed Charlie what do you see on this card. I was very skared even tho I had my rabits foot in my pockit because when I was a kid I always faled tests in school and I spilled ink to. Ⓐ

I told him I saw a inkblot. He said yes and it made me feel good. I thot that was all but when I got up to go he stopped me. He said now sit down Charlie we are not thru yet. Then I dont remember so good but he wantid me to say what was in the ink. I dint see nuthing in the ink but he said there was picturs there other pepul saw some picturs. I coudnt see any picturs. I reely tryed to see. I held the card close up and then far away. Then I said if I had my glases I coud see better I usally only ware my glases in the movies or TV but I said they are in the closit in the hall. I got them. Then I said let me see that card agen I bet Ill find it now.

ANALYZE VISUALS
What is the **mood** of th illustration? Tell how th colors and brush stroke help create that mood.

Ⓐ CHARACTER TRAITS
What can you **infer** abo Charlie's abilities and personality?

DIFFERENTIATED INSTRUCTION

FOR ALL STUDENTS

Expert Groups Encourage students to become subject experts by selecting and researching one of these topics. Students may work independently or in groups. Suggest that they use visuals in their presentations.

- double-blind studies
- methods of measuring intelligence
- criteria for scoring Rorschach tests
- value of subliminal instruction

FOR LESS–PROFICIENT READERS

Use one or more Targeted Passages (pp. 193, 198, 205, 209, 214, 215) to ensure that students focus on key story events, concepts, and skills.

FOR ENGLISH LEARNERS

Options for Reading Provide students with a summary of the story. Explain that what happens to Charlie is told through a series of progress reports that he writes. The language and style of these reports show the increase and then the decline of his intelligence. Have students read the Targeted Passages in groups, using a Reciprocal Teaching strategy.

BEST PRACTICES TOOLKIT—Transparency
Reciprocal Teaching p. A35

BACKGROUND

Rorschach Tests In lines 7–35, Charlie's first experience with a Rorschach test is described. The Swiss psychiatrist Hermann Rorschach developed the test in 1921 to help him make patient diagnoses. The test requires a person to describe what he or she sees in ten inkblots. Some are black or gray (see example on page 192), while others have patches of color. Rorschach evaluated each patient's personality on the basis of several factors, such as the kind of shape that the patient saw and where in the inkblot the perceived image was located. Since Rorschach's time, the science of scoring the test has been refined and standardized to make it a more useful instrument. Other inkblot tests have also been developed.

FOR ENGLISH LEARNERS

Key Academic Vocabulary Have students use New Word Analysis to study this academic vocabulary from the selection: *psychology* (lines 376, 432), *intelligence* (lines 384, 387), *research* (lines 456, 694, 702), *technique* (lines 461, 671, 672, 731), *logical* (lines 745, 780).

 BEST PRACTICES TOOLKIT—Transparency
New Word Analysis p. E8

Prereading For prereading instruction for English learners, see

 BEST PRACTICES TOOLKIT
Scaffolding Reading Instruction pp. 43–46

FOR ADVANCED LEARNERS/PRE–AP

Pre-AP exercises in the bottom channel provide additional challenge for your advanced students. Use them for small groups or individuals.

ADDITIONAL GUIDELINES

For more help with differentiation and tips for classroom management, see

 BEST PRACTICES TOOLKIT
Differentiated Instruction pp. 31–38

READING STRATEGY

B READING A LONG STORY

Possible answer: *He makes a lot of spelling errors, and he shows little understanding of the events going on around him.*

LITERARY ANALYSIS

C CHARACTER TRAITS

Remind students to record their answers in their Y-charts. ***Possible answer:*** *He is very eager to become smart. He is willing to work hard and even to suffer physical pain if necessary.*

If students need help . . . Remind them that sometimes a character's traits are revealed through what other characters say about him or her. Point out in lines 39–41 that Miss Kinnian, Charlie's night school teacher, tells the doctors that he has tried the hardest in school and really wants to learn.

Extend the Discussion What does Miss Kinnian mean when she tells Charlie he is her best student?

I tryed hard but I still coudnt find the picturs I only saw the ink. I told him maybe I need new glases. He rote somthing down on a paper and I got skared of faling the test. I told him it was a very nice inkblot with littel points all around the eges. He looked very sad so that wasnt it. I said please let me try agen. Ill get it in a few minits becaus Im not so fast somtimes. Im a slow reeder too in Miss Kinnians class for slow adults but I'm trying very hard.

He gave me a chance with another card that had 2 kinds of ink spillled on it red and blue.

He was very nice and talked slow like Miss Kinnian does and he explaned it to me that it was a *raw shok*. He said pepul see things in the ink. I said show me where. He said think. I told him I think a inkblot but that wasnt rite eather. He said what does it remind you—pretend somthing. I closd my eyes for a long time to pretend. I told him I pretned a fowntan pen with ink leeking all over a table cloth. Then he got up and went out.

I dont think I passd the *raw shok* test. **B**

progris report 3—martch 7

Dr Strauss and Dr Nemur say it dont matter about the inkblots. I told them I dint spill the ink on the cards and I coudnt see anything in the ink. They said that maybe they will still use me. I said Miss Kinnian never gave me tests like that one only spelling and reading. They said Miss Kinnian told that I was her bestist pupil in the adult nite scool becaus I tryed the hardist and I reely wantid to lern. They said how come you went to the adult nite scool all by yourself Charlie. How did you find it. I said I askd pepul and sumbody told me where I shud go to lern to read and spell good. They said why did you want to. I told them becaus all my life I wantid to be smart and not dumb. But its very hard to be smart. They said you know it will probly be tempirery. I said yes. Miss Kinnian told me. I dont care if it herts. **C**

Later I had more crazy tests today. The nice lady who gave it me told me the name and I asked her how do you spellit so I can rite it in my progris riport. THEMATIC APPERCEPTION TEST.[1] I dont know the frist 2 words but I know what *test* means. You got to pass it or you get bad marks. This test lookd easy becaus I coud see the picturs. Only this time she dint want me to tell her the picturs. That mixd me up. I said the man yesterday said I shoud tell him what I saw in the ink she said that dont make no difrence. She said make up storys about the pepul in the picturs.

I told her how can you tell storys about pepul you never met. I said why shud I make up lies. I never tell lies any more becaus I always get caut.

She told me this test and the other one the raw-shok was for getting personalty. I laffed so hard. I said how can you get that thing from inkblots and fotos. She got sore and put her picturs away. I dont care. It was sily. I gess I faled that test too.

1. **Thematic Apperception** (thĭ-măt'ĭk ăp'ər-sĕp'shən) **Test:** test for analyzing personality on the basis of stories people make up about a series of pictures.

VISUAL VOCABULAR

Rorschach (rôr'shäk') **test** *n.* the name of a personality test that us inkblot designs

B READING A LONG STORY
In what ways are Charl journal entries unique?

C CHARACTER TRAITS
What do lines 41–46 tell you about Charlie's desire to change?

DIFFERENTIATED INSTRUCTION

FOR LESS–PROFICIENT READERS

Reading Strategy Follow-Up: Reading a Long Story Suggest that students use a five-column chart to organize details about the journal entries. The columns should be labeled *March*, *April*, *May*, *June*, and *July*. Tell students that they should record details about Charlie's language, his spelling, and the kinds of information he includes as well as their own observations about his intelligence. Begin a class chart and fill in the first column together.

March
• *Charlie struggles with spelling and grammar. "I dint see nuthing in the ink" (line 15).* • *His progress reports are long. He writes down what happens each day and what people say to him.* • *He doesn't understand a lot of what is happening.*

FOR ENGLISH LEARNERS

Visual Vocabulary

1. Share additional facts about the Rorschach test from the Background note on page 191 of the teacher's edition.
2. Then have students describe what they see in the inkblot shown on this page. Compare students' answers, and talk about why the test would be confusing for Charlie.

Later some men in white coats took me to a difernt part of the hospitil and gave me a game to play. It was like a race with a white mouse. They called the mouse Algernon. Algernon was in a box with a lot of twists and turns like all kinds of walls and they gave me a pencil and a paper with lines and lots of boxes. On one side it said START and on the other end it said FINISH. They said it was *amazed*[2] and that Algernon and me had the same *amazed* to do. I dint see how we could have the same *amazed* if Algernon had a box and I had a paper but I dint say nothing. Anyway there wasnt time because the race started.

One of the men had a watch he was trying to hide so I woudnt see it so I tryed not to look and that made me nervus.

Anyway that test made me feel worser than all the others because they did it over 10 times with difernt *amazeds* and Algernon won every time. I dint know that mice were so smart. Maybe thats because Algernon is a white mouse. Maybe white mice are smarter then other mice. **D**

D POINT OF VIEW
Because this story is told in the **first-person point of view,** you learn about Charlie's thought process directly from him. What do you learn about his mental capacity?

progris riport 4—Mar 8

Their going to use me! Im so exited I can hardly write. Dr Nemur and Dr Strauss had a argament about it first. Dr Nemur was in the office when Dr Strauss brot me in. Dr Nemur was worryed about using me but Dr Strauss told him Miss Kinnian rekemmended me the best from all the people who she was teaching. I like Miss Kinnian becaus shes a very smart teacher. And she said Charlie your going to have a second chance. If you volenteer for this experament you mite get smart. They dont know if it will be perminint but theirs a chance. Thats why I said ok even when I was scared because she said it was an operashun. She said dont be scared Charlie you done so much with so little I think you deserv it most of all.

1 Targeted Passage

So I got scaird when Dr Nemur and Dr Strauss argud about it. Dr Strauss said I had something that was very good. He said I had a good *motor-vation.*[3] I never even knew I had that. I felt proud when he said that not every body with an eye-q[4] of 68 had that thing. I dont know what it is or where I got it but he said Algernon had it too. Algernons *motor-vation* is the cheese they put in his box. But it cant be that because I didnt eat any cheese this week.

Then he told Dr Nemur something I dint understand so while they were talking I wrote down some of the words.

He said Dr Nemur I know Charlie is not what you had in mind as the first of your new brede of intelek** (coudnt get the word) superman. But most people of his low ment** are host** and uncoop** they are usualy dull apath** and hard to reach. He has a good natcher hes intristed and eager to please. **E**

Dr Nemur said remember he will be the first human beeng ever to have his intelijence trippled by surgicle meens.

E CHARACTER TRAITS
What have you learned about Charlie through the comments of Miss Kinnian and the doctors?

2. **amazed:** Charlie's way of writing *a maze.*
3. **motor-vation:** Charlie's way of writing *motivation.*
4. **eye-q:** Charlie's way of writing *IQ* (abbreviation for *intelligence quotient*).

LITERARY ANALYSIS: ***Review***

D POINT OF VIEW

Possible answer: *Charlie does not reason well and does not understand what is going on around him. He interprets what people say very literally, as when he thinks he needs to "find the pictures" in the inkblots.*

Extend the Discussion What are the advantages and disadvantages of a first-person narrator?

BACKGROUND

Intelligence Quotient In line 88, Charlie mentions that his I.Q. is 68. A score below 70 can be an indicator of mental retardation. A score of 100 is, by definition, average. Someone with an I.Q. above 130 would be considered intellectually gifted. If Charlie's I.Q. is tripled, he will have a score of 204, far exceeding the range usually considered brilliant.

LITERARY ANALYSIS

E CHARACTER TRAITS

Remind students to record their ideas in their Y-charts. ***Possible answer:*** *Charlie is good-natured, motivated, and eager to please.*

If students need help . . . Have them reread lines 85–86 and 96, in which Charlie is described directly.

Extend the Discussion What exactly does Dr. Strauss say to Dr. Nemur in lines 93–96? How do his comments further reveal Charlie's character?

FOR LESS–PROFICIENT READERS

1 Targeted Passage [Lines 75–98]

This passage presents the resolution of the first conflict: the doctors have accepted Charlie for their experiment.

- How does Charlie feel when he learns that the doctors are going to use him?
- What will Charlie have to undergo? What do the doctors hope will be the result of their experiment?
- Why do they choose Charlie?

Review: Point of View Remind students that point of view is the perspective from which a story is told. Since Charlie is telling his own story through the progress reports, he is the first-person narrator. Ask students what readers learn and do not learn from a first-person narrator (*they learn only what the narrator experiences, thinks, and feels; they do not learn what other characters feel*). Point out that because Charlie often doesn't understand the events that happen around him, readers must often infer what is really going on.

FOR ENGLISH LEARNERS

Concept Support Point out to students that Charlie writes the way he speaks. He spells words as he hears them. Have students read key passages aloud, keeping this idea about pronunciation in mind. Explain that the spelling and grammatical errors in this part of the story are important because they show Charlie's low intelligence before the operation.

LITERARY ANALYSIS

F CHARACTER TRAITS

Answer: *The fact that Charlie is motivated to learn convinces Dr. Strauss to use him in the experiment.*

If students need help . . . Explain the comparison that Dr. Strauss makes. For Charlie, learning how to read and write with his limited intelligence is as great an achievement as the doctors' learning an advanced theory about time and space without any help.

LITERARY ANALYSIS

G CHARACTER TRAITS

Possible answer: *He wants the operation to help him become smart like other people, so that he is not so different. He also hopes the operation can be used on others to help them become smart.*

Dr Strauss said exakly. Look at how well hes lerned to read and write for his low mentel age its as grate an acheve** as you and I lerning einstines thery of **vity[5] without help. That shows the intenss motor-vation. Its comparat** a tremen** achev** I say we use Charlie. F

I dint get all the words and they were talking to fast but it sounded like Dr Strauss was on my side and like the other one wasnt.

Then Dr Nemur nodded he said all right maybe your right. We will use Charlie. When he said that I got so exited I jumped up and shook his hand for being so good to me. I told him thank you doc you wont be sorry for giving me a second chance. And I mean it like I told him. After the operashun Im gonna try to be smart. Im gonna try awful hard.

F CHARACTER TRAIT
Which of Charlie's trait convince Dr. Strauss to use him in the experiment?

progris ript 5—Mar 10

Im skared. Lots of people who work here and the nurses and the people who gave me the tests came to bring me candy and wish me luck. I hope I have luck. I got my rabits foot and my lucky penny and my horse shoe. Only a black cat crossed me when I was comming to the hospitil. Dr Strauss says dont be supersitis Charlie this is sience. Anyway Im keeping my rabits foot with me.

I asked Dr Strauss if Ill beat Algernon in the race after the operashun and he said maybe. If the operashun works Ill show that mouse I can be as smart as he is. Maybe smarter. Then Ill be abel to read better and spell the words good and know lots of things and be like other people. I want to be smart like other people. If it works perminint they will make everybody smart all over the wurld. G

G CHARACTER TRAIT
What hopes does Charl have for the operation?

They dint give me anything to eat this morning. I dont know what that eating has to do with getting smart. Im very hungry and Dr Nemur took away my box of candy. That Dr Nemur is a grouch. Dr Strauss says I can have it back after the operashun. You cant eat befor a operashun . . .

Progress Report 6—Mar 15

The operashun dint hurt. He did it while I was sleeping. They took off the bandijis from my eyes and my head today so I can make a PROGRESS REPORT. Dr Nemur who looked at some of my other ones says I spell PROGRESS wrong and he told me how to spell it and REPORT too. I got to try and remember that.

I have a very bad memary for spelling. Dr Strauss says its ok to tell about all the things that happin to me but he says I shoud tell more about what I feel and what I think. When I told him I dont know how to think he said try. All the time when the bandijis were on my eyes I tryed to think. Nothing happened. I dont know what to think about. Maybe if I ask him he will tell me how I can think now that Im suppose to get smart. What do smart people think about. Fancy things I suppose. I wish I knew some fancy things alredy.

5. **einstines thery of **vity:** Charlie's way of writing *Einstein's theory of relativity,* the theory of space and time developed by Albert Einstein.

DIFFERENTIATED INSTRUCTION

FOR LESS-PROFICIENT READERS

Concept Support [small-group option] Have students work in small groups to update the left branch of their Y-charts from page 189, using information from lines 1–124. Remind students to make inferences about Charlie's character traits from what he says and does and from what others say about him.

Before Operation
- *motivated*
- *hard-working*
- *limited intelligence*
- *cooperative*
- *gentle*
- *brave*
- *wants to fit in*
- *trusting*

FOR ENGLISH LEARNERS

Culture: Connect

- In lines 111–112, Charlie explains that he has brought his rabbit's foot, a lucky penny, and a horseshoe to the hospital. These are all thought to bring good luck. Still, he is worried, because a black cat crossed his path. According to superstition, this event can bring bad luck.
- Ask students for examples of similar superstitions in their cultures—practices that are thought to ensure good and bad luck.

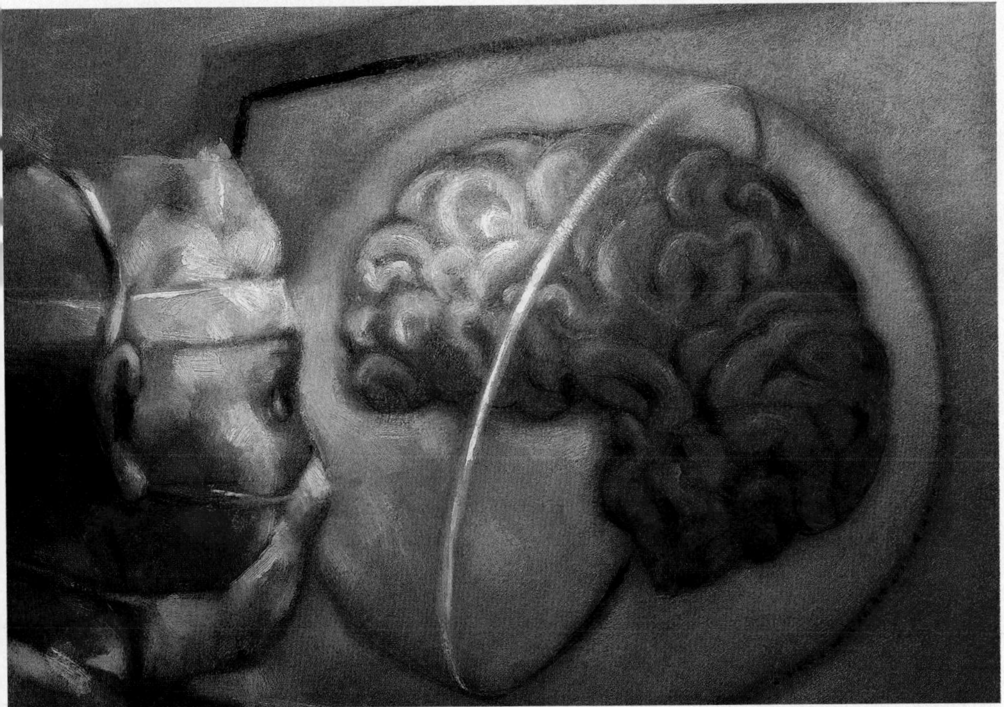

Progress Report 7—mar 19

Nothing is happining. I had lots of tests and different kinds of races with Algernon. I hate that mouse. He always beats me. Dr Strauss said I got to play those games. And he said some time I got to take those tests over again. Those inkblots are stupid. And those pictures are stupid too. I like to draw a picture of a man and a woman but I wont make up lies about people.

I got a headache from trying to think so much. I thot Dr Strauss was my frend but he dont help me. He dont tell me what to think or when Ill get smart. Miss Kinnian dint come to see me. I think writing these progress reports are stupid too. **H**

Progress Report 8—Mar 23

Im going back to work at the factery. They said it was better I shud go back to work but I cant tell anyone what the operashun was for and I have to come to the hospitil for an hour evry night after work. They are gonna pay me mony every month for lerning to be smart.

ANALYZE VISUALS
What is the **connection** between this illustration and what happens to Charlie?

H READING A LONG STORY
In what ways is the March 19 progress report different from the other reports so far? Think about its length and language.

ANALYZE VISUALS

Possible answer: *The illustration shows a surgeon studying a brain. In the story, Charlie has an operation on his brain that increases his intelligence.*

READING STRATEGY

H READING A LONG STORY

Possible answer: *Charlie shows anger, an emotion that he hasn't displayed up to now. He is frustrated that he isn't smart yet and still can't beat Algernon. He is impatient with the tests the scientists are giving him and doesn't see the point of the progress reports.*

Lines 137–149

DISCUSSION PROMPTS

Use these prompts to help students understand the implications of Charlie's feelings after the operation:

Connect How does it feel when you do not get something you have worked for and want very much? *Accept all thoughtful responses.*

Analyze Is the fact that Charlie is showing emotion in this progress report significant? Explain. ***Possible answer:*** *It might indicate that the operation did work. Instead of passively accepting what happens to him and trying to please others, he is now expressing opinions and reacting to the events in his life. Or, the operation may have changed his personality.*

Evaluate Is Charlie's expectation of quick results realistic? Explain. ***Possible answers:***

- *No. Even if his intelligence has increased, it will take time for him to absorb new knowledge and apply it.*
- *Yes. If the surgery has physically altered his brain, he should see some kind of improvement immediately.*

FOR LESS-PROFICIENT READERS

Comprehension Support Remind students that good readers make inferences from details in the text. In line 146, Charlie says that he is going back to work at the factory. Have students explain what *back* indicates and what further information they learn about Charlie's life from this sentence (*he had a job in a factory before the operation*).

FOR ADVANCED LEARNERS/PRE-AP

Evaluate [paired option] Have students think of the first-person narrators that they have encountered in previous readings and consider what makes a narrator reliable or trustworthy. Have students work in pairs to create a checklist of characteristics and then evaluate Charlie as a first-person narrator based on this list. Have pairs share their evaluations in small groups.

LITERARY ANALYSIS

❶ CHARACTER TRAITS

Remind students to write their answers in the "After Operation" section of the chart from page 189. ***Possible answer:*** *Charlie thinks these men are his friends because they always laugh. He is not a good judge of character at this point because he doesn't realize the men are laughing at him in a disrespectful way.*

If students need help . . . Have them reread lines 163–173 and explain in their own words what the men are doing to Charlie. Have students discuss whether the men's behavior is the way friends act.

Lines 174–188

DISCUSSION PROMPTS

Use these prompts to help students understand some of the changes taking place in Charlie:

Recall What is Charlie supposed to do every day after work? Why isn't he doing this? ***Answer:*** *Charlie is supposed to go to the hospital for one hour every day after work. He is getting paid for it. He isn't going because he doesn't want to race with Algernon any more.*

Compare and Contrast Are there any differences between this progress report and those before the operation? Explain. ***Possible answer:*** *There seem to be fewer spelling errors in this report. Also, Charlie expresses his feelings instead of merely listing his own and other people's actions. He shows that he is forming opinions when he questions Dr. Strauss's directions.*

Evaluate How would you describe Charlie's emotional state since the operation? Explain. ***Possible answer:*** *He seems less hopeful. He is disappointed over what he sees as the lack of progress. He is mad at Miss Kinnian for not coming to see him. He doesn't want to cooperate as readily as he did before.*

Im glad Im going back to work because I miss my job and all my frends and all the fun we have there.

Dr Strauss says I shud keep writing things down but I dont have to do it every day just when I think of something or something speshul happins. He says dont get discoridged because it takes time and it happins slow. He says it took a long time with Algernon before he got 3 times smarter then he was before. Thats why Algernon beats me all the time because he had that operashun too. That makes me feel better. I coud probly do that *amazed* faster than a reglar mouse. Maybe some day Ill beat Algernon. Boy that would be something. So far Algernon looks like he mite be smart perminent.

Mar 25 (I dont have to write PROGRESS REPORT on top any more just when I hand it in once a week for Dr Nemur to read. I just have to put the date on. That saves time)

We had a lot of fun at the factory today. Joe Carp said hey look where Charlie had his operashun what did they do Charlie put some brains in. I was going to tell him but I remembered Dr Strauss said no. Then Frank Reilly said what did you do Charlie forget your key and open your door the hard way. That made me laff. Their really my friends and they like me.

Sometimes somebody will say hey look at Joe or Frank or George he really pulled a Charlie Gordon. I dont know why they say that but they always laff. This morning Amos Borg who is the 4 man at Donnegans used my name when he shouted at Ernie the office boy. Ernie lost a packige. He said Ernie for godsake what are you trying to be a Charlie Gordon. I dont understand why he said that. I never lost any packiges. ❶

❶ CHARACTER TRAIT
Why does Charlie think these men are his frier
Note whether he is a good judge of characte
at this point.

Mar 28 Dr Straus came to my room tonight to see why I dint come in like I was suppose to. I told him I dont like to race with Algernon any more. He said I dont have to for a while but I shud come in. He had a present for me only it wasnt a present but just for lend. I thot it was a little television but it wasnt. He said I got to turn it on when I go to sleep. I said your kidding why shud I turn it on when Im going to sleep. Who ever herd of a thing like that. But he said if I want to get smart I got to do what he says. I told him I dint think I was going to get smart and he put his hand on my sholder and said Charlie you dont know it yet but your getting smarter all the time. You wont notice for a while. I think he was just being nice to make me feel good because I dont look any smarter.

Oh yes I almost forgot. I asked him when I can go back to the class at Miss Kinnians school. He said I wont go their. He said that soon Miss Kinnian will come to the hospitil to start and teach me speshul. I was mad at her for not comming to see me when I got the operashun but I like her so maybe we will be frends again.

Mar 29 That crazy TV kept me up all night. How can I sleep with something yelling crazy things all night in my ears. And the nutty pictures. Wow. I dont know what it says when Im up so how am I going to know when Im sleeping.

DIFFERENTIATED INSTRUCTION

FOR ENGLISH READERS

Vocabulary Support Point out the saying *he really pulled a Charlie Gordon* in lines 168–169. Explain to students that *pulled* means "acted like." In other words, when someone does something foolish or makes a mistake, the men at the factory say he is acting like Charlie.

196 UNIT 2: CHARACTER AND POINT OF VIEW

Dr Strauss says its ok. He says my brains are lerning when I sleep and that will help me when Miss Kinnian starts my lessons in the hospitl (only I found out it isnt a hospitil its a labatory. I think its all crazy. If you can get smart when your sleeping why do people go to school. That thing I dont think will work. I use to watch the late show and the late late show on TV all the time and it never made me smart. Maybe you have to sleep while you watch it.

PROGRESS REPORT 9—April 3

Dr Strauss showed me how to keep the TV turned low so now I can sleep. I dont hear a thing. And I still dont understand what it says. A few times I play it over in the morning to find out what I lerned when I was sleeping and I dont think so. Miss Kinnian says Maybe its another langwidge or something. But most times it sounds american. It talks so fast faster than even Miss Gold who was my teacher in 6 grade and I remember she talked so fast I coudnt understand her.

I told Dr Strauss what good is it to get smart in my sleep. I want to be smart when Im awake. He says its the same thing and I have two minds. Theres the *subconscious* and the *conscious*[6] (thats how you spell it). And one dont tell the other one what its doing. They dont even talk to each other. Thats why I dream. And boy have I been having crazy dreams. Wow. Ever since that night TV. The late late late late late show.

I forgot to ask him if it was only me or if everybody had those two minds.

(I just looked up the word in the dictionary Dr Strauss gave me. The word is *subconscious. adj. Of the nature of mental operations yet not present in consciousness; as, subconscious conflict of desires.*) There's more but I still dont know what it means. This isnt a very good dictionary for dumb people like me.

Anyway the headache is from the party. My frends from the factery Joe Carp and Frank Reilly invited me to go with them to Muggsys Saloon for some drinks. I dont like to drink but they said we will have lots of fun. I had a good time.

Joe Carp said I shoud show the girls how I mop out the toilet in the factory and he got me a mop. I showed them and everyone laffed when I told that Mr Donnegan said I was the best janiter he ever had because I like my job and do it good and never come late or miss a day except for my operashun.

I said Miss Kinnian always said Charlie be proud of your job because you do it good.

Everybody laffed and we had a good time and they gave me lots of drinks and Joe said Charlie is a card when hes potted.[7] I dont know what that means but everybody likes me and we have fun. I cant wait to be smart like my best frends Joe Carp and Frank Reilly. **J**

I dont remember how the party was over but I think I went out to buy a newspaper and coffe for Joe and Frank and when I came back there was no one

J POINT OF VIEW
How does hearing about the party from Charlie's **point of view** affect your reaction to his coworkers?

6. **the subconscious** (sŭb-kŏn′shəs) **and the conscious** (kŏn′shəs): psychological terms. *Subconscious* refers to mental activity a person is not aware of; *conscious* refers to mental activity of which a person is aware.

7. **Charlie is a card when he's potted:** Charlie is funny when he's drunk.

Lines 210–214

REINFORCE *KEY IDEA:* KNOWLEDGE

Discuss What do Charlie's actions in this passage reveal about his **knowledge** as compared to before and immediately after the operation? ***Possible answer:*** *He is able to look up a word in a dictionary and understand part of its definition. His grasp of information is increasing greatly.*

LITERARY ANALYSIS: ***Review***

J POINT OF VIEW

Possible answer: *Charlie thinks he is having fun with his coworkers. He misunderstands their actions. This makes their behavior seem even more cruel than if readers weren't aware of Charlie's ignorance.*

FOR LESS-PROFICIENT READERS

Comprehension Support Display a Two-Column Chart to show the contrast between Charlie's perception of events in lines 215–241 and the reality. Discuss what important ideas the readers learn from this episode about Charlie's life.

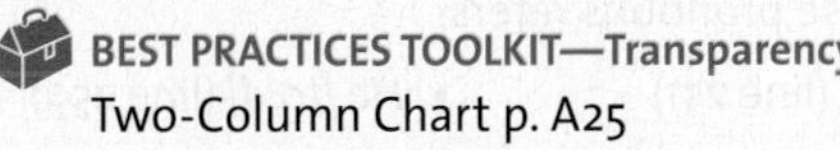
BEST PRACTICES TOOLKIT—Transparency
Two-Column Chart p. A25

Charlie's Perception	*Reality*
They are interested in what he does as a janitor.	*They want to see him make a fool of himself.*
He is having fun with his friends.	*They are using him for their own entertainment.*
Joe and Frank accidentally leave him behind.	*They intentionally run out on Charlie.*

their. I looked for them all over till late. Then I dont remember so good but I think I got sleepy or sick. A nice cop brot me back home. Thats what my landlady Mrs Flynn says.

But I got a headache and a big lump on my head and black and blue all over. I think maybe I fell but Joe Carp says it was the cop they beat up drunks some times. I don't think so. Miss Kinnian says cops are to help people. Anyway I got a bad headache and Im sick and hurt all over. I dont think Ill drink anymore.

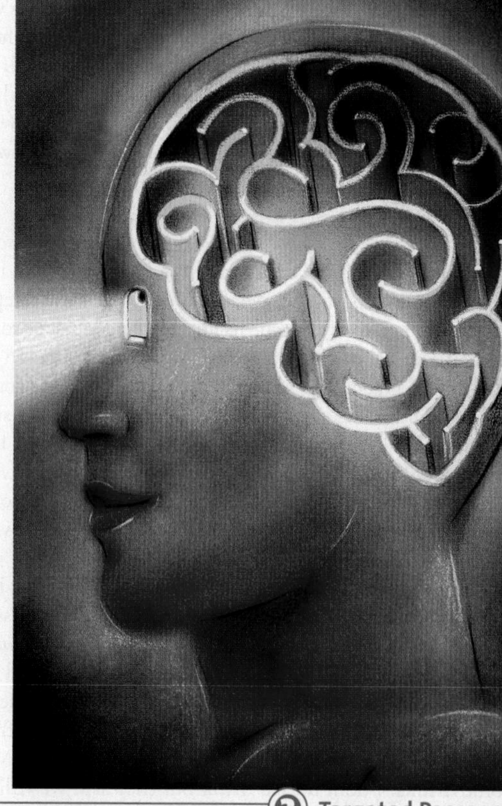

April 6 I beat Algernon! I dint even know I beat him until Burt the tester told me. Then the second time I lost because I got so exited I fell off the chair before I finished. But after that I beat him 8 more times. I must be getting smart to beat a smart mouse like Algernon. But I dont *feel* smarter. **K**

I wanted to race Algernon some more but Burt said thats enough for one day. They let me hold him for a minit. Hes not so bad. Hes soft like a ball of cotton. He blinks and when he opens his eyes their black and pink on the eges.

I said can I feed him because I felt bad to beat him and I wanted to be nice and make frends. Burt said no Algernon is a very specshul mouse with an operashun like mine, and he was the first of all the animals to stay smart so long. He told me Algernon is so smart that every day he has to solve a test to get his food. Its a thing like a lock on a door that changes every time Algernon goes in to eat so he has to lern something new to get his food. That made me sad because if he coudnt lern he woud be hungry.

I dont think its right to make you pass a test to eat. How woud Dr Nemur like it to have to pass a test every time he wants to eat. I think Ill be frends with Algernon. **L**

April 9 Tonight after work Miss Kinnian was at the laboratory. She looked like she was glad to see me but scared. I told her dont worry Miss Kinnian Im not smart yet and she laffed. She said I have confidence in you Charlie the way you struggled so hard to read and right better than all the others. At werst you will have it for a littel wile and your doing somthing for sience.

2 Targeted Passage

K READING A LONG STORY
Note the date on this journal entry. What significant changes have happened in the story since the first entries one month ago?

L CHARACTER TRAITS
In lines 249–266, what does Charlie's treatment of Algernon reveal about his character?

READING STRATEGY

K READING A LONG STORY

***Answer:** Now Charlie can beat Algernon at completing the maze.*

LITERARY ANALYSIS

L CHARACTER TRAITS

Students should record their inferences in the right branch of their Y-charts.
Possible answer:

After Operation
- *gentle*
- *caring*
- *empathetic*

If students need help . . . Write the character traits across the board. Together find details from the text that reveal each trait.

DIFFERENTIATED INSTRUCTION

FOR LESS–PROFICIENT READERS

2 Targeted Passage [Lines 242–266]

This passage presents a turning point: Charlie beats Algernon through the maze.

- What does Charlie's ability to beat Algernon mean?
- How does Charlie feel about his accomplishment?
- What does he think about Algernon now?

FOR ENGLISH LEARNERS

Language: Pronoun Referents [paired option]
Tell students that pronouns may be used to replace nouns that appear earlier in the sentence, paragraph, or story. Ask pairs of students to identify the noun to which each of these pronouns refers:

- *him* (line 251)
- *he [was]* (line 259)
- *He [told]* (line 259)
- *he* (line 265)

We are reading a very hard book. I never read such a hard book before. Its called *Robinson Crusoe* about a man who gets merooned on a dessert Iland. Hes smart and figers out all kinds of things so he can have a house and food and hes a good swimmer. Only I feel sorry because hes all alone and has no frends. But I think their must be somebody else on the iland because theres a picture with his funny umbrella looking at footprints. I hope he gets a frend and not be lonly.

April 10 Miss Kinnian teaches me to spell better. She says look at a word and close your eyes and say it over and over until you remember. I have lots of truble with *through* that you say *threw* and *enough* and *tough* that you dont say *enew* and *tew*. You got to say *enuff* and *tuff*. Thats how I use to write it before I started to get smart. Im confused but Miss Kinnian says theres no reason in spelling.

Apr 14 Finished *Robinson Crusoe*. I want to find out more about what happens to him but Miss Kinnian says thats all there is. *Why*

Apr 15 Miss Kinnian says Im lerning fast. She read some of the Progress Reports and she looked at me kind of funny. She says Im a fine person and Ill show them all. I asked her why. She said never mind but I shoudnt feel bad if I find out that everybody isnt nice like I think. She said for a person who god gave so little to you done more then a lot of people with brains they never even used. I said all my frends are smart people but there good. They like me and they never did anything that wasnt nice. Then she got something in her eye and she had to run out to the ladys room. Ⓜ

Ⓜ CHARACTER TRAITS
What can you **infer** about Miss Kinnian from her conversation with Charlie?

Apr 16 Today, I lerned, the *comma*, this is a comma (,) a period, with a tail, Miss Kinnian, says its importent, because, it makes writing, better, she said, sombeody, coud lose, a lot of money, if a comma, isnt, in the, right place, I dont have, any money, and I dont see, how a comma, keeps you, from losing it,

But she says, everybody, uses commas, so Ill use, them too,

Apr 17 I used the comma wrong. Its punctuation. Miss Kinnian told me to look up long words in the dictionary to lern to spell them. I said whats the difference if you can read it anyway. She said its part of your education so now on Ill look up all the words Im not sure how to spell. It takes a long time to write that way but I think Im remembering. I only have to look up once and after that I get it right. Anyway thats how come I got the word *punctuation* right. (Its that way in the dictionary). Miss Kinnian says a period is punctuation too, and there are lots of other marks to lern. I told her I thot all the periods had to have tails but she said no.

You got to mix them up, she showed? me" how. to mix! them(up,. and now; I can! mix up all kinds" of punctuation, in! my writing? There, are lots! of rules? to lern; but Im gettin'g them in my head.

Lines 272–278

REINFORCE *KEY IDEA:* KNOWLEDGE

Discuss What does Charlie say about the footprints in the illustration? How does this observation show his increased **knowledge?**
Possible answer: *He makes an inference based on the footprints that there is someone else on the island. Making inferences is a higher-level thinking skill that would not have been possible for him a couple of weeks earlier.*

LITERARY ANALYSIS

Ⓜ CHARACTER TRAITS

Possible answer: *Miss Kinnian cares about Charlie. She is upset that the people he thinks are his friends treat him badly and he doesn't know it. She is also worried about the disillusionment he may experience if he does become smart enough to understand that the men at the factory are mean to him.*

If students need help . . .

- Ask students which progress report Miss Kinnian is probably referring to when she tells Charlie that he may find out everyone isn't as nice as he thinks they are (*Progress Report 9, which tells about the work party*). Have students summarize what happens to Charlie at that party.
- Using a Making Inferences chart, guide students to make inferences about Miss Kinnian's character from the details in the text and their own prior knowledge.
  - ***Details from Text:*** *Charlie defends his friends. Miss Kinnian warns him that people may not be as nice as he thinks they are. Miss Kinnian runs out of the room with something in her eye.*
  - ***Prior Knowledge:*** *His friends were mean to him. Miss Kinnian knows that from the progress report.*
  - ***Inference:*** *Miss Kinnian starts to cry because she is sad that people make fun of Charlie and that he doesn't know it. She tries to prepare him to find out that the men at the factory aren't really his friends because she is worried about how he will react.*

 **BEST PRACTICES TOOLKIT—Transparency**
Making Inferences p. A13

FOR ENGLISH LEARNERS

Language: Contractions [mixed-readiness pairs] Remind students that apostrophes can be used to replace letters in contractions. Have students identify the contractions on these two pages that lack apostrophes. List them on the board. Have students work in pairs to rewrite the contractions with the apostrophe in position. Have them also identify the words that form the contractions. Review students' revisions.

FOR ADVANCED LEARNERS/PRE-AP

Compare and Contrast Why does the author choose *Robinson Crusoe* as the book that Charlie reads with Miss Kinnian? Ask students to list and discuss parallels between Charlie's situation and that of Robinson Crusoe, marooned on a deserted island. Encourage students to go beyond the literal similarities to possible metaphorical interpretations for further connections.

Lines 331–357
DISCUSSION PROMPTS

Use these prompts to help students understand what Charlie learns about his so-called friends:

Connect Are Joe and Frank the kinds of friends that Charlie deserves? Explain. *Students will likely say they are not. Charlie is a good-hearted person who should be treated with respect and consideration. He would never hurt Joe or Frank, yet they delight in making fun of him.*

Compare and Contrast Consider what happened the last time Charlie went out with the men from the factory. In what ways are the two evenings the same and different? ***Possible answer:*** *Both times the men from the factory use Charlie to entertain them. Even though he asks for a soft drink this time, they give him alcohol, hoping to get him drunk again. This time, though, Charlie realizes what they are doing to him. He is ashamed and runs away.*

Synthesize What price is Charlie paying for increased knowledge? ***Possible answer:*** *He is losing his innocence and starting to see the flaws in other people and in himself. He suffers disillusionment and hurt.*

One thing I? like about, Dear Miss Kinnian: (thats the way it goes in a business letter if I ever go into business) is she, always gives me' a reason" when—I ask. She's a gen'ius! I wish! I cou'd be smart" like, her;

(Punctuation, is; fun!)

April 18 What a dope I am! I didn't even understand what she was talking about. I read the grammar book last night and it explanes the whole thing. Then I saw it was the same way as Miss Kinnian was trying to tell me, but I didn't get it. I got up in the middle of the night, and the whole thing straightened out in my mind.

Miss Kinnian said that the TV working in my sleep helped out. She said I reached a plateau. Thats like the flat top of a hill.

After I figgered out how punctuation worked, I read over all my old Progress Reports from the beginning. Boy, did I have crazy spelling and punctuation! I told Miss Kinnian I ought to go over the pages and fix all the mistakes but she said, "No, Charlie, Dr. Nemur wants them just as they are. That's why he let you keep them after they were photostated, to see your own progress. You're coming along fast, Charlie."

That made me feel good. After the lesson I went down and played with Algernon. We don't race any more.

April 20 I feel sick inside. Not sick like for a doctor, but inside my chest it feels empty like getting punched and a heartburn at the same time.

I wasn't going to write about it, but I guess I got to, because its important. Today was the first time I ever stayed home from work.

Last night Joe Carp and Frank Reilly invited me to a party. There were lots of girls and some men from the factory. I remembered how sick I got last time I drank too much, so I told Joe I didn't want anything to drink. He gave me a plain coke instead. It tasted funny, but I thought it was just a bad taste in my mouth.

We had a lot of fun for a while. Joe said I should dance with Ellen and she would teach me the steps. I fell a few times and I couldn't understand why because no one else was dancing besides Ellen and me. And all the time I was tripping because somebody's foot was always sticking out.

Then when I got up I saw the look on Joe's face and it gave me a funny feeling in my stomack. "He's a scream," one of the girls said. Everybody was laughing.

Frank said, "I ain't laughed so much since we sent him off for the newspaper that night at Muggsy's and ditched him."

"Look at him. His face is red."

"He's blushing. Charlie is blushing."

"Hey, Ellen, what'd you do to Charlie? I never saw him act like that before."

I didn't know what to do or where to turn. Everyone was looking at me and laughing and I felt naked. I wanted to hide myself. I ran out into the street and

DIFFERENTIATED INSTRUCTION

FOR ENGLISH LEARNERS

Language: Punctuation [mixed-readiness pairs] In lines 295–328, Charlie explains that he is learning the rules for using punctuation. Pair students with more fluent speakers. Have them review the rules for using commas in the pupil edition's Grammar Handbook. Then have students work with their partners to find examples from lines 323–328 that illustrate some of those rules.

Vocabulary: Idioms and Slang [small-group option] Have students work in small groups to figure out the meanings of these words and expressions from context. Ask groups to share their definitions.

- *dope* (line 316), "fool"
- *he's a scream* (line 345), "he's very funny"
- *ditched him* (line 348), "left him"

I threw up. Then I walked home. It's a funny thing I never knew that Joe and Frank and the others liked to have me around all the time to make fun of me.

Now I know what it means when they say "to pull a Charlie Gordon."

I'm ashamed. **N**

N CHARACTER TRAITS
Why is Charlie ashamed now? Why wasn't he ashamed a couple of weeks ago?

PROGRESS REPORT 10

April 21 Still didn't go into the factory. I told Mrs. Flynn my landlady to call and tell Mr. Donnegan I was sick. Mrs. Flynn looks at me very funny lately like she's scared of me.

I think it's a good thing about finding out how everybody laughs at me. I thought about it a lot. It's because I'm so dumb and I don't even know when I'm doing something dumb. People think it's funny when a dumb person can't do things the same way they can.

Anyway, now I know I'm getting smarter every day. I know punctuation and I can spell good. I like to look up all the hard words in the dictionary and I remember them. I'm reading a lot now, and Miss Kinnian says I read very fast. Sometimes I even understand what I'm reading about, and it stays in my mind. There are times when I can close my eyes and think of a page and it all comes back like a picture.

Besides history, geography, and arithmetic, Miss Kinnian said I should start to learn a few foreign languages. Dr. Strauss gave me some more tapes to play while I sleep. I still don't understand how that conscious and unconscious mind works, but Dr. Strauss says not to worry yet. He asked me to promise that when I start learning college subjects next week I wouldn't read any books on psychology—that is, until he gives me permission. **O**

O POINT OF VIEW
How might your understanding of Charlie's progress be different if you knew what others were thinking?

I feel a lot better today, but I guess I'm still a little angry that all the time people were laughing and making fun of me because I wasn't so smart. When I become intelligent like Dr. Strauss says, with three times my I.Q. of 68, then maybe I'll be like everyone else and people will like me and be friendly.

I'm not sure what an *I.Q.* is. Dr. Nemur said it was something that measured how intelligent you were—like a scale in the drugstore weighs pounds. But Dr. Strauss had a big arguement with him and said an I.Q. didn't weigh intelligence at all. He said an I.Q. showed how much intelligence you could get, like the numbers on the outside of a measuring cup. You still had to fill the cup up with stuff.

Then when I asked Burt, who gives me my intelligence tests and works with Algernon, he said that both of them were wrong (only I had to promise not to tell them he said so). Burt says that the I.Q. measures a lot of different things including some of the things you learned already, and it really isn't any good at all.

So I still don't know what I.Q. is except that mine is going to be over 200 soon. I didn't want to say anything, but I don't see how if they don't know *what* it is, or *where* it is—I don't see how they know *how much* of it you've got.

Dr. Nemur says I have to take a *Rorshach Test* tomorrow. I wonder what *that* is.

LITERARY ANALYSIS

N CHARACTER TRAITS

Remind students to record their answers in the chart from page 189. ***Possible answer:*** *He understands his coworkers' true motivations and feels a new emotion, shame, for the first time.*

Extend the Discussion Shame implies wrongdoing on someone's part. Has Charlie done something wrong?

LITERARY ANALYSIS: *Review*

O POINT OF VIEW

Possible answer: *Readers would know if Charlie's progress is what the doctors expected or if it is surprising.*

If students need help . . . Review the other points of view that the author might have used and what different information each narrator might have been able to share.

Extend the Discussion What significant information do readers learn because Charlie narrates this part of the story?

FOR LESS–PROFICIENT READERS

Reading Strategy Follow-Up: Reading a Long Story [paired option] Have students return to the five-column chart and work in pairs to examine details found in the April progress reports. Remind students to think about language and content and use both to make some observations about what is happening to Charlie. Have students share their observations with the class. Add their observations to the class chart.

April
• *Charlie's spelling improves steadily. By the end of the month, he is writing words like "neurosurgeon" correctly.* • *His progress reports include feelings, opinions, and observations, not just a list of what happened and who said what.* • *His punctuation is correct. His sentence structure is more sophisticated.*

April 22 I found out what a *Rorschach* is. It's the test I took before the operation—the one with the inkblots on the pieces of cardboard. The man who gave me the test was the same one.

I was scared to death of those inkblots. I knew he was going to ask me to find the pictures and I knew I wouldn't be able to. I was thinking to myself, if only there was some way of knowing what kind of pictures were hidden there. Maybe there weren't any pictures at all. Maybe it was just a trick to see if I was dumb enough to look for something that wasn't there. Just thinking about that made me sore at him.

"All right, Charlie," he said, "you've seen these cards before, remember?"

"Of course I remember."

The way I said it, he knew I was angry, and he looked surprised. "Yes, of course. Now I want you to look at this one. What might this be? What do you see on this card? People see all sorts of things in these inkblots. Tell me what it might be for you—what it makes you think of."

I was shocked. That wasn't what I had expected him to say at all. "You mean there are no pictures hidden in those inkblots?"

He frowned and took off his glasses. "What?"

"Pictures. Hidden in the inkblots. Last time you told me that everyone could see them and you wanted me to find them too."

He explained to me that the last time he had used almost the exact same words he was using now. I didn't believe it, and I still have the suspicion that he misled me at the time just for the fun of it. Unless—I don't know any more—could I have been *that* feeble-minded?

We went through the cards slowly. One of them looked like a pair of bats tugging at something. Another one looked like two men fencing with swords. I imagined all sorts of things. I guess I got carried away. But I didn't trust him any more, and I kept turning them around and even looking on the back to see if there was anything there I was supposed to catch. While he was making his notes, I peeked out of the corner of my eye to read it. But it was all in code that looked like this:

WF+A DdF-Ad orig. WF-A SF+obj

The test still doesn't make sense to me. It seems to me that anyone could make up lies about things that they didn't really see. How could he know I wasn't making a fool of him by mentioning things that I didn't really imagine? Maybe I'll understand it when Dr. Strauss lets me read up on psychology. Ⓟ

April 25 I figured out a new way to line up the machines in the factory, and Mr. Donnegan says it will save him ten thousand dollars a year in labor and increased production. He gave me a $25 bonus.

I wanted to take Joe Carp and Frank Reilly out to lunch to celebrate, but Joe said he had to buy some things for his wife, and Frank said he was meeting his cousin for lunch. I guess it'll take a little time for them to get

Ⓟ CHARACTER TRAIT
How is Charlie's secon
experience with the
Rorschach test differen
from his first experienc

LITERARY ANALYSIS

Ⓟ CHARACTER TRAITS

Possible answer: *The second time he takes the test, he understands its purpose—to identify what the inkblots make him think of, rather than look for hidden pictures in them.*

If students need help . . . Have them reread lines 12–35 to contrast the first experience with this one.

Lines 433–435
REINFORCE *KEY IDEA:* KNOWLEDGE

Discuss How does Charlie use his newfound **knowledge?** What kind of thinking is he employing here? ***Possible answer:*** *Charlie devises a plan to make the factory operate more efficiently. He uses logic to develop this plan.*

DIFFERENTIATED INSTRUCTION

FOR ENGLISH LEARNERS

Comprehension: Cause and Effect

1. Direct students' attention to lines 433–445. Tell them that this part of the story shows some of the ways in which Charlie's new intelligence affects his life.
2. Distribute copies of the Cause-and-Effect Chain.
3. Fill in the first two boxes together. *(Cause: Charlie's intelligence increases drastically. Effect/Cause: This change scares his coworkers.)*
4. Have pairs complete the chart and share their responses with the class. Then use the details to guide students to see that although having greater intelligence is positive, it can have negative results, too.

BEST PRACTICES TOOLKIT—Transparency
Cause-and-Effect Chain pp. B16, B39

used to the changes in me. Everybody seems to be frightened of me. When I went over to Amos Borg and tapped him on the shoulder, he jumped up in the air.

People don't talk to me much any more or kid around the way they used to. It makes the job kind of lonely.

April 27 I got up the nerve today to ask Miss Kinnian to have dinner with me tomorrow night to celebrate my bonus.

At first she wasn't sure it was right, but I asked Dr. Strauss and he said it was okay. Dr. Strauss and Dr. Nemur don't seem to be getting along so well. They're arguing all the time. This evening when I came in to ask Dr. Strauss about having dinner with Miss Kinnian, I heard them shouting. Dr. Nemur was saying that it was *his* experiment and *his* research, and Dr. Strauss was shouting back that he contributed just as much, because he found me through Miss Kinnian and he performed the operation. Dr. Strauss said that someday thousands of neurosurgeons[8] might be using his technique all over the world.

Dr. Nemur wanted to publish the results of the experiment at the end of this month. Dr. Strauss wanted to wait a while longer to be sure. Dr. Strauss said that Dr. Nemur was more interested in the Chair of Psychology at Princeton[9] than he was in the experiment. Dr. Nemur said that Dr. Strauss was nothing but an **opportunist** who was trying to ride to glory on *his* coattails.

When I left afterwards, I found myself trembling. I don't know why for sure, but it was as if I'd seen both men clearly for the first time. I remember hearing Burt say that Dr. Nemur had a shrew of a wife who was pushing him all the time to get things published so that he could become famous. Burt said that the dream of her life was to have a big shot husband.

Was Dr. Strauss really trying to ride on his coattails?

April 28 I don't understand why I never noticed how beautiful Miss Kinnian really is. She has brown eyes and feathery brown hair that comes to the top of her neck. She's only thirty-four! I think from the beginning I had the feeling that she was an unreachable genius—and very, very old. Now, every time I see her she grows younger and more lovely.

opportunist (ŏp'ər-to͞o'nĭst) *n.* a person who takes advantage of any opportunity, without moral regard, to achieve a goal

8. **neurosurgeons** (no͝or'ō-sûr'jənz): doctors who perform surgery on the brain and nervous system.
9. **Chair of Psychology at Princeton:** head of the psychology department at Princeton University.

Lines 443–478
DISCUSSION PROMPTS

Use these prompts to help students understand how Charlie's operation has changed his perception of others:

Connect Charlie says that he is trembling after he overhears the argument between the two doctors. Would you be upset about this incident if you were Charlie? Why or why not? *Students might say that they would be upset because the doctors are basically arguing over Charlie. Also, he is seeing them as human for the first time and realizing that they are not perfect.*

Analyze Why has Charlie's view of Miss Kinnian changed? ***Possible answer:*** *His intelligence is starting to match and even surpass hers. Therefore, he is seeing her as an equal, not as someone superior to him. Intellectually, he is no longer a child; he is an adult now.*

Synthesize Although Charlie is upset that his coworkers no longer talk to him, what is inevitable about his relationship with them as he becomes smarter? ***Possible answer:*** *He will not have anything in common with them. It will be just as hard to be friends with them when he is smart as it was before the operation, because his greater intelligence will create a gulf between them.*

FOR LESS–PROFICIENT READERS

Concept Support [small-group option] Review students' Y-charts from page 189. Discuss the qualities that Charlie has already revealed since the operation. Then point out how Charlie's interactions with the characters on these pages bring out more of his traits.

1. Assign groups one of these segments of the text to examine: lines 400–432, 433–445, 468–478.
2. Ask them to make inferences about Charlie's character from his own actions, words, and thoughts, and from the way others act toward him.
3. Discuss each group's additions to the chart. *(Lines 400–432: suspicious, critical of his former self, curious; lines 433–445: innovative, kind, understanding, lonely; lines 468–478: insightful, sensitive)*

FOR ENGLISH LEARNERS

Vocabulary: Idioms [paired option] Have students work in pairs to define these idiomatic expressions. Encourage them to use context clues or a dictionary to help them.

- *carried away* (line 423), "excited"
- *got up the nerve* (line 446), "found the courage"
- *ride to glory on his coattails* (line 467), "use someone else's work to gain recognition"
- *big shot* (line 472), "very important"

Lines 479–508

DISCUSSION PROMPTS

Use these prompts to help students explore Miss Kinnian's concerns:

Connect In lines 498–499, Miss Kinnian says that she hopes she was right in advising Charlie to have the operation. Have you ever encouraged someone to take a chance? How did you feel? *Students may say that they felt responsible for the person after encouraging him or her to do something. They may say that they too were anxious and hopeful that everything would turn out all right.*

Analyze Notice that Miss Kinnian does not verbalize her fears. What is she afraid of for Charlie? ***Possible answer:***

- *She may be afraid that his new intelligence will isolate him.*
- *She may fear that he won't be able to handle the strain of his new gifts.*
- *She may fear that the benefits will only be temporary and he will end up worse off than before.*
- *She may wonder about other potential side effects of the operation.*

Evaluate Should Miss Kinnian have encouraged Charlie to have the operation? Explain. ***Possible answers:***

- *Yes. She saw the possibility that Charlie could have a better life and took the risk of advising him to have the operation.*
- *No. She took too much upon herself to change his life, when he didn't seem that unhappy the way he was.*

LITERARY ANALYSIS

Ⓒ CHARACTER TRAITS

Remind students to record their answers in the Y-chart from page 189. ***Possible answer:*** *He assumes the position of an equal in their relationship. He feels the emotion of love. He is able to anticipate what might happen in the future, when he becomes even more intelligent.*

We had dinner and a long talk. When she said that I was coming along so fast that soon I'd be leaving her behind, I laughed.

"It's true, Charlie. You're already a better reader than I am. You can read a whole page at a glance while I can take in only a few lines at a time. And you remember every single thing you read. I'm lucky if I can recall the main thoughts and the general meaning."

"I don't feel intelligent. There are so many things I don't understand."

She took out a cigarette and I lit it for her. "You've got to be a *little* patient. You're accomplishing in days and weeks what it takes normal people to do in half a lifetime. That's what makes it so amazing. You're like a giant sponge now, soaking things in. Facts, figures, general knowledge. And soon you'll begin to connect them, too. You'll see how the different branches of learning are related. There are many levels, Charlie, like steps on a giant ladder that take you up higher and higher to see more and more of the world around you.

"I can see only a little bit of that, Charlie, and I won't go much higher than I am now, but you'll keep climbing up and up, and see more and more, and each step will open new worlds that you never even knew existed." She frowned. "I hope . . . I just hope to God—"

"What?"

"Never mind, Charles. I just hope I wasn't wrong to advise you to go into this in the first place."

I laughed. "How could that be? It worked, didn't it? Even Algernon is still smart."

We sat there silently for a while and I knew what she was thinking about as she watched me toying with the chain of my rabbit's foot and my keys. I didn't want to think of that possibility any more than elderly people want to think of death. I *knew* that this was only the beginning. I knew what she meant about levels because I'd seen some of them already. The thought of leaving her behind made me sad.

I'm in love with Miss Kinnian. Ⓒ

Ⓒ **CHARACTER TRAITS** What new aspects of Charlie's personality are revealed in this scene with Miss Kinnian?

PROGRESS REPORT 11

April 30 I've quit my job with Donnegan's Plastic Box Company. Mr. Donnegan insisted that it would be better for all concerned if I left. What did I do to make them hate me so?

The first I knew of it was when Mr. Donnegan showed me the petition. Eight hundred and forty names, everyone connected with the factory, except Fanny Girden. Scanning the list quickly, I saw at once that hers was the only missing name. All the rest demanded that I be fired.

③ **Targeted Passage**

Joe Carp and Frank Reilly wouldn't talk to me about it. No one else would either, except Fanny. She was one of the few people I'd known who set her mind to something and believed it no matter what the rest of the world

DIFFERENTIATED INSTRUCTION

FOR LESS–PROFICIENT READERS

Comprehension Support Point out the figurative language that Miss Kinnian uses in lines 488–489 and 491–492. In the first simile, she compares Charlie to a giant sponge. He is soaking in knowledge just as a sponge absorbs liquid. The second simile compares learning new things to climbing a ladder. Elicit from students reasons that these similes are appropriate. Ask how they foreshadow what Charlie can expect as he becomes smarter.

FOR ADVANCED LEARNERS/PRE–AP

Synthesize [small-group option] Discuss with students how works of fiction may have more than one theme. Ask students to work in small groups to identify one of the major messages that they think the author is conveying through the characters and events in this story. Ask students to compose a theme statement and identify the evidence from the text that supports it. Have groups present their ideas to the class for evaluation.

204 UNIT 2: CHARACTER AND POINT OF VIEW

proved, said or did—and Fanny did not believe that I should have been fired. She had been against the petition on principle and despite the pressure and threats she'd held out.

"Which don't mean to say," she remarked, "that I don't think there's something mighty strange about you, Charlie. Them changes. I don't know. You used to be a good, dependable, ordinary man—not too bright maybe, but honest. Who knows what you done to yourself to get so smart all of a sudden. Like everybody around here's been saying, Charlie, it's not right."

"But how can you say that, Fanny? What's wrong with a man becoming intelligent and wanting to acquire knowledge and understanding of the world around him?"

She stared down at her work and I turned to leave. Without looking at me, she said: "It was evil when Eve listened to the snake and ate from the tree of knowledge. It was evil when she saw that she was naked. If not for that none of us would ever have to grow old and sick, and die." [10]

Once again now I have the feeling of shame burning inside me. This intelligence has driven a wedge between me and all the people I once knew and loved. Before, they laughed at me and despised me for my ignorance and dullness; now, they hate me for my knowledge and understanding. What in God's name do they want of me?

They've driven me out of the factory. Now I'm more alone than ever before . . .

③ Targeted Passage

ANALYZE VISUALS
What might the flask in this illustration symbolize?

May 15 Dr. Strauss is very angry at me for not having written any progress reports in two weeks. He's justified because the lab is now paying me a regular salary. I told him I was too busy thinking and reading. When I pointed out that writing was such a slow process that it made me impatient with my poor handwriting, he suggested that I learn to type. It's much easier to write now because I can type nearly seventy-five words a minute. Dr. Strauss continually reminds me of the need to speak and write simply so that people will be able to understand me.

I'll try to review all the things that happened to me during the last two weeks. Algernon and I were presented to the *American Psychological Association* sitting in convention

10. **It was evil . . . die:** a reference to the biblical story of Adam and Eve (Genesis 2–3).

Lines 509–533
DISCUSSION PROMPTS

Use these prompts to help students understand what happens at the factory:

Connect If you were Charlie, how would you feel after being presented with the petition? *Students may say that they would feel betrayed and hurt.*

Analyze What is the reason that the workers want Charlie to leave? ***Possible answer:*** *He frightens them because he has suddenly become so smart. He no longer fits into the role he used to occupy, and they don't know how to treat him. He is so much smarter than they are that they feel intimidated.*

Evaluate Who is right about seeking knowledge—Fanny or Charlie? Explain. ***Possible answers:***

- *Charlie is right. Knowledge is good. It is what a person does with it that may turn to evil.*
- *Fanny is right. The pursuit of knowledge may lead to harm for the one engaged in it and for others.*

ANALYZE VISUALS

Possible answer: *The flask might symbolize Charlie, who is filled with knowledge. It is also a symbol of experimentation.*

Lines 534–540
REINFORCE *KEY IDEA:* KNOWLEDGE

Discuss How did Charlie think his life would change once he acquired **knowledge?** How have his recent experiences proven him wrong? ***Possible answer:*** *He thought that having more knowledge would help him fit in better. Now he sees that having more knowledge can be as great a barrier to relationships as having too little.*

FOR LESS–PROFICIENT READERS

③ Targeted Passage [Lines 509–540]

This passage presents a major turning point: Charlie is asked to leave his job at the factory.

- Who signs the petition at the factory?
- What does Fanny say about the way Charlie has changed?
- What is Charlie's reaction to this event? What does the experience show him?

FOR ADVANCED LEARNERS/PRE–AP

Synthesize [small-group option] In lines 530–533, Fanny alludes to the account of Adam and Eve in the book of Genesis in the Bible. Have students form small groups to read this passage of the Bible and discuss Fanny's reference to it.

Lines 576–579
REINFORCE *KEY IDEA:* KNOWLEDGE

Discuss What has Charlie's **knowledge** revealed to him about many people? ***Possible answer:*** *People are not what they seem to be.*

READING STRATEGY

R READING A LONG STORY

Possible answer: *The length and language of this entry reveal a dramatic increase in Charlie's intelligence.*

If students need help . . . Display a T Chart. List some words and phrases from the earlier progress reports in the first column. Then record some key words and phrases from this one in the second column. Have students compare what they see.

Earlier Reports	*May 15 Report*
• *shud rite down* • *dint see nuthing* • *Im a slow reeder* • *intelijence trippled*	• *the specter of self-doubt* • *specialization* • *highly respected psycho-experimentalist*

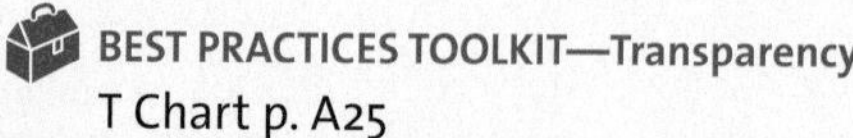

BEST PRACTICES TOOLKIT—Transparency
T Chart p. A25

Extend the Discussion How does Charlie's attitude in this report compare to that in earlier ones?

with the *World Psychological Association* last Tuesday. We created quite a **sensation.** Dr. Nemur and Dr. Strauss were proud of us.

I suspect that Dr. Nemur, who is sixty—ten years older than Dr. Strauss—finds it necessary to see **tangible** results of his work. Undoubtedly the result of pressure by Mrs. Nemur.

Contrary to my earlier impressions of him, I realize that Dr. Nemur is not at all a genius. He has a very good mind, but it struggles under the specter of self-doubt. He wants people to take him for a genius. Therefore, it is important for him to feel that his work is accepted by the world. I believe that Dr. Nemur was afraid of further delay because he worried that someone else might make a discovery along these lines and take the credit from him.

Dr. Strauss on the other hand might be called a genius, although I feel that his areas of knowledge are too limited. He was educated in the tradition of narrow **specialization;** the broader aspects of background were neglected far more than necessary—even for a neuro-surgeon.

I was shocked to learn that the only ancient languages he could read were Latin, Greek, and Hebrew, and that he knows almost nothing of mathematics beyond the elementary levels of the calculus of variations.[11] When he admitted this to me, I found myself almost annoyed. It was as if he'd hidden this part of himself in order to deceive me, pretending—as do many people I've discovered—to be what he is not. No one I've ever known is what he appears to be on the surface.

Dr. Nemur appears to be uncomfortable around me. Sometimes when I try to talk to him, he just looks at me strangely and turns away. I was angry at first when Dr. Strauss told me I was giving Dr. Nemur an inferiority complex.[12] I thought he was mocking me and I'm oversensitive at being made fun of.

How was I to know that a highly respected psycho-experimentalist like Nemur was unacquainted with Hindustani[13] and Chinese? It's **absurd** when you consider the work that is being done in India and China today in the very field of his study.

I asked Dr. Strauss how Nemur could **refute** Rahajamati's attack on his method and results if Nemur couldn't even read them in the first place. That strange look on Dr. Strauss' face can mean only one of two things. Either he doesn't want to tell Nemur what they're saying in India, or else—and this worries me—Dr. Strauss doesn't know either. I must be careful to speak and write clearly and simply so that people won't laugh. R

May 18 I am very disturbed. I saw Miss Kinnian last night for the first time in over a week. I tried to avoid all discussions of intellectual concepts and to keep the conversation on a simple, everyday level, but she just stared at me blankly and asked me what I meant about the mathematical variance equivalent in Dorbermann's *Fifth Concerto.*

sensation (sĕn-sā'sh… *n.* a state of great inte… and excitement

tangible (tăn'jə-bəl) *a…* able to be seen, touch… or understood

specialization (spĕsh'ə-lĭ-zā'shən) *n…* a focus on a particular area of study

absurd (əb-sûrd') *adj.* ridiculously unreasona…

refute (rĭ-fyo͞ot') *v.* to prove as false

R READING A LONG STORY
What do the length and language of the May 15 progress report reveal about Charlie's intelligence? Think ab… how this report differs from those in March and April.

11. **calculus** (kăl'kyə-ləs) **of variations:** a branch of higher mathematics.
12. **inferiority complex:** feelings of worthlessness.
13. **Hindustani** (hĭn'do͞o-stä'nē): a group of languages used in India.

DIFFERENTIATED INSTRUCTION

FOR LESS–PROFICIENT READERS

Comprehension Support [small-group option] To help students understand the effect of Charlie's new intelligence on his relationships, assign Miss Kinnian, Dr. Nemur, Dr. Strauss, or the factory workers to small groups of students. Have them use a Venn Diagram to compare the character's behavior toward Charlie before surgery and after its effects become apparent. Discuss their findings.

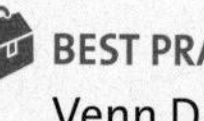

BEST PRACTICES TOOLKIT—Transparency
Venn Diagram p. A26

FOR ADVANCED LEARNERS/PRE–AP

Analyze Point out the interaction between Miss Kinnian and Charlie in lines 594–605. Have students explore how the irony of this situation is related to a possible theme of the story. Ask students to present their insights in class discussion.

When I tried to explain she stopped me and laughed. I guess I got angry, but I suspect I'm approaching her on the wrong level. No matter what I try to discuss with her, I am unable to communicate. I must review Vrostadt's equations on *Levels of Semantic Progression.* I find that I don't communicate with people much any more. Thank God for books and music and things I can think about. I am alone in my apartment at Mrs. Flynn's boarding house most of the time and seldom speak to anyone. S

S CHARACTER TRAITS
How has Charlie's attitude toward socializing changed?

May 20 I would not have noticed the new dishwasher, a boy of about sixteen, at the corner diner where I take my evening meals if not for the incident of the broken dishes.

They crashed to the floor, shattering and sending bits of white china under the tables. The boy stood there, dazed and frightened, holding the empty tray in his hand. The whistles and catcalls from the customers (the cries of "hey, there go the profits!" . . . "*Mazeltov!*" . . . and "well, *he* didn't work here very long . . ." which invariably seems to follow the breaking of glass or dishware in a public restaurant) all seemed to confuse him.

When the owner came to see what the excitement was about, the boy cowered as if he expected to be struck and threw up his arms as if to ward off the blow.

"All right! All right, you dope," shouted the owner, "don't just stand there! Get the broom and sweep that mess up. A broom . . . a broom, you idiot! It's in the kitchen. Sweep up all the pieces."

The boy saw that he was not going to be punished. His frightened expression disappeared and he smiled and hummed as he came back with the broom to sweep the floor. A few of the rowdier customers kept up the remarks, amusing themselves at his expense.

"Here, sonny, over here there's a nice piece behind you . . ."

"C'mon, do it again . . ."

"He's not so dumb. It's easier to break 'em than to wash 'em . . ."

As his vacant eyes moved across the crowd of amused onlookers, he slowly mirrored their smiles and finally broke into an uncertain grin at the joke which he obviously did not understand.

I felt sick inside as I looked at his dull, vacuous smile, the wide, bright eyes of a child, uncertain but eager to please. They were laughing at him because he was mentally retarded.

And I had been laughing at him too.

Suddenly, I was furious at myself and all those who were smirking at him. I jumped up and shouted, "Shut up! Leave him alone! It's not his fault he can't understand! He can't help what he is! But for God's sake . . . he's still a human being!" T

T CHARACTER TRAITS
Why does Charlie defend the dishwasher? Tell what you can **infer** about his personality based on his behavior.

The room grew silent. I cursed myself for losing control and creating a scene. I tried not to look at the boy as I paid my check and walked out without touching my food. I felt ashamed for both of us.

LITERARY ANALYSIS

S CHARACTER TRAITS

Remind students to record their ideas in their Y-charts from page 189. ***Possible answer:*** *He has become more antisocial because of the difficulty of trying to communicate with less-intelligent people.*

LITERARY ANALYSIS

T CHARACTER TRAITS

Possible answer: *He feels empathy for the dishwasher, who reminds Charlie of his former self. His defense of the dishwasher shows that Charlie is a caring and compassionate person.*

FOR LESS–PROFICIENT READERS

Comprehension Support [small-group option] Have students reread lines 160–173, 215–234, and 331–357. Ask small groups to compare Charlie's experiences with the dishwasher's experience in lines 606–632. Discuss the similarities and help students see that Charlie's realization that he used to be just like the boy causes his outburst in lines 634–637.

FOR ENGLISH LEARNERS

Culture: Clarify Explain to students that the expression *mazeltov* (line 612) is Hebrew for "congratulations." Often, this word is shouted out at a Jewish wedding when the groom steps on and breaks a glass. Tell students that here it is used sarcastically, since the breaking of the glasses was accidental.

How strange it is that people of honest feelings and sensibility, who would not take advantage of a man born without arms or legs or eyes—how such people think nothing of abusing a man born with low intelligence. It infuriated me to think that not too long ago I, like this boy, had foolishly played the clown.

And I had almost forgotten.

I'd hidden the picture of the old Charlie Gordon from myself because now that I was intelligent it was something that had to be pushed out of my mind. But today in looking at that boy, for the first time I saw what I had been. *I was just like him!*

Only a short time ago, I learned that people laughed at me. Now I can see that unknowingly I joined with them in laughing at myself. That hurts most of all.

I have often reread my progress reports and seen the illiteracy, the childish naïveté, the mind of low intelligence peering from a dark room, through the keyhole, at the dazzling light outside. I see that even in my dullness I knew that I was inferior, and that other people had something I lacked—something denied me. In my mental blindness, I thought that it was somehow connected with the ability to read and write, and I was sure that if I could get those skills I would automatically have intelligence too.

Even a feeble-minded man wants to be like other men.

A child may not know how to feed itself, or what to eat, yet it knows of hunger.

This then is what I was like. I never knew. Even with my gift of intellectual awareness, I never really knew.

This day was good for me. Seeing the past more clearly, I have decided to use my knowledge and skills to work in the field of increasing human intelligence levels. Who is better equipped for this work? Who else has lived in both worlds? These are my people. Let me use my gift to do something for them. **U**

Tomorrow, I will discuss with Dr. Strauss the manner in which I can work in this area. I may be able to help him work out the problems of widespread use of the technique which was used on me. I have several good ideas of my own.

There is so much that might be done with this technique. If I could be made into a genius, what about thousands of others like myself? What fantastic levels might be achieved by using this technique on normal people? On *geniuses?*

There are so many doors to open. I am impatient to begin.

PROGRESS REPORT 12

May 23 It happened today. Algernon bit me. I visited the lab to see him as I do occasionally, and when I took him out of his cage, he snapped at my hand. I put him back and watched him for a while. He was unusually disturbed and vicious.

May 24 Burt, who is in charge of the experimental animals, tells me that Algernon is changing. He is less cooperative; he refuses to run the maze any more; general motivation has decreased. And he hasn't been eating. Everyone is upset about what this may mean.

U CHARACTER TRAITS How does Charlie's concern for others affect his goals?

4 Targeted Passage

LITERARY ANALYSIS

U CHARACTER TRAITS

Remind students to record their answers in their charts. ***Possible answer:*** *He wants to use his intelligence to help others. This trait is part of who he is.*

Extend the Discussion Why does Charlie use the word *gift* to refer to his increasing intelligence?

DIFFERENTIATED INSTRUCTION

FOR LESS–PROFICIENT READERS

Reading Strategy Follow-Up: Reading a Long Story [small-group option] Review what the class has recorded in the five-column chart. Then have groups work together to examine May's progress reports. Have students share what they observe. Add their details to the class chart.

May
• *Charlie's grammar and spelling are perfect.* • *The language he uses to express himself is very advanced. His writing is well organized and descriptive.* • *He describes events and then reflects upon their significance. His mind is operating at a very high level.*

FOR ADVANCED LEARNERS/PRE–AP

Synthesize Draw students' attention to the metaphor in lines 653–655 that Charlie uses to describe his former state of ignorance. Discuss the ways in which this metaphor is apt. Then ask students to create an original metaphor to express a similar idea. Have students share their figurative language with the class.

208 UNIT 2: CHARACTER AND POINT OF VIEW

May 25 They've been feeding Algernon, who now refuses to work the shifting-lock problem. Everyone identifies me with Algernon. In a way we're both the first of our kind. They're all pretending that Algernon's behavior is not necessarily significant for me. But it's hard to hide the fact that some of the other animals who were used in this experiment are showing strange behavior.

Dr. Strauss and Dr. Nemur have asked me not to come to the lab any more. I know what they're thinking but I can't accept it. I am going ahead with my plans to carry their research forward. With all due respect to both of these fine scientists, I am well aware of their limitations. If there is an answer, I'll have to find it out for myself. Suddenly, time has become very important to me.

④ Targeted Passage

May 29 I have been given a lab of my own and permission to go ahead with the research. I'm on to something. Working day and night. I've had a cot moved into the lab. Most of my writing time is spent on the notes which I keep in a separate folder, but from time to time I feel it necessary to put down my moods and my thoughts out of sheer habit.

I find the *calculus of intelligence* to be a fascinating study. Here is the place for the application of all the knowledge I have acquired. In a sense it's the problem I've been concerned with all my life.

ANALYZE VISUALS
In what way does this illustration **represent** the actions Charlie describes in his May 29 entry?

Lines 676–697

DISCUSSION PROMPTS

Use these prompts to help students understand Charlie's reaction to what is happening with Algernon:

Interpret What might Algernon's odd behavior mean for Charlie? ***Possible answer:*** *Charlie's condition might start to deteriorate, too.*

Analyze What are some possible ways in which Charlie could react to the implications of Algernon's behavior? What does the way he chooses to react reveal about his character? ***Possible answers:*** *He could become depressed and give up hope, or he could become angry and lash out at the doctors and others involved with the project. Instead, he chooses to use the time he has left to try to find a solution. This reaction shows his strength, determination, and spirit.*

Evaluate How would you rate Charlie's chances for success in solving this problem? ***Possible answer:*** *He is more intelligent than anyone else. Plus, he is motivated to save himself. If there is a solution, he will find it.*

ANALYZE VISUALS

Possible answer: *Charlie says that he is applying all the knowledge he has acquired to study his own increase in intelligence. In the illustration, this idea is represented by the way the man is using a fishing rod to pull information out of his head.*

FOR LESS–PROFICIENT READERS

④ Targeted Passage [Lines 676–692]

This passage presents another important turning point: Algernon starts behaving oddly.

- In what ways does Algernon's behavior change?
- Why do people associate Algernon with Charlie?
- What answer does Charlie want to find?

FOR ENGLISH LEARNERS

Vocabulary Support In line 698, Charlie refers to the fascinating study of the *calculus of intelligence*. Explain to students that calculus is a branch of mathematics that deals with limits, rates of change, and the accumulation of quantities. These concepts apply to the experiment in the story because both Charlie's and Algernon's intelligence increased at a very rapid rate. Now Charlie wants to predict how his intelligence will change in the future.

May 31 Dr. Strauss thinks I'm working too hard. Dr. Nemur says I'm trying to cram a lifetime of research and thought into a few weeks. I know I should rest, but I'm driven on by something inside that won't let me stop. I've got to find the reason for the sharp regression in Algernon. I've got to know *if* and *when* it will happen to me.

June 4

Letter to Dr. Strauss (*copy*)

Dear Dr. Strauss:

Under separate cover I am sending you a copy of my report entitled, "The Algernon-Gordon Effect: A Study of Structure and Function of Increased Intelligence," which I would like to have you read and have published.

As you see, my experiments are completed. I have included in my report all of my formulae, as well as mathematical analysis in the appendix. Of course, these should be verified.

Because of its importance to both you and Dr. Nemur (and need I say to myself, too?) I have checked and rechecked my results a dozen times in the hope of finding an error. I am sorry to say the results must stand. Yet for the sake of science, I am grateful for the little bit that I here add to the knowledge of the function of the human mind and of the laws governing the artificial increase of human intelligence.

I recall your once saying to me that an experimental *failure* or the *disproving* of a theory was as important to the advancement of learning as a success would be. I know now that this is true. I am sorry, however, that my own contribution to the field must rest upon the ashes of the work of two men I regard so highly.

Yours truly,
Charles Gordon **V**

encl.: rept.

V READING A LONG STORY
What is different about the June 4 entry? Tell what you learn about Charlie and his future from this section.

June 5 I must not become emotional. The facts and the results of my experiments are clear, and the more sensational aspects of my own rapid climb cannot obscure the fact that the tripling of intelligence by the surgical technique developed by Dr.'s Strauss and Nemur must be viewed as having little or no practical applicability (at the present time) to the increase of human intelligence.

As I review the records and data on Algernon, I see that although he is still in his physical infancy, he has regressed mentally. Motor activity[14] is **impaired;** there is a general reduction of glandular activity; there is an accelerated loss of coordination.

impair (ĭm-pâr') *v.* to weaken; damage

There are also strong indications of progressive amnesia.[15]

As will be seen by my report, these and other physical and mental deterioration syndromes can be predicted with statistically significant results by the application of my formula.

14. **motor activity:** movement produced by use of the muscles.
15. **progressive amnesia** (prə-grĕs'ĭv ăm-nē'zhə): a steadily worsening loss of memory.

READING STRATEGY

V READING A LONG STORY

Possible answer: *The June 4 entry is a letter. Charlie's intelligence is going to decline as Algernon's did.*

If students need help . . . Point out the words *sorry* (lines 717, 723), *failure* (line 721), and *disproving of a theory* (line 722). These words indicate that it is not good news that Charlie is reporting.

DIFFERENTIATED INSTRUCTION

FOR LESS–PROFICIENT READERS

Vocabulary Support [small-group option] Tell students that this part of the story includes several scientific terms to make Charlie's research seem real and impressive. Work with students to identify unfamiliar or challenging words in lines 709–762. Then assign small groups one or two words to look up in a dictionary. Discuss the definitions they locate.

Comprehension Support Point out that Charlie uses figurative language when he says in lines 723–725 that "my own contribution to the field must rest upon the ashes of the work of two men I regard so highly." Explain that Charlie means that his research, based upon the techniques and theories developed by Dr. Nemur and Dr. Strauss, has proven their ideas to be useless.

FOR ENGLISH LEARNERS

Vocabulary: Prefixes [mixed-readiness pairs] Remind students that they can use their knowledge of prefixes to help them define words. Tell them that the prefix *re-* means "again." Have students form pairs and think aloud to show the process they would use to define each of these words, using what they know about the prefix and roots: *research* (line 702), *rechecked* (line 716), *recall* (line 721), *review* (line 734).

The surgical stimulus to which we were both subjected has resulted in an ntensification and acceleration of all mental processes. The unforeseen levelopment, which I have taken the liberty of calling the *Algernon-Gordon Effect,* is the logical extension of the entire intelligence speed-up. The hypothesis here proven may be described simply in the following terms: Artificially increased intelligence deteriorates at a rate of time directly **proportional** to the quantity of the increase.

I feel that this, in itself, is an important discovery.

As long as I am able to write, I will continue to record my thoughts in these progress reports. It is one of my few pleasures. However, by all indications, my own mental deterioration will be very rapid.

I have already begun to notice signs of emotional instability and forgetfulness, the first symptoms of the burn-out.

proportional (prə-pôr'shə-nəl) *adj.* having a constant relation in degree or number

June 10 Deterioration progressing. I have become absent-minded. Algernon died two days ago. Dissection shows my predictions were right. His brain had decreased in weight and there was a general smoothing out of cerebral convolutions as well as a deepening and broadening of brain fissures.[16]

I guess the same thing is or will soon be happening to me. Now that it's definite, I don't want it to happen.

I put Algernon's body in a cheese box and buried him in the back yard. I cried. **W**

W READING A LONG STORY What does Charlie's language in the June 10 entry tell you about what is happening to his intelligence? Think about how this might affect Charlie's attitude toward Algernon's death.

June 15 Dr. Strauss came to see me again. I wouldn't open the door and I told him to go away. I want to be left to myself. I have become touchy and irritable. I feel the darkness closing in. It's hard to throw off thoughts of suicide. I keep telling myself how important this introspective journal will be.

It's a strange sensation to pick up a book that you've read and enjoyed just a few months ago and discover that you don't remember it. I remembered how great I thought John Milton was, but when I picked up *Paradise Lost* I couldn't understand it at all. I got so angry I threw the book across the room.

I've got to try to hold on to some of it. Some of the things I've learned. Oh, God, please don't take it all away.

June 19 Sometimes, at night, I go out for a walk. Last night I couldn't remember where I lived. A policeman took me home. I have the strange feeling that this has all happened to me before—a long time ago. I keep telling myself I'm the only person in the world who can describe what's happening to me.

June 21 Why can't I remember? I've got to fight. I lie in bed for days and I don't know who or where I am. Then it all comes back to me in a flash.

16. **cerebral convolutions** (sĕr'ə-brəl kŏn'-və-lo͞o'shən) . . . **brain fissures** (fĭsh'ərz): cerebral convolutions are ridges or folds on the brain's surface; fissures are grooves that divide the brain into sections.

Lines 729–752

DISCUSSION PROMPTS

Use these prompts to help students understand what will happen to Charlie:

Connect Charlie says he must not become emotional. Would you blame him for being upset? Why or why not? *Students will most likely say that they would not blame him. He knows that he will suffer the same fate as Algernon.*

Analyze What does the progressive amnesia mean for Charlie? ***Possible answer:*** *He will not retain any of the knowledge that he has acquired.*

Synthesize How does Charlie know that his deterioration will be very rapid? ***Possible answer:*** *According to his calculations, the rate of deterioration is directly proportional to the extent of the increase in intelligence. Charlie's intelligence increase was phenomenal; therefore, he will go downhill quickly.*

Lines 742–749

REINFORCE *KEY IDEA:* KNOWLEDGE

Discuss How has Charlie used his **knowledge** to help others? ***Possible answer:*** *He has written a complete report that explains why the experiment did not work. The information in this report can be used to help future scientists and to advance the study of artificially increasing intelligence.*

READING STRATEGY

W READING A LONG STORY

Possible answer: *Charlie's sentences are becoming shorter and simpler, a sign of his mental deterioration. Charlie cannot be objective when he buries Algernon because he knows he will soon die, too. He says, "I cried."*

FOR ADVANCED LEARNERS/PRE–AP

Analyze Ask students to examine the language on these pages, which includes many scientific terms. Have students discuss the effect of this jargon on the reader. Does the language make them forget that the premise of the story is unrealistic?

Synthesize [small-group option] Point out the allusion to *Paradise Lost* in line 769. Explain to students that this is an epic poem narrating the biblical expulsion of Adam and Eve from the Garden of Eden. Ask students to discuss in small groups the significance of the allusion in this part of the story.

LITERARY ANALYSIS: *Review*

⊗ POINT OF VIEW

Possible answer: *Learning about Charlie's deterioration through his own words allows readers to understand his pain in a very direct way. This makes the story especially sad.*

If students need help . . . Read lines 777–783 aloud. Ask students to describe their reactions after hearing the passage.

Extend the Discussion How would the impact of this part of the story be different if someone else told it?

Fugues[17] of amnesia. Symptoms of senility—second childhood. I can watch them coming on. It's so cruelly logical. I learned so much and so fast. Now my mind is deteriorating rapidly. I won't let it happen. I'll fight it. I can't help thinking of the boy in the restaurant, the blank expression, the silly smile, the people laughing at him. No—please—not that again . . . ⊗

⊗ POINT OF VIEW
What effect does lear
about Charlie's feeling
through his own word
have on you?

June 22 I'm forgetting things that I learned recently. It seems to be following the classic pattern—the last things learned are the first things forgotten. Or is that the pattern? I'd better look it up again. . . .

I reread my paper on the *Algernon-Gordon Effect* and I get the strange feeling that it was written by someone else. There are parts I don't even understand.

Motor activity impaired. I keep tripping over things, and it becomes increasingly difficult to type.

June 23 I've given up using the typewriter completely. My coordination is bad. I feel that I'm moving slower and slower. Had a terrible shock today. I picked up a copy of an article I used in my research, Krueger's *Uber psychische Ganzheit,* to see if it would help me understand what I had done. First I thought there was something wrong with my eyes. Then I realized I could no longer read German. I tested myself in other languages. All gone.

June 30 A week since I dared to write again. It's slipping away like sand through my fingers. Most of the books I have are too hard for me now. I get angry with them because I know that I read and understood them just a few weeks ago.

I keep telling myself I must keep writing these reports so that somebody will know what is happening to me. But it gets harder to form the words and remember spellings. I have to look up even simple words in the dictionary now and it makes me impatient with myself.

Dr. Strauss comes around almost every day, but I told him I wouldn't see or speak to anybody. He feels guilty. They all do. But I don't blame anyone. I knew what might happen. But how it hurts.

July 7 I don't know where the week went. Todays Sunday I know because I can see through my window people going to church. I think I stayed in bed all week but I remember Mrs. Flynn bringing food to me a few times. I keep saying over and over Ive got to do something but then I forget or maybe its just easier not to do what I say Im going to do.

I think of my mother and father a lot these days. I found a picture of them with me taken at a beach. My father has a big ball under his arm and my mother is holding me by the hand. I dont remember them the way they are in the picture. All I remember is my father drunk most of the time and arguing with mom about money.

17. **fugues** (fyo͞ogz): psychological states where people seem to act consciously but later have no memory of the action.

Lines 784–806

DISCUSSION PROMPTS

Use these prompts to help students understand the experience that Charlie is undergoing:

Summarize Which of Charlie's functions have been affected so far? ***Answer:*** *His memory, motor activity, coordination, and ability to comprehend are noticeably deteriorating.*

Analyze As Charlie observes his deterioration, what does he know about his condition? ***Possible answer:*** *He knows there is no solution. He knows that he will only get worse.*

Synthesize Could Charlie have comprehended in advance how difficult it would be if the effects of the operation turned out to be temporary? Explain. *Students will likely say no. Before the operation, Charlie had no idea what possessing knowledge and moving to a higher state of intelligence would mean to him.*

DIFFERENTIATED INSTRUCTION

FOR LESS-PROFICIENT READERS

Reading Strategy Follow-Up: Reading a Long Story [small-group option] Discuss the changes that students have seen in Charlie's progress reports since the beginning of the story. Then ask them to work in small groups to identify characteristics of his June reports. Have groups compare observations before adding them to the class chart.

June
• *Charlie is having symptoms of deterioration, but he still spells well and uses correct grammar. His sentences and vocabulary are simpler than in May's reports.* • *He shares his feelings about what he is going through and describes the physical symptoms.*

He never shaved much and he used to scratch my face when he hugged me. My mother said he died but Cousin Miltie said he heard his mom and dad say that my father ran away with another woman. When I asked my mother she slapped my face and said my father was dead. I dont think I ever found out which was true but I dont care much. (He said he was going to take me to see cows on a farm once but he never did. He never kept his promises . . .)

July 10 My landlady Mrs Flynn is very worried about me. She says the way I lay around all day and dont do anything I remind her of her son before she threw him out of the house. She said she doesnt like loafers. If Im sick its one thing, but if Im a loafer thats another thing and she wont have it. I told her I think Im sick.

I try to read a little bit every day, mostly stories, but sometimes I have to read the same thing over and over again because I dont know what it means. And its hard to write. I know I should look up all the words in the dictionary but its so hard and Im so tired all the time.

Then I got the idea that I would only use the easy words instead of the long hard ones. That saves time. I put flowers on Algernons grave about once a week. Mrs Flynn thinks Im crazy to put flowers on a mouses grave but I told her that Algernon was special.

ANALYZE VISUALS
What can you **infer** about what is happening to the man in the picture?

July 14 Its sunday again. I dont have anything to do to keep me busy now because my television set is broke and I dont have any money to get it fixed. (I think I lost this months check from the lab. I dont remember)

I get awful headaches and asperin doesnt help me much. Mrs Flynn knows Im really sick and she feels very sorry for me. Shes a wonderful woman whenever someone is sick.

Lines 831–859
DISCUSSION PROMPTS

Use these prompts to help students understand Charlie's present condition:

Describe What does Charlie do with his time? ***Possible answer:*** *He mostly lies around. His television set is broken, so he can't watch that. He gets bad headaches.*

Compare and Contrast In what ways is Charlie's behavior the same as and different from the way it was before the operation? ***Possible answer:*** *Before the operation, he worked regularly and took care of himself. Now he doesn't have a routine, he is very tired, he doesn't appear to be able to work, and he has trouble with simple tasks such as keeping track of his money.*

Evaluate Is Charlie worse off than he was before the operation or better off? *Students will likely say that Charlie is worse off. First, his deterioration seems to be affecting areas that were okay before. Second, he now must live with the memory of what he used to be able to do.*

ANALYZE VISUALS

Possible answer: *In the illustration, a lightning bolt strikes a man on the head. You can infer that the man has just experienced a flash of brilliance.*

FOR LESS–PROFICIENT READERS

Comprehension Support [small-group option] To illustrate the circular organization of this plot, use a circle diagram with six segments. Together fill in the first three sections, starting at the top and moving in a clockwise direction. Have groups of students complete their charts. Discuss the symmetry of the plot as it is revealed in the diagram.

Charlie's intelligence deteriorates rapidly.
Charlie struggles to learn but is limited by his low intelligence.
Charlie has an operation to increase his intelligence.
Charlie's knowledge increases by leaps and bounds.
Charlie becomes a genius.
Charlie discovers that his intelligence is temporary.

READING STRATEGY

V READING A LONG STORY

Possible answer: *Charlie is no longer using correct punctuation for contractions and direct quotations, and his sentences tend to be either very short or long and rambling. These changes indicate that Charlie is losing his intelligence.*

If students need help . . . Choose a progress report from May and have students compare and contrast the punctuation and sentence structure.

Lines 892–900

DISCUSSION PROMPTS

Use these prompts to help students understand the factory workers' treatment of Charlie:

Connect If you were in Charlie's situation, what do you think would be the hardest part of returning to work at the factory? *Students may say that the hardest part would be facing everyone again and thinking that they might make fun of him again.*

Analyze Why do Frank and Joe defend Charlie? ***Possible answers:*** *They admire him for going through what he has; they feel sorry for him; they feel guilty for their past treatment of him.*

Synthesize Are the factory workers really Charlie's friends now? ***Possible answer:*** *Yes. They see him as a person with courage who has gone through a lot. They no longer want to exploit him for their own amusement.*

July 22 Mrs Flynn called a strange doctor to see me. She was afraid I was going to die. I told the doctor I wasnt too sick and that I only forget sometimes. He asked me did I have any friends or relatives and I said no I dont have any. I told him I had a friend called Algernon once but he was a mouse and we used to run races together. He looked at me kind of funny like he thought I was crazy.

He smiled when I told him I used to be a genius. He talked to me like I was a baby and he winked at Mrs Flynn. I got mad and chased him out because he was making fun of me the way they all used to.

July 24 I have no more money and Mrs Flynn says I got to go to work somewhere and pay the rent because I havent paid for over two months. I dont know any work but the job I used to have at Donnegans Plastic Box Company. I dont want to go back there because they all knew me when I was smart and maybe they'll laugh at me. But I dont know what else to do to get money.

5 Targeted Passage

July 25 I was looking at some of my old progress reports and its very funny but I cant read what I wrote. I can make out some of the words but they dont make sense.

Miss Kinnian came to the door but I said go away I dont want to see you. She cried and I cried too but I wouldnt let her in because I didnt want her to laugh at me. I told her I didn't like her any more. I told her I didn't want to be smart any more. Thats not true. I still love her and I still want to be smart but I had to say that so shed go away. She gave Mrs. Flynn money to pay the rent. I dont want that. I got to get a job.

Please . . . please let me not forget how to read and write . . . V

V READING A LONG STORY
Compare the July 25 progress report to those from previous months How does it help you understand what has happened to Charlie?

July 27 Mr. Donnegan was very nice when I came back and asked him for my old job of janitor. First he was very suspicious but I told him what happened to me then he looked very sad and put his hand on my shoulder and said Charlie Gordon you got guts.

Everybody looked at me when I came downstairs and started working in the toilet sweeping it out like I used to. I told myself Charlie if they make fun of you dont get sore because you remember their not so smart as you once thot they were. And besides they were once your friends and if they laughed at you that doesnt mean anything because they liked you too.

One of the new men who came to work there after I went away made a nasty crack he said hey Charlie I hear your a very smart fella a real quiz kid. Say something intelligent. I felt bad but Joe Carp came over and grabbed him by the shirt and said leave him alone you lousy cracker or Ill break your neck. I didnt expect Joe to take my part so I guess hes really my friend.

Later Frank Reilly came over and said Charlie if anybody bothers you or trys to take advantage you call me or Joe and we will set em straight. I said thanks Frank and I got choked up so I had to turn around and go into the supply room so he wouldnt see me cry. Its good to have friends.

DIFFERENTIATED INSTRUCTION

FOR LESS-PROFICIENT READERS

5 Targeted Passage [Lines 873–900]

This passage presents the falling action: Charlie returns to his old job at the factory.

- What does Charlie do when Miss Kinnian comes to visit?
- What does Mr. Donnegan say when Charlie asks for his old job back? Why?
- What does the new worker say to Charlie? How do both Joe and Frank react?

Reading Strategy Follow-Up: Reading a Long Story [small-group option] Have students work in small groups to identify ways in which the language, spelling, and content of the progress reports in the month of July reveal Charlie's decline. Then add their details to the class chart.

July
• *Charlie has forgotten the rules of punctuation. Example: "but I said go away I dont want to see you" (line 876).*
• *He misspells simple words, such as "reed" and "rite" in line 915.*
• *His reports are like the ones before the operation. He records what people say and do without much analysis.*

July 28 I did a dumb thing today I forgot I wasnt in Miss Kinnians class at the adult center any more like I use to be. I went in and sat down in my old seat in the back of the room and she looked at me funny and she said Charles. I dint remember she ever called me that before only Charlie so I said hello Miss Kinnian Im redy for my lesin today only I lost my reader that we was using. She startid to cry and run out of the room and everybody looked at me and I saw they wasnt the same pepul who use to be in my class.

Then all of a suddin I rememberd some things about the operashun and me getting smart and I said holy smoke I reely pulled a Charlie Gordon that time. I went away before she come back to the room.

Thats why Im going away from New York for good. I dont want to do nothing like that agen. I dont want Miss Kinnian to feel sorry for me. Evry body feels sorry at the factery and I dont want that eather so Im going someplace where nobody knows that Charlie Gordon was once a genus and now he cant even reed a book or rite good.

Im taking a cuple of books along and even if I cant reed them Ill practise hard and maybe I wont forget every thing I lerned. If I try reel hard maybe Ill be a littel bit smarter then I was before the operashun. I got my rabits foot and my luky penny and maybe they will help me.

If you ever reed this Miss Kinnian dont be sorry for me Im glad I got a second chanse to be smart becaus I lerned a lot of things that I never even new were in this world and Im grateful that I saw it all for a littel bit. I dont know why Im dumb agen or what I did wrong maybe its becaus I dint try hard enuff. But if I try and practis very hard maybe Ill get a littl smarter and know what all the words are. I remember a littel bit how nice I had a feeling with the blue book that has the torn cover when I red it. Thats why Im gonna keep trying to get smart so I can have that feeling agen. Its a good feeling to know things and be smart. I wish I had it rite now if I did I woud sit down and reed all the time. Anyway I bet Im the first dumb person in the world who ever found out somthing importent for sience. I remember I did somthing but I dont remember what. So I gess its like I did it for all the dumb pepul like me. ❷

Goodbye Miss Kinnian and Dr. Strauss and evreybody. And P.S. please tell Dr Nemur not to be such a grouch when pepul laff at him and he woud have more frends. Its easy to make frends if you let pepul laff at you. Im going to have lots of frends where I go.

P.P.S. Please if you get a chanse put some flowrs on Algernons grave in the bak yard . . .

⑥ Targeted Passage

❷ **CHARACTER TRAITS**
What does Charlie's attitude toward his experience suggest about the kind of person he is?

Lines 901–915
DISCUSSION PROMPTS

Use these prompts to help students understand why Charlie is leaving New York:

Connect Do you support Charlie's decision to leave New York? Why or why not? *Students may say that, like Charlie, they would not want to be in a place where everyone feels sorry for them. However, they might think it is unwise for Charlie to leave a place where people care about him.*

Analyze What does Charlie's decision reveal about his character? ***Possible answer:*** *He has pride and dignity. He doesn't want to be a burden on other people or cause them pain.*

Synthesize Will Charlie be happier when he leaves New York? Why or why not? ***Possible answer:*** *For a while, he will remember what he once was and what he has lost. That realization will continue to make him sad. But he may at least feel more at peace if he doesn't have to think about other people's reactions to him.*

Lines 924–929
REINFORCE *KEY IDEA:* KNOWLEDGE

Discuss What do readers realize about the potential for Charlie to regain some of his former knowledge? ***Possible answer:*** *No matter how hard he works at it, he will not learn very much. According to his own scientific report, he will suffer the same fate as Algernon.*

LITERARY ANALYSIS

❷ CHARACTER TRAITS

Possible answer: *His positive outlook on the experience suggests that he is truly a good person who wants to help others.*

FOR LESS–PROFICIENT READERS

⑥ Targeted Passage [Lines 916–938]

This passage completes the circle of the plot: Charlie has returned to his pre-operation level of intelligence.

- What do you notice about Charlie's spelling and language in this progress report?
- Why does he tell Miss Kinnian not to be sad?
- What does he hope he can do if he tries hard enough?
- What does he want someone to do for him while he is gone?

Concept Support [small-group option] Have small groups of students complete the third section of their Y-charts, identifying Charlie's traits that remain the same both before and after the operation. Then have the groups share their additions to their charts with the class.

Prereading for this selection is found on pages 188–189.

ANALYZE VISUALS

Activity Does the man in this movie still match your image of Charlie? Explain. *Students may say that he does. He looks about the right age. He has a rather puzzled look on his face. He isn't wearing glasses, however, which Charlie does sometimes. Some students may say that they have pictured Charlie as heavier, taller, bigger, and so on.*

Lines 1–23

LITERARY ANALYSIS

● CHARACTER TRAITS

How does Charlie treat Algernon? What does this behavior reveal about him? ***Possible answer:*** *Charlie talks to Algernon and tries to pet him. These actions show his gentleness and his kind nature.*

Charly[1]

Stirling Silliphant

CHARACTERS
Charlie **Dr. Strauss** **Dr. Nemur** **Alice Kinnian**

Charlie. Boy!

(*He straightens, looks at* Dr. Nemur *and* Dr. Strauss *who stand at one end of the cage.* Alice Kinnian *is just to one side of* Charlie *in a laboratory around which cages containing mice, rats, and monkeys are arranged. Here and there in the background lab assistants are at work.* Dr. Strauss *reaches in a piece of cheese, rewards the mouse.*)

Dr. Strauss. Well, Charlie, what do you think of Algernon?

Charlie (*grinning*). Pretty fancy name for a mouse!

Dr. Strauss. Algernon's a pretty special mouse.

(Charlie *turns back to the cage, rubs the tip of his fingers along the mesh and baby-talks to th mouse.* Algernon *twitches its nose and waggles its whiskers.*)

(*favoring* Dr. Nemur)

Dr. Nemur (*to* Alice). How much does Charl understand about the operation?

Alice Kinnian. Charlie?

(Charlie *looks up.*)

Charlie. Yeh?

Alice Kinnian. What do you remember about the operation we discussed? The reason I brought you here?

Movie still from t 1969 film *Charly*

1. **Charly:** The screenwriter might have chosen to misspell Charlie's name as "Charly" to convey the main character's struggle with spelling.

DIFFERENTIATED INSTRUCTION

FOR LESS–PROFICIENT READERS

Concept Support

- Remind students that the italicized stage directions help them to visualize setting and characters' actions, expressions, and feelings. These parts of the screenplay need to be read as carefully as the dialogue.
- Have students work in pairs to read the first set of stage directions and draw the setting based on the description given. Have students share their sketches. Discuss similarities and differences.

Vocabulary Support Explain to students that in a screenplay, the word *favoring* (lines 19, 52) indicates that a particular actor should face the camera. This places emphasis on the actor's next line of dialogue because he or she will be looking directly at the audience.

BACKGROUND

Charly Although the basic story line of *Charly* is similar to "Flowers for Algernon," several events, characters, and details of setting are different. For example, in the movie, Charlie works in a bakery in Boston, Massachusetts, instead of a box factory in New York City. The character of Dr. Strauss is a woman, Dr. Anna Strauss, as shown in the movie still on this page. Charlie vigorously pursues a romantic relationship with Miss Kinnian, only to be rejected and then accepted when it is too late. Also, in the film version, Charlie rebels by joining a biker gang.

For his part as Charlie in the movie, the actor Cliff Robertson won an Academy Award. Since *Charly* was released in 1968, other versions of the story have been produced, including a made-for-television movie entitled *Flowers for Algernon* in 2000.

FOR ENGLISH LEARNERS

Task Support [small-group option] Divide the students into groups of five. Assign four of the students in the group the role of one of the characters to read aloud. The fifth student will read the stage directions. Then give the students time to act out the scene. The student who reads the stage directions will act as the director.

Lines 28–46

LITERARY ANALYSIS

● CHARACTER TRAITS

In what manner does Charlie give his reasons for wanting the operation? What do his reasons reveal about his character? ***Possible answer:*** *He speaks sincerely and eagerly, knowing that this is his chance to convince the doctors of his worthiness for the operation. His reasons show his desire to improve himself and his willingness to take a risk to do so.*

Lines 64–105

DISCUSSION PROMPTS

Use these prompts to help students understand the importance of the maze race as it is portrayed in the screenplay:

Connect Are you surprised at Charlie's reaction to losing the race to Algernon? Why or why not? *Students may say that they are surprised, because they would expect Charlie to be upset or mad. Instead he shrugs and then smiles at Algernon.*

Analyze What abilities is the maze race testing? Explain. ***Possible answer:*** *It evaluates Charlie's ability to solve problems, reason, learn from his mistakes, and make quick decisions.*

Synthesize What does the maze race reveal about Charlie's candidacy for the operation? ***Possible answer:*** *Although Charlie thinks he has failed the test, in fact, the results probably qualify him. The race shows Charlie to be limited in his abilities but determined. He does not give up even though he is being shocked constantly.*

SELECTION WRAP–UP

REFLECT Ask students how knowing Charlie might affect the lives of other characters.

★ **CRITIQUE** Have students discuss whether the short story would have been improved if other characters' points of view on the events had been included.

READING FLUENCY

Distribute the copy masters and have students practice fluency.

RESOURCE MANAGER—Copy Master
Reading Fluency p. 81

(Charlie *straightens, looks the two doctors straight in the eye—this is his big moment—and the words come now, tumbling.*)

Charlie. All my life I wantid to be smart not dumb. It's very hard to be smart. It's—kind of—slow. I mean, I *try*—but it's—slow. Even when I learn something in Miss Kinnian's class at the Training Center where I try the hardest it's slow—and I ferget. I used to think maybe it's because I talk to myself a lot—you know, I say, hey, Charlie—and stuff like that—but that don't slow me down—because I don't listen to myself.

(*He stops, out of breath, discovers that* Alice—*and the two doctors—still seem to expect more from him.*)

Charlie. Oh—the operashun! The operashun will make me smart. (*a beat—then to* Alice) Is that what you told me?

Alice Kinnian (*softly*). We *hope* it will, Charlie. But nobody knows for sure. Anyway . . . (*looking at the doctors*) . . . the doctors have to talk to a lot of other people too—before they decide who'll be the first to have this operation. (*favoring* Dr. Strauss)

Dr. Strauss. Charlie . . . how would you like to race Algernon?

Charlie (*grinning*). Sure, but . . . (*He looks down at the cage.*)

Charlie. I can't fit in there.

(Dr. Strauss *hands* Charlie *a long metal rod.*)

Dr. Strauss. We call this an electric stylus.

(*She guides* Charlie*'s hand holding the stylus into the open space between the walls of a maze which sits next to* Algernon*'s cage on the long bench before which they stand.*)

Dr. Strauss. When I say START—move the pencil along this line until you come to . . . that place there—the FINISH. If you move the wrong way, you'll get a shock.

(*She causes* Charlie*'s hand to touch the wall of a cul-de-sac.* Charlie *reacts.*)

Dr. Strauss. Did that hurt?

Charlie. Naw.

Dr. Strauss. That shock is a signal . . . it tells you to back up the stylus and go dow another row.

Alice Kinnian. You understand, Charlie?

(Charlie *nods reassuringly, smiles broadly. Thi is FUN.* Dr. Nemur *moves* Algernon *from th finish box to the start box.*)

Dr. Strauss. Ready?

(Charlie, *eager to begin, nods. He holds up his left hand, exhibiting the rabbit's foot.* Alice *sm at him reassuringly.*)

Dr. Strauss. Start.

(Dr. Strauss *waits until she sees that* Charlie *has already begun to guide the stylus, then she lifts the hatch and releases* Algernon. *Camera shots alternate between* Charlie *and* Algerno *as each "runs" his race.* Charlie*'s race is hardt run—it is actually one shock after another, o bafflement piled on top another, one dead end after another—then all too quickly* Algernon *telltale victory squeak is heard.* Charlie *looks over at* Algernon *in the finish box.* Dr. Strau *is feeding him a small piece of cheese. Close-up on* Charlie *as he considers what has just happened. He looks up at* Alice, *who is smiling reassuringly.* Dr. Nemur*'s face is without expression.* Charlie *brings the stylus out of the maze. He shrugs.*)

Charlie. Anybody so stoopid even a little mo can beat him you sure don't want to give hi no operashun. I don't blame you!

(*He puts down the stylus, leans closer to the cag and smiles in wonder at* Algernon.)

Charlie. I dint know mice was so smart.

DIFFERENTIATED INSTRUCTION

FOR ADVANCED LEARNERS/PRE–AP

Synthesize Discuss with students the significance of language in the story that they have just finished. Will Charlie's spoken language in the film carry the same impact as seeing it written on the page? Ask students to debate this question and consider other ways in which the screenplay might show Charlie's transformation.

Compare and Contrast Have students return to lines 61–74 of the story and compare that account of the maze race to the screenplay. What are the strengths of each version? Ask students to support their opinions with examples from the story.

mprehension

1. **Recall** What type of operation does Charlie undergo?
2. **Clarify** Why does Charlie decide to leave New York at the end of the story?
3. **Clarify** In *Charly,* what is the purpose of the electric stylus?

erary Analysis

4. **Identify Character Traits** If you haven't done this yet, fill in the bottom of your Y-chart with traits that Charlie showed throughout the story. How much did the operation change Charlie's character? Use notes on your chart to support your answer.
5. **Understand Plot Elements** The technique of hinting about something that will occur later in a story is called **foreshadowing**. Explain how Algernon's death is an example of this technique.
6. **Analyze a Long Story** This story covers a period of five months. Analyze the progress reports from each of these months to determine the change in Charlie's abilities. Track your results on a graph like the one shown. How quickly did Charlie Gordon's intelligence rise and fall?

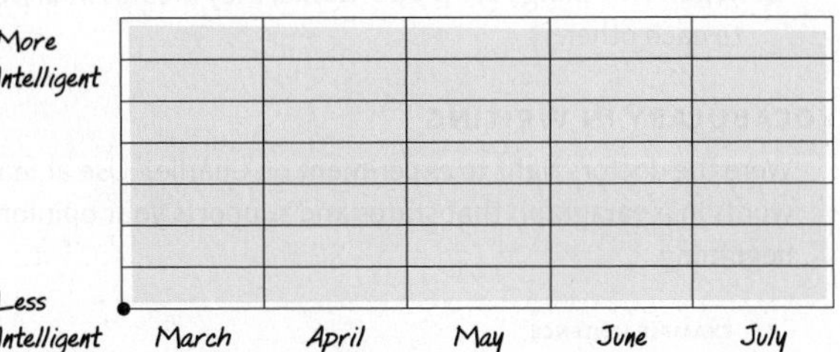

7. **Analyze Parallel Episodes** A **parallel episode** is a repeated element in a story's plot. For example, Charlie races Algernon both before he has the operation and after. Identify at least three other parallel episodes in this story. What is the purpose of repeating these elements?
8. **Compare Texts** Think about the ways that the short story and the screenplay present the scene in which Charlie meets Algernon. What are the similarities and differences? Consider the amount of detail each selection provides.

tension and Challenge

9. **Big Question Activity** Discuss the following question with a small group: Would Charlie have been better off if he had never gained the **knowledge** he did? Consider how he feels at different points in the story.
10. **Literary Criticism** A literary critic wrote that "Flowers for Algernon" has "one of the most perfect and perfectly controlled narrative arcs in the entire history of the short story . . . ." A **narrative arc** is the shape a story's plot takes as it slowly rises, reaches a high point, and then falls to reach a resolution. What do you think the critic meant by this comment?

Practice and Apply

After Reading

For additional support of postreading questions, use these copy masters:

RESOURCE MANAGER—Copy Masters
Reading Check p. 78 (to check understanding of the selection)
Reading a Long Story p. 73 (for practice of reading standards focus)
Question Support p. 79 (After Reading questions adapted for English learners and less-proficient readers)

Additional selection questions are provided for teachers on page 65.

For additional activities to challenge students, see

Power Thinking at **ClassZone.com**

ANSWERS

Comprehension

1. *Charlie has brain surgery to increase his intelligence.*
2. *Charlie doesn't want people to pity him, so he wants to go to a place where no one knew him when he was smart.*
3. *The electric stylus gives a shock when the wrong move is made.*

Literary Analysis

Possible answers:

4. ● **STANDARDS FOCUS Character Traits** *Traits in the third section include curious, kind, hard-working, caring, and gentle. The operation increased Charlie's intelligence and allowed him to feel a wider range of emotions, but it did not change his basic personality.*
5. *Algernon and Charlie had the same kind of operation. When Algernon dies, it foreshadows that Charlie's fate will be the same.*
6. ■ **STANDARDS FOCUS Reading a Long Story** *Students' graphs should show that Charlie's intelligence ascends and reaches its peak in May. By the first week of June, Charlie's deterioration has begun. His intelligence declines back to its pre-operation level by the end of July. The graph should show a perfect arc.*
7. *Other parallel episodes include Charlie's taking the Rorschach test twice with different results, Charlie's going out with his coworkers before and after the operation, and Charlie's being escorted home by a policeman on two different occasions. These episodes show the change in Charlie's intelligence level.*
8. *The screenplay includes more detail about how Charlie reacts when he meets Algernon and about the actual race through the maze. In both the story and the screenplay, Charlie loses to Algernon in this pre-operation race.*

Extension and Challenge

9. *Remind students to support their opinions with evidence from the text.*
10. *The critic means that the story is perfectly balanced. The part of the plot depicting Charlie's increase in intelligence is matched by the part showing his decline. There is a definite turning point when he is at the height of his intellectual powers and Algernon starts to show signs of deterioration.*

ANSWERS

Vocabulary in Context

VOCABULARY PRACTICE

1. *false*
2. *false*
3. *true*
4. *false*
5. *false*
6. *true*
7. *true*
8. *false*

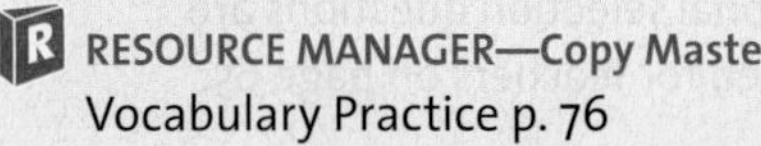

RESOURCE MANAGER—Copy Master
Vocabulary Practice p. 76

VOCABULARY IN WRITING

To help students clarify their opinions, have them discuss the question with a partner. Then ask them to jot down their reasons and scan the vocabulary list to see which choices will help them articulate these ideas.

VOCABULARY STRATEGY: SPECIALIZED VOCABULARY *(also an EL language objective)*

Remind students that they should match any familiar words with their definitions first to help narrow the choices for the remaining terms.

Answers:

1. *(c) an assumption used as the basis for research*
2. *(a) symptoms that characterize a disease or disorder*
3. *(b) a return to a less developed condition*
4. *(d) examining one's own thoughts, feelings, and sensations*

RESOURCE MANAGER—Copy Master
Vocabulary Strategy p. 77

Vocabulary Center at **ClassZone.com**
Additional Vocabulary Activities

Vocabulary in Context

VOCABULARY PRACTICE

Show that you understand the boldfaced words. Decide if each statement is true or false.

absurd, refute, impair, sensation, opportunist, specialization, proportional, tangible

1. Something that causes a **sensation** is not of much interest.
2. A **specialization** means a little knowledge about a lot of things.
3. If something is **absurd,** it's unusual or ridiculous.
4. You cannot touch something that is **tangible.**
5. To **refute** something is to agree with it wholeheartedly.
6. Lack of sleep can **impair** your ability to stay alert.
7. An **opportunist** might take advantage of someone to achieve a goal.
8. When two things are **proportional,** they are not at all related to each other.

VOCABULARY IN WRITING

Were the doctors right to experiment on Charlie? Use at least three vocabulary words in a paragraph that states and supports your opinion. Here is a sample beginning.

EXAMPLE SENTENCE

*Just because research might cause a **sensation** doesn't mean doctors should conduct it.*

VOCABULARY STRATEGY: SPECIALIZED VOCABULARY

Many of the words used in this selection are specialized terms that relate to the study of psychology. Knowing the meanings of these words can help you understand more about this field of study.

PRACTICE Match the word in the first column with its definition in the second column. Use a dictionary if you need help.

1. hypothesis	a. symptoms that characterize a disease or disorder
2. syndrome	b. a return to a less developed condition
3. regression	c. an assumption used as the basis for research
4. introspective	d. examining one's own thoughts, feelings, and sensations

VOCABULARY PRACTICE
For more practice, go to the **Vocabulary Cente** at **ClassZone.com.**

DIFFERENTIATED INSTRUCTION

FOR ENGLISH LEARNERS

Vocabulary Practice Point out the Spanish cognates for several of the vocabulary words: *absurd/absurdo, opportunist/oportunista, refute/refutar, sensation/sensación, specialization/especialización, tangible/tangible.* Remind students to use their knowledge of the cognates to respond to each statement.

FOR ADVANCED LEARNERS/PRE-AP

Vocabulary in Writing Challenge students to develop their paragraph into a speech in which they examine the ethics of the experiment on Charlie. Have students include as many vocabulary words as possible and give their speech to the class.

ading-Writing Connection

xplore the issues raised in "Flowers for Algernon" by responding to these rompts. Then complete the **Grammar and Writing** exercise.

WRITING PROMPTS	SELF-CHECK
A. Short Response: Write a Progress Report What do you think happens to Charlie after the story ends? Write a progress report that Charlie might have written after he left New York. Model the sentence structure, grammar, and spelling in your **one-paragraph report** on the reports in the story.	***A successful report will . . .*** • accurately portray Charlie's character traits • use language that reflects Charlie's intelligence level
B. Extended Response: Evaluate Traits After reading this story, do you think having **knowledge** makes a person happier, kinder, or generally better? Write a **two- or three-paragraph response,** citing as evidence two or more characters.	***A good evaluation will . . .*** • include a statement that answers the question • support the statement with appropriate details

MMAR AND WRITING

OMPARE CORRECTLY The **comparative form** of a modifier is used to compare nly two people or things. For most one-syllable modifiers, add *-er* (brighter, loser) to form the comparative. For most modifiers with two or more syllables, se the word *more* (more important, more easily).

The **superlative form** is used to compare three or more people or things. or most one-syllable modifiers, add *-est* (brightest, closest). For most modifiers vith two or more syllables, use the word *most* (most important, most easily).

Example: Dr. Strauss is closer to being a genius than Dr. Nemur. (*Two things are being compared, and* close *has one syllable.*)

Example: Even the most intelligent person in the world must be unhappy sometimes. (*More than two things are being compared, and* intelligent *has more than one syllable.*)

RACTICE Choose the correct form to complete each sentence.

1. Charlie Gordon becomes (smarter, more smart) than he was before.
2. Dr. Strauss and Dr. Nemur might be the (brightest, most bright) doctors in their field, but they do not always make good decisions.
3. At first, Charlie is (more content, contenter) at his job than at the lab.
4. Miss Kinnian is the person (more, most) worried about Charlie's well-being.

or more help with comparative and superlative forms, see page R58 in the ***rammar Handbook.***

Reading-Writing Connection

WRITING PROMPTS

- For **Prompt A,** discuss the kinds of errors and phrasing that are part of Charlie's style. Then have students outline the ideas that they want to include before they write their paragraphs.
- For **Prompt B,** suggest that students list all of the characters, including Charlie both before and after the operation, and indicate each character's level of knowledge. Then have students circle the ones that they feel are kind, happy, or good, and draw some conclusions about the relationship between knowledge and these qualities, based on their list.

For an extended Reading-Writing Connection activity, see

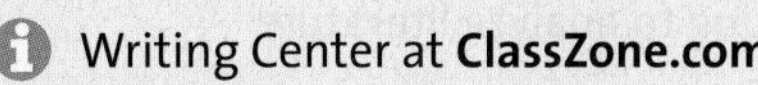

Writing Center at **ClassZone.com**

GRAMMAR AND WRITING

Identify each modifier in the sentences as having one or more syllables before students choose the correct form.

Answers:

1. *smarter*
2. *brightest*
3. *more content*
4. *most*

RESOURCE MANAGER—Copy Master
Compare Correctly p. 80

Assess and Reteach

Assess

RESOURCE MANAGER—Copy Masters
Selection Tests A, B/C pp. 83–84, 85–86

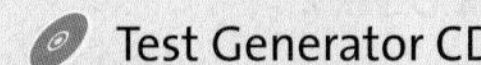

Test Generator CD

Reteach

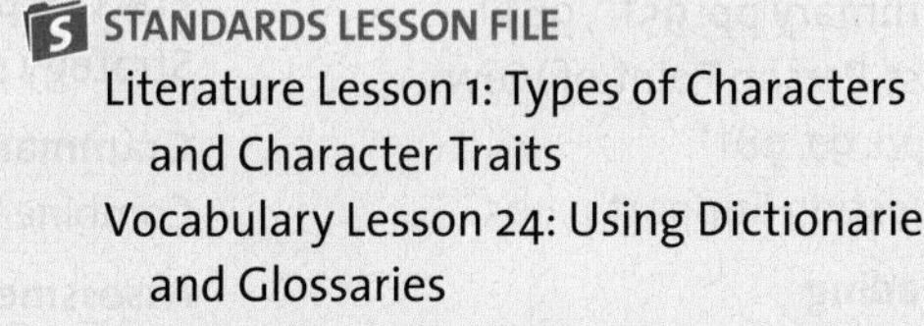

STANDARDS LESSON FILE
Literature Lesson 1: Types of Characters and Character Traits
Vocabulary Lesson 24: Using Dictionaries and Glossaries

FOR LESS–PROFICIENT WRITERS

For Prompt A:

1. As a class, discuss what Charlie might do after he leaves New York. For example, he will need to find a job and might look for another factory to work in. Record some possible ideas on the board.
2. Have students reread the last few paragraphs of the story to remind themselves of Charlie's style before writing their paragraphs independently.

For Prompt B:

1. Have students return to their completed Y-charts and discuss whether Charlie is happier, kinder, or better before or after the operation. Encourage students to give examples from the story.
2. Help students craft a topic sentence, such as *Charlie's increased intelligence does not make him a better or happier person.* Suggest that students use details from the discussion to develop their paragraphs.

Focus and Motivate

OBJECTIVES

Literary Analysis
- explore the key idea of an **opponent**
- identify and analyze first-person point of view
- read a short story

Reading
- draw conclusions

Vocabulary
- build vocabulary for reading and writing
- determine meanings of derivatives by using knowledge of affixes and base words *(also an EL language objective)*
- identify and use the prefixes *fore-* and *mal-* *(also an EL language objective)*

Grammar and Writing
- combine sentences by using coordinating conjunctions
- use writing to analyze literature

SUMMARY

Waverly, the daughter of Chinese immigrants, becomes a chess prodigy. Her parents encourage her talent, but she is embarrassed by her mother's intense interest. After a blow-up in which Waverly accuses her mother of trying to take credit for her successes, she realizes she needs a new strategy to deal with her mother.

Can allies be OPPONENTS?

Discuss the question. To lead into the ***KEY IDEA,*** ask students how people who are supportive can seem like **opponents.** Then have students complete the ***QUICKWRITE*** activity.

Before Reading

Rules of the Game

Short Story by Amy Tan

Can allies be OPPONENTS?

KEY IDEA Family, friends, coaches—these are people who usually want the best for you. Then why can it feel like they're always giving you a hard time? Understanding people's good intentions can be challenging, and it may even feel like your supporters aren't on your side. In "Rules of the Game," find out why a young girl sees her mother—who is her biggest fan—as her main **opponent.**

QUICKWRITE Think of one or two people in your life who want you to be the best you can be. Then write a brief journal entry about your relationship with them. In what ways does their support help you? In what ways does their support make things harder for you?

222

Selection Resources

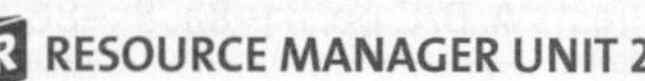

Plan and Teach pp. 87–94

Literary Analysis
Summary pp. 95†*, 96‡*
First-Person Point of View pp. 97, 98†*
Question Support p. 105*

Reading
Draw Conclusions pp. 99, 100†*
Reading Check p. 104
Reading Fluency p. 107

Vocabulary
Study p. 101*
Practice p. 102
Strategy p. 103

Grammar and Writing
Combine Sentences p. 106

Assessment
Selection Tests A, B/C pp. 109*, 111*
Test Generator CD

BEST PRACTICES TOOLKIT

Differentiated Instruction pp. 31–38*
Scaffolding Instruction pp. 43–46*

Graphic Organizers/Strategies
New Word Analysis • Two-Column Chart • Character Traits and Textual Evidence • Common Suffixes • Ask the Experts

Reading Support
Audio Anthology CD*

Technology
Literature, Vocabulary, and Writing Centers at **ClassZone.com**
Write*Smart* CD

* Resources for Differentiation † Also in Spanish ‡ In Haitian Creole and Vietnamese

Teach

ERARY ANALYSIS: FIRST-PERSON POINT OF VIEW

When a writer uses the **first-person point of view,** the narrator is a character in the story—usually the main character. A story is told in the first-person point of view when the narrator

- describes people and events as he or she experiences them
- uses the pronouns *I* and *me* to talk about himself or herself
- doesn't know what other characters are thinking and feeling

As you read, notice how seeing people and events through the narrator's eyes affects your understanding of the selection.

DING SKILL: DRAW CONCLUSIONS

In reading and in life, you often have to **draw conclusions,** or make logical judgments, about things that are not directly stated. Follow these steps to draw a conclusion:

- Gather evidence from the literature.
- Consider your own experience and knowledge.
- Make a judgment that combines both.

As you read, use a chart like the one shown to help you form conclusions about Waverly's relationship with her mother.

Evidence	*My Thoughts*	*Conclusion*
Mrs. Jong scolds Waverly for crying out for salted plums.	*I know parents try to teach their kids how to behave.*	*Mrs. Jong wants Waverly to learn self-control.*

Review: **Visualize**

CABULARY IN CONTEXT

Amy Tan uses the words listed to help her describe one girl's conflicts with her mother. Place each word in the appropriate column of a chart like the one shown.

WORD LIST			
adversary	impart	pungent	
benefactor	malodorous	retort	
concession	ponder	tactic	
foresight			

Know Well	*Think I Know*	*Don't Know at All*

Author Online

Change of Heart The daughter of Chinese immigrants, Amy Tan grew up in California having little interest in her heritage. When she was a teenager, her father and older brother died. Their deaths devastated her, and her rocky relationship with her mother became worse. Tan's mother wanted her to become a doctor or a concert pianist, but Tan became a business writer instead. She later turned to fiction writing as a hobby, which helped her express her emotions about her family and embrace her Chinese heritage as an important part of her identity. Tan's hobby became her new career.

Amy Tan
born 1952

Mother-Daughter Ties Tan wrote "Rules of the Game" for a writing workshop in 1985. She later used it as part of her first novel, *The Joy Luck Club,* which is a series of interconnected stories about four Chinese mothers and their Chinese-American daughters. Tan's family stories have inspired her writing. She once said of her mother, "My books have amounted to taking her stories—a gift to me—and giving them back to her."

MORE ABOUT THE AUTHOR
For more on Amy Tan, visit the **Literature Center** at **ClassZone.com.**

Background

An Old Game Lives On Although the game of chess is hundreds of years old, competitive chess remains a popular pastime today. A special class of players strives for the title of grand master, which only the top 0.02% of tournament players worldwide earn. A player must accumulate at least 2,500 points in tournament play to be recognized as a grand master by the World Chess Federation.

STANDARDS FOCUS

LITERARY ANALYSIS

● FIRST–PERSON POINT OF VIEW

Read this sentence aloud:

Lynn was excited when the famous actor gave her his autograph.

Ask students to rephrase the sentence from the first-person point of view. ***Possible answer:*** *I was excited when the famous actor gave me his autograph.*

CHECK UNDERSTANDING Ask students whether their first-person narrator could say how the actor felt during this scene.

READING SKILL

■ DRAW CONCLUSIONS

Read this passage aloud:

The boy was clearly upset that he had lost the match. His fist clenched his tennis racket as he prepared to throw it. Then he looked over at his older brother. After a moment, he relaxed and told his opponent, "Good match."

Ask: What can you conclude about the brothers? ***Possible answer:*** *The boy respects his older brother, who is his role model for good sportsmanship.*

CHECK UNDERSTANDING Have students draw conclusions about what is happening in the photograph on page 222.

RESOURCE MANAGER—Copy Master
Draw Conclusions p. 99 (for student use while reading the selection)

VOCABULARY SKILL

▲ VOCABULARY IN CONTEXT

DIAGNOSE WORD KNOWLEDGE To determine preteaching needs, have all students complete **Vocabulary in Context.** Check to make sure students have considered all the words and placed them in the chart.

PRETEACH VOCABULARY Use the Vocabulary Study copy master to help students determine the meaning of each boldfaced word.

1. Read aloud the first sentence, emphasizing the boldfaced word.
2. Ask students to look for context clues in the sentence. Discuss possible meanings for *adversary,* such as "opponent."
3. Repeat for the other sentences.
4. Have students work with a partner to answer the questions in Part B.

RESOURCE MANAGER—Copy Master
Vocabulary Study p. 101

For general guidelines on differentiating vocabulary instruction and for alternative vocabulary activities for students not needing vocabulary preteaching, see

BEST PRACTICES TOOLKIT
Scaffolding Vocabulary Instruction pp. 43–46

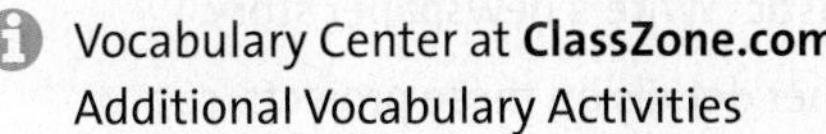

Vocabulary Center at **ClassZone.com**
Additional Vocabulary Activities

Practice and Apply

ANALYZE VISUALS

Possible answer: *The girl's face and the chess pieces closest to her are more in focus than the foreground or background of the photograph. This emphasizes the girl's concentration on her next move in the game and leads the viewer to focus on her.*

LITERARY ANALYSIS

A POINT OF VIEW

Possible answer: *The narrator is a Chinese-American girl. She suggests that her mother has strict rules for proper behavior.*

Lines 1–11

REINFORCE *KEY IDEA:* OPPONENT

Discuss What strategy does Waverly learn to get what she wants from an **opponent?**

Possible answer: *She learns that she cannot use force against a stronger opponent, such as her mother. Instead, she must learn to be patient and wait for the best opportunity to get what she wants. In some cases, the best strategy is simply to play by the rules in the hope of being rewarded by those in power.*

Amy Tan

I was six when my mother taught me the art of invisible strength. It was a strategy for winning arguments, respect from others, and eventually, though neither of us knew it at the time, chess games.

"Bite back your tongue," scolded my mother when I cried loudly, yanking her hand toward the store that sold bags of salted plums. At home, she said, "Wise guy, he not go against wind. In Chinese we say, Come from South, blow with wind—poom!—North will follow. Strongest wind cannot be seen."

The next week I bit back my tongue as we entered the store with the forbidden candies. When my mother finished her shopping, she quietly plucked a small bag of plums from the rack and put it on the counter with the rest of the items. **A**

My mother **imparted** her daily truths so she could help my older brothers and me rise above our circumstances. We lived in San Francisco's Chinatown. Like most of the other Chinese children who played in the back alleys of restaurants and curio shops,[1] I didn't think we were poor. My bowl was always full, three five-course meals every day, beginning with a soup full of mysterious things I didn't want to know the names of.

We lived on Waverly Place, in a warm, clean, two-bedroom flat that sat above a small Chinese bakery specializing in steamed pastries and dim sum.[2]

ANALYZE VISUALS
Note which **details** of
photograph are in foc
and which are blurry.
What effect does this
have on you, the viewe

1 Targeted Passage

A POINT OF VIEW
Identify who is telling this story. What has sh suggested about her relationship with her mother so far?

impart (ĭm-pärt') *v.* to make known; reveal

1. **curio shops:** shops that sell curious or unusual objects.
2. **dim sum:** small portions of a variety of Chinese foods and dumplings.

DIFFERENTIATED INSTRUCTION

FOR ALL STUDENTS

Enhance Learning Styles Provide these independent projects for various learning styles:

- **Visual** Design a chess set.
- **Analytical** Research Chinese immigration to the United States.
- **Linguistic** Write a newspaper story.

For further details on these projects, see

RESOURCE MANAGER
Ideas for Extension pp. 92–93

FOR LESS–PROFICIENT READERS

In combination with the *Audio Anthology CD*, use one or more Targeted Passages (pp. 224, 231, 233) to ensure that students focus on key story events, concepts, and skills.

1 Targeted Passage [Lines 1–11]

This passage introduces the story's main characters: the narrator and her mother.

- What does the narrator's mother teach her at age six?
- Why does the narrator cry one day when she is shopping with her mother?
- How does the narrator end up getting what she wants?

BACKGROUND

The Game of Kings The complex game of chess probably had its origins in India about 1,500 years ago, with a war game called *chaturanga*. As in modern chess, each piece in *chaturanga* had different powers, and the winner of the game was the person whose king was the last one standing.

From India, the game spread east to Asia, and from there to the Middle East. Later, with the spread of Islam, chess came to North Africa, Sicily, and Spain. The Vikings brought the game to Iceland and England, and Slavs brought the game to Russia.

For many centuries, chess was known as "the game of kings" or "the royal game," both because it was popular among the nobility and because it was considered good training for those engaged in warfare. Each culture added its own variations to the game. The rules and set design we are familiar with today became standard in the early 19th century.

Today, chess is no longer just a game for royalty and the upper classes. Players of all ages and all walks of life compete one-on-one, by mail, by e-mail, and on the Internet. Most nations have chess tournaments for both young people and adults, and the outcome of the World Chess Championship is of international interest.

FOR LESS–PROFICIENT READERS

Options for Reading Read the first three paragraphs aloud and make sure students understand the setting and who is telling the story. Then have students read the rest of the selection silently as they listen to the *Audio Anthology CD*. Pause the CD frequently to enable students to make predictions.

FOR ENGLISH LEARNERS

Key Academic Vocabulary Have students use New Word Analysis to study *invisible* (lines 1, 166), *strategy* (line 2), *obvious(ly)* (lines 112, 301), *conclude* (line 150), and *concentrate* (line 278).

BEST PRACTICES TOOLKIT—Transparency
New Word Analysis p. E8

Prereading For prereading instruction for English learners, see

BEST PRACTICES TOOLKIT
Scaffolding Reading Instruction pp. 43–46

FOR ADVANCED LEARNERS/PRE–AP

Pre-AP exercises in the bottom channel provide additional challenge for your advanced students. Use them for small groups or individuals.

ADDITIONAL GUIDELINES

For more help with differentiation and tips for classroom management, see

BEST PRACTICES TOOLKIT
Differentiated Instruction pp. 31–38

In the early morning, when the alley was still quiet, I could smell fragrant red beans as they were cooked down to a pasty sweetness. By daybreak, our flat was heavy with the odor of fried sesame balls and sweet curried chicken crescents. From my bed, I would listen as my father got ready for work, then locked the door behind him, one-two-three clicks.

At the end of our two-block alley was a small sandlot playground with swings and slides well-shined down the middle with use. The play area was bordered by wood-slat benches where old-country people sat cracking roasted watermelon seeds with their golden teeth and scattering the husks to an impatient gathering of gurgling pigeons. The best playground, however, was the dark alley itself. It was crammed with daily mysteries and adventures. My brothers and I would peer into the medicinal herb shop, watching old Li[3] dole out onto a stiff sheet of white paper the right amount of insect shells, saffron-colored seeds, and **pungent** leaves for his ailing customers. It was said that he once cured a woman dying of an ancestral curse that had eluded the best of American doctors. Next to the pharmacy was a printer who specialized in gold-embossed wedding invitations and festive red banners. **B**

Farther down the street was Ping Yuen[4] Fish Market. The front window displayed a tank crowded with doomed fish and turtles struggling to gain footing on the slimy green-tiled sides. A hand-written sign informed tourists, "Within this store, is all for food, not for pet." Inside, the butchers with their bloodstained white smocks deftly gutted the fish while customers cried out their orders and shouted, "Give me your freshest," to which the butchers always protested, "All are freshest." On less crowded market days, we would inspect the crates of live frogs and crabs which we were warned not to poke, boxes of dried cuttlefish, and row upon row of iced prawns, squid, and slippery fish. The sanddabs made me shiver each time; their eyes lay on one flattened side and reminded me of my mother's story of a careless girl who ran into a crowded street and was crushed by a cab. "Was smash flat," reported my mother.

At the corner of the alley was Hong Sing's, a four-table café with a recessed stairwell in front that led to a door marked "Tradesmen." My brothers and I believed the bad people emerged from this door at night. Tourists never went to Hong Sing's, since the menu was printed only in Chinese. A Caucasian man with a big camera once posed me and my playmates in front of the restaurant. He had us move to the side of the picture window so the photo would capture the roasted duck with its head dangling from a juice-covered rope. After he took the picture, I told him he should go into Hong Sing's and eat dinner. When he smiled and asked me what they served, I shouted, "Guts and duck's feet and octopus gizzards!" Then I ran off with my friends, shrieking with laughter as we scampered across the alley and hid in the entryway grotto[5] of the China Gem Company, my heart pounding with hope that he would chase us. **C**

pungent (pŭn′jənt) a sharp or intense

B VISUALIZE
Reread lines 25–36. What words help you picture the neighborhood?

C POINT OF VIEW
Reread lines 49–60. What do the narrator' words and actions tell you about her attitud toward taking risks?

3. **Li** (lē).
4. **Ping Yuen** (bĭng yü′ĕn).
5. **grotto** (grŏt′ō): an artificial structure made to resemble a cave or cavern.

READING STRATEGY: *Review*

B VISUALIZE

Possible answer: *Phrases include* small sandlot playground, slides well-shined down the middle with use, wood-slat benches, gurgling pigeons, dark alley, medicinal herb shop, *and* festive red banners.

LITERARY ANALYSIS

C POINT OF VIEW

Possible answer: *Waverly seems to enjoy taking risks. She plays near a café where she believes "bad people" spend time; she boldly shouts at a man who is taking a picture of her and her friends; she hopes the man will chase them.*

DIFFERENTIATED INSTRUCTION

FOR LESS–PROFICIENT READERS

Review: Visualize Point out that the description of the fish market in lines 37–48 is filled with vivid sensory details. Ask students to close their eyes as you read the passage aloud. Ask them to identify details of sight, sound, touch, taste, and smell in the passage and list these details in separate columns on the board. Then encourage students to draw pictures of the setting.

FOR ENGLISH LEARNERS

Background Explain that this story is set in San Francisco's Chinatown in the 1950s. After World War II, the relaxation of immigration laws and the growth of Communist China led to a major population boom of Chinese immigrants in the region. The narrator's parents were among these immigrants. Today more than 75 percent of Chinatown's residents are foreign-born, and the San Francisco area has one of the largest Chinese populations outside of China.

FOR ADVANCED LEARNERS/PRE–AP

Synthesize After students read page 226, have them think about sensory details that describe their own neighborhood—either past or current—or another neighborhood they visit often. Challenge students to use details that appeal to each of the five senses. Then ask them to use these details in a brief description of the neighborhood.

My mother named me after the street that we lived on: Waverly Place Jong, my official name for important American documents. But my family called me Meimei,[6] "Little Sister." I was the youngest, the only daughter. Each morning before school, my mother would twist and yank on my thick black hair until she had formed two tightly wound pigtails. One day, as she struggled to weave a hard-toothed comb through my disobedient hair, I had a sly thought.

I asked her, "Ma, what is Chinese torture?" My mother shook her head. A bobby pin was wedged between her lips. She wetted her palm and smoothed the hair above my ear, then pushed the pin in so that it nicked sharply against my scalp.

"Who say this word?" she asked without a trace of knowing how wicked I was being. I shrugged my shoulders and said, "Some boy in my class said Chinese people do Chinese torture."

"Chinese people do many things," she said simply. "Chinese people do business, do medicine, do painting. Not lazy like American people. We do torture. Best torture." **D**

My older brother Vincent was the one who actually got the chess set. We had gone to the annual Christmas party held at the First Chinese Baptist Church at the end of the alley. The missionary ladies had put together a Santa bag of gifts donated by members of another church. None of the gifts had names on them. There were separate sacks for boys and girls of different ages.

ANALYZE VISUALS
This photograph shows a Chinese market in San Francisco. How would you describe the **setting?**

D DRAW CONCLUSIONS
How does Waverly feel about her mother fixing her hair?

6. **Meimei** (mā'mā).

ANALYZE VISUALS

Possible answer: *The setting is colorful and filled with many kinds of produce. The signs are written in Chinese, and a few shoppers are examining the produce.*

READING SKILL

D DRAW CONCLUSIONS

Have students record their answers in the chart from page 223. ***Possible answer:***

- ***Evidence:*** *Her mother twists and yanks Waverly's hair and nicks Waverly's scalp with a pin. Waverly brings up the topic of torture.*
- ***My Thoughts:*** *This sort of treatment is painful and unpleasant.*
- ***Conclusion:*** *Waverly doesn't like having her mother fix her hair.*

FOR LESS–PROFICIENT READERS

Comprehension Support [paired option] Students may have some difficulty understanding Mrs. Jong's English. Explain that because she is still learning English, she does not use correct subject-verb agreement, she uses incorrect verb tenses, and she frequently leaves out articles, subjects, or verbs. Model how the sentences would sound in standard English:

- *Was smash flat* (line 48), "She was smashed flat"
- *Who say this word?* (line 72), "Who says this word?"
- *Not lazy like American people* (line 76), "We are not lazy like American people"

Ask pairs to record examples of Mrs. Jong's dialogue in column 1 of a Two-Column Chart. Then have them record their restatements in column 2.

BEST PRACTICES TOOLKIT—Transparency
Two-Column Chart p. A25

READING SKILL

E DRAW CONCLUSIONS

Have students record their answers in the chart from page 223. ***Possible answer:***

- ***Evidence:*** *"She not want it. We not want it."*
- ***My Thoughts:*** *It feels insulting to be given something as a gift that is used and broken.*
- ***Conclusion:*** *Mrs. Jong doesn't like to take other people's castoffs; she's proud.*

Lines 92–125
DISCUSSION PROMPTS

Use these prompts to help students understand the exposition:

Recall What gifts do Waverly and her brothers receive at the party? ***Answer:*** *Waverly receives a package of Life Savers, her brother Winston is given a submarine model, and her brother Vincent receives a chess set.*

Contrast Waverly's mother has two reactions to the gift of the chess set—one at the church, and one at home. What do her different reactions reveal about her character? ***Possible answer:*** *Waverly's mother is polite at the party, but her dismissal of the gift at home shows that she doesn't like accepting used items. She is polite, and she is proud. She feels that her family deserves things that are as nice as other people's.*

Synthesize Waverly's reaction to the chess set is enthusiastic. How do the references to Old Li's magic herbs and Hong Sing's café reflect her enthusiasm? ***Possible answer:*** *She has already described her fascination with Old Li's magic herbs and the secret danger of Hong Sing's café. She has the same feeling of excitement and enthusiasm about the chess set.*

One of the Chinese parishioners had donned a Santa Claus costume and a stiff paper beard with cotton balls glued to it. I think the only children who thought he was the real thing were too young to know that Santa Claus was not Chinese. When my turn came up, the Santa man asked me how old I was. I thought it was a trick question; I was seven according to the American formula and eight by the Chinese calendar. I said I was born on March 17, 1951. That seemed to satisfy him. He then solemnly asked if I had been a very, very good girl this year and did I believe in Jesus Christ and obey my parents. I knew the only answer to that. I nodded back with equal solemnity.

Having watched the other children opening their gifts, I already knew that the big gifts were not necessarily the nicest ones. One girl my age got a large coloring book of biblical characters, while a less greedy girl who selected a smaller box received a glass vial of lavender toilet water. The sound of the box was also important. A ten-year-old boy had chosen a box that jangled when he shook it. It was a tin globe of the world with a slit for inserting money. He must have thought it was full of dimes and nickels, because when he saw that it had just ten pennies, his face fell with such undisguised disappointment that his mother slapped the side of his head and led him out of the church hall, apologizing to the crowd for her son who had such bad manners he couldn't appreciate such a fine gift.

As I peered into the sack, I quickly fingered the remaining presents, testing their weight, imagining what they contained. I chose a heavy, compact one that was wrapped in shiny silver foil and a red satin ribbon. It was a twelve-pack of Life Savers and I spent the rest of the party arranging and rearranging the candy tubes in the order of my favorites. My brother Winston chose wisely as well. His present turned out to be a box of intricate plastic parts; the instructions on the box proclaimed that when they were properly assembled he would have an authentic miniature replica of a World War II submarine.

Vincent got the chess set, which would have been a very decent present to get at a church Christmas party, except it was obviously used and, as we discovered later, it was missing a black pawn and a white knight. My mother graciously thanked the unknown **benefactor,** saying, "Too good. Cost too much." At which point, an old lady with fine white, wispy hair nodded toward our family and said with a whistling whisper, "Merry, merry Christmas."

When we got home, my mother told Vincent to throw the chess set away. "She not want it. We not want it," she said, tossing her head stiffly to the side with a tight, proud smile. My brothers had deaf ears. They were already lining up the chess pieces and reading from the dog-eared instruction book. **E**

I watched Vincent and Winston play during Christmas week. The chessboard seemed to hold elaborate secrets waiting to be untangled. The chessmen were more powerful than Old Li's magic herbs that cured ancestral curses. And my brothers wore such serious faces that I was sure something was at stake that was greater than avoiding the tradesmen's door to Hong Sing's.

"Let me! Let me!" I begged between games when one brother or the other would sit back with a deep sigh of relief and victory, the other annoyed, unable

benefactor (bĕn'ə-făk'tər) *n.* a pe who gives monetary o other aid

E DRAW CONCLUSIC Why does Mrs. Jong w Vincent to throw away chess set?

DIFFERENTIATED INSTRUCTION

FOR LESS–PROFICIENT READERS

Comprehension: Character Traits Help students understand how the narrator's thoughts and actions reveal character traits. Using quotes from page 228, help students fill in a Character Traits and Textual Evidence chart. Guide students to see that Waverly is intuitive, observant, and clever. Encourage them to add to the chart as they read.

BEST PRACTICES TOOLKIT—Transparency
Character Traits and Textual Evidence p. D6

FOR ENGLISH LEARNERS

Culture: Clarify Read aloud lines 86–88. Explain that in the traditional Chinese system for determining a person's age, a child is considered one year old at birth. A person does not become a year older on his or her actual birthday, but at the next New Year, which falls sometime between late January and late February by the Western calendar. So, by the Chinese system, Waverly was one year old at the time of her birth in March 1951 and is eight years old in December of 1958.

to let go of the outcome. Vincent at first refused to let me play, but when I offered my Life Savers as replacements for the buttons that filled in for the missing pieces, he relented. He chose the flavors: wild cherry for the black pawn and peppermint for the white knight. Winner could eat both.

As our mother sprinkled flour and rolled out small doughy circles for the steamed dumplings that would be our dinner that night, Vincent explained the rules, pointing to each piece. "You have sixteen pieces and so do I. One king and queen, two bishops, two knights, two castles, and eight pawns. The pawns can only move forward one step, except on the first move. Then they can move two. But they can only take men by moving crossways like this, except in the beginning, when you can move ahead and take another pawn."

"Why?" I asked as I moved my pawn. "Why can't they move more steps?"

"Because they're pawns," he said.

"But why do they go crossways to take other men? Why aren't there any women and children?"

"Why is the sky blue? Why must you always ask stupid questions?" asked Vincent. "This is a game. These are the rules. I didn't make them up. See. Here. In the book." He jabbed a page with a pawn in his hand. "Pawn. P-A-W-N. Pawn. Read it yourself."

My mother patted the flour off her hands. "Let me see book," she said quietly. She scanned the pages quickly, not reading the foreign English symbols, seeming to search deliberately for nothing in particular.

"This American rules," she concluded at last. "Every time people come out from foreign country, must know rules. You not know, judge say, Too bad, go back. They not telling you why so you can use their way go forward. They say, Don't know why, you find out yourself. But they knowing all the time. Better you take it, find out why yourself." She tossed her head back with a satisfied smile.

SOCIAL STUDIES CONNECTION
Waverly's mother might be suggesting something larger about American rules. Between the years 1882 and 1965, Chinese immigration to the U.S. was restricted. Those who were let into the country were not granted the same rights as other Americans.

I found out about all the whys later. I read the rules and looked up all the big words in a dictionary. I borrowed books from the Chinatown library. I studied each chess piece, trying to absorb the power each contained.

I learned about opening moves and why it's important to control the center early on; the shortest distance between two points is straight down the middle. I learned about the middle game and why **tactics** between two **adversaries** are like clashing ideas; the one who plays better has the clearest plans for both attacking and getting out of traps. I learned why it is essential in the endgame to have **foresight,** a mathematical understanding of all possible moves, and patience; all weaknesses and advantages become evident to a strong adversary and are obscured to a tiring opponent. I discovered that for the whole game one must gather invisible strengths and see the endgame before the game begins.

I also found out why I should never reveal "why" to others. A little knowledge withheld is a great advantage one should store for future use. That is the power of chess. It is a game of secrets in which one must show and never tell.

I loved the secrets I found within the sixty-four black and white squares. I carefully drew a handmade chessboard and pinned it to the wall next to my

tactic (tăk'tĭk) *n.* a maneuver to achieve a goal

adversary (ăd'vər-sĕr'ē) *n.* an opponent

foresight (fôr'sīt) *n.* perception of the significance of events before they have occurred

SOCIAL STUDIES CONNECTION

Chinese immigrant workers came to the United States in the 19th century to work as laborers in railroad construction, mining, and agriculture. As their numbers grew, they came to be perceived as a threat. In 1882, Congress passed the Chinese Exclusion Act, restricting Chinese immigration and preventing Chinese residents from becoming U.S. citizens. The act was finally repealed in 1943.

Lines 150–169
DISCUSSION PROMPTS

Use these prompts to help students understand the story's characters:

Connect Waverly eagerly learns everything she can about chess. When have you been excited in this way about learning something new? *Students should describe similar experiences they have had.*

Analyze How does Waverly's mother feel about "American rules"? In lines 150–154, is she talking about something other than chess? ***Possible answer:*** *She is frustrated because people are expected to know the rules but aren't told what they are. She might be referring to her experience as an immigrant in the United States.*

Speculate Why does Waverly enjoy chess so much? ***Possible answer:*** *She is intrigued by the conflict that takes place on the chessboard. She may feel she is learning lessons about real-life conflict from the game. Or, she may enjoy it simply because she is very good at it.*

FOR ENGLISH LEARNERS

Vocabulary Support [mixed-readiness pairs] Display a chess set and show students how the pieces are set up on a chessboard. Students will probably be familiar with the words *king* and *queen,* but they may need help with *bishop, knight,* and *castle.* Explain that the pawn is the piece with the least value and power. Have mixed-ability partners work to define unfamiliar words or phrases on this page and paraphrase the sentences in which the difficult words and phrases appear.

FOR ADVANCED LEARNERS/PRE–AP

Analyze After students read lines 155–169, have them discuss how each rule or lesson Waverly learns about chess might be interpreted as advice on how to succeed in life. Invite students to rephrase the lessons Waverly learns to make them work as lessons about life. For example, "it's important to control the center early on" (lines 158–159) might be rephrased as "it's important to get an early start on achieving your goals in life."

LITERARY ANALYSIS

F POINT OF VIEW

Possible answer: *Waverly's thoughts reveal that she is very competitive and has a vivid imagination. She is able to sustain her focus on the game while her brothers lose interest.*

REINFORCE *KEY IDEA:* OPPONENT

Discuss Who is Waverly's new **opponent?** In what ways does her opponent actually suport her? ***Possible answer:*** *Waverly's new opponent is an older man called Lau Po. Although he is her opponent and she loses many games to him, Lau Po actually supports her by teaching her new strategies and moves. He also teaches her chess etiquette, and by the end of the summer, Waverly becomes a better chess player because of him.*

ANALYZE VISUALS

Possible answer: *The overhead angle draws viewers' focus to the chessboard.*

bed, where at night I would stare for hours at imaginary battles. Soon I no longer lost any games or Life Savers, but I lost my adversaries. Winston and Vincent decided they were more interested in roaming the streets after school in their Hopalong Cassidy cowboy hats. F

On a cold spring afternoon, while walking home from school, I detoured through the playground at the end of our alley. I saw a group of old men, two seated across a folding table playing a game of chess, others smoking pipes, eating peanuts, and watching. I ran home and grabbed Vincent's chess set, which was bound in a cardboard box with rubber bands. I also carefully selected two prized rolls of Life Savers. I came back to the park and approached a man who was observing the game.

"Want to play?" I asked him. His face widened with surprise and he grinned as he looked at the box under my arm.

"Little sister, been a long time since I play with dolls," he said, smiling benevolently. I quickly put the box down next to him on the bench and displayed my **retort.**

Lau Po,[7] as he allowed me to call him, turned out to be a much better player than my brothers. I lost many games and many Life Savers. But over the weeks, with each diminishing roll of candies, I added new secrets. Lau Po gave me the names. The Double Attack from the East and West Shores. Throwing Stones on the Drowning Man. The Sudden Meeting of the Clan. The Surprise from the Sleeping Guard. The Humble Servant Who Kills the King. Sand in the Eyes of Advancing Forces. A Double Killing Without Blood.

F POINT OF VIEW
What do Waverly's descriptions of her thoughts and actions reveal about her?

retort (rĭ-tôrt') *n.* a quic sharp, witty reply

7. **Lau Po** (lou bō).

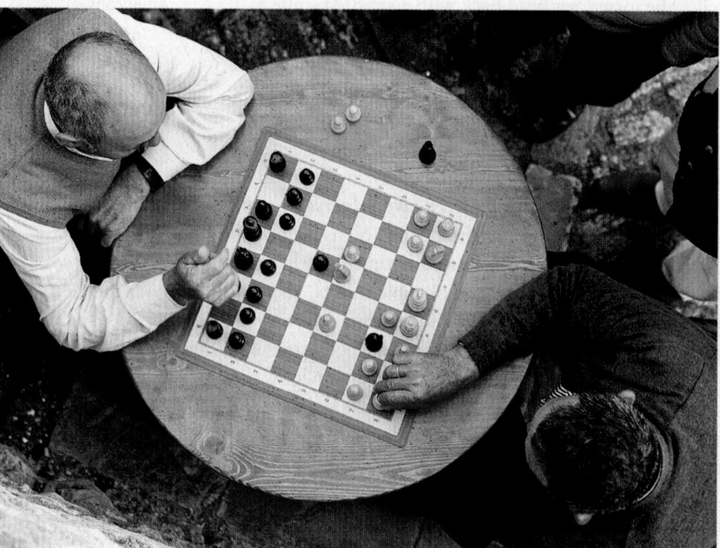

ANALYZE VISUALS
How does the angle at which this photograph was taken affect what you first notice in the picture?

DIFFERENTIATED INSTRUCTION

FOR LESS–PROFICIENT READERS

Reading Skill Follow-Up: Draw Conclusions Have students reread lines 176–187. What conclusions can they draw about Waverly's character from the details in this passage? Have them add to their chart from page 223 to draw conclusions. Remind students to add to their chart as they continue to read the story.

Evidence	*My Thoughts*	*Conclusion*
Waverly asks a man in the park to play chess with her.	*It's dangerous to approach strangers.*	*Waverly is self-confident, daring, and somewhat reckless.*

There were also the fine points of chess etiquette. Keep captured men in neat rows, as well-tended prisoners. Never announce "Check"[8] with vanity, lest someone with an unseen sword slit your throat. Never hurl pieces into the sandbox after you have lost a game, because then you must find them again, by yourself, after apologizing to all around you. By the end of the summer, Lau Po had taught me all he knew, and I had become a better chess player.

A small weekend crowd of Chinese people and tourists would gather as I played and defeated my opponents one by one. My mother would join the crowds during these outdoor exhibition games.[9] She sat proudly on the bench, telling my admirers with proper Chinese humility, "Is luck." **G**

G DRAW CONCLUSIONS Why does Waverly start winning more chess games?

A man who watched me play in the park suggested that my mother allow me to play in local chess tournaments. My mother smiled graciously, an answer that meant nothing. I desperately wanted to go, but I bit back my tongue. I knew she would not let me play among strangers. So as we walked home I said in a small voice that I didn't want to play in the local tournament. They would have American rules. If I lost, I would bring shame on my family. **H**

H POINT OF VIEW Reread lines 208–211. How are Waverly's thoughts and words different from each other? What does this tell you about her?

"Is shame you fall down nobody push you," said my mother.

During my first tournament, my mother sat with me in the front row as I waited for my turn. I frequently bounced my legs to unstick them from the cold metal seat of the folding chair. When my name was called, I leapt up. My mother unwrapped something in her lap. It was her *chang*, a small tablet of red jade which held the sun's fire. "Is luck," she whispered, and tucked it into my dress pocket. I turned to my opponent, a fifteen-year-old boy from Oakland. He looked at me, wrinkling his nose.

2 Targeted Passage

As I began to play, the boy disappeared, the color ran out of the room, and I saw only my white pieces and his black ones waiting on the other side. A light wind began blowing past my ears. It whispered secrets only I could hear.

"Blow from the South," it murmured. "The wind leaves no trail." I saw a clear path, the traps to avoid. The crowd rustled. "Shhh! Shhh!" said the corners of the room. The wind blew stronger. "Throw sand from the East to distract him." The knight came forward ready for the sacrifice. The wind hissed, louder and louder. "Blow, blow, blow. He cannot see. He is blind now. Make him lean away from the wind so he is easier to knock down."

"Check," I said, as the wind roared with laughter. The wind died down to little puffs, my own breath.

My mother placed my first trophy next to a new plastic chess set that the neighborhood Tao society had given to me. As she wiped each piece with a soft cloth, she said, "Next time win more, lose less."

"Ma, it's not how many pieces you lose," I said. "Sometimes you need to lose pieces to get ahead."

8. **check:** a move in chess that places an opponent's king under direct attack.
9. **exhibition games:** public showings or demonstrations.

READING SKILL

G DRAW CONCLUSIONS

Have students record their answers in the chart from page 223. ***Possible answer:***

- ***Evidence:*** *Waverly starts winning more chess games.*
- ***My Thoughts:*** *I know that winning at chess requires study, practice, and dedication.*
- ***Conclusion:*** *Waverly becomes successful at chess because she has an excellent teacher, she practices constantly, and she is motivated to excel.*

LITERARY ANALYSIS

H POINT OF VIEW

Possible answer: *Waverly wants to play in the chess tournament, but she tells her mother she doesn't want to. This shows that Waverly has remembered the lesson from the beginning of the story that if she "bites back her tongue," her mother may give her what she wants.*

If students need help . . . Ask students to reread lines 150–154, in which Waverly's mother expresses her opinion about American rules. Point out that although Mrs. Jong finds the rules perplexing, she also says "Better you take it, find out why yourself." Point out that Waverly is manipulating this proud, stubborn streak in her mother by implying that the American rules might prevent her from winning.

FOR LESS–PROFICIENT READERS

2 Targeted Passage [Lines 206–235]

This passage develops the rising action: Waverly starts playing in chess tournaments.

- Why does Waverly tell her mother that she's afraid of losing in a tournament?
- How does Waverly's mother show her support at the first tournament?
- What does the wind represent as Waverly works to defeat her opponent?
- Why is Waverly's mother dissatisfied with the outcome of the match?

FOR ENGLISH LEARNERS

Vocabulary: Suffixes Point out examples of words with the suffix *-ly* on this page (*proudly, graciously, desperately, frequently*) and identify the base words. Explain that adding the suffix *-ly* to an adjective creates an adverb. Challenge students to create new words by adding the suffix to adjectives. Then use Common Suffixes to help them identify the meanings of additional suffixes.

BEST PRACTICES TOOLKIT—Transparency
Common Suffixes p. E15

Lines 220–230

REINFORCE *KEY IDEA:* OPPONENT

Discuss How does Waverly vanquish her opponents? ***Possible answer:*** *She is completely focused on the game and uses the secrets she learned from Lau Po.*

"Better to lose less, see if you really need."

At the next tournament, I won again, but it was my mother who wore the triumphant grin.

"Lost eight pieces this time. Last time was eleven. What I tell you? Better off lose less!" I was annoyed, but I couldn't say anything. **1**

1 DRAW CONCLUSIC
Why does Waverly fee
she can't correct her
mother?

I attended more tournaments, each one farther away from home. I won all games, in all divisions. The Chinese bakery downstairs from our flat displayed my growing collection of trophies in its window, amidst the dust-covered cakes that were never picked up. The day after I won an important regional tournament, the window encased a fresh sheet cake with whipped-cream frosting and red script saying, "Congratulations, Waverly Jong, Chinatown Chess Champion." Soon after that, a flower shop, headstone engraver, and funeral parlor offered to sponsor me in national tournaments. That's when my mother decided I no longer had to do the dishes. Winston and Vincent had to do my chores.

"Why does she get to play and we do all the work?" complained Vincent.

"Is new American rules," said my mother. "Meimei play, squeeze all her brains out for win chess. You play, worth squeeze towel."

By my ninth birthday, I was a national chess champion. I was still some 429 points away from grand-master status, but I was touted as the Great American Hope, a child prodigy and a girl to boot. They ran a photo of me in *Life* magazine next to a quote in which Bobby Fischer[10] said, "There will never be a woman grand master." "Your move, Bobby," said the caption.

The day they took the magazine picture I wore neatly plaited braids clipped with plastic barrettes trimmed with rhinestones. I was playing in a large high school auditorium that echoed with phlegmy coughs and the squeaky rubber knobs of chair legs sliding across freshly waxed wooden floors. Seated across from me was an American man, about the same age as Lau Po, maybe fifty. I remember that his sweaty brow seemed to weep at my every move. He wore a dark, **malodorous** suit. One of his pockets was stuffed with a great white kerchief on which he wiped his palm before sweeping his hand over the chosen chess piece with great flourish.

malodorous
(măl-ō'dər-əs) *adj.*
having a bad odor

In my crisp pink-and-white dress with scratchy lace at the neck, one of two my mother had sewn for these special occasions, I would clasp my hands under my chin, the delicate points of my elbows poised lightly on the table in the manner my mother had shown me for posing for the press. I would swing my patent leather shoes back and forth like an impatient child riding on a school bus. Then I would pause, suck in my lips, twirl my chosen piece in midair as if undecided, and then firmly plant it in its new threatening place, with a triumphant smile thrown back at my opponent for good measure.

I no longer played in the alley of Waverly Place. I never visited the playground where the pigeons and old men gathered. I went to school, then directly home to learn new chess secrets, cleverly concealed advantages, more escape routes.

10. **Bobby Fischer:** a well-known chess player who, at 15, was the world's youngest grand master.

READING SKILL

1 DRAW CONCLUSIONS

Have students record their answers in the chart from page 223. ***Possible answer:***

- ***Evidence:*** *Waverly has already been unsuccessful at trying to explain the rules of chess to her mother. She has also learned the advantage of "biting back her tongue."*
- ***My Thoughts:*** *Strong-willed people do not tolerate contradiction.*
- ***Conclusion:*** *Waverly knows that it is useless to correct her mother. Waverly will not gain anything by explaining the rules to her mother, and her mother could become angry and punish her.*

Lines 241–257

DISCUSSION PROMPTS

Use these prompts to help students understand Waverly's new circumstances:

Restate How would you restate this comment by Waverly's mother: "Meimei play, squeeze all her brains out for win chess. You play, worth squeeze towel" (lines 251–252)? ***Possible answer:*** *When Meimei plays, she works hard with her mind. When you play, you accomplish nothing, so the only thing you are good for is doing the dishes.*

Infer What does Chinatown's reaction to Waverly's success tell you about the community? ***Possible answer:*** *Local businesses offer to sponsor her, and the bakery displays a decorated cake to congratulate her. In some ways, the community is like an extended family, offering support and congratulations. Her success makes them feel proud.*

Speculate The author describes these events from the first-person point of view but reveals little about Waverly's feelings. How do you think Waverly feels about the photo of herself in *Life* magazine and the magazine's challenge to Bobby Fischer? ***Possible answer:*** *She has shown her confidence and competitive nature. So she is probably excited about it.*

DIFFERENTIATED INSTRUCTION

FOR LESS–PROFICIENT READERS

Review: Visualize Have students reread lines 258–274, paying attention to details that help them create a mental image of the chess match. What details stand out? How does the picture Waverly creates of her opponent contrast with the picture she creates of herself?

FOR ENGLISH LEARNERS

Vocabulary: Cognates [shared-language groups] Have groups scan the story for cognates and report their findings to the class. Spanish cognates on this page include

- *triumphant/triunfante* (line 238)
- *collection/colección* (line 243)
- *trophies/trofeos* (line 243)
- *master/maestro, maestra* (line 254)
- *opponent/oponente* (line 274)

But I found it difficult to concentrate at home. My mother had a habit of standing over me while I plotted out my games. I think she thought of herself as my protective ally. Her lips would be sealed tight, and after each move I made, a soft "Hmmmmph" would escape from her nose.

"Ma, I can't practice when you stand there like that," I said one day. She retreated to the kitchen and made loud noises with the pots and pans. When the crashing stopped, I could see out of the corner of my eye that she was standing in the doorway. "Hmmmph!" Only this one came out of her tight throat. J

My parents made many **concessions** to allow me to practice. One time I complained that the bedroom I shared was so noisy that I couldn't think. Thereafter, my brothers slept in a bed in the living room facing the street. I said I couldn't finish my rice; my head didn't work right when my stomach was too full. I left the table with half-finished bowls and nobody complained.

But there was one duty I couldn't avoid. I had to accompany my mother on Saturday market days when I had no tournament to play. My mother would proudly walk with me, visiting many shops, buying very little. "This my daughter Wave-ly Jong," she said to whoever looked her way.

One day, after we left a shop I said under my breath, "I wish you wouldn't do that, telling everybody I'm your daughter." My mother stopped walking. Crowds of people with heavy bags pushed past us on the sidewalk, bumping into first one shoulder, then another.

"Aiii-ya. So shame be with mother?" She grasped my hand even tighter as she glared at me.

I looked down. "It's not that, it's just so obvious. It's just so embarrassing."

"Embarrass you be my daughter?" Her voice was cracking with anger.

"That's not what I meant. That's not what I said."

"What you say?"

I knew it was a mistake to say anything more, but I heard my voice speaking. "Why do you have to use me to show off? If you want to show off, then why don't you learn to play chess." K

My mother's eyes turned into dangerous black slits. She had no words for me, just sharp silence.

I felt the wind rushing around my hot ears. I jerked my hand out of my mother's tight grasp and spun around, knocking into an old woman. Her bag of groceries spilled to the ground.

"Aii-ya! Stupid girl!" my mother and the woman cried. Oranges and tin cans careened down the sidewalk. As my mother stooped to help the old woman pick up the escaping food, I took off.

I raced down the street, dashing between people, not looking back as my mother screamed shrilly, "Meimei! Meimei!" I fled down an alley, past dark curtained shops and merchants washing the grime off their windows. I sped into the sunlight, into a large street crowded with tourists examining trinkets and souvenirs. I ducked into another dark alley, down another street, up another alley. I ran until it hurt and I realized I had nowhere to go, that I was not running from anything. The alleys contained no escape routes.

J POINT OF VIEW
Reread lines 278–285. How does knowing only Waverly's point of view affect your impression of her mother?

concession (kən-sĕsh'ən) *n.* the act of yielding or conceding

3 Targeted Passage

K DRAW CONCLUSIONS
Why is Waverly embarrassed by her mother's behavior?

LITERARY ANALYSIS

J POINT OF VIEW

Possible answer: *Her mother hovers over Waverly as she practices, not saying much. This creates the impression of critical pressure. Since we don't know what she's thinking, she may seem more critical and formidable than she really is.*

Lines 291–298

REINFORCE *KEY IDEA:* OPPONENT

Discuss Waverly's mother shows her off and embarrasses her. How does this reflect the key idea that our supporters often seem like our **opponents?** ***Possible answer:*** *A supporter's pride can sometimes be so extreme it becomes hurtful or embarrassing. On the other hand, Waverly wants to be supported by her mother but isn't willing to give anything in return.*

READING SKILL

K DRAW CONCLUSIONS

Have students record their answers in the chart from page 223. ***Possible answer:*** *Waverly's mother brings her to many shops, without buying much, and introduces her to whoever will listen. Waverly thinks her mother is using her to feel more important, to "show off."*

FOR LESS–PROFICIENT READERS

3 Targeted Passage [Lines 291–322]

This passage presents the climax of the story as Waverly stands up to her mother.

- How does Waverly's mother act when they are out in public?
- What does Waverly say to her mother?
- How does her mother respond?
- What does Waverly want to escape from?

Comprehension Support [small-group option] Divide half of the class into small groups. Tell them that they will be experts on the story and have them discuss the plot, characters, and theme. Ask the rest of the students to write questions about the story that cannot be answered with a yes-or-no answer. Then convene the expert panel and have students ask them questions.

BEST PRACTICES TOOLKIT
Ask the Experts p. D4

FOR ENGLISH LEARNERS

Vocabulary: Phrasal Verbs Point out these phrasal verbs, explain their meanings, and read the sentences in which they are found. Tell students that context can help them determine the meanings of phrasal verbs. Challenge them to find more phrasal verbs in the story.

- *plotted out* (line 279), "planned"
- *show off* (line 306), "brag"
- *took off* (line 315), "ran, or moved quickly"

ANALYZE VISUALS

In this photograph, the white king is in check. It is in direct opposition to the black queen and is in danger of being taken. Students may say that the photograph creates a feeling of anxiety that is similar to Waverly's mood.

READING STRATEGY: ***Review***

L VISUALIZE

Possible answer: *Images that help readers picture Waverly's walk home include*

- *the quiet alley (line 331)*
- *"the yellow lights shining from our flat like two tiger's eyes in the night" (lines 331–333)*
- *"the sixteen steps to the door" (line 333)*

SELECTION WRAP-UP

REFLECT The story ends with Waverly thinking about her next move. Ask students what they think her next move will be. Have them cite evidence from the story to support their response.

CRITIQUE Have students analyze the effect of the ending. Would they prefer to be told what happens next? Why or why not?

READING FLUENCY

Distribute the copy masters and have students practice fluency.

RESOURCE MANAGER—Copy Master
Reading Fluency p. 107

My breath came out like angry smoke. It was cold. I sat down on an upturned plastic pail next to a stack of empty boxes, cupping my chin with my hands, thinking hard. I imagined my mother, first walking briskly down one street or another looking for me, then giving up and returning home to await my arrival. After two hours, I stood up on creaking legs and slowly walked home.

The alley was quiet and I could see the yellow lights shining from our flat like two tiger's eyes in the night. I climbed the sixteen steps to the door, advancing quietly up each so as not to make any warning sounds. I turned the knob; the door was locked. I heard a chair moving, quick steps, the locks turning—click! click! click!—and then the door opened. **L**

"About time you got home," said Vincent. "Boy, are you in trouble."

He slid back to the dinner table. On a platter were the remains of a large fish, its fleshy head still connected to bones swimming upstream in vain escape. Standing there waiting for my punishment, I heard my mother speak in a dry voice.

"We not concerning this girl. This girl not have concerning for us."

Nobody looked at me. Bone chopsticks clinked against the insides of bowls being emptied into hungry mouths.

I walked into my room, closed the door, and lay down on my bed. The room was dark, the ceiling filled with shadows from the dinnertime lights of neighboring flats.

In my head, I saw a chessboard with sixty-four black and white squares. Opposite me was my opponent, two angry black slits. She wore a triumphant smile. "Strongest wind cannot be seen," she said.

Her black men advanced across the plane, slowly marching to each successive level as a single unit. My white pieces screamed as they scurried and fell off the board one by one. As her men drew closer to my edge, I felt myself growing light. I rose up into the air and flew out the window. Higher and higher, above the alley, over the tops of tiled roofs, where I was gathered up by the wind and pushed up toward the night sky until everything below me disappeared and I was alone.

I closed my eyes and **pondered** my next move.

ANALYZE VISUALS
What is the **mood** of t
photograph?

L VISUALIZE
Reread lines 331–338. What **images** help you picture Waverly's walk home?

ponder (pŏn′dər) *v.* to think or consider caref

DIFFERENTIATED INSTRUCTION

FOR LESS-PROFICIENT READERS

Comprehension Support Make sure students understand the symbolism of the chess match Waverly imagines at the conclusion of the story. Read aloud lines 352–354. Ask students to identify Waverly's opponent in this game. If they have difficulty answering, point out that in line 308, Waverly describes her mother's eyes as "dangerous black slits." Discuss how the chess match parallels the confrontation Waverly has just had with her mother.

Then have students reread the last two sentences of the story. Encourage students to discuss whether they think Waverly really wants to be alone. Ask them what the last sentence suggests about her future relationship with her mother.

FOR ADVANCED LEARNERS/PRE-AP

Evaluate The narrator states in the story's first sentence that her mother taught her "the art of invisible strength." Have students skim the story to identify how Waverly applies that "art," both in chess and in life. Then ask them to discuss what they think Waverly did wrong in dealing with her mother and how she might have better applied the skills her mother taught her. Have students propose an alternative ending to the story to express their ideas.

[Af]ter Reading

[Co]mprehension

1. **Recall** How does Waverly's family get a chess set?
2. **Clarify** What does Waverly learn from the old man in the park?
3. **Clarify** What events cause Waverly to run away from her mother at the market?

[Li]terary Analysis

4. **Visualize** What scene in this story can you picture most vividly? Reread that part of the selection, noting at least three words or phrases that help you visualize the people, places, or events.
5. **Compare and Contrast** Use a Venn diagram like the one shown to compare and contrast Waverly before she learns chess and after she learns chess. How does she change? How does she stay the same?

Before Chess | After Chess

plays with friends

6. **Analyze First-Person Point of View** How would "Rules of the Game" be different if you knew what Waverly's mother was thinking?

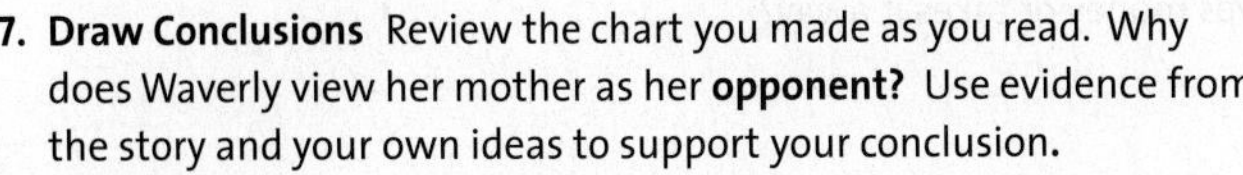

7. **Draw Conclusions** Review the chart you made as you read. Why does Waverly view her mother as her **opponent?** Use evidence from the story and your own ideas to support your conclusion.
8. **Evaluate Conflict** Give one or two reasons why Waverly and her mother might be in conflict with each other. Do you think they treat each other fairly? Explain.

[E]xtension and Challenge

9. **Literary Criticism** Amy Tan once mentioned in an interview that even though "Rules of the Game" is fiction and she never played chess, it is the closest she has come to describing her own life with her mother. She spoke of the "invisible force" her mother taught her. Tan uses the image of the wind throughout the story to represent this invisible force. Look for specific passages in the story in which Tan writes about the wind. With a small group, discuss the wind's effect on Waverly and her chess game.
10. **SOCIAL STUDIES CONNECTION** What challenges did Chinese immigrants face when they moved to the United States in the 1940s and 1950s, as Waverly's mother probably did? Research what it was like for newly arrived people to find jobs and housing and how the government responded to immigration from China. Share your findings with the class.

RESEARCH LINKS
For more on Chinese immigration to the United States, visit the **Research Center** at **ClassZone.com.**

Practice and Apply

After Reading

For additional support of postreading questions, use these copy masters:

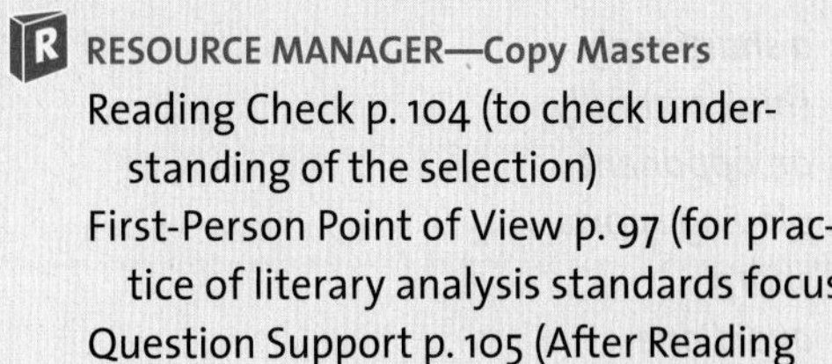

RESOURCE MANAGER—Copy Masters
Reading Check p. 104 (to check understanding of the selection)
First-Person Point of View p. 97 (for practice of literary analysis standards focus)
Question Support p. 105 (After Reading questions adapted for English learners and less-proficient readers)

Additional selection questions are provided for teachers on page 91.

ANSWERS

Comprehension

1. *Waverly's brother receives the chess set as a gift at a church Christmas party.*
2. *Waverly learns about chess rules, secrets, and etiquette.*
3. *Waverly is embarrassed when her mother shows her off in Chinatown.*

Literary Analysis

Possible answers:

4. *Students should choose a scene from Chinatown, the family's flat, or one of the tournaments.*
5. ***Before Chess:** Waverly is curious about everything. She teases her mother.* ***After Chess:** She becomes more serious and focuses mostly on chess. Her relationship with her mother becomes more tense.*
6. ● **STANDARDS FOCUS First-Person Point of View** *We would have a more complete understanding of Waverly's mother and possibly a more critical portrayal of Waverly.*
7. ■ **STANDARDS FOCUS Draw Conclusions** *Waverly feels that her mother doesn't understand her, the game of chess, or her reasons for playing chess. She believes that her mother tries to take credit for her accomplishments.*
8. *The conflict might be due to generational differences, cultural differences, or just different personalities. Students' opinions about how Waverly and her mother treat each other will vary, but should be supported with evidence from the story.*

Extension and Challenge

9. *Waverly's mother first mentions the wind at the beginning of the story. Waverly experiences this invisible force when she plays in chess tournaments. It helps her succeed at chess by whispering "secrets only [Waverly] could hear." At the end of the story, Waverly imagines that the wind helps her escape her mother.*
10.  **SOCIAL STUDIES CONNECTION** *During the 1940s and 1950s, it was difficult for Chinese immigrants to find housing, and many settled in "Chinatowns" in urban areas. It was not until the Civil Rights Movement in the 1960s that the U.S. government took an active role to ensure that Chinese Americans received the basic rights that they were once denied.*

ANSWERS

Vocabulary in Context

VOCABULARY PRACTICE

1. *a sharp reply*
2. *think carefully*
3. *an opponent*
4. *playing sports*
5. *sharp*
6. *avoid one*
7. *giving in*
8. *reveal it*
9. *garbage*
10. *gives money*

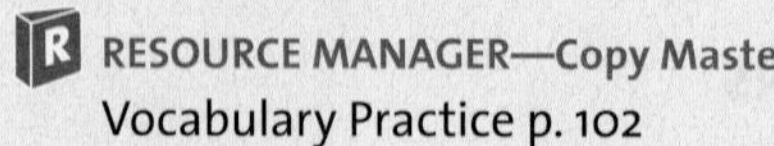

RESOURCE MANAGER—Copy Master
Vocabulary Practice p. 102

VOCABULARY IN WRITING

Encourage students to skim the story to remind themselves of the key events. Then have them choose at least three words to use in their paragraphs.

VOCABULARY STRATEGY: THE PREFIXES *fore-* AND *mal-* *(also an EL language objective)*

- Have students brainstorm a list of words with the prefix *fore-* and another list of words with the prefix *mal-*.
- Encourage students to define the words and use them in sentences.

Answers:

1. *fore-*
2. *mal-*
3. *mal-*
4. *fore-*
5. *fore-*
6. *mal-*

RESOURCE MANAGER—Copy Master
Vocabulary Strategy p. 103

Vocabulary Center at **ClassZone.com**
Additional Vocabulary Activities

Vocabulary in Context

VOCABULARY PRACTICE

Answer each question to show your understanding of the vocabulary words.

adversary
malodorous
benefactor
ponder
concession
pungent
foresight
retort
impart
tactic

1. Is a **retort** a high-pitched sound or a sharp reply?
2. When you **ponder,** do you think carefully or wander around a pond?
3. Which is an **adversary**—an opponent or an advisor?
4. Would a **tactic** help you more in playing sports or watching a movie?
5. Is a **pungent** smell faint or sharp?
6. If a person has **foresight,** is she likely to make a mistake or avoid one?
7. Is a **concession** more like giving in or letting loose?
8. When you **impart** something, do you hide it or reveal it?
9. What is more likely to be **malodorous**—flowers or garbage?
10. Is a **benefactor** someone who gives money or takes it away?

VOCABULARY IN WRITING

Write a paragraph summarizing what happened to Waverly in this story. Use at least three vocabulary words. You could start like this.

EXAMPLE SENTENCE

*At first, Waverly's brothers did not want to **impart** their knowledge of chess to her.*

VOCABULARY STRATEGY: THE PREFIXES *fore-* AND *mal-*

The prefixes *fore-* and *mal-* are used in the vocabulary words *foresight* and *malodorous.* The prefix *fore-* means "in front" or "before," and the prefix *mal-* means "bad" or "badly."

PRACTICE Decide which prefix, *fore-* or *mal-*, should be added to each word to make it match the definition provided.

1. ____ **cast:** to predict the weather conditions in advance
2. ____ **content:** dissatisfied with existing conditions
3. ____ **function:** to function improperly
4. ____ **arm:** part of the arm between the wrist and elbow
5. ____ **word:** a preface or introductory note in a book
6. ____ **practice:** improper treatment of a patient

VOCABULARY PRACTICE
For more practice, go to the **Vocabulary Center** at **ClassZone.com.**

DIFFERENTIATED INSTRUCTION

FOR ENGLISH LEARNERS

Vocabulary Practice [mixed-readiness pairs] Pair students with fluent speakers to answer the questions.

FOR ADVANCED LEARNERS/PRE-AP

Vocabulary Strategy Have students look for clues in the words' definitions. For example, the clues for the words with the *fore-* prefix include "predict" and "preface." The clues for the words with the *mal-* prefix include "dissatisfied" and "improper." Have students use a dictionary to check their answers. Then have them find more words with these prefixes and create a similar exercise. Have students complete each other's exercises.

ading-Writing Connection

Show how well you know the characters in "Rules of the Game" by responding to these prompts. Then complete the **Grammar and Writing** exercise.

WRITING PROMPTS	SELF-CHECK
A. Short Response: Describe a Character What steps does Waverly take to learn the game of chess and improve her skills? Write **one paragraph** to describe how she prepares herself to defeat her **opponents.**	***An effective description will . . .*** • include a topic sentence that introduces the topic • provide details about how Waverly improves her skills
B. Extended Response: Explore Point of View If Waverly's mother were telling the story, what might she say? In **two or three paragraphs,** retell from Waverly's mother's point of view the scenes in which Waverly runs away from the market and then returns home.	***A creative response will . . .*** • use the pronouns *I, me, we,* and *us* • show an understanding of the mother's character

AMMAR AND WRITING

COMBINE SENTENCES Using too many short sentences can make your writing sound choppy. One way to solve this problem is to use a **coordinating conjunction** to combine two shorter sentences. Coordinating conjunctions include the words *for, and, or, nor, but, so,* and *yet.* To combine two sentences, place a comma and a coordinating conjunction between them. Be sure to choose a coordinating conjunction that best shows the relationship between the two ideas.

Original: Waverly wanted salted plums. Her mother wouldn't let her have any.

Revised: Waverly wanted salted plums, but her mother wouldn't let her have any.

PRACTICE Combine the two sentences in each item below using an appropriate coordinating conjunction.

1. Waverly received candy at the Christmas party. Vincent received a chess set.
2. Mrs. Jong wanted Vincent to throw away the chess set. He decided to keep it.
3. Waverly wanted to learn about chess. She watched men play in the park.
4. Mrs. Jong is proud of Waverly's chess skills. Waverly feels like her mother is using her to show off.

*For more help with coordinating conjunctions, see page R63 in the **Grammar Handbook.***

Reading-Writing Connection

WRITING PROMPTS

- For **Prompt A,** have students list three steps Waverly takes. Then have them consider what lessons she learns from these steps.
- For **Prompt B,** have students review the scenes and then use a two-column chart to explain how Waverly's mother might have felt during each scene.

For writing support, see

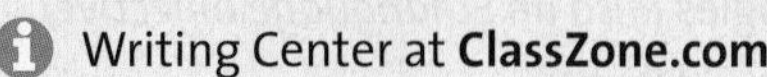

Writing Center at **ClassZone.com**

GRAMMAR AND WRITING

Make sure students understand the different relationships between ideas implied by the various coordinating conjunctions. Then discuss the Practice items:

- In item 1, the second sentence provides additional information.
- In items 2 and 4, the action in the second sentence is the opposite of or contradicts what is indicated in the first sentence.
- The sentences in item 3 express a cause-and-effect relationship.

Possible answers:

1. *Waverly received candy at the Christmas party, and Vincent received a chess set.*
2. *Mrs. Jong wanted Vincent to throw away the chess set, but he decided to keep it.*
3. *Waverly wanted to learn about chess, so she watched men play in the park.*
4. *Mrs. Jong is proud of Waverly's chess skills, yet Waverly feels like her mother is using her to show off.*

RESOURCE MANAGER—Copy Master
Combine Sentences p. 106

DIFFERENTIATED INSTRUCTION

FOR LESS-PROFICIENT WRITERS

For Prompt A:

1. Have students write a topic sentence for the paragraph based on the question.
2. Next, have them write at least one sentence for each step they have listed.
3. In the paragraph's conclusion, students should summarize how these steps help Waverly improve her skills.

For Prompt B:

Students may organize their paragraphs in this way:

- **First paragraph:** Focus on how Waverly's mother reacts when Waverly confronts her on the street.
- **Second paragraph:** Focus on her thoughts and feelings when Waverly runs away.
- **Third paragraph:** Focus on her plans for what she will do and say when Waverly finally returns home.

Assess and Reteach

Assess

RESOURCE MANAGER—Copy Masters
Selection Tests A, B/C pp. 109–110, 111–112

Test Generator CD

Reteach

STANDARDS LESSON FILE
Literature Lesson 11: Types of Point of View
Reading Lesson 9: Drawing Conclusions
Vocabulary Lesson 4: Prefixes

Focus and Motivate

OBJECTIVES

Literary Analysis
- explore the key idea of **identity**
- analyze main character
- read a short story and a vignette

Reading
- set a purpose for reading

Vocabulary
- build vocabulary for reading and writing
- understand the relationship between words in analogies *(also an EL language objective)*

Grammar and Writing
- write a compare-contrast essay

SUMMARY

Both "The Medicine Bag" and "Who Are You Today, María?" explore the role of family and cultural heritage in a character's identity. In "The Medicine Bag," Martin comes to appreciate his Sioux grandfather and feels honored when his grandpa gives him an important heirloom. In "Who Are You Today, María?" María dresses for her school's Who You Are Day. Her outfit celebrates her friendships, her culture, and her close relationship with her Puerto Rican grandmother.

What shows others WHO *we are?*

Discuss the question and the ***KEY IDEA.*** Have students study the image on this page and determine what clues it gives about the girl's cultural **identity.** Then have students work on the ***PICTURE IT*** activity independently.

Comparing Characters

The Medicine Bag

Short Story by Virginia Driving Hawk Sneve

Who Are You Today, María?

Vignette by Judith Ortiz Cofer

What shows others WHO *we are?*

KEY IDEA The clothes we wear, the way we speak, and the traditions we follow are just a few of the ways we show others who we are. Our families and our heritage can also play important roles in shaping our **identity,** which is how we see ourselves and how we want others to see us. In the stories you are about to read, two young people must decide which parts of their identities they want to share with the world.

PICTURE IT Create a collage or drawing that reflects your identity. Think of ways to visually represent your background, the beliefs that are important you, and the meaningful activities and relationships in your life.

238

Selection Resources

RESOURCE MANAGER UNIT 2

Plan and Teach pp. 113–120

Literary Analysis
Summary pp. 121†*, 122‡*; 127†*, 128‡*
Question Support p. 132*

Reading
Set a Purpose for Reading pp. 123, 124†*
Reading Check pp. 126; 131
Reading Fluency p. 134

Vocabulary
Study p. 125*
Practice p. 129
Strategy p. 130

Grammar and Writing
Writing for Assessment p. 133

Assessment
Selection Tests A, B/C pp. 135*, 137*
Test Generator CD

BEST PRACTICES TOOLKIT

Differentiated Instruction pp. 31–38*
Scaffolding Instruction pp. 43–46*

Graphic Organizers/Strategies
Storyboard • Word Questioning • Character Map • Character Traits and Textual Evidence • Timeline

Reading Support
Audio Anthology CD*

Technology
Literature, Vocabulary, and Writing Centers at **ClassZone.com**
Write*Smart* CD

* Resources for Differentiation † Also in Spanish ‡ In Haitian Creole and Vietnamese

LITERARY ANALYSIS: MAIN CHARACTER

Short stories usually focus on one **main character.** Since the plot of the story revolves around this person, understanding him or her is important to understanding the selection as a whole. As you read each of the following stories, get to know the main character just as you would get to know a real person. Ask questions like these:

- Where does the character live, and how does that place affect him or her?
- With whom does the character have important relationships? What are these relationships like?
- What is the character's social background or cultural heritage? How does the character feel about who he or she is?

READING STRATEGY: SET A PURPOSE FOR READING

In this lesson, your **purpose** for reading is to compare two main characters. As you read, begin filling in a chart like the one shown. You will be asked to add to this chart later.

	Martin	*María*
How does his or her environment affect him or her?		
What is his or her relationship with grandparent like?		
What is his or her attitude toward cultural heritage?		

VOCABULARY IN CONTEXT

The words in the box help tell two stories of family relationships. Match each numbered word or phrase with a vocabulary word.

WORD LIST	authentic	conspiracy	sheepishly
	commotion	descendant	unseemly

1. excitement
2. improper
3. son or daughter
4. not fake
5. scheme
6. timidly

Author Online

Virginia Driving Hawk Sneve: Sioux Storyteller Born at the height of the Great Depression, Virginia Driving Hawk Sneve grew up on the Rosebud Sioux reservation in South Dakota. Since her parents often had to leave the reservation to find work, Sneve spent a great deal of time with her grandmothers, whose tales inspired many of her books. Sneve has said that her goal in writing is to present accurate portrayals of Native American life. "The Medicine Bag" describes a tradition in which Native American boys create medicine bags, small pouches that hold items of religious significance and that symbolize the wearer's transition to adulthood.

Virginia Driving Hawk Sneve
born 1933

Judith Ortiz Cofer: A Rich Identity Judith Ortiz Cofer was born in Puerto Rico, but she spent much of her childhood in New Jersey after her father joined the U.S. Navy. When her father was at sea, the family returned to Puerto Rico for extended visits with Cofer's grandmother. At times, Cofer felt that she did not fit in either culture—American or Puerto Rican. She uses her writing to explore the difficulties and rewards of her dual identity.

Judith Ortiz Cofer
born 1952

MORE ABOUT THE AUTHOR
For more on Virginia Driving Hawk Sneve and Judith Ortiz Cofer, visit the **Literature Center** at **ClassZone.com.**

Teach

STANDARDS FOCUS

LITERARY ANALYSIS

● MAIN CHARACTER

Ask students to recall a story they have recently read and identify the main character. Then have students answer the bulleted list of questions on page 239 for the main character.

CHECK UNDERSTANDING Ask pairs of students to take turns describing a main character from a familiar book, film, or television program without mentioning the character by name. Have partners guess the identity of each character from the description.

READING STRATEGY

■ SET A PURPOSE FOR READING

Review with students some of the purposes for reading literature (*to be entertained, to learn about a topic, and so on*). Read the instructions on page 239 together and point out that their purpose for reading these selections is more specific. Discuss the questions in the chart and the insight the answers might provide.

CHECK UNDERSTANDING Ask students to generate other questions they might ask to compare two characters.

RESOURCE MANAGER—Copy Master
Set a Purpose for Reading p. 123 (for student use while reading the selections)

VOCABULARY SKILL

▲ VOCABULARY IN CONTEXT

DIAGNOSE WORD KNOWLEDGE To determine preteaching needs, have all students complete **Vocabulary in Context.** Check their answers.
1. *commotion* **2.** *unseemly* **3.** *descendant* **4.** *authentic* **5.** *conspiracy* **6.** *sheepishly*

PRETEACH VOCABULARY Use the Vocabulary Study copy master to help students determine the meaning of each boldfaced word.

1. Read aloud the first sentence, emphasizing the boldfaced word.
2. Discuss possible meanings for *authentic,* such as "real" or "valuable." Have students note their predictions in the chart.
3. Repeat for each of the other sentences.
4. Have students complete the last column in the chart as they read the selections.

RESOURCE MANAGER—Copy Master
Vocabulary Study p. 125

For general guidelines on differentiating vocabulary instruction and for alternative vocabulary activities for students not needing vocabulary preteaching, see

BEST PRACTICES TOOLKIT
Scaffolding Vocabulary Instruction pp. 43–46

Vocabulary Center at **ClassZone.com**
Additional Vocabulary Activities

Practice and Apply

ANALYZE VISUALS

Possible answer:

- *The man's wrinkled skin tells you he is old.*
- *His high cheekbones and dark eyes suggest that he is Native American.*
- *His determined facial expression suggests that he is strong and courageous.*

About the Art American artist David Behrens (born 1969) majored in illustration at East Carolina University, where he first explored his interest in Native American people and their history. In his paintings, Behrens uses an oil glazing technique that dates back to the Renaissance.

LITERARY ANALYSIS

Ⓐ MAIN CHARACTER

Possible answer: *They wanted to impress their friends by making their grandfather sound glamorous.*

Lines 7–12

REINFORCE *KEY IDEA:* IDENTITY

Discuss What might have been Grandpa's reason for giving authentic Sioux articles to the children? How does this relate to the key idea of **identity?** ***Possible answer:*** *Grandpa likely wanted the children to feel connected to the Sioux people. The items remind the children of their Sioux heritage.*

LITERARY ANALYSIS

Ⓑ MAIN CHARACTER

Possible answer: *He lives in a middle-class suburban neighborhood. There are "fancy little dogs" (line 21) in people's yards.*

The Medicine Bag

Virginia Driving Hawk Sneve

My kid sister Cheryl and I always bragged about our Sioux grandpa, Joe Iron Shell. Our friends, who had always lived in the city and only knew about Indians from movies and TV, were impressed by our stories. Maybe we exaggerated and made Grandpa and the reservation sound glamorous, but when we'd return home to Iowa after our yearly summer visit to Grandpa we always had some exciting tale to tell.

We always had some **authentic** Sioux article to show our listeners. One year Cheryl had new moccasins that Grandpa had made. On another visit he gave me a small, round, flat, rawhide drum which was decorated with a painting of a warrior riding a horse. He taught me a real Sioux chant to sing while I beat the drum with a leather-covered stick that had a feather on the end. Man, that really made an impression. Ⓐ

We never showed our friends Grandpa's picture. Not that we were ashamed of him, but because we knew that the glamorous tales we told didn't go with the real thing. Our friends would have laughed at the picture, because Grandpa wasn't tall and stately like TV Indians. His hair wasn't in braids, but hung in stringy, gray strands on his neck and he was old. He was our great-grandfather, and he didn't live in a tipi, but all by himself in a part log, part tar-paper shack on the Rosebud Reservation in South Dakota. So when Grandpa came to visit us, I was so ashamed and embarrassed I could've died.

There are a lot of yippy poodles and other fancy little dogs in our neighborhood, but they usually barked singly at the mailman from the safety of their own yards. Now it sounded as if a whole pack of mutts were barking together in one place. Ⓑ

ANALYZE VISUALS
What **details** of the ma[n's] face tell you the most about him?

① **Targeted Passage**

authentic (ô-thĕn′tĭk) a[dj.] having a verifiable orig[in;] not counterfeit

Ⓐ MAIN CHARACTER
Why did the narrator and his sister exaggerat[e] when they talked about their grandfather?

Ⓑ MAIN CHARACTER
What **conclusions** can y[ou] draw about the narrato[r's] neighborhood?

Detail of *They Moved Them* (1991), David Behre[ns]. Oil glazing, 9¼″ × 14½″. © David Behre[ns]

DIFFERENTIATED INSTRUCTION

FOR ALL STUDENTS

Hands-On Learning [mixed learning profiles] Have groups create a storyboard for each of the two selections. Each group can choose one of their storyboards as the basis for a movie, radio play, or skit. Display the storyboards and set aside time after reading the selections for groups to perform their productions.

 **BEST PRACTICES TOOLKIT—Transparency**
Storyboard p. C11

FOR LESS–PROFICIENT READERS

In combination with the *Audio Anthology CD*, use one or more Targeted Passages (pp. 240, 244, 247, 248, 250) to ensure that students focus on key story events, concepts, and skills.

① Targeted Passage [Lines 1–20]

This passage introduces the main character, Martin, and provides context for the story.

- How do Martin's friends react to his exaggerated stories about his Sioux grandfather and the "authentic Sioux articles" his grandfather gave him?
- Why doesn't Martin show his grandfather's photo to his friends?
- How does Martin react when his grandfather comes to visit?

BACKGROUND

Lakota Sioux The Lakota Sioux people lived on the Great Plains until the 1870s, when they settled in the Black Hills area of South Dakota. When gold was found in the area, conflict over gold prospecting led to the Black Hills War. Though the Sioux defeated General George Armstrong Custer's 7th Cavalry in a famous battle known as Custer's Last Stand, they were eventually forced to sign a treaty ceding the Black Hills to the United States. Nonetheless, the war continued, culminating in the Massacre at Wounded Knee in 1890, during which U.S. troops killed more than 200 men, women, and children. Now, the Lakota Sioux people primarily live on reservations in South Dakota.

FOR ENGLISH LEARNERS

Key Academic Vocabulary Have students use Word Questioning to study key academic vocabulary from the two selections:

- "The Medicine Bag": *reluctantly* (line 77), *remove* (line 81), *tradition* (line 135), *vision* (lines 219, 224, 230, 249)
- "Who Are You Today, María?": *principal* (lines 4, 16), *communicate* (line 17), *shifts* (line 43), *partner* (line 44), *quoted* (line 65)

BEST PRACTICES TOOLKIT—Transparency
Word Questioning p. E9

Options for Reading Read aloud lines 1–24 and check understanding by asking students to describe the narrator and his grandfather. Then have them continue reading along with the *Audio Anthology CD.*

Prereading For prereading instruction for English learners, see

BEST PRACTICES TOOLKIT
Scaffolding Reading Instruction pp. 43–46

FOR ADVANCED LEARNERS/PRE–AP

Pre-AP exercises in the bottom channel provide additional challenge for your advanced students. Use them for small groups or individuals.

ADDITIONAL GUIDELINES

For more help with differentiation and tips for classroom management, see

BEST PRACTICES TOOLKIT
Differentiated Instruction pp. 31–38

SOCIAL STUDIES CONNECTION

Over 20,000 members of the Sioux tribe live on the Rosebud Reservation in South Dakota. The site's name derives from the many wild rosebuds native to the area.

Lines 28–50
DISCUSSION PROMPTS

Use these prompts to help students understand the significance of the arrival of Martin's grandfather:

Recall How does Grandpa arrive in Martin's neighborhood? ***Answer:*** *Grandpa arrives on foot while the neighborhood dogs bark at him.*

Infer Why does Martin say, "Oh, no! . . . It's Grandpa!" when he sees his grandfather coming? ***Possible answer:*** *Martin thinks Grandpa's appearance doesn't live up to the stories he has told his friends. Martin is afraid his grandpa will embarrass him.*

Analyze How does the way Grandpa greets Martin express his identity? ***Possible answer:*** *Grandpa greets Martin in the formal Sioux manner, shaking his hand and speaking Sioux. This greeting reflects his cultural identity.*

LITERARY ANALYSIS

C MAIN CHARACTER

Possible answer: *Martin is embarrassed about his grandfather's outfit because it looks very out of place in Martin's neighborhood.*

I got up and walked to the curb to see what the **commotion** was. About a block away I saw a crowd of little kids yelling, with the dogs yipping and growling around someone who was walking down the middle of the street.

I watched the group as it slowly came closer and saw that in the center of the strange procession was a man wearing a tall black hat. He'd pause now and then to peer at something in his hand and then at the houses on either side of the street. I felt cold and hot at the same time as I recognized the man. "Oh, no!" I whispered. "It's Grandpa!"

I stood on the curb, unable to move even though I wanted to run and hide. Then I got mad when I saw how the yippy dogs were growling and nipping at the old man's baggy pant legs and how wearily he poked them away with his cane. "Stupid mutts," I said as I ran to rescue Grandpa.

When I kicked and hollered at the dogs to get away, they put their tails between their legs and scattered. The kids ran to the curb where they watched me and the old man.

"Grandpa," I said and felt pretty dumb when my voice cracked. I reached for his beat-up old tin suitcase, which was tied shut with a rope. But he set it down right in the street and shook my hand.

"*Hau,*[1] *Takoza,* Grandchild," he greeted me formally in Sioux.

All I could do was stand there with the whole neighborhood watching and shake the hand of the leather-brown old man. I saw how his gray hair straggled from under his big black hat, which had a drooping feather in its crown. His rumpled black suit hung like a sack over his stooped frame. As he shook my hand, his coat fell open to expose a bright-red, satin shirt with a beaded bolo tie under the collar. His getup wasn't out of place on the reservation, but it sure was here, and I wanted to sink right through the pavement. C

"Hi," I muttered with my head down. I tried to pull my hand away when I felt his bony hand trembling, and looked up to see fatigue in his face. I felt like crying. I couldn't think of anything to say so I picked up Grandpa's suitcase, took his arm, and guided him up the driveway to our house.

Mom was standing on the steps. I don't know how long she'd been watching, but her hand was over her mouth and she looked as if she couldn't believe what she saw. Then she ran to us.

"Grandpa," she gasped. "How in the world did you get here?"

She checked her move to embrace Grandpa and I remembered that such a display of affection is **unseemly** to the Sioux and would embarrass him.

"*Hau,* Marie," he said as he shook Mom's hand. She smiled and took his other arm.

As we supported him up the steps the door banged open and Cheryl came bursting out of the house. She was all smiles and was so obviously glad to see Grandpa that I was ashamed of how I felt.

"Grandpa!" she yelled happily. "You came to see us!"

1. ***Hau*** *Sioux:* hello.

commotion (kə-mō'shə
n. a disturbance

SOCIAL STUDIES CONNECTION

The Rosebud Reservati
in South Dakota

C MAIN CHARACTER
How does Martin feel about his grandfather's outfit?

unseemly (ŭn-sēm'lē) *adj.* inappropriate

DIFFERENTIATED INSTRUCTION

FOR LESS–PROFICIENT READERS

Comprehension Support Have students review lines 1–66 and then help them formulate impressions of Martin. Distribute a Character Map, and have students note how Martin thinks, feels, and acts. Remind them that they may need to finish reading the entire story before they can fill in all the blanks. As students read on, have them add details to their maps.

 **BEST PRACTICES TOOLKIT—Transparency**
Character Map p. D8

FOR ADVANCED LEARNERS/PRE–AP

Study Characterization Challenge advanced learners by having them create a more sophisticated analysis of Martin's character. Distribute copies of the Character Traits and Textual Evidence tool, and have students find quotes from the story that give insight into Martin's character.

 **BEST PRACTICES TOOLKIT—Transparency**
Character Traits and Textual Evidence p. D6

Grandpa smiled and Mom and I let go of him as he stretched out his arms to my 10-year-old sister, who was still young enough to be hugged.

"*Wicincala,*[2] little girl," he greeted her and then collapsed.

He had fainted. Mom and I carried him into her sewing room, where we had a spare bed.

After we had Grandpa on the bed Mom stood there helplessly patting his shoulder.

"Shouldn't we call the doctor, Mom?" I suggested, since she didn't seem to know what to do.

"Yes," she agreed with a sigh. "You make Grandpa comfortable, Martin."

I reluctantly moved to the bed. I knew Grandpa wouldn't want to have Mom undress him, but I didn't want to, either. He was so skinny and frail that his coat slipped off easily. When I loosened his tie and opened his shirt collar, I felt a small leather pouch that hung from a thong around his neck. I left it alone and moved to remove his boots. The scuffed old cowboy boots were tight and he moaned as I put pressure on his legs to jerk them off. **D**

D MAIN CHARACTER
Reread lines 77–82. Which details in these lines indicate that Martin is uneasy around his grandfather?

I put the boots on the floor and saw why they fit so tight. Each one was stuffed with money. I looked at the bills that lined the boots and started to ask about them, but Grandpa's eyes were closed again.

Mom came back with a basin of water. "The doctor thinks Grandpa is suffering from heat exhaustion," she explained as she bathed Grandpa's face. Mom gave a big sigh, "*Oh hinh,* Martin. How do you suppose he got here?"

We found out after the doctor's visit. Grandpa was angrily sitting up in bed while Mom tried to feed him some soup.

"Tonight you let Marie feed you, Grandpa," spoke my dad, who had gotten home from work just as the doctor was leaving. "You're not really sick," he said as he gently pushed Grandpa back against the pillows. "The doctor said you just got too tired and hot after your long trip."

Grandpa relaxed, and between sips of soup, he told us of his journey. Soon after our visit to him Grandpa decided that he would like to see where his only living **descendants** lived and what our home was like. Besides, he admitted **sheepishly,** he was lonesome after we left.

descendant (dĭ-sĕn'dənt) *n.* a person whose descent can be traced to an individual or group

sheepishly (shē'pĭsh-lē) *adv.* meekly; with embarrassment

I knew everybody felt as guilty as I did—especially Mom. Mom was all Grandpa had left. So even after she married my dad, who's a white man and teaches in the college in our city, and after Cheryl and I were born, Mom made sure that every summer we spent a week with Grandpa.

I never thought that Grandpa would be lonely after our visits, and none of us noticed how old and weak he had become. But Grandpa knew and so he came to us. He had ridden on buses for two and a half days. When he arrived in the city, tired and stiff from sitting for so long, he set out, walking, to find us. **E**

E MAIN CHARACTER
Reread lines 99–106. What do you learn about Martin's relationship with his grandfather?

He had stopped to rest on the steps of some building downtown and a policeman found him. The cop, according to Grandpa, was a good man who

2. ***Wicincala*** *Sioux:* girl.

LITERARY ANALYSIS

D MAIN CHARACTER

Possible answer: *Martin doesn't want to undress his grandfather, and he is hesitant to help him remove his boots.*

Extend the Discussion Why might Martin feel uncomfortable in his grandfather's presence?

LITERARY ANALYSIS

E MAIN CHARACTER

Possible answer: *Martin usually sees his grandfather once a week in the summer. He doesn't appear to know his grandfather well or to pay much attention to him: he is surprised to learn he is lonely and has become old and weak.*

If students need help . . . Ask them how often Martin sees his grandfather and what this suggests about how well they might know each other. Then ask students what details about Grandpa the family didn't notice before now.

FOR LESS–PROFICIENT READERS

Reading Strategy Follow-Up: Set a Purpose for Reading Encourage students to update their charts, introduced on page 239, to help them understand Martin. Remind them to look for words that describe Martin's thoughts and feelings.

	Martin
How does his or her environment affect him or her?	• *He notices the difference between his neighborhood and the reservation.* • *He thinks his grandfather doesn't fit in.*
What is his or her relationship with grandparent like?	• *He is embarrassed by his grandfather.*
What is his or her attitude toward cultural heritage?	• *Being Sioux makes him feel different.*

LITERARY ANALYSIS

(F) MAIN CHARACTER

***Possible answer:** Martin is proud of his grandfather for taking such a long journey on his own.*

Lines 117–139

DISCUSSION PROMPTS

Use these prompts to help students understand Martin's grandfather:

Interpret Where does Grandpa hide his money? What personal qualities does he show by this action? ***Possible answer:** He hides his money in his boots. This action suggests that he is old-fashioned and does not have a bank account or credit cards. It also shows that he takes a practical approach to life and doesn't worry whether others might find his behavior unusual.*

Analyze What does Grandpa mean when he says, "Even though the boy bears a white man's name, the medicine bag will be his"? ***Possible answer:** He means that even though Martin is only partly Sioux and lives in a white community, he can still carry on Sioux traditions.*

Synthesize What might Martin learn from his grandfather's example? ***Possible answer:** He might learn to be independent, to save his money, and to follow Sioux traditions.*

LITERARY ANALYSIS

(G) MAIN CHARACTER

***Possible answer:** Martin dreads the time when he will receive the medicine bag. He doesn't want his friends to tease him when they see him wearing it.*

took him to the bus stop and waited until the bus came and told the driver to let Grandpa out at Bell View Drive. After Grandpa got off the bus, he started walking again. But he couldn't see the house numbers on the other side when he walked on the sidewalk so he walked in the middle of the street. That's when all the little kids and dogs followed him.

I knew everybody felt as bad as I did. Yet I was proud of this 86-year-old man, who had never been away from the reservation, having the courage to travel so far alone. (F)

(F) MAIN CHARACTER What is Martin's attitude toward his grandfather's journey?

"You found the money in my boots?" he asked Mom.

"Martin did," she answered, and roused herself to scold. "Grandpa, you shouldn't have carried so much money. What if someone had stolen it from you?"

Grandpa laughed. "I would've known if anyone tried to take the boots off my feet. The money is what I've saved for a long time—a hundred dollars—for my funeral. But you take it now to buy groceries so that I won't be a burden to you while I am here."

"That won't be necessary, Grandpa," Dad said. "We are honored to have you with us and you will never be a burden. I am only sorry that we never thought to bring you home with us this summer and spare you the discomfort of a long trip."

Grandpa was pleased. "Thank you," he answered. "But do not feel bad that you didn't bring me with you for I would not have come then. It was not time." He said this in such a way that no one could argue with him. To Grandpa and the Sioux, he once told me, a thing would be done when it was the right time to do it and that's the way it was.

(2) Targeted Passage

"Also," Grandpa went on, looking at me, "I have come because it is soon time for Martin to have the medicine bag."

We all knew what that meant. Grandpa thought he was going to die and he had to follow the tradition of his family to pass the medicine bag, along with its history, to the oldest male child.

"Even though the boy," he said still looking at me, "bears a white man's name, the medicine bag will be his."

I didn't know what to say. I had the same hot and cold feeling that I had when I first saw Grandpa in the street. The medicine bag was the dirty leather pouch I had found around his neck. "I could never wear such a thing," I almost said aloud. I thought of having my friends see it in gym class, at the swimming pool, and could imagine the smart things they would say. But I just swallowed hard and took a step toward the bed. I knew I would have to take it. (G)

(G) MAIN CHARACTER How does Martin feel about receiving the medicine bag?

But Grandpa was tired. "Not now, Martin," he said, waving his hand in dismissal, "it is not time. Now I will sleep."

So that's how Grandpa came to be with us for two months. My friends kept asking to come see the old man, but I put them off. I told myself that I didn't want them laughing at Grandpa. But even as I made excuses I knew it wasn't Grandpa that I was afraid they'd laugh at.

DIFFERENTIATED INSTRUCTION

FOR LESS–PROFICIENT READERS

(2) Targeted Passage [Lines 128–146]

This passage reveals the reason for Grandpa's visit: he has an important gift for Martin.

- What does Grandpa want to give to Martin? Why is this important to Grandpa?
- What is a medicine bag?
- Why doesn't Martin want to wear the medicine bag? Why does he feel that he has to accept it?

Nothing bothered Cheryl about bringing her friends to see Grandpa. Every day after school started there'd be a crew of giggling little girls or round-eyed little boys crowded around the old man on the patio, where he'd gotten in the habit of sitting every afternoon.

Grandpa would smile in his gentle way and patiently answer their questions, or he'd tell them stories of brave warriors, ghosts, animals, and the kids listened in awed silence. Those little guys thought Grandpa was great.

Finally, one day after school, my friends came home with me because nothing I said stopped them. "We're going to see the great Indian of Bell View Drive," said Hank, who was supposed to be my best friend. "My brother has seen him three times so he oughta be well enough to see us." **H**

When we got to my house Grandpa was sitting on the patio. He had on his red shirt, but today he also wore a fringed leather vest that was decorated with beads. Instead of his usual cowboy boots he had solidly beaded moccasins on his feet that stuck out of his black trousers. Of course, he had his old black hat on—he was seldom without it. But it had been brushed and the feather in the beaded headband was proudly erect, its tip a brighter white. His hair lay in silver strands over the red shirt collar.

I stared just as my friends did and I heard one of them murmur, "Wow!"

Grandpa looked up and when his eyes met mine they twinkled as if he were laughing inside. He nodded to me and my face got all hot. I could tell that he had known all along I was afraid he'd embarrass me in front of my friends.

"*Hau, hoksilas,* boys," he greeted and held out his hand.

My buddies passed in a single file and shook his hand as I introduced them. They were so polite I almost laughed. "How, there, Grandpa," and even a "How-do-you-do, sir."

"You look fine, Grandpa," I said as the guys sat on the lawn chairs or on the patio floor.

"*Hanh,* yes," he agreed. "When I woke up this morning it seemed the right time to dress in the good clothes. I knew that my grandson would be bringing his friends."

"You guys want some lemonade or something?" I offered. No one answered. They were listening to Grandpa as he started telling how he'd killed the deer from which his vest was made.

Grandpa did most of the talking while my friends were there. I was so proud of him and amazed at how respectfully quiet my buddies

H MAIN CHARACTER What bothers Martin about bringing his friends home to meet his grandfather?

ANALYZE VISUALS **Compare** this picture of a medicine bag to the way you imagine the medicine bag in the story. How is it similar?

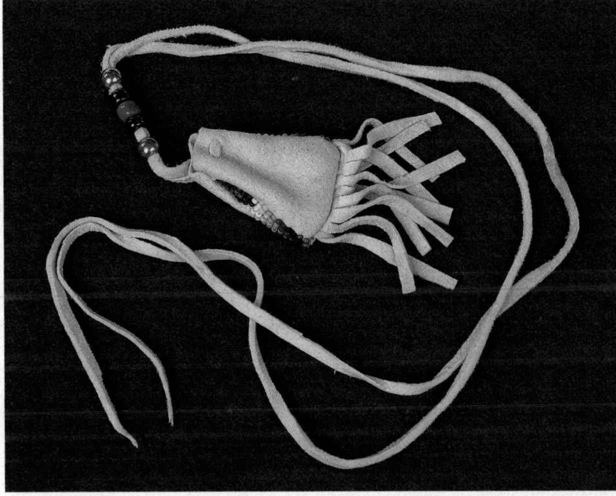

LITERARY ANALYSIS

H MAIN CHARACTER

Possible answer: *Martin worries that his friends will laugh at Grandpa and at him. He is afraid his grandfather will embarrass him.*

Extend the Discussion What happens when Cheryl's friends meet Grandpa? Does this suggest that Martin's fears are justified? Why or why not?

ANALYZE VISUALS

Students' answers will vary. Students may have imagined an older medicine bag than the one shown in the photograph. The story describes a "dirty leather pouch," but the bag in the picture looks new and unworn.

FOR LESS–PROFICIENT READERS

Concept Support After students read lines 159–201, discuss how our expectations of an event often differ from what actually happens. Encourage students to see that Martin's fears about Grandpa and his friends are all unfounded. His own embarrassment causes him to believe that his friends will also find Grandpa embarrassing. Invite students to tell about a time when their expectations about an event turned out to be wrong. What had they expected? What actually happened?

FOR ADVANCED LEARNERS/PRE–AP

Investigate a Tradition [paired option] As students read, have them list the Sioux traditions that appear in the story. These include drumming, storytelling, sweat baths, vision quests, and the medicine bag. Have pairs of students research one tradition and present the results of their research to the class.

were. Mom had to chase them home at supper time. As they left they shook Grandpa's hand again and said to me:

"Martin, he's really great!"

"Yeah, man! Don't blame you for keeping him to yourself."

"Can we come back?" ❶

But after they left, Mom said, "No more visitors for a while, Martin. Grandpa won't admit it, but his strength hasn't returned. He likes having company, but it tires him."

That evening Grandpa called me to his room before he went to sleep. "Tomorrow," he said, "when you come home, it will be time to give you the medicine bag."

I felt a hard squeeze from where my heart is supposed to be and was scared, but I answered, "OK, Grandpa."

All night I had weird dreams about thunder and lightning on a high hill. From a distance I heard the slow beat of a drum. When I woke up in the morning I felt as if I hadn't slept at all. At school it seemed as if the day would never end and, when it finally did, I ran home. ❶

Grandpa was in his room, sitting on the bed. The shades were down and the place was dim and cool. I sat on the floor in front of Grandpa, but he didn't even look at me. After what seemed a long time he spoke.

"I sent your mother and sister away. What you will hear today is only for a man's ears. What you will receive is only for a man's hands." He fell silent and I felt shivers down my back.

"My father in his early manhood," Grandpa began, "made a vision quest to find a spirit guide for his life. You cannot understand how it was in that time, when the great Teton Sioux were first made to stay on the reservation. There was a strong need for guidance from *Wakantanka,* the Great Spirit. But too many of the young men were filled with despair and hatred. They thought it was hopeless to search for a vision when the glorious life was gone and only the hated confines of a reservation lay ahead. But my father held to the old ways.

"He carefully prepared for his quest with a purifying sweat bath and then he went alone to a high butte[3] top to fast and pray. After three days he received his sacred dream—in which he found, after long searching, the white man's iron. He did not understand his vision of finding something belonging to the white people, for in that time they were the enemy. When he came down from the butte to cleanse himself at the stream below, he found the remains of a campfire and the broken shell of an iron kettle. This was a sign which reinforced his dream. He took a piece of the iron for his medicine bag, which he had made of elk skin years before, to prepare for his quest.

"He returned to his village, where he told his dream to the wise old men of the tribe. They gave him the name *Iron Shell,* but neither did they understand the

❶ **MAIN CHARACTER**
Why is Martin proud o
his grandfather?

❶ **MAIN CHARACTER**
How have Martin's
feelings about receivir
the medicine bag
changed?

3. **butte** (byōōt): an abruptly rising hill with sloping sides and a flat top.

LITERARY ANALYSIS

❶ MAIN CHARACTER

Possible answer: *Martin is proud of his grandfather for dressing up in his good clothes and for commanding respect from Martin's friends.*

Extend the Discussion Why do you think Martin is able to see his grandfather more clearly after he sees how much his friends like and respect him? Do you think most young people would act this way? Why or why not?

LITERARY ANALYSIS

❶ MAIN CHARACTER

Possible answer: *Martin now anticipates receiving the bag with excitement and fear, but he no longer seems reluctant.*

Extend the Discussion What do you think contributed to the change in Martin's feelings about receiving the bag?

DIFFERENTIATED INSTRUCTION

FOR LESS–PROFICIENT READERS

Comprehension Support Grandpa's story presents a flashback, a shift in time to story events that occurred in the past. Make sure that students understand the sequence of story events. Display the Timeline transparency and help students create a timeline recording the main story events in chronological order. The first Iron Shell's vision quest (lines 220–236) should be the first event.

BEST PRACTICES TOOLKIT—Transparency
Timeline p. B23

FOR ENGLISH LEARNERS

Language: Punctuation and Print Cues Explain that in stories, each speaker's dialogue begins a new paragraph, and dialogue is surrounded by quotation marks. These clues help readers know that someone is speaking. Explain that sometimes dialogue tags, such as *he said* or *Martin complained,* follow dialogue. Other times, context clues help the reader learn who is speaking. Have students reread lines 199–227 and tell who is speaking in each paragraph.

meaning of the dream. This first Iron Shell kept the piece of iron with him at all times and believed it gave him protection from the evils of those unhappy days.

"Then a terrible thing happened to Iron Shell. He and several other young men were taken from their homes by the soldiers and sent far away to a white man's boarding school. He was angry and lonesome for his parents and the young girl he had wed before he was taken away. At first Iron Shell resisted the teachers' attempts to change him and he did not try to learn. One day it was his turn to work in the school's blacksmith shop. As he walked into the place he knew that his medicine had brought him there to learn and work with the white man's iron.

"Iron Shell became a blacksmith and worked at the trade when he returned to the reservation. All of his life he treasured the medicine bag. When he was old, and I was a man, he gave it to me, for no one made the vision quest any more."

Grandpa quit talking and I stared in disbelief as he covered his face with his hands. His shoulders were shaking with quiet sobs and I looked away until he began to speak again.

"I kept the bag until my son, your mother's father, was a man and had to leave us to fight in the war across the ocean. I gave him the bag, for I believed it would protect him in battle, but he did not take it with him. He was afraid that he would lose it. He died in a faraway place." K

Again Grandpa was still and I felt his grief around me.

"My son," he went on after clearing his throat, "had only a daughter and it is not proper for her to know of these things."

He unbuttoned his shirt, pulled out the leather pouch, and lifted it over his head. He held it in his hand, turning it over and over as if memorizing how it looked.

"In the bag," he said as he opened it and removed two objects, "is the broken shell of the iron kettle, a pebble from the butte, and a piece of the sacred sage." He held the pouch upside down and dust drifted down.

"After the bag is yours you must put a piece of prairie sage within and never open it again until you pass it on to your son." He replaced the pebble and the piece of iron and tied the bag.

I stood up, somehow knowing I should. Grandpa slowly rose from the bed and stood upright in front of me holding the bag before my face. I closed my eyes and waited for him to slip it over my head. But he spoke.

"No, you need not wear it." He placed the soft leather bag in my right hand and closed my other hand over it. "It would not be right to wear it in this time and place where no one will understand. Put it safely away until you are again on the reservation. Wear it then, when you replace the sacred sage."

Grandpa turned and sat again on the bed. Wearily he leaned his head against the pillow. "Go," he said. "I will sleep now."

"Thank you, Grandpa," I said softly and left with the bag in my hands.

That night Mom and Dad took Grandpa to the hospital. Two weeks later I stood alone on the lonely prairie of the reservation and put the sacred sage in my medicine bag. L

K MAIN CHARACTER
What is Martin learning about his heritage?

3 Targeted Passage

L MAIN CHARACTER
What does Martin's return to the reservation suggest about his attitude toward his heritage?

LITERARY ANALYSIS

K MAIN CHARACTER

Possible answer: *Martin is learning about the significance of the medicine bag in his family's history. He is also learning that his family suffered greatly; his great-great-grandfather was separated from his family and forced to attend a white school, and his grandfather died in war.*

If students need help . . . Have students reread lines 241–257. Ask: What stories does Grandpa tell Martin? What does Grandpa want Martin to learn?

LITERARY ANALYSIS

L MAIN CHARACTER

Possible answer: *Martin now takes his heritage seriously and wants to carry on the family traditions.*

Extend the Discussion What do you think Martin does after he puts the sage in his medicine bag?

FOR LESS-PROFICIENT READERS

3 Targeted Passage [Lines 261–282]

This passage concludes the story. Grandpa presents the medicine bag to Martin, who accepts it with gravity.

- What is inside the medicine bag?
- Why does Martin stand up when he receives the medicine bag?
- What happens to Grandpa after he gives Martin the medicine bag?

FOR ADVANCED LEARNERS/PRE-AP

Select an Heirloom [small-group option] Have students choose one item they own that they would like to hand down to their descendents. Encourage students to share with group members a description of the item, what it expresses about their identity, and what it might symbolize to future generations.

SELECTION WRAP-UP

REFLECT Have students discuss how Martin changes during this story.

CRITIQUE Ask students whether Martin acts like a typical young person in this story. Ask students to support their opinions.

READING FLUENCY

Distribute the copy masters and have students practice fluency.

RESOURCE MANAGER—Copy Master
Reading Fluency p. 134

Practice and Apply

Prereading for this selection is found on pages 238–239.

ANALYZE VISUALS

Possible answer: *Because the girl is looking directly at the viewer, she seems self-confident. The flowers in her hair suggest that she is playful.*

About the Art María Sanchez was born in San Salvador, El Salvador, and grew up in Redwood City, California. She has been painting for more than 15 years and is currently studying fine art at the Academy of Art in San Francisco. The artist writes, "My paintings are . . . simple and sometimes familiar expressions of color and form, yet they all tell a story."

Lines 17–19

REINFORCE *KEY IDEA:* IDENTITY

Discuss How does Who You Are Day relate to the key idea of **identity?** ***Possible answer:*** *On this day, students choose outfits that express their identities. They show others who they are and what is important to them.*

LITERARY ANALYSIS

Ⓜ MAIN CHARACTER

Possible answer: *María lives in a diverse community where people from many different cultures reside.*

If students need help . . .

- Review the meaning of *infer* (*"to figure out by using clues in the text and one's own knowledge"*).
- Remind them that María's school is an important part of her community.
- Direct students to reread lines 14–17. Ask them to describe María's school in their own words.

Who Are You Today, María?

Judith Ortiz Cofer

Abuela[1] knocks on my bedroom door. She has come to my room this morning to watch me choose my outfit for Who You Are Day at school. This is a day when we are allowed to dress in clothes that we think tell the world who we really are. (Within reason, our principal warned—no extremes will be tolerated. I hope that her definition of the word *extreme* is the same as my friend Whoopee's. Nothing that she will put on this morning has ever been seen on this planet, much less at school.)

Abuela makes herself comfortable on my bed as I put on my costume of myself made up of pieces of my life. I thought about my Who You Are Day outfit a lot. Mr. Golden told us in English class to think about our choices: are you going to walk around as a joke or as a poem? I have a suspicion that our teachers have allowed us this chance to dress up as ourselves for a reason. Our school is already a united nations, a carnival, and a parade all at once. There are students from dozens of different countries, and we do not always get along. Most of us are too shy to talk to others outside our little circles, and so misunderstandings come up. The principal has tried almost everything. The Who You Are Day is another of her crazy ideas to get us to communicate. In each of my classes, the teacher said, let us know something about what has made you who you are by what you wear to school tomorrow. It all sounds like a **conspiracy** to me. But I like dressing up so I do not complain like the boys have been doing. Most of them hate the idea! Ⓜ

Abuela looks at my choices hanging on the door and shakes her head, smiling, like she did when we went to see *Cats.* It is a smile that says, I do not understand, but if it is important to María, I will bear it the best I can. She is elegant even at 7:00 A.M. in her embroidered silk robe and red velvet slippers. She has wrapped a shawl over her shoulders because she is always cold in our *cueva,*[2] as she calls the apartment. The shawl was handmade by her mother and it is Abuela's most prized possession. As a little girl, I liked to put it over

ANALYZE VISUALS
Based on the **details** in this painting, what impression do you get of the girl?

④ **Targeted Passage**

conspiracy (kən-spîr′ə-sē) *n.* an agreement to perform together an illegal or wrongful act

Ⓜ **MAIN CHARACTER**
What can you **infer** about the community in which María lives?

1. **Abuela** (ä-bwā′lä) *Spanish:* grandmother.
2. ***cueva*** (kwā′vä) *Spanish:* cave.

Frida (2004), María San[chez]. Acrylic on canvas. C[ollection]. Collection. © María San[chez]

DIFFERENTIATED INSTRUCTION

FOR LESS–PROFICIENT READERS

④ Targeted Passage [Lines 1–21]

In this opening passage, María presents her dilemma: she must select an outfit for Who You Are Day at school.

- What is the purpose of Who You Are Day?
- What causes problems in María's school?
- Why does the principal decide to hold this celebration?
- What is María's attitude toward Who You Are Day?

Reading Strategy Follow-Up: Set a Purpose for Reading [paired option] Encourage students to update their charts, introduced on page 239, to help them compare María to Martin. Ask students to list adjectives that describe María as they read. Provide time for students to share their lists with a partner.

BACKGROUND

Textiles in Puerto Rico In the early part of the 20th century, United States companies established a textile industry in Puerto Rico. In textile factories, or *tejidos,* both women and children worked long hours sewing, embroidering, and making lace. In addition to working in these factories, where working conditions were difficult and pay was low, many women took piecework home, hand-sewing exquisite garments for sale overseas.

FOR ENGLISH LEARNERS

Vocabulary Support This selection includes many words related to clothes. Explain that a *fashion statement* (line 47) is something that your clothes express about you. Then have students draw quick sketches to show they know the meanings of these words from the vignette: *robe* (line 25), *slippers* (line 25), *shawl* (line 26), *jacket* (line 40), *platform shoes* (line 45).

FOR ADVANCED LEARNERS/PRE–AP

Synthesize [small-group option] Have students work in small groups to chart references to clothing throughout the story. Invite students to share their charts with other groups and to discuss why the author chose to use clothing as a symbol of identity.

LITERARY ANALYSIS

Ⓝ MAIN CHARACTER

Possible answer: *María has a close, loving relationship with her grandmother.*

If students need help . . . Ask students to reread María's description of her grandmother and to think about what this description reveals.

LITERARY ANALYSIS

Ⓞ MAIN CHARACTER

Possible answer: *María respects her grandmother's Puerto Rican customs and clothing.*

SELECTION WRAP–UP

REFLECT Ask students what message Abuela gives María when she lends María her shawl. Have students explain their responses.

★ CRITIQUE Ask students whether they think the author does a good job of describing María. Ask them to explain why or why not.

my head because the pattern of sequins made a night sky full of stars and because it smelled like Abuela. Ⓝ

Abuela sips from her cup of café con leche[3] as she watches me.

I feel a little strange about being in my underwear in front of her and go in my closet with my choices, which are:

My mother's red skirt that she wore when she had a part in a musical play on the Island. I have played dress-up with it since I was five years old, but it finally fits me perfectly. It is the kind of skirt that opens like an umbrella when you turn in circles.

A top I sewed together from an old sari[4] Uma's mother was going to throw away. It is turquoise blue with silver edges.

And finally, over my sari, I will wear my father's sharkskin[5] suit jacket—it's big on me but I can roll up the sleeves. It is what he likes to wear when he sings at rent parties. Under the light, it changes colors and seems to come alive as the design shifts and moves. Papi says it is great for dancing; you don't even need a partner.

And finally, tall platform shoes we found buried deep in Whoopee's closet, circa 1974, she told me. Whoopee collects antique shoes to go with her science fiction outfits. It is a fashion statement; she will tell anyone who asks. No one knows what the statement means, and that is just fine with Whoopee.

When I part the clothes in my closet and come out like an actor in a play, Abuela's eyes open wide. Before she can say anything, I point to each piece of my outfit and say a name: Mami, Papi, Uma, and Whoopee.

Abuela's face changes as she begins to understand the meaning of my fashion statement.

"Ahora sé quién eres, María, y quién puedes ser, si quieres. Ven acá, mi amor."

Abuela says that she knows who I am and who I may be if I choose. I have heard those words before but I don't remember when or where. Abuela embraces me and kisses my face several times. This is a Puerto Rican thing. It goes on for a while. I close my eyes to wait it out and I suddenly inhale a familiar scent. When I open my eyes, I see a starry sky. Abuela has put her shawl over my head.

"Algo mío para tu día de ser quien eres, mi hija," she tells me. *Something of mine for your day of being who you are.* She is letting me borrow her mother's beautiful shawl! Ⓞ

All day at school, I feel elegant. Whenever anyone tries to make fun of my costume, I think of the words my grandmother quoted to me: *I know who you are and who you may be if you choose.* And when I go into Mr. Golden's class and his eyes ask me, *Who are you today, María?* I will say by the way I walk in, head held high, that today I am a poem.

Ⓝ **MAIN CHARACTER**
What can you **infer** abo
María's relationship wi
her grandmother?

⑤ **Targeted Passage**

Ⓞ **MAIN CHARACTER**
Reread lines 55–63. Wha
is María's attitude towa
her grandmother's Puer
Rican customs and
clothing?

3. **café con leche** (kă-fā kōn lĕch'ā) *Spanish:* coffee with milk.
4. **sari** (sä'rē): a traditional Indian women's garment.
5. **sharkskin:** a synthetic fabric with a smooth, shiny surface.

DIFFERENTIATED INSTRUCTION

FOR LESS–PROFICIENT READERS

⑤ Targeted Passage [Lines 55–68]

This passage concludes the vignette. María has assembled an outfit with items of clothing from people who are important to her. Abuela's shawl completes the ensemble.

- What does Abuela tell María?
- What is the significance of María's borrowing the shawl?
- How does María feel when she goes to school?

FOR ENGLISH LEARNERS

Evaluate Translations Ask the Spanish-speaking students in the class to write their own translations of the Spanish dialogue in lines 54 and 61. Encourage them to compare their translations with those of the author. Were the author's translations complete?

mprehension

1. **Recall** In "The Medicine Bag," why does Martin's grandfather come to visit?
2. **Recall** What does the medicine bag contain?
3. **Represent** Create a sketch of María in her Who You Are Day outfit. Make sure your sketch reflects the details in the selection.

erary Analysis

4. **Make Inferences** In "The Medicine Bag," how do Martin's mother, father, and sister each feel about Grandpa? Cite details from the story to support your answer.
5. **Draw Conclusions** How are Martin's feelings about his grandfather and his Sioux heritage affected by the kind of neighborhood he lives in?
6. **Interpret Ideas** In "Who Are You Today, María?" what do you think María's English teacher means in line 11 when he asks, "are you going to walk around as a joke or as a poem"?
7. **Compare and Contrast** Compare Martin's relationship with Grandpa to María's relationship with Abuela. How are the relationships similar and different?
8. **Analyze Theme** What message about **identity** does each story contain?

mparing Characters

Now that you've read both stories, finish filling in your chart. Then add the final question and answer it, too.

	Martin	*María*
How does his or her environment affect him or her?		
What is his or her relationship with grandparent like?		
What is his or her attitude toward cultural heritage?		
Does the character change in any way? Explain.		

Practice and Apply

After Reading

For additional support of postreading questions, use these copy masters:

RESOURCE MANAGER—Copy Masters
Reading Check pp. 126, 131 (to check understanding of the selections)
Question Support p. 132 (After Reading questions adapted for English learners and less-proficient readers)

Additional selection questions are provided for teachers on page 117.

ANSWERS

Comprehension

1. *Grandfather is lonely. He also thinks he is going to die soon, and he wants to give his medicine bag to Martin.*
2. *The medicine bag contains a piece of an iron kettle, a pebble, and a piece of sage.*
3. *Sketches should show a girl in a skirt, sari top, suit jacket, platform shoes, and shawl.*

Literary Analysis

Possible answers:

4. *Martin's parents feel protective of Grandpa; his sister is proud of Grandpa and eager to introduce him to her friends.*
5. ● **STANDARDS FOCUS Main Character** *At first, Martin is slow to accept his grandfather into his life because his grandfather is so different from the people who live around Martin. He worries he will lose the acceptance of his friends.*
6. *Mr. Golden wants students to think about who they are and take the assignment—and themselves—seriously. He doesn't want kids to make a joke of who they are.*
7. ● **STANDARDS FOCUS Main Character** *For each character, the grandparent is a link to cultural identity. However, Martin has grown up without knowing his grandfather very well. They have a formal relationship and don't show much affection. By contrast, María has grown up around her grandmother, so the two have a casual and close relationship. Abuela is very affectionate, and María loves to be around her.*
8. *"The Medicine Bag": Our cultural heritage is something to be proud of. "Who Are You Today, María?": The people we love all contribute to our identity.*

Comparing Characters

■ **STANDARDS FOCUS Set a Purpose for Reading** ***Possible answer:***

	Martin	María
How does his or her environment affect him or her?	doesn't want to stick out or be different from his neighbors and friends	seems comfortable in many different environments and cultures
What is his or her relationship with grandparent like?	fond but embarrassed, then deeply respectful	close and affectionate, although Abuela sometimes does not understand María
What is his or her attitude toward cultural heritage?	ashamed, scared, and eventually proud	accepting, happy, proud
Does the character change in any way? Explain.	Yes. As he learns more about his grandfather and his heritage, he becomes proud.	No. She has the same accepting attitude about her heritage throughout the story.

ANSWERS

Vocabulary in Context

VOCABULARY PRACTICE

1. *(c) calmness*
2. *(d) proper*
3. *(a) phony*
4. *(c) parent*
5. *(d) boldly*
6. *(b) loyalty*

RESOURCE MANAGER—Copy Master
Vocabulary Practice p. 129

VOCABULARY IN WRITING

Ask students to recall the scene in which Martin receives the medicine bag. Ask them to think about how they would feel if they were in Martin's place. Then have them review the vocabulary list and identify words that could be used to describe their feelings.

VOCABULARY STRATEGY: ANALOGIES *(also an EL language objective)*

Tell students that it can be helpful to state the relationship between an analogy's first two words as a sentence. Then students can insert the remaining word in the same sentence and try to complete it. Model this strategy with the first analogy:

Old *is an antonym of* immature.

Young *is an antonym of* ____.

Answers:

1. *mature*
2. *hinder*
3. *flood*
4. *murky*

RESOURCE MANAGER—Copy Master
Vocabulary Strategy p. 130

Vocabulary Center at **ClassZone.com**
Additional Vocabulary Activities

Vocabulary in Context

VOCABULARY PRACTICE

For each item, choose the word that differs most in meaning from the other words. Refer to a dictionary if you need help.

1. (a) uprising, (b) commotion, (c) calmness, (d) racket
2. (a) unseemly, (b) crude, (c) rude, (d) proper
3. (a) phony, (b) factual, (c) real, (d) authentic
4. (a) heir, (b) descendant, (c) parent, (d) child
5. (a) shyly, (b) self-consciously, (c) sheepishly, (d) boldly
6. (a) conspiracy, (b) loyalty, (c) plot, (d) trickery

authentic | descendant | commotion | sheepishly | conspiracy | unseemly

VOCABULARY IN WRITING

Imagine that Joe Iron Shell is your grandfather. Using two or more vocabulary words, write a paragraph explaining how you feel about receiving the medicine bag. You could start this way.

EXAMPLE SENTENCE

*I **sheepishly** accept the medicine bag.*

VOCABULARY STRATEGY: ANALOGIES

An **analogy** is a relationship between pairs of words. To complete an analogy, identify the relationship between the words in the first pair. The second pair of words must relate to each other in the same way. For example, if the first pair are **antonyms** (words with opposite meanings), the second pair should also be antonyms. If the first pair of words show a **cause-effect relationship,** the second pair of words should show a cause-effect relationship, too.

Analogies are often written as follows—big : small :: soft : rough. If the analogy is read aloud, you would say, "big **is to** small **as** soft **is to** rough."

PRACTICE Choose a word from the box to complete each analogy.

flood | hinder | mature | murky

1. old : immature :: young : ____
2. gather : scatter :: benefit : ____
3. match : fire :: storm : ____
4. bright : drab :: clear : ____

VOCABULARY PRACTICE
For more practice, go to the **Vocabulary Cente** at **ClassZone.com.**

DIFFERENTIATED INSTRUCTION

FOR ENGLISH LEARNERS

Vocabulary Strategy [shared-language pairs] Review with students the meanings of *synonym, antonym, cause,* and *relationship,* and make sure that students understand each word in the analogies. Suggest that they approach each analogy by restating the relationship between the first set of words. For instance: *A match starts a fire, and a storm starts a* ____. Pairs might use their first language to formulate these sentences and then translate them into English.

FOR ADVANCED LEARNERS/PRE–AP

Vocabulary Strategy Challenge students to write analogies using the words from the **Vocabulary Practice** word list. Remind them to use different types of meaning relationships (synonyms, antonyms, cause and effect). Examples:

- commotion : tranquility :: authentic : fake
- descendant : grandson :: ancestor : grandmother
- mistake : sheepish :: success : proud

riting for Assessment

1. READ THE PROMPT

In writing assessments, you will often be asked to compare and contrast main characters from different selections.

PROMPT

In four or five paragraphs, compare and contrast the main characters in "The Medicine Bag" and "Who Are You Today, María?" Consider the environments they came from, their relationships with their grandparents, and their attitudes toward their cultural heritage. In your conclusion, explain whether the characters change in any important ways. Support your response with details from the two stories.

STRATEGIES IN ACTION

1. I need to discuss the **similarities and differences** between the two characters.
2. I need to **give examples** to show how the characters' environments, relationships, and heritage are **alike** or **different**.
3. In the conclusion, I need to **describe** whether the characters change, and if so, how.

2. PLAN YOUR WRITING

Review the chart you filled out on page 251. Use the chart to help you identify the characters' similarities and differences. Then think about how you will set up the body of your essay.

- Do you want to compare the characters' environments in one paragraph, relationships with their grandparents in the next paragraph, and attitudes toward their cultural heritage in a third paragraph?
- Do you want to describe the characters in separate paragraphs and then discuss their similarities and differences in a third paragraph?

I. Introduction
II. Environments they came from
III. Relationships with grandparents
IV. Attitudes toward cultural heritage
V. Conclusion

Once you have decided on an organization, create an outline. Then write a thesis statement that describes the main idea or purpose of your essay.

3. DRAFT YOUR RESPONSE

Introduction Provide the titles and authors of both selections as well as a sentence telling what each is about. Include your thesis statement.
Body Discuss characters' similarities and differences, using your outline as a guide. Support your ideas with story details.
Conclusion Remind readers of your thesis statement. End by noting whether either character changed in any important way.
Revision Make sure your essay answers the question in the writing prompt.

253

Writing for Assessment

1. ***READ THE PROMPT***
   - Read the prompt aloud. Ask volunteers to identify key words and phrases that define the task.
   - Discuss each strategy and have students restate in their own words what they need to do for this assignment.
2. ***PLAN YOUR WRITING***
   - Direct students to use their charts from page 251. The completed chart should include most of the information that they need to write the response.
   - If students need more information, have them brainstorm examples from each story that describe the characters' environments, relationships, and heritage. Then have them reread the beginning and end of each story, focusing on each character's development.
   - Students may prefer to use a block method of comparison, discussing Martin first, then María, and then their similarities and differences.
3. ***DRAFT YOUR RESPONSE***
   - Remind students to write a strong thesis statement.
   - Suggest that students reread their response to ensure it answers the prompt.

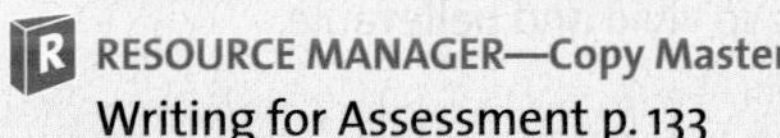
RESOURCE MANAGER—Copy Master
Writing for Assessment p. 133

Assess and Reteach

Assess

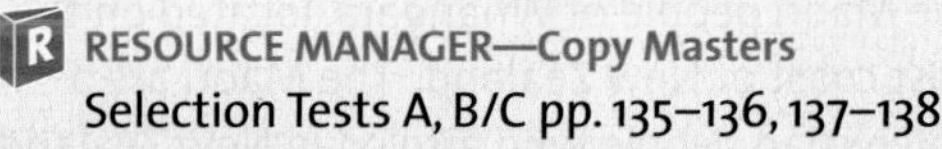
RESOURCE MANAGER—Copy Masters
Selection Tests A, B/C pp. 135–136, 137–138

Test Generator CD

Reteach

STANDARDS LESSON FILE
Literature Lesson 1: Types of Characters and Character Traits
Reading Lesson 12: Comparing and Contrasting
Writing Lesson 29: Comparison-Contrast Essay
Vocabulary Lesson 23: Analogies

DIFFERENTIATED INSTRUCTION

FOR LESS–PROFICIENT WRITERS

Plan Your Writing
Review students' charts from page 251. Discuss the details that best show the characters' similarities and differences. Have students circle those ideas on their charts.

Draft Your Response
Give students this template for their essays:

Introduction: [Character] in [first story] and [character] in [second story] are similar because ____ and different because ____. [Thesis statement.]

Middle paragraphs:
- [Character name] in [first story] lives in [environment]. In contrast, [character name] in [second story] lives in [environment].
- Both characters care about and learn from their grandparents. [Give details.]
- The two characters start out with different attitudes toward their cultural heritage. [Give details.]

Conclusion: [Explain whether the characters change.] [Restate thesis.]

Focus and Motivate

OBJECTIVES

Media Literacy

- explore the key idea of movie **characters**
- identify and analyze visual elements and editing in film
- analyze characterization in film
- create a film scene

SUMMARY

In these clips from the film *Whale Rider,* Paikea is shown in a battle of wills with her grandfather as she tries to participate in his lessons for potential leaders of the tribe. She tries to join his school but is quickly turned away. After that, she secretly observes his lessons from afar. Paikea's grandfather catches her practicing with a traditional fighting stick, and Paikea faces him in calm defiance.

What puts a
CHARACTER *in focus?*

Discuss the question. Ask students what skills they use to learn about people they meet for the first time. Explain that they can use the same skills to learn about fictional **characters** in movies or books. After students read the ***KEY IDEA*** paragraph, invite them to discuss specific fictional characters who are memorable to them and the details that make these characters so vivid and believable.

BACKGROUND

The film *Whale Rider* is based on a novel by Witi Ihimaera. Like fictional Paikea and her family in the film, Ihimaera traces his roots to the Maori people of Whangara, located on the east coast of New Zealand. The Maori are a Polynesian people who arrived in New Zealand long before Europeans. According to legend, a great ancestor by the name of Paikea arrived in eastern New Zealand on the back of a whale more than 1,000 years ago. Whangara chiefs are always a family's first-born male and are believed to be ancient Paikea's direct descendants. In the movie, young Paikea's mother and twin brother die during childbirth, and it is her mother's last request that her surviving child be named after ancient Paikea, the great whale rider.

Media Study

from Whale Rider

Film Clips on *MediaSmart* DVD

What puts a CHARACTER *in focus*

KEY IDEA Think about your favorite fictional **characters.** What is it that draws you to them? Is it the things they say, the way they behave, the lives they lead? As you read about or watch these characters, perhaps you imagine how you would act if you were in their shoes. In this lesson, you'll view two clips from *Whale Rider* to explore the tools filmmakers use to create believable characters.

Background

Out with the Old In *Whale Rider,* a young native New Zealand girl named Paikea, or Pai, must challenge the old ways of her tribe to fulfill her destiny. For over 1,000 years, Paikea's tribe has been ruled by a male. The current chief is Koro, Paikea's grandfather. When Paikea's father refuses his rightful place as chief, Koro must decide who will take his place. Although Paikea is descended from the chief, Koro doesn't believe a girl can lead.

Koro starts a school to train the young men of the tribe in the old ways of their people. He will choose one among them to succeed him. You'll watch the conflict that arises between the determined Paikea and her stubborn grandfather when she tries to join the school.

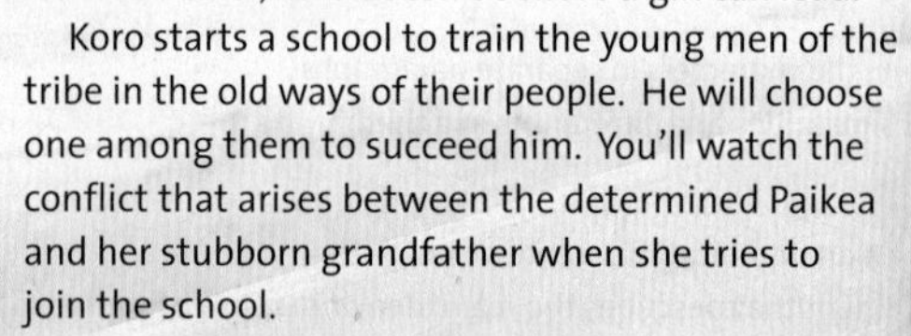

254

Media Study Resources

RESOURCE MANAGER UNIT 2

Plan and Teach pp. 139–142

Media Analysis

Summary pp. 143†*, 144‡*

Viewing Guide p. 145

Close Viewing p. 146

Media Activity p. 147

Produce Your Own Media p. 148

STANDARDS LESSON FILE

Media Lesson 1: Active Viewing Strategies

Media Lesson 4: Analyzing Visuals in Film and TV

Media Lesson 6: Analyzing Editing in Film and TV

Media Center at **ClassZone.com**

MEDIA VIEWING

Media*Smart* DVD

* Resources for Differentiation † Also in Spanish ‡ In Haitian Creole and Vietnamese

edia Literacy: Characters in Movies

The best books and movies develop characters that feel like real people. You laugh with them and cry with them. You're drawn into their stories and you truly care what happens to them. An author provides detail and background through descriptive passages to develop his or her characters. A filmmaker has to rely on his or her camera work, the performances of the actors, and the skills of the film editor to create true-to-life characters.

FILMMAKING TECHNIQUES	STRATEGIES FOR VIEWING
Camera Shots • A **close-up shot** provides a detailed view of a person or object. • A **long shot** provides a wide view of a scene. It can show distance between characters and establish location. • A **reaction shot** shows a person react to what occurred in the previous shot.	• Notice how close-ups focus on facial expressions. Ask yourself what the character might be feeling. • Watch how long shots can reveal relationships. A shot of two people standing apart can show emotional distance. A long shot of one character can single him or her out from a group. • Watch for reaction shots. What does the character's response to an event say about his or her feelings?
Performance • **Physical appearance,** including height, weight, hairstyle, and clothing • **Behavior,** including **facial expressions** and **body language** • **Dialogue,** both what the character says and how he or she says it	• Pay attention to how a main character's appearance provides clues about his or her personality. • Watch a character's posture and facial expressions. These can convey feelings, reactions, or self-image. • Listen to the dialogue. Is the character's tone of voice happy, calm, or angry? What does speech reveal about a character's background and intelligence?
Editing **Editing** is the process of choosing and arranging shots in a sequence. Filmmakers combine the shots they've filmed to create an overall effect on the audience.	• Notice the different types of shots the editor uses. How do they reflect the emotion of the scene? • Watch for reaction shots that are edited into a scene. How do they reveal characters' thoughts and feelings? • Notice how long each shot stays on the screen. How does shot length change as emotion rises in a scene?

MEDIA STUDY: TEACHING OPTIONS

Teaching Option 1: The Basics (1–2 Days)

1. Begin the Media Study using the material provided on pages 254–255.
2. Show the Introduction on Media*Smart.* Then show the First Viewing. As they watch, have students use the Viewing Guide on page 256, along with the corresponding copy master on page 145 of the Resource Manager. Discuss their responses.
3. Return to the pupil edition for the extension activities on page 257.

Teaching Option 2: In-Depth Study (2–3 Days)

1. Begin the Media Study using pages 254–255.
2. Show the Introduction and First Viewing from Media*Smart.*
3. Continue on Media*Smart* with the Media Lessons, using the teacher notes available in the Resources section.
4. Show the Guided Analysis presentation. Have students record their observations on the Student Viewing Guide available in the Resources section from Media*Smart.*
5. Return to the pupil edition, page 257.

Teach

MEDIA LITERACY

Have students refer to any favorite movie characters they mentioned at the beginning of the lesson. Encourage them to think of specific scenes that helped them understand a character. How did these scenes reveal information about the character? Then discuss the chart on page 255.

- **Camera Shots** Ask students to look at the two images on page 255 and identify what type of camera shot each represents. Then have them infer what the director is trying to tell viewers about the character's thoughts, feelings, or relationship with other characters in these shots. Ask students to remember these shots and gather additional information when they view the film clips.
- **Performance** Have students think again about a favorite movie character and recall one or two specific details about his or her
  —physical appearance
  —behavior
  —dialogue or interactions with other characters

  Ask: What do these details reveal about the personality, background, or intelligence of the character?
- **Editing** Explain that scenes in a movie are often shot out of sequence. The job of the director and the film editor includes arranging the shots in the best possible way to tell the story. Tell students that the word *pace* refers to how long each shot stays on the screen. An editor might put together a slow-paced scene with lengthy shots focusing on one or two characters, or a fast-paced scene that includes many quick shots. Ask what effects these two kinds of scenes might have on the viewer.

 Media*Smart* DVD

Practice and Apply

VIEWING GUIDE

1. As students prepare to view the film clips, tell them that they will be asked to explain specific techniques used by filmmakers to create believable characters. Encourage them to watch and listen for these elements:
   - the use of different **camera shots** to reveal the feelings and reactions of characters and to express relationships between characters
   - the relationship between the **physical appearance** and **behavior** of a character and his or her personality and feelings
   - the use of **dialogue** to reveal a character's background, intelligence, and feelings
   - careful **editing** to create an emotional effect with each scene
2. Suggest to students that they watch the clips three or more times to focus on different filmmaking techniques. During the first viewing, students can focus on camera shots. During the second viewing, they should focus on the performances of the main characters. With the third viewing, students should notice the editing. Have students take notes as they watch.

RESOURCE MANAGER—Copy Masters
Viewing Guide p. 145
Close Viewing p. 146
Media Activity p. 147

Media*Smart* DVD

ANSWERS

FIRST VIEWING: Comprehension

1. *Koro says that anger is part of the battle, and the boy must learn to control it.*
2. *Paikea defies Koro by sitting down in the front row even after he tells her to sit in the back. She then spies on the boys' school and practices the skills the boys are learning.*

CLOSE VIEWING: Media Literacy

Possible answers:

3. *Paikea's red shirt makes her stand out from the crowd. Also, she is shown as the only girl in a crowd of boys and men at the beginning of the first clip.*
4. *The reaction shots show the audience that Paikea's grandmother is proud of her for standing up to Koro.*
5. *Viewers see Paikea and the other characters in several different costumes. Also, cutting to different locations indicates that time has passed.*
6. *Students may list these qualities in their diagrams:*
   - ***Koro:** leadership, strictness*
   - ***Both:** strength, intelligence, determination, stubbornness*
   - ***Paikea:** courage, independence, rebelliousness*

MediaSmart DVD

- **Film:** *Whale Rider*
- **Director:** Niki Caro
- **Genre:** Drama
- **Running Time:** 4 minutes

Viewing Guide for
Whale Rider

In these scenes, Koro, the chief, starts to teach the tribe's tradition to the boys of the village. You'll see what happens when Paikea attempts to join the school. As you watch, notice how the directo choice of shots, the actors' performances, and the editing work together to create memorable characters. Pay special attention to the techniques that are used when the emotion rises. Use the questions to analyze the scenes. You may want to view the clips more than once.

NOW VIEW

***FIRST VIEWING:* Comprehension**

1. **Recall** Why doesn't Koro get angry when the boy hits him in the back with his stick?
2. **Clarify** Paikea doesn't say a single word to her grandfather in these scenes. How does she defy his wishes without speaking?

***CLOSE VIEWING:* Media Literacy**

3. **Identify Film Technique** A **long shot** is used to show Paikea's lonelines when she walks away from the group in the beginning of these clips. Find another example from the clips of how the director separates Paikea from the group.
4. **Analyze Shots** Why do you think the director chose to show **reaction shots** of the grandmother when Paikea defies Koro?
5. **Analyze Editing** Even though these scenes are short, they cover severa days in Paikea's life. Cite evidence from the clips that tell you the scenes took place over more than one day.
6. **Compare Characters** Even though Koro and Paikea are at odds throughout these scenes, they are similar in many ways. Compare the two characters by listing descriptive traits of each in a Venn diagram. As a starting point, think of the qualities of a chief that Koro mentions in the scenes: strength, courage, intelligence, and leadership.

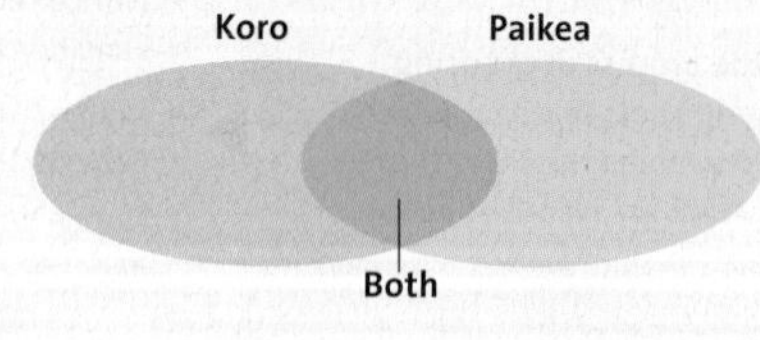

256

rite or Discuss

Evaluate Film In this lesson, you learned some of the techniques filmmakers use to create believable characters. Think about Paikea's predicament. She believes she can be a leader, but she has to defy her grandfather to prove it. Write a paragraph describing how the filmmaking techniques you learned were used in the scene. In your opinion, were the filmmakers successful in making Paikea into a believable character? Think about

- the types of shots the filmmakers use
- the appearance and performance of the actor playing Paikea
- the editing of the scene

oduce Your Own Media

Plan a Scene Imagine you're a movie director. You're planning a scene that is designed to show the relationship between two characters. Create a shot-by-shot description of a two-person scene. You can choose a scene from a story you've read or create your own. Your description should include a brief overall description of what happens in the scene, a list of shots describing what happens in each, and a sketch of each shot.

HERE'S HOW Use these tips to help you plan your scene:

- Remember that conflict drives a story. Consider creating a scene in which your two characters are in a disagreement.
- Include any dialogue that will be spoken in your description of each shot.
- Identify each type of shot you will use. **Close-up shots** are perfect for capturing facial expressions in **reaction shots. Long shots** work better for showing body language and distance between characters.

STUDENT MODEL

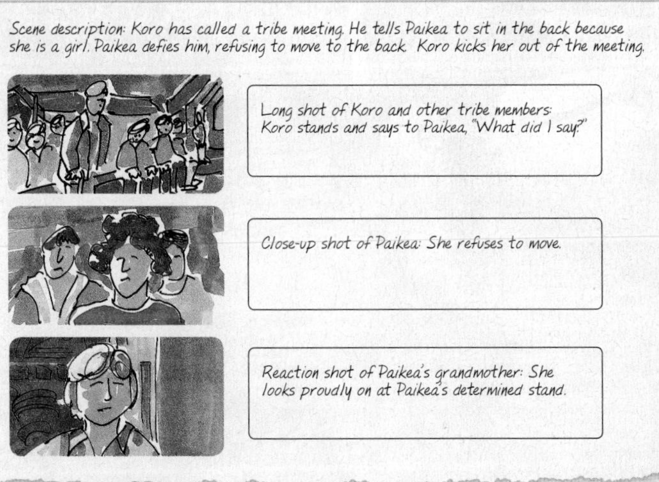

Scene description: Koro has called a tribe meeting. He tells Paikea to sit in the back because she is a girl. Paikea defies him, refusing to move to the back. Koro kicks her out of the meeting.
Long shot of Koro and other tribe members: Koro stands and says to Paikea, "What did I say?"
Close-up shot of Paikea: She refuses to move.
Reaction shot of Paikea's grandmother: She looks proudly on at Paikea's determined stand.

MEDIA TOOLS

For help with creating a shot-by-shot scene description, visit the **Media Center** at **ClassZone.com.**

Tech Tip

If a camera is available, shoot photographs of your classmates acting out your scene in place of the sketches.

Assess and Reteach

Write or Discuss

Evaluate Film In their evaluations, students should focus on the performance of the actor as well as the ways in which the filmmakers edited scenes with various types of camera shots. For example, students might point out the effect of seeing Paikea secretly observe her grandfather's class through a window behind his back. This shot emphasizes Paikea's feeling of being an outsider who is unable to connect with her grandfather in his world. Paikea's facial expressions—which reveal her sadness and disappointment—are crucial to this scene. Students might also point to moments of careful editing, such as the cuts between Koro's, Paikea's, and the grandmother's reactions as Koro and Paikea clash over Paikea's attempt to attend class.

Produce Your Own Media

Rubric A strong plan for a scene should include

- two main characters in a disagreement or other kind of emotional interaction
- dialogue that will be spoken by the scene's main characters
- identification and description of shots that will be used for the scene

RESOURCE MANAGER—Copy Master
Produce Your Own Media p. 148

Media*Smart* DVD

MEDIA STUDY WRAP-UP

Summarize Ask students to summarize the techniques filmmakers use to introduce characters and help viewers understand characters' personalities and feelings. Have them provide specific examples from the *Whale Rider* film clips they have viewed. If necessary, prompt them to focus on the use of camera shots; physical appearance, behavior, and dialogue; and the editing of shots to create effective scenes.

RETEACH

STANDARDS LESSON FILE
Media Lesson 1: Active Viewing Strategies
Media Lesson 4: Analyzing Visuals in Film and TV
Media Lesson 6: Analyzing Editing in Film and TV

Focus and Motivate

OBJECTIVES

Literary Analysis
- explore the key idea of **risk**
- identify and analyze methods of characterization
- read a biography and a letter

Reading
- monitor comprehension

Vocabulary
- build vocabulary for reading and writing
- use context clues to determine word meaning *(also an EL language objective)*

Grammar and Writing
- avoid clauses as fragments by joining dependent and independent clauses
- use writing to analyze literature

SUMMARY

In December of 1851, Harriet Tubman set out from Maryland to lead 11 enslaved people to freedom. On the long, cold walk, she used many methods—including storytelling, urging, and threatening—to keep the fugitives from giving up. Finally, Tubman and her group arrived in St. Catharines, in what is now Ontario, Canada. Over the next six years, Tubman repeated this heroic feat twice a year.

When is a RISK *worth taking?*

Discuss the question. To lead into the ***KEY IDEA,*** ask students to define ***risk*** and to tell what risks the man in the photograph might be taking and why. Discuss when taking a risk might be a good choice. Then have students work on the ***QUICKWRITE*** activity.

Before Reading

from Harriet Tubman: Conductor on the Underground Railroad

Biography by Ann Petry

When is a RISK *worth taking*

KEY IDEA Some people **risk** their lives needlessly looking for a thrill. Others hold themselves back from accomplishment because they are afraid to take a chance. How can you be sure when it's right to put your safety or reputation on the line? In the biography you are about to read, you will meet a woman who took enormous risks to help others because she believed all people have the right to freedom.

QUICKWRITE Think about a time when you took a risk. In a brief paragraph, describe the risk and why you took it. What were the results? Looking back, was the risk worth taking?

258

Selection Resources

RESOURCE MANAGER UNIT 2

Plan and Teach pp. 149–156

Literary Analysis
Summary pp. 157†*, 158‡*
Characterization pp. 159, 160†*
Question Support p. 167*

Reading
Monitor pp. 161, 162†*
Reading Check p. 166
Reading Fluency p. 169

Vocabulary
Study p. 163*
Practice p. 164
Strategy p. 165

Grammar and Writing
Avoid Clauses as Fragments p. 168

Assessment
Selection Tests A, B/C pp. 171*, 173*
Test Generator CD

BEST PRACTICES TOOLKIT

Differentiated Instruction pp. 31–38*
Scaffolding Instruction pp. 43–46*

Graphic Organizers/Strategies
Anticipation Guide • Word Questioning • Making Inferences • Timeline • Character Traits Web • Venn Diagram

Reading Support
Audio Anthology CD*

Technology
Literature, Vocabulary, and Writing Centers at **ClassZone.com**
Write*Smart* CD

* Resources for Differentiation † Also in Spanish ‡ In Haitian Creole and Vietnamese

ERARY ANALYSIS: CHARACTERIZATION

Whether they are describing fictional characters or real people, skillful writers can make you feel as if you've met the person you're reading about. To bring figures to life in this way, writers use the following methods of **characterization:**

- describing the person's physical appearance
- presenting the person's own thoughts, speech, and actions
- revealing other people's reactions to the person
- directly commenting on the person

As you read, pay attention to the methods Ann Petry uses to create a portrait of the biography's subject, Harriet Tubman.

ADING STRATEGY: MONITOR

Have you ever found yourself reading without fully understanding the words in front of you? If so, pause and ask yourself **questions** about confusing parts. When you read to find the answers, you will probably find that more information stays with you.

As you read this biography, take time to note places where you become confused or lose track of ideas. Use a chart like the one shown to record your questions and their answers.

My Questions	*Answers*
How does Harriet Tubman avoid getting caught?	

CABULARY IN CONTEXT

The boldfaced words help Ann Petry tell about one of Harriet Tubman's journeys for freedom. Try to figure out what each word means in the context of its sentence.

1. After days of wear, his shirt was wrinkled and **disheveled.**
2. A good leader can **instill** a feeling of confidence in others.
3. Music can often **evoke** a pleasant memory.
4. Days on their feet made them long to **linger** at each stop.
5. She used clever stories to **cajole** them to take risks.
6. His **sullen** attitude discouraged others in the group.
7. Her positive attitude helped **dispel** their fears.
8. Her **eloquence** helped convince them to follow her.

Author Online

Making History Speak

Ann Petry
1908–1997

The descendant of a runaway slave from Virginia, Ann Petry grew up in a comfortable middle-class household in Old Saybrook, Connecticut. Hers was the only African-American family in town. Despite her father's respected position as the town's pharmacist, Petry experienced racism growing up. Much of her writing describes the struggles of African Americans against prejudice in New England and in Harlem, where she moved in the 1930s. After Petry had a daughter of her own, she became interested in writing for young readers. In addition to her biography of Harriet Tubman, Petry wrote four other books for young people and four books for adults. She said that writing about the lives of real people helped her "make history speak across the centuries." She wanted to remind readers of the important contributions that African-American men and women have made to American history.

MORE ABOUT THE AUTHOR
For more on Ann Petry, visit the **Literature Center** at **ClassZone.com.**

Background

The Underground Railroad In the period before and during the Civil War, many people enslaved in the South fled north to freedom using a secret network of escape routes known as the Underground Railroad. The "conductors" on the Underground Railroad were brave men and women who provided the escaping people with food, hiding places, and guidance to the next "station." Harriet Tubman was one of the most famous of these conductors.

259

Teach

STANDARDS FOCUS

LITERARY ANALYSIS

● CHARACTERIZATION

Write this example on the board:

> Helen is petite. Her skin is dark and smooth, and she wears her hair short. She's one of those people everyone loves. People just want to be near her.

Ask: What methods of characterization do you notice? ***Answer:*** *Methods include describing her appearance, directly commenting on her, and revealing other people's reactions to her.*

CHECK UNDERSTANDING Ask students to identify a method of characterization used in another story they've read.

READING STRATEGY

■ MONITOR

Model the strategy by reading aloud the **Underground Railroad** paragraph on page 259. Then write on the board, "Who were the conductors?" and show how rereading the second sentence reveals the answer (*people who helped others escape slavery*).

CHECK UNDERSTANDING Have students read **Making History Speak** on page 259 and then compose two questions about what they've read.

RESOURCE MANAGER—Copy Master
Monitor p. 161 (for student use while reading the selection)

VOCABULARY SKILL

▲ VOCABULARY IN CONTEXT

DIAGNOSE WORD KNOWLEDGE To determine preteaching needs, have all students complete **Vocabulary in Context.** ***Possible answers:*** **1.** *messy* **2.** *supply gradually* **3.** *summon* **4.** *remain* **5.** *coax* **6.** *sulky* **7.** *drive away* **8.** *ability to speak powerfully*

PRETEACH VOCABULARY Use the Vocabulary Study copy master to help students determine the meaning of each boldfaced word.

1. Read aloud the first sentence, emphasizing the boldfaced word.
2. Ask students to think about the way the word is used and to look for any context clues (*onward*). Discuss possible meanings for *cajole,* such as "coax" or "urge."
3. Repeat for each of the other sentences.
4. Have students complete Part B independently before reading. After reading, have them revise their definitions as needed.

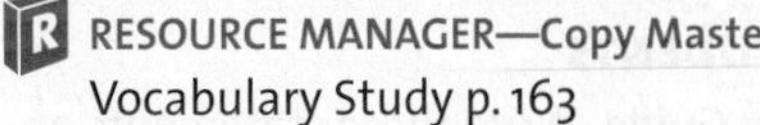

RESOURCE MANAGER—Copy Master
Vocabulary Study p. 163

For general guidelines on differentiating vocabulary instruction and for alternative vocabulary activities for students not needing vocabulary preteaching, see

BEST PRACTICES TOOLKIT
Scaffolding Vocabulary Instruction pp. 43–46

Vocabulary Center at **ClassZone.com**

Practice and Apply

ANALYZE VISUALS

Possible answer:

- *The cross symbolizes Christian faith.*
- *The north star symbolizes guidance.*
- *The portrait of a man might symbolize Tubman's code name, Moses.*
- *Tracks symbolize the Underground Railroad.*
- *There seem to be two suns, one rising and one setting, perhaps symbolizing that Tubman was always moving.*
- *A small house in the distance might symbolize safety and rest.*
- *Tubman's skirt has stripes like the American flag, perhaps symbolizing ideals such as freedom and equality.*

About the Art American artist William H. Johnson (1901–1970) moved to New York when he was 17 years old and put himself through school at the National Academy of Design. His work is known for its folk art influences and stunning use of color.

READING STRATEGY

A MONITOR

Remind students to record questions in their charts. *Responses will vary. Students may wonder who Moses is and what he has to do with Harriet Tubman.*

LITERARY ANALYSIS

B CHARACTERIZATION

Possible answer: *The author says that Moses is stealthy and clever, helping people escape slavery and using the call of the whippoorwill to get their attention.*

Harriet Tubman:

Conductor on the Underground Railroad

Ann Petry

The Railroad Runs to Canada

Along the Eastern Shore of Maryland, in Dorchester County, in Caroline County, the masters kept hearing whispers about the man named Moses, who was running off slaves. At first they did not believe in his existence. The stories about him were fantastic, unbelievable. Yet they watched for him. They offered rewards for his capture. **A**

They never saw him. Now and then they heard whispered rumors to the effect that he was in the neighborhood. The woods were searched. The roads were watched. There was never anything to indicate his whereabouts. But a few days afterward, a goodly number of slaves would be gone from the plantation. Neither the master nor the overseer had heard or seen anything unusual in the quarter.[1] Sometimes one or the other would vaguely remember having heard a whippoorwill call somewhere in the woods, close by, late at night. Though it was the wrong season for whippoorwills. **B**

Sometimes the masters thought they had heard the cry of a hoot owl, repeated, and would remember having thought that the intervals between the low moaning cry were wrong, that it had been repeated four times in succession instead of three. There was never anything more than that to suggest that all was not well in the quarter. Yet when morning came, they invariably discovered that a group of the finest slaves had taken to their heels.

Unfortunately, the discovery was almost always made on a Sunday. Thus a whole day was lost before the machinery of pursuit could be set in motion. The posters offering rewards for the fugitives could not be printed until Monday.

ANALYZE VISUALS
What **symbols** do you notice in this painting?

A MONITOR
What are you wondering about Moses?

1 Targeted Passage

B CHARACTERIZATION
Reread lines 6–13. What does the author tell you about Moses' actions?

1. **quarter:** the area in which enslaved people lived.

Harriet Tubman (1945), William H. Johnson. Oil on paperboard, sheet, 29⅜" × 23⅜". Smithsonian American Art Museum, Washington, D.C.

DIFFERENTIATED INSTRUCTION

FOR ALL STUDENTS

Anticipation Guide Write these statements on the Anticipation Guide. Have students respond to each statement before and after reading.

- The Underground Railroad made use of horse-drawn buggies as well as trains.
- The enslaved people who escaped were safe when they reached New England.
- Harriet Tubman sometimes threatened people with a gun to keep them moving.

BEST PRACTICES TOOLKIT—Transparency
Anticipation Guide p. A14

FOR LESS–PROFICIENT READERS

In combination with the *Audio Anthology CD,* use one or more Targeted Passages (pp. 260, 263, 266, 269) to ensure that students focus on key events and concepts.

1 Targeted Passage [Lines 1–19]

This passage introduces Harriet Tubman but does so by using her code name, Moses.

- Do the masters ever see Moses?
- What do the masters do when they hear the rumors that Moses might be in the neighborhood?
- How do the masters know that Moses has visited?

BACKGROUND

Slavery in the United States Although the first enslaved Africans arrived in Virginia in 1619, the greatest number arrived in the late 1700s to work the cotton fields in the South. By the first half of the 18th century, opposition to slavery, called abolitionism, was growing in the North. President Abraham Lincoln's Emancipation Proclamation of January 1, 1863, ensured that enslaved people would be freed as soon as the Union army won the Civil War. The 13th Amendment to the Constitution officially abolished slavery in the United States in 1865.

FOR ENGLISH LEARNERS

Key Academic Vocabulary Have students use Word Questioning to study this academic vocabulary: from *Harriet Tubman: pursued* (line 59), *aware* (lines 148, 230), *finally* (lines 161, 212); from "Letter to Harriet Tubman": *devotion*.

 BEST PRACTICES TOOLKIT—Transparency
Word Questioning p. E9

FOR ENGLISH LEARNERS

Options for Reading Read aloud lines 1–22 and check understanding by asking students what happens when Moses is nearby. Then have them continue reading along with the *Audio Anthology CD*.

Prereading For prereading instruction for English learners, see

 BEST PRACTICES TOOLKIT
Scaffolding Reading Instruction pp. 43–46

FOR ADVANCED LEARNERS/PRE–AP

Pre-AP exercises in the bottom channel provide additional challenge for your advanced students. Use them for small groups or individuals.

ADDITIONAL GUIDELINES

For more help with differentiation and tips for classroom management, see

 BEST PRACTICES TOOLKIT
Differentiated Instruction pp. 31–38

READING STRATEGY

C MONITOR

Answer: *Leaving on Saturday night gives the escapees a day's head start because on Sundays, the people who are paid to catch them are praying or hunting. Also, posters cannot be printed until Monday.*

READING STRATEGY

D MONITOR

Answer: *Harriet Tubman is Moses.*

Extend the Discussion Explain that Moses is a biblical figure who led the Jews out of slavery in Egypt. Ask students what Tubman and Moses have in common.

ANALYZE VISUALS

Possible answer: *The bright colors convey a hopeful mood, but the images of the people running and of Tubman pointing the way with her enlarged hand convey a fearful mood.*

About the Art Jacob Lawrence (1917–2000) was born in Atlantic City, New Jersey, and grew up in Harlem, New York. He typically used vibrant colors and flattened forms, and he was inspired by the muralist tradition from Mexico. He used his artistic talents as a way to explore his heritage. His paintings are known for telling the stories of African Americans throughout history. Between 1938 and 1940, he created 31 images called *The Harriet Tubman Series.*

The men who made a living hunting for runaway slaves were out of reach, off in the woods with their dogs and their guns, in pursuit of four-footed game, or they were in camp meetings saying their prayers with their wives and families beside them. **C**

Harriet Tubman could have told them that there was far more involved in this matter of running off slaves than signaling the would-be runaways by imitating the call of a whippoorwill, or a hoot owl, far more involved than a matter of waiting for a clear night when the North Star was visible.

In December, 1851, when she started out with the band of fugitives that she planned to take to Canada, she had been in the vicinity of the plantation for days, planning the trip, carefully selecting the slaves that she would take with her.

She had announced her arrival in the quarter by singing the forbidden spiritual—"Go down, Moses, 'way down to Egypt Land"[2]—singing it softly outside the door of a slave cabin, late at night. The husky voice was beautiful even when it was barely more than a murmur borne[3] on the wind. **D**

Once she had made her presence known, word of her coming spread from cabin to cabin. The slaves whispered to each other, ear to mouth, mouth to ear,

2. **"Go down, Moses, 'way down to Egypt Land":** a line from an African-American folk song.
3. **borne:** carried.

C MONITOR
Why does Moses cho
Saturday night to hel
enslaved people esca

D MONITOR
What is Harriet Tubm
relationship to Moses

ANALYZE VISUAL
Consider the colors,
shapes, and figures in
painting. What **mood**
they convey?

Through Forest, Through Rivers, Up Mountains (1967), Jacob Lawrence. Tempera, gouache and pencil on paper, 15¹¹⁄₁₆″ × 26⅞″. Smithsonian Institution, Hirshhorn Museum and Sculpture Garden. © 2007 The Jacob and Gwendolyn Lawrence Foundation, Seattle/Artists Rights Society (ARS), New York.

DIFFERENTIATED INSTRUCTION

FOR LESS–PROFICIENT READERS

Comprehension Support Have students reread lines 20–26. Make sure they understand that the masters hired people to hunt down anyone trying to escape from slavery. Ask students what point the author is trying to make by using the phrase *four-footed game* (line 24).

Possible answer: *She is making the point that some people hunted escaped slave workers as they would hunt animals.*

FOR ENGLISH LEARNERS

Vocabulary: Idioms and Sayings Help students define these idioms and sayings:

- *running off slaves* (lines 3, 28), "helping enslaved people to escape"
- *taken to their heels* (line 19), "run away"
- *sold South* (line 62), "returned to the plantations"
- *holding these things out to them* (lines 67–68), "promising these things"
- *afraid of their own shadows* (line 95), "very nervous or jumpy"

Culture: Clarify Explain to students that a *spiritual* (line 36) is an African-American religious folk song. "Go Down, Moses" was forbidden because slave owners feared it would cause rebellion, such as encouraging enslaved people to escape to freedom.

Moses is here." "Moses has come." "Get ready. Moses is back again." The ones who had agreed to go North with her put ashcake and salt herring in an old bandanna, hastily tied it into a bundle, and then waited patiently for the signal that meant it was time to start.

② Targeted Passage

There were eleven in this party, including one of her brothers and his wife. It was the largest group that she had ever conducted, but she was determined that more and more slaves should know what freedom was like.

She had to take them all the way to Canada. The Fugitive Slave Law[4] was no longer a great many incomprehensible words written down on the country's lawbooks. The new law had become a reality. It was Thomas Sims, a boy, picked up on the streets of Boston at night and shipped back to Georgia. It was Jerry and Shadrach, arrested and jailed with no warning.

She had never been in Canada. The route beyond Philadelphia was strange to her. But she could not let the runaways who accompanied her know this. As they walked along she told them stories of her own first flight, she kept painting vivid word pictures of what it would be like to be free. **E**

E CHARACTERIZATION What do Tubman's words to the runaways tell you about her?

But there were so many of them this time. She knew moments of doubt when she was half-afraid, and kept looking back over her shoulder, imagining that she heard the sound of pursuit. They would certainly be pursued. Eleven of them. Eleven thousand dollars' worth of flesh and bone and muscle that belonged to Maryland planters. If they were caught, the eleven runaways would be whipped and sold South, but she—she would probably be hanged.

They tried to sleep during the day but they never could wholly relax into sleep. She could tell by the positions they assumed, by their restless movements. And they walked at night. Their progress was slow. It took them three nights of walking to reach the first stop. She had told them about the place where they would stay, promising warmth and good food, holding these things out to them as an incentive to keep going. **F**

F MONITOR What questions do you have about the journey?

When she knocked on the door of a farmhouse, a place where she and her parties of runaways had always been welcome, always been given shelter and plenty to eat, there was no answer. She knocked again, softly. A voice from within said, "Who is it?" There was fear in the voice.

She knew instantly from the sound of the voice that there was something wrong. She said, "A friend with friends," the password on the Underground Railroad.

The door opened, slowly. The man who stood in the doorway looked at her coldly, looked with unconcealed astonishment and fear at the eleven **disheveled** runaways who were standing near her. Then he shouted, "Too many, too many. It's not safe. My place was searched last week. It's not safe!" and slammed the door in her face.

disheveled (dĭ-shĕv'əld) *adj.* messy; untidy

She turned away from the house, frowning. She had promised her passengers food and rest and warmth, and instead of that, there would be

4. **Fugitive Slave Law:** a law by which enslaved people who escaped could be recovered by their owners.

LITERARY ANALYSIS

E CHARACTERIZATION

Possible answer: *Using her own experience to inspire the runaways shows that Tubman is clever and determined to succeed.*

READING STRATEGY

F MONITOR

Remind students to record their questions in their charts. ***Possible answer:***

- *How did the runaways stay motivated to keep going?*
- *What did they eat?*
- *What was their mood like?*

Lines 69–80

REINFORCE *KEY IDEA:* RISK

Discuss What does the farmer say when he opens the door? How do his words and actions reflect the **risk** taken by those who helped the runaways? ***Possible answer:*** *The farmer says there are too many runaways and that it's not safe because his home was searched last week. His fearful action, slamming the door in Tubman's face, reflects the grave risk to those who get caught helping the runaways.*

FOR LESS–PROFICIENT READERS

② Targeted Passage [Lines 45–68]

This passage presents the context of Tubman's mission. It indicates why Tubman must take the runaways all the way to Canada and what motivates her to help them.

- What is the Fugitive Slave Law?
- What will happen if the runaways are caught?
- How does Tubman inspire the group to keep going?

Comprehension Support Review with students that making inferences is "reading between the lines," or using personal experience and clues from the text to understand what they read. Distribute copies of the Making Inferences chart. Have students reread lines 48–52 and use the graphic organizer to infer who Thomas Sims and Jerry and Shadrach are.

BEST PRACTICES TOOLKIT—Transparency
Making Inferences p. A13

Lines 98–120
DISCUSSION PROMPTS

Use these prompts to help students understand how Tubman inspires herself and the runaways to keep going:

Recall How much money are the runaways worth? ***Answer:*** *As enslaved laborers, they are worth about $1,000 each, or $11,000.*

Analyze Why do you think Tubman keeps thinking about this dollar amount? ***Possible answer:*** *This may help Tubman stay focused on her mission. Because there are so many runaways and they are worth a lot to their masters, the group is likely being pursued and needs to be very careful.*

Infer Why does Tubman tell the runaways stories about people like Thomas Garrett? ***Possible answer:*** *She wants them to know there are good people in the world. She wants to give them hope and a goal to reach at the end of their struggle.*

SOCIAL STUDIES CONNECTION

The North, with its manufacturing-based economy, was not as reliant on slave labor as the South, which had a mostly farm-based economy. Northerners wanted to ban slavery in the new western states. Southerners saw this as a threat to their own ability to use slave labor and thus as a threat to their livelihood. Southerners finally decided to secede from the Union after the 1860 presidential election when Abraham Lincoln, leader of the anti-slavery Republican party, was elected, even though his name had not appeared on the ballot in ten Southern states.

hunger and cold and more walking over the frozen ground. Somehow she would have to **instill** courage into these eleven people, most of them strangers, would have to feed them on hope and bright dreams of freedom instead of the fried pork and corn bread and milk she had promised them.

instill (ĭn-stĭl′) *v.* to supply gradually

They stumbled along behind her, half-dead for sleep, and she urged them on, though she was as tired and as discouraged as they were. She had never been in Canada but she kept painting wondrous word pictures of what it would be like. She managed to **dispel** their fear of pursuit, so that they would not become hysterical, panic-stricken. Then she had to bring some of the fear back, so that they would stay awake and keep walking though they drooped with sleep.

dispel (dĭ-spĕl′) *v.* to drive away

Yet during the day, when they lay down deep in a thicket, they never really slept, because if a twig snapped or the wind sighed in the branches of a pine tree, they jumped to their feet, afraid of their own shadows, shivering and shaking. It was very cold, but they dared not make fires because someone would see the smoke and wonder about it.

She kept thinking, eleven of them. Eleven thousand dollars' worth of slaves. And she had to take them all the way to Canada. Sometimes she told them about Thomas Garrett, in Wilmington. She said he was their friend even though he did not know them. He was the friend of all fugitives. He called them God's poor. He was a Quaker[5] and his speech was a little different from that of other people. His clothing was different, too. He wore the wide-brimmed hat that the Quakers wear.

SOCIAL STUDIES CONNECTION

In the years leading up to the Civil War, the United States wa bitterly divided abou slavery. Many enslave people in the South escaped all the way to Canada to reach freedom.

She said that he had thick white hair, soft, almost like a baby's, and the kindest eyes she had ever seen. He was a big man and strong, but he had never used his strength to harm anyone, always to help people. He would give all of them a new pair of shoes. Everybody. He always did. Once they reached his house in Wilmington, they would be safe. He would see to it that they were.

She described the house where he lived, told them about the store where he sold shoes. She said he kept a pail of milk and a loaf of bread in the drawer of his desk so that he would have food ready at hand for any of God's poor who should suddenly appear before him, fainting with hunger. There was a hidden room in the store. A whole wall swung open, and behind it was a room where he could hide fugitives. On the wall there were shelves filled with small boxes—boxes of shoes—so that you would never guess that the wall actually opened.

While she talked, she kept watching them. They did not believe her. She could tell by their expressions. They were thinking, New shoes, Thomas Garrett, Quaker, Wilmington—what foolishness was this? Who knew if she told the truth? Where was she taking them anyway?

That night they reached the next stop—a farm that belonged to a German. She made the runaways take shelter behind trees at the edge of the fields before she knocked at the door. She hesitated before she approached the door, thinking, suppose that he, too, should refuse shelter, suppose— Then she

5. **Quaker:** a member of a religious group called the Society of Friends.

DIFFERENTIATED INSTRUCTION

FOR LESS–PROFICIENT READERS

Comprehension Support The stories Tubman tells the runaways interrupt the action and may make it difficult for some students to keep track of the events in the biography. Have students use a Timeline to chart Tubman's journey.

BEST PRACTICES TOOLKIT—Transparency
Timeline p. B23

FOR ENGLISH LEARNERS

Culture: Clarify Lines 99–104 identify Thomas Garrett as a Quaker. Because Quakers were committed to peace, they voluntarily freed their own enslaved workers during the last half of the 18th century. They then became leaders in the movement to abolish slavery entirely.

FOR ADVANCED LEARNERS/PRE–AP

Evaluate Author's Style [small-group option] Encourage students to take turns reading aloud from the biography. Then have students discuss what they notice about the author's style. What does she do to make Harriet Tubman's story interesting and relevant? Are her descriptions and tone effective? What information or descriptions could she have added to make the story more intriguing?

264 UNIT 2: CHARACTER AND POINT OF VIEW

thought, Lord, I'm going to hold steady on to You and You've got to see me through—and knocked softly. **G**

She heard the familiar guttural voice say, "Who's there?"

She answered quickly, "A friend with friends."

He opened the door and greeted her warmly. "How many this time?" he asked.

"Eleven," she said and waited, doubting, wondering.

He said, "Good. Bring them in."

He and his wife fed them in the lamplit kitchen, their faces glowing, as they offered food and more food, urging them to eat, saying there was plenty for everybody, have more milk, have more bread, have more meat.

They spent the night in the warm kitchen. They really slept, all that night and until dusk the next day. When they left, it was with reluctance. They had all been warm and safe and well-fed. It was hard to exchange the security offered by that clean warm kitchen for the darkness and the cold of a December night.

G CHARACTERIZATION
What do Tubman's thoughts suggest about the way she deals with hardship?

"Go On or Die"

Harriet had found it hard to leave the warmth and friendliness, too. But she urged them on. For a while, as they walked, they seemed to carry in them a measure of contentment; some of the serenity and the cleanliness of that big warm kitchen **lingered** on inside them. But as they walked farther and farther away from the warmth and the light, the cold and the darkness entered into them. They fell silent, **sullen**, suspicious. She waited for the moment when some one of them would turn mutinous. It did not happen that night.

linger (lĭng'gər) *v.* to remain or stay longer

sullen (sŭl'ən) *adj.* showing silent resentment; sulky

Two nights later she was aware that the feet behind her were moving slower and slower. She heard the irritability in their voices, knew that soon someone would refuse to go on.

She started talking about William Still and the Philadelphia Vigilance Committee.[6] No one commented. No one asked any questions. She told them the story of William and Ellen Craft and how they escaped from Georgia. Ellen was so fair that she looked as though she were white, and so she dressed up in a man's clothing and she looked like a wealthy young planter. Her husband, William, who was dark, played the role of her slave. Thus they traveled from Macon, Georgia, to Philadelphia, riding on the trains, staying at the finest hotels. Ellen pretended to be very ill—her right arm was in a sling, and her right hand was bandaged, because she was supposed to have rheumatism. Thus she avoided having to sign the register at the hotels for she could not read or write. They finally arrived safely in Philadelphia, and then went on to Boston. **H**

No one said anything. Not one of them seemed to have heard her.

H MONITOR
Why does Tubman tell stories of how other enslaved people escaped?

6. **Philadelphia Vigilance Committee:** fundraising organization that helped people who escaped enslavement.

LITERARY ANALYSIS

G CHARACTERIZATION

Possible answer: *Her thoughts suggest that she deals with hardship by calling on her religious faith to help her stay strong.*

Lines 137–150

DISCUSSION PROMPTS

Use these prompts to help students understand the rising tension among the runaways:

Recall Why is it hard for the runaways to leave the German farmer's house and move on? ***Answer:*** *The runaways have been able to eat and sleep comfortably for the first time on their journey. They have been warm, safe, and well-fed, making a long journey in the cold seem very unappealing.*

Infer Why do you think the runaways fall silent? ***Possible answer:*** *They may fall silent because they are tired, and they miss feeling warm and safe. They may also be worried about how far they still have to go.*

Analyze Why is it important that Tubman remain aware of the runaways' moods at all times? ***Possible answer:*** *To keep the runaways moving, Tubman needs everyone to work together as a team. If one of them "turns mutinous," the group could fall apart and they could all be caught.*

READING STRATEGY

H MONITOR

Possible answer: *She is trying to keep the runaways' spirits up so they will keep walking.*

FOR LESS–PROFICIENT READERS

Comprehension Support [paired option] Have students reread lines 152–162. Then ask pairs to retell the story Tubman tells about William and Ellen Craft and discuss how it might inspire the runaways to keep moving.

FOR ENGLISH LEARNERS

Language: Verb Tenses Remind students that many verbs in English form the past tense by adding *-ed.* Other verbs have irregular past-tense forms. Have students identify the irregular past-tense verbs in lines 125–139:

- *thought* (line 125)
- *heard* (line 127)
- *fed* (line 132)
- *spent, slept* (line 135)
- *left, was* (line 136)

FOR ADVANCED LEARNERS/PRE–AP

Understand Context Have students research the Philadelphia Vigilance Committee and report their findings to the class.

She told them about Frederick Douglass,[7] the most famous of the escaped slaves, of his **eloquence,** of his magnificent appearance. Then she told them of her own first vain effort at running away, **evoking** the memory of that miserable life she had led as a child, reliving it for a moment in the telling.

But they had been tired too long, hungry too long, afraid too long, footsore too long. One of them suddenly cried out in despair, "Let me go back. It is better to be a slave than to suffer like this in order to be free."

She carried a gun with her on these trips. She had never used it—except as a threat. Now as she aimed it, she experienced a feeling of guilt, remembering that time, years ago, when she had prayed for the death of Edward Brodas, the Master, and then not too long afterward had heard that great wailing cry that came from the throats of the field hands, and knew from the sound that the Master was dead.

One of the runaways said, again, "Let me go back. Let me go back," and stood still, and then turned around and said, over his shoulder, "I am going back."

She lifted the gun, aimed it at the despairing slave. She said, "Go on with us or die." The husky low-pitched voice was grim. ❶

He hesitated for a moment and then he joined the others. They started walking again. She tried to explain to them why none of them could go back to the plantation. If a runaway returned, he would turn traitor, the master and the overseer would force him to turn traitor. The returned slave would disclose the stopping places, the hiding places, the cornstacks they had used with the full knowledge of the owner of the farm, the name of the German farmer who had fed them and sheltered them. These people who had risked their own security to help runaways would be ruined, fined, imprisoned.

She said, "We got to go free or die. And freedom's not bought with dust." ❶

This time she told them about the long agony of the Middle Passage[8] on the old slave ships, about the black horror of the holds, about the chains and the whips. They too knew these stories. But she wanted to remind them of the long hard way they had come, about the long hard way they had yet to go. She told them about Thomas Sims, the boy picked up on the streets of Boston and sent back to Georgia. She said when they got him back to Savannah, got him in prison there, they whipped him until a doctor who was standing by watching said, "You will kill him if you strike him again!" His master said, "Let him die!"

Thus she forced them to go on. Sometimes she thought she had become nothing but a voice speaking in the darkness, **cajoling,** urging, threatening. Sometimes she told them things to make them laugh, sometimes she sang to them, and heard the eleven voices behind her blending softly with hers, and then she knew that for the moment all was well with them.

She gave the impression of being a short, muscular, indomitable woman who could never be defeated. Yet at any moment she was liable to be seized by one of those curious fits of sleep, which might last for a few minutes or for hours.

eloquence (ĕl'ə-kwəns) *n.* an abi
to speak powerfully ar
persuasively

evoke (ĭ-vōk') *v.* to cal
forth; to summon

③ Targeted Passage

❶ **CHARACTERIZATIO**
Why does Tubman take
such a drastic action?
Consider what this tell
you about her characte

❶ **CHARACTERIZATIO**
How does Tubman's statement reflect her attitude about the journey?

cajole (kə-jōl') *v.* to urg
gently; to coax

7. **Frederick Douglass:** African-American leader who worked to end slavery.
8. **Middle Passage:** sea route along which enslaved Africans were transported to the Americas.

LITERARY ANALYSIS

❶ CHARACTERIZATION

Possible answers: *Tubman takes such drastic action because the man who wants to return would jeopardize the Underground Railroad and the safety of all the people involved. This passage tells us that Tubman is intelligent and quick-thinking. She understands that one person's actions can have terrible consequences.*

LITERARY ANALYSIS

❶ CHARACTERIZATION

Possible answer: *Her statement reflects her realistic attitude. She knows that the journey is extremely difficult, but she feels freedom is worth risking one's life.*

Lines 193–197

REINFORCE *KEY IDEA:* RISK

Discuss How does Tubman's story about Thomas Sims emphasize the **risk** they've undertaken? ***Possible answer:*** *Tubman's story about how Sims is beaten as his master looks on, not caring if the young boy dies, underscores that Tubman and the others have risked their lives for freedom.*

DIFFERENTIATED INSTRUCTION

FOR LESS–PROFICIENT READERS

③ Targeted Passage [Lines 168–188]

This passage presents a turning point in the journey: one of the runaways threatens to go back, but Harriet Tubman can't allow that.

- Why does the runaway want to turn back?
- What is Harriet Tubman's response?
- Why does she respond this way?

FOR ENGLISH LEARNERS

Culture: Clarify To help students understand the context of the biography, offer them the following background information:

- Frederick Douglass (1818–1895), one of the founders of the U.S. Civil Rights movement, was born a slave. He escaped to the North as a young man. His famous autobiography, *Narrative of the Life of Frederick Douglass,* helped convince many people of the injustice of slavery.
- The Middle Passage was the voyage across the Atlantic Ocean that carried abducted Africans to slave markets in the Americas. Once aboard the ship, the captured people were packed so tightly below deck that there was barely enough room to turn around. The journey took up to three months, depending on the weather. Within this time, many people died from the overcrowded and unsanitary conditions.

Even on this trip, she suddenly fell asleep in the woods. The runaways, ragged, dirty, hungry, cold, did not steal the gun as they might have, and set off by themselves, or turn back. They sat on the ground near her and waited patiently until she awakened. They had come to trust her implicitly, totally. They, too, had come to believe her repeated statement, "We got to go free or die." She was leading them into freedom, and so they waited until she was ready to go on. **K**

K CHARACTERIZATION What do the runaways' actions tell you about Tubman?

Finally, they reached Thomas Garrett's house in Wilmington, Delaware. Just as Harriet had promised, Garrett gave them all new shoes, and provided carriages to take them on to the next stop.

By slow stages they reached Philadelphia, where William Still hastily recorded their names, and the plantations whence they had come, and something of the life they had led in slavery. Then he carefully hid what he had written, for fear it might be discovered. In 1872 he published this record

In Underground Railroad (1967), Jacob Lawrence. Gouache and tempera on paper, 14¼″ × 13″. © 2007 The Jacob and Gwendolyn Lawrence Foundation, Seattle/Artists Rights Society (ARS), New York.

ANALYZE VISUALS What can you **infer** about the people in the painting?

LITERARY ANALYSIS

K CHARACTERIZATION

Possible answer: *The fact that the runaways wait patiently near Tubman shows that she has gained their trust.*

Lines 206–224
DISCUSSION PROMPTS

Use these prompts to help students understand the trust that Harriet Tubman has built up within the group:

Recall What could the runaways do when Tubman suddenly falls asleep in the woods? ***Answer:*** *They could steal her gun and set off by themselves or turn back.*

Analyze Why is it important that Thomas Garrett gives the runaways shoes? ***Possible answer:*** *Tubman has promised the shoes throughout the entire journey. When the promise is fulfilled, it helps strengthen the bond between her and the runaways.*

Speculate What could happen if William Still's writings about the runaways were discovered? ***Possible answer:*** *The Underground Railroad could be in jeopardy, and the people who help the runaways would be in danger.*

ANALYZE VISUALS

Possible answer:

- *The runaways are tired and hungry.*
- *The hosts are caring and kind.*
- *The runaways feel comfortable and relaxed at the hosts' house.*

Students may liken the scene to what the runaways encounter at the Garretts' welcoming home.

FOR LESS-PROFICIENT READERS

Reading Strategy Follow-Up: Monitor
[paired option]

- Have students work in pairs to compare the questions they have added to the chart introduced on page 259. Were there passages both students found difficult? Do they still have questions for which their partner can help them find answers?
- Remind students to continue adding questions and answers to their lists as they come across passages they find difficult or confusing.

My Questions	*Answers*
Why does the first farmer turn away the runaways?	*His place was searched, and he is afraid that there are too many runaways.*
Why does Tubman point her gun at the man?	*If the man returns to slavery, he will risk the lives of the other runaways.*

READING STRATEGY

L MONITOR

Remind students to record their questions in their charts from page 259. ***Possible answer:***

- *What motivates the people to help the escapees?*
- *How many people help the escapees?*

Lines 225–248

DISCUSSION PROMPTS

Use these prompts to help students understand the end of the runaways' journey:

Interpret Why does Tubman feel safer when she reaches New Jersey? ***Possible answer:*** *She probably feels safer because she's in a Northern state. It may be easier for people along the Northern part of the Underground Railroad to help them.*

Speculate How do you think the runaways feel when they stay with Frederick Douglass, a free African American? ***Possible answer:*** *They may feel inspired by his example and thankful for all he does for them.*

LITERARY ANALYSIS

M CHARACTERIZATION

Answer: *Tubman rents a house and lets the fugitives board with her. She finds work for them, encourages them, and begs for them.*

Extend the Discussion Ask students what these actions say about Tubman's feelings toward the fugitives.

in book form and called it *The Underground Railroad.* In the foreword to his book he said: "While I knew the danger of keeping strict records, and while I did not then dream that in my day slavery would be blotted out, or that the time would come when I could publish these records, it used to afford me great satisfaction to take them down, fresh from the lips of fugitives on the way to freedom, and to preserve them as they had given them." L

William Still, who was familiar with all the station stops on the Underground Railroad, supplied Harriet with money and sent her and her eleven fugitives on to Burlington, New Jersey.

Harriet felt safer now, though there were danger spots ahead. But the biggest part of her job was over. As they went farther and farther north, it grew colder; she was aware of the wind on the Jersey ferry and aware of the cold damp in New York. From New York they went on to Syracuse, where the temperature was even lower.

In Syracuse she met the Reverend J. W. Loguen, known as "Jarm" Loguen. This was the beginning of a lifelong friendship. Both Harriet and Jarm Loguen were to become friends and supporters of Old John Brown.[9]

From Syracuse they went north again, into a colder, snowier city—Rochester. Here they almost certainly stayed with Frederick Douglass, for he wrote in his autobiography:

> On one occasion I had eleven fugitives at the same time under my roof, and it was necessary for them to remain with me until I could collect sufficient money to get them to Canada. It was the largest number I ever had at any one time, and I had some difficulty in providing so many with food and shelter, but, as may well be imagined, they were not very fastidious in either direction, and were well content with very plain food, and a strip of carpet on the floor for a bed, or a place on the straw in the barnloft.

Late in December, 1851, Harriet arrived in St. Catharines, Canada West (now Ontario), with the eleven fugitives. It had taken almost a month to complete this journey; most of the time had been spent getting out of Maryland.

That first winter in St. Catharines was a terrible one. Canada was a strange frozen land, snow everywhere, ice everywhere, and a bone-biting cold the like of which none of them had ever experienced before. Harriet rented a small frame house in the town and set to work to make a home. The fugitives boarded with her. They worked in the forests, felling trees, and so did she. Sometimes she took other jobs, cooking or cleaning house for people in the town. She cheered on these newly arrived fugitives, working herself, finding work for them, finding food for them, praying for them, sometimes begging for them. M

Often she found herself thinking of the beauty of Maryland, the mellowness of the soil, the richness of the plant life there. The climate itself made for an ease of living that could never be duplicated in this bleak, barren countryside.

L MONITOR
What do you want to know about the peop
who help the escapee

M CHARACTERIZATIO
How does Tubman help
the fugitives?

9. **Old John Brown:** anti-slavery leader who was executed.

DIFFERENTIATED INSTRUCTION

FOR LESS–PROFICIENT READERS

Comprehension Support Have students update their timelines to include all the events up to reaching St. Catharines, Canada, their final goal. Ask students to name the most important events in the story.

Comprehension Support [small-group option] To aid students' understanding of Harriet Tubman, distribute the Character Traits Web. Have students work in groups to search through the biography and fill out their webs with descriptions of Tubman: her thoughts, behavior, and fears; and others' actions toward her. Have groups present their findings.

BEST PRACTICES TOOLKIT—Transparency
Character Traits Web p. D7

FOR ENGLISH LEARNERS

Vocabulary: Idioms and Sayings The two quotes from original documents by William Still and Frederick Douglass may be difficult for students to understand. Make sure students understand these phrases:

- *in my day* (line 221), "during my lifetime"
- *blotted out* (line 221), "completely destroyed"
- *under my roof* (line 239), "in my house"
- *were well content with* (line 244), "were happy to have"

Harriet and the Promised Land No. 15: Canada Bound (1967), Jacob Lawrence. Gouache and tempera on paper, 16½″ × 28¼″. The University of Michigan Museum of Art. © 2007 The Jacob and Gwendolyn Lawrence Foundation, Seattle/Artists Rights Society (ARS), New York.

In spite of the severe cold, the hard work, she came to love St. Catharines, and the other towns and cities in Canada where black men lived. She discovered that freedom meant more than the right to change jobs at will, more than the right to keep the money that one earned. It was the right to vote and to sit on juries. It was the right to be elected to office. In Canada there were black men who were county officials and members of school boards. St. Catharines had a large colony of ex-slaves, and they owned their own homes, kept them neat and clean and in good repair. They lived in whatever part of town they chose and sent their children to the schools.

When spring came she decided that she would make this small Canadian city her home—as much as any place could be said to be home to a woman who traveled from Canada to the Eastern Shore of Maryland as often as she did.

In the spring of 1852, she went back to Cape May, New Jersey. She spent the summer there, cooking in a hotel. That fall she returned, as usual, to Dorchester County, and brought out nine more slaves, conducting them all the way to St. Catharines, in Canada West, to the bone-biting cold, the snow-covered forests—and freedom.

She continued to live in this fashion, spending the winter in Canada, and the spring and summer working in Cape May, New Jersey, or in Philadelphia. She made two trips a year into slave territory, one in the fall and another in the spring. She now had a definite crystallized purpose, and in carrying it out, her life fell into a pattern which remained unchanged for the next six years. N

ANALYZE VISUALS
What **details** do you notice in this painting that portray the escapees' journey?

(4) **Targeted Passage**

N CHARACTERIZATION
What does the way Tubman lives her life tell you about her?

ANALYZE VISUALS

Possible answer:

- *The snow and the way the escapees are huddled against the cold show the difficulties they had traveling in winter.*
- *The red on the snow could be blood, portraying the long journey on foot.*
- *It is night in the painting, showing that the travelers on the Underground Railroad walked mostly at night.*

LITERARY ANALYSIS

N CHARACTERIZATION

Possible answers:

- *Staying in Canada each winter to help the fugitives shows that she's compassionate.*
- *Working in New Jersey and Philadelphia shows she is practical.*
- *Going into slave territory shows she is brave and committed to freeing more enslaved people.*

SELECTION WRAP–UP

REFLECT Encourage students to consider how reading about Harriet Tubman helped them understand and appreciate her life's work.

CRITIQUE The author couldn't really have known Harriet Tubman's exact thoughts. Ask students what they think about the biographer's imagining Tubman's thoughts and including them in the biography. What does this accomplish? What does the author risk?

READING FLUENCY

Distribute the copy masters and have students practice fluency.

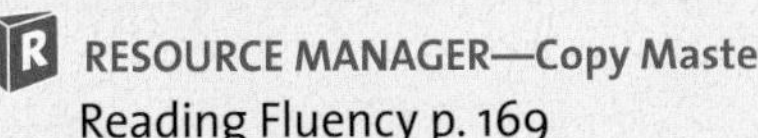
RESOURCE MANAGER—Copy Master
Reading Fluency p. 169

FOR LESS–PROFICIENT READERS

(4) Targeted Passage [Lines 260–282]

This passage discusses the benefits of freedom in St. Catharines and how Harriet Tubman spent the rest of her life.

- What does Harriet Tubman learn about freedom in St. Catharines? What are black men allowed to do in St. Catharines?
- Describe the colony of formerly enslaved people who live in St. Catharines.
- What does Harriet Tubman do every fall and spring for the next six years?

FOR ENGLISH LEARNERS

Comprehension: Comparison [mixed-readiness pairs] Have students reread lines 259–270. Ask what the author is comparing. To help students with this comparison, have them work in pairs to complete a Venn Diagram, comparing and contrasting life in St. Catharines and life as an enslaved person in Maryland.

BEST PRACTICES TOOLKIT—Transparency
Venn Diagram p. A26

DISCUSSION PROMPTS

Use these prompts to help students understand the relationship between Tubman and Douglass:

Infer Why does Douglass write to Tubman? ***Possible answer:*** *Tubman asks Douglass for a "word of commendation" stating that the information presented in her biography is "truthful and trustworthy."*

Analyze How does Frederick Douglass describe the difference between himself and Harriet Tubman? ***Possible answer:*** *He says that he has served the cause in a much more public way, receiving encouragement and approval, while Tubman has worked in private, receiving little, if any, reward.*

Evaluate What does Frederick Douglass think of the risks Harriet Tubman has taken in her quest to free enslaved people? ***Possible answer:*** *He seems to regard her highly for all that she has done, saying that he knows of no one who has gone through more hardship and danger than she.*

Reading for Information

LETTER Frederick Douglass, a vocal African-American statesman and journalist, had a very different style of leadership than Harriet Tubman did. Douglass wrote the following letter when the first biography of Tubman was about to be published.

August 29, 1868

Dear Harriet:

I am glad to know that the story of your eventful life has been written by a kind lady, and that the same is soon to be published. You ask for what you do not need when you call upon me for a word of commendation.[1] I need such words from you far more than you can need them from me, especially where your superior labors and devotion to the cause of the lately enslaved of our land are known as I know them. The difference between us is very marked. Most that I have done and suffered in the service of our cause has been in public, and I have received much encouragement at every step of the way. You, on the other hand, have labored in a private way. I have wrought in the day—you in the night. I have had the applause of the crowd and the satisfaction that comes of being approved by the multitude, while the most that you have done has been witnessed by a few trembling, scarred, and footsore bondmen and women, whom you have led out of the house of bondage, and whose heartfelt "God bless you" has been your only reward. The midnight sky and the silent stars have been the witnesses of your devotion to freedom and of your heroism. Excepting John Brown—of sacred memory—I know of no one who has willingly encountered more perils and hardships to serve our enslaved people than you have. Much that you have done would seem improbable to those who do not know you as I know you. It is to me a great pleasure and a great privilege to bear testimony to your character and your works, and to say to those to whom you may come, that I regard you in every way truthful and trustworthy.

Your friend,

Fredk Douglass

Frederick Douglass

1. **commendation** (kŏm′ən-dā′shən): an expression of praise or recommendation.

DIFFERENTIATED INSTRUCTION

FOR ENGLISH LEARNERS

Option for Reading [mixed-readiness groups] Have students listen to the *Audio Anthology CD* while they read the letter. Have them continue practicing the reading until they become fluent. Then have groups work together to paraphrase the letter, or rewrite it in their own words.

FOR ADVANCED LEARNERS/PRE–AP

Evaluate [small-group option] Have students form small groups to evaluate the various contributions Tubman and Douglass made to the abolitionist cause. While Tubman worked secretly, helping a few hundred people, Douglass worked publicly, speaking out against slavery. Have students discuss the importance of each contribution. Do students think one of them was braver than the other, or were they equally brave in their actions against slavery?

omprehension

1. **Recall** What is the purpose of Harriet Tubman's trips to Maryland?
2. **Clarify** Why does the man at the first stop on the Underground Railroad turn away the group of runaways?
3. **Summarize** How does life for the runaways change in Canada?

terary Analysis

4. **Monitor** Review the chart of questions and answers you made as you read. Which questions added the most to your understanding of the selection? Why?
5. **Identify Anecdote** An **anecdote** is a brief account of an interesting incident. Identify three anecdotes the author uses to describe Harriet Tubman. What do these anecdotes help readers understand about Tubman?
6. **Examine Characterization** Review the four methods of **characterization.** Which method of characterization does Petry use the most in her biography? Tell what you learn about Tubman through this method.
7. **Analyze a Character** Complete a character map for Harriet Tubman like the one shown. Then create a one-sentence description of her.

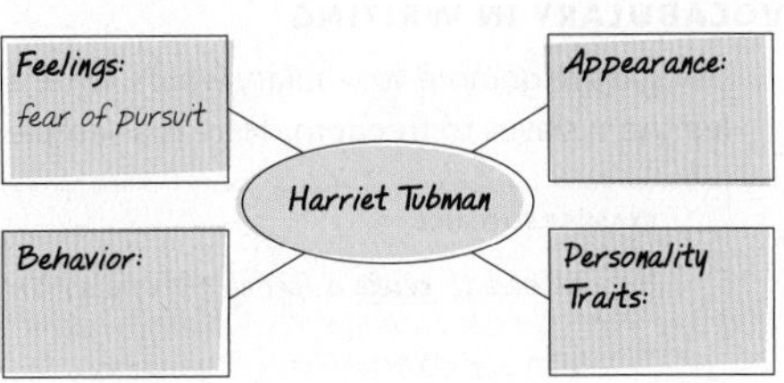

8. **Make Judgments** Read the "Letter to Harriet Tubman" by Frederick Douglass. Why does Douglass believe that Harriet Tubman is "superior" to him? Decide why Douglass might have felt this way, and support your opinion with details from the biography and the letter.

xtension and Challenge

9. **Readers' Circle** Based on the information in the selection, would you have been willing to trust Harriet Tubman with your life? Discuss which of Tubman's qualities make her a good leader and why you might be hesitant to follow her.
10. **SOCIAL STUDIES CONNECTION** Because the Fugitive Slave Law allowed slave owners to recover enslaved people who escaped, Harriet Tubman led escapees on Underground Railroad routes to Canada, where they reached freedom. Research more about the approximately 18 other trips to Canada that Tubman led and present your findings to the class. Consider what continued to motivate her to **risk** her life to help others.

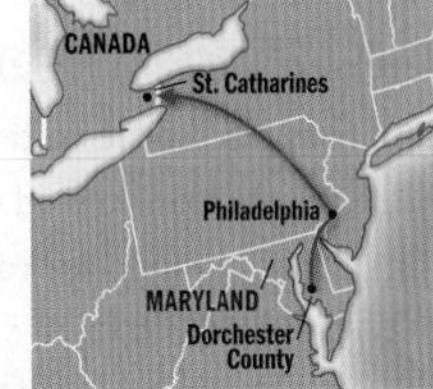

Harriet Tubman's route from Maryland to Canada

RESEARCH LINKS
For more on the Underground Railroad, visit the **Research Center** at **ClassZone.com.**

Practice and Apply

After Reading

For additional support of postreading questions, use these copy masters:

RESOURCE MANAGER—Copy Masters
Reading Check p. 166 (to check understanding of the selection)
Characterization p. 159 (for practice of literary analysis standards focus)
Question Support p. 167 (After Reading questions adapted for English learners and less-proficient readers)

Additional selection questions are provided for teachers on page 153.

For additional activities to challenge students, see

Power Thinking at **ClassZone.com**

ANSWERS

Comprehension

1. *Tubman conducts enslaved people to freedom.*
2. *The man turns away the group because he says it is too large and the authorities have recently searched his home.*
3. *The runaways can earn money, change jobs when they want, vote, serve on juries, hold office, own their own homes, live where they want, and send their children to school.*

Literary Analysis

Possible answers:

4. **STANDARDS FOCUS Monitor** *Students should explain how certain questions helped them understand the selection.*
5. *The author includes many of the anecdotes that Harriet Tubman used to motivate the runaways. For instance, she tells them how William and Ellen Craft escaped from Georgia (lines 152–162) and what happened when Thomas Sims was returned to Georgia (lines 193–197). These anecdotes help readers understand that Tubman is a woman with strong beliefs and perseverance. Through the anecdote about the time Tubman prayed for the death of her old master (lines 172–176), the reader understands what her life was like before she was free and when she might have felt weak and hopeless.*
6. **STANDARDS FOCUS Characterization** *The method that Petry uses the most is to describe Harriet Tubman's behavior. Tubman is strong, clever, and brave.*
7. ***Feelings:*** *fear of pursuit, self-doubt, guilt, hope, weariness.* ***Behavior:*** *helping enslaved people escape, telling stories, instilling courage, threatening people with a gun, singing, earning money.* ***Appearance:*** *short, muscular.* ***Personality Traits:*** *brave, religious, purposeful.* ***Possible sentence:*** *Despite her own fears and weariness, Tubman bravely helped people escape slavery by using stories, threats, and promises to encourage them.*
8. *Douglass might have felt that Tubman was superior to him because his abolition work received a lot of public support and encouragement and did not put him in danger, whereas Tubman's work was done in private, for little reward, and put her in great danger.*

Extension and Challenge

9. *Students' answers will vary. They might note that Tubman's strength, commitment, and bravery would entice them to trust her with their lives.*
10. **SOCIAL STUDIES CONNECTION** *Students should use more than one reliable source to research Tubman's other journeys.*

ANSWERS

Vocabulary in Context

VOCABULARY PRACTICE

1. *linger*
2. *evoke (or instill)*
3. *dispel*
4. *sullen*
5. *disheveled*
6. *cajole*
7. *eloquence*
8. *instill (or evoke)*

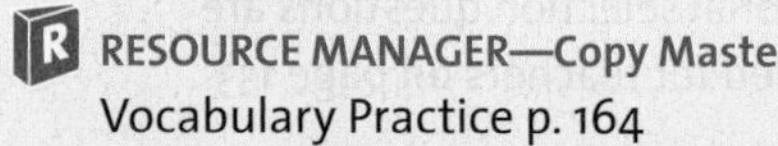

RESOURCE MANAGER—Copy Master
Vocabulary Practice p. 164

VOCABULARY IN WRITING

Ask students to recall what Harriet Tubman did to lead the runaways to freedom. Then have students review the vocabulary list and identify words that could be used to describe her actions.

VOCABULARY STRATEGY: SYNONYMS AS CONTEXT CLUES *(also an EL language objective)*

Guide students to read the sentence carefully for words that describe the boldfaced word. Tell students that sometimes the synonym comes right after a clue word such as *or.*

Possible answers:

1. totally; *"unquestioningly"*
2. undefeatable; *"strong"*
3. satisfaction; *"happiness"*
4. fussy; *"picky"*
5. lure; *"motivation"*
6. unimaginable; *"unknowable, impossible to imagine"*

RESOURCE MANAGER—Copy Master
Vocabulary Strategy p. 165

Vocabulary Center at **ClassZone.com**
Additional Vocabulary Activities

Vocabulary in Context

VOCABULARY PRACTICE

Choose the word from the list that makes the most sense in each sentence.

cajole	evoke	disheveled	instill	dispel	linger	eloquence	sullen

1. Harriet had to make sure that they didn't _____ too long in any one place.
2. She had to work hard to _____ a sense of hope.
3. At times, it was difficult for Harriet to _____ feelings of despair.
4. When she saw the _____ looks on people's faces, she knew it was time for another encouraging story.
5. When they arrived at a destination, they were hungry and their appearance was _____.
6. Harriet often had to _____ the fugitives into moving toward their next stop.
7. Harriet said that Frederick Douglass was a man of great _____.
8. Harriet tried to _____ in the fugitives a sense of responsibility.

VOCABULARY IN WRITING

Using three or more vocabulary words, write a paragraph describing how Harriet led the 11 slaves to freedom. Here is a sample of how you might begin.

> **EXAMPLE SENTENCE**
>
> *Harriet had to* ***evoke*** *a feeling of hope as they walked along on their journey.*

VOCABULARY STRATEGY: SYNONYMS AS CONTEXT CLUES

Context clues are often found in the words and sentences that surround an unfamiliar word. These clues can help you figure out the meaning of the word. A **synonym,** or a word that has a similar definition, can be a context clue. For example, a sentence from the selection refers to "a voice speaking in the darkness, cajoling, urging. . . ." If you know the word *urging,* you can figure out what *cajoling* means because they are synonyms.

PRACTICE Identify the synonyms of each boldfaced word. Then define the word.

1. They had come to trust her **implicitly,** just as they believed in her totally.
2. She was considered **indomitable** because of her undefeatable spirit.
3. Harriet longed for **contentment,** but would never be satisfied until the journey ended.
4. The group was not **fastidious** or fussy about what they ate or where they slept.
5. In the end, the lure of freedom was its own **incentive.**
6. The escape was unimaginable, and the journey almost **incomprehensible.**

VOCABULARY PRACTICE
For more practice, go to the **Vocabulary Cente** at **ClassZone.com.**

DIFFERENTIATED INSTRUCTION

FOR ENGLISH LEARNERS

Vocabulary Practice [mixed-readiness pairs] Make sure students know the meanings of the vocabulary words. Encourage them to review the words and how they are used in the selection. Have pairs identify the correct vocabulary words in the activity.

FOR ADVANCED LEARNERS/PRE-AP

Vocabulary Strategy Challenge students to find synonyms for each of the vocabulary words in the **Vocabulary Practice** activity. Have them use each vocabulary word and its synonym in a sentence.

ading-Writing Connection

Demonstrate your understanding of "Harriet Tubman: Conductor on the Underground Railroad" by responding to these prompts. Then complete the **Grammar and Writing** exercise.

WRITING PROMPTS	SELF-CHECK
A. Short Response: Analyze Motivation Why do you think Harriet Tubman and others who broke the Fugitive Slave Law were willing to take that **risk?** Write a **one-paragraph response,** including details from the biography and the letter from Frederick Douglass.	***An effective analysis will . . .*** • describe the risks that Harriet Tubman took • clearly explain her motivations based on evidence from the texts
B. Extended Response: Write a Character Sketch You learned about Harriet Tubman from the way Ann Petry characterized her. Now it's your turn to describe this historic figure for an elementary school audience. Write a **two- or three-paragraph character sketch** that uses various methods of characterization to capture the personality of Harriet Tubman.	***An interesting character sketch will . . .*** • use at least two methods of characterization • be written in words an elementary school student can understand

AMMAR AND WRITING

AVOID CLAUSES AS FRAGMENTS A clause is a group of words that contains a subject and a verb. An **independent clause** expresses a complete thought and can stand alone as a sentence. A **dependent,** or **subordinate, clause** cannot. Dependent clauses begin with words such as *although, before, because, so that, when, while,* and *that.* To avoid a sentence fragment, join a dependent clause (shown in yellow) to an independent clause.

Original: Harriet Tubman was willing to take risks. Because she wanted everyone to be free.

Revised: Harriet Tubman was willing to take risks because she wanted everyone to be free.

PRACTICE Find four fragments in the following paragraph. Then fix the fragments by combining independent and dependent clauses.

Harriet Tubman would be hanged. If slaveholders caught her. Tubman was willing to kill. So that the Underground Railroad would remain a secret. It made Tubman happy. When former slaves had the right to vote. Although her work was dangerous. She did not ask for any reward.

*For more help with clauses, see page R62 in the **Grammar Handbook.***

Reading-Writing Connection

WRITING PROMPTS

- For **Prompt A,** have students focus on finding specific examples from the biography of the risks Tubman took.
- For **Prompt B,** have students consider what methods of characterization would be most appealing to their audience. Then have them identify details from the text to use as they compose their character sketches.

For an extended Reading-Writing Connection activity, see

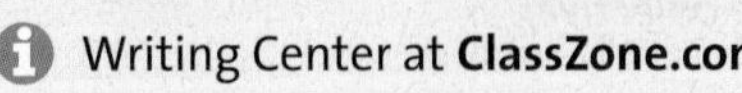
Writing Center at **ClassZone.com**

GRAMMAR AND WRITING

Encourage students to read each sentence aloud. Together, discuss why the fragments are incomplete.

Answers:

Fragments: If slaveholders caught her; So that the Underground Railroad would remain a secret; When former slaves had the right to vote; Although her work was dangerous.

Corrected sentences:

- *Harriet Tubman would be hanged if slave-holders caught her.*
- *Tubman was willing to kill so that the Underground Railroad would remain a secret.*
- *It made Tubman happy when former slaves had the right to vote.*
- *Although her work was dangerous, she did not ask for any reward.*

RESOURCE MANAGER—Copy Master
Avoid Clauses as Fragments p. 168

DIFFERENTIATED INSTRUCTION

FOR LESS–PROFICIENT WRITERS

For Prompt A:

Have students write an introductory sentence describing the risks Tubman took. Encourage them to use the monitoring chart they began on page 259 to identify questions about Tubman's motivation. Then have them explain her motivation based on the evidence they found in the text to answer their questions.

For Prompt B:

1. Have students choose one characteristic of Harriet Tubman from the character map they created in response to **Analyze a Character** on page 271.
2. Then have them write an introductory paragraph that introduces Harriet Tubman.
3. In the second paragraph, students should describe Tubman according to the characteristic they chose, using two methods of characterization.
4. The final paragraph should summarize the character sketch.

Assess and Reteach

Assess

RESOURCE MANAGER—Copy Masters
Selection Tests A, B/C pp. 171–172, 173–174

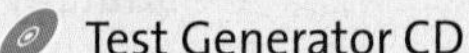
Test Generator CD

Reteach

STANDARDS LESSON FILE
Literature Lesson 3: Characterization
Reading Lesson 2: Monitoring
Writing Lesson 8: Sentence Combining
Vocabulary Lesson 13: Context Clues

Focus and Motivate

OBJECTIVES

Literary Analysis

- explore the key idea of **greatness**
- identify and analyze characteristics of a biography
- read a biography

Reading

- identify main idea and details

Vocabulary

- build vocabulary for reading and writing
- use context to determine the meaning of multiple-meaning words *(also an EL language objective)*

SUMMARY

Abraham Lincoln was a man of contradictions. He was "homely" but could appear handsome when he spoke. He was talkative, but he never expressed his inner feelings. Although not formally educated, he was an eloquent writer and speaker. He was humorous yet melancholy, logical yet superstitious. While some admired his leadership, others criticized him for his lack of experience, and he was very unpopular during the Civil War. This biography explores some of the many facets of Lincoln's character.

What are the signs of GREATNESS?

Discuss the question. To lead into the ***KEY IDEA,*** have students brainstorm qualities of **greatness.** Then have students complete the ***WEB IT*** activity. As they compare their results, ask them whether they agree with the reasons for their classmates' choices.

Before Reading

The Mysterious Mr. Lincoln

Biography by Russell Freedman

What are the signs of GREATNESS?

KEY IDEA People can be noticed for a variety of reasons. A brilliant mind, confident personality, strong work ethic, or generous spirit can make someone shine. When people use these qualities to improve the world and inspire others, they are said to have **greatness.** The biography you are about to read describes the complicated personality—and extraordinary leadership—of one of the greatest U.S. presidents, Abraham Lincoln.

WEB IT Think of two or three people you consider to have qualities of greatness. You can include public figures, friends, or family members. For each person, create a web like the one shown to show the qualities that make him or her great. Then compare your web with your classmates' webs. What qualities come up more than once?

Selection Resources

RESOURCE MANAGER UNIT 2

Plan and Teach pp. 175–182

Literary Analysis
Summary pp. 183†*, 184‡*
Biography pp. 185, 186†*
Question Support p. 193*

Reading
Identify Main Idea and Details pp. 187, 188†*
Reading Check p. 192

Vocabulary
Study p. 189*
Practice p. 190
Strategy p. 191

Assessment
Selection Tests A, B/C pp. 195*, 197*
Test Generator CD

BEST PRACTICES TOOLKIT
Differentiated Instruction pp. 31–38*
Scaffolding Instruction pp. 43–46*

Graphic Organizers/Strategies
Word Questioning • Common Suffixes • Venn Diagram

Reading Support
Audio Anthology CD*

Technology
Literature and Vocabulary Centers at **ClassZone.com**
Write*Smart* CD

* Resources for Differentiation † Also in Spanish ‡ In Haitian Creole and Vietnamese

Teach

STANDARDS FOCUS

LITERARY ANALYSIS

● BIOGRAPHY

Point out the brief biographical sketch of the author on this page. Explain that, like most biographies, it is written in the third person. Discuss what various details reveal about Freedman's character.

CHECK UNDERSTANDING Ask students how reading biographies can help them understand historical figures.

READING SKILL

■ IDENTIFY MAIN IDEA AND DETAILS

Display this paragraph:

> Immigrants have been drawn to the United States for many reasons. Many immigrants come to the United States for jobs or advanced education. Others come to escape political persecution.

Ask: Which sentence is the main idea?

Answer: *The first sentence is the main idea; it makes a general statement. The other sentences support this main idea.*

CHECK UNDERSTANDING Have students identify the main idea of the ***KEY IDEA*** paragraph on page 274.

RESOURCE MANAGER—Copy Master
Identify Main Idea and Details p. 187 (for student use while reading the selection)

ERARY ANALYSIS: BIOGRAPHY

Real people often inspire fascinating pieces of writing. A true account of a person's life that's written by someone else is called a **biography.** Writers of biographies

- use the third-person point of view
- present facts and opinions from a variety of sources
- provide an interpretation of a person's character

As you read this biography, watch for ways Russell Freedman highlights President Lincoln's strengths and weaknesses.

ADING SKILL: IDENTIFY MAIN IDEA AND DETAILS

Nonfiction writing is usually organized around **main ideas,** which are the most important ideas a writer wants to convey about a topic. The writer develops the main ideas through **supporting details,** which can include

- **facts:** statements that can be proven
- **anecdotes:** brief stories that reveal important points
- **quotations:** direct statements from relevant people

Sometimes writers state their main ideas clearly, often at the beginning or end of paragraphs. Other times, you must **infer** the main ideas from the details provided. As you read, note the main ideas and details on a rough outline like the one shown.

I. Lincoln had a distinctive, changing appearance.
A. Tall with long legs
B.
II.

CABULARY IN CONTEXT

The following phrases could have been headlines at the time Abraham Lincoln lived. Replace each boldfaced term with a word or words that means something similar.

1. Southern States **Denounce** the War
2. A **Melancholy** Nation Faces Civil War
3. Soldiers **Defy** the Odds
4. Lincoln to **Patronize** Local Business
5. Exhausted Generals Grow **Listless** as War Rages On
6. Senators **Meddle** in Lincoln's War Plans

Author Online

The Art of Nonfiction

Russell Freedman's father worked for a publishing company and often brought authors home to have dinner with the family. "I wanted to be like them," Freedman says. To improve his writing skills, he got a job as a news reporter. His interest in writing biographies started when he learned about a blind 16-year-old boy who had invented a Braille typewriter. Fascinated by the boy's story, Freedman wrote his first book, *Teenagers Who Made History* (1961). When asked why he specializes in writing nonfiction for young readers, Freedman says he enjoys the challenge of conveying "the spirit and essence of a life."

Russell Freedman
born 1929

Background

Abraham Lincoln Despite being born into a poor family with few opportunities, Abraham Lincoln managed to educate himself. He became a successful lawyer and state politician, but he had even greater ambitions. In 1860, he achieved them; he won the presidency. He steered the country through the long and bloody Civil War (1861–1865), which resulted in an end to slavery in the United States. In April 1865, Lincoln was assassinated by John Wilkes Booth, a southerner who wanted slavery to continue. Lincoln has held an enduring fascination for historians who often find new facets of his personality to examine. As Russell Freedman has pointed out, "Every ten years Lincoln changes character dramatically."

MORE ABOUT THE AUTHOR AND BACKGROUND
To learn more about Russell Freedman and President Lincoln, visit the **Literature Center** at **ClassZone.com.**

VOCABULARY SKILL

▲ VOCABULARY IN CONTEXT

DIAGNOSE WORD KNOWLEDGE To determine preteaching needs, have all students complete **Vocabulary in Context.** ***Possible answers:*** **1.** *Condemn* **2.** *Sad* **3.** *Fight Against* **4.** *Shop at* **5.** *Tired* **6.** *Interfere*

PRETEACH VOCABULARY Use the Vocabulary Study copy master to help students determine which words they already know.

1. Read aloud the first sentence, emphasizing the boldfaced word.
2. Ask students to identify context clues in the sentence (*authority, drive over the speed limit*). Discuss possible meanings for *defy,* such as "disobey."
3. Repeat for the other sentences.
4. Have students work on Part B independently.

RESOURCE MANAGER—Copy Master
Vocabulary Study p. 189

For general guidelines on differentiating vocabulary instruction and for alternative vocabulary activities for students not needing vocabulary preteaching, see

BEST PRACTICES TOOLKIT
Scaffolding Vocabulary Instruction pp. 43–46

Vocabulary Center at **ClassZone.com**
Additional Vocabulary Activities

Practice and Apply

ANALYZE VISUALS

Possible answer: *His expression seems thoughtful and serious, but with a hint of amusement around the mouth and eyes.*

About the Art Lincoln sat for this photograph four days before he was assassinated on April 14, 1865. The photographer, Alexander Gardner (1821–1882), was born in Scotland. He came to the United States around 1856 and was hired by a portrait photographer named Mathew Brady, who would later become famous for his photographs of the Civil War. Gardner helped Brady document the Civil War, and he went on to photograph new settlements in the American West and to make a photographic record of the Native Americans of the Great Plains.

READING SKILL

A MAIN IDEA AND DETAILS

Details should include that the author not only points out that people thought Lincoln was homely, but that Lincoln thought so too. He once referred to his "poor, lean, lank face" (line 8) and laughed at himself often.

LITERARY ANALYSIS

B BIOGRAPHY

Possible answer: *The author quotes a historical source—a Chicago newspaperman who actually knew Lincoln.*

The Mysterious MR. LINCOLN

Russell Freedman

"If any personal description of me is thought desirable, it may be said, I am, in height, six feet, four inches, nearly; lean in flesh, weighing, on average, one hundred and eighty pounds dark complexion, with coarse black hair and grey eyes—no other marks or brands recollected."

ANALYZE VISUALS
Look at this photograph of Lincoln. How would you **describe** the expression on his face?

Abraham Lincoln wasn't the sort of man who could lose himself in a crowd. After all, he stood six feet four inches tall, and to top it off, he wore a high silk hat.

His height was mostly in his long bony legs. When he sat in a chair, he seemed no taller than anyone else. It was only when he stood up that he towered above other men.

At first glance, most people thought he was homely. Lincoln thought so too, referring once to his "poor, lean, lank face." As a young man he was sensitive about his gawky looks, but in time, he learned to laugh at himself. When a rival called him "two-faced" during a political debate, Lincoln replied: "I leave it to my audience. If I had another face, do you think I'd wear this one?" A

According to those who knew him, Lincoln was a man of many faces. In repose,[1] he often seemed sad and gloomy. But when he began to speak, his expression changed. "The dull, **listless** features dropped like a mask," said a Chicago newspaperman. "The eyes began to sparkle, the mouth to smile, the whole countenance[2] was wreathed in animation, so that a stranger would have said 'Why, this man, so angular and solemn a moment ago, is really handsome!'" B

① Targeted Passage

A MAIN IDEA AND DETAILS
Reread lines 7–11. What type of detail does the author use to help conv[ey] Lincoln's appearance? Add this to your outline

listless (lĭst′lĭs) *adj.* lacking energy

B BIOGRAPHY
Who thinks Lincoln is "a man of many faces"? Tell how you know this.

1. **repose** (rĭ-pōz′): the act of resting.
2. **countenance** (koun′tə-nəns): the face; expression of the face.

DIFFERENTIATED INSTRUCTION

FOR ALL STUDENTS

Enhance Learning Styles Provide these independent projects for various learning styles:

- **Interpersonal** Plan a poetry reading.
- **Linguistic** Research and role-play the Lincoln-Douglas debates.
- **Visual** Design a poster or Web site to promote part of Lincoln's campaign in 1860.

For further details on these and other projects, see

RESOURCE MANAGER
Ideas for Extension pp. 180–181

FOR LESS–PROFICIENT READERS

In combination with the *Audio Anthology CD,* use one or more Targeted Passages (pp. 276, 278, 279) to ensure that students focus on key selection events, concepts, and skills.

① Targeted Passage [Lines 1–18]

In this passage, the author's description of Abraham Lincoln shows the impression he made on others.

- Why did Lincoln stand out in a crowd?
- How did Lincoln look? Did he like the way he looked?
- Why did the Chicago newspaperman call Lincoln "really handsome"?

BACKGROUND

Abraham Lincoln With parents who were mostly illiterate, and having had scarcely a year of formal education, Abraham Lincoln was largely self-educated. As a boy, he read such classics as the Bible, John Bunyan's *Pilgrim's Progress,* Daniel Defoe's *Robinson Crusoe,* and Aesop's *Fables.* However, he did not put this learning to work right away.

When he came of age, Lincoln worked for many years at different occupations, including rail-splitter, flatboatman, storekeeper, surveyor, and postmaster. During the Black Hawk War of 1832, he served as a volunteer and later as captain of his company.

Finally, after teaching himself grammar and mathematics, Lincoln decided to study law. He passed the bar exam in 1836 and proceeded to have a successful career. He also became involved in politics, eventually becoming the vice-presidential nominee of the Republican party in 1856.

FOR ENGLISH LEARNERS

Options for Reading Read the first Targeted Passage aloud. Make sure students understand that this biography is not organized chronologically but is rather a portrait of Lincoln's character. Then have students read the rest of the selection silently as they listen to the *Audio Anthology CD.*

Key Academic Vocabulary Have students use Word Questioning to study this academic vocabulary: *debate* (line 10), *partner* (line 29), *logical* (line 62), *approach* (line 63), *military* (lines 69, 70), *conflict* (line 76).

BEST PRACTICES TOOLKIT—Transparency
Word Questioning p. E9

Prereading For prereading instruction for English learners, see

BEST PRACTICES TOOLKIT
Scaffolding Reading Instruction pp. 43–46

FOR ADVANCED LEARNERS/PRE–AP

Pre-AP exercises in the bottom channel provide additional challenge for your advanced students. Use them for small groups or individuals.

ADDITIONAL GUIDELINES

For more help with differentiation and tips for classroom management, see

BEST PRACTICES TOOLKIT
Differentiated Instruction pp. 31–38

READING SKILL

C MAIN IDEA AND DETAILS

Possible answer: *Few, if any, people knew Lincoln well.*

If students need help . . .

- Tell them that the main idea of a paragraph is often located near the beginning of the paragraph.
- Ask them to identify the sentence that tells the important point of this paragraph.
- Have students record their answers as item II in the outline, and suggest that they continue reading to find supporting details.

READING SKILL

D MAIN IDEA AND DETAILS

Possible answer: *The author contrasts Lincoln's unsophisticated, informal speech with his impressive public speaking and knowledge of Shakespeare. This supports the main idea that Lincoln has many sides to his personality.*

Lines 52–57

REINFORCE *KEY IDEA:* GREATNESS

Discuss What was one way in which Lincoln showed **greatness** by inspiring others?
Possible answer: *He was a powerful speaker.*

Lincoln was the most photographed man of his time, but his friends insisted that no photo ever did him justice. It's no wonder. Back then, cameras required long exposures. The person being photographed had to "freeze" as the seconds ticked by. If he blinked an eye, the picture would be blurred. That's why Lincoln looks so stiff and formal in his photos. We never see him laughing or joking.

Artists and writers tried to capture the "real" Lincoln that the camera missed, but something about the man always escaped them. His changeable features, his tones, gestures, and expressions, seemed to **defy** description.

Today it's hard to imagine Lincoln as he really was. And he never cared to reveal much about himself. In company he was witty and talkative, but he rarely betrayed his inner feelings. According to William Herndon, his law partner, he was "the most secretive—reticent—shut-mouthed man that ever lived."

In his own time, Lincoln was never fully understood even by his closest friends. Since then, his life story has been told and retold so many times, he has become as much a legend as a flesh-and-blood human being. While the legend is based on truth, it is only partly true. And it hides the man behind it like a disguise. **C**

The legendary Lincoln is known as Honest Abe, a humble man of the people who rose from a log cabin to the White House. There's no doubt that Lincoln was a poor boy who made good. And it's true that he carried his folksy manners and homespun speech to the White House with him. He said "howdy" to visitors and invited them to "stay a spell." He greeted diplomats while wearing carpet slippers, called his wife "mother" at receptions, and told bawdy[3] jokes at cabinet meetings.

Lincoln may have seemed like a common man, but he wasn't. His friends agreed that he was one of the most ambitious people they had ever known. Lincoln struggled hard to rise above his log-cabin origins, and he was proud of his achievements. By the time he ran for president he was a wealthy man, earning a large income from his law practice and his many investments. As for the nickname Abe, he hated it. No one who knew him well ever called him Abe to his face. They addressed him as Lincoln or Mr. Lincoln.

Lincoln is often described as a sloppy dresser, careless about his appearance. In fact, he **patronized** the best tailor in Springfield, Illinois, buying two suits a year. That was at a time when many men lived, died, and were buried in the same suit.

It's true that Lincoln had little formal "eddication," as he would have pronounced it. Almost everything he "larned" he taught himself. All his life he said "thar" for *there,* "git" for *get,* "kin" for *can.* Even so, he became an eloquent public speaker who could hold a vast audience spellbound, and a great writer whose finest phrases still ring in our ears. He was known to sit up late into the night, discussing Shakespeare's plays with White House visitors. **D**

He was certainly a humorous man, famous for his rollicking stories. But he was also moody and **melancholy,** tormented by long and frequent bouts of depression. Humor was his therapy. He relied on his yarns,[4] a friend observed, to "whistle down sadness."

3. **bawdy** (bô′dē): vulgar.
4. **yarn:** an entertaining tale.

defy (dĭ-fī′) *v.* to bold oppose or resist

C MAIN IDEA AND DETAILS
What is the main idea in this paragraph? Ad to your outline.

2 Targeted Passage

patronize (pā′trə-nīz′) to go to as a customer

D MAIN IDEA AND DETAILS
Note the details about Lincoln's words and actions. What main id do they support?

melancholy (mĕl′ən-kŏl′ē) *adj.* sad; depressed

DIFFERENTIATED INSTRUCTION

FOR LESS–PROFICIENT READERS

2 Targeted Passage [Lines 31–48]

This passage explains why it is difficult to draw an accurate biographical portrait of Lincoln.

- How did Lincoln become a legend?
- Why is Lincoln referred to as "Honest Abe"?
- In what ways did Lincoln seem like a "common man"?
- What were Lincoln's achievements?

Reading Skill Follow-Up: Identify Main Idea and Details [paired option] Have students work in pairs to divide the biography into sections. Each section should have a main idea and supporting details. Then have students place all the main ideas into their outlines before filling in details. *(Possible sections are lines 1–26 [with further details in lines 49–51], lines 27–48, lines 52–64, and lines 65–104.)*

FOR ENGLISH LEARNERS

Vocabulary: Suffixes Point out the words *changeable* (line 25), *talkative* (line 28), *achievements* (line 45), and *humorous* (line 58). Help students identify each base word. Point out how the suffixes change meaning and part of speech. Then distribute copies of Common Suffixes. As students read the selection, ask them to find words with these suffixes and to identify the parts of speech.

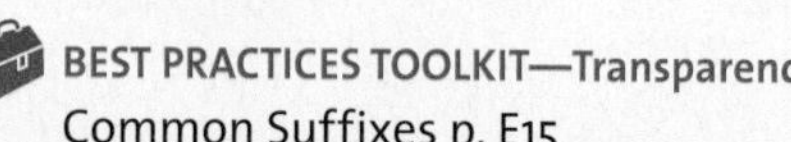

BEST PRACTICES TOOLKIT—Transparency
Common Suffixes p. E15

He had a cool, logical mind, trained in the courtroom, and a practical, commonsense approach to problems. Yet he was deeply superstitious, a believer in dreams, omens, and visions. E

We admire Lincoln today as an American folk hero. During the Civil War, however, he was the most unpopular president the nation had ever known. His critics called him a tyrant, a hick, a stupid baboon who was unfit for his office. As commander in chief of the armed forces, he was **denounced** as a bungling amateur who **meddled** in military affairs he knew nothing about. But he also had his supporters. They praised him as a farsighted statesman, a military mastermind who engineered the Union victory.

Lincoln is best known as the Great Emancipator, the man who freed the slaves. Yet he did not enter the war with that idea in mind. "My paramount object in this struggle *is* to save the Union," he said in 1862, "and is *not* either to save or destroy slavery." As the war continued, Lincoln's attitude changed. Eventually he came to regard the conflict as a moral crusade to wipe out the sin of slavery.

No black leader was more critical of Lincoln than the fiery abolitionist[5] writer and editor Frederick Douglass. Douglass had grown up as a slave. He had won his freedom by escaping to the North. Early in the war, impatient with Lincoln's cautious leadership, Douglass called him "preeminently the white man's president, entirely devoted to the welfare of white men." Later, Douglass changed his mind and came to admire Lincoln. Several years after the war, he said this about the sixteenth president:

"His greatest mission was to accomplish two things: first, to save his country from dismemberment and ruin; and, second, to free his country from the great crime of slavery. . . . taking him for all in all, measuring the tremendous magnitude of the work before him, considering the necessary means to ends, and surveying the end from the beginning, infinite wisdom has seldom sent any man into the world better fitted for his mission than Abraham Lincoln." 

Allan Pinkerton, President Abraham Lincoln, and Major General John A. McClernand at Antietam Battle Site, Maryland. October 3, 1862.

E **BIOGRAPHY**
Which of the qualities described would you expect a great leader to have, and which would you not?

denounce (dĭ-nouns') *v.* to condemn; to criticize

meddle (mĕd'l) *v.* to intrude or interfere

3 **Targeted Passage**

5. **abolitionist** (ăb'ə-lĭsh'ə-nĭst): one who advocated the end of slavery.

LITERARY ANALYSIS

E BIOGRAPHY

Possible answer: *Lincoln's problem-solving skills and logical mind are qualities of a good leader; his superstitious beliefs might not be.*

Lines 72–104
DISCUSSION PROMPTS

Use these prompts to help students analyze Lincoln's character:

Recall Why did Frederick Douglass criticize President Lincoln early in the war? ***Answer:*** *Douglass complained that he was the "white man's president," with only the welfare of white men in mind.*

Summarize Later, Douglass says that "infinite wisdom has seldom sent any man into the world better fitted for his mission than Abraham Lincoln." What was Lincoln's mission, according to Douglass? ***Answer:*** *His mission was to keep the country from splitting apart and to eliminate slavery.*

Evaluate Do you think Lincoln deserves the title Great Emancipator? Why or why not? *Students should support their answers with details from the selection.*

ANALYZE VISUALS

About the Art This photograph was taken on October 3, 1862. President Lincoln had traveled to the battlefield at Antietam to encourage a reluctant Major General John A. McClernand to attack Confederate forces. The man on the left is a detective named Allan Pinkerton.

Activity Compare Lincoln's appearance to that of the other men. What can you conclude about him from his appearance? ***Possible answer:*** *He is wearing formal clothes. He seems strict and determined, and his height makes him appear intimidating.*

SELECTION WRAP-UP

REFLECT Have students share the most interesting or surprising detail they learned about Abraham Lincoln from this biography.

★ **CRITIQUE** This biography includes quotes from Lincoln's friends, third parties, and critics. Ask students what they can learn from such personal accounts that they might not learn from a straightforward descriptive essay.

FOR LESS-PROFICIENT READERS

3 **Targeted Passage [Lines 65–77]**

This passage describes perceptions of Lincoln during the course of the Civil War.

- Why was Lincoln unpopular during the Civil War?
- Why is Lincoln known as the Great Emancipator?
- How did Lincoln's attitude toward slavery change during the course of the war?

FOR ADVANCED LEARNERS/PRE-AP

Compare and Contrast Have students write paragraphs comparing and contrasting Lincoln with another U.S. president. They may organize their ideas in a Venn Diagram. Have students share their paragraphs and discuss what qualities make a good leader.

BEST PRACTICES TOOLKIT—Transparency
Venn Diagram p. A26

Practice and Apply

After Reading

For additional support of postreading questions, use these copy masters:

 RESOURCE MANAGER—Copy Masters

Reading Check p. 192 (to check understanding of the selection)

Biography p. 185 (for practice of literary analysis standards focus)

Question Support p. 193 (After Reading questions adapted for English learners and less-proficient readers)

Additional selection questions are provided for teachers on page 179.

ANSWERS

Comprehension

1. *At that time, people had to sit still for long periods of time while their picture was taken (lines 20–22). If they moved, the picture would be blurred.*
2. *Lincoln originally wanted to preserve the Union.*
3. *Lincoln eventually saw the Civil War as a way to abolish slavery.*

Literary Analysis

Possible answers:

4. **■ STANDARDS FOCUS Identify Main Idea and Details** *Lincoln was a complicated person who accomplished great things.*
5. *Reading Lincoln's own words gives readers an understanding of his sense of humor and his origins. This helps Lincoln seem like a real person. Examples include Lincoln making fun of his appearance (lines 10–11) and saying "howdy" to visitors to the White House.*
6. *Lincoln overcame poverty to become educated and highly successful. He became an eloquent public speaker. He overcame depression. He "engineered the Union victory." His belief in the purpose of the war evolved from simply wanting to preserve the Union to wanting to end slavery.*

After Reading

Comprehension

1. **Recall** According to the author, why does Abraham Lincoln look "so stiff and formal" in photographs?
2. **Recall** What was Lincoln's original reason for entering into the Civil War?
3. **Clarify** What caused Frederick Douglass to change his opinion of Lincoln?

Literary Analysis

4. **Identify Main Idea and Details** Review the outline you filled in as you read. Based on the main ideas and details you noted, what do you think is the overall main idea of the selection?
5. **Analyze Characterization** One method of characterization is to present the way a person talks. Review the quotations from Lincoln that Freedman includes in this biography. In what way do Lincoln's words add to your understanding of his character? Cite one or two specific quotations to support your answer.
6. **Make Judgments** What signs of **greatness** did Lincoln exhibit in his life? Support your response with evidence from the text.
7. **Evaluate Biography** List the strengths and weaknesses of Lincoln in a chart like the one shown. In your opinion, does the author provide a balanced portrait of his subject? Explain.

Strengths	*Weaknesses*
sense of humor	

Extension and Challenge

8. **Readers' Circle** People often say that Abraham Lincoln would have a difficult time winning an election today. Why do you think they say that? Discuss the question with your group. Then decide whether or not you agree. Support your opinion with examples from the biography.
9. **SOCIAL STUDIES CONNECTION** In 1922, President Harding dedicated the Lincoln Memorial, a magnificent structure built in Washington D.C. to honor Abraham Lincoln. Research the memorial to find out what is included within it and what it stands for.

Lincoln Memorial

 **RESEARCH LINKS**
For more about the Lincoln Memorial, visit the **Research Center** at **ClassZone.com.**

7. **● STANDARDS FOCUS Biography** ***Strengths:*** *sense of humor, hardworking, logical mind, talented military strategist.* ***Weaknesses:*** *secretive, little formal education, superstitious.* ***Evaluation:*** *The author presents a balanced portrait by showing the personal problems and difficulties Lincoln overcame and by contrasting his unpopularity during the Civil War with his great popularity today.*

Extension and Challenge

8. *Students should cite details from the biography to support their opinions. They may point out that Lincoln's unusual looks would not show well on television, but that his down-to-earth wit would help him connect with voters.*
9. **SOCIAL STUDIES CONNECTION** *Students may conduct research individually or with a partner. Have students summarize what they learn about the Lincoln Memorial.*

cabulary in Context

ABULARY PRACTICE

or each sentence, choose the vocabulary word that has a similar meaning to the boldfaced word or phrase.

1. It's easy now, after the fact, to say that you **condemn** the awful crime.
2. I **shop regularly at** the corner grocery.
3. Why must you always **interfere** in things that are not your business?
4. He thought it was wrong to **oppose** his parents.
5. That particular music made them feel **sad.**
6. Because he felt so **tired,** he began taking vitamins.

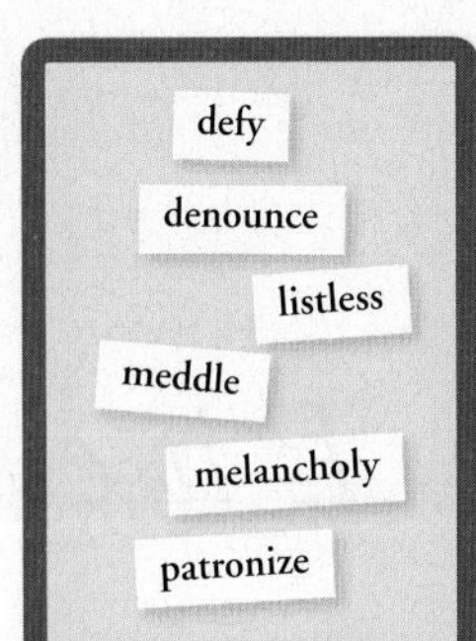

ABULARY IN WRITING

Vhat negative things did people say about President Lincoln when he was in ffice? Use two or more vocabulary words to write your answer in a paragraph. Here is a sample opening sentence.

EXAMPLE SENTENCE

During the Civil War, plenty of people took the opportunity to ***denounce*** *Lincoln's military decisions.*

ABULARY STRATEGY: MULTIPLE-MEANING WORDS

Many English words have more than one meaning. The vocabulary word *patronize* is one of these words. In the selection, *patronize* means "to visit as a customer," but another definition is "to treat in a condescending manner."

PRACTICE Each boldfaced word below has multiple meanings. Read the sentence and figure out the meaning of the boldfaced word based on context clues. Use a dictionary to check your answer. Then find another meaning for the word and use the word in a new sentence.

1. My grandmother knit a sweater using yellow **yarn.**
2. I can **sink** the basketball in the net even when I'm nervous.
3. The **pipe** below the sink was rusty from age.
4. When I am hungry, I **gorge** myself on pancakes and eggs.

VOCABULARY PRACTICE
For more practice, go to the **Vocabulary Center** at **ClassZone.com.**

DIFFERENTIATED INSTRUCTION

FOR ENGLISH LEARNERS

Vocabulary Practice [mixed-readiness pairs] Encourage students to review the definitions of the vocabulary words and to study the context for each word in the story. Pair students with fluent speakers to choose the words that best fit in the sentence.

FOR ADVANCED LEARNERS/PRE–AP

Vocabulary Strategy Challenge students to brainstorm more examples of multiple-meaning words or to find more examples in the selection. Then ask them to write sentences for each word, including in each sentence context clues that show the correct meaning of the word.

ANSWERS

Vocabulary in Context

VOCABULARY PRACTICE

1. *denounce*
2. *patronize*
3. *meddle*
4. *defy*
5. *melancholy*
6. *listless*

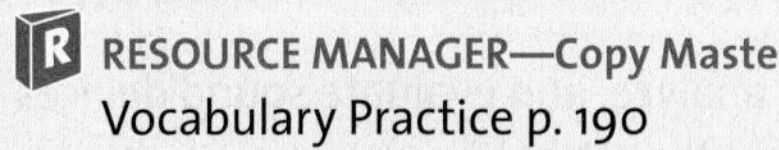

RESOURCE MANAGER—Copy Master
Vocabulary Practice p. 190

VOCABULARY IN WRITING

Suggest that students skim the biography, reviewing how the vocabulary words are used and noting details about Lincoln's reputation. Challenge students to use most of the vocabulary words in their paragraphs.

VOCABULARY STRATEGY: MULTIPLE–MEANING WORDS *(also an EL language objective)*

Possible answers:

1. *"continuous strand of twisted thread used for knitting"; also "entertaining tale" (My grandmother told the children a* ***yarn.****)*
2. *"drop"; also "basin" (I put the dirty dishes in the* ***sink.****)*
3. *"a hollow cylinder or tube"; also "a device used for smoking" (My grandpa coughed after smoking a* ***pipe.****)*
4. *"overeat"; also "a deep, narrow passage with steep, rocky sides" (We climbed the* ***gorge*** *carefully.)*

RESOURCE MANAGER—Copy Master
Vocabulary Strategy p. 191

Vocabulary Center at **ClassZone.com**
Additional Vocabulary Activities

Assess and Reteach

Assess

RESOURCE MANAGER—Copy Masters
Selection Tests A, B/C pp. 195–196, 197–198

Test Generator CD

Reteach

STANDARDS LESSON FILE
Reading Lesson 4: Recognizing Main Idea and Details
Vocabulary Lesson 19: Multiple-Meaning Words

Focus and Motivate

OBJECTIVES

Literary Analysis

- explore the key idea of **persevering**
- identify and analyze methods of characterization
- read narrative poetry, including ballads
- read two poems and a comic strip

Reading

- identify, analyze, and evaluate sound devices (rhyme, rhythm, repetition)

SUMMARY

Both narrative poems celebrate the power of the individual. "Barbara Frietchie," set during the Civil War, tells the story of an elderly woman who boldly stands up for her beliefs and in so doing makes a strong impression on a would-be foe. The title character of "John Henry," a hard-working laborer, wins a contest with his machine counterpart but dies from his superhuman effort.

Is it ever right to GIVE UP?

Discuss the question and introduce the ***KEY IDEA*** by having students define ***persevere.*** Then have students think of someone they know who has continued despite obstacles. Ask volunteers to tell a brief story about what the person did and how he or she was able to persevere. Then have students complete the ***QUICKWRITE*** activity individually.

Before Reading

Barbara Frietchie

Poem by John Greenleaf Whittier

John Henry

Traditional Poem

Is it ever right to GIVE UP?

KEY IDEA Think of a time when you kept trying something without success. Did you get discouraged, or did the experience make you try harder? When some of us might give up, other people find the strength to **persevere.** In the poems you are about to read, you will meet two characters who refuse to take no for an answer.

QUICKWRITE Think of a situation in which you gave up doing something—perhaps playing an instrument or being on a team. Write a brief paragraph explaining the positive and negative consequences of your decision.

282

Selection Resources

RESOURCE MANAGER UNIT 2

Plan and Teach pp. 199–206

Literary Analysis

Characterization in Poetry pp. 207, 208†*

Question Support p. 211*

Reading

Recognize Sound Devices pp. 209, 210†*

Reading Fluency p. 213

Assessment

Selection Tests A, B/C pp. 215*, 217*

 Test Generator CD

BEST PRACTICES TOOLKIT

Differentiated Instruction pp. 31–38*

Graphic Organizers/Strategies

Two-Column Chart • Classification Chart • Think-Pair-Share

Reading Support

Audio Anthology CD*

Technology

Literature Center at **ClassZone.com**

Write*Smart* CD

* Resources for Differentiation † Also in Spanish

RARY ANALYSIS: CHARACTERIZATION IN POETRY

'he two works you are about to read are **narrative poems,** which means they tell a story. Like short stories, narrative poems always feature characters. Poets can bring their characters to life, or **characterize** them, in just a few words. A telling image, a carefully chosen scrap of dialogue, or a striking detail can suggest a great deal about a character's traits, behavior, and values.

As you read "Barbara Frietchie" and "John Henry," pay attention to what the poets' language suggests about the characters. Then note information about each main character n the appropriate part of a graphic like the one shown.

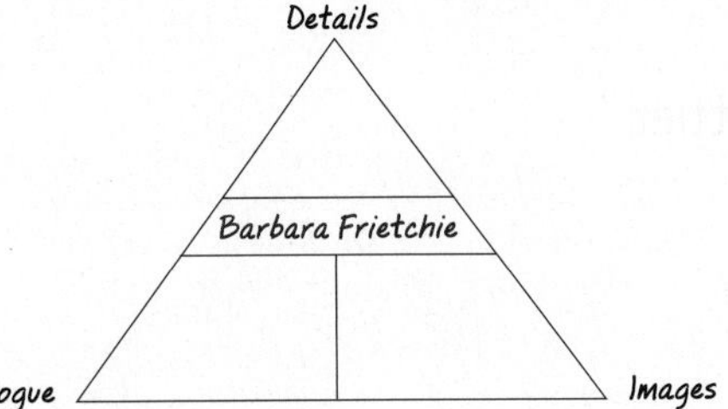

DING SKILL: RECOGNIZE SOUND DEVICES

One way that narrative poems differ from short stories is the extent to which they use **sound devices** to add meaning and interest. The three Rs of sound devices are

- **Rhyme:** the repetition of sounds at the ends of words

  Over the mountains winding down,
  Horse and foot, into Frederick town.

- **Rhythm:** the pattern of stressed and unstressed syllables in the lines of a poem

  She leaned far out on the window-sill

- **Repetition:** repeated sounds, words, or phrases that are used for emphasis

  You must be a steel driving man like me,
  You must be a steel driving man like me.

Reading a poem aloud can help you appreciate the sound devices. As you read "Barbara Frietchie" and "John Henry," notice the effect the devices have on the sound and sense of the poem.

Author Online

Fiery Abolitionist

John Greenleaf Whittier
1807–1892

Although John Greenleaf Whittier had little formal schooling, he was naturally drawn to poetry. His career began in 1826 when a local newspaper published one of his poems, which his older sister had submitted without his knowledge. William Lloyd Garrison, a noted abolitionist, was the newspaper's editor, and his passion for ending slavery affected Whittier. Whittier's poems about the evils of slavery were published in 1846 under the title *Voices of Freedom.*

MORE ABOUT THE AUTHOR
For more on John Greenleaf Whittier, visit the **Literature Center** at **ClassZone.com.**

Background

"Barbara Frietchie" and the Civil War
As an abolitionist, John Greenleaf Whittier strongly supported the Union side in the Civil War. He wrote "Barbara Frietchie" to honor a legendary act of courage. Barbara Frietchie was a citizen of Frederick, Maryland, who was fiercely loyal to the Union. According to legend, as Confederate soldiers marched through the town, she defiantly waved a Union flag.

John Henry It is not known if John Henry actually existed, but the character may have been based on a real steel driver in the early 1870s. Steel drivers used hammers and steel drills to pound holes into mountains. Then explosives blasted deeper into the mountains to create tunnels for railroads. The speed and efficiency of machines like steam drills eventually threatened the livelihood of steel drivers. John Henry's story is often sung as a ballad.

Teach

STANDARDS FOCUS

LITERARY ANALYSIS

● CHARACTERIZATION IN POETRY

Explain that narrative poets must generally use fewer words than short story writers to bring their characters to life. Have students choose a character from a story they've read and identify two details they'd use to characterize him or her in a poem. Students should explain why these details help show the character's traits, behavior, or values.

CHECK UNDERSTANDING Ask students to summarize the methods poets use to bring characters to life.

RESOURCE MANAGER—Copy Master
Characterization in Poetry p. 207 (for student use while reading the poems)

READING SKILL

■ RECOGNIZE SOUND DEVICES

Write this poem on the board:

Who will dare to persevere
When defeat is lurking near?
She who dares to persevere
Scorns defeat and shuts out fear.

Ask students to find examples of repetition and rhyme in the poem. ***Answers:*** *repetition:* dare(s) to persevere, defeat; *rhyme:* persevere, near, fear

CHECK UNDERSTANDING Ask students to tap out the rhythm as you read the poem aloud.

DIFFERENTIATED INSTRUCTION

FOR ALL STUDENTS

Integrated Curriculum For a project that links the poem "Barbara Frietchie" and social studies, have students conduct research on the evolution of the American flag. For further details on this project, see

RESOURCE MANAGER
Ideas for Extension pp. 204–205

FOR LESS–PROFICIENT READERS

Concept Support Tell students that the best way to read poetry is to use punctuation to tell them when to pause. Instead of stopping at the end of every line, which may make comprehension more challenging, encourage students to pause briefly after a comma and slightly longer after a period or a semicolon. Encourage students to read poems aloud to help them gain understanding.

FOR ENGLISH LEARNERS

Option for Reading [paired option] Encourage multiple readings of the poems. Read the poems aloud for students, or have students listen to the poems on the *Audio Anthology CD.* Then have students read each poem aloud to a partner and work together to summarize the narratives.

Practice and Apply

ANALYZE VISUALS

Possible answer: *The flag is tattered and torn. From its condition, you can conclude that the flag was probably carried into battle.*

Lines 1–12

DISCUSSION PROMPTS

Use these questions to help students identify the setting and plot of this narrative poem:

Recall When and where does this poem take place? In lines 1–6, what details paint a picture of the setting? ***Answer:*** *The poem takes place on a September morning in Frederick, Maryland. Setting details include "meadows rich with corn," "clustered spires," hills, and orchards full of fruit.*

Infer What does the word *horde* (line 8) tell you about the size of the approaching Confederate army? ***Answer:*** *It is very large.*

Speculate Given what you know about the setting, why might the soldiers have come to Frederick town? ***Possible answer:*** *The men are hungry (line 8). The land around the town offers much food.*

READING SKILL

A SOUND DEVICES

Possible answers: *rhyme (end words of couplets), rhythm (four stressed syllables in most lines), repetition ("over the mountain[s]" in lines 10 and 11)*

Barbara Frietchie

John Greenleaf Whittier

Up from the meadows rich with corn,
Clear in the cool September morn,

The clustered spires of Frederick stand
Green-walled by the hills of Maryland.

Round about them orchards sweep,
Apple and peach tree fruited deep,

Fair as the garden of the Lord
To the eyes of the famished rebel horde,[1]

On that pleasant morn of the early fall
When Lee[2] marched over the mountain wall;

Over the mountains winding down,
Horse and foot, into Frederick town. **A**

ANALYZE VISUALS
This union flag flew during the Civil War. What **conclusions** can draw about why the f looks the way it does?

A SOUND DEVICES
Which sound devices d you notice in lines 1–12

1. **horde:** a large group or crowd.
2. **Lee:** a general for the Confederate army during the Civil War.

DIFFERENTIATED INSTRUCTION

FOR LESS–PROFICIENT READERS

Vocabulary Support Discuss strategies students can use to tackle unfamiliar words.

- Help them use context clues to infer, in line 8, that *famished* means "hungry" and *rebel* refers to someone in the Confederate army.
- Ask them to look up the word *crimson*, meaning "bright red," in a dictionary.
- Provide them with definitions of *clustered spires* ("*steeples of several churches*") and *garden of the Lord* ("*Garden of Eden*").

FOR ENGLISH LEARNERS

Language: Word Sequence [mixed-readiness pairs] Point out that poets may use unusual word order to help them rhyme words at the ends of lines and maintain a regular rhythm. To illustrate, contrast line 33 (normal: verb follows subject) with line 23 (inverted: verb precedes subject). Pair students with fluent speakers to identify sentences with inverted word order and restate them in normal word order. They may write their answers in a Two-Column Chart.

Inverted Word Order	Normal Word Order
"In her attic window the staff she set" (line 21)	She set the staff in her attic window

BEST PRACTICES TOOLKIT—Transparency
Two-Column Chart p. A25

BACKGROUND

The Stars and Stripes The flag on this page has 33 stars, which dates it to the period between July 4, 1859, and July 3, 1861. The first U.S. flag, adopted by Congress in 1777, had 13 stars and 13 stripes to represent the original 13 colonies. Over the years, the flag was modified as new states joined the Union. However, adding a new stripe for each state eventually became unwieldy, and a naval captain named Samuel C. Reid suggested that the number of stripes be fixed at 13 while a star was added for each new state. In 1818, President James Monroe signed this idea into law. Under the Flag Act of 1818, after a state joined the Union, its star would be officially added to the flag on the following 4th of July.

During the Civil War, the Union flag was altered twice. The 33-star flag that was introduced after Oregon became a state in 1859 was replaced by one with 34 stars in 1861, when Kansas joined the Union. Two years later, several northwestern counties of Virginia left the Confederacy to form the new state of West Virginia, causing a 35th star to appear in the flag's blue field on July 4, 1863.

FOR ENGLISH LEARNERS

Culture: Connect Have students locate the description of the Union flag (lines 13–14) and compare it to the photograph on page 285. Discuss the symbolism of the stars and stripes. Then have students draw or describe the flags of countries with which they have a personal connection. Ask them to explain what the various features of the flag mean.

FOR ADVANCED LEARNERS/PRE–AP

Analyze Style Point out that Whittier often begins his sentences with modifiers, especially long prepositional phrases. Ask students to find examples of these and then identify other aspects of Whittier's style relating to word choice and sound devices. Have students create a Classification Chart to present the main stylistic features of "Barbara Frietchie," along with several examples of each.

 **BEST PRACTICES TOOLKIT—Transparency**
Classification Chart p. B17

LITERARY ANALYSIS

B CHARACTERIZATION

Possible answer: *She is 90 years old and bent over with age. She is "Bravest of all in Frederick town" because she alone is willing to fly the Union flag as the Confederate army approaches.*

READING SKILL

C SOUND DEVICES

Possible answer: *The words at the ends of the lines sound similar but not exactly the same. Students may say that this does not distract them.*

If students need help . . . Read the two lines aloud and then have students say the words *staff* and *scarf.* Explain that a poet's use of words that almost rhyme, but not quite, is called slant rhyme.

Lines 27–36

REINFORCE *KEY IDEA:* PERSEVERE

Discuss What does Barbara Frietchie do and say when the Confederate soldiers shoot at the flag she has displayed on her house? How does Frietchie **persevere** in this scene? ***Possible answer:*** *The soldiers' shots tear apart the flag and break the pole from which it hangs. Frietchie quickly grabs the flag. Then she leans out the window and waves it while challenging Jackson's soldiers to shoot her instead of the flag. She does not give up even though she is face to face with a powerful enemy.*

Forty flags with their silver stars,
Forty flags with their crimson bars,

Flapped in the morning wind: the sun
Of noon looked down, and saw not one.

Up rose old Barbara Frietchie then,
Bowed with her fourscore years and ten;[3]

Bravest of all in Frederick town,
She took up the flag the men hauled down.

In her attic window the staff she set,
To show that one heart was loyal yet. B

Up the street came the rebel tread,
Stonewall Jackson[4] riding ahead.

Under his slouched hat left and right
He glanced; the old flag met his sight.

"Halt!"—the dust-brown ranks stood fast.
"Fire!"—out blazed the rifle-blast.

It shivered the window, pane and sash;
It rent[5] the banner with seam and gash.

Quick, as it fell, from the broken staff
Dame Barbara snatched the silken scarf. C

She leaned far out on the window-sill,
And shook it forth with a royal will.

"Shoot, if you must, this old gray head,
But spare your country's flag," she said.

B CHARACTERIZATI
Reread lines 17–22. What do you learn ab Barbara Frietchie?

C SOUND DEVICES
In lines 31–32, what is different about the us of **rhyme?** Tell what effect this has on you reading of the poem.

3. **fourscore years and ten:** ninety years.
4. **Stonewall Jackson:** a general for the Confederate army during the Civil War.
5. **rent:** tore apart.

DIFFERENTIATED INSTRUCTION

FOR LESS–PROFICIENT READERS

Reading Skill Follow-Up: Recognize Sound Devices [paired option] Have students copy four to six lines from the poem onto a sheet of paper. Then have one partner read a line while the other indicates which syllables are stressed and unstressed, using the marks shown on page 283. Partners should take turns until all the lines are marked. Encourage students to notice patterns in each line.

Comprehension Support [paired option] Lines 13–16 form a complete sentence. Help students understand the events in this brief but important passage (*the townspeople take down their Union flags because they fear the Confederate soldiers*). First, have students read the lines and think about what happens to the flags and why. Then have them share their ideas with partners before discussing them with the group.

BEST PRACTICES TOOLKIT—Transparency
Think-Pair-Share p. A18

FOR ENGLISH LEARNERS

Vocabulary Support [paired option] Have pairs use context clues to define these words:

- *staff* (line 21), "flag pole"
- *tread* (lines 23, 44), "marching"
- *Dame* (line 32), "respectful term of address for an elderly woman"
- *yon* (line 41), "that"
- *tost* (line 45), "tossed"
- *o'er* (line 51), "over"

A shade of sadness, a blush of shame,
Over the face of the leader came;

The nobler nature within him stirred
To life at that woman's deed and word;

"Who touches a hair of yon gray head
Dies like a dog! March on!" he said. **D**

All day long through Frederick street
Sounded the tread of marching feet:

All day long that free flag tost
Over the heads of the rebel host. **E**

Ever its torn folds rose and fell
On the loyal winds that loved it well;

And through the hill-gaps sunset light
Shone over it with a warm good-night.

Barbara Frietchie's work is o'er,
And the Rebel rides on his raids no more.

Honor to her! and let a tear
Fall, for her sake, on Stonewall's bier.[6]

Over Barbara Frietchie's grave,
Flag of Freedom and Union, wave!

Peace and order and beauty draw
Round thy symbol of light and law;

And ever the stars above look down
On thy stars below in Frederick town!

D CHARACTERIZATION
In lines 35–42, what traits and behavior does Barbara Frietchie display that make Stonewall Jackson feel shame?

E SOUND DEVICES
Reread lines 43–46? What does the **repetition** emphasize about the events in Frederick?

6. **bier** (bîr): a stand on which a coffin is placed before a burial.

LITERARY ANALYSIS

D CHARACTERIZATION

Possible answer: *Frietchie shows her bravery and devotion by flying the Union flag and by standing up to Jackson. Jackson feels shame that he has treated such a person poorly. He may also feel shame when Frietchie refers to the Union flag as "your country's flag," because she is implying that Jackson is fighting against his own country.*

READING SKILL

E SOUND DEVICES

Possible answer: *The repetition of "all day long" emphasizes what Frietchie achieved through her defiant action. The flag of the United States waves all day despite the presence of the Confederate troops.*

Lines 51–60

DISCUSSION PROMPTS

Use these prompts to help students understand the poem's setting and point of view:

Interpret How has the setting changed? How can you tell? ***Answer:*** *It is now after the war, and the country is reunited. You can tell because of the detail that "the Rebel rides on his raids no more" and because both Stonewall Jackson and Barbara Frietchie are now dead.*

Analyze What is the speaker's attitude toward Barbara Frietchie's actions? What does the flag she waved represent to the poet? ***Possible answer:*** *The speaker admires Frietchie. The flag represents "Freedom and Union" as well as "light and law."*

FOR LESS–PROFICIENT READERS

Concept Support [paired option] Have students work in pairs to make sure their characterization chart, introduced on page 283, is complete and includes all three types of information. Suggest that they note line numbers for each item they record. Point out that lines 37–40 help to characterize Frietchie by showing the impact her words and actions have on another person.

Details

- *ninety years old; bent over (line 18)*

Dialogue

- *"Shoot, if you must, this old gray head, / But spare your country's flag" (lines 35–36)*

Images

- *rifle-blast, bullets tearing through flag (lines 28–30)*
- *Frietchie's shaking the flag "with a royal will" (line 34)*
- *Jackson's "blush of shame" (line 37)*

FOR ADVANCED LEARNERS/PRE–AP

Characterize Stonewall Jackson [small-group option] Ask students to reread lines 37–46. Have them work in groups of three to complete a characterization chart for Jackson (like the one on page 283). Ask them what words and phrases they would use to describe Jackson as he is depicted in this poem. ***Possible answer:*** *wise, compassionate, thoughtful, ashamed, doubting the rightness of his actions*

Prereading for this poem is found on pages 282–283.

READING SKILL

F SOUND DEVICES

Answer: *The repetition emphasizes John Henry's future occupation as a steel driver.*

Lines 21–25

DISCUSSION PROMPTS

Use these prompts to help students understand the character of John Henry:

Recall What feat is John Henry determined to accomplish? ***Answer:*** *He is determined to beat the steam drill in drilling a hole in the mountain.*

Analyze How does John Henry express his determination to beat the steam drill? ***Answer:*** *He says he'd hammer himself to death before he'd let the drill beat him.*

Speculate Why do you think most tunneling and mining today is done by machines? Do you think people who operate big digging equipment feel the same way about their work as John Henry did? ***Possible answer:*** *Machine work is faster and safer. Students may say the operators, though less physically taxed, still take pride in their work.*

LITERARY ANALYSIS

G CHARACTERIZATION

Possible answer: *John Henry's attitude is determined: he plans to outdo the steam drill even if it kills him.*

John Henry

Traditional

When John Henry was a little boy,
Sitting upon his father's knee,
His father said, "Look here, my boy,
You must be a steel driving man like me,
You must be a steel driving man like me." F

John Henry went up on the mountain,
Just to drive himself some steel.
The rocks was so tall and John Henry so small,
He said lay down hammer and squeal,
He said lay down hammer and squeal.

John Henry had a little wife,
And the dress she wore was red;
The last thing before he died,
He said, "Be true to me when I'm dead,
Oh, be true to me when I'm dead."

John Henry's wife ask him for fifteen cents,
And he said he didn't have but a dime,
Said, "If you wait till the rising sun goes down,
I'll borrow it from the man in the mine,
I'll borrow it from the man in the mine."

John Henry started on the right-hand side,
And the steam drill started on the left.
He said, "Before I'd let that steam drill beat me down,
I'd hammer my fool self to death,
Oh, I'd hammer my fool self to death." G

F SOUND DEVICES
What part of John He[nry's] life does the **repetitio[n]** lines 4–5 emphasize?

G CHARACTERIZATI[ON]
How would you descri[be] John Henry's attitude?

DIFFERENTIATED INSTRUCTION

FOR LESS–PROFICIENT READERS

Comprehension Support Point out that the action in the ballad does not occur in chronological order. Have students point out the stanzas that are out of order (lines 11–15, lines 46–55) and then retell the events of the story in the order in which they occur.

FOR ENGLISH LEARNERS

Reading: Background Clarify what John Henry does for a living—breaking up rock to dig mines and railroad tunnels. Make sketches on the board to show the tools used (sledgehammer and spikelike drill made of steel) and where this work was done (mines and railroad tunnels). Then have two students, one to hammer and one to hold the drill, demonstrate hammering steel to break rock. Ask students to speculate about how strong a steel driving man would be.

The steam drill started at half-past six,
John Henry started the same time.
John Henry struck bottom at half-past eight,
And the steam drill didn't bottom till nine,
And the steam drill didn't bottom till nine.

John Henry said to his captain,
"A man, he ain't nothing but a man,
Before I'd let that steam drill beat me down,
I'd die with the hammer in my hand,
Oh, I'd die with the hammer in my hand."

John Henry said to his shaker,[1]
"Shaker, why don't you sing just a few more rounds?
And before the setting sun goes down,
You're gonna hear this hammer of mine sound,
You're gonna hear this hammer of mine sound."

John Henry hammered on the mountain,
He hammered till half-past three,
He said, "This big Bend Tunnel on the C. & O. road[2]
Is going to be the death of me,
Lord! is going to be the death of me."

John Henry had a little baby boy,
You could hold him in the palm of your hand.
The last words before he died,
"Son, you must be a steel driving man,
Son, you must be a steel driving man." (H)

John Henry had a little woman,
And the dress she wore was red,
She went down the railroad track and never come back,
Said she was going where John Henry fell dead,
Said she was going where John Henry fell dead.

John Henry hammering on the mountain,
As the whistle blew for half-past two,
The last word I heard him say,
"Captain, I've hammered my insides in two,
Lord, I've hammered my insides in two." (I)

(H) CHARACTERIZATION
Why do you think it is important to John Henry that his son follows in his footsteps?

(I) SOUND DEVICES
Read lines 56–57 aloud with a natural **rhythm.** Which syllables are stressed?

---

1. **shaker:** the person who holds the steel drill for the steel driving man and shakes the drill to remove it from the rock.
2. **big Bend . . . road:** Construction work on the Big Bend Tunnel on the Chesapeake & Ohio Railroad in West Virginia took place from 1870 to 1873.

Lines 26–30

REINFORCE *KEY IDEA:* PERSEVERE

Discuss How does John Henry **persevere** in the contest with the steam drill? What is the result? ***Possible answer:*** *He perseveres by hammering fast and hard for two hours. The result is that he reaches "bottom" a half-hour before the steam drill does.*

LITERARY ANALYSIS

(H) CHARACTERIZATION

Possible answer: *John Henry is proud of what he has accomplished. He wants his son to follow the family's traditions and also be the kind of person who never gives up.*

READING SKILL

(I) SOUND DEVICES

Possible answer: *The stressed syllables are* Hen-, ham-, moun-, whis-, blew, half-, *and* two.

SELECTION WRAP–UP

REFLECT Point out that both Barbara Frietchie and John Henry have become American legends. Ask students which character seems more like a real person to them and why.

★ **CRITIQUE** Have students think about how the two poets developed the characters of Barbara Frietchie and John Henry. Were they well-developed and believable? Students should explain why or why not, using examples from the poems for support.

READING FLUENCY

Distribute the copy masters and have students practice fluency.

RESOURCE MANAGER—Copy Master
Reading Fluency p. 213

FOR LESS–PROFICIENT READERS

Concept Support Note that John Henry makes many statements that show how hard he works and how committed he is to the job of driving steel. Ask students to add quotations by John Henry to the dialogue section of their charts from page 283 (*lines 23–25, 32–35, 36–40, 43–45, 49–50, 59–60*). Discuss how these repeated statements give John Henry a larger-than-life quality.

FOR ADVANCED LEARNERS/PRE–AP

Compare and Contrast [small-group option] Have students form small groups to compare and contrast the goal of each main character in the poems. Were the characters both correct to persevere? Why or why not? Which act of perseverance is more understandable? Why? Ask a group member to share students' findings with the class.

JOHN HENRY 289

DISCUSSION PROMPTS

Use these prompts to help students make connections between the cartoon and the ballad "John Henry":

Recall Why is John Henry a childhood hero of the cartoonist? ***Answer:*** *John Henry was a normal person who never gave up.*

Compare How is the cartoon ending different from the ending to the poem? ***Possible answer:*** *In the poem, John Henry dies. In the cartoon, the snow blower showers Bobby with snow. Its power makes him grit his teeth and want to throw a snowball at the man running the machine. The cartoon's ending is funnier and more lighthearted than the poem's ending.*

Evaluate Do you think this cartoon is an effective tribute to John Henry? Why or why not? ***Possible answers:***

- *Yes. It is an effective tribute because it shows a regular person trying to beat a piece of machinery. Although he doesn't win, Bobby is inspired by John Henry to persevere.*
- *No. The humorous tone of the cartoon does not fit the ballad's tragic ending.*

Reading for Information

COMIC STRIP John Henry has been the subject of ballads, children's books, feature films, and more. In this comic, cartoonist John Steventon shows one of the ways he's been inspired by this American folk hero.

SECTION B THE STAR JOURNAL B4

Cartoon Tribute to John Henry

John Henry was a childhood hero of mine, and he was probably one of the biggest influences on who I am and how I live my life. To me, the legend and the man are the same; I still see him as a regular guy who was confident in himself and who never, ever gave up. When he needed a job, he went and got one, convincing the boss that he was the right man for it. And when that job of Steel Driving Man was threatened by automation, he challenged that Steam Drill to a contest and won. Sure, he died in the process, but that just adds to his legend. The point is, he said he would win and did, against all odds. What a role model for young and old alike!

DIFFERENTIATED INSTRUCTION

FOR ENGLISH LEARNERS

Preview Review the main elements of a comic strip before students begin reading. Make sure they understand that a comic strip is read from left to right, starting with the row in the top left corner.

- Have students read the text in the white box, which gives the name of the comic strip, its featured character, and the title of the story that is depicted ("Man vs. Machine").
- Ask them to scan the pictures in the comic strip. Then have them think about the visuals, the title of the story, and the poem they have just read to predict what the comic strip will be about.
- Point out that the story begins with the smaller box in the top right corner.
- Clarify that dialogue bubbles with circles underneath indicate a character's thoughts, while those with an arrow underneath indicate a character's speech.

mprehension

. **Recall** What causes Barbara Frietchie to hold a flag out her window?

. **Clarify** Why does John Henry have a contest with the steam drill?

erary Analysis

. **Make Inferences** Reread lines 23–42 of "Barbara Frietchie." Why do you think Stonewall Jackson decides to protect the woman who defied him?

. **Interpret Symbol** What do you think John Henry's victory over the steam drill **symbolizes,** or stands for beyond its usual meaning?

. **Analyze Ballad** "John Henry" is a **ballad,** a poem that tells a story and was originally meant to be sung. What elements of the poem make it songlike?

. **Compare and Contrast** Using a Venn diagram like the one shown, compare and contrast the characters of Barbara Frietchie and John Henry. Are they more similar or different?

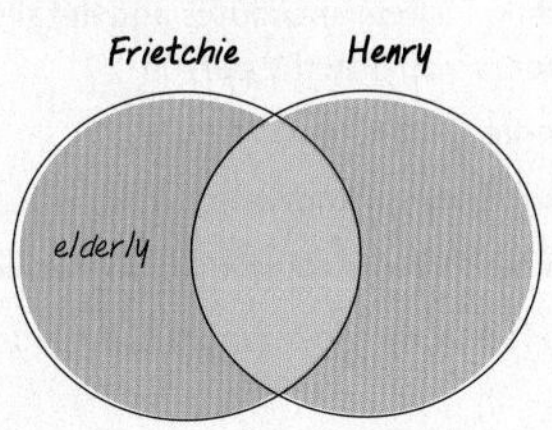

7. **Analyze Characterization** Review the character maps you created as you read. Based on the information you collected, describe each character in detail. What are they like? What do they believe in?

8. **Draw Conclusions** Why do you think Barbara Frietchie and John Henry captured the American imagination? Think about why Americans value the traits these characters display in the poems.

9. **Evaluate Sound Devices** Read several stanzas of each poem aloud. For each poem, tell whether you think the **rhythm, rhyme,** or **repetition** affects the meaning most. Explain your answer.

. **Compare Texts** In the "Cartoon Tribute to John Henry," how does Bobby's encounter with Dr. Dampflok parallel John Henry's experience in the poem?

tension and Challenge

1. **Readers' Circle** Considering the outcome, do you think John Henry was right to **persevere** at his work on the railroad? Explain.

Practice and Apply

After Reading

For additional support of postreading questions, use these copy masters:

RESOURCE MANAGER—Copy Masters
Recognize Sound Devices p. 209 (for practice of reading standards focus)
Question Support p. 211 (After Reading questions adapted for English learners and less-proficient readers)

Additional selection questions are provided for teachers on page 203.

ANSWERS

Comprehension

1. *Frietchie wants to show support for the Union when Confederate soldiers arrive.*
2. *Henry wants to prove that a man using hand tools can outpace the steam drill.*

Literary Analysis

Possible answers:

3. *Jackson may protect Frietchie because he sees her as a model of dedication and courage or because he, too, favors a united country.*
4. *Henry's victory may symbolize the power of the individual or the value of hard work.*
5. *The repetition of whole lines at the end of most stanzas and the generally regular pattern of rhyme make the poem songlike.*
6. ***Differences:*** *Frietchie—elderly, patriotic. Henry—young, strong.* ***Similarities:*** *quick in action, determined, willing to risk their lives for what is important to them.*
7. ● **STANDARDS FOCUS Characterization in Poetry** *Frietchie is a courageous 90-year-old woman who believes in her country. Henry has incredible strength and stamina and believes he can do his job better than any machine.*
8. *Frietchie's patriotism and courage and Henry's determination and hard work are values most Americans share.*
9. ■ **STANDARDS FOCUS Recognize Sound Devices** *"Barbara Frietchie": Rhyme, because the rhyming words help the reader visualize the setting and the characters' actions. "John Henry": Repetition, because the repeated lines in most of the stanzas express Henry's traits or key events.*
10. *Bobby uses old technology (a shovel) to battle new technology (the snow blower), just as John Henry used a hammer to battle the steam drill.*

Extension and Challenge

11. *Many students will admire John Henry's perseverance, because he showed how much one person can accomplish with single-minded determination. Others may say that his perseverance was unwise, because it led to his death. Henry himself presents this view in lines 24–25.*

Assess and Reteach

Assess

RESOURCE MANAGER—Copy Masters
Selection Tests A, B/C pp. 215–216, 217–218

Test Generator CD

Reteach

STANDARDS LESSON FILE
Literature Lesson 3: Characterization
Literature Lesson 20: Rhyme and Rhyme Scheme
Literature Lesson 21: Rhythm and Meter

Focus and Motivate

OBJECTIVES

- analyze a student model that reflects the key traits of a focused description
- use the writing process to produce a focused description of a person or a character
- write using sensory details
- revise and edit, applying a rubric for a focused description
- conduct an interview

WRITER'S ROAD MAP

WRITING PROMPTS 1 AND 2

Suggest that students list some interesting people in their lives as well as memorable literary characters. For each, they should jot down key details that will help them decide which person or character they most want to write about.

ADDITIONAL PROMPTS

Use these prompts for practice with writing focused descriptions of people:

WRITING PROMPT 3

Writing for the Real World Pick a person you know who is a natural leader with strong values. Then act as that person's campaign manager as he or she runs for public office. Write a description that might appear on his or her Web site.

People to Consider

- a peer or a family member
- a teacher or other community member

WRITING PROMPT 4

Writing from a Picture Use your imagination to write a description of a person in a painting or a photograph.

Subjects to Consider

- a model in a magazine photograph
- a person in a painting that appears in an art book or an online museum

For additional writing prompts, see
WriteSmart CD
Writing Center at **ClassZone.com**

KEY TRAITS

Review the six ***KEY TRAITS*** with students, focusing on ideas and organization. Compare the list of traits with the rubric on page 298.

Writing Workshop

Describing a Person

In Unit 2 you read about some incredible people, including Abraham Lincoln and Harriet Tubman. Now you will have a chance to write about someone who fascinates you—either a person you know or a literary character. Read the **Writer's Road Map** and get started describing someone unforgettable.

WRITER'S ROAD MAP

Describing a Person

WRITING PROMPT 1

Writing from Your Life Write a focused description of a person who is important to you. Your description should include anecdotes and details to help your readers visualize the person.

People to Consider

- a friend you know very well
- a person who taught you something important
- a family member who helped you

WRITING PROMPT 2

Writing from Literature The literature in this unit is full of memorable characters. Choose one of the characters you read about and describe that person as clearly as you can.

Characters to Consider

- Greg in "The Treasure of Lemon Brown"
- Charlie in "Flowers for Algernon"
- Waverly in "Rules of the Game"

WRITING TOOLS
For prewriting, revision, and editing tools, visit the **Writing Center** at **ClassZone.com.**

KEY TRAITS

1. IDEAS
- Provides a **focused description** of a clearly identified person or character
- Includes **anecdotes and details** to describe the person
- Uses **dialogue** to show the subject's personality

2. ORGANIZATION
- Has a clear **organization,** with an introduction, a body, and a conclusion
- Uses **transitions** to connect ideas
- Provides any **background information** the reader may need
- **Concludes** by showing why the person is important

3. VOICE
- Has an appropriate and respectful **tone**

4. WORD CHOICE
- Uses **sensory details** to show the reader what the person or character is like

5. SENTENCE FLUENCY
- Varies the **lengths of sentences** to make the description lively and interesting

6. CONVENTIONS
- Uses **correct grammar, spelling, and punctuation**

292 UNIT 2: CHARACTER AND POINT OF VIEW

Writing Workshop Resources

RESOURCE MANAGER UNIT 2
Plan and Teach pp. 219–222
Prewriting–Editing pp. 223–227
Writing Rubric p. 228
Speaking and Listening p. 229
Writing Support p. 230*

STANDARDS LESSON FILE
Writing Lessons 27, 39
Grammar Lesson 15
Speaking and Listening Lessons 9, 10

BEST PRACTICES TOOLKIT
Scaffolding Writing Instruction pp. 43–46*
Cluster Diagram • Observation Chart • Writing Template: Focused Description • Reporter's Questions

TECHNOLOGY

Easy Planner DVD
Writing Center at **ClassZone.com**
Write*Smart* CD

* Resources for Differentiation

t 1: Analyze a Student Model

Madison Delgado
Flaherty Junior High School

Coach Sand's Swimming Lesson

"Are you going to do it, or should we go home for lunch while you make up your mind?" Coach Sand's booming voice shook the diving board as I stood with my knees trembling and toes white and numb from gripping the edge. He was only 17, but planted below me at the side of the pool, he looked even shorter than his 5 feet 6 inches or so and much broader and more muscular—almost like King Kong.

"I'm not afraid of you," I muttered. I *was* afraid of him, though, and so was everyone else.

A group of us had signed up for Coach Sand's Pool School during winter break, thinking that it would be a fun way to improve our swimming and diving. He was the star diver on the high school team and had just gotten a scholarship to the state university. My friends and I had seen him in a few local competitions. We couldn't believe how anyone so short and stocky could turn himself into a graceful arrow that hit the water like a bull's-eye every time.

Coach was the boss of the water and of his students, and he made sure we knew it. The first day, he made us wait for 15 minutes huddled and shivering in our baggy Pool School bathing suits. When he finally came marching into the pool area, he was fully dressed in jeans, cowboy boots, and a black leather jacket. His boot heels cracked the tiles at every step and echoed off the pool walls. Right away, that made us feel scrawny and scared.

"I'm not going to dive into the pool to save any of you," he said, "so listen up and do as I say. You're going to find out that you can swim and dive a lot better than you think you can."

KEY TRAITS IN ACTION

Creates a **focused impression** of Coach Sand with a quotation and highlighted descriptive **details** that show his personality.

Provides important **background information** about the coach's qualifications. Putting this information early in the description is a sign of clear **organization.**

An **anecdote** and **sensory details** make Coach Sand leap off the page.

Teach

Part 1: Analyze a Student Model

Have students read the **Student Model** and **Key Traits in Action.** Then talk about the model, encouraging students to notice specific examples of each trait. You may wish to extend the discussion by using the following activities:

- **Focused Impression** Ask students to summarize the scene described in the opening paragraph. Ask: What impression of Coach Sand does it create? What descriptive details add to this focused impression? ***Possible answer:*** *The writer describes standing on a diving board trying to find the courage to jump off, as Coach Sand tries to get her to jump by mocking her slightly. Readers get the impression that Coach Sand is sarcastic and a bit of a bully. Details that describe his booming voice and his broad, muscular build add to this focused impression.*
- **Sensory Details** Remind students that sensory details are details that appeal to the senses—sight, sound, taste, smell, and touch. Have students identify sensory details in lines 1–22 and tell to which sense each appeals. ***Possible answer:*** *"booming voice" (line 2), sound; "toes white and numb" (line 3), sight and touch; "broader and more muscular—almost like King Kong" (line 6), sight; "a graceful arrow" (line 14), sight; "huddled and shivering in our baggy Pool School bathing suits" (lines 17–18), touch and sight; "jeans, cowboy boots, and a black leather jacket" (lines 19–20), sight; "boot heels cracked the tiles at every step and echoed off the pool walls" (lines 20–21), sound*

DIFFERENTIATED INSTRUCTION

FOR ALL STUDENTS

Student Portfolios Encourage students to save copies of their writing so they can track their progress throughout the year.

For general guidelines on differentiating writing instruction, see

BEST PRACTICES TOOLKIT
Scaffolding Writing Instruction
pp. 43–46

FOR ENGLISH LEARNERS

Language: Skill Words Review these terms:

- *focused impression:* writing that uses descriptive details and quotations to create a clear picture of a person or place
- *organization:* the way in which ideas and details are arranged in a piece of writing
- *anecdote:* a brief story that reveals something about a person or character
- *sensory details:* details that tell how something looks, smells, tastes, sounds, or feels
- *tone:* a writer's attitude toward his or her subject. In this model, the writer uses a respectful tone in describing her experiences with Coach Sand. Share this example from lines 35–39: "What kept us going was his challenge to do more than we thought we could do. Every day for a week, he made us do laps and more laps. Finally, he showed up in a bathing suit one day and climbed up to the high dive. . . . He did a perfect back somersault. . . . We gasped."

- **Dialogue** To illustrate the importance of dialogue in this piece, work with students to look for examples of dialogue that illustrate the personality of Coach Sand and the writer's reaction to his coaching style. Examples include
  —"'Are you going to do it, or should we go home for lunch while you make up your mind?'" (lines 1–2)
  —"'I'm not afraid of you,' I muttered." (lines 7, 41)
  —"'I'm not going to dive into the pool to save any of you,' he said, 'so listen up and do as I say. You're going to find out that you can swim and dive a lot better than you think you can.'" (lines 23–25)
  —"'Way to go,' he said proudly." (line 44)

  Discuss how different this essay would be if the writer had not included dialogue.
- **Conclusion** Explain that the conclusion of an essay should leave readers with a clear understanding of the writer's main idea or purpose for writing. Readers of the model want to know why the writer felt inspired to write about this particular swimming coach. The writer answers this question by showing what she learned from Coach Sand—that she can do more than she thought she could. Also point out that the conclusion takes readers back to the opening scene (line 41 repeats line 7) and tells how it ends.

For interactive student models, see
- Write*Smart* CD
- Writing Center at **ClassZone.com**

My friends and I looked at each other, wondering what we had gotten ourselves into. We were all on the middle school swim team, so we thought that we knew what we could do. Coach Sand disagreed. When my friend Angela raised her hand, Coach barked, "I'll ask the questions around here. Your job is to come up with the answers—or try." Then he lined us all up and had us dive into the pool and swim laps for the next 45 minutes. If anyone stopped to rest or switched to an easy stroke like the sidestroke, he would yell from the deck, "What are you doing, taking a bath? Front crawl, breaststroke, or backstroke."

Highlighted **transition** help the reader see ho ideas are related. **Ton** informal without bein slangy.

What kept us going was his challenge to do more than we thought we could do. Every day for a week, he made us do laps and more laps. Finally, he showed up in a bathing suit one day and climbed up to the high dive without saying a word. He did a perfect back somersault with a double twist and entered the water without a splash. We gasped.

"Okay, you saw that," he said. "Now show me what you can do."

"I'm not afraid of you," I muttered, standing on that diving board. I leaped off and did a simple, clean dive. As I came out of the water, Coach Sand reached down to give me a hand.

Varying the **lengths of sentences** helps to maintain reader intere **Dialogue** helps the rea understand Coach San and the writer's reactic to him.

"Way to go," he said proudly. I had learned his lesson.

Thoughtful **conclusion** shows why the coach is important to this write

2

294 UNIT 2: CHARACTER AND POINT OF VIEW

DIFFERENTIATED INSTRUCTION

FOR ENGLISH LEARNERS

Comprehension: Transitions Use this activity to illustrate how a writer might use transitions to describe a personal experience.

1. Write three or four sentences on the board that describe a recent visit to a store. Use transitional words from the model on pages 293–294. Work with students to underline the transitional words. For example:

   I needed a loaf of bread, so I stopped at the grocery store. When I arrived, the store was crowded. I quickly walked to the bread aisle. Then I walked to the front of the store to wait in line. Finally, I left to go home.
2. Next, use spatial-order words to describe where things are in the store. Have students point out the transitional words and phrases. For example:

   I walked through the door and saw lots of fresh fruit. On the right were strawberries and blueberries. On the left were many kinds of apples. Next to the fruits were the vegetables.
3. Use the copy master to provide students with further practice using transitions.

RESOURCE MANAGER—Copy Master
Writing Support p. 230

rt 2: Apply the Writing Process

REWRITING

Vhat Should I Do?	What Does It Look Like?
. Choose a person or a character. Carefully read the prompts on page 292. Decide which one you will answer. Then list people who are important to you or characters from literature who stick in your mind. Note what is special about each one. (Circle) your first choice. **TIP For Prompt 1, think about people who make you laugh, who annoy you, or who have taught you something. For Prompt 2, think of characters you like or dislike.**	*People* / *Why They Are Important*: *Joe Dean* — *Is always doing something goofy*; *(Coach Sand)* — *Got me to do my best*; *Lily* — *Stood up for me with Mom and Dad*
. Identify the most important impression. Jot down a sentence or two that focuses on what makes this person or character so memorable.	*Coach Sand was really hard on us, but he helped us do more than we ever thought we could.*
. Collect information. Use a cluster diagram to organize details about the person or character's physical appearance, speech, beliefs, thoughts, and actions. Don't forget **anecdotes**—brief stories about the person or character. These can clearly show his or her personality.	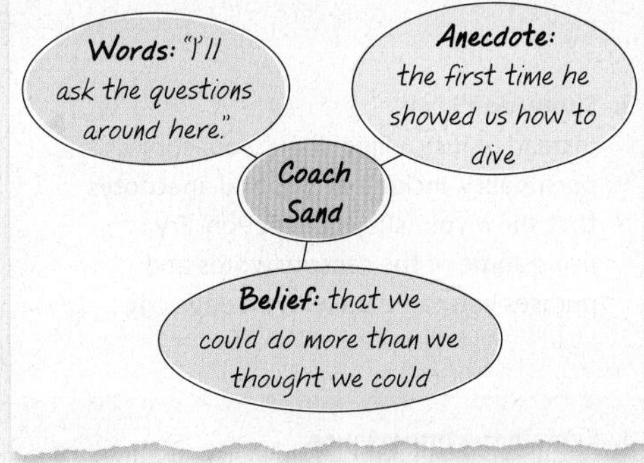
. Brainstorm sensory details. Try to think of specific sights, sounds, smells, tastes, textures, and other qualities associated with the person or character. These will make your writing vivid and distinctive.	*Sights*: • *short and stocky (like King Kong!)*; *Sounds*: • *echo of boot heels off the pool walls* • *booming voice*; *Smells*: • *chlorine* • *Coach's leather jacket*

FOR ENGLISH LEARNERS

Describing a Person Students may use these frames to focus their essays and gather information and sensory details:

The person or character I want to describe is ______. I chose him or her because ______.

In writing about my person or character, I will describe the following:

- sights: ______
- sounds: ______
- smells: ______

My person or character once said ______.

An interesting story about him or her is ______.

Distribute copies of the Observation Chart and encourage students to record details related to the subject they've chosen in the chart. Then they can meet in pairs or small groups to share their charts and talk about their topics.

BEST PRACTICES TOOLKIT—Transparency
Observation Chart p. C7

Practice and Apply

To support students during the writing process, use these copy masters:

RESOURCE MANAGER—Copy Masters
Prewriting–Editing pp. 223–227
Writing Rubric p. 228
Writing Support p. 230 *(for English learners)*

Part 2: Apply the Writing Process

PREWRITING

1. **Choose a person or a character.** If students need help choosing a person or a character, point out the TIP provided with the first step. Encourage them to narrow their list to people and characters who really stand out to them or who generate the strongest feelings. Have students share their top choices with a partner. Partners should identify the most interesting details and ask questions about things that are missing or unclear.
2. **Identify the most important impression.** Students should begin to think about quotations that will create a focused impression. Encourage them to jot down three or four memorable things their person or character once said. Have students meet with their partners to share their quotations.
3. **Collect information.** Encourage students to imagine they are meeting or reading about their person or character for the first time. What is their first impression? What details create and shape this impression?

   BEST PRACTICES TOOLKIT—Transparency
   Cluster Diagram p. B18
4. **Brainstorm sensory details.** Have students work in small groups to make a sensory detail chart related to a person known to everyone in the group, such as a famous actor or athlete. Then have students work individually to complete sensory detail charts for their own essays.

For interactive graphic organizers, see
WriteSmart CD
Writing Center at **ClassZone.com**

DRAFTING

1. **Decide which points to include.** Remind students that every detail should support the main impression of the person or character. Explain that too much detail, or details that aren't as vivid or as interesting as others, can make their essay less focused and less engaging.
2. **Craft an intriguing introduction.** After students experiment with each type of introduction, have them meet in pairs or small groups to share their drafts and use their peers' feedback to figure out which introduction works best.
3. **Show, don't tell.** As students write, they should pause after every paragraph and reread what they've written. As they reread, they can decide whether a sensory detail, an anecdote, or a quote is needed to illustrate a point in a more powerful way.
4. **Explain the importance.** Students should reflect on their introductions and on their details, quotations, and anecdotes. This will help them clarify why their person or character is important and how they should conclude the essay. Point out the TIP to students who have completed their drafts.

For a focused description writing template, see

BEST PRACTICES TOOLKIT—Transparency
Writing Template: Focused Description pp. C16, C30

Write*Smart* CD

Writing Center at **ClassZone.com**

DRAFTING

What Should I Do?	What Does It Look Like?
1. Decide which points to include. How will you support your main impression of the person? Which details or anecdotes will you use to describe each point? Use a chart, list, or outline to get organized.	*Main Points* / *Details* • *scary at first* — • *tough and sarcastic (use examples of what he said)* • *got us to do more than we thought we could* — • *after we saw him dive, wanted to show him what we could do*
2. Craft an intriguing introduction. Try starting with a surprising statement, a quotation, or a description that makes your reader want to know more about the person or character.	**Surprising statement** *Who's afraid of a swimming coach? I was.* **Quotation** *"Are you going to do it, or should we go home for lunch while you make up your mind?"* **Description** *He was 17. He looked like King Kong. His voice shook the diving board under my feet.*
3. Show, don't tell. Instead of just telling about your subject's personality, include details and anecdotes that show your subject in action. Try using some of the sensory words and phrases you came up with on page 295 .	**Telling** *Coach Sand was always very strict.* **Showing** *"I'm not going to dive into the pool to save any of you," he said, "so listen up and do as I say."*
3. Explain the importance. Conclude by making it clear why this person or character matters to you. For example, the writer of the student model realized that her coach was proud of her. **TIP Before you revise, look back at the key traits on page 292 and the rubric and peer-reader questions on page 298.**	*"I'm not afraid of you," I muttered again. I leaped off the board and did a simple, clean dive. As I came out of the water, Coach Sand reached down to give me a hand. "Way to go," he said proudly. I had learned his lesson.*

DIFFERENTIATED INSTRUCTION

FOR LESS–PROFICIENT WRITERS

Organizing Information Share this outline, which matches the organization of the model:

Introduction
- Introduce the subject of the essay with a surprising statement, a quotation, or descriptive details.
- Begin to show why this person or character stands out to you.

Body
- Provide necessary background information.
  —Give facts about who your person or character is.
  —Include sensory details.
- Show your person or character in action.
  —Include dialogue and anecdotes.
  —Add more sensory details.
  —If necessary, include more background information.

Conclusion
- Make it clear why this person or character is special or interesting to you.
- Include a final detail or idea that completes the description of your person or character.

REVISING AND EDITING

What Should I Do?	What Does It Look Like?
1. Stay focused. • Your description should give a focused impression of the person or character. For example, Coach Sand is tough but fair. • Reread your draft. Delete information that wanders from your main point.	*He was the star diver on the high school team and had just gotten a scholarship to the state university.* ~~*Now he is majoring in accounting, and he works part time at a sporting-goods store in Saugus.*~~
2. Provide helpful background information. • Have a peer reader draw a box around parts of your description that don't give enough information. • Add explanations or details that keep your reader from becoming frustrated or confused.	*Then he lined us all up and had us dive into the pool and swim laps for the next 45 minutes. He'd yell from the deck, "What are you doing, taking a bath? Front crawl, breaststroke, or backstroke."* *If anyone stopped to rest or switched to an easy stroke like the sidestroke,*
3. Vary the length of your sentences. • Pick a paragraph and count the number of words in each sentence. Do they all have about the same number of words? Do any sentences begin the same way? • If your writing sounds choppy or droning, revise or combine some sentences to create a pleasing rhythm.	~~*We looked at each other. We wondered what we had gotten ourselves into. All of us were on the middle school swim team. We thought that we knew what we could do. It turned out that Coach Sand disagreed with us.*~~ *My friends and I looked at each other, wondering what we had gotten ourselves into. We were all on the middle school swim team, so we thought that we knew what we could do. Coach Sand disagreed.*
4. Pay attention to tone. • Ask a peer reader to [bracket] any parts of your description that use slang or that seem too informal. • Revise your description so that it is appropriate and respectful throughout. **See page 298:** Ask a Peer Reader	~~*[The dude] did a [wicked] dive. The rest of us were completely [bugging out!!!]*~~ *He did a perfect back somersault with a double twist and entered the water without a splash. We gasped.*

FOR ENGLISH LEARNERS

Revising and Editing Provide an outline to guide students (working with peer readers) through the major steps of a revision.

- The main point of my essay is _________. I deleted the sentence _________ because it did not support my main point.
- I added these descriptive details: _________.
- I am including these transition words: _________.
- I changed the sentence _________ to add more variety. It now reads _________.

FOR ADVANCED LEARNERS/PRE–AP

Synthesize [paired option] Have students form pairs and read each other's focused descriptions. Then have them consider what might happen if the two people or characters met each other. Would they get along? Challenge students to create an anecdote in which the two subjects meet. The story might be funny or dramatic. Have them jot down their anecdote and then share it with other pairs. Students should then discuss what the anecdotes reveal about each subject.

REVISING AND EDITING

1. **Stay focused.** Have students meet with peer readers. Readers should answer these questions: Does the description give a focused impression of a person or character? What is the most important impression? Is there any information that seems to stray from the main point?
2. **Provide helpful background information.** Remind students that they need to keep in mind readers who are not familiar with the person or character they are describing. What details and explanations would these readers need? Suggest that students refer to the **Ask a Peer Reader** questions on page 298 to make sure they have included enough information.
3. **Vary the length of your sentences.** Suggest that students review the model to study how they might add variety to their sentences. They should consider combining ideas to make one long sentence (lines 2–4), adding introductory phrases (lines 17, 21), and using quotations (lines 23–25). They might also use short sentences for dramatic effect (line 39). Encourage students also to observe sentence variety in other selections in the pupil's edition.
4. **Pay attention to tone.** Explain to students that in some cases, slang and other types of informal language can be appropriate and effective for establishing a particular tone. For example, a writer might use a casual conversation between characters to help create a humorous tone. However, too much slang can be distracting and difficult to understand. Language that is overly formal can also be difficult for readers to understand. Formal language can be useful, though, if a writer is trying to establish a somber or admiring tone.

   Give students examples of words and sentences and ask them to tell whether the language is formal or informal. Then have students work with their peer readers to identify formal and informal language in their drafts and decide if the language is appropriate for their intended tone.

For interactive revision tools, see

WriteSmart CD

Writing Center at **ClassZone.com**

Preparing to Publish

Support for meeting the goals in the writing rubric is supplied throughout the **Writing Workshop** on pages 292–297.

For Rubric Bank, see

- Write*Smart* CD
- Writing Center at **ClassZone.com**

Assess and Reteach

After reading and assessing students' focused descriptions, you might use these lessons to reteach key skills:

STANDARDS LESSON FILE

Writing Lesson 27: Descriptive Writing
Writing Lesson 39: Elaborate with Sensory Details
Grammar Lesson 15: *Who, Whom, Whose,* and *Who's*

Preparing to Publish — Describing a Person

Apply the Rubric

A strong description of a person or character . . .

- ☑ uses details to create a focused description
- ☑ uses dialogue, anecdotes, and sensory details to reveal the subject's personality
- ☑ includes helpful background information
- ☑ is sensibly organized
- ☑ uses transitions to show the order of events
- ☑ maintains an appropriate tone
- ☑ varies sentence lengths
- ☑ ends by summarizing why the person is important to the writer

Ask a Peer Reader

- Why is this person or character important to me?
- What else would you like to know about him or her?
- Is my tone appropriate? If not, where are some problem areas?

Stay Away from Clichés

Cliché: I was **scared to death.**
Rewrite: I stood with my knees trembling.
Cliché: The diver was **the best of the best.**
Rewrite: The diver was a graceful arrow who hit the water like a bull's-eye every time.
Cliché: We were **as cold as ice.**
Rewrite: We were huddled and shivering.
Cliché: He was **as strong as an ox.**
Rewrite: He looked like King Kong.

Check Your Grammar

- Use *who* as a subject or a predicate pronoun.

Who suggested that you go to Pool School?
He is the person who coached me.

- Use *whom* for a direct object, indirect object, or object of a preposition.

Whom will you nominate for the award?
They gave whom a diving trophy?

See page R54: Interrogative Pronouns

Writing Online

PUBLISHING OPTIONS
For publishing options, visit the **Writing Center** at **ClassZone.com.**

ASSESSMENT PREPARATION
For writing and grammar assessment practice, go to the **Assessment Center** at **ClassZone.com.**

PEAKING AND LISTENING

Conducting an Interview

Interviewing someone gives you a chance to see the world from another person's perspective.

Planning the Interview

1. **Pick your person.** You can decide to interview the person you wrote about or someone else who interests you. To learn more about your family history, you could interview a relative. You also could think of a subject—like a sport you enjoy—and find someone who knows a great deal about it.

   TIP If you want to practice interviewing before you start your real interview, have a classmate role-play a favorite character from literature.

2. **Set up the interview.** Get in touch with the person face-to-face or by telephone, e-mail, or letter. Ask for permission to conduct an interview. If you want to make a video or audio recording of the interview, mention that as well. Then decide on a time and place. You might agree to meet in a public place, talk by phone, or send instant messages.
3. **Do your research.** Learn all you can about the person beforehand. Make a list of specific questions. Think of questions that can't be answered "yes" or "no." Ask open-ended questions to encourage the person to talk at length about his or her experiences, feelings, and ideas.

Conducting the Interview

1. **Listen carefully and take notes.** Taking notes is important, even if you are recording the interview. Don't be afraid to ask the person to repeat something or to wait while you finish writing.
2. **Ask follow-up questions.** Encourage the person to tell you more. "What happened then?" and "Why do you feel that way?" are good follow-up questions.
3. **Be respectful.** Be attentive and enthusiastic during the interview, and thank the person when you're through. Send a handwritten note or e-card the next day.
4. **Record what you have learned.** Your teacher will explain how to summarize the interview. You might write a summary, produce a partial transcript (a word-for-word re-creation of what was said), or create an audio or video presentation.

See page R84: Evaluate an Interview

SPEAKING AND LISTENING

Ask students to read this page to get an overview of how to plan and conduct an interview.

Rubric A strong interview

- is based on thorough research
- begins with a list of specific, open-ended questions
- avoids questions that can be answered with a simple *yes* or *no*
- includes careful listening and note taking
- makes use of follow-up questions
- must be conducted by an attentive and enthusiastic interviewer
- is followed up with a thank-you note the next day
- is summarized with a written summary, a partial transcript, or an audio or video presentation

RESOURCE MANAGER—Copy Master
Speaking and Listening p. 229

STANDARDS LESSON FILE
Speaking and Listening Lesson 9: Interview
Speaking and Listening Lesson 10: Active Listening

DIFFERENTIATED INSTRUCTION

FOR LESS–PROFICIENT WRITERS

Conducting an Interview To give students a structure to help them prepare questions, distribute copies of the Reporter's Questions transparency. Students can get started by writing six questions, each starting with *Who, What, When, Where, Why,* or *How.* Tell students that these questions will usually be open-ended and will therefore encourage interesting responses.

To provide more support, display the following questions, which students can adapt for their own interviews:

- Whom do you admire the most? Or: Who has taught you the most?
- What was your most memorable, embarrassing, exciting, or frightening experience?
- When did you decide you wanted to be a _________?
- Where were you born? Or: Where did you learn to _________?
- Why do you enjoy (or dislike) _________?
- How did you figure out _________? Or: How do you see your future?

BEST PRACTICES TOOLKIT—Transparency
Reporter's Questions p. C9

Assessment Practice

CHECK READINESS

Read aloud the paragraph under **ASSESS** and explain to students that this is not the full Unit Test but a way for them to check their readiness for it. Then have students examine the skills listed under **REVIEW** and look back in the unit or in the **Student Resource Bank** for any they need to study.

READ THE SELECTIONS

Remind students to keep Unit Goals in mind as they read the passages, paying particular attention to

- point of view
- character and characterization
- their own inferences

To help students focus on **point of view** while reading, encourage them to ask questions such as

- What is one major difference between the way *A Year Down Yonder* and "Luke Baldwin's Vow" are told?
- What do the stories have in common? In what way does point of view affect how you see the characters in the stories?

ANSWER THE QUESTIONS

Direct students to pages R95–R101 of the Test-Taking Handbook to review test-taking strategies. Remind them not to choose the first alternative that seems to fit when answering a multiple-choice question. Instead, students should read through all the choices, eliminate any that are clearly wrong, and then choose the best answer—the one that is most accurate and complete.

Suggest to students that they avoid changing an answer unless they are sure it is incorrect. Tell them that often a first response is the correct one, and that thinking about a question for too long can get them off track. Encourage students to write down the numbers of any questions they want to revisit after they have completed the test. When they return to a question later, they might see their initial response more clearly and make a better decision about keeping it or changing it.

Assessment Practice

Reading Comprehension

ASSESS

The practice test items on the next few pages match skills listed on the Unit Goals page (page 161) and addressed throughout this unit. Taking this practice test will help you assess your knowledge of these skills and determine your readiness for the Unit Test.

REVIEW

After you take the practice test, your teacher can help you identify any skills you need to review.

- Point of View
- Character
- Characterization
- Make Inferences
- Multiple-Meaning Words
- Prefixes
- Verb Tenses
- Comparative and Superlative Forms

ASSESSMENT ONLINE

For more assessment practice and test-taking tips, go to the **Assessment Center** at **ClassZone.com.**

DIRECTIONS *Read these selections and answer the questions that follow.*

from A Year Down Yonder

Richard Peck

As the train pulled out behind me, there came Grandma up the platforn steps. My goodness, she was a big woman. I'd forgotten. And taller still wit her spidery old umbrella held up to keep off the sun of high noon. A fan of white hair escaped the big bun on the back of her head. She drew nearer til she blotted out the day.

You couldn't call her a welcoming woman, and there wasn't a hug in her. She didn't put out her arms, so I had nothing to run into.

Nobody had told Grandma that skirts were shorter this year. Her skirttai brushed her shoes. I recognized the dress. It was the one she put on in hot weather to walk uptown in. Though I was two years older, two years taller t last time, she wasn't one for personal comments. The picnic hamper quiver and she noticed. "What's in there?"

"Bootsie," I said. "My cat."

"Hoo-boy," Grandma said. "Another mouth to feed." Her lips pleated. "And what's that thing?" She nodded to my other hand.

"My radio." But it was more than a radio to me. It was my last touch wi the world.

"That's all we need." Grandma looked skyward. "More noise."

She aimed one of her chins down the platform. "That yours?" She meant the trunk. It was the footlocker Dad had brought home from the Great Wa

"Leave it," she said. "They'll bring it to the house." She turned and trudg away, and I was supposed to follow. I walked away from my trunk, wonderi if I'd ever see it again. It wouldn't have lasted long on the platform in Chica Hot tongs wouldn't have separated me from Bootsie and my radio.

The recession of thirty-seven had hit Grandma's town harder than it had hit Chicago. Grass grew in the main street. Only a face or two showed in the window of The Coffee Pot Cafe. Moore's Store was hurting for trade. Weidenbach's bank looked to be just barely in business.

On the other side of the weedy road, Grandma turned the wrong way, av from her house. Two old slab-sided dogs slept on the sidewalk. Bootsie knew because she was having a conniption in the hamper. And my radio was getti heavier. I caught up with Grandma.

"Where are we going?"

"Going?" she said, the picture of surprise. "Why, to school. You've alread missed pretty nearly two weeks."

DIFFERENTIATED INSTRUCTION

FOR ENGLISH LEARNERS

Assessment Practice: Work Backwards [paired option] Prepare students for the assessment by having them "work backwards," reading the questions before reading the text passages. Have pairs follow these steps to learn unfamiliar words in the test directions and questions:

1. Find words you don't recognize and write each one on an index card.
2. Look up the meaning in a dictionary.
3. Write the meaning on the back of the card.
4. Use your word cards to teach and practice the vocabulary with your partner and another pair.

from Luke Baldwin's Vow

Morley Callaghan

That summer when twelve-year-old Luke Baldwin came to live with his Uncle Henry in the house on the stream by the sawmill, he did not forget that he had promised his dying father he would try to learn things from his uncle; so he used to watch him very carefully.

Uncle Henry, who was the manager of the sawmill, was a big, burly man weighing more than two hundred and thirty pounds, and he had a rough-skinned, brick-colored face. He looked like a powerful man, but his health was not good. He had aches and pains in his back and shoulders which puzzled the doctor. The first thing Luke learned about Uncle Henry was that everybody had great respect for him. The four men he employed in the sawmill were always polite and attentive when he spoke to them. His wife, Luke's Aunt Helen, a kindly, plump, straightforward woman, never argued with him. "You should try and be like your Uncle Henry," she would say to Luke. "He's so wonderfully practical. He takes care of everything in a sensible, easy way."

Luke used to trail around the sawmill after Uncle Henry, not only because he liked the fresh, clean smell of the newly cut wood and the big piles of sawdust, but because he was impressed by his uncle's precise, firm tone when he spoke to the men.

Sometimes Uncle Henry would stop and explain to Luke something about a piece of timber. "Always try and learn the essential facts, son," he would say. "If you've got the facts, you know what's useful and what isn't useful, and no one can fool you."

He showed Luke that nothing of value was ever wasted around the mill. Luke used to listen, and wonder if there was another man in the world who knew so well what was needed and what ought to be thrown away. Uncle Henry had known at once that Luke needed a bicycle to ride to his school, which was two miles away in town, and he bought him a good one. He knew that Luke needed good, serviceable clothes. He also knew exactly how much Aunt Helen needed to run the house, the price of everything, and how much a woman should be paid for doing the family washing. In the evenings Luke used to sit in the living room watching his uncle making notations in a black notebook which he always carried in his vest pocket, and he knew that he was assessing the value of the smallest transaction that had taken place during the day.

ITEM ANALYSIS

COMPREHENSION AND WRITTEN RESPONSE	ITEMS	UNIT PAGES
Point of View	1, 9, 10	162, 169, 223
Character	4, 5, 12, 17, 19	164, 166, 189, 239
Characterization	2, 3, 13, 14, 15, 20	164, 259, 283
Make Inferences	6, 7, 8, 11, 16, 18	169

VOCABULARY	ITEMS	UNIT PAGES
Multiple-Meaning Words	1, 2, 3, 4	281
Prefixes	5, 6, 7	236

WRITING AND GRAMMAR	ITEMS	UNIT PAGES
Verb Tenses	1, 3, 4	181
Comparative and Superlative Forms	2, 5, 6	221

After checking student readiness with this Assessment Practice, you may administer the complete Unit 2 Test in order to more thoroughly evaluate student mastery of unit goals.

FOR LESS–PROFICIENT READERS

Assessment Support Consider these options for completing the **Assessment Practice:**

- Have students "work backwards," reviewing the questions before reading the passages.
- Select random questions in the assessment and have students demonstrate how and where to look for the answers.
- Ask students to locate unfamiliar vocabulary in the assessment. Elicit the meanings of these words from the class.
- Have students record useful test words and definitions in their journals for later reference.
- Read aloud the selections or parts of them to aid in student comprehension.

FOR ENGLISH LEARNERS

Review Academic Vocabulary Display the following terms and examples. Work with students to point out clues in each example that show which point of view it represents.

- *third-person limited point of view:* "Jess was confused by the teacher's instructions, but other students began writing and didn't seem worried."
- *first-person point of view:* "I wrote a long letter to my family. I wanted to tell them about my plans."

ANSWERS

Comprehension

Model a thinking process for answering multiple-choice questions.

1. **D *is correct.*** *A and B can be eliminated because we know the narrator is neither a minor character nor an outside observer: she is fully involved in the action of the story. C is incorrect because the excerpt reveals only the narrator's thoughts.*
2. **C *is correct.*** *We get to know Grandma by reading the narrator's thoughts and feelings as the two interact. We never learn of the townspeople's opinions of Grandma, as in A. B is incorrect because we know only Grandma's words and actions, not her thoughts. D is incorrect because the excerpt doesn't include a detailed description of Grandma's life.*
3. **C *is correct.*** *The narrator's observation that her grandmother does not hug her or express excitement to see her reveals that Grandma is not sentimental. A, B, and D can be eliminated because they refer to the narrator's observations about Grandma's appearance and actions.*
4. **B *is correct.*** *The term* no-nonsense *implies someone who is practical and focused on the business at hand—like Grandma. Her attitude toward the radio (line 18) indicates that she is not easygoing, as in A. Her reaction to the cat (line 14) implies that she is probably not especially generous, as in C. D is incorrect because there is no evidence that she is self-important.*
5. **A *is correct.*** *The narrator's refusal to separate from her cat and her radio (line 24) shows she is strong and determined like her grandmother. B can be eliminated because both characters seem to be serious and not lighthearted. Neither talks a great deal, as in C, and there is no evidence of idealism, as in D.*
6. **C *is correct.*** *The narrator comments on the idea of leaving the trunk unattended in Chicago (line 23), implying that Chicago is her home. Grandma doesn't ban the trunk from her house, as in A, and we have no reason to believe townspeople need items in it, as in B. D is incorrect because Grandma says someone will bring the trunk home for her (line 21).*
7. **D *is correct.*** *The narrator's comment implies that this new place is out of touch with the world she knows. She does not predict her radio will be stolen, as in A; observe that people don't have radios, as in B; or imply that she does not want to make friends, as in C.*
8. **C *is correct.*** *Grandma is practical and unemotional—she is surprised that her granddaughter wouldn't expect to go directly from the train platform to school. Details in the text do not support A, that Grandma thinks school is the most interesting place in town, or B, that she thinks the question is rude. D can be eliminated because there is no indication that the granddaughter never asks questions.*
9. **A *is correct.*** *The opening paragraph indicates that readers will learn about Uncle Henry through Luke's experiences with him. We never get Uncle Henry's observations of himself, as in B. C and D can be eliminated because we also learn about Aunt Helen and the sawmill employees through Luke's eyes.*

Comprehension

DIRECTIONS *Answer these questions about the excerpt from* A Year Down Yonder.

1. You can tell that this story is told from the first person point of view because the narrator
- **A** is a minor character in the story who reveals some information
- **B** is an outside observer rather than a character in the story
- **C** reveals the grandmother's and the girl's thoughts
- **D** uses the pronouns *I* and *me* to refer to herself

2. The author brings Grandma's character to life mainly by revealing
- **A** the townspeople's opinions of Grandma
- **B** Grandma's own thoughts about her granddaughter
- **C** the granddaughter's reactions to Grandma
- **D** a detailed description of Grandma's life

3. The narrator makes you aware that Grandma is not a sentimental person when she says
- **A** "My goodness, she was a big woman."
- **B** "She drew nearer till she blotted out the day."
- **C** "You couldn't call her a welcoming woman, and there wasn't a hug in her."
- **D** "She aimed one of her chins down the platform."

4. Which term best describes Grandma?
- **A** easygoing
- **B** no-nonsense
- **C** generous
- **D** self-important

5. Which character trait do the narrator and her grandmother seem to share?
- **A** determination
- **B** lightheartedness
- **C** talkativeness
- **D** idealism

6. Reread lines 21–23. Why does the narrator wonder if she'll ever see her trunk again?
- **A** Grandma does not want the trunk at her house.
- **B** People in the town could use many of the things in the trunk.
- **C** She comes from a large city, where the trunk could be stolen if left on the platform.
- **D** The trunk is too heavy to carry to Grandma's house.

7. From her comment in lines 16–17 that the radio is "my last touch with the world," you can infer that the narrator
- **A** is afraid that her radio will be stolen
- **B** thinks that people in Grandma's town don have radios
- **C** does not want to make friends in Grandma's town
- **D** feels she has arrived in an isolated place

8. Why is Grandma surprised when the narrato asks, "Where are we going?"
- **A** She expects her granddaughter to know that school is the only interesting place to go in town.
- **B** The question sounds rude to Grandma.
- **C** School has begun, and Grandma thinks that is where her granddaughter belongs.
- **D** Her granddaughter doesn't usually ask questions.

DIRECTIONS *Answer these questions about the excerp from "Luke Baldwin's Vow."*

9. The reader learns about Uncle Henry mainly through the eyes of
- **A** Luke
- **B** Uncle Henry
- **C** Aunt Helen
- **D** the sawmill employees

302

0. You can tell that this excerpt is told from a third-person limited point of view because the narrator
   A is a main character in the story
   B tells about the thoughts and feelings of all of the characters in the story
   C is outside the story and tells what one character sees, thinks, and feels
   D describes his or her own thoughts

1. You can infer that Luke views Uncle Henry with
   A pity
   B irony
   C suspicion
   D admiration

2. What first motivates Luke to watch his uncle carefully?
   A Aunt Helen suggests that it is a good idea to pay attention to his uncle.
   B Luke promised his father that he would try to learn things from his uncle.
   C Uncle Henry knows more about what is needed than anyone else Luke has met.
   D The family wants Luke to succeed as a worker at the sawmill.

3. Which method of characterization is used in lines 13–15 to describe Uncle Henry?
   A a description of his physical appearance
   B another character's opinion of him
   C Uncle Henry's own thoughts about life
   D the author's direct comment about him

4. Uncle Henry's words and actions in lines 20–23 show him to be a
   A strict boss
   B patient teacher
   C fun-loving relative
   D dishonest businessman

5. Luke learns about Uncle Henry mainly by
   A reading his uncle's black notebook
   B listening to Aunt Helen's stories
   C remembering his father's descriptions
   D watching and listening to his uncle

16. From the description of Uncle Henry in this excerpt, you can infer that he is
   A unconcerned about the feelings of other people
   B very shy and forgetful about business dealings
   C careful and smart in his work and personal business
   D confident that he has good health and will live a long time

DIRECTIONS *Answer this question about both selections.*

17. The granddaughter and Luke can both be described as
   A cheerful
   B observant
   C confused
   D spoiled

Written Response

SHORT RESPONSE *Write two or three sentences to answer this question.*

18. Reread lines 8–11 in the excerpt from *A Year Down Yonder.* What can you infer about the grandmother from this description?

19. Reread lines 16–19 in the excerpt from "Luke Baldwin's Vow." What motivates Luke to follow Uncle Henry around the sawmill?

EXTENDED RESPONSE *Write a paragraph to answer this question.*

20. Describe two ways in which Peck brings Grandma's character to life and Callaghan brings Uncle Henry's character to life. Give examples from the excerpts to support your answer.

303

10. C *is correct.* *The narrator reveals the thoughts, feelings, and observations of one character—Luke. A is incorrect because the narrator is outside the story. The thoughts of the other characters are not revealed, as in B. D is incorrect because the narrator reveals Luke's thoughts, not his or her own.*

11. D *is correct.* *Luke's observations show Uncle Henry to be wise and respected by others. A, B, and C can be eliminated because no specific details in the excerpt indicate pity, irony, or suspicion.*

12. B *is correct.* *Before moving, Luke makes a promise to his dying father. It is only later that Aunt Helen suggests observing Uncle Henry, as in A, and Luke begins to admire Uncle Henry's knowledge, as in C. D is incorrect because the excerpt never mentions Luke's being trained to work at the sawmill.*

13. B *is correct.* *In these lines, Aunt Helen gives her opinion of Uncle Henry. The lines do not feature a physical description of Uncle Henry, as in A; Uncle Henry's personal thoughts, as in C; or any direct comments by the author, as in D.*

14. B *is correct.* *Uncle Henry takes the time to teach Luke an important lesson. These lines do not reveal him to be particularly strict, as in A. C is incorrect because he seems serious, not fun-loving. D is incorrect because the lines provide no evidence of dishonesty.*

15. D *is correct.* *Luke observes his uncle working and interacting with others. He does not read a notebook, as in A. B and C can be eliminated because the excerpt does not feature many specific details from Aunt Helen or from Luke's father.*

16. C *is correct.* *Luke's observations reveal the care and intelligence with which Uncle Henry handles work and family matters. A, B, and D can be eliminated because no specific details in the excerpt support these inferences.*

17. B *is correct.* *Both selections are based on the observations of these characters. Their thoughts and actions do not consistently reveal cheerfulness or confusion, as in A and C. D is incorrect because neither character behaves as someone who is spoiled.*

Written Response

Possible short responses:

18. *Grandma is practical and set in her ways. She does not spend a great deal of time thinking about frivolous matters such as what she is wearing.*

19. *Luke enjoys the smell of freshly cut wood. He also likes observing the way Uncle Henry interacts with his employees.*

Possible extended response:

20. *Students could describe Peck's use of dialogue, physical details, and the narrator's observations to bring Grandma's character to life. For example, readers make inferences about Grandma based her imposing figure, her unfashionably long dress, and words such as "Another mouth to feed" (line 14) when she sees the cat. Students could note Callaghan's use of dialogue, observations, and other characters' opinions. For example, Aunt Helen says, "He takes care of everything in a sensible, easy way"(lines 14–15). Luke's observations of his uncle at work and at home support this description.*

ANSWERS

Vocabulary

1. **C *is correct.*** *The context of the story and the word after suggest that Luke follows behind his uncle in the sawmill. A and B can be eliminated because they do not work in the context of the sentence. D is incorrect because it suggests the way a hunter tracks the movements of an animal.*
2. **D *is correct.*** *The mention of steps suggests a raised surface. A can be eliminated because it does not refer to a physical location but to words. We know that Grandma is waiting for a train and not at a place for discussion, as in B; nor is she using a drilling device, as in C.*
3. **B *is correct.*** *The main character has traveled with items in her trunk, which indicates that her trunk is luggage. A is incorrect because a storage compartment is a part of something larger, such as the trunk of a car. C and D can be eliminated because they make no sense in the context of the sentence.*
4. **A *is correct.*** *The narrator indicates that times are hard in Grandma's town and that local businesses need customers. Context clues do not relate to the trade of a single item, as in B; to an occupation, as in C; or to people in a particular field, as in D.*
5. **C *is correct.*** *The narrator indicates that she has seen her grandmother wear the dress before. A and B are incorrect because she did not learn about the dress from someone else and has not forgotten the dress. D is incorrect because she does remember the dress.*
6. **B *is correct.*** *Details in the excerpt illustrate a slow period for businesses. A and C can be eliminated because they do not work in the context of the sentence. D is incorrect because context clues suggest a difficult period, not a period of rest.*
7. **C *is correct.*** *The context paragraph describes all the goods and services Uncle Henry buys to keep the household running. A and B are incorrect because Uncle Henry's activities do not relate to a sudden burst of activity or to immigration. D is incorrect because business profits would be distributed to people involved in the business, which is unrelated to the context.*

Vocabulary

DIRECTIONS *Use context clues and your knowledge of multiple-meaning words to answer the following questions.*

1. Which meaning of the word *trail* is used in line 16 of the excerpt from "Luke Baldwin's Vow"?

"Luke used to trail around the sawmill after Uncle Henry. . . ."

A stream along
B drag heavily
C follow behind
D track closely

2. Which meaning of the word *platform* is used in line 1 of the excerpt from *A Year Down Yonder?*

". . . there came Grandma up the platform steps."

A a statement of principles
B a place for discussion
C a device for drilling
D a raised surface

3. Which meaning of the word *trunk* is used in line 22 of the excerpt from *A Year Down Yonder?*

"I walked away from my trunk, wondering if I'd ever see it again."

A a storage compartment
B a piece of luggage
C a tree stem
D the center of the body

4. Which meaning of the word *trade* is used in line 27 of the excerpt from *A Year Down Yonder?*

"Moore's Store was hurting for trade."

A the customers of a business
B an exchange of one thing for another
C an occupation that requires skilled training
D the people who work in a certain kind of business

DIRECTIONS *Use context clues and your knowledge of prefixes to answer the following questions.*

5. One meaning of the prefix *re-* is "again," and the Latin word *cognoscere* means "to get to know." What is the meaning of the word *recognize* as it is used in line 9 of the excerpt from *A Year Down Yonder?*

"I recognized the dress."

A learned from someone else
B had forgotten once more
C knew from before
D could not remember

6. Another meaning of the prefix *re-* is "back," and the Latin word *cedere* means "to go." What is the meaning of the word *recession* as is used in line 25 of the excerpt from *A Year Down Yonder?*

"The recession of thirty-seven had hit Grandma's town harder than it had hit Chicago."

A the act of performing again
B a period when business activity falls away
C a departing procession
D a short time set aside for rest

7. One meaning of the prefix *trans-* is "transfer." What is the most likely meaning of the word *transaction* as it is used in line 34 of the excerpt from "Luke Baldwin's Vow"?

". . . he knew that he was assessing the value of the smallest transaction that had taken place during the day."

A a sudden burst of activity
B an immigration to a new land
C the passage of goods by sale or barter
D the distribution of the business profits

304

DIFFERENTIATED INSTRUCTION

FOR ENGLISH LEARNERS

Review Academic Vocabulary Remind students that *multiple-meaning words* have different meanings depending on the context in which they are used. In items 1–4, some of the answer choices may be correct definitions of the word, but the word may be used in a completely different way in the story. Therefore, it is especially important to use *context clues,* or information from the surrounding sentences, to choose the correct definition and score a point on the test.

Share this sentence and the possible definitions of *mounted.* Discuss with students how they could select the correct definition (*C*) by using context clues.

Edgar mounted his photographs on the wall.

A. climbed
B. furnished with a horse
C. placed for display
D. prepared and set in motion

Writing & Grammar

DIRECTIONS *Read the passage and answer the questions that follow.*

(1) On October 29, 1929, the stock market will crash, sending the United States into an economic depression. (2) Because it was the more devastating depression ever to afflict the country, it was called the Great Depression. (3) Herbert Hoover, the president at the time, will refuse to provide direct federal relief to the poor. (4) Americans are furious about Hoover's lack of action, and in 1932, the country elected Franklin D. Roosevelt as the new president. (5) Roosevelt was most willing than Hoover was to provide aid. (6) He supplied immediate relief to the poor and aid to farms and businesses. (7) Although a lot of people remained unemployed, their circumstances were more better than they had been before.

1. Choose the correct verb tense to replace the underlined words in sentence 1.
   A is crashing
   B crashed
   C will be crashing
   D has crashed

2. Choose the correct superlative to replace the underlined word in sentence 2.
   A more devastatinger
   B most devastatingest
   C devastatinger
   D most devastating

3. Choose the correct verb tense to replace the underlined words in sentence 3.
   A refused
   B will be refusing
   C is refusing
   D has refused

4. Choose the correct verb tense to replace the underlined word in sentence 4.
   A will be
   B were
   C are becoming
   D have been

5. Choose the correct comparative to replace the underlined words in sentence 5.
   A more willing
   B willingest
   C willinger
   D more willinger

6. Choose the correct comparative to replace the underlined words in sentence 7.
   A best
   B most better
   C betterer
   D better

STOP

305

DIFFERENTIATED INSTRUCTION

FOR ENGLISH LEARNERS

Assessment Support Discuss these terms:

- *verb tense* (items 1, 3, 4)—a form of a verb that tells when the action happens
  —present tense (*she runs, we are sitting, he sings*); present perfect tense (*I have been waiting for a long time*)
  —past tense (*she ran, we were sitting, he sang*); past perfect tense (*I had already been waiting for a long time*)
  —future tense (*she will run, we will sit, he will be singing*)
- *comparative* (items 5, 6)—an adjective that compares two things
  —Jason is *younger* than Ava.
  —This painting is *more interesting* than the other painting.
- *superlative* (item 2)—an adjective that compares three or more things
  —Dara is the *tallest* player on the team.
  —That is the *most creative* idea I have heard today.

ANSWERS

Writing & Grammar

1. **B** ***is correct.*** *Mention of the year 1929 reveals that something from the past is being discussed, so the second part of the clause requires the past tense of the verb* crash. *We can eliminate* A, C, *and* D *because they are verbs in the present, future, and present perfect tenses.*
2. **D** ***is correct.*** Devastating *is a multi-syllable word, so its superlative form is made with the word* most, *not with* -er, *as in* A *and* C, *or with* -est, *as in* B.
3. **A** ***is correct.*** *The phrase* at the time *reveals that the past is still being discussed, and the second clause therefore requires the past tense of the verb* refuse. *We can eliminate* B, C, *and* D *because they are verbs in the future, present, and present perfect tenses.*
4. **B** ***is correct.*** *The second clause of the sentence has a past-tense verb,* elected, *which is a clue that the verb in the first clause should also be past tense. We can eliminate* A, C, *and* D *because they are verbs in the future, present, and present perfect tenses.*
5. **A** ***is correct.*** *The sentence compares two presidents, Roosevelt and Hoover, so a comparative form is required.* B *is incorrect because it uses the superlative suffix* -est *and is also an incorrect form. Since* willing *is a multi-syllable word, its comparative form is made with the word* more *and not with* -er, *as in* C *and* D.
6. **D** ***is correct.*** *The sentence compares two things—life before and after Roosevelt's reforms.* Better *by itself is the correct comparative form of the word* good. A *is incorrect because it is the superlative form of* good. B *can be eliminated because it is an incorrect attempt at creating the superlative form of* good. C *can be eliminated because it incorrectly adds* -er *to a word that is already comparative.*

INTRODUCE *MORE GREAT READS*

In Unit 2, students have discussed a number of big questions. Invite students to tell which question they found most intriguing and why. Then focus attention on the three questions that appear on this page. Discuss the recommended books and their summaries, pointing out how each book connects to the related question. Encourage students to choose one or more of these "great reads" to read independently.

ClassZone.com

To find additional books that match students' interests and ability levels, visit the Literature Center at **ClassZone.com.**

UNIT 2

More Great Reads

Ideas for Independent Reading

Which questions from Unit 2 made an impression on you? Continue exploring them with these books.

What do you cherish?

A Thief in the House of Memory
by Tim Wynne-Jones
Declan barely remembers his mother, but this year the memories have started coming back. Sometimes he thinks he can see and hear her in his old house. Can Declan recall his "real" mom and still trust his dad?

Hope Was Here
by Joan Bauer
Hope and her aunt are starting over again—this time at a diner in small-town Wisconsin. When G.T., the owner, decides to run for mayor even though he has a terminal illness, Hope gets sucked into the campaign.

Song of the Trees
by Mildred D. Taylor
Times are tough for Cassie Logan and her family. They don't even have enough to eat. But when someone offe to buy the trees that have whispered outside of her window for as long as she ca remember, Cassie knows she must protect them.

What shows others who we are?

I, Juan de Pareja
by Elizabeth Borton de Treviño
A man named Juan de Pareja is enslaved in Spain during the 1600s. By watching his owner, a famous artist, Juan learns to paint—a skill forbidden to slaves. If he reveals his true talent, will he be celebrated, or punished?

Stargirl
by Jerry Spinelli
Leo knows Stargirl is different from the rest of Mica High. She has a pet rat and a ukulele and at basketball games she cheers for the other team. When Leo falls in love with her, he likes her just the way she is—at first.

An Innocent Soldier
by Josef Holub
Adam is only 16 when he's forced to serve in Napoleon' army in the place of his employer's son. He is trappe in freezing Russia with a sick lieutenant his own age. Slowly the two boys becom friends, but will they survive

What are the signs of greatness?

The Voice that Challenged a Nation: Marian Anderson and the Struggle for Equal Rights
by Russell Freedman
Marian Anderson was an acclaimed singer, but there were some segregated concert halls that wouldn't let her perform. She helped to erase these barriers.

Sir Walter Raleigh and the Quest for El Dorado
by Marc Aronson
Walter Ralegh was a favorite courtier of Queen Elizabeth. After her death, he tried to regain his glory by returning to South America in search of El Dorado, the fabled city of gold.

Summerland
by Michael Chabon
Ethan is the worst ballplaye in the league. He's called Dog Boy because "he's alwa hoping for a walk." Surprise when a mysterious talent scout chooses him to help save Summerland, the hom of baseball, Ethan hopes he up for the task.

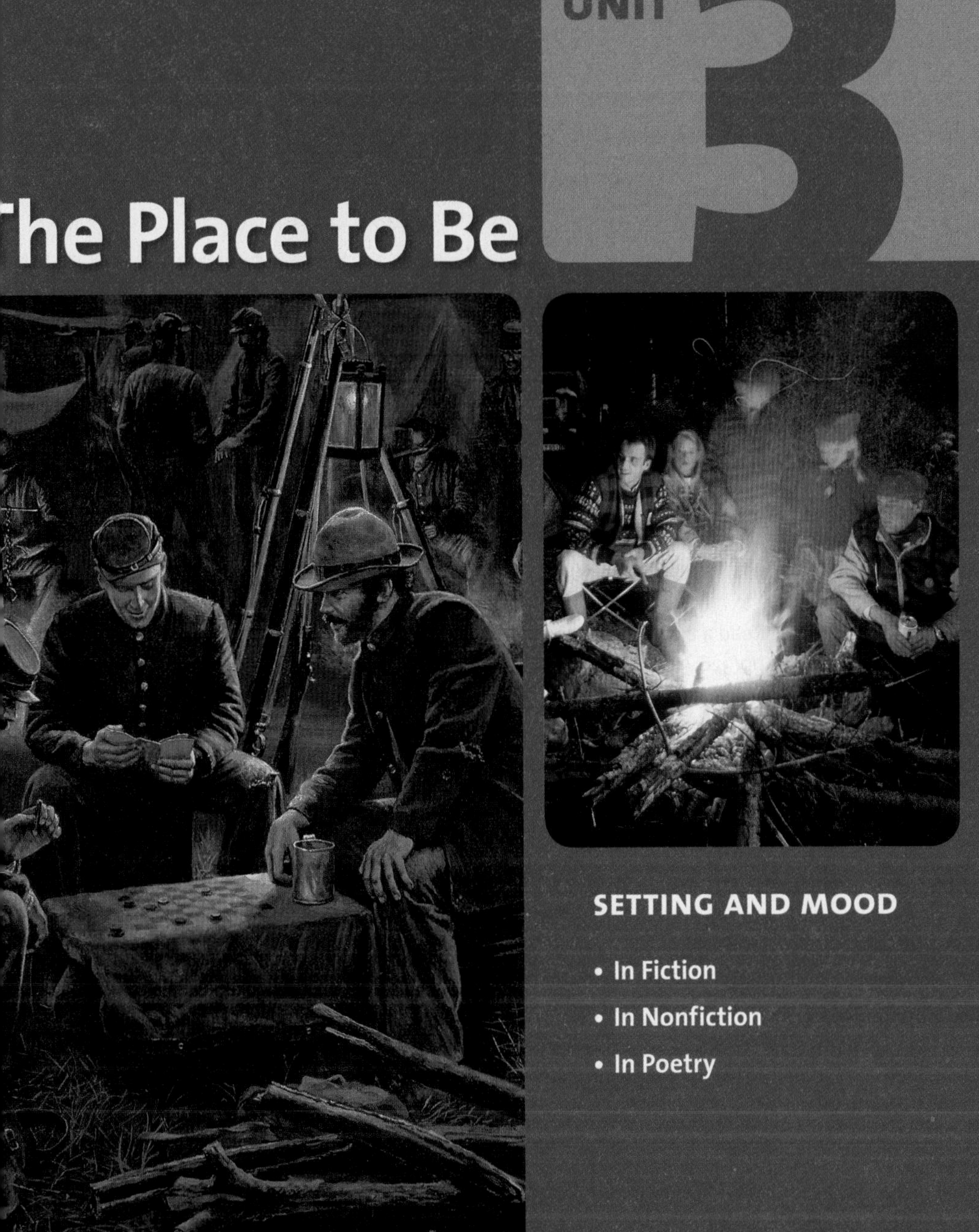

About the Art The painting *Letter from Home* by Mort Kunstler illustrates Ray Bradbury's story "The Drummer Boy of Shiloh." For more information, see page 320 of the teacher's edition.

For help in planning this unit, see

RESOURCE MANAGER UNIT 3
pp. 1–11

INTRODUCE THE UNIT

"Where are you?" we ask our friends when they call. We are always curious about where and when things happen. We wonder about imaginary places, too, and settings in other parts of the world, in the distant past, or far into the future. How can we get to such a world? Reading a good story, we are often carried to another place and time. There, we find out how setting shapes a character's experiences and perceptions. Have students keep these ideas in mind as they think about the pictures on this page. To spark a discussion, ask these questions:

- Where and when might each scene be happening? What clues do you notice that tell you about each setting?
- In what ways do the time and place affect the people in each scene? What do the people in both pictures have in common? In what ways are their situations different?
- What kind of atmosphere, or feeling, does each picture create—for example, happy or sad, exciting or calm? What details contribute to making viewers feel that way?

Discuss how literature helps readers imagine different times and places. In this unit, students will explore how writers create **setting** and **mood** to allow readers, armed with their imaginations, to enter a new world.

UNIT 3

Skills Trace

SKILLS STRAND	Reader's Workshop: Setting and Mood pp. 310–315	*Linked selections* The Drummer Boy of Shiloh pp. 316–325 Short Story *Level: Challenging*	Civil War Journal pp. 326–331 Journal *Level: Average*	Hallucination pp. 332–357 Short Story *Level: Easy*	The Monkey's Paw pp. 358–373 Short Story *Level: Challenging*
Literary Analysis	Setting pp. 310–311, 314–315 Mood pp. 312–315	Setting pp. 317, 320, 321, 322, 324	Form (Journal) pp. 327, 329, 331	Setting and Plot pp. 333, 334, 336, 339, 340, 341, 344, 345, 348, 350, 351, 353, 355	Mood pp. 359, 360, 363, 364, 367, 368, 370, 371
Reading and Informational Texts	Analyze the Literature pp. 311, 313–315	Make Inferences pp. 317, 318, 321, 323, 324 Review: Monitor pp. 321, 323	Read a Primary Source pp. 326, 327, 328, 330, 331 Draw a Conclusion p. 331	Visualize pp. 333, 337, 339, 340, 341, 343, 349, 352, 355 Review: Make Inferences pp. 338, 346 Read a Personal Essay p. 354	Predict pp. 359, 363, 364, 365, 366, 367, 368, 371
Vocabulary		Word Acquisition pp. 317, T317, 325 Context Clues p. T317 Idioms p. 325		Word Acquisition pp. 333, T333, 356 Context Clues p. T333 Homographs p. 356	Word Acquisition pp. 359, T359, 372 Context Clues p. T359 Latin Roots (*cred*) p. 372
Writing, Grammar, and Style				Misplaced Modifiers p. 357	Subject-Verb Agreement with Compound Subjects p. 373
Speaking, Listening, Viewing, and Media	Discuss pp. 310–313	Discuss pp. 316, T318–T323, 324 Analyze Visuals pp. 318, 320	Discuss pp. 326, T327–T330, 331	Discuss pp. 332, T334–T354, 355 Analyze Visuals pp. 334, 338, 343, 347, 351	Discuss pp. 358, T360–T370, 371 Analyze Visuals pp. 360, 365, 369

Assessment-Based Planning: Skills in red are assessed on the Unit 3 Test. **T** = Teacher's Edition page

Great Reads: Roll of Thunder, Hear My Cry pp. 374–379 Historical Novel *Level: Average*	**Going Where I'm Coming From** pp. 380–395 Memoir *Level: Average*	**The Story of an Eyewitness/Letter from New Orleans: Leaving Desire** pp. 396–415 Magazine Articles *Level: Average*	**Mi Madre/ Canyon de Chelly** pp. 416–423 Poems *Level: Easy*	**Writing Workshop: Comparison-Contrast Essay** pp. 424–431
Form (Historical Novel) p. 374	Setting in Nonfiction pp. 381, 382, 385, 387, 389, 390, 393	Scope pp. 397, 399, 400, 401, 403, 404, 405, 406, 407, 408, 409, 410, 411, 412, 413	Imagery pp. 417, 418, 422, 423	
	Connect pp. 381, 384, 385, 386, 389, 393 Read a Poem pp. 391–392	Set a Purpose for Reading pp. 397, 413 Compare Scope of Articles p. 413	Understand Speaker pp. 417, 418, 420, 422, 423	Analyze a Comparison-Contrast Essay pp. 425–426, 430
	Word Acquisition pp. 381, T381, 394 Word Maps p. T381 Base Words p. 394	Word Acquisition pp. 397, T397, 414 Context Clues p. T397 Prefixes (*inter-*) p. 414		
	Subject-Verb Agreement with Indefinite Pronouns p. 395	Write for Assessment p. 415		Write a Comparison-Contrast Essay pp. 424–430 Transitions that Signal Comparisons and Contrasts pp. 428, 430 Sentence Fragments and Run-On Sentences p. 430
Discuss pp. 374, T379	Discuss pp. 380, T382–T392, 393 Analyze Visuals pp. 382, 386, 388	Discuss pp. 396, T398–T412, 413 Role-Play a Newscast p. 396 Analyze Visuals pp. 398, 400, 403, 405, 408, 411	Discuss pp. 416, T418–T422, 423 Analyze Visuals pp. 418, 420	Discuss pp. 424–426 Produce a Power Presentation p. 431

Skills Assessed on the Unit 3 Test:

Literary Analysis
- Identify and analyze setting in fiction and nonfiction
- Identify and analyze mood
- Identify, analyze, and evaluate imagery
- Determine the scope of a selection

Reading and Informational Texts
- Use sensory details to visualize

Vocabulary
- Use context clues to determine the meanings of idioms
- Use context clues to determine the origins and meanings of homographs

Writing, Grammar, and Style
- Write a comparison-contrast essay
- Use transitions to show how ideas are related
- Maintain subject-verb agreement when using compound subjects
- Maintain subject-verb agreement when using indefinite pronouns
- Additional writing and grammar skills

For additional lesson planning help, see **Easy Planner DVD.**

OBJECTIVES

- establish prior knowledge about **setting** and **mood**
- discuss how a writer can spark a reader's **imagination**

Where can IMAGINATION *take you?*

Ask students to think of interesting places in their neighborhood or community. How would they describe those places to someone from another country or another planet? Suggest that they think about the kinds of details that would allow the other person to imagine the place vividly.

ACTIVITY Have students work with partners to make their lists. Remind them that the settings they would like to explore do not have to be contemporary settings. As they share information about the stories with their partners and other classmates, encourage them to discuss the ways in which setting helps them understand plot and characters.

CHECK UNDERSTANDING Have students summarize what they have learned about the ways in which stories can help a reader use **imagination** to visit other times and places.

UNIT 3 Share What You Know

Where can IMAGINATIO *take you*

Close your eyes and picture a place you've always wanted to visit. Maybe you're diving down to a sunken ship, swimming slowly throu the murky waters. Maybe you're in the locker room of your favorite team on the night they won the world championship. Wherever you are, your **imagination** is what takes you there. Good writers know h to spark your imagination and transport you to faraway places or tin

ACTIVITY

- With a partner, make a list called "Stories That Have Taken M Places." In it, include at least four books, stories, or movie with settings that made you feel you had visited another tir or place.
- Make another list called "Places I'd Like to Visit." Include at le four settings you'd like to explore.
- Then question others to see if any of the places you'd like to visit are featured in their "Stories That Have Taken Me Place list. What can your classmates tell you about the places you want to go?

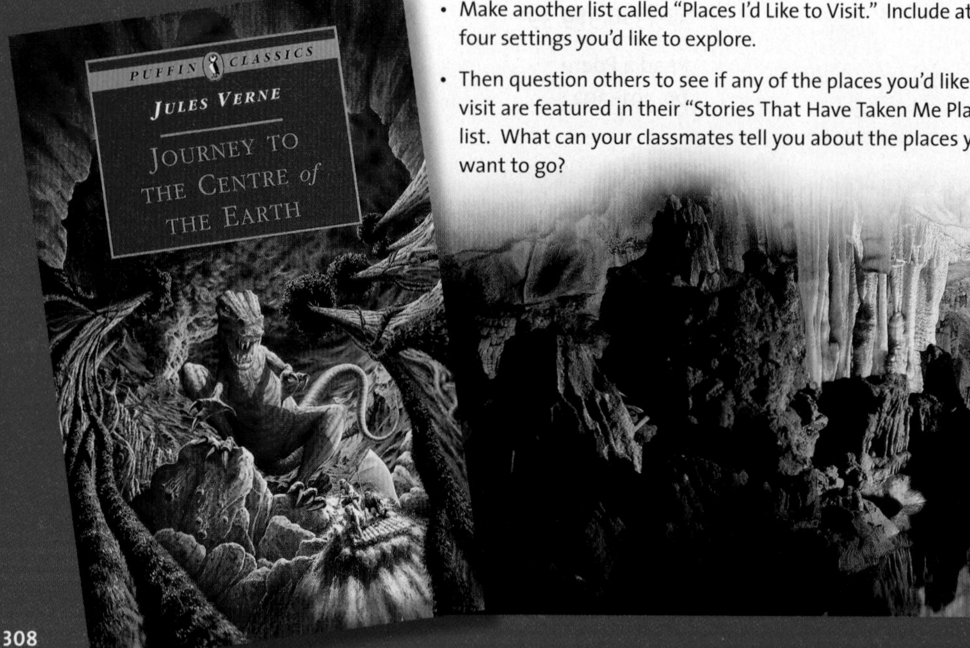

308

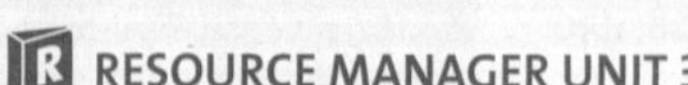

Unit Resources

- RESOURCE MANAGER UNIT 3
- BEST PRACTICES TOOLKIT
- STANDARDS LESSON FILE
- Easy Planner DVD
- Write*Smart* CD
- ClassZone.com
- Audio Anthology CD
- Multi-Language Academic Vocabulary Online
- eEdition CD & Online
- McDougal Littell Assessment System
- Test Generator CD
- Media*Smart* DVD

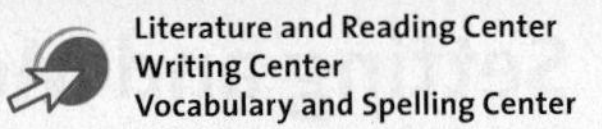

Literature and Reading Center
Writing Center
Vocabulary and Spelling Center

Preview Unit Goals

LITERARY ANALYSIS	• Identify and analyze setting and how setting affects plot • Identify and analyze mood • Identify, analyze, and evaluate imagery
READING	• Develop strategies for reading, including visualizing, predicting, connecting, and setting a purpose for reading • Make inferences • Compare scope of events as presented in two accounts • Read and analyze a primary source
WRITING AND GRAMMAR	• Write a comparison-contrast essay • Maintain subject-verb agreement
SPEAKING, LISTENING, AND VIEWING	• Produce and deliver a power presentation
VOCABULARY	• Use context clues to determine the meaning of idioms and homographs • Use structural analysis to identify base words and affixes • Use knowledge of word roots, base words, and affixes to determine the meaning of words
ACADEMIC VOCABULARY	• setting • imagery • primary source • mood • scope • subject-verb agreement

309

Preview Unit Goals

This page gives an overview of the skills and strategies covered in Unit 3. Point out that each skill strand is a different color, and that throughout the unit, each skill within a strand matches that color. Encourage students to consider their ability to use each skill and strategy as they read this page.

Suggest that students copy the Academic Vocabulary terms in their journals and define them in their own words as they read the unit. Encourage students to use these terms as they discuss and write about the unit's selections.

ADDITIONAL UNIT GOALS

These skills will be taught in this unit but are not the major focus of the unit:

Literary Analysis

- Interpret science fiction
- Compare and contrast the motivations and reactions of characters from different historical eras who confront similar situations or conflicts
- Identify and analyze setting in nonfiction
- Identify, analyze, and compare speakers
- Study a variety of genres: short story, science-fiction story, memoir, historical novel, article, journal

Reading

- Evaluate objectivity of a report

Writing and Grammar

- Avoid misplaced modifiers by placing prepositional phrases close to the words they modify

DIFFERENTIATED INSTRUCTION

FOR ENGLISH LEARNERS

Academic Vocabulary [paired option] Use the Academic Vocabulary copy master to teach *setting, mood, imagery, scope, primary source,* and *subject-verb agreement*.

1. Read each word aloud. Ask students if they have heard any of the words and, if so, in what context. Then read and discuss the examples.
2. Allow students to work in pairs to provide definitions. Then have them complete Part B, and discuss their answers as a class.

Additional Academic Vocabulary [mixed-readiness groups] Use the second copy master to help students study *context clue, idiom, homograph,* and *affix*.

1. As a class, review the definitions.
2. Have students work in small groups to complete the sentences.
3. Have students continue to work in groups to complete Part B.

RESOURCE MANAGER—Copy Masters
Academic Vocabulary p. 9
Additional Academic Vocabulary p. 10

Focus and Motivate

OBJECTIVES

- identify and analyze setting and its effect on plot and characters
- identify and analyze mood
- understand how mood can be conveyed through setting, imagery, and characters' reactions

Teach

Part 1: Setting

Setting Use this activity to extend the discussion and show students the different ways in which setting can influence characters and create conflicts:

- Have students brainstorm a list of stories with which they are familiar.
- Ask them to list the stories in a chart, identifying key details about the setting of each story in a second column.
- Then have students discuss the role of the setting in each story. They should ask themselves: Is the setting just a backdrop for the events of the story, or does it play a larger role? Does the setting affect characters in specific ways? Does it create conflicts?

Story	Setting	Role of Setting
The Hitchhiker	roads between New York and California	Setting makes Adams nervous as he sees the hitchhiker again and again along the road.
Harriet Tubman	United States before the Civil War	Setting creates conflict between Tubman and those who seek to enforce slavery.

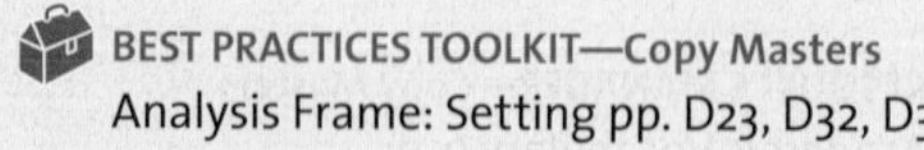

BEST PRACTICES TOOLKIT—Copy Masters
Analysis Frame: Setting pp. D23, D32, D33

UNIT 3
Reader's Workshop

Setting and Mood

Suppose you are immersed in a story about ten castaways stranded on an island. What makes the story such a page-turner? At first, you might credit the intriguin conflicts and characters. However, the setting and the atmosphere may also be responsible for drawing you in. The perilous terrain, the raging storms, the lurkin wildlife—details like these can transport you to the world that a writer describes. Read on to find out how setting and mood can make you feel as if you are there.

Part 1: Setting

You know that the **setting** of a story is the time and place in which the action occurs. The time can be a particular season, year, time of day, or historical period. The place can be anywhere—from a Civil War battlefield to a spaces hurtling toward to Mars.

A writer reveals a setting by describing the details of a time and place. Of he or she also includes descriptions of the characters' clothing and lifestyles. Such descriptions allow readers to visualize a setting in vivid detail.

In some stories, the setting takes center stage, serving as more than just a backdrop for the unfolding action. As this chart shows, a setting can affect t characters or create conflicts for them to endure.

ROLE OF SETTING	EXAMPLE	
Setting can affect characters by • determining the jobs and living conditions available to them • influencing their values, attitudes, and emotions	Small-town rural life had taken its toll on Garrett. He was sick of being around people who had no intention of finishing school or exploring the world. Garrett was determined to do more with his life than settle for a job on his family's farm.	
Setting can create conflicts by • exposing the characters to dangerous weather or natural disasters • making the characters live through difficult time periods, events, or situations, such as poverty or war	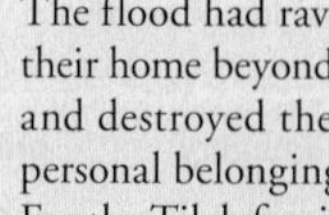 The flood had ravaged their home beyond repair and destroyed their personal belongings. For the Tilak family, the loss was devastating. It would take months, even years, for them to rebuild their lives.	

DIFFERENTIATED INSTRUCTION

FOR ALL STUDENTS

For general guidelines on differentiating instruction, see

BEST PRACTICES TOOLKIT
Differentiated Instruction pp. 31–38

FOR LESS–PROFICIENT READERS

Note Taking Hand out the Note Taking: Setting copy master and have students read page 310 silently. Then have students take notes on the copy master as you discuss the information.

RESOURCE MANAGER—Copy Master
Note Taking p. 15

Analysis Support: Setting [paired option] Ask students to label two Cluster Diagrams *War: Characters* and *Volcanic Explosions: Conflict.* Have pairs read page 311 and record words and phrases related to each passage's setting and its effects on characters and conflict.

BEST PRACTICES TOOLKIT—Transparency
Cluster Diagram p. B18

MODEL 1: SETTING AND CHARACTERS

For Sun-hee's entire life, Korea has been under the rule of the Japanese emperor, who has, by law, forbidden the practicing of Korean customs. When World War II breaks out, life becomes even more difficult for the people of Korea. While no battles are fought on Korean soil, Japanese soldiers patrol the streets, and school classes are replaced by war drills.

from When My Name Was *Keoko* Novel by **Linda Sue Park**

It seemed as if the war would never end. Day after day of too much hard work, not enough food, constant exhaustion—and no chance to make or do anything beautiful. If a war lasts long enough, is it possible that people would completely forget the idea of beauty? That they'd only be able to do what they needed to survive and would no longer remember how to make and enjoy beautiful things?

I was determined not to let this happen to me. At school every day, while I was working with my hands, I let my mind float away to think of something beautiful.

Close Read

1. How has the war affected people's daily lives?
2. Reread the boxed text. How does the narrator fear a long-lasting war could shape people's attitude toward their surroundings?

MODEL 2: SETTING AND CONFLICT

In this science fiction novel, a chain of volcanic explosions has caused ash to seep into the atmosphere. Miles and his family live in Minneapolis, where the air has become increasingly murky.

from Memory Boy Novel by **Will Weaver**

"I'm not leaving," Sarah said, jerking away from me. "Everybody's going to die anyway, so why can't we die in our own house?" She plopped down onto the lawn. Pale pumice[1] puffed up around her and hung in the air like a ghostly double. That was the weird thing about the volcanic ash; it had been falling softly, softly falling, for over two years now—and sometimes it was almost beautiful. Tonight the rock flour suspended in the air made a wide, furry-white halo around the moon. Its giant, raccoon-like eyeball stared down and made the whole neighborhood look X-rayed.

"Nobody's going to die," I said. "Though if we stay in the city, we might," I muttered to myself.

Close Read

1. Find two details that help you to understand the effects of the volcanic explosions on Minneapolis.
2. How do Sarah and Miles each view the conflict that the setting has created for their family?

1. **pumice:** a powdery substance that comes from volcanic glass.

MODEL 1: SETTING AND CHARACTERS

Close Read

Possible answers:

1. *Because of the war, each day in Korea involves "too much hard work, not enough food, constant exhaustion—and no chance to make or do anything beautiful" (lines 1–3).*
2. *According to the narrator, a war that lasts long enough could cause people to forget "how to make and enjoy beautiful things" (lines 5–6). They might only be able to do what is necessary to survive.*

MODEL 2: SETTING AND CONFLICT

Close Read

Possible answers:

1. *Students may cite these details:*
   - *"Pale pumice puffed up around her and hung in the air like a ghostly double." (lines 3–4)*
   - *". . . it had been falling softly, softly falling, for over two years now—and sometimes it was almost beautiful." (lines 4–6)*
   - *"Tonight the rock flour suspended in the air made a wide, furry-white halo around the moon." (lines 6–7)*
   - *"Its giant, raccoon-like eyeball stared down and made the whole neighborhood look X-rayed." (lines 7–8)*
2. *Despite the increasingly thick and murky air, Sarah does not want to flee her own house in the city. She says that everyone is eventually going to die anyway, and she would rather die in her own house. Miles believes they would be safer if they left their home in the city.*

FOR ENGLISH LEARNERS

Concept Support: Setting, Character, and Conflict [mixed-readiness pairs]

1. Review the terms *character* ("a person who takes part in the action of a story") and *conflict* ("a struggle between two forces").
2. Help students identify the setting of each passage on page 311 using clues in the introductory paragraphs, such as "Korea" and "When World War II breaks out."
3. Have students work in pairs to answer the **Close Read** questions.

FOR ADVANCED LEARNERS/PRE-AP

Create Setting Have students write the first paragraphs of two original stories that illustrate how setting can influence characters and create conflict. Students should write one paragraph that introduces a setting that influences one or more characters in some way. Then they should write another paragraph about a setting that creates conflict for one or more characters. Encourage students to share their paragraphs.

Teach

Part 2: Mood

Mood Emphasize to students that a writer's careful choice of words and details determines the mood of a story. In some cases, the same setting could be described in different ways to create different moods. Share these examples:

> Stars and a full moon lit the soft sand of the quiet beach. I was finally alone. I sat at the edge of the water and let the gentle waves wash soothingly over my tired feet. The sound of the moving water almost lulled me to sleep.
>
> I realized I was alone on the dark beach. Only the eerie glow from a full moon lit my way. My toes gripped the rough sand with every step as I hurried away from the icy water. The sound of every crashing wave sent chills up my back.

Have students discuss the differences in the two passages, pointing out specific words and phrases. Encourage them to look for imagery and for details that indicate how each passage makes the reader feel.

CHECK UNDERSTANDING To check students' understanding of mood, ask students to give examples of settings, imagery, or characters' speech or feelings that may create a particular mood. Write three examples of mood on the board, such as *happy, sad,* and *scary.* Have students answer these questions for each mood:

- What kinds of places could help create this mood? What time of the day or year would be most effective in creating the mood?
- What details that appeal to your senses of sight, hearing, touch, taste, and smell would enhance this mood?
- What might characters do or say to build this mood?

Students can give general examples or refer to stories they have read.

Part 2: Mood

The way a writer describes a setting can make you feel as if "you are there," whether "there" is a war-torn country or a city threatened by volcanic explosions. Like setting, mood is responsible for prompting this reaction in you.

Mood is the feeling or atmosphere that a writer creates for readers. A mood can be described as *exciting, somber, terrifying, cheerful, carefree,* or something else. To identify the mood in a work of literature, notice the following elements.

- **Descriptions of Setting** Does the story take place in an abandoned house on a stormy night or on a crowded beach during the summer? The writer's choice of setting and the words he or she uses to describe it can create a mood.
- **Imagery** Writers use **imagery**—language that appeals to your senses of sight, hearing, smell, taste, or touch—to affect your emotions and establish a mood. For instance, images such as *squeals of laughter* and *a rainbow of beach umbrellas* help to convey a cheerful mood.
- **Descriptions of Characters' Speech or Feelings** Pay attention to what the characters say, think, or feel about the setting and the conflict. Are they scared, joyful, or depressed? The characters' reactions often reflect the mood the writer is trying to create.

Examine this graphic. Notice how these three elements work together to create a terrifying mood.

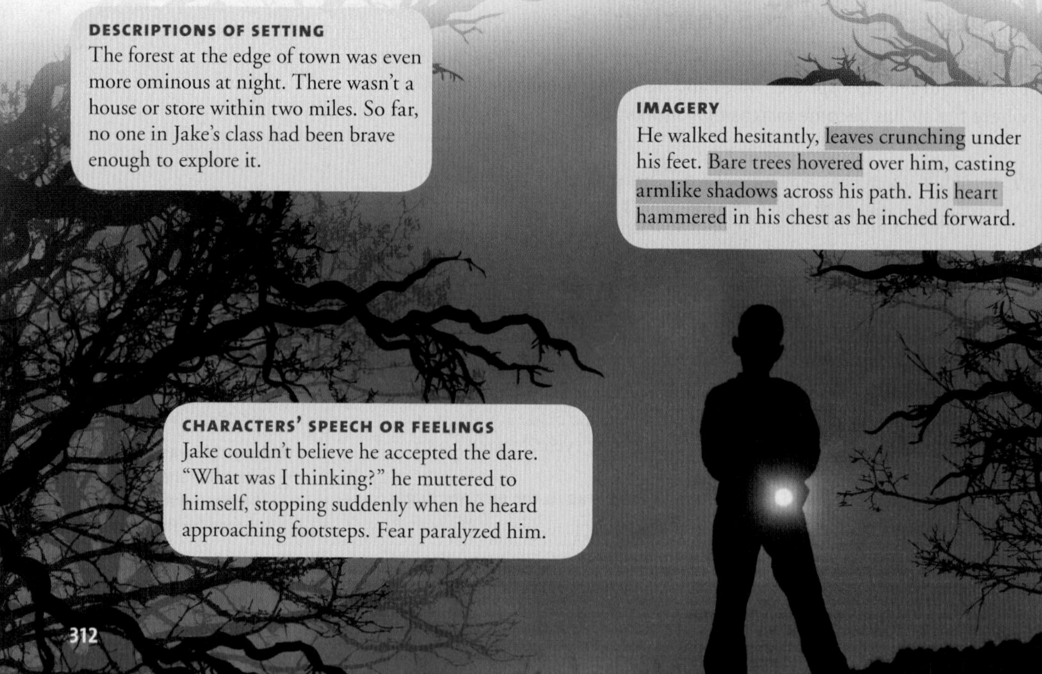

DESCRIPTIONS OF SETTING
The forest at the edge of town was even more ominous at night. There wasn't a house or store within two miles. So far, no one in Jake's class had been brave enough to explore it.
IMAGERY
He walked hesitantly, leaves crunching under his feet. Bare trees hovered over him, casting armlike shadows across his path. His heart hammered in his chest as he inched forward.
CHARACTERS' SPEECH OR FEELINGS
Jake couldn't believe he accepted the dare. "What was I thinking?" he muttered to himself, stopping suddenly when he heard approaching footsteps. Fear paralyzed him.
312

DIFFERENTIATED INSTRUCTION

FOR LESS–PROFICIENT READERS

Note Taking For students who need help with note taking, hand out the Note Taking: Mood copy master. Have students read page 312 silently. Then have students take notes on the copy master as you discuss the information.

RESOURCE MANAGER—Copy Master
Note Taking p. 16

Analysis Support: Mood

1. Display these phrases: *Descriptions of setting; Imagery; Characters' speech or feelings.*
2. Read aloud the excerpts on page 313 as students follow along. Have students stop you each time you encounter an example of one of the elements listed above. Students should write down these details.
3. After you finish reading, discuss the details students noted. Help students use the details to identify the mood of each piece.

MODEL 1: COMPARING MOOD

Set in New England during the Civil War years, *Little Women* follows the lives of the four March sisters. This excerpt describes the day on which Meg, the oldest sister, is to get married. As you read, pay attention to the descriptions of the setting and the roses.

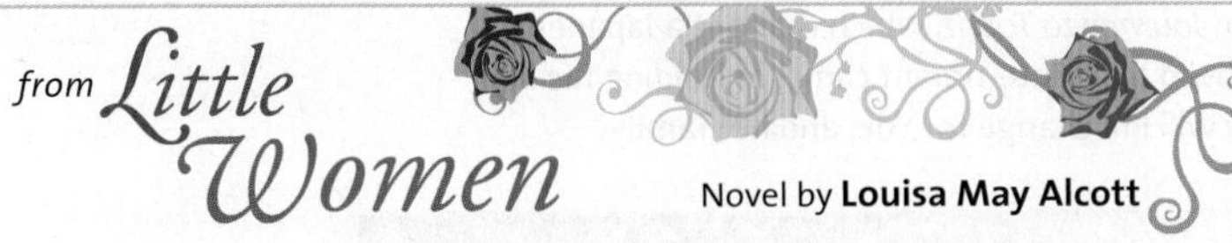

from *Little Women*

Novel by **Louisa May Alcott**

The June roses over the porch were awake bright and early on that morning, rejoicing with all their hearts in the cloudless sunshine, like friendly little neighbors, as they were. Quite flushed with excitement were their ruddy faces, as they swung in the wind, whispering to one another what they had seen; for some peeped in at the dining-room windows, where the feast was spread, some climbed up to nod and smile at the sisters, as they dressed the bride, others waved a welcome to those who came and went on various errands in garden, porch and hall, and all, from the rosiest full-blown flower to the palest baby-bud, offered their tribute of beauty and fragrance to the gentle mistress who had loved and tended them so long.

Close Read

1. In the boxed text, the roses are described as if they were human. What details help you understand the roses' "feelings" about the wedding?
2. What imagery is used to describe the setting?
3. How would you describe the mood of this scene?

MODEL 2: COMPARING MOOD

The mood of this scene is dramatically different from the one you identified in the *Little Women* excerpt. As you read this passage, look closely at the descriptions that help to create this different mood.

from *Max*

Short story by **Chaim Potok**

That night it stormed, and a school bus turned slowly into our small street from the main road, one block away. Our new house was only two blocks from my school, and yellow school buses went up and down the street mornings and afternoons. But never during the night! Now the bus moved carefully along the rain-drenched asphalt, and about fifty feet from our house, it picked up speed. Lying in my bed, I heard the revving of the engine and stepped quickly to the window—in time to see the bus skid from the street and mount the curb, barely missing our sycamore tree. It advanced solemnly, ponderously, as if in slow motion. . . .

Close Read

1. In what ways is this setting different from the one described in *Little Women?*
2. Consider the boxed examples of imagery, as well as the descriptions of the setting. How would you describe the mood?

MODEL 1: COMPARING MOOD

Close Read

Possible answers:

1. *Students may cite these details:*
   - *"rejoicing with all their hearts" (line 2)*
   - *"Quite flushed with excitement were their ruddy faces" (lines 3–4)*
   - *"climbed up to nod and smile at the sisters" (line 6)*
   - *"waved a welcome" (line 7)*
   - *"offered their tribute of beauty and fragrance" (line 9)*
2. *Students may cite these images:*
   - *"June roses over the porch" (line 1)*
   - *"cloudless sunshine" (line 2)*
   - *"some peeped in at the dining-room windows, where the feast was spread" (lines 5–6)*
   - *"some climbed up to nod and smile at the sisters, as they dressed the bride" (lines 6–7)*
   - *"others waved a welcome to those who came and went on various errands in garden, porch, and hall" (lines 7–8)*
   - *"all, from the rosiest full-blown flower to the palest baby-bud, offered their tribute of beauty and fragrance" (lines 8–9)*
3. *The mood is one of happiness, excitement, and celebration.*

MODEL 2: COMPARING MOOD

Close Read

Possible answers:

1. *In this selection, unlike in Model 1, the weather is rainy and stormy and the action takes place at night. The house and its surroundings are not described as being beautiful, as in Model 1. The only mention of the house's landscaping is a line that describes the bus skidding from the street and nearly hitting a sycamore tree.*
2. *The mood in this selection is dreary, tense, and ominous.*

FOR ENGLISH LEARNERS

Analysis Support: Mood [mixed-readiness pairs] To prepare for the **Close Read** questions, have pairs discuss these words and phrases and the feelings associated with them:

- **from *Little Women*:** *bright and early, rejoicing, cloudless sunshine, excitement, welcome, tribute of beauty and fragrance*
- **from *Max*:** *it stormed, rain-drenched asphalt, revving of the engine, skid, solemnly, ponderously*

FOR ADVANCED LEARNERS/PRE-AP

Create Mood Have students rewrite the excerpts on page 313, completely changing the mood of each piece. Challenge students to keep many of the basic details—such as roses and a wedding scene in Model 1 and the school bus and rainy night in Model 2—but to change the descriptive language so it conveys a completely different feeling.

Practice and Apply

Part 3: Analyze the Literature

Close Read

Possible answers:

1. *The scene takes place at an internment camp located in a Utah desert. Details that reveal setting include*
   - *"At the western rim of the desert they could see a tall range of mountains" (lines 2–3)*
   - *"rows and rows of squat tar-papered barracks sitting in a pool of white dust" (lines 5–6)*
   - *"There wasn't a single tree or a blade of grass to break the monotony of the sun-bleached desert." (lines 31–32)*
2. *The camp is ugly and dusty, with people forced to live in rows of unappealing barracks. The apartments are small and close together. There are no trees, so the sun beats down on the camp's residents continuously.*
3. *The mood of the scene is best described as (b) bleak.*

If students need help . . . List for them key words from the boxed lines, such as *engulf, smothering blanket, dreary,* and *monotony.* Talk about the meanings of the words and what feelings and experiences come to mind when they think of these words.

Part 3: Analyze the Literature

Now, you'll use what you've learned about setting and mood to analyze the following two novel excerpts. In each, the main character is seeing his or her new home for the first time.

The first excerpt is from *Journey to Topaz,* which is about a Japanese-American family being moved to an internment camp, or holding facility, during World War II. How will life change for Yuki and her family?

from Journey to Topaz

Novel by **Yoshiko Uchida**

The eager hopeful voices on the bus died down and soon stopped altogether. Mother said nothing more and Yuki herself grew silent. At the western rim of the desert they could see a tall range of mountains, but long before they reached their sheltering shadows the buses made a sharp left turn, and there in the midst of the desert, they came upon rows and rows of squat tar-papered barracks sitting in a pool of white dust that had once been the bottom of a lake. They had arrived at Topaz, the Central Utah War Relocation Center, which would be their new home.

Ken turned to look at Yuki. "Well, here we are," he said dryly. "This is beautiful Topaz."

The minute Yuki stepped off the bus, she felt the white powdery dust of the desert engulf her like a smothering blanket. The Boy Scout Drum and Bugle Corp had come out to welcome the incoming buses, but now they looked like flour-dusted cookies that had escaped from a bakery.

Yuki coughed while one of the team of doctors inspected her throat and then she ran quickly to talk to Emi while Ken finished registering the family.

"We've been assigned to Block 7, Barrack 2, Apartment C," she informed her. "Try to get the room next door."

Emi nodded. "OK, I'll tell Grandma," she said, for they both knew that if anybody could manage such an arrangement, Grandma could.

A boy about Ken's age offered to take them out to their new quarters. He had come in one of the earlier contingents and already knew his way around the big, sprawling barrack city.

"It's a mile square," he explained as they started toward Block 7, and like a guide on a tour he told them all he knew about Topaz.

"There're forty-two blocks and each block has twelve barracks with a mess hall and a latrine-washroom in the center," he pointed out. "When the barracks are all finished and occupied, we'll be the fifth largest city in Utah."

"Imagine!" Mother said.

It sounded impressive, but Yuki thought she had never seen a more dreary place in all her life. There wasn't a single tree or a blade of grass to break the monotony of the sun-bleached desert.

Close Read

1. Where does this scene take place? Find three details that reveal the setting.
2. What conflicts has the setting created for the characters?
3. Reread the boxed lines, which reveal Yuki's first impression of her new home. Which word best describes the mood of this scene?

   a. hopeful
   b. bleak
   c. threatening

DIFFERENTIATED INSTRUCTION

FOR LESS–PROFICIENT READERS

Vocabulary Support Introduce these words from *Journey to Topaz.* Have students read the context for each word and suggest a synonym to replace it.

- *squat* (line 6), "short"
- *barracks* (line 6), "temporary shelters"
- *engulf* (line 12), "cover over"
- *quarters* (line 21), "living space"
- *contingents* (line 22), "groups of people"
- *latrine-washroom* (line 27), "bathroom"
- *monotony* (line 32), "lack of variety"

Analysis Support: Mood

- Read aloud the first two paragraphs from the *Journey to Topaz* excerpt, using your voice to convey the mood. Have students take turns reading aloud paragraphs to complete the excerpt. Then discuss with students what words and phrases helped create the overall mood.
- Repeat the activity with *The House of Dies Drear.* Ask students whether they were surprised by Thomas's reaction to the setting in lines 20–24 and, if so, why.

Now read this excerpt from the novel *The House of Dies Drear.* Thomas Small and his family are driving across states toward their new house, which is rumored to have a long, interesting history. During the Civil War years, the house was owned by an abolitionist who hid fugitive slaves there. How will Thomas react when he sees his new home for the first time?

Novel by **Virginia Hamilton**

Thomas did not wake in time to see the Ohio River. Mr. Small was glad he didn't, for through the gloom of mist and heavy rain, most of its expanse was hidden. What was visible looked much like a thick mud path, as the sedan crossed over it at Huntington.

Thomas lurched awake a long time after. The car went slowly; there was hardly any rain now. His mother spoke excitedly, and Thomas had to shake his head rapidly in order to understand what she was saying.

"Oh dear! My heavens!" Mrs. Small said. "Why it's huge!"

Mr. Small broke in eagerly, turning around to face Thomas. You've waited a long time," he said. "Take a good look, son. There's our new house!"

Thomas looked carefully out of his window. He opened the car door for a few seconds to see better, but found the moist air too warm and soft. The feel of it was not nice at all, and he quickly closed the door. He could see well enough out of the window, and what he saw made everything inside him grow quiet for the first time in weeks. It was more than he could have dreamed.

The house of Dies Drear loomed out of mist and murky sky, not only gray and formless, but huge and unnatural. It seemed to crouch on the side of a hill high above the highway. And it had a dark, isolated look about it that set it at odds with all that was living.

A chill passed over Thomas. He sighed with satisfaction. The house of Dies Drear was a haunted place, of that he was certain.

"Well," Mr. Small said, "what do you think of it, Thomas?"

"It must be the biggest house anyone ever built," Thomas said at last. "And to think—it's our new house! Papa, let's get closer, let's go inside!"

Close Read

1. What clues in the text could help you determine the location of the Small family's new house?
2. What images in lines 16–19 help you to visualize the Small's new house?
3. Pay attention to Thomas's thoughts and speech in lines 11–24. How does he feel about the setting? Support your answer.
4. Review your answers to the preceding two questions. How would you describe the mood of the scene when Thomas first sees the house?

Close Read

Possible answers:

1. *The family crossed over the Ohio River as they traveled to the house. The house is far from the point at which they crossed, because the text says that Thomas awoke a "long time after" they crossed the river. The house was located on the side of a hill high above a highway.*
2. *Students may cite these images:*
   - *"The house . . . loomed out of mist and murky sky, not only gray and formless, but huge and unnatural." (lines 16–17)*
   - *"It seemed to crouch on the side of a hill high above the highway." (lines 17–18)*
   - *"it had a dark, isolated look about it" (line 18)*
3. *When Thomas sees the house, he is clearly impressed by its appearance: "It was more than he could have dreamed" (line 15). He is also described as sighing "with satisfaction" (line 20) as he decides that the house must be haunted. Thomas tells his father, "It must be the biggest house anyone ever built. . . . And to think—it's our new house!" He can't wait to get inside.*
4. *The mood is one of excitement and suspense.*

Assess and Reteach

Assess

Ask students to explain how setting affects characters or creates conflict in one of the excerpts in the lesson. Then ask them to describe one element—such as setting, imagery, or characters' speech or feelings—that reveals the mood of the selection.

Reteach

Use this activity for students who have trouble applying the workshop skills:

1. Divide the class into small groups. Have students review and share the information from their Note Taking copy masters.
2. Have students work together to define setting and mood and to give examples from stories they know.
3. Ask students to then identify setting and mood in at least one of the excerpts in the workshop.

FOR ENGLISH LEARNERS

Language Support: Idioms Help students use context clues to determine the meanings of these idioms. Encourage them to think of their own sentences that show the meanings.

Journey to Topaz

- *died down* (line 1), "became quiet"

The House of Dies Drear

- *more than he could have dreamed* (line 15), "better than he had hoped"
- *at odds with* (lines 18–19), "apart from; in disagreement with"

FOR ADVANCED LEARNERS/PRE–AP

Analyze Setting and Mood Have students write a brief essay analyzing the setting and mood of one of the excerpts on pages 314–315. Students should include a discussion of any conflicts created by setting, the effects of setting on character, and details that create a specific mood. Encourage students to refer to the introductions to the excerpts to inform their discussion of setting and mood.

Focus and Motivate

OBJECTIVES

Literary Analysis
- explore the key idea of **contribution**
- identify and analyze setting
- read a short story

Reading
- make inferences about characters

Vocabulary
- build vocabulary for reading and writing
- use context clues to determine the meanings of idioms *(also an EL language objective)*

SUMMARY

The night before his first battle in the Civil War, a drummer boy lies awake, struggling with his fears and trying not to cry aloud. The General passes by and hears him, however. He stops to talk to the young boy, telling him what an important role he is to play in the battle ahead.

Does every CONTRIBUTION *count?*

Discuss the question and ***KEY IDEA*** with students. Remind them of the saying "Every little bit helps." Ask them for examples of ways that they make a **contribution**—as a family member, a student, a volunteer. Would things run as smoothly without them? Why or why not? Have pairs work on the ***CHART IT*** activity and then discuss their responses.

Before Reading

The Drummer Boy of Shiloh

Short Story by Ray Bradbury

Does every CONTRIBUTION *count?*

KEY IDEA When there are 12 people on the team, and you're not even a starter, you might think that staying for extra practice doesn't matter. But one good assist can make the difference between victory and defeat. In sports, as in many areas of life, every **contribution** counts. You are about to read a short story in which a young drummer boy learns that even he can make a difference.

CHART IT Think of a situation in which one person's contribution affects the outcome. What would happen if that person didn't do his or her part? Create a cause-and-effect chain like the one shown.

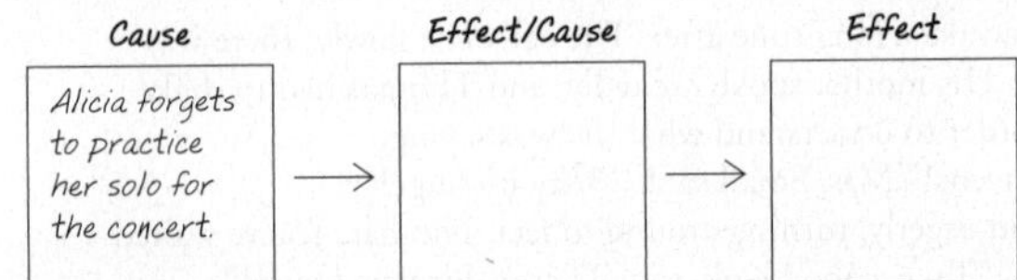

Selection Resources

RESOURCE MANAGER UNIT 3

Plan and Teach pp. 17–24

Literary Analysis
Summary pp. 25†*, 26‡*
Setting pp. 27, 28†*
Question Support p. 35*

Reading
Make Inferences pp. 29, 30†*
Reading Check p. 34
Reading Fluency p. 37

Vocabulary
Study p. 31*
Practice p. 32
Strategy p. 33

Assessment
Selection Tests A, B/C pp. 39*, 41*
Test Generator CD

BEST PRACTICES TOOLKIT

Differentiated Instruction pp. 31–38*
Scaffolding Instruction pp. 43–46*

Graphic Organizers/Strategies
Word Questioning • Cluster Diagram • Cause-and-Effect Diagram (Multiple Effects)

Reading Support
Audio Anthology CD*

Technology
Literature and Vocabulary Centers at **ClassZone.com**
Write*Smart* CD

* Resources for Differentiation † Also in Spanish ‡ In Haitian Creole and Vietnamese

ERARY ANALYSIS: SETTING

The **setting** of a story is the time and place in which events occur. Setting is particularly important in **historical fiction,** which features real places and events from the past and might also include characters based on real people. To give readers a sense of the past, writers of historical fiction

- refer to historically significant events
- use descriptive details that help readers see, hear, and smell what life was like at a different time

As you read, note the ways Ray Bradbury captures what life was like during the Civil War.

DING STRATEGY: MAKE INFERENCES

When you **make inferences** as you read, you make logical guesses based on information in the story and your own knowledge and experience. For example, if a character sighs and puts her face in her hands, you could infer that she is sad. By suggesting rather than stating things directly, a writer can better engage a reader and build suspense.

As you read the story, use a chart like the one shown to note inferences you make about what the drummer boy is feeling. To make these inferences, record details from the story and what you know from your own experience.

Details from the Story	What I Know from Experience	Inference

Review: Monitor

CABULARY IN CONTEXT

These vocabulary words help Ray Bradbury convey what it was like to fight in the Civil War. To see how many you know, match each numbered word or phrase with the word closest in meaning.

WORD LIST	askew	muted	solemn
	legitimately	resolute	strew

1. muffled
2. serious
3. to one side
4. lawfully
5. determined
6. scatter

Author Online

An Idea Man
Fans often ask Ray Bradbury, "Where do you get your ideas?" Bradbury says that he often wakes up with a great idea and immediately turns it into a story. He has written nearly 600 short stories—showing his fans that he's not short on ideas.

Ray Bradbury
born 1920

More than a Science-Fiction Writer
Because much of his work explores the effect of scientific development on human lives, Ray Bradbury is often called a science-fiction writer; however, he doesn't accept this label, and he actually avoids some of the most common technological conveniences. For example, Bradbury does not drive a car or own a computer. In addition to science fiction, he's written plays, mysteries, fantasies, realistic stories and novels, and various types of nonfiction—much of it on an old-fashioned typewriter.

Background

A "Deeply Felt" Story One morning over 40 years ago, Bradbury read in the paper about an actor whose great-grandfather was known as the drummer boy of Shiloh. Struck by the phrase, Bradbury rushed to his typewriter and wrote the first draft of this story in one day. Later, he researched the Civil War and revised the story to make it historically accurate. He says it's one of the most "deeply felt" stories he's ever written. The Battle of Shiloh, upon which this story is based, took place in April, 1862, in southwestern Tennessee. This major battle was the bloodiest yet seen in the U.S.

MORE ABOUT THE AUTHOR AND BACKGROUND
To learn more about Ray Bradbury and the Battle of Shiloh, visit the **Literature Center** at **ClassZone.com.**

THE DRUMMER BOY OF SHILOH 317

Teach

STANDARDS FOCUS

LITERARY ANALYSIS

● SETTING

Write this example on the board:

> The fragile walls of the hut at Bletchley shook with another cold blast of wind. Sara shivered and continued working. They had to crack this code to foil Hitler's planned invasion of Britain.

Ask students to identify the setting.
Answer: *The events take place during winter in a hut at Bletchley during World War II.*

CHECK UNDERSTANDING Ask students to describe the settings of works of historical fiction that they have read.

READING STRATEGY

■ MAKE INFERENCES

Tell students that making inferences is reading between the lines to find clues about characters, setting, and plot. For example, paying attention to a character's behavior helps readers understand the character's inner conflict.

CHECK UNDERSTANDING Ask students to read **Author Online** on page 317 and make inferences about Ray Bradbury.

RESOURCE MANAGER—Copy Master
Make Inferences p. 29 (for student use while reading the selection)

VOCABULARY SKILL

▲ VOCABULARY IN CONTEXT

DIAGNOSE WORD KNOWLEDGE To determine preteaching needs, have all students complete **Vocabulary in Context.** Check students' answers. (**1.** *muted* **2.** *solemn* **3.** *askew* **4.** *legitimately* **5.** *resolute* **6.** *strew*)

PRETEACH VOCABULARY Use the Vocabulary Study copy master to help students determine the meaning of each boldfaced word.

1. Read the first two sentences aloud, emphasizing the boldfaced word.
2. Note the phrases *so many miles away* and *hope that it was loud enough.* Elicit possible meanings for *muted,* such as "quiet."
3. Repeat for the rest of the paragraph.
4. Have students complete Part B independently.

RESOURCE MANAGER—Copy Master
Vocabulary Study p. 31

For general guidelines on differentiating vocabulary instruction and for alternative vocabulary activities for students not needing vocabulary preteaching, see

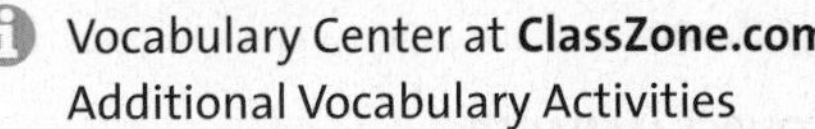
BEST PRACTICES TOOLKIT
Scaffolding Vocabulary Instruction
pp. 43–46

ⓘ Vocabulary Center at **ClassZone.com**
Additional Vocabulary Activities

Practice and Apply

ANALYZE VISUALS

***Possible answer:** He looks young and his uniform looks new and clean, suggesting that he has not had experience in battle.*

About the Art American artist Dale Gallon is both a historian and an artist. Each of his paintings of the Civil War is historically accurate in its details. In fact, he employs a researcher to collect facts on his subject and to write an essay to accompany each print.

READING STRATEGY

A MAKE INFERENCES

Remind students to record their inferences in the chart from page 317. ***Possible answer:** The boy is nervous, and the unexpected sound makes his heart race.*

Lines 9–24

DISCUSSION PROMPTS

Use these prompts to help students understand the setting of the story:

Connect How do you think the drummer boy feels being surrounded by so many people? *Students may recall being in large crowds themselves and may say that it can be overwhelming.*

Analyze The soldiers are described as lying "askew" and "helter-skelter." Why do they lack order? ***Possible answer:** They may be so tired that they have dropped where they stood.*

Speculate What might be foreshadowed by the disordered appearance of the soldiers? ***Possible answer:** The sleeping soldiers might foreshadow the bodies that will litter the field after battle.*

THE Drummer Boy OF Shiloh

RAY BRADBURY

In the April night, more than once, blossoms fell from the orchard trees and lit with rustling taps on the drumskin. At midnight a peach stone left miraculously on a branch through winter, flicked by a bird, fell swift and unseen, struck once, like panic, which jerked the boy upright. In silence he listened to his own heart ruffle away, away, at last gone from his ears and back in his chest again.

After that, he turned the drum on its side, where its great lunar[1] face peered at him whenever he opened his eyes. **A**

His face, alert or at rest, was **solemn.** It was indeed a solemn time and a solemn night for a boy just turned fourteen in the peach field near the Owl Creek not far from the church at Shiloh.

". . . thirty-one, thirty-two, thirty-three . . ."

Unable to see, he stopped counting.

Beyond the thirty-three familiar shadows, forty thousand men, exhausted by nervous expectation, unable to sleep for romantic dreams of battles yet unfought, lay crazily **askew** in their uniforms. A mile yet farther on, another army was **strewn** helter-skelter, turning slow, basting themselves with the thought of what they would do when the time came: a leap, a yell, a blind plunge their strategy, raw youth their protection and benediction.[2]

Now and again the boy heard a vast wind come up, that gently stirred the air. But he knew what it was, the army here, the army there, whispering to itself in the dark. Some men talking to others, others murmuring to themselves, and all so quiet it was like a natural element arisen from south or north with the motion of the earth toward dawn.

1. **lunar** (lōō'nər): of or relating to the moon.
2. **benediction** (bĕn'ĭ-dĭk'shən): a blessing.

ANALYZE VISUALS
What can you **infer** ab
the age and experienc
level of this member o
the Union Army?

A MAKE INFERENCE
Note the boy's reactio
when the peach pit str
the drum. Why do you
think he reacted that v

solemn (sŏl'əm) *adj.* deeply serious

askew (ə-skyōō') *adj.* to one side; awry

strew (strōō) *v.* to spre
here and there; scatte

① Targeted Passage

The Musician, Dale Ga
Courtesy of Gallon Historical
Gettysburg, Pennsylv

DIFFERENTIATED INSTRUCTION

FOR ALL STUDENTS

Anchor Activity Provide opportunities for independent research on the Civil War. Have groups research related topics, such as the causes of the conflict, important battles, notable leaders, and the war's outcome. Have students present oral reports with visuals. For further details on this project, see

RESOURCE MANAGER
Ideas for Extension pp. 22–23

FOR LESS–PROFICIENT READERS

In combination with the *Audio Anthology CD,* use one or more Targeted Passages (pp. 318, 320, 323) to ensure that students focus on key story events, concepts, and skills.

① Targeted Passage [Lines 9–24]

This passage introduces important details about the drummer boy and establishes the setting of the story.

- How old is the drummer boy? Where is he?
- What feeling is the boy experiencing?
- How many soldiers are with the drummer boy in the field?
- What are they all waiting for and thinking about?

BACKGROUND

Drummer Boys In the Civil War and other past military conflicts, drummers played an important role. On the battlefield, drums were used to pass along orders from commanding officers and to indicate where and when the soldiers should move. In addition, drummers regulated the events of the soldiers' day, waking them up in the morning, calling them into formation, and signaling "lights out." Although some drummers were sent to the rear of the lines during the actual battle, others accompanied the troops, playing while under fire.

FOR ENGLISH LEARNERS

Key Academic Vocabulary Have students use Word Questioning to study this academic vocabulary from the selection: *strategy* (line 19), *element* (line 23), *target* (line 90), *focus* (line 132).

BEST PRACTICES TOOLKIT—Transparency
Word Questioning p. E9

Options for Reading Read the first Targeted Passage aloud and discuss what it reveals about character and setting. Then have students read the remainder of the story along with the *Audio Anthology CD*.

Prereading For prereading instruction for English learners, see

BEST PRACTICES TOOLKIT
Scaffolding Reading Instruction pp. 43–46

FOR ADVANCED LEARNERS/PRE–AP

Pre-AP exercises in the bottom channel provide additional challenge for your advanced students. Use them for small groups or individuals.

ADDITIONAL GUIDELINES

For more help with differentiation and tips for classroom management, see

BEST PRACTICES TOOLKIT
Differentiated Instruction pp. 31–38

ANALYZE VISUALS

Possible answer: *Men spent most of their time outdoors, sheltered only by tents. They cooked their food over a fire that was also used to keep them warm. The men passed the time playing games and talking to each other.*

About the Art American artist Mort Künstler (born 1931) turned his attention to the Civil War in the early 1980s. Since that time, his work has been acclaimed for bringing history to life. For this painting, Künstler was inspired by the idea of how precious letters from home were to the soldiers. He made the soldier reading the letter the focal point of the painting and then completed the rest of the scene.

LITERARY ANALYSIS

B SETTING

Possible answer: *Details that indicate the historical setting include the campfires and the bayonets sticking up in the air.*

If students need help . . . Direct them to study the illustration, which will help them visualize the description in lines 30–32. Have them match details in the text with what they can see in the painting and explain how the images show that the setting is from an earlier time.

Extend the Discussion The bayonets are "fixed like eternal lightning." Ask students what effect this simile has on their impression of the setting.

Letter from Home, Mort Künstler. © Mort Künstler, Inc. www.mkunstler.com.

What the men whispered the boy could only guess, and he guessed that it was: Me, I'm the one, I'm the one of all the rest won't die. I'll live through it. I'll go home. The band will play. And I'll be there to hear it.

Yes, thought the boy, that's all very well for them, they can give as good as they get!

For with the careless bones of the young men harvested by night and bindled[3] around campfires were the similarly strewn steel bones of their rifles, with bayonets[4] fixed like eternal lightning lost in the orchard grass. B

Me, thought the boy, I got only a drum, two sticks to beat it, and no shield.

There wasn't a man-boy on this ground tonight did not have a shield he cast, riveted or carved himself on his way to his first attack, compounded of remote but nonetheless firm and fiery family devotion, flag-blown patriotism and cocksure immortality strengthened by the touchstone[5] of very real gunpowder, ramrod, minnieball and flint.[6] But without these last the boy felt his family move yet farther off away in the dark, as if one of those great prairie-burning

3. **bindled:** fastened or wrapped by encircling, as with a belt.
4. **bayonets** (bā′ə-nĕts′): blades adapted to fit the muzzle end of a rifle; used in close combat.
5. **touchstone:** a reference point against which other things are compared or measured.
6. **ramrod, minnieball, and flint:** items used to fire a rifle.

ANALYZE VISUAL
Based on this image, what can you **conclu** about what life was l in a Civil War army ca

2 Targeted Passage

B SETTING
Reread lines 30–32. What **details** help you imagine this particula time and place?

DIFFERENTIATED INSTRUCTION

FOR LESS–PROFICIENT READERS

2 Targeted Passage [Lines 25–33]

This passage presents the major conflict of the story: the drummer boy's fear of going into battle.

- What does the drummer boy mean when he says that the other soldiers "can give as good as they get"? Why can't he?
- What else contributes to the drummer boy's fear of going into battle?

Review: Monitor

- Write these sentence frames on the board: In this part of the story, I learn that ____. I think ____ will happen next.
- Divide the story into sections. After students read each part silently, have them complete the sentence frames. Ask them also to record any questions they have.
- Have students share their questions with the class. Guide students to use strategies such as rereading, skimming, and discussing to find the answers to each.

FOR ADVANCED LEARNERS/PRE–AP

Analyze Style [small-group option] What effect does the author create by repeating the word *bones* in lines 30–32? Discuss how the repetition calls up the image of a graveyard, foreshadowing the destruction of the battle that is to come. Ask small groups to analyze elements of Bradbury's style such as repetition, metaphor, simile, and symbolism. Have them use a three-column chart to record examples, interpret the meaning of each example, and describe the effects on readers.

rains had chanted them away never to return, leaving him with this drum which was worse than a toy in the game to be played tomorrow or some day much too soon. **C**

The boy turned on his side. A moth brushed his face, but it was peach blossom. A peach blossom flicked him, but it was a moth. Nothing stayed put. Nothing had a name. Nothing was as it once was.

If he lay very still, when the dawn came up and the soldiers put on their bravery with their caps, perhaps they might go away, the war with them, and not notice him lying small here, no more than a toy himself. **D**

"Well, by God, now," said a voice.

The boy shut up his eyes, to hide inside himself, but it was too late. Someone, walking by in the night, stood over him.

"Well," said the voice quietly, "here's a soldier crying *before* the fight. Good. Get it over. Won't be time once it all starts."

And the voice was about to move on when the boy, startled, touched the drum at his elbow. The man above, hearing this, stopped. The boy could feel his eyes, sense him slowly bending near. A hand must have come down out of the night, for there was a little rat-tat as the fingernails brushed and the man's breath fanned his face.

"Why, it's the drummer boy, isn't it?"

The boy nodded, not knowing if his nod was seen. "Sir, is that *you?*" he said.

"I assume it is." The man's knees cracked as he bent still closer.

He smelled as all fathers should smell, of salt sweat, ginger tobacco, horse and boot leather, and the earth he walked upon. He had many eyes. No, not eyes, brass buttons that watched the boy. **E**

He could only be, and was, the General.

"What's your name, boy?" he asked.

"Joby," whispered the boy, starting to sit up.

"All right, Joby, don't stir." A hand pressed his chest gently, and the boy relaxed. "How long you been with us, Joby?"

"Three weeks, sir."

"Run off from home or joined **legitimately,** boy?"

Silence.

"Damn-fool question," said the General. "Do you shave yet, boy? Even more of a damn-fool. There's your cheek, fell right off the tree overhead. And the others here not much older. Raw, raw, damn raw, the lot of you. You ready for tomorrow or the next day, Joby?"

"I think so, sir."

"You want to cry some more, go on ahead. I did the same last night."

"*You,* sir?"

"God's truth. Thinking of everything ahead. Both sides figuring the other side will just give up, and soon, and the war done in weeks, and us all home. Well, that's not how it's going to be. And maybe that's why I cried."

C MONITOR
Reread lines 34–42. Do you understand what the man-boys' shields represent? If not, reread this paragraph slowly and refer to the footnotes.

D MAKE INFERENCES
What feelings is the boy experiencing? Include them in your chart, along with the clues that help you infer the feelings.

E SETTING
Reread lines 62–64. What do the **descriptive details** about the General suggest about how men lived in the 1800s?

legitimately
(lə-jĭt'ə-mĭt-lē) *adv.* lawfully

READING STRATEGY: *Review*

C MONITOR

After rereading the paragraph, students should understand that the shields the drummer boy refers to are not real. Their shields are their devotion to their families, their patriotism, their confidence in their immortality, and the strength from knowing that they have guns to protect themselves. These shields give them courage. The drummer boy does not have a gun and feels as though his family is very far away, so he does not feel brave.

READING STRATEGY

D MAKE INFERENCES

Have students record their answers in the chart from page 317. ***Possible answer:***

- ***Details from the Story:*** *The drummer boy feels "his family move yet farther off away in the dark." He calls his drum "worse than a toy," and he hopes that in the morning the other soldiers may leave without him.*
- ***What I Know from Experience:*** *It would be very frightening to go into battle, especially without a gun.*
- ***Inference:*** *The boy feels frightened, resentful, and vulnerable.*

LITERARY ANALYSIS

E SETTING

Possible answer: *The General rides a horse and wears leather boots, both indicators of the time period.*

FOR LESS–PROFICIENT READERS

Reading Strategy Follow-Up: Make Inferences [paired option] Write these details from the story on the board:

- The General checks on his troops at night.
- The General stops to talk to the boy.
- The General tells the drummer boy that he cried the night before.

Have pairs of students use the chart begun on page 317 to make inferences about the General's character.

FOR ENGLISH LEARNERS

Vocabulary Support [mixed-readiness groups] Assign small groups one or two of these military terms to look up in a dictionary. Have students share their definitions.

- *gunpowder* (line 37)
- *ramrod* (line 38)
- *minnieball* (line 38)
- *flint* (line 38)
- *massacre* (line 97)
- *cavalry* (line 126)

SOCIAL STUDIES CONNECTION

The Battle of Shiloh was one of the first major conflicts of the Civil War. Union troops advanced into Tennessee and were heading for the Memphis and Charleston Railroad to disable it. On the way, they camped at Shiloh, expecting to take the offensive. However, the Confederate troops launched a surprise attack that lasted for two days and resulted in over 20,000 casualties, most of them young and inexperienced soldiers. Ultimately, it was a Confederate failure, although both sides took time to recover from their losses.

LITERARY ANALYSIS

F SETTING

Possible answer:

- *There are about 100,000 soldiers gathered from both sides.*
- *The men are inexperienced and need training, but there is no time to prepare them before the battle.*
- *Both sides believe they are right.*
- *Casualties will be numerous.*

Extend the Discussion What attitude about the war is conveyed through the General's speech?

Lines 87–116

DISCUSSION PROMPTS

Use these prompts to help students understand the General's purpose:

Recall Why does the General need Joby? ***Answer:*** *The General needs Joby to help him unite the troops.*

Analyze Why does the General call the drummer boy "the heart of the army"? ***Possible answer:*** *The drummer boy sets the pace for battle in the same way that the heart paces the body.*

Synthesize Based on your prior knowledge, why do you think the General stops to talk to Joby? ***Possible answer:*** *He wants to comfort him and give him courage to face the battle ahead.*

"Yes, sir," said Joby.

The General must have taken out a cigar now, for the dark was suddenly filled with the Indian smell of tobacco unlit as yet, but chewed as the man thought what next to say.

"It's going to be a crazy time," said the General. "Counting both sides, there's a hundred thousand men, give or take a few thousand out there tonight, not one as can spit a sparrow off a tree, or knows a horse clod from a minnieball. Stand up, bare the breast, ask to be a target, thank them and sit down, that's us, that's them. We should turn tail and train four months, they should do the same. But here we are, taken with spring fever and thinking it blood lust, taking our sulphur with cannons instead of with molasses[7] as it should be, going to be a hero, going to live forever. And I can see all of them over there nodding agreement, save the other way around. It's wrong, boy, it's wrong as a head put on hind side front and a man marching backward through life. It will be a double massacre if one of their itchy generals decides to picnic his lads on our grass. More innocents will get shot out of pure Cherokee enthusiasm than ever got shot before. Owl Creek was full of boys splashing around in the noonday sun just a few hours ago. I fear it will be full of boys again, just floating, at sundown tomorrow, not caring where the tide takes them." **F**

The General stopped and made a little pile of winter leaves and twigs in the darkness, as if he might at any moment strike fire to them to see his way through the coming days when the sun might not show its face because of what was happening here and just beyond.

The boy watched the hand stirring the leaves and opened his lips to say something, but did not say it. The General heard the boy's breath and spoke himself.

"Why am I telling you this? That's what you wanted to ask, eh? Well, when you got a bunch of wild horses on a loose rein somewhere, somehow you got to bring order, rein them in. These lads, fresh out of the milkshed, don't know what I know, and I can't tell them: men actually die, in war. So each is his own army. I got to make *one* army of them. And for that, boy, I need you."

"Me!" The boy's lips barely twitched.

"Now, boy," said the General quietly, "you are the heart of the army. Think of that. You're the heart of the army. Listen, now."

And, lying there, Joby listened.

And the General spoke on.

If he, Joby, beat slow tomorrow, the heart would beat slow in the men. They would lag by the wayside.[8] They would drowse in the fields on their muskets.[9] They would sleep forever, after that, in those same fields, their hearts slowed by a drummer boy and stopped by enemy lead.

7. **taking our sulphur with cannons instead of with molasses:** sulphur was an ingredient in gunpowder that was used to fire cannons; at that time sulphur was also used as a tonic or medical treatment. Molasses is a thick, brown syrup, used to mask the unpleasant taste of medicines.
8. **lag by the wayside:** fall behind.
9. **musket:** shoulder gun with a long barrel.

SOCIAL STUDIES CONNECTION

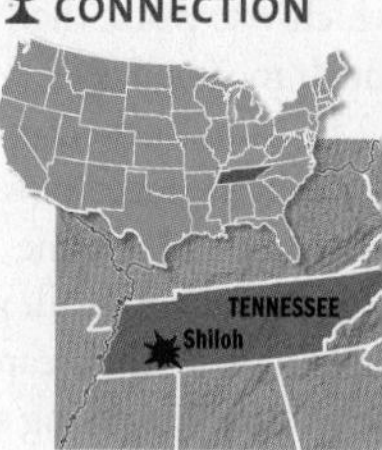

The Battle of Shiloh tc
place near Shiloh Chu
on the banks of Owl C

F SETTING
What do you learn ab
the Civil War from the
General's **dialogue?**

DIFFERENTIATED INSTRUCTION

FOR LESS–PROFICIENT READERS

Concept Support Display a Cluster Diagram. Have small groups work together to contribute details to the chart that reveal the historical setting.

 **BEST PRACTICES TOOLKIT—Transparency**
Cluster Diagram p. B18

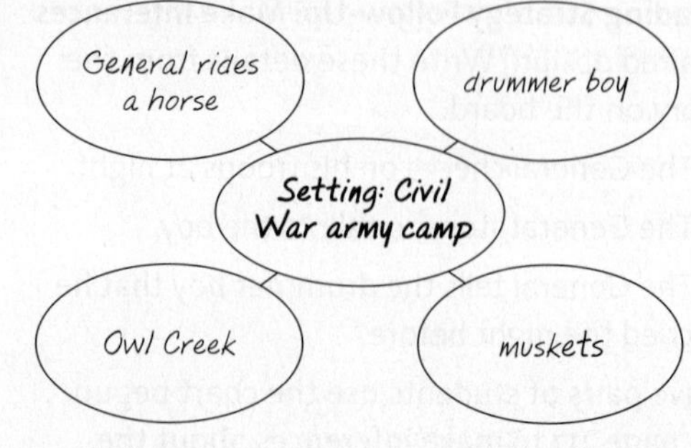

But if he beat a sure, steady, ever faster rhythm, then, then their knees vould come up in a long line down over that hill, one knee after the other, like wave on the ocean shore! Had he seen the ocean ever? Seen the waves rolling n like a well-ordered cavalry charge to the sand? Well, that was it, that's what e wanted, that's what was needed! Joby was his right hand and his left. He ave the orders, but Joby set the pace!

So bring the right knee up and the right foot out and the left knee up and he left foot out. One following the other in good time, in brisk time. Move he blood up the body and make the head proud and the spine stiff and the aw **resolute.** Focus the eye and set the teeth, flare the nostrils and tighten the ands, put steel armor all over the men, for blood moving fast in them does ndeed make men feel as if they'd put on steel. He must keep at it, at it! Long nd steady, steady and long! Then, even though shot or torn, those wounds got n hot blood—in blood he'd helped stir—would feel less pain. If their blood vas cold, it would be more than slaughter, it would be murderous nightmare nd pain best not told and no one to guess. **G**

The General spoke and stopped, letting his breath slack off. Then, after a noment, he said, "So there you are, that's it. Will you do that, boy? Do you now now you're general of the army when the General's left behind?"

The boy nodded mutely.

"You'll run them through for me then, boy?"

"Yes, sir."

"Good. And, God willing, many nights from tonight, many years from iow, when you're as old or far much older than me, when they ask you what ou did in this awful time, you will tell them—one part humble and one part oroud—'I was the drummer boy at the battle of Owl Creek,' or the Tennessee River, or maybe they'll just name it after the church there. 'I was the drummer oy at Shiloh.' Good grief, that has a beat and sound to it fitting for Mr. Longfellow.[10] 'I was the drummer boy at Shiloh.' Who will ever hear those vords and not know you, boy, or what you thought this night, or what you'll hink tomorrow or the next day when we must get up on our legs and *move!*"

The general stood up. "Well, then. God bless you, boy. Good night."

"Good night, sir." **H**

And, tobacco, brass, boot polish, salt sweat and leather, the man moved way through the grass.

Joby lay for a moment, staring but unable to see where the man had gone. He swallowed. He wiped his eyes. He cleared his throat. He settled himself. Then, at last, very slowly and firmly, he turned the drum so that it faced up oward the sky.

He lay next to it, his arm around it, feeling the tremor, the touch, the **muted** hunder as, all the rest of the April night in the year 1862, near the Tennessee River, not far from the Owl Creek, very close to the church named Shiloh, he peach blossoms fell on the drum.

③ Targeted Passage

resolute (rĕz'ə-lo͞ot') *adj.* firm or determined

G MONITOR
Reread lines 119–138. To make sure you understand it, **summarize** the General's advice to Joby.

H MAKE INFERENCES
What can you tell about Joby's feelings toward the General from the way he speaks and listens to him throughout the story?

muted (myo͞o'tĭd) *adj.* muffled; softened

10. **Longfellow:** Henry Wadsworth Longfellow (1807–1882), popular American author of "Paul Revere's Ride" and *The Song of Hiawatha.*

READING STRATEGY: *Review*

G MONITOR

Possible answer: *The General tells Joby to beat a "sure, steady, ever faster rhythm" that will keep the men marching as if they are waves rolling onto the sand. He says that if Joby's drumming is brisk, it will give the soldiers courage, stir their blood, and make their wounds less painful.*

READING STRATEGY

H MAKE INFERENCES

Remind students to record their answers in the chart from page 317. ***Possible answer:***

- ***Details from the Story:*** *Joby listens to him respectfully, and he promises to do his best to support the General in battle.*
- ***What I Know from Experience:*** *In a tough situation, I would admire and respect a man who gives comfort and advice.*
- ***Inference:*** *Joby respects and admires the General and sees him as a father figure.*

Lines 158–165

REINFORCE *KEY IDEA:* CONTRIBUTION

Discuss What does Joby do that shows the General has convinced him that his **contribution** to the army is important? ***Possible answer:*** *Joby turns his drum face up. He also places his arm around the drum.*

SELECTION WRAP-UP

REFLECT Ask students whether they think the General really relies on Joby as much as he says, or if he is merely trying to make him feel needed.

★ CRITIQUE Ask students to evaluate whether the author conveys Joby's feelings clearly. Have students cite evidence to support their opinions.

READING FLUENCY

Distribute the copy masters and have students practice fluency.

RESOURCE MANAGER—Copy Master
Reading Fluency p. 37

FOR LESS-PROFICIENT READERS

③ Targeted Passage [Lines 123–161]

This passage presents the resolution of the drummer boy's conflict.

- What does the General tell Joby he must do during battle? Why?
- Why does the General say that Joby is the general when he is not there?
- What feeling does Joby experience after the General leaves him?

Comprehension Support Distribute copies of the Cause-and-Effect Diagram (Multiple Effects). Direct students to reread lines 123–138, in which the General outlines the effects of the drummer boy's work. Fill in the cause and the first effect together (*cause: the drummer boy beats steadily; effect: the cavalry moves like waves*). Have students complete and compare their charts.

BEST PRACTICES TOOLKIT—Transparency
Cause-and-Effect Diagram pp. B16, B38

Practice and Apply

After Reading

For additional support of postreading questions, use these copy masters:

RESOURCE MANAGER—Copy Masters
Reading Check p. 34 (to check understanding of the selection)
Setting p. 27 (for practice of literary analysis standards focus)
Question Support p. 35 (After Reading questions adapted for English learners and less-proficient readers)

Additional selection questions are provided for teachers on page 21.

For additional activities to challenge students, see

Power Thinking at **ClassZone.com**

ANSWERS

Comprehension

1. *The men whisper that they will survive the battle.*
2. *He hears Joby touch the drum and realizes that it is the drummer boy who is crying.*
3. *The General tells Joby that he needs him to make an army out of the individual men.*

Literary Analysis

Possible answers:

4. ■ **STANDARDS FOCUS Make Inferences** *The General calms Joby and fills him with a quiet confidence and sense of purpose.*
5. ● **STANDARDS FOCUS Setting** *Students' responses should include descriptive details such as "army was strewn helter-skelter" (line 17) and "the army here, the army there, whispering to itself in the dark" (lines 21–22). The General's speech includes references to events such as the boys splashing in Owl Creek.*
6. *At the beginning of the story, the peach pit falling on the drum scares him because it sounds like gunfire. But at the end of the story, after the General's words of encouragement, Joby turns the drum up to the sky because he is no longer scared and because the drum helps him feel that he is an important part of the army.*

After Reading

Comprehension

1. **Recall** At the beginning of the story, what does Joby guess that the men were whispering about?
2. **Clarify** What causes the General to stop and talk with Joby rather than continue walking?
3. **Clarify** According to the General, why was he telling Joby his thoughts about the war?

Literary Analysis

4. **Make Inferences About Characters** Review the chart in which you made inferences about Joby's feelings. Mark the entries that show how Joby felt after the General talked to him. How did the General affect Joby?
5. **Examine Setting** What details of setting help you understand what it was like the night before this Civil War battle? Take notes in a chart like the one shown.

Descriptive Details	*References to Events*
blossoms falling	

6. **Interpret an Event** Reread lines 1–8. Then reread lines 159–161. At the story's end, what does it mean that Joby turns the drum up toward the sky?
7. **Evaluate Historical Fiction** The information about the Civil War that is found in the story can also be found in numerous works of nonfiction. Tell whether you think Bradbury's use of **historical fiction** is an effective way to learn about the kinds of people who fought in the Civil War. Support your opinion with examples from the story.

Extension and Challenge

8. **Big Question Activity** There was no clear winner in the Battle of Shiloh, and nearly 24,000 lives were lost. Given this outcome, do you think the General still would have told Joby that his **contribution** mattered? Discuss your answer in a small group.
9. **SOCIAL STUDIES CONNECTION** Conduct some research about Johnny Clem, a real drummer boy at the Battle of Shiloh, or about another hero or battle of the American Civil War. Share your findings with your classmates.

RESEARCH LINKS
For more about Johnny Clem, visit the **Research Center** at **ClassZone.com.**

7. *Most students will agree that the short story has brought the battle to life and has taught lessons about human relationships in a way that nonfiction texts often do not. Examples will vary but should demonstrate the development of the characters in the story and will probably include dialogue between the General and Joby.*

Extension and Challenge

8. *Students may say that the General knows that the outcome will not be good, but he believes that Joby will play an important role in the way that soldiers face their fate—whether they suffer slowly or die with their blood moving so fast that they feel no pain.*
9. **SOCIAL STUDIES CONNECTION** *Students may choose to do their reports on figures such as Robert E. Lee, Ulysses Grant, or a drummer boy, such as Robert Henry Hendershot.*

:abulary in Context

ABULARY PRACTICE

›r each item, choose the word that differs most in meaning from e other words.

1. (a) legally, (b) legitimately, (c) lawfully, (d) illegally
2. (a) askew, (b) tidy, (c) crooked, (d) awry
3. (a) softened, (b) muted, (c) harsh, (d) indistinct
4. (a) scatter, (b) arrange, (c) jumble, (d) strew
5. (a) bright, (b) heavy, (c) solemn, (d) glum
6. (a) paralyzed, (b) strong, (c) persistent, (d) resolute

askew
legitimately
muted
resolute
solemn
strew

ABULARY IN WRITING

you were the drummer boy, how would you describe the soldiers' camp? rite a one-paragraph journal entry using two or more vocabulary words. ere is a sample beginning.

EXAMPLE SENTENCE

*The General is **solemn** yet kind.*

ABULARY STRATEGY: IDIOMS

n idiom is an expression in which the meaning of the entire phrase is different rom the meaning of the individual words in it. For example, in the story, the eneral says that the marching soldiers would "lag by the wayside" if Joby beat is drum too slowly. The General meant that the soldiers would fall behind. oday we use the phrase "fall by the wayside" to mean the same thing.

You won't be familiar with every idiom you encounter. To figure out the neaning of an idiom you don't understand, use context clues. Also, idioms ppear in some dictionaries. Try looking up the first word of the phrase.

RACTICE Using context clues from the sentences, decide what each diom means.

1. My old computer finally **bit the dust;** it had been working poorly for weeks.
2. Amanda wanted to continue arguing with her sister, but she decided to **leave well enough alone.**
3. I've always been a good dancer, so learning the routine was **a piece of cake.**
4. After signing up for four after-school activities, Max realized that he had **bitten off more than he could chew.**
5. I'm bringing my umbrella, because it's **raining cats and dogs** out there.
6. Maria **let the cat out of the bag** and told Lamar about the surprise party.

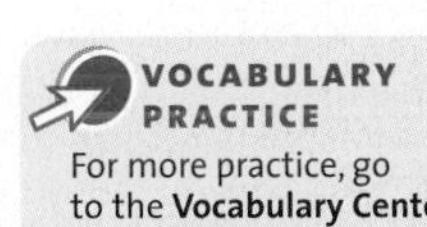

VOCABULARY PRACTICE
For more practice, go to the **Vocabulary Center** at **ClassZone.com.**

ANSWERS

Vocabulary in Context

VOCABULARY PRACTICE

1. *(d) illegally*
2. *(b) tidy*
3. *(c) harsh*
4. *(b) arrange*
5. *(a) bright*
6. *(a) paralyzed*

RESOURCE MANAGER—Copy Master
Vocabulary Practice p. 32

VOCABULARY IN WRITING

Have students reread lines 1–32 and use a web diagram to record sensory details. Tell students to choose vocabulary words that help them express these details in their paragraphs.

VOCABULARY STRATEGY: IDIOMS *(also an EL language objective)*

Have students look up one of the idioms in a dictionary, checking under the major word in the phrase. For example, *let the cat out of the bag* appears under *cat*. Explain that idiom definitions are often found near the end of the dictionary entry.

Possible answers:

1. *stopped working*
2. *give up trying to change something*
3. *easy*
4. *taken on more than is manageable*
5. *raining very hard*
6. *gave away a secret*

RESOURCE MANAGER—Copy Master
Vocabulary Strategy p. 33

Vocabulary Center at **ClassZone.com**
Additional Vocabulary Activities

DIFFERENTIATED INSTRUCTION

FOR ENGLISH LEARNERS

Vocabulary Practice Remind students that words may have more than one meaning. For example, *harsh* can mean "stern" or "severe," but it can also mean "disagreeably loud or vivid." Help students work together to find the multiple meanings of these words and others: *crooked, softened, arrange, bright, heavy*. Discuss which meaning is intended in the grouping in which the word is found.

FOR ADVANCED LEARNERS/PRE-AP

Vocabulary Strategy [small-group option] Have students work together to brainstorm commonly used idioms. Ask them to list as many as they can. Then have them create an illustrated dictionary of idioms.

Assess and Reteach

Assess

RESOURCE MANAGER—Copy Masters
Selection Tests A, B/C pp. 39–40, 41–42

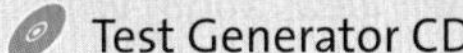

Test Generator CD

Reteach

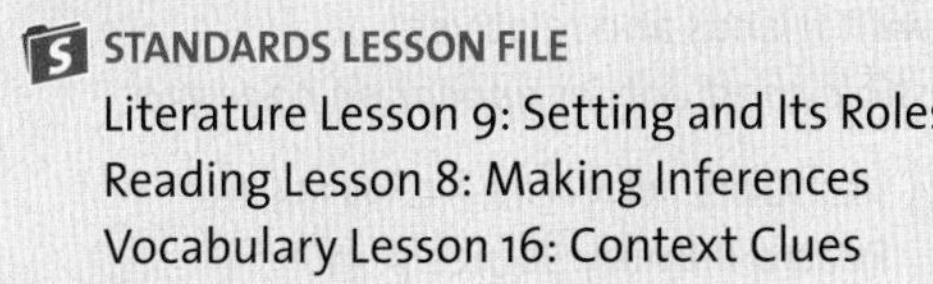

STANDARDS LESSON FILE
Literature Lesson 9: Setting and Its Roles
Reading Lesson 8: Making Inferences
Vocabulary Lesson 16: Context Clues

Focus and Motivate

OBJECTIVES

Reading for Information

- read and analyze a **primary source**
- draw a conclusion
- read journal entries

SUMMARY

In her journal, Louisa May Alcott describes serving as a nurse during the Civil War. At a military hospital near Washington, D.C., she finds purpose and satisfaction in caring for the sick, wounded, and dying soldiers.

What's the Connection?

Write these statements on the Anticipation Guide transparency. Have students respond to each one before and after reading.

- The role of a Civil War nurse was to comfort the wounded and dying.
- Military hospitals during the Civil War were clean and smooth-running places.
- Women did not feel the excitement of the war in the same way that men did.

BEST PRACTICES TOOLKIT—Transparency
Anticipation Guide p. A14

Teach

Skill Focus: Read a Primary Source

Point out that a journal is a **primary source** and provides a window into one particular life and personality as well as a specific time and place in history. Then

- Discuss factors that could shape or limit what information is recorded in a journal, such as the writer's location, age, education, social class, or job.
- Ask students what they might learn from a journal kept by each of the following during the Civil War: a soldier, a teenage girl, a senator, a nurse. Record their responses in a four-column chart on the board.
- Have students share their ideas about why some people in the mid-1800s kept journals. Note that journals were often shared with friends and relatives.

Possible chart entries appear on page 330.

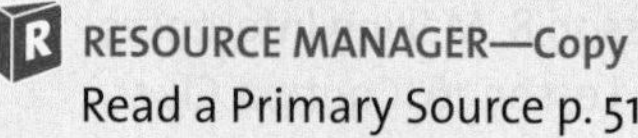
RESOURCE MANAGER—Copy Master
Read a Primary Source p. 51

Reading for Information

Civil War Journal

Journal

Use with *The Drummer Boy of Shiloh*, page 318.

What's the Connection?

Historical fiction such as "The Drummer Boy of Shiloh" can give you an idea about what it was like during the Civil War, but reading about the time period from someone who was actually there can be even more revealing. Louisa May Alcott, who wrote the famous novel *Little Women*, kept a journal during the war years.

Skill Focus: Read a Primary Source

One of the best ways to learn about past events is through **primary sources,** materials that were written or made by people who took part in the events. Journals, photographs, and even personal letters are all examples of primary sources. When you study them, you get direct knowledge, rather than someone else's interpretation, of people, places, and events.

When gathering information from a primary source, it's important to consider what the source is and how its form might limit or affect what it conveys. For example, a business letter is not likely to contain colorful details or gossip. You should also think about other factors that would have shaped the source's contents, such as when and where it was created, for whom, and the creator's position in society.

As you read Alcott's journal entries, keep these considerations in mind. Also note what her journal entries tell you about life during the Civil War. Completing a chart such as the one started here can help.

What is the form and purpose of this text?	*The text is a journal. It was most likely written to reflect on experiences.*
Who was its author? What do you know about her?	*Louisa May Alcott; she was the author of Little Women and other novels.*
When and where was it written?	
What do you already know about life at that time and place?	
Who was its intended audience?	
What does this document reveal about life at the time it was written?	

Selection Resources

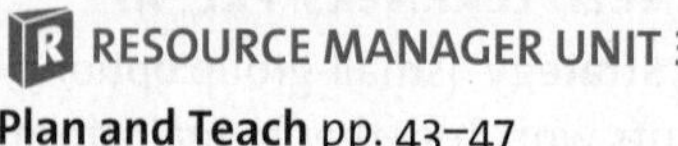
RESOURCE MANAGER UNIT 3

Plan and Teach pp. 43–47

Reading

Summary pp. 49†*, 50‡*
Read a Primary Source pp. 51, 53†*
Reading Check p. 55
Draw a Conclusion pp. 52, 54†*
Question Support p. 56*

Assessment

Selection Tests A, B/C pp. 57*, 59*
Test Generator CD

Reading Support

Audio Anthology CD*

BEST PRACTICES TOOLKIT

Anticipation Guide • Round Robin • Y Chart • Using a Dictionary or Thesaurus Effectively

* Resources for Differentiation † Also in Spanish ‡ In Haitian Creole and Vietnamese

Civil War Journal

Portrait of the author

Louisa May Alcott

FOCUS ON FORM A **journal** is a personal record of thoughts, activities, observations, and feelings. It usually consists of separate, dated entries that appear in chronological order.

861 **A**

pril.—War declared with the South, and our Concord company went to Vashington. A busy time getting them ready, and a sad day seeing them off; for a little town like this we all seem like one family in times like these. At the ation the scene was very dramatic, as the brave boys went away perhaps never come back again.

I've often longed to see a war, and now I have my wish. I long to be a man; but s I can't fight, I will content myself with working for those who can. . . .

A JOURNAL **Preview** the journal entries' headings. In what years were they written?

862 **B**

eptember, October.—War news bad. Anxious faces, beating hearts, and busy ninds.

I like the stir in the air, and long for battle like a warhorse when he smells owder. The blood of the Mays is up!

Jovember.—Thirty years old. Decided to go to Washington as a nurse if I could nd a place. Help needed, and I love nursing, and *must* let out my pent-up nergy in some new way. Winter is always a hard and a dull time, and if I am way there is one less to feed and warm and worry over.

B READ A PRIMARY SOURCE What do you already know about the times in which these entries were written? Add this information to your chart.

DIFFERENTIATED INSTRUCTION

FOR LESS–PROFICIENT READERS

Concept Support Clarify the terms *entry* and *chronological* in the **Focus on Form** note. Then identify the entry for April 1861, noting that both the month and the year are given. Point out that an entry may be just a few lines or several paragraphs. Then ask:

- How many entries are shown in the text for 1862? *(three)*
- In the December 1862 entry, what specific days did Alcott write about in her journal? *(December 11 and 12)*

FOR ENGLISH LEARNERS

Options for Reading After discussing the structure of the journal, have students listen to the *Audio Anthology CD* as they read the selection. If students have trouble with the visually dense text, suggest that they use a 3" x 5" card as a guide when reading. Demonstrate how to align the long edge of the card under the first line of text and move it down the page smoothly, line by line, while reading and listening.

Practice and Apply

FOCUS ON FORM

Journal Discuss with students the purpose and characteristics of a journal. A journal is a primary source that

- records an individual's thoughts and feelings about events in his or her own life
- may include several entries for a single day, one entry daily, or less frequent entries
- is generally handwritten
- often contains details about daily life
- may shed light on historical events

Ask students if they have ever kept a journal. Invite those who have to explain what they gained from the experience.

LITERARY ANALYSIS

A JOURNAL

Answers: *The entries were written between 1861 and 1863.*

INFORMATIONAL ANALYSIS

B READ A PRIMARY SOURCE

Most students will know, or be able to infer, that the Civil War was going on during these years. Students' prior knowledge may include names of major battles, names of political and military leaders, details about flags and military uniforms used by the Union and the Confederacy, types of weapons used, and causes of the war including disagreement about slavery.

If students need help . . . Prompt them to recall what they know by presenting different categories of information. On the board, create a three-column chart with the main heading *Civil War* and the subheadings *War, Politics, and Daily Life.* Then use a Round Robin exercise to elicit what students already know in each area. As needed, suggest narrower categories to encourage students' recall.

 **BEST PRACTICES TOOLKIT—Transparency** Round Robin p. A17

INFORMATIONAL ANALYSIS

C VIEW A PRIMARY SOURCE

Possible answer:

- *Many patients were housed in one big room.*
- *There was not much specialized medical equipment.*
- *Some patients used wheelchairs.*
- *Lighting was supplied by windows and a few gas lamps.*

Extend the Discussion In comparison, what are hospitals like today?

INFORMATIONAL ANALYSIS

D READ A PRIMARY SOURCE

Possible answer: *Alcott spends the day taking care of necessary tasks: having a tooth filled; buying a veil; getting her clothes, pass, money, and parcels together. Her activities suggest that she is a practical person of few needs who cares mostly about being prepared to do the job before her. She is not frivolous or vain.*

I want new experiences, and am sure to get 'em if I go. So I've sent in name, and bide my time writing tales, to leave all snug behind me, and men up my old clothes,—for nurses don't need nice things, thank Heaven!

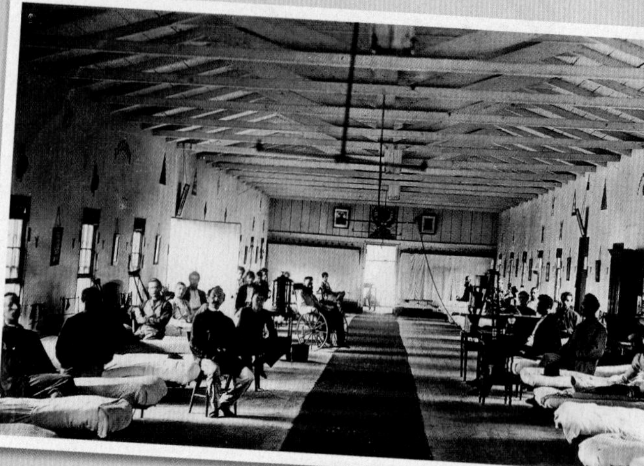

Patients in a military hospital, 1865 C

C VIEW A PRIMARY SOURCE
What do you learn about Civil War hospitals from this photograph?

December.—On the 11th I received a note from Miss H[annah] M. Stever telling me to start for Georgetown next day to fill a place in the Union H Hospital. Mrs. Ropes of Boston was matron, and Miss Kendall of Plymouth a nurse there, and though a hard place, help was needed. I was ready, and w my commander said "March!" I marched. Packed my trunk, and reporte B[oston] that same evening.

We had all been full of courage till the last moment came; then we all b down. I realized that I had taken my life in my hand, and might never see t all again. I said, "Shall I stay, Mother?" as I hugged her close. "No, go! and Lord be with you!" answered the Spartan woman; and till I turned the corner bravely smiled and waved her wet handkerchief on the doorstep. Shall I ever that dear old face again?

So I set forth in the December twilight, with May and Julian Hawthorn escort, feeling as if I was the son of the house going to war.

Friday, the 12th, was a very memorable day, spent in running all over Bos to get my pass, etc., calling for parcels, getting a tooth filled, and buying a vei my only purchase. A. C. gave me some old clothes, the dear Sewalls money myself and boys, lots of love and help; and at 5 P.M., saying "good-by" to a gr of tearful faces at the station, I started on my long journey, full of hope sorrow, courage and plans. D

D READ A PRIMARY SOURCE
Reread lines 33–38. How does Alcott spend her last day in Boston? What do her activities suggest about her needs and values?

DIFFERENTIATED INSTRUCTION

FOR ENGLISH LEARNERS

Language: Punctuation and Print Cues Point out that Alcott frequently uses an ampersand (&) in place of the word *and.* Then discuss the use of ellipses to show that parts of the journal have been omitted. Explain that the omitted text may be of any length, from a sentence to several pages. Tell students that when they see ellipses, they might notice a change in the writer's topic or train of thought because the next part of the text comes from a point further ahead in the journal.

FOR ADVANCED LEARNERS/PRE–AP

Compare Primary Sources Ask students why the photograph's date might explain the neatness and cleanliness of the hospital and the relative health and alertness of the patients. *(The photo was taken near or after the end of the Civil War in 1865.)* Then ask students to compare and contrast the scene shown in the photograph with Alcott's journal description of a hospital ward in 1863 (lines 76–100).

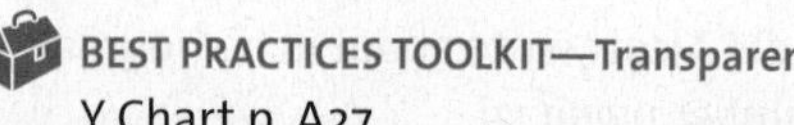

BEST PRACTICES TOOLKIT—Transparency
Y Chart p. A27

A most interesting journey into a new world full of stirring sights and sounds, ew adventures, and an evergrowing sense of the great task I had undertaken.

I said my prayers as I went rushing through the country white with tents, all ive with patriotism, and already red with blood.

A solemn time, but I'm glad to live in it; and am sure it will do me good hether I come out alive or dead.

All went well, and I got to Georgetown one evening very tired. Was kindly elcomed, slept in my narrow bed with two other roommates, and on the morrow egan my new life by seeing a poor man die at dawn, and sitting all day between boy with pneumonia and a man shot through the lungs. A strange day, but I did y best; and when I put mother's little black shawl round the boy while he sat up anting for breath, he smiled and said, "You are real motherly, ma'am." I felt as I was getting on. The man only lay and stared with his big black eyes, and made e very nervous. But all were well behaved; and I sat looking at the twenty strong ces as they looked back at me,—hoping that I looked "motherly" to them; for y thirty years made me feel old, and the suffering round me made me long to omfort every one. . . . E

863

nuary.—I never began the year in a stranger place than this; five hundred miles om home, alone among strangers, doing painful duties all day long, & leading a fe of constant excitement in this greathouse surrounded by 3 or 4 hundred men all stages of suffering, disease & death. Though often home sick, heart sick & orn out, I like it—find real pleasure in comforting tending & cheering these poor ouls who seem to love me, to feel my sympathy though unspoken, & acknowledge y hearty good will in spite of the ignorance, awkwardness, & bashfulness which cannot help showing in so new & trying a situation. The men are docile, respectful, affectionate, with but few exceptions; truly lovable & manly many of them. John uhre a Virginia blacksmith is the prince of patients, & though what we call a ommon man, in education & condition, to me is all that I could expect or ask om the first gentleman in the land. Under his plain speech & unpolished manner seem to see a noble character, a heart as warm & tender as a woman's, a nature esh & frank as any child's. He is about thirty, I think, tall & handsome, mortally ounded & dying royally, without reproach, repining, or remorse. Mrs. Ropes & yself love him & feel indignant that such a man should be so early lost, for hough he might never distinguish himself before the world, his influence & xample cannot be without effect, for real goodness is never wasted.

Mon 4th—I shall record the events of a day as a sample of the days I pend—

Up at six, dress by gas light, run through my ward & fling up the windows hough the men grumble & shiver; but the air is bad enough to breed a pestilence as no notice is taken of our frequent appeals for better ventilation I must do what can. Poke up the fire, add blankets, joke, coax, & command; but continue to pen doors & windows as if life depended on it; mine does, & doubtless many

E JOURNAL
Reread lines 45–55. How does Alcott spend her first day as a nurse? What does she hope and feel?

LITERARY ANALYSIS

E JOURNAL

Answer: *Alcott spends her first day as a nurse watching a man die and nursing a boy with pneumonia and a man shot through the lungs. She hopes that she looks motherly to the men because she wants to be a comfort to them.*

Lines 56–73
DISCUSSION PROMPTS

Use these prompts to help students understand Alcott's early experiences as a Civil War hospital nurse:

Connect How have you felt upon finding yourself in a strange or faraway place? *Students may say they felt excited, ill at ease, confused, curious, or homesick.*

Analyze Alcott's duties are painful, but she finds pleasure in her work as a nurse. What makes her work rewarding? ***Possible answer:*** *She takes pleasure in tending to and cheering up the suffering men and in their affection and acknowledgment of her sympathy and good will.*

Evaluate Do you agree with Alcott that "real goodness is never wasted"? Explain. *Students may say that good people can be an inspiration and comfort to others, no matter how many people they know or how long they live.*

FOR ENGLISH LEARNERS

Vocabulary Support [paired option] Have pairs use context clues to figure out the meanings of these words. Then have them use a dictionary to confirm their guesses.

- *bashfulness* (line 62), "shyness"
- *indignant* (line 71), "angry about something unjust"
- *coax* (line 79), "persuade by pleading"

BEST PRACTICES TOOLKIT
Using a Dictionary or Thesaurus Effectively p. E2

Culture: Clarify Explain that some words used in the journal were common in the mid-1800s but are seldom used today. Share these terms and definitions with students:

- *the morrow* (line 46), "the next day"
- *blacksmith* (line 65), "craftsperson who shapes iron"
- *repining* (line 70), "complaining"
- *gas light* (line 76), "lamp that burns a liquid fuel"
- *pestilence* (line 77), "epidemic disease"

INFORMATIONAL ANALYSIS

F READ A PRIMARY SOURCE

Possible answer:

- ***Hospital conditions:*** *gas lights; bad ventilation; fire for warmth; usually cold, damp, dirty, smelly, chaotic; no proper leadership; good, bad, and indifferent nurses; gruff doctors*
- ***Nurses' routine activities:*** *wake at 6:00 A.M. and dress; open windows and doors, stir fire, rouse men, hand out blankets; breakfast with doctors and nurses of "fried beef, salt butter, husky bread & washy coffee" (lines 86–87); spend morning handing out rations, cutting up food for boys, washing faces, dressing wounds, taking doctor's orders, cleaning, tidying, teaching attendants to make beds and sweep floors, sewing bandages, and fetching pillows, books, and sponges; at noon, help boys eat dinner and then help them write letters; at 5:00 P.M., rush around serving dinner and then give last doses of medication; at 9:00 P.M., day nurses go to bed and night nurses go on duty.*

Skill Focus: Read a Primary Source

Possible answers for the chart on page 326:

When and where was it written?	1861–1863; in Concord, Massachusetts, and Georgetown, D.C.
What do you already know about life at that time and place?	Many soldiers were wounded or killed in battle; people lived without electricity; Lincoln was president; slavery was legal.
Who was its intended audience?	Alcott herself; possibly her family and friends
What does this document reveal about life at the time it was written?	Details about daily life in a military hospital; why one woman became a nurse and how she felt about the experience

another, for a more perfect pestilence-box than this house I never saw—cold, da dirty, full of vile odors from wounds, kitchens, wash rooms, & stables. No compe head, male or female, to right matters, & a jumble of good, bad, & indiffe nurses, surgeons & attendants to complicate the Chaos still more.

After this unwelcome progress through my stifling ward I go to breakfast w what appetite I may; find the inevitable fried beef, salt butter, husky brea washy coffee; listen to the clack of eight women & a dozen men; the first s stupid or possessed of but one idea, the last absorbed in their breakfas themselves to a degree that is both ludicrous and provoking, for all the dishes ordered down the table *full* & returned *empty;* the conversation is entirely am themselves & each announces his opinion with an air of importance frequently causes me to choke in my cup or bolt my meals with undigni speed lest a laugh betray to these pompous beings that a "child's among th takin notes." Till noon I trot, trot, giving out rations, cutting up food for help "boys," washing faces, teaching my attendants how beds are made or floors sw dressing wounds, taking Dr. Fitz Patrick's orders, (privately wishing all the t that he would be more gentle with my big babies,) dusting tables, sew bandages, keeping my tray tidy, rushing up & down after pillows, bed lin sponges, books & directions, till it seems as if I would joyfully pay down a possess for fifteen minutes rest.

At twelve the big bell rings & up comes dinner for the boys who are alw ready for it & never entirely satisfied. Soup, meat, potatoes & bread is the bi fare. Charley Thayer the attendant travels up & down the room serving out rations, saving little for himself yet always thoughtful of his mates & patient woman with their helplessness. When dinner is over some sleep, many read others want letters written. This I like to do for they put in such odd thing express their ideas so comically I have great fun interiorally while as grave possible exteriorally. A few of the men word their paragraphs well & make excel letters. John's was the best of all I wrote. The answering of letters from frie after some one has died is the saddest & hardest duty a nurse has to do.

Supper at five sets every one to running that can run & when that flurry is o all settle down for the evening amusements which consist of newspapers, gos Drs last round, & for such as need them the final doses for the night. At nine bell rings, gas is turned down & day nurses go to bed.

Night nurses go on duty, & sleep & death have the house to themselves. . . .

My work is changed to night watching or half night & half day, from tw to twelve. I like it as it leaves me time for a morning run which is what I nee keep well, for bad air, food, water, work & watching are getting to be too m for me. I trot up & down the streets in all directions, some times to the Heig then half way to Washington, again to the hill over which the long trains of ar wagons are constantly vanishing & ambulances appearing. That way the fight lies, & I long to follow.

F READ A PRIMARY SOURCE
What do you learn about hospital conditions and the nurses' routine activities?

330 UNIT 3: SETTING AND MOOD

DIFFERENTIATED INSTRUCTION

FOR ENGLISH LEARNERS

Vocabulary: Cognates [shared-language groups] Have groups scan the story for cognates and report their findings to the class. Spanish cognates on this page include

- *vile/vil* (line 82)
- *competent/competente* (line 82)
- *chaos/caos* (line 84)
- *ration/ración* (line 94)
- *dose/dosis* (line 113)

FOR ADVANCED LEARNERS/PRE-AP

Apply Journal Form Have students review Alcott's observations and thoughts about the hospital ward in which she works. Then ask them to write a journal entry from the point of view of one of Alcott's patients, such as John Suhre. Have students share their journal entries with another student.

mprehension

. **Recall** When war is declared, how do the people of Concord respond?

. **Summarize** Review Alcott's 1861 and 1862 journal entries. Then, in a few sentences, summarize why Alcott wants to serve as a nurse.

tical Analysis

. **Gather Information from a Primary Source** Reread lines 64–73. Which of John Suhre's qualities does Alcott find most notable? Tell what you learn about her values from her opinions about this soldier.

. **Identify Characteristics of a Journal** If you had stumbled across the original, handwritten version of this journal in a drawer, what characteristics of it would help you identify it as a journal?

ad for Information: Draw a Conclusion

WRITING PROMPT

A **conclusion** is a judgment or belief about something. To reach a solid conclusion, you need to use sound reasoning, evidence, and experience. In a paragraph, state and support a conclusion you have reached about one of the following topics:

- Louisa May Alcott
- Civil War soldiers
- being a nurse in a military hospital
- Civil War military hospitals

To answer this prompt, first identify the topic you would like to focus on. Then follow these steps:

1. Jot down ideas and information about it.
2. Based on this information, reach a conclusion about the topic.
3. Pick out strong support for your conclusion from Alcott's journal, Bradbury's historical fiction, and/or the lesson text.
4. State your conclusion in a topic sentence. Then present your reasons and evidence for arriving at that conclusion.

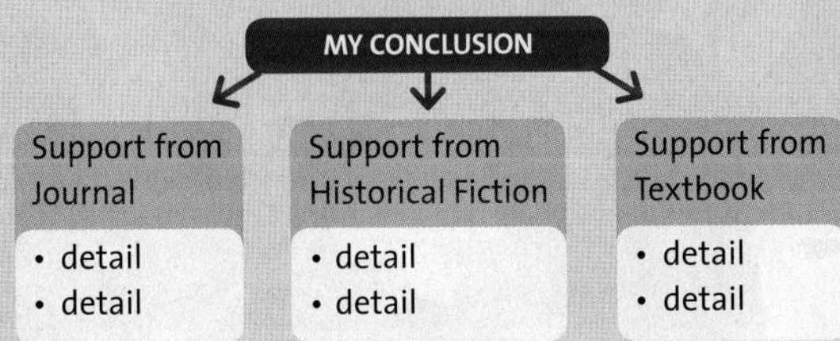

FOR LESS–PROFICIENT WRITERS

Read for Information

- Encourage students to review "The Drummer Boy of Shiloh" before they begin jotting down ideas and information.
- In step 3, if students do not find strong support for their conclusions, tell them to think about revising the conclusion to better fit the evidence.
- Remind students that their topic sentences should be in the form of a broad statement such as "Being a nurse in a Civil War hospital was hard but rewarding work."

FOR ADVANCED LEARNERS/PRE–AP

Read for Information Have students draw a conclusion about each topic listed, instead of just one. Ask them to present their conclusion and support in a four-part graphic organizer of their own design.

Practice and Apply

For additional support of postreading questions, use these copy masters:

RESOURCE MANAGER—Copy Masters
Reading Check p. 55
Question Support p. 56
Draw a Conclusion p. 52
For additional questions, see page 46.

ANSWERS

Comprehension

1. *A company of young soldiers goes off to Washington, D.C. Families help get them ready and say dramatic and tearful good-byes at the train station.*
2. *Alcott longs to see war, to be a man, to fight, and to release her pent-up energy. Serving as a nurse satisfies these longings.*

Critical Analysis

Possible answers:

3. ■ **STANDARDS FOCUS Read a Primary Source** *Alcott says Suhre has little education or refinement but "a noble character, a heart as warm & tender as a woman's, a nature fresh & frank as any child's" (lines 68–69). Although he is dying, he feels no anger or regret. Alcott's esteem for Suhre shows that she values courage.*
4. *Features include dated entries in chronological order, references to real events, and expressions of private thoughts, feelings, observations, and activities.*

Read for Information: Draw a Conclusion

Writing Prompt *Students' conclusions should be clearly stated and supported by reasons and evidence from several sources.*

Assess and Reteach

Assess

RESOURCE MANAGER—Copy Masters
Selection Tests A, B/C pp. 57–58, 59–60
Test Generator CD

Reteach

STANDARDS LESSON FILE
Reading Lesson 9: Drawing Conclusions
Research and Study Skills Lesson 5: Using Primary and Secondary Sources

Focus and Motivate

OBJECTIVES

Literary Analysis
- explore the key idea of **purpose**
- analyze the way in which setting affects plot
- read a short story and a personal essay

Reading
- visualize using sensory details

Vocabulary
- build vocabulary for reading and writing
- use a dictionary to determine the origin of homographs and analyze meaning *(also an EL language objective)*

Grammar and Writing
- avoid misplaced modifiers
- use prepositional phrases to modify nouns or pronouns
- use writing to analyze literature

SUMMARY

Young Sam Chase is a trainee on Energy Planet, working to obtain energy from a neutron star. After hearing that some workers have had hallucinations, Sam goes outdoors to explore. He meets a life-form that communicates its fear that its home will be destroyed by human settlement. Sam persuades the Commander to alter the project's mission.

How do you find your PURPOSE?

To clarify the ***KEY IDEA,*** suggest that having a purpose means knowing you can do something useful with your talents. Direct students' attention to the photograph. Ask them what **purpose** can be served through music. Then have students do the ***QUICKWRITE*** activity.

Before Reading

Hallucination

Short Story by Isaac Asimov

How do you find your PURPOSE?

KEY IDEA Maybe you've heard about a pop star who began performing onstage at the age of three, or about a writer who published her first poem in grade school. Maybe you, too, have always known what your **purpose** is. But most of us have to search, question, and take a few wrong turns before we find out how to put our talents to their best use. In the story you are about to read, a 15-year-old boy discovers his purpose by traveling to a rather unusual place.

QUICKWRITE What might your purpose be? Explore the question by listing the five things you most enjoy doing. Make a separate list of personal qualities that you are proud of, such as kindness, sensitivity, or intelligence. Reflect upon how you can combine these interests and qualities to make a contribution of some sort. Record your reflections in your journal.

332

Selection Resources

RESOURCE MANAGER UNIT 3

Plan and Teach pp. 61–68

Literary Analysis
Summary pp. 69†*, 70‡*
Setting and Plot pp. 71, 72†*
Question Support p. 79*

Reading
Visualize pp. 73, 74†*
Reading Check p. 78
Reading Fluency p. 81

Vocabulary
Study p. 75*
Practice p. 76
Strategy p. 77

Grammar and Writing
Avoid Misplaced Modifiers p. 80

Assessment
Selection Tests A, B/C pp. 83*, 85*
Test Generator CD

BEST PRACTICES TOOLKIT

Differentiated Instruction pp. 31–38*
Scaffolding Instruction pp. 43–46*

Graphic Organizers/Strategies
Read-and-Say-Something • Word Questioning • Venn Diagram • Making Inferences • Comparing Myself to a Character • Word Squares • Sequence Chain • Plot Evaluation • Cluster Diagram

Reading Support
Audio Anthology CD*

Technology
Literature, Vocabulary, and Writing Centers at **ClassZone.com**
Write*Smart* CD

* Resources for Differentiation † Also in Spanish ‡ In Haitian Creole and Vietnamese

Teach

ITERARY ANALYSIS: SETTING AND PLOT

As you probably recall, the time and place in which a story occurs is called the **setting.** When and where a story happens can create a conflict or influence a character's decisions. Therefore, setting can play an important role in a story's **plot,** or sequence of related events. For example, in "The Drummer Boy of Shiloh," a story set on the eve of a Civil War battle, the main character must gather his courage for the next day's fight. As you read "Hallucination," look for ways the story's setting affects its plot.

EADING STRATEGY: VISUALIZE

You're about to read a story that's set on an imaginary planet. How will you be able to understand what the environment is like? One way is to visualize as you read. When you **visualize,** you form mental pictures using details from the story plus your own knowledge and imagination. **Sensory details**—words telling how things look, sound, smell, taste, and feel—can help.

As you read, take note of details that help you form mental pictures. Use a chart like the one shown to sketch your visualizations.

Details	*Visualization*
transparent dome *1,000 meters high* *stretched farther than he could see*	

Review: **Make Inferences**

OCABULARY IN CONTEXT

The boldfaced words help Isaac Asimov tell the story of a boy who discovers his purpose despite opposition. Use context clues to figure out what each word means, and then write a synonym or phrase that means the same.

1. He held a strong **conviction** that something wasn't right.
2. The boy wasn't **insolent;** he tried hard to be respectful.
3. It's difficult to **refrain** from doing something that you enjoy.
4. Losing this game could **diminish** our chances for the finals.
5. Those in **opposition** to the plan were told to keep quiet.
6. She overcame her **inertia** and began seeking a cure.

Author Online

Candy as Inspiration A candy store had an unlikely influence on Isaac Asimov's life and work. The store was a family operation owned by Asimov's father. The new science fiction magazines sold in the store sparked young Asimov's interest in science fiction.

Isaac Asimov
1920–1992

Science Fact and Science Fiction Asimov grew up to combine his interests in both science and science fiction. He earned a PhD in biochemistry and was a well-respected contributor to the field of robotics, the study of robot technology. He was also famous for his dedication to his writing. He often spent 12-hour days in front of his typewriter, and he was able to type more than 90 words per minute. In addition to fiction, Asimov wrote books on a wide variety of topics, including science, math, history, and poetry. In all, Asimov wrote over 450 books, totaling over seven million words.

MORE ABOUT THE AUTHOR
For more on Isaac Asimov, visit the **Literature Center** at **ClassZone.com.**

Background

Science Fiction In science fiction, writers often explore what life might be like in the future. They do so by blending scientific facts and theories and familiar elements of real life with their own ideas to create imaginary worlds and unique situations. Writers of science fiction, including Isaac Asimov, also often use their stories to comment on current political and social conditions.

STANDARDS FOCUS

LITERARY ANALYSIS

● SETTING AND PLOT

Read this example aloud:

The tall-masted ship was stuck in the ice. The frozen sea was as white as the snow-covered land. Each man on board shivered in his thin coat. Each wondered, how would they survive?

Ask students how the setting in this example might influence the plot. ***Possible answer:*** *The men will battle against the ice and cold to stay alive.*

CHECK UNDERSTANDING Ask students to describe a story or movie in which the setting shaped the conflict in the story.

READING STRATEGY

■ VISUALIZE

Tell students that one way to visualize a story is to imagine it as a movie. They should look for descriptive details and make connections between the descriptions and their own experience.

CHECK UNDERSTANDING Ask students what descriptive details they would use to help a reader visualize a flock of geese flying overhead.

RESOURCE MANAGER—Copy Master
Visualize p. 73 (for student use while reading the selection)

VOCABULARY SKILL

▲ VOCABULARY IN CONTEXT

DIAGNOSE WORD KNOWLEDGE To determine preteaching needs, have all students complete **Vocabulary in Context.** *Students' responses will vary.* ***Possible answers:*** **1.** *belief* **2.** *rude* **3.** *hold back* **4.** *decrease* **5.** *resistance* **6.** *idleness*

PRETEACH VOCABULARY Use the Vocabulary Study copy master to help students explore the meaning of each boldfaced word.

1. Read item 1 aloud, emphasizing *refrain.*
2. Point out the context clues *could not* and *interest in them was too great.* Elicit possible meanings for *refrain,* such as "keep from" or "avoid."
3. Have students record their predictions.
4. Repeat the procedure for items 2–6.
5. Have students do Part B independently.

RESOURCE MANAGER—Copy Master
Vocabulary Study p. 75

For general guidelines on differentiating vocabulary instruction and for alternative vocabulary activities for students not needing vocabulary preteaching, see

BEST PRACTICES TOOLKIT
Scaffolding Vocabulary Instruction pp. 43–46

Vocabulary Center at **ClassZone.com**
Additional Vocabulary Activities

Practice and Apply

ANALYZE VISUALS

Possible answer: *This story will probably take place in outer space.*

LITERARY ANALYSIS

Ⓐ SETTING AND PLOT

Possible answer: *The story takes place on Energy Planet. There is a dome large enough to cover a whole community. Sam came to the planet on a spaceship. From these details, it is clear that the story takes place in the distant future.*

Extend the Discussion Have students predict how this aspect of the setting could affect what happens in the story. Record three different predictions on the board and leave them there for future discussion and revision.

HALLUCINATION

ISAAC ASIMOV

PART ONE

Sam Chase arrived on Energy Planet on his fifteenth birthday.

It was a great achievement, he had been told, to have been assigned there, but he wasn't at all sure he felt that at the moment.

It meant a three-year separation from Earth and from his family, while he continued a specialized education in the field, and that was a sobering thought. It was not the field of education in which he was interested, and he could not understand why Central Computer had assigned him to this project, and that was downright depressing.

He looked at the transparent dome overhead. It was quite high, perhaps a thousand meters high, and it stretched in all directions farther than he could clearly see. He asked, "Is it true that this is the only Dome on the planet, sir?"

The information-films he had studied on the spaceship that had carried him here had described only one Dome, but they might have been out-of-date.

Donald Gentry, to whom the question had been addressed, smiled. He was a large man, a little chubby, with dark brown, good-natured eyes, not much hair, and a short, graying beard.

He said, "The only one, Sam. It's quite large, though, and most of the housing facilities are underground, where you'll find no lack of space. Besides, once your basic training is done, you'll be spending most of your time in space. This is just our planetary base." Ⓐ

ANALYZE VISUALS
What can you **infer** from this photograph about where the story will take place?

① **Targeted Passage**

Ⓐ **SETTING AND PLOT**
What have you learned so far about where and when the story takes place?

DIFFERENTIATED INSTRUCTION

FOR ALL STUDENTS

Interest Stations Post suggested projects for students to work on independently.

- **Poster** Research and create a poster on swarm intelligence in insects.
- **Science Fiction** Write a short story that takes place in the future in outer space.
- **Comic Strip** Draw events from the story and combine them in a comic strip.

For further details on these projects, see

RESOURCE MANAGER
Ideas for Extension pp. 66–67

FOR LESS–PROFICIENT READERS

In combination with the *Audio Anthology CD*, use one or more Targeted Passages (pp. 334, 336, 345, 352, 353) to ensure that students focus on key story events, concepts, and skills.

① Targeted Passage [Lines 1–20]

This passage introduces the setting and the story's main character, Sam Chase.

- Why is Sam on Energy Planet?
- Why is Sam depressed about his assignment?
- In what way was the assignment made?
- Where will Sam live on Energy Planet?

BACKGROUND

Neutron Star In the story, Sam Chase is working on a project to obtain energy from a neutron star (lines 33–34). A neutron star is a very compact star that has a mass greater than that of the Sun but is only about 10 miles in diameter. It is so dense that on Earth one piece of a neutron star the size of a sugar cube would weigh as much as a mountain. Because of its density, the force of gravity on a neutron star is millions of times greater than on Earth. Neutron stars also have incredible magnetic fields—up to a thousand trillion times stronger than Earth's.

Scientists believe that a neutron star results from the explosion of a very large star called a supernova. The nearest neutron star is over three light years away from Earth. At least one neutron star is believed to be orbited by a planet.

FOR ENGLISH LEARNERS

Options for Reading [paired option] Have students listen to Part One of the story on the *Audio Anthology CD.* Then divide students into pairs and have them read silently. At the end of each page, have them pause to make a comment to their partner about what they have read. Have pairs write down any questions they cannot answer for later discussion with the whole class.

 BEST PRACTICES TOOLKIT
Read-and-Say-Something p. D3

Key Academic Vocabulary Have students use Word Questioning for *assigned* (lines 2, 7, 86, 155), *environment* (line 63), *investigate* (line 216), *intelligent* (lines 425, 473, 521, 527, 528, 532), and *demonstrate* (line 571).

 BEST PRACTICES TOOLKIT—Transparency
Word Questioning p. E9

Prereading For prereading instruction for English learners, see

BEST PRACTICES TOOLKIT
Scaffolding Reading Instruction pp. 43–46

FOR ADVANCED LEARNERS/PRE–AP

Pre-AP exercises in the bottom channel provide additional challenge for your advanced students. Use them for small groups or individuals.

ADDITIONAL GUIDELINES

For more help with differentiation and tips for classroom management, see

 BEST PRACTICES TOOLKIT
Differentiated Instruction pp. 31–38

Lines 22–31
REINFORCE *KEY IDEA:* PURPOSE

Discuss Does Sam feel he can find his **purpose** in the assignment he has been given? Explain.
Possible answer: *Sam is not sure he will do well in gravitational engineering. This is not the field in which he is most interested.*

LITERARY ANALYSIS

B SETTING AND PLOT

Possible answer: *The humans hope to get close to the neutron star and use it as an energy source.*

"I see, sir," said Sam, a little troubled.

Gentry said, "I am in charge of our basic trainees so I have to study their records carefully. It seems clear to me that this assignment was not your first choice. Am I right?"

Sam hesitated, and then decided he didn't have much choice but to be honest about it. He said, "I'm not sure that I'll do as well as I would like to in gravitational engineering."

"Why not? Surely the Central Computer, which evaluated your scholastic record and your social and personal background can be trusted in its judgments. And if you do well, it will be a great achievement for you, for right here we are on the cutting edge of a new technology."

"I know that, sir," said Sam. "Back on Earth, everyone is very excited about it. No one before has ever tried to get close to a neutron star and make use of its energy."

"Yes?" said Gentry. "I haven't been on Earth for two years. What else do they say about it? I understand there's considerable **opposition?**"

His eyes probed the boy.

Sam shifted uneasily, aware he was being tested. He said, "There are people on Earth who say it's all too dangerous and might be a waste of money."

"Do you believe that?"

"It might be so, but most new technologies have their dangers and many are worth doing despite that. This one is, I think." **B**

"Very good. What else do they say on Earth?"

Sam said, "They say the Commander isn't well and that the project might fail without him." When Gentry didn't respond, Sam said, hastily, "That's what they say."

Gentry acted as though he did not hear. He put his hand on Sam's shoulder and said, "Come, I've got to show you to your Corridor, introduce you to your roommate, and explain what your initial duties will be." As they walked toward the elevator that would take them downward, he said, "What was your first choice in assignment, Chase?"

"Neurophysiology,[1] sir."

"Not a bad choice. Even today, the human brain continues to be a mystery. We know more about neutron stars than we do about the brain, as we found out when this project first began."

"Oh?"

"Indeed! At the start, various people at the base—it was much smaller and more primitive then—reported having experienced hallucinations.[2] They never caused any bad effects, and after a while, there were no further reports. We never found out the cause."

Sam stopped, and looked up and about again, "Was that why the Dome was built, Dr. Gentry?"

1. **neurophysiology** (nŏŏr'ō-fĭz'ē-ŏl'ə-jē): the study of the functions of the nervous system.
2. **hallucination** (hə-lōō'sə-nā'shən): a perception of objects that don't really exist.

opposition (ŏp'ə-zĭsh *n.* the act of opposing resisting

B SETTING AND PLC
Reread lines 28–42. V do the humans hope achieve on Energy Pla

2 Targeted Passag

VISUAL VOCABUL

corridor (kôr'ĭ-dôr') *n* a narrow hallway, ofte with rooms opening onto it.

DIFFERENTIATED INSTRUCTION

FOR LESS–PROFICIENT READERS

2 Targeted Passage [Lines 44–60]

This passage introduces a mystery on Energy Planet and reveals Sam's field of interest.

- What rumor has Sam heard about the Commander of the base?
- What was Sam's first choice of assignment? Describe this field of science.
- What unusual events have been reported at the base?

FOR ENGLISH LEARNERS

Vocabulary Support Relate the word *hallucinations* (line 58) to the common English expression "I thought I was seeing things." Point out that people use this expression when they think they have perceived something real but there is no concrete or external evidence of it. Discuss other ways of conveying the same idea:

- "I saw things that weren't really there."
- "I must have imagined it."
- "It must have been all in my mind."

Visual Vocabulary Point out that corridors exist in most large buildings, such as schools, office buildings, and apartment buildings. On the board, sketch a floor plan that shows several connected corridors with rooms on both sides. Discuss why the people who live in the Dome might find it convenient to organize the underground housing facilities in Corridors.

"No, not at all. We needed a place with a completely Earth-like environment, for various reasons, but we haven't isolated ourselves. People can go outside freely. There are no hallucinations being reported now."

Sam said, "The information I was given about Energy Planet is that there is no life on it except for plants and insects, and that they're harmless."

"That's right, but they're also inedible, so we grow our own vegetables, and keep some small animals, right here under the Dome. Still, we've found nothing hallucinogenic about the planetary life."

"Anything unusual about the atmosphere, sir?"

Gentry looked down from his only slightly greater height and said, "Not at all. People have camped in the open overnight on occasion and nothing has happened. It is a pleasant world. There are streams but no fish, just algae and water-insects. There is nothing to sting you or poison you. There are yellow berries that look delicious and taste terrible but do no other harm. The weather's pretty nearly always good. There are frequent light rains and it is sometimes windy, but there are no extremes of heat and cold." **C**

"And no hallucinations anymore, Dr. Gentry?"

"You sound disappointed," said Gentry, smiling.

Sam took a chance. "Does the Commander's trouble have anything to do with the hallucinations, sir?"

The good nature vanished from Gentry's eyes for a moment, and he frowned. He said, "What trouble do you refer to?"

Sam flushed and they proceeded in silence.

C VISUALIZE Reread lines 66–78. What words help you form a mental picture of Energy Planet? Add these words to your chart.

Sam found few others in the Corridor he had been assigned to, but Gentry explained it was a busy time at the forward station, where the power system was being built in a ring around the neutron star—the tiny object less than ten miles across that had all the mass of a normal star, and a magnetic field of incredible power.

It was the magnetic field that would be tapped. Energy would be led away in enormous amounts and yet it would all be a pinprick, less than a pinprick, to the star's rotational energy, which was the ultimate source. It would take billions of years to bleed off all that energy, and in that time, dozens of populated planets, fed the energy through hyperspace, would have all they needed for an indefinite time.

Sharing his room was Robert Gillette, a dark-haired, unhappy-looking young man. After cautious greetings had been exchanged, Robert revealed the fact that he was sixteen and had been "grounded" with a broken arm, though the fact didn't show since it had been pinned internally.

Robert said, ruefully, "It takes a while before you learn to handle things in space. They may not have weight, but they have **inertia** and you have to allow for that."

inertia (ĭ-nûr'shə) *n.* resistance to motion, action, or change

READING STRATEGY

C VISUALIZE

Possible answer:

- *"no life on it except for plants and insects"*
- *"streams but no fish, just algae and water-insects"*
- *"yellow berries"*
- *"weather's pretty nearly always good"*
- *"light rains and it is sometimes windy"*
- *"no extremes of heat and cold"*

Lines 79–96

DISCUSSION PROMPTS

Use these prompts to help students understand the nature of the neutron-star project:

Analyze Why is the neutron-star project so important? ***Possible answer:*** *It will supply the energy needs of dozens of populated planets for a very long time.*

Speculate In today's world, how many years do you think it will take for humans to actually obtain energy from a neutron star? Explain. *Students may say it will be hundreds or thousands of years because humans so far have not traveled very far in space or developed the special technologies that would be needed.*

BACKGROUND

Inertia Explain that the concept of inertia (line 102) refers to an object's natural tendency to resist change to its state of motion. For example, if you move a book, it will move the few inches that you moved it, but it will not continue moving, as it was not originally in a state of motion.

FOR LESS–PROFICIENT READERS

Vocabulary Support Connect the word *hallucinogenic* (line 70) to *hallucinations* (line 58).

- Point out the common root, which comes from a Latin word meaning "dream."
- Explain that the suffix *-ation* ("action of") indicates a noun, while *-genic* ("producing") indicates an adjective. Give examples of familiar words with these endings, such as *expectation* and *photogenic,* and have students use them in sentences about the story.

FOR ADVANCED LEARNERS/PRE–AP

Compare and Contrast How is Energy Planet similar to and different from Earth? Have students use a Venn Diagram to compare and contrast the two planets. Ask students to share the information in their diagrams and discuss why the similarities and differences might be important to the story.

BEST PRACTICES TOOLKIT—Transparency
Venn Diagram p. A26

Alike: *Both planets have plants and insects, breathable atmosphere, streams, rain, wind.*

Different:

- *Earth has more varieties of life-forms, edible plants, poisonous plants and insects, and extremes of heat and cold.*
- *Energy Planet has no life other than inedible, harmless plants and insects, and no extremes of heat and cold.*

READING SKILL: *Review*

D MAKE INFERENCES

Possible answer: *Robert is concerned that talking about the hallucinations could jeopardize his and Sam's careers.*

If students need help . . . Read lines 121–124 aloud. Point out that

- the breaks in Robert's speech, indicated by the dashes and his use of "uh," suggest that he is uneasy about the reports of hallucinations
- his gruff manner of speaking suggests that he thinks Sam would be foolish to jeopardize his education and career

Sam said, "They always teach you that in—" He was going to say that it was taught in fourth-grade science, but realized that would be insulting, and stopped himself.

Robert caught the implication, however, and flushed. He said, "It's easy to know it in your head. It doesn't mean you get the proper reflexes, till you've practiced quite a bit. You'll find out."

Sam said, "Is it very complicated to get to go outside?"

"No, but why do you want to go? There's nothing there."

"Have you ever been outside?"

"Sure," but he shrugged, and volunteered nothing else.

Sam took a chance. He said, very casually, "Did you ever see one of these hallucinations they talk about?"

Robert said, "*Who* talks about?"

Sam didn't answer directly. He said, "A lot of people used to see them, but they don't anymore. Or so they say."

"So *who* say?"

Sam took another chance. "Or if they see them, they keep quiet about them."

Robert said gruffly, "Listen, let me give you some advice. Don't get interested in these—whatever they are. If you start telling yourself you see—uh—something, you might be sent back. You'll lose your chance at a good education and an important career." **D**

Robert's eyes shifted to a direct stare as he said that.

D MAKE INFERENCE
Why doesn't Robert want to talk about th
hallucinations?

ANALYZE VISUAL
What words would you use to describe th **setting** pictured here

ANALYZE VISUALS

Possible answer: *bare, bleak, lonely*

DIFFERENTIATED INSTRUCTION

FOR LESS–PROFICIENT READERS

Review: Make Inferences Review how to make inferences by making logical guesses based on clues from the text and personal experience. Distribute copies of the Making Inferences chart. Have students work in pairs to reread lines 112–125 and use the graphic organizer to help them figure out why Robert doesn't want to talk about the hallucinations.

 **BEST PRACTICES TOOLKIT—Transparency**
Making Inferences p. A13

FOR ENGLISH LEARNERS

Language: Punctuation and Print Cues [paired option] Discuss and illustrate the print cues students can use to help them follow a conversation when they read:

- The words a character says out loud are enclosed in quotation marks.
- A paragraph indent signals a new speaker.

Have pairs of students read aloud lines 110–119. Ask them to take the roles of the two speakers, paying attention to the quotation marks and paragraph indents.

Sam shrugged and sat down on the unused bunk. "All right for this to be y bed?"

"It's the only other bed here," said Robert, still staring. "The bathroom's to our right. There's your closet, your bureau. You get half the room. There's gym here, a library, a dining area." He paused and then, as though to let ygones be bygones,[3] said, "I'll show you around later." **E**

"Thanks," said Sam. "What kind of a guy is the Commander?"

"He's aces. We wouldn't be here without him. He knows more about yperspatial technology than anyone, and he's got pull with the Space Agency, we get the money and equipment we need."

Sam opened his trunk and, with his back to Robert, said casually, "I nderstand he's not well."

"Things get him down. We're behind schedule, there are cost overruns, and ings like that. Enough to get anyone down."

"Depression, huh? Any connection, you suppose, with—"

Robert stirred impatiently in his seat, "Say, why are you so interested in l this?"

"Energy physics isn't really my deal. Coming here—"

"Well, here's where you are, mister, and you better make up your mind to , or you'll get sent home, and then you won't be anywhere. I'm going to the brary."

Sam remained in the room alone, with his thoughts.

t was not at all difficult for Sam to get permission to leave the Dome. The Corridor-Master didn't even ask the reason until after he had checked him off.

"I want to get a feel for the planet, sir."

The Corridor-Master nodded. "Fair enough, but you only get three hours, ou know. And don't wander out of sight of the Dome. If we have to look or you, we'll find you, because you'll be wearing this," and he held out a ransmitter which Sam knew had been tuned to his own personal wavelength, ne which had been assigned him at birth. "But if we have to go to that rouble, you won't be allowed out again for a pretty long time. And it won't ook good on your record, either. You understand?"

It won't look good on your record. Any reasonable career these days had to nclude experience and education in space, so it was an effective warning. No vonder people might have stopped reporting hallucinations, even if they saw hem. **F**

Even so, Sam was going to have to take his chances. After all, the Central Computer *couldn't* have sent him here just to do energy physics. There was nothing in his record that made sense out of that.

As far as looks were concerned, the planet might have been Earth, some part of Earth anyway, some place where there were a few trees and low bushes and ots of tall grass.

E VISUALIZE
What clues do you get about the boys' living area? Add these details to your chart.

F SETTING AND PLOT
Why is Sam's assignment on Energy Planet so important to his future?

3. **let bygones be bygones:** decide to forget past disagreements.

READING STRATEGY

E VISUALIZE

Possible answer:

- *"It's the only other bed here"*
- *"The bathroom's to your right"*
- *"There's your closet, your bureau"*
- *"There's a gym here, a library, a dining area"*

Lines 133–147

DISCUSSION PROMPTS

Use these prompts to help students understand important background information for the plot:

Recall What problems are affecting the neutron-star project? ***Answer:*** *The project is behind schedule and over budget.*

Infer Why does Robert evade Sam's question about a connection with the Commander's depression? ***Possible answer:*** *The Commander has a lot of authority and knowledge about hyperspatial technology. Robert wants to protect the Commander, as well as his own career.*

Synthesize Why do you think Sam is continuing to ask probing questions about the project? ***Possible answer:*** *He is unsettled by negative comments about the project that he heard back on Earth, and he does not get straight answers from Dr. Gentry or from Robert. His main field of interest is neurophysiology, which makes him curious about the hallucinations. He also wonders whether the Central Computer had a specific reason for assigning him to this project—perhaps to explore the mystery of the hallucinations and the Commander's depression.*

FOR LESS–PROFICIENT READERS

Comprehension Support Explain that *suspense* refers to the tension or excitement readers feel as they wait to find out what will happen next in a story. Point out that the suspense builds in the scene in which Sam talks to Robert (lines 110–146). Ask:

- As you were reading this episode, what questions did you have about what will happen next?
- What statements or details in the text prompted these questions?

FOR ENGLISH LEARNERS

Vocabulary: Idioms and Slang [mixed-readiness pairs] Point out that the dialogue in this story contains casual expressions that the author felt a teenage boy like Sam would be likely to use. Pair students with fluent speakers to define these words and phrases in the context of the dialogue: *Listen* (line 121), *He's aces* (line 133), *he's got pull* (134), *get him down* (line 138), *Say* (line 141), *isn't really my deal* (line 143), *get a feel for* (150).

LITERARY ANALYSIS

F SETTING AND PLOT

Possible answer: *In the world in which Sam lives, experience in space is essential for a good career. He needs to perform well on his assignment so his record will impress future employers.*

READING STRATEGY

G VISUALIZE

Sketches should reflect details from the text. The insect Sam examines is "very small," "hexagonal, bulging above and concave below," with "many short, small legs" that make it seem to move "on tiny wheels." Its wings are "four tiny, feathery objects."

If students need help . . . Supply definitions for *hexagonal* ("having six sides") and *concave* ("rounded inward") and draw pictures on the board to illustrate. Have students locate the context clue for *concave* in lines 171–172 (*bulging above*).

LITERARY ANALYSIS

H SETTING AND PLOT

Possible answer: *Sam observes that the planet has a strange smell. The sky is filled with "lines of clouds" (line 181), the temperature is pleasant, and there is a light wind. The air is damp. The planet also has a few trees and low shrubs, lots of tall grass, and countless flying insects. However, there are no large animals, such as cows. Also, the leaves and grass have an unpleasant smell and taste.*

Extend the Discussion What catches Sam's eye next (lines 204–209)? Do you think he is hallucinating? Explain.

There were no paths and with every cautious step, the grass swayed, and tiny flying creatures whirred upward with a soft, hissing noise of wings.

One of them landed on his finger and Sam looked at it curiously. It was very small and, therefore, hard to see in detail, but it seemed hexagonal, bulging above and concave below. There were many short, small legs so that when it moved it almost seemed to do so on tiny wheels. There were no signs of wings till it suddenly took off, and then four tiny, feathery objects unfurled. G

What made the planet different from Earth, though, was the smell. It wasn't unpleasant, it was just different. The plants must have had an entirely different chemistry from those on Earth; that's why they tasted bad and were inedible. It was just luck they weren't poisonous.

The smell **diminished** with time, however, as it saturated Sam's nostrils. He found an exposed bit of rocky ledge he could sit on and considered the prospect. The sky was filled with lines of clouds, and the Sun was periodically obscured, but the temperature was pleasant and there was only a light wind. The air felt a bit damp, as though it might rain in a few hours.

Sam had brought a small hamper with him and he placed it in his lap and opened it. He had brought along two sandwiches and a canned drink so that he could make rather a picnic of it.

He chewed away and thought: Why should there be hallucinations?

Surely those accepted for a job as important as that of taming a neutron star would have been selected for mental stability. It would be surprising to have even one person hallucinating, let alone a number of them. Was it a matter of chemical influences on the brain?

They would surely have checked that out.

Sam plucked a leaf, tore it in two and squeezed. He then put the torn edge to his nose cautiously, and took it away again. A very acrid, unpleasant smell. He tried a blade of grass. Much the same.

Was the smell enough? It hadn't made him feel dizzy or in any way peculiar.

He used a bit of his water to rinse off the fingers that had held the plants and then rubbed them on his trouser leg. He finished his sandwiches slowly, and tried to see if anything else might be considered unnatural about the planet.

All that greenery. There ought to be animals eating it, rabbits, cows, whatever. Not just insects, innumerable insects, or whatever those little things might be, with the gentle sighing of their tiny feathery wings and the very soft crackle of their munch, munch, munchings of leaves and stalks. H

What if there were a cow—a big, fat cow—doing the munching? And with the last mouthful of his second sandwich between his teeth, his own munching stopped.

There was a kind of smoke in the air between himself and a line of hedges. It waved, billowed, and altered: a very thin smoke. He blinked his eyes, then shook his head, but it was still there.

G VISUALIZE
What details help yo[u] visualize the insects [Sam] discovers? Add a ske[tch] of what you "see" on your chart.

diminish (dĭ-mĭn'ĭsh) to become smaller or

H SETTING AND PLO[T]
What does Sam obser[ve] about the planet?

DIFFERENTIATED INSTRUCTION

FOR LESS–PROFICIENT READERS

Reading Strategy Follow-Up: Visualize [paired option] Have students work in pairs to read lines 168–186 and update their charts from page 333. Remind them to notice words and phrases that appeal to the senses. Ask them if what the reader "sees" is described up close, at a long distance, or somewhere in between. Afterwards, have teams compare their charts and discuss how visualizing helps them understand the story better.

Details	Visualization
"with every cautious step, the grass swayed, and tiny flying creatures whirred upward with a soft, hissing noise of wings" (lines 168–169)	

He swallowed hastily, closed his lunch box, and slung it over his shoulder by s strap. He stood up.

He felt no fear. He was only excited—and curious.

The smoke was growing thicker, and taking on a shape. Vaguely, it looked ke a cow, a smoky, insubstantial shape that he could see through. Was it a allucination? A creation of his mind? He had just been thinking of a cow.

Hallucination or not, he was going to investigate.

With determination, he stepped toward the shape.

ART TWO

Sam Chase stepped toward the cow outlined in smoke on the strange, far planet on which his education and career were to be advanced.

He was convinced there was nothing wrong with his mind. It was the hallucination" that Dr. Gentry had mentioned, but it was no hallucination. ven as he pushed his way through the tall rank[4] grasslike greenery, he noted the lence, and knew not only that it was no hallucination, but what it really *was.*

The smoke seemed to condense and grow darker, outlining the cow more arply. It was as though the cow were being painted in the air.

Sam laughed, and shouted, "Stop! Stop! Don't use me. I don't know a cow ell enough. I've only seen pictures. You're getting it all wrong."

It looked more like a caricature[5] than a real animal and, as he cried out, the utline wavered and thinned. The smoke remained but it was as though an nseen hand had passed across the air to erase what had been written. **I**

I VISUALIZE Close your eyes and picture the cow described here. Add this "picture" to your chart.

Then a new shape began to take form. At first, Sam couldn't quite make out hat it was intended to represent, but it changed and sharpened quickly. He ared in surprise, his mouth hanging open and his hamper bumping emptily gainst his shoulder blade.

The smoke was forming a human being. There was no mistake about it. was forming accurately, as though it had a model it could imitate, and of ourse it did have one, for Sam was standing there.

It was becoming Sam, clothes and all, even the outline of the hamper and he strap over his shoulder. It was another Sam Chase.

It was still a little vague, wavering a bit, insubstantial, but it firmed as hough it were correcting itself, and then, finally, it was steady.

It never became entirely solid. Sam could see the vegetation dimly through , and when a gust of wind caught it, it moved a bit as if it were a tethered alloon. **J**

J SETTING AND PLOT Do you think that what Sam sees is a real part of the planet, or is it a hallucination?

But it was real. It was no creation of his mind. Sam was sure of that.

But he couldn't just stand there, simply facing it. Diffidently, he said, 'Hello, there."

4. **rank:** yielding an excessive crop.
5. **caricature** (kăr′ĭ-kə-cho͝or′): a comic or exaggerated picture.

READING STRATEGY

I VISUALIZE

Students' pictures of the cow should be based on the words and phrases they record from the text, such as "outlined in smoke" (line 218), "as though the cow were being painted in the air" (line 225), and "more like a caricature than a real animal" (line 228).

LITERARY ANALYSIS

J SETTING AND PLOT

Possible answers:

- *It is real. Sam says that it is "no hallucination" (line 221).*
- *It is a hallucination. Sam can see through it, and it sways with the wind. It is not completely solid.*

If students need help . . . Have them tell about experiences of seeing something hazy or unclear at a distance and trying to make out what it was. Did they imagine the thing to be something other than what it really was? Did they feel that their eyes were "playing tricks on them"?

FOR LESS–PROFICIENT READERS

Comprehension Support Read aloud lines 218–237 and ask students to describe what is happening. Make sure students understand that

- Sam is convinced that what he is seeing is no hallucination
- when Sam says, "Don't use me," he is indicating that the smoky form is reading his mind to figure out what a cow looks like
- the form is capable of matching the shape of another being

FOR ADVANCED LEARNERS/PRE–AP

Analyze Character After students finish reading Part One, ask them if they, like Sam, would be excited and curious if they saw a cow materializing out of thin air. Have them use the Comparing Myself to a Character chart to note details about Sam's behavior and attitude and to compare how they might react in a similar situation. Invite students to share their completed charts.

BEST PRACTICES TOOLKIT—Transparency
Comparing Myself to a Character p. D10

Lines 251–285 DISCUSSION PROMPTS

Use these prompts to help students understand how Sam and the Other Sam are able to communicate:

Recall According to Sam, in what way is the Other Sam able to communicate with him? ***Answer:*** *According to Sam, the Other Sam is adjusting the electric currents in his brain cells to make him think of the answers to his own questions.*

Compare How is Sam's "conversation" with the Other Sam similar to or different from the way you communicate? *In students' experiences, it is likely that both parties in the conversation spoke. In Sam's conversation, the Other Sam does not speak but can plant thoughts in Sam's mind. Sam responds to these thoughts with either thoughts or spoken words. They nod when they understand each other.*

Analyze Why is a conversation that involves telepathy hard for Sam to adjust to? ***Possible answer:*** *It takes Sam a while to be able to tell his own thoughts from those imposed from an outside source.*

Somehow, he expected the Other Sam to speak, too, and, indeed, its mouth opened and closed, but no sound came out. It might just have been imitating the motion of Sam's mouth.

Sam said, again, "Hello, can you speak?"

There was no sound but his own voice, and yet there was a tickling in his mind, a **conviction** that they could communicate.

conviction (kən-vĭk's
n. a strong belief

Sam frowned. What made him so sure of that? The thought seemed to pop into his mind.

He said, "Is this what has appeared to other people, human people—my kind—on this world?"

No answering sound, but he was quite sure what the answer to his question was. This had appeared to other people, not necessarily in their own shape, but *something.* And it hadn't worked.

What made him so sure of *that?* Where did these convictions come from in answer to his questions?

Yes, of course, they *were* the answers to his questions. The Other Sam was putting thoughts into his mind. It was adjusting the tiny electric currents in his brain cells so that the proper thoughts would arise.

He nodded thoughtfully at *that* thought, and the Other Sam must have caught the significance of the gesture, for it nodded, too.

It had to be so. First a cow had formed, when Sam had thought of a cow, and then it had shifted when Sam had said the cow was imperfect. The Other Sam could grasp his thoughts somehow, and if it could grasp them, then it could modify them, too, perhaps.

Was this what telepathy[6] was like, then? It was not like talking. It was having thoughts, except that the thoughts originated elsewhere and were not created entirely of one's own mental operations. But how could you tell your own thoughts from thoughts imposed from outside?

Sam knew the answer to that at once. Right now, he was unused to the process. He had never had practice. With time, as he grew more skilled at it, he would be able to tell one kind of thought from another without trouble.

In fact, he could do it now, if he thought about it. Wasn't he carrying on a conversation in a way? He was wondering, and then knowing. The wondering was his own question, the knowing was the Other Sam's answer. Of course it was.

There! The "of course it was," just now, was an answer.

"Not so fast, Other Sam," said Sam, aloud. "Don't go too quickly. Give me a chance to sort things out, or I'll just get confused."

He sat down suddenly on the grass, which bent away from him in all directions.

The Other Sam slowly tried to sit down as well.

6. **telepathy** (tə-lĕp'ə-thē): communication directly from one person's mind to another.

DIFFERENTIATED INSTRUCTION

FOR ADVANCED LEARNERS/PRE–AP

Analyze Author's Intention [small-group option] Sam describes communicating with the Other Sam as "wondering, and then knowing" (line 280). Is it possible that Sam is really talking to himself *about* the Other Sam, rather than communicating directly with an alien through telepathy? In small groups, have students debate whether Asimov is being intentionally ambiguous in this scene. Provide these questions to focus their debates:

- Is Sam having an internal dialogue with himself or is he having an actual, if unusual, conversation with another being?
- Why might the author have left this matter open to question?

Sam laughed. "Your legs are bending in the wrong place."

That was corrected at once. The Other Sam sat down, but remained very stiff from the waist up.

"Relax," said Sam.

Slowly, the Other Sam slumped, flopping a bit to one side, then correcting that. **K**

Sam was relieved. With the Other Sam so willing to follow his lead, he was sure good will was involved. It was! Exactly!

"No," said Sam. "I said, not so fast. Don't go by my thoughts. Let me speak out loud, even if you can't hear me. *Then* adjust my thoughts, so I'll know it's an adjustment. Do you understand?"

He waited a moment and was then sure the Other Sam understood.

Ah, the answer had come, but not right away. Good!

"Why do you appear to people?" asked Sam.

He stared earnestly at the Other Sam, and knew that the Other Sam wanted to communicate with people, but had failed.

No answer to that question had really been required. The answer was obvious. But then, *why* had they failed?

He put it in words. "Why did you fail? You are successfully communicating with me."

ANALYZE VISUALS
What details in this picture help you **visualize** the Other Sam?

K VISUALIZE
What does the Other Sam do to copy Sam's movements? Sketch your mental picture.

ANALYZE VISUALS

Possible answer: *In the picture, there is an exact copy of the seated man directly in front of him. The copy is translucent and smoky, as described in lines 235–244.*

READING STRATEGY

K VISUALIZE

Answer: *The Other Sam tries to sit down on the grass like Sam. The Other Sam sits stiffly at first but then relaxes, like Sam.*

FOR LESS–PROFICIENT READERS

Comprehension Support Students may find it difficult to follow the telepathic dialogue between Sam and the Other Sam. Point out that Sam, too, is confused by this at first. To clarify, assign two students to read aloud lines 295–300. Have one student take the role of the Other Sam and read only the words followed by exclamation points. Make sure students understand that in line 296, the Other Sam is interrupting Sam's thoughts and Sam finds this confusing. So, in lines 297–299, he tells the Other Sam to respond only to his spoken words, not to his thoughts. This helps him more clearly distinguish his own thoughts, conclusions, and questions from the Other Sam's messages.

Lines 319–347
DISCUSSION PROMPTS

Use these prompts to help students understand Sam's interaction with the "alien manifestation":

Restate Why did previous attempts at communication between the Other Sam and the humans fail? ***Answer:*** *The people who saw the "alien manifestation" became frightened, so they were not receptive to its attempts at communicating with them.*

Analyze Does the Other Sam have a moral conscience? How do you know? ***Possible answer:*** *Yes. The Other Sam has the ability to change human minds by force, but this might cause damage. The Other Sam is not willing to harm another mind in order to get what it wants.*

Evaluate Do you think it is reasonable for the Other Sam to feel despair about the presence of humans? Explain. *Students may say it is reasonable because a creature intelligent enough to communicate by telepathy might be able to foresee a chain of cause and effect far into the future.*

LITERARY ANALYSIS

Ⓛ SETTING AND PLOT

Possible answer: *The conflict is between the human beings who built the Dome and the life-forms that live on Energy Planet. The Other Sam believes the planet will be flooded with more and more people and Domes, which will destroy his habitat.*

If students need help . . . Remind them that a conflict is a struggle between two forces that shapes the plot of a story. Have students predict how the author might develop this conflict further.

Extend the Discussion Why, according to the Other Sam, will more and more power stations be built? Do you see any parallels between the situation in the story and energy exploration today?

Sam was beginning to learn how to understand the alien manifestation.[7] It was as if his mind were adapting itself to a new technique of communication, just as it would adapt itself to a new language. Or was Other Sam influencing Sam's mind and teaching him the method without Sam even knowing it was being done?

Sam found himself emptying his mind of immediate thoughts. After he asked his question, he just let his eyes focus at nothing and his eyelids droop, as though he were about to drop off to sleep, and then he knew the answer. There was a little clicking, or something, in his mind, a signal that showed him something had been put in from outside.

He now knew, for instance, that the Other Sam's previous attempts at communication had failed because the people to whom it had appeared had been frightened. They had doubted their own sanity. And because they feared, their minds . . . tightened. Their minds would not receive. The attempts at communication gradually diminished, though they had never entirely stopped.

"But you're communicating with me," said Sam.

Sam was different from all the rest. He had not been afraid.

"Couldn't you have made them not afraid first? Then talked to them?"

It wouldn't work. The fear-filled mind resisted all. An attempt to change might damage. It would be wrong to damage a thinking mind. There had been one such attempt, but it had not worked.

"What is it you are trying to communicate, Other Sam?"

A wish to be left alone. *Despair!*

Despair was more than a thought; it was an emotion; it was a frightening sensation. Sam felt despair wash over him intensely, heavily—and yet it was not part of himself. He felt despair on the surface of his mind, keenly, but underneath it, where his own mind was, he was free of it.

Sam said, wonderingly, "It seems to me as though you're giving up. Why? We're not interfering with you?"

Human beings had built the Dome, cleared a large area of all planetary life and substituted their own. And once the neutron star had its power station—once floods of energy moved outward through hyperspace to power-thirsty worlds—more power stations would be built and still more. Then what would happen to *Home.* (There must be a name for the planet that the Other Sam used but the only thought Sam found in his mind was *Home* and, underneath that, the thought: *ours—ours—ours—*)

This planet was the nearest convenient base to the neutron star. It would be flooded with more and more people, more and more Domes, and their Home would be destroyed. Ⓛ

"But you could change our minds if you had to, even if you damaged a few, couldn't you?"

Ⓛ **SETTING AND PLO**
What **conflict** is being
introduced?

7. **manifestation** (măn′ə-fĕ-stā′shən): an indication of the presence of something.

DIFFERENTIATED INSTRUCTION

FOR ENGLISH LEARNERS

Culture: Connect In lines 309–313, Sam compares the experience of adapting to the way the Other Sam communicates to learning a new language. Have students describe some of their experiences adapting to a new language. Help them notice possible parallels with what Sam experiences, such as his feeling that the other person is speaking too quickly.

FOR ADVANCED LEARNERS/PRE–AP

Synthesize When does science fiction echo real life? Point out that science fiction authors sometimes use their plots to critique the society in which they live. Ask students to review lines 338–363 and then discuss possible parallels between the settlement of Energy Planet by Earth's people and the settlement of North America by Europeans. Encourage groups to discuss whether they agree with the opinion given in lines 353–354.

If they tried, people would find them dangerous. People would work out hat was happening. Ships would approach, and from a distance, use weapons destroy the life on Home, and then bring in People-life instead. This could e seen in the people's minds. People had a violent history; they would stop at othing.

"But what can I do?" said Sam. "I'm just an apprentice. I've just been here a w days. What can I do?"

Fear. Despair.

There were no thoughts that Sam could work out, just the numbing layer of ar and despair.

He felt moved. It was such a peaceful world. They threatened nobody. They idn't even hurt minds when they could. Ⓜ

It wasn't their fault they were conveniently near a neutron star. It wasn't eir fault they were in the way of expanding humanity.

He said, "Let me think."

He thought, and there was the feeling of another mind watching. ometimes his thoughts skipped forward and he recognized a suggestion from utside.

There came the beginning of hope. Sam felt it, but wasn't certain.

He said doubtfully, "I'll try."

③ Targeted Passage

Ⓜ **SETTING AND PLOT**
What have you learned about the beings who inhabit this planet?

He looked at the time-strip[8] on his wrist and jumped a little. Far more time ad passed than he had realized. His three hours were nearly up. "I must go ack now," he said.

He opened his lunch hamper and removed the small thermos of water, rank from it thirstily, and emptied it. He placed the empty thermos under ne arm. He removed the wrappings of the sandwich and stuffed it in his ocket.

The Other Sam wavered and turned smoky. The smoke thinned, dispersed nd was gone.

Sam closed the hamper, swung its strap over his shoulder again and turned oward the Dome.

His heart was hammering. Would he have the courage to go through with is plan? And if he did, would it work?

When Sam entered the Dome, the Corridor-Master was waiting for him and aid, as he looked ostentatiously at his own time-strip, "You shaved it rather ine, didn't you?"

Sam's lips tightened and he tried not to sound **insolent.** "I had three ours, sir."

insolent (ĭn'sə-lənt) *adj.* insulting; arrogant

"And you took two hours and fifty-eight minutes."

"That's less than three hours, sir."

"Hmm." The Corridor-Master was cold and unfriendly. "Dr. Gentry would ike to see you."

8. **time-strip:** watch.

LITERARY ANALYSIS

Ⓜ SETTING AND PLOT

Possible answer: *The beings are peaceful and don't want to hurt humans.*

Extend the Discussion According to the Other Sam, how are "people" different from the beings on Energy Planet?

Lines 381–382

REINFORCE *KEY IDEA:* PURPOSE

Discuss Why does Sam have a sense of **purpose** after his conversation with the Other Sam? ***Possible answer:*** *He understands the harm that will come to the planet as the neutron-star project expands. He is determined to try to save the beings and their home from being destroyed.*

FOR LESS–PROFICIENT READERS

③ Targeted Passage [Lines 350–369]

This passage develops a second conflict as part of the rising action: Sam wants to help the beings save their home.

- What is the likely future of Energy Planet now that humans are there?
- How does the Other Sam feel about this future?
- Why does Sam doubt, at first, that he can help? How does his attitude change?

Comprehension Support Have students reread lines 365–382. Point out that, after receiving "a suggestion from outside," Sam realizes his time is almost up, yet he pauses to open his lunch hamper and remove his thermos and sandwich wrapper. Note that the Other Sam is gone before Sam closes the hamper. Ask students to explain Sam's actions and where the Other Sam went. *(Sam was making room in his hamper for the beings so he could take them into the Dome.)*

READING SKILL: ***Review***

N MAKE INFERENCES

Possible answer: *The Corridor-Master sees Sam as a troublemaker because Sam nearly exceeded his three-hour time limit for being outside the Dome and because Dr. Gentry, who is in charge, wants to see him immediately.*

Lines 404–431

REINFORCE *KEY IDEA:* PURPOSE

Discuss What **purpose** does Dr. Gentry believe he serves in the Dome? ***Possible answer:*** *He believes it is his job to supervise the apprentices and make sure they do not cause trouble. When he notices that the Central Computer has assigned someone to the project who doesn't seem to fit in, he decides to keep an eye on Sam.*

"Yes, sir. What for?"

"He didn't tell me. But I don't like you cutting it that fine your first time out, Chase. And I don't like your attitude either, and I don't like an officer of the Dome wanting to see you. I'm just going to tell you once, Chase—if you're a troublemaker, I won't want you in this Corridor. Do you understand?"

"Yes, sir. But what trouble have I made?"

"We'll find that out soon enough." **N**

N MAKE INFERENC
Why do you think the Corridor-Master believes that Sam is a troublemaker?

Sam had not seen Donald Gentry since their one and only meeting the day the young apprentice had reached the Dome. Gentry still seemed good natured and kindly, and there was nothing in his voice to indicate anything else. He sat in a chair behind his desk, and Sam stood before it, his hamper still bumping his shoulder blade.

Gentry said, "How are you getting along, Sam? Having an interesting time?"

"Yes, sir," said Sam.

"Still feeling you'd rather be doing something else, working somewhere else?"

Sam said, earnestly, "No, sir. This is a good place for me."

"Because you're interested in hallucinations?"

"Yes, sir."

"You've been asking others about it, haven't you?"

"It's an interesting subject to me, sir."

"Because you want to study the human brain?"

"Any brain, sir."

"And you've been wandering about outside the Dome, haven't you?"

"I was told it was permitted, sir."

"It is. But few apprentices take advantage of that so soon. Did you see anything interesting?"

Sam hesitated, then said, "Yes, sir."

"A hallucination?"

"No, sir." He said it quite positively.

Gentry stared at him for a few moments, and there was a kind of speculative hardening of his eyes. "Would you care to tell me what you did see? Honestly."

Sam hesitated again. Then he said, "I saw and spoke to an inhabitant of this planet, sir."

"An intelligent inhabitant, young man?"

"Yes, sir."

Gentry said, "Sam, we had reason to wonder about you when you came. The Central Computer's report on you did not match our needs, though it was favorable in many ways, so I took the opportunity to study you that first day. We kept our collective eye on you, and when you left to wander about the planet on your own, we kept you under observation."

"Sir," said Sam, indignantly. "That violates my right of privacy."

DIFFERENTIATED INSTRUCTION

FOR ADVANCED LEARNERS/PRE-AP

Predict What might the Corridor-Master's labeling of Sam as a troublemaker foreshadow in the story? Have students use the information in Parts One and Two to create a scenario, or projected plot outline, for the remainder of the story. Invite students to share and discuss their scenarios. Tell students to record their predictions and have them check and adjust these predictions as they continue to read.

"Yes, it does, but this is a most vital project and we are sometimes driven to end the rules a little. We saw you talking with considerable animation for a ubstantial period of time."

"I just told you I was, sir."

"Yes, but you were talking to *nothing*, to empty air. You were experiencing a hallucination, Sam!"

ANALYZE VISUALS
What do the details in the photograph suggest about this man's **character?**

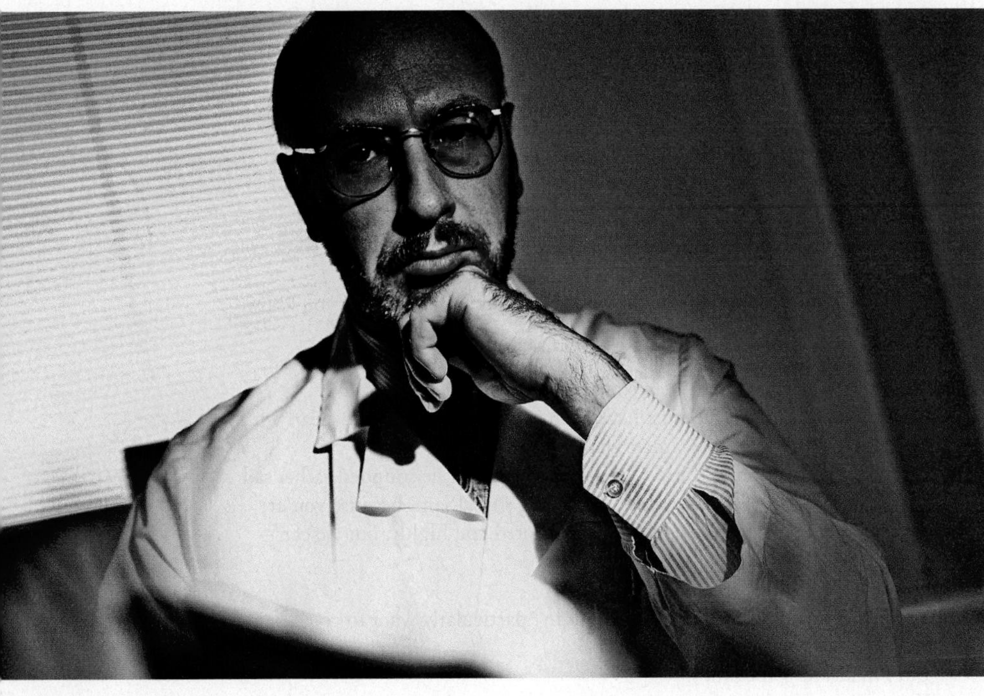

PART THREE

Sam Chase was speechless. A hallucination? It couldn't be a hallucination. Less than half an hour ago, he had been speaking to the Other Sam, had been experiencing the thoughts of the Other Sam. He knew exactly what had happened then, and he was still the same Sam Chase he had been during that conversation and before. He put his elbow over his lunch hamper as though it were a connection with the sandwiches he had been eating when the Other Sam had appeared.

He said, with what was almost a stammer, "Sir—Dr. Gentry—it wasn't a hallucination. It was real."

ANALYZE VISUALS

Possible answer: *His unsmiling face and stern stare suggest that he is unfriendly.*

Lines 406–438
DISCUSSION PROMPTS

Use these prompts to help students understand the opposition Sam faces when he reports his encounter with the Other Sam:

Summarize What do Sam and Dr. Gentry talk about in this scene? ***Answer:*** *Dr. Gentry and Sam discuss what Sam experienced when he was outside the Dome.*

Apply How did Sam's experience with the Other Sam appeal to his interest in neurophysiology? ***Possible answer:*** *Neurophysiology, the study of the nervous system, includes the study of intelligence and the brain. Sam has had an exchange with an unusual form of intelligence.*

Evaluate What opposition does Sam face from Dr. Gentry? Does Dr. Gentry's reaction to Sam's account surprise you? Why or why not? ***Possible answers:*** *Dr. Gentry insists that Sam was talking to thin air—that he saw a hallucination, not an intelligent inhabitant of the planet. Students may say it is surprising that an educated scientist such as Dr. Gentry does not show more curiosity about Sam's discovery. Others may say that they are not surprised that Gentry dismisses Sam's observations, either because Gentry fears for the survival of the neutron-star project or because Sam is young and inexperienced.*

FOR ENGLISH LEARNERS

Vocabulary: Multiple-Meaning Words [mixed-readiness pairs] Have students work in pairs to create a Word Square for *animation* (line 434) based on its meaning in the story. Then have students use this graphic organizer for other words with multiple meanings, such as *flushed* (line 107), *hamper* (line 184), *alien* (line 309), and *grant* (line 559).

Word: *animation* **Translation:** *animado*	**Symbol or Picture:** 
My Meaning: *liveliness* **Dictionary Definition:** *(1) act or process of giving life, motion, or spirit to something; (2) quality of being alive or active; (3) process of preparing animated cartoons*	**Sentence:** *The fans showed their animation by shouting and stomping.*

 **BEST PRACTICES TOOLKIT—Transparency**
Word Squares p. E10

Lines 448–495
DISCUSSION PROMPTS

Use these prompts to help students understand how Sam shows persistence and courage in the face of opposition:

Recall What "proof" does Dr. Gentry have that Sam was not talking to something real outside the Dome? ***Answer:*** *Sam was recorded on a television cassette, which shows him talking to nothing.*

Analyze Why does Sam say that the other apprentices don't tell Dr. Gentry if they have a hallucination? ***Possible answer:*** *If the apprentices do see the beings, they are too frightened to report it because they know it will hurt their careers.*

Evaluate Do you think Sam is wise to insist on a hearing before the Commander? Explain. *Some students may say a meeting with the Commander is his only hope to help the inhabitants of the planet. Others may say Sam's demand is not wise because the Commander will send him home and the official report from the hearing will ruin Sam's career.*

LITERARY ANALYSIS

⊙ SETTING AND PLOT

Possible answer: *Because of his interest in neurophysiology, he is fascinated by the intelligence of the alien life-forms. He wants to save their habitat and continue studying these unusual life-forms.*

Gentry shook his head. "My boy, I saw you talking with animation to nothing at all. I didn't hear what you said, but you were talking. Nothing else was there except plants. Nor was I the only one. There were two other witnesses, and we have it all on record."

"On record?"

"On a television cassette. Why should we lie to you, young man? This has happened before. At the start it happened rather frequently. Now it happens only very rarely. For one thing, we tell the new apprentices of the hallucinations at the start, as I told you, and they generally avoid the planet until they are more acclimated, and then it doesn't happen to them."

"You mean you scare them," blurted out Sam, "so that it's not likely to happen. And they don't tell you if it does happen. But I wasn't scared."

Gentry shook his head. "I'm sorry you weren't, if that was what it would have taken you to keep from seeing things."

"I wasn't seeing things. At least, not things that weren't there."

"How do you intend to argue with a television cassette, which will show you staring at nothing?"

"Sir, what I saw was not opaque. It was smoky, actually; foggy, if you know what I mean."

"Yes, I do. It looked as a hallucination might look, not as reality. But the television set would have seen even smoke."

"Maybe not, sir. My mind must have been focused to see it more clearly. It was probably less clear to the camera than to me."

"It focused your mind, did it?" Gentry stood up, and he sounded rather sad. "That's an admission of hallucination. I'm really sorry, Sam, because you are clearly intelligent, and the Central Computer rated you highly, but we can't use you."

"Will you be sending me home, sir?"

"Yes, but why should that matter? You didn't particularly want to come here."

"I want to stay here *now.*"

"But I'm afraid you cannot."

"You can't just send me home. Don't I get a hearing?"

"You certainly can, if you insist, but in that case, the proceedings will be official and will go on your record, so that you won't get another apprenticeship anywhere. As it is, if you are sent back unofficially, as better suited to an apprenticeship in neurophysiology, you might get that, and be better off, actually, than you are now."

"I don't want that. I want a hearing—before the Commander."

"Oh, no. Not the Commander. He can't be bothered with that."

"It *must* be the Commander," said Sam, with desperate force, "or this Project will fail." ⊙

⊙ SETTING AND PLO
Why does Sam so badl
want to stay on Energy
Planet?

DIFFERENTIATED INSTRUCTION

FOR LESS–PROFICIENT READERS

Vocabulary Support Help students use context clues to figure out the meanings of these words. Invite them to use each word correctly in a sentence and share it with the rest of the class.

- *acclimated* (line 457), "accustomed to a place or situation"
- *opaque* (line 465), "solid"
- *hearing* (line 485), "opportunity to present a case"
- *desperate* (line 487), "moved by despair"

"Unless the Commander gives you a hearing? Why do you say that? Come, you are forcing me to think that you are unstable in ways other than those involved with hallucinations."

"Sir." The words were tumbling out of Sam's mouth now. "The Commander is ill—they know that even on Earth—and if he gets too ill to work, this Project will fail. I did not see a hallucination and the proof is that I know why he is ill and how he can be cured."

"You're not helping yourself," said Gentry.

"If you send me away, I tell you the Project will fail. Can it hurt to let me see the Commander? All I ask is five minutes."

"Five minutes? What if he refuses?"

"*Ask* him, sir. Tell him that I say the same thing that caused his depression can remove it."

"No, I don't think I'll tell him that. But I'll ask him if he'll see you."

The Commander was a thin man, not very tall. His eyes were a deep blue and they looked tired.

His voice was very soft, a little low-pitched, definitely weary. **P**

P VISUALIZE
What does the Commander look like? Note the details that help you picture him, and then sketch him in your chart.

"You're the one who saw the hallucination?"

"It was not a hallucination, Commander. It was real. So was the one *you* saw, Commander." If that did not get him thrown out, Sam thought, he might have a chance. He felt his elbow tightening on his hamper again. He still had it with him.

The Commander seemed to wince. "The one *I* saw?"

"Yes, Commander. It said it had hurt one person. They had to try with you because you were the Commander, and they . . . did damage."

The Commander ignored that and said, "Did you ever have any mental problems before you came here?"

"No, Commander. You can consult my Central Computer record."

Sam thought: *He* must have had problems, but they let it go because he's a genius and they had to have him.

Then he thought: Was that my own idea? Or had it been put there?

The Commander was speaking. Sam had almost missed it. He said, "What you saw can't be real. There is no intelligent life-form on this planet."

"Yes, sir. There is."

"Oh? And no one ever discovered it till you came here, and in three days you did the job?" The Commander smiled very briefly. "I'm afraid I have no choice but to—"

"Wait, Commander," said Sam, in a strangled voice. "We know about the intelligent life-form. It's the insects, the little flying things."

"You say the insects are intelligent?"

FOR LESS–PROFICIENT READERS

Comprehension Support Remind students of the inferences they drew about Sam's emptying of his lunch hamper (lines 370–380). Then point out Sam's thoughts in lines 517–519. What makes Sam think an idea might have been placed in his mind while he is talking to the Commander? *(The beings might be communicating with him from inside the hamper as they eavesdrop on the conversation.)*

READING STRATEGY

P VISUALIZE

Possible answer: *Details in lines 503–505 describe the Commander. He is thin and "not very tall." He has deep blue tired-looking eyes. His voice is "very soft, a little low-pitched, definitely weary."*

If students need help . . . Before students draw their sketch, ask them what tired eyes might look like.

Lines 512–527
DISCUSSION PROMPTS

Use these prompts to help students understand the exchange between Sam and the Commander:

Connect In general, do you think it is hard for a young person to change the mind of an adult? In what way does this help you understand the Commander's reaction to Sam? *Students may say that adults often do not take the comments of young people as seriously as they do those of other adults. The Commander is probably not taking Sam seriously either.*

Infer To what does Sam attribute the Commander's illness? Why does the Commander think that Sam may have "mental problems"? ***Possible answer:*** *Sam claims that the alien life-form he met damaged the Commander's mind when trying to communicate with him. The Commander dismisses this idea and assumes Sam must be mentally unbalanced.*

Synthesize If you were in the Commander's shoes, would you be inclined to believe Sam? Based on your knowledge of life sciences and space exploration, do you think there is intelligent life on distant planets? *Students' responses should refer to the circumstances in the story and what they know about the life sciences and space exploration.*

LITERARY ANALYSIS

Ⓠ SETTING AND PLOT

Possible answer: *When a lot of insects come together in a swarm, their nervous systems combine and interact. In this state, they have the intelligence to communicate with humans.*

If students need help . . . Have students reread lines 529–532. Point out how the image of jigsaw puzzle pieces can help them understand the idea of collective intelligence that Sam is describing. Illustrate Sam's point by sketching interlocking jigsaw pieces on the board. Also, direct students to the visual on this page and point out how it shows that many insects together can form a "smoky" image.

Extend the Discussion Ask students to think back on their answers to the question on page 341 about whether or not Sam is hallucinating. Have they changed their minds? What do they think now?

"Not an individual insect by itself, but they fit together when they want to, like little jigsaw pieces. They can do it in any way they want. And when they do, their nervous systems fit together, too, and build up. A lot of them *together* are intelligent." Ⓠ

The Commander's eyebrows lifted. "That's an interesting idea, anyway. Almost crazy enough to be true. How did you come to that conclusion, young man?"

"By observation, sir. Everywhere I walked, I disturbed the insects in the grass and they flew about in all directions. But once the cow started to form, and I walked toward it, there was nothing to see or hear. The insects were gone. They had gathered together in front of me and they weren't in the grass anymore. That's how I knew."

"You talked with a cow?"

"It was a cow at first, because that's what I thought of. But they had it wrong, so they switched and came together to form a human being—*me*."

"You?" And then, in a lower voice, "Well, that fits anyway."

"Did you see it that way, too, Commander?"

The Commander ignored that. "And when it shaped itself like you, it could talk as you did? Is that what you're telling me?"

"No, Commander. The talking was in my mind."

"Telepathy?"

Ⓠ SETTING AND PLC
Reread lines 529–532. How do the insects communicate with humans?

DIFFERENTIATED INSTRUCTION

FOR ENGLISH LEARNERS

Language: Pronoun Referents

- Point out the pronoun *they* in lines 529–532. Explain that the pronoun the author chose is plural because it refers to the plural word *insects*.
- Then highlight the word *it* in lines 546–547. Explain that at this point the Commander is referring to the many insects that have combined into something that looks like a single human being. Therefore, a singular pronoun, *it*, is appropriate to refer to this being.
- Have students find other examples of *they* and *it* on page 350 and ask them to identify the singular or plural word that is its referent.

"Sort of."

"And what did it say to you, or think to you?"

"It wanted us to **refrain** from disturbing this planet. It wanted us not to ake it over." Sam was all but holding his breath. The interview had lasted nore than five minutes already, and the Commander was making no move to ut an end to it, to send him home.

"Quite impossible."

"Why, Commander?"

"Any other base will double and triple the expense. We're having enough rouble getting grants as it is. Fortunately, it is all a hallucination, young man, nd the problem does not arise." He closed his eyes, then opened them and ooked at Sam without really focusing on him. "I'm sorry, young man. You will e sent back—officially." R

Sam gambled again. "We can't afford to ignore the insects, Commander. They have a lot to give us."

The Commander had raised his hand halfway as though about to give a ignal. He paused long enough to say, "Really? What do they have that they an give us?"

"The one thing more important than energy, Commander. An nderstanding of the brain."

"How do you know that?"

ANALYZE VISUALS
In what ways is the setting captured by this photo different from how you pictured Energy Planet? In what ways is it similar?

refrain (rĭ-frān') *v.* to hold oneself back; to stop

R **SETTING AND PLOT**
Why is it so important to the Commander to remain on the planet?

ANALYZE VISUALS

Students might say that they pictured Energy Planet as a sunny place, since it is a "pleasant world." In the photo, it looks dark. Both the photo and the description of Energy Planet include "lots of tall grass" and numerous tiny flying insects.

LITERARY ANALYSIS

R SETTING AND PLOT

Possible answer: *The project is already having trouble getting funding. If the base is shifted somewhere else, the expense of the project will "double and triple."*

If students need help . . . Explain that the word *grants* (line 559) refers to money awarded for specific purposes, such as the neutron-star project.

FOR LESS–PROFICIENT READERS

Comprehension Support Make sure students understand that the Commander is starting to believe Sam's testimony that the insects are intelligent, but he is opposed to changing the project's base in order to avoid disturbing their planet. Have students complete a Sequence Chain to clarify the plot events that occur during Sam's meeting with the Commander (pages 349–353).

 **BEST PRACTICES TOOLKIT—Transparency**
Sequence Chain pp. B21, B45

READING STRATEGY

S VISUALIZE

Possible answer: *When Sam opens the hamper, a "softly whirring, smoky cloud" comes out (lines 574–575) and forms into the shape of a head that resembles the Commander (lines 581–583).*

If students need help . . . Suggest that students sketch two pictures side by side to show what the insects do.

"I can demonstrate it. I have them here." Sam seized his hamper and swung it forward onto the desk.

"What's that?"

Sam did not answer in words. He opened the hamper, and a softly whirring, smoky cloud appeared.

The Commander rose suddenly and cried out. He lifted his hand high and an alarm bell sounded.

Through the door came Gentry, and others behind him. Sam felt himself seized by the arms, and then a kind of stunned and motionless silence prevailed in the room.

The smoke was condensing, wavering, taking on the shape of a Head, a thin head, with high cheekbones, a smooth forehead and receding hairline. It had the appearance of the Commander.

"I'm seeing things," croaked the Commander.

Sam said, "We're all seeing the same thing, aren't we?" He wriggled and was released. S

Gentry said in a low voice, "Mass hysteria."

"No," said Sam, "it's real." He reached toward the Head in midair, and brought back his finger with a tiny insect on it. He flicked it and it could just barely be seen making its way back to its companions.

No one moved.

Sam said, "Head, do you see the problem with the Commander's mind?"

Sam had the brief vision of a snarl in an otherwise smooth curve, but it vanished and left nothing behind. It was not something that could be easily put into human thought. He hoped the others experienced that quick snarl. Yes, they had. He knew it.

The Commander said, "There is no problem."

Sam said, "Can you adjust it, Head?"

Of course, they could not. It was not right to invade a mind.

Sam said, "Commander, give permission."

The Commander put his hands to his eyes and muttered something Sam did not make out. Then he said, clearly, "It's a nightmare, but I've been in one since—Whatever must be done, I give permission."

Nothing happened.

Or nothing seemed to happen.

And then slowly, little by little, the Commander's face lit in a smile.

He said, just above a whisper, "Astonishing. I'm watching a sun rise. It's been cold night for so long, and now I feel the warmth again." His voice rose high. "I feel wonderful."

The Head deformed at that point, turned into a vague, pulsing fog, then formed a curving, narrowing arrow that sped into the hamper. Sam snapped it shut.

④ **Targeted Passag**

S VISUALIZE
Imagine what the Commander sees wh Sam opens his hampe Sketch this scene in your chart.

DIFFERENTIATED INSTRUCTION

FOR LESS-PROFICIENT READERS

④ **Targeted Passage [Lines 571–616]**

This passage marks the climax and falling action of the story: Sam demonstrates the intelligence of the insects to the Commander and Dr. Gentry, and the Commander decides to change the plans for the project.

- What shape do the flying insects form?
- Who sees what the insects do?
- What change in the Commander's mood occurs after he says, "I give permission"?
- What does the Commander decide to do as a result of Sam's demonstration?

He said, "Commander, have I your permission to restore these little insect-things to their own world?"

"Yes, yes," said the Commander, dismissing that with a wave of his hand. Gentry, call a meeting. We've got to change all our plans." (T)

④ Targeted Passage

(T) **SETTING AND PLOT**
What did the insects do to make the Commander change his plans?

Sam had been escorted outside the Dome by a stolid guard and had then been confined to his quarters for the rest of the day.

It was late when Gentry entered, stared at him thoughtfully, and said, "That was an amazing demonstration of yours. The entire incident has been fed into the Central Computer and we now have a double project—neutron-star energy and neurophysiology. I doubt that there will be any question about pouring money into this project now. And we'll have a group of neurophysiologists arriving eventually. Until then you're going to be working with those little things and you'll probably end up the most important person here."

Sam said, "But will we leave their world to them?"

Gentry said, "We'll have to if we expect to get anything out of them, won't we? The Commander thinks we're going to build elaborate settlements in orbit about this world and shift all operations to them except for a skeleton crew in this Dome to maintain direct contact with the insects—or whatever we'll decide to call them. It will cost a great deal of money, and take time and labor, but it's going to be worth it. No one will question that." (U)

⑤ Targeted Passage

(U) **SETTING AND PLOT**
Reread lines 619–633. What **resolution** have the humans reached regarding their plans for Energy Planet, and for Sam?

Sam said, "Good!"

Gentry stared at him again, longer and more thoughtfully than before.

"My boy," he said, "it seems that what happened came about because you did not fear the supposed hallucination. Your mind remained open, and that was the whole difference. Why was that? Why weren't you afraid?"

Sam flushed. "I'm not sure, sir. As I look back on it, though, it seemed to me I was puzzled as to why I was sent here. I had been doing my best to study neurophysiology through my computerized courses, and I knew very little about astrophysics. The Central Computer had my record, all of it, the full details of everything I had ever studied and I couldn't imagine why I had been sent here.

"Then, when you first mentioned the hallucinations, I thought, 'That must be it. I was sent here to look into it.' I just made up my mind that was the thing I had to do. I had no *time* to be afraid, Dr. Gentry. I had a problem to solve and I—I had faith in the Central Computer. It wouldn't have sent me here, if I weren't up to it."

Gentry shook his head. "I'm afraid I wouldn't have had that much faith in that machine. But they say faith can move mountains, and I guess it did in this case."

LITERARY ANALYSIS

(T) SETTING AND PLOT

Possible answer: *The insects cure the Commander's depression. Their ability to communicate makes the Commander realize that they are important and helps him justify changing the plan for the energy project.*

Lines 619–633
REINFORCE *KEY IDEA:* PURPOSE

Discuss In what way does Sam fulfill the **purpose** given to him by the Central Computer? In what way does his new purpose suit his interest in neurophysiology? ***Possible answer:*** *Sam saved the insects' habitat. Sam's new job will be to study the intelligence of Energy Planet's insect-like inhabitants.*

LITERARY ANALYSIS

(U) SETTING AND PLOT

Possible answer: *The plan now is to have a double project. The humans will keep working to get energy from the neutron star, but they will work from space stations rather than on Energy Planet. A small crew of people will live on the planet to maintain contact with its life-forms. Sam will probably be in charge of the neurophysiology project.*

SELECTION WRAP-UP

REFLECT Ask students to think about why it was important for Energy Planet to have an Earth-like environment. Could Asimov have told the same story, with the same theme, on a planet that was vastly different from Earth?

CRITIQUE Have students consider the life-form that Asimov invented for "Hallucination." Ask whether they find this character intriguing. Compare the Other Sam to other aliens in science fiction stories and films.

READING FLUENCY

Distribute the copy masters and have students practice fluency.

RESOURCE MANAGER—Copy Master
Reading Fluency p. 81

FOR LESS-PROFICIENT READERS

⑤ Targeted Passage [Lines 619–633]

The conflict is fully resolved in this passage.

- What changes will be made to the neutron-star project?
- What role will Sam play?
- In what way will Energy Planet benefit from the changes?

FOR ADVANCED LEARNERS/PRE-AP

Evaluate Plot Invite students to critique the plot of "Hallucination." Have them rate the effectiveness of each stage of the plot—exposition, rising action, climax, falling action, and resolution—on a scale of 1 to 5 and then explain their ratings in a sentence or two. Suggest that students then pair up to compare and discuss their ratings.

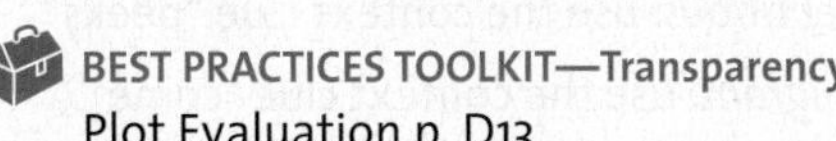

BEST PRACTICES TOOLKIT—Transparency
Plot Evaluation p. D13

DISCUSSION PROMPTS

Use these prompts to help students understand how Asimov became a science fiction writer:

Connect Have you ever felt a sense of purpose to overcome a challenge? In what way does this help you understand Asimov's feeling that he had "something to rise above"? *Students may say that a challenge pushes you to make certain decisions, as Asimov's challenge to succeed at reading and writing pushed him toward being a science fiction writer.*

Analyze What other events caused Asimov to become a science fiction writer? ***Possible answer:*** *Asimov immigrated to the United States, which fueled his desire to succeed at reading and writing. This led him to read science fiction magazines. Asimov's father disapproved of the magazines but gave in because he was preoccupied with the impending birth of Asimov's brother. Asimov was so interested in science fiction that he started writing his own stories.*

BACKGROUND

Science Fiction Magazines The first science fiction magazines were published in the United States. With titles like *Science Wonder Stories* and *Amazing Stories,* both of which appeared in the late 1920s, magazines were the only place readers could find science fiction until the 1950s. Many of the early magazine stories were simply tales of adventure set on imagined planets, and many of the authors were inexperienced writers. Gradually, science and technology became a more important element in the stories, and the literary quality improved as well. Today, apart from a handful of magazines, including *Analog* and *Asimov's Science Fiction,* most science fiction is published in book form.

Reading for Information

PERSONAL ESSAY Much like Sam Chase in "Hallucination," Isaac Asimov found his purpose in a place far from where he was born. When Asimov was three, he and his parents emigrated from Russia to the U.S. His father never fully mastered English, and both father and son wanted the boy to succeed at reading and writing.

from Ellis Island and I

Isaac Asimov

Only in one point did we clash in this matter of reading, and that was over the newsstand in the candy store. I wanted to read the magazines and my father was unalterably opposed. He felt that I would be reading trash and contaminating what he obviously was beginning to think was going to be a first-class mind.

For a while all my arguments fell on deaf ears, and then I discovered science-fiction magazines, which I took surreptitious peeks at while my father was taking his afternoon nap. In particular, I found one called *Science Wonder Stories,* and I pointed out to my father that since the stories were about science, they were bound to be educational.

It was a good time to attack, for my mother was pregnant with what turned out to be my younger brother, and my father was feeling as though he had a lot more on his mind than questions over whether I could read a magazine or not. He gave in.

That started me, at the age of nine, on my career as a science-fiction reader. By the time I was eleven, I felt that I just could not get enough science fiction from the magazines (there were only three, and they came out only once a month), and it struck me that I might write my own.

I didn't quite write science fiction at first, but I managed to get to it when I was fifteen, and by the time I was eighteen I sold a story to one of the magazines and was off and running.

I cannot say how things would have been for me had I not come into the United States as an immigrant. I can't go back and live life over under changed circumstances. Still, as I think about it, it seems to me I needed something to rise above.

To be brief, I'm glad I came here—and I'm glad I had to come here. Life might have been too easy for me if my ancestors had beat me to the punch and had come here on the Mayflower.

354 UNIT 3: SETTING AND MOOD

DIFFERENTIATED INSTRUCTION

FOR LESS–PROFICIENT READERS

Vocabulary Support Guide students in using different strategies to tackle unfamiliar words and terms in the essay:

- *unalterably:* use context clue "opposed"; note *-ly* ending for adverb
- *opposed:* relate to *opposition,* a familiar word from "Hallucination"
- *surreptitious:* use the context clue "peeks"
- *immigrant:* use the context clue "come into the United States"

FOR ENGLISH LEARNERS

Options for Reading Have students listen to the *Audio Anthology CD* and then pair up to read the essay out loud. Suggest that each student read half the essay aloud. The listener should then summarize what was read.

Culture: Clarify Explain these terms from American history:

- *Ellis Island:* immigration station from 1892 to 1954
- *the* Mayflower: ship that carried early English colonists to North America in 1620

nprehension

Recall Why does Sam succeed in communicating with the life forms on Energy Planet?

Recall Why does the Other Sam feel despair?

Clarify Why does Sam bring his lunch box to his meeting with the Commander?

rary Analysis

Visualize Choose three sketches from the chart you completed as you read. For each sketch, tell which parts are based on the author's description and which parts, if any, came from your imagination.

Analyze Setting and Plot How does the setting of "Hallucination" affect the plot of the story? Use examples from the selection to support your answer.

Interpret Science Fiction Writers of science fiction often comment on present society by writing about the future. What message about contemporary culture might Asimov have been communicating with "Hallucination"? Cite evidence from the story to support your interpretation.

Compare Characters Think back to your reading of "The Drummer Boy of Shiloh" on page 318. Although the setting is different from that of "Hallucination," both selections feature teenaged main characters who face big challenges. In a chart like the one shown, compare and contrast these characters in terms of their motivations for taking on the challenge, their traits, and their reactions to events and characters.

	Joby	Sam	Similarities and Differences
Motivations			
Traits			
Reactions			

ension and Challenge

Literary Criticism Isaac Asimov once wrote that, for science fiction writers, "each year sees possible plots destroyed" as real-life technology and information catches up with the imaginary. With a group, discuss whether this means that science fiction written many years ago is no longer relevant. "Hallucination" was written in the last century. Do its messages still hold up today?

Readers' Circle Read the selection "Ellis Island and I" on page 354, taking note of the young Isaac Asimov's personality traits. What characteristics do Asimov and Sam Chase share? How did each young man realize his **purpose?** Share your ideas with a group.

Practice and Apply

After Reading

For additional support of postreading questions, use these copy masters:

RESOURCE MANAGER—Copy Masters
Reading Check p. 78 (to check understanding of the selection)
Setting and Plot p. 71 (for practice of literary analysis standards focus)
Question Support p. 79 (After Reading questions adapted for English learners and less-proficient readers)

Additional selection questions are provided for teachers on page 65.

For additional activities to challenge students, see

Power Thinking at **ClassZone.com**

ANSWERS

Comprehension

1. *Sam is not afraid of the life-forms.*
2. *The Other Sam fears that human beings will take over its planet and destroy it.*
3. *His lunch box contains the insects, his proof that he did not have a hallucination.*

Literary Analysis

Possible answers:

4. **STANDARDS FOCUS Visualize** *Sketches should be mainly based on story details. Students should cite specific words and phrases that are reflected in their sketches.*
5. **STANDARDS FOCUS Setting and Plot** *The setting is a distant planet located near a neutron star. If Sam had not been sent to this planet, he would not have discovered the insects. Because Sam saves the insects' habitat from being destroyed by the humans, Sam receives an important job in neurophysiology.*
6. *Students may say that Asimov was commenting on how exploring for natural resources can have harmful side effects.*
7. *Students may say that although Joby and Sam are motivated in different ways, they share many similarities, such as the fact that they both are young and are searching for their purpose in life.*

   Joby
   - ***Motivations:*** *admires the General and wants to make him proud*
   - ***Traits:*** *unsure of himself; doesn't feel like his work is important; young; feels alone*
   - ***Reactions:*** *is surprised when the General tells him how important he is*

   Sam
   - ***Motivations:*** *wants to figure out why he has been assigned to Energy Planet; wants to convince the Commander that he is right*
   - ***Traits:*** *unsure of himself; inquisitive; intelligent; young; inexperienced*
   - ***Reactions:*** *realizes he is the one who can save the creatures on Energy Planet*

Extension and Challenge

8. *Students may note that the messages provided by science fiction can serve as a reminder of the harmful effects that can be caused by progress in technology, which may become more important as technology is advanced.*
9. *The young Asimov, like Sam Chase, was inquisitive and confident. Sam realized his purpose by investigating a problem related to neurophysiology. Asimov read all the science fiction he could get his hands on, started writing his own stories, and at age 18 sold a story to a science fiction magazine.*

ANSWERS

Vocabulary in Context

VOCABULARY PRACTICE

1. *antonyms*
2. *synonyms*
3. *antonyms*
4. *synonyms*
5. *synonyms*
6. *antonyms*

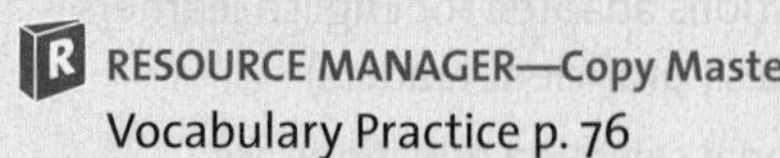

RESOURCE MANAGER—Copy Master
Vocabulary Practice p. 76

VOCABULARY IN WRITING

Ask students to jot down Sam's actions, including his conversations with others. Then have them scan the list to select words that could be used in sentences describing the actions.

VOCABULARY STRATEGY: HOMOGRAPHS

(also an EL language objective)

Point out that homographs are often different parts of speech. Also explain that some homographs have more than two entries in a dictionary.

Definitions may vary but should come from separate dictionary entries to distinguish homographs from multiple-meaning words.
Possible answers:

1. *row: (1) to propel with oars; (2) a noisy quarrel*
2. *well: (1) deep hole in the earth used to obtain water; (2) healthy*
3. *sound: (1) a specific noise; (2) to measure the depth of something*
4. *fine: (1) of very high quality; (2) sum of money paid as a penalty*
5. *wind: (1) moving air; (2) to wrap (something) around a center or another object once or repeatedly*
6. *found: (1) establish; (2) came upon*

RESOURCE MANAGER—Copy Master
Vocabulary Strategy p. 77

Vocabulary Center at **ClassZone.com**
Additional Vocabulary Activities

Vocabulary in Context

VOCABULARY PRACTICE

Decide whether the words in each pair are synonyms (words that mean the same) or antonyms (words that mean the opposite).

1. refrain/persist
2. opposition/resistance
3. inertia/activity
4. diminish/decrease
5. insolent/insulting
6. conviction/doubt

conviction
diminish
inertia
insolent
opposition
refrain

VOCABULARY IN WRITING

Imagine you are Dr. Gentry, writing a report on Sam, a new arrival. How is Sam different from the other humans on Energy Planet? Use two or more vocabulary words to write a one-paragraph report. You might start like this.

EXAMPLE SENTENCE

Sam's ***conviction*** *that the hallucinations are real is disturbing to the others.*

VOCABULARY STRATEGY: HOMOGRAPHS

Homographs are words that are spelled the same but have different meanings, origins, and sometimes pronunciations. The vocabulary word *refrain* is a homograph. Notice the following two different definitions of *refrain:*

refrain[1] (rĭ-frān') *v.* to hold oneself back; restrain

refrain[2] (rĭ-frān') *n.* a phrase or verse repeated at intervals in a poem or song

If you see a word used in a way that is unfamiliar to you, check the dictionary. You'll know a word is a homograph if there are two separate entries for the word.

PRACTICE Use a dictionary to find two or three homographs for each listed word. Note the origin of each word. Then write sentences that show the differences in meaning for each.

1. row	3. sound	5. wind
2. well	4. fine	6. found

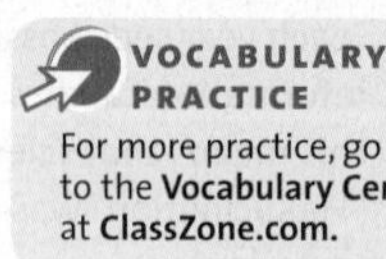

VOCABULARY PRACTICE
For more practice, go to the **Vocabulary Cen**[ter] at **ClassZone.com.**

DIFFERENTIATED INSTRUCTION

FOR LESS–PROFICIENT READERS

Vocabulary Strategy Remind students that some homographs have different pronunciations. Give these examples:

- *row* (rō): "to propel with oars"
  row (rou): "a noisy quarrel"
- *wind* (wĭnd): "moving air"
  wind (wīnd): "to wrap"

Pronounce each homograph and then have students say the word.

FOR ADVANCED LEARNERS/PRE–AP

Vocabulary Practice Challenge students to find as many synonyms as they can for each word and record them in a Cluster Diagram.

BEST PRACTICES TOOLKIT—Transparency
Cluster Diagram p. B18

ading-Writing Connection

Broaden your understanding of "Hallucination" by responding to these prompts. Then complete the **Grammar and Writing** exercise.

WRITING PROMPTS	SELF-CHECK
A. Short Response: Analyze Cause and Effect By the end of the story, Dr. Gentry tells Sam, "You'll probably end up the most important person here." How did Sam gain this position so quickly? In **one paragraph,** describe how Sam's actions made this new opportunity possible.	***A strong analysis will . . .*** • describe the events that led up to Sam's promotion • use specific details and examples from the story
B. Extended Response: Write a Letter Suppose Sam wrote home to describe his experience on Energy Planet. How would he explain how he found his **purpose** there? Write a **one-page letter** from Sam to his parents. Be sure your letter is based on facts from the story.	***A creative letter will . . .*** • identify Sam's **purpose** and summarize the events of the story • tell Sam's experiences from his point of view

AMMAR AND WRITING

AVOID MISPLACED MODIFIERS A **prepositional phrase** consists of a preposition, such as *above, at, for, from, with,* or *on;* its object (a noun or pronoun); and any modifiers of the object.

Example: The massive dome stretched in all directions.

preposition — in; modifier — all; object — directions

When you use a prepositional phrase in your writing, place it close to the word it modifies. Otherwise, you may end up confusing your readers.

Original: From the grass, I saw thousands of tiny insects flying. (*Who or what was in the grass?*)

Revised: I saw thousands of tiny insects flying from the grass. (*The insects were in the grass.*)

PRACTICE Move each misplaced prepositional phrase to the correct place.

1. I wondered why I had been sent to this planet with my background.
2. The smells are different from Earth's smells on this planet.
3. The shape began to look like me in the smoke.
4. The Commander sat in his office behind a desk.

*For more help with misplaced modifiers, see page R59 in the **Grammar Handbook.***

Reading-Writing Connection

WRITING PROMPTS

- For **Prompt A,** encourage students to use a Sequence Chain to identify and order the events that led to Sam's promotion.

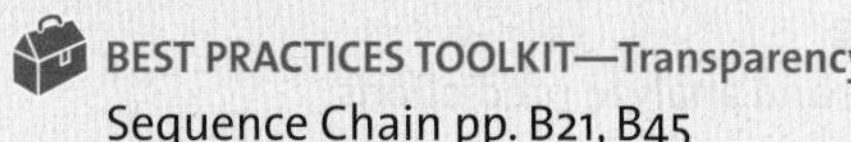

BEST PRACTICES TOOLKIT—Transparency
Sequence Chain pp. B21, B45

- For **Prompt B,** have students review Sam's thoughts about his purpose at the start and at the end of the story. Then have them review Sam's reactions to the rumors he heard, the unusual life-form he met, and the opposition from the Commander.

For an extended Reading-Writing Connection activity, see

Writing Center at **ClassZone.com**

GRAMMAR AND WRITING

Suggest that students read the sentence aloud, identify the prepositional phrase, and then find the word in the sentence that the phrase modifies.

Answers:

1. *I wondered why I, with my background, had been sent to this planet.*
2. *The smells on this planet are different from Earth's smells.*
3. *The shape in the smoke began to look like me.*
4. *The Commander sat behind a desk in his office.*

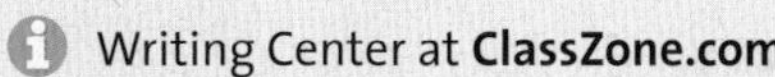

RESOURCE MANAGER—Copy Master
Avoid Misplaced Modifiers p. 80

Assess and Reteach

Assess

RESOURCE MANAGER—Copy Masters
Selection Tests A, B/C pp. 83–84, 85–86

Test Generator CD

Reteach

STANDARDS LESSON FILE
Literature Lesson 9: Setting and Its Roles
Reading Lesson 8: Making Inferences
Vocabulary Lesson 20: Homonyms and Homographs

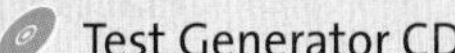

DIFFERENTIATED INSTRUCTION

FOR LESS-PROFICIENT WRITERS

For Prompt A:

1. Have students select three or four key events from the Sequence Chain.
2. After students write a topic sentence, tell them to present the key events they have chosen in chronological order.
3. Suggest that they conclude their paragraph with a statement about Sam's future work.

For Prompt B:

Students may organize their letters this way:

- **First paragraph:** Describe Sam's confusion about his assignment when he arrived on Energy Planet.
- **Second paragraph:** Describe what Sam did to save the insects' habitat and how he applied his interest in neurophysiology.
- **Third paragraph:** Focus on how Sam felt after convincing the Commander about the importance of the insects and state what his new job will be.

Focus and Motivate

OBJECTIVES

Literary Analysis
- explore the key idea of **superstitious**
- identify and analyze mood
- read a short story

Reading
- make and analyze predictions

Vocabulary
- build vocabulary for reading and writing
- use knowledge of the Latin root *cred* to determine meaning *(also an EL language objective)*

Grammar and Writing
- maintain subject-verb agreement when using compound subjects
- use writing to analyze literature

SUMMARY

An old friend, Sergeant-Major Morris, tells the Whites about a monkey's paw that grants three wishes. The Whites use the paw to wish for money, which they get, but as compensation for their son's death. Mrs. White convinces her husband to wish their son back to life. Eventually, Mr. White uses his last wish to end the tragic story.

Are you SUPERSTITIOUS?

To lead into the question and the ***KEY IDEA,*** provide this definition of ***superstitious:*** "believing that some action not connected to a future event can influence the outcome of the event." Ask students what might lead someone to become superstitious. Then have them work on the ***DISCUSS*** activity.

Before Reading

The Monkey's Paw

Short Story by W. W. Jacobs

Are you SUPERSTITIOUS

KEY IDEA Many people say they aren't **superstitious.** But those same people might own a lucky charm or get nervous on Friday the 13th. Usually these superstitions are harmless, but sometimes they can interfere with a person's life. In the selection you are about to read, curiosity about the power of an unusual object brings unexpected consequences.

DISCUSS What kinds of superstitious behaviors do you or people you know believe in? In a small group, brainstorm a list of common superstitions. Then discuss which you think are harmless, and which might cause problems or interfere with someone's life. Share your findings with the class.

358

Selection Resources

RESOURCE MANAGER UNIT 3

Plan and Teach pp. 87–94

Literary Analysis
Summary pp. 95†*, 96‡*
Mood pp. 97, 98†*
Question Support p. 105*

Reading
Predict pp. 99, 100†*
Reading Check p. 104
Reading Fluency p. 107

Vocabulary
Study p. 101*
Practice p. 102
Strategy p. 103

Grammar and Writing
Maintain Subject-Verb Agreement p. 106

Assessment
Selection Tests A, B/C pp. 109*, 111*
Test Generator CD

BEST PRACTICES TOOLKIT

Differentiated Instruction pp. 31–38*
Scaffolding Instruction pp. 43–46*

Graphic Organizers/Strategies
Word Squares • Visualizing • Word Questioning • Read Aloud/Think Aloud • New Word Analysis • Open Mind • Freewriting • Sentence Imitation

Reading Support
Audio Anthology CD*

Technology
Literature, Vocabulary, and Writing Centers at **ClassZone.com**
Write*Smart* CD

* Resources for Differentiation † Also in Spanish ‡ In Haitian Creole and Vietnamese

LITERARY ANALYSIS: MOOD

If you've ever felt nervous or peaceful while reading a book, you've been affected by the story's mood. **Mood** is the feeling or atmosphere the writer creates for the reader. There are as many moods as there are emotions: cheerful, gloomy, anxious, lighthearted—the list goes on. Writers create mood through

- the choice of setting, including time and place
- **imagery**—descriptions that appeal to the reader's senses
- conversations between characters

If you are sensitive to a story's mood, you'll become more involved in the story. As you read "The Monkey's Paw," notice how the story makes you feel and which words or passages make you feel that way.

READING STRATEGY: PREDICT

When you make a **prediction,** you use clues from the selection plus your own knowledge and experience to make a reasonable guess about what will happen. Your guesses won't always be right, but that doesn't matter. Making predictions can help you enjoy reading more, because it keeps you engaged in the story.

As you read, use a chart to record your predictions, what actually happens, and whether your prediction was correct.

My Prediction	Actual Event	Correct? (Yes or No)

VOCABULARY IN CONTEXT

The following words help W. W. Jacobs tell a frightening tale. Choose the word that best completes each sentence.

WORD LIST			
	compensation	fate	peril
	credulity	grimace	resignation

1. The old woman's ____ allowed the stranger to trick her.
2. My creepy neighbor wanted ____ for his broken window.
3. The sailors faced great _____ as the storm approached.
4. His ____ scared the children.
5. Tom sighed with ____ upon realizing he was lost.
6. Had she not been saved, she could have met a terrible ____.

Author Online

Bored at the Bank William Wymark Jacobs grew up on the docks of London, where his father worked as a wharf manager. As a young man, Jacobs was employed at a bank, a job he hated, calling it his "days of captivity." To pass the time, he began writing humorous short stories of ships and sailors. Eventually, he began publishing his stories in magazines and soon became one of the most popular and respected writers of his time.

W. W. Jacobs
1863–1943

A Frightening Classic Though most of Jacobs's stories were humorous, he is most famous for his horror classic "The Monkey's Paw," which has been adapted numerous times for the stage, film, and television. The story's "steady, relentlessly building tension" makes it one of the most widely read horror stories in history.

MORE ABOUT THE AUTHOR
For more on W. W. Jacobs, visit the **Literature Center** at **ClassZone.com.**

Background

The British in India Like most of Jacobs's stories, "The Monkey's Paw" is set in Britain. One of the characters is an officer in the British Army and served in India during the British occupation of the country. The British first arrived in India in the 1600s, when the British East India Company established trading. Their role changed dramatically after the Sepoy Mutiny of 1857–1858, in which Indian soldiers of the British Army revolted. From then on, the British government controlled India through a system of governors and military outposts. As a result, young men went to India to serve in the army. British rule of India ended in 1947, and today, India is an independent nation.

Teach

STANDARDS FOCUS

LITERARY ANALYSIS

● MOOD

Write this example on the board:

As the rising sun sparkled on the lake, small waves lapped energetically against the hull of the boat. My grandmother smiled. "This is the best time of day," she said.

Ask students to describe the mood of the passage and identify the details that create this mood. ***Possible answer:*** *A cheerful mood is created by setting details, the grandmother's smile, and the grandmother's words.*

CHECK UNDERSTANDING Ask students to identify the mood of movies they've seen. What details create each mood?

READING STRATEGY

■ PREDICT

Tell students that when they check their predictions during reading, they can change or modify them based on any new clues they've found in the text.

CHECK UNDERSTANDING After students read the **Background** note, ask them to predict what the monkey's paw is and where it comes from.

RESOURCE MANAGER—Copy Master
Predict p. 99 (for student use while reading the selection)

VOCABULARY SKILL

▲ VOCABULARY IN CONTEXT

DIAGNOSE WORD KNOWLEDGE To determine preteaching needs, have all students complete **Vocabulary in Context.** Check their answers. ***Answers:*** **1.** *credulity* **2.** *compensation* **3.** *peril* **4.** *grimace* **5.** *resignation* **6.** *fate*

PRETEACH VOCABULARY Use the Vocabulary Study copy master to help students predict the meaning of each boldfaced word.

1. Read aloud the first two sentences in Part A, emphasizing the word *credulity.*
2. Point out the context clue *I would believe in anything.* Elicit possible meanings for *credulity,* such as "easy belief."
3. Repeat for the rest of the paragraph.
4. Have students complete Part B independently.

RESOURCE MANAGER—Copy Master
Vocabulary Study p. 101

For general guidelines on differentiating vocabulary instruction and for alternative vocabulary activities for students not needing vocabulary preteaching, see

BEST PRACTICES TOOLKIT
Scaffolding Vocabulary Instruction pp. 43–46

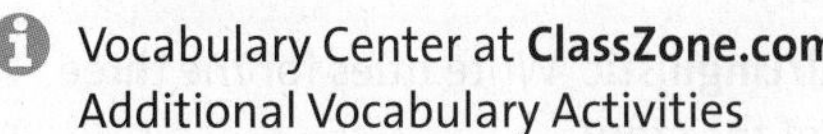

Vocabulary Center at **ClassZone.com**
Additional Vocabulary Activities

Practice and Apply

ANALYZE VISUALS

Possible answer: *The object looks very old. It looks like the skeletal remains of a hand. Based on the title of the story, this object could be a monkey's paw.*

LITERARY ANALYSIS

Ⓐ MOOD

Possible answer: *Words and phrases that describe the setting include*

- *"beastly, slushy, out-of-the-way places"*
- *"Pathway's a bog, and the road's a torrent"*
- *"only two houses in the road are let"*

These details create a dark, forlorn feeling.

THE MONKEY'S PAW

W. W. Jacobs

I

Without, the night was cold and wet, but in the small parlor of Laburnum Villa the blinds were drawn and the fire burned brightly. Father and son were at chess; the former, who possessed ideas about the game involving radical changes, putting his king into such sharp and unnecessary **perils** that it even provoked comment from the white-haired old lady knitting placidly by the fire.

"Hark at the wind," said Mr. White, who, having seen a fatal mistake after it was too late, was amiably[1] desirous of preventing his son from seeing it.

"I'm listening," said the latter, grimly surveying the board as he stretched out his hand. "Check."

"I should hardly think that he'd come tonight," said his father, with his hand poised over the board.

"Mate," replied the son.

"That's the worst of living so far out," bawled Mr. White, with sudden and unlooked-for violence; "of all the beastly, slushy, out-of-the-way places to live in, this is the worst. Pathway's a bog,[2] and the road's a torrent.[3] I don't know what people are thinking about. I suppose because only two houses in the road are let,[4] they think it doesn't matter." Ⓐ

"Never mind, dear," said his wife soothingly; "perhaps you'll win the next one."

ANALYZE VISUALS
What can you **infer** about the object in the photograph? Note the clues you use to make your inference.

peril (pĕr′əl) *n.* danger

Ⓐ **MOOD**
Reread lines 1–18. Not words and phrases tha describe the **setting.** What feelings do thes suggest?

1. **amiably** (ā′mē-ə-blē): in a friendly way.
2. **bog:** a swamp.
3. **torrent** (tôr′ənt): a swift-flowing stream.
4. **let:** rented.

DIFFERENTIATED INSTRUCTION

FOR ALL STUDENTS

Enhance Learning Styles Provide these independent projects for various learning styles:

- **Aural/Kinesthetic** Re-create the mood of "The Monkey's Paw" in a storytelling session.
- **Visual** Create a poster for a movie version of the story.
- **Verbal/Linguistic** Write titles for the three parts of the story.

For further details on these projects, see

RESOURCE MANAGER
Ideas for Extension pp. 92–93

FOR LESS-PROFICIENT READERS

In combination with the *Audio Anthology CD,* use one or more Targeted Passages (pp. 363, 364, 370) to ensure that students focus on key story events, concepts, and skills.

FOR ENGLISH LEARNERS

Options for Reading Read lines 1–20 aloud. Make sure students understand the setting, the mood, and the characters introduced in this passage. Have students read the rest of the selection silently as they listen to the *Audio Anthology CD.* Pause the CD frequently to allow students to reflect and make predictions.

BACKGROUND

Talismans and Amulets In folk traditions around the world, an amulet is a charm or object that is said to protect the person who holds it and bring good luck. A talisman (line 100) is similar to an amulet, but it is thought to bring more than good luck. It may have magical powers and may grant to its holder the power to make a wish that will come true. Talismans and amulets include objects such as gems or stones, coins, pendants, statues, plants, and animals.

CULTURAL CONNECTION

Hinduism The monkey's paw in the story is said to have had a spell put on it by a fakir (line 62). In India, a fakir is a Hindu holy man who has devoted his life to the practice of his religion and may be able to perform miraculous feats. Hinduism is thought to be one of the oldest religions in the world, originating in what is now India in about 3000–2000 B.C. Today, it is the third largest religion and most of the world's Hindus live in India. Talismans and amulets, such as bells, bracelets, and statues, play a part in traditional Hinduism.

FOR ENGLISH LEARNERS

Key Academic Vocabulary Have students use Word Squares to study this academic vocabulary from the selection: *somewhat* (lines 67, 127), *granted* (lines 71, 157, 266), *persisted* (line 73), *depressing* (line 141), *attribute* (line 161).

 **BEST PRACTICES TOOLKIT—Transparency**
Word Squares p. E10

Prereading For prereading instruction for English learners, see

 **BEST PRACTICES TOOLKIT**
Scaffolding Reading Instruction pp. 43–46

FOR ADVANCED LEARNERS/PRE–AP

Pre-AP exercises in the bottom channel provide additional challenge for your advanced students. Use them for small groups or individuals.

ADDITIONAL GUIDELINES

For more help with differentiation and tips for classroom management, see

 **BEST PRACTICES TOOLKIT**
Differentiated Instruction pp. 31–38

Lines 26–45
DISCUSSION PROMPTS

Use these prompts to help students understand who the visitor is and where he has come from:

Interpret Why does Mrs. White say, "Tut, tut!" when she hears the men condoling with each other at the door? ***Possible answer:*** *The men are complaining to each other about the wet weather, and Mrs. White thinks they're making too much of it.*

Analyze Why is Mr. White so excited about Sergeant-Major Morris's visit? ***Possible answer:*** *The sergeant-major brings tales of adventure and excitement into Mr. White's quiet, predictable life. Also, the two were boyhood friends.*

Speculate Why does Sergeant-Major Morris say, "Better where you are"? ***Possible answer:*** *He doesn't seem to have good memories of India. Perhaps something unpleasant happened there.*

Mr. White looked up sharply, just in time to intercept a knowing glance between mother and son. The words died away on his lips, and he hid a guilty grin in his thin gray beard.

"There he is," said Herbert White, as the gate banged loudly and heavy footsteps came toward the door.

The old man rose with hospitable haste, and opening the door, was heard condoling[5] with the new arrival. The new arrival also condoled with himself, so that Mrs. White said, "Tut, tut!" and coughed gently as her husband entered the room, followed by a tall, burly man, beady of eye and rubicund of visage.[6]

"Sergeant-Major Morris," he said, introducing him.

The sergeant-major shook hands, and taking the proffered seat by the fire, watched contentedly while his host brought out drinks and stood a small copper kettle on the fire.

He began to talk, the little family circle regarding with eager interest this visitor from distant parts, as he squared his broad shoulders in the chair and spoke of wild scenes and doughty[7] deeds; of wars and plagues and strange peoples.

"Twenty-one years of it," said Mr. White, nodding at his wife and son. "When he went away, he was a slip of a youth in the warehouse. Now look at him."

"He don't look to have taken much harm," said Mrs. White politely.

"I'd like to go to India myself," said the old man, "just to look round a bit, you know."

"Better where you are," said the sergeant-major, shaking his head. He put down the empty glass, and sighing softly, shook it again.

"I should like to see those old temples and fakirs and jugglers," said the old man. "What was that you started telling me the other day about a monkey's paw or something, Morris?"

"Nothing," said the soldier hastily. "Leastways nothing worth hearing."

"Monkey's paw?" said Mrs. White curiously.

"Well, it's just a bit of what you might call magic, perhaps," said the sergeant-major off-handedly.

His three listeners leaned forward eagerly. The visitor absent-mindedly put his empty glass to his lips and then set it down again. His host filled it for him.

"To look at," said the sergeant-major, fumbling in his pocket, "it's just an ordinary little paw, dried to a mummy."

He took something out of his pocket and proffered it. Mrs. White drew back with a **grimace,** but her son, taking it, examined it curiously.

"And what is there special about it?" inquired Mr. White as he took it from his son, and having examined it, placed it upon the table.

VISUAL VOCABUL

fakir (fə-kîr') *n.* a Mus
or Hindu holy man

grimace (grĭm'ĭs) *n.* a
facial expression of pa
or disgust

5. **condoling** (kən-dōl'ĭng): expressing sympathy.
6. **rubicund** (ro͞o'bĭ-kənd) **of visage** (vĭz'ĭj): with a ruddy complexion.
7. **doughty** (dou'tē): brave.

DIFFERENTIATED INSTRUCTION

FOR ENGLISH LEARNERS

Vocabulary Support Clarify the meanings of these words and expressions for students:

- *Without* (line 1), "outside"
- *Hark at the wind* (line 7), "listen to the wind"
- *proffered* (lines 31, 58), "offered"
- *a slip of a youth* (line 39), "a slender young boy"
- *Leastways* (line 49), "at least"
- *jarred* (line 67), "seemed out of place"
- *is wont to* (line 69), "is accustomed or used to"
- *eyeing him* (line 83), "looking at him"

Visual Vocabulary Have students create visual vocabulary notes for these words from the story:

- *bog* (line 16)
- *talisman* (line 100)
- *antimacassar* (line 119)
- *wardrobe* (line 145)
- *simian* (line 147)

"It had a spell put on it by an old fakir," said the sergeant-major, "a very oly man. He wanted to show that **fate** ruled people's lives, and that those vho interfered with it did so to their sorrow. He put a spell on it so that three eparate men could each have three wishes from it." **B**

His manner was so impressive that his hearers were conscious that their light aughter jarred somewhat.

"Well, why don't you have three, sir?" said Herbert White cleverly.

The soldier regarded him in the way that middle age is wont to regard presumptuous youth. "I have," he said quietly, and his blotchy face whitened.

"And did you really have the three wishes granted?" asked Mrs. White.

"I did," said the sergeant-major, and his glass tapped against his strong teeth.

"And has anybody else wished?" persisted the old lady.

"The first man had his three wishes. Yes," was the reply; "I don't know what he first two were, but the third was for death. That's how I got the paw."

His tones were so grave that a hush fell upon the group.

"If you've had your three wishes, it's no good to you now, then, Morris," said he old man at last. "What do you keep it for?"

The soldier shook his head. "Fancy, I suppose," he said slowly. "I did have some idea of selling it, but I don't think I will. It has caused enough mischief already. Besides, people won't buy. They think it's a fairy tale, some of them; and those who do think anything of it want to try it first and pay me afterward."

"If you could have another three wishes," said the old man, eyeing him keenly, "would you have them?"

"I don't know," said the other. "I don't know."

He took the paw, and dangling it between his forefinger and thumb, suddenly threw it upon the fire. White, with a slight cry, stooped down and snatched it off.

"Better let it burn," said the soldier solemnly.

"If you don't want it, Morris," said the other, "give it to me."

"I won't," said his friend doggedly. "I threw it on the fire. If you keep it, don't blame me for what happens. Pitch it on the fire again like a sensible man." **C**

The other shook his head and examined his new possession closely. "How do you do it?" he inquired.

"Hold it up in your right hand and wish aloud," said the sergeant-major, "but I warn you of the consequences."

"Sounds like the *Arabian Nights*,"[8] said Mrs. White, as she rose and began to set the supper. "Don't you think you might wish for four pairs of hands for me?"

Her husband drew the talisman[9] from his pocket, and then all three burst into laughter as the sergeant-major, with a look of alarm on his face, caught him by the arm.

"If you must wish," he said gruffly, "wish for something sensible." **D**

fate (fāt) *n.* a power that is thought to determine the course of events

B PREDICT
Reread lines 62–65. What role will the monkey's paw play in the story? Describe your prediction in your chart.

1 Targeted Passage

C MOOD
What feeling do you get from the **dialogue** between the Whites and Sergeant-Major Morris?

D PREDICT
What, if anything, do you think Mr. White will wish for? Record your prediction.

8. ***Arabian Nights:*** a famous collection of Asian stories.
9. **talisman** (tăl'ĭs-mən): an object thought to have magical powers.

READING STRATEGY

B PREDICT

Remind students to add their predictions to the charts they began on page 359.
Possible answer: *The characters in the story will make wishes using the monkey's paw. Since "The Monkey's Paw" is the title of the story, it must play a major role in the story's conflict.*

Lines 62–75
REINFORCE *KEY IDEA:* SUPERSTITIOUS

Discuss Do you think the sergeant-major is being **superstitious** about the monkey's paw? Why or why not? ***Possible answers:***

- *Yes, because a monkey's paw cannot contain real power.*
- *No, because he seems to have had some experience with the monkey's paw that justifies his beliefs.*

LITERARY ANALYSIS

C MOOD

Possible answer: *The dialogue adds to the suspenseful mood. The sergeant-major is very vague in his answers about the monkey's paw, but he makes it clear that it can bring only bad luck to those who use it. This makes the reader feel concerned for the Whites, who show interest in the paw.*

READING STRATEGY

D PREDICT

Remind students to add their predictions to the charts they began on page 359.
Students' answers will vary. They may predict that since Mr. White does not believe in the power of the paw, he will wish for something trivial.

FOR LESS-PROFICIENT READERS

Comprehension Support [paired option]
Encourage students to complete a Visualizing web to assist their comprehension of pages 362 and 363. Have them make notes on the web about the setting, the characters, and the characters' relationships. After students have completed their webs, discuss their impressions of the White family.

BEST PRACTICES TOOLKIT—Transparency
Visualizing p. A11

1 Targeted Passage [Lines 62–103]

This passage introduces the source of conflict in the story: the monkey's paw.

- What did the holy man want to show by putting a spell on the monkey's paw?
- What power does the paw have?
- What is the sergeant-major's attitude toward the paw?
- What attitude do the Whites have toward the paw?

Mr. White dropped it back in his pocket, and placing chairs, motioned his friend to the table. In the business of supper the talisman was partly forgotten, and afterward the three sat listening in an enthralled fashion to a second installment of the soldier's adventures in India.

"If the tale about the monkey's paw is not more truthful than those he has been telling us," said Herbert, as the door closed behind their guest, just in time for him to catch the last train, "we shan't make much out of it."

"Did you give him anything for it, Father?" inquired Mrs. White, regarding her husband closely.

"A trifle," said he, coloring slightly. "He didn't want it, but I made him take it. And he pressed me again to throw it away."

"Likely," said Herbert, with pretended horror. "Why, we're going to be rich, and famous, and happy. Wish to be an emperor, Father, to begin with; then you can't be henpecked."

He darted round the table, pursued by the maligned Mrs. White armed with an antimacassar.[10]

Mr. White took the paw from his pocket and eyed it dubiously. "I don't know what to wish for, and that's a fact," he said slowly. "It seems to me I've got all I want."

"If you only cleared the house, you'd be quite happy, wouldn't you?" said Herbert, with his hand on his shoulder. "Well, wish for two hundred pounds, then; that'll just do it."

His father, smiling shamefacedly at his own **credulity,** held up the talisman, as his son, with a solemn face, somewhat marred by a wink at his mother, sat down at the piano and struck a few impressive chords.

"I wish for two hundred pounds," said the old man distinctly. **E**

A fine crash from the piano greeted the words, interrupted by a shuddering cry from the old man. His wife and son ran toward him.

"It moved," he cried, with a glance of disgust at the object as it lay on the floor. "As I wished, it twisted in my hand like a snake."

"Well, I don't see the money," said his son, as he picked it up and placed it on the table, "and I bet I never shall."

"It must have been your fancy, father," said his wife, regarding him anxiously.

He shook his head. "Never mind, though; there's no harm done, but it gave me a shock all the same."

They sat down by the fire again. Outside, the wind was higher than ever, and the old man started nervously at the sound of a door banging upstairs. A silence unusual and depressing settled upon all three, which lasted until the old couple rose to retire for the night. **F**

"I expect you'll find the cash tied up in a big bag in the middle of your bed," said Herbert, as he bade them good-night, "and something horrible squatting up on top of the wardrobe[11] watching you as you pocket your ill-gotten gains."

2 Targeted Passage

credulity (krĭ-do͞o'lĭ-tē) *n.* a disposition to belie[ve] too readily

E PREDICT What do you think will happen as a result of Mr. White's first wish? Record your prediction

F MOOD Reread lines 130–142. Note the **imagery** in these lines. To what senses does it appeal? Explain how i[t] contributes to the moo[d]

10. **antimacassar** (ăn'tĭ-mə-kăs'ər): a cloth placed over an arm or back of a chair.

11. **wardrobe:** a piece of furniture that serves as a closet.

READING STRATEGY

E PREDICT

Before students make a new prediction, have them check the prediction they made on page 363 and record the actual event on their charts. *Students' predictions will vary but should demonstrate an understanding of the potential for danger associated with the monkey's paw.*

LITERARY ANALYSIS

F MOOD

Possible answer: *The images in this passage, such as "shuddering cry," "glance of disgust," and "twisted in my hand like a snake," appeal to the senses of hearing, sight, and touch. They help to create a dark and foreboding mood. They suggest that something evil and strange is associated with the paw.*

If students need help . . . Remind students that imagery consists of words and phrases that appeal to readers' senses. Encourage students to make a picture in their minds as they read this scene and to explore how it makes them feel.

DIFFERENTIATED INSTRUCTION

FOR LESS–PROFICIENT READERS

2 Targeted Passage [Lines 120–142]

This passage presents a key event: Mr. White makes a wish on the monkey's paw.

- Why does Mr. White decide to make a wish?
- What is Herbert's attitude toward the paw?
- What happens when Mr. White uses the paw to make his wish?
- How does the family's mood change after Mr. White wishes on the monkey's paw?

FOR ENGLISH LEARNERS

Vocabulary Support Have students use context clues to determine the meanings of these words and phrases:

- *a trifle* (line 113), "something of little value"
- *pressed me* (line 114), "put pressure on me"
- *cleared the house* (line 123), "didn't owe any money on the house"
- *fancy* (line 136), "imagination"
- *started* (line 140), "jumped"
- *retire* (line 142), "go to bed"

FOR ADVANCED LEARNERS/PRE–AP

Analyze Mood Point out that, beginning on the very first page, the mood of the story alternates between light and dark. Have students identify light and dark passages throughout the story, noting specific details. Invite them to discuss the effect this changing mood has on the reader.

He sat alone in the darkness, gazing at the dying fire, and seeing faces in it. The last face was so horrible and so simian[12] that he gazed at it in amazement. It got so vivid that, with a little uneasy laugh, he felt on the table for a glass containing a little water to throw over it. His hand grasped the monkey's paw, and with a little shiver he wiped his hand on his coat and went up to bed.

ANALYZE VISUALS
What do you see in the fire? How does this **compare** to what Herbert sees?

II

In the brightness of the wintry sun next morning as it streamed over the breakfast table he laughed at his fears. There was an air of prosaic[13] wholesomeness about the room which it had lacked on the previous night, and the dirty, shriveled little paw was pitched on the sideboard[14] with a carelessness which betokened no great belief in its virtues.[15] **G**

G PREDICT
Based on the **mood** of this paragraph, what do you think will happen in Part II? Add this to your chart.

12. **simian** (sĭm′ē-ən): monkey- or ape-like.
13. **prosaic** (prō-zā′ĭk): ordinary.
14. **sideboard:** a piece of furniture used to store linens and dishes.
15. **virtues:** powers.

ANALYZE VISUALS

Possible answer: *There is a monkey's face in the fire. The last face Herbert sees also looks like a monkey.*

Lines 146–150
REINFORCE *KEY IDEA:* SUPERSTITIOUS

Discuss How does this passage show that Herbert is fighting a **superstitious** feeling about the monkey's paw? ***Possible answer:*** *He sees a monkey's face in the fire and he gives a little laugh because he wants to believe it's only his imagination at work. However, when he reaches for water to douse the fire, he grasps the monkey's paw by mistake, and it makes him shiver. He is beginning to fear its power.*

READING STRATEGY

G PREDICT

Remind students to add their predictions to the charts they began on page 359. *Some students may predict that because the mood is lighthearted, something good will happen. Others may have noticed the alternating light and dark mood throughout the story and will predict that something horrible will happen soon.*

FOR LESS–PROFICIENT READERS

Reading Strategy Follow-Up: Predict Have students review the predictions they've made so far in the chart from page 359. Ask students to share some of their predictions. If students are having difficulty formulating predictions, suggest that they use sentence frames such as "I wonder if ____" and "If ____, then ____."

My Prediction	Actual Event	Correct? (Yes or No)
I predict that someone will make a wish on the monkey's paw.	Mr. White makes a wish (line 129).	Yes
I wonder if Mr. White will wish for money.	Mr. White wishes for 200 pounds (line 129).	Yes

Lines 156–190
DISCUSSION PROMPTS

Use these prompts to help students understand each family member's attitude about the power of the monkey's paw:

Interpret Why does Mrs. White say that they were listening to nonsense the night before? ***Possible answer:*** *She doesn't believe wishes can be granted. Even if this one is granted, she questions how 200 pounds could hurt them.*

Analyze Does Mrs. White's statement seem ominous? Why or why not? ***Possible answer:*** *Yes, because after she asks the question about how 200 pounds could hurt Mr. White, readers begin to wonder how it might. The sergeant-major indicated that other people's wishes had had unexpected and unpleasant results.*

Speculate Why do you think the man passes by the Whites' gate three times? ***Possible answer:*** *He may not be sure it is the right house, or he may be uncomfortable about talking to the Whites and is putting it off as long as possible.*

READING STRATEGY

H PREDICT

Have students add this prediction to their charts. *Students' answers will vary, but they should make a connection between the man's visit and Mr. White's wish.*

If students need help . . . Make sure students understand that this visit from a stranger is perceived to be very unusual.

"I suppose all old soldiers are the same," said Mrs. White. "The idea of our listening to such nonsense! How could wishes be granted in these days? And if they could, how could two hundred pounds hurt you, father?"

"Might drop on his head from the sky," said the frivolous[16] Herbert.

"Morris said the things happened so naturally," said his father, "that you might if you so wished attribute it to coincidence."

"Well, don't break into the money before I come back," said Herbert as he rose from the table. "I'm afraid it'll turn you into a mean, avaricious[17] man, and we shall have to disown you."

His mother laughed, and following him to the door, watched him down the road; and returning to the breakfast table, was very happy at the expense of her husband's credulity. All of which did not prevent her from scurrying to the door at the postman's knock, when she found that the post brought a tailor's bill.

"Herbert will have some more of his funny remarks, I expect, when he comes home," she said, as they sat at dinner.

"I dare say," said Mr. White, "but for all that, the thing moved in my hand; that I'll swear to."

"You thought it did," said the old lady soothingly.

"I say it did," replied the other. "There was no thought about it; I had just— What's the matter?"

His wife made no reply. She was watching the mysterious movements of a man outside, who, peering in an undecided fashion at the house, appeared to be trying to make up his mind to enter. In mental connection with the two hundred pounds, she noticed that the stranger was well dressed, and wore a silk hat of glossy newness. Three times he paused at the gate, and then walked on again. The fourth time he stood with his hand upon it, and then with sudden resolution flung it open and walked up the path. Mrs. White at the same moment placed her hands behind her, and hurriedly unfastening the strings of her apron, put that useful article of apparel beneath the cushion of her chair.

She brought the stranger, who seemed ill at ease, into the room. He gazed at her furtively, and listened in a preoccupied fashion as the old lady apologized for the appearance of the room, and her husband's coat, a garment which he usually reserved for the garden. She then waited patiently for him to broach his business, but he was at first strangely silent. **H**

H PREDICT
Reread lines 177–190. Why do you think the man comes to see the Whites?

"I—was asked to call," he said at last, and stooped and picked a piece of cotton from his trousers. "I come from Maw and Meggins."

The old lady started. "Is anything the matter?" she asked breathlessly. "Has anything happened to Herbert? What is it? What is it?"

Her husband interposed. "There, there, mother," he said hastily. "Sit down, and don't jump to conclusions. You've not brought bad news, I'm sure, sir;" and he eyed the other wistfully.

16. **frivolous** (frĭv'ə-ləs): inappropriately silly.
17. **avaricious** (ăv'ə-rĭsh'əs): greedy.

DIFFERENTIATED INSTRUCTION

FOR ENGLISH LEARNERS

Vocabulary Support Have students use Word Questioning to determine the meanings of these words and phrases:

- *break into the money* (line 162), "spend the money"
- *was very happy at the expense of her husband's credulity* (lines 166–167), "joked about her husband's belief (in the paw's power)"
- *ill at ease* (line 186), "uncomfortable, nervous"
- *broach* (line 189), "state"
- *jump to conclusions* (line 196), "make hasty judgments"
- *broke off* (line 204), "stopped speaking"

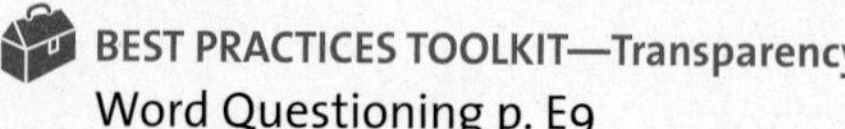

BEST PRACTICES TOOLKIT—Transparency
Word Questioning p. E9

"I'm sorry—" began the visitor.

"Is he hurt?" demanded the mother wildly.

The visitor bowed in assent. "Badly hurt," he said quietly, "but he is not in any pain."

"Oh!" said the old woman, clasping her hands. "Thank goodness for that! Thank—"

She broke off suddenly as the sinister meaning of the assurance dawned upon her and she saw the awful confirmation of her fears in the other's averted face. She caught her breath, and turning to her slower-witted husband, laid her trembling old hand upon his. There was a long silence. **I**

"He was caught in the machinery," said the visitor at length in a low voice.

"Caught in the machinery," repeated Mr. White, in a dazed fashion, "yes."

He sat staring blankly out at the window, and taking his wife's hand between his own, pressed it as he had been wont to do in their old courting days nearly forty years before.

"He was the only one left to us," he said, turning gently to the visitor. "It is hard."

The other coughed, and rising, walked slowly to the window. "The firm wished me to convey their sincere sympathy with you in your great loss," he said, without looking round. "I beg that you will understand I am only their servant and merely obeying orders."

There was no reply; the old woman's face was white, her eyes staring, and her breath inaudible; on the husband's face was a look such as his friend the sergeant might have carried into his first action.

"I was to say that Maw and Meggins disclaim all responsibility," continued the other. "They admit no liability at all, but in consideration of your son's services, they wish to present you with a certain sum as **compensation**."

Mr. White dropped his wife's hand, and rising to his feet, gazed with a look of horror at his visitor. His dry lips shaped the words, "How much?"

"Two hundred pounds," was the answer.

Unconscious of his wife's shriek, the old man smiled faintly, put out his hands like a sightless man, and dropped, a senseless heap, to the floor. **J**

I MOOD
Think about the news the stranger reveals during his conversation with the Whites. What emotions do you feel as a result of this news?

compensation
(kŏm'pən-sā'shən) *n.* something, such as money, received as payment

J PREDICT
Did your prediction about what would result from Mr. White's first wish come true? Add your answer to your chart.

III

In the huge new cemetery, some two miles distant, the old people buried their dead, and came back to a house steeped in shadow and silence. It was all over so quickly that at first they could hardly realize it, and remained in a state of expectation as though of something else to happen—something else which was to lighten this load, too heavy for old hearts to bear.

But the days passed, and expectation gave place to **resignation**—the hopeless resignation of the old, sometimes miscalled apathy. Sometimes they hardly exchanged a word, for now they had nothing to talk about, and their days were long to weariness.

resignation
(rĕz'ĭg-nā'shən) *n.* acceptance of something that is inescapable

LITERARY ANALYSIS

I MOOD

The stranger reveals that Herbert has died. Students may note feelings of sadness, surprise, anxiety, or puzzlement.

Lines 200–229

DISCUSSION PROMPTS

Use these prompts to help students understand the circumstances surrounding Herbert's death:

Interpret What is the "sinister meaning" of the information the stranger brings? ***Answer:*** *He is saying that Herbert has died.*

Infer What does Mr. White mean when he says, "He was the only one left to us"? ***Possible answer:*** *The Whites may have had other children who died. Herbert was the only one still living.*

Synthesize Mr. White does not faint when he is given the news of his son's death. Why does he faint when he hears that the compensation is 200 pounds? ***Possible answer:*** *It is the exact amount he had wished for; he realizes that his wish may have caused his son's death.*

READING STRATEGY

J PREDICT

Students should review their notes about the first wish and reread the text, if necessary, to find out if they were correct.

FOR LESS–PROFICIENT READERS

Comprehension Support [paired option] Review the concept of foreshadowing, when a writer hints about something that will happen later in the story. Have students reread lines 156–161. Ask student pairs to identify and list the phrases that seem to be clues about what happens next. In a class discussion, have students share the clues they noted. Encourage them to add clues to their lists as they continue to read.

FOR ENGLISH LEARNERS

Language: Legal Terminology Make sure students understand that when the man says "Maw and Meggins disclaim all responsibility" and "admit no liability" (lines 222–223), it means that the company feels it is not at fault for Herbert's death. However, the company offers the Whites 200 pounds because their son died while on the job.

It was about a week after that the old man, waking suddenly in the night, stretched out his hand and found himself alone. The room was in darkness, and the sound of subdued weeping came from the window. He raised himself in bed and listened.

"Come back," he said tenderly. "You will be cold."

"It is colder for my son," said the old woman, and wept afresh.

The sound of her sobs died away on his ears. The bed was warm, and his eyes heavy with sleep. He dozed fitfully, and then slept until a sudden wild cry from his wife awoke him with a start.

"*The paw!*" she cried wildly. "The monkey's paw!"

He started up in alarm. "Where? Where is it? What's the matter?"

She came stumbling across the room toward him. "I want it," she said quietly. "You've not destroyed it?" **K**

"It's in the parlor, on the bracket," he replied, marveling. "Why?"

She cried and laughed together, and bending over, kissed his cheek.

"I only just thought of it," she said hysterically. "Why didn't I think of it before? Why didn't *you* think of it?"

"Think of what?" he questioned.

"The other two wishes," she replied rapidly. "We've only had one."

"Was not that enough?" he demanded fiercely.

"No," she cried triumphantly; "we'll have one more. Go down and get it quickly, and wish our boy alive again."

The man sat up in bed and flung the bedclothes from his quaking limbs. "You are mad!" he cried, aghast.

"Get it," she panted; "get it quickly, and wish—Oh, my boy, my boy!"

Her husband struck a match and lit the candle. "Get back to bed," he said unsteadily. "You don't know what you are saying."

"We had the first wish granted," said the old woman feverishly; "why not the second?"

"A coincidence," stammered the old man.

"Go and get it and wish," cried his wife, quivering with excitement.

He went down in the darkness, and felt his way to the parlor, and then to the mantelpiece. The talisman was in its place, and a horrible fear that the unspoken wish might bring his mutilated son before him ere he could escape from the room seized upon him, and he caught his breath as he found that he had lost the direction of the door. His brow cold with sweat, he felt his way round the table, and groped along the wall until he found himself in the small passage with the unwholesome thing in his hand. **L**

Even his wife's face seemed changed as he entered the room. It was white and expectant, and to his fears seemed to have an unnatural look upon it. He was afraid of her.

"*Wish!*" she cried, in a strong voice.

"It is foolish and wicked," he faltered.

"*Wish!*" repeated his wife.

He raised his hand. "I wish my son alive again." **M**

K PREDICT
What do you think Mrs. White plans to do with the paw?

L MOOD
Reread lines 270–276. What **imagery** does th author use to establish the mood in this paragraph?

M PREDICT
Do you think the Whit wish will be granted? Note the clues that influence your answe

READING STRATEGY

K PREDICT

Remind students to add their predictions to the charts they began on page 359. *Students' predictions should reflect an understanding that Mrs. White's desire for the paw is related to Herbert's death. For example, they may predict that Mrs. White will use the paw to wish that Herbert come back to life.*

Lines 248–260

REINFORCE *KEY IDEA:* SUPERSTITIOUS

Discuss Does Mrs. White still think that the power of the monkey's paw is just a **superstitious** belief? Explain. ***Possible answer:*** *No. She sees a connection between wishing on the paw and her son's death, so now she believes that it can bring her son back.*

LITERARY ANALYSIS

L MOOD

Possible answer: *These images contribute to the tense mood of the passage:*

- *the "mutilated son" (line 272)*
- *Mr. White "caught his breath" (line 273)*
- *"His brow cold with sweat" (line 274)*
- *Mr. White "groped" along the wall in the dark (line 275)*
- *Mr. White holds "the unwholesome thing" (line 276)*

READING STRATEGY

M PREDICT

Remind students to add this prediction to the charts they began on page 359. *Students' predictions should show an understanding of what has happened up to this point in the story with regard to the monkey's paw.*

DIFFERENTIATED INSTRUCTION

FOR LESS–PROFICIENT READERS

Comprehension Support [paired option] Model the Read Aloud/Think Aloud strategy to help students understand the change that has come over Mrs. White. Read lines 239–251 and state your understanding of what you've read and your predictions of what will come next. Have pairs repeat this procedure as they read the rest of the page.

BEST PRACTICES TOOLKIT—Transparency
Read Aloud/Think Aloud p. A34

FOR ENGLISH LEARNERS

Vocabulary Support Use New Word Analysis to help students learn and understand these words:

- *marveling* (line 252), "wondering, filled with surprise"
- *quaking* (line 261), "shivering; shaking"
- *ere* (line 272), "before"
- *pulsating* (line 289), "quivering; throbbing"

BEST PRACTICES TOOLKIT—Transparency
New Word Analysis p. E8

The talisman fell to the floor, and he regarded it fearfully. Then he sank trembling into a chair as the old woman, with burning eyes, walked to the window and raised the blind.

He sat until he was chilled with the cold, glancing occasionally at the figure of the old woman peering through the window. The candle-end, which had burned below the rim of the china candlestick, was throwing pulsating shadows on the ceiling and walls, until, with a flicker larger than the rest, it expired.

ANALYZE VISUALS
Describe the **mood** of this photograph. What details contribute to this mood?

ANALYZE VISUALS

Possible answer: *The mood of this image is eerie and unsettling. Details that contribute to the mood include the blurriness, the dark colors, and the shadows on the sinister-looking man in the foreground.*

FOR ADVANCED LEARNERS/PRE–AP

Analyze Character What is Mr. White thinking about as he watches Mrs. White at the window (lines 284–288)? Have students use the Open Mind diagram to explore Mr. White's thoughts, based on what they have learned about him in the story. They may use drawings, words and phrases, complete sentences, or a combination. Invite students to share their completed diagrams.

 **BEST PRACTICES TOOLKIT—Transparency**
Open Mind p. D9

LITERARY ANALYSIS

Ⓝ MOOD

Possible answer: *Sounds that help create the mood include the ticking of the clock, a creaking stair, a squeaky mouse scurrying inside the wall, and the quiet knock on the front door.*

Lines 298–321

DISCUSSION PROMPTS

Use these prompts to help students understand the result of Mr. White's second wish:

Recall What does Mr. White do when he hears the knock on the door? ***Answer:*** *He runs back to his room.*

Infer Why does Mr. White say that the sound is a rat that passed him on the stairs? ***Possible answer:*** *He doesn't want his wife to open the door.*

Synthesize Why do you think Mr. White is afraid of what might be on the other side of the door? ***Possible answer:*** *He understands that the monkey's paw gives you what you wish for, but not in the way you want it. He's afraid that Herbert will be mutilated and grotesque.*

SELECTION WRAP–UP

REFLECT Have students reflect on the change in mood from the opening of the story to the ending. In what way did this contrast heighten the drama of the story?

CRITIQUE Ask students what they think of the author's ability to build suspense. Was he successful in creating interest without giving away too much of the story? Why or why not?

READING FLUENCY

Distribute the copy masters and have students practice fluency.

RESOURCE MANAGER—Copy Master
Reading Fluency p. 107

The old man, with an unspeakable sense of relief at the failure of the talisman, crept back to his bed, and a minute or two afterward the old woman came silently and apathetically beside him.

Neither spoke, but lay silently listening to the ticking of the clock. A stair creaked, and a squeaky mouse scurried noisily through the wall. The darkness was oppressive, and after lying for some time gathering up his courage, he took the box of matches, and striking one, went downstairs for a candle.

At the foot of the stairs the match went out, and he paused to strike another; and at the same moment a knock, so quiet and stealthy as to be scarcely audible, sounded on the front door. Ⓝ

The matches fell from his hand. He stood motionless, his breath suspended until the knock was repeated. Then he turned and fled swiftly back to his room, and closed the door behind him. A third knock sounded through the house.

"*What's that?*" cried the old woman, starting up.

"A rat," said the old man in shaking tones— "a rat. It passed me on the stairs."

His wife sat up in bed listening. A loud knock resounded through the house.

"It's Herbert!" she screamed. "It's Herbert!"

She ran to the door, but her husband was before her, and catching her by the arm, held her tightly.

"What are you going to do?" he whispered hoarsely.

"It's my boy; it's Herbert!" she cried, struggling mechanically. "I forgot it was two miles away. What are you holding me for? Let go. I must open the door."

"Don't let it in," cried the old man, trembling.

"You're afraid of your own son," she cried, struggling. "Let me go. I'm coming, Herbert; I'm coming."

There was another knock, and another. The old woman with a sudden wrench broke free and ran from the room. Her husband followed to the landing, and called after her appealingly as she hurried downstairs. He heard the chain rattle back and the bottom bolt drawn slowly and stiffly from the socket. Then the old woman's voice, strained and panting.

"The bolt," she cried loudly. "Come down. I can't reach it."

But her husband was on his hands and knees groping wildly on the floor in search of the paw. If he could only find it before the thing outside got in. A perfect fusillade[18] of knocks reverberated through the house, and he heard the scraping of a chair as his wife put it down in the passage against the door. He heard the creaking of the bolt as it came slowly back, and at the same moment he found the monkey's paw, and frantically breathed his third and last wish.

The knocking ceased suddenly, although the echoes of it were still in the house. He heard the chair drawn back, and the door opened. A cold wind rushed up the staircase, and a long loud wail of disappointment and misery from his wife gave him courage to run down to her side, and then to the gate beyond. The streetlamp flickering opposite shone on a quiet and deserted road.

Ⓝ **MOOD**
Reread lines 294–30
What sounds help cr
the mood in these
paragraphs?

③ **Targeted Passage**

18. **fusillade** (fyo͞o′sə-läd′): discharge from many guns; a rapid outburst.

DIFFERENTIATED INSTRUCTION

FOR LESS–PROFICIENT READERS

③ **Targeted Passage [Lines 316–332]**

This passage presents the conclusion of the story: Mr. White makes a third wish.

- Why does Mrs. White ask for help?
- Why does Mr. White want to find the monkey's paw?
- What is Mr. White's last wish?

Comprehension Support Make sure students understand the significance of Mrs. White's statement "I forgot it was two miles away" (lines 311–312). Prompt students to recall that the two-mile distance from the cemetery explains why it has taken so long for Mr. White's wish to bring Herbert back.

nprehension

Recall How does Mr. White get the monkey's paw?

Recall What power is the monkey's paw supposed to have?

Clarify Why does Sergeant-Major Morris throw the paw onto the fire?

rary Analysis

Make Inferences At the end of the story, why did the knocking stop so suddenly? Explain.

Examine Predictions Review the chart you created as you read. Did most of your predictions come true? Looking back at the places where your predictions were wrong, notice how W. W. Jacobs tried to surprise readers by giving false clues about what would happen.

Analyze Mood How would you describe this story's mood? Include your answer at the top of a chart like the one shown. Then provide examples of setting descriptions, conversations, and imagery that helped create the mood.

Mood:		
Setting Descriptions:	Conversations:	Imagery:

Draw Conclusions Reread lines 62–65, in which the sergeant-major explains how the monkey's paw supposedly got its power. Based on what you know from your reading of the story, do you think that the paw itself is powerful, or is its power dependent on the **superstitious** nature of the person who possesses it?

ension and Challenge

Creative Response: Art What words or images jumped out at you during your reading of "The Monkey's Paw"? Create a collage of words and images that show the story's mood. Combine pictures from newspapers or magazines with your own writing and sketches.

Reader's Circle Consider what would have happened if Mrs. White had opened the door before her husband made the final wish. Would you have liked to find out what was on the other side of the door? Or is it better for you as a reader not to know? In a small group, discuss your thoughts about the ending of "The Monkey's Paw."

Practice and Apply

After Reading

For additional support of postreading questions, use these copy masters:

RESOURCE MANAGER—Copy Masters

Reading Check p. 104 (to check understanding of the selection)

Mood p. 97 (for practice of literary analysis standards focus)

Question Support p. 105 (After Reading questions adapted for English learners and less-proficient readers)

Additional selection questions are provided for teachers on page 91.

For additional activities to challenge students, see

Power Thinking at **ClassZone.com**

ANSWERS

Comprehension

1. *Mr. White's friend, Sergeant-Major Morris, brings the monkey's paw when he comes to visit. Morris tosses it into the fire, but White pulls it out.*
2. *The paw has the power to grant three wishes to three different men.*
3. *Morris throws the paw into the fire because he believes it will do harm and he wants to destroy it.*

Literary Analysis

Possible answers:

4. *The knocking stops because Mr. White wishes Herbert back to his grave.*
5. ■ **STANDARDS FOCUS Predict** *Students' answers should be based on how well their predictions matched what actually happened in the story.*
6. ● **STANDARDS FOCUS Mood** *The mood of the story is dark, suspenseful, and anxious. Examples:* ***Setting Descriptions:*** *"the night was cold and wet" (line 1), "of all the beastly, slushy, out-of-the-way places to live" (line 15);* ***Conversations:*** *"I don't know what the first two were, but the third was for death" (lines 74–75), "I warn you of the consequences" (line 96);* ***Imagery:*** *"Mrs. White drew back with a grimace" (lines 58–59), "interrupted by a shuddering cry" (lines 130–131), "face was so horrible and so simian" (line 147).*
7. *At first it seems that the monkey's paw derives its power from the superstitious nature of the person who has it. Later, however, it does seem to have real power, because the Whites' first wish is fulfilled even though they don't believe in the paw. On the other hand, Herbert's death and the compensation of 200 pounds could have been a coincidence, and the Whites could have become more superstitious as a result of this coincidence. There is no proof that the knocking on the door is actually Herbert, back from the dead.*

Extension and Challenge

8. *Have students present their collages and explain how the particular words and images they chose relate to the story's mood.*
9. *Students should provide thoughtful reasons for why they prefer one kind of ending over the other. Remind them that "The Monkey's Paw" is a horror story, and have them consider whether the reader's horror is increased or decreased by not knowing exactly what is knocking on the door.*

ANSWERS

Vocabulary in Context

VOCABULARY PRACTICE

1. *(a) safety*
2. *(b) doubt*
3. *(b) resistance*
4. *(c) loss*
5. *(a) choice*
6. *(c) grin*

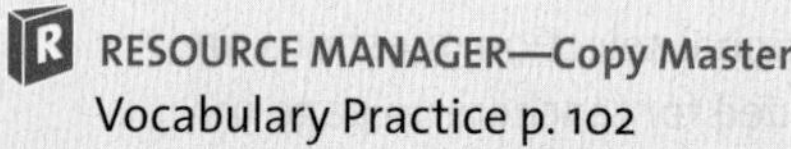

RESOURCE MANAGER—Copy Master
Vocabulary Practice p. 102

VOCABULARY IN WRITING

Ask students to examine their attitudes toward superstitious objects. Would they believe in such a thing as the monkey's paw? Have students review the vocabulary words to see which ones would support their positions about the paw.

VOCABULARY STRATEGY: THE LATIN ROOT *cred* *(also an EL language objective)*

Review with students the meaning of *dis-* (indicates reversal), *in-* (indicates within), and *-ible* (indicates capability or worth). Encourage students to read through all the sentences before they identify the correct answers.

Answers:

1. *credentials*
2. *credo*
3. *credence*
4. *incredible*
5. *discredit*

RESOURCE MANAGER—Copy Master
Vocabulary Strategy p. 103

Vocabulary Center at **ClassZone.com**
Additional Vocabulary Activities

Vocabulary in Context

VOCABULARY PRACTICE

Choose the word in each group that is most nearly opposite in meaning to the boldfaced word.

1. **peril:** (a) safety, (b) risk, (c) hazard
2. **credulity:** (a) simplicity, (b) doubt, (c) openness
3. **resignation:** (a) respect, (b) resistance, (c) acceptance
4. **compensation:** (a) consideration, (b) reward, (c) loss
5. **fate:** (a) choice, (b) destiny, (c) luck
6. **grimace:** (a) frown, (b) scowl, (c) grin

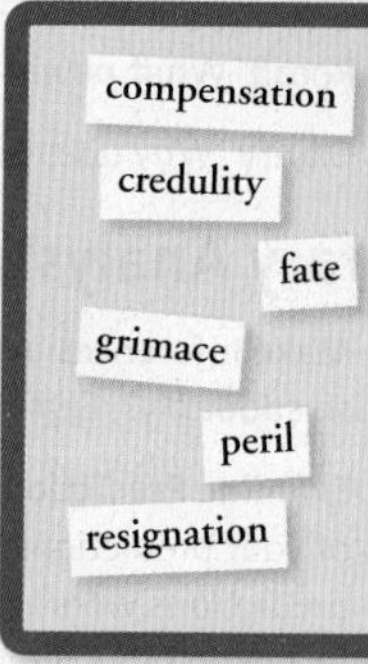

VOCABULARY IN WRITING

If someone offered you a monkey's paw and claimed it had magical powers, how would you respond? Use at least two vocabulary words to write a one-paragraph answer. You might start like this.

EXAMPLE SENTENCE

I don't believe a monkey's paw can change a person's fate.

VOCABULARY STRATEGY: THE LATIN ROOT *cred*

The vocabulary word *credulity* contains the Latin root *cred,* meaning "to believe" or "to trust." A number of commonly used English words are formed using *cred.* To figure out the meanings of unfamiliar words containing *cred,* use your knowledge of the root as well as any context clues provided.

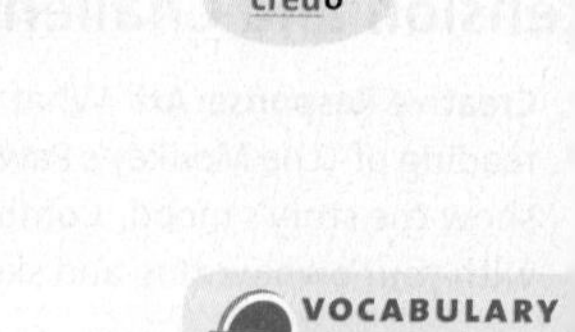

PRACTICE Choose a word from the web to complete each of the following sentences. Use context clues or, if necessary, consult a dictionary.

1. A person must get the proper ______ before he or she is able to teach.
2. Sharon didn't approve of the club's ______, so she didn't join.
3. I gave no ______ to his story, which changed each time he told it.
4. The violinist received several rounds of applause after her ______ performance.
5. They hoped to ______ the candidate by focusing on his lack of experience.

VOCABULARY PRACTICE
For more practice, go to the **Vocabulary Cen** at **ClassZone.com.**

DIFFERENTIATED INSTRUCTION

FOR ENGLISH LEARNERS

Vocabulary Practice For each item in the exercise, have students first define the vocabulary word. If they have difficulty, allow them to refer back to the usage in the story and use context clues and the definition as needed. Then have them look for the word in the set with a meaning that differs most from the meaning of the vocabulary word.

FOR ADVANCED LEARNERS/PRE–AP

Vocabulary Strategy Challenge students to brainstorm more words with the Latin root *cred.* Then have them write a sentence for each word that gives context clues to the word's meaning.

ding-Writing Connection

oaden your understanding of "The Monkey's Paw" by responding to these ompts. Then complete the **Grammar and Writing** exercise.

WRITING PROMPTS	SELF-CHECK
A. Short Response: Examine the Message The fakir wanted to prove "that fate ruled people's lives." Do the events in "The Monkey's Paw" prove this, or is it just a **superstition?** Write **one paragraph** explaining your opinion. Support your ideas with evidence from the text.	***An effective response will . . .*** • offer a clear statement of opinion • include examples from the story as support
B. Extended Response: Rewrite the Ending Suppose Mr. White did not make that last wish. What would have happened when Mrs. White opened the door? In **two or three paragraphs,** write an alternate ending to "The Monkey's Paw." Be sure you use language that fits with the rest of the story.	***A well-written ending will . . .*** • provide an alternate ending that is believable and creative • use a writing style that is similar to W.W. Jacobs's

MMAR AND WRITING

AINTAIN SUBJECT-VERB AGREEMENT A **compound subject** is made up of two or ore subjects joined by a conjunction, such as *and, or,* or *nor.* The conjunction etermines whether you should use a singular or plural verb. If a compound bject is joined by *and,* then it usually takes a plural verb. If a compound bject is joined by *or* or *nor,* then the verb should agree in number with the art closest to it.

Original: Neither Mr. White nor the two men before him finds happiness.

Revised: Neither Mr. White nor the two men before him find happiness. (*The plural verb* find *is correct because the plural noun* men *is closer to it.*)

RACTICE Choose the verb form that agrees with each compound subject.

1. Mr. and Mrs. White (has, have) different feelings about the paw.
2. Neither the paw nor the wishes (has, have) any effect on fate.
3. Herbert and his father (like, likes) to play chess.
4. Either fate or several coincidences (lead, leads) to Herbert's death and the company's compensation.

*or more help with subject-verb agreement with compound subjects, see age R65 in the **Grammar Handbook.***

FOR LESS–PROFICIENT WRITERS

For Prompt A:

1. Guide students in writing a topic sentence that states their opinion.
2. Have students review the story to note examples that support their opinions.
3. Help students use the examples to write sentences that support the topic sentence.

For Prompt B:

- If students are having difficulty with an alternate ending, have them freewrite for ten minutes to generate ideas.
- Use Sentence Imitation to help students analyze W. W. Jacobs's style.

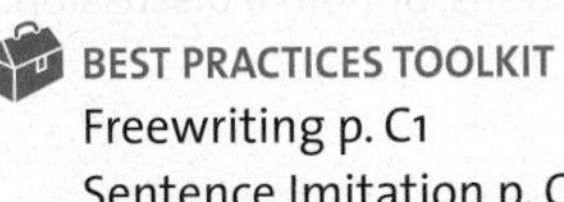

BEST PRACTICES TOOLKIT
Freewriting p. C1
Sentence Imitation p. C2

Reading-Writing Connection

WRITING PROMPTS

- For **Prompt A,** discuss the topic with students. Clarify that Morris said the fakir wanted to prove "that those who interfered with [fate] did so to their sorrow."
- For **Prompt B,** have students review the opening page of the story to get a feel for the author's writing style. Remind them to use imagery to depict the mood.

For an extended Reading-Writing Connection activity, see

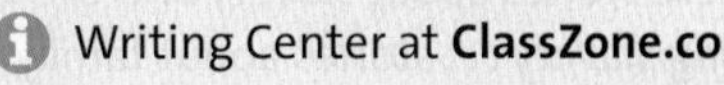

Writing Center at **ClassZone.com**

GRAMMAR AND WRITING

Remind students that the subject is the part of the sentence that tells whom or what the sentence is about. Ask students to identify the subject in this sentence: *My three sons are skiing.*

Answers:

1. *have*
2. *have*
3. *like*
4. *lead*

RESOURCE MANAGER—Copy Master
Maintain Subject-Verb Agreement p. 106

Assess and Reteach

Assess

RESOURCE MANAGER—Copy Masters
Selection Tests A, B/C pp. 109–110, 111–112

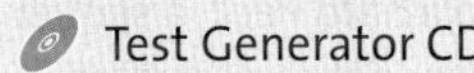

Test Generator CD

Reteach

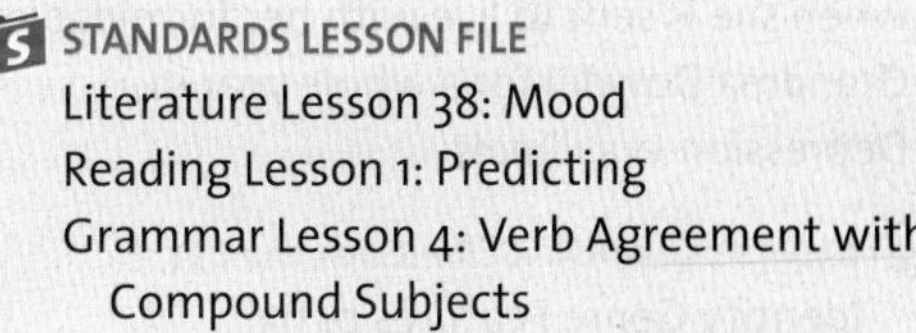

STANDARDS LESSON FILE
Literature Lesson 38: Mood
Reading Lesson 1: Predicting
Grammar Lesson 4: Verb Agreement with Compound Subjects

Introduce

OBJECTIVE

- read historical fiction

Meet Mildred D. Taylor

Mildred D. Taylor has vivid memories of her grandparents' house from her family's annual trips to the South. It was "the house my great-grandfather had built . . . and I remember the adults talking about the past. As they talked I began to visualize all the family who had once known the land, and I felt as if I knew them, too." The stories she listened to, she says, "were stories about slavery and the days following slavery . . . stories about family and friends."

Try a Historical Novel

The best historical novels make readers feel as if they are actually experiencing another time and place. Some writers draw inspiration from their own family histories, as Taylor did for *Roll of Thunder, Hear My Cry.* Others may simply be fascinated by a particular era or event in history. Historical novels that can transport students back in time include

- *Bull Run* by Paul Fleischman, which tells the story of the first major battle in the Civil War through the eyes of 16 narrators with widely different backgrounds and points of view
- *Fever 1793* by Laurie Halse Anderson, about a 16-year-old girl's experiences during the yellow fever epidemic that claimed the lives of 5,000 Philadelphia residents in just three months
- *A Year Down Yonder* by Richard Peck, a sequel to *A Long Way from Chicago* that describes the adventures of 15-year-old Mary Alice when she is sent to live with her formidable Grandma Dowdel for a whole year in Depression-era Illinois

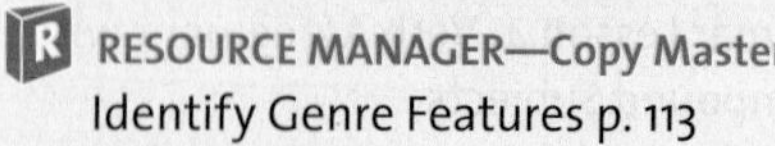

RESOURCE MANAGER—Copy Master
Identify Genre Features p. 113

Great Reads

Roll of Thunder, Hear My Cry

Historical Novel by Mildred D. Taylor

Mildred D. Taylor
born 1943

Other Books by Mildred D. Taylor

- *The Gold Cadillac*
- *The Land*
- *Let the Circle Be Unbroken*
- *The Road to Memphis*

Meet Mildred D. Taylor

Mildred D. Taylor's personal exposure to segregation and bigotry has had a strong influence on her writing. Though Taylor was born in Mississippi, her family moved to the North when she was only three months old. Her father did not want his children to grow up in the racially segregated South. In the Ohio town where she was raised, Taylor was often the only African-American student in her class.

The Taylors returned to the South once a year, however, to visit relatives. The family tradition of sharing stories around bonfires led Taylor to imagine herself as a storyteller. Her father was considered one of the best storytellers in the family, and Taylor credits him for her success: "Without his teachings, without his words, my words would not have been."

Try a Historical Novel

Roll of Thunder, Hear My Cry takes place in Mississippi in the 1930s. Blending fictional characters and events with facts about real places, people, and occurrences, Taylor's **historical novel** transports readers to that time and place.

It wasn't easy to be an African American in the South during the Great Depression. Jobs and food were scarce, and racial tension was high. Many white people viewed African Americans as inferior, and some whites committed acts of violence against them. Taylor creates a vivid picture of what life is like for an African-American family trying to remain united while their community is torn apart.

374

DIFFERENTIATED INSTRUCTION

FOR LESS–PROFICIENT READERS

Reading Support Before students begin reading, review the teaching notes on pages 375–379 and select those that you think would be most helpful to them. You might read the selection aloud, stopping occasionally to share information from the teaching notes, answer questions, or hold a discussion.

Read a Great Book

Cassie Logan and her three brothers—Christopher-John, Stacey, and Little Man—often find themselves struggling to understand why some of the white people in their community treat them so badly. But after the Logan kids pull a prank on the white school's bus driver out of revenge for his mistreatment of them, they soon realize that their actions could have very serious consequences.

from

Roll of THUNDER, Hear My Cry

The room grew quiet again, except for the earthy humming of Big Ma's rich alto voice, the crackle of the hickory fire, and the patter of rain on the roof. Engrossed in a mystery, I was startled when the comfortable sounds were shattered by three rapid knocks on the side door.

Rising quickly, Mama went to the door and called, "Who is it?"

"It's me, ma'am," came a man's gravelly voice. "Joe Avery."

Mama opened the door and Mr. Avery stepped dripping into the room.

"Why, Brother Avery," Mama said, "what are you doing out on a night like this? Come on in. Take off your coat and sit by the fire. Stacey, get Mr. Avery a chair."

"No'm," said Mr. Avery, looking rather nervously over his shoulder into the night. "I ain't got but a minute." He stepped far enough into the room so that he could close the door, then nodded to the rest of us. "Evenin', Miz Caroline, how you t'night?"

"Oh, I'll do, I reckon," said Big Ma, still ironing. "How's Miz Fannie?"

FOR ENGLISH LEARNERS

Read Aloud Preread part of the text and have students continue reading in pairs or small groups. Alternatively, read aloud all or part of the text and stop occasionally to answer questions, hold a discussion, or give an explanation.

Listen to the *Audio Anthology CD* Have students listen to the excerpt as they read along. Then have them read the text independently. Lead them in a follow-up discussion.

Jigsaw Reading [small-group option] Give students an introduction to and a summary of the excerpt. Then have students meet in small groups for Jigsaw Reading. Each student should read part of the excerpt and explain it to the others.

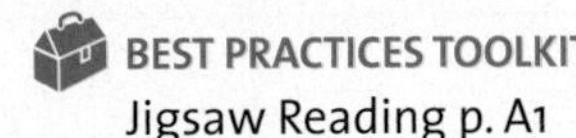

BEST PRACTICES TOOLKIT
Jigsaw Reading p. A1

Read a Great Book

The Logan family in *Roll of Thunder, Hear My Cry* is based on Taylor's own family and the stories she listened to as a child. The true story begins with Taylor's great-grandfather, the son of a white plantation owner and an enslaved woman. Taylor's great-grandfather bought land in Mississippi, which the Taylor family still owns.

Taylor's novel is set in Mississippi in 1933. The Logan children live with their mother and their grandmother, Big Ma, who is their father's mother. They own 400 acres of land that Big Ma's late husband bought. To raise enough money for the mortgage on the land, Papa (David) works on the railroad from just after the spring planting until deep winter. The Logans' land abuts land owned by Harlan Granger, a white man who wants to buy their land from them. The Logans understand, however, that their freedom and independence hinge on land ownership, so they have always rejected Granger's offers.

SHARE WORD MEANINGS

When Cassie is *engrossed* in her mystery (line 3), it means she is giving all of her attention to her book.

SHARE AN FYI

Joe Avery (line 6) works as a sharecropper on Harlan Granger's land. Miz Fannie (lines 16–17) is Mr. Avery's wife. She also works for Granger.

SHARE A READING TIP

The setting of a story influences how its characters speak. Therefore, Taylor's dialogue reflects the way some people spoke in Mississippi in the 1930s. When Mama says "Brother Avery" (line 9), she demonstrates a common African-American and southern custom, calling one's acquaintances "brother" or "sister." Another example of dialect occurs in line 15, when Mr. Avery says, "Evenin', Miz Caroline, how you t'night?"

SHARE A READING TIP

Note the ellipses in lines 18 and 19. When used in the middle of a sentence or phrase, as shown here, ellipses suggest hesitation or uncertainty. When used at the end of a sentence, ellipses indicate that the sentence trails off, perhaps because the speaker cannot or does not want to complete the thought.

A dash at the end of a phrase means that the speaker has been suddenly cut off. In line 29, the children begin to protest, but Mama cuts them off, saying "Hush" and sending them to bed.

"She's fine," he said without dwelling on his wife. "Miz Logan . . . uh, I come to tell you somethin' . . . somethin' important—Mr. Morrison here?"

Mama stiffened. "David. You heard something about David?"

"Oh, no'm," replied Mr. Avery hastily. "Ain't heard nothin' 'bout yo' husband, ma'am."

Mama regarded him quizzically.

"It's . . . it's them again. They's ridin' t'night."

Mama, her face pale and frightened, glanced back at Big Ma; Big Ma held her iron in midair.

"Uh . . . children," Mama said, "I think it's your bedtime."

"But, Mama—" we chorused in protest, wanting to stay and hear who was riding.

"Hush," Mama said sternly. "I said it was time to go to bed. Now go!"

Groaning loudly enough to voice our displeasure, but not loudly enough to arouse Mama's anger, we stacked our books upon the study table and started toward the boys' room.

"Cassie, I said go to bed. That's not your room."

"But, Mama, it's cold in there," I pouted. Usually, we were allowed to build small fires in the other rooms an hour before bedtime to warm them up.

"You'll be warm once you're under the covers. Stacey, take the flashlight with you and light the lantern in your room. Cassie, take the lamp from the desk with you."

I went back and got the kerosene lamp, then entered my bedroom, leaving the door slightly ajar.

"Close that door, Cassie!"

Immediately, the door was closed.

I put the lamp on the dresser, then silently slid the latch off the outside door and slipped onto the wet front porch. I crossed to the boys' room. Tapping lightly, I whispered, "Hey, let me in."

The door creaked open and I darted in. The room was bathed in darkness.

"What they say?" I asked.

"Shhhhh!" came the answer.

I crept to the door leading into Mama's room and huddled beside the boys.

376

The rain softened upon the roof and we could hear Mama asking, "But why? Why are they riding? What's happened?"

"I don't rightly know," said Mr. Avery. "But y'all knows how they is. Anytime they thinks we steppin' outa our *place,* they feels like they gotta stop us. You know what some of 'em done to the Berrys." He paused, then went on bitterly, "It don't take but a little of nothin' to set them devilish night men off."

"But somethin' musta happened," Big Ma said. "How you know 'bout it?"

"All's I can tell ya, Miz Caroline, is what Fannie heard when she was leavin' the Grangers' this evenin'. She'd just finished cleanin' up the supper dishes when Mr. Granger come home with Mr. Grimes—ya know, that white school's bus driver—and two other mens. . . ."

A clap of deafening thunder drowned Mr. Avery's words, then the rain quickened and the conversation was lost.

I grabbed Stacey's arm. "Stacey, they're coming after *us!*"

"What!" squeaked Christopher-John.

"Hush," Stacey said harshly. "And Cassie, let go. That hurts."

"Stacey, somebody musta seen and told on us," I persisted.

"No . . ." Stacey replied unconvincingly. "It couldn't be."

"Couldn't be?" cried Christopher-John in a panic. "Whaddaya mean it couldn't be?"

"Stacey," said Little Man excitedly, "whaddaya think they gonna do to us? Burn us up?"

"Nothin'!" Stacey exclaimed, standing up suddenly. "Now why don't y'all go to bed like y'all s'pose to?"

We were stunned by his attitude. He sounded like Mama and I told him so.

He collapsed in silence by the door, breathing hard, and although I could not see him, I knew that his face was drawn and that his eyes had taken on a haggard look. I touched his arm lightly. "Ain't no call to go blaming yourself," I said. "We all done it."

"But I got us into it," he said listlessly.

"But we all wanted to do it," I comforted.

"Not me!" denied Christopher-John. "All I wanted to do was eat my lunch!"

"Shhhhh," hissed Little Man. "I can hear 'em again."

SHARE AN FYI

When Mama asks why the night men are riding, Mr. Avery replies, "Anytime they thinks we steppin' outa our *place,* they feels like they gotta stop us" (lines 58–59). In the South at the time of this story, and for a long time after, white people in the community took matters of punishment into their own hands. Mobs of men would harass, beat, and sometimes kill African Americans whom they felt had shown disrespect to a white person or done something to threaten the social order. The sheriff in the community typically didn't have much power and simply looked the other way when mobs dispensed "justice" in this way.

SHARE AN FYI

The Berrys, mentioned in line 59, are another African-American family in the community. A mob set fire to three Berry men because one of them supposedly flirted with a white woman. One man died and another was burned beyond recognition.

SHARE WORD MEANINGS

The words *drawn* (line 84) and *haggard* (line 85) are synonyms that mean "tired and worried."

SHARE AN FYI

Mr. Morrison (line 92) is a man who lost his job on the railroad after he got into trouble with some white men. Papa brought him to live with his family and help work the land while he was away. Mr. Morrison lives in a shed on the Logans' property.

SHARE AN FYI

Stacey, 12, is Cassie's older brother. In lines 116–127, he demonstrates that he wants to assume more adult responsibility.

"I'd better go tell Mr. Morrison," Mr. Avery was saying. "He out back?"

"I'll tell him," said Mama.

We could hear the side door open and we scrambled up.

"Cassie, get back to your room quick," Stacey whispered. "They'll probably come check on us now."

"But what'll we do?"

"Nothin' now, Cassie. Them men probably won't even come near here."

"Ya really believe that?" asked Christopher-John hopefully.

"But shouldn't we tell Mama?" I asked.

"No! We can't ever tell nobody!" declared Stacey adamantly. "Now go on, hurry!"

Footsteps neared the door. I dashed onto the porch and hastened back to my own room, where I jumped under the bedcovers with my clothes still on. Shivering, I pulled the heavy patchwork quilts up to my chin.

A few moments later Big Ma came in, leaving the door to Mama's room open. Knowing that she would be suspicious of such an early surrender to sleep, I sighed softly and, making sleepy little sounds, turned onto my stomach, careful not to expose my shirt sleeves. Obviously satisfied by my performance, Big Ma tucked the covers more closely around me and smoothed my hair gently. Then she stooped and started fishing for something under our bed.

I opened my eyes. Now what the devil was she looking for down there? While she was searching, I heard Mama approaching and I closed my eyes again.

"Mama?"

"Stacey, what're you doing up?"

"Let me help."

"Help with what?"

"With . . . with whatever's the matter."

Mama was silent a moment, then said softly, "Thank you, Stacey, but Big Ma and I can handle it."

"But Papa told me to help you!"

"And you do, more than you know. But right now you could help me most by going back to bed. It's a school day tomorrow, remember?"

"But, Mama—"

"If I need you, I'll call you. I promise."

I heard Stacey walk slowly away, then Mama whispering in the doorway, "Cassie asleep?"

378

"Yeah, honey," Big Ma said. "Go on and sit back down. I'll be out in a minute."

Then Big Ma stood up and turned down the wick of the kerosene lamp. As she left the room, my eyes popped open again and I saw her outlined in the doorway, a rifle in her hands. Then she closed the door and I was left to the darkness.

For long minutes I waited, wide awake, wondering what my next move should be. Finally deciding that I should again consult with the boys, I swung my legs over the edge of the bed, but immediately had to swing them back again as Big Ma reentered the room. She passed the bed and pulled a straight-backed chair up to the window. Parting the curtains so that the blackness of the night mixed with the blackness of the room, she sat down without a sound.

I heard the door to the boys' room open and close and I knew that Mama had gone in. I waited for the sound of the door opening again, but it did not come. Soon the chill of the cotton sheets beneath me began to fade and as Big Ma's presence lulled me into a security I did not really feel, I fell asleep.

When I awoke, it was still nightly dark. "Big Ma?" I called. "Big Ma, you there?" But there was no reply from the chair by the window. Thinking that Big Ma had fallen asleep, I climbed from the bed and felt my way to her chair.

She wasn't there.

Keep Reading

You've just gotten a sense of the tense situation the Logan family is in. As one of the few landowning African-American families in the community, the Logans face resentment from many of their white neighbors. Will they be able to hold on to their land through these tough times? Continue reading *Roll of Thunder, Hear My Cry* to find out.

Discuss

SHARE WORD MEANINGS

In line 146, *lulled* means "made to feel peaceful, safe, or sleepy."

Keep Reading

Share these discussion questions with students after they have finished the excerpt. You might use the questions to lead a class discussion or have students form small groups to discuss them.

- Have you read this book? If so, would you recommend it to others? Why? If you haven't read it, what questions are you hoping the rest of the book will answer?
- How would you describe Cassie? What does she say and do in this excerpt that tells you what she's like?
- Who do you think the "night men" (line 61) are? Why are the Logans afraid of them?
- It rains and thunders throughout this selection. Is the author using the weather in a specific way? How? What role do the rain and thunder play in this excerpt?
- Cassie has a distinctive voice. How might the story be different if it were told by an outside observer?

Focus and Motivate

OBJECTIVES

Literary Analysis

- explore the key idea of **belonging**
- identify and analyze setting in nonfiction
- read a memoir and a poem

Reading

- connect own experiences to reading

Vocabulary

- build vocabulary for reading and writing
- use structural analysis to identify base words and affixes *(also an EL language objective)*
- use knowledge of base words and affixes to determine the meanings of words *(also an EL language objective)*

Grammar and Writing

- maintain subject-verb agreement when using indefinite pronouns
- use writing to analyze literature

SUMMARY

In the late 1960s, the author's family moves to Jerusalem, her father's homeland, for a year. During that time, the author attends an Armenian school, makes friends, and struggles with the differences in culture. She misses her life in the United States, but after relocating to Texas, she misses Jerusalem.

Can you BELONG *in two places?*

Discuss the question and the ***KEY IDEA.*** Ask students to think of some of the advantages and disadvantages of feeling a sense of **belonging** to more than one place. Then have students work on the ***QUICKWRITE*** activity.

Before Reading

Going Where I'm Coming From

Memoir by Naomi Shihab Nye

Can you BELONG *in two places?*

KEY IDEA Have you ever heard someone say, "This is where I belong"? What is it about a place that makes you feel a sense of **belonging?** If you spend a lot of time in two different places, such as home and your best friend's house, you may feel equally comfortable in both. The author of the memoir you are about to read discovered that during a year of being away from the United States, she developed a sense of belonging in her new home as well.

QUICKWRITE Think of one or two places where you feel a sense of belonging. What kinds of things make you feel that way—the people, the food, the sights and sounds, the routine? Record your thoughts in your journal.

380

Selection Resources

RESOURCE MANAGER UNIT 3

Plan and Teach pp. 115–122

Literary Analysis

Summary pp. 123†*, 124‡*

Setting in Nonfiction pp. 125, 126†*

Question Support p. 133*

Reading

Connect pp. 127, 128†*

Reading Check p. 132

Vocabulary

Study p. 129*

Practice p. 130

Strategy p. 131

Grammar and Writing

Maintain Subject-Verb Agreement p. 134

Assessment

Selection Tests A, B/C pp. 135*, 137*

Test Generator CD

BEST PRACTICES TOOLKIT

Differentiated Instruction pp. 31–38*

Scaffolding Instruction pp. 43–46*

Graphic Organizers/Strategies

New Word Analysis • Y Chart • Cause-and-Effect Chain • Character Analysis Chart • Read-and-Say-Something • Think-Pair-Share • Cluster Diagram • Sequence Chain

Reading Support

Audio Anthology CD*

Technology

Literature, Vocabulary, and Writing Centers at **ClassZone.com**

Write*Smart* CD

* Resources for Differentiation † Also in Spanish ‡ In Haitian Creole and Vietnamese

RARY ANALYSIS: SETTING IN NONFICTION

'ou might think of **setting,** the time and place in which events occur, as an element of fiction. But setting can be important in nonfiction, too. For example, details about people's customs, beliefs, and day-to-day life are all important to setting. In a memoir, a writer might discuss how these aspects of her childhood home influenced the adult she became.

As you read "Going Where I'm Coming From," notice how the author's identity is shaped by her experiences in her father's homeland.

DING STRATEGY: CONNECT

Sometimes the experiences of people you read about will remind you of events from your own life. When you relate the content of literature to your own experience, you are **connecting** with what you read. By making connections, you can gain new insights into your life and the lives of others around you.

As you read the selection, compare Naomi Shihab Nye's thoughts and experiences with your own. How does this help you better understand her feelings? Take notes in a chart like the one shown.

Author's Experiences	*My Experiences*	*Insights*
She doesn't feel love for her grandmother the first time she meets her.	*I felt shy around my grandmother the first time I visited her in China.*	*Even family bonds can take time to develop.*

CABULARY IN CONTEXT

Nye uses the boldfaced words to help tell her story of living in a new land. Use the context of the numbered sentences to figure out what each word means.

1. The fabric contained a complex and **intricate** design.
2. Mom allowed me to join the team with the **stipulation** that I keep my grades up.
3. In a **valiant** act of bravery, I entered my new classroom.
4. Her father often talked about what it was like to **emigrate** from Mexico to the United States.

Author Online

Combining Cultures Naomi Shihab Nye learned about both Palestinian and American cultures as she was growing up; her mother was born in the United States and her father was born in Palestine. She says that when the other Girl Scouts brought iced cupcakes for treats, she brought dates, apricots, and almonds. In the mid-1960s, Nye and her family moved to a home just outside of Jerusalem. Nye has said that her year there "altered my perception of the universe irrevocably." "Going Where I'm Coming From" is one of many works she's written about her experiences there.

Naomi Shihab Nye born 1952

Building Bridges In her poetry, novels, and essays, Nye encourages people from different cultures to learn to relate to each other. She believes that writers who belong to more than one culture can "build bridges between worlds."

Background

A City Among Valleys Jerusalem is an ancient Middle Eastern city located between the Mediterranean Sea and the Dead Sea. Surrounded by valleys, Jerusalem experiences warm, dry summers and cool winters. Also known as The Holy City, Jerusalem is home to over 700,000 people from a variety of national, religious, and socioeconomic backgrounds. Today, Jerusalem is the capital of the State of Israel. One of the most ancient sections of Jerusalem, the Old City, is divided into four quarters: Armenian, Christian, Jewish, and Muslim.

MORE ABOUT THE AUTHOR AND BACKGROUND

To learn more about Naomi Shihab Nye and Jerusalem, visit the **Literature Center** at **ClassZone.com.**

Teach

STANDARDS FOCUS

LITERARY ANALYSIS

● SETTING IN NONFICTION

Write this example on the board:

> My uncle's new wife sat down at the dinner table. Instantly, my grandmother bustled over. "Ah ah ah! First, you must serve your husband his dinner," she instructed. "Then it is your turn to eat." My aunt blushed deeply.

Ask what custom is an aspect of this setting. ***Answer:*** *The women serve the men's dinner before they eat.*

CHECK UNDERSTANDING Ask students to identify customs or daily practices that would be a part of their memoirs.

READING STRATEGY

■ CONNECT

Ask students if they have been in a situation similar to the aunt's in the example above. If so, how does it help them understand what the aunt must be feeling? *Students may say that when they have not known the right thing to do in a situation, they felt embarrassed, as the aunt does.*

CHECK UNDERSTANDING Ask students to identify characters with whom they've connected and to explain why.

RESOURCE MANAGER—Copy Master

Connect p. 127 (for student use while reading the selection)

VOCABULARY SKILL

▲ VOCABULARY IN CONTEXT

DIAGNOSE WORD KNOWLEDGE To determine preteaching needs, have all students complete **Vocabulary in Context.** *Students' responses will vary.* ***Possible answers:*** 1. *complicated* 2. *condition* 3. *courageous* 4. *move*

PRETEACH VOCABULARY Use the Vocabulary Study copy master to help students create a word map for each boldfaced word.

1. Read the first sentence in Part A aloud.
2. Guide students in creating a word map for *emigrate* like the one shown. Point out that students may not be able to fill in every section for every word.
3. Repeat for each of the other sentences.
4. Have students do Part B independently.

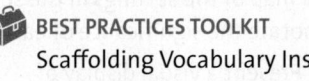

RESOURCE MANAGER—Copy Master

Vocabulary Study p. 129

For general guidelines on differentiating vocabulary instruction and for alternative vocabulary activities for students not needing vocabulary preteaching, see

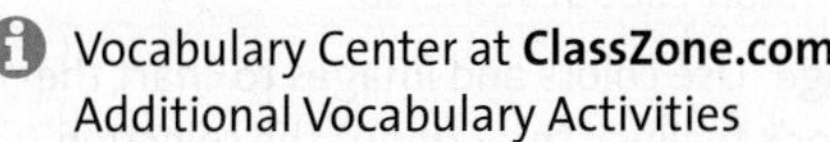

BEST PRACTICES TOOLKIT

Scaffolding Vocabulary Instruction pp. 43–46

Vocabulary Center at **ClassZone.com** Additional Vocabulary Activities

Practice and Apply

ANALYZE VISUALS
Possible answer: *The colors suggest that the setting is exotic, vibrant, and full of life.*

About the Art Palestinian artist Tamam Al-Akhal (born 1935) knows firsthand the plight of a refugee because she was forced to leave her home in Jaffa and reside in a camp in Beirut, Lebanon. She persevered through her art, however, and now is famous for her works, usually done in oil. Some of her most renowned paintings feature the house she had to flee years before.

LITERARY ANALYSIS

A SETTING IN NONFICTION
Possible answer:

- *The grandmother is wearing an embroidered Palestinian dress.*
- *The family moves into a second-story apartment in a stone house surrounded by fields in which sheep are kept.*
- *The author is one of seven girls in the high school, because most local girls go to Arabic-speaking schools after eighth grade.*

Lines 19–23
REINFORCE *KEY IDEA:* BELONGING

Discuss Think about the U.S. culture from which the author comes. What do you think this interview with the counselor does to her sense of **belonging** in her new school? ***Possible answer:*** *After living in the United States, being reprimanded for speaking to boys probably makes the author feel like she is in a very strange and foreign place.*

Going Where I'm Coming From

Naomi Shihab Nye

Shortly after we arrived in Jerusalem, our relatives came to see us at a hotel. Sitti, our grandmother, was very short. She wore a long, thickly embroidered Palestinian dress, had a musical, high-pitched voice and a low, guttural laugh. She kept touching our heads and faces as if she couldn't believe we were there. I had not yet fallen in love with her. Sometimes you don't fall in love with people immediately, even if they're your own grandmother. Everyone seemed to think we were all too thin.

We moved into a second-story flat in a stone house eight miles north of the city, among fields and white stones and wandering sheep. My brother was enrolled in the Friends Girls School and I was enrolled in the Friends Boys School in the town of Ramallah a few miles farther north—it all was a little confused. But the Girls School offered grades one through eight in English and high school continued at the Boys School. Most local girls went to Arabic-speaking schools after eighth grade.

I was a freshman, one of seven girl students among two hundred boys, which would cause me problems a month later. I was called in from the schoolyard at lunchtime, to the office of our counselor who wore shoes so pointed and tight her feet bulged out pinkly on top. **A**

"You will not be talking to them anymore," she said. She rapped on the desk with a pencil for emphasis.

"To whom?"

"All the boy students at this institution. It is inappropriate behavior. From now on, you will speak only with the girls."

ANALYZE VISUALS
What do the colors ir painting suggest abc the **setting?**

A SETTING IN NONFICTION
Reread lines 1–18. What details help yo understand what life was like in Jerusalem

Jerusalem (1984), Tamam Al-Akhal. Pal
Oil on canvas, 50 cm × 70 cm. Private colle

DIFFERENTIATED INSTRUCTION

FOR ALL STUDENTS

Interest Stations Post suggested projects for students to work on independently.

- **Map** Develop a map of the settings in the selection and annotate the significance of each.
- **Bulletin Board** Present a visual display of information about Armenia.
- **Collage** Use colors and images to chart the author's feelings throughout the selection.

For further details on these projects, see

RESOURCE MANAGER
Ideas for Extension pp. 120–121

FOR LESS–PROFICIENT READERS

In combination with the *Audio Anthology CD,* use one or more Targeted Passages (pp. 384, 389, 390) to ensure that students focus on key selection events, concepts, and skills.

FOR ENGLISH LEARNERS

Options for Reading [small-group option] Read aloud lines 1–14. Ask students to predict what kinds of experiences the author will have in Jerusalem. Then have students read the memoir along with the *Audio Anthology CD* or read the Targeted Passages aloud in small groups.

BACKGROUND

Armenia In lines 50–58, the author tells about being enrolled in an Armenian school in Jerusalem. Armenia is a landlocked country bordered by Georgia, Azerbaijan, Turkey, and Iran. It is one of the oldest nations in the world and has had a tumultuous history under the rule of many powers, including Persia, Turkey, Russia, and the Soviet Union. Over the years, deportations and massacres under these governments have forced many Armenians to flee their country. In 1991, however, Armenia finally achieved independence.

Six-Day War In response to hearing of a joint military agreement between its enemies —Egypt, Syria, Jordan, and Iraq—Israel attacked Egypt as a preemptive strike on June 5, 1967. Within six days, Israel had achieved victory and claimed a great deal of territory, including all of Jerusalem, Gaza, and the Sinai Peninsula. This conflict, one of several in the long-running Arab-Israeli hostilities, caused the author and her family to leave Jerusalem (lines 219–224).

FOR ENGLISH LEARNERS

Key Academic Vocabulary Have students use New Word Analysis to study this academic vocabulary from the selection: *grade* (lines 14, 54), *emphasis* (line 20), *transfer* (line 33).

 BEST PRACTICES TOOLKIT—Transparency
New Word Analysis p. E8

Prereading For prereading instruction for English learners, see

 BEST PRACTICES TOOLKIT
Scaffolding Reading Instruction pp. 43–46

FOR ADVANCED LEARNERS/PRE–AP

Pre-AP exercises in the bottom channel provide additional challenge for your advanced students. Use them for small groups or individuals.

ADDITIONAL GUIDELINES

For more help with differentiation and tips for classroom management, see

 BEST PRACTICES TOOLKIT
Differentiated Instruction pp. 31–38

READING STRATEGY

B CONNECT

Remind students to record their responses in their charts from page 381. *Students may say that they protest unfair rules or work to correct them.*

Extend the Discussion Is Nye's reaction similar to or different from the way you might handle this conflict?

SOCIAL STUDIES CONNECTION

The history of Jerusalem has proven to be anything but peaceful. Most recently in the 20th century, the jurisdiction of the city was fought over by Arabs and Israelis. In 1948, as a result of the first Arab-Israeli war, Jerusalem was divided into two sections under control of Israel and Jordan. After the Six-Day War in 1967, Israel claimed control of the entire city.

Lines 50–78

DISCUSSION PROMPTS

Use these prompts to help students understand the author's transfer to a new school:

Connect What would be the hardest adjustment for you if you attended this school? Why? *Students may say that having classes taught in three languages would be difficult. Or, they might say that wearing a uniform would be a difficult adjustment.*

Analyze Why does Nye's father resort to threatening the principal to get her into the school? ***Possible answer:** Nye is not Armenian, but she needs to go to this school because classes are taught in English.*

Evaluate Will Nye try to follow the rules of this school? Explain. ***Possible answers:***

- *Yes. She knows that there are not many options open to her. The experience at the previous school was a shock.*
- *No. She seems unwilling to follow any rules that she does not agree with. The Armenian school is likely to have some rules and customs that are unfamiliar to her. Also, she has already thrown her physics book out the window, which seems rebellious.*

"But there are only six other girls! And I like only one of them!" My friend was Anna, from Italy, whose father ran a small factory that made matches. I'd visited it once with her. It felt risky to walk the aisles among a million filled matchboxes. Later we visited the factory that made olive oil soaps and stacked them in giant pyramids to dry.

"No, thank you," I said. "It's ridiculous to say that girls should only talk to girls. Did I say anything bad to a boy? Did anyone say anything bad to me? They're my friends. They're like my brothers. I won't do it, that's all."

The counselor conferred with the headmaster[1] and they called a taxi. I was sent home with a little paper requesting that I transfer to a different school. The charge: insolence. My mother, startled to see me home early and on my own, stared out the window when I told her.

My brother came home from his school as usual, full of whistling and notebooks. "Did anyone tell you not to talk to girls?" I asked him. He looked at me as if I'd gone goofy. He was too young to know the troubles of the world. He couldn't even imagine them. B

"You know what I've been thinking about?" he said. "A piece of cake. That puffy white layered cake with icing like they have at birthday parties in the United States. Wouldn't that taste good right now?" Our mother said she was thinking about mayonnaise. You couldn't get it in Jerusalem. She'd tried to make it and it didn't work. I felt too gloomy to talk about food.

My brother said, "Let's go let Abu Miriam's chickens out." That's what we always did when we felt sad. We let our fussy landlord's red-and-white chickens loose to flap around the yard happily, puffing their wings. Even when Abu Miriam shouted and waggled his cane and his wife waved a dishtowel, we knew the chickens were thanking us.

My father went with me to the St. Tarkmanchatz Armenian School, a solemnly ancient stone school tucked deep into the Armenian Quarter of the Old City of Jerusalem. It was another world in there. He had already called the school officials on the telephone and tried to enroll me, though they didn't want to. Their school was for Armenian students only, kindergarten through twelfth grade. Classes were taught in three languages: Armenian, Arabic and English, which was why I needed to go there. Although most Arab students at other schools were learning English, I needed a school where classes were actually taught in English—otherwise I would have been staring out the windows triple the usual amount.

The head priest wore a long robe and a tall cone-shaped hat. He said, "Excuse me, please, but your daughter, she is not an Armenian, even a small amount?"

"Not at all," said my father. "But in case you didn't know, there is a **stipulation** in the educational code books of this city that says no student may be rejected solely on the basis of ethnic background, and if you don't accept her, we will alert the proper authorities."

They took me. But the principal wasn't happy about it. The students, however, seemed glad to have a new face to look at. Everyone's name ended in *-ian,*

1. **headmaster:** principal of a private school.

(1) Targeted Passage

B CONNECT
Note Nye's reaction to school's rule about bo and girls. How do yo respond to rules you are unfair?

SOCIAL STUDIES CONNECTION

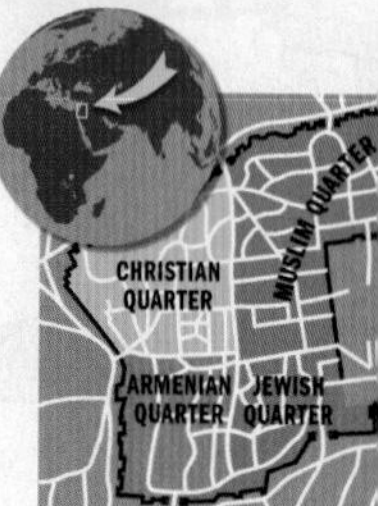

Jerusalem was built around 3000 B.C. Its original name, *Urr Salem,* meant "the land of peace."

stipulation (stĭp'yə-lā'shən) *n.* the act of laying down a condition or agreemer

DIFFERENTIATED INSTRUCTION

FOR LESS–PROFICIENT READERS

(1) Targeted Passage [Lines 29–49]

This passage presents the first signs of the author's conflict with her new setting.

- Why is Nye asked to leave the school? In what way does the experience affect her?
- Are her mother and brother happy in their new home? Explain.
- Why do the author and her brother let the chickens out?

FOR ENGLISH LEARNERS

Culture: Connect In lines 40–44, Nye's mother and brother talk about the food they miss. Her mother cannot find anything to replace mayonnaise, while her brother wants a piece of sugary birthday cake. Ask students if they have ever been in a similar situation. Discuss how substitutes aren't quite the same and why being unable to obtain certain foods or ingredients could increase feelings of homesickness.

.e beautiful, musical Armenian ending—Boghossian, Minassian, Kevorkian, ostomian. My new classmates started calling me Shihabian. We wore uniforms, .vy blue pleated skirts for the girls, white shirts, and navy sweaters. I waited uring the lessons for the English to come around, as if it were a channel on levision. While other students were on the other channels, I scribbled poems in .e margins of my pages, read library books, and wrote a lot of letters filled with .clamation points. All the other students knew all three languages with three ıtirely different alphabets. How could they carry so much in their heads? I felt umbled by my ignorance. One day I felt so frustrated in our physics class—still other language—that I pitched my book out the open window. The professor ıade me go collect it. All the pages had let loose at the seams and were flapping ee into the gutters along with the white wrappers of sandwiches. **C**

Every week the girls had a hands-and-fingernails check. We had to keep our ails clean and trim, and couldn't wear any rings. Some of my new friends would ıvite me home for lunch with them, since we had an hour-and-a-half break and I ved too far to go to my own house.

Their houses were a thousand years old, clustered beehive-fashion behind ıcient walls, stacked and curled and tilting and dark, filled with pictures of ısmiling relatives and small white cloths dangling crocheted[2] edges. We ate pinach pies and white cheese. We dipped our bread in olive oil, as the Arabs id. We ate small sesame cakes, our mouths full of crumbles. They taught me to y "I love you" in Armenian, which sounded like *yes-kay-see-goo-see-rem.* I felt I ad left my old life entirely. **D**

Every afternoon I went down to the basement of the school where the kindergarten lass was having an Arabic lesson. Their desks were pint-sized, their full white smocks ed around their necks. I stuffed my fourteen-year-old self in beside them. They had osy cheeks and shy smiles. They must have thought I was a very slow learner.

More than any of the lessons, I remember the way the teacher rapped the backs f their hands with his ruler when they made a mistake. Their little faces puffed p with quiet tears. This pained me so terribly I forgot all my words. When it ʋas my turn to go to the blackboard and write in Arabic, my hand shook. The indergarten students whispered hints to me from the front row, but I couldn't nderstand them. We learned horribly useless phrases: "Please hand me the ellows[3] for my fire." I wanted words simple as tools, simple as *food* and *yesterday* nd *dreams.* The teacher never rapped my hand, especially after I wrote a letter to he city newspaper, which my father edited, protesting such harsh treatment of oung learners. I wish I had known how to talk to those little ones, but they were ıst beginning their English studies and didn't speak much yet. They were at the ame place in their English that I was in my Arabic.

From the high windows of St. Tarkmanchatz, we could look out over the Old City, the roofs and flapping laundry and television antennas, the pilgrims and hurches and mosques, the olivewood prayer beads and fragrant *falafel*[4] lunch

C CONNECT
Reread lines 69–78. Think of a time when you felt frustrated in class. What did you do to solve the problem?

D SETTING IN NONFICTION
What details help you to picture the Armenian houses and to understand Armenian customs?

2. **crocheted** (krō-shād'): needlework made by looping thread with a hooked needle.
3. **bellows** (bĕl'ōz): an apparatus used for producing a strong current of air.
4. ***falafel*** (fə-lä'fəl): fried balls of ground, spiced chickpeas.

READING STRATEGY

C CONNECT

Remind students to record their responses in their charts from page 381. ***Possible answer:***

- ***Author's Experiences:*** *She gets so frustrated in class that she throws her textbook out the window (lines 75–76).*
- ***My Experiences:*** *When I get frustrated in class, I ask for help from the teacher or another student.*
- ***Insights:*** *The language barrier must have made Nye feel that she couldn't get the help she needed, either from her teacher or from her classmates.*

Lines 79–82

REINFORCE *KEY IDEA:* BELONGING

Discuss How might the actions by the author's classmates affect her sense of **belonging?** ***Possible answer:*** *The other students are hospitable and kind, which might help her feel more at home in her new environment.*

LITERARY ANALYSIS

D SETTING IN NONFICTION

Possible answer:

- *The girls must keep their nails trimmed and cannot wear rings.*
- *The houses are "a thousand years old, clustered beehive-fashion behind ancient walls, stacked and curled and tilting and dark, filled with pictures of unsmiling relatives and small white cloths dangling crocheted edges."*
- *In the Armenian houses, the author eats spinach pies, white cheese, and sesame cakes, and she dips her bread in olive oil.*

Extend the Discussion The author says, "I felt I had left my old life entirely." Does she mean this in a positive or negative way? Explain.

FOR LESS–PROFICIENT READERS

Concept Support [small-group option] Have groups compare their school with St. Tarkmanchatz Armenian School to more fully appreciate the author's experiences. Have students use a Y Chart to organize their details. Encourage them to compare buildings, locations, personnel, classes, rules, and expectations. Then discuss the similarities and differences.

BEST PRACTICES TOOLKIT—Transparency
Y Chart p. A27

FOR ADVANCED LEARNERS/PRE–AP

Make Judgments Have students consider the author's actions so far. She has been asked to leave one school and has written a letter of protest over the teaching methods at another school. As a temporary resident in Jerusalem, is the author showing a lack of respect, or is she just being true to her values? Do visitors to another country have a responsibility to try to fit in, or should they question what they see as wrong? Have students informally debate these questions.

READING STRATEGY

E CONNECT

Remind students to record their responses in their charts from page 381. ***Possible answer:***

- ***Author's Experiences:*** *After seeing the barbed wire separating Jordan from Israel, she has a serious conversation with friends about the fighting in the world.*
- ***My Experiences:*** *When I talk to my friends about serious topics, we sometimes argue or realize that we think the same way.*
- ***Insights:*** *This conversation might make the author feel angry, sad, hopeless, resentful, or introspective.*

ANALYZE VISUALS

Possible answer: *The way they are huddled together shows they have a close relationship. Also, one boy holds another boy's arm to keep him from running away. This shows that the family takes care of one another.*

About the Art Palestinian artist Ismail Shammout (born 1930) focuses his art on the plight of his people, although some of his paintings do depict more positive images of love, beauty, motherhood, community, and nature. He uses oil paints, as in this work, and also watercolors.

stands, the **intricate** interweaving of cultures and prayers and songs and holidays. We saw the barbed wire separating Jordan from Israel then, the bleak, uninhabited strip of no-man's land reminding me how little education saved us after all. People who had differing ideas still came to blows, imagining fighting could solve things. Staring out over the quiet roofs of afternoon, I thought it so foolish. I asked my friends what they thought about it and they shrugged.

"It doesn't matter what we think about it. It just keeps happening. It happened in Armenia too,[5] you know. Really, really bad in Armenia. And who talks about it in the world news now? It happens everywhere. It happens in *your* country one by one, yes? Murders and guns. What can we do?" E

intricate (ĭn'trĭ-kĭt) a
elaborate

E CONNECT
Think of a serious conversation you have had with friends. Based on how you fe afterward, how do yo think Nye might have felt after having this conversation?

5. **It happened in Armenia, too:** Refers to the Armenian massacres of 1915–1923. In response to Russia's use of Armenian troops against the Ottomans in World War I, the Ottoman empire ordered the deportation of 1.75 million Armenians. During the deportation, around a million Armenians were killed or died of starvation.

The Olive Tree (2005), Ismail Shammout. Palestine. Oil on canvas, 60 cm × 80 cm. Private collection.

ANALYZE VISUALS
What can you infer ab this family from the w they are posed in this painting?

DIFFERENTIATED INSTRUCTION

FOR LESS–PROFICIENT READERS

Concept Support Read lines 106–111 aloud. Ask students to sketch the view that the author describes from the window of her school. Have students share their drawings and discuss which details correspond to those in the text.

Sometimes after school, my brother and I walked up the road that led past the crowded refugee camp of Palestinians who owned even less than our modest relatives did in the village. The little kids were stacking stones in empty tin cans and shaking them. We waved our hands and they covered their mouths and laughed. We wore our beat-up American tennis shoes and our old sweatshirts and talked about everything we wanted to do and everywhere else we wished we could go.

"I want to go back to Egypt," my brother said. "I sort of feel like I missed it. Spending all that time in bed instead of exploring—what a waste."

"I want to go to Greece," I said. "I want to play a violin in a symphony orchestra in Austria." We made up things. I wanted to go back to the United States most of all. Suddenly I felt like a patriotic citizen. One of my friends, Sylvie Markarian, had just been shipped off to Damascus, Syria to marry a man who was fifty years old, a widower. Sylvie was exactly my age—we had turned fifteen two days apart. She had never met her future husband before. I thought this was the most revolting thing I had ever heard of. "Tell your parents no thank you," I urged her. "Tell them you *refuse*."

Sylvie's eyes were liquid, swirling brown. I could not see clearly to the bottom of them.

"You don't understand," she told me. "In United States you say no. We don't say no. We have to follow someone's wishes. This is the wish of my father. Me, I am scared. I never slept away from my mother before. But I have no choice. I am going because they tell me to go." She was sobbing, sobbing on my shoulder. And I was stroking her long, soft hair. After that, I carried two fists inside, one for Sylvie and one for me. F

Most weekends my family went to the village to sit with the relatives. We sat and sat and sat. We sat in big rooms and little rooms, in circles, on chairs or on woven mats or brightly covered mattresses piled on the floor. People came in and out to greet my family. Sometimes even donkeys and chickens came in and out. We were like movie stars or dignitaries.[6] They never seemed to get tired of us.

My father translated the more interesting tidbits of conversation, the funny stories my grandmother told. She talked about angels and food and money and people and politics and gossip and old memories from my father's childhood, before he **emigrated** away from her. She wanted to make sure we were going to stick around forever, which made me feel very nervous. We ate from mountains of rice and eggplant on large silver trays—they gave us little plates of our own since it was not our custom to eat from the same plate as other people. We ripped the giant wheels of bread into triangles. Shepherds passed through town with their flocks of sheep and goats, their long canes and cloaks, straight out of the Bible. My brother and I trailed them to the edge of the village, past the lentil fields to the green meadows studded with stones, while the shepherds pretended we weren't there. I think they liked to be alone, unnoticed. The sheep had differently colored dyed bottoms, so shepherds could tell their flocks apart. G

F SETTING IN NONFICTION
Note Nye's reaction to her friend's problem. In what ways is she being affected by her experiences in Jerusalem?

emigrate (ĕm′ĭ-grāt′) *v.* to leave one country and settle in another

G SETTING IN NONFICTION
Reread lines 144–161. What details help create a sense of place?

6. **dignitaries** (dĭg′nĭ-tĕr′ēz): people of high rank or position.

FOR ENGLISH LEARNERS

Vocabulary Support Point out the words *passed* (line 156) and *past* (line 158). Explain that although both words sound the same when they are spoken aloud, they have completely different functions in a sentence. Tell students that *passed* is a verb that means "walked" or "went." *Past* as it is used here is a preposition meaning "beyond in position." Ask students to use each word correctly in a sentence.

Lines 120–125

REINFORCE *KEY IDEA:* BELONGING

Discuss Think about the nature of refugee camps. What point does this reference make about **belonging?** Why do you think the author mentions it here? ***Possible answer:*** *Refugees literally belong nowhere. Their homes have been taken and they have been left with nothing. The author may mention it because she also feels displaced and rootless.*

LITERARY ANALYSIS

F SETTING IN NONFICTION

Possible answer: *Nye is developing a sense of compassion for those who do not have the same freedoms she had in the United States. She is also becoming angry at some of the cultural differences she sees.*

If students need help . . . Use a Cause-and-Effect Chain to help students identify the effects of Sylvie's problem on the author.

Sylvie is forced to marry a 50-year-old man.
↓
Nye is horrified at her friend's lack of freedom.
↓
Nye becomes angry at the culture that treats her friend in this way.

BEST PRACTICES TOOLKIT—Transparency
Cause-and-Effect Chain pp. B16, B39

LITERARY ANALYSIS

G SETTING IN NONFICTION

Possible answer:

- *Woven mats and brightly covered mattresses are piled on the floor.*
- *Chickens and donkeys roam freely.*
- *Rice and eggplant are served on silver trays with wheels of bread ripped into triangles.*
- *Shepherds pass through town with their multicolored flocks.*

ANALYZE VISUALS

Possible answer: *The stone building encompasses the splendor of the busy people, color, and light.*

Lines 162–185
DISCUSSION PROMPTS

Use these prompts to help students understand the author's feelings and her relatives' reactions:

Connect If you were one of the author's relatives, how would you feel if you saw her crying? *Students may say that they would feel concerned and responsible.*

Analyze Why does Nye's father make up excuses for her crying? ***Possible answer:*** *Her father can't tell her relatives that she is crying because she wants to go home. It would hurt their feelings.*

Synthesize Do you agree with Nye's father when he says that later she will "have no idea" what made her so unhappy? Explain. ***Possible answers:***

- *Yes. She is overwhelmed by the differences between Jerusalem and the United States. Later she will come to appreciate these differences and see them as enriching her life.*
- *No. She may look back on the experience as a positive one, but the fact that she has written this vivid memoir describing her feelings shows that she never forgot what made her unhappy.*

In Jerusalem (1997), Ismail Shammout. Palestine. Oil on canvas, 50 cm × 60 cm. Private collection.

During these long, slow, smoke-stained weekends—the men still smoked cigarettes a lot in those days, and the old *taboon,* my family's mounded bread-oven, puffed billowy clouds outside the door—my crying jags began. I cried without any warning, even in the middle of a meal. My crying was usually noiseless but dramatically wet—streams of tears pouring down my cheeks, onto my collar or the back of my hand.

Everything grew quiet.

Someone always asked in Arabic, "What is wrong? Are you sick? Do you wish to lie down?"

My father made **valiant** excuses in the beginning. "She's overtired," he said. "She has a headache. She is missing her friend who moved to Syria. She is homesick just now."

My brother stared at me as if I had just landed from Planet X.

ANALYZE VISUALS
Nye describes the "sto
splendor" of Jerusalem
How does this painting
that description?

valiant (văl′yənt) *adj.* brave

DIFFERENTIATED INSTRUCTION

FOR LESS-PROFICIENT READERS

Reading Strategy Follow-Up: Connect

- Have students review what they have read so far in the selection and record additional connections in their charts. For example, point out the incident in lines 90–93. Have they ever felt similarly out of place?
- Have students share the connections they made. Then help them use these connections to arrive at insights that increase understanding of character or theme.

Author's Experiences	My Experiences	Insights
She has to take Arabic lessons with kindergarten students (lines 90–105).	I just started ice skating, and a lot of the other students are really young.	It's not easy to be a beginner or to be in a situation in which you feel inadequate.

Worst of all was our drive to school every morning, when our car came over the rise in the highway and all Jerusalem lay sprawled before us in its golden, stony splendor pockmarked with olive trees and automobiles. Even the air above the city had a thick, religious texture, as if it were a shining brocade[7] filled with broody incense. I cried hardest then. All those hours tied up in school lay just ahead. My father pulled over and talked to me. He sighed. He kept his hands on the steering wheel even when the car was stopped and said, "Someday, I promise you, you will look back on this period in your life and have no idea what made you so unhappy here."

"I want to go home." It became my anthem. "This place depresses me. It weighs too much. . . . I hate the way people stare at me here." Already I'd been involved in two street skirmishes with boys who stared a little too hard and long. I'd socked one in the jaw and he socked me back. I hit the other one straight in the face with my purse. **H**

"You could be happy here if you tried just a little harder," my father said. "Don't compare it to the United States all the time. Don't pretend the United States is perfect. And look at your brother—he's not having any problems!"

"My brother is eleven years old."

I had crossed the boundary from uncomplicated childhood when happiness was a good ball and a horde of candy-coated Jordan almonds. **I**

One problem was that I had fallen in love with four different boys who all played in the same band. Two of them were even twins. I never quite described it to my parents, but I wrote reams and reams of notes about it on loose-leaf paper that I kept under my sweaters in my closet.

Such new energy made me feel reckless. I gave things away. I gave away my necklace and a whole box of shortbread cookies that my mother had been saving. I gave my extra shoes away to the gypsies. One night when the gypsies camped in a field down the road from our house, I thought about their mounds of white goat cheese lined up on skins in front of their tents, and the wild *oud*[8] music they played deep into the black belly of the night, and I wanted to go sit around their fire. Maybe they could use some shoes.

I packed a sack of old loafers that I rarely wore and walked with my family down the road. The gypsy mothers stared into my shoes curiously. They took them into their tent. Maybe they would use them as vases or drawers. We sat with small glasses of hot, sweet tea until a girl bellowed from deep in her throat, threw back her head, and began dancing. A long bow thrummed across the strings. The girl circled the fire, tapping and clicking, trilling a long musical wail from deep in her throat. My brother looked nervous. He was remembering the belly dancer in Egypt, and her scarf. I felt invisible. I was pretending to be a gypsy. My father stared at me. Didn't I recognize the exquisite oddity of my own life when I sat right in the middle of it? Didn't I feel lucky to be here? Well, yes I did. But sometimes it was hard to be lucky.

(2) **Targeted Passage**

H SETTING IN NONFICTION
Reread lines 175–188. What is it about Jerusalem that makes Nye feel sad and angry?

I CONNECT
Which of your own experiences can help you understand what Nye is feeling?

7. **brocade** (brō-kād'): a heavy fabric with a raised design.
8. ***oud*** (o͞od): a musical instrument resembling a lute.

LITERARY ANALYSIS

H SETTING IN NONFICTION

Possible answer: *She becomes sad when she sees the Jerusalem skyline on her way to school, perhaps because it looks so different from the United States. She is tired of being stared at and has been in fights with boys. Jerusalem depresses her.*

Extend the Discussion What does the author mean when she says that Jerusalem "weighs too much"?

READING STRATEGY

I CONNECT

Remind students to record their responses in their charts from page 381. ***Possible answer:***

- ***Author's Experiences:*** *While talking to her father about her unhappiness about feeling out of place in Israel, she realizes that she is also trying to deal with growing up.*
- ***My Experiences:*** *Sometimes when I feel lonely and confused, I find it difficult to ask my parents for help.*
- ***Insights:*** *The realization that she can no longer be a carefree child is difficult for her to deal with and accept.*

FOR LESS-PROFICIENT READERS

(2) Targeted Passage [Lines 175–194]

This passage reveals the author's conflict: her unhappiness and her difficulty fitting in.

- What does the author do on her way to school? Why?
- Why has the author been in fights?
- Why does her father want her to be more like her brother? Why does she say she can't be more like him?

FOR ADVANCED LEARNERS/PRE-AP

Analyze [paired option] Point out that if the author's personality or character had been different, her perception of her experiences would have been different, too. Have pairs of students analyze her character traits and the impact they have on how she reacts to her year in Jerusalem. Ask students to use the Character Analysis Chart to organize their ideas for presentation in a class discussion.

BEST PRACTICES TOOLKIT—Transparency
Character Analysis Chart p. D5

Lines 201–216
REINFORCE *KEY IDEA:* BELONGING

Discuss What lesson about **belonging** might the gypsies teach the author? ***Possible answer:*** *Gypsies take their culture with them. They don't need a particular geographical location to make them feel that they belong.*

When we left Jerusalem, we left quickly. Left our beds in our rooms and our car in the driveway. Left in a plane, not sure where we were going. The rumbles of fighting with Israel had been growing louder and louder. In the barbed-wire no-man's land visible from the windows of our house, guns cracked loudly in the middle of the night. We lived right near the edge. My father heard disturbing rumors at the newspaper that would soon grow into the infamous Six Day War of 1967. We were in England by then, drinking tea from thin china cups and scanning the newspapers. Bombs were blowing up in Jerusalem. We worried about the village. We worried about my grandmother's dreams, which had been getting worse and worse, she'd told us. We worried about the house we'd left, and the chickens, and the children at the refugee camp. But there was nothing we could do except keep talking about it all.

My parents didn't want to go back to Missouri because they'd already said goodbye to everyone there. They thought we might try a different part of the country. They weighed the virtues of different states. Texas was big and warm. After a chilly year crowded around the small gas heaters we used in Jerusalem, a warm place sounded appealing. In roomy Texas, my parents bought the first house they looked at. My father walked into the city newspaper and said, "Any jobs open around here?"

I burst out crying when I entered a grocery store—so many different kinds of bread. **J**

A letter on thin blue airmail paper reached me months later, written by my classmate, the bass player in my favorite Jerusalem band. "Since you left," he said, "your empty desk reminds me of a snake ready to strike. I am afraid to look at it. I hope you are having a better time than we are."

Of course I was, and I wasn't. *Home* had grown different forever. *Home* had doubled. Back *home* again in my own country, it seemed impossible to forget the place we had just left: the piercing call of the *muezzin*[9] from the mosque[10] at prayer time, the dusky green tint of the olive groves, the sharp, cold air that smelled as deep and old as my grandmother's white sheets flapping from the line on her roof. What story hadn't she finished?

Our father used to tell us that when he was little, the sky over Jerusalem crackled with meteors and shooting stars almost every night. They streaked and flashed, igniting the dark. Some had long golden tails. For a few seconds, you could see their whole swooping trail lit up. Our father and his brothers slept on the roof to watch the sky. "There were so many of them, we didn't even call out every time we saw one."

During our year in Jerusalem, my brother and I kept our eyes cast upwards whenever we were outside at night, but the stars were different since our father was a boy. Now the sky seemed too orderly, stuck in place. The stars had learned where they belonged. Only people on the ground kept changing.

J SETTING IN NONFICTION
Reread lines 217–237. How is Texas different from Jerusalem?

3 Targeted Passage

9. ***muezzin*** (myo͞o-ĕz′ĭn): a crier who calls the Muslim faithful to prayer.
10. **mosque** (mŏsk): a Muslim house of worship.

LITERARY ANALYSIS

J SETTING IN NONFICTION

Possible answer: *Texas is "big and warm." Nye's family no longer has to huddle around a space heater. Houses and jobs are easy to find. In the grocery store, there is a variety of food.*

If students need help . . . Tell students that the details the author includes in lines 231–237 indicate the major differences between the two locations. The words *big, warm,* and *roomy* in reference to Texas suggest that Jerusalem could not be described similarly. The description of how the family purchases a house and finds jobs also sets up a contrast with Jerusalem.

Extend the Discussion Does Texas "weigh too much"? Explain.

Lines 242–247

REINFORCE *KEY IDEA:* BELONGING

Discuss How has the year away changed the author's sense of **belonging?** ***Possible answer:*** *Now that she is in Texas, she misses Jerusalem. She is not quite sure where she belongs.*

SELECTION WRAP-UP

REFLECT Ask students how reading about the author's experiences helped them understand the challenges of living in a different culture.

★ CRITIQUE Ask students if they would like to read about other aspects of Nye's experience. If so, which ones?

DIFFERENTIATED INSTRUCTION

FOR LESS-PROFICIENT READERS

3 Targeted Passage [Lines 238–247]

This passage presents a turning point for the author as she realizes that she has two homes.

- How does the author feel now that she is back in the United States?
- What does Nye keep remembering and wondering? Why?
- What has she learned about belonging?

FOR ADVANCED LEARNERS/PRE-AP

Analyze Theme What message about human nature does the author's experience in this memoir convey? Ask students to examine lines 189–191 and 242–257 for insights to help them write a statement of theme. Have students share their theme statements with the class.

My Father and the Figtree

Naomi Shihab Nye

For other fruits my father was indifferent.
He'd point at the cherry trees and say,
"See those? I wish they were figs."
In the evenings he sat by our beds
weaving folktales like vivid little scarves.
They always involved a figtree.
Even when it didn't fit, he'd stick it in.
Once Joha was walking down the road
and he saw a figtree.
Or, he tied his camel to a figtree and went to sleep.
Or, later when they caught and arrested him,
his pockets were full of figs.

DISCUSSION PROMPTS

Use these prompts to help students understand the constant references to figs by the speaker's father:

Summarize How does the speaker's father feel about figs? ***Answer:*** *He is passionate about them.*

Analyze What is the effect of the father's always including a figtree or figs in his stories? ***Possible answer:*** *The children are constantly reminded of his attachment to figs and their importance in his life. Including a figtree or figs also adds humor.*

Synthesize Does the speaker share her father's feeling about figs? How do you know? ***Possible answer:*** *The speaker's tone is one of amused tolerance as she recounts the many ways her father found to refer to figs. This tone suggests that she doesn't quite see the fascination in the fruit herself.*

FOR LESS–PROFICIENT READERS

Comprehension Support [paired option] Pair students and have them employ a Read-and-Say-Something strategy to explore the poem. Ask students to pause after reading each stanza to discuss the images or ideas and jot down any questions that they have. After they have completed the poem, return to their questions as a class and clarify understanding.

BEST PRACTICES TOOLKIT
Read-and-Say-Something p. D3

FOR ENGLISH LEARNERS

Options for Reading Read the poem aloud, modeling how to follow punctuation cues. Then have students take turns reading the poem to a partner. Or, have them read silently along with the *Audio Anthology CD.*

DISCUSSION PROMPTS

Use these prompts to help students understand the connection between the poem and the key idea of **belonging:**

Recall What is the reaction of the speaker's father to the dried fig? ***Answer:*** *He says it is not the same as picking a large, fat, sweet fig straight from a tree.*

Analyze Why won't the speaker's father plant his own figtree? ***Possible answer:*** *Planting his own tree is not the same as having one already growing on the property. To plant a tree would be like forcing a connection.*

Synthesize Why is the speaker's father so happy when he finds the figtree growing in the garden of his house in Dallas? ***Possible answer:*** *It suggests to him that he has come home and that he does belong in the United States after all.*

At age six I ate a dried fig and shrugged.
"That's not what I'm talking about!" he said,
"I'm talking about a fig straight from the earth—
gift of Allah!—on a branch so heavy
it touches the ground.
I'm talking about picking the largest, fattest,
  sweetest fig
in the world and putting it in my mouth."
(Here he'd stop and close his eyes.)

Years passed, we lived in many houses,
none had figtrees.
We had lima beans, zucchini, parsley, beets.
"Plant one!" my mother said,
but my father never did.
He tended garden half-heartedly, forgot to water,
let the okra get too big.
"What a dreamer he is. Look how many
things he starts and doesn't finish."

The last time he moved, I had a phone call,
my father, in Arabic, chanting a song
I'd never heard. "What's that?"
He took me out to the new yard.
There, in the middle of Dallas, Texas,
a tree with the largest, fattest,
sweetest figs in the world.
"It's a figtree song!" he said,
plucking his fruits like ripe tokens,
emblems, assurance
of a world that was always his own.

DIFFERENTIATED INSTRUCTION

FOR ENGLISH LEARNERS

Task Support [paired option] Adapt the Think-Pair-Share strategy and have students use it to answer selected questions in the Discussion Prompts. Discuss their responses and questions.

 **BEST PRACTICES TOOLKIT—Transparency**
Think-Pair-Share p. A18

FOR ADVANCED LEARNERS/PRE-AP

Analyze [paired option] Ask students to work in pairs to explore the symbolism of the figs and figtree in the poem. Have them develop a Cluster Diagram that displays their insights.

 **BEST PRACTICES TOOLKIT—Transparency**
Cluster Diagram p. B18

392 UNIT 3: SETTING AND MOOD

mprehension

1. **Recall** Why was it necessary for Naomi Shihab Nye to attend the Armenian school after being expelled from her first school?
2. **Clarify** Reread lines 130–143. Why was the author angry about her friend's being sent to Damascus?
3. **Clarify** Why did the family leave Jerusalem?

itical Analysis

4. **Make Connections** Look at the chart you filled in as you read. Which two connections best helped you understand what the author experienced in Jerusalem? Explain.
5. **Examine Setting** Use a web diagram to identify descriptive details that helped convey the **setting** of this selection. Then expand your web to include insights on how this setting affected the author.

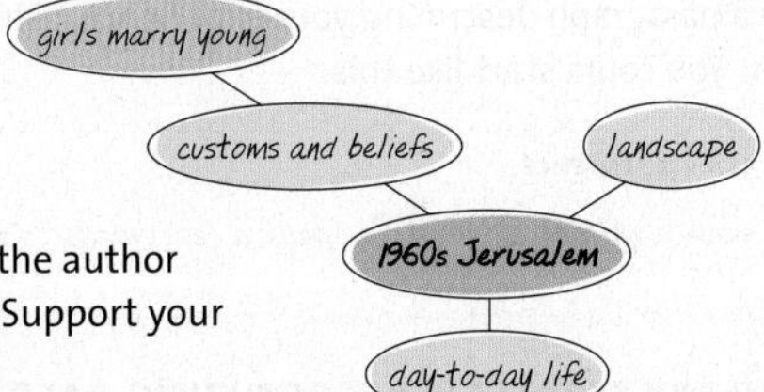

6. **Analyze Memoir** At what point in the selection does the author become aware of a sense of **belonging** in Jerusalem? Support your answer with examples from the memoir.
7. **Compare Literary Works** Nye's father encouraged her to try to be happy in Jerusalem and to learn to appreciate the "exquisite oddity" of her life. What does the poem "My Father and the Figtree" on page 391 reveal about her father's feelings toward living in different places?

tension and Challenge

8. **Creative Project: Music** Naomi Shihab Nye belongs to two cultures. If this memoir were to be made into a television show or a documentary, an appropriate soundtrack might feature American music as well as music from the Middle East. Divide this selection into parts and note which type of music should accompany each part.
9. SOCIAL STUDIES CONNECTION Learn more about Jerusalem—its history, geographical setting, and culture. Present your information in the form of a colorful poster.

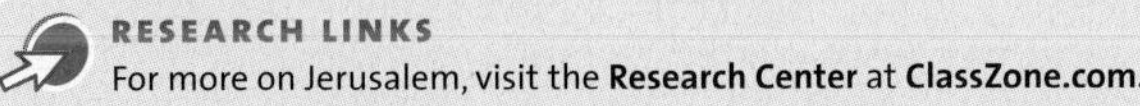
RESEARCH LINKS
For more on Jerusalem, visit the **Research Center** at **ClassZone.com.**

6. *Nye doesn't feel a sense of belonging in Jerusalem until she returns to the United States (lines 242–247). She thinks about the landscape, her grandmother, and the sights and sounds of the city she just left.*
7. *The figtree is a symbol of Nye's father's longing for the place of his birth. He is overjoyed when he finally has a figtree and feels that he is home again.*

Extension and Challenge

8. *Students' musical selections should reflect the setting, events, and feelings in the parts of the memoir that they accompany.*
9. **SOCIAL STUDIES CONNECTION** *Students' posters should be well organized and show evidence of research.*

Practice and Apply

After Reading

For additional support of postreading questions, use these copy masters:

RESOURCE MANAGER—Copy Masters
Reading Check p. 132 (to check understanding of the selection)
Setting in Nonfiction p. 125 (for practice of literary analysis standards focus)
Question Support p. 133 (After Reading questions adapted for English learners and less-proficient readers)

Additional selection questions are provided for teachers on page 119.

For additional activities to challenge students, see

Power Thinking at **ClassZone.com**

ANSWERS

Comprehension

1. *The Armenian school offered classes taught in English.*
2. *Her friend, who was 15 years old, was being forced to marry a much older man.*
3. *The fighting that became known as the Six-Day War of 1967 was starting.*

Critical Analysis

Possible answers:

4. **STANDARDS FOCUS Connect** *Students' answers should refer to specific experiences from the selection.*
5. **STANDARDS FOCUS Setting in Nonfiction** ***Landscape:*** *"houses . . . a thousand years old," churches and mosques, olive groves, fragrant falafel lunch stands.* ***Customs and Beliefs:*** *marriages arranged by parents, weekend family gatherings, strict schools.* ***Day-to-Day Life:*** *spinach pies and white cheese, three different languages taught and spoken in schools, sharing meals from a common plate, sitting on mats on the floor.* ***Insights:*** *The author found the setting foreign at first, and it depressed her. But she finds that Jerusalem is just as much her home as the United States. She can't forget her experiences in Jerusalem and she no longer sees the United States in the same way.*

ANSWERS

Vocabulary in Context

VOCABULARY PRACTICE

1. *false*
2. *true*
3. *true*
4. *false*

 RESOURCE MANAGER—Copy Master
Vocabulary Practice p. 130

VOCABULARY IN WRITING

Suggest that students look back at the memoir and note some of the author's challenges as she tries to fit into her new world. Encourage them to incorporate some of these ideas into their own paragraphs and to review the vocabulary words to see which will fit the sense of their sentences.

VOCABULARY STRATEGY: RECOGNIZING BASE WORDS *(also an EL language objective)*

Remind students that a base word is one that is complete in itself and can stand alone, unlike roots that usually need a prefix or a suffix to make a recognizable word.

Possible answers:

1. *"wearing away"—erode, -sion*
2. *"good judgment or insight"—wise, -dom*
3. *"steering of a ship"—navigate, -ion*
4. *"sequence"—rotate, -ion*
5. *"offer"—propose, -al*

RESOURCE MANAGER—Copy Master
Vocabulary Strategy p. 131

Vocabulary Center at **ClassZone.com**
Additional Vocabulary Activities

Vocabulary in Context

VOCABULARY PRACTICE

Show that you understand the vocabulary words by deciding if each statement is true or false.

1. A **valiant** action is a coward's way out.
2. If a pattern is **intricate,** it has a complicated design.
3. If you are given a **stipulation,** a condition of some kind is involved.
4. People who **emigrate** live in the same country their whole lives.

VOCABULARY IN WRITING

Have you ever moved to a new country? If not, imagine what it must be like. Write a paragraph describing your experience, using two or more vocabulary words. You could start like this.

EXAMPLE SENTENCE

I made a __valiant__ attempt to speak a few words to my new classmates.

VOCABULARY STRATEGY: RECOGNIZING BASE WORDS

To understand an unfamiliar word with affixes (prefixes and suffixes), it helps to identify the base word first. Look within the word for a word that is familiar to you, though the spelling might be different. For example, in the word *emigrate,* you might notice the base word *migrate.* In cases where you do not recognize a base word, you may need to use context clues to figure out the meaning.

PRACTICE Define each boldfaced word. Then give the base word and affixes. Use a dictionary if necessary.

1. The heavy rainfall was causing **erosion** of the soil.
2. He admired the professor for her **wisdom** and knowledge.
3. The most difficult part of the journey was the **navigation** of the river rapids.
4. It was her turn in the **rotation** to take the dog for a walk.
5. Did she accept his **proposal** of marriage?

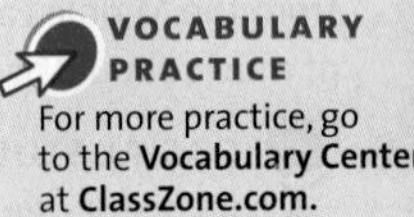
VOCABULARY PRACTICE
For more practice, go to the **Vocabulary Center** at **ClassZone.com.**

DIFFERENTIATED INSTRUCTION

FOR ENGLISH LEARNERS

Vocabulary in Writing Suggest that students narrate their experiences chronologically, using a Sequence Chain to organize the events. Help them write a topic sentence for their paragraph that incorporates one of the vocabulary words, such as *When my family decided to emigrate from ____, I was ____.* Then have them finish their paragraphs based on their charts.

 BEST PRACTICES TOOLKIT—Transparency
Sequence Chain pp. B21, B45

FOR ADVANCED LEARNERS/PRE-AP

Vocabulary Strategy Challenge students to create as many words from each base word as they can. Have students compare lists and define each other's words.

ading-Writing Connection

crease your understanding of "Going Where I'm Coming From" by responding these prompts. Then complete the **Grammar and Writing** exercise.

WRITING PROMPTS	SELF-CHECK
A. Short Response: Analyze the Message Based on Nye's experience, do you think a person can truly **belong** in two places? In **one paragraph,** explain your opinion by citing from the memoir.	***A convincing response will . . .*** • state your position • use details from the text
B. Extended Response: Write a Letter When in Jerusalem, Nye wrote letters to her friends in the U.S. What do you think she said about life in her new country? Write a **two- or three-paragraph letter** that she might have sent.	***A realistic letter will . . .*** • be written in the first-person point of view • contain details about people, places, and events

MMAR AND WRITING

AINTAIN SUBJECT-VERB AGREEMENT Pronouns that do not refer to a specific erson, place, thing, or idea are called **indefinite pronouns.** Some indefinite ronouns are always singular, some are always plural, and some can be either ngular or plural. Here are some common indefinite pronouns.

Singular		Plural		Singular or Plural	
anyone	neither	both	many	any	none
each	something	few	several	most	some

f the pronoun can be singular or plural, use context clues to help you determine what verb to use with it. If the noun that the pronoun refers to is singular, use a ingular verb; if it is plural, use a plural verb.

Original: Most of the students in the school was boys.

Revised: Most of the students in the school were boys.

RACTICE Choose the verb form that agrees with each indefinite pronoun.

1. Both children (misses, miss) their favorite foods from back home.
2. Several students at the Armenian school (likes, like) Naomi.
3. According to dress code, each child (wear, wears) a white smock.
4. Though many of the shepherds are shy, some (wants, want) to talk to people.

or more help with subject-verb agreement with indefinite pronouns, see age R66 in the ***Grammar Handbook.***

Reading-Writing Connection

WRITING PROMPTS

- For **Prompt A,** have students reread lines 242–257. Then have them discuss their opinions with a partner before beginning to write.
- For **Prompt B,** suggest that students return to the web diagram they completed for question 5 on page 393 for details to include in their letters.

For an extended Reading-Writing Connection activity, see

Writing Center at **ClassZone.com**

GRAMMAR AND WRITING

Explain that if an **indefinite pronoun** is followed by a prepositional phrase, the noun in the phrase indicates the pronoun's number. For example:

- *Some of the pie was gone.*
- *Some of the pies were gone.*

In the first sentence, the object of the preposition (*pie*) is singular, so a singular verb is needed. In the second sentence, the object of the preposition is plural, so a plural verb is needed.

Answers:

1. *miss*
2. *like*
3. *wears*
4. *want*

RESOURCE MANAGER—Copy Master
Maintain Subject-Verb Agreement p. 134

Assess and Reteach

Assess

RESOURCE MANAGER—Copy Masters
Selection Tests A, B/C pp. 135–136, 137–138

Test Generator CD

Reteach

STANDARDS LESSON FILE
Literature Lesson 9: Setting and Its Roles
Vocabulary Lesson 1: Word Parts
Grammar Lesson 5: Verb Agreement with Indefinite Pronoun Subjects

FOR LESS–PROFICIENT WRITERS

For Prompt A:

1. Divide students into two groups based on their opinions about whether someone can belong in two places.
2. Have group members support their opinions with details from the memoir and from their own experiences.
3. Help each group craft a topic sentence and then have students independently finish their paragraphs.

For Prompt B:

1. Display the correct friendly letter format.
2. Provide students with the following topic sentences. Have them add details from the memoir to each paragraph.

   Paragraph 1: *My house and school are very different from what I am used to.*

   Paragraph 2: *Each weekend we visit family in the village.*
3. Suggest that students work with a partner to revise their letters.

Focus and Motivate

OBJECTIVES

Elements of Nonfiction
- explore the key idea of a **witness**
- compare the scope of events as presented in two accounts
- read two magazine articles

Reading
- set a purpose for reading

Vocabulary
- build vocabulary for reading and writing
- apply knowledge of the prefix *inter-* to determine word meanings *(also an EL language objective)*
- use knowledge of base words and affixes to determine word meanings *(also an EL language objective)*

Grammar and Writing
- write a compare-contrast essay

SUMMARY

These eyewitness accounts describe the San Francisco earthquake of 1906 and the flooding of New Orleans by Hurricane Katrina in 2005. The account of the earthquake describes its immediate aftermath, while the other focuses on the rescue of one New Orleans resident.

What is the role of a WITNESS?

To lead into the ***KEY IDEA***, ask students if they have ever been a **witness** to a natural disaster. As pairs work on the ***ROLE-PLAY*** activity, encourage them to put themselves in the position of the audience, creating questions and answers about interesting details.

Comparing Articles

The Story of an Eyewitness
Magazine Article by Jack London

Letter from New Orleans: Leaving Desire
Magazine Article by Jon Lee Anderson

What is the role of a WITNESS?

KEY IDEA When events such as natural disasters, crimes, and wars occur, it's important that a **witness** describe what happened so that others can learn from these events. Witnesses have played an important role in reporting everything from local sports to the events in your history textbook. The authors of the accounts you are about to read each witnessed natural disasters. Their writing allowed people from around the world to share in their experiences.

ROLE-PLAY Picture the tornadoes, hurricanes, floods, and snow storms you have seen in the news. Imagine that one of these disasters has just struck your community. With a partner, role-play an evening news broadcast on the disaster. Decide who will be the news reporter and who will be the eyewitness. Then conduct an interview. Remember that your audience will want to know what the disaster looked, sounded, and felt like, as well as how people got hurt or stayed safe.

396

Selection Resources

RESOURCE MANAGER UNIT 3

Plan and Teach pp. 139–146

Elements of Nonfiction
Summary pp. 147†*, 148‡*; 154†*, 155‡*
Question Support p. 157*

Reading
Set a Purpose for Reading pp. 149, 150†*
Reading Check pp. 153; 156
Reading Fluency p. 161

Vocabulary
Study p. 151*
Practice p. 158
Strategy p. 159

Grammar and Writing
Writing for Assessment p. 160

Assessment
Selection Tests A, B/C pp. 163*, 165*
Test Generator CD

BEST PRACTICES TOOLKIT
Differentiated Instruction pp. 31–38*
Scaffolding Instruction pp. 43–46*
Graphic Organizers/Strategies
Reciprocal Questioning • New Word Analysis • Reporter's Questions • Greek and Latin Roots • Venn Diagram • Sequence Chain

Reading Support
Audio Anthology CD*

Technology
Literature, Vocabulary, and Writing Centers at **ClassZone.com**
Write*Smart* CD

* Resources for Differentiation † Also in Spanish ‡ In Haitian Creole and Vietnamese

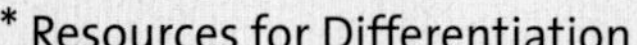

EMENTS OF NONFICTION: SCOPE

When writers choose how much of a subject to focus on, they're deciding on the **scope** of their accounts. The scope can be broad or narrow. For example, an article about Austin, Texas, that focuses on the city's history, economy, and residents has a broad scope. An article that focuses only on the music scene in Austin has a narrow scope.

The following eyewitness accounts describe two different natural disasters. As you read each one, try to determine its scope by considering these questions:

- How well do you get to know the people you meet?
- How much of the disaster area does the writer cover?
- How many events do you learn about? How much time do these events span?

ADING STRATEGY: SET A PURPOSE FOR READING

When you **set a purpose** for reading, you identify what you want to accomplish as you read. Your purpose for reading the following articles is to compare and contrast their scopes. As you read the first account, begin filling in the chart.

	"The Story of an Eyewitness"	*"Letter from New Orleans: Leaving Desire"*
What is the topic?		
Whom does the writer focus on?		
How much of the disaster area does the writer cover?		
Which events does the writer focus on?		

CABULARY IN CONTEXT

These words help the authors capture the impact of a disaster. Create a chart and place each word in the appropriate column.

WORD LIST			
	compel	intermittently	menace
	disconcert	lavishly	vigilantly

Know Well	*Think I Know*	*Don't Know at All*

Author Online

Jack London: Nature Enthusiast Inspired by his experiences as an outdoorsman, sailor, and war correspondent, Jack London became the most popular novelist of his time. He is still known throughout the world for *The Call of the Wild* and *The Sea Wolf.*

Jack London
1876–1916

Jon Lee Anderson: Investigative Journalist Jon Lee Anderson always wanted to be an explorer. Now, as a correspondent for *The New Yorker,* he travels around the world reporting on war, politics, and international affairs.

Jon Lee Anderson
born 1957

MORE ABOUT THE AUTHOR
For more about the authors, visit the **Literature Center** at **ClassZone.com.**

Background

San Francisco Earthquake At 5:12 A.M. on April 18, 1906, a massive earthquake shook San Francisco, setting in motion events that would eventually destroy most of the city. Historians estimate that around 3,000 people died and 250,000 people were left homeless.

Hurricane Katrina Hurricane Katrina hit the Gulf Coast on the morning of August 29, 2005. New Orleans suffered some of the worst damage of the Gulf Coast cities. Heavy flooding there destroyed entire neighborhoods, forced thousands of people to flee the city, and stranded many others in dangerous and unsanitary conditions until they, too, could get out.

397

Teach

STANDARDS FOCUS

ELEMENTS OF NONFICTION

● SCOPE

Write these topics on the board:

- professional sports
- U.S. government
- rock music

Ask students how they could make the scope of each topic narrower. ***Possible answer:*** *sports: specific sport, team, or athlete; U.S. government: leaders, institutions, laws; rock music: specific band or singer*

CHECK UNDERSTANDING Have students describe their community using a broad or narrow scope.

READING STRATEGY

■ SET A PURPOSE FOR READING

Explain that to fulfill a specific purpose for reading, such as comparing the coverage of events, students should pause every two or three paragraphs to consider what they have just read in relation to that purpose. In this case, they should also review and fill in their graphic organizers as they read.

CHECK UNDERSTANDING Have students read the **Author Online** information to compare the two authors.

RESOURCE MANAGER—Copy Master
Set a Purpose for Reading p. 149 (for student use while reading the articles)

VOCABULARY SKILL

▲ VOCABULARY IN CONTEXT

DIAGNOSE WORD KNOWLEDGE To determine preteaching needs, have all students complete **Vocabulary in Context.** After students have placed all the words, note how many they have sorted into the third column.

PRETEACH VOCABULARY Use the Vocabulary Study copy master to help students explore the meaning of each boldfaced word.

1. Have students conceal the word definitions.
2. Read aloud the first sentence, emphasizing the boldfaced word.
3. Discuss possible meanings for *compelled,* such as "forced."
4. Repeat for the other sentences. Then have students check the definitions in column 3.
5. Have students do Part B independently.

RESOURCE MANAGER—Copy Master
Vocabulary Study p. 151

For general guidelines on differentiating vocabulary instruction and for alternative vocabulary activities for students not needing vocabulary preteaching, see

BEST PRACTICES TOOLKIT
Scaffolding Vocabulary Instruction pp. 43–46

Vocabulary Center at **ClassZone.com**
Additional Vocabulary Activities

Practice and Apply

ANALYZE VISUALS

Possible answer: *The image captures a large part of San Francisco. Because the scope of the photograph is broad, the scope of this account will probably also be broad.*

BACKGROUND

San Francisco Earthquakes Before the earthquake of 1906, San Francisco was a bustling, prosperous town, with approximately 350,000 residents. Today, the city's population is more than 700,000 people, and the population of the Bay Area is more than 4 million people.

The earthquake that devastated San Francisco in 1906 had a magnitude of 7.8. Since that time, the largest earthquake to hit the Bay Area, in 1989, was magnitude 6.9. Scientists predict that an even larger earthquake is coming. Seven faults run through the Bay Area, and it is probable that at least one of these will slip in the next 30 years, causing a massive quake.

Attempts have been made to shore up existing buildings and to make new buildings earthquake resistant. Even so, if an earthquake the size of the one that hit San Francisco in 1906 were to occur today, the results would be catastrophic. One estimate is that about 45,000 buildings would be destroyed, and more than 80,000 families would become homeless. A severe earthquake would cause billions of dollars' worth of property damage.

The Story of an Eyewitness

JACK LONDON

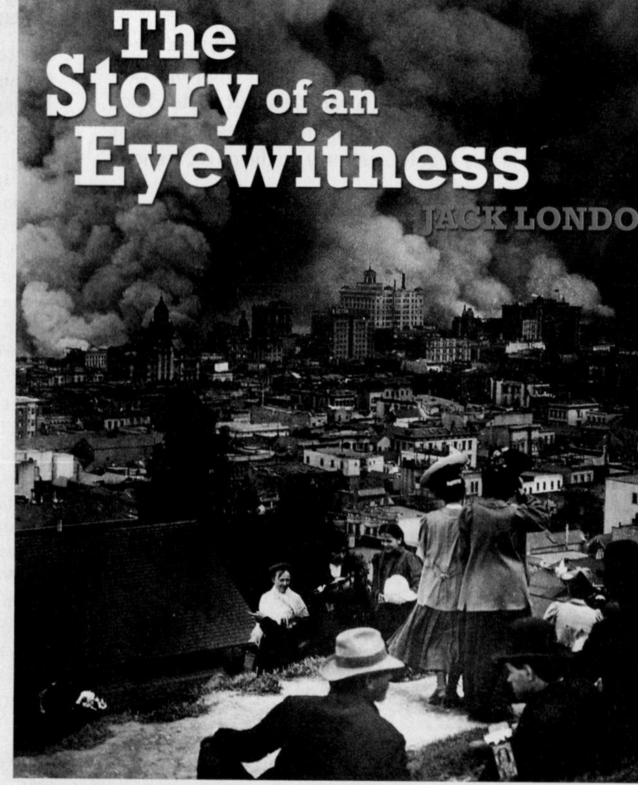

People on Russian Hill look toward San Francisco's downtown.

ANALYZE VISUALS
How much of San Francisco is captured in this image? Based on the **scope** of this photograph, make a **prediction** about the scope of this article.

Upon receipt of the first news of the earthquake, Collier's *telegraphed to M Jack London—who lives only forty miles from San Francisco—requesting him to go to the scene of the disaster and write the story of what he saw. M London started at once, and he sent the following dramatic description of t tragic events he witnessed in the burning city.*

Targeted Passage ①

The earthquake shook down in San Francisco hundreds of thousands of dollars worth of walls and chimneys. But the conflagration[1] that followed burned up hundreds of millions of dollars' worth of property. T is no estimating within hundreds of millions the actual damage wrought Not in history has a modern imperial city been so completely destroyed.

1. **conflagration** (kŏn'flə-grā'shən): a large destructive fire.

398 UNIT 3: SETTING AND MOOD

DIFFERENTIATED INSTRUCTION

FOR ALL STUDENTS

Learning Center Set up a learning center with books, pictures, and newspaper and magazine articles on natural disasters such as earthquakes, hurricanes, floods, and volcanic eruptions. Provide a variety of independent projects, such as creating a timeline of natural disasters in human history and designing a brochure for emergency preparedness.

FOR LESS–PROFICIENT READERS

In combination with the *Audio Anthology CD,* use one or more Targeted Passages (pp. 398, 404, 405, 412) to ensure that students focus on key selection details, concepts, and skills.

① Targeted Passage [Introduction–Line 5]

This passage explains the writer's purpose and describes the extent of the devastation.

- Who was Jack London?
- Why did London go to San Francisco?
- Which caused more damage in San Francisco—the earthquake or the fires?
- What does London say about the actual damage that was wrought?

Comprehension Support Clarify how dynamite was used to try to contain the fire (lines 36–41). The firefighters blew up buildings to create walls of rubble to prevent the fire from spreading.

an Francisco is gone. Nothing remains of it but memories and a fringe
dwelling houses on its outskirts. Its industrial section is wiped out. Its
usiness section is wiped out. Its social and residential section is wiped out.
he factories and warehouses, the great stores and newspaper buildings, the
otels and the palaces of the nabobs,[2] are all gone. Remains only the fringe
dwelling houses on the outskirts of what was once San Francisco. **A**

Within an hour after the earthquake shock the smoke of San Francisco's
urning was a lurid[3] tower visible a hundred miles away. And for three
ays and nights this lurid tower swayed in the sky, reddening the sun,
arkening the day, and filling the land with smoke.

On Wednesday morning at a quarter past five came the earthquake. A
inute later the flames were leaping upward. In a dozen different quarters
outh of Market Street, in the working-class ghetto, and in the factories,
res started. There was no opposing the flames. There was no organization,
o communication. All the cunning adjustments of a twentieth century city
ad been smashed by the earthquake. The streets were humped into ridges
nd depressions, and piled with the debris of fallen walls. The steel rails
ere twisted into perpendicular and horizontal angles. The telephone and
legraph systems were disrupted. And the great water-mains had burst. All
e shrewd contrivances[4] and safeguards of man had been thrown out of
ear by thirty seconds' twitching of the earth-crust.

he Fire Made Its Own Draft

y Wednesday afternoon, inside of twelve hours, half the heart of the city
as gone. At that time I watched the vast conflagration from out on the bay.
was dead calm. Not a flicker of wind stirred. Yet from every side wind was
ouring in upon the city. East, west, north, and south, strong winds were
lowing upon the doomed city. The heated air rising made an enormous
acuum. Thus did the fire of itself build its own colossal chimney through
he atmosphere. Day and night this dead calm continued, and yet, near to
he flames, the wind was often half a gale, so mighty was the vacuum.

Wednesday night saw the destruction of the very heart of the city.
ynamite was **lavishly** used, and many of San Francisco's proudest
ructures were crumbled by man himself into ruins, but there was no
ithstanding the onrush of the flames. Time and again successful
ands were made by the fire-fighters, and every time the flames flanked[5]
round on either side or came up from the rear, and turned to defeat

A SCOPE
How much of the city is Jack London describing in this paragraph?

lavishly (lăv'ĭsh-lē) *adv.* extravagantly

2. **nabobs** (nä'bŏbz'): people of wealth and prominence.
3. **lurid** (lŏŏr'ĭd): glowing with the glare of fire through a haze.
4. **contrivances** (kən-trī'vən-sĕz): acts of clever planning.
5. **flanked** (flăngk'd): placed at the side of.

ELEMENTS OF NONFICTION

A SCOPE

Remind students to record details in their charts from page 397. ***Possible answer:*** *He describes the entire city, including the outskirts.*

Lines 1–26
DISCUSSION PROMPTS

Use these prompts to help students understand the scope of the account and the writer's early impressions:

Recall What sections of the city were destroyed by the earthquake and fire? ***Answer:*** *The industrial, business, social, and residential areas were destroyed.*

Analyze Why didn't the fire department respond to the fire right away? ***Possible answer:*** *The streets were blocked with debris, water mains were ruptured, and firefighters couldn't communicate with each other.*

Evaluate What effect is created by the parallel sentence structures in lines 7–8 and 19–20? ***Possible answer:*** *The repetitions emphasize the extent of the devastation and the inadequacy of the response.*

Synthesize What broader conclusions can you draw from London's statement that "All the shrewd contrivances and safeguards of man had been thrown out of gear by thirty seconds' twitching of the earth-crust" (lines 24–26)? ***Possible answer:*** *Human achievements are no match for the power of nature.*

FOR ENGLISH LEARNERS

Options for Reading [paired option] Have students listen to the *Audio Anthology CD* as they read the selections silently and then work in pairs to practice Reciprocal Questioning. Ask them to take turns asking questions to recall, predict, clarify, and summarize what they are reading. Help students make their questions clearer or more specific if necessary.

BEST PRACTICES TOOLKIT
Reciprocal Questioning p. A3

Key Academic Vocabulary Have students use New Word Analysis for this academic vocabulary in "The Story of an Eyewitness": *abandon* (line 91), *estimated* (line 201).

BEST PRACTICES TOOLKIT—Transparency
New Word Analysis p. E8

Prereading For prereading instruction for English learners, see

BEST PRACTICES TOOLKIT
Scaffolding Reading Instruction pp. 43–46

FOR ADVANCED LEARNERS/PRE–AP

Pre-AP exercises in the bottom channel provide additional challenge for your advanced students. Use them for small groups or individuals.

ADDITIONAL GUIDELINES

For more help with differentiation and tips for classroom management, see

BEST PRACTICES TOOLKIT
Differentiated Instruction pp. 31–38

ANALYZE VISUALS

Possible answer: *The tremors were powerful enough to split the street apart.*

ELEMENTS OF NONFICTION

B SCOPE

Possible answer: *London describes the extremes of property damage, acts of heroism, and the number of victims of the earthquake and fire.*

ELEMENTS OF NONFICTION

C SCOPE

Remind students to record details in their charts from page 397. ***Possible answer:*** *So far, London has described crowds. This suggests that the scope of his account is broad.*

ANALYZE VISUALS
What can you **infer** from this photo about the strength of the San Francisco earthquake?

the hard-won victory. An enumeration[6] of the buildings destroyed would be a directory of San Francisco. An enumeration of the buildings undestroyed would be a line and several addresses. An enumeration of the deeds of heroism would stock a library and bankrupt the Carnegie medal fund. An enumeration of the dead will never be made. All vestiges[7] of them were destroyed by the flames. The number of the victims of the earthquake will never be known. South of Market Street, where the loss of life was particularly heavy, was the first to catch fire. B

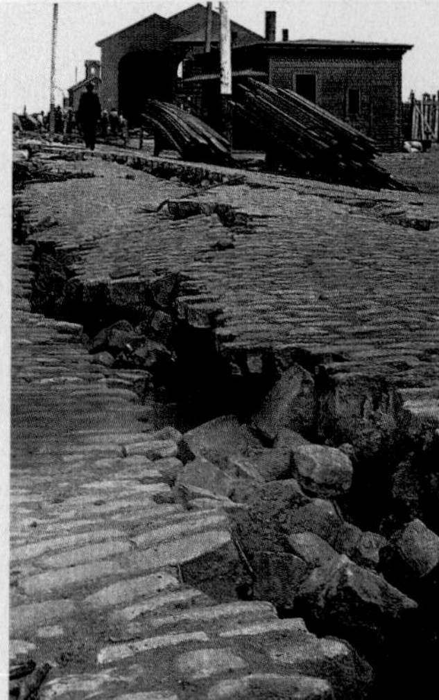
A street along San Francisco's waterfront, cracked during the earthquake

B SCOPE
What aspects of the disaster is London describing?

Remarkable as it may seem, Wednesday night while the whole city crashed and roared into ruin, was a quiet night. There were no crowds. There was no shouting and yelling. There was no hysteria, no disorder. passed Wednesday night in the path of the advancing flames, and in a those terrible hours I saw not one woman who wept, not one man who excited, not one person who was in the slightest degree panic stricken.

Before the flames, throughout the night, fled tens of thousands of homeless ones. Some were wrapped in blankets. Others carried bundles bedding and dear household treasures. Sometimes a whole family was harnessed to a carriage or delivery wagon that was weighted down with their possessions. Baby buggies, toy wagons, and go-carts were used as trucks, while every other person was dragging a trunk. Yet everybody w gracious. The most perfect courtesy obtained. Never in all San Francis history were her people so kind and courteous as on this night of terror

A Caravan of Trunks

All night these tens of thousands fled before the flames. Many of them, th poor people from the labor ghetto, had fled all day as well. They had left t homes burdened with possessions. Now and again they lightened up, fling out upon the street clothing and treasures they had dragged for miles. C

C SCOPE
So far, has London described individuals or crowds? Tell what this suggests about the scope of his account.

6. **enumeration** (ĭ-nōō′mə-rā′shən): the act of counting or listing one by one.
7. **vestiges** (vĕs′tĭj-əs): visible signs that something once existed.

DIFFERENTIATED INSTRUCTION

FOR LESS–PROFICIENT READERS

Comprehension Support Display a map of San Francisco to help students track the spread of the fire and the other events described in the article.

FOR ENGLISH LEARNERS

Language: Syntax [mixed-readiness pairs] Point out that this article was written about 100 years ago, and the style and syntax are somewhat old-fashioned. For example, London frequently places verbs, adverbs, and prepositional phrases before the subject. Some languages, such as Spanish, have similar syntactical constructions, so London's style may be more accessible to speakers of these languages.

Have pairs work together to rewrite the sentences that have unusual syntax in standard modern English. Examples include

- *Remains only the fringe . . .* (lines 10–11)
- *Thus did the fire of itself build its own colossal chimney . . .* (lines 32–33)
- *Before the flames . . . fled tens of thousands of homeless ones.* (lines 66–67)
- *Everywhere were trunks with across them lying . . .* (lines 80–82)

They held on longest to their trunks, and over these trunks many a trong man broke his heart that night. The hills of San Francisco are steep, nd up these hills, mile after mile, were the trunks dragged. Everywhere vere trunks with across them lying their exhausted owners, men and vomen. Before the march of the flames were flung picket lines of soldiers. And a block at a time, as the flames advanced, these pickets retreated. One f their tasks was to keep the trunk-pullers moving. The exhausted reatures, stirred on by the **menace** of bayonets,[8] would arise and struggle p the steep pavements, pausing from weakness every five or ten feet.

Often, after surmounting a heart-breaking hill, they would find another vall of flame advancing upon them at right angles and be **compelled** to hange anew the line of their retreat. In the end, completely played out, fter toiling for a dozen hours like giants, thousands of them were ompelled to abandon their trunks. Here the shopkeepers and soft nembers of the middle class were at a disadvantage. But the working-men lug holes in vacant lots and backyards and buried their trunks.

menace (mĕn′ĭs) *n.* a possible danger; threat

compel (kəm-pĕl′) *v.* to pressure by force

The Doomed City

At nine o'clock Wednesday evening I walked down through the very heart of he city. I walked through miles and miles of magnificent buildings and owering skyscrapers. Here was no fire. All was in perfect order. The police atrolled the streets. Every building had its watchman at the door. And yet it vas doomed, all of it. There was no water. The dynamite was giving out. And t right angles two different conflagrations were sweeping down upon it. **D**

At one o'clock in the morning I walked down through the same section. Everything still stood intact. There was no fire. And yet there was a hange. A rain of ashes was falling. The watchmen at the doors were gone. The police had been withdrawn. There were no firemen, no fire-engines, o men fighting with dynamite. The district had been absolutely bandoned. I stood at the corner of Kearney and Market, in the very nnermost heart of San Francisco. Kearney Street was deserted. Half a lozen blocks away it was burning on both sides. The street was a wall of lame. And against this wall of flame, silhouetted sharply, were two United States cavalrymen sitting on their horses, calmly watching. That was all. Not another person was in sight. In the intact heart of the city, two roopers sat [on] their horses and watched. **E**

D SCOPE
Reread lines 94–95. What time of day is it when London is making his observations? As you continue reading, look for other references to the time.

E SCOPE
Why might London have chosen to describe the same section of downtown twice?

Spread of the Conflagration

Surrender was complete. There was no water. The sewers had long since been pumped dry. There was no dynamite. Another fire had broken out

8. **bayonets** (bā′ə-nĕts′): blades that fit on the end of rifles and are used as weapons.

ELEMENTS OF NONFICTION

D SCOPE
Answer: *It is nine o'clock in the evening.*

ELEMENTS OF NONFICTION

E SCOPE
Possible answer: *London shows how quickly the fire transformed a peaceful and protected neighborhood into one that was abandoned and destroyed.*

FOR LESS–PROFICIENT READERS

Comprehension Support Help students visualize the change that took place within the four-hour period described in lines 94–111. Read the passage aloud and ask students to imagine that they are walking through this section of the city with Jack London. Have them identify the words in the passage that appeal to their senses.

FOR ENGLISH LEARNERS

Vocabulary: Multiple-Meaning Words Help students use context clues to understand the various meanings of the word *heart* on this page. The expressions *broke his heart* (line 79) and *heart-breaking hill* (line 87) refer to the extreme emotions of sadness and despair. The expressions *heart of the city* (lines 94–95) and *innermost heart* (line 106) describe the center of the city. Ask students if they can think of any other expressions that include the word *heart.*

THE STORY OF AN EYEWITNESS 401

Lines 134–142

REINFORCE *KEY IDEA:* WITNESS

Discuss London spoke to one of the people on the street, urging the man to flee. How is a reader affected when a **witness** becomes part of the narrative? ***Possible answer:*** *The events become real and more personal to the reader.*

Lines 129–155

DISCUSSION PROMPTS

Use these prompts to help students understand London's changing perspective:

Connect The owner of the house on whose steps London sat was "cool and cheerful and hospitable" (line 150), although he was about to lose all of his valuable property to the fire. Why do you think people have different reactions to disaster? How would you have reacted in the homeowner's place? *Students should cite details from the passage in their responses.*

Analyze How did the conflagration affect the victims' perceptions of what things were worth? Give examples. ***Possible answer:*** *None of the old standards applied. One man was willing to spend $1,000 for a team of horses; another man was worth $30,000 one day and nothing the next; the wealthy homeowner was about to lose his valuable possessions but did not seem very upset about the loss.*

Evaluate What does this eyewitness account reveal that a third-person account might not convey? ***Possible answer:*** *It gives a much more personal view of the disaster, showing how specific individuals reacted as the fire advanced.*

further uptown, and now from three sides conflagrations were sweepir down. The fourth side had been burned earlier in the day. In that dire stood the tottering walls of the Examiner Building, the burned-out Ca Building, the smoldering ruins of the Grand Hotel, and the gutted, devastated, dynamited Palace Hotel.

The following will illustrate the sweep of the flames and the inabilit men to calculate their spread. At eight o'clock Wednesday evening I pa through Union Square. It was packed with refugees. Thousands of the had gone to bed on the grass. Government tents had been set up, supp was being cooked, and the refugees were lining up for free meals.

At half past one in the morning three sides of Union Square were in flames. The fourth side, where stood the great St. Francis Hotel, was s holding out. An hour later, ignited from top and sides the St. Francis w flaming heavenward. Union Square, heaped high with mountains of trunks, was deserted. Troops, refugees, and all had retreated.

A Fortune for a Horse!

It was at Union Square that I saw a man offering a thousand dollars fo team of horses. He was in charge of a truck piled high with trunks fro some hotel. It had been hauled here into what was considered safety, a the horses had been taken out. The flames were on three sides of the Square and there were no horses.

Also, at this time, standing beside the truck, I urged a man to seek safety in flight. He was all but hemmed in by several conflagrations. H was an old man and he was on crutches. Said he: "Today is my birthda Last night I was worth thirty thousand dollars. I bought some delicate and other things for my birthday dinner. I have had no dinner, and all own are these crutches."

I convinced him of his danger and started him limping on his way. hour later, from a distance, I saw the truck-load of trunks burning mer in the middle of the street.

On Thursday morning at a quarter past five, just twenty-four hours a the earthquake, I sat on the steps of a small residence on Nob Hill. With sat Japanese, Italians, Chinese, and negroes—a bit of the cosmopolitan flotsam[9] of the wreck of the city. All about were the palaces of the nabob pioneers of Forty-nine.[10] To the east and south at right angles, were advancing two mighty walls of flame.

9. **flotsam** (flŏt'səm): floating wreckage after a ship has sunk.

10. **pioneers of Forty-nine:** reference to the pioneers who came to San Francisco during the Calif gold rush in 1849.

DIFFERENTIATED INSTRUCTION

FOR LESS–PROFICIENT READERS

Vocabulary: Phrasal Verbs Point out these phrasal verbs, read the sentences in which they are found, and explain their meaning. Tell students that context can help them determine the meanings of phrasal verbs. Challenge them to find more phrasal verbs in the two articles.

- *holding out* (line 126), "not surrendering"
- *hemmed in* (line 135), "trapped on all sides"
- *broke through* (lines 161–162), "became free; appeared"

roops walk east along Market Street as the Call Building burns in the distance.

ANALYZE VISUALS
Which **detail** from this photograph best helps you understand the devastation to the city?

I went inside with the owner of the house on the steps of which I sat. He was cool and cheerful and hospitable. "Yesterday morning," he said, "I was worth six hundred thousand dollars. This morning this house is all I have left. It will go in fifteen minutes. He pointed to a large cabinet. "That is my wife's collection of china. This rug upon which we stand is a present. It cost fifteen hundred dollars. Try that piano. Listen to its tone. There are few like it. There are no horses. The flames will be here in fifteen minutes." F

Outside the old Mark Hopkins residence a palace was just catching fire. The troops were falling back and driving the refugees before them. From every side came the roaring of flames, the crashing of walls, and the detonations of dynamite.

F SCOPE
Reread lines 129–155. What do you notice about how these people are described?

The Dawn of the Second Day

I passed out of the house. Day was trying to dawn through the smoke-pall.[11] A sickly light was creeping over the face of things. Once only the sun broke through the smoke-pall, blood-red, and showing a quarter its usual size. The smoke-pall itself, viewed from beneath, was a rose color that pulsed and fluttered with lavender shades. Then it turned to mauve and yellow and dun.[12] There was no sun. And so dawned the second day on stricken San Francisco.

An hour later I was creeping past the shattered dome of the City Hall. Than it there was no better exhibit of the destructive force of the earthquake. Most of the stone had been shaken from the great dome, leaving standing the naked framework of steel. Market Street was piled high with the wreckage, and across the wreckage lay the overthrown pillars of the City Hall shattered into short crosswise sections.

11. **pall** (pôl): a covering that darkens or covers.
12. **dun** (dŭn): dull brownish gray.

ANALYZE VISUALS
Possible answer: *The wide field of view shows a large section of the city in flames and filled with smoke.*

ELEMENTS OF NONFICTION

F SCOPE

Possible answer: *The people are described by race, social status, and economic class.*

If students need help . . . Point out that each paragraph in this section describes a separate individual, such as the man who tried to buy a team of horses, the man on crutches, and the homeowner; or a group, such as the "cosmopolitan flotsam" (lines 145–146) who sat on the steps of a house.

FOR LESS–PROFICIENT READERS

Vocabulary: Multiple-Meaning Words Point out the words *left* (line 152), *present* (line 153), *passed* (line 160), and *quarter* (line 162) on this page. Have students use a dictionary to find at least two meanings for each of these words and check the pronunciation for each meaning. Have them write sentences using the words twice—once for each meaning.

FOR ADVANCED LEARNERS/PRE–AP

Visualize Read lines 160–171 aloud, and have students draw a picture or create a painting inspired by the description in the passage. Encourage them to incorporate some or all of the colors in the description. Have students share their drawings and paintings and vote for the one that they think best captures the mood of the passage.

ELEMENTS OF NONFICTION

G SCOPE

Remind students to add details to their charts from page 397. ***Possible answer:*** *The main event is the "conflagration," or fire, that began after the earthquake.*

ELEMENTS OF NONFICTION

H SCOPE

Possible answer: *Readers don't learn much about what took place Thursday and Friday. They learn only that the firefighters made their last great stand to protect what little remained of the city and that the flames were finally conquered.*

ELEMENTS OF NONFICTION

I SCOPE

Possible answer: *London describes what happened to the refugees: some camped around the city, some crowded into surrounding cities and towns, and others left the peninsula. He refers to how the railroads, government, bankers, businessmen, relief societies, and people throughout the United States came to their aid.*

SELECTION WRAP-UP

REFLECT Ask students whether London drew them into the events and made them feel connected to the refugees. Or, did they feel like outsiders while reading the account?

CRITIQUE Have students discuss whether they were satisfied with the scope of the coverage. What additional information did they wish the writer had included?

READING FLUENCY

Distribute the copy masters and have students practice fluency.

RESOURCE MANAGER—Copy Master
Reading Fluency p. 161

This section of the city, with the exception of the Mint and the Post Office, was already a waste of smoking ruins. Here and there through smoke, creeping warily under the shadows of tottering walls, emerged occasional men and women. It was like the meeting of the handful of survivors after the day of the end of the world.

Beeves Slaughtered and Roasted

On Mission Street lay a dozen steers, in a neat row stretching across t street just as they had been struck down by the flying ruins of the earthquake. The fire had passed through afterward and roasted them The human dead had been carried away before the fire came. At ano place on Mission Street I saw a milk wagon. A steel telegraph pole ha smashed down sheer through the driver's seat and crushed the front wheels. The milk cans lay scattered around.

All day Thursday and all Thursday night, all day Friday and Friday night, the flames still raged on.

Friday night saw the flames finally conquered, though not until Rus Hill and Telegraph Hill had been swept and three-quarters of a mile of wharves and docks had been licked up. G

G SCOPE What is the main event London tracked from beginning to end?

The Last Stand

Targeted Passage 2

The great stand of the fire-fighters was made Thursday night on Van N Avenue. Had they failed here, the comparatively few remaining houses of the city would have been swept. Here were the magnificent residence of the second generation of San Francisco nabobs, and these, in a solid zone, were dynamited down across the path of the fire. Here and there flames leaped the zone, but these fires were beaten out, principally by t use of wet blankets and rugs. H

H SCOPE How much do you learn about what took place Thursday and Friday?

San Francisco, at the present time, is like the crater of a volcano, arou which are camped tens of thousands of refugees. At the Presidio[13] alone at least twenty thousand. All the surrounding cities and towns are jamm with the homeless ones, where they are being cared for by the relief committees. The refugees were carried free by the railroads to any point they wished to go, and it is estimated that over one hundred thousand people have left the peninsula on which San Francisco stood. The government has the situation in hand, and, thanks to the immediate rel given by the whole United States, there is not the slightest possibility of famine. The bankers and business men have already set about making preparations to rebuild San Francisco. I

I SCOPE What information about the disaster does London provide in this last paragraph?

13. **Presidio** (prĭ-sē′dē-ō′): a historic military post in San Francisco.

DIFFERENTIATED INSTRUCTION

FOR LESS-PROFICIENT READERS

2 Targeted Passage [Lines 189–206]

This passage concludes the selection: the writer describes the disaster's aftermath and makes an assessment about the city's future.

- What happened on Thursday night after the earthquake?
- Where did the refugees from San Francisco go? Who cared for them?
- Who set out to rebuild the city?

FOR ADVANCED LEARNERS/PRE-AP

Synthesize Have students role-play an interview between a reporter and one of the firefighters who battled the fires in San Francisco. Encourage them to refer to events in the article and to use the Reporter's Questions: *Who? What? When? Where? Why?* and *How?*

BEST PRACTICES TOOLKIT—Transparency
Reporter's Questions p. C9

404 UNIT 3: SETTING AND MOOD

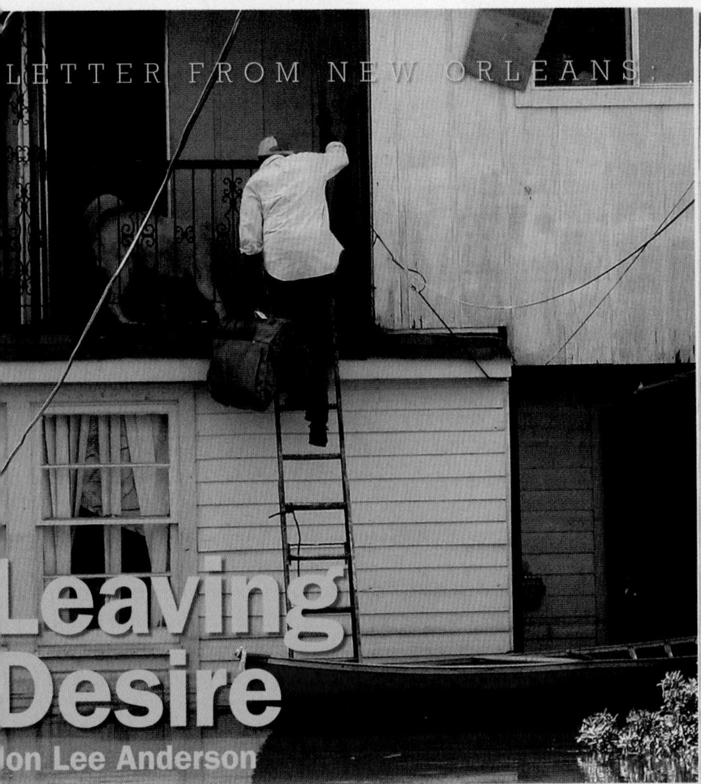

ANALYZE VISUALS
This photo shows Lionel Petrie, a man trapped in the flooding that occurred after Hurrican Katrina hit, climbing down into the floodwaters. What **questions** come to mind as you look at this image?

When I first saw Lionel Petrie, he was standing on the second-story porch of his house, at the junction of Desire Street and North unny Friend, in the Ninth Ward of New Orleans. The house was built wood, with white siding and peach trim. Petrie, an African-American ith salt-and-pepper hair and a mustache, appeared to be in his sixties. A rge Akita[1] was standing next to him, ears perked **vigilantly.** The two of em looked out from across the fenced-in expanse of the front yard. Petrie as clearly an organized man: a painter's ladder was dangling from the iling of the porch, and a clutch of orange life vests hung within reach of fibreglass canoe that was tethered to the house. The canoe bobbed on the rface of the stinking black water that filled the street and had engulfed ost of the first floor of the house. The spiked parapet of a wrought-on fence poked up about eight inches above the waterline, etching out a ormal square that separated the house from the street. Ⓐ

③ Targeted Passage

vigilantly (vĭj'ə-lənt-lē) *adv.* in a state of alertness; watchfully

Ⓐ SCOPE
What is this paragraph about? Note the kind of details provided about the subject.

1. **Akita** (ä-kē'tə): a breed of Japanese hunting dog.

Practice and Apply

Prereading for this selection is found on page 397.

ANALYZE VISUALS

Students may wonder how far the man will have to go in the boat before he gets to safety, whether any of his family or friends are still in the house, and whether he'll ever be able to return to his home.

About the Art This photograph of Lionel Petrie, the subject of Anderson's article, was taken by rescuer Shawn Alladio. It is one of the hundreds of photographs she took as she rescued hurricane victims in New Orleans.

ELEMENTS OF NONFICTION

Ⓐ SCOPE

Possible answer: *This paragraph is about Anderson's first impressions of Lionel Petrie. It contains specific details about Petrie's appearance and his house.*

FOR LESS–PROFICIENT READERS

Reading Strategy Follow-Up: Set a Purpose for Reading Read the first paragraph aloud. Have students identify the topic of the selection and write it in the third column of the chart from page 397. Then, as they read, have students answer the other questions in the chart, recording words and phrases that support their answers.

③ Targeted Passage [Lines 1–14]

This passage establishes the setting of the article and introduces its subject.

- What is this article about?
- Where did the writer see Lionel Petrie? What was Petrie doing?
- What do the details tell you about what happened?

FOR ENGLISH LEARNERS

Key Academic Vocabulary Have students use New Word Analysis to study this academic vocabulary in "Letter from New Orleans: Leaving Desire": *team* (lines 69, 70), *community* (line 95), *priority* (line 169).

 **BEST PRACTICES TOOLKIT—Transparency**
New Word Analysis p. E8

BACKGROUND

The Flooding of New Orleans After Hurricane Katrina tore through the Gulf Coast on August 29, 2005, several levees and floodwalls protecting New Orleans gave way, and approximately 80 percent of the city was flooded. On September 23–24, Hurricane Rita passed southwest and west of the city, and several levees that had been shored up failed again. It took a few weeks for all of the water to be pumped out of New Orleans, particularly from low-lying areas like the Ninth Ward.

Although many residents had fled before the hurricane arrived, thousands remained and were stranded for several days, many of them in dire straits without food, water, or medical care. States around the country opened shelters for evacuees from the Gulf Coast. Many evacuees from New Orleans who lost their homes and jobs because of the hurricane ultimately decided not to return to the city.

Lines 20–37
REINFORCE *KEY IDEA:* WITNESS

Discuss Why do you think Jon Lee Anderson wanted to join Alladio on her rescue mission? Do you think his presence as a **witness** might be useful? ***Possible answer:*** *He wanted to get a close-up look at the effect of the hurricane and flood on the residents of New Orleans. His presence might be useful because he can then give a clear, unbiased picture of what he saw.*

Discuss In what way does Alladio use what she has **witnessed** to help her persuade Lionel Petrie to leave his house? ***Possible answer:*** *Alladio has been elsewhere in New Orleans and has seen the extent of the devastation. Based on what she's seen, she is able to persuade Petrie that he might die if he stays in his house.*

Petrie's house was different from those of his neighbors, most of wh were small brick row houses, or rundown clapboard houses that had d porches flush with the street. His was set far back in the lot, and had self-possessed air about it. Near the fence, in what must have been the driveway, the hoods of two submerged cars and a truck could be seen.

I was seated in the back of a four-person Yamaha WaveRunner that was piloted by Shawn Alladio, an energetic woman in her forties, with long blond hair, from Whittier, California. Eight days had passed sinc Hurricane Katrina made landfall, and Alladio was out on a search for trapped survivors and for what rescuers were calling "holdouts"—resid who didn't want to leave their homes—in one of the poorest and wors parts of the city, the Ninth Ward, in eastern New Orleans.

Alladio maneuvered the WaveRunner so that we were alongside Pet fence, and, after calling out a greeting to him, she asked him if he war to leave; he waved politely in response, but shook his head. She told hi that the floodwater was toxic and that he would soon become sick. He something in reply, but we couldn't hear him because of the rumble of WaveRunner's idling engine. Alladio turned the ignition key off.

Petrie explained that his wife and son and daughter had left the city car, heading for Baton Rouge, the day before Katrina hit. He didn't kr where his family was now, and, if he left, they wouldn't know where h was. He said that he intended to wait for them to come back, and for t waters to go down.

Alladio told him that the authorities were not allowing people to retu to this part of New Orleans, and that it might be a month before the wa receded. He listened carefully, nodded, and replied that he had stocks of and some water; that he'd be all right—he'd wait. He patted his dog's h "Thank you, but I'll be fine," he said. Alladio tried again. "I can promis that you will *not* see your family if you stay here," she told him; it was m likelier that he would pass out and die from the fumes from the water. **B**

B SCOPE
What do you learn about Petrie's situation and his attitude toward it?

He asked whether she would promise that he would be able to join his family.

Alladio paused, and said to me quietly, "I can't promise him that. If turn him over to the authorities, like the other evacuees, he could end anywhere in the country."

Turning back to Petrie, she asked, "If I drive you to Baton Rouge m will you come with me?"

"You would take me yourself?" he asked.

"Yes," she said. "I promise. Today, when I am done with my work, I take you there."

Petrie took a step back on his porch. He raised his head thoughtfully and asked, "Can I take my dog with me?"

ELEMENTS OF NONFICTION

B SCOPE

Possible answer: *Petrie's situation is serious. His family left their home before Katrina hit. If he leaves with Alladio, he risks not finding them again. If he stays, he risks getting sick or dying from the toxic water. He seems calm when Alladio tells him that he might be there a month before the waters go down.*

DIFFERENTIATED INSTRUCTION

FOR ENGLISH LEARNERS

Reading: Background Explain that a WaveRunner (line 20) is a small watercraft with a powerful engine. Most watercraft in this category are for one or two people, and smaller models require the operator to stand up. The model described in the selection has seating for four people. You might ask a student to locate a photograph on the Internet to share with the class.

Language: Print and Punctuation Cues Read aloud lines 22–26, emphasizing the pauses indicated by the dashes as well as the text set off in quotation marks. Explain that long sentences containing dashes can first be read without the information that is enclosed. Next, point out the ellipses at the end of line 87. Explain that ellipses are sometimes used to indicate pauses, but that in this case, and elsewhere throughout the article, they signify that text has been omitted.

406 UNIT 3: SETTING AND MOOD

"Oh, God," Alladio said under her breath. "I hate this." Then she said him, "I am so sorry, Mr. Petrie, but, no, they won't allow us to take out nimals. You will have to leave him here."

Petrie gripped the railing of the porch and leaned over again, in a kind f slow, sustained forward lurch, his head down. Then he nodded and id, "O.K."

Alladio told Petrie to prepare a small bag with his essential belongings, to y goodbye to his dog and, if he wanted, put out some food and water for im. She would be back in an hour to pick him up; in the meantime, she eeded to see if there were more people who needed evacuating. He said, O.K.," and waved, and went back inside the house. The dog followed him. **C**

Alladio had arrived in New Orleans on Saturday, September 3rd, with a team of California rescue workers and a small flotilla[2] of donated VaveRunners. She and her team were loosely attached to a task force sent y the State of California, but were mostly on their own. We had met at a aging area underneath an elevated section of Interstate 10. As I arrived, vacuees were being brought out of the water to a slightly raised stretch f land where railroad tracks ran under the highway. A boat came up and eposited an elderly black couple. Rescuers carried the woman, who was vearing a denim skirt, a T-shirt, and gold earrings, and sat her down on fallen telephone pole. She rocked back and forth, with one hand raised, nd murmured, "I just want to tell you—thank you, Jesus." Her husband valked over unsteadily to join her. They had stayed at home until just efore the hurricane, and then gone to their church. As the water rose, they ook refuge in the choir loft. They stayed there for eight days, drinking the vater the storm washed in. "We were down to our last two crackers," she aid. Another man was brought over, shaking, and speaking incoherently. The only words I could make out were "I'm still alive."

After putting on chest waders to protect ourselves from the fetid[3] loodwaters—which Alladio warned me were "really gnarly"—we set off y boat from Interstate 10. . . .

We passed cargo yards, electrical pylons,[4] and houses with tar-paper oofs that had water halfway up the windows, and other houses that vere completely submerged. When we came to the intersection of Louisa treet and Higgins Boulevard, the street signs were at eye level and the raffic lights were barely above the surface of the water. We passed a house vith a shattered plate-glass window. Peering down into the living room,

2. **flotilla** (flō-tĭl'ə): a small fleet of ships
3. **fetid** (fĕ'tĭd): having an offensive odor..
4. **electrical pylons** (pī'lŏnz'): steel towers supporting electrical wires.

C SCOPE
Reread lines 50–67. What does the conversation between Alladio and Petrie reveal about the kind of person Alladio is?

ELEMENTS OF NONFICTION

C SCOPE

Possible answer: *It shows that she is firm, persuasive, and compassionate.*

If students need help . . . Point out lines 50–54. Discuss how she reacts not only as a dispassionate rescuer but also as a caring volunteer. She is willing to drive Petrie to Baton Rouge, and she is very sorry to leave Petrie's dog behind.

Lines 68–99

DISCUSSION PROMPTS

Use these prompts to help students visualize the setting:

Recall Where did Anderson meet Alladio?
Answer: *They met at a staging area under an elevated section of the interstate highway.*

Draw Conclusions Why do you think the floodwaters are "fetid" and "gnarly"?
Possible answer: *They are probably contaminated with sewage, chemicals, and garbage.*

Evaluate Why does the writer include these details about what he sees from the boat?
Possible answer: *They convey how deep the floodwaters are and how dangerous their situation is.*

FOR ENGLISH LEARNERS

Vocabulary: Word Associations [paired activity] Have pairs use context clues to figure out the meanings of these phrases:

- *task force* (line 70), "a group of people assigned to a specific job or project"
- *staging area* (line 72), "the center of operations"
- *chest waders* (line 85), "high waterproof boots"
- *eye level* (line 91), "straight ahead"

FOR ADVANCED LEARNERS/PRE–AP

Use Word Roots Remind students that many words in English have Greek and Latin roots. Three words with Latin roots on this spread are

- *maneuvered* (line 27), from *manu operare,* "to work by hand"
- *toxic* (line 30), from *toxicum,* "a poison"
- *evacuees* (line 48), from *vacuare,* "to make empty"

Display the Greek and Latin Roots transparencies and have students look up other words with these roots in a dictionary. Have them work with a partner to use all these words in a sentence.

 **BEST PRACTICES TOOLKIT—Transparencies**
Greek and Latin Roots pp. E20, E21, E22

ELEMENTS OF NONFICTION

Ⓓ SCOPE

Possible answer:

- ***Sights:*** *helicopters dumping water on fires, columns of brown and gray smoke, towers of downtown New Orleans*
- ***Sounds:*** *helicopters clattering overhead*
- ***Smells:*** *floodwater smelling of oil and raw sewage, rotting garbage, and death*

ANALYZE VISUALS

Possible answer: *The black, opaque water is deep enough that it almost covers the car in front of the pink house and engulfs the entire neighborhood. In the foreground, an electric pole stands in the water. Lionel Petrie is trapped in his house by the dangerous water that surrounds him.*

I saw a sofa floating near a framed photo of Muhammad Ali standing triumphantly over Sonny Liston. At a community swimming pool, a lifeguard seat poked just above the waters. We passed a rowboat carry two white men and being towed by a black man with dreadlocks, up t neck in water. Later, we saw them again; all three were in the boat no and were paddling with broken street signs.

It was a clear, hot day, and the floodwater smelled strongly of oil an raw sewage, and stung the eyes. There were other smells, from islands rotting garbage, and, **intermittently,** as elsewhere in the city, the smel of death. Helicopters had been clattering overhead all morning, some of them dumping buckets of water on house fires that had broken out everywhere. Scudding[5] columns of brown and gray smoke shot up fro half a dozen points around the city. The towers of downtown New Or were visible in the distance. Ⓓ

intermittently (ĭn'tər-mĭt'nt-lē) *adv.* stopping and starting at intervals

Ⓓ SCOPE
What sights, sounds, and smells does the author describe?

ANALYZE VISUALS
In what way does this image help you understand the seriousness of Lionel Petrie's situation?

A New Orleans neighborhood lies under several feet of water.

Until the nineteenth century, the Ninth Ward was a swamp, and, ev after it became home to a black and immigrant white community, and was drained (in that order), it was periodically devastated by flooding. During Hurricane Betsy, in 1965, it was hit harder than most of the ci and was underwater for days. The neglect of the Ninth Ward by the ci government was notorious; well into the twentieth century, it lacked adequate sewers and clean water. The Norman Rockwell image that th Ninth Ward inspired was that of the first grader Ruby Bridges, a tiny b

5. **scudding** (skŭd'ĭng): skimming along swiftly.

DIFFERENTIATED INSTRUCTION

FOR ENGLISH LEARNERS

Vocabulary: Cognates [shared-language groups] Have groups scan the selection for cognates and report their findings to the class. Spanish cognates on this page include

- *community/comunidad* (line 95)
- *island/isla* (line 101)
- *column/columna* (line 105)
- *dozen/docena* (line 106)
- *distance/distancia* (line 107)

;irl in a white dress, who was led to school by federal marshals past jeering vhite crowds—a chapter in a violent desegregation struggle that divided he city in the nineteen-sixties. In the next decades, many of the white esidents of the Ninth Ward left; by the time Katrina hit, almost all the tudents in the school that Ruby Bridges integrated were black.

At 2037 Desire, a block past Petrie's home, three people stood on the second-floor porch of a large wooden house: a bulky young woman n a white blouse, with dyed orange hair, and tattoos on one arm; a young nan with copper skin in a lilac polo shirt . . . and an old man who was bare-hested except for a pair of red suspenders. The ground floor was flooded and sign above it said, "Winner Supermarket—ATM Inside." Alladio hailed hem and repeated the argument that she had made to Petrie. The young nan said that his name was Theron Green, and that he and his father, Alfred Green, the old man, and his fiancée—Trinell Sanson, the tattooed woman—vere fine, and were planning to stay. They also had a friend inside the house, hey said. Theron Green spoke in a thick local accent, and his eyes were alert nd suspicious. He was clearly anxious for us to leave. "We feel comfortable, afe in our own house here," he said. "Anyway, I don't want no looters coming here." Alladio told him that there would soon be forced evacuations, but Green was adamant. "I'll wait till they force me out, then," he said. Trinell Sanson said, "We're fine. If it gets too bad, we'll catch the helicopter.". . .

Alladio warned me not to get spattered by the floodwater. "The people who have been in this are going to get sick," she said. The Environmental Protection Agency had teams out taking water samples to check for toxins, nd the rumor—apparently unfounded—was that entire districts were so contaminated that they would have to be razed, along with hundreds of housands of vehicles. The people who lived there might not realize it, she said, "but once they leave they are never going to see their homes again.". . .

When we returned to Petrie's house, he was packed and waiting for us on the second-floor porch, dressed in slacks, a fresh unbuttoned shirt over a T-shirt, and a Marine Corps baseball cap. He leaned down to his dog, took both its ears in his hands and caressed them, and then told the dog to go inside. Petrie climbed into the canoe and began paddling over to us. The dog reemerged on the balcony, appearing **disconcerted** and watchful. Petrie did not look back. He came alongside the fence and we helped him first with a bag and then with a little black case that he said had his wife's Bible in it. "I know she'd want me to bring that," he said. He climbed onto the WaveRunner behind me. Alladio gave the vessel a little power, and we began moving off. E

disconcert (dĭs'kən-sûrt') *v.* to ruffle; to frustrate by throwing into disorder

E **SCOPE**
What event has this article focused on so far?

Lines 137–154
DISCUSSION PROMPTS

Use these prompts to help students understand the context of Petrie's rescue:

Describe What do you learn about the extent of the damage from the description? ***Possible answer:*** *The damage from the flooding is citywide.*

Infer What can you infer from Lionel Petrie's appearance and actions as he prepares to leave? ***Possible answer:*** *He wears a Marine Corps hat, so he probably had been in the Marines. He is affectionate with the dog, caressing its ears, so he probably is sad to leave it behind.*

Synthesize How does the description of the setting support Alladio's earlier statement to Petrie: "I can promise you that you will *not* see your family if you stay here" (lines 42–43)? ***Possible answer:*** *The description shows that it is impossible for his family to return home. There is more water than Petrie had realized.*

ELEMENTS OF NONFICTION

E SCOPE

Remind students to record details in their charts from page 397. ***Possible answer:*** *So far, this article has focused on the rescue of Lionel Petrie.*

FOR ADVANCED LEARNERS/PRE–AP

Compare and Contrast [paired option] Have pairs of students compare and contrast the experiences of the survivors of the San Francisco earthquake and Hurricane Katrina, based on the details in the two articles. Have them record their ideas in a Venn Diagram.

BEST PRACTICES TOOLKIT—Transparency
Venn Diagram p. A26

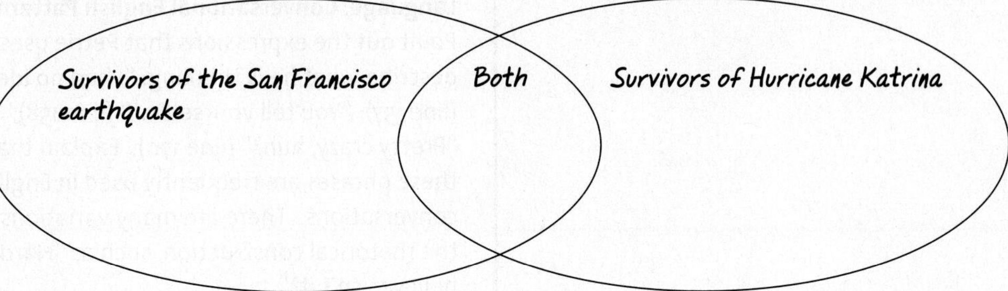

BACKGROUND

Lionel Petrie's Dog Three days after rescuing Lionel Petrie from his flooded house, Shawn Alladio returned to New Orleans and rescued his dog, Kita, whom Petrie had had to leave behind.

As we made our way down Desire, Petrie looked around him at th devastation, his neighbors' houses submerged in water. He said, "Oh, God. I had no idea."

I asked him why he hadn't left earlier. "You tell yourself that the wat are going to recede, and when they don't one day you say maybe they w the next," he answered.

The waters had subsided somewhat after the initial surge, he said. Then he had noticed, as the days went by, that there was an ebb and fl to them, as if a tide were moving in and out. To his mind, the city had become part of Lake Pontchartrain. He had heard on the radio about t levees breaking. When the electricity went out, he had listened to the r each night, but had turned it off after a little while, to save his batteries

As we spoke, he seemed to be trying to make sense of his own reacti to the catastrophe. He had understood logically that he was stranded a in danger, and yet he had decided that his first priority was to remain a prepare the house for his family's return: "Pretty crazy, huh? I even sta repairing my roof." About a third of the roof had been torn away by th hurricane, and he had worked for several days patching it up while the lay underwater. . . .

When we passed Theron Green's house, he and his father and his fiancée waved and smiled at Petrie. . . .

Petrie told me that he was worried about his aunt Willa Mae Butler: "She's about eighty-two, and lives on Bartholomew Street. I'm worried she's dead, because this time she said she wasn't going."

As we travelled slowly back toward Interstate 10, avoiding debris and downed electrical lines, Petrie began calling out landmarks. He had liv in the neighborhood his entire life. As a child, he had lived on Louisa Street. He pointed to a building that he said was the primary school he attended from kindergarten through eighth grade. . . . **F**

F SCOPE
How much of New Orleans is this article covering? Tell how you know.

By now, he was reconciled to his rescue. "I think the good Lord sent to me," he said. "I am looking forward to seeing my wife!" Her name w Mildred. He was sixty-four and Mildred was sixty-one. They had marr when she was seventeen and he was twenty. "Everyone said we wouldn' last, but we've been together forty-five years, and this is the first time w have been apart.". . .

After we landed, Shawn Alladio went out on one more tour of the neighborhood to see if there was anyone else to bring in. While w waited for her to return, Petrie and I sat in my rented van in the shade under Interstate 10. Nearby, rescuers stripped down and washed in solutions of water and bleach. . . .

ELEMENTS OF NONFICTION

F SCOPE

Remind students to record details in their charts from page 397. ***Possible answer:*** *Anderson covers a very limited part of the disaster area—primarily the Ninth Ward and a staging area near Interstate 10. His article is focused on details about Petrie's rescue and the Ninth Ward.*

DIFFERENTIATED INSTRUCTION

FOR ENGLISH LEARNERS

Language: Conversational English Patterns
Point out the expressions that Petrie uses to describe what he is thinking: "I had no idea" (line 157); "You tell yourself . . ." (line 158); "Pretty crazy, huh?" (line 170). Explain that these phrases are frequently used in English conversations. There are many variations of the rhetorical construction, such as "Hard to believe, isn't it?"

A man crosses a flooded New Orleans street.

ANALYZE VISUALS
What **details** in this photograph help you understand how deep the water is?

Petrie told me about his own children. Lionel, his namesake, forty-three years old, had been in the Marine Corps for fifteen years and served in the first Gulf War. He had been an aviation mechanic, but when he got out he couldn't get a job, so he went back to school, at the University of New Orleans, where he was pursuing an undergraduate degree when the hurricane arrived. Lionel owned two houses, one just blocks away from Petrie's, which he rented out. Petrie's second son, Bruce, who was thirty-eight, had also been a marine, had an accounting degree, and worked as a shelter supervisor for Girls and Boys Town. Bruce had driven out of the city with his wife and children before Katrina. Petrie smiled when he spoke of his daughter, Crystal, who was twenty-one. She was studying nursing in New Orleans. Lionel had driven her and their mother out of the city. G

Petrie hadn't gone to college; he got hired at a shipyard right after high school. After a couple of years, he decided to train as a welder. "For a year, I went to welders' school from 8 A.M. to noon and worked at American Marine from 6 P.M. until 6 A.M. Got my certificate as a certified welder around 1962. I went to several places looking for a job as a welder, but never got hired." When, in 1965, Petrie went to apply for a job at Equitable Equipment, near his home, he saw white welders being hired even as he was told that the only openings were for laborers. He contacted the local N.A.A.C.P. and filed a complaint with the newly formed Equal Employment Opportunity Commission. "They took an interest in my case, and I was the first black to be hired as a skilled worker by Equitable," he said. "I would sit down to eat my lunch and the white guys would go

G SCOPE
What do you learn about Petrie in this paragraph?

ANALYZE VISUALS

Possible answer: *The water is up to the man's waist and almost up to the car's windows.*

ELEMENTS OF NONFICTION

G SCOPE

Possible answer:

- *Petrie has three children: Lionel, Bruce, and Crystal.*
- *His older son, Lionel, served as a Marine in the first Gulf War and has recently gone back to school to get his college degree.*
- *His son Bruce was also a Marine, has an accounting degree, and works at Girls and Boys Town. He is married and has kids.*
- *Petrie's daughter, Crystal, is 21 and is studying nursing in New Orleans.*
- *All of Petrie's children, his grandchildren, and his wife got out of the city before Hurricane Katrina arrived.*

FOR ENGLISH LEARNERS

Background: Culture To aid student comprehension of lines 207–218, share these explanations of unfamiliar terms:

- *N.A.A.C.P.* (line 215) is an abbreviation for the National Association for the Advancement of Colored People—an organization that protects the rights of minorities in the United States. It was founded in 1909 and continues to be influential today.
- The U.S. Equal Employment Opportunity Commission (lines 215–216) is an organization that helps protect people from discrimination in the workplace. The EEOC was established in 1965 and has played a key role in developing better workplace practices nationwide.

ELEMENTS OF NONFICTION

H SCOPE

Possible answer: *Alladio is leaving the next day, because the volunteers are no longer needed. We also know that she keeps her promise to drive Petrie to Baton Rouge.*

ELEMENTS OF NONFICTION

I SCOPE

Answer: *The events take place over the course of one and a half days.*

SELECTION WRAP–UP

REFLECT Have students think about the way the writer portrays Shawn Alladio in this article. Does he seem to admire Alladio? How can you tell?

★ **CRITIQUE** Have students evaluate whether the writer should have given more information about his own role in the events as well as his reaction to them.

sit somewhere else. I didn't care—I was just there to do my job." After working for a decade at Equitable, and then at Kaiser Aluminum unti 1983, when it shut down its Louisiana operations, he decided to set up own business, Petrie Iron and Construction. He didn't have insurance, though, and he figured that he'd lost everything.

H SCOPE What information do you get about Alladio?

Later that evening, Alladio drove Petrie and me to Baton Rouge in a rented pickup, towing her WaveRunner behind her. She had been that forced evacuations would begin soon, and that the operation woul shift toward law enforcement. She was leaving the next day. **H**

Targeted Passage 4

In his exhaustion, Petrie had not been able to remember any telepho numbers, but, as we drove along, cell-phone numbers for his son Bruce his daughter came back to him. I handed him my phone, and a minut later I heard him say, "They're in Memphis!"

When he hung up, he said that his wife and daughter were staying i Memphis at a cousin's house. Lionel had already found some temporar factory work. Bruce was staying with his wife's family, in Kentucky. W Mae Butler, Petrie's aunt, was alive and in Texas. Bruce was going to lo on the Internet for a flight for his father from Baton Rouge to Memph

A little while later, as we drove into the night, Petrie said reflectively "I don't know if I want to go back to New Orleans—seeing it how it w I don't think I do." He doubted, from what he had seen, that much of it could ever be rebuilt. "The first thing I picture now is the water I sa when I was coming out," he said.

A few minutes afterward, Bruce called back to say that the next availa flight was in three days' time. Alladio suggested that we try the Greyhou station instead. It was already late when we arrived at the scruffy littl bus station in Baton Rouge, full of refugees from New Orleans. I joined long line of people waiting for information and tickets. Half an hour late it had barely moved. A man and a woman were arguing, and when th stationmaster called for passengers for Houston, I heard the man tell her, don't care what you say—I'm getting on that bus." After he left, the wom leaned against a pillar and wiped her eyes. A tall man with a stack of relig tracts was reciting Psalms from memory, and a woman made subdued sou of agreement or said, "That's right," in a rhythmic cadence. Two policem patrolled the station; there were a number of young men who looked stre wise and seemed to be loitering among the waiting passengers.

Around midnight, Bruce called again. He had resolved to drive dow from Kentucky to get his father. He would leave shortly with his wife, Donna. Lionel Petrie would wait for them in the Greyhound station. B thought that if he and Donna took turns driving they could make the in twelve hours. They were there by noon the next day. **I**

I SCOPE Over what span of time did the events in this account take place?

DIFFERENTIATED INSTRUCTION

FOR LESS–PROFICIENT READERS

4 Targeted Passage [Lines 224–241]

This passage describes how Petrie gets back in touch with his family.

- Where did Alladio drive Petrie?
- Was Alladio returning to New Orleans? Why or why not?
- What did Petrie learn about his family? Where did they go?
- What did Petrie say about returning to New Orleans? Why did he feel this way?

Comprehension Support Have students complete a Sequence Chain for the events mentioned in the article, including the hurricane, Petrie's family leaving New Orleans, Petrie's own rescue, and the reuniting of the family. Help students understand that the narrative is not told in chronological order, so they will need to reorder the events in the correct sequence.

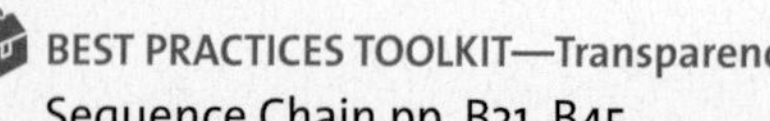

BEST PRACTICES TOOLKIT—Transparency
Sequence Chain pp. B21, B45

mprehension

1. **Recall** In "The Story of an Eyewitness," how much of San Francisco does Jack London say was destroyed by the earthquake and the fire that came afterward?
2. **Clarify** What span of time does London's account cover?
3. **Clarify** In "Letter from New Orleans," why is Lionel Petrie reluctant to leave his home?

itical Analysis

4. **Examine Scope** Which passage in "The Story of an Eyewitness" best helped you understand the extent of the tragedy that struck San Francisco? Explain.
5. **Evaluate Objectivity** An **objective** report is one that is fair, neutral, and evenhanded. Do you think that Jack London's account is objective? Cite evidence from the text to support your opinion.
6. **Make Judgments** The authorities forced thousands of people to leave behind their pets during the evacuation of New Orleans. Was it right to ask people to abandon their pets? Why or why not?
7. **Evaluate Accounts** Think about the two articles you have just read. Which account do you think is more powerful? Explain your opinion.

mparing Articles

Now that you've read both articles, finish filling in your chart. Then add the final question, and answer it, too.

	"The Story of an Eyewitness"	"Letter from New Orleans: Leaving Desire"
What is the topic?	the San Francisco earthquake of 1906	
Whom does the writer focus on?		
How much of the disaster area does the writer cover?		
Which events does the writer focus on?		
How would you describe the scope of the account?		

Practice and Apply

After Reading

For additional support of postreading questions, use these copy masters:

RESOURCE MANAGER—Copy Masters
Reading Check pp. 153, 156 (to check understanding of the selections)
Question Support p. 157 (After Reading questions adapted for English learners and less-proficient readers)

Additional selection questions are provided for teachers on page 143.

ANSWERS

Comprehension

1. *London says that most of San Francisco was destroyed by the earthquake and the fire.*
2. *London's article covers three days.*
3. *Petrie was afraid that if he left, his family would have no way to find him.*

Critical Analysis

Possible answers:

4. ● **STANDARDS FOCUS Scope** *Students should cite a specific passage in the article and explain how it helped them understand the devastation.*
5. *The majority of students will likely respond that London's article is objective because it describes heroic deeds, emotionally charged events, and riveting images with calm detachment and an absence of judgment. Evidence given will vary.*
6. *Help students recognize that such decisions are difficult and can only be judged as either wise and prudent or hasty and insensitive much later, when all the facts are known.*
7. *Accept all reasonable answers. Some students will choose "The Story of an Eyewitness" because of the dramatic descriptions of the raging fires and cracks in the earth. Other students will choose "Letter from New Orleans," perhaps because it seems more personal and they can identify more with a recent event.*

Comparing Articles

■ **STANDARDS FOCUS Set a Purpose for Reading**

"The Story of an Eyewitness"

- ***Topic:*** *San Francisco earthquake of 1906*
- ***Whom is focused on:*** *firefighters, troops, refugees, and three individuals*
- ***Disaster area covered:*** *Market Street, Kearney Street, Union Square, Nob Hill, Mission Street, Russian Hill, Telegraph Hill, Van Ness Avenue*
- ***Which events are focused on:*** *the earthquake, fires, the destruction of the city, and the refugees fleeing the city*
- ***Scope:*** *broad*

"Letter from New Orleans: Leaving Desire"

- ***Topic:*** *effect of Hurricane Katrina on New Orleans*
- ***Whom is focused on:*** *Lionel Petrie and Shawn Alladio*
- ***Disaster area covered:*** *Lionel Petrie's house; part of New Orleans's Ninth Ward; a staging area near Interstate 10*
- ***Which events are focused on:*** *the rescue of Lionel Petrie*
- ***Scope:*** *narrow*

ANSWERS

Vocabulary in Context

VOCABULARY PRACTICE

1. *elegant*
2. *something to avoid*
3. *you confuse them*
4. *you are forcing them*
5. *alert*
6. *thunder*

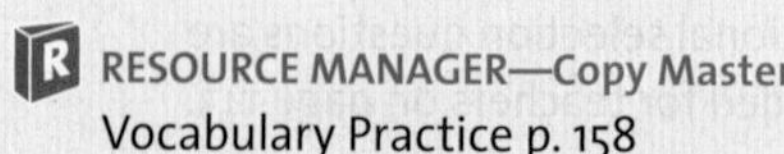

VOCABULARY IN WRITING

Have students review how each vocabulary word is used in the text to help them write what they might have experienced.

VOCABULARY STRATEGY: THE PREFIX *inter-* *(also an EL language objective)*

As they work through the exercise, suggest that students first focus on defining the base word or root word. Then they can put that definition together with the meaning for *inter-* to write the definition.

Answers:

1. *switched into the place of each other*
2. *to unite or join closely as by hooking or dovetailing*
3. *of, relating to, or involving two or more nations*
4. *between two extremes or in a middle position or state*
5. *connecting two or more states*

RESOURCE MANAGER—Copy Master
Vocabulary Strategy p. 159

Vocabulary Center at **ClassZone.com**
Additional Vocabulary Activities

Vocabulary in Context

VOCABULARY PRACTICE

Answer each question to show your understanding of the vocabulary words.

1. Would a **lavishly** decorated home be simple or elegant?
2. Is a **menace** something to avoid or to look forward to?
3. If you **disconcert** people, do you confuse them or calm them?
4. If you **compel** people to do something, are you forcing them or inviting them?
5. Would a person who watches **vigilantly** be alert or distracted?
6. Which sound would be heard **intermittently**—thunder or a steady siren?

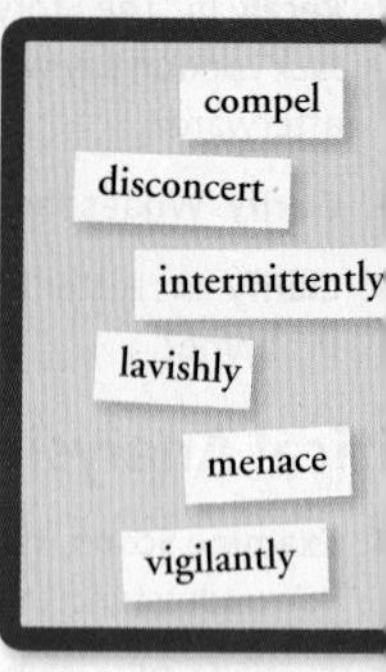

VOCABULARY IN WRITING

Imagine you volunteered to help in New Orleans after the hurricane. Using at least two vocabulary words, describe what you might have experienced. Here is a sample beginning.

EXAMPLE SENTENCE

The hurricane was a ***menace*** *to the city.*

VOCABULARY STRATEGY: THE PREFIX *inter-*

A prefix is a word part attached to the beginning of a base word or root word. When a prefix is added, a new word is formed. The vocabulary word *intermittently* contains the prefix *inter-*, which means "between," added to the Latin word meaning "to let go." If you know the meaning of a prefix, it can help you figure out the meaning of an unfamiliar word, especially if you consider the word's context.

PRACTICE The boldfaced words all contain the prefix *inter-*. Use your knowledge of this prefix and the base word to write a definition for each word. Remember to use context clues or a dictionary if you need help.

1. The twins looked so similar, they could be **interchanged** and no one would know.
2. The puzzle pieces **interlock** so that they won't come apart.
3. An **international** commission was established to study world hunger.
4. I have to pass the **intermediate** course before I can move on to the advanced level.
5. We took the **interstate** highway on our drive from New York to Ohio.

VOCABULARY PRACTICE
For more practice, go to the Vocabulary Cent
at ClassZone.com.

DIFFERENTIATED INSTRUCTION

FOR ENGLISH LEARNERS

Vocabulary Practice [mixed-readiness pairs] Encourage students who are having trouble to review the definitions and context of the vocabulary words in the selections. Pair struggling students with fluent speakers to answer the six questions.

FOR ADVANCED LEARNERS/PRE–AP

Vocabulary Strategy Have students rewrite the sentences using different context clues. Next, have them cover up the boldfaced word and challenge a partner to choose the right word for each sentence.

iting for Assessment

. READ THE PROMPT

The two articles you've just read cover similar subjects in different ways. In writing assessments, you might be asked to compare such selections.

PROMPT

"The Story of an Eyewitness" and "Letter from New Orleans: Leaving Desire" are both eyewitness accounts of natural disasters. In four or five paragraphs, contrast the scope, or range of focus, of each article's disaster coverage. Use details from the articles to explain the differences between how people, places, and events are covered. Also explain how you think the scope affects the reader.

◀ STRATEGIES IN ACTION

1. I need to ***identify the range of focus*** of each article.
2. I need to ***state the differences*** between the articles' scopes.
3. I need to ***support my statement with examples*** about people, places, and events.
4. I need to ***explain the effect*** of each article's scope on the reader.

. PLAN YOUR WRITING

To identify the scope of each reporter's disaster coverage, review the chart you completed. Write a thesis statement that tells how each article's scope differs. Then think about how you will set up the body of your response.

- Option A: In one paragraph, describe the scope of the first article's coverage of people, places, and events. In the next paragraph, describe the other article's scope.
- Option B: In one paragraph, contrast the way each article covers people. In the next paragraph, contrast the way each covers places. In the third, contrast the number of events covered.

I. Introduction
II. Scope of first article
III. Scope of second article
IV. Conclusion

Once you have decided on your approach, create an outline to organize your details.

. DRAFT YOUR RESPONSE

Introduction Provide the titles and authors of both articles, a brief description of what each article is about, and your thesis statement.

Body With your outline as a guide, discuss the differences in the scope of each article, using details about the writers' coverage of people, places, and events as support.

Conclusion Restate your thesis statement, and leave your reader with a final thought about the role that scope plays in each of these articles.

Revision Double-check to make sure your thesis statement clearly presents the ideas you develop in your body paragraphs.

Writing for Assessment

1. *READ THE PROMPT*

Read the prompt aloud. Ask volunteers to identify key words and phrases that define the task (*contrast the scope, explain the differences, affects the reader*).

2. *PLAN YOUR WRITING*

- Have students refer to their completed charts from page 413 as they plan their writing.
- After students have decided how to organize their response, have them write key details in the appropriate sections of their outline.
- Have students use their notes to create a strong thesis statement. Give them an example: "The scope of London's coverage of the San Francisco earthquake is broad, while the scope of Anderson's coverage is quite narrow, focusing on the effect of Hurricane Katrina on one person." Explain that this thesis statement belongs in an introductory paragraph.

3. *DRAFT YOUR RESPONSE*

Remind students to begin each body paragraph with a strong topic sentence. For example: "London's coverage of the 1906 San Francisco earthquake is broad in scope, with a breathtaking view of the disaster."

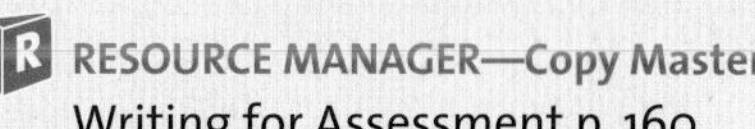

RESOURCE MANAGER—Copy Master
Writing for Assessment p. 160

Assess and Reteach

Assess

RESOURCE MANAGER—Copy Masters
Selection Tests A, B/C pp. 163–164, 165–166

Test Generator CD

Reteach

STANDARDS LESSON FILE
Informational Texts Lesson 11: Compare Treatment, Organization, and Scope
Writing Lesson 29: Comparison-Contrast Essay
Vocabulary Lesson 1: Word Parts
Vocabulary Lesson 4: Prefixes

DIFFERENTIATED INSTRUCTION

FOR LESS–PROFICIENT WRITERS

Draft Your Response Provide a template to help students structure their responses.

Introduction

- Give the titles and names of the writers.
- Make a thesis statement.

Body

- Explain the scope of the first article. Describe the treatment of people, places, and events.
- Explain the scope of the second article. Describe the treatment of people, places, and events.
- Point out differences in coverage of people, places, and events.

Conclusion

- Restate your thesis.
- Explain how the scope of each article affects the reader.

Focus and Motivate

OBJECTIVES

Literary Analysis
- explore the key idea of the **earth**
- identify, analyze, and evaluate imagery
- read two poems

Reading
- identify, analyze, and compare speakers

SUMMARY

In "Mi Madre," the speaker compares the earth to a loving mother. In "Canyon de Chelly," the speaker describes exploring the canyon and recounts a young son's wonder and pleasure in the joy of discovery.

What gifts does the EARTH *provide?*

Discuss the question with students. To lead into the ***KEY IDEA,*** ask them to think about which of the **earth's** resources they have used in the last 24 hours. How would their lives be different without access to these resources? What other, intangible gifts does the earth offer? Next, have small groups work on the ***LIST IT*** activity. Suggest that they consider uses for these resources in the areas of energy, food, housing, medicine, recreation, and transportation.

Before Reading

Mi Madre

Poem by Pat Mora

Canyon de Chelly

Poem by Simon J. Ortiz

What gifts does the EARTH *provide?*

KEY IDEA It's not hard to appreciate nature when you're taking a walk on a sunny day or swimming at a scenic beach. But the **earth** gives us many gifts that we may not always recognize. The gas that warms our homes, the concrete we use to pave our sidewalks, even the paper we write on—these things are all precious resources provided to us by the earth. The poets whose works you're about to read share their appreciation for the earth's gifts through words.

LIST IT The earth's resources can be used in multiple ways. In a small group, choose one of the resources shown, and brainstorm at least five ways we can use it. Did you discover any new uses for these resources? Share your list with the class.

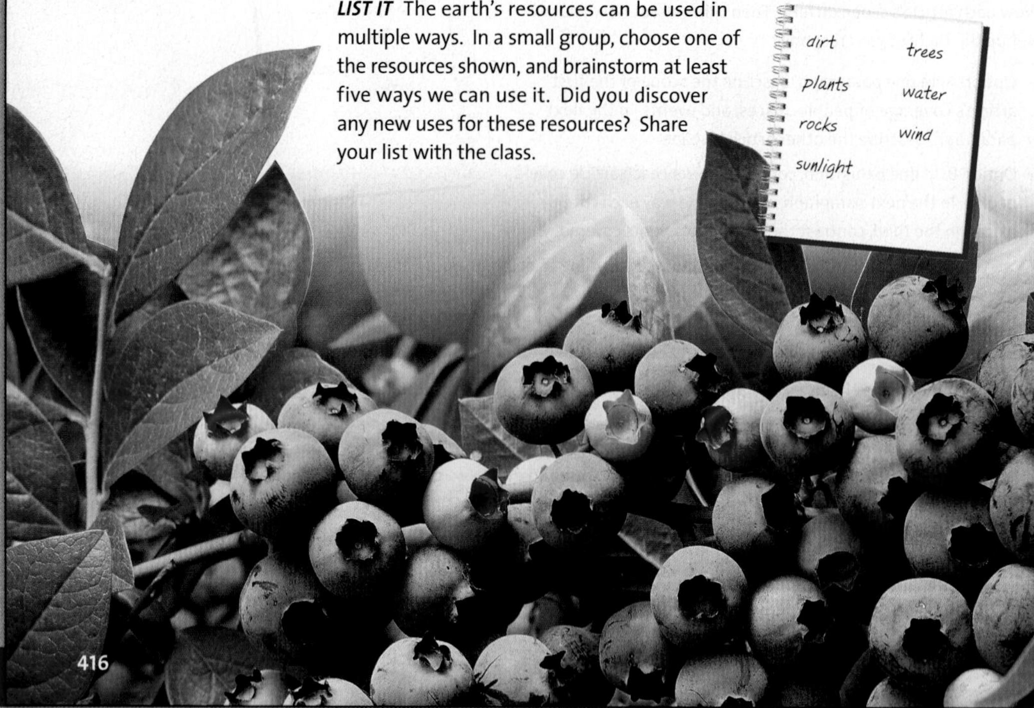

Selection Resources

RESOURCE MANAGER UNIT 3

Plan and Teach pp. 167–174

Literary Analysis
Imagery pp. 175, 176†*
Question Support p. 179*

Reading
Understand Speaker pp. 177, 178†*
Reading Fluency p. 180

Assessment
Selection Tests A, B/C pp. 181*, 183*
Test Generator CD

BEST PRACTICES TOOLKIT

Differentiated Instruction pp. 31–38*

Graphic Organizers/Strategies
Read-and-Say-Something • Linear Array • Two-Column Chart • Venn Diagram

Reading Support
Audio Anthology CD*

Technology
Literature Center at **ClassZone.com**
Write*Smart* CD

* Resources for Differentiation † Also in Spanish

RARY ANALYSIS: IMAGERY

he use of description that makes something seem real or easy
o imagine is called **imagery.** Poets create imagery by using words and phrases that appeal to our senses of sight, hearing, mell, taste, and touch. Paying attention to imagery can enable ou to "experience" a poem as if you were there. For example, ook at the following lines from "Mi Madre":

say tease me.
he sprinkles raindrops in my face on a sunny day.

he image "sprinkles raindrops" appeals to the sense of touch, vhile "sunny day" appeals to the sense of sight. If you combine hese images in your mind, you can almost share in this scene. s you read "Mi Madre" and "Canyon de Chelly," use a word veb to keep track of these and other examples of imagery.

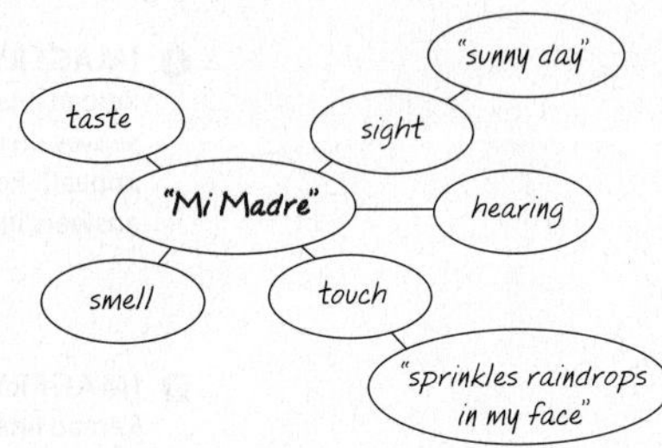

DING SKILL: UNDERSTAND SPEAKER

n poetry, the **speaker** is the voice that "talks" to the reader and elates the ideas presented in the poem from a specific point of view. It is important to understand that the speaker is not he same as the poet. For example, a poet may choose to write bout a subject from the perspective of a child. In that case, the deas that are expressed are those of the child, not necessarily he poet. As you read "Mi Madre" and "Canyon de Chelly," look or clues that will help you decide who each speaker is and how e or she feels about the subject of the poem.

Author Online

Pat Mora: Literacy Advocate The granddaughter of Mexican immigrants, Pat Mora realized early in her writing career that her cultural heritage was "a source of pride." Her books celebrate family, the desert in which she grew up, and the Mexican-American experience. Her children's books frequently feature Latino characters, because she believes that children of all backgrounds should see themselves reflected in the books they read.

Pat Mora
born 1942

Simon J. Ortiz: Native New Mexican Raised on New Mexico's Acoma Pueblo, Simon Ortiz is regarded as one of today's greatest Native-American writers. His work frequently focuses on having a sense of place. "You have to have it," Ortiz says. "Otherwise you are drifting." Ortiz hopes that all people can learn from his poetry. "I tell you about me and my world," he says, "so you may be able to see yourself."

Simon J. Ortiz
born 1941

MORE ABOUT THE AUTHOR
For more on Pat Mora and Simon J. Ortiz, visit the **Literature Center** at **ClassZone.com.**

Background

Arizona's Canyon de Chelly (pronounced *shā*) is home to a Navajo tribal community that has preserved this sacred land for centuries. The canyon, now a national park, is known for its stunning landscapes, tribal artifacts, and rock paintings.

Teach

STANDARDS FOCUS

LITERARY ANALYSIS

● IMAGERY

Read this example aloud:

> The day was bright and cold. A feathery blanket of snow covered the wintry city.

To what sense or senses does the image appeal? ***Possible answer:*** *It appeals to the senses of sight ("bright," "blanket") and touch ("cold," "feathery").*

CHECK UNDERSTANDING Ask students how imagery helps them "experience" this scene.

RESOURCE MANAGER—Copy Master
Imagery p. 175 (for student use while reading the poems)

READING SKILL

■ UNDERSTAND SPEAKER

Ask students to name three possible speakers in a poem about a mother and a child. ***Possible answer:*** *the mother, the child, or an outside observer*

CHECK UNDERSTANDING Have students identify the speakers of the last two or three poems they have read.

DIFFERENTIATED INSTRUCTION

FOR ALL STUDENTS

For general guidelines on differentiating instruction, see

BEST PRACTICES TOOLKIT
Differentiated Instruction pp. 31–38

FOR LESS–PROFICIENT READERS

Concept Support Tell students that both of these poems reflect the speakers' feelings about the **earth.** As students read, suggest that they ask themselves the following questions:

- Who are the characters in the poems? *(the speakers, the desert in "Mi Madre," the son of the speaker in "Canyon de Chelly")*
- How do the speakers feel about the earth? How can you tell? *(Both speakers feel affection and gratitude. They describe the gifts the earth has given them.)*

FOR ENGLISH LEARNERS

Options for Reading [paired option] Have students listen to the *Audio Anthology CD* while they read along with the poems. Then have students do the Read-and-Say-Something activity with a partner, commenting on images, phrases, and ideas that struck them as they read.

BEST PRACTICES TOOLKIT
Read-and-Say-Something p. D3

Practice and Apply

ANALYZE VISUALS

Students might say that they pictured a cactus like the one in the painting. However, they might not have pictured the flowers, trees, and colors found in the painting.

About the Art This painting by American artist Isabel Bronson Cartwright (1885–1966), called *Prickly Pear*, illustrates the image in line 2 of the poem. The flowers will eventually turn into a sweet, red, fleshy fruit called *tuna* in Spanish. *Tuna* is a popular food in Mexico.

LITERARY ANALYSIS

A IMAGERY

Possible answer:

- ***taste and touch:** "red prickly pear on a spiked cactus"*
- ***touch and sight:** "sprinkles raindrops in my face on a sunny day"*
- ***hearing:** "shouts thunder"*
- ***sight:** "flashes lightning"*

LITERARY ANALYSIS

B IMAGERY

***Possible answer:** The image suggests comfort, protection, and warmth.*

If students need help . . . Direct students' attention to footnote 1 and point out that many people associate these feelings with their mothers.

READING SKILL

C SPEAKER

***Possible answer:** The speaker has many needs, and the desert helps fulfill those needs. The speaker loves and appreciates nature.*

MI MADRE[1]

Pat Mora

I say feed me.
She serves red prickly pear on a spiked cactus.

I say tease me.
She sprinkles raindrops in my face on a sunny day.

I say frighten me.
She shouts thunder, flashes lightning. A

I say comfort me.
She invites me to lay on her firm body.

I say heal me.
She gives me *manzanilla, orégano, dormilón.*[2]

I say caress me.
She strokes my skin with her warm breath. B

I say make me beautiful.
She offers turquoise for my fingers, a pink blossom for my hair. C

I say sing to me.
She chants lonely women's songs of femaleness.

I say teach me.
She endures: glaring heat
numbing cold
frightening dryness.

She: the desert
She: strong mother.

1. **Mi Madre** (mē mä'drā) *Spanish:* my mother.
2. ***manzanilla, orégano, dormilón*** (măn'zə-nē'yə, ə-rĕg'ə-nō', dôr-mē-lōn') *Spanish:* sweet-smelling herbs that can be used to make home medicines.

ANALYZE VISUAL
Compare this paintin[g] with your own ment[al] image of the desert. Are the images simila[r] or different?

A IMAGERY
Reread lines 1–6. To w[hat] senses do these imag[es] appeal? Record your answers in your word[...]

B IMAGERY
Reread lines 11–12. W[hat] feelings does this ima[ge] suggest?

C SPEAKER
What type of person [is] the speaker? How do you know?

Prickly Pear, Isabel Bronson Cartw[right]. Oil on canvas. Private colle[ction]. © Peter Harholt/Super[Stock]

DIFFERENTIATED INSTRUCTION

FOR LESS–PROFICIENT READERS

Comprehension Support Discuss the structure of the poem. Point out that nearly all of the stanzas (except the last) are couplets with the same structure. In the first line of each couplet, the speaker "says" something. In the second line, "She" (the desert) responds with various actions. Encourage students to look for patterns as they read poetry. Explain that this will increase their enjoyment and understanding of what they read.

FOR ENGLISH LEARNERS

Vocabulary Support [mixed-readiness pairs] Have students complete Linear Arrays for some or all of the following words in the poem: *prickly, shouts, invites, gives, warm, beautiful, endures.* Suggest that students use the same part of speech in each array. Discuss the nuances of meaning in each array.

 **BEST PRACTICES TOOLKIT—Transparency**
Linear Array p. E7

BACKGROUND

The American Southwest The region known as the American Southwest includes Arizona, New Mexico, and parts of Texas, Oklahoma, Colorado, Utah, Nevada, and California. Known for its dryness, the region has high mountains, dry plains, sandstone deposits, and deserts. For the most part, the region's climate is hot and arid.

CULTURAL CONNECTION

Southwest Culture The American Southwest was originally inhabited by Native American groups who lived off the land as farmers, hunters, and herders. Spanish settlers from Mexico came to the region in the 1600s, looking for gold. Many stayed to farm the land. Anglo settlers came to the region from the eastern United States in the 1800s, looking for land and economic opportunity. The cultures of the American Southwest today, particularly those of New Mexico and Arizona, are a blend of these three influences.

FOR ENGLISH LEARNERS

Language: Punctuation and Print Cues Point out the italics used for the Spanish words in line 10. Explain that non-English words are usually italicized to indicate they are from another language. Encourage Spanish speakers who are familiar with the herbs mentioned here to describe their characteristics and uses. Next, point out the colons in lines 18 and 21–22. Explain that the colons indicate emphasis. Discuss what the poet is emphasizing in these lines.

FOR ADVANCED LEARNERS/PRE–AP

Synthesize Ask students to choose five couplets and rewrite the second line of each one with a focus on where they live. Invite students to share their couplets with the rest of the class.

ANALYZE VISUALS

Some students may conclude that it is a painting because the background is blurry and indistinct. Others may say that it could be a photograph that was taken from far away (perhaps with a digital zoom) or that was simply shot out of focus.

Lines 1–7

REINFORCE *KEY IDEA:* EARTH

Discuss What gifts of the **earth** does the speaker appreciate in these lines? ***Possible answer:*** *The speaker appreciates the feel of the stone and the sight of the blue skies, as well as the earth's enduring quality.*

READING SKILL

D SPEAKER

Possible answer: *The speaker is in awe of the canyon and has a son.*

CANYON DE CHELLY

Simon J. Ortiz

Lie on your back on stone,
the stone carved to fit
the shape of yourself.
Who made it like this,
knowing that I would be along
in a million years and look
at the sky being blue forever?

My son is near me. He sits
and turns on his butt
and crawls over to stones,
picks one up and holds it,
and then puts it into his mouth.
The taste of stone.
What is it but stone,
the earth in your mouth.
You, son, are tasting forever. D

ANALYZE VISUALS
Is this a photograph or a painting? Tell what led you to your answer and why others might **conclude** differently.

D SPEAKER
What do you know abc the speaker of this poe

DIFFERENTIATED INSTRUCTION

FOR LESS–PROFICIENT READERS

Reading Skill Follow-Up: Understand Speaker Discuss "Mi Madre" and have students use the first column of a Two-Column Chart to record what they learned about the speaker. As students read "Canyon de Chelly," have them write what they learn about its speaker in the second column of the chart. Ask these questions to help students think about the poems' speakers:

- What is each speaker's attitude toward his or her subject?
- What might each speaker want the reader to know?

BEST PRACTICES TOOLKIT—Transparency Two-Column Chart p. A25

Lines 1–16

DISCUSSION PROMPTS

Use these prompts to help students develop insight into the poem's meaning:

Recall What is the speaker doing in the first stanza? ***Answer:*** *The speaker is lying on a rock and looking at the sky.*

Infer What can you infer about the speaker's son from this description? What details help you make that inference? ***Possible answer:*** *The son is still very young—perhaps a baby or toddler. He crawls and puts things in his mouth, in the way that very young children do.*

Evaluate The last line of each stanza (lines 7 and 16) ends with the word *forever.* What is the effect of that repetition? What does it tell you about the speaker's feelings toward the canyon? ***Possible answer:*** *The repetition calls attention to the vast size and extreme age of the canyon, putting the small, mortal speaker and the boy in sharp contrast. This implies that the speaker is in awe of the canyon.*

FOR LESS–PROFICIENT READERS

Concept Support Help students identify the images in the first two stanzas of the poem. Ask them to determine to which senses these images appeal. Then have them add the images to the word webs they began on page 417.

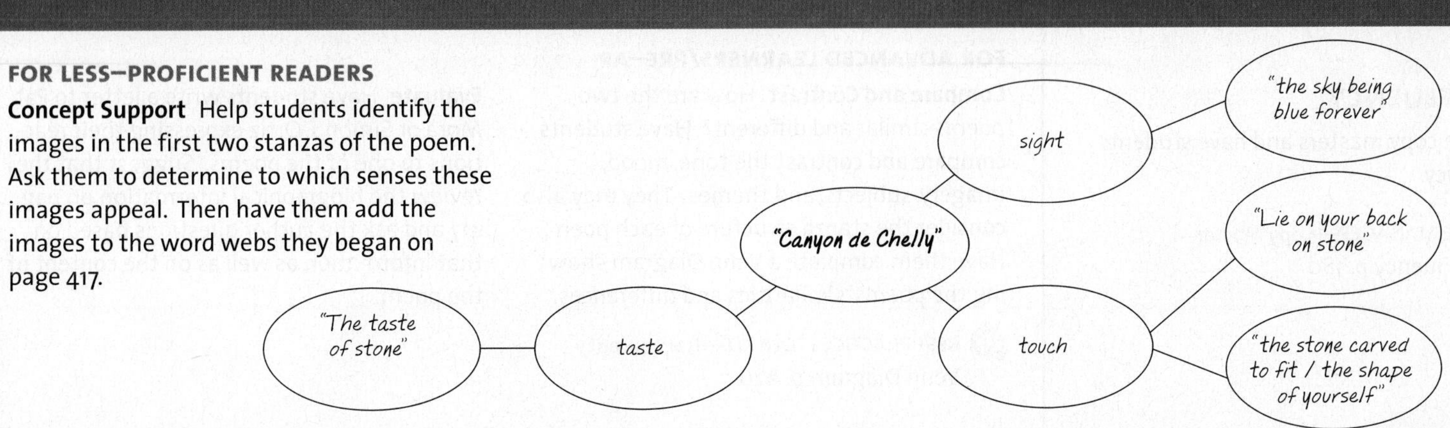

LITERARY ANALYSIS

E IMAGERY

Possible answer:

- ***touch:*** *"wind moves softly"*
- ***hearing:*** *"laughs with the wind"; "gasps and laughs"*

These images suggest happiness and peacefulness.

READING SKILL

F SPEAKER

Possible answer: *The speaker wants to teach the boy about nature and share a connection to the earth.*

SELECTION WRAP–UP

REFLECT Have students explain which speaker they most identified with and why.

★ CRITIQUE Discuss the different structures of the poems. Ask students how the structure of each poem complements its content and theme.

READING FLUENCY

Distribute the copy masters and have students practice fluency.

RESOURCE MANAGER—Copy Master
Reading Fluency p. 180

We walk to the edge of cliff
and look down into the canyon.
On this side, we cannot see
the bottom cliff edge but looking
further out, we see fields,
sand furrows, cottonwoods.
In winter, they are softly gray.
The cliffs' shadows are distant,
hundreds of feet below;
we cannot see our own shadows.
The wind moves softly into us.
My son laughs with the wind;
he gasps and laughs. E

We find gray root, old wood,
so old, with curious twists
in it, curving back into curves,
juniper, piñon, or something
with hard, red berries in spring.
You taste them, and they are sweet
and bitter, the berries a delicacy
for bluejays. The plant rooted
fragilely into a sandy place
by a canyon wall, the sun bathing
shiny, pointed leaves.

My son touches the root carefully,
aware of its ancient quality.
He lays his soft, small fingers on it
and looks at me for information.
I tell him: wood, an old root,
and around it, the earth, ourselves. F

E IMAGERY
Reread lines 27–29. Add the images in th lines to your web. W emotions do these images suggest?

F SPEAKER
Reread lines 41–46. W do you think the spea brings his son to the canyon?

DIFFERENTIATED INSTRUCTION

FOR ADVANCED LEARNERS/PRE–AP

Compare and Contrast How are the two poems similar and different? Have students compare and contrast the tone, mood, imagery, subjects, and themes. They may also consider the stanza structure of each poem. Have them complete a Venn Diagram showing the poems' similarities and differences.

BEST PRACTICES TOOLKIT—Transparency
Venn Diagram p. A26

Evaluate Have students write a letter to Pat Mora or Simon J. Ortiz expressing their reactions to one of the poems. Suggest that they review the biographical information on page 417 and ask the author questions based on that information as well as on the content of the poem.

422 UNIT 3: SETTING AND MOOD

mprehension

1. **Recall** In "Mi Madre," how does the desert heal the speaker?
2. **Recall** In "Canyon de Chelly," what two things does the speaker's son taste?
3. **Represent** Reread lines 13–14 from "Mi Madre" and lines 17–22 from "Canyon de Chelly." Choose one of these groups of lines and sketch the image created in your mind.

erary Analysis

4. **Interpret Poem** In "Mi Madre," the speaker refers to the desert as a "strong mother." How is the desert in the poem like a mother?
5. **Make Inferences** Reread the first three lines of "Canyon de Chelly." To whom do you think the speaker is talking? Why do you think so?
6. **Compare and Contrast Speakers** Using a Y-chart like the one shown, fill in the top part with what you know about each speaker's relationship to the **earth.** Include the gifts he or she receives from it and how he or she feels about it. How are these relationships similar? Then cross out the similarities and write them in the bottom part.

"Mi Madre" | "Canyon de Chelly" | Similarities

7. **Evaluate Imagery** Both "Mi Madre" and "Canyon de Chelly" are about real places the poets have visited. Review the imagery webs you created. Which poem's imagery best helped you to picture the subject of the poem?

tension and Challenge

8. **Creative Project: Poetry** Think of a place in the outdoors that you enjoy. Jot down notes about how the place looks, smells, feels, sounds, or tastes. Then write a poem about the place. Be sure to include **imagery** that appeals to at least three of the five senses.
9. **SOCIAL STUDIES CONNECTION** The Navajo, or Diné, make up the largest Native American nation in the United States. Research their history and traditions, including their preservation of Canyon de Chelly as a national landmark. Share your findings with a group.

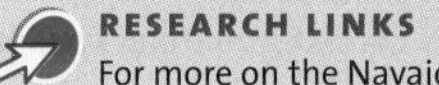

RESEARCH LINKS
For more on the Navajo, visit the **Research Center** at **ClassZone.com.**

Practice and Apply

After Reading

For additional support of postreading questions, use these copy masters:

RESOURCE MANAGER—Copy Masters
Understand Speaker p. 177 (for practice of reading standards focus)
Question Support p. 179 (After Reading questions adapted for English learners and less-proficient readers)

Additional selection questions are provided for teachers on page 171.

ANSWERS

Comprehension

1. *The desert gives the speaker* manzanilla, orégano, *and* dormilón.
2. *The speaker's son tastes stone and forever.*
3. *Students' sketches should include key images from these lines.*

Literary Analysis

Possible answers:

4. *The desert is like a mother because she feeds, plays with, comforts, adorns, and teaches her children. She helps heal her children's injuries and sicknesses.*
5. *Students may say that the speaker is talking to the reader, because the speaker says "yourself." They may also say the speaker is talking to his son, because much of the poem is about the speaker teaching his son about the canyon.*
6. **STANDARDS FOCUS Understand Speaker** ***"Mi Madre":*** *the desert fulfills needs and gives gifts of food, healing, comfort, and beauty; the speaker learns from the desert; the desert is like a mother.* ***"Canyon de Chelly":*** *the speaker is awed by the canyon, which provides a connection to the past and gives gifts of plants and the wind; the speaker wants to share the canyon with his son.* ***Similarities:*** *parent/child relationship; the earth provides necessities for the speakers; they feel connected to the earth.*
7. **STANDARDS FOCUS Imagery** *Answers will vary but should include images that appeal to the senses.*

Extension and Challenge

8. *Encourage students to record their notes in a web like the one on page 417.*
9. **SOCIAL STUDIES CONNECTION** *Students may wish to explore the Web sites of the Navajo nation and Canyon de Chelly for information.*

Assess and Reteach

Assess

RESOURCE MANAGER—Copy Masters
Selection Tests A, B/C pp. 181–182, 183–184

Test Generator CD

Reteach

STANDARDS LESSON FILE
Literature Lesson 19: Speaker
Literature Lesson 28: Imagery

Focus and Motivate

OBJECTIVES

- analyze a student model that reflects the key traits of a comparison-contrast essay
- use the writing process to compare and contrast two subjects
- revise and edit, applying a rubric for a strong comparison-contrast essay
- produce and deliver a power presentation

WRITER'S ROAD MAP

WRITING PROMPTS 1 AND 2

Help students choose a prompt by describing memorable selections they have read. Students might also brainstorm key details about two places, people, or events. Remind them that the two selections or subjects they choose should have both similarities and differences.

ADDITIONAL PROMPTS

Use these prompts for practice with writing comparison-contrast essays:

WRITING PROMPT 3

Writing from the Real World Write a review that compares and contrasts the features, strengths, and weaknesses of two news sources.

Subjects to Consider
- two national magazines
- two local newspapers
- two television news broadcasts

WRITING PROMPT 4

Writing About Fine Art Focus on two paintings, photographs, or illustrations that appear in your textbook, in an art book from the library, or at an online museum. Compare and contrast the two pieces.

Subjects to Consider
- two paintings from the same era
- a historical and a contemporary political cartoon
- two photographs or paintings that depict similar scenes in different ways

KEY TRAITS

Review the ***KEY TRAITS*** with students, focusing primarily on ideas and organization. Compare the list of traits with the rubric on page 430.

Writing Workshop

Comparison-Contrast Essay

In Unit 3 and in your own life, you have encountered people and situations that almost beg to be compared. To write an essay that compares or contrasts two real or fictional people, places, or events, start with the **Writer's Road Map.**

WRITER'S ROAD MAP

Comparison-Contrast Essay

WRITING PROMPT 1

Writing from Literature Write an essay that compares or contrasts two selections that you have read this year. Concentrate on key aspects such as setting, people or characters, events, or the writer's style. Your essay should give your reader a new understanding of the selections.

Selections to Compare
- "The Monkey's Paw" and "The Tell-Tale Heart"
- "Going Where I'm Coming From" and "My First Free Summer"
- "Mi Madre" and "My Father and the Fig Tree"

WRITING PROMPT 2

Writing from Your Life Write a comparison-contrast essay about two places, people, or events that are familiar, important, or interesting to you. Explain why you chose those two subjects.

Subjects to Compare
- two after-school hangouts
- two people who are important to you
- family rituals from two different cultures

WRITING TOOLS
For prewriting, revision, and editing tools, visit the **Writing Center at ClassZone.com.**

KEY TRAITS

1. *IDEAS*
- Identifies the **subjects** being compared and contrasted
- Presents a **thesis statement** that identifies similarities or differences
- Supports key points with **examples**

2. *ORGANIZATION*
- Includes an **introduction** that holds the reader's attention
- Has a clear **organizational pattern**
- Uses **transitions** to show how ideas are related
- Sums up the key points in a **conclusion** that also explains why the subjects are important

3. *VOICE*
- Consistently uses language that is **appropriate** for the audience and purpose

4. *WORD CHOICE*
- Uses **precise words** to explain similarities and differences

5. *SENTENCE FLUENCY*
- Varies **sentence beginnings**

6. *CONVENTIONS*
- Uses **correct grammar, spelling, and punctuation**

Writing Workshop Resources

 RESOURCE MANAGER UNIT 3

Plan and Teach pp. 185–188
Prewriting–Editing pp. 189–193
Writing Rubric p. 194
Publishing with Technology p. 195
Writing Support p. 196*

STANDARDS LESSON FILE

Writing Lesson 29
Grammar Lessons 1, 2
Media Lessons 19, 22

 BEST PRACTICES TOOLKIT

Scaffolding Writing Instruction pp. 43–46*
Venn Diagram • Two-Column Chart • Y Chart • Writing Template: Compare and Contrast • Analysis Frames: Author's Craft, Character, Setting

TECHNOLOGY

Easy Planner DVD

Writing Center at **ClassZone.com**

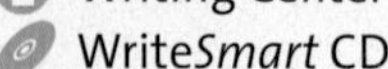

Write*Smart* CD

* Resources for Differentiation

t 1: Analyze a Student Model

Tyler Kurcewski
West Fairview
Intermediate School

Different Worlds, Similar Challenges

Nobody ever said life was easy. In fact, it's really about proving that you can face challenges. This is clear in the short stories "The Drummer Boy of Shiloh" by Ray Bradbury and "Hallucination" by Isaac Asimov. Although the main characters of these stories live on different planets during different centuries, both successfully face tremendous challenges.

The settings of these two stories are completely different. "The Drummer Boy of Shiloh" takes place during the Civil War. It begins with a description that sounds almost like a poem: "In the April night, more than once, blossoms fell from the orchard trees and lighted with rustling taps on the drumskin." The exact place is a field where a major battle will be fought the next day. "Hallucination," on the other hand, is set on Energy Planet—somewhere in the universe, sometime far in the future. To make things more like home, the Earth people have built a "transparent dome overhead. It was quite high, perhaps a thousand meters high, and it stretched in all directions farther than he could clearly see." Young Earthlings get specialized training on this planet.

Although the two main characters are in totally different places and times, they are similar in several key ways. Both are young teenagers. The drummer boy, Joby, has just turned 14, and we learn that he is too young to shave. We learn in the first sentence of "Hallucination" that Sam is 15. Both boys are also away from home: Joby has run away to join the army, and Sam is on Energy Planet because Central Computer sent him there. In addition, they both have difficult challenges to deal with. Joby may die in battle the next day. Sam must solve the mystery of the hallucinations that nobody wants to talk about.

KEY TRAITS IN ACTION

Appealing, straight-forward **introduction** states the **subjects** of the comparison. Highlighted **thesis statement** spells out the main similarities and differences.

Organizational pattern is logical, discussing setting in both stories and then moving on to characters in both stories. Quotations and other **examples** help the reader understand how the settings differ.

Teach

Part 1: Analyze a Student Model

Have students read the **Student Model** and **Key Traits in Action.** Then discuss the model, drawing attention to examples of each trait. To reinforce students' understanding of the key traits, use these activities:

- **Introduction** Ask students to identify the subjects to be compared and contrasted. According to the thesis statement, what are the specific similarities and differences between the subjects? ***Possible answer:*** *The subjects are the short stories "The Drummer Boy of Shiloh" and "Hallucination." According to the thesis statement, the characters in the stories are different because they "live on different planets during different centuries," but they are similar because they "both successfully face tremendous challenges."*
- **Organizational Pattern** To highlight the organizational pattern of the model, have students identify the topic sentence of each body paragraph. ***Answers:***
  - *—Paragraph 2: "The settings of these two stories are completely different." (line 6)*
  - *—Paragraph 3: "Although the two main characters are in totally different places and times, they are similar in several key ways." (lines 17–18)*
  - *—Paragraph 4: "The way these two characters handle their challenges is very different, though." (lines 27–28)*
  - *—Paragraph 5: "By the end of the stories, though, both Joby and Sam accept their challenges and face them with courage." (lines 34–35)*

DIFFERENTIATED INSTRUCTION

FOR ALL STUDENTS

Student Portfolios Encourage students to save copies of their writing so they can track their progress throughout the year.

For general guidelines on differentiating writing instruction, see

BEST PRACTICES TOOLKIT
Scaffolding Writing Instruction
pp. 43–46

FOR ENGLISH LEARNERS

Language: Skill Words Write these terms on the board and review them with students:

- *introduction:* the section that begins an essay, where the writer first describes the subject, or main idea, of the essay
- *thesis statement:* one or two sentences that tell the main idea of an essay
- *organizational pattern:* the way ideas and details are arranged or presented
- *precise words:* words that fit the purpose of an essay and tell readers exactly what the writer means. In the model, precise words help readers understand the main characters of the two stories (lines 28–33): "Joby seems weak and frightened. He's afraid to die and lies crying in the dark. . . . In sharp contrast, Sam is confident and determined. He ignores the assignment he's been sent to work on and investigates . . . on his own."

- **Transitions** Remind students that transitions are words and phrases that show how ideas are connected. Help students identify transitions in the model. Ask these questions:
  —How does the writer smoothly connect the first and second paragraphs on page 426? ***Possible answer:*** *In the first paragraph (lines 27–33), the writer discusses differences in the ways the characters react to challenges. The second paragraph (lines 34–47) begins, "By the end of the stories, though, both Joby and Sam. . . ." The words* though *and* both *signal that this paragraph will discuss similarities rather than differences. The writer goes on to describe ways in which both characters handle challenges with courage.*
  —What transitional words and phrases are used in lines 34–52? ***Possible answer:*** *"though" (line 34), "both" (line 34), "but" (line 38), "In the end" (line 45), "however" (line 50), "Both" (line 50)*
- **Precise Words** Explain that precise words help readers visualize images and actions and better understand a writer's ideas. Work with students to find more examples of precise words in lines 34–47. ***Possible answer:*** *"Calmly and bravely" (line 40), "insect-like creatures" (line 43), "cure the Commander and save the power station" (lines 46–47)*

For interactive student models, see

WriteSmart CD

Writing Center at **ClassZone.com**

The way these two characters handle their challenges is very different, though. Joby seems weak and frightened. He's afraid to die and lies crying in the dark. There's not much he can do except worry and wait for morning to come and the battle to begin. In sharp contrast, Sam is confident and determined. He ignores the assignment he's been sent to work on and investigates the hallucinations on his own.

By the end of the stories, though, both Joby and Sam accept their challenges and face them with courage. In "The Drummer Boy of Shiloh," the general gives Joby the confidence he needs, telling him he is "the heart of the army. . . . the general of the army when the General's left behind." The story ends before the battle begins, but we know that Joby's attitude has changed. Turning his drum to face the sky shows that he is no longer afraid of the sound of blossoms falling on it. Calmly and bravely, he has decided to march to war. In "Hallucination," Sam uses his intuition and almost superhuman intelligence to solve the mystery. He quickly learns how to communicate with the planet's insect-like creatures and realizes that "previous attempts at communication had failed because the people . . . had been frightened." In the end, he discovers how these beings create the hallucinations. Making this discovery helps to cure the Commander and save the power station.

The settings of the short stories "The Drummer Boy of Shiloh" and "Hallucination" span history and the universe. The main characters in the stories are very much alike, however. Both of them learn to face the challenges in their lives. Their courage inspires us and encourages us to face our own challenges.

A **transition** alerts the reader to an importa[nt] difference between t[he] characters.

Uses a variety of **sentence beginnings** [to] hold the reader's inte[rest].

Precise words are clea[r] and **appropriate** for th[e] writer's purpose and for his audience (his classmates and teach[er]).

Conclusion summariz[es] the main points. The highlighted phrase explains the importan[ce] of the stories.

2

DIFFERENTIATED INSTRUCTION

FOR ENGLISH LEARNERS

Comprehension: Transitions Have students study the chart of transitional words and phrases on page 430. Then use this activity to give them practice with transitions:

1. Show students pictures of two vehicles, such as a van and a pick-up truck.
2. Display sentences that compare and contrast the vehicles, and work with students to underline the transitions.

The van has many seats, but the truck has only two seats. (difference)

Both vehicles have four tires. (similarity)

The van has four doors. In contrast, the truck has only two doors. (difference)

A van is useful. It holds many people. The truck is also useful. However, the truck can carry more boxes and tools than people. (similarity, difference)

3. Hold up two new pictures. You might choose two buildings or two animals.
4. Repeat the exercise, this time asking students to provide the sentences using transitional words and phrases.
5. Use the copy master to provide students with further practice using transitions.

RESOURCE MANAGER—Copy Master
Writing Support p. 196

Part 2: Apply the Writing Process

PREWRITING

What Should I Do?	What Does It Look Like?
1. Analyze the prompt. Choose a prompt from page 424 and study it carefully. Draw a (circle) around the type of writing it asks you to do. Underline the purpose of your writing. If the prompt doesn't tell you who your audience is, assume that you are writing for your teacher and classmates.	***WRITING PROMPT*** Write an (essay) that compares or contrasts two selections that you have read this year. Concentrate on key aspects such as setting, people or characters, events, or the writer's style. Your essay should give your reader a new understanding of the selections. *I liked the stories about the drummer boy and the kid on the alien planet. I think my teacher and classmates would enjoy reading more about them, too.*
2. Note similarities and differences. Use a Venn diagram or a chart to keep track of comparisons and contrasts. **TIP If you have trouble thinking of interesting, important similarities and differences, choose two other subjects.**	*"Drummer Boy"*: • *set during the Civil War* • *Joby is scared.* *Both*: • *teenage boys* • *facing challenges* *"Hallucination"*: • *set in the future* • *Sam is confident.*
3. List your key points and find examples that support them. Write down the main similarities and differences between your subjects. Then look for facts, examples, and quotations to back up your ideas. If you use quotations, be sure to copy the words exactly.	***Key point:*** *Both characters meet their challenges.* ***Support:*** • *Joby bravely waits for battle. He knows he is "the heart of the army."* • *Sam figures out what the hallucinations are. He's really smart.*
4. Draft a thesis statement. Tell your reader which subjects you're comparing, and then briefly describe their main similarities and differences. You can change your thesis statement as you draft and revise.	*I am comparing "The Drummer Boy of Shiloh" by Ray Bradbury and "Hallucination" by Isaac Asimov. The stories seem totally different at first, but it turns out that both main characters have to face bad situations.*

FOR ENGLISH LEARNERS

Listing Key Points and Writing a Thesis Statement Give students these frames to help them identify the key points they want to make and draft a thesis statement:

- My subjects are ________ and ________.
- Key Point 1: My subjects are alike because both ________ and ________.
- Examples that support this point include ________.
- Key Point 2: My subjects are different in these ways: ________ and ________.
- Examples that support this point include ________.
- My thesis statement is: ________.

Also provide copies of graphic organizers that students can use to gather ideas and details.

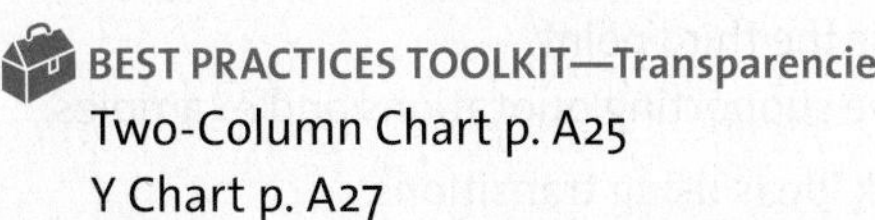

BEST PRACTICES TOOLKIT—Transparencies
Two-Column Chart p. A25
Y Chart p. A27

Practice and Apply

To support students during the writing process, use these copy masters:

RESOURCE MANAGER—Copy Masters
Prewriting–Editing pp. 189–193
Writing Rubric p. 194
Writing Support p. 196 *(for English learners)*

Part 2: Apply the Writing Process

PREWRITING

1. **Analyze the prompt.** Students who have selected the same prompt can meet in pairs or small groups to discuss their goals as they begin writing. Encourage them to share their topic ideas and help each other identify some of the details they might include in their essays. They should focus on ideas and details that best serve the purpose of the selected prompt.
2. **Note similarities and differences.** Have students continue working in pairs or small groups. Students can work together to use Venn Diagrams for generating and organizing ideas on their subjects. If students are having trouble coming up with enough information, point out the TIP in step 2.

   BEST PRACTICES TOOLKIT—Transparency
   Venn Diagram p. A26
3. **List your key points and find examples that support them.** Have students create a chart in which they organize their key ideas and any supporting facts, examples, and quotations they could potentially use. Once they have gathered all their information in the chart, they can choose a few of the strongest supporting examples for each point to use in their essays.
4. **Draft a thesis statement.** Ask each student to share a working thesis statement with a partner or small group. Students can help each other clarify what they want to say in their essays.

For interactive graphic organizers, see
WriteSmart CD
Writing Center at **ClassZone.com**

DRAFTING

1. **Organize your ideas.** Discuss advantages and challenges of each organizational pattern. For example, specific comparisons might become lost in a subject-by-subject organization, with each subject being discussed separately. In a point-by-point organization, it is easier to stay focused on similarities and differences. However, the writer must work hard to use transitions so that comparisons are clear. If students are having trouble deciding which type of organization to use, encourage them to read the TIP in step 1.
2. **Back up your key points.** Have students list statements about their subjects. Then encourage them to review each statement and think of different ways they can "show" readers what they mean with details and quotations.
3. **Use transitions to link ideas.** Remind students that transitional words are key to helping readers follow the main points of a comparison-contrast essay. Suggest that students practice writing sentences for their essays using transitional words and phrases from the chart on page 430.

For a comparison-contrast essay writing template, see

BEST PRACTICES TOOLKIT—Transparencies
Writing Template: Compare and Contrast pp. C16, C25, C26

Write*Smart* CD

Writing Center at **ClassZone.com**

DRAFTING

What Should I Do?	What Does It Look Like?
1. Organize your ideas. Here are two ways to organize your essay. The writer of the model used point-by-point organization. **Subject by subject**—Discuss all the points about one subject and then all the points about the other. **Point by point**—Discuss your key points one by one, showing how they relate to each subject. **TIP Try out each organization and use the one that works better for your essay.**	**SUBJECT-BY-SUBJECT ORGANIZATION** *Subject A: "Drummer Boy"* *Setting: U.S. during Civil War* *Main character: Joby, a frightened teen* *Challenge: to face a battle* *Subject B: "Hallucination"* *Setting: on Energy Planet in future* *Main character: Sam, a confident teen* *Challenge: to solve a mystery* **POINT-BY-POINT ORGANIZATION** *Point 1: Setting* *"Drummer Boy": U.S. during Civil War* *"Hallucination": Energy Planet, the future* *Point 2: Main Character* *"Drummer Boy": teen Joby at war, afraid* *"Hallucination": teen Sam away from Earth, confident* *Point 3: Challenge* *"Drummer Boy": a battle* *"Hallucination": a mystery*
2. Back up your key points. Instead of just telling readers "Sam is really smart," show them by giving details and quotations from the story.	*Sam uses his intuition and almost superhuman intelligence to solve the mystery.* — Key point *He quickly learns to communicate with the planet's insect-like creatures and realizes that "previous attempts at communication had failed because the people . . . had been frightened."* — Details and quotation
3. Use transitions to link ideas. Use words such as *both* and *similarly* to show how ideas are alike. Try *however, though,* or *on the other hand* to show differences. Placing some transitions at the beginning of your sentences will help give your writing variety. **See page 430:** Add Transitions	*The way these two characters handle their challenges is very different, though. Joby seems weak and frightened. He's afraid to die and lies crying in the dark. There's not much he can do except worry and wait for morning to come and the battle to begin. In sharp contrast, Sam is confident and determined.*

DIFFERENTIATED INSTRUCTION

FOR LESS–PROFICIENT WRITERS

Organizing Information Provide this outline and explain that it represents the organization of the **Student Model.** Encourage students to follow this outline as they plan and write their own comparison-contrast essays.

Introduction
- Introduce the subjects of the comparison.
- State clearly the main similarities and differences between the subjects.

Body Paragraphs—Point-by-Point
- Discuss the first point.
  —Give supporting quotations and examples.
  —Link ideas using transitions.
- Discuss the second point.
  —Give supporting quotations and examples.
  —Link ideas using transitions.
- Discuss the third point.
  —Give supporting quotations and examples.
  —Link ideas using transitions.

Conclusion
- Mention again the subjects of the essay.
- Summarize your main points.
- Include a final detail or idea that illustrates why you chose your subjects and what readers can learn from them.

REVISING AND EDITING

What Should I Do?	What Does It Look Like?
1. Create a thought-provoking introduction. • Reread the first sentence of your introduction. Ask yourself if it makes you want to read on. • If not, add a question, an interesting detail, or a surprising quotation.	*Nobody ever said life was easy. In fact, it's really about proving that you can face challenges. This is clear in* ~~*I am comparing*~~ *the short stories "The Drummer Boy of Shiloh" by Ray Bradbury and "Hallucination" by Isaac Asimov.*
2. Clarify your thesis. • [Bracket] the statement that explains the main similarities and differences of your subjects. • Revise it if necessary so that it clearly and concisely states the key points of your essay.	[~~*The stories seem totally different at first, but it turns out that both main characters have to face bad situations.*~~] *Although the main characters of these stories live on different planets during different centuries, both successfully face tremendous challenges.*
3. Be precise. • Underline any vague words, such as *nice, really, bad,* and *thing.* • Replace those words with specific terms that tell your reader exactly what you mean. **TIP** **Try replacing boring verbs (*ran* and *talk*) with precise ones (*fled* and *chatter*).**	*He ignores the* ~~*thing*~~ *assignment he's been sent to work on and* ~~*does the research*~~ *investigates the hallucinations on his own.*
4. Make your conclusion memorable. • Ask a peer reader to read your conclusion and tell you why you chose those two subjects to compare and contrast. • If the reason isn't clear, add details to make sure readers understand the subjects' importance to you. **See page 430:** Ask a Peer Reader	*The settings of the short stories "The Drummer Boy of Shiloh" and "Hallucination" span history and the universe. The main characters in the stories are very much alike, however. Both of them learn to face the challenges in their lives. Their courage inspires us and encourages us to face our own challenges.*

FOR ENGLISH LEARNERS

Creating an Introduction Have students use these prompts to help them create a solid introduction:

- The main idea of my essay is ________.
- I chose my subjects because ________.
- The first sentence of my introduction could be ________. To make it more interesting, I could add
  —a question such as ________
  —an interesting detail such as ________
  —a quotation like "________"

FOR ADVANCED LEARNERS/PRE–AP

Expand Analysis Ask students to explore literature selections in depth using an Analysis Frame for Author's Craft, Character, or Setting. Based on their focused analyses, students can generate ideas for more challenging thesis statements.

BEST PRACTICES TOOLKIT—Copy Masters
Analysis Frames p. D23; Author's Craft pp. D26, D27; Character pp. D28, D29; Setting pp. D32, D33

REVISING AND EDITING

1. **Create a thought-provoking introduction.** Suggest that students experiment with different types of introductions—one that incorporates a quotation, one that features a question, and one that makes use of an interesting detail. Then have them meet in pairs or small groups to figure out which one works best.
2. **Clarify your thesis.** Have students return to their thesis statement after they have drafted the body of their essay to make sure the essay they've written actually supports their statement about the main similarities and differences of their subjects. If it does not, students should decide if they need a revised thesis statement or more supporting information throughout the essay.
3. **Be precise.** Have students work in pairs or small groups to identify vague words in their essays. Before they begin, suggest they brainstorm a list of precise verbs and adjectives to serve as a model. They might consider verbs that describe the way a person moves across a room, or adjectives that describe foods they do or don't like.

   Point out the **TIP** provided with step 3. Tell students that they might need to review an essay more than once to notice all the places in which a precise word could improve a sentence.
4. **Make your conclusion memorable.** Encourage students to look back at their introductions to be sure their conclusions are focused and in agreement with their thesis statements. Students might experiment with different endings and present their peer reader with choices. For example, students can try moving sentences around or adding different kinds of details.

For interactive revision tools, see

- Write*Smart* CD
- Writing Center at **ClassZone.com**

Preparing to Publish

Support for meeting the goals in the writing rubric is supplied throughout the **Writing Workshop** on pages 424–429.

For Rubric Bank, see

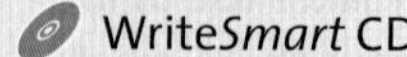

WriteSmart CD

Writing Center at **ClassZone.com**

Assess and Reteach

After reading and assessing students' comparison-contrast essays, you might use these lessons to reteach key skills:

STANDARDS LESSON FILE

Writing Lesson 29: Comparison-Contrast Essay

Grammar Lesson 1: Avoiding Sentence Fragments

Grammar Lesson 2: Avoiding Run-Ons

Preparing to Publish — Comparison-Contrast Essay

Apply the Rubric

A strong comparison-contrast essay . . .

- ☑ has an attention-getting introduction that names the subjects being compared or contrasted
- ☑ points out the main similarities and differences of the subjects in a thesis statement
- ☑ Supports key points with quotations and other examples
- ☑ uses transitions to print out important comparisons or contrasts
- ☑ is logically organized
- ☑ varies sentence beginnings
- ☑ uses precise words and language suited to the audience and purpose
- ☑ concludes by summarizing key points and telling why the subjects are important

Ask a Peer Reader

- What is the strongest and clearest point that I made?
- Do any points need more explanation? If so, which ones?
- Why do you think I chose these subjects?

Add Transitions

To Compare	To Contrast
also	although
by comparison	in contrast
in addition to	nevertheless
likewise	on the other hand
similarly	unlike

Check Your Grammar

- To correct a sentence fragment, add whatever the sentence is missing—a subject, a verb, or both.

  He discovers
  ^How these beings create the hallucinations.

See page R64: Correcting Fragments

- Add punctuation to separate run-ons into individual sentences.

  Joby seems weak and frightened. he's afraid to die and lies crying in the dark.

See pages R64–R65: Correcting Run-on Sentences

Writing Online

PUBLISHING OPTIONS
For publishing options, visit the **Writing Center** at **ClassZone.com.**

ASSESSMENT PREPARATION
For writing and grammar assessment practice, go to the **Assessment Center** at **ClassZone.com.**

Producing a Power Presentation

You can turn your essay into a power presentation. In other words, use a computer to create slides of the main points you made, and then present your work to an audience.

Planning the Presentation

1. **Focus on your most important ideas.** Use a software program to make a slide for your introduction and another for your conclusion. Then create a slide for each of the key points you made in your essay. Each slide should have a headline and two to four short bullet points.
2. **Decide how you want your presentation to look.** You can select a template of preset fonts and colors or choose your own. Make sure the type is easy to read, even from the back of the room. You can add graphics or animations to make your slides more appealing, but be sure that the main focus stays on the words.

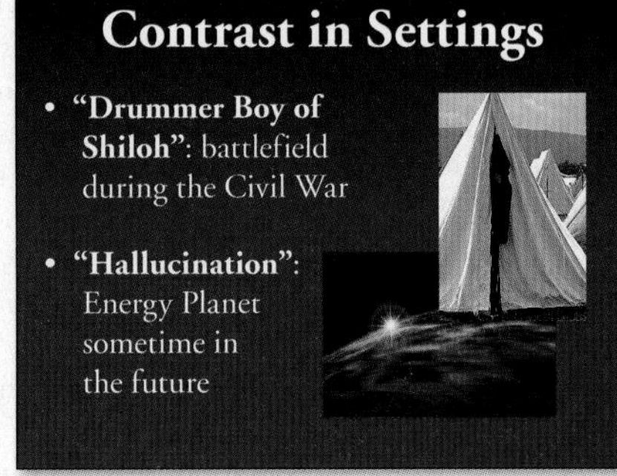

Contrast in Settings
• "Drummer Boy of Shiloh": battlefield during the Civil War
• "Hallucination": Energy Planet sometime in the future

3. **Try it out.** Work with the projection equipment until you're comfortable using it. Practice glancing at the slides and using the words like an outline to help you expand on your ideas.

Delivering the Presentation

1. **Make it lively and interesting.** Don't just read the words on your slides. Instead, add examples and explanations that will interest your audience and help them understand your ideas. Look at people in various parts of the room as you speak.
2. **Ask for feedback.** When you have finished, ask for feedback and constructive criticism. Think about what you might do differently for your next presentation.

PUBLISHING WITH TECHNOLOGY

Ask students to read this page to get an overview of how to produce a power presentation.

Before students begin working, review this rubric with them so that they understand their goals:

Rubric A strong power presentation

- includes a slide for the introduction and a slide for the conclusion
- includes a slide with a headline and two to four short bullet points for each key point
- uses type that is easy for an audience to read
- is lively and interesting
- goes beyond words on the page to include examples and illustrations
- is delivered by a presenter who speaks directly to audience members throughout the room as he or she speaks
- ends with a request for audience feedback

RESOURCE MANAGER—Copy Master
Publishing with Technology p. 195

STANDARDS LESSON FILE
Media Lesson 19: Analyzing Visuals
Media Lesson 22: Creating a Power Presentation

DIFFERENTIATED INSTRUCTION

FOR LESS–PROFICIENT WRITERS

Producing a Power Presentation Have students compare the sample slide on page 431 to lines 6–16 on page 425. Note that

- the text is condensed so that the key information can be presented visually
- pictures replace long descriptive passages
- bullets and different type styles make the slide easy to read

Direct students' attention to lines 17–26 on page 425. Work with them to adapt this information for another slide. Prompt them with questions such as

- What should the headline be?
- What key points should appear beneath the headline?
- In what way will text be presented so it is easy to read from a distance?
- What graphics or animations might make the slide more interesting?

Possible text for slide:
Similarities in Characters

- *young teenagers*
- *away from home*
- *face difficult challenges*

For more practice, ask students to adapt lines 27–33 on page 426 into a slide on their own.

CHECK READINESS

Read aloud the paragraph under **ASSESS** and stress to students that this is not the full Unit Test but a way for them to check their readiness for it. Then have students examine the skills listed under **REVIEW** and look back in the unit or in the **Student Resource Bank** for any they need to study.

READ THE SELECTIONS

Remind students to keep Unit Goals in mind as they read the passages, paying particular attention to

- setting
- mood
- imagery
- what they visualize as they read

To help students focus on **setting** while reading, encourage them to ask questions such as

- How would you describe the settings of "The Apprentice" and *Year of the Black Pony?* What do the two settings have in common? In what ways do they differ?
- What role does setting play in the two excerpts? In what ways do the settings affect the action of the stories and add to their drama?

ANSWER THE QUESTIONS

Direct students to pages R95–R101 of the Test-Taking Handbook to review test-taking strategies. Remind them not to choose the first alternative that seems to fit when answering a multiple-choice question. Instead, students should read through all the choices, eliminate any that are clearly wrong, and then choose the best answer—the one that is most accurate and complete.

Explain that an important part of successfully completing a test is budgeting time. Encourage students to look over the entire test and think about how much time they will need for each section. If they know from the start that a particular section will be challenging for them, they can budget more time for the difficult section and try to move more quickly through sections they feel more confident about.

Assessment Practice

Reading Comprehension

ASSESS

The practice test items on the next few pages match skills listed on the Unit Goals page (page 309) and addressed throughout this unit. Taking this practice test will help you assess your knowledge of these skills and determine your readiness for the Unit Test.

REVIEW

After you take the practice test, your teacher can help you identify any skills you need to review.

- Setting
- Mood
- Imagery
- Visualize
- Idioms
- Homographs
- Subject-Verb Agreement

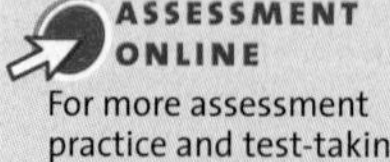

ASSESSMENT ONLINE

For more assessment practice and test-taking tips, go to the **Assessment Center** at **ClassZone.com.**

DIRECTIONS *Read these selections and answer the questions that follow.*

from The Apprentice

Dorothy Canfield Fisher

And now, this afternoon, when he was six months old, tall, rangy, power standing up far above her knee, nearly to her waist, she didn't know where he was. But of course he must be somewhere around. He always was. She composed her face to look natural and went downstairs to search the house He was probably asleep somewhere. She looked every room over carefully. mother was nowhere visible. It was safe to call him again, to give the specia piercing whistle which always brought him racing to her, the white-feather plume of his tail waving in elation that she wanted him.

But he did not answer. She stood still on the front porch to think.

Could he have gone up to their special place in the edge of the field whe the three young pines, their branches growing close to the ground, made a triangular, walled-in space, completely hidden from the world? Sometimes went up there with her. When she lay down on the dried grass to dream, h too lay down quietly, his head on his paws, his beautiful eyes fixed adoring on her. He entered into her every mood. If she wanted to be quiet, all right he did too.

It didn't seem as though he would have gone alone there. Still—She lope up the steep slope of the field rather fast, beginning to be anxious.

No, he was not there. She stood, irresolutely, in the roofless, green-walle triangular hide-out, wondering what to do next.

Then, before she knew what thought had come into her mind, its emotional impact knocked her down. At least her knees crumpled under h Last Wednesday the Wilsons had brought their sheep down to the home fa from the upper pasture! She herself had seen them on the way to school, an like an idiot had not thought of Rollie. She had seen them grazing on the river meadow.

She was off like a racer at the crack of the starting pistol, her long, strong legs stretched in great leaps, her pigtails flying. She took the short cut dowr the upper edge of the meadow, regardless of the brambles. Their thorn-spik wiry stems tore at her flesh, but she did not care. She welcomed the pain. It was something she was doing for Rollie, for her Rollie.

She was tearing through the pine woods now, rushing down the steep, stony path, tripping over roots, half-falling, catching herself just in time, nc slackening her speed. She burst out on the open knoll above the river mead calling wildly, "Rollie, here, Rollie, here, boy! here! here!" She tried to whis

DIFFERENTIATED INSTRUCTION

FOR ENGLISH LEARNERS

Assessment Practice: Work Backwards

[paired option] Prepare students for the assessment by having them "work backwards," reading the questions before reading the text passage. Have pairs follow these steps to learn unfamiliar words in the test directions and questions:

1. Find words you don't recognize and write each one on an index card.
2. Look up the meaning in a dictionary.
3. Write the meaning on the back of the card.
4. Use your word cards to teach and practice the vocabulary with your partner and another pair.

but she was crying too hard to pucker her lips. She had not, till then, known she was crying.

There was nobody to see or hear her. Twilight was falling over the bare knoll. The sunless evening wind slid down the mountain like an invisible river, engulfing her in cold. Her teeth began to chatter. "Here, Rollie, here, boy, here!" She strained her eyes to look down into the meadow to see if the sheep were there. She could not be sure. She stopped calling him as if he were a dog, and called out his name despairingly, as if he were her child, "Rollie! oh, *Rollie*, where are you!"

from Year of the Black Pony

Walt Morey

I was late. I took off from the house running fast as I could. I rounded the barn, crossed the pasture, and started up the long slope that led to the top of Christmas Ridge. I ran until my throat was dry and my heart felt like it was about to jump from my rib cage. Then the slope turned steep. I quit running and climbed the rest of the way.

The spine of Christmas Ridge is about fifty feet wide. It stretches for miles splitting the valley almost down the middle. There's an odd nest of big rocks up there about thirty feet high. I climbed to the topmost one and stretched out on my stomach. The valley rolled away beneath me, a spring-green carpet of new grass speckled with clumps of trees and brush. In the middle stood our typical homesteader's board-and-bat cabin, the two outbuildings, and the pattern of fences and gates.

My breathing gradually settled back to normal and my heart stopped pounding. I kept listening and looking. There was nothing. I was too late. I was about to get up and leave when I heard it. A faint rumble rode the morning silence like the roll of distant thunder. It swelled in volume. I got to my knees in excitement. My heart was hammering again.

They burst around a shoulder of the ridge a hundred yards away—fifteen or twenty horses running hard. They were Sam Fletcher's young stock that he let run loose on the open range. They followed the ridge every morning to feed in some distant part of the valley. At night a hired hand rode out and drove them home.

I had eyes for only one. The black pony in the lead. He ran like he loved being free. His head was up, sharp ears forward, black mane and tail flying in the wind. The sun made his black coat glisten like satin. The big muscles

ITEM ANALYSIS

COMPREHENSION AND WRITTEN RESPONSE	ITEMS	UNIT PAGES
Setting	1, 7, 8	310, 317, 333, 381
Mood	2, 4, 6, 9, 12, 17	312, 359
Imagery	5, 10, 13, 14	417
Visualize	3, 11, 14, 15, 16	333

VOCABULARY	ITEMS	UNIT PAGES
Idioms	1, 2, 3, 4	325
Homographs	5, 6, 7	356

WRITING AND GRAMMAR	ITEMS	UNIT PAGES
Subject-Verb Agreement	1, 2, 3, 4, 5, 6	373, 395

FOR LESS–PROFICIENT READERS

Assessment Support Consider these options for completing the **Assessment Practice:**

- Have students "work backwards," reviewing the questions before reading the passages.
- Select random questions in the assessment and have students demonstrate how and where to look for the answers.
- Ask students to locate unfamiliar vocabulary in the assessment. Elicit the meanings of these words from the class.
- Have students record useful test words and definitions in their journals for later reference.
- Read the selections or parts of them aloud to aid in student comprehension.

McDougal Littell Assessment System

After checking student readiness with this Assessment Practice, you may administer the complete Unit 3 Test in order to more thoroughly evaluate student mastery of unit goals.

ANSWERS

Comprehension

Model a thinking process for answering multiple-choice questions.

1. **D *is correct.*** *Details reveal a rural setting with fields, forests, and farms. We can eliminate* A *and* B *because the narrator never mentions neighbors, buildings, or businesses—details that would indicate a suburban or city environment.* C *is incorrect because details about pine trees, open meadows, and the cold do not fit with a tropical forest.*
2. **C *is correct.*** *The words* anxious *and* irresolutely *create tension because they reveal that the narrator is nervous and unsure of what to do next.* A *and* B *are incorrect because when they occur the girl is still unsure Rollie is missing and does not yet feel nervous.* D *is incorrect because the details are part of her memory of a time when she was not feeling tense.*
3. **C *is correct.*** *Her panic is causing her to run frantically, without regard for her own safety.* A, B, *and* D *can be eliminated because she is not actually running at the moments they occur.*
4. **D *is correct.*** *Details show the tender, or loving, relationship between Rollie and the narrator.* A *is incorrect because there is nothing eerie about the special place—the narrator feels completely comfortable there.* B *is incorrect because details focus on the connection between Rollie and the narrator, not on a general feeling of peacefulness.* C *is incorrect because the details do not indicate nervousness.*
5. **C *is correct.*** *The narrator feels the thorny stems tearing at her skin.* A *can be eliminated because it is visual and does not include words related to touch.* B *is incorrect because this image appeals to a reader's sense of hearing, not touch.* D *is incorrect because it does not relate to the sense of touch.*
6. **B *is correct.*** *The narrator is alone in the darkening knoll, growing ever more fearful that she will not find Rollie.* A *and* D *are incorrect because she feels the opposite of calm and lighthearted.* C *is incorrect because the narrator is still frantically searching for Rollie and has no time to feel weary.*

across shoulders and legs rippled like light flashes on water. They pounded past right under the rock where I crouched. I watched until they were out of sight. The whole thing took maybe two minutes.

Every Saturday since the winter weather had broken I'd climbed up here to watch that pony pass. The sight of him did something to me I've never quite been able to explain. He was more than tremendous strength and speed and beauty of motion. He set me dreaming.

Comprehension

DIRECTIONS *Answer these questions about the excerpt from "The Apprentice."*

1. From the descriptive details used in this excerpt, you can tell that the story's setting is a
   - **A** landscaped suburban community with grassy yards
   - **B** large city park with trees and meadows
   - **C** tropical forest with dense undergrowth
   - **D** mountainous area of fields, forests, and farms
2. Which phrases contribute to the tense mood in the excerpt?
   - **A** "probably asleep somewhere"; "completely hidden from the world"
   - **B** "safe to call him"; "special piercing whistle"
   - **C** "beginning to be anxious"; "She stood, irresolutely"
   - **D** "on the way to school"; "grazing on the river"
3. Which phrase helps you visualize the girl running frantically in search of Rollie?
   - **A** "the special piercing whistle" (lines 6–7)
   - **B** "wondering what to do next" (line 20)
   - **C** "tripping over roots, half-falling" (line 33)
   - **D** "strained her eyes to look down" (line 41)
4. Reread lines 10–16. The description of the special place where the girl and Rollie like to go helps create a mood of
   - **A** eeriness
   - **B** peacefulness
   - **C** nervousness
   - **D** tenderness
5. Which image appeals to the reader's sense of touch?
   - **A** "steep slope of the field" (line 18)
   - **B** "crack of the starting pistol" (line 27)
   - **C** "thorn-spiked wiry stems" (lines 29–30)
   - **D** "the open knoll" (line 34)
6. The description of the setting in lines 38–42 creates a mood that is
   - **A** calm
   - **B** fearful
   - **C** weary
   - **D** lighthearted

DIRECTIONS *Answer these questions about the excerpt from* Year of the Black Pony.

7. The setting for this excerpt is
   - **A** the top of Christmas Ridge
   - **B** a valley far from Christmas Ridge
   - **C** a pasture near Christmas Ridge
   - **D** the barn at the foot of Christmas Ridge

434

7. **A *is correct.*** *The narrator describes climbing to the top of the ridge. We can eliminate* B *because the narrator looks down on the valley beneath him from Christmas Ridge;* C *and* D *are incorrect because the main action does not take place in a pasture or in a barn.*
8. **D *is correct.*** *The narrator describes the "spring-green carpet of new grass" (lines 9–10) and mentions that the horses run loose "every morning" (line 20).* A, B, *and* C *are incorrect because these details eliminate fall, summer, winter, and any time of day except morning.*
9. **B *is correct.*** *Readers are in suspense wondering where the narrator is going and why he needs to run. We can eliminate* A *because the narrator is not being playful but is trying urgently to get somewhere.* C *and* D *are incorrect because the details provided do not indicate despair or confidence.*

8. The event described in the excerpt takes place on a
A fall afternoon
B summer night
C winter evening
D spring morning

9. In line 1, the narrator says, "I was late. I took off from the house running fast as I could." These statements create a mood of
A playfulness
B suspense
C despair
D confidence

10. The imagery in lines 15–17 appeals to the reader's sense of
A hearing
B sight
C smell
D taste

11. Which description helps you visualize the black pony running with the herd?
A "Sam Fletcher's young stock" (line 19)
B "mane and tail flying in the wind" (lines 24–25)
C "big muscles across shoulders and legs" (lines 25–26)
D "more than tremendous strength" (line 31)

12. The words *burst, flashes,* and *pounded* are used in the excerpt to help create feelings of
A confusion
B excitement
C panic
D terror

DIRECTIONS *Answer these questions about both selections.*

13. Imagery in both excerpts helps you visualize
A untamed animals
B mysterious characters
C hilly, countryside settings
D destructive forces in nature

14. The authors help you picture the characters mainly through
A detailed descriptions of their actions
B conversations between characters
C words that name the characters' feelings
D the animals' awareness of the characters

Written Response

SHORT RESPONSE *Write two or three sentences to answer these questions.*

15. Identify two sensory details in lines 6–12 in the excerpt from *Year of the Black Pony* that help you visualize the setting. To which of your senses do they appeal?

16. Which sensory details in the excerpt help you visualize Rollie's appearance in "The Apprentice"? Give two quotations from the excerpt to support your answer.

EXTENDED RESPONSE *Write a paragraph to answer this question.*

17. Describe how the mood of the excerpt from "The Apprentice" changes as the girl looks for Rollie.

GO ON

10. A *is correct.* *A "rumble . . . like the roll of distant thunder" appeals to the reader's sense of hearing.* B, C, *and* D *are incorrect because we cannot see, smell, or taste a rumble.*

11. B *is correct.* *The image of the flying mane and tail helps readers see the horse running. We can eliminate* A *because it refers to the horses as a group.* C *and* D *are incorrect because they do not specifically describe the look of the pony running with the herd.*

12. B *is correct.* *These words reveal the excitement the narrator feels as he watches the herd running. Concrete details describing the scene give no indication of confusion, panic, or terror, making* A, C, *and* D *incorrect.*

13. C *is correct.* *In both excerpts, characters walk up steep slopes in country settings.* A *is incorrect because the first excerpt is about a family pet and not an untamed animal. Neither story includes images of mysterious characters, as in* B, *or destructive natural forces, as in* D.

14. A *is correct.* *Both excerpts focus primarily on the narrators' actions.* B *is incorrect because neither narrator talks to other characters.* C *is incorrect because there are few words naming the characters' feelings, and such words would not be very helpful for visualizing.* D *can be eliminated because neither excerpt gives the animals' point of view.*

Written Response

Possible short responses:

15. *Sensory details in lines 6–12 include Christmas Ridge "splitting the valley almost down the middle" (line 7) and the valley as "a spring-green carpet of new grass speckled with clumps of trees and brush" (lines 9–10). These details appeal to readers' sense of sight.*

16. *Sensory details that help readers visualize Rollie include those describing his size—"tall, rangy, powerful, standing up far above her knee, nearly to her waist" (lines 1–2)—and those describing his wagging tail—"the white-feathered plume . . . waving in elation" (lines 7–8).*

Possible extended response:

17. *The response should describe the narrator's growing feelings of concern, her sense of panic, and finally, her sadness and despair. At first she says "But of course he must be somewhere around" (line 3) as she looks in every room and whistles for him. She wonders if he is in their special place, but she doesn't think he would go there alone. At that point, "She [lopes] up the steep slope of the field rather fast, beginning to be anxious" (lines 17–18) and "[stands], irresolutely, . . . wondering what to do next" (lines 19–20). The thought that he might have run away, following sheep, causes her knees to crumple under her (line 22) and she "[is] off like a racer" (line 27). She takes a shortcut even though brambles scratch her legs. The narrator frantically calls out Rollie's name and tries to whistle but realizes "she [is] crying too hard to pucker her lips" (line 36). Finally, as daylight slips away, she feels despair and calls out to Rollie in desperation (lines 42–44).*

ANSWERS

Vocabulary

1. **D *is correct.*** *The narrator is searching each room for her dog. She does not need to try to remember each room, as in* A*; fail to notice each room, as in* B*; or describe each room, as in* C.
2. **C *is correct.*** *The rest of the sentence, which tells of the narrator "running fast as I could," indicates that* took off *means "moved quickly." The context does not support the meaning "subtracted from," "became popular," or "imitated humorously," making* A, B, *and* D *incorrect.*
3. **D *is correct.*** *A hired hand is someone who is paid to "lend a hand," or work, for someone else. A family member would not be hired, making* A *incorrect. Since the hired hand rides into the valley, he or she must be a person, eliminating* B. *A manager would be less likely to perform this task than a laborer, eliminating* C.
4. **B *is correct.*** *The context of the paragraph supports the idea that the narrator is especially interested in one horse. We can eliminate* A *and* C *because there is no evidence that the narrator is planning to buy a horse or needs glasses.* D *is incorrect because it does not make sense with the next sentence, "The black pony in the lead."*
5. **B *is correct.*** *In both instances,* tearing *refers to moving quickly.* A *and* C *are incorrect because they both refer to a ripping apart of two things. We can eliminate* D *because it refers to tears formed in the eyes, as in crying.*
6. **D *is correct.*** *In both instances,* steep *is used to describe a sharp slope.* A *is incorrect because it refers to something that is extremely difficult.* B *is incorrect because it uses* steep *to describe an unreasonably high price.* C *can be eliminated because it refers to soaking a teabag in water to release its flavors.*
7. **C *is correct.*** *Both sentences describe a current of outdoor air.* A *is incorrect because it refers to walking a curving path.* B *is incorrect because it uses* wind *to mean "breath."* D *is incorrect because in this context* wind *is breath that is used to make sounds on instruments with mouthpieces.*

Vocabulary

DIRECTIONS *Use context clues and your knowledge of idioms to answer the following questions.*

1. In line 5 of "The Apprentice," the girl "looked every room over carefully." The idiom *looked over* means
   A tried to remember
   B failed to notice
   C described
   D examined
2. In line 1 of *Year of the Black Pony,* the idiom *took off* means
   A subtracted from
   B became popular
   C moved quickly
   D imitated humorously
3. In line 21 of *Year of the Black Pony,* the idiom *hired hand* refers to a
   A family member
   B young horse
   C manager
   D paid laborer
4. In line 23 of *Year of the Black Pony,* the narrator says, "I had eyes for only one." The idiom *had eyes for* means that the narrator
   A could afford to buy just one horse
   B was interested in one particular horse
   C needed glasses to see the herd
   D watched the horses every day

DIRECTIONS *Use context clues and your knowledge of homographs to answer the following questions.*

> She was tearing though the pine woods nov rushing down the steep, stony path, trippin over roots, half-falling, catching herself just in time, not slackening her speed.

5. Which sentence uses *tearing* as it is used in line 32 of "The Apprentice"?
   A Jake began tearing the wrapping paper from his birthday gift.
   B Nora was tearing around her room in a great hurry.
   C Jealousy was tearing their friendship apart.
   D Madison blinked her eyes to stop them from tearing.
6. Which sentence uses *steep* as it is used in li 32 of "The Apprentice"?
   A Raising a child is a steep undertaking.
   B The price of those sneakers seems steep.
   C Steep the tea bag in boiling water.
   D The steep cliffs were impossible to clim

> The sunless evening wind slid down the mountain like an invisible river, engulfing her in cold.

7. Which sentence uses *wind* as it is used in l 39 of "The Apprentice"?
   A She had to wind a path through the de forest.
   B The plunge into icy water knocked the wind out of him.
   C As he stepped outside, the gentle wind lingered on his face.
   D Trumpets and saxophones are wind instruments.

436

DIFFERENTIATED INSTRUCTION

FOR ENGLISH LEARNERS

Review Academic Vocabulary Make sure students understand these terms before they work on items 1–7:

- An *idiom* is an expression that means something different from what the words literally say. Examples include
  —*break a leg* ("I wish you good luck")
  —*wild goose chase* ("a journey or effort that is useless")
  —*cut to the chase* ("get to the main point of what you are saying")
- *Homographs* are words that have the same spellings but different meanings and sometimes different pronunciations. Examples include
  —*well* ("in good health" or "a deep hole in the earth from which water is drawn")
  —*bow* ("to bend forward" or "a type of knot")
  —*project* ("a task" or "to throw forward")

Writing & Grammar

DIRECTIONS *Read the passage and answer the questions that follow.*

(1) Ancient Egyptians regarded the cat as a sacred animal. (2) Cats was the protectors of grain, killing any rats or other animals that might eat this staple of the Egyptian diet. (3) Anyone who either purposely or accidentally killed a cat were put to death. (4) Egyptians so revered the animal that many Egyptian goddesses took the form of a cat. (5) Mafdet, Sekhmet, and Bastet is examples of ancient Egyptian cat goddesses. (6) Neither Mafdet nor Sekhmet were quite as celebrated as Bastet, though. (7) Beauty, fertility, and motherhood was three of the qualities for which Egyptians worshipped Bastet. (8) In the city of Bubastis, Egyptians would hold a yearly festival to celebrate her. (9) There and in Memphis, large cemeteries was devoted to the burial of mummified cats.

1. To maintain subject-verb agreement in sentence 2, change the underlined verb to
   A were
   B has been
   C am
   D is

2. To maintain subject-verb agreement in sentence 3, change the underlined verb to
   A are
   B was
   C have been
   D am

3. To maintain subject-verb agreement in sentence 5, change the underlined verb to
   A was
   B am
   C are
   D has been

4. To maintain subject-verb agreement in sentence 6, change the underlined verb to
   A was
   B am
   C are
   D have been

5. To maintain subject-verb agreement in sentence 7, change the underlined verb to
   A were
   B is
   C has been
   D am

6. To maintain subject-verb agreement in sentence 9, change the underlined verb to
   A am
   B is
   C has been
   D were

STOP

437

ANSWERS

Writing & Grammar

1. **A** ***is correct.*** Cats *is a plural subject and must have a plural verb, and the action is in the past tense.* B *is incorrect because it is present perfect tense—implying an action that is ongoing.* C *and* D *are incorrect because they are both present-tense forms of* to be *that agree with singular subjects.*
2. **B** ***is correct.*** Anyone *is a singular indefinite pronoun and so must have a singular verb.* A, C, *and* D *are incorrect because they are all present tenses, and the action is in the past tense.*
3. **C** ***is correct.*** *The compound subject of this sentence needs a plural, present-tense form of* to be. A *is incorrect because it is singular and past tense.* B *and* D *are incorrect because they both agree with singular subjects.*
4. **A** ***is correct.*** *Use of* neither *and* nor *in the subject means that the verb must be singular. The verb must also be past tense. We can eliminate* B *because it needs a first-person subject.* C *is incorrect because it is a present-tense verb.* D *is incorrect because it is a present perfect verb.*
5. **A** ***is correct.*** *The verb must agree in number with the compound subject, and it must be past tense. The verb cannot be singular and present tense, as in* B, *or present perfect, as in* C. *We can eliminate* D *because it is in the present tense and needs a first-person subject.*
6. **D** ***is correct.*** *The verb must be past tense and must agree with a plural subject. We can eliminate* A *because the sentence does not have a first-person subject.* B *is incorrect because it is singular and in the present tense.* C *is incorrect because it is the present perfect tense.*

DIFFERENTIATED INSTRUCTION

FOR ENGLISH LEARNERS

Assessment Support: Subject-Verb Agreement Items 1–6 involve forms of the verb *to be,* some of which use the helping verb *to have.* Review with students the forms of these verbs.

Subject	Present Tense	Past Tense
I, we	have	had
you	have	had
he, she, it	has	had
they	have	had

Subject	Present Tense	Past Tense
I	am	was
you	are	were
he, she, it	is	was
we	are	were
you (plural)	are	were
they	are	were

INTRODUCE *MORE GREAT READS*

In Unit 3, students have discussed a number of big questions. Invite students to tell which question they found most intriguing and why. Then focus attention on the three questions that appear on this page. Discuss the recommended books and their summaries, pointing out how each book connects to the related question. Encourage students to choose one or more of these "great reads" to read independently.

ClassZone.com

To find additional books that match students' interests and ability levels, visit the Literature Center at **ClassZone.com.**

Ideas for Independent Reading

Which questions from Unit 3 made an impression on you? Continue exploring them with these books.

How do you find your purpose?

The Boxer
by Kathleen Karr

In 1880s New York, 15-year-old Johnny is the one who has to work to feed his family. One night he sees a sign promising five dollars to anyone willing to fight, and suddenly he's a boxer. Will he win enough to get his family out of the tenements?

Full Tilt
by Neal Shusterman

Focused, steady Blake has had one purpose his whole life: to keep his impulsive brother Quinn out of trouble. When Quinn steals Blake's ticket for a mysterious carnival, Blake goes to save his brother—again. But maybe Blake is the one who needs help.

Olive's Ocean
by Kevin Henkes

Soon after Olive's death, Martha is given a page f Olive's journal. The two were never friends, but w Martha realizes they had in common, she begins t life differently. She spen the summer at the ocean trying to fulfill Olive's dre

What is the role of a witness?

Run, Boy, Run
by Uri Orlev

Srulik is only eight when he manages to escape from the Nazi-controlled ghetto into the Polish countryside. His father tells him he must forget who he is and do anything necessary to fit in and survive. But forgetting comes at a cost.

Iqbal
by Francesco D'Adamo

Everything changes at the carpet factory when 13-year-old Iqbal is chained to a loom next to Fatima. Iqbal tells the children their owner will never release them, but he promises to escape. If Iqbal does get free, should he try to help his friends and risk recapture?

Fish
by L. S. Matthews

Tiger's family moved fror their home country to a drought-stricken village t a clinic. They stay until th civil war forces them to l but the borders have clos and only a treacherous tr over the mountains will b them to safety.

What gifts does the earth provide?

Four Wings and a Prayer
by Sue Halpern

Every fall, millions of butterflies form an orange and black wave that rolls down from Canada or New York all the way to Mexico. Every spring a new generation of butterflies returns to their parents' homes. How do the butterflies know where to go?

Saving the Planet and Stuff
by Gail Gauthier

As an intern at an environmental magazine in Vermont, Michael must live without a car, TV, or air conditioning. He thinks about quitting, but instead he stays and learns about business, composting, and himself.

Tofu and T. rex
by Greg Leitich Smith

Freddie was protesting the treatment of her new school's mascot, a live bul when the football field caught fire. She's been se back to Chicago to live wit her cousin and grandfathe Can a vegetarian survive l with two meat-eaters?

438 UNIT 3: SETTING AND MOOD

UNIT 4

A World of Meaning

THEME AND SYMBOL

- In Fiction
- In Poetry
- In Drama
- In Media

439

About the Art The painting on the left, *The Moon and the Abandoned Old Woman* by Tsukioka Yoshitoshi, illustrates "The Wise Old Woman," a Japanese folk tale retold by Yoshiko Uchida. See page 468 of the teacher's edition for more information.

For help in planning this unit, see

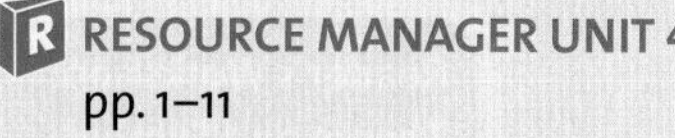
RESOURCE MANAGER UNIT 4 pp. 1–11

INTRODUCE THE UNIT

People around the world share many of the same dreams, beliefs, and fears. They imagine the future and hope for positive change. They worry about their relationships, families, and careers, and about the many forces in the world that are beyond their control. They are torn between the desire to help others and their selfish or fearful instincts. All people seek meaning in the actions and choices of others, in the given situations of the world, and in their own lives. These are universal **themes** in the human experience, and they are at the center of many stories, poems, and plays. An entire world of meaning awaits readers who explore these themes. Invite students to think about these ideas as they discuss the pictures on this page. To spark a discussion, ask

- What is happening in the painting and the photograph?
- What meaning can you find in each image?
- What do mountains usually represent? What do they mean in these pictures?

Discuss how literature can help students gain insight into life. In this unit, students will learn how writers from different cultural backgrounds use **symbols** and other literary elements to convey **theme** in various genres.

UNIT 4

Skills Trace

SKILLS STRAND	**Reader's Workshop: Theme and Symbol** pp. 442–447	**Gil's Furniture Bought & Sold** pp. 448–453 Anecdote *Level: Easy*	**Pandora's Box** pp. 454–461 Greek Myth *Level: Challenging*	**The Old Grandfather and His Little Grandson/ The Wise Old Woman** pp. 462–475 Russian Folk Tale/ Japanese Folk Tale *Level: Easy*	**My Mother Pieced Quilts/quilting** pp. 476–483 Poems *Level: Average*
Literary Analysis	Theme and Symbol pp. 442–447	Symbol pp. 449, 450, 452	Theme pp. 455, 458, 459, 460	Universal Theme pp. 463, 464, 466, 468, 471, 472, 473	Symbol in Poetry pp. 477, 478, 480, 481, 482
Reading and Informational Texts	Analyze the Literature pp. 443, 445–447	Make Inferences pp. 449, 450, 452	Strategies for Reading a Myth pp. 455, 456, 458, 459, 460	Set a Purpose for Reading pp. 463, 473 Compare Universal Themes p. 473	Draw Conclusions pp. 477, 478, 480, 481, 482
Vocabulary	Academic Vocabulary pp. 442, 444		Word Acquisition pp. 455, T455, 461 Context Clues p. T455 Reference Aids p. 461	Word Acquisition pp. 463, T463, 474 Word Maps p. T463 Suffixes (*-ly*) p. 474	
Writing, Grammar, and Style		Subject-Verb Agreement Using Prepositional Phrases p. 453		Write for Assessment p. 475	Active and Passive Voice p. 483
Speaking, Listening, Viewing, and Media	Discuss pp. 442–444	Discuss pp. 448, T450–T451, 452 Analyze Visuals p. 450	Discuss pp. 454, T456–T459, 460 Analyze Visuals p. 456	Discuss pp. 462, T464–T472, 473 Analyze Visuals pp. 464, 466, 468, 470	Discuss pp. 476, T478–T481, 482 Analyze Visuals pp. 478, 481

Assessment-Based Planning: Skills in red are assessed on the Unit 4 Test. **T** = Teacher's Edition page

Linked selections			
The Diary of Anne Frank pp. 484–543 Drama *Level: Average*	**Beyond *The Diary of Anne Frank*** pp. 544–553 Newspaper Article, Interview *Level: Average*	**Media Study:** *from* **Anne Frank Remembered** pp. 554–557 Film Clips	**Writing Workshop: Short Story** pp. 558–565
Theme pp. 485, T488, T491, T495, T496, T499, T501, T504, T506, T508, T509, T512, T513, T516, T517, T518, T519, 521, T525, T526, T527, T530, T531, T532, T534, T535, T537, T538, T539, T540, 542	Form (Interview) pp. 547, 553		
Story Mapping pp. 485, T486, T490, T493, T496, T501, T504, T507, T509, T517, T518, 521, T522, T526, T528, T534, T536, T537, T538, T539, T540, 542 Read a Diary Entry p. 520	Synthesize pp. 544, 545, 546, 548, 549, 550, 551, 552, 553 Make a Generalization p. 553		Analyze a Short Story pp. 559–560, 564
Word Acquisition pp. 485, T485 Context Clues p. T485		Academic Vocabulary (Film) p. 555	
Capitalization p. 543			Write a Short Story pp. 558–564 Questions for Developing a Story p. 564 Verb Tenses p. 564
Discuss pp. 484, T486–T519, 521, T522–T541, 542 Blocking p. T505 Costume Design p. T523 Analyze Visuals pp. T487, T501, T505, T511, T514, T527, T533, T541	Discuss pp. 544, T545–T552, 553	Discuss pp. 554, 557 Analyze Elements of a Documentary pp. 555–556 Strategies for Viewing a Documentary p. 555 Create a Visual Timeline p. 557	Discuss pp. 558–560 Produce a Video p. 565

Skills Assessed on the Unit 4 Test:

Literary Analysis
- Identify and interpret symbol
- Identify and analyze theme

Reading and Informational Texts
- Make inferences
- Draw conclusions

Vocabulary
- Use a thesaurus to find synonyms and use them correctly in sentences
- Use knowledge of suffixes to determine the meanings of words

Writing, Grammar, and Style
- Write a short story
- Capitalize correctly (languages, countries and nationalities, ethnicities, political parties, religions)
- Use active voice
- Additional writing and grammar skills

For additional lesson planning help, see **Easy Planner DVD.**

OBJECTIVES

- establish prior knowledge about **theme**
- discuss how literature can teach readers important lessons about life

What are life's hidden MESSAGES?

Discuss with students the insights that literature can give them about their own lives. Ask them why they think certain themes—for example, friendship, work, freedom, and family—are universal. Have they ever experienced the same kinds of changes, or learned the same lessons, as characters in stories?

ACTIVITY Ask students to jot down some notes in answer to each question. Then have students meet in small groups to discuss their insights. If any two students chose the same movie, or if students are familiar with each other's choices, have them brainstorm other possible themes. Point out that one story or movie can have many themes, and that each reader or viewer may notice and respond to different themes.

CHECK UNDERSTANDING Have students summarize what they have learned about **theme.**

UNIT 4 ***Share What You Know***

What are life's hidden MESSAGES

What's the best story you've ever read? Chances are you enjoye the story not just for its characters or plot but for its **theme,** or message about life and human nature. All great stories have a them whether it's about the value of friendship, the bonds of a family love, or the triumph of good over evil. A story's characters grow an change because of what they learn through their experiences. As the characters learn these life lessons, you as a reader grow, too.

ACTIVITY You may not have given it much thought, but your favor movies have probably offered you valuable messages. Recall a mov that you love, and then answer these questions to help you ident its theme.

- What lessons, if any, do the characters learn?
- If there is a battle or struggle, who wins and who loses? Why?
- What did you learn from this movie that you can apply to your own life?

440

Unit Resources

- RESOURCE MANAGER UNIT 4
- BEST PRACTICES TOOLKIT
- STANDARDS LESSON FILE
- Easy Planner DVD
- Write*Smart* CD
- ClassZone.com
- Audio Anthology CD
- Multi-Language Academic Vocabulary Online
- eEdition CD & Online
- McDougal Littell Assessment System
- Test Generator CD
- Media*Smart* DVD

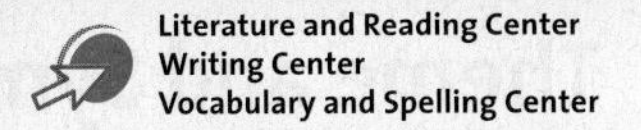

Literature and Reading Center
Writing Center
Vocabulary and Spelling Center

Preview Unit Goals

LITERARY ANALYSIS	• Identify and interpret symbols in poetry • Identify and analyze theme • Identify, analyze, and compare universal themes • Use a story map to analyze plot development
READING	• Make inferences and draw conclusions • Synthesize information and make generalizations • Set a purpose for reading
WRITING AND GRAMMAR	• Write a short story • Use active voice • Capitalize proper names correctly
SPEAKING, LISTENING, AND VIEWING	• Identify and analyze the elements of a documentary • Compare and contrast information and events in print and nonprint sources • Produce a video
VOCABULARY	• Use reference aids to find synonyms • Use knowledge of root words and affixes to determine meanings of words
ACADEMIC VOCABULARY	• symbol • theme • universal theme • synthesize

DIFFERENTIATED INSTRUCTION

FOR ENGLISH LEARNERS

Academic Vocabulary [small-group option] Use the Academic Vocabulary copy master to introduce these terms that students will use throughout the unit: *symbol, theme, universal theme, synthesize.*

- Have students work in groups to discuss the definitions and complete the sentences.
- Allow students to work individually or in groups to complete Part B.

Additional Academic Vocabulary [paired option] Use the second copy master to teach the terms *inference, conclusion, generalization, documentary, synonym,* and *affix.* Read each term aloud and discuss the examples. Then have pairs fill in the missing words of the definitions. Challenge them to brainstorm additional examples. Have students complete Part B individually or with a partner.

RESOURCE MANAGER—Copy Masters
Academic Vocabulary p. 9
Additional Academic Vocabulary p. 10

Preview Unit Goals

This page provides an overview of the skills and strategies covered in Unit 4. Each skill strand is a different color. Remind students that throughout the unit, this color coding lets them know what kinds of skills they are studying. As they read this page, encourage students to think about each skill or strategy and how well they are able to use it.

Suggest that students copy the Academic Vocabulary terms in their journals and define them in their own words as they read the unit. Encourage students to use these terms as they discuss and write about the selections.

ADDITIONAL UNIT GOALS

These skills will be taught in this unit but are not the major focus of the unit:

Literary Analysis
- Use story elements to identify theme
- Identify parallel episodes
- Identify internal and external conflicts
- Identify subplot
- Identify climax and resolution
- Identify and analyze flashback
- Study a variety of genres: anecdote, Greek myth, Russian folk tale, Japanese folk tale, play, poetry, diary entry, interview, newspaper article

Reading
- Develop strategies for reading myths

Writing and Grammar
- Maintain subject-verb agreement when using prepositional phrases

Speaking, Listening, and Viewing
- Interpret information presented in a non-print source
- Create a visual timeline

Vocabulary
- Use synonyms of words in sentences

Focus and Motivate

OBJECTIVES

- identify and interpret symbol
- use story elements to identify theme
- identify and analyze theme

Teach

Part 1: What's the Big Idea?

Universal Theme Explain that universal themes are found not only in literature but also in fine arts and performing arts. Help students think of examples of themes in contemporary music, movies, paintings, or other art forms. Discuss which themes are universal.

Symbol Tell students that to identify symbols in a story, they should look for people, places, activities, or objects about which the main character has strong feelings. A story's narrator may also give clues to symbols.

Have students brainstorm a list of stories they know. List these in a chart. Then ask students to identify symbols in the stories and explain what the symbols represent.

Story	Symbol	What Symbol Represents
"Clean Sweep"	Mrs. Leonardo's book	connection to family and past

CHECK UNDERSTANDING Have students identify symbols they encounter in their daily lives, such as flags, a peace symbol, and so on.

 BEST PRACTICES TOOLKIT—Copy Masters

Analysis Frame: Theme pp. D23, D34, D35

UNIT 4

Reader's Workshop

Theme and Symbol

What makes a story memorable? Long after you've forgotten the names of the characters and the events of the plot, you'll likely remember the theme—the big idea at the heart of the story. A **theme** is a message about life or human nature that a writer wants you to understand. In this unit, you'll discover that themes in literature can give you insights into events, issues, and relationships in your life.

Part 1: What's the Big Idea?

Friendship, war, and family are subjects that people of all ages and in all parts o the world think about. Writers—past and present—have considered these subj too, exploring them in stories, poems, and plays. Some writers communicate unique themes, messages that are specific to a particular time, place, or situatic Others express **universal themes**—big ideas that show up again and again in literature of all time periods and cultures. "Friends help each other through tou times" and "People must learn from their mistakes" are two universal themes.

Whether it is universal or one of a kind, a theme is often communicated through different elements in a story, such as the characters, setting, and conflict. A writer may also use symbols to hint at a theme. A **symbol** is an object, activity, place, or person that stands for something beyond itself.

Notice how the theme is communicated in the following example.

THEME
LIVE IN THE PRESENT, NOT THE PAST.

Character

The main character is **14-year-old Eva,** who has recently moved with her family to a new city. **Sullen and angry,** Eva desperately misses her friends back home.

Setting

Eva can't stand the thought of exploring an **unfamiliar city** and an **intimidating school.** Being in this new setting reminds her of what she left behind.

Symbol

Eva shuts herself in her room all day, looking through old yearbooks and e-mailing her friends. **Eva's room symbolizes the past,** where she remains trapped and isolated from the world.

Conflicts

Eva gets upset when he parents suggest that sh make new friends. She a feels hurt when **her frie don't e-mail very often.**

Resolution: Eventually, Eva realizes that she mu move on. While she can hold onto the past in her memories, she has to liv in the present.

DIFFERENTIATED INSTRUCTION

FOR ALL STUDENTS

For general guidelines on differentiating instruction, see

 BEST PRACTICES TOOLKIT

Differentiated Instruction pp. 31–38

FOR LESS–PROFICIENT READERS

Note Taking Hand out the Note Taking: What's the Big Idea? copy master and have students read page 442 silently. Then have students take notes on the copy master as you discuss the information.

 RESOURCE MANAGER—Copy Master

Note Taking p. 15

Elements of Theme Have students discuss ways in which the details of character, setting, symbol, and conflicts at the bottom of page 442 contribute to the theme "Live in the present, not the past." Point out that the symbol of Eva's room is central to the theme of the story—it is the place where she lives in the past. Have students brainstorm symbols that might stand for the past in a story about their own lives.

MODEL: THEME AND SYMBOL

Alfred is a high-school dropout who is barely staying out of trouble with the law. One night after getting beaten up, he steps into a gym to see if he can join the neighborhood boxing club. As he talks to Mr. Donatelli, the gym owner, about the challenges of training as a fighter, Alfred realizes Mr. Donatelli may be talking about more than just boxing.

from

THE CONTENDER

Novel by **Robert Lipsyte**

"How far did you go in school?"

"Eleventh grade."

"What happened?"

"I quit."

"Why?"

"Didn't seem like any reason to stay."

"What makes you think you won't quit here too?"

Alfred swallowed. He suddenly wished he hadn't come up the steps, that he was somewhere else, anywhere. He thought of the cave.

"Well?"

"I want to be somebody."

"Everybody is somebody."

"Somebody special. A champion."

Donatelli's thin lips tightened. "Everybody wants to be a champion. That's not enough. You have to start by wanting to be a contender, the man coming up, the man who knows there's a good chance he'll never get to the top, the man who's willing to sweat and bleed to get up as high as his legs and his brains and his heart will take him. That must sound corny to you."

"No."

"It's the climbing that makes the man. Getting to the top is an extra reward."

"I want to try."

Donatelli shrugged. "Boxing is a dying sport. People aren't much interested anymore. They want easy things like television, bowling, car rides. Get yourself a good job. Finish high school. Go at night if you have to."

"I'll try hard."

"Talk it over with your parents."

"I don't have any. I live with my aunt."

The pale blue eyes came around again. They seemed softer now. But the voice was still cold and flat. "It's not easy trying to become a contender. It's never any fun in the beginning. It's hard work, you'll want to quit at least once every day. If you quit before you really try, that's worse than never starting at all."

Close Read

1. Reread the boxed text. What conflict is set up?
2. What is Alfred's goal? What does Mr. Donatelli think about that goal?
3. Given what Mr. Donatelli says in lines 14–20, what do you think boxing might symbolize to him?
4. Reread lines 29–31. What lesson might Alfred learn from training as a boxer? State this lesson as a theme.

MODEL: THEME AND SYMBOL

Close Read

Possible answers:

1. *The conflict is between Alfred, who has quit school, and Mr. Donatelli, who is challenging Alfred's commitment to training.*
2. *Alfred wants to be "somebody"—a champion (line 13). Mr. Donatelli thinks that wanting to be a champion is not enough, that Alfred should first want to become a contender (lines 14–18). Alfred must be willing to struggle toward a goal even though he might never reach it.*
3. *Boxing might symbolize the struggles and challenges presented by life. Having a good life means being willing to push oneself as hard and as far as possible.*
4. *Alfred's lesson, and the theme of the story, might be stated, "What matters most is the effort we put into achieving our goals, rather than the achievement of the goals themselves."*

FOR ENGLISH LEARNERS

Concept Support: Theme [mixed-readiness groups] Have students point out the statement of theme in the story (lines 29–31). Then ask mixed-readiness groups to discuss whether or not they agree with the theme. Encourage them to give examples to explain their points of view, using the statement of theme in the story as a model. For example: *If you quit learning to ride a bicycle because it is hard, then you have been wasting your time.*

FOR ADVANCED LEARNERS/PRE–AP

Apply [small-group option] Have students work to complete a Story Frame for an original story with the same theme as *The Contender.* Encourage them to include possible symbols that could be used to support the theme. Have students share their ideas in small groups, evaluating the symbols they have chosen and suggesting others that could work in the story.

BEST PRACTICES TOOLKIT—Transparency
Story Frame p. C10

READER'S WORKSHOP 443

Teach

Part 2: Identifying Theme

Theme Read aloud this passage:

Marla and Joseph had been good friends since the third grade, when Marla moved to the city with her family. They rode to school on the bus together every morning, but one day Joseph wasn't there. Marla was worried, so she called him when she got home that afternoon.

"What happened to you today?" she asked. "I can't believe you missed the math test, especially since we studied so hard together over the weekend."

Joseph was silent for a moment. Finally, he said, "My grandmother died yesterday, so I stayed home from school."

"Don't move," Marla said. "I'll be right there." She dropped everything and hurried over to Joseph's apartment. There, she gave him a big hug, and they sat and talked together for hours.

Then ask students the following questions:

- What is the topic? ***Possible answer:*** *friendship*
- What is the theme? ***Possible answer:*** *Good friends help each other through hard times.*
- Is the theme implied, or is it directly stated? ***Answer:*** *It is implied. Readers must infer the theme from Marla's words and actions.*

Part 2: Identifying Theme

Sometimes the theme of a story is stated directly by the narrator or a character. More often, the theme is implied, which means you have to do some digging to uncover it. It helps to look closely at the characters, the plot, and other clues when you're trying to identify a story's theme. The questions in the chart, as well as these reminders, can help you discover the message.

- The theme is not the topic of a story, but the writer's message *about* the topic. While a topic can be described in a word or two, it can take one or two sentences to express a theme. For example, "first impressions" is a topic. "First impressions aren't always right" is a theme.
- Some works of literature have multiple themes, but one may stand out more than the others.
- Different people can interpret the same story differently.

CLUES TO THEME

TITLE
The title of a story can suggest an important idea or symbol. Ask:
- What in the story does the title refer to?
- What idea or symbol does the title highlight?
- Could the title have more than one meaning?

CHARACTERS
Characters can reflect theme by how they act or what they learn. Ask:
- What do the main character's actions and thoughts tell you about him or her?
- How does the character change?
- What lessons does the character learn?

PLOT AND CONFLICT
A story revolves around conflicts that are central to the theme. Ask:
- What conflicts do the characters face?
- How are the conflicts resolved?

SETTING
Setting can connect to a theme because of what it means to the characters or to readers. Ask:
- How does the setting affect the characters or influence their actions?
- What might the setting represent to readers?

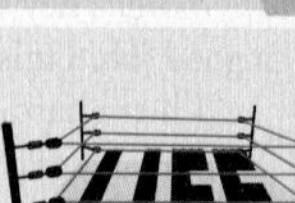

IMPORTANT STATEMENTS
The narrator or a character may make statements that hint at the theme. Ask:
- What key statements are made in the story?
- Could any statement be reworded as an overall theme?

SYMBOLS
A symbol can convey a theme because of what it means to the main character. Ask:
- Does anything seem to stand for something beyond itself?
- What might the symbol mean to the main character? What might it represent to readers?

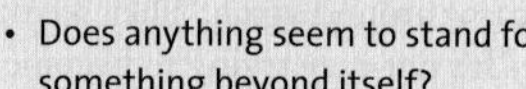

DIFFERENTIATED INSTRUCTION

FOR LESS–PROFICIENT READERS

Note Taking For students who need help with note taking, hand out the Note Taking: Identifying Theme copy master. Read and discuss the information on page 444. Assist students, as needed, in completing the copy master.

 **RESOURCE MANAGER—Copy Master**
Note Taking p. 16

Analysis Support [paired option] Once they have identified the clues to theme in the Note Taking activity, have students work with a partner to analyze each of the clues to theme in *The Contender.* For each clue, have them ask each other the questions in the chart on page 444. Then have them draw conclusions about the theme of the story.

Practice and Apply

Part 3: Analyze the Literature

Connie is not crazy about spending time with her Puerto Rican grandmother—her *abuela.* What lesson will Connie learn when her grandmother comes to visit? As you read, use what you've learned to uncover the theme of this story.

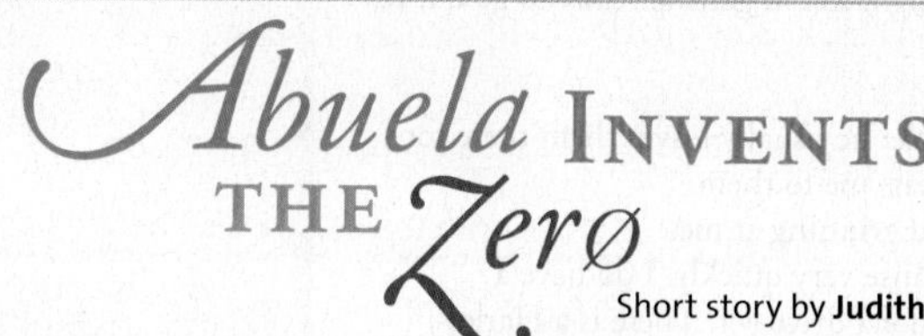

Short story by **Judith Ortiz Cofer**

"You made me feel like a zero, like a nothing," she says in Spanish, *un cero, nada.* She is trembling, an angry little old woman lost in a heavy winter coat that belongs to my mother. And I end up being sent to my room, like I was a child, to think about my grandmother's idea of math.

It all began with Abuela coming from the Island[1] for a visit—her first time in the United States. My mother and father paid her way here so that she wouldn't die without seeing snow, though if you asked me, and nobody has, the dirty slush in this city is not worth the price of a ticket. But I guess she deserves some kind of award for having had ten kids and survived to tell about it. My mother is the youngest of the bunch. Right up to the time when we're supposed to pick up the old lady at the airport, my mother is telling me stories about how hard times were for la familia on la isla,[2] and how *la abuela* worked night and day to support them after their father died of a heart attack. I'd die of a heart attack too if I had a troop like that to support. Anyway, I had seen her only three or four times in my entire life, whenever we would go for somebody's funeral. I was born here and I have lived in this building all my life. But when Mami says, "Connie, please be nice to Abuela. She doesn't have too many years left. Do you promise me, Constancia?"—when she uses my full name, I know she means business. So I say, "Sure." Why wouldn't I be nice? I'm not a monster, after all.

So we go to Kennedy[3] to get la abuela and she is the last to come out of the airplane, on the arm of the cabin attendant, all wrapped up in a black shawl. He hands her over to my parents like she was a package sent airmail. It is January, two feet of snow on the ground, and she's wearing a shawl over a thin black dress. That's just the start.

Once home, she refuses to let my mother buy her a coat because it's a waste of money for the two weeks she'll be in *el Polo Norte*, as she calls New Jersey, the North Pole. So since she's only four feet eleven inches tall, she walks around in my mother's big black coat looking ridiculous. I try to walk far behind them in public so that no one will think we're together. I plan to

1. **the Island:** Puerto Rico.
2. **la familia on la isla:** the family on the island.
3. **Kennedy:** John F. Kennedy International Airport.

Close Read

1. Examine the title of the story and reread the first paragraph. What symbol do you predict will be central to the theme?
2. Reread the boxed details, in which Connie shares her thoughts about her grandmother. Based on these details, how would you describe Connie?
3. What conflicts do you think might arise for Connie during her grandmother's visit?

Part 3: Analyze the Literature

Close Read

Possible answers:

1. *The number zero will likely be a symbol that relates to the story's theme.*
2. *Connie is disrespectful to older people, referring to her grandmother as "the old lady" (line 11). She has never had to take on much responsibility and is not very compassionate or sensitive.*
3. *She might experience a conflict with her grandmother, who belongs to a world Connie doesn't understand or value. She might also face an internal conflict over how she relates to her grandmother.*

FOR LESS–PROFICIENT READERS

Vocabulary Support Introduce these words from "Abuela Invents the Zero." Have students read the context for each word and suggest a synonym to replace it.

- *shawl* (line 24), "wrap"
- *escort* (line 34), "accompany"
- *compromise* (line 41), "agreement"
- *drenched* (line 69), "soaked"
- *cringe* (line 99), "cower"

FOR ENGLISH LEARNERS

Concept Support: Clues to Theme Write these clues to theme on the board and have students identify them by analyzing the title and the first paragraph:

- Title *("Abuela Invents the Zero")*
- Characters *(narrator, grandmother)*
- Conflict *(between the narrator and her grandmother)*
- Symbol *(the number zero)*

Close Read

4. ***Possible answer:*** *Connie is resentful that she has to take her grandmother to church on Sunday. She is embarrassed by her grandmother's appearance (lines 54–56) and worries about what other churchgoers will think when they see her and her grandmother together. She is impatient and frustrated (lines 62–68).*

stay very busy the whole time she's with us so that I won't be asked to take her anywhere, but my plan is ruined when my mother comes down with the flu and Abuela absolutely *has* to attend Sunday mass. . . . My father decides that he should stay home with my mother and that I should escort la abuela to church. He tells me this on Saturday night as I'm getting ready to go out to the mall with my friends.

"No way," I say.

I go for the car keys on the kitchen table: he usually leaves them there for me on Friday and Saturday nights. He beats me to them.

"No way," he says, pocketing them and grinning at me.

Needless to say, we come to a compromise very quickly. I do have a responsibility to Sandra and Anita, who don't drive yet. There is a Harley-Davidson fashion show at Brookline Square that we *cannot* miss.

"The mass in Spanish is at ten sharp tomorrow morning, *entiendes?*" My father is dangling the car keys in front of my nose and pulling them back when I try to reach for them. He's really enjoying himself.

"I understand. Ten o'clock. I'm out of here." I pry his fingers off the key ring. He knows that I'm late, so he makes it just a little difficult. Then he laughs. I run out of our apartment before he changes his mind. I have no idea what I'm getting myself into.

Sunday morning I have to walk two blocks on dirty snow to retrieve the car. I warm it up for Abuela as instructed by my parents, and drive it to the front of our building. My father walks her by the hand in baby steps on the slippery snow. The sight of her little head with a bun on top of it sticking out of that huge coat makes me want to run back into my room and get under the covers. I just hope that nobody I know sees us together. I'm dreaming, of course. The mass is packed with people from our block. It's a holy day of obligation and everyone I ever met is there.

I have to help her climb the steps, and she stops to take a deep breath after each one, then I lead her down the aisle so that everybody can see me with my bizarre grandmother. If I were a good Catholic, I'm sure I'd get some purgatory[4] time taken off for my sacrifice. She is walking as slow as Captain Cousteau[5] exploring the bottom of the sea, looking around, taking her sweet time. Finally she chooses a pew, but she wants to sit in the *other* end. It's like she had a spot picked out for some unknown reason, and although it's the most inconvenient seat in the house, that's where she has to sit. So we squeeze by all the people already sitting there, saying, "Excuse me, please, *con permiso*, pardon me," getting annoyed looks the whole way. By the time we settle in, I'm drenched in sweat. I keep my head down like I'm praying so as not to see or be seen. She is praying loud, in Spanish, and singing hymns at the top of her creaky voice.

4. **purgatory:** spiritual place in which souls purify themselves of sin before going to heaven.
5. **Captain Cousteau:** Jacques Yves Cousteau (zhäk ēv ko͝o-stō′) (1910–1997), a French underwater explorer, film producer, and author.

Close Read

4. How would you desc Connie's attitude tow and treatment of he grandmother? Supp your answer.

DIFFERENTIATED INSTRUCTION

FOR LESS–PROFICIENT READERS

Analysis Support: Theme [paired option] Have students list details describing the appearance, actions, speech, and thoughts of Connie and her grandmother in lines 51–87. Next, have them discuss with a partner what these details reveal about the author's message. At this point in the story, what do they think the story's theme might be?

FOR ENGLISH LEARNERS

Language Support: Idioms Help students use context clues to determine the meanings of these idioms in the story. Ask volunteers to act out or mime the meanings.

- *beats me to them* (line 39), "gets them first"
- *ten sharp* (line 44), "exactly ten o'clock"
- *taking her sweet time* (lines 63–64), "moving very slowly"
- *shooting daggers* (line 81), "glaring"
- *frozen to my seat* (line 85), "can't move"

I ignore her when she gets up with a hundred other people to go take communion.[6] I'm actually praying hard now—that this will all be over soon. But the next time I look up, I see a black coat dragging around and around the church, stopping here and there so a little gray head can peek out like a periscope on a submarine. There are giggles in the church, and even the priest has frozen in the middle of a blessing, his hands above his head like he is about to lead the congregation in a set of jumping jacks.

I realize to my horror that my grandmother is lost. She can't find her way back to the pew. I am so embarrassed that even though the woman next to me is shooting daggers at me with her eyes, I just can't move to go get her. I put my hands over my face like I'm praying, but it's really to hide my burning cheeks. I would like for her to disappear. I just know that on Monday my friends, and my enemies, in the barrio[7] will have a lot of senile-grandmother jokes to tell in front of me. I am frozen to my seat. So the same woman who wants me dead on the spot does it for me. She makes a big deal out of getting up and hurrying to get Abuela.

The rest of the mass is a blur. All I know is that my grandmother kneels the whole time with her hands over *her* face. She doesn't speak to me on the way home, and she doesn't let me help her walk, even though she almost falls a couple of times.

When we get to the apartment, my parents are at the kitchen table, where my mother is trying to eat some soup. They can see right away that something is wrong. Then Abuela points her finger at me like a judge passing a sentence on a criminal. She says in Spanish, "You made me feel like a zero, like a nothing." Then she goes to her room.

I try to explain what happened. "I don't understand why she's so upset. She just got lost and wandered around for a while," I tell them. But it sounds lame, even to my own ears. My mother gives me a look that makes me cringe and goes in to Abuela's room to get her version of the story. She comes out with tears in her eyes.

"Your grandmother says to tell you that of all the hurtful things you can do to a person, the worst is to make them feel as if they are worth nothing."

I can feel myself shrinking right there in front of her. But I can't bring myself to tell my mother that I think I understand how I made Abuela feel. I might be sent into the old lady's room to apologize, and it's not easy to admit you've been a jerk—at least, not right away with everybody watching. So I just sit there not saying anything.

My mother looks at me for a long time, like she feels sorry for me. Then she says, "You should know, Constancia, that if it wasn't for this old woman whose existence you don't seem to value, you and I would not be here."

That's when *I'm* sent to *my* room to consider a number I hadn't thought much about—until today.

6. **communion:** the part of a Christian service in which bread and wine are consumed in memory of Christ's sacrifice.

7. **barrio:** Spanish-speaking community or neighborhood.

Close Read

5. Why do you think the author chose a church as the setting for this scene? How might she want you to react to Connie's behavior there?

6. What lesson has Connie learned from the conflict with her grandmother? Where on this page do you see this lesson directly stated as a theme?

7. What new understanding of the word *zero* does Connie now have? What understanding do you have of the story's title?

Close Read

Possible answers:

5. *A church is a place where people are encouraged to practice kindness. Connie's behavior—her embarrassment and her unwillingness to help her grandmother—contradict that message. The author may want readers to feel that Connie's behavior is unacceptable.*
6. *Connie has learned that her actions can hurt other people. The lesson is directly stated in lines 101–102: "[O]f all the hurtful things you can do to a person, the worst is to make them feel as if they are worth nothing."*
7. *Connie understands that the word zero can describe a person's feeling of being neglected and treated as if he or she were invisible. The title reflects the lesson Connie learns from her grandmother.*

Assess and Reteach

Assess

Ask students to identify the clues to theme in the story: title, characters, setting, conflict, symbol, and important statements.

Reteach

Use this activity for students who have trouble applying the workshop skills:

1. Have pairs of students review their Note Taking copy masters.
2. Ask students to discuss whether or not the theme of "Abuela Invents the Zero" is a universal theme and to give reasons for their answers.
3. Have them discuss what these things in the story might symbolize, and how each symbol could be related to a theme: the grandmother's black shawl (line 22), Sunday mass (line 33), the car keys (line 38).

FOR ADVANCED LEARNERS/PRE-AP

Synthesize Have students write a brief letter to Connie expressing their feelings about her actions and her attitudes toward her grandmother. In their letters, they should give examples from their own experience about what it feels like to be treated poorly and the consequences they have experienced from their poor treatment of others. If they wish, students may share their letters with a partner.

Focus and Motivate

OBJECTIVES

Literary Analysis

- explore the key idea of what makes something **priceless**
- identify and interpret symbols
- read an anecdote

Reading

- make inferences

Grammar and Writing

- maintain subject-verb agreement when using prepositional phrases
- use writing to analyze literature

SUMMARY

In this short vignette from Sandra Cisneros's critically acclaimed *The House on Mango Street,* the narrator and her sister Nenny visit a junk shop. While there, Nenny discovers a music box. Much to the dismay of the narrator, who feels embarrassed by her sudden desire to own the music box, Nenny asks the shop owner how much it costs. His reply? Not for sale.

What makes something PRICELESS?

To help students better understand the ***KEY IDEA,*** ask them if only material things can be considered **priceless.** Can a special friendship be priceless? Why or why not? What other nonmaterial items would students consider priceless? Then have students work on the ***QUICKWRITE*** activity independently. In addition to writing about a prized possession, invite students to present their object to the class or act out something that has meaning to them and explain its significance.

Before Reading

Gil's Furniture Bought & Sold

Anecdote by Sandra Cisneros

What makes something PRICELESS?

KEY IDEA Perhaps you've heard a painting or antique described as **priceless.** In many cases, this means that the item is worth so much money that the amount can't be guessed at. But sometimes an object is priceless because it is worth more than money to the person who owns it. The anecdote you are about to read is a short account of a priceless object turning up in an unexpected place.

QUICKWRITE Describe your most prized possession and tell why it is special to you. Then consider if there are any circumstances under which you might give away or sell this object.

448

Selection Resources

RESOURCE MANAGER UNIT 4

Plan and Teach pp. 17–24

Literary Analysis

Summary pp. 25†*, 26‡*

Symbol pp. 27, 28†*

Question Support p. 32*

Reading

Make Inferences pp. 29, 30†*

Reading Check p. 31

Reading Fluency p. 35

Grammar and Writing

Maintain Subject-Verb Agreement p. 33

Assessment

Selection Tests A, B/C pp. 37*, 39*

Test Generator CD

BEST PRACTICES TOOLKIT

Differentiated Instruction pp. 31–38*

Scaffolding Instruction pp. 43–46*

Graphic Organizers/Strategies

Predicting • Think-Pair-Share • Character Map

Reading Support

Audio Anthology CD*

Technology

Literature and Writing Centers at **ClassZone.com**

Write*Smart* CD

* Resources for Differentiation † Also in Spanish ‡ In Haitian Creole and Vietnamese

RARY ANALYSIS: SYMBOL

When you see an American flag, you probably think of more than the fabric it's made of and its pattern of stars and stripes. The flag represents something much bigger—the United States of America. When a person, place, or thing stands for something beyond itself, it is called a **symbol.**

Writers often use symbols to quickly communicate complex ideas. For example, a sunrise can symbolize a new beginning, or a rose can stand for love. To recognize a symbol in literature, ask yourself questions such as these:

What object appears repeatedly?

How do the characters react to this object?

What big ideas does the story address, and how does this object relate to them?

As you read "Gil's Furniture Bought & Sold," consider how an important object is used as a symbol.

DING SKILL: MAKE INFERENCES

Skilled readers know they must "read between the lines" to make logical guesses about what a writer means but does not say directly. This process is called **making inferences,** and it can help you to understand the characters in a story. Follow these steps to make an inference:

- Gather details or evidence from the story.
- Consider your own experience and knowledge.
- Form an opinion based on both.

As you read, use a chart like the one shown to make inferences about the three characters in the selection.

Details from Story	*What I Know*	*Inference About Character*

Author Online

A Bilingual Beginning

Sandra Cisneros
born 1954

Sandra Cisneros grew up in Chicago, the only daughter in a Mexican-American family with seven children. She spoke English to her mother and Spanish to her father, and she even thought the two languages were the same when she was very young. She was fascinated with the sound of words, especially those found in fairy tales and fantasy stories, such as *Alice in Wonderland.* The strange and fancy words in the pages of these books were quite different from those she heard every day at home and in her poor neighborhood. Cisneros dreamed of escaping her neighborhood and becoming a writer. She credits her mother with helping her achieve this goal.

"I've Followed My Gut and My Heart"

In order to earn a living, Cisneros decided she should work as an English teacher and write in her free time. The poetry and short fiction she produced revealed her unique voice, created from the influences of Latino and American culture. Her first novel, *The House on Mango Street,* was published in 1984 and helped make her a best-selling author. Her work often deals with struggles, such as alienation, poverty, and dual cultural loyalties. Cisneros's stories and poems have won many awards. She has said of her success, "In everything I've done in my life, including all the choices I've made as a writer, I've followed my gut and my heart."

MORE ABOUT THE AUTHOR
For more on Sandra Cisneros, visit the **Literature Center** at **ClassZone.com.**

Teach

STANDARDS FOCUS

LITERARY ANALYSIS

● SYMBOL

Explain that not all symbols are universal, like the U.S. flag; some symbols work only in the context in which they are presented. Writers can turn almost any person, place, or thing into a symbol to convey a particular meaning or message. Display these examples and ask what each image might symbolize:

- a person turning into a bird and flying away *(freedom, joy)*
- a dungeon with thick walls and bars in the windows *(confinement, despair)*

CHECK UNDERSTANDING Ask students to read the Cisneros quote on page 449. What do *my gut* and *my heart* symbolize?

READING SKILL

■ MAKE INFERENCES

Tell students: A man is standing in front of a restaurant. He paces back and forth and keeps glancing at his watch. Ask: How do you think he is feeling? ***Possible answer:*** *impatient, annoyed, nervous*

CHECK UNDERSTANDING Ask students what clues they used from what you said and from their own knowledge to make their inferences.

RESOURCE MANAGER—Copy Master
Make Inferences p. 29 (for student use while reading the selection)

DIFFERENTIATED INSTRUCTION

FOR ALL STUDENTS

For general guidelines on differentiating instruction, see

BEST PRACTICES TOOLKIT
Differentiated Instruction pp. 31–38

FOR LESS-PROFICIENT READERS

Predict Have students look at the art on page 451. Discuss what the illustration reveals about the story's setting. Then ask students to predict, on the basis of this illustration as well as the story's title, what might happen in the anecdote.

BEST PRACTICES TOOLKIT—Transparency
Predicting p. A10

FOR ENGLISH LEARNERS

Prereading For prereading instruction for English learners, see

BEST PRACTICES TOOLKIT
Scaffolding Reading Instruction pp. 43–46

Options for Reading Read the anecdote aloud. (A reading is also available on the *Audio Anthology CD.*) Have students use Think-Pair-Share to answer important questions about the selection.

BEST PRACTICES TOOLKIT—Transparency
Think-Pair-Share p. A18

Practice and Apply

ANALYZE VISUALS

Possible answer: *It would be easy to knock something over while shopping, and it would be difficult to find a specific item.*

READING SKILL

A MAKE INFERENCES

Possible answer: *They don't have much money, and they like to browse through the unusual merchandise.*

READING SKILL

B MAKE INFERENCES

Possible answer: *Nenny is outgoing. The narrator is quiet; she observes more than she speaks. The store's owner is also quiet and doesn't mind being left alone.*

LITERARY ANALYSIS

C SYMBOL

Possible answer: *The narrator is very moved by the songs the music box plays, and Nenny wants to buy the music box.*

Lines 15–28

DISCUSSION PROMPTS

Use these prompts to help students understand the narrator and Nenny:

Recall What does the narrator think the music box will look like? ***Answer:*** *She expects it to be a pretty, painted music box with a ballerina inside.*

Analyze What does the narrator's response to the music box tell you about her? ***Possible answer:*** *She has deep feelings and appreciates beautiful music.*

Infer Reread lines 24–27. Why do you think the narrator thinks Nenny is even "stupider" than herself? ***Possible answer:*** *The narrator understands that the music box is priceless, but Nenny doesn't and tries to buy it.*

Line 28

REINFORCE *KEY IDEA:* PRICELESS

Discuss Why do you think the music box is **priceless** to the old man? ***Possible answer:*** *He appreciates the special quality of music that the box produces.*

There is a junk store. An old man owns it. We bought a used refrigerator from him once, and Carlos sold a box of magazines for a dollar. The store is small with just a dirty window for light. He doesn't turn the lights on unless you got money to buy things with, so in the dark we look and see all kinds of things, me and Nenny. Tables with their feet upside-down and rows and rows of refrigerators with round corners and couches that spin dust in the air when you punch them and a hundred T.V.'s that don't work probably. Everything is on top of everything so the whole store has skinny aisles to walk through. You can get lost easy. **A**

The owner, he is a black man who doesn't talk much and sometimes if you didn't know better you could be in there a long time before your eyes notice a pair of gold glasses floating in the dark. Nenny who thinks she is smart and talks to any old man, asks lots of questions. Me, I never said nothing to him except once when I bought the Statue of Liberty for a dime. **B**

But Nenny, I hear her asking one time how's this here and the man says, This, this is a music box, and I turn around quick thinking he means a *pretty* box with flowers painted on it, with a ballerina inside. Only there's nothing like that where this old man is pointing, just a wood box that's old and got a big brass record in it with holes. Then he starts it up and all sorts of things start happening. It's like all of a sudden he let go a million moths all over the dusty furniture and swan-neck shadows and in our bones. It's like drops of water. Or like marimbas only with a funny little plucked sound to it like if you were running your fingers across the teeth of a metal comb.

And then I don't know why, but I have to turn around and pretend I don't care about the box so Nenny won't see how stupid I am. But Nenny, who is stupider, already is asking how much and I can see her fingers going for the quarters in her pants pocket. **C**

This, the old man says shutting the lid, this ain't for sale. ❧

ANALYZE VISUALS
Look at the way objects are arranged in the store pictured on page 451. What can you **infer** abou what it would be like to shop there?

A MAKE INFERENCES
Why do you think the narrator and Nenny shop at a junk store?

B MAKE INFERENCES
Reread lines 10–14. What can you assume about each character's personality from the details in this paragraph?

C SYMBOL
How do the narrator and Nenny react to th music box?

DIFFERENTIATED INSTRUCTION

FOR ENGLISH LEARNERS

Language: Conversational English Patterns
Remind students that writers sometimes use conversational English to show how people actually speak. Read aloud lines 5–7 and point out that this is a sentence fragment without a verb. Then read aloud lines 22–23 and note that the sentence begins with a conjunction. Work with students to find other examples where the author breaks the rules of standard, written English to make the narrator sound like a real girl.

FOR ADVANCED LEARNERS/PRE–AP

Analyze Similes Have students explore the similes in lines 20–23 and reflect on their meaning. Challenge students to express one of the comparisons using similes of their own. Once they have rewritten the similes, invite students to share and compare them. Discuss which ones work the best.

BACKGROUND

The House on Mango Street The novel from which this selection is excerpted, *The House on Mango Street,* is no ordinary novel. It is made up of 44 related vignettes—short literary sketches—narrated by Esperanza Cordero, a young girl coming of age in a Chicago barrio. Her family recently moved to a new house on Mango Street, but Esperanza longs for a house of her own where she will have the privacy she so desires. Many of the vignettes, including "Gil's Furniture Bought & Sold," center on Esperanza's neighborhood, which she explores with her friends and her younger sister, Nenny.

SELECTION WRAP–UP

REFLECT Ask students which character they would like to know more about and why.

CRITIQUE Have students reread the last line of the anecdote. Then ask what the wording of this line adds to the overall effect of the selection.

READING FLUENCY

Distribute the copy masters and have students practice fluency.

RESOURCE MANAGER—Copy Master
Reading Fluency p. 35

FOR LESS–PROFICIENT READERS

Reading Skill Follow-Up: Make Inferences
Review the details students have recorded in their charts from page 449. Remind students to list several story details for each of the three characters in the first column, and what they already know from their own life in the second column. Model how to make inferences about the man. Then prompt students to make inferences about the other characters.

Details from Story	What I Know	Inference About Character
quiet old man owns junk store likes beautiful music tries to save money by turning lights off	reminds me of my grandfather	He is a deep thinker.

Practice and Apply

After Reading

For additional support of postreading questions, use these copy masters:

RESOURCE MANAGER—Copy Masters

Reading Check p. 31 (to check understanding of the selection)

Symbol p. 27 (for practice of literary analysis standards focus)

Question Support p. 32 (After Reading questions adapted for English learners and less-proficient readers)

Additional selection questions are provided for teachers on page 21.

ANSWERS

Comprehension

1. *The family bought a used refrigerator from the junk store.*
2. *The store is dark and the man is quiet.*
3. *The store is dark, crowded, dusty, and full of many different kinds of items.*

Literary Analysis

Possible answers:

4. **■ STANDARDS FOCUS Make Inferences** *The three characters are all interested in old items that don't cost a lot of money. Nenny wanted to buy the old music box and didn't understand its importance to the old man. The narrator felt the beauty in the music and realized it was an important item to the old man. The old man loved the music and could not part with the music box.*
5. **● STANDARDS FOCUS Symbol** *The music box symbolizes beauty that is found in unexpected places.*
6. *The narrator feels strong emotions when she hears the music, and she turns away so Nenny won't notice. This shows that she is a very private person.*
7. ***Narrator:*** *thoughtful and quiet, doesn't talk to the old man;* ***Both:*** *seem to be about the same age, come from the same neighborhood, enjoy searching for bargains;* ***Nenny:*** *outgoing and talkative, asks the old man many questions*
8. *The junk store is an appropriate setting to discover something priceless because it is full of old, unexpected things that probably had a lot of meaning to people at some time. Still, it is surprising to find something of value in a store that is dark, dusty, and cluttered with "junk." It is more common to find priceless objects in a museum or in a very expensive shop.*

Extension and Challenge

9. *Students' collages should include the type of objects typically found at a junk store.*
10. *Students' presentations should reflect an understanding of how a disc music box works as well as why the phonograph replaced the music box as a main source of musical entertainment.*

After Reading

Comprehension

1. **Recall** What item did the narrator's family buy from the junk store in the past?
2. **Clarify** Why is it sometimes hard to know that the owner is in the store?
3. **Summarize** In your own words, describe the appearance of the junk store.

Literary Analysis

4. **Make Inferences** Review the chart you created as you read the anecdote. Based on these inferences, why do you think each character reacted to the music box the way he or she did? Give details from the anecdote to support your answer.
5. **Interpret a Symbol** What does the music box **symbolize?** Explain why you think so.
6. **Draw Conclusions** What do you think the narrator means when she says, "I have to turn around and pretend I don't care about the box so Nenny won't see how stupid I am"? Consider what this tells you about her personality.
7. **Compare and Contrast Characters** Using a Venn diagram like the one shown, compare and contrast the narrator and Nenny. As you fill in the diagram, note how they interact with the storeowner.

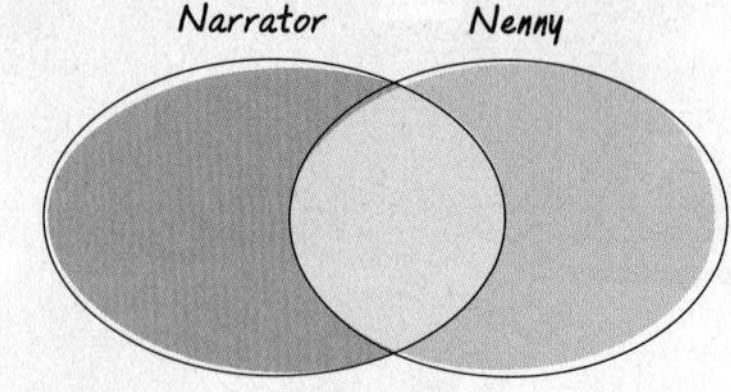

8. **Evaluate a Setting** A story's **setting** can affect your expectations about what is going to happen. Reread lines 1–9. In what ways is the junk store an appropriate setting for the characters to discover something **priceless?** In what ways is the setting surprising?

Extension and Challenge

9. **Creative Project: Art** Think about the description of the junk store and the various items for sale there. Then make a collage of items you would expect to find in the store. You can cut out pictures from magazines and newspapers or include your own sketches.
10. **Inquiry and Research** Music boxes were once popular objects for people to have in their homes. The music box described in this story is a disc music box. Research more about disc music boxes and how they work. Also research how the popularity of the phonograph affected the music box industry in the early 1900s. Present your findings to the class.

RESEARCH LINKS
For more on music boxes, visit the **Research Center** at **ClassZone.com.**

ading-Writing Connection

how your understanding of the characters in "Gil's Furniture Bought & Sold" by esponding to these prompts. Then complete the **Grammar and Writing** exercise.

WRITING PROMPTS	SELF-CHECK
A. Short Response: Write a Dialogue Imagine what the narrator and Nenny talked about after they left the junk store. Write a **half-page dialogue** that captures what they may have said. Be sure to use language that matches the personalities of the characters.	***A creative dialogue will . . .*** • include details about their experience in the store • reveal differences between the two characters through what they say
B. Extended Response: Analyze a Character What did you learn about the junk store's owner based on his store, his behavior, and his words? Write **two or three paragraphs** describing the type of man he seems to be. Be sure to consider why the music box is **priceless** to him.	***A detailed analysis will . . .*** • support general statements about the man with evidence from the anecdote • make inferences about why he values the music box

AMMAR AND WRITING

AINTAIN SUBJECT-VERB AGREEMENT You may recall that subjects and verbs nust agree in number. That rule remains true even when a subject and a verb ave a **prepositional phrase** between them. The subject of a sentence is never ound in a prepositional phrase. If you are having a problem deciding whether o use a singular or plural verb in a sentence that contains a prepositional phrase, nentally block out the phrase. This will help you determine what the subject of he sentence is and whether it needs a singular or plural verb.

Example: The items in the junk shop are too numerous to count. (*The subject is* items, *not* shop, *so the sentence needs the plural verb* are.)

PRACTICE Choose the verb form that agrees with the subject in each sentence.

1. A box of books (was, were) one item that got sold to the owner of the store.
2. Refrigerators in the aisle (create, creates) a problem.
3. The owner's impression of the kids (are, is) that they aren't actually going to buy anything.
4. A handful of quarters (are, is) all that Nenny has to spend.

For more help with subject-verb agreement, see page R65 in the ***Grammar Handbook.***

Reading-Writing Connection

WRITING PROMPTS

- For **Prompt A,** have students work in pairs to brainstorm what the two characters might have said after leaving the junk store. Afterwards, each pair can role-play the part of one of the characters to make sure the dialogue is true to their character's personality.
- For **Prompt B,** have students create a Character Map for the junk store's owner. Suggest that they begin their analysis with a physical description and then move on to personality traits.

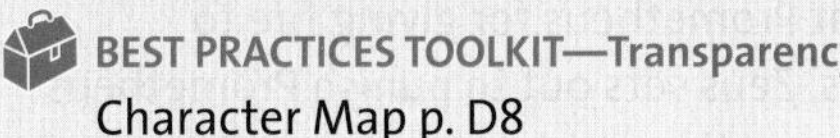

BEST PRACTICES TOOLKIT—Transparency
Character Map p. D8

For writing support, see

Writing Center at **ClassZone.com**

GRAMMAR AND WRITING

Suggest that students cover up the prepositional phrase in each sentence and then see which verb sounds best in the shortened sentence structure.

Answers:

1. *was*
2. *create*
3. *is*
4. *is*

RESOURCE MANAGER—Copy Master
Maintain Subject-Verb Agreement p. 33

Assess and Reteach

Assess

RESOURCE MANAGER—Copy Masters
Selection Tests A, B/C pp. 37–38, 39–40

Test Generator CD

Reteach

STANDARDS LESSON FILE
Literature Lesson 31: Symbol and Symbolism
Reading Lesson 8: Making Inferences
Grammar Lesson 7: Inverted Sentences and Intervening Phrases

DIFFERENTIATED INSTRUCTION

FOR LESS—PROFICIENT WRITERS

For Prompt A:

Review these rules of writing dialogue:

- Set off speakers' words in quotation marks.
- Start a new paragraph with each new speaker.
- Identify the speakers.

Write this sentence on the board as a visual reminder of the basic rules of dialogue: *"I can't believe he wouldn't sell me that music box," Nenny complained.*

For Prompt B:

1. Have students work on the Character Map in pairs.
2. Have students write their paragraphs using ideas from their maps. The first paragraph should describe what the man looks and sounds like. The second paragraph should explore what he says and does. The final paragraph should explain what these traits and actions have helped students infer about why the music box is priceless to the store's owner.

Focus and Motivate

OBJECTIVES

Literary Analysis
- explore the key idea of **curiosity**
- identify and analyze theme
- read a Greek myth

Reading
- develop strategies for reading myths

Vocabulary
- build vocabulary for reading and writing
- use reference aids to find synonyms and use synonyms in sentences *(also an EL language objective)*

SUMMARY

Angry at Prometheus for giving fire to humans, Zeus sets out to punish Prometheus' brother and the entire human race. He sends Pandora, the perfect woman, to be Epimetheus' bride. Epimetheus distrusts Zeus and warns Pandora never to open the box of magic that Zeus has sent as a dowry. Eventually, the curious Pandora opens the box, releasing War, Cruelty, Envy, and a host of other evils. Last to emerge is Hope, suggesting that perhaps all is not lost.

Is CURIOSITY *a gift or a curse?*

Discuss the question. To lead into the ***KEY IDEA,*** ask students to define ***curiosity.*** Ask them what they are curious about. How might the future be different if everyone suddenly lost their curiosity? Then have small groups work on the ***LIST IT*** activity.

Before Reading

Pandora's Box

Greek Myth Retold by Louis Untermeyer

Is CURIOSITY *a gift or a curse?*

KEY IDEA Have you ever heard the saying "Curiosity killed the cat"? This statement implies that **curiosity** can be dangerous. But curiosity has also led scientists to discover cures for diseases and journalists to ask important questions that inform the public. As you read the following myth, decide whether curiosity is presented as a desirable trait to have.

LIST IT Does curiosity lead to more benefits than it does problems? Or is it the other way around? With a small group of classmates, choose a side. In two minutes, come up with as many examples as possible to illustrate your point. Then see which side has more responses.

454

Selection Resources

RESOURCE MANAGER UNIT 4

Plan and Teach pp. 41–48

Literary Analysis
Summary pp. 49†*, 50‡*
Theme pp. 51, 52†*
Question Support p. 59*

Reading
Reading a Myth pp. 53, 54†*
Reading Check p. 58
Reading Fluency p. 60

Vocabulary
Study p. 55*
Practice p. 56
Strategy p. 57

Assessment
Selection Tests A, B/C pp. 61*, 63*
Test Generator CD

BEST PRACTICES TOOLKIT

Differentiated Instruction pp. 31–38*
Scaffolding Instruction pp. 43–46*

Graphic Organizers/Strategies
Word Questioning • Cluster Diagram

Reading Support
Audio Anthology CD*

Technology
Literature and Vocabulary Centers at **ClassZone.com**
Write*Smart* CD

* Resources for Differentiation † Also in Spanish ‡ In Haitian Creole and Vietnamese

ERARY ANALYSIS: THEME

Writers often share with their readers messages about life or human nature—for example, love may come when you least expect it. This type of message is called a **theme.** Writers can either state a theme directly or allow readers to figure it out on their own. To infer a selection's theme, readers can look at important details or symbols. In the myth you are about to read, pay attention to a mysterious box and its contents to help you determine the theme.

ADING STRATEGY: READING A MYTH

Thousands of years ago, before anyone had microscopes or even books, people explained the world through stories called **myths.** Most myths

- were passed along through word of mouth
- feature gods or other supernatural beings who often show such human characteristics as anger and love
- reveal the consequences of human errors
- explain how something came to be

In order to understand a myth's significance, think beyond its basic story and consider what the characters, their actions, and the objects represent. As you read "Pandora's Box," take notes in a chart like the one shown.

What human qualities do the gods display?	
What kind of behavior does Pandora demonstrate?	
What do the contents of the box represent?	

CABULARY IN CONTEXT

The boldfaced words help Louis Untermeyer tell the story of Pandora. Using context clues in each sentence, try to figure out what each word means.

1. The gods **adorn** her with special gifts.
2. She could no longer **restrain** her curiosity.
3. Zeus' **subtle** punishment was not immediately obvious.
4. Her beauty and charm helped **ensnare** his attention.

Author Online

Jeweler and Poet Louis Untermeyer, son of a wealthy jewelry manufacturer, dreamed of becoming a concert pianist. At age 15, however, he dropped out of high school and went to work for his father. He spent the next 22 years in the family business, working as a salesman, designer, and then vice president. During this time he also wrote and published many poems and puns.

Louis Untermeyer 1885–1977

Translator and Anthologist In 1923, Untermeyer quit the jewelry business and went to Europe for two years to study. After he returned to the United States, he became a writer, lecturer, and teacher. One of his friends was American poet Robert Frost. Untermeyer edited many poetry anthologies that became popular textbooks in schools. He also became a respected translator, adapting myths and stories for the contemporary American audience.

MORE ABOUT THE AUTHOR
For more on Louis Untermeyer, visit the **Literature Center** at **ClassZone.com.**

Background

The Gods' Soap Opera Many of the best-known myths, such as "Pandora's Box," come from ancient Greece. The Greek gods were a lively, passionate bunch. Zeus, king of the gods, ruled the heavens and earth from Mount Olympus. In one myth, Prometheus, a lesser god, gives humans fire against Zeus' will. Furious, Zeus condemns Prometheus to be chained for eternity to a rock. But as you'll see in the myth you're about to read, Zeus wasn't done punishing Prometheus yet. Now he's going to pick on Prometheus' brother, Epimetheus.

Teach

STANDARDS FOCUS

LITERARY ANALYSIS

● THEME

Ask students what the myth might be about, based on the ***KEY IDEA*** paragraph on page 454. What lesson about life might such a story teach? ***Possible answer:*** *The lesson might be that curiosity can get you into trouble or that curiosity can lead to wonderful new discoveries.*

CHECK UNDERSTANDING Ask students to identify themes in stories or movies they know.

READING STRATEGY

■ READING A MYTH

Point out that myths help show the qualities that are valued by a society. In Greek myths, the gods have the same qualities or character traits as humans, and they suffer the consequences of their actions as humans do. Explain that by paying attention to what happens in myths, readers can learn lessons about values and consequences.

CHECK UNDERSTANDING Ask students what gods in myths might be able to do that humans would not be capable of.

RESOURCE MANAGER—Copy Master
Reading a Myth p. 53 (for student use while reading the selection)

VOCABULARY SKILL

▲ VOCABULARY IN CONTEXT

DIAGNOSE WORD KNOWLEDGE To determine preteaching needs, have all students complete **Vocabulary in Context.** *Students' responses will vary.* ***Possible answers:*** **1.** *enhance* **2.** *hold back* **3.** *unnoticeable* **4.** *capture*

PRETEACH VOCABULARY Use the Vocabulary Study copy master to help students predict the meaning of each boldfaced word, using context clues.

1. Read item 1 aloud, emphasizing *adorn.*
2. Point out the phrase *qualities that would make her the perfect woman.* Elicit possible meanings for *adorn,* such as "to improve."
3. Have students record their predictions.
4. Repeat the procedure for items 2–4.
5. Have students check their predictions as they read the myth.

RESOURCE MANAGER—Copy Master
Vocabulary Study p. 55

For general guidelines on differentiating vocabulary instruction and for alternative vocabulary activities for students not needing vocabulary preteaching, see

BEST PRACTICES TOOLKIT
Scaffolding Vocabulary Instruction pp. 43–46

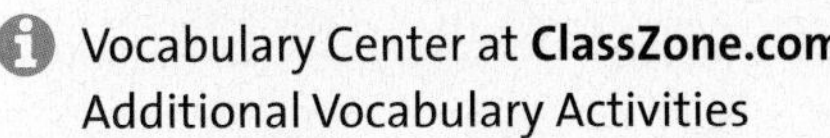

Vocabulary Center at **ClassZone.com**
Additional Vocabulary Activities

Practice and Apply

Lines 10–15
DISCUSSION PROMPTS

Use these prompts to help students understand the author's use of sensory language:

Recall What elements does Hephaestus add to the river clay? ***Answer:*** *He adds the fragrance of a river rose, the sweetness of honey, the smoothness of a silver dolphin, the voices of larks and lake-water, the color of sunrise on snow, and the warmth of a sunny May morning.*

Analyze Which of the five senses does each element appeal to? ***Possible answer:***

- *fragrance of a rose—smell*
- *sweetness of honey—taste*
- *smoothness of a dolphin, warmth of a sunny May morning—touch*
- *voices of larks and lake-water—hearing*
- *color of sunrise on snow—sight*

Synthesize Why is it significant that Hephaestus chooses to add these five elements to the clay? ***Possible answer:*** *Each of the elements accounts for one of the five senses, making Pandora appealing in every way that humans can relate to her.*

READING STRATEGY

A READING A MYTH

Possible answer: *The gods display sympathy, daring, rebelliousness, the desire for revenge, cruelty, and craftiness.*

ANALYZE VISUALS

Possible answer:

- *She treasures the box.*
- *She is protective of the box.*
- *She knows opening the box is wrong and fears someone will see her.*

Retold by Louis Untermeyer

Prometheus had thought about mankind with such sympathy that he had dared to steal the needed fire from Olympus,[1] and for this he was grievously punished by Zeus.[2] But the lord of Olympus did not think this cruelty was enough. Prometheus had a brother, Epimetheus, and though he was harmless and slow-witted, Zeus extended his displeasure to him. He did not punish Epimetheus as brutally as he had done his brother; he had a more **subtle** plan. It was a scheme which would not only affect Epimetheus but also the whole race of human beings whom Prometheus had dared to help and who were living happily and untroubled. **A**

Zeus ordered Hephaestus, the smith and artisan of the gods, to make a woman out of the materials of earth. Hephaestus took some river clay that had flakes of gold in it and began to make a lovely girl. In with the clay he mixed the fragrance of a river rose, the sweetness of Hymettus[3] honey, the smoothness of a silver dolphin, the voices of larks and lake-water, the color of sunrise on snow, the warmth of a sunny morning in May. Then he summoned

subtle (sŭt'l) *adj.* sligh
difficult to detect

A READING A MYTH
Think about the gods have met so far. Wha human characteristics do they have? Add th information to your c

ANALYZE VISUALS
Based on the woman' expression and body language, what can y **infer** about her attitu toward the box?

1. **Olympus** (ə-lĭm'pəs): home of the mythical Greek gods.
2. **Zeus** (zo͞os): father of the Greek gods; ruler of the heavens.
3. **Hymettus** (hī-mĕt'əs): a mountain ridge near Athens, Greece.

456 UNIT 4: THEME AND SYMBOL

Pandora, Helen Stratton. From *A Book of*
by Jean Lang. Mary Evans/Edwin Wa

DIFFERENTIATED INSTRUCTION

FOR ALL STUDENTS

Enhance Learning Styles Provide these independent projects for students with various learning styles:

- **Spatial** Draw a diagram of the story plot on large poster board. Begin with Prometheus' theft of fire.
- **Visual** Create a poster to illustrate the evils that flew out of Pandora's box. Include an image of Hope in the center of the poster.
- **Linguistic** Write an alternative ending to the story and include a surprise twist.

FOR LESS–PROFICIENT READERS

In combination with the *Audio Anthology CD*, use one or more Targeted Passages (pp. 458, 459) to ensure that students focus on key story events, concepts, and skills.

BACKGROUND

Prometheus Prometheus' first kindness toward humans centered around the sacrifices people made to Zeus. Prometheus tricked Zeus into accepting the bones and fat of the sacrifices, leaving the meat for the humans. This angered Zeus, causing him to deny Prometheus' request to provide humans with fire. In one version of the story, Prometheus steals fire from the hearth of Zeus and brings it to Earth hidden in a stalk of fennel weed. In another, Prometheus takes fire from the forge of Hephaestus. In yet another story, he lights his torch at the chariot of the sun to bring fire to humans.

CULTURAL CONNECTION

Fire Myths Many cultures have myths that explain how humankind received fire. In African mythology, a small boy uses a long stick to light a lamp for the Creator God. He wraps the stick in leaves so the fire won't burn out before he can return to Earth with it. In the myths of the Nez Percé Indians, the Great Power keeps fire in big black bags in the sky. A young boy manages to shoot one of the bags with an arrow, and the burning arrow delivers fire to the Nez Percé people when it falls to Earth. In the mythology of Mexico, Opossum offers to bring fire to a village in return for a promise that the villagers will never eat him. Opossum then convinces Lady Fire to allow him to warm himself by her fire. After he gets close enough for his tail to catch fire, he runs back to the village, sharing fire with others along the way. This myth also explains why opossums have no hair on their tails.

FOR ENGLISH LEARNERS

Key Academic Vocabulary Have students use Word Questioning for these words: *scheme* (line 7), *finally* (lines 16, 84), *grant* (lines 17, 49), *conduct* (line 32), *benefited* (line 55).

 BEST PRACTICES TOOLKIT—Transparency
Word Questioning p. E9

Prereading For prereading instruction for English learners, see

 BEST PRACTICES TOOLKIT
Scaffolding Reading Instruction pp. 43–46

Options for Reading Read the first paragraph aloud and make sure students understand that Prometheus' theft of fire and his punishment for that act occurred before the story opens. Also, make sure students realize that Epimetheus is being punished for no other reason than because he is Prometheus' brother. Then have students read along with the *Audio Anthology CD.*

FOR ADVANCED LEARNERS/PRE–AP

Pre-AP exercises in the bottom channel provide additional challenge for your advanced students. Use them for small groups or individuals.

ADDITIONAL GUIDELINES

For more help with differentiation and tips for classroom management, see

 BEST PRACTICES TOOLKIT
Differentiated Instruction pp. 31–38

READING STRATEGY

B READING A MYTH

Possible answer: *The gods Zeus and Hephaestus, the Four Winds, and the goddesses Aphrodite, Athene, and Hera collaborate in creating Pandora.*

LITERARY ANALYSIS

C THEME

Possible answer: *The contents will be harmful, not only to Epimetheus but also to humankind.*

Lines 48–51

REINFORCE *KEY IDEA:* CURIOSITY

Discuss Based on his advice about the box, do you think Epimetheus understands the trait of **curiosity?** ***Possible answer:*** *He doesn't understand curiosity; he thinks that if Pandora puts the box out of sight she will not think about it. He doesn't realize that allowing Pandora to keep the box will eventually lead to her opening it.*

the Four Winds to breathe life into the new creation. Finally he called upon the goddesses to complete the work and grant the glowing figure a touch of their own powers.

"Hephaestus has given her beauty," said Aphrodite,[4] "but I shall make her more beautiful by adding the spark of love. It will shine in her eyes, and everyone that looks on her will be enchanted."

"I shall make her wise," said Athene.[5] "She shall be able to choose between false and true, between what men value and what she must know is worthless."

"I shall make her a woman, a puzzle to every man," said Hera, the wife of Zeus. "I shall make her a real woman, for I shall give her the gift of curiosity." B

Smiling, the goddesses **adorned** her, and when Zeus beheld her grace, her garland of gold, and the glory of her endowments, he was as charmed as though he had been a mortal. "We will call her Pandora," he said, "Pandora, the All-Gifted. She shall become the bride of Epimetheus. But she shall not go empty-handed. She shall bring with her a casket, a box of magic as her dowry.[6] And Hermes, my messenger, shall conduct her to earth."

Epimetheus could not understand why the gods had become concerned about him. He was dazzled by Hermes, and it was some time before he could believe that the exquisite creature brought by the messenger god was meant for him. Even after Hermes departed in a flashing cloud and Pandora stood blushing beside him, he was perturbed. He remembered how often his brother Prometheus had warned him, "Do not trust the gods. And beware especially of Zeus and anything he may send you." However, when Pandora looked in his eyes and smiled, he was, as Aphrodite had predicted, enchanted and **ensnared.** Yet, even as he took her in his arms, he cautioned her.

"We have reason to fear the gods," said Epimetheus, "and also their gifts," he added, pointing to the casket.

"But this is my dowry," murmured Pandora. "Zeus himself filled it with magic as a present for us. See how beautifully it is carved and painted. Look at the silver hinges and the great gold clasp that fastens it." C

"Keep it well fastened," said Epimetheus, "otherwise I shall never rest easy. I do not know what the casket may contain, and I do not want to know. Promise me one thing. Never open the box. It is, I grant, a beautiful thing, too beautiful to destroy, and we will keep it. But hide it. Put it not only out of your sight but out of your mind. Then we shall both be content."

Happy that she could keep her dowry, Pandora put it under the bed and turned to her husband with love. And so for a long time nothing disturbed their married life and their continual joy in each other.

But, though Pandora benefited from the goddesses' gifts of beauty and wisdom, the gift of Hera had not been given in vain. For quite a while,

B READING A MYTH
What supernatural be
were involved in the
creation of Pandora?

adorn (ə-dôrn') *v.* to enhance or decorate

① **Targeted Passag**

ensnare (ĕn-snâr') *v.* to take or catch in something

C THEME
What can you **infer** ab
the contents of the bo
based on Zeus' desire
revenge?

4. **Aphrodite** (ăf'rə-dī'tē): Greek goddess of love and beauty.
5. **Athene** (ə-thē'nē): Greek goddess of wisdom; sometimes spelled *Athena.*
6. **dowry** (dou'rē): money or property a bride brings to a marriage.

DIFFERENTIATED INSTRUCTION

FOR LESS-PROFICIENT READERS

① **Targeted Passage [Lines 33–54]**

This passage sets up the story's main conflict.

- What warning did Prometheus give Epimetheus?
- In what way does Epimetheus ignore the warning? In what way does he obey it?
- How does Pandora react when Epimetheus tells her not to open the box?
- What does Pandora promise Epimetheus?

Reading Strategy Follow-Up: Reading a Myth [paired option] Have pairs read lines 19–54 and update their charts from page 455.

- **What human qualities do the gods display?** *sympathy, daring, desire for revenge, cruelty, cunning; and appreciation of love, wisdom, and curiosity*
- **What kind of behavior does Pandora demonstrate?** *enchanted by the box, protests not being able to open the box, obeys her husband, tries to be a good wife*

FOR ENGLISH LEARNERS

Vocabulary: Synonyms Have pairs of students use context clues to locate in the selection synonyms for the first word in each of the following word pairs:

- *grant* (line 17); *give* (line 25)
- *casket* (line 31); *box* (line 31)
- *beautiful* (line 20); *exquisite* (line 35)
- *gifts* (line 42); *present* (line 45)

458 UNIT 4: THEME AND SYMBOL

andora **restrained** her curiosity about the wonderful casket. But with the assing of time she could not help wondering what it might contain. After all, was *her* dowry, and she had a right to see what the greatest of the gods had onferred upon her. Then, ashamed of her weakness, she put the idea from her, nd thought only of her delight in her home with Epimetheus.

One day, however, the curiosity, so long stifled, overmastered her. "I shall nly lift the lid," she said to herself, "and snatch a moment's glimpse of what nay be inside. No matter what I see, I won't touch a thing. Surely there can e no harm in that." **D**

> **restrain** (rĭ-strān') *v.* to hold back; to control

> **D READING A MYTH** What prompts Pandora to look inside the box?

Anxiously, as though she were being watched, she tiptoed to her room. Gently getting down on her hands and knees, she drew the casket from under he bed. Half fearfully and half eagerly she lifted the lid. It was only a moment nd the lid was up only an inch, but in that moment a swarm of horrible hings flew out. They were noisome,[7] abominably colored, and evil-looking, or they were the spirits of all that was evil, sad, and hurtful. They were War nd Famine, Crime and Pestilence, Spite and Cruelty, Sickness and Malice, Envy, Woe, Wickedness, and all the other disasters let loose in the world.

2 Targeted Passage

Hearing Pandora's scream, Epimetheus rushed in. But it was too late. He and Pandora were set upon and stung, and the evil spirits flew off to ttack the rest of mankind. **E**

> **E READING A MYTH** What happens to humanity as a result of Pandora's actions?

"It is all my fault," cried Pandora. "If I had thought more about your warning and less about my own desires, I could have controlled my curiosity."

"The fault is mine," said Epimetheus. "I should have burned the box." Then e added, for the poison of Malice was already taking effect, "After all, you are what you are—only a woman—and what else could one expect of a woman."

Disconsolate[8] that she had brought so harmful a dowry to Epimetheus as well as to all other men and women, Pandora wept. It was hours before she et her husband comfort her. Finally, after she grew quiet, they heard a faint ound inside the box.

"Lift the lid again," said Epimetheus. "I think you have released the worst. Perhaps something else, something better, is still there."

He was right. At the bottom of the box was a quivering thing. Its body was mall; its wings were frail; but there was a radiance about it. Somehow Pandora knew what it was, and she took it up, touched it carefully, and showed it to Epimetheus. "It is Hope," she said.

"Do you think it will live?" asked Epimetheus.

"Yes," answered Pandora. "I am sure it will. Somehow I know that it will outlive War and Sickness and the other evils. And," she added, watching he shining thing rise and flutter about the room, "it will never leave us for ong. Even if we lose sight of it, it will be there." **F**

> **F THEME** How does the winged creature relate to the other things in the box?

She was no longer downhearted as Hope spread its wings and went out nto the world.

7. **noisome** (noi'səm): offensive.
8. **disconsolate** (dĭs-kŏn'sə-lĭt): gloomy.

READING STRATEGY

D READING A MYTH

Remind students to record Pandora's behavior in their charts from page 455. ***Possible answer:*** *She is overwhelmed by her own curiosity.*

READING STRATEGY

E READING A MYTH

Have students record the contents of the box in their charts. ***Possible answer:*** *Pandora unleashes on humanity the evil spirits of war, famine, crime, and other disasters.*

LITERARY ANALYSIS

F THEME

Possible answer: *The winged creature represents hope, and it is the only thing that can outlive the evil spirits.*

SELECTION WRAP–UP

CRITIQUE Ask students to evaluate the author's use of dialogue in this retelling of the myth. Does it make the story more or less appealing to modern-day audiences?

READING FLUENCY

Distribute the copy masters and have students practice fluency.

RESOURCE MANAGER—Copy Master
Reading Fluency p. 60

FOR LESS–PROFICIENT READERS

2 Targeted Passage [Lines 66–98]

This passage reveals the climax and resolution of the story.

- What happens when Pandora opens the box?
- Why does Epimetheus first blame himself and then Pandora for the horrible thing that has occurred?
- In what way is the problem resolved at the end of the story?

FOR ADVANCED LEARNERS/PRE–AP

Analyze Blame [paired option] Have pairs use a Cluster Diagram to decide who is to blame for war, crime, sickness, and other evils in the world according to the myth. Instruct them to write "Who is to blame?" in the center oval. In the second level of ovals, tell them to name characters who might be blamed. In the third level, they should list reasons. Then ask each pair of students to defend their choice.

BEST PRACTICES TOOLKIT—Transparency
Cluster Diagram p. B18

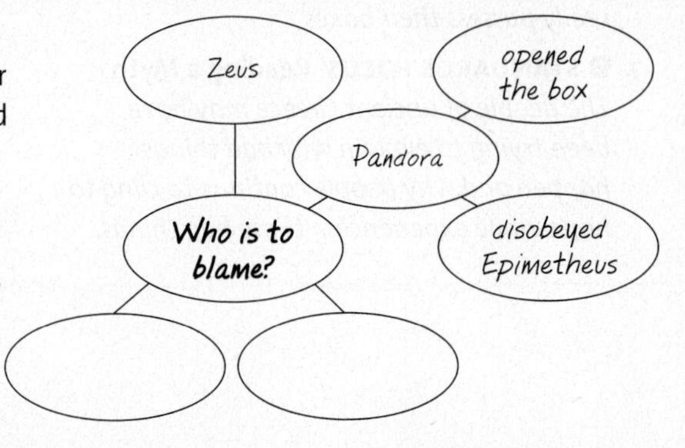

Practice and Apply

After Reading

For additional support of postreading questions, use these copy masters:

RESOURCE MANAGER—Copy Masters

Reading Check p. 58 (to check understanding of the selection)

Theme p. 51 (for practice of literary analysis standards focus)

Question Support p. 59 (After Reading questions adapted for English learners and less-proficient readers)

Additional selection questions are provided for teachers on page 45.

ANSWERS

Comprehension

1. *Zeus is angry with Epimetheus' brother Prometheus for giving fire to humankind. He knows that by making Epimetheus and all of humankind suffer, he will be adding to Prometheus' punishment.*
2. *Pandora is both excited to see Zeus' gift and worried because she's been warned that a gift from the gods cannot be trusted.*
3. *Students' drawings should represent details from the story.*

Literary Analysis

Possible answers:

4. *Hera believes that women are naturally curious, so Pandora needs curiosity in order to be like other women.*
5. **STANDARDS FOCUS Theme** *The theme this myth conveys is that humankind will always have hope, despite all the bad things that may happen in the world.*
6. ***Music Box:*** *meant to bring pleasure;* ***Pandora's Box:*** *meant to cause suffering;* ***Similarities:*** *both boxes are beautiful; both arouse curiosity; owners cannot really possess their boxes*
7. **STANDARDS FOCUS Reading a Myth** *The people of ancient Greece may have been trying to explain why bad things happen and why people continue to cling to hope while experiencing these bad things.*

After Reading

Comprehension

1. **Recall** Why does Zeus punish Epimetheus?
2. **Clarify** Why does Pandora open the box with a mixture of fear and eagerness?
3. **Represent** Create a drawing that represents what happens when Pandora opens the box.

Literary Analysis

4. **Interpret a Line** Reread lines 25–26. Why does having **curiosity** make Pandora "real"?
5. **Identify Theme** What is the theme of this myth? Consider the message about life the author conveys through events surrounding the box.
6. **Compare and Contrast Symbols** Use a Y-chart like the one shown to compare and contrast the box in "Pandora's Box" to the music box in "Gil's Furniture Bought & Sold." Think about the role the boxes play in the myth and the anecdote.

Music Box | Pandora's Box | Similarities

7. **Examine a Myth** Review the chart you made as you read. Based on the information you collected, what do you think the people of ancient Greece were trying to explain through this myth?

Extension and Challenge

8. **SOCIAL STUDIES CONNECTION** The phrase "Pandora's box" is widely used in the English language to describe an action that can have many negative consequences. Research why the atomic bomb developed by the United States has been called a "Pandora's box," and explain the connection to the myth. Present your findings to the class.

A mushroom cloud rises into the sky after a 1954 test of a nuclear device.

RESEARCH LINKS
For more on the atomic bomb, visit the **Research Center** at **ClassZone.com.**

Extension and Challenge

8. **SOCIAL STUDIES CONNECTION** *Students' research should reflect the idea that the atomic bomb brought misery to hundreds of thousands of people in Japan during World War II and that its consequences on the environment may not be detected for hundreds of years. Development of the bomb led to even more lethal bombs. Both the bomb and the myth convey the idea that one can never tell how far-reaching his or her actions might be.*

cabulary in Context

CABULARY PRACTICE

Choose the word from the list that makes the most sense in each sentence.

1. Zeus had a ____ plan for Epimetheus.
2. The goddesses wanted to ____ Pandora with gold garlands.
3. Aphrodite predicted that Pandora would ____ Epimetheus.
4. Epimetheus warned Pandora to ____ her interest in the casket.

adorn
ensnare
restrain
subtle

CABULARY IN WRITING

Why did Zeus decide to get back at Prometheus by picking on Epimetheus? Using two or more vocabulary words, write a paragraph describing what might have been going through his mind. You might start like this.

EXAMPLE SENTENCE

*Zeus could not **restrain** his desire for revenge.*

CABULARY STRATEGY: USING REFERENCE AIDS

Synonyms are words with similar meanings. For example, a synonym for *restrain* is *stifle.* When you're writing, you can use the following reference aids to help you find a more precise or powerful word to express an idea:

- a **thesaurus**—a book that lists words related to each other in meaning. An electronic thesaurus tool is also found on many word processing programs.

  restrain *verb* check, detain, stifle, suppress

- a **dictionary**—a book that lists words in alphabetical order and gives their definitions and pronunciations. Synonyms are listed after the definition of some words.

  restrain (rĭ-strān') *v.* **-strained, -strain•ing, -strains** to hold back or keep in check; control: *couldn't restrain the tears.* **syn** CHECK, DETAIN, STIFLE, SUPPRESS

PRACTICE Use a reference aid to find a synonym for each word. Note the synonym as well as the reference aid you used to find it. Then use each synonym in a sentence that matches its shade of meaning.

1. frail 2. methodical 3. scheme 4. invigorate

VOCABULARY PRACTICE
For more practice, go to the **Vocabulary Center** at **ClassZone.com.**

ANSWERS

Vocabulary in Context

VOCABULARY PRACTICE

1. *subtle*
2. *adorn*
3. *ensnare*
4. *restrain*

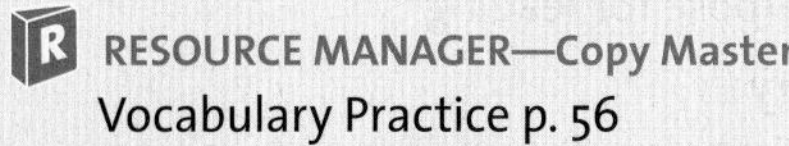

RESOURCE MANAGER—Copy Master
Vocabulary Practice p. 56

VOCABULARY IN WRITING

Ask students to recall the details of the trouble between Zeus and Prometheus. Then have them review the vocabulary list and identify words that could be used to explain why Zeus punished Epimetheus.

VOCABULARY STRATEGY: USING REFERENCE AIDS *(also an EL language objective)*

Remind students that when choosing synonyms from a reference aid, they should use the synonym in the context to make sure it has the correct shade of meaning.

Students' sentences will vary but should reflect each synonym's shade of meaning. ***Possible synonyms:***

1. *weak*
2. *organized*
3. *plan*
4. *energize*

RESOURCE MANAGER—Copy Master
Vocabulary Strategy p. 57

Vocabulary Center at **ClassZone.com**
Additional Vocabulary Activities

DIFFERENTIATED INSTRUCTION

FOR ENGLISH LEARNERS

Vocabulary Practice Before students begin the exercise, have them cover the word box. Ask them to fill in the blank in each sentence with any word that makes sense to them, based on their knowledge of the story. Then have them see if they can find a synonym in the word box for each word they used.

FOR ADVANCED LEARNERS/PRE–AP

Vocabulary Strategy Ask students to write dictionary entries for *adorn, ensnare,* and *subtle,* basing their entries on the example provided on the page. Then have them compare their answers to the definition found in a dictionary.

Assess and Reteach

Assess

RESOURCE MANAGER—Copy Masters
Selection Tests A, B/C pp. 61–62, 63–64

Test Generator CD

Reteach

STANDARDS LESSON FILE
Literature Lesson 13: Theme
Vocabulary Lesson 24: Using Dictionaries and Glossaries

Focus and Motivate

OBJECTIVES

Literary Analysis
- explore the key idea of **respect**
- identify, analyze, and compare universal themes
- read a Russian folk tale and a Japanese folk tale

Reading
- set a purpose for reading

Vocabulary
- build vocabulary for reading and writing
- determine meanings of derivatives by using knowledge of root words and affixes *(also an EL language objective)*

Grammar and Writing
- write a compare-contrast essay

SUMMARY

In "The Old Grandfather and His Little Grandson," an old man is mistreated by his son and his son's wife. When the couple's son indicates that he will treat them in the same way when they are old, they are kinder to the old man. In "The Wise Old Woman," a farmer hides his mother after a lord decrees that old people must be sent away to die. When the wisdom of the farmer's mother saves the village, the lord rescinds his decree.

How well do we treat our ELDERS?

To lead into the ***KEY IDEA,*** ask students to suggest ways in which our society **respects** people. Then have pairs work on the ***LIST IT*** activity.

Comparing Theme

The Old Grandfather and His Little Grandson

Russian Folk Tale Retold by Leo Tolstoy

The Wise Old Woman

Japanese Folk Tale Retold by Yoshiko Uchida

How well do we treat our ELDERS?

KEY IDEA Think about all the things the elderly people you know have done in their long lives. They've probably cared for their families, made contributions on the job or in the community, and witnessed events that are now part of history. Do you think they get the **respect** they deserve from younger generations? The two folk tales you are about to read explore reasons why our elders have earned special treatment.

LIST IT Create a list of three to five things that you can do to honor the wisdom and experience of someone from an older generation. Remember that a small gesture can have a big impact.

462

Selection Resources

RESOURCE MANAGER UNIT 4

Plan and Teach pp. 65–72

Literary Analysis
Summary pp. 73†*, 74‡*; 80†*, 81‡*
Question Support p. 83*

Reading
Set a Purpose for Reading pp. 75, 76†*
Reading Check pp. 78; 82
Reading Fluency p. 79

Vocabulary
Study p. 77*
Practice p. 84
Strategy p. 85

Grammar and Writing
Writing for Assessment p. 86

Assessment
Selection Tests A, B/C pp. 87*, 89*
Test Generator CD

BEST PRACTICES TOOLKIT

Differentiated Instruction pp. 31–38*
Scaffolding Instruction pp. 43–46*

Graphic Organizers/Strategies
New Word Analysis • Common Prefixes • Words with Multiple Meanings • Cause-and-Effect Chain • Reporter's Questions • Common Suffixes

Reading Support
Audio Anthology CD*

Technology
Literature, Vocabulary, and Writing Centers at **ClassZone.com**
Write*Smart* CD

* Resources for Differentiation † Also in Spanish ‡ In Haitian Creole and Vietnamese

RARY ANALYSIS: UNIVERSAL THEME

lmost every culture has its **folk tales,** simple stories passed own through generations by word of mouth. Even though he cultures themselves may be different in many ways, the ales often focus on the same basic ideas about life and how o behave. As a result, many folk tales have a **universal theme,** r a message that is meaningful to people living in any country nd at any time.

The two folk tales in this lesson come from different ountries and cultures, yet they express a similar theme. o identify their universal theme, pay attention to the haracters, their actions, and the consequences of their actions.

DING STRATEGY: SET A PURPOSE FOR READING

n this lesson, your **purpose for reading** is to compare two folk ales and to identify the universal theme they share. To do this, s you read take notes in a chart like the one shown. Later on, ou will be asked to do more with this chart.

	"The Old Grandfather and His Little Grandson"	"The Wise Old Woman"
Who are the important characters?	*elderly character:* *unkind characters:* *other characters:*	*elderly character:* *unkind characters:* *other characters:*
How is the elderly character mistreated?		
What motivates characters to stop this mistreatment?		

ABULARY IN CONTEXT

n "The Wise Old Woman," Yoshiko Uchida uses these words to describe a cruel lord and the people who suffer under his rule. Test your knowledge of each word by matching it with the numbered term closest in meaning.

WORD LIST arrogant bewilderment deceive haughtily

1. proudly 2. superior 3. astonishment 4. mislead

Author Online

Leo Tolstoy: Russian Novelist Russian writer Leo Tolstoy wanted to produce literature that would help people adopt simple, religious lives. Tolstoy created some of the world's best-known novels, including *War and Peace* and *Anna Karenina.* He also wrote short stories, dramas, essays, and adaptations. As he grew older, Tolstoy imposed increasingly strict rigors on himself in order to live what he saw as a good life. He became isolated from his wife and 13 children. In 1910, while escaping his family by train, Tolstoy developed pneumonia and died. His works live on as literary classics.

Leo Tolstoy
1828–1910

Yoshiko Uchida: Japanese-American Author The daughter of Japanese immigrants, Yoshiko Uchida grew up in California feeling different from her white classmates. This difference became more obvious after the bombing of Pearl Harbor in 1941. Government officials sent her father to an internment camp. Uchida and her family were later interned with him. She wrote many books for children that drew on her experience. She said, "I want to dispel the stereotypic image still held by many non-Asians about the Japanese and write about them as real people."

Yoshiko Uchida
1921–1992

MORE ABOUT THE AUTHOR
For more on Leo Tolstoy and Yoshiko Uchida, visit the **Literature Center** at **ClassZone.com.**

463

Teach

STANDARDS FOCUS

LITERARY ANALYSIS

● UNIVERSAL THEME

Ask students which of the following statements expresses a universal theme:

Good deeds are rewarded.
Farming is hard work.
Leo Tolstoy wrote great novels.

Answer: *Good deeds are rewarded.*

CHECK UNDERSTANDING Ask students to name two folk tales or stories that have the same universal theme.

READING STRATEGY

■ SET A PURPOSE FOR READING

Explain that to fulfill a specific purpose for reading, such as comparing folk tales, students should pause during reading to ask themselves questions and to review and fill in their graphic organizers.

CHECK UNDERSTANDING Ask students to name other kinds of graphic organizers they might use when their purpose for reading is to compare two stories.

RESOURCE MANAGER—Copy Master
Set a Purpose for Reading p. 75
(for student use while reading the selections)

VOCABULARY SKILL

▲ VOCABULARY IN CONTEXT

DIAGNOSE WORD KNOWLEDGE To determine preteaching needs, have all students complete **Vocabulary in Context.** Check students' answers. ***Answers:*** **1.** *haughtily* **2.** *arrogant* **3.** *bewilderment* **4.** *deceive*

PRETEACH VOCABULARY Use the Vocabulary Study copy master to help students create a word map for each boldfaced word.

1. Read the first sentence in Part A aloud.
2. Guide students in creating a word map for *arrogant* like the one shown. Point out that students may not be able to fill in every section for every word.
3. Repeat the procedure for each of the remaining words.

RESOURCE MANAGER—Copy Master
Vocabulary Study p. 77

For general guidelines on differentiating vocabulary instruction and for alternative vocabulary activities for students not needing vocabulary preteaching, see

BEST PRACTICES TOOLKIT
Scaffolding Vocabulary Instruction pp. 43–46

Vocabulary Center at **ClassZone.com**
Additional Vocabulary Activities

Practice and Apply

ANALYZE VISUALS
Possible answer: *The dark, bluish-gray color creates a somber mood.*

About the Art Spanish artist Pablo Picasso (1881–1973) was one of the 20th century's most prolific artists. Picasso was influential in the development of Cubism and Surrealism, and during his long career he created sculptures, book illustrations, and murals. *Old Beggar with a Boy* was painted during his Blue Period (1901–1904), which was characterized by melancholy themes. This painting captures the universal quality of affection experienced by many grandparents and their grandchildren. It also conveys the vulnerability of old age.

LITERARY ANALYSIS

Ⓐ UNIVERSAL THEME
Possible answer: *They treat him with coldness, cruelty, and disrespect.*

LITERARY ANALYSIS

Ⓑ UNIVERSAL THEME
Possible answer: *They realize that they, too, will one day be old and will want to be treated with respect instead of scorn. They also realize that their cruel example has taught their son the wrong lesson about how elders should be treated.*

Extend the Discussion Do you think the man and his wife would have had this realization on their own? Why or why not?

The Old Grandfather and His Little Grandson

Retold by Leo Tolstoy

The grandfather had become very old. His legs would not carry him, his eyes could not see, his ears could not hear, and he was toothless. When he ate, bits of food sometimes dropped out of his mouth. His son and his son's wife no longer allowed him to eat with them at the table. He had to eat his meals in the corner near the stove.

One day they gave him his food in a bowl. He tried to move the bowl closer; it fell to the floor and broke. His daughter-in-law scolded him. She told him that he spoiled everything in the house and broke their dishes, and she said that from now on he would get his food in a wooden dish. The old man sighed and said nothing. Ⓐ

A few days later, the old man's son and his wife were sitting in their hut, resting and watching their little boy playing on the floor. They saw him putting together something out of small pieces of wood. His father asked him, "What are you making, Misha?"

The little grandson said, "I'm making a wooden bucket. When you and Mamma get old, I'll feed you out of this wooden dish."

The young peasant and his wife looked at each other and tears filled their eyes. They were ashamed because they had treated the old grandfather so meanly, and from that day they again let the old man eat with them at the table and took better care of him. ~ Ⓑ

ANALYZE VISUALS
How does color affect mood of this picture?

① Targeted Passage

Ⓐ UNIVERSAL THEME
How do the man and his wife treat the grandfather?

Ⓑ UNIVERSAL THEME
What have the man and his wife realized about themselves?

Beggar and a Boy (1903), Pablo Picasso. C canvas, 125 cm × 92 cm. Pushkin Museum, Mo © Bridgeman Art Library. © 2007 Estate of Picasso/Artists Rights Society (ARS), New

DIFFERENTIATED INSTRUCTION

FOR ALL STUDENTS

Enhance Learning Styles Provide these independent projects for various learning styles:

- **Linguistic** Write two speeches for the lord of the village.
- **Visual** Select woodblock prints to illustrate the stories.
- **Analytical** Analyze and evaluate themes of folk tales.

For further details on these and other projects, see

RESOURCE MANAGER
Ideas for Extension pp. 70–71

FOR LESS–PROFICIENT READERS
In combination with the *Audio Anthology CD*, use one or more Targeted Passages (pp. 464, 466, 470, 472) to ensure that students focus on key story events, concepts, and skills.

① Targeted Passage [Lines 6–20]
This passage shows the turning point of the story.

- Why does the daughter-in-law decide that the old man must get his food in a wooden dish?
- What does the grandson do and say? How does this make his parents feel?
- How are things different at the end of the story?

BACKGROUND

Folk Tales Folk tales began as an oral tradition and continue to be a vital part of many cultures today. Folk tales spread around the world as people moved from one place to another and blended with folk tales people heard in the new locations. Interestingly, many cultures that have never interacted have folk tales with similar plots, motifs, and universal themes. This shows that no matter how different people are, they share basic experiences, concerns, and values.

FOR ENGLISH LEARNERS

Options for Reading [small-group option] Read the first folk tale aloud, pausing frequently to monitor students' comprehension. For the second folk tale, have students read along with the *Audio Anthology CD* in small groups. Encourage students to pause the CD frequently to check their understanding and discuss any questions they have.

Key Academic Vocabulary Have students use New Word Analysis for these words in "The Wise Old Woman": *task* (lines 84, 97), *finally* (line 145), *abandon* (line 150).

 BEST PRACTICES TOOLKIT—Transparency
New Word Analysis p. E8

Prereading For prereading instruction for English learners, see

 BEST PRACTICES TOOLKIT
Scaffolding Reading Instruction pp. 43–46

FOR ADVANCED LEARNERS/PRE-AP

Pre-AP exercises in the bottom channel provide additional challenge for your advanced students. Use them for small groups or individuals.

ADDITIONAL GUIDELINES

For more help with differentiation and tips for classroom management, see

 BEST PRACTICES TOOLKIT
Differentiated Instruction pp. 31–38

Lines 3–6
REINFORCE *KEY IDEA:* RESPECT

Discuss The young lord does not **respect** old people because they are not able to work for a living. Thus he thinks they are not useful. Is working for a living the only way that people can be useful? What are some other reasons that we respect people? ***Possible answer:*** *No, working for a living is not the only way a person can be useful. We respect people for what they have accomplished in their lives, for the knowledge and wisdom that they have, and for the kindness that they show to others.*

LITERARY ANALYSIS

C UNIVERSAL THEME

Possible answer: *He says he has no use for old people—they are neither useful nor able to work. He wants the village filled with young people.*

ANALYZE VISUALS

Possible answer: *The setting is a busy street in a Japanese village. The street, lined with huts, slopes down to a lake, and small mountains lie in the distance.*

About the Art This woodblock print of a village street was created by the artist Hiroshige III, who became well known for his prints of Japanese landscapes. He is also known for his depiction of modernization in the 19th century. Hiroshige III was the pupil of the master Hiroshige I, who died in 1858.

THE WISE OLD WOMAN

Retold by Yoshiko Uchida

Many long years ago, there lived an **arrogant** and cruel young lord who ruled over a small village in the western hills of Japan.

"I have no use for old people in my village," he said **haughtily.** "They are neither useful nor able to work for a living. I therefore decree[1] that anyone over seventy-one must be banished[2] from the village and left in the mountains to die."

"What a dreadful decree! What a cruel and unreasonable lord we have," the people of the village murmured. But the lord fearfully punished anyone who disobeyed him, and so villagers who turned seventy-one were tearfully carried into the mountains, never to return.

Gradually there were fewer and fewer old people in the village and soon they disappeared altogether. Then the young lord was pleased.

"What a fine village of young, healthy and hard-working people I have," he bragged. "Soon it will be the finest village in all of Japan." C

arrogant (ăr'ə-gənt) *ad* displaying a sense of self-importance

haughtily (hô'tə-lē) *adv* proudly; scornfully

2 Targeted Passage

C UNIVERSAL THEME
Why does the young l decide that old people must be banished?

ANALYZE VISUALS
How would you describ the **setting** shown in th picture?

1. **decree** (dĭ-krē'): to make an order; an order that has the force of law.
2. **banished:** forced to leave a country or a place.

Village Street (1875), Hiroshige III. From the se *Famous Places on the Tokaido: a Record of the Pr of Reform.* © Asian Art & Archaeology, Inc./Co

DIFFERENTIATED INSTRUCTION

FOR LESS–PROFICIENT READERS

2 Targeted Passage [Lines 1–12]

This passage sets the stage for the conflict in the folk tale.

- What does the lord who rules the village think about old people?
- What does he order the villagers to do?
- What feelings do the villagers experience about the lord's order? Do they obey him?
- In what way does the village change as a result of the lord's order?

FOR ADVANCED LEARNERS/PRE–AP

Predict [small-group option] Have students make predictions about what will happen in the story, based on the title, their reading of the first page, and their understanding of universal themes in folk tales. Have them write their predictions in their notebooks, along with a statement of the universal theme that would be expressed in their predicted story. When they finish the story, ask students to share their predictions in small groups and discuss how accurate they were.

BACKGROUND

Ubasuteyama In the time period during which this folk tale is set, Ubasuteyama (literally, "old woman-abandoning mountain") was practiced. Elderly family members, sometimes at the orders of village officials, were carried away to a mountain and left to die from exposure, starvation, and dehydration. Drought, a shortage of food, and overpopulation were some of the reasons for the practice.

Many Japanese legends and poems are based on Ubasuteyama. It was also the subject of a 1958 film by director Kinoshita Keisuke titled *The Ballad of Narayama.* The film won the top prize at the Cannes film festival.

FOR LESS–PROFICIENT READERS

Reading Strategy Follow-Up: Set a Purpose for Reading Read lines 1–18 aloud. Ask students to identify the important characters in the folk tale and have them record the information in the chart from page 463. As they continue to read, have students answer the other questions in the chart.

FOR ENGLISH LEARNERS

Vocabulary: Prefixes Remind students that the prefix *dis-* indicates a reversal or absence. Examples of words with this prefix are *disobeyed* (line 9) and *disappeared* (line 12). Use Common Prefixes to help students identify the meanings of additional prefixes as they read, such as *un-*, which means "not."

 **BEST PRACTICES TOOLKIT—Transparency**
Common Prefixes p. E14

THE WISE OLD WOMAN 467

SOCIAL STUDIES CONNECTION

Most Japanese live in the lowlands, near rivers or the ocean. The majority of Japan's large cities began as ports (Kobe, Yokohama, Nagasaki) or as "castle towns" (Tokyo). The location of castle towns made it possible for rulers to oversee and control major transportation routes. The towns profited from trade and were well defended against invaders.

LITERARY ANALYSIS

D UNIVERSAL THEME

Possible answer: *The son cannot bear to leave his mother alone in the mountains to die, especially when she shows her love for him by marking the path so he will not get lost on his way back.*

ANALYZE VISUALS

Possible answer: *The way is steep, and the moon shows that it is nighttime.*

About the Art The subject of this woodblock print by Tsukioka Yoshitoshi (1839–1892) is exactly the same as that of the folk tale—the Japanese practice of Ubasuteyama. For more information, see the Background note on page 467 of the teacher's edition.

Now there lived in this village a kind young farmer and his aged mother. They were poor, but the farmer was good to his mother, and the two of them lived happily together. However, as the years went by, the mother grew older, and before long she reached the terrible age of seventy-one.

"If only I could somehow **deceive** the cruel lord," the farmer thought. But there were records in the village books and every one knew that his mother had turned seventy-one.

Each day the son put off telling his mother that he must take her into the mountains to die, but the people of the village began to talk. The farmer knew that if he did not take his mother away soon, the lord would send his soldiers and throw them both into a dark dungeon to die a terrible death.

"Mother—" he would begin, as he tried to tell her what he must do, but he could not go on.

Then one day the mother herself spoke of the lord's dread decree. "Well, my son," she said, "the time has come for you to take me to the mountains. We must hurry before the lord sends his soldiers for you." And she did not seem worried at all that she must go to the mountains to die.

"Forgive me, dear mother, for what I must do," the farmer said sadly, and the next morning he lifted his mother to his shoulders and set off on the steep path toward the mountains. Up and up he climbed, until the trees clustered close and the path was gone. There was no longer even the sound of birds, and they heard only the soft wail of the wind in the trees. The son walked slowly, for he could not bear to think of leaving his old mother in the mountains. On and on he climbed, not wanting to stop and leave her behind. Soon, he heard his mother breaking off small twigs from the trees that they passed.

"Mother, what are you doing?" he asked.

"Do not worry, my son," she answered gently. "I am just marking the way so you will not get lost returning to the village."

The son stopped. "Even now you are thinking of me?" he asked, wonderingly.

The mother nodded. "Of course, my son," she replied. "You will always be in my thoughts. How could it be otherwise?"

At that, the young farmer could bear it no longer. "Mother, I cannot leave you in the mountains to die all alone," he said. "We are going home and no matter what the lord does to punish me, I will never desert you again." D

So they waited until the sun had set and a lone star crept into the silent sky. Then in the dark shadows of night, the farmer carried his mother down the hill and they returned quietly to their little house. The farmer dug a deep hole in the floor of his kitchen and made a small room where he could hide his mother. From that day, she spent all her time in the secret room and the farmer carried meals to her there. The rest of the time, he was careful to work in the fields and act as though he lived alone. In this way, for almost two years, he kept his mother safely hidden and no one in the village knew that she was there.

deceive (dĭ-sēv') *v.* to cause to believe what not true; to mislead

SOCIAL STUDIES CONNECTION

Japan is a string of several thousand islan off the east coast of th continent of Asia. Muc of Japan consists of hil and mountains.

D UNIVERSAL THEM
Why does the son de to disobey the decree even though he migh be punished?

ANALYZE VISUALS
Based on this picture, what can you **conclud** about the journey up the mountain?

DIFFERENTIATED INSTRUCTION

FOR ENGLISH LEARNERS

Vocabulary: Homographs and Multiple-Meaning Words Have students use Words with Multiple Meanings to figure out the correct meanings of these words in the context of the folk tale:

- *fine* (line 13): often used to mean "a sum of money imposed as a penalty," here it means "of superior quality"
- *close* (line 35): often used to mean "to shut," here it means "with little space between"
- *bear* (line 37): often used to mean "a large animal," here it means "tolerate or endure"
- *desert* (line 49): often used to mean "a dry, barren region," here it means "to leave"

Point out the different pronunciations of *close* and *desert* when the meaning changes.

 **BEST PRACTICES TOOLKIT—Transparency**
Words with Multiple Meanings p. E31

The Moon and the Abandoned Old Woman (1891), Yoshitoshi. © Asian Art & Archaeology, Inc./Corbis.

Lines 15–58

DISCUSSION PROMPTS

Use these prompts to help students understand the motivations and consequences of the farmer's actions:

Connect The son puts off taking his mother into the mountains to die. Then, after they set out, he walks very slowly. How do you feel when you are forced to do something you don't want to do? *Students may reply that they feel uneasy, unhappy, and filled with guilt, like the farmer in the story.*

Infer What can you infer from this passage about the relationship between the farmer and his mother? How does this help you understand the farmer's internal conflict? ***Possible answer:*** *The farmer and his mother love each other and take care of each other. The farmer is forced to abandon his mother rather than take care of her. This makes him feel desperate and guilty.*

Speculate Why do you think the author includes the details that describe the sound of the wind in the trees (line 36) and the image of the star rising in the sky (lines 50–51)? ***Possible answer:*** *The wailing wind mirrors the farmer's feelings of sadness, and the star creeping "into the silent sky" mirrors the way he and his mother return to the village.*

FOR LESS–PROFICIENT READERS

Comprehension: Cause and Effect Review cause and effect, and then distribute the Cause-and-Effect Chain for students to fill out. Help students understand the chain of events leading to the farmer's decision to return with his mother to the village.

 **BEST PRACTICES TOOLKIT—Transparency**
Cause-and-Effect Chain pp. B16, B39

FOR ADVANCED LEARNERS/PRE–AP

Synthesize Challenge students to write a poem based on the images in this woodblock print. They can write the poem from the first- or third-person point of view, in either a narrative or a free-verse form. When they have finished, invite volunteers to share their poems. Discuss how the poems capture or complement the mood of the image.

ANALYZE VISUALS

Possible answer: *The man has an aggressive stance, leaning forward with his hands on his hips. He has a furrowed brow, staring eyes, and a frown. These details give the impression that he is fierce and aggressive.*

About the Art This woodcut print of a Japanese actor playing the role of a pirate, also by Tsukioka Yoshitoshi, shows what Lord Higa might have looked like.

Lines 59–79

DISCUSSION PROMPTS

Use these prompts to help students understand the plot's rising action:

Recall What task does Lord Higa give the villagers? What does he say will happen if they are unable to complete the task? ***Answer:*** *He tells them to bring him a box with a thousand ropes of ash. If they cannot do this, he will conquer the village.*

Draw Conclusions Why do you think the wise men are unable to solve the problem posed by Lord Higa? ***Possible answer:*** *They are young and don't have the wisdom of experience that comes with age.*

Evaluate When faced with the prospect of a new lord, the farmer worries about his mother. Do you think his worry is justified? Why or why not? ***Possible answer:*** *It is justified because the new lord might impose even more suffering on the people of the village. Both lords are cruel.*

Moon, Tsukioka Yoshitoshi. From the *Snow, Moon and Flower* Series. © Christie's Images Ltd.

Then one day there was a terrible commotion among the villagers for Lord Higa of the town beyond the hills threatened to conquer their village and make it his own.

"Only one thing can spare you," Lord Higa announced. "Bring me a box containing one thousand ropes of ash and I will spare your village."

The cruel young lord quickly gathered together all the wise men of his village. "You are men of wisdom," he said. "Surely you can tell me how to meet Lord Higa's demands so our village can be spared."

But the wise men shook their heads. "It is impossible to make even one rope of ash, sire," they answered. "How can we ever make one thousand?"

"Fools!" the lord cried angrily. "What good is your wisdom if you cannot help me now?"

And he posted a notice in the village square offering a great reward of gold to any villager who could help him save their village.

But all the people in the village whispered, "Surely, it is an impossible thing, for ash crumbles at the touch of the finger. How could anyone ever make a rope of ash?" They shook their heads and sighed, "Alas, alas, we must be conquered by yet another cruel lord."

The young farmer, too, supposed that this must be, and he wondered what would happen to his mother if a new lord even more terrible than their own came to rule over them.

When his mother saw the troubled look on his face, she asked, "Why are you so worried, my son?"

ANALYZE VISUALS
What **details** about th
man's appearance aff
your impression of his
personality?

③ **Targeted Passag**

DIFFERENTIATED INSTRUCTION

FOR LESS-PROFICIENT READERS

③ **Targeted Passage [Lines 59–76]**

This passage introduces a problem—Lord Higa threatens the village.

- What threat does Lord Higa make? What demands does he make?
- Whom does the young lord ask for help in meeting Lord Higa's demands? What is the result?
- What do the villagers predict will happen next?

FOR ENGLISH LEARNERS

Vocabulary: Cognates [shared-language groups] Have groups scan the story for cognates and report their findings to the class. Spanish cognates on this page include

- *commotion/conmoción* (line 59)
- *conquer/conquistar* (line 60)
- *announced/anunció* (line 62)
- *offering/ofreciendo* (line 71)
- *supposed/supuso* (line 77)

So the farmer told her of the impossible demand made by Lord Higa if the illage was to be spared, but his mother did not seem troubled at all. Instead ne laughed softly and said, "Why, that is not such an impossible task. All one as to do is soak ordinary rope in salt water and dry it well. When it is burned, will hold its shape and there is your rope of ash! Tell the villagers to hurry nd find one thousand pieces of rope."

The farmer shook his head in amazement. "Mother, you are wonderfully vise," he said, and he rushed to tell the young lord what he must do. **E**

E UNIVERSAL THEME What do you learn about the old woman from the way she solves the village's problem?

"You are wiser than all the wise men of the village," the lord said when he eard the farmer's solution, and he rewarded him with many pieces of gold. 'he thousand ropes of ash were quickly made and the village was spared.

In a few days, however, there was another great commotion in the village as ord Higa sent another threat. This time he sent a log with a small hole that urved and bent seven times through its length, and he demanded that a single iece of silk thread be threaded through the hole. "If you cannot perform this ısk," the lord threatened, "I shall come to conquer your village."

The young lord hurried once more to his wise men, but they all shook their eads in **bewilderment**. "A needle cannot bend its way through such curves," hey moaned. "Again we are faced with an impossible demand."

bewilderment (bĭ-wĭl'dər-mənt) *n.* the state of being confused or astonished

"And again you are stupid fools!'" the lord said, stamping his foot npatiently. He then posted a second notice in the village square asking the illagers for their help.

Once more the young farmer hurried with the problem to his mother in her ecret room.

"Why, that is not so difficult," his mother said with a quick smile. "Put ome sugar at one end of the hole. Then, tie an ant to a piece of silk thread and ut it in at the other end. He will weave his way in and out of the curves to get o the sugar and he will take the silk thread with him."

"Mother, you are remarkable!" the son cried, and he hurried off to the lord vith the solution to the second problem.

Once more the lord commended the young farmer and rewarded him with nany pieces of gold. "You are a brilliant man and you have saved our village gain," he said gratefully.

But the lord's troubles were not over even then, for a few days later Lord Higa sent still another demand. "This time you will undoubtedly fail and then shall conquer your village," he threatened. "Bring me a drum that sounds vithout being beaten."

"But that is not possible," sighed the people of the village. "How can anyone nake a drum sound without beating it?"

This time the wise men held their heads in their hands and moaned, "It is opeless. It is hopeless. This time Lord Higa will conquer us all."

LITERARY ANALYSIS

E UNIVERSAL THEME

Possible answer: *The old woman is wise and clever.*

Lines 112–114

REINFORCE *KEY IDEA:* RESPECT

Discuss Does the young lord **respect** the farmer? Explain. ***Possible answer:*** *Yes. Because the farmer has saved the village twice, the young lord rewards the farmer with gold and tells him he is brilliant.*

FOR LESS–PROFICIENT READERS

Comprehension Support Have students create drawings or models of the three problems and solutions—the rope, the log, and the drum. Ask students if they can think of other possible solutions to the problems. Discuss their answers.

FOR ADVANCED LEARNERS/PRE–AP

Synthesize [paired option] Breaking news! Have students work with a partner to write a television news "Special Report," describing the threat by Lord Higa and how the young lord, the wise men, and the villagers respond to the threat. To organize the report, have students develop a list of Reporter's Questions.

 **BEST PRACTICES TOOLKIT—Transparency** Reporter's Questions p. C9

LITERARY ANALYSIS

F UNIVERSAL THEME

Possible answer: *The old woman has the wisdom of experience, which allows her to solve the problems.*

LITERARY ANALYSIS

G UNIVERSAL THEME

Possible answer: *The young lord learns that old people possess wisdom and experience and should be valued and treated with respect.*

The young farmer hurried home breathlessly. "Mother, Mother, we must solve another terrible problem or Lord Higa will conquer our village!" And he quickly told his mother about the impossible drum.

His mother, however, smiled and answered, "Why, this is the easiest of them all. Make a drum with sides of paper and put a bumblebee inside. As it tries to escape, it will buzz and beat itself against the paper and you will have a drum that sounds without being beaten." F

The young farmer was amazed at his mother's wisdom. "You are far wiser than any of the wise men of the village," he said, and he hurried to tell the young lord how to meet Lord Higa's third demand.

When the lord heard the answer, he was greatly impressed. "Surely a young man like you cannot be wiser than all my wise men," he said. "Tell me honestly, who has helped you solve all these difficult problems?"

The young farmer could not lie. "My lord," he began slowly, "for the past two years I have broken the law of the land. I have kept my aged mother hidden beneath the floor of my house, and it is she who solved each of your problems and saved the village from Lord Higa."

He trembled as he spoke, for he feared the lord's displeasure and rage. Surely now the soldiers would be summoned to throw him into the dark dungeon. But when he glanced fearfully at the lord, he saw that the young ruler was not angry at all. Instead, he was silent and thoughtful, for at last he realized how much wisdom and knowledge old people possess.

"I have been very wrong," he said finally. "And I must ask the forgiveness of your mother and of all my people. Never again will I demand that the old people of our village be sent to the mountains to die. Rather, they will be treated with the respect and honor they deserve and share with us the wisdom of their years." G

And so it was. From that day, the villagers were no longer forced to abandon their parents in the mountains, and the village became once more a happy, cheerful place in which to live. The terrible Lord Higa stopped sending his impossible demands and no longer threatened to conquer them, for he too was impressed. "Even in such a small village there is much wisdom," he declared, "and its people should be allowed to live in peace."

And that is exactly what the farmer and his mother and all the people of the village did for all the years thereafter.

F UNIVERSAL THEM
Why do you think th
old woman is able t
solve all the problem
created by Lord Higa
demands?

(4) Targeted Passag

G UNIVERSAL THEM
What lesson does th
young lord learn?

SELECTION WRAP–UP

REFLECT Ask students to think about which character in the folk tales they find most sympathetic. If they could say one thing to that character, what would it be?

CRITIQUE Point out that both folk tales have happy endings. Ask students to imagine an alternate ending to either or both of the folk tales. Would such an ending support the universal theme? Why or why not?

READING FLUENCY

Distribute the copy masters and have students practice fluency.

RESOURCE MANAGER—Copy Master
Reading Fluency p. 79

DIFFERENTIATED INSTRUCTION

FOR LESS–PROFICIENT READERS

(4) Targeted Passage [Lines 136–155]

This passage presents the folk tale's resolution.

- What does the farmer admit to the young lord?
- In what way does he think the lord will respond? In what way does the lord actually respond?
- In what way is life in the village different after the young lord lifts his decree?

FOR ENGLISH LEARNERS

Vocabulary: Suffixes Point out examples of words on this page with the suffix *-ful,* which means "full of" (*fearful[ly], thoughtful, cheerful*) and identify the base words. Explain that the addition of this suffix changes nouns to adjectives. Challenge students to create new words by adding the suffix to other nouns. Then use Common Suffixes to help them identify the meanings of other suffixes.

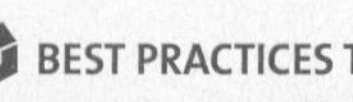

BEST PRACTICES TOOLKIT—Transparency
Common Suffixes p. E15

...mprehension

Recall In "The Old Grandfather and His Little Grandson," whose action shames the couple into treating the grandfather better?

Recall In "The Wise Old Woman," what is the young lord's decree?

Clarify What causes Lord Higa to spare the village?

...erary Analysis

Analyze Motives In "The Old Grandfather and His Little Grandson," why do you think the son and his wife react so negatively to the grandfather's accident?

Compare and Contrast Characters Reread lines 1–49 of "The Wise Old Woman." How are the young lord and the young farmer different? In your answer, be sure to describe each character's traits.

Identify Parallel Episodes In folk tales, events often happen in threes. There may be three wishes or three tasks, for example. These repeated events are called **parallel episodes.** What parallel episodes can you find in "The Wise Old Woman"?

...mparing Universal Theme

...ow that you have read both tales, finish filling in your chart. Finally, add the ...uestion about universal theme to your chart and write your answer.

	"The Old Grandfather and His Little Grandson"	"The Wise Old Woman"
Who are the important characters?	elderly character: unkind characters: other characters:	elderly character: unkind characters: other characters:
How is the elderly character mistreated?		
What motivates characters to stop this mistreatment?		
What is the universal theme?		

Practice and Apply

After Reading

For additional support of postreading questions, use these copy masters:

RESOURCE MANAGER—Copy Masters
Reading Check pp. 78, 82 (to check understanding of the selections)
Question Support p. 83 (After Reading questions adapted for English learners and less-proficient readers)
Additional selection questions are provided for teachers on page 69.

ANSWERS

Comprehension

1. *The young grandson's action shames his parents into treating the grandfather better.*
2. *The young lord decrees that when villagers reach the age of 71, they must be taken into the mountains to die.*
3. *Lord Higa is impressed that the villagers are able to meet his demands, so he decides that they should be allowed to live in peace.*

Literary Analysis

Possible answers:

4. *The grandfather irritates them and they feel he is an unpleasant nuisance; they cannot identify with his problems; they worry about how others may see them.*
5. *The young lord decrees that old people should be left to die. He does not think they are worthy of living. He is cruel, thoughtless, and greedy. The young farmer risks his own life to save his mother. He is brave, selfless, and caring.*
6. *The three parallel episodes are centered around Lord Higa's three demands. With each demand, the wise men and the villagers fail to find a solution, the farmer asks his mother, and the mother solves the problem.*

Comparing Universal Theme

● **STANDARDS FOCUS** Universal Theme

■ **STANDARDS FOCUS** Set a Purpose for Reading

"The Old Grandfather and His Little Grandson"

- **Who are the important characters?** *elderly grandfather, unkind son and daughter-in-law, grandson*
- **How is the elderly character mistreated?** *He is scolded and made to eat from a wooden bowl.*
- **What motivates characters to stop this mistreatment?** *The grandson makes a wooden bucket for his parents to eat from when they are older, thus shaming them.*

"The Wise Old Woman"

- **Who are the important characters?** *elderly mother, unkind young lord, son*
- **How is the elderly character mistreated?** *The young lord decrees that she must be sent from the village at age 71 to die in the mountains.*
- **What motivates characters to stop this mistreatment?** *The young lord reverses his decree when the old woman solves three problems, thus saving the village from being conquered.*

Both

- **What is the universal theme?** *Our elders deserve to be treated with respect.*

ANSWERS

Vocabulary in Context

VOCABULARY PRACTICE

1. *(b) modestly*
2. *(a) understanding*
3. *(b) humble*
4. *(c) guide*

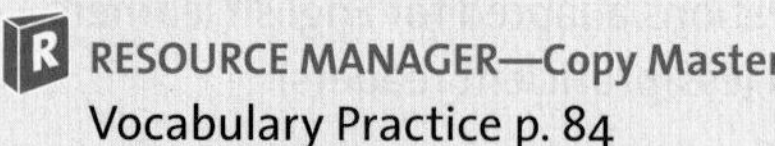

RESOURCE MANAGER—Copy Master
Vocabulary Practice p. 84

VOCABULARY IN WRITING

Challenge students to use each vocabulary word in a paragraph from the young lord's perspective. Encourage them to use as much detail as possible in each sentence.

VOCABULARY STRATEGY: THE SUFFIX *-ly*

(also an EL language objective)

Remind students that the spelling of some words changes when the suffix *-ly* is added to form an adverb. For example, when *-ly* is added to the word *happy,* the *y* is replaced by an *i* to form *happily.* Remind students to use a dictionary to check spelling when they are using suffixes to create new words.

Possible answers:

1. *cruelly; In the beginning of the story, the young lord acted cruelly.*
2. *tearfully; Tearfully, the son took his mother into the mountains.*
3. *angrily; The lord angrily asked the villagers for help.*
4. *happily; The old woman happily provided her son with the answers.*

RESOURCE MANAGER—Copy Master
Vocabulary Strategy p. 85

Vocabulary Center at **ClassZone.com**
Additional Vocabulary Activities

Vocabulary in Context

VOCABULARY PRACTICE

Choose the word in each group that is most nearly opposite in meaning to the boldfaced word.

1. **haughtily:** (a) snobbishly, (b) modestly, (c) indifferently
2. **bewilderment:** (a) understanding, (b) confusion, (c) shock
3. **arrogant:** (a) smug, (b) humble, (c) aloof
4. **deceive:** (a) outsmart, (b) scam, (c) guide

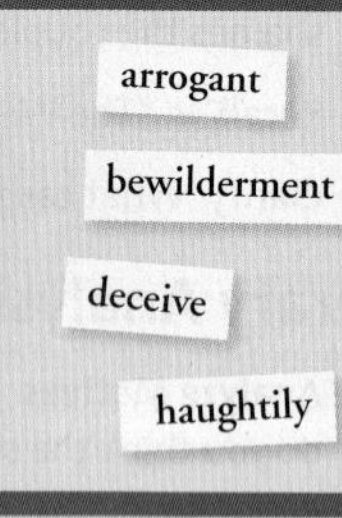

VOCABULARY IN WRITING

Write a paragraph from the young lord's perspective, explaining the lesson he learned. Include at least two vocabulary words. Here is a sample of how you might begin.

EXAMPLE SENTENCE

*When I learned how wise the old woman was, I felt truly ashamed I had been so **arrogant**.*

VOCABULARY STRATEGY: THE SUFFIX *-ly*

A suffix is a word part that can be added to the end of a root or base word. Sometimes a suffix is used to change a word's part of speech. For example, when the suffix *-ly* is added to the end of the word *haughty,* it forms the adverb *haughtily.* When an adjective ends in *-y,* as *haughty* does, the *y* changes to *i* before *-ly* is added.

PRACTICE Change each boldfaced adjective to an adverb by adding the suffix *-ly.* Then rephrase each sentence so it makes sense.

1. In the beginning of the story, the young lord was **cruel.**
2. The **tearful** son had to take his mother into the mountains.
3. The **angry** lord asked the villagers for help.
4. The old woman was **happy** to provide her son with the answers.

VOCABULARY PRACTICE
For more practice, go to the **Vocabulary Cen**
at **ClassZone.com.**

DIFFERENTIATED INSTRUCTION

FOR ENGLISH LEARNERS

Vocabulary Practice [mixed-readiness pairs]

1. Pair students with more fluent readers to define all of the words in each set.
2. Then have students locate each boldfaced word in the folk tale and replace it with the words in the set.
3. Use the context clues to help them choose the word in each set that differs most from the meaning of the boldfaced word.

FOR ADVANCED LEARNERS/PRE–AP

Vocabulary Strategy Have students find other words in the folk tales with the suffix *-ly* and use the words to write sentences describing the characters.

Writing for Assessment

1. READ THE PROMPT

In writing assessments, you will often be asked to compare and contrast two works that share a similar theme.

PROMPT

The folk tales "The Old Grandfather and His Little Grandson" and "The Wise Old Woman" express the same universal theme in different ways. In four to five paragraphs, compare and contrast the ways in which the folk tales convey their message. Include details from the tales to support your response.

STRATEGIES IN ACTION

1. I have to make sure I understand the **message** expressed by these folk tales.
2. I need to identify the **similarities and differences** in how the tales get the message across.
3. I should support my ideas using **information** from the two tales.

2. PLAN YOUR WRITING

Review your chart to identify the universal theme and the way each folk tale expresses it. Then think about how you will set up the body of your response.

- Option A: In one paragraph, describe how the universal theme is conveyed in the first folk tale; in the next paragraph, describe how this theme is conveyed in the second folk tale; in a third paragraph, discuss similarities and differences.
- Option B: In one paragraph, compare the elderly characters; in a second paragraph, compare the mistreatment of the elderly characters; in a third paragraph, compare the motivations for ending the mistreatment.

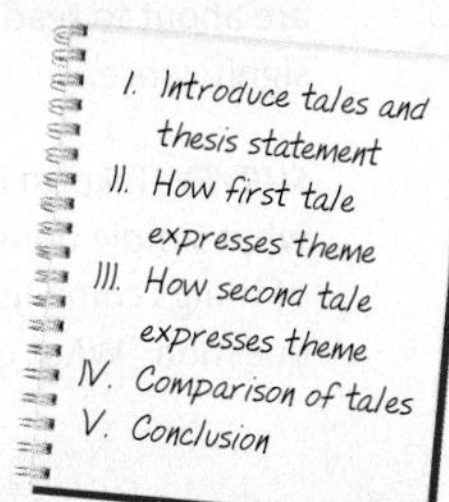

I. Introduce tales and thesis statement
II. How first tale expresses theme
III. How second tale expresses theme
IV. Comparison of tales
V. Conclusion

Once you have decided on the organization, outline your essay. Then write a thesis statement that describes the main idea of your essay.

3. DRAFT YOUR RESPONSE

Introduction Give the titles and authors of the tales. Provide a sentence telling what each tale is about. State the universal theme and include your thesis statement.
Body Using your outline as a guide, discuss how each folk tale conveys the universal theme. Use details from the tales to support your ideas.
Conclusion End each essay by restating the universal theme and your thesis statement. Explain whether the values conveyed by these tales are still important.
Revision Make sure you clearly identify the tale you are discussing in each paragraph.

DIFFERENTIATED INSTRUCTION

FOR LESS–PROFICIENT WRITERS

Draft Your Response Provide students with a template to structure their responses, such as this one for Option A:

Introduction
- Give titles of folk tales.
- Make thesis statement.

Body
- Explain how the universal theme is conveyed in the first folk tale: describe the elderly characters, their mistreatment, and the motivation for ending it.
- Repeat the previous step for the second folk tale.
- Compare and contrast how each folk tale's message is conveyed.

Conclusion
- Restate thesis.
- Draw conclusions about universal theme.

Writing for Assessment

1. ***READ THE PROMPT***
   Read the prompt aloud. Ask volunteers to identify key words and phrases that define the task (*compare and contrast, include details*).
2. ***PLAN YOUR WRITING***
   - Have students refer to the chart they have completed as they plan their writing.
   - After students have decided how to organize their response, have them write key details in the appropriate sections of their outlines.
3. ***DRAFT YOUR RESPONSE***
   - Have students use their outline to create a strong thesis statement. Give them an example: "The universal theme in the folk tales is conveyed through the actions the characters take in response to conflict."
   - Remind students to begin each body paragraph with a strong topic sentence.
   - List transitions on the board that can be used to strengthen the unity within each paragraph and between paragraphs, such as *in addition, on the other hand, in contrast,* and *finally.*

RESOURCE MANAGER—Copy Master
Writing for Assessment p. 86

Assess and Reteach

Assess

RESOURCE MANAGER—Copy Masters
Selection Tests A, B/C pp. 87–88, 89–90

Test Generator CD

Reteach

STANDARDS LESSON FILE
Literature Lesson 13: Theme
Reading Lesson 12: Comparing and Contrasting
Writing Lesson 29: Comparison-Contrast Essay
Vocabulary Lesson 1: Word Parts

Focus and Motivate

OBJECTIVES

Literary Analysis
- explore the key idea of **meaning**
- identify and interpret symbol in poetry
- read poetry

Reading
- draw conclusions

Grammar and Writing
- use the active voice
- use writing to analyze literature

SUMMARY

In "My Mother Pieced Quilts," the speaker reflects on her mother's quilts, the pieces of which represent a tapestry of the family's life and the mother's care. The quilts will be passed from generation to generation. In "quilting," the speaker compares two worlds—the world of art, where a mother and daughter quilt together, and the world of science, where alchemists mumble over cold stone. The speaker wonders if these two worlds will ever meet.

What gives MEANING *to simple things?*

Discuss the question. To lead into the ***KEY IDEA,*** ask students to think about what gives **meaning** to their lives. Encourage them to think about family, friends, special interests or hobbies, and so on. Have students work on the ***SURVEY*** activity. Then ask if they think our society values simple things. Why? Is it important to value simple things?

Before Reading

My Mother Pieced Quilts

Poem by Teresa Palomo Acosta

quilting

Poem by Lucille Clifton

What gives MEANING *to simple things?*

KEY IDEA Is there a song that reminds you of a particular time or place in your life? Perhaps there is a food that makes you think of a special person or holiday. Simple things like these can have a unique **meaning** when they represent something more. In the poems you are about to read, you'll see how simple things can have personal significance.

SURVEY Take an informal survey of five to ten classmates to find out what simple things have the most meaning for them. What types of things come up most often? As a class, create an answer to the question "What gives meaning to simple things?"

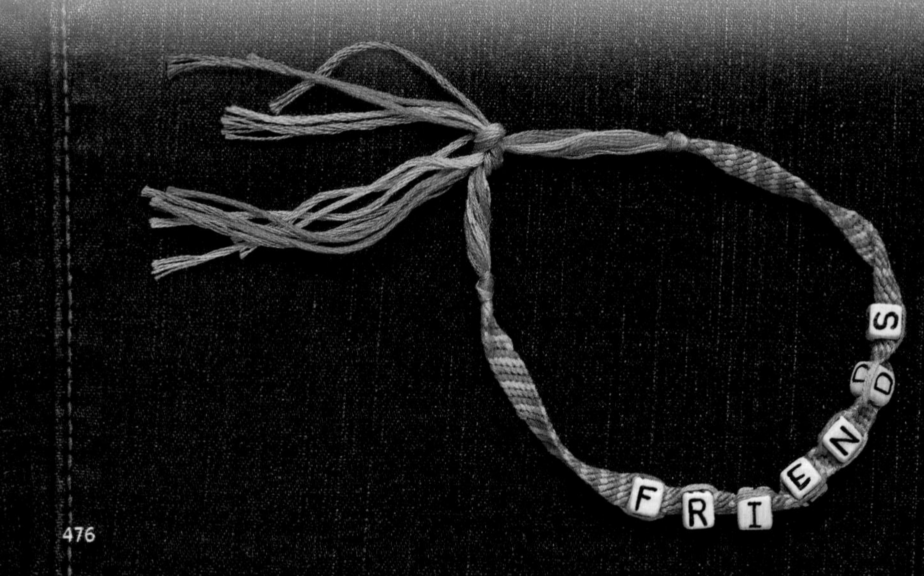

476

Selection Resources

RESOURCE MANAGER UNIT 4

Plan and Teach pp. 91–98

Literary Analysis
Symbol in Poetry pp. 99, 100†*
Question Support p. 103*

Reading
Draw Conclusions pp. 101, 102†*
Reading Fluency p. 105

Grammar and Writing
Use the Active Voice p. 104

Assessment
Selection Tests A, B/C pp. 107*, 109*
Test Generator CD

BEST PRACTICES TOOLKIT

Differentiated Instruction pp. 31–38*

Graphic Organizers/Strategies
Cluster Diagram • Draw It • Drawing Conclusions • Think-Pair-Share • Writing Template: Reflective Essay

Reading Support
Audio Anthology CD*

Technology
Literature and Writing Centers at **ClassZone.com**
Write*Smart* CD

* Resources for Differentiation † Also in Spanish

LITERARY ANALYSIS: SYMBOL IN POETRY

Symbols are people, places, and things that stand for something beyond themselves. Writers often use them to convey complex ideas in a few words. For example, in the poems you are about to read, quilts and quilting represent something more significant than an object or activity. To understand these symbols, use the following tips:

- Think about the big ideas each line or stanza expresses. Ask: *What message about families, art, or other big topics is the poem communicating?*
- Pay attention to the poet's word choice. Ask: *Which words have positive associations? Which have negative associations?*
- Notice how the symbol relates to the big ideas in the poem. Ask: *In what way do quilts or quilting help convey the poem's message?*

As you read, use graphics like the ones shown to write down clues that help you understand each symbol. You'll finish filling in the graphics later.

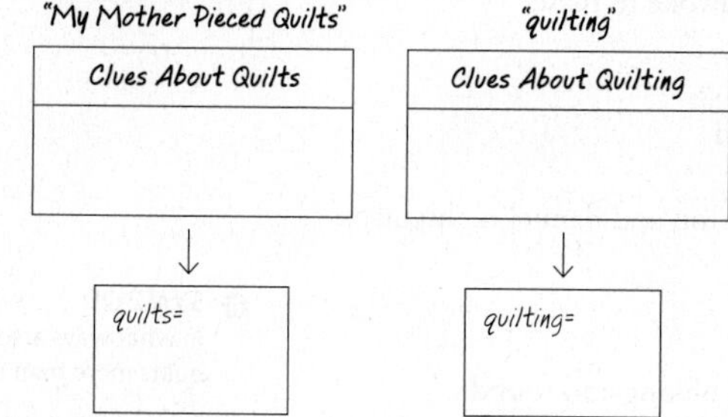

READING SKILL: DRAW CONCLUSIONS

You often must **draw conclusions** to understand the message a poet is trying to share. A conclusion is a belief you arrive at or a logical judgment you make by combining your inferences about the poem with your personal knowledge and experience.

To help you draw a conclusion, you can fill in a statement like this: "I believe _____ because _____ and _____." For example, "I believe the daughter respects her mother because she seems awed by her mother's talent and because I know from experience how important adult role models are." As you read "My Mother Pieced Quilts" and "quilting," fill in your own statements to draw conclusions about the value of quilting.

Author Online

Teresa Palomo Acosta: Women's Advocate Teresa Palomo Acosta grew up in central Texas, where she enjoyed listening to her grandfather tell colorful stories about her family's history in Mexico and Texas. Acosta's work as a writer springs from her desire to tell stories about people who don't usually appear in literature. In particular, she writes about the lives and struggles of Mexican-American women in the past and present. Widely recognized for her efforts in support of women, she's been named an Outstanding Woman in the Arts.

Teresa Palomo Acosta born 1949

Lucille Clifton: Creating Beautiful Poems Lucille Clifton grew up in the state of New York and was the first in her family to finish high school and attend college. Her poetry often deals with her African-American roots and having strength through difficult times. She believes writing poetry explores what it means to be human. "Poetry doesn't have to be pretty," she said, "but it must be beautiful." Clifton has won many awards for her work, including the National Book Award and an Emmy Award.

Lucille Clifton born 1936

MORE ABOUT THE AUTHOR
For more on Teresa Palomo Acosta and Lucille Clifton, visit the **Literature Center** at **ClassZone.com.**

Teach

STANDARDS FOCUS

LITERARY ANALYSIS

● SYMBOL IN POETRY

Discuss how symbols can suggest an author's intent in a poem and can lead to an exploration of the poem's theme. Ask students to predict what the quilts may symbolize in the two poems they are about to read and what themes the poets might explore. *Students' responses will vary. They may suggest that quilts could symbolize home and family. The themes may have to do with love and memories.*

CHECK UNDERSTANDING Select an object in the classroom and have students brainstorm ideas that it could symbolize.

RESOURCE MANAGER—Copy Master
Symbol in Poetry p. 99 (for student use while reading the poems)

READING SKILL

■ DRAW CONCLUSIONS

Explain that most poets don't directly state what a poem is about, so readers have to draw conclusions to explore a poem's meaning. Discuss how readers may draw different conclusions based on differing backgrounds and experiences.

CHECK UNDERSTANDING Ask students to explain in their own words what it means to draw conclusions.

DIFFERENTIATED INSTRUCTION

FOR ALL STUDENTS

For general guidelines on differentiating instruction, see

BEST PRACTICES TOOLKIT
Differentiated Instruction pp. 31–38

FOR LESS–PROFICIENT READERS

Concept Support Record strategies for reading poetry in a class Cluster Diagram. Then have groups of students read one of the poems aloud and try out the strategies. Ask students which strategies worked best and why.

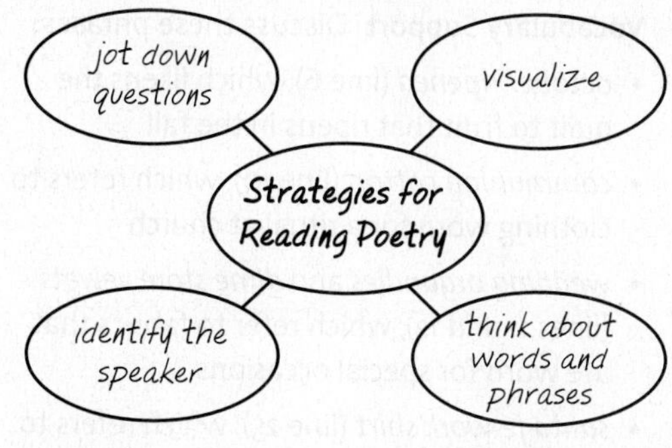

BEST PRACTICES TOOLKIT—Transparency
Cluster Diagram p. B18

FOR ENGLISH LEARNERS

Options for Reading Have students read each poem aloud or follow along as they listen to the *Audio Anthology CD*. Then have students use Draw It to begin to analyze the symbols in the two poems.

BEST PRACTICES TOOLKIT
Draw It p. A2

Practice and Apply

ANALYZE VISUALS

Possible answer: *The quilt shows a bird, gloves, butterflies, buttons, houses, a sun, a baby dress, and flowers. The baby dress and houses may symbolize the quiltmaker's past. The gloves may symbolize caring and warmth. The sun, butterflies, and flowers may symbolize the natural world.*

About the Art Jane Burch Cochran, who lives near the small town of Rabbit Hash, Kentucky, wants people to find their own meanings in her image-filled quilts. She stitches gloves into many of her quilts, using them to symbolize hands searching for answers.

Lines 1–9

REINFORCE *KEY IDEA:* MEANING

Discuss How can something that was originally "just meant as covers" take on more **meaning** the longer one has it? *Students' responses will vary. The details of the quilt and the memories associated with the details may become evident only on close examination over a long period of time.*

LITERARY ANALYSIS

A SYMBOL

Possible answer: *The quilts represent the mother's hard work and include fabrics that represent parts of the family's life.*

If students need help . . . Work together to identify details in the poem that are symbols for the family's life, such as "communion cotton" and "wedding organdies."

READING SKILL

B DRAW CONCLUSIONS

Possible answer: *The mother was skilled and in control as she made quilts, just as she nurtured and directed her family.*

My Mother Pieced Quilts

Teresa Palomo Acosta

they were just meant as covers
in winters
as weapons
against pounding january winds

but it was just that every morning I awoke to these
october ripened canvases
passed my hand across their cloth faces
and began to wonder how you pieced
all these together
these strips of gentle communion cotton and flannel nightgowns
wedding organdies
dime store velvets **A**

how you shaped patterns square and oblong and round
positioned
balanced
then cemented them
with your thread
a steel needle
a thimble

how the thread darted in and out
galloping along the frayed edges, tucking them in
as you did us at night
oh how you stretched and turned and re-arranged
your michigan spring faded curtain pieces
my father's santa fe work shirt
the summer denims, the tweeds of fall **B**

ANALYZE VISUAL
What recognizable objects can you find i[n] this quilt? Tell what e[ach] might **symbolize** to t[he] quiltmaker.

A SYMBOL
In what ways are the quilts more than cove[rs]

B DRAW CONCLUSI[ONS]
How does the mother['s] skill in making the qui[lt] mirror her role in the family?

American Childhood (1995), Jane Burch Coc[hran]. Fabric, beads, buttons, paint, baby dress, gloves, 53"

DIFFERENTIATED INSTRUCTION

FOR LESS–PROFICIENT READERS

Vocabulary Support Discuss these phrases:

- *october ripened* (line 6), which likens the quilt to fruit that ripens in the fall
- *communion cotton* (line 10), which refers to clothing worn for a ritual at church
- *wedding organdies* and *dime store velvets* (lines 11 and 12), which refer to fabrics that are worn for special occasions
- *santa fe work shirt* (line 25), which refers to a shirt worn by someone who works for the Santa Fe Railroad

FOR ENGLISH LEARNERS

Vocabulary: Figurative Language [mixed-readiness pairs] Have pairs of students interpret the meanings of these phrases:

- *as weapons* (line 3), "as a means of keeping out the cold"
- *their cloth faces* (line 7), "the surface of the quilt"
- *cemented* (line 16), "sewed together firmly"
- *galloping along the frayed edges* (line 21), "quickly stitching together scraps of cloth"

BACKGROUND

Quilting Quilting is a method of sewing two layers of fabric on both sides of a warmer layer, like a sandwich. In the United States, it developed as a unique form that serves both function (warmth) and art—the creative use of patterns and fabrics. In the 17th and 18th centuries, fabric was in short supply in the United States, so piecing together a quilt from leftovers was economical and practical.

Enslaved women in the South sewed and quilted for the owners of plantations. Although not much is known about the quilts made for their own families, simple quilts were probably sewn from the scraps. Certain quilting patterns, such as Underground Railroad, Jacob's Ladder, North Star, and Slave Chain, commemorate those who fled for their freedom on the Underground Railroad.

The crazy quilt, a patchwork using various sizes of fabric sewn together in no definite pattern, became popular in the late 1800s in Europe and Asia and was then brought to the United States. It allows the quilter to use every scrap of fabric left over from other projects.

Quilts have been used as clothing in colder climates around the world, but now they are chiefly used as bedcovers or decorations. They are often made to celebrate an event, such as a birth or a wedding, and quilters often sew images into their quilts to symbolize complex ideas, such as a heart for love.

FOR LESS–PROFICIENT READERS

Comprehension Support Tell students that because the poem has no punctuation or capitalization, readers must pay close attention to other clues to the poem's structure. Point out the repeated word *how* in lines 8, 13, 20, and 23. Explain that each time the word appears, it introduces a new thought or memory that the speaker wonders about or feels amazed by. In line 27, the introductory phrase *in the evening* signals the start of a new section of the poem.

Concept Support [small-group option] Have students work in small groups to add clues to the charts introduced on page 477 about the symbols used in lines 1–26. Students may identify these clues:

- "as weapons / against pounding january winds" (lines 3–4)
- "tucking them in / as you did us at night" (lines 21–22)
- "the summer denims, the tweeds of fall" (line 26)

FOR ADVANCED LEARNERS/PRE–AP

Analyze Figurative Language [small-group option] Have students work in small groups to identify and categorize examples of figurative language from the poem. Ask students to decide which is the most memorable or vivid image in the poem. Have them discuss why it is so effective.

Lines 27–37

REINFORCE *KEY IDEA:* MEANING

Discuss How does the speaker communicate the **meaning** this moment holds? ***Possible answer:*** *The speaker says "lounging on your arm," evoking the memory of a warm and loving relationship between the speaker and her mother.*

Extend the Discussion Ask students to think of a simple thing that has special meaning for them. Invite them to present the object to the class or to act out something that has meaning to them and explain its significance.

LITERARY ANALYSIS

C SYMBOL

Possible answer: *The quilt represents various seasons, holidays, happy events, and sad occasions, such as the speaker's grandmother's funeral.*

READING SKILL

D DRAW CONCLUSIONS

Possible answer: *The speaker compares the mother to a river current and to an army commander on horseback. The mother is described as being able to conjure up vivid memories from the family's past. The speaker is in awe of her mother's ability to re-create both happy and sad memories through her quilting.*

LITERARY ANALYSIS

E SYMBOL

Possible answer: *The quilts represent the history of the family. They "sing on" by continuing to tell the story of the family as they are passed on through generations.*

in the evening you sat at your canvas
—our cracked linoleum floor the drawing board
me lounging on your arm
and you staking out the plan:
whether to put the lilac purple of easter against the red plaid
of winter-going-
into-spring
whether to mix a yellow with blue and white and paint the
corpus christi noon when my father held your hand
whether to shape a five-point star from the
somber black silk you wore to grandmother's funeral **C**

you were the river current
carrying the roaring notes
forming them into pictures of a little boy reclining
a swallow flying
you were the caravan master at the reins
driving your threaded needle artillery[1] across the mosaic[2]
cloth bridges
delivering yourself in separate testimonies.[3]

oh mother you plunged me sobbing and laughing
into our past
into the river crossing at five
into the spinach fields
into the plainview cotton rows
into tuberculosis wards
into braids and muslin[4] dresses
sewn hard and taut to withstand the thrashings of twenty-five years **D**

stretched out they lay
armed/ready/shouting/celebrating

knotted with love
the quilts sing on **E**

C SYMBOL
Reread lines 31–37. W
parts of life do the fa
in the quilt represent

D DRAW CONCLUS
Think about the imag
the **speaker** uses as s
describes her mothe
What is the speaker's
attitude toward her
mother?

E SYMBOL
What does the **speak**
mean when she says
quilts sing on"? Cons
how the quilt represe
the family itself.

1. **artillery** (är-tĭl'ə-rē): large weapons that are operated by crews.
2. **mosaic** (mō-zā'ĭk): a picture or design created when small colored pieces of stone or tile are set into a surface.
3. **testimonies** (tĕs'tə-mō'nēz): declarations.
4. **muslin** (mŭz'lĭn): sturdy cotton fabric.

DIFFERENTIATED INSTRUCTION

FOR LESS–PROFICIENT READERS

Reading Skill Follow-Up: Draw Conclusions [small-group option] Ask students to work in small groups to read lines 27–57 and fill in a Drawing Conclusions chart with statements from the poem and their own inferences. Explain that although the poem doesn't include "facts," the words are the speaker's truth. Discuss students' conclusions.

BEST PRACTICES TOOLKIT—Transparency
Drawing Conclusions p. A28

FOR ENGLISH LEARNERS

Culture: Clarify Make sure students understand these references from the poem:

- *canvas* (line 27): fabric that is stretched over a frame and used by artists to paint on
- *linoleum* (line 28): a hard-surface floor covering that was used in homes in the mid-1900s
- *corpus christi* (line 35): a town in Texas

quilting

Lucille Clifton

Crossing Borders (1995), Deidre Scherer. Fabric and thread. © Deidre Scherer.

somewhere in the unknown world
a yellow eyed woman
sits with her daughter
quilting.

some other where
alchemists[1] mumble over pots.
their chemistry stirs
into science. their science
freezes into stone. F

in the unknown world
the woman
threading together her need
and her needle
nods toward the smiling girl
remember
this will keep us warm. G

how does this poem end?
do the daughters' daughters quilt?
do the alchemists practice their tables?
do the worlds continue spinning
away from each other forever?

ANALYZE VISUALS
What might the gesture in this picture **symbolize?**

F **DRAW CONCLUSIONS**
Does the **speaker** present the place where the alchemists are in a positive or negative way? Tell what words in this stanza make you think so.

G **SYMBOL**
How is the world where the mother and daughter quilt different from the alchemists' world?

1. **alchemist** (ăl′kə-mĭst): a chemist who tries to turn metals into gold.

ANALYZE VISUALS

Possible answer: *The gesture of two hands clasping might symbolize warmth, love, comfort, and caring.*

About the Art Deidre Scherer studied painting at the Rhode Island School of Design and has worked with fabric since the late 1970s. Her quilts have a painterly quality and her fiber work focuses on issues of age and mortality, presenting death as a natural part of life.

READING SKILL

F DRAW CONCLUSIONS

Possible answer: *The speaker presents the alchemists' world in a negative way. The word* mumble *(line 6) suggests that what they are talking about is not very important. The phrase* freezes into stone *(line 9) suggests a cold, impersonal world.*

LITERARY ANALYSIS

G SYMBOL

Possible answer: *The world where the mother and daughter quilt is a warmer and friendlier place that depends on human interaction and connections.*

Extend the Discussion Do you think the speaker is making a fair comparison between the two worlds? Why or why not?

SELECTION WRAP-UP

REFLECT Ask students whether these poems changed the way they think about quilts and quilting. If so, how?

CRITIQUE The two poems focus on the same topic in different ways. Ask students which poem appeals to them more, and to explain why.

READING FLUENCY

Distribute the copy masters and have students practice fluency.

RESOURCE MANAGER—Copy Master
Reading Fluency p. 105

FOR LESS-PROFICIENT READERS

Concept Support [small-group option] Have students add clues to their charts from page 477 about the symbols in the poem "quilting." Students may identify these clues:

- "the unknown world" (lines 1, 10)
- "some other where" (line 5)
- "their science / freezes into stone" (lines 8–9)
- "threading together her need / and her needle" (lines 12–13)
- *"this will keep us warm"* (line 16)
- "how does this poem end?" (line 17)

After students have filled in their charts, have them use Think-Pair-Share to explore what the symbols in both poems stand for.

BEST PRACTICES TOOLKIT—Transparency
Think-Pair-Share p. A18

Practice and Apply

After Reading

For additional support of postreading questions, use these copy masters:

RESOURCE MANAGER—Copy Masters
Draw Conclusions p. 101 (for practice of reading standards focus)
Question Support p. 103 (After Reading questions adapted for English learners and less-proficient readers)

Additional selection questions are provided for teachers on page 95.

ANSWERS

Comprehension

1. *The quilts were meant for covers in winter.*
2. *The mother considers making a star out of the black silk.*
3. *The alchemists are trying to change the properties of metals to advance science.*

Literary Analysis

Possible answers:

4. *Students should choose three descriptive phrases from the poem, such as "october ripened canvases," "strips of gentle communion cotton," "dime store velvets," "shaped patterns square and oblong and round," and "red plaid."*
5. *For the mother, quilting might fulfill a need to keep warm, to create something artistic and beautiful, to share the experience with her daughter, and to pass along her knowledge so her daughter also can realize the beauty and function of quilting.*
6. *The poem contrasts the world of art and the world of science. The world of art is presented as a warm, personal place, while the world of science is presented as cold and impersonal. The worlds might be moving apart because as each world focuses on advancing, there is less to connect them to each other.*
7. ● **STANDARDS FOCUS Symbol in Poetry** *In "My Mother Pieced Quilts," the quilts symbolize the family's history. In "quilting," the act of quilting symbolizes art.*
8. ■ **STANDARDS FOCUS Draw Conclusions** ***Practical:*** *keeps people warm;* ***Creative:*** *gives people a chance to choose and arrange fabric in a way that has personal meaning for them; allows people to make something beautiful;* ***Social:*** *brings people together in both the creation and the use of the quilt. The value in making quilts depends on individuals, but it can fulfill a desire to create and to provide for others.*

Extension and Challenge

9. *Students' responses will vary. Encourage students to think about people who are important to them, sports and hobbies they enjoy, favorite memories, clothes they like, and favorite simple things that have meaning in their lives. Students may choose to create a "crazy quilt" that doesn't have a strict design, or they may create a geometric quilt pattern.*

After Reading

Comprehension

1. **Recall** What were the quilts in "My Mother Pieced Quilts" meant for?
2. **Recall** In "My Mother Pieced Quilts," what does the mother consider doing with the black silk from the grandmother's funeral?
3. **Summarize** Describe the alchemists' work in "quilting."

Literary Analysis

4. **Visualize** In "My Mother Pieced Quilts," the poet uses vivid language to create a picture of the fabrics, patterns, and colors of the quilts. What three descriptive phrases best help you visualize the quilts?
5. **Clarify a Line** In "quilting," the mother threads together "her need and her needle." What need might quilting fulfill for the mother? Think about why it's important for her to share the experience with her daughter.
6. **Interpret a Question** In "quilting," the poem ends with the following question: "do the worlds continue spinning away from each other forever?" Think about how the worlds are contrasted in the poem. Why might they be moving apart? Explain your answer.
7. **Analyze Symbols** Finish filling in your graphics with any additional clues to the meanings of "quilts" and "quilting" in the two poems. In "My Mother Pieced Quilts," what do the quilts symbolize? In "quilting," what does the act of quilting symbolize? Write the answers in your graphic.
8. **Draw Conclusions** In a chart like the one shown, list examples from the poems of the practical, creative, and social reasons for quilting. Based on this list, what can you conclude about the value in making quilts?

	Reasons for Quilting
Practical	
Creative	
Social	

Extension and Challenge

9. **Creative Project: Art** If you were to make a quilt to represent your life, what would it look like? Think about the fabrics, colors, and designs you would choose and their **meaning** to you. Then make a collage of your quilt.

482 UNIT 4: THEME AND SYMBOL

ading-Writing Connection

)elve deeper into "My Mother Pieced Quilts" and "quilting" by responding o these prompts. Then complete the **Grammar and Writing** exercise.

WRITING PROMPTS	SELF-CHECK
A. Short Response: Describe a Relationship In what way is the mother-daughter relationship central to the message in the poem "quilting"? In a **one-paragraph description,** explain why the mother wants to quilt with her daughter.	***An effective description will . . .*** • explain the importance of quilting to the mother • reveal how quilting connects the generations
B. Extended Response: Write a Speech Imagine a museum has decided to show the quilts described in "My Mother Pieced Quilts." The speaker of the poem has been asked to discuss her mother's work. Write a **one-page speech** in which the speaker explains to the audience how the quilts were created and what they **mean** to her.	***A successful speech will . . .*** • include details about how the quilts were made and what some of the squares represent • reflect the relationship between the mother and daughter

AMMAR AND WRITING

USE THE ACTIVE VOICE Verbs can be in either the active voice or passive voice. n a sentence that uses the **active voice,** the subject *performs* the verb's action. n a sentence that uses the **passive voice,** the subject *receives* the verb's action. The passive voice tends to make sentences dull and weak, so you should use the active voice whenever possible.

Passive: The quilt was sewn together by my mother. (*The subject* quilt *receives the action of the verb phrase* was sewn.)

Active: My mother sewed the quilt together. (*The subject* mother *performs the action of the verb* sewed.)

PRACTICE Rewrite each of these sentences in the active voice.

1. The quilts were worked on every night by my mother.
2. I am reminded of my fifth birthday by this piece of pink satin.
3. The denim that's used in the quilt was worn by my father.
4. Our family was warmed and comforted by my mother's quilts.

For more help with active and passive voice, see page R57 in the ***Grammar Handbook.***

Reading-Writing Connection

WRITING PROMPTS

- For **Prompt A,** encourage students to review their response to question 5 on page 482 about the mother threading together "her need and her needle."
- For **Prompt B,** have students use the Reflective Essay template to help them note details about the poem.

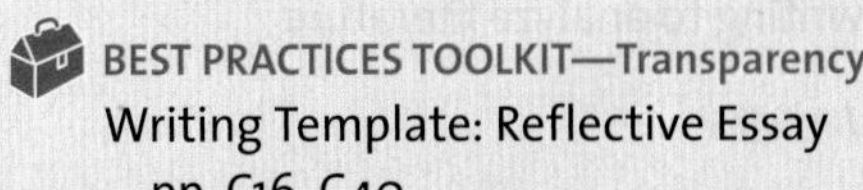

BEST PRACTICES TOOLKIT—Transparency
Writing Template: Reflective Essay pp. C16, C40

For writing support, see

Writing Center at **ClassZone.com**

GRAMMAR AND WRITING

Tell students that to change the sentences from passive to active voice they need to

- first identify the subject that *receives* the verb's action in each sentence
- then rewrite the sentence so that the subject *performs* the action

Answers:

1. *My mother worked on the quilts every night.*
2. *This piece of pink satin reminds me of my fifth birthday.*
3. *My father wore the denim that's used in the quilt.*
4. *My mother's quilts warmed and comforted our family.*

RESOURCE MANAGER—Copy Master
Use the Active Voice p. 104

DIFFERENTIATED INSTRUCTION

FOR LESS–PROFICIENT WRITERS

For Prompt A:

1. Have students identify why quilting is important to the mother.
2. Have students think about why a mother would want to share this skill with her daughter.
3. Encourage students to explain how quilting connects the mother and the daughter.

For Prompt B:

1. Together, draft a thesis statement that describes the quilts in general and summarizes what they mean to the speaker.
2. Help students organize their speech into paragraphs. **Paragraph 1:** Describe the quilts. **Paragraph 2:** Describe how the quilts were made. **Paragraph 3:** Examine the relationship between the daughter and her mother.
3. Make sure students include a closing paragraph.

Assess and Reteach

Assess

RESOURCE MANAGER—Copy Masters
Selection Tests A, B/C pp. 107–108, 109–110

Test Generator CD

Reteach

STANDARDS LESSON FILE
Literature Lesson 31: Symbol and Symbolism
Reading Lesson 9: Drawing Conclusions

Focus and Motivate

OBJECTIVES

Literary Analysis
- explore the key idea of **impact**
- identify and analyze theme
- read a play and a diary entry

Reading
- use a story map to analyze plot development

Grammar and Writing
- capitalize correctly
- use writing to analyze literature

SUMMARY

This play tells the story of the two years Anne Frank spent living secretly in the attic of a warehouse with her family and several others during World War II. While in hiding, they struggle with hunger, severe restrictions on their activities, and the fear that if they are discovered, they will be sent to Nazi concentration camps. Eventually, they are found and sent to different camps. After the war ends, the only survivor, Mr. Frank, returns to the attic and finds Anne's diary, which becomes the record of their experiences.

What IMPACT *will you have on the world?*

Discuss the question and the ***KEY IDEA*** with students. Ask them to identify a person who has had a positive **impact** on their lives. In what ways have they been changed by knowing or observing this person? Would they want to affect someone else similarly? Then have students work on the ***QUICKWRITE*** activity.

Before Reading

The Diary of Anne Frank

Drama by Frances Goodrich and Albert Hackett

What IMPACT *will you have on the world?*

KEY IDEA Everyone makes an **impact** on the world in some way. National leaders or sports heroes may inspire millions, while the rest of us can influence a smaller circle of friends and family through our actions, our beliefs, or our commitments. Whether you make your mark quietly or boldly, a life well lived can be a guide to others. In the play you're about to read, a young girl doesn't realize that the thoughts she expresses in her diary will later influence readers all over the world.

QUICKWRITE People of all ages make important contributions to the world. What impact do you now have on others? What impact do you hope to have later in your life? Write your ideas in a brief journal entry. Think about how education and life experience might affect your goals for the future.

Selection Resources

RESOURCE MANAGER UNIT 4

Plan and Teach pp. 111–118

Literary Analysis
Summary pp. 119, 120†*, 121‡*, 122‡*
Theme pp. 123, 124†*
Question Support pp. 128*, 130*

Reading
Story Mapping pp. 125, 126†*
Reading Check p. 129
Reading Fluency p. 132

Vocabulary
Study p. 127*

Grammar and Writing
Capitalize Correctly p. 131

Assessment
Selection Tests A, B/C pp. 133*, 135*
Test Generator CD

BEST PRACTICES TOOLKIT

Differentiated Instruction pp. 31–38*
Scaffolding Instruction pp. 43–46*

Graphic Organizers/Strategies
Reciprocal Teaching • New Word Analysis • Words with Multiple Meanings • Read Aloud/Think Aloud • Venn Diagram • Cause-and-Effect Graphics • Sequence Chain • T Chart • Round Robin • Plot Diagram

Reading Support
Audio Anthology CD*

Technology
Literature, Vocabulary, and Writing Centers at **ClassZone.com**
Write*Smart* CD

* Resources for Differentiation † Also in Spanish ‡ In Haitian Creole and Vietnamese

ERARY ANALYSIS: THEME

The play you are about to read is based on a diary written by Anne Frank, a teenager who spent more than two years hiding from the Nazis. When Anne's diary was published, readers around the world were profoundly touched that, despite all she had been through, she still believed people were good at heart.

When the playwrights adapted Anne's diary, they used her belief in the essential goodness of people as one of the work's **themes,** or messages about life. As you read, notice how Anne's thoughts and feelings, as well as the characters' relationships with each other, work together to express this theme.

DING SKILL: STORY MAPPING

As you know, a road map can be a useful tool to help you get someplace. Similarly, a **story map** can help you understand what you're reading. It shows how a story's parts fit together and how the action moves from one event to another. As you read *The Diary of Anne Frank,* complete a story map like the one shown.

The Diary of Anne Frank

Setting: ______

Characters: ______ ______ ______ ______

Problem: ______

Events: ______ ______ ______ ______

Resolution: ______

CABULARY IN CONTEXT

The following words help the playwrights capture Anne's experiences. To see how many you know, try to match each word from the list with the word or phrase closest in meaning.

WORD LIST			
	apprehension	fortify	remorse
	disgruntled	indignantly	unabashed
	foreboding	pandemonium	

1. wild uproar
2. displeased
3. worry
4. angrily
5. strengthen
6. sinking feeling
7. bold
8. sorrow

Author On|ine

From Comedies to Drama Screenwriting team Frances Goodrich and Albert Hackett were a married couple known for their upbeat comedies and musicals. In the late 1940s, they began working on a drama that would take eight years to complete. Their play, *The Diary of Anne Frank,* was based on Anne Frank's diary entries. As part of their research, the couple traveled to Amsterdam to interview Anne's father and to see the family's hiding place. Their play adaptation won a Pulitzer Prize in 1956.

Frances Goodrich 1890–1984

Albert Hackett 1900–1995

Background

Anne Frank's Diary Anne Frank and her family were Jewish citizens of Germany. When the Nazi party, led by Adolf Hitler, came to power in 1933, the Nazis blamed the country's problems on the Jews. Jews were stripped of their rights. Many were eventually sent to concentration camps where more than 6 million Jews died in what became known as the Holocaust. The Franks moved to the Netherlands to escape persecution, but the Nazis invaded that country in 1940. In order to survive, Anne's family went into hiding when she was 13 years old. They hid in attic rooms behind Mr. Frank's office, and several other Jews joined them. In this "Secret Annex," Anne kept a diary about her life in hiding. More than two years later, the group's worst fears came true when the Nazis found them. Everyone who had been living there was sent to concentration camps. Anne's diary was discovered later.

MORE ABOUT THE AUTHOR AND BACKGROUND

To learn more about the authors and the Holocaust, visit the **Literature Center** at **ClassZone.com.**

Teach

STANDARDS FOCUS

LITERARY ANALYSIS

● THEME

Tell students that to identify theme, they should also look at dialogue, changes in characters, and characters' actions.

CHECK UNDERSTANDING Have students predict dialogue, actions, relationships, changes in characters, and Anne's thoughts and feelings that might express themes.

READING SKILL

■ STORY MAPPING

Write this example on the board:

On a frigid winter day, Grasshopper ran out of food. Just then, Ant came by carrying some grain. Grasshopper begged her to give him some. Ant smiled and invited Grasshopper into her warm home for a meal.

Have students identify setting, character, problem, events, and resolution. ***Possible answer:*** *Setting: cold winter day; Characters: Ant and Grasshopper; Problem: Grasshopper's hunger; Events: Ant walks by, Grasshopper asks for food; Resolution: Ant invites him for a meal*

CHECK UNDERSTANDING Have students organize the details they identified in a story map.

RESOURCE MANAGER—Copy Master
Story Mapping p. 125 (for student use while reading the selection)

VOCABULARY SKILL

▲ VOCABULARY IN CONTEXT

ANSWERS **1.** *pandemonium* **2.** *disgruntled* **3.** *apprehension* **4.** *indignantly* **5.** *fortify* **6.** *foreboding* **7.** *unabashed* **8.** *remorse*

PRETEACH VOCABULARY To preteach vocabulary, use the Vocabulary Study copy master. Supply these definitions as needed:

indignantly (ĭn-dĭg′nənt-lē) *adv.* angrily

disgruntled (dĭs-grŭn′tld) *adj.* unhappy

foreboding (fôr-bō′dĭng) *n.* a sense of impending misfortune

remorse (rĭ-môrs′) *n.* sorrow; regret

unabashed (ŭn′ə-băsht′) *adj.* obvious; bold

apprehension (ăp′rĭ-hĕn′shən) *n.* nervousness

fortify (fôr′tə-fī′) *v.* to make strong

pandemonium (păn′də-mō′nē-əm) *n.* wild uproar or noise

RESOURCE MANAGER—Copy Master
Vocabulary Study p. 127

For general guidelines on differentiating vocabulary instruction and for alternative vocabulary activities for students not needing vocabulary preteaching, see

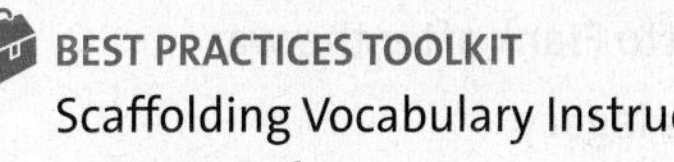

BEST PRACTICES TOOLKIT
Scaffolding Vocabulary Instruction pp. 43–46

Vocabulary Center at **ClassZone.com**

Practice and Apply

READING SKILL

STORY MAPPING

What is the setting of this play? (Have students record important details in their story map from page 485.) ***Answer:***

- *Amsterdam, 1942–1945*
- *the top floor of a warehouse and office building*
- *three rooms and a small attic*

BACKGROUND

The Secret Annex In July 1942, Anne Frank and her family went into hiding in a small attic area hidden behind Otto Frank's office. The entrance to the area, which they called the Secret Annex, lay behind a movable bookcase. It was in these close quarters that Anne Frank, her family, the "Van Daans" (actually Hermann Van Pels, his wife, and their son, Peter—Otto Frank changed their names when he published Anne's diary), and "Mr. Dussel" (actually Fritz Pfeffer) lived fearfully for two years, hoping and praying for liberation.

THE Diary OF Anne Frank

Frances Goodrich and Albert Hackett

CHARACTERS

SECRET ANNEX RESIDENTS

Anne Frank
Margot Frank
Mr. Frank
Mrs. Frank
Peter Van Daan
Mr. Van Daan
Mrs. Van Daan
Mr. Dussel

WORKERS IN MR. FRANK'S BUSINESS

Miep Gies (mēp gēs)
Mr. Kraler (krä'lər)

The Time. *July 1942–August 1944, November 1945*
The Place. *Amsterdam, the Netherlands*

The scene remains the same throughout the play. It is the top floor of a warehouse and office building in Amsterdam, Holland. The sharply peaked roof of the building is outlined against a sea of other rooftops, stretching away into the distance. Nearby is the belfry of a church tower, the Westertoren, whose carillon rings out the hours. Occasionally faint sounds float up from below: the voices of children playing in the street, the tramp of marching feet, a boat whistle from the canal.

The three rooms of the top floor and a small attic space above are exposed to our view. The largest of the rooms is in the center, with two small rooms, slightly raised, on either side. On the right is a bathroom, out of sight. A narrow steep flight of stairs at the back leads up to the attic. The rooms [are] *sparsely furnished with a few chairs, cots, a table* [or] *two. The windows are painted over, or covered u*[nder] *makeshift blackout curtains. In the main room th*[ere] *is a sink, a gas ring for cooking and a wood-burn*[ing] *stove for warmth.*

The room on the left is hardly more than a clo[set.] *There is a skylight in the sloping ceiling. Directly under this room is a small steep stairwell, with st*[eps] *leading down to a door. This is the only entrance from the building below. When the door is opene*[d] *we see that it has been concealed on the outer side by a bookcase attached to it.*

The Diary of Anne Frank, starring Natalie Portman as Anne, ran on Broadway at the Music Box Theatre from December 1997 to June 1998.

DIFFERENTIATED INSTRUCTION

FOR ALL STUDENTS

Expert Groups Encourage individual students or groups to choose one of these topics on which to become experts. Have students present their findings to the class.

- the Holocaust
- the life of Otto Frank after the war
- Anne Frank's legacy
- invasion of Normandy
- rationing in Europe during World War II

FOR LESS–PROFICIENT READERS

In combination with the *Audio Anthology CD*, use one or more Targeted Passages (pp. 490, 492, 502, 506, 517, 526, 534, 537, 539, 540) to ensure that students focus on key events, concepts, and skills.

FOR ENGLISH LEARNERS

Options for Reading Provide students with a summary of the play. Then have them read the Targeted Passages aloud in small groups or have them listen to part or all of the play along with the *Audio Anthology CD*. Use Reciprocal Teaching with students to help them increase their comprehension and keep track of important ideas.

 **BEST PRACTICES TOOLKIT—Transparency**
Reciprocal Teaching p. A35

BACKGROUND

Star of David Point out the yellow stars worn by the actors in this photograph. Between the 17th and 19th centuries, the star became associated with the Jewish faith, although the symbol itself dates back to ancient times. One interpretation of its meaning is that it represents the shield of David, which is a sign of God's protection. (David was the Israelite king who united the kingdom of Israel during his reign from about 1000 to 962 B.C.) The star is seen on synagogues, the flag of Israel, and Jewish tombstones. During World War II, Jews were forced to wear the star as a means of identification to enable the Nazis to more easily enforce their policies of segregation and persecution.

ANALYZE VISUALS

About the Art Photographer Joan Marcus knows her way around Broadway. After graduating from George Washington University, she worked as a photographer at the Kennedy Center to earn money for graduate school. Her job there led her into photography as a full-time career. For over 25 years, she has specialized in taking photographs of stage productions. Her artistry is seen in the scenes she captures here of the 1997–1998 Broadway production of *The Diary of Anne Frank*, starring Natalie Portman.

ADDITIONAL TEACHING OPPORTUNITY

Lighting Often, lighting becomes one of the most important tools that a director can use to set the mood of a scene in a play. Directors can use a variety of techniques to make a play's lighting effective. For example, various levels of light, such as direct spotlights, shadows, and partial darkness, can create specific moods.

Have students examine the photograph on page 487. What elements are emphasized by the lighting? What mood does the lighting create? *Students may say that the stars the actors are wearing stand out because they are illuminated by a shaft of light. One actor's hands, gripping a bundle of some sort, are also highlighted. The dim lighting creates a gloomy or depressing feeling.*

FOR ENGLISH LEARNERS

Key Academic Vocabulary In Act One, have students analyze *tension* (lines 276, 999), *schedule* (lines 1306, 1363), *adjust* (line 1332), and *concentration* (line 2024).

BEST PRACTICES TOOLKIT—Transparency
New Word Analysis p. E8

Prereading For prereading instruction for English learners, see

BEST PRACTICES TOOLKIT
Scaffolding Reading Instruction pp. 43–46

FOR ADVANCED LEARNERS/PRE–AP

Pre-AP exercises in the bottom channel provide additional challenge for your advanced students. Use them for small groups or individuals.

ADDITIONAL GUIDELINES

For more help with differentiation and tips for classroom management, see

BEST PRACTICES TOOLKIT
Differentiated Instruction pp. 31–38

Lines 47–54

LITERARY ANALYSIS

● THEME

Why is Mr. Frank planning to leave Amsterdam? How does he describe himself? ***Possible answer:*** *Mr. Frank does not want to face the memories that Amsterdam holds for him. He describes himself as a "bitter old man" (line 52).*

If students need help . . . Remind them that changes in character can help bring out theme. Comparing Mr. Frank at the beginning and end of the play will help reveal the playwrights' message.

Extend the Discussion What questions does Mr. Frank's dialogue raise for the audience?

Lines 53–76

DISCUSSION PROMPTS

Use these prompts to help students understand the events in Scene 1:

Interpret How does Mr. Frank feel toward Miep? Do you know why? ***Possible answer:*** *Mr. Frank feels grateful to Miep. It is not yet clear what Miep and Mr. Kraler did for him.*

Analyze Why might Mr. Frank tell Miep to burn the papers she found? ***Possible answer:*** *They remind him of a time he does not want to remember.*

Synthesize Note the date of Anne's diary entry in relationship to the time in which this scene is set. What might Anne's diary explain? ***Possible answer:*** *Anne's first diary entry is dated July 6, 1942, three years before the scene is set. Her diary might explain what has happened in the meantime and why Mr. Frank feels as he does.*

The curtain rises on an empty stage. It is late afternoon November, 1945.

The rooms are dusty, the curtains in rags. Chairs and tables are overturned.

The door at the foot of the small stairwell swings open. Mr. Frank *comes up the steps into view. He is a gentle, cultured European in his middle years. There is still a trace of a German accent in his speech.*

He stands looking slowly around, making a supreme effort at self-control. He is weak, ill. His clothes are threadbare.

After a second he drops his rucksack on the couch and moves slowly about. He opens the door to one of the smaller rooms, and then abruptly closes it again, turning away. He goes to the window at the back, looking off at the Westertoren as its carillon strikes the hour of six, then he moves restlessly on.

From the street below we hear the sound of a barrel organ and children's voices at play. There is a many-colored scarf hanging from a nail. Mr. Frank *takes it, putting it around his neck. As he starts back for his rucksack, his eye is caught by something lying on the floor. It is a woman's white glove. He holds it in his hand and suddenly all of his self-control is gone. He breaks down, crying.*

We hear footsteps on the stairs. Miep Gies *comes up, looking for* Mr. Frank. Miep *is a Dutch girl of about twenty-two. She wears a coat and hat, ready to go home. She is pregnant. Her attitude toward* Mr. Frank *is protective, compassionate.*

Miep. Are you all right, Mr. Frank?

Mr. Frank (*quickly controlling himself*). Yes, Miep, yes.

Miep. Everyone in the office has gone home . . . It's after six. (*then pleading*) Don't stay up here, Mr. Frank. What's the use of torturing yourself like this?

Mr. Frank. I've come to say good-bye . . . I'm leaving here, Miep.

Miep. What do you mean? Where are you goin Where?

Mr. Frank. I don't know yet. I haven't decided.

Miep. Mr. Frank, you can't leave here! This is y home! Amsterdam is your home. Your busines here, waiting for you . . . You're needed here . . Now that the war is over, there are things that

Mr. Frank. I can't stay in Amsterdam, Miep. It too many memories for me. Everywhere there's something . . . the house we lived in . . . the school . . . that street organ playing out there . I'm not the person you used to know, Miep. I'm a bitter old man. (*breaking off*) Forgive me I shouldn't speak to you like this . . . after all t you did for us . . . the suffering . . .

Miep. No. No. It wasn't suffering. You can't say we suffered. (*As she speaks, she straightens a chai which is overturned.*)

Mr. Frank. I know what you went through, you and Mr. Kraler. I'll remember it as long as I liv (*He gives one last look around.*) Come, Miep.

(*He starts for the steps, then remembers his rucksa going back to get it.*)

Miep (*hurrying up to a cupboard*). Mr. Frank, did you see? There are some of your papers her (*She brings a bundle of papers to him.*) We foun them in a heap of rubbish on the floor after . . after you left.

Mr. Frank. Burn them.

(*He opens his rucksack to put the glove in it.*)

Miep. But, Mr. Frank, there are letters, notes . .

Mr. Frank. Burn them. All of them.

Miep. Burn *this?*

(*She hands him a paperbound notebook.*)

Mr. Frank (*quietly*). Anne's diary. (*He opens the diary and begins to read.*) "Monday, the sixth of July, nineteen forty-two." (*to* Miep) Nineteen

DIFFERENTIATED INSTRUCTION

FOR LESS–PROFICIENT READERS

Comprehension Support Review these elements of drama with students. Have them give examples of each from lines 1–76.

- *stage directions:* instructions to actors, directors, and others working on a play. They appear in italics and help readers understand action, setting, characters' gestures, facial expressions, and tone of voice.
- *dialogue:* conversation between characters that develops plot, character, and theme
- *acts:* major divisions of a play, similar to chapters in a book
- *scenes:* divisions of acts. A new scene indicates a change in the time or place of the action.

488 UNIT 4: THEME AND SYMBOL

489

ADDITIONAL TEACHING OPPORTUNITY

Set Design Explain that set design is the creation of the setting of a play. Point out that the designers for the set shown on page 489 built a second level on the stage. This platform indicates the attic part of the Annex. Its open design means that the audience can see the action on both levels without the need for elaborate set changes.

Tell students that depending upon the play and the way the director interprets it, the set design might either be realistic or require the audience to use imagination. Ask students how they would describe this set and why. Would they change any elements? ***Possible answer:*** *This set design is realistic. The props and the arrangement of the furnishings make the set look like an ordinary living space. The window in the attic also looks realistic. If students say that they would modify any elements of the set, ask them to explain their reasoning.*

FOR LESS–PROFICIENT READERS

Concept Support Use these steps to prepare students for reading the play:

1. Return to page 486. Pronounce the characters' names and clarify their relationships.
2. Read aloud relevant background notes in the pupil and teacher's editions to clarify why the Franks are in hiding.
3. Explain the structure of the play—that it moves from the present (1945) to the past and then back.

FOR ENGLISH LEARNERS

Language: Punctuation Cues Point out the ellipses in lines 34–70. Remind students that an ellipsis tells the reader that the speaker has paused, perhaps because he or she does not know how to express an idea. An ellipsis might also indicate that the speaker's voice trails off before continuing with a related thought. Read some of the lines to students to demonstrate the effect of ellipses on speech patterns and rhythms. Discuss how the ellipses make the dialogue sound realistic.

Lines 97–116

READING SKILL

STORY MAPPING

What problem do the Franks face? How do they react? (Remind students to record this problem on their story maps.) ***Possible answer:*** *To remain safe from the Nazis, the Franks must go into hiding.*

If students need help . . . Remind them of the historical context of the play. Jews are being taken away to concentration camps or being put to death. The Franks are hiding in an effort to survive.

BACKGROUND

Amsterdam in 1942 To explain why the Franks suddenly go into hiding, tell students that by 1942, life in Amsterdam for the Jewish population had become increasingly restricted, and the threat of deportation to forced labor camps was becoming a reality. In July 1942, Margot Frank received a notice that she would soon be sent to a work camp. Shortly after, the Frank family decided it was time to move into the hidden quarters behind Mr. Frank's business that he had been preparing for over a year.

forty-two. Is it possible, Miep? . . . Only three years ago. (*As he continues his reading, he sits down on the couch.*) "Dear Diary, since you and I are going to be great friends, I will start by telling you about myself. My name is Anne Frank. I am thirteen years old. I was born in Germany the twelfth of June, nineteen twenty-nine. As my family is Jewish, we emigrated to Holland when Hitler came to power."

(*As* Mr. Frank *reads on, another voice joins his, as if coming from the air. It is* Anne's Voice.)

Mr. Frank and Anne. "My father started a business, importing spice and herbs. Things went well for us until nineteen forty. Then the war came, and the Dutch capitulation, followed by the arrival of the Germans. Then things got very bad for the Jews."

(Mr. Frank's Voice *dies out.* Anne's Voice *continues alone. The lights dim slowly to darkness. The curtain falls on the scene.*)

Anne's Voice. You could not do this and you could not do that. They forced Father out of his business. We had to wear yellow stars.[1] I had to turn in my bike. I couldn't go to a Dutch school any more. I couldn't go to the movies, or ride in an automobile, or even on a streetcar, and a million other things. But somehow we children still managed to have fun. Yesterday Father told me we were going into hiding. Where, he wouldn't say. At five o'clock this morning Mother woke me and told me to hurry and get dressed. I was to put on as many clothes as I could. It would look too suspicious if we walked along carrying suitcases. It wasn't until we were on our way that I learned where we were going. Our hiding place was to be upstairs in the building where Father used to have his business. Three other people were coming in with us . . . the Van Daans and their son Peter . . . Father knew the Van Daans but we had never met them . . .

(*During the last lines the curtain rises on the scene. The lights dim on.* Anne's Voice *fades out.*)

(1) Targeted Passage

Scene 2

It is early morning, July, 1942. The rooms are bare, as before, but they are now clean and orderly.

Mr. Van Daan, *a tall, portly man in his late forties, is in the main room, pacing up and down, nervously smoking a cigarette. His clothes and overcoat are expensive and well cut.*

Mrs. Van Daan *sits on the couch, clutching her possessions, a hatbox, bags, etc. She is a pretty woma in her early forties. She wears a fur coat over her other clothes.*

Peter Van Daan *is standing at the window of the room on the right, looking down at the street below. He is a shy, awkward boy of sixteen. He wears a cap a raincoat, and long Dutch trousers, like "plus fours At his feet is a black case, a carrier for his cat.*

The yellow Star of David is conspicuous on all of their clothes.

Mrs. Van Daan (*rising, nervous, excited*). Something's happened to them! I know it!

Mr. Van Daan. Now, Kerli!

Mrs. Van Daan. Mr. Frank said they'd be here at seven o'clock. He said . . .

Mr. Van Daan. They have two miles to walk. You can't expect . . .

Mrs. Van Daan. They've been picked up. That's what's happened. They've been taken . . .

(Mr. Van Daan *indicates that he hears someone coming.*)

Mr. Van Daan. You see?

(Peter *takes up his carrier and his schoolbag, etc., and goes into the main room as* Mr. Frank *comes up the stairwell from below.* Mr. Frank *looks much younger now. His movements are brisk, his manner confident. He wears an overcoat and carries his hat and a small cardboard box. He crosses to the* Van Daans, *shaking hands with each of them.*)

Mr. Frank. Mrs. Van Daan, Mr. Van Daan, Peter (*then, in explanation of their lateness*) There were

1. **yellow stars:** the six-pointed Stars of David that the Nazis ordered all Jews to wear for identification.

DIFFERENTIATED INSTRUCTION

FOR LESS–PROFICIENT READERS

(1) Targeted Passage [Lines 88–116]

This passage introduces elements of setting and establishes the major conflict of the play.

- How does Anne's life change after 1940?
- Why won't her father tell her where the family is going?
- Why does Anne have to wear as many clothes as possible?
- Where is Anne's family's hiding place?
- Who else is going into hiding with them?

Review: Flashback Review the definition of *flashback* with students (*interruption of the action to present events that took place at an earlier time*). Tell students that most of the action in this play takes place in the flashback sequence. Have students think of other works they have read that have used this device, such as *The Hitchhiker.* Then remind them to review the stage directions and the dialogue to discover where the flashback begins.

oo many of the Green Police[2] on the streets . . . we had to take the long way around.

Up the steps come Margot Frank, Mrs. Frank, Miep [*not pregnant now*] *and* Mr. Kraler. *All of them carry bags, packages, and so forth. The Star of David is conspicuous on all of the* Franks' *clothing.* Margot *is eighteen, beautiful, quiet, shy.* Mrs. Frank *is a young mother, gently bred, reserved. She, like* Mr. Frank, *has a slight German accent.* Mr. Kraler *is a Dutchman, dependable, kindly.*

As Mr. Kraler *and* Miep *go upstage to put down their parcels,* Mrs. Frank *turns back to call* Anne.)

Mrs. Frank. Anne?

(Anne *comes running up the stairs. She is thirteen, quick in her movements, interested in everything, mercurial in her emotions. She wears a cape, long wool socks and carries a schoolbag.*)

Mr. Frank (*introducing them*). My wife, Edith. Mr. and Mrs. Van Daan (Mrs. Frank *hurries over, shaking hands with them.*) . . . their son, Peter . . . my daughters, Margot and Anne.

(Anne *gives a polite little curtsy as she shakes* Mr. Van Daan*'s hand. Then she immediately starts off on a tour of investigation of her new home, going upstairs to the attic room.* Miep *and* Mr. Kraler *are putting the various things they have brought on the shelves.*)

Mr. Kraler. I'm sorry there is still so much confusion.

Mr. Frank. Please. Don't think of it. After all, we'll have plenty of leisure to arrange everything ourselves.

Miep (*to* Mrs. Frank). We put the stores of food you sent in here. Your drugs are here . . . soap, linen here.

Mrs. Frank. Thank you, Miep.

Miep. I made up the beds . . . the way Mr. Frank and Mr. Kraler said. (*She starts out.*) Forgive me. I have to hurry. I've got to go to the other side of town to get some ration books[3] for you.

Mrs. Van Daan. Ration books? If they see our names on ration books, they'll know we're here.

Mr. Kraler. There isn't anything . . .

Miep. Don't worry. Your names won't be on them. (*as she hurries out*) I'll be up later.

Together

Mr. Frank. Thank you, Miep.

Mrs. Frank (*to* Mr. Kraler). It's illegal, then, the ration books? We've never done anything illegal.

Mr. Frank. We won't be living here exactly according to regulations. (*As* Mr. Kraler *reassures* Mrs. Frank, *he takes various small things, such as matches, soap, etc., from his pockets, handing them to her.*)

Mr. Kraler. This isn't the black market,[4] Mrs. Frank. This is what we call the white market . . . helping all of the hundreds and hundreds who are hiding out in Amsterdam.

(*The carillon is heard playing the quarter-hour before eight.* Mr. Kraler *looks at his watch.* Anne *stops at the window as she comes down the stairs.*)

Anne. It's the Westertoren!

Mr. Kraler. I must go. I must be out of here and downstairs in the office before the workmen get here. (*He starts for the stairs leading out.*) Miep or I, or both of us, will be up each day to bring you food and news and find out what your needs are. Tomorrow I'll get you a better bolt for the door at the foot of the stairs. It needs a bolt that you can throw yourself and open only at our signal. (*to* Mr. Frank) Oh . . . You'll tell them about the noise?

Mr. Frank. I'll tell them.

Mr. Kraler. Good-bye then for the moment. I'll come up again, after the workmen leave.

Mr. Frank. Good-bye, Mr. Kraler.

Mrs. Frank (*shaking his hand*). How can we thank you? (*The others murmur their good-byes.*)

2. **Green Police:** the Nazi police who wore green uniforms.
3. **ration books:** books of stamps or coupons issued by the government in wartime. With these coupons, people could purchase scarce items, such as food, clothing, and gasoline.
4. **black market:** a system for selling goods illegally, in violation of rationing and other restrictions.

Lines 198–211

LITERARY ANALYSIS

● THEME

Why do you think Miep and Mr. Kraler are helping the Franks and the Van Daans? What risks are they taking? ***Possible answer:*** *Miep and Mr. Kraler are Mr. Frank's employees. They may be helping the Franks because they think highly of Mr. Frank or because they are opposed to what is happening in Holland. Most likely, if they are caught, they will be imprisoned or killed.*

FOR LESS–PROFICIENT READERS

Comprehension Support [small-group option] Point out that this scene provides many details about the characters. Because changes in characters help bring out theme, it is important to know what they are like before they begin their ordeal. Have students work in small groups to pick out details of appearance and personality from the stage directions and dialogue in lines 119–313. Record the descriptions in a class chart.

Character	Act One, Scene 2
Mr. Van Daan	portly, well-dressed, gracious, willing to give up his room for the Franks, helped Mr. Frank when he first arrived in Holland
Miep	helpful, courageous, polite, trustworthy

FOR ADVANCED LEARNERS/PRE–AP

Analyze Plot Structure What is the effect of building the story through flashback rather than straightforward chronological order? Ask students to consider how the stage directions and dialogue in Scene 1 affect their expectations and understanding as they move into the events of July 1942. Have students discuss their ideas.

THE DIARY OF ANNE FRANK: ACT ONE 491

Lines 296–313

DISCUSSION PROMPTS

Use these prompts to help students understand the relationship between the Van Daans and the Franks:

Connect The hiding place has very limited space. Think about a time you might have spent in a crowded living arrangement. Do you think inviting the Van Daans was an easy decision for Mr. Frank to make? Explain. *Students may say that it was a hard decision. It will make their situation more uncomfortable than it already was.*

Analyze What is the reason that Mr. Frank invites the Van Daans? What does this decision reveal about his character? ***Possible answer:*** *He is grateful to Mr. Van Daan for helping him when Mr. Frank first arrived in Holland. This shows that Mr. Frank is a generous, gracious man who doesn't forget another person's kindness toward him.*

Evaluate Do you think Mr. Frank should have invited the Van Daans? *Students may say that he was right to invite them because Mr. Van Daan helped Mr. Frank when he needed it. Others may say that he should not have invited them. Their presence puts the Franks in greater danger.*

Mr. Kraler. I never thought I'd live to see the day when a man like Mr. Frank would have to go into hiding. When you think—(*He breaks off, going out.* Mr. Frank *follows him down the steps, bolting the door after him. In the interval before he returns,* Peter *goes over to* Margot, *shaking hands with her. As* Mr. Frank *comes back up the steps,* Mrs. Frank *questions him anxiously.*)

Mrs. Frank. What did he mean, about the noise?

Mr. Frank. First let us take off some of these clothes. (*They all start to take off garment after garment. On each of their coats, sweaters, blouses, suits, dresses, is another yellow Star of David.* Mr. *and* Mrs. Frank *are underdressed quite simply. The others wear several things, sweaters, extra dresses, bathrobes, aprons, nightgowns, etc.*)

Mr. Van Daan. It's a wonder we weren't arrested, walking along the streets . . . Petronella with a fur coat in July . . . and that cat of Peter's crying all the way.

Anne (*as she is removing a pair of panties*). A cat?

Mrs. Frank (*shocked*). Anne, please!

Anne. It's all right. I've got on three more. (*She pulls off two more. Finally, as they have all removed their surplus clothes, they look to* Mr. Frank, *waiting for him to speak.*)

Mr. Frank. Now. About the noise. While the men are in the building below, we must have complete quiet. Every sound can be heard down there, not only in the workrooms, but in the offices too. The men come at about eight-thirty, and leave at about five-thirty. So, to be perfectly safe, from eight in the morning until six in the evening we must move only when it is necessary, and then in stockinged feet. We must not speak above a whisper. We must not run any water. We cannot use the sink, or even, forgive me, the w.c.[5] The pipes go down through the workrooms. It would be heard. No trash . . . (Mr. Frank *stops abruptly as he hears the sound of marching feet from the street below. Everyone is motionless, paralyzed with fear.* Mr. Frank *goes quietly into the room on the right to look down out of the window.* Anne *runs after him, peering out with him. The tramping feet pass without stopping. The tension is relieved.* Mr. Frank, *followed by* An[ne] *returns to the main room and resumes his instructi[ons] to the group.*) . . . No trash must ever be thrown out which might reveal that someone is living up here . . . not even a potato paring. We must burn everything in the stove at night. This is the way we must live until it is over, if we are to survive.

(*There is silence for a second.*)

Mrs. Frank. Until it is over.

Mr. Frank (*reassuringly*). After six we can move about . . . we can talk and laugh and have our supper and read and play games . . . just as we would at home. (*He looks at his watch.*) And now I think it would be wise if we all went to our rooms, and were settled before eight o'clock. Mrs. Van Daan, you and your husband will be upsta[irs]. I regret that there's no place up there for Peter. But he will be here, near us. This will be our common room, where we'll meet to talk and eat and read, like one family.

Mr. Van Daan. And where do you and Mrs. Frank sleep?

Mr. Frank. This room is also our bedroom.

Mrs. Van Daan. That isn't right. We'll sleep here and you take the room upstairs. } *Together*

Mr. Van Daan. It's your place. }

Mr. Frank. Please. I've thought this out for weeks. It's the best arrangement. The only arrangement.

Mrs. Van Daan (*to* Mr. Frank). Never, never can we thank you. (*then to* Mrs. Frank) I don't know what would have happened to us, if it hadn't been for Mr. Frank.

Mr. Frank. You don't know how your husband helped me when I came to this country . . . knowing no one . . . not able to speak the language. I can never repay him for that. (*going to* Van Daan) May I help you with your things?

5. **w.c.:** water closet; toilet.

② Targeted Passage

DIFFERENTIATED INSTRUCTION

FOR LESS–PROFICIENT READERS

② Targeted Passage [Lines 258–295]

This passage builds understanding of the conflict: it will be an enormous struggle to live restricted lives to avoid capture by the Nazis.

- What rules will the Franks and Van Daans have to follow while in hiding?
- Why must they follow these rules strictly?
- What happens after six o'clock each night?

FOR ENGLISH LEARNERS

Language: Pronoun Referents [mixed-readiness groups] Tell students that sometimes the noun or phrase that a pronoun refers to is not specifically stated. The speaker might think the listener understands what he or she is talking about. Or, the referent might be found much earlier in the conversation. Help students increase their comprehension of the dialogue by having small groups work together to find the referents for these pronouns:

- *he* (line 240)—*Mr. Kraler*
- *It* (line 269)—*the noise of the water*
- *it* (line 282)—*the war*
- *That* (line 299)—*the Franks sleeping in the common room*
- *It's* (line 302)—*the Annex*
- *this* (line 303)—*the plans for the living arrangements*

Have groups share the referents they have identified.

Mr. Van Daan. No. No. (*to* Mrs. Van Daan) Come along, *liefje*.[6]

Mrs. Van Daan. You'll be all right, Peter? You're not afraid?

Peter (*embarrassed*). Please, Mother.

(*They start up the stairs to the attic room above.* Mr. Frank *turns to* Mrs. Frank.)

Mr. Frank. You too must have some rest, Edith. You didn't close your eyes last night. Nor you, Margot.

Anne. I slept, Father. Wasn't that funny? I knew it was the last night in my own bed, and yet I slept soundly.

Mr. Frank. I'm glad, Anne. Now you'll be able to help me straighten things in here. (*to* Mrs. Frank *and* Margot) Come with me . . . You and Margot rest in this room for the time being. (*He picks up their clothes, starting for the room on the right.*)

Mrs. Frank. You're sure . . . ? I could help . . . And Anne hasn't had her milk . . .

Mr. Frank. I'll give it to her. (*to* Anne *and* Peter) Anne, Peter . . . it's best that you take off your shoes now, before you forget. (*He leads the way to the room, followed by* Margot.)

Mrs. Frank. You're sure you're not tired, Anne?

Anne. I feel fine. I'm going to help Father.

Mrs. Frank. Peter, I'm glad you are to be with us.

Peter. Yes, Mrs. Frank.

(Mrs. Frank *goes to join* Mr. Frank *and* Margot.)

(*During the following scene* Mr. Frank *helps* Margot *and* Mrs. Frank *to hang up their clothes. Then he persuades them both to lie down and rest. The* Van Daans *in their room above settle themselves. In the main room* Anne *and* Peter *remove their shoes.* Peter *takes his cat out of the carrier.*)

Anne. What's your cat's name?

Peter. Mouschi.[7]

Anne. Mouschi! Mouschi! Mouschi! (*She picks up the cat, walking away with it. To* Peter.) I love cats. I have one . . . a darling little cat. But they made me leave her behind. I left some food and a note for the neighbors to take care of her . . . I'm going to miss her terribly. What is yours? A him or a her?

Peter. He's a tom. He doesn't like strangers.

(*He takes the cat from her, putting it back in its carrier.*)

Anne (***unabashed***). Then I'll have to stop being a stranger, won't I? Is he fixed?

Peter (*startled*). Huh?

Anne. Did you have him fixed?

Peter. No.

Anne. Oh, you ought to have him fixed—to keep him from—you know, fighting. Where did you go to school?

Peter. Jewish Secondary.

Anne. But that's where Margot and I go! I never saw you around.

Peter. I used to see you . . . sometimes . . .

Anne. You did?

Peter. . . . in the school yard. You were always in the middle of a bunch of kids. (*He takes a penknife from his pocket.*)

Anne. Why didn't you ever come over?

Peter. I'm sort of a lone wolf. (*He starts to rip off his Star of David.*)

Anne. What are you doing?

Peter. Taking it off.

Anne. But you can't do that. They'll arrest you if you go out without your star.

(*He tosses his knife on the table.*)

Peter. Who's going out?

Anne. Why, of course! You're right! Of course we don't need them any more. (*She picks up his knife and starts to take her star off.*) I wonder what our friends will think when we don't show up today?

Peter. I didn't have any dates with anyone.

6. ***liefje*** (lēf'yə) *Dutch:* little darling.

7. **Mouschi** (mo͝o'shē)

Lines 119–347

READING SKILL

STORY MAPPING

What is the first major event of Scene 2? (Have students record their answers on their story maps.) ***Possible answer:*** *The Van Daans and the Franks gather in the Annex, which is to be their home until the end of the war, and get settled.*

Lines 350–355

REINFORCE *KEY IDEA:* IMPACT

Discuss What happened to Anne's cat? What does this make you realize about the **impact** of the war? ***Possible answer:*** *Anne had to leave her cat behind and hope that the neighbors would take care of it. Students may say that this detail makes them realize how much people had to sacrifice during the war and how devastating it was to every aspect of family life.*

Lines 356–388

DISCUSSION PROMPTS

Use these prompts to help students understand the character traits of Anne and Peter:

Connect What would be the first thing you would do in Anne's situation? *Students may say that they, too, would try to get to know the other people.*

Compare and Contrast In what ways are Peter and Anne the same or different? Explain, using details from the text. ***Possible answer:*** *Anne is chatty and seems quite social. According to Peter, she is always surrounded by friends. She wonders what her friends will think about her absence. Peter is quiet and less outgoing. He calls himself a "lone wolf" and says he has no plans with friends. He also doesn't seem to want to share his cat with Anne.*

Synthesize Based on what you learn about the two characters, what do you think each will find the most difficult about their living situation? ***Possible answer:*** *Anne will miss her friends. Peter will find it hard to adjust to the lack of privacy.*

FOR LESS–PROFICIENT READERS

Comprehension Support Review the differences between Anne and Peter as developed in lines 356–388. Have students add these details to the chart they started on page 491. Then ask students to use the details about both to predict how Anne and Peter will get along with each other.

FOR ENGLISH LEARNERS

Vocabulary: Multiple Meanings [mixed-readiness pairs] Use the word *throw* from line 223 to model the strategy for defining multiple-meaning words. Point out that the word *bolt* and the phrase *open yourself* suggest that *throw* might mean "lock" or "close." Use a dictionary to confirm this definition. Have pairs define these words: *run* (line 267), *take* (line 300), *fixed* (line 360).

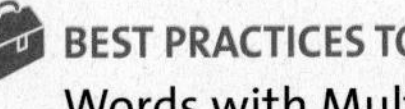

BEST PRACTICES TOOLKIT—Transparency
Words with Multiple Meanings p. E31

ADDITIONAL TEACHING OPPORTUNITY

Casting Discuss with students the fact that many casting decisions are made on the basis of the requirements of the part. The director of the production that this photograph was taken from chose to stage this play realistically. Therefore, the director had to consider the age, character traits, and physical attributes of the real-life characters. Have students take another look at the photographs of Anne on page 484 and think about what they have learned about Anne and Peter from the stage directions and the dialogue. Ask students if they think that Anne and Peter were well cast in this production. Why or why not? *Students may say that the actors portraying both Anne and Peter seem the right age and have a look of innocence about them that is suitable for their roles.*

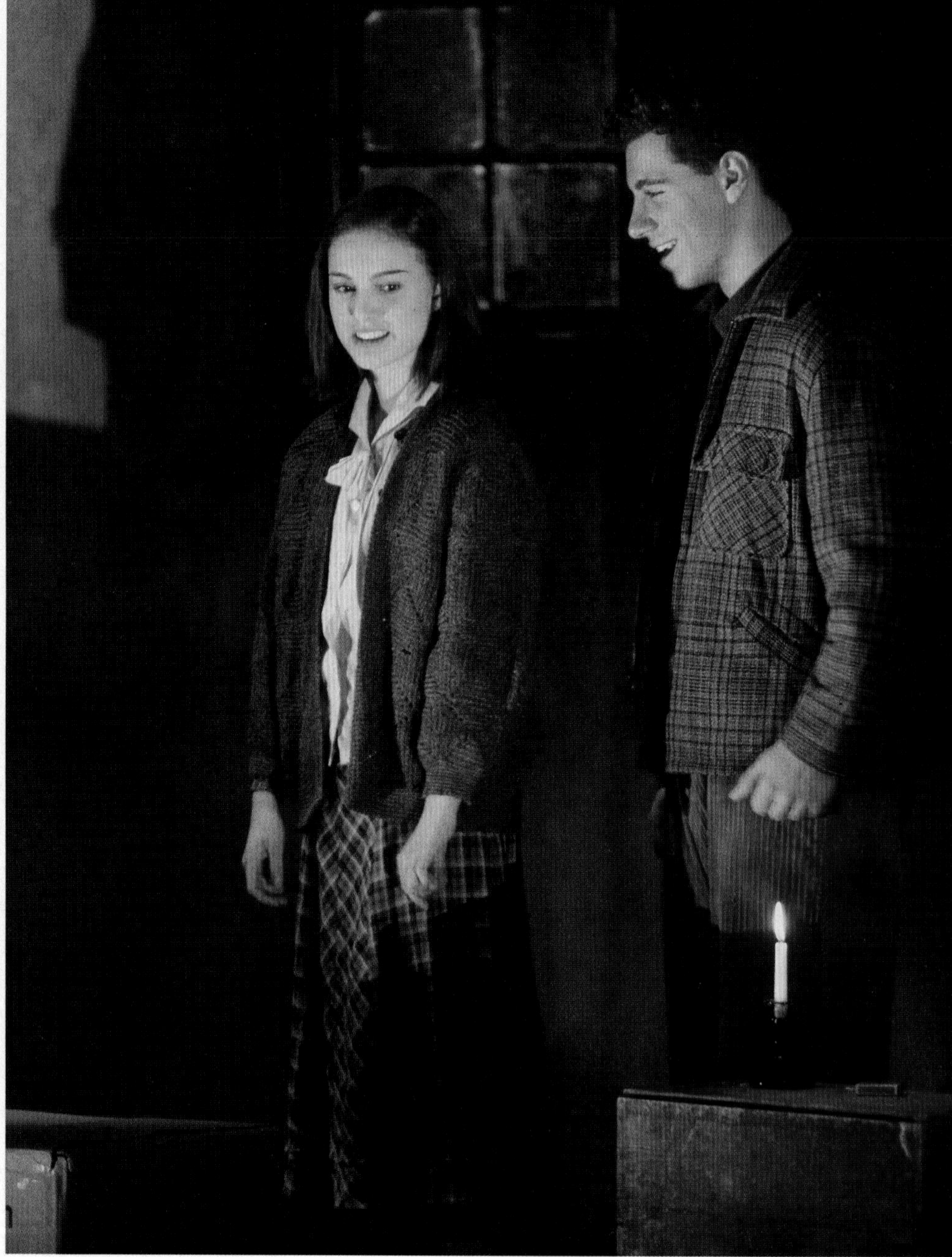

nne. Oh, I did. I had a date with Jopie to go and 'ay ping-pong at her house. Do you know Jopie e Waal?[8]

eter. No.

nne. Jopie's my best friend. I wonder what ie'll think when she telephones and there's no nswer? . . . Probably she'll go over to the house . . . wonder what she'll think . . . we left everything s if we'd suddenly been called away . . . breakfast ishes in the sink . . . beds not made . . . (*As she ulls off her star, the cloth underneath shows clearly he color and form of the star.*) Look! It's still there! Peter *goes over to the stove with his star.*) What're ou going to do with yours?

eter. Burn it.

nne (*She starts to throw hers in, and cannot.*) It's unny, I can't throw mine away. I don't know why.

eter. You can't throw . . . ? Something they randed you with . . . ? That they made you wear o they could spit on you?

nne. I know. I know. But after all, it *is* the Star f David, isn't it?

In the bedroom, right, Margot *and* Mrs. Frank *re lying down.* Mr. Frank *starts quietly out.*)

eter. Maybe it's different for a girl.

Mr. Frank *comes into the main room.*)

Ar. Frank. Forgive me, Peter. Now let me see. We must find a bed for your cat. (*He goes to a upboard.*) I'm glad you brought your cat. Anne vas feeling so badly about hers. (*getting a used mall washtub*) Here we are. Will it be comfortable n that?

eter (*gathering up his things*). Thanks.

Ar. Frank (*opening the door of the room on the left*). And here is your room. But I warn you, Peter, you an't grow any more. Not an inch, or you'll have o sleep with your feet out of the skylight. Are you ungry?

eter. No.

Mr. Frank. We have some bread and butter.

Peter. No, thank you.

Mr. Frank. You can have it for luncheon then. And tonight we will have a real supper . . . our first supper together.

Peter. Thanks. Thanks.

(*He goes into his room. During the following scene he arranges his possessions in his new room.*)

Mr. Frank. That's a nice boy, Peter.

Anne. He's awfully shy, isn't he?

Mr. Frank. You'll like him, I know.

Anne. I certainly hope so, since he's the only boy I'm likely to see for months and months.

(Mr. Frank *sits down, taking off his shoes.*)

Mr. Frank. Annele,[9] there's a box there. Will you open it? (*He indicates a carton on the couch.* Anne *brings it to the center table. In the street below there is the sound of children playing.*)

Anne (*as she opens the carton*). You know the way I'm going to think of it here? I'm going to think of it as a boarding house. A very peculiar summer boarding house, like the one that we—(*She breaks off as she pulls out some photographs.*) Father! My movie stars! I was wondering where they were! I was looking for them this morning . . . and Queen Wilhelmina! How wonderful!

Mr. Frank. There's something more. Go on. Look further. (*He goes over to the sink, pouring a glass of milk from a thermos bottle.*)

Anne (*pulling out a pasteboard-bound book*). A diary! (*She throws her arms around her father.*) I've never had a diary. And I've always longed for one. (*She looks around the room.*) Pencil, pencil, pencil, pencil. (*She starts down the stairs.*) I'm going down to the office to get a pencil.

Mr. Frank. Anne! No! (*He goes after her, catching her by the arm and pulling her back.*)

Anne (*startled*). But there's no one in the building now.

8. **Jopie de Waal** (yō'pē də väl')

9. **Annele/Anneke:** a nickname for Anne.

BACKGROUND

Queen Wilhelmina In line 453, Anne exclaims happily that her father has brought her photograph of Queen Wilhelmina. Queen Wilhelmina ruled the Netherlands from 1890 to 1948. When the Germans invaded, she left for England with her family and her cabinet. For the duration of the war, she ruled in exile, broadcasting messages to her people urging them not to give up hope that they would soon be liberated. Having her photograph symbolizes Anne's resistance against the German presence.

Lines 446–453

LITERARY ANALYSIS

● THEME

In what way is Anne going to view her experience in hiding? What does this reveal about her outlook on life? ***Possible answer:*** *Anne says that she is going to pretend she is staying in a peculiar boardinghouse. Her attitude toward the experience shows that she is optimistic and cheerful. She is willing to make the best of a bad situation.*

If students need help . . . Use a Read Aloud/Think Aloud strategy to help students make inferences about Anne's character from what she says.

BEST PRACTICES TOOLKIT—Transparency
Read Aloud/Think Aloud p. A34

Extend the Discussion How does Anne's attitude suggest a possible theme?

Lines 454–462

LITERARY ANALYSIS

● THEME

What does the choice of gift show about Mr. Frank's relationship with Anne? ***Possible answer:*** *Mr. Frank gives Anne a diary, something that she has always wanted. This shows his thoughtfulness as well as the special bond that he shares with his daughter.*

DIFFERENTIATED INSTRUCTION

FOR ENGLISH LEARNERS

Culture: Clarify

- Tell students that a *boardinghouse* (line 448) is a kind of guest house in which visitors have their own bedrooms but eat meals together at the same time and at the same table.
- Explain that the photographs that are referred to in line 450 are similar to posters of movie or music stars that teens might hang on their walls today.

FOR ADVANCED LEARNERS/PRE–AP

Analyze [small-group option] Why is a diary an appropriate gift to give Anne in particular or to anyone in her situation? Ask students to think about the purpose of a diary and what it implies about the present and the future. Then have them explore its suitability based on what they know of Anne's personality. Have students organize their ideas in webs and present them in small groups.

Lines 467–476

READING SKILL

STORY MAPPING

What does Anne realize about the idea of "going into hiding"? ***Possible answer:*** *Anne begins to understand that she can never leave the Annex. For an indefinite period, she can't see her friends, listen to the radio, or go outside.*

If students need help . . . Take this opportunity to have them connect to Anne's experience and feelings. Ask them to imagine that they must live in the classroom indefinitely. What they need will be brought in, but they can never go out the door. How would they feel?

Lines 528–549

LITERARY ANALYSIS

THEME

How does Anne view Miep and Mr. Kraler? How do you think they influence her attitude? ***Possible answer:*** *She admires them for their courage and cheerfulness in the face of extreme danger. The fact that she comments on their behavior suggests that she is influenced by them and may try to follow their example.*

Mr. Frank. It doesn't matter. I don't want you ever to go beyond that door.

Anne (*sobered*). Never . . . ? Not even at nighttime, when everyone is gone? Or on Sundays? Can't I go down to listen to the radio?

Mr. Frank. Never. I am sorry, Anneke. It isn't safe. No, you must never go beyond that door.

(*For the first time* Anne *realizes what "going into hiding" means.*)

Anne. I see.

Mr. Frank. It'll be hard, I know. But always remember this, Anneke. There are no walls, there are no bolts, no locks that anyone can put on your mind. Miep will bring us books. We will read history, poetry, mythology. (*He gives her the glass of milk.*) Here's your milk. (*With his arm about her, they go over to the couch, sitting down side by side.*) As a matter of fact, between us, Anne, being here has certain advantages for you. For instance, you remember the battle you had with your mother the other day on the subject of overshoes? You said you'd rather die than wear overshoes. But in the end you had to wear them? Well now, you see, for as long as we are here you will never have to wear overshoes! Isn't that good? And the coat that you inherited from Margot, you won't have to wear that any more. And the piano! You won't have to practice on the piano. I tell you, this is going to be a fine life for you!

(Anne*'s panic is gone.* Peter *appears in the doorway of his room, with a saucer in his hand. He is carrying his cat.*)

Peter. I . . . I . . . I thought I'd better get some water for Mouschi before . . .

Mr. Frank. Of course.

(*As he starts toward the sink the carillon begins to chime the hour of eight. He tiptoes to the window at the back and looks down at the street below. He turns to* Peter, *indicating in pantomime that it is too late.* Peter *starts back for his room. He steps on a creaking board. The three of them are frozen for a minute in fear. As* Peter *starts away again,* Anne *tiptoes over to him and pours some of the milk from her glass into the saucer for the cat.* Peter *squats on the flo putting the milk before the cat.* Mr. Frank *gives* Anne *his fountain pen, and then goes into the ro at the right. For a second* Anne *watches the cat, t she goes over to the center table, and opens her di*

In the room at the right, Mrs. Frank *has sat u quickly at the sound of the carillon.* Mr. Frank *co in and sits down beside her on the settee, his arm comfortingly around her.*

Upstairs, in the attic room, Mr. *and* Mrs. Van Daan *have hung their clothes in the closet and are now seated on the iron bed.* Mrs. Van Daan *leans back exhausted.* Mr. Van Daan *fans her with a newspaper.*

Anne *starts to write in her diary. The lights di out, the curtain falls.*

In the darkness Anne's Voice *comes to us again faintly at first, and then with growing strength.*)

Anne's Voice. I expect I should be describing wh it feels like to go into hiding. But I really don't know yet myself. I only know it's funny never t be able to go outdoors . . . never to breathe fresh air . . . never to run and shout and jump. It's th silence in the nights that frightens me most. Ev time I hear a creak in the house, or a step on th street outside, I'm sure they're coming for us. T days aren't so bad. At least we know that Miep Mr. Kraler are down there below us in the offic Our protectors, we call them. I asked Father wh would happen to them if the Nazis found out t were hiding us. Pim said that they would suffer same fate that we would . . . Imagine! They kn this, and yet when they come up here, they're always cheerful and gay as if there were nothing the world to bother them . . . Friday, the twenty first of August, nineteen forty-two. Today I'm going to tell you our general news. Mother is unbearable. She insists on treating me like a bal which I loathe. Otherwise things are going bett The weather is . . .

(*As* Anne's Voice *is fading out, the curtain rises on the scene.*)

DIFFERENTIATED INSTRUCTION

FOR LESS-PROFICIENT READERS

Comprehension Support Remind students that the major conflict in the play leads to other conflicts or problems.

- Review the two types of conflict. *(External conflict is a struggle between a character and an outside force, such as nature, another character, or society. Internal conflict is a struggle within the character.)*
- Have small groups reread lines 528–549 and identify internal and external conflicts.

External Conflict	Internal Conflict
• Anne's mother treats her like a baby. • Anne is in danger of being found by the Nazis.	• Anne fears they will be discovered. • Anne misses going outside.

FOR ADVANCED LEARNERS/PRE-AP

Evaluate [small-group option] Is Mr. Frank's point about mental freedom in lines 477–480 a valid one? Ask students to write a few sentences in which they react to his words, citing their own experiences or beliefs. Have students share their statements in small groups.

Scene 3

It is a little after six o'clock in the evening, two months later.

Margot *is in the bedroom at the right, studying.* Mr. Van Daan *is lying down in the attic room above.*

The rest of the "family" is in the main room. Anne *and* Peter *sit opposite each other at the center table, where they have been doing their lessons.* Mrs. Frank *is on the couch.* Mrs. Van Daan *is seated with her fur coat, on which she has been sewing, in her lap. None of them are wearing their shoes.*

Their eyes are on Mr. Frank, *waiting for him to give them the signal which will release them from their day-long quiet.* Mr. Frank, *his shoes in his hand, stands looking down out of the window at the back, watching to be sure that all of the workmen have left the building below.*

After a few seconds of motionless silence, Mr. Frank *turns from the window.*

Mr. Frank (*quietly, to the group*). It's safe now. The last workman has left. (*There is an immediate stir of relief.*)

Anne (*Her pent-up energy explodes.*) WHEE!

Mrs. Frank (*startled, amused*). Anne!

Mrs. Van Daan. I'm first for the w.c. (*She hurries off to the bathroom.* Mrs. Frank *puts on her shoes and starts up to the sink to prepare supper.* Anne *sneaks* Peter*'s shoes from under the table and hides them behind her back.* Mr. Frank *goes in to* Margot*'s room.*)

Mr. Frank (*to* Margot). Six o'clock. School's over.

(Margot *gets up, stretching.* Mr. Frank *sits down to put on his shoes. In the main room* Peter *tries to find his.*)

Peter (*to* Anne). Have you seen my shoes?

Anne (*innocently*). Your shoes?

Peter. You've taken them, haven't you?

Anne. I don't know what you're talking about.

Peter. You're going to be sorry!

Anne. Am I? (Peter *goes after her.* Anne, *with his shoes in her hand, runs from him, dodging behind her mother.*)

Mrs. Frank (*protesting*). Anne, dear!

Peter. Wait till I get you!

Anne. I'm waiting! (Peter *makes a lunge for her. They both fall to the floor.* Peter *pins her down, wrestling with her to get the shoes.*) Don't! Don't! Peter, stop it. Ouch!

Mrs. Frank. Anne! . . . Peter!

(*Suddenly* Peter *becomes self-conscious. He grabs his shoes roughly and starts for his room.*)

Anne (*following him*). Peter, where are you going? Come dance with me.

Peter. I tell you I don't know how.

Anne. I'll teach you.

Peter. I'm going to give Mouschi his dinner.

Anne. Can I watch?

Peter. He doesn't like people around while he eats.

Anne. Peter, please.

Peter. No! (*He goes into his room.* Anne *slams his door after him.*)

Mrs. Frank. Anne, dear, I think you shouldn't play like that with Peter. It's not dignified.

Anne. Who cares if it's dignified? I don't want to be dignified.

(Mr. Frank *and* Margot *come from the room on the right.* Margot *goes to help her mother.* Mr. Frank *starts for the center table to correct* Margot*'s school papers.*)

Mrs. Frank (*to* Anne). You complain that I don't treat you like a grownup. But when I do, you resent it.

Anne. I only want some fun . . . someone to laugh and clown with . . . After you've sat still all day and hardly moved, you've got to have some fun. I don't know what's the matter with that boy.

Lines 563–570

REINFORCE *KEY IDEA:* IMPACT

Discuss How does the location of their hiding place have an **impact** on the lives of the Franks and the Van Daans? ***Possible answer:*** *They are forced to remain silent and move very little from eight in the morning until six at night.*

Lines 571–611

DISCUSSION PROMPTS

Use these prompts to help students understand the realities of life in hiding:

Connect How would you feel if you had to be quiet from eight in the morning until six at night? What would be the first thing you would do at six o'clock? *Students might say that they would feel restless and trapped. The minute they could, they might shout or jump around, as Anne does.*

Compare and Contrast How are the interactions between the characters different from the way they were at first? ***Possible answer:*** *The characters were quite stilted and polite to each other at first. They seem less formal now. Mrs. Van Daan openly claims the bathroom, and Anne and Peter wrestle.*

Speculate Why do you think Peter behaves the way he does toward Anne? *Students may say that Anne's chattiness and constant need for his attention is annoying him. Other students might think that Peter has a crush on Anne.*

FOR LESS–PROFICIENT READERS

Concept Support [small-group option] To help students appreciate the restrictions on the lives of Anne and the others, have them work in small groups to diagram the location of the Annex in relationship to the offices that Miep, Mr. Kraler, and the workers occupy during the day. Discuss students' diagrams and talk about the pros and cons of hiding in a functional office building as opposed to an abandoned structure.

Lines 665–682

DISCUSSION PROMPTS

Use these prompts to help students understand the characters of Mrs. Van Daan and Mrs. Frank:

Connect What feelings do you think Peter is experiencing when his mother calls Anne his "little girl friend"? How would you feel? *Students will probably say that he is embarrassed and wishes his mother wouldn't say things like that. Whether he has feelings for Anne or not, it is embarrassing to be teased.*

Analyze In what way would you describe Mrs. Van Daan, based on her comments? ***Possible answer:*** *She is tactless and insensitive to the feelings of her son. Also, she is unaware of the effect that her words might have on the Franks.*

Speculate What feelings do you think Mrs. Frank has about the direction of the conversation? Why? ***Possible answer:*** *Mrs. Frank deliberately changes the subject, which suggests that the direction of the conversation makes her feel uncomfortable. She has already scolded Anne for behaving in an undignified manner and may not feel that a relationship between Anne and Peter in the current situation should be encouraged or discussed. Or, perhaps she is being sensitive to Peter's feelings.*

Mr. Frank. He isn't used to girls. Give him a little time.

Anne. Time? Isn't two months time? I could cry. (*catching hold of* Margot) Come on, Margot . . . dance with me. Come on, please.

Margot. I have to help with supper.

Anne. You know we're going to forget how to dance . . . When we get out we won't remember a thing.

(*She starts to sing and dance by herself.* Mr. Frank *takes her in his arms, waltzing with her.* Mrs. Van Daan *comes in from the bathroom.*)

Mrs. Van Daan. Next? (*She looks around as she starts putting on her shoes.*) Where's Peter?

Anne (*as they are dancing*). Where would he be!

Mrs. Van Daan. He hasn't finished his lessons, has he? His father'll kill him if he catches him in there with that cat and his work not done. (Mr. Frank *and* Anne *finish their dance. They bow to each other with extravagant formality.*) Anne, get him out of there, will you?

Anne (*at* Peter's *door*). Peter? Peter?

Peter (*opening the door a crack*). What is it?

Anne. Your mother says to come out.

Peter. I'm giving Mouschi his dinner.

Mrs. Van Daan. You know what your father says. (*She sits on the couch, sewing on the lining of her fur coat.*)

Peter. For heaven's sake, I haven't even looked at him since lunch.

Mrs. Van Daan. I'm just telling you, that's all.

Anne. I'll feed him.

Peter. I don't want you in there.

Mrs. Van Daan. Peter!

Peter (*to* Anne). Then give him his dinner and come right out, you hear? (*He comes back to the table.* Anne *shuts the door of* Peter's *room after her and disappears behind the curtain covering his closet.*)

Mrs. Van Daan (*to* Peter). Now is that any way t talk to your little girl friend?

Peter. Mother . . . for heaven's sake . . . will you please stop saying that?

Mrs. Van Daan. Look at him blush! Look at hin

Peter. Please! I'm not . . . anyway . . . let me alo will you?

Mrs. Van Daan. He acts like it was something to ashamed of. It's nothing to be ashamed of, to h a little girl friend.

Peter. You're crazy. She's only thirteen.

Mrs. Van Daan. So what? And you're sixteen. Just perfect. Your father's ten years older than I am. (Mr. Frank) I warn you, Mr. Frank, if this war la much longer, we're going to be related and then

Mr. Frank. *Mazeltov!*[10]

Mrs. Frank (*deliberately changing the conversation* I wonder where Miep is. She's usually so promp

(*Suddenly everything else is forgotten as they hear sound of an automobile coming to a screeching sto in the street below. They are tense, motionless in th terror. The car starts away. A wave of relief sweeps over them. They pick up their occupations again.* Anne *flings open the door of* Peter's *room, makin a dramatic entrance. She is dressed in* Peter's *cloth* Peter *looks at her in fury. The others are amused.*)

Anne. Good evening, everyone. Forgive me if I don't stay. (*She jumps up on a chair.*) I have a friend waiting for me in there. My friend Tom. Tom Cat. Some people say that we look alike. But Tom has the most beautiful whiskers, and I have only a little fuzz. I am hoping . . . in time

Peter. All right, Mrs. Quack Quack!

Anne (*outraged—jumping down*). Peter!

Peter. I heard about you . . . How you talked so much in class they called you Mrs. Quack Quack. How Mr. Smitter made you write a composition . . . "'Quack, quack,' said Mrs. Quack Quack."

10. **Mazeltov!** (mä'zəl tôf') *Hebrew:* Congratulations!

DIFFERENTIATED INSTRUCTION

FOR LESS-PROFICIENT READERS

Comprehension Support Tell students that during the rising action of the plot, they can expect more conflicts to develop. These struggles increase the tension and suspense and may make the outcome of the major problem more uncertain. Anne introduces some of the conflicts in lines 528–549. Ask small groups to identify additional internal and external conflicts in lines 627–775 and add them to the chart they started on page 496.

External Conflict	Internal Conflict
• Anne teases Peter. • Mr. Van Daan wants Peter to study more. • Mrs. Frank is upset at Anne's behavior.	• Anne worries that she will forget how to dance or how to be young and carefree.

FOR ENGLISH LEARNERS

Concept Support Draw students' attention to lines 683–690. These stage directions describe the characters' reactions to hearing a speeding car pull up outside. Explain that each time there is an unusual noise or the sound of a car or truck stopping, they fear that it is the Nazis, coming to arrest them. If the car moves on, as this one does, then they can relax once again.

nne. Well, go on. Tell them the rest. How it was) good he read it out loud to the class and then :ad it to all his other classes!

eter. Quack! Quack! Quack . . . Quack . . .)uack . . .

Anne *pulls off the coat and trousers.*)

nne. You are the most intolerable, insufferable oy I've ever met!

She throws the clothes down the stairwell. Peter *goes lown after them.*)

eter. Quack, quack, quack!

Ars. Van Daan (*to* Anne). That's right, Anneke! ;ive it to him!

nne. With all the boys in the world . . . Why had to get locked up with one like you! . . .

eter. Quack, quack, quack, and from now on stay ut of my room!

As Peter *passes her,* Anne *puts out her foot, tripping im. He picks himself up, and goes on into his room.*)

Ars. Frank (*quietly*). Anne, dear . . . your hair. *She feels* Anne's *forehead.*) You're warm. Are you eeling all right?

nne. Please, Mother. (*She goes over to the center able, slipping into her shoes.*)

Ars. Frank (*following her*). You haven't a fever, ave you?

nne (*pulling away*). No. No.

Ars. Frank. You know we can't call a doctor ere, ever. There's only one thing to do . . . vatch carefully. Prevent an illness before it comes. et me see your tongue.

nne. Mother, this is perfectly absurd.

Ars. Frank. Anne, dear, don't be such a baby. Let ne see your tongue. (*As* Anne *refuses,* Mrs. Frank *ppeals to* Mr. Frank.) Otto . . . ?

Ar. Frank. You hear your mother, Anne. (Anne *licks out her tongue for a second, then turns away.*)

Ars. Frank. Come on—open up! (*as* Anne *opens ier mouth very wide*) You seem all right . . . but erhaps an aspirin . . .

Mrs. Van Daan. For heaven's sake, don't give that child any pills. I waited for fifteen minutes this morning for her to come out of the w.c.

Anne. I was washing my hair!

Mr. Frank. I think there's nothing the matter with our Anne that a ride on her bike, or a visit with her friend Jopie de Waal wouldn't cure. Isn't that so, Anne?

(Mr. Van Daan *comes down into the room. From outside we hear faint sounds of bombers going over and a burst of ack-ack.*)

Mr. Van Daan. Miep not come yet?

Mrs. Van Daan. The workmen just left, a little while ago.

Mr. Van Daan. What's for dinner tonight?

Mrs. Van Daan. Beans.

Mr. Van Daan. Not again!

Mrs. Van Daan. Poor Putti! I know. But what can we do? That's all that Miep brought us.

(Mr. Van Daan *starts to pace, his hands behind his back.* Anne *follows behind him, imitating him.*)

Anne. We are now in what is known as the "bean cycle." Beans boiled, beans en casserole, beans with strings, beans without strings . . .

(Peter *has come out of his room. He slides into his place at the table, becoming immediately absorbed in his studies.*)

Mr. Van Daan (*to* Peter). I saw you . . . in there, playing with your cat.

Mrs. Van Daan. He just went in for a second, putting his coat away. He's been out here all the time, doing his lessons.

Mr. Frank (*looking up from the papers*). Anne, you got an excellent in your history paper today . . . and very good in Latin.

Anne (*sitting beside him*). How about algebra?

Mr. Frank. I'll have to make a confession. Up until now I've managed to stay ahead of you in algebra. Today you caught up with me. We'll leave it to Margot to correct.

Lines 688–722

REINFORCE *KEY IDEA:* IMPACT

Discuss What **impact** are the months of hiding starting to have on Anne and the others? ***Possible answer:*** *Anne's energy can't be contained, and she becomes boisterous. Her behavior in this instance is directed at Peter, who becomes very annoyed with her and retaliates by bringing up her nickname from school.*

Lines 748–751

LITERARY ANALYSIS

● THEME

Why does Mr. Frank say "there's nothing the matter with our Anne that a ride on her bike, or a visit with her friend . . . wouldn't cure"? ***Possible answer:*** *Mr. Frank is defending Anne against the criticism of the others. He is also trying to keep the peace and remind everyone to have a little tolerance and patience for each other.*

Extend the Discussion What is Mr. Frank's role among the residents in the Annex?

FOR ENGLISH LEARNERS

Vocabulary: Idioms and Sayings Idiomatic expressions are used to make the dialogue sound realistic. Have small groups of students use context clues to define these:

- *clown with* (line 624), "play with"
- *kill him* (line 643), "become very angry with him"
- *Give it to him!* (line 716), "scold him"
- *gets fresh* (line 828), "becomes too bold"
- *an angel* (lines 861–862), "a good person"

Culture: Clarify

- Explain that in lines 691–696, Anne refers to Peter's slight moustache when she talks about "a little fuzz." He responds by calling her "Mrs. Quack Quack," a name used at school to describe Anne's habit of talking so much. Tell students that *quack* is supposed to mimic the sound of a duck.
- In lines 731–738, Mrs. Frank asks to see Anne's tongue. A coated tongue was thought to be an indication of sickness.

THE DIARY OF ANNE FRANK: ACT ONE 499

Lines 804–850
DISCUSSION PROMPTS

Use these prompts to help students understand the dynamics within the Van Daan family:

Connect If you were in hiding, would you rather live with the Franks or the Van Daans? *Most students will probably say that they would prefer to live with the Franks. They may say that Mr. Frank seems to be more capable of keeping everyone calm than Mr. or Mrs. Van Daan.*

Compare In what way are the Franks different from the Van Daans? *Students may say that the Franks seem much more agreeable than the Van Daans and that the Franks seem like a more good-natured family. They may also note that although Anne complains about her mother treating her like a baby, they do not fight like the Van Daans, who seem to bicker constantly.*

Synthesize What are the various sources of tension within the Van Daan family? ***Possible answer:*** *Mr. Van Daan is annoyed with Peter for not doing his schoolwork. He makes Peter feel like "a dunce." Mrs. Van Daan tries to protect Peter from his father, which aggravates Mr. Van Daan. Peter is embarrassed by his mother.*

Anne. Isn't algebra *vile,* Pim!

Mr. Frank. Vile!

Margot (*to* Mr. Frank). How did I do?

Anne (*getting up*). Excellent, excellent, excellent, excellent!

Mr. Frank (*to* Margot). You should have used the subjunctive here . . .

Margot. Should I? . . . I thought . . . look here . . . I didn't use it here . . . (*The two become absorbed in the papers.*)

Anne. Mrs. Van Daan, may I try on your coat?

Mrs. Frank. No, Anne.

Mrs. Van Daan (*giving it to* Anne). It's all right . . . but careful with it. (Anne *puts it on and struts with it.*) My father gave me that the year before he died. He always bought the best that money could buy.

Anne. Mrs. Van Daan, did you have a lot of boy friends before you were married?

Mrs. Frank. Anne, that's a personal question. It's not courteous to ask personal questions.

Mrs. Van Daan. Oh I don't mind. (*to* Anne) Our house was always swarming with boys. When I was a girl we had . . .

Mr. Van Daan. Oh, God. Not again!

Mrs. Van Daan (*good-humored*). Shut up! (*Without a pause, to* Anne. Mr. Van Daan *mimics* Mrs. Van Daan, *speaking the first few words in unison with her.*) One summer we had a big house in Hilversum. The boys came buzzing round like bees around a jam pot. And when I was sixteen! . . . We were wearing our skirts very short those days and I had good-looking legs. (*She pulls up her skirt, going to* Mr. Frank.) I still have 'em. I may not be as pretty as I used to be, but I still have my legs. How about it, Mr. Frank?

Mr. Van Daan. All right. All right. We see them.

Mrs. Van Daan. I'm not asking you. I'm asking Mr. Frank.

Peter. Mother, for heaven's sake.

Mrs. Van Daan. Oh, I embarrass you, do I? We I just hope the girl you marry has as good. (*th* Anne) My father used to worry about me, wit many boys hanging round. He told me, if any them gets fresh, you say to him . . . "Rememb Mr. So-and-So, remember I'm a lady."

Anne. "Remember, Mr. So-and-So, remember I'm a lady." (*She gives* Mrs. Van Daan *her coat.*)

Mr. Van Daan. Look at you, talking that way i front of her! Don't you know she puts it all do in that diary?

Mrs. Van Daan. So, if she does? I'm only tellir the truth!

(Anne *stretches out, putting her ear to the floor, listening to what is going on below. The sound of the bombers fades away.*)

Mrs. Frank (*setting the table*). Would you mind Peter, if I moved you over to the couch?

Anne (*listening*). Miep must have the radio on.

(Peter *picks up his papers, going over to the couc beside* Mrs. Van Daan.)

Mr. Van Daan (*accusingly, to* Peter). Haven't yo finished yet?

Peter. No.

Mr. Van Daan. You ought to be ashamed of your

Peter. All right. All right. I'm a dunce. I'm a hopeless case. Why do I go on?

Mrs. Van Daan. You're not hopeless. Don't talk that way. It's just that you haven't anyone to he you, like the girls have. (*to* Mr. Frank) Maybe could help him, Mr. Frank?

Mr. Frank. I'm sure that his father . . . ?

Mr. Van Daan. Not me. I can't do anything wit him. He won't listen to me. You go ahead . . . you want.

Mr. Frank (*going to* Peter). What about it, Peter Shall we make our school coeducational?

Mrs. Van Daan (*kissing* Mr. Frank). You're an angel, Mr. Frank. An angel. I don't know why I didn't meet you before I met that one there.

DIFFERENTIATED INSTRUCTION

FOR ENGLISH LEARNERS

Vocabulary Support Tell students that the expression *Mr. So-and-So* in line 829 is used in place of a name when the specific name is not remembered or known.

Concept Support Explain to students that in lines 915–917, Anne appears to be talking to Miep, but Miep is not really there. Rather, Anne is imitating the way the Franks and the Van Daans treat Miep and rely on her for everything.

FOR ADVANCED LEARNERS/PRE–AP

Analyze [small-group option] Discuss with students how conversation and behavior can provide insights into characters' inner thoughts. Ask students to look at what Anne, Mrs. Frank, and Mrs. Van Daan say and do in the first part of this scene. What do their actions and words show about their secret fears, apart from the overwhelming worry about surviving? Ask students to make inferences based on the evidence in the text and to discuss their ideas in small groups.

500 UNIT 4: THEME AND SYMBOL

Iere, sit down, Mr. Frank . . . (*She forces him* *own on the couch beside* Peter.) Now, Peter, you sten to Mr. Frank.

Ir. Frank. It might be better for us to go into Peter's oom. (Peter *jumps up eagerly, leading the way.*)

Irs. Van Daan. That's right. You go in there, Peter. ou listen to Mr. Frank. Mr. Frank is a highly ducated man. (*As* Mr. Frank *is about to follow* eter *into his room,* Mrs. Frank *stops him and wipes* *he lipstick from his lips. Then she closes the door* *fter them.*)

nne (*on the floor, listening*). Shh! I can hear a nan's voice talking.

Ir. Van Daan (*to* Anne). Isn't it bad enough here vithout your sprawling all over the place? (Anne *its up.*)

Irs. Van Daan (*to* Mr. Van Daan). If you didn't moke so much, you wouldn't be so bad-tempered.

Ir. Van Daan. Am I smoking? Do you see me moking?

Irs. Van Daan. Don't tell me you've used up all hose cigarettes.

Ir. Van Daan. One package. Miep only brought ne one package.

Irs. Van Daan. It's a filthy habit anyway. It's a ood time to break yourself.

Ir. Van Daan. Oh, stop it, please.

Irs. Van Daan. You're smoking up all our money. ou know that, don't you?

Ir. Van Daan. Will you shut up? (*During this,* Mrs. Frank *and* Margot *have studiously kept their* *yes down. But* Anne, *seated on the floor, has been* *ollowing the discussion interestedly.* Mr. Van Daan *urns to see her staring up at him.*) And what are ou staring at?

Anne. I never heard grownups quarrel before. thought only children quarreled.

Mr. Van Daan. This isn't a quarrel! It's a discussion. And I never heard children so rude before.

Anne (*rising,* ***indignantly***). *I,* rude!

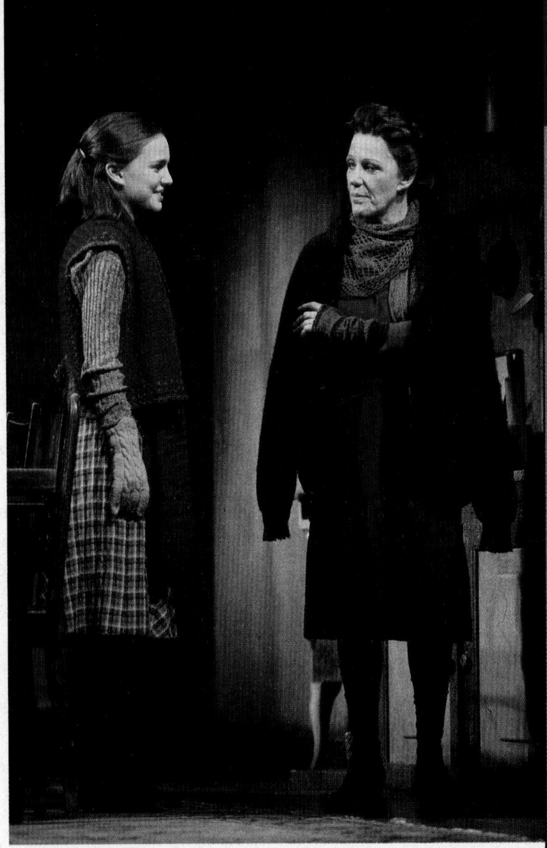

Mr. Van Daan. Yes!

Mrs. Frank (*quickly*). Anne, will you get me my knitting? (Anne *goes to get it.*) I must remember, when Miep comes, to ask her to bring me some more wool.

Margot (*going to her room*). I need some hairpins and some soap. I made a list. (*She goes into her bedroom to get the list.*)

Mrs. Frank (*to* Anne). Have you some library books for Miep when she comes?

Anne. It's a wonder that Miep has a life of her own, the way we make her run errands for us. Please, Miep, get me some starch. Please take my hair out and have it cut. Tell me all the latest news, Miep.

ANALYZE VISUALS

Activity What are the costumes worn by the actors in this photograph meant to suggest about conditions in the Annex? ***Possible answer:*** *There isn't enough heat, so they wear layers of clothing to keep warm.*

Lines 877–898

READING SKILL

STORY MAPPING

What happens in this passage? What do the interactions between the characters show about how living in hiding is affecting Mr. Van Daan? (Have students record important details in their story map from page 485.) ***Possible answer:*** *Mr. Van Daan is becoming increasingly difficult to please. He criticizes Anne and fights with his wife. He is feeling the strain of living in hiding.*

Extend the Discussion How does the conflict between Mr. and Mrs. Van Daan affect the others? In what way could Mr. Van Daan's actions and behaviors represent a theme of the play?

FOR LESS–PROFICIENT READERS

Comprehension Support Tell students that one of the methods the playwrights use to bring out the characters' traits is contrast. Use a Venn Diagram to help students compare Mr. Frank and Mr. Van Daan and their reactions to being in hiding, using their words and actions from lines 739–904.

BEST PRACTICES TOOLKIT—Transparency
Venn Diagram p. A26

Mr. Frank
- *supports wife's decisions about Anne*
- *sensitive to Anne's feelings*
- *happy to help Peter*

Both
living in hiding

Mr. Van Daan
- *makes fun of wife; argues with her*
- *criticizes Peter and Anne*
- *mostly concerned about his own needs*

Lines 924–990
DISCUSSION PROMPTS

Use these prompts to help students understand more about the interactions of the characters:

Connect Would you find Anne annoying if you had to live with her in the Annex? Why or why not? *Some students might say that Anne brings a little life into the dreariness of everyone's existence. She is high-spirited, but she is also young. Others may say that she could get on people's nerves, especially if they were already tense.*

Compare Based on the dialogue of the Van Daans, how are the two characters alike? ***Possible answer:*** *Both are dramatic and emotional. They say what they think and feel.*

Evaluate Do you think Mrs. Van Daan is justified in the way she reacts to Anne? *Students might say that Mrs. Van Daan overreacts. She has a right to be upset because her coat is her most precious possession, but her words are unnecessarily harsh.*

(*She goes over, kneeling on the couch beside* Mrs. Van Daan.) Did you know she was engaged? His name is Dirk, and Miep's afraid the Nazis will ship him off to Germany to work in one of their war plants. That's what they're doing with some of the young Dutchmen . . . they pick them up off the streets—

Mr. Van Daan (*interrupting*). Don't you ever get tired of talking? Suppose you try keeping still for five minutes. Just five minutes. (*He starts to pace again. Again* Anne *follows him, mimicking him.* Mrs. Frank *jumps up and takes her by the arm up to the sink, and gives her a glass of milk.*)

Mrs. Frank. Come here, Anne. It's time for your glass of milk.

Mr. Van Daan. Talk, talk, talk. I never heard such a child. Where is my . . . ? Every evening it's the same, talk, talk, talk. (*He looks around.*) Where is my . . . ?

Mrs. Van Daan. What're you looking for?

Mr. Van Daan. My pipe. Have you seen my pipe?

Mrs. Van Daan. What good's a pipe? You haven't got any tobacco.

Mr. Van Daan. At least I'll have something to hold in my mouth! (*opening* Margot's *bedroom door*) Margot, have you seen my pipe?

Margot. It was on the table last night. (Anne *puts her glass of milk on the table and picks up his pipe, hiding it behind her back.*)

Mr. Van Daan. I know. I know. Anne, did you see my pipe? . . . Anne!

Mrs. Frank. Anne, Mr. Van Daan is speaking to you.

Anne. Am I allowed to talk now?

Mr. Van Daan. You're the most aggravating . . . The trouble with you is, you've been spoiled. What you need is a good old-fashioned spanking.

Anne (*mimicking* Mrs. Van Daan). "Remember, Mr. So-and-So, remember I'm a lady." (*She thrusts the pipe into his mouth, then picks up her glass of milk.*)

Mr. Van Daan (*restraining himself with difficu*
Why aren't you nice and quiet like your sister
Margot? Why do you have to show off all the
time? Let me give you a little advice, young la
Men don't like that kind of thing in a girl. Yo
know that? A man likes a girl who'll listen to
once in a while . . . a domestic girl, who'll kee
her house shining for her husband . . . who lo
to cook and sew and . . .

Anne. I'd cut my throat first! I'd open my vei
I'm going to be remarkable! I'm going to Pari

Mr. Van Daan (*scoffingly*). Paris!

Anne. . . . to study music and art.

Mr. Van Daan. Yeah! Yeah!

Anne. I'm going to be a famous dancer or
singer . . . or something wonderful. (*She mak*
a wide gesture, spilling the glass of milk on the f
coat in Mrs. Van Daan*'s lap.* Margot *rushes qu*
over with a towel. Anne *tries to brush the milk*
with her skirt.)

Mrs. Van Daan. Now look what you've done . .
you clumsy little fool! My beautiful fur coat r
father gave me . . .

Anne. I'm so sorry.

Mrs. Van Daan. What do you care? It isn't you
. . . So go on, ruin it! Do you know what that c
cost? Do you? And now look at it! Look at it!

Anne. I'm very, very sorry.

Mrs. Van Daan. I could kill you for this. I cou
just kill you! (Mrs. Van Daan *goes up the stair*
clutching the coat. Mr. Van Daan *starts after he*

Mr. Van Daan. Petronella . . . *liefje! Liefje!* . . .
Come back . . . the supper . . . come back!

Mrs. Frank. Anne, you must not behave in that way.

Anne. It was an accident. Anyone can have an accident.

Mrs. Frank. I don't mean that. I mean the answering back. You must not answer back. They are our guests. We must always show the

(3) Targeted Passage

DIFFERENTIATED INSTRUCTION

FOR LESS-PROFICIENT READERS

(3) Targeted Passage [Lines 924–988]

This passage develops the rising action.

- In what way does Anne annoy Mr. Van Daan?
- What does Anne do with Mr. Van Daan's pipe?
- What does Mr. Van Daan say that Anne needs?
- What does this passage show about conditions in the Annex at this point?

FOR ADVANCED LEARNERS/PRE-AP

Evaluate Is the strain of living in hiding changing the characters or just bringing out their true natures? Have students cite evidence from the play to support their answers to this question. Then have students informally debate the issue in class.

greatest courtesy to them. We're all living under terrible tension. (*She stops as* Margot *indicates that* Van Daan *can hear. When he is gone, she continues.*) That's why we must control ourselves . . . You don't hear Margot getting into arguments with them, do you? Watch Margot. She's always courteous with them. Never familiar. She keeps her distance. And they respect her for it. Try to be like Margot.

Anne. And have them walk all over me, the way they do her? No, thanks!

Mrs. Frank. I'm not afraid that anyone is going to walk all over you, Anne. I'm afraid for other people, that you'll walk on them. I don't know what happens to you, Anne. You are wild, self-willed. If I had ever talked to my mother as you talk to me . . .

Anne. Things have changed. People aren't like that any more. "Yes, Mother." "No, Mother." "Anything you say, Mother." I've got to fight things out for myself! Make something of myself!

Mrs. Frank. It isn't necessary to fight to do it. Margot doesn't fight, and isn't she . . . ?

Anne (*violently rebellious*). Margot! Margot! Margot! That's all I hear from everyone . . . how wonderful Margot is . . . "Why aren't you like Margot?"

Margot (*protesting*). Oh, come on, Anne, don't be so . . .

Anne (*paying no attention*). Everything she does is right, and everything I do is wrong! I'm the goat around here! . . . You're all against me! . . . And you worst of all!

(*She rushes off into her room and throws herself down on the settee, stifling her sobs.* Mrs. Frank *sighs and starts toward the stove.*)

Mrs. Frank (*to* Margot). Let's put the soup on the stove . . . if there's anyone who cares to eat. Margot, will you take the bread out? (Margot *gets the bread from the cupboard.*) I don't know how we can go on living this way . . . I can't say a word to Anne . . . she flies at me . . .

Margot. You know Anne. In half an hour she'll be out here, laughing and joking.

Mrs. Frank. And . . . (*She makes a motion upwards, indicating the* Van Daans.) . . . I told your father it wouldn't work . . . but no . . . no . . . he had to ask them, he said . . . he owed it to him, he said. Well, he knows now that I was right! These quarrels! . . . This bickering!

Margot (*with a warning look*). Shush. Shush.

(*The buzzer for the door sounds.* Mrs. Frank *gasps, startled.*)

Mrs. Frank. Every time I hear that sound, my heart stops!

Margot (*starting for* Peter*'s door*). It's Miep. (*She knocks at the door.*) Father?

(Mr. Frank *comes quickly from* Peter*'s room.*)

Mr. Frank. Thank you, Margot. (*as he goes down the steps to open the outer door*) Has everyone his list?

Margot. I'll get my books. (*giving her mother a list*) Here's your list. (Margot *goes into her and* Anne*'s bedroom on the right.* Anne *sits up, hiding her tears, as* Margot *comes in.*) Miep's here.

(Margot *picks up her books and goes back.* Anne *hurries over to the mirror, smoothing her hair.*)

Mr. Van Daan (*coming down the stairs*). Is it Miep?

Margot. Yes. Father's gone down to let her in.

Mr. Van Daan. At last I'll have some cigarettes!

Mrs. Frank (*to* Mr. Van Daan). I can't tell you how unhappy I am about Mrs. Van Daan's coat. Anne should never have touched it.

Mr. Van Daan. She'll be all right.

Mrs. Frank. Is there anything I can do?

Mr. Van Daan. Don't worry.

(*He turns to meet* Miep. *But it is not* Miep *who comes up the steps. It is* Mr. Kraler, *followed by* Mr. Frank. *Their faces are grave.* Anne *comes from the bedroom.* Peter *comes from his room.*)

Mrs. Frank. Mr. Kraler!

Mr. Van Daan. How are you, Mr. Kraler?

Lines 995–1032

DISCUSSION PROMPTS

Use these prompts to help students explore Anne's character traits:

Connect Margot and Anne have different ways of coping with their situations. Would you react more like Margot or more like Anne? Explain. *Some students might say that they would be quiet like Margot so that they would not cause any problems. Others might say that they would be more outspoken like Anne to make sure that others wouldn't take advantage of them.*

Analyze Why don't Anne and her mother get along? ***Possible answer:*** *Mrs. Frank is quiet and gentle, like Margot. She wants Anne to have more self-control. But Anne wants to "fight things out."*

Synthesize What is Anne feeling that motivates her to act as she does? ***Possible answer:*** *Anne is growing up and no longer wants to be treated as a baby. She is fearful that her youth will be spent hiding away and that she won't be able to "make something" of herself.*

FOR LESS–PROFICIENT READERS

Concept Support [paired option] Point out that not all conflicts in the play affect the resolution of the major conflict, the ability of the characters to remain safe from the Nazis. However, some do. Review the conflicts identified so far in the play and ask pairs of students to pick out any that they think might place the Franks and Van Daans in jeopardy. ***Possible answer:*** *Mr. Van Daan's hostile behavior might lead to his being asked to leave the Annex.*

Comprehension Support Tell students that connecting to the way characters feel and act can sometimes help readers understand what is happening more clearly. Ask students to identify parts of the play to which they have a strong reaction—of sympathy, anger, or empathy. Then have students take turns reading the chosen passage aloud and explaining why they feel as they do. Discuss how connecting affects their appreciation of the story.

THE DIARY OF ANNE FRANK: ACT ONE 503

Lines 1094–1113

READING SKILL

■ STORY MAPPING

What request does Mr. Kraler make that will change the lives of the characters? (Have students record their response on their story maps from page 485.) ***Possible answer:*** *He asks that Mr. Frank allow Mr. Dussel, a Jewish dentist, to move into the Annex.*

If students need help . . . Discuss how this event is related to the major conflict.

Lines 1120–1139

LITERARY ANALYSIS

● THEME

How do the different characters react to the news of Mr. Dussel's arrival? ***Possible answer:*** *Mr. Frank immediately agrees that he must come. Mr. Van Daan worries about how an extra person will affect the food supply. Mrs. Frank is fine with the decision but worries about where he will sleep. Peter offers to give up his bed for the newcomer and sleep on the floor. Anne proposes that she and Margot change their sleeping arrangements with Peter and Mr. Dussel.*

Extend the Discussion What drives Mr. Van Daan's reaction?

Lines 1146–1155
REINFORCE *KEY IDEA:* IMPACT

Discuss What is the immediate **impact** of Mr. Dussel's arrival on Anne and the others? ***Possible answer:*** *The immediate effect is to disrupt the sleeping arrangements. Margot moves into the main room with her parents. Anne must share her room with Mr. Dussel.*

Margot. This is a surprise.

Mrs. Frank. When Mr. Kraler comes, the sun begins to shine.

Mr. Van Daan. Miep is coming?

Mr. Kraler. Not tonight.

(Kraler *goes to* Margot *and* Mrs. Frank *and* Anne, *shaking hands with them.*)

Mrs. Frank. Wouldn't you like a cup of coffee? . . . Or, better still, will you have supper with us?

Mr. Frank. Mr. Kraler has something to talk over with us. Something has happened, he says, which demands an immediate decision.

Mrs. Frank (*fearful*). What is it?

(Mr. Kraler *sits down on the couch. As he talks he takes bread, cabbages, milk, etc., from his briefcase, giving them to* Margot *and* Anne *to put away.*)

Mr. Kraler. Usually, when I come up here, I try to bring you some bit of good news. What's the use of telling you the bad news when there's nothing that you can do about it? But today something has happened . . . Dirk . . . Miep's Dirk, you know, came to me just now. He tells me that he has a Jewish friend living near him. A dentist. He says he's in trouble. He begged me, could I do anything for this man? Could I find him a hiding place? . . . So I've come to you . . . I know it's a terrible thing to ask of you, living as you are, but would you take him in with you?

Mr. Frank. Of course we will.

Mr. Kraler (*rising*). It'll be just for a night or two . . . until I find some other place. This happened so suddenly that I didn't know where to turn.

Mr. Frank. Where is he?

Mr. Kraler. Downstairs in the office.

Mr. Frank. Good. Bring him up.

Mr. Kraler. His name is Dussel . . . Jan Dussel.

Mr. Frank. Dussel . . . I think I know him.

Mr. Kraler. I'll get him. (*He goes quickly down the steps and out.* Mr. Frank *suddenly becomes conscious of the others.*)

Mr. Frank. Forgive me. I spoke without consul you. But I knew you'd feel as I do.

Mr. Van Daan. There's no reason for you to consult anyone. This is your place. You have a right to do exactly as you please. The only thi I feel . . . there's so little food as it is . . . and t take in another person . . .

(Peter *turns away, ashamed of his father.*)

Mr. Frank. We can stretch the food a little. It's only for a few days.

Mr. Van Daan. You want to make a bet?

Mrs. Frank. I think it's fine to have him. But, Otto, where are you going to put him? Where

Peter. He can have my bed. I can sleep on the floor. I wouldn't mind.

Mr. Frank. That's good of you, Peter. But your room's too small . . . even for *you.*

Anne. I have a much better idea. I'll come in here with you and Mother, and Margot can ta Peter's room and Peter can go in our room wit Mr. Dussel.

Margot. That's right. We could do that.

Mr. Frank. No, Margot. You mustn't sleep in that room . . . neither you nor Anne. Mouschi has caught some rats in there. Peter's brave. He doesn't mind.

Anne. Then how about *this?* I'll come in here w you and Mother, and Mr. Dussel can have my

Mrs. Frank. No. No. *No!* Margot will come in here with us and he can have her bed. It's the only way. Margot, bring your things in here. Help her, Anne.

(Margot *hurries into her room to get her things.*)

Anne (*to her mother*). Why Margot? Why can' I come in here?

Mrs. Frank. Because it wouldn't be proper for Margot to sleep with a . . . Please, Anne. Don' argue. Please. (Anne *starts slowly away.*)

Mr. Frank. (*to* Anne). You don't mind sharing your room with Mr. Dussel, do you, Anne?

DIFFERENTIATED INSTRUCTION

FOR LESS–PROFICIENT READERS

Concept Support Use a T Chart to help students see the relationship of characters' actions to the development of a major theme of the play. Fill in the first column with details about the positive actions of various characters in Scenes 2 and 3. Then have students work in groups to explain how each example brings out the idea that people are really good at heart.

BEST PRACTICES TOOLKIT—Transparency
T Chart p. A25

Characters' Actions	*Connection to Theme*
• Mr. Frank invites the Van Daans and then Mr. Dussel to share the hiding place.	• Mr. Frank wants to save as many people as he can, despite the hardship.
• Miep and Mr. Kraler help the Franks.	• They are willing to risk their lives to help.
• Peter offers his bed to Mr. Dussel.	• Peter values his privacy but gives up his bed for a stranger.

Anne. No. No, of course not.

Mr. Frank. Good. (Anne *goes off into her bedroom, helping* Margot. Mr. Frank *starts to search in the cupboards.*) Where's the cognac?

Mrs. Frank. It's there. But, Otto, I was saving it in case of illness.

Mr. Frank. I think we couldn't find a better time to use it. Peter, will you get five glasses for me?

(Peter *goes for the glasses.* Margot *comes out of her bedroom, carrying her possessions, which she hangs behind a curtain in the main room.* Mr. Frank *finds the cognac and pours it into the five glasses that* Peter *brings him.* Mr. Van Daan *stands looking on sourly.* Mrs. Van Daan *comes downstairs and looks around at all the bustle.*)

Mrs. Van Daan. What's happening? What's going on?

Mr. Van Daan. Someone's moving in with us.

Mrs. Van Daan. In here? You're joking.

Margot. It's only for a night or two . . . until Mr. Kraler finds him another place.

Mr. Van Daan. Yeah! Yeah!

(Mr. Frank *hurries over as* Mr. Kraler *and* Dussel *come up.* Dussel *is a man in his late fifties, meticulous, finicky . . . bewildered now. He wears a raincoat. He carries a briefcase, stuffed full, and a small medicine case.*)

Mr. Frank. Come in, Mr. Dussel.

Mr. Kraler. This is Mr. Frank.

Dussel. Mr. Otto Frank?

Mr. Frank. Yes. Let me take your things. (*He takes the hat and briefcase, but* Dussel *clings to his medicine case.*) This is my wife Edith . . .

FOR LESS–PROFICIENT READERS

Comprehension Support [small-group option] Examine the consequences of having Mr. Dussel move in. Have small groups of students work on a Cause-and-Effect Diagram. Fill in one or two of the effects together (***Cause:*** *Mr. Dussel moves in.* ***Effects:*** *Anne must share a room with him; Margot must move into the main room; the rations must be stretched*). Discuss group responses.

BEST PRACTICES TOOLKIT—Transparency
Cause-and-Effect Diagram pp. B16, B38

FOR ADVANCED LEARNERS/PRE–AP

Analyze What do you think Anne would really like to say to her father in line 1158? Remind students that Anne is not a sophisticated teen. She might not know what her mother is hinting at in lines 1153–1154. What might Anne think instead? How will her perception of her mother's actions affect their relationship? Ask students to discuss their ideas and suggest other ways that this situation might have been handled.

Lines 1159–1179

DISCUSSION PROMPTS

Use these prompts to help students understand the significance of Mr. Frank's actions:

Connect If you were Mr. Frank, what would you be concerned about in this situation? *Students might say that they would want Mr. Dussel to feel welcome, not like an unwanted outsider.*

Analyze Based on Mr. Van Daan's comments, what conflict might arise from the arrival of Mr. Dussel? ***Possible answer:*** *There could be friction among the others.*

Speculate Cognac is a kind of liquor that can be used for medicinal purposes or to celebrate something positive. Why does Mr. Frank demand that they have some now? ***Possible answer:*** *He wants the arrival of Mr. Dussel to be seen as a positive event. He wants to smooth the ruffled feathers of the Van Daans.*

ANALYZE VISUALS

Activity Have small groups of students write a few lines of dialogue that might explain why everyone is looking at Peter. Have them keep the speech patterns of the characters in mind. *Students' dialogues will vary but should suggest a scenario that is plausible in the context of the play.*

ADDITIONAL TEACHING OPPORTUNITY

Blocking In theater, the actors' movements are usually carefully planned. The way actors move around the stage is referred to as blocking. Often, an actor's movements can convey as much as his or her words.

Ask students to study the photograph on page 505. What do they think the actors' movements in this scene could convey about the scene itself, or about the characters? *Students may say that the way the actors are positioned around their new guest conveys excitement. Anne looks especially interested in the newcomer, Mr. Dussel, because of the way her entire body is leaning forward, the smile on her face, and her arms stretched forward as though she is welcoming him.*

Lines 1202–1212

LITERARY ANALYSIS

● THEME

What is Mr. Kraler's explanation for why he helps the Franks and the Van Daans? ***Possible answer:*** *He does not consider himself heroic. Rather, he says that he simply does not like the Nazis.*

Lines 1228–1244

REINFORCE *KEY IDEA:* IMPACT

Discuss In what condition did the Franks leave their house? What was the **impact** on their friends and neighbors? ***Possible answer:*** *The Franks left the house in disorder, as if they had gone suddenly. Mr. Frank put the address of a place in Switzerland in the wastebasket. As a result, friends and neighbors thought the Franks had escaped to Switzerland.*

BACKGROUND

Swiss Neutrality In lines 1243–1244, Anne tells her father that his plan worked. People thought the family had escaped to Switzerland. This would seem plausible for two reasons. First, Mr. Frank's mother lived in Switzerland. Also, during World War II, Switzerland maintained a policy of neutrality, meaning that it was prepared to defend itself but would not participate in the war. Consequently, Germany did not invade Switzerland, and it became a stopping point for refugees on their way to other countries.

Mr. and Mrs. Van Daan . . . their son, Peter . . . and my daughters, Margot and Anne.

(Dussel *shakes hands with everyone.*)

Mr. Kraler. Thank you, Mr. Frank. Thank you all. Mr. Dussel, I leave you in good hands. Oh . . . Dirk's coat.

(Dussel *hurriedly takes off the raincoat, giving it to* Mr. Kraler. *Underneath is his white dentist's jacket, with a yellow Star of David on it.*)

Dussel (*to* Mr. Kraler). What can I say to thank you . . . ?

Mrs. Frank (*to* Dussel). Mr. Kraler and Miep . . . They're our life line. Without them we couldn't live.

Mr. Kraler. Please. Please. You make us seem very heroic. It isn't that at all. We simply don't like the Nazis. (*to* Mr. Frank, *who offers him a drink*) No, thanks. (*then going on*) We don't like their methods. We don't like . . .

Mr. Frank (*smiling*). I know. I know. "No one's going to tell us Dutchmen what to do with our damn Jews!"

Mr. Kraler (*to* Dussel). Pay no attention to Mr. Frank. I'll be up tomorrow to see that they're treating you right. (*to* Mr. Frank) Don't trouble to come down again. Peter will bolt the door after me, won't you, Peter?

Peter. Yes, sir.

Mr. Frank. Thank you, Peter. I'll do it.

Mr. Kraler. Good night. Good night.

Group. Good night, Mr. Kraler. We'll see you tomorrow, (*etc., etc.*)

(Mr. Kraler *goes out with* Mr. Frank. Mrs. Frank *gives each one of the "grownups" a glass of cognac.*)

Mrs. Frank. Please, Mr. Dussel, sit down.

(Mr. Dussel *sinks into a chair.* Mrs. Frank *gives him a glass of cognac.*)

Dussel. I'm dreaming. I know it. I can't believe my eyes. Mr. Otto Frank here! (*to* Mrs. Frank) You're not in Switzerland then? A woman told me . . . She said she'd gone to your house . . . door was open, everything was in disorder, di in the sink. She said she found a piece of pap in the wastebasket with an address scribbled it . . . an address in Zurich. She said you mus have escaped to Zurich.

Anne. Father put that there purposely . . . just so people would think that very thing!

Dussel. And you've been here all the time?

Mrs. Frank. All the time . . . ever since July.

(Anne *speaks to her father as he comes back.*)

Anne. It worked, Pim . . . the address you left Mr. Dussel says that people believe we escape to Switzerland.

Targeted Passage ④

Mr. Frank. I'm glad . . . And now let's have a li drink to welcome Mr. Dussel. (*Before they can drink,* Mr. Dussel *bolts his drink.* Mr. Frank *s and raises his glass.*) To Mr. Dussel. Welcome. We're very honored to have you with us.

Mrs. Frank. To Mr. Dussel, welcome.

(*The* Van Daans *murmur a welcome. The "grou ups" drink.*)

Mrs. Van Daan. Um. That was good.

Mr. Van Daan. Did Mr. Kraler warn you that won't get much to eat here? You can imagine three ration books among the seven of us . . . now you make eight.

(Peter *walks away, humiliated. Outside a street organ is heard dimly.*)

Dussel (*rising*). Mr. Van Daan, you don't reali what is happening outside that you should warn me of a thing like that. You don't realize what's going on . . . (*As* Mr. Van Daan *starts his characteristic pacing,* Dussel *turns to speak t the others.*) Right here in Amsterdam every da hundreds of Jews disappear . . . They surroun a block and search house by house. Children come home from school to find their parents gone. Hundreds are being deported . . . peopl that you and I know . . . the Hallensteins . . . the Wessels . . .

DIFFERENTIATED INSTRUCTION

FOR LESS–PROFICIENT READERS

④ Targeted Passage [Lines 1245–1271]

This passage increases tension and suspense as life gets more difficult in the Annex.

- How does Mr. Frank welcome Mr. Dussel?
- What is Mr. Van Daan's warning to Mr. Dussel? Of whom is he really thinking?
- What is Peter's reaction to his father's comment?
- What does Mr. Dussel say is happening to the Jews in Amsterdam?

FOR ADVANCED LEARNERS/PRE–AP

Analyze [small-group option] Point out lines 1258–1259. Discuss with students how many of the stage directions describe noises heard outside on the street. Ask students why the playwrights intersperse those stage directions with what is happening in the Annex. What message are they conveying? In small-group discussions, have students identify the playwrights' purpose and support their interpretation.

506 UNIT 4: THEME AND SYMBOL

Mrs. Frank (*in tears*). Oh, no. No!

Dussel. They get their call-up notice . . . come to the Jewish theatre on such and such a day and hour . . . bring only what you can carry in a rucksack. And if you refuse the call-up notice, then they come and drag you from your home and ship you off to Mauthausen.[11] The death camp!

Mrs. Frank. We didn't know that things had got so much worse.

Dussel. Forgive me for speaking so.

Anne (*coming to* Dussel). Do you know the de Waals? . . . What's become of them? Their daughter Jopie and I are in the same class. Jopie's my best friend.

Dussel. They are gone.

Anne. Gone?

Dussel. With all the others.

Anne. Oh, no. Not Jopie!

(*She turns away, in tears.* Mrs. Frank *motions to* Margot *to comfort her.* Margot *goes to* Anne, *putting her arms comfortingly around her.*)

Mrs. Van Daan. There were some people called Wagner. They lived near us . . . ?

Mr. Frank (*interrupting, with a glance at* Anne). I think we should put this off until later. We all have many questions we want to ask . . . But I'm sure that Mr. Dussel would like to get settled before supper.

Dussel. Thank you. I would. I brought very little with me.

Mr. Frank (*giving him his hat and briefcase*). I'm sorry we can't give you a room alone. But I hope you won't be too uncomfortable. We've had to make strict rules here . . . a schedule of hours . . . We'll tell you after supper. Anne, would you like to take Mr. Dussel to his room?

Anne (*controlling her tears*). If you'll come with me, Mr. Dussel? (*She starts for her room.*)

Dussel (*shaking hands with each in turn*). Forgive me if I haven't really expressed my gratitude to all of you. This has been such a shock to me. I'd always thought of myself as Dutch. I was born in Holland. My father was born in Holland, and my grandfather. And now . . . after all these years . . . (*He breaks off.*) If you'll excuse me.

(Dussel *gives a little bow and hurries off after* Anne. Mr. Frank *and the others are subdued.*)

Anne (*turning on the light*). Well, here we are.

(Dussel *looks around the room. In the main room* Margot *speaks to her mother.*)

Margot. The news sounds pretty bad, doesn't it? It's so different from what Mr. Kraler tells us. Mr. Kraler says things are improving.

Mr. Van Daan. I like it better the way Kraler tells it.

(*They resume their occupations, quietly.* Peter *goes off into his room. In Anne's room,* Anne *turns to* Dussel.)

Anne. You're going to share the room with me.

Dussel. I'm a man who's always lived alone. I haven't had to adjust myself to others. I hope you'll bear with me until I learn.

Anne. Let me help you. (*She takes his briefcase.*) Do you always live all alone? Have you no family at all?

Dussel. No one. (*He opens his medicine case and spreads his bottles on the dressing table.*)

Anne. How dreadful. You must be terribly lonely.

Dussel. I'm used to it.

Anne. I don't think I could ever get used to it. Didn't you even have a pet? A cat, or a dog?

Dussel. I have an allergy for fur-bearing animals. They give me asthma.

Anne. Oh, dear. Peter has a cat.

Dussel. Here? He has it here?

Anne. Yes. But we hardly ever see it. He keeps it in his room all the time. I'm sure it will be all right.

---

11. **Mauthausen** (mout'hou'zən): a Nazi concentration camp in Austria.

Lines 1273–1293

READING SKILL

STORY MAPPING

What bad news does Anne find out from Mr. Dussel? ***Possible answer:*** *Anne finds out that her best friend has been taken away by the Nazis.*

Lines 1311–1317

REINFORCE *KEY IDEA:* IMPACT

Discuss What has been the **impact** of the day's events on Mr. Dussel? Why does he feel this way? ***Possible answer:*** *Mr. Dussel is in shock. He has always thought of himself as Dutch because his family has lived in Holland for so long. He feels betrayed and lost.*

FOR LESS–PROFICIENT READERS

Comprehension Support [small-group option] Point out that one of the effects of having Mr. Dussel move in will most likely be to increase tension among the characters. Ask students to work together to predict what conflicts might arise from his presence in the Annex, based on lines 1330–1348.

FOR ENGLISH LEARNERS

Vocabulary: Idioms and Sayings [mixed-readiness pairs] Have students work in pairs to define these expressions:

- *I leave you in good hands* (line 1195), "you will be taken care of"
- *They're our lifeline* (line 1203), "their actions keep us alive"
- *get settled* (line 1299), "arrange his belongings"
- *bear with me* (line 1333), "be patient"

FOR ADVANCED LEARNERS/PRE–AP

Analyze [paired option] Ask students to imagine the emotions that each character feels upon hearing the news that Mr. Dussel brings. Do the characters feel guilt? Relief? Greater fear? Assign pairs of students one or more of the characters. Ask them to infer the emotions the character feels and why those feelings would be consistent with his or her character as it is revealed in the play. Have pairs share their insights.

THE DIARY OF ANNE FRANK: ACT ONE 507

Lines 1351–1378

LITERARY ANALYSIS

● THEME

How does Anne treat Mr. Dussel? ***Possible answer:*** *She is helpful, kind, and considerate.*

Extend the Discussion Why does Anne behave as she does toward Mr. Dussel?

Lines 1393–1425

DISCUSSION PROMPTS

Use these prompts to help students identify important points in Anne's diary entry:

Connect Have you ever had to share a room? Based on your experience, what kinds of disagreements do you think Anne and Mr. Dussel might have? *Students may say that the characters might argue over keeping the room tidy, who should get space on the dresser, or when each person gets the room to him- or herself.*

Analyze Is it surprising that Anne and Mr. Dussel do not get along? Explain. ***Possible answer:*** *It is not surprising. Mr. Dussel presented himself as a man who has always lived alone and doesn't like commotion. Living with Anne in such close quarters is bound to get on his nerves.*

Synthesize Compare what Mr. Dussel tells Anne in lines 1393–1396 with the reality of their coexistence. What important idea is brought out by the difference between word and deed? ***Possible answer:*** *People cannot always live up to their own expectations.*

Dussel. Let us hope so.

(*He takes some pills to* ***fortify*** *himself.*)

Anne. That's Margot's bed, where you're going to sleep. I sleep on the sofa there. (*indicating the clothes hooks on the wall*) We cleared these off for your things. (*She goes over to the window.*) The best part about this room . . . you can look down and see a bit of the street and the canal. There's a houseboat . . . you can see the end of it . . . a bargeman lives there with his family . . . They have a baby and he's just beginning to walk and I'm so afraid he's going to fall into the canal some day. I watch him . . .

Dussel (*interrupting*). Your father spoke of a schedule.

Anne (*coming away from the window*). Oh, yes. It's mostly about the times we have to be quiet. And times for the w.c. You can use it now if you like.

Dussel (*stiffly*). No, thank you.

Anne. I suppose you think it's awful, my talking about a thing like that. But you don't know how important it can get to be, especially when you're frightened . . . About this room, the way Margot and I did . . . she had it to herself in the afternoons for studying, reading . . . lessons, you know . . . and I took the mornings. Would that be all right with you?

Dussel. I'm not at my best in the morning.

Anne. You stay here in the mornings then. I'll take the room in the afternoons.

Dussel. Tell me, when you're in here, what happens to me? Where am I spending my time? In there, with all the people?

Anne. Yes.

Dussel. I see. I see.

Anne. We have supper at half past six.

Dussel (*going over to the sofa*). Then, if you don't mind . . . I like to lie down quietly for ten minutes before eating. I find it helps the digestion.

Anne. Of course. I hope I'm not going to be t much of a bother to you. I seem to be able to everyone's back up.

(Dussel *lies down on the sofa, curled up, his ba to her.*)

Dussel. I always get along very well with child My patients all bring their children to me, because they know I get on well with them. So don't you worry about that.

(Anne *leans over him, taking his hand and sha it gratefully.*)

Anne. Thank you. Thank you, Mr. Dussel.

(*The lights dim to darkness. The curtain falls o scene.* Anne's Voice *comes to us faintly at first, then with increasing power.*)

Anne's Voice. . . . And yesterday I finished Cissy Van Marxvelt's latest book. I think sh is a first-class writer. I shall definitely let my children read her. Monday the twenty-first c September, nineteen forty-two. Mr. Dussel and I had another battle yesterday. Yes, Mr. Dussel! According to him, nothing, I repeat nothing, is right about me . . . my appearanc my character, my manners. While he was goi on at me I thought . . . sometime I'll give yo such a smack that you'll fly right up to the ceiling! Why is it that every grownup thinks h knows the way to bring up children? Particula the grownups that never had any. I keep wishing that Peter was a girl instead of a boy Then I would have someone to talk to. Margo a darling, but she takes everything too seriousl To pause for a moment on the subject of Mr Van Daan. I must tell you that her attempts flirt with Father are getting her nowhere. Pi thank goodness, won't play.

(*As she is saying the last lines, the curtain rises o the darkened scene.* Anne's Voice *fades out.*)

DIFFERENTIATED INSTRUCTION

FOR LESS–PROFICIENT READERS

Reading Skill Follow-Up: Story Mapping As a class, review students' story maps. Discuss how the events on the map are directly related to the central problem.

Setting: *the secret annex of a warehouse in Amsterdam, 1942–1945*

Characters: *Frank family, Van Daan family, Mr. Dussel, Miep, Mr. Kraler*

Problem: *The characters must endure the hardships of living in hiding in order to be safe from the Nazis.*

Events:

1. The Franks and the Van Daans gather in the Annex.

2. Mr. Dussel moves into the Annex.

Scene 4

It is the middle of the night, several months later. The stage is dark except for a little light which comes through the skylight in Peter*'s room.*

Everyone is in bed. Mr. *and* Mrs. Frank *lie on the couch in the main room, which has been pulled out to serve as a makeshift double bed.*

Margot *is sleeping on a mattress on the floor in the main room, behind a curtain stretched across for privacy. The others are all in their accustomed rooms.*

From outside we hear two drunken soldiers singing "Lili Marlene." A girl's high giggle is heard. The sound of running feet is heard coming closer and then fading in the distance. Throughout the scene there is the distant sound of airplanes passing overhead.

A match suddenly flares up in the attic. We dimly see Mr. Van Daan. *He is getting his bearings. He comes quickly down the stairs, and goes to the cupboard where the food is stored. Again the match flares up, and is as quickly blown out. The dim figure is seen to steal back up the stairs.*

There is quiet for a second or two, broken only by the sound of airplanes, and running feet on the street below.

Suddenly, out of the silence and the dark, we hear Anne *scream.*

Anne (*screaming*). No! No! Don't . . . don't take me!

(*She moans, tossing and crying in her sleep. The other people wake, terrified.* Dussel *sits up in bed, furious.*)

Dussel. Shush! Anne! Anne, for God's sake, shush!

Anne (*still in her nightmare*). Save me! Save me!

(*She screams and screams.* Dussel *gets out of bed, going over to her, trying to wake her.*)

Dussel. For God's sake! Quiet! Quiet! You want someone to hear?

(*In the main room* Mrs. Frank *grabs a shawl and pulls it around her. She rushes in to* Anne, *taking her in her arms.* Mr. Frank *hurriedly gets up, putting on his overcoat.* Margot *sits up, terrified.* Peter*'s light goes on in his room.*)

Mrs. Frank (*to* Anne, *in her room*). Hush, darling, hush. It's all right. It's all right. (*over her shoulder to* Dussel) Will you be kind enough to turn on the light, Mr. Dussel? (*back to* Anne) It's nothing, my darling. It was just a dream.

(Dussel *turns on the light in the bedroom.* Mrs. Frank *holds* Anne *in her arms. Gradually* Anne *comes out of her nightmare, still trembling with horror.* Mr. Frank *comes into the room, and goes quickly to the window, looking out to be sure that no one outside had heard* Anne*'s screams.* Mrs. Frank *holds* Anne, *talking softly to her. In the main room* Margot *stands on a chair, turning on the center hanging lamp. A light goes on in the* Van Daan*'s room overhead.* Peter *puts his robe on, coming out of his room.*)

Dussel (*to* Mrs. Frank, *blowing his nose*). Something must be done about that child, Mrs. Frank. Yelling like that! Who knows but there's somebody on the streets? She's endangering all our lives.

Mrs. Frank. Anne, darling.

Dussel. Every night she twists and turns. I don't sleep. I spend half my night shushing her. And now it's nightmares!

(Margot *comes to the door of* Anne*'s room, followed by* Peter. Mr. Frank *goes to them, indicating that everything is all right.* Peter *takes* Margot *back.*)

Mrs. Frank (*to* Anne). You're here, safe, you see? Nothing has happened. (*to* Dussel) Please, Mr. Dussel, go back to bed. She'll be herself in a minute or two. Won't you, Anne?

Dussel (*picking up a book and a pillow*). Thank you, but I'm going to the w.c. The one place where there's peace! (*He stalks out.* Mr. Van Daan, *in underwear and trousers, comes down the stairs.*)

Lines 1442–1447

READING SKILL

STORY MAPPING

What is Mr. Van Daan doing? In what way will his action affect others? (Have students record their answers on their story maps.) ***Possible answer:*** *Mr. Van Daan is creeping downstairs to steal food. By taking food, he is depriving others of their fair share.*

If students need help . . . Have them think about what will happen if food runs out. In what way would that affect the outcome of the play?

Extend the Discussion In what way was this event foreshadowed in earlier scenes?

Lines 1484–1502

LITERARY ANALYSIS

THEME

In what way do the various characters react to Anne's nightmare? ***Possible answer:*** *Anne's family and Peter are concerned and hurry to check on her. Mr. Dussel seems mostly concerned that the noise will endanger everyone and keep him awake.*

FOR LESS–PROFICIENT READERS

Concept Support Have students identify additional conflicts that arise in this first part of the scene. Discuss which conflicts are potentially serious and why.

FOR ENGLISH LEARNERS

Vocabulary Support [mixed-readiness pairs] Explain that in lines 1442–1447 Mr. Van Daan is stealing food, or taking what doesn't belong to him. He is also described in line 1447 as a "dim figure" that "is seen to steal back up the stairs." Tell students that in this context, *steal* means "to move sneakily or silently." Have pairs of students use both meanings of the word in sentences.

THE DIARY OF ANNE FRANK: ACT ONE 509

Lines 1537–1560
REINFORCE *KEY IDEA:* IMPACT

Discuss What is one way in which the strain of living in hiding has had an **impact** on the relationships in the Frank family? ***Possible answer:*** *The relationship between Anne and her mother has grown more difficult. Anne has increasingly turned to her father for comfort. Both Mr. Frank and Margot have had to function as peacemakers in their family.*

Mr. Van Daan (*to* Dussel). What is it? What happened?

Dussel. A nightmare. She was having a nightmare!

Mr. Van Daan. I thought someone was murdering her.

Dussel. Unfortunately, no.

(*He goes into the bathroom.* Mr. Van Daan *goes back up the stairs.* Mr. Frank, *in the main room, sends* Peter *back to his own bedroom.*)

Mr. Frank. Thank you, Peter. Go back to bed.

(Peter *goes back to his room.* Mr. Frank *follows him, turning out the light and looking out the window. Then he goes back to the main room, and gets up on a chair, turning out the center hanging lamp.*)

Mrs. Frank (*to* Anne). Would you like some water? (Anne *shakes her head.*) Was it a very bad dream? Perhaps if you told me . . . ?

Anne. I'd rather not talk about it.

Mrs. Frank. Poor darling. Try to sleep then. I'll sit right here beside you until you fall asleep. (*She brings a stool over, sitting there.*)

Anne. You don't have to.

Mrs. Frank. But I'd like to stay with you . . . very much. Really.

Anne. I'd rather you didn't.

Mrs. Frank. Good night, then. (*She leans down to kiss* Anne. Anne *throws her arm up over her face, turning away.* Mrs. Frank, *hiding her hurt, kisses* Anne*'s arm.*) You'll be all right? There's nothing that you want?

Anne. Will you please ask Father to come.

Mrs. Frank (*after a second*). Of course, Anne dear. (*She hurries out into the other room.* Mr. Frank *comes to her as she comes in.*) *Sie verlangt nach Dir!*[12]

Mr. Frank (*sensing her hurt*). Edith, *Liebe, schau . . .*[13]

Mrs. Frank. *Es macht nichts! Ich danke dem liebe Herrgott, dass sie sich wenigstens an Dich wende wenn sie Trost braucht! Geh hinein, Otto, sie ist g hysterisch vor Angst.*[14] (*as* Mr. Frank *hesitates*) *G zu ihr.*[15] (*He looks at her for a second and then g get a cup of water for* Anne. Mrs. Frank *sinks d on the bed, her face in her hands, trying to keep f sobbing aloud.* Margot *comes over to her, putting arms around her.*) She wants nothing of me. Sh pulled away when I leaned down to kiss her.

Margot. It's a phase . . . You heard Father . . . Most girls go through it . . . they turn to thei fathers at this age . . . they give all their love t their fathers.

Mrs. Frank. You weren't like this. You didn't sh me out.

Margot. She'll get over it . . . (*She smooths the for* Mrs. Frank *and sits beside her a moment as* Mrs. Frank *lies down. In* Anne*'s room* Mr. Fra *comes in, sitting down by* Anne. Anne *flings he arms around him, clinging to him. In the distan we hear the sound of ack-ack.*)

Anne. Oh, Pim. I dreamed that they came to g us! The Green Police! They broke down the d and grabbed me and started to drag me out t way they did Jopie.

Mr. Frank. I want you to take this pill.

Anne. What is it?

Mr. Frank. Something to quiet you.

(*She takes it and drinks the water. In the main room* Margot *turns out the light and goes back to her bed.*)

Mr. Frank (*to* Anne). Do you want me to read to you for a while?

---

12. ***Sie verlangt nach Dir*** (zē fer-längt′ näKH dîr) *German*: She is asking for you.
13. ***Liebe, schau*** (lē′bə shou′) *German*: Dear, look.
14. ***Es macht . . . vor Angst*** (ĕs mäKHt′ nĭKHts′! ĭKH dängk′ə dām lē′bən hĕr′gôt′, däs zē zĭKH′ vān′ĭKH-shtənz än dĭKH′ vĕn′dət, vĕn zē trôst′ brouKHt′! gā hĭn-īn′, ôt′tô; zē ĭst gänts hü-stĕr′ĭsh fôr ängst′) *German*: It's all right. I thank dear God that at least she turns to you when she needs comfort. Go in, Otto; she is hysterical with fear.
15. ***Geh zu ihr*** (gā′ tso͞o îr′) *German*: Go to her.

DIFFERENTIATED INSTRUCTION

FOR LESS–PROFICIENT READERS

Comprehension Support As a class, discuss and chart the sequence of events in lines 1426–1570 to help students understand how many of the characters' actions take place simultaneously on different parts of the stage. Use a Sequence Chain. Point out that much of the action is described in the stage directions.

 **BEST PRACTICES TOOLKIT—Transparency**
Sequence Chain pp. B21, B45

FOR ADVANCED LEARNERS/PRE–AP

Analyze [small-group option] What purpose does the German dialogue in lines 1536–1543 serve? Ask students to explore why the playwrights might have chosen to have the characters conduct this conversation in German. Have students discuss their ideas in small groups.

ANALYZE VISUALS

Activity In what way is this scene consistent with what just happened in the play? ***Possible answer:*** *Mr. Frank appears to be comforting Anne. He has his arm around her as if to protect her. She looks sad and has obviously turned to him for reassurance.*

THE DIARY OF ANNE FRANK: ACT ONE 511

Lines 1605–1624

LITERARY ANALYSIS

THEME

Why does Anne review the events of her day each night? ***Answer:*** *She wants to become a better person, so she thinks about what she has done throughout the day.*

If students need help . . . Make sure they see that Anne searches her conscience each night in an effort to become a better person. Lead students to see how Anne's action relates to the theme—that even under extreme circumstances, it is possible and important to keep trying to bring out one's inner goodness.

Extend the Discussion Do you think that Anne considers herself to be a person who is good at heart?

BACKGROUND

The Allies The principal "Allies" consisted of the United States, Great Britain, France, the Soviet Union, and China; these Allied nations were at the forefront of the war against the "Axis powers," which consisted of Germany, Italy, and Japan. It was the Allied nations who first liberated and shut down many of the Nazi concentration camps, including Bergen-Belsen in April 1945.

Lines 1625–1650

DISCUSSION PROMPTS

Use these prompts to help students understand more about what the characters are experiencing:

Connect If you had been in hiding for as long as Anne and the others have, what would you want to do? *Students might say that they would want a special food or they would want to see their friends or just take a walk outside.*

Analyze Why does Mr. Frank think more frequent air raids is a good sign? ***Possible answer:*** *The air raids show that the Allies have not stopped trying to defeat Germany.*

Synthesize In what way do you think good news about the war affects conditions in the Annex? ***Possible answer:*** *Hearing good news most likely lifts the spirits of the residents. They might find it easier to get along with each other while they are more hopeful.*

Anne. No. Just sit with me for a minute. Was I awful? Did I yell terribly loud? Do you think anyone outside could have heard?

Mr. Frank. No. No. Lie quietly now. Try to sleep.

Anne. I'm a terrible coward. I'm so disappointed in myself. I think I've conquered my fear . . . I think I'm really grown-up . . . and then something happens . . . and I run to you like a baby . . . I love you, Father. I don't love anyone but you.

Mr. Frank (*reproachfully*). Annele!

Anne. It's true. I've been thinking about it for a long time. You're the only one I love.

Mr. Frank. It's fine to hear you tell me that you love me. But I'd be happier if you said you loved your mother as well . . . She needs your help so much . . . your love . . .

Anne. We have nothing in common. She doesn't understand me. Whenever I try to explain my views on life to her she asks me if I'm constipated.

Mr. Frank. You hurt her very much just now. She's crying. She's in there crying.

Anne. I can't help it. I only told the truth. I didn't want her here . . . (*then, with sudden change*) Oh, Pim, I was horrible, wasn't I? And the worst of it is, I can stand off and look at myself doing it and know it's cruel and yet I can't stop doing it. What's the matter with me? Tell me. Don't say it's just a phase! Help me.

Mr. Frank. There is so little that we parents can do to help our children. We can only try to set a good example . . . point the way. The rest you must do yourself. You must build your own character.

Anne. I'm trying. Really I am. Every night I think back over all of the things I did that day that were wrong . . . like putting the wet mop in Mr. Dussel's bed . . . and this thing now with Mother. I say to myself, that was wrong. I make up my mind, I'm never going to do that again. Never! Of course I may do something worse . . . but a least I'll never do *that* again! . . . I have a nicer s Father . . . a sweeter, nicer side. But I'm scared show it. I'm afraid that people are going to laug me if I'm serious. So the mean Anne comes to outside and the good Anne stays on the inside, I keep on trying to switch them around and ha the good Anne outside and the bad Anne insid and be what I'd like to be . . . and might be . . . only . . . only . . . (*She is asleep.* Mr. Frank *watc her for a moment and then turns off the light, an starts out. The lights dim out. The curtain falls o scene.* Anne's Voice *is heard dimly at first, and th with growing strength.*)

Anne's Voice. . . . The air raids are getting wors They come over day and night. The noise is terrifying. Pim says it should be music to our e The more planes, the sooner will come the end the war. Mrs. Van Daan pretends to be a fatalis What will be, will be. But when the planes con over, who is the most frightened? No one else b Petronella! . . . Monday, the ninth of Novembe nineteen forty-two. Wonderful news! The Allie have landed in Africa. Pim says that we can loo for an early finish to the war. Just for fun he ask each of us what was the first thing we wanted to do when we got out of here. Mrs. Van Daan lo to be home with her own things, her needle-po chairs, the Beckstein piano her father gave her . the best that money could buy. Peter would lik to go to a movie. Mr. Dussel wants to get back his dentist's drill. He's afraid he is losing his tou For myself, there are so many things . . . to ride bike again . . . to laugh till my belly aches . . . to have new clothes from the skin out . . . to have hot tub filled to overflowing and wallow in it fo hours . . . to be back in school with my friends

(*As the last lines are being said, the curtain rises the scene. The lights dim on as* Anne's Voice *fad away.*)

DIFFERENTIATED INSTRUCTION

FOR ENGLISH LEARNERS

Vocabulary Support Tell students that the *air raids* referred to in line 1625 are bombing attacks from Allied planes. By destroying enemy headquarters and factories that made weapons, the Allies hoped to bring about Germany's surrender.

Vocabulary: Cognates Remind students to use their knowledge of cognates to help them define unfamiliar words throughout the play. Spanish speakers may recognize these words:

- *fatalist/fatalista* (line 1629)
- *sanctify/santificar* (line 1659)
- *tyranny/tiranía* (line 1672)
- *oppression/opresión* (line 1673)

Scene 5

It is the first night of the Hanukkah[16] *celebration.* Mr. Frank *is standing at the head of the table on which is the Menorah.*[17] *He lights the Shamos, or servant candle, and holds it as he says the blessing. Seated listening is all of the "family," dressed in their best. The men wear hats,* Peter *wears his cap.*

Mr. Frank (*reading from a prayer book*). "Praised be Thou, oh Lord our God, Ruler of the universe, who has sanctified us with Thy commandments and bidden us kindle the Hanukkah lights. Praised be Thou, oh Lord our God, Ruler of the universe, who has wrought wondrous deliverances for our fathers in days of old. Praised be Thou, oh Lord our God, Ruler of the universe, that Thou has given us life and sustenance and brought us to this happy season." (Mr. Frank *lights the one candle of the Menorah as he continues.*) "We kindle this Hanukkah light to celebrate the great and wonderful deeds wrought through the zeal with which God filled the hearts of the heroic Maccabees, two thousand years ago. They fought against indifference, against tyranny and oppression, and they restored our Temple to us. May these lights remind us that we should ever look to God, whence cometh our help." Amen. [Pronounced O-mayn.]

All. Amen.

(Mr. Frank *hands* Mrs. Frank *the prayer book.*)

Mrs. Frank (*reading*). "I lift up mine eyes unto the mountains, from whence cometh my help. My help cometh from the Lord who made heaven and earth. He will not suffer thy foot to be moved. He that keepeth thee will not slumber. He that keepeth Israel doth neither slumber nor sleep. The Lord is thy keeper. The Lord is thy shade upon thy right hand. The sun shall not smite thee by day, nor the moon by night. The Lord shall keep thee from all evil. He shall keep thy soul. The Lord shall guard thy going out and thy coming in, from this time forth and forevermore." Amen.

All. Amen.

(Mrs. Frank *puts down the prayer book and goes to get the food and wine.* Margot *helps her.* Mr. Frank *takes the men's hats and puts them aside.*)

Dussel (*rising*). That was very moving.

Anne (*pulling him back*). It isn't over yet!

Mrs. Van Daan. Sit down! Sit down!

Anne. There's a lot more, songs and presents.

Dussel. Presents?

Mrs. Frank. Not this year, unfortunately.

Mrs. Van Daan. But always on Hanukkah everyone gives presents . . . everyone!

Dussel. Like our St. Nicholas' Day.[18] (*There is a chorus of "no's" from the group.*)

Mrs. Van Daan. No! Not like St. Nicholas! What kind of a Jew are you that you don't know Hanukkah?

Mrs. Frank (*as she brings the food*). I remember particularly the candles . . . First one, as we have tonight. Then the second night you light two candles, the next night three . . . and so on until you have eight candles burning. When there are eight candles it is truly beautiful.

Mrs. Van Daan. And the potato pancakes.

Mr. Van Daan. Don't talk about them!

Mrs. Van Daan. I make the best *latkes*[19] you ever tasted!

Mrs. Frank. Invite us all next year . . . in your own home.

Mr. Frank. God willing!

Mrs. Van Daan. God willing.

---

16. **Hanukkah** (hä'nə-kə): a Jewish holiday, celebrated in December and lasting eight days.
17. **Menorah** (mə-nôr'ə): a candleholder with nine branches, used in the celebration of Hanukkah.
18. **St. Nicholas's Day:** December 6, the day that Christian children in the Netherlands receive gifts.
19. **latkes** (lät'kəz): potato pancakes.

BACKGROUND

Hanukkah In 165 B.C., Judas Maccabee overthrew the Syrians, who had invaded Judea, seized the Jews' holy temple in Jerusalem, and forced the Jews to relinquish their rituals. After repairing and rededicating the temple, Judas ordered a celebration. According to the Talmud, a collection of scholarly Jewish writing, enough lamp oil was found to keep the menorah in the temple burning for only one day. However, it continued to burn for eight days, thus establishing the Hanukkah tradition of adding one lit candle each night until there are eight.

Lines 1667–1676

LITERARY ANALYSIS

THEME

What message do the words of the prayer convey to those listening? ***Possible answer:*** *The prayer gives hope that oppression and tyranny can be overcome.*

FOR ENGLISH LEARNERS

Vocabulary Support [small-group option] To help students understand the language used in lines 1657–1690, have them work in small groups to define some of the terms. Encourage them to use context clues and a dictionary. Discuss the definitions they find.

- *Thou* (line 1658), "you"
- *Thy* (line 1659), "your"
- *bidden* (line 1660), "instructed to do something"
- *wrought* (line 1662), "made"
- *whence* (line 1675), "from where"
- *cometh* (line 1675), "comes"
- *mine* (line 1679), "my"
- *keepeth* (line 1683), "keeps"
- *thee* (line 1683), "you"
- *doth* (line 1684), "does"
- *smite* (line 1686), "strike, hit"

FOR ADVANCED LEARNERS/PRE–AP

Analyze Point out Mr. Dussel's comment in line 1703. Discuss how ironic it is that he is being persecuted for being Jewish when, in fact, he is unaware of Jewish traditions and celebrates the Dutch holidays and customs. Then ask students to think about how this irony conveys a message about the actions of the Germans and their persecution of different groups of people throughout World War II. Have students share their insights.

THE DIARY OF ANNE FRANK: ACT ONE 513

ANALYZE VISUALS

Activity What is the mood conveyed by this photograph? What helps create this feeling? ***Possible answer:*** *The mood is happy and relaxed. The actors are smiling and turned to face each other.*

Margot. What I remember best is the presents we used to get when we were little . . . eight days of presents . . . and each day they got better and better.

Mrs. Frank (*sitting down*). We are all here, alive. That is present enough.

Anne. No, it isn't. I've got something . . .

(*She rushes into her room, hurriedly puts on a little hat improvised from the lamp shade, grabs a satchel bulging with parcels and comes running back.*)

Mrs. Frank. What is it?

Anne. Presents!

Mrs. Van Daan. Presents!

Dussel. Look!

Mr. Van Daan. What's she got on her head?

Peter. A lamp shade!

Anne (*She picks out one at random*). This is for Margot. (*She hands it to* Margot, *pulling her t her feet.*) Read it out loud.

Margot (*reading*).

"You have never lost your temper.
You never will, I fear,
You are so good.
But if you should,
Put all your cross words here."

(*She tears open the package.*)

A new crossword puzzle book! Where did you get it?

DIFFERENTIATED INSTRUCTION

FOR LESS–PROFICIENT READERS

Concept Support [small-group option] Remind students that character is a key to theme. Because Anne is a central character, her thoughts and actions are particularly important in the development of the play's message. Have students work in small groups to review the play and find examples of Anne's words and actions that support the major theme of the play. Have them contribute their details to a class web.

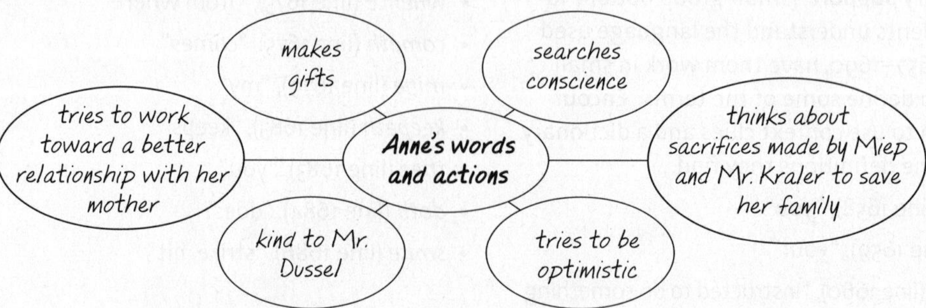

Anne. It isn't new. It's one that you've done. But I rubbed it all out, and if you wait a little and forget, you can do it all over again.

Margot (*sitting*). It's wonderful, Anne. Thank you. You'd never know it wasn't new.

(*From outside we hear the sound of a streetcar passing.*)

Anne (*with another gift*). Mrs. Van Daan.

Mrs. Van Daan (*taking it*). This is awful . . . I haven't anything for anyone . . . I never thought . . .

Mr. Frank. This is all Anne's idea.

Mrs. Van Daan (*holding up a bottle*). What is it?

Anne. It's hair shampoo. I took all the odds and ends of soap and mixed them with the last of my toilet water.

Mrs. Van Daan. Oh, Anneke!

Anne. I wanted to write a poem for all of them, but I didn't have time. (*offering a large box to* Mr. Van Daan) Yours, Mr. Van Daan, is *really* something . . . something you want more than anything. (*as she waits for him to open it*) Look! Cigarettes!

Mr. Van Daan. Cigarettes!

Anne. Two of them! Pim found some old pipe tobacco in the pocket lining of his coat . . . and we made them . . . or rather, Pim did.

Mrs. Van Daan. Let me see . . . Well, look at that! Light it, Putti! Light it.

(Mr. Van Daan *hesitates.*)

Anne. It's tobacco, really it is! There's a little fluff in it, but not much.

(*Everyone watches intently as* Mr. Van Daan *cautiously lights it. The cigarette flares up. Everyone laughs.*)

Peter. It works!

Mrs. Van Daan. Look at him.

Mr. Van Daan (*spluttering*). Thank you, Anne. Thank you.

(Anne *rushes back to her satchel for another present.*)

Anne (*handing her mother a piece of paper*). For Mother, Hanukkah greeting. (*She pulls her mother to her feet.*)

Mrs. Frank (*She reads.*) "Here's an I.O.U. that I promise to pay. Ten hours of doing whatever you say. Signed, Anne Frank." (Mrs. Frank, *touched, takes* Anne *in her arms, holding her close.*)

Dussel (*to* Anne). Ten hours of doing what you're told? *Anything* you're told?

Anne. That's right.

Dussel. You wouldn't want to sell that, Mrs. Frank?

Mrs. Frank. Never! This is the most precious gift I've ever had!

(*She sits, showing her present to the others.* Anne *hurries back to the satchel and pulls out a scarf, the scarf that* Mr. Frank *found in the first scene.*)

Anne (*offering it to her father*). For Pim.

Mr. Frank. Anneke . . . I wasn't supposed to have a present! (*He takes it, unfolding it and showing it to the others.*)

Anne. It's a muffler . . . to put round your neck . . . like an ascot, you know. I made it myself out of odds and ends . . . I knitted it in the dark each night, after I'd gone to bed. I'm afraid it looks better in the dark!

Mr. Frank (*putting it on*). It's fine. It fits me perfectly. Thank you, Annele.

(Anne *hands* Peter *a ball of paper, with a string attached to it.*)

Anne. That's for Mouschi.

Peter (*rising to bow*). On behalf of Mouschi, I thank you.

Anne (*hesitant, handing him a gift*). And . . . this is yours . . . from Mrs. Quack Quack. (*as he holds it gingerly in his hands*) Well . . . open it . . . Aren't you going to open it?

Lines 1794–1804

REINFORCE *KEY IDEA:* IMPACT

Discuss What kind of **impact** does Anne's present to her mother have? Why? ***Possible answer:*** *Anne's mother is very touched by the gift because it shows Anne's thoughtfulness and also because it might be Anne's way of showing her mother that she wants to improve their relationship.*

FOR LESS–PROFICIENT READERS

Comprehension Support Draw students' attention to lines 1809–1811. Ask students to explain Mr. Frank's comment "I wasn't supposed to have a present!" ***Possible answer:*** *He was in on the plan and did not expect to get a gift himself.*

FOR ENGLISH LEARNERS

Vocabulary Support Tell students that the initials *I.O.U.* in line 1794 stand for and sound like the words *I owe you*. An I.O.U. is usually a written note acknowledging that one person owes another something and is promising to pay it. In this case, Anne is saying that her gift to her mother is the payment of ten hours of service at any time in the future.

THE DIARY OF ANNE FRANK: ACT ONE 515

Lines 1824–1852
DISCUSSION PROMPTS

Use these prompts to help students understand Anne and Peter's relationship:

Connect What would you be thinking if you were Peter waiting for your gift from Anne? *Students might say that, like Peter, they would be worried that the present would be a joke.*

Analyze Anne is described as hesitant before she gives Peter his gift. Why do you think she pauses and appears uncertain? ***Possible answer:*** *She may not be sure he will like the gift. She may be afraid of the reactions of the others. She may be embarrassed.*

Speculate What might Peter's lack of comment and Anne's choice of gift suggest about their interaction, compared to earlier in the play? ***Possible answer:*** *The fact that Anne gives Peter a serious and thoughtful gift and that Peter accepts it without saying something sarcastic suggests that their relationship has matured.*

Lines 1728–1880
LITERARY ANALYSIS
● THEME

After seeing the presents that Anne gives to everyone, does your opinion of her change? Why or why not? *Students may say that their opinion does not change, because they have thought all along that she has a good heart. Some students may say that her effort to make just the right gift for each person shows her sensitive nature.*

Peter. I'm scared to. I know something's going to jump out and hit me.

Anne. No. It's nothing like that, really.

Mrs. Van Daan (*as he is opening it*). What is it, Peter? Go on. Show it.

Anne (*excitedly*). It's a safety razor!

Dussel. A what?

Anne. A razor!

Mrs. Van Daan (*looking at it*). You didn't make that out of odds and ends.

Anne (*to* Peter). Miep got it for me. It's not new. It's second-hand. But you really do need a razor now.

Dussel. For what?

Anne. Look on his upper lip . . . you can see the beginning of a mustache.

Dussel. He wants to get rid of that? Put a little milk on it and let the cat lick it off.

Peter (*starting for his room*). Think you're funny, don't you.

Dussel. Look! He can't wait! He's going in to try it!

Peter. I'm going to give Mouschi his present! (*He goes into his room, slamming the door behind him.*)

Mr. Van Daan (*disgustedly*). Mouschi, Mouschi, Mouschi.

(*In the distance we hear a dog persistently barking.* Anne *brings a gift to* Dussel.)

Anne. And last but never least, my roommate, Mr. Dussel.

Dussel. For me? You have something for me? (*He opens the small box she gives him.*)

Anne. I made them myself.

Dussel (*puzzled*). Capsules! Two capsules!

Anne. They're ear-plugs!

Dussel. Ear-plugs?

Anne. To put in your ears so you won't hear me when I thrash around at night. I saw them advertised in a magazine. They're not real ones . . . I made them out of cotton and candl wax. Try them . . . See if they don't work . . . see if you can hear me talk . . .

Dussel (*putting them in his ears*). Wait now unt I get them in . . . so.

Anne. Are you ready?

Dussel. Huh?

Anne. Are you ready?

Dussel. Good God! They've gone inside! I can' get them out! (*They laugh as* Mr. Dussel *jumps about, trying to shake the plugs out of his ears. Finally he gets them out. Putting them away.*) Thank you, Anne! Thank you!

Mr. Van Daan. A real Hanukkah!

Mrs. Van Daan. Wasn't it cute of her?

Mrs. Frank. I don't know when she did it.

Margot. I love my present.

Togeth

Anne (*sitting at the table*). And now let's have t song, Father . . . please . . . (*to* Dussel) Have y heard the Hanukkah song, Mr. Dussel? The s is the whole thing! (*She sings.*) "Oh, Hanukka Oh Hanukkah! The sweet celebration . . . "

Mr. Frank (*quieting her*). I'm afraid, Anne, we shouldn't sing that song tonight. (*to* Dussel) It's a song of jubilation, of rejoicing. One is ap to become too enthusiastic.

Anne. Oh, please, please. Let's sing the song. I promise not to shout!

Mr. Frank. Very well. But quietly now . . . I'll k an eye on you and when . . .

(*As* Anne *starts to sing, she is interrupted by* Du *who is snorting and wheezing.*)

Dussel (*pointing to* Peter). You . . . You! (Peter *coming from his bedroom, ostentatiously holding bulge in his coat as if he were holding his cat, an*

DIFFERENTIATED INSTRUCTION

FOR ADVANCED LEARNERS/PRE–AP

Analyze Have students use the equation to show what the gifts signify about Anne's relationship with each recipient. Then ask students to predict how Anne's thoughtfulness might change her relationship with various members of the "family."

Recipient		Gift		Anne's Relationship with Recipient
Mr. Dussel	+	*earplugs*	=	*Anne knows she is noisy and that this bothers Mr. Dussel.*

dangling Anne*'s present before it.*) How many times . . . I told you . . . Out! Out!

Mr. Van Daan (*going to* Peter). What's the matter with you? Haven't you any sense? Get that cat out of here.

Peter (*innocently*). Cat?

Mr. Van Daan. You heard me. Get it out of here!

Peter. I have no cat. (*Delighted with his joke, he opens his coat and pulls out a bath towel. The group at the table laugh, enjoying the joke.*)

Dussel (*still wheezing*). It doesn't need to be the cat . . . his clothes are enough . . . when he comes out of that room . . .

Mr. Van Daan. Don't worry. You won't be bothered any more. We're getting rid of it.

Dussel. At last you listen to me. (*He goes off into his bedroom.*)

Mr. Van Daan (*calling after him*). I'm not doing it for you. That's all in your mind . . . all of it! (*He starts back to his place at the table.*) I'm doing it because I'm sick of seeing that cat eat all our food.

Peter. That's not true! I only give him bones . . . scraps . . .

Mr. Van Daan. Don't tell me! He gets fatter every day! Damn cat looks better than any of us. Out he goes tonight!

Peter. No! No!

Anne. Mr. Van Daan, you can't do that! That's Peter's cat. Peter loves that cat.

Mrs. Frank (*quietly*). Anne.

Peter (*to* Mr. Van Daan). If he goes, I go.

Mr. Van Daan. Go! Go!

Mrs. Van Daan. You're not going and the cat's not going! Now please . . . this is Hanukkah . . . Hanukkah . . . this is the time to celebrate . . . What's the matter with all of you? Come on, Anne. Let's have the song.

Anne (*singing*). "Oh, Hanukkah! Oh, Hanukkah! The sweet celebration."

Mr. Frank (*rising*). I think we should first blow out the candle . . . then we'll have something for tomorrow night.

Margot. But, Father, you're supposed to let it burn itself out.

Mr. Frank. I'm sure that God understands shortages. (*before blowing it out*) "Praised be Thou, oh Lord our God, who hast sustained us and permitted us to celebrate this joyous festival."

(*He is about to blow out the candle when suddenly there is a crash of something falling below. They all freeze in horror, motionless. For a few seconds there is complete silence.* Mr. Frank *slips off his shoes. The others noiselessly follow his example.* Mr. Frank *turns out a light near him. He motions to* Peter *to turn off the center lamp.* Peter *tries to reach it, realizes he cannot and gets up on a chair. Just as he is touching the lamp he loses his balance. The chair goes out from under him. He falls. The iron lamp shade crashes to the floor. There is a sound of feet below, running down the stairs.*)

Mr. Van Daan (*under his breath*). God Almighty! (*The only light left comes from the Hanukkah candle.* Dussel *comes from his room.* Mr. Frank *creeps over to the stairwell and stands listening. The dog is heard barking excitedly.*) Do you hear anything?

Mr. Frank (*in a whisper*). No. I think they've gone.

Mrs. Van Daan. It's the Green Police. They've found us.

Mr. Frank. If they had, they wouldn't have left. They'd be up here by now.

Mrs. Van Daan. I know it's the Green Police. They've gone to get help. That's all. They'll be back!

Mr. Van Daan. Or it may have been the Gestapo,[20] looking for papers . . .

(5) **Targeted Passage**

20. **Gestapo** (gə-stä′pō): the Nazi secret police force, known for its terrorism and brutality.

Lines 1917–1930

LITERARY ANALYSIS

THEME

What is Mr. Van Daan's attitude toward Mouschi? Why? ***Possible answer:*** *Mr. Van Daan hates the cat. He thinks it eats too much food.*

Lines 1953–1964

READING SKILL

STORY MAPPING

What major event occurs at the end of the Hanukkah celebration? (Remind students to record this event on their story maps.) ***Possible answer:*** *They hear a crash from down below in the warehouse. Then, as Peter reaches to turn off the light, he falls from the chair upon which he is balanced with a loud crash. Whoever is downstairs hears it and runs away.*

If students need help . . . Have them discuss in pairs how this event relates to the major problem or conflict of the play.

FOR LESS–PROFICIENT READERS

(5) **Targeted Passage [Lines 1949–1980]**

This passage presents a major complication in the rising action: the hiding place may have been discovered.

- What is the group's first reaction when they hear the noise from downstairs? Why?
- What does Peter do that increases the tension?
- Who does Mrs. Van Daan think it is?
- If someone heard the "family" in the Annex, what could happen next?

Comprehension Support [small-group option] Have students work in small groups to predict how this event will affect their life in hiding. Have them use what they already know about the characters' states of mind and behavior and then make a logical guess about the effect of additional stress on them. Have students share their predictions.

Lines 2006–2052

LITERARY ANALYSIS

● THEME

How do the characters react to this crisis? What theme is conveyed by their behavior? ***Possible answer:*** *Mr. Frank goes downstairs to investigate. Mrs. Van Daan becomes hysterical. Mr. Van Daan becomes abusive and rough. Peter offers to go down after Mr. Frank, showing his courage. Mrs. Frank prays, while Anne worries about her father. Margot fearfully and obediently clings to her parents. Their behavior reveals that a crisis brings out the best in some people and the worst in others.*

If students need help . . . Use a three-column chart to clarify theme.

Column 1: Helpful Behavior

- Mr. Frank investigates.
- Peter offers to go after Mr. Frank.

Column 2: Unhelpful Behavior

- Mr. Van Daan is abusive.
- Mrs. Van Daan panics.

Column 3: Theme

- Some people are helpful in a crisis, while others simply create more problems.

Lines 2053–2059

READING SKILL

■ STORY MAPPING

Who is the intruder in the warehouse? How does Mr. Frank know? ***Answer:*** *A thief was in the warehouse. The cash box and the radio have been taken. Also, the street door is wide open.*

Mr. Frank (*interrupting*). Or a thief, looking for money.

Mrs. Van Daan. We've got to do something . . . Quick! Quick! Before they come back.

Mr. Van Daan. There isn't anything to do. Just wait.

(Mr. Frank *holds up his hand for them to be quiet. He is listening intently. There is complete silence as they all strain to hear any sound from below. Suddenly* Anne *begins to sway. With a low cry she falls to the floor in a faint.* Mrs. Frank *goes to her quickly, sitting beside her on the floor and taking her in her arms.*)

Mrs. Frank. Get some water, please! Get some water!

(Margot *starts for the sink.*)

Mr. Van Daan (*grabbing* Margot). No! No! No one's going to run water!

Mr. Frank. If they've found us, they've found us. Get the water. (Margot *starts again for the sink.* Mr. Frank, *getting a flashlight*) I'm going down.

(Margot *rushes to him, clinging to him.* Anne *struggles to consciousness.*)

Margot. No, Father, no! There may be someone there, waiting . . . It may be a trap!

Mr. Frank. This is Saturday. There is no way for us to know what has happened until Miep or Mr. Kraler comes on Monday morning. We cannot live with this uncertainty.

Margot. Don't go, Father!

Mrs. Frank. Hush, darling, hush. (Mr. Frank *slips quietly out, down the steps and out through the door below.*) Margot! Stay close to me.

(Margot *goes to her mother.*)

Mr. Van Daan. Shush! Shush!

(Mrs. Frank *whispers to* Margot *to get the water.* Margot *goes for it.*)

Mrs. Van Daan. Putti, where's our money? Get our money. I hear you can buy the Green Police off, so much a head. Go upstairs quick! Get th money!

Mr. Van Daan. Keep still!

Mrs. Van Daan (*kneeling before him, pleading*). Do you want to be dragged off to a concentra camp? Are you going to stand there and wait them to come up and get you? Do something, I tell you!

Mr. Van Daan (*pushing her aside*). Will you kee still! (*He goes over to the stairwell to listen.* Peter *goes to his mother, helping her up onto the sofa. There is a second of silence, then* Anne *can stand no longer.*)

Anne. Someone go after Father! Make Father come back!

Peter (*starting for the door*). I'll go.

Mr. Van Daan. Haven't you done enough?

(*He pushes* Peter *roughly away. In his anger agai his father* Peter *grabs a chair as if to hit him wit it, then puts it down, burying his face in his han* Mrs. Frank *begins to pray softly.*)

Anne. Please, please, Mr. Van Daan. Get Fathe

Mr. Van Daan. Quiet! Quiet!

(Anne *is shocked into silence.* Mrs. Frank *pulls closer, holding her protectively in her arms.*)

Mrs. Frank (*softly, praying*). "I lift up mine eyes u the mountains, from whence cometh my help. help cometh from the Lord who made heaven a earth. He will not suffer thy foot to be moved . He that keepeth thee will not slumber . . ." (*Sh stops as she hears someone coming. They all watch door tensely.* Mr. Frank *comes quietly in.* Anne *ru to him, holding him tight.*)

Mr. Frank. It was a thief. That noise must have scared him away.

Mrs. Van Daan. Thank God.

Mr. Frank. He took the cash box. And the radio He ran away in such a hurry that he didn't sto to shut the street door. It was swinging wide

DIFFERENTIATED INSTRUCTION

FOR ENGLISH LEARNERS

Concept Support Use a Cause-and-Effect Chain to help students understand the importance of the events in lines 1953–2086.

BEST PRACTICES TOOLKIT—Transparency Cause-and-Effect Chain pp. B16, B39

Cause: *There is a crash downstairs.*

→ ***Effect/Cause:*** *Peter stands on a chair to turn off the light and his chair crashes to the floor.*

→ ***Effect/Cause:*** *Thief runs away but knows that there are people upstairs in the warehouse.*

→ ***Effect:*** *Group fears the thief will tell someone.*

open. (*A breath of relief sweeps over them.*) I think it would be good to have some light.

Margot. Are you sure it's all right?

Mr. Frank. The danger has passed. (Margot *goes to light the small lamp.*) Don't be so terrified, Anne. We're safe.

Dussel. Who says the danger has passed? Don't you realize we are in greater danger than ever?

Mr. Frank. Mr. Dussel, will you be still!

(Mr. Frank *takes* Anne *back to the table, making her sit down with him, trying to calm her.*)

Dussel (*pointing to* Peter). Thanks to this clumsy fool, there's someone now who knows we're up here! Someone now knows we're up here, hiding!

Mrs. Van Daan (*going to* Dussel). Someone knows we're here, yes. But who is the someone? A thief! A thief! You think a thief is going to go to the Green Police and say . . . I was robbing a place the other night and I heard a noise up over my head? You think a thief is going to do that?

Dussel. Yes. I think he will.

Mrs. Van Daan (*hysterically*). You're crazy! (*She stumbles back to her seat at the table.* Peter *follows protectively, pushing* Dussel *aside.*)

Dussel. I think some day he'll be caught and then he'll make a bargain with the Green Police . . . if they'll let him off, he'll tell them where some Jews are hiding!

(*He goes off into the bedroom. There is a second of appalled silence.*)

Mr. Van Daan. He's right.

Anne. Father, let's get out of here! We can't stay here now . . . Let's go . . .

Mr. Van Daan. Go! Where?

Mrs. Frank (*sinking into her chair at the table*). Yes. Where?

Mr. Frank (*rising, to them all*). Have we lost all faith? All courage? A moment ago we thought that they'd come for us. We were sure it was the end. But it wasn't the end. We're alive, safe. (Mr. Van Daan *goes to the table and sits.* Mr. Frank *prays.*) "We thank Thee, oh Lord our God, that in Thy infinite mercy Thou hast again seen fit to spare us." (*He blows out the candle, then turns to* Anne.) Come on, Anne. The song! Let's have the song! (*He starts to sing.* Anne *finally starts falteringly to sing, as* Mr. Frank *urges her on. Her voice is hardly audible at first.*)

Anne (*singing*). "Oh, Hanukkah! Oh, Hanukkah! The sweet . . . celebration . . . " (*As she goes on singing, the others gradually join in, their voices still shaking with fear.* Mrs. Van Daan *sobs as she sings.*)

Group. "Around the feast . . . we . . . gather
In complete . . . jubilation . . .
Happiest of sea . . . sons
Now is here.
Many are the reasons for good cheer."

(Dussel *comes from the bedroom. He comes over to the table, standing beside* Margot, *listening to them as they sing.*)

"Together
We'll weather
Whatever tomorrow may bring."

(*As they sing on with growing courage, the lights start to dim.*)

"So hear us rejoicing
And merrily voicing
The Hanukkah song that we sing.
Hoy!"

(*The lights are out. The curtain starts slowly to fall.*)

"Hear us rejoicing
And merrily voicing
The Hanukkah song that we sing."

(*They are still singing, as the curtain falls.*)

The Curtain Falls.

Lines 2062–2086

REINFORCE *KEY IDEA:* IMPACT

Discuss According to Mr. Dussel, what **impact** will this incident have on their safety? ***Possible answer:*** *He believes that the thief will bargain with the police if he is caught. He may offer to tell them where Jews are hiding.*

Lines 2090–2106

LITERARY ANALYSIS

THEME

What does Mr. Frank say to encourage the others? How do his words and example affect them? ***Possible answer:*** *Mr. Frank tells the others that instead of fearing what may never happen, they should rejoice at what did happen. They are still safe, even though moments before they thought they would be discovered. His common sense and show of courage enable the rest of them to rise to the occasion.*

SELECTION WRAP-UP

REFLECT Ask students in what way Mr. Dussel influences the interactions among characters in the Annex. What theme is brought out by his presence?

CRITIQUE Ask students if they think the portrayal of the characters and their situation is realistic enough. If not, what might the playwrights add or remove?

READING FLUENCY

Distribute the copy masters and have students practice fluency.

RESOURCE MANAGER—Copy Master
Reading Fluency p. 132

FOR LESS–PROFICIENT READERS

Comprehension Support

1. Have students review their first impressions of the characters from Scene 2 that they recorded in the chart from page 491.
2. Have them add a third column to record details about appearances and personalities in Scene 3 and Scene 4. Students might find it helpful to review the details they recorded in the various graphic organizers on pages 501, 504, and 514.
3. Then have groups decide which characters seem the same and which appear different from their first impression.
4. Discuss the lessons that might be taken from the apparent changes in character.

DISCUSSION PROMPTS

Use these prompts to help students connect the real Anne Frank with her character in the play:

Connect Both the real Anne and the character reserve their most private thoughts for their diaries. How do you think the real Anne might feel about the fact that her diary is so widely read? *Students may say that she would be embarrassed. However, she might also be glad that her story is being told and that what she and others went through is remembered.*

Compare and Contrast Reread lines 1594–1624 in the play. Based on your reading of the diary entry, is this a conversation that the real Anne might have had? ***Possible answer:*** *Yes. The real Anne also struggles with the conflict between her feelings and the way she wants to appear and behave. She says, "I have to hold my head up high and put a bold face on things, but the thoughts keep coming anyway."*

Evaluate Do you think the playwrights portrayed Anne realistically? Explain. *Students will likely say yes. By using some of her exact words, the playwrights convey her personality. They also show her most important character traits, as revealed in this entry. For example, she tried to meet her trials bravely; she constantly struggled to be a better person; she was mercurial, up one minute and down the next.*

BACKGROUND

Anne's Characters In the first paragraph, students may be confused by the reference to Mrs. Kleiman. Explain to students that the real names of the workers who helped the Franks and the people who went into hiding with them are not used in the play. For example, the Van Daans were actually the Van Pels. Also, some of the characters are combinations of more than one real-life person. The other name that may seem confusing to students is "Kitty," the recipient of Anne's diary entries. Although it is unknown exactly why Anne chose to refer to her diary as "Kitty," all Anne really wanted was one true, best friend; "Kitty" turned out to be her best friend, with whom she could share everything.

Reading for Information

DIARY ENTRY Anne Frank's diary entries give readers an intimate understanding of what was going through her mind while she was in hiding. This entry from December 1943 describes her conflicting emotions about life in the Annex.

Friday, December 24, 1943

Dear Kitty,

As I've written you many times before, moods have a tendency to affect us quite a bit here, and in my case it's been getting worse lately. *"Himmelhoch jauchzend, zu Tode betrübt"*[1] certainly applies to me. I'm "on top of the world" when I think of how fortunate we are and compare myself to other Jewish children, and "in the depths of despair" when, for example, Mrs. Kleiman comes by and talks about Jopie's hockey club, canoe trips, school plays and afternoon teas with friends.

I don't think I'm jealous of Jopie, but I long to have a really good time for once and to laugh so hard it hurts. We're stuck in this house like lepers, especially during winter and the Christmas and New Year's holidays. Actually, I shouldn't even be writing this, since it makes me seem so ungrateful, but I can't keep everything to myself, so I'll repeat what I said at the beginning: "Paper is more patient than people."

Whenever someone comes in from outside, with the wind in their clothes and the cold on their cheeks, I feel like burying my head under the blankets to keep from thinking, "When will we be allowed to breathe fresh air again?" I can't do that—on the contrary, I have to hold my head up high and put a bold face on things, but the thoughts keep coming anyway. Not just once, but over and over.

Believe me, if you've been shut up for a year and a half, it can get to be too much for you sometimes. But feelings can't be ignored, no matter how unjust or ungrateful they seem. I long to ride a bike, dance, whistle, look at the world, feel young and know that I'm free, and yet I can't let it show. Just imagine what would happen if all eight of us were to feel sorry for ourselves or walk around with the discontent clearly visible on our faces. Where would that get us? . . .

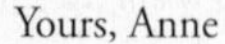

Yours, Anne

1. ***"Himmelhoch jauchzend, zu Tode betrübt":*** A famous line from Goethe: "On top of the world, or in the depths of despair."

DIFFERENTIATED INSTRUCTION

FOR LESS–PROFICIENT READERS

Comprehension Support Ask students to skim Anne's journal entry again. Then ask them to review their charts and notes that they have made about Anne while reading. Encourage students to use a T Chart to compare the character of Anne in the play to the real Anne as shown through the diary entry.

BEST PRACTICES TOOLKIT—Transparency
T Chart p. A25

FOR ENGLISH LEARNERS

Options for Reading [small-group option] Have students follow along silently as they listen to the *Audio Anthology CD.* Then have students work in small groups and answer some or all of the discussion prompts, rereading passages as necessary.

er Reading

mprehension

1. **Recall** How do the people in the Annex get food and other supplies?
2. **Recall** Why do some of the people in the Annex complain about Anne?
3. **Clarify** Why does Mr. Frank say that the loud air raids should be music to the ears of those hiding in the attic?

erary Analysis

4. **Interpret a Character's Words** What does Anne mean when she writes in her diary, "Paper is more patient than people"? Cite specific examples from the play that explain Anne's attitude.
5. **Examine Your Story Map** Look over your story map and make sure it's complete so far. What is the last major event in this act? What do you predict might happen in Act Two as a result of this event?
6. **Understand Conflicts** A conflict in literature is a struggle between two opposing forces. An **external conflict** is a struggle between a character and society, another character, or a force of nature. An **internal conflict** is a struggle within a character's mind. In a chart like the one shown, include the external and internal conflicts you notice so far in the play. Circle the one or two conflicts you think are the main ones.

External Conflicts	Internal Conficts

7. **Identify Subplot** A **subplot** is an additional, or secondary, plot in a work of literature. The subplot contains its own conflict, often separate from the main conflicts of the story. What is one subplot that has been introduced in Act One?
8. **Analyze Theme** Which characters help the most to develop the theme that people are good at heart? Consider actions of people both inside and outside the Secret Annex. Do any other characters make you question the play's theme? Explain.

tension and Challenge

9. **Readers' Circle** Review the diary entry included on page 520. Anne admits she sometimes feels like burying her head under the blankets. Yet she holds her head up high and puts a "bold face on things." What **impact** do you think her behavior had on those around her? Discuss this question with a small group.

Practice and Apply

After Reading

For additional support of postreading questions, use these copy masters:

RESOURCE MANAGER—Copy Masters
Theme p. 123 (for practice of literary analysis standards focus)
Question Support p. 128 (After Reading questions adapted for English learners and less-proficient readers)
Additional selection questions are provided for teachers on page 115.

For additional activities to challenge students, see

Power Thinking at **ClassZone.com**

ANSWERS

Comprehension

1. *Miep and Mr. Kraler bring them supplies.*
2. *Anne talks a lot and sometimes uses her pent-up energy to play pranks on the other residents of the Annex, which leads to arguments with them.*
3. *He believes that the more airplanes that come, the sooner the war will be over.*

Literary Analysis

Possible answers:

4. *She means that her diary will not scold her for expressing her thoughts. Students should give examples of Anne being scolded for sharing her thoughts.*
5. ■ **STANDARDS FOCUS Story Mapping** *The last major event in this act is Mr. Frank finding that a thief broke in downstairs. The thief might have heard Peter falling off the chair as he tried to turn off the light. This event might lead to the discovery of the Annex and the people living there.*
6. ***External Conflicts:*** *persecution of the Jews by the Nazis; arguments between residents of the Annex; the thief's possible discovery of the hiding place; Mr. Dussel's allergy to Peter's cat.* ***Internal Conflicts:*** *Mr. Frank's feelings of anger and bitterness upon returning to the Annex in Scene 1; Anne's longing to be outside; Anne's fear of being discovered; Anne's struggle to be a better person; Mrs. Frank's distress over her conflict with Anne; Mr. Van Daan's hunger*
7. *The growing relationship between Anne and Peter is one subplot. Anne's conflict with her mother is another.*
8. ● **STANDARDS FOCUS Theme** *Characters who help develop the theme are Miep, Mr. Kraler, Anne, Margot, Mr. Frank, Mrs. Frank, and Peter. Mr. and Mrs. Van Daan and Mr. Dussel could make readers question the play's theme, as could the whole context of the Nazi persecution of Jews during World War II.*

Extension and Challenge

9. *Students should bring out the point that Anne makes when she questions what would happen if all eight of them showed their despair. Putting on a brave face will raise the spirits of the others or at least remind them to try to be brave themselves.*

Practice and Apply

Lines 3–20

READING SKILL

STORY MAPPING

In what way has the setting changed from the last scene of Act One? In what way has it stayed the same? ***Answer:*** *It is now January 1944, a few weeks later than the end of the first act. In total, it is now almost a year and half since Anne and the others went into hiding. The location is the same, however.*

Lines 37–58

READING SKILL

STORY MAPPING

Why is everyone startled when the buzzer rings? How do they react when they realize who it is? ***Possible answer:*** *It is a Saturday, so they are not expecting visitors. Until Miep identifies herself, they are not sure who it is. When they do realize it is Miep and Mr. Kraler, they are thrilled.*

Lines 74–78

DISCUSSION PROMPTS

Use these prompts to help students focus on the significance of Peter's missing cat:

Connect What feelings would you have if you had a pet and it disappeared? What feelings do you think Peter is experiencing over Mouschi's absence? *Students may say that they would miss their pet and be worried that it was hurt. Peter probably misses Mouschi even more since he is stuck in the Annex, and he probably feels anxious because he can't go search for him.*

Analyze Is it a complete surprise that Mouschi is missing? Why or why not? ***Possible answer:*** *No. In lines 1917–1931 of Act One, Mr. Van Daan says that he is going to get rid of the cat. Mr. Dussel encourages him to do so.*

Speculate What do you think happened to Mouschi? *Students may speculate that Mr. Van Daan or Mr. Dussel deliberately left the skylight in Peter's room open so that the cat could climb out or that one of them took the cat down to the door and let it out.*

In the darkness we hear Anne's Voice, *again reading from the diary.*

Anne's Voice. Saturday, the first of January, nineteen forty-four. Another new year has begun and we find ourselves still in our hiding place. We have been here now for one year, five months and twenty-five days. It seems that our life is at a standstill.

The curtain rises on the scene. It is late afternoon. Everyone is bundled up against the cold. In the main room Mrs. Frank *is taking down the laundry which is hung across the back.* Mr. Frank *sits in the chair down left, reading.* Margot *is lying on the couch with a blanket over her and the many-colored knitted scarf around her throat.* Anne *is seated at the center table, writing in her diary.* Peter, Mr. *and* Mrs. Van Daan, *and* Dussel *are all in their own rooms, reading or lying down.*

As the lights dim on, Anne's Voice *continues, without a break.*

Anne's Voice. We are all a little thinner. The Van Daans' "discussions" are as violent as ever. Mother still does not understand me. But then I don't understand her either. There is one great change, however. A change in myself. I read somewhere that girls of my age don't feel quite certain of themselves. That they become quiet within and begin to think of the miracle that is taking place in their bodies. I think that what is happening to me is so wonderful . . . not only what can be seen, but what is taking place inside. Each time it has happened I have a feeling that I have a sweet secret. (*We hear the chimes and then a hymn being played on the carillon outside.*) And in spite of any pain, I long for the time when I shall feel that secret within me again.

(*The buzzer of the door below suddenly sounds. Everyone is startled,* Mr. Frank *tiptoes cautiously to the top of the steps and listens. Again the buzzer sounds, in* Miep*'s V-for-Victory signal.*)

Mr. Frank. It's Miep! (*He goes quickly down the s to unbolt the door.* Mrs. Frank *calls upstairs to th* Van Daans *and then to* Peter.)

Mrs. Frank. Wake up, everyone! Miep is here! (Anne *quickly puts her diary away.* Margot *sits up, pulling the blanket around her shoulders.* Mr. Dussel *sits on the edge of his bed, listening,* ***disgruntled.*** Miep *comes up the steps, followed b* Mr. Kraler. *They bring flowers, books, newspaper etc.* Anne *rushes to* Miep, *throwing her arms affectionately around her.*) Miep . . . *and* Mr. Kraler . . . What a delightful surprise!

Mr. Kraler. We came to bring you New Year's greetings.

Mrs. Frank. You shouldn't . . . you should have at least one day to yourselves. (*She goes quickly to the stove and brings down teacups and tea for all of them.*)

Anne. Don't say that, it's so wonderful to see th (*sniffing at* Miep*'s coat*) I can smell the wind an the cold on your clothes.

Miep (*giving her the flowers*). There you are. (*then to* Margot, *feeling her forehead*) How are y Margot? . . . Feeling any better?

Margot. I'm all right.

Anne. We filled her full of every kind of pill so won't cough and make a noise. (*She runs into h room to put the flowers in water.* Mr. *and* Mrs. V Daan *come from upstairs. Outside there is the sou of a band playing.*)

Mrs. Van Daan. Well, hello, Miep. Mr. Kraler.

Mr. Kraler (*giving a bouquet of flowers to* Mrs. Va Daan). With my hope for peace in the New Ye

Peter (*anxiously*). Miep, have you seen Mousch Have you seen him anywhere around?

Miep. I'm sorry, Peter. I asked everyone in the neighborhood had they seen a gray cat. But the said no.

(Mrs. Frank *gives* Miep *a cup of tea.* Mr. Frank *comes up the steps, carrying a small cake on a plat*

Mr. Frank. Look what Miep's brought for us!

Mrs. Frank (*taking it*). A cake!

DIFFERENTIATED INSTRUCTION

FOR LESS-PROFICIENT READERS

Comprehension Support Have students review their story maps and other charts from Act One. Then use a Round Robin strategy to have students take turns explaining important events, conflicts, or characters' behaviors from the first part of the play. Use this opportunity to clarify misconceptions and to answer any questions.

BEST PRACTICES TOOLKIT—Transparency
Round Robin p. A17

ADDITIONAL TEACHING OPPORTUNITY

Costume Design Tell students that even though the costumes may look simple, a great deal of thought goes into the outfits that the actors wear. In a play such as this one, the clothing must look authentic and match the setting. This includes the economic circumstances of the characters as well as the time period in which the action takes place. It would not make sense for Anne to be wearing sneakers, for example. In fact, it would distract the audience from the events unfolding on stage.

The articles of clothing worn by the characters might also be used to reveal some aspects of personality. The fact that Mrs. Van Daan brings a luxurious fur coat into hiding reveals her love of material possessions. Ask students to discuss in what way the clothing worn in this photograph conveys a sense of the time period and the circumstances of the characters. ***Possible answer:*** *Mr. Kraler is carrying a hat. All of the actors are wearing multiple layers of clothing, including scarves, even though they are inside, showing that it is cold in the Annex. The women wear skirts or suits rather than slacks, and the men are also dressed formally in comparison to today's styles.*

Lines 79–141
DISCUSSION PROMPTS

Use these prompts to help students understand the conflict over the cake:

Connect The inhabitants of the Annex are very excited to eat the cake. Would you feel the same if you were in their position? Why? *Students might say that they would be excited, too. First of all, food is so scarce that any addition is welcome. Second, they have not had a treat like cake for an entire year because of the rationing. Third, it makes the day seem special.*

Analyze Based on what you know about Mr. and Mrs. Van Daan, do you believe Mr. Dussel's accusation that Mrs. Van Daan cuts bigger portions for her husband? Explain. ***Possible answer:*** *Yes. Mr. Van Daan is very concerned about food. Mrs. Van Daan might do this to try to keep him happy.*

Synthesize How do the characters' reactions to Miep's gift show their true natures? ***Possible answer:*** *Miep refuses any cake, which is consistent with her generosity and selflessness. Mr. Van Daan tries to get more cake for himself by saying that Margot doesn't want any, showing himself to be greedy and grasping. Anne defends Margot, which reveals her sense of justice. Mrs. Frank continues to ask Miep to have some, showing her gracious nature. Mr. Frank tries to keep the peace among everyone.*

Lines 150–160
REINFORCE *KEY IDEA:* IMPACT

Discuss What **impact** has Mouschi's disappearance had on the inhabitants of the Annex? ***Possible answer:*** *Mr. Dussel is happy. Peter is distraught and on edge.*

Mr. Van Daan. A cake! (*He pinches* Miep*'s cheeks gaily and hurries up to the cupboard.*) I'll get some plates.

(Dussel, *in his room, hastily puts a coat on and starts out to join the others.*)

Mrs. Frank. Thank you, Miepia. You shouldn't have done it. You must have used all of your sugar ration for weeks. (*giving it to* Mrs. Van Daan) It's beautiful, isn't it?

Mrs. Van Daan. It's been ages since I even saw a cake. Not since you brought us one last year. (*without looking at the cake, to* Miep) Remember? Don't you remember, you gave us one on New Year's Day? Just this time last year? I'll never forget it because you had "Peace in nineteen forty-three" on it. (*She looks at the cake and reads.*) "Peace in nineteen forty-four!"

Miep. Well, it has to come sometime, you know. (*as* Dussel *comes from his room*) Hello, Mr. Dussel.

Mr. Kraler. How are you?

Mr. Van Daan (*bringing plates and a knife*). Here's the knife, *liefje.* Now, how many of us are there?

Miep. None for me, thank you.

Mr. Frank. Oh, please. You must.

Miep. I couldn't.

Mr. Van Daan. Good! That leaves one . . . two . . . three . . . seven of us.

Dussel. Eight! Eight! It's the same number as it always is!

Mr. Van Daan. I left Margot out. I take it for granted Margot won't eat any.

Anne. Why wouldn't she!

Mrs. Frank. I think it won't harm her.

Mr. Van Daan. All right! All right! I just didn't want her to start coughing again, that's all.

Dussel. And please, Mrs. Frank should cut the cake.

Mr. Van Daan. What's the difference?
Mrs. Van Daan. It's not Mrs. Frank's cake, is it, Miep? It's for all of us.
} *Together*

Dussel. Mrs. Frank divides things better.

Mrs. Van Daan (*going to* Dussel). What are you trying to say?
Mr. Van Daan. Oh, come on! Stop wasting time!
} *Togeth*

Mrs. Van Daan (*to* Dussel). Don't I always give everybody exactly the same? Don't I?

Mr. Van Daan. Forget it, Kerli.

Mrs. Van Daan. No. I want an answer! Don't I?

Dussel. Yes. Yes. Everybody gets exactly the same . . . except Mr. Van Daan always gets a lit bit more.

(Mr. Van Daan *advances on* Dussel, *the knife sti in his hand.*)

Mr. Van Daan. That's a lie!

(Dussel *retreats before the onslaught of the* Van Daans.)

Mr. Frank. Please, please! (*then to* Miep) You see what a little sugar cake does to us? It goes right our heads!

Mr. Van Daan (*handing* Mrs. Frank *the knife*). Here you are, Mrs. Frank.

Mrs. Frank. Thank you. (*then to* Miep *as she goe to the table to cut the cake*) Are you sure you wo have some?

Miep (*drinking her tea*). No, really, I have to go in a minute.

(*The sound of the band fades out in the distance.*)

Peter (*to* Miep). Maybe Mouschi went back to house . . . they say that cats . . . Do you ever ge over there . . . ? I mean . . . do you suppose you could . . . ?

Miep. I'll try, Peter. The first minute I get I'll tr But I'm afraid, with him gone a week . . .

Dussel. Make up your mind, already someone h had a nice big dinner from that cat!

(Peter *is furious, inarticulate. He starts toward* Dussel *as if to hit him.* Mr. Frank *stops him.* Mrs. Frank *speaks quickly to ease the situation.*)

Mrs. Frank (*to* Miep). This is delicious, Miep!

Mrs. Van Daan (*eating hers*). Delicious!

DIFFERENTIATED INSTRUCTION

FOR LESS–PROFICIENT READERS

Comprehension Support

1. Point out that this scene shows that there are still many unresolved conflicts among the inhabitants of the Annex.
2. Have students identify the internal and external conflicts that are revealed in lines 21–160. ***Possible answer:*** *Internal: Peter misses Mouschi. External: Mr. Dussel antagonizes everyone. Mr. Van Daan tries to get more food by taking others' shares. Miep and Mr. Kraler still risk their lives to help them. The residents of the Annex are still threatened by the Nazis. The Van Daans still argue. Anne and her mother continue to disagree.*
3. Ask students, what, if any, conflicts have been resolved at this point in the play. ***Possible answer:*** *Mr. Dussel is no longer bothered by Mouschi because the cat has disappeared.*
4. Remind students to look for resolutions to the unresolved conflicts as they read further.

Mr. Van Daan (*finishing it in one gulp*). Dirk's in luck to get a girl who can bake like this!

Miep (*putting down her empty teacup*). I have to run. Dirk's taking me to a party tonight.

Anne. How heavenly! Remember now what everyone is wearing, and what you have to eat and everything, so you can tell us tomorrow.

Miep. I'll give you a full report! Good-bye, everyone!

Mr. Van Daan (*to* Miep). Just a minute. There's something I'd like you to do for me. (*He hurries off up the stairs to his room.*)

Mrs. Van Daan (*sharply*). Putti, where are you going? (*She rushes up the stairs after him, calling hysterically.*) What do you want? Putti, what are you going to do?

Miep (*to* Peter). What's wrong?

Peter (*his sympathy is with his mother*). Father says he's going to sell her fur coat. She's crazy about that old fur coat.

Dussel. Is it possible? Is it possible that anyone is so silly as to worry about a fur coat in times like this?

Peter. It's none of your darn business . . . and if you say one more thing . . . I'll, I'll take you and I'll . . . I mean it . . . I'll . . .

(*There is a piercing scream from* Mrs. Van Daan *above. She grabs at the fur coat as* Mr. Van Daan *is starting downstairs with it.*)

Mrs. Van Daan. No! No! No! Don't you dare take that! You hear? It's mine! (*Downstairs* Peter *turns away, embarrassed, miserable.*) My father gave me that! You didn't give it to me. You have no right. Let go of it . . . you hear?

(Mr. Van Daan *pulls the coat from her hands and hurries downstairs.* Mrs. Van Daan *sinks to the floor, sobbing. As* Mr. Van Daan *comes into the main room the others look away, embarrassed for him.*)

Mr. Van Daan (*to* Mr. Kraler). Just a little—discussion over the advisability of selling this coat. As I have often reminded Mrs. Van Daan, it's very selfish of her to keep it when people outside are in such desperate need of clothing . . . (*He gives the coat to* Miep.) So if you will please to sell it for us? It should fetch a good price. And by the way, will you get me cigarettes. I don't care what kind they are . . . get all you can.

Miep. It's terribly difficult to get them, Mr. Van Daan. But I'll try. Good-bye.

(*She goes.* Mr. Frank *follows her down the steps to bolt the door after her.* Mrs. Frank *gives* Mr. Kraler *a cup of tea.*)

Mrs. Frank. Are you sure you won't have some cake, Mr. Kraler?

Mr. Kraler. I'd better not.

Mr. Van Daan. You're still feeling badly? What does your doctor say?

Mr. Kraler. I haven't been to him.

Mrs. Frank. Now, Mr. Kraler! . . .

Mr. Kraler (*sitting at the table*). Oh, I tried. But you can't get near a doctor these days . . . they're so busy. After weeks I finally managed to get one on the telephone. I told him I'd like an appointment . . . I wasn't feeling very well. You know what he answers . . . over the telephone . . . Stick out your tongue! (*They laugh. He turns to* Mr. Frank *as* Mr. Frank *comes back.*) I have some contracts here . . . I wonder if you'd look over them with me . . .

Mr. Frank (*putting out his hand*). Of course.

Mr. Kraler (*He rises.*) If we could go downstairs . . . (Mr. Frank *starts ahead,* Mr. Kraler *speaks to the others.*) Will you forgive us? I won't keep him but a minute. (*He starts to follow* Mr. Frank *down the steps.*)

Margot (*with sudden* ***foreboding***). What's happened? Something's happened! Hasn't it, Mr. Kraler?

(Mr. Kraler *stops and comes back, trying to reassure* Margot *with a pretense of casualness.*)

Mr. Kraler. No, really. I want your father's advice . . .

Margot. Something's gone wrong! I know it!

Lines 179–210

DISCUSSION PROMPTS

Use these prompts to help students understand what is happening between Mr. and Mrs. Van Daan:

Connect With whom do you sympathize in this situation—Mr. or Mrs. Van Daan? *Students might say that they sympathize with Mrs. Van Daan. The coat is very special to her, and the memories associated with it help her get through difficult times. Others might sympathize with Mr. Van Daan, who is being practical.*

Analyze Why does Mr. Van Daan want the money? ***Possible answer:*** *He wants Miep to buy him more cigarettes.*

Evaluate Who do you think feels worse about the "discussion" about the fur coat—the Van Daans or the others? ***Possible answer:*** *The others are probably more embarrassed about what they have witnessed than the Van Daans. The Van Daans regularly argue, so they must not be self-conscious about it.*

Lines 221–230

LITERARY ANALYSIS

● THEME

What is Mr. Kraler's attitude toward his illness? ***Possible answer:*** *He seems to be quite calm about it. He makes a joke out of the fact that he cannot get an appointment with his doctor.*

Extend the Discussion How does Mr. Kraler's joke reveal his courage?

FOR ENGLISH LEARNERS

Vocabulary: Idioms and Sayings [mixed-readiness groups] Have students work together to define these expressions:

- *have to run* (lines 165–166), "must leave"
- *crazy about that old fur coat* (lines 180–181), "likes the coat a lot"
- *fetch a good price* (line 206), "be worth a lot of money to a buyer"
- *keep him* (line 234), "delay him"

Lines 254–274

READING SKILL

■ STORY MAPPING

What complication has arisen in the office that might affect those hiding in the Annex? (Have students record this event in their story maps from page 485.) ***Answer:*** *One of the employees in the warehouse might know that the Franks are hiding in the Annex. He asked about the Franks, mentioned the door behind the bookcase, and then requested more money from Mr. Kraler.*

Lines 303–310

LITERARY ANALYSIS

● THEME

Mr. Kraler did not tell his wife the real reason for his visit to the office. Why hasn't he confided in her? ***Possible answer:*** *He may not want to risk anyone else knowing about the Franks. He may not want his wife to know anything that would put her in danger or cause to worry.*

Lines 321–324

REINFORCE *KEY IDEA:* IMPACT

Discuss What does Margot's remark reveal about the **impact** this time in hiding has had on her? ***Possible answer:*** *Margot says she wishes that whatever is going to happen would just happen. Her comment shows how the suspense and constant fear are wearing on her.*

Mr. Frank (*coming back, to* Mr. Kraler). If it's something that concerns us here, it's better that we all hear it.

Mr. Kraler (*turning to him, quietly*). But . . . the children . . . ?

Mr. Frank. What they'd imagine would be worse than any reality.

(*As* Mr. Kraler *speaks, they all listen with intense* ***apprehension.*** Mrs. Van Daan *comes down the stairs and sits on the bottom step.*)

Mr. Kraler. It's a man in the storeroom . . . I don't know whether or not you remember him . . . Carl, about fifty, heavy-set, near-sighted . . . He came with us just before you left.

Mr. Frank. He was from Utrecht?

Mr. Kraler. That's the man. A couple of weeks ago, when I was in the storeroom, he closed the door and asked me . . . how's Mr. Frank? What do you hear from Mr. Frank? I told him I only knew there was a rumor that you were in Switzerland. He said he'd heard that rumor too, but he thought I might know something more. I didn't pay any attention to it . . . but then a thing happened yesterday . . . He'd brought some invoices to the office for me to sign. As I was going through them, I looked up. He was standing staring at the bookcase . . . your bookcase. He said he thought he remembered a door there . . . Wasn't there a door there that used to go up to the loft? Then he told me he wanted more money. Twenty guilders[1] more a week.

Mr. Van Daan. Blackmail!

Mr. Frank. Twenty guilders? Very modest blackmail.

Mr. Van Daan. That's just the beginning.

Dussel (*coming to* Mr. Frank). You know what I think? He was the thief who was down there that night. That's how he knows we're here.

Mr. Frank (*to* Mr. Kraler). How was it left? What did you tell him?

Mr. Kraler. I said I had to think about it. What shall I do? Pay him the money? . . . Take a chance on firing him . . . or what? I don't know.

Dussel (*frantic*). For God's sake don't fire him! Pay him what he asks . . . keep him here where you can have your eye on him.

Mr. Frank. Is it so much that he's asking? What they paying nowadays?

Mr. Kraler. He could get it in a war plant. But t isn't a war plant. Mind you, I don't know if he really knows . . . or if he doesn't know.

Mr. Frank. Offer him half. Then we'll soon find out if it's blackmail or not.

Dussel. And if it is? We've got to pay it, haven't Anything he asks we've got to pay!

Mr. Frank. Let's decide that when the time come

Mr. Kraler. This may be all my imagination. You get to a point, these days, where you suspect everyone and everything. Again and again . . . on some simple look or word, I've found myself . . .

(*The telephone rings in the office below.*)

Mrs. Van Daan (*hurrying to* Mr. Kraler). There's telephone! What does that mean, the telephone ringing on a holiday?

Mr. Kraler. That's my wife. I told her I had to go over some papers in my office . . . to call me then when she got out of church. (*He starts out.*) I'll offer him half then. Good-bye . . . we'll hope for the best!

(*The group call their good-byes half-heartedly.* Mr. Frank *follows* Mr. Kraler, *to bolt the door below. During the following scene,* Mr. Frank *con back up and stands listening, disturbed.*)

Dussel (*to* Mr. Van Daan). You can thank your s for this . . . smashing the light! I tell you, it's jus a question of time now. (*He goes to the window a the back and stands looking out.*)

Margot. Sometimes I wish the end would come . . . whatever it is.

Mrs. Frank (*shocked*). Margot!

(Anne *goes to* Margot, *sitting beside her on the co with her arms around her.*)

Margot. Then at least we'd know where we were

⑥ **Targeted Passage**

1. **guilders** (gĭl′dərz): the basic monetary unit of the Netherlands at the time.

DIFFERENTIATED INSTRUCTION

FOR LESS–PROFICIENT READERS

⑥ **Targeted Passage [Lines 254–310]**

This passage presents another threat to the group's safety: an employee might know about the Annex.

- Why does Mr. Kraler think that Carl knows about the Franks?
- What does Mr. Frank suggest that Mr. Kraler do? What does Mr. Dussel advise?
- When will they know if the threat is real?

FOR ENGLISH LEARNERS

Comprehension: Cause and Effect To help students understand the concept of blackmail, display a cause-and-effect chart such as this one and work together to complete it:

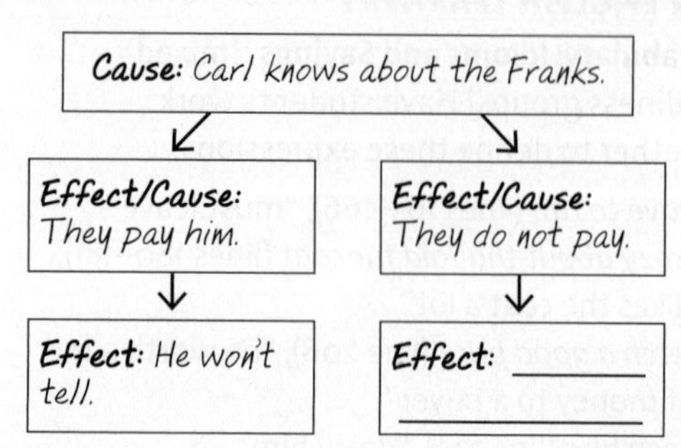

Cause: Carl knows about the Franks.
Effect/Cause: They pay him.
Effect/Cause: They do not pay.
Effect: He won't tell.
Effect: ______

Mrs. Frank. You should be ashamed of yourself! Talking that way! Think how lucky we are! Think of the thousands dying in the war, every day. Think of the people in concentration camps.

Anne (*interrupting*). What's the good of that? What's the good of thinking of misery when you're already miserable? That's stupid!

Mrs. Frank. Anne!

(As Anne *goes on raging at her mother,* Mrs. Frank *tries to break in, in an effort to quiet her.*)

Anne. We're young, Margot and Peter and I! You grownups have had your chance! But look at us . . . If we begin thinking of all the horror in the world, we're lost! We're trying to hold onto some kind of ideals . . . when everything . . . ideals, hopes . . . everything, are being destroyed! It isn't our fault that the world is in such a mess! We weren't around when all this started! So don't try to take it out on us!

(*She rushes off to her room, slamming the door after her. She picks up a brush from the chest and hurls it to the floor. Then she sits on the settee, trying to control her anger.*)

Mr. Van Daan. She talks as if we started the war! Did we start the war? (*He spots* Anne's *cake. As he starts to take it,* Peter *anticipates him.*)

Peter. She left her cake. (*He starts for* Anne's *room with the cake. There is silence in the main room.* Mrs. Van Daan *goes up to her room, followed by* Van Daan. Dussel *stays looking out the window.* Mr. Frank *brings* Mrs. Frank *her cake. She eats it slowly, without relish.* Mr. Frank *takes his cake to* Margot *and sits quietly on the sofa beside her.* Peter *stands in the doorway of* Anne's *darkened room, looking at her, then makes a little movement to let her know he is there.* Anne *sits up, quickly, trying to hide the signs of her tears.* Peter *holds out the cake to her.*) You left this.

Anne (*dully*). Thanks.

(Peter *starts to go out, then comes back.*)

Peter. I thought you were fine just now. You know just how to talk to them. You know just how to say it. I'm no good . . . I never can think . . . especially when I'm mad . . . That Dussel . . . when he said that about Mouschi . . . someone eating him . . . all I could think is . . . I wanted to hit him. I wanted to give him such a . . . a . . . that he'd . . . That's what I used to do when there was an argument at school . . . That's the way I . . . but here . . . And an old man like that . . . it wouldn't be so good.

Anne. You're making a big mistake about me. I do it all wrong. I say too much. I go too far. I hurt people's feelings . . .

(Dussel *leaves the window, going to his room.*)

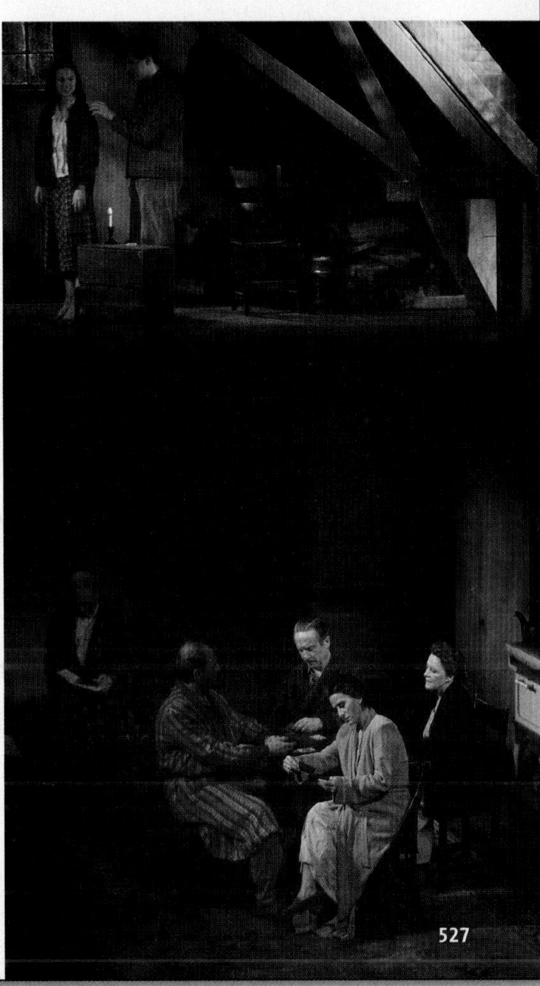

527

Lines 325–343

LITERARY ANALYSIS

THEME

Is Anne's approach to dealing with the situation different from her mother's? Explain. ***Possible answer:*** *Thinking about what others are suffering helps Mrs. Frank feel grateful for what she has. Anne prefers to think about her hopes and dreams.*

Lines 344–374

LITERARY ANALYSIS

THEME

Why does Peter go to Anne's room? What change is seen in their relationship here? ***Possible answer:*** *Peter notices his father eyeing Anne's cake and takes it to her. This action and the conversation they have show that they are resolving their conflict.*

ANALYZE VISUALS

Activity Ask students what impressions of life in the Annex are created by this photograph of the stage. ***Possible answer:*** *There is a lot of activity going on, even if it is only playing cards or talking. The photograph creates a vivid sense of the number of people who have to share a small space and the routines they have developed to cope with their situation.*

FOR LESS–PROFICIENT READERS

Comprehension Support [small-group option] Direct students' attention to lines 365–374. Tell them that this might be considered a turning point in the relationship between Anne and Peter. Ask small groups of students to paraphrase, or put into their own words, what Peter is saying here. Then discuss what this conversation might signal and what insights into Peter's character his words reveal.

FOR ADVANCED LEARNERS/PRE–AP

Make Judgments Does Mr. Frank or Mr. Dussel have the best plan for dealing with Carl? Is there another solution? Have students identify the steps they would use to solve the problem. Remind them to consider all of the implications of blackmail and its possible consequences. Then have students share their problem-solving plan.

Lines 407–442

DISCUSSION PROMPTS

Use these prompts to help students gain insight into Anne's and Peter's characters through their conversation:

Connect Whom do you talk to about your problems? In what way do you think Anne will feel after this conversation with Peter? *Students might say that she will feel less alone and isolated in her situation.*

Analyze What changes are evident in both Anne and Peter? ***Possible answer:*** *Anne is more mature, as shown in her willingness to have a conversation with Peter, not just talk at him or try to antagonize him. Peter has grown, too. He is less self-conscious and better able to see Anne's good qualities.*

Speculate In what way will this new solidarity affect the dynamics in the Annex? Explain. ***Possible answer:*** *This new relationship might ease tension in many ways. Anne will have someone to talk to about her mother, and Peter will be able to confide his feelings about his parents and Mr. Dussel. So, they both might become easier to live with.*

Lines 454–477

READING SKILL

STORY MAPPING

What two events occur that affect the inhabitants of the Annex greatly? (Remind students to record their answers on their story maps from page 485.) ***Answer:*** *The suppliers of the ration books have been arrested, so Miep no longer has the coupons to obtain extra food. Also, Mr. Kraler is in the hospital.*

Peter. I think you're just fine . . . What I want to say . . . if it wasn't for you around here, I don't know. What I mean . . .

(Peter *is interrupted by* Dussel*'s turning on the light.* Dussel *stands in the doorway, startled to see* Peter. Peter *advances toward him forbiddingly.* Dussel *backs out of the room.* Peter *closes the door on him.*)

Anne. Do you mean it, Peter? Do you really mean it?

Peter. I said it, didn't I?

Anne. Thank you, Peter!

(*In the main room* Mr. *and* Mrs. Frank *collect the dishes and take them to the sink, washing them.* Margot *lies down again on the couch.* Dussel, *lost, wanders into* Peter*'s room and takes up a book, starting to read.*)

Peter (*looking at the photographs on the wall*). You've got quite a collection.

Anne. Wouldn't you like some in your room? I could give you some. Heaven knows you spend enough time in there . . . doing heaven knows what . . .

Peter. It's easier. A fight starts, or an argument . . . I duck in there.

Anne. You're lucky, having a room to go to. His lordship is always here . . . I hardly ever get a minute alone. When they start in on me, I can't duck away. I have to stand there and take it.

Peter. You gave some of it back just now.

Anne. I get so mad. They've formed their opinions . . . about everything . . . but we . . . we're still trying to find out . . . We have problems here that no other people our age have ever had. And just as you think you've solved them, something comes along and bang! You have to start all over again.

Peter. At least you've got someone you can talk to.

Anne. Not really. Mother . . . I never discuss anything serious with her. She doesn't understand. Father's all right. We can talk about everything . . . everything but one thing. Mother. He simply won't talk about her. I don't think you can be really intimate with anyone if he holds someth back, do you?

Peter. I think your father's fine.

Anne. Oh, he is, Peter! He is! He's the only one who's ever given me the feeling that I have any sense. But anyway, nothing can take the place school and play and friends of your own age . . or near your age . . . can it?

Peter. I suppose you miss your friends and all.

Anne. It isn't just . . . (*She breaks off, staring up at him for a second.*) Isn't it funny, you and I? Here we've been seeing each other every minut for almost a year and a half, and this is the first time we've ever really talked. It helps a lot to ha someone to talk to, don't you think? It helps yo to let off steam.

Peter (*going to the door*). Well, any time you wa to let off steam, you can come into my room.

Anne (*following him*). I can get up an awful lot steam. You'll have to be careful how you say th

Peter. It's all right with me.

Anne. Do you mean it?

Peter. I said it, didn't I?

(*He goes out.* Anne *stands in her doorway looking after him. As* Peter *gets to his door he stands for a minute looking back at her. Then he goes into his room.* Dussel *rises as he comes in, and quickly pa him, going out. He starts across for his room.* Ann *sees him coming, and pulls her door shut.* Dussel *turns back toward* Peter*'s room.* Peter *pulls his do shut.* Dussel *stands there, bewildered, forlorn.*

The scene slowly dims out. The curtain falls on scene. Anne's Voice *comes over in the darkness . . faintly at first, and then with growing strength.*)

Anne's Voice. We've had bad news. The people from whom Miep got our ration books have be arrested. So we have had to cut down on our fo Our stomachs are so empty that they rumble an make strange noises, all in different keys. Mr. V Daan's is deep and low, like a bass fiddle. Mine high, whistling like a flute. As we all sit around

DIFFERENTIATED INSTRUCTION

FOR LESS–PROFICIENT READERS

Reading Skill Follow-Up: Story Mapping [small-group option] Review the events added to the story map in this act so far (*an employee seems to be blackmailing Mr. Kraler; the ration book suppliers have been arrested; Mr. Kraler has been hospitalized*). Have small groups chart the effects of each event on the residents of the Annex and on the resolution of the central conflict. Have groups present their charts.

Events	Effects
Carl seems to be blackmailing Mr. Kraler.	• increases tension and worry • If Carl tells, they may be discovered.
The ration book suppliers have been arrested.	• The group will have less to eat. • Tempers may flare. • They may not survive in hiding.
Mr. Kraler has been hospitalized.	• Miep becomes totally responsible for them. • removes a source of help and security

vaiting for supper, it's like an orchestra tuning ıp. It only needs Toscanini[2] to raise his baton and ve'd be off in the Ride of the Valkyries.[3] Monday, he sixth of March, nineteen forty-four. Mr. Kraler s in the hospital. It seems he has ulcers. Pim says ve are his ulcers. Miep has to run the business nd us too. The Americans have landed on the outhern tip of Italy. Father looks for a quick inish to the war. Mr. Dussel is waiting every day or the warehouse man to demand more money. Have I been skipping too much from one subject o another? I can't help it. I feel that spring is oming. I feel it in my whole body and soul. I feel ıtterly confused. I am longing . . . so longing . . . or everything . . . for friends . . . for someone o talk to . . . someone who understands . . . omeone young, who feels as I do . . .

As these last lines are being said, the curtain rises on he scene. The lights dim on. Anne's Voice *fades out.*)

Scene 2

It is evening, after supper. From outside we hear he sound of children playing. The "grownups," with he exception of Mr. Van Daan, *are all in the main oom.* Mrs. Frank *is doing some mending,* Mrs. Van Daan *is reading a fashion magazine.* Mr. Frank *is going over business accounts.* Dussel, *in his dentist's acket, is pacing up and down, impatient to get into his bedroom.* Mr. Van Daan *is upstairs working on a piece of embroidery in an embroidery frame.*

In his room Peter *is sitting before the mirror, smoothing his hair. As the scene goes on, he puts on his tie, brushes his coat and puts it on, preparing himself meticulously for a visit from* Anne. *On his wall are now hung some of* Anne's *motion picture stars.*

In her room Anne *too is getting dressed. She stands before the mirror in her slip, trying various ways of dressing her hair.* Margot *is seated on the sofa, hemming a skirt for* Anne *to wear.*

In the main room Dussel *can stand it no longer. He comes over, rapping sharply on the door of his and* Anne*'s bedroom.*

Anne (*calling to him*). No, no, Mr. Dussel! I am not dressed yet. (Dussel *walks away, furious, sitting down and burying his head in his hands.* Anne *turns to* Margot.) How is that? How does that look?

Margot (*glancing at her briefly*). Fine.

Anne. You didn't even look.

Margot. Of course I did. It's fine.

Anne. Margot, tell me, am I terribly ugly?

Margot. Oh, stop fishing.

Anne. No. No. Tell me.

Margot. Of course you're not. You've got nice eyes . . . and a lot of animation, and . . .

Anne. A little vague, aren't you?

(*She reaches over and takes a brassière out of* Margot*'s sewing basket. She holds it up to herself, studying the effect in the mirror. Outside,* Mrs. Frank, *feeling sorry for* Dussel, *comes over, knocking at the girls' door.*)

Mrs. Frank (*outside*). May I come in?

Margot. Come in, Mother.

Mrs. Frank (*shutting the door behind her*). Mr. Dussel's impatient to get in here.

Anne (*still with the brassière*). Heavens, he takes the room for himself the entire day.

Mrs. Frank (*gently*). Anne, dear, you're not going in again tonight to see Peter?

Anne (*dignified*). That is my intention.

Mrs. Frank. But you've already spent a great deal of time in there today.

Anne. I was in there exactly twice. Once to get the dictionary, and then three-quarters of an hour before supper.

Mrs. Frank. Aren't you afraid you're disturbing him?

Anne. Mother, I have some intuition.

2. **Toscanini** (tŏs'kə-nē'nē): Arturo Toscanini, a famous Italian orchestral conductor.
3. **Ride of the Valkyries** (văl-kîr'ēz): a moving passage from an opera by Richard Wagner, a German composer.

Lines 521–534
REINFORCE *KEY IDEA:* IMPACT

Discuss What **impact** do Anne's visits to Peter's room have on her mother? ***Possible answer:*** *Her mother is uncomfortable with the frequency of Anne's visits. She may see it as improper that her daughter is alone with Peter in his room. Also, she fears that Anne is disturbing Peter.*

FOR ENGLISH LEARNERS

Vocabulary: Idioms and Sayings [mixed-readiness pairs] Have pairs of students use context clues to define these expressions:

- *duck in* (line 401), "escape into" or "hide in"
- *take it* (line 405), "listen to criticism"
- *gave some of it back* (line 406), "told them what you thought"
- *holds something back* (lines 420–421), "doesn't share thoughts and feelings"
- *let off steam* (line 435), "express true feelings"
- *run the business* (line 466), "keep the business going"
- *fishing* (line 509), "looking for compliments"

THE DIARY OF ANNE FRANK: ACT TWO 529

Lines 568–589

LITERARY ANALYSIS

● **THEME**

How does Margot's reaction to Anne and Peter's relationship show her good nature?
Possible answer: *She is not jealous of her sister's happiness, even though her life does not offer much in the way of diversion. She is just happy for Anne.*

Mrs. Frank. Then may I ask you this much, Anne. Please don't shut the door when you go in.

Anne. You sound like Mrs. Van Daan! (*She throws the brassière back in* Margot*'s sewing basket and picks up her blouse, putting it on.*)

Mrs. Frank. No. No. I don't mean to suggest anything wrong. I only wish that you wouldn't expose yourself to criticism . . . that you wouldn't give Mrs. Van Daan the opportunity to be unpleasant.

Anne. Mrs. Van Daan doesn't need an opportunity to be unpleasant!

Mrs. Frank. Everyone's on edge, worried about Mr. Kraler. This is one more thing . . .

Anne. I'm sorry, Mother. I'm going to Peter's room. I'm not going to let Petronella Van Daan spoil our friendship.

(Mrs. Frank *hesitates for a second, then goes out, closing the door after her. She gets a pack of playing cards and sits at the center table, playing solitaire. In* Anne*'s room* Margot *hands the finished skirt to* Anne. *As* Anne *is putting it on,* Margot *takes off her high-heeled shoes and stuffs paper in the toes so that* Anne *can wear them.*)

Margot (*to* Anne). Why don't you two talk in the main room? It'd save a lot of trouble. It's hard on Mother, having to listen to those remarks from Mrs. Van Daan and not say a word.

Anne. Why doesn't she say a word? I think it's ridiculous to take it and take it.

Margot. You don't understand Mother at all, do you? She can't talk back. She's not like you. It's just not in her nature to fight back.

Anne. Anyway . . . the only one I worry about is you. I feel awfully guilty about you.

(*She sits on the stool near* Margot, *putting on* Margot*'s high-heeled shoes.*)

Margot. What about?

Anne. I mean, every time I go into Peter's room, I have a feeling I may be hurting you. (Margot *shakes her head.*) I know if it were me, I'd be w I'd be desperately jealous, if it were me.

Margot. Well, I'm not.

Anne. You don't feel badly? Really? Truly? You're not jealous?

Margot. Of course I'm jealous . . . jealous that you've got something to get up in the morning for . . . But jealous of you and Peter? No.

(Anne *goes back to the mirror.*)

Anne. Maybe there's nothing to be jealous of. Maybe he doesn't really like me. Maybe I'm jus taking the place of his cat . . . (*She picks up a p of short white gloves, putting them on.*) Wouldn't you like to come in with us?

Margot. I have a book.

(*The sound of the children playing outside fades out. In the main room* Dussel *can stand it no longer. He jumps up, going to the bedroom door and knocking sharply.*)

Dussel. Will you please let me in my room!

Anne. Just a minute, dear, dear Mr. Dussel. (*Sh picks up her Mother's pink stole and adjusts it elegantly over her shoulders, then gives a last look in the mirror.*) Well, here I go . . . to run the gauntlet.[4] (*She starts out, followed by* Margot.)

Dussel (*as she appears—sarcastic*). Thank you so much.

(Dussel *goes into his room.* Anne *goes toward* Pe *room, passing* Mrs. Van Daan *and her parents a center table.*)

Mrs. Van Daan. My God, look at her! (Anne *pays attention. She knocks at* Peter*'s door.*) I don't know what good it is to have a son. I never see him. H wouldn't care if I killed myself. (Peter *opens the and stands aside for* Anne *to come in.*) Just a min Anne. (*She goes to them at the door.*) I'd like to sa a few words to my son. Do you mind? (Peter *an* Anne *stand waiting.*) Peter, I don't want you stay up till all hours tonight. You've got to have your sleep. You're a growing boy. You hear?

4. **to run the gauntlet:** to endure a series of troubles or difficulties.

DIFFERENTIATED INSTRUCTION

FOR LESS–PROFICIENT READERS

Comprehension Support [paired option] Point out that Anne and Peter's friendship has created some new conflicts. Have pairs identify new external and internal conflicts caused by Anne's visits to Peter. ***Possible answer:*** *External: Mrs. Van Daan criticizes Anne for visiting Peter's room. Internal: Anne worries about hurting Margot. Mrs. Van Daan resents the loss of her son's attention. Mrs. Frank is uncomfortable with Mrs. Van Daan's criticism.*

FOR ADVANCED LEARNERS/PRE–AP

Make Judgments [small-group option] What shows true goodness of spirit—a grand heroic gesture or consistent small sacrifices for others? Ask students to consider the theme in view of the glimpse into daily life under great pressure that the play reveals. Have students present and defend their opinions in small groups.

Mrs. Frank. Anne won't stay late. She's going to bed promptly at nine. Aren't you, Anne?

Anne. Yes, Mother . . . (*to* Mrs. Van Daan) May we go now?

Mrs. Van Daan. Are you asking me? I didn't know I had anything to say about it.

Mrs. Frank. Listen for the chimes, Anne dear.

(*The two young people go off into* Peter*'s room, shutting the door after them.*)

Mrs. Van Daan (*to* Mrs. Frank). In my day it was the boys who called on the girls. Not the girls on the boys.

Mrs. Frank. You know how young people like to feel that they have secrets. Peter's room is the only place where they can talk.

Mrs. Van Daan. Talk! That's not what they called it when I was young.

(Mrs. Van Daan *goes off to the bathroom.* Margot *settles down to read her book.* Mr. Frank *puts his papers away and brings a chess game to the center table. He and* Mrs. Frank *start to play. In* Peter*'s room,* Anne *speaks to* Peter*, indignant, humiliated.*)

Anne. Aren't they awful? Aren't they impossible? Treating us as if we were still in the nursery.

(*She sits on the cot.* Peter *gets a bottle of pop and two glasses.*)

Peter. Don't let it bother you. It doesn't bother me.

Anne. I suppose you can't really blame them . . . they think back to what *they* were like at our age. They don't realize how much more advanced we are . . . When you think what wonderful discussions we've had! . . . Oh, I forgot. I was going to bring you some more pictures.

Peter. Oh, these are fine, thanks.

Anne. Don't you want some more? Miep just brought me some new ones.

Peter. Maybe later. (*He gives her a glass of pop and, taking some for himself, sits down facing her.*)

Anne (*looking up at one of the photographs*). I remember when I got that . . . I won it. I bet Jopie that I could eat five ice-cream cones. We'd all been playing ping-pong . . . We used to have heavenly times . . . we'd finish up with ice cream at the Delphi, or the Oasis, where Jews were allowed . . . there'd always be a lot of boys . . . we'd laugh and joke . . . I'd like to go back to it for a few days or a week. But after that I know I'd be bored to death. I think more seriously about life now. I want to be a journalist . . . or something. I love to write. What do you want to do?

Peter. I thought I might go off some place . . . work on a farm or something . . . some job that doesn't take much brains.

Anne. You shouldn't talk that way. You've got the most awful inferiority complex.

Peter. I know I'm not smart.

Anne. That isn't true. You're much better than I am in dozens of things . . . arithmetic and algebra and . . . well, you're a million times better than I am in algebra. (*with sudden directness*) You like Margot, don't you? Right from the start you liked her, liked her much better than me.

Peter (*uncomfortably*). Oh, I don't know.

(*In the main room* Mrs. Van Daan *comes from the bathroom and goes over to the sink, polishing a coffee pot.*)

Anne. It's all right. Everyone feels that way. Margot's so good. She's sweet and bright and beautiful and I'm not.

Peter. I wouldn't say that.

Anne. Oh, no, I'm not. I know that. I know quite well that I'm not a beauty. I never have been and never shall be.

Peter. I don't agree at all. I think you're pretty.

Anne. That's not true!

Peter. And another thing. You've changed . . . from at first, I mean.

Anne. I have?

Peter. I used to think you were awful noisy.

Anne. And what do you think now, Peter? How have I changed?

Peter. Well . . . er . . . you're . . . quieter.

Lines 605–636

DISCUSSION PROMPTS

Use these prompts to help students understand Mrs. Van Daan's reaction:

Connect If you were Anne, would visiting Peter be worth the criticism? Why or why not? *Students might say that they would continue their visits just on principle. Others might say that they would meet in the common room or not visit as frequently, because they wouldn't want to hear the comments.*

Compare and Contrast How has Mrs. Van Daan's attitude toward Anne's friendship with Peter changed from earlier in the play? Reread lines 672–679 in Act One to compare. ***Possible answer:*** *Mrs. Van Daan seemed to encourage Anne's pursuit of Peter in the beginning. She called Anne his "little girl friend." Now she seems resentful of their friendship and tries to discourage it.*

Speculate What might account for Mrs. Van Daan's attitude? Explain. ***Possible answer:*** *Mrs. Van Daan is jealous of the attention that Anne gets from Peter. Earlier, Mrs. Van Daan may have felt involved in their relationship. Now, they shut her out.*

Lines 653–664

LITERARY ANALYSIS

● THEME

How does Anne think she has changed? ***Possible answer:*** *Anne says that she is more serious now. Before, socializing was important to her. Now, she thinks she would tire of that activity in a short time.*

If students need help . . . Ask them to think about what has changed Anne (*living under difficult circumstances and fearing for her life*). Then guide them to identify a theme that might be taken from the change in Anne. ***Possible answer:*** *Great stress or undergoing a crisis can change someone's priorities.*

FOR ENGLISH LEARNERS

Language: Comparisons Discuss the use of subjective and objective pronouns in comparisons. Display and explain these examples:

- *You're much better than I am* (lines 671–672). The pronoun *I* is used because it is the subject of the verb *am*.
- *Right from the start you liked her . . . much better than* [you liked] *me* (lines 675–676). *Me* is used because it is the object of the verb *liked*. The bracketed phrase is understood as part of the sentence structure.

Have students work together to choose the correct pronoun in these sentences:

1. Anne is noisier than (he, him) is. *(he)*
2. Mrs. Frank has trouble understanding Anne. Mrs. Frank understands Margot better than (she, her). *(her)*
3. The comments bother Peter less than they bother (she, her). *(her)*
4. Anne shares a room, but Peter has his own room. Anne has less privacy than (he, him). *(he)*

Lines 739–754

LITERARY ANALYSIS

● THEME

How does Anne's uncertainty about the future affect her attitude about her life in the present? ***Possible answer:*** *Because she doesn't know if she even has a future, she is eager to take advantage of the present and experience what she can before it is too late.*

Extend the Discussion Is Anne's attitude realistic under the circumstances? Explain.

(*In his room* Dussel *takes his pajamas and toilet articles and goes into the bathroom to change.*)

Anne. I'm glad you don't just hate me.

Peter. I never said that.

Anne. I bet when you get out of here you'll never think of me again.

Peter. That's crazy.

Anne. When you get back with all of your friends, you're going to say . . . now what did I ever see in that Mrs. Quack Quack.

Peter. I haven't got any friends.

Anne. Oh, Peter, of course you have. Everyone has friends.

Peter. Not me. I don't want any. I get along all right without them.

Anne. Does that mean you can get along without me? I think of myself as your friend.

Peter. No. If they were all like you, it'd be different.

(*He takes the glasses and the bottle and puts them away. There is a second's silence and then* Anne *speaks, hesitantly, shyly.*)

Anne. Peter, did you ever kiss a girl?

Peter. Yes. Once.

Anne (*to cover her feelings*). That picture's crooked. (Peter *goes over, straightening the photograph.*) Was she pretty?

Peter. Huh?

Anne. The girl that you kissed.

Peter. I don't know. I was blindfolded. (*He comes back and sits down again.*) It was at a party. One of those kissing games.

Anne (*relieved*). Oh. I don't suppose that really counts, does it?

Peter. It didn't with me.

Anne. I've been kissed twice. Once a man I'd never seen before kissed me on the cheek when he picked me up off the ice and I was crying. And the other was Mr. Koophuis, a friend of Father's who kissed my hand. You wouldn't say those counted, would you?

Peter. I wouldn't say so.

Anne. I know almost for certain that Margot would never kiss anyone unless she was engaged to them. And I'm sure too that Mother never touched a man before Pim. But I don't know . . . things are so different now . . . What do you think? Do you think a girl shouldn't kiss anyone except if she's engaged or something? It's so hard to try to think what to do, when here we are with the whole world falling around our ears and you think . . . well . . . you don't know what's going to happen tomorrow and . . . What do you think?

Peter. I suppose it'd depend on the girl. Some girl anything they do's wrong. But others . . . well . . . it wouldn't necessarily be wrong with them. (*The carillon starts to strike nine o'clock.*) I've always thought that when two people . . .

Anne. Nine o'clock. I have to go.

Peter. That's right.

Anne (*without moving*). Good night.

(*There is a second's pause, then* Peter *gets up and moves toward the door.*)

Peter. You won't let them stop you coming?

Anne. No. (*She rises and starts for the door.*) Sometime I might bring my diary. There are so many things in it that I want to talk over with you. There's a lot about you.

Peter. What kind of things?

Anne. I wouldn't want you to see some of it. I thought you were a nothing, just the way you thought about me.

Peter. Did you change your mind, the way I changed my mind about you?

Anne. Well . . . You'll see . . .

(*For a second* Anne *stands looking up at* Peter*, longing for him to kiss her. As he makes no move she turns away. Then suddenly* Peter *grabs her awkwar in his arms, kissing her on the cheek.* Anne *walks ou dazed. She stands for a minute, her back to the peop in the main room. As she regains her poise she goes to her mother and father and* Margot*, silently kissing them. They murmur their good nights to her. As she* *s about to open her bedroom door, she catches sight of* /Irs. Van Daan. *She goes quickly to her, taking her* *ice in her hands and kissing her first on one cheek* *nd then on the other. Then she hurries off into her* *oom.* Mrs. Van Daan *looks after her, and then looks* *ver at* Peter*'s room. Her suspicions are confirmed.*)

Irs. Van Daan (*She knows.*) Ah hah!

(*The lights dim out. The curtain falls on the scene.* *n the darkness* Anne's Voice *comes faintly at first* *nd then with growing strength.*)

nne's Voice. By this time we all know each other o well that if anyone starts to tell a story, the rest an finish it for him. We're having to cut down till further on our meals. What makes it worse, he rats have been at work again. They've carried ff some of our precious food. Even Mr. Dussel vishes now that Mouschi was here. Thursday, the wentieth of April, nineteen forty-four. Invasion ever is mounting every day. Miep tells us that eople outside talk of nothing else. For myself, ife has become much more pleasant. I often go to 'eter's room after supper. Oh, don't think I'm in ove, because I'm not. But it does make life more bearable to have someone with whom you can exchange views. No more tonight. P.S. . . . I must be honest. I must confess that I actually live for the next meeting. Is there anything lovelier than to sit under the skylight and feel the sun on your cheeks and have a darling boy in your arms? I admit now that I'm glad the Van Daans had a son and not a daughter. I've outgrown another dress. That's the third. I'm having to wear Margot's clothes after all. I'm working hard on my French and am now reading *La Belle Nivernaise.*

(*As she is saying the last lines—the curtain rises on the scene. The lights dim on, as* Anne's Voice *fades out.*)

Scene 3

It is night, a few weeks later. Everyone is in bed. There is complete quiet. In the Van Daans' *room a match flares up for a moment and then is quickly put out.* Mr. Van Daan, *in bare feet, dressed in underwear and trousers, is dimly seen coming stealthily down the stairs and into the main room, where* Mr. *and* Mrs.

533

Lines 800–810

REINFORCE *KEY IDEA:* IMPACT

Discuss What **impact** have Anne's visits to Peter had on her life? ***Possible answer:*** *She describes her life as much more pleasant now. She has a renewed sense of purpose and new energy. He has made her believe in a future.*

ANALYZE VISUALS

Activity Does this photograph capture the personality of Anne as she is portrayed in the play? Why or why not? *Students may say that it does. Anne has been described as sprawling on the floor as the actress is in the photograph. The actress also appears intent on her writing, which is characteristic of Anne.*

DIFFERENTIATED INSTRUCTION

FOR ENGLISH LEARNERS

Vocabulary Support Remind students that Anne writes in her diary as if she is writing a letter to a friend. In line 804, she includes a *P.S.* Explain that these initials stand for *postscript,* a message that comes after the main text. Tell students that using *P.S.* indicates that the writer has thought of something else he or she wants to add.

FOR ADVANCED LEARNERS/PRE–AP

Analyze Review the definition of *dramatic irony* (*the audience knows something that the characters do not*). Discuss how dramatic irony can increase suspense, heighten interest, and add complications to a plot. Then have students find examples of dramatic irony in the play up to this point. Have them record the examples and describe how each affects their understanding and appreciation of the play. They might begin by looking at lines 792–796. Have students share their results.

Speculate [small-group option] Under different circumstances, would the relationship between Peter and Anne be likely to last? Have students examine what they know about them and their interactions and then form their opinion supported by reasons and evidence from the text. Have students discuss the question in small groups.

Lines 816–839

READING SKILL

■ STORY MAPPING

What have the residents of the Annex just discovered? (Remind students to record the event in their story maps.) ***Answer:*** *Mr. Van Daan has been stealing food.*

Lines 858–880

REINFORCE *KEY IDEA:* IMPACT

Discuss Why does Mr. Van Daan's theft have such a strong **impact** on Mrs. Frank? ***Possible answer:*** *Mrs. Frank feels betrayed. She cannot believe someone would take food away from his own child. In addition, Mrs. Frank is worn down by her own years of deprivation. She is just as hungry as everyone else.*

Lines 881–894

LITERARY ANALYSIS

● THEME

Why do you think Mr. Frank doesn't support his wife's demand that the Van Daans leave? ***Possible answer:*** *He knows that they would soon be caught by the Nazis, and he may want to give Mr. Van Daan another chance. He may also think that the security of the rest of them might be compromised if the Van Daans left.*

If students need help . . . Work together to create a list of Mr. Frank's actions throughout the play (*invites the Van Daans and Mr. Dussel to share the Annex, brings Anne's photographs and gives her a diary, comforts Anne, investigates the noise in the warehouse*). Point out how each of his actions shows him to be compassionate and levelheaded. To agree that the Van Daans should leave would go against his character traits.

Targeted Passage ⑦

Frank *and* Margot *are sleeping. He goes to the food safe and again lights a match. Then he cautiously opens the safe, taking out a half-loaf of bread. As he closes the safe, it creaks. He stands rigid.* Mrs. Frank *sits up in bed. She sees him.*

Mrs. Frank (*screaming*). Otto! Otto! *Komme schnell!*[5]

(*The rest of the people wake, hurriedly getting up.*)

Mr. Frank. *Was ist los? Was ist passiert?*[6]

(Dussel, *followed by* Anne, *comes from his room.*)

Mrs. Frank (*as she rushes over to* Mr. Van Daan). *Er stiehlt das Essen!*[7]

Dussel (*grabbing* Mr. Van Daan). You! You! Give me that.

Mrs. Van Daan (*coming down the stairs*). Putti . . . Putti . . . what is it?

Dussel (*his hands on* Van Daan*'s neck*). You dirty thief . . . stealing food . . . you good-for-nothing . . .

Mr. Frank. Mr. Dussel! For God's sake! Help me, Peter!

(Peter *comes over, trying, with* Mr. Frank, *to separate the two struggling men.*)

Peter. Let him go! Let go!

(Dussel *drops* Mr. Van Daan, *pushing him away. He shows them the end of a loaf of bread that he has taken from* Van Daan.)

Dussel. You greedy, selfish . . . !

(Margot *turns on the lights.*)

Mrs. Van Daan. Putti . . . what is it?

(*All of* Mrs. Frank*'s gentleness, her self-control, is gone. She is outraged, in a frenzy of indignation.*)

Mrs. Frank. The bread! He was stealing the bread!

Dussel. It was you, and all the time we thought it was the rats!

Mr. Frank. Mr. Van Daan, how could you!

Mr. Van Daan. I'm hungry.

Mrs. Frank. We're all of us hungry! I see the chil[d] getting thinner and thinner. Your own son Peter I've heard him moan in his sleep, he's so hungry And you come in the night and steal food that should go to them . . . to the children!

Mrs. Van Daan (*going to* Mr. Van Daan *protectively*). He needs more food than the rest [of] us. He's used to more. He's a big man.

(Mr. Van Daan *breaks away, going over and sitti[ng] on the couch.*)

Mrs. Frank (*turning on* Mrs. Van Daan). And you . . . you're worse than he is! You're a mothe[r] and yet you sacrifice your child to this man . . this . . . this . . .

Mr. Frank. Edith! Edith!

(Margot *picks up the pink woolen stole, putting i[t] over her mother's shoulders.*)

Mrs. Frank (*paying no attention, going on to* Mrs Van Daan). Don't think I haven't seen you! Alw[ays] saving the choicest bits for him! I've watched y[ou] day after day and I've held my tongue. But not any longer! Not after this! Now I want him to g[o]! I want him to get out of here!

Mr. Frank. Edith!

Mr. Van Daan. Get out of here?

Mrs. Van Daan. What do you mean?

} *Togethe[r]*

Mrs. Frank. Just that! Take your things and get o[ut]

Mr. Frank (*to* Mrs. Frank). You're speaking in anger. You cannot mean what you are saying.

Mrs. Frank. I mean exactly that!

(Mrs. Van Daan *takes a cover from the* Franks' *be[d] pulling it about her.*)

Mr. Frank. For two long years we have lived here, side by side. We have respected each other's rights . . . we have managed to live in peace. Are we now going to throw it all away? I know this will never happen again, will it, Mr. Van Daan?

5. ***Komme schnell!*** (kôm'e shnĕl') *German*: Come quickly!
6. ***Was ist los? Was ist passiert?*** (väs ĭst lôs'? väs ĭst päsērt'?) *German*: What's the matter? What has happened?
7. ***Er stiehlt das Essen!*** (ĕr shtēlt' däs ĕs'ən) *German*: He is stealing food!

DIFFERENTIATED INSTRUCTION

FOR LESS–PROFICIENT READERS

⑦ **Targeted Passage [Lines 851–894]**

This passage shows the conflict among the Annex residents reaching a peak after the discovery that Mr. Van Daan is stealing food.

- How is Mrs. Frank's behavior different from the way she usually acts?
- What does she demand that Mr. Van Daan do? Why?
- What is Mr. Frank's reaction?

FOR ENGLISH LEARNERS

Comprehension Support Make sure students understand that for the characters, a mystery has been cleared up. They thought that rats were to blame for missing amounts of food. Now, having caught Mr. Van Daan in the act of stealing, they understand that he has probably been taking food for a while. Encourage students to predict what might happen to Mr. Van Daan.

Mr. Van Daan. No. No.

Mrs. Frank. He steals once! He'll steal again!

(Mr. Van Daan, *holding his stomach, starts for the bathroom.* Anne *puts her arms around him, helping him up the step.*)

Mr. Frank. Edith, please. Let us be calm. We'll all go to our rooms . . . and afterwards we'll sit down quietly and talk this out . . . we'll find some way . . .

Mrs. Frank. No! No! No more talk! I want them to leave!

Mrs. Van Daan. You'd put us out, on the streets?

Mrs. Frank. There are other hiding places.

Mrs. Van Daan. A cellar . . . a closet. I know. And we have no money left even to pay for that.

Mrs. Frank. I'll give you money. Out of my own pocket I'll give it gladly. (*She gets her purse from a shelf and comes back with it.*)

Mrs. Van Daan. Mr. Frank, you told Putti you'd never forget what he'd done for you when you came to Amsterdam. You said you could never repay him, that you . . .

Mrs. Frank (*counting out money*). If my husband had any obligation to you, he's paid it, over and over.

Mr. Frank. Edith, I've never seen you like this before. I don't know you.

Mrs. Frank. I should have spoken out long ago.

Dussel. You can't be nice to some people.

Mrs. Van Daan (*turning on* Dussel). There would have been plenty for all of us, if *you* hadn't come in here!

Mr. Frank. We don't need the Nazis to destroy us. We're destroying ourselves.

(*He sits down, with his head in his hands.* Mrs. Frank *goes to* Mrs. Van Daan.)

Mrs. Frank (*giving* Mrs. Van Daan *some money*). Give this to Miep. She'll find you a place.

Anne. Mother, you're not putting *Peter* out. Peter hasn't done anything.

Mrs. Frank. He'll stay, of course. When I say I must protect the children, I mean Peter too.

(Peter *rises from the steps where he has been sitting.*)

Peter. I'd have to go if Father goes.

(Mr. Van Daan *comes from the bathroom.* Mrs. Van Daan *hurries to him and takes him to the couch. Then she gets water from the sink to bathe his face.*)

Mrs. Frank (*while this is going on*). He's no father to you . . . that man! He doesn't know what it is to be a father!

Peter (*starting for his room*). I wouldn't feel right. I couldn't stay.

Mrs. Frank. Very well, then. I'm sorry.

Anne (*rushing over to* Peter). No, Peter! No! (Peter *goes into his room, closing the door after him.* Anne *turns back to her mother, crying.*) I don't care about the food. They can have mine! I don't want it! Only don't send them away. It'll be daylight soon. They'll be caught . . .

Margot (*putting her arms comfortingly around* Anne). Please, Mother!

Mrs. Frank. They're not going now. They'll stay here until Miep finds them a place. (*to* Mrs. Van Daan) But one thing I insist on! He must never come down here again! He must never come to this room where the food is stored! We'll divide what we have . . . an equal share for each! (Dussel *hurries over to get a sack of potatoes from the food safe.* Mrs. Frank *goes on, to* Mrs. Van Daan.) You can cook it here and take it up to him.

(Dussel *brings the sack of potatoes back to the center table.*)

Margot. Oh, no. No. We haven't sunk so far that we're going to fight over a handful of rotten potatoes.

Dussel (*dividing the potatoes into piles*). Mrs. Frank, Mr. Frank, Margot, Anne, Peter, Mrs. Van Daan, Mr. Van Daan, myself . . . Mrs. Frank . . .

(*The buzzer sounds in* Miep's *signal.*)

Mr. Frank. It's Miep! (*He hurries over, getting his overcoat and putting it on.*)

Margot. At this hour?

Mrs. Frank. It is trouble.

Lines 897–899

LITERARY ANALYSIS

● THEME

Why do you think Mr. Van Daan feels ill? What does this reaction show about him? ***Possible answer:*** *Mr. Van Daan realizes the enormity of his actions. He feels disgusted with himself. This reaction shows that he still has a conscience and can feel remorse.*

Extend the Discussion Will Mr. Van Daan steal again? Why or why not?

Lines 831–971
DISCUSSION PROMPTS

Use these prompts to help students understand the feelings of various characters:

Connect Which character has the reaction that you might have in a similar situation? *Students may say that they would feel as outraged as Mrs. Frank and would want the Van Daans to leave. Some might try to calm everyone down, as Mr. Frank does. Others might feel horrified that the Van Daans are to be thrown out, like Anne and Margot. Some students might react like Mr. Dussel.*

Analyze What is Mr. Dussel's motivation for his behavior during this crisis? ***Possible answer:*** *He is looking out for himself. He wants to ensure his survival, no matter what.*

Analyze Explain what Mr. Frank means when he says, "We don't need the Nazis to destroy us. We're destroying ourselves." ***Possible answer:*** *He means that the only way they can survive is if they cooperate. If the group becomes torn by anger and disagreement, then they are lost.*

FOR LESS–PROFICIENT READERS

Concept Support [small-group option] Use a Cause-and-Effect Diagram (Multiple Effects) to explore the negative consequences of Mrs. Frank's demand that the Van Daans leave the Annex. Have small groups think of the effects on the Van Daans, those left behind, and Miep. Record ideas on the class chart.

 **BEST PRACTICES TOOLKIT—Transparency**
Cause-and-Effect Diagram pp. B16, B38

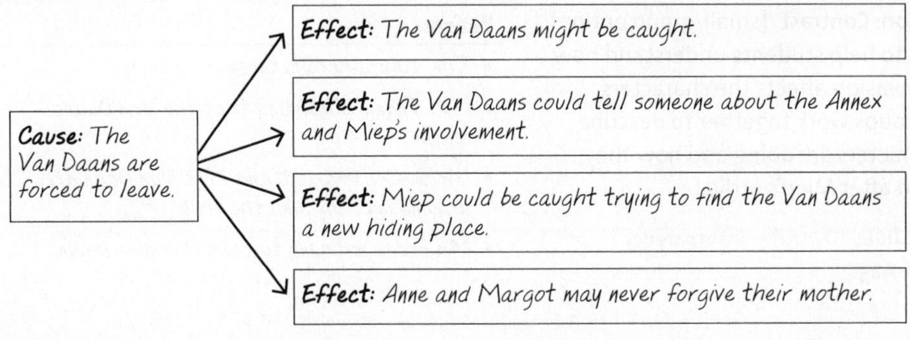

Cause: The Van Daans are forced to leave.
Effect: The Van Daans might be caught.
Effect: The Van Daans could tell someone about the Annex and Miep's involvement.
Effect: Miep could be caught trying to find the Van Daans a new hiding place.
Effect: Anne and Margot may never forgive their mother.

BACKGROUND

Normandy Invasion In line 993, Miep rushes into the Annex with news of the invasion. The invasion of Normandy took place on June 6, 1944. Over 6,000 vessels left British ports to cross the channel to France, while overhead 13,000 planes dropped bombs and parachutists. The battle for Normandy took two months, but by August, Allied troops had liberated much of France and were on their way to reclaiming western Europe from German occupation.

Lines 999–1019

REINFORCE *KEY IDEA:* IMPACT

Discuss What **impact** does the news of the invasion have on the characters? ***Possible answer:*** *Hostility is forgotten as Mrs. Frank hugs Mr. Van Daan and Mr. Dussel embraces Mrs. Van Daan. The others sing and parade around the room.*

Lines 992–1028

READING SKILL

STORY MAPPING

What does the invasion of Normandy mean for the residents of the Annex? (Remind students to record the event on their story maps.) ***Possible answer:*** *The invasion means that the end of the war is a possibility, not just a hope. It means that their ordeal may be over soon.*

Mr. Frank (*as he starts down to unbolt the door*). I beg you, don't let her see a thing like this!

Mr. Dussel (*counting without stopping*). . . . Anne, Peter, Mrs. Van Daan, Mr. Van Daan, myself . . .

Margot (*to* Dussel). Stop it! Stop it!

Dussel. . . . Mr. Frank, Margot, Anne, Peter, Mrs. Van Daan, Mr. Van Daan, myself, Mrs. Frank . . .

Mrs. Van Daan. You're keeping the big ones for yourself! All the big ones . . . Look at the size of that! . . . And that! . . .

(Dussel *continues on with his dividing.* Peter, *with his shirt and trousers on, comes from his room.*)

Margot. Stop it! Stop it!

(*We hear* Miep*'s excited voice speaking to* Mr. Frank *below.*)

Miep. Mr. Frank . . . the most wonderful news! . . . The invasion has begun!

Mr. Frank. Go on, tell them! Tell them!

(Miep *comes running up the steps, ahead of* Mr. Frank. *She has a man's raincoat on over her nightclothes and a bunch of orange-colored flowers in her hand.*)

Miep. Did you hear that, everybody? Did you hear what I said? The invasion has begun! The invasion!

(*They all stare at* Miep, *unable to grasp what she is telling them.* Peter *is the first to recover his wits.*)

Peter. Where?

Mrs. Van Daan. When? When, Miep?

Miep. It began early this morning . . .

(*As she talks on, the realization of what she has said begins to dawn on them. Everyone goes crazy. A wild demonstration takes place.* Mrs. Frank *hugs* Mr. Van Daan.)

Mrs. Frank. Oh, Mr. Van Daan, did you hear that?

(Dussel *embraces* Mrs. Van Daan. Peter *grabs a frying pan and parades around the room, beating on it, singing the Dutch National Anthem.* Anne *and* Margot *follow him, singing, weaving in and out among the excited grownups.* Margot *breaks away to take the flowers from* Miep *and distribute them to everyone. While this* **pandemonium** *is going on* Mrs. Frank *tries to make herself heard above th excitement.*)

Mrs. Frank (*to* Miep). How do you know?

Miep. The radio . . . The B.B.C.! They said th landed on the coast of Normandy!

Peter. The British?

Miep. British, Americans, French, Dutch, Pole Norwegians . . . all of them! More than four thousand ships! Churchill spoke, and General Eisenhower! D-Day they call it!

Mr. Frank. Thank God, it's come!

Mrs. Van Daan. At last!

Miep (*starting out*). I'm going to tell Mr. Krale This'll be better than any blood transfusion.

Mr. Frank (*stopping her*). What part of Norman did they land, did they say?

Miep. Normandy . . . that's all I know now . . . I'll be up the minute I hear some more! (*She g hurriedly out.*)

Mr. Frank (*to* Mrs. Frank). What did I tell you? What did I tell you?

(Mrs. Frank *indicates that he has forgotten to bo the door after* Miep. *He hurries down the steps.* Mr. Van Daan, *sitting on the couch, suddenly breaks into a convulsive sob. Everybody looks at him, bewildered.*)

Mrs. Van Daan (*hurrying to him*). Putti! Putti! What is it? What happened?

Mr. Van Daan. Please. I'm so ashamed.

(Mr. Frank *comes back up the steps.*)

Dussel. Oh, for God's sake!

Mrs. Van Daan. Don't, Putti.

Margot. It doesn't matter now!

Mr. Frank (*going to* Mr. Van Daan). Didn't you hear what Miep said? The invasion has come! We're going to be liberated! This is a time to celebrate!

(*He embraces* Mrs. Frank *and then hurries to the cupboard and gets the cognac and a glass.*)

Mr. Van Daan. To steal bread from children!

DIFFERENTIATED INSTRUCTION

FOR LESS-PROFICIENT READERS

Comprehension: Contrast [small-group option] Use a T Chart to help students understand how word of the invasion affects the characters. Have small groups work together to describe what the characters are doing and how they act before and after Miep's arrival.

BEST PRACTICES TOOLKIT—Transparency
T Chart p. A25

Before	*After*
• *The atmosphere is tense.*	• *Everyone is wildly happy.*
• *Mrs. Frank is insisting that the Van Daans leave.*	• *Mrs. Frank hugs Mr. Van Daan.*
• *Mr. Dussel, Margot, and Mrs. Van Daan are arguing over dividing the food.*	• *Mr. Dussel hugs Mrs. Van Daan.*
• *Mr. Frank is trying to calm everyone down.*	• *Mr. Van Daan sobs because he is ashamed.*
	• *Mr. Frank gets cognac to celebrate.*

Ⓑ Targeted Passage

Mrs. Frank. We've all done things that we're ashamed of.

Anne. Look at me, the way I've treated Mother . . . so mean and horrid to her.

Mrs. Frank. No, Anneke, no.

(Anne *runs to her mother, putting her arms around her.*)

Anne. Oh, Mother, I was. I was awful.

Mr. Van Daan. Not like me. No one is as bad as me!

Dussel (*to* Mr. Van Daan). Stop it now! Let's be happy!

Mr. Frank (*giving* Mr. Van Daan *a glass of cognac*). Here! Here! *Schnapps! L'chaim!*[8]

(Van Daan *takes the cognac. They all watch him. He gives them a feeble smile.* Anne *puts up her fingers in a V-for-Victory sign. As* Van Daan *gives an answering V-sign, they are startled to hear a loud sob from behind them. It is* Mrs. Frank, *stricken with* ***remorse.*** *She is sitting on the other side of the room.*)

Mrs. Frank (*through her sobs*). When I think of the terrible things I said . . .

(Mr. Frank, Anne, *and* Margot *hurry to her, trying to comfort her.* Mr. Van Daan *brings her his glass of cognac.*)

Mr. Van Daan. No! No! You were right!

Mrs. Frank. That I should speak that way to you! . . . Our friends! . . . Our guests! (*She starts to cry again.*)

Dussel. Stop it, you're spoiling the whole invasion!

(*As they are comforting her, the lights dim out. The curtain falls.*)

Anne's Voice (*faintly at first and then with growing strength*). We're all in much better spirits these days. There's still excellent news of the invasion. The best part about it is that I have a feeling that friends are coming. Who knows? Maybe I'll be back in school by fall. Ha, ha! The joke is on us! The warehouse man doesn't know a thing and we are paying him all that money! . . . Wednesday, the second of July, nineteen forty-four. The invasion seems temporarily to be bogged down. Mr. Kraler has to have an operation, which looks bad. The Gestapo have found the radio that was stolen. Mr. Dussel says they'll trace it back and back to the thief, and then, it's just a matter of time till they get to us. Everyone is low. Even poor Pim can't raise their spirits. I have often been downcast myself . . . but never in despair. I can shake off everything if I write. But . . . and that is the great question . . . will I ever be able to write well? I want to so much. I want to go on living even after my death. Another birthday has gone by, so now I am fifteen. Already I know what I want. I have a goal, an opinion.

(*As this is being said—the curtain rises on the scene, the lights dim on, and* Anne's Voice *fades out.*)

Scene 4

It is an afternoon a few weeks later . . . Everyone but Margot *is in the main room. There is a sense of great tension.*

Both Mrs. Frank *and* Mr. Van Daan *are nervously pacing back and forth,* Dussel *is standing at the window, looking down fixedly at the street below.* Peter *is at the center table, trying to do his lessons.* Anne *sits opposite him, writing in her diary.* Mrs. Van Daan *is seated on the couch, her eyes on* Mr. Frank *as he sits reading.*

The sound of a telephone ringing comes from the office below. They all are rigid, listening tensely. Mr. Dussel *rushes down to* Mr. Frank.

Dussel. There it goes again, the telephone! Mr. Frank, do you hear?

Mr. Frank (*quietly*). Yes. I hear.

Dussel (*pleading, insistent*). But this is the third time, Mr. Frank! The third time in quick succession! It's a signal! I tell you it's Miep, trying to get us! For some reason she can't come to us and she's trying to warn us of something!

8. ***Schnapps!*** (shnäps) *German*: Brandy! ***L'chaim!*** (lə KHä'yĭm) *Hebrew*: To life!

Lines 1071–1086

LITERARY ANALYSIS

● THEME

What does Mrs. Frank's remorse show about her previous outburst? ***Possible answer:*** *Her outrage at Mr. Van Daan was fueled by exhaustion and tension. Now that some of the anxiety has been relieved, she is back to her normal self, which is more tolerant and forgiving.*

Lines 1090–1112

READING SKILL

■ STORY MAPPING

What mixture of good and bad news does Anne's diary entry contain? ***Possible answer:*** *The residents of the Annex now believe that they have been paying Carl for nothing; he is unaware of their presence in the warehouse. Although that is good news, it is offset by the bad news that Mr. Kraler needs to have an operation and the invasion is not moving forward very quickly. Also, the stolen radio has been recovered, which means the thief might be found.*

If students need help . . . Have them return to lines 1949–2086 in Act One. Remind them that the thief heard them in the Annex and might use that information to help himself if he is caught.

FOR LESS–PROFICIENT READERS

Ⓑ **Targeted Passage [Lines 1058–1087]**

This passage presents the resolution of the conflict caused by the discovery of Mr. Van Daan's theft.

- How do you know that Mrs. Frank has forgiven Mr. Van Daan?
- What does Anne say to her mother? Why?
- Why does Mrs. Frank begin to cry?
- Will the residents find it easier to be nice to each other from now on? Why or why not?

FOR ADVANCED LEARNERS/PRE-AP

Analyze Irony Just as real life is often ironic, so is there irony in many of the circumstances of this play, including this scene. Have students chart the irony they find and discuss its effect on readers' appreciation of events and characters and on the communication of theme.

Analyze Mood What is the mood of the opening passage of Scene 4? Ask students to describe the mood and explain how the playwrights create this atmosphere through their choice of words and phrases.

Lines 1139–1164

READING SKILL

■ STORY MAPPING

Why are the residents of the Annex so tense? (Have students record what is happening in this part of the play on their story maps.) ***Possible answer:*** *The phone keeps ringing, Miep has not been to see them for three days, and the workers haven't shown up at the warehouse, even though it is a Friday.*

Lines 1165–1193

DISCUSSION PROMPTS

Use these prompts to help students understand the build-up of suspense in this scene:

Connect Would you answer the phone? Why or why not? *Students might say that they would, to end the suspense of not knowing who it is. Others might say that they would not, in case it was a trick.*

Analyze How are the reactions of the characters consistent with their behavior up to now? ***Possible answer:*** *Mr. Van Daan blames Mrs. Van Daan for the situation they are in. Mrs. Van Daan is hysterical. They argue with each other as they have in the past. Mr. Dussel plunges into action, just as he did in the conflict over the food. Mr. Frank tries to keep everyone calm.*

Synthesize Why do you think Miep has not visited in three days and the workers did not show up on a Friday? ***Possible answer:*** *The Nazis may have discovered the hiding place and will not allow people into the area.*

Lines 1204–1217

LITERARY ANALYSIS

● THEME

What is Anne's purpose in this speech? ***Possible answer:*** *She is trying to cheer Peter up.*

Mr. Frank. Please. Please.

Mr. Van Daan (*to* Dussel). You're wasting your breath.

Dussel. Something has happened, Mr. Frank. For three days now Miep hasn't been to see us! And today not a man has come to work. There hasn't been a sound in the building!

Mrs. Frank. Perhaps it's Sunday. We may have lost track of the days.

Mr. Van Daan (*to* Anne). You with the diary there. What day is it?

Dussel (*going to* Mrs. Frank). I don't lose track of the days! I know exactly what day it is! It's Friday, the fourth of August. Friday, and not a man at work. (*He rushes back to* Mr. Frank, *pleading with him, almost in tears.*) I tell you Mr. Kraler's dead. That's the only explanation. He's dead and they've closed down the building, and Miep's trying to tell us!

Mr. Frank. She'd never telephone us.

Dussel (*frantic*). Mr. Frank, answer that! I beg you, answer it!

Mr. Frank. No.

Mr. Van Daan. Just pick it up and listen. You don't have to speak. Just listen and see if it's Miep.

Dussel (*speaking at the same time*). For God's sake . . . I ask you.

Mr. Frank. No. I've told you, no. I'll do nothing that might let anyone know we're in the building.

Peter. Mr. Frank's right.

Mr. Van Daan. There's no need to tell us what side you're on.

Mr. Frank. If we wait patiently, quietly, I believe that help will come.

(*There is silence for a minute as they all listen to the telephone ringing.*)

Dussel. I'm going down. (*He rushes down the steps.* Mr. Frank *tries ineffectually to hold him.* Dussel *runs to the lower door, unbolting it. The telephone stops ringing.* Dussel *bolts the door and comes slowly back up the steps.*) Too late. (Mr. Frank *goes to* Margo[t and] Anne*'s bedroom.*)

Mr. Van Daan. So we just wait here until we die

Mrs. Van Daan (*hysterically*). I can't stand it! I'll kill myself! I'll kill myself!

Mr. Van Daan. For God's sake, stop it!

(*In the distance, a German military band is hear[d] playing a Viennese waltz.*)

Mrs. Van Daan. I think you'd be glad if I did! I think you want me to die!

Mr. Van Daan. Whose fault is it we're here? (M[rs.] Van Daan *starts for her room. He follows, talkin[g] at her.*) We could've been safe somewhere . . . in America or Switzerland. But no! No! You wouldn't leave when I wanted to. You couldn't leave your things. You couldn't leave your precious furniture.

Mrs. Van Daan. Don't touch me!

(*She hurries up the stairs, followed by* Mr. Van Daan. Peter, *unable to bear it, goes to his room.* Anne *looks after him, deeply concerned.* Dussel *returns to his post at the window.* Mr. Frank *co[mes] back into the main room and takes a book, tryin[g to] read.* Mrs. Frank *sits near the sink, starting to pe[el] some potatoes.* Anne *quietly goes to* Peter*'s room, closing the door after her.* Peter *is lying face dow[n] on the cot.* Anne *leans over him, holding him in [her] arms, trying to bring him out of his despair.*)

Anne. Look, Peter, the sky. (*She looks up throug[h] the skylight.*) What a lovely, lovely day! Aren't t[he] clouds beautiful? You know what I do when it seems as if I couldn't stand being cooped up for [one] more minute? I *think* myself out. I think myse[lf] on a walk in the park where I used to go with Pim. Where the jonquils and the crocus and t[he] violets grow down the slopes. You know the m[ost] wonderful part about *thinking* yourself out? Yo[u] can have it any way you like. You can have ros[es] and violets and chrysanthemums all blooming [at] the same time . . . It's funny . . . I used to take [it] all for granted . . . and now I've gone crazy ab[out] everything to do with nature. Haven't you?

DIFFERENTIATED INSTRUCTION

FOR LESS–PROFICIENT READERS

Concept Support To help students understand the dramatic structure of the play, display a Plot Diagram. Have students refer to their story maps and identify the events that are part of the rising action. Record them on the diagram to illustrate how the events lead to the climax. Have students use their prior knowledge and text evidence to predict what the climactic event will be.

BEST PRACTICES TOOLKIT—Transparency
Plot Diagram p. D12

Possible events for the plot diagram:

1. *Franks and Van Daans move to the Annex.*
2. *Mr. Dussel joins them.*
3. *Thief in the warehouse hears them.*
4. *Carl seems to be blackmailing Mr. Kraler.*
5. *Mr. Kraler is hospitalized and the ration book suppliers are arrested.*
6. *Mr. Van Daan is found stealing food.*
7. *They receive news of the invasion.*
8. *Miep is absent and the warehouse is deserted.*

Peter. I've just gone crazy. I think if something doesn't happen soon . . . if we don't get out of here . . . I can't stand much more of it!

Anne (*softly*). I wish you had a religion, Peter.

Peter. No, thanks! Not me!

Anne. Oh, I don't mean you have to be Orthodox[9] . . . or believe in heaven and hell and purgatory and things . . . I just mean some religion . . . it doesn't matter what. Just to believe in something! When I think of all that's out there . . . the trees . . . and flowers . . . and seagulls . . . when I think of the dearness of you, Peter . . . and the goodness of the people we know . . . Mr. Kraler, Miep, Dirk, the vegetable man, all risking their lives for us every day . . . When I think of these good things, I'm not afraid any more . . . I find myself, and God, and I . . .

(Peter *interrupts, getting up and walking away.*)

Peter. That's fine! But when I begin to think, I get mad! Look at us, hiding out for two years. Not able to move! Caught here like . . . waiting for them to come and get us . . . and all for what?

Anne. We're not the only people that've had to suffer. There've always been people that've had to . . . sometimes one race . . . sometimes another . . . and yet . . .

Peter. That doesn't make me feel any better!

Anne (*going to him*). I know it's terrible, trying to have any faith . . . when people are doing such horrible . . . But you know what I sometimes think? I think the world may be going through a phase, the way I was with Mother. It'll pass, maybe not for hundreds of years, but some day . . . I still believe, in spite of everything, that people are really good at heart.

Peter. I want to see something now . . . Not a thousand years from now! (*He goes over, sitting down again on the cot.*)

Anne. But, Peter, if you'd only look at it as part of a great pattern . . . that we're just a little minute in the life . . . (*She breaks off.*) Listen to us, going at each other like a couple of stupid grownups! Look at the sky now. Isn't it lovely? (*She holds out her hand to him.* Peter *takes it and rises, standing with her at the window looking out, his arms around her.*) Some day, when we're outside again, I'm going to . . .

(9) Targeted Passage

(*She breaks off as she hears the sound of a car, its brakes squealing as it comes to a sudden stop. The people in the other rooms also become aware of the sound. They listen tensely. Another car roars up to a screeching stop.* Anne *and* Peter *come from* Peter*'s room.* Mr. *and* Mrs. Van Daan *creep down the stairs.* Dussel *comes out from his room. Everyone is listening, hardly breathing. A doorbell clangs again and again in the building below.* Mr. Frank *starts quietly down the steps to the door.* Dussel *and* Peter *follow him. The others stand rigid, waiting, terrified.*

In a few seconds Dussel *comes stumbling back up the steps. He shakes off* Peter*'s help and goes to his room.* Mr. Frank *bolts the door below, and comes slowly back up the steps. Their eyes are all on him as he stands there for a minute. They realize that what they feared has happened.* Mrs. Van Daan *starts to whimper.* Mr. Van Daan *puts her gently in a chair, and then hurries off up the stairs to their room to collect their things.* Peter *goes to comfort his mother. There is a sound of violent pounding on a door below.*)

Mr. Frank (*quietly*). For the past two years we have lived in fear. Now we can live in hope.

(*The pounding below becomes more insistent. There are muffled sounds of voices, shouting commands.*)

Men's Voices. *Auf machen! Da drinnen! Auf machen! Schnell! Schnell! Schnell! etc., etc.*[10]

(*The street door below is forced open. We hear the heavy tread of footsteps coming up.* Mr. Frank *gets two school bags from the shelves, and gives one to* Anne *and the other to* Margot. *He goes to get a bag for* Mrs. Frank. *The sound of feet coming up grows*

9. **Orthodox:** Orthodox Jews who strictly observe Jewish laws and traditions.

10. **Auf machen! . . . Schnell!** (ouf' mäzкн'ən! dä drĭn'ən! ouf' mäкн'ən! shnĕl! shnĕl! shnĕl!) *German:* Open up! Inside there! Open up! Quick! Quick! Quick!

Lines 1223–1234

LITERARY ANALYSIS

THEME

Who are the people who have helped Anne and the others? How does the thought of them affect Anne? ***Possible answer:*** *She names Mr. Kraler, Miep, Miep's fiancé Dirk, and the vegetable man as having helped them. She says the thought of what they have done helps her not to be afraid.*

Lines 1245–1252

LITERARY ANALYSIS

THEME

How does Anne's experience with her mother influence her view of what is happening in the world? ***Possible answer:*** *Even though she loves her mother and has not meant to hurt her, Anne knows that she has been very cruel to her. She believes that world events are similar—people are doing hurtful things that are wrong, but it is just a phase and it will pass.*

Lines 1265–1303

READING SKILL

STORY MAPPING

What is the climax of the plot? (Have students record this event on their story maps.) ***Possible answer:*** *The discovery of the hiding place is the moment of highest tension and the point at which the outcome of the play can be foreseen.*

FOR LESS–PROFICIENT READERS

(9) Targeted Passage [Lines 1265–1297]

This passage presents the climax of the plot: the Nazis discover the hiding place.

- What noise is heard outside that indicates they may be in danger?
- Whom do the voices and footsteps coming up the stairs belong to?
- Why does Mr. Frank get bags for Anne, Margot, and Mrs. Frank?

FOR ADVANCED LEARNERS/PRE–AP

Synthesize [small-group option] In lines 1287–1288, Mr. Frank says, "For the past two years we have lived in fear. Now we can live in hope." Ask students to respond to that quotation in a short paragraph. Have them share what they have written in small groups.

Analyze Theme [small-group option] What other messages might be taken from the characters' experiences throughout the play? Ask students to work in groups to develop a theme statement related to one of the major topics of the play, such as war, the effects of stress on people, the strength of the human spirit, courage, faith, and family. Have students volunteer their statements and discuss the evidence from the text that conveys this message.

Lines 1347–1368

READING SKILL

■ STORY MAPPING

What happens after the soldiers take the group away? ***Possible answer:*** *They are sent to concentration camps. Only Mr. Frank survives.*

BACKGROUND

Anne's Fate Everyone in the Annex was first taken to a transit camp in Holland, where they spent a few weeks before being sent to Auschwitz in Poland. In Auschwitz they were separated by gender. Anne never saw her father again. Later she and Margot were sent on to Bergen-Belsen, a camp in Germany. There they both contracted typhus and died a few weeks before the Allies liberated the camp in April 1945.

Lines 1323–1328

LITERARY ANALYSIS

● THEME

In what way has Mr. Frank changed from the first scene of the play? How does this change support the major theme? ***Possible answer:*** *After reading Anne's positive and optimistic vision of the world, Mr. Frank is no longer bitter or angry. Her words help him see the world differently and restore the goodness in his heart.*

louder. Peter *comes to* Anne, *kissing her good-bye, then he goes to his room to collect his things. The buzzer of their door starts to ring.* Mr. Frank *brings* Mrs. Frank *a bag. They stand together, waiting. We hear the thud of gun butts on the door, trying to break it down.*

Anne *stands, holding her school satchel, looking over at her father and mother with a soft, reassuring smile. She is no longer a child, but a woman with courage to meet whatever lies ahead.*

The lights dim out. The curtain falls on the scene. We hear a mighty crash as the door is shattered. After a second Anne's Voice *is heard.)*

Anne's Voice. And so it seems our stay here is over. They are waiting for us now. They've allowed us five minutes to get our things. We can each take a bag and whatever it will hold of clothing. Nothing else. So, dear Diary, that means I must leave you behind. Good-bye for a while. P.S. Please, please, Miep, or Mr. Kraler, or anyone else. If you should find this diary, will you please keep it safe for me, because some day I hope . . .

(*Her voice stops abruptly. There is silence. After a second the curtain rises.*)

Scene 5

It is again the afternoon in November, 1945. The rooms are as we saw them in the first scene. Mr. Kraler *has joined* Miep *and* Mr. Frank. *There are coffee cups on the table. We see a great change in* Mr. Frank. *He is calm now. His bitterness is gone. He slowly turns a few pages of the diary. They are blank.*

Mr. Frank. No more. (*He closes the diary and puts it down on the couch beside him.*)

Miep. I'd gone to the country to find food. When I got back the block was surrounded by police . . .

Mr. Kraler. We made it our business to learn how they knew. It was the thief . . . the thief who told them.

(Miep *goes up to the gas burner, bringing back a of coffee.*)

Mr. Frank (*after a pause*). It seems strange to say this, that anyone could be happy in a concentration camp. But Anne was happy in the camp in Holland where they first took us. After two years of being shut up in these rooms she could be out . . . out in the sunshine and the fresh air that she loved.

Miep (*offering the coffee to* Mr. Frank). A little more?

Mr. Frank (*holding out his cup to her*). The new of the war was good. The British and America were sweeping through France. We felt sure that they would get to us in time. In Septemb we were told that we were to be shipped to Poland . . . The men to one camp. The wome to another. I was sent to Auschwitz. They wen to Belsen. In January we were freed, the few of who were left. The war wasn't yet over, so it too us a long time to get home. We'd be sent her and there behind the lines where we'd be safe Each time our train would stop . . . at a siding or a crossing . . . we'd all get out and go from group to group . . . Where were you? Were yo at Belsen? At Buchenwald? At Mauthausen? Is possible that you knew my wife? Did you ever s my husband? My son? My daughter? That's ho I found out about my wife's death . . . of Marg the Van Daans . . . Dussel. But Anne . . . I stil hoped . . . Yesterday I went to Rotterdam. I'd heard of a woman there . . . She'd been in Belse with Anne . . . I know now.

(*He picks up the diary again, and turns the page back to find a certain passage. As he finds it we h* Anne's Voice.)

Anne's Voice. In spite of everything, I still beli that people are really good at heart.

(Mr. Frank *slowly closes the diary.*)

Mr. Frank. She puts me to shame. (*They are sile The Curtain Falls.*

⑩ **Targeted Passage**

DIFFERENTIATED INSTRUCTION

FOR LESS–PROFICIENT READERS

⑩ Targeted Passage [Lines 1331–1368]

This passage ties up loose ends of the plot.

- Why had Miep stayed away from the Annex?
- Who told the soldiers of their hiding place?
- Where were the residents of the Annex taken? Then what happened to them?
- Why does it take Mr. Frank so long to get home after he has been freed?
- How does he find out what happened to his family?

Concept Support Use a web diagram to complete discussion of theme. Place the statement *People are good at heart* in the center and have students volunteer ways in which that idea is supported in Act Two. They should include these and other examples: *Miep baked a cake with all of her sugar, Margot was kind to Anne regarding Peter, Mr. Frank defended the Van Daans, Mrs. Frank forgave Mr. Van Daan, and Anne attempted to cheer up Peter.*

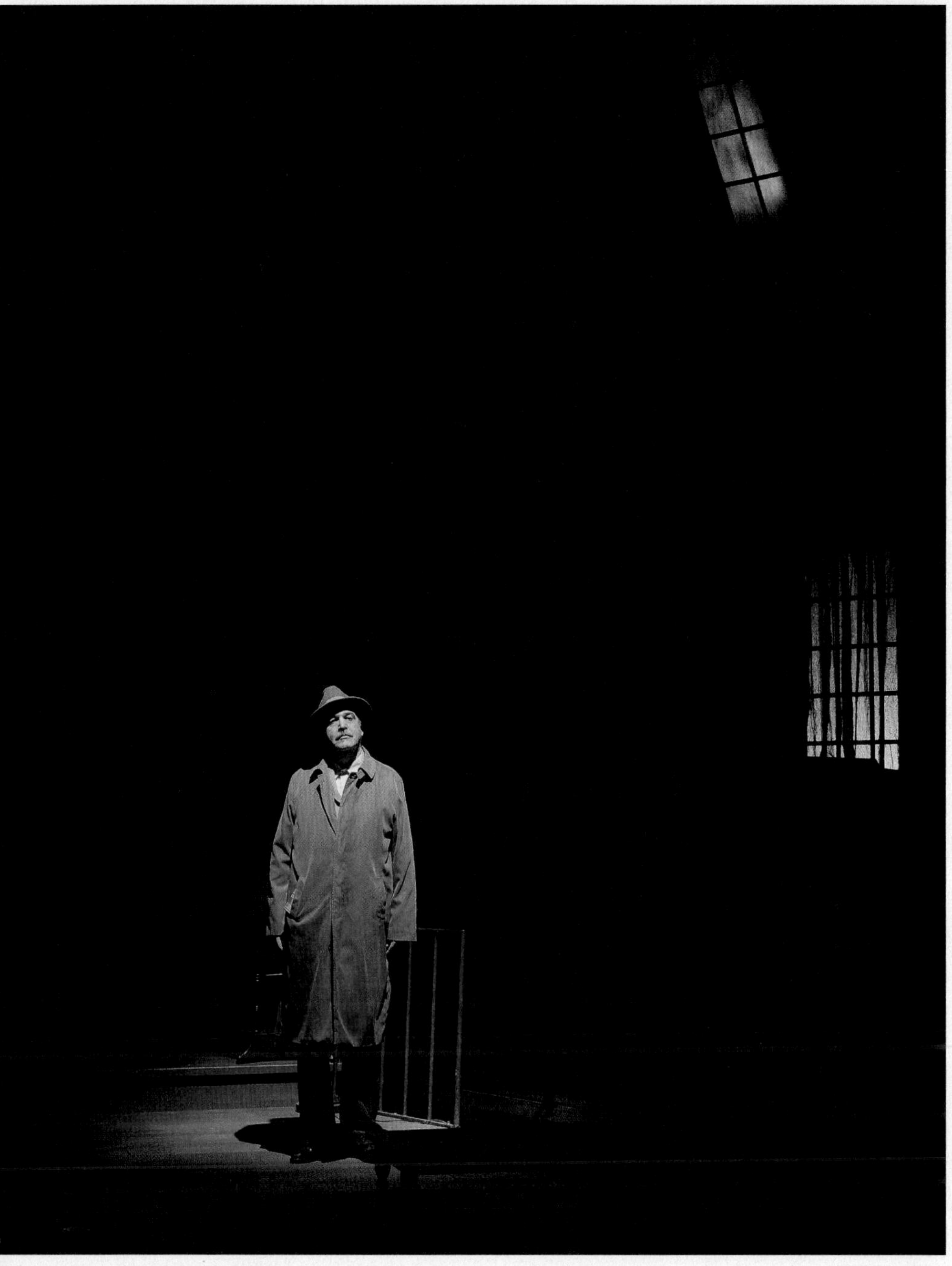

ANALYZE VISUALS

Activity Have students compare this photograph with the one on page 523 that begins the act. How does the contrast emphasize the message of the photograph on this page? ***Possible answer:*** *The photograph on page 523 is filled with people and light. The inhabitants are still together and because they are alive, they still have hope. In the final photograph, the darkness creates a mood of sadness or finality, while the solitary figure of Mr. Frank emphasizes his loss.*

SELECTION WRAP-UP

REFLECT Ask students what makes the fate of Anne and the others particularly hard to accept.

CRITIQUE Ask students whether the play develops the hardships suffered by Anne and the others fully enough. Have students explain their responses.

FOR LESS–PROFICIENT READERS

Reading Skill Follow-Up: Story Mapping

[small-group option] Have students work in small groups to review their story maps for accuracy and discuss problem areas or inconsistencies. Be sure to include these events from the end of Act Two: *The group receives word of the invasion. Miep does not appear for three days, and the warehouse is deserted. The Nazis discover the Annex and take everyone away.*

Practice and Apply

After Reading

For additional support of postreading questions, use these copy masters:

RESOURCE MANAGER—Copy Masters

Reading Check p. 129 (to check understanding of the selection)

Theme p. 123 (for practice of literary analysis standards focus)

Question Support p. 130 (After Reading questions adapted for English learners and less-proficient readers)

Additional selection questions are provided for teachers on page 115.

For additional activities to challenge students, see

Power Thinking at **ClassZone.com**

After Reading

Comprehension

1. **Recall** Who was stealing the bread in the Annex?
2. **Clarify** According to Margot, why don't Anne and her mother get along?
3. **Summarize** Why does the man from the storeroom request extra money?

Literary Analysis

4. **Complete Your Story Map** Review your story map and make sure you're satisfied. Then circle the event you consider to be the climax of the play, and add the play's resolution. Remember the **climax** is the point of highest action, and the **resolution** is the point at which the conflict is resolved.
5. **Draw Conclusions** Mrs. Van Daan doesn't need her fur coat in the attic. Why does she react so strongly when Mr. Van Daan wants to sell it?
6. **Interpret Characters' Actions** Why do Anne and Mrs. Frank apologize to each other after hearing about the invasion of Normandy? Think about what **impact** the circumstances might have had on their attitudes.
7. **Analyze Flashback** A flashback is a scene from an earlier time that interrupts the ongoing action of a story. Most of the play takes place during the war years, but the first and last scene take place after the war. Make a timeline like the one shown that clarifies the order in which important events happen. How does reading about the events out of order affect your understanding?

8. **Evaluate Theme** At the end of Act Two, Anne shares with Peter her ideas about the tragic events they have been hearing about. She says, "I think the world may be going through a phase . . . . It'll pass." How do Anne's ideas illustrate the theme of the play? How does Peter react to her ideas?

Extension and Challenge

9. **Creative Project: Drama** With a small group of classmates, choose a scene that supports the play's theme and practice acting it out. When you perform for the class, explain why you chose the scene you did.
10. **SOCIAL STUDIES CONNECTION** Many Jews in Europe escaped their countries or went into hiding when the Nazis came to power. Research one of the following people to find out how ordinary people tried to save themselves from the Nazis: Yettie Mendels, Erika Van Hesteren, Alfred Lessing, and Joseph Heinrich. Present your findings to the class.

RESEARCH LINKS
For more on the Holocaust, visit the **Research Center** at **ClassZone.com.**

ANSWERS

Comprehension

1. *Mr. Van Daan was stealing the bread.*
2. *They don't get along because they are too different. It is not in Mrs. Frank's nature to fight or stand up for herself as Anne does.*
3. *Mr. Kraler thinks the man wants money for keeping quiet about the Franks.*

Literary Analysis

Possible answers:

4. **STANDARDS FOCUS Story Mapping** *The climax is when the Nazis find the hiding place. This resolves the major conflict of the play, although Mr. Frank's return to the Annex after the war might be considered a resolution as he comes to accept what happened and we find out what happened to the characters.*
5. *To Mrs. Van Daan, her coat represents her life of comfort and security before the war.*
6. *They realize that their problems with each other are petty. The invasion makes them feel more optimistic about the chance of being rescued.*
7. *Seeing Mr. Frank bitter and disillusioned makes readers want to know about the events that brought him to this point.*
8. **STANDARDS FOCUS Theme** *Anne's words show her optimism and belief in the fundamental goodness of people. Peter, thinking about their experiences in the past two years, is more skeptical and cannot quite trust in the implicit goodness of human nature.*

Extension and Challenge

9. *Students should choose an appropriate scene and act it out meaningfully. Their performances should show evidence of rehearsal.*
10. **SOCIAL STUDIES CONNECTION** *Many of those who hid during World War II had to move quite frequently, such as Yettie Mendels. Suggest that students first create a timeline of the person's life during this period and then fill in important details.*

ading-Writing Connection

ncrease your understanding of *The Diary of Anne Frank* by responding to these rompts. Then complete the **Grammar and Writing** exercise.

WRITING PROMPTS	SELF-CHECK
A. Short Response: Describe a Relationship Anne's relationship with Peter is an important subplot in the play. Write a **one-paragraph description** that summarizes her changing feelings toward Peter. Consider how having a peer to talk to helped Anne cope with conflict both inside and outside the Annex.	***An effective description will . . .*** • describe Anne's feelings toward Peter at different points in the play • support statements with quotations from the characters
B. Extended Response: Evaluate a Legacy Why do you think Anne Frank's diary has made an **impact** on countless readers around the world? Write **two or three paragraphs** explaining why readers might identify with Anne and draw inspiration from her life.	***An insightful evaluation will . . .*** • describe Anne's personality • convey your ideas about why Anne's outlook on life is inspiring and unique

AMMAR AND WRITING

APITALIZE CORRECTLY Languages, nationalities, ethnicities, political parties, nd religions should always be capitalized. Here are some examples:

anguages—English, Spanish, Russian, Chinese

ountries and Nationalities—Mexico, Canada, Irish, South African

thnicities—Hispanic, Native American, Caucasian, Asian

olitical Parties—Democrats, Republicans, Socialists, Nazis

eligions—Judaism, Islam, Christianity, Buddhism

Example: Although the Franks lived in Holland, their first language was German.

RACTICE Rewrite the following sentences, correcting any errors in apitalization. A sentence may contain more than one error.

1. Not all germans wanted the nazis to be in control.
2. For many europeans, it was dangerous to practice judaism.
3. Because they were jewish, the Franks fled to holland to escape persecution.
4. Anne Frank's diary was translated into many languages, including english.

*or more help with capitalization, see page R51 in the **Grammar Handbook.***

DIFFERENTIATED INSTRUCTION

FOR LESS–PROFICIENT WRITERS

For Prompt A:

1. Have students revisit lines 688–722 in Act One and lines 365–442 and 637–776 in Act Two to find out how Anne feels about Peter in the beginning, middle, and end of the play.
2. Discuss what students find out. Then give them a basic outline for their paragraphs: *In the beginning, Anne thinks Peter _____.* *In the middle, Anne feels Peter _______.* *By the end, Anne sees Peter as _______.*

For Prompt B:

1. Reread Anne's diary entries aloud and together identify and record important quotations or ideas about her.
2. Have small groups decide which three or four examples they connect to most strongly and why.
3. Help students form a topic sentence: *Readers today can still connect to Anne Frank's feelings and her experiences.* Then have them complete their paragraphs.

Reading-Writing Connection

WRITING PROMPTS

- For **Prompt A,** suggest that students revisit these lines to find out how Anne's feelings about Peter change throughout the play: Act One: 348–440, 585–611, 688–722, 1824–1843; Act Two: 365–442, 637–776, 1204–1264.
- For **Prompt B,** suggest that students look back at Anne's diary entries at the end of each scene. Have them use a T Chart to identify aspects of Anne's personality and experience to which others might connect.

BEST PRACTICES TOOLKIT—Transparency
T Chart p. A25

For an extended Reading-Writing Connection activity, see

Writing Center at **ClassZone.com**

GRAMMAR AND WRITING

Remind students to check a dictionary if they are not sure whether to capitalize a word.

Answers:

1. *Not all Germans wanted the Nazis to be in control.*
2. *For many Europeans, it was dangerous to practice Judaism.*
3. *Because they were Jewish, the Franks fled to Holland to escape persecution.*
4. *Anne Frank's diary was translated into many languages, including English.*

RESOURCE MANAGER—Copy Master
Capitalize Correctly p. 131

Assess and Reteach

Assess

RESOURCE MANAGER—Copy Masters
Selection Tests A, B/C pp. 133–134, 135–136

Test Generator CD

Reteach

STANDARDS LESSON FILE
Literature Lesson 5: Elements of Plot
Literature Lesson 13: Theme

Focus and Motivate

OBJECTIVES

Reading for Information

- synthesize information
- make a generalization
- read a newspaper article and an interview

SUMMARY

The author of "A Diary from Another World" writes about her visits to Anne Frank's hiding place and reflects on what Anne may have thought about during her life in hiding. An interview with one of Anne's close childhood friends describes the Franks' disappearance, life in Amsterdam after the Nazi occupation, details about the concentration camps, and her encounters with Anne at Bergen-Belsen.

What's the Connection?

Use a KWL chart to prepare students for the selections. Ask students to brainstorm what they already know about Anne Frank, the Holocaust, and World War II. Add their information to the first column of the chart. Then invite students to discuss what confuses them and what they hope to learn from the article and the interview. Write their questions in the second column of the chart. After students have read the selections, have them volunteer information for the third column.

BEST PRACTICES TOOLKIT—Transparency
KWL: Know, Want to Know, Learned p. A21

Teach

Skill Focus: Synthesize

Ask students to consider the following questions as they fill in the chart:

- Which account(s) give information about life in a German concentration camp?
- Which account(s) give information about life for Jewish families living in Amsterdam?
- In what way do the article and the interview fill in gaps in your impressions of Anne Frank and her experience?

Possible chart entries appear on page 552.

RESOURCE MANAGER—Copy Master
Synthesize p. 145

Reading for Information

Beyond *The Diary of Anne Frank*

- Newspaper Article, page 545
- Interview, page 547

Use with *The Diary of Anne Frank,* page 486.

What's the Connection?

In *The Diary of Anne Frank,* you learned what life in hiding was like for Anne and her family. Now you will read accounts from two Holocaust survivors that will tell you more about Anne, Nazi-occupied Amsterdam, and the concentration camp where the Franks were sent.

Skill Focus: Synthesize

Reading a play, diary, or book about a topic can teach you a great deal. However, you can seldom get a complete picture from any one source. To fully understand something, you have to **synthesize,** or connect facts, details, and ideas from different sources in order to form new ideas about the topic.

In this lesson, you will synthesize what you have already learned from *The Diary of Anne Frank* and one of Anne's diary entries (page 520) with information and impressions from two more sources. Your goal is to develop a fuller picture of what life was like for Jewish families in Nazi-occupied Amsterdam and in the Bergen-Belsen concentration camp.

To begin, use a chart like the one shown to record what you've learned from the play and from Anne's diary entry. Then read the next selections to add to your knowledge and fill in gaps in your understanding. Continue filling in the chart with what you learn about life under the Nazis.

	Life for a Jewish family hiding in Amsterdam	Life for a Jewish family living openly in Amsterdam	Life in a German concentration camp	Impressions of Anne Frank
The Diary of Anne Frank & Anne's December 1943 diary entry				
"A Diary from Another World"				
from *The Last Seven Months of Anne Frank*				

Selection Resources

RESOURCE MANAGER UNIT 4

Plan and Teach pp. 137–141

Reading
Summary pp. 143†*, 144‡*
Synthesize pp. 145, 147†*
Reading Check p. 149
Make a Generalization pp. 146, 148†*
Question Support p. 150*

Assessment
Selection Tests A, B/C pp. 151*, 153*
Test Generator CD

Reading Support
Audio Anthology CD*

BEST PRACTICES TOOLKIT
KWL: Know, Want to Know, Learned • Common Suffixes • Word Questioning • Think-Pair-Share • Sequence Chain

* Resources for Differentiation † Also in Spanish ‡ In Haitian Creole and Vietnamese

A Diary from Another World

Gerda Weissmann Klein

"On Friday, June 12, I woke up at 6 A.M. and—small wonder—it was my birthday. I received a warm welcome from my cat and masses of things from Mummy and Daddy . . ."

Any 13-year-old girl could have written that on her birthday. As it happens these words appear in a diary which was one of the "masses of things" and in which Anne Frank wrote: "I hope I shall be able to confide in you completely, as I have never been able to do in anyone before . . ."

She thought that what she would write in her diary would be for her eyes alone, so she committed her innermost thoughts to it. She thought that perhaps in the very distant future—when she might have children, or even grandchildren, that they might on a rainy afternoon find their grandmother's old diary. . . .

Alas, Anne Frank died as a young girl, for no other reason than that she was Jewish. The Nazis invaded Holland, as they did most other European countries, and anyone who loved freedom and equality and was free of prejudice became an enemy of the Nazi regime. . . .

I visited Anne Frank's house the other day. Actually, I visited it twice—once alone at night when it was tightly closed, the inside shrouded in darkness. It conveyed then the eerie feeling of a tomb in which Anne's unfulfilled dreams had been dreamed during many lonely nights. . . .

Then I returned during the daytime, as the sun shone brightly and the carillon[1] from the nearby clock tower, of which Anne had written, was just playing a merry tune. In the bright sunlight, I heard music playing, saw boats moving on the canal and observed people walking by.

Across the canal I noticed a boutique, saw some young people looking at sweaters. Two kids in jeans rode on bicycles. Life was going on, even as it must have gone on while she lived there. **A**

Front of Anne Frank House, Amsterdam, the Netherlands

A SYNTHESIZE
What are Gerda Weissmann Klein's impressions of Anne Frank's house and neighborhood?

1. **carillon** (kăr′ə-lŏn′): set of tuned bells in a tower.

Practice and Apply

BACKGROUND

Gerda Weissmann Klein Like Anne Frank, Gerda Weissmann was a teenager when she lost her freedom. In 1942, Nazis took her from her home in Poland and sent her to a forced-labor camp. In 1945, after three years of forced labor, Gerda was forced to go with the Nazis as they fled from the advancing Soviet army. At the time of her rescue, the day before her 21st birthday, she weighed 68 pounds. Gerda's family and friends all perished in the Holocaust. She later married her liberator, a U.S. Army lieutenant named Kurt Klein, and the two dedicated their lives to teaching others tolerance and hope.

INFORMATIONAL ANALYSIS

A SYNTHESIZE

Possible answer: *When she first visits the house at night, her impression is that of an eerie tomb. When she returns in the daytime, her impressions are positive. She sees the sun shining brightly and hears church bells and other music. She sees people and boats, and she can imagine Anne looking out on her life as it used to be.*

DIFFERENTIATED INSTRUCTION

FOR LESS–PROFICIENT READERS

Concept Support Explain that most newspaper journalists aim to be neutral, or objective, by presenting only facts. However, the writer of this article also presents her impressions and opinions. Ask students to look for words and phrases that signal the writer's opinions. ***Possible answer:*** *"It conveyed then the eerie feeling of a tomb" (lines 35–36); "I found it sadder during the daytime" (lines 53–54); "Through understanding, let us assure that . . ." (lines 100–101)*

FOR ENGLISH LEARNERS

Options for Reading Be sure students understand the term *synthesize.* Explain that they synthesize information when they get it from more than one source. For example, if they learn about an event by reading a newspaper, watching a TV news broadcast, and looking online, then they are synthesizing. Preview the selection titles and ask students what they expect to learn about Anne Frank from the selections. Students may then read along with the *Audio Anthology CD.*

READING FOR INFORMATION 545

Lines 60–97

DISCUSSION PROMPTS

Use these prompts to help students understand the author's perspective on Anne Frank's experience:

Connect Anne Frank wishes she could take part in the same world as everyone else. What "ordinary things" in your life would you miss if you were confined to a hiding place like Anne? *Students may mention spending time with friends, playing sports, going to the mall, and other everyday activities.*

Infer What can you infer about Anne from the description of the pictures hanging over her bed? ***Possible answer:*** *The pictures of movie stars and a chimpanzee's birthday party show that Anne enjoys glamour and humor.*

Speculate Gerda Weissmann Klein is a survivor of the Holocaust. What do you think motivated her to visit Anne Frank's hiding place in Amsterdam? ***Possible answer:*** *She may have wanted to honor Anne's memory and find out how Anne's experiences were similar to and different from her own.*

INFORMATIONAL ANALYSIS

B SYNTHESIZE

Have students record their answers in the chart from page 544. ***Possible answer:*** *Anne's thoughts are very much like those of other young people. She wants to live a normal life filled with pleasure, friends, and ordinary activities such as going to school or to the movies. The description of the building where Anne hid gives insight into how cramped her daily life was and how she could clearly see life on the street but never be part of it.*

Actually, I found it sadder during the daytime, for the night at least seemed to shut out the rest of the world, whereas during the day everything revolved around the silent, subdued girl who so desperately wanted to be a part of that stream of life.

What did she think about in those tiny rooms where shutters had to be closed in the daytime? She tells us that often the heat became oppressive from the tiny stove on which the families cooked their meals. We know that the toilet could not be flushed in the daytime, lest the neighbors would be alerted to the existence of the hiding place.

What did Anne Frank think about as she sat on her bed during those perilous days looking at the pictures of American movie stars and a picture of a chimpanzee's birthday party which still hangs there today?

Her diary tells us that she thought not of fame, nor wealth, nor greatness. She thought rather how much she would want to run downstairs into the ti garden where sunflowers now bloo against the fence, instead of having glimpse them from far above.

She thought of touching them a running through a meadow in t spring, of buying an ice cream cone fro a vendor on a hot summer afternoon.

She thought of ordinary thing such as going to school with other kid She thought of dressing up and beir able to go to the movies.

In short, she thought of all t things which millions of kids do eve day and find boring. But to Anne, wh occasionally dared to climb to the ro to see the sky and the patch of worl below, that world was as remote as t evening star. B

This is the legacy she left us, t understanding of things all of us tal for granted. Through understandin let us assure that all people everywhe can live in freedom so that a book lik *The Diary of Anne Frank* will never b written again as a true story.

B SYNTHESIZE
Reread lines 76–97. What new insights about Anne's thoughts do you get from this article?

Anne Frank's diary

DIFFERENTIATED INSTRUCTION

FOR ENGLISH LEARNERS

Vocabulary: Suffixes [mixed-readiness pairs] Remind students that the suffix *-ous* means "filled with." Point out the word *perilous* in line 72. Explain that the word *peril* is a noun meaning "danger" and that adding the suffix *-ous* forms an adjective meaning "filled with danger." Then have pairs use Common Suffixes to identify and define other words with suffixes on this page (including *oppressive, existence, greatness, vendor,* and *occasionally*).

 **BEST PRACTICES TOOLKIT—Transparency**
Common Suffixes p. E15

Key Academic Vocabulary Have students use Word Questioning to study these words from "A Diary from Another World": *regime* (line 30), *whereas* (line 56), *assure* (line 101).

 **BEST PRACTICES TOOLKIT—Transparency**
Word Questioning p. E9

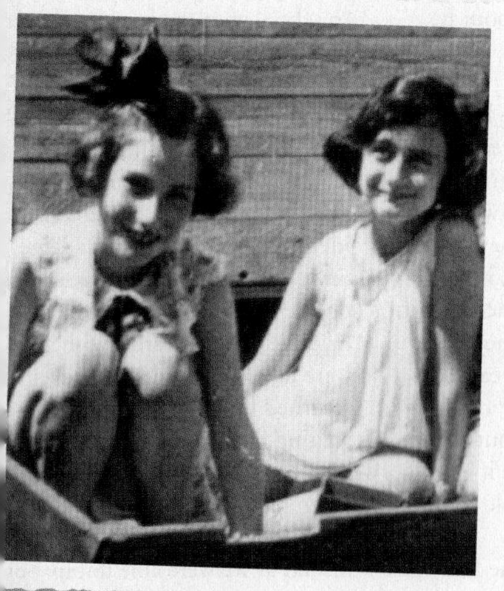

Hannah Elisabeth Pick-Goslar and Anne Frank

rom

The Last Seven Months of Anne Frank

nterview with Hannah Elisabeth Pick-Goslar

Willy Lindwer

Mr. Frank's factory, Opekta, produced a substance for naking jam. My mother always got he old packages as a gift. Soon after chool let out, my mother sent me to he Franks' house to get the scale because she wanted to make jam. t was a beautiful day.

I went as usual to the Franks' ouse and rang and rang and rang, but no one opened the door. I didn't know why no one answered. I rang again, and finally, Mr. Goudsmit, a tenant, opened the door. G

"What do you want? What have you come for?" he asked in astonishment.

"I've come to borrow the scale."

"Don't you know that the entire Frank family has gone to Switzerland?"

F FOCUS ON FORM

An **interview** is a meeting in which one person asks another about his or her thoughts, feelings, insights, or experiences. In this interview, which was conducted for a television documentary about Anne Frank, the questions asked by Willy Lindwer have been omited. Only Pick-Goslar's answers are printed.

G INTERVIEW

On the basis of the photograph and what you've read so far, what do you think might be the relationship between Hannah and Anne?

FOCUS ON FORM

Interview Discuss with students the purpose and characteristics of an interview. This type of writing

- informs or explains
- tells the point of view of the interviewee
- can either include both the questions and the answers from an interview or include only the answers

Have students look for Pick-Goslar's point of view as they read the interview.

BACKGROUND

A Close Friend Anne Frank refers several times in her diary to her friend "Lies Goosens." This is actually Hannah Elisabeth Pick-Goslar. The families of the two girls were neighbors and good friends. Anne's father, who survived the Holocaust, changed the names of people in her diary before it was published.

LITERARY ANALYSIS

G INTERVIEW

Possible answer: *They seem to be good friends who have a lot of fun together and whose families are very close.*

FOR LESS-PROFICIENT READERS

Comprehension Support Have students answer these questions as they read:

- Who is being interviewed? What relationship did this person have with Anne Frank?
- What did Pick-Goslar think had happened to the Franks? What actually happened?

Have students use Think-Pair-Share to answer selected Discussion Prompts.

 BEST PRACTICES TOOLKIT—Transparency
Think-Pair-Share p. A18

FOR ADVANCED LEARNERS/PRE-AP

Analyze [small-group option] Have students discuss these questions involving the opening passage in the interview (lines 1–28):

- What can you tell from this passage about the relationship between the Franks and the Pick-Goslars?
- In what way does the opening of the interview differ from the opening of Klein's article (page 545)? In what way is it similar?
- What does Mr. Goudsmit's reaction reveal about life in Nazi-occupied Amsterdam?

INFORMATIONAL ANALYSIS

D SYNTHESIZE

Have students record their answers in the chart from page 544. ***Possible answer:*** *Jews had to wear yellow stars and carry cards that identified them as Jewish. If they were stopped on the street and found to be Jewish, they were often taken away and never seen again.*

Lines 29–70

DISCUSSION PROMPTS

Use these prompts to help students understand daily life in Amsterdam during the Nazi occupation:

Recall What did Pick-Goslar's family do to avoid being harmed by the Nazis? ***Answer:*** *They obtained false Paraguayan passports.*

Infer What likely happened to Pick-Goslar's missing schoolmates and to others who disappeared? ***Possible answer:*** *The missing children could have been taken by the Nazis, left the country, or gone into hiding with their families, as Anne Frank did.*

Speculate Pick-Goslar says that the Frank family spent a year getting ready to go into hiding. What kinds of preparations might they have had to make? ***Possible answer:*** *They would have had to arrange a place to hide, invent a story to cover their disappearance, and find people willing to secretly bring them food and other supplies.*

D SYNTHESIZE
After the Franks went into hiding, what happened to other Jews in Amsterdam?

I didn't know anything about it. "Why?" I asked.

He didn't know either.

This was a bolt out of the blue. Why had they gone to Switzerland? The only connection the Frank family had with Switzerland was that Otto Frank's mother lived there.

But later it appeared that, in fact, the family had always reckoned that it would get worse for Jews. They had been preparing for a whole year to go into hiding. We didn't know anything about this. You can't talk about something like that. Because if anyone talked, then the whole affair would go amiss. . . .

I believe that Anne was the first girlfriend that I lost. It was, of course, very frightening, but we began to get used to the idea. When I went back to school after the summer, fewer children came to class every day.

We stayed in Amsterdam almo full year longer, until June 20, 19 and all this time things were getti worse and worse. Jews had to wea yellow star. We had an *Ausweis* (a identification card), with a large " on it—for Jew. People were stopp on the street: "May I see your *Ausweis?*" If you were Jewish, you were taken away and you never returned home. And a mother waiting for her child would ask herself: Where is my child? Have taken her away? . . . **D**

So far, my family had been luc insofar as we were able to buy Sou American citizenship through an uncle in Switzerland. We were expatriates. That's why it was

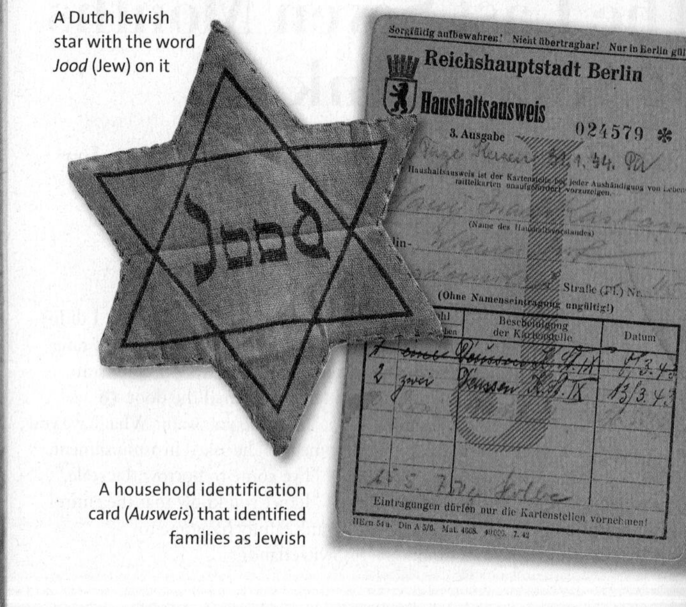

A Dutch Jewish star with the word *Jood* (Jew) on it

A household identification card (*Ausweis*) that identified families as Jewish

DIFFERENTIATED INSTRUCTION

FOR ENGLISH LEARNERS

Vocabulary: Idioms and Sayings Explain these expressions to students, and then help students use them in original sentences:

- *a bolt out of the blue* (line 24), "surprising, sometimes upsetting information"
- *go amiss* (line 37), "not happen as planned"
- *didn't have the heart* (lines 84–85), "did not want to cause pain"
- *went from door to door* (lines 93–94), "visited each house in a neighborhood"

FOR ADVANCED LEARNERS/PRE-AP

Synthesize [paired option] Have students briefly role-play an interview with Pick-Goslar's teacher, discussing the changing mood in Amsterdam and her thoughts and feelings about the disappearance of more and more of her students.

›ossible. We got passports from 'araguay. Laughing, my father said, You'd better know something about 'araguay in case they ask." So I earned the name of the capital, sunción. I didn't know anything lse, but no one ever asked me nything.

Because of these passports we ould still go out for a while longer vithout trembling in fear, but you ever knew what would happen omorrow. . . .

So we continued to live, with ittle to eat and with a great deal of ear, but at least we were at home. n October, my mother died during hildbirth. The baby was born dead. That was in Anne's diary. Someone old Anne that our baby had died, ›ut not that my mother had died oo. They probably didn't have the eart to tell her. . . . **E**

Everything went along fine until une 20, 1943, when there was the ›ig roundup in Amsterdam-South. On that day, the Germans started something new. At five o'clock in the morning while everyone was asleep they blocked off all the southern part of Amsterdam. They went from door to door, rang, and asked:

"Do Jews live here?"

"Yes."

"You have fifteen minutes; take a backpack, put a few things in it, and get outside quickly."

That was our neighborhood, so we had to pack too. A passport no longer helped. We had a quarter of an hour, and we had to go with them. . . .

So we were taken to Westerbork. My father ended up in a very large barracks. My sister and I were put in an orphanage, where, they said, there was more to eat. My father had known the director of the orphanage when he was in Germany. My little sister wasn't there very long. She became seriously ill and had to have operations on both ears. She was in the hospital for almost the entire time that we were in Westerbork. . . .

5 3 September 4 · Blatt

JUDENTRANSPORT AUS DEN NIEDERLANDEN - LAGER WESTERBORK

Haeftlinge

301.	Engers	Isidor	30.4. 93	Kaufmann
302	Engers	Leonard	15.6. 20	Lamdarbeiter
303	Franco	Manfred	1.5. 05	Verleger
304.	Frank	Arthur	22.8. 81	Kaufmann
305.	Frank	Isaac	29.11.87	Installateur
306.	Frank	Margot	16.2. 26	ohne
307.	Frank	Otto	12.5. 89	Kaufmann
308.	Frank-Hollaender	Edith	16.1. 00	ohne
309.	Frank	Anneliese	12.6. 29	ohne
310.	v.Franck	Sara	27.4. 02	Typistin
311.	Franken	Rozanna	16.5. 96	Landarbeiter
312.	Franken-Weyand	Johanna	24.12.96	Landbauer
313.	Franken	Hermann	12.5.34	ohne
314.	Franken	Louis	10.8. 17	Gaertner
315.	Franken	Rosalina	29.3. 27	Landbau
316.	Frankfort	Alex	14.11.19	Dr.i.d.Oekonomie

The Franks' names on a transport list from the Westerbork transit camp

E SYNTHESIZE
Reread lines 58–85. What strategies did Jews living openly use to survive? What hardships did they endure?

INFORMATIONAL ANALYSIS

E SYNTHESIZE

Have students record their answers in the chart from page 544. ***Possible answer:*** *Strategies included buying passports from another country and pretending to be expatriates, as Pick-Goslar's family did. They endured constant fear and hunger.*

Extend the Discussion Why do you think there was a shortage of food in Amsterdam?

FOR LESS–PROFICIENT READERS

Comprehension Support Point out that, in the interview, Pick-Goslar frequently uses dialogue to convey information. Remind students that writers use quotation marks to set off dialogue. Model looking for quotation marks and the introductory sentences that explain who is speaking. Help students identify the change of speakers in the narrative. Then read aloud lines 86–99, and ask students to tell who is speaking in lines 95–99.

FOR ADVANCED LEARNERS/PRE–AP

Synthesize Have students write ideas for a short story set in Nazi-occupied Amsterdam. Their notes should include details from the play, Anne Frank's diary entry, Klein's article, and this interview. Encourage students to give a brief description of each character and to outline a rough plot for their stories.

INFORMATIONAL ANALYSIS

F SYNTHESIZE

Possible answer: *In this incident, a woman offers to take care of Pick-Goslar's sister even though the woman is already taking care of seven children under very difficult conditions. This kindness and generosity is an illustration of the theme of the play—that deep down, people are basically good.*

Extend the Discussion Remind students of Anne Frank's words from page 540 of the play: "In spite of everything, I still believe that people are really good at heart." Ask them to recall other examples of human behavior—from Anne's diary or elsewhere—that illustrate this theme.

Lines 134–204

DISCUSSION PROMPTS

Use these prompts to help students understand Pick-Goslar's experiences at Bergen-Belsen:

Recall According to Pick-Goslar, what happened to concentration camp prisoners who became sick? ***Answer:*** *Anyone who got sick was taken away to a hospital so they wouldn't infect others in the camp.*

Infer Why do you think so many people in the concentration camps became sick? ***Possible answer:*** *They lived close together in unsanitary conditions, so infections spread easily. They also endured poor nutrition and had inadequate clothing to withstand the cold weather, which made them more vulnerable to illness.*

Speculate What might happen next in Pick-Goslar's narrative? How might the excerpt end? ***Possible answer:*** *Since the title is* The Last Seven Months of Anne Frank, *Pick-Goslar must be reunited with Anne before Anne dies. Since Pick-Goslar is telling her story, she must survive her experiences in the camps either by escaping or by being liberated.*

F SYNTHESIZE
Reread lines 148–162. What is the relationship between this incident and the **theme** of the play?

On February 15, 1944, we were transported to Bergen-Belsen. . . . When we arrived, our clothes weren't taken away and families weren't separated. My father and my sister stayed with me. We slept in different places, but we could see each other every evening. The trip took—I don't remember precisely—two or three days to get to Bergen-Belsen. . . .

In Bergen-Belsen, it was very cold in the winter. We soon found that out. Because we had been arrested in June we hadn't thought about winter clothes. Especially me, a young girl, who had to do her own packing. But what I had brought, I kept.

My sister had a large bandage on her head because she had had surgery on her ears in Westerbork. The first day we arrived in Bergen-Belsen, I got jaundice. The policy of the Germans was: whoever got sick had to go to the hospital; otherwise, all the others could be infected. I didn't know what to do with my little sister. My father was confined in another barracks and I couldn't take her to him. He also had to work, so that wouldn't have worked out.

So there I was and didn't know what to do. This situation showed me that there were very special people in that camp. I told an old lady that I was at my wits' end: "Tomorrow morning, I have to go to the hospital and my little sister is sick."

Two hours later, a woman came, who said, "My name is Abrahams. Mrs. Lange told me that you were here and that you don't know what to do with your sister. I have seven children; give her to me; then we'll just have one more little child with us." F

And that's how it worked out. The next morning her daughter, who seemed to be about my age, came and took the little girl with Meanwhile, my father was able to visit me. We were together with t family until the end. To this day have stayed on friendly terms wit them. . . .

One day, we looked in the direction where there hadn't been any barracks and saw that tents h suddenly appeared there. . . . The barbed-wire fence was built throu the middle of the camp and filled with straw so that we couldn't see other side. But we were, of course very close to each other, because t camp wasn't large. All those peop from the tents were taken to the barracks on the other side. In spit of the German guards on the high watchtowers, we tried to make contact. . . .

One of my acquaintances, an o woman, came up to me one day. "Do you know, there are some Du people there. I spoke to Mrs. Van Daan." The woman had known he from before, and she told me that Anne was there. She knew that I k Anne.

"Go over to the barbed-wire fe and try to talk to her." And, of course, I did. In the evening, I sto by the barbed-wire fence and bega to call out. And quite by chance M Van Daan was there again. I asked her, "Could you call Anne?"

She said, "Yes, yes, wait a minu I'll go to get Anne. I can't get Mar she is very, very ill and is in bed."

DIFFERENTIATED INSTRUCTION

FOR LESS-PROFICIENT READERS

Comprehension Support [paired option] Have partners create a Sequence Chain of events described so far in the interview.

Hannah visits the Franks' house and learns they have moved to Switzerland. → *Hannah returns to school in the fall, and many children do not come to class.* →

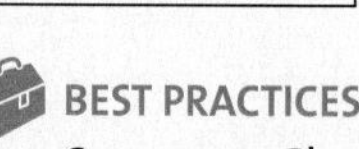

BEST PRACTICES TOOLKIT—Transparency
Sequence Chain pp. B21, B45

FOR ENGLISH LEARNERS

Vocabulary: Cognates [shared-language groups] Have groups scan the story for cognates and report their findings to the class. Spanish cognates on this page include

- *transported/transportado* (line 118)
- *surgery/cirugía* (line 136)
- *infected/infectado* (line 141)
- *situation/situación* (line 149)

A sign posted by the British army outside the Bergen-Belsen concentration camp

But naturally I was much more interested in Anne, and I waited there a few minutes in the dark.

Anne came to the barbed-wire fence—I couldn't see her. The fence and the straw were between us. There wasn't much light. Maybe I saw her shadow. It wasn't the same Anne. She was a broken girl. I probably was, too, but it was so terrible. She immediately began to cry, and she told me, "I don't have any parents anymore."

I remember that with absolute certainty. That was terribly sad, because she couldn't have known anything else. She thought that her father had been gassed right away. But Mr. Frank looked very young and healthy, and of course the Germans didn't know how old everybody was who they wanted to gas, but selected them on the basis of their appearance. Someone who looked healthy had to work, but another who might even be younger, but who was sick or looked bad, went directly to the gas chamber. **G**

I always think, if Anne had known that her father was still alive, she

G SYNTHESIZE
What happened to Jewish people in the concentration camps who looked healthy? What happened to those who were sick or looked ill?

BACKGROUND

Bergen-Belsen Established in 1943, Bergen-Belsen was one of several Nazi concentration camps in Germany. Originally, it was designed to hold Jews who could be exchanged for German prisoners of war. No gas chambers were built at Bergen-Belsen, but it was still a deadly place. Although originally designed to hold no more than 10,000 prisoners, by the end of the war it held about 60,000 prisoners, many of whom, like Anne Frank, had been in Polish camps like Auschwitz. In the first few months of 1945, more than 35,000 people died at Bergen-Belsen from exhaustion, starvation, and various diseases, including a typhus epidemic.

British troops arrived in Bergen-Belsen on April 15, 1945, but they were too late to save the lives of approximately 28,000 prisoners who died within the next few weeks. Soon after their arrival, the British troops buried the dead in mass graves and burned the camp's rat-infested buildings to the ground to prevent the spread of disease.

After liberation, Bergen-Belsen became a camp for displaced Jews, most of whom later emigrated to Israel.

INFORMATIONAL ANALYSIS

G SYNTHESIZE

Have students record their answers in the chart from page 544. ***Answer:*** *People who looked healthy were forced to work; the rest were sent to the gas chamber.*

FOR ADVANCED LEARNERS/PRE–AP

Synthesize Have students brainstorm an additional set of questions they would like to ask in a follow-up interview with Hannah Elisabeth Pick-Goslar. When framing their questions, they may also refer to the information in Anne Frank's diary or in Gerda Weissmann Klein's newspaper article.

Describe Ask students to imagine that they are onlookers during the encounter between Hannah and Anne at the barbed-wire fence. Have them write a paragraph describing the scene. What details might an onlooker notice that Hannah might not?

INFORMATIONAL ANALYSIS

H SYNTHESIZE

Possible answer: *Anne is starving and cold, and her head has been shaved. She doesn't have any clothes. Her sister is very ill, and she believes both her parents are dead.*

INFORMATIONAL ANALYSIS

I SYNTHESIZE

Possible answer: *Life at Bergen-Belsen is very grim. Its prisoners are starving, sick, and cold. Some prisoners help each other as much as they can. Others will do anything, including stealing food, to survive.*

Skill Focus: Synthesize

Possible answers for the chart on page 544:

- ***Hiding in Amsterdam: Row 1:*** *cramped, no privacy, bickering, fear, stuck inside with no fresh air, longing to do normal things;* ***Row 2:*** *hot hiding place, desire for ordinary things and a normal life;* ***Row 3:*** *tells about going into hiding but doesn't describe it*
- ***Living openly in Amsterdam: Row 1:*** *Mr. Dussel tells how Jews disappear after Nazi searches;* ***Row 2:*** *Anne imagines what it would be like to live openly, Klein provides picture of ordinary life in the streets;* ***Row 3:*** *having to wear a yellow star and carry identification cards, get false passports, feel fear and hunger, roundups of Jews*
- ***German concentration camp: Row 1:*** *mentions the death camps but doesn't describe them;* ***Row 2:*** *no information;* ***Row 3:*** *very cold, not enough food, Anne's head was shaved, many people sick, some people helped each other, others stole food, people transferred between camps and to different sections within camps, received Red Cross packages*
- ***Impressions of Anne Frank: Row 1:*** *Anne is bright, curious, determined, outspoken, and creative; she is a romantic who has faith in humanity; she is frustrated and sad and longs for a normal life; she must hide her sadness;* ***Row 2:*** *a spirited girl who desired things that many people take for granted;* ***Row 3:*** *weakened and sad, "a broken girl"*

might have had more strength to survive, because she died very shortly before the end—only a few days before [liberation]. But maybe it was all predestined.

So we stood there, two young girls, and we cried. I told her about my mother. She hadn't known that; she only knew that the baby had died. And I told her about my little sister. I told her that my father was in the hospital. He died two weeks later; he was already very sick. She told me that Margot was seriously ill and she told me about going into hiding because I was, of course, extremely curious.

"But what are you doing here? You were supposed to be in Switzerland, weren't you?" And then she told me what had happened. That they didn't go to Switzerland at all and why they had said that; so that everyone should think that they had gone to her grandmother's.

Then she said, "We don't have anything at all to eat here, almost nothing, and we are cold; we don't have any clothes and I've gotten very thin and they shaved my hair." That was terrible for her. She had always been very proud of her hair. It may have grown back a bit in the meantime, but it certainly wasn't the long hair she'd had before, which she playfully curled around her fingers. It was much worse for them than for us. I said, "They didn't take away our clothes." That was our first meeting. **H**

Then for the first time—we had already been in the camp for more than a year; we arrived in February 1944, and this was February 1945—we received a very small Red Cross package: my sister, my father, and A very small package, the size of a book, with *knäckebrot* (Scandinav crackers), and a few cookies. You imagine how little that was. My s always says, "But Mama, that was something really very special." Bu in those days we really collected everything, half a cookie, a sock, a glove—anything that gave a little warmth or something to eat. My friends also gave me something fo Anne. I certainly couldn't have thrown a large package over the barbed-wire fence; not that I had but that wouldn't have been possi at all.

We agreed to try to meet the ne evening at eight o'clock—I believe still had a watch. And, in fact, I succeeded in throwing the package over.

But I heard her screaming, and I called out, "What happened?"

And Anne answered, "Oh, the woman standing next to me caugh and she won't give it back to me."

Then she began to scream.

I calmed her down a bit and sai "I'll try again but I don't know if I be able to." We arranged to meet again, two or three days later, and was actually able to throw over another package. She caught it; th was the main thing.

After these three or four meetin at the barbed-wire fence in Bergen Belsen, I didn't see her again, beca the people in Anne's camp were transferred to another section in Bergen-Belsen. That happened around the end of February. **I**

That was the last time I saw An alive and spoke to her.

H SYNTHESIZE
What do you learn about Anne's circumstances from this first meeting?

I SYNTHESIZE
By the end of this account, what have you learned about life in Bergen-Belsen?

DIFFERENTIATED INSTRUCTION

FOR LESS–PROFICIENT READERS

Concept Support [paired option] Have pairs complete the chart from page 544. Encourage students to scan each source and any notes they've taken to make sure that they have included the most relevant details. Tell them that some of the spaces in the chart may remain blank if a source does not cover a particular topic.

FOR ADVANCED LEARNERS/PRE–AP

Synthesize [small-group option] Have groups find additional examples of articles and interviews about Anne Frank, the experiences of Jews in Amsterdam, and Bergen-Belsen. Ask each student to choose a source and share its information with other group members. Then have students synthesize the information and present any new details to the class.

Comprehension

1. **Recall** For what occasion does Anne Frank receive her diary?
2. **Summarize** Briefly describe Hannah Elisabeth Pick-Goslar's experiences in Bergen-Belsen before she reconnects with Anne.

Critical Analysis

3. **Evaluate a Source** Gerda Weissmann Klein, the author of "A Diary from Another World," is Jewish. When she was 15, Nazis invaded her home country, Poland. She was forced to work as a slave laborer in German factories. Her entire family was killed in the Holocaust. What effect does Klein's background have on the way you view the information in the article?
4. **Analyze an Interview** Pick-Goslar has a unique view of Anne. Explain why that is. What new information about Anne and her family do you learn from Pick-Goslar's account?
5. **Synthesize** What were the physical and emotional effects of living in a Nazi-occupied country as a Jew? What survival techniques allowed people to withstand the hardships they did? Refer to the chart you filled in as you read, and support your answer with evidence from at least three selections.

Read for Information: Make a Generalization

WRITING PROMPT

Identify an important life lesson you take away from these Jewish families' experiences. Support your response with evidence from the selections.

To respond to this prompt, you will have to make a generalization. A **generalization** is a broad statement about a topic that follows logically from solid evidence. To arrive at your generalization, follow these steps:

1. Review the information you gathered in your chart, jotting down any general statements about life or human nature that this information suggests to you.
2. Pick the most convincing statement you have jotted down and rephrase it as a life lesson. To do this, begin with a phrase such as "It is human nature to . . ."
3. Review the evidence for your generalization to make sure it comes from more than one source and supports your statement.
4. In a paragraph, state the life lesson you've identified. Then present evidence for this generalization.

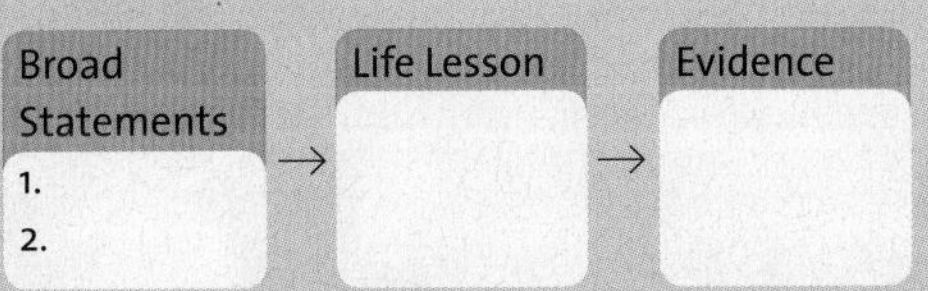

Practice and Apply

For additional support of postreading questions, use these copy masters:

RESOURCE MANAGER—Copy Masters
Reading Check p. 149
Question Support p. 150
Make a Generalization p. 146

For additional questions, see page 140.

ANSWERS

Comprehension

1. *Anne receives the diary on her birthday.*
2. *Pick-Goslar and her sister are separated from their father. They are helped by another family.*

Critical Analysis

3. *Klein knows what it was like to live in peril. She shared some of Anne Frank's feelings and experiences. This makes the article believable and strong.*
4. *Pick-Goslar remembers Anne from when they were childhood friends and also talked to Anne shortly before she died. The interview reveals that Anne was hungry and cold at Bergen-Belsen and her spirits were very low. Her sister was ill, and she thought her parents had both died. Anne died just a few days before the camp was liberated.*
5. **STANDARDS FOCUS Synthesize** *People often went hungry. They feared being taken away by the Nazis. Some went into hiding or acquired false documents.*

Read for Information: Make a Generalization

Writing Prompt *Students' generalizations should be supported by evidence from more than one source.*

FOR LESS–PROFICIENT WRITERS

Read for Information

1. Ask students to review their charts and state two or three ideas about life or human nature suggested by their entries.
2. To choose the most convincing statement, suggest that students read their statements to a partner and elicit feedback.
3. Guide students in giving specific examples from the accounts to support their generalizations and life lessons.

FOR ADVANCED LEARNERS/PRE–AP

Read for Information Have students write a second paragraph in which they refer to the life lesson they have identified as the justification for a course of action or change of attitude about a controversial social issue. Tell them to use evidence to support the life lesson. Then invite volunteers to share their paragraphs and lead a discussion about what makes each one persuasive.

Assess and Reteach

Assess

RESOURCE MANAGER—Copy Masters
Selection Tests A, B/C pp. 151–152, 153–154

Test Generator CD

Reteach

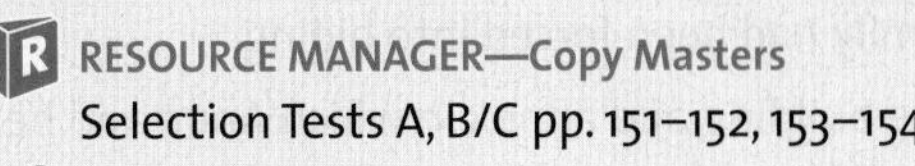

STANDARDS LESSON FILE
Reading Lesson 10: Making Generalizations
Reading Lesson 14: Synthesizing Information

Focus and Motivate

OBJECTIVES

Media Literacy

- explore the key idea of **history**
- identify and analyze the elements of a documentary
- interpret information presented in a nonprint source
- compare and contrast information and events in print and nonprint sources
- create a visual timeline

SUMMARY

The first clip from *Anne Frank Remembered* gives a tour of the Frank family's secret annex and a reading from Anne's diary in which she describes its rooms. The second clip explains how her diary came to be published and the great success it achieved. The third clip shows footage of Anne looking out an Amsterdam window, childhood photos of her, and another poignant reading from her diary.

Can films make HISTORY *fresh?*

Discuss the question. Ask students to refer to any historical films or TV shows they have seen. After students read the ***KEY IDEA,*** invite them to discuss famous figures in **history** they would like to meet or know more about. Then focus on students' perceptions of Anne Frank and what they hope a biographical documentary might reveal about her life.

BACKGROUND

The Frank family left their homeland of Germany in 1933, when the Nazi party came to power there. The family had several happy years in Amsterdam before the German army invaded in 1940 and introduced discriminatory policies against Jews. By 1942, Anne and her family had been forced into hiding.

The building and annex in which Anne and her family lived for two years is now the site of a popular museum. Visitors can view Anne's diary as well as other original letters, documents, and objects; walk the rooms of the annex (shown in the documentary); and learn about history. The museum also sponsors activities that address current social issues and promote tolerance.

Media Study

from Anne Frank Remembered

Film Clips on *MediaSmart DVD*

Can films make HISTORY *fresh?*

KEY IDEA Have you ever wanted to meet a famous figure from **history?** We can learn the facts about a famous person's life, but we can't know what it would be like to sit down and talk to him or her. In this lesson, you'll watch a biographical documentary about Anne Frank. You'll explore how the filmmakers try to bring you into Anne's world and give you a sense of what she was really like.

Background

Behind the Symbol Anne Frank's diary has sold over 31 million copies in approximately 67 languages. She has become an enduring symbol of the tragedy of the Holocaust. But behind that symbol was a real girl, a teenager trapped for two years in a small hiding place with seven other people.

Anne Frank Remembered is a documentary that explores the life and death of the girl behind the symbol. The film takes viewers inside the Franks' hidden annex, revealing what it was like to live in such cramped quarters. It also tells the story of Anne's diary, and how her private thoughts became the book that has touched readers throughout the world.

554

Media Study Resources

RESOURCE MANAGER UNIT 4

Plan and Teach pp. 155–158

Media Analysis

Summary pp. 159†*, 160‡*
Viewing Guide p. 161
Close Viewing p. 162
Media Activity p. 163
Produce Your Own Media p. 164

STANDARDS LESSON FILE

Media Lesson 1: Active Viewing Strategies
Media Lesson 4: Analyzing Visuals in Film and TV
Media Lesson 5: Analyzing Sound in Film and TV
Media Lesson 7: Evaluating Films and TV Shows

Media Center at **ClassZone.com**

MEDIA VIEWING

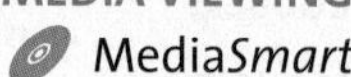
Media*Smart* DVD

* Resources for Differentiation † Also in Spanish ‡ In Haitian Creole and Vietnamese

edia Literacy: Documentary

A **documentary** is a nonfiction film that often presents social, political, or historical subject matter. Famous historical figures make good subjects for documentaries, because the filmmakers can tell the story of both the individual and the time period. To create a documentary, filmmakers often gather **primary sources,** firsthand information such as diaries, photographs, and eyewitness accounts. They then combine these materials with **voice-over narration** and, often, a **re-enactment** of scenes or settings to re-create the times for viewers.

FEATURES OF A DOCUMENTARY

Footage is recorded material that gives information about a subject. It includes film clips, photographs, news reports, and interviews. Footage from a particular time period can show viewers what life was like back then.

Voice-over narration is the voice of an unseen speaker that is heard in a documentary. The voice-over tells the subject's story and explains the footage. **Primary sources,** such as diary entries, can also be read as part of the voice-over narration.

Re-enactment is the re-creation of key events or important settings. Filmmakers shoot scenes or settings using sets, props, actors, and costumes. They try to re-create the subject's story as realistically as possible.

STRATEGIES FOR VIEWING

- Identify the different types of **footage.** Notice how the filmmakers combine primary source footage with footage they shoot themselves, such as interviews and re-enactments, to tell the whole story.
- Think about the purpose of the **voice-over narration.** Different narrators can present different sides of someone's personality.
- Notice the type of information you learn from any **re-enactments.** Re-enactments are often used in historical documentaries. Think about why the filmmakers might have chosen to present the information in this way.

MEDIA STUDY: TEACHING OPTIONS

Teaching Option 1: The Basics (1–2 Days)

1. Begin the Media Study using the material provided on pages 554–555.
2. Show the Introduction on Media*Smart*. Then show the First Viewing. As they watch, have students use the Viewing Guide on page 556, along with the corresponding copy master on page 161 of the Resource Manager. Discuss their responses.
3. Return to the pupil's edition for the extension activities on page 557.

Teaching Option 2: In-Depth Study (2–3 Days)

1. Begin the Media Study using pages 554–555.
2. Show the Introduction and First Viewing from Media*Smart*. Continue on Media*Smart* with the Media Lessons, using the teacher notes in the Resources section.
3. Show the Guided Analysis presentation. Have students record their observations on the Student Viewing Guide available in the Resources section from Media*Smart*.
4. Return to the pupil's edition, page 557.

Teach

MEDIA LITERACY: DOCUMENTARY

Have students again refer back to any historical films and documentaries they have seen. Ask them to recall how information was presented in these films. Was there firsthand information such as photographs and eyewitness accounts? Did a speaker explain what was happening in the documentary? Share information about documentaries you have seen. Then discuss the chart on page 555.

- **Footage** Ask students to think about the power of having actual footage from a particular time period or event. Ask: What is the purpose of including primary source footage such as old film clips or photographs? What effect might these images have on viewers? Have students think about distant historical events for which there are no photographs or film footage. Do students relate to these events any differently than they do to more recent events for which there is footage?
- **Voice-over Narration** Explain that voice-over narration is necessary to provide additional facts and explain what viewers are seeing. Tell students that filmmakers must choose their narrators carefully, as the sound of a narrator's voice and the narrator's attitude toward the subject of the documentary can affect how people interpret the information. Have different students read aloud the same passage from this lesson to demonstrate the effect of different reading styles. Students might experiment with volume and try emphasizing different words.
- **Re-enactment** Have students examine the photograph on page 555, which depicts the kitchen area of the secret annex in which Anne Frank and her family lived. Note that everyday items such as pots and pans, a teapot, and a painting on the wall have been added to the scene to re-create the original setting. Ask: Why have people gone to the trouble of adding these items? Do you think viewers can relate more easily to the historical people and their situation when they see such items rather than just an empty room? Explain.

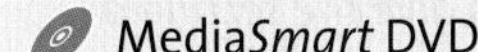

Media*Smart* DVD

Practice and Apply

VIEWING GUIDE

1. As students prepare to view the clips from the documentary, explain to them that they will be asked to point out specific elements used by the filmmakers. Encourage them to observe the following:
   - the use of **primary source footage** such as diary pages, photographs, and film footage
   - **voice-over narration** that includes two distinctly different narrators
   - use of **re-enactment** to re-create the setting of the secret annex
2. Suggest that students view the clips more than once. When watching them for the first time, they should watch and listen for information. During the second viewing, students should take notes about the voice-over narration and the way the film-makers present footage and information. Encourage students to think about why filmmakers included certain scenes and footage and why the documentary uses two narrators.

RESOURCE MANAGER—Copy Masters
Viewing Guide p. 161
Close Viewing p. 162
Media Activity p. 163

Media*Smart* DVD

ANSWERS

FIRST VIEWING: Comprehension

1. *A newspaper article written about the diary by a friend of a friend of Otto Frank caught the attention of a publisher.*
2. *Primary source materials include the readings from Anne's diary, the photographs of Anne and the rest of the Frank family, the film footage of Anne at the window, and the newspaper article about the diary.*

CLOSE VIEWING: Media Literacy

Possible answers:

3. *The filmmakers may have wanted to re-create the Franks' annex as realistically as possible, but also to give the setting a feeling of impermanence. The fading away of the food and furniture creates a ghostlike feeling—a reminder of the Franks' fate.*
4. *The male narrator tells Anne's story, and the female narrator reads from Anne's diary. This allows the viewer to know instantly when a diary excerpt is being read, and it gives a more personal feeling to the diary entries.*
5. *In showing footage of Anne when she was alive, filmmakers may have wanted to end the film on a touching note and to show how Anne continues to live on through her words. The shot also serves as a reminder that Anne was a living, breathing child and not just a mythical figure associated with words on a page.*

***MediaSmart* DVD**
- **Film:** *Anne Frank Remembered*
- **Director:** Jon Blair
- **Voice-over Narrators:** Kenneth Branagh and Glenn Close
- **Genre:** Documentary
- **Running Time:** 4 minutes

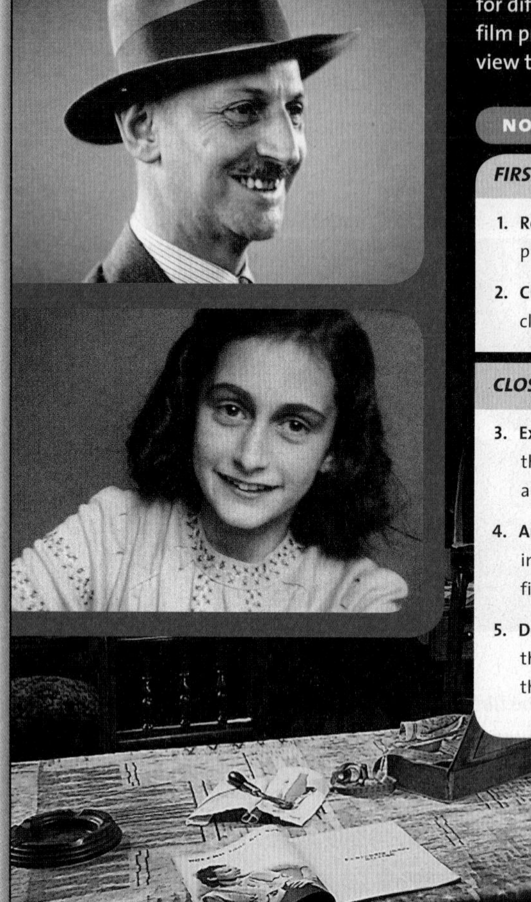

Viewing Guide for
Anne Frank Remembered

You'll view three clips from *Anne Frank Remembered.* They reveal the Franks' secret annex in Amsterdam, the story of the publicatio of the diary, and the only known moving footage of Anne Frank. A you view the clips, think about how the documentary features ad freshness to her story. You'll hear two different **voice-over narrat** Notice the different types of information you learn from each. Wa for different types of **footage** and any **re-enactment** of setting the film provides. Before answering these questions, you may want t view the clip more than once.

NOW VIEW

***FIRST VIEWING:* Comprehension**

1. **Recall** After Otto Frank had such trouble getting Anne's diary published, what finally caused a publisher to step forward?
2. **Clarify** Give two examples of **primary source** material used in the clips you viewed.

***CLOSE VIEWING:* Media Literacy**

3. **Examine the Visuals** Think about the **re-enactment** of the setting of the secret annex. Why do you think the filmmakers show the food and furniture fading away to leave empty rooms?
4. **Analyze Voice-over Narration** Think about the different types of information the two **voice-over narrators** provide. Why might the filmmakers have decided to use two narrators rather than one?
5. **Determine Filmmakers' Purpose** The clip of Anne Frank standing at the window is from the end of the documentary. What effect do you think the filmmakers intended this clip to have on viewers?

rite or Discuss

Compare the Texts Think about the impression you had of Anne Frank from the play you read. Now think about the documentary clips you viewed. Write a brief comparison of the Anne you read about in the play and the Anne described in the film. Which is most effective at going beyond the symbol and revealing what you believe to be the real Anne Frank? Think about the following:

- the documentary footage of the actual secret annex where the Franks hid
- how the play portrays Anne's personality
- the footage of Anne at the window, and the voice-over reading of her diary

oduce Your Own Media

Create a Visual Timeline When filmmakers plan a biographical documentary, they look closely at their subject's entire life story. They decide what events to include in the documentary and what to leave out. Imagine you're planning a documentary about a friend's life. Choose five or six events in that person's life, and create a visual timeline depicting these events. Your timeline should include a photograph or drawing and a caption for each event.

MEDIA TOOLS

For help with creating a timeline, visit the **Media Center** at **ClassZone.com.**

HERE'S HOW Here are a few suggestions for preparing your visual timeline:

- Start by choosing the events you want to show. Choose the most exciting and interesting things that have happened to your friend.
- Collect or take photographs to illustrate each event. You might want to have your friend **re-enact** a favorite event, such as a time he or she won a contest.
- Write a brief sentence for each picture that describes the event depicted.
- Arrange your pictures on a board in chronological order.

STUDENT MODEL

Tech Tip

If available, use a computer software program to present your timeline.

Assess and Reteach

Write or Discuss

Compare the Texts To help students get started, encourage them to make a two-column chart in which they can record their thoughts about the play and the documentary. Students should think about which piece best helped them understand Anne Frank as a person. Students may conclude that both pieces were effective in different ways. For example, the play provides a dramatization of Anne actually interacting with family and friends in the annex. In the documentary, however, viewers get a better sense of how small and cramped the living quarters were. The documentary also presents actual photos and footage of Anne. Students might mention that in the play they see a writer's or an actor's portrayal of Anne, while the documentary brings Anne's actual words to life through voice-over narration.

Produce Your Own Media

Rubric A strong visual timeline should have

- five or six photographs or drawings that depict important events in a person's life
- a brief sentence describing each event on the timeline
- pictures arranged on a board in chronological order

RESOURCE MANAGER—Copy Master
Produce Your Own Media p. 164

Media*Smart* DVD

MEDIA STUDY WRAP-UP

Summarize Ask students to summarize the elements filmmakers use to create effective documentaries. Ask them to refer to specific examples from the *Anne Frank Remembered* clips. If necessary, remind them to focus on the use of footage, voice-over narration, and re-enactment.

RETEACH

STANDARDS LESSON FILE

Media Lesson 1: Active Viewing Strategies
Media Lesson 4: Analyzing Visuals in Film and TV
Media Lesson 5: Analyzing Sound in Film and TV
Media Lesson 7: Evaluating Films and TV Shows

Focus and Motivate

OBJECTIVES

- analyze a student model that reflects the key traits of a short story
- use the writing process to produce a short story
- revise and edit, using a rubric for short-story writing
- produce a video

WRITER'S ROAD MAP

WRITING PROMPTS 1 AND 2

Help students brainstorm plots, conflicts, and characters and review themes from stories in the unit. Encourage them to develop plots rich in conflict with at least two interesting characters that will hold readers' attention.

ADDITIONAL PROMPTS

Use these prompts for practice with writing short stories:

WRITING PROMPT 3

Writing from a Picture Look in books and magazines for a painting or other work of art that you find intriguing. Then freewrite about details in the work—people, setting, events—that might be part of a good story. Finally, review what you have written and choose the character(s), setting, and central conflict for your short story.

WRITING PROMPT 4

Writing from the Real World Write a short story based on a news story. Use details about interesting people, ideas, and events as a springboard for your characters, plot, and setting.

Sources of News Stories

- a newspaper or magazine article
- a news-oriented Web site
- a television or radio broadcast

For additional writing prompts, see

- Write*Smart* CD
- Writing Center at **ClassZone.com**

KEY TRAITS

Review the six ***KEY TRAITS*** with students, focusing primarily on ideas, organization, and word choice. Compare these traits with the rubric on page 564.

Writing Workshop

Short Story

What did you like best about the stories you read this year—the characters, the suspense, or maybe the satisfying endings? In this workshop, you will weave your own tale of adventure, mystery, triumph, or woe. Follow the **Writer's Road Map** to learn how.

WRITER'S ROAD MAP

Short Story

WRITING PROMPT 1

Writing from Your Imagination Write a short story that has an interesting plot. Make sure that your story includes a conflict and at least two characters.

Plots to Consider:

- Two people adopt an unusual dog.
- An alien lands on the school football field.
- A family gets locked in at the local natural history museum.

WRITING PROMPT 2

Writing from Literature Choose a "big question" from this unit that really made you think. Then write a short story inspired by that question. Create a plot, conflict, setting, and at least two characters to hold your reader's attention.

Questions to Make You Think:

- What makes something priceless? ("Gil's Furniture Bought and Sold")
- Is curiosity a gift or a curse? ("Pandora's Box")
- What impact will you have on the world? (*The Diary of Anne Frank*)

WRITING TOOLS
Go to the **Writing Center** at **Classzone.com** for interactive models, publishing ideas, and other support for this workshop.

KEY TRAITS

1. *IDEAS*
- Has an intriguing **plot** and at least two **characters**
- Develops and resolves a **central conflict**
- Includes **descriptive details** that reveal the setting and characters
- Uses **dialogue** to show characters' personalities

2. *ORGANIZATION*
- **Introduces** the characters, setting, or action in a way that gets the reader's attention
- Follows a clear **sequence of events**
- Resolves the conflict in a convincing **conclusion**

3. *VOICE*
- Shows the writer's unique **style**

4. *WORD CHOICE*
- Includes **sensory language** to help readers imagine the fictional world

5. *SENTENCE FLUENCY*
- Varies **sentence lengths**

6. *CONVENTIONS*
- Uses **correct grammar, spelling, and punctuation**

Writing Workshop Resources

RESOURCE MANAGER UNIT 4

Plan and Teach pp. 165–168
Prewriting–Editing pp. 169–173
Writing Rubric p. 174
Publishing with Technology p. 175
Writing Support p. 176*

STANDARDS LESSON FILE

Writing Lessons 1, 14, 27, 28, 48
Grammar Lesson 16
Media Lesson 20

BEST PRACTICES TOOLKIT

Scaffolding Writing Instruction pp. 43–46*
Plot Diagram • Character Traits Web • Analysis Frames • Writing Template: Short Story • Cluster Diagram • Sequence Chain • Storyboard

TECHNOLOGY

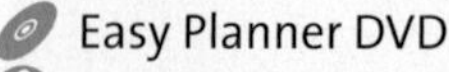

- Easy Planner DVD
- Writing Center at **ClassZone.com**
- Write*Smart* CD

* Resources for Differentiation

rt 1: Analyze a Student Model

James Pickford
Eldridge Middle School

Flight Patterns

Working with Joe on the science project hadn't been Samuel's idea. Joe was a good kid, but he was the school soccer star, not the school science star. Samuel loved science but didn't think he was any good at sports. So when Ms. Krunkner shouted, "Joe and Samuel, you're up!" Samuel wondered for the twentieth time why she had ever put them on the same team.

Samuel, who hated standing in front of the class, shuffled to the front of the room as Joe walked confidently to the starting line that Ms. Krunkner had taped on the floor. Joe was holding the paper airplane that Samuel had designed.

"Joe, are you launching it?" Ms. Krunkner asked.

"Yeah. Is that okay, Samuel?" Joe asked.

After Samuel nodded a timid yes, Ms. Krunkner gave Samuel the tape measure so he could measure how far the plane flew.

"You have three tries, but all of them will count toward your average," Ms. Krunkner said.

Joe cranked his arm back and threw the plane fast—it looped straight up, back toward Joe, and then forward only a few feet before it hit the ground. Samuel measured the distance. It was barely five feet. The class started laughing. Samuel brought the plane back to Joe, who looked embarrassed.

"Throw it as level to the ground as you can," Samuel said.

"That's what I'm trying to do," Joe said.

Joe threw it again, and again it did a dramatic loop and crashed six feet away. Samuel picked it up and smoothed the nose, which had gotten a little crunched, and made sure the wings were evenly folded.

KEY TRAITS IN ACTION

Introduces three **characters** and a **central conflict** (Samuel is nervous about working with Joe).

Develops an interesting **plot** with a clear **sequence of events.**

Teach

Part 1: Analyze a Student Model

Have students read the **Student Model** and **Key Traits in Action.** Then discuss the model with the class, pointing out specific examples of each key trait. You may also wish to incorporate these activities:

- **Introduction** Tell students that a story can begin in several ways. For example:

Dialogue	"Joe and Samuel, you're up!"
Description of Setting	The atmosphere in the packed classroom was tense.
Flashback	Thinking back on the day Ms. Krunkner had given the assignment, Samuel couldn't understand why she had paired him with Joe.

  Ask students which of the alternative openings they might suggest for the model, and why.

- **Central Conflict** Remind students that there are two kinds of conflict—internal and external. Give them these examples:

  —**Internal:** Joanne is nervous about giving an oral report.

  —**External:** Joanne gets into an argument with her brother.

  As they read the model, have students identify examples of internal and external conflict.

DIFFERENTIATED INSTRUCTION

FOR ALL STUDENTS

Student Portfolios Encourage students to save copies of their writing so that they can track their progress throughout the year.

For general guidelines on differentiating writing instruction, see

BEST PRACTICES TOOLKIT
Scaffolding Writing Instruction pp. 43–46

FOR ENGLISH LEARNERS

Language: Skill Words Write these terms on the board and review them with students:

- *conflict:* the problem or obstacle that stands in the way of the things a character wants
- *plot:* the main events of a story, including conflict. For example, a story's plot may involve a conflict between two friends who are arguing about which of them should ask a boy to a school dance. By the end of the story, the plot will be resolved one way or the other—one of the girls will ask the boy to the dance, or neither of them will.
- *sequence of events:* the order in which things happen in a story. A plot's sequence of events usually begins with the introduction of a conflict and ends with a resolution of that conflict.

- **Sensory Language** To illustrate the effectiveness of sensory language, write this sentence pair on the board:

  The winter day was dark and cold.

  Snowflakes whirred in the dim light of an icy winter morning.

  Have students discuss differences between the two sentences. Ask them to point out the words that appeal to the senses of sight, hearing, and touch in the second sentence and discuss how the second sentence helps the reader imagine the scene more vividly.

- **Conclusion** Explain that there are as many ways to end short stories as there to begin them. Ask students to look through the model and, with a partner, brainstorm other ways the writer might have ended the story. For example, the writer might have ended with a conversation between Joe and Samuel, or Samuel might not have caught the Frisbee and yet still have been included in the game.

For interactive student models, see

WriteSmart CD

Writing Center at **ClassZone.com**

ADDITIONAL TEACHING OPPORTUNITY

Writer's Attitude Point out that a story often reveals the writer's attitude toward the subject of the story. Have students identify the subject of this story and infer what the writer might have wanted to say about it. ***Possible answer:*** *The subject is an event that gives a shy person more confidence in himself. The author's attitude may be that although trying new things can be scary, the experience can give a person greater self-confidence once it's all over.*

"Samuel, you do it this time," Joe said.

"What?" Samuel said, panicking.

"You throw it!" Joe whispered, refusing to take the plane out of Samuel's hands.

"Come on, boys," Ms. Krunkner said.

Samuel's heart was racing as he stepped up to the line. As he raised the plane up above his shoulder, he paused for an instant to imagine it flying smoothly in a straight line. Then he pulled his arm back and launched the plane gently forward. It sailed smoothly to the opposite wall. When Samuel heard his classmates cheering, he let out the breath that he realized he'd been holding.

"Very nice, Samuel," Ms. Krunkner said. As the boys returned to their places, some kids high-fived them.

Samuel was in a great mood for the rest of the day. He felt as if people were looking at him with admiration.

At the end of the day, as Samuel walked by the soccer field, Joe called out, "Hey Samuel! Come and play Frisbee with us." Samuel started to say he wasn't good at sports, but Joe just smiled.

A second later, someone threw the Frisbee right at Samuel. Samuel put his hands up and caught it. He looked at the Frisbee and realized that making it fly would be all about getting it to spin and stay level. He held it flat and flicked his wrist to throw the Frisbee back. It soared over the grass and straight into waiting hands. He didn't even have to think about it; it just felt right. It was a good day for new flight patterns.

2

Descriptive details (highlighted) and lots of **dialogue** are important parts of this writer's **style.**

Highlighted **sensory language** helps the reader understand Samuel's emotions. Varied **sentence lengths** add interest and sophistication.

Satisfying, thoughtful **conclusion** shows how Samuel is changing.

DIFFERENTIATED INSTRUCTION

FOR ENGLISH LEARNERS

Comprehension: Transitions [mixed-readiness pairs] If students are not familiar with the transitional words they need to show the sequence of events in a short story, give them these examples:

- **Before** Joey knocked on the door . . .
- When Joey **first** entered the room . . .
- **Then** Joey looked for . . .
- **Until** Joey heard Evangeline's voice . . .
- **After** Joey thought about . . .
- **Next,** Joey asked Evangeline . . .
- **Eventually,** Joey realized . . .
- **Finally,** Joey told Evangeline . . .
- **At last,** Evangeline explained to Joey . . .

Have students work with more fluent partners to complete several of the above statements, linking them together to create a very brief story with a clear sequence of events.

 **RESOURCE MANAGER—Copy Master**
Writing Support p. 176

rt 2: Apply the Writing Process

REWRITING

What Should I Do?	What Does It Look Like?
1. Find an idea. Start with a list. Jot down any story elements that come to mind, such as characters (two brothers?), settings (a dark cave?), and conflicts (a longstanding feud?). Put a star next to one or more that interest you. **TIP** You can also get started by asking "what if" questions. See page 564 for some examples.	see chart below

Characters	Settings	Conflicts
Jill and her dad	Griffin Park	different personalities*
Samuel and Joe*	the cafeteria	the MVP award
Billy and his team	Avon Beach	conscience and peer pressure
my sister and me	science class*	

2. Create a story map.
A successful story has characters, setting, and a **plot**—a sequence of events that leads to a climax. To make sure that your idea is truly a story rather than just a description, make a story map, an outline, or a flow chart.

See page 24: Plot at a Glance

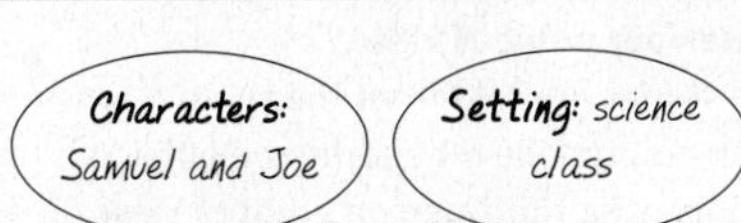

Conflict: different personalities; also Samuel's insecurity

Event 1: Ms. Krunkner calls on Joe and Samuel to demonstrate their project.

Event 2: Joe messes up twice.

Event 3: Samuel succeeds.

Event 4: Joe invites Samuel to play Frisbee, and Samuel succeeds again.

Solution or Ending: Samuel has new confidence.

3. Add interest to your characters.
Jot down some details about your characters, such as what they say, how they look, and how they act.

Samuel	Joe
• shy, good student, quiet	• confident and strong
• hates being in front of the class	• soccer star
• smart, likes science	• nice guy, no attitude

Practice and Apply

To support students during the writing process, use these copy masters:

RESOURCE MANAGER—Copy Masters
Prewriting–Editing pp. 169–173
Writing Rubric p. 174
Writing Support p. 176 *(for English learners)*

Part 2: Apply the Writing Process

PREWRITING

1. **Find an idea.** Point out the three-column chart and explain that students will be creating a chart with the same heads. Discuss the options that the writer of the student model considered, and then point out the TIP provided with step 1. Have students create their own charts and brainstorm "what if?" questions about the characters, settings, and conflicts they have listed. Then have them choose the combination that yields them the most interesting possibilities.
2. **Create a story map.** In addition to a story map, some students may find it useful to complete a Plot Diagram. Emphasize that the conflict must be resolved by the story's conclusion.

BEST PRACTICES TOOLKIT—Transparency
Plot Diagram p. D12

3. **Add interest to your characters.** Point out that the two characters in the student model have nearly opposite qualities, which makes the conflict between them more intense. Suggest that students develop contrasts between the characters in their stories.

For interactive graphic organizers, see
WriteSmart CD
Writing Center at **ClassZone.com**

FOR ENGLISH LEARNERS

Task Support: Gathering Details [mixed-readiness pairs] Have students use a Character Traits Web to gather details about their characters' personalities, appearance, and actions. Suggest that they fill in the web in their home language and then work with a more fluent speaker to brainstorm English words and phrases to express their ideas.

BEST PRACTICES TOOLKIT—Transparency
Character Traits Web p. D7

FOR ADVANCED LEARNERS/PRE-AP

Analyze Challenge students to develop more complex plots and characters for their short stories. Analysis Frames can help them generate ideas. Students may use the Core Analysis Frame for fiction, as well as more detailed frames for character and plot.

BEST PRACTICES TOOLKIT—Copy Masters
Analysis Frames p. D23
Fiction pp. D24, D25
Character pp. D28, D29
Plot pp. D30, D31

DRAFTING

1. **Grab your reader's attention.** Suggest that students write two or three versions of their opening to see which one works best. Remind them of techniques they can use to capture a reader's interest:
   - Begin with a surprising statement that gets the reader interested in the story.
   - Begin with dialogue.
   - Begin with a vivid description of the character(s) or the setting.
   - Begin with a flashback or statement of conflict (as in the student model).
2. **Choose your point of view.** Review the advantages and disadvantages of each point of view.
   - Third-person: describes events in a more detached voice; shows the thoughts and feelings of more than one character
   - First-person: draws the reader into the narrator's world; shows the thoughts and feelings of only one character

   To help students choose the best point of view for their stories, encourage them to write the same passage in each point of view and then choose the one they prefer.
3. **Bring your characters to life.** Suggest that students take notes on a "back story" for each character. Encourage them to explore where the characters live, what their families are like, and what important events have influenced their lives. This will help students give better descriptions of their characters.
4. **Make the conflict clear.** Have students work with a partner to state and evaluate the conflict in their stories and to explain how they plan to resolve it. Before students begin to revise, point out the TIP provided with step 4.

For a short story writing template, see

BEST PRACTICES TOOLKIT—Transparency
Writing Template: Short Story pp. C16, C42

Write*Smart* CD

Writing Center at **ClassZone.com**

DRAFTING

What Should I Do?	*What Does It Look Like?*
1. Grab your reader's attention. Write an opening that says, "Read me!" Try starting with a surprising statement, a bit of dialogue, sensory language, or a conflict.	**A surprising statement** *"Get me out of here!" Samuel thought.* **Sensory details** *Samuel's cheeks and the tips of his ears burned with embarrassment.* **A conflict** *Working with Joe on the science project hadn't been Samuel's idea.*
2. Choose your point of view. Some stories are told from the third-person point of view by someone outside the story. The third-person point of view uses pronouns such as *he, she,* and *they.* Other stories are told in the first-person point of view. The narrator is a character in these stories and uses the pronoun *I.*	**Third-person point of view** *Samuel nodded a timid yes.* **First-person point of view** *I nodded a timid yes.*
3. Bring your characters to life. Realistic dialogue and precise descriptive details can give your reader clues about the characters' ages, thoughts, interests, and personalities.	*"Samuel, you do it this time," Joe said.* *"What?" Samuel said, panicking.* *"You throw it!" Joe whispered, refusing to take the plane out of Samuel's hands.*
4. Make the conflict clear. If you haven't got a conflict, you haven't got a story. Be sure the problem or conflict is clear and that the plot centers on how it is resolved. **TIP Before you revise, look back at the key traits on page 558 and the rubric and peer-reader questions on page 564.**	*Samuel wondered for the twentieth time why she had ever put them on the same team.* *The class started laughing. Samuel brought the plane back to Joe, who looked embarrassed.*

DIFFERENTIATED INSTRUCTION

FOR LESS–PROFICIENT WRITERS

Organizing Information The student model is a good example of short story organization. Point out that most stories present events in the order in which they occur, unless there is a flashback. Provide this model to help students organize their stories:

Exposition
- Introduce the characters, the setting, and the central conflict.

Rising Action and Climax
- Develop the conflict.
- Give more details about the characters.
- Include dialogue—the exact words that characters say.
- Create a sequence of events that leads to a climax.

Resolution
- Show how the conflict ends.

REVISING AND EDITING

What Should I Do?	What Does It Look Like?
1. Check the sequence. • Remember to show or tell your reader how one event leads to the next. • Underline places where you should add transitional or other words and phrases to help your reader follow the sequence of events.	After Samuel nodded a timid yes. Ms. Krunkner gave Samuel the tape measure. He could measure how far the plane flew. so
2. Improve the dialogue. • Ask a peer reader to [bracket] dialogue that sounds too formal or so slangy that your audience may not understand it. • Revise the dialogue until it is realistic and convincing. You can include fragments and grammatical errors if that's how your characters would actually talk. **See page 564:** Ask a Peer Reader	~~"Joe, [will you be the one who will launch the paper airplane that you have made?"] Ms. Krunkner asked.~~ ~~["Yes, if that is all right with Samuel,"] Joe said.~~ "Joe, are you launching it?" Ms. Krunkner asked. "Yeah. Is that okay, Samuel?" Joe asked.
3. Focus on the details. • Put a box around your strongest details, whether those are sensory or descriptive. • Add or revise details to tell your reader more about the setting, characters, and events.	[Samuel's heart was racing] as he stepped up to the line. ~~It was a good throw, so Samuel felt relief.~~ When Samuel heard his classmates cheering, he let out the breath that he realized he'd been holding.
4. Solve the conflict. • Reread your last few paragraphs. Did you resolve the central conflict? • Create an ending that solves the problem and satisfies the reader. For example, you might show how a character has changed.	He looked at the Frisbee and realized that making it fly would be all about getting it to spin and stay level. He held it flat and flicked his wrist to throw the Frisbee back. It soared over the grass and straight into waiting hands. He didn't even have to think about it; it just felt right. It was a good day for new flight patterns.

FOR LESS–PROFICIENT WRITERS

Check the Sequence Have students use a Sequence Chain to make sure that the events in their stories follow logically from one to another. When they have written their main events in the chart, suggest that they consider whether all the events are clearly related by cause and effect. If not, they might need to add explanation or intermediate events to fill in the gaps.

BEST PRACTICES TOOLKIT—Transparency
Sequence Chain pp. B21, B45

FOR ENGLISH LEARNERS

Task Support: Focus on the Details [mixed-readiness pairs] Have students work in pairs to revise the following sentences by adding sensory or descriptive details. Ask students to share their sentences and compare their revisions. Could they use any of the descriptive words in their stories?

- Jeremy was tired.
- His bedroom was messy.
- The race was long and boring.
- He had a strange dream.

REVISING AND EDITING

1. **Check the sequence.** Help students think of other words and phrases that could substitute for the transitions in the example. Discuss how fluency with transitional words and phrases not only helps develop a story's sequence of events but also makes the text more coherent. In the example, the original version has three short, choppy sentences; the transitions make the text flow smoothly by showing how events and ideas are related.
2. **Improve the dialogue.** Have students review the dialogue in other stories in the unit, identifying examples of fragments and grammatical errors. Discuss whether students think this makes the dialogue more realistic. Then have students make a list of their own characters' main traits. Would their characters speak formally or informally? Which characters would be most likely to talk a lot, and which ones would probably speak very little?
3. **Focus on the details.** Have students review the sensory details highlighted on page 560 of the student model. Then ask them to use a Cluster Diagram to gather additional details of sight, hearing, touch, taste, and smell that will make their stories more vivid and interesting.

   BEST PRACTICES TOOLKIT—Transparency
   Cluster Diagram p. B18
4. **Solve the conflict.** Suggest that peer readers review each other's stories to determine whether the problem has been solved and whether the ending is satisfying. Then have them make suggestions for improvement. This might involve revising the story's sequence of events and the development of conflict throughout the story.

For interactive revision tools, see
- Write*Smart* CD
- Writing Center at **ClassZone.com**

Preparing to Publish

Support for meeting the goals in the writing rubric is supplied throughout the **Writing Workshop** on pages 558–563.

For Rubric Bank, see

- Write*Smart* CD
- Writing Center at **ClassZone.com**

Assess and Reteach

After reading and assessing students' short stories, you might use these lessons to reteach key skills:

STANDARDS LESSON FILE

Writing Lesson 1: Finding a Writing Idea
Writing Lesson 14: Sequence and Chronological Order
Writing Lesson 27: Descriptive Writing
Writing Lesson 28: Short Story
Writing Lesson 48: Writing Dialogue
Grammar Lesson 16: Basic Verb Tenses

Preparing to Publish Short Story

Apply the Rubric

A strong short story . . .

- ☑ creates interest starting with the first sentence
- ☑ has a well-developed plot with a logical sequence of events
- ☑ presents, develops, and resolves a central conflict
- ☑ uses descriptive details, sensory language, and dialogue to enliven the characters, setting, and events
- ☑ varies sentence lengths
- ☑ shows the writer's distinctive style
- ☑ has a satisfying, believable conclusion

Ask a Peer Reader

- What is the conflict in my story? How is it resolved?
- Is the dialogue believable? If not, how could I improve it?
- Is the sequence unclear at any point? If so, where?
- How would you describe the main character or characters?

"What If" Questions

What if a character got lost in the woods, in a city, or in a huge amusement park?

What if a game or a field trip didn't go as plann[ed] because of a conflict between two characters?

What if someone discovered a secret that could change a life?

What if two people had to race against time to reach safety?

What if a character woke up one morning as a different person, an animal, or a space alien?

Check Your Grammar

- Most stories use the past tense to tell what happened.

> *Samuel shuffled to the front of the room.*
> *Joe was the school's soccer star.*

- Most dialogue uses some form of the present tense.

> *"Joe, are you launching it?"*
> *"That's what I'm trying to do," said Joe.*

Writing Online

PUBLISHING OPTIONS
For publishing options, visit the **Writing Center** at **ClassZone.com.**

ASSESSMENT PREPARATION
For writing and grammar assessment practice, go to the **Assessment Center** at **ClassZone.com.**

564 UNIT 4: THEME AND SYMBOL

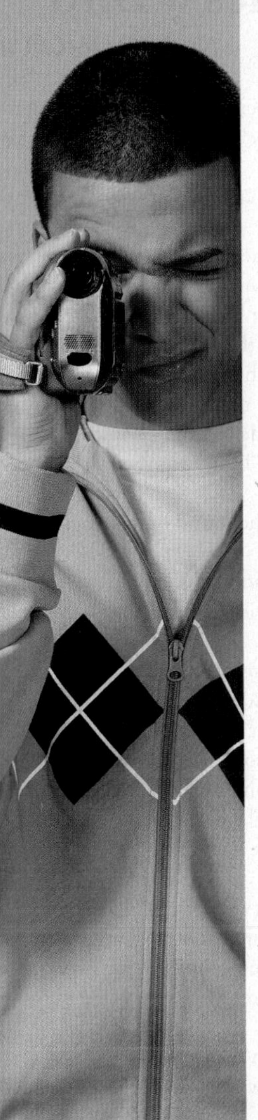

Producing a Video

You can make a video of the story you wrote or of any story or scene from this unit.

Planning the Video

1. **Write a script.** Turning a story into a script almost always involves adding dialogue. Often, it also means adding a narrator who supplies background information. Remember that a script also includes stage directions as well as ideas for sound effects (sometimes abbreviated as *SFX*) and music.
2. **Create a storyboard.** Plan your video by making simple sketches of each scene.
3. **Find actors and props.** Ask classmates to act in and narrate your video. Gather any props you will need.

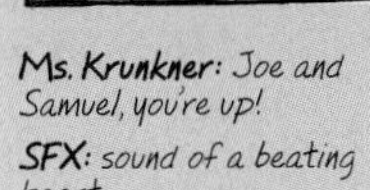

Ms. Krunkner: Joe and Samuel, you're up!
SFX: sound of a beating heart

Narrator: Samuel's heart is racing.
SFX: sound of heart grows louder

Producing the Video

1. **Shoot the footage.** Include different kinds of shots, such as close-ups, medium shots, and long shots. Try using different camera angles. Your goal is to tell a story that it is both clear and interesting.
2. **Wrap it up.** Use editing software to put the scenes in the right order and to add a title screen and credits. Remember, it's more important to tell a good story that your audience can follow easily than to stay close to the original. Don't hesitate to cut or to add.
3. **Show your masterpiece.** Screen your video for your classmates and invited guests. If you wish, hold a comments and questions session afterward. Ask your audience for feedback on what they liked and didn't like about your video.

PUBLISHING WITH TECHNOLOGY

Ask students to read this page to get an overview of how to produce a video.

Before students begin working, review this rubric with them so that they understand their goals:

Rubric An effective video

- is based on a script that can include dialogue, stage directions, background information, and sound effects
- has been planned with a storyboard
- involves actors and props
- includes different kinds of shots and camera angles
- is well edited

RESOURCE MANAGER—Copy Master
Publishing with Technology p. 175

STANDARDS LESSON FILE
Media Lesson 20: Producing a Video

DIFFERENTIATED INSTRUCTION

FOR LESS–PROFICIENT WRITERS

Planning a Video

1. Explain that a video must be carefully planned, telling the story but also including elements such as sound effects, dialogue, and stage directions to make it clear what is happening. A video should also be sketched out in advance on a storyboard so that the sequence of events is clear.
2. As students write their scripts, have them consider these questions:
   - Does the story contain enough dialogue for the script, or do I need to write more?
   - Can the characters' emotions be shown with sound effects? If so, what kinds of sound effects could I use?
   - What other kinds of sound effects can I incorporate into my script?
   - Does my video need a narrator? If so, which parts of the story should be told or explained by the narrator?
   - What actions do the characters in the story perform? What stage directions will describe these actions to the actors?
3. Have students use a Storyboard to develop an outline for their video. The storyboard should indicate key dialogue and narration.

BEST PRACTICES TOOLKIT—Transparency
Storyboard p. C11

Assessment Practice

CHECK READINESS

Read aloud the paragraph under **ASSESS** and stress to students that this is not the full Unit Test but a way for them to check their readiness for it. Then have students examine the skills listed under **REVIEW** and look back in the unit or in the **Student Resource Bank** for any skills they need to study.

READ THE SELECTION

Remind students to keep Unit Goals in mind as they read the passage, paying particular attention to

- themes
- symbols
- conclusions they draw while reading

To help students focus on **theme** while reading, encourage them to ask questions such as

- What is the major conflict? In what way is it resolved?
- What are the effects of the conflict and its resolution on the characters? What lessons do the characters learn?

ANSWER THE QUESTIONS

Direct students to pages R95–R101 of the Test-Taking Handbook to review test-taking strategies. Remind students not to choose the first alternative that seems to fit when answering a multiple-choice question. Instead, they should read through all the choices, eliminate any that are clearly wrong, and then choose the best answer—the one that is most accurate and complete.

Tell students that they may need to refer back to the selection to find an answer to a question or to confirm a response. Explain that they should not waste time rereading the entire passage. Rather, they should think about where in the passage the answer may be located and skim quickly, looking for key words that echo the question or one of the answer choices. When they identify the relevant part of the text, they should read it more closely to find the details they need.

Assessment Practice

Reading Comprehension

ASSESS

The practice test items on the next few pages match skills listed on the Unit Goals page (page 441) and addressed throughout this unit. Taking this practice test will help you assess your knowledge of these skills and determine your readiness for the Unit Test.

REVIEW

After you take the practice test, your teacher can help you identify any skills you need to review.

- Theme
- Symbol
- Draw Conclusions
- Thesaurus
- Suffixes
- Capitalization: Countries, Languages, and Ethnicities
- Active Voice

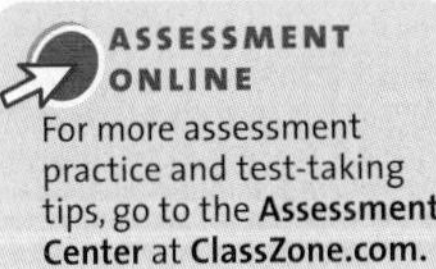

For more assessment practice and test-taking tips, go to the **Assessment Center** at **ClassZone.com.**

DIRECTIONS *Read this selection and answer the questions that follow.*

A Blind Man Catches a Bird

Alexander McCall Smit

A young man married a woman whose brother was blind. The young man was eager to get to know his new brother-in-law and so he asked him if he would like to go hunting with him.

"I cannot see," the blind man said. "But you can help me see when we are out hunting together. We can go."

The young man led the blind man off into the bush. At first they followed path that he knew and it was easy for the blind man to tag on behind the othe After a while, though, they went off into thicker bush, where the trees grew closely together and there were many places for the animals to hide. The blinc man now held on to the arm of his sighted brother-in-law and told him many things about the sounds that they heard around them. Because he had no sigh he had a great ability to interpret the noises made by animals in the bush.

"There are warthogs around," he would say, "I can hear their noises over there."

Or: "That bird is preparing to fly. Listen to the sound of its wings unfolding."

To the brother-in-law, these sounds were meaningless, and he was most impressed at the blind man's ability to understand the bush although it must have been for him one great darkness.

They walked on for several hours, until they reached a place where they could set their traps. The blind man followed the other's advice, and put his trap in a place where birds might come for water. The other man put his trap a short distance away, taking care to disguise it so that no bird would know th it was there. He did not bother to disguise the blind man's trap, as it was hot and he was eager to get home to his new wife. The blind man thought that h had disguised his trap, but he did not see that he had failed to do so and any bird could tell that there was a trap there.

They returned to their hunting place the next day. The blind man was excited at the prospect of having caught something, and the young man had to tell him to keep quiet, or he would scare all the animals away. Even before they reached the traps, the blind man was able to tell that they had caught something.

"I can hear birds," he said. "There are birds in the traps."

When he reached his trap, the young man saw that he had caught a small

DIFFERENTIATED INSTRUCTION

FOR ENGLISH LEARNERS

Assessment Practice: Work Backwards

[paired option] Prepare students for the assessment by having them read the questions before reading the passage. Have pairs follow these steps to learn unfamiliar words in the test directions and questions:

1. Find words you don't recognize and write each one on an index card.
2. Look up the meaning in a dictionary.
3. Write the meaning on the back of the card.
4. Use your word cards to teach and practice the vocabulary with your partner and another pair of students.

ird. He took it out of the trap and put it in a pouch that he had brought with im. Then the two of them walked towards the blind man's trap.

"There is a bird in it," he said to the blind man. "You have caught a bird too."

As he spoke, he felt himself filling with jealousy. The blind man's bird was narvelously colored, as if it had flown through a rainbow and been stained by ne colors. The feathers from a bird such as that would make a fine present for is new wife, but the blind man had a wife too, and she would also want the eathers.

The young man bent down and took the blind man's bird from the trap. Then, quickly substituting his own bird, he passed it to the blind man and put he colored bird into his own pouch.

"Here is your bird," he said to the blind man. "You may put it in your ouch."

The blind man reached out for the bird and took it. He felt it for a moment, is fingers passing over the wings and the breast. Then, without saying nything, he put the bird into his pouch and they began the trip home.

On their way home, the two men stopped to rest under a broad tree. As they at there, they talked about many things. The young man was impressed with he wisdom of the blind man, who knew a great deal, although he could see othing at all.

"Why do people fight with one another?" he asked the blind man. It was question which had always troubled him and he wondered if the blind man ould give him an answer.

The blind man said nothing for a few moments, but it was clear to the oung man that he was thinking. Then the blind man raised his head, and it eemed to the young man as if the unseeing eyes were staring right into his oul. Quietly he gave his answer.

"Men fight because they do to each other what you have just done to me."

The words shocked the young man and made him ashamed. He tried to hink of a response, but none came. Rising to his feet, he fetched his pouch, ook out the brightly colored bird and gave it back to the blind man.

The blind man took the bird, felt over it with his fingers, and smiled.

"Do you have any other questions for me?" he asked.

"Yes," said the young man. "How do men become friends after they have ought?"

The blind man smiled again.

"They do what you have just done," he said. "That's how they become riends again."

ITEM ANALYSIS

COMPREHENSION AND WRITTEN RESPONSE	ITEMS	UNIT PAGES
Theme	1, 2, 7, 16	442, 444, 455, 463, 485
Symbol	3, 5, 8, 12, 15, 16	442, 449, 477
Draw Conclusions	4, 6, 9, 10, 11, 13, 14	477

VOCABULARY	ITEMS	UNIT PAGES
Thesaurus	1, 2, 3	461
Suffixes	4, 5, 6	474

WRITING AND GRAMMAR	ITEMS	UNIT PAGES
Capitalization: Countries, Languages, and Ethnicities	1, 3	543
Active Voice	2, 4, 5	483

FOR LESS–PROFICIENT READERS

Assessment Support Consider these options for completing the **Assessment Practice:**

- Have students work backwards, reviewing the questions before reading the passage.
- Select random questions in the assessment and have students demonstrate how and where to look for the answers.
- Ask students to locate unfamiliar vocabulary in the assessment. Elicit the meanings of these words from the class.
- Have students jot down useful testing words and definitions in their journals for later reference.
- Read the selection or parts of it aloud to aid in student comprehension.

McDougal Littell
Assessment System

After checking student readiness with this Assessment Practice, you may administer the complete Unit 4 Test in order to more thoroughly evaluate student mastery of unit goals.

ANSWERS

Comprehension

Model a thinking process for answering multiple-choice questions.

1. **C *is correct.*** *In lines 70–72, the blind man says that the young man's return of the bird has restored their friendship. The young man's action shows a desire to make things right. There is no evidence to support A. The young man's motive is jealousy (line 38), not the need to feel smart. B and D are incorrect because they do not convey messages about life or human nature.*
2. **D *is correct.*** *One major theme involves the insight that the blind man possesses in place of physical sight. A, B, and C are unrelated to the themes developed by the story's plot, symbols, and characters.*
3. **B *is correct.*** *By the end of the story, the young man has learned a life lesson. A is incorrect because the blind man does not propose the hunt; the young man does. The ideas in C and D are not supported by the details in the story.*
4. **A *is correct.*** *The sentence in lines 11–12 develops a cause-and-effect relationship between lack of sight and acute hearing. Because the young man can see, he has not trained himself to listen closely. B is incorrect because interpreting the animals' noises is not the same as speaking their language. C is incorrect because neither man would be able to hear if the sounds were muffled. D is unsupported by details in the story.*
5. **D *is correct.*** *In lines 22–24, the young man is described as carefully disguising his trap so that it might deceive the birds. Later, he also deceives his brother-in-law. A, B, and C are contradicted by the young man's care in disguising his trap.*
6. **A *is correct.*** *Lines 55–57 indicate that the first question has always bothered the young man, suggesting that he wants to know more about people and relationships. B is incorrect because, in line 25, the young man is described as being eager to return to his wife. C is incorrect because he is already impressed with the blind man's wisdom (lines 52–54). There is no evidence to suggest that he is feeling argumentative, making D incorrect.*
7. **A *is correct.*** *The young man's action of switching the birds is dishonest and could have led to conflict between the two men. B is incorrect, although the blind man's willingness to forgive in lines 70–72 suggests this theme later in the story. C is incorrect because the young man's actions, not his words, could have led to a fight. D is irrelevant to the question of why people fight; it relates instead to solving conflicts.*
8. **A *is correct.*** *The young man is impressed with the blind man's wisdom (lines 52–54), and he learns an important life lesson from him. The events of the story do not especially show the blind man's strength or courage, making B and C incorrect. D applies to the young man (line 38), not to his brother-in-law.*
9. **C *is correct.*** *He thinks that the feathers from the bird would make a fine present for his wife (lines 40–41). A is incorrect because his wife would be displeased if she found out that her husband did not help her brother set a good trap. B and D are unrelated to pleasing his wife.*

Comprehension

DIRECTIONS *Answer these questions about "A Blind Man Catches a Bird."*

1. Which statement expresses the overall theme of the story?
   - **A** People cheat others because it makes them feel smart.
   - **B** People should rely more on their hearing than on their sight.
   - **C** True friendship depends on respect and fairness.
   - **D** Hunting is a good way to learn about animal behavior.
2. Which quotation conveys one of the story's themes?
   - **A** "At first they followed a path that he knew and it was easy for the blind man to tag on behind the other." (lines 6–7)
   - **B** "The blind man followed the other's advice, and put his trap in a place where birds might come for water." (line 21–22)
   - **C** "When he reached his trap, the young man saw that he had caught a small bird." (lines 34–35)
   - **D** "The young man was impressed with the wisdom of the blind man, who knew a great deal, although he could see nothing at all." (lines 52–54)
3. The hunting trip could be a symbol of the
   - **A** wisdom of a person who is blind
   - **B** search for what is important in life
   - **C** human struggle to control nature
   - **D** difficulty of living without sight
4. The sounds in the bush are meaningless to the young man because
   - **A** his ability to see limits his ability to listen
   - **B** he cannot speak the language of the animals
   - **C** a thick growth of trees muffles every sound
   - **D** the blind man is talking in a loud voice
5. The disguised trap might symbolize the young man's
   - **A** carelessness
   - **B** foolishness
   - **C** laziness
   - **D** deceitfulness
6. From the two questions that he asks the b man in lines 55 and 68–69, you can conc that the young man is
   - **A** trying to understand human nature
   - **B** having problems with his new wife
   - **C** testing the blind man's intelligence
   - **D** looking for something to argue about
7. Which theme is suggested by the blind m answer to the question about why people fight?
   - **A** Dishonesty ruins people's relationships.
   - **B** Friends must be willing to forgive.
   - **C** People should think before they speak.
   - **D** Compromise will solve most problems.
8. Which quality might the blind man symbolize?
   - **A** wisdom
   - **B** strength
   - **C** courage
   - **D** jealousy
9. You can conclude that the young man is e to please his new wife when he
   - **A** does not help the blind man disguise hi bird trap
   - **B** is impressed that the blind man can understand the animals' sounds
   - **C** steals the colorful bird so that she can h its feathers
   - **D** asks his brother-in-law why people figh

568

Why is the blind man silent when he realizes that the young man has cheated him by switching the birds?

A He plans to catch another bird to replace the small one.
B He is waiting for the right moment to talk calmly with his brother-in-law.
C He knows that the young man will be punished later.
D He plans to tell the young man's wife what happened.

Reread lines 55–64. You can conclude that the young man is shocked at the response to his question because he

A thinks the blind man doesn't know that the young man cheated him
B expects the blind man to politely ignore his question
C knows the blind man doesn't understand his question
D believes that he has a right to take the beautiful bird

What does the colorful bird symbolize to the men in the story?

A bad luck
B a valued prize
C a happy memory
D broken promises

You can conclude that the young man gives the colorful bird to the blind man in order to

A restore their friendship
B show his generosity
C please his new wife
D avoid an argument

Written Response

SHORT RESPONSE *Write two or three sentences to answer each question.*

14. Even though he doesn't know how to set a trap, the blind man catches a beautiful bird. What conclusion can you draw from that incident?

15. What might the blindness in the story symbolize? In what ways are the two characters blind?

EXTENDED RESPONSE *Write a paragraph to answer this question.*

16. Explain the connection between one symbol and one theme in the story.

GO ON

10. B *is correct.* *Because the blind man eventually does mention it, a correct conclusion would be that he is waiting for the right time.* A *is incorrect; there is nothing in the text to suggest that they will reset the traps.* C *and* D *are unsupported by evidence in the story.*

11. A *is correct.* *The young man is "shocked" and "ashamed" (line 63), suggesting that he would not have taken the bird if he thought he might be found out.* B, C, *and* D *are unsupported by the story.*

12. B *is correct.* *Both men desire the colorful bird, suggesting that it represents something of value.* A, C, *and* D *do not match the bird's symbolism in the story.*

13. A *is correct.* *The young man is ashamed and wants to repair the damage he did with his action.* B *is incorrect because the bird rightfully belongs to the blind man.* C *and* D *may be results of his action but not his motivation for doing it.*

Written Response

Possible short responses:

14. *The blind man may lack the skills of his brother-in-law, but he has wisdom. Readers may conclude that wisdom is more important in life than mere ability. It leads to a richer, more fulfilling life.*

15. *One character is physically blind but possesses insight. The other character has sight but lacks the ability to see what is right.*

Possible extended response:

16. *Students' paragraphs should*

- *explain one symbol in the story, such as the hunting trip, the trap, or the bird*
- *show how the symbol helps bring out one of the themes, such as the importance of insight to living a meaningful existence, the importance of respect and honesty in human relationships, or the rewards that come from living wisely and honestly*
- *support their connection with details from the text*

DIFFERENTIATED INSTRUCTION

FOR ENGLISH LEARNERS

Review Academic Vocabulary Review the definitions of these terms with students:

- *theme:* a message about life or human nature that is communicated by a literary work, often revealed through changes in the characters or through lessons they learn
- *symbol:* a person, place, object, or action that stands for something beyond itself
- *conclusion:* a logical statement or guess, based on information in the text and prior knowledge

Use this passage to model how to identify symbols (*turkey symbolizes generosity, hug symbolizes parents' acceptance*), draw conclusions (*hug supports the conclusion that parents are proud of the narrator*), and infer theme (*it is better to give than to receive*):

> "I gave away our Thanksgiving turkey to Lena's family," I confessed. My parents looked at each other. Then they hugged me and said that they hoped I liked peanut butter sandwiches with gravy. We later agreed that they weren't bad!

ANSWERS

Vocabulary

1. **C *is correct.*** *The phrase from the story is "tag on behind the other." Since the two characters are walking into the bush, the logical meaning is "follow." A is incorrect because the blind man is not in pursuit of the other character. B and D are incorrect because they do not fit the context of the sentence.*
2. **A *is correct.*** *The young man placed the trap "a short distance away," meaning a length of a few yards. B, C, and D do not make sense in the context of the sentence.*
3. **B *is correct.*** *As the two men return to their traps, the blind man is excited about the possibility of having caught a bird. A does not make sense in the context of the story. C is incorrect because it implies that the blind man can see that he has caught a bird. D is incorrect because it suggests an opinion about an idea, which does not fit the context.*
4. **C *is correct.*** *The blind man has the ability or talent to interpret the noises. A and B are incorrect because both words indicate a wish to do something rather than the ability to do it. D is incorrect because having intelligence is not related to interpreting noises.*
5. **D *is correct.*** *The suffix -less means "without." Therefore,* meaningless *means "without meaning" or "impossible to understand." A, B, and C do not reflect the definition of* meaning *or -less.*
6. **C *is correct.*** *Admiration and wonder are closely related. Therefore, if something inspires admiration, it often causes wonder. A, B, and D are unrelated to the definition of* marvel.

Vocabulary

DIRECTIONS *Use context clues and the thesaurus entries to answer the following questions.*

> **tag:** *verb.* call, identify, brand, label, follow, trail, chase

1. Which word could be substituted for the word *tag* as it is used in line 7?
   - **A** chase
   - **B** identify
   - **C** follow
   - **D** call

> **distance:** *noun.* space, coldness, separation, gap, length, remoteness

2. Which word could be substituted for the word *distance* as it is used in line 23?
   - **A** length
   - **B** separation
   - **C** remoteness
   - **D** coldness

> **prospect:** *noun.* customer, chance, hope, possibility, scene, view

3. Which word could be substituted for the word *prospect* as it is used in line 29?
   - **A** customer
   - **B** possibility
   - **C** scene
   - **D** view

DIRECTIONS *Use context clues and your knowledg of suffixes to answer the following questions.*

4. The word *able* means "having the power o skill to do something." What is the most li meaning of the word *ability* as it is used in line 12?
   - **A** feeling
   - **B** desire
   - **C** talent
   - **D** intelligence
5. The word *meaning* refers to "something th one wishes to convey, especially by languag What is the most likely meaning of the wo *meaningless* as it is used in line 17?
   - **A** easily overlooked
   - **B** beautifully melodic
   - **C** not worth listening to
   - **D** impossible to understand
6. The word *marvel* means "one that inspires admiration." What is the most likely mean of the word *marvelously* as it is used in line
   - **A** in a lighthearted manner
   - **B** with a reddish tint
   - **C** in a way that causes wonder
   - **D** with unattractive colors

DIFFERENTIATED INSTRUCTION

FOR ENGLISH LEARNERS

Test-Taking Strategies: Word Replacement [mixed-readiness pairs] Model how to answer question 1 by using these steps. Then have student pairs follow the same strategy to answer questions 2 and 3.

1. Return to the passage and read the sentence in which the word to be defined is found.
2. Mentally identify a synonym for the word.
3. Find the answer choice that is closest in meaning to that word.
4. Substitute the choice back into the original sentence to see if it makes sense.

Writing & Grammar

DIRECTIONS *Read this passage and answer the questions that follow.*

(1) South Africa's current population descends from african, asian, and european settlers. (2) More than 1,500 years ago, the Transvaal region of South Africa was settled by members of the Bantu language group. (3) In 1652, the Dutch became the first Europeans to settle in South Africa. (4) Though dutch was the dominant language throughout the 1700s, english and a new language, known as afrikaans, later became the official languages of south africa. (5) Today, 11 official languages are recognized by the government. (6) The Zulu, the Xhosa, and the Sotho are just some of the African ethnic groups who speak these languages. (7) Respect for the many other languages spoken in the country is encouraged in the constitution.

1. Which words should be capitalized in sentence 1?
   A african, european
   B asian
   C european, settlers
   D african, asian, european

2. Choose the correct way to rewrite sentence 2 in the active voice.
   A The Transvaal region of South Africa was settled by members of the Bantu language group more than 1,500 years ago.
   B The Transvaal region of South Africa was settled more than 1,500 years ago by members of the Bantu language group.
   C More than 1,500 years ago, members of the Bantu language group settled the Transvaal region of South Africa.
   D The Transvaal region of South Africa was first settled by members of the Bantu language group more than 1,500 years ago.

3. Which words should be capitalized in sentence 4?
   A dutch, english
   B dutch, english, afrikaans, south africa
   C afrikaans, south africa
   D english

4. Choose the correct way to rewrite sentence 5 in the active voice.
   A Today, 11 official languages are being recognized by the government.
   B Eleven official languages are now recognized by the government.
   C Today, the government recognizes 11 official languages.
   D A total of 11 official languages are recognized today by the government.

5. Choose the correct way to rewrite sentence 7 in the active voice.
   A Respect is encouraged in the constitution for the many other languages spoken in the country.
   B The constitution encourages respect for the many other languages spoken in the country.
   C In the constitution, respect is encouraged for the many other languages spoken in the country.
   D Use of the many other languages spoken in the country is respected in the constitution.

STOP

ANSWERS

Writing & Grammar

1. **D is correct.** *All of the words referring to people of particular ethnicities should be capitalized. A, B, and C are incorrect because they do not include all of those words. C is also incorrect because the word ancestors is a common noun and should not be capitalized.*
2. **C is correct.** *In the active voice, the subject (members) performs the action of settling, and the direct object (*Transvaal region*) receives it. A, B, and D are incorrect because* Transvaal region *is the subject of each sentence, so these rewrites are still in the passive voice.*
3. **B is correct.** *The three languages should be capitalized as well as the country of South Africa. A, C, and D are incorrect because they do not include all of the words that should be capitalized.*
4. **C is correct.** *The subject,* government, *performs the action of recognizing. A, B, and D are all in the passive voice and are therefore incorrect.*
5. **B is correct.** *The subject,* constitution, *performs the action of encouraging respect. A, C, and D are in the passive voice and are therefore incorrect.*

DIFFERENTIATED INSTRUCTION

FOR ENGLISH LEARNERS

Assessment Support: Capitalization [mixed-readiness pairs] Review these rules:

- Capitalize languages, nationalities, and ethnicities: *English, Spanish, Portuguese, American, Colombian, Hispanic, Mandarin*
- Capitalize continents and political units: *Asia, North America, United States, Argentina*

Then have pairs correct these sentences:

We moved to this Country, brazil, when I was ten. My mother is japanese, and my father is canadian.

Assessment Support: Active and Passive Voice Discuss these terms:

- *active voice:* a verb form in which the subject performs the action and the direct object receives the action. Example: *The musician played the piano brilliantly.*
- *passive voice:* a verb form in which the subject receives the action of the verb. The passive form uses *to be* as a helping verb. Example: *The piano was played brilliantly by the musician.*

Then have students rewrite these sentences in either the passive or the active voice:

- The audience was stunned by the talent of the actors. *(The talent of the actors stunned the audience.)*
- The girl did her homework right after school. *(The homework was done by the girl right after school.)*
- The home-run ball was caught by a spectator at the game. *(A spectator at the game caught the home-run ball.)*

INTRODUCE *MORE GREAT READS*

In Unit 4, students have discussed a number of big questions. Invite students to tell which question they found most intriguing and why. Then focus attention on the three questions that appear on this page. Discuss the recommended books and their summaries, pointing out how each book connects to the related question. Encourage students to choose one or more of these "great reads" to read independently.

ClassZone.com

To find additional books that match students' interests and ability levels, visit the Literature Center at **ClassZone.com.**

Ideas for Independent Reading

Which questions from Unit 4 made an impression on you? Continue exploring them with these books.

Is curiosity a gift or a curse?

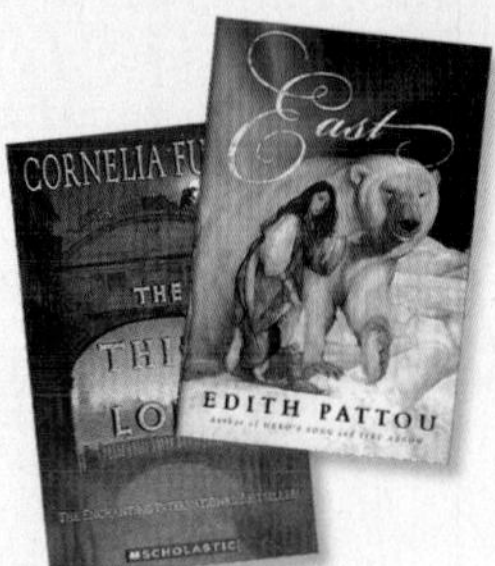

East
by Edith Pattou

Rose was born curious. When a white bear shows up and asks her to go with him so her family can prosper, teenaged Rose agrees. She doesn't realize that living with a bear is only the beginning of a longer journey.

Mable Riley: A Reliable Record of Humdrum, Peril, and Romance
by Marthe Jocelyn

The year is 1901, and Mable hopes she'll have an adventure when she moves away with her sister. At first, life remains boring. But everything changes when Mable meets the neighbor.

The Thief Lord
by Cornelia Funke

Prosper and Bo have run a to Venice to escape their a and uncle. They are taken by the Thief Lord, a maske boy who leads a band of children. When the Thief Lord accepts a mysterious assignment, the adventur of the band get complicat

How well do we treat our elders?

The Cay
by Theodore Taylor

Phillip and his mother escape the German invasion of Curaçao on a freighter, but the boat is torpedoed. Phillip wakes up on a life raft with a cat and a West Indian named Timothy. Will Phillip be able to survive with only an old man for support?

A Step from Heaven
by An Na

Young Ju is only four when her family moves to the U.S. from Korea. At first, everyone is happy, but then her parents start fighting again. Young Ju has been raised to respect her elders, but she knows that sometimes her father isn't right. What should she do?

The Not-So-Star-Spangled Life of Sunita Sen
by Mitali Perkins

When Sunita's grandparen visit from India, her life changes. For one thing, sh can't have boys over anym She has to find a way to ac her family and still fit in.

What impact will you have on the world?

The Book Thief
by Markus Zusak

Liesel is a little girl the first time she meets Death in Nazi Germany. The second time, she's a book thief, stealing books and reading them to anyone who needs to listen. Later, she writes her own story. This is the book Death wants you to hear.

The Merlin Conspiracy
by Diana Wynne Jones

Roddy and Grundo are just teenagers in the Royal Court. No one but an outsider will believe them when they warn of a conspiracy against the king. Can three young magicians win a battle to keep the magic in the multiverse?

Be the Difference: A Beginner's Guide to Changing the World
by Danny Seo

At 12, Danny Seo inspired thousands of students to join him in an environmer movement. Ten years late he wrote this book. Read advice about how teenage can improve the world.

UNIT 5

Painting with Words

POETRY

573

For help in planning this unit, see

RESOURCE MANAGER UNIT 5 pp. 1–11

INTRODUCE THE UNIT

Although we may not think of ourselves as artists, every time we use words to describe a person, place, thing, idea, or feeling, we paint a mental picture. Words provide the palette of colors, and our voice, pen, or keyboard is the paintbrush. The best part is that each picture can be original because there is no end to the ways in which words can be arranged on our canvas.

Illustrate the idea of painting pictures with words by having pairs of students write a description of someone eating a juicy apple. Have students compare images to show the versatility of words. Then have them look carefully at the art on page 573 and complete these activities in small groups:

- Write down words and phrases that "paint" each image.
- Arrange the words and phrases to convey the essence of each picture. Use either complete sentences or phrases.
- Consider how the words look on the page as well as what they mean. Read aloud what you have written to see if it has a pleasing sound.

Have groups share their word paintings. Guide them to see that they have written poems. **Poetry** is the most concentrated form of painting with words. In this unit, students will learn more about the techniques that poets use to make their works masterpieces.

About the Art The copper engraving *La Promenade en Mer* by Jean Plichart appears with the poem "Boots of Spanish Leather" by Bob Dylan. See page 639. The photograph of shells appears on page 609 as an illustration for Alice Walker's poem "We Alone."

UNIT 5

Skills Trace

SKILLS STRAND	Reader's Workshop: Appreciating Poetry pp. 576–581	Simile: Willow and Ginkgo/ Introduction to Poetry pp. 582–587 Poems *Level: Average*	Macavity: The Mystery Cat/ Vermin pp. 588–595 Poems *Level: Average*	the lesson of the moth/Identity pp. 596–603 Poems *Level: Easy*	It's all I have to bring today—/ We Alone pp. 604–611 Poems *Level: Average*	Speech to the Young: Speech to the Progress-Toward/Mother to Son pp. 612–617 Lyric Poems *Level: Easy*
Literary Analysis	Form and Speaker pp. 576–577, 581 Sound Devices pp. 578–579, 581 Imagery and Figurative Language pp. 580–581	Stanza pp. 583, 584, 587 Metaphor and Simile pp. 583, 584, 586, 587	Couplet pp. 589, 592, 594	Free Verse pp. 597, 600, 602 Speaker pp. 597, 598, 600, 601, 602	Recurring Theme pp. 605, 606, 608, 610	Lyric Poetry pp. 613, 616, 617 Sound Devices pp. 613, 614, 616, 617
Reading and Informational Texts	Analyze the Literature pp. 577, 579, 581	Visualize pp. 583, 586, 587	Analyze Figurative Language pp. 589, 590, 592, 593, 594	Clarify Meaning pp. 597, 598, 601, 602	Set a Purpose for Reading pp. 605, 610 Compare Recurring Theme p. 610	Make Inferences pp. 613, 614, 617
Vocabulary	Academic Vocabulary pp. 576–578, 580		Word Acquisition pp. 589, T589, 595 Context Clues p. T589 Word Origins p. 595			
Writing, Grammar, and Style				Commas in a Series and Between Adjectives p. 603	Write for Assessment p. 611	
Speaking, Listening, Viewing, and Media	Discuss pp. 576–580	Discuss pp. 582, T584–T586, 587 Analyze Visuals p. 584	Discuss pp. 588, T590–T593, 594 Analyze Visuals p. 590	Discuss pp. 596, T598–T601, 602 Analyze Visuals p. 598	Discuss pp. 604, T606–T609, 610 Analyze Visuals pp. 606, 608	Discuss pp. 612, T614–T616, 617 Analyze Visuals pp. 614, T616

 Assessment-Based Planning: Skills in red are assessed on the Unit 5 Test. **T** = Teacher's Edition page

On the Grasshopper and Cricket/ Ode on Solitude pp. 618–623 Sonnet/Ode *Level: Challenging*	*Linked selections* **One More Round/ Not My Bones** pp. 624–631 Poems *Level: Average/ Challenging*	*from* **Fortune's Bones** pp. 632–635 Book Excerpt *Level: Average*	**Boots of Spanish Leather/*from* The Song of Hiawatha** pp. 636–647 Ballad/Epic *Level: Easy/Challenging*	**Writing Workshop: Personal Response to a Poem** pp. 648–655
Traditional Forms pp. 619, 622, 623 Rhyme Scheme pp. 619, 620, 623	Word Choice pp. 625, 626, 628, 630		Narrative Poetry pp. 637, 638, 639, 640, 643, 645, 646 Rhythm and Meter pp. 637, 639, 642, 645, 646	
Paraphrase pp. 619, 620, 622, 623	Strategies for Reading Poetry pp. 625, 627, 629, 630	Form (Notes) pp. 633, 635 Outline pp. 632, 633, 634, 635 Support an Opinion p. 635	Summarize pp. 637, 638, 642, 643, 646	Analyze a Personal Response to a Poem pp. 649–650, 654
	Word Acquisition pp. 625, T625, 631 Context Clues p. T625 Latin Roots (*carn*) p. 631			
			Punctuation of Titles p. 647	Write a Personal Response to a Poem pp. 648–654 Punctuation of Quotations from Poems p. 654
Discuss pp. 618, T620–T622, 623 Analyze Visuals p. 620	Discuss pp. 624, T626–T629, 630 Analyze Visuals pp. 627, T628	Discuss pp. 632, T633–T634, 635	Discuss pp. 636, T638–T645, 646 Analyze Visuals pp. 638, 640, 644	Discuss pp. 648–650 Give an Oral Interpretation of a Poem p. 655

Skills Assessed on the Unit 5 Test:

Literary Analysis

- Identify and analyze figurative language, including similes, metaphors, extended metaphors, and personification
- Analyze stanzas in poetry and compare the length and meaning of stanzas
- Identify and analyze sound devices, including rhyme scheme, rhythm, repetition, assonance, alliteration
- Analyze speaker

Reading and Informational Texts

- Paraphrase lines of poetry
- Support an opinion

Vocabulary

- Use knowledge of word origins to help determine word meanings
- Use knowledge of Latin roots to help determine word meanings

Writing, Grammar, and Style

- Write a personal response to a poem
- Use commas correctly with items in a series and between adjectives
- Punctuate titles correctly by using quotation marks and italics
- Additional writing and grammar skills

For additional lesson planning help, see **Easy Planner DVD.**

OBJECTIVES

- establish prior knowledge about **poems**
- discuss the characteristics of a poem

What makes a POEM?

Ask students to share their experiences in writing a **poem.** Have them think about what they would do if they were to write one today. In what way would their approach be different than it was when they were younger? Lead students to draw some conclusions about what makes a poem.

ACTIVITY Before students answer the questions, review some of the poems that they have read in the past to help them compose their lists. Then, after pairs have met, ask them to share their answers to the questions on page 574 in small groups. Have groups use each other's ideas to put together their definition of a poem. Compare meanings and choose common elements to include in a class definition.

CHECK UNDERSTANDING Have students summarize what they have learned about the nature of a **poem.**

UNIT 5 **Share What You Know**

What makes a POEM?

Have you ever tried to write a **poem?** If so, you probably had to th about what a poem is. Is it lines that rhyme? Pictures painted wit words? Toe-tapping rhythms? A poem can be all of these things– none of them.

ACTIVITY Poetry is everywhere—in our favorite songs, the nurser rhymes we read as children, and even in some television commerc With a partner, make a list of poems that you have read or heard. Then answer the following questions:

- Did you find poetry in any unexpected places?
- What do these poems have in common?
- How do the words create mental pictures?
- Do these poems rhyme, or have rhythm?

Once you've answered these questions, see if you can define a poe

574

Unit Resources

- RESOURCE MANAGER UNIT 5
- BEST PRACTICES TOOLKIT
- STANDARDS LESSON FILE
- Easy Planner DVD
- Write*Smart* CD
- ClassZone.com
- Audio Anthology CD
- Multi-Language Academic Vocabulary Online
- eEdition CD & Online
- McDougal Littell Assessment System
- Test Generator CD
- Media*Smart* DVD

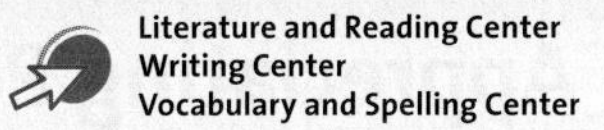

Literature and Reading Center
Writing Center
Vocabulary and Spelling Center

Preview Unit Goals

LITERARY ANALYSIS	• Identify and analyze figurative language • Identify, analyze, and compare length and meaning of stanzas • Identify and analyze sound devices • Identify, analyze, and compare rhyme schemes • Analyze repetition in poetry • Identify and analyze rhythm and meter and their effects • Identify and analyze speaker
READING	• Develop strategies for reading, including visualizing, clarifying, and setting a purpose for reading • Paraphrase lines in poetry • Outline information • Support an opinion
WRITING AND GRAMMAR	• Write a personal response to a poem • Use commas and other punctuation correctly
SPEAKING, LISTENING, AND VIEWING	• Give an oral interpretation of a poem
VOCABULARY	• Use knowledge of word roots and word origins to help determine word meaning
ACADEMIC VOCABULARY	• figurative language • sound devices • stanza • rhyme scheme

DIFFERENTIATED INSTRUCTION

FOR ENGLISH LEARNERS

Academic Vocabulary Use the Academic Vocabulary copy master to introduce these terms: *figurative language, sound devices, stanza, rhyme scheme.*

1. Read each term and definition aloud.
2. Allow students to work in pairs to complete the chart activities and Part B.
3. Reconvene to review students' responses.

Additional Academic Vocabulary Use the second copy master to help students study these terms from the unit: *couplet, free verse, lyric poetry, metaphor, narrative poetry, repetition, rhythm, simile.* Read each word and explanatory sentence aloud. As a class, define each term. Then have pairs work on Part B. Review their responses.

RESOURCE MANAGER—Copy Masters
Academic Vocabulary p. 9
Additional Academic Vocabulary p. 10

Preview Unit Goals

Note the color-coding used to show the different types of skills on page 575, which should be familiar to students from previous units. Read the unit goals aloud as students follow along. Ask them which skills and strategies they have used in the past and which are new to them. Then suggest that they record questions about the skills in their journals and look for answers as they work through the unit.

Have students write the Academic Vocabulary terms in their journals and suggest that they add a definition for each term as they come across it in their reading. Encourage students to use these terms when they talk about their work in Unit 5.

ADDITIONAL UNIT GOALS

These skills will be taught in this unit but are not the major focus of the unit:

Literary Analysis

- Identify and analyze stanzas in poetry, including couplets
- Identify similes and metaphors
- Identify and analyze tone in poetry
- Compare traditional forms of poetry with free verse
- Analyze and evaluate free verse
- Identify and compare recurring themes
- Identify and analyze symbols
- Identify and analyze dialect in poetry
- Identify examples of soft rhyme
- Identify imagery in poetry
- Analyze and compare word choice in poetry
- Identify onomatopoeia
- Study a variety of genres: free verse, lyric poetry, narrative poetry, author's notes

Reading

- Make inferences
- Summarize poetry

Writing and Grammar

- Write a comparison-contrast essay

Focus and Motivate

OBJECTIVES

- identify and analyze elements of poetic form, including lines and stanzas
- identify and analyze a poem's speaker
- compare traditional form with free verse
- identify and analyze sound devices, imagery, and figurative language

Teach

Part 1: The Basics

Form Explain that each stanza in a poem contributes to the poem's overall message. The end of a stanza usually signifies the end of one thought or impression and the beginning of a new one. Use this activity to give students practice analyzing stanzas:

- Read aloud the poems on page 576, pausing after each stanza.
- Have students identify the main idea or impression created by each stanza and then list their responses in a Two-Column Chart.

Stanza	Main Idea or Impression
"The Geese," stanza 1	Speaker's father notices call of geese each fall
"The Geese," stanza 2	Father lies awake, imagining he can fly with the geese
"Street Corner Flight," stanza 1	Two boys in a city hold white pigeons in their hands
"Street Corner Flight," stanza 2	The boys gently release the birds, which fly away

 **BEST PRACTICES TOOLKIT—Transparency**
Two-Column Chart p. A25

Speaker Help students identify the speakers of the poems on page 576. Point out that the speaker of "The Geese" could be either the poet or a character created by the poet. Discuss how a first-person speaker might change the impact of "Street Corner Flight."

 **BEST PRACTICES TOOLKIT—Copy Masters**
Core Analysis Frame: Poetry pp. D23, D36, D37
Analysis Frame: Poetic Form and Structure pp. D23, D42, D43

UNIT 5 Reader's Workshop

Appreciating Poetry

The poet Robert Frost once said that a poem "begins in delight and ends in wisdo While many poems are entertaining, a poem can also have the power to change you see the world. Whether it follows a set pattern or bends all the rules, each p uses language in a new way to communicate its message.

Part 1: The Basics

What do you see when you look at a poem? One difference between a poem and a short story is the **form,** or the structure of the writing. All poems are broken up into **lines.** The length of each line and where it breaks, or ends, contribute to the poem's meaning and sound. Lines often appear in groups, c **stanzas.** The stanzas work together to convey the overall message of the poe

Some poems follow the rules of a traditional form. For example, a poem might have a specific number of lines and stanzas or a regular pattern of rhyt and rhyme. Other poems are unconventional, with no recognizable patterns. A poet might even choose to use incorrect grammar or spelling to create a particular sound or to emphasize meaning.

Just as a story has a narrator, a poem has a voice that "talks" to readers. This voice, or **speaker,** is sometimes a fictional character rather than the poet

Take a look at the following poems. Which is traditional? Which is unconventional? Which one has a distinct speaker?

EXAMPLE 1

from **"The Geese"**
Poem by **Richard Peck**

My father was the first to hear
The passage of the geese each fall,
Passing above the house so near
He'd hear within his heart their call.

And then at breakfast time he'd say:
"The geese were heading south last
night,"
For he had lain awake till day,
Feeling his earthbound soul take flight.

EXAMPLE 2

from **"Street Corner Flight"**
Poem by **Norma Landa Flores**

From this side . . .
of their concrete barrio
two small boys hold
fat white pigeons
trapped in their trembling hands.

Then,
gently,
not disturbing
their powers of flight,
release them
into the air.

DIFFERENTIATED INSTRUCTION

FOR ALL STUDENTS

For general guidelines on differentiating instruction, see

 **BEST PRACTICES TOOLKIT**
Differentiated Instruction pp. 31–38

FOR LESS–PROFICIENT READERS

Note Taking Use the copy master Note Taking: Poetry Basics to help students understand, record, and retain the information on page 576.

 **RESOURCE MANAGER—Copy Master**
Note Taking p. 15

Analysis Support Help students explore the form of an unconventional poem.

- Point out that the lines in "Street Corner Flight" are of varying lengths, and some lines are indented.
- Discuss the shape of the poem's stanzas. Point out that each stanza resembles the pattern of birds in flight.
- Ask students to discuss the ways form and meaning are connected in this poem.

MODEL 1: TRADITIONAL FORM

In this traditional poem, the speaker reflects on the return of night at the end of a day. Read it aloud to help you identify the characteristics of its form.

from

Good-Night

Poem by **Robert Louis Stevenson**

When the bright lamp is carried in,
The sunless hours again begin;
O'er all without, in field and lane,
The haunted night returns again.

Now we behold the embers flee
About the firelit hearth; and see
Our faces painted as we pass,
Like pictures, on the window-glass.

Close Read

1. How many lines are in each stanza?
2. In the first stanza, rhyming pairs are highlighted. Identify the rhyming words in the second stanza. What pattern do you see?

MODEL 2: FREE VERSE

In this unconventional poem—called a **free verse** poem—the poet lets the ideas drive where each line breaks and when each stanza ends.

That Day

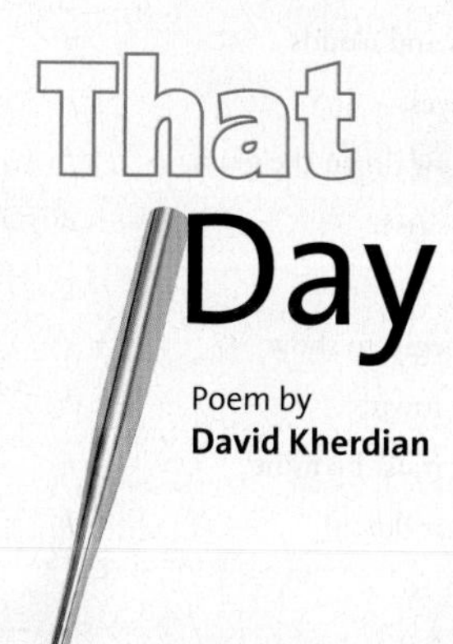

Poem by **David Kherdian**

Just once
my father stopped on the way
into the house from work
and joined in the softball game
we were having in the street,
and attempted to play in *our*
game that *his* country had never
known.

Just once
and the day stands out forever
in my memory
as a father's living gesture
to his son,
that in playing even the fool
or clown, he would reveal
that the lines of their lives
were sewn from a tougher fabric
than the son had previously known.

Close Read

1. How does the form of this poem differ from that of "Good-Night"?
2. Notice the short lengths of the boxed lines. What might the poet be trying to emphasize by isolating and repeating this phrase?
3. What do you learn about the speaker of this poem?

MODEL 1: TRADITIONAL FORM

Close Read

Possible answers:

1. *There are four lines in each stanza.*
2. *The rhyming words are* flee/see *and* pass/glass. *Both stanzas have the same pattern of rhyme: the first two lines rhyme with each other and the last two lines rhyme with each other (aabb).*

MODEL 2: FREE VERSE

Close Read

Possible answers:

1. *The line lengths are irregular, there are no rhyming words, and each stanza has a different number of lines.*
2. *By isolating and repeating the phrase "Just once," he might be trying to emphasize how special the event was to the speaker.*
3. *The speaker is the son of an immigrant.*

FOR ENGLISH LEARNERS

Language Support Help students use context clues to determine the meanings of these words and phrases in "Good-Night":

- *sunless hours* (line 2), "nighttime"
- *O'er all without* (line 3), "everywhere outside"
- *behold the embers flee / About the firelit hearth* (lines 5–6), "watch sparks fly from the fire indoors"

FOR ADVANCED LEARNERS/PRE–AP

Apply [paired option] Have students work with partners to discuss how they might recast "Good-Night" as a free verse poem. Encourage them to experiment with varying line lengths, breaking up the stanzas, and ending lines with non-rhyming words. Then have them discuss how form influences the meaning and impact of a poem. For example, how might the poem's effect on the reader change if *When* (line 1), *Now* (line 5), or other words were placed on lines by themselves?

READER'S WORKSHOP 577

Part 2: Poetic Elements

Rhythm and Rhyme Explain that the rhythm of a poem may be regular, as in "Good-Night" on page 577 and "Afternoon on a Hill" on page 578, or it may be more natural and conversational, as in "That Day" on page 577.

Point out that poets often use rhyme at the ends of lines to connect ideas and to reinforce the rhythm of a poem. Have a volunteer read aloud "Afternoon on a Hill," emphasizing the rhyming words and the sing-song rhythm. Point out that only the second and fourth lines of each stanza end with a rhyming word, but that these words come at the end of sentences or complete thoughts. Discuss how this structure helps the poem flow in a natural way.

Repetition, Alliteration, and Assonance Tell students that songs also use sound devices to create meaning. Have students brainstorm examples of song lyrics they know, and write these lyrics on the board. Help students identify examples of repetition, alliteration, and assonance in the songs.

CHECK UNDERSTANDING Have students find poems in previous units and ask them to identify examples of rhythm, rhyme, repetition, alliteration, and assonance.

Part 2: Poetic Elements

Like different colors of paint or the notes on a musical scale, language can be arranged to create a desired effect. For example, short, choppy lines can produce a fast-paced pounding beat, while long, rhythmic lines can create a soothing melody. Poets manipulate the words and lines in their writing, fully conscious of how their work will sound when read aloud and how it will make readers feel. Sound devices, imagery, and figurative language are important tools of the trade.

SOUND DEVICES

Poets choose words not only for their meaning, but also for their sounds. The sound of a word or line can help emphasize meaning or create a musical quality. Here are some examples of sound devices poets use.

SOUND DEVICES	EXAMPLE
RHYTHM the pattern of stressed (´) and unstressed (˘) syllables in each line. A regular pattern of rhythm is called meter.	"Afternoon on a Hill" Poem by **Edna St. Vincent Millay**
RHYME the repetition of sounds at the ends of words, as in *sun* and *one*. Rhyme scheme is the pattern that the end-rhyming words follow. To identify rhyme scheme, assign a letter to each sound, as shown here.	I will be the gladdest thing *a* Under the sun! *b* I will touch a hundred flowers *c* And not pick one. *b*
REPETITION the use of a word, phrase, line, or sound more than once, such as the repeated use of the phrase *I will*	I will look at cliffs and clouds *d* With quiet eyes, *e* Watch the wind bow down the grass, *f* And the grass rise. *e*
ALLITERATION the repetition of consonant sounds at the beginning of words, such as the *m* in *mark*, *must*, and *mine*	And when lights begin to show *g* Up from the town, *h* I will mark which must be mine, *i* And then start down! *h*
ASSONANCE the repetition of vowel sounds in words that don't end with the same consonant, such as the *ow* sound in *bow* and *down*	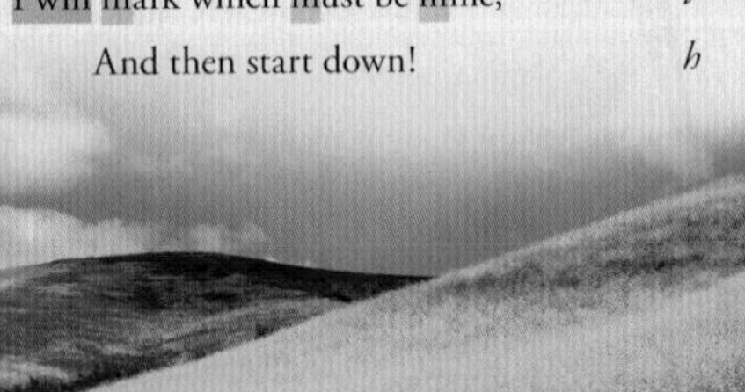

DIFFERENTIATED INSTRUCTION

FOR LESS–PROFICIENT READERS

Note Taking For students who need help with note taking, hand out the Note Taking: Poetic Elements copy master. Read and discuss the information on page 578. Assist students, as needed, in completing the copy master.

RESOURCE MANAGER—Copy Master
Note Taking p. 16

FOR ADVANCED LEARNERS/PRE–AP

Compare and Contrast Have students compare and contrast the rhythm of the poems on pages 577 and 578. Ask them to explain how the rhythm of each poem suits its speaker and the meaning the poet is trying to communicate. To record their ideas, they may use a Comparison Matrix with separate columns for *speaker* and *meaning*.

 **BEST PRACTICES TOOLKIT—Transparency**
Comparison Matrix p. A24

MODEL 1: RHYTHM AND RHYME

Read this traditional poem aloud, listening for its rhythm and rhyme.

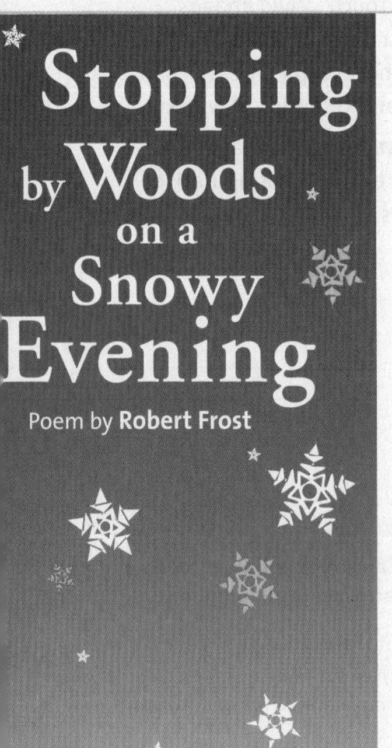

Whose woods these are I think I know.
His house is in the village, though;
He will not see me stopping here
To watch his woods fill up with snow.

My little horse must think it queer
To stop without a farmhouse near
Between the woods and frozen lake
The darkest evening of the year.

He gives his harness bells a shake
To ask if there is some mistake.
The only other sound's the sweep
Of easy wind and downy flake.

The woods are lovely, dark and deep,
But I have promises to keep,
And miles to go before I sleep,
And miles to go before I sleep.

Close Read

1. Stressed (´) and unstressed (˘) syllables are marked in the first stanza. Read the second stanza out loud. Does it follow the same pattern as the first stanza?
2. The end rhymes in the first stanza are highlighted. Examine the end rhymes in the other stanzas to figure out the rhyme scheme.

MODEL 2: ALLITERATION AND REPETITION

This unconventional poem uses alliteration and repetition to help emphasize meaning. Make sure to read the lines all the way across.

from Chrysalis Diary

Poem by **Paul Fleischman**

November 13:

Cold told me
to fasten my feet
to this branch,

to dangle upside down
from my perch,

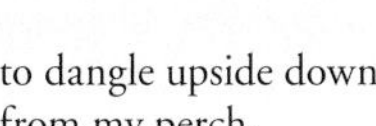

to shed my skin,

to cease being a caterpillar

and I have obeyed.
and I have obeyed.

Close Read

1. The alliteration in the boxed line helps to create a sense of the caterpillar's strong grip. Find another example of alliteration.
2. What does the repetition in the last line help emphasize?
3. Who is the speaker of the poem?

MODEL 1: RHYTHM AND RHYME

Close Read

Possible answers:

1. *Yes, the second stanza follows the same metrical pattern as the first stanza.*
2. *The rhyme scheme of the poem is aaba, bbcb, ccdc, dddd.*

MODEL 2: ALLITERATION AND REPETITION

Close Read

Possible answers:

1. *Another example of alliteration is in line 5: "to dangle upside down."*
2. *It emphasizes the irresistible natural forces that cause the transformation of the caterpillar.*
3. *The speaker of the poem is a caterpillar that is turning into a butterfly.*

FOR ENGLISH LEARNERS

Analysis Support: Rhyme Read "Stopping by Woods on a Snowy Evening" aloud to students, emphasizing the rhyming words as you read. Help students think of synonyms for each of these words. Then read the poem aloud again, substituting the synonyms for the rhyming words. Have students discuss why the version that uses rhyme is more appealing.

FOR ADVANCED LEARNERS/PRE–AP

Synthesize [paired option] Challenge students to list details for a brief poem about an animal. Encourage them to think of terms and phrases that use alliteration and assonance. For example, a poem about a lizard might include phrases such as "sun-speckled" and "dreaming near a stream." Have students share their lists with a partner and brainstorm terms and phrases that might be repeated or rhyme with other words.

IMAGERY AND FIGURATIVE LANGUAGE

Imagery Tell students that as they read a poem or listen to someone read it aloud, they should pay close attention to the images or word pictures the poem creates. What sights, smells, sounds, tastes, or textures come to mind? What feelings do the images evoke?

Have students explore imagery that can be used to describe objects and ideas such as these: love, fear, the moon, trees, an animal, a city street. Have them use copies of the Cluster Diagram transparency to record details about these things that appeal to the senses of sight, hearing, smell, touch, and taste. When they have completed their diagrams, have students share their details with the class. Lead a discussion about ways in which imagery makes the descriptions more vivid and appealing.

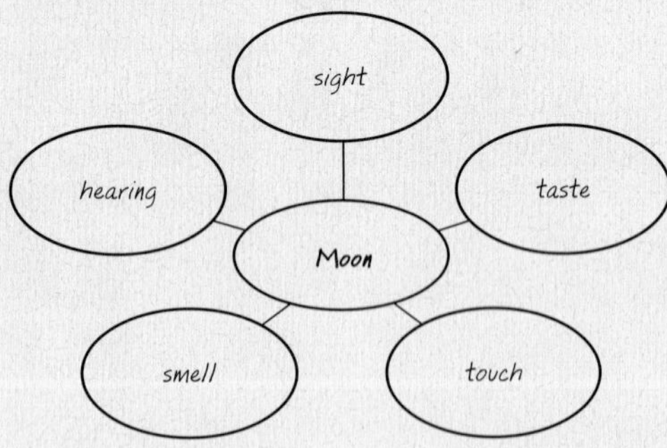

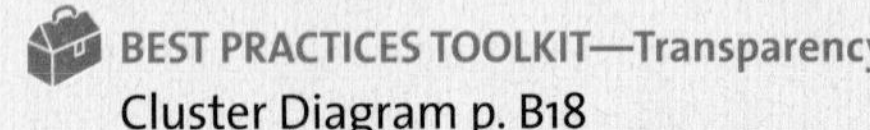

Cluster Diagram p. B18

Figurative Language Explain that similes, metaphors, and personification all make a comparison between two things that are different in most ways. A poet can exploit the one quality shared by two things to create a fresh and interesting description. Have students develop their own figurative language to describe these items:

- **Similes:** The screaming baby was like _______. The baby's father was as _______ as _______.
- **Metaphor:** The spilled milk was a(n) _______.
- **Personification:** The bitterly cold wind _______.

IMAGERY AND FIGURATIVE LANGUAGE

In addition to sound devices, poets use **imagery,** or language that appeals to one or more of your senses—sight, hearing, smell, taste, and touch. Vivid images help readers to more clearly understand what a poet describes. In "Stopping by Woods on a Snowy Evening," for example, images like "the sweep / Of easy wind and downy flake" help you to visualize the scene and hear the sounds of winter.

One way poets create imagery is by using **figurative language,** or imaginative descriptions that are not literally true. Notice how these examples of figurative language help you to picture ordinary things in new ways.

SIMILE

a comparison of two things using the word *like* or *as*

The sun spun like
a tossed coin.
It whirled on the azure sky,
it clattered into the horizon,
it clicked in the slot,
and neon-lights popped
and blinked "Time expired,"
as on a parking meter.

—"Sunset"
by Oswald Mbuyiseni Mtshali

METAPHOR

a comparison of two things that does not include the word *like* or *as*

In the pond in the park
all things are doubled:
Long buildings hang and
wriggle gently. Chimneys
are bent legs bouncing
on clouds below.

—from "Water Picture"
by May Swenson

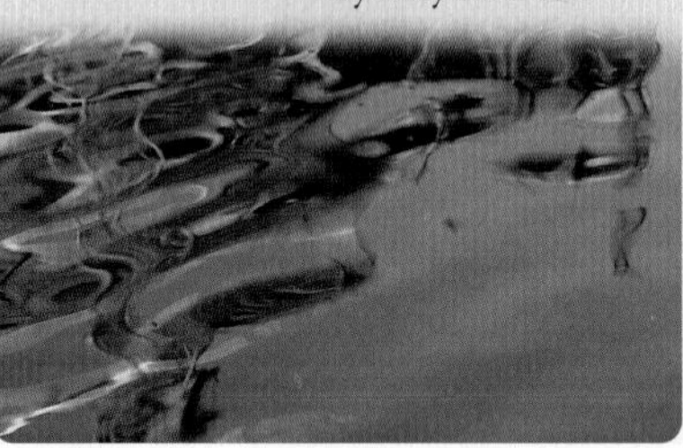

PERSONIFICATION

a description of an object, animal, or idea as if it has human qualities and emotions

When I opened the door
I found the vine leaves
speaking among themselves in abundant
whispers.
My presence made them
hush their green breath,
embarrassed, the way
humans stand up, buttoning their jackets,
acting as if they were leaving anyway, as if
the conversation had ended
just before you arrived.

—from "Aware"
by Denise Levertov

DIFFERENTIATED INSTRUCTION

FOR LESS–PROFICIENT READERS

Comprehension Support: Figurative Language

- Have students review the examples of simile, metaphor, and personification on page 580. Then have them use a Two-Column Chart to record what is being compared in each example.
- Ask students to brainstorm words that describe the feelings the figurative language in each poem creates for them.

Figurative Language	Comparison
simile	*sun compared to a coin*
metaphor	*chimneys compared to bent knees*
personification	*vine leaves compared to people whispering*

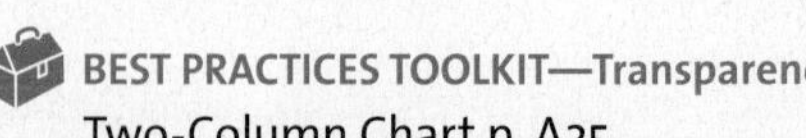

Two-Column Chart p. A25

rt 3: Analyze the Literature

In "Lineage," Margaret Walker uses many different poetic elements to describe the speaker's admiration for her ancestors. Using what you've learned in this workshop, analyze the form, sound devices, and language in this poem. Notice how all these elements work together to communicate a powerful message.

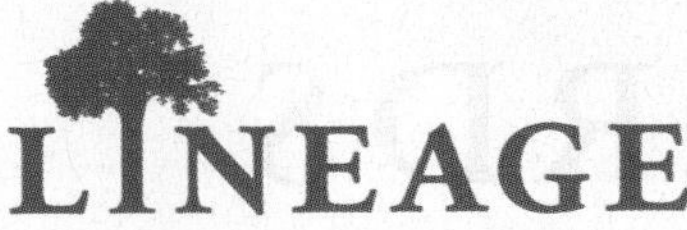

LINEAGE

Poem by **Margaret Walker**

My grandmothers were strong.
They followed plows and bent to toil.
They moved through fields sowing seed.
They touched earth and grain grew.
They were full of sturdiness and singing.
My grandmothers were strong.

My grandmothers are full of memories
Smelling of soap and onions and wet clay
With veins rolling roughly over quick hands
They have many clean words to say.
My grandmothers were strong.
Why am I not as they?

Close Read

1. What is traditional about the form of this poem?
2. One example of alliteration is boxed. Find two more examples.
3. The poem's first line is repeated two more times and helps to emphasize an important message. How is strength defined in the poem?
4. Find four images that help you picture the grandmothers. What sense does each image appeal to?
5. How would you describe the speaker of this poem? Think about the qualities she admires in her grandmothers and how she sees herself in relation to them.

Practice and Apply

Part 3: Analyze the Literature

Close Read

Possible answers:

1. *It has two stanzas of equal length. The second stanza has a rhyme pattern.*
2. *"grain grew" (line 4), "Smelling of soap" (line 8), "rolling roughly" (line 9)*
3. *Strength in the poem is physical and mental.*
4. *"bent to toil" (line 2)—sight; "touched earth" (line 4)—touch; "singing" (line 5)—hearing; "soap and onions and wet clay" (line 8)—smell; "veins rolling roughly over quick hands" (line 9)—sight*
5. *The speaker is unsure of herself. She admires her grandmothers, but their strength came from physical labor and their rich memories. She does not feel that she has either of these.*

Assess and Reteach

Assess

Organize small groups and assign one poem from pages 576–581 to each group member. Then have students meet to discuss and compare the forms, speakers, sound devices, imagery, and figurative language in the poems.

Reteach

Use this activity for students who have trouble applying the workshop skills:

1. Pair students and have them find and list examples of form, speaker, sound devices, imagery, and figurative language in the poems.
2. Review students' Note Taking copy masters. Clarify terms and concepts, illustrating each one with concrete examples.

FOR ADVANCED LEARNERS/PRE–AP

Analyze [paired option] Have students work with partners to discuss these questions about "Lineage" on page 581:

- The poet mentions the smells of "soap and onions and wet clay." What activities are evoked by these smells? What additional imagery could describe these activities?
- Why was the photograph on page 581 chosen to illustrate this poem? What other images might you choose to illustrate it?
- Notice the punctuation in the poem. Every line in the first stanza ends with a period. In what way does this affect the rhythm of the stanza when you read it aloud? In what way does the lack of end punctuation in the first three lines of the second stanza, along with the rhyming words in lines 8, 10, and 12, signal a shift in meaning?

Focus and Motivate

OBJECTIVES

Literary Analysis

- explore the key idea of using **words** to create images
- identify similes and metaphors
- identify and compare length and meaning of stanzas
- read poetry

Reading

- visualize

SUMMARY

"Simile: Willow and Ginkgo" uses similes to compare the graceful willow tree with the ungainly ginkgo tree. Although the speaker appreciates the beauty of the willow, the speaker's heart belongs to the determined ginkgo. In "Introduction to Poetry," the speaker asks readers to enjoy and fully experience poetry rather than "beating it with a hose / to find out what it really means."

How can WORDS *create pictures?*

Discuss the question and the ***KEY IDEA.*** Ask students to describe their experiences of seeing a film based on a book they've read. What **words** in the book helped them imagine the characters, setting, and events? What images in the movie were similar to or different from their mental images? After students have discussed their experiences, have pairs work on the ***QUICKWRITE*** activity.

Before Reading

Simile: Willow and Ginkgo

Poem by Eve Merriam

Introduction to Poetry

Poem by Billy Collins

How can WORDS *create pictures?*

KEY IDEA Have you ever seen the movie version of a book you've already read? Then you probably have had the experience of being surprised when a character didn't look the way you had pictured him or her. **Words** can create such distinct and powerful images that what you imagine while reading can seem as "real" as what you see. The poems you are about to read might help you see words themselves in a fresh, new way.

QUICKWRITE Choose a photograph from a magazine. Try to think of the way the pictured item might feel, sound, smell, or taste, in addition to how it appears. In a brief paragraph, create a vivid description of the image. Read your paragraph to a partner and ask which words best help him or her picture what you're describing. Then show the image.

582

Selection Resources

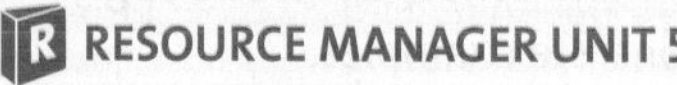

RESOURCE MANAGER UNIT 5

Plan and Teach pp. 17–24

Literary Analysis

Metaphor and Simile pp. 25, 26†*

Question Support p. 29*

Reading

Visualize pp. 27, 28†*

Reading Fluency p. 30

Assessment

Selection Tests A, B/C pp. 31*, 33*

Test Generator CD

BEST PRACTICES TOOLKIT

Differentiated Instruction pp. 31–38*

Graphic Organizer

Sequence Chain

Reading Support

Audio Anthology CD*

Technology

Literature Center at **ClassZone.com**

Write*Smart* CD

* Resources for Differentiation † Also in Spanish

ETIC FORM: STANZA

Many poems are divided into **stanzas,** or groupings of two or more lines that form a unit. In poetry, a stanza serves a similar purpose to a paragraph in prose. Stanzas may be used to separate ideas, add emphasis, or create a certain appearance on the page.

ERARY ANALYSIS: METAPHOR AND SIMILE

Have you ever heard an expression that didn't mean exactly what it said? The expression probably contained figurative language. **Figurative language** consists of words used in an imaginative way to communicate meaning beyond their strict definition. Two types of figurative language are

- **Similes,** which use *like* or *as* to compare two unlike things. For example: *The frozen lake is like glass.*
- **Metaphors,** which make comparisons without the words *like* or *as.* For example: *All the world is a stage.*

As you read the following poems, look for examples of metaphors and similes and note how the poets use them to create an emotional response, present vibrant images, or express complex ideas with a few words.

ADING SKILL: VISUALIZE

One way to help yourself enjoy the richness of a poem is to take the time to **visualize** the words, or form pictures in your mind. To visualize, pay attention to details that help you imagine how something looks, sounds, smells, feels, or even tastes. Combine these details with your own knowledge and experiences. As you read these poems, keep track of what you visualize in a chart like the one shown.

What I Visualize	*Words and Phrases That Helped*
dark, jerky lines	*"crude sketch"*

Author Online

Eve Merriam: Always a Poet Eve Merriam began writing poetry when she was about eight years old, and she never considered any other career. "It's like . . . oxygen," she said, "when I hear rhymes and word play." Although at times during her life she was forced to take other jobs, she continued writing poetry. Her first collection of poetry for adults, *Family Circle,* won the 1946 Yale Younger Poets Prize. Later in her career, Merriam focused on sharing her love of language with children, eventually publishing 24 books of poetry for young readers.

Eve Merriam 1916–1992

Billy Collins: America's Most Popular Poet In the United States, even the top poets can be unknown to most of the public. Billy Collins, however, is well known and well loved. His rise to fame began when Collins became a regular guest on radio programs, where his humor and welcoming manner won him a loyal following. He has since become one of the best-selling poets of his generation and regularly attracts standing-room-only crowds to his poetry readings. When he served as the Poet Laureate of the United States from 2001 to 2003, he created the 180 Project, which provided high schools across the country with poems to be read along with daily announcements. His goal was to make poetry part of everyday life for young people.

Billy Collins born 1941

MORE ABOUT THE AUTHOR
For more on these poets, visit the **Literature Center** at **ClassZone.com.**

Teach

STANDARDS FOCUS

POETIC FORM

● STANZA

Have students turn to pages 284–289. Ask them to compare and contrast the stanzas in "Barbara Frietchie" and "John Henry." ***Possible answer:*** *In both poems, every stanza has the same number of lines. Those in "Barbara Frietchie" have two lines, while those in "John Henry" have five lines.*

CHECK UNDERSTANDING Ask students whether the stanzas in the two poems separate ideas, add emphasis, or create a pattern on the page.

LITERARY ANALYSIS

● METAPHOR AND SIMILE

Write these examples on the board:

1. My puppy is a tiny tornado.
2. His eyes are like the ocean.

Ask: Which sentence is a simile? Which is a metaphor? How do you know? ***Answer:*** *Sentence 1 is a metaphor, and sentence 2 is a simile. Both compare two unrelated things, but the simile uses* like.

CHECK UNDERSTANDING Ask students to rewrite the example simile on page 583 as a metaphor, and the example metaphor as a simile.

READING SKILL

■ VISUALIZE

Read aloud this sentence: *The night sky sparkled with jewels.* Ask: What pictures formed in your mind? What words helped you visualize? ***Possible answer:*** *I pictured a clear night with many stars. The words* night sky, sparkled, *and* jewels *helped me form this image.*

CHECK UNDERSTANDING Ask students what they visualize when they read the simile *The frozen lake is like glass.*

RESOURCE MANAGER—Copy Master
Visualize p. 27 (for student use while reading the poems)

DIFFERENTIATED INSTRUCTION

FOR ALL STUDENTS

Enhance Learning Styles Provide independent projects for various learning styles.

- **Visual** Sketch items from nature.
- **Verbal** Explore nature poetry.
- **Logical** Investigate the *ginkgo biloba* tree.

For further details on these projects, see

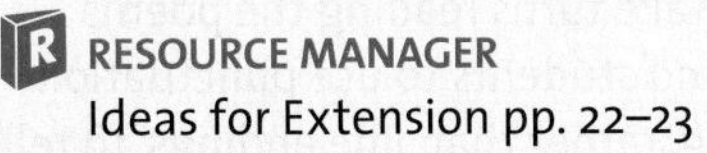

RESOURCE MANAGER
Ideas for Extension pp. 22–23

FOR LESS–PROFICIENT READERS

Concept Support Identify strategies for reading poetry on a class Sequence Chain. Have students apply the steps to the poems.

1. Read the poem aloud.
2. Visualize the images.
3. Identify the speaker.
4. Analyze key words and phrases.
5. Think about the message or theme.

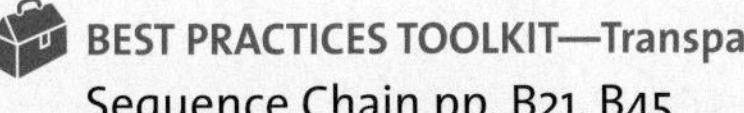

BEST PRACTICES TOOLKIT—Transparency
Sequence Chain pp. B21, B45

Practice and Apply

ANALYZE VISUALS

Possible answer: *The leaf of a ginkgo tree appears at the top of the image, mirroring the ginkgo leaves at the bottom of the image.*

About the Art Born in Japan, artist Atsuko Kato has lived in Germany for more than 22 years. She and her husband, Kunihiko Kato, also an artist, take inspiration from nature, calling it an "infinite creative source." Atsuko enjoys growing plants, an interest that is reflected in her work; the ginkgo is a motif in many of her paintings.

LITERARY ANALYSIS

Ⓐ METAPHOR AND SIMILE

Possible answer:

- *willow: "sleek as a velvet-nosed calf"; "branches are like silken thread"*
- *ginkgo: "leathery as an old bull"; branches "like stubby rough wool"*

If students need help . . . Suggest that they begin by looking for the words *like* and *as* to find the similes.

POETIC FORM

Ⓑ STANZA

Possible answer: *The poet started a new stanza when she changed the subject from describing the willow to describing the ginkgo. Also, all the other stanzas before line 17 are four lines long, so she was being consistent.*

Extend the Discussion The last stanza is only two lines long. Which purpose or purposes might this serve: to separate ideas, to add emphasis, or to create a particular appearance on the page?

Lines 1–22

REINFORCE *KEY IDEA:* WORDS

Discuss Which **words** in this poem appeal to the sense of sound? ***Possible answer:*** *The words in the second stanza appeal to the sense of sound. "The willow's music is like a soprano" (line 5), while "The ginkgo's tune is like a chorus" (line 7).*

Simile: *Willow* and *Ginkgo*

EVE MERRIAM

The willow is like an etching,
Fine-lined against the sky.
The ginkgo is like a crude sketch,
Hardly worthy to be signed.

The willow's music is like a soprano,
Delicate and thin.
The ginkgo's tune is like a chorus
With everyone joining in.

The willow is sleek as a velvet-nosed calf;
The ginkgo is leathery as an old bull.
The willow's branches are like silken thread;
The ginkgo's like stubby rough wool. Ⓐ

The willow is like a nymph with streaming hair;
Wherever it grows, there is green and gold and fair.
The willow dips to the water,
Protected and precious, like the king's favorite daughter.

The ginkgo forces its way through gray concrete;
Like a city child, it grows up in the street.
Thrust against the metal sky,
Somehow it survives and even thrives. Ⓑ

My eyes feast upon the willow,
But my heart goes to the ginkgo.

ANALYZE VISUALS
What **motif,** or repeat element, do you notic in this image?

Ⓐ METAPHOR AND SIMILE
In lines 9–12, what sim are used to describe th willow? What similes describe the ginkgo?

Ⓑ STANZA
Why do you think the poet started a new stanza at line 17?

Light–I (1992), Atsuko K
Oil on board, 100 cm × 70

DIFFERENTIATED INSTRUCTION

FOR ENGLISH LEARNERS

Vocabulary Support

- Explain that an etching (line 1) is a print in which the artist uses acid to make a design on a metal plate, which is then used to make a print. Guide students to look for a clue in line 2 that hints at this meaning.
- Explain that a soprano (line 5) is a singer with a high-pitched voice. Have students use the word *soprano* in an original sentence.

Options for Reading Read each poem aloud, or play the readings from the *Audio Anthology CD.* Encourage students to listen carefully and note any words or phrases that are unfamiliar. Help students define these words. Then reread the poem and stop for questions or discussion. Finally, ask students to take turns reading the poems aloud. Remind students to use punctuation and meaning, rather than line endings, to tell them when to pause.

BACKGROUND

Willow and Ginkgo Trees Willow trees, with their graceful, drooping branches, generally grow near water. These deciduous trees have narrow, pointed leaves.

Ginkgo trees can be traced to prehistoric times. With stubby stems and fan-shaped leaves, the deciduous ginkgo has a very different appearance from the willow. Ginkgo trees may be male or female. A nut with a foul-smelling seed coat grows from the female ginkgo.

FOR ENGLISH LEARNERS

Vocabulary Support Show students photos of a willow and a ginkgo to support their understanding of these two very different trees. Lead students in a choral reading of the poem and use the photos to point out the specific parts of each tree.

FOR ADVANCED LEARNERS/PRE–AP

Write a Simile Poem [paired option] Have students work in pairs to write their own simile poem comparing and contrasting two people, places, or things. Each student might write about one of the items to be compared. Then partners can combine their descriptions to create a poem.

ANALYZE VISUALS

About the Art Painter Ben McLaughlin (born 1969) studied fine art and printmaking in London. His work has been described as "post-cards from the edge of the everyday world."

READING SKILL

C VISUALIZE

Possible answer: *"hold it up to the light / like a color slide" (lines 2–3): touch, sight; "press an ear against its hive" (line 4): touch, hearing, sight*

LITERARY ANALYSIS

D METAPHOR AND SIMILE

Possible answer: *The poem is compared to a person being tortured.*

Lines 1–16

DISCUSSION PROMPTS

Use these prompts to help students understand the poem's message and speaker:

Connect The speaker asks that people do various things with a poem. What do you do with a poem when you read it? *Students may say they think about what the poem means or visualize the images.*

Analyze What metaphor does the speaker introduce in lines 5–6? What does it mean? ***Possible answer:*** *The speaker introduces the metaphor of a mouse in a maze, urging the reader to get lost in poetry.*

Synthesize Think about the poem's title and the art on page 586. What job might the speaker have? Whom does the speaker want to approach poetry differently? ***Possible answer:*** *The speaker is a teacher who wants students to appreciate the beauty and fun of a poem instead of just analyzing its meaning.*

SELECTION WRAP-UP

★ **CRITIQUE** Ask students why they think the poets chose to divide the stanzas the way they did.

READING FLUENCY

Distribute the copy masters and have students practice fluency.

RESOURCE MANAGER—Copy Master
Reading Fluency p. 30

Introduction *to* Poetry

BILLY COLLINS

Wednesday 6: Rain, slowly clearing eastwards (2001), Ben McLaughlin. Oil board, 20.3 cm × 20.3 cm. Private collection. © Bridgeman Art Library.

I ask them to take a poem
and hold it up to the light
like a color slide

or press an ear against its hive. C

I say drop a mouse into a poem
and watch him probe his way out,

or walk inside the poem's room
and feel the walls for a light switch.

I want them to waterski
across the surface of a poem
waving at the author's name on the shore.

But all they want to do
is tie the poem to a chair with rope
and torture a confession out of it. D

They begin beating it with a hose
to find out what it really means.

C VISUALIZE
Reread lines 1–4. What words help you visualize what the poet describes? To which senses do these details appeal?

D METAPHOR AND SIMILE
In lines 12–14, what metaphor is used to describe the poem?

DIFFERENTIATED INSTRUCTION

FOR LESS-PROFICIENT READERS

Reading Skill Follow-Up: Visualize [paired option] Have students take turns listening to a partner read the poem aloud. While they listen, students should close their eyes and focus on the images in the poem. Remind students to listen for words and phrases that appeal to their senses. Then have students use the chart introduced on page 583 to record what they visualized.

FOR ADVANCED LEARNERS/PRE-AP

Choose Illustrations [small-group option] Tell students to choose a different illustration for this poem. Have students work in small groups to analyze the poem and choose an image they think reflects its imagery or message. Students can use books, magazines, and online resources to find the illustration. Students should be ready to explain their choices.

ter Reading

mprehension

1. **Recall** In "Simile: Willow and Ginkgo," which tree does the speaker think is more beautiful?
2. **Recall** What does the speaker in "Introduction to Poetry" want readers to do on the surface of a poem?

erary Analysis

3. **Visualize** Review the chart you made as you read. Select two examples that were especially effective in helping you make visualizations. What **words** helped you "see" images in your mind?
4. **Identify Simile and Metaphor** For each poem, identify as many figurative comparisons as you can. In a chart like the one shown, list what is being described and what it is compared to. Then identify whether the comparison is a simile or a metaphor.

"Introduction to Poetry"			
Line(s)	What Is Being Described	What It Is Compared To	Simile or Metaphor
2–3	poem	color slide	simile

5. **Interpret a Line** Reread the last two lines of "Simile: Willow and Ginkgo." Why do you think the speaker's "heart goes to the ginkgo"? Support your answer with words and phrases from the poem.
6. **Compare Stanzas** Look back at the stanzas in "Introduction to Poetry." How are the poem's stanzas alike? How are they different? Consider their length as well as their content.
7. **Analyze Tone** In "Introduction to Poetry," the **tone,** or the expression of a writer's attitude toward the subject, changes partway through the poem. Identify where this change occurs. How do the poet's word choice and imagery signal the change?

tension and Challenge

8. **Literary Criticism** Billy Collins has described his poetry as "reader-friendly, hospitable, congenial, welcoming." Do you agree? Use details from "Introduction to Poetry" to support your opinion.
9. **Creative Project: Poem** Write your own short poem describing what the experience of reading poetry is like for you. Include at least one **metaphor** and one **simile.**

Practice and Apply

After Reading

For additional support of postreading questions, use these copy masters:

RESOURCE MANAGER—Copy Masters
Metaphor and Simile p. 25 (for practice of literary analysis standards focus)
Question Support p. 29 (After Reading questions adapted for English learners and less-proficient readers)

Additional selection questions are provided for teachers on page 21.

ANSWERS

Comprehension

1. *The speaker thinks the willow is more beautiful but has a greater love for the ginkgo.*
2. *The speaker wants readers to waterski across it, waving at the author's name on the shore.*

Literary Analysis

Possible answers:

3. **■ STANDARDS FOCUS Visualize** *The words* forces *and* gray concrete *helped me visualize the ginkgo tree bursting up through hard ground. The words* mouse *and* probe *helped me visualize a mouse in a maze.*
4. **● STANDARDS FOCUS Metaphor and Simile** *"Simile: Willow and Ginkgo" contains only similes. A willow is compared to a an etching (lines 1–2), a soprano (lines 5–6), a calf (line 9), silken thread (line 11), a nymph (lines 13–14), and the king's favorite daughter (lines 15–16). A ginkgo is compared to a crude sketch (lines 3–4), a chorus (lines 7–8), an old bull (line 10), stubby wool (line 12), and a city child (lines 17–20). In "Introduction to Poetry," a simile compares a poem to a color slide (lines 1–3). Metaphors compare a poem to a beehive (line 4), a maze (lines 5–6), a dark room (lines 7–8), a lake (lines 9–11), and a torture victim (lines 12–14).*
5. *The speaker sees the willow's beauty, but his or her "heart goes to the ginkgo" because it is scrappy and tough like a "city child."*
6. **● STANDARDS FOCUS Stanza** *Each stanza introduces a new metaphor, except for stanza 7, which extends the torture metaphor. The stanzas vary from one to three lines long.*
7. *Until line 12, the word choice and imagery (relating to waterskiing and mice, for example) are lighthearted and gentle. In line 12, the imagery grows dark and violent (describing torture and beating).*

Extension and Challenge

8. *Collins's imagery is accessible and welcoming; waterskiing, light switches, mazes, and hives are familiar to readers.*
9. *Poems should describe students' experience and feature at least one metaphor and simile.*

Assess and Reteach

Assess

RESOURCE MANAGER—Copy Masters
Selection Tests A, B/C pp. 31–32, 33–34

Test Generator CD

Reteach

STANDARDS LESSON FILE
Literature Lesson 18: Structure of Poetry
Literature Lesson 29: Simile and Metaphor

Focus and Motivate

OBJECTIVES

Literary Analysis
- explore the key idea of **animals**
- identify and analyze couplets
- read poetry

Reading
- identify and analyze figurative language, including personification and extended metaphor

Vocabulary
- build vocabulary for reading and writing
- use knowledge of word origins to help determine meanings of words *(also an EL language objective)*

SUMMARY

The title character of "Macavity: The Mystery Cat" is a criminal feline who sneaks about causing mischief and mayhem but never gets caught. In "Vermin," the speaker's hard-to-pin-down thoughts are compared to a quickly vanishing mouse.

What's the smartest ANIMAL?

Discuss the question with students. To lead into the ***KEY IDEA,*** ask students to think about **animals** they or someone they know have owned. How intelligent were these animals? Were students ever surprised by their intelligence? Next, have small groups work on the ***LIST IT*** activity. Suggest that they come up with at least two qualities for each animal. Ask which qualities, if any, the animals share with each other.

Before Reading

Macavity: The Mystery Cat

Poem by T. S. Eliot

Vermin

Poem by E. B. White

What's the smartest ANIMAL?

KEY IDEA Cats can escape from peculiar places. Dogs can learn tricks. Chimpanzees can communicate in sign language. All **animals** can appear to be intelligent at times. In the poems that follow, you will read about a couple of animals that are too clever to be caught—no matter how hard people try.

LIST IT Certain qualities are often associated with specific **animals.** For example, loyalty is a trait displayed by dogs. With a group, identify what the animals listed are known for. Did other groups come up with similar ideas?

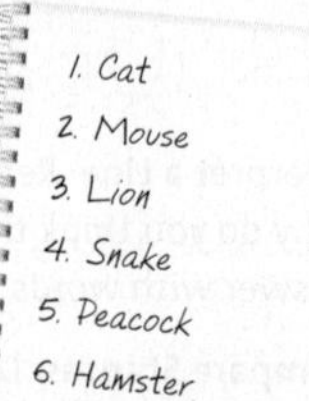

588

Selection Resources

RESOURCE MANAGER UNIT 5

Plan and Teach pp. 35–42

Literary Analysis
Couplet pp. 43, 44†*
Question Support p. 50*

Reading
Analyze Figurative Language pp. 45, 46†*
Reading Fluency p. 51

Vocabulary
Study p. 47*
Practice p. 48
Strategy p. 49

Assessment
Selection Tests A, B/C pp. 53*, 55*
Test Generator CD

BEST PRACTICES TOOLKIT

Differentiated Instruction pp. 31–38*
Scaffolding Instruction pp. 43–46*

Graphic Organizers/Strategies
Two-Column Chart • Freewriting

Reading Support
Audio Anthology CD*

Technology
Literature and Vocabulary Centers at **ClassZone.com**
Write*Smart* CD

* Resources for Differentiation   † Also in Spanish

LITERARY ANALYSIS: COUPLET

"Macavity: The Mystery Cat" is written in **couplets,** or rhymed pairs of lines. The lines in each couplet usually have the same or a similar number of syllables. As you read, use a chart like the one shown to record the rhymes T. S. Eliot uses to construct a poem made up entirely of couplets.

Stanza	Rhymes
1	Paw, Law despair, there
2	

READING SKILL: ANALYZE FIGURATIVE LANGUAGE

You may recall that **figurative language** refers to words used in an imaginative rather than literally true way to express ideas. The following poems contain these types of figurative language:

- **Personification** gives human qualities to an animal, object, or idea.
- **Extended metaphors** develop a comparison of two unlike things throughout several lines, multiple stanzas, or an entire poem.

As you read, identify the type of figurative language used in each poem and consider the ideas it conveys.

VOCABULARY IN CONTEXT

The words in Column A help T. S. Eliot and E. B. White portray memorable animals in their poems. Match each word in Column A to the word in Column B that is closest in meaning.

Column A	Column B
1. bafflement	a. pest
2. depravity	b. courtesy
3. fiend	c. immorality
4. levitation	d. confusion
5. suavity	e. rising
6. vermin	f. monster

Author Online

T. S. Eliot
1888–1965

T. S. Eliot: Distinguished Poet While attending Harvard University, Thomas Stearns Eliot wrote several poems that would become among the most famous in the English language, including "The Love Song of J. Alfred Prufrock." Although most of the poetry Eliot wrote was very complex, he also had a lifelong interest in children's nonsense verse. In letters to his godson, Eliot first created the amusing animal poems that would become *Old Possum's Book of Practical Cats.* This collection, which includes "Macavity: The Mystery Cat," was published in 1939. It became the basis for the Broadway musical *CATS!*

E. B. White
1899–1985

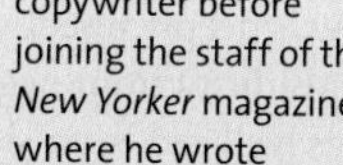

E. B. White: Always a Writer At age nine, Elwyn Brooks White won a prize for a poem about a mouse. He published his first magazine article at age 12. He was a newspaper reporter and an advertising copywriter before joining the staff of the *New Yorker* magazine, where he wrote essays, poems, and humor pieces. Some of White's most memorable characters are animals. As an adult, White invented a tale about a mouse with human parents. Generations have grown up with that children's classic—*Stuart Little*—as well as *Charlotte's Web,* a story of friendship between a spider and a pig.

MORE ABOUT THE AUTHOR
For more on these poets, visit the **Literature Center** at **ClassZone.com.**

589

Teach

STANDARDS FOCUS

LITERARY ANALYSIS

● COUPLET

Write the following couplet on the board and ask a volunteer to read it aloud:

Tiger, tiger, burning bright
In the forests of the night

Ask students how they can tell that this is a couplet. ***Answer:*** *The two lines rhyme and have the same number of syllables.*

CHECK UNDERSTANDING Ask students to find rhyming couplets in other poems from the pupil's edition.

RESOURCE MANAGER—Copy Master
Couplet p. 43 (for student use while reading the poems)

READING SKILL

■ ANALYZE FIGURATIVE LANGUAGE

Give students the following example: A storm is compared to a nightmare from the beginning to the end of a poem. Ask: Is this an example of personification or extended metaphor? How can you tell? ***Answer:*** *It is an extended metaphor. The comparison extends across the entire poem. There is no mention of human qualities in the comparison.*

CHECK UNDERSTANDING Have students brainstorm ideas for personification and extended metaphors based on the animals in the ***LIST IT*** activity.

VOCABULARY SKILL

▲ VOCABULARY IN CONTEXT

DIAGNOSE WORD KNOWLEDGE To determine preteaching needs, have all students complete **Vocabulary in Context.** Check students' answers. ***Answers:*** **1.** *d* **2.** *c* **3.** *f* **4.** *e* **5.** *b* **6.** *a*

PRETEACH VOCABULARY Help students explore the meaning of each boldfaced word on the Vocabulary Study copy master.

1. Read aloud the first sentence, emphasizing the boldfaced word.
2. Ask students to think about the way the word is used. Discuss possible meanings for *bafflement,* such as "confusion."
3. Repeat the procedure for the other sentences.
4. Have students write the sentences in Part B independently. Encourage them to use the sentences to tell a story.

RESOURCE MANAGER—Copy Master
Vocabulary Study p. 47

For general guidelines on differentiating vocabulary instruction and for alternative vocabulary activities for students not needing vocabulary preteaching, see

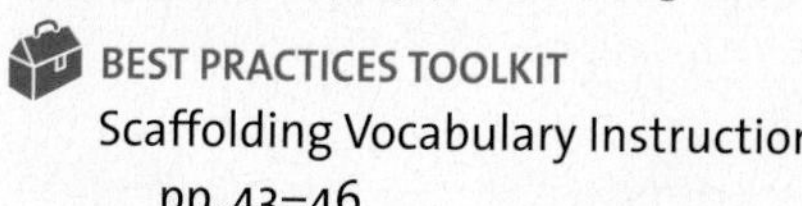

BEST PRACTICES TOOLKIT
Scaffolding Vocabulary Instruction pp. 43–46

Vocabulary Center at **ClassZone.com**
Additional Vocabulary Activities

Practice and Apply

ANALYZE VISUALS

Possible answer: *The cat's traits might include focus, balance, strength, and the ability to land on its feet.*

Lines 5–10

REINFORCE *KEY IDEA:* ANIMALS

Discuss In what way is Macavity very smart? Can you think of other **animals** that have the same kind of intelligence as Macavity?

Possible answer: *Macavity is smart because he hides after he has done something that will get him in trouble. Dogs have similar intelligence; they also hide when they have done something wrong.*

READING SKILL

A FIGURATIVE LANGUAGE

Possible answer:

- *"His brow is deeply lined with thought" (line 13).*
- *"[H]is whiskers are uncombed" (line 14).*

MACAVITY: The Mystery Cat

T. S. Eliot

Macavity's a Mystery Cat: he's called the Hidden Paw—
For he's the master criminal who can defy the Law.
He's the **bafflement** of Scotland Yard,[1] the Flying Squad's[2] despair:
For when they reach the scene of crime—*Macavity's not there!*

Macavity, Macavity, there's no one like Macavity,
He's broken every human law, he breaks the law of gravity.
His powers of **levitation** would make a fakir[3] stare,
And when you reach the scene of crime—*Macavity's not there!*
You may seek him in the basement, you may look up in the air—
But I tell you once and once again, *Macavity's not there!*

Macavity's a ginger cat, he's very tall and thin;
You would know him if you saw him, for his eyes are sunken in.
His brow is deeply lined with thought, his head is highly domed;
His coat is dusty from neglect, his whiskers are uncombed.
He sways his head from side to side, with movements like a snake;
And when you think he's half asleep, he's always wide awake. **A**

ANALYZE VISUALS
What **traits** might the cat in the photograph possess?

bafflement (băf'əl-mə
n. confusion; puzzlem

levitation (lĕv'ĭ-tā'sh
n. the act of rising into the air and floating

A FIGURATIVE LANGUAGE
What human physical qualities does the poet give to Macavity?

1. **Scotland Yard:** police headquarters in London, England.
2. **the Flying Squad:** a group of highly skilled detectives in London's police force.
3. **fakir** (fə-kîr'): a Muslim or Hindu holy person who may perform magic tricks.

DIFFERENTIATED INSTRUCTION

FOR ALL STUDENTS

Enhance Learning Styles Provide independent projects for various learning styles.

- ***Linguistic*** Write a poem using personification.
- ***Visual*** Illustrate a poem's stanzas.
- ***Analytical*** Research animal intelligence.

For further details on these projects, see

RESOURCE MANAGER
Ideas for Extension pp. 40–41

FOR ENGLISH LEARNERS

Options for Reading Have students listen to the *Audio Anthology CD* while they read along with the poems. Then have students do choral readings of the poems.

Prereading For prereading instruction for English learners, see

BEST PRACTICES TOOLKIT
Scaffolding Reading Instruction
pp. 43–46

BACKGROUND

Animal Intelligence How intelligent are animals? Intelligence can be defined in many ways: as the ability to learn, to use language, to solve problems, to mimic behavior, to develop and use technology, to think strategically and abstractly, to innovate, or to deceive. Many animals have one or more of these abilities.

Some primates, such as baboons, orangutans, and chimpanzees, are capable of abstract thinking. Other intelligent mammals include dolphins, which can follow complex instructions, and rats, which can learn to follow mazes and solve puzzles.

Many birds are also very clever. Ravens, for example, can solve complicated puzzles, and crows in New Caledonia use tools (sticks) to get food (insect larvae in rotten wood). Other birds, such as pigeons and parrots, can learn to name or count different objects.

Some species have a kind of social intelligence. Honeybees, for example, are able to precisely communicate and learn the location of food sources from each other.

FOR ENGLISH LEARNERS

Language: Punctuation and Print Cues Before they begin reading, have students skim the poem and point out italicized text, dashes, and unusually capitalized words. Explain that the capitals and italics indicate emphasis, the dash can show forward motion or an important pause, and the repeated, italicized phrase *Macavity's not there!* is like the chorus of a song, which is also repeated.

FOR ADVANCED LEARNERS/PRE–AP

Evaluate Sound Devices [small-group option] Remind students that this poem was written for children. Have students find the sound devices Eliot uses in his poem (*rhyme, rhythm, alliteration*) and discuss how these might contribute to the humorous tone and help make the poem appealing to young children. Encourage students to discuss their ideas with the class.

ADDITIONAL GUIDELINES

For more help with differentiation and tips for classroom management, see

BEST PRACTICES TOOLKIT
Differentiated Instruction pp. 31–38

LITERARY ANALYSIS

B COUPLET

Have students record their answers in the chart from page 589. ***Answer:*** *The fifth stanza has three couplets. The rhyming words are* cards/Yard's, rifled/stifled, *and* repair/there.

READING SKILL

C FIGURATIVE LANGUAGE

Possible answer: *Macavity has the human personality traits of cleverness, wickedness, and deceitfulness. Details that reveal these traits include the following:*

- *He is called a "master criminal" who outsmarts various human law enforcement agencies (lines 1–4).*
- *"He's outwardly respectable. (They say he cheats at cards.)" (line 21)*
- *He's known for "deceitfulness and suavity" (line 36) and for "wicked deeds" (line 39).*

Lines 21–42

DISCUSSION PROMPTS

Use these prompts to help students understand the poem's humor:

Summarize Of what crimes is Macavity accused in lines 23–26? ***Answer:*** *He is accused of looting the food cupboard, stealing jewels, drinking all the milk, smothering dogs, and breaking greenhouse glass and trellises.*

Analyze In what ways does Eliot exaggerate to add to the humor of the poem? Give an example. ***Possible answer:*** *Eliot's exaggeration creates a level of ridiculousness that readers will find amusing. Examples include Macavity's breaking "every human law" and even "the law of gravity" (line 6).*

Synthesize What does the comparison of Macavity to Napoleon tell you about Macavity's relationship to other cats? ***Possible answer:*** *Like Napoleon, he has immense power; other cats are probably afraid of him.*

Macavity, Macavity, there's no one like Macavity,
For he's a **fiend** in feline shape, a monster of **depravity.**
You may meet him in a by-street, you may see him in the square—
But when a crime's discovered, then *Macavity's not there!*

He's outwardly respectable. (They say he cheats at cards.)
And his footprints are not found in any file of Scotland Yard's.
And when the larder's[4] looted, or the jewel-case is rifled,[5]
Or when the milk is missing, or another Peke's[6] been stifled,[7]
Or the greenhouse glass is broken, and the trellis past repair—
Ay, there's the wonder of the thing! *Macavity's not there!* B

And when the Foreign Office find a Treaty's gone astray,
Or the Admiralty[8] lose some plans and drawings by the way,
There may be a scrap of paper in the hall or on the stair—
But it's useless to investigate—*Macavity's not there!*
And when the loss has been disclosed, the Secret Service say:
"It *must* have been Macavity!"—but he's a mile away.
You'll be sure to find him resting, or a-licking of his thumbs,
Or engaged in doing complicated long division sums.

Macavity, Macavity, there's no one like Macavity,
There never was a Cat of such deceitfulness and **suavity.**
He always has an alibi, and one or two to spare:
At whatever time the deed took place—MACAVITY WASN'T THERE!
And they say that all the Cats whose wicked deeds are widely known
(I might mention Mungojerrie, I might mention Griddlebone)
Are nothing more than agents for the Cat who all the time
Just controls their operations: the Napoleon[9] of Crime! C

fiend (fēnd) *n.* a demo
an evil spirit

depravity (dĭ-prăv'ĭ-t
n. moral corruption

B COUPLET
How many couplets make up the fifth stan What rhyming words e each pair of lines? Rec them in your chart.

suavity (swä'vĭ-tē) *n.* graceful, politeness

C FIGURATIVE LANGUAGE
What human personali traits does Macavity ha

4. **larder** (lär'dər): a food storage cupboard.
5. **rifled** (rī'fəld): robbed; plundered.
6. **Peke** (pēk): a Pekinese dog.
7. **stifled** (stī'fəld): killed by smothering.
8. **Admiralty** (ăd'mər-əl-tē): the British government department that once was in charge of Britain's navy.
9. **Napoleon** (nə-pō'lē-ən): a French emperor (1804–1814/1815) who conquered much of Europe.

DIFFERENTIATED INSTRUCTION

FOR LESS–PROFICIENT READERS

Reading Skill Follow-Up: Analyze Figurative Language Have students use a Two-Column Chart to record details of personification in "Macavity: The Mystery Cat."

Details	*Human Qualities Suggested by the Details*
Macavity is "outwardly respectable," but "They say he cheats at cards." (line 21)	*dishonest, sneaky*

BEST PRACTICES TOOLKIT—Transparency
Two-Column Chart p. A25

FOR ENGLISH LEARNERS

Vocabulary: Cognates [shared-language groups] Have groups scan the selection for cognates and report their findings to the class. Spanish cognates on this page include

- *feline/felino* (line 18)
- *crime/crimen* (line 20)
- *treaty/tratado* (line 27)
- *paper/papel* (line 29)
- *agents/agentes* (line 41)

VERMIN

E. B. White

The mouse of Thought infests[1] my head.
He knows my cupboard and the crumb.
Vermin! I despise[2] vermin.
I have no trap, no skill with traps,
No bait, no hope, no cheese, no bread—
I fumble with the task to no avail.[3]
I've seen him several times lately.
He is too quick for me,
I see only his tail. **D**

vermin (vûr'mĭn) *n., pl.* destructive and annoying insects and small animals, such as cockroaches and rats

D FIGURATIVE LANGUAGE
What two things are compared in this poem?

1. **infests** (ĭn-fĕstz'): lives in or overruns in large numbers.
2. **despise** (dĭ-spīz'): dislike intensely.
3. **to no avail:** without success; uselessly.

FOR LESS-PROFICIENT READERS

Comprehension Support To make sure that students understand the poem's extended metaphor, ask these questions:

- What is another way of stating the idea in line 2? *(He knows how I think.)*
- What task does the speaker "fumble with"? *(the task of trapping the mouse/thought)*
- In what way is the speaker's thought like vermin—a pest? *(The thought won't go away, but he also can't catch it.)*

FOR ADVANCED LEARNERS/PRE-AP

Synthesize Have students brainstorm ideas for another extended metaphor to describe thought. If students have trouble coming up with a metaphor, suggest that they use Freewriting to explore possibilities. Have students share their ideas with the class.

BEST PRACTICES TOOLKIT
Freewriting p. C1

READING SKILL

D FIGURATIVE LANGUAGE

Answer: *The poem compares the speaker's thoughts and a mouse.*

Extend the Discussion What does the use of the word *infests* (line 1) show about the speaker's attitude toward his thoughts?

Lines 1–9 REINFORCE *KEY IDEA:* ANIMALS

Discuss What other **animals** could be compared to different kinds of thoughts that people have? *Students should make relevant comparisons to various kinds of thoughts, such as angry, reassuring, anxious, joyful, and repetitive thoughts.*

SELECTION WRAP-UP

REFLECT Encourage students to think about what Macavity and the mouse have in common. How does the intelligence of these animals compare with human intelligence?

CRITIQUE Have students think about the way each poet's word choice conveys his feelings about the subject of his poem.

READING FLUENCY

Distribute the copy masters and have students practice fluency.

RESOURCE MANAGER—Copy Master
Reading Fluency p. 51

Practice and Apply

After Reading

For additional support of postreading questions, use these copy masters:

RESOURCE MANAGER—Copy Masters
Analyze Figurative Language p. 45 (for practice of reading standards focus)
Question Support p. 50 (After Reading questions adapted for English learners and less-proficient readers)

Additional selection questions are provided for teachers on page 39.

ANSWERS

Comprehension

1. *Macavity fools and confuses the English police (Scotland Yard).*
2. *The speaker sees the mouse's tail.*
3. *Sketches should reflect most of the following details: ginger color, tall, thin, sunken eyes, lined brow, domed head, dusty coat, uncombed whiskers.*

Literary Analysis

Possible answers:

4. ● **STANDARDS FOCUS Couplet** *No. Seven couplets include* there *as a rhyming word, but Eliot pairs it with a different word each time. Likewise,* Macavity *is a repeated rhyming word, but Eliot pairs it with three different words.*
5. ■ **STANDARDS FOCUS Analyze Figurative Language** *Macavity is clever and wicked. He has an unkempt appearance and engages in theft, deception, and murder. Details include the following:*
   - ***Behavior:*** *"cheats at cards" (line 21); steals food, jewels, and milk (lines 23–24); murders dogs (line 24); destroys property (line 25); steals important papers (lines 27–32); arranges alibis (line 37); organizes the "wicked deeds" of other cats (lines 39–42)*
   - ***Personality:*** *"outwardly respectable" (line 21); intelligent enough to perform "complicated long division sums" (line 34); known for "deceitfulness and suavity" (line 36)*
   - ***Appearance:*** *has a brow "deeply lined with thought" (line 13); allows his whiskers to go "uncombed" (line 14)*
6. *I try to catch the mouse, without success. Or, I don't know how to control my thoughts.*
7. ■ **STANDARDS FOCUS Analyze Figurative Language** *The speaker's head (where thoughts live) is compared to a cupboard (where vermin live), and the speaker has none of the tools required to catch a mouse or his own thoughts. At the end of the poem, the speaker compares a disappearing thought with a glimpse of the mouse's tail. The speaker is frustrated by thoughts that escape him—like the mouse.*

Extension and Challenge

8. *Students should compare the traits they wrote in the* **LIST IT** *activity with those of the animals in the poems. Some poems may include both personification and metaphor.*

After Reading

Comprehension

1. **Recall** Who does Macavity fool and confuse?
2. **Recall** What part of the mouse does the speaker see in "Vermin"?
3. **Represent** Reread lines 11–14 of "Macavity: the Mystery Cat." Based on this description, make a sketch of Macavity. Label your sketch to show what details from the poem you included.

Literary Analysis

4. **Examine Couplets** Review the chart you used to record the rhymes in "Macavity: The Mystery Cat." Does T. S. Eliot repeat any rhymes?
5. **Analyze Personification** What do you learn about Macavity from the personification used in the poem? Use a web like the one shown to collect details about the cat's human appearance, behavior, and personality.

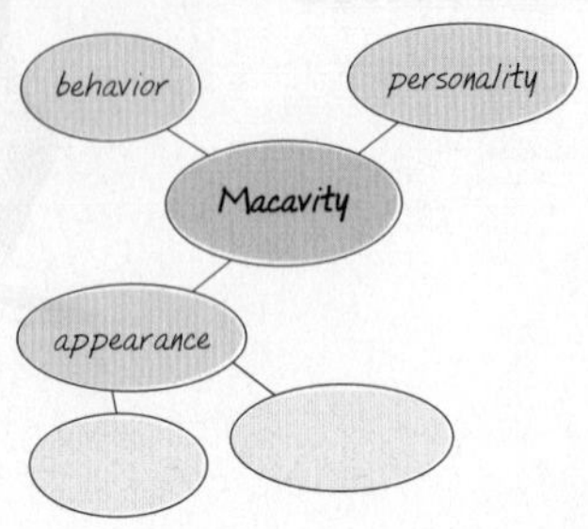

6. **Interpret a Line** In poetry, a word or line can have more than one meaning. In "Vermin," the speaker says "I fumble with the task to no avail." What different ways can you interpret this?
7. **Draw Conclusions from Extended Metaphor** In "Vermin," identify two similarities between the speaker's thoughts and a mouse. What does this comparison suggest about the speaker's attitude toward his own thoughts?

Extension and Challenge

8. **Big Question Activity** Review the list you created on page 588. How do the traits you assigned to cats and mice compare with the traits displayed by the **animals** in the poems? Write your own poem about one of the animals on the list. Make sure you use either **personification** or **metaphor** to explore ideas or add humor.

cabulary in Context

CABULARY PRACTICE

Decide whether the words in each pair are synonyms (words with similar meanings) or antonyms (words with opposite meanings).

bafflement
levitation
depravity
suavity
fiend
vermin

1. depravity/saintliness
2. levitation/ascent
3. bafflement/puzzlement
4. suavity/awkwardness
5. vermin/pest
6. fiend/beast

CABULARY IN WRITING

Do you know any creatures that share qualities with either the cat or mouse described in these poems? If not, imagine one. Use at least two vocabulary words to write a **one-paragraph description** of the animal. You could start this way.

EXAMPLE

My cat Katrina is a ***fiend*** *and a thief. She is always stealing small items such as hair clips and rubber bands.*

CABULARY STRATEGY: WORD ORIGINS

Like people and countries, words have their own histories. A good way to understand a word's current meaning is to learn about its history, or **etymology.** For example, the word *suavity,* which means "graceful politeness" comes from the Latin word *suvis,* which means "delightful, sweet."

A word's origin can be found in most dictionaries and can reveal a great deal about a word's meaning. For example, look at the etymology in this dictionary entry:

neighbor (nā'bər) *n.* One who lives near or next to another [from Old English *nēahgebūr: nēah,* near + *gebūr,* dweller]

PRACTICE Look up the etymology of each of these words in the dictionary. Write the word's origin and explain how knowing the word's history can help you remember its meaning.

1. hippopotamus
2. hybrid
3. dinosaur
4. sports
5. calendar

VOCABULARY PRACTICE
For more practice, go to the **Vocabulary Center** at **ClassZone.com.**

ANSWERS

Vocabulary in Context

VOCABULARY PRACTICE

1. *antonyms*
2. *synonyms*
3. *synonyms*
4. *antonyms*
5. *synonyms*
6. *synonyms*

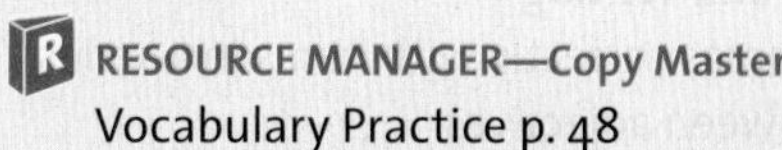

RESOURCE MANAGER—Copy Master
Vocabulary Practice p. 48

VOCABULARY IN WRITING

Have students identify two or three key qualities of each animal. Challenge them to use as many of the vocabulary words as they can in their paragraphs.

VOCABULARY STRATEGY: WORD ORIGINS

(also an EL language objective)

Remind students that English has borrowed heavily from other languages, including Greek, Latin, Spanish, French, and Italian.

Possible answers:

1. *Greek:* hippos *(horse);* potamos *(river)*
2. *Latin:* hibrida *(mongrel)*
3. *Greek:* deinos *(terrible); sauros (lizard)*
4. *Old French:* desport *(pleasure)*
5. *Latin:* kalendarium *(account book)*

RESOURCE MANAGER—Copy Master
Vocabulary Strategy p. 49

Vocabulary Center at **ClassZone.com**
Additional Vocabulary Activities

DIFFERENTIATED INSTRUCTION

FOR ENGLISH LEARNERS

Vocabulary Practice [mixed-readiness pairs] Have English learners work with more fluent partners to review the definitions and context of the vocabulary words in the poems. Encourage pairs to write sentences using the synonyms and the antonyms and then practice their pronunciation by reading them aloud.

FOR ADVANCED LEARNERS/PRE-AP

Vocabulary Strategy [paired option] Have pairs look up the etymologies of this lesson's vocabulary words. Then display the transparencies and discuss how analyzing the origins of English words can help students expand their vocabulary. Have students create a glossary of words from the poems with etymologies, definitions, and pronunciations.

Assess and Reteach

Assess

RESOURCE MANAGER—Copy Masters
Selection Tests A, B/C pp. 53–54, 55–56

Test Generator CD

Reteach

STANDARDS LESSON FILE
Literature Lesson 18: Structure of Poetry
Literature Lesson 29: Simile and Metaphor
Literature Lesson 30: Personification
Vocabulary Lesson 25: Etymologies

Focus and Motivate

OBJECTIVES

Literary Analysis
- explore the key idea of **beauty**
- identify and analyze stanzas in poetry
- analyze and evaluate free verse
- identify and analyze speaker
- read free verse

Reading
- clarify meaning

Grammar and Writing
- use commas correctly with items in a series and between adjectives
- use writing to analyze literature

SUMMARY

Archy, the cockroach speaker of "the lesson of the moth," asks a moth why he wishes to burn himself in a flame or on a light bulb. The moth replies that he would rather experience a moment of intense happiness and be a part of beauty than live a long life of boredom. The speaker of "Identity" wishes to be a weed rather than a flower because a weed's life is better; while flowers are plucked by greedy hands, weeds are left alone.

Does BEAUTY *matter?*

Discuss the question. To lead into the ***KEY IDEA,*** ask students how they define ***beauty.*** Then have them comment on the study described on page 596. Do students agree that they judge the beauty of strangers differently from the beauty of people they know? Why might this be the case? Then have students complete the ***SURVEY*** activity.

Before Reading

the lesson of the moth
Poem by Don Marquis

Identity
Poem by Julio Noboa

Does BEAUTY *matter?*

KEY IDEA What is our standard of **beauty?** A recent study found that people judged the beauty of strangers differently than they judged the beauty of people they knew. With strangers, people took into account only physical appearance. With familiar faces, the participants considered characteristics such as intelligence, courage, and dependability. The speakers in the poems you're about to read have their own ideas about beauty.

SURVEY Survey your classmates to find out what five or six characteristics they think make someone beautiful. List the ten answers that were given most often, and then separate them into internal and external characteristics. According to your survey, is beauty only skin deep?

Selection Resources

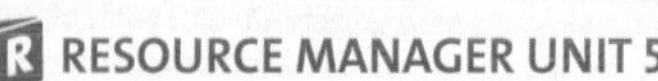

RESOURCE MANAGER UNIT 5

Plan and Teach pp. 57–64

Literary Analysis
Speaker pp. 65, 66†*
Question Support p. 69*

Reading
Clarify Meaning pp. 67, 68†*
Reading Fluency p. 71

Grammar and Writing
Use Commas Correctly p. 70

Assessment
Selection Tests A, B/C pp. 73*, 75*
Test Generator CD

BEST PRACTICES TOOLKIT

Differentiated Instruction pp. 31–38*

Graphic Organizers/Strategies
Think-Pair-Share • Read Aloud/Think Aloud • Two-Column Chart • Core Analysis Frame: Poetry • Open Mind

Reading Support
Audio Anthology CD*

Technology
Literature and Writing Centers at **ClassZone.com**
Write*Smart* CD

* Resources for Differentiation † Also in Spanish

TIC FORM: FREE VERSE

t is often said that to write poetry, you first have to learn the rules—then you can break them. **Free verse** is poetry that "breaks the rules" because it does not contain regular patterns of rhythm or rhyme. However, writers of free verse often use repetition and other sound devices to emphasize meaning. As you read, notice the way the poems sound like everyday speech.

RARY ANALYSIS: SPEAKER

n a poem, the voice that "talks" to the reader is called the **speaker.** Readers often assume that the speaker and the poet are the same, but this is not always true. The speaker may be a character created by the poet. For example, the speaker in "the lesson of the moth" is a cockroach named Archy. As you read each poem, think about the speaker's point of view.

DING SKILL: CLARIFY MEANING

Just as poets use words, rhythm, and rhyme to create certain effects, they also use line breaks, stanzas, and punctuation to help emphasize ideas. For example, look at the way the punctuation and line and stanza breaks in the first stanza of "Identity" affect meaning.

Let them be as flowers,
always watered, fed, guarded, admired,
but harnessed to a pot of dirt.

In the first two lines, commas cause you to pause and linger on words that are associated with positive feelings. However, the third line, which ends with a period, abruptly undercuts the comforting words the speaker associates with flowers. Because the stanza ends with this line, it emphasizes that the speaker sees confinement where others see beauty. As you study each poem, think about the way the line breaks, stanzas, and punctuation affect the way you read and understand it. Use a graphic organizer like the one shown to note these elements and the effects they create.

Elements	Used?	Effect
line and stanza breaks	yes	separate positive and negative ideas
commas		
end marks (question marks, periods, etc.)		

Author Online

Don Marquis: Talented Newsman Don Marquis published novels and worked as a screenwriter, but he was mainly a newspaper writer. A daily column in the *New York Evening Sun* led Marquis to create a character called Archy the cockroach, who filled column space with short lines and helped Marquis see life from a different perspective. "the lesson of the moth" is one of many poems Marquis wrote in the voice of Archy. Marquis pretended that Archy wrote his verses on the typewriter during the night. Marquis explained the lack of capitalization in the poems by saying that Archy never learned to use the shift key. Although Marquis's poems are mainly remembered for their humor, they also allowed him to comment on society.

Don Marquis
1878–1937

Julio Noboa: Poet and Educator Julio Noboa was born in the Bronx. He credits his Puerto Rican father and a high-school English teacher with encouraging him to write. Noboa wrote "Identity" when he was in eighth grade. The poem was inspired by Noboa's feelings after a break up with a girlfriend, an experience that he says encouraged him to think "about what's really important to me." Today Noboa is a college professor and writes more newspaper columns and scholarly papers than poetry.

Julio Noboa
born 1949

MORE ABOUT THE AUTHOR
For more on these poets, visit the **Literature Center** at **ClassZone.com.**

DIFFERENTIATED INSTRUCTION

FOR ALL STUDENTS
For general guidelines on differentiating instruction, see

BEST PRACTICES TOOLKIT
Differentiated Instruction pp. 31–38

FOR LESS–PROFICIENT READERS
Concept Support Have students use Think-Pair-Share to answer selected questions about each poem and to fill in their Clarifying Meaning charts from page 597.

BEST PRACTICES TOOLKIT—Transparency
Think-Pair-Share p. A18

FOR ENGLISH LEARNERS
Options for Reading Provide students with small sticky notes. Read the poems aloud. Then have students read along as they listen to the poems on the *Audio Anthology CD.* Have students place sticky notes next to passages they have difficulty understand-ing. Clarify these passage in a small-group discussion.

Teach

STANDARDS FOCUS

POETIC FORM

● FREE VERSE

Write this example on the board:

"Beauty Within"

Beauty within
beats
beauty outside; beauty
outside cannot exist
without
beauty within.

Ask students how they can tell this is free verse. ***Answer:*** *The words do not rhyme and there is no regular rhythm.*

CHECK UNDERSTANDING Ask students what repetition the poet used to emphasize meaning.

LITERARY ANALYSIS

● SPEAKER

Ask students what they can infer about the speaker of "Beauty Within." ***Possible answer:*** *The speaker cares more about inner beauty than outer beauty.*

CHECK UNDERSTANDING Ask students how the speaker would respond to the question *Does beauty matter?*

READING SKILL

■ CLARIFY MEANING

Delete the punctuation from "Beauty Within" and ask students how doing so makes the poem harder to read. ***Possible answer:*** *Without the semicolon, it's hard to tell where one idea ends and the next one begins.*

CHECK UNDERSTANDING Ask students what strategies they could use to clarify the meaning of a poem.

RESOURCE MANAGER—Copy Master
Clarify Meaning p. 67 (for student use while reading the poems)

Practice and Apply

ANALYZE VISUALS

***Possible answer:** The lightbulb might symbolize beauty and excitement.*

LITERARY ANALYSIS

A SPEAKER

***Possible answer:** He is curious; he is not a human because he can talk to moths.*

READING SKILL

B CLARIFY MEANING

***Possible answer:** "Why do you fellows pull this stunt?" I asked him. "Because it is the conventional thing for moths, or why? If that had been an uncovered candle instead of an electric light bulb, you would now be a small, unsightly cinder. Have you no sense?"*

If students need help . . . Suggest that they read the stanza aloud. Have them note where they pause and consider punctuating those pauses with either periods or question marks. Remind them to punctuate dialogue—the questions the speaker asks the moth—with quotation marks.

the lesson of the moth

Don Marquis

i was talking to a moth
the other evening
he was trying to break into
an electric light bulb
and fry himself on the wires **A**

why do you fellows
pull this stunt i asked him
because it is the conventional[1]
thing for moths or why
if that had been an uncovered
candle instead of an electric
light bulb you would
now be a small unsightly cinder[2]
have you no sense **B**

plenty of it he answered
but at times we get tired
of using it
we get bored with the routine

ANALYZE VISUALS
What might the light bulb **symbolize?**

A SPEAKER
What are your first impressions of the speaker?

B CLARIFY MEANINC
Imagine that this stan
was punctuated like regular text. Where would the punctuatio
appear?

1. **conventional:** customary; usual; accepted.
2. **cinder:** a piece of burned material.

DIFFERENTIATED INSTRUCTION

FOR LESS–PROFICIENT READERS

Comprehension Support Tell students that the first word of the poem, *i*, refers to the poem's speaker, a cockroach named Archy. Point out that the poem includes personification. Review personification—a technique that gives human qualities to animals, objects, or ideas—and ask students to find examples in the poem.

FOR ENGLISH LEARNERS

Language: Punctuation and Print Cues [paired option] Point out that in a poem, a complete thought sometimes ends in the middle or even near the beginning of a line. Use Read Aloud/Think Aloud to model how to identify complete thoughts within the first few stanzas of the poem. Have pairs of students apply the strategy to the rest of the poem.

BEST PRACTICES TOOLKIT—Transparency
Read Aloud/Think Aloud p. A34

BACKGROUND

Moths and Light Many people are curious about why moths are attracted to lights. One hypothesis is that moths, who often migrate, use starlight and the moon to help them navigate. They may mistake a light bulb for the moon.

Lines 1–14
DISCUSSION PROMPTS

Use these prompts to help students understand the speaker's questions:

Recall To whom is the speaker addressing these questions? ***Answer:*** *The speaker is talking to a moth.*

Summarize What is the speaker's main question to the moth? ***Answer:*** *The speaker wants to know why the moth wants to "fry himself" on a light bulb.*

Analyze How would you describe the speaker's attitude toward the moth at this point in the poem? Give examples to support your response. ***Possible answer:*** *The speaker is condescending and thinks the moth is ridiculous for flying into the light. Examples from the poem include*

- *"why do you fellows / pull this stunt" (lines 6–7)*
- *"conventional / thing for moths" (lines 8–9)*
- *"small unsightly cinder" (line 13)*
- *"have you no sense" (line 14)*

FOR LESS–PROFICIENT READERS

Reading Skill Follow-Up: Clarifying Meaning Ask students to point out which stanzas tell the words of the speaker (*stanzas 1, 2, 4, and 5*) and which tell the words of the moth (*stanza 3*). Explain that the page break after line 18 is not meant to be a true break in the stanza. Guide students to see that the poet uses stanza breaks to help readers tell who is speaking. Have students note this information on the chart from page 597.

FOR ENGLISH LEARNERS

Language: Pronoun Referents Write the pronouns *I, he, you,* and *it* on the board. Remind students that pronouns replace nouns. Give students a Two-Column Chart with pronouns from the poem listed in the left column. Have students read the poem, note the pronouns from the chart, and record the nouns to which they refer in the right column.

BEST PRACTICES TOOLKIT—Transparency
Two-Column Chart p. A25

Pronoun	Noun
i (lines 1, 7, 43, 51, 52)	Archy
he (line 3)	a moth
you (lines 12, 14)	the moth
it (lines 15, 17)	sense
he (line 15)	the moth
it (line 23)	fire
they (line 41)	human beings
him (line 43)	the moth

Lines 25–37

REINFORCE *KEY IDEA:* BEAUTY

Discuss Based on the moth's response to the speaker, how do you think he would answer the question *Does **beauty** matter?* ***Possible answer:*** *The moth would likely say that beauty is all that matters—he is so passionate about the beauty of the fire that he is willing to die for it. He says that "it is better to be a part of beauty / for one instant and then to cease to / exist than to exist forever / and never be a part of beauty" (lines 34–37).*

POETIC FORM

C FREE VERSE

Possible answer: *Phrases like* plenty of it *(line 15) and* come easy go easy *(line 39) sound like the way people really talk. "[I]t is better to be happy / for a moment / and be burned up with beauty / than to live a long time / and be bored all the while" (lines 25–29) sounds more philosophical and literary than the way most people really speak.*

LITERARY ANALYSIS

D SPEAKER

Possible answer: *The speaker compares himself with the moth by stating that he disagrees with the moth. He says he "would rather have / half the happiness and twice / the longevity" (lines 48–50).*

Extend the Discussion Archy and the moth disagree over whether it is more important to experience beauty or to live a long life. Are there other answers to this question besides those offered by the two characters?

and crave beauty
and excitement
fire is beautiful
and we know that if we get
too close it will kill us
but what does that matter
it is better to be happy
for a moment
and be burned up with beauty
than to live a long time
and be bored all the while
so we wad all our life up
into one little roll
and then we shoot the roll
that is what life is for
it is better to be a part of beauty
for one instant and then to cease to
exist than to exist forever
and never be a part of beauty
our attitude toward life
is to come easy go easy
we are like human beings
used to be before they became
too civilized to enjoy themselves **C**

and before i could argue him
out of his philosophy
he went and immolated[3] himself
on a patent[4] cigar lighter
i do not agree with him
myself i would rather have
half the happiness and twice
the longevity[5] **D**

but at the same time i wish
there was something i wanted
as badly as he wanted to fry himself

—archy

C FREE VERSE In what ways do the l[ines] in this stanza sound l[ike] the way people really talk? In what ways d[o] they sound different?

D SPEAKER In what way does the speaker compare him[self] to the moth?

3. **immolated** (ĭm′ə-lātd′): killed as a sacrifice.
4. **patent** (păt′nt): patented; covered by a lawful grant that gives the inventor the exclusive right to manufacture an item for a certain time period.
5. **longevity** (lŏn-jĕv′ĭ-tē): length of life.

DIFFERENTIATED INSTRUCTION

FOR LESS–PROFICIENT READERS

Comprehension Support To help students understand the moth's philosophy, work with them to add correct punctuation to lines 15–42. Then help them clarify the moth's reason for flying into fire—he craves beauty, and to him, fire is beautiful; he is willing to give up his life to have an instant of being a part of the fire's beauty.

Concept Support To ensure students understand the poem, including its structure, work as a group to complete the Core Analysis Frame for poetry. Modify the list of questions as necessary to meet your students' needs. Point out to students that they can use these types of questions whenever they read poetry to get a deeper understanding and appreciation of the poem.

BEST PRACTICES TOOLKIT—Copy Masters
Core Analysis Frame: Poetry pp. D23, D36, D37

FOR ADVANCED LEARNERS/PRE–AP

Debate [small-group option] Have students form two debate teams, one representing Archy's view that longevity is more important than beauty and one representing the moth's view that beauty is more important. Give students time to develop support for their side, including quotes from the poems. Then hold a formal debate. Have teams choose two or three presenters, while you act as moderator. Ask class members to evaluate each group's ideas.

DENTITY

Julio Noboa

The Mountain (1991), Albert Herbert. Oil on canvas, 50.8 cm × 61 cm. Private collection. © Bridgeman Art Library.

Let them be as flowers,
always watered, fed, guarded, admired,
but harnessed to a pot of dirt.

I'd rather be a tall, ugly weed,
clinging on cliffs, like an eagle
wind-wavering above high, jagged rocks. **E**

To have broken through the surface of stone
to live, to feel exposed to the madness
of the vast, eternal sky.
To be swayed by the breezes of an ancient sea,
carrying my soul, my seed beyond the mountains
of time
or into the abyss[1] of the bizarre.

I'd rather be unseen, and if,

then shunned[2] by everyone
than to be a pleasant-smelling flower,
growing in clusters in the fertile valley
where they're praised, handled, and plucked
by greedy, human hands. **F**

I'd rather smell of musty, green stench
than of sweet, fragrant lilac.
If I could stand alone, strong and free,
I'd rather be a tall, ugly weed.

E SPEAKER
Reread lines 1–6. How does the speaker's view of himself or herself contrast with the way the speaker views "them"?

F CLARIFY MEANING
Reread lines 13–18, paying attention to the commas. What effect do they have on the way you read this stanza?

1. **abyss:** a seemingly bottomless space.
2. **shunned:** deliberately avoided; shut out.

LITERARY ANALYSIS

E SPEAKER
Possible answer: *The speaker sees himself or herself as an ugly weed and sees "them" as well-tended flowers harnessed to a pot.*

READING SKILL

F CLARIFY MEANING
Students may say that the commas made them slow down and pause frequently.

Lines 1–22
DISCUSSION PROMPTS

Use these prompts to help students understand the speaker's thoughts about flowers and weeds:

Interpret What does the speaker admire about a weed? ***Possible answer:*** *The speaker admires the weed's independence and strength.*

Analyze What does the speaker think is one drawback to being beautiful? ***Possible answer:*** *Beautiful people attract the attention of others, which gets them into stifling, dependent relationships.*

Evaluate Does the speaker make a convincing argument that it's better to be a weed than to be a flower? Explain. *Some students may say that the speaker makes a strong case for the value of independence over beauty. Others may say that the speaker secretly envies the "flowers" who enjoy an easy life surrounded by friends.*

SELECTION WRAP-UP

REFLECT Ask students what questions they would like to ask the speaker of "Identity," and why.

★ CRITIQUE Have students consider which poem more effectively answers the question *Does beauty matter?* Ask them to explain their choice.

READING FLUENCY

Distribute the copy masters and have students practice fluency.

RESOURCE MANAGER—Copy Master
Reading Fluency p. 71

FOR LESS-PROFICIENT READERS

Understand Metaphors Help students recognize the poet's use of metaphor throughout "Identity." Remind students that a metaphor is a comparison of two unlike things that have some quality in common. Help students identify the main metaphors: the comparisons of a weed to an adventurous, strong person, and a flower to a beautiful person who does not have freedom or a place of his or her own.

FOR ENGLISH LEARNERS

Vocabulary Support Point out the following words in the last stanza, which all relate to smell. Help students define the words and describe the difference between how the speaker thinks a weed and a lilac smell. Then have students use each word in an original sentence.

- *musty, stench* (line 19)
- *sweet, fragrant* (line 20)

Practice and Apply

After Reading

For additional support of postreading questions, use these copy masters:

RESOURCE MANAGER—Copy Masters

Speaker p. 65 (for practice of literary analysis standards focus)

Question Support p. 69 (After Reading questions adapted for English learners and less-proficient readers)

Additional selection questions are provided for teachers on page 61.

ANSWERS

Comprehension

1. *Moths "crave beauty / and excitement."*
2. *Student sketches will vary but should reflect details from "Identity."*

Literary Analysis

Possible answers:

3. *The speaker learns that although he values longevity over happiness, he does wish he shared some of the moth's passion. Students should cite lines 47–53 as evidence.*
4. *There is a stanza break each time a different character speaks or there is a new thought. Pauses that would usually be punctuated with a comma or an end mark are indicated by line breaks.*
5. *The speaker wants to be strong, free, and independent and doesn't want to be safe, beautiful, and admired.*
6. **■ STANDARDS FOCUS Clarify Meaning** *Responses should present an understanding of how, in free verse, punctuation and line and stanza breaks help readers better understand a poem.*
7. **● STANDARDS FOCUS Speaker** *The moth thinks beauty is worth the price of death. The speaker in "Identity" would happily give up beauty in order to gain freedom. Their views are similar in that both value the freedom to live an exciting life. Their views are different in that the moth views beauty as exciting, while the speaker in "Identity" thinks that beauty stifles excitement.*

After Reading

Comprehension

1. **Recall** According to "the lesson of the moth," why do moths fly toward light?
2. **Represent** Create a sketch that shows the differences between the flower and the weed described in "Identity." Make sure your sketch reflects at least two specific details from the poem.

Literary Analysis

3. **Make Inferences** What does the **speaker** learn about himself in "the lesson of the moth"? Support your response with evidence from the poem.
4. **Examine Stanza** In "the lesson of the moth," how does the poet use **stanzas** to help you follow the conversation between the cockroach and the moth?
5. **Analyze Metaphor** What kind of person does the speaker in "Identity" want to be? What kind of person does he not want to be?
6. **Clarify Meaning** Refer to the charts you created as you read. For each poem, tell whether the line breaks, the stanzas, or the punctuation did the most to help you understand the poem's meaning. Explain what and how that element helped you understand.
7. **Compare and Contrast Views** In "the lesson of the moth," what is the moth's attitude about the price of **beauty?** In "Identity," what is the speaker's attitude about the price of beauty? Explain whether you think their views are more similar or more different.
8. **Evaluate Free Verse** Use a chart like the one shown to list examples of rhyme, repetition, or other sound devices, such as **alliteration** (the repetition of consonant sounds at the beginning of words). What images or ideas do these devices emphasize?

	"the lesson of the moth"	*"Identity"*
Rhyme		
Repetition		
Sound Devices		

Extension and Challenge

9. **SCIENCE CONNECTION** How do the qualities of real cockroaches and moths correspond to the poetic creations Don Marquis presents in "the lesson of the moth"? Research to find out about each creature's habits and life span. Display your findings in a poster, and be ready to explain how the poem does—or does not—relate to reality.

Cockroach

RESEARCH LINKS
For more on cockroaches and moths, visit the **Research Center** at **ClassZone.com.**

8. **● STANDARDS FOCUS Free Verse** *"The lesson of the moth" uses repetition (*beauty, exist*), and alliteration (*burned, beauty, bored*). The repetition of beauty evokes the moth's dancing at it, fluttering ever nearer. "Identity" uses repetition (*I'd rather*) and sound devices: alliteration (*clinging/cliffs, soul/seed*), assonance (*weed/eagle, broken/exposed, madness/vast*). The assonance conveys the sheer size of freedom, and the repetition lends conviction to the argument. Neither poem uses rhyme.*

Extension and Challenge

9. **SCIENCE CONNECTION** *Students' posters should point out the differences between the real qualities of moths and cockroaches and the poetic qualities used in "the lesson of the moth," including the obvious—these insects do not talk—and the more subtle, such as the real reasons moths might be attracted to light.*

ading-Writing Connection

:ontinue to explore the meaning of "the lesson of the moth" and "Identity" by esponding to these prompts. Then complete the **Grammar and Writing** exercise.

WRITING PROMPTS	SELF-CHECK
A. Short Response: Answer the Big Question Choose one of the "characters" from the poems—Archy, the moth, or the speaker in "Identity." Write **a paragraph** answering the question, "Does **beauty** matter?" from the point of view of this character.	***An effective answer will . . .*** • use the first person pronoun "I" • express the character's personality and perspective
B. Extended Response: Identify Emotions A critic once wrote that Don Marquis was "remarkable for his ability to intertwine the humorous and the melancholy [sad]." How does "the lesson of the moth" display this ability? Write a **two- or three-paragraph response.**	***A strong response will . . .*** • show an understanding of the poem's meaning • cite both funny and serious lines and images

AMMAR AND WRITING

USE COMMAS CORRECTLY By using commas properly, you can avoid confusing your readers. When writing a sentence that lists **items in a series,** insert a comma after every item except the last one. (A series consists of three or more items.) Also insert a comma between two or more **adjectives** of equal rank that modify the same noun.

Original: Both the moth in "the lesson of the moth" and the speaker in "Identity" find beauty in unusual surprising places.

Revised: Both the moth in "the lesson of the moth" and the speaker in "Identity" find beauty in unusual, surprising places.

PRACTICE Insert commas where needed in the following sentences.

1. The moth would rather take risks get injured and die young than be bored.
2. He thinks that the dangerous exciting heat of fire is beautiful.
3. I wouldn't mind being unseen shunned and alone like a weed.
4. Unlike flowers, weeds are strong free and independent.

For more help with using commas correctly, see page R49 in the ***Grammar Handbook.***

Reading-Writing Connection

WRITING PROMPTS

- For **Prompt A,** suggest students choose their character by deciding which character has the most to say about the question or which character's opinion best reflects the students' own point of view.
- For **Prompt B,** distribute copies of the Two-Column Chart. Suggest that students record examples of funny lines and images in the first column and more serious lines and images in the second column.

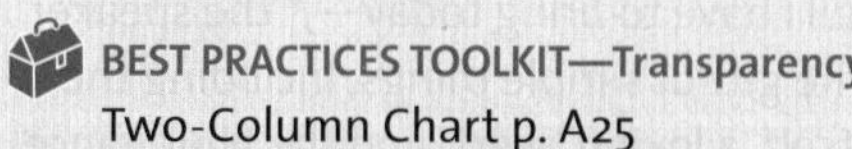

BEST PRACTICES TOOLKIT—Transparency
Two-Column Chart p. A25

For writing support, see

Writing Center at **ClassZone.com**

GRAMMAR AND WRITING

Clarify that a series takes the form *A, B, and C.* The items may be nouns, verbs, adjectives, or adverbs. Work with students to help them identify the appropriate placement of commas in each practice sentence.

Answers:

1. *The moth would rather take risks, get injured, and die young than be bored.*
2. *He thinks that the dangerous, exciting heat of fire is beautiful.*
3. *I wouldn't mind being unseen, shunned, and alone like a weed.*
4. *Unlike flowers, weeds are strong, free, and independent.*

RESOURCE MANAGER—Copy Master
Use Commas Correctly p. 70

Assess and Reteach

Assess

RESOURCE MANAGER—Copy Masters
Selection Tests A, B/C pp. 73–74, 75–76

Test Generator CD

Reteach

STANDARDS LESSON FILE
Literature Lesson 18: Structure of Poetry
Literature Lesson 19: Speaker
Grammar Lesson 20: Missing or Misplaced Commas

DIFFERENTIATED INSTRUCTION

FOR LESS–PROFICIENT WRITERS

For Prompt A:

Once students have selected their character, have them complete the Open Mind organizer. Encourage students to reread the appropriate poem and tell what their character thinks and feels about the question. Have students use their ideas as the basis for their paragraph.

BEST PRACTICES TOOLKIT—Transparency
Open Mind p. D11

For Prompt B:

Have students work on their Two-Column Charts in pairs. Help students develop a topic sentence about Marquis's ability to use both funny and serious ideas in one poem. Have students write three paragraphs using their charts: The first should introduce the poem; the second should describe Marquis's humor; the third should describe the poet's ability to be serious.

Focus and Motivate

OBJECTIVES

Literary Analysis
- explore the key idea of **wealth**
- identify and compare recurring theme
- read poetry

Reading
- set a purpose for reading

Grammar and Writing
- write a compare-contrast essay

SUMMARY

In "It's all I have to bring today—," the speaker offers the gift of simple things, including the poem itself, a loving heart, and the abundance of nature. In "We Alone," the speaker compares the value of gold, or money, with other kinds of wealth. She concludes that common, plentiful things should be valued as highly as gold.

Can you be RICH *without money?*

Discuss the question. To lead into the ***KEY IDEA,*** ask students to think about people they know or know about who are wealthy. Are these people happy? If so, are they happy because of what their material **wealth** brings them or for some other reason? As pairs work on the ***QUICKWRITE*** activity, encourage students to think of personal qualities that bring wealth to their lives, such as imagination, generosity, and curiosity. If they had to choose between these immaterial things and wealth, what would they choose?

Comparing Theme

It's all I have to bring today—

Poem by Emily Dickinson

We Alone

Poem by Alice Walker

Can you be RICH *without money?*

KEY IDEA If you hear that people are wealthy, you probably think they have a lot of money. Perhaps you imagine that they own expensive things like jewels, antiques, and designer goods. But does **wealth** always have to refer to material objects? The poets whose works you are about to read would like us to find riches in more common places.

QUICKWRITE What types of non-material things do you consider part of your wealth? Family? Friends? Pets? With a small group, discuss the everyday things that can lend richness to your life.

604

Selection Resources

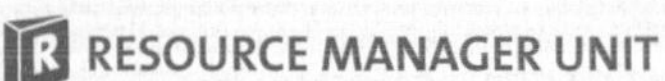

RESOURCE MANAGER UNIT 5

Plan and Teach pp. 77–84

Literary Analysis
Question Support p. 87*

Reading
Set a Purpose for Reading pp. 85, 86†*
Reading Fluency p. 90

Grammar and Writing
Writing for Assessment p. 89

Assessment
Selection Tests A, B/C pp. 91*, 93*
Test Generator CD

BEST PRACTICES TOOLKIT

Differentiated Instruction pp. 31–38*

Graphic Organizers/Strategies
Cluster Diagram • Read-and-Say-Something

Reading Support
Audio Anthology CD*

Technology
Literature and Writing Centers at **ClassZone.com**
Write*Smart* CD

* Resources for Differentiation † Also in Spanish

ERARY ANALYSIS: RECURRING THEME

You already know that the message of a literary work is called the theme. When the same message is found in different works, it is called a **recurring theme.** The following poems were written in different centuries by poets of different cultures and backgrounds, but they express a similar idea: common things should be considered valuable. As you read, notice how each poet develops this recurring theme. Pay attention to

- the speaker's feelings and beliefs
- important statements the speaker makes
- images and details that stand out
- repeated words and phrases

ADING STRATEGY: SET A PURPOSE FOR READING

Your **purpose for reading** the two poems is to compare the way the poets communicate the recurring theme. After you've read the poems once, go back and read them again. This time, take notes in a chart like the one shown.

Recurring Theme: Common things should be considered valuable.		
	"It's all I have to bring today—"	*"We Alone"*
What strong feelings or beliefs does the speaker express?		
Which images and details stand out?		
Which words and phrases are repeated?		

Author Online

Emily Dickinson: An Unsung Talent

Emily Dickinson
1830–1886

In 1862, Emily Dickinson read an announcement in a magazine asking for the work of new poets. Dickinson sent several of her poems to the editor, asking him if her work "breathed." The editor thought she had talent, but he didn't like her use of rhythm, and he asked her to correct her punctuation and capitalization. Dickinson didn't. Instead, she kept the poems in a box. After her death, her sister found this wealth of poems and had them published. Dickinson is now considered one of America's greatest poets.

Alice Walker: Ground-Breaker

Alice Walker
born 1944

Alice Walker was born in a small town in Georgia where her part-Cherokee mother and African-American father worked as tenant farmers. Although the family did not have much money, Walker's parents "worshipped reading" and made sure there was always a wealth of books in the house. Walker began writing in a notebook around age eight. She also made up many stories that she never put on paper, because she feared if she wrote them her brothers might find them and make fun of her. Today, Alice Walker is a world-renowned author and was the first African-American woman to win the Pulitzer Prize in fiction.

MORE ABOUT THE AUTHOR
For more on on these poets, visit the **Literature Center** at **ClassZone.com.**

605

Teach

STANDARDS FOCUS

LITERARY ANALYSIS

● RECURRING THEME

Ask students to identify selections from previous units with a common theme. ***Possible answer:*** *"The Old Grandfather and His Little Grandson" and "The Wise Old Woman" (Old people should be treated with respect.); "The Treasure of Lemon Brown" and "Rules of the Game" (It can be hard to get along with our parents, even when they want to help us.)*

CHECK UNDERSTANDING Have students identify details from the selections that reveal the recurring themes.

READING STRATEGY

■ SET A PURPOSE FOR READING

Point out that the questions in the chart reflect the bulleted items for analyzing theme in a poem. Tell students that the chart will help them identify differences as well as similarities in the two poets' approaches to the theme.

CHECK UNDERSTANDING Have students read the biographies on page 605 with the purpose of comparing and contrasting the two poets' lives. Ask students to tell two similarities or differences they noted.

RESOURCE MANAGER—Copy Master
Set a Purpose for Reading p. 85 (for student use while reading the poems)

DIFFERENTIATED INSTRUCTION

FOR ALL STUDENTS

For general guidelines on differentiating instruction, see

BEST PRACTICES TOOLKIT
Differentiated Instruction pp. 31–38

FOR LESS–PROFICIENT READERS

Concept Support [small-group option] Identify the characteristics of poetic structure in a class Cluster Diagram. Then have groups read the poems aloud and discuss which characteristics they find.

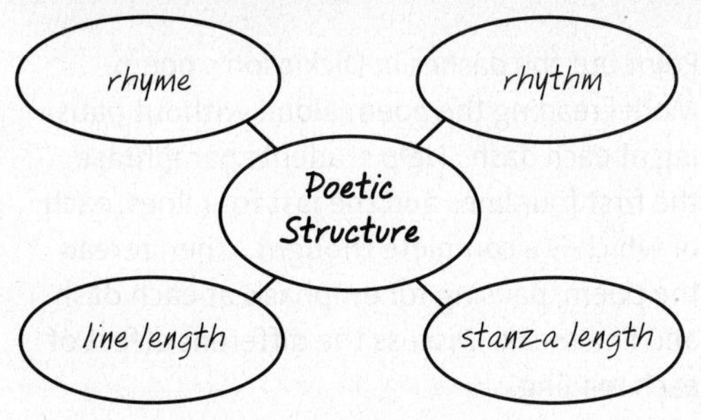

BEST PRACTICES TOOLKIT—Transparency
Cluster Diagram p. B18

FOR ENGLISH LEARNERS

Options for Reading [paired activity] Have students listen to the *Audio Anthology CD* while they read along with the poems. Then have students do the Read-and-Say-Something activity with a partner, commenting on images, phrases, and ideas that struck them as they read the poems.

BEST PRACTICES TOOLKIT
Read-and-Say-Something p. D3

Practice and Apply

ANALYZE VISUALS

***Possible answer:** The setting, with its brightly colored flowers, might create a feeling of warmth, peacefulness, and pleasure.*

Lines 1–4
REINFORCE *KEY IDEA:* WEALTH

Discuss Where does the speaker find **wealth?** Explain. ***Possible answer:** The speaker finds wealth in his or her love ("my heart") and in the beauty of nature ("all the fields," "all the meadows wide").*

LITERARY ANALYSIS

Ⓐ RECURRING THEME

***Answer:** The images are of fields (line 3), wide meadows (line 4), bees (line 7), and clover (line 8).*

Extend the Discussion Point out that *Bees* and *Clover* are the only words (other than the first words of each line) that are capitalized in the poem. Challenge students to explain why the capitalization of these words might be significant.

It's all I have to bring today—

Emily Dickinson

It's all I have to bring today—
This, and my heart beside—
This, and my heart, and all the fields—
And all the meadows wide—
Be sure you count—should I forget
Some one the sum could tell—
This, and my heart, and all the Bees
Which in the Clover dwell. Ⓐ

ANALYZE VISUALS
How might you feel if you were in the **settin**[g] depicted in this pictur[e]

Ⓐ RECURRING THEM[E]
What images of nature you find in the poem?

DIFFERENTIATED INSTRUCTION

FOR LESS–PROFICIENT READERS

Comprehension Support

- Some of the poem's syntax is old-fashioned and may confuse students. Dickinson sometimes reverses the placement of nouns and modifiers ("meadows wide" [line 4]) or inverts the usual syntax of words and phrases ("Which in the Clover dwell" [line 8]). Help students rephrase these examples using modern word order.
- Point out the dashes in Dickinson's poem. Model reading the poem aloud without pausing at each dash. Help students paraphrase the first four lines and the last four lines, each of which is a complete thought. Then reread the poem, pausing for emphasis at each dash and line break. Discuss the different effect of each reading.
- Make sure students understand that the dashes in lines 5 and 6 set off a parenthetical remark that can be omitted to clarify the grammatical structure of lines 5–8. The speaker says that "you" should count the poem, the speaker's heart, and the bees and clover among the things "I have to bring today." In case the speaker forgets to mention one of these things, "you" can check the speaker's math against the total sum.

Lines 1–8
DISCUSSION PROMPTS

Use these prompts to help students understand and apply the theme of the poem:

Connect If you had no material wealth to give someone you love, what other gifts could you give that person? *Students' responses will vary. Tokens of love that do not cost a lot of money include acts of kindness and homemade gifts.*

Infer What is the speaker of the poem like? Which details make you think so? ***Possible answer:*** *The speaker is generous and loves the natural world. The speaker makes a gift of his or her heart and all the beauty of nature.*

Analyze In what way is the first line of the poem ironic? ***Possible answer:*** *The phrase* all I have to bring today *suggests something small and sounds almost apologetic. In fact, the speaker's gift is an abundant one.*

FOR LESS–PROFICIENT READERS

Reading Strategy Follow Up: Set a Purpose for Reading [paired option] Have students work in pairs to answer the questions in the chart from page 605 to consider how Dickinson communicates the theme of her poem. Have them record their answers in their own charts. (See page 610 of the teacher's edition for possible answers.)

FOR ADVANCED LEARNERS/PRE–AP

Create a Dialogue Have students imagine a conversation that might take place between the speaker and the person addressed as "you" in the poem. Challenge them to rephrase the ideas in the poem in conversational English and to write a brief dialogue that includes the other person's reactions. Invite students to read their dialogues aloud with a partner for the class.

We Alone

Alice Walker

We alone can devalue gold
by not caring
if it falls or rises
in the marketplace.
Wherever there is gold
there is a chain, you know,
and if your chain
is gold
so much the worse
for you. **B**

Feathers, shells
and sea-shaped stones
are all as rare.

This could be our revolution:
To love what is plentiful
as much as
what is scarce. **C**

ANALYZE VISUALS
To what objects does the light draw attention?

B RECURRING THEME
How does the speaker feel about the value of gold?

C RECURRING THEME
Reread lines 14–17 and paraphrase the speaker's statement.

ANALYZE VISUALS

Possible answer: *The light draws attention to parts of the sea urchins, shells, and coral, highlighting their various textures.*

LITERARY ANALYSIS

B RECURRING THEME

Possible answer: *The speaker doesn't think gold has great value. Words and phrases that show the speaker's feelings include* not caring, chain, *and* so much the worse / for you.

LITERARY ANALYSIS

C RECURRING THEME

Possible answer: *People could change the world if they decided to treasure everyday things ("what is plentiful") as much as they treasure rare things ("what is scarce").*

If students need help . . . Discuss the word *revolution,* explaining that it can refer not only to the overthrow of a government but also to a profound and significant change in thought and behavior.

Lines 5–10
REINFORCE *KEY IDEA:* WEALTH

Discuss How might the speaker respond to this question: Can you have **wealth** without money? ***Possible answer:*** *The speaker would respond that yes, you can have wealth without money, because many beautiful objects are available to all people, whether they have money or not.*

DIFFERENTIATED INSTRUCTION

FOR LESS–PROFICIENT READERS

Comprehension Support Encourage students to use punctuation, rather than line breaks, to tell them when to pause as they read. Ask for four volunteers to read aloud "We Alone." Have the first student read one sentence and then stop to allow the next student to read the second sentence. After they have read the poem once, have the students repeat the reading, this time with greater fluency.

FOR ENGLISH LEARNERS

Vocabulary: Prefixes [mixed-readiness pairs] Point out the word *devalue* in the first line of the poem, and explain that the prefix *de-* means "do or make the opposite of." Then have them discuss how people can "devalue gold / by not caring." Encourage pairs to use a dictionary to find several more words with this prefix. Have them practice writing sentences using these words.

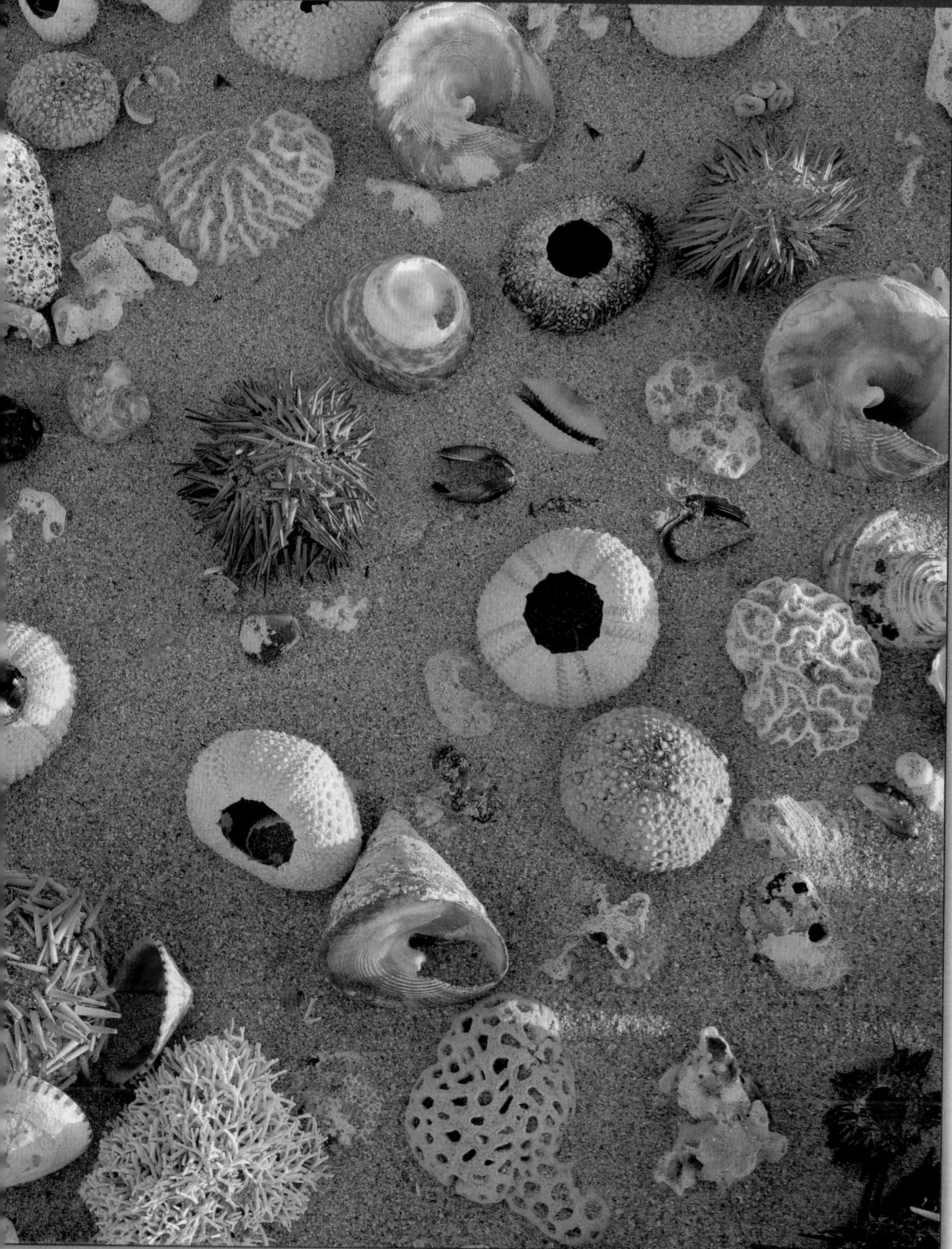

BACKGROUND

Gold The metal gold has been prized for thousands of years. Artisans from Minos, Egypt, Assyria, and other ancient civilizations valued gold for its beauty, and they used it to make jewelry and other decorative items. For centuries, kings and explorers sought gold to fill their treasuries.

Gold is still valued for its beauty, but it is also important to the international monetary system as a universally accepted currency for exchange. Although the gold standard no longer exists, nations still accept gold as a means of international payment.

Most gold is found in alluvial deposits (deposits made by flowing water) and in rock. Today the leading producers of gold are Australia, Canada, China, Russia, South Africa, and the United States.

SELECTION WRAP–UP

REFLECT Ask students to think about the two speakers' ideas about wealth. What does each speaker value?

CRITIQUE Have students consider the way each poet uses line breaks and punctuation. Ask: Which style do you find most effective, and why?

READING FLUENCY

Distribute the copy masters and have students practice fluency.

RESOURCE MANAGER—Copy Master
Reading Fluency p. 90

FOR ADVANCED LEARNERS/PRE–AP

Hypothesize [small-group option] Have students meet in small groups to discuss these questions. Ask a speaker from each group to share the group's ideas with the class.

- How would the world be different if there were no money, but if instead people acquired the goods and services they needed through a barter system?
- What would the advantages and disadvantages of such a system be?

Synthesize [small-group option] Challenge students to find other selections that have a theme similar to that of the poems they have just read. Have students discuss these questions in small groups and then share their ideas with the class:

- Why might this theme be a popular one for writers to explore in their work?
- In what ways might this theme reflect the role that writers and other artists play in our society?

Practice and Apply

After Reading

For additional support of postreading questions, use this copy master:

RESOURCE MANAGER—Copy Master
Question Support p. 87 (After Reading questions adapted for English learners and less-proficient readers)

Additional selection questions are provided for teachers on page 81.

ANSWERS

Comprehension

1. *The speaker brings "this" (which could be the poem), the speaker's own heart, fields and meadows, and bees.*
2. *People can decrease gold's value by not caring if it falls or rises in the marketplace.*
3. *"Feathers, shells / and sea-shaped stones" are as rare as gold.*

Literary Analysis

Possible answers:

4. *Students might visualize a woman walking in a meadow on a bright day, carrying flowers, and talking to a loved one.*
5. *"This" must be something whose value comes from within. It might refer to the speaker, who immediately offers his or her heart right after saying the word. It might also be the poem, a humble offering that expresses the speaker's point of view.*
6. *The speaker places a high value on the offered gifts; as a result, he or she probably feels wealthy.*
7. *The chain symbolizes enslavement. It conveys the idea that material things (such as gold) do not free us but instead hold us back.*
8. *"Plentiful" things might include ordinary, abundant objects such as shells and leaves that are beautiful and bring us joy.*
9. *The tone of Dickinson's poem is light and personal; its subject is the gifts of nature and the heart. Walker's poem has a more serious tone because it deals with society's attitude toward material things. The mention of gold and the marketplace evokes material wealth and inequality. The poem concludes with a more positive tone; Walker suggests that everyone is capable of loving what is plentiful.*

After Reading

Comprehension

1. **Recall** In "It's all I have to bring today—," what does the speaker bring?
2. **Recall** According to the speaker in "We Alone," how can people decrease the value of gold?
3. **Recall** In "We Alone," what items in nature are as rare as gold?

Literary Analysis

4. **Visualize** What mental pictures did you create as you read "It's all I have to bring today—"? Describe how you visualized the speaker, the setting, and the situation in this poem.
5. **Interpret Poetry** In "It's all I have to bring today—," the word *this* is repeated in lines 2, 3, and 7. What do you think *this* might refer to—the speaker, the poem, or something else? Support your ideas.
6. **Make Inferences** Do you think the speaker in "It's all I have to bring today—" feels **wealthy?** Explain your answer.
7. **Analyze Symbol** A symbol is a person, place, or thing that stands for something beyond itself. In "We Alone," what ideas does the chain represent? Support your response.
8. **Draw Conclusions** Reread the last stanza of "We Alone." What are some "plentiful" things that we should love as much as or more than the scarce things?
9. **Evaluate Tone** The tone of a poem is the poet's or speaker's attitude toward the subject. Do the two poems have the same tone or different tones? Support your answer with details from each poem.

Comparing Recurring Theme

Now that you've read both poems, finish filling in your chart. Then start thinking about the similarities and differences in how the poems express the theme.

Recurring Theme: Common things in life should be considered valuable.		
	"It's all I have to bring today—"	*"We Alone"*
What strong feelings or beliefs does the speaker express?	*She offers only her heart and nature's beauty.*	*The worth of gold is determined by people.*
Which images and details stand out?		
Which words and phrases are repeated?		

Comparing Recurring Theme

STANDARDS FOCUS Set a Purpose for Reading

	"It's all I have to bring today—"	*"We Alone"*
What strong feelings or beliefs does the speaker express?	*She offers only her heart and nature's beauty.*	*The worth of gold is determined by people.*
Which images and details stand out?	*"all the fields," "the meadows wide," "all the Bees / Which in the Clover dwell"*	*the gold chain; "Feathers, shells / and sea-shaped stones"*
Which words and phrases are repeated?	*"This, and my heart"; "all"*	*"gold," "chain"*

Writing for Assessment

1. READ THE PROMPT

You've just read two poems that express similar ideas about wealth. In writing assessments, you will often be asked to compare literary selections that differ in some ways but share a recurring theme.

PROMPT

"It's all I have to bring today—" and "We Alone" express this theme: common things should be considered valuable. In four or five paragraphs, compare and contrast how this theme is expressed in the poems. Focus on the speakers, images, and use of repetition in each poem. Use details from the poems to support each point.

STRATEGIES IN ACTION

1. I should make sure I understand how each poem expresses the **message**.
2. I need to identify the **similarities and differences** in how the poems develop the message.
3. I must support my ideas using **quotations** from the poems.

2. PLAN YOUR WRITING

Review your chart, thinking about the way each poem conveys the theme. Make sure you can cite words and phrases to support your notes. Then think about how you will set up your response.

- Option A: In one paragraph, describe how the recurring theme is developed in the first poem; in the next paragraph, describe how this theme is developed in the second poem; in a third paragraph, discuss similarities and differences in how the poems develop the theme.
- Option B: In one paragraph, compare how the speakers contribute to the theme; in a second paragraph, compare the use of imagery; in a third paragraph, compare the use of repetition.

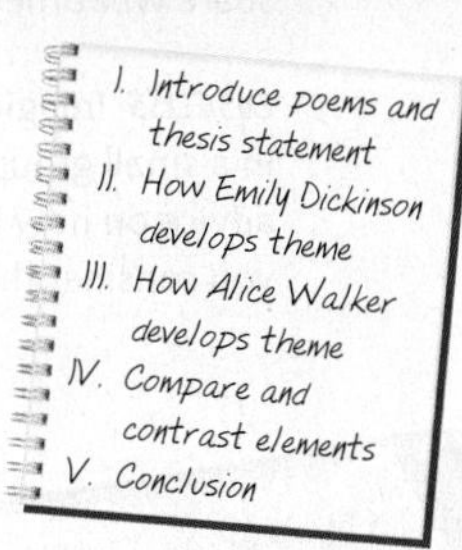

I. Introduce poems and thesis statement
II. How Emily Dickinson develops theme
III. How Alice Walker develops theme
IV. Compare and contrast elements
V. Conclusion

Now, outline your essay. Then write a thesis statement that describes your main idea.

3. DRAFT YOUR RESPONSE

Introduction Include the titles and the poets' names. State the theme and your thesis.
Body Using your outline and the details in your chart, describe how each poem develops the recurring theme. Include details from the poems to support your ideas.
Conclusion End your essay by restating the recurring theme and your thesis. Include a final thought about why this theme is important.
Revision Make sure the poem details you cite truly support your ideas. Gather additional support from the poems if necessary.

DIFFERENTIATED INSTRUCTION

FOR LESS-PROFICIENT WRITERS

Draft Your Response Provide these suggestions to help students structure their responses:

Introduction
- Give titles and names of poets.
- State your thesis.

Body
- Explain how first poet develops theme.
  —Describe speaker and images.
  —Describe use of repetition.
- Explain how second poet develops theme.
  —Describe speaker and images.
  —Describe use of repetition.
- Describe similarities in the ways the two poets develop the theme.
- Describe differences in the ways the two poets develop the theme.

Conclusion
- Restate thesis.

Writing for Assessment

1. ***READ THE PROMPT***
   Read the prompt aloud. Ask volunteers to identify key words and phrases that define the task (*theme, four or five paragraphs, compare and contrast, speakers, images, repetition, details*).

2. ***PLAN YOUR WRITING***
   - Have students use the notes in their charts from page 605 to create a strong thesis statement.
   - After students have decided how to organize their response, have them write key details in the appropriate sections of their outlines.

3. ***DRAFT YOUR RESPONSE***
   - Remind students to begin each body paragraph with a strong topic sentence.
   - List transitions on the board that might strengthen the unity within each paragraph and between paragraphs, such as *in addition, unlike, in contrast,* and *similarly.*

RESOURCE MANAGER—Copy Master
Writing for Assessment p. 89

Assess and Reteach

Assess

RESOURCE MANAGER—Copy Masters
Selection Tests A, B/C pp. 91–92, 93–94

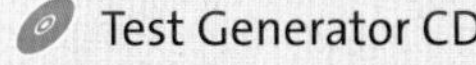

Test Generator CD

Reteach

STANDARDS LESSON FILE
Literature Lesson 13: Theme
Writing Lesson 29: Comparison-Contrast Essay

Focus and Motivate

OBJECTIVES

Literary Analysis
- explore the key idea of **advice**
- analyze and evaluate lyric poetry
- identify and analyze sound devices (assonance, alliteration)
- read lyric poetry

Reading
- make inferences

SUMMARY

Both poems convey the idea that one needs determination to face life's obstacles. "Speech to the Young: Speech to the Progress-Toward" encourages young people to think positively and to enjoy life. In "Mother to Son," the speaker is a mother who has persevered through a difficult life. She urges her son not to give up when life becomes hard.

What is good ADVICE?

Discuss the question. Lead into the ***KEY IDEA*** by encouraging students to think about **advice** they have received from adults they know. Who gave the advice? What advice did they give you? Ask how they determined whether the advice was good enough to follow. Then have small groups of students do the ***DISCUSS*** activity.

Before Reading

Speech to the Young
Speech to the Progress-Toward

Poem by Gwendolyn Brooks

Mother to Son

Poem by Langston Hughes

What is good ADVICE?

KEY IDEA Suggestions about how to improve your grades or how to approach the new guy at school can be welcome, but how do you know if it's good **advice?** Sometimes it depends on who gives it. Is it someone who has been there and learned from his or her own experience? Is it someone who cares about you or has a stake in the outcome? In the two poems you are about to read, the speakers share what they have learned with a younger generation.

DISCUSS Imagine you need to bring up your grade in science class. In a small group, brainstorm a list of three people you would ask for advice on how to improve your study habits and grade and tell why you consider these people a good source for advice.

{ 38 } ADVICE
stella says....
Dear Stella,
My best friend isn't speaking to me anymore, and I don't know why. We've been friends since kindergarten, but lately, she ignores me and spends all her time with these other girls who are more popular than me. I really want to be friends with her again, but I don't know how to get her to like me. What should I do?
—Confused, 14
Dear Confused,
That's a tough question! You have a right to be confused. Sometimes friendships fall apart, and it's hard to tell why. But don't blame

612

Selection Resources

RESOURCE MANAGER UNIT 5

Plan and Teach pp. 95–102

Literary Analysis
Sound Devices pp. 103, 104†*
Question Support p. 107*

Reading
Make Inferences pp. 105, 106†*

Assessment
Selection Tests A, B/C pp. 109*, 111*
Test Generator CD

BEST PRACTICES TOOLKIT

Differentiated Instruction pp. 31–38*

Graphic Organizers/Strategies
Think-Pair-Share • Making Inferences • Two-Column Chart

Reading Support
Audio Anthology CD*

Technology
Literature Center at **ClassZone.com**
Write*Smart* CD

* Resources for Differentiation † Also in Spanish

ETIC FORM: LYRIC POETRY

If you're a poet and you want to share your deepest feelings on a topic such as love, death, or the power of nature, what kind of poem would you write? A good choice would be a **lyric poem.** Lyric poems

- are short
- have a single speaker who expresses personal thoughts and feelings
- focus on a single, strong idea

ERARY ANALYSIS: SOUND DEVICES

Writers use sound devices to create a musical quality and to call attention to certain words. **Alliteration** is the repetition of consonant sounds at the beginning of words. Notice the repeated *w* sound in the following example:

When the wind whispers

Another sound device based on repetition is **assonance**, in which a vowel sound is repeated in two or more syllables.

Poetry is old, ancient, goes back far.

As you read the following poems, notice the alliteration and assonance and think about the effect of these sound devices.

ADING STRATEGY: MAKE INFERENCES

As you try to understand the speakers and the advice they give in these two poems, look for clues that hint at their experiences, attitudes, and personality. Combine these clues with your own knowledge or experience to **make inferences,** logical guesses about what the poet doesn't state directly. Use inference equations like the one shown to record your inferences about the speakers.

The title of the poem is "Speech to the Young."	+	Older people like to give advice.	=	Speaker is an older person.

Author Online

Gwendolyn Brooks: Young Talent As a budding young poet, Gwendolyn Brooks went to hear Langston Hughes give a speech at her church. Brooks's mother insisted that she show some of her work to Hughes. He read her poems on the spot and told her she had talent. "That did mean a lot to a sixteen-year-old girl," Brooks later said. Brooks went on to achieve great fame as a poet. As Poet Laureate of Illinois, she used her own money to fund literary awards for young writers.

Gwendolyn Brooks
1917–2000

Langston Hughes: World Traveler Langston Hughes was voted "class poet" at his high school in Cleveland, Ohio. After graduation, Hughes visited his father, who was living in Mexico. During the trip, Hughes wrote "The Negro Speaks of Rivers." It remains one of his best-known works. Hughes continued to see the world, traveling extensively in Africa and Europe. The poetry he sent home helped build his literary reputation. Hughes described the people he wrote about as "beaten and baffled, but determined not to be wholly beaten." Some African-American critics disapproved of his choice of subject matter, but Hughes felt that "the masses of our people had as much in their lives to put into books as did those more fortunate ones."

Langston Hughes
1902–1967

MORE ABOUT THE AUTHOR
For more on these poets, visit the **Literature Center** at **ClassZone.com.**

Teach

STANDARDS FOCUS

POETIC FORM

● LYRIC POETRY

Have students read the titles of the two poems in this lesson. Ask them how the titles can help them predict that both poems are lyric poems. ***Possible answer:*** *The word* speech *in the title of the Brooks poem suggests that a single speaker will share his or her thoughts on a topic. "Mother to Son" suggests that the speaker, a mother, will express her personal thoughts or feelings.*

CHECK UNDERSTANDING Ask students what topics they might write about in a lyric poem.

LITERARY ANALYSIS

● SOUND DEVICES

Display these examples and have students identify each as either alliteration or assonance:

He crooned a tune about a blue moon. *(assonance)*

He sang sincerely to his sweetheart, Sally. *(alliteration)*

CHECK UNDERSTANDING Ask students to say the vowel sound or consonant sound that is repeated in each example.

READING STRATEGY

■ MAKE INFERENCES

Copy the inference equation on the board and add these labels: *What the Poem Says, What I Know, Inference.* Then read the "equation" aloud using words from the labels: "The poem is titled 'Speech to the Young,' so I infer that the speaker is an older person."

CHECK UNDERSTANDING Clip magazine images of people doing various activities. Have students make inferences about what the people are doing.

RESOURCE MANAGER—Copy Master
Make Inferences p. 105 (for student use while reading the poems)

DIFFERENTIATED INSTRUCTION

FOR ALL STUDENTS

For general guidelines on differentiating instruction, see

BEST PRACTICES TOOLKIT
Differentiated Instruction pp. 31–38

FOR LESS-PROFICIENT READERS

Concept Support [small-group option]
Discuss the characteristics of lyric poetry and record them in a class chart. Then have groups of students read the poems aloud and discuss the features they find.

FOR ENGLISH LEARNERS

Option for Reading [mixed-readiness pairs]
Have students listen to each poem on the *Audio Anthology CD.* Then have students use Think-Pair-Share to discuss the important ideas in the poem and to ask questions about any unfamiliar words or phrases.

BEST PRACTICES TOOLKIT—Transparency
Think-Pair-Share p. A18

Practice and Apply

ANALYZE VISUALS

Possible answer: *You can infer that they do not have a close relationship because they stand apart from each other and are not even painted with the same color palette.*

LITERARY ANALYSIS

A SOUND DEVICES

Possible answer: *Examples of alliteration include*

- Say, sun-slappers, self-soilers (*lines 1–4*)
- harmony-hushers (*line 5*), hard home-run (*line 9*)

If students need help . . . Remind them that alliteration refers to the use of words that begin with the same consonant sounds, such as *long life.*

READING STRATEGY

B MAKE INFERENCES

Possible answer: *The speaker expresses an attitude of optimism about everyday life as a joyful experience. The message may be paraphrased, "Enjoy the present; do not live for the future or in the past."*

If students need help . . . Point out that modern poets often play with the rules of language. Brooks, for example, uses the preposition *along* as if it were a noun in the sentence *Live in the along.* Stress that for Brooks, this word means "doing," "process," or "present moment."

Extend the Discussion Think of a "battle won" or a goal for your future. Do you think enjoying life as it unfolds is more or less important than achieving this goal?

Lines 10–12

REINFORCE *KEY IDEA:* ADVICE

Discuss Do you agree with the **advice** the speaker gives in these lines? *Students may agree that enjoying life in the present is important but may say that personal victories and goals are also important. Perhaps the best strategy is to set goals but not to become so focused on achieving them that you ignore all the amazing things that happen every day.*

Speech to the Young Speech to the Progress-Toward

(Among them Nora and Henry III)

Gwendolyn Brooks

Say to them,
say to the down-keepers,
the sun-slappers,
the self-soilers,
the harmony-hushers,
"Even if you are not ready for day
it cannot always be night."
You will be right.
For that is the hard home-run. A

Live not for battles won.
Live not for the-end-of-the-song.
Live in the along. B

ANALYZE VISUALS
What can you **infer** abo[ut] the relationship betwe[en] the girl and the woman [in] the picture?

A SOUND DEVICES
How many examples o[f] **alliteration** can you fin[d] in the first stanza?

B MAKE INFERENCES
What attitude does th[e] speaker express in line[s] 10–12?

New Dreams (2002), Ernest Crichlow. Lithograph, 24¾" × 16¾". Phot[o] Maureen Turci, Mojo Portfolio. Courtesy of the Estate of Ernest Crich[low].

DIFFERENTIATED INSTRUCTION

FOR LESS–PROFICIENT READERS

Comprehension Support Point out that Brooks uses repetition in her poem. Explain that poets repeat sounds and words to emphasize important ideas. Ask these questions:

- What verbs does the poet repeat? ***Answer:*** *say, live*
- Why might Brooks have chosen to repeat these words? ***Possible answer:*** *She feels it is important for people to embrace life and to tell others how they wish to live.*

FOR ENGLISH LEARNERS

Vocabulary Support Help students understand the vocabulary in lines 2–5. Explain that when Brooks refers to "down-keepers," she may mean people who stay "down" or who keep others down. Help students define *sun-slappers, self-soilers,* and *harmony-hushers.* Students should recognize that these are all people who focus on the negative aspects of life. Then help students paraphrase lines 6–7 so they can understand Brooks's message.

BACKGROUND

Etymology of *Lyric* The word *lyric* comes from the Greek word for *lyre,* a stringed instrument that was plucked by musicians and singers. The related word *lyrics* refers to the words of a song. Like songs, lyric poems express the emotions and thoughts of one speaker. The use of sound devices adds to the musical quality of lyric poems.

Lines 1–9

DISCUSSION PROMPTS

Use these prompts to help students understand Brooks's poem:

Connect In what way do the "down-keepers," "sun-slappers," "self-soilers," and "harmony-hushers" affect your life? *Students may say that such people have a negative influence. Their constant negativity makes everyone feel sad and hopeless.*

Speculate What problem might the poet have seen in real life that she wanted to address with this poem? ***Possible answer:*** *She may have noticed that negative attitudes were affecting young people she knew and preventing them from enjoying life. She may have wanted to share her wisdom that life is too short to focus only on problems.*

FOR LESS–PROFICIENT READERS

Reading Strategy Follow-Up: Make Inferences Ask students to make an inference about why the speaker calls adopting the advice a "hard home-run" (line 9). Help them create an inference equation like the one shown on page 613.

The advice is called a "hard home-run."	+	In baseball, a home run helps win the game.	=	Following the advice can lead to success in life.

BEST PRACTICES TOOLKIT—Transparency
Making Inferences p. A13

FOR ADVANCED LEARNERS/PRE–AP

Apply [small-group option] Have students form groups to identify the "down-keepers," "sun-slappers," "self-soilers," and "harmony-hushers" they see in their world. Have them focus on people and messages in the media that reach millions of young people every day. When they have made a list of these influences, have them discuss ways to escape their potentially harmful effects. Then invite students to share their ideas in a class discussion.

ANALYZE VISUALS

Possible answer: *The woman seems quiet, and her intense stare suggests that she is focused and determined.*

LITERARY ANALYSIS

Ⓒ SOUND DEVICES

Answer: *The assonance is created by the words* goin', no, So, *and* don't.

POETIC FORM

Ⓓ LYRIC POETRY

Possible answer: *Life can be difficult and confusing, but it's important to keep moving ahead.*

If students need help . . . Read aloud lines 15–20 and have students summarize the advice that the speaker (the mother) gives to her son. Explain that this advice is the speaker's main idea.

SELECTION WRAP-UP

REFLECT Ask students what advice they would give if they were writing a poem to a younger person. What experiences might they relate?

★ CRITIQUE Have students explain which of these poems they found more convincing, and why.

Mother to Son

Langston Hughes

Lady, Ernest Crichlow. Etching, 22" × 18". Courtesy of the Estate of Ernest Crichlow.

Well, son, I'll tell you:
Life for me ain't been no crystal stair.
It's had tacks in it,
And splinters,
And boards torn up,
And places with no carpet on the floor—
Bare.
But all the time
I'se been a-climbin' on,
And reachin' landin's,
And turnin' corners,
And sometimes goin' in the dark
Where there ain't been no light.
So boy, don't you turn back. Ⓒ
Don't you set down on the steps
'Cause you finds it's kinder hard.
Don't you fall now—
For I'se still goin', honey,
I'se still climbin',
And life for me ain't been no crystal stair. Ⓓ

ANALYZE VISUALS
What personality **traits** would you expect the woman in the painting to have?

Ⓒ SOUND DEVICES
Notice the **assonance** created by the use of t long *o* sound in lines 12- What words contain th sound?

Ⓓ LYRIC POETRY
What is the main idea the speaker is expressi about her life?

DIFFERENTIATED INSTRUCTION

FOR LESS-PROFICIENT READERS

Culture: Clarify Point out that much of "Mother to Son" is written in a dialect that reflects the speech patterns of some African Americans at the time the poem was written. Explain that one trait of this dialect is dropping the letter *g* at the end of words that end in *-ing.* Have students point out examples (*climbin', reachin', landin's, turnin',* and *goin'*).

Be sure students understand these examples of dialect and their equivalent in standard English:

- *ain't been no* (lines 2, 13, 20), "has not been a"
- *I'se* (lines 9, 18, 19), "I have" or "I am"
- *a-climbin' on* (line 9), "continuing to climb"
- *set down* (line 15), "sit down"
- *kinder* (line 16), "kind of; somewhat"

FOR ENGLISH LEARNERS

Task Support Help students identify words with the vowel *o* in lines 12–14. Point out that words with this vowel may have different sounds, as in *no* and *boy.* Ask students to listen carefully for vowel sounds as you read lines 12–14 aloud. In a Two-Column Chart, record words with the long *o* sound in one column and those with a different *o* sound in the other.

 **BEST PRACTICES TOOLKIT—Transparency**
Two-Column Chart p. A25

ter Reading

mprehension

1. **Recall** In "Speech to the Young," what does the speaker tell the young to say?
2. **Recall** What two things does the speaker in "Speech to the Young" say we should *not* live for?
3. **Represent** Create a sketch of the stairway described by the speaker in "Mother to Son."

terary Analysis

4. **Interpret Meaning** What does the speaker in "Speech to the Young" mean by "Even if you are not ready for the day/it cannot always be night"?
5. **Examine Dialect** In "Mother to Son," words such as *ain't* and *kinder* are examples of **dialect,** the particular way language is used in a certain place or by a certain group of people. What does Hughes's use of dialect help you to understand about the speaker?
6. **Identify Figurative Language** What **metaphor** is used throughout "Mother to Son"? What does it tell you about the mother's life and how she has responded to it?
7. **Make Inferences About the Speakers** In your own words, describe how you picture the speaker in each poem. Use the inference equations you made as you read to help you.
8. **Analyze Sound Devices** For each poem, use a chart like the one shown to record the instances of **alliteration** and **assonance.** Which poem makes greater use of these sound devices?

"Speech to the Young"	
Alliteration	Assonance
say/sun-slappers/self-soilers	

9. **Evaluate Lyric Poetry** Which lyric poem gives you a more hopeful feeling? Explain your choice.

xtension and Challenge

10. **Readers' Circle** In a group, discuss the **advice** each speaker gives. Which speaker's advice do you think is best? Why?

Practice and Apply

After Reading

For additional support of postreading questions, use these copy masters:

RESOURCE MANAGER—Copy Masters
Sound Devices p. 103 (for practice of literary analysis standards focus)
Question Support p. 107 (After Reading questions adapted for English learners and less-proficient readers)

Additional selection questions are provided for teachers on page 99.

ANSWERS

Comprehension

1. *"Even if you are not ready for day / it cannot always be night" (lines 6–7).*
2. *In lines 10–11, the speaker says not to live for "battles won" or "the-end-of-the-song."*
3. *Sketches should reflect details mentioned in the poem such as tacks, splinters, boards torn up, places with no carpet, multiple landings, and corners to turn.*

Literary Analysis

Possible answers:

4. *The speaker means there's a bright side to life.*
5. *The use of dialect shows that the speaker is most likely an African American.*
6. *The mother's life is compared to climbing an uncomfortable and treacherous stairway. This metaphor suggests that her life has been hard but that she has kept going.*
7. ● **STANDARDS FOCUS Make Inferences** *Students may picture the speaker in "Speech to the Young" as a spunky woman who looks at you directly and speaks clearly. They may picture the speaker in "Mother to Son" as an older woman with a careworn face who moves slowly but steadily.*
8. ● **STANDARDS FOCUS Sound Devices**
   - ***"Speech to the Young": Alliteration:*** *say/sun-slappers/self-soilers; harmony-hushers/hard home-run* ***Assonance:*** *say/day/always; night/right; song/along*
   - ***"Mother to Son": Alliteration:*** *tell/tacks/torn/time/turnin'; don't/don't/down/don't* ***Assonance:*** *goin'/no/So/don't/don't/don't/goin'*
   - ***Conclusion:*** *The Hughes poem makes greater use of both sound devices.*
9. ● **STANDARDS FOCUS Lyric Poetry** *Students may say the Brooks poem gives them a more hopeful feeling because the speaker focuses more on the positive message. The speaker in the Hughes poem seems weighed down by life's difficulties.*

Extension and Challenge

10. *Students should cite examples from their own experience in their responses.*

Assess and Reteach

Assess

RESOURCE MANAGER—Copy Masters
Selection Tests A, B/C pp. 109–110, 111–112

Test Generator CD

Reteach

STANDARDS LESSON FILE
Literature Lessons 17, 22, 23
Reading Lesson 8

Focus and Motivate

OBJECTIVES

Literary Analysis
- explore the key idea of **form**
- identify and analyze traditional forms of poetry
- identify and compare rhyme schemes
- read lyric poetry

Reading
- paraphrase lines of poetry

SUMMARY

In "On the Grasshopper and Cricket," the speaker reflects on the sound of the grasshopper on a summer day—"the poetry of earth"—and the song of a cricket behind a stove on a winter evening, which brings to mind the memory of summer. In "Ode on Solitude," the speaker describes and celebrates a life of rural solitude, in which the land and the animals provide everything a person needs.

When does FORM *matter?*

Discuss the question. To lead into the ***KEY IDEA,*** ask students to think about where they see examples of **form.** Do they see form in nature? in billboards and other advertisements? in various dances? Have them consider why it might be valuable to work within certain forms, whether in science, art, or athletics. Then have students work on the ***LIST IT*** activity.

Before Reading

On the Grasshopper and Cricket

Poem by John Keats

Ode on Solitude

Poem by Alexander Pope

When does FORM *matter?*

KEY IDEA "Bend from the waist." "Lift your chin." "Hold your arms like this." Learning almost any new skill—swinging a bat or a tennis racket, swimming and diving, cartwheeling or dancing—involves learning **form.** In the poems you are about to read, two of the most well-respected poets in the English language use traditional poetic forms to create meaning.

LIST IT Make a list of activities that involve **form.** Rank them in order of which requires the most attention to form.

1. Ballroom dancing
2. Baseball
3. Writing
4. Painting

618

Selection Resources

RESOURCE MANAGER UNIT 5

Plan and Teach pp. 113–120

Literary Analysis
Rhyme Scheme pp. 121, 122†*
Question Support p. 125*

Reading
Paraphrase pp. 123, 124†*

Assessment
Selection Tests A, B/C pp. 127*, 129*
Test Generator CD

BEST PRACTICES TOOLKIT
Differentiated Instruction pp. 31–38*

Graphic Organizers/Strategies
Visualizing • Think-Pair-Share • Jigsaw Reading

Reading Support
Audio Anthology CD*

Technology
Literature Center at **ClassZone.com**
Write*Smart* CD

* Resources for Differentiation † Also in Spanish

ETIC FORM: TRADITIONAL FORMS

The poems that follow are examples of two traditional **forms,** or types. Both are **lyric poems,** or short poems in which a speaker expresses personal thoughts and feelings.

- "On the Grasshopper and Cricket" is a **sonnet**—a lyric poem with 14 lines and regular patterns of rhyme and rhythm.
- "Ode on Solitude" is an **ode,** a type of lyric poem that deals with an important topic.

TERARY ANALYSIS: RHYME SCHEME

Rhyme scheme is the pattern of rhyming words at the ends of a poem's lines. You can use letters to identify rhyme scheme. Write the letter *a* next to the first rhyming word and all words that rhyme with it. Then write the letter *b* next to the second rhyming word and the words that rhyme with it, and so on.

Happy the man, whose wish and care a
A few paternal acres bound, b
Content to breathe his native air a
In his own ground. b

The letter *a* identifies all the words at the ends of lines that rhyme with *care.* The letter *b* indicates all the words that rhyme with *bound.* After your first reading of each of these poems, read it a second time and note the rhyme scheme in a chart.

"On the Grasshopper and Cricket"

Line	Rhyme Scheme
1	a
2	

ADING STRATEGY: PARAPHRASE

Since these poems use language in a way that is seldom heard today, they can be challenging to read. One good way to make sure you understand what you read is to **paraphrase** it, or restate it in your own words.

As you read the poems, look for punctuation marks that show where a thought begins and ends. Then check your understanding by paraphrasing the idea. If you still find a thought difficult to "translate," reread the lines slowly and use the context and a dictionary to decode important words that you don't know.

Author Online

John Keats: A Short, Creative Life John Keats lost both his parents when he was a child. His guardian wanted him to be a doctor, but when Keats went to London to study, he met a group of young writers and abandoned a medical career to pursue his poetry. He was remarkably creative, writing four of his most famous poems in a single month. In 1818, Keats's brother died of tuberculosis. The following year, Keats began to show the same symptoms and soon became too ill to write. He died at the age of 25. In his three-year writing career, Keats created a body of work whose quality is greater than that of Shakespeare or Wordsworth at the same age.

John Keats
1795–1821

Alexander Pope: Living on Poetry Alexander Pope suffered from severe headaches, and later in life, asthma. In addition, he was Catholic, which at that time meant that he could not attend universities. None of this stopped him from his studies. Pope mostly educated himself, learning Latin and Greek. His translations were so successful they made Pope the first English poet able to live off of his work. He is famous for his poetry, essays, and satires. Lines from his essays—such as "To err is human, to forgive, divine"—have become part of the English language.

Alexander Pope
1688–1744

MORE ABOUT THE AUTHOR
For more on these poets, visit the **Literature Center** at **ClassZone.com.**

619

DIFFERENTIATED INSTRUCTION

FOR ALL STUDENTS

For general guidelines on differentiating instruction, see

 BEST PRACTICES TOOLKIT
Differentiated Instruction pp. 31–38

FOR ENGLISH LEARNERS

Options for Reading Have students listen to the poems on the *Audio Anthology CD.* Have students use the Visualizing strategy to help them create mental images as they follow along.

 BEST PRACTICES TOOLKIT—Transparency
Visualizing p. A11

Teach

STANDARDS FOCUS

POETIC FORM

TRADITIONAL FORMS

Point out that the sonnet requires a strict adherence to form, while the ode offers more leeway. Ask students to recall the lyrics of a typical song. What form or pattern does the song follow? ***Possible answer:*** *Many songs follow the form of verse, chorus, verse, chorus, and so on. Within the verses and the chorus, there may be rhyming words at the end of each line.*

CHECK UNDERSTANDING Ask students to explain how sonnets and odes differ from free verse.

LITERARY ANALYSIS

RHYME SCHEME

Point out that a rhyme scheme may use words that sound similar but do not rhyme exactly, such as *stop* and *clock.* This is called soft rhyme.

CHECK UNDERSTANDING Have students turn to poems they've already read and identify rhyme schemes.

 RESOURCE MANAGER—Copy Master
Rhyme Scheme p. 121 (for student use while reading the poems)

READING STRATEGY

PARAPHRASE

Write this example on the board and ask students to paraphrase it:

On this planet we've found many four-legged creatures. Their bodies are covered with fur. Some speak with a woof, some neigh, and some meow. There are also two-legged creatures who enjoy the company of the four-legged ones.

Possible answer: *A visitor from another planet says they've found four-legged, furry animals including dogs, cats, and horses on Earth. Humans like these animals.*

CHECK UNDERSTANDING Ask students to paraphrase a familiar television ad.

Practice and Apply

LITERARY ANALYSIS

A RHYME SCHEME

Remind students to use their charts from page 619 to determine the rhyme scheme. ***Answer:*** *The rhyme scheme is abba.*

READING STRATEGY

B PARAPHRASE

Possible answer: *On a silent, cold winter night, a cricket near the stove begins to sing. The cricket's song reminds the speaker, who is dozing off near the stove, of the grasshopper in summer.*

Lines 1–14

DISCUSSION PROMPTS

Use these prompts to help students understand the poem's main idea:

Recall Why aren't the birds singing when the grasshopper sings? ***Answer:*** *The grasshopper sings in the heat of the day, while the birds cool off and rest in the shade of the trees.*

Interpret What idea is repeated in the poem? What does it mean? ***Possible answer:*** *The idea that "The poetry of earth is never dead" (line 1) is repeated in line 9: "The poetry of earth is ceasing never." Nature's poetry is the sound of living creatures celebrating the joy of being alive in every season. When one creature stops singing, another begins to sing, so the poetry never dies.*

ANALYZE VISUALS

Possible answer: *The image suggests a mood of stillness and expectation. It also creates a feeling of mystery because so much of the scene is shrouded in darkness.*

ON THE *Grasshopper* AND *Cricket*

John Keats

The poetry of earth is never dead:
When all the birds are faint with the hot sun,
And hide in cooling trees, a voice will run
From hedge to hedge about the new-mown mead; **A**
That is the Grasshopper's—he takes the lead
In summer luxury,—he has never done
With his delights; for when tired out with fun
He rests at ease beneath some pleasant weed.
The poetry of earth is ceasing never:
On a lone winter evening, when the frost
Has wrought[1] a silence, from the stove there shrills
The Cricket's song, in warmth increasing ever,
And seems to one in drowsiness half lost,
The Grasshopper's among some grassy hills. **B**

A RHYME SCHEME
How would you describe the rhyme scheme in lines 1–4? Note that *mead* is a shortened form of *meadow,* so is pronounced mĕd.

B PARAPHRASE
How would you paraphrase lines 10–12? Now read lines 13–14. What does the cricket's song remind the speaker of?

ANALYZE VISUALS
What **mood** does this image suggest?

1. **wrought** (rôt): made; produced.

DIFFERENTIATED INSTRUCTION

FOR LESS–PROFICIENT READERS

Comprehension Support [paired option] Have students use Think-Pair-Share to discuss these questions:

- What details might describe a hot summer day and a cozy winter evening?
- What do a grasshopper and a cricket sound like? (Note: A brief search on the Internet will provide a sample of each.)

BEST PRACTICES TOOLKIT—Transparency
Think-Pair-Share p. A18

FOR ENGLISH LEARNERS

Vocabulary Support [mixed-readiness pairs] Have pairs use context clues to figure out the meanings of these phrases:

- *are faint with the hot sun* (line 2), "feel weak because the sun is so hot"
- *a voice will run* (line 3), "a chirp is heard"
- *new-mown mead* (line 4), "recently cut meadow"
- *at ease* (line 8), "calmly, comfortably"
- *in drowsiness half lost* (line 13), "almost asleep"

BACKGROUND

Keats's Inspiration In December 1816, John Keats and a fellow poet named Leigh Hunt challenged each other to write a sonnet about a grasshopper and a cricket. Each wrote his sonnet within 15 minutes.

FOR LESS–PROFICIENT READERS

Concept Support [small-group option] Explain to students that this type of sonnet (a Petrarchan sonnet) usually has one of the following rhyme schemes:

- first eight lines: *abbaabba*
- last six lines: *cdecde, cdccdc,* or *cdedce*

Have students work in small groups to record the rhyme scheme of the poem in their charts from page 619.

FOR ADVANCED LEARNERS/PRE–AP

Analyze Theme [paired option] Have students work in pairs to select a line from one of the poems that best expresses the poem's theme. Ask students to state the theme in their own words and cite details from the poem that support the theme. Invite students to share and compare their work.

ANALYZE VISUALS

About the Art Artist Gary Ernest Smith (born 1942) is a contemporary realist who lives near Highland, Utah. He is both a painter and a sculptor. His works convey the simple essence of his subjects, which are often inspired by his rural upbringing. He says, "Large bold shapes, with minimal detail, are the substance of my work. Most of the detailing in my pictures is 'implied' rather than painted."

READING STRATEGY

C PARAPHRASE

Possible answer: *The speaker's herds of cows or goats give him milk to drink, the fields give wheat for bread, his sheep provide wool for clothing, and the trees give both shade and wood for the fire.*

POETIC FORM

D TRADITIONAL FORMS

Possible answer: *Words and phrases that develop the theme of solitude include* unseen, unknown; unlamented; Steal from the world; *and* not a stone / Tell where I lie.

Extend the Discussion How does the last stanza provide a culmination of the theme of solitude?

Lines 1–20

REINFORCE *KEY IDEA:* FORM

Discuss Ask students what they notice about the **form** of the poem. How does the poem's form affect its meaning? ***Possible answer:*** *The poem contains five stanzas of four lines each. The fourth line is short. Students may say that the short lines suggest solitude.*

SELECTION WRAP-UP

REFLECT Ask students in what ways they came to appreciate these challenging poems after they took time to reread, paraphrase, and discuss them.

★ CRITIQUE Ask students to think about the speaker's message in "Ode on Solitude." Do they agree with the message about self-reliance and being alone? Why or why not?

Ode on Solitude

Alexander Pope

Barn at Cove, Oregon (2005), Gary Ernest Smith. Oil on canvas, 30″ × 4(

Happy the man whose wish and care
A few paternal[1] acres bound,
Content to breathe his native[2] air,
In his own ground.

Whose herds with milk, whose fields with bread,
Whose flocks supply him with attire,
Whose trees in summer yield him shade,
In winter fire. **C**

Blest, who can unconcern'dly find
Hours, days, and years slide soft away,
In health of body, peace of mind,
Quiet by day,

Sound sleep by night; study and ease,
Together mixt; sweet recreation;
And Innocence, which most does please
With meditation.

Thus let me live, unseen, unknown,
Thus unlamented[3] let me die,
Steal from the world, and not a stone
Tell where I lie. **D**

C PARAPHRASE
In the second stanza, what do the speaker's herds, fields, flocks, an trees provide for him? State the answer in yo own words.

D TRADITIONAL FORMS
What words and phras in the last stanza help develop the theme of solitude?

1. **paternal** (pə-tûr′nəl): received from a father.
2. **native:** being one's own because of one's birthplace.
3. **unlamented** (ŭn-lə-mĕnt′ĕd): not missed; not mourned for.

DIFFERENTIATED INSTRUCTION

FOR LESS-PROFICIENT READERS

Reading Strategy Follow-Up: Paraphrase [small-group option] Ask students to work in Jigsaw groups to read a stanza of the poem and write a paraphrase of it. Encourage students to discuss their ideas and use context clues and a dictionary to translate the meanings of difficult passages and words. Have groups share their paraphrases.

BEST PRACTICES TOOLKIT
Jigsaw Reading p. A1

FOR ENGLISH LEARNERS

Vocabulary Support Make sure students understand these words and phrases:

- *A few paternal acres bound* (line 2), "is limited to a small piece of land left to him by his father"
- *unconcern'dly* (line 9), "showing no worry"
- *mixt* (line 14), "mixed"
- *Innocence* (line 15), "a state of being pure"
- *steal* (line 19), "to sneak away"

622 UNIT 5: POETRY

er Reading

mprehension

1. **Recall** In "On the Grasshopper and Cricket," which insect represents summer? Which insect represents winter?
2. **Recall** Name three of the things that, according to the speaker in "Ode on Solitude," make man happy.

erary Analysis

3. **Examine Imagery** You remember that imagery consists of words or phrases that appeal to the senses. Use a web to record imagery from "On the Grasshopper and Cricket." To which senses does the poet appeal?

smell
taste
hearing
"On the Grasshopper and Cricket"
touch
sight
hot sun

4. **Identify Soft Rhyme** Sometimes a poet cannot find words that fit a poem's rhyme scheme *and* express the correct meaning. In such a case, a poet might use a **soft rhyme,** words that share one or more sounds but do not actually rhyme. What example of a soft rhyme do you find in "Ode on Solitude"?
5. **Paraphrase Poetry** Choose two especially challenging lines from each poem and "translate" them in your own words. What does each paraphrase help you to understand about the poem?
6. **Understand Traditional Forms** According to the bulleted definitions on page 619, what characteristics of its form does each poem show?
7. **Compare and Contrast Rhyme Scheme** Look back at the chart you made for each poem's rhyme scheme. Which poem's rhyme scheme is more complex? Explain.

tension and Challenge

8. **Readers' Circle** Alexander Pope wrote the first draft of "Ode on Solitude" around 1700. How do you think the speaker's idea of happiness might be different if the poem were rewritten today? Explain.

Practice and Apply

After Reading

For additional support of postreading questions, use these copy masters:

RESOURCE MANAGER—Copy Masters
Paraphrase p. 123 (for practice of reading standards focus)
Question Support p. 125 (After Reading questions adapted for English learners and less-proficient readers)

Additional selection questions are provided for teachers on page 117.

ANSWERS

Comprehension

1. *The grasshopper represents summer. The cricket represents winter.*
2. *Things that can make a man happy include living on his own land (lines 3–4); having animal herds for milk, fields for growing food, and flocks of sheep for clothing (lines 5–6); enjoying good health (line 11); peace of mind (line 11); good sleep (line 13); and time for study and relaxation (lines 13–14).*

Literary Analysis

Possible answers:

3. ***Touch:** hot sun, cooling trees, frost, warm stove; **Sight:** hedges, new-mown meadow, pleasant weed, grassy hills; **Hearing:** grasshopper's voice, silence, cricket's shrill*
4. *Examples of soft rhyme include* bread/shade *(lines 5 and 7).*
5. **■ STANDARDS FOCUS Paraphrase** *"On the Grasshopper and Cricket," lines 5–6: The grasshopper excels at enjoying summer. "Ode on Solitude," lines 9–10: A man who can let time go by without worry is very fortunate.*
6. **● STANDARDS FOCUS Traditional Forms** *"On the Grasshopper and Cricket" has 14 lines and a regular pattern of rhyme and rhythm. "Ode on Solitude" treats the topic of solitude in a serious, thoughtful way.*
7. **● STANDARDS FOCUS Rhyme Scheme** *"On the Grasshopper and Cricket" has a more complex rhyme scheme in which certain rhymes recur over a number of lines. In "Ode on Solitude," the rhyme pattern is repeated in each four-line stanza.*

Extension and Challenge

8. *Some students may say that although the world has changed greatly since Pope wrote this poem, the happiness that solitude can provide has not changed. Some students may say that the kind of solitude that gives the speaker so much happiness does not exist any longer. However, the speaker might find different things to be happy about, such as the freedom to create one's own solitude in the midst of the much more complicated world of today.*

Assess and Reteach

Assess

RESOURCE MANAGER—Copy Masters
Selection Tests A, B/C pp. 127–128, 129–130
Test Generator CD

Reteach

STANDARDS LESSON FILE
Literature Lessons 15, 16, 17, 20
Research and Study Skills Lesson 12

Focus and Motivate

OBJECTIVES

Literary Analysis
- explore the key idea of feeling **free**
- analyze and compare word choice in poetry
- analyze repetition in poetry
- read two poems

Reading
- read poetry

Vocabulary
- build vocabulary for reading and writing
- use knowledge of the Latin root *carn* to help determine word meaning *(also an EL language objective)*

SUMMARY

In the form of a work song, "One More Round" points out that while work in itself is rewarding, work derived from slave labor is destructive to the human spirit. In "Not My Bones," the speaker declares that what gives humans their individual identities is not their bodies but their minds and souls.

When do you feel most FREE?

Discuss the question. To lead into the ***KEY IDEA,*** ask students to imagine what it might feel like to lose their sense of freedom. How would their outlook on life change if they could not read a book, play a game, go to school, or have a conversation with a friend without obtaining someone's consent? Ask if people who have no physical freedom can still be **free** in other ways. Then have students work on the ***QUICKWRITE*** activity.

Before Reading

One More Round

Poem by Maya Angelou

Not My Bones

Poem by Marilyn Nelson

When do you feel most FREE?

KEY IDEA Riding a skateboard or a bike or a horse makes many people feel physically **free.** Reading a book can liberate the mind to explore the universe. Watching fireworks on the Fourth of July might remind us that we live in a country of many freedoms. The following poems convey the feelings of those who have found freedom at long last.

QUICKWRITE When have you felt most free? Think of two or three times and either describe them or sketch them in your journal. Try to explain why these situations gave you a sense of freedom.

Selection Resources

RESOURCE MANAGER UNIT 5

Plan and Teach pp. 131–138

Literary Analysis
Word Choice pp. 139, 140†*
Question Support p. 146*

Reading
Read Poetry pp. 141, 142†*
Reading Fluency p. 147

Vocabulary
Study p. 143*
Practice p. 144
Strategy p. 145

Assessment
Selection Tests A, B/C pp. 149*, 151*
Test Generator CD

BEST PRACTICES TOOLKIT
Differentiated Instruction pp. 31–38*
Scaffolding Instruction pp. 43–46*

Graphic Organizers/Strategies
Pair-Share • Venn Diagram

Reading Support
Audio Anthology CD*

Technology
Literature and Vocabulary Centers at **ClassZone.com**
Write*Smart* CD

* Resources for Differentiation † Also in Spanish

RARY ANALYIS: WORD CHOICE

To express complicated thoughts and feelings in just a few lines, poets must make every word count. So a poet's **word choice,** or use of words, is particularly important.

For example, in "Not My Bones," Marilyn Nelson writes "The soul runs free. It roams the night sky's mute geometry." Why did she choose these words when she could have written, "The soul flies among the stars in the sky"? Perhaps because the words *mute geometry* suggests a quiet order to the universe.

As you read each poem, look for similarly interesting, unusual, or striking words, and consider why the poet might have chosen them. Record your thoughts on a chart like the one shown.

Striking Words	*Why Poet Might Have Chosen*
mute geometry	*to suggest a quiet, planned universe*

DING STRATEGY: READ POETRY

One way poems can make an impact is through their use of **repetition,** a technique in which a sound, word, phrase, or line is repeated to emphasize an important idea or to create a pattern throughout the poem. Repetition also helps to reinforce meaning and to create an appealing rhythm. For example, look at the first lines of "Not My Bones":

I was not this body,
I was not these bones.

By repeating *I was not,* the speaker emphasizes her strong feelings. Try reading the poems aloud to get a better sense of how repetition helps create meaning and rhythm.

CABULARY IN CONTEXT

The following words help poet Marilyn Nelson explain how an enslaved person can find freedom. To see how many you know, use the words to complete the sentences.

WORD LIST	converge	cosmic	essential	incarnation

1. Abolitionist groups ____ to fight slavery.
2. Some believe that each soul has more than one ____.
3. Freedom of speech is ____ to a democracy.
4. Astronomers' work is to understand the ____ order.

Author Online

Maya Angelou: Silence to Star

Maya Angelou born 1928

At the age of seven, Maya Angelou went through a difficult time and stopped talking for five years. A family friend not only taught her the importance of the spoken word but also encouraged her to write. Since then, Angelou has written poetry, autobiographies, plays, screenplays, children's books, and even a cookbook. As her fame has grown, she has become an important public figure, mixing with presidents, television and movie stars, and other internationally recognized artists.

Marilyn Nelson: Early Promise

Marilyn Nelson born 1946

Marilyn Nelson's sixth-grade teacher predicted that Nelson would become a famous writer. The teacher was right. Nelson's books of poetry have won many awards, including the Newbery Honor. The poem "Not My Bones" comes from the book *Fortune's Bones: The Manumission Requiem,* which Nelson wrote to honor the memory of Fortune, an enslaved person who died in 1798. Nelson was commissioned to write the book by the Mattatuck Museum in Connecticut after the descendents of Fortune's owners donated his skeleton to the institution. Nelson has said she is motivated by the desire "to talk about finding pride . . . in people who triumphed over slavery."

MORE ABOUT THE AUTHOR
For more on these poets, visit the **Literature Center** at **ClassZone.com.**

Teach

STANDARDS FOCUS

LITERARY ANALYSIS

● WORD CHOICE

Have students give examples of times when it's important to choose their words carefully. *Students' examples might include defending an opinion or giving constructive criticism.*

CHECK UNDERSTANDING Ask students to discuss differences in meaning between the words in each pair: *silent/quiet, belief/opinion, follow/chase.* When would they choose to use each word?

RESOURCE MANAGER—Copy Master
Word Choice p. 139 (for student use while reading the poems)

READING STRATEGY

■ READ POETRY

Ask students to think of a song that has a chorus or refrain. Discuss the purpose that the refrain serves and point out that repetition of the refrain serves the same purpose in music as repetition does in poetry: it emphasizes a particular feeling or idea and creates a rhythm.

CHECK UNDERSTANDING Ask students to think of situations when they might use repetition in everyday speech. Discuss the effect of using repetition.

VOCABULARY SKILL

▲ VOCABULARY IN CONTEXT

DIAGNOSE WORD KNOWLEDGE To determine preteaching needs, have all students complete **Vocabulary in Context.** ***Answers:*** **1.** *converge* **2.** *incarnation* **3.** *essential* **4.** *cosmic*

PRETEACH VOCABULARY Use the Vocabulary Study copy master to help students explore the meaning of each boldfaced word.

1. Read item 1 aloud, emphasizing *converge.*
2. Point out the phrase *to plan the dance.* Elicit possible meanings for *converge,* such as "get together." Have students record their predicted meanings in the chart.
3. Repeat for items 2–4. Then remind students to check their predicted meanings as they read the poems.

RESOURCE MANAGER—Copy Master
Vocabulary Study p. 143

For general guidelines on differentiating vocabulary instruction and for alternative vocabulary activities for students not needing vocabulary preteaching, see

BEST PRACTICES TOOLKIT
Scaffolding Vocabulary Instruction pp. 43–46

Vocabulary Center at **ClassZone.com**
Additional Vocabulary Activities

Practice and Apply

Lines 1–5
DISCUSSION PROMPTS
Use these prompts to help students understand the speaker's meaning:

Interpret In lines 1–2, what is the speaker saying about work? ***Possible answer:*** *The speaker is saying that work can provide a particular kind of satisfaction that nothing else can.*

Analyze What does the speaker mean by "I was born to work up to my grave"? ***Possible answer:*** *The speaker expects to work until he or she dies. The speaker can scarcely imagine a life without work.*

Compare What is the difference between being born to work up to one's grave and spending one's life working as a slave? ***Possible answer:*** *Most people must work their entire lives in order to survive. Free people can make choices about their work, but enslaved people are denied choice and may be forced to work past the point of endurance.*

LITERARY ANALYSIS

A WORD CHOICE

Possible answer:

Striking Words	*Why Poet Might Have Chosen*
drove steel, stood guard	to show that the speaker's parents worked hard
holler 'cause	to reflect the dialect spoken by the family
graves, worked-out slaves	to express the tragedy of a life lived in slavery

ONE MORE ROUND

Maya Angelou

There ain't no pay beneath the sun
As sweet as rest when a job's well done.
I was born to work up to my grave
But I was not born
To be a slave.

One more round
And let's heave it down,
One more round
And let's heave it down.

Papa drove steel and Momma stood guard,
I never heard them holler 'cause the work was hard.
They were born to work up to their graves
But they were not born
To be worked-out slaves. **A**

One more round
And let's heave it down,
One more round
And let's heave it down.

Brothers and sisters know the daily grind,[1]
It was not labor made them lose their minds.
They were born to work up to their graves
But they were not born
To be worked-out slaves.

1. **grind:** a labor-intensive routine.

A WORD CHOICE
Reread the third stanz[a]. What words stand out to you? Note what the words and phrases ma[ke] you think of and then a[dd] them to your chart.

DIFFERENTIATED INSTRUCTION

FOR ALL STUDENTS
For general guidelines on differentiating instruction, see

BEST PRACTICES TOOLKIT
Differentiated Instruction pp. 31–38

FOR LESS–PROFICIENT READERS
Reading Strategy Follow-Up: Read Poetry Read the poem aloud and have students read stanzas 2, 4, 6, and 8 chorally. Ask them why enslaved laborers might have sung similar lines while they worked.

FOR ENGLISH LEARNERS
Options for Reading [paired option] Have students listen to each poem on the *Audio Anthology CD.* Then have students use a Pair-Share strategy to answer questions about each work.

BEST PRACTICES TOOLKIT—Transparency
Pair-Share p. A18

Aspiration (1936), Aaron Douglas. Oil on canvas, 60″ × 60″.

One more round
And let's heave it down,
One more round
And let's heave it down.

And now I'll tell you my Golden Rule,[2]
I was born to work but I ain't no mule.
I was born to work up to my grave
But I was not born
To be a slave.

One more round
And let's heave it down,
One more round
And let's heave it down. **B**

ANALYZE VISUALS
What **symbols** do you see in this painting?

B READ POETRY
This poem is modeled after songs workers sang as they labored. What stanzas remind you of a song?

2. **Golden Rule:** the biblical teaching that one should behave towards others as one wants others to behave towards oneself.

ANALYZE VISUALS

Possible answer:

- *factory symbolizing industry or paid labor*
- *city symbolizing human achievement*
- *globe symbolizing geography or astronomy*
- *drawing tools symbolizing architecture*
- *beaker symbolizing science*
- *book symbolizing education or knowledge*
- *upraised, shackled arms symbolizing slavery*
- *star symbolizing the North Star, which was used to guide enslaved people to freedom on the Underground Railroad*

About the Art *Aspiration* is one of four murals painted by African-American artist Aaron Douglas (1898–1979) for the Texas Centennial Exposition in 1936. Active in the Harlem Renaissance, Douglas spoke passionately about creating art that uniquely represents African-American culture: "Let's bare our arms and plunge them deep through laughter, through pain, through sorrow, through hope, through disappointment, into the very depths of the souls of our people. . . . Then let's sing it, dance it, write it, paint it."

READING STRATEGY

B READ POETRY

Possible answer: *The second, fourth, sixth, and eighth stanzas, which repeat the same lines, are like the refrain of a song.*

FOR ENGLISH LEARNERS

Reading: Background Explain that in the 1800s, railroads were built across the United States. The phrase *Papa drove steel* (line 10) refers to laying railroad tracks. This heavy labor was done by strong men who dug and graded the land, blasted through rocks, and used heavy hammers to drive the steel tracks into place. Invite students to speculate about what "Momma stood guard" over. ***Possible answer:*** *the family's home and children*

Vocabulary: Dialect Point out that the word *ain't* (lines 1 and 29) is a nonstandard contraction for "am not," "are not," "is not," "has not," or "have not." Also explain to students that *'cause* (line 11) is a nonstandard contraction meaning "because." Challenge students to substitute formal English usage in each of these lines. Also point out the word *holler* in line 11 and explain that it means "yell" or "complain."

ONE MORE ROUND 627

ANALYZE VISUALS

About the Art Medical illustrator William B. Westwood painted Fortune's image after a careful study of a life-size re-creation of Fortune's body based on his skeleton. Fortune's clothes in the painting are modeled after the clothing African Americans wore in the 1700s.

Activity What information might a skeleton reveal that would enable an artist to visualize the person as he or she appeared in life? ***Possible answer:*** *The skeleton would indicate the person's height and proportions, age, physical trauma such as broken bones, and the general shape of the face.*

LITERARY ANALYSIS

C WORD CHOICE

Possible answer: *Lines 3–6 mean that a human being is made of molecules that come together only for as long as the person lives; then they move on. This idea is supported in lines 9–14 by the phrases* brief incarnations, clouds in clothes, bore light passed on, *and* while it was in my hands it was called by my name.

NOT MY BONES

Marilyn Nelson

Fortune (2001), William B. Westwood. © William B. Westwood.

I was not this body,
I was not these bones.
This skeleton was just my
temporary home.
Elementary molecules[1] **converged** for a breath,
then danced on beyond my individual death.
And I am not my body,
I am not my body.

We are brief **incarnations,**
we are clouds in clothes.
We are water respirators,
we are how earth knows.
I bore[2] light passed on from an original flame;
while it was in my hands it was called by my name.
But I am not my body,
I am not my body. C

1. **elementary molecules:** the smallest, most basic particles of substances.
2. **bore:** carried; transported.

converge (kən-vûrj') *v.* to come together in o place; meet

incarnation (ĭn'-kär-nā'-shən) *n.* a bodily form

C WORD CHOICE
Reread lines 3–6. Wha are they saying about our physical bodies? What words in lines 9- suggest the same idea Add these to your char

DIFFERENTIATED INSTRUCTION

FOR LESS–PROFICIENT READERS

Concept Support [paired option] Have pairs read lines 9–16 and update their charts from page 625.

Striking Words	Why Poet Might Have Chosen
brief incarnations; clouds in clothes; water respirators	to create vivid images and a sense of oneness with nature

FOR ENGLISH LEARNERS

Vocabulary: Cognates [shared-language pairs] Have pairs scan the poem for cognates. Spanish cognates on this page include

- *skeleton/esqueleto* (line 3)
- *temporary/temporal* (line 4)
- *elementary/elemental* (line 5)
- *molecules/moléculas* (line 5)
- *converge/converger* (line 5)
- *individual/individual* (line 6)
- *respirators/respiradores* (line 11)

You can own a man's body,
but you can't own his mind.
That's like making a bridle
to ride on the wind.
I will tell you one thing, and I'll tell you true:
Life's the best thing that can happen to you.
But you are not your body,
you are not your body.

You can own someone's body,
but the soul runs free.
It roams the night sky's
mute geometry.
You can murder hope, you can pound faith flat,
but like weeds and wildflowers, they grow right back.
For you are not your body,
you are not your body.

You are not your body,
you are not your bones.
What's **essential** about you
is what can't be owned.
What's essential in you is your longing to raise
your itty-bitty voice in the **cosmic** praise.
For you are not your body,
you are not your body.

Well, I woke up this morning just so glad to be free,
glad to be free, glad to be free.
I woke up this morning in restful peace.
For I am not my body,
I am not my bones.
I am not my body,
glory hallelujah, not my bones,
I am not my bones. D

essential (ĭ-sĕn'shəl) *adj.* having the qualities that give something its true identity

cosmic (kŏz'mĭk) *adj.* universal; infinitely large

D READ POETRY
What lines in this poem have been most often repeated?

Lines 25–32
REINFORCE *KEY IDEA:* FREE

Discuss In what way is Fortune **free** today? ***Possible answer:*** *According to the poem, Fortune's soul runs free.*

Lines 33–48
DISCUSSION PROMPTS

Use these prompts to help students understand the speaker's meaning:

Recall Who is the speaker in this poem? What does the speaker think about his body? ***Possible answer:*** *The speaker is the spirit of an enslaved person who has died. He thinks that his physical body is not essential.*

Infer What does the speaker think about human beings' place in the universe? ***Possible answer:*** *The speaker thinks that in the scheme of things, we are very small.*

Evaluate What effect does the poem's point of view have on the message? ***Possible answer:*** *The point of view of an enslaved person who has finally achieved freedom lends authority to the message.*

READING STRATEGY

D READ POETRY

Answer: *"I am not my body" (lines 7, 8, 15, 16, 44, 46); "you are not your body" (lines 23, 24, 31, 32, 33, 39, 40)*

SELECTION WRAP–UP

REFLECT Ask students how the two speakers' attitudes about enslavement are alike and different.

★ CRITIQUE Point out that Nelson uses more figurative language than Angelou. Ask: Which style do you prefer? Why?

READING FLUENCY

Distribute the copy masters and have students practice fluency.

RESOURCE MANAGER—Copy Master
Reading Fluency p. 147

FOR ADVANCED LEARNERS/PRE–AP

Compare and Contrast [paired option] Have students work in pairs to analyze the style of each poet, focusing on aspects such as development of speaker and mood, line length, rhythm, rhyme, and word choice. Pairs should use a Venn Diagram to organize their ideas. Then have them share their findings with the class.

BEST PRACTICES TOOLKIT—Transparency
Venn Diagram p. A26

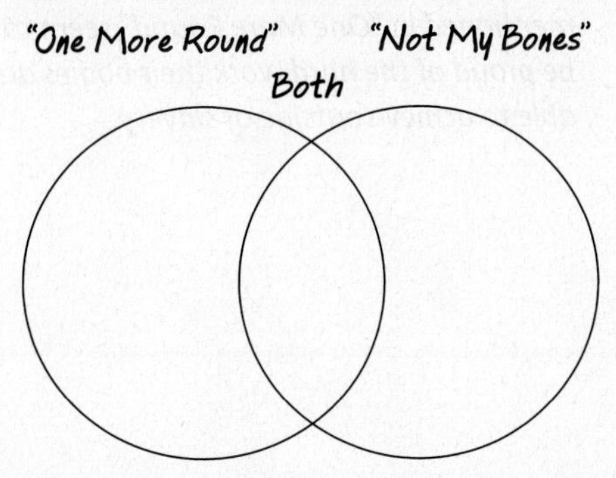

Practice and Apply

After Reading

For additional support of postreading questions, use these copy masters:

RESOURCE MANAGER—Copy Masters
Read Poetry p. 141 (for practice of reading standards focus)
Question Support p. 146 (After Reading questions adapted for English learners and less-proficient readers)
Additional selection questions are provided for teachers on page 135.

ANSWERS

Comprehension

1. *The speaker's Golden Rule is "I was born to work but I ain't no mule" (line 29).*
2. *The speaker says that hope and faith grow back (lines 29–30).*

Literary Analysis

Possible answers:

3. *Working hard is something that the characters accept without question, but they do not accept being "worked-out" as slaves.*
4. *A person's mind and soul are not physical; therefore, they cannot be owned.*
5. **STANDARDS FOCUS Read Poetry** ***"One More Round":*** *"One more round / and let's heave it down" stresses that life is filled with hard work and echoes the repetitive nature of manual labor. It may also express the speaker's desire to "heave down" the legacy of slavery.* ***"Not My Bones":*** *The lines "I am not my body" and "you are not your body" emphasize that one's physical being does not reflect the essence of what makes one human.*
6. **STANDARDS FOCUS Word Choice** *Responses should include examples of Angelou's simple diction and Nelson's more complex diction and use of imagery, and they should link each poet's word choice to the subject matter and theme.*
7. *Students who choose Angelou's poem may support their choice by referring to its rebellious tone; those who choose Nelson's poem may mention its vivid imagery.*
8. *Some students may respond that they would not agree, because the people mentioned in "One More Round" seem to be proud of the hard work their bodies are able to achieve outside of slavery.*

Extension and Challenge

9. *Answers will vary. Students' songs can be set to any melody but should reflect the content of the poem and a complementary rhythm.*

After Reading

Comprehension

1 **Recall** In "One More Round," what is the speaker's "Golden Rule"?

2. **Recall** According to the speaker in "Not My Bones," what happens when hope is murdered and faith is pounded flat?

Literary Analysis

3. **Interpret Poetry** Using a word web like the one shown, note important phrases about work associated with the people mentioned in "One More Round." What distinction does the speaker draw between work and slavery?

4. **Make Inferences** Why does the speaker in "Not My Bones" feel that a person's mind and soul cannot be owned?
5. **Analyze Repetition** For each poem, identify the two phrases or sections that are repeated most frequently. How do these repeated words contribute to the poems' meaning?
6. **Compare Word Choice** Review the charts you made as you read the poems. Make a generalization, or overall statement, about each poet's word choice. What is different about the words chosen for each poem?
7. **Evaluate Theme** Which poem's theme do you think conveys a greater sense of **freedom?** Support your response with details from the poem.
8. **Draw Conclusions** Do you think the people mentioned in "One More Round" would agree with the speaker of "Not My Bones" that "you are not your body"? Explain why or why not.

Extension and Challenge

9. **Creative Project: Music** Work with a small group to create a song from "One More Round." Practice reading the poem aloud, using desks, pencils, or other classroom materials as drums to keep the rhythm. Perform your piece for the class.

Vocabulary in Context

VOCABULARY PRACTICE

Choose the letter of the word that means the same, or nearly the same, as the boldfaced word.

1. two streams **converge:** (a) rise, (b) separate, (c) meet, (d) flow
2. **cosmic** ideas: (a) fascinating, (b) universal, (c) mistaken, (d) weird
3. **essential** elements: (a) dissimilar, (b) toxic, (c) similar, (d) basic
4. a brief **incarnation:** (a) meeting, (b) lifetime, (c) quarrel, (d) vacation

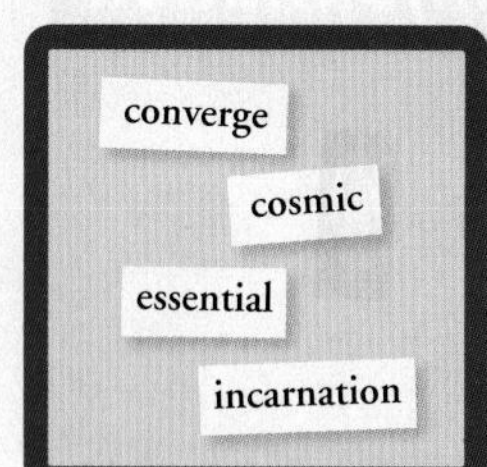

VOCABULARY IN WRITING

Do you think Marilyn Nelson is right when she says that people are not their bodies? Write a paragraph explaining your opinion. Use at least two vocabulary words in your paragraph. You could start this way.

EXAMPLE SENTENCE

I agree with Nelson when she says that each person's soul is an ***essential*** *part of him or her.*

VOCABULARY STRATEGY: THE LATIN ROOT *carn*

The vocabulary word *incarnation* comes from the Latin root *carn*, which means "flesh." *Carn* (combined with other word parts) appears in a number of English words. To determine the meaning of a word that contains this root, use context clues—the words and sentences around the word—as well as your knowledge of the root's meaning.

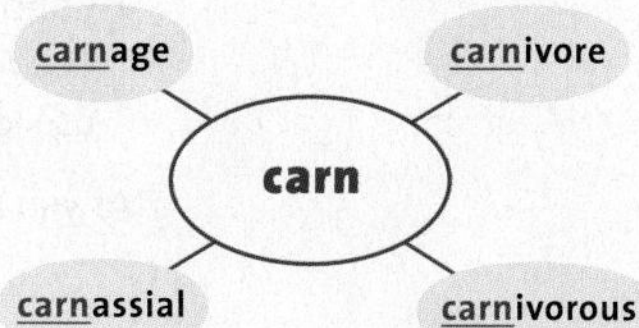

PRACTICE Choose the word from the web that best completes each sentence. Be ready to explain how the root *carn* helps to give each word its meaning.

1. Tyrannosaurus Rex was a huge ____ that devoured other dinosaurs.
2. The wolf is a ____ mammal that lives and hunts in a pack.
3. Drunk drivers cause ____ on U.S. highways.
4. Molars are ____ teeth, because they are adapted for chewing meat.

VOCABULARY PRACTICE
For more practice, go to the Vocabulary Center at ClassZone.com.

DIFFERENTIATED INSTRUCTION

FOR ENGLISH LEARNERS

Vocabulary in Writing Before they begin to write, review with students the definition of each vocabulary word. Display the definitions on the board so that students can refer to them while they write.

FOR ADVANCED LEARNERS/PRE-AP

Vocabulary Strategy Ask students to figure out the link between the Latin root *carn* and the following words, without using a dictionary. Then have them use a dictionary to confirm their conclusions.

- *carnival,* "a time of merrymaking before the period of Lent in the Christian calendar, during which people do not eat meat"
- *carnation,* "a pink-colored flower whose color could resemble flesh"
- *chili con carne,* "a Mexican dish with meat"

ANSWERS

Vocabulary in Context

VOCABULARY PRACTICE

1. *(c) meet*
2. *(b) universal*
3. *(d) basic*
4. *(b) lifetime*

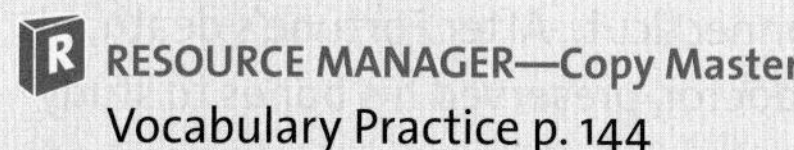

RESOURCE MANAGER—Copy Master
Vocabulary Practice p. 144

VOCABULARY IN WRITING

Ask students to recall the arguments the speaker uses in support of this statement. Then have them review the vocabulary list and identify words that could be used to express their own opinions.

VOCABULARY STRATEGY: THE LATIN ROOT *carn* *(also an EL language objective)*

Have students cover the web while they read each sentence, completing the sentence with a word that makes sense in the context. Then have them find the word on the web that could be used as a synonym for their word.

Answers:

1. *carnivore*
2. *carnivorous*
3. *carnage*
4. *carnassial*

RESOURCE MANAGER—Copy Master
Vocabulary Strategy p. 145

Vocabulary Center at **ClassZone.com**
Additional Vocabulary Activities

Assess and Reteach

Assess

RESOURCE MANAGER—Copy Masters
Selection Tests A, B/C pp. 149–150, 151–152

Test Generator CD

Reteach

STANDARDS LESSON FILE
Literature Lesson 34: Repetition and Parallelism
Literature Lesson 36: Word Choice and Diction
Vocabulary Lesson 1: Word Parts

Focus and Motivate

OBJECTIVES

Reading for Information
- outline
- support an opinion
- read author's notes

SUMMARY

An enslaved man named Fortune managed a farm in Connecticut. After Fortune's death, his master, a doctor, preserved his bones to study human anatomy. In the 1930s, the bones were given to a museum. By then no one knew whose they were. In the 1990s, historians linked the bones to Fortune, and scientists determined his cause of death.

What's the Connection?

Write these statements on the Anticipation Guide transparency. Have students respond to each one before and after reading.

- Enslaved people in the North owned nothing and were often separated from their families.
- Doctors in the late 1700s knew little about human anatomy.
- Attitudes about what is proper to display in museums have changed in recent years.

 **BEST PRACTICES TOOLKIT—Transparency**
Anticipation Guide p. A14

Teach

Skill Focus: Outline

Share these **outlining** tips with students:

- Use brief phrases, but make sure they are easily understood. Example: "Father of two sons and two daughters" is clear, while "Father two sons daughters" is not.
- Ignore or summarize minor details. Example: The fact that Fortune probably ran his master's farm is important. The type of crops is less important and could be omitted from an outline.
- Supply words that help categorize the facts. Example: The words *Status, Circumstances,* and *Death* clarify subtopics *A, B,* and *C.*
- See page R4 of the Reading Handbook for more tips.

Possible outline entries appear on pages 633–634 in boxed Outline notes.

RESOURCE MANAGER—Copy Master
Outline p. 161

Reading for Information

Fortune's Bones

Book Excerpt

Use with "Not My Bones," page 628.

What's the Connection?

The poem "Not My Bones" was inspired by the real life of Fortune, an enslaved person. Now learn more about this man and about what happened to his bones after he died.

Skill Focus: Outline

When you read nonfiction, do you find it hard to remember the main facts and ideas? Taking notes in the form of an outline can help you.

An **outline** is a way of summarizing the main topics, subtopics, and details in a text. If the text has headings and subheadings, those will probably tell you the main topics and subtopics to cover. If, as in "Fortune's Bones," there are no headings, see if you can use the topic sentence of each paragraph to identify the main topics. Next, follow these steps:

- Write the main topics as short phrases or sentences beside Roman numerals, leaving plenty of space below each Roman numeral entry.
- Underneath each Roman numeral entry, jot down related subtopics, using capital letters to order them.
- Continue adding information according to the level of its importance. Use Arabic numbers for entries below the capital letters. If necessary, use lowercased letters for details beneath the numbers.

As you read the following book excerpt, complete the outline started here.

Fortune

I. Fortune before he was bones in a Connecticut museum
  A. Status: A husband, father, baptized Christian, and a slave
    1. Husband to Dinah
    2. Father of two sons and two daughters
      a.
      b.
    3.
    4.
  B. Circumstances: When and where he lived and what he did
    1.
    2.
    3.
  C. Death: Fortune died in 1798 at about the age of 60.
II. Fortune's bones
  A. Dr. Porter preserved Fortune's bones to study the human skeleton.
  B.

Selection Resources

RESOURCE MANAGER UNIT 5

Plan and Teach pp. 153–157

Reading
Summary pp. 159†*, 160‡*
Outline pp. 161, 163†*
Reading Check p. 165
Support an Opinion pp. 162, 164†*
Question Support p. 166*

Assessment
Selection Tests A, B/C pp. 167*, 169*
Test Generator CD

Reading Support
Audio Anthology CD*

BEST PRACTICES TOOLKIT
Anticipation Guide • Round Robin/Roundtable

* Resources for Differentiation † Also in Spanish ‡ In Haitian Creole and Vietnamese

Practice and Apply

from **Fortune's Bones**

Notes by Pamela Espeland

A sculptor used information about Fortune's bones to create this reconstruction of Fortune's face.

Before Fortune was bones in a Connecticut museum, he was a husband, a father, a baptized Christian, and a slave.

His wife's name was Dinah. His sons were Africa and Jacob. His daughters were Mira and Roxa. He was baptized in an Episcopal church, which did not make him free. His master was Dr. Preserved Porter, a physician who specialized in setting broken bones. **A**

They lived in Waterbury, Connecticut, in the late 1700s. Dr. Porter had a 75-acre farm, which Fortune probably ran. He planted and harvested corn, rye, potatoes, onions, apples, buckwheat, oats, and hay. He cared for the cattle and hogs.

Unlike many slaves, who owned little or nothing and were often separated from their families, Fortune owned a small house near Dr. Porter's home. He and Dinah and their children lived together. **B**

When Dr. Porter died in 1803, he left an estate that was worth about $7,000—a lot of money for the time. The estate included Fortune's widow, Dinah, and their son Jacob. Fortune had died in 1798.

According to Connecticut's Act of Gradual Emancipation, children born to enslaved parents after March 1, 1784, were to be freed when they reached age 21. Jacob was 18. By law, he could be enslaved for another three years.

In Dr. Porter's will, he left Dinah to his wife, Lydia. He gave Jacob to his daughter Hannah. **C**

No one knows what happened to Africa, Mira, and Roxa.

FOCUS ON FORM
You're about to read the notes that accompany "Not My Bones" and Marilyn Nelson's other poems about Fortune. These **notes** provide facts and additional information about Fortune's life and his bones.

A OUTLINE
What information do you learn about Fortune's sons? About his daughters? Add these details next to lowercase letters *a* and *b* on your outline.

B OUTLINE
When and where did Fortune live? Under subtopic *B*, note this information next to numbers *1* and *2*. Next to number *3*, include information about the work Fortune did.

C NOTES
What facts about slavery in the northern United States do you learn from these notes?

FOCUS ON FORM

Notes Discuss the purpose and characteristics of notes in a book. Point out that these notes

- comment on or help explain the contents of the book in which they appear
- can have various styles
- may be supplied by the author of the book or by a critical reader

INFORMATIONAL ANALYSIS

A OUTLINE

Possible answer:

I. Fortune before he was bones . . .
A. Status
1. Husband to Dinah
2. Father of two sons and two daughters
a. Sons: Africa and Jacob
b. Daughters: Mira and Roxa

Extend the Discussion Use the information in lines 4–6 to complete numbers 3 and 4 in the outline. ***Possible answer:***

3. Baptized in an Episcopal church
4. Property of Dr. Preserved Porter, a doctor who specialized in setting broken bones

INFORMATIONAL ANALYSIS

B OUTLINE

Possible answer:

B. Circumstances
1. In the late 1700s
2. In Waterbury, Connecticut, with his wife and children in their own small house on Dr. Porter's property
3. Probably ran Dr. Porter's farm

ELEMENTS OF NONFICTION

C NOTES

Possible answer: *When a slave owner died, his or her enslaved workers could be passed on to other family members. Connecticut passed a law that called for children born to enslaved parents after March 1, 1784, to be freed when they turned 21.*

If students need help . . . Define *estate* (line 14) as "all the property a person owns at the time of his or her death" and *emancipation* (line 17) as "the process or act of freeing a person."

DIFFERENTIATED INSTRUCTION

FOR LESS–PROFICIENT READERS

Concept Support

- Point out that outlining involves condensing information. However, if a key fact is stated simply and briefly in the text, it can be transferred directly to an outline.
- If an outline entry is becoming too long, students should check to see if they can shorten it or break it into more than one entry at the same level.
- Illustrate these approaches with examples from subtopics *A* and *B* in section *I*.

FOR ENGLISH LEARNERS

Language: Pronoun Referents Point out the use of *his* twice in lines 20–21. Guide students to see that this pronoun is male and singular and thus refers to Dr. Porter. Note that *his* is the possessive form, showing ownership. To help students sort the four other names mentioned in the sentence, identify Lydia and Hannah as Porter's wife and daughter. Then have students identify Dinah and Jacob as Fortune's wife and son by referring back to line 3.

INFORMATIONAL ANALYSIS

D OUTLINE

Possible answer:

A. Dr. Porter preserved Fortune's bones to study the human skeleton.

1. Porter's two doctor sons studied the skeleton.

2. Four more generations of Porters used it to learn the names of the bones.

3. Another Porter relative took part of the skeleton to a college class.

4. Someone wrote "Larry" on the skull.

Lines 26–30

DISCUSSION PROMPT

Evaluate Was keeping Fortune's bones a good decision? *Students may say it was, since so many people learned from studying the bones. However, Fortune's family probably would have wanted to give him a proper burial.*

INFORMATIONAL ANALYSIS

E OUTLINE

Possible answer:

B. Over time, the skeleton was lost and found.

C. In 1933, a descendant of Dr. Porter's gave the bones to Mattatuck Museum.

1. The museum sent the bones to Europe.

2. The museum displayed the skeleton.

3. The museum put the skeleton into storage out of respect in 1970.

INFORMATIONAL ANALYSIS

F OUTLINE

Possible answer:

D. The skeleton was identified by historians in the 1990s; then archaeologists and anthropologists studied it.

1. Study showed that, during his labors, Fortune suffered various injuries.

2. He probably died from a quick, sudden injury that may have snapped a vertebra in his neck.

Most slaves who died in Waterbury in the 1700s were buried in one of the town's cemeteries. When Fortune died, he wasn't buried. Instead, Dr. Porter preserved Fortune's skeleton to further the study of human anatomy.

Dr. Porter had been a bonesetter for many years, but he'd never had a skeleton to study. He had two sons who were also doctors. They could learn from the skeleton, too.

Fortune was about 60 at the time of his death and, in spite of his injuries in relatively good health. His skeleton was sturdy and complete. . . .

Four more generations of Porters became physicians, and the skeleton stayed in the family. Porter children, grandchildren, and great-grandchildren used i to learn the names of the bones. This was their earliest medical training.

Sally Porter Law McGlannan, the last Porter doctor, remembered playi with the skeleton as a young girl. . . . Another family member, Leander Law once brought part of Fortune's skeleton to a college physiology class.

At some point—no one knows exactly when—"Larry" was written on th skull. Fortune's name was forgotten for nearly a century. **D**

D OUTLINE
Reread lines 26–38. What else happened to the skeleton while it stayed in the family? Add these details under section *II*, letter *A*. Number each detail you include.

Over the years, the skeleton was lost and found. It was boarded up in an att then discovered by a crew of workers hired to renovate an old building.

In 1933, Sally Porter Law McGlannan gave the bones to the Mattatuck Museum. The museum sent the bones to Europe to be assembled for display The skeleton hung in a glass case in the museum for decades, fascinating adults and frightening children.

Many stories were invented about the skeleton. Some said that "Larry" was Revolutionary War hero—maybe even George Washington. Some said he f to his death. Some said he drowned. Some said he was killed trying to escap Some thought he had been hanged.

One Waterbury resident remembers, "Larry was the thing to see when yo go to the museum. I don't think anybody ever envisioned that this was truly a human being." **E**

E OUTLINE
Reread lines 39–51, and note the topic sentences. Turn the topic sentences of the first two paragraphs in this section into capital-lettered entries *B* and *C*. Then, beneath *C*, add details about the skeleton's "life" as museum property.

In 1970, the skeleton, still called "Larry," was taken out of its case and put int storage. Times had changed. The museum now believed that displaying th skeleton was disrespectful. It wasn't just a bunch of bones. It was the remain of someone's son, maybe someone's father.

The skeleton rested for more than 25 years. Then, in the 1990s, historian searched local records and found a slave named Fortune. Archaeologists and anthropologists studied the bones, which started giving up their secrets. Th bones told how Fortune labored, suffered, and died: A quick, sudden injury like whiplash, may have snapped a vertebra in his neck. He did not drown o fall from a cliff. He was not hanged. **F**

But he was free.

F OUTLINE
When did scholars learn more about the bones? Include this information on your outline next to the letter *D*. Underneath, number the details about what scholars learned.

DIFFERENTIATED INSTRUCTION

FOR LESS–PROFICIENT READERS

Concept Support Have students discuss how notes about Fortune's bones might differ, in form and content, from a magazine article on the same topic. List their comments in a chart on the board. ***Possible answer:***

- ***Notes:*** *plain, matter-of-fact style with simple sentences; limited visuals*
- ***Magazine article:*** *author's personal style, with more complex sentences, catchy leads, interesting vocabulary, quotations from experts, and so on; more visuals*

Concept Support If students copy the outline, have them leave space under subtopics *A* and *B* in section *II* for the numbered points they'll be adding. Also tell them to add letters *C* and *D* with space under each for details.

FOR ENGLISH LEARNERS

Culture: Connect Invite students with connections to non-Western cultures to discuss attitudes in those cultures toward using human remains for educational or scientific purposes.

[Co]mprehension

1. **Recall** Where did Fortune live?
2. **Recall** Who gave Fortune's skeleton to the museum? What was her relationship to Fortune?
3. **Clarify** How did the museum learn how Fortune died?

[Cr]itical Analysis

4. **Refine Your Outline** Review your outline. If it's missing any important topics or details, add them now. What could someone learn about Fortune just from reading the capital letter headings of your outline?
5. **Evaluate Notes** Reread "Not My Bones" on pages 628–629. Compare the understanding of Fortune that you get from this poem with the understanding of him that you get from the accompanying notes. What might be the strengths of a book that combines poems with historical notes?

[Re]ad for Information: Support an Opinion

WRITING PROMPT

In the afterword of *Fortune's Bones,* Marie Galbraith, the executive director of the Mattatuck Museum, writes:

> "When the Fortune Project began, the committee members felt strongly that Fortune's remains should be buried. Now they are divided on this issue, as are visitors to the museum's exhibit 'Fortune's Story/Larry's Legacy.'"

What do you think should be done with Fortune's bones? Should the skeleton be buried, or should it be kept on display? Support your opinion with reasons and evidence, including details from the poem and the notes.

To answer this prompt, first decide what your opinion is. Then follow these steps:

1. Briefly state your opinion of what should be done with Fortune's skeleton.
2. Jot down the reasons for your opinion and gather evidence to support those reasons, including information from the poem and notes.
3. In a paragraph, state your opinion in a sentence or two. Then support it with clearly stated reasons and evidence.

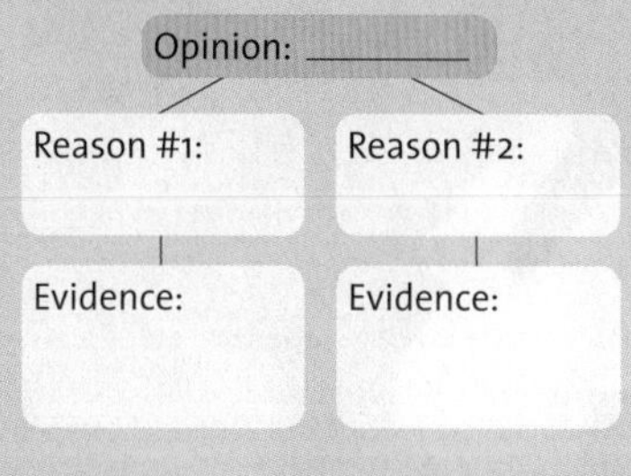

Practice and Apply

For additional support of postreading questions, use these copy masters:

RESOURCE MANAGER—Copy Masters
Reading Check p. 165
Question Support p. 166
Support an Opinion p. 162
For additional questions, see page 156.

ANSWERS

Comprehension

1. *Fortune lived in Waterbury, Connecticut, on a farm owned by Dr. Preserved Porter.*
2. *Sally Porter Law McGlannan, Dr. Porter's great-granddaughter, gave Fortune's skeleton to the museum.*
3. *Anthropologists and archaeologists studied Fortune's bones and found that he died of a sudden injury that broke his neck.*

Critical Analysis

Possible answers:

4. **STANDARDS FOCUS Outline** *Fortune was a husband, a father, a baptized Christian, and a slave. He died in 1798 at the age of 60. Dr. Porter preserved Fortune's bones to study human anatomy. Over the years, the skeleton was lost and found. In 1933, a descendant of Porter's gave the bones to a museum. They were identified and studied in the 1990s.*
5. *Such a book could supply two perspectives that complement each other. The poems could explore the personal or emotional significance of the subject, while the notes could answer readers' questions about historical facts and context.*

Read for Information: Support an Opinion

Writing Prompt *Opinions should be clearly stated and supported by reasons and evidence.*

Assess and Reteach

Assess

RESOURCE MANAGER—Copy Masters
Selection Tests A, B/C pp. 167–168, 169–170
Test Generator CD

Reteach

STANDARDS LESSON FILE
Reading Lesson 4: Recognizing Main Idea and Details

FOR LESS–PROFICIENT WRITERS

Read for Information

- Before students begin, ask them to review lines 52–55 to understand why the museum decided in the 1970s to remove the skeleton from view.
- Then have them think about how they would feel, or have felt, when looking at the bones of a long-dead human in a museum.
- Suggest that students talk about their views and evidence with another student before writing.

FOR ADVANCED LEARNERS/PRE–AP

Apply [small-group option] What is the proper way to handle human remains on display in museums? Point out that this issue has also been a concern of Native American groups. Have students find an article on the Internet that examines this controversy. Ask them to outline the article and then use their outline to share what they learned in a small-group Roundtable.

BEST PRACTICES TOOLKIT—Transparency
Round Robin/Roundtable p. A17

Focus and Motivate

OBJECTIVES

Literary Analysis

- explore the key idea of a **story**
- identify and analyze rhythm and meter and their effects
- identify, analyze, and evaluate characteristics of narrative poetry
- read narrative poetry

Reading

- summarize poetry

Grammar and Writing

- punctuate titles correctly by using quotation marks and italics
- use writing to analyze literature

SUMMARY

In Dylan's ballad "Boots of Spanish Leather," a conflict develops between the speakers when one sails away to Spain. The traveler's repeated offer to send back an exotic gift makes the one left behind realize that their love is lost. In Longfellow's epic *The Song of Hiawatha,* young Hiawatha learns about the ways of nature from his grandmother. After befriending all the birds and beasts, however, he must hunt and kill his first deer.

When do poems tell a STORY?

Introduce the question and discuss the ***KEY IDEA.*** Have students recall "John Henry" (page 288) as one example of a poem that tells a **story.** Assist students in identifying the setting, main character, and plot. Follow up by having small groups do the ***DISCUSS*** activity.

Before Reading

Boots of Spanish Leather

Poem by Bob Dylan

from The Song of Hiawatha

Poem by Henry Wadsworth Longfellow

When do poems tell a STORY?

KEY IDEA When you hear the word **story,** you might think of plots that unfold in short stories, novels, or movies. But some of the first stories that people told to each other took on the form of poetry. Ever since, some writers have used the stanzas, rhythm, and rhyme of poetry to tell about characters, setting, and conflict. The following two works are examples of stories told in poetic form.

DISCUSS Think of a poem or song you know that tells a story. For your group, summarize the story in your own words. How many of your classmates can guess the original work?

636

Selection Resources

RESOURCE MANAGER UNIT 5

Plan and Teach pp. 171–178

Literary Analysis
Rhythm and Meter pp. 179, 180†*
Question Support p. 183*

Reading
Summarize pp. 181, 182†*

Grammar and Writing
Punctuate Titles Correctly p. 184

Assessment
Selection Tests A, B/C pp. 185*, 187*
Test Generator CD

BEST PRACTICES TOOLKIT

Differentiated Instruction pp. 31–38*

Graphic Organizers/Strategies
Think-Pair-Share • Two-Column Chart • Read Aloud/Think Aloud • Whip Around

Reading Support
Audio Anthology CD*

Technology
Literature and Writing Centers at **ClassZone.com**
Write*Smart* CD

* Resources for Differentiation † Also in Spanish

POETIC FORM: NARRATIVE POETRY

The two poems that follow are examples of specific types of **narrative poetry,** or poetry that tells a story.

- "Boots of Spanish Leather" is a **ballad,** a narrative poem that is meant to be sung and focuses on a single tragic event.
- *The Song of Hiawatha* is an **epic,** a long narrative poem about the life of a hero whose actions reflect the values of the group he or she belongs to.

Like all narrative poems, ballads and epics contain characters, plot, and setting.

ITERARY ANALYSIS: RHYTHM AND METER

One way that poetry differs from prose is the extent to which it features rhythm and meter. **Rhythm** is the pattern of stressed (´) and unstressed (˘) syllables in a line of poetry. Narrative poetry often has a regular, repeated pattern of rhythm, which is called **meter.**

Rhythm and meter create the overall tempo or pace of a poem. They give poems their musical sound and help poets to emphasize certain words or phrases. For example, notice the soothing, regular rhythm in the following lines from *The Song of Hiawatha:*

By the shores of Gitche Gumee,
By the shining Big-Sea-Water,

As you read the poems, listen for the way rhythm and meter create emphasis and add a musical effect.

EADING STRATEGY: SUMMARIZE

When you **summarize,** you briefly retell the main ideas and most important details of a piece of writing in your own words. Summarizing narrative poetry can help you make sure you understand the characters' feelings, thoughts, and actions. As you read each poem, use a graphic organizer like the one shown to help yourself identify the most important ideas of each stanza or section.

Stanza/Section	*Main Idea*	*Detail(s)*
1	*A woman lives in the forest by the water.*	*Her name is Nokomis.*

Author Online

Bob Dylan: A Poet of His Times In the 1960s, Bob Dylan burst onto the folk music scene in New York City. He quickly became famous as the voice of his generation. But the young man, who was born Robert Zimmerman in a Minnesota mining town, was not content to be labeled. He disappointed many of his early fans when he began to play rock music. He confused others when he left the rock scene to pursue a religious path. And all the while, drawing from both classic literature and traditional American music, he wrote lyrics widely recognized as important poems.

Bob Dylan
born 1941

Henry Wadsworth Longfellow: American Legend Henry Wadsworth Longfellow introduced American landscapes, history, and culture to a wide readership. Many of his works draw from the history of European Americans; *The Song of Hiawatha* was one of the first literary works in English to treat Native-American themes with respect. The real Hiawatha was a Native American chief credited with helping to make peace among warring tribes. Longfellow's hero was a combination of this historical figure and other people the poet learned about through researching the traditions of various Native American groups.

Henry Wadsworth Longfellow
1807–1882

MORE ABOUT THE AUTHOR
For more on these poets, visit the **Literature Center** at **ClassZone.com.**

Teach

STANDARDS FOCUS

POETIC FORM

● NARRATIVE POETRY

Point out that ballads are often about ordinary people, while epics celebrate cultural heroes. Ask students to name possible subjects for a ballad and an epic. ***Possible answer:*** *Ballad: a sports hero, a firefighter, or a local person. Epic: a national or world leader, a military hero, or a founding member of a society.*

CHECK UNDERSTANDING Ask students how they would decide whether a person is a good subject for a ballad or an epic.

LITERARY ANALYSIS

● RHYTHM AND METER

Display this saying from Ben Franklin:

Early to bed and early to rise
Makes a man healthy, wealthy, and wise.

Lightly tap out the rhythm of the words as you say them. Then add the marks for the stressed and unstressed syllables. Note that you are using slightly louder and longer taps for the stressed syllables.

CHECK UNDERSTANDING Ask students to identify stressed and unstressed syllables in the proverb "An apple a day keeps the doctor away."

READING STRATEGY

■ SUMMARIZE

Ask students to reread the ***KEY IDEA*** paragraph on page 636 and summarize the main idea of the paragraph in one sentence. ***Possible answer:*** *Poems that tell stories have characters, setting, and conflict.*

CHECK UNDERSTANDING Have students summarize a favorite song or a poem they have read.

RESOURCE MANAGER—Copy Master
Summarize p. 181 (for student use while reading the poems)

DIFFERENTIATED INSTRUCTION

FOR ALL STUDENTS

For general guidelines on differentiating instruction, see

BEST PRACTICES TOOLKIT
Differentiated Instruction pp. 31–38

FOR LESS-PROFICIENT READERS

Concept Support Review the characteristics of narrative poetry: setting, characters, and plot. Ask students to use a three-column chart to take notes on these story elements as they read the poems.

FOR ENGLISH LEARNERS

Options for Reading [paired option] Read each poem aloud or play the readings that are available on the *Audio Anthology CD.* Have students use a Think-Pair-Share strategy to answer important questions about each work.

BEST PRACTICES TOOLKIT—Transparency
Think-Pair-Share p. A18

Practice and Apply

ANALYZE VISUALS

Possible answer: *The dark blue colors in the foreground suggest a sorrowful or bleak mood. In the background, the mix of orange, red, gray, and blue suggests an angry or excited mood.*

POETIC FORM

A NARRATIVE POETRY

Possible answer: *The speaker in the first stanza is leaving home on a ship. The speaker in the second stanza is staying behind. Both speakers use the phrase* my own true love *to refer to the other speaker.*

If students need help . . . Point out that the use of italics in alternate stanzas on this page highlights the fact that there are two different speakers in the ballad.

READING STRATEGY

B SUMMARIZE

Remind students to add their answers to the chart from page 637. ***Possible answer:***

- ***Stanza/Section:*** *4*
- ***Main Idea:*** *The speaker does not want the gift.*
- ***Detail(s):*** *The speaker wants only the sweet kiss of his beloved.*

Extend the Discussion If you were the one left behind, would you share the speaker's attitude? Explain.

Lines 1–20

REINFORCE *KEY IDEA:* STORY

Discuss What **story** elements are evident in this poem so far? Explain. ***Possible answer:***

- ***Characters:*** *the two speakers*
- ***Plot:*** *One of the speakers is going away.*
- ***Conflict:*** *The speaker who is leaving wants to send a gift because she might be gone for a long time. The other speaker does not want the gift, but would rather have his "own true love" nearby.*
- ***Setting:*** *One of the speakers will be sailing to Spain.*

Boots of Spanish Leather

Bob Dylan

Oh, I'm sailin' away my own true love,
I'm sailin' away in the morning.
Is there something I can send you from across the sea,
From the place that I'll be landing?

No, there's nothin' you can send me, my own true love,
There's nothin' I wish to be ownin'.
Just carry yourself back to me unspoiled,
From across that lonesome ocean. **A**

Oh, but I just thought you might want something fine
Made of silver or of golden,
Either from the mountains of Madrid[1]
Or from the coast of Barcelona.[2]

Oh, but if I had the stars from the darkest night
And the diamonds from the deepest ocean,
I'd forsake[3] them all for your sweet kiss,
For that's all I'm wishin' to be ownin'. **B**

That I might be gone a long time
And it's only that I'm askin',
Is there something I can send you to remember me by,
To make your time more easy passin'.

ANALYZE VISUALS
What is the **mood** of t
painting? Explain hov
the colors contribute t
that mood.

A NARRATIVE POET
Reread the first two
stanzas. What do you
know about the speak
in the first stanza? Wh
is the speaker in the
second?

B SUMMARIZE
What is this speaker's
attitude toward the
offered gift?

1. **Madrid** (mə-drĭd'): the capital of Spain, located in the central part of the country.
2. **Barcelona** (bär'-sə-lōnə): a northeastern Spanish city, located on the Mediterranean Sea coast.
3. **forsake** (fôr-sāk'): to give up (something that was formerly precious).

DIFFERENTIATED INSTRUCTION

FOR ENGLISH LEARNERS

Language: Direct Address Point out that the two speakers are addressing each other directly, as shown by their use of the pronoun *you* and the noun phrase *my own true love.* To clarify, give students some everyday examples of direct address:

- I brought you a present, Sam.
- Thank you, my friend.

La Promenade en Mer (1988), Jean Plichart. Copper engraving. © SuperStock.

Oh, how can, how can you ask me again,
It only brings me sorrow.
The same thing I want from you today,
I would want again tomorrow. **C**

I got a letter on a lonesome day,
It was from her ship a-sailin',
Saying I don't know when I'll be comin' back again,
It depends on how I'm a-feelin'.

Well, if you, my love, must think that-a-way,
I'm sure your mind is roamin'.
I'm sure your heart is not with me,
But with the country to where you're goin'.

So take heed, take heed of the western wind,
Take heed of the stormy weather.
And yes, there's something you can send back to me,
Spanish boots of Spanish leather. **D**

C NARRATIVE POETRY
What is the **conflict** between the two speakers, or characters?

D RHYTHM AND METER
Reread lines 33–36 aloud. Which words are emphasized by the repetition and rhythm?

POETIC FORM

C NARRATIVE POETRY

Possible answer: *One speaker wants to travel to Spain; the other wants them to be together.*

If students need help . . . Ask students to scan lines 13–16 to find out what the speaker means by the phrase *The same thing I want from you today* (line 23).

LITERARY ANALYSIS

D RHYTHM AND METER

Possible answer: *The repetition of the phrase* take heed *emphasizes that the character left behind still cares deeply about the other. The change in rhythm in the final line and the repetition of the word* Spanish *emphasizes the speaker's change of attitude about the gift and the goodbye.*

Line 1–36
DISCUSSION PROMPTS

Use these prompts to help students understand the poem's setting and conflict:

Recall Where is the first speaker going? ***Answer:*** *to Spain*

Analyze Does this story take place in the present or the past? What details provide clues to the setting? ***Possible answer:*** *It takes place in the past. Clues are that crossing the ocean requires sailing in a ship, and long-distance communication is by letter.*

Compare The character who is left behind uses the word *lonesome* twice, in lines 8 and 25. Does the other character also feel lonesome? Explain. ***Possible answer:*** *The character who is sailing away never mentions feeling lonesome and seems to be caught up in what lies ahead in another country.*

ADDITIONAL TEACHING OPPORTUNITY

Geography and History On a world map, show students the location of Spain in relation to North America. Discuss why being separated from a loved one by an ocean would have been harder to endure in the past than it is today.

FOR LESS–PROFICIENT READERS

Comprehension Support To help students understand lines 25–28, explain that in the days when all long-distance communication was by letter, sailing ships coming and going across the ocean sometimes crossed paths, especially near ports. When they did, passengers could transfer letters they had written from one ship to the other, to be carried back to the place they had left.

FOR ADVANCED LEARNERS/PRE–AP

Analyze Story Ending Have students discuss whether the speaker in the last stanza is really interested in "Spanish boots of Spanish leather," or the last two lines are an example of irony—saying one thing but meaning another. What is the speaker really saying to his or her beloved? Ask students to write a paragraph that analyzes the ending of the story. Have them share their paragraphs and discuss their views.

ANALYZE VISUALS

Possible answer: *The person shows a peaceful reverence of the moon and stars.*

About the Art Joe Geshick (born 1943) studied art in New York in the late 1970s and now lives and works in northern Minnesota. Of Ojibwe descent, Geshick uses earth tones, simple lines, and rich textures to explore Native American traditions and spirituality in his work. He says, "I use a semi-abstract approach in the creation of these paintings because it is important to me not to violate the sacredness of the actual ceremonies. I encourage the viewer to relate to my work from personal experience."

POETIC FORM

E NARRATIVE POETRY

Answer: *The setting is by the shores of Gitche Gumee at the wigwam of Nokomis in front of a dark forest.*

The Song of Hiawatha

Henry Wadsworth Longfellow

By the shores of Gitche Gumee,
By the shining Big-Sea-Water,
Stood the wigwam of Nokomis,
Daughter of the Moon, Nokomis.
Dark behind it rose the forest,
Rose the black and gloomy pine trees,
Rose the firs with cones upon them;
Bright before it beat the water,
Beat the clear and sunny water,
Beat the shining Big-Sea-Water. **E**
There the wrinkled old Nokomis
Nursed the little Hiawatha,
Rocked him in his linden[1] cradle,
Bedded soft in moss and rushes,
Safely bound with reindeer sinews;
Stilled his fretful wail by saying,
"Hush! the Naked Bear will hear thee!"
Lulled him into slumber, singing,
"Ewa-yea! my little owlet!
Who is this, that lights the wigwam?
With his great eyes lights the wigwam?
Ewa-yea! my little owlet!"
Many things Nokomis taught him
Of the stars that shine in heaven;
Showed him Ishkoodah, the comet,

ANALYZE VISUALS
What is the attitude of the person in this painting?

E NARRATIVE POETRY
What is the **setting** of this poem?

1. **linden** (lĭn′dən): made of wood from a linden tree.

Communion, Joe Geshick. © Joe Gesh

DIFFERENTIATED INSTRUCTION

FOR ENGLISH LEARNERS

Culture: Connect Ask students to compare Hiawatha's grandmother, Nokomis, to an older person who is special to them. Have them note the way Nokomis treats Hiawatha as a child and what she teaches him. Guide students to use a Two-Column Chart to compare the qualities and behavior of Nokomis and the qualities and behavior of the person they know.

BEST PRACTICES TOOLKIT—Transparency
Two-Column Chart p. A25

Vocabulary Support Use Read Aloud/Think Aloud to show how students can use context to figure out the meanings of these words:

- *wigwam* (lines 3, 20, 21), "rounded hut used by Native Americans in the Great Lakes region"
- *rushes* (line 14), "marsh plants with hollow stems"
- *sinews* (line 15), "cordlike tissues that connect muscle to bone"
- *fretful* (line 16), "troubled"

For example, have students read line 14 and point out that rushes might be plants that grow in the same place that moss does. Then ask students to work in pairs to find the complete or exact meaning of each word in a dictionary. Have them agree on the best way to restate the dictionary meaning in their own words.

BEST PRACTICES TOOLKIT—Transparency
Read Aloud/Think Aloud p. A34

BACKGROUND

Hiawatha Remind students that the character of Hiawatha is based in part on a real Onondagan chief who was possibly a Mohawk by birth. Point out that the Onondaga lived in what is now central and northern New York State. Ask students to use this information and a map of the United States to speculate about what "Big-Sea-Water" may refer to (*one of the Great Lakes*).

FOR LESS–PROFICIENT READERS

Reading Strategy Follow-Up: Summarize [paired option] Have students work in pairs to read lines 11–22 and update their charts, introduced on page 637. Point out that each section begins with an indented line, and remind students to look for the main idea of each section and the details that support that idea. Note that the main idea for section 1 appears on page 637.

Stanza/Section	*Main Idea*	*Detail(s)*
section 1 (lines 1–10)	*A woman lives in the forest by the water.*	*Her name is Nokomis.*
section 2 (lines 11–22)	*Nokomis takes care of and comforts a baby.*	*The baby is Hiawatha. Hiawatha is the light of Nokomis's life.*

READING STRATEGY

F SUMMARIZE

Remind students to add their answers to their charts from page 637. ***Possible answer:*** *Nokomis teaches Hiawatha about stars and constellations in the night sky and the stories associated with them.*

If students need help . . . Read the section aloud. Then ask students to name, or infer, the things that Nokomis shows Hiawatha. These include "the stars" (line 24), "the comet" (line 25), the northern lights (lines 27–30), and the Milky Way (lines 31–34).

LITERARY ANALYSIS

G RHYTHM AND METER

Answer: *Yes, the rhythm is regular. Each line has eight syllables, of which the first, third, fifth, and seventh are stressed.*

If students need help . . . Have them tap the rhythm with their thumb and index finger, making a louder sound with the thumb, as the class does a choral reading of lines 42–53.

Extend the Discussion In what way does the rhythm Longfellow uses relate to the musical culture of many Native American groups?

Ishkoodah, with fiery tresses;[2]
Showed the Death-Dance of the spirits,
Warriors with their plumes and war-clubs,
Flaring far away to northward
In the frosty nights of Winter;
Showed the broad white road in heaven,
Pathway of the ghosts, the shadows,
Running straight across the heavens,
Crowded with the ghosts, the shadows. **F**
At the door on summer evenings
Sat the little Hiawatha;
Heard the whispering of the pine-trees,
Heard the lapping of the waters,
Sounds of music, words of wonder;
"Minne-wawa!" said the pine-trees,
"Mudway-aushka!" said the water.
Saw the firefly, Wah-wah-taysee,
Flitting through the dusk of evening,
With the twinkle of its candle
Lighting up the brakes[3] and bushes,
And he sang the song of children,
Sang the song Nokomis taught him:
"Wah-wah-taysee, little firefly,
Little, flitting, white-fire insect,
Little, dancing, white-fire creature,
Light me with your little candle,
Ere upon my bed I lay me,
Ere in sleep I close my eyelids!" **G**
Saw the moon rise from the water
Rippling, rounding from the water,
Saw the flecks and shadows on it,
Whispered, "What is that, Nokomis?"
And the good Nokomis answered:
"Once a warrior, very angry,
Seized his grandmother, and threw her
Up into the sky at midnight;
Right against the moon he threw her;
'Tis her body that you see there."
Saw the rainbow in the heaven,
In the eastern sky, the rainbow,
Whispered, "What is that, Nokomis?"

F SUMMARIZE
Each new section of th
poem begins with an indented line. What is main idea of this secti
Add it to your chart.

G RHYTHM AND ME
Read lines 42–53 aloud tapping your pencil to their rhythm. Is the rhythm regular?

2. **tresses:** long locks or ringlets of hair.
3. **brakes:** areas overgrown with dense bushes; thickets.

DIFFERENTIATED INSTRUCTION

FOR ENGLISH LEARNERS

Culture: Clarify Tell students that most of the Native American words Longfellow uses come from the Ojibwe language used by groups who lived in the upper Great Lakes region. Pronounce several of the words, have students say the words after you, and ask students to use context to infer what the words mean. Discuss how the words add authenticity to the poem. Then have students scan the rest of the poem to identify and pronounce other Native American words.

FOR ADVANCED LEARNERS/PRE-AP

Analyze Rhythm and Meter [small-group option] Have small groups compare the rhythm in lines 35–41 of *The Song of Hiawatha* with the rhythm in lines 5–8 of "Boots of Spanish Leather." Have the groups

- write out the lines and mark the stressed and unstressed syllables
- describe the rhythm in each excerpt, noting whether it applies to the whole poem

And the good Nokomis answered:
"'Tis the heaven of flowers you see there
All the wildflowers of the forest,
All the lilies of the prairie,
When on earth they fade and perish,
Blossom in that heaven above us."
  When he heard the owls at midnight,
Hooting, laughing in the forest,
"What is that?" he cried in terror,
"What is that," he said, "Nokomis?"
And the good Nokomis answered:
"That is but the owl and owlet,
Talking in their native language,
Talking, scolding at each other." **H**
  Then the little Hiawatha
Learned of every bird its language,
Learned their names and all their secrets:
How they built their nests in Summer,
Where they hid themselves in Winter;
Talked with them whene'er he met them,
Called them "Hiawatha's Chickens."
  Of all beasts he learned the language,
Learned their names and all their secrets:
How the beavers built their lodges,
Where the squirrels hid their acorns,
How the reindeer ran so swiftly,
Why the rabbit was so timid,
Talked with them whene'er he met them,
Called them "Hiawatha's Brothers." **I**
  Then Iagoo, the great boaster,
He the marvelous storyteller,
He the traveler and the talker,
He the friend of old Nokomis,
Made a bow for Hiawatha;
From a branch of ash he made it,
From an oak bough made the arrows,
Tipped with flint,[4] and winged with feathers
And the cord he made of deerskin.
  Then he said to Hiawatha:
"Go, my son, into the forest,
Where the red deer herd together.

H NARRATIVE POETRY
Nokomis, Hiawatha's grandmother, raises him as her own. What kind of relationship do the woman and boy seem to have?

I SUMMARIZE
Reread lines 81–95. What does Hiawatha learn in this section?

4. **flint:** a hard, gray or black quartz.

POETIC FORM

H NARRATIVE POETRY

Possible answer: *Hiawatha and Nokomis have a close, supportive relationship. Nokomis patiently answers his questions about the natural world.*

READING STRATEGY

I SUMMARIZE

Have students record their answers in the chart from page 637. ***Possible answer:*** *Hiawatha learns to understand the animals, including how they live and their special abilities.*

Lines 64–95

DISCUSSION PROMPTS

Use these prompts to help students understand the theme of the poem:

Summarize What kinds of questions does Hiawatha ask Nokomis? ***Answer:*** *Hiawatha asks questions about things in nature, such as rainbows and the sound of owls.*

Analyze The young Hiawatha calls the animals "Hiawatha's Brothers." What does this tell you about how he thinks about them? ***Possible answer:*** *He feels a kinship with the animals.*

Synthesize You read on page 637 that Longfellow's poem was one of the first works written in English that expressed respect for Native American cultures. What aspects of Hiawatha's culture does the poet seem to admire? ***Possible answer:*** *He admires the culture's intimate understanding of and respect for the natural world.*

FOR LESS–PROFICIENT READERS

Reading Strategy Follow-Up: Summarize

[paired option] Have students work in pairs to read sections 11 and 12 (lines 96–109) and record the main ideas and important details in their Summarize charts from page 637. Encourage them to take notes in their own words.

Stanza/Section	Main Idea	Detail(s)
section 11 (lines 96–104)	Iagoo makes a bow for Hiawatha.	Iagoo is a great storyteller. The bow and arrow are made from parts of trees and animals.
section 12 (lines 105–109)	Iagoo tells Hiawatha to kill a great deer.	Iagoo tells Hiawatha to go into the forest.

THE SONG OF HIAWATHA 643

ANALYZE VISUALS

Possible answer: *The painting suggests that people and animals are one; that they are connected.*

Lines 110–132

DISCUSSION PROMPTS

Have students use these prompts to help them analyze Hiawatha's actions in the poem:

Connect What tends to be your response when you are asked to take on an adult responsibility like Hiawatha? *Students may say they become serious and pay attention to what they are doing.*

Analyze What feelings does Hiawatha experience as he walks into the forest with his bow and arrow? ***Possible answer:*** *He feels proud and confident.*

Synthesize Recall what Hiawatha learned in lines 81–95. In what way might his knowledge of the animals help him as a hunter? ***Possible answer:*** *His knowledge of their habits will help him get close to the animal he is tracking.*

Deer Spirit Helper, Joe Geshick. Oil. © Joe Geshick.

Kill for us a famous roebuck,
Kill for us a deer with antlers!"
Forth into the forest straightway
All alone walked Hiawatha
Proudly, with his bow and arrows;
And the birds sang round him, o'er him,
"Do not shoot us, Hiawatha!"
Sang the robin, the Opechee,
Sang the bluebird, the Owaissa,
"Do not shoot us, Hiawatha!"
Up the oak tree, close beside him,
Sprang the squirrel, Adjidaumo,
In and out among the branches,
Coughed and chattered from the oak tree,
Laughed, and said between his laughing,
"Do not shoot me, Hiawatha!"
And the rabbit from his pathway
Leaped aside, and at a distance
Sat erect upon his haunches,
Half in fear and half in frolic,
Saying to the little hunter,
"Do not shoot me, Hiawatha!"
But he heeded[5] not, nor heard them,
For his thoughts were with the red deer;
On their tracks his eyes were fastened,

ANALYZE VISUALS
What does the paintir suggest about the relationship between people and animals?

5. **heeded:** listened to and considered; paid attention to.

DIFFERENTIATED INSTRUCTION

FOR LESS–PROFICIENT READERS

Concept Support Ask students to refer to their Summarize charts and the three-column chart they started on page 637 of the teacher's edition to review the setting, characters, and plot of *The Song of Hiawatha.* Name one of these story elements. Then give students a moment to jot down a related detail from the poem. Ask students to share their details. When all students have answered, briefly summarize the information the class has presented.

 **BEST PRACTICES TOOLKIT**
Whip Around p. B1

FOR ENGLISH LEARNERS

Language: Punctuation Point out the comma in line 115. Explain that this comma signals an *appositive,* a word or phrase that renames the noun that the comma follows. Thus *Opechee* renames, or means the same thing as, *robin.* Ask students to find and explain appositives in lines 116 and 119.

Leading downward to the river,
To the ford across the river,
And as one in slumber walked he.
    Hidden in the alder bushes,
There he waited till the deer came,
Till he saw two antlers lifted,
Saw two eyes look from the thicket,
Saw two nostrils point to the windward,
And a deer came down the pathway,
Flecked with leafy light and shadow.
And his heart within him fluttered,
Trembled like the leaves above him,
Like the birch leaf palpitated,
As the deer came down the pathway. Ⓙ
    Then, upon one knee uprising,
Hiawatha aimed an arrow;
Scarce a twig moved with his motion,
Scarce a leaf was stirred or rustled,
But the wary roebuck started,
Stamped with all his hooves together,
Listened with one foot uplifted,
Leaped as if to meet the arrow;
Ah! the singing, fatal arrow,
Like a wasp it buzzed and stung him!
    Dead he lay there in the forest,
By the ford across the river,
Beat his timid heart no longer;
But the heart of Hiawatha
Throbbed and shouted and exulted,[6]
As he bore the red deer homeward,
And Iagoo and Nokomis
Hailed his coming with applauses.
    From the red deer's hide Nokomis
Made a cloak for Hiawatha,
From the red deer's flesh Nokomis
Made a banquet to his honor.
All the village came and feasted,
All the guests praised Hiawatha,
Called him Strong-Heart, Soan-ge-taha!
Called him Loon-Heart, Mahn-go-taysee! Ⓚ

Ⓙ **RHYTHM AND METER**
Reread lines 136–146. How does the meter help convey the **suspense** of a hunt?

Ⓚ **NARRATIVE POETRY**
What **conflict** does Hiawatha face? How is it resolved?

6. **exulted** (ĭg-zŭltʹd): rejoiced; felt jubilant and triumphant.

LITERARY ANALYSIS

Ⓙ RHYTHM AND METER

Possible answer: *The meter propels the reader forward, as if running toward the hunt.*

Lines 130–156

REINFORCE *KEY IDEA:* STORY

Discuss What aspects of Hiawatha's character are highlighted in the **story** of his first hunt, in lines 130–156? ***Possible answer:*** *The story emphasizes Hiawatha's concentration (lines 130–131), tracking skill (line 132–133), patience (lines 136–137), self-control (lines 141–146), and marksmanship (lines 155–156).*

POETIC FORM

Ⓚ NARRATIVE POETRY

Possible answer: *Hiawatha faces a conflict with the wild deer he is hunting because he regards all the beasts of the forest as his brothers (line 95). This conflict is resolved when Hiawatha kills the deer with his bow and arrow (lines 155–156) and rejoices at the success of his hunt (lines 160–162).*

SELECTION WRAP-UP

REFLECT What is a possible theme for each poem? Which details support each theme?

★ **CRITIQUE** Point out the different styles of the two poems. Ask: Which style do you like best, and why?

FOR LESS-PROFICIENT READERS

Comprehension Support Ask students to close their eyes and listen as you read aloud lines 136–156. Tell them to listen for details that appeal to the senses and use these to visualize what is happening in the poem. After reading, have students open their eyes. Ask them what details stand out in their mind as they reflect on what they visualized.

FOR ADVANCED LEARNERS/PRE-AP

Analyze Sound Elements Have students review Longfellow's epic poem and Dylan's ballad to analyze the sound elements of rhyme, repetition, and alliteration in each poem. Ask students to create a graphic organizer to organize their findings. Have them write an example of each sound element on the board and explain it to the class.

THE SONG OF HIAWATHA 645

Practice and Apply

After Reading

For additional support of postreading questions, use these copy masters:

RESOURCE MANAGER—Copy Masters

Rhythm and Meter p. 179 (for practice of literary analysis standards focus)

Question Support p. 183 (After Reading questions adapted for English learners and less-proficient readers)

Additional selection questions are provided for teachers on page 175.

ANSWERS

Comprehension

1. *At the beginning, the speaker left behind wants the other speaker to come back safely. At the end, the speaker wants boots of Spanish leather.*
2. *Nokomis, his grandmother, raises him.*
3. *The village celebrates Hiawatha's success in killing his first deer.*

Literary Analysis

Possible answers:

4. ■ **STANDARDS FOCUS Summarize *"Boots of Spanish Leather":*** *The main character's true love travels to Spain, probably never to return.* **The Song of Hiawatha:** *Hiawatha is taught to respect the natural world and proves himself a skillful hunter.*
5. *Examples include "whispering" (line 37), "lapping" (line 38), and "buzzed" (line 156).*
6. *The speaker realizes that his true love isn't interested in returning to him. He says to her, "your mind is roamin'" and "your heart is not with me" (lines 30–31).*
7. ● **STANDARDS FOCUS Rhythm and Meter** *Students may mark the lines as follows:*

   Showed the broad white road in heaven,
   Pathway of the ghosts, the shadows,
   Running straight across the heavens,
   Crowded with the ghosts, the shadows.

   The rest of the poem follows this same pattern of alternating stressed and unstressed syllables.

After Reading

Comprehension

1. **Recall** What does the speaker who is left behind in "Boots of Spanish Leather" want at the beginning of the poem? At the end?
2. **Recall** Who raises Hiawatha?
3. **Clarify** What does the village celebrate at the end of *The Song of Hiawatha?*

Literary Analysis

4. **Summarize Poetry** Look back at the graphic organizers you made as you read. Which stanzas or sections contain the most important information? Summarize each poem in a few sentences.
5. **Identify Onomatopoeia** When the sound of a word suggests its meaning, such as "splat," it is called onomatopoeia. Find three examples of onomatopoeia in *The Song of Hiawatha.*
6. **Make Inferences** In "Boots of Spanish Leather," why does the speaker change his mind about wanting a gift? What may he have realized?
7. **Examine Rhythm and Meter** Copy lines 31–34 of *The Song of Hiawatha* and mark the stressed and unstressed syllables as in the example on page 637. What pattern does the rhythm follow? Note whether the rest of the poem follows the same rhythm or different ones.
8. **Draw Conclusions about an Epic** The heroes in epic poems often represent values important to the culture they come from. What values does Hiawatha stand for? Note them on a graphic like the one shown. Also give examples that support each value.

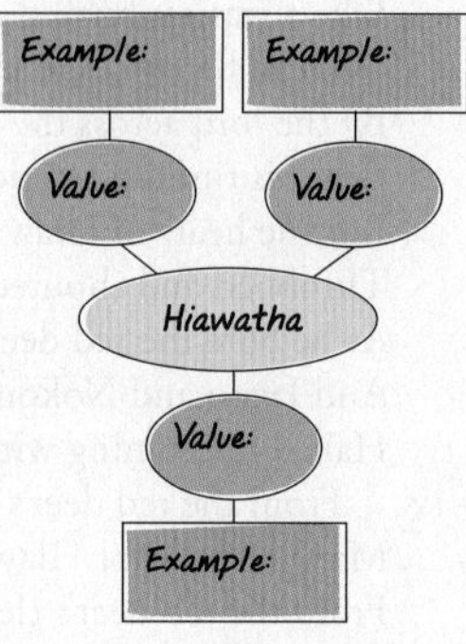

9. **Evaluate Narrative Poems** Did the **stories** these poems told satisfy you in the same way a good short story does? Explain your answer, making sure to consider whether the poems created memorable characters, suspenseful plots, and rewarding resolutions.

Extension and Challenge

10. **Literary Criticism** In his diary, Longfellow wrote, "I have at length hit upon a plan for a poem on the American Indians which seems to me the right one, and the only. It is to weave together their beautiful traditions into a whole. . . ." Do you think it was a good idea for him to blend different tribal traditions to create his epic? With a group, discuss the value of this poem.

8. ***Value 1:*** *Respect for the knowledge of elders. Example: Nokomis shares important knowledge with Hiawatha as a child.* ***Value 2:*** *Respect for nature. Example: Hiawatha learns the languages of all the animals.* ***Value 3:*** *Skillful hunting. Example: Hiawatha kills the deer instantly, and humanely, with a single arrow.*
9. ● **STANDARDS FOCUS Narrative Poetry** *Students should support their opinions by explaining what made the settings, characters, and plots memorable or appealing.*

Extension and Challenge

10. *Students may say that because Longfellow is a poet, not a journalist, he has the "license" to weave together various traditions rather than treating them separately or focusing on just one. They may also note that Longfellow treats Native American themes with sensitivity and respect. Other students may argue that Longfellow may give readers inaccurate ideas about Native Americans.*

[R]eading-Writing Connection

Increase your appreciation of "Boots of Spanish Leather" and *The Song of Hiawatha* by responding to these prompts. Then complete the **Grammar and Writing** exercise.

WRITING PROMPTS	SELF-CHECK
A. Short Response: Analyze a Character How does Hiawatha change during this part of the epic? Write a **one-paragraph response** in which you compare the traits of the very young Hiawatha in the beginning of the excerpt to those of the growing boy at the end.	***A well-written response will . . .*** • include a clear statement about how Hiawatha changes over the course of the poem • cite words, phrases, and events from the poem that reveal Hiawatha's traits
B. Extended Response: Write a Short Story Choose one of these poems and rewrite it as a **one-or-two page short story** that would appeal to teenagers today. Change or add details about the setting, characters, and conflict. Consider using dialogue to make the events seem real.	***An engaging short story will . . .*** • contain interesting characters • present a problem that the characters face

[G]RAMMAR AND WRITING

PUNCTUATE TITLES CORRECTLY A title is punctuated according to the type of work it is. Use **quotation marks** for the titles of shorter works, such as articles, short stories, essays, and songs. Use **italics** (or underlining) for the titles of longer works, such as books, plays, magazines, newspapers, and movies. Note that the titles of short poems receive quotation marks, while the titles of epic poems like *The Song of Hiawatha* receive italics.

Example: Longfellow's research for his epic poem *The Song of Hiawatha* came from the book *The Hiawatha Legends.*

PRACTICE Rewrite each sentence, correctly punctuating the titles.

1. Bob Dylan's song Boots of Spanish Leather talks about the pain of separation.
2. Longfellow wrote another epic poem entitled Evangeline: A Tale of Acadie.
3. Longfellow also wrote the short poem Paul Revere's Ride.
4. Let Us Read Longfellow is an article from the newspaper The Wall Street Journal.

For more help with punctuating titles, see page R50 in the ***Grammar Handbook.***

DIFFERENTIATED INSTRUCTION

FOR LESS–PROFICIENT WRITERS

For Prompt A:

Students may organize paragraphs this way:

- **Opening sentence:** Make a broad statement about how Hiawatha changes.
- **Body:** Describe young Hiawatha's qualities, with supporting details. Then describe him as an older boy, giving examples. Use a transition to contrast the descriptions.
- **Closing sentence:** Describe how Hiawatha's qualities will help him as a leader.

For Prompt B:

- Suggest that students use an omniscient narrator, as in *The Song of Hiawatha,* and begin their story with a scene that involves the main character and reveals the character's traits.
- Quickly establish the setting.
- Tell students that they can invent additional details about the characters and conflict, but these details should be consistent with the story.

Reading-Writing Connection

WRITING PROMPTS

- For **Prompt A,** tell students to skim the poem and record details in a two-column chart about what Hiawatha is like at the poem's beginning (lines 1–95) and end (lines 96–172). Have them review their details to make generalizations about the very young Hiawatha and the growing boy.
- For **Prompt B,** have students refer to their Summarize charts from page 637 to collect details about the setting, characters, and plot. Suggest that students build on these details to develop their stories.

For writing support, see

Writing Center at **ClassZone.com**

GRAMMAR AND WRITING

Suggest that students read each sentence aloud and look for a clue word that indicates whether the work mentioned is short or long.

Answers:

1. Bob Dylan's song "Boots of Spanish Leather" talks about the pain of separation.
2. Longfellow wrote another epic poem entitled *Evangeline: A Tale of Acadie.*
3. Longfellow also wrote the short poem "Paul Revere's Ride."
4. "Let Us Read Longfellow" is an article from the newspaper *The Wall Street Journal.*

RESOURCE MANAGER—Copy Master
Punctuate Titles Correctly p. 184

Assess and Reteach

Assess

RESOURCE MANAGER—Copy Masters
Selection Tests A, B/C pp. 185–186, 187–188

Test Generator CD

Reteach

STANDARDS LESSON FILE
Literature Lesson 17: Narrative vs. Lyric Poetry
Literature Lesson 21: Rhythm and Meter
Research and Study Skills Lesson 13: Summarizing

Focus and Motivate

OBJECTIVES

- analyze a student model that reflects the key traits of a personal response to a poem
- use the writing process to respond to a poem
- revise and edit, applying a rubric for writing a personal response to a poem
- give an oral interpretation of a poem

WRITER'S ROAD MAP

WRITING PROMPTS 1 AND 2

Help students choose a prompt by brainstorming a list of familiar poems and song lyrics. Students can jot down notable details beside each title.

ADDITIONAL PROMPTS

Use these prompts for practice with writing personal responses to a poem:

WRITING PROMPT 3

Writing for the Real World Write a review of a song or jingle used in an advertisement. It can be one that you think works well in the ad or one that falls short of what it is trying to accomplish.

Subjects to Consider:

- a short jingle created to sell a product or service
- a popular or classic song repurposed to sell a product or service

WRITING PROMPT 4

Writing from Historical or Current Events Write a personal response to a poem inspired by historical or current events and issues.

Poems to Consider:

- a poem that conveys a particular perspective on a war
- a poem inspired by an issue such as civil rights or immigration

For additional writing prompts, see

WriteSmart CD

Writing Center at **ClassZone.com**

KEY TRAITS

Review the six ***KEY TRAITS*** with students, focusing primarily on ideas and organization. Compare the list of traits with the rubric on page 654.

Writing Workshop

Personal Response to a Poem

Laughter, sadness, confusion, anger—the poems in this unit may have made you f all these emotions and more. A good way to share your personal response is to pu it in writing. The **Writer's Road Map** can show you how.

WRITER'S ROAD MAP

Personal Response to a Poem

WRITING PROMPT 1

Writing from Literature Choose a poem that you liked, disliked, or found puzzling. Write a personal response that explains why the poem made you react so strongly. Briefly describe the poem so readers will understand your response.

Poems to Explore

- "Stopping by Woods on a Snowy Evening"
- "Mother to Son"

WRITING PROMPT 2

Writing for the Real World Write an essay about a song lyric that has special meaning for you. Include explanations and quotations from the lyric so readers will understand why the song matters to you.

Types of Music to Explore

- love songs
- rap
- traditional songs of a culture

WRITING TOOLS

For prewriting, revision, and editing tools, visit the **Writing Center** at **ClassZone.com.**

KEY TRAITS

1. *IDEAS*
- Clearly presents an **overall response** to the poem or song
- Supports key points with **explanations and quotations**

2. *ORGANIZATION*
- **Identifies** the poem or song in the introduction
- Provides enough **information** about the work so readers can understand the response
- Uses **transitional words and phrases** to connect ideas
- **Summarizes** the response in a conclusion

3. *VOICE*
- Maintains a **tone** that shows the writer's honest response

4. *WORD CHOICE*
- Uses **precise literary terms** when describing the poem or song

5. *SENTENCE FLUENCY*
- Varies **sentence lengths**

6. *CONVENTIONS*
- Uses **correct grammar, spelling, and punctuation**

Writing Workshop Resources

RESOURCE MANAGER UNIT 5

Plan and Teach pp. 189–192
Prewriting–Editing pp. 193–197
Writing Rubric p. 198
Speaking and Listening p. 199
Writing Support p. 200*

STANDARDS LESSON FILE

Writing Lessons 33, 38, 46
Speaking and Listening Lesson 8

BEST PRACTICES TOOLKIT

Scaffolding Writing Instruction pp. 43–46*
Freewriting • Spider Map • Writing Template: Responding to Literature

TECHNOLOGY

 Easy Planner DVD
Writing Center at **ClassZone.com**
 WriteSmart CD

* Resources for Differentiation

rt 1: Analyze a Student Model

Susan Liang
Martin Luther King, Jr. Middle School

What "Identity" Taught Me

"I'd rather be a tall, ugly weed." These words shocked me when I first read them in Julio Noboa's poem "Identity." Why would anybody choose to be something that people want to destroy? By the time I finished reading the poem, though, I understood the poet's message. The clear, powerful imagery in the poem helped me see that the speaker just wants to be himself, no matter what other people think. I realized that I want to be independent, too.

The first stanza of the poem is an unusual simile that compares people and plants: "Let them be as flowers," beautiful but "harnessed to a pot of dirt." Using the pronoun *them* shows that the speaker doesn't identify with these people—he is setting himself apart from them. He doesn't want to be fussed over and admired like some flowers in a pot. I had never thought about flowers as dependent before. What kind of plant would the speaker want to be? I wondered.

The second and third stanzas of the poem answered my question. The speaker tells us that he would rather be a weed. I always thought of weeds as ugly and unwanted, but his descriptions helped me think about them differently. He describes weeds as free and strong—"clinging on cliffs" and able to break through rocks. Unlike potted flowers, weeds aren't bound by anything. They face "the vast eternal sky" and are "beyond the mountains of time." That's total, unlimited freedom. The speaker is saying that being independent is much better than being admired. I agree.

KEY TRAITS IN ACTION

Appealing introduction **identifies** the poem's title and author.

The rest of the opening paragraph clearly states a positive **overall response** to the poem.

Uses **precise literary terms** (highlighted) and gives extensive **information** about the poem to help the reader understand the response.

Transitional words signal important contrasts. Varied **sentence lengths** give the writing a pleasing rhythm.

Teach

Part 1: Analyze a Student Model

Have students read the **Student Model** and **Key Traits in Action.** Discuss specific examples of each trait found in the model. You may also wish to use these activities:

- **Overall Response** Point out the writer's use of a quotation to begin the essay. The quotation becomes a springboard for a description of her overall response. Ask: What was the writer's first response to the idea expressed by the quotation? What did the poem's imagery eventually help her understand about the poem and about herself? ***Possible answer:*** *The writer was shocked by the idea that someone would choose to be something that others choose to destroy. The poem's imagery helped her understand that the speaker wants the freedom to be himself. The writer realizes that she, too, wants to be independent.*
- **Transitional Words** Remind students that transitional words and phrases show how ideas are related; a contrasting relationship is just one example. Ask these questions:
  —In what way does the writer connect the third and fourth paragraphs? ***Possible answer:*** *In the third paragraph, the writer describes how she begins to understand the poet's point of view. The sentence in lines 24–25 is a transition that indicates the fourth paragraph will give more examples to support the ideas in the third paragraph.*
  —What other transition words signaling contrasts are used in the essay? ***Possible answer:*** *"however" (line 28), "though" (line 32), "but" (line 34)*

DIFFERENTIATED INSTRUCTION

FOR ALL STUDENTS

Student Portfolios Encourage students to save copies of their writing so that they can track their progress throughout the year.

For general guidelines on differentiating writing instruction, see

BEST PRACTICES TOOLKIT
Scaffolding Writing Instruction
pp. 43–46

FOR ENGLISH LEARNERS

Language: Skill Words Write these terms on the board and review them with students:

- *overall response:* a reader's thoughts and feelings about a poem as a whole
- *precise literary terms:* words used to identify specific parts of a poem, such as *stanza* (groups of related lines), *simile* (comparison using *like* or *as*), and *speaker* (the voice in a poem)
- *tone:* a writer's attitude toward a topic, revealed in his or her choice of words
- *quotations:* exact words taken from the poem. Share this example (lines 18–21) and discuss the way quotations are used to support statements about the poem:

  He describes weeds as free and strong—"clinging on cliffs" and able to break through rocks. Unlike potted flowers, weeds aren't bound by anything. They face "the vast eternal sky" and are "beyond the mountains of time." That's total, unlimited freedom.

- **Explanations and Quotations** Point out that the writer's response includes a combination of her own explanations of the ideas found in the poem and direct quotations that reveal the speaker's ideas. For example, in line 25, the writer explains that the speaker "points out that flowers aren't left alone." She then includes a quotation (line 26) that uses the speaker's own words to support this idea. Ask students: What does the writer say to introduce and explain the speaker's statement that he'd "rather be unseen"? ***Possible answer:*** *"The speaker doesn't seem to mind being ignored" (lines 29–30).*
- **Tone** Remind students that tone is a writer's attitude toward a topic. This writer wants to share her response to the poem "Identity" with others. Therefore, she writes in an "open, honest tone" about the way the poem affected her. For example, she says in lines 27–28 that a description of flowers "made me remember how I felt when my parents or teachers nagged at me." Ask students to find two other examples that reveal this tone. ***Possible answer:*** *"I can remember so many times when I wanted to do one thing, but I did something else just to make people like me" (lines 33–35); "The poem made me envy the speaker's strength and want to be like him" (lines 40–41).*

For interactive student models, see

WriteSmart CD

Writing Center at **ClassZone.com**

The next stanza gave me even more reasons to agree with the speaker. He points out that flowers aren't left alone. They are smelled, "praised, handled, and plucked / by greedy, human hands." This description made me remember how I felt when my parents or teachers nagged at me to do this or that. People ignore weeds, however, because they don't think weeds are worth anything. The speaker doesn't seem to mind being ignored. In fact, he says he'd "rather be unseen."

Explanations and quotations from the poem support the key point about flowers nc being left alone. Sharir responses this way creates an open, hones **tone.**

In the next stanza, the speaker admits that weeds can smell bad. He doesn't seem to think that's a problem, though. It's important to be who you are, he explains, no matter what other people think. I can remember so many times when I wanted to do one thing, but I did something else just to make people like me. It sounds as if the speaker doesn't do that. He insists that being himself matters more to him than anything else. All he wants to do is "stand alone, strong and free."

Reading "Identity" made me think about who I am and who I want to be. By comparing different kinds of people with flowers and weeds, Noboa made me see the plants and myself in a new way. The poem made me envy the speaker's strength and want to be like him. It helped me realize that I care too much about other people's opinions. I, too, would rather be a tall, ugly weed than a pampered flower.

Conclusion **summarizes** how the student reacte to the poem and what she learned from reading it.

2

DIFFERENTIATED INSTRUCTION

FOR ENGLISH LEARNERS

Comprehension: Transitions Use this activity to show how a writer uses transitions to signal contrasts and similarities:

1. Display these paragraphs that give a person's response to two different places:

   I love going to the lake or taking walks in the woods. Both the lake and the woods are peaceful. My best friend Ana, however, likes being in busy cities.

   I think cities are noisy and crowded. This doesn't bother Ana, though. She says they are exciting. There is always something to see and do, but there are also parks and other places to sit and relax. Although I understand, I still like the woods.

2. Have students point out the transitional words. Then work with them to write more sentences about the country or the city. Use transitional words to signal contrasts and similarities.
3. Show students photographs or illustrations of two different settings or structures. Ask them to compare and contrast the pictures using transitional words and phrases.
4. Use the copy master to provide students with further practice using transitions.

RESOURCE MANAGER—Copy Master
Writing Support p. 200

...rt 2: Apply the Writing Process

PREWRITING

What Should I Do?	What Does It Look Like?
1. Choose a poem or song. Reread the prompts on page 648 and decide whether you will write about a poem or a song. Once you have a poem or song in mind, read it or listen to it several times. Then make a chart that lists quotations from the work and your reactions, questions, and comments.	**Lines from "Identity"** / **Questions and Comments** "I'd rather be a tall, ugly weed" — Huh? Who wants to be a weed? flowers "praised, handled, and plucked / by greedy, human hands" — This reminds me of when Mom nags me—too much attention. "If I could stand alone, strong, and free" — I think this means that it's better to be independent than admired.
2. Freewrite about your reactions. Write down thoughts and feelings about the poem or song as they occur to you. TIP **If your reactions to this song or poem are too personal to share with your classmates and teacher, go back to step 1 and choose another work.**	"Identity" made me realize how much I try to please other people even though I know I shouldn't worry so much about what others think of me. Why can't I just be free to be whoever I am? If that means being ugly and smelly, oh well. Flowers = pretty but helpless, dependent on others to take care of them I never thought that I would want to be like a weed! It sure is a different way of looking at things.
3. Find support for your ideas. Keep your reactions in mind as you read the poem or listen to the song again. List specific quotations and examples that support those reactions.	*Main idea:* Weeds are free and independent. *Support:* • not "harnessed to a pot of dirt" like flowers • "beyond the mountains of time" • "unseen" or "shunned by everyone" (that means totally ignored)

FOR ENGLISH LEARNERS

Personal Response to a Poem Have students use these sentence frames to focus their ideas as they prepare to write:

- The title of my poem or song is ________.
- I chose this poem or song because ________.
- One important idea in the poem or song is ________.
- Details or quotations that support this idea include ________, ________, and ________.

Finding Support for Ideas [paired option] Show students how to use a Spider Map to record the main idea of a poem, related ideas, and supporting details or quotations. Have them meet in pairs to share their maps and talk about their poems.

BEST PRACTICES TOOLKIT—Transparency
Spider Map p. B22

Practice and Apply

To support students during the writing process, use these copy masters:

RESOURCE MANAGER—Copy Masters
Prewriting–Editing pp. 193–197
Writing Rubric p. 198
Writing Support p. 200 *(for English learners)*

Part 2: Apply the Writing Process

PREWRITING

1. **Choose a poem or song.** If students are trying to decide between two or more poems and songs, suggest that they make a brief chart for each work under consideration. Students can then review quotations and their reactions, questions, and comments relating to each work and decide which would be the most interesting subject for a written personal response. Students could meet in pairs or small groups to share their charts and get feedback.
2. **Freewrite about your reactions.** Ask students to try to write without stopping for a period of time. This will help them to tap into all their thoughts and feelings about a poem or song and get their ideas down on paper. If students find that most of their reactions are highly personal in nature, point out the TIP in step 2. Remind students that the teacher and peer readers will be reading their response, so they should write one they are comfortable sharing.

   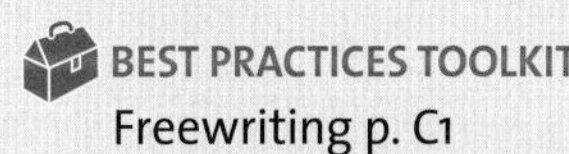
   BEST PRACTICES TOOLKIT
   Freewriting p. C1
3. **Find support for your ideas.** Tell students that they can also begin by writing down memorable quotations or details and then describe their reactions to each one. They should try to explain what each quotation or detail means to them, how it makes them feel, or what question it raises.

For interactive graphic organizers, see
WriteSmart CD
Writing Center at **ClassZone.com**

DRAFTING

1. **Make your introduction surprising or appealing.** To help students get started, explain that words and details from the poem or song that appeal to them might also pique the interest of their readers. Encourage students to choose what they feel is the most interesting or unique detail, line, or idea from the poem or song and try to incorporate it in a first draft of their introduction. If students are still having trouble deciding what kind of introduction to create, point out the TIP in step 1.
2. **Organize your ideas.** Suggest to students that they first write down the most important ideas they want to share and then try to organize them. For each idea, they should note quotations or examples they plan to use for support.

BEST PRACTICES TOOLKIT—Transparency
Writing Template: Responding to Literature pp. C16, C41

3. **Explain why you reacted the way you did.** Have students meet in pairs to exchange papers. Partners should read each other's work and mark places where additional quotations and examples might be needed for clarity. Before students begin to revise their final papers, suggest that they review their work based on the TIP in step 3.

Write*Smart* CD

Writing Center at **ClassZone.com**

DRAFTING

What Should I Do?	*What Does It Look Like?*
1. Make your introduction surprising or appealing. Try to get your reader interested right away. Then give the title and author of the work and state your overall response to it. **TIP** **You may need to try two or three different introductions before you find the right one.**	**Ask a question** *Why would anybody want to be a weed?* **Include a surprising quotation** *"I'd rather be a tall, ugly weed." These words shocked me.* **Provide an imaginative description** *Imagine a tall weed growing on the edge of a rocky, isolated cliff.*
2. Organize your ideas. An informal outline can help you plan your essay. You can begin with the most important idea and then write about the next most important idea, and so on. You can also discuss ideas as they appear in the work, from beginning to end.	***Main message:*** *The speaker just wants to be himself.* ***First stanza:*** *simile: other people are like flowers, "harnessed to a pot of dirt" (So what kind of plant would the speaker be?)* ***Second and third stanzas:*** *Speaker is free like a weed.* ***Fourth stanza:*** *Flowers get "praised, handled, and plucked."* ***Fifth stanza:*** *Weeds smell bad, and people ignore them; speaker would "rather be unseen."* ***Conclusion:*** *The poem helped me realize that I want to be more like the speaker—less concerned with what other people think of me.*
3. Explain why you reacted the way you did. Don't just tell readers your response to the work. Show them by including specific examples and quotations. **See page 654:** Check Your Grammar **TIP** **Before you revise, look back at the key traits on page 648 and the rubric and peer-reader questions on page 654.**	*The first part of the poem is an unusual simile that compares people and plants: "Let them be as flowers," beautiful but "harnessed to a pot of dirt."* — Key idea *Using the pronoun <u>them</u> shows that the man doesn't identify with these people—he is setting himself apart from them. He doesn't want to be fussed over and admired like some flowers in a pot.* — Support

DIFFERENTIATED INSTRUCTION

FOR LESS–PROFICIENT WRITERS

Organizing Information To help students organize information for their responses, provide this frame:

Introduction
- Grab readers' attention with an interesting question, a surprising quotation, or an imaginative description.
- Identify the poem's title and author.
- State your overall response to the poem or song.

Body—Option 1
- Describe what you feel is the most important idea from the poem or song and include one quotation or example to support the idea.
- Discuss other ideas in the order of their importance to you and include quotations or examples to support each idea.

Body—Option 2
- Begin with the first idea from the poem or song and include one quotation or example to support the idea.
- Discuss other ideas in the order in which they appear in the poem or song and include quotations or examples to support each idea.

Conclusion
- Summarize your reaction to the poem.
- Explain why the poem is memorable to you or what it taught you.

REVISING AND EDITING

What Should I Do?	What Does It Look Like?
1. Strengthen your introduction. • Does your introduction reach out and grab readers, name the work, and state your overall response? • If not, rewrite your opening and add any missing information.	in Julio Noboa's poem "Identity." "I'd rather be a tall, ugly weed." These words shocked me when I first read them. Why would anybody choose to be something that people want to destroy? By the time I finished reading the poem, though, I understood the poet's message. The clear, powerful imagery in the poem helped me see that the speaker just wants to be himself, no matter what other people think. I realized that I want to be independent, too.
2. Use correct literary terms. • (Circle) the literary terms you included. • If you have few or no circles, add terms such as *speaker, stanza, rhythm, imagery, simile,* and *metaphor.* **See page 654:** Literary Terms	stanza The first ~~part~~ of the poem is an unusual (simile) that compares people and plants: "Let them be as flowers," beautiful but "harnessed to a pot of dirt." Using the pronoun them shows that the ~~man~~ doesn't identify with these people—he is setting himself apart from them. speaker
3. Pay attention to sentence length. • Find the longest and the shortest sentences in your response. Count the number of words in each. • If most of your sentences are about the same length, divide or combine some to give your reader some variety.	~~He describes weeds as free and strong. They are "clinging on cliffs." They can even break through rocks.~~ He describes weeds as free and strong—"clinging on cliffs" and able to break through rocks.
4. Make logical connections. • Ask a peer reader to draw a [box] around sentences that are not connected logically. • Add transitions as needed to make the relationship between the ideas clear. **See page 654:** Ask a Peer Reader	[Reading "Identity" made me think about who I am and who I want to be. Noboa made me see the plants and myself in a new way.] By comparing different kinds of people with flowers and weeds,

REVISING AND EDITING

1. **Strengthen your introduction.** Allow students to meet in pairs to share introductions. Peer readers should work together to figure out the strengths of their introductions and also how they might be revised or reorganized to be more effective.
2. **Use correct literary terms.** Remind students that precise literary terms give their readers important information and help them understand elements of the poem. Encourage students to review how literary terms are used in the model. Then have them look back at their own responses and mark places where literary terms could be added.
3. **Pay attention to sentence length.** Tell students that reading their responses aloud can also help them figure out if they need more sentence variety. If most of their sentences sound short and choppy, they should combine some of them to make their response read more smoothly. If their sentences are mostly long and there are few places to pause and take a breath, then some of the longer sentences might need to be divided. Students can work in pairs to read their papers aloud and decide what sentences should be revised.
4. **Make logical connections.** Remind students to put themselves in the place of a reader who is not familiar with their personal response. Statements that seem logical to a person who has spent a great deal of time reading and thinking about their personal response might not be as clear to a person who does not have the same prior knowledge. They should keep this in mind as they work with their peer reader. Encourage students to refer back to the model and other essays in the pupil's edition to see how writers use transitions to connect and clarify ideas.

For interactive revision tools, see

- Write*Smart* CD
- Writing Center at **ClassZone.com**

FOR LESS–PROFICIENT WRITERS

Sentence Length Discuss this example to show how students might combine a section of short sentences:

> The cats were sleeping. They were curled up together. They were purring softly.
>
> *(The cats were sleeping, curled up together and purring softly.)*

Help students look for sentences in their personal responses that might be either combined or divided.

FOR ADVANCED LEARNERS/PRE–AP

Compare and Contrast Have students write a personal response to two poems with either similar ideas or contrasting ideas. Students might choose two poems they love, dislike, or find puzzling for the same reasons. Or, they might locate two poems that stand out for their differences. For example, the poems might represent two different attitudes toward life. Students can explain why one attitude appeals to them over another, using examples and quotations from each poem.

Preparing to Publish

Support for meeting the goals in the writing rubric is supplied throughout the **Writing Workshop** on pages 648–653.

For Rubric Bank, see

WriteSmart CD

Writing Center at **ClassZone.com**

Assess and Reteach

After reading and assessing students' personal responses, you might use these lessons to reteach key skills:

STANDARDS LESSON FILE

Writing Lesson 33: Writing about Literature

Writing Lesson 38: Show, Don't Tell

Writing Lesson 46: Choosing a Tone

Preparing to Publish

Personal Response to a Poem

Apply the Rubric

A strong personal response to a poem . . .

- ☑ introduces the essay by identifying the poem or song
- ☑ presents an overall response to the work
- ☑ gives readers enough information so they can understand the writer's reaction
- ☑ includes quotations that support the key ideas
- ☑ uses literary terms accurately
- ☑ maintains a tone that matches the writer's honest response
- ☑ uses transitions to connect the ideas
- ☑ varies sentence lengths
- ☑ concludes with a concise summary

Ask a Peer Reader

- In your own words, what was my overall response to this poem or song?
- Where could I add transitions to connect ideas?
- Which of my points is most memorable? Why?

Literary Terms

free verse—poetry without regular patterns of rhyme and rhythm
imagery—words and phrases that appeal to the reader's five senses
metaphor—a comparison that does not use *like* or *as*
rhythm—beat caused by stressed and unstressed syllables
simile—a comparison that uses *like* or *as*
speaker—the voice that "talks" to the reader, similar to a narrator in fiction
stanza—group of two or more lines that form a unit in a poem

Check Your Grammar

When you quote poems or songs, copy the words exactly and put quotation marks at the beginning and end. Show where one line ends and another begins by using a slash (/).

They are smelled, "praised, handled, and plucked / by greedy, human hands."

Writing Online

PUBLISHING OPTIONS
For publishing options, visit the **Writing Center** at **ClassZone.com.**

ASSESSMENT PREPARATION
For writing and grammar assessment practice, go to the **Assessment Center** at **ClassZone.com.**

Oral Interpretation of a Poem

Part of the power of poetry is the sound of the spoken words. Giving an oral interpretation of your poem will let your audience hear that power for themselves.

Planning the Oral Interpretation

1. **Practice reciting the poem aloud.** Try pausing, speeding up, or speaking more softly or loudly to stress the deeper meaning of the poem. Appropriate gestures or facial expressions also may help your audience understand the words. For example, for the line, "I'd rather be a tall, ugly weed," you might stand up as tall as you can.
2. **Mark up a copy of the poem.** Leave extra space between the lines so you can add notes about using gestures or facial expressions. Highlight places where you plan to change your volume or speed.

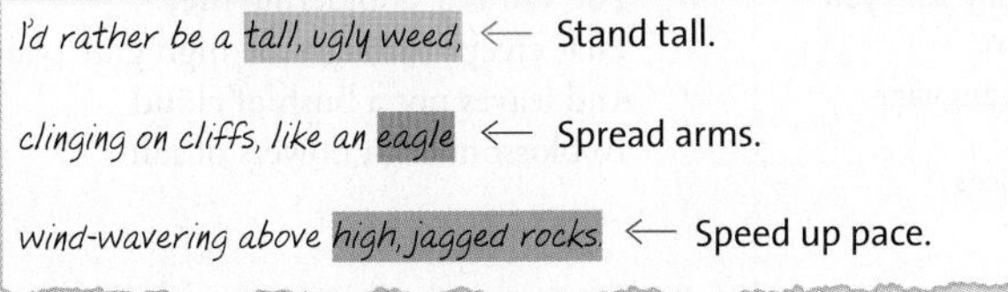

I'd rather be a tall, ugly weed, ← Stand tall.
clinging on cliffs, like an eagle ← Spread arms.
wind-wavering above high, jagged rocks. ← Speed up pace.

3. **Refine your delivery.** Run through your presentation several times in front of a mirror or with an audience of friends or family members. Ask for feedback on how well you convey the message of the poem.

Giving the Oral Interpretation

1. **Show your audience that you enjoy sharing this poem.** Speak normally, but loudly enough to be heard at the back of the room. If you use gestures, make them seem as natural as possible.
2. **Make eye contact.** Don't keep your eyes on your script. Instead, look up frequently and focus on people in various parts of the room.
3. **Get your audience involved.** Ask for questions or comments on your oral interpretation. This information can help you improve your next presentation.

See page R82: Evaluate an Oral Interpretation

SPEAKING AND LISTENING

Ask students to read this page to get an overview of how to give an oral interpretation of a poem.

Before students begin working, review this rubric with them so that they understand their goals:

Rubric A strong oral interpretation

- is delivered with changes in speed and volume that stress the meaning of the poem
- includes appropriate gestures or facial expressions
- is well planned, shaped by the reader's notes on where to incorporate gestures, facial expressions, and changes in volume and speed
- has been practiced several times and improved based on audience feedback
- holds the attention of an audience through the reader's use of eye contact
- ends with a request for audience questions and comments

RESOURCE MANAGER—Copy Master
Speaking and Listening p. 199

STANDARDS LESSON FILE
Speaking and Listening Lesson 8: Oral Interpretation

DIFFERENTIATED INSTRUCTION

FOR LESS–PROFICIENT WRITERS

Oral Interpretation of a Poem

Have students look at the sample notes for reading "Identity" shown on page 655. Note that

- the reader plans to stand as tall as possible when saying, "I'd rather be a tall, ugly weed," to express pride in being a tall weed
- the reader will illustrate the word *eagle* by spreading his or her arms far apart
- the reader will speed up the pace of the reading to stress the idea of the weed wavering in the wind above jagged rocks

Have students plan for the oral interpretation of the poem they've chosen. Encourage them to consider these questions:

- Where can I use gestures—such as standing tall or slouching, smiling or frowning, or moving in a certain way?
- Where should I read faster or slower? For example, a line describing something stressful, frightening, or exciting might be read rapidly.
- Where should I read loudly or softly to stress an idea or a mood?

Assessment Practice

CHECK READINESS

Read aloud the paragraph under **ASSESS** and stress to students that this is not the full Unit Test but a way for them to check their readiness for it. Then have students examine the skills listed under **REVIEW** and look back in the unit or in the **Student Resource Bank** for any they need to study.

READ THE SELECTIONS

Remind students to keep unit goals in mind as they read the poems, paying particular attention to

- figurative language
- speaker
- sound devices
- stanzas
- ways they could paraphrase lines in their own words

To help students focus on **speaker** while reading, encourage them to ask questions such as

- In the poem, is the voice that addresses the reader the poet or a fictional character?
- What is the speaker's situation?
- What emotions does the speaker feel? Why?

ANSWER THE QUESTIONS

Direct students to pages R95–R101 of the Test-Taking Handbook to review test-taking strategies. Remind them not to choose the first alternative that seems to fit when answering a multiple-choice question. Instead, students should read through all the choices, eliminate any that are clearly wrong, and then choose the best answer—the one that is most accurate and complete.

When checking their answers, students may be tempted to look for patterns in the answer choices. For example, they might assume because the last two answers have been *C*, the next answer will have to be a different letter. Explain that test preparers take special care to avoid creating patterns in answer choices. Tell students they should not waste time looking for patterns; instead, they should simply make sure they have chosen the best answer to each question.

Assessment Practice

Reading Comprehension

ASSESS
The practice test items on the next few pages match skills listed on the Unit Goals page (page 575) and addressed throughout this unit. Taking this practice test will help you assess your knowledge of these skills and determine your readiness for the Unit Test.

REVIEW
After you take the practice test, your teacher can help you identify any skills you need to review.

- Figurative Language
- Speaker
- Sound Devices
- Paraphrase
- Stanzas
- Latin Words and Roots
- Word Origins
- Commas
- Punctuation of Titles

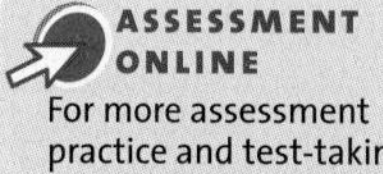

ASSESSMENT ONLINE
For more assessment practice and test-taking tips, go to the **Assessment Center** at **ClassZone.com.**

DIRECTIONS *Read these poems and answer the questions that follow.*

An Indian Summer Day on the Prairie

Vachel Lindsay

In the Beginning

The sun is a huntress young,
The sun is a red, red joy,
The sun is an Indian girl,
Of the tribe of the Illinois.

Mid-Morning

The sun is a smoldering fire,
That creeps through the high gray plain,
And leaves not a bush of cloud
To blossom with flowers of rain.

Noon

The sun is a wounded deer,
That treads pale grass in the skies,
Shaking his golden horns,
Flashing his baleful eyes.

Sunset

The sun is an eagle old,
There in the windless west.
Atop of the spirit-cliffs
He builds him a crimson nest.

DIFFERENTIATED INSTRUCTION

FOR ENGLISH LEARNERS

Assessment Practice: Work Backwards
[paired option] Prepare students for the assessment by having them read the questions before they read the poems. Have pairs follow these steps to learn unfamiliar words in the test directions and questions:

1. Find words you don't recognize and write each one on an index card.
2. Look up the meaning of the words in a dictionary.
3. Write the meaning on the back of the card.
4. Use your word cards to teach and practice the vocabulary with your partner and another pair.

The Sunflowers

Mary Oliver

Come with me
into the field of sunflowers.
Their faces are burnished disks,
their dry spines

creak like ship masts,
their green leaves,
so heavy and many,
fill all day with the sticky

sugars of the sun.
Come with me
to visit the sunflowers,
they are shy

but want to be friends;
they have wonderful stories
of when they were young—
the important weather,

the wandering crows.
Don't be afraid
to ask them questions!
Their bright faces,

which follow the sun,
will listen, and all
those rows of seeds—
each one a new life!—

hope for a deeper acquaintance;
each of them, though it stands
in a crowd of many,
like a separate universe,

GO ON

ITEM ANALYSIS

COMPREHENSION AND WRITTEN RESPONSE	ITEMS	UNIT PAGES
Figurative Language	1, 5, 6, 11, 13	580, 583, 589
Speaker	9, 10, 12, 18	576, 597
Sound Devices	7, 8, 16	578–579, 613, 619, 637
Paraphrase	3, 14, 17	619
Stanzas	2, 4, 15, 19	576, 583

VOCABULARY	ITEMS	UNIT PAGES
Latin Words and Roots	6, 7, 8	631
Word Origins	1, 2, 3, 4, 5	595

WRITING AND GRAMMAR	ITEMS	UNIT PAGES
Commas	2, 3, 5	603
Punctuation of Titles	1, 4, 6	647

FOR LESS–PROFICIENT READERS

Assessment Support Consider these options for completing the **Assessment Practice:**

- Have students "work backwards," reviewing the questions before reading the poems.
- Select random questions in the assessment and have students demonstrate how and where to look for the answers.
- Ask students to locate unfamiliar vocabulary in the assessment. Elicit the meanings of these words from the class.
- Have students record useful testing words and definitions in their journals for later reference.
- Read the poems or parts of them aloud to aid in student comprehension.

After checking student readiness with this Assessment Practice, you may administer the complete Unit 5 Test in order to more thoroughly evaluate student mastery of unit goals.

ANSWERS

Comprehension

Model a thinking process for answering multiple-choice questions.

1. **C *is correct.*** *In lines 1–4, the sun is described as a young Indian huntress.* A and B *can be eliminated because each choice references more than one person or thing, whereas the stanza uses the singular article "a."* D *is incorrect because it is not a personification.*
2. **A *is correct.*** *Each stanza is a single sentence that describes the sun at a particular time of day.* B *is incorrect because there is nothing unusual about the appearance of the stanzas.* C *is incorrect because each stanza has one sentence, not four.* D *is incorrect because each stanza has four lines, not five.*
3. **B *is correct.*** *Lines 5–8 describe the effect of the midmorning sun: it burns off the clouds.* A *is incorrect because the sun is compared to a fire, but there is no mention of the plain's being on fire.* C *can be eliminated because the stanza is titled "Mid-Morning," not "Noon."* D *is incorrect because the word* bush *in line 7 refers figuratively to clouds, not to actual bushes.*
4. **B *is correct.*** *The second and fourth lines of each stanza rhyme, while the first and third lines do not.* A, C, *and* D *are incorrect because they do not match this pattern.*
5. **A *is correct.*** *Line 9 says, "The sun is a wounded deer."* B *and* D *are incorrect because although these phrases appear in the stanza, they are not compared directly to the sun.* C *is incorrect because the sun is one element of the noon sky, but the sun is not compared to the noon sky.*
6. **B *is correct.*** *The stanza title and the words "The sun is an eagle" explain this metaphor.* A, C, *and* D *are incorrect because there are no details in the stanza to support them.*
7. **A *is correct.*** *The vowels in* sun, huntress, *and* young *have the same sound.* B, C, *and* D *can be eliminated because none of these choices has repeating vowel sounds.*
8. **B *is correct.*** *The initial consonant sound is repeated in the words* windless *and* west. A, C, *and* D *are incorrect because none of these choices has a repeated initial consonant sound.*
9. **C *is correct.*** *The speaker is trying to show what the sunflowers have in common with people.* A *is incorrect because the poem does not have a particularly humorous tone.* B *is incorrect because the speaker gives the sunflowers positive human qualities and does not point out weaknesses.* D *is incorrect because personification does not affect the lyrical, or song-like, qualities of a poem.*
10. **A *is correct.*** *The speaker says, "Come with me / into the field of sunflowers."* B *is incorrect because the parts of the sunflower are described figuratively, so readers are not learning scientific facts.* C *and* D *can be eliminated because although these ideas are hinted at, they do not involve an invitation from the speaker to the reader.*
11. **C *is correct.*** *The sunflower spines are said to "creak like ship masts" in lines 4–5.* A *and* B *can be eliminated because they refer to visual images, not to sound.* D *is incorrect because it refers to smell, not to sound.*
12. **B *is correct.*** *The speaker is addressing readers.* A, C, *and* D *are all part of the scene that the speaker is describing.*

is lonely, the long work
of turning their lives
into a celebration
is not easy. Come

and let us talk with those modest faces,
the simple garments of leaves,
the coarse roots in the earth
so uprightly burning.

Comprehension

DIRECTIONS *Answer these questions about "An Indian Summer Day on the Prairie."*

1. In the first stanza, the sun is personified as
   - **A** a tribe from Illinois
   - **B** three red planets
   - **C** a girl who is hunting
   - **D** the beginning of the day
2. With each stanza in this poem, the poet develops
   - **A** one idea in a single sentence
   - **B** an unusual appearance on the page
   - **C** several images in four sentences
   - **D** a list of unrelated ideas in five lines
3. Which statement is the best paraphrase of lines 5–8?
   - **A** The sun's strong rays set the plain on fire during midmorning.
   - **B** By midmorning, the fiery sun is so hot that it burns away the rain clouds.
   - **C** The sun at noon is so red that it looks like a fire in the sky.
   - **D** The midmorning sun is drying up the bushes on the plain.
4. The pattern of rhyming words in every stanza of this poem is
   - **A** *abba*
   - **B** *abcb*
   - **C** *abab*
   - **D** *abcc*
5. The extended metaphor in lines 9–12 compares the sun to
   - **A** a wounded deer
   - **B** pale grass
   - **C** the noon sky
   - **D** golden horns
6. In lines 13–16, the eagle building his nest is a metaphor for the
   - **A** western sky
   - **B** setting sun
   - **C** wild deer
   - **D** prairie hunters
7. Which line from the poem contains an example of assonance?
   - **A** "The sun is a huntress young"
   - **B** "The sun is a smoldering fire"
   - **C** "And leaves not a bush of cloud"
   - **D** "Shaking his golden horns"
8. Which line from the poem contains an example of alliteration?
   - **A** "The sun is an Indian girl"
   - **B** "There in the windless west"
   - **C** "Atop of the spirit-cliffs"
   - **D** "The sun is an eagle old"

658

ECTIONS *Answer these questions about e Sunflowers."*

By giving the sunflowers human qualities, the speaker in the poem is
A creating a humorous image
B emphasizing human weaknessses
C expressing a connection with nature
D making the poem more lyrical

The poem's speaker is asking readers to
A go along on a visit to the sunflowers
B learn about the different parts of a sunflower
C be strong, like sunflowers in a field
D celebrate life, like each seed of a sunflower

The simile in lines 1–7 compares the sound of the sunflower stalks to the
A shape of human faces
B sight of burnished disks
C noise made by ship masts
D smell of green leaves

The speaker's exclamation in lines 18–19, "Don't be afraid to ask them questions!" is directed to the
A sunflowers C crows
B readers D sun

The simile in lines 26–29 compares each sunflower to a "separate universe" to emphasize its
A isolation C short life
B loyalty D weakness

Which statement is the best paraphrase of lines 29–32: "the long work / of turning their lives / into a celebration / is not easy"?
A Water helps sunflower seeds grow.
B Sunflowers are beautiful and useful.
C It takes time for seeds to become sunflowers.
D Sunflowers can teach us about having fun.

15. Which statement best describes the four-line stanzas in this poem?
A The pattern of indented lines connects the ideas from stanza to stanza.
B Each stanza contains a single idea that is unrelated to the ideas of the other stanzas.
C The stanzas have a simple rhyme scheme that emphasizes the rhythm of the poem.
D The length of every line follows the same pattern in each stanza.

DIRECTIONS *Answer this question about both selections.*

16. To give their descriptions of a bright summer day a musical quality, both poets use
A metaphors and similes
B assonance and alliteration
C rhyming lines
D free verse

Written Response

SHORT RESPONSE *Write two or three sentences to answer each question.*

17. Paraphrase the speaker's invitation in lines 10–17 of "The Sunflowers."

18. What can you tell about the speaker of "The Sunflowers" from the statements made in the poem?

EXTENDED RESPONSE *Write a paragraph to answer this question.*

19. What do the stanza titles tell you about "An Indian Summer Day on the Prairie"? What story is told by the four stanzas together?

GO ON

659

DIFFERENTIATED INSTRUCTION

FOR ENGLISH LEARNERS

Review Academic Vocabulary Review the definitions of these terms with students:

- *personification:* a description that gives human qualities to an object or idea
- *stanza:* a group of lines in a poem similar to a paragraph in prose writing
- *paraphrase:* a restatement in different, often simpler words
- *metaphor:* a comparison that says one thing is something else, as in "The sound of the ocean was a friendly voice in my ear."
- *assonance:* the repetition of vowel sounds within words, as in "waves of rain"
- *alliteration:* the repetition of initial consonant sounds, as in "pickled peppers"
- *speaker:* the voice that talks to readers in a poem
- *simile:* a comparison that uses *like* or *as*, as in "The river was like a long snake slithering through the land."

13. A *is correct.* *The idea of isolation is reinforced by the word "lonely" in line 29.* B, C, *and* D *are not supported by the context.*

14. C *is correct.* *The lines are part of the sentence begun in line 20 about the rows of seeds.* A *is incorrect because the need for water is not mentioned in these lines.* B *and* D *are not supported by the context.*

15. A *is correct.* *Throughout the poem, ideas flow from one stanza to the next. Therefore,* B *is incorrect.* C *can be eliminated because the poem does not have a rhyme scheme.* D *is incorrect because it is the indents, not the line lengths, that follow the same pattern in every stanza.*

16. B *is correct.* *Both poems contain assonance and alliteration.* A *is incorrect because metaphors and similes do not contribute to the musical qualities of a poem.* C *is incorrect because "The Sunflowers" does not contain rhyming lines.* D *is incorrect because both poems have regular patterns of stanza structure.*

Written Response

Possible short responses:

17. *Come with me to make friends with the shy sunflowers and listen to their stories about growing up in the fields.*

18. *The speaker is imaginative, takes pleasure in the simple beauty of nature's creations, and wants to share the joy and insights gained by observing nature.*

Possible extended response:

19. *Students should point out that the stanza titles provide a chronology of a day on the prairie during Indian Summer. The story that is told by the four stanzas together is the story of the sun's progression across the sky. In the morning, the sun is strong and eager, like a young huntress. At midmorning it is like a spreading fire that banishes the clouds from the sky. At noon, it is like a wounded deer, flashing golden energy as it crosses the sky. By sunset, the sun is tired, like an old eagle, building a fiery resting place in the western sky.*

ANSWERS

Vocabulary

1. **D *is correct.*** Crimson *means "red."* A, B, *and* C *can be eliminated because their meanings have no connection to an insect used to make a red dye, and their spellings are not similar to* qirmiz.
2. **C *is correct.*** *Something that is smoldering is creating smoke.* A, B, *and* D *are incorrect because none of these words is related to smoke.*
3. **A *is correct.*** Baleful *means "harmful or ominous," and its spelling is similar to* bealu. B *is incorrect because although being wounded could cause misery, there is no similarity between the spellings of* wounded *and* bealu. C *and* D *can be eliminated because neither of these words has a meaning related to misery.*
4. **C *is correct.*** Burnished *means "polished."* A, B, *and* D *are incorrect because their meanings are not related to brownness or to being polished.*
5. **B *is correct.*** *A garment is a piece of clothing, or adornment.* A, C, *and* D *can be eliminated because none of these words relates to the meaning of adornment, nor do they have roots similar to* garnir.
6. **D *is correct.*** *To be acquainted with someone is to know the person.* A *and* C *can be eliminated because neither of these words has a meaning related to knowing.* B *is incorrect because while we know our friends, the spelling of* friends *has no similarity to that of* accognoscere.
7. **C *is correct.*** *To separate is to keep apart.* A, B, *and* D *can be eliminated because none of these words has this meaning and none has a root similar to* separare.
8. **C *is correct.*** *The spelling of* universe *indicates a possible combination of* unus *and* vertere. A, B, *and* D *have spellings that do not reflect these Latin words.*

Vocabulary

DIRECTIONS *Use context clues and the explanations of word origins to answer the following questions.*

1. Which word in "An Indian Summer Day on the Prairie" comes from *qirmiz,* the Arabic word for an insect that is used to produce a red dye?
   A sun **C** pale
   B golden **D** crimson
2. Which word in "An Indian Summer Day on the Prairie" comes from *smorian,* an Old English word that means "to smoke"?
   A shaking **C** smoldering
   B flashing **D** spirit
3. Which word in "An Indian Summer Day on the Prairie" comes from *bealu,* an Old English word that means "misery"?
   A baleful **C** young
   B wounded **D** bush
4. Which word in "The Sunflowers" comes from *brun,* a Germanic word that means "brown, polished"?
   A sunflower **C** burnished
   B bright **D** burning
5. Which word in "The Sunflowers" comes from *garnir,* a Old French word that means "to equip, adorn"?
   A green **C** coarse
   B garment **D** modest

DIRECTIONS *Use your knowledge of Latin words … roots to answer the following questions.*

6. Which word in "The Sunflowers" comes f… *accognoscere,* a Latin word that means "to know perfectly"?
   A visit
   B friends
   C celebration
   D acquaintance
7. Which word in "The Sunflowers" comes f… *separare,* a Latin word that means "apart"?
   A rows
   B uprightly
   C separate
   D wandering
8. Which word in "The Sunflowers" comes fr… the Latin words *unus,* which means "one," and *vertere,* which means "to turn"?
   A lonely
   B rotating
   C universe
   D wonderful

660

DIFFERENTIATED INSTRUCTION

FOR ENGLISH LEARNERS

Review Word Origins Discuss these tips to help students determine word origins:

- Compare the meaning of the root word that is provided in the question to the meanings of the words provided as answer choices.
- If you are unsure of the meaning of an answer choice, refer back to the poem and use context clues to help you determine the meaning.
- The spelling of the English word should be similar to the root word; it should have at least some of the same consonants.

Ask students which of these words in "An Indian Summer Day on the Prairie" comes from *flour,* a Middle English word that means "blossom": *joy, flower, bush, grass.* Point out that *flower* is the only choice that includes the consonants *f, l,* and *r.* Also, *flower* is a synonym of *blossom.*

riting & Grammar

CTIONS *Read this passage and answer the questions that follow.*

(1) Last winter I read the article Bringing Back the Prairie in Audubon magazine. (2) I told my mom dad and brother that I wanted to plant a prairie in our backyard. (3) I hoped to plant yellow foxtail, prairie cordgrass and cattail sedge. (4) My brother offered to build a pond after he read Carl Sandburg's short poem Young Bullfrogs. (5) He wanted big green bullfrogs to visit our backyard! (6) Before we began planting our small prairie, we all read the book Where the Sky Began: Land of the Tallgrass Prairie to learn as much as we could about what to plant.

Choose the correct way to punctuate the article and magazine titles in sentence 1.

A *Bringing Back the Prairie* and *Audubon*
B "Bringing Back the Prairie" and *Audubon*
C *Bringing Back the Prairie* and "Audubon"
D "Bringing Back the Prairie" and "Audubon"

Choose the correct way to punctuate sentence 2 with commas.

A I told, my mom dad and brother that I wanted, to plant a prairie in our backyard.
B I told my mom, dad, and brother that I wanted to plant a prairie in our backyard.
C I told my mom, dad, and brother, that I wanted to plant a prairie in our backyard.
D I told my mom dad and brother that I wanted to plant a prairie, in our backyard.

Choose the correct way to punctuate sentence 3 with commas.

A I hoped to plant yellow foxtail, prairie cordgrass and cattail, sedge.
B I hoped to plant yellow foxtail prairie cordgrass and, cattail sedge.
C I hoped to plant, yellow foxtail prairie cordgrass and cattail sedge.
D I hoped to plant yellow foxtail, prairie cordgrass, and cattail sedge.

4. Choose the correct way to punctuate the title of the poem in sentence 4.

A *Young Bullfrogs*
B *"Young Bullfrogs"*
C "Young Bullfrogs"
D "Young" Bullfrogs

5. Choose the correct way to punctuate sentence 5 with commas.

A He wanted big, green bullfrogs to visit our backyard!
B He wanted, big green bullfrogs to visit our backyard!
C He wanted big, green, bullfrogs to visit our backyard!
D He wanted big green bullfrogs, to visit our backyard!

6. Choose the correct way to punctuate the book title in sentence 6.

A "Where the Sky Began: Land of the Tallgrass Prairie"
B *Where the Sky Began:* Land of the Tallgrass Prairie
C *Where the Sky Began: Land of the Tallgrass Prairie*
D *"Where the Sky Began: Land of the Tallgrass Prairie"*

STOP

661

DIFFERENTIATED INSTRUCTION

FOR ENGLISH LEARNERS

Assessment Support Use these tips and examples to discuss the use of commas, quotation marks, and italics:

- *comma* (items 2, 3, 5): Use a comma after each item in a series except the last item.
  —Keesha, Leora, and Tina met after school.
  —I ate a fresh, delicious salad for lunch.
- *quotation marks* (items 1, 4, 6): Use quotation marks to enclose titles of short stories, poems, songs, and magazine articles.
  —"Flying Cows" is the title of my poem.
  —"Saving the Wetlands" is the featured article in this magazine.
- *italics* (items 1, 4, 6): Use italics for titles of books, magazines, newspapers, plays, paintings, and ships.
  —*Little Women* is my favorite book.
  —I just got a subscription to *National Geographic* magazine.

ANSWERS

Writing & Grammar

1. **B *is correct.*** *The article title is set off by quotation marks and the magazine title is in italics.* A *is incorrect because both titles are in italics.* C *is incorrect because the article title is in italics and the magazine title is set off by quotation marks.* D *is incorrect because both titles are set off by quotation marks.*
2. **B *is correct.*** *Each item in the series is followed by a comma.* A *can be eliminated because commas are incorrectly placed after verbs. In* C, *the comma after* brother *is incorrect.* D *is missing the series commas and has an incorrect comma after* prairie.
3. **D *is correct.*** *Each item in the series (a two-word noun phrase) is followed by a comma. The commas in* A, B, *and* C *do not separate the items in the list.*
4. **C *is correct.*** *The title of a short poem should be set off by quotation marks. We can eliminate* A *and* B *because the title appears in italics. We can eliminate* D *because both words of the title should be enclosed by the quotation marks.*
5. **A *is correct.*** *Two adjectives in a series are separated by a comma.* B *is incorrect because the comma separates the verb from its object.* C *is incorrect because* green *should not be separated from the noun it modifies.* D *is incorrect because no comma is needed before the infinitive phrase.*
6. **C *is correct.*** *Book titles should be set in italics. We can eliminate* A *because the title is enclosed in quotation marks.* B *is incorrect because part of the title—the subtitle—is not in italics.* D *is incorrect because although the title is in italics, it is also enclosed in quotation marks.*

INTRODUCE *MORE GREAT READS*

In Unit 5, students have discussed a number of big questions. Invite students to tell which question they found most intriguing and why. Then focus attention on the three questions that appear on this page. Discuss the recommended books and their summaries, pointing out how each book connects to the related question. Encourage students to choose one or more of these "great reads" to read independently.

ClassZone.com

To find additional books that match students' interests and ability levels, visit the Literature Center at **ClassZone.com.**

Ideas for Independent Reading

Which questions from Unit 5 made an impression on you? Continue exploring them with these books.

Does beauty matter?

Uglies
by Scott Westerfeld

In the future, all 16-year-olds have an operation that makes them "beautiful." Most of the younger Uglies can't wait until it's their turn for the operation, but a girl named Shay rebels against being the same as everyone else. Will her friend Tally help her or betray her?

Criss Cross
by Lynne Rae Perkins

Debbie and Hector are 14 years old, and they'd like their appearance to reflect the interesting people they hope they're becoming. How will these important changes happen? It's not always clear, but by the end of the summer, a great deal will be different.

Margaux with an X
by Ronald Koertge

Margaux is dazzlingly beautiful and very popula
She's also miserable. Mos
of the boys in school have
crushes on her, but she's
only interested in Danny.
A shabby-looking outcast,
Danny shares her love of
language and helps her cc
with problems at home.

Can you be rich without money?

Colibrí
by Ann Cameron

Years ago, a fortune teller told Uncle that Rosa would make him rich. They have been traveling through Guatemala ever since, begging and cheating people to get money and food. Now that Rosa is older, lying to people is harder, and Uncle is getting impatient.

The Black Pearl
by Scott O'Dell

When Ramon finds the Pearl of Heaven, everyone comes to look at it, and his father gives the pearl to the church. Some people think the jewel brings bad luck because it belongs to the Manta Diable. When misfortune hits the village, only Ramon can fix it.

A Year Down Yonder
by Richard Peck

It's the Depression, and
people are broke. Mary Ali
is sent to live in rural Illino
with her eccentric Grandm
Dowdell. Grandma has ha
like "borrowing" the Sherif
boat or Old Man Nyquist's
apples, which seem to ma
life a little easier.

When do you feel most free?

The Upstairs Room
by Johanna Reiss

Annie is only six when Hitler comes to power in Germany and starts making laws that punish the Jews. Annie is glad she lives in Holland so her family is safe, but as the German army gets stronger, how long will Annie's safety last?

Let Me Play: The Story of Title IX, the Law That Changed the Future of Girls in America
by Karen Blumenthal

Before 1972, many girls weren't able join a soccer team or enter medical school. Finally, the people fighting against this injustice won, and the law was changed.

The Warrior Heir
by Cinda Williams Chim

Every day Jack takes medic
for his heart condition. Or
day he forgets, and it's the
best day of his life. Sudde
he's faster and stronger. H
finds out he's really a mag
warrior and his "medicine'
was hiding him from peop
who want to kill him.

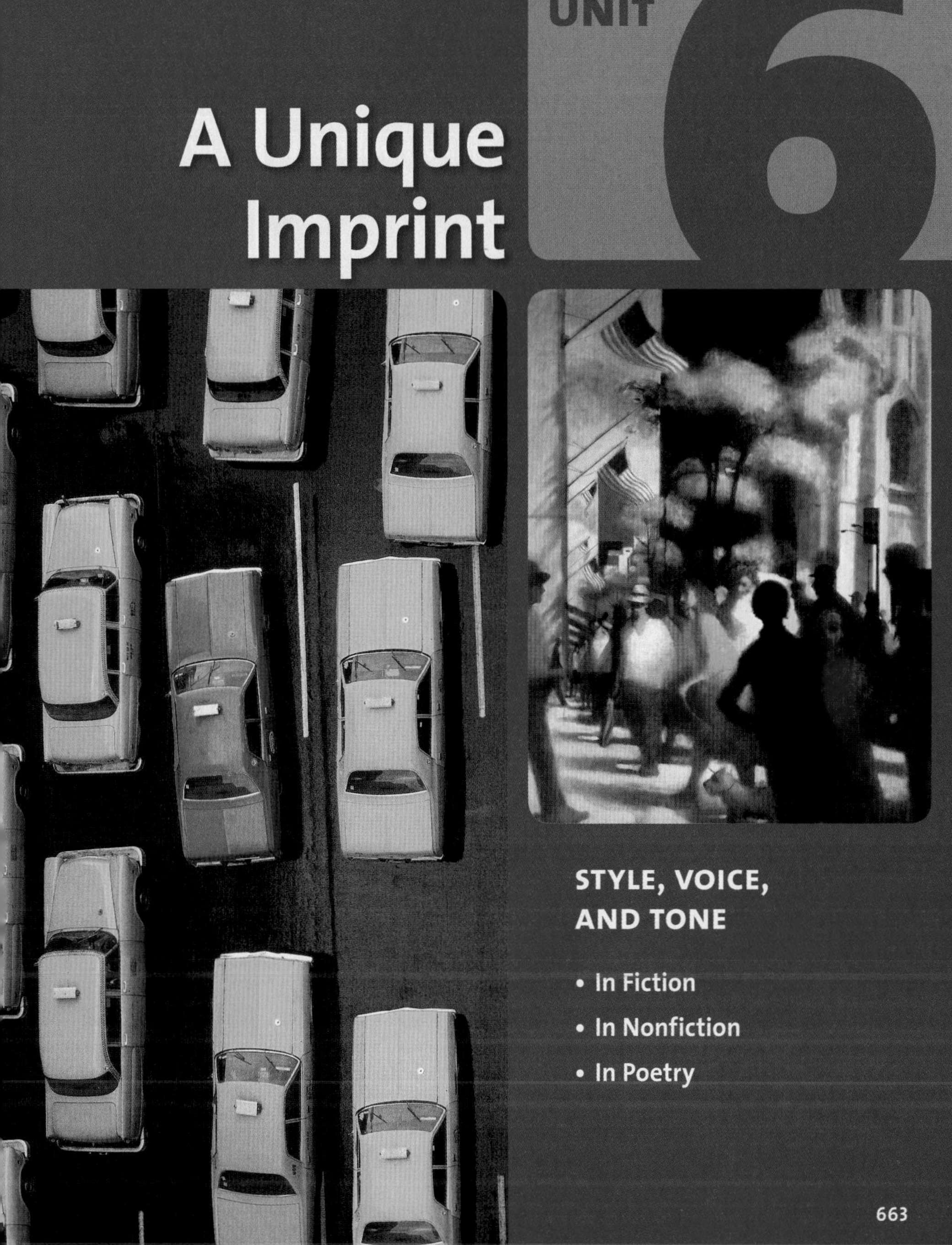

For help in planning this unit, see

RESOURCE MANAGER UNIT 6 pp. 1–11

INTRODUCE THE UNIT

No two fingerprints are alike. Each has its own pattern of ridges that loop, arch, or whorl to form a unique imprint that marks us as individuals. Our individuality is affirmed in other ways as well, some more apparent than our fingerprints. Use these questions to guide a discussion about style:

- Examine the painting on page 663. What do you notice about the way the artist has created this scene? If you saw another painting by the same artist, what techniques or perspectives might help you recognize the artist's style?
- Look at the image of the cars. Are a person's individual qualities always as visible as the image suggests? Explain.
- What modes of expression can help a person convey his or her uniqueness?
- In what ways do you show who you are and what is important to you?

Tell students that in this unit, they will examine different writers' **styles.** They will learn how elements of style contribute to **tone** and **voice** to create a writer's unique imprint. Analyzing these facets of the writer's craft will, in turn, make students more conscious of their own literary style.

About the Art Bill Jacklin's painting *The Promenade, Fifth Avenue* illustrates the story "New York Day Women" by Edwidge Danticat. For more information, see page 674 of the teacher's edition.

UNIT 6

Skills Trace

SKILLS STRAND	Reader's Workshop: Style, Voice, and Tone pp. 666–671	New York Day Women pp. 672–681 Short Story *Level: Average*	Linked selections: The Lady, or the Tiger? pp. 682–693 Short Story *Level: Challenging*	Linked selections: The Monty Hall Debate pp. 694–697 Newspaper Article *Level: Average*	Great Reads: *from* Kira-Kira pp. 698–703 Coming-of-Age Novel *Level: Average*
Literary Analysis	Style pp. 666–667, 670–671 Voice pp. 666–667 Tone pp. 668–671	Style pp. 673, 674, 676, 677, 678, 679	Tone pp. 683, 684, 686, 688, 689, 692		Form (Coming-of-Age Novel) p. 698
Reading and Informational Texts	Analyze the Literature pp. 667, 669–671	Identify Sequence pp. 673, 674, 677, 678, 679	Paraphrase pp. 683, 686, 687, 688, 691, 692	Use a Graphic Aid pp. 694, 695, 696, 697 Synthesize p. 697	
Vocabulary	Academic Vocabulary pp. 666, 668	Word Acquisition pp. 673, T673, 680 Context Clues p. T673 Multiple-Meaning Words p. 680	Word Acquisition pp. 683, T683, 693 Context Clues p. T683 Connotation and Denotation p. 693		
Writing, Grammar, and Style		Concise Writing Using Appositives p. 681			
Speaking, Listening, Viewing, and Media	Discuss pp. 666–669	Discuss pp. 672, T674–T678, 679 Analyze Visuals p. 674	Discuss pp. 682, T684–T691, 692 Analyze Visuals pp. 684, T687, 690	Discuss pp. 694, T695–T696, 697	Discuss pp. 698, T703

Assessment-Based Planning: Skills in red are assessed on the Unit 6 Test. **T** = Teacher's Edition page

from **Roughing It** pp. 704–715 Memoir *Level: Challenging*	**Us and Them** pp. 716–727 Personal Essay *Level: Average*	**O Captain! My Captain!/ I Saw Old General at Bay** pp. 728–733 Poems *Level: Average*	**Western Wagons/ The Other Pioneers** pp. 734–741 Poems *Level: Average*	**Writing Workshop: Literary Analysis** pp. 742–749
Voice pp. 705, 708, 709, 710, 711, 712	Irony pp. 717, 718, 720, 723, 724, 725 Review: Tone p. 721	Style in Poetry pp. 729, 730, 732, 733	Tone (in Poetry) pp. 735, 736, 738, 739, 740	
Monitor pp. 705, 706, 708, 710, 712 Read a Newspaper Article p. 715	Evaluate pp. 717, 721, 722, 723, 725	Understand Historical Context pp. 729, 730, 732, 733	Set a Purpose for Reading pp. 735, 740 Compare Tone p. 740	Analyze a Literary Analysis pp. 743–744, 748
Word Acquisition pp. 705, T705, 713 Word Maps p. T705 Latin Roots (*leg*) p. 713	Word Acquisition pp. 717, T717, 726 Context Clues p. T717 Idioms p. 726			
Formation of Compound Sentences p. 714	Formation of Complex Sentences p. 727		Write for Assessment p. 741	Write a Literary Analysis pp. 742–748 Parallel Structure p. 748 Misplaced Modifiers p. 748
Discuss pp. 704, T706–T711, 712, T715 Analyze Visuals pp. 706, 709, T710	Discuss pp. 716, T718–T724, 725 Analyze Visuals pp. 718, 723	Discuss pp. 728, T730–T732, 733 Analyze Visuals pp. 730, T732	Discuss pp. 734, T736–T739, 740 Analyze Visuals pp. 736, 739	Discuss pp. 742–744 Create an Online Database p. 749

Skills Assessed on the Unit 6 Test:

Literary Analysis
- Identify, analyze, and evaluate style (diction, imagery, sentence structure)
- Identify and analyze tone (language, speaker, sound devices)
- Identify and analyze irony

Reading and Informational Texts
- Identify sequence using signal words
- Analyze voice
- Evaluate

Vocabulary
- Use knowledge of Latin roots to determine the meanings of words
- Use context to understand idioms

Writing, Grammar, and Style
- Write a literary analysis essay
- Use appositives and appositive phrases to write concisely
- Form a compound sentence by joining two simple sentences (or independent clauses)
- Form a complex sentence by joining an independent and a dependent clause
- Additional writing and grammar skills

For additional lesson planning help, see **Easy Planner DVD.**

OBJECTIVES

- establish prior knowledge about **style**
- analyze the style of a creative individual and discuss the impact of the person's style

What's in STYLE?

Ask students to examine the photographs on page 664. Challenge them to identify as many individuals as they can and to assign an approximate date to each picture. Then ask students which aspects of each person's clothing, make-up, and hairstyle are in style today and which are definitely not in style. Are there any elements of style that seem appealing even though they are not currently in fashion?

ACTIVITY After students have completed the activity, guide them to see that in developing their own style, they may adapt some characteristics of other people's style and reject other elements. Writing is a good example. As students read the works of writers with different styles, they will get valuable ideas for expanding the scope and power of their own writing.

CHECK UNDERSTANDING Have students define **style** based on what they have just read and discussed.

UNIT 6 *Share What You Know*

What's in STYLE?

How do you decide what clothes to put on in the morning, or how to arrange your hair? You might follow current trends, or you migh[t] draw on the fashions of years past to create a unique look. Whatev[er] you choose, your appearance reflects your personal **style,** the way y[ou] express yourself to others. Writers, filmmakers, songwriters, and arti[sts] have their own ways of expressing themselves, too. Their style inclu[des] the way they use elements of their craft to communicate ideas.

ACTIVITY With a partner, think of an author, actor, singer, or artist whose style you and your partner both like. What about this person' work makes it unique? Answer the following questions:

- What three things come to mind first when you think of this person's creations?
- What sets this person apart?
- What words would you use to describe his or her style?

After answering these questions, discuss whether this person's style has influenced your own style, and how.

664

Unit Resources

- RESOURCE MANAGER UNIT 6
- BEST PRACTICES TOOLKIT
- STANDARDS LESSON FILE
- Easy Planner DVD
- Write*Smart* CD
- ClassZone.com
- Audio Anthology CD
- Multi-Language Academic Vocabulary Online
- eEdition CD & Online
- McDougal Littell Assessment System
- Test Generator CD
- Media*Smart* DVD

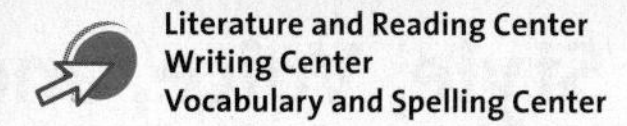
Literature and Reading Center
Writing Center
Vocabulary and Spelling Center

Preview Unit Goals

LITERARY ANALYSIS	• Identify, analyze, and evaluate style, including diction, imagery, and sentence structure • Compare and contrast style • Identify and analyze voice, irony, and tone
READING	• Evaluate information and opinions • Use and interpret graphic aids • Synthesize information • Identify sequence using signal words
WRITING AND GRAMMAR	• Write a literary analysis essay • Write concisely by using appositives and appositive phrases • Form compound and complex sentences
SPEAKING, LISTENING, AND VIEWING	• Create an online database
VOCABULARY	• Use context to help determine meaning of idioms and multiple-meaning words • Understand connotative and denotative meanings of words • Use knowledge of Latin word roots to help determine word meaning
ACADEMIC VOCABULARY	• style • literary analysis • voice • tone • synthesize • irony

Preview Unit Goals

This page provides an overview of the skills and strategies that students will be learning and applying in Unit 6. Review each goal. Ask students which skills they have used in the past. Which are new to them? Then suggest that students record questions about these skills and goals in their journals and look for answers as they work through the unit.

Have students write the Academic Vocabulary terms in their journals and add the definition of each term as they come across it in their reading. Encourage students to use these terms as they discuss and write about the selections in the unit.

ADDITIONAL UNIT GOALS

These skills will be taught in this unit but are not the major focus of the unit:

Literary Analysis
- Compare and contrast tone
- Compare and contrast poems, including imagery, speaker, sound devices, and tone
- Study a variety of genres: short story, memoir, personal essay, poetry, newspaper article

Reading
- Monitor reading
- Set a purpose for reading
- Recognize historical context
- Paraphrase

Writing and Grammar
- Write a comparison-contrast essay
- Punctuate appositive phrases correctly

Vocabulary
- Use knowledge of the Latin root *leg* to help determine word meaning

DIFFERENTIATED INSTRUCTION

FOR ENGLISH LEARNERS

Academic Vocabulary [paired option] Use the Academic Vocabulary copy master to introduce the vocabulary terms: *style, tone, literary analysis, synthesize, voice, irony.*

1. Read each word aloud and work together to complete the definition.
2. Allow students to work in pairs to complete the third column of the chart and Part B.
3. Reconvene to review students' responses.

Additional Academic Vocabulary [paired option] Use the second copy master to help students study these terms from the unit: *appositive, database, historical context, hyperbole, monitor, paraphrase, speaker.* Read each word and explanatory sentence aloud. As a class, define each term. Then have pairs work on Part B. Review their responses.

RESOURCE MANAGER—Copy Masters
Academic Vocabulary p. 9
Additional Academic Vocabulary p. 10

Focus and Motivate

OBJECTIVES

- identify, analyze, and evaluate elements of style (word choice, sentence structure, and imagery)
- compare and contrast style
- compare and contrast tone

Teach

Part 1: What Is Style?

Style Survey students about their favorite selections from the text. Point out that everyone has different preferences, and that their individual reactions have a lot to do with each author's style—whether or not they like the way the writer uses words, literary devices, and other elements.

Word Choice Ask students what words could be substituted for the highlighted ones to create a more formal style in the Kingston excerpt. ***Possible answer:*** *"I did not attempt," "increased the rate of"*

Sentence Structure Read aloud the excerpt from "Dancing Miranda" and discuss how the long, flowing sentence gives the impression of movement and energy. Ask a volunteer to recite a version of the passage using shorter sentences and discuss the effect.

Imagery Tell students that some authors' styles are characterized by few images while others rely heavily on imagery. The kinds of images chosen often reveal an author's perspective on life.

Have students fill out a chart like this one with examples from and descriptions of their favorite selection. Then have them summarize the author's style.

"Raymond's Run"

Word Choice	Sentence Structure	Imagery
"as any fool can see," "cause he's not quite right"	mostly short, simple sentences	"a little girl with skinny arms and a squeaky voice"

 BEST PRACTICES TOOLKIT—Copy Masters
Analysis Frame: Author's Craft pp. D23, D26, D27

UNIT 6
Reader's Workshop

Style, Voice, and Tone

Think about the last time you read an e-mail from a friend. Could you almost "hear" that friend talking to you? Perhaps the e-mail contained phrases your friend often uses, or expressed an attitude that is typical of him or her. The personality that comes across in any piece of writing—whether it's a friend's e-mail or a classic novel—is the **voice.** The voice can belong to the writer or to a narrator. Either way, it is created through the writer's one-of-a-kind style.

Part 1: What Is Style?

"The rosy fingertips of dawn spread delicately across the sky." "The sun bounced into view like a giant rubber ball." *How* something is said often affects a reader as much as *what* is being said. In literature, how something is said is called the **style.** A writer's style can be described using such words as *formal, conversational,* or *journalistic.* Style is created through a combination of elements, including word choice, sentence structure, and imagery.

ELEMENTS OF STYLE	EXAMPLES	
Word Choice Is the writing packed with conversational words and slang, or elegant, formal phrases? Precise, vivid, casual, formal—the kinds of words a writer uses can help to create style.	**The simple, informal language in this sentence helps to create a conversational style.** I didn't try to shout over the helicopters; they chopped up sound and the air, and whupped up heartbeats. —from *The Fifth Book of Peace* by Maxine Hong Kingston	
Sentence Structure One element of style is **sentence structure,** the lengths and types of sentences a writer uses. Some writers are noted for crafting long, complex sentences. Others are noted for using short, simple ones.	**This long sentence reflects a flowing, descriptive style and gives you a sense of the character's energy.** Miranda gave her mother a quick smile and bounded forward in great skipping leaps up the ramp, across the red and gold carpet in the lobby, down the long side aisle and up the steps onto the stage. —from "Dancing Miranda" by Diane de Anda	
Imagery Words and phrases that appeal to readers' senses create memorable **images.** The kinds and amount of images a writer uses can help to define his or her style.	**This writer layers on image after image, creating a poetic style that reflects the rhythm of the sea.** Beyond the sails stretched the sky itself, as blue as a baby's bluest eyes, while the greenish sea, crowned with lacy caps of foaming white, rushed by with unrelenting speed. —from *The True Confessions of Charlotte Doyle* by Avi	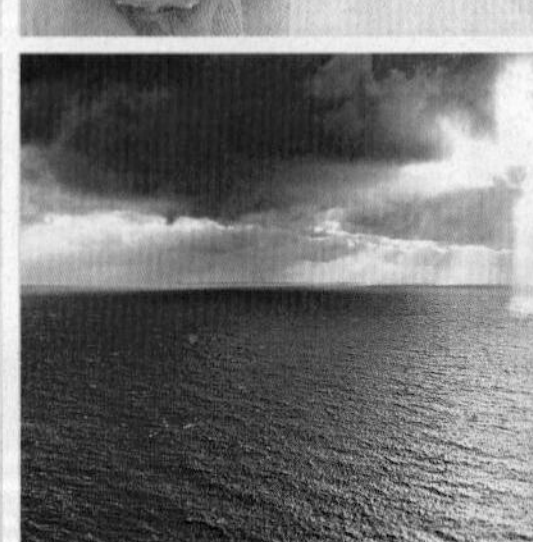

DIFFERENTIATED INSTRUCTION

FOR ALL STUDENTS

For general guidelines on differentiating instruction, see

 BEST PRACTICES TOOLKIT
Differentiated Instruction pp. 31–38

FOR LESS-PROFICIENT READERS

Note Taking Use the Note Taking: What Is Style? copy master to help students record and remember the information on page 666.

 RESOURCE MANAGER—Copy Master
Note Taking p. 15

Elements of Style

1. Display the first paragraph of an Edgar Allan Poe story, such as "The Tell-Tale Heart," "The Cask of Amontillado," or "The Pit and the Pendulum."
2. Model for students how to analyze the style by examining word choice, sentence structure and length, and imagery. Guide students to see that all of these elements contribute to the formal, highly descriptive, and dark style that is characteristic of Poe.

MODEL 1: COMPARING STYLE

In this excerpt, Rita Williams-Garcia uses a conversational, humorous style to convey the narrator's dread of a family meal. As you read, look closely at the author's word choice—the element that helps to create this style.

from Food from the *Outside*

Short story by **Rita Williams-Garcia**

My sister, brother, and I didn't have a dog, but we sure could have used one around dinnertime. Our dog would never have had to beg for table scraps, for we promised sincerely in our mealtime prayers always to feed Rover the main course. It wouldn't have been so much for love of dog, but for survival. You see, our mother, known throughout the neighborhood as "Miss Essie," was still refining her cooking skills. Until we could persuade our parents to let us have a dog, we sat at the dinner table with wax sandwich bags hidden in our pockets, especially when Miss Essie served "Hackensack," our code word for mystery stew.

Close Read

1. Find two examples of words and phrases in this excerpt that sound like casual conversation.
2. Reread the boxed details. Would you describe the narrator's voice as humorous, sincere, sarcastic, or something else? Explain.

MODEL 2: COMPARING STYLE

C. S. Lewis uses a more formal, descriptive style to write about an elaborate feast in the enchanted world of Narnia.

from The Voyage of the *Dawn Treader*

Novel by **C. S. Lewis**

On the table itself there was set out such a banquet as had never been seen, not even when Peter the High King kept his court at Cair Paravel. There were turkeys and geese and peacocks, there were boars' heads and sides of venison, there were pies shaped like ships under full sail or like dragons and elephants, there were ice puddings and bright lobsters and gleaming salmon, there were nuts and grapes, pineapples and peaches, pomegranates and melons and tomatoes. There were flagons[1] of gold and silver and curiously-wrought[2] glass; and the smell of the fruit and the wine blew toward them like a promise of all happiness.

1. **flagons:** vessels used for holding wine; flasks.
2. **curiously-wrought:** strangely crafted.

Close Read

1. How would you describe the structure of the author's sentences?
2. One element of Lewis's style is his use of imagery. Two examples have been boxed. Find three more examples.
3. What is the most striking stylistic difference between how the two authors describe a meal? Support your answer.

MODEL 1: COMPARING STYLE

Close Read

Possible answers:

1. *The phrases "we sure could have used one" in line 1 and "You see" in lines 4–5 sound as if the narrator is speaking directly to the reader.*
2. *The narrator's voice is humorous. The exaggeration about surviving family meals and the detail about the children's "code word for mystery stew" poke fun at their mother's cooking skills.*

If students need help . . . Remind them that voice refers to the personality of the speaker or writer—in this case, the story's narrator—as it is expressed through word choice, sentence structure, and imagery.

MODEL 2: COMPARING STYLE

Close Read

Possible answers:

1. *The sentences are long, listing the many extravagant foods at a banquet. The author repeats the phrase "there were," which gives structure to the paragraph and also emphasizes the large number of items on the table.*
2. *Other examples of imagery include "pies shaped . . . like dragons and elephants" (line 4), "bright lobsters" (line 5), "flagons of gold and silver and curiously-wrought glass" (line 7), and "the smell of the fruit and the wine blew toward them like a promise of all happiness" (lines 8–9).*
3. *C. S. Lewis's style is lavishly descriptive and somewhat formal, focusing on the sights of the heaping banquet table. Williams-Garcia focuses more on the emotions of the diners, using a humorous, informal style to convey her message.*

FOR ENGLISH LEARNERS

Concept Support: Style

- Read each excerpt aloud to help students hear the differences in style.
- Then work together to pick out words and phrases in the first selection that create a humorous, casual style and words and phrases in the second that contribute to the more formal, descriptive style.

FOR ADVANCED LEARNERS/PRE–AP

Analyze Style [paired option] Have students choose two or three samples of their own writing. Ask them to exchange the samples with a partner. Then have each student analyze the other's style, examining word choice, sentence structure, and imagery. Ask students to summarize their ideas about their partner's style and return the samples with their analysis. Have pairs discuss whether they agree with the conclusion drawn by their partner.

READER'S WORKSHOP 667

Teach

Part 2: Tone

Point out that unlike someone who is speaking—who can use voice expression, volume, and pace to convey tone—a writer can rely only on words. Therefore, readers must pay close attention to the words, images, details, and literary devices that a writer chooses in order to infer the writer's attitude about the subject.

Explain that writers use tone to help achieve their purpose and convey their message. Read both excerpts aloud. Then discuss how Myers's tone in the first excerpt illustrates how important basketball was to him when he was 11 years old. In the second excerpt, Sleator's humorous, negative tone helps readers understand the dismay and dread he felt as a student in PE class and also his adult perspective on the situation.

CHECK UNDERSTANDING Ask students to explain the ways in which a writer's style (including choice of words and details) can reveal his or her tone.

Part 2: Tone

Another important element of style is **tone**—a writer's attitude toward a subject. The tone of a piece of writing might be described using words such as *humorous, sarcastic, mocking, admiring, serious,* or *sympathetic.* One way to determine a writer's tone is to look at the specific words, phrases, and details he or she chooses to include.

Take a look at these two excerpts. In each, the writer conveys a very specific attitude toward sports.

COMPARING TONE

Walter Dean Myers

By the time I was eleven, basketball had entered my life. I knew I was going to be a star and I could dream about myself playing in the NBA. My strength was my outside shot and in my dreams I always made the last, desperate shot that swished through the net just as the buzzer sounded.

—from "Daydreams"

Myers uses an **optimistic, confident tone** to express his attitude toward his basketball abilities.

- Myers's choice of words reveals his dreamy optimism.
- Details convey the author's confidence.

William Sleator

I was always the last one picked for teams. I was so used to it that it didn't bother me. I was always way out in left field or right field or whichever field it is that balls hardly ever go to, and I lived in fear that a ball would come my way and I'd have to try to catch the thing and it would hit me on the head or I'd drop it. PE was the worst thing about school.

—from "The Masque of the Red Death"

Sleator uses a **negative, yet humorous tone** to express his attitude toward PE class.

- Words and phrases let readers know exactly how Sleator felt about playing baseball in PE class.
- The details reveal the author's sense of humor about his experience, as well as explain *why* PE class was so terrible.

668

DIFFERENTIATED INSTRUCTION

FOR LESS–PROFICIENT READERS

Note Taking [paired option] Hand out the Note Taking: Tone copy master. Read and discuss the top of page 668. As a class, complete the first item on the copy master. Then have students form pairs to complete the page.

 RESOURCE MANAGER—Copy Master
Note Taking p. 16

Identify Tone [small-group option] Display these sentence frames:

On Monday nights, my family eats liver and onions. I _____ that meal. The _____ of the meat cooking and the _____ of the boiling onions and butter make me _____.

Remind students that a writer's tone toward his or her subject is determined by the choice of words and details. Ask small groups to experiment with tone by substituting words and phrases to create an excited tone and then a disgusted one. Have them compare results.

MODEL 1: COMPARING TONE

The narrator of this novel, a teenaged boy, thinks back on helping a neighbor with her lawn. Read on to find out how he felt about this experience.

from *Bird*

Novel by **Angela Johnson**

I used to mow old Mrs. Pritchard's lawn when I was eight. She had one of those old mowers that was hard as anything to push through all the grass in her backyard. She said she didn't like the gas mowers because they stunk and scared all the birds away.

I wouldn't have done it for anybody else, but she always had lemonade out for me, then she'd feed me the best peach cobbler I ever tasted. I didn't tell her, but I'd have mowed that big yard for nothing but some of that cobbler. I'm easy that way.

Close Read

1. What words and phrases in the boxed lines help you to understand the boy's feelings about helping Mrs. Pritchard?
2. Which word pair best describes the tone revealed in the boxed lines?
   a. warm, nostalgic
   b. resentful, bitter
   c. biting, sarcastic

MODEL 2: COMPARING TONE

In her memoir, Haven Kimmel recalls a time in her childhood when she was strongly encouraged to do good deeds for other people. As you read about Kimmel's first attempt to do something good, think about how you would describe her attitude, or tone.

from

Nonfiction by **Haven Kimmel**

I spent every afternoon stalking good works. My first victim was Agnes Johnson who was 164 years old. Her skin, impatient for her to get it over with and die, appeared to be sliding down off her body into a pool around her ankles. She was older than dirt, but feisty. She insisted on cutting her own grass every week with an ancient push mower. For years I'd seen her out there, pushing against the mower as if it were a huge rock, her skinny arms quivering, her lips trembling, a thin film of sweat shining on the place most people had an upper lip. I'd never paid her much mind, but on this particular day I realized I'd hit the jackpot. Ordinarily I'd have rather run naked into a rose bush than cut grass; at my own house I suggested a few times a week that we get a goat or some other furry grazing thing to live in the backyard. (I thought a goat was an especially clever choice because they could also eat our empty tin cans.) So if I mowed Agnes Johnson's yard, I could probably avoid doing any more good deeds until I myself was flat-out old.

Close Read

1. Examine the boxed words. Are these words you would typically associate with doing good deeds? Explain.
2. Identify three details that help you understand Kimmel's feelings about helping Agnes Johnson.
3. What word would you use to describe the author's tone, or attitude, toward doing good deeds?

MODEL 1: COMPARING TONE

Close Read

Possible answers:

1. *The phrases "I wouldn't have done it for anybody else," "she'd feed me the best peach cobbler I ever tasted," and "I'd have mowed that big yard for nothing but some of that cobbler" convey the narrator's willingness to help Mrs. Pritchard and his affection for her and her peach cobbler.*
2. *The word pair that best describes the tone of the passage is (a)* warm, nostalgic.

MODEL 2: COMPARING TONE

Close Read

Possible answers:

1. *No, the words* stalking *and* victim *are not usually associated with good deeds. They sound threatening rather than generous.*
2. *Details such as "My first victim was Agnes Johnson who was 164 years old" (lines 1–2), "on this particular day I realized I'd hit the jackpot" (lines 8–9), and "if I mowed Agnes Johnson's yard, I could probably avoid doing any more good deeds until I myself was flat-out old" (lines 13–14) convey the tone of the author toward his subject.*
3. *The word* determined *describes the author's tone. Although he would "rather run naked into a rose bush than cut grass," he wants to mow Agnes Johnson's lawn because he has committed himself to doing good works.*

FOR ENGLISH LEARNERS

Reading Support: Tone [mixed-readiness groups]

1. Read both selections aloud to students, defining words such as *cobbler* and *feisty.* Convey the tone of each selection through voice expression.
2. Divide students into small groups. Have them work on the **Close Read** questions.
3. Review their responses as a class.

Practice and Apply

Part 3: Analyze the Literature

Close Read

Possible answers:

1. *Examples of imagery include*
   - *"loitering around the fringes of the action" (lines 8–9)*
   - *"the ball rocketing across the field, missing the goal by what looked like about half a mile" (lines 11–12)*
   - *"swollen to the size of a baked ham" (line 19)*
2. *Details that contribute to the humorous, self-mocking tone include*
   - *"We would, I imagined, become sweethearts, get engaged, eventually marry, and live happily ever after" (lines 4–6)*
   - *"missing the goal by what looked like about half a mile" (line 12)*
   - *"I was on the grass . . . giving my full attention to learning the nature of agony" (lines 14–15)*
   - *"After nearly a week of character-building, I limped back to school" (line 23)*
   - *"And she, very properly, decided the right thing to do was never to speak to me again" (lines 24–25)*
3. *The voice in this excerpt conveys the impression of someone who is able to laugh at himself and see humor in incidents that show him in an unflattering light.*

Part 3: Analyze the Literature

Both of the following selections are about romance and the anxiety that it can spark. Though the excerpts share a similar topic, each reveals its writer's distinct personality.

The first excerpt is from an essay Lloyd Alexander wrote about his earliest experience with dating—or, rather, not dating. As you read, look for examples of the elements of style that you have studied in this workshop.

from **THE Truth ABOUT THE WORLD**

Essay by **Lloyd Alexander**

My first date never happened. When I finally built up enough nerve, I dared to ask one of the girls in my ninth-grade class to go to some kind of dance or other—I don't remember exactly; it was long ago. To my amazement, she accepted. For myself, I always thought in large, long-range terms. We would, I imagined, become sweethearts, get engaged, eventually marry, and live happily ever after.

Friday afternoon, the day before the glorious event, our gym teacher ordered us outdoors to play soccer. I usually preferred loitering around the fringes of the action, but when the ball bounded straight at me, I seized the moment to give it the mightiest kick in school history.

I noticed a couple of things. For one, I glimpsed the ball rocketing across the field, missing the goal by what looked like about half a mile; for another, [I saw an expression of despondency and long suffering on the face of the gym teacher.] By then, I was on the grass, trying to hold my left foot in both hands and giving my full attention to learning the nature of agony.

A couple of classmates hauled me to the nurse's office. My mother had to be summoned. She took me home in our ancient Plymouth and phoned the doctor (they made house calls in those days). He examined my foot, now swollen to the size of a baked ham. [He assured me I would live. I was sorry to hear that.]

The date, of course, was off. My mother took charge of canceling it; I hadn't the heart to do it myself. In those days, pain was supposed to build character. After nearly a week of character-building, I limped back to school. I was too ashamed even to look at my might-have-been date. And she, very properly, decided the right thing to do was never to speak to me again.

Close Read

1. One element of Alexander's style is his use of imagery. Find two examples of imagery in the excerp
2. The [boxed] details hel create a humorous, se mocking tone. Identi two other details that reflect this tone.
3. Based on the voice yo "heard" as you read, h would you describe th author's personality?

DIFFERENTIATED INSTRUCTION

FOR LESS–PROFICIENT READERS

Analysis Support: Style [paired option] Before students answer the **Close Read** questions, have pairs find examples of each style element in the passage. Review their responses.

Elements of Style	*Alexander's Style*	*Examples*
word choice	*powerful verbs, precise nouns*	*amazement, loitering, bounded, seized, despondency*
sentence structure	*long, descriptive sentences*	*"We would, I imagined, become sweethearts, get engaged, eventually marry, and live happily ever after."*
imagery	*vivid and humorous*	*"swollen to the size of a baked ham"*
details	*make fun of the incident and himself*	*"missing the goal by what looked like about half a mile"*

The following excerpt is from a novel, so the voice you "hear" belongs to the narrator—a teenager named Leo. Here, Leo describes an awkward early encounter with his future girlfriend, who calls herself Stargirl. As you read, consider what elements help to create the author's style.

Novel by **Jerry Spinelli**

At first it was enough just to see the house. Then I began to wonder if she was inside. I wondered what she could be doing. Light came from every window I could see. There was a car in the driveway. The longer I hung around, the closer I wanted to be. I crossed the street and practically dashed past the house. As I went by, I scooped up a stone from the yard. I went up the street, turned, and looked at her house in the distance.

I whispered to the salt-sprinkled sky, "That's where Stargirl Caraway lives. She likes me."

I headed back toward the house. The street, the sidewalks were deserted. The stone was warm in my hand. This time I walked slowly as I approached. I felt strange. My eyes fixed on a triangle of light in a curtained window. I saw a shadow on a yellow wall. I seemed to be drifting, footless, into the light.

Suddenly the front door opened. I dived behind the car in the driveway and crouched by the rear fender. I heard the door close. I heard steps. The steps matched the movement of a long shadow cast down the driveway. My breath stopped. The shadow stopped. I felt both ridiculous and weirdly, perfectly placed, as if crouching by that car was precisely what life had in store for me at that moment.

Her voice came from beyond the shadow. "Remember when you followed me into the desert that day after school?"

Absurdly, I debated whether to answer, as if doing so would—what? Give me away? I leaned into the smooth metal of the fender. It never occurred to me to stand, to show myself. Hours seemed to pass before I finally croaked, "Yes."

"Why did you turn around and go back?"

Her tone was casual, as if she held conversations every night with people crouching behind the car in the driveway.

Close Read

1. Spinelli's writing includes rich imagery that helps readers to visualize the setting. Find three examples.
2. Describe the structures of the boxed sentences. What effect do you think Spinelli was trying to achieve through this stylistic choice?
3. Which word pair best describes the tone revealed in lines 7–12 and 16–18?
   a. sarcastic and bitter
   b. romantic and dreamy
   c. sad and serious
4. Compare Spinelli's writing with Alexander's. How are the authors' styles similar or different?

FOR LESS–PROFICIENT READERS

Analysis Support: Style [small-group option] Have students work in small groups to create a T Chart to compare and contrast Spinelli's word choice, imagery, sentence structure, and tone with Alexander's.

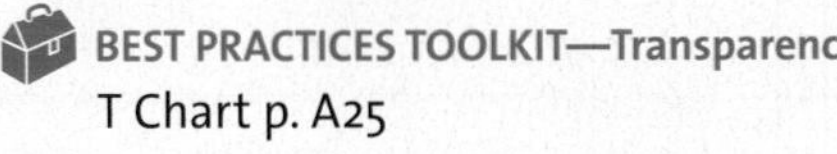

BEST PRACTICES TOOLKIT—Transparency
T Chart p. A25

FOR ADVANCED LEARNERS/PRE–AP

Extend the Passage Ask students to add another paragraph or two to the excerpt from *Stargirl.* Challenge them to imitate the style of the author and re-create the voice of the narrator while picking up the plot thread. Have students then take turns reading what they've written to the class. Have the class vote on the one that best captures the style, tone, and voice of the original excerpt.

Close Read

Possible answers:

1. *Imagery such as "Light came from every window I could see," "I whispered to the salt-sprinkled sky," and "My eyes fixed on a triangle of light in a curtained window" helps the readers to visualize the setting.*
2. *The sentences are short and simple to give the effect that Stargirl's appearance is sudden and that Leo is nervous.*
3. *The word pair that best describes the tone of the passage is (b)* romantic and dreamy.
4. *Both authors use simple, informal language and imagery to write about romance and the anxiety it can cause. While Alexander reveals a humorous, self-mocking attitude toward romance in his essay that conveys a real experience from his life, Spinelli creates a romantic and dreamy tone in his fictional story about Stargirl and Leo. Spinelli also includes short, simple sentences to show his character's anxiety.*

Assess and Reteach

Assess

Have students explain how style and tone contribute to voice.

Reteach

For students who cannot apply the workshop skills to the excerpts, try these options:

1. Have small groups meet to review their Note Taking copy masters together.
2. Choose three short passages from the text that illustrate distinctive styles. Write phrases describing each style on the board. Have students work together to match each phrase to the passage it describes. Discuss their choices.

Focus and Motivate

OBJECTIVES

Literary Analysis
- explore the key idea of **perception**
- identify, analyze, and evaluate style
- read a short story

Reading
- identify sequence using signal words

Vocabulary
- build vocabulary for reading and writing
- use context to define multiple-meaning words *(also an EL language objective)*

Grammar and Writing
- combine sentences and write concisely by using appositives and appositive phrases
- punctuate appositive phrases correctly
- use writing to analyze literature

SUMMARY

While on her lunch hour, Suzette spots her mother, a Haitian immigrant, strolling through Manhattan. Suzette follows undetected as her usually timid mother navigates the busy city streets with ease and ends up at a park, where she has been hired as a "day woman" to watch a child while his mother goes jogging. After an hour of surveillance, Suzette gains a new appreciation for her mother.

Who is the REAL *you?*

Discuss the question. To lead into the ***KEY IDEA,*** name a celebrity and ask volunteers to tell how they **perceive** that person. Point out that individual perceptions of the same person may be very different. Then have students work on the ***QUICKWRITE*** activity.

Before Reading

New York Day Women

Short Story by Edwidge Danticat

Who is the REAL *you?*

KEY IDEA At first, it might seem silly to wonder who you really are. But do you act the same around your teachers as you do around your friends? And do your grandparents **perceive** the same person your friends see? We all have different sides to ourselves. In the story you are about to read, a young woman discovers a side of her mother she never knew existed.

QUICKWRITE Think of three or four people who know you in different ways—for example, your best friend, a teacher, a parent, and an enemy. What adjectives would each person use to describe you? How would you describe yourself? Jot down your thoughts about whether anyone perceives the real you.

672

Selection Resources

RESOURCE MANAGER UNIT 6

Plan and Teach pp. 17–24

Literary Analysis
Summary pp. 25†*, 26‡*
Style pp. 27, 28†*
Question Support p. 35*

Reading
Identify Sequence pp. 29, 30†*
Reading Check p. 34
Reading Fluency p. 37

Vocabulary
Study p. 31*
Practice p. 32
Strategy p. 33

Grammar and Writing
Write Concisely p. 36

Assessment
Selection Tests A, B/C pp. 39*, 41*
Test Generator CD

BEST PRACTICES TOOLKIT

Differentiated Instruction pp. 31–38*
Scaffolding Instruction pp. 43–46*

Graphic Organizers/Strategies
Word Questioning • Character Map

Technology

Literature, Vocabulary, and Writing Centers at **ClassZone.com**
Write*Smart* CD

* Resources for Differentiation † Also in Spanish ‡ In Haitian Creole and Vietnamese

TERARY ANALYSIS: STYLE

Each of us has a unique style, or way of dressing, acting, and speaking. In literature, **style** is a writer's way of expressing himself or herself. Style does not refer to what is said, but rather how it is said. Writers show style through the choices they make about the following things:

- Word choice and **imagery**—descriptive words and phrases that appeal to the senses. Notice Edwidge Danticat's descriptions.
- Presentation—the way the story appears on the page. Notice Danticat's use of line spacing, italics, and typographical symbols.
- Sentence structure. Notice Danticat's purposeful use of sentence fragments.

EADING SKILL: IDENTIFY SEQUENCE

Sequence is the order in which events occur in a story. To help yourself keep track of the order, look for signal words and phrases, such as *today, that morning, as, now, an hour later, then,* and *before.*

In the story you are about to read, the narrator relates present-day events while reflecting on conversations and incidents from the past. Keep track of the sequence of present-day events by recording them in a sequence chart like the one shown.

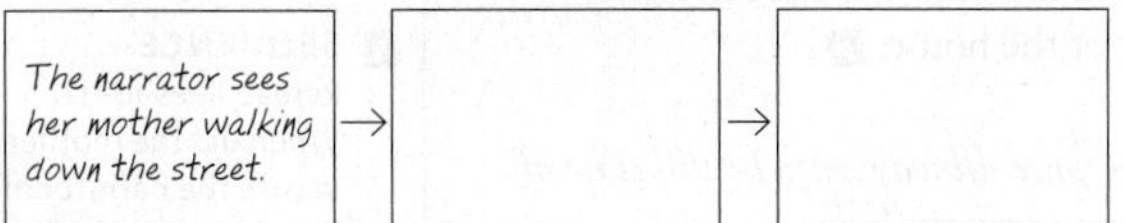
The narrator sees her mother walking down the street.

OCABULARY IN CONTEXT

The following boldfaced words help Danticat show how people sometimes don't really understand each other. To see how many words you know, restate each sentence, using a different word or phrase for the boldfaced word.

1. Pablo can **mesmerize** people with his charm, so they forget he isn't reliable.
2. Jenny's only **offense** is that she brags too much.
3. My **pursuit** of the truth only left me more confused.
4. I **contemplate** joining the game, but no one expects me to, so I don't.
5. I doubt that the feisty Emily will **surrender** easily.

Author On|ine

Edwidge Danticat born 1969

A New Home in New York Writer Edwidge Danticat (ĕd'wēj dăn'tē-kä) emigrated from Haiti to Brooklyn, New York, when she was 12. Danticat had a hard time adjusting to life in New York. Her classmates made fun of her clothing, hairstyle, and Haitian accent. To escape from the loneliness she felt during this time, Danticat wrote stories about her home country. Over her career, Danticat has published several novels and short story collections, most of which involve Haitian culture and characters.

Krik? Krak! During her childhood, Danticat heard many Haitian stories. Storytellers begin their tales by asking the audience, "Krik?" If the audience is ready, they will respond with an excited "Krak!" This exchange of words became the title of Danticat's first collection of short stories, in which "New York Day Women" appears.

MORE ABOUT THE AUTHOR For more on Edwidge Danticat, visit the **Literature Center** at **ClassZone.com.**

Background

A Haven for Haitians Danticat's homeland is one of the most densely populated and least developed countries in the Western hemisphere. This small country in the West Indies has been ruled by brutal dictators for much of its history. Hundreds of thousands of Haitians, including Danticat's family, have fled to the United States. Many have settled in Brooklyn, a borough of New York City. According to the 2000 census, over 200,000 Haitians and Haitian Americans live there. In some Brooklyn schools, Haitian children make up 75 percent of the population.

Teach

STANDARDS FOCUS

LITERARY ANALYSIS

● STYLE

Read aloud the following sentences. Explain that each conveys basically the same information. Ask students in what ways the writers' styles differ.

- Crowds of cheering onlookers gathered on this sunny day to celebrate the union of the prince and his lovely bride.
- Tons of people showed up to watch the prince get married.

Possible answer: *The first writer's style is formal and descriptive, while the second is more casual and less descriptive.*

CHECK UNDERSTANDING Ask: In what ways might a journalist's style differ from that of a short story writer or a poet?

READING SKILL

■ IDENTIFY SEQUENCE

Have students read **A New Home in New York** in **Author Online** on page 673. Ask: What phrases signal the sequence of events in Danticat's life? ***Answer:*** *"when she was 12," "during this time," "Over her career"*

CHECK UNDERSTANDING Have students create a sequence chart to show their actions this morning.

RESOURCE MANAGER—Copy Master Identify Sequence p. 29 (for student use while reading the selection)

VOCABULARY SKILL

▲ VOCABULARY IN CONTEXT

DIAGNOSE WORD KNOWLEDGE To determine preteaching needs, have all students complete **Vocabulary in Context.** *Students' responses will vary.* ***Possible answers:*** **1.** *impress* **2.** *fault* **3.** *chasing after* **4.** *consider carefully* **5.** *give in*

PRETEACH VOCABULARY Use the Vocabulary Study copy master to help students determine the meaning of each boldfaced word.

1. Read the first pair of sentences in Part A aloud, emphasizing *contemplate.*
2. Point out the context phrases *which size to buy* and *instead of automatically refusing to consider it.* Elicit possible meanings for *contemplate,* such as "to think about."
3. Repeat the procedure for items b–e.
4. Have students complete Part B on their own.

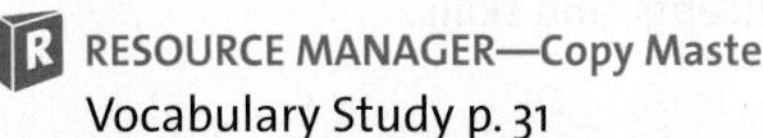
RESOURCE MANAGER—Copy Master Vocabulary Study p. 31

For general guidelines on differentiating vocabulary instruction and for alternative vocabulary activities for students not needing vocabulary preteaching, see

BEST PRACTICES TOOLKIT Scaffolding Vocabulary Instruction pp. 43–46

Vocabulary Center at **ClassZone.com** Additional Vocabulary Activities

Practice and Apply

ANALYZE VISUALS

Possible answer: *The figure is alone and standing in the shadows, perhaps waiting or looking for someone.*

About the Art British artist Bill Jacklin (born 1943) visited New York City in 1985 and found the sights and sounds of the city, along with its variety of people from different cultures, so exciting that he decided to move there. Soon after, Jacklin began painting what he called "Urban Portraits" of the city. Jacklin's bustling city landscapes, such as the one portrayed in *The Promenade, Fifth Avenue,* contain areas of light and dark, causing the scenes to be both recognizable and unfamiliar to viewers at the same time. Jacklin's paintings are featured in museums around the world.

READING SKILL

Ⓐ SEQUENCE

Answer: *The mother made the accusations earlier that day. The signal phrases "who I left at home that morning" (line 10) and "as I dash out of the house" (line 12) tell when the event happened.*

LITERARY ANALYSIS

Ⓑ STYLE

Possible answer: *Repeated phrases include "my mother, who" and "whether or not." The story might be about the narrator's relationship with her mother.*

NEW YORK DAY WOMEN

Edwidge Danticat

Today, walking down the street, I see my mother. She is strolling with a happy gait, her body thrust toward the DON'T WALK sign and the yellow taxicabs that make forty-five-degree turns on the corner of Madison and Fifty-seventh Street.

I have never seen her in this kind of neighborhood, peering into Chanel and Tiffany's and gawking at the jewels glowing in the Bulgari[1] windows. My mother never shops outside of Brooklyn. She has never seen the advertising office where I work. She is afraid to take the subway, where you may meet those young black militant street preachers who curse black women for straightening their hair.

Yet, here she is, my mother, who I left at home that morning in her bathrobe, with pieces of newspapers twisted like rollers in her hair. My mother, who accuses me of random **offenses** as I dash out of the house. Ⓐ

❖

Would you get up and give an old lady like me your subway seat? In this state of mind, I bet you don't even give up your seat to a pregnant lady.

❖

My mother, who is often right about that. Sometimes I get up and give my seat. Other times, I don't. It all depends on how pregnant the woman is and whether or not she is with her . . . husband and whether or not *he* is sitting down. Ⓑ

As my mother stands in front of Carnegie Hall,[2] one taxi driver yells to another, "What do you think this is, a dance floor?"

My mother waits patiently for this dispute to be settled before crossing the street.

❖

In Haiti when you get hit by a car, the owner of the car gets out and kicks you for getting blood on his bumper.

❖

ANALYZE VISUALS
What can you **infer** abo
the central silhouetted figure?

① **Targeted Passage**

offense (ə-fĕns') *n.* a violation of a moral or social code; a sin

Ⓐ **SEQUENCE**
Reread lines 10–12. When did the mother accuse the narrator of "random offenses"? Tell how you know.

Ⓑ **STYLE**
Reread lines 10–17. Note any **repetition** of words or phrases. Based on this repetition, what do you think will be the subject of this story?

1. **Chanel** (shə-nĕl'); Tiffany's; Bulgari (bo͝ol' gä-rē): very expensive shops that sell luxury goods such as designer clothing, perfume, glassware, and jewelry.
2. **Carnegie Hall** (kär'nə-gē hôl): a famous concert hall in New York City.

The Promenade, Fifth Avenue (198
Bill Jacklin. Oil on canv
243.6 cm × 182.7 cm. Private collectio

DIFFERENTIATED INSTRUCTION

FOR ALL STUDENTS

Enhance Learning Styles Provide independent projects for various learning styles.

- **Interpersonal** Work in a group to research Haitian proverbs.
- **Visual** Create a mural that depicts the sequence of events in the story.
- **Linguistic** Write a personal narrative about a time when your perception of a person changed.

For further details on these projects, see

RESOURCE MANAGER
Ideas for Extension pp. 22–23

FOR LESS–PROFICIENT READERS

Use one or more Targeted Passages (pp. 674, 677, 678) to ensure that students focus on key events, concepts, and skills.

① Targeted Passage [Lines 1–22]

This passage introduces the story's narrator and her mother as well as the setting in New York City.

- Who is the narrator of the story?
- Where does the narrator see her mother? Why does this surprise the narrator?
- What does the narrator think of her mother? Explain.
- Whose words are in italics?

BACKGROUND

Immigration in New York City New York City is the destination for immigrants from all over the world, making it a culturally diverse and exciting place to live. Since 2000, nearly half a million people have emigrated to New York City. In 2005, immigrants and their children accounted for at least 60 percent of the city's 8 million people.

Lines 1–22

DISCUSSION PROMPTS

Use these prompts to help students understand the difference between the narrator's mother and the narrator's perception of her mother:

Recall In what way does the narrator describe her mother in lines 5–9? ***Answer:*** *She describes her mother as someone who is too timid to deal with life in New York City.*

Infer What can you infer about the narrator's mother from lines 1–4? ***Possible answer:*** *She has strolled these streets before. She is enjoying walking around the city.*

Speculate After reading the mother's statement in lines 21–22, why do you think it is important to her that the narrator give up her seat in the subway? ***Possible answer:*** *It is important to the mother that the narrator behave politely and value all human life. She does not want the narrator to be immune to the suffering of others and to act cruelly.*

FOR ENGLISH LEARNERS

Key Academic Vocabulary Have students use Word Questioning to study these academic vocabulary words: *random* (line 12), *channel* (line 29), *occurs* (line 98).

BEST PRACTICES TOOLKIT—Transparency
Word Questioning p. E9

Prereading For prereading instruction for English learners, see

BEST PRACTICES TOOLKIT
Scaffolding Reading Instruction pp. 43–46

FOR ADVANCED LEARNERS/PRE–AP

Pre-AP exercises in the bottom channel provide additional challenge for your advanced students. Use them for small groups or individuals.

ADDITIONAL GUIDELINES

For more help with differentiation and tips for classroom management, see

BEST PRACTICES TOOLKIT
Differentiated Instruction pp. 31–38

SOCIAL STUDIES CONNECTION

New York City New York City is divided into five boroughs, or districts: Manhattan, Staten Island, Brooklyn, Queens, and the Bronx. Manhattan is located on a 12-mile-long island between the East River and the Hudson River. It is the main business, cultural, and entertainment center for the city, and includes Central Park, which is about two and a half miles long and half a mile wide. The borough of Staten Island, just south of Manhattan, is a residential community, reached by ferry from the southern tip of Manhattan. The Bronx is almost due north of Manhattan and is also mainly residential. Stretching about 118 miles to the east is Long Island, which includes the boroughs of Brooklyn and Queens. Brooklyn, which is about three times as large as Manhattan, is located on the southwestern tip of Long Island. Brooklyn is mainly a bedroom community, where people who work in busy Manhattan live. On the northern tip of Long Island is Queens, home of LaGuardia International Airport and the New York Mets' Shea Stadium.

LITERARY ANALYSIS

C STYLE

Possible answer: *Danticat may have chosen to show the mother's words in italics to emphasize them. The italics also clearly separate the mother's words and ideas from her daughter's, stressing the differences between the two women.*

My mother who laughs when she says this and shows a large gap in her mouth where she lost three more molars to the dentist last week. My mother, who at fifty-nine, says dentures are okay.

❖

You can take them out when they bother you. I'll like them. I'll like them fine.

❖

Will it feel empty when Papa kisses you?

❖

Oh no, he doesn't kiss me that way anymore.

❖

My mother, who watches the lottery drawing every night on channel 11 without ever having played the numbers.

❖

A third of that money is all I would need. We would pay the mortgage, and your father could stop driving that taxicab all over Brooklyn.

❖

I follow my mother, **mesmerized** by the many possibilities of her journey. Even in a flowered dress, she is lost in a sea of pinstripes[3] and gray suits, high heels and elegant short skirts, . . . sneakers, dashing from building to building.

My mother, who won't go out to dinner with anyone.

❖

If they want to eat with me, let them come to my house, even if I boil water and give it to them.

❖

My mother, who talks to herself when she peels the skin off poultry.

❖

Fat, you know, and cholesterol. Fat and cholesterol killed your aunt Hermine. C

❖

My mother, who makes jam with dried grapefruit peel and then puts in cinnamon bark that I always think is cockroaches in the jam. My mother, whom I have always bought household appliances for, on her birthday. A nice rice cooker, a blender.

I trail the red orchids in her dress and the heavy faux[4] leather bag on her shoulders. Realizing the ferocious pace of my **pursuit,** I stop against a wall to rest. My mother keeps on walking as though she owns the sidewalk under her feet.

As she heads toward the Plaza Hotel,[5] a bicycle messenger swings so close to her that I want to dash forward and rescue her, but she stands dead in her tracks[6] and lets him ride around her and then goes on.

SOCIAL STUDIES CONNECTION

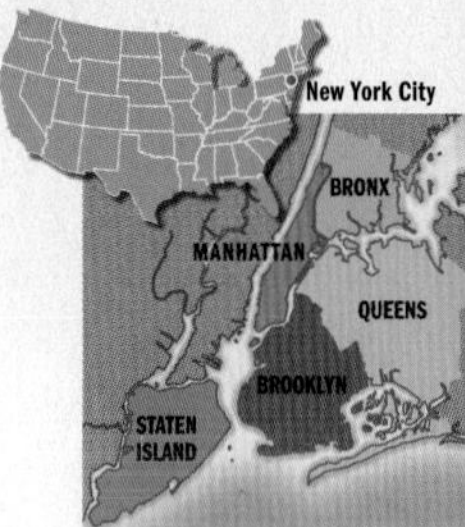

New York City is divided into five boroughs, or municipalities. The family in the story lives in Brooklyn. The narrator and her mother are now in Manhattan.

mesmerize (mĕz'mə-rīz') *v.* to spellbind; to enthrall

C STYLE Why do you think Dantica[t] chooses to show the mother's words in italics?

pursuit (pər-so͞ot') *n.* the act of chasing

3. **pinstripes:** fabrics with very thin stripes, usually used to make business suits.
4. **faux** (fō): artificial but meant to look genuine.
5. **Plaza Hotel:** a world-renowned hotel located near Central Park in New York City.
6. **dead in her tracks:** perfectly still.

DIFFERENTIATED INSTRUCTION

FOR LESS–PROFICIENT READERS

Reading Skill Follow-Up: Identify Sequence

Have students work in pairs to read lines 33–50 and update the charts that were introduced on page 673. Remind students to look for events that are taking place in the story's present. Allow them to record the events on their charts. Afterward, have students compare their sequence charts for accuracy.

The narrator sees her mother walking down the street. → *The narrator follows her mother, watching out for her mother's flowered dress.* → *The narrator slows down and rests against a wall.* → *A bicycle messenger almost runs into her mother.*

676 UNIT 6: STYLE, VOICE, AND TONE

My mother stops at a corner hot-dog stand and asks for something. The vendor hands her a can of soda that she slips into her bag. She stops by another vendor selling sundresses for seven dollars each. I can tell that she is looking at an African print dress, **contemplating** my size. I think to myself, Please Ma, don't buy it. It would be just another thing I would bury in the garage or give to Goodwill.

contemplate (kŏn'təm-plāt') *v.* to consider carefully and at length

❖

Why should we give to Goodwill when there are so many people back home who need clothes? We save our clothes for the relatives in Haiti.

❖

Twenty years we have been saving all kinds of things for the relatives in Haiti. I need the place in the garage for an exercise bike.

❖

You are pretty enough to be a stewardess. Only dogs like bones.

❖

This mother of mine, she stops at another hot-dog vendor's and buys a frankfurter that she eats on the street. I never knew that she ate frankfurters. With her blood pressure, she shouldn't eat anything with sodium.[7] She has to be careful with her heart, this day woman.[8]

❖

I cannot just swallow salt. Salt is heavier than a hundred bags of shame.

❖

She is slowing her pace, and now I am too close. If she turns around, she might see me. I let her walk into the park before I start to follow again. **D**

My mother walks toward the sandbox in the middle of the park. There a woman is waiting with a child. The woman is wearing a leotard with biker's shorts and has small weights in her hands. The woman kisses the child good-bye and **surrenders** him to my mother, then she bolts off, running on the cemented stretches in the park.

The child given to my mother has frizzy blond hair. His hand slips into hers easily, like he's known her for a long time. When he raises his face to look at my mother, it is as though he is looking at the sky.

My mother gives this child the soda that she bought from the vendor on the street corner. The child's face lights up as she puts . . . a straw in the can for him. This seems to be a conspiracy just between the two of them. **E**

My mother and the child sit and watch the other children play in the sandbox. The child pulls out a comic book from a knapsack with Big Bird on the back. My mother peers into his comic book. My mother, who taught herself to read as a little girl in Haiti from the books that her brothers brought home from school.

My mother, who has now lost six of her seven sisters in Ville Rose[9] and has never had the strength to return for their funerals.

❖

D SEQUENCE
Reread lines 66–67. What words help you understand the sequence of events?

② Targeted Passage

surrender (sə-rĕn'dər) *v.* to give up possession or control to another

E STYLE
Reread lines 68–78. Danticat uses vivid **imagery** in this passage. Which images do you think best illustrate the special relationship between the narrator's mother and the boy?

7. **sodium** (sō'dē-əm): salt.
8. **day woman:** a woman who is employed as a housekeeper or babysitter but does not live in her employer's home.
9. **Ville Rose** (vĭl rōz): a fictional Haitian town.

Lines 51–60
DISCUSSION PROMPTS

Use these prompts to help students understand the relationship between the narrator and her mother:

Connect The narrator and her mother have different tastes in clothing. What styles do you and your friends like that the adults you know do not, and vice versa? *Students should give examples of clothing, jewelry, hairstyles, and so on that reflect the tastes of different generations.*

Infer What can you infer about the difference between the priorities of the narrator and her mother from lines 58–59? ***Possible answer:** Her mother is concerned about her relatives, while the narrator is concerned about her weight.*

Analyze What does the mother mean when she says, "Only dogs like bones"? ***Possible answer:** She means that her daughter should not be so concerned about losing weight.*

READING SKILL

D SEQUENCE

***Answer:** The words* now, before, *and* again *help readers understand the sequence of events.*

LITERARY ANALYSIS

E STYLE

***Possible answer:** These images illustrate the relationship: "His hand slips into hers easily," "as though he is looking at the sky," "child's face lights up," and "a conspiracy just between the two of them."*

FOR LESS–PROFICIENT READERS

② Targeted Passage [Lines 66–75]

This passage reveals the first details about the mother's job as a day woman.

- Why does the narrator's mother slow down?
- Why does the woman in biker's shorts give her child to the narrator's mother?
- What evidence shows that the narrator's mother has spent time with the child before?

FOR ADVANCED LEARNERS/PRE–AP

Analyze Character [small-group option]
While the narrator follows her mother all over Manhattan, she observes her mother's activities and, at the same time, creates a vivid image of her mother for readers. Invite small groups to discuss these questions: *When the narrator discovers that her mother is babysitting, do you think she feels jealous? What you think the narrator's relationship with her mother was like when she was a child? What is their relationship like now, and how might it change in the future?*

Lines 66–84
REINFORCE *KEY IDEA:* PERCEIVE

Discuss In what way does the little boy **perceive** the mother differently from the narrator? ***Possible answer:** The boy perceives her as a special friend. The narrator perceives her as a timid and set-in-her-ways immigrant who does not fit in well in a big city.*

NEW YORK DAY WOMEN 677

READING SKILL

F SEQUENCE

Possible answer: *The narrator's statement "My lunch hour is long since gone" (line 91) indicates that she has been watching her mother for over an hour.*

Lines 98–100

REINFORCE *KEY IDEA:* PERCEIVE

Discuss In what way do these lines sum up the change in how the narrator **perceives** her mother? ***Possible answer:*** *The lines indicate that the mother has changed so much in the narrator's eyes that she is no longer certain who her mother is.*

LITERARY ANALYSIS

G STYLE

Possible answer: *The structure is a sentence fragment, which Danticat frequently uses to echo the narrator's thought processes or speech patterns.*

SELECTION WRAP-UP

REFLECT Encourage students to consider why the author cast the mother and daughter as immigrants rather than native-born Americans. Ask what they learned about the immigrant experience from the characters.

★ CRITIQUE Have students think about the way the author developed the relationship between the narrator and her mother without ever having them converse face to face. Do students feel as if they have a good understanding of the relationship? Have students cite story evidence to support their opinions.

READING FLUENCY

Distribute the copy masters and have students practice fluency.

R RESOURCE MANAGER—Copy Master
Reading Fluency p. 37

Many graves to kiss when I go back. Many graves to kiss.

❖

She throws away the empty soda can when the child is done with it. I wait and watch from a corner until the woman in the leotard and biker's shorts returns, sweaty and breathless, an hour later. My mother gives the woman back her child and strolls farther into the park.

I turn around and start to walk out of the park before my mother can see me. My lunch hour is long since gone. I have to hurry back to work. I walk through a cluster of joggers, then race to a *Sweden Tours* bus. I stand behind the bus and take a peek at my mother in the park. She is standing in a circle, chatting with a group of women who are taking other people's children on an afternoon outing. They look like a Third World[10] Parent-Teacher Association meeting.

I quickly jump into a cab heading back to the office. Would Ma have said hello had she been the one to see me first? **F**

③ Targeted Passage

F SEQUENCE
How long has the narrator been watching her mother? Tell how you know.

As the cab races away from the park, it occurs to me that perhaps one day I would chase an old woman down a street by mistake and that old woman would be somebody else's mother, who I would have mistaken for mine.

❖

Day women come out when nobody expects them.

❖

Tonight on the subway, I will get up and give my seat to a pregnant woman or a lady about Ma's age.

My mother, who stuffs thimbles in her mouth and then blows up her cheeks like Dizzy Gillespie[11] while sewing yet another Raggedy Ann[12] doll that she names Suzette after me. **G**

G STYLE
Reread lines 104–106. In what way does the structure of this sentenc represent Danticat's styl

❖

I will have all these little Suzettes in case you never have any babies, which looks more and more like it is going to happen.

❖

My mother, who sews lace collars on my company softball T-shirts when she does my laundry.

❖

Why, you can't look like a lady playing softball?

❖

My mother, who never went to any of my Parent-Teacher Association meetings when I was in school.

❖

You're so good anyway. What are they going to tell me? I don't want to make you ashamed of this day woman. Shame is heavier than a hundred bags of salt.

---

10. **Third World:** the developing nations of Africa, Asia, and Latin America.
11. **Dizzy Gillespie** (dĭz′ē gə-lĕs′pē): an American trumpet player, bandleader, and composer (1917–1993) whose cheeks ballooned out when he played.
12. **Raggedy Ann:** a red-haired rag doll and fictional character who was the subject of several children's books.

DIFFERENTIATED INSTRUCTION

FOR LESS-PROFICIENT READERS

③ Targeted Passage [Lines 86–97]

This passage concludes the main action of the plot as the narrator stops watching her mother and heads back to work.

- What happens when the woman in the leotard and biker's shorts returns?
- What does the narrator's mother have in common with the other women in the park?
- Why doesn't the narrator continue to watch her mother?

FOR ADVANCED LEARNERS/PRE-AP

Analyze Repetition The narrator's mother is referred to as "my mother" many times throughout the story. Ask students to discuss what the repetition of this phrase adds to the meaning of the story. In addition, have them consider why the author chose not to include the mother's name.

ter Reading

omprehension

1. **Recall** What does the narrator's mother do for a living?
2. **Clarify** Why is the narrator, Suzette, surprised to see her mother?
3. **Clarify** Why doesn't Suzette go up to greet her mother?

terary Analysis

4. **Examine Characterization** How does Edwidge Danticat bring the mother's character to life? Using a character map like the one shown, record details from the story that describe the mother's appearance, beliefs and values, and actions.

Mother
Appearance | Beliefs and Values | Actions

5. **Examine Sequence** Review the sequence chart you made while reading. Under each square, note what Suzette seems to feel about her mother at that point in the story. In what way does Suzette's **perception** of her mother change from the beginning to the end of the story?
6. **Draw Conclusions** In the beginning of the story Suzette admits that she might not give up her seat on a bus to an older or pregnant woman. Yet by the story's end, she changes her mind. What do you think causes this change?
7. **Make Judgments** Reread lines 114–115. Do you think Suzette is ashamed of her mother? Why or why not? Support your answer with examples from the story.
8. **Evaluate Style** Choose a passage from the story that you think is a good example of Danticat's style. You may wish to look for a passage in which Danticat uses **imagery,** unique sentence structures, or **repetition.** Why did you pick the passage that you did?

tension and Challenge

9. **Readers' Circle** Should Suzette have approached her mother, and if so, what should she have said? Why do you think the mother never told Suzette about her trips to Manhattan? Discuss these questions with a small group.
10. **SOCIAL STUDIES CONNECTION** Although the action in "New York Day Women" occurs in Manhattan, Suzette and her mother actually live in Brooklyn. Research the people, landmarks, geography, and history of these two boroughs, and create a poster contrasting the two. Present your poster to your class.

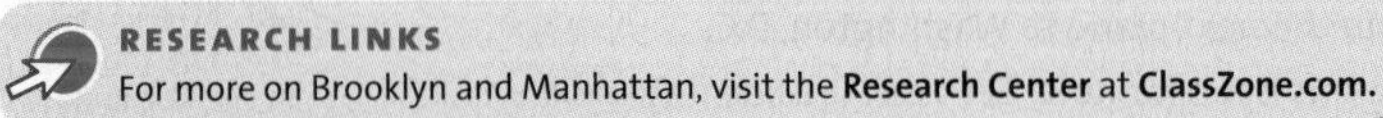
RESEARCH LINKS
For more on Brooklyn and Manhattan, visit the **Research Center** at **ClassZone.com.**

Practice and Apply

After Reading

For additional support of postreading questions, use these copy masters:

RESOURCE MANAGER—Copy Masters
Reading Check p. 34 (to check understanding of the selection)
Style p. 27 (for practice of literary analysis standards focus)
Question Support p. 35 (After Reading questions adapted for English learners and less-proficient readers)

Additional selection questions are provided for teachers on page 21.

ANSWERS

Comprehension

1. *She works as a day woman, a woman who is hired by the day to babysit for another woman's child.*
2. *Suzette believed that her mother never left Brooklyn.*
3. *Suzette is surprised by her mother's actions and wants to see where she is going.*

Literary Analysis

Possible answers:

4. ***Appearance:*** *wears a flowery dress; carries faux leather bag; has gapped teeth.* ***Beliefs and Values:*** *thinks daughter should give up her subway seat to those in need; wants to help her relatives in Haiti; does not believe skinny women are more attractive.* ***Actions:*** *walks down the street "with a happy gait"; watches the lottery drawing every night; buys soda for the child.*
5. **STANDARDS FOCUS Identify Sequence** *Suzette's feelings include the following: she is surprised that her mother is in the city; she is amazed at how well she handles crowds; she is afraid she will be hit by a bike; she thinks her mother does not understand her taste in clothing; she is surprised that her mother eats a hotdog; she sees that her mother is admired by the child; she sees that her mother enjoys talking with her friends. By the end of the story, Suzette has more respect for her mother.*
6. *Seeing her mother in a different light gives Suzette more respect for her mother's opinion.*
7. *Accept any answer that states a clear position and uses story examples to support that position.*
8. **STANDARDS FOCUS Style** *Accept any answer that cites a passage that conveys Danticat's style and provides a reason for choosing that passage.*

Extension and Challenge

9. *Students' discussions should support their opinion with evidence from the story.*
10. **SOCIAL STUDIES CONNECTION** *Students' posters should reflect the differences between the two boroughs found in their research.*

ANSWERS

Vocabulary in Context

VOCABULARY PRACTICE

1. *(b) consider*
2. *(a) fascinate*
3. *(c) chasing*
4. *(b) give up*
5. *(a) wrongdoing*

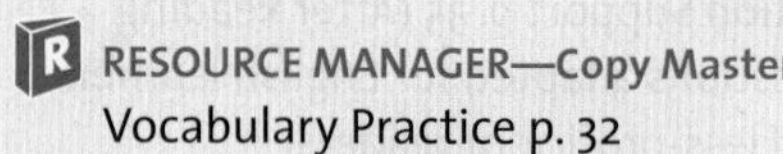

RESOURCE MANAGER—Copy Master
Vocabulary Practice p. 32

VOCABULARY IN WRITING

Suggest that students review the vocabulary words to see which ones could be used to describe what they might learn from following someone for a day.

VOCABULARY STRATEGY: MULTIPLE-MEANING WORDS *(also an EL language objective)*

Possible answers:

1. *jolts—"stops suddenly"; "motion"*
2. *complete cycle—"play one more"; "chess"*
3. *reserve—"a seat on the next plane"*
4. *postpone—"for now"; "put it aside until next week"*
5. *possible access—"open"; "opportunity"*

RESOURCE MANAGER—Copy Master
Vocabulary Strategy p. 33

Vocabulary Center at **ClassZone.com**
Additional Vocabulary Activities

Vocabulary in Context

VOCABULARY PRACTICE

Choose the letter of the word or phrase that means the same, or nearly the same, as the boldfaced word or phrase.

1. **contemplate** a decision: (a) disregard, (b) consider, (c) ignore, (d) avoid
2. **mesmerize** an audience: (a) fascinate, (b) bore, (c) puzzle, (d) disappoint
3. **pursuit** of a criminal: (a) arrest, (b) imprisonment, (c) chasing, (d) pardon
4. **surrender** her valuables: (a) purchase, (b) give up, (c) hide, (d) hold
5. a minor **offense:** (a) wrongdoing, (b) injury, (c) argument, (d) accomplishment

contemplate
mesmerize
offense
pursuit
surrender

VOCABULARY IN WRITING

What do you think you would learn if you followed someone you knew for a day? Write a paragraph explaining your answer. Use at least two vocabulary words in your paragraph. You could start this way.

EXAMPLE SENTENCE

As my mother enters the coffee shop, I ***contemplate*** *following her, but I decide to stay outside instead.*

VOCABULARY STRATEGY: MULTIPLE-MEANING WORDS

Many English words have more than one meaning. For example, you might know that *offense* is a term used in sports that means "those players whose primary responsibility it is to score." But you might not be familiar with its meaning in this selection: "a violation of a moral or social code."

If a word does not make sense to you, look at the words around it for clues to other possible meanings. For example:

My mother, who accuses me of random offenses as I dash out of the house.

Would the mother be more likely to accuse the narrator of a sports-related move, or of a moral or social mistake? Based on the context of the sentence, you can conclude that the second definition is correct. For further help with multiple-meaning words, check a dictionary.

PRACTICE Define the boldfaced words. Identify context clues that helped you understand the meaning of each.

1. The bus stops suddenly, and the motion **jerks** me out of a deep sleep.
2. Although we were tired, Michael and I decided to play one more **round** of chess.
3. Please **book** me a seat on the next plane to Washington, D.C.
4. I think we need to **table** this issue for now. Let's put it aside until next week.
5. These new circumstances open a **window** of opportunity for us.

VOCABULARY PRACTICE
For more practice, go to the **Vocabulary Center** at **ClassZone.com.**

DIFFERENTIATED INSTRUCTION

FOR ENGLISH LEARNERS

Vocabulary in Writing Ask students to write a sentence about each of these topics:

- something they have contemplated doing
- something that mesmerizes them
- something they are currently in pursuit of
- something they have surrendered in the last week
- an action or behavior that they consider an offense

FOR ADVANCED LEARNERS/PRE-AP

Vocabulary Strategy Challenge students to list words that have three or more meanings. Then have them switch lists with another student and provide the various definitions of the words.

eading-Writing Connection

Get to know the characters in "New York Day Women" better by responding to these prompts. Then complete the **Grammar and Writing** exercise.

WRITING PROMPTS	SELF-CHECK
A. Short Response: Write a Character Sketch What do you learn about Suzette as she pursues her mother? Make inferences about her age, appearance, occupation, and personality. Then write a **one-paragraph character sketch** of her.	***A thorough description will . . .*** • include details about Suzette's life and personality • cite specific details from the story that helped you make inferences about her
B. Extended Response: Write A Scene Imagine that Suzette tells her mother what she saw and how her **perceptions** of her mother have changed as a result of this experience. How does the mother respond? Is she upset? surprised? relieved? Write a **two- or three-paragraph scene** about the encounter.	***An engaging scene will . . .*** • be based on details about both characters • use words and phrases appropriate to each character

AMMAR AND WRITING

WRITE CONCISELY An **appositive** is a noun or pronoun that identifies or renames another noun or pronoun. An **appositive phrase** is made up of an appositive and its modifiers. You can make your writing more concise by using an appositive or appositive phrase to combine two sentences into one.

Original: The mother works in Manhattan. She is a native of Haiti.

Revised: The mother, a native of Haiti, works in Manhattan. (A native of Haiti *is an appositive phrase that identifies* mother.)

Place commas before and after an appositive phrase when it adds extra, nonessential information about the noun or pronoun that precedes it, as in the example above.

PRACTICE In each item, combine the two sentences by changing the second sentence to an appositive phrase.

1. Suzette works in Manhattan. She is a resident of Brooklyn.
2. Suzette doesn't give her subway seat to older passengers. She is the narrator.
3. The mother babysits children. She is a day woman.
4. The mother waits to cross the street. She is a patient woman.

For more help with appositive phrases, see page R61 in the ***Grammar Handbook.***

DIFFERENTIATED INSTRUCTION

FOR LESS–PROFICIENT WRITERS

For Prompt A:

1. Have students write sentences summarizing each aspect of their Character Map.
2. After students write an opening sentence that states their main idea, tell them to organize their supporting sentences to present a full description of Suzette. They may need to combine sentences or add transitions to make the text flow logically.

For Prompt B:

Students may want to organize their scenes in this way:

- **First paragraph:** Introduce the setting and the situation.
- **Second paragraph**: Focus on Suzette's confession and her mother's reaction.
- **Third paragraph:** Focus on the way Suzette's perception of her mother has changed.

Reading-Writing Connection

WRITING PROMPTS

- For **Prompt A,** encourage students to create a Character Map about Suzette based on what they recall from the story. Then suggest that they select the most interesting details for their paragraphs.

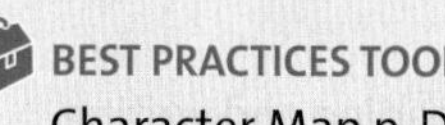

BEST PRACTICES TOOLKIT—Transparency
Character Map p. D8

- For **Prompt B,** suggest that students review the italicized text in the selection to help them write dialogue that reflects the mother's personality and values.

For writing support, see

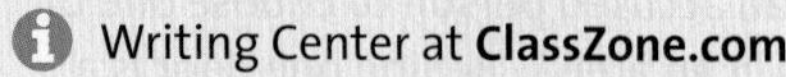

Writing Center at **ClassZone.com**

GRAMMAR AND WRITING

Explain that the second sentence in each item provides additional nonessential information about the subject of the first sentence. Because the information is not essential to the sentence, it should be set off by commas.

Answers:

1. *Suzette, a resident of Brooklyn, works in Manhattan.*
2. *Suzette, the narrator, doesn't give her subway seat to older passengers.*
3. *The mother, a day woman, babysits children.*
4. *The mother, a patient woman, waits to cross the street.*

RESOURCE MANAGER—Copy Master
Write Concisely p. 36

Assess and Reteach

Assess

RESOURCE MANAGER—Copy Masters
Selection Tests A, B/C pp. 39–40, 41–42

Test Generator CD

Reteach

STANDARDS LESSON FILE
Literature Lesson 40: Style
Reading Lesson 6: Recognizing Sequence and Chronological Order
Vocabulary Lesson 19: Multiple-Meaning Words

Focus and Motivate

OBJECTIVES

Literary Analysis
- explore the key idea of **decisions**
- identify and analyze tone
- read a short story

Reading
- paraphrase

Vocabulary
- build vocabulary for reading and writing
- understand connotative and denotative meanings of words *(also an EL language objective)*

SUMMARY

A king dispenses a barbaric form of justice by requiring an accused person to choose one of two doors in an arena. Behind one door is a tiger who will maul the person to death, and behind the other is a beautiful lady who will marry him. When the king discovers that a commoner loves his daughter, he punishes him in the arena. The princess knows what is behind each door, and she signals her lover which door to choose. The story leaves readers to decide what is behind that door.

How do you make DECISIONS?

Discuss the question. To lead into the ***KEY IDEA,*** discuss the kinds of **decisions** students might have to make. Which are most important? As groups work on the ***SURVEY*** activity, ask students how they might combine decision-making methods to help them make an especially difficult choice.

Before Reading

The Lady, or the Tiger?

Short Story by Frank R. Stockton

How do you make DECISIONS?

KEY IDEA How we make **decisions** depends on the situation. A simple coin toss can help you decide who goes first when playing a video game. But you wouldn't want to flip a coin when making a more important choice, such as which sport to play or which high school to attend. In the story you are about to read, a decision has life-or-death consequences.

SURVEY Working with a small group, create a list of ways people commonly make decisions. Survey the class to learn how others choose what course to follow. Add more methods to the list as people mention them. What methods come up most often? Which do you think are most effective?

How Do You Make Decisions?	
List Pros and Cons	//
Talk to Parents	////

682

Selection Resources

RESOURCE MANAGER UNIT 6

Plan and Teach pp. 43–50

Literary Analysis
Summary pp. 51†*, 52‡*
Tone pp. 53, 54†*
Question Support p. 61*

Reading
Paraphrase pp. 55, 56†*
Reading Check p. 60
Reading Fluency p. 62

Vocabulary
Study p. 57*
Practice p. 58
Strategy p. 59

Assessment
Selection Tests A, B/C pp. 63*, 65*
Test Generator CD

BEST PRACTICES TOOLKIT

Differentiated Instruction pp. 31–38*

Scaffolding Instruction pp. 43–46*

Graphic Organizers/Strategies
Personal Word List • New Word Analysis • Linear Array • T Chart • Sentence Imitation • Setting Diagram

Reading Support
Audio Anthology CD*

Technology
Literature and Vocabulary Centers at **ClassZone.com**
Write*Smart* CD

* Resources for Differentiation † Also in Spanish ‡ In Haitian Creole and Vietnamese

ERARY ANALYSIS: TONE

Writers often express an attitude, or **tone,** toward the subject, setting, or characters they're writing about. A tone can often be described with one word, such as angry, proud, or playful. Just as knowing a friend's attitude can help you decide whether she's serious or joking, knowing a writer's tone can help you grasp his or her message. To help you determine Frank R. Stockton's tone, pay attention to the words and details he uses to describe

- the **characters—**Do his descriptions of them suggest whether he thinks they're smart or foolish, kind or cruel?
- the **setting—**Does he admire the society's customs?
- the **plot events—**Does his language show that he takes the events seriously, or not?

ADING STRATEGY: PARAPHRASE

One good way to understand and remember what you read is to **paraphrase** it, or restate the writer's language in your own words. To paraphrase, follow these steps:

- Reread the passage, looking for the main ideas.
- Define unfamiliar words using context clues or a dictionary.
- Restate important ideas and details in your own words. A good paraphrase should be about as long as the original text.

As you read, paraphrase difficult sections in your notebook.

Line Numbers	*Paraphrase*
1–4	*Long ago, there lived a rough, cruel king. He had been influenced by forward-thinking cultures, but he was still uncivilized.*

CABULARY IN CONTEXT

The following words help reveal Stockton's opinion of his characters. How many do you know? Make a chart like the one shown, putting each word in the appropriate column.

WORD LIST			
	anguished	conventional	progressiveness
	aspire	devious	subordinate
	assert	impartial	waver

Know Well	*Think I Know*	*Don't Know at All*

Author Online

Full of Fairy Tales

Frank R. Stockton
1834–1902

Though today Frank R. Stockton's most popular story is "The Lady, or the Tiger?" many of his other works were widely read during his lifetime. Born near Philadelphia, Pennsylvania, Stockton began writing fairy tales as a child, later claiming that he did so because "my mind was full of them."

Literary Sensation While still in high school, Stockton won a short story contest sponsored by a magazine. Later on in life, Stockton wrote stories for both adults and children. "The Lady, or the Tiger?" caused a sensation among the American public. The ending was debated in high schools, and Stockton received hundreds of letters from people seeking the solution. Unfortunately, Stockton did not like the story as much as his readers did; he felt it did not represent his best work.

MORE ABOUT THE AUTHOR
For more on Frank R. Stockton, visit the **Literature Center** at **ClassZone.com.**

Background

Historic Arena Much of the action in "The Lady, or the Tiger?" takes place in an amphitheater. One of the most famous amphitheaters in history is the Colosseum, built during the Roman empire in the year A.D. 72. Capable of seating 50,000 people, this massive structure featured three levels of seating, wood floors, and an innovative canvas roof that brought in cool air from the outside. The Colosseum was the scene of gruesome "games" involving slaves, prisoners, or animals fighting gladiators (professionally trained swordsmen) to the death. Although lightning and earthquakes destroyed large parts of the Colosseum over the years, much of it still stands today.

Teach

STANDARDS FOCUS

LITERARY ANALYSIS

● TONE

Read aloud this example:

> Learning to tie your shoes wasn't too difficult, was it? You'd think you could learn to clean your room once in a while!

Ask students to describe the author's tone in these sentences. ***Possible answer:*** *The tone is critical and sarcastic.*

CHECK UNDERSTANDING Have students identify clues in the sentences that suggest the tone.

READING STRATEGY

■ PARAPHRASE

Have students paraphrase the three paragraphs under **Author Online** on page 683. Remind them to identify main ideas and supporting details.

CHECK UNDERSTANDING Ask students to give examples of texts (such as scientific articles and poems with antiquated syntax) in which paraphrasing would be especially useful for improving comprehension.

RESOURCE MANAGER—Copy Master
Paraphrase p. 55 (for student use while reading the selection)

VOCABULARY SKILL

▲ VOCABULARY IN CONTEXT

DIAGNOSE WORD KNOWLEDGE To determine preteaching needs, have all students complete **Vocabulary in Context.** *Students should review the words and place them in the appropriate columns.*

PRETEACH VOCABULARY Use the Vocabulary Study copy master to help students use context clues to predict the meaning of each boldfaced word.

1. Read item 1 aloud, emphasizing the boldfaced word *anguished.*
2. Point out the words *unlucky, wailing,* and *mourned.* Elicit possible meanings for *anguished,* such as "distressed."
3. Have students record the predicted meaning in column 2 of the chart.
4. Repeat the procedure for items 2–9.
5. Have students fill in column 3 of their charts after reading the story.

RESOURCE MANAGER—Copy Master
Vocabulary Study p. 57

For general guidelines on differentiating vocabulary instruction and for alternative vocabulary activities for students not needing vocabulary preteaching, see

BEST PRACTICES TOOLKIT
Scaffolding Vocabulary Instruction pp. 43–46

Vocabulary Center at **ClassZone.com**

Practice and Apply

Lines 1–12

REINFORCE *KEY IDEA:* DECISIONS

Discuss Do you think the king has trouble making **decisions?** Why or why not? ***Possible answer:*** *The king does not have trouble making decisions. He is so arrogant that he does not consult anyone but himself.*

LITERARY ANALYSIS

Ⓐ TONE

Possible answer: *Terms such as "semi-barbaric," "florid," "untrammeled," "exuberant fancy," and "bland" suggest that the author does not have much respect for the king; in fact, he seems to find him ridiculous.*

ANALYZE VISUALS

Possible answer: *The grand buildings suggest that the kingdom is wealthy. Its people seem to enjoy celebrations and lively public events.*

About the Art Lawrence Alma-Tadema (1836–1912) was a Dutch-born British artist who specialized in elegant scenes of everyday life in ancient Greece and Rome. He is noted for his precise images, which are similar to photographs. This painting depicts a procession of women and children carrying flowers while enthusiastic spectators cheer from above.

The Lady, or the Tiger?

Frank R. Stockton

In the very olden time, there lived a semi-barbaric king, whose ideas, though somewhat polished and sharpened by the **progressiveness** of distant Latin neighbors, were still large, florid,[1] and untrammeled,[2] as became the half of him which was barbaric.[3] He was a man of exuberant fancy, and, withal, of an authority so irresistible that, at his will, he turned his varied fancies into facts. He was greatly given to self-communing;[4] and, when he and himself agreed upon anything, the thing was done. When every member of his domestic and political systems moved smoothly in its appointed course, his nature was bland and genial; but whenever there was a little hitch, and some of his orbs got out of their orbits, he was blander and more genial still, for nothing pleased him so much as to make the crooked straight, and crush down uneven places. Ⓐ

Among the borrowed notions by which his barbarism had become semifixed was that of the public arena, in which, by exhibitions of manly and beastly valor, the minds of his subjects were refined and cultured.

progressiveness (prə-grĕs'ĭv-nĭs) *n.* the state of advancing towa[rd] better conditions or nev[w] policies, ideas, or metho[ds]

Ⓐ TONE

Based on the words he uses to describe the kin[g], how do you think Stock[ton] feels about this characte[r]?

ANALYZE VISUALS

What do the details in this painting help you **infer** about the kingdom and its people?

1. **florid** (flôr'ĭd): very ornate; flowery.
2. **untrammeled** (ŭn-trăm'əld): not limited or restricted.
3. **barbaric** (bär-bâr'ĭk): marked by crudeness or lack of restraint in taste, style, or manner.
4. **self-communing:** the act of "talking" things over with oneself only.

Spring (1894), Lawrence Alma-Tadema. Oi[l on] canvas, 70¼" × 31½". The J. Paul Getty Muse[um], Los Angeles. (72.PA.3). © J. Paul Getty Tr[ust]

DIFFERENTIATED INSTRUCTION

FOR ALL STUDENTS

Enhance Learning Styles Provide independent projects for various learning styles.

- **Linguistic** Write another ending to the story.
- **Visual** Create a storyboard for a film.
- **Interpersonal** Discuss moral dilemmas.

For further details on these projects, see

RESOURCE MANAGER

Ideas for Extension pp. 48–49

FOR LESS–PROFICIENT READERS

In combination with the *Audio Anthology CD*, use one or more Targeted Passages (pp. 686, 688, 689, 691) to ensure that students focus on key events, concepts, and skills.

Vocabulary Support The story is filled with challenging vocabulary. As students read, encourage them to add new words to a Personal Word List.

BEST PRACTICES TOOLKIT

Personal Word List p. E2

BACKGROUND

Roman Law In line 3, Stockton refers to the king's "distant Latin neighbors." This is probably a reference to Latin-speaking Rome, which grew from a small settlement in present-day Italy in 753 B.C. to a powerful empire that controlled all the lands bordering the Mediterranean Sea by A.D. 100. The "barbaric" games in the Roman amphitheaters included the spectacles of captives, slaves, and gladiators fighting to the death and, as in this story, condemned criminals being killed by wild animals.

The "progressiveness" (line 2) of these same Latin neighbors included the development of legal systems and governmental institutions that influenced the development of modern societies. In some ways, however, the Roman legal system was not especially enlightened. Accused persons had few protections. For example, if they refused to confess, they could be kept in jail for a long time, perhaps indefinitely, and could also be tortured.

FOR ENGLISH LEARNERS

Comprehension Support [mixed-readiness pairs] Stockton uses complex syntax and wordy descriptions. To help students become familiar with his style, have pairs study the first paragraph together. They might look up difficult vocabulary, experiment with syntax, invert words, and move parts of sentences around to clarify meaning. Suggest they use the same strategies as they continue to read.

Key Academic Vocabulary Have students use New Word Analysis to study *tradition* (line 30), *element* (lines 75, 159), *community* (line 77), *selected* (lines 98, 140), *intense* (line 123), and *presume* (line 204).

BEST PRACTICES TOOLKIT—Transparency
New Word Analysis p. E8

Prereading For prereading instruction for English learners, see

BEST PRACTICES TOOLKIT
Scaffolding Reading Instruction pp. 43–46

FOR ADVANCED LEARNERS/PRE–AP

Pre-AP exercises in the bottom channel provide additional challenge for your advanced students. Use them for small groups or individuals.

ADDITIONAL GUIDELINES

For more help with differentiation and tips for classroom management, see

BEST PRACTICES TOOLKIT
Differentiated Instruction pp. 31–38

BACKGROUND

Ruins of amphitheaters can be found all over the former Roman Empire. Studying the ruins has helped archaeologists learn more about the ancient civilization. The largest of the Roman amphitheaters is the Colosseum, which once held up to 50,000 people and remains a popular tourist attraction today.

READING STRATEGY

B PARAPHRASE

Have students record their answers in the chart from page 683. ***Possible answer:*** *When a subject was accused of a crime, that person's fate would be decided in a public arena. Although the king borrowed the design of the arena, he invented its unique purpose. Above all else, the king preferred to be amused rather than follow tradition, and he tried to expand his barbaric thoughts and ideals.*

But even here the exuberant and barbaric fancy **asserted** itself. The arena of the king was built, not to give the people an opportunity of hearing the rhapsodies of dying gladiators, nor to enable them to view the inevitable conclusion of a conflict between religious opinions and hungry jaws, but for purposes far better adapted to widen and develop the mental energies of the people. This vast amphitheater, with its encircling galleries, its mysterious vaults, and its unseen passages, was an agent of poetic justice, in which crime was punished, or virtue rewarded, by the decrees of an impartial and incorruptible chance.

When a subject was accused of a crime of sufficient importance to interest the king, public notice was given that on an appointed day the fate of the accused person would be decided in the king's arena—a structure which well deserved its name; for, although its form and plan were borrowed from afar, its purpose emanated solely from the brain of this man, who, every barleycorn a king,[5] knew no tradition to which he owed more allegiance than pleased his fancy, and who ingrafted on every adopted form of human thought and action the rich growth of his barbaric idealism. **B**

When all the people had assembled in the galleries and the king, surrounded by his court, sat high up on his throne of royal state on one side of the arena, he gave a signal, a door beneath him opened, and the accused subject stepped out into the amphitheater. Directly opposite him, on the other side of the enclosed space, were two doors, exactly alike and side by side. It was the duty and the privilege of the person on trial to walk directly to these doors and open one of them. He could open either door he pleased; he was subject to no guidance or influence but that of the aforementioned **impartial** and incorruptible chance. If he opened the one, there came out of it a hungry tiger, the fiercest and most cruel that could be procured, which immediately sprang upon him and tore him to pieces, as a punishment for his guilt. The moment that the case of the criminal was thus decided, doleful iron bells were clanged, great wails went up from the hired mourners posted on the outer rim of the arena, and the vast audience, with bowed heads and downcast hearts, wended slowly their homeward way, mourning greatly that one so young and fair, or so old and respected, should have merited so dire a fate.

But if the accused person opened the other door, there came forth from it a lady, the most suitable to his years and station that his majesty could select among his fair subjects; and to this lady he was immediately married, as a reward for his innocence. It mattered not that he might already possess a wife and family, or that his affections might be engaged upon an object of his own selection: the king allowed no such **subordinate** arrangements to interfere with his great scheme of retribution and reward. The exercises, as in the other instance, took place immediately and in the arena. Another door opened beneath the king, and a priest, followed by a band of choristers

assert (ə-sûrt') *v.* to ac[t] forcefully; to take char[ge]

VISUAL VOCABULA[RY]

amphitheater (ăm'fə-thē'ə-tər) *n.* an arena where contests a[nd] spectacles are held

B PARAPHRASE Reread lines 25–32. Paraphrase this passag[e]. Was the amphitheater used in the same way i[n] this kingdom as it was elsewhere? Explain.

impartial (ĭm-pär'shəl) *adj.* not partial or biase[d]; unprejudiced

① Targeted Passage

subordinate (sə-bôr'dn-ĭt) *adj.* secondary; belonging to a lower rank

5. **every barleycorn a king:** a playful exaggeration of the expression "every ounce a king," meaning "thoroughly kingly." (Grains of barley were formerly used as units of measurement.)

DIFFERENTIATED INSTRUCTION

FOR LESS–PROFICIENT READERS

① Targeted Passage [Lines 25–52]

This passage describes the setting and explains the king's system of justice.

- Why would a person be brought to the king's arena?
- What choice must an accused person make?
- What is behind each door?
- What do the king and the other spectators conclude about the accused person based on which door he chooses?

FOR ENGLISH LEARNERS

Visual Vocabulary Make sure students understand that an amphitheater is a round structure with tiers of seats rising upward from an arena where some kind of spectacle or entertainment takes place. Discuss contemporary amphitheaters and arenas with which students may be familiar, such as stadiums and outdoor theaters.

and dancing maidens blowing joyous airs on golden horns and treading an epithalamic measure,[6] advanced to where the pair stood, side by side; and the wedding was promptly and cheerily solemnized.[7] Then the gay brass bells rang forth their merry peals, the people shouted glad hurrahs, and the innocent man, preceded by children strewing flowers on his path, led his bride to his home.

This was the king's semi-barbaric method of administering justice. Its perfect fairness is obvious. The criminal could not know out of which door would come the lady: he opened either he pleased, without having the slightest idea whether, in the next instant, he was to be devoured or married. On some occasions the tiger came out of one door and on some out of the other. The decisions of this tribunal[8] were not only fair, they were positively determinate: the accused person was instantly punished if he found himself guilty; and, if innocent, he was rewarded on the spot, whether he liked it or not. There was no escape from the judgments of the king's arena. **C**

C PARAPHRASE
Reread lines 64–72. How would you explain the king's "perfect" system of justice? Add this to your notebook.

6. **treading an epithalamic** (ĕp′ə-thə-lā′mĭk) **measure:** dancing to wedding music.
7. **solemnized** (sŏl′əm-nīzd′): celebrated or observed with dignity.
8. **tribunal** (trī-byo͞o′nəl): something that has the power to determine guilt or innocence.

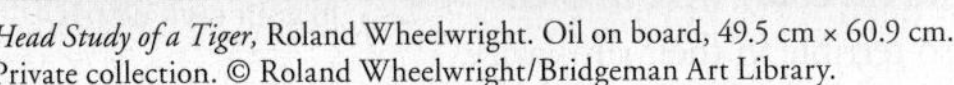

Head Study of a Tiger, Roland Wheelwright. Oil on board, 49.5 cm × 60.9 cm. Private collection. © Roland Wheelwright/Bridgeman Art Library.

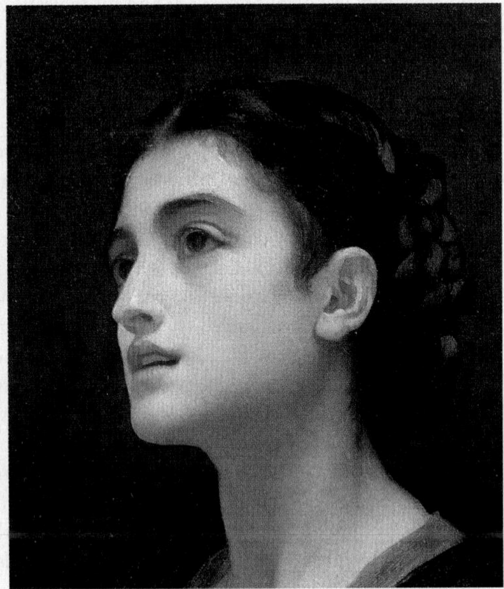

Detail of *Study of a Lady,* Frederic Leighton. Oil on canvas, 25.5 cm × 19 cm. Private collection. © Bridgeman Art Library.

READING STRATEGY

C PARAPHRASE

Have students record their answers in the chart from page 683. ***Possible answer:*** *The king's method of dispensing justice was fair. The accused was perfectly free to choose one door or the other. If he chose the door with a tiger, he was devoured and proven guilty. If he chose the door with the maiden, he would be declared innocent and be wedded to her instantly as a reward. The king's system is "perfect" because justice is swift, absolute, and the accused's choice.*

ANALYZE VISUALS

About the Art Roland Wheelwright (1870–1955) was born in Australia but moved to England when he was very young. He is well known for illustrating children's books and for his paintings of historical subjects, many of which included horses. He also illustrated the work of several writers, including Charles Dickens and Sir Walter Scott.

English painter Frederic Leighton (1830–1896) was interested in biblical and mythological subjects. He was extremely popular during his lifetime, so much so that Queen Victoria bought one of his paintings.

Activity Do the expressions of the tiger and the lady correspond with their description in the story? Support your response with evidence from the story. ***Possible answer:*** *The tiger in the painting looks alert but calm, unlike the "fiercest and most cruel" beast described in lines 41–42. The lady in the painting more closely resembles "the woman who blushed and trembled" behind the other door (line 150).*

FOR ENGLISH LEARNERS

Vocabulary Support [mixed-readiness pairs] Have pairs of students complete a Linear Array for some or all of these words from pages 686–687: *vast* (line 21), *cruel* (line 42), *innocence* (line 52), *joyous* (line 58), *shouted* (line 61). Encourage students to use a dictionary or thesaurus to help them as needed.

BEST PRACTICES TOOLKIT—Transparency
Linear Array p. E7

Vocabulary: Word Associations [mixed-readiness pairs] Have pairs of students use context clues to figure out the meanings of these word combinations:

- *downcast hearts* (line 46), "sad feelings"
- *subordinate arrangements* (line 54), "lesser plans"
- *blowing joyous airs* (line 58), "playing happy songs"
- *positively determinate* (lines 69–70), "unable to be changed"

Lines 80–109
DISCUSSION PROMPTS

Use these prompts to help students understand the characters and the rising action:

Recall In what way is the king's daughter like her father? ***Answer:*** *She is emotional, overbearing, and somewhat barbaric.*

Infer What can you infer about the king's character based on his reaction to learning that his daughter loves a commoner? ***Possible answer:*** *The king is intolerant, inflexible, and vengeful. He is also cruel, not caring about his daughter's feelings.*

Speculate Which do you think the king loves more—his daughter or his system of justice? ***Possible answer:*** *The king loves his system of justice more because he ignores his daughter's feelings and looks forward to being entertained.*

LITERARY ANALYSIS

(D) TONE

Possible answer: *Though Stockton says this was the first case in which a commoner had ever dared to love a royal person, he also calls the romance "conventional." This story line is familiar from the oldest of tales.*

If students need help . . . Ask them whether Stockton's statement that "never before had a subject dared to love the daughter of a king" is literally true.

READING STRATEGY

(E) PARAPHRASE

Have students record their answers in the chart from page 683. ***Possible answer:*** *Everyone knew that the young man had loved the princess. However, this fact did not interfere with the king's plan to implement his favorite system of justice. No matter what happened to the young man, he would no longer be a problem for the king. The king would enjoy watching and finding out whether the young man's love for his daughter was right or wrong.*

The institution was a very popular one. When the people gathered together on one of the great trial days, they never knew whether they were to witness a bloody slaughter or a hilarious wedding. This element of uncertainty lent an interest to the occasion which it could not otherwise have attained. Thus, the masses were entertained and pleased, and the thinking part of the community could bring no charge of unfairness against this plan; for did not the accused person have the whole matter in his own hands?

(2) **Targeted Passage**

This semi-barbaric king had a daughter as blooming as his most florid fancies, and with a soul as fervent[9] and imperious[10] as his own. As is usual in such cases, she was the apple of his eye and was loved by him above all humanity. Among his courtiers was a young man of that fineness of blood and lowness of station common to the **conventional** heroes of romance who love royal maidens. This royal maiden was well satisfied with her lover, for he was handsome and brave to a degree unsurpassed in all this kingdom; and she loved him with an ardor that had enough of barbarism in it to make it exceedingly warm and strong. This love affair moved on happily for many months, until one day the king happened to discover its existence. He did not hesitate nor **waver** in regard to his duty in the premises. The youth was immediately cast into prison, and a day was appointed for his trial in the king's arena. This, of course, was an especially important occasion; and his majesty, as well as all the people, was greatly interested in the workings and development of this trial. Never before had such a case occurred; never before had a subject dared to love the daughter of a king. In after-years such things became commonplace enough, but then they were, in no slight degree, novel and startling. (D)

conventional (kən-vĕn'shə-nəl) *adj.* conforming to establis[hed] practice or accepted standards; traditional

waver (wā'vər) *v.* to exhibit indecision; to hesitate

The tiger-cages of the kingdom were searched for the most savage and relentless beasts, from which the fiercest monster might be selected for the arena; and the ranks of maiden youth and beauty throughout the land were carefully surveyed by competent judges, in order that the young man might have a fitting bride in case fate did not determine for him a different destiny. Of course, everybody knew that the deed with which the accused was charged had been done. He had loved the princess, and neither he, she, nor any one else thought of denying the fact; but the king would not think of allowing any fact of this kind to interfere with the workings of the tribunal, in which he took such great delight and satisfaction. No matter how the affair turned out, the youth would be disposed of; and the king would take an aesthetic[11] pleasure in watching the course of events, which would determine whether or not the young man had done wrong in allowing himself to love the princess. (E)

(D) TONE
Reread lines 91–96. Stockton describes the citizens as being "grea[tly] interested" in the "nov[el] and startling" events that are unfolding. In what way might this description be **ironic,** stating the opposite of what Stockton believes

(E) PARAPHRASE
Reread lines 102–109. What is the young man['s] fate? Rewrite this pass[age] in your own words.

The appointed day arrived. From far and near the people gathered, and thronged the great galleries of the arena, and crowds, unable to gain admittance, massed themselves against its outside walls. The king and his court were in their places, opposite the twin doors,—those fateful portals, so terrible in their similarity.

9. **fervent** (fûr'vənt): having or showing great emotion or zeal.
10. **imperious** (ĭm-pîr'ē-əs): arrogantly domineering or overbearing.
11. **aesthetic** (ĕs-thĕt'ĭk): concerning the artistic appreciation of beauty.

DIFFERENTIATED INSTRUCTION

FOR LESS–PROFICIENT READERS

(2) **Targeted Passage [Lines 80–96]**

This passage gives details of the story's main characters and rising action.

- What is the king's daughter like?
- Who does the king's daughter love? What kind of person is he?
- What does the king do when he finds out about the love affair?

FOR ENGLISH LEARNERS

Vocabulary: Cognates [shared-language groups] Have groups scan the selection for cognates. Spanish cognates on this page include

- *barbarism/barbarismo* (line 87)
- *prison/prisión* (line 90)
- *majesty/majestad* (line 92)
- *savage/salvaje* (line 97)
- *judges/juezes* (line 100)
- *destiny/destino* (line 101)
- *portals/portales* (line 113)

All was ready. The signal was given. A door beneath the royal party opened, and the lover of the princess walked into the arena. Tall, beautiful, fair, his appearance was greeted with a low hum of admiration and anxiety. Half the audience had not known so grand a youth had lived among them. No wonder the princess loved him! What a terrible thing for him to be there!

As the youth advanced into the arena, he turned, as the custom was, to bow to the king: but he did not think at all of that royal personage; his eyes were fixed upon the princess, who sat to the right of her father. Had it not been for the moiety[12] of barbarism in her nature, it is probable that lady would not have been there; but her intense and fervid[13] soul would not allow her to be absent on an occasion in which she was so terribly interested. From the moment that the decree had gone forth, that her lover should decide his fate in the king's arena, she had thought of nothing, night or day, but this great event and the various subjects connected with it. Possessed of more power, influence, and force of character than any one who had ever before been interested in such a case, she had done what no other person had done—she had possessed herself of the secret of the doors. She knew in which of the two rooms, that lay behind those doors, stood the cage of the tiger, with its open front, and in which waited the lady. Through these thick doors, heavily curtained with skins on the inside, it was impossible that any noise or suggestion should come from within to the person who should approach to raise the latch of one of them; but gold, and the power of a woman's will, had brought the secret to the princess. F

And not only did she know in which room stood the lady ready to emerge, all blushing and radiant, should her door be opened, but she knew who the lady was. It was one of the fairest and loveliest of the damsels of the court who had been selected as the reward of the accused youth, should he be proved innocent of the crime of **aspiring** to one so far above him; and the princess hated her. Often had she seen, or imagined that she had seen, this fair creature throwing glances of admiration upon the person of her lover, and sometimes she thought these glances were perceived and even returned. Now and then she had seen them talking together; it was but for a moment or two, but much can be said in a brief space; it may have been on most unimportant topics, but how could she know that? The girl was lovely, but she had dared to raise her eyes to the loved one of the princess; and, with all the intensity of the savage blood transmitted to her through long lines of wholly barbaric ancestors, she hated the woman who blushed and trembled behind that silent door. G

When her lover turned and looked at her, and his eyes met hers as she sat there paler and whiter than anyone in the vast ocean of anxious faces about her, he saw, by that power of quick perception which is given to those whose souls are one, that she knew behind which door crouched the tiger, and behind

F TONE
Reread lines 119–136. What is Stockton's attitude toward the princess? Tell what words and details in the passage reveal this attitude.

aspire (ə-spīr') *v.* to have a great ambition or an ultimate goal; to desire strongly

3 Targeted Passage

G TONE
Stockton frequently refers to barbarism in this story. What does this reveal about his attitude toward the characters?

12. **moiety** (moi'ĭ-tē): a portion.
13. **fervid** (fûr'vĭd): passionate.

LITERARY ANALYSIS

F TONE

Possible answer: *The words "barbarism," "intense and fervid," and "force of character," along with the fact that she attends the occasion and uses her power and influence to find out what is behind each door, reveal that Stockton thinks the princess is dangerous and possibly unstable. At the same time, he gives her credit for having uncommon determination and strength.*

LITERARY ANALYSIS

G TONE

Possible answer: *The word* barbaric *describes a passionate and rash person who is neither reasonable nor moral. It is used to describe both the king and his daughter. The word has a negative connotation, suggesting that Stockton has contempt for these characters.*

Lines 114–151
DISCUSSION PROMPTS

Use these prompts to help students understand the turning point of the story:

Recall What is the audience's reaction to the young man when he enters the arena? ***Answer:*** *They admire his beauty and feel anxious about his fate.*

Infer Stockton tells the reader that the princess hates the lady behind the door. In what way might this affect her feelings about the outcome of the trial? ***Possible answer:*** *The princess might prefer to see her lover dead than married to a woman she hates.*

Evaluate The king is certain that the young man will be "disposed of" regardless of which door he chooses. Do you share the king's certainty at this point in the story? What twists and turns in the plot might surprise the king? *Students may say that they do share the king's certainty, because either the princess's lover will be devoured, or married off—either way, he will not be with the princess. But students may also note that the princess could beg her father to let her marry him, if he was not devoured. The princess could also run away with her lover, or threaten her father in some way.*

FOR LESS–PROFICIENT READERS

3 Targeted Passage [Lines 127–151]

This passage describes complications in the plot: the princess knows what lies behind each door and the identity of the lady.

- What information does the princess have?
- Who is the lady standing behind the door?
- What are the princess's feelings about this lady? Why does she feel this way?

Reading Strategy Follow-Up: Paraphrase
[paired option] Have students reread lines 137–151, and then ask them to work in pairs to paraphrase this passage. Remind them to note main ideas and to look up definitions of difficult vocabulary words in a dictionary. Have students fill in the chart from page 683 with their paraphrase of the passage. Remind them to add to their chart as they continue reading.

which stood the lady. He had expected her to know it. He understood her nature, and his soul was assured that she would never rest until she had made plain to herself this thing, hidden to all other lookers-on, even to the king. The only hope for the youth in which there was any element of certainty was based upon the success of the princess in discovering this mystery; and the moment he looked upon her, he saw she had succeeded, as in his soul he knew she would succeed.

Then it was that his quick and anxious glance asked the question: "Which?" It was as plain to her as if he shouted it from where he stood. There was not an instant to be lost. The question was asked in a flash; it must be answered in another.

Cleopatra (about 1888), John W. Waterhouse. Oil on canvas, 65.4 cm × 56.8 cm. © 2002 Christie's Images Limited.

ANALYZE VISUALS
Does the person in thi painting match your ic of the princess in the story? Explain why or why not.

ANALYZE VISUALS

Students who think the princess in the painting and the one in the story are alike will probably cite the woman's expression, posture, and the dark shadows covering her eyes, which can be interpreted as sullen and somewhat threatening. Her right hand is also positioned in a way that would allow her to signal to her lover.

About the Art John William Waterhouse (1849–1917) was born in Rome but spent most of his life in London. Early in his career, he painted works based on classical themes. In later years, he was influenced by a popular Pre-Raphaelite theme—that of the "femme fatale," a woman who is considered to be dangerously seductive. This painting of Cleopatra was commissioned in 1887 by a London weekly for an exhibit of paintings of women in Shakespeare's plays.

DIFFERENTIATED INSTRUCTION

FOR LESS–PROFICIENT READERS

Concept Support Have students reread lines 137–151 and 182–197. Then have them complete two T Charts listing the benefits and drawbacks of each choice the princess is considering. Encourage them to discuss their lists with a partner, exploring whether or not there might be additional factors that are not explicitly stated in the story.

 **BEST PRACTICES TOOLKIT—Transparency**
T Chart p. A25

FOR ADVANCED LEARNERS/PRE–AP

Analyze Style Use the Sentence Imitation strategy to help students improve their writing. Begin by reading aloud lines 182–184 and 196–197. Point out the syntax of the two sentences, and model writing sentences using similar syntax. Then ask students to write sentences about a difficult decision they or someone else has made, imitating Stockton's style.

 **BEST PRACTICES TOOLKIT**
Sentence Imitation p. C2

Her right arm lay on the cushioned parapet[14] before her. She raised her hand and made a slight, quick movement toward the right. No one but her lover saw her. Every eye but his was fixed on the man in the arena.

He turned, and with a firm and rapid step he walked across the empty space. Every heart stopped beating, every breath was held, every eye was fixed immovably upon that man. Without the slightest hesitation, he went to the door on the right and opened it.

④ Targeted Passage

Now, the point of the story is this: Did the tiger come out of that door, or did the lady?

The more we reflect upon this question, the harder it is to answer. It involves a study of the human heart which leads us through **devious** mazes of passion, out of which it is difficult to find our way. Think of it, fair reader, not as if the decision of the question depended upon yourself, but upon that hot-blooded, semi-barbaric princess, her soul at a white heat beneath the combined fires of despair and jealousy. She had lost him, but who should have him? H

devious (dē′vē-əs) *adj.* departing from the straight or direct course

H **PARAPHRASE**
Reread lines 176–181. What is Stockton saying to his readers? Paraphrase this passage in your notebook.

How often, in her waking hours and in her dreams, had she started in wild horror, and covered her face with her hands as she thought of her lover opening the door on the other side of which waited the cruel fangs of the tiger!

But how much oftener had she seen him at the other door! How in her grievous reveries[15] had she gnashed her teeth, and torn her hair, when she saw his start of rapturous[16] delight as he opened the door of the lady! How her soul had burned in agony when she had seen him rush to meet that woman, with her flushing cheek and sparkling eye of triumph; when she had seen him lead her forth, his whole frame kindled with the joy of recovered life; when she had heard the glad shouts from the multitude, and the wild ringing of the happy bells; when she had seen the priest, with his joyous followers, advance to the couple, and make them man and wife before her very eyes; and when she had seen them walk away together upon their path of flowers, followed by the tremendous shouts of the hilarious multitude, in which her one despairing shriek was lost and drowned!

Would it not be better for him to die at once, and go to wait for her in the blessed regions of semi-barbaric futurity?

And yet, that awful tiger, those shrieks, that blood!

Her decision had been indicated in an instant, but it had been made after days and nights of **anguished** deliberation. She had known she would be asked, she had decided what she would answer, and, without the slightest hesitation, she had moved her hand to the right.

anguished (ăng′gwĭsht) *adj.* tormented; distressed

The question of her decision is one not to be lightly considered, and it is not for me to presume to set myself up as the one person able to answer it. And so I leave it with all of you: Which came out of the opened door—the lady, or the tiger?

14. **parapet** (păr′ə-pĭt): a low railing at the edge of a balcony.
15. **reveries** (rĕv′ə-rēz): daydreams.
16. **rapturous** (răp′chər-əs): filled with great joy; ecstatic.

FOR LESS-PROFICIENT READERS

④ **Targeted Passage [Lines 167–206]**

This passage contains the story's surprise ending: there is no resolution to the plot.

- What door does the princess's lover open? Why does he choose that door?
- What does the author ask readers to do?
- What problem did the princess face?
- What decision do you think the princess made? Why do you think so?

FOR ADVANCED LEARNERS/PRE-AP

Synthesize [paired option] Have students work with a partner to design sets for a dramatization of the story. Suggest that they use the illustrations to gather information about the architecture in the time period in which the story takes place and the Setting Diagram to organize their ideas.

BEST PRACTICES TOOLKIT—Transparency
Setting Diagram p. D14

Lines 152–173
REINFORCE *KEY IDEA:* DECISIONS

Discuss What can you infer about the young man based on the way he communicates with the princess and his **decision** to open the door on the right? ***Possible answer:*** *The fact that he does not show "the slightest hesitation" suggests that he is confident the princess loves him deeply and will give him the correct information to save his life.*

READING STRATEGY

H PARAPHRASE

Have students record their answers in the chart from page 683. ***Possible answer:*** *Thinking hard about the question makes it even more difficult to answer. Love and human nature are extremely difficult to understand. Readers must approach the question from the princess's point of view. She is filled with despair and jealousy. If she can't have him, who should?*

Lines 174–197
REINFORCE *KEY IDEA:* DECISIONS

Discuss What **decision** do you think the princess might have made if she had not known which lady was behind the door? *Students may say it would be more likely that she would point to the door with the lady if the lady weren't someone she knew and hated.*

SELECTION WRAP-UP

REFLECT Have students think of a time when they or someone they know had to make an important decision. What advice would they give to one or more of the story's characters about making a wise decision?

CRITIQUE Ask students if they would have enjoyed a clear resolution to the plot more than the open-ended conclusion. Why?

READING FLUENCY

Distribute the copy masters and have students practice fluency.

RESOURCE MANAGER—Copy Master
Reading Fluency p. 62

Practice and Apply

After Reading

For additional support of postreading questions, use these copy masters:

RESOURCE MANAGER—Copy Masters
Reading Check p. 60 (to check understanding of the selection)
Tone p. 53 (for practice of literary analysis standards focus)
Question Support p. 61 (After Reading questions adapted for English learners and less-proficient readers)

Additional selection questions are provided for teachers on page 47.

For additional activities to challenge students, see

Power Thinking at **ClassZone.com**

ANSWERS

Comprehension

1. *The king's system is popular with the citizens. They enjoy being entertained by the "trial" and the unpredictable outcome.*
2. *The young man, a commoner, has fallen in love with the king's daughter.*
3. *Diagrams should include appropriate details from the story, such as a huge arena with the king sitting up high on a throne. Underneath his throne is a door from which the accused appears. On the opposite side of the arena are two doors, behind which are the tiger and the lady.*

Literary Analysis

Possible answers:

4. *The ending is surprising because Stockton goes into great detail about the princess's anguish as she makes her decision but does not reveal which door the princess chooses. Readers would have expected that, as in most stories, the resolution of the conflict would be revealed.*
5. ● **STANDARDS FOCUS** **Tone** *Students will most likely choose sarcastic, serious, or playful. Accept all well-supported answers that give examples of word choice and descriptive details.*
6. ■ **STANDARDS FOCUS** **Paraphrase** *Responses should show an understanding that paraphrasing helps them better understand and remember the story.*
7. *The king's system is not just. It depends entirely on chance and not on reason. An accused man—whether guilty or innocent—might end up married to a woman that he does not want to marry. There is an equal chance that he will be eaten by a tiger.*
8. *Some students will argue that the princess's obvious love for the young man would prompt her to save his life and point him toward the door with the lady. Others may argue that her fiery temperament and jealous nature would lead her to choose the door with the tiger.*

Extension and Challenge

9. *Students might say that the choice of the lady reveals a belief that humans are basically good. On the other hand, the choice of the tiger reveals a belief that humans are basically selfish.*
10. *Before writing their scenes, students should review the details of the princess's thoughts and behavior in the story. Her words and the way they are delivered should reflect her personality and her strong feelings.*

After Reading

Comprehension

1. **Recall** How do the citizens of the kingdom feel about the king's method of justice?
2. **Recall** What "crime" has the young man committed?
3. **Represent** Reread lines 21–24 and 33–63. Create a diagram of the arena. Use information from the story to include at least three labels in your diagram.

Literary Analysis

4. **Examine a Story's Ending** What was surprising about the way "The Lady, or the Tiger?" ended? Why did you expect something different?
5. **Identify Tone** Choose the one word from the following list that you think best describes the tone of the story: *sarcastic, sad, serious, playful, bitter, anxious, sentimental,* or *curious.* Write the word in the top of a chart like the one shown. Fill in your chart with words and details about the characters, setting, and situation in the story that support your choice.

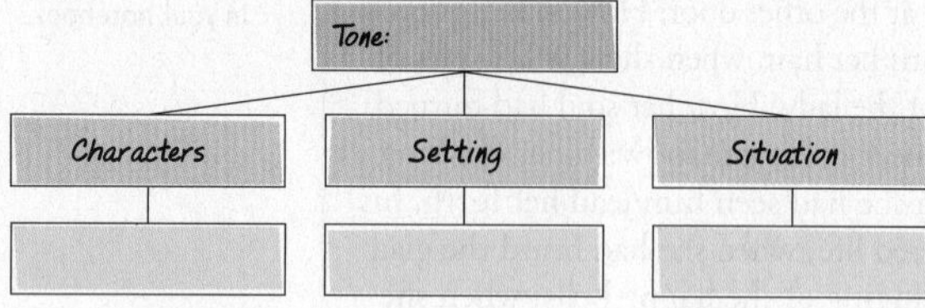

6. **Explore Paraphrasing** Choose two of the passages you paraphrased in your notebook. What crucial information did you gain from paraphrasing these passages that helped you understand the story?
7. **Evaluate** Describe the king's system of "justice." Is there anything just, or fair, about it? Explain.
8. **Draw Conclusions** Based on what you know about the princess, which door do you think she **decides** on? Use details from the selection to support your response.

Extension and Challenge

9. **Literary Criticism** Frank R. Stockton once said, "If you decide which it was—the lady or the tiger—you find out what kind of person you are yourself." What might your interpretation of the story show you about yourself and your view of human nature?
10. **Creative Response: Writing** Why do you think the princess didn't stand up for her beloved? If she had done so, what might she have said to her father? Write a scene in which the princess defends the man she loves against the king's accusations.

Vocabulary in Context

VOCABULARY PRACTICE

Choose the word in each group that is most nearly opposite in meaning to the boldfaced word.

1. **impartial:** (a) unbiased, (b) fair, (c) prejudiced, (d) objective
2. **assert:** (a) deny, (b) claim, (c) declare, (d) stress
3. **subordinate:** (a) beneath, (b) second-in-command, (c) presiding, (d) assisting
4. **conventional:** (a) customary, (b) unusual, (c) accepted, (d) traditional
5. **waver:** (a) hesitate, (b) falter, (c) pause, (d) continue
6. **devious:** (a) straightforward, (b) cunning, (c) sneaky, (d) deceitful
7. **aspire:** (a) plan, (b) hope, (c) attempt, (d) fail
8. **anguished:** (a) tormented, (b) pained, (c) miserable, (d) pleased
9. **progressiveness:** (a) narrow-mindedness, (b) forward-thinking, (c) acceptance, (d) tolerance

anguished
aspire
assert
conventional
devious
impartial
progressiveness
subordinate
waver

VOCABULARY IN WRITING

What makes the princess in this tale different from most fairy-tale princesses that you have read about? Write a paragraph explaining your answer. Use at least two vocabulary words in your paragraph. You could start this way.

EXAMPLE SENTENCE

*Unlike most fairy-tale heroines, this princess is **devious** in nature.*

VOCABULARY STRATEGY: CONNOTATION AND DENOTATION

A **denotation** is the literal meaning of a word—that is, the definition found in a dictionary. A word's **connotation** is a feeling or attitude linked with a word. Connotations have a big impact on the meaning a word conveys. For example, the vocabulary word *conventional* means "traditional." But it also connotes "old-fashioned" or "unimaginative." Recognizing connotations will help you identify the tone of what you read.

PRACTICE Show the difference in the connotations of the word pairs by writing a sentence for each word.

1. bland/simple
2. youthful/immature
3. fierce/strong
4. disagree/clash
5. cunning/smart
6. adventurous/reckless
7. smell/stench
8. grueling/challenging

VOCABULARY PRACTICE
For more practice, go to the **Vocabulary Center** at **ClassZone.com.**

DIFFERENTIATED INSTRUCTION

FOR ENGLISH LEARNERS

Vocabulary Practice Ask students if they can recall how each word was used in the story. If necessary, allow them to refer back to the usage in the story and use those context clues to help them choose the word in each set that differs most from the meaning of the boldfaced word. Help students break the vocabulary words down into parts, identifying prefixes, suffixes, roots, and base words that may also give hints to the words' meanings.

FOR ADVANCED LEARNERS/PRE–AP

Vocabulary Strategy [paired option] Challenge students to create a crossword puzzle in which the clues include words with strong connotations and the answers are words with similar denotations but different connotations. (A sample clue is "A nicer way to say someone is *overbearing*." Answer: *strong-willed*) They can use the words from the ***PRACTICE*** exercise as well as others. Have them exchange puzzles with a partner and solve them.

ANSWERS

Vocabulary in Context

VOCABULARY PRACTICE

1. *(c) prejudiced*
2. *(a) deny*
3. *(c) presiding*
4. *(b) unusual*
5. *(d) continue*
6. *(a) straightforward*
7. *(d) fail*
8. *(d) pleased*
9. *(a) narrow-mindedness*

RESOURCE MANAGER—Copy Master
Vocabulary Practice p. 58

VOCABULARY IN WRITING

Have students review the descriptions of the princess on pages 688, 689, and 691 and make a list of her major traits. Then have them list the traits of more familiar fairy-tale princesses and analyze the differences.

VOCABULARY STRATEGY: CONNOTATION AND DENOTATION *(also an EL language objective)*

Give students more practice by providing them with these words and challenging them to find words with opposite connotations: *beastly, doleful, florid, competent.*

*Students' sentences should include context clues that show the difference in connotations. Example sentences: Without seasoning, the soup was **bland** and tasteless. Using a few fresh vegetables from the garden, she made a **simple** but satisfying stew.*

RESOURCE MANAGER—Copy Master
Vocabulary Strategy p. 59

Vocabulary Center at **ClassZone.com**
Additional Vocabulary Activities

Assess and Reteach

Assess

RESOURCE MANAGER—Copy Masters
Selection Tests A, B/C pp. 63–64, 65–66

Test Generator CD

Reteach

STANDARDS LESSON FILE
Literature Lesson 39: Tone
Research and Study Skills Lesson 12: Paraphrasing
Vocabulary Lesson 17: Denotation and Connotation

THE LADY, OR THE TIGER? 693

Focus and Motivate

OBJECTIVES

Reading for Information
- use a graphic aid
- synthesize
- read a math article

SUMMARY

This article describes a debate about a popular game show called "Let's Make a Deal." A contestant is invited to choose one of three doors, hoping to win the big prize behind one of them. Once the host, Monty Hall, reveals which of the remaining two doors does not have the big prize, a contestant must decide whether to stick with his or her original choice or change. The "Monty Hall debate" is whether the contestant has better odds of winning by standing firm or by changing. The experts, including Hall, prove that changing gives better odds.

What's the Connection?

Use an Anticipation Guide to prepare students for the article. Write these statements on the transparency. Tell students that some statements might be false. Have students respond to each statement before and after reading the article.

- Mathematicians always agree about how to solve problems.
- Probability is the chance that something will happen or will not happen.
- Many games are based on probability.

 **BEST PRACTICES TOOLKIT—Transparency**
Anticipation Guide p. A14

Teach

Skill Focus: Use a Graphic Aid

Ask students to consider these questions as they read the article and analyze the diagram:

- What do the three boxes in the second row represent? Do "you" know what is behind your chosen door at this point?
- What do the shaded boxes represent?
- What do you get if you choose a door with a goat behind it and then change your choice?

When students have finished reading the article, review the diagram.

RESOURCE MANAGER—Copy Master
Use a Graphic Aid p. 75

Reading for Information

The Monty Hall Debate

Newspaper Article

Use with "The Lady, or the Tiger?" page 684.

What's the Connection?

In "The Lady, or the Tiger?" you read about a man who had to make a life-or-death choice between two doors. The following article is about a similar (though far less serious) decision faced by contestants of "Let's Make a Deal," a television game show popular in the 1960s and 1970s.

Skill Focus: Use a Graphic Aid

"Let's Make a Deal," host Monty Hall became famous for asking contestants to guess which of three doors hid a big prize. After a contestant picked a door, Hall would open one of the other two doors to show that the prize wasn't behind it. Then he'd give the contestants a choice: Do you want to change your guess to the other door or stick to the door you originally picked?

The article you're about to read explains why one choice is better than the other. The explanation is somewhat complicated, but the diagram shown here can help you understand it. Like other **graphic aids,** this diagram provides a visual representation of ideas. Copy it into your notebook, so you can write on it if you want to. Then refer to the diagram as you read the article, and use these tips to help you interpret it:

- Use symbols such as arrows to help you follow the diagram.
- Pay attention to labels that identify specific details, and relate them to what you read in the article.
- Look for patterns in the use of shading. For example, does one type of information always get shaded a certain way?

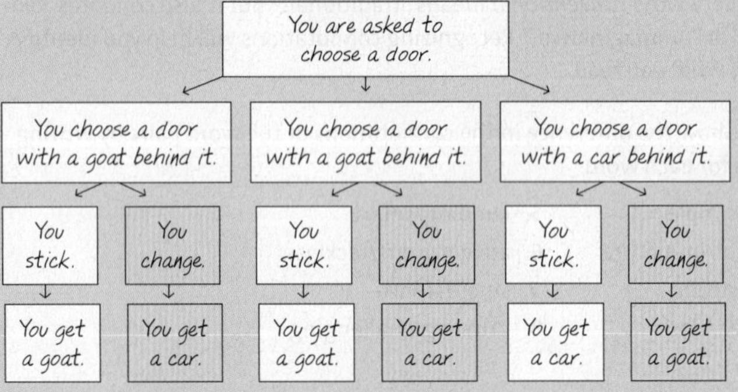

Selection Resources

RESOURCE MANAGER UNIT 6

Plan and Teach pp. 67–71

Reading
Summary pp. 73†*, 74‡*
Use a Graphic Aid pp. 75, 77†*
Reading Check p. 79
Synthesize pp. 76, 78†*
Question Support p. 80*

Assessment
Selection Tests A, B/C pp. 81*, 83*
Test Generator CD

Reading Support
Audio Anthology CD*

BEST PRACTICES TOOLKIT
Anticipation Guide • Reciprocal Teaching

* Resources for Differentiation † Also in Spanish ‡ In Haitian Creole and Vietnamese

SECTION C THE NEW YORK TIMES C3

The Monty Hall Debate

John Tierney

Marilyn vos Savant, a magazine columnist who is listed in the *Guinness Book of World Records* for highest IQ, was once asked this question:

Suppose you're on a game show, and you're given the choice of three doors: Behind one door is a car; behind the others, goats. You pick a door, say No. 1, and the host, who knows what's behind the other doors, opens another door, say No. 3, which has a goat. He then says to you, "Do you want to stick with your original choice or pick door No. 2?" Is it to your advantage to take the switch?

Ms. vos Savant's answer was that you should always change and pick the other door, because the chances are two in three that there will be a car behind that door. Since she gave her answer, Ms. vos Savant estimates she has received 10,000 letters, the great majority disagreeing with her. . . . Of the critical letters she received, close to 1,000 carried signatures with Ph.D.'s, and many were on letterheads of mathematics and science departments. . . . **A**

A GRAPHIC AID Notice how the description in lines 6–13 is represented in the diagram you copied. What do the first and second rows of the diagram show? What do the third and fourth rows show?

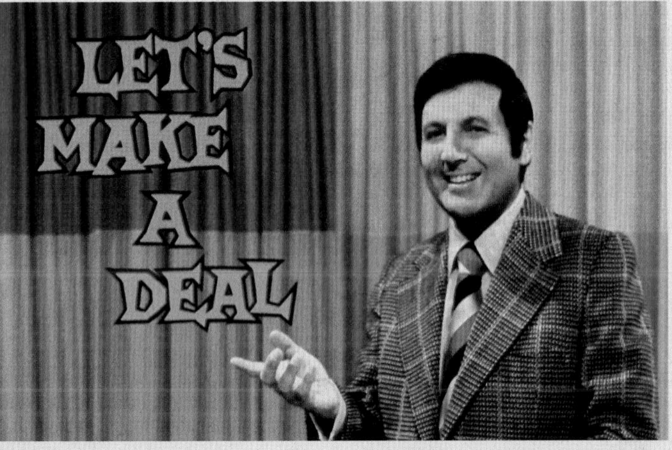

Monty Hall hosted "Let's Make A Deal" from 1963 to 1976.

Practice and Apply

INFORMATIONAL ANALYSIS

A GRAPHIC AID

Possible answer: *The first row represents the choice you are given. The second row shows each of your possible choices. The third row shows the two options you have after viewing the goat behind another door: "you stick" or "you change." The fourth row shows the outcome of each possible choice with regard to the door chosen at the outset.*

BACKGROUND

The Debate John Tierney's 1991 article in the *New York Times,* from which this selection is excerpted, stated the following: "[Marilyn vos Savant's] answer . . . has been debated in the halls of the C.I.A. and the barracks of fighter pilots in the Persian Gulf. It has been analyzed by mathematicians at M.I.T. and computer programmers at Los Alamos National Laboratory in New Mexico. It has been tested in classes ranging from second grade to graduate level at more than 1,000 schools across the country." Vos Savant first proposed her solution to the "Monty Hall problem" in a 1990 column. In *The Power of Logical Thinking,* published in 1997, she addresses the problem more extensively. Many years later, the debate continues to fascinate math experts and students of logic.

A Game of Chance During every taping of "Let's Make a Deal," about eight members of the studio audience were chosen to play. These contestants, called "Traders," brought odd or humorous items from home to start the dealing. Monty Hall, the show's host, made numerous deals. Sometimes he would offer contestants money to buy back the prizes they had already chosen. Another challenge was that prizes were sometimes disguised. For example, Traders might be invited to buy a garbage can. They had no way of knowing whether it contained actual garbage or, for example, a mink coat. The Big Deal of the Day took place near the end of the show. Traders would choose either Door #1, Door #2, or Door #3, and Monty Hall would often try to make a deal to get them to switch.

DIFFERENTIATED INSTRUCTION

FOR LESS–PROFICIENT READERS

Comprehension Support

1. Help students understand these elements of the introduction (lines 1–30):
   - the question vos Savant is asked
   - the reason she gives for her answer
   - the reaction to her answer
2. Have students discuss their initial reactions to vos Savant's answer. Does it seem logical? Why?

FOR ENGLISH LEARNERS

Options for Reading [paired option] Have students listen to the *Audio Anthology CD* as they follow along in the text and then work in pairs to practice Reciprocal Teaching. Ask them to take turns asking questions to clarify, predict, and summarize the main ideas in what they are reading. Help students make their questions clearer or more specific if necessary.

BEST PRACTICES TOOLKIT—Transparency Reciprocal Teaching p. A35

INFORMATIONAL ANALYSIS

B GRAPHIC AID

***Possible answer:** The shading helps readers distinguish the "you stick" responses and their outcomes from the "you change" responses and their outcomes. The shading in the last row shows that changing leads to a two-in-three chance of getting a car instead of a one-in-three chance.*

Lines 31–87

DISCUSSION PROMPTS

Use these prompts to help students understand the explanation of the correct answer to the "Monty Hall debate":

Recall What odds did vos Savant's critics think a contestant had if he or she decided to switch? ***Possible answer:** They believed the probability was one in two that the contestant, by switching, would get the car.*

Analyze In lines 72–81, the writer describes Monty Hall testing the theory in his home. What were the results of the test? Were they exactly two in three? What conclusions can you draw from this test? ***Possible answer:** After playing several rounds, Monty Hall confirmed that the odds of winning are higher if the contestant switches doors. In one case, the odds were actually four out of five (eight cars and two goats). A conclusion is that when multiple rounds of the game are played, the odds are not always exact, but the ratio of cars to goats is always higher if the contestant switches.*

Synthesize In what way might the producers of "Let's Make a Deal" have benefited from confusion about the odds? ***Possible answer:** Contestants who believed they had a 50/50 chance by "sticking" were reluctant to switch. So, they lost more frequently, and the game show didn't give away as many big prizes.*

Skill Focus: Use a Graphic Aid

Review the chart with students and make sure they all know how to interpret it. Discuss the answers to the questions on page 694 of the teacher's edition. Clarify and restate the answers as necessary. Ask: Has the article clarified the diagram, and vice versa?

B GRAPHIC AID
Reread lines 64–71. What does the shading on the chart on page 694 indicate?

Robert Sachs, a professor of mathematics at George Mason University in Fairfax, Va., expressed the prevailing view that there was no reason to switch doors.

"You blew it!" he wrote. "Let me explain: If one door is shown to be a loser, that information changes the probability of either remaining choice—*neither of which has any reason to be more likely*—to $\frac{1}{2}$. As a professional mathematician, I'm very concerned with the general public's lack of mathematical skills. Please help by confessing your error and, in the future, being more careful.". . .

Monty Hall, the game show host who actually gave contestants this choice on "Let's Make a Deal," said he was not surprised at the experts' insistence that the probability was one out of two. "That's the same assumption contestants would make on the show after I showed them there was nothing behind one door," he said. "They'd think the odds on their door had now gone up to one in two, so they hated to give up the door no matter how much money I offered.[1] By opening one of the other doors we were applying pressure.". . .

Mr. Hall said he realized the contestants were wrong, because the odds on Door 1 were still only one in three even after he opened another door. Since the only other place the car could be was behind Door 2, the odds on that door must now be two in three. **B**

Sitting at his dining room table, Mr. Hall quickly conducted ten rounds of the game as this contestant tried the non-switching strategy. The result was four cars and six goats. Then for the next ten rounds the contestant tried switching doors, and there was a dramatic improvement: eight cars and two goats. A pattern was emerging.

"So her answer's right: you should switch," Mr. Hall said, reaching the same conclusion as the tens of thousands of students who conducted similar experiments at Ms. vos Savant's suggestion. That conclusion was also reached eventually by many of her critics in academia, although most did not bother to write letters of retraction. Dr. Sachs, whose letter was published in her column, was one of the few with the grace to concede his mistake.

"I wrote her another letter," Dr. Sachs said, "telling her that after removing my foot from my mouth I'm now eating humble pie.[2] I vowed as penance to answer all the people who wrote to castigate[3] me. It's been an intense professional embarrassment.". . .

1. **how much money I offered:** Monty Hall would sometimes increase the drama of the show by offering contestants money to change their minds about whether to switch doors.
2. **after removing my foot . . . eating humble pie:** after making a careless comment I'm now forced to make an embarrassing apology.
3. **castigate** (kăs'tĭ-gāt'): severely criticize.

DIFFERENTIATED INSTRUCTION

FOR LESS–PROFICIENT READERS

Concept Support [paired option] To help students internalize the concepts in the article, suggest that they play the game with a partner. They can play with any three items, two of which are the same. As they play, encourage students to refer to the diagram on page 694. Suggest that they play ten rounds each of "sticking" and "changing," keeping track of their results. Then discuss whether their test has supported vos Savant's answer.

FOR ADVANCED LEARNERS/PRE–AP

Investigate Tell students that several books and Web sites address the "Monty Hall problem." Most of the Web sites offer both explanations of the problem and simulated games. Challenge students to explore the Web sites and play the games. Suggest that they identify and explore other variables that support vos Savant's theory, and then share their findings with the class.

omprehension

1. **Recall** Who is Marilyn vos Savant?
2. **Recall** Did most people who wrote to Ms. vos Savant agree or disagree with her answer to the Monty Hall problem?
3. **Clarify** Reread lines 36–41. According to Robert Sachs, what does Ms. vos Savant fail to realize?

itical Analysis

4. **Understand a Graphic Aid** How does the shading on the diagram help you understand that a contestant has a two-in-three chance of getting a car if he or she changes doors? Also explain how the shading reveals what the chance of getting the car is if the contestant sticks with his or her original choice.

ead for Information: Synthesize

WRITING PROMPT

Imagine your best friend is about to go on a game show like "Let's Make a Deal." Since you have seen the show before, you understand that the host knows which door the car is behind. Sometimes he offers contestants money to influence their decision. What advice should you give your friend so that he or she chooses the winning door? Synthesize what you've learned about decision-making from the short story, this article, and your life to answer this question. Then write a letter in which you present your friend with guidelines about making the right decision. Be sure to support your advice with details and examples.

When you **synthesize,** you combine information from various sources to gain a better understanding of a subject. Following these steps can help you synthesize:

1. Reflect on what you learned about decision-making from the story, the article, and your life.

2. Jot down the most important considerations about decision-making that you found in these sources.
3. Write a letter in which you present these considerations as guidelines for choosing the winning door. Support each guideline you offer with an example from your life, the article, or "The Lady, or the Tiger?"

Practice and Apply

For additional support of postreading questions, use these copy masters:

 RESOURCE MANAGER—Copy Masters
Reading Check p. 79
Question Support p. 80
Synthesize p. 76
For additional questions, see page 70.

ANSWERS

Comprehension

1. *She is a magazine columnist who is listed in the* Guinness Book of World Records *for having the highest IQ. Her correct answer to the Monty Hall problem sparked heated debate among math experts.*
2. *The majority disagreed with her.*
3. *Sachs claims that she fails to realize that both options are equally likely to be a winner. That is, both doors now have a one-in-two chance of opening to a car.*

Critical Analysis

4. ■ **STANDARDS FOCUS Use a Graphic Aid** *There are three shaded boxes in the bottom row of the diagram. Two boxes contain a car, while one contains a goat. In other words, 2/3 of the boxes contain cars. In the unshaded boxes, 2/3 contain goats, and only 1/3 (one box) contains a car.*

Read for Information: Synthesize

Writing Prompt *Strong answers will explain that the method one uses to make a decision depends upon the nature of the decision; will provide more than one or two guidelines for making decisions; will support guidelines with examples from the story, the article, and personal experiences; and will format the letter correctly.*

FOR LESS–PROFICIENT WRITERS

Read for Information

1. Ask students to reread "The Lady, or the Tiger?", review the diagram on page 694, and reflect on their personal experiences with decision-making.
2. To help students identify the most important points, have them share their notes with a partner and elicit feedback.
3. Guide students in supporting guidelines with examples from their own experience, the article, the diagram, or the story.

FOR ADVANCED LEARNERS/PRE–AP

Read for Information Have students develop their letter into a short article that they might submit to the school newspaper. In the article, have them expand on the guidelines in the letter and include more details and examples. Invite volunteers to read their articles aloud, and then have the class vote for the article that is clearest and easiest to follow.

Assess and Reteach

Assess

RESOURCE MANAGER—Copy Masters
Selection Tests A, B/C pp. 81–82, 83–84

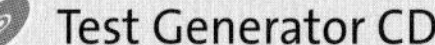
Test Generator CD

Reteach

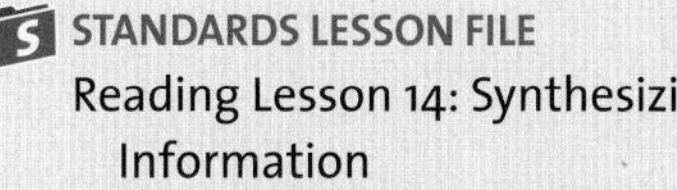
STANDARDS LESSON FILE
Reading Lesson 14: Synthesizing Information
Informational Texts Lesson 24: Diagrams

Introduce

OBJECTIVE

- read a coming-of-age novel

Meet Cynthia Kadohata

Kadohata says one important source of her "writing energy" is travel. Traveling throughout the United States and focusing on its beautiful landscapes puts her in touch with her true self. Kadohata says, "I have to be in touch with this real, essential me whenever I sit down to write." Another source of joy and inspiration in Kadohata's life is her family, which includes her son Sammy, adopted in 2004 from Kazakhstan, and her Doberman pinscher Shika Kojika. Kadohata got Shika in 2002 through a rescue organization for homeless Dobermans.

Try a Coming-of-Age Novel

Emphasize the fact that central to a coming-of-age novel is a challenge that forever changes a character. The challenge might relate primarily to an adventure, a journey, a conflict among characters, or a quiet struggle within one character.

The 1960 novel *To Kill a Mockingbird* by Harper Lee is one of the most famous American coming-of-age novels of the 20th century. The child narrator, Scout Finch, lives through a difficult period in which her lawyer father angers their pre–civil rights era Southern community when he defends an African-American man falsely accused of a crime. At the same time, Scout and her brother meet and befriend a man who has long been an outcast in their community. These experiences represent struggles that change Scout—teaching her about racial justice, tolerance, and the importance of standing up for one's beliefs.

Other well-known coming-of-age novels include Robert Cormier's *The Chocolate War,* in which a boy learns a hard lesson about human nature when he tries to stand up to his classmates, and Mark Twain's *The Adventures of Huckleberry Finn,* about a young boy's journey down the Mississippi River.

RESOURCE MANAGER—Copy Master
Identify Genre Features p. 85

Great Reads

Kira-Kira

Coming-of-Age Novel by Cynthia Kadohata

Cynthia Kadohata
born 1956

Other Books by Cynthia Kadohata

- *The Floating World*
- *The Glass Mountains*

Meet Cynthia Kadohata

Like the main character's family in *Kira-Kira,* Cynthia Kadohata's family moved often so that her parents could seek work. They lived in Illinois, Arkansas, Georgia, and Michigan before finally settling in California. Kadohata, a Japanese American, often did not feel like she fit in during her childhood. "I remember a little girl asking me something like, 'Are you black or white?'" she says. "I really stumbled for an answer. I said, 'I don't know.'" But since then, Kadohata has come to embrace her cultural identity. Today, she is often viewed as one of the great voices in Asian-American writing.

Although she majored in journalism in college, in her early 20s Kadohata began to appreciate the power of fiction. "I had always thought that nonfiction represented the 'truth,'" she explains, "but . . . I realized you could say things with fiction that you couldn't say any other way." Kadohata set out to become a fiction writer and was determined to succeed. She received 25 rejection letters before *The New Yorker* finally published one of her stories, launching her career as an award-winning author. *Kira-Kira* is her first young-adult novel.

Try a Coming-of-Age Novel

At what point do you leave your childhood fears behind and boldly take on greater responsibilities? When a child is faced with a challenging situation or difficult decision, he or she often has to grow up very quickly. A novel that centers on a young person's path to greater maturity is called a **coming-of-age novel.** *Kira-Kira,* which follows the life of its young narrator, is an example of this type of novel.

698

DIFFERENTIATED INSTRUCTION

FOR LESS–PROFICIENT READERS

Reading Support Before students begin reading, review the teaching notes on pages 699–703 and select those that you think would be most helpful to them. You might read the selection aloud with students and discuss the relevant notes. Stop occasionally to answer questions, give an explanation, or hold a discussion.

Read a Great Book

Katie Takeshima thinks her older sister, Lynn, is a genius—partly because Lynn sees the world in such a unique way. Lynn finds beauty in ordinary things and teaches Katie to see them *kira-kira,* or glittering, too. The family business is far from being a shining success, however; and when Katie's parents get down to their last $600, they decide it's time to move on. As the family prepares to leave Iowa in order for Mr. and Mrs. Takeshima to pursue better job opportunities in Georgia, Katie wonders how their lives will change.

from

KIRA-KIRA

We were poor, but in the way Japanese are poor, meaning we never borrowed money from anyone, period. Meaning once a year we bought as many fifty-pound bags of rice as we could afford, and we didn't get nervous again about money until we reached our last bag. Nothing went to waste in our house. For breakfast my parents often made their *ochazuke*—green tea mixed with rice—from the crusty old rice at the bottom of the pot. For our move to Georgia, Dad and Uncle loaded up the truck with all the bags of rice that we hadn't sold at the store. I watched my parents look at the rice in the truck, and I could see that the rice made them feel good. It made them feel safe.

I liked to see them that way, especially my mother, who never seemed to feel safe. My mother was a delicate, rare, and beautiful flower. Our father told us that. She weighed hardly more than Lynn. She was so delicate that if you bumped into her accidentally, you could bruise her. She fell down a single stair once, and she broke her leg. To her that was proof even a single stair could present peril. When I would approach even a single stair, she would call out, "Be careful!"

699

Read a Great Book

According to Kadohata, Katie evolves into a character who wants to learn more about herself and others and to grow as a person. Much of Katie's growth as a person comes from her relationship with her sister, which is central to *Kira-Kira.* Lynn proves to have a tremendous influence on Katie. At one point in the novel, Katie writes of her sister, "Lynn could take a simple, everyday object like a box of Kleenex and use it to prove how amazing the world is." In this excerpt, in which the sisters are experiencing together a traumatic change, readers can begin to see the bond between the girls and subtle ways in which Katie follows her older sister's lead and looks to her sister for answers.

SHARE AN FYI

Many Japanese people make *ochazuke* as a way to use leftover rice. In Kyoto, Japan, *ochazuke* is known as *bubuzuke.* If a host asks a guest if he or she would like to have some *bubuzuke,* it means the visit is over and the guest has likely overstayed his or her welcome.

FOR ENGLISH LEARNERS

Read Aloud Preread part of the excerpt and have students continue reading in pairs or small groups. Alternatively, read aloud all or part of the excerpt and stop occasionally to answer questions, hold a discussion, or give an explanation.

Listen to the *Audio Anthology CD* Have students listen to the excerpt as they read along. Then have them read the text independently. Lead them in a follow-up discussion.

Readers Theater [small-group option]

1. Have students first read the excerpt independently or in pairs.
2. Then read aloud from the text for two or three minutes to demonstrate how to read descriptions and dialogue fluently and with expression.
3. Divide the class into small groups. Assign the roles of Katie (the narrator), Lynn, Mrs. Takeshima, Mr. Takeshima, and Uncle Katsuhisa. Because it is the largest role, you might split the role of Katie among two or more students. Students should use sticky notes to identify their lines.
4. Have each group read the selection aloud as you walk from group to group, monitoring fluency and offering assistance.

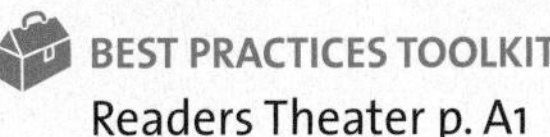

BEST PRACTICES TOOLKIT
Readers Theater p. A1

SHARE A READING TIP

Explain that Japanese words such as *"Shizukani!"* (lines 26 and 27) are inserted into the text to reflect the family's cultural identity. Demonstrate for students how the words should be pronounced or work with students to look up their pronunciations.

SHARE WORD MEANINGS

When Katie says Bera-Bera "sassed" her (line 49), she means he made disrespectful remarks. Katie is giving her stuffed toy the personality of a spirited child her own age.

Our mother didn't like us to run or play or climb, because it was dangerous. She didn't like us to walk in the middle of our empty street, because you never knew. She didn't want us to go to college someday, because we might get strange ideas. She liked peace and quiet. My father used to say, "Shhhh. Your mother is taking a bath." Or, "Quiet down, girls, your mother is drinking tea." We never understood why we couldn't make noise while our mother was doing anything at all. My mother's favorite thing to tell us, in her iron-rimmed singsong voice, was *"Shizukani!"* That means "Hush!"

She never said *"Shizukani!"* to my father. She made him food and rubbed his feet, and for this he let her handle all the money. Lynn said our mother probably knew a special foot-rubbing technique that made men silly. My father loved my mother a lot. That made *me* feel safe.

The night before we moved, my father and uncle sat on a tree stump across the road. Lynn and I peeked out at them before we got in bed. My uncle talked and talked, and my father listened and listened. Sometimes they both laughed loudly.

"What are they talking about?" I said.

"Women," Lynn said knowingly.

"What are they saying about women?"

"That the pretty ones make them giggle."

"Oh. Good night."

"Good night!"

Our mother came into the bedroom in the middle of the night, the way she always did, to make sure we were asleep. As usual, Lynn was asleep and I was awake. If I was awake, I usually pretended to be asleep so as not to get in trouble. But tonight I said, "Mom?"

"It's late, why are you up?"

"I can't sleep without Bera-Bera." Bera-Bera was my favorite stuffed animal, which my mother had packed in a box. Bera-Bera talked too much, laughed too loudly, and sometimes sassed me, but still I loved him.

"Someday you won't even remember Bera-Bera." She said this gently, and as if the thought made her a little sad. The thought made me a little sad too. She kissed my forehead and left. Outside I could

hear noises: "Yah! Ooooh-YAH!" Et cetera. Lynn was sound asleep. I got up and watched Uncle Katsuhisa spit. My father no longer sat on the tree stump. It was just Uncle Katsuhisa out there. He was a madman, for sure.

We left Iowa at dusk the next evening. We had meant to leave in the morning but got a little behind schedule for several reasons:

1. I couldn't find the box with Bera-Bera, and I was convinced he was lost. Naturally, I had to have hysterics.
2. My parents misplaced their six hundred dollars.
3. Lynn couldn't find her favorite sweater with embroidered flowers. Naturally, she had to have hysterics.
4. Uncle Katsuhisa fell asleep, and we thought it would be rude to wake him.

Uncle woke up on his own. My parents found their money. But Lynn and I didn't find our items, so naturally, we continued our hysterics. Finally, my mother said, "We must leave or I don't know what!" She looked at Lynn and me crying. "Maybe you girls should keep your uncle company while he drives."

"Oh, no," said Uncle. "I wouldn't want to deprive you of their delightful company."

"No," said my mother. "I wouldn't want you to be lonely."

So we climbed into the noisy truck with our noisy uncle. Then we cried so much that our uncle refused to drive with us anymore. He pulled to the side of the highway. Then we got in our parents' car and cried so much that they pulled over and flipped a coin with Uncle Katsuhisa. Uncle lost, so we got back in the truck with him.

Lynn and I were perfectly happy in Iowa. I did not see why we had to move to a new job that my father had told us would be the hardest work he had ever done. I did not see why we had to move to a southern state where my father said you could not understand a word people said

SHARE AN FYI

The state of Iowa is more than 500 miles north and west of the state of Georgia. Driving between the two states today, without stopping, would take the family roughly 8 hours.

SHARE A READING TIP

The narrator's description of "hysterics" (lines 60 and 63)—uncontrollable, exaggerated outbursts—reflects the voice of someone looking back on events of the past with a sense of humor. Katie is making fun of the fact that she and her sister were being overly dramatic. Students should look for other examples of this voice as they read.

SHARE A READING TIP

Point out that lines 97–99 illustrate the relationship between Katie and her older sister. Katie takes her cues from Lynn, and the two are close companions.

SHARE AN FYI

In the United States, chewing and spitting tobacco has most often been associated with baseball players. However, today most professional ballplayers opt not to chew tobacco because of its terrible health effects. Many ballplayers have taken to chewing and spitting sunflower seeds instead.

because of their southern accents. I did not see why we had to leave our house for a small apartment.

After awhile Lynn and I ran out of tears and sat glumly in the truck with Uncle Katsuhisa. I knew if I thought of Bera-Bera, I would cry. But I had nothing else to do, so I thought of him. He was half dog, half rabbit, and he had orange fur. He was my best friend next to Lynn.

"I want Bera-Bera!" I cried out.

Lynn cried out, "I want my sweater!" We both burst into tears.

It was a warm night. Whenever we paused in our crying, the only other sound inside the truck was the sound of my uncle smacking his chewing tobacco. I dreaded to know what would happen when he spit out that tobacco. Now he rolled down the window, and I thought the Great Spit was about to come. Instead, he looked at us slyly.

"I could teach you girls how to spit like a master," he said.

My sister squinted at him. She stopped crying. So did I. I could tell she thought it might be fun to learn how to spit like a master. So did I. Our mother would kill us. Lynn said, "Maybe."

He belched very loudly, then glanced at us. I realized his belch was preparation for spitting. I swallowed some air and burped. So did Lynn. Then Uncle Katsuhisa's throat rumbled. The rumbling got louder and louder. Even over the sound of the motor, it seemed like a war was going on in his throat. Lynn and I tried to rumble our throats like him.

"Hocka-hocka-hocka!" he said.

Lynn and I copied him: "Hocka-hocka-hocka!"

"Geh-geh-geh!"

"Geh-geh-geh!"

He turned to his open window, and an amazing wad of brown juice flew from his mouth. The brown juice was like a bat bursting out of a cave. We turned around to watch it speed away. A part of me hoped it would hit the car behind us, but it didn't. I leaned over Lynn and out the passenger window. "Hyaaahhhh!" I said, and a little trickle of saliva fell down my chin.

No one spoke. For some reason the silence made me start crying again. As if Uncle Katsuhisa couldn't restrain himself, he started singing my name over and over, "Katie, Katie, Katie . . ." Then he sang

Katie songs to the tunes of "Row, Row, Row Your Boat," "America the Beautiful," "Kookaburra," and some songs I didn't recognize. For instance, he sang, "Oh, Katie, Kate, for spacious skies, for Katie Katie Kate." He made me giggle. It was almost as if someone were tickling me. For a while I forgot about Bera-Bera.

Lynn smiled with satisfaction. I knew this was because she liked for me to be happy. The wind hit our hair as Uncle Katsuhisa continued to sing Katie songs. I looked outside over a field and tried to find the *Sode Boshi,* the kimono sleeve in the sky where Uncle Katsuhisa said westerners see the constellation Orion. Then my uncle began to sing Lynnie songs.

She laughed and laughed and laughed.

Keep Reading

The Takeshimas are on their way to a new life in a small Georgia town, where there are very few other Japanese Americans. How different will things be for them there? As you continue to read *Kira-Kira,* you will see the family through times of great joy and times of deep sorrow. Through it all, Katie continues to follow her sister's example by looking for beauty in the world around her. Read along as Katie's experiences in Georgia help her to grow into a thoughtful young woman.

Discuss

SHARE AN FYI

The kookaburra featured in the popular song of the same name (line 119) is an Australian bird. In the song, the kookaburra eats "gum drops," or drops of sap that form on the gum tree in which the bird sits.

SHARE AN FYI

In astronomy, Orion (line 127) is a constellation named for a mythological Greek hunter. This grouping of stars, especially the three bright stars said to form Orion's belt, is recognized in cultures throughout the world. Sode Boshi, a Japanese interpretation of the constellation, refers to the wide sleeve of a kimono—a traditional Japanese robe.

Keep Reading

Share these discussion questions with students after they have finished the excerpt. You might use the questions to lead a class discussion or have students form small groups to discuss them.

- What do you find most interesting about the Takeshima family?
- How do you think Katie and Lynn will adjust to their new life in Georgia, based on what you've learned about them?
- How do you think the relationship between Katie and Lynn will factor into the rest of the book?
- What do you know about Katie's relationship with her mother, and what role do you think this relationship might play in the rest of the book?

ADDITIONAL TEACHING OPPORTUNITY

Evaluate Opinions Have students find book reviews for the novel *Kira-Kira.* Point out that they can use book reviews to determine whether they might enjoy reading a particular book. Note that they can also use this strategy with films. Have students practice by finding and reading a film review as well. With both the book and the film reviews, guide students in identifying and evaluating opinions expressed rather than taking them at face value.

Focus and Motivate

OBJECTIVES

Literary Analysis

- explore the key idea of **exaggerate**
- identify and analyze voice (complex sentences with descriptions, hyperbole, and understatement)
- read a memoir and a newspaper article

Reading

- monitor (adjust rate, reread)

Vocabulary

- build vocabulary for reading and writing
- use knowledge of the Latin root *leg* to help determine word meaning *(also an EL language objective)*

Grammar and Writing

- form compound sentences by joining two simple sentences (or independent clauses)
- use writing to analyze literature

SUMMARY

In this humorous memoir, Twain relates his adventures in a variety of occupations, from grocery clerk to silver miner, before finding his niche as a city reporter with a small Virginia newspaper. In this job, he discovers he has a special talent for creating "stirring news" by embellishing the truth.

Why do we EXAGGERATE?

To expand on the ***KEY IDEA,*** have students read the cartoon. Ask them what Snoopy **exaggerates.** *(He describes walking across the sandbox as a trip through a desert.)* Is his exaggeration more interesting than the truth? Then have students do the ***DISCUSS*** activity.

Before Reading

from Roughing It

Memoir by Mark Twain

Why do we EXAGGERATE?

KEY IDEA "It takes me forever to walk to school." "I have about a million hours of homework to do." "My backpack must weigh two hundred pounds." Have you ever found yourself saying something like this, even when you know it's not accurate? We all **exaggerate** at times. In the memoir you are about to read, Mark Twain uses exaggeration not only to make us laugh, but also to make us think.

DISCUSS How good are you at exaggerating? Choose a simple event—your trip to the grocery store, or yesterday's band practice. Tell the story in its basic form, with no exaggeration. Then tell the story again, this time exaggerating the events and descriptive details. Did your exaggeration make the second version more fun to hear? Or did it push the limits of believability too far? Share your stories with your group and let them decide.

Peanuts by Charles Schulz

HERE'S THE WORLD FAMOUS SERGEANT-MAJOR OF THE FOREIGN LEGION LEADING HIS TROOPS ON A MISSION

AS THEY LEAVE CIVILIZATION, THEY APPROACH THE DESERT WITH ITS MILES AND MILES OF BURNING SAND...
© 1983 United Feature Syndicate, Inc. 8-5
WELL, MAYBE THREE OR FOUR FEET

Peanuts, Charles Schulz. August 5, 1983. © United Feature Syndicate, Inc.

704

Selection Resources

RESOURCE MANAGER UNIT 6

Plan and Teach pp. 87–94

Literary Analysis

Summary pp. 95†*, 96‡*

Voice pp. 97, 98†*

Question Support p. 105*

Reading

Monitor pp. 99, 100†*

Reading Check p. 104

Reading Fluency p. 107

Vocabulary

Study p. 101*

Practice p. 102

Strategy p. 103

Grammar and Writing

Form Compound Sentences p. 106

Assessment

Selection Tests A, B/C pp. 109*, 111*

Test Generator CD

BEST PRACTICES TOOLKIT

Differentiated Instruction pp. 31–38*

Scaffolding Instruction pp. 43–46*

Graphic Organizers/Strategies

Knowledge Rating • Cluster Diagram • T Chart

Reading Support

Audio Anthology CD*

Technology

Literature, Vocabulary, and Writing Centers at **ClassZone.com**

Write*Smart* CD

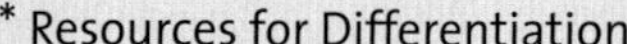

* Resources for Differentiation † Also in Spanish ‡ In Haitian Creole and Vietnamese

ERARY ANALYSIS: VOICE

In literature, **voice** refers to a writer's unique use of language. The way a writer chooses words, constructs sentences, and expresses ideas makes his or her personality come through on the page. As you read, look for the ways Mark Twain achieves his humorous voice through

- complex sentences containing amusing descriptions
- **hyperbole,** or exaggeration
- **understatement,** or downplaying something's importance

ADING STRATEGY: MONITOR

Twain uses long sentences and old-fashioned vocabulary. To make sure you understand what he's saying, **monitor** yourself, or pause to check your understanding. If you're not clear about what you just read, try these strategies:

- **Adjust your reading rate** by slowing down when you get to long, complicated sentences and passages.
- **Use context clues** or a dictionary to figure out the meaning of archaic (old-fashioned) vocabulary.
- **Note descriptive details** to help you picture characters, events, and settings.
- **Reread difficult passages** to help clarify information.

As you read, use a chart to note the line numbers of difficult passages and the strategies you used to understand them.

Confusing Lines	What They Mean	How I Figured It Out

CABULARY IN CONTEXT

Twain uses the following words in a humorous way. To see how many you know, match each word with its synonym, the word closest to it in meaning.

WORD LIST			
	array	legitimate	sensational
	conspicuous	livelihood	tolerable
	contrive	rigid	yield

1. occupation
2. inflexible
3. shocking
4. surrender
5. assortment
6. valid
7. invent
8. adequate
9. obvious

Author On|ine

Mark Twain
1835–1910

Growing Up on the River When Samuel Clemens was four years old, his family moved to Hannibal, Missouri, a small town on the Mississippi River. Clemens grew up fascinated by the river, traveling its waters in homemade rafts, playing in swimming holes, and exploring nearby woods and caves. His carefree childhood days ended at 11, however, when his father died of pneumonia. In order to support his family, Clemens left school and worked for a newspaper and printing firm.

Looking for Adventure In 1853, Clemens left Hannibal to seek his fortune mining along the Amazon River. But Clemens never made it to the Amazon. On his journey south he befriended a steamboat captain, and for four years he sailed the Mississippi River. After a brief stint in the Confederate Army during the Civil War, Clemens moved to Nevada and began writing for a local paper. It was during this time that he assumed the pen name "Mark Twain," a term that means "two fathoms deep," or water that is deep enough for a riverboat to navigate safely.

The Start of a Legend Mark Twain made a name for himself traveling around the world and writing newspaper columns about his adventures. His humorous voice captured the hearts of American readers, and before long, Twain was a household name. His book *Roughing It* contains essays about his travels and work experiences, all told in his signature way.

MORE ABOUT THE AUTHOR
For more on Mark Twain, visit the **Literature Center** at **ClassZone.com.**

Teach

STANDARDS FOCUS

LITERARY ANALYSIS

● VOICE

Write these sentences on the board:

I'm so happy I could kiss a pig.
At 99 degrees, it's a wee bit hot outside.

Ask students which sentence uses hyperbole and which uses understatement. ***Answer:*** *The first sentence uses hyperbole; the second is an understatement.*

CHECK UNDERSTANDING Ask students to write and share their own examples of hyperbole and understatement.

READING STRATEGY

■ MONITOR

Ask students to reread the first box of the Peanuts cartoon. Point out that if they don't understand Snoopy's statement the first time they read it, they can reread it at a slower rate. Demonstrate this, and then think aloud as you picture the scene Snoopy is imagining. Point out that the words *sergeant-major, legion, troops,* and *mission* suggest a military scene.

CHECK UNDERSTANDING Ask volunteers to explain ways the monitoring strategies have helped them understand what they have read in the past.

RESOURCE MANAGER—Copy Master
Monitor p. 99 (for student use while reading the selection)

VOCABULARY SKILL

▲ VOCABULARY IN CONTEXT

DIAGNOSE WORD KNOWLEDGE To determine preteaching needs, have all students complete **Vocabulary in Context.** ***Answers:*** **1.** *livelihood* **2.** *rigid* **3.** *sensational* **4.** *yield* **5.** *array* **6.** *legitimate* **7.** *contrive* **8.** *tolerable* **9.** *conspicuous*

PRETEACH VOCABULARY Use the Vocabulary Study copy master to help students explore the meaning of each boldfaced word.

1. Read aloud the first sentence in Part A.
2. Help students create a word map for *livelihood.* Point out that they may not be able to fill in every box for every word.
3. Repeat the procedure for each of the other sentences.
4. Have students complete Part B independently.

RESOURCE MANAGER—Copy Master
Vocabulary Study p. 101

For general guidelines on differentiating vocabulary instruction and for alternative vocabulary activities for students not needing vocabulary preteaching, see

BEST PRACTICES TOOLKIT
Scaffolding Vocabulary Instruction pp. 43–46

Vocabulary Center at **ClassZone.com**
Additional Vocabulary Activities

Practice and Apply

READING STRATEGY

A MONITOR

Remind students to record their answers in the chart from page 705. ***Possible answer:*** *Twain needed to support himself because his father died and left Twain deeply in debt.*

If students need help . . . Point out that students can clarify Twain's long sentences by breaking them down into smaller, meaningful parts. Show this on the board by writing the sentence on several lines, breaking at logical points. Then discuss the meaning of each part.

ANALYZE VISUALS

Possible answer: *The wastebasket full of pages suggests that Twain rewrote his drafts many times; the images surrounding him suggest that he had many ideas swirling around in his head.*

About the Art This colored engraving of Samuel Langhorne Clemens, titled "The Author and His Memories," dates from 1880.

ROUGHING IT

Mark Twain

What to do next?

It was a momentous question. I had gone out into the world to shift for myself,[1] at the age of thirteen (for my father had indorsed[2] for friends, and although he left us a sumptuous legacy of pride in his fine Virginian stock and its national distinction, I presently found that I could not live on that alone without occasional bread to wash it down with). **A** I had gained a **livelihood** in various vocations, but had not dazzled anybody with my successes; still the list was before me, and the amplest liberty in the matter of choosing, provided I wanted to work—which I did not, after being so wealthy. I had once been a grocery clerk, for one day, but had consumed so much sugar in that time that I was relieved from further duty by the proprietor;[3] said he wanted me outside, so that he could have my custom. I had studied law an entire week, and then given it up because it was so prosy and tiresome. I had engaged briefly in the study of blacksmithing, but wasted so much time trying to fix the bellows so that it would blow itself, that the master turned me adrift in disgrace, and told me I would come to no good. I had been a bookseller's clerk for a while, but the customers bothered me so much I could not read with any comfort, and so the proprietor gave me a furlough and forgot

A MONITOR
Why did Twain need to support himself at a young age? Rephrase the information in parenthesis to find out.

livelihood (līv'lē-ho͝od') *n.* a means of support; a way of making a living

1 Targeted Passage

ANALYZE VISUALS
What does this image of Mark Twain suggest about his **writing process**?

1. **shift for myself:** take care of myself.
2. **indorsed** (ĭn-dôrsd'): endorsed; signed financial documents; perhaps this means that Twain's father backed up friends' unwise financial schemes, and lost all of his own money as a result.
3. **proprietor** (prə-prī'ĭ-tər): one who owns and manages a business.

DIFFERENTIATED INSTRUCTION

FOR ALL STUDENTS

Journals After asking the question "What to do next?" Twain recounts his experiences with a variety of jobs, humorously explaining that none seemed suitable for him. Ask students to reflect in their journals on what people should consider when they look for a job. What kind of job do they hope to have one day? What skills will they need for that job? What steps should they take to acquire those skills?

FOR LESS–PROFICIENT READERS

In combination with the *Audio Anthology CD*, use one or more Targeted Passages (pp. 706, 711) to ensure that students focus on key events, concepts, and skills.

1 Targeted Passage [Lines 2–18]

This passage introduces Twain and sets up the problem of finding the right occupation.

- What is Twain's motivation for trying to find a job?
- What jobs did Twain try when he was young?
- What did Twain's job experiences have in common?
- Was Twain successful at any of the jobs he mentions?

BACKGROUND

Newspapers By the mid-1800s, around the time Twain got his first job as a reporter, newspapers were increasing in popularity. Advances in technology, including mechanized typesetting, high-speed printing, and telegraph and telephone communications, helped increase circulation and reduce the price of a single copy. Big-city newspapers printed up to 50,000 copies a day, which sold for a few pennies apiece. In addition to about 400 daily papers, around 3,000 weeklies were being printed in the United States by mid-century.

FOR ENGLISH LEARNERS

Key Academic Vocabulary Have students use Knowledge Rating to study these words: *achievements* (line 25), *resolved* (line 47), *editor(s)* (lines 52, 58, 75, 86, 88, 108), *publication* (line 95), *compensation* (line 130), *occupation* (line 150).

BEST PRACTICES TOOLKIT—Transparency
Knowledge Rating p. E3

Prereading For prereading instruction for English learners, see

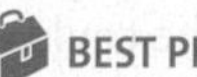

BEST PRACTICES TOOLKIT
Scaffolding Reading Instruction pp. 43–46

FOR ADVANCED LEARNERS/PRE–AP

Pre-AP exercises in the bottom channel provide additional challenge for your advanced students. Use them for small groups or individuals.

ADDITIONAL GUIDELINES

For more help with differentiation and tips for classroom management, see

BEST PRACTICES TOOLKIT
Differentiated Instruction pp. 31–38

LITERARY ANALYSIS

B VOICE

***Possible answer:** Twain says, "But my prescriptions were unlucky . . . sell more stomach-pumps . . ." This is an understatement because he is downplaying the fact that many people were sickened by the medicines he gave them.*

Lines 47–48

REINFORCE *KEY IDEA:* EXAGGERATE

Discuss In what two ways does Twain **exaggerate** in these lines? ***Possible answer:*** *First, Twain says he would rather starve than take up mining again. Second, he compares digging and tossing rock and dirt, which falls back on his head, to making a target of himself and shooting at it.*

READING STRATEGY

C MONITOR

Suggest that students record their answers in their charts from page 705. ***Possible answer:** Twain got a job offer from the* Enterprise *because for some time he had been writing letters to the paper. The paper printed his letters, so the editors must have liked his writing. Students may say they used the strategy of rereading the passage to find the explanation.*

to put a limit to it. I had clerked in a drug store part of a summer, but my prescriptions were unlucky, and we appeared to sell more stomach-pumps than soda-water. So I had to go. I had made of myself a **tolerable** printer, under the impression that I would be another Franklin some day, but somehow had missed the connection thus far. There was no berth[4] open in the Esmeralda *Union,* and besides I had always been such a slow compositor[5] that I looked with envy upon the achievements of apprentices of two years' standing; and when I took a "take," foremen were in the habit of suggesting that it would be wanted "some time during the year." I was a good average St. Louis and New Orleans pilot and by no means ashamed of my abilities in that line; wages were two hundred and fifty dollars a month and no board[6] to pay, and I did long to stand behind a wheel again and never roam any more—but I had been making such a fool of myself lately in grandiloquent letters home about my blind lead and my European excursion that I did what many and many a poor disappointed miner had done before; said, "It is all over with me now, and I will never go back home to be pitied—and snubbed." I had been a private secretary, a silver-miner and a silver-mill operative, and amounted to less than nothing in each, and now— B

tolerable (tŏl'ər-ə-bəl) *adj.* fairly good; passab

B VOICE
Reread lines 19–21. Where does Twain use **understatement** in this passage?

What to do next?

I **yielded** to Higbie's appeals and consented to try the mining once more. We climbed far up on the mountainside and went to work on a little rubbishy claim of ours that had a shaft on it eight feet deep. Higbie descended into it and worked bravely with his pick till he had loosened up a deal of rock and dirt, and then I went down with a long-handled shovel (the most awkward invention yet **contrived** by man) to throw it out. You must brace the shovel forward with the side of your knee till it is full, and then, with a skillful toss, throw it backward over your left shoulder. I made the toss, and landed the mess just on the edge of the shaft and it all came back on my head and down the back of my neck. I never said a word, but climbed out and walked home. I inwardly resolved that I would starve before I would make a target of myself and shoot rubbish at it with a long-handled shovel. I sat down, in the cabin, and gave myself up to solid misery—so to speak. Now in pleasanter days I had amused myself with writing letters to the chief paper of the territory, the Virginia *Daily Territorial Enterprise,* and had always been surprised when they appeared in print. My good opinion of the editors had steadily declined; for it seemed to me that they might have found something better to fill up with than my literature. I had found a letter in the post-office as I came home from the hillside, and finally I opened it. Eureka! [I never did know what Eureka meant, but it seems to be as proper a word to heave in as any when no other that sounds pretty offers.] It was a deliberate offer to me of Twenty-five Dollars a week to come up to Virginia and be city editor of the *Enterprise.* C

yield (yēld) *v.* to give in to another

contrive (kən-trīv') *v.* to invent or fabricate, especially by improvisat

C MONITOR
How did Twain get a jo offer from the *Enterpris* Note the strategy you used to find this answe

4. **berth:** job.
5. **compositor** (kəm-pŏz'ĭ-tər): a worker who sets type for a printing business.
6. **board:** meals.

DIFFERENTIATED INSTRUCTION

FOR LESS–PROFICIENT READERS

Concept Support

- Help students identify the techniques that Twain uses to achieve humor in lines 19–21 (*understatement*), 24–27 (*hyperbole*), and 47–48 (*hyperbole*).
- Point out that another way in which Twain achieves humor is by poking fun at himself. For example, in lines 49–54, he says that he doesn't think much of any group that values his work.

FOR ENGLISH LEARNERS

Language: Clarify Clarify these phrases and terms for students:

- *he could have my custom* (line 12), "he could have me as a customer"
- *another Franklin* (line 22), "as good a printer as Ben Franklin, the leading printer and newspaper publisher in colonial America"
- *when I took a "take"* (line 25), "when I took a turn (at setting type)"
- *grandiloquent* (line 31), "filled with fancy and grand language"
- *humiliation* (line 66), "loss of dignity or pride"
- *proprietor* (line 88), "owner-manager of a business"
- *desperado* (line 125), "outlaw"
- *saloon* (line 126), "place where alcoholic drinks are sold and drunk"
- *trifle* (line 127), "something of little importance"

708 UNIT 6: STYLE, VOICE, AND TONE

I would have challenged the publisher in the "blind lead" days—I wanted to fall down and worship him, now. Twenty-five Dollars a week—it looked like bloated luxury—a fortune, a sinful and lavish waste of money. But my transports[7] cooled when I thought of my inexperience and consequent unfitness for the position—and straightway, on top of this, my long **array** of failures rose up before me. Yet if I refused this place I must presently become dependent upon somebody for my bread, a thing necessarily distasteful to a man who had never experienced such a humiliation since he was thirteen years old. Not much to be proud of, since it is so common—but then it was all I had to *be* proud of. So I was scared into being a city editor. I would have declined, otherwise. Necessity is the mother of "taking chances." I do not doubt that if, at that time, I had been offered a salary to translate the Talmud[8] from the original Hebrew, I would have accepted—albeit with diffidence and some misgivings—and thrown as much variety into it as I could for the money. D

array (ə-rā') *n.* a large number of items

D VOICE
Reread lines 69–72. Where is **hyperbole** used in this passage?

7. **transports:** joyful excitement.
8. **Talmud** (täl'mo͝od): a collection of ancient writings by rabbis; this is the basis of Orthodox Jewish law.

ANALYZE VISUALS
Identify which man in the illustration is Mark Twain. How does the drawing of him **compare** with your mental image?

LITERARY ANALYSIS

D VOICE

Possible answer: *Twain uses hyperbole when he says he would have accepted any job for a good salary, even one for which he was clearly unqualified. Twain is emphasizing how desperate he was to find work. The humor of this passage lies in imagining Twain attempting to translate the Talmud when he doesn't know Hebrew.*

ANALYZE VISUALS

Possible answer: *We can assume based on his prominence in the illustration that the man standing is Mark Twain. Like the man in the drawing, Twain "secured a more conservative costume" and did not wear a revolver (lines 79–81).*

About the Art The engravings on this page and on page 710 are original illustrations from the 1897 edition of *Roughing It.*

FOR ENGLISH LEARNERS

Vocabulary Support [mixed-readiness groups] Make copies of the paragraph on page 709 for students. Have them individually circle any words that are unfamiliar. Then place students in small groups. Ask them to use context and prior knowledge to define as many circled words as they can. Then have them check the definitions in a dictionary. Ask each student to compile a personal list of challenging words, along with their definitions, and practice using them.

FOR ADVANCED LEARNERS/PRE–AP

Analyze Language Challenge students to rewrite lines 59–72 in their own words. Tell them their paraphrase should contain all the basic information that is in the original. Suggest that students read aloud their paraphrases in a small group and note similarities and differences. (Explain that *"blind lead" days* is a reference to Twain's days as a prospector, when he might have struck it rich if he had finished his part of the job.)

ANALYZE VISUALS

Activity Ask students which of Twain's adventures the picture may relate to and what the picture suggests about his skills as a horseman. ***Possible answer:*** *The picture may relate to his mining days in the West. It suggests he was not a very good horseman.*

READING STRATEGY

E MONITOR

Remind students to record their responses in the chart from page 705. *Students might read slowly, use context clues, note descriptive details, or reread the passage.*

Lines 87–109

DISCUSSION PROMPTS

Use these prompts to help students understand Twain's approach to journalism:

Recall What are two effects of reporting that sticks to the facts? ***Answer:*** *People have confidence in the news; the newspaper gains a good reputation.*

Infer What does Twain think of the chief editor and his advice? Explain. ***Possible answer:*** *He respects him and values his advice. He shows this by saying that the name "Goodman" describes him well and by saying that "to this day" he evaluates reporting based on Goodman's advice.*

Compare How does Twain's reporting as a city editor match up to Goodman's standards? ***Possible answer:*** *It doesn't; Twain exaggerates and makes up information for his stories.*

I went up to Virginia and entered upon my new vocation. I was a rusty-looking city editor, I am free to confess—coatless, slouch hat, blue woolen shirt, pantaloons stuffed into boot-tops, whiskered half down to the waist, and the universal navy revolver slung to my belt. But I secured a more conservative costume and discarded the revolver. I had never had occasion to kill anybody, nor ever felt a desire to do so, but had worn the thing in deference to popular sentiment, and in order that I might not, by its absence, be offensively **conspicuous,** and a subject of remark. But the other editors, and all the printers, carried revolvers. I asked the chief editor and proprietor (Mr. Goodman, I will call him, since it describes him as well as any name could do) for some instructions with regard to my duties, and he told me to go all over town and ask all sorts of people all sorts of questions, make notes of the information gained, and write them out for publication. And he added: **E**

"Never say 'We learn' so-and-so, or 'It is reported,' or 'It is rumored,' or 'We understand' so-and-so, but go to headquarters and get the absolute facts, and then speak out and say 'It *is* so-and-so.' Otherwise, people will not put confidence in your news. Unassailable[9] certainty is the thing that gives a newspaper the firmest and most valuable reputation."

It was the whole thing in a nutshell; and to this day, when I find a reporter commencing his article with "We understand," I gather a suspicion that he has not taken as much pains to inform himself as he ought to have done. I moralize well, but I did not always practise well when I was a city editor; I let fancy get the upper hand of fact too often when there was a dearth[10] of news. I can never forget my first day's experience as a reporter. I wandered about town questioning everybody, boring everybody, and finding out that nobody knew anything. At the end of five hours my note-book was still barren. I spoke to Mr. Goodman. He said:

"Dan used to make a good thing out of the hay-wagons in a dry time when there were no fires or inquests. Are there no hay-wagons in from the Truckee?

conspicuous (kən-spĭk'yo͞o-əs) *adj.* easy to notice; obvious

E MONITOR Reread lines 73–95. Do you find any of these sentences difficult to understand? If so, choose a strategy to help you clarify their meaning.

9. **unassailable** (ŭn'ə-sā'lə-bəl): impossible to dispute or disprove; undeniable.
10. **dearth** (dûrth): a scarce supply; a lack.

DIFFERENTIATED INSTRUCTION

FOR LESS–PROFICIENT READERS

Reading Strategy Follow-Up: Monitor [paired option] As students read pages 710–711, remind them to reread any passages that are confusing. In their charts from page 705, have them record the line numbers of these passages. Remind them to look for details or context clues that can help them figure out what the lines mean, and to write the meaning in column 2. In column 3, have them briefly note their strategies.

Confusing Lines	What They Mean	How I Figured It Out
Lines 81-86	I wore the revolver because everyone else did, and I didn't want to stand out.	Reread slowly. Used context clues ("deference to popular sentiment," "conspicuous").

If there are, you might speak of the renewed activity and all that sort of thing, in the hay business, you know. It isn't **sensational** or exciting, but it fills up and looks business-like."

sensational (sĕn-sā'shə-nəl) *adj.* intended to arouse strong curiosity or interest, especially through exaggerated details

I canvassed the city again and found one wretched old hay-truck dragging in from the country. But I made affluent use of it. I multiplied it by sixteen, brought it into town from sixteen different directions, made sixteen separate items of it, and got up such another sweat about hay as Virginia City had never seen in the world before.

This was encouraging. Two nonpareil[11] columns had to be filled, and I was getting along. Presently, when things began to look dismal again, a desperado killed a man in a saloon and joy returned once more. I never was so glad over any mere trifle before in my life. I said to the murderer:

"Sir, you are a stranger to me, but you have done me a kindness this day which I can never forget. If whole years of gratitude can be to you any slight compensation, they shall be yours. I was in trouble and you have relieved me nobly and at a time when all seemed dark and drear. Count me your friend from this time forth, for I am not a man to forget a favor." **F**

F VOICE
Do you think Twain really responded to the murder in this way? Explain your answer.

If I did not really say that to him I at least felt a sort of itching desire to do it. I wrote up the murder with a hungry attention to details, and when it was finished experienced but one regret—namely, that they had not hanged my benefactor on the spot, so that I could work him up too.

Next I discovered some emigrant-wagons[12] going into camp on the plaza and found that they had lately come through the hostile Indian country and had fared rather roughly. I made the best of the item that the circumstances permitted, and felt that if I were not confined within **rigid** limits by the presence of the reporters of the other papers I could add particulars that would make the article much more interesting. However, I found one wagon that was going on to California, and made some judicious inquiries of the proprietor. When I learned, through his short and surly answers to my cross-questioning, that he was certainly going on and would not be in the city next day to make trouble, I got ahead of the other papers, for I took down his list of names and added his party to the killed and wounded. Having more scope here, I put this wagon through an Indian fight that to this day has no parallel in history. **G**

rigid (rĭj'ĭd) *adj.* inflexible; strict

G VOICE
Reread lines 137–148. What **amusing descriptions** does Twain use to explain his article about the emigrant-wagons?

My two columns were filled. When I read them over in the morning I felt that I had found my **legitimate** occupation at last. I reasoned within myself that news, and stirring news, too, was what a paper needed, and I felt that I was peculiarly endowed[13] with the ability to furnish it. Mr. Goodman said that I was as good a reporter as Dan. I desired no higher commendation. With encouragement like that, I felt that I could take my pen and murder all the immigrants on the plains if need be, and the interests of the paper demanded it. ∾

legitimate (lə-jĭt'ə-mĭt) *adj.* genuine; authentic

2 Targeted Passage

11. **nonpareil** (nŏn'pə-rĕl'): unequalled; peerless.
12. **emigrant-wagons** (ĕm'ĭ-grənt): wagons in which pioneers rode on their way to settle in the West.
13. **peculiarly endowed** (pĭ-kyōōl'yər-lē ĕn-doud'): specifically supplied with a talent or quality.

LITERARY ANALYSIS

F VOICE

Possible answer: *Twain is not really glad about the murder, but he is happy to have a newsworthy event to write about. He creates humor by contrasting his response to the event with the expected reaction.*

LITERARY ANALYSIS

G VOICE

Possible answer: *Amusing descriptions include*

- *"I took down his list of names and added his party to the killed and wounded" (lines 146–147).*
- *"I put this wagon through an Indian fight that to this day has no parallel in history" (lines 147–148).*

SELECTION WRAP-UP

REFLECT Ask students whether the information in *Roughing It* makes them think they would like being a newspaper reporter. Have them explain.

CRITIQUE Ask which part of *Roughing It* the students found most amusing. Why?

READING FLUENCY

Distribute the copy masters and have students practice fluency.

RESOURCE MANAGER—Copy Master
Reading Fluency p. 107

FOR LESS-PROFICIENT READERS

2 Targeted Passage [Lines 149–155]

In this passage, Twain explains that he has discovered his true calling in life.

- What kind of news does Twain think the newspaper needs?
- What praise does Mr. Goodman, the chief editor, give Twain?
- How does this encouragement affect Twain's plans for his future?

FOR ADVANCED LEARNERS/PRE-AP

Analyze Character Have students develop a personality profile of Mark Twain. Ask them to use a Cluster Diagram to record details about him. Then have them add descriptive adjectives and phrases based on those details. Ask students to present an oral summary of their profile, using their Cluster Diagram for reference.

BEST PRACTICES TOOLKIT—Transparency
Cluster Diagram p. B18

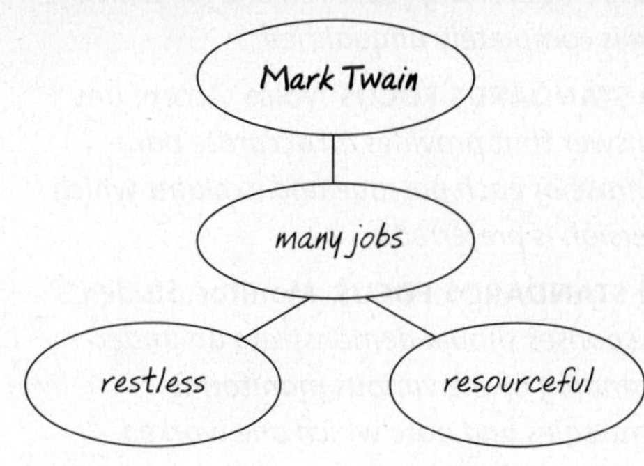

Practice and Apply

After Reading

For additional support of postreading questions, use these copy masters:

RESOURCE MANAGER—Copy Masters

Reading Check p. 104 (to check understanding of the selection)

Voice p. 97 (for practice of literary analysis standards focus)

Question Support p. 105 (After Reading questions adapted for English learners and less-proficient readers)

Additional selection questions are provided for teachers on page 91.

ANSWERS

Comprehension

1. *He eats too many sweets, reads instead of helping customers, and gives out prescriptions that make people sick.*
2. *He decides he would rather starve.*
3. *He fleshes out his stories by inserting incidents that never happened.*

Literary Analysis

Possible answers:

4. ***Exaggeration #1:** "I inwardly resolved that I would starve before I would make a target of myself" (line 47); **Inference:** The author is desperate to find a line of work that suits him. **Exaggeration #2:** "Twenty-five Dollars a week . . . a fortune, a sinful and lavish waste of money" (lines 60–61); **Inference:** Because the author has so much debt and can't hold a job, any amount of money looks like a fortune to him. **Exaggeration #3:** "if . . . I had been offered a salary to translate the Talmud from the original Hebrew, I would have accepted" (lines 70–71); **Inference:** The author is desperate for any job, even one for which he is completely unqualified.*
5. ● **STANDARDS FOCUS Voice** *Accept any answer that provides an accurate paraphrase of each passage and explains which version is preferred.*
6. ■ **STANDARDS FOCUS Monitor** *Students' responses should demonstrate an understanding of the various monitoring strategies and note which one worked best with the selection.*

After Reading

Comprehension

1. **Recall** Why does Mark Twain lose his jobs at the grocery store, bookstore, and drugstore?
2. **Recall** What does Twain decide about mining as an occupation?
3. **Clarify** How does Twain fill up his two newspaper columns?

Literary Analysis

4. **Make Inferences** Although an **exaggeration** may be misleading, it often contains a grain of truth. Skim the selection for three examples of exaggeration that provide information about the author. In a diagram like the one shown, present the examples and tell what you can infer from each one.

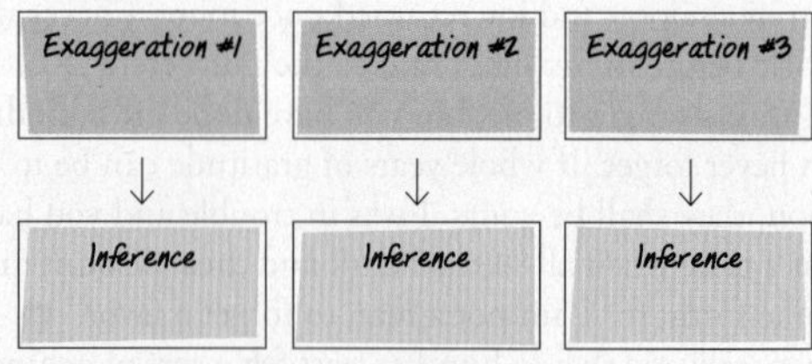

5. **Analyze Voice** Long sentences containing amusing descriptions, hyperbole, and understatement are typical of Twain's unique voice. Find three sentences that you think are particularly funny or effective. Then, rewrite each sentence in a more straightforward way. Which version do you like better?
6. **Examine Monitoring** Review the list you kept while reading. Which monitoring strategy helped you best understand and enjoy *Roughing It?* Explain, and give examples.
7. **Draw Conclusions About Style** Reread lines 2–10. Based on what you know about Twain, why do you think he uses such long, complicated sentences?
8. **Make Judgments** A **memoir** is a form of autobiographical nonfiction in which an author shares part of his or her life story. Memoirs are assumed to be based on fact. Given Twain's generous use of exaggeration, do you think it is fair to label *Roughing It* a memoir? Why or why not?

Extension and Challenge

9. **Creative Response: Art** If *Roughing It* were made into a movie, which parts would draw viewers to the theater? Design a movie poster that illustrates the scenes or characters most likely to attract an audience. Be sure to create an interesting slogan to entice people to see the movie.
10. **Speaking and Listening** With a partner, create a mock interview with Mark Twain. First, brainstorm a list of questions a reporter would ask Twain, based on the information he provides in *Roughing It.* Then, with one person acting as the reporter and one as Twain, conduct the interview in front of the rest of the class. Try to stay true to the selection, and to Twain's voice, by adding humor and **exaggeration** to Twain's responses.

7. *Twain's style may reflect a talkative nature and love of storytelling as well as the more formal prose style of the 19th century.*
8. *Some students may say that because the piece involves fabrications and exaggerations, it should not be called a memoir. Others will say exaggeration is simply a part of Twain's unique voice, and the piece should be considered a memoir because it is based on real events and reveals the author's true character.*

Extension and Challenge

9. *Posters might depict Twain in his various jobs, looking rough when he applies to be a reporter, interviewing the murderer, or imagining a fight between pioneers and Indians. Slogans should be attention-getting and should accurately reflect the memoir's tone and content.*
10. *Interviews should feature questions about key events. The student playing Twain should capture his love of exaggeration and his humorous outlook.*

ocabulary in Context

CABULARY PRACTICE

Synonyms have a similar meaning, and **antonyms** have opposite or nearly opposite meanings. Decide whether the words in each pair are synonyms or antonyms.

1. rigid/permissive
2. tolerable/acceptable
3. conspicuous/noticeable
4. livelihood/occupation
5. legitimate/wrong
6. yield/resist
7. array/variety
8. sensational/understated
9. contrive/invent

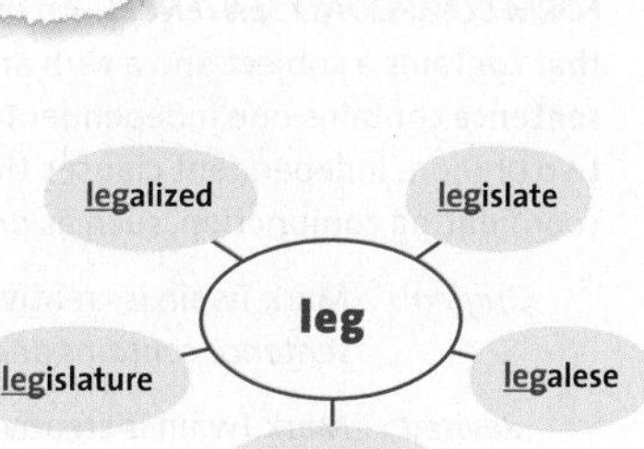

CABULARY IN WRITING

Sometimes we exaggerate to make dull stories more interesting. Think of a boring chore that you are required to do. Write an exaggerated description of how you handle this task. Use at least two vocabulary words in your paragraph. You could start this way.

EXAMPLE SENTENCE

Although it's been several years since I cleaned my room, I find the mess ***tolerable.***

CABULARY STRATEGY: THE LATIN ROOT *leg*

The vocabulary word *legitimate* comes from the Latin root *leg*, which means "law." *Leg* (combined with other word parts) appears in a number of English words. To understand the meaning of a word that contains this root, use context clues and your knowledge of the root's meaning.

leg: legalized, legislate, legislature, legalese, legislators

PRACTICE Choose the word from the web that best completes each sentence. Then explain how the root *leg* helps to give each word its meaning.

1. The document was written in ____, but I finally figured out what it meant.
2. Each region's voters elect one member of our state ____.
3. Dad e-mailed Representative Lee and asked her to help ____ some tough new environmental laws.
4. Senators are ____ who propose laws in Congress.
5. California abolished the death penalty and then ____ it again.

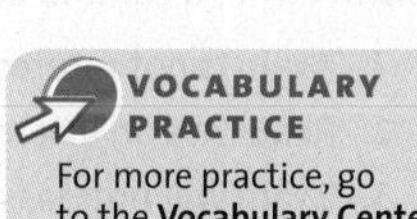

VOCABULARY PRACTICE
For more practice, go to the **Vocabulary Center** at **ClassZone.com.**

DIFFERENTIATED INSTRUCTION

FOR LESS–PROFICIENT READERS

Vocabulary Practice [paired option] Suggest that students create a flash card for each vocabulary word, with the word on one side and a synonym on the other side. Encourage them to "flash" the cards with two different partners. The first time they should show the side with the vocabulary word and ask their partner for a synonym. The second time, they should show the synonym and ask the partner to state the vocabulary word.

FOR ADVANCED LEARNERS/PRE–AP

Vocabulary Strategy [small-group option] Invite groups to expand the word web for the Latin root *leg* by adding additional examples. Have them provide a definition for each example they add and ask them to check their definitions in a dictionary. Challenge students to use the words in sentences.

ANSWERS

Vocabulary in Context

VOCABULARY PRACTICE

1. *antonyms*
2. *synonyms*
3. *synonyms*
4. *synonyms*
5. *antonyms*
6. *antonyms*
7. *synonyms*
8. *antonyms*
9. *synonyms*

RESOURCE MANAGER—Copy Master
Vocabulary Practice p. 102

VOCABULARY IN WRITING

Suggest that students review each word in the boxed list before they begin to write. Tell them to try to work in one or two of these words as they write about their chore. If they cannot, suggest they write the paragraph and then review it to look for places where they could substitute or add one of the vocabulary words.

VOCABULARY STRATEGY: THE LATIN ROOT *leg* *(also an EL language objective)*

- Say each word in the diagram aloud. Ask students to define any of the words they recognize.
- Help them identify each word as a noun or a verb and decide whether a noun or a verb is called for in each ***PRACTICE*** sentence. Then scan the choices in the diagram.

Answers:

1. *legalese*
2. *legislature*
3. *legislate*
4. *legislators*
5. *legalized*

RESOURCE MANAGER—Copy Master
Vocabulary Strategy p. 103

Vocabulary Center at **ClassZone.com**
Additional Vocabulary Activities

Reading-Writing Connection

WRITING PROMPTS

- For **Prompt A,** suggest that students identify statements that reveal Twain's attitude toward work, make inferences, and then generalize from these inferences.
- For **Prompt B,** have students list Phillips's commandments and then take notes on how Twain approached at least two articles.

For writing support, see

Writing Center at **ClassZone.com**

GRAMMAR AND WRITING

Suggest that students determine the relationship between the sentences in each pair. If the sentences show cause and effect, they might be joined by a semicolon or by the word *so.* If the relationship is one of opposites, they might be joined using *but* or *yet.* If one sentence adds information to the other, *and* can be used to join them.

Possible answers:

1. *Twain is not interested in hard work, yet he needs a job to support himself.*
2. *Twain has an interesting way with words, but he tells too many tall tales.*
3. *Twain will not pass his journalism class; he does not follow the rules of ethical writing.*
4. *Twain should conduct better research, and he should not exaggerate his articles for the sake of selling newspapers.*

RESOURCE MANAGER—Copy Master
Form Compound Sentences p. 106

Assess and Reteach

Assess

RESOURCE MANAGER—Copy Masters
Selection Tests A, B/C pp. 109–110, 111–112

Test Generator CD

Reteach

STANDARDS LESSON FILE
Literature Lesson 40: Style
Reading Lesson 2: Monitoring
Vocabulary Lesson 1: Word Parts
Grammar Lesson 20: Missing or Misplaced Commas

Reading-Writing Connection

Broaden your understanding of *Roughing It* by responding to these prompts. Then complete the **Grammar and Writing** exercise.

WRITING PROMPTS	SELF-CHECK
A. Short Response: Explore Author's Attitude A writer's voice reveals his or her unique attitudes and beliefs. Based on your reading of *Roughing It,* how do you think Mark Twain feels about work? In **one paragraph,** describe Twain's attitude toward work.	***A strong response will . . .*** • use examples from the selection • contain a clear statement of opinion
B. Extended Response: Write an Evaluation Imagine that John McCandlish Phillips, author of "The Simple Commandments of Journalistic Ethics" on page 715, is Twain's teacher. How would he evaluate Twain's reporting techniques, including his use of **exaggeration?** Write a **half-page evaluation** of Twain's news articles from Phillips's point of view.	***An effective evaluation will . . .*** • include a statement of opinion about Twain's work as a reporter • provide Twain with advice on how to write ethically

GRAMMAR AND WRITING

FORM COMPOUND SENTENCES An **independent clause** is a group of words that contains a subject and a verb and can stand alone as a sentence. A **simple sentence** contains one independent clause. A **compound sentence** contains two or more independent clauses that are joined either by a comma and a coordinating conjunction, such as *and, but, or, so,* or *yet,* or by a semicolon.

Original: Mark Twain is creative. He's a good writer. (*Each simple sentence contains one independent clause.*)

Revised: Mark Twain is creative, and he's a good writer. (*The compound sentence contains two independent clauses that are joined by a comma and a coordinating conjunction.*)

PRACTICE Create a compound sentence by joining the two simple sentences with either a comma and a coordinating conjunction or a semicolon.

1. Twain is not interested in hard work. He needs a job to support himself.
2. Twain has an interesting way with words. He tells too many tall tales.
3. Twain will not pass his journalism class. He does not follow the rules of ethical writing.
4. Twain should conduct better research. He should not exaggerate his articles for the sake of selling newspapers.

*For more help with independent clauses and simple and compound sentences, see pages R62 and R63 in the **Grammar Handbook.***

DIFFERENTIATED INSTRUCTION

FOR LESS–PROFICIENT WRITERS

For Prompt A:

1. Tell students to begin by presenting an opinion statement.
2. Then have students support their opinion with three examples of Twain's comments about work and conclude the paragraph.

For Prompt B:

1. Suggest that students use a T Chart to take notes on pages 710–711 of the memoir and the article on page 715.
2. Ask students to describe Twain's work in the first paragraph, providing examples for support. In the next paragraph, ask them to give ethical guidelines for reporting the news. In a final paragraph, ask them to point out ways Twain could improve his reporting techniques.

BEST PRACTICES TOOLKIT—Transparency
T Chart p. A25

Reading for Information

NEWSPAPER ARTICLE You wouldn't know it from reading about Mark Twain's behavior, but most journalists actually follow a code of ethics, or fairness. In this article, a former *New York Times* writer explains this code to student journalists.

SECTION A THE STAR JOURNAL A3

The Simple Commandments of Journalistic Ethics

John McCandlish Phillips

. . . Long after my years in news reporting, I have had repeated occasions to speak to young or aspiring journalists. With rare exceptions, the matter they have wanted most to hear about is reportorial ethics. . . .

Here is the core of what I tell aspiring journalists about the question they so reliably pose:

In journalistic usage, you shall be as accurate and balanced and fair, and as faithful to pinned-down facts, as you possibly can be. The right does not exist to put anything whatever between quotation marks that are not words as they were spoken, to 97 percent word accuracy. Misquotation or fabricated quotation is lying in print—a terrible disservice to those abused by the license taken. It does not help when the act is careless rather than deceitful.

You will not lie. You will not distort. You will not make things up.

You will not embroider your story for effect.

If you get into investigative reporting, never let your suspicions run one-eighth of an inch ahead of your facts—solid, fully ascertained evidence that conclusively verifies the suspicions that promoted the investigation.

Newspapers and broadcast news must—and they do—report accusations made by public figures against other such figures. When the newspaper itself levels the accusation, and presents its supporting case, it is much more deeply hurtful to the accused than the former is.

Always remember that, in public accusation, the irreducible, primary, essential requirement is that it be factually accurate. If it truly is, you have every right to take it to print or on air, and things will likely be better for it.

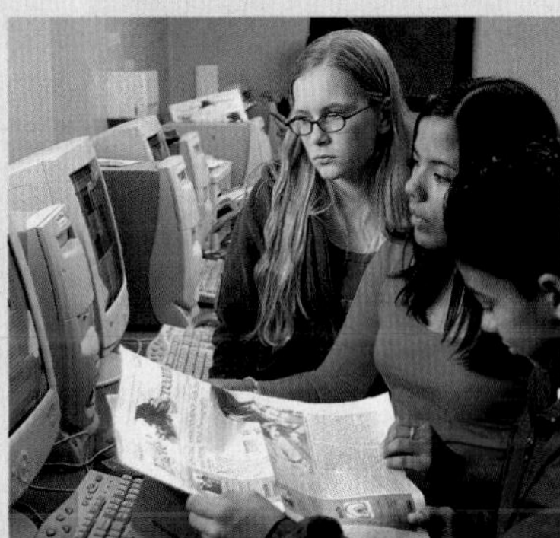

Students design a school newspaper.

This selection provides support for Writing Prompt B on page 714. You can also use it as a mini-lesson on reading for information.

READING FOR INFORMATION

This newspaper article will help students put Mark Twain's dubious journalistic practices into perspective. Ask students to pretend they are Twain and write a paragraph from the first-person point of view discussing their opinion of journalism ethics.

DISCUSSION PROMPTS

Use these prompts to help students understand the principles of good journalism:

Connect Why is behaving ethically important? *Students may say that ethical behavior shows respect for other people and creates a climate of trust.*

Analyze What are two examples of "lying in print"? ***Possible answer:*** *misquoting someone, making up a quotation*

Speculate Why does Phillips make a special point of telling journalists to be careful when presenting accusations made by public figures against other public figures? ***Possible answer:*** *Such accusations can ruin a person's career.*

DIFFERENTIATED INSTRUCTION

FOR ENGLISH LEARNERS

Vocabulary Support Before students read the selection or listen to the *Audio Anthology CD*, provide the following definitions:

- *ethics*, "rules of appropriate behavior"
- *misquotation*, "incorrect statement of a person's words"
- *fabricated*, "invented"
- *embroider*, "add fanciful details"
- *ascertained*, "discovered"

FOR ADVANCED LEARNERS/PRE–AP

Extrapolate Key Points Have students discuss these questions:

- Are some of the commandments more important than others? Explain.
- In what ways are Phillips's commandments similar to or different from those of Mr. Goodman, Twain's editor?
- Why are journalistic ethics important to society?

Focus and Motivate

OBJECTIVES

Literary Analysis
- explore the key idea of **normal**
- identify and analyze irony
- read a personal essay

Reading
- evaluate information and opinions

Vocabulary
- build vocabulary for reading and writing
- use context to determine the meanings of idioms *(also an EL language objective)*

Grammar and Writing
- form a complex sentence by joining an independent and a dependent clause
- use writing to analyze literature

SUMMARY

In this essay, the author describes his fascination as a young boy with a family on his street. They do not watch television, and he pities their isolation and ignorance of popular culture. His feelings turn to dislike, however, when they come trick-or-treating the day after Halloween and he is forced to give some of his own candy to them.

What's really NORMAL?

Discuss the question and the ***KEY IDEA.*** Ask students if they think ***normal*** is, indeed, a relative term. In other words, can someone be normal in one setting and abnormal in another? Have students share their opinions before they begin the ***DISCUSS*** activity.

Before Reading

Us and Them

Personal Essay by David Sedaris

What's really NORMAL?

KEY IDEA Imagine a town where everyone dyes his or her hair purple and spends free time either at puppet shows or raising ferrets. If someone moves in who has brown hair and loves video games and soccer, would he or she be considered **normal?** What we mean by that word often depends on where we are and who we're with. In the selection you are about to read, a young boy is fascinated by a family that doesn't seem normal.

DISCUSS How do you define *normal?* Think about things like the way you and your friends and family dress, the music you listen to, and the activities you participate in. Create a definition for the word *normal* based on these observations, and compare it with classmates' definitions. Is everyone's view of *normal* the same?

Selection Resources

RESOURCE MANAGER UNIT 6

Plan and Teach pp. 113–120

Literary Analysis
Summary pp. 121†*, 122‡*
Irony pp. 123, 124†*
Question Support p. 131*

Reading
Evaluate pp. 125, 126†*
Reading Check p. 130

Vocabulary
Study p. 127*
Practice p. 128
Strategy p. 129

Grammar and Writing
Form Complex Sentences p. 132

Assessment
Selection Tests A, B/C pp. 133*, 135*
Test Generator CD

BEST PRACTICES TOOLKIT

Differentiated Instruction pp. 31–38*
Scaffolding Instruction pp. 43–46*

Graphic Organizers/Strategies
Reciprocal Teaching • Word Questioning • T Chart • Cluster Diagram

Reading Support
Audio Anthology CD*

Technology
Literature, Vocabulary, and Writing Centers at **ClassZone.com**
Write*Smart* CD

* Resources for Differentiation † Also in Spanish ‡ In Haitian Creole and Vietnamese

ERARY ANALYSIS: IRONY

Have you ever stayed up late to study for a test, only to find out that the test was postponed? Many people would call this turn of events ironic. **Irony** is a contrast between what is expected and what actually exists or happens. Irony can make a piece of literature tragic, thoughtful, or funny, depending upon the writer's goal. Types of irony include

- **situational irony,** which is a contrast between what is expected to happen and what actually does happen
- **verbal irony,** which occurs when someone states one thing and means another
- **dramatic irony,** which happens when readers know more about a situation or a character in a story than the characters do

As you read, record examples of irony in a chart as shown.

Example	Type of Irony	Why It's Ironic

Review: Tone

ADING SKILL: EVALUATE

When you **evaluate,** you make judgments about the author's opinions, actions, or statements. Forming opinions on what you read makes you think about what's right and wrong, and why. As you read, judge whether the young David Sedaris's thoughts and actions seem sensible, fair, and accurate.

CABULARY IN CONTEXT

The way Sedaris uses the following boldfaced words helps create the ironic **tone** of his story. Use context clues in each sentence to figure out the meaning of the boldfaced terms.

1. Lucy doesn't **merit** an invitation to my party.
2. Don't **imply** that you believe me if you really don't.
3. Carmen, don't **inflict** your terrible music on me!
4. Although I disagree, I won't **interfere** with your decision.
5. I **attribute** John's grades to hard work and dedication.
6. Taylor tosses her papers **indiscriminately** into her bag.
7. There's no way Mom can **accommodate** all of us in her tiny car.
8. If you **provoke** me, I will likely argue with you.

Author Online

A Man of Many Jobs David Sedaris has had several odd jobs over the years, including apple picking, house painting, performance art, and apartment cleaning. But a humorous essay he wrote about his experiences working as an elf in a department store's holiday display launched his writing career. After reading "The SantaLand Diaries" on National Public Radio, Sedaris became an instant hit, and since then his books have sold millions of copies. His inspiration comes from the diaries he has kept for over 30 years, in which he records his intelligent, funny, and emotional observations on everyday life.

David Sedaris
born 1957

Literary Rock Star Sedaris frequently tours the U.S. and Europe, reading his essays and short stories to sold-out concert halls. These appearances give Sedaris a chance to meet his fans and also to improve his writing. He often reads unpublished essays, revising them based on the crowd's reaction.

Family Secrets Many of Sedaris's essays are about the people in his life. His book *Dress Your Family in Corduroy and Denim,* from which this essay was taken, contains thoughts on his family and childhood. In one essay, he writes that his family is afraid to tell him anything important for fear that their stories will end up in his next book. Most of their conversations, he says, begin with the words "You have to swear you will never repeat this." Fortunately for his readers, Sedaris doesn't make those promises.

MORE ABOUT THE AUTHOR
For more on David Sedaris, visit the **Literature Center** at **ClassZone.com.**

Teach

STANDARDS FOCUS

LITERARY ANALYSIS

● IRONY

Write this example on the board and ask students what kind of irony it uses:

> For once, I was going to get to school on time. Within minutes of my alarm ringing, I was ready and walking out the door, waving goodbye to my puzzled parents. An hour later, I trudged back in to find them laughing hysterically. I had forgotten it was Saturday.

Answer: *The irony is situational. The narrator rushes to school, only to find out that it's not a school day.*

CHECK UNDERSTANDING Ask students to identify examples of irony from previous selections they have read.

RESOURCE MANAGER—Copy Master
Irony p. 123 (for student use while reading the selection)

READING SKILL

■ EVALUATE

Tell students that evaluating is a skill they use frequently in daily life. For example, when they decide what to have for lunch, they are judging the merits of each choice and deciding what is right for them.

CHECK UNDERSTANDING Ask students to identify other circumstances in which they evaluate something or someone.

VOCABULARY SKILL

▲ VOCABULARY IN CONTEXT

DIAGNOSE WORD KNOWLEDGE To determine preteaching needs, have all students complete **Vocabulary in Context.** *Responses will vary.* ***Possible answers:*** **1.** *deserve* **2.** *suggest* **3.** *force* **4.** *get involved* **5.** *credit* **6.** *carelessly* **7.** *fit* **8.** *goad*

PRETEACH VOCABULARY Use the Vocabulary Study copy master to help students explore the meaning of each boldfaced word.

1. Read aloud the first sentence.
2. Ask students to identify clues to the meaning of *accommodate,* such as *small front hall* and *barely.* Discuss possible meanings for *accommodate,* such as "fit."
3. Repeat the procedure for items 2–8.
4. Have students complete the chart in Part B independently.

RESOURCE MANAGER—Copy Master
Vocabulary Study p. 127

For general guidelines on differentiating vocabulary instruction and for alternative vocabulary activities for students not needing vocabulary preteaching, see

BEST PRACTICES TOOLKIT
Scaffolding Vocabulary Instruction pp. 43–46

Vocabulary Center at **ClassZone.com**
Additional Vocabulary Activities

Practice and Apply

LITERARY ANALYSIS

Ⓐ IRONY

Have students record this first example of irony in their charts from page 717. ***Possible answer:***

- ***Example:*** *Sedaris says he could make friends if he wanted to, but it isn't the right time (lines 9–10).*
- ***Type of Irony:*** *verbal*
- ***Why It's Ironic:*** *Sedaris is obviously unable to make friends at this point in his life, but this comment makes it seem as if it is his choice.*

If students need help . . . Review the definition of verbal irony. The author is saying one thing, but the truth is something different.

Extend the Discussion What does the comment reveal about Sedaris's personality at this point in his life?

ANALYZE VISUALS

Possible answer: *The dark, gray colors on the outside contrast with the red lampshade and bright lights beaming from inside the house. It seems that everything is normal outside, but something very interesting is happening inside.*

About the Art The painting on page 719 is representative of the work of American artist Ryan Kapp (born 1973), who often depicts framed windows and scenes of light amidst darkness. He is inspired by personal photographs and by illustrations from magazines.

David Sedaris

When my family first moved to North Carolina, we lived in a rented house three blocks from the school where I would begin the third grade. My mother made friends with one of the neighbors, but one seemed enough for her. Within a year we would move again and, as she explained, there wasn't much point in getting too close to people we would have to say good-bye to. Our next house was less than a mile away, and the short journey would hardly **merit** tears or even good-byes, for that matter. It was more of a "see you later" situation, but still I adopted my mother's attitude, as it allowed me to pretend that not making friends was a conscious[1] choice. I could if I wanted to. It just wasn't the right time. Ⓐ

Back in New York State, we had lived in the country, with no sidewalks or streetlights; you could leave the house and still be alone. But here, when you looked out the window, you saw other houses, and people inside those houses. I hoped that in walking around after dark I might witness a murder, but for the most part our neighbors just sat in their living rooms, watching TV. The only place that seemed truly different was owned by a man named Mr. Tomkey, who did not believe in television. This was told to us by our mother's friend, who dropped by one afternoon with a basketful of okra.[2] The woman did not editorialize[3]—rather, she just presented her information, leaving her listener to make of it what she might. Had my mother said, "That's the craziest thing I've ever heard in my life," I assume that the friend would have agreed, and had she said, "Three cheers for Mr. Tomkey," the friend likely would have agreed as well. It was a kind of test, as was the okra.

merit (mĕr′ĭt) *v.* to deserve

Ⓐ IRONY
Reread lines 6–10. When Sedaris says he could make friends if h wanted to, what does he actually mean?

ANALYZE VISUALS
Note the colors used in this painting. Why do y think the artist chose t **contrast** the inside and outside of the house in this way?

1. **conscious:** deliberate.
2. **okra** (ō′krə): edible pods used in soups and as a vegetable.
3. **editorialize** (ĕd′ĭ-tôr′ē-əl-īz′): to give one's own opinions on a topic.

Detail of *Outside In* (2004), Ryan Kapp. Oi canvas on panel, 18″ × 24″. © Ryan Ka

DIFFERENTIATED INSTRUCTION

FOR ALL STUDENTS

Interest Stations Post suggested projects for students to work on independently.

- **Comic Strip** Illustrate one of the incidents in the author's life in the form of a comic strip.
- **Poster** Use images and text to explore the concept of "normal."
- **Oral Report** Research the influence of television on people's lives.

For further details on these projects, see

RESOURCE MANAGER
Ideas for Extension pp. 142–143

FOR LESS-PROFICIENT READERS

In combination with the *Audio Anthology CD*, use one or more Targeted Passages (pp. 720, 721, 724) to ensure that students focus on key events, concepts, and skills.

FOR ENGLISH LEARNERS

Options for Reading [small-group option] Read aloud lines 1–23 to familiarize students with the author's style. Explain that in this essay the author is describing a period in his childhood. Have students read the rest of the essay along with the *Audio Anthology CD* and use a Reciprocal Teaching strategy in small groups to increase their comprehension of plot and literary techniques in nonfiction.

BEST PRACTICES TOOLKIT—Transparency
Reciprocal Teaching p. A35

BACKGROUND

Television in the 1960s The first televisions were sold in 1939, but the trend did not truly catch on until the late 1940s. At the time in which the essay is set, the mid-1960s, over 90 percent of households in the United States had a television. Although color television had been invented a decade or so earlier, these sets were very expensive, so most families had sets that showed only black-and-white images.

FOR ENGLISH LEARNERS

Key Academic Vocabulary Have students use Word Questioning to study *grade* (lines 3, 62, 63), *attitude* (line 8), *compensate* (line 35), *ignorant* (line 66), and *shift* (lines 196, 199).

 BEST PRACTICES TOOLKIT—Transparency
Word Questioning p. E9

Prereading For prereading instruction for English learners, see

 BEST PRACTICES TOOLKIT
Scaffolding Reading Instruction pp. 43–46

FOR ADVANCED LEARNERS/PRE–AP

Pre-AP exercises in the bottom channel provide additional challenge for your advanced students. Use them for small groups or individuals.

ADDITIONAL GUIDELINES

For more help with differentiation and tips for classroom management, see

 BEST PRACTICES TOOLKIT
Differentiated Instruction pp. 31–38

LITERARY ANALYSIS

B IRONY

Remind students to record this example of irony in their charts from page 717. ***Possible answer:*** *The mother claims that she does not believe in television, but then she watches the news "and whatever [comes] on after the news," showing that she has no real objection to it.*

Lines 38–58

DISCUSSION PROMPTS

Use these prompts to help students understand the significance of Sedaris's behavior in this passage:

Connect Would you have recommended to Sedaris that he spy on the Tomkeys to satisfy his curiosity? Why or why not? *Students may say that they would have recommended other approaches, such as making friends with them. Spying on the Tomkeys is sneaky, wrong, and odd.*

Analyze Based on his comments about the Tomkeys, what role does television play in Sedaris's life? ***Possible answer:*** *His comments indicate that his standards for judging others and his ideas about what is normal come from television.*

Synthesize What is the irony of Sedaris's evaluation of the Tomkeys? ***Possible answer:*** *The irony is that Sedaris and his family seem to be the odd ones compared to the Tomkeys, whose lack of dependence on television allows them to interact with each other and make their own decisions about how to live their lives.*

Lines 63–67

REINFORCE *KEY IDEA:* NORMAL

Discuss To Sedaris, what defines a **normal** person? ***Possible answer:*** *To Sedaris, a normal person is one who watches television and who behaves the way people do on TV.*

To say that you did not believe in television was different from saying that you did not care for it. Belief **implied** that television had a master plan and that you were against it. It also suggested that you thought too much. When my mother reported that Mr. Tomkey did not believe in television, my father said, "Well, good for him. I don't know that I believe in it, either."

"That's exactly how I feel," my mother said, and then my parents watched the news, and whatever came on after the news. B

imply (ĭm-plī') *v.* to express indirectly

B IRONY
Reread lines 29–30. What's the difference between what the mother says and what she does?

Word spread that Mr. Tomkey did not own a television, and you began hearing that while this was all very well and good, it was unfair of him to **inflict** his beliefs upon others, specifically his innocent wife and children. It was speculated that just as the blind man develops a keener sense of hearing, the family must somehow compensate for their loss. "Maybe they read," my mother's friend said. "Maybe they listen to the radio, but you can bet your boots they're doing *something.*"

inflict (ĭn-flĭkt') *v.* to deal out something unpleasant or burdensome; to impose

I wanted to know what this something was, and so I began peering through the Tomkeys' windows. During the day I'd stand across the street from their house, acting as though I were waiting for someone, and at night, when the view was better and I had less chance of being discovered, I would creep into their yard and hide in the bushes beside their fence.

(1) Targeted Passage

Because they had no TV, the Tomkeys were forced to talk during dinner. They had no idea how puny their lives were, and so they were not ashamed that a camera would have found them uninteresting. They did not know what attractive was or what dinner was supposed to look like or even what time people were supposed to eat. Sometimes they wouldn't sit down until eight o'clock, long after everyone else had finished doing the dishes. During the meal, Mr. Tomkey would occasionally pound the table and point at his children with a fork, but the moment he finished, everyone would start laughing. I got the idea that he was imitating someone else, and wondered if he spied on us while we were eating.

When fall arrived and school began, I saw the Tomkey children marching up the hill with paper sacks in their hands. The son was one grade lower than me, and the daughter was one grade higher. We never spoke, but I'd pass them in the halls from time to time and attempt to view the world through their eyes. What must it be like to be so ignorant and alone? Could a normal person even imagine it? Staring at an

---

DIFFERENTIATED INSTRUCTION

FOR LESS–PROFICIENT READERS

(1) Targeted Passage [Lines 31–42]

This passage begins to build understanding of Sedaris's relationship with the Tomkeys.

- In what way do the neighbors react when they find out that the Tomkeys don't watch television?
- Why does Sedaris decide to spy on the Tomkeys?
- What do Sedaris's actions reveal about his personality?

FOR ADVANCED LEARNERS/PRE-AP

Analyze Author's Purpose [small-group option] Point out to students the irony of Sedaris's depiction of himself in this essay, focusing particularly on lines 38–71. Ask students to discuss in small groups what the author's ironic self-portrayal reveals about his purpose for writing this essay.

Elmer Fudd[4] lunch box, I tried to divorce myself from[5] everything I already knew: Elmer's inability to pronounce the letter *r,* his constant pursuit of an intelligent and considerably more famous rabbit. I tried to think of him as just a drawing, but it was impossible to separate him from his celebrity. **C**

One day in class a boy named William began to write the wrong answer on the blackboard, and our teacher flailed her arms, saying, "Warning, Will. Danger, danger." Her voice was synthetic and void of emotion, and we laughed, knowing that she was imitating the robot in a weekly show about a family who lived in outer space. The Tomkeys, though, would have thought she was having a heart attack. It occurred to me that they needed a guide, someone who could accompany them through the course of an average day and point out all the things they were unable to understand. I could have done it on weekends, but friendship would have taken away their mystery and **interfered** with the good feeling I got from pitying them. So I kept my distance.[6] **D**

C TONE
Reread lines 43–71. What words and images reveal Sedaris's attitude toward the Tomkeys?

interfere (ĭn'tər-fîr') *v.* to create an obstacle

D EVALUATE
Do you think Sedaris is right to keep his distance? Explain.

In early October the Tomkeys bought a boat, and everyone seemed greatly relieved, especially my mother's friend, who noted that the motor was definitely secondhand. It was reported that Mr. Tomkey's father-in-law owned a house on the lake and had invited the family to use it whenever they liked. This explained why they were gone all weekend, but it did not make their absences any easier to bear. I felt as if my favorite show had been canceled.

Halloween fell on a Saturday that year, and by the time my mother took us to the store, all the good costumes were gone. My sisters dressed as witches and I went as a hobo. I'd looked forward to going in disguise to the Tomkeys' door, but they were off at the lake, and their house was dark. Before leaving, they had left a coffee can full of gumdrops on the front porch, alongside a sign reading DON'T BE GREEDY. In terms of Halloween candy, individual gumdrops were just about as low as you could get. This was evidenced by the large number of them floating in an adjacent dog bowl. It was disgusting to think that this was what a gumdrop might look like in your stomach, and it was insulting to be told not to take too much of something you didn't really want in the first place. "Who do these Tomkeys think they are?" my sister Lisa said.

2 Targeted Passage

The night after Halloween, we were sitting around watching TV when the doorbell rang. Visitors were infrequent at our house, so while my father stayed behind, my mother, sisters, and I ran downstairs in a group, opening the door to discover the entire Tomkey family on our front stoop. The parents looked as they always had, but the son and daughter were dressed in costumes—she as a ballerina and he as some kind of a rodent with terry-cloth ears and a tail made from what looked to be an extension cord. It seemed they had spent the previous evening isolated at the lake and had missed the opportunity

4. **Elmer Fudd** (ĕl'mər fŭd): a cartoon character who is always chasing after Bugs Bunny; Fudd mispronounces the *r* sound as *w,* as in "wascally wabbit."
5. **divorce myself from:** separate myself from.
6. **kept my distance:** kept myself emotionally distant.

LITERARY ANALYSIS: *Review*

C TONE

Possible answer: *Phrases that develop Sedaris's tone of pity for the Tomkeys and his own feelings of superiority include*

- *"forced to talk during dinner" (line 44)*
- *"no idea how puny their lives were" (lines 44–45)*
- *"not ashamed that a camera would have found them uninteresting" (lines 46–47)*
- *"attempt to view the world through their eyes" (lines 64–65)*
- *"ignorant and alone" (line 66)*

If students need help . . . Read these lines aloud, emphasizing words and phrases that contribute to the tone, to enable students to hear Sedaris's tone.

READING SKILL

D EVALUATE

Possible answer: *Students will likely say that he is wrong to keep his distance. He could be friends with the Tomkeys if he wanted to be, but he is less interested in them as people than as a means of amusement and a curiosity.*

FOR LESS-PROFICIENT READERS

2 Targeted Passage [Lines 82–99]

This passage develops understanding of Sedaris's attitude toward the Tomkeys.

- How does Sedaris feel when the Tomkeys begin going to the lake each weekend? Why?
- Why does Sedaris look forward to going to the Tomkeys' house for Halloween? Why is he disappointed when he arrives?

FOR ENGLISH LEARNERS

Culture: Clarify Explain that in lines 88–99, Sedaris is making a judgment on the kind of candy left out by the Tomkeys. To his family, a couple of gumdrops, which are little chewy jellies, cannot compare to a miniature chocolate bar or a roll of hard candy. In addition, the author and his sister see it as a sign that the Tomkeys are insensitive and out of touch.

Vocabulary: Compound Words [mixed-readiness groups] Review the definition of a compound word. Then have students work in small groups to find as many compound words as they can in lines 24–106. Have them list the words and define them using their knowledge of the word parts and context clues. Have groups compare their lists and definitions.

to observe[7] Halloween. "So, well, I guess we're trick-or-treating *now,* if that's okay," Mr. Tomkey said.

I **attributed** their behavior to the fact that they didn't have a TV, but television didn't teach you everything. Asking for candy on Halloween was called trick-or-treating, but asking for candy on November first was called begging, and it made people uncomfortable. This was one of the things you were supposed to learn simply by being alive, and it angered me that the Tomkeys didn't understand it. **E**

"Why, of course it's not too late," my mother said. "Kids, why don't you . . . run and get . . . the candy."

"But the candy is gone," my sister Gretchen said. "You gave it away last night."

"Not *that* candy," my mother said. "The other candy. Why don't you run and go get it?"

"You mean *our* candy?" Lisa said. "The candy that we *earned?*"

This was exactly what our mother was talking about, but she didn't want to say this in front of the Tomkeys. In order to spare their feelings, she wanted them to believe that we always kept a bucket of candy lying around the house, just waiting for someone to knock on the door and ask for it. "Go on, now," she said. "Hurry up."

My room was situated right off the foyer, and if the Tomkeys had looked in that direction, they could have seen my bed and the brown paper bag marked MY CANDY. KEEP OUT. I didn't want them to know how much I had, and so I went into my room and shut the door behind me. Then I closed the curtains and emptied my bag onto the bed, searching for whatever was the crummiest. All my life chocolate has made me ill. I don't know if I'm allergic or what, but even the smallest amount leaves me with a blinding headache. Eventually, I learned to stay away from it, but as a child I refused to be left out. The brownies were eaten, and when the pounding began I would blame the grape juice or my mother's cigarette smoke or the tightness of my glasses—anything but the chocolate. My candy bars were poison but they were brand-name, and so I put them in pile no. 1, which definitely would not go to the Tomkeys.

Out in the hallway I could hear my mother straining for something to talk about. "A boat!" she said. "That sounds marvelous. Can you just drive it right into the water?"

"Actually, we have a trailer," Mr. Tomkey said. "So what we do is back it into the lake."

"Oh, a trailer. What kind is it?"

"Well, it's a *boat* trailer," Mr. Tomkey said.

"Right, but is it wooden or, you know . . . I guess what I'm asking is what *style* trailer do you have?"

Behind my mother's words were two messages. The first and most obvious was "Yes, I am talking about boat trailers, but also I am dying." The second, meant only for my sisters and me, was "If you do not immediately step forward

7. **observe:** to celebrate.

attribute (ə-trĭb'yo͞ot) *v.* to relate to a certain cause

E EVALUATE
Is Sedaris's reaction to the late trick-or-treaters appropriate?

READING SKILL

E EVALUATE

Possible answer: *His angry reaction is not really reasonable. The Tomkeys aren't doing anything wrong.*

Extend the Discussion Why does this incident upset Sedaris so much?

Lines 121–131

REINFORCE *KEY IDEA:* NORMAL

Discuss In what way do Sedaris and his sisters respond to their mother's request? Is their reaction **normal**? ***Possible answer:*** *Sedaris and his sisters don't want to give up their candy. Many children would react the same way.*

DIFFERENTIATED INSTRUCTION

FOR LESS–PROFICIENT READERS

Concept Support [small-group option] Review the three types of irony, encouraging students to give examples of each type. Then have small groups reread lines 110–138 and ask them to find examples of irony. Discuss students' responses and record them in the class chart from page 717.

Example	*Type of Irony*	*Why It's Ironic*
The mother tells the children to get the candy (lines 116–117).	*dramatic*	*The children and readers know there is no candy, but the Tomkeys do not.*
"The candy that we earned?" (line 121)	*verbal*	*Asking for candy, whether on Halloween or on November 1, is not working for it or earning it.*

ANALYZE VISUALS
What's the first thing you notice in this photograph? Now look at the photo more carefully and tell what new **details** you see.

with that candy, you will never again experience freedom, happiness, or the possibility of my warm embrace."

I knew that it was just a matter of time before she came into my room and started collecting the candy herself, grabbing **indiscriminately,** with no regard to my rating system. Had I been thinking straight, I would have hidden the most valuable items in my dresser drawer, but instead, panicked by the thought of her hand on my doorknob, I tore off the wrappers and began cramming the candy bars into my mouth, desperately, like someone in a contest. Most were miniature, which made them easier to **accommodate,** but still there was only so much room, and it was hard to chew and fit more in at the same time. The headache began immediately, and I chalked it up to[8] tension. F

My mother told the Tomkeys she needed to check on something, and then she opened the door and stuck her head inside my room. "What . . . are you doing?" she whispered, but my mouth was too full to answer. "I'll just be a moment," she called, and as she closed the door behind her and moved toward my bed, I began breaking the wax lips and candy necklaces pulled from pile no. 2. These were the second-best things I had received, and while it hurt to destroy them, it would have hurt even more to give them away. I had just started to mutilate a miniature box of Red Hots when my mother pried them from my hands, accidentally finishing the job for me. BB-size pellets clattered onto the floor, and as I followed them with my eyes, she snatched up a roll of Necco wafers. G

indiscriminately (ĭn′dĭ-skrĭm′ə-nĭt-lē) *adv.* without making careful distinctions or choices

accommodate (ə-kŏm′ə-dāt) *v.* to make room for

F IRONY
What actually causes Sedaris's headache? Tell why this is ironic.

G EVALUATE
What positive or negative qualities is Sedaris displaying?

8. **chalked it up to:** identified its cause or source as.

ANALYZE VISUALS

Students might say that they notice the brown paper bag first. They might say that at second glance, they see licorice, lollipops, half-eaten candy bars, and candy wrappers.

LITERARY ANALYSIS

F IRONY

Remind students to add their answer to their charts from page 717. ***Possible answer:*** *The chocolate causes Sedaris's headache. This is ironic because he knows that chocolate makes him sick, but he eats it anyway to prevent it from falling into the hands of the Tomkeys. Then he blames something else as the cause.*

READING SKILL

G EVALUATE

Possible answer: *Sedaris's actions show him to be greedy, selfish, and immature.*

Lines 153–171
DISCUSSION PROMPTS

Use these prompts to help students understand Sedaris's personality:

Connect If you did not want to share your candy, what would you do? *Students may say that they would hide it or give what they didn't like to their mother.*

Analyze If the children at the door had been anyone other than the Tomkeys, would Sedaris's reaction have been the same? ***Possible answer:*** *He may have tried to save his best candy for himself but would not have destroyed the candy in "pile no. 2."*

Synthesize Based on your understanding of the situation and of Sedaris's feelings about the Tomkeys, what emotions would you say are triggering Sedaris's response? ***Possible answer:*** *His emotions include anger about having to give away his candy as well feeling that his way of life is threatened by the odd behavior of the Tomkeys.*

FOR LESS–PROFICIENT READERS

Reading Skill Follow-Up: Evaluate Point out to students that when they recommend a movie to a friend, they measure it against standards, or criteria, that they have for evaluating movies. Have small groups of students use a list of criteria to evaluate Sedaris's maturity, based on his behavior in lines 127–171. Students might wish to use a chart such as this one.

Criteria	*Yes*	*Somewhat*	*No*
makes good decisions			
acts responsibly			
understands the situations of others			
willing to share			

Lines 175–180

REINFORCE *KEY IDEA:* NORMAL

Discuss Is Sedaris's mother's reaction **normal** under these circumstances? Explain. ***Possible answer:*** *Yes. She is angry with her son for being selfish and for making her wait with the Tomkeys.*

LITERARY ANALYSIS

Ⓗ IRONY

Possible answer: *It is ironic because curiosity is not a gift. Sedaris gives nothing of himself, not even his friendship. When he does have a chance to share, he does the opposite, hoarding and gorging to avoid having to give anything to the Tomkeys.*

SELECTION WRAP–UP

REFLECT Ask students what Sedaris's perspective on this part of his childhood reveals about the way he has changed.

★ CRITIQUE Have students explain whether the events in the essay are presented in a way that makes them relevant to the lives of readers. Why or why not?

"Not those," I pleaded, but rather than words, my mouth expelled chocolate, chewed chocolate, which fell onto the sleeve of her sweater. "Not those. Not those."

She shook her arm, and the mound of chocolate dropped . . . upon my bedspread. "You should look at yourself," she said. "I mean, *really* look at yourself."

Along with the Necco wafers she took several Tootsie Pops and half a dozen caramels wrapped in cellophane. I heard her apologize to the Tomkeys for her absence, and then I heard my candy hitting the bottom of their bags.

"What do you say?" Mrs. Tomkey asked.

And the children answered, "Thank you."

While I was in trouble for not bringing my candy sooner, my sisters were in more trouble for not bringing theirs at all. We spent the early part of the evening in our rooms, then one by one we eased our way back upstairs, and joined our parents in front of the TV. I was the last to arrive, and took a seat on the floor beside the sofa. The show was a Western, and even if my head had not been throbbing, I doubt I would have had the wherewithal[9] to follow it. A posse of outlaws crested a rocky hilltop, squinting at a flurry of dust advancing from the horizon, and I thought again of the Tomkeys and of how alone and out of place they had looked in their dopey costumes. "What was up with that kid's tail?" I asked.

"Shhhh," my family said.

For months I had protected and watched over these people, but now, with one stupid act, they had turned my pity into something hard and ugly. The shift wasn't gradual, but immediate, and it **provoked** an uncomfortable feeling of loss. We hadn't been friends, the Tomkeys and I, but still I had given them the gift of my curiosity. Wondering about the Tomkey family had made me feel generous, but now I would have to shift gears and find pleasure in hating them. The only alternative was to do as my mother had instructed and take a good look at myself. This was an old trick, designed to turn one's hatred inward, and while I was determined not to fall for it, it was hard to shake the mental picture snapped[10] by her suggestion: here is a boy sitting on a bed, his mouth smeared with chocolate. He's a human being, but also he's a pig, surrounded by trash and gorging himself so that others may be denied. Were this the only image in the world, you'd be forced to give it your full attention, but fortunately there were others. This stagecoach, for instance, coming round the bend with a cargo of gold. This shiny new Mustang convertible. This teenage girl, her hair a beatiful mane, sipping Pepsi through a straw, one picture after another, on and on until the news, and whatever came on after the news. ∾ Ⓗ

provoke (prə-vōk') *v.* to cause; to bring up

③ **Targeted Passage**

Ⓗ IRONY
Reread lines 198–210. Why is it ironic for Seda to say he felt generous toward the Tomkeys?

9. **wherewithal** (wâr'wĭth-ôl'): ability.

10. **mental picture snapped:** an imagined picture brought quickly to mind, like a snapshot, a quickly taken photograph.

DIFFERENTIATED INSTRUCTION

FOR LESS–PROFICIENT READERS

③ Targeted Passage [Lines 194–210]

This passage presents Sedaris's new attitude toward the Tomkeys.

- What changes Sedaris's feelings toward the Tomkeys?
- What is his view of them now? Why?
- Why doesn't he want to think about his own image? What helps him put the image out of his mind?

Review: Tone

- Review the definition of *tone* with students (*"a writer's attitude toward a subject"*). Remind them that tone is conveyed through the writer's choice of words and images.
- Read lines 201–205 aloud. Ask students what images or words affect them strongly (*smeared, pig, surrounded by trash, gorging himself*). Record these on the board and have students use the clues to identify the author's tone as he looks back at himself.

724 UNIT 6: STYLE, VOICE, AND TONE

omprehension

1. **Recall** Why did the young Sedaris begin spying on the Tomkeys?
2. **Recall** Why were the Tomkeys unable to trick-or-treat on Halloween?
3. **Clarify** Why did Mrs. Sedaris want to give her children's candy to the Tomkey children?

terary Analysis

4. **Identify Judgments** The young Sedaris had strong opinions about many things that the Tomkeys did or said. Look through the essay and find at least three places where he makes a positive or negative statement about the family. What do you learn about Sedaris from the judgments he makes? Is his behavior toward the Tomkeys fair? Explain your answer using examples from the selection.
5. **Analyze Irony** This essay was written by an adult looking back on his childhood. Review the chart you made while reading. Which examples of irony show that Sedaris is making fun of himself and his family? Explain.
6. **Draw Conclusions** Reread lines 164–168. Why is it so difficult for Sedaris to share his candy with the Tomkeys? What might have happened if he had chosen to share?
7. **Evaluate Attitudes** Review the passages in which Sedaris mentions television. What are the good and bad things about the role it plays in his and his family's lives? Note them on a scale like the one shown. Then explain whether you think there's anything wrong with the way the Sedarises use TV.

Good	Bad
3. ______	3. ______
2. ______	2. ______
1. ______	1. ______

tension and Challenge

8. **Speaking and Listening** David Sedaris has said that he likes to "paint mental pictures" for the people who listen to his essays on the radio. In a small group, take turns reading portions of "Us and Them" out loud. As one person reads, the others should listen for images that particularly stand out to them. Then discuss whether it's more fun to read the essay or hear it, and why.
9. **Readers' Circle** Comedian Joe Ancis once said, "The only **normal** people are the ones you don't know very well." Do you think that Sedaris would agree with this quote? Do you agree? Share your conclusions with the class.

Practice and Apply

After Reading

For additional support of postreading questions, use these copy masters:

RESOURCE MANAGER—Copy Masters

Reading Check p. 130 (to check understanding of the selection)

Evaluate p. 125 (for practice of reading standards focus)

Question Support p. 131 (After Reading questions adapted for English learners and less-proficient readers)

Additional selection questions are provided for teachers on page 117.

For additional activities to challenge students, see

Power Thinking at **ClassZone.com**

ANSWERS

Comprehension

1. *Sedaris wanted to know what the Tomkeys did for entertainment since they did not have a television.*
2. *The Tomkeys had been away for the weekend and missed Halloween.*
3. *Mrs. Sedaris didn't want to be rude to the Tomkeys. She wanted to be hospitable.*

Literary Analysis

Possible answers:

4. *Statements that students select should support the idea that Sedaris did not understand people well at this stage of his life and was selfish, easily offended, and strongly influenced by television. His behavior was unfair to the Tomkeys, who were probably nice people.*
5. ● **STANDARDS FOCUS Irony** *Most examples in the chart show Sedaris making fun of himself. He makes fun of his inability to make friends, his parents saying things they don't mean, his greed, and his belief that he was being generous to the Tomkeys when, in fact, the opposite was true.*
6. *He thinks the Tomkeys are odd and does not want to share with them. If he had, he might have become friends with them and discovered that they were interesting people.*
7. ■ **STANDARDS FOCUS Evaluate** ***Good:*** *Sedaris understands references to television shows and has a point of common interest with classmates. His family watches television together.* ***Bad:*** *While his family watches television, they do not interact. The standards of television become his own. He assumes that anyone who does not own a television is not normal.*

Extension and Challenge

8. *Students may say that hearing the essay read aloud enables them to appreciate the tone more fully, which, in turn, helps them visualize the events more clearly.*
9. *Encourage students to reach a consensus in their groups and to support their opinions with evidence from the essay or their own experiences.*

ANSWERS

Vocabulary in Context

VOCABULARY PRACTICE

1. *false*
2. *true*
3. *false*
4. *true*
5. *false*
6. *false*
7. *true*
8. *true*

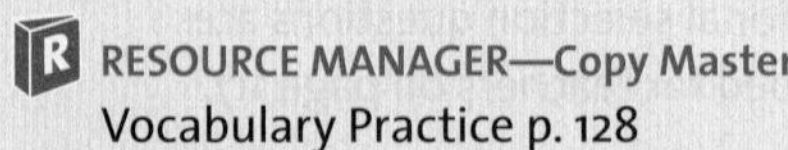

RESOURCE MANAGER—Copy Master
Vocabulary Practice p. 128

VOCABULARY IN WRITING

Suggest that students brainstorm possible choices and then use a T Chart to contrast their first impression with their later understanding of the person. After students have collected their details, they can review the vocabulary list and identify words that will help them express their ideas.

BEST PRACTICES TOOLKIT—Transparency
T Chart p. A25

VOCABULARY STRATEGY: IDIOMS *(also an EL language objective)*

- Point out these idioms in the selection: *bet your boots* (lines 36–37), *as low as you could get* (line 94).
- Model how to define them using context clues before students work on the exercise.

Possible answers:

1. *at the drop of a hat—"immediately"*
2. *up to something—"secretly planning something"*
3. *hang in there—"don't give up"*
4. *fell on deaf ears—"made no impact because no one was listening"*
5. *take five—"take a short break"*

RESOURCE MANAGER—Copy Master
Vocabulary Strategy p. 129

Vocabulary Center at **ClassZone.com**
Additional Vocabulary Activities

Vocabulary in Context

VOCABULARY PRACTICE

Show that you understand the meaning of each boldfaced word by deciding *true* or *false* for each statement.

1. A small car can easily **accommodate** six passengers.
2. Moving away can **provoke** homesickness.
3. Winning a competition does not **merit** congratulations.
4. If someone looks tired, we might **attribute** this to lack of sleep.
5. To **imply** that someone is wrong means to tell that person, "You are wrong."
6. Work experience and confidence usually **interfere** with a successful job search.
7. Someone who buys shoes **indiscriminately** may not try them on first.
8. If you **inflict** your views on others, you are forcing people to listen to you.

VOCABULARY IN WRITING

How many people have you formed the wrong opinion about? Write a paragraph explaining how your first impression of someone was wrong. Use at least two vocabulary words in your paragraph. You could start this way.

> **EXAMPLE SENTENCE**
>
> *The first time I met Richard, I **attributed** his unusual style to his being strange.*

VOCABULARY STRATEGY: IDIOMS

An **idiom** is an expression that has a different meaning from its literal meaning. For example, in this essay Sedaris says that when he got a headache, he "chalked it up to tension." *Chalked it up to* is an idiomatic expression that means "identified the cause as." There is no actual chalk or chalkboard involved.

If you encounter an unfamiliar idiom, you can often use context clues to figure out its meaning. Otherwise, look up the first word of the expression in a dictionary, where you will often find idioms explained in the entry.

PRACTICE Identify the idiom in each sentence and give a definition for it.

1. We expected her to be shy, but she'd tell you her life story at the drop of a hat.
2. Josh is definitely up to something—I can tell by the expression on his face.
3. Although I was tired during practice, my coach told me to hang in there.
4. Cynthia was unhappy with the store's service, but her complaints fell on deaf ears.
5. In order to get the exhausted cast through the last hour of rehearsal, the director told them to take five.

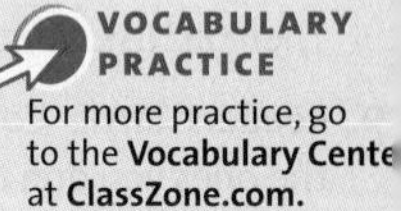

VOCABULARY PRACTICE
For more practice, go to the **Vocabulary Cente** at **ClassZone.com.**

DIFFERENTIATED INSTRUCTION

FOR ENGLISH LEARNERS

Vocabulary Practice [mixed-readiness pairs] Have students work in pairs to rewrite each sentence, replacing the vocabulary word with a paraphrase of the definition. For example, *A small car easily has room for six passengers.* Then have them complete the exercise by identifying the statements as true or false.

FOR ADVANCED LEARNERS/PRE–AP

Vocabulary Strategy [small-group option] Have students work in small teams to create several of their own idioms. Encourage them to be imaginative and to combine elements of other idioms if they wish. Have each team write sentences on the board that help to illustrate the meanings of their idioms. Then have the class try to define the new idioms.

ading-Writing Connection

Continue exploring "Us and Them" by responding to the prompts. Then complete the **Grammar and Writing** exercise.

WRITING PROMPTS	SELF-CHECK
A. Short Response: Write a Journal Sedaris often wondered what life must have been like for the Tomkeys. What did they do since they didn't watch TV? Write a **one-paragraph journal entry** from the perspective of one of the Tomkey children, describing a **normal** day in your household.	***A creative journal entry will . . .*** • describe the members of the Tomkey family • use information from the essay to add details to the narrative
B. Extended Response: Analyze the Message What do you think Sedaris learned from his experience with the Tomkeys? What might he want others to learn? In **two or three paragraphs,** analyze the message of "Us and Them," using examples from the selection.	***An effective analysis will . . .*** • clearly state the message of the essay • refer to specific scenes, lines, and details

AMMAR AND WRITING

FORM COMPLEX SENTENCES A **complex sentence** contains one independent clause and one or more dependent clauses. An **independent clause** can stand alone as a sentence. A **dependent clause** is a group of words that contains a subject and a verb but cannot stand alone as a sentence. Dependent clauses begin with words such as *after, because, even though, since, until, where,* and *who.* By adding one of these words or phrases to an independent clause, you make it dependent. The dependent clause can then be combined with an independent clause to form a complex sentence.

Original: We don't own a television. My family still has fun together.

Revised: Even though we don't own a television, my family still has fun together. (*This is now one complex sentence.*)

PRACTICE In each item, change one independent clause to a dependent clause. Then combine the clauses to form a complex sentence.

1. My family doesn't have a TV. We spend more time talking to each other.
2. We also spend time at the lake house. My brother catches a lot of fish.
3. Sometimes I wish we had a TV. The kids at school make fun of us.
4. We moved to this neighborhood last year. I've made a few friends.

For more help with dependent clauses and complex sentences, see page R64 in the ***Grammar Handbook.***

DIFFERENTIATED INSTRUCTION

FOR LESS–PROFICIENT WRITERS

For Prompt A:

- Use a Cluster Diagram to brainstorm activities that the Tomkey children might have enjoyed. Have students select two or three of the ideas to use in their entries.
- Have students review the essay to find details that describe the Tomkey family. Help students add two of these details to their journal entries.

BEST PRACTICES TOOLKIT—Transparency
Cluster Diagram p. B18

For Prompt B:

- Discuss possible themes as a class. For example, one message might be that being different doesn't mean being inferior. Have the class choose a theme on which they can agree. Then have small groups find evidence from the text to support this interpretation of theme.
- Discuss the supporting details, listing them on the board. Have students write their paragraphs independently.

Reading-Writing Connection

WRITING PROMPTS

- For **Prompt A,** have students brainstorm activities other than watching television that children might do. Suggest that they organize their journal entries chronologically.
- For **Prompt B,** suggest that students list important details from the selection and work in small groups to draw conclusions about possible lessons.

For an extended Reading-Writing Connection activity, see

Writing Center at **ClassZone.com**

GRAMMAR AND WRITING

- Tell students to identify the relationship between the ideas in the sentences to help them decide which should be dependent. For example, there may be a cause-and-effect or sequential relationship.
- Tell students that a comma often separates the independent and dependent clauses.

Possible answers:

1. *Because my family doesn't have a TV, we spend more time talking to each other.*
2. *We also spend time at the lake house, where my brother catches a lot of fish.*
3. *Sometimes I wish we had a TV, because the kids at school make fun of us.*
4. *Since we moved to this neighborhood last year, I've made a few friends.*

RESOURCE MANAGER—Copy Master
Form Complex Sentences p. 132

Assess and Reteach

Assess

RESOURCE MANAGER—Copy Masters
Selection Tests A, B/C pp. 133–134, 135–136

Test Generator CD

Reteach

STANDARDS LESSON FILE
Literature Lesson 35: Irony
Literature Lesson 39: Tone
Vocabulary Lesson 22: Idioms

Focus and Motivate

OBJECTIVES

Literary Analysis

- explore the key idea of **cost**
- identify and analyze style in poetry (imagery, repetition, irony)
- read poetry

Reading

- recognize historical context

SUMMARY

"O Captain! My Captain!" laments the death of President Abraham Lincoln, portraying him as the fallen captain of a ship that has ridden out the storm of the Civil War. In "I Saw Old General at Bay," the speaker describes a desperate moment in a battle, when a general calls for volunteers to run the enemy lines. Many step forward, and those that are chosen "depart with cheerfulness, freely risking their lives."

What is the COST *of victory?*

Discuss the question. To lead into the ***KEY IDEA,*** ask students to think about a world conflict currently in the news. Have them discuss the **cost** of that conflict. Ask: Under what circumstances is a military victory worth the price of suffering and destruction? Then have students work on the ***QUICKWRITE*** activity.

Before Reading

O Captain! My Captain!
I Saw Old General at Bay

Poems by Walt Whitman

What is the COST *of victory?*

KEY IDEA Triumph often comes with consequences. For example, the Union victory in the Civil War preserved the United States and ended slavery, but these outcomes came at a **cost.** Almost 700,000 people died, countless others suffered, and enormous amounts of property were destroyed. In the two poems you are about to read, Walt Whitman reflects on the great cost of victory in the Civil War.

QUICKWRITE Wars are not the only events in which winning takes a toll. We all have had personal victories that cost us in one way or another. For example, suppose you and your best friend have an argument over an issue that is very important to both of you. You might win the argument, but lose your friend in the process. In your journal, write about a time in your life when victory had a price. Was what you won worth the cost? Explain.

728

Selection Resources

RESOURCE MANAGER UNIT 6

Plan and Teach pp. 137–144

Literary Analysis

Style in Poetry pp. 145, 146†*

Question Support p. 149*

Reading

Understand Historical Context pp. 147, 148†*

Reading Fluency p. 150

Assessment

Selection Tests A, B/C pp. 151*, 153*

Test Generator CD

BEST PRACTICES TOOLKIT

Differentiated Instruction pp. 31–38*

Graphic Organizers/Strategies

Think-Pair-Share • New Word Analysis • Visualizing • Venn Diagram

Reading Support

Audio Anthology CD*

Technology

Literature Center at **ClassZone.com**

Write*Smart* CD

* Resources for Differentiation † Also in Spanish

ERARY ANALYSIS: STYLE IN POETRY

Walt Whitman is known for his uniquely American **style,** or way of using language to express ideas. One thing that makes Whitman's style stand out is his unconventional use of language. He often didn't follow traditional rules of line length and rhyme as other poets of his time did. In addition, Whitman often wrote about politics and current events, topics the poets who came before him tended to avoid. The following elements are also part of Whitman's style:

- strong **imagery,** or words and phrases that appeal to the reader's five senses
- **repetition** of a sound, word, phrase, or line for emphasis
- **irony,** or a contrast between what is expected and what actually happens

As you read "O Captain! My Captain!" and "I Saw Old General at Bay," use a chart like the one shown to help you identify these elements of the legendary poet's style.

	"O Captain! My Captain!"	"I Saw Old General at Bay"
Imagery		
Repetition		
Irony		

ADING SKILL: UNDERSTAND HISTORICAL CONTEXT

As with other works of literature, Whitman's poems become easier to understand once you know their **historical context,** the real events and people that influenced them. Whitman wrote "O Captain! My Captain!" and "I Saw Old General at Bay" as a way of expressing his thoughts and feelings about the Civil War. Before you begin the two poems, read the **Background** on this page. The information can help you better appreciate Whitman's message.

Author Online

An American Voice Poet Walt Whitman is considered one of America's most beloved and original writers. The poems in his collection *Leaves of Grass* were the first to be written in free verse, which means they did not contain regular patterns of rhythm and rhyme. Whitman's poetry was praised by a few critics in his lifetime, but many others did not like it. As a result, his work did not become popular until after his death.

Walt Whitman
1819–1892

Background

The "Good Gray Poet" When his brother George, a Union soldier, was injured in battle in 1862, Whitman went to Virginia to care for him. Whitman was moved by the sight of the injured soldiers and decided to stay in Washington, D.C., volunteering in army hospitals. Friends often referred to Whitman as the "Good Gray Poet" because of his charity toward the troops.

A Poet in Mourning On April 14, 1865, only five days after the end of the Civil War, President Abraham Lincoln was assassinated because of his antislavery beliefs. Whitman was a great admirer of Lincoln's. He wrote "O Captain! My Captain!" to capture the sense of tragedy that overwhelmed the nation upon Lincoln's death. The poem "I Saw Old General at Bay" was published in a collection called *Drum Taps,* which included many poems expressing Whitman's feelings about the war.

MORE ABOUT THE AUTHOR AND BACKGROUND
To learn more about Walt Whitman and the Civil War, visit the **Literature Center** at **ClassZone.com.**

729

Teach

STANDARDS FOCUS

LITERARY ANALYSIS

● STYLE IN POETRY

Read this line aloud:

Cawing loudly, a crow flew over the silent battlefield.

Ask students if this is an example of imagery, repetition, or irony. How can they tell? ***Answer:*** *It is an example of imagery, with details that appeal to the senses of sight and hearing.*

CHECK UNDERSTANDING Ask students to describe examples of imagery, repetition, or irony from other poems they have read.

RESOURCE MANAGER—Copy Master
Style in Poetry p. 145 (for student use while reading the poems)

READING SKILL

■ UNDERSTAND HISTORICAL CONTEXT

Ask students to summarize the **Background** information on this page. Then challenge them to make statements about Walt Whitman and Abraham Lincoln that reflect the historical background.

CHECK UNDERSTANDING Ask students how historical context has helped them understand other literary works, such as "Paul Revere's Ride" (page 134), *The Diary of Anne Frank* (page 486), "One More Round" (page 626), or "Not My Bones" (page 628).

DIFFERENTIATED INSTRUCTION

FOR ALL STUDENTS
For general guidelines on differentiating instruction, see

BEST PRACTICES TOOLKIT
Differentiated Instruction pp. 31–38

FOR LESS–PROFICIENT READERS
Concept Support Tell students that the poems both reflect the speakers' feelings about the cost of victory. As they read, have students ask themselves these questions:

- What emotions does each speaker express?
- Does the speaker of "O Captain! My Captain!" feel that the final results of the Civil War were worth the cost?
- Does the speaker of "I Saw Old General at Bay" feel that winning the battle is worth the cost to the individual soldiers?

FOR ENGLISH LEARNERS
Options for Reading [paired option] Have students listen to the *Audio Anthology CD* while they read along with the poems. Then have them use the Think-Pair-Share strategy to answer important questions about each poem.

BEST PRACTICES TOOLKIT—Transparency
Think-Pair-Share p. A18

Practice and Apply

READING SKILL

A HISTORICAL CONTEXT

Possible answer: *The captain is Abraham Lincoln, and his ship is the United States.*

LITERARY ANALYSIS

B STYLE IN POETRY

Have students record their answers in the chart from page 729. ***Possible answer:*** *The irony is in the contrast between the crowd's joy over the end of the war and the sight of the slain captain.*

LITERARY ANALYSIS

C STYLE IN POETRY

Have students record their answers in the chart from page 729. ***Possible answer:*** *Imagery includes "hear the bells," "flag is flung," "bugle trills," "bouquets and ribbon'd wreaths," "shores a-crowding," and "eager faces turning."*

Extend the Discussion Notice Whitman's use of repetition in the poem. What image is repeated in the second stanza? What effect does that create?

ANALYZE VISUALS

Possible answer: *The dark, muted colors and the serious expression on Lincoln's face suggest a sad, solemn mood.*

About the Art For more than 20 years, Wendy Allen has painted images of Abraham Lincoln. Allen describes Lincoln's face as "calm yet haunting, protective yet remote . . . the subject I choose to paint over and over again."

Lines 1–24

REINFORCE *KEY IDEA:* COST

Discuss What clues indicate that the speaker feels the **cost** of Abraham Lincoln's death was personal as well as national? ***Possible answer:*** *The speaker refers to Lincoln repeatedly as "my captain" and also as "dear father" (line 13) and "My father" (line 18). While the crowd celebrates the end of the war, the speaker cradles the captain's head (lines 14, 18) and privately mourns his death.*

O Captain! My Captain!

Walt Whitman

O Captain! my Captain! our fearful trip is done,
The ship has weather'd every rack,[1] the prize we sought[2] is won, **A**
The port is near, the bells I hear, the people all exulting,
While follow eyes the steady keel,[3] the vessel grim and daring:
    But O heart! heart! heart!
        O the bleeding drops of red,
            Where on the deck my Captain lies,
                Fallen cold and dead. **B**

O Captain! my Captain! rise up and hear the bells;
Rise up—for you the flag is flung[4]—for you the bugle trills,
For you bouquets and ribbon'd wreaths—for you the shores
    a-crowding,
For you they call, the swaying mass, their eager faces turning;
    Here Captain! dear father!
        This arm beneath your head!
            It is some dream that on the deck,
                You've fallen cold and dead. **C**

My Captain does not answer, his lips are pale and still,
My father does not feel my arm, he has no pulse nor will,
The ship is anchor'd safe and sound, its voyage closed and done,
From fearful trip the victor ship comes in with object won;
    Exult O shores, and ring O bells!
        But I with mournful tread,[5]
            Walk the deck my Captain lies,
                Fallen cold and dead.

A HISTORICAL CONTE
Given what you read in the Background on page 729, who do you think is the captain, an what is his ship?

B STYLE IN POETRY
Reread lines 1–8. In wh way does the descripti of the rejoicing crowds help emphasize the tragedy and **irony** of the captain's death?

C STYLE IN POETRY
Reread lines 9–16. Wh **imagery** does Whitma use to convey the peop adoration of their lead Add these images to y chart.

ANALYZE VISUALS
What words would yo use to describe the mo of this painting?

1. **rack:** a mass of wind-driven clouds.
2. **sought** (sôt): searched for; tried to gain.
3. **keel:** the main part of a ship's structure.
4. **flung:** suddenly put out.
5. **tread** (trĕd): footsteps.

Lincoln 2, Wendy Allen. Oil on canvas. © Wendy A

DIFFERENTIATED INSTRUCTION

FOR ENGLISH LEARNERS

Vocabulary Support Have students use the New Word Analysis strategy to explore the meanings of these words:

- *fearful* (line 1), "causing fear; frightening"
- *weather'd* (line 2), "survived"
- *port* (line 3), "place where ships anchor or find shelter"
- *exulting* (line 3), "rejoicing; celebrating"
- *vessel* (line 4), "ship"
- *bouquets* (line 11), "bunches of flowers"
- *pulse* (line 18), "rhythmical throbbing of arteries caused by regular contractions of the heart; sign of life"
- *anchor'd* (line 19), "secured; held fast"
- *victor* (line 20), "winning"
- *object* (line 20), "goal"

BEST PRACTICES TOOLKIT—Transparency
New Word Analysis p. E8

BACKGROUND

Assassination and Reconstruction Abraham Lincoln was shot by a Confederate supporter as he watched a play in Washington, D.C. He was the first U.S. president to be assassinated.

Some historians believe that Reconstruction would have been very different if Lincoln had lived. Andrew Johnson, who succeeded Lincoln, was a Southerner who believed that blacks were inferior to whites. At the beginning of Reconstruction, he did not pressure states to give African Americans the right to vote. These states passed Black Codes that denied African Americans civil and voting rights.

FOR LESS–PROFICIENT READERS

Comprehension Support Distribute the Visualizing transparency and ask students to close their eyes as you read the poem aloud. Then ask them to fill in the diagram with details from the poem.

BEST PRACTICES TOOLKIT—Transparency Visualizing p. A11

FOR ADVANCED LEARNERS/PRE–AP

Synthesize Have students write a brief announcement of Lincoln's death to be delivered by the speaker of the poem to "the swaying mass" (line 12) of people who are celebrating the end of the war. Remind students to consider what they have learned about the poem's historical context when composing the announcement. Ask volunteers to deliver their announcements, and encourage listeners to discuss what it would have felt like to hear the news of Lincoln's death.

LITERARY ANALYSIS

D STYLE IN POETRY

Have students record their answers in the chart from page 729. ***Possible answer:*** *Imagery includes "Old as he was" and "his gray eyes yet shone out in battle like stars."*

READING SKILL

E HISTORICAL CONTEXT

Possible answer: *As a hospital volunteer, Whitman knew what dangers the soldiers would be facing.*

ANALYZE VISUALS

Activity Why do you think the artist chose to make the general's figure dark and indistinct? What details would you emphasize to portray the general from the poem? ***Possible answer:*** *The general is depicted as mysterious and alone. Portrayals of the general from the poem might focus on his shining eyes or his weathered face.*

SELECTION WRAP–UP

REFLECT Have students discuss how their knowledge of the historical context helped them identify with the poems' speakers.

★ CRITIQUE Ask students to describe ways in which the form (stanzas, line length, rhyme, repetition) of each poem effectively mirrors its content.

READING FLUENCY

Distribute the copy masters and have students practice fluency.

RESOURCE MANAGER—Copy Master
Reading Fluency p. 150

I Saw Old General at Bay

Walt Whitman

I saw old General at bay,
(Old as he was, his gray eyes yet shone out in battle like stars,) **D**
His small force was now completely hemm'd[1] in, in his works,
He call'd for volunteers to run the enemy's lines, a desperate emergency,
I saw a hundred and more step forth from the ranks, but two or three were selected,
I saw them receive their orders aside, they listen'd with care, the adjutant[2] was very grave,
I saw them depart with cheerfulness, freely risking their lives. **E**

D STYLE IN POETRY Reread line 2. What descriptive words and details help you understand what the general looks like?

E HISTORICAL CONTE Reread the last line. Which of Whitman's experiences best helps you interpret it?

1. **hemm'd:** hemmed; surrounded or enclosed.
2. **adjutant** (ăj'ə-tənt): a staff officer who helps a commanding officer with administrative affairs.

Detail of *Major General John Sedgwick Monument,* Wendy Allen. Oil on canvas, 40″ × 30″. © Wendy Allen.

DIFFERENTIATED INSTRUCTION

FOR LESS–PROFICIENT READERS

Reading Skill Follow-Up: Understand Historical Context Help students connect what they know about the Civil War with the key idea of **cost** by using the background notes on page 317, the story "The Drummer Boy of Shiloh" (pages 318–323), Louisa May Alcott's journal (pages 327–330), and the background notes on page 729. Ask students to consider these questions:

- Does Whitman accurately describe the devastation of the Civil War?
- Compare "O Captain! My Captain!" with "The Drummer Boy of Shiloh." Which piece do you connect with more, and why?

FOR ADVANCED LEARNERS/PRE–AP

Compare and Contrast Have students compare and contrast the tone, mood, imagery, subject, and theme of each poem. They may also consider the poems' stanza structures. Have them complete a Venn Diagram showing the poems' similarities and differences.

BEST PRACTICES TOOLKIT—Transparency
Venn Diagram p. A26

ter Reading

mprehension

1. **Recall** What does the speaker of "O Captain! My Captain!" see on the deck of the ship?
2. **Clarify** What "desperate emergency" did the old general face?
3. **Clarify** For what did the general need volunteers?

terary Analysis

4. **Apply Historical Context** Knowing the historical context of a poem often helps you understand the figurative language that is used. In "O Captain! My Captain!" Walt Whitman uses an **extended metaphor,** a comparison of two unlike things that unfolds throughout several lines or stanzas, or even an entire poem. How does knowing about Whitman's life and times help you identify the metaphor? Create a chart to list the elements of the metaphor and what each element represents.

Element	What It Represents
captain	President Lincoln
fearful trip	
ship	
prize	
storm	
arrival of the ship at port	

5. **Make Inferences** Reread the last line of "I Saw Old General at Bay." What do the volunteers' attitudes say about the general?
6. **Understand Elegy** An **elegy** is an extended, thoughtful poem in which the speaker reflects upon death—often in tribute to a person who has died recently. Which of the two poems best fits this definition? Support your answer with examples from the poem you chose.
7. **Analyze Style** Review the chart you made while reading. Note the places Whitman uses imagery, repetition, and irony. How do these elements emphasize both the **cost** of the war and the greatness of those who led the Union to victory?

tension and Challenge

8. **Creative Project: Art** What pictures might help others to understand these poems? Choose one of the poems and look online for pictures or clip art that help capture its **mood.** Assemble the images in the form of a collage.
9. SOCIAL STUDIES CONNECTION Find out more about the Civil War. Create a poster showing the causes, benefits, and cost of the war, and present your poster to the class.

RESEARCH LINKS
For more on the Civil War, visit the **Research Center** at **ClassZone.com.**

Practice and Apply

After Reading

For additional support of postreading questions, use these copy masters:

RESOURCE MANAGER—Copy Masters
Understand Historical Context p. 147 (for practice of reading standards focus)
Question Support p. 149 (After Reading questions adapted for English learners and less-proficient readers)

Additional selection questions are provided for teachers on page 141.

ANSWERS

Comprehension

1. *The captain lies dead on the deck.*
2. *The general's troops were "hemm'd in," or surrounded by enemy forces.*
3. *He needed them to run the enemy's lines.*

Literary Analysis

Possible answers:

4. **STANDARDS FOCUS Understand Historical Context** *Students' charts should include the following information: captain—President Lincoln; fearful trip—Civil War; ship—the United States; prize—winning the war; storm—battles; arrival of the ship at port—the end of the war.*
5. *The volunteers respect and trust the general. They are willing to risk their lives to carry out his plan to win the battle.*
6. *"O Captain! My Captain!" is an elegy, a tribute to President Lincoln. In lines 13–16, "Captain" and "dear father" refer to President Lincoln. The images of his death include "You've fallen cold and dead."*
7. **STANDARDS FOCUS Style in Poetry** *The cost of the war is shown in "O Captain! My Captain!" through somber images that depict the captain "fallen cold and dead." In "I Saw Old General at Bay," the phrase "freely risking their lives" shows the cost of war. Imagery that captures Lincoln's greatness includes "for you the flag is flung—for you the bugle trills" (line 10). In "I Saw Old General at Bay," the detail "his gray eyes shone out in battle like stars" suggests that he is passionate and brave. Students' examples should show how repetition and irony convey similar ideas.*

Extension and Challenge

8. *Before students begin their search, encourage them to freewrite about colors and images evoked by the poem's mood.*
9. **SOCIAL STUDIES CONNECTION** *Suggest that students produce a summary that explains how the images show the causes, benefits, and costs of the war.*

Assess and Reteach

Assess

RESOURCE MANAGER—Copy Masters
Selection Tests A, B/C pp. 151–152, 153–154

Test Generator CD

Reteach

STANDARDS LESSON FILE
Literature Lesson 28: Imagery
Literature Lesson 34: Repetition and Parallelism
Literature Lesson 35: Irony
Literature Lesson 40: Style

Focus and Motivate

OBJECTIVES

Literary Analysis
- explore the key idea of **pioneers**
- identify and analyze tone (language, speaker, sound devices)
- compare and contrast poems (images, speaker, sound devices, tone)
- read poetry

Reading
- set a purpose for reading

Grammar and Writing
- write a compare-contrast essay

SUMMARY

Both poems describe the settlement of the West, but from different perspectives. "Western Wagons" is about the pioneers who traveled west from the eastern United States, while "The Other Pioneers" is about the pioneers who came north from New Spain—present-day Mexico—to settle in the Southwest region.

What makes a PIONEER?

Discuss the question with students. To lead into the ***KEY IDEA,*** ask students whether **pioneers** are different from other people who move from one place to another. If so, what sets them apart? Encourage students to think about the many opportunities pioneers seek, and the risks they are sometimes forced to take. As groups work on the ***LIST IT*** activity, encourage students to identify those pioneers they most admire and would most like to emulate.

Comparing Tone

Western Wagons

Poem by Rosemary and Stephen Vincent Benét

The Other Pioneers

Poem by Roberto Félix Salazar

What makes a PIONEER?

KEY IDEA Many of us are satisfied with where we live and what we do. Others have a more restless spirit. They want to build a path toward new ways of living or thinking. What are these **pioneers** searching for? The poems you're about to read describe two different groups that broke new ground.

LIST IT Who do you think of as a pioneer? Maybe it's someone you've met in real life, or someone you've read about in a history book or news article. Brainstorm with your group to create a list of pioneers—in science, art, sports, and other fields—who have made discoveries or developed new ways of thinking. Next to each name, tell why you included him or her.

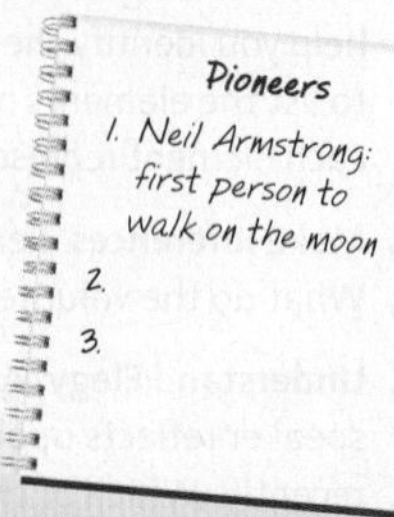

Pioneers
1. Neil Armstrong: first person to walk on the moon
2.
3.

734

Selection Resources

RESOURCE MANAGER UNIT 6

Plan and Teach pp. 155–162

Literary Analysis
Question Support p. 165*

Reading
Set a Purpose for Reading pp. 163, 164†*
Reading Fluency p. 167

Grammar and Writing
Writing for Assessment p. 166

Assessment
Selection Tests A, B/C pp. 169*, 171*
Test Generator CD

BEST PRACTICES TOOLKIT
Differentiated Instruction pp. 31–38*

Graphic Organizers/Strategies
Cluster Diagram • Read-and-Say-Something

Reading Support
Audio Anthology CD*

Technology
Literature and Writing Centers at **ClassZone.com**
Write*Smart* CD

* Resources for Differentiation † Also in Spanish

TERARY ANALYSIS: TONE

Poems tell about all kinds of subjects—love, nature, and memorable people, to name a few. The **tone** of a poem is the poet's attitude toward the subject. All literary elements can contribute to tone. For example, word choice, imagery, sound devices, and the choice of speaker (or voice that tells the poem) can suggest a tone that is optimistic, gloomy, or proud.

The poems in this lesson describe two different groups of pioneers. Use the following strategies to identify each poet's attitude toward the pioneers:

- Notice the **language** the poet uses. Do the images and descriptive words seem sad, joyful, or something else?
- Think about the **speaker.** How does he or she seem to feel about the subject?
- Consider any **sound devices.** How does the use of repetition, rhyme, or rhythm affect the poem?

EADING STRATEGY: SET A PURPOSE FOR READING

Your **purpose for reading** "Western Wagons" and "The Other Pioneers" is to identify the tone of each poem and then to compare and contrast the tones. First, read the poems all the way through to understand what they are about. What's your first impression of each poet's attitude toward the subject? Now reread the poems, using a chart like the one shown to note any clues to the tone. Later you will add to this chart.

Shared Subject: Pioneers in Early America		
	"Western Wagons"	*"The Other Pioneers"*
What images, words, and phrases tell about the pioneers and their actions?		
How does the speaker feel?		
What sound devices, if any, does the poet use? How do they affect the poem?		

Author Online

Rosemary and Stephen Vincent Benét: A Literary Family Stephen Vincent Benét grew up in a family of writers. He published his first book when he was just 17. In 1920, Benét met Rosemary Carr, a journalist. Stephen and Rosemary often combined their writing talents, especially in children's books that brought American history to life.

Rosemary Carr Benét 1898?–1962

Stephen Vincent Benét 1898–1943

Roberto Félix Salazar: Paying Tribute Salazar was born in Laredo, Texas, a town close to the border between Mexico and the United States. In "The Other Pioneers" he celebrates his heritage and honors the contributions of his Spanish ancestors.

Roberto Félix Salazar born 1913–1996

Background

O Pioneers! Between 1840 and 1861, over 300,000 people headed west toward California and Oregon, some looking for gold, others for the perfect spot of land. Even before this, Spanish pioneers came to North America looking for good farming land and the promise of a better life.

MORE ABOUT THE AUTHOR AND BACKGROUND
To learn more about the authors and the American frontier, visit the **Literature Center** at **ClassZone.com.**

Teach

STANDARDS FOCUS

LITERARY ANALYSIS

● TONE

Read aloud these lines:

"Out in the West, he died in vain!"
His son wept, but would not explain.

Ask students to describe the tone of these lines. If necessary, prompt them by asking what event has taken place "Out in the West" and what feelings the speaker seems to have about this event. ***Possible answer:*** *The tone is sad and mournful.*

CHECK UNDERSTANDING Ask students to identify the clues to tone in the poem's lines.

READING STRATEGY

■ SET A PURPOSE FOR READING

Explain that to fulfill a specific purpose for reading, such as comparing tone, students should read the poems more than once. They may also need to adjust their reading rate and pause to fill in their graphic organizers as they read.

CHECK UNDERSTANDING Ask students to set a purpose for reading the **Author Online** information and use reading strategies to achieve the purpose.

RESOURCE MANAGER—Copy Master
Set a Purpose for Reading p. 163 (for student use while reading the poems)

DIFFERENTIATED INSTRUCTION

FOR ALL STUDENTS

For general guidelines on differentiating instruction, see

BEST PRACTICES TOOLKIT
Differentiated Instruction pp. 31–38

FOR LESS-PROFICIENT READERS

Concept Support [small-group option] Identify various kinds of sound devices in a class Cluster Diagram. Then have groups of students read the poems aloud and discuss the sound devices they hear and their effects.

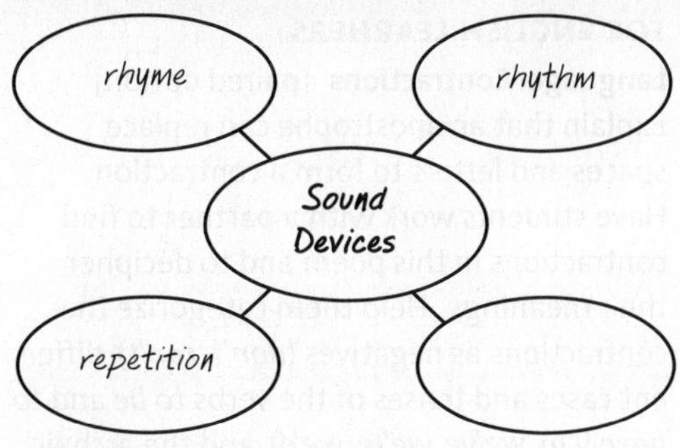

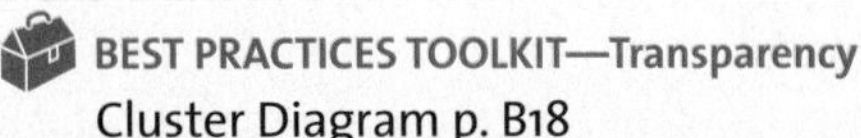

BEST PRACTICES TOOLKIT—Transparency
Cluster Diagram p. B18

FOR ENGLISH LEARNERS

Options for Reading [paired activity] Have students listen to the *Audio Anthology CD* while they read the poems. Then have students do the Read-and-Say-Something activity with a partner, commenting on images, phrases, and ideas that struck them as they read.

BEST PRACTICES TOOLKIT
Read-and-Say-Something p. D3

Practice and Apply

ANALYZE VISUALS

Possible answer: *Some students might say that the setting—wide open plains and vast skies—evokes a feeling of adventure and excitement. The group is traveling toward the light, leaving the darkness behind them.*

About the Art American painter Newell Convers Wyeth (1882–1945) created thousands of illustrations as well as many large murals, still lifes, and landscape paintings. He traveled to the American West several times, drawn by the same countryside that had drawn the pioneers. In 1907, he was described in *Outing Magazine* as "one of our greatest, if not our *greatest*, painter of American outdoor life."

LITERARY ANALYSIS

Ⓐ TONE

Possible answer: *The speaker admires the pioneers' determination but also notes their recklessness. Supporting words and phrases include "get rich out there or die!" (line 4) and "The cowards never started" (line 9).*

LITERARY ANALYSIS

Ⓑ TONE

Possible answer: *Adjectives that describe the rhyme and rhythm might include* light, upbeat, quick-moving, *and* enthusiastic.

Extend the Discussion In what ways do the rhythm and rhyme make the poem song-like, with a light, carefree feeling?

Western Wagons

Rosemary and Stephen Vincent Benét

They went with axe and rifle, when the trail was still to blaze,[1]
They went with wife and children, in the prairie-schooner[2] days,
With banjo and with frying pan—Susanna, don't you cry![3]
For I'm off to California to get rich out there or die!

We've broken land and cleared it, but we're tired of where we are.
They say that wild Nebraska is a better place by far.
There's gold in far Wyoming, there's black earth in Ioway,
So pack up the kids and blankets, for we're moving out today!

The cowards never started and the weak died on the road,
And all across the continent the endless campfires glowed.
We'd taken land and settled—but a traveler passed by—
And we're going West tomorrow—Lordy, never ask us why! Ⓐ

We're going West tomorrow, where the promises can't fail.
O'er the hills in legions, boys, and crowd the dusty trail!
We shall starve and freeze and suffer. We shall die, and tame the lands.
But we're going West tomorrow, with our fortune in our hands. Ⓑ

ANALYZE VISUALS
What feeling does this **setting** evoke for you? Tell what elements of the painting contribute to that feeling.

Ⓐ TONE
How does the speaker seem to feel about the pioneers and the decisions they made? Tell which words and phrases help you know.

Ⓑ TONE
Reread the poem aloud, paying attention to the **rhyme** and **rhythm.** What adjectives would you use to describe them?

1. **blaze:** to show a trail by cutting marks into trees.
2. **prairie schooner** (prâr'ē skōō'nər): a covered wagon, which looks like a schooner (ship) sailing across the prairie.
3. **Susanna, don't you cry:** lyrics from a traditional song.

Detail of *Covered Wagons Heading We*[st] N. C. Wyeth. Oil on canv[as]. © Bridgeman Art Libra[ry]

Lines 13–16
REINFORCE *KEY IDEA:* PIONEERS

Discuss What are these **pioneers** seeking? What are they willing to give up to achieve their goal? ***Possible answer:*** *They're seeking their fortunes, or hoping to have success in life. They're willing to suffer and even die in pursuit of their goal.*

DIFFERENTIATED INSTRUCTION

FOR ENGLISH LEARNERS

Language: Contractions [paired option] Explain that an apostrophe can replace spaces and letters to form a contraction. Have students work with a partner to find contractions in this poem and to decipher their meanings. Help them categorize the contractions as negatives (*don't, can't*), different cases and tenses of the verbs *to be* and *to have* (*I'm, we've, we're, we'd*), and the archaic form *o'er.*

Vocabulary: Cognates [shared-language groups] Have groups scan the poems for cognates and report their findings to the class. Spanish cognates in this poem include

- *rich/rico, -a* (line 4)
- *cowards/cobardes* (line 9)
- *continent/continente* (line 10)
- *promises/promesas* (line 13)
- *suffer/sufrir* (line 15)
- *fortune/fortuna* (line 16)

BACKGROUND

Settlers of the West In the early to mid-1800s, the size of the United States more than doubled due to the acquisition of land in the American West and Southwest through the Louisiana Purchase, the annexation of Texas, and the Gadsden Purchase from Mexico. In the 1840s, the federal government began to give this newly acquired land to homesteaders for little or no money, and in 1862, the Homestead Act allowed people to live on 160 acres of unclaimed land for five years, at which point the land became theirs. Within approximately 40 years, about 375,000 farms had been established west of the Mississippi—altogether, nearly 274 million acres were claimed. Also swelling the population of the West, gold seekers poured into California after the discovery of gold there in 1848.

However, the settlement of these lands had in fact begun long before—in the 1600s—when the Spanish established missions throughout the region. Then, in the 18th century, migration from present-day Mexico to the Southwest began as a result of a system of land grants from New Spain to potential settlers in New Mexico and elsewhere in the region.

R LESS–PROFICIENT READERS

ading Strategy Follow Up: Set a Purpose for ading Ask students what the images, words l phrases, and sound devices tell them about speaker's feelings toward the subject. Have m record their answers to the questions in chart from page 735.

FOR ADVANCED LEARNERS/PRE–AP

Synthesize [small-group option] Have students use the two poems as a starting point for a discussion of what daily life might have been like for pioneers. Encourage them to consider all aspects of the pioneer's life by thinking about what it would be like to

- say goodbye to friends and family
- travel long distances by foot, horse, or wagon
- go for days with little or no food
- have little privacy, if any
- suffer other physical hardships

Ask a volunteer to share the group's thoughts with the class.

The *Other* Pioneers

Roberto Félix Salazar

Now I must write
Of those of mine who rode these plains
Long years before the Saxon[1] and the Irish came.
Of those who plowed the land and built the towns
And gave the towns soft-woven Spanish names.
Of those who moved across the Rio Grande[2]
Toward the hiss of Texas snake and Indian yell.
Of men who from the earth made thick-walled homes
And from the earth raised churches to their God.
And of the wives who bore them sons
And smiled with knowing joy. **C**

They saw the Texas sun rise golden-red with promised wealth
And saw the Texas sun sink golden yet, with wealth unspent.
"Here," they said. "Here to live and here to love."
"Here is the land for our sons and the sons of our sons."
And they sang the songs of ancient Spain
And they made new songs to fit new needs.
They cleared the brush and planted the corn
And saw green stalks turn black from lack of rain.
They roamed the plains behind the herds
And stood the Indian's cruel attacks.
There was dust and there was sweat.
And there were tears and the women prayed. **D**

1. **Saxon** (săk'sən): British.
2. **Rio Grande** (rē'ō grănd'): a river that flows through Colorado, New Mexico, and Texas, and forms part of the United States/Mexican border; its name means "big river."

C TONE
Reread lines 1–11. What words and **images** describe the pioneers ar their actions? Tell which qualities of the pioneers are highlighted by this description.

D TONE
Which words and phrase help you understand the speaker's feelings towar the pioneers?

LITERARY ANALYSIS

C TONE

Possible answer: *The words and images "rode these plains," "plowed the land," "built the towns," "soft-woven Spanish names," "thick-walled homes," "raised churches," and "bore them sons" highlight the hardworking, practical, and spiritual qualities of the pioneers.*

LITERARY ANALYSIS

D TONE

Possible answer: *The speaker seems to respect and admire the pioneers. Details that show these feelings include "they made new songs to fit new needs," "stood the Indian's cruel attacks," "There was dust and there was sweat," and "there were tears."*

Lines 1–23
DISCUSSION PROMPTS

Use these prompts to help students explore the theme of the poem:

Connect Most pioneers knew they might never see their homes again. How might it feel to leave your old life behind—forever? *Students' responses will vary but may include feelings of sadness and fear.*

Analyze What is the "promised wealth" that is "unspent"? ***Possible answer:*** *The wealth is an abundant future.*

Synthesize What gives the pioneers strength? Explain your answer. ***Possible answer:*** *The pioneers gain strength from religion, from the land, from prevailing despite setbacks, and from the hope of providing a better future for their children.*

DIFFERENTIATED INSTRUCTION

FOR LESS–PROFICIENT READERS
Vocabulary Support

1. Point out the word *stood* in line 21. Explain that it is a shortened version of *withstood,* the past tense of *withstand,* which means "to successfully resist or endure."
2. Explain that the word *stalwart* in line 28 means "physically strong" or "firm and resolute."
3. Check understanding by having students use each word in an original sentence.

FOR ENGLISH LEARNERS
Language: Modifiers [mixed-readiness pairs] Point out the compound adjectives *soft-woven, thick-walled,* and *golden-red.* Have students work with more fluent speakers to create additional compound adjectives from words in the poem (such as *knowing, ancient, new, green, broad, tall,* and *gentle*) and use them in sentences.

The Vaquero (about 1851), Hugo Wilhelm Arthur Nahl. Oil on canvas mounted on masonite. Courtesy of the Oakland Museum of California Kahn Collection (A65.57).

And the years moved on.
Those who were first placed in graves
Beside the broad mesquite and the tall nopal.[3]
Gentle mothers left their graces and their arts
And stalwart fathers pride and manly strength.
Salinas, de la Garza, Sánchez, García,
Uribe, Gonzálaz, Martinez, de León:
Such were the names of the fathers.
Salinas, de la Garza, Sánchez, García,
Uribe, Gonzálaz, Martinez, de León:
Such are the names of the sons. E

ANALYZE VISUALS
How do you think the artist feels about the subject of this painting?

E TONE
Reread lines 29–34. What idea is emphasized by the **repetition** in these lines?

3. **mesquite** (mĕ-skēt'), **nopal** (nō'pəl): plants native to the southwestern United States.

ANALYZE VISUALS

Possible answer: *The artist may admire the riders' skill and enthusiasm and the beauty of the horses.*

About the Art Born in Germany, artist Hugo Wilhelm Arthur Nahl (1833–1889) came to the United States in 1849 seeking adventure. With his brother, he lived in New York City for two years and then went west to California during the California Gold Rush. His paintings included many dramatic scenes like the one portrayed here.

LITERARY ANALYSIS

E TONE

Possible answer: *The repetition emphasizes the idea that the strength and courage of the first pioneers is a legacy for their descendants.*

SELECTION WRAP-UP

REFLECT Ask students to think about the ways in which the authors use the themes of death and rebirth in the two poems. What is the importance of these themes in terms of the life of a pioneer?

CRITIQUE Point out that "Western Wagons" has a strict rhyme scheme, while "The Other Pioneers" does not. Ask students which style appeals to them more, and why.

READING FLUENCY

Distribute the copy masters and have students practice fluency.

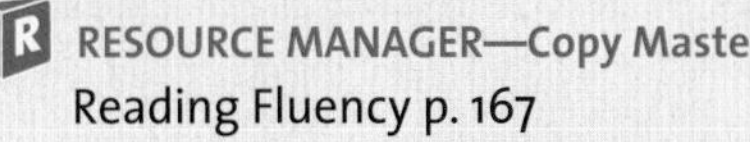

RESOURCE MANAGER—Copy Master
Reading Fluency p. 167

FOR ENGLISH LEARNERS

Language: Verb Tenses [mixed-readiness pairs] Explain that English contains many verbs with irregular past forms and that students should try to memorize these. Review the past-tense forms of some irregular verbs found in this poem. These include *rode, came, built, made, bore, saw, sang, stood,* and *left.* Pair English learners with fluent speakers and have them write two sentences for each verb, one using the present tense and one using the past.

FOR ADVANCED LEARNERS/PRE-AP

Synthesize [mixed learning profiles] Encourage linguistic and musical learners to set the words of one of these poems to music. Suggest that linguistic learners find a line in the poem that could be a refrain. Challenge musical learners to create a melody, pace, and rhythm consistent with the tone of the poem. Invite volunteers to share their songs with the class and elicit feedback.

Practice and Apply

After Reading

For additional support of postreading questions, use this copy master:

RESOURCE MANAGER—Copy Master
Question Support p. 165 (After Reading questions adapted for English learners and less-proficient readers)

Additional selection questions are provided for teachers on page 159.

ANSWERS

Comprehension

1. *The pioneers are taking axes, rifles, banjos, frying pans, and blankets.*
2. *The "other pioneers" were the Spanish pioneers who settled in the southwestern United States.*

Literary Analysis

Possible answers:

3. *The speaker is a pioneer who is heading west to California to seek his fortune. He or she has heard rumors about the good land and gold in the western states. The phrase "to get rich out there or die" shows that the speaker is determined to succeed but knows the journey will be difficult.*
4. *One example is the repetition of "we're going West tomorrow," which emphasizes the pioneers' determination.*
5. *The people were hoping to settle in a new land and to pass down that land through generations of descendants.*
6. *Salazar feels the accomplishments of the Spanish settlers have been overshadowed by the later pioneers. His purpose might be to make sure that his ancestors are remembered and honored.*
7. *Both groups of pioneers are brave and hardworking, but the pioneers in "Western Wagons" seem more interested in adventure and gold than the pioneers in Salazar's poem. The pioneers in "The Other Pioneers" want to find a place to settle down and build homes for themselves and future generations.*

After Reading

Comprehension

1. **Recall** In "Western Wagons," what things are the pioneers taking with them?
2. **Clarify** Who were the "other pioneers"?

Literary Analysis

3. **Make Inferences about Speaker** What do you know about the feelings and situation of the speaker in "Western Wagons"? Cite specific lines from the poem to support your answer.
4. **Analyze Repetition** Look for examples of repetition in "Western Wagons." What ideas are emphasized through the use of repetition?
5. **Interpret Poetry** Reread lines 12–15 of "The Other Pioneers." What were the people hoping for from their new home?
6. **Draw Conclusions about Purpose** What might have been Salazar's purpose for writing "The Other Pioneers"?
7. **Compare and Contrast** Compare and contrast the **pioneers** in "Western Wagons" and "The Other Pioneers." How are the pioneers' traits and attitudes the same? How are they different? Consider their ideas about home, moving, and future generations.

Comparing Tone

Now that you've read both poems, finish filling in your chart. Then add—and answer—the final question.

Shared Subject: Pioneers in Early America		
	"Western Wagons"	*"The Other Pioneers"*
What images, words, and phrases tell about the pioneers and their actions?		
How does the speaker feel?		
What sound devices, if any, does the poet use? How do they affect the poem?		
What is the tone of the poem?		

Comparing Tone

● **STANDARDS FOCUS** Tone

■ **STANDARDS FOCUS** Set a Purpose for Reading

"Western Wagons"

Row 1: *"We've broken land and cleared it," "endless campfires glowed," "taken land and settled," "starve and freeze and suffer," "die, and tame the lands";* ***Row 2:*** *happy, enthusiastic, fearless, reckless;* ***Row 3:*** *Rhyme and rhythm create an entertaining sing-song quality, while repetition of "we're going West tomorrow" emphasizes the pioneers' determination;* ***Row 4:*** *enthusiastic, admiring*

"The Other Pioneers"

Row 1: *"plowed the land," "built the towns," "raised churches," "bore them sons," "cleared the brush and planted the corn," "dust . . . sweat," "Gentle mothers," "stalwart fathers," "pride and manly strength";* ***Row 2:*** *proud, honored, determined;* ***Row 3:*** *Repetition of lines beginning with* and, of those, *and* here *emphasizes determination, while repetition of the pioneers' last names emphasizes the pioneers' legacy;* ***Row 4:*** *proud, respectful*

Writing for Assessment

1. READ THE PROMPT

You just read two poems about pioneers. In writing assessments, you may be asked to compare and contrast the tone of selections such as these that share a similar subject.

PROMPT

"Western Wagons" and "The Other Pioneers" both tell about pioneers, but the tone of the poems is not identical. In four or five paragraphs, compare and contrast the tone of each poem and describe how this tone is developed through imagery, word choice, sound devices, and speakers. Use quotations from the poems to support your ideas.

STRATEGIES IN ACTION

1. I need to describe the **attitude** toward pioneers expressed in each poem and tell how this attitude is shown.
2. I need to tell how the attitudes are **similar and different**.
3. I must support my ideas using **examples** from the poems.

2. PLAN YOUR WRITING

Review the chart you filled out and note the similarities and differences between the tones of the two poems and the way they're conveyed. Make sure you have enough quotations and examples to support your ideas. Then think about how you will set up the body of your response.

- Option A: In one paragraph, describe the tone of the first poem and explain how it was created. In the next paragraph, describe the tone of the second poem and explain how it is similar and different from the tone of the first.
- Option B: In one paragraph, compare how speaker and word choice contribute to the tone. In a second paragraph, compare how sound devices and imagery contribute to the tone.

Choose an option. Then outline your essay and write a thesis statement.

I. Introduce poems and thesis statement
II. Tone in "Western Wagons"
III. Tone in "The Other Pioneers" and how it compares
IV. Conclusion

3. DRAFT YOUR RESPONSE

Introduction Give the titles of the poems, the poets' names, and your thesis statement.
Body Follow your outline to describe the tone of each poem and explain the similarities and differences between the poems. Include details from the poems to support your ideas.
Conclusion End your essay by restating your thesis statement. You might also include your thoughts about which poem's tone made the strongest impression on you and why.
Revision Make sure the quotations you cite are correctly punctuated with quotation marks.

DIFFERENTIATED INSTRUCTION

FOR LESS-PROFICIENT WRITERS

Draft Your Response Provide this outline to help students structure their responses:

Introduction

- Give the poem titles and poets' names.
- State your thesis.

Body

- Explain the first poet's attitude.
  — Describe the speaker's feelings.
  — Explain how word choice, imagery, and sound devices contribute to tone.
- Explain the second poet's attitude.
  — Describe the speaker's feelings.
  — Explain how word choice, imagery, and sound devices contribute to tone.
- Explain how the poets' attitudes are similar and different.

Conclusion

- Restate your thesis.

Writing for Assessment

1. ***READ THE PROMPT***

   Read the prompt aloud. Ask volunteers which key words and phrases define the task (*compare and contrast, tone, use quotations*).

2. ***PLAN YOUR WRITING***

   - Have students use the notes in their charts from page 735 to create a strong thesis statement.
   - After students have decided how to organize their response, have them write key details in the appropriate sections of their outlines.

3. ***DRAFT YOUR RESPONSE***

   - Remind students to begin each body paragraph with a strong topic sentence. Explain that all the details in the paragraph should support the topic sentence.
   - List transitions on the board that might strengthen the unity within each paragraph and between paragraphs, such as *in addition, unlike, in contrast,* and *similarly.*

RESOURCE MANAGER—Copy Master
Writing for Assessment p. 166

Assess and Reteach

Assess

RESOURCE MANAGER—Copy Masters
Selection Tests A, B/C pp. 169–170, 171–172

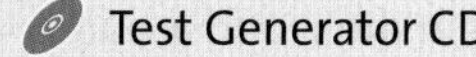

Test Generator CD

Reteach

STANDARDS LESSON FILE
Literature Lesson 39: Tone
Reading Lesson 12: Comparing and Contrasting

Focus and Motivate

OBJECTIVES

- analyze a student model that reflects the key traits of a literary analysis essay
- use the writing process to write a literary analysis essay
- revise and edit, applying a rubric for writing a strong literary analysis essay
- create an online database

WRITER'S ROAD MAP

WRITING PROMPTS 1 AND 2

Help students choose a prompt by writing down the titles and notable details of their favorite selections from the unit. Students might also brainstorm a list of memorable stories from other sources.

ADDITIONAL PROMPTS

Use these prompts for practice with writing a literary analysis:

WRITING PROMPT 3

Writing from Children's Literature Choose a children's story and write an essay that analyzes its most distinctive elements.

Stories to Consider:

- a retelling of a classic fairy tale
- a story that you liked to hear as a child
- a story with an intriguing plot, an unforgettable main character, or a timeless theme

WRITING PROMPT 4

Writing from the Oral Tradition People throughout history have told stories to teach lessons and explain the world around them. Choose a traditional tale and write an essay in which you describe its elements and analyze why it is meaningful.

Tales to Consider:

- folk tales from different cultures
- myths from different cultures

For additional writing prompts, see

Write*Smart* CD

Writing Center at **ClassZone.com**

KEY TRAITS

Review the six ***KEY TRAITS*** with students, focusing primarily on ideas, organization, and word choice. Compare the list of traits with the rubric on page 748.

Writing Workshop

Literary Analysis

In this unit, you looked closely at style, voice, and other literary elements that make writing distinctive. In this workshop, you will examine literary elements that make a work especially meaningful or enjoyable to you. Use the **Writer's Road Map** as your guide.

WRITER'S ROAD MAP

Literary Analysis

WRITING PROMPT 1

Writing from Literature Choose a selection from this unit and write an essay that helps a reader understand it more deeply. Focus on one or two literary elements, such as plot, characters, setting, or mood.

Selections to Consider

- "The Lady, or the Tiger?"
- "New York Day Women"
- "Us and Them"

WRITING PROMPT 2

Writing from the Real World Think of a memorable story you have viewed or read. Write an essay in which you describe the story and analyze the reasons that it is meaningful to you.

Sources of Stories

- television shows with particular settings, such as a police station or a hospital
- movies with exciting or surprising plots
- magazine articles that describe real-life adventures

WRITING TOOLS
For prewriting, revision, and editing tools, visit the **Writing Center** at **ClassZone.com.**

KEY TRAITS

1. *IDEAS*
- Presents a **thesis statement** that identifies the main idea of the analysis
- Supports key points with **evidence,** such as quotations and details

2. *ORGANIZATION*
- **Identifies the title and author** of the work in a thought-provoking introduction
- Provides **details** as needed to give the reader background information
- Uses **transitions** to connect ideas
- **Summarizes** the analysis in a conclusion and makes a broad judgment about the work

3. *VOICE*
- Uses language that is **appropriate** for the audience and purpose

4. *WORD CHOICE*
- Uses **precise words** to examine the work

5. *SENTENCE FLUENCY*
- Varies **sentence structures**

6. *CONVENTIONS*
- Uses **correct grammar, spelling, and punctuation**

Writing Workshop Resources

RESOURCE MANAGER UNIT 6

Plan and Teach pp. 173–176
Prewriting–Editing pp. 177–181
Writing Rubric p. 182
Publishing with Technology p. 183
Writing Support p. 184*

STANDARDS LESSON FILE

Writing Lessons 9, 19, 21, 22, 33, 44
Media Lessons 17, 18, 21

BEST PRACTICES TOOLKIT

Scaffolding Writing Instruction pp. 43–46*
Main Idea and Details • Cluster Diagram • Writing Template: Literary Analysis

TECHNOLOGY

Easy Planner DVD
Writing Center at **ClassZone.com**
Write*Smart* CD

* Resources for Differentiation

art 1: Analyze a Student Model

Ramón Cepero
Oxford Charter School

Fancy Is Funnier Than Fact

"I let fancy get the upper hand of fact too often," Mark Twain explains in *Roughing It.* What he means is that he likes to tell a few tall tales. He also likes to skip over or change some of the facts, which makes his writing style surprising and funny. In *Roughing It,* Twain uses irony and exaggeration to create humor.

Twain begins by listing several jobs that he has already tried and lost. Each failure is funny because Twain uses irony to describe what really happened. For instance, Twain remembers working in a bookstore. He says he spent all his time there reading. He adds that the customers "bothered" him by interrupting his reading. It's funny to think of someone who is bothered by having to work at his job. When Twain tells about being a clerk in a drug store, he says his "prescriptions were unlucky." He adds that, as a result, "we appeared to sell more stomach-pumps than soda-water." This description is humorous, even though readers probably feel sorry for the customers who got sick taking medicine that was supposed to make them better.

The way Twain describes his time as a reporter is laugh-out-loud funny. For example, his boss tells Twain to write about hay-wagons that come into the city. Twain finds only one hay-wagon, but he turns it into a whopping sixteen news stories. He explains how he did it this way: "I multiplied [the one hay-wagon] by sixteen, brought it into town from sixteen different directions, made sixteen separate items of it, and got up such another sweat about hay as Virginia City had never seen in the world before." One story about a hay-wagon sounds boring, but Twain's sixteen stories, as well as the big "sweat about hay" in Virginia City, sound funny.

KEY TRAITS IN ACTION

Begins with a thought-provoking introduction that identifies the work's **title and author,** as well as a clear **thesis statement.**

Varies **sentence structures** and uses **appropriate** language.

Provides **details** that add needed background information. Supports the thesis with **evidence.**

Teach

Part 1: Analyze a Student Model

Have students read the **Student Model** and **Key Traits in Action.** Discuss the model, pointing out specific examples of each trait. You may also wish to use these activities:

- **Thesis Statement** Remind students that the thesis statement tells the essay's main idea, which will be supported by further ideas and evidence in the body of the essay. Have students locate the thesis statement in lines 4–5. Ask them how they might expect the body of the essay to be organized, based on the thesis statement. ***Possible answer:*** *The writer might first give examples of Twain's use of irony and then give examples of his use of exaggeration.*
- **Sentence Structure** Display this passage and ask a student to read it aloud:

  He says he spent all his time reading. He says that the customers "bothered him." He says his "prescriptions were unlucky" when he was a clerk in a drug store.

  Then have students compare the passage to lines 9–13 of the model. Discuss how the writer varies sentence structure. Ask: How does varied sentence structure improve the essay? ***Possible answer:*** *Varying sentence structures makes the essay less repetitive and more interesting to read.*

DIFFERENTIATED INSTRUCTION

FOR ALL STUDENTS

Student Portfolios Encourage students to save copies of their writing so they can track their progress throughout the year.

For general guidelines on differentiating writing instruction, see

BEST PRACTICES TOOLKIT
Scaffolding Writing Instruction
pp. 43–46

FOR ENGLISH LEARNERS

Language: Skill Words Write these terms on the board and review them with students:

- *thesis statement:* sentence that tells the main idea of an essay
- *sentence structures:* the different ways sentences can be put together. For example: "I went to the park after dinner" or "After dinner, I went to the park."
- *appropriate:* suited to a particular situation. For example, slang is usually not appropriate in an essay written for school.
- *evidence:* details that help prove a statement is true or help readers draw conclusions. Writers often use the phrases *for example* and *for instance* to introduce supporting evidence. In line 8 of the model, "For instance" introduces evidence for the writer's claim that "Each failure is funny because Twain uses irony to describe what really happened" (lines 7–8).

- **Transitions** Point out the writer's use of transitions throughout the model. Ask these questions:

  How does the writer smoothly connect the third and fourth paragraphs of the essay on pages 743–744? ***Possible answer:*** *The writer introduces the topic of Twain's job as a reporter in the third paragraph. He begins the fourth paragraph with "Later in the narrative, Twain tells another tall tale about his work as a reporter." The transitions indicate that he will continue the discussion of Twain as a reporter with further examples.*

  What transition words and phrases are used in lines 31–37? ***Possible answer:*** *"This is funny because" (line 31), "but" (line 32), "Then" (line 33), "but" (line 37)*

- **Precise Words** Have students note the highlighted precise words in lines 31–33. Discuss how these words help readers visualize and understand what the writer describes. Point out that in a literary analysis essay, it is important to use correct literary terms, such as *plot, conflict, character, speaker, foreshadowing,* and so on. Have students skim the rest of the model essay to find more examples of precise words. ***Possible answer:*** *"surprising and funny" (line 4), "irony and exaggeration" (line 5), "He adds" (lines 9, 13), "He explains" (line 20), "laugh-out-loud funny" (lines 17–18), "narrative" (lines 27, 39), "tall tale" (line 27), "desperate" (line 28), "inventing" (line 39), "hilarious and worthwhile" (line 43)*

  Then work with students to brainstorm a list of other precise nouns and verbs they might use in their essays. Start by having them think of precise words that might replace vague words such as *good, said,* and *went.* ***Possible answer:*** *sparkling, spectacular, stunning, whispered, shouted, suggested, skipped, jogged, galloped, crept*

For interactive student models, see

WriteSmart CD

Writing Center at **ClassZone.com**

Later in the narrative, Twain tells another tall tale about his work as a reporter. He explains that one day he was desperate because there was nothing to write about. Then he found out that an outlaw had killed a man in a saloon. Twain says that "joy returned once more. I never was so glad." This is funny because it's so ridiculous. Twain might have been a little relieved that there was news to write about, but he couldn't have been joyful. Then Twain surprises the reader by explaining how he wrote a letter to the outlaw. He told the man, "You have done me a kindness this day which I can never forget." Twain can't really be thinking of murder as a kindness or a personal favor. He is just glad to get some news, but the irony about his "joy" makes it funny.

Uses **transitions** effectively.

Precise words help to make the analysis clear and logical.

In *Roughing It,* Twain turns his experiences with work into a funny narrative about failing at jobs, getting fired, inventing "news," and finally finding a "legitimate occupation" as a writer. He uses irony and exaggeration and lets "fancy get the upper hand of fact too often" as he tells about his work life. Twain's many exaggerations make *Roughing It* a hilarious and worthwhile read.

Lively conclusion **summarizes** the analysis and makes a broad judgment about the work.

2

DIFFERENTIATED INSTRUCTION

FOR ENGLISH LEARNERS

Comprehension: Transitions Write three or four sentences on the board that demonstrate using transitions to respond to a reading and work with students to underline the transitional words. For example:

> At first, the main character is excited because he has new neighbors. Then he learns the neighbors are unfriendly. Later in the story, readers learn that the new neighbors are hiding something. The author gives clues, but we don't learn the truth until the end of the story.

Then have students write three or four sentences about a character or story they know well. Encourage them to use at least three transitions to connect their ideas.

Use the copy master to provide students with further practice using transitions.

 **RESOURCE MANAGER—Copy Master**
Writing Support p. 184

Part 2: Apply the Writing Process

PREWRITING

What Should I Do? / **What Does It Look Like?**

1. Reread or re-view the work you chose.
One way to find an idea or focus is to go back over the piece you have chosen and examine its literary elements, such as its characters, dialogue, setting, or style. List examples of each element.

Element	Examples
Repetition	"What to do next?"; repeated failures at various jobs
Language	long sentences; fancy words (proprietor, dearth, excursion)
Exaggeration	the drugstore sold more stomach pumps than soda water; one hay-wagon turns into sixteen hay-wagons

2. Develop a working thesis.
For Prompt 1, your thesis should name one or two literary elements and explain how they affect the meaning of the work. For Prompt 2, your thesis should tell the reader why the work matters to you.

Working thesis:
Twain exaggerates a lot, and that makes a funny narrative.

3. Craft a strong introduction.
Your opening paragraph should grab the reader's attention and state the thesis clearly and completely.

TIP **Strong introductions include quotations, surprising statements, or questions.**

Start with a question:
Why is Mark Twain's writing so funny?
Start with a quotation:
"I let fancy get the upper hand of fact too often."
Start with a surprising statement:
One hay-wagon can become sixteen news stories in the hand of a clever and devious reporter.

4. Find evidence to support your thesis.
Prove your thesis by referring directly to the details of the work. For example, the writer of the student model wanted to figure out what made *Roughing It* so funny. He analyzed the work and found several examples of irony.

Key point: Twain uses irony.
Supporting evidence:
- *doesn't like working in a bookstore because customers bother him instead of letting him read*
- *reacts to murder with "joy" and says, "I was never so glad"*

Practice and Apply

To support students during the writing process, use these copy masters:

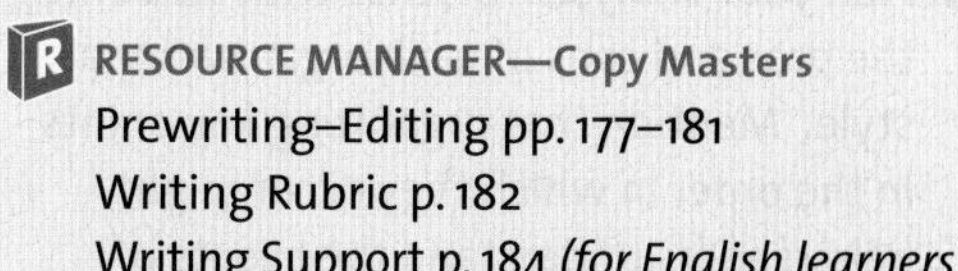

RESOURCE MANAGER—Copy Masters
Prewriting–Editing pp. 177–181
Writing Rubric p. 182
Writing Support p. 184 *(for English learners)*

Part 2: Apply the Writing Process

PREWRITING

1. **Reread or re-view the work you chose.** Students can decide between two potential subjects by charting the literary elements of both. They can then decide which piece would make the most interesting essay. If identifying specific literary elements for any given piece is too challenging, they should look for another subject.
2. **Develop a working thesis.** Students should identify what they want to say about the work they've chosen. Remind them that they may need to revise their thesis once they begin writing, but it is helpful to have at least a working thesis in place as they begin writing and organizing their thoughts.
3. **Craft a strong introduction.** Encourage students to experiment with different ways of beginning their essays. If students need ideas, point out the TIP in step 3. Give students time to meet in pairs or small groups to share first drafts of introductions and get feedback.
4. **Find evidence to support your thesis.** Students should isolate each of the major points they want to make and then figure out what details they will use to support it. Suggest that they use a graphic organizer to record their main ideas and supporting details.

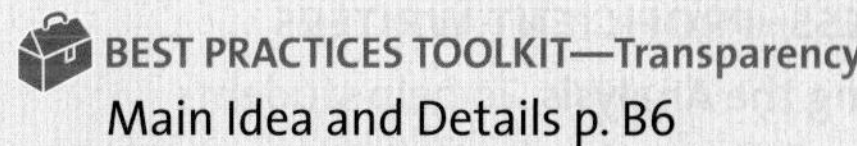

BEST PRACTICES TOOLKIT—Transparency
Main Idea and Details p. B6

For interactive graphic organizers, see
Write*Smart* CD
Writing Center at **ClassZone.com**

FOR ENGLISH LEARNERS

Developing a Working Thesis [mixed-readiness pairs] Have students use these frames to focus on the literary elements of the piece they have chosen. Remind students that they should focus on one or two important literary elements.

- I want to write about the work ________ by ________.
- I chose this piece because ________.
- The main idea I want to share with readers about this piece is ________.
- I will focus on this/these literary element(s): ________.
- This/These element(s) are important to the piece because ________.

Distribute copies of the Cluster Diagram and encourage students to record details and quotations related to each literary element. Have students meet with partners to discuss their diagrams and draft thesis statements.

BEST PRACTICES TOOLKIT—Transparency
Cluster Diagram p. B18

DRAFTING

1. **Plan your analysis.** Discuss with students the pros and cons of each organizational style. Mention that organizing key points in the order in which they occur might help readers understand the events of the literary work being described. On the other hand, arranging key points in order of importance might help grab readers' attention at the start and give emphasis to the most important ideas. Students might create two brief preliminary outlines in which they try both ways of organizing their information. They can then pick the one that seems to make the most sense.
2. **Consider your audience.** Have students share early drafts with a partner to find out if they have included enough background information. Students should encourage their partners to circle sections of the essay that need more explanation.
3. **Back up your points with evidence.** Tell students that each statement they make should have at least one supporting detail or quotation. Peer readers should help each other identify places where more evidence is needed. Point out the TIP before students begin revising their drafts.

BEST PRACTICES TOOLKIT—Transparency
Writing Template: Literary Analysis pp. C16, C32

Write*Smart* CD

Writing Center at **ClassZone.com**

DRAFTING

What Should I Do?	What Does It Look Like?
1. Plan your analysis. The writer of the student model discussed each key point in the order it appeared in Twain's narrative. If you prefer, you could discuss your key points in order of importance—putting the most important key point either first or last.	***Order of appearance in the narrative:*** *1. Jobs Twain tried and failed at* *2. Early event in Twain's career as a newspaperman* *3. Later event in Twain's career as a newspaperman* ***Order of importance:*** *1. Greatest example: response to saloon killing* *2. Another example: stories about hay-wagons* *3. Another example: early jobs*
2. Consider your audience. Your audience may not be familiar with the work you are analyzing. Remember to add background information to help readers follow your points.	*Twain is a good storyteller, and he is so funny. For example, his boss tells Twain to write about hay-wagons that come into the city. Twain finds only one hay-wagon, but he turns it into a whopping sixteen news stories. He explains how he did it this way: "I multiplied [the one hay-wagon] by sixteen, brought it into town from sixteen different directions, made sixteen separate items of it, and got up such another sweat about hay as Virginia City had never seen in the world before." One story about a hay-wagon sounds boring, but Twain's sixteen stories, as well as the big "sweat about hay" in Virginia City, sound funny.*
3. Back up your points with evidence. You need to prove each key point that you make. You can do this with evidence, such as a few well-chosen details or quoted words. TIP **Before you revise, look back at the key traits on page 742 and the rubric and peer-reader questions on page 748.**	*Each failure is funny. That's because Twain uses exaggeration and irony.* — *Key point* *For instance, Twain remembers working in a bookstore. He says he spent all his time there reading. He adds that the customers "bothered" him by interrupting his reading. It's funny to think of someone who is bothered by having to work at his job.* — *Support*

DIFFERENTIATED INSTRUCTION

FOR LESS–PROFICIENT WRITERS

Planning the Analysis To help students organize information for their literary analysis essays, provide this sample outline:

Introduction
- Begin with a question, quotation, or surprising statement.
- Identify the work's title and author.
- Present a clear thesis statement.

Body
- Discuss the first key point.
  —Provide evidence (examples, quotations) to support the point.
  —Explain how the evidence relates to the key point and the main idea of the essay.
- Transition to the second key point.
  —Provide evidence (examples, quotations) to support the point.
  —Explain how the evidence relates to the key point and the main idea of the essay.
- Continue describing key points, either in the order in which they appear in the work or in order of importance.

Conclusion
- Discuss the meaning of the work. Reflect back on your introduction.
- Explain why the piece matters to you or why it is important.

REVISING AND EDITING

What Should I Do?	What Does It Look Like?
1. Improve how you start. • Reread your opening sentence. Ask yourself: Will this interest my reader? • (Circle) the author's name and the title of the work. Add this information if it is missing. • [Bracket] your thesis. Make it as clear and specific as possible.	~~(Mark Twain) likes to tell tall tales. He also likes to change some of the facts in his story. [Twain exaggerates a lot, and that makes a funny narrative.]~~ *"I let fancy get the upper hand of fact too often," Mark Twain explains in Roughing It. What he means is that he likes to tell a few tall tales. He also likes to skip over or change some of the facts, which makes his writing style surprising and funny. In Roughing It, Twain uses exaggeration to create humor.*
2. Use exact, specific words. • Consider replacing some of your weak, state-of-being verbs, such as *is* and *might be*, with action verbs. • Also, think about replacing dull, tired modifiers, such as *really, very,* and *so*, with more specific words.	~~Twain is a good storyteller, and he is so funny.~~ *The way Twain describes his time as a reporter is laugh-out-loud funny.*
3. Vary your sentences. • Highlight places where you have used several simple sentences in a row. • Revise to include a mix of sentence structures that make your analysis more sophisticated.	~~Twain lists several jobs. He has already tried and lost each one. Each failure is funny. That's because Twain uses exaggeration and irony.~~ *Twain begins by listing several jobs that he has already tried and lost. Each failure is funny because Twain uses exaggeration and irony to tell what really happened.*
4. Tell why it matters. • Ask a peer reader to point out statements in your conclusion that discuss the meaning or impact of the work. • Add a reflection on the work if one is needed. **See page 748:** Ask a Peer Reader	*Twain turns his experiences with work into a funny narrative about failing at jobs, getting fired, inventing "news," and finally finding a "legitimate occupation" as a writer. He exaggerates and lets "fancy get the upper hand of fact too often" as he tells about his work life. Twain's many exaggerations make Roughing It a hilarious and worthwhile read.*

FOR ENGLISH LEARNERS

Revising and Editing [paired option] Allow students to work with a peer reader to revise their writing. Provide this outline:

- I will improve how I start my essay by adding/changing ________.
- I replaced the weak or dull words ________ with these words: ________.
- I added a mix of sentence types. Here is an example: ________.
- This statement from my conclusion discusses the meaning of the work: ________.

FOR ADVANCED LEARNERS/PRE–AP

Analyzing Two Works Invite students to write an analysis that focuses on the literary elements of two similar or contrasting works. For example, Mark Twain's *Roughing It* might be paired with another work that uses a similar style of humorous exaggeration or irony. Or, it might be paired with a work that explores similar themes with a different style of humor or with no humor at all. Explain that comparing and contrasting two works can emphasize the main features of both works.

REVISING AND EDITING

1. **Improve how you start.** Have students form pairs for peer reading. Students in each pair should be honest with each other in making recommendations and in answering these specific questions: Does the first paragraph interest me and make me want to continue reading? Why or why not? Do I know right away the author's name and the title of the work being discussed? Is the thesis statement clear?
2. **Use exact, specific words.** Discuss why "laugh-out-loud funny" is more specific than "so funny." Then have students look through their essays to identify verbs and adjectives that might be replaced with more interesting ones.
3. **Vary your sentences.** Suggest that students read their essays aloud. If the writing sounds choppy and repetitive, then they likely have too many simple sentences and need to consider ways of revising them. Have students revisit the model essay to see how the writer incorporates sentence variety. For example, point out that the writer uses introductory phrases (line 8), complex sentences (lines 7–8), direct quotations (lines 12–14), and compound sentences (line 19–20) throughout the essay.
4. **Tell why it matters.** Have students reread their thesis statements. Explain that their concluding statements should echo the ideas expressed at the beginning of the essay, but with a new twist or insight. Encourage them to experiment with different ways of discussing the meaning of the work and reflecting on the work. Turn students' attention to the conclusion of the model and point out the way the writer uses quotations from the work to reinforce key ideas.

For interactive revision tools, see

- Write*Smart* CD
- Writing Center at **ClassZone.com**

Preparing to Publish

Support for meeting the goals in the writing rubric is supplied throughout the **Writing Workshop** on pages 742–747.

For Rubric Bank, see

- Write*Smart* CD
- Writing Center at **ClassZone.com**

Assess and Reteach

After reading and assessing students' literary analysis essays, you might use these lessons to reteach key skills:

STANDARDS LESSON FILE

Writing Lesson 9: Creating Sentence Variety
Writing Lesson 19: Transitions
Writing Lesson 21: Writing a Thesis Statement
Writing Lesson 22: Writing Introductions
Writing Lesson 33: Writing About Literature
Writing Lesson 44: Using Precise Words

Preparing to Publish Literary Analysis

Apply the Rubric

A strong literary analysis . . .

- ☑ has an attention-getting introduction that identifies the title and author of the work being analyzed
- ☑ presents a clear, specific thesis
- ☑ supports key points with evidence
- ☑ provides background information so the reader can understand the analysis
- ☑ varies sentence structures
- ☑ uses transitions, appropriate language, and precise words
- ☑ concludes by summarizing the key ideas and reflecting on the work's effect or importance

Ask a Peer Reader

- What is my thesis?
- How well do I support each main point I make? Do I need to add details or quotations?
- Where in my conclusion do I explain what effect the work had on me?

Check Your Grammar

- Make sure that elements in your sentences are parallel. For example, phrases that serve the same purpose in a sentence should take the same form.

> *Twain likes to tell tall tales, skip over some of the facts, and ~~exaggerating~~ exaggerate some of the details.*

> *Roughing It is a funny narrative about failing at jobs, getting fired, inventing "news," and ~~how he finds~~ finding work.*

See page R64: Parallel Structure

- Do not misplace modifiers. Remember to follow the modifying phrase directly with the noun or pronoun it modifies.

> *~~In a saloon, Twain found out that an outlaw had killed a man.~~*
> *Twain found out that an outlaw had killed a man in a saloon.*

See page R59: Misplaced Modifiers

Writing Online

PUBLISHING OPTIONS
For publishing options, visit the **Writing Center** at **ClassZone.com.**

ASSESSMENT PREPARATION
For writing and grammar assessment practice, go to the **Assessment Center** at **ClassZone.com.**

PUBLISHING WITH TECHNOLOGY

Creating an Online Database

You and your classmates can publish your work by building an online database. The database you create could house your literary analyses as well as other reviews that give your opinions on books, movies, video games, or restaurants.

Preparing the Scene

1. **Decide on the content.** Determine what your database will include.
2. **Plan the organization of the database.** Decide how you will organize the database—perhaps by type of review or by keyword. Will you provide an index, a FAQ (that's a Frequently Asked Questions section), or a way for users to submit feedback?
3. **Sketch your home page.** Be sure that your home page shows the name of your site and has clear, easy-to-use navigation buttons. Add interest to your home page with graphics and color.
4. **Create credits.** On your home page, provide a link that says "About This Site" or otherwise signals information about site contents. Then list the site's creators, including all authors, as well as credits for all visuals.

   TIP Remember to get permission for anything you include on the site. This includes your classmates' permission to upload their work, as well as permission for any visuals, sound effects, or other items you import.

Producing the Database

1. **Use an authoring program.** Find out what software your school offers for building Web sites. Your school's computer specialist may offer a quick lesson in how to use it to import text and visuals. Otherwise, consult the Help menu, the manual, or an online tutorial for guidance.
2. **Ask peers to try out an early version of the database.** Find out what works well and what needs revising. Be sure to proofread the text, too.
3. **Upload it.** Work with the computer specialist at your school to make your database available on the Web.

PUBLISHING WITH TECHNOLOGY

Ask students to read this page to get an overview of how to plan and produce an online database of their literary analyses and other writings.

Before students begin working, review this rubric with them so that they understand their goals:

Rubric A strong online database has

- clear organization
- a home page with the name of the site and easy-to-use navigation buttons
- interesting graphics and color
- a link to information about site contents, including a list of the site's creators and credits for visuals
- a system that has been tested and proven to work well
- content that has been proofread

RESOURCE MANAGER—Copy Master
Publishing with Technology p. 183

STANDARDS LESSON FILE
Media Lesson 17: Understanding the Basics of Web Sites
Media Lesson 18: Evaluating Web Sites
Media Lesson 21: Creating a Web Site

DIFFERENTIATED INSTRUCTION

FOR LESS–PROFICIENT WRITERS

Creating an Online Database Review the steps for creating an online database on page 749. Then offer students additional support through each step of the project.

- Explain to students the options for their databases. Discuss the benefits of being able to access their writings easily.
- Direct students to other databases available online and discuss their organization and features.
- Work with students to make a list of features they might want to include.
- Allow students to work on databases in pairs or small groups. You might assign students with less computer experience to work with students who are more knowledgeable.
- Give students ample time for sharing their ideas and proofreading each other's work.

Assessment Practice

CHECK READINESS

Read aloud the paragraph under **ASSESS** and stress to students that this is not the full Unit Test but a way for them to check their readiness for it. Then have students examine the skills listed under **REVIEW** and look back in the unit or in the **Student Resource Bank** for any they need to study.

READ THE SELECTION

Remind students to keep Unit Goals in mind as they read the passage, paying particular attention to

- style
- sequence
- irony
- tone

To help students focus on **style** while reading, encourage them to ask questions such as

- Does the author use formal or informal language?
- Does the sentence structure emphasize certain ideas or feelings?
- What images does the author use to appeal to the reader's senses?

ANSWER THE QUESTIONS

Direct students to pages R95–R101 of the Test-Taking Handbook to review test-taking strategies. Remind them not to choose the first alternative that seems to fit when answering a multiple-choice question. Instead, students should read through all the choices, eliminate any that are clearly wrong, and then choose the best answer—the one that is most accurate and complete.

If students have budgeted their time well, they will have time to check their answers. Encourage students to review their answers, making sure that each answer they have chosen matches up correctly to the question. They should also check that their answer choices are clearly marked and that for each question they have marked only one answer.

Assessment Practice

Reading Comprehension

ASSESS

The practice test items on the next few pages match skills listed on the Unit Goals page (page 665) and addressed throughout this unit. Taking this practice test will help you assess your knowledge of these skills and determine your readiness for the Unit Test.

REVIEW

After you take the practice test, your teacher can help you identify any skills you need to review.

- Style
  - Word Choice
  - Sentence Structure
  - Imagery
- Sequence
- Irony
- Tone
- Idioms
- Latin Words and Roots
- Appositive Phrases
- Compound and Complex Sentences

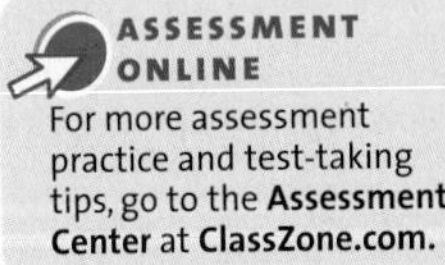

ASSESSMENT ONLINE

For more assessment practice and test-taking tips, go to the **Assessment Center at ClassZone.com.**

DIRECTIONS *Read this selection and answer the questions that follow.*

A Hike in New York City

Sam Levenson

At least once each summer we kids went off on a hike, but never without strong opposition from Mama. When it came to the open road, Mama had a closed mind.

Her method of discouraging us from venturing into the unknown was to make the entire project appear ridiculous:

"You're going on a what?"

"We're going on a hike."

"What's a hike?" Mama would ask.

When we started to explain it, the whole idea did in fact become ridiculous.

"We go walking, Ma."

"Walking? For that you have to leave home? What's the matter with walking right here? You walk; I'll watch."

"You don't understand, Ma. We take lunch along."

"I'll give you lunch here, and you can march right around the table," and she would start singing a march, clapping her hands rhythmically.

"Ma, we climb mountains in the woods."

She couldn't understand why it was so much more enjoyable to fall off a mountain than off a fire escape.

"And how about the wild animals in the woods?"

"Wild animals? What kind of wild animals?"

"A bear, for instance. A bear could eat you up."

"Ma, bears don't eat little children."

"Okay. So he won't eat you, but he could take a bite and spit it out! I'm telling you now, if a wild animal eats you up don't come running to me. And who's going with you?"

"Well, there's Georgie—"

"Georgie! Not him! He's a real wild animal!" She then went on to list all the conditions for the trip. "And remember one thing, don't tear your pants, and remember one thing, don't eat wild berries and bring me home the cramps, an remember one thing, don't tell me tomorrow morning that you're too tired to go to school, and remember one thing, wear boots, a sweater, warm underwea and an umbrella, and a hat, and remember one thing, if you should get lost in the jungle, call up so I'll know you're all right. And don't dare come home without color in your cheeks. I wish I was young and free like you. Take soap."

DIFFERENTIATED INSTRUCTION

FOR ENGLISH LEARNERS

Assessment Practice: Work Backwards

[paired option] Prepare students for the assessment by having them read the questions before they read the text passage. Have pairs follow these steps to learn unfamiliar words in the test directions and questions:

1. Find words you don't recognize and write each one on an index card.
2. Look up the meaning of the word in a dictionary.
3. Write the meaning on the back of the card.
4. Use your word cards to teach and practice the vocabulary with your partner and another pair of students.

Since the consent was specifically granted for the next day only, that night none of us slept. There was always a chance that it might rain. Brother Albert stayed at the crystal set[1] all night like a ship's radio operator with his earphones on, listening to weather bulletins and repeating them aloud for the rest of us. "It's clearing in Nebraska. Hot air masses coming up from the Gulf. They say it's good for planting alfalfa. Storm warning off the coast of Newfoundland. It's drizzling in Montreal."

At 6:00 A.M. we were ready for Operation Hike, rain or shine, but we had to wait for Papa to get up. We didn't need his permission, but we did need his blanket.

Into the valley of Central Park we marched, bowed down with knapsacks, flashlights, a compass-mirror (so you could tell not only where you were lost but who was lost), a thermos bottle (semi-automatic—you had to fill it but it emptied by itself), and an ax. Onward! Forward! Upward! Philip was always the leader. He was the one to get lost first. Jerry was the lookout. He would yell, "Look out!" and fall off the cliff. None of us knew how long we were supposed to march. We went on because we didn't know what to do if we stopped. One brave coward finally spoke up. "I can't go on anymore. The heat is killing me. Let's start the fire here."

No hike was complete without Georgie and his Uncle Bernie's World War I bugle. This kid had lungs like a vacuum cleaner. With him outside the walls of Jericho, they could have sent the rest of the army home. He used to stand on a hill and let go a blast that had the Staten Island ferries running into each other.

Lunch, naturally, had been packed in a shoe box—sandwiches, fruit, cheese, and napkins all squashed together neatly. The lid would open by itself every twenty minutes for air.

It happened every time, the Miracle of the Sandwiches. One kid always got a "brilliant idea." "Hey, I got a brilliant idea. I'm tired of my mother's sandwiches. Let's everybody trade sandwiches." All the kids exchanged sandwiches, and miraculously we all ended up with salami.

Albert was the true nature lover. "You know, you can learn a lot about human nature from the ants," he always said as he lifted up rock after rock to study his favorite insects. And he was right. While he was studying the ants, someone swiped his apple.

We came home with color in our cheeks—green. To make sure we could go again, we didn't forget Mama. We brought her a bouquet. She took one whiff and broke out in red blotches.

GO ON

1. **crystal set:** a radio.

ITEM ANALYSIS

COMPREHENSION AND WRITTEN RESPONSE	ITEMS	UNIT PAGES
Style	3, 6, 7, 8, 10, 11, 12, 17	664, 666, 673, 729
Word Choice	6, 10	666, 673
Sentence Structure	3, 11	666, 673
Imagery	8, 12	666, 673, 729
Sequence	1, 2, 15	673
Irony	7, 13, 14, 16	717, 729
Tone	4, 5, 9	668, 683, 735

VOCABULARY	ITEMS	UNIT PAGES
Idioms	1, 2, 3, 4	726
Latin Words and Roots	5, 6, 7	713

WRITING AND GRAMMAR	ITEMS	UNIT PAGES
Appositive Phrases	1, 4	681
Compound and Complex Sentences	2, 3	714, 727

FOR LESS–PROFICIENT READERS

Assessment Support Consider these options for completing the **Assessment Practice:**

- Have students "work backwards," reviewing the questions before reading the passage.
- Select random questions in the assessment and have students demonstrate how and where to look for the answers.
- Ask students to locate unfamiliar vocabulary words in the assessment. Elicit the meanings of these words from the class.
- Have students record useful testing words and definitions in their journals for later reference.
- Read the selection or parts of it aloud to aid in student comprehension.

After checking student readiness with this Assessment Practice, you may administer the complete Unit 6 Test in order to more thoroughly evaluate student mastery of unit goals.

ANSWERS

Comprehension

Model a thinking process for answering multiple-choice questions.

1. **C *is correct.*** *A can be eliminated because Albert listens to the weather reports the night before the hike. B is incorrect because they are ready at six o'clock, but they must wait to get Papa's blanket. D is incorrect because they didn't eat lunch until they were on their hike.*
2. **C *is correct.*** *It is the only choice with phrases that tell when something happened. A, B, and D are incorrect because each one contains a phrase that tells where something happened but no phrases that indicate when.*
3. **D *is correct.*** *Scanning the selection reveals a mix of long and short sentences, so A, B, and C can be eliminated.*
4. **B *is correct.*** *Sentence 2 uses word play to contrast the terms "open road" and "closed mind." A can be eliminated because it is simply a statement of fact. C and D are incorrect because they do not include humor.*
5. **B *is correct.*** *The ironic comment in the second sentence sets the humorous tone. A can be eliminated because the author uses a mix of long and short sentences. C and D are incorrect because the author does not use specialized vocabulary or detailed descriptions.*
6. **D *is correct.*** *Mama uses the phrase "and remember one thing" to precede her warnings to the children. A is incorrect because Mama is allowing them to go on the hike, which shows she is not angry. B can be eliminated because Mama's warnings are not given in a specific order. C is incorrect because Mama is not excited about the hike.*
7. **C *is correct.*** *It is verbal irony because if the children get lost, they will not be "all right." There are no details to support A or B, and D is incorrect because it is not ironic to call the New York City park a jungle.*
8. **A *is correct.*** *Mama can be pictured clapping her hands, and the reader can imagine the sound of the clapping and the singing. B, C, and D are incorrect because none of them include images that appeal to the sense of hearing.*

Comprehension

DIRECTIONS *Answer these questions about "A Hike in New York City."*

1. When do the children set out on their hike?
   - **A** before Albert hears the weather report
   - **B** at six o'clock in the morning
   - **C** after they get Papa's blanket
   - **D** as soon as they eat lunch
2. Which words and phrases from the passage help the reader follow the order of events?
   - **A** at least, in the woods
   - **B** on a hike, right here
   - **C** that night, at 6:00 A.M.
   - **D** open road, rain or shine
3. One element of the author's style is his use of
   - **A** mostly short sentences
   - **B** mostly long sentences
   - **C** all short sentences
   - **D** a mix of long and short sentences
4. Which one of the first four sentences in the passage tells you this will be a funny story?
   - **A** sentence 1
   - **B** sentence 2
   - **C** sentence 3
   - **D** sentence 4
5. The author sets the tone by using
   - **A** long sentences
   - **B** ironic comments
   - **C** specialized vocabulary
   - **D** detailed descriptions
6. In lines 28–32, the repetition of the phrase "and remember one thing" has the effect of
   - **A** creating an angry tone
   - **B** clarifying the sequence of events
   - **C** building excitement for the hike
   - **D** emphasizing Mama's many worries
7. In lines 32–33, Mama says "if you should get lost in the jungle, call up so I'll know you're all right." This statement is ironic because
   - **A** it is easy to get lost in a big city park
   - **B** Mama is afraid that the children will get lo
   - **C** the children are not all right if they are lo
   - **D** the New York City park is not a jungle
8. Which image appeals to the reader's sense of sight and hearing?
   - **A** Mama "singing a march, clapping her hands rhythmically"(line 15)
   - **B** Albert at the crystal set "with his earphor on" (lines 37–38)
   - **C** the children "bowed down with knapsack (line 45)
   - **D** lunch items "squashed together neatly" in a shoe box (line 59)

752

9. **D *is correct.*** *The phrases compare the ordinary events to important, dramatic events. A is incorrect because the phrases express a sophisticated point of view. B is incorrect because it is the narrator, not Mama, who uses the phrases. C can be eliminated because the interpretations of the phrases are clear.*
10. **B *is correct.*** *These are words that are likely to be used in everyday conversation. A can be eliminated because long, multisyllabic words are usually not informal. C and D can be eliminated because these are neutral words that are neither formal nor informal.*
11. **A *is correct.*** *The exclamation points indicate excitement, and the words convey positive feelings. B and C can be eliminated because there are no details to support a fear of getting lost or a need for their mother. D can be eliminated because there are no details to support the idea that they are anxious to climb a hill.*
12. **A *is correct.*** *These lines describe how Georgie played the bugle. Lines 55–57 indicate that he played very loudly. They do not describe how he spoke, as in B; his feelings about playing the bugle, as in C; or the cleanliness of his lungs, as in D.*

The phrases "Operation Hike" and "the Miracle of the Sandwiches" are funny because they

A express a child's innocent point of view
B show Mama's concern for her children
C can be interpreted in different ways
D make everyday events seem important

Which words in the passage help to create an informal style?

A opposition, ridiculous, rhythmically
B kids, swiped, squashed
C hike, walk, marched
D coward, insects, bouquet

With the exclamations "Onward! Forward! Upward!" in line 48, the author emphasizes the boys'

A excitement about the hike
B fear of getting lost
C need for their mother
D interest in climbing a hill

In line 55, the image that compares Georgie's lungs to a vacuum cleaner shows that he

A has strong lungs
B speaks very loudly
C likes to play the bugle
D has dirt in his lungs

In line 62, the quotation marks around "brilliant idea" suggest that this phrase is an example of

A understatement
B verbal irony
C vivid imagery
D symbolism

14. Reread lines 69–71. What is ironic about the children's gift to Mama?

A The children bring Mama a gift so that she will let them go hiking again.
B The children find flowers in Central Park to bring to Mama.
C Mama has an allergic reaction to the bouquet.
D Mama is surprised by the children's gift.

15. Which event happens last in the passage?

A The children exchange sandwiches.
B Someone steals Albert's apple.
C Mama breaks out in red blotches.
D Georgie plays his uncle's bugle.

Written Response

SHORT RESPONSE *Write two or three sentences to answer this question.*

16. Find two examples of irony in the passage and identify each as situational, verbal, or dramatic irony.

EXTENDED RESPONSE *Write a paragraph to answer this question.*

17. The author's writing style turns his remembrance into a funny story. Give two examples of his humor, and explain how the words, images, or sentences in the examples contribute to the humor.

13. B *is correct.* *The phrase is ironic because the narrator does not really consider the idea to be brilliant.* A *is incorrect because the word* brilliant *indicates overstatement rather than understatement.* C *and* D *are incorrect because there is no imagery or symbolism in the phrase.*

14. C *is correct.* *The children want to please Mama, but their gift makes her break out in a rash.* A, B, *and* D *can be eliminated because these events are not the opposite of what is expected or planned.*

15. C *is correct.* *Mama breaks out in a rash when she sniffs the bouquet the children have brought her from their hike.* A, B, *and* D *can be eliminated because all of these events take place before the children return home from the hike.*

Written Response

Possible short response:

16. *An example of situational irony is when the kids exchange sandwiches because one kid is tired of his mother's sandwiches, but they all end up with salami (lines 62–64), or when one of the children says he is too hot to go on and suggests starting a fire (lines 52–53). An example of verbal irony is the description of the lunch items as "all squashed together neatly" (lines 58–59), since they cannot be both "squashed together" and neat. An example of dramatic irony is when Mama suggests that a bear will eat the kids (line 21). The reader knows it is unlikely that the kids will meet a bear in a park in New York City.*

Possible extended response:

17. *Students could cite the author's use of word play in lines 2–3, the use of exaggeration in Mama's objections to the hike, her list of conditions, and the names "Operation Hike," and "the Miracle of the Sandwiches." They might also cite the images of the hikers loaded down with equipment, bumbling through Central Park (lines 45–51) and Georgie blowing a bugle blast that causes ferries to collide (lines 56–57). Students could note Levenson's use of irony to contrast the children's serious attitude about their hike and the ridiculous things they do.*

DIFFERENTIATED INSTRUCTION

FOR ENGLISH LEARNERS

Assessment Vocabulary Review these terms before students answer questions:

- *style:* an author's way of writing, including his or her choice of words, use of long or short sentences, and use of imagery
- *imagery:* words that help readers see, hear, smell, taste, or feel what a writer is describing
- *tone:* a writer's attitude toward a subject, such as serious, sarcastic, or humorous
- *ironic:* containing an example of situational, verbal, or dramatic irony
- *situational irony:* when something happens that is the opposite of what is expected
- *verbal irony:* when a writer or a character says the opposite of what he or she really means
- *dramatic irony:* when readers know something that a character in a story does not know

ANSWERS

Vocabulary

1. **B *is correct.*** *The word* least *in the idiom is related to* less. *A can be eliminated because it indicates "equal to." "At least" means that some summers the family went hiking only once, making C incorrect. D is incorrect because* roughly *is vague and does not work with the precise word* once.
2. **C *is correct.*** *Mama has a closed mind with regard to the open road. A can be eliminated because it does not work in the context of the sentence. B is incorrect because it suggests a cause-and-effect relationship for which there are no supporting details. D is incorrect because it suggests an event that does not make sense in the context of the passage.*
3. **D *is correct.*** *Georgie produces a sound that causes ferries to collide. A and B are incorrect because Georgie purposely carries his uncle's bugle. C can be eliminated because it does not make sense in the context of the sentence.*
4. **A *is correct.*** *Red blotches appear on Mama's skin. Context clues do not relate to trying to avoid the blotches, as in B; to worrying about them, as in C; or to scratching at them, as in D.*
5. **B *is correct.*** *Mama is against the idea of the hike. A is incorrect because the context does not show that she punishes the children. C is incorrect because the text does not express the idea of being influenced by something. D is incorrect because the context shows that Mama does not approve of the hike.*
6. **B *is correct.*** *People laugh at ideas that are silly. A can be eliminated because Mama wants to discourage the kids and would not want to make the project appear enjoyable. C is incorrect because it doesn't work in the context of the sentence. D can be eliminated because it does not express the meaning of "to laugh."*
7. **D *is correct.*** *The children could not explain how they all ended up with salami. A is incorrect because it does not work in the context of the sentence. B and C are incorrect because they do not convey the meaning of "to wonder at."*

Vocabulary

DIRECTIONS *Use context clues and your knowledge of idioms to answer the following questions.*

1. In line 1, the narrator says that the children in his family went hiking "at least once each summer." The idiom *at least* means
A as much as
B not less than
C more than
D roughly

2. In lines 2–3, the narrator says, "When it came to the open road, Mama had a closed mind." The idiom *when it came to* means
A in addition to
B because of
C with regard to
D upon arriving at

3. In line 57, Georgie "let go a blast" on his uncle's bugle. The idiom *let go* means
A was scared by
B forgot about
C left alone
D blew forcefully

4. In line 71, the narrator says that his mother "broke out" when she sniffed the bouquet. The idiom *broke out* means
A developed a rash
B tried to avoid
C worried about
D scratched at

DIRECTIONS *Use context clues and your understan of Latin words and roots to answer the following questions.*

5. The prefix *ob-* means "against," and the Lat word *ponere* means "to put." What is the meaning of the word *opposition* in line 2?
A punishment
B resistance
C influence
D approval

6. The Latin word *ridere* means "to laugh." What is the meaning of the word *ridiculous* in line 5?
A enjoyable
B silly
C realistic
D unusual

7. The Latin word *mirari* means "to wonder a What is the meaning of the word *miraculou* in line 64?
A with great curiosity
B without even trying
C by any means possible
D in a way that cannot be explained

DIFFERENTIATED INSTRUCTION

FOR ENGLISH LEARNERS

Review Academic Vocabulary Remind students that an idiom is an expression that has a different meaning from its literal meaning. Suggest that looking for context clues can help them figure out the meanings of idioms. Note that sometimes visualizing the images that an idiom suggests can give clues to meaning. Provide these additional context sentences to help students figure out the meanings of the idioms in items 1–4:

- Chinh ate at least three slices of pizza, and maybe more.
- Mom liked animals, but when it came to getting a puppy, she said no.
- When I saw that huge spider on my pillow, I let go a loud scream.
- After touching the poison ivy, Dayana's hand broke out in itchy red bumps.

'riting & Grammar

ECTIONS *Read this passage and answer the questions that follow.*

(1) Central Park occupies 843 acres of land in New York City. (2) It is the most visited park in the nation. (3) When the city bought the land in the mid 1800s, it had to be cleared of farms, livestock, and open sewers. (4) The city held a competition for the new park's design. (5) Officials chose a plan. (6) The completed park looked natural. (7) It consisted of artificial lakes and imported trees and shrubs. (8) Now the park is a popular spot for bird watching. (9) It is an oasis for migrating birds.

. How might you use an appositive phrase to combine sentences 1 and 2?

A Central Park is the most visited park in the nation and occupies 843 acres of land in New York City.
B The most visited park in the nation is Central Park, and it occupies 843 acres of land in New York City.
C Central Park, the most visited park in the nation, occupies 843 acres of land in New York City.
D Occupying 843 acres of land in New York City, Central Park is the most visited park in the nation.

. How might you combine sentences 4 and 5 to form one compound sentence?

A The city held a competition for the new park's design, choosing a plan.
B The city held a competition for the new park's design, and officials chose a plan.
C After the city held a competition for the new park's design, officials chose a plan.
D The city held a competition for the new park's design and chose a plan.

3. How might you combine sentences 6 and 7 to form one complex sentence?

A The completed park looked natural, but it consisted of artificial lakes and imported trees and shrubs.
B Though the completed park looked natural, it consisted of artificial lakes and imported trees and shrubs.
C The completed park looked natural but consisted of artificial lakes and imported trees and shrubs.
D The completed park looked natural, consisting of artificial lakes and imported trees and shrubs.

4. How might you use an appositive phrase to combine sentences 8 and 9?

A Migrating birds now make the park an oasis and a popular spot for bird watching.
B Because it is an oasis for migrating birds, the park is now a popular spot for bird watching.
C The park, an oasis for migrating birds, is now a popular spot for bird watching.
D The park is an oasis for migrating birds, so now it is a popular spot for bird watching.

ANSWERS

Writing & Grammar

1. **C *is correct.*** *The phrase "the most visited park in the nation" is an appositive for "Central Park" and is correctly set off by commas. Choices* A, B, *and* D *do not contain an appositive phrase.*
2. **B *is correct.*** *It contains two independent clauses.* A, C, *and* D *are incorrect because none of them contain two independent clauses.*
3. **B *is correct.*** *It contains one dependent and one independent clause. We can eliminate* A *because it is a compound sentence.* C *and* D *are incorrect because neither contains both a dependent and an independent clause.*
4. **C *is correct.*** *The phrase "an oasis for migrating birds" is an appositive for "The park." Choices* A, B, *and* D *do not contain an appositive phrase.*

DIFFERENTIATED INSTRUCTION

FOR ENGLISH LEARNERS

Assessment Support Discuss these terms:

- *appositive phrase* (items 1, 4)—a noun phrase that identifies or renames another noun or pronoun in the sentence
  —Ira, my cousin, is a mountain climber.
  —An experienced mountain climber, he loves the outdoors.
- *compound sentence* (item 2)—two independent clauses, often joined by the conjunction *and, or, but,* or *nor*
  —We might hike, or we might go swimming.
  —Mama told us we could go hiking, but she said we had to be home early.
- *complex sentence* (item 3)—one independent clause and one dependent clause, which may begin with a word such as *after, because, although, since, until, where,* or *who*
  —Because I often get lost, I always carry a compass.
  —Yesterday I went to the gym, where I worked out for two hours.

INTRODUCE *MORE GREAT READS*

In Unit 6, students have discussed a number of big questions. Invite students to tell which question they found most intriguing and why. Then focus attention on the three questions that appear on this page. Discuss the recommended books and their summaries, pointing out how each book connects to the related question. Encourage students to choose one or more of these "great reads" to read independently.

ClassZone.com

To find additional books that match students' interests and ability levels, visit the Literature Center at **ClassZone.com**.

Ideas for Independent Reading

Which questions from Unit 6 made an impression on you? Continue exploring them with these books.

How do you make decisions?

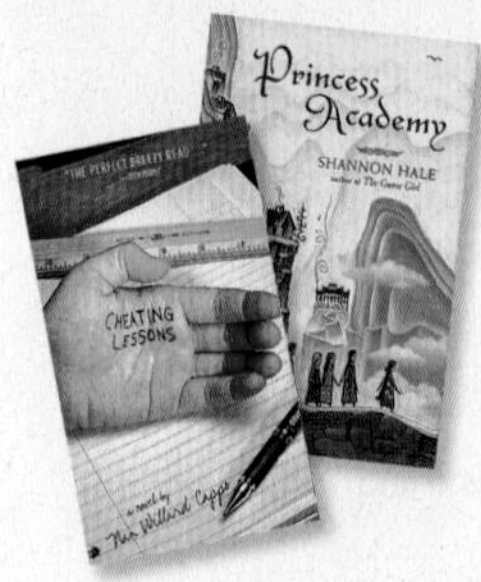

Cheating Lessons
by Nan Willard
Wickham High will finally compete against fancy Pinehurst at the State Quiz Bowl. Bernadette can't wait to crush the other team until she realizes there's no way her school honestly aced the test. She has to decide between telling a lie or hurting friends.

Good Brother, Bad Brother: The Story of Edwin Booth and John Wilkes Booth
by James Cross Giblin
Two brothers grow up together. Both become well-known actors like their father, but one goes on to kill the President of the United States. What happened?

Princess Academy
by Shannon Hale
The king's priests have decreed that the next princess will come from tiny Mount Eskel. Suddenly, all the girls in the village have to go to school. Miri decides she has to be the best student. But what will Miri do if the prince chooses her?

What's really normal?

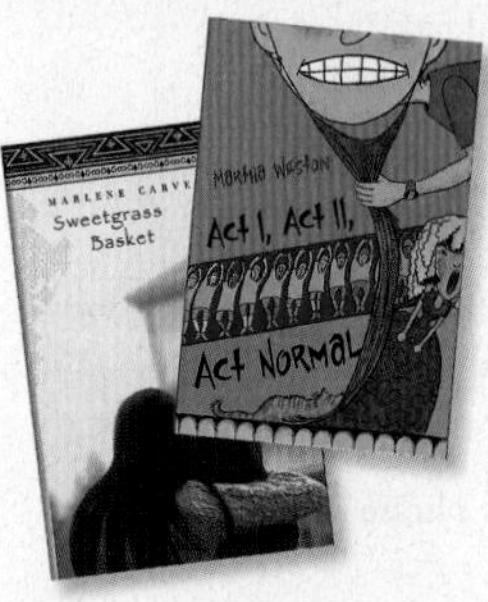

Act I, Act II, Act Normal
by Martha Weston
Topher has been waiting for three years to be the lead in the 8th grade play. Too bad this year's production is Rumpelstiltskin, the Musical, written by geeky Samantha. Topher takes the role, but will the school bully and the touchy leading lady ruin it for him?

Sweetgrass Basket
by Marlene Carvell
In the early 1900s, Mattie and Sarah are forced to go to a boarding school for Native American children. They're told it's their best chance for a "normal" life. Now far from home, the two girls have to figure out how to survive and keep their traditions.

Hans Christian Andersen: His Fairy Tale Life
by Hjordis Varmer and Lilian Brogger
Everyone knows Andersen's fairy tales, but did you know he was obsessed with fame? He begged rich men, a princess, and even the king, until someone would support his dream to write and act.

What makes a pioneer?

China's Son: Growing Up in the Cultural Revolution
by Da Chen
Da Chen suffers in 1960s China, which is run by communists. His father is often in labor camps and his brothers and sisters work in the fields. Then Da gets the chance to apply for college. Will life finally get better?

Guinea Pig Scientists
by Leslie Dendy and Mel Boring
Scientists who experiment on themselves are brave and sometimes foolhardy. We wouldn't know how the digestive system worked, what animal spread yellow fever, or how to build safer cars without these people.

O Pioneers!
by Willa Cather
Alexandra is only 16 when her father dies and leaves her in charge of their failing homestead on the Nebraska prairies. Her brothers agree to listen to her advice, but will they let her put the farm deeper in debt to chase her father's dream?

UNIT 7

Our Place in the World

HISTORY, CULTURE, AND THE AUTHOR

- In Fiction
- In Nonfiction
- In Media
- In Poetry

757

About the Art The painting *Los Comaradas del Barrio* by Jesse Treviño illustrates Gary Soto's memoir "One Last Time." Page 818 of the teacher's edition provides more information. The photograph of Hawaii's Diamond Head and Waikiki Beach appears with the excerpt from *Dreams from My Father* by Barack Obama. See page 837.

For help in planning this unit, see

RESOURCE MANAGER UNIT 7 pp. 1–11

INTRODUCE THE UNIT

We are all "citizens of the world," sharing many basic traits, but our personal identity is much more specific. The country we live in, the ethnic and religious groups we belong to, and the experiences we share with people close to us—each of these helps define our unique place in the world. Think about your background. Where are your parents and grandparents from? What language or languages did you hear growing up? What are the most important values in your family or community? In what ways does your daily life reflect the place and time where you live? Many authors think about these questions. They write about what they know, drawing on their family and cultural backgrounds for inspiration.

Invite students to think about these ideas as they discuss the pictures on this page. Ask these questions:

- Look closely at the painting on the left. What is the neighborhood like? What impression do you get of the boys and their relationship to each other? If you asked one of the boys to tell you about this day, what might he remember?
- Do you recognize the place shown in the photograph? If you grew up in this place, what kinds of experiences might you have? In what ways might this place influence the way you see the world?

Discuss how literature can help students connect with other cultures and identify with people from other times and places. In this unit, students will learn how **history** and **culture** influence **authors** as they write.

UNIT 7

Skills Trace

SKILLS STRAND	**Reader's Workshop: History, Culture, and the Author** pp. 760–765	**The Snapping Turtle** pp. 766–781 Short Story *Level: Easy*	**Out of Bounds** pp. 782–799 Short Story *Level: Challenging*	**Pecos Bill** pp. 800–809 Tall Tale *Level: Average*	**Great Reads:** *from* **The Pearl** pp. 810–815 Novella *Level: Average*	**One Last Time** pp. 816–829 Memoir *Level: Average*
Literary Analysis	Influence of Writer's Background pp. 760–761, 764–765 Historical and Cultural Influences pp. 762–765	Influence of Author's Background pp. 767, 768, 771, 772, 774, 778, 779	Cultural Conflict pp. 783, 784, 787, 788, 791, 794, 795, 797	Tall Tale pp. 801, 802, 804, 805, 806, 807, 808, 809	Form (Novella) p. 810	Author's Perspective pp. 817, 818, 821, 823, 824, 825, 827
Reading and Informational Texts	Analyze the Literature pp. 761, 763–765	Compare and Contrast pp. 767, 770, 771, 775, 777, 779	Make Inferences pp. 783, 786, 789, 790, 791, 792, 796, 797	Visualize pp. 801, 802, 805, 808, 809		Analyze Sensory Details pp. 817, 820, 823, 824, 825, 827 Read a Poem p. 826
Vocabulary	Academic Vocabulary p. 762	Word Acquisition pp. 767, T767, 780 Context Clues—General p. T767; Analogies p. 780	Word Acquisition pp. 783, T783, 798 Context Clues p. T783 Homographs p. 798			Word Acquisition pp. 817, T817, 828 Context Clues—General p. T817; Similes p. 828
Writing, Grammar, and Style		Compound-Complex Sentences p. 781	Colons p. 799			Semicolons p. 829
Speaking, Listening, Viewing, and Media	Discuss pp. 760–763	Discuss pp. 766, T768–T778, 779 Analyze Visuals pp. 768, 773, 776	Discuss pp. 782, T784–T796, 797 Analyze Visuals pp. 784, 793, 795	Discuss pp. 800, T802–T808, 809 Analyze Visuals pp. 802, T807	Discuss pp. 810, T815	Discuss pp. 816, T818–T826, 827 Analyze Visuals pp. 818, 822

Assessment-Based Planning: Skills in red are assessed on the Unit 7 Test. **T** = Teacher's Edition page

Linked selections: *from* **Dreams from My Father** pp. 830–845 Autobiography *Level: Challenging*	*from* **Out of Many, One** pp. 846–849 Speech *Level: Average*	**Media Study: Political Cartoons** pp. 850–853 Image Collection	**I Want to Write/Sit-Ins** pp. 854–859 Poems *Level: Easy*	**Writing Workshop: Cause-and-Effect Essay** pp. 860–867
Autobiography pp. 831, 832, 836, 838, 839, 841, 842, 844	Characteristics of a Speech pp. 847, 849		Historical Context pp. 855, 857, 858	
Recognize Cause-and-Effect Relationships pp. 831, 835, 836, 839, 841, 842, 843, 844	Identify Treatment pp. 846, 848, 849 Compare and Contrast p. 849		Analyze Repetition pp. 855, 856, 857, 858 Read a Book Excerpt p. 859	Analyze a Cause-and-Effect Essay pp. 861–862, 866
Word Acquisition pp. 831, T831, 845 Context Clues p. T831 Denotation and Connotation p. 845				
				Write a Cause-and-Effect Essay pp. 860–866 Commas After Introductory Words or Phrases p. 866
Discuss pp. 830, T832–T843, 844 Analyze Visuals pp. 832, 837, 840, 843	Discuss pp. 846, T847–T848, 849	Discuss pp. 850, 853 Analyze the Visual Aspects of Political Cartoons pp. 851–852 Create a Political Cartoon p. 853	Discuss pp. 854, T856–T857, 858, T859 Analyze Visuals p. 856, 857	Discuss pp. 860–862 Create a Multimedia Presentation p. 867

Skills Assessed on the Unit 7 Test:

Literary Analysis
- Identify and analyze the influence of an author's background
- Identify and analyze author's perspective (tone, direct statements, emphasis)
- Identify, analyze, and interpret an autobiography

Reading and Informational Texts
- Make inferences
- Identify and analyze cause-and-effect relationships
- Compare and contrast ideas and information
- Identify treatment

Vocabulary
- Use context to determine the meanings of homographs
- Distinguish between connotative and denotative meanings of words

Writing, Grammar, and Style
- Write a cause-and-effect essay
- Combine sentences to form one compound-complex sentence
- Use colons correctly after letter greetings and before lists of items
- Use semicolons correctly to separate parts of a series
- Additional writing and grammar skills

For additional lesson planning help, see **Easy Planner DVD.**

OBJECTIVES

- establish prior knowledge about history and **culture**
- discuss the influence of an author's history and culture

What SHAPES *who we are?*

Discuss with students how their culture—at a national or on a personal level—contributes to their identity. In a conversation with someone from the future, how would students describe their culture and the ways in which it has influenced their outlook on life?

ACTIVITY Suggest that students begin by brainstorming details about people, places, and events and listing these in separate columns of a chart or list. Then have them explore the Web, magazines, and other sources to find images that remind them of the influences that have shaped them. In their collages, they may also want to include texts that are important to them—everything from song lyrics to family sayings.

CHECK UNDERSTANDING Have students summarize what they have learned about how history and **culture** shape an author's perspective.

UNIT 7 Share What You Know

What SHAPES *who we are?*

If you were to write a book about your life, where would you begin? If you're like many authors and artists, what you say would probably reflect the influence of your family, friends, and **culture.** Although you can't always see it, culture plays an important part in shaping your world. The language you speak, the holidays you celebrate, the games you play, and the music you listen to are all part of your culture.

ACTIVITY What parts of your history and culture influence you the most? Think about the important people, places, and events in your life. Then reflect on your family's traditions and your own taste in entertainment. Make a collage out of images and mementos that symbolize what shapes you.

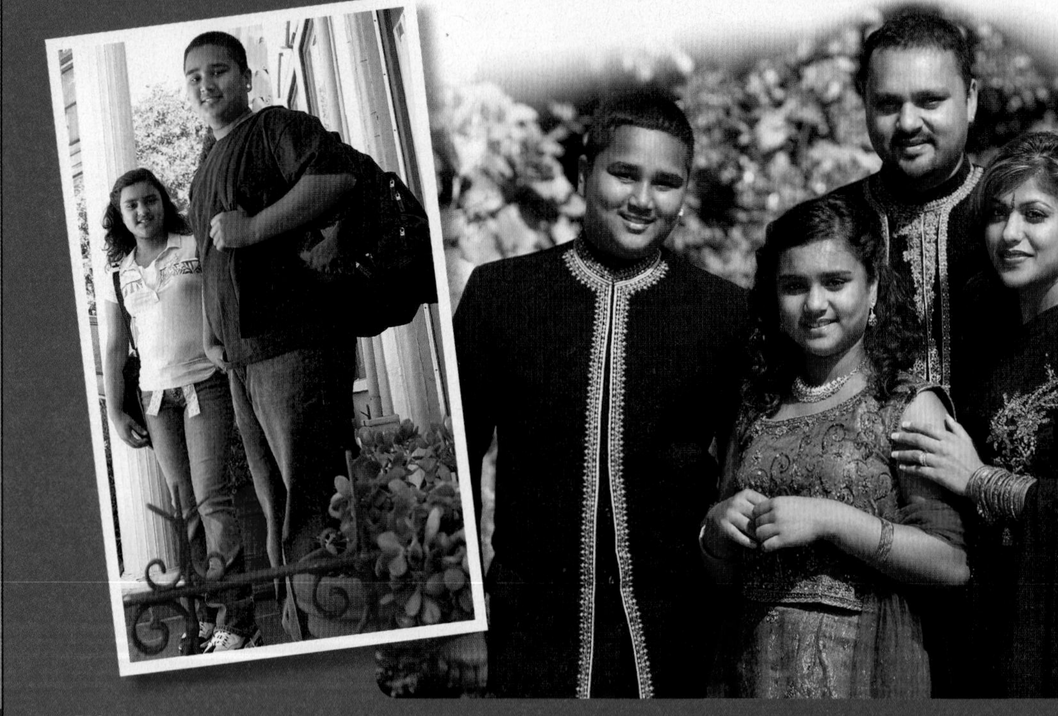

758

Unit Resources

- RESOURCE MANAGER UNIT 7
- BEST PRACTICES TOOLKIT
- STANDARDS LESSON FILE
- Easy Planner DVD
- Write*Smart* CD
- ClassZone.com
- Audio Anthology CD
- Multi-Language Academic Vocabulary Online
- eEdition CD & Online
- McDougal Littell Assessment System
- Test Generator CD
- Media*Smart* DVD

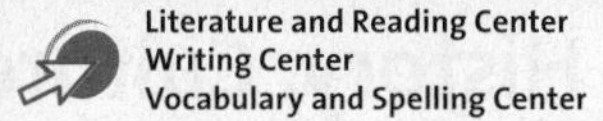

Literature and Reading Center
Writing Center
Vocabulary and Spelling Center

Preview Unit Goals

LITERARY ANALYSIS	• Identify and analyze influence of writer's background • Identify and analyze historical and cultural context of selections • Identify and analyze author's perspective • Identify and analyze characteristics of an autobiography
READING	• Make inferences • Identify and analyze cause-and-effect relationships • Identify and analyze treatment of an idea • Compare and contrast
WRITING AND GRAMMAR	• Write a cause-and-effect essay • Combine sentences to form a compound-complex sentence • Use colons and semicolons correctly
SPEAKING, LISTENING, AND VIEWING	• Identify visual aspects of illustrations • Compare different points of view in nonprint media sources • Deliver a multimedia presentation
VOCABULARY	• Use context to determine the meaning of homographs • Distinguish between connotative and denotative meanings of words
ACADEMIC VOCABULARY	• author's background • cultural context • author's perspective • cause-and-effect • historical context • treatment

Preview Unit Goals

This page provides an overview of the skills and strategies covered in this unit. Each skill strand is a different color. Remind students that throughout the unit, this color coding lets them know what kinds of skills they are studying. As they read this page, encourage students to think about each skill or strategy and their ability to use it.

Suggest that students copy the Academic Vocabulary terms in their journals and define them in their own words as they read the unit. Encourage students to use these terms as they discuss and write about the selections.

ADDITIONAL UNIT GOALS

These skills will be taught in this unit but are not the major focus of the unit:

Literary Analysis

- Identify and analyze cultural conflicts
- Identify and analyze characteristics of a tall tale
- Identify and analyze repetition
- Identify and analyze imagery
- Evaluate a speech
- Identify characteristics of a keynote speech
- Study a variety of genres: short story, tall tale, memoir, autobiography, poetry, speech

Reading

- Visualize

Writing and Grammar

- Use transition words to signal causes and effects

Speaking, Listening, and Viewing

- Compare and contrast the style of illustrators
- Create an interview plan
- Create a multimedia presentation

Vocabulary

- Analyze analogies to infer literal and figurative meanings of words
- Use similes as context to determine the meanings of unfamiliar words

DIFFERENTIATED INSTRUCTION

FOR ENGLISH LEARNERS

Academic Vocabulary Use the Academic Vocabulary copy master to introduce these terms: *author's background, author's perspective, historical context, cultural context, cause-and-effect, treatment.*

- Have students work in groups to discuss the examples and write definitions in Part A.
- Allow students to work individually or in pairs to complete Part B.

Additional Academic Vocabulary Use the second copy master to teach the terms *inference, sentence combining, compare and contrast, homograph,* and *connotative and denotative meanings.* Read each term aloud and discuss the definition. Then have students work in groups to complete the sentences. Have students complete Part B individually or with a group.

RESOURCE MANAGER—Copy Masters
Academic Vocabulary p. 9
Additional Academic Vocabulary p. 10

Focus and Motivate

OBJECTIVES

- identify and analyze the influence of a writer's background on his or her work
- identify and analyze the historical and cultural contexts of a selection

Teach

Part 1: A Writer's Background

To illustrate the influence of background on a writer's work, have students freewrite briefly on an assigned topic, such as music, vacations, or sports. Then have volunteers describe what they wrote and why. Guide students to see that the diversity of their responses is due in large part to their backgrounds, including previous experiences. For example, if music is a part of one student's family traditions, he or she may have described a holiday celebration associated with songs or music. If another student recently attended a rock concert, that might have been his or her focus.

Have students exchange their freewrites with a partner and ask these questions about their partner's work:

- What is the topic?
- What have you learned about the writer?
- What evidence do you see of the writer's experiences, values, and culture?
- Why do you think the writer wrote what he or she did?

 BEST PRACTICES TOOLKIT—Copy Masters
Analysis Frame: Literary Nonfiction
pp. D23, D50, D51

UNIT 7
Reader's Workshop

History, Culture, and the Author

Have you ever heard the lyrics to a song and wondered what motivated the musician to write them? If you found out that an athlete had once overcome a serious illness, would that make his or her best season even more impressive? What about a work of literature—do you ever wonder what inspired its creation? In this workshop, you'll learn about different factors that can affect writers. By examining the layers of a writer's experience, you can "read into" literature with far more insight.

Part 1: A Writer's Background

You are the unique product of many factors, including your heritage, family life, national identity, and economic status. Just as all these factors shape your ideas and beliefs, they influence writers as well. Writers may not consciously realize it, but their personal backgrounds affect not only what they choose to write about but how they express their ideas.

For instance, consider "Eating Together," a poem that paints a touching picture of a close-knit family. First, read the poem itself. Then go back and read the background on Li-Young Lee to discover how knowledge about the author's family adds extra meaning to the poem.

Eating Together

Poem by **Li-Young Lee**

BACKGROUND Li-Young Lee was born to Chinese parents in Jakarta, Indonesia, in 1957. The family moved many times during Lee's childhood—often to avoid anti-Chinese sentiments—before settling in the United States. Lee's poetry frequently focuses on his close-knit, traditional Chinese family, and many poems express the poet's grief over his father's death.

In the steamer is the trout
seasoned with slivers of ginger,
two sprigs of green onion, and sesame oil.
We shall eat it with rice for lunch,
brothers, sister, my mother who will
taste the sweetest meat of the head,
holding it between her fingers
deftly, the way my father did
weeks ago. Then he lay down
to sleep like a snow-covered road
winding through pines older than him,
without any travelers, and lonely for no one.

QUESTIONS TO

What evidence of the heritage and customs
The Asian family desc the poem seems close and traditional, much Lee's own family.

What might have bee author's motivation f this poem?
Lee may have wanted express his feelings a father's death and to on how his father's ab has affected his famil

DIFFERENTIATED INSTRUCTION

FOR ALL STUDENTS
For general guidelines on differentiating instruction, see

 BEST PRACTICES TOOLKIT
Differentiated Instruction pp. 31–38

FOR LESS–PROFICIENT READERS
Note Taking Hand out the Note Taking: A Writer's Background copy master and ask students to read page 760 silently. Then have them record their notes on the copy master as you discuss the information.

 RESOURCE MANAGER—Copy Master
Note Taking p. 15

FOR ENGLISH LEARNERS
Reading Support: *Audio Anthology CD* Have students listen to "Eating Together" and "Dusting" on the *Audio Anthology CD* before beginning discussion of each poem. Encourage students to read along silently as they listen.

MODEL 1: ANALYZING A POEM

Read this poem a first time, without knowing anything about the author behind the words and ideas. How would you describe the speaker?

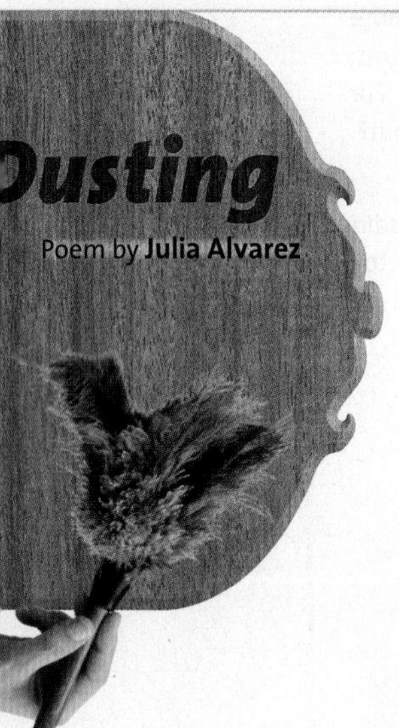

Each morning I wrote my name
on the dusty cabinet, then crossed
the dining table in script, scrawled
in capitals on the backs of chairs,
practicing signatures like scales
while Mother followed, squirting
linseed[1] from a burping can
into a crumpled-up flannel.

She erased my fingerprints
from the bookshelf and rocker,
polished mirrors on the desk
scribbled with my alphabets.
My name was swallowed in the towel
with which she jeweled the table tops.
The grain surfaced in the oak
and the pine grew luminous.
But I refused with every mark
to be like her, anonymous.

1. **linseed:** yellowish oil made from flax seeds, often used to help preserve the shine of natural wood furniture.

Close Read

1. What images does Alvarez use to help you visualize the actions of the speaker and her mother? Find three examples.
2. Think about what the speaker means by what she says in the boxed lines. How is she different from her mother?

MODEL 2: THE WRITER'S BACKGROUND

Read this background information about Julia Alvarez. Then go back and read the poem a second time.

Julia Alvarez was born in New York in 1950. When she was three months old, her parents returned with her to their native country, the Dominican Republic. However, the family came back to the United States for political reasons when Alvarez was ten years old. Alvarez grew up speaking Spanish, with English as a second language. Her mother worked as a housekeeper and, as a young girl, Alvarez would often go with her mother to work. Alvarez has said, "As I followed my mother cleaning house, washing and ironing clothes, rolling dough, I was using the material of my housebound girl life to claim my woman's legacy." Alvarez later became a writer and continues to share her childhood experiences in her works.

Close Read

1. In what way does the background information help you to better understand the poem?
2. What connection can you draw between the last two lines of the poem and Alvarez's career?

FOR LESS–PROFICIENT READERS

Analysis Support: Speaker

- Remind students that the speaker of a poem is like the narrator in a piece of fiction. The speaker is created by the poet to express the ideas in the poem.
- Tell students that even though the speaker may be similar to the poet, the two should not be confused as the same person. It is not Julia Alvarez who is the speaker in the poem "Dusting" but the voice of someone who resembles her in some ways.

FOR ADVANCED LEARNERS/PRE–AP

Analyze [paired option] Have students work in pairs to locate another poem by Julia Alvarez that reflects some aspect of her life. Have pairs analyze the influence of her background on the work and present both the poem and their analysis to the class. Encourage students to do additional research on Alvarez's life if necessary.

MODEL 1: ANALYZING A POEM

Close Read

Possible answers:

1. *The image "practicing signatures like scales" (line 5) helps readers picture the speaker's enthusiastic efforts to make her mark. In contrast, images such as "Mother followed, squirting / linseed from a burping can / into a crumpled-up flannel" (lines 6–8) and "My name was swallowed in the towel / with which she jeweled the table tops" (lines 13–14) reveal the mother's efforts to erase the speaker's scrawls.*
2. *The speaker wants to make her mark on the world and have her name be seen and heard by others. In contrast, the speaker's mother doesn't leave her own marks; rather, she tries to make the furniture look as if no one has touched it.*

MODEL 2: THE WRITER'S BACKGROUND

Close Read

Possible answers:

1. *The background reveals that "Dusting" is autobiographical. Like the speaker, a young Alvarez went to work with her mother, who was a housekeeper. Alvarez says that she "was using the material of my housebound girl life to claim my woman's legacy" (lines 12–13). The speaker's actions reflect Alvarez's own attitude and ambitions.*
2. *Like the speaker who "refused with every mark / to be like [her mother], anonymous," Alvarez—a well-known writer—is anything but anonymous.*

If students need help . . . Display a Two-Column Chart. Together, list significant details about Alvarez's life in the first column. Then identify the ideas in the poem that correspond to each detail.

BEST PRACTICES TOOLKIT—Transparency
Two-Column Chart p. A25

READER'S WORKSHOP 761

Part 2: Historical and Cultural Influences

Tell students that some stories are not closely related to a particular historical or cultural context. For example, it is not clear exactly when and where Joan Bauer's story "Clean Sweep" (page 64) takes place, because the values and traditions exhibited by the characters are not tied to any specific time period or culture. Other works, however, are inspired by or grow out of a particular context, such as *The Diary of Anne Frank* (page 486). Display a web such as this one and point out to students how the historical and cultural context of the play establish the setting, drive the plot, and inform the theme.

Historical and Cultural Context of *The Diary of Anne Frank*

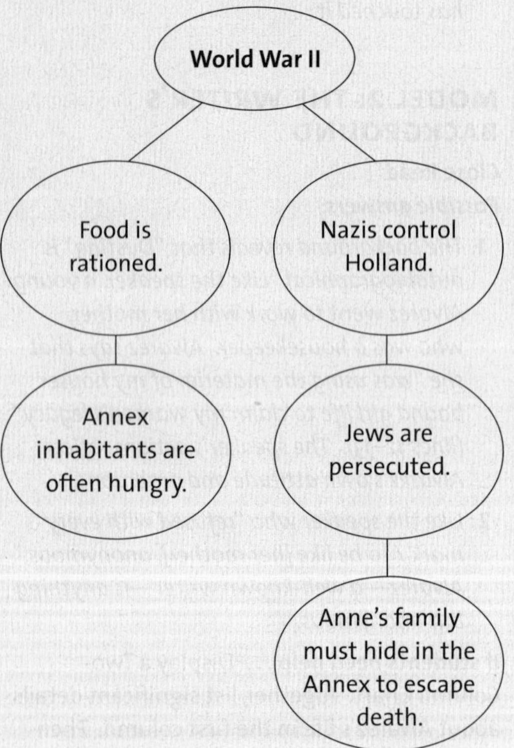

Have students read the background on James Baldwin and then the excerpt from his short story before discussing the ways in which the historical and cultural context of the story affects its setting, characters, conflict, and theme.

CHECK UNDERSTANDING Have students identify other works of fiction with strong historical or cultural contexts.

Part 2: Historical and Cultural Influences

Knowing about a writer's personal background can help you to appreciate his or her work more fully. Similarly, knowing the **historical and cultural contexts** in which the work was written can help you interpret and analyze that work more accurately. **Historical and cultural contexts** refer to the events, social problems, traditions, and values that may have influenced the author and the writing. For example, what events and issues of the time was the author concerned about? How are those concerns reflected in the writing?

Take a look at this excerpt from a story by James Baldwin. Notice how reading the background and answering some questions can give you new insights into Baldwin's vivid descriptions.

from Sonny's Blues

Short story by **James Baldwin**

BACKGROUND In the early 1900s, African Americans were encouraged to move to Manhattan's Harlem neighborhood, partly to shelter them from emerging racial conflicts in other neighborhoods. By 1920, Harlem was populated almost exclusively by African Americans. Though the 1920s became known as the Harlem Renaissance because of the blossoming of jazz music, writing, and art in the African-American community, it was also a time of economic hardship. Since many landlords in other areas refused to rent apartments to African Americans, landlords in Harlem often took advantage of their tenants by charging high rents.

"Sonny's Blues" was published in 1957, reflecting James Baldwin's firsthand knowledge of the neighborhood in which he grew up. Throughout most of the twentieth century, Harlem was known for being troubled by crime and poverty as well as being a prominent African-American cultural community.

The narrator and his brother are returning to the neighborhood of their youth:

Houses exactly like the houses of our past yet dominated the landscape, boys exactly like the boys we once had been found themselves smothering in these houses, came down into the streets for light and air and found themselves encircled by disaster. Some escaped the trap, most didn't. Those who got out always left something of themselves behind, as some animals amputate a leg and leave it in the trap. It might be said, perhaps, that I had escaped, after all, I was a schoolteacher; or that Sonny had, he hadn't lived in Harlem for years. Yet, as the cab moved uptown through streets which seemed, with a rush, to darken with dark people, and as I covertly studied Sonny's face, it came to me that what we both were seeking through our separate cab windows was that part of ourselves which had been left behind.

QUESTIONS TO ASK

What social problems are reflected in the writing? Baldwin uses words and phrases like "smothering," "encircled by disaster," and "the trap" to describe the poverty-stricken Harlem neighborhood of his youth.

What might have prompted the author to write this story? Baldwin may have wanted to explore why former residents of Harlem who "escaped the trap" still feel so connected to the neighborhood in which they grew up.

762

DIFFERENTIATED INSTRUCTION

FOR LESS–PROFICIENT READERS

Note Taking [paired option] Hand out the Note Taking: Historical and Cultural Influences copy master. Read and discuss page 762. As a class, complete the first item on the copy master. Then have students form pairs to complete the page.

RESOURCE MANAGER—Copy Master
Note Taking p. 16

Identify Historical Context [small-group option] In preparation for answering the questions on page 763, have students first read lines 1–6 of **Model 2** and then work in small groups to create a timeline of significant events in World War II. Compare timelines. Make sure students understand that although France and Britain were allies at the start of the war, the German occupation made France a hostile territory to Allied forces from 1940 to 1944.

MODEL 1: ANALYZING FICTION

In this story, a British pilot wakes up in a French hospital during World War II. Find out what he's thinking about as a nurse tends to him. First, read this excerpt and answer the **Close Read** questions. Then read the background that follows.

from

Beware of the Dog

Short story by **Roald Dahl**

"I believe there's someone coming down to see you from the Air Ministry after breakfast," she went on. "They want a report or something. I expect you know all about it. How you got shot down and all that. I won't let him stay long, so don't worry."

He did not answer. She finished washing him and gave him a toothbrush and some toothpowder. He brushed his teeth, rinsed his mouth, and spat the water out into the basin.

Later she brought him his breakfast on a tray, but he did not want to eat. He was still feeling weak and sick and he wished only to lie still and think about what had happened. And there was a sentence running through his head. It was a sentence which Johnny, the Intelligence Officer of his squadron, always repeated to the pilots every day before they went out. He could see Johnny now, leaning against the wall of the dispersal hut with his pipe in his hand, saying, "And if they get you, don't forget, just your name, rank, and number. Nothing else. For God's sake, say nothing else."

Close Read

1. What do you learn about the pilot in this passage?
2. The hospital staff is being kind to the pilot, but he believes they are only trying to get information from him. Which words and phrases convey his anxiety?

MODEL 2: HISTORICAL AND CULTURAL CONTEXT

The following background helps to explain why a British pilot would be nervous about waking up in a French hospital.

World War II began with Germany's 1939 invasion of Poland, which caused Britain and France to declare war on Germany. By 1941, German forces had occupied France and much of Western Europe, but Great Britain was still fighting back. Other countries joined the war on both sides of the conflict, dividing into the Axis forces and the Allies. France was not liberated from German occupation until 1944.

Roald Dahl joined the British Royal Air Force in 1939. He became a fighter pilot and flew missions over North Africa, Greece, and the Middle East during the war. After his plane crashed in Egypt, he spent six months in a hospital, recovering from a head injury. When he was asked later to share his experiences, Dahl's career as a writer began. "Beware of the Dog" was published in 1944.

Close Read

1. What exactly is the pilot worried about? Explain how the background helps you to understand his situation.
2. In your opinion, is Dahl's tone in the story sympathetic to the pilot? Explain.

MODEL 1: ANALYZING FICTION

Close Read

Possible answers:

1. *Readers learn that the pilot has recently been shot down and that someone from the Air Ministry may be visiting the hospital to interview him about the incident. The pilot seems anxious about this potential visit. He knows that he's not supposed to divulge too much information.*
2. *Words and phrases that convey the pilot's anxiety include "did not want to eat" (line 8), "feeling weak and sick" (line 9), "a sentence running through his head" (lines 10–11), and "'Nothing else. For God's sake, say nothing else'" (line 15).*

If students need help . . . Make sure they understand that, in a war, an intelligence officer is concerned with preventing the enemy from learning information and with trying to get as much information, or intelligence, from the enemy as possible.

MODEL 2: HISTORICAL AND CULTURAL CONTEXT

Close Read

Possible answers:

1. *At this point during the war, France was occupied by Germany. Knowing this, the pilot might be wary of sharing information about his mission with anyone in France, for fear that critical information could end up in the hands of Britain's enemy.*
2. *Dahl's tone is sympathetic, as evidenced by the extent to which he lets readers inside the character's head to share the pilot's anxieties. Like the character in the story, Dahl was a fighter pilot in World War II and suffered a head injury after a plane crash. Dahl may have a sympathetic tone because he was in a situation similar to the pilot's.*

FOR LESS–PROFICIENT READERS

Analysis Support: Writer's Background

[small-group option] As a class, reread lines 7–14 of **Model 2.** Have students list the author's experience in the first column of a Two-Column Chart. Then have small groups return to the story and identify the parts that show the influence of or are related to the author's own experience. Have students list in the second column of the chart the parts they have identified.

BEST PRACTICES TOOLKIT—Transparency

Two-Column Chart p. A25

FOR ADVANCED LEARNERS/PRE–AP

Analyze [paired option] Have students work in pairs to analyze the historical and cultural context of a work of fiction that they have read previously. Ask students to present their analysis in a diagram or chart.

Practice and Apply

Part 3: Analyze the Literature

Have students read the background information on page 764 and note significant details of the writer's background as well as facts about the historical and cultural context of "Origami."

Part 3: Analyze the Literature

Before reading "Origami," read the following background information about the author, Susan K. Ito, and the topics mentioned in her story.

BACKGROUND

Crafting Words and Mending Old Wounds

Susan K. Ito

Seeking to Belong As a child, Susan K. Ito often struggled with her sense of identity. She says, "I felt like I was the only one of my kind: mixed-race, adopted, only child." She often found herself envying women who were full-blooded Japanese, since she was only part Japanese. When she began taking literature and creative writing classes in graduate school, Ito felt like she had found where she belonged: "I was finally immersing myself in the world that I'd longed to be in forever: the world of words." Life as a Japanese American and the struggle for a sense of belonging have been the focus of much of her writing.

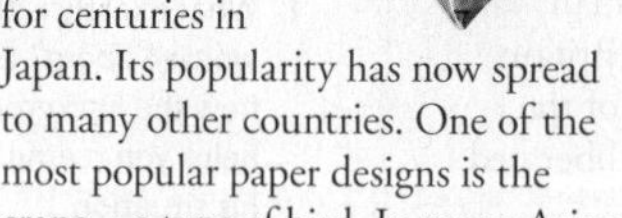

Peace Cranes "Origami" is named after a paper-folding craft that has been practiced for centuries in Japan. Its popularity has now spread to many other countries. One of the most popular paper designs is the crane—a type of bird. In many Asian countries, the crane is a symbol of peace. Many people from around the world send paper cranes to a memorial in Hiroshima, Japan, every year. It is done in memory of those who died there during World War II and as an expression of the senders' wish for world peace.

Japanese Internment During World War II, nations were divided between the Axis and Allied forces. In 1941 Japan—a member of the Axis powers—bombed the U.S. military base at Pearl Harbor in Honolulu, Hawaii, prompting the United States to declare war on Japan. Four years later, the United States dropped atomic bombs on two Japanese cities: Hiroshima and Nagasaki.

Americans were fearful of another attack within their borders. As a precaution, Japanese immigrants and Americans of Japanese ancestry were sent to and held in facilities called internment camps in order to isolate them from the rest of the American public. The largest camp was the Tule Lake Segregation Center in California. At the time, limiting the rights of one ethnic group was viewed as being done in service of the greater good of the American public. The last internment camp closed in 1948. However, it was not until 1988 that the U.S. government issued its first official apology for its treatment of Japanese Americans during World War II.

Japanese internment camp in Santa Anita, California

DIFFERENTIATED INSTRUCTION

FOR LESS–PROFICIENT READERS

Analysis Support: Context [small-group option] Have students read the background information on this page and take notes on these three topics using a Main Idea and Details chart.

- author's life
- origami cranes
- Japanese internment camps

Have groups volunteer their details to complete a class chart to be displayed during the reading of the selection on page 765.

BEST PRACTICES TOOLKIT—Transparency
Main Idea and Details p. B6

The narrator of this short story views herself as an outsider struggling to prove that she belongs. As you read this excerpt, consider how the background information enhances your understanding of the story.

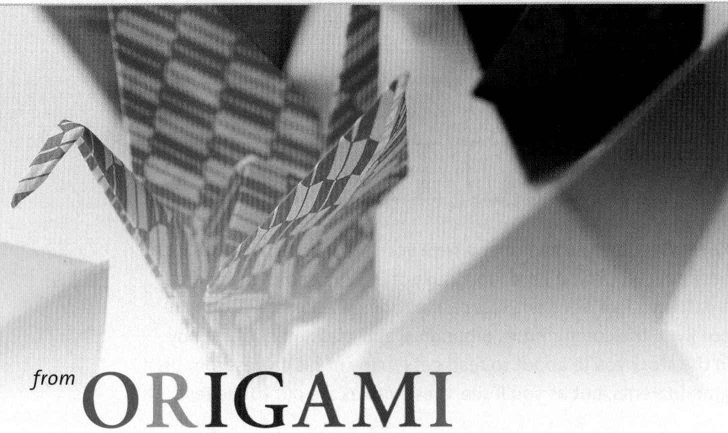

from ORIGAMI

Short story by **Susan K. Ito**

I take my place, hesitantly, among the group of Japanese women, smile back at the ones who look up from their task to nod at me. Their words float around me like alphabet soup, familiar, comforting, but nothing that I clearly understand. The long cafeteria table blooms with folded paper birds of all colors: royal purple, light gray, a small shimmering silver one. They're weaving an origami wreath for Sunday's memorial service, a thousand cranes for the souls of those who died at Tule Lake's internment camp.

I spread the square of sky-blue paper flat under my hands, then fold it in half. So far, this is easy. I'm going to follow all the directions. It's going to be a perfect crane, *tsuru,* flying from my palm. Fold again, then flip that side of the triangle under to make a box. Oh no. What? I didn't get that. I'm lost. The women around me keep creasing, folding, spreading, their fingers moving with easy grace. My thumbs are huge, thick, in the way of these paper wings that are trying to unfold but can't.

My heart rises and flutters, beating against its cage in panic, in confusion. I try to retrace my steps, turn the paper upside down, in reverse. It's not working. I want to crumple the paper into a blue ball, an origami rock.

But instead I unfold the paper with damp, shaking fingers. I persevere. *Gambaro.* Don't give up. I'm going to make this crane if it kills me. I'm going to prove that I can do this thing, this Japanese skill. I'm going to pull the coordination out of my blood, make it flow into my fingers. I have to.

But what if I can't? Then it only proves the thing that I fear the most, don't want to believe. That I'm not really Japanese. That I'm just an imposter, a fake, a watered-down, inauthentic K-mart version of the real thing.

Close Read

1. Reread the boxed text. How does the background enhance your reading of this passage?
2. Why does the narrator feel insecure in this situation? Support your answer.
3. Does Ito seem to sympathize with the narrator? Explain.
4. Which details show you that the narrator admires people who are Japanese?
5. Which details in the background help you understand why Ito might have chosen to write this story?

Close Read

Possible answers:

1. *The background information explains the peace cranes, why they are being created for a memorial service, and Japanese internment at the Tule Lake War Segregation Center in California.*
2. *The narrator feels insecure because she can't seem to make a perfect crane. Unlike those around her who are working "with easy grace" (lines 12–13), the narrator feels clumsy, with her "huge, thick" thumbs (line 13).*
3. *Ito's tone is sympathetic toward her narrator. The author reveals the narrator's fears, vulnerabilities, and admirable determination to persevere in the face of failure.*
4. *The narrator describes the Japanese women's words as "familiar, comforting" (line 3) and their movements as having a skilled, "easy grace" (line 13). The narrator fears that she will be perceived as "an imposter, a fake, a watered-down, inauthentic K-mart version" (lines 23–24).*
5. *The background on Ito reveals that she, like the narrator, has struggled with her own sense of identity. As a Japanese American, Ito envied full-blooded Japanese, much as the narrator admires the women who fold cranes around her.*

Assess and Reteach

Assess

Have students explain the cultural context of the story "Origami."

Reteach

Have groups of students choose one of the selections in the workshop and do a Read Aloud/Think Aloud exercise, analyzing the ways in which the writer's background or the historical and cultural context are apparent.

 **BEST PRACTICES TOOLKIT—Transparency**
Read Aloud/Think Aloud p. A34

FOR LESS–PROFICIENT READERS

Analysis Support: Background [paired option] Before students answer the **Close Read** questions, have them work in pairs on a Venn Diagram comparing the ways in which the narrator in "Origami" is like the author. After students have completed their diagrams, discuss the differences and similarities.

 **BEST PRACTICES TOOLKIT—Transparency**
Venn Diagram p. A26

FOR ENGLISH LEARNERS

Language Support: Figurative Expressions Discuss the meanings of these expressions:

- *Their words float around me like alphabet soup* (lines 2–3): Many people are talking, and the narrator hears only some of the words.
- *The long cafeteria table blooms with folded paper birds* (line 4): The table is heaped with colorful origami cranes.
- *I didn't get that. I'm lost.* (line 11): The narrator didn't understand the directions and is confused.

Focus and Motivate

OBJECTIVES

Literary Analysis
- explore the key idea of **values**
- identify and analyze the influence of an author's background
- read a short story

Reading
- compare and contrast characters

Vocabulary
- build vocabulary for reading and writing
- analyze analogies to infer literal and figurative meanings of words *(also an EL language objective)*

Grammar and Writing
- combine sentences to form compound-complex sentences
- use writing to analyze literature

SUMMARY

Sonny lives with his grandparents, who teach him respect for the earth and for animals. One day, Sonny goes fishing and then decides to explore a reservoir. There, he captures a snapping turtle, which he plans to sell. He later changes his mind when he realizes that the turtle was getting ready to lay its eggs.

Where do we get our VALUES?

Discuss the question. To lead into the ***KEY IDEA,*** ask students to describe the **values** the parents in the photograph might be teaching their children. After students complete the ***LIST IT*** activity, ask them how their values affect their everyday choices.

Before Reading

The Snapping Turtle

Short Story by Joseph Bruchac

Where do we get our VALUES?

KEY IDEA Do you remember where you learned that honesty is the best policy? Or that hard work pays off? We get our **values** from a patchwork of different sources, including important people in our lives, the communities around us, and mass media. The boy in the story you're about to read gets many of his values from his grandparents, but as you'll see, these values are put to the test.

LIST IT Take one minute to list some of the values that are important to you. Circle the value that most influences how you live your life. Then, as a class, generate a list that reflects the group's responses, and discuss where you learned these values.

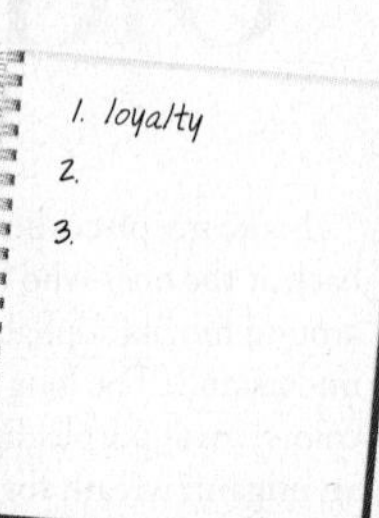

766

Selection Resources

RESOURCE MANAGER UNIT 7

Plan and Teach pp. 17–24

Literary Analysis
Summary pp. 25†*, 26‡*
Influence of Author's Background pp. 27, 28†*
Question Support p. 35*

Reading
Compare and Contrast pp. 29, 30†*
Reading Check p. 34
Reading Fluency p. 37

Vocabulary
Study p. 31*
Practice p. 32
Strategy p. 33

Grammar and Writing
Form Compound-Complex Sentences p. 36

Assessment
Selection Tests A, B/C pp. 39*, 41*
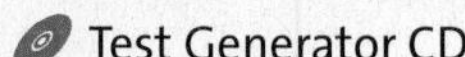 Test Generator CD

BEST PRACTICES TOOLKIT

Differentiated Instruction pp. 31–38*
Scaffolding Instruction pp. 43–46*

Graphic Organizers/Strategies
Reciprocal Questioning • New Word Analysis • Words with Multiple Meanings • Ask the Experts • Jigsaw Reading • Common Prefixes • Common Suffixes

Reading Support
Audio Anthology CD*

Technology
Literature, Vocabulary, and Writing Centers at **ClassZone.com**
Write*Smart* CD

* Resources for Differentiation † Also in Spanish ‡ In Haitian Creole and Vietnamese

LITERARY ANALYSIS: INFLUENCE OF AUTHOR'S BACKGROUND

An author's background, including life experiences and cultural heritage, shapes his or her way of looking at the world and often affects what he or she writes. For example, Joseph Bruchac was raised by his grandparents, one of whom was Native American. Many of his stories, in turn, have Native American characters and reflect Native American values.

Before you read, learn more about Bruchac from the biography on this page. Then, as you read, notice how Bruchac's characters reflect his own cultural heritage, beliefs and values, and life story.

READING SKILL: COMPARE AND CONTRAST

When you **compare** two or more things, you identify ways in which they are alike. When you **contrast** them, you find ways in which they are different. Thinking about characters' similarities and differences can help you recognize their qualities and values. In "The Snapping Turtle," you will compare and contrast

- the narrator and other boys
- the narrator's grandmother and grandfather

As you read, use Venn diagrams to compare and contrast these characters' attitudes, backgrounds, and values.

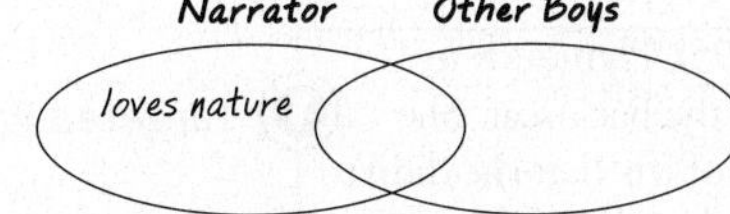

VOCABULARY IN CONTEXT

The boldfaced words help Bruchac tell about a boy's relationship with nature. Try restating each sentence, using a different word or phrase for the boldfaced word.

1. My **philosophy** is "Leave nothing but footprints."
2. The memorial garden seemed to give the hero **immortality.**
3. Amy and I like to **traipse** around the meadow.
4. I have no **inclination** to go indoors when it's nice outside.
5. It takes **craftiness** to successfully trick a raccoon.
6. I **cache** my camping gear behind a tree while I hike.
7. Following their **migration** route, the geese flew north.
8. The thick undergrowth made the forest **impregnable.**
9. The **basking** sunbather enjoyed the afternoon breeze.
10. **Undaunted,** the bird flew on in search of food.

Author Online

Writer and Storyteller Joseph Bruchac was raised by his grandparents in the foothills of New York State's Adirondack Mountains, in a house built by his grandfather. After leaving home to study literature, Bruchac returned to his hometown. He and his wife now live in the house where he grew up. Bruchac has published many books of stories and poetry, and he founded his own publishing company, the Greenfield Review Press. In addition to being an author, Bruchac is a well-known professional storyteller, performing the traditional stories of the Native Americans of the Northeast.

Joseph Bruchac
born 1942

Hidden Heritage Bruchac's grandfather was part Native American. He was descended from the Abenaki (ä'bə-nä'kē), a group that originally lived in New England and southern Canada. Bruchac did not discover this heritage until he was a teenager, because his grandfather feared that he would be discriminated against if he revealed his Native American roots. Although Bruchac did not know it at the time, his grandfather raised him with traditional Abenaki values. The Abenaki believe in honoring their elders, treating the earth with respect by not wasting its resources, and sharing food and possessions with others.

MORE ABOUT THE AUTHOR
For more on Joseph Bruchac, visit the **Literature Center** at **ClassZone.com.**

Teach

STANDARDS FOCUS

LITERARY ANALYSIS

● INFLUENCE OF AUTHOR'S BACKGROUND

Have students read the author information on page 767. Then have them give examples of the kinds of characters that might reflect the influence of Bruchac's background, especially the values passed on by his grandfather. ***Possible answer:*** *hunters who respect nature, old people who tell stories, social workers*

CHECK UNDERSTANDING Ask what kinds of characters might reflect students' own cultural heritage, beliefs, and values.

READING SKILL

■ COMPARE AND CONTRAST

Use a Venn diagram to compare and contrast two characters from another short story the class has read, such as

- Gretchen and Squeaky from "Raymond's Run" (p. 34)
- Katie and Benjamin from "Clean Sweep" (p. 64)
- Laurence and Eddy from "The Great Rat Hunt" (p. 120)

CHECK UNDERSTANDING Ask students what clues indicate the similarities and differences between characters.

RESOURCE MANAGER—Copy Master
Compare and Contrast p. 29 (for student use while reading the story)

VOCABULARY SKILL

▲ VOCABULARY IN CONTEXT

DIAGNOSE WORD KNOWLEDGE To determine preteaching needs, have all students complete **Vocabulary in Context.** ***Possible answers:***
1. *viewpoint* **2.** *never-ending life* **3.** *wander* **4.** *desire* **5.** *cleverness* **6.** *hide* **7.** *relocation* **8.** *impossible to enter* **9.** *lounging* **10.** *unafraid*

PRETEACH VOCABULARY Use the Vocabulary Study copy master as follows:

1. Read aloud the first sentence, emphasizing the boldfaced word.
2. Ask students to look for context clues. Discuss possible meanings for *basking,* such as "lying still in the hot sun."
3. Repeat for the other sentences.
4. Have students work with a partner to answer the questions in Part B.

RESOURCE MANAGER—Copy Master
Vocabulary Study p. 31

For general guidelines on differentiating vocabulary instruction and for alternative vocabulary activities for students not needing vocabulary preteaching, see

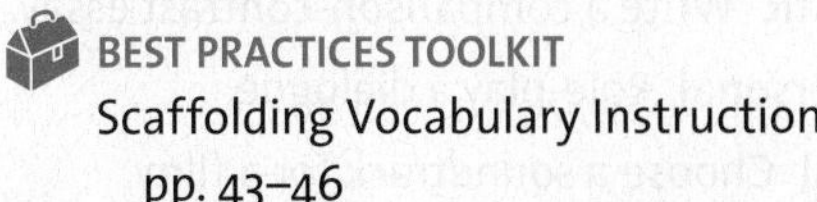
BEST PRACTICES TOOLKIT
Scaffolding Vocabulary Instruction pp. 43–46

Vocabulary Center at **ClassZone.com**
Additional Vocabulary Activities

Practice and Apply

ANALYZE VISUALS

Possible answer:

- *Most of the painting is in shades of green and blue except for the human figure. This has the effect of drawing viewers' attention to the child, who seems very small in comparison to the natural surroundings.*
- *The patch of light blue at the bottom of the painting helps viewers notice how the sky and trees are reflected in the water.*

About the Art British artist Lincoln Seligman (born 1950) studied law, but he soon discovered that the legal profession did not suit him. From the age of 30, he devoted himself to art. In addition to painting, his talents extend to sculpting in fabric, steel, bronze, and stone. Many of his murals and sculptures are large pieces that have been commissioned to enrich the atriums of modern buildings in a number of countries.

Lines 10–22

REINFORCE *KEY IDEA*: VALUES

Discuss What **values** do you think Sonny learns from watching his grandmother work in the flower garden and drive through Greenfield? ***Possible answer:*** *He learns the values of respect for nature, generosity, and sharing.*

LITERARY ANALYSIS

Ⓐ AUTHOR'S BACKGROUND

Possible answer: *Caring for her iris plants and sharing them with others to ensure that many different types of iris will survive show that she believes in treating the earth with respect.*

THE SNAPPING TURTLE

Joseph Bruchac

My grandmother was working in the flower garden near the road that morning when I came out with my fishing pole. She was separating out the roots of iris. As far as flowers go, she and I were agreed that iris had the sweetest scent. Iris would grow about anywhere, shooting up green sword-shaped leaves like the mythical soldiers that sprang from the planted teeth of a dragon. But iris needed some amount of care. Their roots would multiply so thick and fast that they could crowd themselves right up out of the soil. Spring separating and replanting were, as my grandmother put it, just the ticket.[1]

ANALYZE VISUALS
What **effect** does the artist's use of color have on what you notice in the painting?

① Targeted Passage

Later that day, I knew, she would climb into our blue 1951 Plymouth to drive around the back roads of Greenfield, a box of iris in the back seat. She would stop at farms where she had noticed a certain color of iris that she didn't have yet. Up to the door she would go to ask for a root so that she could add another splash of color to our garden. And, in exchange, she would give that person, most often a flowered-aproned and somewhat elderly woman like herself, some of her own iris.

It wasn't just that she wanted more flowers herself. She had a **philosophy**. If only one person keeps a plant, something might happen to it. Early frost, insects, animals, Lord knows what. But if many have that kind of plant, then it may survive. Sharing meant a kind of **immortality**. I didn't quite understand it then, but I enjoyed taking those rides with her, carrying boxes and cans and flowerpots with new kinds of iris back to the car. Ⓐ

"Going fishing, Sonny?" she said now.

Of course, she knew where I was going. Not only the evidence of the pole in my hand, but also the simple facts that it was a Saturday morning in late May and I was a boy of ten, would have led her to that natural conclusion. But she had to ask. It was part of our routine.

philosophy (fĭ-lŏs'ə-fē) *n.* a system of values or beliefs

immortality (ĭm'ôr-tăl'ĭ-tē) *n.* the condition of having an endless life

Ⓐ AUTHOR'S BACKGROUND
Which of the grandmother's thoughts and actions show that she believes in treating the earth with respect?

1. **just the ticket:** the perfect solution.

Child Fishing (1989), Lincoln Seligman. Private collection. © Bridgeman Art Library

DIFFERENTIATED INSTRUCTION

FOR ALL STUDENTS

Enhance Learning Styles Provide independent projects for various learning styles.

- **Linguistic** Write a comparison-contrast essay.
- **Interpersonal** Role-play a dialogue.
- **Musical** Choose a soundtrack for a film version of the story.
- **Analytical** Research different types of turtles.

For further details on these projects, see

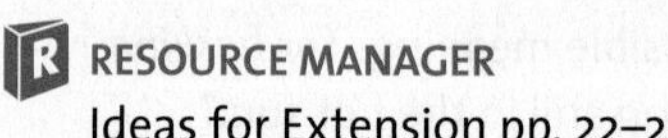

RESOURCE MANAGER
Ideas for Extension pp. 22–23

FOR LESS-PROFICIENT READERS

In combination with the *Audio Anthology CD,* use one or more Targeted Passages (pp. 768, 772, 774, 775, 778) to ensure that students focus on key story events, concepts, and skills.

① Targeted Passage [Lines 10–27]

This passage introduces the narrator's grandmother and describes her values.

- What does Sonny's grandmother trade with others?
- What does she believe about the way people should take care of plants?
- What does she ask Sonny? Why does she already know the answer to the question?

BACKGROUND

The Abenaki The Abenaki were a confederacy of Native American tribes in upstate New York, northern New England, and southern Canada. They organized the confederacy to fight and protect themselves against another group of tribes—the Iroquois Confederacy.

For food, the Abenaki hunted, fished, and grew corn (maize). They lived in wigwams—several families sharing each building. During the 20th century, the population of the Abenaki was about 5,000. Today the Abenaki population is growing, and there is a renewed dedication to their cultural traditions.

FOR ENGLISH LEARNERS

Options for Reading [paired option] Have students follow along with the *Audio Anthology CD.* Then have pairs of students use a Reciprocal Questioning strategy to take turns recalling, predicting, clarifying, or summarizing what they are reading.

 BEST PRACTICES TOOLKIT
Reciprocal Questioning p. A3

Key Academic Vocabulary Have students use New Word Analysis to study these words from the selection: *survive* (line 20), *indicate* (line 32), *routes* (line 191), *focus* (line 281), *generation(s)* (lines 325, 335).

 BEST PRACTICES TOOLKIT—Transparency
New Word Analysis p. E8

Prereading For prereading instruction for English learners, see

 BEST PRACTICES TOOLKIT
Scaffolding Reading Instruction pp. 43–46

FOR ADVANCED LEARNERS/PRE–AP

Pre-AP exercises in the bottom channel provide additional challenge for your advanced students. Use them for small groups or individuals.

ADDITIONAL GUIDELINES

For more help with differentiation and tips for classroom management, see

 BEST PRACTICES TOOLKIT
Differentiated Instruction pp. 31–38

"Un-hun," I answered, as I always did. "Unless you and Grampa need some help." Then I held my breath, for though my offer of aid had been sincere enough, I really wanted to go fishing.

Grama thrust her foot down on the spading[2] fork, carefully levering out a heavy clump of iris marked last fall with a purple ribbon to indicate the color. She did such things with half my effort and twice the skill, despite the fact I was growing, as she put it, like a weed. "No, you go on along. This afternoon Grampa and I could use some help, though."

"I'll be back by then," I said, but I didn't turn and walk away. I waited for the next thing I knew she would say.

"You stay off of the state road, now."

In my grandmother's mind, Route 9N, which came down the hill past my grandparents' little gas station and general store on the corner, was nothing less than a Road of Death. If I ever set foot on it, I would surely be as doomed as our four cats and two dogs that met their fates there.

"Runned over and kilt," as Grampa Jesse put it.

Grampa Jesse, who had been the hired man for my grandmother's parents before he and Grama eloped, was not a person with book learning like my college-educated grandmother. His family was Abenaki Indian, poor but honest hill people who could read the signs in the forest, but who had never **traipsed** far along the trails of schoolhouse ways. Between Grama's books and Grampa's practical knowledge, some of which I was about to apply to bring home a mess of[3] trout, I figured I was getting about the best education a ten-year-old boy could have. I was lucky that my grandparents were raising me. **B**

traipse (trāps) *v.* to walk or tramp around

B COMPARE AND CONTRAST
Reread lines 44–51. What differences does the narrator point out between Grama and Grampa?

"I'll stay off the state road," I promised. "I'll just follow Bell Brook."

Truth be told, the state road made me a little nervous, too. It was all too easy to imagine myself in the place of one of my defunct pets, stunned by the elephant bellow of a tractor-trailer's horn, looking wild-eyed up to the shiny metal grill; the thud, the lightning-bolt flash of light, and then the eternal dark. I imagined my grandfather shoveling the dirt over me in a backyard grave next to that of Lady, the collie, and Kitty-kitty, the gray cat, while my grandmother dried her eyes with her apron and said, "I told him to stay off that road!"

I was big on knowledge but very short on courage in those years. I mostly played by myself because the other kids my age from the houses and farms scattered around our rural township regarded me as a Grama's boy who would tell if they were to tie me up and threaten to burn my toes with matches, a ritual required to join the local society of pre-teenage boys. A squealer. And they were right.

I didn't much miss the company of other kids. I had discovered that most of them had little interest in the living things around them. They were noisier than Grampa and I were, scaring away the rabbits that we could creep right

2. **spading:** digging.
3. **a mess of:** an amount of (food).

READING SKILL

B COMPARE AND CONTRAST

Have students record their answers in a Venn diagram as introduced on page 767. ***Possible answer:*** *Grama is college educated. Grampa has little formal education but much practical knowledge, and he is an Abenaki Indian.*

DIFFERENTIATED INSTRUCTION

FOR ENGLISH LEARNERS

Vocabulary: Cognates [shared-language groups] Have groups scan the story for cognates and report their findings to the class. Spanish cognates on this page include

- *sincere/sincero, -a* (line 29)
- *nervous/nervioso, -a* (line 53)
- *eternal/eterno, -a* (line 56)
- *imagined/imaginé (line 57)*
- *courage/coraje* (line 61)
- *discovered/descubierto* (line 67)

Comprehension: Idioms [mixed-readiness pairs] Have students work in pairs to figure out the meanings of these and other phrases in the selection. Then help students use them in original sentences:

- *met their fates* (line 42), "were killed"
- *book learning* (line 45), "formal education"
- *was big on* (line 61), "had a lot of"
- *was . . . short on* (line 61), "had little"
- *squealer* (line 65), "someone who tells"

up on. Instead of watching the frogs catching flies with their long, gummy tongues, those boys wanted to shoot them with their BB guns. I couldn't imagine any of them having the patience or **inclination** to hold out a hand filled with sunflower seeds, as Grampa had showed me I could, long enough for a chickadee to come and light on an index finger.

Even fishing was done differently when I did it Grampa's way. I knew for a fact that most of those boys would go out and come home with an empty creel. They hadn't been watching for fish from the banks as I had in the weeks before the trout season began, so they didn't know where the fish lived. They didn't know how to keep low, float your line in, wait for that first tap, and then, after the strike that bent your pole, set the hook. And they never said thank-you to every fish they caught, the way I remembered to do. **C**

Walking the creek edge, I set off downstream. By mid-morning, my bait can of moss and red earthworms that Grampa and I had dug from the edge of our manure pile was near empty. I'd gone half a mile and had already caught seven trout. All of them were squaretails, native brook trout whose sides were patterned with a speckled rainbow of bright circles—red, green, gold. I'd only kept the ones more than seven inches long, and I'd remembered to wet my hand before taking the little ones off the hook. Grasping a trout with a dry hand would abrade the slick coat of natural oil from the skin and leave it open for infection and disease.

As always, I'd had to keep the eyes in the back of my head open just as Grampa had told me to do whenever I was in the woods.

"Things is always hunting one another," he'd said.

And he was right. Twice, at places where Bell Brook swung near Mill Road I'd had to leave the stream banks to take shelter when I heard the ominous crunch of bicycle tires on the gravel. Back then, when I was ten, I was smaller than the other boys my age. I made up for it by being harder to catch. Equal parts of **craftiness** and plain old panic at being collared by bullies I viewed as close kin to Attila the Hun[4] kept me slipperier than an eel.

From grapevine tangles up the bank, I'd watched as Pauly Roffmeier, Ricky Holstead, and Will Backus rolled up to the creek, making more noise than a herd of hippos, to plunk their own lines in. Both times, they caught nothing. It wasn't surprising, since they were talking like jaybirds, scaring away whatever fish might have been within half a mile. And Will kept lighting matches and throwing them down to watch them hiss out when they struck the water. Not to mention the fact that I had pulled a ten-inch brook trout out of the first hole and an eleven incher out of the second before they even reached the stream. **D**

I looked up at the sky. I didn't wear a watch then. No watch made by man seemed able to work more than a few days when strapped to my wrist. It was a common thing on my Grampa's side of the family. "We jest got too much 'lectricity in us," he explained.

inclination (ĭn-klə-nā'shən) *n.* a tendency to prefer one thing over another

VISUAL VOCABULARY

creel: a basket used to carry caught fish

C AUTHOR'S BACKGROUND
Reread lines 67–81. Which of the narrator's habits and attitudes reflect his Abenaki heritage?

craftiness (krăf'tē-nĕs) *n.* deviousness or deception

D COMPARE AND CONTRAST
Reread lines 100–108. How is the boys' approach to fishing different from that of the narrator?

4. **Attila the Hun:** a barbarian leader who successfully invaded the Roman Empire in the A.D. 400s.

FOR ENGLISH LEARNERS

Visual Vocabulary Tell students that creels are baskets made of wicker—a material made of thin, flexible twigs woven together to make baskets or furniture.

FOR ADVANCED LEARNERS/PRE–AP

Create Similes Point out the simile *talking like jaybirds* (line 103). Discuss the way in which this vivid comparison captures an essential quality of the bird and makes it easier to see, hear, and feel what is being described. Have students write their own similes, and then hold a contest in which students vote for the best simile.

Lines 39–74

DISCUSSION PROMPTS

Use these prompts to help students understand the narrator's background:

Recall How is the narrator different from other kids his age? ***Answer:*** *He is respectful of nature and is not as noisy and rambunctious as the other kids.*

Infer From what you've read thus far, with whom do you think the narrator spends most of his time? ***Possible answer:*** *He probably spends most of his time with his grandparents or with animals. He says he doesn't "much miss the company of other kids."*

Interpret What does the narrator mean when he says he "was big on knowledge but very short on courage in those years" (line 61)? ***Possible answer:*** *He means he has learned a lot from his educated grandmother and his practical grandfather, but he is too fearful to venture onto the state road or to play with the other boys in the township.*

LITERARY ANALYSIS

C AUTHOR'S BACKGROUND

Possible answer: *He uses his Abenaki grandfather's fishing method, and he treats the earth with respect by thanking the fish that he catches.*

READING SKILL

D COMPARE AND CONTRAST

Have students record their answers in the Venn diagram from page 767. ***Possible answer:*** *The boys are impatient and loud, and they throw matches into the water, scaring the fish away. They do not catch any fish. The narrator, on the other hand, is quiet and respectful of his surroundings, and he is successful at catching fish.*

THE SNAPPING TURTLE 771

Lines 113–148
DISCUSSION PROMPTS

Use these prompts to help students understand the story's rising action:

Recall What is the narrator's plan for crossing the road? Is he following his grandmother's instructions? ***Answer:*** *He decides to cross under the road, in a culvert. Technically, he is not going against his grandmother's wishes, but for all intents and purposes, he is.*

Infer Based on the narrator's reaction, do you think he is frightened when he encounters the spider in the culvert? Cite evidence. ***Possible answer:*** *He is surprised but not afraid. In fact, he addresses the spider courteously, apologizing for disturbing it. Then he passes it carefully, but without anxiety.*

Synthesize In line 145, the narrator says that walking through the culvert "was like passing from one world into another." Based on what you already know about the narrator, what might these two worlds be? ***Possible answer:*** *He is passing from the world of fear into courage, from the world of the familiar to the unfamiliar, from the world of his grandparents to the world of the other boys.*

Lines 120–123
REINFORCE *KEY IDEA:* VALUES

Discuss What exchange does the narrator make with the crows and jays? What Abenaki **values** does this exchange represent? ***Possible answer:*** *In exchange for the fish entrails, the birds will trust the narrator and not be afraid. This exchange represents the value of respecting the earth and not wasting its resources.*

LITERARY ANALYSIS

Ⓔ AUTHOR'S BACKGROUND

Possible answer: *The narrator demonstrates the effect of his Abenaki heritage by respecting nature—talking to the spider and trying not to disturb it.*

If students need help . . . Have students review the information about the author's Abenaki heritage on page 767.

Without a watch, I could measure time by the sun. I could see it was about ten. I had reached the place where Bell Brook crossed under the state road. Usually I went no further than this. It had been my boundary for years. But somewhere along the way I had decided that today would be different. I think perhaps a part of me was ashamed of hiding from the other boys, ashamed of always being afraid. I wanted to do something that I'd always been afraid to do. I wanted to be brave.

I had no need to fish further. I had plenty of trout for our supper. I'd cleaned them all out with my Swiss Army knife, leaving the entrails[5] where the crows and jays could get them. If you did that, the crows and jays would know you for a friend and not sound the alarm when they saw you walking in the woods. I sank the creel under water, wedged it beneath a stone. The water of the brook was deep and cold and I knew it would keep the flesh of the trout fresh and firm. Then I **cached** my pole and bait can under the spice bushes. As I looked up at the highway, Grama's words came back to me:

② **Targeted Passage**

cache (kăsh) *v.* to store in a hiding place

"Stay off the state road, Sonny."

"*Under,*" I said aloud, "is not *on.*"

Then, taking a deep breath, bent over at the waist, I waded into the culvert[6] that dove under the Road of Death. I had gone no more than half a dozen steps before I walked into a spider web so strong that it actually bounced me back. I splashed a little water from the creek up onto it and watched the beads shape a pattern of concentric circles. The orb-weaver sat unmoving in a corner, one leg resting on a strand of the web. She'd been waiting for the vibration of some flying creature caught in the sticky strands of her net. Clearly, I was much more than she had hoped for. She sat there without moving. Her wide back was patterned with a shape like that of a red and gold hourglass. Her compound eyes, jet black on her head, took in my giant shape. Spiders gave some people the willies.[7] I knew their bite would hurt like blue blazes, but I still thought them graced with great beauty.

"Excuse me," I said. "Didn't mean to bother you."

The spider raised one front leg. A nervous reaction, most likely, but I raised one hand back. Then I ducked carefully beneath the web, entering an area where the light was different. It was like passing from one world into another. I sloshed through the dark culvert, my fingertips brushing the rushing surface of the stream, the current pushing at my calves. My sneakered feet barely held their purchase[8] on the ridged metal, slick with moss. Ⓔ

Ⓔ **AUTHOR'S BACKGROUND**
What effect might the narrator's heritage have on his reaction to the spider? Explain.

When I came out the other side, the sunlight was blinding. Just ahead of me the creek was overarched with willows. They were so thick and low that there was no way I could pass without either going underwater or breaking a way through the brush. I wasn't ready to do either. So I made my way up the

5. **entrails** (ĕn′trālz′): the internal organs.
6. **culvert** (kŭl′vərt): a drain that passes under a road.
7. **the willies:** a feeling of fear and/or disgust.
8. **held their purchase:** gripped; refrained from slipping.

DIFFERENTIATED INSTRUCTION

FOR LESS–PROFICIENT READERS

② **Targeted Passage [Lines 113–142]**

This passage describes a turning point as the narrator decides to cross under the state road.

- What does the narrator want to do, and why?
- What does the narrator do with the fish he has caught?
- In what way does the narrator plan to cross the highway?
- What does the narrator find in the culvert? What is his reaction?

Comprehension Support Help students understand that the dialogue on this page has three different purposes: Sonny is recalling his grandmother's words (line 128), talking to himself (line 129), and addressing the spider (line 142).

Bridge Over Weekeepeemee (1974), Mark Potter. Oil on canvas. Private collection. © Bridgeman Art Library.

bank, thinking to circle back and pick up the creek farther down. For what purpose, I wasn't sure, aside from just wanting to do it. I was nervous as a hen yard when a chicken hawk is circling overhead. But I was excited, too. This was new ground to me, almost a mile from home. I'd gone farther from home in the familiar directions of north and west, into the safety of the woods, but this was different: Across the state road, in the direction of town; someone else's hunting territory. I stayed low to the ground and hugged the edges of the brush as I moved. Then I saw something that drew me away from the creek: The glint of a wider expanse of water. The Rez, the old Greenfield Reservoir.

I'd never been to the Rez, though I knew the other boys went there. As I'd sat alone on the bus, my bookbag clasped tightly to my chest, I'd heard them talk about swimming there, fishing for bass, spearing bullfrogs five times as big as the little frogs in Bell Brook.

I knew I shouldn't be there, yet I was. Slowly I moved to the side of the wide trail that led to the edge of the deep water, and it was just as well that I did: Their bikes had been stashed in the brush down the other side of the path. They'd been more quiet than usual. I might have walked up on them if I hadn't heard a voice. . . .

ANALYZE VISUALS
Compare the scene in this painting with the way you picture the culvert in the story. What are the similarities and differences?

ANALYZE VISUALS

Possible answer: *The painting shows a structure with a highway passing over it, which is similar to the culvert in the story. However, the narrator needs to bend at the waist (line 130) to walk through the culvert, while the structure in the painting seems to have a much higher ceiling. Also, the culvert in the story is made of "ridged metal" (line 148) rather than concrete. It is probably a large, round pipe.*

About the Art Much of the work of Mark Potter (1929–1995) is of landscapes. Several include human-made elements such as train tracks or bridges, like the bridge shown here.

FOR ENGLISH LEARNERS

Vocabulary: Multiple-Meaning Words
Explain that many words in English have more than one meaning, depending on the context in which they are used. Examples on this page include *ground, state, brush,* and *chest.* Have students use the strategies on the Words with Multiple Meanings transparency to define these words. Challenge them to identify other such words in the story.

BEST PRACTICES TOOLKIT—Transparency
Words with Multiple Meanings p. E31

FOR ADVANCED LEARNERS/PRE–AP

Synthesize The narrator finds beauty in all aspects of nature, even a spider living in a culvert. Have students reread lines 130–148 and then brainstorm details of a special place in nature. Encourage them to make a list of details that appeal to the five senses. To extend the activity, have students use the details to write haiku.

Lines 189–196
REINFORCE *KEY IDEA:* VALUES

Discuss In the spring, the narrator and his grandparents pick up migrating turtles on the road so that they will not be killed by cars. What **values** is the narrator learning from this annual tradition? ***Possible answer:*** *He is learning to prioritize caring for other creatures.*

I picked up some of the dark mud with my fingertips and drew lines across my cheeks. Grampa had explained it would make me harder to see. Then I slid to a place where an old tree leaned over the bank, cloaked by the cattails that grew from the edge of the Rez. I made my way out on the trunk and looked. . . .

"It's not gonna come up," Ricky said. He picked up something that looked like a makeshift spear. "You lied."

"I did not. It was over there. The biggest snapper I ever saw." Will shaded his eyes with one hand and looked right in my direction without seeing me. "If we catch it, we could sell it for ten dollars to that man on Congress Street. They say snapping turtles have seven different kinds of meat in them."

"Hmph," Pauly said, throwing his own spear aside. "Let's go find something else to do."

One by one, they picked up their fishing poles and went back down the path. I waited without moving, hearing their heavy feet on the trail and then the rattle of their bike chains. . . . All I could think of was that snapping turtle.

I knew a lot about turtles. There were mud turtles and map turtles. There was the smart orange-legged wood turtle and the red-eared slider with its cheeks painted crimson as if it was going to war. Every spring Grama and Grampa and I would drive around, picking up those whose old **migration** routes had been cut by the recent and lethal ribbons of road. Spooked by a car, a turtle falls into that old defense of pulling head and legs and tail into its once **impregnable** fortress. But a shell does little good against the wheels of a Nash or a DeSoto.[9]

Some days we'd rescue as many as a dozen turtles, taking them home for a few days before releasing them back into the wild. Painted turtles, several as big as two hands held together, might nip at you some, but they weren't really dangerous. And the wood turtles would learn in a day or so to reach out for a strawberry or a piece of juicy tomato and then leave their heads out for a scratch while you stroked them with a finger.

Snappers though, they were different. Long-tailed, heavy-bodied and short-tempered, their jaws would gape wide and they'd hiss when you came up on them ashore. Their heads and legs were too big to pull into their shells and they would heave up on their legs and lunge forward as they snapped at you. They might weigh as much as fifty pounds, and it was said they could take off a handful of fingers in one bite. There wasn't much to recommend a snapping turtle as a friend. F

Most people seemed to hate snappers. Snappers ate the fish and the ducks; they scared swimmers away. Or I should say that people hated them alive. Dead, they were supposed to be the best-eating turtle of all. *Ten dollars,* I thought. *Enough for me to send away to the mail-order pet place and get a pair of real flying squirrels.* I'd kept that clipping from *Field and Stream* magazine

9. **Nash . . . DeSoto:** car brands that were popular during the 1950s.

(3) **Targeted Passag**

migration (mī-grā'shə
n. the act of changing location seasonally (us here as an adjective)

impregnable (ĭm-prĕg'nə-bəl) *adj.* impossible to enter by force

F AUTHOR'S BACKGROUND
Do you think Bruchac h had experiences simila to those the narrator describes here? Explai your answer.

LITERARY ANALYSIS

F AUTHOR'S BACKGROUND

Students might infer that the author has had some of the experiences he writes about. He knows a lot about turtles, and he describes them in great detail.

Extend the Discussion Do you think the narrator and his grandparents would rescue a snapping turtle from the road, even though it is not a friendly creature? Why or why not?

DIFFERENTIATED INSTRUCTION

FOR LESS–PROFICIENT READERS

(3) Targeted Passage [Lines 171–186]

This passage introduces the snapping turtle, the focus of the story's main conflict.

- Whom does the narrator overhear at the reservoir?
- What are the boys talking about?
- Why does the narrator stay at the Rez?

Reading Skill Follow-Up: Compare and Contrast [paired option] Have student pairs read lines 171–196 and update their Venn diagrams from page 767, comparing and contrasting the narrator and the other boys. Remind students to look for ways in which the characters' attitudes, backgrounds, and values are similar or different.

thumbtacked over my bed for four months now. A sort of plan was coming into my mind. G

People were afraid of getting bit by snappers when they were swimming. But from what I'd read, and from what Grampa told me, they really didn't have much to worry about.

"Snapper won't bother you none in the water," Grampa said. If you were even to step on a snapping turtle resting on the bottom of a pond, all it would do would be to move away. On land, all the danger from a snapper was to the front or the side. From behind, a snapper couldn't get you. Get it by the tail, you were safe. That was the way.

And as I thought, I kept watch. And as I kept watch, I kept up a silent chant inside my mind.

Come here, I'm waiting for you.
Come here, I'm waiting for you.

G COMPARE AND CONTRAST
What does the narrator have in common with Will, one of the other boys?

Before long, a smallish log that had been sticking up farther out in the pond began to drift my way. It was, as I had expected, no log at all. It was a turtle's head. I stayed still. The sun's heat beat on my back, but I lay there like a **basking** lizard. Closer and closer the turtle came, heading right into water less than waist deep. It was going right for shore, for the sandy bank bathed in sun. I didn't think about why then, just wondered at the way my wanting seemed to have called it to me.

basking (băsk'ĭng) *adj.* warming oneself pleasantly, as in sunlight

When it was almost to shore, I slid into the water on the other side of the log I'd been waiting on. The turtle surely sensed me, for it started to swing around as I moved slowly toward it, swimming as much as walking. But I lunged and grabbed it by the tail. Its tail was rough and ridged, as easy to hold as if coated with sandpaper. I pulled hard and the turtle came toward me. I stepped back, trying not to fall and pull it on top of me. My feet found the bank, and I leaned hard to drag the turtle out, its clawed feet digging into the dirt as it tried to get away. A roaring hiss like the rush of air from a punctured tire came out of its mouth, and I stumbled, almost losing my grasp. Then I took another step, heaved again, and it was mine.

Or at least it was until I let go. I knew I could not let go. I looked around, holding its tail, moving my feet to keep it from walking its front legs around to where it would snap at me. It felt as if it weighed a thousand pounds. I could only lift up the back half of its body. I started dragging it toward the creek, fifty yards away. It seemed to take hours, a kind of dance between me and the great turtle, but I did it. I pulled it back through the roaring culvert, water gushing over its shell, under the spider web, and past my hidden pole and creel. I could come back later for the fish. Now there was only room in the world for Bell Brook, the turtle, and me.

The long passage upstream is a blur in my memory. I thought of salmon leaping over falls and learned a little that day how hard such a journey must be.

(4) **Targeted Passage**

READING SKILL

G COMPARE AND CONTRAST

Have students record their answers in the Venn diagram from page 767. ***Possible answer:*** *They both think about how much money the snapping turtle might be worth.*

Lines 218–252

DISCUSSION PROMPTS

Use these prompts to help students understand the narrator's actions:

Recall When he catches the turtle, what part of its body does the narrator hold on to? Why? ***Answer:*** *He holds on to the tail so that the turtle can't swing around and bite him.*

Analyze What do you think the narrator will do with the turtle once he gets it home? Provide evidence from the story to support your prediction. *Some students may think he will sell it because he has his heart set on buying the flying squirrels, while others may think he will change his mind and return it to its habitat.*

Speculate Based on what you know about the values of the narrator's grandparents, what might they think about the narrator's decision to capture and sell a turtle? ***Possible answer:*** *Considering their respect for nature and their desire to help all animals, his grandparents would probably disapprove of the narrator's actions.*

FOR LESS–PROFICIENT READERS

(4) Targeted Passage [Lines 234–254]

This passage develops the conflict between the narrator and the snapping turtle.

- By what method does the narrator catch the turtle?
- What is the turtle's response? What sound does it make?
- Why is it so difficult for the narrator to get the turtle to the creek?
- To what does the narrator compare his journey?

FOR ENGLISH LEARNERS

Language: Conversational English Patterns

Point out the double negative in line 218 and give other examples (*haven't got none, didn't hardly*). Explain that in some languages, such as Spanish, double negatives are often used for emphasis. Encourage Spanish speakers to give some examples. Then explain that in standard English, the use of double negatives is considered incorrect, although it is used in some dialects. The author uses it here to show the way Grampa speaks.

When I rounded the last bend and reached the place where the brook edged our property, I breathed a great sigh. But I could not rest. There was still a field and the back yard to cross.

My grandparents saw me coming. From the height of the sun it was now mid-afternoon, and I knew I was dreadful late.

"Sonny, where have you . . . ?" began Grama.

Then she saw the turtle.

"I'm sorry. It took so long because of . . ." I didn't finish the sentence because the snapping turtle, **undaunted** by his backward passage, took that opportunity to try once more to swing around and get me. I had to make three quick steps in a circle, heaving at its tail as I did so.

undaunted (ŭn-dôn'tĭ) *adj.* not discouraged; courageous

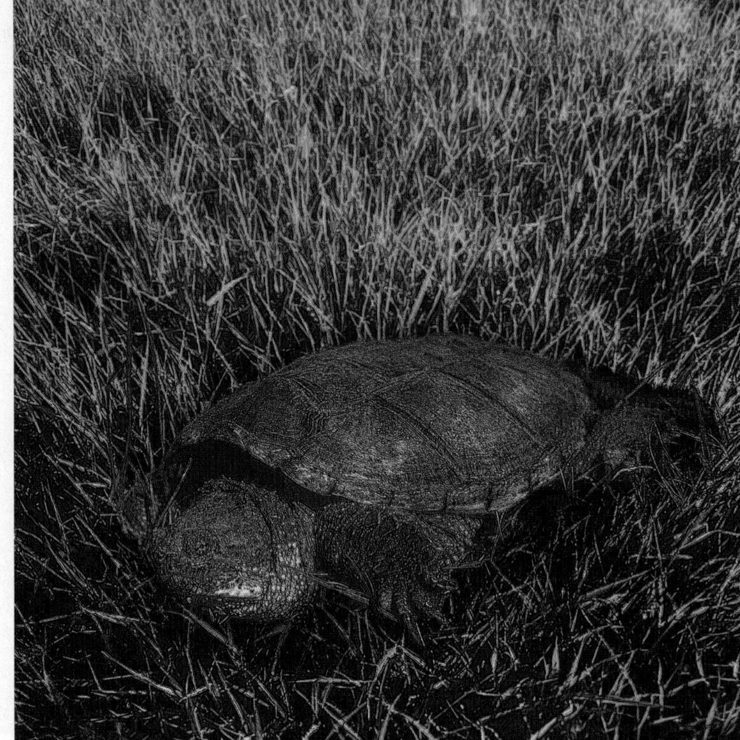

ANALYZE VISUALS
What **details** on the snapping turtle do you notice most? What details are difficult to see?

ANALYZE VISUALS

Possible answer: *The turtle's large head and one front claw are clearly visible. Its tail is mostly hidden, however, and it is difficult to tell how large the turtle is because there are no other objects close by for comparison.*

DIFFERENTIATED INSTRUCTION

FOR LESS–PROFICIENT READERS

Comprehension Support

- Point out the use of ellipses on these two pages. Explain that sometimes ellipses indicate that text has been left out. In line 295, for example, the ellipsis replaces words that have been omitted from the original version of the story. In lines 260 and 262, however, the author uses ellipses to indicate unfinished sentences.
- [small-group option] Form small groups from half of the class. Tell them that they will be experts on the story and ask them to discuss the plot, characters, and theme. While these groups are meeting, ask the rest of the students to write questions about the story that require more than a yes or no answer. Then convene the expert panel and have students ask and answer questions.

BEST PRACTICES TOOLKIT
Ask the Experts p. D4

FOR ENGLISH LEARNERS

Language: Punctuation Point out the series of hyphens used to create an adjective and idiomatic expression: "all-too-familiar tail" (line 276). Explain that hyphens can combine the words in a phrase to create a single adjective. Examples include "ten-year-old boy" and "easy-to-learn instructions."

"Nice size turtle," Grampa Jesse said.

My grandmother looked at me. I realized then I must have been a sight. Wet, muddy, face and hands scratched from the brush that overhung the creek.

"I caught it at the reservoir," I said. I didn't think to lie to them about where I'd been. I waited for my grandmother to scold me. But she didn't.

"Jesse," she said, "Get the big washtub."

My grandfather did as she said. He brought it back and then stepped next to me.

"Leave go," he said.

My hands had a life of their own, grimly determined never to let loose of that all-too-familiar tail, but I forced them to open. The turtle flopped down Before it could move, my grandfather dropped the big washtub over it. All was silent for a minute as I stood there, my arms aching as they hung by my side. Then the washtub began to move. My grandmother sat down on it and it stopped.

She looked at me. So did Grampa. It was wonderful how they could focus their attention on me in a way that made me feel they were ready to do whatever they could to help. **H**

"What now?" Grama said.

"I heard that somebody down on Congress Street would pay ten dollars for a snapping turtle."

"Jack's," Grampa said.

My grandmother nodded. "Well," she said, "if you go now you can be back in time for supper. I thought we were having trout." She raised an eyebrow at me.

"I left them this side of the culvert by 9N," I said. "Along with my pole."

"You clean up and put on dry clothes. Your grandfather will get the fish."

"But I hid them."

My grandmother smiled. "Your grandfather will find them." And he did.

An hour later, we were on the way to Congress Street. . . . In the 1950s, Congress Street was like a piece of Harlem[10] dropped into an upstate town. We pulled up in front of Jack's, and a man who looked to be my grandfather's age got up and walked over to us. His skin was only a little darker than my grandfather's, and the two nodded to each other.

My grandfather put his hand on the trunk of the Plymouth.

"What you got there?" Jack said.

"Show him, Sonny."

I opened the trunk. My snapping turtle lifted up its head as I did so.

"I heard you might want to buy a turtle like this for ten dollars," I said.

Jack shook his head. "Ten dollars for a little one like that? I'd give you two dollars."

I looked at my turtle. Had it shrunk since Grampa wrestled it into the trunk?

H COMPARE AND CONTRAST
Reread lines 266–283. What similar qualities do Grama and Grampa display?

10. **Harlem:** a New York City neighborhood that was and is largely African American.

FOR ENGLISH LEARNERS

Language: Conversational English Patterns [mixed-readiness groups] Point out that some of the dialogue on this page is abbreviated; that is, certain words are left out. Examples are

- *Nice size turtle* (line 266), "That's a nice-sized turtle."
- *Leave go* (line 274), "Let it go."
- *What now?* (line 284), "What should we do now?"
- *What you got there?* (line 301), "What have you got there?"

Assign mixed-readiness Jigsaw Reading groups to find more examples of these speech patterns in the rest of the story. Ask each group to fill in missing words in the dialogue they identify and report back to the class.

BEST PRACTICES TOOLKIT
Jigsaw Reading p. A1

Lines 266–289

REINFORCE *KEY IDEA:* VALUES

Discuss In what way do Grama and Grampa set aside their **values** to help the narrator? Why might they do this? ***Possible answer:*** *They set aside their respect for all living creatures to help the narrator catch and sell the turtle. They might do this to teach the narrator a lesson or to show him that they trust him to make his own choices.*

READING SKILL

H COMPARE AND CONTRAST

Have students record their answers in the Venn diagram introduced on page 767. ***Possible answer:*** *Grama and Grampa are both supportive, understanding, and helpful.*

Lines 260–294

DISCUSSION PROMPTS

Use these prompts to help students describe the narrator's grandparents:

Summarize How do the narrator's grandparents react when he comes home with the turtle? What do they do to help him? ***Possible answer:*** *They don't scold him, as he expects. Instead, they trap the turtle under a washtub and ask the narrator what he plans to do.*

Infer Why do you think the narrator's grandmother doesn't scold him for going to the reservoir? *Students may say that she is relieved he is safe and that she wants him to use the values she's taught him to make his own decisions.*

Synthesize The narrator's grandmother is confident that his grandfather will find the fish that the narrator has hidden. Based on what you know about Grampa, why do you think she is so confident about this? ***Possible answer:*** *She knows that Grampa has practical knowledge and that he taught Sonny how to fish, so he will know where to look for the hidden fish.*

“That’s not enough,” I said.

“Three dollars. My last offer.”

I looked at Grampa. He shrugged his shoulders.

“I guess I don’t want to sell it,” I said.

“All right,” Jack said. “You change your mind, come on back.” He touched his hat with two fingers and walked back over to his chair in the sun.

As we drove back toward home, neither of us said anything for a while. Then my grandfather spoke.

“Would five dollars’ve been enough?”

“No,” I said.

“How about ten?”

I thought about that. “I guess not.”

“Why you suppose that turtle was heading for that sandbank?” Grampa said.

I thought about that, too. Then I realized the truth of it.

“It was coming out to lay its eggs.”

“Might be.”

I thought hard then. I’d learned it was never right for a hunter to shoot a mother animal, because it hurt the next generation to come. Was a turtle any different? ❶

“Can we take her back?” I asked.

“Up to you, Sonny.”

And so we did. Gramp drove the Plymouth right up the trail to the edge of the Rez. He held a stick so the turtle would grab onto it as I hauled her out of the trunk. I put her down and she just stayed there, her nose a foot from the water but not moving.

“We’ll leave her,” Grampa said. We turned to get into the car. When I looked back over my shoulder, she was gone. Only ripples on the water, widening circles rolling on toward other shores like generations following each other, like my grandmother’s flowers still growing in a hundred gardens in Greenfield, like the turtles still seeking out that sandbank, like this story that is no longer just my own but belongs now to your memory, too. ❧

⑤ Targeted Passage

❶ AUTHOR’S BACKGROUND
What lesson does the narrator learn? Tell how this lesson relates to Bruchac’s values.

LITERARY ANALYSIS

❶ AUTHOR’S BACKGROUND

Possible answer: *The narrator learns that the turtle’s life is priceless and that killing a mother turtle would hurt generations to come. According to Abenaki beliefs, you shouldn’t kill mother animals.*

Extend the Discussion Have students evaluate the statement in lines 324–325. Do they agree with it? Why or why not?

SELECTION WRAP–UP

REFLECT Ask students whether the resolution of the plot—the return of the turtle to the reservoir—surprised them. Is this ending foreshadowed? If so, how?

★ CRITIQUE Have students evaluate the setting of the story. How clearly is the setting developed? What is the effect of the setting on the plot? Have students cite examples to support their answers.

READING FLUENCY

Distribute the copy masters and have students practice fluency.

RESOURCE MANAGER—Copy Master
Reading Fluency p. 37

DIFFERENTIATED INSTRUCTION

FOR LESS–PROFICIENT READERS

⑤ Targeted Passage [Lines 314–338]

This passage resolves the conflict as the narrator decides what to do with the turtle.

- What does the narrator realize about the turtle? What action does he decide to take?
- What help does the narrator’s grandfather give him?
- What happens to the turtle at the end of the story?

FOR ADVANCED LEARNERS/PRE–AP

Evaluate Have students write a one- or two-paragraph letter to Joseph Bruchac, expressing their reaction to “The Snapping Turtle.” Invite them to explain to Bruchac how their values are similar to or different from those held by the characters in the story.

After Reading

Comprehension

1. **Recall** What actions does the narrator take to make sure he fishes responsibly?
2. **Recall** Why does the narrator decide to cross under the state road?
3. **Represent** How does the narrator get the snapping turtle out of the water? Reread lines 234–243, and sketch the scene.

Literary Analysis

4. **Visualize** How well does Joseph Bruchac help you visualize the characters, events, and settings in the story? Choose a passage that you find visually descriptive and explain what words and phrases help you picture the scene.
5. **Make Inferences About Relationships** Describe the narrator's relationship with his grandparents. Do you think the other boys in the story would have similar relationships with the adults in their lives? Explain your answer.
6. **Compare and Contrast Characters** What are the similarities and differences between Grama and Grampa? Consider their backgrounds, **values,** and traits. Use the notes from one of your Venn diagrams to help you answer the question, and cite evidence from the story.
7. **Analyze Influence of Author's Background** Reread Bruchac's biography on page 767 to remind you of his Abenaki beliefs. In what ways does "The Snapping Turtle" reflect these values? In a graphic like the one shown, give examples from the story.

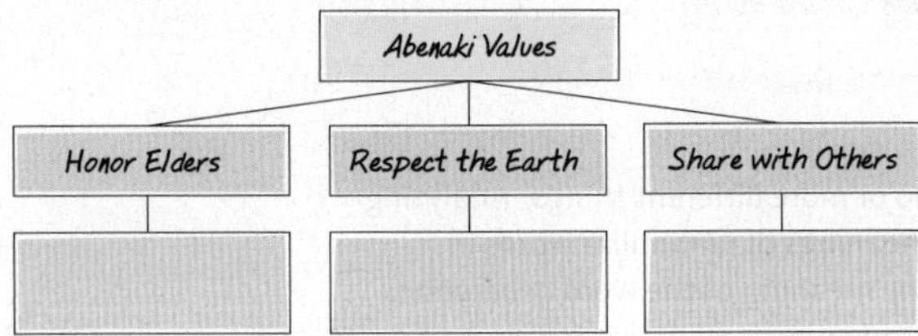

8. **Evaluate the Ending** Reread the last paragraph of the story. How well do you think it wraps up the **plot** and summarizes the **theme?** Refer to specific phrases in the paragraph as you explain your answer.

Extension and Challenge

9. **Inquiry and Research** In Native American cultures, stories are often used to teach children. Find a retelling of a Native American story, perhaps from one of Joseph Bruchac's collections, and present it to the class. Explain what lesson it is meant to teach.

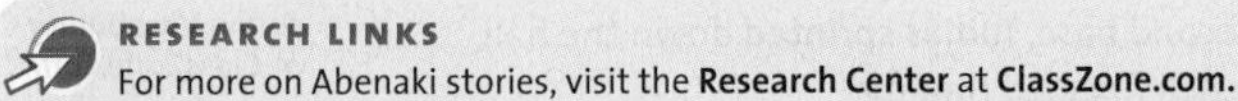

RESEARCH LINKS
For more on Abenaki stories, visit the **Research Center** at **ClassZone.com.**

Practice and Apply

After Reading

For additional support of postreading questions, use these copy masters:

RESOURCE MANAGER—Copy Masters
Reading Check p. 34 (to check understanding of the selection)
Influence of Author's Background p. 27 (for practice of literary analysis standards focus)
Question Support p. 35 (After Reading questions adapted for English learners and less-proficient readers)

Additional selection questions are provided for teachers on page 21.

ANSWERS

Comprehension

1. *He is quiet and respectful of the environment, wets his hand before touching the fish so he doesn't harm their skin, and catches only enough for dinner.*
2. *He decides to take a risk and do something he wouldn't ordinarily do.*
3. *Sketches should show a boy dragging a large snapping turtle out of the water by its tail.*

Literary Analysis

Possible answers:

4. *Students should cite a specific passage from the story with details that help them visualize characters, events, and settings.*
5. *The narrator loves his grandparents, learns from them, respects them, and helps them. The other boys would probably have different relationships with adults. They are not respectful of animals and torture people their own age. Therefore, they probably are not respectful of adults either.*
6. ■ **STANDARDS FOCUS Compare and Contrast** *Grama has more formal education than Grampa. While Grampa is Abenaki and Grama is not, both believe in treating the earth with respect and sharing their knowledge and resources with others.*
7. ● **STANDARDS FOCUS Influence of Author's Background** ***Honor Elders:*** *The narrator considers his grandparents' advice before acting and contributes to the needs of the household.* ***Respect the Earth:*** *The narrator tries not to disturb animals.* ***Share with Others:*** *The narrator plans to share the hidden fish with his grandparents. Grama shares her irises.*
8. *The story closes with a passage about sharing, a common theme throughout the story. The ending effectively wraps up the plot by having the narrator learn an important life lesson and returning the turtle to the water. He realizes that sharing is an essential part of life—sharing between generations, sharing flowers, and sharing stories.*

Extension and Challenge

9. *Tell students that, in addition to other works by Bruchac, examples of retellings can be found in collections of Native American tales and mythology.*

ANSWERS

Vocabulary in Context

VOCABULARY PRACTICE

1. *(b) slyness*
2. *(a) stroll*
3. *(c) conceal*
4. *(a) relocation*
5. *(c) impenetrable*
6. *(b) desire*
7. *(a) sunbathing*
8. *(b) unafraid*
9. *(c) permanence*
10. *(a) belief*

RESOURCE MANAGER—Copy Master
Vocabulary Practice p. 32

VOCABULARY IN WRITING

Suggest that students begin by rereading the passages that describe ways in which the narrator and the other boys interact with nature. Then have students brainstorm how they would respond to a similar situation. Review words and phrases that can be used to make comparisons, such as *like, unlike, in the same way as,* and *differently.* Challenge students to use as many of the vocabulary words in their paragraphs as possible.

VOCABULARY STRATEGY: ANALOGIES *(also an EL language objective)*

Explain that analogies always have two parts: one part contains the word being identified and the other part makes the comparison.

Possible answers:

1. *"no longer existing"*
2. *"flimsy, temporary"*
3. *"took care of; nurtured"*
4. *"ran very fast"*

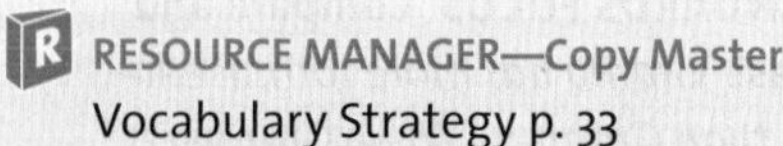
RESOURCE MANAGER—Copy Master
Vocabulary Strategy p. 33

Vocabulary Center at **ClassZone.com**
Additional Vocabulary Activities

Vocabulary in Context

VOCABULARY PRACTICE

Choose the word in each group that is closest in meaning to the boldfaced word.

1. **craftiness:** (a) intelligence, (b) slyness, (c) dishonesty
2. **traipse:** (a) stroll, (b) slither, (c) bounce
3. **cache:** (a) spend, (b) waste, (c) conceal
4. **migration:** (a) relocation, (b) nesting, (c) settlement
5. **impregnable:** (a) frightening, (b) unguarded, (c) impenetrable
6. **inclination:** (a) wisdom, (b) desire, (c) strength
7. **basking:** (a) sunbathing, (b) swimming, (c) cooking
8. **undaunted:** (a) unhurt, (b) unafraid, (c) uncaring
9. **immortality:** (a) birth, (b) death, (c) permanence
10. **philosophy:** (a) belief, (b) style, (c) story

basking
inclination
cache
migration
craftiness
philosophy
immortality
traipse
impregnable
undaunted

VOCABULARY IN WRITING

Using at least two vocabulary words, write a paragraph telling about your own views on nature. You may want to compare yourself with the boys in the story. You could start this way.

EXAMPLE SENTENCE

Unlike the narrator, I don't have an ***inclination*** *toward fishing.*

VOCABULARY STRATEGY: ANALOGIES

An analogy compares similar aspects of two or more different things. Analyzing an analogy is one way of figuring out the meanings of unfamiliar words in context. For example, you can determine the meaning of the word *generations* from the thing it is compared to in this passage:

> *Only ripples on the water, widening circles rolling on toward other shores like* ***generations*** *following each other. . . .* (lines 334–336)

PRACTICE Use the comparison in each sentence to help you understand the boldfaced word.

1. **Defunct** Web sites are like ghost towns that once bustled with life.
2. Like a **makeshift** shelter, a flimsy excuse soon falls apart.
3. Carmina **tended** to the mold she was growing for the science fair the way a mother bird looks after her nest.
4. Like a baseball player stealing second base, Tomás **sprinted** down the hall and slid into his seat just as the bell finished ringing.

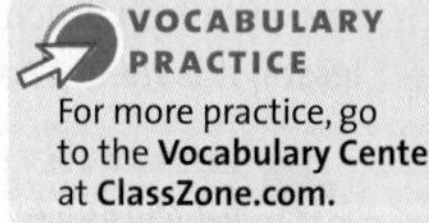
VOCABULARY PRACTICE
For more practice, go to the **Vocabulary Center** at **ClassZone.com.**

DIFFERENTIATED INSTRUCTION

FOR LESS–PROFICIENT READERS

Vocabulary Practice Point out that several of the vocabulary words, as well as the answer choices, have prefixes or suffixes that can give clues to their meaning. These include *-ness, dis-, -tion, re-, -ment, im-, un-, in-,* and *-ence.* Use Common Prefixes and Common Suffixes to review these word parts.

BEST PRACTICES TOOLKIT—Transparencies
Common Prefixes p. E14
Common Suffixes p. E15

FOR ADVANCED LEARNERS/PRE–AP

Vocabulary Strategy [paired option] Have partners create analogies using several of the vocabulary words. Each student should then analyze his or her partner's analogies. For analogies that aren't clear, have partners brainstorm other comparisons.

780 UNIT 7: HISTORY, CULTURE, AND THE AUTHOR

Reading-Writing Connection

Demonstrate your understanding of "The Snapping Turtle" by responding to these prompts. Then complete the **Grammar and Writing** exercise.

WRITING PROMPTS	SELF-CHECK
A. Short Response: Write a Letter Think about the narrator's relationship with his grandparents. Then imagine the narrator as an adult. Write a **one-paragraph letter** in which the grown-up narrator expresses his appreciation to his grandparents for raising him.	***A well-written letter will . . .*** • sound like it's written by an adult • use details to show why the narrator is appreciative
B. Extended Response: Examine Values Do you think that modern American society respects the Native American **values** described in Joseph Bruchac's story? Explain why or why not in a **two- or three-paragraph response.**	***An insightful response will . . .*** • include a clear position statement • demonstrate an understanding of Abenaki values

GRAMMAR AND WRITING

FORM COMPOUND-COMPLEX SENTENCES A **compound-complex sentence** contains two or more independent clauses and one or more dependent clauses. (Recall that a dependent clause cannot stand alone as a sentence and is introduced by words such as *after, because, if,* and *though.*) Compound-complex sentences can help add variety to writing by allowing short, related sentences to be combined.

Original: I did something wrong. You were ready to help. You made me feel safe.

Revised: Though I did something wrong, you were ready to help, and you made me feel safe.

PRACTICE In each item, combine the sentences to form one compound-complex sentence. Use the first word in parentheses to join two independent clauses. Use the second word to change one sentence to a dependent clause.

1. You wanted to add a new color to both your garden and hers. You'd ask the woman for her iris roots. You'd give her some of your own. *(and, if)*
2. I was going to sell the turtle. I didn't. I remembered your lessons. *(but, after)*
3. We'd catch turtles. Then we'd release them. You didn't want them to die. *(and, because)*
4. The other boys couldn't catch fish. We could. We were quiet. *(but, because)*

For more help with compound-complex sentences, see page R64 in the ***Grammar Handbook.***

Reading-Writing Connection

WRITING PROMPTS

- For **Prompt A,** have students brainstorm two or three lessons the narrator learns from his grandparents that he might value as an adult.
- For **Prompt B,** have students list Abenaki values and ask themselves which of these values, if any, are respected in modern American society.

For writing support, see

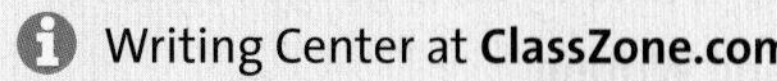

Writing Center at **ClassZone.com**

GRAMMAR AND WRITING

Have students point out the dependent clause and the independent clauses in the revised example sentence before working on the **Practice** activity.

Answers:

1. *If you wanted to add a new color to both your garden and hers, you'd ask the woman for her iris roots, and you'd give her some of your own.*
2. *I was going to sell the turtle, but I didn't after I remembered your lessons.*
3. *We'd catch turtles, and then we'd release them because you didn't want them to die.*
4. *The other boys couldn't catch fish, but we could because we were quiet.*

RESOURCE MANAGER—Copy Master
Form Compound-Complex Sentences p. 36

Assess and Reteach

Assess

RESOURCE MANAGER—Copy Masters
Selection Tests A, B/C pp. 39–40, 41–42

Test Generator CD

Reteach

STANDARDS LESSON FILE
Literature Lesson 41: Author's Perspective
Reading Lesson 12: Comparing and Contrasting
Vocabulary Lesson 23: Analogies

DIFFERENTIATED INSTRUCTION

FOR LESS–PROFICIENT WRITERS

For Prompt A:

1. Suggest that students write an introductory sentence that tells the purpose of the letter: to express appreciation.
2. Next, have them write at least one sentence about each lesson the narrator learned from his grandparents and appreciates as an adult.

For Prompt B:

Students may organize their responses in this way:

- **First paragraph:** Include a clear position statement.
- **Second paragraph:** Describe Abenaki values.
- **Third paragraph:** Explain which Abenaki values, if any, are respected in modern American society.

Focus and Motivate

OBJECTIVES

Literary Analysis
- explore the key idea of telling **right** from wrong
- identify and analyze cultural conflicts
- read a short story

Reading
- make inferences

Vocabulary
- build vocabulary for reading and writing
- use context to determine the meaning of homographs *(also an EL language objective)*

Grammar and Writing
- use colons correctly
- use writing to analyze literature

SUMMARY

Squatters displaced by flooding have built a camp below Rohan's hilltop house in South Africa. After some robberies, the house owners decide to stop sharing water so that the squatters will leave. One day, Solani, a boy from the camp, comes to the door asking for water. Rohan helps Solani carry the water to the camp, where Solani's mother is giving birth. The boys form a connection, and Rohan learns to see the squatters differently.

How do you know what's RIGHT?

Discuss the question. To lead into the ***KEY IDEA,*** ask students whether it is ever **right** to break a law. As they work on the ***DISCUSS*** activity, ask them to explain which rules or laws they think should be changed and why.

Before Reading

Out of Bounds

Short Story by Beverley Naidoo

How do you know what's RIGHT?

KEY IDEA Can you think of a situation when you weren't sure what to do? If so, you know that it's not always easy to tell **right** from wrong. Sometimes you must rely on your internal compass to guide your behavior. In this story, a boy decides to disobey a rule in order to help someone in need.

DISCUSS What purpose do rules serve in families and society? When might rules have to be changed? Discuss these questions with a small group.

Selection Resources

RESOURCE MANAGER UNIT 7

Plan and Teach pp. 43–50

Literary Analysis
Summary pp. 51†*, 52‡*
Cultural Conflict pp. 53, 54†*
Question Support p. 61*

Reading
Make Inferences pp. 55, 56†*
Reading Check p. 60

Vocabulary
Study p. 57*
Practice p. 58
Strategy p. 59

Grammar and Writing
Use Colons Correctly p. 62

Assessment
Selection Tests A, B/C pp. 63*, 65*
Test Generator CD

BEST PRACTICES TOOLKIT

Differentiated Instruction pp. 31–38*
Scaffolding Instruction pp. 43–46*

Graphic Organizers/Strategies
Word Questioning • Open Mind • Common Suffixes • Character Map

Reading Support
Audio Anthology CD*

Technology
Literature, Vocabulary, and Writing Centers at **ClassZone.com**
Write*Smart* CD

* Resources for Differentiation † Also in Spanish ‡ In Haitian Creole and Vietnamese

ERARY ANALYSIS: CULTURAL CONFLICT

When you read a story set in another country, knowing about the area's history and culture can be important background. It can help you to understand the characters' behavior and the cultural conflicts that unfold. A **cultural conflict** is a struggle that arises because of the differing values, customs, or circumstances between groups of people. For example, if a story is set in a place where one religious group has been fighting against another, parents might be angry if their child becomes friends with someone from outside their group.

"Out of Bounds" takes place in South Africa. As you read the selection, think about how South Africa's history and culture affect the conflicts. The background on this page will provide you with some of the information you need.

ADING SKILL: MAKE INFERENCES

Fiction writers do not always make direct statements about characters or the cultures in which they live. Instead, writers provide certain details and expect readers to combine these details with their own knowledge to "read between the lines" of a story. This process of forming logical guesses is called **making inferences.** As you read, use a chart like the one shown to record your inferences about the characters and their culture.

Evidence from Story	*My Knowledge*	*Inference*
Father tops wall with wire.		

CABULARY IN CONTEXT

The boldfaced words help Beverley Naidoo describe a society influenced by its history of racial injustice. Using context clues, try to write a definition for each word.

1. Afraid to go to a school where they would be teased, the boys **straggle** behind their older brother.
2. The flood could **maroon** many people on rooftops.
3. Members of the newer **sect** didn't agree with people from the orthodox church.
4. The Africans fought **vigorously** for equality.
5. The peace talks gave people a **glimmer** of hope.
6. The evening news was interesting enough to **engross** him.
7. We watched the energized boy **bound** up the hill.
8. Poor communication will **hamper** efforts to get along.

Author Online

Writing for Justice
Beverley Naidoo grew up in Johannesburg, South Africa, when the country was racially segregated. It wasn't until she went to college that she recognized the injustice of the laws. After she moved to England, she decided to write children's books that speak honestly about South African society. She published her first book, *Journey to Jo'burg,* in 1984. It was banned in her home country until 1991.

Beverley Naidoo
born 1943

Background

Apartheid South Africa is the southernmost country on the African continent. The nation is ethnically diverse, with whites forming the smallest group. However, up until 1994, whites ruled the country under a system called apartheid (apartness). Apartheid was based on segregation between the races. The white government classified non-whites into three groups. Africans made up the largest group but had the fewest rights. "Coloureds" (people of mixed race) and those of Indian descent were granted limited rights in 1984. The government decided where each group could live, conduct business, or own land. The effects of apartheid continue to influence South African society today. Africans, on average, remain poorer and have less access to education than other groups.

Storms and Floods "Out of Bounds" is set in 2000. That year, severe storms devastated southern Africa. Floods swept away schools, roads, crops, and livestock. About 540,000 people were left homeless.

MORE ABOUT THE AUTHOR AND BACKGROUND
To learn more about Beverley Naidoo and South Africa, visit the **Literature Center** at **ClassZone.com.**

Teach

STANDARDS FOCUS

LITERARY ANALYSIS

● CULTURAL CONFLICT

Discuss the many conflicts that can arise among people from different cultures—about religion, politics, limited resources, and so on. Ask students to read the **Apartheid** note on page 783 and predict the cultural conflicts they might read about in a story set in South Africa. ***Possible answer:*** *racial prejudice, conflicts over land, or economic justice*

CHECK UNDERSTANDING Ask students to give a brief plot synopsis of a movie, television program, or book that examines cultural conflict.

READING SKILL

■ MAKE INFERENCES

Explain that making inferences can help students guess a character's values. For example, if students read that a character goes to jail for refusing to obey an unjust law, they could infer that the character values fairness above his or her own comfort and security.

CHECK UNDERSTANDING Ask students what clues might help them infer that a character feels angry, afraid, or confused.

RESOURCE MANAGER—Copy Master
Make Inferences p. 55 (for student use while reading the selection)

VOCABULARY SKILL

▲ VOCABULARY IN CONTEXT

DIAGNOSE WORD KNOWLEDGE To determine preteaching needs, have all students complete **Vocabulary in Context.** ***Possible answers:*** **1.** *follow* **2.** *trap* **3.** *religious group* **4.** *energetically* **5.** *hint* **6.** *absorb* **7.** *run quickly* **8.** *thwart*

PRETEACH VOCABULARY Use the Vocabulary Study copy master to help students explore the meaning of each boldfaced word.

1. Have students conceal the Definition column.
2. Read aloud the first sentence, emphasizing the boldfaced word.
3. Ask students to think about the way the word is used. Discuss possible meanings for *bounding,* such as "running quickly."
4. Repeat for the other sentences, and then have students check their definitions.
5. Have students write the sentences in Part B independently.

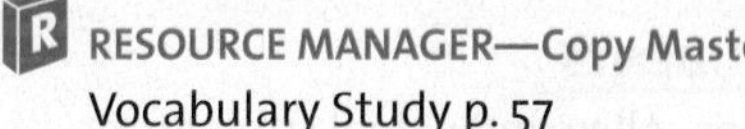

RESOURCE MANAGER—Copy Master
Vocabulary Study p. 57

For general guidelines on differentiating vocabulary instruction and for alternative vocabulary activities for students not needing vocabulary preteaching, see

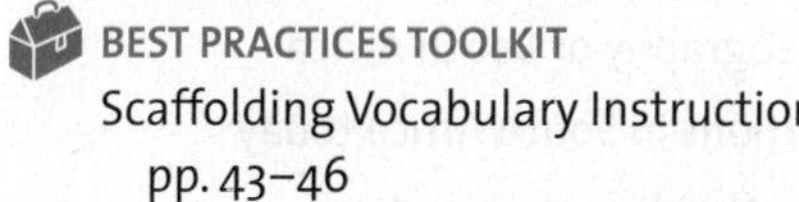

BEST PRACTICES TOOLKIT
Scaffolding Vocabulary Instruction pp. 43–46

Vocabulary Center at **ClassZone.com**

Practice and Apply

ANALYZE VISUALS

Possible answer: *While all the buildings are angular and geometrical, the house at the top of the hill is more colorful and elaborate. It appears to belong to someone who is wealthier than the people who live at the base of the hill.*

LITERARY ANALYSIS

Ⓐ CULTURAL CONFLICT

Possible answer: *They feel that the squatters don't belong. They don't trust the squatters and don't want them there (Rohan's father puts up additional bricks on their garden wall and tops it with barbed wire to keep them out). The mother's comment indicates that she doesn't feel sympathy for the squatters.*

OUT OF BOUNDS

Beverley Naidoo

Out of bounds.

That's what his parents said as soon as the squatters[1] took over the land below their house. Rohan's dad added another meter of thick concrete bricks to their garden wall and topped it with curling barbed wire. He certainly wasn't going to wait for the first break-in and be sorry later. They lived on the ridge of a steep hill with the garden sloping down. Despite the high wall, from his bedroom upstairs, Rohan could see over the spiked-wire circles down to the place where he and his friends used to play. The wild fig trees under which they had made their hideouts were still there. They had spent hours dragging planks, pipes, sheets of metal and plastic—whatever might be useful—up the hill from rubbish tipped in a ditch below. The first squatters pulled their hideouts apart and used the same old scraps again for their own constructions. Rohan could still see the "ski slope"—the red earth down which he and his friends had bumped and flown on a couple of old garbage can lids. The squatters used it as their road up the hill. Now it looked like a crimson scar cut between the shacks littering the hillside.

"There's only one good thing about this business," Ma said after the back wall was completed. "We won't have to wash that disgusting red dust out of your clothes any more!" Ⓐ

ANALYZE VISUALS
Compare the house at the top of the hill with the buildings below. What similarities and differences do you not

① Targeted Passage

Ⓐ CULTURAL CONFLI
In lines 1–19, what do y learn about the family' feelings toward the squatters?

1. **squatters:** people who occupy public land in order to gain ownership of it.

DIFFERENTIATED INSTRUCTION

FOR ALL STUDENTS

Expert Groups Allow individual students or groups to select one of these topics to research and present to the class:

- the Boer War
- apartheid
- urban geography of South Africa
- race relations in South Africa today
- post-apartheid elected leaders
- Truth and Reconciliation Commission

FOR LESS–PROFICIENT READERS

In combination with the *Audio Anthology CD*, use one or more Targeted Passages (pp. 784, 790, 794, 796) to ensure that students focus on key story events, concepts, and skills.

① Targeted Passage [Lines 1–16]

This passage introduces the setting of the story and the main character, Rohan.

- Who lives below Rohan's house?
- What does Rohan's father add to the garden wall? Why?
- What materials did the first squatters use to build their homes?
- What did Rohan and his friends use the "ski slope" for? What do the squatters use it for?

BACKGROUND

Cities in Post-Apartheid South Africa The passage of the Groups Areas Act in 1950 led to the segregation of the business and residential areas of South African cities and towns. Africans, "coloureds," and Asians were forced to live on reserves, or "homelands," which were designated for each ethnic group. Most of these were established far from South Africa's major cities. Non-whites also lived on the periphery of the cities in segregated public housing called "townships." People were crowded into very small areas relative to the size of their populations, and most residents experienced high unemployment and poor living conditions.

After apartheid ended, people were free to live wherever they wished. Huge numbers of people moved to the cities from rural areas, hoping to find jobs and a better quality of life. The cities, however, were not prepared for these migrants. Because of a severe shortage of affordable housing, the migrants built squatters' camps, where many still live in unsanitary conditions and without clean water.

In some cases, the government has been forced to supply housing to squatters. Unfortunately, this housing is often far from the urban areas where most of the jobs are found.

FOR ENGLISH LEARNERS

Options for Reading Read the first Targeted Passage aloud. Make sure students understand the setting of the story. Then have students read the rest of the selection silently as they listen to the *Audio Anthology CD*. Pause the CD frequently to enable students to make predictions.

Key Academic Vocabulary Have students use Word Questioning to study these words: *couple* (lines 14, 22, 276, 281, 295), *uniform* (lines 65, 172), *adult* (lines 151, 167), *vehicles* (line 241), *structure* (line 290).

BEST PRACTICES TOOLKIT—Transparency
Word Questioning p. E9

Prereading For prereading instruction for English learners, see

BEST PRACTICES TOOLKIT
Scaffolding Reading Instruction pp. 43–46

FOR ADVANCED LEARNERS/PRE–AP

Pre-AP exercises in the bottom channel provide additional challenge for your advanced students. Use them for small groups or individuals.

ADDITIONAL GUIDELINES

For more help with differentiation and tips for classroom management, see

BEST PRACTICES TOOLKIT
Differentiated Instruction pp. 31–38

Rohan said nothing. How could he explain what he had lost?

At first, some of the squatter women and children came up to the houses with buckets asking for water. For a couple of weeks his mother opened the gate after checking that no men were hanging around in the background. She allowed the women to fill their buckets at the outside tap. Most of her neighbors found themselves doing the same. Torrential rains and floods had ushered in the new millennium by sweeping away homes, animals and people in the north of the country. The television was awash with pictures of homeless families and efforts to help them. No one knew from where exactly the squatters had come. But as Ma said, how could you refuse a woman or child some water?

It wasn't long before all that changed. The first complaint of clothes disappearing off the washing line came from their new neighbors. The first African family, in fact, to move in among the Indians on Mount View. No one had actually seen anyone but everyone was suspicious including the neighbor, Mrs. Zuma.

"You can't really trust these people, you know," Mrs. Zuma tutted[2] when she came to ask if Ma had seen anyone hanging around. However, it was when thieves broke into old Mrs. Pillay's house, grabbed the gold thali from around her neck, and left her with a heart attack that views hardened. Young men could be seen hanging around the shacks. Were some of them not part of the same gang? Mrs. Pillay's son demanded the police search through the settlement immediately. But the police argued they would need more evidence and that the thieves could have come from anywhere. **B**

A new nervousness now gripped the house owners on top of the hill. Every report of theft, break-in, or car hijacking, anywhere in the country, led to another conversation about the squatters on the other side of their garden walls.

At night Rohan peered through the bars of his window before going to sleep. Flickering lights from candles and lamps were the only sign that people were living out there in the thick darkness. In the daytime, when Ma heard the bell and saw that it was a woman or child with a bucket, she no longer answered the call.

All the neighbors were agreed. Why should private house owners be expected to provide water for these people? That was the Council's job. If the squatters were refused water, then perhaps they would find somewhere else to put up their shacks. A more suitable place. Or even, go back to where they came from. **C**

The squatters did not go away. No one knew from where they managed to get their water or how far they had to walk. On the way to school, Rohan and his dad drove past women walking with buckets on their heads.

2. **tutted:** made a "tut tut" sound with the tongue to express annoyance.

VISUAL VOCABULA

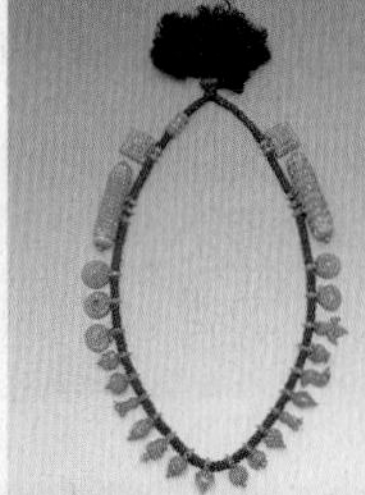

thali *n.* necklace given b a groom to his bride at a Hindu wedding ceremo

B MAKE INFERENCES
What ethnicity is Rohan family?

C MAKE INFERENCES
How does crime affect the residents' attitude toward the squatters?

READING SKILL

B MAKE INFERENCES

Have students record their answers in the chart from page 783. ***Answer:*** *Rohan's family is Indian.*

If students need help . . . Point out line 33, which mentions "the Indians on Mount View," and the reference to the theft of a gold thali from a neighbor (lines 38–39). Make sure students know that Hinduism is a religion that developed on the Indian subcontinent.

READING SKILL

C MAKE INFERENCES

Have students record their answers in the chart from page 783. ***Possible answer:*** *The residents who once felt sorry for the squatters and provided them with water become afraid and stop helping them.*

Lines 53–57

REINFORCE *KEY IDEA:* RIGHT

Discuss The house owners decide to stop giving the squatters access to their water. Do you think the house owners made the **right** decision? Why or why not? *Some students may argue that the house owners made the right decision because they need to protect their property. Others may argue that the house owners should give the squatters water and other assistance.*

DIFFERENTIATED INSTRUCTION

FOR ENGLISH LEARNERS

Visual Vocabulary On their wedding day, the Hindu groom ties the thali around his bride's neck. Elicit information from students from other cultures about their cultures' wedding customs. Do the bride and groom give each other gifts? What rituals are performed before, during, and after the wedding ceremonies?

"These people are tough as ticks! You let them settle and it's impossible to get them out," complained Dad. "Next thing they'll be wanting our electricity."

But Rohan wasn't really listening. He was scanning the line of African children who **straggled** behind the women and who wore the black and white uniform of Mount View Primary, his old school. He had been a pupil there until his parents had moved him to his private school in Durban[3] with its smaller classes, cricket pitch, and its own rugby ground.[4] Most of the African children at Mount View had mothers who cleaned, washed, and ironed for the families on top of the hill. But since the New Year they had been joined by the squatter children and each week the line grew longer.

straggle (străg'əl) *v.* to spread out in a scattered group

The queue[5] of traffic at the crossroads slowed them down, giving Rohan more time to find the "wire car" boy. He was looking for a boy who always steered a wire car in front of him with a long handle. He was about his own age—twelve or thirteen perhaps—and very thin and wiry himself. What interested Rohan was that the boy never had the same car for more than two or three days. Nor had he ever seen so many elaborate designs simply made out of wire, each suggesting a different make of car. They were much more complicated than the little wire toys in the African Crafts shop at the mall. D

D CULTURAL CONFLICT
What differences between Rohan's life and the life of the "wire car" boy are illustrated in lines 63–78?

3. **Durban** (dûr'bən): a city in South Africa.
4. **cricket pitch** and **rugby ground:** playing fields for ballgames that originated in England.
5. **queue** (kyo͞o): a waiting line.

787

LITERARY ANALYSIS

D CULTURAL CONFLICT
Possible answer: *Rohan goes to private school and travels by car. The "wire car" boy goes to public school and has to walk.*

Lines 58–78
DISCUSSION PROMPTS

Use these prompts to help students learn more about the story's setting and how it appears to the main character:

Recall Why is Rohan's old school, Mount View Primary, becoming so crowded? ***Answer:*** *The squatter children have begun to attend the school.*

Compare What do Rohan and the "wire car" boy have in common? ***Possible answer:*** *They are about the same age and they both like wire cars.*

Synthesize Rohan's new school has smaller classes and offers more sports. In what other ways is it probably different from his old school? Why else do you think Rohan's parents might have moved him to a private school? ***Possible answer:*** *The school probably does not have many African pupils or squatter children attending. Rohan's parents might have moved him to a private school so that he would not come in contact with squatter children.*

FOR ENGLISH LEARNERS

Comprehension Support For students who may be confused, explain that the Indians referred to in the story are Asians, not American Indians or Native Americans. Point out India and South Africa on a world map and explain that both of these countries were once British colonies.

FOR ADVANCED LEARNERS/PRE–AP

Synthesize Have students think about their neighborhood—either past or current—or another neighborhood that they visit often. What are their neighbors like? Do any of the characters in the story remind them of these neighbors? Have them write a brief sketch describing their neighborhood and drawing comparisons to the setting of the story.

LITERARY ANALYSIS

Ⓔ CULTURAL CONFLICT

***Possible answer:** Rohan wants to regain his playground, while his father thinks crime will decrease if the squatters leave.*

SOCIAL STUDIES CONNECTION

Mozambique borders South Africa on the coast of the Indian Ocean. As students read about the news story that Rohan and his mother watch (lines 90–116), note that Cyclone Eline hit Mozambique in February 2000 with wind gusts of 160 mph, flooding much of the country. An estimated 800,000 people were affected all over the country by the devastating storm, but the most significant damage was in the southern part of the country. This storm caused some of the worst flooding in Mozambique's history.

Lines 90–119

DISCUSSION PROMPTS

Use these prompts to help students understand the story's rising action:

Recall What event do Rohan and his mother watch unfolding on television? ***Answer:** They watch a news report of flooding in Mozambique and the rescue of a mother and her baby, who was just born in a tree.*

Infer How does Rohan's mother respond to Rohan's question about what they will do if the cyclone comes near their home? What does her response reveal about her mixed emotions toward the squatters? ***Possible answer:** She responds that she and Rohan will be all right, but she is worried that the squatters will "get it." She wants the government to help. Her response reveals that she is concerned about the squatters but doesn't want to help them personally.*

Speculate Why might Rohan's mother be more sympathetic to the flood victims in Mozambique than to the plight of her neighbors in the squatters' camp? ***Possible answer:** The squatters are much closer to home and threaten her comfort and security. With the Mozambicans, she can be sympathetic but not have to get involved.*

"Hey, cool!" Rohan whistled. "See that, Dad?" The boy must have heard because he glanced toward them. His gaze slid across the silver hood of their car toward the trunk but didn't rise up to look at Rohan directly.

"It's a Merc[6]—like ours, Dad! What a beaut! Do you think—"

"*Don't* think about it, son! You want us to stop and ask how much he wants, don't you?"

Rohan half frowned, half smiled. How easily his father knew him!

"No way! If we start buying from these people, we'll be encouraging them! That's not the message we want them to get now, is it?"

Rohan was quiet. He couldn't argue with his dad's logic. If the squatters moved away, he and his friends could get their territory back again. Ⓔ

Ⓔ CULTURAL CONFLIC
Reread lines 83–89. Hov is Rohan's reason for wanting the squatters tc leave different from tha of his father?

Rohan returned home early from school. A precious half day. In the past he would have spent it in his hideout. Instead he flicked on the television. News. As his finger hovered over the button to switch channels, the whirr of a helicopter invaded the living room.

"Hey, Ma! Look at this!"

Ma appeared from the kitchen, her hands cupped, white and dusty with flour. On the screen, a tight human knot swung at the end of a rope above a valley swirling with muddy water.

"A South African Air Force rescue team today saved a baby from certain death just an hour after she was born in a tree. Her mother was perched in the tree over floodwaters that have devastated Mozambique. The mother and her baby daughter were among the lucky few. Many thousands of Mozambicans are still waiting to be lifted to safety from branches and rooftops. They have now been **marooned** for days by the rising water that has swallowed whole towns and villages."

SOCIAL STUDIES CONNECTION

Racial tension in South Africa and Mozambique affected the response tc the flooding.

maroon (mə-ro͞on') *v.* to leave behind in a plac from which there is little hope of escape

"Those poor people! What a place to give birth!" Ma's floury hands almost looked ready to cradle a baby.

Rohan was watching how the gale from the rotors[7] forced the leaves and branches of the tree to open like a giant flower until the helicopter began to lift. Members of the mother's family still clung desperately to the main trunk. Rohan saw both fear and determination in their eyes.

He and Ma listened to the weather report that followed. Although Cyclone Eline was over, Cyclone Gloria[8] was now whipping up storms across the Indian Ocean and heading toward Mozambique. Where would it go next? Durban was only down the coast. Rohan had seen a program about a **sect** who believed the new millennium would mark the end of the world. They were convinced that the floods were a sign that The End was beginning.

sect (sĕkt) *n.* a religious group

"What if the cyclone comes here, Ma?"

---

6. **Merc:** short for Mercedes, a brand of car.
7. **rotors** (rō'tərz): helicopter blades.
8. **Cyclone Eline, Cyclone Gloria:** tropical storms that struck in 2000.

DIFFERENTIATED INSTRUCTION

FOR ENGLISH LEARNERS

Language: Conversational English Patterns
Point out the expressions *Hey, cool!* (line 79), *What a beaut!* (line 82), and *No way!* (line 86). Explain that *beaut* is a shortened version of *beauty*. Tell students that these and similar exclamations are frequently used in dialogue. Have students use context to help them determine what each expression means.

Language: Print Cues [paired option]
Point out the three uses of italics on pages 788–789: *Don't* in line 83, *rotis* in line 120, and *Tough as ticks* in line 134. Explain that, in the first example, italics are used for emphasis in dialogue; in the second, to indicate a non-English word; and in the third, to indicate an unspoken thought. Have students work with a partner to find other examples of italicized text in the story and to determine how and why it is used.

"No, we'll be all right son. But that lot out there will get it. The government really should do something." Ma nodded in the direction of the squatters.

"Now, let me finish these *rotis*[9] for your sister!"

Ma returned to her bread making. When she had finished, she wanted Rohan to come with her to his married sister's house. He pleaded to stay behind.

"I've got homework to do, Ma! I'll be fine."

"You won't answer the door unless it's someone we know, will you?"

"No, Ma!" he chanted. Ma said the same thing every time.

Alone in the house, Rohan daydreamed at his desk. He was close enough to the window to see down the hill. What if there was so much rain that a river formed along the road below! As the water rose, people would have to abandon their shacks to climb higher up. They would be trapped between the flood below and the torrents above. In assembly they had heard the story of Noah building the ark. Perhaps it wasn't just a story after all. Perhaps the people had tried to cling on to the tops of trees as tightly as those they had seen on television.

Tough as ticks.

The phrase popped into his mind. Wasn't that what his dad had said about the squatters? Yet the one sure way to get rid of ticks was to cover them in liquid paraffin.[10] Drown them. A terrible thought. He should push it right away. **F**

F MAKE INFERENCES Note the change in Rohan's attitude toward the squatters. What has caused this change?

Rohan was about to stretch out for his math book when a figure caught his eye on the old ski slope. It was the thin wiry boy, but he wasn't pushing a car this time. He was carrying two large buckets, one on his head, the other by his side. He descended briskly down the slope and turned along the road in the opposite direction to that taken by the women who carried buckets on their heads. Rohan followed the figure until he went out of sight, then forced himself to open his book.

The bell rang just as he was getting interested in the first question. Nuisance! He hurried to the landing. If someone was standing right in front of the gate, it was possible to see who it was from the window above the stairs. He stood back, careful not to be seen himself. It was the same boy, an empty container on the ground each side of him! Didn't he know not to come to the house up here? But he was only a child, and it looked as if he just wanted some water. It would be different if it were an adult or a complete stranger. Rohan's daydream also made him feel a little guilty. He could see the boy look anxiously through the bars, his hand raised as if wondering whether to ring the bell again. Usually when the boy was pushing his wire car on the way to school, he appeared relaxed and calm.

By the time the bell rang a second time, Rohan had decided. He hurried downstairs but slowed himself as he walked outside toward the gate.

9. ***rotis*** (rō'tēs): Indian flatbreads that are cooked on a griddle.

10. **paraffin** (păr'ə-fĭn): wax.

READING SKILL

F MAKE INFERENCES

Have students record their answers in the chart from page 783. ***Possible answer:***

- ***Evidence from Story:*** *Rohan sees how the Mozambicans are affected by the floods.*
- ***My Knowledge:*** *When I see people suffering, I feel sorry for them.*
- ***Inference:*** *Rohan understands how vulnerable the squatters are and feels sorry for them.*

Lines 126–157

DISCUSSION PROMPTS

Use these prompts to help students analyze the main character and identify his internal conflict:

Restate Why does Rohan try to "push away" his daydream? ***Answer:*** *He is bothered by the terrible thought he has about getting rid of the squatters by drowning them.*

Analyze Do you think Rohan would have answered the door if it were any other squatter? ***Possible answer:*** *Rohan would not have opened the door for an adult or a squatter who was a "complete stranger" (line 151). Most likely, Rohan answered the door for the boy because they have so much in common, which makes Rohan feel as if he knows him.*

Evaluate Why do you think the author included this scene with Rohan's daydream? ***Possible answer:*** *Rohan daydreams about suffering that can occur as a result of natural disaster and human cruelty. This adds suspense to the story and explains why Rohan isn't sure if he should obey his mother or answer the door.*

FOR ENGLISH LEARNERS

Clarify: Culture

- Not all students will understand the reference to "The End" in line 116. According to biblical prophecy, the end of the world will be foretold by natural disasters such as floods. Elicit other religious stories or myths with which students might be familiar that contain devastating events such as floods or earthquakes.
- Another biblical reference is found in lines 130–131. Explain that the story of Noah is found in the book of Genesis in the Bible. According to the story, Noah was told to build an ark—a large boat—and to bring on board two of every creature in the world. Once Noah had completed the ark, God caused it to rain for 40 days and 40 nights, drowning every other living thing on Earth. Only Noah, his family, and the creatures on board the ark survived.

"What do you want?" Rohan tried not to show that he recognized the boy.

"I need water for my mother. Please." The boy held his palms out in front of him as if asking for a favor. "My mother—she's having a baby—it's bad—there's no more water. Please."

This was an emergency. Not on television but right in front of him. Still Rohan hesitated. His parents would be extremely cross that he had put himself in this situation by coming to talk to the boy. Weren't there stories of adults who used children as decoys to get people to open their gates so they could storm in? He should have stayed inside. Should he tell the boy to go next door where there would at least be an adult? But the boy had chosen to come here. Perhaps he had seen Rohan watching him from the car and knew this was his house.

"We stay there." The boy pointed in the direction of the squatter camp. "I go to school there." He pointed in the direction of Mount View Primary. He was trying to reassure Rohan that it would be OK to open the gate. He was still in his school uniform but wore a pair of dirty-blue rubber sandals. His legs were as thin as sticks.

"Isn't there a doctor with your mother?" It was such a silly question that as soon as it was out, Rohan wished he could take it back. If they could afford a doctor, they wouldn't be squatters on a bare hillside. The boy shook his head **vigorously**. If he thought it was stupid, he didn't let it show on his troubled face.

vigorously (vĭg'ər-əs-lē) *adv.* energetically

"Wait there!" Rohan returned to the house. The button for the electric gate was inside the front door. The boy waited while the wrought-iron bars slowly rolled back. **G**

G MAKE INFERENCES
Why do you think Roha[n] decides to open the gat[e]

"OK. Bring your buckets over here." Rohan pointed to the outside tap. The buckets clanked against each other as the boy jogged toward him.

"Thank you," he said quietly.

The unexpected softness in his voice had a strange effect on Rohan. It sounded so different from his own bossy tone. Suddenly he felt a little ashamed. This was the same boy whose wire cars he admired! If he were still at Mount View Primary they would probably be in the same class. They might even have been friends, and he would be learning how to make wire cars himself. Why had he spoken so arrogantly? It was really only a small favor that was being asked for. The water in the bucket gurgling and churning reminded Rohan of the water swirling beneath the Mozambican woman with her baby. *Her* rescuer had been taking a really big risk but hadn't looked big headed.[11] He had just got on with the job.

2 Targeted Passage

When both buckets were full, the boy stooped to lift one on to his head. Rohan saw his face and neck muscles strain under the weight. How would he manage to keep it balanced and carry the other bucket too?

"Wait! I'll give you a hand." Rohan's offer was out before he had time to think it through properly. If the boy was surprised, he didn't show it. All his energy seemed to be focused on his task. Rohan dashed into the kitchen to grab the spare set of keys. Ma would be away for another hour at least. He

11. **big headed:** conceited.

READING SKILL

G MAKE INFERENCES

Have students record their answers in the chart from page 783. ***Possible answer:***

- ***Evidence from Story:*** *Rohan has seen the boy before and knows the two share an interest in wire cars. The boy goes to his former school. He asks whether the boy's mother has a doctor.*
- ***My Knowledge:*** *When I have something in common with a person, I'm more likely to help him or her. When I ask stupid questions, I feel embarrassed.*
- ***Inference:*** *He is sympathetic, he is not afraid of the boy, and he is embarrassed for asking a stupid question.*

Lines 181–204

REINFORCE *KEY IDEA:* RIGHT

Discuss Rohan's parents would not want him to help the boy. Do you think he makes the **right** decision to help the boy despite his parents' wishes? ***Possible answers:***

- *Yes, he is making the right decision. The boy's mother needs water, and Rohan's parents are selfish not to help the squatters.*
- *No, he is not making the right decision. He has no idea what trouble he might get into if he helps the boy. His parents are right to protect their family by keeping the squatters out.*

DIFFERENTIATED INSTRUCTION

FOR LESS-PROFICIENT READERS

2 Targeted Passage [Lines 158–198]

This passage describes the main character's internal conflict about helping a squatter.

- What favor does the boy ask of Rohan? Why does he ask this favor?
- Why is Rohan nervous about opening the gate?
- Why does Rohan feel ashamed about the way he talks to the boy at first?
- What does Rohan offer to do?

FOR ENGLISH LEARNERS

Vocabulary: Idioms Explain that students can use context clues to unlock the meaning of some idiomatic expressions. One example is in line 197: "I'll give you a hand." Help students understand that the idiom means "I will help you." Point out that Rohan has just seen the boy struggle to lift the heavy buckets, and then he rushes into the kitchen to get the spare set of keys. Then help students use context clues to define "He caught the boy's eye" (line 209).

790 UNIT 7: HISTORY, CULTURE, AND THE AUTHOR

would be back soon, and she need never know. It was only after the gate clicked behind them that Rohan remembered the neighbors. If anyone saw him, they were bound to ask Ma what he was doing with a boy from the squatter camp. He crossed the fingers of one hand. **H**

At first Rohan said nothing. Sharing the weight of the bucket, he could feel the strain all the way up from his fingers to his left shoulder. When they reached the corner and set off down the hill, the bucket seemed to propel them forward. It was an effort to keep a steady pace. Rohan glanced at the container on the boy's head, marveling at how he kept it balanced. He caught the boy's eye.

"How do you do that? You haven't spilled a drop!"

The boy gave a **glimmer** of a smile.

"You learn."

Rohan liked the simple reply. He should ask the boy about the cars. This was his chance, before they turned into the noisy main road and reached the squatter camp.

"I've seen you with wire cars. Do you make them yourself?"

"Yes—and my brother."

"You make them together? Do you keep them all?"

"My brother—he sells them at the beach." The boy waved his free hand in the direction of the sea. "The tourists—they like them." **I**

"Your cars are better than any I've seen in the shops! Do you get lots of money for them?"

"Mmhh!" The boy made a sound something between a laugh and a snort. Rohan realized that he had asked another brainless question. Would they be staying in a shack if they got lots of money? Rohan had often seen his own father bargaining to get something cheaper from a street hawker.[12] He tried to cover his mistake.

"There's a shop in the mall where they sell wire cars. They charge a lot and yours are a hundred times better!"

"We can't go there. The guards—they don't let us in."

Rohan knew the security guards at the entrance to the mall. Some of them even greeted his parents with a little salute. Rohan had seen poor children hanging around outside. They offered to push your trolley,[13] to clean your car—anything for a few cents. Sometimes Ma gave an orange or an apple from her shopping bag to a child. Other times she would just say "No thank you" and wave a child away. Ma never gave money. . . . Rohan had never thought what it would be like to be chased away. How did the guards decide who could enter? How could the boy and his brother go and show the lady in the African Crafts shop his cars if they weren't allowed in? **J**

Rohan was quiet as they reached the main road and turned toward the squatter camp. The noise of vehicles roaring past was deafening. He never normally walked down here. Not by himself nor with anyone else. His family

H CULTURAL CONFLICT
What is Rohan's biggest fear about leaving the house to help the boy?

glimmer (glĭm′ər) *n.* a faint sign

I MAKE INFERENCES
Reread lines 208–220. What are some of the boy's **character traits**?

J CULTURAL CONFLICT
Reread lines 230–239. How are Rohan and the boy treated differently by the society in which they live?

12. **hawker:** seller.
13. **trolley:** shopping cart.

LITERARY ANALYSIS

H CULTURAL CONFLICT

Possible answer: *Rohan's biggest fear is that his mother will find out that he's helped the boy.*

READING SKILL

I MAKE INFERENCES

Have students record their answers in the chart from page 783. ***Possible answer:***

- ***Evidence from Story:*** *The boy and his brother make wire cars, which they sell to tourists.*
- ***My Knowledge:*** *People who make crafts that tourists will buy are artistic and talented. People who make and sell things are resourceful.*
- ***Inference:*** *The boy is artistic, talented, and resourceful.*

LITERARY ANALYSIS

J CULTURAL CONFLICT

Possible answer: *Rohan can go wherever he wants and his family is treated with respect by the security guards, while the boy is not even allowed into the mall.*

Extend the Discussion What kinds of discrimination exist in American society? What might you do to help eliminate such discrimination?

FOR ADVANCED LEARNERS/PRE-AP

Write Interview Questions Rohan asks the boy many questions. What additional questions would students like to ask him? Have students write a list of interview questions. Encourage them to write open-ended questions—ones that can be answered with more than just a yes or no response.

Analyze Character Distribute copies of the Open Mind transparency. Have students fill in the diagram with thoughts and feelings that the boy from the squatters' camp might be having up to this point. Suggest that they review details in the story that give clues about the boy's thoughts and personality. When they have completed their diagrams, have them draw conclusions about this character.

BEST PRACTICES TOOLKIT—Transparency
Open Mind p. D11

went everywhere by car. With all the locks down, of course. The only people who walked were poor people. His eyes were drawn to a group of young men walking toward them. They were still some distance away, but already Rohan began to feel uneasy. They were coming from the crossroads that his dad always approached on full alert. Rohan knew how his father jumped the red lights when the road was clear, especially at night. Everyone had heard stories of gangs who hijacked cars waiting for the lights to change.

The handle had begun to feel like it was cutting into his fingers. The boy must have sensed something because he signaled to Rohan to lower the bucket. For a few seconds they each stretched their fingers.

"It's too far? You want to go?" The boy was giving him a chance to change his mind. To leave and go back home. He had already helped carry the water more than half the way. He could make an excuse about the time. But the thought of running back to the house along the road on his own now worried him.

"No, it's fine. Let's go." Rohan heard a strange brightness in his own voice. He curled his fingers around the handle again. **K**

As they drew nearer the men, Rohan felt their gaze on him and suddenly his head was spinning with questions. Why on earth had he offered to help carry the water? What did he think he was doing coming down here? And he hadn't even yet entered the squatter camp itself!

"We go here." The boy's voice steadied him a little.

Rohan turned and stared up at his old ski slope. He felt the force of the young men's eyes on his back as he and the boy began to ascend the rough track. Someone behind called out something in Zulu[14] and, without turning, the boy shouted back.

The words flew so quickly into one another that Rohan didn't pick up any even though he was learning Zulu in school. They must be talking about him, but he was too embarrassed—and frightened—to ask. He could feel his heart pumping faster and told himself it was because of the stiff climb. He needed to concentrate where he put each foot. The track was full of holes and small stones. A quick glance over his shoulder revealed that the young men had also entered the squatter camp but seemed to be heading for a shack with a roof covered in old tires on the lower slope. A couple of them were still watching. He must just look ahead and control his fear. As long as he was with the boy, he was safe, surely? **L**

A bunch of small children appeared from nowhere, giggling and staring. He couldn't follow their chatter but heard the word *"iNdiya!"* The boy ignored them until a couple of children started darting back and forth in front of them, sweeping up the red dust with their feet.

"Hambani!" Rohan could hear the boy's irritation as he waved them away. But the darting and dancing continued just out of reach.

K MAKE INFERENCES
What do you think gives Rohan renewed determination to help?

L MAKE INFERENCES
Reread lines 269–278. What is Rohan afraid of

14. **Zulu** (zo͞o'lo͞o): the language of the Zulu, a Bantu people of South Africa.

READING SKILL

K MAKE INFERENCES

Have students record their answers in the chart from page 783. ***Possible answer:***

- ***Evidence from Story:*** *Rohan thinks about running home alone along the road.*
- ***My Knowledge:*** *I'd be afraid to walk home by myself in this situation.*
- ***Inference:*** *He realizes there is no easy way to turn back, so he resolves to keep going.*

BACKGROUND

South African Languages The boy and the young men speak to each other in Zulu (lines 267–268). Tell students that South Africans speak a number of languages. The native African population is divided into four basic language groups. Two other major languages —Afrikaans and English—are spoken by white South Africans. Other South Africans speak Portuguese, Italian, and various Asian languages. Discuss the challenges that can exist when several languages are spoken in a community. Have students from various language groups discuss their experience.

READING SKILL

L MAKE INFERENCES

Have students record their answers in the chart from page 783. ***Possible answer:***

- ***Evidence from Story:*** *Rohan doesn't understand Zulu, the young men are staring at him, and the track is very rough.*
- ***My Knowledge:*** *Being in unfamiliar surroundings can be frightening.*
- ***Inference:*** *He is afraid that his unfamiliar surroundings might be unsafe.*

DIFFERENTIATED INSTRUCTION

FOR ENGLISH LEARNERS

Vocabulary: Cognates [shared-language groups] Have groups scan the story for cognates and report their findings to the class. Spanish cognates on this page include

- *especially/especialmente* (line 248)
- *strange/extraño, -a* (line 258)
- *force/fuerza* (line 265)
- *ascend/ascender* (line 266)
- *concentrate/concentrarse* (line 273)
- *appeared/aparecieron* (line 279)

"Hambani-bo!" This time the boy's voice deepened to a threat, and the cluster of children pulled aside with one or two mischievous grins. Beads of sweat had begun trickling down the boy's face. With his own skin prickling with sticky heat, Rohan wondered at the wiry strength of the boy whose back, head, and bucket were still perfectly upright as they mounted the hill.

"It's that one—we stay there." The boy, at last, pointed to a structure of corrugated iron,[15] wood, and black plastic a little further up. It was not far from the old fig trees. For a moment Rohan thought he would say something about his hideout which the first squatters had pulled down. But he stopped himself. Maybe the boy had even been one of them!

As they drew nearer, they heard a woman moaning and a couple of other women's voices that sounded as if they were comforting her. The boy lowered the bucket swiftly from his head and pushed aside a plywood sheet, the door to his home.

ANALYZE VISUALS
What do you think life is like in the **setting** pictured?

15. **corrugated** (kôr'ə-gā'tĭd) **iron:** sheet iron with parallel ridges.

793

ANALYZE VISUALS

Possible answer: *Life is crowded and uncomfortable. There would be little chance for privacy, and the shacks would do little to protect people from the elements.*

Lines 243–289
DISCUSSION PROMPTS

Use these prompts to help students analyze the external conflict Rohan faces in the squatters' camp:

Connect Have you ever been in an unfamiliar place that made you feel as afraid as Rohan does near the squatters' camp? In what way does this help you understand Rohan's feelings? *Students should describe unfamiliar places that have made them feel afraid and explain how it is similar to Rohan's situation.*

Infer The Zulu words of the boy and the young men are not translated for the reader. What might they be saying to each other? ***Possible answer:*** *The young men may be telling the boy he shouldn't have brought Rohan to the camp, and the boy may be explaining that Rohan is helping him carry water.*

Speculate Rohan gains a new perspective from carrying a heavy bucket and walking along the road. What new perspective might the boy from the squatters' camp gain from his interaction with Rohan? ***Possible answer:*** *He may realize that the homeowners can be compassionate and respectful.*

Lines 292–294
REINFORCE *KEY IDEA:* RIGHT

Discuss Rohan realizes that the boy might have been one of the squatters who pulled down his hideout. What feelings do you think Rohan experiences about this? Do you think he makes the **right** choice not to mention this incident to the boy? *Students may think that although Rohan misses his hideout, he understands that the squatters had no other materials to build their shelters. They may say that Rohan makes the right choice in not mentioning the hideout because complaining about losing a hideout when the squatters have lost so much would be insensitive.*

FOR ENGLISH LEARNERS

Vocabulary: Phrasal Verbs [mixed-readiness pairs] Explain that a phrasal verb is a verb combined with a preposition. Point out two phrasal verbs on this page: *pulled aside* (line 286), which means "parted" or "separated," and *pulled down* (line 293), which means "destroyed." Tell students that several phrasal verbs contain the word *pull*. Share the following list of phrasal verbs and their meanings, and challenge students to work with a more fluent partner to write sentences. They may use various tenses of the verbs in their sentences.

- *pull in,* "arrive"
- *pull off,* "succeed"
- *pull over,* "stop at the side of the road"
- *pull through,* "recover"
- *pull out,* "leave"

Rohan wasn't sure what to do. He knew he couldn't follow. The sounds from within scared him. The moans were rapid and painful. . . .

Rohan folded his arms tightly, trying not to show how awkward he felt. The little children were still watching but keeping their distance. They could probably also hear the cries. It would be hard to keep anything private here. The only other people nearby were two gray-haired men sitting on boxes a little lower down the hill. One of them was bent over an old-fashioned sewing machine placed on a metal drum, a makeshift table. Normally Rohan would have been very curious to see what he was stitching, but now he was just grateful that both men were **engrossed** in talking and didn't seem interested in him.

engross (ĕn-grōs') *v.* to completely occupy

He turned to look up the hill—toward his house and the others at the top protected by their walls with wires, spikes, and broken bottles. When he had hidden in his hideout down here, he had always loved the feeling of being safe yet almost in his own separate little country. But that had been a game and he could just hop over the wall to return to the other side. Surrounded now by homes made out of scraps and other people's leftovers, this place seemed a complete world away from the houses on the hill. In fact, how was he going to get home? If he didn't leave soon, Ma would be back before him. Would the boy at least take him part of the way through the squatter camp? He needed him to come outside so that he could ask him.

(3) **Targeted Passage**

"What do you want here?"

Rohan spun around. A man with half-closed eyes and his head tilted to one side stood with his hands on his hips, surveying Rohan from head to foot. His gaze lingered for a moment on Rohan's watch.

"I . . . I brought water with . . . with . . ." Rohan stammered. He hadn't asked the boy his name! Panic-stricken, he pointed to the door of the shack. The man stepped forward, and Rohan stumbled back against the wall of corrugated iron. The clattering brought the boy to the door. The man immediately switched into loud, fast Zulu. The boy spoke quietly at first, but when the man's voice didn't calm down, the boy's began to rise too. Even when he pointed to the bucket and Rohan, the man's face remained scornful. Rohan was fully expecting to be grabbed when a sharp baby's cry interrupted the argument. The boy's face lit up, and the man suddenly fell silent. Rohan's heart thumped wildly as the man's eyes mocked him before he turned and walked away. (M)

(M) **CULTURAL CONFLICT** Why do you think the man is scornful and mocks Rohan with his eyes?

Rohan folded his arms tightly, trying not to shake. Before he could say anything, a lady appeared behind the boy, placing a hand on his shoulder.

"You have a little sister!" She smiled at the boy and then at Rohan. She looked friendly but tired. Her cheeks shone as if she too had been perspiring. It was obviously hard work helping to deliver a baby.

"Tell your mother thank you for the water. You really helped us today."

Rohan managed to smile back.

"It's OK." His voice came out strangely small.

"Solani will take you back now—before it gets dark."

Rohan felt a weight lifting. He did not need to ask.

LITERARY ANALYSIS

(M) CULTURAL CONFLICT

Possible answer: *The man might resent Rohan's privileged lifestyle, and he doesn't like Rohan's being in the squatters' camp.*

Extend the Discussion In what way does the man's behavior resemble that of Rohan's father?

Lines 335–342

REINFORCE *KEY IDEA:* RIGHT

Discuss How does Rohan know for sure that he made the **right** decision in helping Solani?

Possible answer: *He finds out that the baby was born safely. The woman who helped Solani's mother deliver the baby thanks him for the water. She also repays his kindness by sending Solani to walk him home.*

DIFFERENTIATED INSTRUCTION

FOR LESS–PROFICIENT READERS

(3) **Targeted Passage [Lines 309–338]**

This passage shows the climax of the story and the development of the main character.

- What does Rohan see as he looks up the hill?
- What does Rohan worry about?
- Who confronts Rohan? What is this person's attitude toward Rohan?
- What happens to end the tense situation between Rohan and the man?

FOR ENGLISH LEARNERS

Vocabulary: Suffixes Point out these words: *immediately* (line 326), *quietly* (line 327), *wildly* (line 331), *tightly* (line 333), *suspiciously* (line 352), *rapidly* (lines 364–365). Explain that adding *-ly* to an adjective creates an adverb. Challenge students to create new words by adding *-ly* to other adjectives. Then use Common Suffixes to help them understand other suffixes and words that contain them.

 **BEST PRACTICES TOOLKIT—Transparency**
Common Suffixes p. E15

The sun was getting lower and made long rodlike shadows leap beside them as they scrambled down the slope. Knowing the boy's name made Rohan feel a little easier, and he wondered why he hadn't asked him earlier. He told Solani his own, and the next thing he was telling him about riding on garbage can lids down the ski slope. Solani grinned.

"It's good! But this place—it's a road now. We can't do it. The people will be angry if we knock someone down."

Rohan understood that. But what he didn't understand was why the man with scornful eyes had been so angry with him. And why had those other young men looked at him so suspiciously? He decided to ask Solani.

"They don't know you. Sometimes people come and attack us. So if a stranger comes, they must always check first."

When they reached the road, neither spoke. The hometime traffic would have drowned their voices anyway. Rohan thought about what Solani had said about him being a stranger. Surely they knew that he was from one of the houses on top of the hill. The houses that also did not welcome strangers. Like the squatters. **N**

They parted at the top of the hill. Rohan was anxious to reach the house before his mother returned, and Solani was eager to see his baby sister. Opening the electronic gates, Rohan was relieved that his mother's car was neither in the yard nor the garage. He dashed upstairs to his room and peered out of the window over to the squatter camp. The evening was falling very rapidly. His mother would be home any minute—and his dad. Neither liked to drive in the dark if they could help it.

ANALYZE VISUALS
Note the boy's expression and body language. What can you **infer** about his mood?

N CULTURAL CONFLICT
What do Rohan's neighborhood and the squatters' camp have in common?

ANALYZE VISUALS

Students may infer that the boy is feeling solemn and shy.

About the Art Steve McCurry (born 1950), the photographer of this boy in Mauritania, has captured images of war and civil conflict in many countries around the world. These include Iran, Iraq, the Philippines, Lebanon, Cambodia, the former Yugoslavia, and Afghanistan. About his work, he says, "Most of my images are grounded in people. I look for the unguarded moment, the essential soul peeking out, experience etched on a person's face. I try to convey what it is like to be that person, a person caught in a broader landscape, that you could call the human condition."

LITERARY ANALYSIS

N CULTURAL CONFLICT

Possible answer: *Both communities are fearful of strangers.*

FOR LESS-PROFICIENT READERS

Reading Skill Follow-Up: Make Inferences
[paired option] Remind students that they make inferences based on two things: what they read in the story and what they know. Have pairs reread lines 309–325 and use the graphic organizer to help them determine why Rohan didn't think earlier to introduce himself and ask Solani for his name.

Evidence from Story	*My Knowledge*	*Inference*
From the time he offered to help Solani, Rohan has been nervous about his safety and his parents finding out about the incident.	*Being nervous can keep someone from reaching out to another person. A person might not think to learn a stranger's name.*	*Although he was willing to help Solani carry the water, Rohan thought of him as a stranger.*

Rohan fixed his eyes on the deep crimson scar, hoping to see Solani climbing the slope. How strange to think that he had been there himself less than half an hour ago. In that other world. Yes! There was Solani! A tiny, wiry figure **bounding** up the hill. Not **hampered** this time with a container of water on his head. Rohan watched Solani weave through other figures traveling more slowly until three quarters of the way up the hill, he darted off and disappeared into the darkening shadow that was his home.

bound (bound) *v.* to le[ap] forward

hamper (hăm′pər) *v.* to prevent the free movement of

Rohan surprised his parents by joining them for the eight o'clock news. The story about the rescue of mother and baby from the floods in Mozambique was repeated.

"Sophia Pedro and her baby daughter Rositha were among the lucky few. Many thousands of Mozambicans are still waiting to be lifted to safety. . . ."

This time the reporter added their names. Rohan observed the mother more closely. Had she also cried and moaned like Solani's mother? With the roaring waters underneath, how many people had heard her? **O**

"It's nice to see these South African soldiers doing some good," said Ma when the news was finished.

Rohan wished he could say what he too had done that afternoon. But he feared the storm that it would let loose and went upstairs to his bedroom. Before slipping between his sheets, he peered out once again through the bars at the hill swallowed up by the night. He thought he saw a light still flickering in Solani's home and wondered how many people were tucked inside the sheets of iron, plastic, and wood. He prayed that Cyclone Gloria would keep well away.

Next morning, the glint of metal beside the gate caught his eye from the front door. His dad was reversing the car out of the garage. Rohan ran across the drive. There, just inside the gate, was a wire car. A small, perfect Merc! Who could it be from, except Solani? He must have slipped it through the bars of the gate in the early morning. Quickly Rohan pushed it behind a cluster of scarlet gladioli. If his parents saw it, they would want to know from where it had come. They would discover he had gone out of bounds. . . . Well, so had Solani! Each of them had taken a risk. He needed time to think. In the meantime, the car would have to be his secret. Their secret. His and Solani's.

O MAKE INFERENCES
Why has Rohan becom[e] more interested in the news?

④ Targeted Passage

READING SKILL

O MAKE INFERENCES

Have students record their answers in the chart from page 783. ***Possible answer:***

- ***Evidence from Story:*** *Rohan has experienced the birth of Solani's sister under difficult circumstances.*
- ***My Knowledge:*** *When people feel connected to others, they are more interested in what happens to them.*
- ***Inference:*** *Rohan now sees the mother and baby on the news as real people that he cares about.*

SELECTION WRAP-UP

REFLECT Rohan's father distrusts the squatters, and the people in the camp distrust Rohan. Throughout the course of the story, however, Rohan and Solani come to trust each other. Ask students if they think the two boys will be able to bridge the distrust between their families and communities. Or, is the prejudice and fear too deeply entrenched?

★ CRITIQUE Have students evaluate the author's decision to tell the story from Rohan's point of view. How would the story have been different if it were told from another point of view, such as Solani's or Rohan's father's?

DIFFERENTIATED INSTRUCTION

FOR LESS-PROFICIENT READERS

④ Targeted Passage [Lines 374–400]

This passage contains the resolution of the story.

- What does Rohan think about as he watches the news with his parents?
- Does Rohan tell his parents what he has done? Why or why not?
- What does Rohan find the next morning?
- Why does he decide to keep Solani's gift a secret?

FOR ADVANCED LEARNERS/PRE-AP

Character Map [paired option] Distribute copies of the Character Map. Check students' understanding of the journey Rohan has made from the beginning to the end of the story by having them complete the map. Then have them discuss with a partner whether or not they identify with Rohan. Would they have reacted similarly to the events of the story?

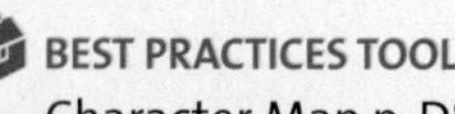
BEST PRACTICES TOOLKIT—Transparency
Character Map p. D8

796 UNIT 7: HISTORY, CULTURE, AND THE AUTHOR

After Reading

Comprehension

1. **Recall** Why doesn't Rohan go to his hideout anymore?
2. **Recall** Where has Rohan seen Solani before Solani comes to his house?
3. **Represent** Make a sketch showing Rohan's house and the squatters' camp. Think about what these places look like and where they are in relation to one another. Use descriptions in the story to guide you.

Literary Analysis

4. **Make Inferences About Characters** Review your chart of inferences about the characters and their culture. Why does Rohan think it's the **right** decision to help Solani? Name three reasons why these two boys might be drawn together.
5. **Analyze Cultural Conflict** What causes the residents of Mount View to discriminate against the squatters? Consider what you know about the history and culture of South Africa as well as events in the story's plot. Record your response in a diagram like the one shown.

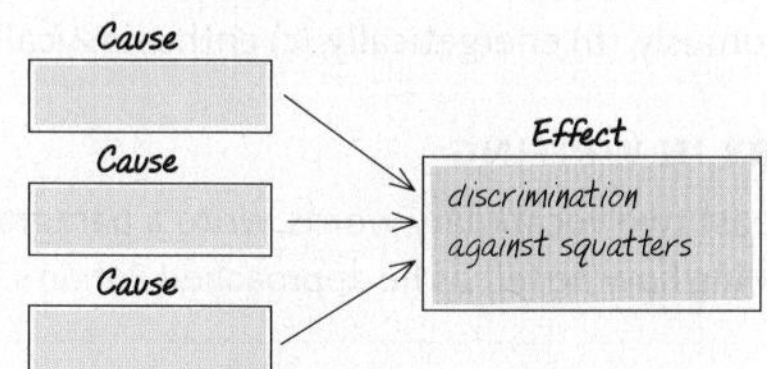

6. **Evaluate Attitudes** Describe the attitudes of Rohan's mother and father toward the squatters. Do you think they are prejudiced against Africans? Then consider Rohan's experience in the squatters' camp. Do you think the Africans are prejudiced against him? Explain your responses, citing evidence from the story.
7. **Make Judgments** Who do you think took the greater risk by going out of bounds—Rohan or Solani? Explain your answer.
8. **Predict** Do you think that Rohan and Solani will be able to maintain their friendship? Why or why not?

Extension and Challenge

9. **Literary Criticism** As a child, Beverley Naidoo didn't notice that she lived in an unfair society. "It was like being brought up to be a horse with blinkers," she has said. "Luckily when I left school, I met people who challenged me . . . and I was able to take off the blinkers." How do Rohan's experiences in "Out of Bounds" reflect the author's background?
10. **SOCIAL STUDIES CONNECTION** Research Nelson Mandela's role in ending the system of apartheid in South Africa. Why is he considered an inspirational leader?

RESEARCH LINKS
For more on Nelson Mandela, visit the **Research Center** at **ClassZone.com.**

Nelson Mandela

Practice and Apply

After Reading

For additional support of postreading questions, use these copy masters:

RESOURCE MANAGER—Copy Masters

Reading Check p. 60 (to check understanding of the selection)

Cultural Conflict p. 53 (for practice of literary analysis standards focus)

Question Support p. 61 (After Reading questions adapted for English learners and less-proficient readers)

Additional selection questions are provided for teachers on page 47.

ANSWERS

Comprehension

1. *Squatters have taken over the land where Rohan's hideout used to be.*
2. *Rohan has seen Solani in the street with his wire cars.*
3. *Sketches should show the solidity of Rohan's house and the temporary nature of the camp. They should also show Rohan's house on top of the hill and the camp below it.*

Literary Analysis

Possible answers:

4. **STANDARDS FOCUS Make Inferences** *Rohan has seen Solani before, and Solani seems to genuinely need help. The boys might be drawn together because they are the same age, and if Rohan were still attending the local school, they probably would have been in the same class. They are also both interested in wire cars.*
5. **STANDARDS FOCUS Cultural Conflict** *Causes of discrimination: legacy of apartheid—Indians and Africans mostly live separately; high crime rates—residents worry that having poor people nearby will increase crime; neighborhood crimes—residents think the squatters' camp is the source of these crimes; competition for resources—residents resent the squatters asking for water.*
6. *Rohan's parents display signs of prejudice toward the squatters, although his mother has some sympathy for the poor and seems to have good intentions. (She gives them water and thinks something should be done to help them.) His father, however, expresses no sympathy. He builds the garden wall higher and discourages his son from helping the poor. The squatters also show signs of prejudice against Rohan when they make negative assumptions about him.*
7. *Some students might say Rohan took the greater risk, because he has been taught that poor people will attack or rob him. Others may say Solani took the bigger risk by entering an area where he was unwelcome and where he may have been falsely accused of a crime.*
8. *Students might say that class differences would make maintaining a friendship difficult for the boys.*

Extension and Challenge

9. *Students should look at the ways in which Rohan's journey "takes off the blinkers" and lets him see that he lives in an unfair society.*
10. **SOCIAL STUDIES CONNECTION** *Encourage students to learn about Mandela's activities before his imprisonment and how he became a force for change in South Africa.*

ANSWERS

Vocabulary in Context

VOCABULARY PRACTICE

1. *(d) stroll*
2. *(b) distract*
3. *(d) excess*
4. *(b) free*
5. *(a) maroon*
6. *(d) everyone*
7. *(b) lead*
8. *(d) weakly*

RESOURCE MANAGER—Copy Master
Vocabulary Practice p. 58

VOCABULARY IN WRITING

Give students sentence frames such as the following to help them write from Solani's point of view and use vocabulary words in their sentences.

My family's health is ________ by our lack of clean water. *(hampered)*

I feel ________ in the squatters' camp. *(marooned)*

VOCABULARY STRATEGY: HOMOGRAPHS

(also an EL language objective)

Challenge students to write another sentence that uses a different definition for each word.

Possible answers:

1. *group*
2. *herded*
3. *wrinkled*
4. *circular openings in the centers of the irises*
5. *cattle*

RESOURCE MANAGER—Copy Master
Vocabulary Strategy p. 59

Vocabulary Center at **ClassZone.com**
Additional Vocabulary Activities

Vocabulary in Context

VOCABULARY PRACTICE

For each item, choose the word that differs most in meaning from the other words. Refer to a dictionary if you need help.

1. (a) bound, (b) leap, (c) spring, (d) stroll
2. (a) engross, (b) distract, (c) involve, (d) interest
3. (a) glimmer, (b) trace, (c) fraction, (d) excess
4. (a) hamper, (b) free, (c) prevent, (d) hinder
5. (a) maroon, (b) rescue, (c) save, (d) retrieve
6. (a) sect, (b) denomination, (c) group, (d) everyone
7. (a) straggle, (b) lead, (c) scatter, (d) dawdle
8. (a) vigorously, (b) energetically, (c) enthusiastically, (d) weakly

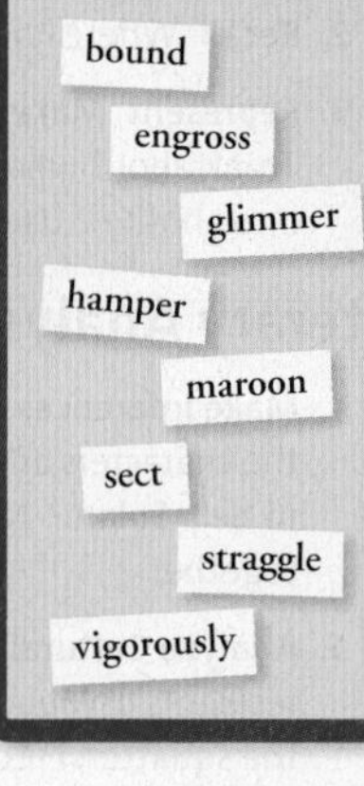

bound
engross
glimmer
hamper
maroon
sect
straggle
vigorously

VOCABULARY IN WRITING

Using at least two vocabulary words, write a paragraph from Solani's point of view telling how he felt as he approached Rohan's house to ask for water.

EXAMPLE SENTENCE

*I was afraid, but I couldn't let that **hamper** me because my mother needed water.*

VOCABULARY STRATEGY: HOMOGRAPHS

Homographs are words that look the same but have different meanings, origins, and sometimes pronunciations. For example, in the phrase "out of bounds," *bounds* means "boundaries." However, in the sentence "Solani bounds up the hill," *bounds* means "springs forward."

If a familiar-looking word does not make sense to you, look at the words around it for context clues to other possible meanings. For further help, check a dictionary.

PRACTICE Use context clues to define the boldfaced words. Then check your definitions in a dictionary and note the word's origin.

1. She said goodbye to him in front of a **bank** of elevators.
2. The goatherd **drove** his flock up the hill.
3. Great-Grandma's **lined** face shows her age.
4. Your **pupils** grow tiny when you step into bright sunlight.
5. Cowhands herded longhorn **steers** into a corral.

VOCABULARY PRACTICE
For more practice, go to the **Vocabulary Center** at **ClassZone.com.**

DIFFERENTIATED INSTRUCTION

FOR ENGLISH LEARNERS

Vocabulary Practice [mixed-readiness pairs] Encourage students having trouble with the exercise to review the definitions and context of the words in the selections. Pair English learners with fluent speakers to identify the word that differs most in meaning from the others in each set.

FOR ADVANCED LEARNERS/PRE–AP

Vocabulary Strategy Have students find more examples of homographs in the selection. Then have them compare their lists to find out who identified the most homographs. Remind them to check their words in a dictionary to make sure each homograph pair has two separate entries.

eading-Writing Connection

Demonstrate your understanding of "Out of Bounds" by responding to these prompts. Then complete the **Grammar and Writing** exercise.

WRITING PROMPTS	SELF-CHECK
A. Short Response: Write a Journal Entry How has reading this story affected your beliefs about whether it's **right** to go "out of bounds" to help another person? Write a **one-paragraph journal entry** explaining how the story changed your thinking or confirmed your beliefs.	***A well-written entry will . . .*** • state your original ideas about whether it's ever good to go out of bounds • use examples from the story to explain why your thinking changed or stayed the same
B. Extended Response: Create a Community Plan How could the residents of Mount View improve their relationship with the squatters? Write a **two- or three-paragraph plan** to help the two communities better understand one another.	***A strong plan will . . .*** • reflect an understanding of the relationship between the communities in the story • present several ideas to bring the two communities together

AMMAR AND WRITING

USE COLONS CORRECTLY A **colon** should be placed after a formal greeting in a business letter (*To Whom It May Concern:*) and before a list of items (*I had the following foods for breakfast: eggs, toast, and cereal*). When using a colon to introduce a list, avoid placing it directly after a verb or a preposition. Instead, insert the colon after a noun or after the words *the following*.

Original: The squatters suffer from: poverty, homelessness, and a lack of water.

Revised: The squatters suffer from the following: poverty, homelessness, and a lack of water. (*Inserting* the following *after the preposition* from *makes use of the colon correct.*)

PRACTICE Rewrite the following letter, correcting the colon errors.

Dear Mount View residents
To improve our relationship with the squatters, we are recommending that residents provide squatters with: food, water, and blankets. Also, we request that these professionals offer aid to the squatters, doctors, nurses, and teachers. From the walls, please remove: wire, spikes, and broken glass.

*For more help with using colons correctly, see page R50 in the **Grammar Handbook**.*

DIFFERENTIATED INSTRUCTION

FOR LESS–PROFICIENT WRITERS

For Prompt A:

1. Have students write a topic sentence for the paragraph based on the question.
2. Next, have them write a sentence for each of the original ideas they listed.
3. Then have them write at least one sentence for each original idea, explaining whether their ideas have changed.
4. Finally, have them write sentences that explain the way the examples from the story changed or confirmed their beliefs.

For Prompt B:

Students may organize their plans in this way:

- **First paragraph:** Students should write a thesis statement and describe the most serious problems between the residents of Mount View and the squatters' community.
- **Second paragraph:** Students should propose two or three solutions.
- **Third paragraph:** Students should conclude with a description of how their plan will bring the two communities together.

Reading-Writing Connection

WRITING PROMPTS

- For **Prompt A,** have students write one or two of their original ideas. Then have them provide at least two examples from the story and explain the way they affected their beliefs.
- For **Prompt B,** have students list two or three problems and then list possible solutions.

For writing support, see

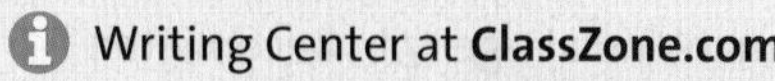
Writing Center at **ClassZone.com**

GRAMMAR AND WRITING

Remind students that a formal letter is often addressed to an organization or to a person with whom the writer does not have a personal relationship. A friendly letter, in contrast, is usually addressed to a friend or relative, and a comma is used after the greeting (for example, *Dear Rohan,*).

Possible answer:

Dear Mount View residents:

To improve our relationship with the squatters, we are recommending that residents provide squatters with food, water, and blankets. Also, we request that these professionals offer aid to the squatters: doctors, nurses, and teachers. From the walls, please remove the following: wire, spikes, and broken glass.

RESOURCE MANAGER—Copy Master
Use Colons Correctly p. 62

Assess and Reteach

Assess

RESOURCE MANAGER—Copy Masters
Selection Tests A, B/C pp. 63–64, 65–66

Test Generator CD

Reteach

STANDARDS LESSON FILE
Literature Lesson 9: Setting and Its Roles
Reading Lesson 8: Making Inferences
Vocabulary Lesson 20: Homonyms and Homographs

Focus and Motivate

OBJECTIVES

Literary Analysis
- explore the key idea of **folk heroes**
- identify and analyze characteristics of a tall tale
- read a tall tale

Reading
- visualize

SUMMARY

Pecos Bill is reared by coyotes in Texas until he joins humankind at age 17 to become the greatest cowboy ever. Because of his superhuman strength and courage, Bill becomes the leader of the Hell's Gate Gang and controls the entire Southwest. During a drought, he ropes a cyclone and wrings water from it. Later, he marries a tough cowgirl, Slue-foot Sue, who is bucked into the sky by Bill's horse on their wedding day. Bill tries to lasso her but is pulled up into the sky too. They both end up on the moon, where they now live with their family.

What is a FOLK HERO?

Discuss the question. To help students better understand the ***KEY IDEA,*** have them name real people they consider heroes and explain what qualities make them heroic. List these qualities on the board, and then have students come up with a class definition of *hero*. Discuss how this definition is similar to and different from the description of **folk heroes** on page 800. Then have students work on the ***DISCUSS*** activity.

Before Reading

Pecos Bill

Tall Tale Retold by Mary Pope Osborne

What is a FOLK HERO?

KEY IDEA A steel-driving man who defeats a machine through hard work and perseverance. An outlaw who steals from the rich to give to the poor. A cowgirl who can circle the moon. Every culture has its **folk heroes,** characters whose courage, generosity, or accomplishments inspire ordinary people. Some folk heroes are real people or are based on the lives of real people; others are invented to symbolize the values of a particular culture. In the tall tale you are about to read, you will meet a fictional American folk hero known for his strength and bravery.

DISCUSS Imagine you were on a committee to select a folk hero to speak at your school. In small groups, choose a real person or a character you've read about who would inspire you and your classmates. What qualities does this person possess that make him or her a folk hero? What topics would you like to see this person address at your school?

800

Selection Resources

RESOURCE MANAGER UNIT 7

Plan and Teach pp. 67–74

Literary Analysis
Summary pp. 75†*, 76‡*
Tall Tale pp. 77, 78†*
Question Support p. 82*

Reading
Visualize pp. 79, 80†*
Reading Check p. 81
Reading Fluency p. 83

Assessment
Selection Tests A, B/C pp. 85*, 87*
Test Generator CD

BEST PRACTICES TOOLKIT
Differentiated Instruction pp. 31–38*
Scaffolding Instruction pp. 43–46*
Graphic Organizers/Strategies
New Word Analysis • T Chart

Reading Support
Audio Anthology CD*

Technology
Literature Center at **ClassZone.com**
Write*Smart* CD

* Resources for Differentiation † Also in Spanish ‡ In Haitian Creole and Vietnamese

ERARY ANALYSIS: TALL TALE

Folk heroes often appear in **tall tales,** which are humorous stories about impossible events. Many of these stories were originally passed down from generation to generation by being told out loud. Some of them even started off with a kernel of truth, but as you'll see, they aren't exactly realistic. Tall tales have these characteristics:

- The hero or heroine is often larger than life, which means he or she is bigger, louder, stronger, or stranger than any real person could be.
- Problems are solved in humorous ways.
- **Hyperbole,** or exaggeration, is used to emphasize the main character's qualities and create humor.

As you read, note how these characteristics apply to "Pecos Bill."

ADING STRATEGY: VISUALIZE

Tall tales are funny and action-packed. To enjoy them fully, it helps to **visualize,** or picture in your mind, the incredible events in the story as you read about them. To visualize, focus on descriptions that appeal to your senses, especially those of sight, sound, and touch. Use these sensory details to form a mental picture of the characters and action. As you read, use a chart like the one shown to note descriptive words and phrases that help you visualize the tall tale.

Character or Event	Descriptive Words or Phrases
Little Bill falls out of the wagon.	"sat there in the dirt" "rattle off in a cloud of dust"

Author Online

Finding Her Way
After graduating from college, Mary Pope Osborne decided to explore the world. She traveled around Europe, the Middle East, and southern Asia. She slept outdoors and bathed in rivers in Iraq, Afghanistan, and India. And, she says, she was "terrified" almost the whole time. She survived an earthquake and a riot, only to end up sick in a hospital, all alone and far from home. While she rested, she read J. R. R. Tolkien's *The Lord of the Rings* series. She identified with Tolkien's hero, Frodo, whose dangerous journey seemed to resemble her own. Says Osborne, "Ultimately Frodo's courage and powers of endurance became mine," which helped her recover from her illness and make her way home. Eventually, she began writing children's stories for fun and discovered her new career.

Mary Pope Osborne
born 1949

MORE ABOUT THE AUTHOR
For more on Mary Pope Osborne, visit the **Literature Center** at **ClassZone.com.**

Background

Tall Tales and the American Frontier
Tall tales are often set on the American frontier—large parts of the West and Southwest that had small populations in the 19th century. Life on the frontier was often adventurous and free-spirited, and sharing stories became an important social activity. Tall tales may have started as bragging contests held by ranch hands on the frontier. As they tried to outdo each other, they exaggerated stories about their abilities more and more. The achievements described in tall tales often center around the characteristics of courage, determination, and cleverness, all of which were needed to survive on the frontier.

DIFFERENTIATED INSTRUCTION

FOR ALL STUDENTS

Expert Groups Encourage individual students or groups to choose one of the following topics on which to become experts. Have students share their findings with the class.

- coyotes
- western Texas
- folk tales from different cultures

FOR LESS–PROFICIENT READERS

In combination with the *Audio Anthology CD,* use one or more Targeted Passages (pp. 804, 806, 808) to ensure that students focus on key events, concepts, and skills.

FOR ENGLISH LEARNERS

Prereading For prereading instruction for English learners, see

BEST PRACTICES TOOLKIT
Scaffolding Reading Instruction pp. 43–46

Teach

STANDARDS FOCUS

LITERARY ANALYSIS

● TALL TALE

Read this passage aloud and ask students which details indicate a tall tale:

> Mary Sue, the greatest vet in Texas, needed to examine a sick cat named Harry, but Harry had climbed into the tallest tree in town and refused to budge. Luckily, Mary Sue was as tall as that tree and could look Harry square in the eyes. Using cat talk, she convinced him to calm down and then gently reached out and grabbed him. She walked the 50 miles back to her clinic petting Harry, who purred and fell asleep in her hand.

Possible answer: *Mary Sue's height makes her larger than life. Her ability to talk "cat" and her 50-mile walk to and from the clinic are examples of hyperbole. The way the problem is solved is both strange and humorous—Mary Sue simply looks the cat in the eye and reasons with it before plucking it from the tree.*

CHECK UNDERSTANDING Ask students to explain in their own words what makes a story a tall tale.

READING STRATEGY

■ VISUALIZE

Read aloud the **Author Online** information on page 801 and ask students what words or phrases help them visualize Osborne's travels. ***Possible answer:*** *"slept outdoors," "bathed in rivers," "an earthquake and a riot," "in a hospital, all alone," "dangerous journey"*

CHECK UNDERSTANDING Ask students to identify words and phrases in the tall tale on this page that help them visualize Mary Sue and her actions.

RESOURCE MANAGER—Copy Master
Visualize p. 79 (for student use while reading the selection)

Practice and Apply

ANALYZE VISUALS

Students may mention these humorous details:

- *the fierce snake wrapped around Bill's arm*
- *the horse riding on top of Bill*
- *Bill riding a mountain lion, complete with a saddle*

LITERARY ANALYSIS

Ⓐ TALL TALE

Possible answer: *Bill's toughness is clearly exaggerated—he "teethed on horseshoes" and "played with grizzly bears" (line 5). His father's need for space and his impulsiveness are also exaggerated—he feels crowded when new neighbors settle 50 miles away, and so the family packs up and moves west before sundown.*

Extend the Discussion Why do you think the author might have chosen to begin the story with such exaggerations? What do they tell you about the characters and the plot?

READING STRATEGY

Ⓑ VISUALIZE

Have students record their answers in the chart from page 801. ***Possible answer:***

Character or Event	*Descriptive Words or Phrases*
Bill and his brothers fight and Bill falls from the wagon.	*"clattered," "desolate land," "crushing heat," "wallop," "going at one another tooth and nail," "kerplop," "sun-scorched desert"*

Lines 4–19

REINFORCE *KEY IDEA:* FOLK HEROES

Discuss What qualities of a **folk hero** does baby Bill already display? ***Possible answer:*** *Folk heroes often display larger-than-life qualities. Baby Bill is extraordinarily strong: he uses horseshoes for teething rings, plays with grizzly bears, and beats up his older brothers. He is also extraordinarily brave: he doesn't cry when he falls out of the wagon or when his family leaves him all alone in the desert.*

RETOLD BY MARY POPE OSBORNE

Ask any coyote near the Pecos River in western Texas who was the best cowboy who ever lived, and he'll throw back his head and howl, "Ah-hooo!" If you didn't know already, that's coyote language for *Pecos Bill.*

When Pecos Bill was a little baby, he was as tough as a pine knot. He teethed on horseshoes instead of teething rings and played with grizzly bears instead of teddy bears. He could have grown up just fine in the untamed land of eastern Texas. But one day his pappy ran in from the fields, hollering, "Pack up, Ma! Neighbors movin' in fifty miles away! It's gettin' too crowded!"

Before sundown Bill's folks loaded their fifteen kids and all their belongings into their covered wagon and started west. Ⓐ

As they clattered across the desolate land of western Texas, the crushing heat nearly drove them all crazy. Baby Bill got so hot and cross that he began to wallop[1] his big brothers. Pretty soon all fifteen kids were going at one another tooth and nail.[2] Before they turned each other into catfish bait, Bill fell out of the wagon and landed *kerplop* on the sun-scorched desert. Ⓑ

The others were so busy fighting that they didn't even notice the baby was missing until it was too late to do anything about it.

Well, tough little Bill just sat there in the dirt, watching his family rattle off in a cloud of dust, until an old coyote walked over and sniffed him.

"Goo-goo!" Bill said.

Now it's an amazing coincidence, but "Goo-goo" happens to mean something similar to "Glad to meet you" in coyote language. Naturally the old coyote figured he'd come across one of his own kind. He gave Bill a big lick and picked him up by the scruff of the neck and carried him home to his den.

ANALYZE VISUALS
What **details** make this illustration humorous?

Ⓐ TALL TALE
Which of young Bill's an his father's qualities are exaggerated?

Ⓑ VISUALIZE
Reread lines 11–15. What words and phrases help you picture the scene?

1. **wallop** (wŏl′ əp): to beat up.
2. **tooth and nail:** very fiercely.

Illustrations by Michael McCur

DIFFERENTIATED INSTRUCTION

FOR ENGLISH LEARNERS

Key Academic Vocabulary Have students use New Word Analysis to study these words from the story: *coincidence* (line 21), *ignorant* (line 58), *appreciate* (line 62), *revealed* (line 111), *creating* (line 139), *area* (line 139).

 **BEST PRACTICES TOOLKIT—Transparency** New Word Analysis p. E8

Options for Reading Read aloud the first three paragraphs of the selection. Discuss with students what they learn about Pecos Bill and the setting. Then have students follow along as they listen to the rest of the selection on the *Audio Anthology CD.* Pause the CD frequently to enable students to identify details of plot, setting, and character, as well as key characteristics of tall tales.

BACKGROUND

Cowboy History Spanish ranchers in Mexico employed the first cowboys during the 16th century. Because the ranches covered vast areas of land, the ranchers could let their cattle roam. They trained local Native Americans to herd the cattle on the open range. These early cowboys were called *vaqueros,* after *vaca,* Spanish for "cow."

Cattle Drives and "Pecos Bill" Before railroads reached the Texas rangelands, trail drives were the best way to move cattle to railroad stations for transport to markets in other parts of the United States. Cowboys herded millions of longhorn cattle over dusty trails from the mid-1860s to the mid-1880s. Edward O'Reilly, inspired by the stories of this rugged trail life and by tales of Paul Bunyan—another folk hero—wrote the first Pecos Bill tall tale in 1923. Other writers made more and more imaginative additions to O'Reilly's original tale.

FOR ENGLISH LEARNERS

Vocabulary: Dialect Students may not be familiar with the dialect used in this story. Share or elicit the meanings of these words and help students use them in original sentences. Then have students note other instances of dialect in the story and write an original sentence using each word or phrase.

- *hollering* (line 7), "yelling"
- *folks* (line 9), "parents"
- *feller* (line 48), "man"
- *critter* (lines 77, 95), "animal"

FOR ADVANCED LEARNERS/PRE-AP

Pre-AP exercises in the bottom channel provide additional challenge for your advanced students. Use them for small groups or individuals.

ADDITIONAL GUIDELINES

For more help with differentiation and tips for classroom management, see

BEST PRACTICES TOOLKIT
Differentiated Instruction pp. 31–38

LITERARY ANALYSIS

C TALL TALE

Possible answer: *The resolution is humorous because Bill is raised by coyotes, which is something that could not happen in real life.*

Bill soon discovered the coyote's kinfolk were about the wildest, roughest bunch you could imagine. Before he knew it, he was roaming the prairies with the pack. He howled at the moon, sniffed the brush, and chased lizards across the sand. He was having such a good time, scuttling about naked and dirty on all fours, that he completely forgot what it was like to be a human. **C**

Pecos Bill's coyote days came to an end about seventeen years later. One evening as he was sniffing the sagebrush, a cowpoke[3] came loping by on a big horse. "Hey, you!" he shouted. "What in the world are you?"

Bill sat on his haunches and stared at the feller.

"What *are* you?" asked the cowpoke again.

"Varmint,"[4] said Bill hoarsely, for he hadn't used his human voice in seventeen years.

"No, you ain't!"

"Yeah, I am. I got fleas, don't I?"

"Well, that don't mean nothing. A lot of Texans got fleas. The thing varmints got that you ain't got is a tail."

"Oh, yes, I do have a tail," said Pecos Bill.

"Lemme see it then," said the cowpoke.

Bill turned around to look at his rear end, and for the first time in his life he realized he didn't have a tail.

"Dang," he said. "But if I'm not a varmint, what am I?"

"You're a cowboy! So start acting like one!"

Bill just growled at the feller like any coyote worth his salt[5] would. But deep down in his heart of hearts he knew the cowpoke was right. For the last seventeen years he'd had a sneaking suspicion that he was different from that pack of coyotes. For one thing, none of them seemed to smell quite as bad as he did. **D**

So with a heavy heart he said good-bye to his four-legged friends and took off with the cowpoke for the nearest ranch.

C TALL TALE
Baby Bill gets separated from his family. What's humorous about the way this problem gets solved?

1 Targeted Passage

D TALL TALE
Reread lines 39–52. Which lines, if any, are funny to you? Explain why.

Acting like a human wasn't all that easy for Pecos Bill. Even though he soon started dressing right, he never bothered to shave or comb his hair. He'd just throw some water on his face in the morning and go around the rest of the day looking like a wet dog. Ignorant cowpokes claimed Bill wasn't too smart. Some of the meaner ones liked to joke that he wore a ten-dollar hat on a five-cent head.

The truth was Pecos Bill would soon prove to be one of the greatest cowboys who ever lived. He just needed to find the kind of folks who'd appreciate him. One night when he was licking his dinner plate, his ears perked up. A couple of ranch hands were going on about a gang of wild cowboys.

3. **cowpoke:** cowhand; cattle herder.
4. **varmint:** wild and/or vicious animal.
5. **worth his salt:** worthy of respect.

LITERARY ANALYSIS

D TALL TALE

Students might note these funny situations:

- *Bill sniffs the sagebrush and sits on his haunches (lines 31–34).*
- *Bill thinks he's a wild animal (lines 35–37).*
- *The cowboy says that many Texans have fleas (line 40).*
- *Bill realizes for the first time that he doesn't have a tail (lines 44–45).*
- *Bill notices that he smells worse than the coyotes (lines 51–52).*

DIFFERENTIATED INSTRUCTION

FOR LESS-PROFICIENT READERS

1 Targeted Passage [Lines 25–54]

This passage presents a humorous turning point in which Bill realizes he is not a coyote.

- What is Bill's life with the coyotes like?
- How long has Bill lived with the coyotes?
- Why is Bill's voice hoarse?
- What "fact" does Bill provide to prove he is a coyote?
- What finally convinces Bill that he is not a coyote? What does he do as a result?

FOR ENGLISH LEARNERS

Language: Conversational English Patterns

Explain that in conversation, people often do not speak in complete sentences. Point out the following examples of dialogue and help students fill in the missing words:

- *"Neighbors movin' in fifty miles away!"* (line 8)
- *"Varmint"* (line 36)
- *"The Hell's Gate Gang"* (line 70)
- *"Sounds like my kind of folks"* (line 72)

804 UNIT 7: HISTORY, CULTURE, AND THE AUTHOR

"Yep. Those fellas are more animal than human," one ranch hand was saying.

"Yep. Them's the toughest bunch I ever come across. Heck, they're so tough, they can kick fire out of flint rock[6] with their bare toes!"

"Yep. 'N' they like to bite nails in half for fun!"

"Who are these fellers?" asked Bill.

"The Hell's Gate Gang," said the ranch hand. "The mangiest, meanest, most low-down bunch of low-life varmints that ever grew hair."

"Sounds like my kind of folks," said Bill, and before anyone could holler whoa, he jumped on his horse and took off for Hell's Gate Canyon.

Bill hadn't gone far when disaster struck. His horse stepped in a hole and broke its ankle.

"Dang!" said Bill as he stumbled up from the spill. He draped the lame critter around his neck and hurried on.

After he'd walked about a hundred more miles, Bill heard some mean rattling. Then a fifty-foot rattlesnake reared up its ugly head and stuck out its long, forked tongue, ready to fight.

"Knock it off, you scaly-hided fool. I'm in a hurry," Bill said.

The snake didn't give a spit for Bill's plans. He just rattled on.

Before the cussed varmint could strike, Bill had no choice but to knock him cross-eyed. "Hey, feller," he said, holding up the dazed snake. "I like your spunk. Come go with us." Then he wrapped the rattler around his arm and continued on his way.

After Bill had hiked another hundred miles with his horse around his neck and his snake around his arm, he heard a terrible growl. A huge mountain lion was crouching on a cliff, getting ready to leap on top of him.

"Don't jump, you mangy bobtailed[7] fleabag!" Bill said.

Well, call any mountain lion a mangy bobtailed fleabag, and he'll jump on your back for sure. After this one leaped onto Bill, so much fur began to fly that it darkened the sky. Bill wrestled that mountain lion into a headlock, then squeezed him so tight that the big cat had to cry uncle.[8] **E**

When the embarrassed old critter started to slink off, Bill felt sorry for him. "Aw, c'mon, you big silly," he said. "You're more like me than most humans I meet."

He saddled up the cat, jumped on his back, and the four of them headed for the canyon, with the mountain lion screeching, the horse neighing, the rattler rattling, and Pecos Bill hollering a wild war whoop. **F**

When the Hell's Gate Gang heard those noises coming from the prairie, they nearly fainted. They dropped their dinner plates, and their faces turned as white as bleached desert bones. Their knees knocked and their six-guns shook.

"Hey, there!" Bill said as he sidled up to their campfire, grinning. "Who's the boss around here?"

E TALL TALE
What can you **infer** about Bill's abilities from the feats he performs in lines 76–94?

F VISUALIZE
Reread lines 98–100. What words help you see and hear the action?

6. **flint rock:** a very hard, fine-grained quartz that sparks when struck with steel.
7. **bobtailed:** having a very short tail or one that has been bobbed (cut short).
8. **cry uncle:** give up fighting; admit that one has been beaten.

LITERARY ANALYSIS

E TALL TALE

Possible answer: *Bill is extremely strong and brave.*

If students need help . . . Review what it means to infer. Remind students that to infer means to "read between the lines" by making logical guesses based on the text and their own experiences.

READING STRATEGY

F VISUALIZE

Have students record their answers in their charts from page 801. ***Possible answer:***

- ***See:*** *"saddled up the cat, [and] jumped on his back" (line 98)*
- ***Hear:*** *"screeching," "neighing," "rattling," and "hollering" (lines 99–100)*

If students need help . . . Review the descriptions in lines 98–100. Help students find sensory details, and have them tell which senses they appeal to.

Lines 74–100
DISCUSSION PROMPTS

Use these prompts to help students understand the humor in this part of the story:

Recall List three examples of exaggerated or impossible details in this passage. ***Possible answer:*** *Bill hikes 100 miles with a horse around his neck, "fifty-foot rattlesnake" (line 79), "so much fur began to fly that it darkened the sky" (lines 92–93)*

Analyze What is funny about why the mountain lion attacks Bill? ***Possible answer:*** *The lion attacks because of Bill's insult. It is funny to think of a mountain lion taking offense at being insulted by a person.*

Evaluate The many examples of exaggeration in this passage are intended to add humor to the story. Do you think the author succeeds in creating humor in this scene? Why or why not? *Some students may believe that the scene is funny because of the many exaggerations. Others may believe that too many exaggerations at once cause readers to stop paying close attention to them and therefore miss the intended humor.*

FOR LESS–PROFICIENT READERS

Reading Strategy Follow-Up: Visualize
[paired option] Remind students that descriptive details can help them visualize characters as well as events. Have pairs read lines 63–73 and update their charts from page 801. Tell students to look for words and phrases that describe the wild cowboys called the Hell's Gate Gang. Interested students might use the details to make quick sketches of the cowboys to share with the class.

Character or Event	Descriptive Words or Phrases
Hell's Gate Gang	"more animal than human," "tough," "kick fire . . . with their bare toes," "bite nails in half for fun," "mangiest, meanest, most low-down bunch of low-life varmints that ever grew hair"

A nine-foot feller with ten pistols at his sides stepped forward and in a shaky voice said, "Stranger, I was. But from now on, it'll be you."

"Well, thanky, pardner," said Bill. "Get on with your dinner, boys. Don't let me interrupt."

Once Bill settled down with the Hell's Gate Gang, his true genius revealed itself. With his gang's help, he put together the biggest ranch in the southwest. He used New Mexico as a corral and Arizona as a pasture. He invented tarantulas and scorpions as practical jokes. He also invented roping. Some say his rope was exactly as long as the equator; others argue it was two feet shorter. **G**

Things were going fine for Bill until Texas began to suffer the worst drought in its history. It was so dry that all the rivers turned as powdery as biscuit flour. The parched grass was catching fire everywhere. For a while Bill and his gang managed to lasso water from the Rio Grande.[9] When that river dried up, they lassoed water from the Gulf of Mexico.

No matter what he did, though, Bill couldn't get enough water to stay ahead of the drought. All his horses and cows were starting to dry up and blow away like balls of tumbleweed. It was horrible.

Just when the end seemed near, the sky turned a deep shade of purple. From the distant mountains came a terrible roar. The cattle began to stampede, and a huge black funnel of a cyclone appeared, heading straight for Bill's ranch.

The rest of the Hell's Gate Gang shouted, "Help!" and ran.

But Pecos Bill wasn't scared in the least. "Yahoo!" he hollered, and he swung his lariat and lassoed that cyclone around its neck.

Bill held on tight as he got sucked up into the middle of the swirling cloud. He grabbed the cyclone by the ears and pulled himself onto her back. Then he let out a whoop and headed that twister across Texas.

The mighty cyclone bucked, arched, and screamed like a wild bronco. But Pecos Bill just held on with his legs and used his strong hands to wring the rain out of her wind. He wrung out rain that flooded Texas, New Mexico, and Arizona, until finally he slid off the shriveled-up funnel and fell into California. The earth sank about two hundred feet below sea level in the spot where Bill landed, creating the area known today as Death Valley. **H**

"There. That little waterin' should hold things for a while," he said, brushing himself off.

After his cyclone ride, no horse was too wild for Pecos Bill. He soon found a young colt that was as tough as a tiger and as crazy as a streak of lightning. He named the colt Widow Maker and raised him on barbed wire and dynamite. Whenever the two rode together, they back-flipped and somersaulted all over Texas, loving every minute of it.

(2) Targeted Passage

G TALL TALE Which of Bill's characteristics and achievements are exaggerated in lines 110–115?

H TALL TALE Tall tales sometimes explain how natural phenomena came to be. What do lines 134–139 explain?

9. **Rio Grande** (rē'ō grănd'): a river that forms part of the U.S.-Mexican border.

LITERARY ANALYSIS

G TALL TALE

Possible answer: *The size of Bill's ranch; his invention of tarantulas, scorpions, and roping; and length of his rope are all exaggerated.*

LITERARY ANALYSIS

H TALL TALE

Answer: *The lines explain how Death Valley came to be. Bill created a valley when he fell to the earth after riding the cyclone.*

Lines 110–141

DISCUSSION PROMPTS

Use these prompts to help students understand Bill's next set of adventures:

Connect Based on what you've learned about Bill so far, would you want to befriend him? Why or why not? *Some students may want to befriend Bill because he could protect them from everything, even natural disasters. Others may say Bill gets himself into too many dangerous situations and is too wild.*

Infer Why do you think the leader of the Hell's Gate Gang immediately makes Bill the gang's leader? ***Possible answer:*** *When Bill approaches with the snake, the mountain lion, and the horse, the leader can tell Bill is wilder and tougher than he is.*

Evaluate What language does the author use to explain why the cyclone is not terrifying to Bill? ***Possible answer:*** *The author compares the cyclone to a wild animal, which Bill is used to taming: "Bill held on tight" and "grabbed the cyclone by the ears and pulled himself onto her back." "The mighty cyclone bucked, arched, and screamed like a wild bronco. But Pecos Bill just held on with his legs. . . ." This language explains why Bill is not afraid of the cyclone: he simply treats it like an animal.*

DIFFERENTIATED INSTRUCTION

FOR LESS–PROFICIENT READERS

(2) Targeted Passage [Lines 110–139]

This passage develops the legend of Pecos Bill by describing some of his astounding feats.

- What is unusual about Bill's ranch?
- What things does Bill invent?
- What problem does the drought cause for Bill? What is his solution to the problem?
- What happens when Bill finally slides off the cyclone?

FOR ENGLISH LEARNERS

Vocabulary Support Discuss the following terms that relate to the American Southwest:

- *to lasso* (line 119), "to capture with a long rope that has a loop at one end, usually used to catch horses and cattle"
- *tumbleweed* (line 123), "a plant with many branches that breaks off from its roots at the end of the growing season and is rolled about by the wind"
- *stampede* (line 126), "a sudden rush of a large number of frightened animals"

One day when Bill and Widow Maker were bouncing around the Pecos River, they came across an awesome sight: a wild-looking, red-haired woman riding on the back of the biggest catfish Bill had ever seen. The woman looked like she was having a ball, screeching, "Ride 'em, cowgirl!" as the catfish whipped her around in the air. ❶

"What's your name?" Bill shouted.

"Slue-foot[10] Sue! What's it to you?" she said. Then she war-whooped away over the windy water.

Thereafter all Pecos Bill could think of was Slue-foot Sue. He spent more and more time away from the Hell's Gate Gang as he wandered the barren cattle-lands, looking for her. When he finally found her lonely little cabin, he was so love-struck he reverted to some of his old coyote ways. He sat on his haunches in the moonlight and began a-howling and ah-hooing.

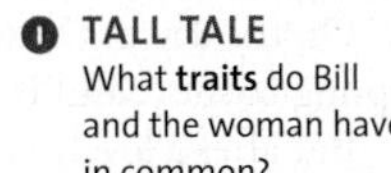

❶ **TALL TALE**
What **traits** do Bill and the woman have in common?

10. **slue** (slo͞o): to rotate, turn sharply, or pivot.

LITERARY ANALYSIS

❶ TALL TALE

Possible answer: *They are both wild, like to ride wild animals, and enjoy life.*

If students need help . . . Work with them to identify Bill's traits. Write students' ideas on the board. Then read aloud lines 147–151. Ask students what details about the woman reveal qualities similar to Bill's.

ANALYZE VISUALS

Activity After students have finished the story, have them tell what scene this image depicts. Then ask them to reread lines 147–154 and 182–188 and tell how closely the image matches their visualization of Slue-foot Sue and the scene in which she and Bill fly to the moon. ***Possible answer:*** *The image depicts the scene in which Bill lassos Sue after she is thrown from Bill's wild bronco and they are catapulted into space. Students may note that Sue does not look as wild as they had imagined after reading lines 148–154.*

FOR ADVANCED LEARNERS/PRE–AP

Analyze Figurative Language [small-group option] Have students form small groups to identify and discuss how the author heightens the absurdity and humor of the tall tale by using figurative language, including similes and personification. Ask students to create a T Chart to note and analyze the examples they find.

BEST PRACTICES TOOLKIT—Transparency
T Chart p. A25

Example of Figurative Language	*What It Describes*
"a young colt that was as tough as a tiger and as crazy as a streak of lightning" (lines 143–144)	*Bill's new horse; shows that the horse is strong and wild*

Well, the good news was that Sue had a bit of coyote in her too, so she completely understood Bill's language. She stuck her head out her window and ah-hooed back to him that she loved him, too. Consequently Bill and Sue decided to get married.

On the day of the wedding Sue wore a beautiful white dress with a steel-spring bustle,[11] and Bill appeared in an elegant buckskin suit.

But after a lovely ceremony, a terrible catastrophe occurred. Slue-foot Sue got it into her head that she just had to have a ride on Bill's wild bronco, Widow Maker.

"You can't do that, honey," Bill said. "He won't let any human toss a leg over him but me."

"Don't worry," said Sue. "You know I can ride anything on four legs, not to mention what flies or swims." **J**

Bill tried his best to talk Sue out of it, but she wouldn't listen. She was dying to buck on the back of that bronco. Wearing her white wedding dress with the bustle, she jumped on Widow Maker and kicked him with her spurs.

Well, that bronco didn't need any thorns in his side to start bucking to beat the band. He bounded up in the air with such amazing force that suddenly Sue was flying high into the Texas sky. She flew over plains and mesas,[12] over canyons, deserts, and prairies. She flew so high that she looped over the new moon and fell back to earth.

But when Sue landed on her steel-spring bustle, she rebounded right back into the heavens! As she bounced back and forth between heaven and earth, Bill whirled his lariat[13] above his head, then lassoed her. But instead of bringing Sue back down to earth, he got yanked into the night sky alongside her!

Together Pecos Bill and Slue-foot Sue bounced off the earth and went flying to the moon. And at that point Bill must have gotten some sort of foothold in a moon crater—because neither he nor Sue returned to earth. Not ever.

Folks figure those two must have dug their boot heels into some moon cheese and raised a pack of wild coyotes just like themselves. Texans'll tell you that every time you hear thunder rolling over the desolate land near the Pecos River, it's just Bill's family having a good laugh upstairs. When you hear a strange ah-hooing in the dark night, don't be fooled—that's the sound of Bill howling *on* the moon instead of *at* it. And when lights flash across the midnight sky, you can bet it's Bill and Sue riding the backs of some white-hot shooting stars. **K**

J TALL TALE
Do you think Sue will succeed in riding Wido Maker? Why or why nc

3 Targeted Passage

K VISUALIZE
Reread lines 191–198. Note the descriptive details in this passage. What do they help you picture?

11. **bustle** (bŭs′əl): a springy steel framework worn under the back of a woman's skirt to make it puff out.
12. **mesas** (mā′səs): high, flat-topped areas of land.
13. **lariat** (lăr′ē-ət): a rope with a slip-knotted loop at one end that a cowhand throws over an animal's head or body and pulls tight.

LITERARY ANALYSIS

J TALL TALE

Students who say that Sue will be able to ride Widow Maker may argue that because she and Bill share many qualities, she might also share the ability to ride the horse. Others may agree with Bill, who knows that no other person but him can ride the bronco, and may note the ominous name of the animal, Widow Maker.

READING STRATEGY

K VISUALIZE

Have students record their answers in their charts from page 801. ***Possible answer:*** *The details describe where Bill's family lives now (on the moon) and what their life is like (they ride "the backs of some white-hot shooting stars").*

SELECTION WRAP–UP

REFLECT Ask students to explain whether Pecos Bill is a likeable character.

★ CRITIQUE Have students evaluate whether the ending of this story fits the criteria of a tall tale.

READING FLUENCY

Distribute the copy masters and have students practice fluency.

R RESOURCE MANAGER—Copy Master
Reading Fluency p. 83

DIFFERENTIATED INSTRUCTION

FOR LESS–PROFICIENT READERS

3 Targeted Passage [Lines 173–198]

This passage concludes the story by describing what happens to Bill and Sue.

- What does Sue insist on doing after the wedding ceremony? What happens to her?
- What does Bill do to save Sue? What happens to him?
- Where do people think Bill and Sue are now?
- In what way do Texans use the story of Bill and Sue to explain thunder?

FOR ADVANCED LEARNERS/PRE–AP

Imitate the Author's Style Have students write a new ending to the story. Students should write one short paragraph explaining what happens after line 176, when Sue jumps on Widow Maker. Encourage students to imitate the author's style, including humor and exaggeration. Ask volunteers to share their new endings with the class.

fter Reading

omprehension

1. **Recall** Why does a coyote decide to take care of Bill?
2. **Clarify** How does Bill become the leader of the Hell's Gate Gang?
3. **Summarize** How do Bill and Sue end up leaving Earth and living in the sky?

iterary Analysis

4. **Examine a Tall Tale** In what ways does "Pecos Bill" exhibit the characteristics of a tall tale? Review the characteristics on page 801. Give examples from the story to support each one.
5. **Visualize** Review the chart you filled in as you read. What person or event did you picture most clearly? Tell what descriptions and sensory details helped you. Overall, how well do you think the author helped you visualize the story? Explain.
6. **Analyze Characterization** How does the author help you get to know what Pecos Bill is like? Use a character map to show what you learn about Bill through each of the four methods of characterization.

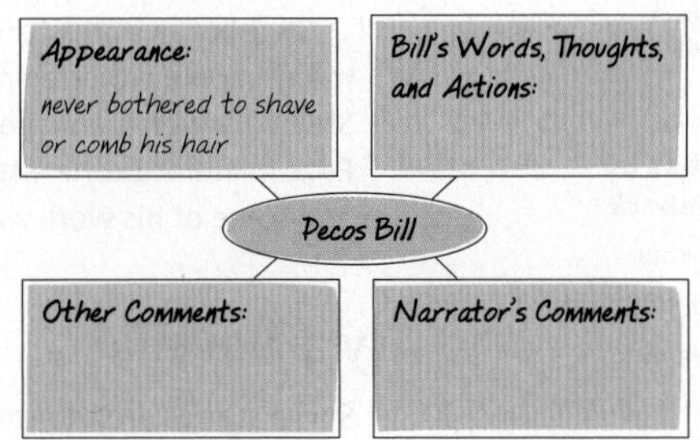

7. **Draw Conclusions** Why do you think Pecos Bill became a **folk hero** in American culture? Consider what his personal characteristics and achievements might represent to people.

xtension and Challenge

8. **Creative Project: Comic Strip** The incredible characters and events in tall tales have much in common with cartoons. Choose one of the events described in "Pecos Bill." Create a three- to four-panel comic strip that illustrates this event.
9. **SOCIAL STUDIES CONNECTION** What were the lives of cowboys in the 19th century really like? Research the topic, and then compare your findings with the life of Pecos Bill in the story. Are there similarities?

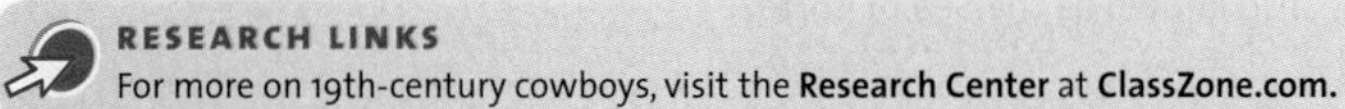

RESEARCH LINKS
For more on 19th-century cowboys, visit the Research Center at ClassZone.com.

Practice and Apply

After Reading

For additional support of postreading questions, use these copy masters:

RESOURCE MANAGER—Copy Masters
Reading Check p. 81 (to check understanding of the selection)
Tall Tale p. 77 (for practice of literary analysis standards focus)
Question Support p. 82 (After Reading questions adapted for English learners and less-proficient readers)

Additional selection questions are provided for teachers on page 71.

ANSWERS

Comprehension

1. *The coyote mistakes Bill's "Goo-goo!" for coyote language and thinks Bill is a coyote.*
2. *Bill intimidates the Hell's Gate Gang with all the wild animals he brings with him, so the gang makes him their leader.*
3. *Widow Maker throws Sue into the air, and every time she lands, she bounces back up on her steel-spring bustle. When Bill tries to lasso her, he gets pulled into the sky, too.*

Literary Analysis

Possible answers:

4. ● **STANDARDS FOCUS Tall Tale** *Bill and Sue are larger than life. Bill solves problems (the drought, being attacked by a snake and a mountain lion) in humorous ways. Bill's characteristics (strength, bravery, determination, cowboy skills) are exaggerated, as are Sue's.*
5. ■ **STANDARDS FOCUS Visualize** *Students should name the person or event they pictured most clearly and the descriptions that helped them do so. They should also make an overall judgment about how well the author helped them visualize the tale.*
6. ***Appearance:*** *looks like a wet dog, has strong hands, wears an elegant buckskin suit;* ***Bill's Words, Thoughts, and Actions:*** *teethes on horseshoes, carries his horse, defeats a mountain lion and a snake;* ***Other Comments:*** *"claimed Bill wasn't too smart";* ***Narrator's Comments:*** *"the best cowboy who ever lived," "true genius," "Bill wasn't scared"*
7. *Bill has great strength, bravery, and ingenuity—qualities many Americans value.*

Extension and Challenge

8. *An effective cartoon should be based solely on details from the text, include at least three panels, and demonstrate an understanding of the sequence of events.*
9. **SOCIAL STUDIES CONNECTION** *Students' findings should reflect a basic understanding of cowboy culture, as well as the similarities between real cowboys and those from the tall tale.*

Assess and Reteach

Assess

RESOURCE MANAGER—Copy Masters
Selection Tests A, B/C pp. 85–86, 87–88

Test Generator CD

Reteach

STANDARDS LESSON FILE
Literature Lesson 1: Types of Characters and Character Traits

Introduce

OBJECTIVE

- read a novella

Meet John Steinbeck

Steinbeck decided he wanted to be a writer when he was a teenager, and he spent many hours alone, crafting his stories and poems. This calling to be a writer went hand in hand with his wish to confront social problems and to give voice to people facing a variety of struggles. Steinbeck's commitment to understanding people and societies fueled his interest in travel throughout his life. One of his last great adventures was a three-month journey across the United States in a camper with his poodle, Charley—meeting people and getting to know the character and values of the nation. He was at different times pleased and angered by what he found. He recorded his thoughts about the people and places he encountered. Later, he published these writings in the book *Travels with Charley in Search of America* (1962).

Try a Novella

Explain that the novella first appeared in Italy during the Middle Ages (circa A.D. 476–1453), and that it influenced the development of both the novel and the short story. Most of the world's classic novellas deal with significant issues or struggles, such as people learning life lessons or embarking on important journeys. Novellas are often tightly structured and rely on imagery and symbolism to create meaning. For example, the pearl in the title of Steinbeck's novella is an important symbol in the story.

Other well-known novellas include Leo Tolstoy's *The Death of Ivan Ilyich,* about a dying man who realizes he never fully lived his life; Herman Melville's *Billy Budd,* a study of good and evil through a tragic incident at sea; Joseph Conrad's *Heart of Darkness,* in which a man on a journey questions human nature; and Franz Kafka's *The Metamorphosis,* in which a salesman wakes up one day to find he has become a giant insect.

RESOURCE MANAGER—Copy Master
Identify Genre Features p. 89

Great Reads

The Pearl

Novella by John Steinbeck

John Steinbeck
1902–1968

Other Books by John Steinbeck

- *Cannery Row*
- *The Grapes of Wrath*
- *The Red Pony*
- *Travels with Charley*

Meet John Steinbeck

John Steinbeck grew up in Salinas, California. Some of his earliest jobs were in sugar factories and ranches in this fertile area of the state. He worked alongside many Mexican Americans, and he gained respect for their culture and sympathized with their tough living and working conditions. Later, he lived in Mexico for a time, which made him even more aware of how poverty affects people's lives. Even after achieving success, he never flaunted his wealth. He lived simply and traveled often.

Steinbeck wrote stories about the poor at a time when many people preferred not to think about such things. Though Steinbeck won many prominent awards, including the 1962 Nobel Prize in literature, he also received hate mail from some readers, and some of his work was even banned.

Try a Novella

Some stories are too short to be called novels but too long to be called short stories. These fall into the category of the **novella,** a story ranging from about 50 to 100 pages in length. Being limited in length, a novella usually focuses on a particular situation or conflict and has fewer characters than a novel.

Some of John Steinbeck's best-known works are novellas. The brief form allows his stories to seem simple while conveying powerful themes. He based his novella *The Pearl* on a Mexican parable, a traditional story that is meant to teach a lesson. He heard it while traveling around the Gulf of California, also known as the Sea of Cortez.

810

DIFFERENTIATED INSTRUCTION

FOR LESS–PROFICIENT READERS

Reading Support Before students begin reading, review the teaching notes on pages 811–814 and select those that you think would be most helpful to them. You might read the selection aloud with students and discuss relevant notes as you read. Stop occasionally to answer questions, give an explanation, or hold a discussion about some aspect of the story.

Read a Great Book

"If this story is a parable, perhaps everyone takes his own meaning from it and reads his own life into it." So begins the story of Kino, the poor fisherman, his wife, Juana, their baby, Coyotito, and the great pearl that was found and lost again. When Coyotito is stung by a scorpion, Kino and Juana travel from their village to take him to the nearest doctor. However, being poor, they are unable to pay for treatment and are turned away. But once they have a large pearl in their possession, the greedy doctor makes a house call, hoping to get a share of the profits.

from

The Pearl

"It is as I thought," he said. "The poison has gone inward and it will strike soon. Come look!" He held the eyelid down. "See—it is blue." And Kino, looking anxiously, saw that indeed it was a little blue. And he didn't know whether or not it was always a little blue. But the trap was set. He couldn't take the chance.

The doctor's eyes watered in their little hammocks. "I will give him something to try to turn the poison aside," he said. And he handed the baby to Kino.

Then from his bag he took a little bottle of white powder and a capsule of gelatine. He filled the capsule with the powder and closed it, and then around the first capsule he fitted a second capsule and closed it. Then he worked very deftly. He took the baby and pinched its lower lip until it opened its mouth. His fat fingers placed the capsule far back on the baby's tongue, back of the point where he could spit it out, and then from the floor he picked up the little pitcher of pulque and gave Coyotito a drink, and it was done. He looked again at the baby's eyeball and he pursed his lips and seemed to think.

811

Read

Read a Great Book

John Steinbeck's discomfort with wealth was reflected in his modest lifestyle and is expressed through characters and situations in his writings. In *The Pearl,* Steinbeck shows that while the idea of wealth is attractive, in practice it can bring corruption and unwanted complications. In this excerpt, for example, the doctor is distracted from his main responsibilities as a caregiver by his greed. At the same time, Kino's life is suddenly gripped by suspicion and fear as he realizes he must guard the pearl.

The excerpt also illustrates Steinbeck's belief in a bond between people and nature. While growing up in California's Salinas Valley, a fertile farming area, Steinbeck developed an appreciation for nature. He felt that characters should be viewed against the backdrop of their environments. He wrote, "The trees and the muscled mountains are the world—but not the world apart from man—the world and man—the one inseparable unit. . . ." Readers can also observe this idea in his rich descriptions of Kino's environment.

SHARE AN FYI

The scorpion, a relative of the spider with a poisonous stinger, is often a symbol of evil in legends and fables. In most cases, a scorpion's sting will not cause death. However, it can be fatal to babies and elderly people.

SHARE WORD MEANINGS

Pulque (line 16) is a thick beverage made in Mexico from the juice of an agave plant known as the maguey. The maguey was a sacred and important plant in ancient Mexico.

FOR ENGLISH LEARNERS

Read Aloud Preread part of the excerpt aloud and then have students continue reading in pairs or small groups. Alternatively, read aloud the entire excerpt, stopping occasionally to answer questions, lead a discussion, or give an explanation.

Listen to the *Audio Anthology CD* Have students listen to the excerpt as they read along. Then have them read the text independently. Lead them in a follow-up discussion.

Jigsaw Reading [small-group option] Have students meet in small groups for Jigsaw Reading. Each student should read part of the excerpt and explain it to the others. Before students meet in their groups, review the introductory paragraph on page 811 and make sure students understand the context of the excerpt. Point out that the first lines of dialogue in the excerpt are the doctor's.

BEST PRACTICES TOOLKIT
Jigsaw Reading p. A1

SHARE WORD MEANINGS

An *estuary* (line 44) is a body of water where a river meets the sea and where fresh and salt water mix. Historically, villages and cities have grown up around estuaries because they make travel and trade convenient.

SHARE A READING TIP

Point out Steinbeck's rich description of a school of large fish attacking a school of small fish and of night hawks hunting the night mice (lines 44–51). This is an example of the way Steinbeck shows his characters' connectedness with nature. In addition, the paragraph is thematically important, as it reflects the idea of the big and powerful stalking and harming those who are less powerful.

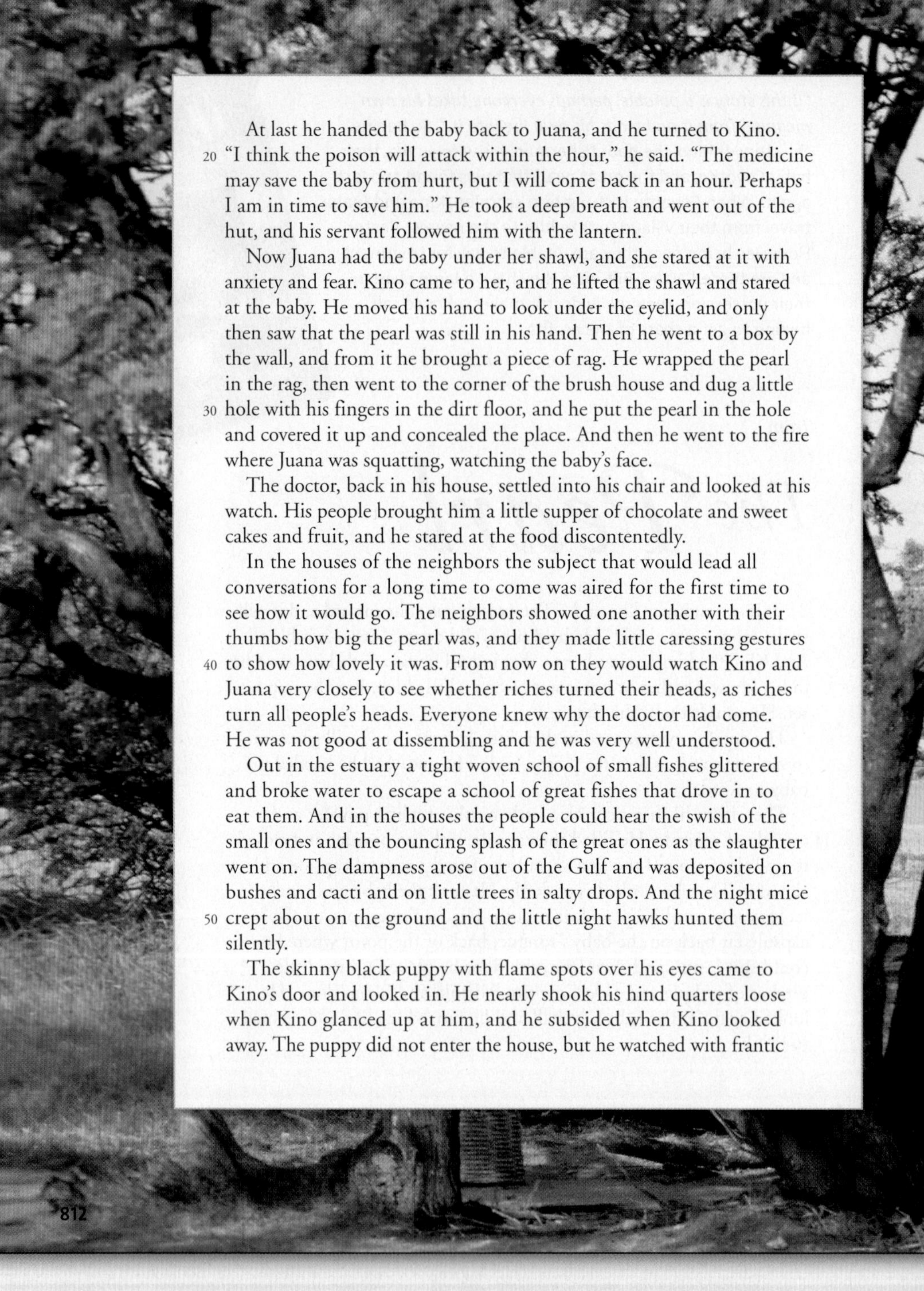

At last he handed the baby back to Juana, and he turned to Kino. "I think the poison will attack within the hour," he said. "The medicine may save the baby from hurt, but I will come back in an hour. Perhaps I am in time to save him." He took a deep breath and went out of the hut, and his servant followed him with the lantern.

Now Juana had the baby under her shawl, and she stared at it with anxiety and fear. Kino came to her, and he lifted the shawl and stared at the baby. He moved his hand to look under the eyelid, and only then saw that the pearl was still in his hand. Then he went to a box by the wall, and from it he brought a piece of rag. He wrapped the pearl in the rag, then went to the corner of the brush house and dug a little hole with his fingers in the dirt floor, and he put the pearl in the hole and covered it up and concealed the place. And then he went to the fire where Juana was squatting, watching the baby's face.

The doctor, back in his house, settled into his chair and looked at his watch. His people brought him a little supper of chocolate and sweet cakes and fruit, and he stared at the food discontentedly.

In the houses of the neighbors the subject that would lead all conversations for a long time to come was aired for the first time to see how it would go. The neighbors showed one another with their thumbs how big the pearl was, and they made little caressing gestures to show how lovely it was. From now on they would watch Kino and Juana very closely to see whether riches turned their heads, as riches turn all people's heads. Everyone knew why the doctor had come. He was not good at dissembling and he was very well understood.

Out in the estuary a tight woven school of small fishes glittered and broke water to escape a school of great fishes that drove in to eat them. And in the houses the people could hear the swish of the small ones and the bouncing splash of the great ones as the slaughter went on. The dampness arose out of the Gulf and was deposited on bushes and cacti and on little trees in salty drops. And the night mice crept about on the ground and the little night hawks hunted them silently.

The skinny black puppy with flame spots over his eyes came to Kino's door and looked in. He nearly shook his hind quarters loose when Kino glanced up at him, and he subsided when Kino looked away. The puppy did not enter the house, but he watched with frantic

812

interest while Kino ate his beans from the little pottery dish and wiped it clean with a corncake and ate the cake and washed the whole down with a drink of pulque.

Kino was finished and was rolling a cigarette when Juana spoke sharply. "Kino." He glanced at her and then got up and went quickly to her for he saw fright in her eyes. He stood over her, looking down, but the light was very dim. He kicked a pile of twigs into the fire hole to make a blaze, and then he could see the face of Coyotito. The baby's face was flushed and his throat was working and a little thick drool of saliva issued from his lips. The spasm of the stomach muscles began, and the baby was very sick.

Kino knelt beside his wife. "So the doctor knew," he said, but he said it for himself as well as for his wife, for his mind was hard and suspicious and he was remembering the white powder. Juana rocked from side to side and moaned out the little Song of the Family as though it could ward off the danger, and the baby vomited and writhed in her arms. Now uncertainty was in Kino, and the music of evil throbbed in his head and nearly drove out Juana's song.

The doctor finished his chocolate and nibbled the little fallen pieces of sweet cake. He brushed his fingers on a napkin, looked at his watch, arose, and took up his little bag.

The news of the baby's illness traveled quickly among the brush houses, for sickness is second only to hunger as the enemy of poor people. And some said softly, "Luck, you see, brings bitter friends." And they nodded and got up to go to Kino's house. The neighbors scuttled with covered noses through the dark until they crowded into Kino's house again. They stood and gazed, and they made little comments on the sadness that this should happen at a time of joy, and they said, "All things are in God's hands." The old women squatted down beside Juana to try to give her aid if they could and comfort if they could not.

Then the doctor hurried in, followed by his man. He scattered the old women like chickens. He took the baby and examined it and felt its head. "The poison it has worked," he said. "I think I can defeat it. I will try my best." He asked for water, and in the cup of it he put three drops of ammonia, and he pried open the baby's mouth and poured it down. The baby spluttered and screeched under the

SHARE A READING TIP

Suggest to students that they pay special attention to the neighbors, who have an important literary function. They act almost as a single character, commenting on the main action of the story, revealing the opinions and beliefs of the community, and predicting the ultimate fate of the main characters.

SHARE AN FYI

A pearl is a small, hard mass formed by certain mollusks, or shellfish. Pearls were one of the first items from nature that people valued for their beauty and rarity. Diving for pearls is an ancient tradition that has existed in many parts of the world. Natural pearls form in only a small percentage of mollusks, but today people also cultivate pearls. This process involves implanting a small bead inside an oyster's shell around which the animal develops a pearl.

SHARE A READING TIP

Point out Steinbeck's sensory details in lines 124–139. Tell students to be aware of details (such as "the distant barking of dogs" and "the creeping of the breeze") that are carefully chosen to reflect Kino's uneasiness and to foreshadow, or hint at, future events.

treatment, and Juana watched him with haunted eyes. The doctor spoke a little as he worked. "It is lucky that I know about the poison of the scorpion, otherwise—" and he shrugged to show what could have happened.

But Kino was suspicious, and he could not take his eyes from the doctor's open bag, and from the bottle of white powder there. Gradually the spasms subsided and the baby relaxed under the doctor's hands. And then Coyotito sighed deeply and went to sleep, for he was very tired with vomiting.

The doctor put the baby in Juana's arms. "He will get well now," he said. "I have won the fight." And Juana looked at him with adoration.

The doctor was closing his bag now. He said, "When do you think you can pay this bill?" He said it even kindly.

"When I have sold my pearl I will pay you," Kino said.

"You have a pearl? A good pearl?" the doctor asked with interest.

And then the chorus of the neighbors broke in. "He has found the Pearl of the World," they cried, and they joined forefinger with thumb to show how great the pearl was.

"Kino will be a rich man," they clamored. "It is a pearl such as one has never seen."

The doctor looked surprised. "I had not heard of it. Do you keep this pearl in a safe place? Perhaps you would like me to put it in my safe?"

Kino's eyes were hooded now, his cheeks were drawn taut. "I have it secure," he said. "Tomorrow I will sell it and then I will pay you."

The doctor shrugged, and his wet eyes never left Kino's eyes. He knew the pearl would be buried in the house, and he thought Kino might look toward the place where it was buried. "It would be a shame to have it stolen before you could sell it," the doctor said, and he saw Kino's eyes flick involuntarily to the floor near the side post of the brush house.

When the doctor had gone and all the neighbors had reluctantly returned to their houses, Kino squatted beside the little glowing coals in the fire hole and listened to the night sound, the soft sweep of the little waves on the shore and the distant barking of dogs, the creeping of the breeze through the brush house roof and the soft speech of his neighbors in their houses in the village. For these people do not sleep soundly all night; they awaken at intervals and talk a little and then go to sleep again. And after a while Kino got up and went to the door of his house.

He smelled the breeze and he listened for any foreign sound of secrecy or creeping, and his eyes searched the darkness, for the music of evil was sounding in his head and he was fierce and afraid. After he had probed the night with his senses he went to the place by the side post where the pearl was buried, and he dug it up and brought it to his sleeping mat, and under his sleeping mat he dug another little hole in the dirt floor and buried the pearl and covered it up again.

And Juana, sitting by the fire hole, watched him with questioning eyes, and when he had buried his pearl she asked, "Who do you fear?" ∾

Keep Reading

Is Kino right to fear that something bad is going to happen now that he has the "Pearl of the World"? As you continue to read the novella, you'll follow Kino and Juana as they seek their fortune, dodging danger at every turn. Discover how finding the pearl will change their lives forever.

Discuss

Keep Reading

Share these discussion questions with students after they have finished the excerpt. You might use the questions to lead a class discussion or have students form small groups to discuss them.

- Have you read this novella? If yes, would you recommend it to others? Why or why not? If you haven't read it, what questions are you hoping the rest of the book will answer?
- What do you find most interesting about Kino, his family, and his community?
- What is your opinion of the doctor? Do you think he will play a role in the rest of the book? Explain.
- Do you agree with Kino's neighbors that "Luck, you see, brings bitter friends" (line 79)? Do details in this excerpt make you feel as though Kino and his family will face hard times or good times as a result of the pearl? Explain.
- The excerpt ends with Juana asking Kino, "Who do you fear?" Who or what does he fear, and why?

Focus and Motivate

OBJECTIVES

Literary Analysis
- explore the key idea of **jobs**
- identify and analyze author's perspective
- read a memoir and a poem

Reading
- analyze sensory details

Vocabulary
- build vocabulary for reading and writing
- use similes as context to determine the meanings of unfamiliar words *(also an EL language objective)*

Grammar and Writing
- use semicolons correctly to separate parts of a series
- use writing to analyze literature

SUMMARY

In this memoir, Gary Soto recalls the tedious field work he did as a teenager. At first he is excited about picking grapes, but he soon realizes it is backbreaking work for very little money. His next job is chopping cotton, which he prefers because he earns more and feels "tough." The next fall, however, when there is no money for school clothes, Soto returns to the grape fields "one last time."

What can you learn from a JOB?

Discuss the question. Lead into the ***KEY IDEA*** by asking students what kinds of **jobs** they've had. What are the benefits and drawbacks of having a job? After students complete the ***QUICKWRITE,*** have them share their ideas.

Before Reading

One Last Time

Memoir by Gary Soto

What can you learn from a JOB?

KEY IDEA Does the thought of taking out the trash make you groan? Would you rather stay in bed than deliver newspapers on a rainy morning? Lots of times, **jobs** don't sound fun. But they can teach important lessons and help you figure out your goals for the future. In this memoir, the author discovers that finding out what he doesn't want to do is almost as important as finding out what he does want to do.

QUICKWRITE What have you learned from a job? Whether it was inside or outside your home, describe a job you've had or a chore you've done and the lessons you took away from it.

816

Selection Resources

RESOURCE MANAGER UNIT 7

Plan and Teach pp. 91–98

Literary Analysis
Summary pp. 99†*, 100‡*
Author's Perspective pp. 101, 102†*
Question Support p. 109*

Reading
Analyze Sensory Details pp. 103, 104†*
Reading Check p. 108
Reading Fluency p. 111

Vocabulary
Study p. 105*
Practice p. 106
Strategy p. 107

Grammar and Writing
Use Semicolons Correctly p. 110

Assessment
Selection Tests A, B/C pp. 113*, 115*
Test Generator CD

BEST PRACTICES TOOLKIT

Differentiated Instruction pp. 31–38*

Scaffolding Instruction pp. 43–46*

Graphic Organizers/Strategies
Word Questioning • Venn Diagram • Writing Template: Compare and Contrast • Writing Template: Persuasive Writing

Reading Support
Audio Anthology CD*

Technology
Literature, Vocabulary, and Writing Centers at **ClassZone.com**
Write*Smart* CD

* Resources for Differentiation † Also in Spanish ‡ In Haitian Creole and Vietnamese

ERARY ANALYSIS: AUTHOR'S PERSPECTIVE

Your view of the world is based on the people you know, the places you've lived, and the experiences you've had. Similarly, an **author's perspective**—the way a writer looks at a topic—is shaped by his or her experiences, environment, and values.

In his memoir, Gary Soto describes his teenage years working as a field laborer. As you read, look for clues to help you identify Soto's perspective on his work.

ADING STRATEGY: ANALYZE SENSORY DETAILS

Does it ever feel like you're actually seeing or hearing the experiences described on the page? If so, it's probably because of the author's expert use of sensory details. **Sensory details** are words and phrases that appeal to a reader's five senses. By using such details, a writer helps the reader create vivid mental pictures of settings, people, and events.

For example, in "One Last Time" Soto describes a bus that "started off in slow chugs"—a detail that helps you "hear" the rickety old bus. As you read, look for two or three details that appeal to each sense and record them in a web.

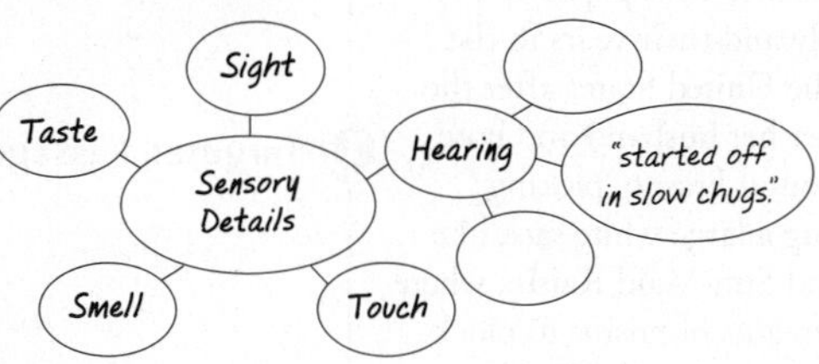

CABULARY IN CONTEXT

The words in Column A help Soto describe his jobs. See how many you know by matching each word to the word or phrase in Column B that is closest in meaning.

Column A	Column B
1. ramble	a. weak
2. foreman	b. angry
3. grope	c. workers' boss
4. stoop	d. bend over at the waist
5. contractor	e. unpleasant situation
6. irate	f. awkwardly grab for
7. feeble	g. talk on and on
8. predicament	h. one who provides services for a price

Author Online

Saved by Poetry

Gary Soto
born 1952

Born to parents of Mexican descent, Gary Soto grew up in Fresno, California. When Soto was five years old, his father died in an industrial accident, which left Soto feeling alone and confused. Struggling in school, he assumed he would lead a life much like that of his parents, who worked at picking crops and other low-paying jobs. However, he chose to enroll in college. Soto planned to study geography, but in his second year, he stumbled across a book of modern American poetry. This book changed his goals for the future. Soto was inspired to become a writer and began studying literature. Writing poetry and prose helped him reflect on his life and express himself in a new way.

Writing from Experience Soto began writing for young readers in the 1990s. In his poetry and fiction, he draws on his personal experience in books such as *Baseball in April and Other Stories* (1990), which describes the joys and challenges of Mexican-American boys and girls living in California. Soto also began writing biographies and other nonfiction. He says the greatest challenge of writing nonfiction is "making it exciting," although he adds that any reader who claims to be bored by the book should "cut grapes for a season. Then he or she will know boredom."

MORE ABOUT THE AUTHOR
For more on Gary Soto, visit the **Literature Center** at **ClassZone.com**.

Teach

STANDARDS FOCUS

LITERARY ANALYSIS

● AUTHOR'S PERSPECTIVE

Point out the last sentence of **Writing from Experience** on page 817. Ask students: From what perspective does Soto write about picking grapes? In what ways do you think his perspective will affect what he writes? ***Possible answer:*** *Soto is able to write from the perspective of someone who has actually picked grapes. Soto's description of grape picking will likely not be favorable.*

CHECK UNDERSTANDING Ask students from what perspective they might write about having a job.

READING STRATEGY

■ ANALYZE SENSORY DETAILS

Ask students what senses this sentence appeals to: *The green and yellow lawn mower roared loudly as I strained to control its path across the lawn.* ***Possible answers:*** *sight ("green and yellow lawn mower," "path across the lawn"); sound ("roared loudly"); touch ("strained," "control")*

CHECK UNDERSTANDING Ask students what kinds of sensory details might be included in a story about picking grapes.

RESOURCE MANAGER—Copy Master
Analyze Sensory Details p. 103 (for student use while reading the selection)

VOCABULARY SKILL

▲ VOCABULARY IN CONTEXT

DIAGNOSE WORD KNOWLEDGE To determine preteaching needs, have all students complete **Vocabulary in Context.** ***Answers:*** **1.** *g* **2.** *c* **3.** *f* **4.** *d* **5.** *h* **6.** *b* **7.** *a* **8.** *e*

PRETEACH VOCABULARY Use the Vocabulary Study copy master to help students use context clues to predict the meaning of each boldfaced word.

1. Read item 1 aloud, emphasizing *contractors.*
2. Point out the word *hired* and the phrase *to install new electrical wiring and plumbing.* Elicit possible meanings for *contractors,* such as "paid professionals."
3. Repeat the procedure for items 2–8.
4. Have students do Part B on their own.

RESOURCE MANAGER—Copy Master
Vocabulary Study p. 105

For general guidelines on differentiating vocabulary instruction and for alternative vocabulary activities for students not needing vocabulary preteaching, see

BEST PRACTICES TOOLKIT
Scaffolding Vocabulary Instruction pp. 43–46

Vocabulary Center at **ClassZone.com**
Additional Vocabulary Activities

Practice and Apply

ANALYZE VISUALS

Possible answer: *You can infer that the boys are friends: their postures indicate closeness, and their clothes are all similar.*

About the Art Jesse Treviño (born 1946) studied art in New York City. After losing his right arm during the Vietnam War, Treviño had to learn to draw all over again. The artist focuses much of his work on Latin-American culture.

LITERARY ANALYSIS

Ⓐ AUTHOR'S PERSPECTIVE

Possible answer: *The people in the movie remind him of his relatives, and he thinks about their difficult lives.*

Lines 1–23

DISCUSSION PROMPTS

Use these prompts to help students understand the attitude Soto's family had toward work:

Describe How would you describe Soto's grandmother? ***Possible answer:*** *She was a hard worker. She picked crops dragging a large white sack behind her, and she worked packing raisins for many years.*

Infer Based on the number and types of jobs Soto's grandmother held, what can you infer about her attitude toward work when she came to the United States? ***Possible answer:*** *She knew she would have to work hard to have a better life.*

Synthesize What is Soto's attitude toward his mother's job? Do you think such an attitude is typical of children? ***Possible answer:*** *Soto does not understand why his mother complains at the end of a work day, nor does he realize the importance of behaving himself so that she can focus on her work. Students will probably agree that Soto's attitude is typical of a young child.*

One Last Time

GARY SOTO

Yesterday I saw the movie *Gandhi*[1] and recognized a few of the people—not in the theater but in the film. I saw my relatives, dusty and thin as sparrows, returning from the fields with hoes balanced on their shoulders. The workers were squinting, eyes small and veined, and were using their hands to say what there was to say to those in the audience with popcorn. . . . I didn't have any, though. I sat thinking of my family and their years in the fields, beginning with Grandmother who came to the United States after the Mexican revolution[2] to settle in Fresno where she met her husband and bore children, many of them. She worked in the fields around Fresno, picking grapes, oranges, plums, peaches, and cotton, dragging a large white sack like a sled. She worked in the packing houses, Bonner and Sun-Maid Raisin, where she stood at a conveyor belt passing her hand over streams of raisins to pluck out leaves and pebbles. For over twenty years she worked at a machine that boxed raisins until she retired at sixty-five. Ⓐ

Grandfather worked in the fields, as did his children. Mother also found herself out there when she separated from Father for three weeks. I remember her coming home, dusty and so tired that she had to rest on the porch before she trudged inside to wash and start dinner. I didn't understand the complaints about her ankles or the small of her back, even though I had been in the grape fields watching her work. With my brother and sister I ran in and out of the rows; we enjoyed ourselves and pretended not to hear Mother scolding us to sit down and behave ourselves. A few years later, however, I caught on when I went to pick grapes rather than play in the rows.

ANALYZE VISUALS
What can you **infer** abo[ut] the boys based on thei[r] posture and clothing?

① **Targeted Passage**

Ⓐ **AUTHOR'S PERSPECTIVE**
What does Soto think about when he sees th[e] working people in the movie? As you continu[e] reading, notice how hi[s] family history affects h[is] view of field work.

1. ***Gandhi*** (gän'dē): a 1982 film biography of Mohandas Gandhi (1869–1948), an Indian spiritual and political leader who, through nonviolent struggle, forced England to grant India's independence.
2. **Mexican revolution** (1910–1920): an armed conflict during which revolutionaries overthrew Mexico's longtime dictator and reformed the government.

Detail of *Los Comarada[s]* *Barrio* (1976), Jesse Treviño. Acryl[ic on] canvas, 36" × 48". Collection of the a[rtist]

DIFFERENTIATED INSTRUCTION

FOR ALL STUDENTS

Enhance Learning Styles Provide independent projects such as these for various learning styles:

- **Musical** Compose a song Soto might sing to himself to make field work less boring.
- **Visual** Design a poster from a fruit or vegetable grower's perspective encouraging people to work in the fields.
- **Verbal** Create and perform a speech that expresses Soto's thoughts.

FOR LESS–PROFICIENT READERS

In combination with the *Audio Anthology CD*, use one or more Targeted Passages (pp. 818, 821, 823, 825) to ensure that students focus on key events, concepts, and skills.

① Targeted Passage [Lines 1–23]

This passage describes the work history of Soto's family.

- Whom does Soto think about when he sees the movie *Gandhi*? In what way are his relatives like the people in the movie?

BACKGROUND

Mexican Immigration Unemployment, violence, and political unrest around the time of the Mexican Revolution (1910–1920) caused the first wave of Mexican migration to the United States. Some Mexicans became citizens; others were migrant workers who returned home after seasonal work. Many had experience working the agricultural fields of Mexico, so they readily found jobs as farm workers. Both World War I (1914–1917) and World War II (1939–1945) encouraged Mexican immigration because many American men were overseas fighting, causing huge shortages in the workforce. The labor of Mexicans during the war years filled an important need. Their service enabled the country to keep running, which helped the United States in its war efforts.

CULTURAL CONNECTION

Mexican Americans Tell students that there are many famous Mexican Americans who have made a significant impact on American culture, such as acclaimed author Sandra Cisneros. She is the author of multiple books and essays, including *The House on Mango Street, Woman Hollering Creek,* and *My Wicked, Wicked Ways.* In 1995, Cisneros won the MacArthur Foundation Fellowship.

Invite students to share their knowledge of ways people from their own or other cultures have contributed to American culture.

- What jobs do Soto's grandparents do?
- Why does Soto's mother complain about her ankles and the small of her back?
- What experience does Soto say helped him understand his mother's complaints?

FOR ENGLISH LEARNERS

Key Academic Vocabulary Have students use Word Questioning to study these words: *revolution* (line 8), *labor* (lines 136, 140, 232), *inspect* (line 178), *corporations* (line 215).

BEST PRACTICES TOOLKIT—Transparency
Word Questioning p. E9

Prereading For prereading instruction for English learners, see

BEST PRACTICES TOOLKIT
Scaffolding Reading Instruction pp. 43–46

FOR ADVANCED LEARNERS/PRE–AP

Pre-AP exercises in the bottom channel provide additional challenge for your advanced students. Use them for small groups or individuals.

ADDITIONAL GUIDELINES

For more help with differentiation and tips for classroom management, see

BEST PRACTICES TOOLKIT
Differentiated Instruction pp. 31–38

Lines 24–48
DISCUSSION PROMPTS

Use these prompts to help students understand Soto's initial attitude toward picking grapes:

Recall What is Soto's attitude toward picking grapes as the day begins? Why? ***Answer:*** *Soto is excited because he thinks he will make a lot of money.*

Analyze Why do you think Soto's mother does not comment on Soto's ramblings about making money and buying her a tea pot? ***Possible answer:*** *Soto's mother probably knows that picking grapes is not an easy job and that even an experienced picker cannot make as much money as he dreams of making.*

Speculate What might happen because Soto has decided to pick grapes as rapidly as he can? ***Possible answer:*** *He might end up making a lot of money, or he might become tired and end up making less money than if he'd worked steadily.*

READING STRATEGY

B SENSORY DETAILS

Students might include these details:

- ***Touch:*** *"fighting the snap and whip of vines" (line 37), "groping for grapes" (line 38), "groping, cutting, and tugging" (line 42), "raked the grapes with my hands" (line 43), "jumped back under the vine on my knees" (line 44), "cut, pulled hard, and stopped to gather the grapes" (lines 46–47), "tossing them like popcorn into my mouth" (line 48)*
- ***Sight:*** *"pan brimmed with bunches" (line 38), "spilled like jewels from a pirate's chest" (lines 40–41), "five trays gleaming" (line 46)*

Mother and I got up before dawn and ate quick bowls of cereal. She drove in silence while I **rambled** on how everything was now solved, how I was going to make enough money to end our misery and even buy her a beautiful copper tea pot, the one I had shown her in Long's Drugs. When we arrived I was frisky and ready to go, self-consciously aware of my grape knife dangling at my wrist. I almost ran to the row the **foreman** had pointed out, but I returned to help Mother with the grape pans and jug of water. She told me to settle down and reminded me not to lose my knife. I walked at her side and listened to her explain how to cut grapes; bent down, hands on knees, I watched her demonstrate by cutting a few bunches into my pan. She stood over me as I tried it myself, tugging at a bunch of grapes that pulled loose like beads from a necklace. "Cut the stem all the way," she told me as last advice before she walked away, her shoes sinking in the loose dirt, to begin work on her own row.

I cut another bunch, then another, fighting the snap and whip of vines. After ten minutes of **groping** for grapes, my first pan brimmed with bunches. I poured them on the paper tray, which was bordered by a wooden frame that kept the grapes from rolling off, and they spilled like jewels from a pirate's chest. The tray was only half filled, so I hurried to jump under the vines and begin groping, cutting, and tugging at the grapes again. I emptied the pan, raked the grapes with my hands to make them look like they filled the tray, and jumped back under the vine on my knees. I tried to cut faster because Mother, in the next row, was slowly moving ahead. I peeked into her row and saw five trays gleaming in the early morning. I cut, pulled hard, and stopped to gather the grapes that missed the pan; already bored, I spat on a few to wash them before tossing them like popcorn into my mouth. B

So it went. Two pans equaled one tray—or six cents. By lunchtime I had a trail of thirty-seven trays behind me while Mother had sixty or more. We met about halfway from our last trays, and I sat down with a grunt, knees wet from kneeling on dropped grapes. I washed my hands with the water from the jug, drying them on the inside of my shirt sleeve before I opened the paper bag for the first sandwich, which I gave to Mother. I dipped my hand in again to unwrap a sandwich without looking at it. I took a first bite and chewed it slowly for the tang of mustard. Eating in silence I looked straight ahead at the vines, and only when we were finished with cookies did we talk.

"Are you tired?" she asked.

"No, but I got a sliver from the frame," I told her. I showed her the web of skin between my thumb and index finger. She wrinkled her forehead but said it was nothing.

"How many trays did you do?"

I looked straight ahead, not answering at first. I recounted in my mind the whole morning of bend, cut, pour again and again, before answering a **feeble** "thirty-seven." No elaboration, no detail. Without looking at me she told me how she had done field work in Texas and Michigan as a child. But I had a difficult time listening to her stories. I played with my grape knife, stabbing it

ramble (răm′bəl) *v.* to t at length and aimlessly

foreman (fôr′mən) *n.* t leader of a work crew

grope (grōp) *v.* to reach about with uncertainty

B SENSORY DETAILS What details in lines 37- help you understand th experience of cutting grapes? Add this information to your we

feeble (fē′bəl) *adj.* wea or faint

DIFFERENTIATED INSTRUCTION

FOR LESS–PROFICIENT READERS

Reading Strategy Follow-Up: Analyze Sensory Details [paired option] Review the five senses with students, and remind them to add descriptions to their sensory detail webs (from page 817) as they read. Have pairs scan pages 820–821 looking for sensory details to add to their webs. ***Possible answer:***

- ***Sight:*** *"the web of skin between my thumb and index finger" (lines 59–60), "knife sticking up like a small, leafless plant" (line 69)*
- ***Hearing:*** *"sat down with a grunt" (line 51)*
- ***Touch:*** *"knees wet from kneeling on dropped grapes" (lines 51–52), "afternoon heat" (line 96)*
- ***Taste:*** *"tang of mustard" (line 56)*
- ***Smell:*** *no examples*

into the ground, but stopped when Mother reminded me that I had better not lose it. I left the knife sticking up like a small, leafless plant. She then talked about school, the junior high I would be going to that fall, and then about Rick and Debra, how sorry they would be that they hadn't come out to pick grapes because they'd have no new clothes for the school year. She stopped talking when she peeked at her watch, a bandless one she kept in her pocket. She got up with an *"Ay, Dios,"*[3] and told me that we'd work until three, leaving me cutting figures in the sand with my knife and dreading the return to work.

Finally I rose and walked slowly back to where I had left off, again kneeling under the vine and fixing the pan under bunches of grapes. By that time, 11:30, the sun was over my shoulder and made me squint and think of the pool at the Y.M.C.A. where I was a summer member. I saw myself diving face first into the water and loving it. I saw myself gleaming like something new, at the edge of the pool. I had to daydream and keep my mind busy because boredom was a terror almost as awful as the work itself. My mind went dumb with stupid things, and I had to keep it moving with dreams of baseball and would-be girlfriends. I even sang, however softly, to keep my mind moving, my hands moving. **C**

I worked less hurriedly and with less vision. I no longer saw that copper pot sitting squat on our stove or Mother waiting for it to whistle. The wardrobe that I imagined, crisp and bright in the closet, numbered only one pair of jeans and two shirts because, in half a day, six cents times thirty-seven trays was two dollars and twenty-two cents. It became clear to me. If I worked eight hours, I might make four dollars. I'd take this, even gladly, and walk downtown to look into store windows on the mall and long for the bright madras[4] shirts from Walter Smith or Coffee's, but settling for two imitation ones from Penney's.

That first day I laid down seventy-three trays while Mother had a hundred and twenty behind her. On the back of an old envelope, she wrote out our numbers and hours. We washed at the pump behind the farm house and walked slowly to our car for the drive back to town in the afternoon heat. That evening after dinner I sat in a lawn chair listening to music from a transistor radio while Rick and David King played catch. I joined them in a game of pickle, but there was little joy in trying to avoid their tags because I couldn't get the fields out of my mind: I saw myself dropping on my knees under a vine to tug at a branch that wouldn't come off. In bed, when I closed my eyes, I saw the fields, yellow with kicked up dust, and a crooked trail of trays rotting behind me. **D**

The next day I woke tired and started picking tired. The grapes rained into the pan, slowly filling like a belly, until I had my first tray and started my second. So it went all day, and the next, and all through the following week, so that by the end of thirteen days the foreman counted out, in tens mostly, my pay of fifty-three dollars. Mother earned one hundred and forty-eight dollars. She wrote this on her envelope, with a message I didn't bother to ask her about.

C AUTHOR'S PERSPECTIVE
What do Soto's statements about work in lines 75 and 81–82 tell you about his attitude toward field work?

2 Targeted Passage

D AUTHOR'S PERSPECTIVE
What effect does the author's work environment have on his life away from work?

3. ***Ay, Dios*** (ī dē-ōs') *Spanish:* "Oh, God."
4. **madras** (măd'rəs): cotton cloth, usually with a plaid pattern.

Lines 69–72
REINFORCE *KEY IDEA:* JOBS

Discuss Why do you think Soto's mother tells him that his brother and sister will regret not having summer **jobs?** ***Possible answer:*** *Soto's mother may be trying to encourage Soto by reminding him that he will get new clothes, while his siblings will not.*

LITERARY ANALYSIS

C AUTHOR'S PERSPECTIVE

Possible answer: *Soto's statements about "dreading the return to work" and having to daydream to avoid the boredom "almost as awful as the work itself" indicate that he has a negative attitude toward field work: he finds it tedious.*

Lines 85–92
REINFORCE *KEY IDEA:* JOBS

Discuss What does Soto learn about the **job** on his first day of work? ***Possible answer:*** *Soto learns that picking grapes is hard, boring, low-paying work.*

LITERARY ANALYSIS

D AUTHOR'S PERSPECTIVE

Possible answer: *His work environment has a negative effect because he is unable to stop thinking about his job, which prevents him from having fun and from sleeping.*

FOR LESS–PROFICIENT READERS

2 Targeted Passage [Lines 85–92]

This passage describes the change Soto experiences during the afternoon of his first day of picking grapes.

- Why is Soto working less hurriedly now?
- What goals has he given up? Why?
- What new goals is he willing to settle for?

FOR ENGLISH LEARNERS

Culture: Clarify Clarify the following terms for students:

- A *pump* (line 95) is an outdoor water faucet that is hooked to an underground well.
- A *transistor radio* (line 97) is a small radio that can be held in one's hand or carried in one's pocket.
- *Pickle* (line 98) is a baseball game that often has only three players: a runner and two fielders. The fielders throw the ball back and forth and try to tag, or touch, the runner before he or she takes the next base.

ANALYZE VISUALS

***Possible answer:** A shopping district might be a difficult place for Soto to spend time because he cannot afford to buy all the nice clothes he sees.*

About the Art Emigdio Vasquez is famous for his colorful murals, many of which can be found in Orange County, California. Vasquez's murals reflect his Hispanic heritage, including a tribute to Mexican-American farm leader César Chávez. Vasquez is also a teacher; he says, "I am there to give [students] instruction and ideas . . . to let their artistry flow."

Lines 119–135
DISCUSSION PROMPTS

Use these prompts to help students understand Soto's inner conflict about picking grapes:

Recall What choice does Soto make at age 15? ***Answer:** He would rather wear old clothes than pick grapes.*

Analyze Why do you think Soto feels he may have made a mistake? ***Possible answer:** He would like to have new clothes and can have them only if he works.*

Speculate Do you think Soto is actually able to fool his classmates by arranging his wardrobe to make it seem larger than it actually is? ***Possible answer:** He probably does not fool them because most of his clothes are old and out-of-style.*

La Calle Cuatro (2001), Emigdio Vasquez. Oil on canvas, 22″ × 28″. © Emigdio Vasquez.

ANALYZE VISUALS
Why might a **setting** lik
that in the picture be a
difficult place for Soto
spend time?

The next day I walked with my friend Scott to the downtown mall where we drooled over the clothes behind fancy windows, bought popcorn, and sat at a tier of outdoor fountains to talk about girls. Finally we went into Penney's for more popcorn, which we ate walking around, before we returned home without buying anything. It wasn't until a few days before school that I let my fifty-three dollars slip quietly from my hands, buying a pair of pants, two shirts, and a maroon T-shirt, the kind that was in style. At home I tried them on while Rick looked on enviously; later, the day before school started, I tried them on again wondering not so much if they were worth it as who would see me first in those clothes.

Along with my brother and sister I picked grapes until I was fifteen, before giving up and saying that I'd rather wear old clothes than **stoop** like a Mexican. Mother thought I was being stuck-up, even stupid, because there would be no clothes for me in the fall. I told her I didn't care, but when Rick and Debra rose at five in the morning, I lay awake in bed feeling that perhaps I had made a mistake but unwilling to change my mind. That fall Mother bought me two pairs of socks, a packet of colored T-shirts, and underwear. The T-shirts would help, I thought, but who would see that I had new underwear and socks? I wore a new T-shirt on the first day of school, then an old shirt on Tuesday, then another T-shirt on Wednesday, and on Thursday an old Nehru shirt[5] that was embarrassingly out of style. On Friday I changed into the corduroy pants my brother had handed down to me and slipped into my last new T-shirt. I worked like a magician, blinding my classmates, who were all clothes conscious and small-time social climbers, by arranging my wardrobe to make it seem larger than it really was. But by spring I had to do something—my blue jeans were almost silver and my shoes had lost their form, puddling like black ice around my feet. That spring of my sixteenth year,

stoop (sto͞op) *v.* to bend forward and down from the waist or the middle of the back

5. **Nehru** (nā′ro͞o) **shirt:** an Indian-style shirt with a stand-up collar.

DIFFERENTIATED INSTRUCTION

FOR ENGLISH LEARNERS

Comprehension: Sequence [paired option] Tell students that in a memoir, events are recounted in a sequence, often in the order in which they happened. Point out that "The next day" that Soto describes on this page (beginning in line 109) is the day that follows Soto's last day of grape picking. Instruct students to work in pairs to find the phrases Soto uses in lines 109–141 to indicate the order in which events occur, such as *Finally, before,* and *a few days before school.*

FOR ADVANCED LEARNERS/PRE–AP

Evaluate Details [small-group option] Tell students that much of Soto's writing is aimed at young adults. Have students form small groups and review the story for details Soto might have included to appeal to this audience. Ask them to evaluate Soto's ability to appeal to young adults. What details does he include that many young adults would connect to? Which details, if any, might young adults not care about? Ask a volunteer to share the group's conclusions with the class.

Rick and I decided to take a labor bus to chop cotton. In his old Volkswagen, which was more noise than power, we drove on a Saturday morning to West Fresno—or Chinatown as some call it—parked, walked slowly toward a bus, and stood gawking at the . . . blacks, Okies,[6] *Tejanos*[7] with gold teeth, . . . Mexican families, and labor **contractors** shouting "Cotton" or "Beets," the work of spring. **E**

We boarded the "Cotton" bus without looking at the contractor who stood almost blocking the entrance. . . . We boarded scared. . . . We sat . . . looking straight ahead, and only glanced briefly at the others who boarded, almost all of them broken and poorly dressed in loudly mismatched clothes. Finally when the contractor banged his palm against the side of the bus, the young man at the wheel, smiling and talking in Spanish, started the engine, idled it for a moment while he adjusted the mirrors, and started off in slow chugs. Except for the windshield there was no glass in the windows, so as soon as we were on the rural roads outside Fresno, the dust and sand began to be sucked into the bus, whipping about like **irate** wasps as the gravel ticked about us. We closed our eyes, clotted up our mouths that wanted to open with embarrassed laughter because we couldn't believe we were on that bus with those people and the dust attacking us for no reason. **F**

When we arrived at a field we followed the others to a pickup where we each took a hoe and marched to stand before a row. Rick and I, self-conscious and unsure, looked around at the others who leaned on their hoes or squatted in front of the rows, almost all talking in Spanish, joking . . . all waiting for the foreman's whistle to begin work. Mother had explained how to chop cotton by showing us with a broom in the backyard.

"Like this," she said, her broom swishing down weeds. "Leave one plant and cut four—and cut them! Don't leave them standing or the foreman will get mad."

The foreman whistled and we started up the row stealing glances at other workers to see if we were doing it right. But after awhile we worked like we knew what we were doing, neither of us hurrying or falling behind. But slowly the clot of men, women, and kids began to spread and loosen. Even Rick pulled away. I didn't hurry, though. I cut smoothly and cleanly as I walked at a slow pace, in a sort of funeral march. My eyes measured each space of cotton plants before I cut. If I missed the plants, I swished again. I worked intently, seldom looking up, so when I did I was amazed to see the sun, like a broken orange coin, in the east. It looked blurry, unbelievable, like something not of this world. I looked around in amazement, scanning the eastern horizon that was a taut line jutted with an occasional mountain. The horizon was beautiful, like a snapshot of the moon, in the early light of morning, in the quiet of no cars and few people. **G**

contractor (kŏn'trăk'tər) *n.* one who agrees to provide services for a specific price

E AUTHOR'S PERSPECTIVE
Reread lines 119–141. What reasons does Soto give for rejecting field work? Tell why his views change.

irate (ī-rāt') *adj.* very angry

F SENSORY DETAILS
Reread lines 142–154. What words and phrases help you feel, hear, and see what it was like to ride the "Cotton" bus?

③ Targeted Passage

G SENSORY DETAILS
What sensory details does Soto use to help you see the beauty of his surroundings?

6. **Okies** (ō'kēz): people from Oklahoma and other midwestern states who moved to California to find work during the Great Depression of the 1930s.
7. ***Tejanos*** (tā-hä'nōs): Texans of Mexican ancestry.

ADDITIONAL TEACHING OPPORTUNITY

Regional Labels During the 1930s, at the height of the Great Depression, a drought struck the Plains region of the central United States. People migrated west to California with hopes of jobs and land; victims of the Dust Bowl in Oklahoma moved in such large numbers that they were called "Okies" (line 139) by reporters. Ask students to identify the way the label "Okie" reflects the setting of the memoir in Fresno, California.

LITERARY ANALYSIS

E AUTHOR'S PERSPECTIVE

Possible answer: *Soto rejects field work because he doesn't want to "stoop like a Mexican," or do hard work. He changes his mind because he needs to earn money so that he can buy new clothes.*

READING STRATEGY

F SENSORY DETAILS

Have students record their answers in the web from page 817. ***Possible answer:***

- ***Touch:*** *"dust and sand . . . whipping about" (lines 150–151), "dust attacking us" (line 154)*
- ***Hearing:*** *"the contractor banged his palm against the side of the bus" (line 146), "talking in Spanish" (line 147), "slow chugs" (line 148), "gravel ticked about us" (line 151)*
- ***Sight:*** *"others who boarded . . . broken and poorly dressed in loudly mismatched clothes" (lines 144–145), "no glass in the windows" (line 149), "dust and sand began to be sucked into the bus" (lines 150–151)*

READING STRATEGY

G SENSORY DETAILS

Have students record their answers in the web from page 817. ***Possible answer:*** *He describes the sun as "blurry" and "like a broken orange coin" and the horizon as being "a taut line jutted with an occasional mountain" and "beautiful, like a snapshot of the moon."*

FOR LESS–PROFICIENT READERS

③ Targeted Passage [Lines 142–172]

This passage describes the author's experience on the first morning of his second job.

- What feelings do Soto and Rick experience as they board the bus and as they wait to begin work? Why do they feel this way?
- Who taught the boys to chop cotton? What method did she use to teach them?
- Describe the way Soto works in the cotton field. What might be his attitude toward chopping cotton?

FOR ENGLISH LEARNERS

Language: Phrasal Verbs [paired option]
Tell students that a phrasal verb, or a verb followed by a preposition or an adverb, has a different meaning than the verb alone. Have student pairs read the sentences containing these phrasal verbs: *giving up* (line 120), *changed into* (lines 129–130), *handed down* (line 130), *slipped into* (line 130), and *pulled away* (line 168). Ask students to use context or reference materials to define each verb. Encourage them to look for other phrasal verbs as they read.

The foreman trudged in boots in my direction, stepping awkwardly over the plants, to inspect the work. No one around me looked up. We all worked steadily while we waited for him to leave. When he did leave, with a feeble complaint addressed to no one in particular, we looked up smiling under straw hats and bandanas.

By 11:00, our lunch time, my ankles were hurting from walking on clods[8] the size of hardballs. My arms ached and my face was dusted by a wind that was perpetual, always busy whipping about. But the work was not bad, I thought. It was better, so much better, than picking grapes, especially with the hourly wage of a dollar twenty-five instead of piece work. Rick and I walked sorely toward the bus where we washed and drank water. Instead of eating in the bus or in the shade of the bus, we kept to ourselves by walking down to the irrigation canal[9] that ran the length of the field, to open our lunch of sandwiches and crackers. We laughed at the crackers, which seemed like a cruel joke from our Mother, because we were working under the sun and the last thing we wanted was a salty dessert. We ate them anyway and drank more water before we returned to the field, both of us limping in exaggeration. Working side by side, we talked and laughed at our **predicament** because our Mother had warned us year after year that if we didn't get on track in school we'd have to work in the fields and then we would see. We mimicked Mother's whining voice and smirked at her smoky view of the future in which we'd be trapped by marriage and screaming kids. We'd eat beans and then we'd see. **H**

Rick pulled slowly away to the rhythm of his hoe falling faster and smoother. It was better that way, to work alone. I could hum made-up songs or songs from the radio and think to myself about school and friends. At the time I was doing badly in my classes, mainly because of a difficult stepfather, but also because I didn't care anymore. All through junior high and into my first year of high school there were those who said I would never do anything, be anyone. They said I'd work like a donkey and marry the first Mexican girl that came along. I was reminded so often, verbally and in the way I was treated at home, that I began to believe that chopping cotton might be a lifetime job for me. If not chopping cotton, then I might get lucky and find myself in a car wash or restaurant or junkyard. But it was clear; I'd work, and work hard. **I**

I cleared my mind by humming and looking about. The sun was directly above with a few soft blades of clouds against a sky that seemed bluer and more beautiful than our sky in the city. Occasionally the breeze flurried and picked up dust so that I had to cover my eyes and screw up my face. The workers were hunched, brown as the clods under our feet, and spread across the field that ran without end—fields that were owned by corporations, not families.

I hoed trying to keep my mind busy with scenes from school and pretend girlfriends until finally my brain turned off and my thinking went fuzzy with boredom. I looked about, no longer mesmerized by the beauty of the

predicament (prĭ-dĭk'ə-mənt) *n.* an unpleasant situation from which it is difficult to free oneself

H SENSORY DETAILS Which detail in lines 182–198 most helps you feel what it was like to be with Soto and Rick that day?

I AUTHOR'S PERSPECTIVE How might Soto's experiences at school and home affect his expectations for himself?

8. **clods:** hardened clumps of soil.
9. **irrigation canal:** a ditch that brings water to crops.

READING STRATEGY

H SENSORY DETAILS

Have students record their answers in the web from page 817. *Answers will vary. Some students may choose the details that describe how sore Soto and Rick were. Others might choose the details that describe Soto and Rick eating lunch together or talking about their mother.*

LITERARY ANALYSIS

I AUTHOR'S PERSPECTIVE

***Possible answer:** He may set low expectations for himself based on others' comments that he would never amount to anything.*

DIFFERENTIATED INSTRUCTION

FOR LESS–PROFICIENT READERS

Vocabulary Support Remind students that they can often use context clues to learn the meaning of a new word. Ask students the following questions about vocabulary in the memoir:

- Line 177: Based on the phrases "in boots" and "stepping awkwardly," what do you think *trudged* means?
- Line 184: Based on the phrase "always busy whipping about," what do you think *perpetual* means?
- Line 186: Based on the phrases "hourly wage" and "instead of" what do you think *piece work* is?

FOR ENGLISH LEARNERS

Vocabulary: Idioms and Sayings Point out and ask students to define the following idioms and sayings from the memoir:

- *kept to ourselves* (line 188), "stayed away from others"
- *get on track* (line 195), "do better"
- *Working side by side* (lines 193–194), "working next to each other"
- *work like a donkey* (line 205), "work hard"
- *ate my words* (line 259), "took back what I said"

landscape, . . . no longer dreaming of the clothes I'd buy with my pay. My eyes followed my chopping as the plants, thin as their shadows, fell with each strike. I worked slowly with ankles and arms hurting, neck stiff, and eyes stinging from the dust and the sun that glanced off the field like a mirror.

By quitting time, 3:00, there was such an excruciating pain in my ankles that I walked as if I were wearing snowshoes. Rick laughed at me and I laughed too, embarrassed that most of the men were walking normally and I was among the first timers who had to get used to this work. "And what about you . . ." I came back at Rick. His eyes were meshed red and his long hippie hair was flecked with dust and gnats and bits of leaves. We placed our hoes in the back of a pickup and stood in line for our pay, which was twelve fifty. I was amazed at the pay, which was the most I had ever earned in one day, and thought that I'd come back the next day, Sunday. This was too good.

Instead of joining the others in the labor bus, we jumped in the back of a pickup when the driver said we'd get to town sooner and were welcome to join him. We scrambled into the truck bed to be joined by a heavy-set and laughing *Tejano* whose head was shaped like an egg, particularly so because the bandana he wore ended in a point on the top of his head. He laughed almost demonically as the pickup roared up the dirt path, a gray cape of dust rising behind us. On the highway, with the wind in our faces, we squinted at the fields as if we were looking for someone. The *Tejano* had quit laughing but was smiling broadly, occasionally chortling tunes he never finished. I was scared of him, though Rick, two years older and five inches taller, wasn't. If the *Tejano* looked at him, Rick stared back for a second or two before he looked away to the fields. **J**

I felt like a soldier coming home from war when we rattled into Chinatown. People leaning against car hoods stared, their necks following us, owl-like; . . . Chinese grocers stopped brooming their storefronts to raise their cadaverous faces at us. We stopped in front of the Chi Chi Club where Mexican music blared from the juke box and cue balls cracked like dull ice. The *Tejano,* who was dirty as we were, stepped awkwardly over the side rail, dusted himself off with his bandana, and sauntered into the club. **K**

Rick and I jumped from the back, thanked the driver who said *de nada*[10] and popped his clutch, so that the pickup jerked and coughed blue smoke. We returned smiling to our car, happy with the money we had made and pleased that we had, in a small way, proved ourselves to be tough; that we worked as well as other men and earned the same pay.

We returned the next day and the next week until the season was over and there was nothing to do. I told myself that I wouldn't pick grapes that summer, saying all through June and July that it was for Mexicans, not me. When August came around and I still had not found a summer job, I ate my words, sharpened my knife, and joined Mother, Rick, and Debra for one last time.

J SENSORY DETAILS
Reread lines 234–243. What details help you understand what the *Tejano* looks like and sounds like as he rides in the truck?

K AUTHOR'S PERSPECTIVE
Why does Soto feel like "a soldier coming home from war"?

4 Targeted Passage

10. ***de nada*** (də nä'də) *Spanish:* "You're welcome—it's nothing."

READING STRATEGY

J SENSORY DETAILS

Have students record their answers in the web from page 817. ***Possible answer:***

- ***Tejano looks like:*** *"heavy-set and laughing," "head was shaped like an egg," "bandana he wore ended in a point on the top of his head"*
- ***Tejano sounds like:*** *"laughed almost demonically," "chortling tunes he never finished"*

LITERARY ANALYSIS

K AUTHOR'S PERSPECTIVE

Possible answer: *He believes he has experienced something difficult and dangerous.*

If students need help . . . Have students describe how Soto is feeling. Then, elicit descriptions of what a soldier might feel like and make comparisons between Soto and a soldier.

SELECTION WRAP-UP

REFLECT Encourage students to think about the ways in which Soto's field-work experiences might have helped him become a successful writer.

CRITIQUE Ask students whether they think all readers can appreciate "One Last Time" or whether the story appeals mostly to those who have done field work. Have students explain their responses.

READING FLUENCY

Distribute the copy masters and have students practice fluency.

RESOURCE MANAGER—Copy Master
Reading Fluency p. 111

FOR LESS-PROFICIENT READERS

4 Targeted Passage [Lines 244–260]

This passage concludes the memoir and clarifies the meaning of the title.

- What do people do when the pickup drives into Chinatown?
- Why are Rick and Soto happy when they return to their car?
- What does Soto do "one last time" in August?

FOR ADVANCED LEARNERS/PRE-AP

Compare and Contrast Distribute the Venn Diagram and challenge students to write a paragraph comparing and contrasting Soto's first day picking grapes with his first day chopping cotton. Students might consider:

- In what ways do the circumstances differ?
- In what ways is Soto's attitude different?
- What are the effects of each job?

BEST PRACTICES TOOLKIT—Transparency
Venn Diagram p. A26

DISCUSSION PROMPTS

Use these prompts to help students understand the connection between what Soto learns from field work and the cycle described in "How Things Work":

Connect How might working hard at a job affect your spending habits? *Answers will vary, but students may note that they'd be more frugal after working hard for their money.*

Synthesize Consider what "task" the speaker is referring to in line 5 of the poem. When does young Soto complete this task in his memoir? When does he not? ***Possible answer:*** *The task of people in a consumer society is to earn and spend money. Soto completes this task when he works and buys school clothes; he doesn't complete it when he chooses to stay home and wear old clothes rather than pick grapes.*

Speculate What advice about money might the speaker in the poem give young Soto? ***Possible answer:*** *The speaker might tell young Soto that spending money is important because it gives others a chance to earn and spend money.*

Connect: Poem

How Things Work

GARY SOTO

Today it's going to cost us twenty dollars
To live. Five for a softball. Four for a book,
A handful of ones for coffee and two sweet rolls,
Bus fare, rosin[1] for your mother's violin.
We're completing our task. The tip I left
For the waitress filters down
Like rain, wetting the new roots of a child
Perhaps, a belligerent cat that won't let go
Of a balled sock until there's chicken to eat.
As far as I can tell, daughter, it works like this:
You buy bread from a grocery, a bag of apples
From a fruit stand, and what coins
Are passed on helps others buy pencils, glue,
Tickets to a movie in which laughter
Is thrown into their faces.
If we buy a goldfish, someone tries on a hat.
If we buy crayons, someone walks home with a broom.
A tip, a small purchase here and there,
And things just keep going. I guess.

1. **rosin** (rŏz′ĭn): a substance derived from tree sap that is used to increase sliding friction on stringed instruments' bows.

DIFFERENTIATED INSTRUCTION

FOR LESS–PROFICIENT READERS

Comprehension Support Clarify Soto's descriptions in the poem.

- In lines 5–7, Soto uses both a simile ("the tip . . . filters down like rain") and a metaphor ("wetting the new roots of a child") to describe the way money circulates.
- In lines 14–15, Soto uses the phrase "laughter is thrown into their faces" to suggest the way a movie can cause an audience to laugh.

FOR ENGLISH LEARNERS

Option for Reading Have students listen to the *Audio Anthology CD* while they read along with the poem. Then do an echo reading of the poem with students. Help students paraphrase the poem to make sure they understand what the speaker is saying and that the speaker is talking to his daughter.

826 UNIT 7: HISTORY, CULTURE, AND THE AUTHOR

fter Reading

omprehension

1. **Recall** What does Gary Soto dream of buying his mother?
2. **Recall** What does Soto think about when he is bored at work?
3. **Summarize** Describe Soto's first day chopping cotton.

iterary Analysis

4. **Make Inferences** How might Soto's family history affect his thoughts and feelings about working in the fields? Cite evidence from the story and the biography on page 817 to support your response.
5. **Analyze Sensory Details** Review the sensory details you noted in your web. What single detail best captures for you what it was like to pick grapes or chop cotton?
6. **Compare and Contrast** Which does Soto like more, picking grapes or chopping cotton? Note the similarities and differences between the two jobs. Then explain why Soto prefers the one he does.
7. **Examine Author's Perspective** In what ways does Gary Soto's perspective toward work change throughout the selection? Consider what happens to Soto's dreams the longer he works in the fields. Track his attitude toward his jobs on a timeline like the one shown. Record his positive feelings above the line and negative feelings below the line.

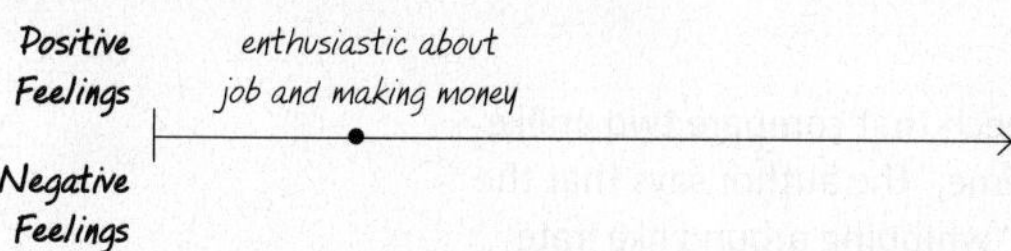

8. **Compare Literary Works** Think about Gary Soto's childhood experiences as a field laborer. What effect might they have had on the view of money he expresses in his poem "How Things Work" on page 826? Explain.

xtension and Challenge

9. **Big Question Activity** What might Soto say he learned from his **jobs** working in the fields? Respond to the Quickwrite activity on page 816 as if you were Soto.
10. **Readers' Circle** Writers choose titles for their selections very carefully. Why do you think Gary Soto titled this memoir "One Last Time"? Reread the last paragraph of the memoir and think about the ideas Soto emphasizes. Then, in small groups, brainstorm other possible titles. Share your best idea with the class.

Practice and Apply

After Reading

For additional support of postreading questions, use these copy masters:

RESOURCE MANAGER—Copy Masters

Reading Check p. 108 (to check understanding of the selection)

Author's Perspective p. 101 (for practice of literary analysis standards focus)

Question Support p. 109 (After Reading questions adapted for English learners and less-proficient readers)

Additional selection questions are provided for teachers on page 95.

ANSWERS

Comprehension

1. *Soto dreams of buying his mother a copper tea pot.*
2. *He thinks about the pool, baseball, and girls.*
3. *After an uncomfortable bus ride to the fields, he works intently in the morning, lunches with his brother, fights boredom and pain in the afternoon, and then is pleased with his work and the money he has earned.*

Literary Analysis

Possible answers:

4. *Because his relatives' lives as fieldworkers were so hard (lines 9–11, 15–20), Soto knows the difficulty of field work and may advise people to further their education to avoid it.*
5. **STANDARDS FOCUS Analyze Sensory Details** *Answers will vary. Students' answers should describe the experience of picking grapes or chopping cotton.*
6. *Soto prefers chopping cotton. Both jobs are physically demanding and boring. Chopping cotton pays more, allows him to see the beauty around him, and makes him feel tough.*
7. **STANDARDS FOCUS Author's Perspective** *Soto starts out being enthusiastic about picking grapes because of the money he will earn. He quickly gets bored and discouraged and lets go of the dream of buying lots of clothes. At first, Soto is self-conscious about chopping cotton. Then he gets caught up in the work and enjoys the beautiful scenery. However, while he makes more money and feels tough, this job is still tiring and boring. Soto eventually decides to pick grapes one last time when no other work is available.*
8. *Working in the field for little money enabled Soto to buy clothes for school, so he understands that even small amounts of money mean a lot to the working poor.*

Extension and Challenge

9. *"I learned that field work is boring, exhausting, and poorly paid, so I decided to go to college to avoid having to do physical labor as an adult."*
10. *Students' title ideas will vary. Soto may have chosen the title based on his decision to return to the grape fields one last time, in the hope that by the next year, he will have found a better job.*

ANSWERS

Vocabulary in Context

VOCABULARY PRACTICE

1. *false*
2. *true*
3. *false*
4. *true*
5. *true*
6. *false*
7. *true*
8. *true*

RESOURCE MANAGER—Copy Master
Vocabulary Practice p. 106

VOCABULARY IN WRITING

Suggest that students review the vocabulary words and identify the ones with negative connotations. In what way might these words be used to describe a terrible summer job?

VOCABULARY STRATEGY: SIMILES *(also an EL language objective)*

To reinforce the way that similes make comparisons between unlike things, discuss these examples from the selection:

- "my relatives, dusty and thin as sparrows" (lines 2–3)
- "a bunch of grapes that pulled loose like beads from a necklace" (lines 34–35)
- "the knife sticking up like a small, leafless plant" (line 69)
- "the sun, like a broken orange coin" (lines 171–172)

Possible answers:

1. *expanded*
2. *running without moving*
3. *with great concentration*
4. *lit up*
5. *agonizing*

RESOURCE MANAGER—Copy Master
Vocabulary Strategy p. 107

Vocabulary Center at **ClassZone.com**
Additional Vocabulary Activities

Vocabulary in Context

VOCABULARY PRACTICE

Show that you understand the vocabulary words by telling whether each statement is true or false.

1. Someone who **rambles** on about a topic gets right to the point.
2. It is a **foreman**'s job to tell workers what to do.
3. Someone who **gropes** for an item finds it right away.
4. If you drop something on the floor, you can **stoop** to pick it up.
5. **Contractors** supply labor and materials for a project.
6. Most people feel **irate** on their birthdays.
7. A **feeble** voice is difficult to hear.
8. Having two appointments at the same time might be called a **predicament.**

contractor
feeble
foreman
grope
irate
predicament
ramble
stoop

VOCABULARY IN WRITING

What is the worst summer job you can imagine? Using at least two vocabulary words, write a paragraph describing your first day.

EXAMPLE SENTENCE

*The labor **contractor** hired us to work.*

VOCABULARY STRATEGY: SIMILES

Writers sometimes use **similes,** or figures of speech that compare two unlike things using the words *like* or *as.* In "One Last Time," the author says that the dust and sand flying into their moving bus was "whipping around like irate wasps." This simile helps readers imagine what it would feel like to be riding in the bus.

Similes can also provide context clues to help you figure out unfamiliar word meanings. If you know that "whipping around" implies fast, curving motion and that *wasps* move more quickly when they're angered, then you can figure out that *irate* means "very angry."

PRACTICE Use the simile in each sentence as a context clue to help you define the boldfaced word.

1. His **elaborate** story was as layered as a wedding cake.
2. The **idling** engine purred like a lazy kitten.
3. She stared at me as **intently** as a cat watches a bird.
4. The lightning **illuminated** the sky like a fireworks display.
5. Her **excruciating** sense of homesickness felt like physical pain.

VOCABULARY PRACTICE
For more practice, go to the **Vocabulary Cente[r]** at **ClassZone.com.**

DIFFERENTIATED INSTRUCTION

FOR ENGLISH LEARNERS

Vocabulary Strategy Encourage Spanish-speaking students to use their knowledge of cognates to help them remember the definitions of these words:

- *elaborated/elaborado*
- *intently/atento*
- *illuminated/iluminado*

FOR ADVANCED LEARNERS/PRE–AP

Vocabulary Strategy Challenge students to create new sentences with different similes that define the boldfaced words. Have students share their similes with a partner. Alternatively, you might have students write similes using the vocabulary words *ramble, feeble, grope,* and *stoop.*

828 UNIT 7: HISTORY, CULTURE, AND THE AUTHOR

eading-Writing Connection

Deepen your appreciation of "One Last Time" by responding to the prompts. Then complete the **Grammar and Writing** exercise.

WRITING PROMPTS	SELF-CHECK
A. Short Response: Write a Letter to the Editor Do you think children under the age of 16 should be allowed to work **jobs** harvesting crops? Write a **one-paragraph letter to the editor** of a newspaper, expressing your opinion.	***A strong letter will . . .*** • clearly state your position for or against the issue • give reasons that support your opinion
B. Extended Response: Compare Narrators Gary Soto in "One More Time" and the narrator in "The Snapping Turtle" (page 766) are both deeply affected by their cultural heritage. In a **two- or three-paragraph response,** compare and contrast how their heritages influence their actions.	***An effective comparison will . . .*** • identify each person's heritage and how he feels about it • support your points with evidence from the selections

RAMMAR AND WRITING

USE SEMICOLONS CORRECTLY When there are commas within parts of a series, you must use a **semicolon** to separate the parts.

Original: Some children need to earn money to buy bus tokens, clothing, and school supplies, such as pencils, paper, and notebooks.

Revised: Some children need to earn money to buy bus tokens; clothing; and school supplies, such as pencils, paper, and notebooks. (*Because one part of the series contains commas, a semicolon should separate the parts.*)

PRACTICE In the following sentences, insert semicolons as needed.

1. Not all parents can afford to buy food, clothing, and other necessities, pay for their children's education, and maintain a roof over their heads.
2. Hard work teaches children responsibility, independence, and self-respect, enables them to earn a living, and instructs them in the value of money.
3. Children should be able to work on farms if they attend school, don't handle pesticides, machinery, or dangerous animals, and are paid a decent wage.
4. A job harvesting crops provides children with exercise, sunshine, and clean air, gets them away from TV, and teaches them to appreciate their food.

For more help with semicolons, see page R49 in the ***Grammar Handbook.***

Reading-Writing Connection

WRITING PROMPTS

- For **Prompt A,** encourage students to list the pros and cons of children under the age of 16 having jobs. Then have students take a position and support it with details from their list.
- For **Prompt B,** suggest that students review both stories and use the Compare and Contrast writing template to plan their responses.

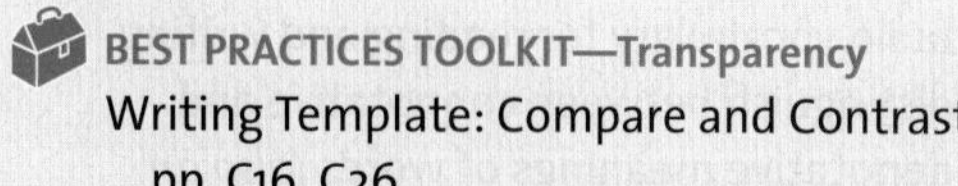

BEST PRACTICES TOOLKIT—Transparency
Writing Template: Compare and Contrast pp. C16, C26

For writing support, see

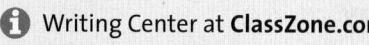

Writing Center at **ClassZone.com**

GRAMMAR AND WRITING

Write the original sentence from page 829 on the board. Circle the three parts of the series and point out that only one of them has commas within it. Discuss how the semicolons in the revised sentence clarify what the three items in the series are and make the sentence easier to understand.

Answers: *Semicolons should be placed after the following words:*

1. *necessities, education*
2. *self-respect, living*
3. *school, animals*
4. *air, TV*

RESOURCE MANAGER—Copy Master
Use Semicolons Correctly p. 110

Assess and Reteach

Assess

RESOURCE MANAGER—Copy Masters
Selection Tests A, B/C pp. 113–114, 115–116

Test Generator CD

Reteach

STANDARDS LESSON FILE
Literature Lesson 29: Simile and Metaphor
Literature Lesson 41: Author's Perspective
Vocabulary Lesson 14: Context Clues

DIFFERENTIATED INSTRUCTION

FOR LESS-PROFICIENT WRITERS

For Prompt A:

1. Distribute the Persuasive Writing template and suggest that students fill in at least two reasons and then add supporting details from their pros and cons list.
2. Tell students to select their most strongly supported reason to use in their letters.

BEST PRACTICES TOOLKIT—Transparency
Writing Template: Persuasive Writing pp. C16, C35

For Prompt B:

Suggest that students write a three-paragraph response using the block method of comparing and contrasting.

- **First paragraph:** Focus on the ways Soto is affected by his cultural heritage.
- **Second paragraph:** Focus on the ways the narrator in "The Snapping Turtle" is affected.
- **Third paragraph:** Express the similarities and differences between Soto and the narrator in "The Snapping Turtle."

Focus and Motivate

OBJECTIVES

Literary Analysis

- explore the key idea of what makes you **proud**
- identify, analyze, and interpret an autobiography
- read an autobiography

Reading

- identify and analyze cause-and-effect relationships

Vocabulary

- build vocabulary for reading and writing
- distinguish between connotative and denotative meanings of words *(also an EL language objective)*

SUMMARY

Ten-year-old Barack Obama is one of only two African-American children in his grade at an elite private school in Hawaii. Obama struggles with feeling different from his classmates. His fear and isolation lead him to spend much of his spare time watching television with his grandparents, until a month-long visit from his Kenyan father changes his perspective and helps him see the value of hard work and his cultural heritage.

What makes you PROUD?

Discuss the question with students. To lead into the ***KEY IDEA,*** ask students to discuss why people might want to be like everyone else. Have them consider the benefits of being **proud** of their differences. Then have students work independently on the ***SKETCH IT*** activity.

Before Reading

from Dreams from My Father

Autobiography by Barack Obama

What makes you PROUD?

KEY IDEA No other person in the world is exactly like you. Even identical twins develop distinct personalities and interests. But so often, instead of being **proud** of their uniqueness, people want to "fit in" by trying to be like everyone else. In this autobiography, Barack Obama describes how, as a child, he began to take pride in his family heritage—the very thing that made him feel different from most of his classmates.

SKETCH IT What has been your proudest moment? It doesn't have to involve something others recognize as a major accomplishment. It just has to be meaningful to you. Make a sketch that reflects details of this moment and how you felt. If you're struggling to think of an example, make a drawing of a goal you have for yourself and what it might be like to achieve it.

830

Selection Resources

RESOURCE MANAGER UNIT 7

Plan and Teach pp. 117–124

Literary Analysis
Summary pp. 125†*, 126‡*
Autobiography pp. 127, 128†*
Question Support p. 135*

Reading
Recognize Cause-and-Effect Relationships pp. 129, 130†*
Reading Check p. 134
Reading Fluency p. 136

Vocabulary
Study p. 131*
Practice p. 132
Strategy p. 133

Assessment
Selection Tests A, B/C pp. 137*, 139*
Test Generator CD

BEST PRACTICES TOOLKIT

Differentiated Instruction pp. 31–38*
Scaffolding Instruction pp. 43–46*

Graphic Organizers/Strategies
Word Questioning • Read-and-Say-Something • Spider Map

Reading Support
Audio Anthology CD*

Technology
Literature and Vocabulary Centers at **ClassZone.com**
Write*Smart* CD

* Resources for Differentiation † Also in Spanish ‡ In Haitian Creole and Vietnamese

LITERARY ANALYSIS: AUTOBIOGRAPHY

An **autobiography** is the true story of a person's life, told by that person. Autobiographies share the following characteristics:

- They are told from the first-person point of view.
- They focus on significant people and events in the writer's life.
- They express the ways those people and events affected the writer.

This excerpt from Barack Obama's autobiography describes a visit from his father. As you read, pay attention to the details that reveal the relationship between father and son.

READING SKILL: RECOGNIZE CAUSE-AND-EFFECT RELATIONSHIPS

Why do people do the things they do? Why do they feel the way they feel? Understanding **cause-and-effect relationships** between actions, events, and feelings can give you greater insight into the people you read about. In Barack Obama's autobiography, not every cause-and-effect relationship is stated directly. Sometimes you will have to look deeper to notice when one or more things are responsible for causing another.

As you read, notice how Obama's emotions affect his actions. For each important cause-and-effect relationship, create a graphic like the one shown.

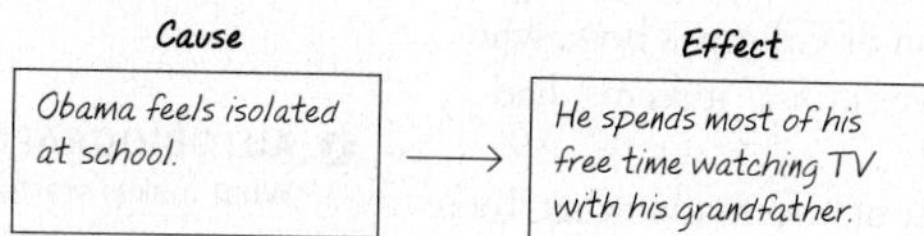

Cause
Obama feels isolated at school.
Effect
He spends most of his free time watching TV with his grandfather.

VOCABULARY IN CONTEXT

Barack Obama uses the following words to tell about his boyhood visit with his father. How well do you know these words? Place each one in the correct column of a chart like the one shown.

WORD LIST			
	dowdy	novelty	refuge
	inevitable	opaque	volatile
	irretrievably	recuperation	

Know Well	Think I Know	Don't Know at All

Author Online

A Cultural Mix
Barack Obama once described himself as a "skinny kid with a funny name." *Barack* means "blessing" in Swahili, a language spoken in Kenya and other African countries. Obama was named after his father, who was Kenyan. Obama's parents met at the University of Hawaii. There, Obama Sr. was the first-ever African student. Obama's mother, who is white, was originally from Kansas. Their marriage was short-lived, and Obama's father eventually moved back to Kenya. His mother remarried and took Obama to live with her new husband in Indonesia for four years. At age ten, Obama returned to Hawaii, where his grandparents helped raise him.

Barack Obama
born 1961

A Life of Service After graduating from Columbia University in New York City, Obama worked as a community organizer in Chicago, helping people affected by unemployment. He then attended Harvard Law School. He was offered jobs working for an important judge and in high-powered law firms, but instead he chose to return to Chicago to practice civil-rights law. In 1997, Obama entered politics, becoming an Illinois state senator representing Chicago's south side. In 2004, Obama was elected to the United States Senate. That same year, he wrote and presented the keynote speech at the Democratic National Convention, an important meeting at which the Democratic Party declares its candidate for president. The speech and Obama's delivery of it were widely praised.

MORE ABOUT THE AUTHOR
For more on Barack Obama, visit the **Literature Center** at **ClassZone.com.**

Teach

STANDARDS FOCUS

LITERARY ANALYSIS

AUTOBIOGRAPHY

Explain that authors of autobiographies cannot include all the details of their lives, so they focus on important events that changed them in some way. Have students think of a famous person and tell one event the person might include in his or her autobiography and why.

CHECK UNDERSTANDING Ask students to name significant people or events they might include in their own autobiographies.

READING SKILL

RECOGNIZE CAUSE-AND-EFFECT RELATIONSHIPS

Tell students that recognizing cause-and-effect relationships will help them understand why things happen. Have students tell one or more possible effects of the following causes:

- It rained on the day of the pool party.
- Maria studied hard for her test.
- Jamal was very impressed by the surgeon who spoke to his class.

CHECK UNDERSTANDING Have students name a cause-and-effect relationship in their own lives.

RESOURCE MANAGER—Copy Master
Recognize Cause-and-Effect Relationships p. 129 (for student use while reading the selection)

VOCABULARY SKILL

VOCABULARY IN CONTEXT

DIAGNOSE WORD KNOWLEDGE To determine preteaching needs, have all students complete **Vocabulary in Context.** *Students' responses will vary.*

PRETEACH VOCABULARY Use the Vocabulary Study copy master to help students predict the meaning of each boldfaced word, using context clues.

1. Read item 1 aloud, emphasizing *dowdy.*
2. Point out the phrase *compared to the youthful, popular styles the other girls wore.* Elicit possible meanings for *dowdy,* such as "out of style."
3. Have students record their predictions.
4. Repeat the procedure for items 2–8.

RESOURCE MANAGER—Copy Master
Vocabulary Study p. 131

For general guidelines on differentiating vocabulary instruction and for alternative vocabulary activities for students not needing vocabulary preteaching, see

BEST PRACTICES TOOLKIT
Scaffolding Vocabulary Instruction pp. 43–46

Vocabulary Center at **ClassZone.com**
Additional Vocabulary Activities

Practice and Apply

ANALYZE VISUALS

Possible answer: *The brightly decorated Hawaiian patterns of the clothes stand out, as do the big smiles on the children's faces. Students may also note that most of the children besides Obama are either Caucasian or Asian.*

LITERARY ANALYSIS

Ⓐ AUTOBIOGRAPHY

Possible answer: *Obama wants to make friends; his family hopes that Obama's attending the prestigious school will raise the family status.*

Lines 1–22

REINFORCE *KEY IDEA:* PROUD

Discuss In what ways is it evident that Gramps and Toot are **proud** of sending Obama to Punahou School? ***Possible answer:*** *They tell everyone about his admission (lines 2–5). Toot and Gramps set aside time to read the information about the school (lines 12–22).*

Dreams from My Father

BARACK OBAMA

ANALYZE VISUALS
Look at Obama's actual class picture. What **details** about Obama and his classmates stand out the most?

As the summer drew to a close, I became increasingly restless to start school. My main concern was finding companions my own age; but for my grandparents, my admission into Punahou Academy heralded the start of something grand, an elevation in the family status that they took great pains to let everyone know. Started by missionaries[1] in 1841, Punahou had grown into a prestigious prep school, an incubator for island elites. Its reputation had helped sway my mother in her decision to send me back to the States: It hadn't been easy to get me in, my grandparents told her; there was a long waiting list, and I was considered only because of the intervention of Gramps's boss, who was an alumnus (my first experience with affirmative action,[2] it seems, had little to do with race). . . . Ⓐ

With my admission notice had come a thick packet of information that Toot[3] set aside to pore over one Saturday afternoon. "Welcome to the Punahou family," the letter announced. A locker had been assigned to me; I was enrolled in a meal plan unless a box was checked; there was a list of things to buy—a uniform for physical education, scissors, a ruler, number two pencils, a calculator (optional). Gramps spent the evening reading the entire school catalog, a thick book that listed my expected progression through the next seven years—the college prep courses, the extracurricular activities, the traditions of well-rounded excellence. With each new item, Gramps grew more and more animated; several times he got up, with his thumb saving his place, and headed toward the room where Toot was reading, his voice full of amazement: "Madelyn, get a load of this!"

Ⓐ AUTOBIOGRAPHY
What makes starting school such an important event for Obama and his family?

1. **missionaries:** people who travel to distant places and spread their religion.
2. **affirmative action:** a system in which employers and schools give preference to members of minority groups in order to make up for past discrimination.
3. **Toot:** Obama's name for his grandmother.

DIFFERENTIATED INSTRUCTION

FOR ALL STUDENTS

Anchor Activity Provide opportunities for independent learning on the political career of Barack Obama. Have individual students or groups research how Obama entered politics and what he has accomplished as a public servant.

For further details on this project, see

RESOURCE MANAGER
Ideas for Extension pp. 122–123

FOR LESS–PROFICIENT READERS

In combination with the *Audio Anthology CD,* use one or more Targeted Passages (pp. 834, 836, 840, 843) to ensure that students focus on key events, concepts, and skills.

FOR ENGLISH LEARNERS

Prereading For prereading instruction for English learners, see

BEST PRACTICES TOOLKIT
Scaffolding Reading Instruction pp. 43–46

BACKGROUND

Punahou School Punahou has 3,700 students in kindergarten through twelfth grade, making it the largest private school in the United States. The campus grounds consist of more than 40 buildings, three of which are libraries. Of its 400 graduates each year, 99 percent go on to college.

CULTURAL CONNECTION

Hawaii Hawaii is one of the most ethnically diverse states in the nation. In Hawaii, there is no one ethnic group that makes up 51 percent or more of the population, so you could say that everyone is a minority! However, Asians and Caucasians make up the majority of the population. Native Hawaiians, Pacific Islanders, and African Americans make up the rest of the population. Invite students to share the ethnic make-up of other states with which they are more familiar.

FOR ENGLISH LEARNERS

Key Academic Vocabulary Have students use Word Questioning to study these words: *isolation* (line 78), *image(s)* (lines 151, 225, 231), *interactions* (line 218), *assignments* (line 261), *exposed* (line 298).

BEST PRACTICES TOOLKIT—Transparency
Word Questioning p. E9

Options for Reading [paired option] Read aloud page 832 and make sure students understand the setting and the events so far. Then have students listen to the rest of the selection on the *Audio Anthology CD* as they follow along. Students may work in pairs and pause the CD at the end of each page to discuss important points and raise questions.

BEST PRACTICES TOOLKIT
Read-and-Say-Something p. D3

FOR ADVANCED LEARNERS/PRE–AP

Pre-AP exercises in the bottom channel provide additional challenge for your advanced students. Use them for small groups or individuals.

ADDITIONAL GUIDELINES

For more help with differentiation and tips for classroom management, see

BEST PRACTICES TOOLKIT
Differentiated Instruction pp. 31–38

SOCIAL STUDIES CONNECTION

Kenya Kenya, whose capital is Nairobi, is about twice the size of the state of Nevada. English is its official language, but Swahili is the language spoken most often by Kenyans. Most Kenyans are farmers, producing goods for both local and foreign markets. The country's national parks and animal reserves are rich with wildlife, many of which are endangered, and tourists visit Kenya to see animals they may never see anywhere else on Earth. The Luo tribe, to which Obama's father belonged, is the third largest ethnic group in Kenya. The Luo played an important part in helping Kenya gain independence from Great Britain, which ruled the country from 1895 to 1963. Like other Kenyans today, many Luo are farmers, but because most live along the shores of Lake Victoria on Kenya's western border, many also fish for a living.

So it was with a great rush of excitement that Gramps accompanied me on my first day of school. He had insisted that we arrive early, and Castle Hall, the building for the fifth and sixth graders, was not yet opened. A handful of children had already arrived, busy catching up on the summer's news. We sat beside a slender Chinese boy who had a large dental retainer strapped around his neck.

"Hi there," Gramps said to the boy. "This here's Barry. I'm Barry's grandfather. You can call me Gramps." He shook hands with the boy, whose name was Frederick. "Barry's new."

"Me too," Frederick said, and the two of them launched into a lively conversation. I sat, embarrassed, until the doors finally opened and we went up the stairs to our classroom. At the door, Gramps slapped both of us on the back.

"Don't do anything I would do," he said with a grin.

"Your grandfather's funny," Frederick said as we watched Gramps introduce himself to Miss Hefty, our homeroom teacher.

"Yeah. He is."

We sat at a table with four other children, and Miss Hefty, an energetic middle-aged woman with short gray hair, took attendance. When she read my full name, I heard titters break across the room. Frederick leaned over to me.

"I thought your name was Barry."

"Would you prefer if we called you Barry?" Miss Hefty asked. "Barack is such a beautiful name. Your grandfather tells me your father is Kenyan. I used to live in Kenya, you know. Teaching children just your age. It's such a magnificent country. Do you know what tribe your father is from?"

Her question brought on more giggles, and I remained speechless for a moment. When I finally said "Luo," a sandy-haired boy behind me repeated the word in a loud hoot, like the sound of a monkey. The children could no longer contain themselves, and it took a stern reprimand from Miss Hefty before the class would settle down and we could mercifully move on to the next person on the list.

I spent the rest of the day in a daze. A redheaded girl asked to touch my hair and seemed hurt when I refused. A ruddy-faced boy asked me if my father ate people. When I got home, Gramps was in the middle of preparing dinner.

"So how was it? Isn't it terrific that Miss Hefty used to live in Kenya? Makes the first day a little easier, I'll bet."

I went into my room and closed the door.

The **novelty** of having me in the class quickly wore off for the other kids, although my sense that I didn't belong continued to grow. The clothes that Gramps and I had chosen for me were too old-fashioned; the Indonesian sandals that had served me so well in Djakarta[4] were **dowdy.** Most of my

SOCIAL STUDIES CONNECTION

Kenya is a country of great ethnic diversity.

① **Targeted Passage**

novelty (nŏv'əl-tē) *n.* t quality of being new

dowdy (dou'dē) *adj.* out of style; shabby

4. **Djakarta** (jə-kär'tə): the capital city of Indonesia, an island nation in Southeast Asia; sometimes spelled *Jakarta.*

DIFFERENTIATED INSTRUCTION

FOR LESS–PROFICIENT READERS

① **Targeted Passage [Lines 40–59]**

This passage describes how the other students treat Obama on his first day of school.

- What is the other students' reaction when they hear Obama's name and the name of his father's tribe?
- What does the ruddy-faced boy ask Obama?
- In what way does Obama's day differ from the way Gramps thinks it went?

Reading Skill Follow-Up: Recognize Cause-and-Effect Relationships [paired option] Encourage students to create graphic organizers like the one on page 831 to help them see the cause-and-effect relationships in Obama's story. Have pairs note the events that occur on Obama's first day at Punahou (causes) and how these events affect Obama (effects). Help students see how these events contribute to Obama's sense that he doesn't belong there.

Cause		Effect
Gramps accompanies Obama to school and talks with Frederick.	→	*Obama is embarrassed.*

classmates had been together since kindergarten; they lived in the same neighborhoods, in split-level homes with swimming pools; their fathers coached the same Little League teams; their mothers sponsored the bake sales. Nobody played soccer or badminton or chess, and I had no idea how to throw a football in a spiral or balance on a skateboard. **B**

B CAUSE AND EFFECT
What are some of the causes of Obama's discomfort around his classmates?

A ten-year-old's nightmare. Still, in my discomfort that first month, I was no worse off than the other children who were relegated to the category of misfits—the girls who were too tall or too shy, the boy who was mildly hyperactive, the kids whose asthma excused them from PE.

There was one other child in my class, though, who reminded me of a different sort of pain. Her name was Coretta, and before my arrival she had been the only black person in our grade. She was plump and dark and didn't seem to have many friends. From the first day, we avoided each other but watched from a distance, as if direct contact would only remind us more keenly of our isolation.

Finally, during recess one hot, cloudless day, we found ourselves occupying the same corner of the playground. I don't remember what we said to each other, but I remember that suddenly she was chasing me around the jungle gyms and swings. She was laughing brightly, and I teased her and dodged this way and that, until she finally caught me and we fell to the ground breathless. When I looked up, I saw a group of children, faceless before the glare of the sun, pointing down at us.

"Coretta has a boyfriend! Coretta has a boyfriend!"

The chants grew louder as a few more kids circled us.

"She's not my g-girlfriend," I stammered. I looked to Coretta for some assistance, but she just stood there looking down at the ground. "Coretta's got a boyfriend! Why don't you kiss her, mister boyfriend?"

"I'm not her boyfriend!" I shouted. I ran up to Coretta and gave her a slight shove; she staggered back and looked up at me, but still said nothing. "Leave me alone!" I shouted again. And suddenly Coretta was running, faster and faster, until she disappeared from sight. Appreciative laughs rose around me. Then the bell rang, and the teachers appeared to round us back into class. **C**

C CAUSE AND EFFECT
Reread lines 91–96. What causes Obama to push Coretta away?

For the rest of the afternoon, I was haunted by the look on Coretta's face just before she had started to run: her disappointment, and the accusation. I wanted to explain to her somehow that it had been nothing personal; I'd just never had a girlfriend before and saw no particular need to have one now. But I didn't even know if that was true. I knew only that it was too late for explanations, that somehow I'd been tested and found wanting; and whenever I snuck a glance at Coretta's desk, I would see her with her head bent over her work, appearing as if nothing had happened, pulled into herself and asking no favors.

READING SKILL

B CAUSE AND EFFECT

Remind students to record their answers in the graphic from page 831. ***Possible answer:*** *Obama's classmates laugh at him and ask rude and ignorant questions, making him feel that he doesn't fit in.*

READING SKILL

C CAUSE AND EFFECT

Remind students to record their answers in the graphic from page 831. ***Possible answer:*** *The students' pointing and chanting "Coretta has a boyfriend!" causes Obama to push Coretta away. He feels embarrassed and misunderstood.*

FOR ENGLISH LEARNERS

Language: Pronoun Referents Explain to students that pronouns, such as *she, he, it, we,* and *they* replace nouns in sentences. Have students point out the pronouns in these lines and tell what noun each refers to:

- line 40 *(we: Frederick and Obama)*
- line 41 *(she: Miss Hefty)*
- line 75 *(she: Coretta)*
- line 76 *(we: Coretta and Obama)*
- line 97 *(I: Obama)*

FOR ADVANCED LEARNERS/PRE–AP

Discuss Point of View [small-group option] Remind students that readers see the anecdote about Coretta only from Obama's point of view. Have small groups of students discuss how the story might have been different if told from different points of view: Coretta's and the other children's. What details might they have included? How might they have viewed the event differently from Obama? Ask a volunteer to summarize the discussion for the class.

My act of betrayal bought me some room from the other children, and like Coretta, I was mostly left alone. I made a few friends, learned to speak less often in class, and managed to toss a wobbly football around. But from that day forward, a part of me felt trampled on, crushed, and I took **refuge** in the life that my grandparents led. After school let out, I would walk the five blocks to our apartment; if I had any change in my pockets, I might stop off at a newsstand run by a blind man, who would let me know what new comics had come in. Gramps would be at home to let me into the apartment, and as he lay down for his afternoon nap, I would watch cartoons and sitcom reruns. At four-thirty, I would wake Gramps and we would drive downtown to pick up Toot. My homework would be done in time for dinner, which we ate in front of the television. There I would stay for the rest of the evening, negotiating with Gramps over which programs to watch, sharing the latest snack food he'd discovered at the supermarket. At ten o'clock, I went to my room (Johnny Carson came on at that time, and there was no negotiating around that), and I would fall asleep to the sounds of Top 40 music on the radio. **D**

Nested in the soft, forgiving bosom of America's consumer culture, I felt safe; it was as if I had dropped into a long hibernation. I wonder sometimes how long I might have stayed there had it not been for the telegram Toot found in the mailbox one day.

"Your father's coming to see you," she said. "Next month. Two weeks after your mother gets here. They'll both stay through New Year's."

She carefully folded the paper and slipped it into a drawer in the kitchen. Both she and Gramps fell silent, the way I imagine people react when the doctor tells them they have a serious, but curable, illness. For a moment the air was sucked out of the room, and we stood suspended, alone with our thoughts.

"Well," Toot said finally, "I suppose we better start looking for a place where he can stay."

Gramps took off his glasses and rubbed his eyes.

"Should be one heck of a Christmas."

Over lunch, I explained to a group of boys that my father was a prince. "My grandfather, see, he's a chief. It's sort of like the king of the tribe, you know . . . like the Indians. So that makes my father a prince. He'll take over when my grandfather dies."

"What about that?" one of my friends asked as we emptied our trays into the trash bin. "I mean, will you go back and be a prince?"

"Well . . . if I want to, I could. It's sort of complicated, see, 'cause the tribe is full of warriors. Like Obama . . . that means 'Burning Spear.' The men in our tribe all want to be chief, so my father has to settle these feuds before I can come." **E**

refuge (rĕf′yo͞oj) *n.* a source of comfort in times of trouble

② Targeted Passage

D AUTOBIOGRAPHY
What role do television and radio play in Obama's daily life as a child?

E CAUSE AND EFFECT
Why might Obama tell exaggerated or untrue stories about his father?

LITERARY ANALYSIS

D AUTOBIOGRAPHY

Possible answer: *TV and radio keep Obama occupied, helping to ease his loneliness.*

Lines 126–135

DISCUSSION PROMPTS

Use these prompts to help students understand how Obama and his grandparents react to news of a visit by Obama's father:

Recall What information does the telegram provide? ***Answer:*** *It tells the family that Obama's father is coming for a visit.*

Compare Why do you think Obama compares his grandparents' reaction to news of the visit to learning that they have "a serious, but curable, illness"? ***Possible answer:*** *If you had a serious but curable illness, you would worry but know that eventually things would return to normal. Obama realizes his grandparents aren't thrilled about the visit but know that eventually their lives will return to normal.*

Speculate What do you think Gramps means in line 135? ***Possible answer:*** *He means that Christmas will be challenging because the visit will involve close contact between people who haven't seen one another for a long time.*

READING SKILL

E CAUSE AND EFFECT

Remind students to record their answers in the graphic from page 831. ***Possible answer:*** *Obama might hope the stories will impress his classmates and cause them to like him.*

DIFFERENTIATED INSTRUCTION

FOR LESS–PROFICIENT READERS

② Targeted Passage [Lines 105–125]

This passage explains the effect of Obama's betrayal of Coretta.

- What effect does the incident with Coretta have on Obama's relationships with other students? Does he feel good about this?
- What is Obama's relationship with Gramps like during this time?
- What is Obama's routine? Why is this routine comforting to him?

FOR ADVANCED LEARNERS/PRE–AP

Analyze Metaphor [small-group option] Ask students to consider why Obama compares his situation to being "Nested in the soft, forgiving bosom of America's consumer culture" (line 122). Have groups discuss these questions:

- What part of the American consumer culture is Obama referring to?
- What about this type of culture is soft? What is forgiving?

836 UNIT 7: HISTORY, CULTURE, AND THE AUTHOR

As the words tumbled out of my mouth, and I felt the boys re-adjust to me, more curious and familiar as we bumped into each other in the line back to class, a part of me really began to believe the story. But another part of me knew that what I was telling them was a lie, something I'd constructed from the scraps of information I'd picked up from my mother. After a week of my father in the flesh, I had decided that I preferred his more distant image, an image I could alter on a whim—or ignore when convenient. If my father hadn't exactly disappointed me, he remained something unknown, something **volatile** and vaguely threatening.

My mother had sensed my apprehension in the days building up to his arrival—I suppose it mirrored her own—and so, in between her efforts to prepare the apartment we'd sublet for him, she would try to assure me that the reunion would go smoothly. She had maintained a correspondence with him throughout the time we had been in Indonesia, she explained, and he knew all about me. Like her, my father had remarried, and I now had five brothers and one sister living in Kenya. He had been in a bad car accident, and this trip was part of his **recuperation** after a long stay in the hospital.

"You two will become great friends," she decided. . . .

ANALYZE VISUALS
Look at this picture of Honolulu in 1972. What are some features of the **setting** where Obama grew up?

volatile (vŏl′ə-tl) *adj.* difficult to define or pin down; unpredictable

recuperation (rĭ-ko͞o′pə-rā′shən) *n.* a return to health or strength; recovery

ANALYZE VISUALS

***Possible answer:** The setting includes beautiful beaches and high-rise hotels or apartments overlooking the ocean.*

About the Art This photograph shows a view of Honolulu's Waikiki Beach, a two-mile stretch of coastline fronted by hotels and tourist attractions. Hawaii's most famous landmark, Diamond Head, rises in the background. Diamond Head's peak sits on the rim of an extinct volcanic crater and is protected from commercial development.

Lines 146–163
DISCUSSION PROMPTS

Use these prompts to help students understand Obama's attitudes toward others:

Connect Do you think friends who are "bought" with false claims can be true friends? *Students might feel that a true friend is one who likes the other person for what he or she truly is, not for something he or she claims to be.*

Analyze Why does Obama prefer an image of his father that he can "alter on a whim"? What does this say about Obama at this point in his life? ***Possible answer:** Obama does not want to accept his father's shortcomings. This suggests that young Obama believes his parents should be perfect.*

Speculate What behavior might Obama's father display during his visit to cause Obama to view him as "unknown, . . . volatile and vaguely threatening"? ***Possible answer:** Obama's father might behave more like an authority figure than a warm, caring parent.*

FOR ENGLISH LEARNERS

Vocabulary: Multiple-Meaning Words [mixed-readiness pairs] Explain that some words in English are spelled and pronounced the same but have different meanings. Have pairs find the multiple-meaning words shown in the first column of this chart and fill in columns 2 and 3 with the word's meaning in the selection and another meaning for the word. Tell students to watch for other multiple-meaning words as they continue reading.

Multiple-Meaning Word	Meaning in Selection	Alternate Meaning
act (line 105)	"action"	"play a role"
room (line 105)	"space"	"area in a home"
rest (line 116)	"remainder"	"relax"
settle (line 144)	"resolve"	"sink"

The big day finally arrived, and Miss Hefty let me out early from class, wishing me luck. I left the school building feeling like a condemned man. My legs were heavy, and with each approaching step toward my grandparents' apartment, the thump in my chest grew louder. When I entered the elevator, I stood without pressing the button. The door closed, then reopened, and an older Filipino man who lived on the fourth floor got on.

"Your grandfather says your father is coming to visit you today," the man said cheerfully. "You must be very happy." **F**

F AUTOBIOGRAPHY
How does Obama feel about seeing his father? Compare this with how other people think he feels.

When—after standing in front of the door and looking out across the Honolulu skyline at a distant ship, and then squinting at the sky to watch sparrows spiral through the air—I could think of no possible means of escape, I rang the doorbell. Toot opened the door.

"There he is! Come on, Bar . . . come meet your father."

And there, in the unlit hallway, I saw him, a tall, dark figure who walked with a slight limp. He crouched down and put his arms around me, and I let my arms hang at my sides. Behind him stood my mother, her chin trembling as usual.

"Well, Barry," my father said. "It is a good thing to see you after so long. Very good."

He led me by the hand into the living room, and we all sat down.

"So, Barry, your grandmama has told me that you are doing very well in school."

I shrugged.

"He's feeling a little shy, I think," Toot offered. She smiled and rubbed my head.

"Well," my father said, "you have no reason to be shy about doing well. Have I told you that your brothers and sister have also excelled in their schooling? It's in the blood, I think," he said with a laugh.

I watched him carefully as the adults began to talk. He was much thinner than I had expected, the bones of his knees cutting the legs of his trousers in sharp angles; I couldn't imagine him lifting anyone off the ground. Beside him, a cane with a blunt ivory head leaned against the wall. He wore a blue blazer, and a white shirt, and a scarlet ascot.[5] His horn-rimmed glasses reflected the light of the lamp so that I couldn't see his eyes very well, but when he took the glasses off to rub the bridge of his nose, I saw that they were slightly yellow, the eyes of someone who's had malaria[6] more than once. There was a fragility about his frame, I thought, a caution. . . . After an hour or so, my mother suggested that he looked tired and should take a nap, and he agreed. He gathered up his travel bag, then stopped in mid-stride and began to fish around in it, until he finally pulled out three wooden figurines—a lion, an elephant, and an ebony[7] man in tribal dress beating a drum—and handed them to me. **G**

G AUTOBIOGRAPHY
What are Obama's first impressions of his father?

---

5. **ascot** (ăs'kət): a neck scarf worn knotted so that its ends lie flat, one upon the other.
6. **malaria** (mə-lâr'ē-ə): a serious disease that is spread by mosquitoes and causes fever and chills.
7. **ebony** (ĕb'ə-nē): a hard, black wood grown in Africa.

LITERARY ANALYSIS

F AUTOBIOGRAPHY

Possible answer: *Obama is nervous about seeing his father, while other people assume he is happy about the visit.*

Lines 183–190

REINFORCE *KEY IDEA:* PROUD

Discuss What quality in his children makes Obama's father **proud?** ***Possible answer:*** *Their ability to do well in school makes him proud.*

LITERARY ANALYSIS

G AUTOBIOGRAPHY

Possible answer: *To Obama, his father appears thin and frail. He carries a cane and wears a blazer, shirt, and ascot. Obama notices that his father's eyes are slightly yellow, indicating that he has had malaria.*

DIFFERENTIATED INSTRUCTION

FOR ENGLISH LEARNERS

Vocabulary Support Lines 191–199 describe Obama's father's appearance. Help students visualize Obama's father by defining these vocabulary words from the selection:

- *Trousers* are long pants.
- A *cane* is a walking stick; the *ivory* head of the cane is carved from the tusk of an elephant.
- A *blazer* is a sport coat or dress jacket.
- *Horn-rimmed glasses* have thick frames made of natural horn or tortoise shell or a man-made imitation.

FOR ADVANCED LEARNERS/PRE-AP

Sensory Details Encourage students to notice that Obama uses many sensory details in his autobiography. Have students use a Spider Map to note the sensory details used to describe the events leading up to Obama's meeting with his father.

 **BEST PRACTICES TOOLKIT—Transparency**
Spider Map p. B22

838 UNIT 7: HISTORY, CULTURE, AND THE AUTHOR

"Say thank you, Bar," my mother said.

"Thank you," I muttered.

My father and I both looked down at the carvings, lifeless in my hands. He touched my shoulder.

"They are only small things," he said softly. Then he nodded to Gramps, and together they gathered up his luggage and went downstairs to the other apartment.

A month. That's how long we would have together, the five of us in my grandparents' living room most evenings, during the day on drives around the island or on short walks past the private landmarks of a family: the lot where my father's apartment had once stood; the remodeled hospital where I had been born; my grandparents' first house in Hawaii, before the one on University Avenue, a house I had never known. There was so much to tell in that single month, so much explaining to do; and yet when I reach back into my memory for the words of my father, the small interactions or conversations we might have had, they seem **irretrievably** lost. Perhaps they're imprinted too deeply, his voice the seed of all sorts of tangled arguments that I carry on with myself, as impenetrable now as the pattern of my genes, so that all I can perceive is the worn-out shell. My wife offers a simpler explanation—that boys and their fathers don't always have much to say to each other unless and until they trust—and this may come closer to the mark, for I often felt mute before him, and he never pushed me to speak. I'm left with mostly images that appear and die off in my mind like distant sounds: his head thrown back in laughter at one of Gramps's jokes as my mother and I hang Christmas ornaments; his grip on my shoulder as he introduces me to one of his old friends from college; the narrowing of his eyes, the stroking of his sparse goatee, as he reads his important books. **H**

Images, and his effect on other people. For whenever he spoke—his one leg draped over the other, his large hands outstretched to direct or deflect attention, his voice deep and sure, cajoling and laughing—I would see a sudden change take place in the family. Gramps became more vigorous and thoughtful, my mother more bashful; even Toot, smoked out of the foxhole of her bedroom, would start sparring with him about politics or finance, stabbing the air with her blue-veined hands to make a point. It was as if his presence had summoned the spirit of earlier times and allowed each of them to reprise his or her old role; as if Dr. King had never been shot, and the Kennedys continued to beckon the nation, and war and riot and famine were nothing more than temporary setbacks, and there was nothing to fear but fear itself. **I**

It fascinated me, this strange power of his, and for the first time I began to think of my father as something real and immediate, perhaps even permanent.

irretrievably
(ĭr'ĭ-trē'və-blē) *adv.* permanently; in a manner that cannot be reversed

H AUTOBIOGRAPHY
Reread lines 211–230. Why is this month with his father so important to Obama? Note the memories of his father that are most vivid to him.

I CAUSE AND EFFECT
What effect does Obama's father have on members of the family?

LITERARY ANALYSIS

H AUTOBIOGRAPHY

Possible answer: *Obama has only one short month to spend with his father, so he feels pressure to share a lot with him. The memories that are the most vivid are pictures of single moments with his father: his father's head thrown back in laughter, the grip of his father's hand on his shoulder, the narrowing of his father's eyes, and his father stroking his goatee.*

READING SKILL

I CAUSE AND EFFECT

Remind students to record their answers in the graphic from page 831. ***Possible answer:*** *He energizes them. Rather than watching television and sticking to their usual, quiet routine, they respond to Obama's father by laughing, being more thoughtful, or arguing with him.*

FOR LESS–PROFICIENT READERS

Comprehension Support Be sure students understand the sequence of events in lines 211–230. Remind them that Obama is recalling the events of his childhood as an adult. In lines 222–224, he refers to an explanation his present-day wife has offered about his relationship with his father. Lines 225–230 relate his efforts as an adult to remember the small interactions and conversations he had with his father during the visit, which occurred when Obama was ten.

FOR ENGLISH LEARNERS

Culture: Clarify Explain to students that this part of Obama's autobiography takes place in the early 1970s, after three important tragic events in U.S. history. To clarify lines 237–242, share these facts:

- Dr. Martin Luther King Jr. was an important African-American civil rights leader who was assassinated in April 1968.
- John F. Kennedy was president of the United States until his assassination in 1963.
- Kennedy's brother Robert was running for president in 1968 when in June of that year he was assassinated.
- The phrase "nothing to fear but fear itself" is from a famous speech made by President Franklin D. Roosevelt in 1933. At that time, the United States was in the midst of a serious economic depression, and the new president offered a vision of hope for the future.

Lines 245–263

DISCUSSION PROMPTS

Use these prompts to help students understand the conflict between Obama's father and his mother and grandparents:

Recall What is the source of the argument in this scene? ***Answer:*** *Obama's mother and grandparents believe Obama should be allowed to watch a television cartoon, but his father believes he should be in his room studying.*

Infer What can you infer about the values of Obama's father from this incident? ***Possible answer:*** *He believes children should work hard all the time. He does not believe watching television is a worthwhile pursuit.*

Evaluate Do you think Obama's father's expectations are realistic? Explain. *Students might think that Obama's father expects too much of a ten-year-old boy.*

ANALYZE VISUALS

Possible answer: *The similarities are the Christmas tree (line 227) and the cartoon playing on the television,* How the Grinch Stole Christmas *(lines 249–250), which the adults are arguing about.*

After a few weeks, though, I could feel the tension around me beginning to build. Gramps complained that my father was sitting in his chair. Toot muttered, while doing the dishes, that she wasn't anybody's servant. My mother's mouth pinched, her eyes avoiding her parents, as we ate dinner. One evening, I turned on the television to watch a cartoon special—*How the Grinch Stole Christmas*—and the whispers broke into shouts.

"Barry, you have watched enough television tonight," my father said. "Go in your room and study now, and let the adults talk."

Toot stood up and turned off the TV. "Why don't you turn the show on in the bedroom, Bar."

"No, Madelyn," my father said, "that's not what I mean. He has been watching that machine constantly, and now it is time for him to study."

My mother tried to explain that it was almost Christmas vacation, that the cartoon was a Christmas favorite, that I had been looking forward to it all week. "It won't last long."

"Anna, this is nonsense. If the boy has done his work for tomorrow, he can begin on his next day's assignments. Or the assignments he will have when he returns from the holidays." He turned to me. "I tell you, Barry, you do not work as hard as you should. Go now, before I get angry at you."

(3) **Targeted Passage**

ANALYZE VISUALS
Compare the scene in the photograph with th
way you imagine Toot and Gramps' apartment
What are the similaritie

DIFFERENTIATED INSTRUCTION

FOR LESS–PROFICIENT READERS

(3) **Targeted Passage [Lines 245–263]**

This passage reveals a turning point in which the family tensions turn into an open argument.

- For what reasons is Obama's father's visit beginning to wear on the other adults?
- In what way do the adults' attitudes toward television differ?
- What does Obama's father expect of Obama as a student?

Reading Skill Follow-Up: Recognize Cause-and-Effect Relationships [paired option] Have pairs read pages 840–841 and update their graphic organizers from page 831. Remind students to look for people and events Obama has mentioned and the effect they have on him.

Cause	Effect
Tensions are building in the household. →	Obama becomes caught in an argument between his father and the other adults.

I went to my room and slammed the door, listening as the voices outside grew louder, Gramps insisting that this was his house, Toot saying that my father had no right to come in and bully everyone, including me, after being gone all this time. I heard my father say that they were spoiling me, that I needed a firm hand, and I listened to my mother tell her parents that nothing ever changed with them. We all stood accused, and even after my father left and Toot came in to say that I could watch the last five minutes of my show, I felt as if something had cracked open between all of us, goblins rushing out of some old, sealed-off lair. Watching the green Grinch on the television screen, intent on ruining Christmas, eventually transformed by the faith of the doe-eyed creatures who inhabited Whoville, I saw it for what it was: a lie. I began to count the days until my father would leave and things would return to normal. J

J CAUSE AND EFFECT What causes tension in the family?

The next day, Toot sent me down to the apartment where my father was staying to see if he had any laundry to wash. I knocked, and my father opened the door, shirtless. Inside, I saw my mother ironing some of his clothes. Her hair was tied back in a ponytail, and her eyes were soft and dark, as if she'd been crying. My father asked me to sit down beside him on the bed, but I told him that Toot needed me to help her, and left after relaying the message. Back upstairs, I had begun cleaning my room when my mother came in.

"You shouldn't be mad at your father, Bar. He loves you very much. He's just a little stubborn sometimes."

"Okay," I said without looking up. I could feel her eyes follow me around the room until she finally let out a slow breath and went to the door.

"I know all this stuff is confusing for you," she said. "For me, too. Just try to remember what I said, okay?" She put her hand on the doorknob. "Do you want me to close the door?"

I nodded, but she had been gone for only a minute when she stuck her head back into the room.

"By the way, I forgot to tell you that Miss Hefty has invited your father to come to school on Thursday. She wants him to speak to the class."

I couldn't imagine worse news. I spent that night and all of the next day trying to suppress thoughts of the **inevitable**: the faces of my classmates when they heard about mud huts, all my lies exposed, the painful jokes afterward. Each time I remembered, my body squirmed as if it had received a jolt to the nerves. K

inevitable (ĭn-ĕv′ĭ-tə-bəl) *n.* that which cannot be avoided or prevented

K AUTOBIOGRAPHY Why is Obama afraid to have his father visit his class?

I was still trying to figure out how I'd explain myself when my father walked into our class the next day. Miss Hefty welcomed him eagerly, and as I took my seat I heard several children ask each other what was going on. I became more desperate when our math teacher, a big, no-nonsense Hawaiian named Mr. Eldredge, came into the room, followed by thirty confused children from his homeroom next door.

READING SKILL

J CAUSE AND EFFECT

Remind students to record their answers in the graphic from page 831. ***Possible answer:*** *Obama's father accuses Obama's mother and grandparents of spoiling his son. This disapproval causes Obama and the other family members to feel angry and resentful.*

LITERARY ANALYSIS

K AUTOBIOGRAPHY

Possible answer: *Obama fears his father will embarrass him and reveal Obama was lying about his father's being a chief.*

FOR ENGLISH LEARNERS

Language: Punctuation and Print Cues Point out Obama's use of colons on this page (lines 274 and 297). Explain to students that colons signal readers that an explanation about an independent clause follows. To help clarify this, ask students what explanation follows the colon in each sentence. For further discussion, guide students to other instances of colon use in the story: page 832, lines 7 and 22; page 835, line 98; page 839, lines 213 and 226.

FOR ADVANCED LEARNERS/PRE–AP

Analyze [small-group option] Have small groups discuss these questions relating to Obama's statement that the ending of *How the Grinch Stole Christmas* is "a lie." Ask a volunteer to share the group's findings.

- Who is the Grinch in Obama's story?
- Who are the "doe-eyed creatures who inhabited Whoville"?
- In what ways might the evening's events make Obama believe the story is a lie?

BACKGROUND

The Eunoto Ceremony The Masai people of Kenya perform the initiation ceremony described by Obama's father (lines 315–316). Boys in their early teens, known as junior warriors, guard the tribe's houses and tend its cattle herds. Traditionally, to become senior warriors, the boys take part in the Eunoto ceremony. This centuries-old ritual lasts four days, and during that time, the boys are required to kill a lion using only spears. At the end of the ceremony, each boy's hair, which has not been cut since birth, is shaved by his mother, and the new senior warriors may then marry and begin raising families. The Eunoto ceremony has been outlawed by the Kenyan government, along with the killing of lions, but many Masai warriors continue to follow tribal tradition.

Lines 307–323
REINFORCE *KEY IDEA:* PROUD

Discuss Why is Miss Hefty **proud** after Obama's father finishes speaking? ***Possible answer:*** *She feels a special connection with Kenya since she once taught there, and she believes Obama's father did a good job of presenting this unique culture to her students.*

READING SKILL

Ⓛ CAUSE AND EFFECT

Remind students to record their answers in the graphic from page 831. ***Possible answer:*** *The talk impresses the class and causes Coretta to feel "simple satisfaction" (line 332).*

LITERARY ANALYSIS

Ⓜ AUTOBIOGRAPHY

Possible answer: *Obama begins to see his father in a different, more positive light and, as a result, starts looking up to him and seeking his approval.*

"We have a special treat for you today," Miss Hefty began. "Barry Obama's father is here, and he's come all the way from Kenya, in Africa, to tell us about his country."

The other kids looked at me as my father stood up, and I held my head stiffly, trying to focus on a vacant point on the blackboard behind him. He had been speaking for some time before I could finally bring myself back to the moment. He was leaning against Miss Hefty's thick oak desk and describing the deep gash in the earth where mankind had first appeared. He spoke of the wild animals that still roamed the plains, the tribes that still required a young boy to kill a lion to prove his manhood. He spoke of the customs of the Luo, how elders received the utmost respect and made laws for all to follow under great-trunked trees. And he told us of Kenya's struggle to be free, how the British had wanted to stay and unjustly rule the people, just as they had in America; how many had been enslaved only because of the color of their skin, just as they had in America; but that Kenyans, like all of us in the room, longed to be free and develop themselves through hard work and sacrifice.

When he finished, Miss Hefty was absolutely beaming with pride. All my classmates applauded heartily, and a few struck up the courage to ask questions, each of which my father appeared to consider carefully before answering. The bell rang for lunch, and Mr. Eldredge came up to me.

"You've got a pretty impressive father."

The ruddy-faced boy who had asked about cannibalism said, "Your dad is pretty cool."

And off to one side, I saw Coretta watch my father say good-bye to some of the children. She seemed too intent to smile; her face showed only a look of simple satisfaction. Ⓛ

Ⓛ CAUSE AND EFFECT What effect does Obama's father's talk have on the class?

Two weeks later he was gone. In that time, we stand together in front of the Christmas tree and pose for pictures, the only ones I have of us together, me holding an orange basketball, his gift to me, him showing off the tie I've bought him ("Ah, people will know that I am very important wearing such a tie"). At a Dave Brubeck[8] concert, I struggle to sit quietly in the dark auditorium beside him, unable to follow the spare equations of sound that the performers make, careful to clap whenever he claps. For brief spells in the day I will lie beside him, the two of us alone in the apartment sublet from a retired old woman whose name I forget, the place full of quilts and doilies and knitted seat covers, and I read my book while he reads his. He remains **opaque** to me, a present mass; when I mimic his gestures or turns of phrase, I know neither their origins nor their consequences, can't see how they play out over time. But I grow accustomed to his company. Ⓜ

opaque (ō-pāk') *adj.* hidden; difficult or impossible to understand

Ⓜ AUTOBIOGRAPHY In what ways has Obama's relationship with his father changed during their visit?

The day of his departure, as my mother and I helped him pack his bags, he unearthed two records, forty-fives, in dull brown dust jackets.

8. **Dave Brubeck** (bro͞o'bĕk): an American jazz pianist and composer whose music was very popular during the 1960s.

DIFFERENTIATED INSTRUCTION

FOR ENGLISH LEARNERS

Culture: Clarify Explain to students that lines 318–319 refer to the American Revolution from 1775 to 1783, when the colonies went to war with Great Britain to gain their independence. Lines 319–320 refer to the years 1619–1865 in American history, when African Americans were enslaved by white people. Slavery ended after the Civil War, which took place from 1861 to 1865.

FOR ADVANCED LEARNERS/PRE–AP

Evaluate Author's Style Point out that Obama shifts to the present tense in lines 333–345. Have students write a short paragraph in response to these questions:

- Why might Obama have chosen to describe these two weeks using the present tense?
- How does the shift to present tense affect the presentation of the information?
- In what other ways does Obama emphasize the importance of the last two weeks of the visit?

ANALYZE VISUALS
What **details** of this stereo does the photographer focus on?

"Barry! Look here—I forgot that I had brought these for you. The sounds of your continent."

It took him a while to puzzle out my grandparents' old stereo, but finally the disk began to turn, and he gingerly placed the needle on the groove. A tinny guitar lick opened, then the sharp horns, the thump of drums, then the guitar again, and then the voices, clean and joyful as they rode up the back beat, urging us on.

"Come, Barry," my father said. "You will learn from the master." And suddenly his slender body was swaying back and forth, the lush sound was rising, his arms were swinging as they cast an invisible net, his feet wove over the floor in off-beats, his bad leg stiff but his rump high, his head back, his hips moving in a tight circle. The rhythm quickened, the horns sounded, and his eyes closed to follow his pleasure, and then one eye opened to peek down at me and his solemn face spread into a silly grin, and my mother smiled, and my grandparents walked in to see what all the commotion was about. I took my first tentative steps with my eyes closed, down, up, my arms swinging, the voices lifting. And I hear him still: As I follow my father into the sound, he lets out a quick shout, bright and high, a shout that leaves much behind and reaches out for more, a shout that cries for laughter. ~ N

(4) Targeted Passage

N CAUSE AND EFFECT
Reread lines 355–366. What feelings does his father's music and dancing create in Obama?

ANALYZE VISUALS

Possible answer: *The photographer focuses on the arm that holds the needle and the turntable of the record player.*

READING SKILL

N CAUSE AND EFFECT

Remind students to record their answers in the graphic from page 831. ***Possible answer:*** *The music and dancing cause Obama to feel connected to his father and his heritage.*

SELECTION WRAP-UP

REFLECT Have students compare and contrast the adult Obama's attitude toward his father with the child Obama's attitude.

CRITIQUE Ask students whether Obama's reflections on his thoughts and actions as a child add to or detract from their enjoyment of the story. Do students admire Obama's honesty or like him less for what he admits about himself?

READING FLUENCY

Distribute the copy masters and have students practice fluency.

RESOURCE MANAGER—Copy Master
Reading Fluency p. 136

FOR LESS-PROFICIENT READERS

(4) Targeted Passage [Lines 348–366]

This passage concludes the story of Obama's father's visit.

- What music is on the record?
- What does Obama's father do once the music starts?
- Why do you think Obama's father invites Obama to dance with him?

FOR ENGLISH LEARNERS

Culture: Clarify Explain to students that "forty-fives" (line 347) were audio recordings used before tape players or CD players. A 45 RPM record featured two songs, one on each side. A "guitar lick" (line 352) is a short guitar solo that is often improvised, or made up on the spur of the moment, by the guitarist. The "back beat" (line 353) of a song is the accent on the second and fourth beat of a measure in 4/4 time and is characteristic of rock music.

Practice and Apply

After Reading

Comprehension

1. **Recall** Why is Miss Hefty interested in Obama's Kenyan heritage?
2. **Clarify** Why does Obama's father object to the young Obama watching television?
3. **Summarize** What does Obama's father discuss in his speech to Obama's class?

Literary Analysis

4. **Identify Cultural Values** Note things about American culture that Obama values as a child. As an adult looking back on his life, do you think Obama is critical of the way he spent his own time? Explain why or why not.
5. **Interpret Autobiography** Do you think Obama grows close to his father during their one-month visit? Cite details from the autobiography to support your opinion about their relationship.
6. **Examine Cause-and-Effect Relationships** Review the cause-and-effect graphics you created as you read. Create one more that shows the overall effect Obama's father's visit had on Obama.

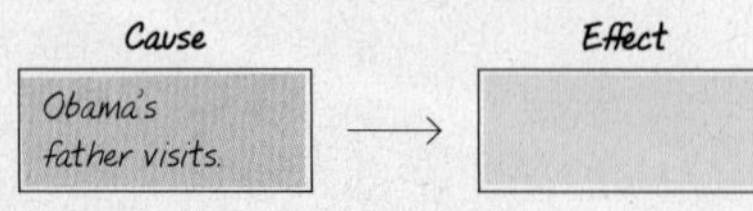

7. **Analyze a Symbolic Event** Reread lines 73–104. Obama calls his rejection of Coretta a "betrayal." What might this event symbolize, beyond Obama's desire to be left alone by the other students?
8. **Draw Conclusions** How does the title *Dreams from My Father* relate to this selection? What dreams do you think Obama's father inspired in Obama? Consider how Obama's feelings of **pride** changed during the visit.

Extension and Challenge

9. **Literary Criticism** Barack Obama has said of *Dreams from My Father*, "I see my book as part of my politics. . . . Policy [official government planning] has to be guided by facts, but to move people you have to tell stories." Why might people be moved by Obama's personal story? Why might they relate to him?
10. **SOCIAL STUDIES CONNECTION** Research more about the history, beliefs, and culture of the Luo tribe in Kenya. Then make a poster that summarizes the key points of what you learned.

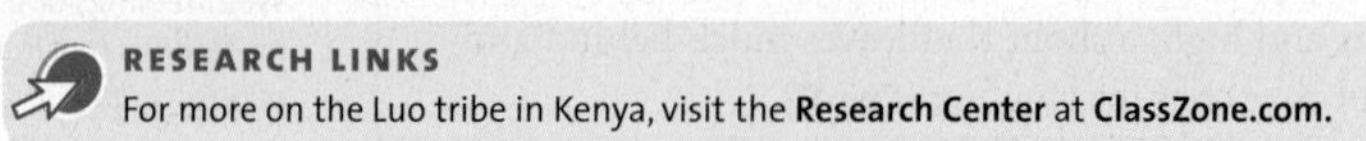
RESEARCH LINKS
For more on the Luo tribe in Kenya, visit the **Research Center** at **ClassZone.com.**

After Reading

For additional support of postreading questions, use these copy masters:

RESOURCE MANAGER—Copy Masters
Reading Check p. 134 (to check understanding of the selection)
Autobiography p. 127 (for practice of literary analysis standards focus)
Question Support p. 135 (After Reading questions adapted for English learners and less-proficient readers)

Additional selection questions are provided for teachers on page 121.

For additional activities to challenge students, see

Power Thinking at **ClassZone.com**

ANSWERS

Comprehension

1. *Miss Hefty once lived and taught in Kenya.*
2. *Obama's father feels that TV is distracting his son from his studies.*
3. *Obama's father describes the history and culture of Kenya.*

Literary Analysis

Possible answers:

4. *Obama values comic books, TV, and popular music. As an adult, he describes the way he spent his time as "a long hibernation," implying he believes his mind was not as engaged as it should have been.*
5. **STANDARDS FOCUS Autobiography** *Although Obama still finds his father "opaque," he admires him and tries to be like him. These details suggest that the two have formed a bond.*
6. **STANDARDS FOCUS Recognize Cause-and-Effect Relationships** *Obama's father's visit causes young Obama to view himself in a new way, to be proud of his Kenyan heritage, and to value learning and more active pursuits than watching television.*
7. *Because Coretta is the only other African-American student, the event might symbolize Obama's rejection of his heritage.*
8. *The dreams Obama's father inspired in Obama may have been to reach his potential, to work hard, and to strive for civil rights for African Americans. Obama becomes more proud of his heritage after hearing his father speak at school.*

Extension and Challenge

9. *People might be moved by the fact that Obama was somewhat of an outcast at his school and had to endure the cruelty and stereotypical attitudes of the other students. Many readers will relate to the fact that his parents were divorced and that he did not always get along with or understand his father.*
10. **SOCIAL STUDIES CONNECTION** *Students' posters should summarize the key points of their research on the Luo tribe.*

ocabulary in Context

OCABULARY PRACTICE

Answer each question to show your understanding of the vocabulary words.

1. Are **dowdy** clothes stylish or unstylish?
2. If you try to change the **inevitable,** are you likely to succeed?
3. If an item is **irretrievably** lost, is it possible or impossible to find?
4. If having guests over is a **novelty,** is it typical or unusual?
5. If an idea seems **opaque** to you, is that idea easy or difficult to understand?
6. During a **recuperation,** do you get better or worse?
7. Is a rabbit more likely to take **refuge** in its burrow or in an open field?
8. If someone has a **volatile** personality, are the person's actions difficult or easy to predict?

dowdy
inevitable
irretrievably
novelty
opaque
recuperation
refuge
volatile

OCABULARY IN WRITING

Using at least two vocabulary words, write a paragraph from young Obama's point of view that explains how he feels when his family argues about his television habits.

EXAMPLE SENTENCES

After a tense evening at the apartment, I want to take ***refuge*** *in the comfort of my room.*

OCABULARY STRATEGY: DENOTATION AND CONNOTATION

A word's **denotation** is its dictionary definition, but many words have additional ideas and feelings associated with them. These associations, or shades of meaning, are called **connotations**. Connotations can be positive or negative. For example, the words *clever* and *conniving* have different connotations. *Clever* describes someone who is creative and smart, while *conniving* implies the person is manipulative and dishonest. To fully understand what you read, it is important to recognize word connotations.

PRACTICE Each pair of phrases uses words with similar meanings but different connotations. Use each phrase in a sentence that reflects the word's connotation.

1. a unique gift
   a bizarre gift
2. the stubborn child
   the persistent child
3. a rowdy audience
   a lively audience
4. to control a situation
   to manipulate a situation

VOCABULARY PRACTICE
For more practice, go to the **Vocabulary Center** at **ClassZone.com.**

DIFFERENTIATED INSTRUCTION

FOR ENGLISH LEARNERS

Vocabulary Practice Encourage students to return to the story to see how each vocabulary word is used in context. Doing so will help students answer the questions in the exercise.

FOR ADVANCED LEARNERS/PRE-AP

Vocabulary Strategy Challenge students to replace the words in question with other suitable words that have similar meanings and connotations. Example: a *surprising* gift; a *shocking* gift.

ANSWERS

Vocabulary in Context

VOCABULARY PRACTICE

1. *unstylish*
2. *no*
3. *impossible to find*
4. *unusual*
5. *difficult to understand*
6. *you get better*
7. *in its burrow*
8. *difficult to predict*

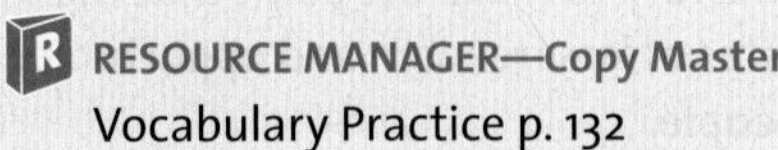

RESOURCE MANAGER—Copy Master
Vocabulary Practice p. 132

VOCABULARY IN WRITING

Suggest that students review the vocabulary words to see which ones could be used to describe Obama's feelings when his family argues about his television habits.

VOCABULARY STRATEGY: DENOTATION AND CONNOTATION *(also an EL language objective)*

To reinforce the concept, discuss whether each of these vocabulary words has a positive or negative connotation: *dowdy, refuge, volatile.*

Students' sentences should reflect the following connotations:

1. *unique—positive; bizarre—negative*
2. *stubborn—negative; persistent—positive*
3. *rowdy—negative; lively—positive*
4. *control—positive; manipulate—negative*

RESOURCE MANAGER—Copy Master
Vocabulary Strategy p. 133

Vocabulary Center at **ClassZone.com**
Additional Vocabulary Activities

Assess and Reteach

Assess

RESOURCE MANAGER—Copy Masters
Selection Tests A, B/C pp. 137–138, 139–140

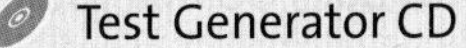

Test Generator CD

Reteach

STANDARDS LESSON FILE
Reading Lesson 7: Recognizing Cause and Effect
Vocabulary Lesson 17: Denotation and Connotation

Focus and Motivate

OBJECTIVES

Reading for Information

- identify treatment, including form, purpose, and tone
- compare and contrast portrayals
- identify characteristics of a keynote speech
- read a speech

SUMMARY

In his keynote speech at the 2004 Democratic National Convention, Barack Obama relates his family history to make the point that the United States offers freedom and opportunity to all its people.

What's the Connection?

Write these statements on the Anticipation Guide transparency. Have students respond to each one before and after reading.

- Obama's mother grew up in Kansas before her family moved to Hawaii.
- People everywhere have the same basic dreams for their children.
- The greatness of the United States lies mainly in its military power.

BEST PRACTICES TOOLKIT—Transparency
Anticipation Guide p. A14

Teach

Skill Focus: Identify Treatment

Use the following tips to guide students through the process of identifying Obama's treatment of his subject matter:

- **For what purpose(s) is the selection written?** Guide students to lines 30–34. Ask: What is Obama's purpose in sharing his personal story? Why should others care?
- **What is the writer's primary purpose?** Have students read **Focus on Form** on page 847 of the pupil's edition.
- **What is the writer's tone?** Have students consider these questions:
  —**Lines 1–2:** What words does Obama use to describe Illinois?
  —**Lines 10–12:** What words does Obama use to describe the United States?

Possible chart entries appear on page 848.

RESOURCE MANAGER—Copy Master
Identify Treatment p. 149

Reading for Information

Out of Many, One

Speech

Use with *Dreams from My Father*, page 832.

What's the Connection?

The autobiography you just read provides insight into what Barack Obama's family life was like when he was growing up. Now see how Obama describes his family background in the beginning of a keynote political speech he gave at the 2004 Democratic National Convention.

Skill Focus: Identify Treatment

Three writers know they have to write about the first day of middle school. One writer writes a funny newspaper column about an embarrassing moment she had when she started sixth grade. Another writer describes the first day of sixth grade in a letter to her grandmother. A third writer creates an e-mail that gives students tips on how to find their way around the new middle school. How can such a variety of writings come from the same topic? It's because writers can handle the same subject matter in very different ways.

The way a topic is handled is called its treatment. The writer's purpose, or reason for writing, helps determine a work's treatment. So does the form the writing takes and the tone, or attitude the writer expresses about the topic. In order to identify a writer's treatment, ask yourself the following questions:

- **What form does the writing take?** For example, is it a newspaper column, a personal letter, or a business memo?
- **For what purpose(s) is the selection written?** Is it written to entertain, to express ideas and feelings, to inform, or to inspire? If there is more than one purpose, which is primary?
- **What is the writer's tone, or attitude toward the subject?** For example, the tone of a selection might be described as mocking, optimistic, or serious.

In the following excerpt of "Out of Many, One," Obama's topic is his family background. As you read, identify Obama's treatment of this topic by completing a chart such as the one begun here.

	"Out of Many, One"
What form does the writing take?	*speech*
For what purpose(s) is the selection written? What is the writer's primary purpose?	
What is the writer's tone?	

Selection Resources

RESOURCE MANAGER UNIT 7

Plan and Teach pp. 141–145

Reading

Summary pp. 147†*, 148‡*
Identify Treatment pp. 149, 151†*
Reading Check p. 153
Compare and Contrast pp. 150, 152†*
Question Support p. 154*

Assessment

Selection Tests A, B/C pp. 155*, 157*

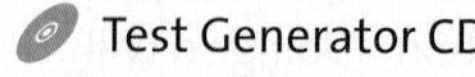
Test Generator CD

Reading Support

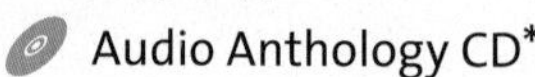
Audio Anthology CD*

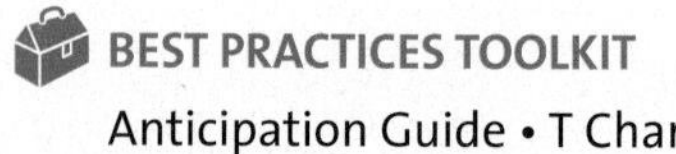
BEST PRACTICES TOOLKIT
Anticipation Guide • T Chart

* Resources for Differentiation † Also in Spanish ‡ In Haitian Creole and Vietnamese

from Out of Many, One

by Barack Obama

Barack Obama at the 2004 Democratic National Convention

FOCUS ON FORM
A **speech** is a talk or public address that is meant to be heard by an audience. A **keynote speech** is one that reflects the key points of a group's ideas and policies.

On behalf of the great state of Illinois, crossroads of a nation, Land of Lincoln, let me express my deepest gratitude for the privilege of addressing this convention. **A**

Tonight is a particular honor for me because—let's face it—my presence on this stage is pretty unlikely. My father was a foreign student, born and raised in a small village in Kenya. He grew up herding goats, went to school in a tin-roof shack. His father—my grandfather—was a cook, a domestic servant to the British.

But my grandfather had larger dreams for his son. Through hard work and perseverance my father got a scholarship to study in a magical place, America, that shone as a beacon of freedom and opportunity to so many who had come before.

A SPEECH
What words or phrases help you know that this is a speech?

DIFFERENTIATED INSTRUCTION

FOR LESS–PROFICIENT READERS

Concept Support Clarify the terms *public* and *policies* in the **Focus on Form** note. Then ask: Based on the photo, who are the public in Obama's audience? ***(Possible answer:*** *adults of various ages and races, both men and women)* What might be a political party's policy on an issue like immigration? ***(Possible answer:*** *The party might support limiting immigration, strengthening the country's borders, or helping more immigrants become citizens.)*

FOR ENGLISH LEARNERS

Culture: Clarify Explain that Obama gave this speech in July of 2004. The following November, he was elected to the U.S. Senate from the state of Illinois. Point out Illinois on a map and tell students that it is a national crossroads (line 1) because major waterways and other transportation routes link it to the East, West, and Gulf coasts as well as to the Midwest. Illinois is the birthplace of Abraham Lincoln (lines 1–2), the 16th president of the United States.

Practice and Apply

BACKGROUND

The Democratic National Convention The Democratic Party was formed in 1792 and held its first convention in 1832. Conventions are held every four years. The two main purposes of the convention are to nominate the party's presidential candidate and to adopt a new party platform. A party platform explains the party's position on issues such as education, health care, and national security. In 2004, when Barack Obama delivered the keynote speech, the Democrats nominated Senator John Kerry of Massachusetts to run for president.

FOCUS ON FORM

Speech Discuss with students the purpose and characteristics of a keynote speech. At national party conventions, this kind of speech

- is delivered by a person who represents and can articulate the core values of the party
- is meant to appeal both to enthusiastic party members and to a wider audience watching the speech on television
- can advance the career of the speaker by exposing him or her to a national audience

Ask students why they think the Democratic Party might have chosen Barack Obama to deliver the keynote speech in 2004.

LITERARY ANALYSIS

A SPEECH
Possible answer: *"the privilege of addressing this convention"*

Lines 1–12

DISCUSSION PROMPTS

Use these prompts to help students examine Obama's statements:

Interpret Why does Obama describe the United States as "a magical place"? ***Possible answer:*** *It is "magical" because people with limited futures can come here and reach their potential.*

Analyze Why might Obama mention that Illinois is known as the "Land of Lincoln"? ***Possible answer:*** *President Abraham Lincoln abolished slavery, thus granting African Americans the freedom to reach their potential. Part of Obama's heritage is African.*

While studying here, my father met my mother. She was born in a town on the other side of the world, in Kansas. Her father worked on oil rigs and farms through most of the Depression. The day after Pearl Harbor my grandfather signed up for duty; joined Patton's army, marched across Europe. Back home, my grandmother raised their baby and went to work on a bomber assembly line. After the war, they studied on the G.I. Bill, bought a house through F.H.A., and later moved west all the way to Hawaii in search of opportunity. And they, too, had big dreams for their daughter. A common dream, born of two continents.

My parents shared not only an improbable love, they shared an abiding faith in the possibilities of this nation. They would give me an African name, Barack, or "blessed," believing that in a tolerant America your name is no barrier to success. They imagined me going to the best schools in the land, even though they weren't rich, because in a generous America you don't have to be rich to achieve your potential. **B**

They are both passed away now. And yet, I know that, on this night, they look down on me with great pride.

I stand here today, grateful for the diversity of my heritage, aware that my parents' dreams live on in my two precious daughters. I stand here knowing that my story is part of the larger American story, that I owe a debt to all of those who came before me, and that, in no other country on Earth, is my story even possible. **C**

Tonight, we gather to affirm the greatness of our nation—not because of the height of our skyscrapers, or the power of our military, or the size of our economy. Our pride is based on a very simple premise, summed up in a declaration made over two hundred years ago: "We hold these truths to be self-evident, that all men are created equal. That they are endowed by their Creator with certain inalienable rights. That among these are life, liberty, and the pursuit of happiness."

That is the true genius of America—a faith in simple dreams, an insistence on small miracles. That we can tuck in our children at night and know that they are fed and clothed and safe from harm. That we can say what we think, write what we think, without hearing a sudden knock on the door. That we can have an idea and start our own business without paying a bribe. That we can participate in the political process without fear of retribution, and that our votes will be counted, at least most of the time.

This year, in this election, we are called to reaffirm our values and our commitments, to hold them against a hard reality and see how we are measuring up to the legacy of our forbearers and the promise of future generations.

B IDENTIFY TREATMENT
How would you describe Obama's **tone** as he talks about his parents?

C IDENTIFY TREATMENT
Reread lines 30–34. What do these lines suggest about Obama's main purpose for sharing his family background?

INFORMATIONAL ANALYSIS

B IDENTIFY TREATMENT

Possible answers: *Obama's tone is one of admiration and love.*

Extend the Discussion Do you agree that in the United States, a person's name is "no barrier to success"?

INFORMATIONAL ANALYSIS

C IDENTIFY TREATMENT

Possible answer: *The lines suggest that Obama shared his family background to point out the common ground that exists between his family and every family in the United States. The lines also point out what makes the United States special.*

Extend the Discussion Do you feel you share a common ground with Obama's family? Why or why not?

Skill Focus: Identify Treatment

Possible answers for the chart on page 846:

	"Out of Many, One"
What form does the writing take?	*speech*
For what purpose(s) is the selection written? What is the writer's primary purpose?	*Obama's purpose is to entertain, to express ideas and feelings, and to inspire. Since Obama is delivering the keynote speech at the 2004 Democratic National Convention, his primary purpose is to reflect the ideas and policies of the Democratic Party.*
What is the writer's tone?	*admiring; proud; grateful; optimistic*

DIFFERENTIATED INSTRUCTION

FOR ENGLISH LEARNERS

Vocabulary Support Define the following key words and phrases for students:

- *tolerant* (line 24), "accepting"
- *achieve your potential* (line 27), "be the best you can be"
- *premise* (line 37), "basic idea"
- *inalienable* (line 40), "not able to be taken away"
- *retribution* (line 47), "punishment"
- *reaffirm our values and our commitments* (lines 49–50), "recall our beliefs and goals"

FOR ADVANCED LEARNERS/PRE–AP

Apply [small-group option] Ask students to locate a copy of the keynote speech from the 2004 Republican National Convention. In what ways do the two parties differ in their ideas and policies? In what ways are they similar? Have students discuss their findings in small groups.

omprehension

1. **Recall** According to Obama, why was it "pretty unlikely" that he would end up giving an important speech at a national political convention?
2. **Clarify** What do Obama's parents and grandparents all have in common?

ritical Analysis

3. **Identify Treatment** Review the chart you completed as you read. In your own words, define Obama's treatment of his family in this speech.
4. **Identify Repetition** Identify one important word, phrase, or idea that Obama repeats in his speech. What does the repetition help Obama emphasize?
5. **Evaluate a Speech** In your opinion, was it appropriate for Obama to share so much about his personal history in his **keynote speech?** Support your answer.

ead for Information: Compare and Contrast

WRITING PROMPT

In a paragraph, compare and contrast Barack Obama's portrayal of his family in this speech with the portrayal in his autobiography.

Remember that when you **compare and contrast,** you identify the ways in which two or more things are alike and different. To get started, follow these steps:

1. Review each selection and note the main points and most important details Obama includes about each family member.
2. Identify the similarities and differences between the way the family members are portrayed in the speech and autobiography.
3. In a sentence, make a general statement about the similarities and differences in the portrayals. Support your statement with specific examples. Then draw a conclusion about the differences you have noticed.

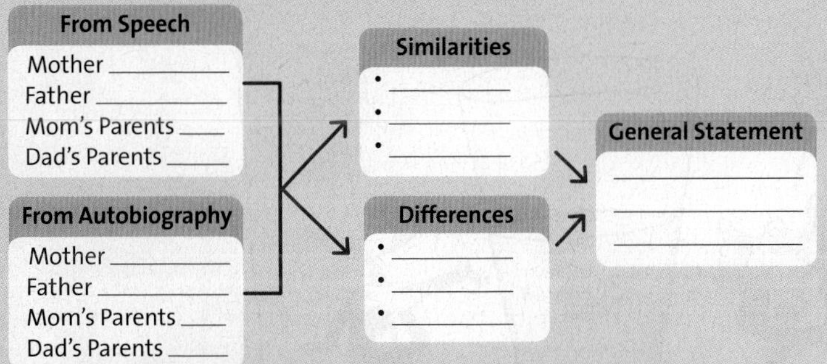

Practice and Apply

For additional support of postreading questions, use these copy masters:

RESOURCE MANAGER—Copy Masters
Reading Check p. 153
Question Support p. 154
Compare and Contrast p. 150
For additional questions, see page 144.

ANSWERS

Comprehension

1. *Obama's father grew up in Kenya herding goats. His grandfather was a servant to British colonials in Africa.*
2. *Obama's parents and grandparents all had dreams for their children.*

Critical Analysis

Possible answers:

3. **STANDARDS FOCUS Identify Treatment** *Obama's treatment of his family in the speech is full of admiration and gratitude. Since the main purpose of the speech is to reflect the Democratic party's ideas and policies, he also treats his personal story as a symbol for America.*
4. *The repetition of dreams (lines 9, 20, 42) helps Obama emphasize the idea that in the United States, everyone has the opportunity to reach his or her potential.*
5. *Some students might say that a speech to a national political convention should discuss issues that affect the nation as a whole. Others might point out that Obama uses the story of his family to make a general point about the United States itself.*

Read for Information: Compare and Contrast

Writing Prompt *Students' paragraphs should be clearly stated and supported by examples from both selections.*

FOR LESS–PROFICIENT WRITERS

Read for Information

- Suggest that students use a T Chart to record details about each family member from both selections.
- Tell students to circle details that are similar in both columns of the chart and underline those that are different. Have them select the two most important similarities and differences to discuss in their paragraphs.
- Solicit ideas from students on general statements that could be made about the similarities and differences.

Details About Obama's Father

Speech	*Autobiography*
was born and raised in a small village in Kenya	*lived in Kenya*
herded goats	*energizing*

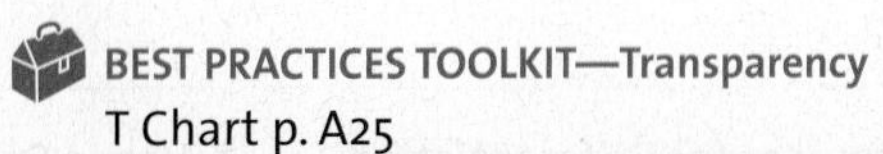
BEST PRACTICES TOOLKIT—Transparency
T Chart p. A25

Assess and Reteach

Assess

RESOURCE MANAGER—Copy Masters
Selection Tests A, B/C pp. 155–156, 157–158
Test Generator CD

Reteach

STANDARDS LESSON FILE
Reading Lesson 3: Determining Author's Purpose

Focus and Motivate

OBJECTIVES

Media Literacy

- explore the key idea of how cartoons can make political **statements**
- identify visual aspects of cartoons
- compare and contrast cartoonists' styles
- compare different points of view in nonprint media sources
- create a political cartoon

SUMMARY

The 1984 cartoon "Acid Rain" comments on the harmful effects of acid rain. Uncle Sam reaches out to catch a drop of rain, only to have it burn a hole through his hand. The 1890 cartoon "The Silver Sun of Prosperity" provides a positive view of the Sherman Silver Purchase Act. Uncle Sam is shown proudly holding an enormous silver dollar.

Can CARTOONS *have a point?*

Discuss the question. After students read the ***KEY IDEA*** paragraph, discuss how images, such as those used in cartoons, might be used to make a **statement** about government and society. Ask students to describe cartoons they've seen. Do any of these cartoons have a meaningful message alongside the humor?

BACKGROUND

Tell students that one of the most famous political cartoonists in American history, Thomas Nast (1840–1902), is remembered for proving just how much influence a skilled cartoonist can have over politics and public opinion. Nast's cartoons attacked serious government corruption that existed in his day. For example, Nast is credited with the ousting of politician William Marcy Tweed, an 1860s Democratic boss of New York City who cheated the city out of millions of dollars.

Today, people recognize that political cartoonists can still have a great deal of influence. On October 16, 2006, well-known political cartoonists from around the world met at the United Nations to discuss and debate their rights, roles, and responsibilities as journalists in the 21st century. The program was called "Cartooning for Peace."

Media Study

Political Cartoons

Image Collection on ***MediaSmart*** **DVD**

Can CARTOONS *have a point?*

KEY IDEA In the United States, everyone can express an opinion, and there are countless ways opinions are expressed. In this lesson, you'll look at how images and words can be carefully combined to make timely **statements** about American life.

Background

Cartoon Comments A **political cartoon** is a humorous drawing that makes a comment about a political issue or an event. Political cartoons usually appear on the editorial pages of newspapers, alongside writings that express opinions. These cartoons can reflect current topics in a funny or serious way.

The following cartoon presents two characters who might look familiar. In political cartoons, the elephant often appears as the symbol of the Republican Party and the donkey stands for the Democratic Party. These characters often represent two sides of an issue. In this case, though, does the cartoonist seem to think that either side is correct?

© 2006 Larry Wright. The Detroit News. All Rights Reserved. caglecartoons.com

850

Media Study Resources

 **RESOURCE MANAGER UNIT 7**

Plan and Teach pp. 159–162

Media Analysis

Summary pp. 163†*, 164‡*

Viewing Guide p. 165

Close Viewing p. 166

Media Activity p. 167

Produce Your Own Media p. 168

STANDARDS LESSON FILE

Media Lesson 3: Influence of Media on Society

Media Lesson 19: Analyzing Visuals

Media Center at **ClassZone.com**

MEDIA VIEWING

Media*Smart* DVD

* Resources for Differentiation † Also in Spanish ‡ In Haitian Creole and Vietnamese

edia Literacy: Messages in Political Cartoons

For any cartoon, the cartoonist's aim is to include images and details that help you figure out his or her message. One of the most enduring images in political cartoons is the figure of Uncle Sam. Political cartoonists use him as a symbol for the United States. His appearance may vary from cartoon to cartoon. However, he's usually easy to recognize, and the message he communicates is tied to a national issue. Use the following strategies to analyze political cartoons.

STRATEGIES FOR ANALYZING A POLITICAL CARTOON

© Frank Evers/Courtesy New York Daily News.

Identify the subject.
Look for labels. Any words you see might be used to identify people, groups, or events. What label appears in this cartoon?

Identify symbols and specific details.
Almost every detail in a political cartoon is carefully chosen to communicate part of the message. What key symbols and images appear in this cartoon?

Look for exaggeration.
Just as in ordinary comics, the humor in political cartoons is delivered often through exaggeration. In this political cartoon, what details appear to be extreme or unusual?

Figure out the point of view.
In any political cartoon, look for clues to the cartoonist's point of view. Are characters portrayed positively or negatively? Are their actions admirable, foolish, or criminal?

Notice how the art elements are used to catch the eye and to create certain effects.

- Political cartoons usually appear in black and white. When you spot any other color, consider what the cartoonist is highlighting and what message he or she is communicating.
- **Lines** convey certain moods. Straight lines can signal an issue is serious. Curvy lines convey playfulness.
- To get your attention, cartoonists exaggerate **shapes,** often making objects appear to be larger than life. Most often, cartoonists exaggerate by changing the **sizes** of familiar objects or of labels.

MEDIA STUDY: TEACHING OPTIONS

Teaching Option 1: The Basics (1–2 Days)

1. Begin the Media Study using the material provided on pages 850–851.
2. Show the Introduction on Media*Smart.* As they watch, have students use the Viewing Guide on page 852, along with the corresponding copy master on page 165 of the Resource Manager. Discuss their responses.
3. Return to the pupil's edition for the extension activities on page 853.

Teaching Option 2: In-Depth Study (2–3 Days)

1. Begin the Media Study using pages 850–851.
2. Show the Introduction from Media*Smart.* Then continue on Media*Smart* with the Media Lessons, using the teacher notes in the Resources section.
3. Show the Guided Analysis presentation. Have students record their observations on the Student Viewing Guide available in the Resources section from Media*Smart.*
4. Return to the pupil's edition, page 853.

Teach

MEDIA LITERACY

Discuss with students the people and issues that are likely topics of political cartoons today. Then discuss the chart on page 851.

- **Subject** Ask students to find the label in this cartoon. Would the meaning of the cartoon be clear without this label? If necessary, clarify that acid rain is a form of pollution. The burning of fossil fuels releases gases that mix with water in the atmosphere. The resulting acid rain can have a harmful effect on waterways, forests, and even buildings.
- **Symbols and Details** Make sure students understand that Uncle Sam represents the United States. Ask: What details in the cartoon are striking? ***Possible answer:*** *Uncle Sam's quizzical expression and the raindrop that has gone through his hand*
- **Exaggeration** Students should identify the large hole in Uncle Sam's hand, apparently caused by a single drop of acid rain, as an example of exaggeration.
- **Point of View** Ask students what they think is the cartoonist's perspective on acid rain. Does he think it is a serious issue or just something to joke about? ***Possible answer:*** *The cartoonist uses humor to point out that acid rain is a more serious issue than many people realize.*
- **Art Elements** Ask students whether they think this cartoon could be enhanced by the addition of **color.** If they could add color to just one part of the cartoon, where would they add it, and why?

  Ask students whether the **lines** in this cartoon are mostly straight or mostly curvy (*straight*). What is the most striking use of a straight line, and what message does it suggest? ***Possible answer:*** *The straight line of the falling raindrop suggests that acid rain is a serious issue.*

  Have students consider the cartoonist's use of **shape** and **size.** What element in the drawing is larger than it would be in real life, and what does this emphasize? ***Possible answer:*** *Uncle Sam's hand is enlarged, drawing attention to the acid raindrop that has burned a hole through his palm.*

MediaSmart DVD

Practice and Apply

VIEWING GUIDE

1. As students prepare to take a close look at the political cartoons, tell them that they will be asked to identify and explain specific elements used to express the ideas of the cartoonists. Encourage them to observe these elements:
   - labels, symbols, and other details that convey the cartoonist's message and point of view
   - the use of exaggeration to create humor and to make a statement
   - the use of **color** in one of the cartoons to express a particular feeling
   - **lines** drawn to suggest a specific mood or impression
   - **shapes** that are exaggerated or unusual in **size** to capture attention and express an idea
2. Tell students it is difficult to notice everything about a piece of art in a single viewing. Suggest that they first look at the cartoons for meaning. Then have them study the cartoons more closely, focusing on one or two specific elements at a time. At this point students should figure out how the cartoonists used specific techniques to express ideas.

RESOURCE MANAGER—Copy Masters
Viewing Guide p. 165
Close Viewing p. 166
Media Activity p. 167

Media*Smart* DVD

ANSWERS

***FIRST VIEWING:* Comprehension**

1. *Uncle Sam's hand and the drop of rain appear unusually large.*
2. *The silver dollar is enormous and the focal point of the cartoon.*

***CLOSE VIEWING:* Media Literacy**

Possible answers:

3. *The size of the raindrop and the damage it causes, as well as the look of confusion on Uncle Sam's face, are all exaggerations in order to make a point.*
4. *The political cartoon might be commenting on the fact that people in the United States are ignorant about the dangers and effects of acid rain.*
5. *A dignified Uncle Sam is shown high above a busy city, holding up an enormous silver dollar with a look of pride and accomplishment. He symbolizes the people of the United States, the prosperity of the nation, and the positive influence the Sherman Silver Purchase Act will supposedly have on the nation. The cartoonist uses bright colors such as yellow, orange, and white to suggest sunlight; exaggerates the size of the coin and the size of Uncle Sam; and makes prominent the text* United States of America *on the coin. The man tipping his hat seems to be waving to a cheering crowd, emphasizing the idea that passing the bill is a triumph. The cartoonist also uses a moving train, boats, farmers, and many buildings to indicate a healthy economy.*

***MediaSmart* DVD**
- **Selection 1:** "Acid Rain"
- **Cartoonist:** Frank Evers
- **Selection 2:** "The Silver Sun of Prosperity"
- **Cartoonist:** Bernard Gillam
- **Genre:** Political Cartoons

Viewing Guide for
Political Cartoons

Use the DVD to see larger versions of the political cartoons. As yo
examine each one, think about when it was created and the issue
comments on. The political cartoon on page 851 was published a
time when the effects of acid rain first became a topic in the new
The cartoon here first appeared in 1890, when the U.S. Congres
passed the Sherman Silver Purchase Act. This act called for the government to put more money into circulation by purchasing more silver than ever before.

Think about the way Uncle Sam is drawn in each political carto
and the images and words each cartoonist uses to make a comme
Use these questions to help you interpret the messages.

NOW VIEW

***FIRST VIEWING:* Comprehension**

1. **Identify** Name any object that appears unusually large in size in the "Acid Rain" political cartoon.
2. **Clarify** Apart from the title, "The Silver Sun of Prosperity," what help you to understand the subject of this political cartoon?

***CLOSE VIEWING:* Media Literacy**

3. **Identify Exaggeration** In the "Acid Rain" political cartoon, what looks exaggerated about the appearance of Uncle Sam and the rain?
4. **Analyze the Message** In "Acid Rain," Uncle Sam seems to be a bit confused. What comment might the political cartoonist be making by drawing Uncle Sam in this way?
5. **Analyze the Message** The political cartoonist of "The Silver Sun of Prosperity" was in favor of the Sherman Silver Act. What evidence do you see of this in the political cartoon? Think about
   - Uncle Sam's action in the cartoon and what he symbolizes
   - the color choices and the use of text and exaggeration
   - the specific objects the cartoonist chose to depict

852

Write or Discuss

Compare Political Cartoons You've seen how the image of Uncle Sam has spanned generations. The political cartoons in this lesson were created at different times to address different issues. How else are they alike or different? Write a brief comparison-contrast paragraph that describes at least two more differences. Think about

- whether the political cartoon includes many details or only a few
- the message of each political cartoon
- whether each cartoonist uses color

Produce Your Own Media

Create a Political Cartoon Choose an issue that you think would make a good subject for your own **political cartoon.** This issue may be something that affects your school, your neighborhood, or the entire nation. The basic rule is to choose an issue that's familiar to your audience and that is important enough for them to care about. It may help you to briefly discuss your ideas with your teacher.

HERE'S HOW Use these suggestions in making your political cartoon:

- What details could you use to represent the issue?
- What might you exaggerate in the image to highlight your point?
- Draw attention to the most important part of your image through the use of art elements. For example, make the person or object that matters most larger in size than the other objects.
- Draw or label the people or objects in the political cartoon so that they're easy to recognize. You can also use speech balloons to show what a character is saying. Make sure there are reasons for using any words you include.

STUDENT MODEL

MEDIA TOOLS

For help with creating a political cartoon, visit the **Media Center** at **ClassZone.com.**

Tech Tip

If available, use a software program to make a slideshow of the cartoons in your class.

Assess and Reteach

Write or Discuss

Compare Political Cartoons To help students begin, suggest that they write their ideas in a Venn Diagram. Students might point out any of the following differences: "Acid Rain" is simple with few details, while "The Silver Sun of Prosperity" is highly detailed; the message of "Acid Rain" is negative or cautionary, while the message of "Silver Sun" is positive and hopeful; "Acid Rain" is in black and white, while "Silver Sun" makes use of color; "Acid Rain" shows Uncle Sam looking confused, while "Silver Sun" shows him appearing proud and confident. The cartoons are similar in the way they depict Uncle Sam's style of dress and general appearance, and in their use of Uncle Sam as a symbol of the United States.

 **BEST PRACTICES TOOLKIT—Transparency**
Venn Diagram p. A26

Produce Your Own Media

Rubric A strong political cartoon should

- address an important issue that affects people
- include details that represent the cartoon's subject and possibly exaggerated images to highlight a point
- make use of art elements to draw attention to the most important part of an image
- feature people or objects that are labeled or otherwise easy to recognize

RESOURCE MANAGER—Copy Master
Produce Your Own Media p. 168

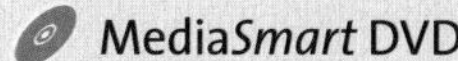

Media*Smart* DVD

MEDIA STUDY WRAP–UP

Summarize Ask students to summarize the elements political cartoonists use to express ideas. Have them provide specific examples from the two cartoons featured in this lesson. If necessary, prompt them to discuss the cartoonists' use of labels, symbols, exaggeration, color, lines, shape, and size to express ideas.

RETEACH

STANDARDS LESSON FILE
Media Lesson 3: Influence of Media on Society
Media Lesson 19: Analyzing Visuals

Focus and Motivate

OBJECTIVES

Literary Analysis

- explore the key idea of **injustice**
- identify and analyze historical context
- read poetry and a book excerpt

Reading

- identify and analyze repetition

SUMMARY

The poem "I Want to Write" describes the speaker's longing to capture the songs of her people: their stories, their pain, and their beauty. "Sit-Ins" addresses the first students who participated in a sit-in at a Woolworth's department store in 1960. The poem celebrates the students' "courage and faith, convictions, and intelligence," as well as their efforts to achieve justice and awaken the consciences of the people who make and enforce unjust laws. The book excerpt from *A Dream of Freedom* provides further details about the Woolworth's protest.

How can we fight INJUSTICE?

Discuss the question. To lead into the ***KEY IDEA,*** ask students what words and images come to mind when they think of the word ***injustice.*** Discuss students' ideas and how students feel when they witness injustice. Then have students complete the ***LIST IT*** activity in small groups.

Before Reading

I Want to Write
Sit-Ins

Poems by Margaret Walker

How can we fight INJUSTICE?

KEY IDEA A girl is blamed for someone else's mistake. A boy is accused because of the color of his skin. People are denied rights because of the group they belong to, or they are put into danger because of what they believe. Witnessing **injustice** can make you feel angry, powerless, or even physically sick. But there are ways to fight back. In the poems you're about to read, Margaret Walker celebrates working for what's right.

LIST IT How can people fight injustice? With a small group, brainstorm a list of ways people can help make the world a fairer place. Then compare your lists with those of other groups. Who came up with the most examples? Who came up with ideas no one else did?

854

Selection Resources

RESOURCE MANAGER UNIT 7

Plan and Teach pp. 169–176

Literary Analysis

Historical Context pp. 177, 178†*

Question Support p. 181*

Reading

Analyze Repetition pp. 179, 180†*

Reading Fluency p. 182

Assessment

Selection Tests A, B/C pp. 183*, 185*

Test Generator CD

BEST PRACTICES TOOLKIT

Differentiated Instruction pp. 31–38*

Graphic Organizers/Strategies

Think-Pair-Share

Reading Support

Audio Anthology CD*

Technology

Literature Center at **ClassZone.com**

Write*Smart* CD

* Resources for Differentiation † Also in Spanish

LITERARY ANALYSIS: HISTORICAL CONTEXT

Just as a writer's cultural background can affect his or her work, the time period in which a writer lives also can influence his or her subject matter and attitude. When you look at literature in its **historical context,** you consider what was happening in society at the time a piece of writing was created.

Margaret Walker wrote the two poems you are about to read in different decades. She wrote "I Want to Write" in the 1930s and "Sit-Ins" in the 1960s. First study the background on this page, and read the excerpt from *A Dream of Freedom* on page 859. Then, as you read the poems, try to connect historical events with Margaret Walker's words.

READING SKILL: ANALYZE REPETITION

Sound devices can add interest and appeal to all types of poems, whether long, short, funny, or serious. One of the sound devices used in Walker's poems is **repetition,** in which a sound, word, phrase, or line is repeated for emphasis or unity. To understand the effect of repetition in a poem, follow these steps:

- Write down repeated words, phrases, or lines.
- Think about what ideas these repeated elements emphasize.
- Notice how the repetition relates to the poem's overall message.

As you read each poem, record examples of repetition in a chart like the one shown, and describe the effect each has on your understanding of Walker's ideas.

Repetition	*Effect*

Author Online

Privilege and Pain Margaret Walker had a middle-class upbringing in the South at a time when many African Americans weren't so lucky. Her parents' jobs provided a nice income, but the family still suffered from discrimination. In an interview, she recalled the effects of racial prejudice: "Before I was 10, I knew what it was to step off the sidewalk to let a white man pass; otherwise he might knock me off. . . ."

Margaret Walker
1915–1998

For Her People While Walker was growing up in the 1920s, an African-American cultural movement called the Harlem Renaissance was flourishing in New York City. Walker discovered the works of these new writers when she was 11 years old. Already showing a gift for writing, Walker knew that she, too, wanted to tell the stories of African Americans. Encouraged by poet Langston Hughes, Walker went to college in the North in 1932. Ten years later, Yale University published her first collection of poetry, *For My People.*

Background

Civil Rights In the South, "Jim Crow" laws kept blacks and whites separated in public places, such as schools and restaurants. In the 1960s, Martin Luther King Jr. and other leaders organized nonviolent protests against segregation. Tactics included boycotts (refusing to buy products from companies that supported segregation) and sit-ins (peacefully demanding service at segregated businesses).

MORE ABOUT THE AUTHOR AND BACKGROUND
To learn more about Margaret Walker and the civil rights movement, visit the **Literature Center** at **ClassZone.com.**

Teach

STANDARDS FOCUS

LITERARY ANALYSIS

● HISTORICAL CONTEXT

Read aloud the author and background information on page 855. Ask students how writing during the civil rights movement might have influenced Walker's poetry. ***Possible answer:*** *Her poems might deal with the injustice experienced by African Americans or their attempts to fight this injustice.*

CHECK UNDERSTANDING Ask students to identify the historical context of a well-known story, such as *The Diary of a Young Girl* by Anne Frank. How does the historical context affect events in the book?

READING SKILL

■ ANALYZE REPETITION

Read these lines aloud:

We get no looks; we hide in books.
We roll our eyes; we snub the boys.
We get no looks; we hide in books.
We're out of sight; we cry at night.

Have students point out the repetition in these lines. What do they think the poet is trying to emphasize by using repetition here? ***Possible answer:*** *The word* we *and the line "We get no looks; we hide in books" are repeated. Repeating* we *emphasizes the group experience. Repeating the line emphasizes how the girls deal with their upset feelings.*

CHECK UNDERSTANDING Ask students to identify songs or nursery rhymes that include repetition. Discuss the effect of the repetition in each example.

RESOURCE MANAGER—Copy Master
Analyze Repetition p. 179 (for student use while reading the poems)

DIFFERENTIATED INSTRUCTION

FOR ALL STUDENTS

For general guidelines on differentiating instruction, see

BEST PRACTICES TOOLKIT
Differentiated Instruction pp. 31–38

FOR LESS–PROFICIENT READERS

Comprehension Support Be sure students are familiar with figurative language and understand how it is used in poetry. Explain that figurative language is words and phrases used in ways other than their ordinary meanings. Figurative language might include metaphors (implied comparisons) and similes (direct comparisons using *like* or *as*). This type of language is not meant to be taken literally. For example, if a poet writes, "The sky is on fire," she might mean that the sunset turns the sky red, not that there is an actual fire. To help students with comprehension, assist them in identifying and explaining figurative language in the Walker poems.

I WANT TO WRITE / SIT–INS 855

Practice and Apply

Lines 1–10
DISCUSSION PROMPTS

Use these prompts to help students understand the speaker's message:

Restate In your own words, tell what the speaker means by "I want to catch the last floating strains from their sob-torn throats." ***Possible answer:*** *I want to write down the songs of my grief-stricken people.*

Analyze What might the speaker mean by "I want to frame their dreams into words; their souls into notes"? ***Possible answer:*** *The speaker wants to write or tell about the dreams and "souls" of African-American people so that their stories will be told.*

Evaluate In addition to emphasizing an idea, what sound effect does the repetition in this poem create? ***Possible answer:*** *The repetition creates rhythm and makes the poem sound like one of the "songs" the speaker wants to write.*

ANALYZE VISUALS

Possible answer: *The girl has a calm, friendly, and thoughtful expression. She might have a kind and curious personality.*

READING SKILL
A REPETITION

Possible answer: *The repetition of "I want" and "to write" emphasizes the speaker's desire to describe the African-American experience.*

Illustration by Jérôme Lagarrigue.

I Want to Write

Margaret Walker

I want to write
I want to write the songs of my people.
I want to hear them singing melodies in the dark.
I want to catch the last floating strains[1] from their sob-torn throats.
I want to frame their dreams into words; their souls into notes.
I want to catch their sunshine laughter in a bowl;
fling dark hands to a darker sky
and fill them full of stars
then crush and mix such lights till they become
a mirrored pool of brilliance in the dawn. A

ANALYZE VISUALS
Look at the image on this page. **Describe** the expression on the girl's face. What do you think her personality is like?

A REPETITION
Note the phrase in this poem that is repeated. What idea does it emphasize?

1. **strains:** tunes.

DIFFERENTIATED INSTRUCTION

FOR LESS–PROFICIENT READERS

Reading Skill Follow-Up: Analyze Repetition [paired option] To help students better understand the purpose of repetition in the poem, have them work in pairs to begin filling in their charts from page 855.

Repetition	*Effect*
"I want to write"	*Repeating this phrase in the first two lines emphasizes the speaker's longing to capture the African-American experience in words.*

FOR ENGLISH LEARNERS

Options for Reading Have students follow along as they listen to the poems on the *Audio Anthology CD*. Have students use Think-Pair-Share to answer important questions about each work, including the questions on pages 856 and 857 of the pupil's edition.

 **BEST PRACTICES TOOLKIT—Transparency**
Think-Pair-Share p. A18

Illustration by Jérôme Lagarrigue.

Sit-Ins

Margaret Walker

Greensboro, North Carolina, in the Spring of 1960

You were our first brave ones to defy their dissonance of hate
With your silence
With your willingness to suffer
Without violence
Those first bright young to fling your names across pages
Of new southern history
With courage and faith, convictions, and intelligence **B**
The first to blaze a flaming path for justice
And awaken consciences
Of these stony ones.

Come, Lord Jesus, Bold Young Galilean[1]
Sit Beside this Counter, Lord, with Me! **C**

ANALYZE VISUALS
What can you **infer** about why the woman and child might be walking away from the counter?

B REPETITION
Reread lines 1–7. What does the repetition help you to understand about the people Walker is describing?

C HISTORICAL CONTEXT
What historical details does Walker cite in the poem?

1. **Galilean** (găl′ə-lē′ən): According to the Bible, Jesus lived near the Sea of Galilee, in Israel.

ANALYZE VISUALS

Possible answer: *They might be walking away because they are not allowed to be served at a "whites-only" counter.*

About the Art Jérôme Lagarrigue was born in Paris, France, in 1973 and now lives in both Paris and New York, where he paints landscapes and portraits. He illustrated *Freedom Summer,* a children's book about two boys' experience the summer after the passing of the Civil Rights Act of 1964, which outlawed discrimination based on race, color, gender, religion, or national origin. For these illustrations, he received the Coretta Scott King/John Steptoe award for new talent.

READING SKILL

B REPETITION

Possible answer: *The repetition emphasizes the traits of the protesters—they were courageous, smart, and determined to protest in a peaceful manner.*

LITERARY ANALYSIS

C HISTORICAL CONTEXT

Possible answer: *The nonviolent protest in Greensboro, North Carolina, in the spring of 1960 attracted national attention.*

Lines 1–12

REINFORCE *KEY IDEA:* INJUSTICE

Discuss How do you think the speaker of "Sit-Ins" would respond to the question *How can we fight* ***injustice?*** Cite evidence from the poem. ***Possible answer:*** *The speaker would say we can fight injustice "Without violence" and "With courage and faith, convictions, and intelligence."*

SELECTION WRAP-UP

CRITIQUE Which poem addresses the idea of injustice most effectively? Explain.

READING FLUENCY

Distribute the copy masters and have students practice fluency.

RESOURCE MANAGER—Copy Master
Reading Fluency p. 182

FOR ENGLISH LEARNERS

Vocabulary Support Be sure students understand the meaning of these words as they are used in "Sit-Ins." Explain that some words are being used figuratively.

- *defy* (line 1), "to challenge or rebel"
- *dissonance* (line 1), "disagreement"
- *fling* (line 5), "toss"
- *convictions* (line 7), "confidence"
- *consciences* (line 9), "senses of right and wrong"

FOR ADVANCED LEARNERS/PRE-AP

Identify Symbolism [small-group option] Point out references to light and dark in the two poems. Have small groups discuss how the poet uses references to lightness and darkness as symbols. Encourage students to share their findings with the class.

Practice and Apply

After Reading

For additional support of postreading questions, use these copy masters:

RESOURCE MANAGER—Copy Masters
Historical Context p. 177 (for practice of literary analysis standards focus)
Question Support p. 181 (After Reading questions adapted for English learners and less-proficient readers)
Additional selection questions are provided for teachers on page 173.

ANSWERS

Comprehension

1. *The speaker wants to write about the experiences of African Americans.*
2. *The sit-in protesters have bravery, a willingness to suffer, determination, faith, convictions, and intelligence.*

Literary Analysis

Possible answers:

3. ***Hearing:*** *"songs," "singing melodies," "last floating strains from their sob-torn throats";* ***Sight:*** *"in the dark," "fling dark hands to a darker sky / and fill them full of stars," "mirrored pool of brilliance";* ***Touch:*** *"catch their sunshine laughter," "crush and mix." These images indicate that the people the speaker wants to write about have difficult lives but remain full of dreams, laughter, and hope.*
4. **● STANDARDS FOCUS Historical Context** *In the 1930s, Southern African Americans were segregated by Jim Crow laws. In the North, African Americans did not escape discrimination. Walker protests racial injustice by writing of the "dark" conditions in which African Americans lived and describing her hope for a better, more just future for her people.*
5. *The "stony ones" might be people who do not want to change old unjust laws.*
6. *Students may mention the specific details about the sit-in described in the book excerpt—who the protesters were, where the protest took place, and how people responded. The poem emphasizes the bravery and other positive qualities of the protesters and helps readers understand the social significance of their actions.*

After Reading

Comprehension

1. **Recall** In "I Want to Write," what does the speaker want to write about?
2. **Recall** In "Sit-Ins," what qualities do the people participating in the sit-ins have?

Literary Analysis

3. **Understand Imagery** Recall that imagery consists of words and phrases that appeal to readers' senses. In a chart like the one shown, note the images in "I Want to Write" that appeal to the senses of hearing, sight, and touch. What do these images help you to understand about the people Walker wants to write about?

Hearing	Sight	Touch
"singing melodies"		

4. **Examine Historical Context** Margaret Walker writes, "I want to write the songs of my people." Tell what you know about conditions and events that affected African Americans in the 1930s. How might Walker have been trying to protest racial **injustice** in "I Want to Write"? Support your answer with quotations from the poem.
5. **Interpret a Passage** In "Sit-Ins," Walker describes those participating in the sit-ins as "The first to blaze a flaming path for justice/And awaken consciences/Of these stony ones." Who might the "stony ones" be? Think about the qualities the word *stony* suggests.
6. **Compare Texts** What information in the excerpt from *A Dream of Freedom* does the most to help you understand the poem "Sit-Ins"? What details do you get in the poem that help you understand the book excerpt? Explain.
7. **Analyze Repetition** Look at the chart you completed as you read. Decide which poem makes greater use of repetition. What is the overall effect of this repetition on your understanding of Walker's ideas?

Extension and Challenge

8. **Big Question Activity** Review the list you came up with on page 854. After reading the poems and the book excerpt, do you have anything you want to add to the list? With your group, decide which method you think would be most effective in achieving justice.
9.  **SOCIAL STUDIES CONNECTION** Research another major event in the civil rights movement, such as the Montgomery Bus Boycott or the March on Washington. How did people participating in these events hope to achieve justice? In a presentation to the class, explain the event and its significance.

RESEARCH LINKS
For more on the civil rights movement, visit the **Research Center** at **ClassZone.com.**

7. **■ STANDARDS FOCUS Analyze Repetition** *"I Want to Write" uses more repetition. The repetition of "I want to" emphasizes how important Walker thinks it is to represent African Americans' struggles and hopes.*

Extension and Challenge

8. *Students' responses should demonstrate a deeper understanding of ways to overcome injustice, particularly nonviolent methods.*
9. **SOCIAL STUDIES CONNECTION** *Students should explain the significance of the event and participants' goals.*

Assess and Reteach

Assess

RESOURCE MANAGER—Copy Masters
Selection Tests A, B/C pp. 183–184, 185–186

 Test Generator CD

Reteach

STANDARDS LESSON FILE
Literature Lesson 34: Repetition and Parallelism
Literature Lesson 41: Author's Perspective

Reading for Information

BOOK EXCERPT In 1960, four African-American college students decided to protest racial segregation in a new way. This book excerpt describes their bold actions and how the students inspired others to join their cause.

from *A Dream of Freedom*

BY DIANE McWHORTER

Four protesters sit at a whites-only lunch counter at Woolworth's.

On the last day of January 1960, a North Carolina teenager named Ezell Blair Jr. announced to his mother, "Mom, we are going to do something tomorrow that may change history, that might change the world." Blair attended a black college in Greensboro called North Carolina Agricultural and Technical. On Monday afternoon, February 1, he and three A&T classmates, Franklin McCain, David Richmond, and Joseph McNeil, went downtown to Woolworth's department store, took a seat at the lunch counter, and ordered a doughnut and coffee.

"I'm sorry," said the waitress, "we don't serve you here."

Though white-only lunch counters were a fact of southern life, one of the students replied, "We just beg to disagree with you." Before sitting down, they had deliberately bought some school supplies. Holding up a receipt, they pointed out that they had just been served at a nearby cash register. One of the most insulting hypocrisies of segregation was that stores in the South, as Franklin McCain put it, "don't separate your money in this cash register, but, no, please don't step down to the hot dog stand."

The youths sat at the counter for an hour. They were heckled by a black dishwasher, and stared at by a white policeman. An elderly white woman cheered in a loud whisper: "You should have done it ten years ago!"

The store manager turned off the lights at five-thirty, half an hour before closing time. "By then," McCain recalled, "we had the confidence, my goodness, of a Mack truck." In a week, the Greensboro Four had grown to hundreds. Within two months, protests had taken place in 125 cities in nine states. . . .

The sit-ins, as the lunch counter campaign became known, sparked a freedom flame.

This selection provides support for question 6 on page 858. You can also use it as a mini-lesson on reading for information.

READING FOR INFORMATION

Point out that this excerpt is from *A Dream of Freedom*, a nonfiction book that gives information about the civil rights movement from 1954 to 1968. Have students preview the excerpt by reading the introduction and by looking at the photograph and reading its caption. Ask them what they think they might learn about in this article. ***Possible answer:*** *This selection might provide information about the four college students and how they protest. The photograph and caption explain that the protest took place at a lunch counter at Woolworth's.*

DISCUSSION PROMPTS

Use these prompts to help students learn about the sit-in:

Recall In what way do the students respond to the waitress who says, "I'm sorry, we don't serve you here"? ***Answer:*** *Before sitting down, the students bought school supplies. They show the receipt to the waitress and explain that they were just "served" at another cash register in the store.*

Analyze What hypocrisy of segregation does Franklin McCain point out? Why is this an act of hypocrisy? ***Possible answer:*** *Stores will take the money of African Americans but will not let them eat in their stores. This is a hypocrisy because the stores are willing to make money off people whom they are not willing to treat fairly.*

Evaluate What is the effect of the author's choice to include three different ways people reacted to the students while they sat at the counter? ***Possible answer:*** *The effect is powerful; it shows that the students stayed resolute no matter how people responded to them.*

DIFFERENTIATED INSTRUCTION

FOR ENGLISH LEARNERS

Vocabulary Support Be sure students are familiar with these vocabulary words before they read the selection:

- *deliberately*, "on purpose"
- *insulting*, "offensive"
- *hypocrisies*, "double standards; words or actions that are not consistent"
- *segregation*, "separation, such as by race or by gender"
- *heckled*, "booed; jeered at"

FOR ADVANCED LEARNERS/PRE–AP

Speculate [small-group option] After students have read this article, have them discuss how these four African-American college students "changed history." Ask them to speculate about why the experience of the first sit-in gave the young men "the confidence . . . of a Mack truck." What might have been empowering about the experience? Why might it have led to many more protests? In what other ways might the protest have inspired people?

Focus and Motivate

OBJECTIVES

- analyze a student model that reflects the key traits of a cause-and-effect essay
- use the writing process to write a cause-and effect essay
- use transition words to signal causes and effects
- revise and edit, using a rubric
- create a multimedia presentation on a cause-and-effect relationship

WRITER'S ROAD MAP

WRITING PROMPTS 1 AND 2

To generate ideas for the first prompt, have some small groups review local and national newspapers to find current events. Have others brainstorm historical events. List topics from each group on the board. For the second prompt, review selections in this unit together, discussing the cause-and-effect relationships they present.

ADDITIONAL PROMPTS

Use these prompts for more practice writing cause-and-effect essays:

WRITING PROMPT 3

Writing from Your Life Choose an important accomplishment or failure in your life and write about the events that caused it.

Ideas to Consider

- winning an award
- learning a new skill or sport
- losing the trust of someone close

WRITING PROMPT 4

Writing from Science Explore the causes of a condition affecting the physical world.

Ideas to Consider

- greenhouse effect
- famine
- extinction of species

For additional writing prompts, see

WriteSmart CD

Writing Center at **ClassZone.com**

KEY TRAITS

Review the six ***KEY TRAITS*** with students, focusing primarily on ideas, organization, and word choice. Compare the list of traits with the rubric on page 866.

Writing Workshop

Cause-and-Effect Essay

In this unit, you learned the effects that some early experiences had on Gary Soto, Barack Obama, and other writers. Check out the **Writer's Road Map** and begin writing about a cause-and-effect relationship that is important to you.

WRITER'S ROAD MAP

Cause-and-Effect Essay

WRITING PROMPT 1

Writing from the Real World Write an essay about a cause-and-effect relationship that you think is important or interesting. Make sure you can show clearly how one event caused another event to happen.

Topics to Consider

- a natural event, such as a hurricane or a storm
- a historical event, such as the California gold rush
- a community event, such as building a skate park

WRITING PROMPT 2

Writing from Literature Literature can be full of cause-and-effect relationships. Write an essay that traces a cause-and-effect relationship in a literary work.

Literature to Consider

- experiencing how others live ("Out of Bounds")
- the effects of political protest ("Sit-Ins")
- the power of dreams ("Out of Many, One")

WRITING TOOLS

For prewriting, revision, and editing tools, visit the **Writing Center at ClassZone.com.**

KEY TRAITS

1. *IDEAS*
- Identifies a true **cause-and-effect relationship**
- Presents a **thesis statement** that explains the connection between causes and effects
- Uses facts, examples, and other **details** to **support** each cause and effect

2. *ORGANIZATION*
- Presents causes and effects in a sensible **order**
- Uses **transitions** to show the relationship between effects and causes
- Has an attention-getting **introduction** and a **conclusion** that summarizes the cause-and-effect relationship

3. *VOICE*
- Uses a **tone** that is appropriate for the audience and purpose

4. *WORD CHOICE*
- Uses **precise language** to explain each cause and effect

5. *SENTENCE FLUENCY*
- Uses a variety of **sentence types** (statements, questions, and exclamations)

6. *CONVENTIONS*
- Uses **correct grammar, spelling, and punctuation**

Writing Workshop Resources

RESOURCE MANAGER UNIT 7

Plan and Teach pp. 187–190
Prewriting–Editing pp. 191–195
Writing Rubric p. 196
Publishing with Technology p. 197
Writing Support p. 198*

STANDARDS LESSON FILE

Writing Lessons 9, 16, 19, 21, 30, 40, 44
Grammar Lesson 20
Media Lesson 22

BEST PRACTICES TOOLKIT

Scaffolding Writing Instruction pp. 43–46*
Cause-and-Effect Diagrams • Cluster Diagram • Writing Template: Cause and Effect • Storyboard

TECHNOLOGY

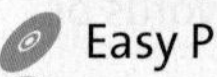

Easy Planner DVD

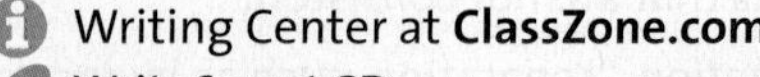

Writing Center at **ClassZone.com**

Write*Smart* CD

* Resources for Differentiation

Part 1: Analyze a Student Model

Chris Hawkins
Danvers Intermediate School

Why Is It So Noisy?

One afternoon last week, I was sitting in the park, trying to relax. I had gone there because I thought the sound of the wind in the trees and the waves on the shore of the lake would help get my mind off a problem that was bothering me. What I heard instead wasn't soothing natural sounds, but noise, noise, and more noise. The blaring car horns, beeping trucks, squealing bus brakes, shrieking ambulance sirens, and barking dogs made me even more nervous than I was before. "I can't even hear myself think!" I shouted. This kind of noise pollution is everywhere, and it's not just annoying—it's harmful because it may lead to hearing loss.

Traffic sounds like the ones I heard in the park are the major cause of noise pollution. Just think how much noise a passing car, truck, bus, train, or motorcycle makes. Can you imagine hearing dozens of them at once? It doesn't take much imagination, because we actually experience that racket every time we go outside. Don't look up for relief, either. According to the Council on the Environment of New York City, an airplane 2,000 feet away makes a noise as loud as a car blowing its horn just a step away. The sound of a jet taking off can actually cause buildings near an airport to vibrate, so just imagine what it does to our bodies.

Another cause of noise pollution is machinery like jackhammers, bulldozers, leaf blowers, and lawnmowers. As anyone who lives in the city or suburbs knows, the annoying vibrations from these machines can have immediate and dramatic effects. The noise interrupts our thoughts, makes conversations difficult, and can even be painful to our ears.

KEY TRAITS IN ACTION

Introduction includes an anecdote that gets the reader interested.

Thesis states a **cause-and-effect relationship:** excessive noise leads to harm.

Specific **details** and a fact **support** the idea that noise pollution is a serious issue. The writer varies **sentence types** by including a question.

Entire essay follows a logical **order.** The writer has already discussed the major cause of noise pollution and moves on to other sources in this paragraph. Use of the words *cause* and *effect* help to make the ideas clear.

Teach

Part 1: Analyze a Student Model

Have students read the **Student Model** and **Key Traits in Action.** Then discuss the model with the class, focusing on specific examples of each trait. You may also wish to incorporate these activities:

- **Thesis** Tell students that developing a thesis statement is one of the first steps in the writing process. It establishes the focus for the essay, not only identifying the main idea but presenting an attitude toward that main idea (*noise pollution is harmful*).

  Point out that the thesis statement in the model is found at the end of the introductory paragraph. Ask students why this is a logical place to insert the thesis. ***Possible answer:*** *In this position, the thesis statement provides a natural transition or bridge into the body of the essay. It also prepares readers for what they are going to learn in the essay.*
- **Supporting Details** List the kinds of details that a writer might use to support and develop the main idea: facts, statistics, incidents, examples, sensory details, quotations. Have students work with a partner to find each type of detail in the student model. ***Possible answer:*** *facts (lines 14–16, 29–33), statistics (lines 33–34), incidents (lines 1–7), examples (lines 19–20), sensory details (lines 5–7), quotations (lines 7–8)*
- **Sentence Types** Have students locate declarative, interrogative, and imperative sentences in lines 10–18. ***Possible answer:***
  - —***declarative:*** *"Traffic sounds . . . noise pollution." "It doesn't take much imagination . . . go outside." "According to the Council . . . step away." "The sound of a jet taking off . . . to our bodies."*
  - —***interrogative:*** *"Can you imagine hearing dozens of them at once?"*
  - —***imperative:*** *"Just think how much . . . makes." "Don't look up for relief, either."*

  What is the effect of varying sentence types? ***Possible answer:*** *Presenting information in different kinds of sentences helps keep readers' attention and avoid monotony.*

DIFFERENTIATED INSTRUCTION

FOR ALL STUDENTS

Student Portfolios Encourage students to save copies of their writing so they can track their progress throughout the year.

For general guidelines on differentiating writing instruction, see

BEST PRACTICES TOOLKIT
Scaffolding Writing Instruction
pp. 43–46

FOR ENGLISH LEARNERS

Language: Skill Words Review these terms:

- *thesis:* sentence in an essay that defines the writer's purpose
- *cause-and-effect relationship:* one event leads to another. Example: I made the soccer team because I practiced all year.
- *supporting details:* facts, examples, reasons, quotations, or statistics that prove the main idea
- *order:* organization of details
- *tone:* the writer's attitude about the subject

- **Precise Language** Write this sentence on the board: The noise level at a lot of events can be loud. Then write the sentence in lines 24–25 of the student model next to it. Ask students to contrast the effect of the general statement with the precise language used in the model. ***Possible answer:*** *The sentence in the model is more effective. By identifying specific events that expose people to noise pollution, the writer proves that it is everywhere and that everyone is affected. The examples show that noise pollution is a part of daily recreational activities.*
- **Transitions** Remind students that transitions show relationships between ideas. The words and phrases on page 866 are particularly useful for identifying cause-and-effect relationships. Ask students to find examples of these transitions and any others that indicate cause and effect in the model essay. ***Possible answer:*** *"because" (line 13), "so" (line 18), "As a result" (line 27), "If" (line 32), "caused by" (line 34)*
- **Conclusion** Discuss other ways that a cause-and-effect essay might be concluded. For example, the writer might comment on the ideas that he or she has presented, speculate about further effects, or incorporate a relevant quotation.

For interactive student models, see

WriteSmart CD

Writing Center at **ClassZone.com**

When it's loud, music becomes noise, too. The noise level at concerts, arcades, parties, and other events can be almost deafening. We have actually gotten so used to blaring music that it doesn't even seem loud to us. As a result, when we listen to music at home, or even through headphones, we turn the volume way up.

The effects of all this noise pollution are frightening. According to an article I read in the *Danvers Ledger,* "Loud noises can actually destroy the cells inside our ears." The longer we're exposed to the noise and the louder it is, the worse the damage will be. If these cells are destroyed, there is no way to restore them or our hearing. The House Ear Institute estimates that almost 10 million Americans suffer from hearing loss caused by noise.

Living in the world means dealing with noise. However, since we understand the causes of noise pollution, we can try to prevent its harmful effects. We can avoid noisy environments as much as possible and wear earplugs or earmuffs when we're in construction zones or at the airport. We can turn down our TVs, DVD and CD players, computers, and personal music players. Finally, we need to tell other people about the dangers of noise pollution and start doing what we can to prevent it—now.

Highlighted **precise language** makes the causes and effects clear.

Highlighted **transition** brings attention to one effect that loud music has on people.

The word *we* helps to create a **tone** that makes the reader feel comfortable. **Conclusion** summarizes the causes of noise pollution and suggests ways to minimize its harmful effects.

DIFFERENTIATED INSTRUCTION

FOR ENGLISH LEARNERS

Comprehension: Transitions

- Display these sentences. Have students fill in the blanks with transitions from page 866.
  - —Pumpkins were small this year _______ of the dry summer. *(because)*
  - —I overslept this morning. _______ I missed my bus. *(As a result, Consequently)*
  - —_______ Jorge gets extra help, he will do better in school. *(If)*
- Display this chart. Have pairs match causes and effects and write sentences, underlining each transitional word or phrase.

Causes	Effects
• if more than ten people come to dinner • roads were closed • my dog was muddy • because of the rain	• the picnic was cancelled • so I gave him a bath • we won't have enough food • as a result, traffic backed up

Possible answer:

If more than ten people come to dinner, we won't have enough food.

Roads were closed. As a result, traffic backed up.

My dog was muddy, so I gave him a bath.

Because of the rain, the picnic was cancelled.

RESOURCE MANAGER—Copy Master
Writing Support p. 198

Part 2: Apply the Writing Process

PREWRITING

What Should I Do?	What Does It Look Like?
1. Decide on the right topic for you. Think of events in your life or the world that made you ask yourself "Why did that happen?" or "What happened after that?" List the ideas that come to mind. (Circle) the topic that interests you most. **TIP** **Grouping your ideas into categories can help you focus.**	See the My World / The Wider World list below.
2. Use a flow chart to explore causes and effects. Ask yourself if the events are true causes and effects. One event may follow another but not be caused by it. "I went out without drying my hair and caught pneumonia" is an example of a **false cause.** Germs cause illness; wet hair does not.	See the flow chart below.
3. Draft a thesis statement. Write a sentence explaining the main points you want to make about the cause-and-effect relationship.	***Working thesis statement*** *Our world is definitely not a quiet place, and the noise pollution we experience every day is annoying and can also cause hearing problems.*
4. Collect details in support of your key points. Look for facts, statistics, quotations, and anecdotes to support the statements you make about causes and effects.	***Key point:*** *Noise pollution is damaging.* ***Evidence:*** • *Danvers Ledger reports, "Loud noises can actually destroy the cells inside our ears."* • *According to the House Ear Institute, almost 10 million Americans have loss of hearing due to noise.*

My World	*The Wider World*
• *Sid's skateboarding accident*	• *melting glaciers*
• *Leslie wanting to get a dog*	• *(noise pollution)*
• *getting lost during school field trip*	• *lowering the voting age to 16*
• *earning my blue belt in judo*	• *stereotypes of teenagers*

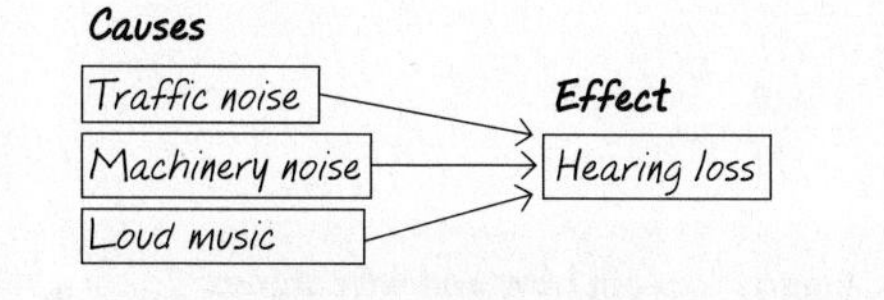

Practice and Apply

To support students during the writing process, use these copy masters:

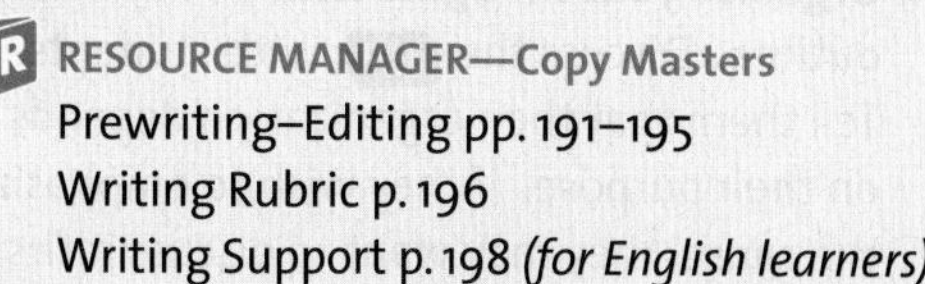

RESOURCE MANAGER—Copy Masters
Prewriting–Editing pp. 191–195
Writing Rubric p. 196
Writing Support p. 198 *(for English learners)*

Part 2: Apply the Writing Process

PREWRITING

1. **Decide on the right topic for you.** Have groups of students brainstorm topics to add to those in the text. If they have trouble choosing only one topic, suggest that students put the circled topics in order of priority and choose the topic at the top of the list. Then point out the TIP.
2. **Use a flow chart to explore causes and effects.** Tell students that although the flow chart in the text shows several causes leading to one effect, they may choose to approach their topic by examining a single cause and multiple effects. Display the two Cause-and-Effect Diagrams to illustrate the two ways of exploring causes and effects. Then have students freewrite on their topic to establish whether they have multiple causes or effects. Have students work individually to complete their charts.

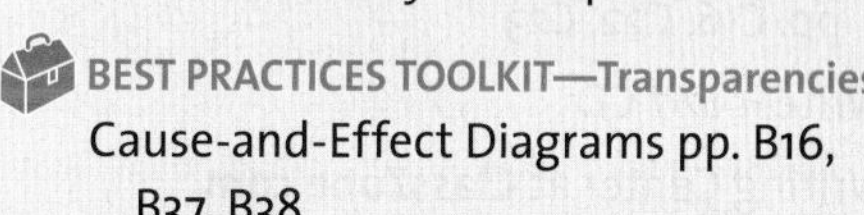

BEST PRACTICES TOOLKIT—Transparencies
Cause-and-Effect Diagrams pp. B16, B37, B38

3. **Draft a thesis statement.** Have students share their thesis statement with a partner. Have partners evaluate whether the statement clearly identifies the main idea and establishes the purpose of the essay.
4. **Collect details in support of your key points.** In addition to print and electronic resources, students might acquire information through personal interviews, brainstorming, and observation. Tell students that if they find it difficult to gather enough support, they may want to broaden or narrow their focus.

For interactive graphic organizers, see
WriteSmart CD
Writing Center at **ClassZone.com**

FOR ENGLISH LEARNERS

Identifying True Causes and Effects Write these statements on the board:

- If you exceed the speed limit, you may receive a ticket.
- I lost my lucky pen, so I failed the test.
- The heavy smog caused her to have an asthma attack.
- Since he is the middle child, he likes sports.

Have students identify each cause-and-effect relationship as true or false. Discuss the logic behind their evaluations.

Drafting a Thesis Statement [paired option] Help students write a strong thesis statement by displaying these prompts:

- I am going to write about ______.
- I am going to show that ______ causes ______.
- My feeling about this topic is ______.

Then have students work in pairs to develop a thesis statement that states the topic and their attitude toward it. Have them use lines 8–9 of the student model as an example.

DRAFTING

1. **Organize your thoughts with an informal outline.** Discuss the TIP with students. Tell them that their organization depends on their purpose. If they wish to emphasize the cause, they may want to discuss it first, as the writer of the student model does. If they wish to emphasize the effect, then they might start by identifying it before focusing on the cause.
2. **Clearly explain how and why things happen.** Before students write their body paragraphs, suggest that they use a Cluster Diagram to record and organize their details for each cause and effect.

   BEST PRACTICES TOOLKIT—Transparency
   Cluster Diagram p. B18
3. **Leave your reader with something to think about.** Review the key traits, rubric, and peer-reader questions together, as the TIP suggests. Then have students write a draft of their conclusion. Have them set it aside and then return to it later to see what changes they might make to improve it.

For cause-and-effect essay writing templates, see

BEST PRACTICES TOOLKIT—Transparencies
Writing Template: Cause and Effect pp. C16, C22, C23

Write*Smart* CD

Writing Center at **ClassZone.com**

DRAFTING

What Should I Do?	What Does It Look Like?
1. Organize your thoughts with an informal outline. This writer described the major causes of noise pollution and then discussed its most significant effect. You can also present the effects first and then analyze their causes. **TIP Try different ways of organizing your essay and choose the one that works best for you.**	***Introduction*** *Discuss how noise affects my life* *Thesis: Noise pollution annoying and damaging* ***Most important cause: Traffic*** *Cars, buses, trains, airplanes* ***Second most important cause: Machinery*** *Jackhammers, bulldozers, leaf blowers, lawnmowers* ***Third most important cause: Music*** *Concerts, parties, personal music players* ***Most important effect: Hearing loss*** *Permanent damage to ear cells; 10 million Americans affected* ***Conclusion*** *Need to take action to prevent harmful effects of noise pollution*
2. Clearly explain how and why things happen. Remember the details you collected in step 4 on the previous page? Include those and other specific, relevant details to help your reader understand the cause-and-effect relationship.	*Another cause of noise pollution is machinery like jackhammers, bulldozers, leaf blowers, and lawnmowers. As anyone who lives in the city or suburbs knows, the annoying vibrations from these machines can interrupt our thoughts, make conversations difficult, and even be painful to our ears.*
3. Leave your reader with something to think about. Your conclusion should use fresh, new language to summarize the causes and effects. If possible, it should also show how the topic is important to the reader's life or suggest what the reader can do to change the situation. **TIP Before revising, look back at the key traits on page 860 and the rubric and peer-reader questions on page 866.**	*We understand the causes of noise pollution, so we can try to prevent its harmful effects. We can avoid noisy environments as much as possible and turn down our personal music players. Finally, we need to tell other people about the dangers of noise pollution and start doing what we can to prevent it—now.*

DIFFERENTIATED INSTRUCTION

FOR LESS–PROFICIENT WRITERS

Organizing the Essay [small-group option]

1. Display the two Cause-and-Effect writing template transparencies. Point out similarities and differences in how they are organized and discuss the use of each.
2. Have students review their causes, effects, and significant details to help them decide which template to use.
3. Distribute copies of the templates and have students work on them in class. Check their progress occasionally.
4. After students complete their templates, have them gather in small groups to discuss their work. Encourage group members to give each other feedback on developing and organizing their ideas.
5. Tell students that each part of the template corresponds to a paragraph in their essay. The thesis belongs in the introductory paragraph, and each cause or effect box will become a body paragraph. Allow time for questions before students begin writing.

REVISING AND EDITING

What Should I Do?	What Does It Look Like?
1. Have a classmate review your introduction. • Ask a peer reader if the first few sentences of your essay make him or her want to read on. • If the answer is no, try eliminating sentences that give little information or adding an interesting detail, quotation, question, or anecdote. **See page 866:** Ask a Peer Reader	*~~My essay is about noise pollution because I think it is very important. This issue is getting worse.~~* *One afternoon last week, I was sitting in the park, trying to relax. I had gone there because I thought the sound of the wind in the trees and the waves on the shore of the lake would help get my mind off a problem that was bothering me. What I heard instead wasn't soothing natural sounds, but noise, noise, and more noise.*
2. Evaluate your supporting information. • [Bracket] the facts and examples that illustrate your key points. • Consider adding quotations, statistics, or other details that make your statements easy to understand.	*Don't look up for relief, either. [~~Jet planes make a terrible racket.~~] According to the Council on the Environment of New York City, an airplane 2,000 feet away makes a noise as loud as a car blowing its horn just a step away.*
3. Use transitions wisely. • Underline the transitional words and phrases you used to make the relationship between causes and effects clear. • Think about adding transitions such as *however, since,* and *as a result* to show how ideas are connected. **See page 866:** Add Transitional Words	*~~We understand the causes of noise pollution, so we can try to prevent its harmful effects.~~ Living in the world means dealing with noise. However, since we understand the causes of noise pollution, we can try to prevent its harmful effects.*
4. Add a question or exclamation where appropriate. • Reread your essay. Do all your sentences end with periods? • Consider including an exclamation or a question for a change of pace. **TIP** Use exclamations and questions sparingly to avoid sounding overexcited or confused.	*Just think how much noise a passing car, truck, bus, train, or motorcycle makes. ~~Then~~ Can you imagine hearing dozens of them at once ~~.~~?*

REVISING AND EDITING

1. **Have a classmate review your introduction.** Have students examine the first paragraphs of several essays in the pupil's edition. Ask them to identify ways that the authors capture readers' attention. Write some of these techniques on the board and challenge students to incorporate them in their essays.

   As an alternative, have students meet with a partner to talk about why they first became interested in their topic. Have partners jot down some of the ideas and work with each other to include them in their introductory paragraphs.

2. **Evaluate your supporting information.** Have partners exchange essays and mark where more details should be inserted. Also have them identify details that seem unrelated to the main idea.

3. **Use transitions wisely.** Suggest that students read their essays aloud to themselves or to a partner to hear where more transitions should be added.

4. **Add a question or exclamation where appropriate.** Have students highlight or underline questions and exclamations in their drafts to see if they have included enough sentence variety. Then read the **TIP** with students.

For interactive revision tools, see

- Write*Smart* CD
- Writing Center at **ClassZone.com**

FOR ENGLISH LEARNERS

Task Support [paired option] Review the four types of sentences with students. Provide some examples of each.

- *declarative:* states a fact or idea
- *imperative:* gives a command
- *interrogative:* asks a question
- *exclamatory:* shows an emotion

Then have students work in pairs to rewrite each of these sentences as the type indicated:

- Can you believe that car exhaust is a major cause of air pollution? (declarative) *A major cause of air pollution is car exhaust.*
- One way to reduce noise pollution is to turn down the volume of your car stereo. (imperative) *Turn down the volume of your car stereo.*
- People accept stereotypes without questioning them. (interrogative) *Should people accept stereotypes without questioning them?*

FOR ADVANCED LEARNERS/PRE–AP

Experiment with Introductions Challenge students to write two or three introductions for their essays, using different methods of capturing readers' attention. They might include a quotation in one, an anecdote in another, and begin a third with a question that leads into some background information. Students may share their introductions with a partner and together identify the most effective one.

WRITING WORKSHOP 865

Preparing to Publish

Support for meeting the goals in the writing rubric is supplied throughout the **Writing Workshop** on pages 860–865.

For Rubric Bank, see

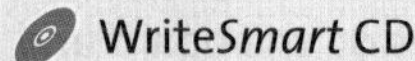

WriteSmart CD

Writing Center at **ClassZone.com**

Assess and Reteach

After reading and assessing students' essays, you might use these lessons to reteach key skills:

STANDARDS LESSON FILE

- Writing Lesson 9: Creating Sentence Variety
- Writing Lesson 16: Cause-and-Effect Order
- Writing Lesson 19: Transitions
- Writing Lesson 21: Writing a Thesis Statement
- Writing Lesson 30: Cause-and-Effect Essay
- Writing Lesson 40: Elaborate with Facts and Statistics
- Writing Lesson 44: Using Precise Words
- Grammar Lesson 20: Missing or Misplaced Commas

Preparing to Publish Cause-and-Effect Essay

Apply the Rubric

A strong cause-and-effect essay . . .

- ☑ has an intriguing introduction
- ☑ explains an actual cause-and-effect relationship rather than simply showing how one event follows another
- ☑ includes a thesis statement
- ☑ uses transitions to signal important causes and effects
- ☑ supports key ideas with examples, quotations, or other details
- ☑ is organized logically
- ☑ uses precise words to help readers understand the causes and effects
- ☑ includes an occasional question or exclamation for variety
- ☑ maintains an appropriate tone
- ☑ summarizes the causes and effects in a compelling conclusion

Ask a Peer Reader

- How can I improve my introduction?
- Which causes or effects need more explanation?
- Which point that I made was most interesting, surprising, or disturbing? Why?

Add Transitional Words

Cause	Effect
because	as a result
if	consequently
provided that	so
since	then
	therefore

Check Your Grammar

Use a comma to set off an introductory word or phrase.

One afternoon last week, I was sitting in the park.

As a result, we turn the volume way up when we listen to music at home.

However, we can try to prevent the harmful effects of noise pollution.

See page R49: Quick Reference: Punctuation

Writing Online

PUBLISHING OPTIONS

For publishing options, visit the **Writing Center** at **ClassZone.com.**

ASSESSMENT PREPARATION

For writing and grammar assessment practice, go to the **Assessment Center** at **ClassZone.com.**

Creating a Multimedia Presentation

Now that you have traced a cause-and-effect relationship, share that information with others by creating a multimedia presentation.

Planning the Presentation

1. **Decide on your technology.** Ask your school's media specialist about doing a power presentation, a slide show, or an interactive display.
2. **Think about the visuals and audio.** You may be able to present supporting evidence through spoken words, video clips, photographs, animations, maps, charts, or graphs. Consider adding music or sound effects to get your message across.

Sound effect: loud jet engines
Voiceover: What does this sound do to your ears?

3. **Create a storyboard.** Sketch exactly what your audience will see and hear. Include details about text, voiceovers, music, effects, and other images and sounds.

Delivering the Presentation

1. **Put it all together.** Scan or download all of your images and sounds onto a computer. Record voiceovers and insert them in the proper places. Create title screens, text, and any other elements you want to include.

   TIP Be sure to get permission for words, images, or audio that you did not create yourself.
2. **Share your results.** Deliver your presentation to an audience or invite small groups to explore it on their own.
3. **Find out what others thought.** Ask your audience for positive and negative comments on your presentation. Use the feedback to improve your next presentation.

PUBLISHING WITH TECHNOLOGY

Have students read this page for an overview of how to prepare a multimedia presentation in which they present a cause-and-effect relationship.

Before students begin working, review this rubric with them so that they understand their goals:

Rubric A strong multimedia presentation

- clearly presents a cause-and-effect relationship
- uses a variety of media, such as words, video clips, photographs, and other graphics, to convey the message
- is developed from a well-planned storyboard
- shows evidence of logical organization
- has been edited for clarity and smoothness
- ends with a request for audience feedback that can be used to improve the next presentation

RESOURCE MANAGER—Copy Master
Publishing with Technology p. 197

STANDARDS LESSON FILE
Media Lesson 22: Creating a Power Presentation

DIFFERENTIATED INSTRUCTION

FOR LESS–PROFICIENT WRITERS

Planning the Presentation [paired option]

1. Distribute copies of the Storyboard. Have students sketch out what they would like to include in their presentations.
2. Remind students to stay focused on the major cause-and-effect relationships they developed in their essays.
3. Then have students meet with a partner and decide what graphics and sound effects will help bring out their ideas. Have them decide whether or not they need to write a script for a narrator.
4. Review the TIP with students, explaining exactly which materials require permission and how to obtain images or sound effects that belong to the public domain.
5. Have pairs then present their storyboards in small groups and discuss possible improvements.
6. Then pair students with a partner who is knowledgeable about computers to help them put their presentations together in their final form.

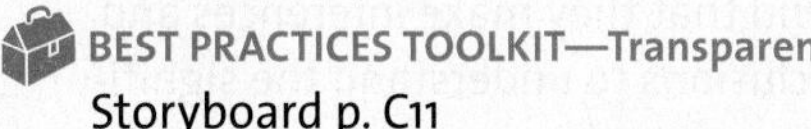

BEST PRACTICES TOOLKIT—Transparency
Storyboard p. C11

Assessment Practice

CHECK READINESS

Read aloud the paragraph under **ASSESS** and stress to students that this is not the full Unit Test, but a way for them to check their readiness for it. Then have students examine the skills listed under **REVIEW** and look back in the unit or in the **Student Resource Bank** for any skills they need to study.

READ THE SELECTIONS

Remind students to keep Unit Goals in mind as they read the passages, paying particular attention to

- author's background
- author's perspective
- characteristics of autobiography
- their own inferences
- causes and effects

To help students focus on the **author's background** while reading, encourage them to ask questions such as

- What facts do you learn about the author from reading his autobiography?
- What connections can you see between the author's background and the content and style of his writing?

ANSWER THE QUESTIONS

Direct students to pages R95–R101 of the Test-Taking Handbook to review test-taking strategies. Remind students not to choose the first alternative that seems to fit when answering a multiple-choice question. Instead, they should read through all the choices, eliminate any that are clearly wrong, and then choose the best answer—the one that is most accurate and complete.

Remind students to use active reading strategies on test passages. Encourage them to preview each passage—looking at the title, the first paragraph, and text features—to get an overview of the content. Tell them to ask themselves questions and take notes on scrap paper as they read. Suggest that they pause frequently to summarize what they've read. If they are confused, they should reread the sentence or paragraph before moving on. Finally, recommend that they make inferences and draw conclusions to understand the significance of details in the text.

Assessment Practice

Reading Comprehension

ASSESS

The practice test items on the next few pages match skills listed on the Unit Goals page (page 759) and addressed throughout this unit. Taking this practice test will help you assess your knowledge of these skills and determine your readiness for the Unit Test.

REVIEW

After you take the practice test, your teacher can help you identify any skills you need to review.

- Author's Background
- Author's Perspective
- Autobiography
- Make Inferences
- Cause and Effect
- Homographs
- Denotation and Connotation
- Compound-Complex Sentences
- Colons
- Semicolons

ASSESSMENT ONLINE

For more assessment practice and test-taking tips, go to the **Assessment Center** at **ClassZone.com.**

DIRECTIONS Caught by the Sea *is an autobiography, and* The Voyage of the *Frog is a novel. Read these excerpts and answer the questions that follow.*

from Caught by the Sea

Gary Paulsen

The motor suddenly became an intrusion, an ugly sound, and as soon as I was past the jetties and was in open ocean I killed it. For a few seconds, half a minute, we moved on in silence by inertia, coasting from the energy the moto had given us, and then it died and I felt the breeze again on my face as I looke to the rear. It was pushing at the back edge of the sail and I pulled the tiller over to steer off the wind a bit and felt the sail fill. The boat moved differentl now, started the dance with the wind and water and moonlight as she heeled slightly and took on life, personality. We glided along in near silence, the only sound the soft gurgle of water along the hull.

I did not dare to walk forward in the dark and put up the jib, having never done it before, but she sailed pretty well on the mainsail alone and we kept ou course, moving at three or four knots by the speedometer in the cockpit, until daylight some four hours away, when the wind stopped, entirely, and left the dawning ocean as still as a pond and me marooned some twelve miles offsho

I didn't care. I was completely enraptured by what had happened to me. I lowered the mainsail and sat peacefully drifting around in circles, feeling at home, truly at home.

For the entire morning there was no wind, and while I might have had enoug gas to motor partway back to the harbor, there was something wrong about usin it on such a beautiful morning. I made a small pot of oatmeal on the little stove and some instant coffee and ate breakfast in the cockpit, letting the morning su warm me; then I pulled my sleeping bag out of the cabin and laid it in the cockp and took a small sleep while the boat rocked gently on the swells.

A sound awakened me an hour or so later and I looked over the side to see th boat surrounded by swarms of small fish, maybe anchovies or herring. No soon did I spot them than pelicans came in and began crash-diving around the boat and then other seabirds arrived, and within minutes a huge pod of dolphins, hundreds of them, showed up. The dolphins began working the school of bait fish, sweeping back and forth like happy wolves, thrashing the water with their tails, perhaps to stun the fish. Then they ate them by the thousands.

While I lay in the calm, all around the boat the sea seethed with life. After the dolphins came some sharks, three or four on call to clean up the debris from the slaughter. In half an hour they were gone, moving off, following the schools of small fish and dolphins and flocks of seabirds.

868 UNIT 7: HISTORY, CULTURE, AND THE AUTHOR

DIFFERENTIATED INSTRUCTION

FOR ENGLISH LEARNERS

Assessment Practice: Work Backwards

[paired option] Prepare students for the assessment by having them read the questions before reading the passages. Have pairs follow these steps to learn unfamiliar words in the test directions and questions:

1. Find words you don't recognize and write each one on an index card.
2. Look up the meaning in a dictionary.
3. Write the meaning on the back of the card.
4. Use your word cards to teach and practice the vocabulary with your partner and another pair of students.

"Amazing," I said aloud. It was amazing that I would be greeted on the sea with such enthusiasm, amazing that on one of the most populated coasts in the world, near a metropolis that stretched nearly two hundred miles from San Diego to Santa Barbara, where nearly eighteen million people jammed the freeways and sidewalks, I would be completely alone with the sea and my boat; amazing that the planet still held such a place.

from The Voyage of the *Frog*

Gary Paulsen

And at two in the morning he saw the light in the water. He saw it first to the stern. In his wake, in the silent bubbles left by the *Frog* moving through the water, there was a rippled, dotted line of eerie light glowing up from the water. It was blue-green, seemed to come from down in the water, and at first it startled and frightened him. But then he remembered hearing about it.

Small animals in the water, microscopic organisms, sometimes phosphoresced—gave off light almost like lightning bugs—when disturbed. He must be going through a mass of them. In back of the *Frog* was a long line of blue light, fading as the water settled down again.

He tied the tiller off, leaned over the side, and looked toward the front where the bow cut a wave that curled over.

"Ohhh . . ." It slipped out of his mouth unbidden, almost a sigh of amazement. The boat was moving through blue fire, blue fire in the night. The bow wave was a rolling curve of blue light, sparkled with bits of green that seemed to want to crawl up the side of the boat and then fold back and over, splashing out in ripples and droplets of light.

It could not be as beautiful as it was—not be that beautiful and be real. It was so bright and shining a thing that the *Frog* seemed to be moving through, a lake of cold fire, and as he watched he saw a form move beneath the boat, caught in the blue glow of the bow wave, a torpedo form that shot forward with an incredible burst of speed. He saw first the glowing curved line around the head of the creature and the line showed him that it was the front of a dolphin. All in seconds, in short parts of seconds, he saw the head and the body moving forward beneath the boat and then it exploded—the dolphin blew out of the water in front of the boat.

It rose in a clean curve just in front of the bowsprit, five, six feet out of the water in a leap of joy that only dolphins can make, carrying with it a shroud of splashing blue-green fire that whirled and spiraled in the darkness to follow

ITEM ANALYSIS

COMPREHENSION AND WRITTEN RESPONSE	ITEMS	UNIT PAGES
Author's Background	8, 14, 16	760, 767
Author's Perspective	3, 5, 15, 17	817
Autobiography	1, 2, 7	831
Make Inferences	5, 11, 13	783
Cause and Effect	4, 6, 9, 10, 12	831

VOCABULARY	ITEMS	UNIT PAGES
Homographs	1, 2, 3, 4	798
Denotation and Connotation	5, 6, 7	845

WRITING AND GRAMMAR	ITEMS	UNIT PAGES
Compound-Complex Sentences	1, 4	781
Colons	2, 3	799
Semicolons	5	829

FOR LESS–PROFICIENT READERS

Assessment Support Consider these options for completing the **Assessment Practice:**

- Have students "work backwards," reviewing the questions before reading the passages.
- Select random questions in the assessment and have students demonstrate how and where to look for the answers.
- Ask students to locate unfamiliar vocabulary in the assessment. Elicit the meanings of these words from the class.
- Have students jot down useful testing words and definitions in their journals for later reference.
- Read the selections or parts of them aloud to aid in student comprehension.

McDougal Littell Assessment System

After checking student readiness with this Assessment Practice, you may administer the complete Unit 7 Test in order to more thoroughly evaluate student mastery of unit goals.

ANSWERS

Comprehension

Model a thinking process for answering multiple-choice questions.

1. **B *is correct.*** *The passage describes an experience Paulsen once had while sailing on the ocean.* A *and* C *are incorrect because there is no mention of other people in the excerpt.* D *is incorrect because the passage does not address Paulsen's decision to become a writer.*
2. **C *is correct.*** *A major characteristic of an autobiography is the use of first-person point of view.* A *is incorrect because Paulsen does reveal his thoughts.* B *is incorrect because the idea of being alone is not related to the autobiographical genre.* D *is incorrect because Paulsen does not mention his childhood.*
3. **A *is correct.*** *The word* peacefully *and the phrase "at home, truly at home" convey Paulsen's enjoyment of his experience.* B *and* D *can be eliminated because they describe his actions but do not convey an attitude.* C *is incorrect because it shows trepidation rather than joy.*
4. **B *is correct.*** *He writes that the sound of the motor "became an intrusion, an ugly sound" (line 1). These words support the idea that the noise of the motor bothered him.* A, C, *and* D *are unsupported by details in the passage.*
5. **B *is correct.*** *This sentence shows his awareness of and sensitivity to his setting.* A *is incorrect because there are no others to disturb.* C *is incorrect because if he were learning how to operate the boat, he would most likely have the motor on.* D *is unsupported by any details in the passage.*
6. **C *is correct.*** *In lines 24–25, Paulsen describes the arrival of swarms of small fish. Soon after, the pelicans and dolphins arrive to feed on the fish, and finally the sharks come to clean up the debris.* A *is incorrect because this incident takes place during the day. Because Paulsen is on his boat, his smell would not draw predators to the area, making* B *incorrect.* D *is incorrect because the motor is still turned off.*

the dolphin up, over and down, back into the water and plunging in green light back to the depths beneath the *Frog.*

David was frozen with it, did not know how long he stayed with one hand reaching up as if to touch where the dolphin had been, touch the curve of blue fire. It was all there and gone—just as suddenly gone as if it had never been—and his breath burst suddenly out into the night.

He looked back, expecting to see the dolphin as the boat went over it but there was nothing.

Comprehension

DIRECTIONS *Answer these questions about the excerpt from* Caught by the Sea.

1. Which characteristic of an autobiography can you identify in this excerpt?

A It shows how Paulsen was affected by the people in his life.
B It focuses on a memorable event in Paulsen's life.
C It reveals what other people think about Paulsen.
D It explains why Paulsen decided to become a writer.

2. One clue that this excerpt is from an autobiography is that the author

A does not reveal his thoughts
B stresses how alone he is on his boat
C uses the first person point of view
D discusses his childhood experiences

3. Which sentence tells you that Paulsen enjoys his sailing experience?

A "I lowered the mainsail and sat peacefully drifting around in circles, feeling at home, truly at home."
B "I made a small pot of oatmeal on the little stove and some instant coffee and ate breakfast in the cockpit. . . ."
C "I did not dare to walk forward in the dark and put up the jib. . . ."
D "While I lay in the calm, all around the boat the sea seethed with life."

4. Reread lines 1–5. Paulsen turns off the motor of his boat because he

A has to save fuel
B is bothered by its noise
C senses danger ahead
D doesn't want to scare the fish

5. In lines 19–20, Paulsen writes that there is "something wrong" about using the motor on a beautiful morning. What can you infer about him from this statement?

A He worries about disturbing others.
B He enjoys the peaceful setting.
C He is learning how to operate the boat.
D He is hiding from someone.

6. What attracts the seabirds, dolphins, and sharks to the waters around the boat?

A light from the moon
B the smell of a human
C swarms of small fish
D the sound of the boat's motor

7. If *Caught by the Sea* were a biography instead of an autobiography, the excerpt might have left out

A Paulsen's expression of his feelings
B facts about weather conditions
C information on the boat's location
D a description of the animals that surround the boat

7. **A *is correct.*** *A biographer does not have direct access to the subject's thoughts and feelings. A biography would include details about observable events and conditions, however, making* B, C, *and* D *incorrect.*
8. **C *is correct.*** *Paulsen's close observation of the ocean is reflected in the excerpt's setting. The third-person point of view and the chronology of events are not informed by Paulsen's background as an outdoorsman, making* A *and* D *incorrect.* B *can be eliminated because there is no conflict revealed in the excerpt.*
9. **A *is correct.*** *The text directly states that David is "startled and frightened" by the eerie light he sees. Therefore,* B, C, *and* D *are incorrect.*
10. **B *is correct.*** *As David recalls, small organisms give off phosphorescence when disturbed. Therefore, the boat must be stirring them up.* A, C, *and* D *are unsupported by details in the passage.*

RECTIONS *Answer these questions about the excerpt om* The Voyage of the *Frog.*

8. Paulsen's experience as an outdoorsman is reflected in the story's
   A point of view C setting
   B conflict D chronology

9. At first, the "eerie light glowing up from the water" in lines 3–5 causes David to feel
   A scared C alone
   B giddy D confused

10. Reread lines 6–9. Why are the small animals in the water giving off light?
   A Their bright light helps them locate food.
   B The movement of the boat stirs them up.
   C They sense that predators are nearby.
   D They are signaling to other fish in the water.

11. Reread lines 26–34. You can infer that David holds his breath when he sees the dolphin because he
   A plans to capture the dolphin
   B does not want to disturb the dolphin
   C is amazed at the sight of the dolphin
   D thinks that the dolphin might hurt him

12. When he sees the leaping dolphin and the glowing water around it, David
   A tries to sail after the dolphin
   B reaches out as if to touch what he sees
   C hides in the bow of the boat
   D shouts out in disbelief

13. The presence of a dolphin suggests that the *Frog* is sailing in
   A an ocean C a pond
   B a stream D a river

DIRECTIONS *Refer to both selections to answer this question.*

14. The excerpt from *The Voyage of the* Frog reflects which experience in Paulsen's background?
   A staying up all night to watch the sunrise
   B getting an unexpected glimpse of sea animals
   C cooking and sleeping on a boat
   D learning how to operate a sailboat

Written Response

SHORT RESPONSE *Write two or three sentences to answer the questions.*

15. Name two things Paulsen finds amazing in the excerpt from *Caught by the Sea.* Use quotations from the excerpt to support your answer.

16. Choose one experience described in *The Voyage of the* Frog that is similar to Paulsen's experiences in *Caught by the Sea,* and explain the similarity between the two.

EXTENDED RESPONSE *Write a paragraph to answer this question.*

17. Reread lines 1–9 and 15–17 in *Caught by the Sea.* What effect does his sailing experience have on Paulsen? Support your answer with examples from the excerpt.

11. C ***is correct.*** *The lavish description of the dolphin's path as "blue-green fire that whirled and spiraled in the darkness" supports the idea that David is too amazed to even breathe until the dolphin is out of sight. Then, "his breath burst suddenly out into the night." A, B, and D are unsupported by details in the passage.*

12. B ***is correct.*** *In lines 31–32, David is described as staying with "one hand reaching up as if to touch where the dolphin had been." A is incorrect because line 35 describes him as looking back to see the dolphin, not sailing after it. C is unsupported by the text. D is incorrect because David holds his breath until the dolphin has disappeared.*

13. A ***is correct.*** *Dolphins are found in large bodies of salt water, eliminating B, C, and D.*

14. B ***is correct.*** *In real life, Paulsen is amazed by the fish, birds, dolphins, and sharks he sees, and David is captivated by the sight of the dolphin leaping out of the ocean. David does not see the sunrise in the excerpt, making A incorrect. C and D are not reflected in the novel excerpt, so they are also incorrect.*

Written Response

Possible short responses:

15. *In lines 35–40, Paulsen says he is amazed that he "would be greeted on the sea with such enthusiasm," by his ability to be so "completely alone with the sea" while so close to a densely populated metropolis, and by the fact that "the planet still [holds] such a place."*

16. *Both Paulsen and his character derive amazement and pleasure from the spectacle of sea life that they witness while out on a sailboat.*

Possible extended response:

17. *Students' paragraphs should develop the idea that Paulsen's experiences bring him inner peace, greater sensitivity to the rhythms of life on the sea, and a feeling of amazement.*

ANSWERS

Vocabulary

1. **B *is correct.*** *The word* pod *in the passage refers to a large group of marine mammals.* A *and* C *are incorrect because, in each of these sentences,* pod *refers to a small vehicle that carries people or equipment. In* D, pod *refers to the protective casing around eggs, making it incorrect also.*
2. **C *is correct.*** *In both the passage and this sentence,* wake *means "the swell of waves caused by the movement of a ship through the water."* A *is incorrect because it uses the idiomatic expression* in their wake *to mean "left behind by an event."* B *is incorrect because it uses* wake *to mean "a vigil over a dead person."* D *is incorrect because* wake *is used as a verb meaning "to regain consciousness after sleeping."*
3. **D *is correct.*** *In both the passage and this sentence,* bow *refers to the front of a boat or ship.* A *is incorrect because, in this sentence,* bow *means "a gesture of bending forward from the waist in acknowledgment of applause."* B *can be eliminated because it uses* bow *to mean "a ribbon tied in a decorative knot."* C *is incorrect because, in this sentence,* bow *refers to a weapon used to propel an arrow through the air.*
4. **A *is correct.*** Fold *in this sentence means "to bend over" or "to crease," which matches the meaning in the passage.* B *is incorrect because it uses* fold *to mean "to close a business."* Fold *in* C *means "a fenced enclosure for animals," while in* D, *it refers to a family group or community.*
5. **C *is correct.*** *The tails of the dolphins were* thrashing *the water to stun the fish, conveying the idea that the movement is powerful or forceful.* A, B, *and* D *do not fit the context of the sentence.*
6. **C *is correct.*** *As Paulsen "lay in the calm" of his boat, life "seethed" around him, suggesting a contrast between the author's stillness and the marine animals' energetic movement.* A, B, *and* D *do not fit the context of the sentence.*
7. **A *is correct.*** *The dolphin "blew out of the water," moving with great speed.* B, C, *and* D *do not fit the context of the sentence.*

Vocabulary

DIRECTIONS *Use context clues and your knowledge of homographs to answer the following questions.*

1. Which sentence uses *pod* as it is used in line 27 of the excerpt from *Caught by the Sea?*

"... within minutes a huge pod of dolphins, hundreds of them, showed up."

A The divers descended to the ocean floor in a small pod.
B A pod of gray whales was visible from the shore.
C The pod separated from the spacecraft during reentry.
D Some insects lay eggs in clusters that are called pods.

2. Which sentence uses *wake* as it is used in line 2 of the excerpt from *The Voyage of the* Frog?

"In his wake, in the silent bubbles left by the *Frog* moving through the water. . . ."

A The floodwaters ruined every house and barn in their wake.
B After the admiral died, the sailors held his wake at sea.
C A small boat can be swamped in the wake of a larger ship.
D Some of the passengers on the cruise ship did not wake up until noon.

3. Which sentence uses *bow* as it is used in line 11 of the excerpt from *The Voyage of the* Frog?

"He tied the tiller off, leaned over the side, and looked toward the front where the bow cut a wave that curled over."

A The pianist took a bow after her performance.
B He wrapped a big blue bow across the boat.
C It is hard to catch fish with a bow and arrow.
D I saw the sunrise from the bow of the ship.

4. Which sentence uses *fold* as it is used in line of the excerpt from *The Voyage of the* Frog?

"The bow wave was a rolling curve of blue light, sparkled with bits of green that seeme to want to crawl up the side of the boat and then fold back and over. . . ."

A You can fold the newspaper so it will fit into your backpack.
B The owner had to fold his company because he was leaving the city.
C The farmer kept his sheep in a large fold behind the barn.
D The grandparents welcomed the new bab into the fold.

DIRECTIONS *Use context clues and your knowledge o denotation and connotation to answer the following questions.*

5. The word *thrashing* in line 29 of the excerpt from *Caught by the Sea* has a connotation of

A sadness **C** forcefulness
B intelligence **D** rudeness

6. The denotation of the word *seethed* in line 31 of the excerpt from *Caught by the Sea* is "bubbled or foamed." What is its connotation?

A secrecy **C** movement
B gentleness **D** happiness

7. The word *exploded* in line 24 of the excerpt from *The Voyage of the* Frog has a connotation of

A speed **C** heaviness
B hardness **D** clumsiness

872

DIFFERENTIATED INSTRUCTION

FOR ENGLISH LEARNERS

Review Academic Vocabulary [paired option] Review the definitions of these terms:

- *homographs:* words with the same spelling but different meanings. Example:
  —"No sooner did I spot [the fish] than pelicans came." (lines 25–26)
  —What is that spot on the tablecloth?
- *denotation*—the dictionary definition of a word. For example, *spot* in the first sentence means "see" or "notice." *Spot* in the second sentence means "mark."
- *connotation*—feelings or thoughts that a particular word suggests. For example, *stain* and *blemish* have stronger negative connotations than *spot.*

Have pairs complete these activities:

- Write two sentences using the homograph *light* with different meanings. Give the denotation of *light* in each sentence.
- Replace these underlined words with words that have similar meanings but more positive connotations: *The cat was scrawny. The boy was reckless.*

Writing & Grammar

DIRECTIONS *Read this passage and answer the questions that follow.*

(1) Dolphins live in water. (2) Many people think of them as fish. (3) They are actually mammals. (4) The following are different types of dolphins the bottle-nosed dolphin, the common dolphin, and the white-sided dolphin. (5) All dolphins share the following characteristics smooth skin, flippers, and a blowhole. (6) Dolphins have no sense of smell. (7) They have a keen sense of hearing. (8) They can detect sounds that humans cannot. (9) Dolphins have been trained to perform in amusement parks, zoos, and aquariums, to retrieve objects, and to guard military ships.

1. Choose the correct way to combine sentences 1, 2, and 3 into one compound-complex sentence.
   - **A** Dolphins live in water, so many people think of them as fish, but they are actually mammals.
   - **B** Dolphins live in water, and many people think of them as fish, but they are actually mammals.
   - **C** Because dolphins live in water, many people think of them as fish, but they are actually mammals.
   - **D** Dolphins are actually mammals living in water, although many people think of them as fish.

2. In sentence 4, a colon should be placed after which word?
   - **A** following
   - **B** are
   - **C** of
   - **D** dolphins

3. In sentence 5, a colon should be placed after which word?
   - **A** share
   - **B** following
   - **C** characteristics
   - **D** skin

4. Choose the correct way to combine sentences 6, 7, and 8 into one compound-complex sentence.
   - **A** Though dolphins have no sense of smell, they have a keen sense of hearing, and they can detect sounds that humans cannot.
   - **B** Having no sense of smell but a keen sense of hearing, dolphins can detect sounds that humans cannot.
   - **C** Dolphins have no sense of smell but a keen sense of hearing, enabling them to detect sounds that humans cannot.
   - **D** Despite having no sense of smell, dolphins have a keen sense of hearing, detecting sounds that humans cannot.

5. In sentence 9, a semicolon should be placed after which words?
   - **A** to, aquariums, objects
   - **B** parks, zoos, aquariums, objects
   - **C** perform, retrieve, guard
   - **D** aquariums, objects

STOP

ANSWERS

Writing & Grammar

1. **C *is correct.*** *The conjunction* Because *introduces a dependent clause, and the conjunction* but *joins two independent clauses, making this a compound-complex sentence.* A *and* B *are compound sentences.* D *is a complex sentence but not compound.*
2. **D *is correct.*** *The colon introduces a list. Therefore, it should be placed before the list of dolphin types.* A, B, *and* C *are incorrect because a colon placed after any of these words would interrupt the sentence.*
3. **C *is correct.*** *Placing the colon after* characteristics *introduces the list.* A *and* B *are incorrect because a colon would interrupt the sentence if placed after either word.* D *is incorrect because "smooth skin" is one of the items in the list and should not be separated from the others.*
4. **A *is correct.*** *There are two independent clauses as well as one dependent clause.* B *is incorrect because it has only one independent clause,* dolphins can detect sounds. C *and* D *both include one independent clause and no dependent clauses, so they are neither compound nor complex.*
5. **D *is correct.*** *For clarity, semicolons may separate items in a list that contain commas. Therefore, semicolons belong after the phrase "to perform in amusement parks, zoos, and aquariums" and the phrase "to retrieve objects."* A, B, *and* C *are incorrect because semicolons placed after* to, parks, zoos, *or any of the verbs would interrupt the phrases in the list.*

DIFFERENTIATED INSTRUCTION

FOR ENGLISH LEARNERS

Assessment Support: Compound-Complex Sentences Discuss these terms:

- *independent clause:* has a subject and a verb and expresses a complete thought. Example: *The dolphins ate the fish.*
- *dependent clause:* has a subject and a verb but does not express a complete thought. Examples: *after the dolphin leaped; which we knew already; whoever sailed the boat*
- *compound-complex sentence:* a sentence with at least two independent clauses and one or more dependent clauses. Example: *He had sailed for many years, but the storm was the worst in history, and even he did not dare sail through it.*

Have students identify which sentence is compound-complex and explain why:

- The experience of sailing inspired him to write a poem, which he later published.
- If you stay on deck during the short trip, you should be able to avoid seasickness, and you might enjoy yourself more. *(compound-complex)*

INTRODUCE *MORE GREAT READS*

In Unit 7, students have discussed a number of big questions. Invite students to tell which question they found most intriguing and why. Then focus attention on the three questions that appear on this page. Discuss the recommended books and their summaries, pointing out how each book connects to the related question. Encourage students to choose one or more of these "great reads" to read independently.

ClassZone.com

To find additional books that match students' interests and ability levels, visit the Literature Center at **ClassZone.com.**

UNIT 7

More Great Reads

Ideas for Independent Reading

Which questions from Unit 7 made an impression on you? Continue exploring them with these books.

Where do we get our values?

Betsy and the Emperor
by Staton Rabin

After years at boarding school, 14-year-old Betsy is back home on St. Helena. Her family is hosting a special "guest": Napoleon, the former emperor of France, is a prisoner at Betsy's house. What can an ex-emperor and a rebellious teenager have in common?

Lizzie Bright and the Buckminster Boy
by Gary D. Schmidt

People in Phippsburg, Maine, don't like it when Turner befriends Lizzie Bright, who lives in a nearby African-American settlement. When the town evicts Lizzie's community, Turner helps fight back.

Part of Me
by Kimberly Willis Holt

Raised in Louisiana during t Great Depression, Rose nev gets to college, but she trie to pass on her love of books her children and grandchild Although not all of them follow in her footsteps, the family stories help each generation stay strong.

What can you learn from a job?

Code Talker
By Joseph Bruchac

World War II is raging, and Ned wants to help. He joins the Marines and becomes a secret Navajo code talker. He helps create a code that can't be cracked, and then uses it to send and receive messages in the midst of battle. Will Ned survive the fighting?

Gathering Blue
by Lois Lowry

In the future, when society is in ruins from disasters, a crippled orphan like Kira is often destined to die. But Kira's weaving skills are discovered, and suddenly she's important. If only her new job didn't bring with it serious problems.

Ghost Boy
Iain Lawrence

Harold is an albino, and in h small town he's an outcast When the circus comes to town, Harold leaves with it immediately accepted by members of the sideshow. He soon finds out that even the circus, he and his friend are considered strange.

How can we fight injustice?

Stop The Train!
by Geraldine McCaughrean

In 1893, people came to Florence, Oklahoma, searching for a stake in a new prairie town. Now the Red Rock Railroad Company refuses to stop in Florence. The new town is sure to die unless the settlers can find a way to get the train to stop.

The Outcasts of 19 Schuyler Place
by E.L. Konigsburg

Margaret Rose is happy to be rescued from Camp Talequa by her uncles. But they seem to accept that the town wants to destroy the three beautiful towers they built in the backyard. Someone has to save these works of art.

Warriors Don't Cry
by Melba Pattillo Beals

Melba Pattillo Beals was on of the nine African-America teenagers who integrated the Little Rock Central High School in 1957. In this mem she describes both the viole protesters she faced as well as the people and ideals tha gave her courage and hope.

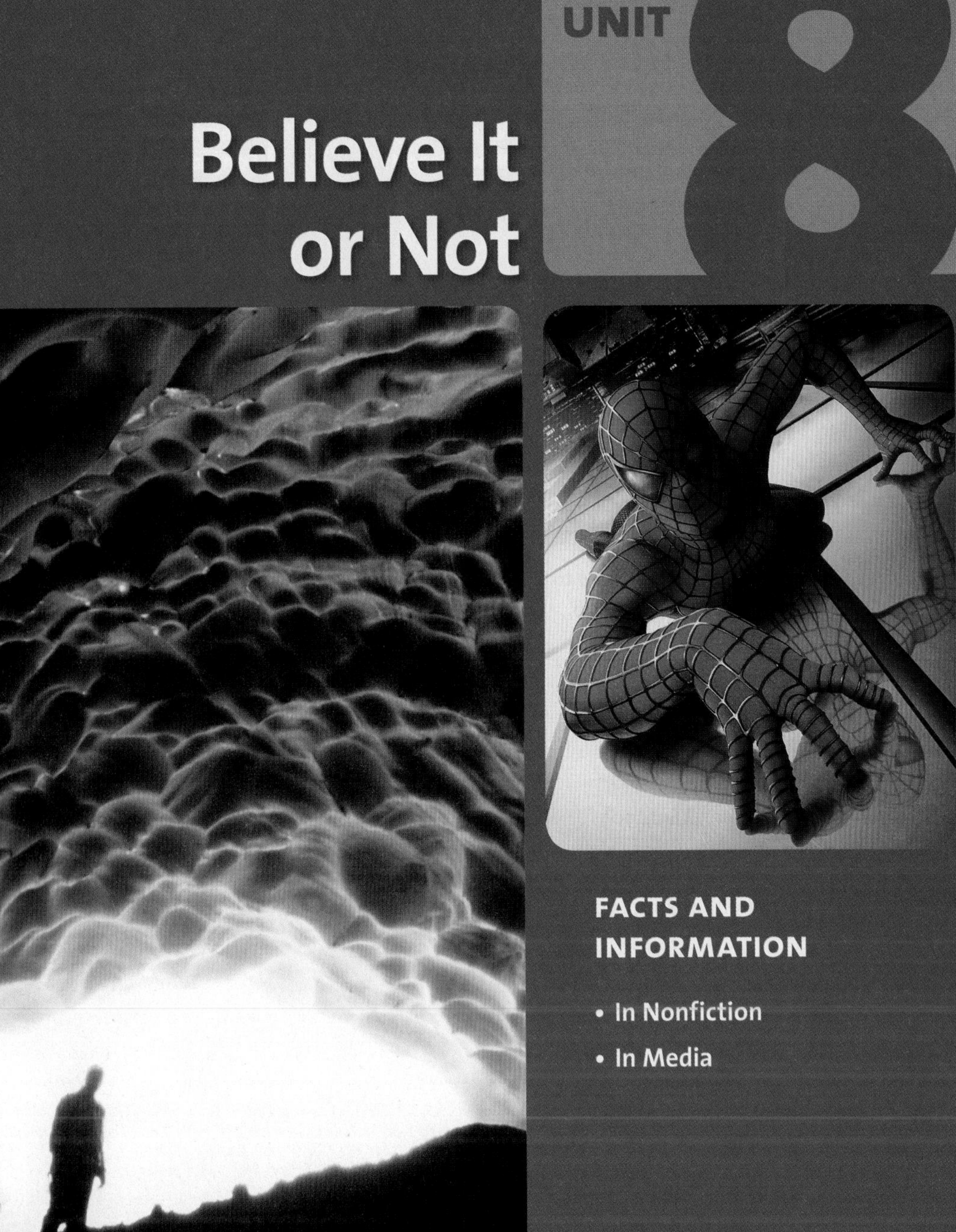

About the Art The photograph on the left illustrates "Over the Top: The True Adventures of a Volcano Chaser" by Renee Skelton. See pages 900–901 for more information. The image on the right illustrates "The Spider Man Behind *Spider-Man*" by Bijal P. Trivedi; see page 887 of the pupil's edition.

For help in planning this unit, see
RESOURCE MANAGER UNIT 8
pp. 1–11

INTRODUCE THE UNIT

Do you believe it? Or not? Every day scientists discover strange facts about the natural world—fantastic details that seem more like science fiction than reality. For example, consider these facts:

1. Some creatures living on the dark sea floor generate their own fluorescent light.
2. The human body contains billions if not trillions of cells, each one a small factory.
3. Strong evidence suggests that there was once water—and possibly life—on Mars.

Equally strange facts await those who explore history, human psychology, and culture. Where do we go to learn more about these and other topics? How can we tell which sources are most reliable? Invite students to think about these ideas as they discuss the pictures on this page. Use these questions to spark a discussion:

- Look closely at the photograph on the left. Do you think this is a real place, or is it a movie set? Where can you find more information about what you see in the photograph? Do you trust the sources that provide the information? Why or why not?
- Can you identify the figure in the illustration on the right? What facts about spiders do you think the creators of *Spider-Man* incorporated into this character?

Discuss the kinds of **facts** that students can learn by reading nonfiction. Tell students that in this unit they will learn new and fascinating **information** about the world.

UNIT 8

Skills Trace

SKILLS STRAND	**Reader's Workshop: Reading Informational Text** pp. 878–883	**The Spider Man Behind *Spider-Man*** pp. 884–893 Feature Article *Level: Easy*	**Over the Top: The True Adventures of a Volcano Chaser** pp. 894–903 Magazine Article *Level: Average*	**Media Study: News Reports** pp. 904–907 TV Newscast Clip, Magazine Article	**Interview with a Songcatcher** pp. 908–917 Interview *Level: Average*
Reading and Informational Texts	Identify and Use Text Features pp. 878–879, 883 Identify Main Idea and Supporting Details pp. 880–883 Take Notes p. 882 Analyze the Literature pp. 879, 881, 883	Analyze Text Features pp. 885, 886, 889, 891 Summarize pp. 885, 886, 889, 890, 891	Interpret and Evaluate Graphic Aids pp. 895, 897, 898, 900, 902 Review: Text Features p. 900 Adjust Reading Rate to Purpose pp. 895, 896, 898, 899, 901, 902		Analyze an Interview pp. 909, 910, 912, 914, 916 Distinguish Between Fact and Opinion pp. 909, 911, 912, 913, 914, 915, 916
Vocabulary	Academic Vocabulary pp. 878, 880	Word Acquisition pp. 885, T885, 892 Context Clues p. T885 Base Words p. 892	Word Acquisition pp. 895, T895, 903 Word Maps p. T895 Word Origins p. 903	Academic Vocabulary (News Reports) p. 905	Word Acquisition pp. 909, T909, 917 Context Clues p. T909 Denotation and Connotation p. 917
Writing, Grammar, and Style		Capitalization of Titles p. 893			
Speaking, Listening, Viewing, and Media	Discuss pp. 878–882	Discuss pp. 884, T886–T890, 891 Analyze Visuals p. 887	Discuss pp. 894, T896–T901, 902	Discuss pp. 904, 907 Interpret How Information Is Presented in News Reports pp. 905–906 Analyze News Sources pp. 905–907 Create an Interview Plan p. 907	Discuss pp. 908, T910–T915, 916 Analyze Visuals pp. 911, 915

Assessment-Based Planning: Skills in red are assessed on the Unit 8 Test. **T** = Teacher's Edition page

Kabul's Singing Sensation pp. 918–927 Magazine Article *Level: Challenging*	Robo-Legs/Eureka: Scientific Twists of Fate pp. 928–937 Magazine Article/ Online Article *Level: Average*	Great Reads: *from* An American Plague: The True and Terrifying Story of the Yellow Fever Epidemic of 1793 pp. 938–943 History Book *Level: Challenging*	Writing Workshop: Problem-Solution Essay pp. 944–951
Identify a Feature Article and Its Characteristics pp. 919, 921, 923, 924, 925 Identify Main Idea and Details pp. 919, 922, 923, 925	Identify Author's Purpose pp. 929, 931, 932, 933, 934, 936 Monitor pp. 929, 931, 932, 934, 935, 936	Form (History Book) p. 938	Analyze a Problem-Solution Essay pp. 945–946, 950
Word Acquisition pp. 919, T919, 926 Context Clues p. T919 Suffixes That Form Adjectives p. 926	Word Acquisition pp. 929, T929, 937 Word Maps p. T929 Latin Roots (*pend*) p. 937		
Commas After Introductory Words and Phrases p. 927			Write a Problem-Solution Essay pp. 944–950 Logical Fallacies p. 950 Subject-Verb Agreement with Indefinite Pronoun Subjects p. 950
Discuss pp. 918, T920–T924, 925 Analyze Visuals p. 920	Discuss pp. 928, T930–T935, 936 Analyze Visuals p. 930	Discuss pp. T938, T943	Discuss pp. 944–946 Give an Oral Report p. 951

Skills Assessed on the Unit 8 Test:

Reading and Informational Texts

- Identify main idea and supporting details
- Summarize main ideas in an article
- Use text features to locate and comprehend information
- Interpret and evaluate graphic aids
- Distinguish between fact and opinion
- Identify author's purpose

Vocabulary

- Use knowledge of base words and affixes to help determine word meaning
- Use knowledge of suffixes to help determine word meaning

Writing, Grammar, and Style

- Write a problem-solution essay
- Capitalize titles correctly
- Use commas correctly after introductory words and phrases
- Additional writing and grammar skills

For additional lesson planning help, see **Easy Planner DVD.**

UNIT 8 Share What You Know

OBJECTIVES

- establish prior knowledge about gathering **facts**
- discuss various sources of information

Where do you get your FACTS?

Ask students where they go to find information—everything from the least expensive brand of shampoo to the names of U.S. presidents. If someone asked them to recommend the best source for these facts, how would they respond?

ACTIVITY As students analyze where they get their information, point out that they probably turn to some sources more than others. For example, some students might always begin their research with the Internet. Others might consult almanacs or encyclopedias or ask a knowledgeable person, such as a librarian. For each source they identify, suggest that students create a web diagram showing the kinds of information about which that source is likely to be most authoritative and reliable.

CHECK UNDERSTANDING Have students summarize what they have learned about how and where to locate **facts** and information.

Where do you get your FACTS?

You don't go a single day without needing to gather some **facts.** With message boards, magazines, books, and directories all offering you information, where do you turn when you need an answer you can count on? It depends on what kind of facts you're looking for, and what you need to know.

ACTIVITY Work with a partner to analyze where you get your information.

- Make a list of five or six facts that you might look for in a typical day.
- Next to each fact, write one or more sources in which you might find it.
- Share your list with others. Do you get most of your facts from printed material, from the Internet, or from somewhere else?
- Discuss which of these sources are most trustworthy and which are easiest to use.

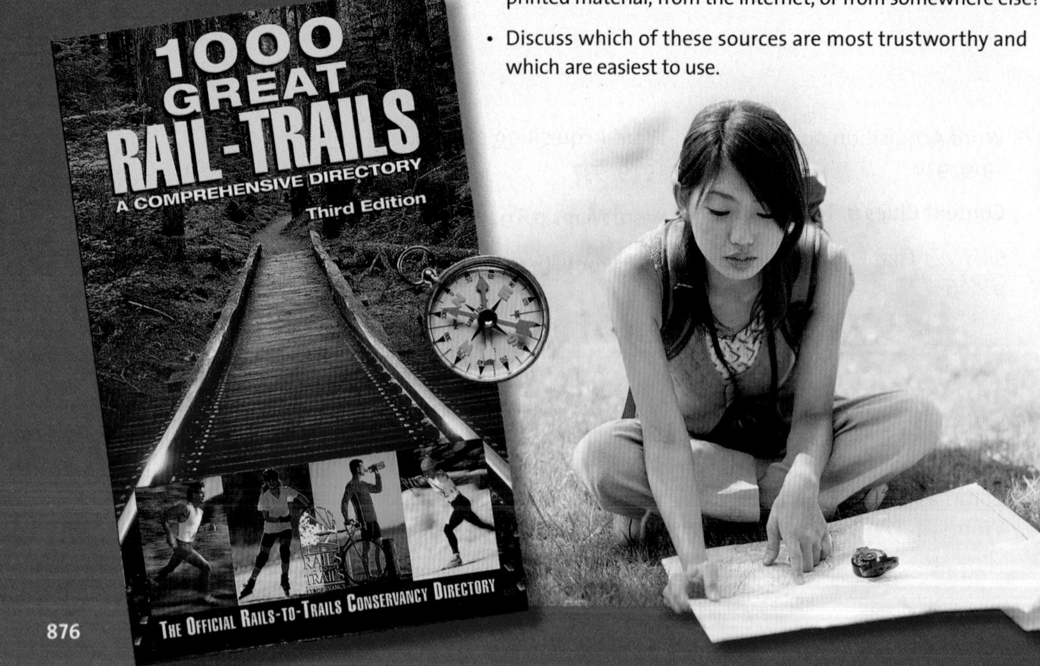

876

Unit Resources

- RESOURCE MANAGER UNIT 8
- BEST PRACTICES TOOLKIT
- STANDARDS LESSON FILE
- Easy Planner DVD
- Write*Smart* CD
- ClassZone.com
- Audio Anthology CD
- Multi-Language Academic Vocabulary Online
- eEdition CD & Online
- McDougal Littell Assessment System
- Test Generator CD
- Media*Smart* DVD

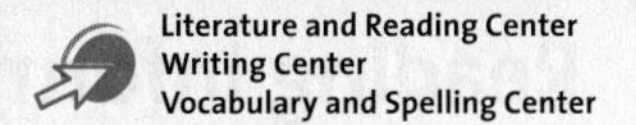

Literature and Reading Center
Writing Center
Vocabulary and Spelling Center

Preview Unit Goals

READING	• Identify main idea and supporting details • Identify and analyze author's purpose • Distinguish between fact and opinion • Adjust reading rate to purpose • Summarize main ideas in an article • Take notes • Use text features to comprehend and locate information • Interpret and evaluate graphic aids
WRITING AND GRAMMAR	• Write a problem-solution essay • Capitalize titles correctly • Use commas correctly after introductory words and phrases
SPEAKING, LISTENING, AND VIEWING	• Interpret how events and information are presented in the news • Compare how different media cover the same event • Deliver an oral report
VOCABULARY	• Apply knowledge of base words, affixes, and root words to determine the meaning of words • Use word origins to help understand how other languages have influenced English word meaning
ACADEMIC VOCABULARY	• main idea • supporting details • summarize • text features • graphic aids

DIFFERENTIATED INSTRUCTION

FOR ENGLISH LEARNERS

Academic Vocabulary [small-group option] Use the Academic Vocabulary copy master to introduce these terms: *main idea, supporting details, summarize, text features, graphic aids.*

- Have students work in groups to discuss the definitions in Part A and to complete the sentences.
- Allow students to work individually or in pairs to complete Part B.

Additional Academic Vocabulary [paired option] Use the second copy master to teach the terms *author's purpose, fact and opinion,* and *word origins.* Discuss the example Word Square, and invite students to provide additional examples and definitions. Then have students work with a partner to fill in the remaining Word Squares. Challenge them to find multiple examples to illustrate each term.

RESOURCE MANAGER—Copy Masters
Academic Vocabulary p. 9
Additional Academic Vocabulary p. 10

Preview Unit Goals

This page provides an overview of the skills and strategies covered in this unit. Each skill strand is a different color. Throughout the unit, this color coding lets students know what kinds of skills they are studying. As they read this page, encourage students to think about each skill or strategy and how well they are able to use it.

Suggest that students copy the Academic Vocabulary terms in their journals. As they read the unit, encourage them to define these terms in their own words and record them. Point out that the best way for students to learn these terms is to use them frequently as they discuss and write about the selections in the unit.

ADDITIONAL UNIT GOALS

These skills will be taught in this unit but are not the major focus of the unit:

Elements of Nonfiction
- Identify and analyze characteristics and content of an interview
- Identify form and characteristics of a feature article
- Study a variety of genres: historical novel, feature article, magazine article, interview, online article

Reading
- Monitor comprehension by questioning, visualizing, and rereading

Writing and Grammar
- Avoid using logical fallacies

Speaking, Listening, and Viewing
- Identify formats of news reports
- Create an interview plan

Vocabulary
- Use structural analysis to identify base words and affixes
- Distinguish between connotative and denotative meanings of words
- Use knowledge of the Latin root *pend* to help determine word meanings

Focus and Motivate

OBJECTIVES

- identify text features
- identify main ideas and supporting details
- take notes on a newspaper or magazine article

Teach

Part 1: Text Features

In the first column of a three-column chart, list the text features identified on this page, including *titles, subheadings, captions, sidebars, boldfaced words, bulleted lists,* and *links.* Then have students think of other text features with which they are familiar, such as *italicized words, footnotes, graphic aids, icons,* and *numbered lists.* Add their terms to the chart. Have students write explanations and definitions of each feature in the second column, using the information in the text as well as their prior knowledge.

Ask students to look through their textbook to find examples of each text feature that they have listed. Have them record the example and page number in the third column of their chart. Review their charts together.

Text Feature	Explanation	Example
titles	identify topic of article or book	"The Other Riders," page 141
subheadings	identify topic of a section of text	"Rumors of a March on Concord," page 141

 BEST PRACTICES TOOLKIT—Transparency
Three-Column Journal p. B10

CHECK UNDERSTANDING Have students explain what they learn about the content of the workshop from previewing the text features on pages 878–883.

UNIT 8
Reader's Workshop

Reading Informational Text

You are living in an age of information. In a matter of minutes, you can find magazine articles, Web sites, and blogs on just about any topic, from global warming to cell-phone technology. But how can you be sure you're getting the most out of what you're reading? What's the best way to wade through all those facts and figures? Learning a few strategies can help you navigate through a sea of information, find answers to your questions, and remember what you've learned.

Part 1: Text Features

Time is money in the fast-paced, modern world. So, it's important to be able to find information quickly when you're searching through Web sites, books, and magazines. One way to locate useful information at a glance is to notice the text features writers use. **Text features** include titles, subheadings, captions, sidebars, boldfaced words, bulleted lists, and links. These elements allow you to see the most important ideas without having to read every word.

Consider the following article from the back of a "Fun Facts" pamphlet. By scanning the text features, you can anticipate what information the article include before deciding to read further.

1 The **title** reveals the topic of the article—the history of hot dogs.

2 **Subheadings** highlight what each section of the article is about.

3 A **sidebar** provides more information.

4 A **bulleted list** presents information in an easy-to-read format.

Hot Dogs in Europe 2

There are several different theories about the origin of the hot dog. Traditionally, Frankfurt-am-Main, Germany, is credited with originating the frankfurter.

Hot Dog Specialties 3

4
- In the South, people like their hot dogs "dragged through the garden" with a cole-slaw type topping.
- New Yorkers like their hot dogs served with steamed onions and pale yellow mustard.
- Folks in Kansas City enjoy hot dogs with sauerkraut and Swiss cheese.

All-American Dogs

Another story points to the Louisiana Purchase Exposition in 1904. A concessionaire sold hot dogs as plain sausages, and provided customers with white gloves for easier eating. After the gloves were not returned, he consulted a baker, who designed the "hot dog bun" to protect eaters' fingers.

One of the more credible stories comes from Barry Popick, a prominent hot dog historian at Roosevelt University. He claims the term began appearing in college magazines in the 1890s. Yale students kept referring to wagons selling hot sausages in buns outside their dorms as "dog wagons." It didn't take long for the use of the word *dog* to become "hot dog."

DIFFERENTIATED INSTRUCTION

FOR ALL STUDENTS

For general guidelines on differentiating instruction, see

 BEST PRACTICES TOOLKIT
Differentiated Instruction pp. 31–38

FOR LESS-PROFICIENT READERS

Note Taking Hand out the Note Taking: Text Features copy master and ask students to read page 878 silently. Then have them take notes during your class discussion.

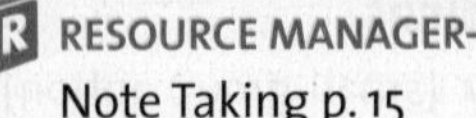
RESOURCE MANAGER—Copy Master
Note Taking p. 15

Recognize Text Features Have students find these text features in the article on page 879:

- title
- subheadings
- sidebar

Model for students how to use these features to preview the content of the article.

MODEL: TEXT FEATURES

Skim the text features in this Web article. What information do you think the article will provide? Now read the full article and answer the questions.

DANGER from the Sky

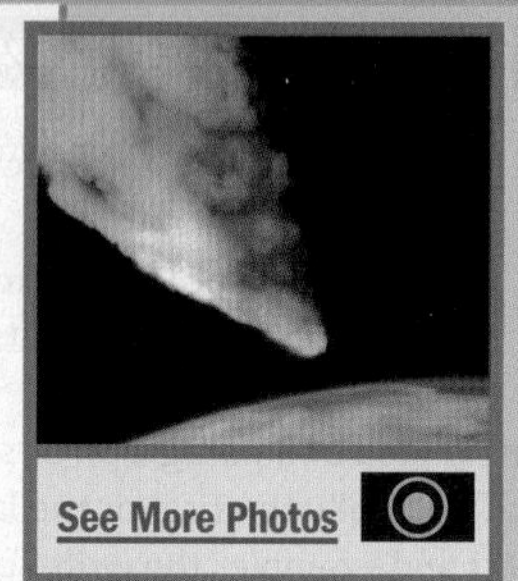

That's not Swiss cheese up there. The **craters** that cover much of the Moon's surface were caused by collisions with space objects billions of years ago. In 1953 an astronomer even caught on film the bright flash of an object hitting the Moon. With so much evidence of objects hitting our nearest neighbor, scientists wonder when another large object from space will strike our planet.

Impacts on Earth

Earth's **atmosphere** protects us from collisions with small objects, which burn up in the air. However, when a large object strikes Earth, the atmosphere can spread the effects of the impact far beyond the crater. A large collision may throw dust high into the air, where it can be carried around the globe. The dust can block sunlight for months and sharply lower global temperatures.

About 65 million years ago, a large space object struck Earth. At about the same time, most species of organisms died out, including the dinosaurs. Many scientists think that the results of this collision caused the global devastation.

Risk of a Meteorite Collision

When will the next space object hit Earth? A collision is probably occurring as you read this sentence. Tiny particles hit Earth's atmosphere all the time. Some of these particles have enough mass to make it through the atmosphere.

Objects that reach Earth's surface are called **meteorites**. Most meteorites splash harmlessly into the ocean or hit unpopulated areas. However, every few years a meteorite damages a home or other property.

—by Miguel Lopez

TRACKING ASTEROIDS

Although Earth is unlikely to have a major collision with a space object anytime soon, scientists feel the danger is too great to ignore. They are using telescopes to find large, rocky space objects called **asteroids**. After locating an asteroid, they use computer models to predict its path.

Close Read

1. If you were doing a report on meteorites, would this article be useful to you? Explain which text feature helped you find the answer.
2. Summarize the information that appears under the subheading *Impacts on Earth.* Write another subheading that the author could have used.
3. What additional information does the sidebar provide?

MODEL: TEXT FEATURES

Close Read

Possible answers:

1. *Yes, this article would be a helpful reference. The boldfaced term* meteorites *(line 25) helps readers quickly locate the useful information. In an electronic format, this underlined term would also be a link to further information.*
2. *The section explains that Earth's atmosphere protects the planet from collisions with small objects. Whereas smaller objects burn up in the air before hitting the ground, larger objects have a more significant impact. Many scientists believe that a collision with a large object happened 65 million years ago, causing the extinction of dinosaurs and other organisms. Other possible subheadings for this section include "Collisions with Earth," "Collisions Large and Small," or "Earth's Collision Course."*
3. *The sidebar explains the methods that scientists use to determine the paths of asteroids and thus monitor the potential danger they pose to Earth.*

FOR ENGLISH LEARNERS

Language Support: Cognates Point out cognates in the article that Spanish-speaking students might recognize:

- *crater/cráter* (lines 1, 12)
- *collision/colisión* (lines 3, 10, 12, 17, 18, 20)
- *planet/planeta* (line 8)
- *meteorite/meteorito* (lines 25, 27)

Have students look for other cognates as they read.

FOR ADVANCED LEARNERS/PRE–AP

Synthesize Have students add one or more text features to the article "Danger from the Sky." For example, they might locate a photograph of a meteorite or crater and include a caption, add a bulleted list to summarize or introduce new information, present a graph, or insert footnotes with explanations of technical or specialized terms. Invite students to share the additional text features and discuss their functions.

Teach

Part 2: Main Idea and Supporting Details

Topic and Main Idea Make sure students understand that the main idea establishes what the writer wants to say about the topic. Ask students to identify the topic of a movie that they have seen recently, such as teen romance or car racing. Then ask them to state the main idea of the movie—for example, "Unrequited love leads to heartache" or "Reckless actions fuel disaster."

Supporting Details Ask students to list types of supporting details in addition to facts and examples. ***Possible answer:*** *reasons, sensory details, analogies, explanations, statistics*

Implied or Stated Main Ideas Explain that readers should form their own main idea statement as they read a nonfiction work. If a sentence within the text matches their version, then it means that the writer has chosen to state the main idea in a topic sentence. Tell students that text features such as titles, subheadings, and boldfaced words can help readers determine both topic and main idea.

CHECK UNDERSTANDING Ask students to explain the relationship between a topic, a main idea, and supporting details.

Part 2: Main Idea and Supporting Details

After you preview a text, you're ready to examine it more closely. The following strategies can help you to better understand what you are reading and gather the information you need.

IDENTIFYING MAIN IDEAS

The **topic** of a piece of nonfiction is what the text is about. A topic can usually be stated in a word or two, such as *pets* or *dog training.* The **main idea** is the most important idea that a writer wants to share about a topic. The main idea might be the focus of a single paragraph, a section, or the entire article. For example, a main idea might be "The most important factor in dog training is consistent communication."

	LENGTH	EXAMPLE
TOPIC	one or two words	dog training
MAIN IDEA	sentence	The most important factor in dog training is consistent communication.

Often, the main idea of a paragraph or section is directly stated in a **topic sentence,** which is usually the first or the last sentence in that paragraph or section. The facts and examples the writer provides as support for the main idea are called **supporting details.** Sometimes, the main idea is implied, which means it's not directly stated. In that case, you need to **infer** the main idea by looking for what the supporting details add up to. Identifying the main idea of each section or paragraph can help you determine the main idea of the entire article.

Examine this paragraph from "Danger from the Sky." Notice how the main idea and supporting details work together to form a paragraph. The main idea of this paragraph can help you figure out the main idea of the entire article—that our risk of a major collision with space objects is low.

> Although Earth is unlikely to have a major collision with a space object anytime soon, scientists feel the danger is too great to ignore. They are using telescopes to find large, rocky space objects called asteroids. After locating an asteroid, they use computer models to predict its path.

Notice that the **main idea** is direct[ly] stated: The danger of a major collision between Earth and a spac[e] object, though unlikely, is too grea[t] to ignore.

These facts **support** the main idea by explaining what scientist[s] are doing to predict dangerous collisions.

DIFFERENTIATED INSTRUCTION

FOR LESS–PROFICIENT READERS

Note Taking [paired option] Hand out the Note Taking: Main Idea and Supporting Details copy master. Read and discuss pages 880 and 882. As a class, respond to the first questions on the copy master. Then have students work in pairs to complete the page.

RESOURCE MANAGER—Copy Master
Note Taking p. 16

Identify Main Idea Display this paragraph:

A dog is standing at the window. His ears perk up, and he begins to bark. His tail is wagging, and his bark is loud but unhurried. He is saying that a friend from the neighborhood is passing by. Suddenly, the tone changes. His bark becomes urgent and high-pitched, telling his humans that he is ready to meet the threat he sees outside. Once the danger has passed, he decides it is time for a snack. He utters short, abrupt barks that say, "I'm hungry!"

Work with students to identify the main idea of this paragraph, using sentence frames such as these:

- This paragraph is about ________. *(dogs barking)*
- From the supporting details, I learn that ________. *(a dog can bark in many ways, and each way means something different)*
- Therefore, the main idea of this paragraph is that ________. *(dogs bark in different ways to communicate different messages)*

MODEL 1: MAIN IDEA AND DETAILS

Read this article about a lifelike robot created by a Korean scientist.

Female Android Debuts

Article by **Victoria Gilman**

These school-age tots seem to be making friends with EveR-1, a female android that made her debut in South Korea. The robot was built by Baeg Moon-hong, a senior researcher with the Division for Applied Robot Technology at the Korea Institute of Industrial Technology in Ansan, just south of Seoul.

Children check out Korean android EveR-1.

Meet EveR-1 EveR-1 is designed to resemble a Korean female in her early 20s. Fifteen motors underneath her silicon skin allow her to express a limited range of emotions, and a 400-word vocabulary enables her to hold a simple conversation. The android weighs 110 pounds and would stand 5 feet, 3 inches tall—if she could stand. EveR-1 can move her arms and hands, but her lower half is immobile.

Not Alone Researchers at Osaka University in Japan unveiled their own life-size female android, Repliee Q1. That robot could "speak," and gesture and even appeared to breathe but, like EveR-1, was only mobile from the waist up.

Close Read

1. The main idea of the *Meet EveR-1* section is boxed. Identify the details that support it.
2. What is the main idea of the section with the subheading *Not Alone?*

MODEL 2: MAIN IDEA AND DETAILS

This article is about deadly poisons. Skim the title and the subheading, and answer the first **Close Read** question. Then read the article more closely to help you answer the second question.

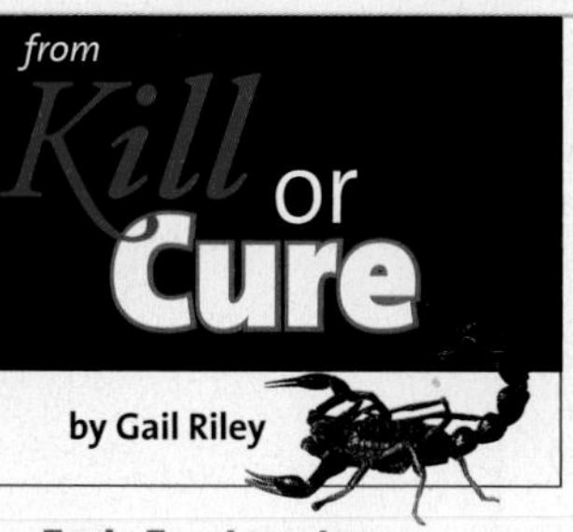

Night falls in an Israeli desert. A cockroach skitters across the sand. Suddenly, a scorpion grabs the cockroach in its pincers. It injects searing venom into its victim through its stinger. The venom causes paralysis. The cockroach cannot move. It can do nothing to fend off the scorpion's attack.

Toxic Treatments

It's hard to believe, but the deadly venom that paralyzed the cockroach can be used to heal rather than harm. Scientists are experimenting with the Israeli scorpion's venom. Some of them believe it has the power to shrink brain tumors. For hundreds of years, scientists have been experimenting with poisons extracted from animals and plants. They have found that the same toxins that can injure or kill can also be used to treat health problems.

Close Read

1. Based on the title and the subheading, what do you think the main idea of the article will be?
2. Identify the main idea that the boxed sentences are supporting.

MODEL 1: MAIN IDEA AND DETAILS

Close Read

Possible answers:

1. *Supporting details include*
   - *she can express a limited range of emotions*
   - *she can hold a simple conversation*
   - *she weighs 110 pounds and would be five feet, three inches tall if she could stand up*
2. *Researchers in Japan have created a life-sized female android, too.*

MODEL 2: MAIN IDEA AND DETAILS

Close Read

Possible answers:

1. *The main idea of the article could be that certain poisonous substances may double as cures for illnesses.*
2. *"Scientists are experimenting with the Israeli scorpion's venom" (lines 12–13).*

FOR ENGLISH LEARNERS

Concept Support: Main Idea and Supporting Details [small-group option] Before students work on the **Close Read** questions, give them additional practice in identifying main ideas and supporting details. Write these statements on the board. Tell them that each set of statements contains a main idea and several supporting details. Have small groups of students label each statement accordingly.

- Indoor cats cannot get into fights with other neighborhood felines.
- They are protected from parasites and diseases that they might pick up outside.
- Being hit by a car is another danger for cats that roam outdoors.
- In addition, cats might eat something they shouldn't if they are unsupervised outside.
- Keeping a cat indoors all the time can help prevent many problems. *(main idea)*

- The color of Stargazer lilies is like creamy strawberry ice cream.
- These lilies have a perfume that is strong but not overpowering.
- Stargazer lilies are popular because of their many attractive traits. *(main idea)*
- Stargazers require little care to grow strong and sturdy in the garden.

Take Notes Tell students to use text features to guide their note-taking process. For example, subheadings indicate a transition to a new main idea and set of supporting details, so the reader should start a new section of notes. Bulleted or numbered lists may summarize important facts. Boldfaced terms most likely need to be recorded and defined or explained.

Using the article on page 879, demonstrate how to use text features to guide note taking. Point out that the divisions and subheadings of the main article, not including the sidebar, show development of three main ideas. This provides the overall organization for a set of notes. Each main idea has its own supporting details. Display this example for lines 1–8:

I. Danger from collision with space objects threatens Earth as well as the Moon.
   - A. The Moon's craters have been caused by objects hitting its surface.
   - B. Scientists wonder when another space object will strike Earth.

Explain how the method of note taking depends on the organization of the text and the reader's purpose for reading. For example, if someone reading the android article on page 881 wants to remember information about both robots, the outline on page 882 would be most helpful. If the reader wants to compare the two robots, the Y-chart would work better.

Review other graphic organizers and note-taking formats, such as

BEST PRACTICES TOOLKIT—Transparencies
- Venn Diagram p. A26
- Main Idea and Details p. B6
- Classification Chart p. B17
- Sequence Chain pp. B21, B45
- Spider Map p. B22
- Timeline p. B23

CHECK UNDERSTANDING Have students summarize the purposes of taking notes.

TAKING NOTES

Have you ever read an article on a fascinating subject—talking robots or life-saving poisons, for example—and later realized that you couldn't recall a single thing about it? Taking notes as you read can help you retain the main ideas and imprint them on your memory. There's something about finding, organizing, and recording the most critical information that can really help you learn.

Your notes can take any number of forms, including an outline, a bulleted list, or a graphic organizer, such as a word web or a Y-chart. The form you use isn't as important as the information you include. As you read, try to determine what information is most important, then restate it in your own words.

Notice how information from one of the articles you just read can be organized in two different ways.

OUTLINE

I. EveR-1 resembles a Korean female in her 20s.
- *A. Made in South Korea*
- *B. Can show emotion, talk, and move her arms*
- *C. Can only move the top half of her body*

II. Repliee Q1 is another life-size female android.
- *A. Made in Japan*
- *B. Can talk, move her arms, and looks like she's breathing*
- *C. Can only move the top half of her body*

GRAPHIC ORGANIZER

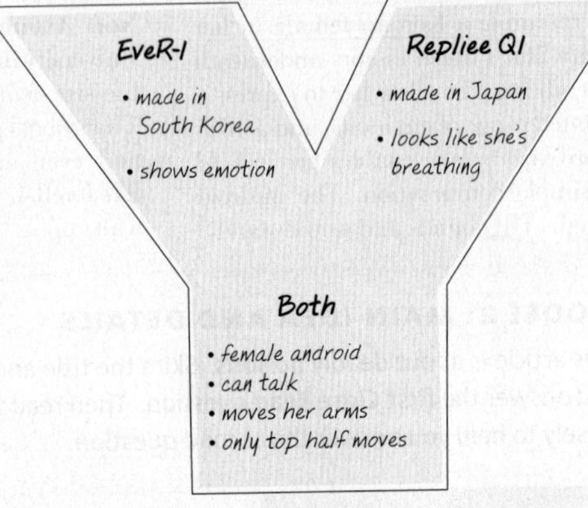

If you own the book, newspaper, or magazine you are reading, you might use a highlighter to mark the main ideas and supporting details. If you don't own the text, you can use colored sticky notes to flag important information. Just make sure to remove them after you've finished organizing your notes.

Both South Korea and Japan have developed life-like female androids. Only the top half of each android moves. (from Science News, B20)

** I wonder if other robots are in development. What will new advances in technology bring?*

882

DIFFERENTIATED INSTRUCTION

FOR LESS–PROFICIENT READERS

Take Notes Have students return to page 881. Ask them to take notes on **Model 2,** choosing the method that they think will work best. After students have finished, ask them to share their notes and describe the approach that they took.

FOR ENGLISH LEARNERS

Reading Support: Read Aloud [small-group option] Read the article on page 883 aloud before students read it independently. Have them work on the **Close Read** questions in small groups.

Part 3: Analyze the Text

Preview this article and answer the first **Close Read** question. Then read the article more closely, using the other questions to help you take notes.

THE Great Chicago Fire OF 1871

Magazine article by **Michael Burgan**

RECIPE FOR DISASTER Chicago in 1871 was already a big city, bustling with more than 334,000 residents. Its streets, sidewalks, and most of its buildings were made of wood. Hay and straw were inside every barn. To make the situation worse, people used candles and oil lamps.

Fires had been common that year because of the dry weather. The Chicago Fire Department was overworked and underequipped. On Saturday, October 7, firefighters began putting out a fire that wiped out four city blocks. It took them 16 hours. By Sunday evening the men were exhausted. Then around 8:45 P.M., a fire began in the barn of Patrick and Catherine O'Leary.

"EVERYTHING WENT WRONG"

Human error then made a bad situation worse. One firefighter later said, "From the beginning of that fatal fire, everything went wrong!" A watchman atop the courthouse saw smoke rising from the O'Leary barn, but he assumed it was coming from the previous fire. When he finally realized a new fire was blazing, he misjudged its location. His assistant sent a message to the fire stations, but he mistakenly directed horse-drawn fire wagons to a location about a mile from the burning barn. When the fire department finally reached the barn, its equipment was no match for the blaze. The new fire raged on.

OUT OF CONTROL

As the fire blazed, there arose a deafening roar—wood crackling as flames devoured it, cries for help, explosions from oil and gas tanks, the crash of falling buildings. The fire department could do nothing to stop the fire. Around 4 A.M. the next day, the fire destroyed the city's waterworks, shutting off water to the fire hydrants. Firefighters had to drag water in buckets from Lake Michigan and the Chicago River. City officials made a desperate call for help to other cities, but their forces arrived too late. The fire kept burning—totally out of control.

THE AFTERMATH

The Great Fire burned until October 10, when rain finally fell. Thousands of buildings had been destroyed. About 300 people had died in the blaze, and more than 100,000 were left homeless.

Close Read

1. Preview the title and subheadings. What information do you think this article will provide?
2. Describe the main idea that the boxed details support. Copy the main idea and details into your notebook. Add letters as necessary.

   I.
   A.
   B.

3. The main idea of the second section is listed here. Copy it into your notebook, along with the supporting details.

   II. *Human error made a bad situation even worse.*
   A.
   B.

4. Identify the main idea and details in the third and fourth sections. Add the information to your outline.

   III.
   A.
   B. *The fire destroyed the city's waterworks.*
   IV.
   A. *300 people died.*
   B.

Practice and Apply

Part 3: Analyze the Text

Close Read

Possible answers:

1. *The article will tell about the Great Chicago Fire of 1871—how it started, how it was handled, and how it affected the city.*
2. *Outline for first section:*
   - **I.** *For a variety of reasons, Chicago in 1871 was a "recipe for disaster."*
     - **A.** *Buildings were made of wood.*
     - **B.** *Hay and straw filled every barn.*
     - **C.** *People used candles and oil lamps.*
     - **D.** *The weather was dry.*
     - **E.** *The fire department was overworked and underequipped. By Sunday evening, the firefighters were exhausted from putting out another fire.*
3. *Outline for second section:*
   - **A.** *The person who first spotted the fire misidentified its source and location.*
   - **B.** *Firefighters wasted valuable time going to the wrong location.*
   - **C.** *When the firefighters finally arrived on the scene, they didn't have the equipment to match the fire.*
4. *Outline for last sections:*
   - **III.** *The fire blazed out of control.*
     - **A.** *There was a deafening roar caused by explosions, falling buildings, and people's cries for help.*
     - **C.** *Forces from other cities arrived too late.*
   - **IV.** *The fire had very damaging consequences for the city and its people.*
     - **B.** *Thousands of buildings were destroyed.*

FOR ADVANCED LEARNERS/PRE–AP

Synthesize Have students use a graphic organizer to take notes on the article on page 883. Tell them that their chart or diagram should reflect the major organizational pattern of the article. Ask students to present their organizers to the class and explain how their choice helps them see and remember the relationships among ideas more clearly.

Assess and Reteach

Assess

Provide students with a brief nonfiction article. Ask them to identify text features as well as the main idea and supporting details.

Reteach

Meet with small groups to review students' note-taking copy masters. Clarify terms and concepts, illustrating each one with concrete details from "The Great Chicago Fire of 1871" or another brief work of nonfiction.

READER'S WORKSHOP 883

Focus and Motivate

OBJECTIVES

Elements of Nonfiction
- explore the key idea of a **career**
- use text features to locate and comprehend information
- read a feature article

Reading
- summarize main ideas in an article

Vocabulary
- use structural analysis to identify base words and affixes *(also an EL language objective)*
- determine meanings of derivatives by applying knowledge of meanings of base words and affixes *(also an EL language objective)*

Grammar and Writing
- correctly capitalize titles of books, movies, articles, songs, magazines, and other works
- use writing to analyze nonfiction

SUMMARY

Entomologist Steven Kutcher studies the behavior of insects and then adapts that behavior for movies, television, commercials, and music videos. His goal is to educate the public about the fascinating world of insects.

What is your DREAM JOB?

Discuss the question. To lead into the ***KEY IDEA,*** ask students what constitutes a dream **career.** Is it the work itself? the hours? the pay? the location? the coworkers? Then have students work on the ***SURVEY*** activity.

Before Reading

The Spider Man Behind *Spider-Man*

Feature Article by Bijal P. Trivedi

What is your DREAM JOB?

KEY IDEA Ever since you were little, people have probably asked you what you want to be when you grow up. Now that you're older and know yourself better, your dream job might be coming into focus. Is it a job that would take you outdoors? Onto a movie set? Into a sports arena? Your ideal **career** probably reflects your individual talents, interests, and personality. In the following article, you'll read about a man who turned his passion into a dream job.

SURVEY Interview several classmates to find out what their dream jobs would be. Ask these students why they chose the jobs they did. How do their dream careers compare to your own?

Name	*Dream Job*	*Why?*
Kayla	*Veterinarian*	*1. Likes taking care of animal* *2. Gets good grades in scien* *3. Enjoys learning about animals*

884

Selection Resources

RESOURCE MANAGER UNIT 8

Plan and Teach pp. 17–24

Elements of Nonfiction
Summary pp. 25†*, 26‡*
Text Features pp. 27, 28†*
Question Support p. 35*

Reading
Summarize pp. 29, 30†*
Reading Check p. 34
Reading Fluency p. 37

Vocabulary
Study p. 31*
Practice p. 32
Strategy p. 33

Grammar and Writing
Capitalize Correctly p. 36

Assessment
Selection Tests A, B/C pp. 39*, 41*
Test Generator CD

BEST PRACTICES TOOLKIT
Differentiated Instruction pp. 31–38*
Scaffolding Instruction pp. 43–46*

Graphic Organizers/Strategies
Word Questioning

Reading Support
Audio Anthology CD*

Technology
Literature, Vocabulary, and Writing Centers at **ClassZone.com**
Write*Smart* CD

* Resources for Differentiation † Also in Spanish ‡ In Haitian Creole and Vietnamese

EMENTS OF NONFICTION: TEXT FEATURES

Nonfiction articles often contain **text features,** design elements that help organize the material and identify key ideas. Common text features include

- **headings**—the title of the article
- **subheadings**—headings that signal the beginning of a new topic or section within a written piece
- **sidebars**—additional information set in a box alongside, below, or within an article
- **bulleted lists**—lists of items of equal value or importance. This list of text features is an example of a bulleted list.

Recognizing text features can help you find information. As you read "The Spider Man Behind *Spider-Man*," notice how the text features clue you in to the topics and key ideas.

ADING STRATEGY: SUMMARIZE

Have you ever told a friend about a movie you just saw? If so, you probably gave your friend a summary. When you **summarize** a piece of writing, you briefly retell the main ideas or key points. Summarizing is a way to check your understanding, and it can help you remember information. As you read "The Spider Man Behind *Spider-Man*," use a chart to take notes on the key points. Later, you'll use these notes to summarize the article.

What Steven Kutcher Does	His Training and Background	His Spider-Man Experience

CABULARY IN CONTEXT

The boldfaced words help the author describe one man's interesting career. Try using context clues to figure out what each word means.

1. He has the **perseverance** necessary to finish the job.
2. Bill is an **engaging** person whom everyone likes.
3. Maria has the **potential** to become a first-rate scientist.
4. Ashley's watercolor **rendition** of her dream earned praise from her art teacher.

Author Online

A Love of Science Bijal Trivedi (bĭj′əl trē-vä′dē) became fascinated with dinosaurs at the age of nine. Soon after, she transferred her interest to the space shuttle and astronomy. From an early age, it was clear that Trivedi's dream job would involve science.

Bijal P. Trivedi
born 1970

Exciting Places and Discoveries Trivedi studied science in college and earned master's degrees in both biology and science journalism. Because Trivedi didn't want to work in a lab, she became a science writer. She has written for magazines such as *National Geographic, Popular Science,* and *Wired.* She says, "Being a science writer is a bit like being Indiana Jones—you get to travel with lots of smart scientists to exciting places and then write stories about their discoveries." Trivedi has won several awards for her journalism.

MORE ABOUT THE AUTHOR
For more on Bijal P. Trivedi, visit the **Literature Center** at **ClassZone.com.**

Background

The Amazing Spider-Man In 1962, writer Stan Lee and artist Steve Ditko created the character of Peter Parker, a teenager who gains spider-like powers through the bite of a radioactive spider and becomes Spider-Man. Spider-Man first appeared in an issue of *Amazing Fantasy* by Marvel Comics and then gained a comic book series all his own. *The Amazing Spider-Man* comics have been popular ever since. In the movies about the superhero, CGI, or computer-generated imagery, made it appear that Peter Parker could swing from one tall building to another, stick to walls, and do other incredible feats that only a Spider-Man could do.

Teach

STANDARDS FOCUS

ELEMENTS OF NONFICTION

● TEXT FEATURES

Ask students to examine page 885. Which text features are present on this page? ***Possible answer: Headings:*** *Elements of Nonfiction: Text Features, Reading Strategy: Summarize, Vocabulary in Context, Background* ***Subheadings:*** *A Love of Science, Exciting Places and Discoveries, The Amazing Spider-Man* ***Sidebar:*** *Author Online* ***Bulleted list:*** *under Elements of Nonfiction*

CHECK UNDERSTANDING Ask students when writers might use a bulleted list and why.

READING STRATEGY

■ SUMMARIZE

Read the **Background** paragraph aloud. Then ask students: What are the main ideas of the paragraph? ***Possible answer:*** *In 1962, Lee and Ditko created Spider-Man comics. In the movie, computer-generated imagery makes it appear that Parker is doing Spider-Man tricks.*

CHECK UNDERSTANDING Have students summarize a TV show they've watched or a book or an article they've read.

RESOURCE MANAGER—Copy Master
Summarize p. 29 (for student use while reading the selection)

VOCABULARY SKILL

▲ VOCABULARY IN CONTEXT

DIAGNOSE WORD KNOWLEDGE To determine preteaching needs, have all students complete **Vocabulary in Context.** ***Possible answers:*** **1.** *determination* **2.** *friendly* **3.** *ability* **4.** *version*

PRETEACH VOCABULARY Use the Vocabulary Study copy master to help students use context clues to predict the meaning of each boldfaced word.

1. Read the two sentences in item 1 aloud, emphasizing *engaging.*
2. Point out the context clues *made many friends* and *earned him many tips.* Elicit possible meanings for *engaging,* such as "likable" or "charming."
3. Have students record their predictions.
4. Repeat the procedure for items 2–4.
5. Have students complete Part B on their own.

RESOURCE MANAGER—Copy Master
Vocabulary Study p. 31

For general guidelines on differentiating vocabulary instruction and for alternative vocabulary activities for students not needing vocabulary preteaching, see

BEST PRACTICES TOOLKIT
Scaffolding Vocabulary Instruction pp. 43–46

Vocabulary Center at **ClassZone.com**

Practice and Apply

READING STRATEGY

A SUMMARIZE

Students should record their answers in the column titled "What Steven Kutcher Does."

Possible answer:

- *gets cockroaches to run and flip over*
- *gets beetles, cockroaches, and spiders to crawl toward something*
- *makes bees swarm indoors*
- *repairs butterfly wings*
- *makes a wasp fly into an actor's mouth*

ELEMENTS OF NONFICTION

B TEXT FEATURES

Possible answer: *how and when Kutcher developed a passion for insects that led to his career training bugs for Hollywood*

Lines 11–21

DISCUSSION PROMPTS

Use these prompts to help students understand how Kutcher's interest in insects influenced his career choice:

Recall What early experiences influenced Kutcher's career choice? ***Answer:*** *catching fireflies; spending summers in the Catskills*

Analyze What does Kutcher mean when he says his experiences in nature "lit a fire within me"? ***Possible answer:*** *The experiences aroused his life-long interest in bugs.*

Evaluate Not getting into his chosen Ph.D. program could have devastated Kutcher. What did he decide to do instead? What does this tell you about him? ***Possible answer:*** *He decided to reevaluate his career options. He is determined and practical.*

THE SPIDER MAN BEHIND SPIDER-MAN

Bijal P. Trivedi

Targeted Passage ①

A SUMMARIZE What are some of Kutcher's unique skills? Record them in your chart.

B TEXT FEATURES On the basis of this **subheading** and what you've read so far, what information do you expect to find in this section?

Entomologist Steven Kutcher is the spider man behind *Spider-Man*. "He's the guy to call in Hollywood when you need insects—he is the ultimate insect trainer," says Robin Miller, property master for the movie *Spider-Man*.

"I know how to get a cockroach to run across the floor and flip onto its back. I can get cockroaches, beetles, and spiders to crawl to a quarter four feet away on cue. I can make bees swarm indoors and I can repair butterfly wings," says Kutcher. He has even made a live wasp fly into an actor's mouth. "I study insect behavior, and learn what they do and then adapt the behavior to what the director wants," says Kutcher. **A**

Passion for Bugs B

Kutcher's love of insects began as a toddler when he collected fireflies in New York. But he was also influenced by very "positive early childhood experiences in nature" when his family would spend summers in the Catskills.[1] "Something about seeing fish, catching butterflies, lit a fire within me," says Kutcher.

Kutcher followed his passion for bugs and studied entomology in college, receiving his B.S. from the University of California, Davis, and later an M.A. in biology—with an emphasis on entomology,[2] insect behavior, and ecology[3] from the California State University in Long Beach. He had planned to pursue a Ph.D.,[4] but when he wasn't accepted at the graduate school of his choice he decided to reevaluate his career options.

1. **Catskills** (kăt'skĭlz'): the Catskill Mountain region in New York state. It is a popular vacation area.
2. **entomology** (ĕn'tə-mŏl'ə-jē): the study of insects.
3. **ecology** (ĭ-kŏl'ə-jē): the study of relationships among living things and their environment.
4. **B.S.; M.A.; Ph.D.:** Bachelor of Science, an undergraduate degree; Master of Arts, a graduate degree; Doctor of Philosophy, a graduate degree that is usually more time-consuming and difficult to earn than a master's degree.

DIFFERENTIATED INSTRUCTION

FOR ALL STUDENTS

Enhance Learning Styles Provide independent projects for various learning styles.

- **Visual** Create a cartoon strip.
- **Interpersonal** Role-play an interview.
- **Analytical** Speculate on the reasons for some people's fear of insects.

For further details on these projects, see

RESOURCE MANAGER
Ideas for Extension pp. 22–23

FOR LESS–PROFICIENT READERS

In combination with the *Audio Anthology CD*, use one or more Targeted Passages (pp. 886, 888, 890) to ensure students focus on key facts, concepts, and skills.

① Targeted Passage [Lines 1–21]

This passage introduces Kutcher and his work.

- What does Kutcher do for a living?
- What childhood experiences inspired Kutcher to become an entomologist?
- What event in Kutcher's life made him reevaluate his career options?

Reading Strategy Follow-Up: Summarize Ask students in which column of the chart from page 885 they would place the information in lines 11–21 (*His Training and Background*). Then have them record key facts in their charts. ***Possible answer:*** *Kutcher had positive childhood experiences in nature; he received a BS in entomology and an MA in biology with an emphasis on insect behavior.*

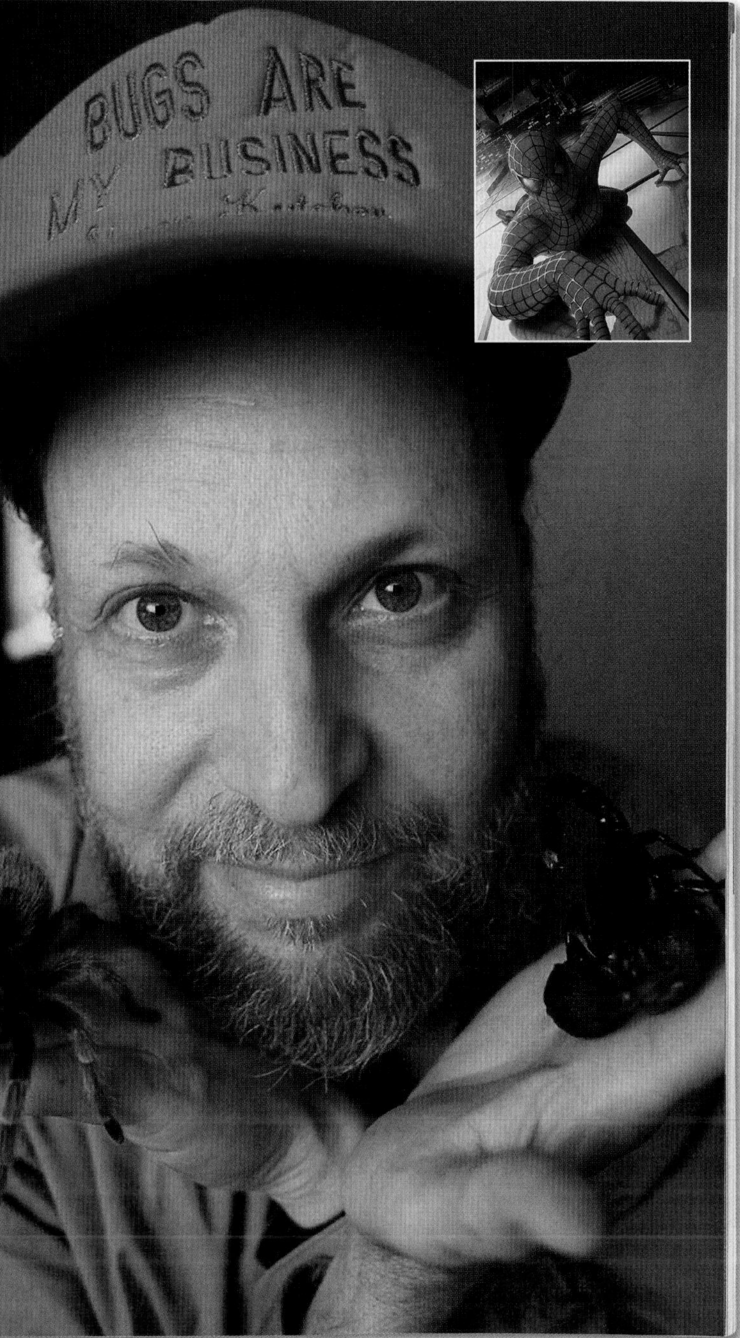

ANALYZE VISUALS
Based on this photo of Steven Kutcher, what can you **infer** about his interests and personality?

BACKGROUND

Instinct or Intelligence? Scientists have long thought that insects' behavior is based on instinct, or how bugs' brains are "wired." Researchers at the University of Montana wanted to find out if bees' behavior could be influenced by something besides instinct. They injected tiny amounts of chemicals found in explosives into bees' feeders. Within two days, the bees began associating the smell of the chemicals with food. As a result, they were able to locate buried landmines simply by picking up the scent of the explosives. The researchers hope someday to be able to use honeybees instead of humans or dogs to locate these and other dangerous weapons.

CULTURAL CONNECTION

Cultural Entomology Cultural entomology is the study of the effects insects have had on human culture over the centuries. In ancient Greece, the writer Aesop based many of his fables on lessons that could be learned from insects. In African mythology, Anansi the spider, actually an arachnid rather than an insect, was a great trickster, while in some Native American tales, a spider woman created Earth. Invite students to share knowledge of cultural entomology from other cultures.

ANALYZE VISUALS

Possible answer: *Kutcher's expression suggests he is confident; his funny hat indicates he has a sense of humor and is interested in bugs; the fact that he's holding bugs suggests that he finds them intriguing and is not scared of them.*

FOR ENGLISH LEARNERS

Options for Reading Provide a brief introduction to the selection to make sure students understand the concept of entomology. Then have students read along with the *Audio Anthology CD.*

Prereading For prereading instruction for English learners, see

 **BEST PRACTICES TOOLKIT**
Scaffolding Reading Instruction pp. 43–46

Key Academic Vocabulary Have students use Word Questioning to study these words from the selection: *option(s)* (lines 21, 52), *job* (lines 25, 28, 29), *create* (line 46), *contacted* (line 53), *design* (line 78).

BEST PRACTICES TOOLKIT—Transparency
Word Questioning p. E9

FOR ADVANCED LEARNERS/PRE-AP

Pre-AP exercises in the bottom channel provide additional challenge for your advanced students. Use them for small groups or individuals.

ADDITIONAL GUIDELINES
For more help with differentiation and tips for classroom management, see

 **BEST PRACTICES TOOLKIT**
Differentiated Instruction pp. 31–38

Lines 11–26

REINFORCE *KEY IDEA:* CAREER

Discuss In what ways is Kutcher's **career** his dream job? ***Possible answer:*** *Kutcher has been interested in insects since he was a child. His job allows him to work with insects on a daily basis and requires him to use his knowledge of insect behavior to get insects to "perform."*

BACKGROUND

Forensic Entomology Besides the typical tasks listed in the sidebar on pages 888–889, some entomologists, known as forensic entomologists, use insect evidence to help solve crimes. Probably the first incidence of forensic entomology took place in a village in China in 1235 A.D. A murder had been committed, and it was believed that the murder weapon had been a sickle, a curved blade with a handle used for cutting grain, grass, or weeds. All the villagers were required to bring their sickles to the local death investigator, who then displayed them for all to see. While the sickles looked the same, one was different: it attracted flies because the human tissue of the murder victim had stuck to the blade during the murder. The owner of the sickle confessed to the crime.

Forensic entomology consists of these three general areas:

- **Medicolegal** focuses on solving cases involving sudden death and includes methods by which time, site, and cause of death are determined.
- **Urban** deals with insects that affect humans and their immediate environments.
- **Stored products** concentrates on insects that infest items such as food or kitchen products.

Targeted Passage ②

One day he received a call from his former academic advisor asking him to baby-sit 3,000 locusts that were to be used for the movie *Exorcist 2.* Kutcher had to place the locusts wherever they were needed, including on the stars Richard Burton and Linda Blair. That was his first job, and it has been Hollywood creepy crawlies ever since.

After doing a long survey of movies Kutcher found that about one third of all movies had an insect in it. "I saw immediate job **potential,**" Kutcher says.

Almost 25 years after his first job Kutcher now holds an impressive list of movie, television, music video, and commercial credits that include his biggest movie, *Arachnophobia,* the comedy-thriller in which a California town is overrun with deadly spiders. He also supervised the bug and spider stunts in *Alien, Contact, Jurassic Park, Pacific Heights,* and *Wild Wild West.*

"He is a very observant and **engaging** guy," says Lucinda Strub, a special effects person who worked with Kutcher on *Arachnophobia.* "One of his main goals is to educate the public about how fascinating and interesting insects are. He is really out to teach people about bugs," says Strub, who then . . . clarified that "of course spiders are not bugs, they are arachnids."

potential (pə-tĕn'shəl) *n.* the ability to grow or develop

engaging (ĕn-gāj'ĭng) *adj.* charming; likeable

perseverance (pûr'sə-vîr'əns) *n.* steady persistence in sticking to a course of action

So You Want to Be an Entomologist?

Do you get grossed out when you see a spider or earwig[5] crawling up your wall? Or does the spider's web and the inchworm's movement fascinate you? If the latter question describes you, then entomology could be the perfect career for you.

Entomologists study the classification, life cycle, and habits of insects and related life forms, and plan and implement insect surveys and pest management programs. They also investigate ways to control insect pests and manage beneficial insects such as plant pollinators,[6] insect parasites, and insect predators.

Interests and Skills

Entomologists need the intellect, curiosity, creativity, patience, and **perseverance** required to pursue answers to complex research questions about bugs. Because there are thousands and thousands of insect species, entomologists must also have a good memory. Entomologists must be able to work well both independently and as part of a team.

5. **earwig** (îr-wĭg'): an insect that has two pincers protruding from the rear of its abdomen.
6. **pollinators** (pŏl'ə-nāt'tərs): animals that carry pollen from one plant to another, causing the plants to produce fruit.

DIFFERENTIATED INSTRUCTION

FOR LESS—PROFICIENT READERS

② Targeted Passage [Lines 22–34]

This passage describes how Kutcher got his start in movies.

- Who gave Kutcher his first job in a movie? What was the job?
- What information led Kutcher to conclude that there was a potential career for him in movies?
- In addition to movies, what other media has Kutcher worked in?

FOR ENGLISH LEARNERS

Vocabulary: Cognates Encourage Spanish-speaking students to use their knowledge of cognates to define these words:

- *entomology/entomologia* (line 16)
- *potential/potencial* (line 28)
- *arachnid/arácnido* (line 39)
- *beneficial/beneficioso* (sidebar)
- *parasite/parásito* (sidebar)
- *predator/depredador* (sidebar)
- *creative/creativo* (line 84)

Even with his busy filmmaking schedule, Kutcher still finds time to teach once a week at a local community college. He also started the annual Insect Fair at the Los Angeles Arboretum. **C**

The Perfect Match

Kutcher's most recent challenge has been finding the perfect spider for the movie *Spider-Man*. . . . The concept designer for the movie produced a computer **rendition** that combined traits of up to four arachnids to create an image of the mutant spider that bites Peter Parker (a.k.a. Spider-Man) and endows him with spider powers. **D**

"I was given this drawing of a spider that didn't exist and told to find a real spider that matched it," says Miller, whose responsibilities include assembling all the props in the entire film. The spider resembled a black widow, which wasn't an option because its bite is too dangerous.

Miller contacted Steven Kutcher and showed him the picture. Kutcher then arranged a "spider Olympics" for *Spider-Man* director Sam Raimi. Kutcher brought in different types of spiders to showcase the talents of each, says Miller. "He literally had the spiders doing tricks." One spider

Typical Tasks

- Study the evolution of insects
- Discover and describe new species of insects
- Conduct research into the impact and control of insect pest problems
- Conduct field and laboratory tests of pesticides to evaluate their effect on different species of insects under different conditions
- Curate museum insect collections
- Prepare publications that make it possible to identify insect, spider, mite, and tick species
- Coordinate public awareness and education programs **E**

AVERAGE EARNINGS

Maximum Salary: **$71,270**

Average Salary: **$47,740**

Entry Level Salary: **$29,260**

Educational Paths

Students interested in a career working with insects should prepare for college by taking a variety of science classes. Many students get a general undergraduate degree in biology or zoology[7] and then specialize in entomology at the post-graduate level. For those wishing to lead research teams or teach at the university level, a Ph.D. is a requirement. **F**

7. **zoology** (zō͞o-ŏl'ə-jē): the study of animals.

C SUMMARIZE
Reread lines 22–42. What are two of the most important pieces of information you get from these paragraphs? Add them to your chart.

rendition (rĕn-dĭsh'ən) *n.* a pictorial representation; an interpretation

D TEXT FEATURES
Reread the **subheading** and first sentence of this section. What "perfect match" does the subheading refer to?

E TEXT FEATURES
What does this **bulleted list** help you better understand?

F TEXT FEATURES
What does the information presented in the blue **sidebar** add to your understanding of Steven Kutcher and his career?

BACKGROUND

Athletic Spiders Like Spider-Man, spiders are amazingly athletic. Jumping spiders can leap up to 50 times the length of their bodies. To match that feat, a human would have to jump almost 300 feet from a standstill. The European house spider can cover a distance 330 times the length of its body in 10 seconds. That's like a person running the length of more than six football fields. Bola spiders use a thread of silk to lasso their prey, and net-casting spiders throw a web over passing insects. The long-bodied cellar spider can twirl around so fast in its web that it becomes a blur to predators.

READING STRATEGY

C SUMMARIZE

Students should record their answers in the column titled "What Steven Kutcher Does." ***Possible answer:***

- *Kutcher is an experienced insect trainer.*
- *He educates people about bugs.*

ELEMENTS OF NONFICTION

D TEXT FEATURES

Possible answer: *The "perfect match" refers to the spider Kutcher found to play the mutant spider in the movie* Spider-Man.

ELEMENTS OF NONFICTION

E TEXT FEATURES

Possible answer: *The bulleted list helps readers better understand the typical tasks of an entomologist.*

ELEMENTS OF NONFICTION

F TEXT FEATURES

Possible answer: *The information in the blue sidebar explains what the average entomologist does. It also points out how unique Kutcher's job is because he did not follow the usual paths most entomologists follow.*

FOR ADVANCED LEARNERS/PRE–AP

Analyze [small-group option] Have groups discuss these questions regarding the bulleted list of an entomologist's typical tasks. Encourage them to present their conclusions to the class by creating a poster that summarizes their ideas.

- What scientific or societal value does each task have?
- Based on these tasks, what other fields are probably affected by the work of entomologists?
- What do you think might be the most important task of an entomologist in today's world? Why?

READING STRATEGY

G SUMMARIZE

Students should record their answers in the column titled "His *Spider-Man* Experiences." ***Possible answer:*** *Kutcher had to find the perfect spider, paint it to resemble the spider in Spider-Man comics, and train it to do what the property master wanted it to do.*

ADDITIONAL TEACHING OPPORTUNITY

Fiction and Nonfiction Ask students in what ways this article is different from a piece of fiction. In what ways is it similar? ***Possible answer:*** *The article is different from fiction because it provides factual information about a real person instead of characters, setting, and plot that are imaginary. The writer is required to quote people accurately, whereas an author of fiction can have his or her characters say anything. Both the article and a piece of fiction tell about the events in the life of an intriguing person; however, Kutcher's adventures will continue, while the adventures of the characters in a piece of fiction typically end on the last page.*

SELECTION WRAP-UP

SYNTHESIZE Ask students to determine, based on Kutcher's career, what they think he wants to teach people about insects. ***Possible answer:*** *Kutcher may want to teach people that insects are predictable in their behavior, since most of their behavior is instinctual, and that insects have a place in our culture.*

★ **CRITIQUE** Ask students whether this article provided them with enough information about entomology to either consider or reject it as a possible career. What information did they find most useful?

READING FLUENCY

Distribute the copy masters and have students practice fluency.

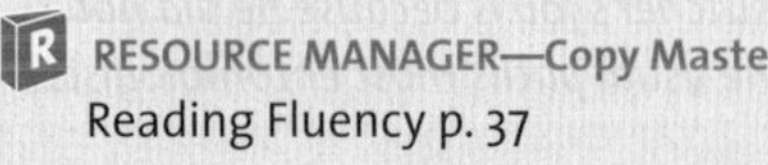

RESOURCE MANAGER—Copy Master
Reading Fluency p. 37

could jump, another was able to spin webs very quickly, and yet another was able to produce a drag line and essentially swing out of the way—all activities that Spider-Man can do.

The spider that Raimi selected was *Steatoda grossa,* a brown spider with a smooth, swollen body and thin twiggy legs. The problem was that the color was wrong, "we needed a spider that had metallic blue and a radioactive[8] red-orange color to it," says Miller.

The answer was spider makeup. Originally Kutcher wanted to make an entire costume for the spider, but the timing came down to the wire and he finally settled on body paint. "I had to find a non-toxic[9] paint, design a little harness to hold the spider as he was painted, and supervise the artist painting *Steatoda.*"

The *Steatoda grossa* spider

Targeted Passage 3

"I need the spider to go from A to B to C and Steve can train it to do that," says Miller, who has worked with Kutcher on several movies. "He is very creative; he can figure out how to get the creature to do what he wants while being very delicate," says Strub.

Why, in this age of computer-generated special effects, did the director simply not animate the spider? "The real thing always looks best, especiall[y] when it fills the whole movie screen," says Miller. And computer-generate[d] graphics are very expensive, although the scene where the mutant spider bites Peter Parker is computer-generated.

"People find me, and I'm off on these adventures," says Kutcher, "problem solving, and exploring, and teaching, and educating people abo[ut] insects." But Steven Kutcher's hat best describes his life, his love, and his philosophy: "Bugs are my business." G

G SUMMARIZE
What crucial jobs did Kutcher perform in the making of *Spider-Man?* Add these to the appropriate section of your chart.

8. **radioactive** (rā'dē-ō-ăk'tĭv): exhibiting radiation emissions that possibly result from a nuclear explosion.
9. **non-toxic:** not poisonous or otherwise life-threatening.

DIFFERENTIATED INSTRUCTION

FOR LESS-PROFICIENT READERS

3 Targeted Passage [Lines 82–94]

This passage concludes the article.

- What does Miller's quote tell you about Kutcher's techniques?
- Why did the director decide to use a real spider rather than an animated one?
- During which scene did the director decide to use special effects? Why might he have done so?
- In what way is Kutcher's career an adventure?

Comprehension Support Have students complete this chart of problems and solutions:

Lines 63–73	**Problem:** *Spider was the wrong col* **Solution:**
Lines 73–77	**Problem:** *Kutcher ran out of time to make a costume.* **Solution:**
Lines 77–81	**Problem:** **Solution:** *Kutcher designed a harnes to hold the spider.*

fter Reading

omprehension

1. **Recall** What was Steven Kutcher's first experience on a movie set?
2. **Recall** Why did the makers of *Spider-Man* want to use a real spider instead of a computer-generated spider for most of the spider scenes?
3. **Clarify** Why was it such a challenge for Kutcher to find the perfect spider for the movie *Spider-Man?*

ritical Analysis

4. **Examine Text Features** Which text features help you find the following pieces of information? Note your answers in a chart like the one shown.

Information	*Text Feature That Helps You Find It*
Broad focus of the article	
Kutcher's interest in bugs	
Typical tasks performed by entomologists	
General information about entomologists	

5. **Compare Summaries** Using the chart you made as you read, write a summary of the entire article. Next, trade summaries with a classmate. Compare the summary you received with the article to see if the summary is complete. Share your findings with your classmate, and then revise your own summary as needed.
6. **Make Generalizations** A generalization is a broad statement about a group of people or a topic. Based on the information given in the article and the sidebar, what's one generalization you can make about the kind of people who become entomologists?
7. **Draw Conclusions** Reread lines 11–15 and 35–42. Why do you think Kutcher wants other people to have a better understanding of insects?

xtension and Challenge

8. **Big Question Activity** What was your answer to the big question on page 884? Using books or the Internet, find out what skills or education you might need for this **career.** Present this information in a format similar to the sidebar on pages 888–889.
9. **Creative Project: Music** Alone or in a small group, create a song or rap from the point of view of an insect who "works" for Steven Kutcher. Look back at the article to help you recall some of the things these creatures have been trained to do and Kutcher's attitude toward what some people call "creepy crawlies." Share your song or rap with the class.

Practice and Apply

After Reading

For additional support of postreading questions, use these copy masters:

RESOURCE MANAGER—Copy Masters

Reading Check p. 34 (to check understanding of the selection)

Text Features p. 27 (for practice of elements of nonfiction standards focus)

Question Support p. 35 (After Reading questions adapted for English learners and less-proficient readers)

Additional selection questions are provided for teachers on page 21.

ANSWERS

Comprehension

1. *Kutcher's first job was to "baby-sit 3,000 locusts" for the movie* Exorcist 2 *(line 23).*
2. *The filmmakers wanted to use a real spider because the real thing looks best and because computer-generated graphics are expensive.*
3. *It was a challenge because the spider the filmmakers wanted does not exist. Kutcher had to find a spider that featured traits of four different spiders and that wasn't poisonous.*

Critical Analysis

Possible answers:

4. ● **STANDARDS FOCUS** **Text Features**
   - ***Broad focus of the article:*** *heading*
   - ***Kutcher's interest in bugs:*** *subheadings*
   - ***Typical tasks performed by entomologists:*** *bulleted list*
   - ***General information about entomologists:*** *sidebar*
5. ■ **STANDARDS FOCUS** **Summarize** *Students' summaries should include what Steven Kutcher does, his training and background, and his* Spider-Man *experience.*
6. *Entomologists are smart and able to remember a lot of facts. They can work both independently and with others. They are inquisitive and dedicated. They have an interest in bugs.*
7. *Kutcher had a positive experience with insects as a child. If people understand insects better, they might view insects more positively.*

Extension and Challenge

8. *Responses will vary. Students' sidebars should reflect their research and include the skills and/or education needed for their dream jobs.*
9. *Students' song or rap should be written from an insect's point of view and accurately recall the information in the story.*

ANSWERS

Vocabulary in Context

VOCABULARY PRACTICE

1. *antonyms*
2. *synonyms*
3. *antonyms*
4. *synonyms*

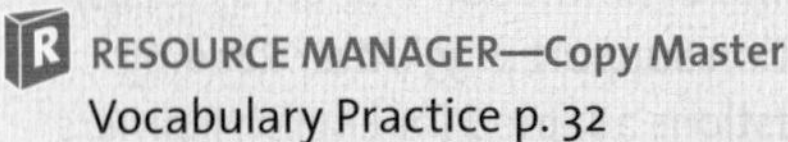

RESOURCE MANAGER—Copy Master Vocabulary Practice p. 32

VOCABULARY IN WRITING

Suggest that students review the vocabulary words to see which ones could be used to explain why they would be good job candidates.

VOCABULARY STRATEGY: RECOGNIZING BASE WORDS *(also an EL language objective)*

Remind students that base words often change their spelling when a suffix is added. For example, a final *y* may change to *i*, or a final *e* may be dropped before the suffix.

Possible answers:

1. *clarify: "make clear"; clarification: "something that clears up confusion or misunderstanding"*
2. *assemble: "gather"; assemblage: "a gathering"*
3. *class: "a group whose members have something in common"; classification: "the grouping of things into categories"*
4. *employ: "hire or put to work"; unemployment: "a lack of work"*
5. *adapt: "adjust to certain conditions"; adaptations: "adjustments made for certain conditions"*

RESOURCE MANAGER—Copy Master Vocabulary Strategy p. 33

Vocabulary Center at **ClassZone.com** Additional Vocabulary Activities

Vocabulary in Context

VOCABULARY PRACTICE

Decide whether the words in each pair are synonyms (words with similar meanings) or antonyms (words with opposite meanings).

1. perseverance/laziness
2. rendition/interpretation
3. engaging/disagreeable
4. potential/promise

VOCABULARY IN WRITING

Imagine that you are applying for a job as Steven Kutcher's assistant. What makes you a good candidate? Using at least two vocabulary words, write a paragraph telling Kutcher why he should hire you. You might start this way.

EXAMPLE SENTENCE

*Because of my **perseverance**, I earned top grades in school.*

VOCABULARY STRATEGY: RECOGNIZING BASE WORDS

To understand an unfamiliar word that has affixes (prefixes and suffixes), it helps to identify the base word first. Look within the word for a word that is familiar to you, even though the spelling may be different. For example, in the word *engaging*, you might notice the base word *engage*. In cases where you do not recognize a base word, using context clues may help you to figure out the meaning.

PRACTICE Find the base word in each boldfaced word. Think about its meaning. Then try to define the whole word. Use a dictionary if necessary.

1. If you do not understand an idea, ask your teacher for **clarification.**
2. President Lincoln spoke to a small **assemblage.**
3. My **classification** system is based on size, shape, and color.
4. Mayor Diaz will give a speech about the city's high **unemployment** rate.
5. What **adaptations** help desert plants to cope with their environment?

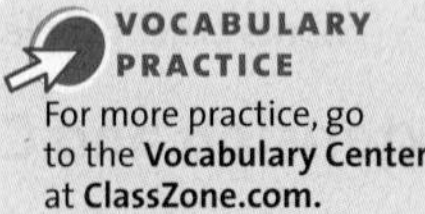

VOCABULARY PRACTICE

For more practice, go to the **Vocabulary Center** at **ClassZone.com.**

DIFFERENTIATED INSTRUCTION

FOR ENGLISH LEARNERS

Vocabulary Practice Ask students if they can remember how each vocabulary word was used in the article. If necessary, allow them to refer to the usage in the selection and use context clues to help them determine which pairs are synonyms and which are antonyms.

FOR ADVANCED LEARNERS/PRE-AP

Vocabulary Practice Challenge students to come up with synonyms for the antonym pairs (items 1 and 3) and antonyms for the synonym pairs (items 2 and 4). Have students share their ideas with a partner.

Reading-Writing Connection

Explore Steven Kutcher's career further by responding to these prompts. Then complete the **Grammar and Writing** exercise.

WRITING PROMPTS	SELF-CHECK
A. Short Response: Describe the Subject In the article "The Spider Man Behind *Spider-Man*," Steven Kutcher is described by several people who have worked with him on movie sets. Using your own words, combine these accounts into a **one-paragraph description** of Kutcher.	***A thorough description will . . .*** • not include direct quotes but will restate the information given • give details about Kutcher's talents, skills, and interests
B. Extended Response: Write a Job Advertisement Imagine that you are a movie director looking to hire someone to train insects for your next film. What type of person do you want to hire? Write a **two- or three-paragraph advertisement** giving the education, skills, and interests needed for this **career.** Include a subheading for each section.	***A strong advertisement will . . .*** • incorporate details from the article and sidebar about the education and skills needed • give a description of the job, including the name of the movie and a brief summary of its plot

GRAMMAR AND WRITING

CAPITALIZE CORRECTLY The **titles** of books, movies, articles, songs, magazines, and other works should be correctly capitalized. When writing titles, always capitalize the first and last words and all other important words within the title. Unless they appear as the first or last words in the title, articles, coordinating conjunctions, and prepositions of fewer than five letters should not be capitalized.

Original: *the Top Careers For Science Majors*

Revised: *The Top Careers for Science Majors*

PRACTICE Rewrite each title, correcting the capitalization errors.

1. The amazing spider-Man
2. Field Guide To North American Insects And Spiders
3. Movie magic: Creating Special Effects For The Big Screen
4. National geographic

For more help with capitalizing titles, see page R51 in the ***Grammar Handbook.***

Reading-Writing Connection

WRITING PROMPTS

- For **Prompt A,** suggest that students begin by listing the traits people attribute to Kutcher. Then students should use a thesaurus to locate synonyms for those traits and use those synonyms in their paragraphs.
- For **Prompt B,** suggest that students review the article, filling in a chart with three headings: *Education, Skills,* and *Interests.* Instruct students to refer to the chart as they write the advertisement.

For writing support, see

Writing Center at **ClassZone.com**

GRAMMAR AND WRITING

Point out that pronouns and verbs should be capitalized in titles, even those with few letters, such as *my, our, is,* and *are.* Work with students to brainstorm examples of words that should not be capitalized in titles.

- Articles: *a, an, the*
- Coordinating conjunctions: *and, but, or, yet*
- Prepositions: *with, on, for, in*

Answers:

1. *The Amazing Spider-Man*
2. *Field Guide to North American Insects and Spiders*
3. *Movie Magic: Creating Special Effects for the Big Screen*
4. *National Geographic*

RESOURCE MANAGER—Copy Master
Capitalize Correctly p. 36

DIFFERENTIATED INSTRUCTION

FOR LESS–PROFICIENT WRITERS

For Prompt A:

1. Have students write sentences describing Kutcher's interests and experience.
2. Suggest that students begin the paragraph with a generalization about Kutcher, such as "Steven Kutcher is a well-known bug trainer" or "Steven Kutcher knows bugs."
3. Instruct students to follow the generalization with the descriptive sentences they wrote, adding transitions as needed.

For Prompt B:

Suggest that students write a two-paragraph advertisement. The first paragraph should focus on information about the movie and the specific duties the person will perform. The second paragraph should list the job requirements.

Assess and Reteach

Assess

RESOURCE MANAGER—Copy Masters
Selection Tests A, B/C pp. 39–40, 41–42

Test Generator CD

Reteach

STANDARDS LESSON FILE
Informational Texts Lesson 1: Text Features
Research and Study Skills Lesson 13: Summarizing
Vocabulary Lesson 1: Word Parts

Focus and Motivate

OBJECTIVES

Elements of Nonfiction
- explore the key idea of **danger**
- interpret and evaluate graphic aids
- read a magazine article

Reading
- adjust reading rate to purpose (skim, scan, reread)

Vocabulary
- build vocabulary for reading and writing
- use word origins as an aid to understanding the historical influence on English word meaning *(also an EL language objective)*

SUMMARY

Carsten Peter is a photojournalist drawn to capturing images of dramatic events, such as volcanic eruptions. This article describes two of his adventures in pursuit of spectacular photographs: first, dropping into the rumbling crater of a volcano in the South Pacific; and second, exploring chambers formed by erupting volcanoes under Iceland's glaciers.

Why do people seek DANGER?

Discuss the question. To lead into the ***KEY IDEA,*** ask students why **danger** might be thrilling to some people and terrifying to others. As students work on the ***WEB IT*** activity, suggest the following examples of dangerous activities: race-car driving, tornado chasing, deep-sea diving, skateboarding, and spelunking (exploring caves).

Before Reading

Over the Top: The True Adventures of a Volcano Chaser

Magazine Article by Renee Skelton

Why do people seek DANGER?

KEY IDEA Most people avoid danger. They buckle their seat belts when they fly on a plane. They take care not to anger mean dogs, not to swim where there are sharks, not to walk on thin ice. But then there are other people—the ones who dream of skydiving and who soar through half-pipes on their skateboards. The man featured in the article you're about to read belongs to this group. He's willing to risk his life to photograph mysteries of the earth.

WEB IT What dangerous activities are also popular pastimes? What is it about these activities that makes people willing to risk their safety? Use a web to explore the reasons why these activities can be viewed as both fun and dangerous.

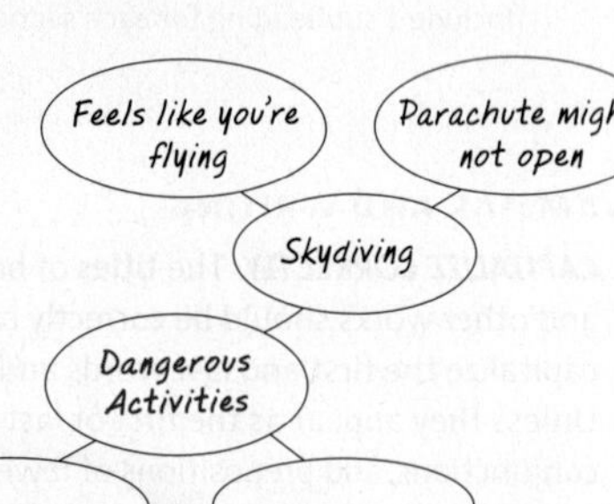

Selection Resources

RESOURCE MANAGER UNIT 8

Plan and Teach pp. 43–50

Elements of Nonfiction
Summary pp. 51†*, 52‡*
Graphic Aids pp. 53, 54†*
Question Support p. 61*

Reading
Adjust Reading Rate to Purpose pp. 55, 56†*
Reading Check p. 60
Reading Fluency p. 62

Vocabulary
Study p. 57*
Practice p. 58
Strategy p. 59

Assessment
Selection Tests A, B/C pp. 63*, 65*
Test Generator CD

BEST PRACTICES TOOLKIT
Differentiated Instruction pp. 31–38*
Scaffolding Instruction pp. 43–46*

Graphic Organizers/Strategies
New Word Analysis • Word Questioning • Venn Diagram

Reading Support
Audio Anthology CD*

Technology
Literature and Vocabulary Centers at **ClassZone.com**
Write*Smart* CD

* Resources for Differentiation † Also in Spanish ‡ In Haitian Creole and Vietnamese

LEMENTS OF NONFICTION: GRAPHIC AIDS

If you've read a magazine article lately, chances are you've come across a **graphic aid,** a visual representation of information. Writers use graphic aids to highlight or summarize important concepts and to explain things in fewer words. Common graphic aids include photographs, maps, diagrams, graphs, and timelines.

As you read "Over the Top: The True Adventures of a Volcano Chaser," note the graphic aids that are included. What do they help you understand? Take notes in a chart like the one shown.

Type of Graphic Aid	*What It Explains*

Review: **Text Features**

EADING STRATEGY: ADJUST READING RATE TO PURPOSE

Effective readers change the speed at which they read to suit their purpose. Try this as you read the following article.

When your purpose is to	Adjust your rate like this
Get an overview of the article	**Skim** before you begin. This involves **quickly** reading the title, subheadings, and any graphic aids.
Find key words or particular information	**Scan** the text. This involves moving your eyes **quickly** over the text, looking for the words or information you need.
Gain a full understanding of something, or clarify information	Read the material at a **slower** pace, and **reread** if necessary.

To use the best strategy for your purpose, stay mindful of why you're reading and whether you need to adjust your rate.

OCABULARY IN CONTEXT

The following vocabulary words help Renee Skelton tell about a man with a dangerous job. To see how many you know, match each word with its numbered synonym.

WORD LIST	cavernous	pinnacle	searing
	labyrinth	scale	straddle

1. climb **3.** top **5.** maze
2. vast **4.** span **6.** hot

Background

Renee Skelton: A Well-Versed Writer
Freelance writer Renee Skelton has written books and articles on topics ranging from American history to climate change. She lives in New Jersey and is a frequent contributor to *National Geographic Kids.*

Background

Sharing Science
National Geographic, first published in 1888, is one of the world's best-known magazines. It's especially known for its colorful, detailed photographs of geographic regions and the people who live there. The photos are taken by some of the world's best photojournalists, people who present a news story primarily through photographs. These men and women travel the globe with their cameras, seeking out fascinating and sometimes dangerous locations.

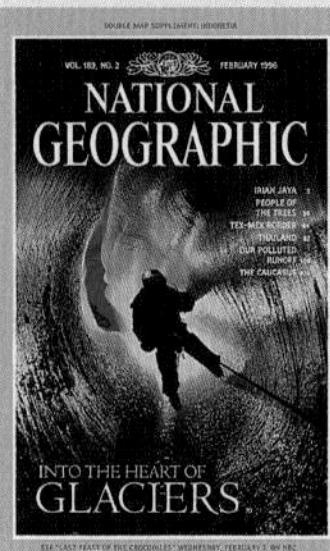

Exploring the Unknown In the article you are about to read, photojournalist Carsten Peter visits an active volcano and chambers beneath glacial ice. No stranger to dangerous situations, Peter has captured stunning images of glaciers, caves, and tornadoes for the pages of *National Geographic.* Why is he so attracted to the dangerous natural wonders he photographs? "I'm most interested in the unknown," he says.

BUILDING BACKGROUND
To learn more about Carsten Peter and *National Geographic*, visit the **Literature Center** at **ClassZone.com.**

895

Teach

STANDARDS FOCUS

ELEMENTS OF NONFICTION

● GRAPHIC AIDS

Ask students these questions:

- Would photographs be useful graphic aids in an article about telescopes? Why or why not? ***Possible answer:*** *Yes; they could show the telescopes themselves and also the images captured by the telescopes.*
- In what kind of article might you find a map? ***Possible answer:*** *an article about history, geography, or travel*

CHECK UNDERSTANDING Have students give examples of information that could be presented in a diagram, a timeline, or a graph.

RESOURCE MANAGER—Copy Master
Graphic Aids p. 53 (for student use while reading the selection)

READING STRATEGY

■ ADJUST READING RATE TO PURPOSE

Have students practice adjusting their reading rate while reading the **Background** on page 895. First have them identify their purpose. Then encourage them to skim the column, scan the text, and then read the full column more slowly.

CHECK UNDERSTANDING Have students tell what they learned from skimming the column, scanning the text, and then reading the full column more slowly.

VOCABULARY SKILL

▲ VOCABULARY IN CONTEXT

DIAGNOSE WORD KNOWLEDGE To determine preteaching needs, have all students complete **Vocabulary in Context.** ***Answers:*** **1.** *scale* **2.** *cavernous* **3.** *pinnacle* **4.** *straddle* **5.** *labyrinth* **6.** *searing*

PRETEACH VOCABULARY Use the Vocabulary Study copy master to help students determine the words they already know.

1. Read the first sentence in Part A aloud.
2. Guide students in creating a word map for *cavernous.* Point out that students may not be able to fill in every section of the map for every word.
3. Repeat for each of the other sentences.
4. Have students complete Part B independently.

RESOURCE MANAGER—Copy Master
Vocabulary Study p. 57

For general guidelines on differentiating vocabulary instruction and for alternative vocabulary activities for students not needing vocabulary preteaching, see

BEST PRACTICES TOOLKIT
Scaffolding Vocabulary Instruction pp. 43–46

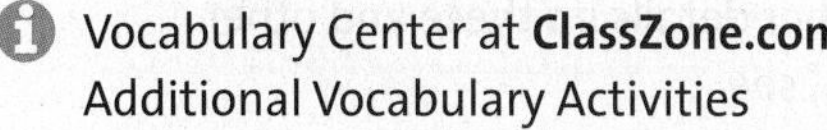

Vocabulary Center at **ClassZone.com**
Additional Vocabulary Activities

Practice and Apply

READING STRATEGY

A ADJUST READING RATE

Possible answer: *The article's title suggests that it will describe the adventures of a "volcano chaser." Students will read about the "Boiling Pit" (line 24) and the "Fire and Ice" (line 59) that this person has encountered. The photographs show that the "volcano chaser" is a photographer, and the map shows that he has traveled all over the world. Other graphic aids and accompanying captions provide both detailed and general information about volcanoes.*

REINFORCE *KEY IDEA:* DANGER

Discuss How far do the people in this photograph seem to be from the erupting volcano? What kind of **danger** might they be in? ***Possible answer:*** *They seem to be very close to the volcano. They might be in danger from the heat, lava, or ash.*

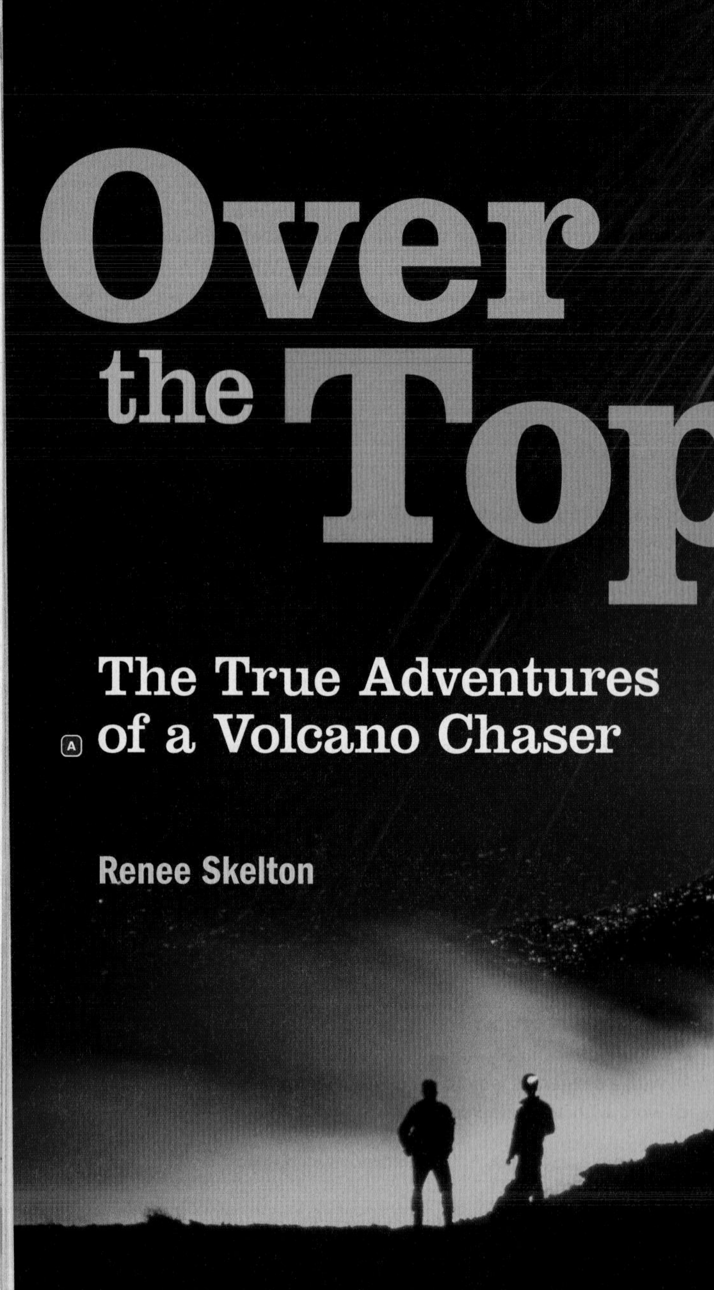

A ADJUST READING RATE
What can you expect to learn from this article? Take a minute to **skim** the selection and make some predictions about what you'll be reading.

896 UNIT 8: FACTS AND INFORMATION

DIFFERENTIATED INSTRUCTION

FOR ALL STUDENTS

Enhance Learning Styles Provide independent projects for various learning styles.

- **Visual** Create a photo exhibit.
- **Analytical** Research Iceland's geography.
- **Linguistic** Write a letter of application.

For further details on these and other projects, see

RESOURCE MANAGER
Ideas for Extension pp. 48–49

FOR LESS–PROFICIENT READERS

In combination with the *Audio Anthology CD,* use one or more Targeted Passages (pp. 898, 899, 901) to ensure that students focus on key events, concepts, and skills.

Comprehension Support Point out that the text on page 897, which begins with an oversized letter, is actually the first paragraph in the article. It does not look like the text in the rest of the article because it is part of the design of the spread. Read the paragraph to students, and ask them to tell how the writer gets readers' attention with this first paragraph. ***Possible answer:*** *She describes Carsten Peter's dangerous actions, what could possibly go wrong, and how terrifying these actions would be for most people.*

Dangling from a climber's rope, Carsten Peter slowly lowers himself into the fiery throat of Ambrym volcano. One slip, or a direct blast of hot, poisonous gas from the boiling lava lake below, and this descent could be his last. For most people this would have been terror time.

Ⓑ

Ⓑ **GRAPHIC AIDS**
What does this **photograph** suggest about what the article will focus on?

BACKGROUND

By the Numbers These facts about volcanoes emphasize their fascinating, destructive power:

- Mount St. Helens's 1980 explosion was heard from 200 miles away.
- 92,000 people died after the 1815 explosion of Tambora, a volcano in Indonesia, and the resulting tidal wave.
- About 20 feet of ash and pumice buried the city of Pompeii during the Mount Vesuvius eruption in A.D. 79.
- Approximately 24 volcanoes are erupting on Earth at any given time.

ELEMENTS OF NONFICTION

Ⓑ GRAPHIC AIDS

Have students record their answers in a chart like the one on page 895. ***Possible answer:***

Type of Graphic Aid	What It Explains
photograph on pages 896–897	It suggests that the article will describe the danger of photographing volcanoes up close.

FOR ENGLISH LEARNERS

Options for Reading Read the first Targeted Passage aloud. Make sure students understand that this article is about one person's experience with volcanoes and is not an article about volcanoes in general. Then have students read the rest of the selection silently as they listen to the *Audio Anthology CD.*

Key Academic Vocabulary Have students use New Word Analysis to study these words: *attached* (lines 35, 53), *device* (line 37), *intense* (line 47), *challenge* (line 61), *potential* (line 80), *region* (line 81).

 **BEST PRACTICES TOOLKIT—Transparency**
New Word Analysis p. E8

Prereading For prereading instruction for English learners, see

 **BEST PRACTICES TOOLKIT**
Scaffolding Reading Instruction pp. 43–46

FOR ADVANCED LEARNERS/PRE–AP

Pre-AP exercises in the bottom channel provide additional challenge for your advanced students. Use them for small groups or individuals.

ADDITIONAL GUIDELINES
For more help with differentiation and tips for classroom management, see

BEST PRACTICES TOOLKIT
Differentiated Instruction pp. 31–38

ELEMENTS OF NONFICTION

C GRAPHIC AIDS

Have students record their answers in a chart like the one on page 895. ***Possible answer:***

Type of Graphic Aid	What It Explains
map and caption on page 898	It shows some of the many places where Peter has explored volcanoes.

REINFORCE *KEY IDEA:* DANGER

Discuss Because he knows he will face **danger,** what precautions does Peter probably take when preparing for an expedition? ***Possible answer:*** *He probably assembles a skilled team, brings safety equipment and protective gear, and gets into shape for the physical challenges he will face.*

READING STRATEGY

D ADJUST READING RATE

Possible answer: *The tallest volcano on Earth is Mauna Kea, in Hawaii. It is 30,000 feet high.*

If students need help . . . As they scan the captions, have them look for the phrase *tallest volcano.*

Extend the Discussion In what way is scanning for specific information like using a search engine to search the Internet?

---

scale (skāl) *v.* to climb up or over; ascend

Targeted Passage ①

But for Peter it was all in a day's work. The daredevil photographer roams the world, **scaling** mountains and dropping into erupting volcanoes to photograph these fiery mountains at their most frightening—and most beautiful. Does he get scared? "Sure," Peter says. "You wouldn't be normal if you didn't get scared." But volcanoes are a window into Earth's scorching center. And for Peter, peering through that window with his camera is worth the risk.

Peter's adventures keep him globe-trotting. The map shows a few of the places he has explored volcanoes. C

C GRAPHIC AIDS
Look carefully at the **map** and its caption. What facts does it offer that you don't get from the text?

Into a Boiling Pit

Ambrym is a tiny South Pacific island that consists of a flat-topped volcano. The volcano erupted violently about 2,000 years ago. The explosion left the

Long Ago
Mount Vesuvius's[1] eruption in A.D. 79 buried two Roman cities, killing 16,000 people.

Loud
The 1883 explosion of Krakatoa, a volcano in Indonesia,[2] was heard 3,000 miles away.

Up There
Mauna Kea, in Hawaii, is the world's tallest volcano. It is 30,000 feet high.

Ring
Most volcanoes are concentrated around the edge of the Pacific Ocean, in the "Ring of Fire."

Blown Away
In mere seconds, whole forests of trees around Mount St. Helens,[3] Washington, were flattened in 1980. Trees 165 feet tall were blown down like toothpicks by the force of the volcano's eruption.

Out There
The biggest volcano in our solar system is Olympus Mons on Mars. It is 17 miles high. D

D ADJUST READING RATE
What is the tallest volcano on Earth? **Scan** these captions to find the answer.

1. **Mount Vesuvius** (vĭ-so͞o′vē-əs): a volcano located in southern Italy.
2. **Indonesia** (ĭn-dō-nē′zhə): an island nation located in Southeast Asia.
3. **Mount St. Helens:** volcano located in southern Washington state.

DIFFERENTIATED INSTRUCTION

FOR LESS–PROFICIENT READERS

① **Targeted Passage [Lines 9–23]**

This passage explains what motivates Peter to pursue his dangerous work.

- What does Peter do to get close enough to erupting volcanoes to photograph them?
- Does Peter ever feel frightened by the dangerous aspects of his work?
- What makes the danger of Peter's job worth the risk?

Review: Text Features Review text features with students. These include headings, subheadings, sidebars, and bulleted or numbered lists. Have students find examples of these text features in the article. Then ask them to study the yellow sidebar on this page. Point out the headings and the arrows, and explain that the arrows indicate which photographs illustrate which paragraphs.

FOR ADVANCED LEARNERS/PRE–AP

Evaluate the Writer's Style [small-group option] Have small groups evaluate the writer's style: How well does she use sensory details, suspense, and quotations to present Peter's story? Ask students to share their findings, using specific details as support.

seven-and-one-half-mile-wide caldera, or wide crater, that now forms its top. Peter hoped to use one of the vent openings in Ambrym's caldera as a porthole into the volcano's fiery center.

When Peter arrived at Ambrym, the volcano was rumbling, its craters belching steam, gas, and ash. He and his group set out right away, hacking through dense jungle and climbing 4,000 feet up the side of the volcano. They emerged from the jungle onto the caldera's rim—a moonscape of boulders and gray-black ash.

After several days of exploring the caldera's surface, Peter decided to descend into Marum, one of Ambrym's pitlike craters. Wearing protective gear, he attached one end of a climbing rope to an anchor hammered into the ground and the other end to his descent device. Peter then disappeared over the edge of Marum's clifflike rim, camera equipment mounted on his helmet and tethered to his back and waist. Peter descended 1,000 feet down the face of the crater's steep walls, as heat rising from the **searing** lava lake blasted him. Pockets of gas and water trapped in the lava expanded and exploded, sending out booms that echoed and shook the crater walls. "The Earth was trembling all around me," Peter says. "And I felt the vibrations all through my body." **E**

Peter had to be careful. A sharp rock could have cut his rope, dropping him into the **cavernous** pit. Tremors[4] could have pried boulders from the cliff above, sending them crashing down on an arm or leg. Peter paused partway down, clutching the rope as volcanic ash stung his eyes and intense heat and sound from the blasting lava rose around him. "If the volcano had exploded then, it would have been the last eruption I ever saw," he says. He drew as close as possible to the spitting, belching lava lake at the bottom. Glowing lava bombs were bursting like fireworks from its surface as Peter snapped photos all night.

4. **tremors** (trĕm'ərz): shaking or vibrating of the earth.

Peter captures images of the 2002 eruption of Mount Etna in Sicily.

searing (sîr'ĭng) *adj.* hot enough to burn, char, or scorch

② Targeted Passage

E ADJUST READING RATE
What steps did Peter take to safely descend into the crater? Reread lines 34–40 and note Peter's process.

cavernous (kăv'ər-nəs) *adj.* as deep or vast as a cavern, or a large cave

READING STRATEGY

E ADJUST READING RATE

Possible answer:

- *First, Peter and his team hiked around the volcano, exploring the surface to find a safe place for Peter's descent.*
- *Then, Peter decided to descend into Marum, one of Ambrym's craters.*
- *Next, he put on protective gear, attached himself to a climbing rope that was anchored into the ground, and lowered himself into the crater.*

Lines 30–51
DISCUSSION PROMPTS

Use these prompts to help students explore the actions Peter takes to obtain his photographs:

Recall Why did Peter climb into the crater of the volcano? ***Answer:*** *He wanted to take photographs of the volcano from the inside.*

Infer What kind of help do you think Peter's group provided on this expedition? ***Possible answer:*** *They probably helped him take care of his equipment, explored the caldera's surface with him, and helped him decide where and when to descend into the crater. They would also have helped him if he'd had trouble climbing in or out of the crater.*

Evaluate Why do you think the writer quotes Peter throughout the article? ***Possible answer:*** *She interviewed Peter for the article, and she uses quotations from her interview to show readers exactly what Peter is thinking as he pursues life-threatening activities.*

FOR LESS–PROFICIENT READERS

② **Targeted Passage [Lines 34–51]**

This passage provides an example of the kind of dangerous risk that Peter takes.

- Where does Peter decide to enter into Ambrym?
- How far down into the crater does he descend? What does he see, hear, and feel there?
- What does he do after he gets as close as he can to the surface of the lava?

FOR ENGLISH LEARNERS

Vocabulary: Suffixes [mixed-readiness pairs] Point out the words *pitlike* (line 35) and *clifflike* (line 38). Explain that the suffix *-like,* when added to a noun, creates an adjective that makes a comparison. In these examples, the volcano's craters are compared to pits, and the rim of a crater is compared to a cliff. Have students work with more fluent partners to create adjectives using the suffix *-like* with nouns from the selection.

FOR ADVANCED LEARNERS/PRE–AP

Write Descriptive Sentences [paired option] Have students find active verbs used on this page to describe the volcano (*rumbling, belching, blasted, expanded, exploded, trembling, spitting, bursting*). To give students practice writing descriptive sentences with vivid verbs, challenge them to write a short paragraph using as many of these words as they can. Then have students share their paragraphs with a partner.

ELEMENTS OF NONFICTION: *Review*

F TEXT FEATURES

Possible answer: *The subheading helps readers predict that the section will describe volcanoes in cold climates.*

ELEMENTS OF NONFICTION

G GRAPHIC AIDS

Have students record their answers in a chart like the one on page 895. ***Possible answer:***

Type of Graphic Aid	*What It Explains*
diagram on page 900	*It shows the heat and energy that gather in the mantle and crust. It helps readers visualize Peter's position, which is just above the conduit through which the lava bursts when the volcano explodes.*

ELEMENTS OF NONFICTION

H GRAPHIC AIDS

Have students record their answers in a chart like the one on page 895. ***Possible answer:***

Type of Graphic Aid	*What It Explains*
photos and captions on pages 900–901	*They show how dangerous Peter's career is because he is willing to get so close to unpredictable natural forces. They also show that his photography is beautiful and unique.*

The next morning, exhausted, Peter attached his rope and pulled himself up to safety on Marum's rim. It was time to leave Ambrym for new adventures.

F TEXT FEATURES
Based on this **subheading**, what can you predict about the content of this section?

Fire and Ice F

Half a world away in Iceland,[5] the challenge was more ice than fire. Because of Iceland's location, many volcanoes are hidden below its thick glacial ice. Iceland **straddles** the mid-Atlantic ridge, where two of the plates that form Earth's crust are pulling apart. The results are frequent tremors and volcanic eruptions. When volcanoes under Iceland's glaciers erupt, they burn through ice at the glacier's base. Escaping heat carves out spectacular formations under the ice.

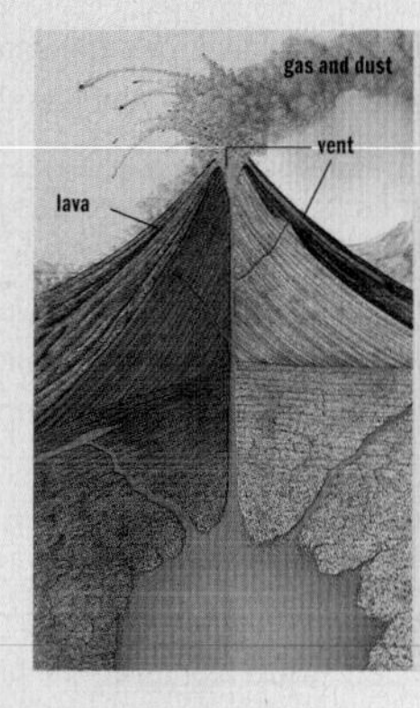

Signs That "It's Gonna Blow!"

1. In and around a volcano, the frequency and intensity of earthquakes increase.
2. The ground at the eruption site deforms or bulges.
3. The amount of gas released by the volcano increases.

G

G GRAPHIC AIDS
What does this **diagram** add to your understanding of the danger Peter faces while photographing Ambrym?

straddle (străd'l) *v.* to be on both sides of

5. **Iceland:** an island nation located in the North Atlantic Ocean near the Arctic Circle.

H Intense heat from a volcano created this ice cave inside a glacier in Iceland.

H GRAPHIC AIDS
What do these **photos** and captions add to your understanding of Peter's career?

DIFFERENTIATED INSTRUCTION

FOR LESS–PROFICIENT READERS

Reading Strategy Follow-Up: Adjust Reading Rate to Purpose Have students skim pages 900–901, quickly reading the subheading and examining the graphic aids to get an overview of the content. Then have them scan the "Fire and Ice" section to find out what Peter's goal was while in Iceland. Finally, have students read this section at a slower pace to gain a full understanding of the dangers Peter faced. Remind them to refer to the chart on page 895 to clarify the strategy.

FOR ENGLISH LEARNERS

Vocabulary Support Use Word Questioning to teach the following vocabulary:

- *glacial* (line 65), "freezing"
- *ridge* (line 65), "a long narrow chain of hills or mountains"
- *tremors* (line 67), "shaking movements"
- *carves out* (line 68), "cuts out"
- *spectacular* (line 69), "impressive"

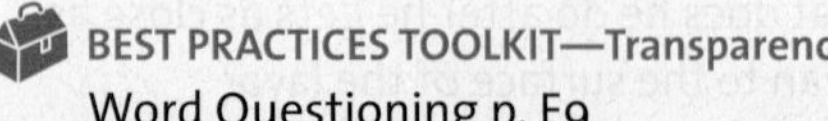

BEST PRACTICES TOOLKIT—Transparency
Word Questioning p. E9

Peter's goal was to photograph these underground wonders. After a jolting jeep ride over part of the glacier, Peter continued on foot—leaping crevasses, sloshing through icy rivers of meltwater, and scrambling over jagged ice **pinnacles**. "The heat created chambers inside the ice we were passing over," says Peter. "We had to be very careful." Peter found that out the hard way. Crossing an area of ice that looked solid, Peter stepped on a thin section and crashed through into a hidden river of icy water. He struggled to keep his head and cameras above water. The cameras didn't make it. Luckily Peter did, thanks to two friends who pulled him out of the frigid water.

Exploring the surface ice, Peter discovered a collapsed ice chamber that led to a **labyrinth** of ice caves and tunnels inside the glacier. "It was beautiful, but we were in potential danger because the chamber could have collapsed at any time," Peter says. "Also, we were in a region where earthquakes and floods are common occurrences." But using carbide[6] lights to illuminate the dark tunnels, Peter took incredible photos of the formations in the glacier's frozen heart. **1**

As you read this, Peter is probably perched on the rim of another volcano, camera in hand. He's withstanding heat from 2,200 degrees Fahrenheit lava flows and dodging deadly clouds of gas to get close to nature at its most extreme. Earth's geology continues to fascinate him. "Volcanoes are very powerful," he says. "When you feel these eruptions, it's the greatest experience you can have."

pinnacle (pĭn'ə-kəl) *n.* a peak; a pointed top

③ Targeted Passage

labyrinth (lăb'ə-rĭnth') *n.* a maze; an intricate structure of interconnected passages

1 ADJUST READING RATE
What three things posed a danger to Peter as he explored the ice chamber? **Scan** lines 78–82 to find the answer.

6. **carbide** (kär'bīd'): a very hard material made partly of carbon.

Peter lowers himself through a heat vent in Iceland's Grímsvötn volcano.

READING STRATEGY

1 ADJUST READING RATE

Possible answer: *Three dangerous things are earthquakes, floods, and the fact that the chamber could collapse at any time.*

SELECTION WRAP-UP

REFLECT Ask students if they would enjoy accompanying Peter on his expeditions. Why or why not?

CRITIQUE Discuss the graphic aids in the article. Did the article have a good balance between graphic aids and text?

READING FLUENCY

Distribute the copy masters and have students practice fluency.

RESOURCE MANAGER—Copy Master
Reading Fluency p. 62

FOR LESS-PROFICIENT READERS

③ Targeted Passage [Lines 70–83]

This passage describes the dangers Peter encounters in Iceland.

- Why does Peter have to be careful as he crosses the ice? What dangers does he encounter?
- What does Peter find under the surface ice?
- Why is the ice chamber dangerous?

FOR ADVANCED LEARNERS/PRE-AP

Synthesize Have students list ideas for a poem based on the photographs in the article.

Compare and Contrast Have students use a Venn Diagram to compare and contrast the two expeditions described in the article.

BEST PRACTICES TOOLKIT—Transparency
Venn Diagram p. A26

Possible answer:

- ***Ambrym:*** *volcanic crater; hot*
- ***Both:*** *below the surface; life-threatening; Peter accompanied by others; took incredible photographs*
- ***Iceland:*** *ice chambers; cold; falls into icy water*

Practice and Apply

After Reading

Comprehension

1. **Recall** What could have killed or injured Carsten Peter as he photographed inside the Ambrym volcano?
2. **Recall** What did Peter go to Iceland to photograph?
3. **Represent** Using the information provided by the captions on page 898, draw a simple timeline that shows the order in which three famous volcanoes erupted.

Critical Analysis

4. **Analyze Reading Rate** What part of the article did you read most quickly? When did you have to change your reading rate? Explain which strategy you found most useful as you read.
5. **Draw Conclusions** Why do you think Carsten Peter feels it is important to photograph volcanoes in spite of the **danger** involved?
6. **Compare and Contrast** In what ways are the careers of Steven Kutcher ("The Spider Man Behind *Spider-Man*," page 886) and Carsten Peter alike? In what ways are they different? Complete a Y-chart like the one shown to compare and contrast the two men and their careers. Record the differences in the top part of the Y, and the similarities in the bottom.

Kutcher
Peter
Similarities

7. **Evaluate Graphic Aids** Look back at the chart you made as you read. What information do you get from the graphic aids? Would this information have been more or less clear if it had been included with the main text but without any visuals? Explain.

Extension and Challenge

8. **Readers' Circle** Carsten Peter obviously believes that the risks he takes are worth the results. Imagine that he is a member of your family, such as your brother, uncle, or father. Would you support his choices, or would you urge him to find a safer career? Discuss your ideas.
9. **SCIENCE CONNECTION** How are volcanoes formed? What causes them to erupt? Research these questions about volcanoes, and ask one additional question of your own. Present your findings to the class in the form of a "slide show," either on paper or the computer.

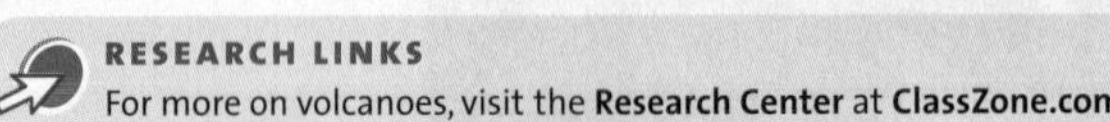

RESEARCH LINKS
For more on volcanoes, visit the Research Center at ClassZone.com.

After Reading

For additional support of postreading questions, use these copy masters:

RESOURCE MANAGER—Copy Masters

Reading Check p. 60 (to check understanding of the selection)

Adjust Reading Rate to Purpose p. 55 (for practice of reading standards focus)

Question Support p. 61 (After Reading questions adapted for English learners and less-proficient readers)

Additional selection questions are provided for teachers on page 47.

ANSWERS

Comprehension

1. *A sharp rock could have cut Peter's rope, sending him falling into the lava. Falling boulders could have crushed his arm or leg. The volcano also could have exploded at any time.*
2. *Peter went to Iceland to photograph the ice formations that are carved into the glaciers by heat from underground volcanoes.*
3. *Timelines should show the names and eruption dates of the volcanoes mentioned in captions: Mount Vesuvius, A.D. 79; Krakatoa, 1883; Mount St. Helens, 1980.*

Critical Analysis

Possible answers:

4. **● STANDARDS FOCUS Adjust Reading Rate to Purpose** *Students should refer to specific strategies listed in the chart on page 895 and explain which ones they found most useful.*
5. *Peter probably feels that it is important for people to learn about volcanoes and the only way most people can see what is happening under the surface of the earth is through photography.*
6. *Students should provide this information: Kutcher trains insects for movies, works on movie sets, teaches people about bugs, and has an education in entomology. Peter photographs volcanoes, travels all over the world, seeks adventure. Similarities: Both men encounter danger in their careers. Their careers are unique. They entertain and inform people through their work.*
7. **● STANDARDS FOCUS Graphic Aids** *Students may say the graphic aids helped them visualize the information in the main text. If the information had just been presented as text within the article, it would not have been as clear.*

Extension and Challenge

8. *Suggest that students scan the article to find Peter's explanations about why he likes to do what he does. Have them take these explanations into account as they respond to the question.*
9. **SCIENCE CONNECTION** *When choosing an additional question, students might review the photographs of volcanoes and the descriptions of Peter's adventures. Encourage students to incorporate visuals in their presentations.*

ocabulary in Context

OCABULARY PRACTICE

For each item, choose the word that differs most in meaning from the other words. Refer to a dictionary if you need help.

1. (a) searing, (b) scorching, (c) frigid, (d) sweltering
2. (a) descend, (b) scale, (c) climb, (d) ascend
3. (a) slant, (b) tilt, (c) straddle, (d) lean
4. (a) maze, (b) labyrinth, (c) network, (d) beeline
5. (a) gaping, (b) shallow, (c) deep, (d) cavernous
6. (a) pinnacle, (b) bottom, (c) base, (d) foot

OCABULARY IN WRITING

Using at least two vocabulary words, write a paragraph about a daring sport or exciting hobby that you've tried or want to try. You might start like this.

EXAMPLE SENTENCE

*I was terrified as we climbed slowly to the **pinnacle** of the mountain.*

OCABULARY STRATEGY: WORD ORIGINS

Many common words in the English language have interesting histories. For example, the vocabulary word *scale* comes from the Latin word *scalae,* meaning "ladder." It makes sense, then, that to scale something means to climb it.

You can find a word's **etymology,** or the history of the word, in most dictionaries. Understanding etymologies can help you connect the word's meaning to something you already know. Here is an example of an etymology:

expand (ĭk-spănd') *v.* to become greater in size, quantity, volume, or scope [Middle English *expanden,* to spread out, from Latin *expandere: ex- + pandere,* to spread]

PRACTICE Look up the etymology of each word in the dictionary. Write the word's origin, and tell how knowing the word's history can help you remember its meaning.

1. intense
2. grief
3. sparse
4. glacier
5. danger

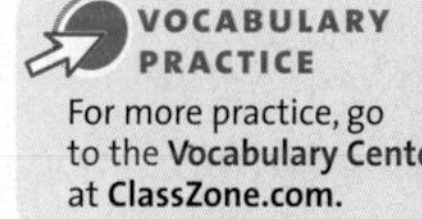
VOCABULARY PRACTICE
For more practice, go to the **Vocabulary Center** at **ClassZone.com.**

DIFFERENTIATED INSTRUCTION

FOR ENGLISH LEARNERS

Vocabulary Practice Make sure students know how to pronounce the vocabulary words in the lesson. Point out that English—unlike some other languages—has few rules for stressing syllables, and that students can find pronunciation information in a dictionary. Review how to interpret stress marks in a pronunciation.

FOR ADVANCED LEARNERS/PRE–AP

Vocabulary Strategy Challenge students to use a dictionary to find the origins of words in the instructions for this activity—for example, *language, vocabulary, climb, history,* and *dictionary.* Have them discuss how they can connect the etymologies of these words to something they already know.

ANSWERS

Vocabulary in Context

VOCABULARY PRACTICE

1. *(c) frigid*
2. *(a) descend*
3. *(c) straddle*
4. *(d) beeline*
5. *(b) shallow*
6. *(a) pinnacle*

RESOURCE MANAGER—Copy Master
Vocabulary Practice p. 58

VOCABULARY IN WRITING

Explain that the words do not necessarily have to be used literally. For example, *labyrinth* could be used to describe a complex process.

VOCABULARY STRATEGY: WORD ORIGINS

(also an EL language objective)

Explain that many words can have a single origin. For example, the word *intense,* which has a Latin origin, is related to the words *intensity, intensify,* and *intensive.*

Possible answers:

1. *intense*—Latin, *intensus* ("stretched," "intent")
2. *grief*—Middle English, *grever* ("to harm"), from Latin, *gravāre* ("to burden")
3. *sparse*—Latin, *sparsus* ("scattered")
4. *glacier*—Old French, *glace* ("ice")
5. *danger*—Middle English, *daunger* ("power," "peril"), from Latin *dominus* ("lord," "master")

RESOURCE MANAGER—Copy Master
Vocabulary Strategy p. 59

Vocabulary Center at **ClassZone.com**
Additional Vocabulary Activities

Assess and Reteach

Assess

RESOURCE MANAGER—Copy Masters
Selection Tests A, B/C pp. 63–64, 65–66

Test Generator CD

Reteach

STANDARDS LESSON FILE
Informational Texts Lessons 1, 21–24
Vocabulary Lesson 25

Focus and Motivate

OBJECTIVES

Media Literacy

- explore the key idea of **quotes** in news reports
- identify formats of news reports
- interpret how events and information are presented in news reports
- compare how different media cover the same event
- create an interview plan

SUMMARY

Both the TV newscast "Deep Impact" and the magazine article "A Grand Slam" are about NASA's launching of a space probe to hit a comet and gather information about it. The TV newscast includes footage of the comet explosion, sound bites from scientists involved in the project, and an interview with a CBS News space analyst. The magazine article provides a description of the experiment, supported by direct and paraphrased quotes from scientists involved in the project.

What's the SOURCE?

Discuss the question. Ask students to name sources they consult for information about current events. Then talk about sources used by reporters to create news stories. Have students read the ***KEY IDEA*** paragraph. Discuss the purpose of **quotes** in news reporting, and ask students what quotes from different sources add to a news report.

BACKGROUND

A comet is a small object that orbits the sun. When a comet gets close enough to the sun, icy materials at its center, or nucleus, are vaporized. This is what gives comets their characteristic feature—an envelope of dust particles and gases that sometimes form long "tails." Today, air pollution and bright lights make comets challenging to view from Earth without telescopes. In ancient times, however, bright comets were clearly visible and were subjects of both fascination and confusion. Because they appeared suddenly and unexpectedly, people often feared them and saw them as signs of impending trouble.

Media Study

News Reports

TV Newscast Clip/Magazine Article on *MediaSmart* DVD

What's the SOURCE?

KEY IDEA Recall a time you watched a TV news report in which someone was making statements to a reporter. What was the circumstance? Did the statements appear to be ones you could trust? In news reporting, it's not just the events that matter but what people have to say about them. In this lesson, you'll see how **quotes** can help you fully understand a news event.

Background

Fireworks in Space July 4, 2005, was a day of celebration at the National Aeronautics and Space Administration (NASA). As part of a major mission called "Deep Impact," NASA launched a space probe that hit a comet so hard, it burrowed through its surface—then exploded. Scientists and engineers cheered as the probe's nearby mother ship transmitted images of the spectacular event. NASA realized it had gathered a wealth of scientific data about the comet that would help in future research.

To explore how news reporters gather and support their facts, you'll watch a TV newscast and read a magazine article that cover this remarkable event.

904

Media Study Resources

RESOURCE MANAGER UNIT 8

Plan and Teach pp. 67–70

Media Analysis

Summary pp. 71†*, 72‡*
Viewing Guide p. 73
Close Viewing p. 74
Media Activity p. 75
Produce Your Own Media p. 76

STANDARDS LESSON FILE

Media Lessons 8, 9, 10, 11, 12

Media Center at **ClassZone.com**

MEDIA VIEWING

 Media*Smart* DVD

* Resources for Differentiation † Also in Spanish ‡ In Haitian Creole and Vietnamese

Media Literacy: Sources in the News

In the world of news, a **source** is a person who provides information for a news report. A reporter usually uses one or more sources while creating a news report. In printed news, the reporter includes **quotations,** the words spoken by the sources to the reporter. In a TV or radio newscast, the quoted statements are called **sound bites,** which are edited from interviews with the sources. Here are the types of sources usually quoted in the news.

TYPES OF SOURCES

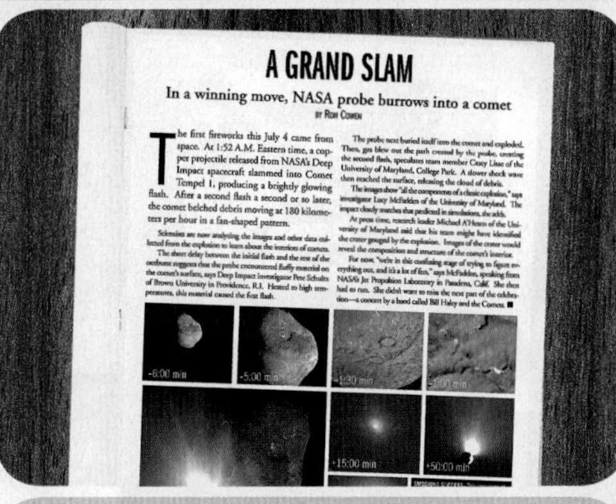

A GRAND SLAM

In a winning move, NASA probe burrows into a comet

BY RON COWEN

The first fireworks this July 4 came from space. At 1:52 A.M. Eastern time, a copper projectile released from NASA's Deep Impact spacecraft slammed into Comet Tempel 1, producing a brightly glowing flash. After a second flash a second or so later, the comet belched debris moving at 180 kilometers per hour in a fan-shaped pattern.

Scientists are now analyzing the images and other data collected from the explosion to learn about the interiors of comets.

The short delay between the initial flash and the rest of the outburst suggests that the probe encountered fluffy material on the comet's surface, says Deep Impact investigator Pete Schultz of Brown University in Providence, R.I. Heated to high temperatures, this material caused the first flash.

The probe next buried itself into the comet and exploded. Then, gas blew out the path created by the probe, creating the second flash, speculates team member Carey Lisse of the University of Maryland, College Park. A slower shock wave then reached the surface, releasing the cloud of debris.

The images show "all the components of a classic explosion," says investigator Lucy McFadden of the University of Maryland. The impact closely matches that predicted in simulations, she adds.

At press time, research leader Michael A'Hearn of the University of Maryland said that his team might have identified the crater gouged by the explosion. Images of the crater would reveal the composition and structure of the comet's interior.

For now, "we're in this confusing stage of trying to figure everything out, and it's a lot of fun," says McFadden, speaking from NASA's Jet Propulsion Laboratory in Pasadena, Calif. She then had to run. She didn't want to miss the next part of the celebration—a concert by a band called Bill Haley and the Comets. ■

-6:00 min | -5:00 min | -1:30 min | -1:00 min | +15:00 min | +50:00 min

Witnesses
These are the people who are present at the time of an event or who are directly affected by it.

Experts
Often experts are quoted after an event occurs. They're qualified to share their knowledge about what happened.

Officials
These sources are authority figures, those who represent the government, a business, and so on.

Sources as Counterpoints
One source may give one side of an event or an issue. In the same report, another source may have a very different view.

STRATEGIES FOR ANALYZING SOURCES

- Identify a source by name and determine his or her role.
- Question why a source is included in a news report. Ask yourself: What is this source helping me to understand about the event?
- Be aware that what you're hearing or reading is not the entire interview. Think about how the sound bites or quotations support certain facts.
- In reports that include countering or opposing sources, check to see that the two sides are **balanced** or are represented equally. It's important that a news report be neutral and fair to all sides.

MEDIA STUDY: TEACHING OPTIONS

Teaching Option 1: The Basics (1–2 Days)

1. Begin the Media Study using the material provided on pages 904–905.
2. Show the Introduction on Media*Smart*. Have students use the Viewing Guide on page 906, along with the corresponding copy master on page 73 of the Resource Manager. Discuss their responses.
3. Return to the pupil's edition for the extension activities on page 907.

Teaching Option 2: In-Depth Study (2–3 Days)

1. Begin the Media Study using pages 904–905.
2. Show the Introduction and First Viewing from Media*Smart*.
3. Continue on Media*Smart* with the Media Lessons, using the teacher notes.
4. Show the Guided Analysis presentation. Have students record their observations on the Student Viewing Guide available in the Resources section from Media*Smart*.
5. Return to the pupil's edition, page 907.

Teach

MEDIA LITERACY

Review the role of **sources** in the news. Mention two or three general news topics—such as the aftermath of a natural disaster, the results of a close election, or the closing of a museum or library due to lack of funds. Ask students to suggest types of sources that might be included in credible news stories about these topics. Then discuss the chart on page 905.

- **Sources in TV Newscasts** Ask students to discuss ways in which sound bites are incorporated into TV news reports. You might have students role-play sound bites on various topics, such as school lunches, local weather, or another topic they know about or have a strong opinion about.
- **Effect of Sound Bites** Discuss why it is useful to see and hear a source speaking about a topic. Explain that sound bites can be used to express emotions—such as sadness or excitement—that surround a particular event. Viewers can also make judgments based on the tone or behavior of a witness, official, or expert featured in a sound bite.
- **Sources in Print News** Read aloud a brief portion of a newspaper, magazine, or online news article that contains quoted statements. To demonstrate the power of the quotations, read the excerpt once without the quotes and a second time with the quotes.
- **Effect of Quotes** Ask students why quotes from sources might improve print news reports and make them more believable, even if the writer already includes all the necessary information in the text. Discuss the impact of using sources as counterpoints.

  You might also mention that a writer sometimes includes descriptive details about how something was said or what the speaker was doing as he or she made a statement. For example, "'We've never seen anything like this before,' she said excitedly as she pointed to the sky." Or, "'This event really brings the community together,' the mayor shouted over the noise of the crowd."

MediaSmart DVD

Practice and Apply

VIEWING GUIDE

1. As students prepare to view the TV news clip and read the magazine article, explain to them that they will be asked to examine the types of sources used in both pieces. Encourage students to observe these elements:
   - how **sources** are used to support specific information
   - the effect of **sound bites** and their placement in the newscast
   - the article's use of **quotations** to support ideas and provide information
2. Suggest that students watch the newscast and read the article more than once. The first reading or viewing should be for the purpose of gathering general information about the event. Then, students should study each piece more closely, focusing on its use of sources. Encourage students to take notes as they encounter and analyze sound bites and quotes.

RESOURCE MANAGER—Copy Masters
Viewing Guide p. 73
Close Viewing p. 74
Media Activity p. 75

MediaSmart DVD

ANSWERS

***FIRST VIEWING:* Comprehension**

1. *The animation is remarkable because it closely matches what actually happened, despite the fact that scientists were not certain when they created it exactly what would happen.*
2. *The article identifies Pete Schultz as a Deep Impact investigator from Brown University.*

***CLOSE VIEWING:* Media Literacy**

Possible answers:

3. *The sound bites support the factual information that is presented. The people speaking also expand on the information and express why the results of the experiment are exciting and important.*
4. *The writer may have wanted to include only the most essential scientific facts from each person's interview, or to rephrase technical language in simpler terms that would be comprehensible to his audience.*
5. *Possible chart entries are provided. Students may note that the pieces feature some of the same sources, relying mostly on people involved with the mission. Only the TV newscast includes independent analysis by a person not directly involved in the project.*

	Sources
"Deep Impact"	• Peter Schultz, Deep Impact co-investigator • Mike A'Hearn, Deep Impact principal investigator • Bill Harwood, CBS News space analyst
"A Grand Slam"	• Pete Schultz, Deep Impact investigator • team member Casey Lisse • investigator Lucy McFadden • research leader Michael A'Hearn

MediaSmart DVD

- **News Format 1:** "Deep Impact"
- **Reporter:** Bill Whitaker
- **Genre:** TV newscast
- **Running Time:** 2.5 minutes
- **News Format 2:** "A Grand Slam"
- **Reporter:** Ron Cowen
- **Genre:** Magazine article

Viewing Guide for
News Reports

You'll watch the CBS network news report that first aired at the tim of the event. Then you'll read an article that appeared a few days later in the weekly newsmagazine *Science News.* As you examine each one, look for the people who make statements. Take notes about the sources or about any striking feature of each format. Answer these questions to help analyze the news reports.

NOW VIEW

***FIRST VIEWING:* Comprehension**

1. **Clarify** NASA had created an animated model, or simulation, of the comet explosion. According to the TV newscast, what makes the simulation remarkable?
2. **Recall** Which one of the sources is an investigator from Brown University?

***CLOSE VIEWING:* Media Literacy**

3. **Analyze TV Sources** In the "Deep Impact" news report, each **sound bite** is included after a certain amount of factual information is presented. Why do you think the news report is edited in this way?
4. **Analyze Print Sources** The sources who are quoted in the magazine article are quoted directly or are **paraphrased.** This means the reporter has restated what he was told in his own words. In a science-related article, why might he have chosen to paraphrase?
5. **Compare News Sources** Use a chart like this to identify and compare the types of sources of both news reports.

	Sources
"Deep Impact"	
"A Grand Slam"	

906

Write or Discuss

Evaluate Sources You encountered a number of sources in the TV newscast and in the magazine article. Now choose one of the news reports and make your own statement. In a short paragraph, tell how effectively you think the sources are used. Consider:

- what types of individuals are used as sources
- your basic impressions of these sources
- what the sources helped you to understand in the news report

Produce Your Own Media

Create an Interview Plan In small groups, brainstorm at least three possible news stories to cover in your school or neighborhood. Once these are determined, imagine you're a team of reporters preparing to interview different sources for the news reports. Use your ideas to help you create an **interview plan.** This plan will help you to determine the most likely people to contact for an interview. It can also help you prepare interview questions.

HERE'S HOW To help you devise your interview plan, use these tips.

- For this planning stage, list the possible sources. Jot down a detail that describes that person's connection to the news story.
- For each source, jot down questions that you think would clearly relate to the news story.
- Try to create questions that are open-ended. The best sound bites start with questions like these. Avoid questions that lead to a simple "yes" or "no" response.

STUDENT MODEL

Possible News Stories:
• *the opening of a school's time capsule from 1990*
• *the new neighborhood garden project*
Sources:
Mr. Camacho—He originally installed the time capsule.
Ms. Evans—School principal
Tara Sebring and Jamal Humphrey—They've assembled a new capsule.
Possible Questions:
• *Why now for opening the capsule?*
• *Will there be some sort of ceremony to mark the opening?*
• *What does the new capsule contain?*

MEDIA TOOLS

For help with creating a interview plan, visit the **Media Center** at **ClassZone.com.**

Tech Tip

If available, record your interview plans as electronic files.

Assess and Reteach

Write or Discuss

Evaluate Sources Encourage students to begin by reviewing the news report that will be their focus. Students can make a chart to organize their information and ideas about various sources in the piece. A student focusing on the TV newscast might mention that sound bites from people involved in the mission helped them understand its importance and appreciate the excitement surrounding it. A student focusing on the magazine article might mention that paraphrased quotes from Pete Schulz and Michael A'Hearn reveal key information. Direct quotes by investigator Lucy McFadden help readers understand scientists' eagerness to analyze all the new information the mission has made available to them.

Produce Your Own Media

Rubric A strong interview plan should include

- descriptions of three possible news stories
- a list of possible sources
- questions for each source that relate clearly to the news story
- questions that are open-ended to encourage strong sound bites and quotes

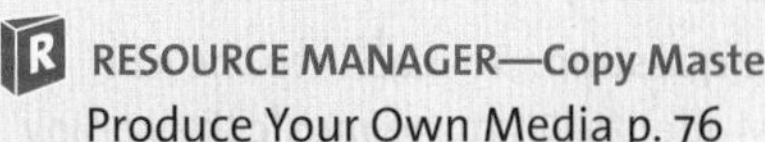
RESOURCE MANAGER—Copy Master
Produce Your Own Media p. 76

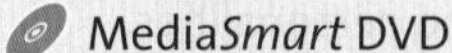
Media*Smart* DVD

MEDIA STUDY WRAP-UP

Summarize Ask students to summarize the types of sources used in news reports and the ways in which sources are used. Encourage them to refer to specific examples from the TV newscast "Deep Impact" and the magazine article "A Grand Slam." If necessary, guide them to discuss the use and placement of sound bites and quotations in the pieces. For example, students might point out that each sound bite in "Deep Impact" supports and expands on a certain amount of factual information.

RETEACH

STANDARDS LESSON FILE

Media Lesson 8: Understanding the Basics of News Reporting
Media Lesson 9: Analyzing TV News
Media Lesson 10: Analyzing Print and Online News
Media Lesson 11: Comparing News Formats
Media Lesson 12: Evaluating News Reports

Focus and Motivate

OBJECTIVES

Elements of Nonfiction
- explore the key idea of **music**
- identify and analyze the characteristics and content of an interview
- read an interview

Reading
- distinguish between fact and opinion

Vocabulary
- build vocabulary for reading and writing
- distinguish between connotative and denotative meanings of words *(also an EL language objective)*

SUMMARY

In this interview, ethnomusicologist Henrietta Yurchenco describes the beginning of her career in Mexico, the challenges she has faced, and what she has learned about the way music bridges differences between people who don't understand each other's languages. She also discusses the political aspect of music and the continued importance of making field recordings.

What does MUSIC *say about us?*

Discuss the question. To lead into the ***KEY IDEA,*** ask students what the **music** they enjoy says about their tastes and personalities. As students work on the ***CHART IT*** activity, encourage them to give reasons to support or refute each statement.

Before Reading

Interview with a Songcatcher

Interview by Brian Handwerk

What does MUSIC *say about us?*

KEY IDEA Imagine someone you've never met, who knows nothing about you but your three favorite songs. What could she guess about you based on this information? Could she tell what you think is important? what makes you happy? what makes you sad? In the following interview, journalist Brian Handwerk talks to a woman who has made a career of learning about other people through their **music.**

CHART IT Copy this chart in a notebook. Then decide whether you agree or disagree with each statement. After you read "Interview with a Songcatcher," you'll revisit this chart.

Anticipation Guide

	Before Reading	*After Reading*
People with different tastes in music probably don't have much else in common.		
The words of a song are not as important as the melody.		
Politics and social conditions have little impact on a culture's music.		

908

Selection Resources

RESOURCE MANAGER UNIT 8

Plan and Teach pp. 77–84

Elements of Nonfiction
Summary pp. 85†*, 86‡*
Interview pp. 87, 88†*
Question Support p. 95*

Reading
Distinguish Fact and Opinion pp. 89, 90†*
Reading Check p. 94

Vocabulary
Study p. 91*
Practice p. 92
Strategy p. 93

Assessment
Selection Tests A, B/C pp. 97*, 99*
Test Generator CD

BEST PRACTICES TOOLKIT
Differentiated Instruction pp. 31–38*
Scaffolding Instruction pp. 43–46*

Graphic Organizers/Strategies
Reciprocal Teaching • Word Questioning • Common Suffixes • Linear Array

Reading Support
Audio Anthology CD*

Technology
Literature and Vocabulary Centers at **ClassZone.com**
Write*Smart* CD

* Resources for Differentiation † Also in Spanish ‡ In Haitian Creole and Vietnamese

LEMENTS OF NONFICTION: INTERVIEW

If you've ever read an entertainment magazine, you have probably read an interview. An **interview** is a conversation between two people in which one person asks questions and the other responds. An interview

- often includes both the reporter's questions and the interviewee's responses
- typically provides long, uninterrupted quotations that give readers a sense of the person speaking

As you read "Interview with a Songcatcher," notice how the format of the interview helps you follow who is speaking.

EADING SKILL: DISTINGUISH FACT AND OPINION

A **fact** is a statement that can be proved true from personal observations, by consulting a reliable source such as an encyclopedia, or even by conducting an experiment. An **opinion** is a statement that cannot be proved because it expresses a person's feelings, thoughts, or beliefs.

Fact: *The Chicago White Sox won the 2005 World Series.*

Opinion: *The Chicago White Sox are a great team.*

When you read nonfiction, it's important to distinguish between facts that you can rely on and opinions about which people could disagree. To practice telling the difference, use a chart to note at least four facts and four opinions as you read this interview.

Statement	*Fact or Opinion?*

OCABULARY IN CONTEXT

The words in column A help one woman tell how she's learned about people's music. Match each word with the word in column B that you think is closest in meaning.

Column A	Column B
1. circumstance	a. undeveloped
2. composer	b. innermost
3. informant	c. situation
4. intimate	d. distant
5. primitive	e. songwriter
6. remote	f. speaker

Author Online

Brian Handwerk
born 1970

Writing That Travels the Globe Freelance writers like Brian Handwerk don't work for one particular newspaper or magazine. They get to write for a variety of publications on a range of topics. For example, Handwerk has written articles on the environment, politics, and scientific discoveries. His articles have been printed in publications around the globe. He says, "One of the best parts of the job is being able to interview amazing people like Henrietta Yurchenco . . . I'm lucky to be able to meet people like her through my writing."

Background

Ethnomusicology Each culture has a unique way of expressing itself through music. The study of ethnomusicology (ĕth'nō-myōō'zĭ-kŏl'ə-jē) is dedicated to preserving the music of all the world's cultures. Ethnomusicologists—also called songcatchers—travel to remote areas to record music from different groups. In addition to studying songs and instruments, songcatchers also study the ideas and methods that lead to the creation of music. For example, Henrietta Yurchenco (hĕn-re-ĕt'ə yûr-chĕn'kō), the songcatcher featured in this interview, spent two years studying and recording music in isolated areas of Mexico and Guatemala. Today, a number of universities and colleges offer courses in ethnomusicology.

MORE ABOUT THE AUTHOR AND BACKGROUND
To learn more about Brian Handwerk and songcatching, visit the **Literature Center** at **ClassZone.com.**

Teach

STANDARDS FOCUS

ELEMENTS OF NONFICTION

● INTERVIEW

Ask students to discuss interviews they have seen on television—of musicians, politicians, or other celebrities. Then have students read **Author Online** and create a list of questions they would ask Brian Handwerk if they had a chance to interview him.

CHECK UNDERSTANDING Have students explain how an interview differs from a typical conversation.

READING SKILL

■ DISTINGUISH FACT AND OPINION

Read the following statements, and have students identify them as fact or opinion:

- Rap is a modern form of music. *(fact)*
- Classical music is boring. *(opinion)*
- Many bands have drummers. *(fact)*

CHECK UNDERSTANDING Challenge students to rewrite the two fact statements as opinions and the opinion statement as a fact.

RESOURCE MANAGER—Copy Master
Distinguish Fact and Opinion p. 89 (for student use while reading the selection)

VOCABULARY SKILL

▲ VOCABULARY IN CONTEXT

DIAGNOSE WORD KNOWLEDGE To determine preteaching needs, have all students complete **Vocabulary in Context.** ***Answers:*** **1.** *c* **2.** *e* **3.** *f* **4.** *b* **5.** *a* **6.** *d*

PRETEACH VOCABULARY Use the Vocabulary Study copy master to help students use context clues to uncover word meanings.

1. Read aloud the first sentence, emphasizing the boldfaced word.
2. Ask students to think about the way the word is used. Discuss possible meanings for *circumstances,* such as "conditions" or "situations."
3. Repeat for the remaining sentences.
4. Have students write the sentences in Part B independently. Encourage them to use the sentences to tell a story.

RESOURCE MANAGER—Copy Master
Vocabulary Study p. 91

For general guidelines on differentiating vocabulary instruction and for alternative vocabulary activities for students not needing vocabulary preteaching, see

BEST PRACTICES TOOLKIT
Scaffolding Vocabulary Instruction pp. 43–46

Vocabulary Center at **ClassZone.com**
Additional Vocabulary Activities

Practice and Apply

ELEMENTS OF NONFICTION

Ⓐ INTERVIEW

Possible answer: *Handwerk is asking this question. In an interview, the interviewer asks the questions, and the interviewee gives the answers. We can assume that Handwerk is the interviewer because his name is under the title and the title indicates that he is going to interview a "songcatcher."*

Lines 1–11
DISCUSSION PROMPTS

Use these prompts to help students relate to Yurchenco's personality and interests:

Connect Yurchenco became interested in world music while working at a radio station in New York. What work or learning have you done that has made you want to explore something more deeply? *Accept all thoughtful responses.*

Infer One of Yurchenco's friends is the painter Rufino Tamayo (line 9). What can you infer from this fact about Yurchenco's general interests? ***Possible answer:*** *She is interested in a variety of art and artists, not just music and musicians.*

Evaluate Yurchenco says that most of the events in her life resulted from "just a set of funny circumstances." Do you think circumstances alone can explain a 60-year career? Why or why not? *Some students may agree that the random situations people find themselves in determine their destiny. Others may point out that Yurchenco's interest in music had already led to a job at a radio station, so she put herself in a position to have other music-related opportunities.*

Ethnomusicologist Henrietta Yurchenco spent over 60 years traveling the world in search of the unrecorded music of small cultural groups. Yurchenco recorded the music of various groups and tribes in Mexico, Central and South America, Spain, and Morocco. Her collection of world music is now housed in the United States Library of Congress, preserved for future generations of music lovers.

Targeted Passage ①

You've had such an incredible career, how did it all begin? Ⓐ

To tell you the truth, I think that most of the things that happened to me in life happened with absolutely no plan whatsoever—just a set of funny **circumstances**.

When I was working at WNYC [radio station] I was introduced to music from around the world, because everyone came to WNYC. I played artists like Woody Guthrie, Leadbelly, Pete Seeger,[1] and I also played music from all around the world. I was curious, you know, just plain curiosity.

One of our friends, the great Mexican painter Rufino Tamayo, called my husband and I and said "We're driving to Mexico, do you want to go?" We did. We drove from New York to Mexico and it changed my life.

Ⓐ INTERVIEW Who is asking this question? Tell how you know.

circumstance (sûr'kəm-stăns') *n.* a condition that affects or relates to an event or series of events

1. **Woody Guthrie; Leadbelly; Pete Seeger:** American folksingers and composers.

DIFFERENTIATED INSTRUCTION

FOR ALL STUDENTS

Enhance Learning Styles Provide these independent projects for students with various learning styles:

- **Linguistic** Write a letter from Yurchenco describing her experiences.
- **Analytical** Explore the American Folklife Center of the Library of Congress.
- **Musical/Interpersonal** Organize a world music party.

For further details on these projects, see

RESOURCE MANAGER
Ideas for Extension pp. 82–83

FOR LESS-PROFICIENT READERS

In combination with the *Audio Anthology CD,* use one or more Targeted Passages (pp. 910, 913, 915) to ensure that students focus on key facts, concepts, and skills.

① Targeted Passage [Introduction and Lines 1–11]

This passage gives an overview of Yurchenco's career and describes how it began.

- Where has Yurchenco recorded music?
- Where was she first introduced to music from around the world?
- What kind of work did Yurchenco do in New York City?
- Why did she first go to Mexico?

K FORWARD STOP REFRESH HOME PRINT

Henrietta Yurchenco shows off her early recording equipment.

It was in Mexico where you first began field recording of remote tribes?

Yes, because of a chance letter from the Library of Congress. I was doing radio programs for the Inter-American Indian Institute. . . . Dr. [Manuel] Gamio, the head of that institute, said, "We've received a letter from the Library of Congress. They'll send equipment and a little money. Are you interested?" **B**

I almost bit his hand off. I said, "I'll do it!" He was telling me about sleeping on the ground, long trips by animals, deadly scorpions, et cetera, but I wasn't listening. I didn't care. That's what I did for the next two years in Mexico and Guatemala.[2]

Were the practical aspects as difficult as advertised? Dealing with cumbersome early equipment, for example?

It was a horror. . . . People have asked me, "You went so far into those <u>remote</u> areas with just one recording machine?" One machine? I was thankful

2. **Guatemala** (gwä'tə-mä'lə): a country in northern Central America.

ANALYZE VISUALS
What do the **details** in this photograph suggest about Henrietta Yurchenco's interests and personality?

B FACT AND OPINION
Yurchenco states that the Library of Congress offered money and equipment to the Inter-American Indian Institute to record tribes in Mexico. Is this a fact or an opinion? Explain.

remote (rĭ-mōt') *adj.* located far away

ANALYZE VISUALS

Possible answer: *The recorder suggests that Yurchenco is interested in music. The decorations in her apartment, her style of dress, and her smile indicate that she has a lively, curious personality.*

READING SKILL

B FACT AND OPINION

Have students record their answers in a chart like the one shown on page 909.

Possible answer:

Statement	Fact or Opinion?
"They'll send equipment and a little money."	Fact: This could be proved by consulting the records of the Library of Congress.

BACKGROUND

Library of Congress Founded in 1800 in Washington, D.C., the Library of Congress (line 17) is the world's largest library, containing more than 130 million items. These include manuscripts, books and other printed materials, photographs, music and other recordings, and maps. Many of these materials are available to researchers in Washington, D.C., and over the Internet.

FOR ENGLISH LEARNERS

Options for Reading [paired option] Read the first Targeted Passage aloud. Clarify that it includes an introduction, a question, and an answer. Then have students continue reading along with the *Audio Anthology CD.* After listening to each section, have partners use Reciprocal Teaching to summarize, generate questions, clarify, and make predictions about the remaining sections of the interview.

BEST PRACTICES TOOLKIT—Transparency
Reciprocal Teaching p. A35

Key Academic Vocabulary Have students use Word Questioning to study these words: *institute* (lines 15, 16), *aspects* (lines 23, 113), *area(s)* (lines 26, 72), *culture* (lines 38, 102), *community* (lines 50, 65).

BEST PRACTICES TOOLKIT—Transparency
Word Questioning p. E9

Prereading For prereading instruction for English learners, see

BEST PRACTICES TOOLKIT
Scaffolding Reading Instruction pp. 43–46

FOR ADVANCED LEARNERS/PRE–AP

Pre-AP exercises in the bottom channel provide additional challenge for your advanced students. Use them for small groups or individuals.

ADDITIONAL GUIDELINES

For more help with differentiation and tips for classroom management, see

BEST PRACTICES TOOLKIT
Differentiated Instruction pp. 31–38

ELEMENTS OF NONFICTION

C INTERVIEW

Possible answer: *These lines reveal that Yurchenco was very brave because she slept on the ground even though she was terrified of scorpions. They also show that she was adventurous, flexible, and not bothered by living in rugged conditions.*

Extend the Discussion In what ways does someone's personality influence his or her career choice? What other careers might attract people with personalities like Yurchenco's?

READING SKILL

D FACT AND OPINION

Have students record their answers in the chart from page 909. ***Possible answer:*** *You could interview other people who were there, read journals written by Yurchenco and others, or study photographs from her trips.*

BACK FORWARD STOP REFRESH HOME PRINT

Yurchenco poses with Tzotzil Maya musicians in 1942.

to have one. . . . At one point the cord broke when we were way into the mountains. My photographer was with me on that trip and he just held it together with his hands. He stayed absolutely still, didn't move an inch and it was a perfect recording.

On most of the trips we had a big car motor for power. We had to carry gasoline, the machine, and the aluminum or even steel discs. That's all we had so we just hauled it everywhere. The only thing that really terrified me was deadly scorpions. It's not comfortable sleeping on the ground when you know those things are around—but it was a great adventure. C

Some places I had help from missionaries,[3] some places I was alone with 200 pounds of equipment. Don't ask me how it worked sometimes. D

How difficult was it for you to understand the culture of these remote communities?

When I was in Mexico I visited some very **primitive** and isolated people who had had no contact with mainstream society for many years. I swear I saw animal sacrifices and curing ceremonies that were thousands of years old. I discovered what there was of pre-Hispanic[4]

C INTERVIEW
Reread lines 33–35. What do they reveal about Yurchenco's personality?

D FACT AND OPINION
Reread lines 36–37. What might you do to verify these statements as facts?

primitive (prĭm'ĭ-tĭv) *adj.* of or relating to a nonindustrial, often tribal, culture

3. **missionaries** (mĭsh'ə-nĕr'ēz): people who are sent to do religious work in foreign countries.
4. **pre-Hispanic** (prē-hĭ-spăn'ĭk): related to an era before Spanish conquerors arrived in the Americas.

DIFFERENTIATED INSTRUCTION

FOR ENGLISH LEARNERS

Vocabulary: Suffixes [mixed-readiness pairs] Point out the words *photographer* (line 28), *informants* (line 48), and *anthropologists* (line 56), and help students identify the base words (*photograph, inform, anthropology*). Explain that some suffixes, when added to certain nouns and verbs, create words describing people. These suffixes include *-er, -or, -ist, -ant,* and *-ian.* Tell students that the spelling of the base word frequently changes, as in the word *anthropologists.*

1. Have students work with a more fluent partner to use these suffixes to create more words that describe people. Encourage students to use a dictionary to check the spellings of the words.
2. Have students use Common Suffixes to help them identify the meanings of additional suffixes and understand unfamiliar words.

BEST PRACTICES TOOLKIT—Transparency
Common Suffixes p. E15

music and dance at that time among 14 different tribes. After some of the recordings these people died and the younger people did not really learn the stuff. . . .

People in the field have to be very careful because they're told things but shouldn't believe them. You have to look behind the words. **Informants** might tell you what you want to hear, or not tell you something that the community won't want you to hear. So you have to be very careful, and really observe. . . .

informant (ĭn-fôr′mənt) *n.* one who gives information

How are you able to do that as an outsider with a lot of recording equipment?

② Targeted Passage

First of all it was easy because, as you've no doubt noticed, I'm a woman. So I'm not threatening and they did not regard a woman as threatening. Secondly, I never asked direct questions. Anthropologists[5] go into the field with questions. I didn't, I just went with hugs and kisses and asked "Will you please sing for me?" When you ask about music it means, "She's interested, she likes me, she respects me." And I've never met a people who didn't respond to that.

The Yaquis,[6] for example, who were known as a very warlike tribe, were absolutely marvelous. They were poets; their stuff was gorgeous. I said to the chieftain, "I want to get the words for all these songs"; he said, "We'll come together before you leave and we'll write it all down so you get it right." Well, the entire tribe came to this little community center, babies, women, grandparents, everyone. We sweltered in there, it was 100 degrees, but we got it all down. **E**

You had to be a good listener. I've sat on many, many a porch with women of all kinds and colors and just asked "So what happened after that?"

E FACT AND OPINION What two opinions does Yurchenco express about the Yaquis? Tell what words led you to this conclusion.

Was the lack of a common language a problem?

I never found that there was a distance between them and me because I didn't understand their language. To this day I travel to one area of Mexico that has a rich musical heritage. I've been going there since 1942, and the

5. **anthropologists** (ăn′thrə-pŏl′ə-jĭsts): scientists who study the origin, behavior, and cultural development of humans.

6. **Yaquis** (yä′kēs): a native people of Sonora, Mexico, who settled mainly along the Yaqui River.

Lines 40–46
REINFORCE *KEY IDEA:* MUSIC

Discuss Why do you think the younger people Yurchenco refers to here did not learn the **music** of their elders? ***Possible answer:*** *They might have been more aware of and interested in contemporary culture and music than in traditional tribal culture.*

READING SKILL

E FACT AND OPINION

Have students record their answers in the chart from page 909. ***Possible answer:***

Statement	Fact or Opinion?
"The Yaquis . . . were absolutely marvelous. . . . their stuff was gorgeous."	Opinion: Adjectives such as "marvelous" and "gorgeous" are subjective, that is, not everyone may agree with Yurchenco's assessment of the Yaquis and their music.

FOR LESS-PROFICIENT READERS

② Targeted Passage [Lines 52–69]

This passage describes how Yurchenco faced the challenge of being an outsider.

- Why were people willing to talk to Yurchenco and share their music with her?
- What information did Yurchenco get from the Yaqui people? What did she do to get it?
- What question has Yurchenco asked many times?

FOR ENGLISH LEARNERS

Vocabulary Support Point out the word *field* in line 47. Explain that, in anthropology, the word has a very specific meaning: the area or setting where an anthropologist studies a particular culture. The word can also be used to describe a profession or interest, as in the *field of biology.* On a more literal level, a *field* is a large, level piece of land. Common usage includes *soccer field* and *field of corn.*

INTERVIEW WITH A SONGCATCHER 913

ELEMENTS OF NONFICTION

F INTERVIEW

Possible answer: *Yurchenco approaches her work by forming close relationships with the people she works with. They see her as a friend, and they know that she respects them.*

Extend the Discussion What are some ways in which people communicate thoughts and feelings without using words?

READING SKILL

G FACT AND OPINION

Have students record their answers in the chart from page 909. ***Possible answer:*** *This statement cannot be verified as a fact. It expresses Yurchenco's opinion about the value of music.*

Lines 77–100

DISCUSSION PROMPTS

Use these prompts to help students understand Yurchenco's values:

Connect Yurchenco describes bonding with strangers who share a love of music. Have you ever had this experience—with music or another shared interest? What was it like? *Students' responses should be thoughtful and include details of their experiences.*

Evaluate Paraphrase Yurchenco's comments in lines 97–100. Do you agree with her idea? ***Possible answers:*** *Yes; you have to know what's going on socially and politically in order to fully understand popular music. No; most popular music can be understood without knowing this context.*

BACK FORWARD STOP REFRESH HOME PRINT

composer (kəm-pō′zər) *n.* one who creates musical pieces

F INTERVIEW
What does this response to the question reveal about Yurchenco's approach to her work?

G FACT AND OPINION
Reread the first sentence of this paragraph. Can you verify this statement as fact?

wife of the main Indian **composer** there doesn't speak Spanish. Every time she sees me we just hug, and she kisses me and cries. They know whether you respect them and you don't need words. F

It's better to use music than bombs to win friendships. When we were in Morocco[7] the last time most of the Jews had left for other countries. We were sitting in Tangier[8] in a café, and a little ensemble was playing Arabic music. I went up to them and I said, "We are musicians from New York." They got up, gave us hugs and kisses, and said, "Please sit down and we'll play for you." It's a wonderful bond. There's nothing more emotional than the arts and music. G

There's a voice to be heard through that emotion as well?

The song to me is the basic human expression. It tells you things, or avoids telling you things, or disguises things, but you have to look at what it means.

There's so much study of folk music and typically there's not much study of the words. It's like going to the opera for many people, and they don't have the ghost of an idea what it's about. They just hear the music. But if that's what the composer had meant he would have just written, you know, "Blah, blah, blah." Music itself tells you things but so do the words. You have to look at the meaning. . . .

You've always been attuned to the political aspect of music as well.

I'm concerned with more than music. I'm concerned with the society, with the people more than anything. When I hear popular music I have to consider the social and political things that are going on in order to understand it. It's the same with any music around the world, but that fact is very often neglected.

I'm not a romantic; I'm political. These romantics say "We must preserve the precious culture." But at the cost of poverty and ignorance? Is that what you want? That's what it means. Life changes, and with modern communications, roads, and infrastructure a lot of things will

7. **Morocco** (mə-rŏk′ō): a country in northwest Africa. It has coastlines on the Mediterranean Sea and the Atlantic Ocean.

8. **Tangier** (tăn-jîr′): a northern Moroccan city.

DIFFERENTIATED INSTRUCTION

FOR LESS–PROFICIENT READERS

Reading Skill Follow-Up: Distinguish Fact and Opinion [paired option] Have partners reread lines 101–106. Tell them to identify one fact and one opinion in the passage. Remind students to refer to the chart on page 909 to clarify the strategy. ***Possible answer:*** *Fact: "Life changes, and . . . a lot of things will disappear, of course." Opinion: "But maybe people's lives will be better."*

FOR ADVANCED LEARNERS/PRE–AP

Expand Vocabulary [paired option] Ask students to work with a partner to identify synonyms of these words: *cries, respect, wonderful, disguises, neglected.* Then have them check their answers in a dictionary, thesaurus, or synonym finder. Challenge them to find antonyms, as well. Finally, have them complete a Linear Array using these synonyms and antonyms to expand their vocabulary.

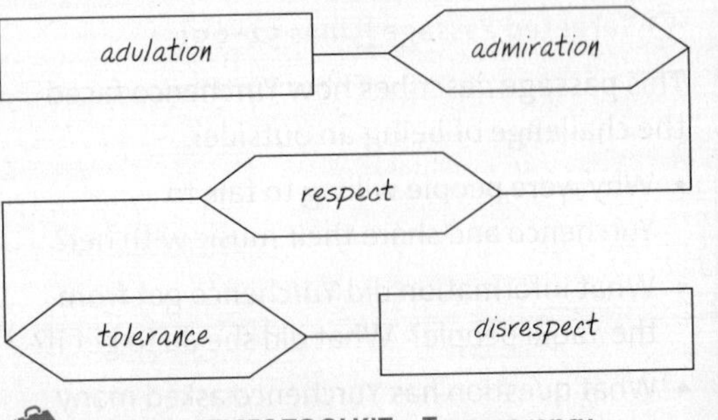

BEST PRACTICES TOOLKIT—Transparency
Linear Array p. E7

CK FORWARD STOP REFRESH HOME PRINT

disappear, of course. But maybe people's lives will be better—I don't just talk about music as if it were surrounded by a moat[9] or something.

Why is the work of field recordings important, and why is it important to preserve and distribute these voices of the past 100-odd years?

It's our history. We have a written history. There are books for political history, the formation of nations, political and social struggles. But music is one of the most intimate expressions. Through music you become knowledgeable of the intimate aspects of life that aren't told in books. It's important because the people themselves tell you; it's not someone's interpretation. History books are written by the victors, but songs are the people's own words and melodies. That's what makes music a very powerful tool to understand people. H

9. **moat** (mōt): a water-filled ditch that surrounds and protects a castle, fortress, or town.

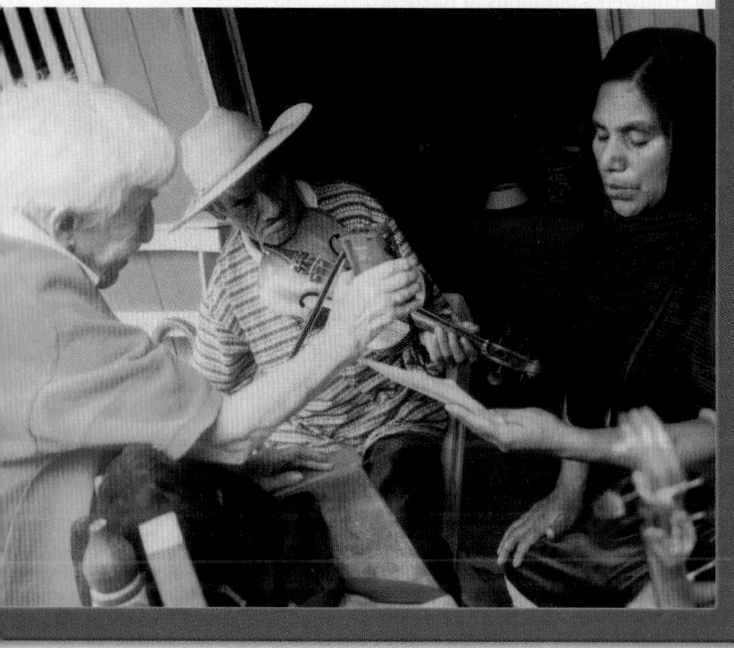

(3) Targeted Passage

intimate (ĭn'tə-mĭt) *adj.* relating to one's deepest nature

H FACT AND OPINION
Find one fact and one opinion in this paragraph. How were you able to identify each?

ANALYZE VISUALS
What can you **infer** from this photo about the way Yurchenco relates to the people she meets?

READING SKILL

H FACT AND OPINION

Have students record their answers in the chart from page 909. ***Possible answer:***

Statement	Fact or Opinion?
"There are books for political history, the formation of nations, political and social struggles."	Fact: Books on these topics can be found at the library, at a bookstore, or online.
"That's what makes music a very powerful tool to understand people."	Opinion: It cannot be proved. Some people may think that music doesn't help people understand each other.

ANALYZE VISUALS

Possible answer: *Yurchenco's posture in the photograph suggests she is deeply interested in what the man she's talking to has to say. From this, you can infer that she uses her curiosity and warmth to connect with the people she visits.*

SELECTION WRAP-UP

REFLECT Yurchenco says that songs are "people's own words and melodies," while history books interpret events from the point of view of the "victors." Ask students who are the victors she is referring to and whether they agree with her ideas.

★ **CRITIQUE** Have students evaluate the format of the selection. What are the advantages and disadvantages of the interview format?

FOR LESS-PROFICIENT READERS

(3) Targeted Passage [Lines 107–117]

In this passage, Yurchenco draws conclusions based on her experience and shares her opinions about music and politics.

- According to Yurchenco, what does music share that books are unable to express?
- Who writes the history books?
- Who creates songs?
- Why does Yurchenco think it is important to preserve these songs?

FOR ADVANCED LEARNERS/PRE-AP

Evaluate Have students write a short letter to Handwerk in which they evaluate the interview. Suggest that they include two statements of positive feedback praising specific questions Handwerk asked or reflecting on Yurchenco's responses. Challenge students to include two constructive suggestions for improvement. For example, when could Handwerk have asked follow-up questions about a particular topic?

Practice and Apply

After Reading

Comprehension

1. **Recall** How did Henrietta Yurchenco begin recording tribal music?
2. **Clarify** Why does Yurchenco think music can tell more about a culture than history books?
3. **Summarize** Reread lines 70–83. How is Yurchenco able to communicate with people who don't speak her language?

Critical Analysis

4. **Describe a Songcatcher** What type of person is Henrietta Yurchenco? Using a chart like the one shown, write three adjectives that describe Yurchenco's personality. Expand your chart using one statement from the interview that supports each adjective.

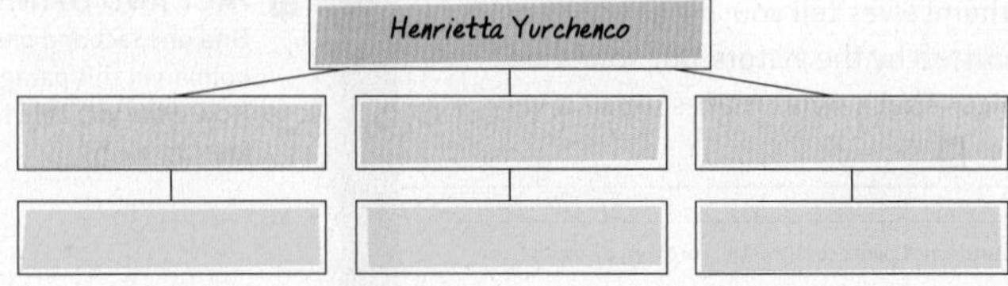

5. **Analyze an Interview** Reread Handwerk's questions to Yurchenco. What do these questions tell you about his interest in or prior knowledge of songcatching?
6. **Evaluate Fact and Opinion** Look back at the facts and opinions you recorded as you read. Then exchange your list with a partner. Does he or she agree with you about which statements are facts and which are opinions?
7. **Make Judgments** Look again at the questions Handwerk asked Yurchenco. Were they good choices? Why or why not? If you were to continue the **interview,** what are another two questions you would ask?

Extension and Challenge

8. **Big Question Activity** Go back to the anticipation guide you started before reading. Now, fill in the "After Reading" column. Have any of your opinions about **music** changed after reading this interview? Explain.
9. **Creative Project: Music** Imagine that Henrietta Yurchenco came to your class. What music would you play for her to let her know what it's like to be a student your age in the United States today? With a group, come up with a list of five songs. They can be songs written by recording artists, or songs written by one or all of you. Next to each song, explain why you chose it.

After Reading

For additional support of postreading questions, use these copy masters:

RESOURCE MANAGER—Copy Masters
Reading Check p. 94 (to check understanding of the selection)
Interview p. 87 (for practice of elements of nonfiction standards focus)
Question Support p. 95 (After Reading questions adapted for English learners and less-proficient readers)

Additional selection questions are provided for teachers on page 81.

ANSWERS

Comprehension

1. *The Inter-American Indian Institute received a letter from the Library of Congress offering equipment and money to record music. The head of the institute offered the job to Yurchenco.*
2. *Yurchenco believes only "victors," or the most powerful in society, tell their story in history books. Through music, many people in a culture can tell their story.*
3. *Yurchenco communicates with people through hugs and kisses and by showing them respect.*

Critical Analysis

Possible answers:

4. ***Determined/Eager:*** *"I almost bit his hand off. I said, 'I'll do it.'"* ***Brave:*** *"It's not comfortable sleeping on the ground when you know those things [scorpions] are around—but it was a great adventure."* ***Warm/Compassionate:*** *"Every time she sees me we just hug, and she kisses me and cries."*
5. ● **STANDARDS FOCUS Interview** *Handwerk's first question (line 1) shows both his interest in and prior knowledge of songcatching and Yurchenco's contribution to the field. His question about "cumbersome early equipment" (line 24) also reveals his background knowledge about songcatching.*
6. ■ **STANDARDS FOCUS Distinguish Fact and Opinion** *Answers will vary. Students should provide support for each detail they labeled as fact or opinion.*
7. *Students will most likely say that Handwerk's questions were good because they enabled Yurchenco to talk about her career and her beliefs. Students should add questions that would elicit information not included in the interview (for example, more about Yurchenco's musical background and the places she visited).*

Extension and Challenge

8. *If students' opinions have changed, have them identify details from the interview that contributed to the change.*
9. *As they choose the songs, have students make sure that they find as diverse a collection as possible, representing different regions of the country and different musical styles.*

ocabulary in Context

OCABULARY PRACTICE

Show that you understand the boldfaced vocabulary words by telling whether each statement is true or false.

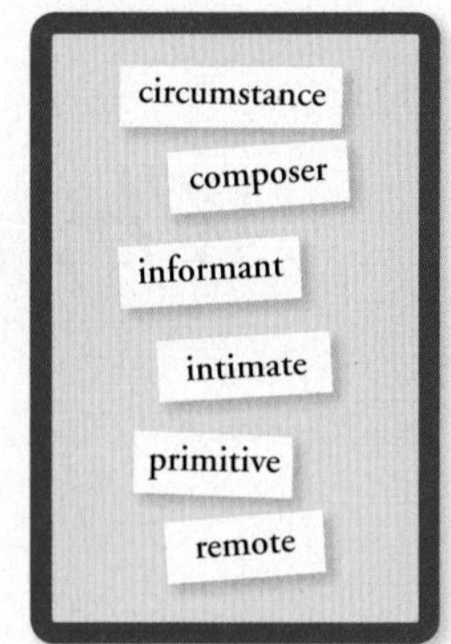

1. A **remote** village is far away from other communities.
2. A **composer** is someone who writes plays.
3. Most European cultures are **primitive.**
4. An **informant** is the same as a liar.
5. Most people share **intimate** details about their lives with no one but family members and friends.
6. A **circumstance** is a person who bosses others around.

OCABULARY IN WRITING

If Henrietta Yurchenco were to write the story of her career as a songcatcher, what might she say? Write the introductory paragraph of Yurchenco's memoir. You might start like this.

EXAMPLE SENTENCE

*My first trip was to a **remote** village in Mexico.*

OCABULARY STRATEGY: DENOTATION AND CONNOTATION

A word's **denotation** is the basic definition found in a dictionary. Its **connotation** is a feeling or attitude linked with that word. Connotations can influence the meaning a word conveys. For example, the vocabulary word *primitive* means "of or relating to a nonindustrial, often tribal, culture." But the word has also come to mean "unsophisticated" or "crude." Recognizing connotations can help you understand the opinions of the people you read about.

PRACTICE Replace each boldfaced word with another word with a similar meaning, but a negative connotation.

1. Marcus's dog is **overweight** because the family feeds it too much.
2. Even after she left the room, Lia's perfume left an odd **scent** in the air.
3. The **elderly** woman moved slowly as she crossed the street.
4. Michael is so **clever.** He always gets his way.
5. I can't be friends with Cynthia. Her attitude is **unpleasant.**

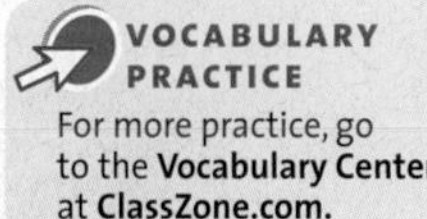

For more practice, go to the **Vocabulary Center** at **ClassZone.com.**

ANSWERS

Vocabulary in Context

VOCABULARY PRACTICE

1. *true*
2. *false*
3. *false*
4. *false*
5. *true*
6. *false*

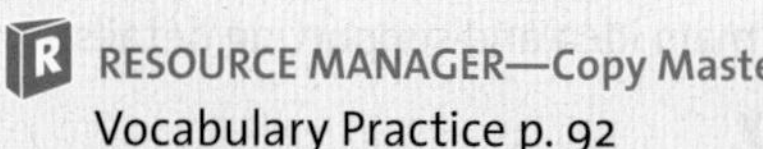

RESOURCE MANAGER—Copy Master
Vocabulary Practice p. 92

VOCABULARY IN WRITING

Suggest that students skim the interview and note key events from Yurchenco's career and her thoughts about them. They should then decide which of these events and thoughts might best be described by the vocabulary words. Challenge students to use at least half of the vocabulary words in their paragraphs.

VOCABULARY STRATEGY: DENOTATION AND CONNOTATION *(also an EL language objective)*

Remind students to consider what they have already learned about an author or speaker to help them identify the connotations of the words they use.

Possible answers:

1. *chubby*
2. *stench*
3. *old*
4. *sly*
5. *obnoxious*

RESOURCE MANAGER—Copy Master
Vocabulary Strategy p. 93

Vocabulary Center at **ClassZone.com**
Additional Vocabulary Activities

DIFFERENTIATED INSTRUCTION

FOR ENGLISH LEARNERS

Vocabulary Practice [mixed-readiness pairs] Encourage students who are having trouble to review the definitions and context of the vocabulary words in the selection. Have them work with a more fluent partner to pinpoint the context clue in each sentence that will tell them whether the sentence is true or false.

FOR ADVANCED LEARNERS/PRE-AP

Vocabulary Strategy [paired option] Have partners work together to brainstorm several words with strong connotations, both positive and negative, which can be used to describe music. Have them use these words in a paragraph about people who love music.

Assess and Reteach

Assess

RESOURCE MANAGER—Copy Masters
Selection Tests A, B/C pp. 97–98, 99–100

Test Generator CD

Reteach

STANDARDS LESSON FILE
Reading Lesson 5: Distinguishing Fact from Opinion
Vocabulary Lesson 17: Denotation and Connotation

Focus and Motivate

OBJECTIVES

Elements of Nonfiction
- explore the key idea of **singing**
- identify form and characteristics of feature articles
- read a magazine article

Reading
- identify main idea and supporting details

Vocabulary
- build vocabulary for reading and writing
- use structural analysis to identify base words and suffixes that form adjectives *(also an EL language objective)*
- determine meanings of derivatives by applying knowledge of meanings of base words and affixes *(also an EL language objective)*

Grammar and Writing
- use commas correctly after introductory words and phrases
- use writing to analyze literature

SUMMARY

"Kabul's Singing Sensation" focuses on 13-year-old Mirwais Najrabi, a young singer in war-torn Afghanistan who uses his voice to inspire fellow Afghans.

Why do we SING?

Discuss the question and the ***KEY IDEA*** of **singing.** Do a quick survey to find out how many students like to sing and how many don't and discuss the results. Then have students work on the ***WEB IT*** activity and invite them to share and compare their webs.

Before Reading

Kabul's Singing Sensation

Magazine Article by Tim McGirk

Why do we SING?

KEY IDEA Think about the last time you **sang.** Was it at a birthday party? during choir practice? on the street with a group of friends? Whether it's to celebrate, lift someone's spirits, or express joy, almost everyone belts out a tune at some point or another. In the article you're about to read, you'll meet a boy whose singing helps relieve the suffering of his country.

WEB IT People sing for a variety of reasons. Fill in a web like the one shown with places and events where people sing or hear singing. What do you think is the most common reason to sing?

918

Selection Resources

RESOURCE MANAGER UNIT 8

Plan and Teach pp. 101–108

Elements of Nonfiction
Summary pp. 109†*, 110‡*
Feature Article pp. 111, 112†*
Question Support p. 119*

Reading
Identify Main Idea and Details pp. 113, 114†*
Reading Check p. 118
Reading Fluency p. 121

Vocabulary
Study p. 115*
Practice p. 116
Strategy p. 117

Grammar and Writing
Use Commas Correctly p. 120

Assessment
Selection Tests A, B/C pp. 123*, 125*
Test Generator CD

BEST PRACTICES TOOLKIT

Differentiated Instruction pp. 31–38*
Scaffolding Instruction pp. 43–46*

Graphic Organizers/Strategies
Anticipation Guide • Word Questioning • New Word Analysis • Distinguishing Fact and Opinion • Freewriting

Reading Support
Audio Anthology CD*

Technology
Literature, Vocabulary, and Writing Centers at **ClassZone.com**
Write*Smart* CD

* Resources for Differentiation † Also in Spanish ‡ In Haitian Creole and Vietnamese

EMENTS OF NONFICTION: FEATURE ARTICLE

What was the last article you read in a magazine or newspaper? If it was a piece about a favorite celebrity or about skate parks around the country, what you read was probably a feature article. A **feature article** is an article that

- focuses on a person or topic of human interest, rather than a current news event
- often includes language and imagery that appeal to emotions
- often gives only one perspective on a story

As you read "Kabul's Singing Sensation," notice how the author helps you understand the difficult life of one young Afghan singer.

ADING SKILL: IDENTIFY MAIN IDEA AND DETAILS

Nonfiction writers usually organize their writing around **main ideas,** the most important ideas they want to share about a topic. Sometimes these main ideas are stated directly, often at the beginning of a section or paragraph. Other times they may merely be implied, or suggested. **Supporting details,** such as facts or examples, help to illustrate main ideas.

The article you are about to read contains several main ideas supported by details. Use an outline like the one shown to record supporting details for each main idea.

I. *History and politics of Afghanistan*
   A.
   B.
II. *Difficulties faced by Mirwais and his family*
   A.
   B.

OCABULARY IN CONTEXT

Tim McGirk uses the following words to describe the challenges faced by a young musician. How many words do you know? Make a chart like the one shown, putting each vocabulary word in the appropriate column.

WORD LIST

edict	immaculate	transcendent
exile	puritanical	virtuoso

Know Well	*Think I Know*	*Don't Know at All*

Author Online

Danger and Determination
Reporters who travel to dangerous areas of the world often have difficult decisions to make. How bold or how careful should they be in order to get information? Tim McGirk, a reporter for *Time* magazine, has had to answer this question himself.

Tim McGirk
born 1952

In 2001, McGirk had to decide whether to visit an island in the Philippines where rebels held kidnapped tourists and journalists and sometimes killed them. Because of the dangers involved, he chose not go to the island. However, since 1976, McGirk has covered his share of difficult assignments, including reporting on the people and situations in Latin America and in war-torn areas of the Middle East.

Background

Turbulent Times The late 20th century saw years of civil unrest in Afghanistan, a landlocked country in southern Asia. The Taliban, a violent Muslim extremist group, captured control of the country in the 1990s. The group imposed strict rules on the Afghan people, based on its extreme interpretation of Islam. Under the Taliban's rule, Afghan girls lost their right to an education, art and sports were outlawed, and even music was banned. Those who violated the Taliban's rules were often brutally punished. The Taliban fell out of power after a 2001 invasion by the United States and its allies. A new government was created, and people in certain parts of the country again enjoyed some of the freedoms they had missed for years.

MORE ABOUT THE AUTHOR AND BACKGROUND
To learn more about Tim McGirk and Afghanistan, visit the **Literature Center** at **ClassZone.com.**

Teach

STANDARDS FOCUS

ELEMENTS OF NONFICTION

● FEATURE ARTICLE

Ask students to identify the elements of a feature article in this example:

> Shayna Lopez always knew she wanted to be an actress. With fierce determination and luck, she reached her goal at the tender age of eight, landing a role in the film *Make Believe.*

Possible answer: *It focuses on one person and includes language that appeals to readers' emotions ("fierce determination," "tender age of eight").*

CHECK UNDERSTANDING Ask students why writers of feature articles use emotional language and imagery.

READING SKILL

■ IDENTIFY MAIN IDEA AND DETAILS

Have students identify the main idea in the example paragraph. Ask if it is stated or implied. ***Answer:*** *"Shayna Lopez always knew she wanted to be an actress." It is stated.*

CHECK UNDERSTANDING Have students identify details that support the main idea of the example paragraph.

RESOURCE MANAGER—Copy Master
Identify Main Idea and Details p. 113 (for student use while reading the selection)

VOCABULARY SKILL

▲ VOCABULARY IN CONTEXT

DIAGNOSE WORD KNOWLEDGE To determine preteaching needs, have all students complete **Vocabulary in Context.** *Students' answers will vary.*

PRETEACH VOCABULARY Use the Vocabulary Study copy master to help students determine the meaning of each boldfaced word.

1. Read aloud the first sentence, emphasizing the boldfaced word.
2. Ask students to think about the way the word is used. Discuss possible meanings for *edict,* such as "law."
3. Repeat the procedure for each of the remaining sentences.
4. Have students complete the chart in Part B independently.

RESOURCE MANAGER—Copy Master
Vocabulary Study p. 115

For general guidelines on differentiating vocabulary instruction and for alternative vocabulary activities for students not needing vocabulary preteaching, see

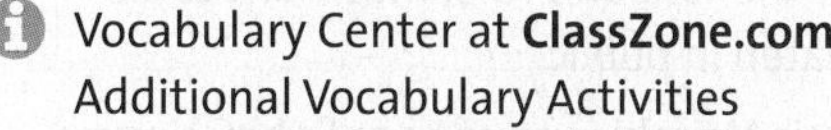

BEST PRACTICES TOOLKIT
Scaffolding Vocabulary Instruction pp. 43–46

Vocabulary Center at **ClassZone.com**
Additional Vocabulary Activities

Practice and Apply

BACKGROUND

Islamic Traditions and Customs Mirwais Najrabi lives in Afghanistan, which is a Muslim country. The article includes numerous references to Islamic customs and their impact on daily life. Share these facts with students:

- One-fifth of the world's population is Muslim. There are approximately 30 million Muslims in Afghanistan.
- Ramadan (line 86) is the holiest month in the Muslim calendar. According to Muslim belief, the holy book of God, the Quran, was revealed in the month of Ramadan. During Ramadan, observant Muslims fast from dawn until sunset every day, practice acts of charity, and refrain from gossip and other negative behaviors.
- The Quran provides instruction for every detail of a Muslim's daily life.
- *Islam* is the Arabic word for submission to the will of God (Allah).

ANALYZE VISUALS

Possible answer: *His expression is filled with emotion. His eyes look sad, as if he is singing a sad song.*

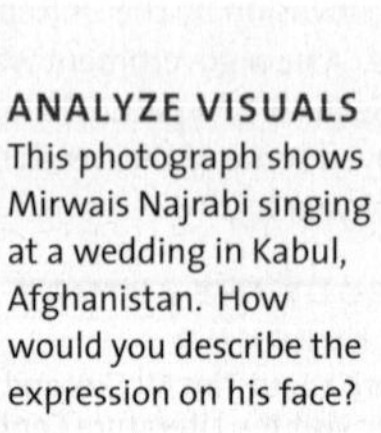

ANALYZE VISUALS
This photograph shows Mirwais Najrabi singing at a wedding in Kabul, Afghanistan. How would you describe the expression on his face?

DIFFERENTIATED INSTRUCTION

FOR ALL STUDENTS

Anticipation Guide Write these statements on an Anticipation Guide and have students respond to them before and after reading:

- Singing has only recently become popular in Afghanistan.
- Under the Taliban's rule, musicians could be beaten in public.
- Mirwais Najrabi, one of Kabul's boy singers, is as popular as a rock star.

 BEST PRACTICES TOOLKIT—Transparency
Anticipation Guide p. A14

FOR LESS–PROFICIENT READERS

In combination with the *Audio Anthology CD,* use one or more Targeted Passages (pp. 922, 924) to ensure that students focus on the article's main ideas and supporting details.

FOR ENGLISH LEARNERS

Options for Reading [small-group option] Read aloud lines 1–11. Compare the written description of Mirwais's appearance with the photograph of the singer. Then have students continue reading in small groups as they listen to the *Audio Anthology CD.*

920 UNIT 8: FACTS AND INFORMATION

Kabul's Singing Sensation

TIM McGIRK

It's midnight, long past bedtime for most children. But in a poor, war-ravaged neighborhood of Kabul,[1] more than 300 men are gathered at a wedding party to listen to the singing of Mirwais Najrabi, a pale, chestnut-haired 13-year-old. He performs in an open courtyard, under the night sky, to an audience that has endured so much suffering and grief over years of oppression, war, and mayhem. Yet for this brief, **transcendent** moment, their burden is lifted by the exquisite purity of the boy's voice. **A**

With his jaunty, Bollywood-style[2] haircut and white embroidered tunic, Mirwais looks as though he would warble like a pretty songbird, but his singing is forceful and worldly, as if he has already seen it all. And he has. Tonight, he croons folksongs of impossible love, betrayal, and heroism that flow from the depths of Afghanistan's tragic history. . . . Two men leap up to dance, circling each other like angry cobras. They turn aggressive and are pulled apart. . . . When performances get wild, says Mirwais, he tells himself: "I must not be scared, never."

transcendent (trăn-sĕn′dənt) *adj.* being above the material world

A FEATURE ARTICLE
Reread lines 1–8. What words and phrases suggest that you are reading a feature article?

1. **Kabul** (kä′bo͝ol): Afghanistan's capital city.
2. **Bollywood** (bŏl′ē-wo͝od′): the Indian film industry. The name combines the names *Hollywood* (center of the U.S. film industry) and *Bombay* (the former name for Mumbai, a large Indian city).

ELEMENTS OF NONFICTION

A FEATURE ARTICLE

Possible answer: *"poor, war-ravaged neighborhood," "Mirwais Najrabi, a pale, chestnut-haired 13-year-old," "under the night sky," "an audience that has endured so much suffering and grief," "transcendent moment," "exquisite purity of the boy's voice"*

If students need help . . . Have them review the characteristics of feature articles on page 919.

Lines 1–16
REINFORCE *KEY IDEA:* SINGING

Discuss What do you think Mirwais would say is his purpose in **singing?** Use evidence from the article to support your answer. ***Possible answer:*** *Mirwais might say his purpose is to inspire the Afghan people. Evidence from the text includes "audience that has endured so much suffering" (line 5), "burden is lifted by the exquisite purity of the boy's voice" (lines 7–8), and "he croons folksongs . . . that flow from the depths of Afghanistan's tragic history" (lines 12–13).*

FOR ENGLISH LEARNERS

Key Academic Vocabulary Have students use Word Questioning to study these words: *brief* (line 6), *tradition* (lines 27, 48), *regime* (line 28), *range* (line 50).

BEST PRACTICES TOOLKIT—Transparency
Word Questioning p. E9

Prereading For prereading instruction for English learners, see

BEST PRACTICES TOOLKIT
Scaffolding Reading Instruction pp. 43–46

FOR ADVANCED LEARNERS/PRE–AP

Pre-AP exercises in the bottom channel provide additional challenge for your advanced students. Use them for small groups or individuals.

ADDITIONAL GUIDELINES

For more help with differentiation and tips for classroom management, see

BEST PRACTICES TOOLKIT
Differentiated Instruction pp. 31–38

READING SKILL

B MAIN IDEA

Students should add their details under section *II* of their outlines. ***Possible answer:***

A. Death of Mirwais's father when Mirwais was five years old

B. Explosions of mortars and rockets near their home in the Char-Deh neighborhood of Kabul

Lines 27–38

DISCUSSION PROMPTS

Use these prompts to help students understand life under the Taliban regime:

Recall What did the Taliban do to musicians? Why? ***Answer:*** *They arrested and beat musicians because they believed music was "un-Islamic."*

Infer What would the Taliban have done to Mirwais's family if they had found the hidden instruments? Support your response with evidence from the text. ***Possible answer:*** *The Taliban authorities would have arrested and beaten the family; they may even have killed them for their act of defiance against the regime. Evidence from the text includes "many musicians arrested and beaten" (line 29) and Nur-ul-Haq's statement that they were afraid the Taliban would kill them (lines 35–36).*

Synthesize Based on the family's actions during the Taliban regime, what conclusions can you draw about their feelings about music? ***Possible answer:*** *They are so passionate about music that they were willing to risk their lives by committing the "crime" of burying their instruments to prevent them from being destroyed.*

Note that Afghanistan is a mountainous country.

Targeted Passage ①

exile (ĕk'sīl') *n.* enforced removal from one's native country

B MAIN IDEA What details help you understand the difficulties Mirwais has faced? Add these details to your outline.

puritanical (pyŏŏr-ĭ-tăn'ĭ-kəl) *adj.* strictly observant of religious practices; sternly moral

edict (ē'dĭkt') *n.* a command from those in power

The soulful melancholy in Mirwais's voice is the product of hard times. He may be only 13, but he has already suffered greatly, and this, he says, may have helped him capture the anguish that many Afghans have endure in the last 25 years of scorching battle and **exile.** "I sing what I feel," he says with a child's simplicity. His father was a famous musician who died when Mirwais was only five years old. The family had the misfortune of living in the Char-Deh neighborhood of Kabul on the front line between two warring commanders; as mortars and rockets exploded around them, Mirwais and his brothers risked their lives every day just to draw water from a communal well. B

Boy vocalists, long a part of Afghan tradition, were once silenced completely by the **puritanical** Taliban regime, which regarded song as un-Islamic and had many musicians arrested and beaten. When the Taliban seized power, one of their first **edicts** was to ban music. They ransacked the Afghan Radio and Television station, decorating nearby trees and rosebushes with streamers of ripped-out audiotape. (Brave technicians, however, sealed thousands of Afghan records and tapes behind a false wall at the studio, which the Taliban never found.) "We were afraid that the Taliban would kill us," recalls Mirwais's older

DIFFERENTIATED INSTRUCTION

FOR LESS–PROFICIENT READERS

① Targeted Passage [Lines 17–26]

This passage explores one of the selection's main ideas: the connection between Mirwais's difficult life and the "soulful melancholy" in his voice.

- What happened to Mirwais's father?
- What makes Mirwais's neighborhood so dangerous?
- What does Mirwais mean when he says, "I sing what I feel"?

FOR ENGLISH LEARNERS

Vocabulary Support Use New Word Analysis to teach these words:

- *melancholy* (line 17), "sadness"
- *anguish* (line 19), "deep sadness"
- *endured* (line 19), "suffered"
- *misfortune* (line 22), "bad luck"
- *vocalists* (line 27), "singers"
- *ransacked* (line 31), "searched"

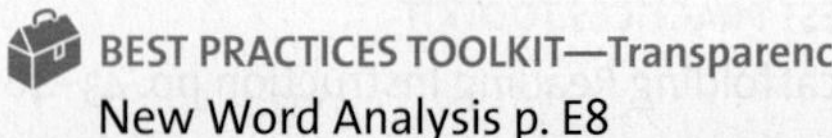
BEST PRACTICES TOOLKIT—Transparency
New Word Analysis p. E8

brother Nur-ul-Haq, a tabla[3] player who says dozens of artists were beaten in public by Taliban zealots. So the family buried their musical instruments under a chicken coop in the garden. Another brother left to sell flowers in Iran, while Nur-ul-Haq hawked carpets in Pakistan. Mirwais, who was just five years old when the Taliban took over, stayed in Kabul with his mother. **C**

As a toddler, Mirwais showed no interest in music. It wasn't until he was six, a year after his father's death, that anyone even heard him sing. According to Nur-ul-Haq, Mirwais had never hummed or whistled until the day when he climbed a pomegranate tree in the garden and sang to his mother. His voice was a revelation. She immediately apprenticed him to a music teacher, Ustaad Amin Jan Mazari, who listened to him and took him on for free. In the South Asian tradition of gurus and disciples,[4] Mirwais lived with his teacher "like a son," recalls Mazari. He did household chores and spent hours each day practicing the broad range of vocal scales found in classical Afghan music. Mirwais came to revere his master. Today, when they meet, the boy's face glows, and he bows to touch his teacher's feet. "He has good talent," says Mazari, "and, by the kindness of Allah, when Mirwais is 40 years old or so, with practice, he will become great."

. . . After the Taliban were defeated, singers began wandering back from exile in Europe and the U.S. to a tumultuous welcome, and Kabul's **virtuosos** unearthed the instruments they buried in their gardens. Songs now blast from Kabul shops, and more than a dozen radio stations flourish around the country. Mirwais, one of the first to sing in public after the Taliban's ouster,[5] is at the front of this revival. Despite his youth, he recognizes the enormity of the change. In the old days, he says, "If the Taliban caught me, they would have shaved my head. And only Allah knows what other punishments I would have faced." **D**

Remaining a singer until adulthood may be a challenge. Already, Mirwais works punishing hours, often singing until 3:00 A.M. and then rising late to ride his bicycle—whose handlebars have sprouted a bouquet of artificial flowers—to a dirt-floor schoolhouse that has no doors or windows to ward off the icy winter winds. Mirwais sits there with other drably uniformed boys, a bright kid with a sad smile. The schoolyard is full of toughs, and he knows better than to show off his one luxury, a new cell phone in which he's stored dozens of jangling tunes. **E**

C MAIN IDEA
How did the Taliban enforce the ban on music? Note the details that helped you answer this question.

virtuoso (vûr'cho͞o-ō'sō) *n.* a musician with excellent abilities, techniques, and/or an attractive personal style

D MAIN IDEA
Reread lines 56–65. How did Kabul change with the Taliban out of power? Add these details to your outline.

E FEATURE ARTICLE
Identify two examples of strong **imagery** used in this paragraph. What do they help you better understand about Mirwais's daily life?

3. **tabla** (tä'blə): a small hand drum of northern India.
4. **gurus and disciples** (go͝o-ro͞oz', dĭ-sī'pəls): spiritual or religious teachers and their students, who respect them very much.
5. **ouster** (ous'tər): the state of being ejected or forced out.

READING SKILL

C MAIN IDEA

Students should add the main idea and supporting details to their outlines.

Possible answer:

III. Ban on music by the Taliban regime

- *A. Arrests and beatings of musicians*
- *B. Ransacking of radio and TV stations*
- *C. Destruction of audiotape*

READING SKILL

D MAIN IDEA

Possible answer:

V. Change after the Taliban regime ousted

- *A. The return of musicians to Kabul*
- *B. Musical instruments in full view*
- *C. Songs played in shops*
- *D. Music on the radio*
- *E. Mirwais, the first to sing in public*

ELEMENTS OF NONFICTION

E FEATURE ARTICLE

Possible answer: *Examples of imagery include*

- *"handlebars have sprouted a bouquet of artificial flowers" (lines 68–69)*
- *"dirt-floor schoolhouse" (line 69)*
- *"icy winter winds" (line 70)*
- *"drably uniformed" (line 71)*
- *"a bright kid with a sad smile" (line 71)*
- *"dozens of jangling tunes" (line 73)*

These images show the contrast between the gritty reality of Mirwais's daily life and his positive attitude that allows him to take joy in the beauty of flowers and music.

FOR LESS–PROFICIENT READERS

Reading Skill Follow-Up: Identify Main Idea and Details [paired option] Have students work in pairs to update their outlines from page 919. Ask them to reread lines 42–55 to find the main idea of this section and add it to their outlines. Then have them list the details in the paragraph that support this main idea. Remind students to continue updating their outlines as they read the article.

Possible answer:

IV. Mirwais's talent

- *A. Recognition by his mother when he was six*
- *B. Apprenticeship under Ustaad Mazari*
- *C. Living with Mazari as a son*
  1. *Chores*
  2. *Practice*

ELEMENTS OF NONFICTION

F FEATURE ARTICLE

Possible answer: *Opinions: "Among the boy singers, Mirwais is tops" (line 81), "His performance blew the other contestants off the stage" (lines 89–90). The writer does not try to be objective; he does not profile any of Mirwais's competitors or interview people who are fans of other singers or who do not like or approve of Mirwais's music.*

If students need help . . . Review the differences between facts and opinions. Then work with students to complete the Distinguishing Fact and Opinion transparency.

BEST PRACTICES TOOLKIT—Transparency
Distinguishing Fact and Opinion p. A29

Extend the Discussion Why do you think writers of feature articles include their opinions about their subjects?

SELECTION WRAP–UP

REFLECT Ask students what details in the article helped them understand how important music is to Mirwais.

CRITIQUE Ask students if the writer provided enough background to help them understand why Mirwais is Kabul's "singing sensation."

READING FLUENCY

Distribute the copy masters and have students practice fluency.

RESOURCE MANAGER—Copy Master
Reading Fluency p. 121

Young artists like Mirwais have several advantages over their older rivals. The . . . clarity of their voices blends harmoniously with the Afghan rabab, an ancient, 19-stringed instrument that is a cross between a sitar and a mandolin.[6] And because he is still a boy, Mirwais is allowed at weddings to sing for both men and women, whose parties are strictly segregated. This will last until Mirwais turns 15 and is considered a man, no longer to be trusted around unveiled women.[7]

Targeted Passage ②

Among the boy singers, Mirwais is tops, though he has a 14-year-old rival, Wali Fateh Ali Khan, a favorite of former King Zahir Shah. But among the common folk, Mirwais is considered the best. He and his three-piece band—a tabla drummer and rabab and harmonium[8] players—were booked every night during the three-month wedding season prior to the holy month of Ramadan, when the partying stops. His crowning achievement came last September, when he won a famous singing contest at Kabul's Park Cinema. That day, Mirwais appeared in an **immaculate** white suit, handling the audience with the casual manner of a mite-sized Sinatra.[9] His performance blew the other contestants off the stage. F

immaculate (ĭ-măk'yə-lĭt) *adj.* spotless; very clean

F FEATURE ARTICLE
Identify one **opinion** given in this paragraph. Does the author try to be objective, or unbiased, in this article?

6. **sitar** (sĭ-tär'); **mandolin** (măn'də-lĭn'): two guitarlike string instruments.
7. **unveiled women:** Some Muslims (followers of Islam) believe that women should wear veils to hide themselves from all men except close family members.
8. **harmonium** (här-mo'nē-əm): an organlike keyboard instrument.
9. **Sinatra** (sə-nä'trə): Frank Sinatra (1915–1998). American singer and actor known for his beautiful voice.

Mirwais practices with his music teacher, Ustaad Mazari (center).

DIFFERENTIATED INSTRUCTION

FOR LESS–PROFICIENT READERS

② Targeted Passage [Lines 81–90]

This passage concludes the article by highlighting how extremely successful Mirwais is as a boy singer.

- Who is Wali Fateh Ali Khan?
- What did Mirwais do every night before the month of Ramadan?
- What is Mirwais's "crowning acheivement"?
- What do the common folk think about Mirwais?

FOR ADVANCED LEARNERS/PRE-AP

Make Judgments Have students participate in an informal classroom debate on these questions: Is the writer's tone, or attitude toward the subject, appropriate for discussing this topic? Why or why not? Challenge students to provide details from the text to support their positions.

fter Reading

omprehension

1. **Recall** When did Mirwais first sing?
2. **Recall** From whom did Mirwais receive his musical training?
3. **Recall** What advantages do younger singers have over older singers in Afghanistan?

ritical Analysis

4. **Summarize Main Ideas and Details** Look back at the outline you created while reading "Kabul's Singing Sensation." Based on the main ideas and details you noted, summarize the article.
5. **Examine Word Choice** What does Mirwais's voice sound like? Look back at the article and find words and **imagery** that help you "hear" Mirwais's voice.
6. **Analyze Quotations** A quotation is a direct statement made by someone. Lines 16, 20, and 63–65 contain three quotations from Mirwais. What do these quotations tell you about the young singer?
7. **Evaluate a Feature Article** Do you think Mirwais Najrabi is a good subject for a human-interest piece? Explain why most people would—or would not—be interested in reading about him.

xtension and Challenge

8. **Readers' Circle** What if **singing** were banned in this country? How would you react to this decision? What would you be willing to risk to preserve music? Consider how Mirwais and his family reacted to life under the Taliban as you discuss these and other questions.
9. SOCIAL STUDIES CONNECTION What is the current state of Afghanistan? What is life like for those who live there? Research the social and political climate of Afghanistan. Share your findings with the class.

A family rides on horseback through the mountains of Afghanistan.

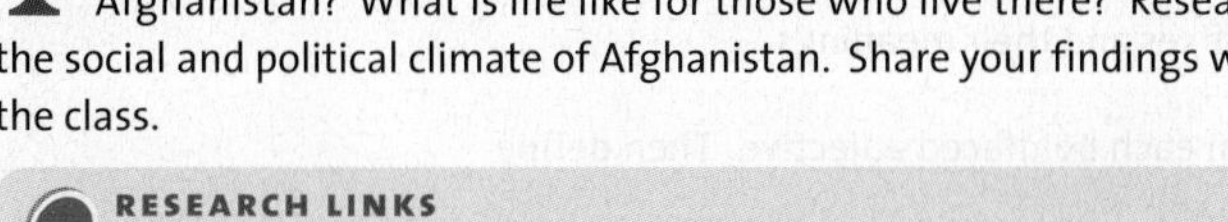

RESEARCH LINKS
For more on Afghanistan, visit the **Research Center** at **ClassZone.com.**

Practice and Apply

After Reading

For additional support of postreading questions, use these copy masters:

RESOURCE MANAGER—Copy Masters
Reading Check p. 118 (to check understanding of the selection)
Feature Article p. 111 (for practice of elements of nonfiction standards focus)
Question Support p. 119 (After Reading questions adapted for English learners and less-proficient readers)

Additional selection questions are provided for teachers on page 105.

ANSWERS

Comprehension

1. *He first sang when he was six years old.*
2. *Mirwais received his training from a music teacher, Ustaad Amin Jan Mazari.*
3. *Younger singers have voices that "blend harmoniously" with Afghan instruments. Also, young boys are allowed to sing at weddings for both men and women, whose parties are segregated (men over the age of 15 are not allowed to go to women's parties).*

Critical Analysis

Possible answers:

4. **STANDARDS FOCUS Identify Main Idea and Details** *Summaries should clearly state the main ideas and the most important supporting details. Example: Mirwais Najrabi is a talented young singer who has struggled to be successful in the aftermath of the Taliban's rule of Afghanistan.*
5. *Words and phrases used to describe Mirwais's voice include "exquisite purity" (line 7), "forceful and worldly" (line 11), "soulful melancholy" (line 17), "a revelation" (line 46), "clarity" (line 75), and "blends harmoniously" (line 75).*
6. *The quotations show that Mirwais is brave and that he is passionate about his music.*
7. **STANDARDS FOCUS Feature Article** *Accept any answer that states a position and provides specific reasons why Mirwais is or is not a good subject.*

Extension and Challenge

8. *Students' responses should reflect their personal attachment to music. Their responses should also compare the family's actions when music was banned with how students think they would respond to such a ban.*
9. **SOCIAL STUDIES CONNECTION** *Students' responses should demonstrate an understanding of the current situation in Afghanistan, including the type of government and the social climate.*

ANSWERS

Vocabulary in Context

VOCABULARY PRACTICE

1. *(b) a king's order*
2. *(a) being sent away*
3. *(c) without dirt*
4. *(b) like a group with strict rules*
5. *(b) rising above*
6. *(c) a musical star*

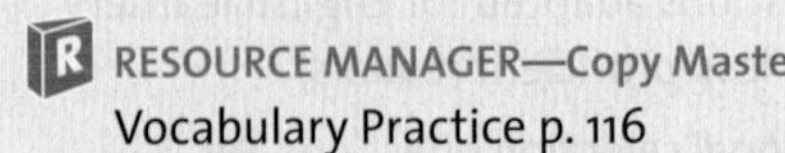
RESOURCE MANAGER—Copy Master
Vocabulary Practice p. 116

VOCABULARY IN WRITING

Suggest that before they start writing, students review the vocabulary words to see which ones would most likely be used to describe their favorite singer.

VOCABULARY STRATEGY: SUFFIXES THAT FORM ADJECTIVES *(also an EL language objective)*

- Have students divide each boldfaced word into parts (base word and suffix).
- Point out that all the suffixes listed in the chart have the same meaning.

Answers:

1. *joy, "causing joy"*
2. *sphere, "like a sphere"*
3. *expect, "having to do with expecting or waiting"*
4. *algebra, "having to do with algebra"*
5. *consider, "showing kindness to others"*

RESOURCE MANAGER—Copy Master
Vocabulary Strategy p. 117

Vocabulary Center at **ClassZone.com**
Additional Vocabulary Activities

Vocabulary in Context

VOCABULARY PRACTICE

Note the letter of the item that you might associate with each boldfaced word.

1. **edict:** (a) a friend's suggestion, (b) a king's order, (c) a polite request
2. **exile:** (a) being sent away, (b) being imprisoned, (c) having to pay a fine
3. **immaculate:** (a) without decorations, (b) without wrinkles, (c) without dirt
4. **puritanical:** (a) like a new school principal, (b) like a group with strict rules, (c) like a popular athletic coach
5. **transcendent:** (a) sinking down, (b) rising above, (c) solving problems
6. **virtuoso:** (a) a beginning violinist, (b) an off-key singer, (c) a musical star

edict
exile
immaculate
puritanical
transcendent
virtuoso

VOCABULARY IN WRITING

Tim McGirk used emotional language and imagery to describe Mirwais's voice. How would you describe your favorite singer? Using at least two vocabulary words, write a one-paragraph review of his or her music. You might start like this.

EXAMPLE SENTENCE

*Although he's only 16 years old, Chris is already a hip-hop **virtuoso**.*

VOCABULARY STRATEGY: SUFFIXES THAT FORM ADJECTIVES

A **suffix** is a word part that can be added to a root or base word to form a new word. Some suffixes, such as *-ical* in *puritanical,* can be added to nouns to form adjectives. Others, such as *-ent* in *transcendent,* can be added to verbs to form adjectives. If you can recognize the root or base word in a word with a suffix, you can often figure out the entire word's meaning. Consult the chart for common adjective suffixes and their meanings.

Suffix	Meaning
-ant, -ate, -ent, -ic, -ical, -ous	like; having to do with; showing; causing

PRACTICE Identify the base word in each boldfaced adjective. Then define the adjective.

1. Yesterday I received the **joyous** news that my grandmother will be coming to visit.
2. Like the earth, the moon is roughly **spherical.**
3. As he waits for his food, our dog wears an **expectant** expression.
4. Can you solve **algebraic** problems?
5. Mrs. Pine is a **considerate** host who makes sure that her guests are comfortable.

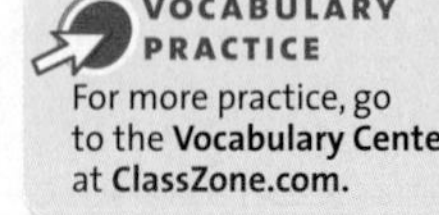
VOCABULARY PRACTICE
For more practice, go to the **Vocabulary Center** at **ClassZone.com.**

DIFFERENTIATED INSTRUCTION

FOR ENGLISH LEARNERS

Vocabulary in Writing Suggest that students model their opening sentence on the example sentence. Provide a sentence frame to help students write the next part of their responses:

His/Her music makes me feel ___________ *because* ___________.

Then have students write one or two more sentences to finish their responses.

FOR ADVANCED LEARNERS/PRE–AP

Vocabulary Strategy [small-group option] Assign groups of students one of the suffixes. Challenge groups to list as many words with the suffix as they can. Have them use their knowledge of the suffix's meaning or a dictionary to define each word they identify.

Reading-Writing Connection

Demonstrate your understanding of "Kabul's Singing Sensation" by responding to these prompts. Then complete the **Grammar and Writing** exercise.

WRITING PROMPTS	SELF-CHECK
A. Short Response: Write an Explanation Why do you think Mirwais and other Afghan musicians were willing to risk their lives for music? Write a **one-paragraph explanation** of Mirwais's possible motivation.	***A clear explanation will . . .*** • show an understanding of Mirwais's background and personality • consider the role music plays in culture
B. Extended Response: Write a Letter Music can connect people across distance and culture. Write a **two- or three-paragraph letter** to Mirwais expressing your reactions to the article you just read. Then share with him some of your own experiences and thoughts about **singing** and music.	***A successful letter will . . .*** • clearly state your opinion about what you read in the article • make connections between yourself and Mirwais

GRAMMAR AND WRITING

USE COMMAS CORRECTLY Be sure to insert commas after **introductory words and phrases** to avoid possible confusion. Place commas immediately after introductory words, such as *finally* and *afterwards,* and after introductory phrases.

Original: In Afghanistan the Taliban ransacked the Afghan Radio and Television station.

Revised: In Afghanistan, the Taliban ransacked the Afghan Radio and Television station.

PRACTICE In each sentence, add commas where they are needed.

1. Since the age of four I've played the trumpet.
2. Over the summer my friends and I formed a singing group.
3. After reading the article I wanted to hear your music.
4. Fortunately you were not harmed by the Taliban.

*For more help with commas, see page R49 in the **Grammar Handbook.***

DIFFERENTIATED INSTRUCTION

FOR LESS–PROFICIENT WRITERS

For Prompt A:

1. Discuss what motivated Mirwais and other Afghans to risk their lives for music.
2. List students' ideas on the board.
3. Help students use the ideas on the board to form a topic sentence.
4. Have students skim the article for information about Mirwais's background and personality to include in the supporting sentences.

For Prompt B:

Suggest that students write two-paragraph letters. They might organize their letters in this way:

- **First paragraph:** Use freewriting notes to express a personal reaction to the article.
- **Second paragraph:** Use freewriting notes to describe personal experiences and thoughts about singing and music and their connection to Mirwais.

Reading-Writing Connection

WRITING PROMPTS

- For **Prompt A,** point out that students should begin their explanation with a topic sentence that explains Mirwais's motivation. Remind students that they need to provide examples and details from the selection to support their topic sentence.
- For **Prompt B,** have students freewrite on their reaction to the article as well as their own experiences and thoughts about singing.

BEST PRACTICES TOOLKIT
Freewriting p. C1

For writing support, see
Writing Center at **ClassZone.com**

GRAMMAR AND WRITING

- Note that many introductory phrases are also prepositional phrases, such as *In Afghanistan* and *Among the singers.*
- Remind students that a prepositional phrase consists of a preposition (*in, among*), its object (*Afghanistan, singers*), and any modifiers (*the*).

Answers:

1. *Since the age of four, I've played the trumpet.*
2. *Over the summer, my friends and I formed a singing group.*
3. *After reading the article, I wanted to hear your music.*
4. *Fortunately, you were not harmed by the Taliban.*

RESOURCE MANAGER—Copy Master
Use Commas Correctly p. 120

Assess and Reteach

Assess

RESOURCE MANAGER—Copy Masters
Selection Tests A, B/C pp. 123–124, 125–126

Test Generator CD

Reteach

STANDARDS LESSON FILE
Reading Lesson 4: Recognizing Main Idea and Details
Vocabulary Lesson 7: Suffixes

Focus and Motivate

OBJECTIVES

Elements of Nonfiction
- explore the key idea of **science**
- identify and analyze author's purpose
- read a magazine article and an online article

Reading
- monitor comprehension by questioning, visualizing, and rereading

Vocabulary
- build vocabulary for reading and writing
- use knowledge of the Latin root *pend* to help determine word meanings *(also an EL language objective)*

SUMMARY

These articles discuss some of the scientific breakthroughs that have allowed people to lead longer, better lives. Through personal stories and facts, "Robo-Legs" explores how robotic prosthetic limbs provide increased mobility for many amputees, in some cases blurring the line between human and machine. "Eureka: Scientific Twists of Fate" explores the relationship between luck and scientific talent, using the discoveries of penicillin and the cure for smallpox as examples.

How has SCIENCE *changed our lives?*

Have students read the question and the ***KEY IDEA***. Ask the class to brainstorm a list of breakthroughs in **science.** Ask students in what ways each breakthrough has changed people's lives. Then have students work on the ***QUICKWRITE*** activity.

Before Reading

Robo-Legs

Magazine Article by Michel Marriott

Eureka: Scientific Twists of Fate

Online Article

How has SCIENCE *changed our lives?*

KEY IDEA The next time you answer a cell phone, turn on a light, or take your asthma medicine, think about the knowledge that was needed to create these things. **Science** has made it possible for doctors, engineers, and inventors to develop technologies and medicines that make our lives healthier and more convenient. In the following articles, you'll read about some of the amazing scientific breakthroughs that have allowed people to lead longer, better lives.

QUICKWRITE What is one scientific development that you feel you could not live without? Think beyond obvious technological gadgets such as your computer or cell phone. Write one paragraph telling what a day might be like if this discovery had never taken place.

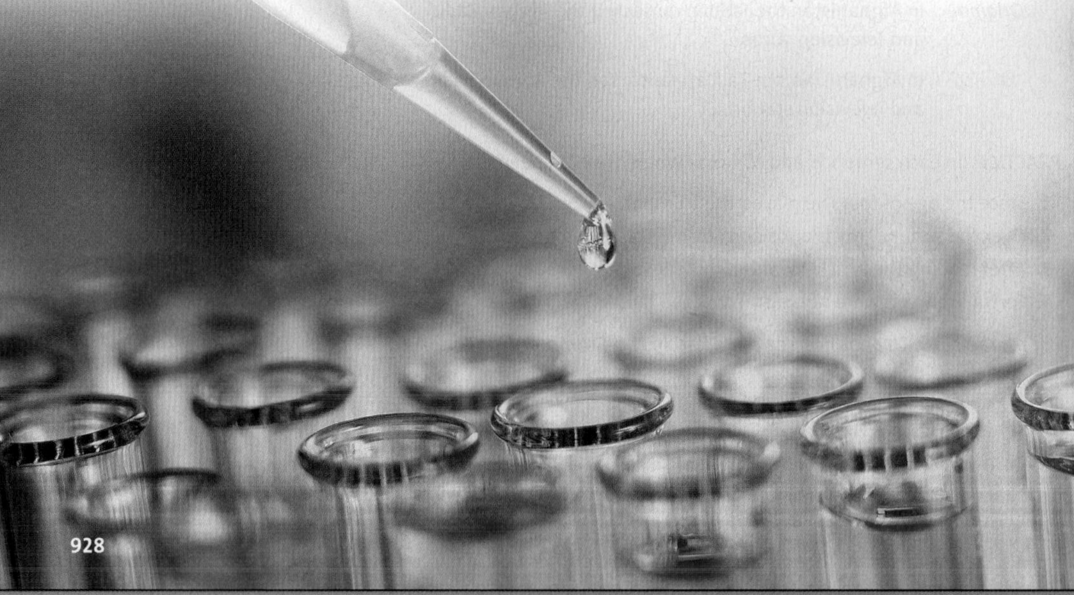

928

Selection Resources

RESOURCE MANAGER UNIT 8

Plan and Teach pp. 127–134

Elements of Nonfiction
Summary pp. 135†*, 136‡*
Author's Purpose pp. 137, 138†*
Question Support p. 145*

Reading
Monitor pp. 139, 140†*
Reading Check p. 144
Reading Fluency p. 146

Vocabulary
Study p. 141*
Practice p. 142
Strategy p. 143

Assessment
Selection Tests A, B/C pp. 147*, 149*
Test Generator CD

BEST PRACTICES TOOLKIT
Differentiated Instruction pp. 31–38*
Scaffolding Instruction pp. 43–46*

Graphic Organizers/Strategies
New Word Analysis • Jigsaw Reading • Concept Cards

Reading Support
Audio Anthology CD*

Technology
Literature and Vocabulary Centers at **ClassZone.com**
WriteSmart CD

* Resources for Differentiation † Also in Spanish ‡ In Haitian Creole and Vietnamese

LEMENTS OF NONFICTION: AUTHOR'S PURPOSE

When you write an e-mail to a friend, you often do so with a purpose—to tell him or her about your day, or to inquire about this weekend's plans. An **author's purpose** is his or her reason for writing a certain piece. That reason might be to persuade, to entertain, to inform or explain, or to express his or her thoughts and feelings. Although a writer may have more than one reason for writing, usually one purpose stands out.

You can figure out an author's purpose by examining the author's subject, **tone,** and words. For example, a serious piece about the environment is probably meant to inform or persuade. Your reaction to a piece is also a good indicator. If you laugh out loud while reading an essay, then the author's purpose is probably to entertain. As you read the following articles, try to identify each author's purpose.

EADING STRATEGY: MONITOR

When you **monitor** your reading, you pause to check your comprehension of the material. To monitor effectively, pause frequently and try the following strategies:

- **Ask questions** about the information presented.
- **Visualize,** or picture, events and details described.
- **Reread** passages that you find confusing.

Use a chart like the one shown to help you monitor.

Where I Paused	What Confused Me	How I Clarified the Information

OCABULARY IN CONTEXT

How many of the boldfaced words do you know? Use context clues to figure out a definition for each.

1. People who lose an **appendage** can still exercise.
2. The pollution could **contaminate** the water supply.
3. **Infectious** diseases can be transmitted quickly.
4. I need **keener** eyesight to thread the needle.
5. Roberto gains **mobility** by using a wheelchair.
6. The infection was **pervasive** throughout her body.
7. Mrs. Blake needed **rehabilitation** following knee surgery.
8. The scientist's **serendipitous** discovery led to a cure.

Author Online

A Born Communicator Michel Marriott says that he was "practically born talking." As a child, he talked all the time, and eventually he began writing out his thoughts on paper. Through his work at his school newspaper, Marriott realized that journalism was a good career choice. Since then, Marriott has worked for the *Washington Post, Newsweek,* and *The New York Times*, covering a variety of topics, including technology, fashion, and urban crime. In 1995, director Spike Lee produced *New Jersey Drive,* a film based on Marriott's series of articles about the desperate lives of young car thieves. The series was nominated for a Pulitzer Prize.

Michel Marriott
born 1954

MORE ABOUT THE AUTHOR
For more on Michel Marriott, visit the **Literature Center** at **ClassZone.com.**

Background

Marvelous Medical Inventions Throughout history, scientists and inventors have worked to make life better for those with physical disabilities. The first eyeglasses were created in the 1200s. The first hearing aids, called "trumpets," were invented in the early 1800s. Prosthetics, used to replace missing arms and legs, were made of wood or metal as long ago as the days of ancient Rome. In medieval times, a knight who lost an arm could be fitted with a metal prosthetic that held a shield during battle. In the 1800s, wooden legs were fashioned to resemble real legs. They included springs and sockets to allow movement. Today, scientists draw on robotics and a better understanding of the human body to create prosthetics that are very similar to real limbs.

929

Teach

STANDARDS FOCUS

ELEMENTS OF NONFICTION

● AUTHOR'S PURPOSE

Write this example on the board:

Did you know that chicken pox is a deadly disease? The good news: a vaccination is now available. Some people refuse to be vaccinated for fear the vaccination itself will make them ill, but research studies have proven that the risk of dying from the disease far outweighs the risks from the vaccine.

Ask: What is the author's purpose? ***Possible answer:*** *to persuade people to get vaccinated for chicken pox*

CHECK UNDERSTANDING Ask students what genres authors might use if their purpose is to inform readers.

READING STRATEGY

■ MONITOR

Ask students why asking questions about a difficult passage can help them make sense of it. ***Possible answer:*** *Asking a question about what confuses you can help you focus your reading on finding an answer.*

CHECK UNDERSTANDING Have students read **Author Online** and ask questions to clarify the information.

RESOURCE MANAGER—Copy Master
Monitor p. 139 (for student use while reading the selections)

VOCABULARY SKILL

▲ VOCABULARY IN CONTEXT

DIAGNOSE WORD KNOWLEDGE To determine preteaching needs, have all students complete **Vocabulary in Context.** ***Possible answers:*** **1.** *arm or leg* **2.** *to make dirty or impure* **3.** *able to be passed from person to person* **4.** *sharper; more highly developed* **5.** *the ability to move around* **6.** *widespread* **7.** *special exercises in order to recover from an injury* **8.** *lucky*

PRETEACH VOCABULARY Use the Vocabulary Study copy master to help students explore the meaning of each boldfaced word.

1. Read aloud the first sentence, emphasizing the boldfaced word.
2. Discuss possible meanings for *appendage,* such as "limb." Work with students to create a word map for *appendage.*
3. Repeat for each of the other sentences.
4. Have students complete Part B on their own.

RESOURCE MANAGER—Copy Master
Vocabulary Study p. 141

For general guidelines on differentiating vocabulary instruction and for alternative vocabulary activities for students not needing vocabulary preteaching, see

BEST PRACTICES TOOLKIT
Scaffolding Vocabulary Instruction pp. 43–46

Vocabulary Center at **ClassZone.com**

Practice and Apply

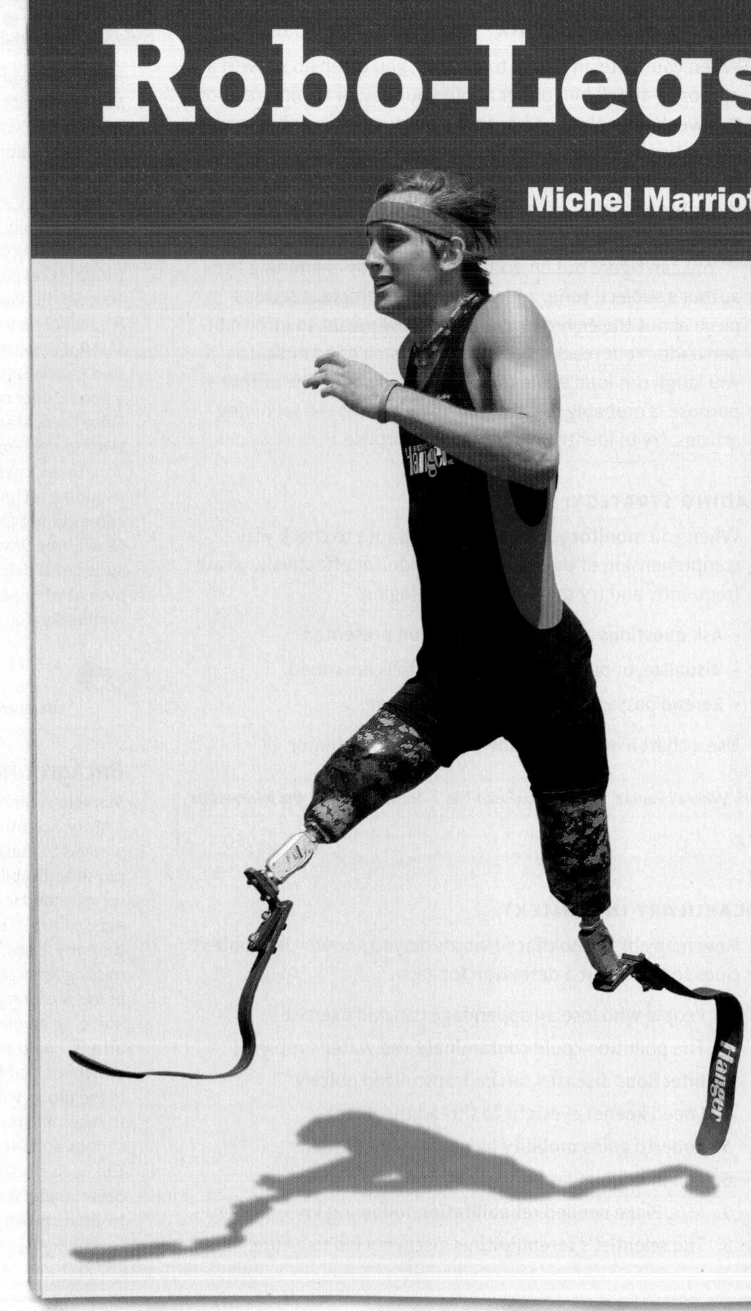

ANALYZE VISUALS
This photo shows Cameron Clapp competing at the 2005 Endeavor Games. Based on his body language and facial expression, what can you **conclude** about Clapp's personality?

ANALYZE VISUALS

Possible answer: *His body language suggests that he is energetic and determined. The smile on his face suggests that he has an optimistic personality.*

DIFFERENTIATED INSTRUCTION

FOR ALL STUDENTS

Enhance Learning Styles Provide these projects for various learning styles:

- **Interpersonal** Write and perform an interview with Cameron Clapp.
- **Visual** Create a comic strip.
- **Linguistic** Write a persuasive essay.

For further details on these projects, see

 RESOURCE MANAGER
Ideas for Extension pp. 132–133

FOR ENGLISH LEARNERS

Key Academic Vocabulary Use New Word Analysis to teach these terms in "Robo-Legs": *generation(s)* (lines 11, 42), *technology(ies)* (lines 12, 15, 16, 18, 21, 38). In "Eureka": *research* (lines 12, 32), *benefits* (line 46).

 BEST PRACTICES TOOLKIT—Transparency
New Word Analysis p. E8

Prereading For prereading instruction for English learners, see

 BEST PRACTICES TOOLKIT
Scaffolding Reading Instruction pp. 43–46

Options for Reading [small-group option] Have students silently read along as they listen to the *Audio Anthology CD*. Then divide students into Jigsaw Reading groups and assign one Targeted Passage to each group. When groups can read their passages fluently, have them do a choral reading for the class and conduct a discussion of each passage's main idea.

 BEST PRACTICES TOOLKIT
Jigsaw Reading p. A1

New prosthetic limbs[1] are providing increased ***mobility*** *for many amputees—and blurring the line between humans and machines*

mobility (mō-bĭl'ĭ-tē) *n.* the capability of moving from place to place

With his blond hair, buff torso, and megawatt smile, Cameron Clapp is in many ways the typical California teenager. There are, however, a few things that set him apart: For starters, this former skater boy is now making his way through life on a pair of shiny, state-of-the-art[2] robotic legs. **A**

"I make it look easy," he says.

Clapp, 19, lost both his legs above the knee and his right arm just short of his shoulder after getting hit by a train almost five years ago near his home in Grover Beach, California. Following years of **rehabilitation** and a series of prosthetics, each more technologically advanced than the last, he has become part of a new generation of people who are embracing breakthrough technologies as a means of overcoming their own bodies' limitations.

"I do have a lot of motivation and self-esteem," Clapp says, "but I might look at myself differently if technology was not on my side."

The technology he's referring to is the C-Leg. Introduced by Otto Bock HeathCare, a German company that makes advanced prosthetics, the C-Leg combines computer technology with hydraulics. Sensors monitor how the leg is being placed on the ground, and microprocessors[3] guide the limb's hydraulic system, enabling it to imitate a natural step. It literally does the walking for the walker. The technology, however, is not cheap; a single C-Leg can cost more than $40,000. **B**

The C-Leg is one of the examples of how blazing advancements, including tiny programmable microprocessors, lightweight materials, and **keener** sensors, are restoring remarkable degrees of mobility to amputees, says William Hanson, president of . . . a Massachusetts company that specializes in developing and distributing advanced prosthetic arms and hands.

A AUTHOR'S PURPOSE
Reread lines 1–5. Based on the information presented so far, what one or two purposes do you think the author has for writing?

rehabilitation (rē'hə-bĭl'ĭ-tā'shən) *n.* the process of restoring someone to physical capability, usually through exercise and physical therapy

B MONITOR
Examine lines 16–21. What words and phrases help you **visualize** Clapp's legs? Compare your mental image with the photo on page 930.

keener (kēn'ər) *adj.* more acutely sensitive

① Targeted Passage

1. **prosthetic limbs** (prŏs-thĕt'ĭk lĭmz): artificial arms and legs.
2. **state-of-the-art**: made using the newest technology available.
3. **microprocessors:** tiny computer parts that operators can program, or give new instructions to.

ELEMENTS OF NONFICTION

A AUTHOR'S PURPOSE

Possible answer: *The author wants to inform readers about new technology (prosthetic limbs). The author also wants to entertain readers with phrases like "buff torso, and megawatt smile" (line 1) and "skater boy" (line 4).*

READING STRATEGY

B MONITOR

Possible answer: *The details "C-Leg" (line 16), "combines computer technology with hydraulics" (line 18), "sensors monitor" (line 18), and "microprocessors guide the limb's hydraulic system" (lines 19–20) help readers visualize Clapp's legs. Students' responses will vary as to how closely their mental images match the photograph on page 930.*

If students need help . . .

- Ask them to think about how the name of the prosthetic, *C-Leg*, relates to its structure. Can they see the shape of the letter *c* in the device?
- Clarify that a hydraulic system uses fluid under pressure to do work—for example, to lift a car so that mechanics can work on it from below. Help them find the cylinder-shaped hydraulic systems in the photograph on page 930.

FOR LESS–PROFICIENT READERS

In combination with the *Audio Anthology CD*, use one or more Targeted Passages (pp. 931, 933, 934) to ensure that students focus on each article's key concepts and skills.

① Targeted Passage [Lines 16–28]

This passage describes the technology behind the "robo-legs."

- What is the C-Leg?
- What does the C-Leg combine with computer technology?
- In what ways is the C-Leg an advancement over previous prosthetic devices?

Concept Cards Give students an index card for each article. Ask them to skim each article, looking only at headings, subheadings, captions, and other text features. Have them write on the card their predictions about what the article will be about. Remind students to check and revise their predictions after reading.

BEST PRACTICES TOOLKIT—Transparency
Concept Cards p. A19

FOR ADVANCED LEARNERS/PRE–AP

Pre-AP exercises in the bottom channel provide additional challenge for your advanced students. Use them for small groups or individuals.

ADDITIONAL GUIDELINES

For more help with differentiation and tips for classroom management, see

BEST PRACTICES TOOLKIT
Differentiated Instruction pp. 31–38

Lines 29–34

REINFORCE *KEY IDEA:* SCIENCE

Discuss What is one way in which **science** has affected the world of sports? What rules might be needed to make sure some competitors in the Endeavor Games don't have an unfair advantage? ***Possible answer:*** *The science of prosthetic limbs has led to the creation of sporting events for people who have lost arms and legs. Events like the Endeavor Games would need to have rules about the technology athletes use, so that expensive devices like the C-Leg wouldn't give some athletes an advantage over others who don't have them.*

ELEMENTS OF NONFICTION

C AUTHOR'S PURPOSE

Possible answer: *The author provides these details to inform readers about ways in which technology allows people who are missing limbs to continue participating in their favorite activities, like walking, running, and swimming.*

READING STRATEGY

D MONITOR

Remind students to record their responses in their charts from page 929. *Accept all reasonable responses. Students may have questions about the paragraph's vocabulary or about the concept of the blurred line between humans and machines.*

Clapp's prosthetic legs feature several attachments to suit different purposes.

Three Sets of Legs

For example, Clapp, who remains very involved in athletics despite his condition, has three different sets of specialized prosthetic legs: one for walking, one for running, and one for swimming. He put all of them to use at the Endeavor Games in Edmond, Oklahoma—an annual sporting event for athletes with disabilities—where he competed in events like the 200-meter dash and the 50-yard freestyle swim. **C**

C AUTHOR'S PURPOSE Why do you think the author included facts about Clapp's three sets of prosthetic legs?

Man or Machine?

But increased mobility is only part of the story. Something more subtle, and possibly far-reaching, is also occurring: The line that has long separated human beings from the machines that assist them is blurring, as complex technologies become a visible part of the people who depend upon them. **D**

D MONITOR What **questions** do you have after reading this paragraph? Decide whether to reread or read on for answers.

Increasingly, amputees, especially young men like Clapp, and soldiers who have lost limbs in Afghanistan and Iraq, are choosing not to hide their

DIFFERENTIATED INSTRUCTION

FOR LESS–PROFICIENT READERS

Reading Strategy Follow-Up: Monitor [paired option] Have students work in pairs to update their charts from page 929. Ask pairs to choose a difficult passage from page 932 or 933 to clarify. Encourage partners to talk about the passage and to share what each finds difficult about it. Then have pairs work together to decide what strategy they will use to help them clarify this information.

Where I Paused	What Confused Me	How I Clarified the Information
Lines 36–39	I don't understand what the author means about lines blurring.	I asked questions and then read on to clarify the information.
Lines 50–59	I'm confused about what happened at the party.	I visualized the scene.

prosthetics under clothing as previous generations did. Instead, some of the estimated 1.2 million amputees in the United States—more than two-thirds of whom are men—proudly polish and decorate their electronic limbs for all to see. . . .

Many young people, especially those who have been using personal electronics since childhood, are comfortable recharging their limbs' batteries in public and plugging their prosthetics into their computers to adjust the software, Hanson says.

Nick Springer, 20, a student at Eckerd College in St. Petersburg, Florida, who lost his arms and legs to meningitis when he was 14, recalls doing just that at a party when the lithium-ion batteries[4] for his legs went dead.

"I usually get 30 hours out of them before I have to charge them again," he says. "But I didn't charge them up the day before."

Terminator Legs

When his legs ran out of power, he spent most of his time sitting on a couch talking to people while his legs were plugged into an electrical outlet nearby. According to Springer, no one at the party seemed to care, and his faith in his high-tech **appendages** appears unfazed. "I love my Terminator[5] legs," he says. E

Springer also remembers going to see *Star Wars: Episode III—Revenge of the Sith* with his father. While he liked the movie, he found the final scenes—in which Anakin Skywalker loses his arms and legs in a light-saber battle and is rebuilt with fully functional prosthetics to become the infamous Darth Vader—a little far-fetched.

"We have a long way to go before we get anything like that," he says. "But look how far humanity has come in the past decade. Who knows? The hardest part is getting the ball rolling. We pretty much got it rolling."

Nick Springer plays hockey with the help of specially-made prosthetics. © Dith Pran/New York Times/Redux.

appendage (ə-pĕn'dĭj) *n.* a body part, such as an arm or leg, that is attached to the main part of the body

E AUTHOR'S PURPOSE
Reread lines 55–59. What do you think is Marriott's attitude toward the subject of today's prosthetics and the people who use them?

2 Targeted Passage

4. **lithium-ion batteries** (lĭth'ē-əm–ī'ŏn' băt'ə-rēz): very light, small batteries with a great deal of energy packed into a small space.
5. **Terminator:** a robotic character in a 1984 film, *The Terminator.*

ELEMENTS OF NONFICTION

E AUTHOR'S PURPOSE

Possible answer: *Marriott's attitude, or tone, is lighthearted when he describes Nick Springer. He also has a tone of wonder or amazement when describing the technology Springer uses.*

If students need help . . . Remind them that an author's tone, or attitude toward a subject, can often be described in one word, such as *happy, admiring, bitter,* or *upbeat.* Suggest that students skim the article for details and descriptions the author uses when describing the prosthetics and the people who use them, such as "blazing advancements" (line 23) and "his faith in his high-tech appendages appears unfazed" (line 58).

Lines 40–59
DISCUSSION PROMPTS

Use these prompts to help students understand how young amputees feel about their high-tech prosthetics:

Summarize Summarize Nick Springer's experience at the party. ***Possible answer:*** *While at a party, the batteries for his prosthetic legs died. He plugged them into an electrical outlet to recharge the batteries, and in the meantime sat on a couch talking to people. The other party-goers didn't appear to think anything of it.*

Analyze What do you think explains the differences between the way today's amputees feel about their prosthetics and the way amputees in past generations felt? ***Possible answer:*** *The difference in people's attitudes toward their prosthetics may reflect changes in society. Society today has access to more information, which might make people more accepting of others with various handicaps.*

Speculate Why do you think over two-thirds of amputees are men? ***Possible answer:*** *Military personnel lose limbs during times of war, and the majority of people in the military are men. Also, men make up a higher proportion of the industrial workforce, and accidents involving industrial jobs could cause the loss of a limb.*

FOR LESS–PROFICIENT READERS

2 Targeted Passage [Lines 60–78]

This passage concludes the article with a comparison of real life to a science-fiction movie scene.

- In the movie *Star Wars: Episode III,* what happens to Anakin Skywalker after he loses his arms and legs?
- Why does Nick Springer find this scene "a little far-fetched"?
- What does Springer mean when he says, "We pretty much got it [the ball] rolling"?

FOR ENGLISH LEARNERS

Vocabulary Support Discuss with students the meanings of these words and phrases. Then work together to use them in new sentences.

- *amputees* (line 40), "people who have lost limbs"
- *functional* (line 66), "usable"
- *far-fetched* (line 69), "hard to believe"
- *humanity* (line 73), "people"
- *getting the ball rolling* (lines 76–77), "starting the process"

BACKGROUND

Smallpox Smallpox was originally called *variola,* from the Latin word for "spotted." A hallmark of the disease is the small raised bumps that appear on victims' bodies. While 30 percent of victims have died, survivors of the disease include Abraham Lincoln and Joseph Stalin.

Due to a worldwide vaccination campaign, the last known case of smallpox occurred in 1977, in Somalia. The last known case in the United States was in 1949. Even so, smallpox was responsible for an estimated 300 to 500 million deaths in the 20th century. Currently, vaccinations for smallpox are not available for the general population in the United States, but vaccinations are required for some U.S. military personnel.

Eureka *Eureka,* which is from the Greek word for "I have found (it)," is a term used when someone is excited about a new discovery. It gained fame during the California Gold Rush of 1849, when prospectors would shout "Eureka!" upon finding gold. The word actually dates back to the third century B.C., when Archimedes, the Greek mathematician, engineer, and physicist, exclaimed *"Heureka!"* after figuring out the formula for determining the purity of gold. Help students see why the author used this word in the article's title.

ELEMENTS OF NONFICTION

Ⓐ AUTHOR'S PURPOSE

Possible answer: *The author wants to inform readers about scientific discoveries that happened by accident. Based on the lighthearted tone of the introduction, it seems that the author also wants to entertain readers.*

If students need help . . . Read aloud the first paragraph of the article. As you read, emphasize details and descriptions that help readers determine the author's tone.

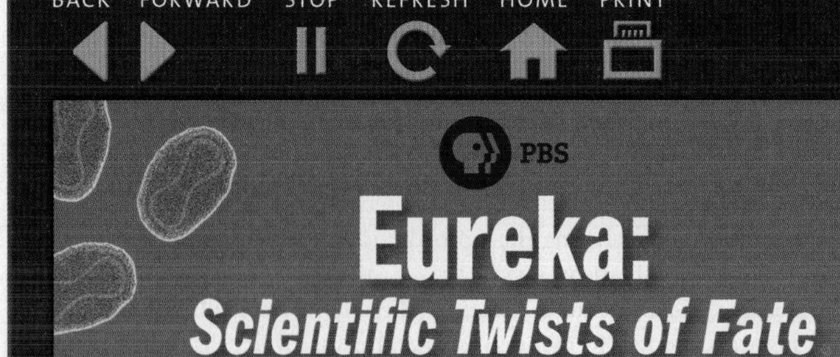

BACK FORWARD STOP REFRESH HOME PRINT
PBS
Eureka:
Scientific Twists of Fate

Targeted Passage 

Ⓐ AUTHOR'S PURPOSE Based on the tone of this paragraph and the information presented, what do you think might be the purpose or purposes of this article?

. . . We are all familiar with the tale of Newton's apple. While sitting in his orchard one day in 1665, Isaac Newton's[1] curiosity was sparked by a falling apple, leading him to "discover" the law of gravity. As doubtful as the story sounds, writings by Newton and his contemporaries verify the incident. Though science often seems an orderly and methodical process, history is dotted with surprising discoveries such as these. Were they merely luck? Or the results of a gifted mind? Actually, a bit of both. Sometimes scientific discoveries come from the most unexpected places, when talented people are watching out for them. Here are two examples of similarly **serendipitous** finds. Ⓐ

serendipitous (sĕr′ən-dĭp′ĭ-təs) *adj.* found by fortunate accident

The Smallpox Cure

In the late 1700s, Edward Jenner, a young English doctor-in-training, was told by a local milkmaid that she was safe from smallpox[2] because she had already had cowpox. Like its deadly cousin, cowpox also produced painful blisters, yet doctors had not made a connection between the two diseases. After extensive research, Jenner discovered that what she said was true—milkmaids exposed to a common strain of cowpox almost never contracted smallpox.

Jenner's supervising physicians took little interest in his findings. Then, in 1796, he injected a young boy named James Phipps with tissue taken from a cowpox blister on a milkmaid's hand. He then exposed the boy to the deadly smallpox virus. So **pervasive** and devastating was this disease at the time that the boy's family was willing to take this unimaginable risk. But their gamble paid off. Young James remained completely healthy, and the vaccination process was born.

pervasive (pər-vā′sĭv) *adj.* present throughout

Jenner's idea opened the door not only to the eradication of smallpox but to the subsequent perfection of the immunization procedure by Louis Pasteur.[3] The modern

1. **Isaac Newton:** mathematician and scientist (1642–1727) who developed the theory of gravity.
2. **smallpox:** a highly infectious, often fatal disease characterized by high fevers and blisters that leave pockmarks on the skin.
3. **Louis Pasteur** (lo͞o′ē păs-tûr′): French chemist (1822–1895) who founded modern microbiology and developed several life-saving vaccines.

DIFFERENTIATED INSTRUCTION

FOR LESS–PROFICIENT READERS

③ Targeted Passage [Lines 1–8]

This passage presents the article's main idea: "Sometimes scientific discoveries come from the most unexpected places, when talented people are watching out for them."

- What is "the tale of Newton's apple"?
- What is the topic of this article?
- Does the author think science's surprising discoveries were merely luck?
- What does the author mean by "similarly serendipitous finds"?

FOR ENGLISH LEARNERS

Vocabulary: Cognates Remind students to look for cognates as they read this article. Spanish cognates on pages 934–935 include

- *curiosity/curiosidad* (line 2)
- *gravity/gravedad* (line 3)
- *methodical/metódico* (line 5)
- *inject/inyectar* (line 16)
- *cultivate/cultivar* (line 33)
- *microbe/microbio* (line 36)
- *antibiotic/antibiótico* (line 48)

CK FORWARD STOP REFRESH HOME PRINT

term "vaccine," from the Latin word for "cow," honors Jenner and his life-saving inspiration. . . . **B**

Alexander Fleming

B MONITOR
Reread the subheading of this section. Based on this, what question about smallpox should you be able to answer? If you can't answer this question for yourself, **reread** lines 9–25.

Penicillin

Arguably the most important medical discovery of the 20th century came about purely by accident. Throughout the 1920s, Scottish scientist Alexander Fleming was searching for a cure for **infectious** disease, the major cause of death throughout much of human history. As part of his research, Fleming was cultivating several species of bacteria in separate petri dishes.

infectious (ĭn-fĕk'shəs) *adj.* capable of being transmitted by infection

One day, Fleming noticed that a mold had **contaminated** the petri dish containing the bacteria *Staphylococcus,* a common microbe responsible for a variety of ailments ranging from the earaches to deadly post-operative infections. But before tossing away the moldy dish, Fleming realized that the intruder had actually killed off much of the bacteria culture.

contaminate (kən-tăm'ə-nāt') *v.* to make impure or unclean through contact

The tiny, wind-born mold spore must have landed in the *Staphylococcus* colony during a brief moment Fleming had uncovered the dish. Fleming isolated the mold and identified it as a member of the genus *Penicillium.* He called the antibiotic substance it secreted penicillin.

Fleming's further investigation found that penicillin killed off several, but not all, strains of the disease-causing microbes he was growing in his lab. Had the penicillium contaminated a different dish, Fleming might never have discovered its medicinal benefits.

Additionally, Fleming found penicillin was non-toxic to humans and animals. Realizing the strategic advantage in possessing the world's first antibiotic, the U.S. and Britain joined forces to mass-produce the drug, and treated thousands of Allied troops wounded in the D-Day invasion of Europe. It has saved countless lives ever since. In 1945, Fleming shared the Nobel Prize in Medicine for his work on the "Wonder Drug" penicillin. . . . **C**

C MONITOR
Why is penicillin important? Reread this section if you don't know the answer.

Serendipity or Smarts?

Each of these examples of serendipity helped advance the scope of human knowledge by great leaps and bounds. But these accidents and twists of fate are not quite as random as they seem. Each discovery occurred in the presence of a well-trained intellect. . . . As Louis Pasteur once said, "In the fields of observation, chance favors only the prepared mind."

READING STRATEGY

B MONITOR

Remind students to record their responses in their charts from page 929. *Students should be able to answer this question: How was the cure for smallpox discovered?*

READING STRATEGY

C MONITOR

Possible answer: *Penicillin kills bacteria and is safe in most humans and animals. It has saved countless lives.*

Lines 26–51

DISCUSSION PROMPTS

Use this prompt to help students understand how penicillin was discovered:

Analyze Why does the author consider the discovery of penicillin one of the "scientific twists of fate"? Do you agree? Explain.
Possible answer: *He considers it a twist of fate because Fleming was not investigating mold spores to find out if they could be used to fight disease. Rather, Fleming noticed that a mold spore that had blown into a petri dish by accident was killing the bacteria in the dish, which led him to isolate penicillin from the mold. Some students will agree this was a twist of fate since it was luck that caused the mold to land in the right petri dish. Some may argue that it was more than just fate; Fleming's response needs to be acknowledged as well.*

SELECTION WRAP-UP

REFLECT Ask students which article they find more relevant to their lives, and why.

★ **CRITIQUE** Have students tell which article they would suggest to a friend who wanted to learn more about how science has changed people's lives, and why.

READING FLUENCY

Distribute the copy masters and have students practice fluency.

RESOURCE MANAGER—Copy Master
Reading Fluency p. 146

FOR ENGLISH LEARNERS

Vocabulary: Specialized Terms [paired option] Have pairs use context clues and a dictionary to define these medical terms:

- *strain* (line 13), "type or kind"
- *immunization* (line 22), "vaccination; the injection of a weakened form of a bacterium into the body to help the body develop defenses to fight off the bacterium"
- *bacteria* (line 34), "germs; tiny, one-celled organisms that can cause illness"
- *ailments* (line 36), "illnesses"

FOR ADVANCED LEARNERS/PRE-AP

Make Judgments [paired option] Explain to students that writers often spend a great deal of time deciding on the titles and subheadings for articles such as the two in this lesson. Ask students to work in pairs to come up with an alternative title and subheadings for one of the articles. Remind them that their titles need to grab readers' attention so that they will want to read the entire article. Have pairs share their changes with the class. Discuss how effective students' changes are.

Practice and Apply

After Reading

For additional support of postreading questions, use these copy masters:

RESOURCE MANAGER—Copy Masters

Reading Check p. 144 (to check understanding of the selection)

Author's Purpose p. 137 (for practice of elements of nonfiction standards focus)

Question Support p. 145 (After Reading questions adapted for English learners and less-proficient readers)

Additional selection questions are provided for teachers on page 131.

ANSWERS

Comprehension

1. *The C-Leg's sensors monitor how the leg is placed on the ground, while microprocessors guide the limb to move in the correct way.*
2. *The current generation of amputees is not ashamed of their prosthetic limbs. They display them proudly.*
3. *Phipps's family was willing to risk his exposure to smallpox because of the potential to prevent the disease from spreading and causing further devastation.*

Critical Analysis

Possible answers:

4. *The author wants to share with readers how important technology is becoming in our lives. Humans and robotics are combining in new ways, and we have yet to see the full impact of these developments.*
5. *Pasteur means that in science, discoveries are often made though luck, but someone must be observant and follow up on it for discoveries to happen. Examples: Edward Jenner paid attention when he heard about a woman who had been exposed to cowpox and was immune to smallpox. He followed up and found a vaccine for smallpox. Alexander Fleming was observant when he noticed the effect that mold had on bacteria. He used this information to discover penicillin.*
6. ■ **STANDARDS FOCUS Monitor** *Accept all answers that point to specific examples and techniques that helped students clarify information in the articles.*
7. ● **STANDARDS FOCUS Author's Purpose** *The main purpose of "Robo-Legs" is to inform readers about advancements in prosthetic technology. The main purpose of "Eureka" is to inform readers about how commonly known medical advancements were discovered by accident.*
8. *The articles are both about amazing scientific discoveries. They aim to inform and entertain the reader. The authors both use entertaining anecdotes to "hook" readers, and they describe the discoveries with a lighthearted tone. The articles were presented in a single lesson to show that articles about slightly different subjects can accomplish the same purpose.*

Extension and Challenge

9. *Students' responses might reflect personal experiences with serious medical conditions, such as cancer. Allow students the option of writing in a journal instead of discussing with a group.*
10. **SCIENCE CONNECTION** *Students' responses should demonstrate an understanding of the variety of ways robotics are used today.*

After Reading

Comprehension

1. **Recall** How does the C-Leg described in "Robo-Legs" work?
2. **Summarize** According to "Robo-Legs," what is different about the way young amputees feel about their prosthetic limbs?
3. **Clarify** James Phipps is mentioned in "Eureka: Scientific Twists of Fate." Why was his family willing to risk his exposure to the smallpox virus?

Critical Analysis

4. **Examine the Message** Reread the first paragraph of "Robo-Legs" as well as lines 23–28 and 35–39. Based on the information stated and the descriptive words and phrases used, what do you think is the message the author wants to share about **science** and technology?
5. **Interpret Quotation** "Eureka: Scientific Twists of Fate" contains this quote from Louis Pasteur: "In the fields of observation, chance favors only the prepared mind." What does he mean? Use examples from the article to support your answer.
6. **Evaluate Monitoring Techniques** Look back at the chart you created as you read. Which strategy best helped you understand the articles? Explain.
7. **Analyze Authors' Purposes** Reflect back on your reading of both articles. What's the author's main purpose in "Robo-Legs"? What is the main purpose of "Eureka: Scientific Twists of Fate"? Give examples from each selection to support your answers.
8. **Compare Texts** Use a Venn diagram like the one shown to record similarities and differences between the articles. Consider the subject matter, purpose, and tone of each article. Why do you think these two articles were presented together in a single lesson?

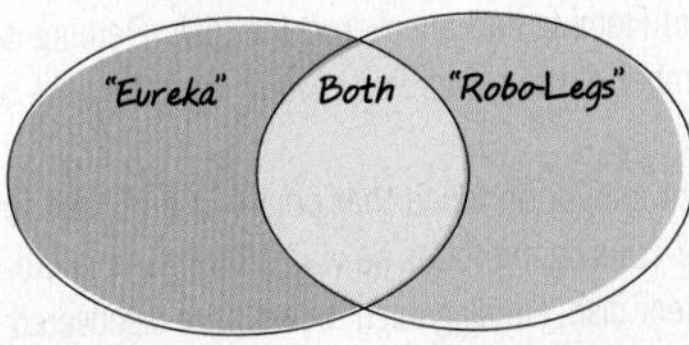

Extension and Challenge

9. **Readers' Circle** Both "Robo-Legs" and "Eureka: Scientific Twists of Fate" describe medical advancements that have helped people lead better lives. What problems would you like science to solve? Discuss your answer with a small group.
10. **SCIENCE CONNECTION** Robotics has become an exciting and popular field of scientific study. Other than prosthetics, what is another way robotics is being used today? Research to find an answer. Then present your findings to the class.

RESEARCH LINKS
For more on robotics, visit the **Research Center** at **ClassZone.com.**

936 UNIT 8: FACTS AND INFORMATION

Vocabulary in Context

VOCABULARY PRACTICE

Answer each question to show your understanding of the vocabulary words.

appendage · mobility · contaminate · pervasive · infectious · rehabilitation · keener · serendipitous

1. Which is an **appendage,** a boy's back or his leg?
2. Which can **contaminate** your dinner, bacteria or salt?
3. Which are **infectious,** colds or injuries?
4. If your eyesight gets **keener,** does it get better or worse?
5. Which provides **mobility,** an armchair or a car?
6. If an attitude is **pervasive,** do many people share it or just a few?
7. Would you need **rehabilitation** to recover from a broken leg, or from a cold?
8. If you make a **serendipitous** discovery, are you lucky or unlucky?

VOCABULARY IN WRITING

How has medical technology helped you or someone you know? Write a paragraph describing the way medical advancements improve people's quality of life. You might start like this.

> **EXAMPLE SENTENCE**
>
> *My grandmother's wheelchair provides her with* ***mobility****.*

VOCABULARY STRATEGY: THE LATIN ROOT *pend*

The vocabulary word *appendage* contains the Latin root *pend,* which means "hang." Many English words contain this root. To figure out the meaning of words with this root, use context clues and your knowledge of the root's meaning.

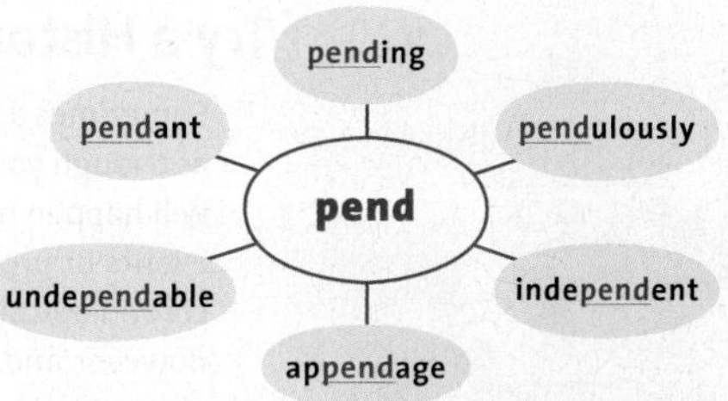

PRACTICE Choose the word from the web that best completes each sentence. Then explain how the root *pend* relates to the meaning of the word.

1. If an employee is ____, he will not keep his job very long.
2. Dogs are pack animals, so they hate being left alone; however, cats are fairly ____ creatures.
3. She wore a diamond____ around her neck.
4. The detective has several cases ____, but none of them are resolved.
5. The elephant's trunk swung ____ from side to side.

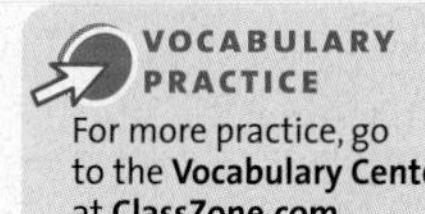

For more practice, go to the **Vocabulary Center** at **ClassZone.com.**

DIFFERENTIATED INSTRUCTION

FOR ENGLISH LEARNERS

Vocabulary Practice Make sure students can pronounce all the vocabulary words in this lesson. Remind them that dictionaries include pronunciation information for each word. Review how to interpret stress marks in a dictionary entry.

FOR ADVANCED LEARNERS/PRE–AP

Vocabulary Strategy Challenge students to list as many words with the root *pend* as they can. Have them use their knowledge of the root's meaning or a dictionary to define each word they list. Then have students compare their lists.

ANSWERS

Vocabulary in Context

VOCABULARY PRACTICE

1. *his leg*
2. *bacteria*
3. *colds*
4. *it gets better*
5. *a car*
6. *many people*
7. *from a broken leg*
8. *lucky*

RESOURCE MANAGER—Copy Master
Vocabulary Practice p. 142

VOCABULARY IN WRITING

Have students jot down ideas for their paragraphs. Then suggest that they review the vocabulary words to see which ones they might use in their writing.

VOCABULARY STRATEGY: THE LATIN ROOT *pend* *(also an EL language objective)*

Remind students to use context clues to decide which word best fits in each sentence.

Possible answers:

1. *undependable: You can "hang onto" a dependable person, but not on an undependable one.*
2. *independent: An independent creature does not "hang on" (depend on) others.*
3. *pendant: It "hangs on" the neck.*
4. *pending: The cases are still "hanging," or unresolved.*
5. *pendulously: The trunk hangs loosely, so it can sway from side to side.*

RESOURCE MANAGER—Copy Master
Vocabulary Strategy p. 143

Vocabulary Center at **ClassZone.com**
Additional Vocabulary Activities

Assess and Reteach

Assess

RESOURCE MANAGER—Copy Masters
Selection Tests A, B/C pp. 147–148, 149–150

Test Generator CD

Reteach

STANDARDS LESSON FILE
Literature Lesson 39: Tone
Reading Lesson 2: Monitoring
Vocabulary Lesson 1: Word Parts

OBJECTIVE

- read a history book

Meet Jim Murphy

Murphy has expressed his creativity and love of words in various ways throughout his life. As a child, he enjoyed writing and illustrating his own comic books. In high school and college, he wrote many poems and short stories that were published in school journals. Murphy stopped writing when he began working in publishing as a children's book editor. After spending many years editing and sometimes rewriting the work of others, he decided to try to develop a writing career. Murphy's first book, published in 1978, was called *Weird and Wacky Inventions.* Murphy's favorite part of his job is doing the research for his books. He says, "It's like being a detective—hunting out what *really* took place, trying to find those odd, interesting and sometimes bizarre details I like to include in my books."

Try a History Book

Point out to students the difference between a history book like those of Jim Murphy and a work of historical fiction. Murphy uses real historical details to create stories that sometimes read like exciting adventure novels. However, the people he names are people who actually lived, and their words come from actual journals, memoirs, and other firsthand accounts. A work of historical fiction, on the other hand, is a book in which the setting and other details are grounded in historical fact while most or all of the characters and dialogue are fictional.

Explain that even though history books are factual accounts, the interpreting and retelling of historical events is often influenced by the ideas and beliefs of the researcher or writer. A skilled history writer like Murphy must be able to understand the meaning and importance of historical events, connect with people of the past, and tell their stories in a compelling way.

RESOURCE MANAGER—Copy Master
Identify Genre Features p. 151

An American Plague:
The True and Terrifying Story of the Yellow Fever Epidemic of 1793

History Book by Jim Murphy

Jim Murphy
born 1947

Other Books by Jim Murphy

- *Blizzard!: The Storm That Changed America*
- *The Great Fire*
- *A Young Patriot: The American Revolution as Experienced by One Boy*

Meet Jim Murphy

Jim Murphy didn't read much as a child. It wasn't until a high school teacher told his class that they weren't allowed to read a particular novel that Murphy became inspired to read. At first, he did it just to be rebellious. Murphy says that as he continued to read, he developed a love of history, because it enabled him to "visit many different times and places in the past."

Today, Murphy is the award-winning author of over 25 books about American history. He finds his work rewarding, and he especially enjoys the research stage of each project. He seeks out eyewitness accounts of events and loves to uncover the vivid details that add drama and emotion to his work. "One of my goals in writing about events from the past is to show that children weren't just observers of our history," Murphy says. "They were actual participants and sometimes did amazing and heroic things."

Try a History Book

Sometimes a nonfiction book can be so enthralling, it's almost as though you are reading a suspense novel, wondering what will happen next. History books tell about a series of important events or provide details about one major event, often in chronological order. Some history books start with the outcome, however, and then back up to show readers how it came about.

938

DIFFERENTIATED INSTRUCTION

FOR LESS–PROFICIENT READERS

Reading Support Before students begin reading, review the teaching notes on pages 939–943 and select those that you think would be most helpful to them. You might read the selection aloud with students and discuss the relevant notes. Stop occasionally to answer questions, give an explanation, or hold a discussion.

Read a Great Book

In 1793, Philadelphia, Pennsylvania, was the nation's capital. It was also a city at the mercy of an invisible enemy. In this vivid account of the yellow fever epidemic, Jim Murphy highlights some of the conditions in Philadelphia at that time and shows how those conditions contributed to the spread of a deadly disease.

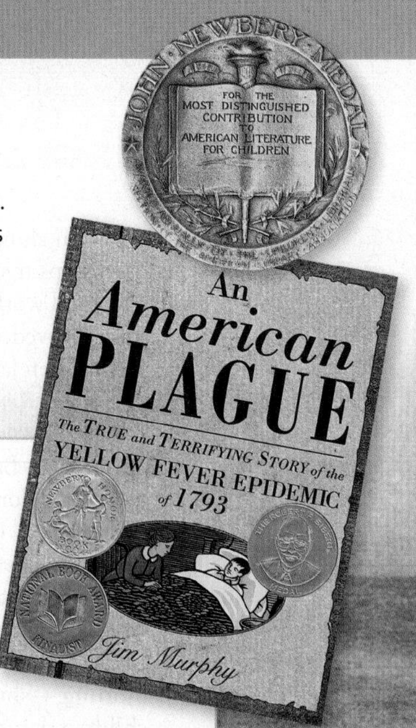

from

An American Plague:

The True and Terrifying Story of the Yellow Fever Epidemic of 1793

Saturday, August 3, 1793. The sun came up, as it had every day since the end of May, bright, hot, and unrelenting. The swamps and marshes south of Philadelphia had already lost a great deal of water to the intense heat, while the Delaware and Schuylkill Rivers had receded to reveal long stretches of their muddy, root-choked banks. Dead fish and gooey vegetable matter were exposed and rotted, while swarms of insects droned in the heavy, humid air.

In Philadelphia itself an increasing number of cats were dropping dead every day, attracting, one Philadelphian complained, "an amazing number of flies and other insects." Mosquitoes were everywhere, though their high-pitched whirring was particularly loud near rain barrels, gutters, and open sewers.

These sewers, called "sinks," were particularly ripe this year. Most streets in the city were unpaved and had no system of covered sewers and pipes to channel water away from buildings. Instead, deep holes were dug at various street corners to collect runoff water and anything else that might be washed along. Dead animals were routinely tossed into this soup, where everything decayed and sent up noxious bubbles to foul the air.

939

Read

Read a Great Book

Murphy says that one thing all his nonfiction books have in common is voice. He explains, "A dramatic situation is nice, but history really comes alive when I can use the firsthand accounts—excerpts from letters, memoirs, journals, diaries, and recollections—of people who were actually there. These voices help readers experience events as if they were actually there." In reading this excerpt from *An American Plague*, students will understand what Murphy means. The author's account of the onset of the yellow fever epidemic gives the perspectives and personal stories of several prominent community members. Murphy also names some of the earliest victims of the disease. Because of this style, readers are never distant from the real people who experienced this devastating event.

SHARE AN FYI

Yellow fever is an infectious tropical disease transmitted by mosquitoes and characterized by high fevers and internal bleeding. The name of the disease comes from the yellowish color of the skin and eyes often seen in seriously infected people.

SHARE A READING TIP

To give students a better sense of the book's setting, suggest that they find a map of Pennsylvania in an atlas. Students can locate the southeastern city of Philadelphia and the Delaware and Schuylkill Rivers in eastern Pennsylvania.

FOR ENGLISH LEARNERS

Read Aloud Read aloud all or part of the excerpt and stop occasionally to answer questions, hold a discussion, or give an explanation. Another option is to read part of the excerpt aloud and then have students continue reading in pairs or small groups.

Listen to the *Audio Anthology CD* Have students listen to the excerpt as they read along. Then have them read the text independently. Lead them in a follow-up discussion.

Jigsaw Reading [small-group option] Have students meet in small groups for Jigsaw Reading. Each student should read part of the excerpt and explain it to the others. Before students meet in their groups, spend time introducing and summarizing the excerpt. Answer any questions about the selection's challenging vocabulary.

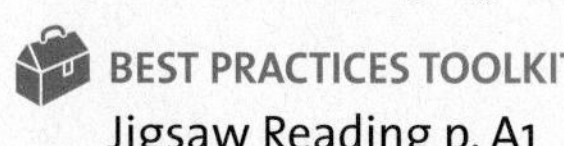

BEST PRACTICES TOOLKIT
Jigsaw Reading p. A1

SHARE WORD MEANINGS

In the 18th century, Philadelphia emerged as a major port city and a center for trade and shipbuilding. Murphy establishes setting using these terms related to ships and trade:

- *casks* (line 21), sturdy cylindrical containers for holding liquids
- *hold* (line 21), a ship's storage area
- *stevedores* (line 22), men whose job is to load and unload ships
- *sloop* (line 24), a single-masted sailing ship

SHARE AN FYI

Santo Domingo (line 24) was the early name of Hispaniola Island in the Caribbean Sea, an island shared today by the nations of Haiti and the Dominican Republic. It is also the name of a city founded on the island in 1496 by Bartholomew Columbus, brother of Christopher Columbus. Today this city is the capital of the Dominican Republic.

SHARE A READING TIP

Statements in quotation marks (as in lines 30–31) that appear throughout the selection are actual quotes from primary sources such as journals and letters.

Down along the docks lining the Delaware, cargo was being loaded onto ships that would sail to New York, Boston, and other distant ports. The hard work of hoisting heavy casks into the hold was accompanied by the stevedores' usual grunts and muttered oaths.

The men laboring near Water Street had particular reason to curse. The sloop *Amelia* from Santo Domingo had anchored with a cargo of coffee, which had spoiled during the voyage. The bad coffee was dumped on Ball's Wharf, where it putrefied in the sun and sent out a powerful odor that could be smelled over a quarter mile away. Benjamin Rush, one of Philadelphia's most celebrated doctors and a signer of the Declaration of Independence, lived three long blocks from Ball's Wharf, but he recalled that the coffee stank "to the great annoyance of the whole neighborhood."

Despite the stench, the streets nearby were crowded with people that morning—ship owners and their captains talking seriously, shouting children darting between wagons or climbing on crates and barrels, well-dressed men and women out for a stroll, servants and slaves hurrying from one chore to the next. Philadelphia was then the largest city in North America, with nearly 51,000 inhabitants; those who didn't absolutely have to be indoors working had escaped to the open air to seek relief from the sweltering heat.

Many of them stopped at one of the city's 415 shops, whose doors and windows were wide open to let in light and any hint of a cooling breeze. The rest continued along, headed for the market on High Street.

Here three city blocks were crowded with vendors calling their wares while eager shoppers studied merchandise or haggled over weights and prices. Horse-drawn wagons clattered up and down the cobblestone street, bringing in more fresh vegetables, squawking chickens, and squealing pigs. People commented on the stench from Ball's Wharf, but the market's own ripe blend of odors—of roasting meats, strong cheeses, days-old sheep and cow guts, dried blood, and horse manure—tended to overwhelm all others.

One and a half blocks from the market was the handsomely refurbished mansion of Robert Morris, a wealthy manufacturer who had used his fortune to help finance the Revolutionary War. Morris was lending this house to George and Martha Washington and had moved himself into another, larger one he owned just up the block. Washington was then president of the United States, and Philadelphia was the temporary capital of the young nation and the center of its federal government. Washington spent the day at home in a small, stuffy office

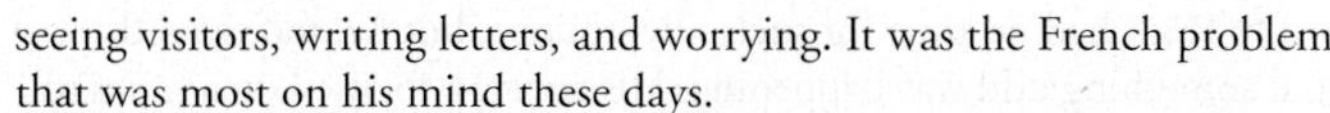

seeing visitors, writing letters, and worrying. It was the French problem that was most on his mind these days.

Not so many years before, the French monarch, Louis XVI, had sent money, ships, and soldiers to aid the struggling Continental Army's fight against the British. The French aid had been a major reason why Washington was able to surround and force General Charles Cornwallis to surrender at Yorktown in 1781. This military victory eventually led to a British capitulation three years later and to freedom for the United States—and lasting fame for Washington.

Then, in 1789, France erupted in its own revolution. The common people and a few nobles and churchmen soon gained complete power in France and beheaded Louis XVI in January 1793. Many of France's neighbors worried that similar revolutions might spread to their countries and wanted the new French republic crushed. Soon after the king was put to death, revolutionary France was at war with Great Britain, Holland, Spain, and Austria.

Naturally, the French republic had turned to the United States for help, only to have President Washington hesitate. Washington knew that he and his country owed the French an eternal debt. He simply wasn't sure that the United States had the military strength to take on so many formidable foes.

Many citizens felt Washington's Proclamation of Neutrality was a betrayal of the French people. His own secretary of state, Thomas Jefferson, certainly did, and he argued bitterly with Treasury Secretary Alexander Hamilton over the issue. Wasn't the French fight for individual freedom, Jefferson asked, exactly like America's struggle against British oppression? . . .

While Washington worried, the city's taverns, beer gardens, and coffeehouses—all 176 of them—were teeming with activity that Saturday. There men, and a few women, lifted their glasses in toasts and singing and let the hours slip away in lively conversation. Business and politics and the latest gossip were the favorite topics. No doubt the heat, the foul stink from Ball's Wharf, and the country's refusal to join with France were discussed and argued over at length.

In all respects it seemed as if August 3 was a very normal day, with business and buying and pleasure as usual.

Oh, there were a few who felt a tingle of unease. For weeks an unusually large supply of wild pigeons had been for sale at the market. Popular folklore suggested that such an abundance of pigeons always brought with it unhealthy air and sickness.

SHARE AN FYI

General Charles Cornwallis (line 64) was a commander of the British forces during the Revolutionary War. His surrender in Yorktown, Virginia, led to the end of the war.

SHARE AN FYI

The Proclamation of Neutrality (line 80) was an announcement that the United States would not take part in France's revolution.

SHARE A READING TIP

Encourage students to notice how the author establishes the details of everyday life in the community before the disease took hold. This is so that readers will later understand how much the fever disrupted and changed ordinary life.

SHARE AN FYI

The "breaking of the Sabbath" (line 110) refers to a failure to follow religious rules regarding behavior on Sundays, the Christian day of rest.

Dr. Rush had no time for such silly notions, but he, too, sensed that something odd was happening. His concern focused on a series of illnesses that had struck his patients throughout the year—the mumps in January, jaw and mouth infections in February, scarlet fever in March, followed by influenza in July. "There was something in the heat and drought," the good doctor speculated, "which was uncommon, in their influence upon the human body."

The Reverend J. Henry C. Helmuth of the Lutheran congregation, too, thought something was wrong in the city, though it had nothing to do with sickness of the body. It was the souls of its citizens he worried about. "Philadelphia . . . seemed to strive to exceed all other places in the breaking of the Sabbath," he noted. . . .

Rush and Helmuth would have been surprised to know that their worries were turning to reality on August 3. For on that Saturday a young French sailor rooming at Richard Denny's boarding house, over on North Water Street, was desperately ill with a fever. Eighteenth-century record keeping wasn't very precise, so no one bothered to write down his name. Besides, this sailor was poor and a foreigner, not the sort of person who would draw much attention from the community around him. All we know is that his fever worsened and was accompanied by violent seizures, and that a few days later he died.

Other residents at Denny's would follow this sailor to the grave—a Mr. Moore fell into a stupor and passed away, Mrs. Richard Parkinson expired on August 7, next the lodging house owner and his wife, Mary, and then the first sailor's roommate. Around the same time, two people in the house next to Denny's died of the same severe fever.

Eight deaths in the space of a week in two houses on the same street . . . but the city did not take notice. Summer fevers were common visitors to all American cities in the eighteenth century, and therefore not headline news. Besides, Denny's was located on a narrow out-of-the-way street—really more an alley than a street. "It is much confined," a resident remarked, "ill-aired, and, in every respect, is a disagreeable street." Things happened along this street all the time—sometimes very bad things—that went unnoticed by the authorities and the rest of the population.

So the deaths did not disrupt Philadelphia much at all. Ships came and went; men and women did chores, talked, and sought relief from the heat and insects; the markets and shops hummed with activity; children played; and the city, state, and federal governments went about their business.

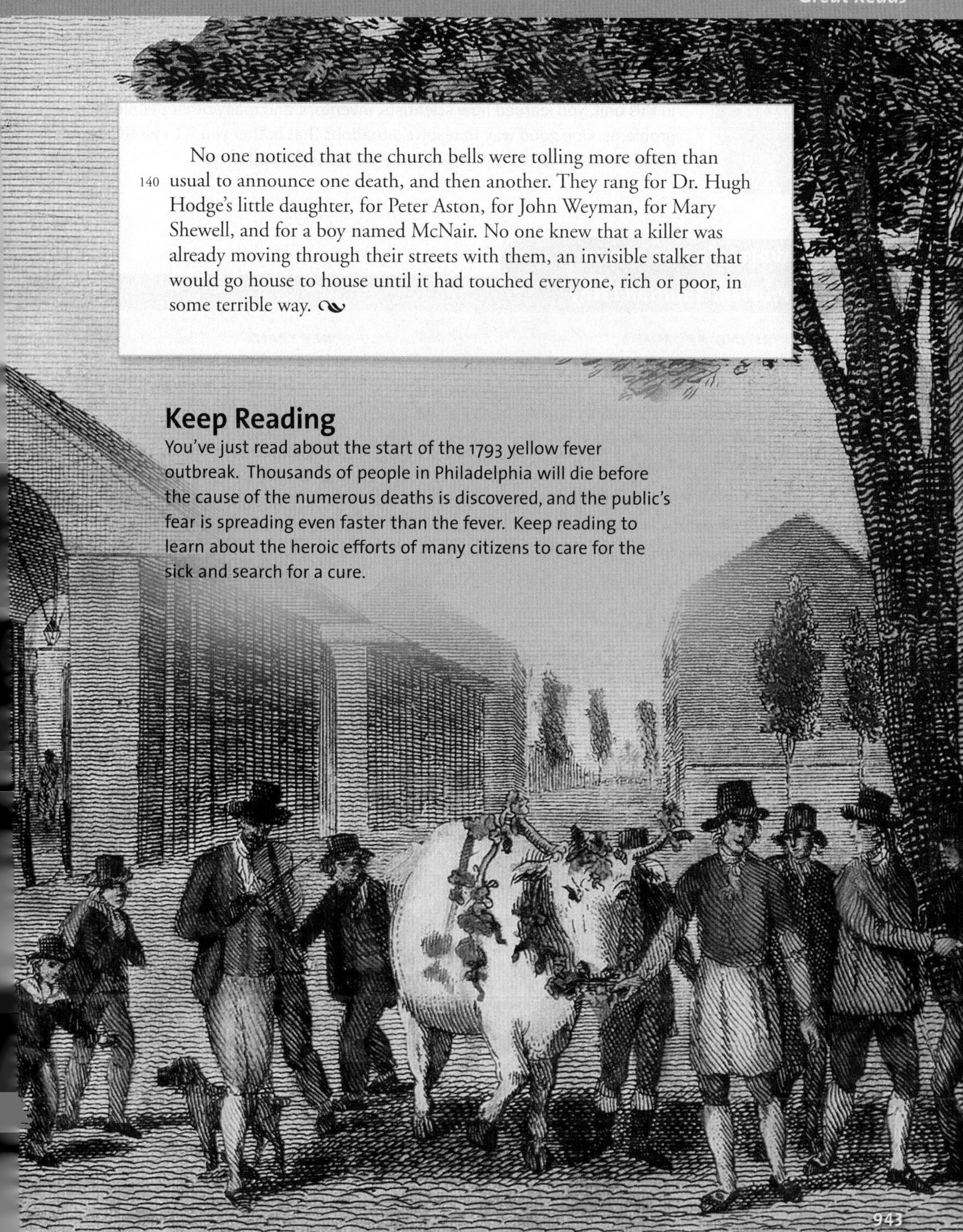

No one noticed that the church bells were tolling more often than usual to announce one death, and then another. They rang for Dr. Hugh Hodge's little daughter, for Peter Aston, for John Weyman, for Mary Shewell, and for a boy named McNair. No one knew that a killer was already moving through their streets with them, an invisible stalker that would go house to house until it had touched everyone, rich or poor, in some terrible way.

Keep Reading

You've just read about the start of the 1793 yellow fever outbreak. Thousands of people in Philadelphia will die before the cause of the numerous deaths is discovered, and the public's fear is spreading even faster than the fever. Keep reading to learn about the heroic efforts of many citizens to care for the sick and search for a cure.

Discuss

SHARE A READING TIP

Point out the way the author uses descriptive language to make the account more gripping for readers (lines 139–145). In this instance, he uses personification, giving the disease human traits.

Keep Reading

Share these discussion questions with students after they have finished reading the excerpt. You might use the questions to lead a class discussion or have students form small groups to discuss them.

- Have you read the rest of this book? If yes, would you recommend it to others? Why? If you haven't yet read the book, what more are you hoping to learn about this time period?
- What details of this historical account do you find most interesting? Why?
- Why do you think the author mentions the thoughts and feelings of specific people? Does this help draw you in as a reader? Explain.
- In what ways do you think people might react when the disease completely takes hold of the community?

Focus and Motivate

OBJECTIVES

- analyze a student model that reflects the key traits of a problem-solution essay
- use the writing process to write a problem-solution essay
- avoid using logical fallacies
- revise and edit, using a rubric for a strong problem-solution essay
- give an oral report on a problem and solution

WRITER'S ROAD MAP

WRITING PROMPTS 1 AND 2

Help students generate ideas for the first prompt by asking them what they would change about the world if they could. Then review the selections in this unit and discuss the problem each one presents.

ADDITIONAL PROMPTS

Use these prompts for more practice writing problem-solution essays:

WRITING PROMPT 3

Writing from the Media Think about the kinds of problems faced by movie or TV characters. Choose one that affects many people or that interests you.

Ideas to Consider

- bullying in school
- peer pressure
- family conflicts

WRITING PROMPT 4

Writing About Health Find out more about the causes, effects, and possible solutions related to health issues that today's teens confront.

Ideas to Consider

- stress
- eating disorders
- substance abuse

For additional writing prompts, see

Write*Smart* CD

Writing Center at **ClassZone.com**

KEY TRAITS

Review the six ***KEY TRAITS*** with students, focusing primarily on ideas and organization. Compare the list of traits with the rubric on page 950.

Writing Workshop

Problem-Solution Essay

In this unit, you learned how scientists, inventors, and many other people face problems. One good way to resolve situations that bother you is to write a problem-solution essay. To learn more, consult the **Writer's Road Map.**

WRITER'S ROAD MAP

Problem-Solution Essay

WRITING PROMPT 1

Writing for the Real World Choose a problem that really interests you. Write an essay in which you explain the problem, examine its causes, and explore possible solutions.

Problems to Explore

- stereotypes of teenagers
- environmental issues
- overcrowding in the school lunchroom
- cheating in professional sports

WRITING PROMPT 2

Writing from Literature Every selection in this unit deals with solving a problem. Choose one of the problems you read about in the unit. Write an essay identifying the problem and describing a solution.

Selections to Explore

- "The Spider Man Behind *Spider-Man*" (training insects)
- "Interview with a Songcatcher" (recording and preserving world music)
- "Robo-Legs" (providing mobility for amputees)

WRITING TOOLS
For prewriting, revision, and editing tools, visit the **Writing Center** at **ClassZone.com.**

KEY TRAITS

1. *IDEAS*
- **States the problem** in a clearly worded thesis
- Explains the **causes and effects** of the problem
- Discusses different **solutions**
- Gives **details** to help explain the solution to the problem

2. *ORGANIZATION*
- Makes the importance of the problem clear in the **introduction**
- Uses **transitions** to connect ideas
- **Concludes** by summing up the best solution

3. *VOICE*
- Maintains a **tone** that is suited to topic, audience, and purpose

4. *WORD CHOICE*
- Uses **precise words** to express the problem and solution

5. *SENTENCE FLUENCY*
- Varies **sentence beginnings**

6. *CONVENTIONS*
- Uses **correct grammar, spelling, and punctuation**

Writing Workshop Resources

RESOURCE MANAGER UNIT 8

Plan and Teach pp. 153–156
Prewriting–Editing pp. 157–161
Writing Rubric p. 162
Speaking and Listening p. 163
Writing Support p. 164*

STANDARDS LESSON FILE

Writing Lessons 16, 19, 21, 22, 23, 31, 44
Grammar Lesson 5
Speaking and Listening Lesson 1

BEST PRACTICES TOOLKIT

Scaffolding Writing Instruction pp. 43–46*
Problem and Solution Charts • KWL: Know, Want to Know, Learned • Cause-and-Effect Chain • Writing Template: Problem-Solution Essay • Main Idea and Details

TECHNOLOGY

Easy Planner DVD
Writing Center at **ClassZone.com**

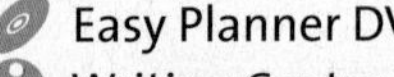

Write*Smart* CD

* Resources for Differentiation

Part 1: Analyze a Student Model

Alicia M. Fiore
LaSalle Academy

Our Public Pool: Problem or Solution?

I always look forward to summer vacation, but this year, I'm even more excited than usual. Swimming is my favorite sport, and I just learned that the new public pool in Madison Park will be finished ahead of schedule. Best of all, it will open the day after school closes. I was really excited until I learned that users have to pay an expensive membership fee. Unless we can find a way to make the pool available to the whole community, many of my friends and I will have a long, hot summer vacation.

According to the dictionary, the word *public* means "relating to people in general." To me, that definition means that a public pool should be open to everybody, not just to everybody who can pay the membership fee. The problem is not just what the pool is called, though. What the community needs is a pool that really is available to every citizen.

I know that building a pool is expensive. Once it is built, it has to be treated with chemicals and cleaned regularly to make sure the water is safe for people to swim in. Someone has to water and mow the grass in the sunbathing area. Then there are lifeguards, locker-room attendants, and snack-bar workers who must be paid. Our community needs to find money to cover these expenses. However, charging the public a large fee to cover these expenses prevents many citizens from enjoying the pool.

A solution to this problem will have to satisfy both the people who want to use the pool and the ones who run it. One possibility would be for the town to raise taxes to cover the costs of operating the pool. If other people are like my parents, though, they think their taxes are already much too high. For this reason, raising taxes probably wouldn't work.

KEY TRAITS IN ACTION

Introduction shows the importance of the topic. Highlighted thesis **states the problem.**

Varies **sentence beginnings** to hold the reader's interest.

Describes the **causes** of the problem (having a pool is expensive) and an important **effect** (the community must find a way to pay for it).

Presents a possible **solution.** Highlighted **transitions** help connect the ideas showing the disadvantages of this option.

Teach

Part 1: Analyze a Student Model

Have students read the **Student Model** and **Key Traits in Action.** Then discuss the model, focusing on specific examples of each trait. You might also use these activities:

- **Introduction** Remind students that an effective introduction should grab readers' attention. A startling statistic, a question, or an interesting anecdote can accomplish this purpose. Ask students why they think the writer of the model begins her essay as she does. ***Possible answer:*** *Because the writer begins by describing how and why the pool is so important to her, readers can sympathize with her dilemma and are interested in how she might solve it.*
- **Causes** Have students list the causes of the problem. ***Possible answer:*** *Factors that contribute to the cost of a public pool include the necessary chemicals, maintenance, and staff.* Ask students how including these causes affects readers' understanding of the problem and their impression of the writer. ***Possible answer:*** *Readers understand the dimensions of the problem more clearly. By listing these causes, the writer shows herself to be informed about her topic.*
- **Solution** Ask students what the phrase "One possibility" (line 23) suggests about the solution presented in this paragraph. ***Possible answer:*** *This phrase suggests that the writer has more than one solution in mind. This is only one of her ideas.*

DIFFERENTIATED INSTRUCTION

FOR ALL STUDENTS

Student Portfolios Encourage students to save copies of their writing so they can track their progress throughout the year.

For general guidelines on differentiating writing instruction, see

BEST PRACTICES TOOLKIT
Scaffolding Writing Instruction
pp. 43–46

FOR ENGLISH LEARNERS

Language: Skill Words Write these terms on the board and review them with students:

- *problem:* conflict or difficulty that needs to be solved. (*I don't have enough money to buy a new bike.*)
- *solution:* strategy to solve a problem. (*I will get a job after school to earn money to buy a bike.*)
- *cause:* event or action that leads to another event. (*The heavy rains caused the landslide.*)
- *effect:* direct or logical outcome of an event or action. (*Flooding also resulted from the heavy rains.*)
- *tone:* attitude of the writer toward his or her subject. A writer's tone might be sarcastic, approving, or bitter, for example, and is conveyed through a writer's choice of words, details, and literary devices. (*The town dump is an eyesore, a festering boil on the landscape.*)

- **Details** Have students identify the examples and other specific details that the writer offers in this paragraph. Discuss the impact of including these details.
- **Precise Words** Tell students that using nouns and adjectives in place of pronouns or inserting modifying phrases will help convey their point more effectively. Have them replace the underlined words in these sentences with more precise ones:
  - —Those under ten should get some free swims. *(Children, four free swims a week)*
  - —Someone must be on duty at the pool constantly. *(A lifeguard)*
  - —A public pool should be available to all. *(all members of the community)*
- **Tone** Ask students which words in lines 32–38 help convey the matter-of-fact and honest tone. ***Possible answer:*** *The words and phrases "could be," "probably feel good," and "I know" convey an honest and sincere attitude. This tone makes readers feel that the writer is working with them to come up with the best solution.*
- **Conclusion** Point out that this writer identifies a specific action that she wants readers to take. Tell students that a conclusion might also explain the results of implementing a solution or predict what will happen if the problem is not solved.

For interactive student models, see

WriteSmart CD

Writing Center at **ClassZone.com**

Another option would be for the community government to sponsor fundraising events like car washes, bake sales, cleanup days, and concerts. People like to get together and donate their time for a good cause, so these fundraisers could be successful. They would be one-time events, however, and the pool would need money coming in regularly to stay open.

Proposes a second possible solution and gives **details** about its advantages and disadvantages.

Here's a better solution. The town could still charge a membership fee for those who can pay, but open the pool to everyone at certain times. Free swims could be scheduled one or two days a week, a few hours every day, or any time the temperature rises above a certain point. Community members who can afford the fee would probably feel good about giving other people the chance to use the pool, too. I know my friends and I would be thrilled.

Precise words make the third possible solution easy to understand. Matter-of-fact, honest **tone** is suited to the audience—the writer's classmates and neighbors.

There is a simple, effective solution to the problem of the new public pool—free swims. With your support, I know it will work. Just sign the petition posted outside the town hall and give everyone the chance to kick back, cool off, and float through the summer.

Concludes by summarizing the best solution, telling the reader how to help make it happen, and describing how enjoyable using the pool will be for everyone.

2

946 UNIT 8: FACTS AND INFORMATION

DIFFERENTIATED INSTRUCTION

FOR ENGLISH LEARNERS

Comprehension: Transitions [small-group option]

1. Write the first paragraph of the model on the board, underlining these transitions: *but* (line 1), *and* (line 2), *best of all* (line 4), *after* (line 4), *until* (line 5), *unless* (line 6).
2. Work with students to identify the function of each transition (*but—contrast; and, best of all—elaboration; after, until—sequence; unless—cause and effect*).
3. Have students work in small groups to find other examples of each type of transition in the essay. ***Possible answer:***
   - —***cause and effect:*** *however (line 20), if (line 24), so (line 29)*
   - —***comparison and contrast:*** *not just (lines 11, 12), though (lines 13, 25), however (line 30), but (line 33)*
   - —***elaboration:*** *for this reason (line 26), another (line 27), too (line 37)*
   - —***sequence:*** *once (line 15), then (line 18)*

To provide students with further practice using transitions, use this copy master:

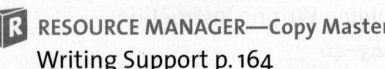

RESOURCE MANAGER—Copy Master
Writing Support p. 164

Part 2: Apply the Writing Process

PREWRITING

What Should I Do?	What Does It Look Like?
1. Choose a prompt. Reread the prompts on page 944. Pick the one that interests you. Look it over carefully, (circling) all the details you need to cover in your essay.	***WRITING PROMPT*** *Choose a problem that really interests you. Write an (essay) in which you (explain the problem), (examine its causes), and (explore possible solutions).* *I can think of many interesting problems, but I need to write about one that really can be solved.*
2. Focus on a problem. Make a list of problems from your life or from something that you have read. Group them in categories to help you come up with ideas. Underline the problem that will be the focus of your essay.	see chart below
3. Try out a variety of solutions. Think about the problem you have chosen. Alone or with a friend, brainstorm possible solutions. Consider the advantages and disadvantages of each. **TIP If you have trouble thinking of solutions that will work, choose another problem to write about.**	*Pool fees* — *Have free swims.* / *Find volunteers to work there.* / *Use tax money.* / *Try fundraiser events.*
4. Find support for your best solution. It's not enough to tell your reader, "I'm sure my solution will work." For Prompt 1, list facts, reasons, and other details that show why the solution you propose is the best one. For Prompt 2, find evidence in the literature that explains why the solution was successful or unsuccessful.	***Have free swims at certain times.*** • *Town will get the fees it needs from people who can pay.* • *People will feel good about helping others.* • *Everybody will be able to enjoy the pool.* • *BUT . . . how would free swims work?*

Family	*Community*	*Environment*
• *arguments with parents*	• *new public pool requires fee*	• *litter in parks*
• *too many chores*	• *ban on certain dog breeds*	• *West Nile virus*

FOR ENGLISH LEARNERS

Focusing on a Problem Display these prompts to help students choose a topic and explore possible solutions:

- I think _______ is a big problem today.
- It is a problem because ________.
- It affects ________.
- This problem could be solved by ________, ________, or ________.
- This is a good solution because _______.

FOR ADVANCED LEARNERS/PRE–AP

Research Challenge students to choose a problem about which they would like to learn more. To direct their research, suggest that they first fill in a KWL chart with what they know about the problem and what they would like to discover.

BEST PRACTICES TOOLKIT—Transparency
KWL: Know, Want to Know, Learned p. A21

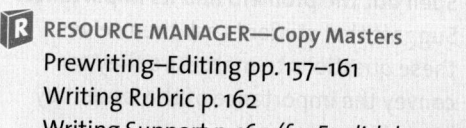

Practice and Apply

To support students during the writing process, use these copy masters:

RESOURCE MANAGER—Copy Masters
Prewriting–Editing pp. 157–161
Writing Rubric p. 162
Writing Support p. 164 *(for English learners)*

Part 2: Apply the Writing Process

PREWRITING

1. Choose a prompt. Compare and contrast the two prompts to help students make their choice. The first prompt requires students to analyze an original problem and think of solutions. The second draws from reading that they have already done.

2. Focus on a problem. Have students skim local and national newspapers and add ideas to the chart on page 947. Or, suggest that students interview teachers or administrators to find out about school issues.

Before students choose their topics, suggest that they fill in Problem and Solution Charts for the topics that interest them the most. This will help them see which topics require research and decide whether they want to pursue them or choose topics that are based on their prior knowledge and personal experience.

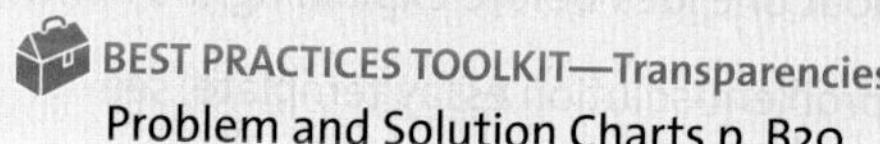
BEST PRACTICES TOOLKIT—Transparencies
Problem and Solution Charts p. B20

3. Try out a variety of solutions. Tell students that the solutions they list do not have to be their final ideas. As the TIP suggests, they just need to make sure they have enough substance for an essay. Students might add ovals to the web with possible advantages and disadvantages or create a separate chart.

4. Find support for your best solution. Have students meet in small groups to discuss their problems and theoretical solutions. Group members should generate ideas to support each proposal.

For interactive graphic organizers, see
WriteSmart CD
Writing Center at **ClassZone.com**

DRAFTING

1. Spell out the problem and its importance. Suggest that students ask themselves these questions to make sure they can convey the importance of the issue they have chosen:

- Whom does this problem affect?
- Why should this problem be solved?

2. Explain the problem's causes and effects. Encourage students to use a Cause-and-Effect Chain to analyze the dimensions of the problem before they draft this part of the essay.

BEST PRACTICES TOOLKIT—Transparency
Cause-and-Effect Chain pp. B16, B39

3. Describe several possible solutions. Tell students to organize their description of each solution similarly. In other words, if they begin by describing the advantages of each solution, they should continue in this pattern. Remind them to include specific details about each solution.

4. Decide on a structure for your essay. Tell students that presenting the best solution last is a good strategy since it helps readers remember it. The order of the other solutions might be determined by their relationship to each other. Does one lead into another? Is it necessary to know about one idea before explaining the next?

For a problem-solution essay template, see

BEST PRACTICES TOOLKIT—Transparency
Writing Template: Problem-Solution Essay pp. C16, C36

Write*Smart* CD

Writing Center at **ClassZone.com**

DRAFTING

What Should I Do?	*What Does It Look Like?*
1. Spell out the problem and its importance. Before you can propose a solution, you need to make sure that your reader understands exactly what the problem is and why it matters.	*I was really excited about the new public pool until I learned that users have to pay an expensive membership fee. Unless we can find a way to make the pool available to the whole community, many of my friends and I will have a long, hot summer vacation.*
2. Explain the problem's causes and effects. Write about factors that led to the problem and results of those factors. Make sure that there are logical connections between causes and effects.	*Building and maintaining a pool is expensive. As a result, our community needs to find money to cover those expenses. However, charging the public a large fee prevents many citizens from enjoying the pool.*
3. Describe several possible solutions. Think about the solutions you came up with when you were brainstorming. Choose two or three and describe them for your reader.	*One possibility would be for the town to raise taxes to cover the costs of operating the pool.* — Possible solution *If other people are like my parents, though, they think their taxes are already much too high.* — Why it won't work
4. Decide on a structure for your essay. Make an informal outline of your key points. Describe the problem first. Then you can discuss possible solutions and end with the one you think is best, as this writer did. Or, if you prefer, explain the best solution first and then address the ones that you believe are not as strong.	***Problem:*** *Fee prevents everybody from using public pool.* ***Possible solution A:*** *Raise taxes (but they are too high already).* ***Possible solution B:*** *Hold fund-raisers (but they wouldn't be a regular source of money).* ***Proposed solution C:*** *Have free swims (the best solution because money comes in from people who can afford it, and everybody gets a chance to use the pool).*

948 UNIT 8: FACTS AND INFORMATION

DIFFERENTIATED INSTRUCTION

FOR LESS–PROFICIENT WRITERS

Deciding on a Structure Provide students with this plan for structuring their essays:

Paragraph 1 (Introduction)
- State the problem.
- Explain whom it affects and why it is important to solve.

Paragraph 2
- Explain causes of the problem.
- Describe effects.

Paragraph 3
- State first solution.
- Explain advantages and disadvantages.

Paragraph 4
- State second solution (the better one of the two).
- Explain advantages and disadvantages.

Paragraph 5 (Conclusion)
- Restate problem and best solution.
- Suggest action or plan for implementing solution.

REVISING AND EDITING

What Should I Do?	What Does It Look Like?
1. Clarify with transitions. • Ask a peer reader to underline sentences that don't seem to be connected logically. • If your essay has underlines, add a transition or other information to show the logical relationship between ideas. **See page 950:** Ask a Peer Reader	People like to get together and donate their time for a good cause, ~~and also~~ so these fund-raisers could be successful. They would be one-time events, however, and the pool would need money coming in regularly to stay open.
2. Strengthen supporting details. • Draw a box around statements that lack details or that contain information not connected to your key ideas. • Replace with information that makes your case stronger.	~~Lots of people work at the pool.~~ The pool has to be treated with chemicals and cleaned regularly to make sure the water is safe for people to swim in. Someone has to water and mow the grass in the sunbathing area. Then there are lifeguards, locker-room attendants, and snack-bar workers who must be paid. Our community needs to find money to cover these expenses.
3. Be on the lookout for vague statements. • Circle statements such as "Something has to be done," "This is really important," or "It's a serious problem." • Revise using specific words that explain your ideas clearly.	~~It just doesn't make sense.~~ What the community needs is a pool that really is available to every citizen.
4. Make your conclusion complete. • Be sure that your conclusion sums up the problem and reiterates the solution that you believe is best. • Depending on your topic, you may want to add a call to action. That's when you tell your reader what to do about the problem.	There is a simple, effective solution to the problem of the new public pool—free swims. With your support, I know it will work. Just sign the petition posted outside the town hall and give everyone the chance to kick back, cool off, and float through the summer.

REVISING AND EDITING

1. **Clarify with transitions.** Have peer readers take turns reading their partner's essay aloud to help them hear where transitions should be inserted. Point out that in the example on page 949, the insertion of *so* clarifies the cause-and-effect relationship necessary for understanding the writer's argument.
2. **Strengthen supporting details.** Remind students that including strong topic sentences will help them focus the details in their paragraphs and eliminate irrelevant facts or ideas. Have students return to the **Student Model** and identify the topic sentences in paragraphs 2, 3, and 4. Discuss the way in which the details in these paragraphs relate to and develop the main idea stated in the topic sentence.
3. **Be on the lookout for vague statements.** Have peer readers circle all pronouns, including personal and indefinite. Have partners then work together to make sure that there is an obvious antecedent for each pronoun. If not, students should replace the pronoun with a specific noun.
4. **Make your conclusion complete.** Have students exchange their conclusions with a partner and provide feedback, keeping in mind the ideas presented on page 949.

For interactive revision tools, see

WriteSmart CD

Writing Center at **ClassZone.com**

FOR LESS–PROFICIENT WRITERS

Strengthening Supporting Details

1. Help students identify the main idea and supporting details in lines 15–21 of the model. Display a Main Idea and Details chart, fill in the main idea, and have students provide details from the paragraph.
2. Suggest that students create a similar chart as they plan each body paragraph of their essays.

A pool is expensive.
- It must be treated with chemicals and cleaned regularly.
- Someone has to take care of the sunbathing area.
- Lifeguards, locker-room attendants, and snack bar workers must be paid.

BEST PRACTICES TOOLKIT—Transparency
Main Idea and Details p. B6

FOR ADVANCED LEARNERS/PRE–AP

Synthesize Invite students to write a letter to the editor about their problem and solution, adapting the form and content of their essay to fit this genre. Remind them to supplement their research if necessary and to keep their audience in mind as they review their details and vocabulary. Their explanation of the problem, its significance, and a proposed solution should be clear and concise.

Preparing to Publish

Support for meeting the goals in the writing rubric is supplied throughout the **Writing Workshop** on pages 944–949.

For Rubric Bank, see

- Write*Smart* CD
- Writing Center at **ClassZone.com**

Assess and Reteach

After reading and assessing students' essays, you might use these lessons to reteach key skills:

STANDARDS LESSON FILE

- Writing Lesson 16: Cause-and-Effect Order
- Writing Lesson 19: Transitions
- Writing Lesson 21: Writing a Thesis Statement
- Writing Lesson 22: Writing Introductions
- Writing Lesson 23: Writing Conclusions
- Writing Lesson 31: Problem-Solution Essay
- Writing Lesson 44: Using Precise Words
- Grammar Lesson 5: Verb Agreement with Indefinite Pronoun Subjects

Preparing to Publish Problem-Solution Essay

Apply the Rubric

A strong problem-solution essay . . .

- ☑ begins by describing the problem and why it matters
- ☑ presents a logical thesis statement
- ☑ explains the causes and effects of the problem
- ☑ proposes several solutions
- ☑ supports the best solution with details and explanations
- ☑ connects ideas with transitions
- ☑ has a tone that suits the audience and purpose
- ☑ uses precise words to express ideas
- ☑ varies sentence beginnings
- ☑ concludes with a summary of the problem and the best solution

Ask a Peer Reader

- Why is this problem important to me?
- Which of my ideas need better logical connections?
- What other solutions to this problem can you think of?

Avoid Logical Fallacies

Circular reasoning—supporting a statement merely by repeating it in different words ("Access to the pool is crucial because it is really, really important.")

Either/or fallacy—suggesting that there are only two choices in a situation that really offers more options ("Either the pool is free for everyone or our summer vacation is ruined.")

Overgeneralization—a generalization that is too broad to be valid ("Everyone loves to swim, so the pool should be free to all.")

Check Your Grammar

Use correct singular or plural verb forms with indefinite pronoun subjects.

Everyone is excited about the pool. (singular)

Most of the pool area is paved. (singular)

Most of the swimmers pay the fee. (plural)

Many of the swimmers pay the fee. (plural)

See page R66: Indefinite Pronouns as Subjects

Writing Online

PUBLISHING OPTIONS
For publishing options, visit the **Writing Center** at **ClassZone.com.**

ASSESSMENT PREPARATION
For writing and grammar assessment practice, go to the **Assessment Center** at **ClassZone.com.**

SPEAKING AND LISTENING

Giving an Oral Report

In Unit 8, you read nonfiction that described a variety of problems, and you wrote a problem-solution essay. To inform people about a problem that bothers you—the one you wrote about or a different one—present it as an oral report.

Planning the Oral Report

1. **Choose the points you will cover.** Find out to whom you will be speaking, what audience members already know about the problem, and how long you are expected to speak. Think about what questions your listeners might ask and how you will answer them.
2. **Find visuals to include.** Collect or create drawings, photographs, maps, charts, spreadsheets, or other graphics to make your report more interesting and informative.

> *Possible Solutions to Pool Fees*
>
> *Raise taxes.* ☹
> - *Taxes are already high.*
> - *People will never agree.*

3. **Practice presenting your report.** Run through your report several times in front of a practice audience. This practice will help you weave your visuals into your presentation and smooth out your delivery.

Delivering the Oral Report

1. **Relate to your audience.** Be relaxed and look directly at your audience when speaking. Move your eyes around the room so everyone feels included.
2. **Speak loudly and clearly at a natural speed.** Don't be afraid to pause to think or take a breath.
3. **Use gestures and facial expressions.** Move your arms, hands, and head to stress what you are saying. Facial expressions can also convince listeners that you care about the problem.
4. **Ask for feedback.** Invite listeners to tell you what they thought of your presentation. Listen carefully to their comments and use them to improve your next oral report.

SPEAKING AND LISTENING

Have students read this page for an overview of how to prepare and present an oral report in which they inform their audience about a problem and a possible solution.

Before students begin working, review this rubric with them so that they understand their goals:

Rubric A strong oral report
- clearly explains the problem and one or more solutions
- incorporates necessary background information
- addresses possible questions or concerns
- uses pictures or other visual aids to help the audience understand the topic
- shows evidence of frequent rehearsal
- is delivered smoothly with ample eye contact
- is told with good pacing—neither too slow nor too fast—and appropriate volume
- includes facial and voice expression as well as gestures
- ends with a request for audience feedback

RESOURCE MANAGER—Copy Master
Speaking and Listening p. 163

STANDARDS LESSON FILE
Speaking and Listening Lesson 1: Preparing and Presenting a Speech

DIFFERENTIATED INSTRUCTION

FOR LESS–PROFICIENT WRITERS

Planning the Presentation Suggest that students follow these steps to adapt their essays into the form of an oral report:

1. Print each of these parts of the essay on the front of a large index card: the introduction (including statement of problem and its importance), the causes and effects, the explanation of the first solution, the explanation of the second solution, and the conclusion. Number the cards.
2. Highlight important words and phrases that should be emphasized.
3. Insert cues on the cards to indicate when to show the visual aid.

Delivering the Oral Report [paired option] Have students practice with a partner, using their cards or the copy of the report that they plan to use for their formal presentation. Have partners provide feedback on these aspects:

- eye contact *(How can this be improved?)*
- voice volume *(Can the speaker be heard at all times?)*
- pace *(Is the speed at which the speaker presents the report appropriate?)*
- facial expressions and gestures *(Does the speaker appear interested and enthusiastic?)*
- organization of the content *(Is the report easy to follow?)*

Assessment Practice

CHECK READINESS

Read aloud the paragraph under **ASSESS** and stress to students that this is not the full Unit Test but a way for them to check their readiness for it. Then have students examine the skills listed under **REVIEW** and look back in the unit or in the **Student Resource Bank** for any they need to study.

READ THE SELECTION

Remind students to keep unit goals in mind as they read the passage, paying particular attention to

- text features
- graphic aids
- ways information could be summarized
- main ideas and supporting details

To help students focus on **text features** while reading, encourage them to ask questions such as

- What do the subheadings reveal about the content?
- In what way do graphic aids such as charts or tables extend or clarify information given in the text?
- Do photographs and captions give additional information or clarify text information?

ANSWER THE QUESTIONS

Direct students to pages R95–R101 of the Test-Taking Handbook to review test-taking strategies. Remind them not to choose the first alternative that seems to fit when answering a multiple-choice question. Instead, they should read through all the choices, eliminate any that are clearly wrong, and then choose the best answer—the one that is most accurate and complete.

Before students begin reading, encourage them to skim the questions that follow the passage. Point out that knowing what kinds of questions they will need to answer can help them focus their reading and quickly identify important facts and details.

Assessment Practice

Reading Comprehension

ASSESS
The practice test items on the next few pages match skills listed on the Unit Goals page (page 877) and addressed throughout this unit. Taking this practice test will help you assess your knowledge of these skills and determine your readiness for the Unit Test.

REVIEW
After you take the practice test, your teacher can help you identify any skills you need to review.

- Text Features
- Graphic Aids
- Summarize
- Main Ideas and Supporting Details
- Suffixes
- Base Words
- Introductory Commas
- Capitalization of Titles

ASSESSMENT ONLINE
For more assessment practice and test-taking tips, go to the **Assessment Center** at **ClassZone.com.**

DIRECTIONS *Read this selection and answer the questions that follow.*

from Odd Couples

Amy Sarver

Living in the wild can be hard. Finding food and staying safe aren't easy. Each day, animals struggle to survive in their habitats. Not all animals get by on their own. Some animals form a close partnership with other kinds of animals. These pairings are called symbiotic relationships.

In a symbiotic relationship, the animals depend on each other. One animal helps the other meet its needs. Sounds good, right? Not always. Some animals are not very kind to their partners. In some cases, one animal meets its needs but hurts its partner. Sounds crazy, but it does happen. Take ticks, for exampl These insects guzzle blood to live. To get blood, they attach themselves to other kinds of animals. Ticks do not help their hosts. Instead, they can pass germs that cause disease. In other relationships, animals don't treat their partners so poorly. Both animals benefit, or get help, from living with the other animal. Check out how animals pair up to survive.

Keeping Clean

Small animals called cleaner shrimps have found a way of helping fish at coral reefs. As their name suggests, the shrimps clean the fish. Here's how it works. The shrimps hang out at what scientists call a cleaning station. A fish stops by. Then a shrimp climbs onto the fish. The shrimp even steps into the fish's mouth. The shrimp uses its tiny claws to pick stuff off the fish's body. That can include dead skin, tiny pieces of food, and wee creatures that can hurt the fish. The fish gets a nice cleaning. The shrimp enjoys a tasty meal of fish trash.

Small birds called plovers are also in the cleaning business. They have big customers—crocodiles. Crocs have long snouts filled with sharp teeth. Cleaning them is tricky. That's where the plover comes in. When a croc opens its mouth, the plover hops right in. The croc does not snap its snout shut. Instead, it lets the plover eat small, harmful animals attached to the crocodile's teeth. The plover gets an easy meal. The croc gets clean teeth.

Sweet Success

Some animals need each other because they like the same food. Take the honeyguide bird and the ratel. They live on grasslands in Africa. Both animals love honey. Yet each has a problem getting some. The bird can find a beehive, but can't open it. The ratel can open a hive, but doesn't know how to find one

DIFFERENTIATED INSTRUCTION

FOR ENGLISH LEARNERS

Assessment Practice: Work Backwards
[paired option] Prepare students for the assessment by having them "work backwards"; that is, they should read the questions before they read the text passage. Have pairs follow these steps to learn unfamiliar words in the test directions and questions:

1. Find words you don't recognize and write each one on an index card.
2. Look up the meaning in a dictionary.
3. Write the meaning on the back of the card.
4. Use your word cards to teach and practice the vocabulary with your partner and another pair.

So the two animals team up. The bird flies over the grasslands, looking for hives. When it spots one, it swoops down and makes noise. The sound tells the ratel to come eat. The ratel uses its sharp claws to tear apart the hive. It gobbles up most of the honey-covered mess. Then the honeyguide bird enjoys finishing off the leftovers.

Clowning Around

Land and sky animals aren't the only ones that work together. So do some sea animals. One of the oddest couples is made up of the sea anemone and the clownfish. You might think sea anemones look like plants, but they are really hungry animals. They attach themselves to a rock or a coral reef. There they wait for a fish to swim by. Then they sting it with their tentacles. The stunned fish is then pulled into the sea anemone's hidden mouth. Still, one daring fish makes its home among sea anemones. It's the clownfish. This orange-and-white fish isn't kidding around. Its body is shielded by a thick layer of mucus. The slime protects the clownfish from the sea anemone's dangerous, stinging tentacles. The clownfish is also a good neighbor. It helps the sea anemone by luring in fish. When a hungry fish spots a colorful clownfish, it darts toward it. The clownfish safely swims under the anemone's tentacles. If the hungry fish follows, it gets stung. Then it becomes the anemone's next meal. The brave clownfish not only reels in fish food, it chases away fish that might eat an anemone. So the clownfish and anemone help keep each other fed and safe.

Instead of searching the sky for insects, the oxpecker bird catches a ride aboard large animals such as the antelope. In return, the bird picks ticks and other pests off the animal's body.

Clownfish live safely among sea anemones. They lure edible fish into the anemones' deadly tentacles and chase away harmful ones.

A Different Way of Life

All animals want to do one thing—survive in the wild. Some do that by living alone. Others live in flocks, herds, hives, packs, or schools. Some animals, both large and small, know the best way to stay alive is to live with or near other kinds of animals. At first glance, these teammates don't seem to make sense. If you look more closely, you'll soon learn that these animals help one another find food, shelter, and safety. They make the most of their various differences. These unlikely partners pair up to get the most out of life.

ITEM ANALYSIS

COMPREHENSION AND WRITTEN RESPONSE	ITEMS	UNIT PAGES
Text Features	2, 4, 10, 11	878, 885
Graphic Aids	3, 9, 10	895
Summarize	1, 7, 11	885
Main Ideas and Supporting Details	5, 6, 8	880, 919

VOCABULARY	ITEMS	UNIT PAGES
Suffixes	1, 2, 3, 4	926
Base Words	5, 6, 7, 8	892

WRITING AND GRAMMAR	ITEMS	UNIT PAGES
Introductory Commas	1, 2, 5	927
Capitalization of Titles	3, 4, 6	893

FOR LESS-PROFICIENT READERS

Assessment Support Consider these options for completing the **Assessment Practice:**

- Have students review the questions before reading the passage.
- Select random questions in the assessment and have students demonstrate how and where to look for the answers.
- Ask students to locate unfamiliar vocabulary in the assessment. Elicit the meanings of these words from the class.
- Have students record useful testing words and definitions in their journals for later reference.
- Read the selection or parts of it aloud to aid in student comprehension.

After checking student readiness with this Assessment Practice, you may administer the complete Unit 8 Test in order to more thoroughly evaluate student mastery of unit goals.

ANSWERS

Comprehension

Model a thinking process for answering multiple-choice questions.

1. **D *is correct.*** *This statement summarizes the information given in the text about both cleaner shrimps and plovers. A can be eliminated because the plovers do not set up cleaning stations. B is incorrect because it applies only to the shrimps and not to the plovers. C is incorrect because it is not supported by the text.*
2. **C *is correct.*** *Neither the honeyguide bird nor the ratel can get honey on its own. A can be eliminated because finding a beehive does not mean success for the honeyguide bird until the ratel opens the hive. B can be eliminated because sending a signal does not guarantee access to honey. D is incorrect because it describes success only for the ratel, but the main idea of the paragraph is that by working together, both animals get honey.*
3. **A *is correct.*** *The photograph shows why someone "might think that sea anemones look like plants" (line 43). B is incorrect because the photograph does not clearly show the clownfish's layer of mucus. C and D are incorrect because the photograph does not show any other fish besides the clownfish.*
4. **B *is correct.*** *The chart defines parasitism as a relationship in which one species benefits while the other is harmed, and the article says that ticks can pass along harmful germs as they suck the blood of their hosts (lines 8–11). A can be eliminated because the shrimp helps the fish it cleans (lines 15–22). C is incorrect because the ratel has a mutually beneficial relationship with the honeyguide bird (lines 30–38). Similarly, D is incorrect because the clownfish and the sea anemone have a relationship that matches the chart's definition of mutualism, not parasitism.*
5. **D *is correct.*** *Plovers and crocodiles both benefit from their relationship. A is incorrect because the article describes the tick as harming its host (lines 8–11). The chart describes the tapeworm as parasitic and the trumpetfish as having a commensal relationship with soft coral, making B and C incorrect.*

SYMBIOTIC INTERACTIONS		
Type of Relationship	**Example**	**Interaction**
Mutualism: both species benefit	bees and flowers	Bees gather nectar from flowers; they spread pollen that the flowers need to reproduce.
	aphids and ants	Aphids provide ants with sweet liquid; ants protect aphids from predators.
Commensalism: one species benefits; the other is not affected	trumpetfish and soft coral	Coral gives the trumpetfish camouflage for hunting; coral is unharmed.
	lichens and trees	Lichens live on trees; trees are unharmed.
Parasitism: one species benefits; the other is harmed	tapeworms and pigs	The tapeworm lives in the intestines of a host, such as a pig; it causes sickness in the host.
	mistletoe and trees	Mistletoe takes food from trees; the trees are damaged.

Comprehension

DIRECTIONS *Answer these questions about the article "Odd Couples."*

1. Which statement best summarizes the information in lines 15–28?

A Some animals set up cleaning stations where they get food from other animals that stop by.
B There isn't much food in the ocean, so shrimp need to eat fish trash.
C Birds such as plovers have learned from shrimp how to get food out of another animal's mouth.
D Sometimes, one animal gets food by cleaning another animal, so both animals benefit.

2. Reread lines 30–38. The term "sweet success" in the subheading (line 29) refers to what happens when the

A honeyguide bird finds a beehive
B honeyguide bird makes loud noises to attract the ratel
C honeyguide bird and the ratel work together to get honey
D ratel tears up the beehive and eats most of the honey

3. Which fact in the article does the photograph of the clownfish help you understand?

A Sea anemones look like plants.
B The clownfish is shielded by a layer of mucus.
C A hungry fish gets stung when it darts toward a clownfish.
D The clownfish chases away fish that might eat the anemones.

6. **D *is correct.*** *The main idea is that some animals form close partnerships and "help one another find food, shelter, and safety" (lines 66–67). Although A, B, and C are true, they do not express the main idea.*
7. **D *is correct.*** *It restates the main idea of the paragraph. A can be eliminated because it is a supporting detail but does not restate the main idea. B and C are not supported by information in the paragraph.*
8. **B *is correct.*** *The clownfish gains safety and the sea anemone gets food. A and C are not supported by the text. D is a true statement about parasitic relationships, but it is not supported by the mutually beneficial relationship between the clownfish and the sea anemone.*
9. **A *is correct.*** *The bird cleans pests off the antelope. B is incorrect because the "Sweet Success" section is about animals who like the same food. C is incorrect because "Clowning Around" is devoted to the relationship between the clownfish and the sea anemone. D can be eliminated because "A Different Way of Life" is the article's conclusion—another specific example would be out of place in this summary paragraph.*

4. Reread the definitions in the chart. Which animal mentioned in the article has a parasitic relationship with another animal?
   - A shrimp
   - B tick
   - C ratel
   - D clownfish

5. According to the article, an unlikely couple can form a relationship that helps both partners. Which two species described in the selection best illustrate that idea?
   - A tick and antelope
   - B tapeworm and pig
   - C trumpetfish and soft coral
   - D plover and crocodile

6. Which detail helps you understand the main idea of the article?
   - A The honeyguide bird and the ratel both live on grasslands in Africa.
   - B Many animals survive in the wild by living together in flocks or herds.
   - C Crocodiles have longs snouts with sharp teeth that are difficult to clean.
   - D The cleaner shrimp enjoys a meal while removing harmful creatures from a fish.

7. Which statement best summarizes lines 61–68?
   - A Many animals live together in groups of their own species, such as flocks, herds, or schools.
   - B The strongest animals survive in the wild by living alone.
   - C Wild animal behavior is difficult to predict and often makes little sense.
   - D Animals use different survival strategies, including teaming up with unlikely partners.

8. The relationship between the clownfish and the sea anemone supports the idea that
   - A a few animals form partnerships to have fun together
   - B in some symbiotic relationships, both animals benefit from forming a partnership
   - C animals that form partnerships survive better than animals that get by on their own
   - D in some symbiotic relationships, one animal meets its needs but hurts its partner

9. Reread the caption with the antelope photograph. Under which subheading in the article would you add a paragraph about the antelope and the oxpecker bird?
   - A Keeping Clean
   - B Sweet Success
   - C Clowning Around
   - D A Different Way of Life

Written Response

SHORT RESPONSE *Write two or three sentences to answer this question.*

10. Choose an animal pair from either photograph. Where would you place that pair in the chart: under mutualism, commensalism, or parasitism? Explain your answer.

EXTENDED RESPONSE *Write a paragraph to answer this question.*

11. Summarize the key points presented in the chart. Give one example of each type of symbiotic interaction to support your answer.

GO ON

Written Response

Possible short response:

10. *Both the antelope/oxpecker bird relationship and the clownfish/sea anemone relationship would be categorized under mutualism. The chart defines mutualism as a relationship in which both species benefit. The oxpecker bird rids the antelope of pests while getting food for itself. The clownfish gains protection from predators while it lures food for the sea anemone and chases away the anemone's predators.*

Possible extended response:

11. *Students' summaries should include the definitions of mutualism, commensalism, and parasitism provided in the chart. For each category of symbiotic relationship, they should select one example from the chart or from the article and explain why it illustrates the concept. For example, they might cite the relationship between aphids and ants as an example of mutualism because both species benefit. The relationship between a trumpetfish and soft coral is an example of commensalism because the fish benefits while the coral is neither harmed nor helped. The relationship between a tapeworm and a pig is an example of parasitism because the tapeworm benefits while the pig is harmed.*

DIFFERENTIATED INSTRUCTION

FOR ENGLISH LEARNERS

Review Academic Vocabulary On the board, write these academic vocabulary terms. Then give the definitions in random order and have students match them to the terms. Challenge students to give examples of each term.

- *summarize:* to restate the most important information from a passage in one's own words, in a shortened form
- *fact:* a statement that can be proved
- *main idea:* the most important idea in a paragraph or passage
- *detail:* a word, phrase, or sentence that tells something about the main idea
- *chart:* a visual or graphic way of organizing information
- *caption:* descriptive phrase, sentence, or sentences placed near a photograph

ANSWERS

Vocabulary

1. **D is correct.** *The sentence describes pairings, or partnerships.* A, B, and C *are not supported by the context.*
2. **B is correct.** *The context explains that the anemone stings the fish before pulling it into its mouth, which suggests that the fish has been paralyzed.* A, C, and D *can be eliminated because these words describe mental states that would not help the anemone eat its prey.*
3. **A is correct.** *The animals have many differences, making them "unlikely partners."* B, C, and D *can be eliminated because they do not make sense in the context of the passage.*
4. **C is correct.** *Clownfish lure fish that sea anemones can eat "and chase away harmful ones." The caption does not suggest that the fish are injured or hungry, making* A and B *incorrect. Although the fish may be pleasant tasting,* D *is not the best answer because the caption contrasts edible fish with "harmful ones."*
5. **B is correct.** *Tiny organisms can hurt the fish.* A, C, and D *can be eliminated because they do not make sense in the context of the passage.*
6. **C is correct.** *The animals in symbiotic relationships are "unlikely partners" because they are so different from one another.* A, B, and D *are incorrect because they do not make sense in the context.*
7. **D is correct.** *Flowers need pollen to make seeds and generate offspring.* A, B, and C *are all vague phrases that do not make sense in the context.*
8. **A is correct.** *Ants protect aphids from other organisms that would eat them.* B, C, and D *can be eliminated because they do not suggest a reason why the aphids would need protection.*

Vocabulary

DIRECTIONS *Use context clues and your knowledge of suffixes to answer the following questions.*

1. What is the meaning of the word *symbiotic* as it is used in line 4?
   A staying alert to danger
   B competing for food
   C acting in an aggressive way
   D having a close association
2. What is the meaning of the word *stunned* as it is used in line 46?
   A confused
   B paralyzed
   C astonished
   D bored
3. What is the meaning of the word *various* as it is used in line 67?
   A many
   B changing
   C extreme
   D consistent
4. What is the meaning of the word *edible* as it is used in the caption with the clownfish photograph?
   A injured
   B hungry
   C safe to eat
   D pleasant tasting

DIRECTIONS *Use context clues and your knowledge of base words to answer the following questions.*

5. What is the meaning of the word *creatures* in line 20?
   A domestic animals
   B living organisms
   C imaginary beings
   D artistic life forms
6. What is the meaning of the word *differences* as it is used in line 68?
   A disagreements or arguments
   B comparisons
   C the ways of being unlike
   D unsure reactions
7. What is the meaning of the word *reproduce* as it is used to describe the bee-pollen interaction in the chart?
   A do something again
   B imitate an action
   C begin a process
   D generate offspring
8. What is the meaning of the word *predators* as it is used to describe the aphid-ant interaction in the chart?
   A organisms that live by hunting or catching others
   B animals that lived before humans existed
   C those that make their presence known in advance
   D groups that help each other survive

956

DIFFERENTIATED INSTRUCTION

FOR ENGLISH LEARNERS

Review Academic Vocabulary Point out the terms *suffixes* and *base words* in the directions. Discuss the meanings of these terms and tell students that knowing the meanings of suffixes and base words can help them determine the meanings of unfamiliar words they encounter.

- *suffix:* word part placed at the end of a base word to change the word's tense, person, or number, or to change the meaning of the base word. Examples:
  — *-ed:* indicates a past-tense verb, which may be used as an adjective
  — *-ible:* able, likely
  — *-ic:* relating to
  — *-ous:* marked by, state or quality of
- *base word:* word that stands alone and is complete in itself. Examples:
  — *create:* to bring into being
  — *differ:* to be unlike
  — *prey:* to hunt (another animal) for food
  — *produce:* to make

Writing & Grammar

DIRECTIONS *Read this passage and answer the questions that follow.*

(1) In 1921 Margaret Bourke-White received her first camera. (2) She would go on to became a renowned photojournalist in the next decade. (3) During the Great Depression Bourke-White photographed the South. (4) Her haunting images later appeared in the book *You have seen their Faces.* (5) Bourke-White also photographed Russia during World War II, documenting it in her book *shooting the Russian war.* (6) In the late 1940s Bourke-White spent two years in India. (7) Her photographs from this trip appeared in the book *halfway to Freedom: A Report on the new India.*

1. Choose the correct way to punctuate sentence 1 with a comma.

A In 1921, Margaret Bourke-White received her first camera.
B In 1921 Margaret, Bourke-White received her first camera.
C In 1921 Margaret Bourke-White received, her first camera.
D In 1921 Margaret Bourke-White received her first, camera.

2. Choose the correct way to punctuate sentence 3 with a comma.

A During the Great Depression Bourke-White, photographed the South.
B During the Great Depression Bourke-White photographed, the South.
C During the Great Depression, Bourke-White photographed the South.
D During the Great, Depression Bourke-White photographed the South.

3. Choose the correct way to capitalize the title in sentence 4.

A *You have seen Their Faces*
B *You Have Seen their faces*
C *You Have Seen their Faces*
D *You Have Seen Their Faces*

4. Choose the correct way to capitalize the title in sentence 5.

A *Shooting the Russian war*
B *Shooting the Russian War*
C *shooting the Russian War*
D *Shooting The Russian War*

5. Choose the correct way to punctuate sentence 6 with a comma.

A In the late 1940s, Bourke-White spent two years in India.
B In the late 1940s Bourke-White, spent two years in India.
C In the late 1940s Bourke-White spent two, years in India.
D In the late 1940s Bourke-White spent two years, in India.

6. Choose the correct way to capitalize the title in sentence 7.

A *Halfway to Freedom: A Report on the new India*
B *Halfway To Freedom: A Report On The New India*
C *Halfway to Freedom: A Report On the New India*
D *Halfway to Freedom: A Report on the New India*

STOP

957

DIFFERENTIATED INSTRUCTION

FOR ENGLISH LEARNERS

Assessment Support Discuss the use of commas with introductory phrases and the correct capitalization of titles.

- *introductory comma* (items 1, 2, 5): Use a comma after an adverbial phrase—one that tells how or when.
  —Before snapping the picture, she checked the camera settings.
  —In the early 1800s, women in the United States had few rights.
- *capitalization of titles* (items 3, 4, 6): Capitalize the first word and all important words in titles. Do not capitalize articles (*a, an, the*) or prepositions of fewer than five letters (*at, in, for*) unless they are the first word of the title.
  —*To the Lighthouse*
  —*You Can't Take It with You*

ANSWERS

Writing & Grammar

1. **A *is correct.*** *The introductory phrase is set off by a comma.* B *is incorrect because the comma separates the subject's first and last names.* C *is incorrect because the comma separates the verb and its object.* D *is incorrect because the comma separates an adjective from the noun it modifies.*
2. **C *is correct.*** *The introductory phrase is set off by a comma.* A *is incorrect because the comma separates the subject from the verb.* B *is incorrect because the comma separates a verb from its object.* D *is incorrect because the comma separates an adjective from the noun it modifies.*
3. **D *is correct.*** *Each important word is capitalized, including nouns, pronouns, verbs, and adjectives. We can eliminate* A, B, *and* C *because each has one or more important words that are not capitalized.*
4. **B *is correct.*** *Each important word is capitalized.* A *and* C *are incorrect because each has one important word that is not capitalized (*war *and* shooting*).* D *is incorrect because the article (*The*) is capitalized.*
5. **A *is correct.*** *The introductory phrase is set off by a comma. We can eliminate* B *because the comma separates the subject from the verb.* C *is incorrect because the comma separates an adjective from the noun it modifies.* D *is incorrect because the comma creates a confusing pause before the last phrase.*
6. **D *is correct.*** *Each important word is capitalized. We can eliminate* A *because the adjective* new *is not capitalized.* B *is incorrect because all the articles and prepositions are capitalized.* C *is incorrect because the preposition* On *is capitalized; only prepositions of five letters or more should be capitalized.*

INTRODUCE *MORE GREAT READS*

In Unit 8, students have discussed a number of big questions. Invite students to tell which question they found most intriguing and why. Then focus attention on the three questions that appear on this page. Discuss the recommended books and their summaries, pointing out how each book connects to the related question. Encourage students to choose one or more of these "great reads" to read independently.

ClassZone.com

To find additional books that match students' interests and ability levels, visit the Literature Center at **ClassZone.com.**

Ideas for Independent Reading

Which questions from Unit 8 made an impression on you? Continue exploring them with these books.

What is your dream job?

Dare to Dream! 25 Extraordinary Lives
by Sandra McLeod Humphrey
Some of the world's most famous athletes, scientists, artists, and politicians had to overcome serious obstacles to achieve success. This book tells the real-life stories of people who beat the odds.

Come Back to Afghanistan: A California Teenager's Story
by Said Hyder Akbar and Susan Burton
After the fall of the Taliban government, Said and his father returned to Afghanistan. Said tells what it was like to be a teenager working to rebuild a country.

Stonecutter
by Leander Watts
It's 1835, and 14-year-old Albion is learning to be a stonecutter. His big break comes when he's hired to do the stonework at a new estate. When he gets there, he finds a creepy, half-finished mansion. Something isn't right.

Why do people seek danger?

Mortal Engines
by Philip Reeve
What could an assassin, a third-class historian, and a rich man's daughter ever have in common? They are all teenagers who are willing to risk their safety to solve the mystery that threatens to destroy the world.

Eragon
by Christopher Paolini
Eragon lives a quiet life on a farm until he finds a dragon's egg. After it hatches, Eragon's peaceful childhood comes to a violent end. He realizes it's his fate to become a dragon rider and join in the war against the evil King Galbatorix.

The Gadget
by Paul Zindel
Thirteen-year-old Stephen escapes war-torn London to live with his father, who is a scientist on a secret military base in New Mexico. Stephe is determined to learn all he can about the "gadget" his father is working on, but at what price?

What does music say about us?

The Black Canary
by Jane Louise Curry
James's parents think he will become a musician like them, but that is the one thing he knows he doesn't want. His opinion changes when he finds a portal to another time. He's stuck in the 1600s, and he can't go home until he develops his musical gifts.

Mountain Solo
by Jeanette Ingold
Tess is a violin prodigy, but after a disastrous concert she vows to give up music. She goes to live with her dad and his new wife in Montana. Can the mystery surrounding a young musician from the pioneer days help her figure out her own truth?

This Land Was Made for You and Me: The Life an Songs of Woody Guthri
by Elizabeth Partridge
Woody Guthrie was a songwriter who traveled the country, singing about people struggling to get by. His own life was difficult, to but he inspired people from many generations.

958 UNIT 8: FACTS AND INFORMATION

State Your Case

ARGUMENT AND PERSUASION

- In Nonfiction
- In Media
- In Literature

959

About the Art The photograph on the left appears with Rick Reilly's opinion piece "The Weak Shall Inherit the Gym." (See page 989.) The photograph of the polar bear appears on page 970 with the article "Zoos: Myth and Reality" by Rob Laidlaw.

For help in planning this unit, see

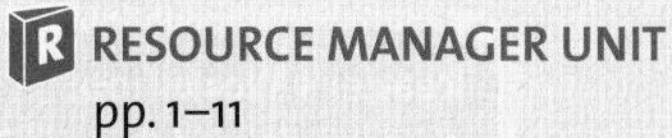
RESOURCE MANAGER UNIT 9
pp. 1–11

INTRODUCE THE UNIT

Ask students what it means to "state your case." Elicit from them the idea that stating one's case means presenting a position or an opinion on an issue and backing it up with reasons and evidence. The goal is to convince someone else to accept one's own point of view on the issue.

Have volunteers share times when they have successfully stated their case. Discuss what techniques or strategies helped them win their arguments. Then ask students to examine the two photographs on this page and consider these questions:

- Imagine that you are the girl on the left. What case might you have presented to convince your parents to let you play hockey?
- What argument might be supported by the photograph on the right? What elements of this photograph make it a convincing piece of evidence?

Discuss with students which details led to their conclusions. Tell students that for every argument that is made, someone else has a different viewpoint. In the future, it is likely that students will need to argue for an important cause, evaluate the logic of others' arguments, or persuade someone else to accept a certain belief. The selections in this unit will help them understand more about the skills of developing a successful **argument** and using effective **persuasion.**

Skills Trace

SKILLS STRAND	Reader's Workshop: Argument and Persuasion pp. 962–967	Zoos: Myth and Reality/ Zoos Connect Us to the Natural World pp. 968–979 Online Article/Opinion Piece *Level: Challenging*	Media Study: Movie Ad Campaign pp. 980–983 Movie Advertisements	Position on Dodgeball in Physical Education/The Weak Shall Inherit the Gym pp. 984–993 Position Statement/ Opinion Piece *Level: Average*
Literary Analysis				
Reading and Informational Texts	Elements of an Argument pp. 962–963, 966–967 Persuasive Techniques pp. 964–967 Analyze the Literature pp. 963, 965–967	Argument pp. 969, 970, 971, 973, 974, 975, 976, 977 Distinguishing Between Fact and Opinion pp. 969, 971, 972, 974, 976, 977		Persuasive Techniques pp. 985, 986, 987, 988, 990, 991 Set a Purpose for Reading pp. 985, 991 Compare Persuasive Techniques p. 991
Vocabulary	Academic Vocabulary pp. 962, 964	Word Acquisition pp. 969, T969, 978 Context Clues p. T969 Greek Roots (*exo*) p. 978	Academic Vocabulary (Ads) p. 981	Word Acquisition pp. 985, T985, 992 Context Clues p. T985 Latin Words (*gressus*) p. 992
Writing, Grammar, and Style		Capitalization p. 979		Write for Assessment p. 993
Speaking, Listening, Viewing, and Media	Discuss pp. 962–965	Discuss pp. 968, T970–T976, 977 Analyze Visuals pp. 970, 975	Discuss pp. 980, 983 Analyze and Evaluate an Ad Campaign pp. 981–983 Create Your Own Ad Campaign p. 983	Discuss pp. 984, T986–T990, 991 Analyze Visuals pp. 987, 989

 Assessment-Based Planning: Skills in red are assessed on the Unit 9 Test. **T** = Teacher's Edition page

The Sanctuary of School pp. 994–1001 Essay *Level: Easy*	**Educating Sons/ The First Americans** pp. 1002–1009 Speech/Letter *Level: Average*	**St. Crispian's Day Speech** pp. 1010–1015 Drama Excerpt *Level: Challenging*	**Writing Workshop: Persuasive Essay** pp. 1016–1023
		Persuasion in Literature pp. 1011, 1012, 1014	
Analyze Author's Purpose pp. 995, 996, 998, 999, 1000 Identify Cause-and-Effect Relationships pp. 995, 997, 998, 1000	Analyze the Influence of Historical Context pp. 1003, 1004, 1007, 1008 Identify Comparisons and Contrasts pp. 1003, 1006, 1007, 1008	Paraphrase pp. 1011, 1012, 1014	Analyze a Persuasive Essay pp. 1017–1018, 1022
Word Acquisition pp. 995, T995, 1001 Word Maps p. T995 Related Words p. 1001	Word Acquisition pp. 1003, T1003, 1009 Context Clues—General p. T1003; Antonyms p. 1009		
		Sentence Structure (Parallelism) p. 1015	Write a Persuasive Essay pp. 1016–1022 Emotional Appeals pp. 1021, 1022 Active Voice p. 1022
Discuss pp. 994, T996–T999, 1000 Analyze Visuals p. 997	Discuss pp. 1002, T1004–T1007, 1008 Analyze Visuals p. 1005	Discuss pp. 1010, T1012–T1013, 1014 Analyze Visuals p. 1012	Discuss pp. 1016–1018 Deliver a Persuasive Speech p. 1023

Skills Assessed on the Unit 9 Test:

Reading and Informational Texts
- Distinguish between facts and opinions
- Identify causes and effects
- Identify comparisons and contrasts
- Identify author's purpose
- Identify elements of an argument (claim, support, counterargument)
- Identify and analyze persuasive techniques

Vocabulary
- Use knowledge of Greek and Latin words and roots to help determine word meanings
- Determine meanings of related words by applying knowledge of word roots, base words, and affixes

Writing, Grammar, and Style
- Write a persuasive essay
- Capitalize correctly names of organizations, businesses, and institutions
- Use parallelism to link related ideas in writing
- Additional writing and grammar skills

For additional lesson planning help, see **Easy Planner DVD.**

OBJECTIVES

- establish prior knowledge about ways to **persuade**
- discuss qualities that make someone or something convincing

Whom can you BELIEVE?

Read the paragraph aloud. Ask students to list other instances in which they are the targets of persuasion. Have them discuss why it is important to consider carefully the sources that they choose to believe. What might happen if they place their trust in a company, person, or product that is not credible? Ask students if they have ever been persuaded to do something that they shouldn't have. What did they learn from the experience?

ACTIVITY Have students take turns describing ads that they have found convincing. Ask them to explain why, using the bulleted questions as a guide. Encourage students to consider ways in which the visual elements and language also contribute to the effectiveness of an ad. Based on students' discussion, generate a class list of the common factors that determine persuasiveness. Discuss which of these qualities are reliable criteria for helping them decide what to believe.

CHECK UNDERSTANDING Distribute a print ad to students. Have them point out elements designed to **persuade** them and evaluate the ad's overall credibility.

UNIT 9 *Share What You Know*

Whom can you BELIEV

As soon as you wake up in the morning, you're surrounded by peopl groups, and corporations trying to influence the way you think or act. To **persuade** you to buy a brand of shoes, a company runs an ad showing a great athlete wearing the same pair as he sinks a jump shot. To encourage you to sell T-shirts for a fundraiser, the class president starts the morning announcements by offering a prize to the student who sells the most. Meanwhile, a friend begs you to work with her instead of with your usual partner. How can you be sure you're doing what's best for you?

ACTIVITY Think about a time when an advertisement persuaded you to buy a product. What influenced your decision to believe that company's claims? Consider the following questions:

- Were you familiar with that company's products?
- What did the advertisement tell you that you did not hear from competing companies' ads?
- Did the company use celebrity endorsements, statistics, or other persuasive techniques to convince you to buy its product?

960

Unit Resources

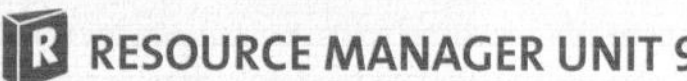
RESOURCE MANAGER UNIT 9

BEST PRACTICES TOOLKIT

STANDARDS LESSON FILE

Easy Planner DVD

Write*Smart* CD

ClassZone.com

Audio Anthology CD

Multi-Language Academic Vocabulary Online

eEdition CD & Online

McDougal Littell Assessment System

Test Generator CD

Media*Smart* DVD

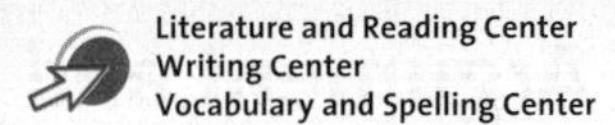

Preview Unit Goals

READING	• Identify and analyze elements of an argument • Identify and analyze persuasive techniques • Analyze the effectiveness of persuasive techniques • Distinguish between and evaluate facts and opinions • Identify and analyze author's purpose • Identify and analyze comparisons and contrasts • Identify and analyze the historical context of a text • Identify and analyze tone
WRITING AND GRAMMAR	• Write a persuasive essay • Use parallelism to link related ideas • Capitalize names correctly
SPEAKING, LISTENING, AND VIEWING	• Analyze and evaluate an ad campaign • Recognize persuasive techniques in media messages • Deliver a persuasive speech
VOCABULARY	• Use knowledge of word roots, base words, and affixes to help determine word meaning • Use antonyms as context clues to determine word meaning
ACADEMIC VOCABULARY	• argument • fact and opinion • historical context • tone • author's purpose • persuasive techniques

Preview Unit Goals

Read the unit goals aloud as students follow along. Point out the various skills that they will be developing in this unit. Ask them which skills they have used in the past. Which are new to them? Then suggest that they record questions about these skills and goals in their journals and look for answers as they work through the unit.

Have students write the Academic Vocabulary terms in their journals, and suggest that they add the definition of each word as they come across it in their reading. Encourage students to use these terms when they talk about their work in this unit.

ADDITIONAL UNIT GOALS

These skills will be taught in this unit but are not the major focus of the unit:

Reading
- Set a purpose for reading
- Identify and analyze cause-and-effect relationships
- Identify and analyze an overgeneralization
- Paraphrase
- Identify and analyze irony
- Read a variety of genres: drama excerpt, article, opinion piece, position statement, essay, speech, letter

Speaking, Listening, and Viewing
- Analyze the relationship between advertising and media
- Analyze the effect of different techniques that target a specific audience
- Create an ad campaign

Vocabulary
- Use structural analysis to identify words

DIFFERENTIATED INSTRUCTION

FOR ENGLISH LEARNERS

Academic Vocabulary [paired option] Use the Academic Vocabulary copy master to introduce the vocabulary terms, including *argument* and *historical context.*

1. Read each term and the corresponding sentences aloud. Work together to define each term.
2. Allow students to work in pairs to complete the sentences in Part B.
3. Reconvene to review students' responses.

Additional Academic Vocabulary [paired option] Use the second copy master to teach these terms from the unit: *affixes, appeal by association, claim, emotional appeal, ethical appeal, loaded language, parallelism.* Read each term and definition aloud. Then have students complete the chart and work on Part B in pairs before reviewing their responses.

RESOURCE MANAGER—Copy Masters
Academic Vocabulary p. 9
Additional Academic Vocabulary p. 10

Focus and Motivate

OBJECTIVES

- identify and analyze elements of an argument
- identify and analyze persuasive techniques

Teach

Part 1: Elements of an Argument

Claim and Support Have students select an editorial from a newspaper. Display the Summary Frame: Argumentation and work with the class to evaluate the editorial. Ask students to identify the claim and the supporting evidence. How well does the evidence support the claim? If students aren't sure, have them restate the claim and the evidence in their own words.

BEST PRACTICES TOOLKIT—Transparency
Summary Frame: Argumentation p. B11

Counterargument Using the same editorial, ask students whether it acknowledges the opposing viewpoint and provides a counterargument, an argument made to disprove or answer the opposing viewpoint. Point out that a counterargument isn't necessary in making an argument, but including one can strengthen the argument. If the editorial does not have a counterargument, challenge students to provide one.

CHECK UNDERSTANDING Ask students to summarize in their own words the basic parts of an argument.

UNIT 9
Reader's Workshop

Argument and Persuasion

Persuasive messages are everywhere—on buses and billboards, on television and the Web, even on cereal boxes and candy wrappers. Using direct or subtle techniques, these messages tell you what to wear, what to buy, and what to think. How can you sift through all the pitches, claims, and pizzazz, and make sure you figure out what's really important? In this workshop, you'll learn how to separate the substance of these messages from what's simply a sugar coating.

Part 1: Elements of an Argument

The word *argument* doesn't always refer to two people having a disagreement. In formal speaking and writing, an **argument** is a claim supported by reasons and evidence. Sound arguments appeal to logic, not to emotions. A strong argument

- presents a **claim,** or the writer's position on a problem or an issue. The claim might be stated directly ("Vitamins are good for you.") or indirectly ("Take your vitamins—feel the difference."). The claim often appears in the introduction, conclusion, or title of an argument.
- provides **support,** or the reasons and evidence that back up the claim. Support can include facts, statistics, examples, and quotations from experts.
- anticipates what people with the opposing viewpoint might say and counter their objections by offering further evidence to support the claim.

Look closely at the elements of an argument in this poster.

1 **Claim:** The title of the poster states its claim: One person can make a difference.

2 **Support 1:** Giving a few hours of your time will build a stronger community.

3 **Support 2:** Volunteering will make you a better person.

4 Notice that an opposing viewpoint is addressed and countered: No effort is a wasted effort.

1 **ONE PERSON CAN MAKE A DIFFERENCE!**

Want to make a difference? Volunteer!

2 **Public service builds a stronger community.** Consider volunteering a couple of hours each week—as a tutor, activities leader, or coach—to help others.

3 **Serving others will give you a sense of self-satisfaction.** You'll also grow as an individual. Come see what you can do.

4 **Don't let anyone convince you that one person can't make a difference.** No effort is a wasted effort!

DIFFERENTIATED INSTRUCTION

FOR ALL STUDENTS

For general guidelines on differentiating instruction, see

BEST PRACTICES TOOLKIT
Differentiated Instruction pp. 31–38

FOR LESS-PROFICIENT READERS

Note Taking Hand out the Note Taking: Elements of an Argument copy master and ask students to read page 962 silently. Then have them record their notes on the copy master as you discuss the information.

RESOURCE MANAGER—Copy Master
Note Taking p. 15

Identify Support Write the terms *fact, statistic, example, anecdote,* and *quotation* on slips of paper and put them in a bag. Ask a student to draw a term from the bag and provide a definition or an example. The student should then select a classmate to repeat the process.

MODEL: ELEMENTS OF AN ARGUMENT

The author of this essay makes a case against junk food by focusing on one example. As you read this excerpt, try to identify the author's claim. What reasons and evidence does he provide as support for his position?

from Why Can't I Live on *French Fries?*

Essay by **Richard J. Roberts**

So what's so bad about stuffing yourself with nothing but French fries all the time, anyway? Simple: Pretty soon you'll be missing important nutrients. Let's start with vitamins. The body does not need much of them, but in most cases, it cannot produce them. Potatoes contain mostly vitamin C and hardly any other vitamin. No vitamin K, for example, which is needed to form a scab when you're bleeding so that the bleeding stops. And no vitamin A, needed for the eyes to function properly. Not enough vitamin A, and you'll see even less well at night than everyone else. Over the long run, a lack of vitamin A can even cause blindness. Many children in Africa suffer from it.

If you were to eat only French fries, your teeth would also slowly go bad and your bones would become brittle. That's because potatoes do not contain enough calcium, and your bones need calcium throughout your life, not just while you're growing. Besides, all those mountains of fries would overload you with sodium, because they're often too salty, and salt contains sodium. It's important that your body maintain a good sodium balance, because otherwise, it can't regulate its body temperature very well, but too much sodium causes high blood pressure in some people.

French fries also contain little protein. Proteins are critical. They are the true bearers of life. The cells from which most living creatures are built consist mostly of proteins. Without proteins, for example, you would not have any muscles. . . .

We chemists and doctors still know far too little about nutrition and its effects on health. This is why every person has to find out for him- or herself what's good for each. But one thing I can guarantee: You'll get into trouble if you always eat nothing but French fries. By the way, I myself would love to wolf down French fries every day. But I, too, have to restrain myself and should stick to the advice that I've given you here.

Close Read

1. Reread the title and lines 1–2. What is the author's claim?
2. In the boxed lines, the author explains that a person needs vitamins that are not found in French fries. What examples does he use to support this reason?
3. In lines 10–21, the author offers three other reasons to support his claim. Restate these reasons in your own words.
4. What does the author do in the last paragraph to strengthen his argument?

MODEL: ELEMENTS OF AN ARGUMENT

Close Read

Possible answers:

1. *The author's claim is that if you eat nothing but French fries, you will be missing important nutrients.*
2. *Examples the author provides of vitamins not found in French fries include vitamin K (line 5), which helps to stop bleeding; and vitamin A (line 7), needed for night vision and good eye health.*
3. *The author provides the following reasons: (1) Potatoes lack calcium, which is needed for strong teeth and bones. (2) French fries are often very salty, which can upset the body's sodium balance and cause high blood pressure. (3) French fries lack protein, which is important for muscle development.*
4. *The author acknowledges that he, too, would love to eat French fries every day. By including this information, he strengthens his argument by anticipating what the opposing viewpoint might say ("Why not eat French fries? They taste so good!") and countering it by saying that he knows his health and nutrition depend on sticking to his advice.*

FOR LESS–PROFICIENT READERS

Analysis Support: Examples [paired option]
Explain that supporting examples are often stated as cause-and-effect relationships. Have partners work together to use a Cause-and-Effect Diagram to analyze the three effects of eating nothing but French fries that are stated in the essay.

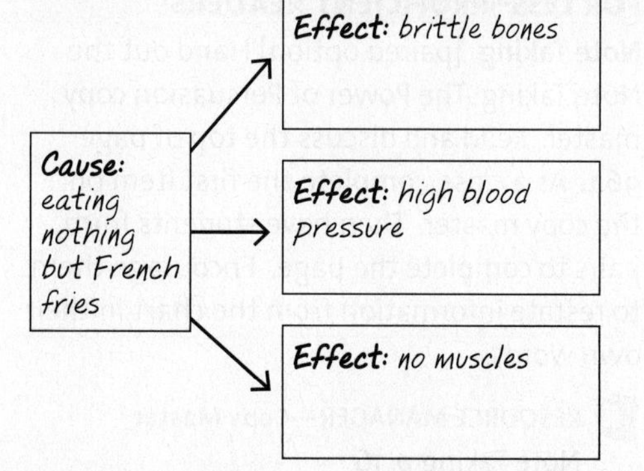

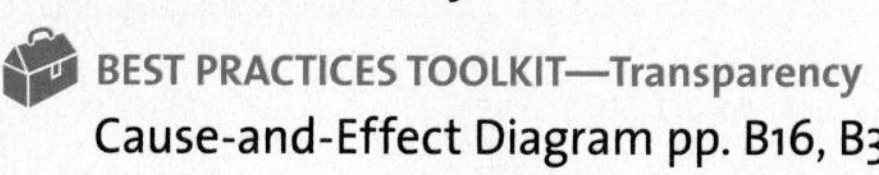

BEST PRACTICES TOOLKIT—Transparency
Cause-and-Effect Diagram pp. B16, B38

READER'S WORKSHOP 963

Teach

Part 2: The Power of Persuasion

Appeals by Association Discuss the examples of each kind of appeal by association on page 964. Point out that, in order to be persuasive, a person or organization that uses this technique must choose carefully the kind of associations they make. For example, a company selling expensive cars probably would not choose a singer popular among teenagers to give a testimonial—most adult customers wouldn't even know who the singer is. Work with the class to brainstorm appeals by association that would work well in these situations:

- A company wants teenagers to buy its brand of shoes.
- A local environmental organization is looking for volunteers to join a clean-up effort.
- A middle-school student is running for class president.
- The school's literary magazine needs more students to submit poems, stories, and essays for the next issue.

Emotional Appeals Explain that persuasive techniques may appeal to a wide variety of emotions, needs, or desires. Share this list with students and work with them to provide an example of an appropriate appeal for each:

- adventure
- comfort
- creativity
- patriotism
- friendship
- power
- courage
- pride
- gratitude
- duty

CHECK UNDERSTANDING Have students close their books. Read aloud each example from the chart and have students identify the persuasive technique it represents.

BEST PRACTICES TOOLKIT—Copy Masters
Analysis Frame: Persuasion pp. D23, D46, D47

Part 2: The Power of Persuasion

Who can ignore the pleading expression on the face of a starving child or a description of an injured animal whose survival depends on *you?* Effective writers, speakers, and advertisers know how to pull your heartstrings. They try to influence your feelings and actions using **persuasive techniques,** such as the ones shown here. While these techniques can enhance strong arguments, they can also mask the flaws in weak ones. That's why it's important for you to recognize these techniques for what they are. Use this chart as a guide.

PERSUASIVE TECHNIQUES	EXAMPLES
Appeals by Association	
Bandwagon Appeal Taps into people's desire to belong	Millions of teens have made City Jeanz part their wardrobe. What are you waiting for?
Snob Appeal Taps into people's need to feel superior to others	Join the Brookside Club for Seasoned Skiiers—because you're *way beyond* the beginner slopes.
Testimonial Relies on the backing of a celebrity, an expert, or a satisfied customer	As a supermodel, it's important for me to have a great smile. Brite Strips whiten your teeth without the wait.
Transfer Connects a product, a candidate, or a cause with a positive image or idea	Vote for cleaner air. Vote for Tony Leonard.
Appeal to Values	
Ethical Appeal Tries to gain moral support for a claim by linking the claim to a widely accepted value	If you believe that every child deserves a good education, support the Great Minds Organization.
Emotional Appeals	
Appeal to Fear Makes people feel as if their safety, security, or health is in danger	How clean are the hotel rooms you're staying in? You'll be shocked by what our documentary reveals.
Appeal to Pity Taps into people's compassion for others	For the cost of one cup of coffee a day, you could save a life.
Word Choice	
Loaded Language Uses words with strongly positive or negative connotations to stir people's emotions	The alley next to the parking lot is dark and dangerous. Vote to increase the number of street lamps in our neighborhood. Residents deserve to feel safe and protected.

964 UNIT 9: ARGUMENT AND PERSUASION

DIFFERENTIATED INSTRUCTION

FOR LESS–PROFICIENT READERS

Note Taking [paired option] Hand out the Note Taking: The Power of Persuasion copy master. Read and discuss the top of page 964. As a class, complete the first item on the copy master. Then have students form pairs to complete the page. Encourage them to restate information from the chart in their own words.

RESOURCE MANAGER—Copy Master
Note Taking p. 16

FOR ADVANCED LEARNERS/PRE–AP

Brainstorm Loaded Language [small-group option] Ask students to work together to brainstorm examples of words with positive and negative connotations. Have them use the words to create reference charts to display in the classroom.

MODEL 1: PERSUASION IN TEXT

This article challenges the positive concept of competition. What techniques does the author use to persuade you to adopt her position?

from

Against Competition

Newspaper article by **Gayle Heaney**

Our society uses sports metaphors for almost every aspect of life: Gear up, go for the goal, score one for the team! But studies show that the competitive spirit we admire can also have negative effects on a person—especially if the pressure to compete is instilled at a young age.

Young children often place excessive value on how they perform and can be emotionally devastated if they fail. Consider, for example, if a boy feels pressured to succeed in a particular sport. If he is unable to improve his skills, his self-esteem will disintegrate. If anyone criticizes his performance, he magnifies the criticism and views himself as a failure in everything.

In adults, competition can cause a person's stress levels to skyrocket. High stress levels can have damaging and dangerous consequences because they often lead to high blood pressure or to uncontrollable outbursts of anger. Road rage is turning our nation's highways into battlefields. Sports events often turn into violent fistfights, either on the field or in the crowd. Is this the kind of behavior we should be modeling for our children?

Close Read

1. Notice the highlighted examples of loaded language in the boxed sentence. Find two other examples of loaded language.
2. Reread lines 10–15. Which type of emotional appeal is the author using?

MODEL 2: PERSUASION IN ADVERTISING

Persuasion is a key factor in the advertisements you see on television, in magazines, and on product packaging. What techniques do you notice in this promotional poster?

ANNUAL SPORTS CHALLENGE:
June 20–26

Do *you* have what it takes to be a champion? Let us show you.

"I DIDN'T HAVE THE NERVE TO TRY OUT FOR THE SOCCER TEAM LAST YEAR. BUT THE SPORTS CHALLENGE PROGRAM HELPED ME BUILD MY SKILLS IN A FUN, CHALLENGING ENVIRONMENT. NOW I HAVE THE CONFIDENCE I NEED TO COMPETE—AND SUCCEED."

JEANNIE, AGE 14

Close Read

1. Which type of appeal by association does this poster use?
2. Describe the intended effect of the poster on readers.

MODEL 1: PERSUASION IN TEXT

Close Read

Possible answers:

1. *Other examples of loaded language include "disintegrate" (line 8), "failure" (line 9), "damaging, dangerous" (line 11), "uncontrollable" (line 12), and "violent" (line 14).*
2. *The author is using an appeal to fear. She is trying to scare readers into supporting her claim by talking about the "damaging, dangerous" consequences of competition.*

MODEL 2: PERSUASION IN ADVERTISING

Close Read

Possible answers:

1. *The poster uses a testimonial from a 14-year-old girl who participated in the Annual Sports Challenge program and had a positive experience. Some students may also say that the poster employs a transfer appeal by associating the program with the positive idea of being a champion.*
2. *The poster is intended to make the reader believe that the Sports Challenge program can make anyone a champion. It serves as a competitive challenge ("Do you have what it takes to be a champion?"). The advertisers may want other young people to accept the challenge by showing that they, like Jeannie, have what it takes. Also, advertisers may want viewers to decide to join the Annual Sports Challenge so they can be like the athletic, positive 14-year-old girl who is quoted.*

FOR ENGLISH LEARNERS

Concept Support: Loaded Language To help students understand the concept of loaded language, examine the negative connotations of the loaded language in **Model 1.** Then provide a more neutral substitute for each example and invite students to compare and contrast the connotations.

- *disintegrate* (line 8), "fall apart into tiny pieces"; neutral—*decline,* "fall back"
- *damaging, dangerous* (line 11), "destructive, harmful"; neutral—*negative,* "undesirable"
- *uncontrollable* (line 12), "wild and explosive"; neutral—*sudden,* "without warning"
- *violent* (line 14), "marked by great physical force"; neutral—*heated,* "marked by excited feelings"

Practice and Apply

Part 3: Analyze the Texts

Close Read

Possible answers:

1. *The claim is that "Raising the driving age will punish all young drivers for the mistakes of a few of their peers" (lines 3–4).*
2. *The author offers the following reasons and evidence as support for his claim: (1) In the United States, people follow the principle "innocent until proven guilty." By raising the driving age, we are labeling all teens guilty before they've done anything wrong. (2) Studies show that inexperience, not age, causes accidents, so raising the driving age won't necessarily solve any problems. (3) Teens need to be able to drive to get where they need to go. It's a major disruption to take their mobility away from them.*
3. *The author says that taking driving privileges away from teens is no more logical than taking those privileges away from men of all ages, since men are statistically more likely to kill other people while driving than women are.*

Part 3: Analyze the Texts

Now you'll apply what you've learned in this workshop as you analyze two texts—an editorial and a poster. Both texts are about the legal driving age. As you read each text, try to identify the claim, the support, and any persuasive techniques that are used.

Should the Driving Age Be Raised to 18?

NO!

Editorial by **Alex Koroknay-Palicz**
National Youth Rights Association

If your neighbor robs a bank, should you go to jail? No. If your classmate gets in an accident, should your driver's license be taken away? Of course not. Neither situation is fair. Raising the driving age will punish all young drivers for the mistakes of a few of their peers.

In this country we live by the principle of innocent until proven guilty. Those who want to raise the driving age have labeled teens guilty before they've gotten in an accident or before they've even stepped into a car. They believe that just because of your birth date, you are dangerous and must be punished by having your ability to drive taken from you.

Those who favor raising the driving age say that statistics show teenagers are more likely to get into accidents than adults. What they don't say is that statistics also show that men of all ages are 77 percent more likely to kill someone while driving than women. If people want to save lives by raising the driving age, then how about saving lives by allowing only women to drive?

Except raising the driving age won't save lives. Studies show that it is inexperience, not age, that causes accidents. Raising the driving age will just create inexperienced, accident-prone drivers at 18 instead of 16.

Teens need the ability to drive just as much as anyone else—to get to school, to get to work, to get to sports or band practice, or just to go out with their friends. Cars are necessary for mobility in this country. Taking that away is a large disruption to the lives of teenagers—for no good reason.

Close Read

1. The title tells you which side of the issue the author falls on, but the claim of his argument is stated in the first paragraph. What is the author's claim?
2. What reasons and evidence does the authc provide as support for h claim?
3. The author presents an opposing viewpoint in the boxed lines. In your own words, restate his response to this opposition.

DIFFERENTIATED INSTRUCTION

FOR LESS–PROFICIENT READERS

Analysis Support: Argument [paired option] Have partners read the editorial, stopping after each paragraph to ask and answer questions about the author's argument and the supporting evidence. Then have them answer the **Close Read** questions.

FOR ADVANCED LEARNERS/PRE–AP

Analyze Opposing Viewpoint Have a volunteer read aloud the editorial as a presentation for a TV op-ed segment. Ask students to listen to identify the opposing viewpoint. Then have them prepare a rebuttal to the editorial by using persuasive techniques to state the opposing argument. Invite volunteers to role-play a TV presentation of their rebuttals.

The creators of this public-service poster offer a different viewpoint on the same issue. What techniques are used to get you to see their side?

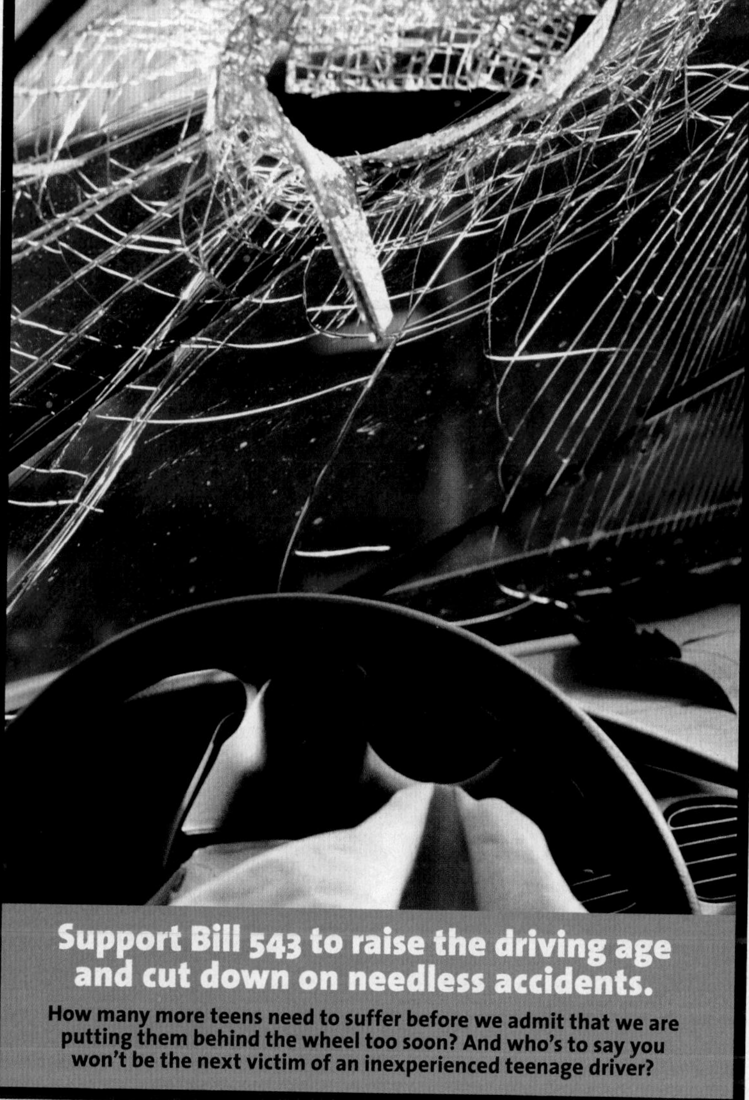

Support Bill 543 to raise the driving age and cut down on needless accidents.
How many more teens need to suffer before we admit that we are putting them behind the wheel too soon? And who's to say you won't be the next victim of an inexperienced teenage driver?

Close Read

1. Examine the text and photograph used in this ad. What emotional appeal is being used?
2. In what way does this ad use the technique of transfer?

Close Read

Possible answers:

1. *This public-service poster uses an appeal to fear by suggesting that many teens will be killed, injured, or traumatized because they are put behind the wheel too soon. Also, the ad attempts to scare viewers by suggesting that they could be the victims of a teenage drunk driver.*
2. *The ad uses transfer by attempting to connect Bill 543 (raising the driving age) with the positive notion of preventing "needless accidents."*

Assess and Reteach

Assess

Have students briefly summarize the claim, supporting examples, and persuasive techniques of the "Support Bill 543" poster.

Reteach

For students who cannot apply the workshop skills to "Support Bill 543," try these options:

1. Pair students with classmates who have grasped the lesson. Have each pair create flashcards that contain questions and answers about the claim, supporting examples, and persuasive techniques used in the poster.
2. Meet with small groups to review students' Note Taking copy masters. Clarify terms and concepts, illustrating each one with concrete examples from editorials and advertisements students have read.

FOR LESS–PROFICIENT READERS

Analysis Support: Persuasion in Text and Advertising [paired option] Have pairs of students use a Two-Column Chart to list the elements of the editorial "Should the Driving Age Be Raised to 18?—No!" and of the "Support Bill 543" poster. Ask them to include the claim, examples of support, the opposing viewpoint (if any), and persuasive techniques.

Editorial: "Should the Driving Age Be Raised to 18? No!"	*Poster: "Support Bill 543"*
Claim: Raising the driving age punishes all young drivers for the mistakes of a few.	*Claim: Supporting Bill 543 to raise the driving age will cut down on needless accidents.*
Support:	*Support:*
Opposing viewpoint:	*Opposing viewpoint: (none)*
Persuasive techniques:	*Persuasive techniques:*

 **BEST PRACTICES TOOLKIT—Transparency**
Two-Column Chart p. A25

Focus and Motivate

OBJECTIVES

Elements of Nonfiction
- explore the key idea of **wildlife**
- identify and analyze elements of an argument
- read an article and an opinion piece

Reading
- distinguish and evaluate fact and opinion

Vocabulary
- build vocabulary for reading and writing
- use knowledge of the Greek root *exo* to help determine word meaning *(also an EL language objective)*

Grammar and Writing
- capitalize correctly names of organizations, institutions, stores, and companies
- use writing to analyze literature

SUMMARY

The author of "Zoos: Myth and Reality" criticizes zoos for failing to provide consistently humane treatment to animals in captivity. In contrast, the author of "Zoos Connect Us to the Natural World" claims that the care of animals in zoos has improved and that zoos play a major role in conservation and in educating people about wildlife.

Should WILDLIFE *stay wild?*

Discuss the question. To lead into the ***KEY IDEA,*** ask students to identify the ideal conditions for **wildlife** living in captivity. As groups work on the ***LIST IT*** activity, encourage them to draw on their experience of visiting zoos and knowledge of wildlife.

Before Reading

Zoos: Myth and Reality

Online Article by Rob Laidlaw

Zoos Connect Us to the Natural World

Opinion Piece by Michael Hutchins

Should WILDLIFE *stay wild?*

KEY IDEA Close your eyes and picture an elephant. Are you picturing it in the zoo or in the wild? As humans inhabit more and more of the earth's land, some species of **wildlife** are more likely to be found in captivity than in their natural habitat. But is this a good thing? The writers of the selections you're about to read have different views on whether or not zoos are good for humans and animals.

LIST IT With a group, make a list of the good things and bad things about zoos. Do the pros outnumber the cons, or vice versa? Tell whether you think zoos are a good idea.

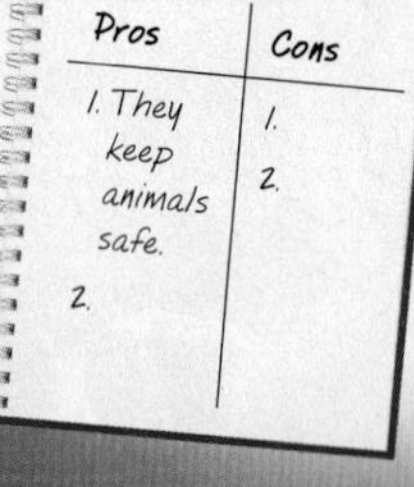

Pros
Cons
1. They keep animals safe.
2.
1.
2.

968

Selection Resources

RESOURCE MANAGER UNIT 9

Plan and Teach pp. 17–24

Elements of Nonfiction
Summary pp. 25†*, 26‡*
Argument pp. 27, 28†*
Question Support p. 35*

Reading
Distinguish Fact and Opinion pp. 29, 30†*
Reading Check p. 34
Reading Fluency p. 37

Vocabulary
Study p. 31*
Practice p. 32
Strategy p. 33

Grammar and Writing
Capitalize Correctly p. 36

Assessment
Selection Tests A, B/C pp. 39*, 41*
Test Generator CD

BEST PRACTICES TOOLKIT
Differentiated Instruction pp. 31–38*
Scaffolding Instruction pp. 43–46*

Graphic Organizers/Strategies
New Word Analysis • Personal Word List • Common Suffixes • T Chart

Reading Support
Audio Anthology CD*

Technology
Literature, Vocabulary, and Writing Centers at **ClassZone.com**
Write*Smart* CD

* Resources for Differentiation † Also in Spanish ‡ In Haitian Creole and Vietnamese

LEMENTS OF NONFICTION: ARGUMENT

When you express an opinion on an issue or problem and support it with evidence and reasons, you are presenting an **argument.** An effective argument provides

- a **claim,** or the writer's position on the issue or problem
- **support,** or any material that helps to prove a claim
- a **counterargument,** or an argument made to disprove or answer another viewpoint.

As you read, notice how the authors build their arguments using claims, support, and counterarguments.

EADING SKILL: DISTINGUISH FACT AND OPINION

To decide if an argument is convincing, you need to be able to tell the difference between a statement of fact and a writer's opinion. A **fact** is a statement that can be proved through a personal observation, an eyewitness account, a reliable source, a scientific experiment, or a discussion with an expert. An **opinion** can vary from person to person. It cannot be proved because it expresses a belief, feeling, or thought. As you read each selection, list three important facts and three strong opinions.

"Zoos: Myth and Reality"	
Facts:	*Opinions:*
1.	*1.*
2.	*2.*

OCABULARY IN CONTEXT

The words in Column A help the authors develop arguments about zoos. See how many you know by matching each word to the item in Column B that comes closest to its meaning.

Column A	Column B
1. propaganda	**a.** unusual
2. deprivation	**b.** corresponding position
3. futility	**c.** stark
4. sterile	**d.** uselessness
5. languish	**e.** biased information
6. counterpart	**f.** use for selfish reasons
7. exotic	**g.** weaken
8. exploit	**h.** a lack of

Author On|ine

Rob Laidlaw: Wildlife Guardian

Rob Laidlaw
born 1959

Rob Laidlaw has dedicated himself to improving the conditions of animals in captivity. He is co-founder and Executive Director of Zoocheck Canada, an animal protection charity. Laidlaw has inspected close to 1,000 zoos, circuses, and wildlife displays throughout Canada and the United States. He has worked with Canada's government on establishing standards for zoos. Laidlaw also worked on developing a humane stray dog program, and he investigated Canada's role in the international pet reptile trade. Laidlaw shares his knowledge about animals through writing. He has published articles about all kinds of wildlife, from wild horses and polar bears to the red-eared slider and the black rhino.

Michael Hutchins: Animal Caretaker

Michael Hutchins
born 1951

As the executive director of The Wildlife Society, Michael Hutchins has traveled to more than 33 countries. His efforts have involved trapping and tagging mountain goats in the Olympic Mountains, scuba diving with manta rays, and tracking jaguars. He has published many articles, books, and reports on the relationships between animals and their environments and on conservation.

MORE ABOUT THE AUTHOR
For more on Rob Laidlaw and Michael Hutchins, visit the **Literature Center** at **ClassZone.com.**

969

Teach

STANDARDS FOCUS

ELEMENTS OF NONFICTION

● ARGUMENT

Read this passage aloud:

> More schools should adopt dress codes. Students in schools with dress codes worry less about status and can focus better on their studies. They also spend less time and money on clothing.

Ask students: What claim does this writer make? What ideas provide support for the claim? ***Possible answer:*** *Claim: More schools should adopt dress codes. Support: Students worry less about status, focus more on studies, and save time and money.*

CHECK UNDERSTANDING Have students write a counterargument on the topic of dress codes.

READING SKILL

■ DISTINGUISH FACT AND OPINION

Return to the argument about dress codes and ask students to identify the facts and the opinion. Ask students what evidence or sources they might use to verify the facts.

CHECK UNDERSTANDING Have students write fact and opinion statements about wildlife.

RESOURCE MANAGER—Copy Master
Distinguish Fact and Opinion p. 29 (for student use while reading the selections)

VOCABULARY SKILL

▲ VOCABULARY IN CONTEXT

DIAGNOSE WORD KNOWLEDGE To determine preteaching needs, have all students complete **Vocabulary in Context.** ***Possible answers:*** **1.** *e* **2.** *h* **3.** *d* **4.** *c* **5.** *g* **6.** *b* **7.** *a* **8.** *f*

PRETEACH VOCABULARY Use the Vocabulary Study copy master to help students determine the meaning of vocabulary words from context.

1. Read aloud the first two sentences, emphasizing the boldfaced word.
2. Discuss possible meanings for *propaganda,* such as "slanted information."
3. Repeat the procedure for each boldfaced word in the passage.
4. Have students match each word with its definition in Part B.

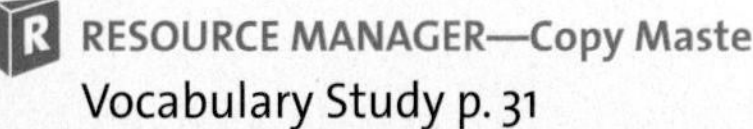
RESOURCE MANAGER—Copy Master
Vocabulary Study p. 31

For general guidelines on differentiating vocabulary instruction and for alternative vocabulary activities for students not needing vocabulary preteaching, see

BEST PRACTICES TOOLKIT
Scaffolding Vocabulary Instruction pp. 43–46

Vocabulary Center at **ClassZone.com**
Additional Vocabulary Activities

Practice and Apply

ANALYZE VISUALS

Students may say that the bear looks sad, thoughtful, or lonely. Accept all reasonable responses.

BACKGROUND

History of Zoos The purpose of most modern zoos is to entertain and educate the public and to study animals, often with a goal of helping to preserve endangered species. The earliest zoos, however, were probably collections of animals in the process of being domesticated. The world's earliest recorded collection of captive animals, created in about 4500 B.C. in present-day Iraq, held only pigeons. In India, elephants were first confined around 2500 B.C.

The Greeks collected and studied animals from as early as the seventh century B.C., and by the fourth century B.C., most Greek city-states probably had zoos. Ancient Roman zoos also kept animals to be used in public spectacles, such as gladiatorial games.

The modern practice of creating and maintaining zoos began in 1752 with the building of the Imperial Menagerie at the Schönbrunn Palace in Vienna, Austria. This menagerie is still open to the public today. By the mid-19th century, zoos existed all over the world. Today there are more than 1,000 public zoos worldwide.

ELEMENTS OF NONFICTION

Ⓐ ARGUMENT

Possible answer: *He claims that zoo animals live miserable lives.*

ANALYZE VISUALS
If you were to assign human qualities to this polar bear, what would they be?

Targeted Passage ①

propaganda
(prŏp′ə-găn′də) *n.* information that supports a certain cause

deprivation
(dĕp′rə-vā′shən) *n.* the condition of not having one's needs met; a lack of

Ⓐ ARGUMENT
What is the author's **claim** about zoos? Remember that a claim is a position or opinion, not a fact.

In recent years, zoos have become the target of intense public scrutiny and criticism. In response, many have tried to repackage themselves as institutions devoted to wildlife conservation, public education, and animal welfare. But most zoos fail to live up to their own **propaganda** and vast numbers of zoo animals continue to endure lives of misery and **deprivation**. Ⓐ

Nearly every zoo, from the smallest amateur operation to the largest professional facilities, claims to be making important contributions to conservation, usually through participation in endangered species captive propagation initiatives and public education programming. The zoo world buzzword[1] of the moment is "conservation."

Yet, with an estimated 10,000 organized zoos worldwide, representing tens of thousands of human workers and billions of dollars in operating budgets, only a tiny percentage allocate the resources necessary to

1. **buzzword:** a word or phrase connected with a specialized field or group that sounds important or technical and is usually used to impress those outside the group.

DIFFERENTIATED INSTRUCTION

FOR ALL STUDENTS

Learning Center Set up a learning center with books, pictures, and newspaper and magazine articles about the care of wildlife in zoos and other facilities around the world. Provide a variety of independent projects, such as studying zoo design, researching the history of zoos, and learning about a career as a zoologist or veterinarian.

FOR LESS–PROFICIENT READERS

In combination with the *Audio Anthology CD,* use one or more Targeted Passages (pp. 970–971, 973, 974, 976) to ensure that students focus on key selection facts, concepts, and skills.

① Targeted Passage [Lines 1–16]

This passage states the author's claim and provides some factual support for his argument.

- In what ways have zoos tried to repackage themselves?
- What is life like for many zoo animals?
- What claims do most zoos make?
- What do many zoos spend most of their money on?

BACK FORWARD STOP REFRESH HOME PRINT

participate in captive propagation initiatives, and fewer still provide any real support for the *in situ*[2] protection of wildlife and their natural habitat.

So far, the record on reintroductions to the wild is dismal. Only 16 species have established self-sustaining populations in the wild as a result of captive breeding efforts, and most of those programs were initiated by government wildlife agencies—not zoos. The contribution of zoos in this regard has been minimal, and often involves supplementing existing wild populations with a small number of captive-born individuals who are ill-prepared for life in the wild. **B**

As the **futility** of captive breeding as a major conservation tool becomes evident to those in the industry, many zoos are now turning to education to justify themselves. Yet, zoos claim that they teach visitors about wildlife conservation and habitat protection, and their contention that they motivate members of the public to become directly involved in wildlife conservation work doesn't stand up to scrutiny. The truth is that scant empirical evidence exists to prove that the primary vehicle for education in most zoos—the animal in the cage—actually teaches anyone anything. In fact, viewing animals in cages may be counterproductive educationally by conveying the wrong kinds of messages to the public. Also, the legions[3] of conservationists that zoos should have produced, if their claims were true, have never materialized. **C**

Humane Treatment

But there is one issue about which there appears to be widespread agreement—at least in principle. So long as wild animals are kept in captivity, they ought to be treated humanely.

Studies have shown that animals can suffer physically, mentally, and emotionally. For this reason, captive environments must be complex enough to compensate for the lack of natural freedom and choice, and they must facilitate expression of natural movement and behavior patterns. This principle has been widely espoused by the modern zoo community in various articles, books, and television documentaries. **D**

Yet despite the best of intentions or claims, most animals in zoos in North America are still consigned to lead miserable lives in undersized,

2. ***in situ*** (ĭn sē'to͞o): a Latin phrase; in zoology, it refers to studying an animal without removing it from its natural habitat.
3. **legions** (lē'jənz): large numbers.

① Targeted Passage

B FACT AND OPINION
Reread lines 17–23. Identify the opinion and the facts. Do the facts support the author's opinion?

futility (fyo͞o-tĭl'ĭ-tē) *n.* uselessness

C ARGUMENT
Reread lines 26–35. What **counterargument** does the author present against the zoos' claims?

D FACT AND OPINION
Reread lines 39–44. What sources does the author cite here? Explain whether these sources sound reliable to you.

READING SKILL

B FACT AND OPINION

Have students record the facts and opinion in the chart from page 969. ***Possible answer:***

"Zoos: Myth and Reality"	
Facts:	*Opinions:*
• Only 16 species have been successfully reintroduced to the wild through captive breeding programs. *• Most programs were run by wildlife agencies, not zoos.* *• Some zoos have put unprepared captive-born animals in the midst of wild populations.*	*"The record on reintroductions to the wild is dismal."*

Most students will say the facts support the author's opinion.

ELEMENTS OF NONFICTION

C ARGUMENT

Possible answer: *His counterargument is that "viewing animals in cages" at zoos does little to educate the public and might even send the wrong message about wildlife conservation and habitat protection. Also, zoos have not produced "legions of conservationists" to prove their claim.*

READING SKILL

D FACT AND OPINION

Possible answer: *He cites "studies" but does not provide specific references. Students may say this lack of specific citations makes the sources sound unreliable.*

FOR ENGLISH LEARNERS

Key Academic Vocabulary Have students use New Word Analysis for these words in "Zoos: Myth and Reality": *professional* (lines 8, 70), *evident* (line 25), *environments* (lines 40, 99).

BEST PRACTICES TOOLKIT—Transparency
New Word Analysis p. E8

Prereading For prereading instruction for English learners, see

BEST PRACTICES TOOLKIT
Scaffolding Reading Instruction pp. 43–46

FOR ADVANCED LEARNERS/PRE–AP

Pre-AP exercises in the bottom channel provide additional challenge for your advanced students. Use them for small groups or individuals.

ADDITIONAL GUIDELINES

For more help with differentiation and tips for classroom management, see

BEST PRACTICES TOOLKIT
Differentiated Instruction pp. 31–38

ZOOS: MYTH AND REALITY 971

READING SKILL

E FACT AND OPINION

Possible answer: *It is a statement of fact, because the size of the exhibits in the past and present can be verified and compared. Students should add the fact to the chart they began on page 969.*

Lines 53–66

DISCUSSION PROMPTS

Use these prompts to help students follow Laidlaw's argument:

Restate What fault does Laidlaw find with many of the new Arctic polar bear exhibits? ***Answer:*** *They are made of artificial materials to look good, but they do not take into account the needs of the animals.*

Compare and Contrast In what ways are the new exhibits like the old ones? In what way are they different? ***Possible answer:*** *Superficially, the exhibits seem to be more roomy and humane. However, many of them are nearly as small and sterile as the old ones.*

Synthesize What would Laidlaw's ideal zoo exhibit for polar bears be like? In general, what kind of exhibits do you think he would recommend for all wildlife in zoos? ***Possible answer:*** *The ideal exhibit for polar bears would resemble their natural Arctic ice and tundra habitat. In general, he would recommend creating zoo exhibits that are as similar as possible to the animals' habitats in the wild.*

BACK FORWARD STOP REFRESH HOME PRINT

impoverished enclosures, both old and new, that fail to meet their biological and behavioral needs. Many in the zoo industry will bristle[4] at this statement and point to numerous improvements in the zoo field. They'll claim they've shifted from menagerie-style[5] entertainment centers where animals were displayed in barred, **sterile,** biologically irrelevant cages, to kinder, gentler, more scientifically-based kinds of institutions.

sterile (stĕr′əl) *adj.* barren; lacking vitality

But many of the "advances" in zoo animal housing and husbandry are superficial and provide little benefit to the animals. For example, the many new, heavily promoted, Arctic "art deco" polar bear exhibits that are springing up in zoos across the continent consistently ignore the natural biology and behavior of these animals. The artificial rockwork and hard floor surfaces typically resemble a Flintstones movie set more than the natural Arctic ice and tundra habitat of polar bears. These exhibits are made for the public and dupe them into believing things are getting better. What they really achieve is more misery and deprivation.

In addition, many new exhibits are hardly larger than the sterile, barred cages of days gone by. And one look at the prison-like, off-display holding and service areas in most zoos, where many animals spend a good portion of their lives, is proof of the hypocrisy of zoo claims that things are better for the animals than they were in the past. E

E FACT AND OPINION Reread the sentence that begins at line 63. Is this statement a fact or an opinion? Tell how you know.

Behind the Invisible Bars

If not all is well behind the invisible bars of North America's more luxurious zoos, a more transparent problem is found in the hundreds of substandard roadside zoos that dot the continent. These amateurish operations fall far below any professional standard and do nothing but cause misery and death to thousands of animals.

My own investigations have revealed animals in visible distress lying unprotected from the full glare of the hot summer sun; primates in barren cages with no opportunity to climb; groups of black bears begging for marshmallows as they sit in stagnant moats of excrement-filled water, scarred and wounded from fighting; nocturnal[6] animals kept without shade or privacy; animals without water; and the list goes on and on.

4. **bristle** (brĭs′əl): to show annoyance or anger.
5. **menagerie** (mə-năj′ə-rē): a collection of live wild animals on display.
6. **nocturnal** (nŏk-tûr′nəl): habitually active at night and asleep during the daytime.

DIFFERENTIATED INSTRUCTION

FOR LESS–PROFICIENT READERS

Comprehension Support Students may need extra support with the challenging vocabulary in this selection. As they read, encourage students to look up words in a dictionary and add new words and their definitions to a Personal Word List.

BEST PRACTICES TOOLKIT
Personal Word List p. E2

FOR ENGLISH LEARNERS

Vocabulary Support [mixed-readiness pairs] Have students work in pairs to define

- *husbandry* (line 53), "good, careful management of resources"
- *superficial* (line 54), "for appearance only; not real or substantial"
- *dupe* (line 60), "deceive; trick"
- *hypocrisy* (line 65), "saying one thing when the opposite is true"
- *dot* (line 69), "appear all over"

Many zoos, including those that meet industry guidelines, also annually produce a predictable surplus in animals that often end up in the hands of private collectors, animal auctions, circuses and novelty acts, substandard zoos, and even "canned hunt" operations where they're shot as trophies.

A look at compliance with the zoo industry's own standards (which in the author's view do not necessarily constitute adequate standards) demonstrates how bad the situation really is. Of the estimated 200 public display facilities in Canada, only 26—slightly more than 10 percent—have been deemed to meet the standards of the Canadian Association of Zoos and Aquariums (CAZA).

In the U.S., out of the 1,800–2,000 licensed exhibitors of wild animals (which includes biomedical research institutions, breeding facilities, small exhibitors, travelling shows, educational programs using live animals, zoos and aquariums), about 175 are accredited by the American Zoo and Aquarium Association (AZA), equivalent to less than 10 percent of all facilities. (F)

Times are changing, and with them, public attitudes. Increasingly, members of the public find the confinement of animals in substandard conditions offensive. Zoos across the continent are feeling the pressure. They have to accept that if wild animals are to be kept in captivity, their needs must be met.

Are there good captive environments where the biological and behavioral needs of animals are being satisfied? The answer is yes. A recent Zoocheck Canada survey of black bear and gray wolf facilities in North America revealed a number of outstanding exhibits where the animals displayed an extensive range of natural movements and behaviors. But they are few and far between.

Can zoos make a useful contribution to conservation and education? Again, the answer is yes. The Durrell Wildlife Conservation Trust (Jersey Zoo) in the U.K., for example, clearly shows that zoos can become leaders in conservation education and wildlife protection. But few actually do.

I can't understand why the more responsible segments of the zoo industry have not come to their senses and acknowledged the obvious—the present state of zoos is untenable. Either zoos can voluntarily adopt humane policies and practices, push for the closure of substandard facilities, and participate in advocating for laws to help wildlife, or they can be dragged kicking and screaming into the new millennium. It's their choice.

(F) ARGUMENT
Explain whether these statistics prove the author's claim.

(2) Targeted Passage

ELEMENTS OF NONFICTION

(F) ARGUMENT

Possible answer: *Yes, the statistics give specific examples of the lack of compliance with standards. These examples show how bad the situation is.*

Lines 94–98
REINFORCE *KEY IDEA:* WILDLIFE

Discuss In what way do public attitudes affect treatment of **wildlife** in zoos? ***Possible answer:*** *People put pressure on zoos to provide natural habitats for wildlife and to improve the conditions in which they live.*

FOR LESS-PROFICIENT READERS

(2) Targeted Passage [Lines 99–115]

In this passage, the author draws conclusions based on his arguments and describes possible solutions to the problem he has described.

- Does the author think there are good zoos?
- What do the good exhibits provide?
- What does the author say the zoo industry should acknowledge?
- What actions does the author say the zoo industry should take?

Reading Skill Follow-Up: Distinguish Fact and Opinion Have students reread lines 99–108. Ask them to identify two opinions in the passage (*there are some good captive environments; zoos can make a useful contribution to conservation*) and decide whether the opinions are supported by facts. Remind students to add their answers to the chart they began on page 969.

FOR ADVANCED LEARNERS/PRE-AP

Analyze Style Point out Laidlaw's use of questions and answers in the paragraphs that begin with lines 99 and 105. Ask students why he might have included these paragraphs. Have them consider these questions:

- What effect is created by the repetition of "the answer is yes"?
- In what way do these paragraphs affect the tone of the article?
- What is the effect on the argument?

ZOOS: MYTH AND REALITY 973

ELEMENTS OF NONFICTION

G ARGUMENT

Possible answer: It will probably argue that zoos have a positive impact on people's lives.

READING SKILL

H FACT AND OPINION

Possible answer: Yes, the information can be verified. Students may add these facts to their charts:*

- *Gorillas in zoos today are typically kept in large, naturalistic settings.*
- *In such settings, gorillas form social groups as they do in the wild.*
- *They also live longer than wild gorillas.*

Extend the Discussion What could you do to verify these facts about gorillas? What would be the best sources of reliable information?

G ARGUMENT
You can often identify the writer's **claim** by reading the title. What do you think this opinion piece will argue?

languish (lăng'gwĭsh) *v.* to lose strength and vitality

counterpart (koun'tər-pärt') *n.* one that has the same functions and traits as another

H FACT AND OPINION
Reread lines 32–42. Can this information be verified? Once you decide whether this statement is a fact or opinion, add it to your chart.

Targeted Passage 3

2G THE BOSTON GLOBE OPINIO

Zoos Connect Us to the Natural World

Michael Hutchin

The scene of Little Joe, the curious young gorilla out of his zoo exhibit wandering through Franklin Park,[1] certainly sold papers last month. But less well covered was the very real success that our nation's best zoos have had in nurturing the animals who live within their walls.

At the turn of the last century, gorillas—these strange, human-like creatures from "darkest Africa"—still flourished in the wild and thoroughly captivated the American public. But once relocated from their jungle habitat, gorillas **languished.** Zoos found it impossible to keep the animals alive for more than a few weeks since little was known about the natural history of gorillas. Even as late as the 1960s and '70s, most zoo gorillas were kept singly or in pairs in small, sterile concrete and tile cages and fed inappropriate foods. But things began to change as information from field and zoo biologists brought more understanding of both the physiological and psychological needs of these remarkable creatures.

Gorillas in today's zoos are typically kept in large, naturalistic exhibits, maintained in appropriate social groupings, fed nutritionally appropriate diets, and provided wit excellent veterinary care. The resul is that zoo gorillas exhibit behavior similar to their wild **counterparts,** reproduce consistently, and live longer on average than they do in nature. H

In fact, recent advances in exhibit design, animal nutrition, genetic management, and veterinary medicine have revolutionized animal welfare and care in our zoos. Today, more thar 90 percent of mammals housed in accredited[2] facilities were born in zoos and not taken from the wild. They are under the charge of animal curators and caretakers wh are trained professionals, with bot academic and practical experience. Furthermore, accredited zoos have

1. **Franklin Park:** a Boston, Massachusetts, park that has a zoo in it.
2. **accredited** (ə-krĕd'ĭt-əd): meeting certain standards that have been set by a respected authority (in this case, the American Zoo and Aquarium Association).

DIFFERENTIATED INSTRUCTION

FOR LESS–PROFICIENT READERS

3 Targeted Passage [Lines 20–48]

This passage gives supporting details for the author's argument, focusing primarily on changes in the treatment of gorillas.

- What kind of treatment did zoo gorillas receive in the 1960s and 1970s?
- What led to changes in this treatment?
- How are zoo gorillas treated today?
- What recent advances have changed the treatment of animals in zoos?

FOR ENGLISH LEARNERS

Vocabulary: Word Associations [paired option]
Have pairs of students use context clues to figure out the meanings of these word combinations:

- *appropriate social groupings* (lines 34–35), "the way animals naturally live together"
- *nutritionally appropriate* (lines 35–36), "best food for that particular animal"
- *revolutionized animal welfare* (line 47), "made major changes in the care of animals"

ANALYZE VISUALS
What **conclusions** can you draw about the impact this encounter might have on the girl?

become "learning organizations" that constantly strive to improve the lives and health of the animals in their care. I

So why should we have gorillas or any other wild animals in zoos today? Before speculating about the role of these institutions in contemporary society, I must first draw a distinction between accredited zoos and other kinds of facilities that keep wild animals for public display. All of my statements are focused exclusively on the 213 facilities accredited by the American Zoo and Aquarium Association. AZA members undergo a detailed peer-review[3] process, which is more comprehensive than existing local, state, or federal regulations.

At a time when children learn more about the world around them from television and computers than from personal experience, modern zoos—and aquariums, for that matter—offer fun, safe opportunities to view living wild animals up close and personal. In 2002, over 140 million people visited AZA zoos and aquariums, more than attended all professional baseball, football, basketball, and ice hockey games combined. Modern zoological parks provide us a wonderful opportunity to build awareness and appreciation of wildlife in an increasingly urbanized populace—a group that is becoming progressively disconnected from the natural world. J

Only a small percentage of our nation's citizens can afford to travel to **exotic** locations to view wild tigers, elephants, or giant pandas

I ARGUMENT
What criticisms is the author addressing in this paragraph? Paraphrase his **counterargument.**

J ARGUMENT
Reread lines 77–96. Which sentence provides support for the author's **claim?** Which is a restatement of his claim?

exotic (ĭg-zŏt′ĭk) *adj.* foreign; unusual; exciting

3. **peer-review:** evaluation by equals (in this case, other zoo officials).

ANALYZE VISUALS

Students may say that the encounter will be a happy memory for the girl; it may encourage her to learn more about seals; and it may cause her to visit the zoo again and to support its programs and activities.

ELEMENTS OF NONFICTION

I ARGUMENT

Possible answer: *The author is addressing the criticism that zoos keep animals in exhibits unlike their natural habitats and that they are not well cared for. His counterargument is that 90 percent of mammals in accredited facilities were born in captivity. Also, zoos are run by professionals who have studied the animals in their care and continue to learn ways to improve the animals' lives.*

ELEMENTS OF NONFICTION

J ARGUMENT

Possible answer: *The sentence beginning with "In 2002," supports the author's claim; the sentence beginning with "Modern zoological parks" restates the author's claim.*

Lines 77–84

REINFORCE *KEY IDEA:* WILDLIFE

Discuss In what way does the author think children benefit from viewing **wildlife** in zoos?

Possible answer: *He says that children—who get much of their information from television and computers—are able to see a living wild animal firsthand at a zoo.*

FOR ENGLISH LEARNERS

Vocabulary: Cognates [shared-language groups] Have groups scan the story for cognates and report their findings to the class. Spanish cognates on pages 974–975 include

- *creatures/criaturas* (line 11)
- *maintained/mantenido* (line 34)
- *veterinary/veterinario* (line 46)
- *exclusively/exclusivamente* (line 70)
- *facilities/facilidades* (line 71)
- *percentage/porcentaje* (line 97)

FOR ADVANCED LEARNERS/PRE–AP

Analyze Argument Have students reread lines 61–76. Point out that Hutchins has chosen to focus on only a small number of accredited facilities. Remind students that Laidlaw, in his article, makes the point that unaccredited facilities outnumber these nine to one. He takes these numbers into account when evaluating the quality of zoos and other facilities. Lead a discussion about how the conclusions each author draws depend on the parameters he establishes for his argument.

READING SKILL

K FACT AND OPINION

Possible answer: *To verify this information, you would have to experience a zoo or survey people who have.*

READING SKILL

L FACT AND OPINION

Have students record their answers in their charts from page 969. ***Possible answer:***

"Zoos Connect Us . . ."	
Facts:	*Opinions:*
• Last year, 1,400 field conservation, educational, and scientific projects were sponsored in over 80 countries. *• Projects included butterflies in Ohio, wildlife in Africa, and marine mammals and sea turtles.*	*"The best zoos include conservation, education, and science among their core missions."*

ELEMENTS OF NONFICTION

M ARGUMENT

Possible answer: *He puts forth the opposing viewpoint that zoos exploit animals for financial gain. As a counterargument, he cites his own experiences with dedicated zoo professionals.*

SELECTION WRAP-UP

REFLECT Discuss the ways in which opinion pieces can influence readers—by educating them about an issue, by changing their minds about an issue, or by motivating them to take action. Have students explain how they were influenced by reading the selections.

CRITIQUE Discuss the strikingly different opening of each article. Which opening do students find more effective?

READING FLUENCY

Distribute the copy masters and have students practice fluency.

RESOURCE MANAGER—Copy Master
Reading Fluency pp. 37–38

---

or to dive with sharks or moray eels. Zoos provide exhilarating experiences that can't be replicated on two-dimensional television or computer screens. Seeing, smelling, and in some cases even touching real, live animals is a powerful experience. K

The best zoos include conservation, education, and science among their core missions,[4] and the animals in their collections can be viewed as ambassadors for their counterparts in the wild. Many species are endangered or threatened and would have little chance of survival without human intervention. Increasingly, zoos are playing an important role in those efforts. Last year alone, AZA member institutions supported 1,400 field conservation[5] and associated educational and scientific projects in over 80 countries worldwide. These ranged from restoring habitat for endangered Karner blue butterflies[6] in Ohio to attempting to curb the illegal, commercial harvest of wildlife for meat in Africa to rehabilitating injured marine mammals and sea turtles and returning them to the sea. L

Some critics have characterized zoos and aquariums as "**exploiting**" animals for personal financial gain, but that's not true of the professionals I know. As a curatorial intern at New York's Bronx Zoo/Wildlife Conservation Society in the late 1980s, I went on rounds with the staff veterinarians as they cared for sick and injured animals. They worked long hours for comparatively little pay, and their dedication was inspiring. I also witnessed animal keepers weeping over the loss of their favorite animals and spending their own money to attend training programs to improve their knowledge and skills. M

In my opinion, a society that values wildlife and nature should support our best zoos and aquariums. Habitat conservation is the key to saving endangered species, and professionally managed zoos and aquariums and their expert, dedicated staffs play a vital role by supporting on-the-ground conservation efforts and by encouraging people to care for and learn about wildlife and nature.

Zoos and aquariums are reinventing themselves, but while many are in the process of rebuilding their aging infrastructures, still others retain vestiges of the past or have been hit hard by recent state or local budget cuts. Good zoos and aquariums are invaluable community assets, and they deserve our attention and enthusiastic support.

K FACT AND OPINION
Reread lines 102–108. How would you verify this information?

L FACT AND OPINION
Find one statement of fact and one opinion in this paragraph.

exploit (ĕk'sploit') *v.* to use for selfish purposes

M ARGUMENT
What opposing viewpoint does the author present? What is his **counterargument?**

Targeted Passage ④

4. **core missions:** central goals and beliefs.
5. **field conservation:** conservation of wild organisms in their natural habitats (not in zoos).
6. **Karner blue butterflies:** endangered butterflies of the northern U.S. and Canada.

DIFFERENTIATED INSTRUCTION

FOR LESS-PROFICIENT READERS

④ Targeted Passage [Lines 134–174]

This passage begins with a description of the author's personal experience and ends with a summary of his argument.

- What did the author experience when he was an intern at the Bronx Zoo? In what way did that experience shape his opinions?
- According to the author, what is the best way to save endangered species?
- What kinds of problems do some zoos and aquariums still have?

FOR ENGLISH LEARNERS

Vocabulary: Suffixes Point out words on this page with the suffix *-tion* (*conservation, education, collection[s], intervention,* and *institution[s]*). Help students identify the base words. Use Common Suffixes to help them identify the meanings. Ask students to think of other words with the suffix *-tion* and explore their meanings.

BEST PRACTICES TOOLKIT—Transparency
Common Suffixes p. E15

After Reading

Comprehension

1. **Recall** According to "Zoos: Myth and Reality," what often happens to surplus animals from zoos?
2. **Recall** According to "Zoos Connect Us to the Natural World," how do zoos benefit people?
3. **Clarify** What kind of action does each author call for?

Critical Analysis

4. **Analyze Arguments** For each selection, identify the author's **claim.** Note the claim in a graphic organizer like the one shown. Then list three reasons or pieces of evidence the author uses to support his claim.

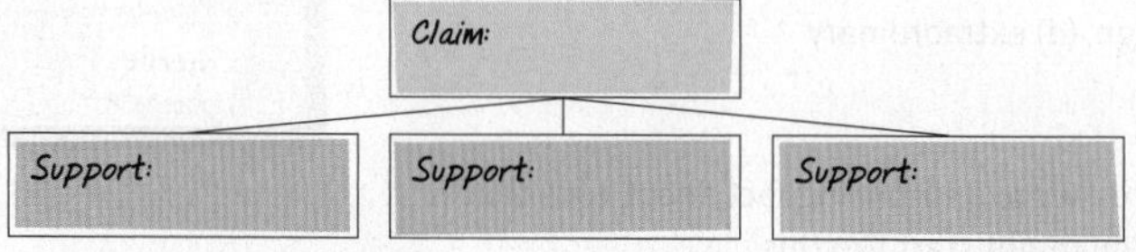

5. **Compare Scope** Tell whether the article or the opinion piece has the broadest scope, meaning the greatest range of coverage. Consider especially the number of zoos each selection refers to. Do you think the broader scope makes the selection more or less convincing? Explain.
6. **Evaluate Fact and Opinion** Review the lists you made of facts and opinions from the two selections. In your view, what is the single most convincing fact and the single most convincing opinion? Explain why you think so.

Extension and Challenge

7. **Speaking and Listening** Form two teams, one representing Rob Laidlaw and one representing Michael Hutchins. Then, with your team, answer the question "Should wildlife stay wild?" from the perspective of your author. Debate the question with the other team, using support from the two selections.
8. **Inquiry and Research** Learn more about a zoo that you've visited or heard about. Is it accredited? What kind of background do the employees have? How are they trained? How are the animals housed and cared for? Research to find answers, and discuss your findings with the class. Share your opinions on whether the zoo is keeping **wildlife** safe.

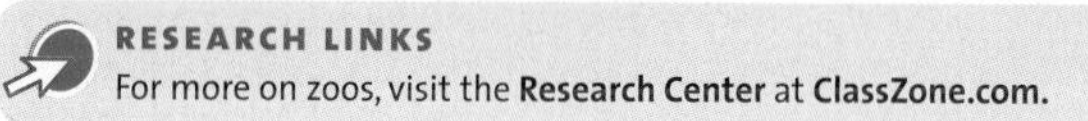
RESEARCH LINKS
For more on zoos, visit the **Research Center** at **ClassZone.com.**

Practice and Apply

After Reading

For additional support of postreading questions, use these copy masters:

RESOURCE MANAGER—Copy Masters
Reading Check p. 34 (to check understanding of the selections)
Argument p. 27 (for practice of elements of nonfiction standards focus)
Question Support p. 35 (After Reading questions adapted for English learners and less-proficient readers)

Additional selection questions are provided for teachers on page 21.

ANSWERS

Comprehension

1. *Surplus animals often end up with private collectors, animal auctions, circuses, substandard zoos, and are even used in hunts.*
2. *Zoos educate people about animals and give people the experience of personal contact.*
3. *Laidlaw calls for the accredited, responsible zoos to encourage humane treatment of wildlife. Hutchins calls for more support of zoos.*

Critical Analysis

Possible answers:

4. ● **STANDARDS FOCUS Argument** ***Laidlaw: Claim****—Most zoo animals live miserable lives.* ***Support****—Animals can suffer physically, mentally and emotionally. Zoo habitats don't meet animals' biological and behavioral needs. Surplus zoo animals are sold into inhumane conditions.* ***Hutchins: Claim****—Zoos provide a way for people to connect to nature.* ***Support****—Zoos provide educational opportunities and allow people to interact with animals. More people visit zoos than sporting events. Most people can't afford to interact with wildlife in exotic locations; zoos make interaction possible. In one year, through the support of zoos, people were able to implement 1,400 field conservation and educational projects in 80 countries worldwide.*
5. *Laidlaw's article discusses all zoos; Hutchins's opinion piece discusses only accredited zoos. Laidlaw's article seems more convincing because he's looking at a bigger picture.*
6. ■ **STANDARDS FOCUS Distinguish Fact and Opinion** *Suggest that students compare their lists with a partner to identify the most convincing facts and opinions and discuss their reasons for their choices.*

Extension and Challenge

7. *As they are preparing for the debate, encourage students to anticipate counterarguments and prepare an effective response.*
8. *Suggest that students use the Internet to begin their research. Have them reread the articles to help them develop criteria about how zoos can keep wildlife safe.*

ANSWERS

Vocabulary in Context

VOCABULARY PRACTICE

1. *(c) enjoy*
2. *(a) exploit*
3. *(a) hope*
4. *(c) lush*
5. *(d) wealth*
6. *(b) truth*
7. *(a) boss*
8. *(a) ordinary*

RESOURCE MANAGER—Copy Master
Vocabulary Practice p. 32

VOCABULARY IN WRITING

Have students review the facts they listed as they read the articles and identify two or three facts that they found most surprising.

VOCABULARY STRATEGY: THE GREEK ROOT *exo* (also an EL language objective)

As students look up the words in the dictionary, encourage them to look up each base word to learn about its origin. Tell students that they can also use context clues to choose the right word.

Answers:

1. *exosphere*
2. *exocarp*
3. *exodus*
4. *exoskeleton*

RESOURCE MANAGER—Copy Master
Vocabulary Strategy p. 33

Vocabulary Center at **ClassZone.com**
Additional Vocabulary Activities

Vocabulary in Context

VOCABULARY PRACTICE

For each item, choose the word that differs most in meaning from the other words.

1. (a) suffer, (b) languish, (c) enjoy, (d) endure
2. (a) exploit, (b) aid, (c) help, (d) befriend
3. (a) hope, (b) uselessness, (c) futility, (d) meaninglessness
4. (a) unadorned, (b) desolate, (c) lush, (d) sterile
5. (a) suffering, (b) deprivation, (c) lack, (d) wealth
6. (a) persuasion, (b) truth, (c) propaganda, (d) bias
7. (a) boss, (b) equal, (c) peer, (d) counterpart
8. (a) ordinary, (b) exotic, (c) foreign, (d) extraordinary

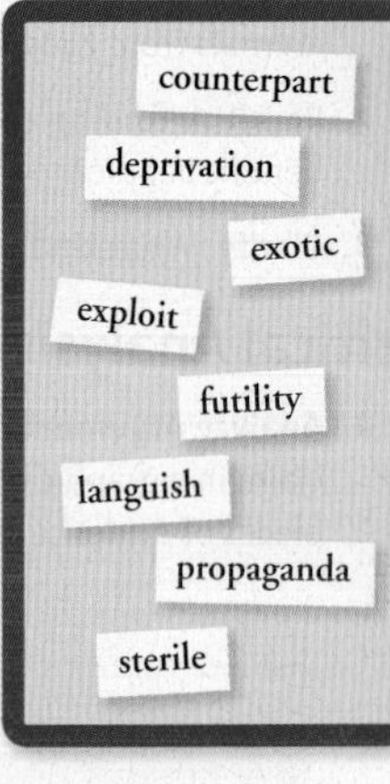

counterpart
deprivation
exotic
exploit
futility
languish
propaganda
sterile

VOCABULARY IN WRITING

Using at least two vocabulary words, write a surprising fact about zoos that you learned from the selections. You might start like this.

> **EXAMPLE SENTENCE**
> *I learned that the majority of zoo animals __languish__ in uncomfortable, inappropriate environments.*

VOCABULARY STRATEGY: THE GREEK ROOT *exo*

The vocabulary word *exotic* contains the Greek root *exo*, which means "outside" or "external." You can use your understanding of this root along with context clues to help you to figure out the meaning of other words formed from *exo*.

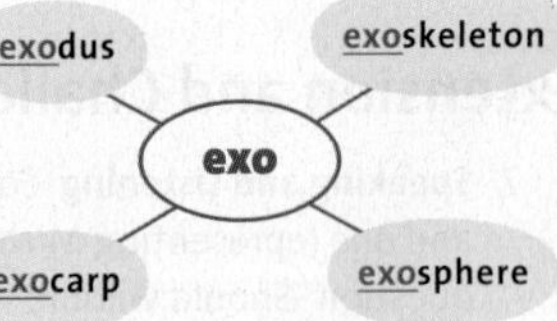

PRACTICE Use a dictionary to look up each word that appears in the web. Then decide which word best completes each sentence. Be ready to explain how the meaning of the root is reflected in each word.

1. The earth's _____ protects it from much of the sun's ultraviolet radiation.
2. A peach's fuzzy _____ holds in the juicy fruit.
3. There was a mass _____ of fans from the stadium after the concert.
4. A beetle's _____ is like armor, protecting it from predators and weather.

VOCABULARY PRACTICE
For more practice, go to the **Vocabulary Center** at **ClassZone.com.**

DIFFERENTIATED INSTRUCTION

FOR ENGLISH LEARNERS

Vocabulary Practice [mixed-readiness pairs] Pair students with fluent speakers to help choose the word in each set that differs most from the meaning of the other three words. Encourage students who are having trouble to review the definitions and context of the vocabulary words in the selections.

FOR ADVANCED LEARNERS/PRE-AP

Vocabulary Strategy [paired option] Have students consult a dictionary to find as many words as possible with the root *exo*. Challenge them to create a crossword puzzle with those words. Then have them exchange puzzles with a partner and solve them. Allow pairs to use a dictionary as needed to help them solve the puzzles.

978 UNIT 9: ARGUMENT AND PERSUASION

Reading-Writing Connection

Demonstrate your understanding of the arguments in "Zoos: Myth and Reality" and "Zoos Connect Us to the Natural World" by responding to these prompts. Then complete the **Grammar and Writing** exercise.

WRITING PROMPTS	SELF-CHECK
A. Short Response: Letter to the Editor What argument would you make about **wildlife** in captivity? Write a **one-paragraph letter to the editor,** supporting or criticizing a zoo, circus, or other place that houses wild animals.	***A convincing letter to the editor will . . .*** • make your position clear • include a call to action
B. Extended Response: Compare Perspectives Look back at the authors' biographies on page 969. How do you think each author's experience has influenced his opinion of zoos? Write **two or three paragraphs** comparing the authors' perspectives, or the ideas and values that influence their viewpoints.	***A successful comparison will . . .*** • clearly state each author's opinion • connect each author's experience to his opinion

GRAMMAR AND WRITING

CAPITALIZE CORRECTLY In your writing, remember to **capitalize** all the important words in the names of organizations, institutions, stores, and companies. Do not capitalize words such as *hospital, school, company, church,* and *college* when they are not used as parts of the official names.

Original: The university of texas is one of the many Universities offering zoology classes.

Revised: The University of Texas is one of the many universities offering zoology classes.

PRACTICE Correct the capitalization errors in the following sentences.

1. I believe the lincoln park zoo is teaching people to value wildlife.
2. The Zoo's habitats are safer for animals than the danger of the wild.
3. The durrell wildlife conservation trust actually protects wildlife.
4. Some circuses might not have high standards, but ringling brothers and barnum and bailey circus is trying to improve.

For more help with capitalization, see page R51 in the ***Grammar Handbook.***

DIFFERENTIATED INSTRUCTION

FOR LESS–PROFICIENT WRITERS

For Prompt A:
Suggest that students begin their letters with a position statement, such as

- I believe that zoos are __________ because __________.
- Animal captivity is __________ because __________.

Encourage students to do research online to find facts that will support their opinions on animal captivity.

For Prompt B:
Students may organize their paragraphs in this way:

- **First paragraph:** State the first author's opinion, connecting the opinion to the author's experience.
- **Second paragraph:** State the second author's opinion, connecting the opinion to the author's experience.
- **Third paragraph:** Compare the authors' perspectives and draw a conclusion.

Reading-Writing Connection

WRITING PROMPTS

- For **Prompt A,** have students write a position statement and list two or three examples they can use to support their position. Have them list several actions from which they can choose a call to action.
- For **Prompt B,** have students use a T Chart to list the information about each author. Have them circle the key factors that they think have influenced each author's opinions.

BEST PRACTICES TOOLKIT—Transparency
T Chart p. A25

For writing support, see
Writing Center at **ClassZone.com**

GRAMMAR AND WRITING

Point out that learning to distinguish between proper and common nouns will help students capitalize correctly.

Answers:

1. *I believe the Lincoln Park Zoo is teaching people to value wildlife.*
2. *The zoo's habitats are safer for animals than the danger of the wild.*
3. *The Durrell Wildlife Conservation Trust actually protects wildlife.*
4. *Some circuses might not have high standards, but Ringling Brothers and Barnum and Bailey Circus is trying to improve.*

RESOURCE MANAGER—Copy Master
Capitalize Correctly p. 36

Assess and Reteach

Assess

RESOURCE MANAGER—Copy Masters
Selection Tests A, B/C pp. 39–40, 41–42

Test Generator CD

Reteach

STANDARDS LESSON FILE
Reading Lesson 5: Distinguishing Fact from Opinion
Informational Texts Lesson 14: Elements of an Argument
Vocabulary Lesson 9: Greek Roots and Combining Forms

Focus and Motivate

OBJECTIVES

Media Literacy

- explore the key idea of using marketing techniques to build **anticipation**
- analyze and evaluate an ad campaign, including its use of persuasive techniques
- analyze the relationship between advertising and media
- analyze the effects of various techniques that target different audiences
- create an ad campaign

SUMMARY

In the teaser trailer for *Star Wars: Episode III,* an ominous image of Darth Vader rising leads into a montage of explosive, emotional scenes. The full-length trailer gives more details about the story—the struggles of Anakin Skywalker, his attraction to the dark side, the distrust of people around him, and his ultimate transformation. The ad campaign also includes two movie posters—one featuring a striking image of Darth Vader and the other showing a collage of grim-faced characters around two shadowy figures who are fighting.

How do ads create BUZZ?

Discuss the question. Have students name favorite movies and recall the previews and ads created to get people excited about them. Then ask students to read the ***KEY IDEA*** paragraph. Identify features of specific ads and previews that build people's **anticipation.**

BACKGROUND

The *Star Wars* series, based on stories by George Lucas, began in 1977 with what is now known as *Star Wars: Episode IV—A New Hope.* The winner of seven Academy Awards and one of the most profitable movies of all time, it features a cast of characters anchored firmly in popular culture, including Luke Skywalker and Darth Vader. The series now includes six films: two sequels to the original film, *Episode V—The Empire Strikes Back* (1980) and *Episode VI—Return of the Jedi* (1983); and three prequels: *Episode I—The Phantom Menace* (1999), *Episode II—Attack of the Clones* (2002), and *Episode III—Revenge of the Sith* (2005).

Media Study

Movie Ad Campaign

Movie Advertisements on ***MediaSmart*** DVD

How do ads create BUZZ?

KEY IDEA Think about the last movie you just couldn't wait to see. How did you find out about it? Did you watch a preview that made it look exciting? Maybe you saw ads while surfing the Internet or passed billboards on the way to school. In this lesson, you'll explore how advertisers use these marketing techniques to build a sense of **anticipation** for an upcoming movie release.

Background

Coming Soon . . . Movie studios know that sometimes a commercial is not enough to persuade their target audience to see an upcoming film. They use a series of different types of ads to create excitement, so that not only will you run out to see the movie; you'll also tell your friends about it. In effect, you become part of the studio's ad campaign. This word of mouth is powerful, as people are more likely to trust the opinion of someone they know over the razzle-dazzle of a commercial. A movie is said to have **buzz** around it when it gets people excited enough to spread the word.

You'll look at advertisements for the movie *Star Wars: Episode III—Revenge of the Sith* to see how advertisers try to create buzz.

Media Study Resources

 **RESOURCE MANAGER UNIT 9**

Plan and Teach pp. 43–46

Media Analysis

Summary pp. 47†*, 48‡*

Viewing Guide p. 49

Close Viewing p. 50

Media Activity p. 51

Produce Your Own Media p. 52

STANDARDS LESSON FILE

Media Lesson 14: Analyzing Production Techniques in Advertising

Media Lesson 15: Analyzing Persuasive Techniques in Advertising

Media Lesson 16: Evaluating Ads

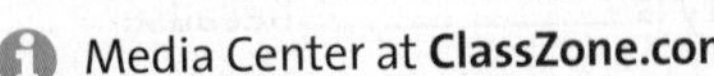
Media Center at **ClassZone.com**

MEDIA VIEWING

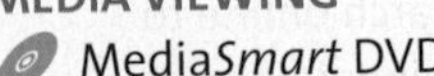
Media*Smart* DVD

* Resources for Differentiation † Also in Spanish ‡ In Haitian Creole and Vietnamese

Media Literacy: Persuasion in Ads

An **ad campaign** is a series of advertisements for a single product or brand. The ads appear over time and in several different forms. Movie studios use carefully chosen visual and sound techniques in each ad to persuade their target audience. The image you see in a **print ad** should evoke the movie's mood as much as the music that plays in a **trailer.** Here are some of the types of advertisements that studios use.

FEATURES OF AN AD CAMPAIGN

Trailers are movie ads that show selected scenes from a film. Trailers usually appear a few months before the movie opens. They persuade viewers to see the movie by showing the most exciting, funny, or touching moments from the film.

Teaser Trailers are shorter, flashier trailers made to build anticipation. Teasers often come out long before the movie is released. They're short because they're designed to make you curious.

Print Ads include billboards, posters, magazine, and newspaper ads. Print ads play a large role in many movie ad campaigns. They often persuade with a **tagline,** or memorable phrase that sums up the movie, and a single image meant to evoke a feeling about the film.

Promotional Web Site is a Web site created to advertise the movie. Movie Web sites often include trailers, cast and crew information, games, and information about the making of the film. They're often designed to draw the audience's interest with an interactive experience.

STRATEGIES FOR ANALYZING MOVIE ADS

Whether you're looking at a print ad, a trailer, or a promotional Web site, think about how the ad creates anticipation and excitement about the film.

- Determine the target audience. Think about who is most likely to see the movie and consider how the ad is directed at that group.
- Consider the visual and sound techniques used. Think about why each image or sound was chosen and the effect that each has on the viewer.
- Notice how the different ads work together to create an overall feeling about the film. The early ads are usually designed to spark curiosity. The later ads then build on that curiosity, providing more information about the film.

MEDIA STUDY: TEACHING OPTIONS

Teaching Option 1: The Basics (1–2 Days)

1. Begin the Media Study using the material provided on pages 980–981.
2. Show the Introduction on Media*Smart.* Then show the First Viewing. As they watch, have students use the Viewing Guide on page 982, along with the corresponding copy master on page 49 of the Resource Manager. Discuss their responses.
3. Return to the pupil's edition for the extension activities on page 983.

Teaching Option 2: In-Depth Study (2–3 Days)

1. Begin the Media Study using pages 980–981.
2. Show the Introduction and First Viewing from Media*Smart.* Continue on Media*Smart* with the Media Lessons, using the teacher notes in the Resources section.
3. Show the Guided Analysis presentation. Have students record their observations on the Student Viewing Guide available in the Resources section from Media*Smart.*
4. Return to the pupil's edition, page 983.

Teach

MEDIA LITERACY

Encourage students to extend the discussion they began on page 980, focusing on ad campaigns they have seen for various movies. Ask: What specific visual and sound techniques were used to stimulate interest in popular adventure movies, comedies, and tearjerkers? Were these ads effective? Why or why not? Then discuss the chart on page 981.

- **Trailers** Explain that trailers are often shown before the start of a feature film in a theater. Ask students to examine the still from a movie trailer shown on page 981. What do the actors' poses, the expressions on their faces, and the props say about the film? What kinds of sounds might you expect to hear in the background? Then ask students to pick one of their favorite movies and jot down some scenes and sounds they would include in a trailer for the film.
- **Teaser Trailers** Have students again focus on a favorite movie. If they were planning a teaser trailer, what moments of the film would they highlight? What sounds would they include? What questions would they try to raise in the minds of viewers? Encourage students to share and compare ideas for teaser trailers for familiar films.
- **Print Ads** Draw students' attention to the movie poster on page 981. What feelings is it meant to evoke? *(fear, dread, excitement)* What details in the poster create these feelings? *(threatening image of Darth Vader with an outstretched, grasping hand; red flames and darkness)* What is the **tagline?** What does it tell potential viewers? *("Rise Lord Vader" tells viewers that the imposing figure in the poster, Lord Vader, will rise to power in the film.)*
- **Promotional Web Site** Ask students if they have ever gone to a movie Web site. Encourage them to discuss what kinds of information they found and whether this information increased their interest in the film. Ask students to think about the information they might put on a Web site advertising their favorite film. Then encourage them to go online and research some Web sites for current movies.

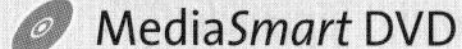 Media*Smart* DVD

Practice and Apply

VIEWING GUIDE

1. As students prepare to examine the movie **trailers** and posters for *Star Wars: Episode III—Revenge of the Sith,* explain to them that they will be asked to identify and analyze persuasive techniques used by the movie studio to attract viewers. Encourage students to observe these elements:
   - the effect of visual and sound techniques
   - the use of words and images in the **posters**
   - the overall effect of the **ad campaign**—the **trailers** and posters combined
2. Ask students to view the trailers and the posters more than once in order to analyze them carefully. After the first viewing, they should describe their general impressions. During subsequent viewings, they should describe specific elements such as sound, visuals, and mood.

RESOURCE MANAGER—Copy Masters
Viewing Guide p. 49
Close Viewing p. 50
Media Activity p. 51

Media*Smart* DVD

ANSWERS

***FIRST VIEWING:* Comprehension**

1. *The teaser provides very little information about the plot of the movie. Viewers learn only that it will have a lot of action and that Darth Vader will play a central role.*
2. *According to the trailer, the main characters are Anakin Skywalker (the young man with blond hair); his mentor, the Chancellor (the old man); and Obi Wan Kenobi (the red-haired man with the beard).*

***CLOSE VIEWING:* Media Literacy**

Possible answers:

3. *The dramatic music adds to the excitement of the visuals.*
4. *"Rise Lord Vader" poster: The image of Darth Vader with flames behind him gives the impression that the movie will be exciting, fantastic, and dark. Vader is clearly a villain, and the world he inhabits is fiery and dangerous. "Episode III" poster: It's clear that the movie is a space fantasy that will include lots of action and fighting. The grim determination on each of the characters' faces suggests that the stakes will be high and that the movie will be more serious than funny. The collage of images suggests that the story will be epic in scope.*
5. *The teaser is geared toward building general excitement about the film without giving much information about the plot. It makes viewers want to know more about the film. The full-length trailer gives the audience an idea of what the story is about. We learn that it revolves around Anakin Skywalker and his turn to the dark side of the Force. It makes viewers want to see the film and know more about the characters and the story.*
6. *Viewers would likely say that the movie is a space epic with lots of action and adventure. It's about good versus evil and one man's temptation to turn to the dark side. The movie will be exciting, action-packed, and enhanced with many special effects.*

***MediaSmart* DVD**
- **Selection 1:** *Star Wars: Episode III—Revenge of the Sith* teaser trailer
- **Selection 2:** movie trailer
- **Selection 3:** movie posters

Viewing Guide for
Movie Ad Campaign

View the DVD to examine the ad campaign used for the movie *Star Wars: Episode III—Revenge of the Sith.* You'll examine a **teaser traile** a full-length **trailer,** and the visuals and words of **print ads.** As you look at each selection, consider how it attempts to persuade you to see and talk about the film. Jot down the impressions you get of th movie from each selection. Then think about the overall effect of th ad campaign. Use these questions to help you analyze it.

NOW VIEW

***FIRST VIEWING:* Comprehension**

1. **Clarify** What do you learn about the plot of the movie from the **teaser?**
2. **Identify** According to the full-length **trailer,** who are the main characters in *Star Wars: Episode III?*

***CLOSE VIEWING:* Media Literacy**

3. **Analyze Music** What effect does the music in the **teaser** have on the viewer?
4. **Analyze Images** What impressions do you get about *Star Wars: Episode III* from the images on the **posters?**
5. **Compare Trailers** Compare and contrast the **teaser** and the full-length **trailer.** How does your response to each differ?
6. **Interpret the Effect** Think about the effect the **ad campaign** may have had on potential moviegoers when the movie was released. Based on the materials you viewed, how do you think these people would have described the movie to their friends?

982

Write or Discuss

Evaluate the Ad Campaign You've explored how advertisers attempt to create buzz. Think about the ads you examined for *Star Wars: Episode III—Revenge of the Sith.* What parts of the ad campaign did you find effective? Write an opinion statement describing whether or not you think the ad campaign would create buzz among you and your friends today. Think about

- whether the **teaser trailer** sparks your curiosity
- the details you learn about the movie from the full-length **trailer**
- your overall impression of the movie from all of the selections you viewed

Produce Your Own Media

Create Your Own Ad Campaign Imagine your favorite short story or novel has just been made into a movie. You've been asked to plan an **ad campaign** that will get people buzzing about it. Working with one or two other students, draw **storyboards** for a **teaser trailer** and a full-length **trailer,** and draw a **poster** for the film.

HERE'S HOW Use these tips as you create your ad campaign:

- Remember that a storyboard is made up of drawings and brief descriptions of what happens in each shot.
- Think about the most exciting aspects of the story you choose. What will get people talking about the movie?
- For your poster, use an image that represents the overall feeling you want people to get from the film.
- Consider what music you want to play during your teaser trailer.

MEDIA TOOLS

For help with creating an ad campaign, visit the **Media Center** at **ClassZone.com.**

STUDENT MODEL

Tech Tip

If a camera is available, take photos of classmates dressed as characters and use a computer graphics program to create your poster.

Assess and Reteach

Write or Discuss

Evaluate the Ad Campaign Have students view the trailers and the posters again before they begin their evaluations. Each student should then describe his or her overall impression of the movie, supported by concrete details from the components of the ad campaign. For example, students might say the teaser trailer sparks their curiosity with strong music, glimpses of fighting, looks of anguish on the faces of characters, and the ominous rising of Darth Vader. Students should also refer to details provided by the full-length trailer—such as scenes that reveal the movie will revolve around the struggles of Anakin Skywalker, his path toward the dark side, and the reactions of people around him.

Produce Your Own Media

Rubric A strong ad campaign should include

- storyboards with a drawing and a description of each shot in the trailers
- trailers that highlight the most exciting or interesting parts of the movie
- a poster that represents the overall feeling of the film
- suggestions for music that will enhance the trailers

RESOURCE MANAGER—Copy Master
Produce Your Own Media p. 52

Media*Smart* DVD

MEDIA STUDY WRAP-UP

Summarize Ask students to summarize the techniques used by advertisers to attract people to movies. Encourage them to refer to specific examples from the trailers and the posters for *Star Wars: Episode III.* As needed, guide them to discuss sound and visual techniques in the trailers, such as background music, sound effects, and excerpts from key movie scenes. Students should also refer to words and images in the posters.

RETEACH

STANDARDS LESSON FILE

Media Lesson 14: Analyzing Production Techniques in Advertising
Media Lesson 15: Analyzing Persuasive Techniques in Advertising
Media Lesson 16: Evaluating Ads

Focus and Motivate

OBJECTIVES

Elements of Nonfiction
- explore the key idea of **games**
- identify and analyze persuasive techniques
- identify and analyze tone
- read a position statement and an opinion piece

Reading
- set a purpose for reading

Vocabulary
- build vocabulary for reading and writing
- use knowledge of the Latin word *gressus* to help determine word meaning *(also an EL language objective)*

Grammar and Writing
- write a compare-contrast essay

SUMMARY

In its position statement, the National Association for Sport and Physical Education gives reasons why dodgeball is not appropriate for K–12 gym classes. In contrast, Rick Reilly argues in his opinion piece that dodgeball teaches students valuable life skills and provides a safe outlet for aggression.

Are all GAMES *worth playing?*

To lead into the ***KEY IDEA***, ask students to think about the types of **games** they play. These might include sports, board games, or video games. Then have them complete the ***LIST IT*** activity. Afterwards, students can form new groups to discuss the reasons they assigned games to the lists as they did.

Comparing Persuasive Techniques

Position on Dodgeball in Physical Education

Position Statement by the National Association for Sport and Physical Education

The Weak Shall Inherit the Gym

Opinion Piece by Rick Reilly

Are all GAMES *worth playing?*

KEY IDEA Games are supposed to be fun, right? But have you ever watched a customer at a carnival game spend 20 or 30 dollars trying to win a cheap stuffed animal? Seeing this might make you question not only how fun it is, but also whether or not all **games** are worth playing. You're about to read two very different opinions on whether the game of dodgeball is fun or torture for those who play it.

LIST IT Work with a group to make two lists. On the first, list five or more games you think are worth playing. On the second, list five or more games you think are not worth the time, money, or risk. Compare your lists with others'. Were there any games that appeared on both the good and not-so-good lists?

984

Selection Resources

RESOURCE MANAGER UNIT 9

Plan and Teach pp. 53–60

Elements of Nonfiction
Summary pp. 61†*, 62‡*
Question Support p. 69*

Reading
Set a Purpose for Reading pp. 63, 64†*
Reading Check p. 68
Reading Fluency p. 71

Vocabulary
Study p. 65*
Practice p. 66
Strategy p. 67

Grammar and Writing
Writing for Assessment p. 70

Assessment
Selection Tests A, B/C pp. 73*, 75*
Test Generator CD

BEST PRACTICES TOOLKIT
Differentiated Instruction pp. 31–38*
Scaffolding Instruction pp. 43–46*

Graphic Organizers/Strategies
Word Questioning

Reading Support
Audio Anthology CD*

Technology
Literature, Vocabulary, and Writing Centers at **ClassZone.com**
Write*Smart* CD

* Resources for Differentiation † Also in Spanish ‡ In Haitian Creole and Vietnamese

LEMENTS OF NONFICTION: PERSUASION

A logical, well-supported argument can be very persuasive. But writers often rely on more than facts to convince readers. Sometimes they express an attitude, or **tone** toward their subject, in order to win your support. Writers might also use **persuasive techniques** such as these:

- **Emotional appeals**—the use of words, descriptions, or images that call forth strong feelings, such as pity, fear, or anger.
  If this law doesn't pass, innocent puppies will continue to be horribly mistreated in puppy mills.
- **Ethical appeals**—attempts to gain moral support for a claim by linking the claim to a widely accepted value.
  We need this law because animals deserve decent treatment.

As you read, notice the ways the authors try to convince you.

EADING STRATEGY: SET A PURPOSE FOR READING

When you **set a purpose** for reading, you decide what you want to accomplish as you read. In this lesson, your purpose is to compare and contrast the persuasive techniques used in two selections. Filling in a chart like the one begun here can help. Use line numbers to tell where the appeals are.

	"Position on Dodgeball in Physical Education"	"The Weak Shall Inherit the Gym"
What emotional appeals does the writer use?	Appeal to pity: lines 34–35	
What ethical appeals does the writer use?		
What is the writer's tone? How does it affect you?		

OCABULARY IN CONTEXT

The boldfaced words help to convey opinions about playing dodgeball. Try to figure out each word's meaning.

1. If you witness someone cheating, report the **impropriety.**
2. Students are not **adequately** prepared for competition.
3. We were able to **eliminate** the other players one by one.
4. One great player can **annihilate** an entire opposing team.
5. Is dodgeball a safe way to take out **aggression?**
6. The school is going to **ban** the game.

Author Online

Funny Man with Serious Talent Many *Sports Illustrated* readers turn to the last page of their magazine first in order to read Rick Reilly's weekly column "Life of Reilly." The column, along with his novels and essay collections, has earned Reilly the reputation as "one of the funniest humans on the planet." Reilly has written about everything from ice-skating to the Iditarod, the Alaskan dog race. His adventures include facing fastballs from eight-time All-Star pitcher Nolan Ryan, cycling with seven-time Tour de France winner Lance Armstrong, and playing 108 holes of golf in one day. He began his sports writing career as a sophomore at the University of Colorado, taking phoned- in high-school volleyball scores for his hometown newspaper. After graduation, he moved on to stints at the *Denver Post* and the *Los Angeles Times*, eventually landing at *Sports Illustrated* in 1985. He has been voted National Sportswriter of the Year 10 times.

Rick Reilly
born 1958

National Association for Sport and Physical Education The NASPE is made up of gym teachers, coaches, athletic directors, athletic trainers, sport management professionals, researchers, and college faculty. The association provides a way for all of these professionals to help one another to improve physical education in schools. By researching, developing standards, and spreading information, NASPE helps students learn about fitness and stay active all their lives.

MORE ABOUT THE AUTHOR
For more on Rick Reilly and the National Association for Sport and Physical Education, visit the **Literature Center** at **ClassZone.com.**

985

Teach

STANDARDS FOCUS

ELEMENTS OF NONFICTION

● PERSUASION

Write these headings on the board: *Emotional Appeals, Ethical Appeals, Other.* Ask students to brainstorm ways they could convince a friend to see one movie over another. Record students' suggestions under the appropriate headings. ***Possible answers:*** *Emotional: "It's a really exciting movie." "Your favorite actor is in it." Ethical: "It's my turn to pick the movie." "We need to support the local theater." Other: "I'll buy the popcorn."*

CHECK UNDERSTANDING Ask students what persuasive techniques they are exposed to in their everyday lives.

READING STRATEGY

■ SET A PURPOSE FOR READING

Explain that to fulfill a specific purpose for reading, students may have to adjust their reading rate, reread passages, and pause to review their graphic organizers.

CHECK UNDERSTANDING Ask students to set a purpose for reading **Author Online** and to notice the adjustments they make to meet that purpose.

RESOURCE MANAGER—Copy Master
Set a Purpose for Reading p. 63
(for student use while reading the selections)

VOCABULARY SKILL

▲ VOCABULARY IN CONTEXT

DIAGNOSE WORD KNOWLEDGE To determine preteaching needs, have all students complete **Vocabulary in Context.** ***Possible answers:*** 1. *wrongdoing* 2. *completely* 3. *get rid of* 4. *destroy* 5. *anger* 6. *not allow*

PRETEACH VOCABULARY Use the Vocabulary Study copy master to help students explore the meaning of each boldfaced word.

1. Read item 1 aloud, emphasizing *adequately.*
2. Point out the phrase *asked her teacher for additional help.* Elicit predicted meanings for *adequately,* such as "fully."
3. Have students record their predictions.
4. Repeat the procedure for items 2–6.
5. Have students check their predicted meanings as they read the selections.

RESOURCE MANAGER—Copy Master
Vocabulary Study p. 65

For general guidelines on differentiating vocabulary instruction and for alternative vocabulary activities for students not needing vocabulary preteaching, see

BEST PRACTICES TOOLKIT
Scaffolding Vocabulary Instruction pp. 43–46

Vocabulary Center at **ClassZone.com**
Additional Vocabulary Activities

Practice and Apply

Position on Dodgeball in Physical Education

National Association for Sport and Physical Education

impropriety (ĭm'prə-prī'ĭ-tē) *n.* an unsuitable or inappropriate act or quality

Targeted Passage ①

With the recent release of both a movie and television show about dodgeball, debate about the game's merits and **improprieties** has escalated in the media and on the NASPE listserv.[1] Thus, the National Association for Sport and Physical Education (NASPE) would like to reiterate its position about including dodgeball in school physical education programs.

NASPE believes that dodgeball is **not** an appropriate activity for K–12 school physical education programs. The purpose of physical education is to provide students with:

- The knowledge, skills, and confidence needed to be physically active for a lifetime
- A daily dose of physical activity for health benefits
- Positive experiences so that kids want to be physically active outside of physical education class and throughout their lifetime

The goals of physical education can be obtained through a wide variety of appropriate physical activities. Ⓐ

Ⓐ **PERSUASION**
What is the NASPE's position on dodgeball in school physical education programs?

Getting and keeping children and adolescents active is one of the biggest challenges facing parents and youth leaders.

- 61.5% of children aged 9–13 years do not participate in any organized physical activity during their non-school hours and 22.6% do not engage in any free-time physical activity.
- One-third of high school students are not **adequately** active and over 10% do not participate in any physical activity at all.
- 16% of U.S. youth aged 6–19 are overweight—triple the proportion of 25 years ago. Ⓑ

adequately (ăd'ĭ-kwĭt-lē) *adv.* enough to satisfy a requirement or meet a need

Ⓑ **PERSUASION**
Reread lines 18–24. Based on these lines, how would you describe the **tone** of this document?

According to NASPE's *Appropriate Practices for Elementary School Physical Education* (2000), "in a quality physical education class teachers involve ALL children in activities that allow them to participate actively, both physically and mentally. Activities such as relay races, dodgeball, and

1. **listserv** (lĭst-sûrv): an e-mail list that allows a group of people to hold a discussion by writing to each other via the Internet.

ELEMENTS OF NONFICTION

Ⓐ PERSUASION

Possible answer: *The NASPE's position is that dodgeball should not be included in K–12 physical education programs.*

ELEMENTS OF NONFICTION

Ⓑ PERSUASION

Students will likely find the tone serious, authoritative, and objective.

DIFFERENTIATED INSTRUCTION

FOR ALL STUDENTS

Expert Groups Encourage groups of students to select one of these topics to research and then share their information with the class:

- the NASPE
- Rick Reilly
- physical education activities
- the history of dodgeball

FOR LESS-PROFICIENT READERS

In combination with the *Audio Anthology CD*, use one or more Targeted Passages (pp. 986, 988) to ensure that students focus on key concepts and skills.

① **Targeted Passage [Lines 1–15]**

This passage establishes the reasons the NASPE thinks it is important to take a position on dodgeball and explains the purpose of physical education.

- What recent developments have caused the NASPE to restate its position on dodgeball in school physical education programs?
- What is the NASPE's position on dodgeball?
- According to the NASPE, what is the purpose of physical education?

FOR ENGLISH LEARNERS

Prereading For prereading instruction for English learners, see

BEST PRACTICES TOOLKIT
Scaffolding Reading Instruction pp. 43–46

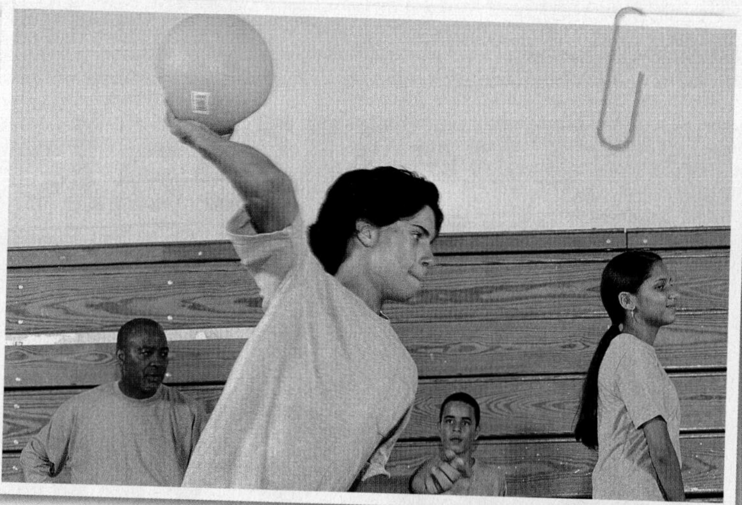

ANALYZE VISUALS
How many people pictured on this dodgeball team appear to be getting exercise?

elimination tag provide limited opportunities for everyone in the class, especially the slower, less agile students who need the activity the most."

The students who are **eliminated** first in dodgeball are typically the ones who most need to be active and practice their skills. Many times these students are also the ones with the least amount of confidence in their physical abilities. Being targeted because they are the "weaker" players, and being hit by a hard-thrown ball, does not help kids to develop confidence.

eliminate (ĭ-lĭm'ə-nāt') *v.* to remove from consideration by defeating

The arguments most often heard in favor of dodgeball are that it allows for the practice of important physical skills—and kids like it.

- Dodgeball does provide a means of practicing some important physical skills—running, dodging, throwing, and catching. However, there are many activities that allow practice of these skills without using human targets or eliminating students from play.
- Some kids may like it—the most skilled, the most confident. But many do not! Certainly not the student who gets hit hard in the stomach, head, or groin. And it is not appropriate to teach our children that you win by hurting others. C

C PERSUASION
Reread lines 42–45. What kind of **emotional appeal** is being made? What is the **ethical appeal?**

In a recent article about the new GSN (games network) TV show called "Extreme Dodgeball," there is talk of "developing and executing extreme strategies to **annihilate** opponents" and the use of terms such as "throw-to-kill ratios," and "headshots." NASPE asks, "Is this the type of game that you want children to be exposed to?"

annihilate (ə-nī'ə-lāt') *v.* to completely destroy or defeat

ANALYZE VISUALS

Possible answer: *Only one person seems to be getting exercise—the boy throwing the ball.*

BACKGROUND

Dodgeball Although there are different versions of dodgeball, there are usually six to ten players on each team, and the object is to eliminate the other team's players. Each team gets three eight-inch rubber-coated foam balls, which they throw at the opposing players. Players are eliminated if they are hit by a live ball (one that has not touched the ground), if they drop a live ball, or if an opposing player catches a live ball that they have thrown. Play continues until one team is eliminated.

ELEMENTS OF NONFICTION

C PERSUASION

Possible answer: *The emotional appeal (lines 42–44) focuses on students who get hurt playing the game. The ethical appeal (lines 44–45) is that it is wrong to teach children that they can win by hurting others.*

If students need help . . . Read lines 38–45 aloud to allow them to hear the change in tone.

Lines 46–50
REINFORCE *KEY IDEA:* GAMES

Discuss Extreme dodgeball seems to be a serious, hard-hitting **game.** Why might players think it is worth the risk? ***Possible answer:*** *Players may be attracted to the action and the intense competition.*

FOR LESS–PROFICIENT READERS

Reading Strategy Follow-Up: Set a Purpose for Reading Have students use the chart from page 985 to record details about persuasive techniques in this selection.

- ***Emotional appeals:*** *Appeal to pity, lines 31–35, 42–45*
- ***Ethical appeals:*** *Appeal to fairness, lines 25–30, 38–43*
- ***Tone and effect:*** *Tone is serious, authoritative, and objective; readers feel assured by writer's knowledge*

FOR ENGLISH LEARNERS

Key Academic Vocabulary Have groups complete Word Questioning charts for these words from "Position on Dodgeball": *physical* (lines 4, 5, and elsewhere throughout selection), *appropriate* (lines 6, 15, 44), *participate* (lines 18, 22).

BEST PRACTICES TOOLKIT—Transparency
Word Questioning p. E9

FOR ADVANCED LEARNERS/PRE–AP

Pre-AP exercises in the bottom channel provide additional challenge for your advanced students. Use them for small groups or individuals.

ADDITIONAL GUIDELINES
For more help with differentiation and tips for classroom management, see

BEST PRACTICES TOOLKIT
Differentiated Instruction pp. 31–38

POSITION ON DODGEBALL IN PHYSICAL EDUCATION 987

ELEMENTS OF NONFICTION

D PERSUASION

Possible answer: *The phrases "Not to alarm you" and "America is going softer than left-out butter" establish a sarcastic and humorous tone.*

ELEMENTS OF NONFICTION

E PERSUASION

Possible answer: *Williams thinks dodgeball "encourages the best to pick on the weak." Reilly responds sarcastically, pretending to be shocked to learn that there are actually weak and strong people in the world. He also points out that dodgeball is a child's first chance to find out whether he or she is strong or weak and learn how to deal with it.*

Lines 12–14

REINFORCE *KEY IDEA:* GAMES

Discuss Do you think **games** that teach players that they are weak are worth playing? Explain. *Some students may feel that such games are worthwhile because learning about weaknesses can enable a person to improve. Other students might believe that the purpose of playing games should be to have fun, so games that point out weaknesses should be avoided.*

OPINION

The Weak Shall Inherit the Gym

Rick Reilly

Not to alarm you, but America is going softer than left-out butter. Exhibit 9,137: Schools have started banning dodgeball.

I kid you not. Dodgeball has been outlawed by some school districts in New York, Texas, Utah and Virginia. Many more are thinking about it, like Cecil County, Md., where the school board wants to **ban** any game with "human targets." D

Human targets? What's tag? What's a snowball fight? What's a close play at second? Neil Williams, a physical education professor at Eastern Connecticut State, says dodgeball has to go because it "encourages the best to pick on the weak." Noooo! You mean there's weak in the world? There's strong? Of course there is, and dodgeball is one of the first opportunities in life to figure out which one you are and how you're going to deal with it. E

We had a bully, Big Joe, in our seventh grade. Must have weighed 225 pounds, . . . We also had a kid named Melvin, who was so thin we could've faxed him from class to class. I'll never forget the dodgeball game in which Big Joe had a ball in each hand and one sandwiched

ban (băn) *v.* to prohibit

D PERSUASION
What words and phrases in the first sentence make Rick Reilly's **tone** immediately clear?

Targeted Passage ②

E PERSUASION
Why does Neil Williams object to dodgeball? Describe Reilly's response to this objection.

DIFFERENTIATED INSTRUCTION

FOR LESS–PROFICIENT READERS

② Targeted Passage [Lines 8–14]

This passage introduces Reilly's argument against banning dodgeball.

- What point is Reilly making in lines 8–9?
- Is Reilly being sincere in lines 11–12? Explain.
- According to Reilly, what is the value of dodgeball?

FOR ADVANCED LEARNERS/PRE–AP

Hyperbole Ask students to explain the purpose of Reilly's use of hyperbole, or exaggeration, in lines 16–17. *(Reilly is injecting humor into the piece.)* Then challenge students to use hyperbole to create their own description of Melvin or Big Joe.

ANALYZE VISUALS
Is the girl in the photo wearing the appropriate amount of protective gear? Why or why not?

ANALYZE VISUALS

Possible answer: *The girl seems to be wearing too much protective gear to be able to move. However, it is unlikely that she could get hurt.*

REINFORCE *KEY IDEA:* GAMES

Discuss In what way might the NASPE react to the **game** the girl in the photo is playing? In what way might Rick Reilly respond? ***Possible answer:*** *The NASPE might disapprove of any game that requires so much protective equipment because it indicates that the player is a human target. Reilly would probably respond by pointing out that the girl is totally protected, so there's little chance she can get hurt. Reilly might even wonder if so much equipment is necessary.*

FOR ENGLISH LEARNERS

Language: Conversational English Patterns
Point out that Reilly uses informal, conversational language to help establish his tone of sarcastic disbelief. He sometimes uses sentence fragments, leaving out words that can be inferred from the context. For example:

- *Human targets?* (line 8): The repetition of this term from line 7, followed by examples of tag and snowball fights, emphasizes that Reilly thinks the term *human targets* is a ridiculous exaggeration.
- *You mean there's weak in the world?* (line 11): The verb *do* is understood at the beginning of the line; the noun *people* is understood after the adjective *weak.*
- *Must have weighed 225 pounds* (lines 15–16): The pronoun *he* is understood at the beginning of the sentence.

Lines 15–22
REINFORCE *KEY IDEA:* GAMES

Discuss Why might the **game** of dodgeball be appealing to Big Joe? to Melvin? ***Possible answer:*** *Big Joe might see the game as a chance to bully kids "legally." Melvin might see it as a chance to get back at bullies like Big Joe.*

ELEMENTS OF NONFICTION

F PERSUASION

Possible answer: *Reilly uses the idea that growing up sheltered does nothing to prepare kids for the competitiveness of the real world. He seems to have little respect for workers in fast-food restaurants.*

ELEMENTS OF NONFICTION

G PERSUASION

Answers will vary. Students may cite the modification or banning of existing games or the creation of silly new games.

SELECTION WRAP–UP

REFLECT Ask students what kind of dodgeball player Reilly might have been in school, based on what they know about him. Then ask in what way his background might affect his stance on dodgeball.

★ **CRITIQUE** Ask students if they were persuaded to agree with the author of either selection. If so, what elements of the argument convinced them? If not, what was lacking in one or both of the arguments?

READING FLUENCY

Distribute the copy masters and have students practice fluency.

R RESOURCE MANAGER—Copy Master
Reading Fluency p. 71

---

aggression (ə-grĕsh′ən) *n.* hostile or destructive behavior or action

F PERSUASION
What widely accepted value does Reilly use to make an **ethical appeal?** Consider whether he seems to respect the job of filling chalupas.

G PERSUASION
Reread lines 34–51. Sometimes writers try to convince you that a position is wrong because it could result in a ridiculous outcome. Identify one ridiculous outcome proposed by Reilly in lines 34–51.

between his knees, firing at our side like a human tennis-ball machine, when, all of a sudden, he got plunked. . . . Joe whirled around to see who'd done it and saw that it was none other than Melvin, all 83 pounds of him, most of it smile.

Some of these . . . whiners say dodgeball is inappropriate in these violent times. Are you kidding? Dodgeball is one of the few times in life when you get to let out your **aggressions,** no questions asked. We don't need less dodgeball in schools, we need more!

I know what all these . . . parents want. They want their Ambers and their Alexanders to grow up in a cozy womb of noncompetition, where everybody shares tofu[1] and Little Red Riding Hood and the big, bad wolf set up a commune.[2] Then their kids will stumble out into the bright light of the real world and find out that, yes, there's weak and there's strong and teams and sides and winning and losing. You'll recognize those kids. They'll be the ones filling up chalupas.[3] Very noncompetitive. F

But Williams and his fellow whiners aren't stopping at dodgeball. In their Physical Education Hall of Shame they've also included duck-duck-goose and musical chairs. Seriously. So, if we give them dodgeball, you can look for these games to be banned next:

Tag. Referring to any child as *it* is demeaning and hurtful. Instead of the child hollering, "You're it!" we recommend, "You're special!"

Baseball. Involves wrong-headed notions of *stealing, errors* and gruesome *hit-and-run.* Players should always be safe, never out.

Capture the flag. Mimics war.

Kick the can. Unfair to the can.

If we let these PC twinkies[4] have their way, we'll be left with:

Duck-duck-duck. Teacher spends the entire hour patting each child softly on the head.

Upsy down. The entire class takes turns fluffing the gym teacher's pillow before her nap.

Swedish baseball. Players are allowed free passage to first, second or third, where they receive a relaxing two-minute massage from opposing players. G

1. **tofu** (tō′fo͞o): a protein-rich soybean curd that many vegetarians eat in place of meat.
2. **commune** (kŏm′yo͞on′): a cooperative community in which a group of people who are not necessarily related live and work together.
3. **chalupas** (chə-lo͞o′päs): fried tortillas filled with meat, a Mexican dish similar to tacos that is served at several U.S. fast-food chains.
4. **PC twinkies:** Reilly's expression for people who are too concerned (politically correct) with offending others by words or actions.

DIFFERENTIATED INSTRUCTION

FOR ENGLISH LEARNERS

Reading: Background Explain these games referred to in lines 35–36:

- *duck-duck-goose:* Players sit in a circle, except for one person who is "it." The "it" person walks around the circle, tapping each player on the head and calling each a duck. Then the "it" person chooses one player to call a goose. The goose gets up and chases the "it" person, who tries to reach the goose's chair before being tagged. If the "it" person is tagged, he or she must sit in the center of the circle until another player takes his or her place. The goose becomes "it," and the game continues.
- *musical chairs:* Six players walk around five chairs to the sound of music. When the music stops, players sit down. The player left without a chair is eliminated. A chair is removed, and the game continues with the remaining players.

990 UNIT 9: ARGUMENT AND PERSUASION

Comprehension

1. **Recall** What reason does the NASPE give for once again announcing its position on dodgeball in school physical education programs?
2. **Clarify** Reread lines 15–22 of "The Weak Shall Inherit the Gym." What did dodgeball do for Melvin?

Critical Analysis

3. **Identify Persuasive Technique** Often writers use **loaded language,** or words with strong positive or negative associations, to influence readers. Reread lines 46–50 of "Position on Dodgeball." Identify the loaded language used to create an **appeal to fear.**
4. **Examine Name-Calling** Attempting to discredit a position or idea by attacking people associated with it is name-calling. Find examples of name-calling in "The Weak Shall Inherit the Gym." Does it make Reilly's argument more or less convincing? Give reasons for your answer.
5. **Analyze Tone** What is Reilly's tone, or attitude toward opponents of dodgeball? Explain how this tone might persuade readers to share his opinion of the **game.**
6. **Make Judgments** A **stereotype** is an overgeneralization about a person or group. In your opinion, is Reilly guilty of stereotyping? Explain.
7. **Evaluate** After reading these two positions on dodgeball, would you say it is a game worth playing? Explain why or why not.

Comparing Persuasive Techniques

Now that you've read "Position on Dodgeball in Physical Education" and "The Weak Shall Inherit the Gym," finish filling in your chart. Then add and answer the final question.

	"Position on Dodgeball in Physical Eduction"	"The Weak Shall Inherit the Gym"
What emotional appeals does the writer use?	Appeal to pity: lines 34–35	
What ethical appeals does the writer use?		
What is the writer's tone? How does it affect you?		
What does the writer rely upon most to persuade—emotional appeals, ethical appeals, or tone?		

	"Position on Dodgeball . . ."	"The Weak Shall Inherit . . ."
What emotional appeals does the writer use?	Appeal to pity: lines 34–35, 42–45	Appeal to fear: lines 1–4, 44–51
What ethical appeals does the writer use?	Appeal to fairness: lines 25–30, 38–43	Appeal to children's needs: lines 11–14, 23–26, 27–33
What is the writer's tone? How does it affect you?	Tone is serious, authoritative, and objective; readers may feel assured by the writer's knowledge.	Tone is sarcastic, humorous, and scornful; readers may feel either offended or inspired by his approach.
What does the writer rely upon most to persuade—emotional appeals, ethical appeals, or tone?	ethical appeals	tone

Practice and Apply

After Reading

For additional support of postreading questions, use these copy masters:

RESOURCE MANAGER—Copy Masters
Reading Check p. 68 (to check understanding of the selections)
Question Support p. 69 (After Reading questions adapted for English learners and less-proficient readers)

Additional selection questions are provided for teachers on page 57.

ANSWERS

Comprehension

1. *The debate over dodgeball has resurfaced as a result of both a movie and a television show that focus on the game.*
2. *Dodgeball gave Melvin a chance to get back at a bully and boosted his confidence.*

Critical Analysis

Possible answers:

3. ● **STANDARDS FOCUS Persuasion** *Loaded language includes "extreme strategies," "annihilate opponents," "throw-to-kill ratios," and "headshots."*
4. *Examples include "whiners" (lines 23, 34) and "PC twinkies" (line 44). Students may feel that the name-calling weakens the argument because it is an immature tactic.*
5. *Reilly's tone is scornful and sarcastic. This tone might make readers reluctant to side with "whiners," who are considered weak.*
6. *Reilly is stereotyping people who oppose playing dodgeball in schools. He makes sweeping generalizations about their motives, their lifestyles, the names they choose for their children, and their goals for their families.*
7. *Accept all well-supported and clearly explained responses.*

Comparing Persuasive Techniques

■ **STANDARDS FOCUS Set a Purpose for Reading** *Students should be able to support their answers to the final question with reasons and evidence from the text. Possible chart entries are provided.*

Vocabulary in Context

VOCABULARY PRACTICE

Synonyms are words that have similar meanings, and **antonyms** are words that have opposite meanings. Decide whether the words in each pair are synonyms or antonyms.

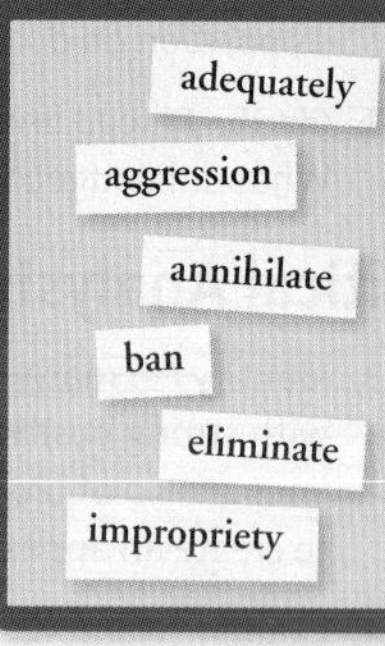

1. adequately—insufficiently
2. aggression—ferocity
3. annihilate—destroy
4. ban—legalize
5. eliminate—banish
6. impropriety—rudeness

VOCABULARY IN WRITING

What gym class activity would you like to see either added to or banned from your school? Using at least two vocabulary words, write a short paragraph in which you explain your opinion. You might start like this.

> **EXAMPLE SENTENCE**
>
> *I would **ban** dodgeball from physical education classes.*

VOCABULARY STRATEGY: THE LATIN WORD *gressus*

The vocabulary word *aggression* comes from the Latin word *gressus*, which means "to go." Many English words have the same origin. To figure out the meaning of words with this history, use context clues and your knowledge of the meaning of *gressus*.

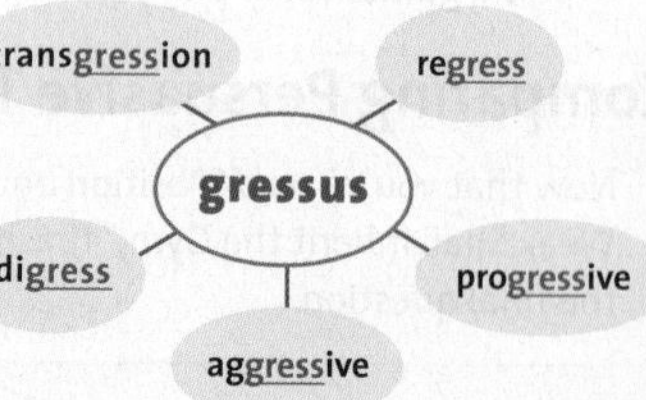

PRACTICE Choose the word from the web that best completes each sentence. Then explain how the word *gressus* relates to the meaning of the word.

1. The trainer works with ____ dogs to make them gentler and more obedient.
2. Many dogs will ____ if they don't get constant social interaction.
3. Stealing a car is a serious _____, so car thieves receive harsh penalties.
4. Please stick to the topic and do not _____.
5. The Renaissance was a _____ time period in which the arts flourished and scientists made important discoveries.

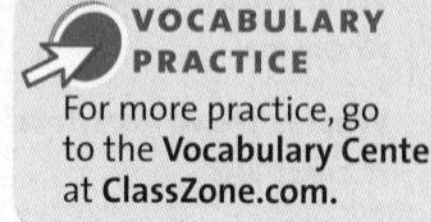

For more practice, go to the **Vocabulary Center** at **ClassZone.com.**

ANSWERS

Vocabulary in Context

VOCABULARY PRACTICE

1. *antonyms*
2. *synonyms*
3. *synonyms*
4. *antonyms*
5. *synonyms*
6. *synonyms*

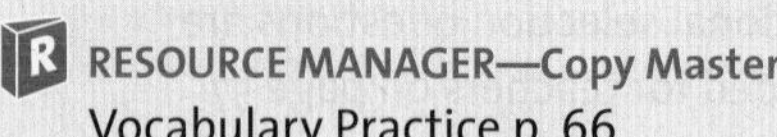
RESOURCE MANAGER—Copy Master
Vocabulary Practice p. 66

VOCABULARY IN WRITING

Suggest that students think of at least two good reasons for adding or banning a particular gym class activity. Then have them review the vocabulary words to see which ones they could use to explain their opinions.

VOCABULARY STRATEGY: THE LATIN WORD *gressus* *(also an EL language objective)*

Review the meanings of these prefixes and suffixes:

Prefixes	Suffixes
ag- = to, toward *di-* = two *pro-* = forward *re-* = again *trans-* = across	*-ion* = state of *-ive* = inclined to

Possible answers:

1. *aggressive—Aggressive dogs go toward those they are attacking.*
2. *regress—Dogs who regress go back to their old, untrained, way of behaving.*
3. *transgression—A transgression is a movement away from accepted behavior and toward unaccepted behavior.*
4. *digress—One who digresses moves in a second direction—away from a topic.*
5. *progressive—A progressive time period is one in which there is movement toward enlightenment.*

RESOURCE MANAGER—Copy Master
Vocabulary Strategy p. 67

Vocabulary Center at **ClassZone.com**
Additional Vocabulary Activities

DIFFERENTIATED INSTRUCTION

FOR ENGLISH LEARNERS

Vocabulary Practice Encourage Spanish-speaking students to use their knowledge of cognates to help them remember the definitions of the vocabulary words:

- *adequately* (*adecuadamente*)
- *aggression* (*agresión*)
- *annihilate* (*aniquilar*)
- *eliminate* (*eliminar*)
- *impropriety* (*impropiedad*)

FOR ADVANCED LEARNERS/PRE-AP

Vocabulary Strategy Challenge students to create additional practice items with other words that come from the Latin word *gressus* and have them explain how *gressus* relates to the meaning of each English word.

Writing for Assessment

1. READ THE PROMPT

The two selections you've just read support opposite sides of the same issue. In writing assessments, you might be asked to compare or contrast such selections.

PROMPT

"Position on Dodgeball in Physical Education" and "The Weak Shall Inherit the Gym" each express a position on whether dodgeball should be played in school. In four or five paragraphs, contrast the tone and persuasive techniques in each selection. Use details from the selections to explain the differences in how these techniques are used to persuade readers.

STRATEGIES IN ACTION

1. I need to **identify the tone and types of appeals** used in each selection.
2. I need to **state the differences** in the writers' use of tone and persuasive techniques.
3. I need to **support my statements with examples** from the selections.

2. PLAN YOUR WRITING

To make sure you understand the persuasive techniques each writer uses, review the chart you completed. Write a thesis statement identifying the differences in their methods of persuasion. Then consider how to organize your response.

- **Option A:** In one paragraph, describe the tone and persuasive techniques the writer of the position paper relies upon. In the next paragraph, describe the tone and persuasive techniques the writer of the editorial relies upon.
- **Option B:** In one paragraph, contrast each writer's tone. In the next paragraph, contrast their emotional appeals. In a third, contrast their ethical appeals and any other techniques they use to persuade.

I. Introduction
II. Tone and persuasive techniques in first selection
III. Tone and persuasive techniques in second selection
IV. Conclusion

Once you have decided on your approach, create an outline to organize your details.

3. DRAFT YOUR RESPONSE

Introduction Provide the titles and authors of both selections, a brief description of each author's position, and your thesis statement.
Body Using your outline as a guide, compare the tone and persuasive techniques used in the two selections. Include details from the selections to illustrate your statements.
Conclusion Restate your thesis statement, and leave your reader with a final thought about the persuasion used in each of these selections.
Revision Double-check to make sure your thesis statement clearly presents the ideas you develop in your body paragraphs.

Writing for Assessment

1. ***READ THE PROMPT***
   - Read the prompt aloud. Ask volunteers to identify key words and phrases that define the task.
   - Discuss each strategy. Help students brainstorm a list of words they could use to describe an author's tone, such as *authoritative* or *mocking*. Then help them brainstorm a list of words they could use to describe an author's persuasive techniques, such as *name-calling* or *ethical appeal*.
2. ***PLAN YOUR WRITING***
   - Direct students to use their charts from page 985. Their charts should include most of the information they need to write a response.
   - Guide students to focus on the development of tone and use of persuasive techniques and not to stray into a contrast of the reasons the authors provide for their position.
3. ***DRAFT YOUR RESPONSE***
   - Remind students to begin each body paragraph with a strong topic sentence.
   - List transitions on the board that will help students tie ideas together both within and between paragraphs, such as *on the other hand, besides, for example,* and *as a result*.

RESOURCE MANAGER—Copy Master
Writing for Assessment p. 70

Assess and Reteach

Assess

RESOURCE MANAGER—Copy Masters
Selection Tests A, B/C pp. 73–74, 75–76

Test Generator CD

Reteach

STANDARDS LESSON FILE
Literature Lesson 39: Tone
Reading Lesson 12: Comparing and Contrasting
Informational Texts Lesson 15: Persuasive Techniques
Writing Lesson 29: Comparison-Contrast Essay
Vocabulary Lesson 12: Word Families and Derivatives

DIFFERENTIATED INSTRUCTION

FOR LESS–PROFICIENT WRITERS

Draft Your Response Give students this template:

Introduction: [Author] expresses the position that [summary of author's position on whether dodgeball should be played in school] in [title]. On the other hand, [author] expresses the position that [summary of author's position on whether dodgeball should be played in school] in [title]. Both writers use persuasive techniques and tone to convince their readers.

Body

- [First author] uses [persuasive technique]. [Provide examples.] [Transition], [first author] uses a(n) [adjective] tone. [Provide examples.]
- [Second author] uses [persuasive technique]. [Provide examples.] [Transition], [second author] uses a(n) [adjective] tone. [Provide examples.]

Conclusion: [Restate thesis.] [End with a final thought about the persuasive techniques and tone used in each selection.]

Focus and Motivate

OBJECTIVES

Elements of Nonfiction
- explore the key idea of **relationships**
- identify and analyze author's purpose
- read an essay

Reading
- identify and analyze cause-and-effect relationships

Vocabulary
- build vocabulary for reading and writing
- determine meanings of related words by applying knowledge of word roots, base words, and affixes *(also an EL language objective)*
- use structural analysis to identify words *(also an EL language objective)*

SUMMARY

In "The Sanctuary of School," Lynda Barry recalls how, when she was a child, her school provided for her the support and sense of safety that were often lacking in her home life. Barry argues that the sense of belonging schools can provide to children is as important as the knowledge that they impart.

Why do we need SCHOOLS?

Have students read the question and the ***KEY IDEA.*** Discuss and define the "new three Rs": rigor, relevance, and **relationships.** Ask students if they agree that today's schools need to focus on relationships. Then have students work in groups to ***DISCUSS*** what they think are schools' most important tasks.

Before Reading

The Sanctuary of School

Essay by Lynda Barry

Why do we need SCHOOLS?

KEY IDEA Traditionally, a school's most basic function was to teach the "three Rs": reading, writing, and 'rithmetic. More recently, Bill Gates, founder of the Microsoft Corporation, suggested that today's schools need to focus on three new "Rs": rigor, relevance, and **relationships**. In the essay you're about to read, Lynda Barry describes how the relationships made all the difference in her life.

DISCUSS With a small group, discuss what you think are a school's three most important tasks. Write them down and share them with your class. How many ideas have to do with the classroom and lessons? How many are tied to something less academic?

994

Selection Resources

RESOURCE MANAGER UNIT 9

Plan and Teach pp. 77–84

Elements of Nonfiction
Summary pp. 85†*, 86‡*
Author's Purpose pp. 87, 88†*
Question Support p. 95*

Reading
Identify Cause and Effect pp. 89, 90†*
Reading Check p. 94

Vocabulary
Study p. 91*
Practice p. 92
Strategy p. 93

Assessment
Selection Tests A, B/C pp. 97*, 99*
Test Generator CD

BEST PRACTICES TOOLKIT

Differentiated Instruction pp. 31–38*
Scaffolding Instruction pp. 43–46*

Graphic Organizers/Strategies
Jigsaw Reading • New Word Analysis • Analysis Frame: Persuasion

Reading Support
Audio Anthology CD*

Technology
Literature and Vocabulary Centers at **ClassZone.com**
Write*Smart* CD

* Resources for Differentiation   † Also in Spanish   ‡ In Haitian Creole and Vietnamese

LEMENTS OF NONFICTION: AUTHOR'S PURPOSE

Writers usually have one or more **purposes** when they sit down to write, and they carefully select strategies to achieve these purposes. In this essay, Lynda Barry's purpose is to persuade us to value and support public schools. As you read, analyze the way that Barry uses a personal experience from her childhood to make her larger point. Pay attention to the effect that her words, details, and images have on you.

EADING SKILL: IDENTIFY CAUSE AND EFFECT

A **cause** is an event or action that directly results in another event. An **effect** is the direct outcome of an event or action. For example, if your school bus gets a flat tire, that could be the cause of your being late for school. Being late is the effect. Sometimes signal words will alert you to causes (*because, since*) and effects (*as a result, therefore*). Other times, you'll have to make the connection for yourself.

As you read this essay, look for the conditions in Barry's environment that cause her to behave the way she does. Each time you recognize a cause-and-effect relationship, create a diagram like the one shown.

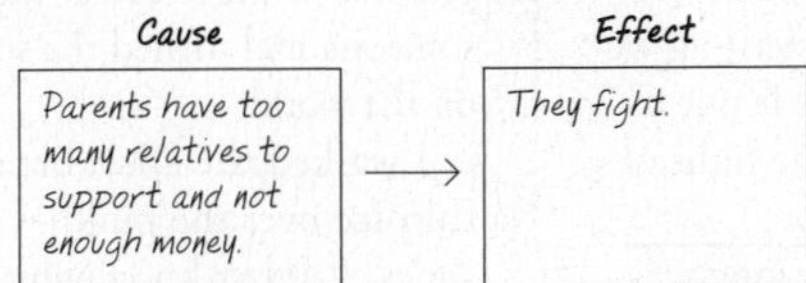

OCABULARY IN CONTEXT

The boldfaced words help Lynda Barry to convey what she felt about school when she was a little girl. To see how many of them you know, restate each sentence, using a different word or phrase for the boldfaced term.

1. A **neglectful** student forgets to do her homework.
2. Children thrive in loving, **secure** homes.
3. Our school doesn't look unique or exciting on the outside, but inside it is anything but **nondescript**.
4. On a hot day, an air-conditioned classroom is a **sanctuary**.

Author Online

Difficult Childhood Lynda Barry never felt that she "fit in"—not with her classmates at school, nor with either side of her parents' Filipino and Norwegian-Irish families. An excellent student, Barry became the first member of her family to attend college. There she began drawing quirky comic strips based on her own life experiences and publishing them in her school's student newspaper.

Lynda Barry
born 1956

Comic Strip Success After college, Barry struggled to decide what to do with her life and how to support herself. Cartoonist and writer Matt Groening (creator of *The Simpsons* television series) had been a college classmate of Barry's. Through Groening, the *Chicago Reader* newspaper learned of Barry's work and hired her to draw a weekly comic strip. Soon, her comic strips "Girls and Boys," "Ernie Pook's Comeek," and "Modern Romance" gained her a nationwide following. She has also published plays and novels, including *The Good Times Are Killing Me* and *Cruddy: An Illustrated Novel.* Her childhood continues to have a big effect on her art. Childhood, she says, is "where all our motivations, feelings, and opinions come from."

MORE ABOUT THE AUTHOR
For more on Lynda Barry, visit the **Literature Center** at **ClassZone.com.**

Teach

STANDARDS FOCUS

ELEMENTS OF NONFICTION

● AUTHOR'S PURPOSE

Write this example on the board:

One time in sixth grade, my class took an important math test. I finished early and thought I'd check the answers that the kids sitting on either side of me wrote. For one question, they both wrote the same answer, but it was different from mine. I changed my answer to match theirs. When we got our tests back, I found out that my original answer had been correct!

Ask: What might be the author's purpose in sharing this personal story? ***Possible answer:*** *to persuade people not to cheat*

CHECK UNDERSTANDING Ask students why writers use personal experiences as a strategy for persuading readers.

READING SKILL

■ IDENTIFY CAUSE AND EFFECT

Have students identify a cause-and-effect relationship in the Author's Purpose example. ***Possible answer:*** *Cause: The author copied an answer from other students. Effect: The author got the item wrong.*

CHECK UNDERSTANDING Have students identify cause-and-effect relationships in the **Author Online** information about Lynda Barry.

RESOURCE MANAGER—**Copy Master**
Identify Cause and Effect p. 89 (for student use while reading the selection)

VOCABULARY SKILL

▲ VOCABULARY IN CONTEXT

DIAGNOSE WORD KNOWLEDGE To determine preteaching needs, have all students complete **Vocabulary in Context.** ***Possible answers:*** **1.** *careless* **2.** *safe* **3.** *ordinary* **4.** *refuge*

PRETEACH VOCABULARY Use the Vocabulary Study copy master to help students determine the meaning of each boldfaced word.

1. Read aloud the first sentence, emphasizing *sanctuary.*
2. Discuss possible meanings, such as "place of safety and comfort."
3. Create a word map for *sanctuary.*
4. Repeat for each of the other sentences.
5. Have students complete Part B independently.

RESOURCE MANAGER—**Copy Master**
Vocabulary Study p. 91

For general guidelines on differentiating vocabulary instruction and for alternative vocabulary activities for students not needing vocabulary preteaching, see

BEST PRACTICES TOOLKIT
Scaffolding Vocabulary Instruction pp. 43–46

Vocabulary Center at **ClassZone.com**
Additional Vocabulary Activities

Practice and Apply

Lines 15–26
REINFORCE *KEY IDEA:* RELATIONSHIPS

Discuss What do you learn about Barry's **relationship** with her brother in this passage? ***Possible answer:*** *They seem to have a close relationship because when they have to give up their room to visiting relatives, they enjoy spending time together watching TV.*

Lines 27–46
DISCUSSION PROMPTS

Use these prompts to help students understand Barry's feelings and behavior when she sneaks out of her house:

Connect What surprises you most about Barry's actions in the morning? *Students may be surprised that a 7-year-old would sneak out of the house and wouldn't be frightened of walking to school alone in the dark.*

Interpret Why does Barry use the simile "as if someone had turned the sound off on the world" (lines 36–38)? ***Possible answer:*** *The simile compares the stillness outside to Barry's experience watching television with the sound off.*

Speculate Barry describes her panic as a feeling of being "lost." What might be causing her to feel this way? ***Possible answer:*** *Barry feels "lost" in her home, where her parents are fighting and she keeps "losing" her bedroom to relatives.*

ELEMENTS OF NONFICTION

Ⓐ AUTHOR'S PURPOSE

Possible answer: *She wanted to escape from an unhappy home.*

The New York Times

The Sanctuary of School

LYNDA BARRY

sanctuary (săngk'cho͞o-ĕr'ē) *n.* a place of refuge

Targeted Passage ①

I was seven years old the first time I snuck out of the house in the dark. It was winter and my parents had been fighting all night. They were short on money and long on relatives who kept "temporarily" moving into our house because they had nowhere else to go.

My brother and I were used to giving up our bedroom. We slept on the couch, something we actually liked because it put us that much closer to the light of our lives, our television.

At night when everyone was asleep, we lay on our pillows watching it with the sound off. We watched Steve Allen's[1] mouth moving. We watched Johnny Carson's[2] mouth moving. We watched movies filled with gangsters shooting machine guns into packed rooms, dying soldiers hurling a last grenade and beautiful women crying at windows. Then the sign-off finally came and we tried to sleep.

The morning I snuck out, I woke up filled with a panic about needing to get to school. The sun wasn't quite up yet but my anxiety was so fierce that I just got dressed, walked quietly across the kitchen and let myself out the back door.

It was quiet outside. Stars were still out. Nothing moved and no one was in the street. It was as if someone had turned the sound off on the world.

I walked the alley, breaking thin ice over the puddles with my shoes. I didn't know why I was walking to school in the dark. I didn't think about it. All I knew was a feeling of panic, like the panic that strikes kids when they realize they are lost. Ⓐ

Ⓐ AUTHOR'S PURPOSE
What can you **infer** about Barry's reason for walking to school in the dark?

That feeling eased the moment I turned the corner and saw the dark outline of my school at the top of the hill. My school was made up of about 15 **nondescript**

nondescript (nŏn'dĭ-skrĭpt') *adj.* lacking unique qualities

1. **Steve Allen:** (1921–2000) actor, comedian, songwriter, and author who hosted popular TV variety shows in the 1950s and 60s.
2. **Johnny Carson:** (1925–2005) comedian who hosted a late-night TV show, *The Tonight Show*, from 1962 to 1992.

996 UNIT 9: ARGUMENT AND PERSUASION

DIFFERENTIATED INSTRUCTION

FOR ALL STUDENTS

Enhance Learning Styles Provide these independent projects for students with various learning styles:

- **Creative** Create a cartoon about a relationship.
- **Visual** Create a poster illustrating four quotations from the essay.
- **Linguistic** Interview adults and report on schools in an earlier era.

For further details on these projects, see

RESOURCE MANAGER
Ideas for Extension pp. 82–83

FOR LESS–PROFICIENT READERS

In combination with the *Audio Anthology CD*, use one or more Targeted Passages (pp. 996, 999) to ensure that students focus on the selection's key events, concepts, and skills.

① Targeted Passage [Lines 1–14]

This opening passage provides clues about Barry's relationship with her family.

- At what age does Barry sneak out of her house for the first time?
- Why are her parents fighting?
- Why must Barry and her brother often give up their bedroom?
- Do Barry and her brother mind giving up their room? Why or why not?

ANALYZE VISUALS
This illustration by Lynda Barry accompanied the essay when it was originally published in a supplement to *The New York Times*. What can you **conclude** about the young Barry's relationship to school?

portable classrooms set down on a fenced concrete lot in a rundown Seattle[3] neighborhood, but it had the most beautiful view of the Cascade Mountains. You could see them from anywhere on the playfield and you could see them from the windows of my classroom—Room 2. **B**

B CAUSE AND EFFECT
Reread lines 47–50. What causes Barry to feel less panicked?

3. **Seattle:** a city in west central Washington state.

ANALYZE VISUALS

Possible answer: *Her tight embrace of the schoolhouse and her assertion that she is "home" indicate that she loves school and feels comfortable there. School gives her a sense of belonging.*

READING SKILL

B CAUSE AND EFFECT

Remind students to record their answers in the diagram from page 995. ***Possible answer:*** *The sight of her school eases her panic.*

If students need help . . . Discuss the differences between a cause and its effect. Explain that the question itself provides the effect: Barry feels less panicked. Have students reread the passage to look for the cause of this change in her feelings. Work with students to create a cause-and-effect diagram.

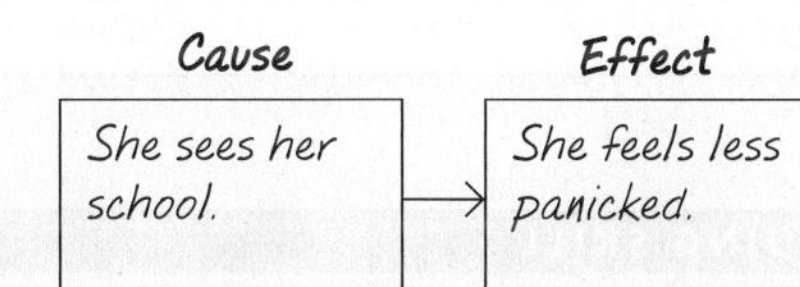

FOR ENGLISH LEARNERS

Options for Reading [small-group option] Have students silently read along as they listen to the *Audio Anthology CD*. Then divide students into Jigsaw groups and assign one Targeted Passage to each group. When groups can read their passage fluently, have them do a choral reading for the class. Encourage them to discuss the main idea of the passage.

BEST PRACTICES TOOLKIT
Jigsaw Reading p. A1

Key Academic Vocabulary Have students use New Word Analysis for these words: *temporarily* (lines 6, 174), *survival* (line 72), *financial* (line 73), *depression* (line 78).

BEST PRACTICES TOOLKIT—Transparency
New Word Analysis p. E8

Prereading For prereading instruction for English learners, see

BEST PRACTICES TOOLKIT
Scaffolding Reading Instruction pp. 43–46

FOR ADVANCED LEARNERS/PRE-AP

Pre-AP exercises in the bottom channel provide additional challenge for your advanced students. Use them for small groups or individuals.

ADDITIONAL GUIDELINES

For more help with differentiation and tips for classroom management, see

BEST PRACTICES TOOLKIT
Differentiated Instruction pp. 31–38

READING SKILL

C CAUSE AND EFFECT

Remind students to record their answers in the diagram from page 995. ***Possible answer:*** *They are too worried about their own problems to realize she is missing.*

ELEMENTS OF NONFICTION

D AUTHOR'S PURPOSE

Possible answer: *School is important to children like Barry and her brother because it is the only place where people pay attention to them.*

ELEMENTS OF NONFICTION

E AUTHOR'S PURPOSE

Possible answer: *The people who work at the school are kind and caring, and Barry trusts them.*

READING SKILL

F CAUSE AND EFFECT

Remind students to record their answers in the diagram from page 995. ***Possible answer:*** *Being at school makes Barry feel calm and secure.*

C CAUSE AND EFFECT
What causes Barry's parents not to notice she is missing?

D AUTHOR'S PURPOSE
Reread lines 74–86. What connection does Barry make between herself, other children, and the importance of school?

E AUTHOR'S PURPOSE
What are your impressions of the janitor and the teachers, and of Barry's relationships with them?

secure (sĭ-kyŏŏr') *adj.* safe; protected; free from fear or anxiety

F CAUSE AND EFFECT
Reread lines 119–131. Describe the effect that being in school has on Barry.

I walked over to the monkey bars and hooked my arms around the cold metal. I stood for a long time just looking across Rainier Valley.[4] The sky was beginning to whiten and I could hear a few birds.

In a perfect world my absence at home would not have gone unnoticed. I would have had two parents in a panic to locate me, instead of two parents in a panic to locate an answer to the hard question of survival during a deep financial and emotional crisis. C

But in an overcrowded and unhappy home, it's incredibly easy for any child to slip away. The high levels of frustration, depression and anger in my house made my brother and me invisible. We were children with the sound turned off. And for us, as for the steadily increasing number of neglected children in this country, the only place where we could count on being noticed was at school. D

"Hey there, young lady. Did you forget to go home last night?" It was Mr. Gunderson, our janitor, whom we all loved. He was nice and he was funny and he was old with white hair, thick glasses and an unbelievable number of keys. I could hear them jingling as he walked across the playfield. I felt incredibly happy to see him.

He let me push his wheeled garbage can between the different portables as he unlocked each room. He let me turn on the light and raise the window shades and I saw my school slowly come to life. I saw Mrs. Holman, our scho secretary, walk into the office without her orange lipstick on yet. She waved.

I saw the fifth-grade teacher, Mr. Cunningham, walking under the breezeway eating a hard roll. He waved.

And I saw my teacher, Mrs. Clai LeSane, walking toward us in a red coat and calling my name in a very happy and surprised way, and suddenly my throat got tight and my eyes stung and I ran toward her crying. It was something that surprised us both. E

It's only thinking about it now, 28 years later, that I realize I was crying from relief. I was with my teacher, and in a while I was going to sit at my desk, with my crayons and pencils and books anc classmates all around me, and for the next six hours I was going to enjoy a thoroughly **secure**, warm and stable world. It was a world I absolutely relied on. Without it, I don't know where I would have gone that morning. F

Mrs. LeSane asked me what wa wrong and when I said, "Nothing, she seemingly left it at that. But sh asked me if I would carry her purs for her, an honor above all honors, and she asked if I wanted to come into Room 2 early and paint.

4. **Rainier Valley:** a section of southeast Seattle.

DIFFERENTIATED INSTRUCTION

FOR LESS–PROFICIENT READERS

Reading Skill Follow-Up: Identify Cause and Effect Read aloud lines 87–96. Model the strategy by asking, "Why does everyone love the janitor?" Explain that "everyone loves the janitor" is an effect. Write this effect in the right-hand box of a cause-and-effect diagram. Invite students to find the cause and add it to the diagram.

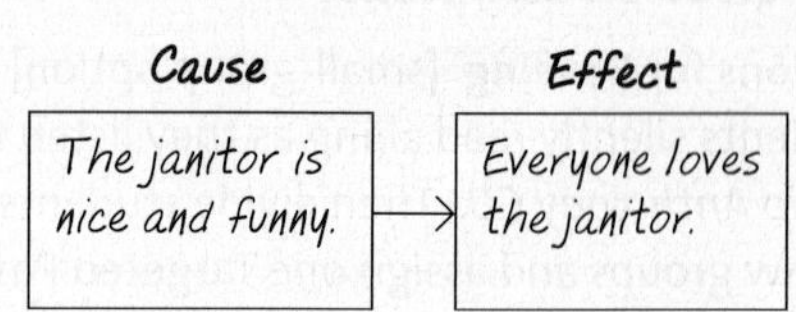

She believed in the natural healing power of painting and drawing for troubled children. In the back of her room there was always a drawing table and an easel with plenty of supplies, and sometimes during the day she would come up to you for what seemed like no good reason and quietly ask if you wanted to go to the back table and "make some pictures for Mrs. LeSane." We all had a chance at it—to sit apart from the class for a while to paint, draw and silently work out impossible problems on 11 × 17 sheets of newsprint.

Drawing came to mean everything to me. At the back table in Room 2, I learned to build myself a life preserver that I could carry into my home. **G**

We all know that a good education system saves lives, but the people of this country are still told that cutting the budget for public schools is necessary, that poor salaries for teachers are all we can manage and that art, music and all creative activities must be the first to go when times are lean.

Before- and after-school programs are cut and we are told that public schools are not made for baby-sitting children. If parents are **neglectful** temporarily or permanently, for whatever reason, it's certainly sad, but their unlucky children must fend for themselves. Or slip through the cracks.[5] Or wander in a dark night alone.

We are told in a thousand ways that not only are public schools not important, but that the children who attend them, the children who need them most, are not important either. We leave them to learn from the blind eye of a television, or to the mercy of "a thousand points of light"[6] that can be as far away as stars.

I was lucky. I had Mrs. LeSane. I had Mr. Gunderson. I had an abundance of art supplies. And I had a particular brand of neglect in my home that allowed me to slip away and get to them. But what about the rest of the kids who weren't as lucky? What happened to them?

By the time the bell rang that morning I had finished my drawing and Mrs. LeSane pinned it up on the special bulletin board she reserved for drawings from the back table. It was the same picture I always drew—a sun in the corner of a blue sky over a nice house with flowers all around it.

Mrs. LeSane asked us to please stand, face the flag, place our right hands over our hearts and say the Pledge of Allegiance. Children across the country do it faithfully. I wonder now when the country will face its children and say a pledge right back. **H**

5. **slip through the cracks:** become lost or harmed due to negligence.
6. **"a thousand points of light":** volunteers and charities—a metaphor from a 1989 speech by then-President George H. W. Bush.

(2) Targeted Passage

G AUTHOR'S PURPOSE
Reread lines 156–160. What do you think Barry means when she says she learned to build herself "a life preserver"?

neglectful (nĭ-glĕkt'fəl) *adj.* characterized by a failure to properly care for someone or something

H AUTHOR'S PURPOSE
Reread lines 161–215. Which sentence best sums up Barry's purpose?

ELEMENTS OF NONFICTION

G AUTHOR'S PURPOSE

Possible answer: *Drawing allows Barry to express herself and work out her problems, and it makes her feel special. This makes Barry's argument (that public school can help neglected children) more convincing.*

ELEMENTS OF NONFICTION

H AUTHOR'S PURPOSE

Possible answer: *"I wonder now when the country will face its children and say a pledge right back."*

Extend the Discussion Restate Barry's purpose in your own words.

SELECTION WRAP-UP

REFLECT Ask students what questions they would like to ask the author, and why.

CRITIQUE Ask students if they feel Barry's purpose has been accomplished or if they feel the essay should have included more details. Have them explain what kinds of additional details the author might have included.

FOR LESS-PROFICIENT READERS

(2) Targeted Passage [Lines 161–198]

In this passage, Barry argues that public schools need to take care of neglected children.

- What does Barry say the "people of this country are still [being] told"? Who is "telling" us this information?
- Does Barry think that providing before- and after-school programs is a good idea? Why?
- Why does Barry think that she was luckier than "the rest of the kids"?

FOR ADVANCED LEARNERS/PRE-AP

Analyze Persuasive Techniques [small-group option] Distribute copies of the Analysis Frame for persuasion. Have students discuss the questions in small groups. Then have them conclude by summarizing their findings for the rest of the class.

BEST PRACTICES TOOLKIT—Copy Masters
Analysis Frame: Persuasion pp. D23, D46, D47

Practice and Apply

After Reading

For additional support of postreading questions, use these copy masters:

RESOURCE MANAGER—Copy Masters

Reading Check p. 94 (to check understanding of the selection)

Author's Purpose p. 87 (for practice of elements of nonfiction standards focus)

Question Support p. 95 (After Reading questions adapted for English learners and less-proficient readers)

Additional selection questions are provided for teachers on page 81.

ANSWERS

Comprehension

1. *Barry walks to her school.*
2. *She cries out of relief because she feels she is in a safe place.*

Critical Analysis

Possible answers:

3. ● **STANDARDS FOCUS Identify Cause and Effect** *Students may say that the most important cause-and-effect relationship is that being in school causes Barry to feel less panicked. Barry draws a direct relationship between the quality of a child's school and a child's well-being.*
4. ***Line 17:*** *TV;* ***Lines 36–38:*** *the world outside;* ***Lines 80–81:*** *Barry and her brother at home. The image is powerful to Barry because it expresses her feelings of being ignored.*
5. *She wants Americans to "pledge" that they will make quality public school available for all students.*
6. ● **STANDARDS FOCUS Author's Purpose** *Some students may believe that many children share Barry's situation and will therefore find her argument convincing. Others may say that she overgeneralizes and does not provide enough evidence that schools should provide to all children the kind of benefits she describes.*
7. *Accept all reasonable answers. Example: Barry might not have gone on to college and become a successful cartoonist if she hadn't had the opportunity to participate in creative activities at school.*

After Reading

Comprehension

1. **Recall** Where does Lynda Barry go after she sneaks out of her house?
2. **Clarify** Why does Barry cry when she sees Mrs. LeSane?

Critical Analysis

3. **Examine Cause and Effect** Look back at the cause-and-effect diagrams you created as you read. Which cause-and-effect relationship do you think is most important to Barry's argument in favor of public schools?
4. **Interpret Imagery** Skim pages 996 and 998, and note the three places where Barry describes someone or something as having "the sound turned off." In a graphic like the one shown, tell what she is referring to in each case. Why do you think the image is so powerful to Barry?

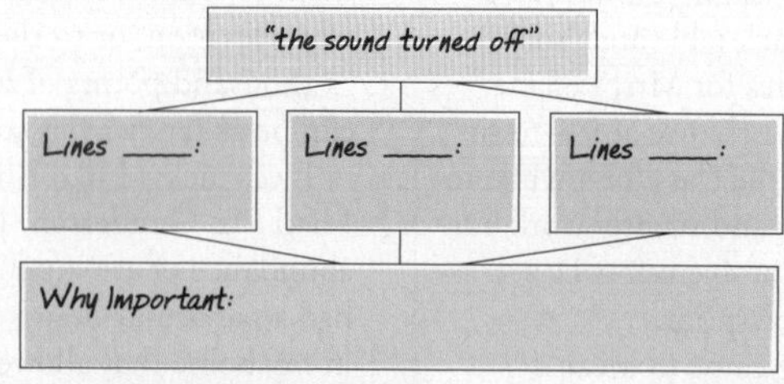

5. **Make Inferences** Reread the last paragraph of the essay. What is the "pledge" that Barry wants Americans to make to schoolchildren?
6. **Analyze Author's Purpose** The evidence Barry offers to persuade the reader comes from a single source—her personal experience. Generalizing from a single experience can be considered **overgeneralization.** Would you say Barry's argument is effective, or is her experience is too narrow to achieve her purpose? Explain.
7. **Draw Conclusions** How might Barry's life have been different if she hadn't had creative activities at school?

Extension and Challenge

8. **Big Question Activity** Revisit the notes you took on page 994. With your group, discuss whether reading Lynda Barry's essay changed your opinion about schools' three most important tasks.
9. **Inquiry and Research** Lynda Barry's essay encourages us to support public schools for the education and important **relationships** they offer to all students. Find out about the purpose of public education in the United States. When were public schools established and why? How are they funded? On the basis of what you find out, decide whether Barry's expectations for schools are reasonable.

RESEARCH LINKS
For more on public education in the United States, visit the **Research Center** at **ClassZone.com.**

Extension and Challenge

8. *Some students may find that reading the essay has changed their opinions; those who listed tasks similar to those Barry discusses in her essay may find that their opinions have not changed.*
9. *Students' opinions about whether Barry's expectations for schools are reasonable should be based on their research into the purposes of public education, as well as how they are funded, rather than personal beliefs.*

Vocabulary in Context

VOCABULARY PRACTICE

Choose the letter of the term that is most closely related to the boldfaced word.

1. **sanctuary**: (a) playground, (b) forest, (c) refuge
2. **nondescript:** (a) plain, (b) ugly, (c) beautiful
3. **secure:** (a) free, (b) safe, (c) loose
4. **neglectful:** (a) cruel, (b) bossy, (c) inattentive

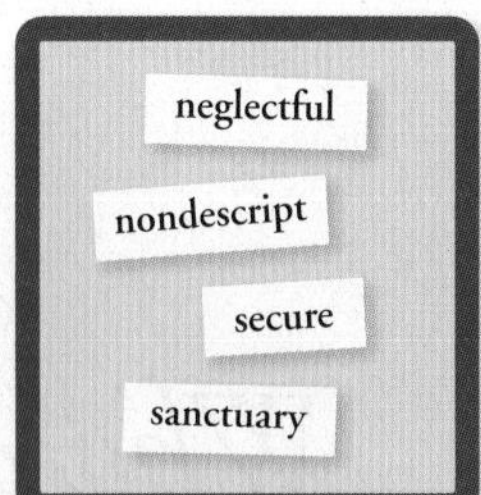

VOCABULARY IN WRITING

Using at least two vocabulary words, describe a place you consider a "sanctuary." You might start like this.

EXAMPLE SENTENCE

The tree house my brothers and I built has become our __sanctuary__.

VOCABULARY STRATEGY: RELATED WORDS

One strategy that can help you figure out the meaning of an unfamiliar word is to look for a relationship between it and a word you already know. For example, if you don't know the meaning of the word *nondescript*, you might recognize a similarity between that word and the word *descriptive*. You can then guess that *nondescript* has something to do with how much there is to describe.

PRACTICE Identify a word you know that relates to each numbered word. Then guess at the definition for the numbered word. Check your definition in a dictionary, and write a sentence using the word.

1. criminology
2. humanitarian
3. logistical
4. inconsolable
5. disenchantment
6. elongation

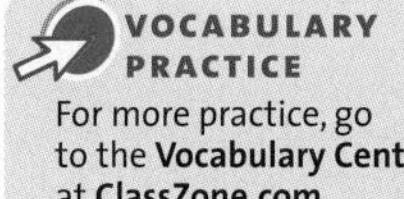

VOCABULARY PRACTICE
For more practice, go to the **Vocabulary Center** at **ClassZone.com.**

DIFFERENTIATED INSTRUCTION

FOR ENGLISH LEARNERS

Vocabulary Practice Make sure students understand the meaning of the phrase "most closely related" in the directions. Explain that one strategy for answering multiple-choice questions is to first eliminate any obviously wrong answers. If students still have difficulty choosing the correct term, allow them to return to the selection to find the definition of the boldfaced word.

FOR ADVANCED LEARNERS/PRE–AP

Vocabulary Strategy Challenge students to list as many words related to each of the numbered words as they can. Then have students choose one related word for each numbered word to include in a sentence. Have them include enough context clues so that others can determine the meaning of the related word just by reading the sentence. Ask students to exchange their sentences with a partner to see if their context clues are sufficient for defining the word.

ANSWERS

Vocabulary in Context

VOCABULARY PRACTICE

1. *(c) refuge*
2. *(a) plain*
3. *(b) safe*
4. *(c) inattentive*

RESOURCE MANAGER—Copy Master
Vocabulary Practice p. 92

VOCABULARY IN WRITING

Have students jot down ideas for their description and then decide which vocabulary words they might use in their writing.

VOCABULARY STRATEGY: RELATED WORDS

(also an EL language objective)

Suggest that students look for the root of each vocabulary word and then identify words that have the same root.

Possible answers:

1. *criminal; "the scientific study of criminal behavior and corrections"*
2. *human; "one who is devoted to the promotion of human welfare"*
3. *logic; "relating to the management of the details of an operation"*
4. *console; "impossible to console"*
5. *enchant; "state of being freed from illusion or false belief"*
6. *long; "the act of making longer"*

RESOURCE MANAGER—Copy Master
Vocabulary Strategy p. 93

Vocabulary Center at **ClassZone.com**
Additional Vocabulary Activities

Assess and Reteach

Assess

RESOURCE MANAGER—Copy Masters
Selection Tests A, B/C pp. 97–98, 99–100

Test Generator CD

Reteach

STANDARDS LESSON FILE
Reading Lesson 3: Determining Author's Purpose
Reading Lesson 7: Recognizing Cause and Effect
Vocabulary Lesson 12: Word Families and Derivatives

Focus and Motivate

OBJECTIVES

Elements of Nonfiction
- explore the key idea of what's **important**
- identify and analyze the influence of historical context
- read a speech and a letter

Reading
- identify and analyze comparisons and contrasts

Vocabulary
- build vocabulary for reading and writing
- use antonyms as context clues to determine word meaning *(also an EL language objective)*

SUMMARY

In his 1744 speech "Educating Sons," Iroquois Chief Canasatego thanks English colonists for their offer to educate Iroquois boys, but he points out that a university education would not prepare them for Iroquois life. In "The First Americans," the Grand Council Fire of American Indians urges the mayor of Chicago to correct the negative stereotypes and inaccuracies about Native Americans in textbooks.

Who decides what's IMPORTANT?

Discuss the question and the ***KEY IDEA*** of what's **important** to learn in school. Who decides what should be taught in schools? Should students have a say in the decision? Why or why not? After students work as a class on the ***SURVEY*** activity, give them the opportunity to move to a different corner if they have changed their mind about the most important thing they have learned in school.

Before Reading

Educating Sons
Speech by Chief Canasatego

The First Americans
Letter by the Grand Council Fire of American Indians

Who decides what's IMPORTANT?

KEY IDEA Not everyone agrees on what we should teach or on how it should be taught. Often what is considered **important** to learn depends on where and when we're living. For example, the speech and letter that follow were written before Native American cultures received much respect from European Americans. Native American leaders have had to argue that their culture, language, history, and way of life are useful knowledge.

SURVEY As a class, make a list of the most **important** and useful things you've learned in school. Vote on the top four and post them in the four corners of your classroom. Then go stand under the one that you consider most important. Why did you choose what you did? Present your reasons to the class.

1002

Selection Resources

RESOURCE MANAGER UNIT 9

Plan and Teach pp. 101–108

Elements of Nonfiction
Summary pp. 109†*, 110‡*
Historical Context pp. 111, 112†*
Question Support p. 119*

Reading
Identify Comparisons and Contrasts pp. 113, 114†*
Reading Check p. 118

Vocabulary
Study p. 115*
Practice p. 116
Strategy p. 117

Assessment
Selection Tests A, B/C pp. 121*, 123*
Test Generator CD

BEST PRACTICES TOOLKIT
Differentiated Instruction pp. 31–38*
Scaffolding Instruction pp. 43–46*

Graphic Organizers/Strategies
Word Questioning

Reading Support
Audio Anthology CD*

Technology
Literature and Vocabulary Centers at **ClassZone.com**
Write*Smart* CD

* Resources for Differentiation † Also in Spanish ‡ In Haitian Creole and Vietnamese

ELEMENTS OF NONFICTION: HISTORICAL CONTEXT

You'll understand the following selections better if you consider their **historical context**. This means thinking about the conditions and events that caused the authors to say or write what they did. The Background information on this page provides some historical context. As you read the speech and letter that follow, keep this information in mind.

READING SKILL: IDENTIFY COMPARISONS AND CONTRASTS

Writers often make their points by **comparing** and **contrasting** two subjects, pointing out the similarities and differences between them. For example, in the arguments you're about to read, the authors compare and contrast what is taught to young people with what the authors think should be taught. To help you keep track of the arguments, create a chart for each selection.

"Educating Sons"	
What Is Taught	*What Should Be Taught*

VOCABULARY IN CONTEXT

The following words help convey some Native Americans' viewpoints on education in the United States. To see how many you know, use the words to complete the sentences.

WORD LIST	decline	oratory	savage
	esteem	sacred	treacherous

1. For the Lakota people, the Black Hills region is a _____ place with deep religious significance.
2. Because of his famous speech "I will fight no more forever," Chief Joseph is known for his brilliant _____.
3. To call someone a _____ is to say that he is uncivilized.
4. Because the United States broke so many treaties, most Native Americans viewed the government as _____.
5. Many Cherokees chose to _____ offers by the government and were forcibly removed from their land.
6. In most Native cultures, grandparents are held in high _____ and treated with respect.

Author Online

A Man of Influence Chief Canasatego of the Onondaga Tribe was an influential leader in the Iroquois Confederacy, a group of tribes in the upper New York State area. Benjamin Franklin used Canasatego's ideas in his early plans for colonial union.

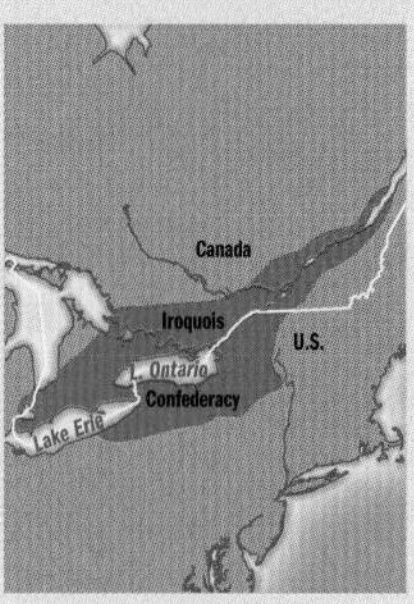

Background

A "No Thank You" Speech In the 1700s, the British and the French were competing for land and resources in North America. English colonists thought that by offering Iroquois boys the chance to attend the university in Virginia, they would convince the Iroquois to support their side. The Iroquois, however, didn't want to send their sons to the school, for reasons made clear in Chief Canasatego's 1744 speech.

The Grand Council Fire of American Indians In 1927, Mayor William Hale Thompson of Chicago raised a protest against school textbooks he believed presented history in a way that was prejudiced in favor of Great Britain. The mayor wanted to revise textbooks to be what he called "100 percent American." The members of the Grand Council Fire of American Indians—led by its president Scott H. Peters, a Chippewa Indian—wanted to point out that the British were not the only group portrayed inaccurately in textbooks. They wrote a letter asking the mayor to change texts to reflect the perspectives and accomplishments of Native Americans. They wore full ceremonial dress and war paint when presenting the mayor with their letter.

MORE ABOUT THE AUTHOR AND BACKGROUND
To learn more about Chief Canasatego and the Grand Council Fire of American Indians, visit the **Literature Center** at **ClassZone.com.**

1003

Teach

STANDARDS FOCUS

ELEMENTS OF NONFICTION

● HISTORICAL CONTEXT

Have students read the **Background** information and summarize the conditions and events that caused the authors to write each selection they are about to read.

CHECK UNDERSTANDING Ask students how understanding the historical context might affect their understanding and appreciation of each selection.

READING SKILL

■ IDENTIFY COMPARISONS AND CONTRASTS

Remind students that one way to identify comparisons and contrasts is to look for transition words that signal comparisons (*also, likewise, similarly*) and contrasts (*but, however, despite*).

CHECK UNDERSTANDING Ask students to brainstorm a list of transition words that signal comparisons and contrasts.

 RESOURCE MANAGER—Copy Master
Identify Comparisons and Contrasts p. 113 (for student use while reading the selections)

VOCABULARY SKILL

▲ VOCABULARY IN CONTEXT

DIAGNOSE WORD KNOWLEDGE To determine preteaching needs, have all students complete **Vocabulary in Context.** ***Answers:*** **1.** *sacred* **2.** *oratory* **3.** *savage* **4.** *treacherous* **5.** *decline* **6.** *esteem*

PRETEACH VOCABULARY Use the Vocabulary Study copy master to help students determine the meaning of each boldfaced word.

1. Read aloud the first sentence, emphasizing the boldfaced word.
2. Ask students to think about the way the word is used. Discuss possible meanings for *decline,* such as "turn down."
3. Repeat for each of the other sentences.
4. Have students complete the chart in Part B independently.

 RESOURCE MANAGER—Copy Master
Vocabulary Study p. 115

For general guidelines on differentiating vocabulary instruction and for alternative vocabulary activities for students not needing vocabulary preteaching, see

BEST PRACTICES TOOLKIT
Scaffolding Vocabulary Instruction pp. 43–46

Vocabulary Center at **ClassZone.com**
Additional Vocabulary Activities

Practice and Apply

Lines 1–7
DISCUSSION PROMPTS

Use these prompts to help students understand Chief Canasatego's message:

Recall What evidence does Chief Canasatego have that the colonists' intentions are good? ***Possible answer:*** *The colonists respect their colleges and are willing to spend their own money to educate the Iroquois boys.*

Infer Notice the warm, appreciative tone of lines 1–4. Why do you think Canasatego begins his speech in this way? ***Possible answer:*** *He understands that an effective way to begin a persuasive speech is to appeal to the vanity of the audience.*

Interpret What does Canasatego mean when he says, "But you who are so wise must know that different nations have different conceptions of things"? ***Possible answer:*** *People as wise as those who made the offer must understand that Onondaga society has different values from theirs and different ideas about education.*

ELEMENTS OF NONFICTION

Ⓐ HISTORICAL CONTEXT

Possible answer: *Onondaga life was physically demanding and required survival skills such as the ability to hunt and build shelter; Chief Canasatego's society needed to prepare its young men to be hunters, warriors, and councilors.*

If students need help . . . Read aloud lines 10–15. Ask: If such men are "good for nothing," then what qualities would make a man useful? What does this tell you about the way the Onondaga live?

EDUCATING SONS

Chief Canasatego

esteem (ĭ-stēm') *v.* to regard with respect

We know you highly **esteem** the kind of learning taught in these colleges. And the maintenance of our young men, while with you, would be very expensive to you. We're convinced, therefore, that you mean to do us good by your proposal, and we thank you heartily. But you who are so wise must know that different nations have different conceptions of things. And you will not, therefore, take it amiss[1] if our ideas of this kind of education happens not to be the same with yours.

Targeted Passage ①

Ⓐ **HISTORICAL CONTEXT** What can you **infer** about Chief Canasatego's Onondaga society?

We have had some experience of it. Several of our young people were formerly brought up in the colleges of the northern province. They were instructed in all your sciences. But when they came back to us, they were bad runners, ignorant of every means of living in the woods, unable to bear either cold or hunger, knew neither how to build a cabin, take a deer, or kill an enemy, spoke our language imperfectly, and therefore were neither fit for hunters nor warriors nor councilors. They were totally good for nothing. Ⓐ

decline (dĭ-klīn') *v.* to politely refuse

We are, however, not the less obliged[2] for your kind offer, though we **decline** accepting. To show our grateful sense of it, if the gentlemen of Virginia will send us a dozen of their sons, we would take great care in their education, instruct them in all we know, and make men of them.

1. **take it amiss:** be offended.
2. **obliged** (ə-blījd'): grateful or indebted.

DIFFERENTIATED INSTRUCTION

FOR ALL STUDENTS

Expert Groups Encourage groups of students to become experts on one of these topics. Students should then present their findings, using visuals as appropriate.

- Black Partridge
- Native Americans' contributions during World War I
- Shabbona
- Chief Canasatego

For further details on this project, see

RESOURCE MANAGER
Ideas for Extension pp. 104–105

FOR LESS-PROFICIENT READERS

In combination with the *Audio Anthology CD*, use one or more Targeted Passages (pp. 1004, 1006) to ensure that students focus on key concepts and skills in the selections.

① Targeted Passage [Lines 8–19]

In this passage, Chief Canasatego outlines his reasons for declining the colonists' offer.

- What experience helps Canasatego predict what will happen to the Iroquois boys if the Iroquois accept the offer?
- What does he mean when he says, "They were totally good for nothing"?
- Reread lines 16–19. What point does Chief Canasatego make in the conclusion of his speech?

ANALYZE VISUALS
What three **adjectives** best describe the boy in this photograph?

ANALYZE VISUALS

Possible answer:

- *strong*
- *proud*
- *impressive*

Lines 8–15
REINFORCE *KEY IDEA:* IMPORTANT

Discuss Why do you think the Iroquois and the colonists have such different ideas about what type of education is **important** for turning boys into men? ***Possible answer:*** *The two groups have extremely different lifestyles, so what the colonists consider to be important, such as knowledge of the sciences, is not useful in the Iroquois culture, which requires an intimate and practical knowledge of the natural world for survival.*

ADDITIONAL TEACHING OPPORTUNITY

Hidden Agenda Remind students that a text can have more than one layer of meaning. In fiction, the events of the plot are one layer, and themes are another layer. In a speech such as Chief Canasatego's, the apparent message can coexist with a hidden agenda. Ask students to identify the more obvious and superficial reason for the speech as well as its hidden agenda. ***Possible answer:*** *The apparent message is a polite decline of the colonists' offer. The hidden agenda is a commentary on how poorly the white man's education served Iroquois boys in the past and a condemnation of such a soft, impractical education for young men.*

FOR ENGLISH LEARNERS

Options for Reading Read the first Targeted Passage aloud. Make sure students understand the historical context in which the speech was given. Then have students read the entire speech and the letter silently as they listen to the *Audio Anthology CD.*

Prereading For prereading instruction for English learners, see

 **BEST PRACTICES TOOLKIT**
Scaffolding Reading Instruction pp. 43–46

Key Academic Vocabulary Have students use Word Questioning to study these words: in "Educating Sons," *convinced* (line 3), *instructed* (line 10), *ignorant* (line 11); in "The First Americans," *incidents* (line 10), *designs* (line 33), *culture* (line 67).

BEST PRACTICES TOOLKIT—Transparency
Word Questioning p. E9

FOR ADVANCED LEARNERS/PRE–AP

Pre-AP exercises in the bottom channel provide additional challenge for your advanced students. Use them for small groups or individuals.

ADDITIONAL GUIDELINES

For more help with differentiation and tips for classroom management, see

 **BEST PRACTICES TOOLKIT**
Differentiated Instruction pp. 31–38

READING SKILL

B COMPARISONS AND CONTRASTS

Possible answer:

What Is Taught
• *Native American victories are portrayed as massacres.*
• *Native Americans are described as violent, murderous, and treacherous.*
• *The textbooks say that Native Americans were always fighting each other.*

Lines 1–23

DISCUSSION PROMPTS

Use these prompts to help students understand the Grand Council's motivation for writing the letter:

Recall Based on the historical context you read on page 1003, why does the Grand Council point out that Native Americans are "the only ones, truly, that are 100 percent"? ***Answer:*** *This is a reference to Mayor Thompson's campaign to make textbooks "100 percent American."*

Analyze What is the effect of using the term *massacre* instead of *battle* to refer to a Native American victory? ***Possible answer:*** *The word* massacre *has a negative connotation, suggesting a brutal slaughter of innocent people. The word* battle *suggests a legitimate struggle between opposing sides of a conflict. The use of* massacre *makes Native Americans seem savage and immoral and ignores any legitimate reasons they might have had for fighting.*

Evaluate In lines 22–23, the Grand Council says, "It is true that we had our own small battles." What is the effect of this admission on the Grand Council's persuasive argument? ***Possible answer:*** *This admission allows the Grand Council to provide a counterargument that strengthens the Grand Council's argument.*

The First Americans

The Grand Council Fire of American Indians

DECEMBER 1, 1927

TO THE MAYOR OF CHICAGO:—

You tell all white men "America First." We believe in that. We are the only ones, truly, that are 100 percent. We therefore ask you while you are teaching school children about America First, teach them truth about the First Americans.

We do not know if school histories are pro-British, but we do know that they are unjust to the life of our people—the American Indian. They call all white victories, battles, and all Indian victories, massacres. The battle with Custer[1] has been taught to school children as a fearful massacre on our part. We ask that this, as well as other incidents, be told fairly. If the Custer battle was a massacre, what was Wounded Knee?[2]

Targeted Passage ②

History books teach that Indians were murderers—is it murder to fight in self-defense? Indians killed white men because white men took their lands, ruined their hunting grounds, burned their forests, destroyed their buffalo. White men penned our people on reservations, then took away the reservations. White men who rise to protect their property are called patriots—Indians who do the same are called murderers.

White men call Indians **treacherous**—but no mention is made of broken treaties on the part of the white man. White men say that Indians were always fighting. It was only our lack of skill in white man's warfare that led to our defeat. An Indian mother prayed that her boy be a great medicine man[3] rather than a great warrior. It is true that we had our own small battles, but in the main we were peace-loving and home-loving. **B**

White men called Indians thieves—and yet we lived in frail skin lodges and needed no locks or iron bars. White men call Indians **savages.** What is civilization? Its marks are a noble religion and philosophy, original arts, stirring music, rich history and legend. We had these. Then we were not savages, but a civilized race.

We made blankets that were beautiful that the white man with all his machinery has never been able to duplicate. We made baskets that

treacherous (trĕch'ər-əs) *adj.* not to be relied on; untrustworthy

B COMPARISONS AND CONTRASTS
Reread lines 6–23. According to the Grand Council Fire members, what do textbooks teach about Native Americans? Add this information to your chart.

savage (săv'ĭj) *n.* a person regarded as primitive or uncivilized

1. **Custer:** George Armstrong Custer (1839–1876), a U.S. cavalry officer who fought Sioux and Cheyenne warriors at Little Bighorn; Custer was killed and his army was wiped out.
2. **Wounded Knee:** a creek in South Dakota where U.S. troops massacred about 200 Native Americans on December 29, 1890.
3. **medicine man:** a Native-American holy man and healer.

1006 UNIT 9: ARGUMENT AND PERSUASION

DIFFERENTIATED INSTRUCTION

FOR LESS-PROFICIENT READERS

② Targeted Passage [Lines 7–28]

In this passage, the Grand Council explains the inaccuracies in textbooks.

- According to the Grand Council, in what way are Native Americans represented in textbooks?
- According to the Grand Council, why did Native Americans fight and kill white men?
- According to the Grand Council, what led to the Native Americans' defeat?
- According to the Grand Council, what makes the Native Americans a civilized race?

FOR ADVANCED LEARNERS/PRE-AP

Analyze Style [small-group option] Have students work in small groups to skim the letter for places where the Grand Council poses questions for readers, such as "What is civilization?" (lines 25–26). Ask groups to discuss whether the questions help or hurt the argument. In what ways? Invite groups to share their opinions with the class.

were beautiful. We wove in beads and colored quills, designs that were not just decorative motifs, but were the outward expression of our very thoughts. We made pottery—pottery that was useful and beautiful as well. Why not make school children acquainted with the beautiful handicrafts in which we were skilled? Put in every school Indian blankets, baskets, pottery.

We sang songs that carried in their melodies all the sounds of nature—the running of waters, the sighing of winds, and the calls of the animals. Teach these to your children that they may come to love nature as we love it.

We had our statesmen—and their **oratory** has never been equalled. Teach the children some of these speeches of our people, remarkable for their brilliant oratory.

We played games—games that brought good health and sound bodies. Why not put these in your schools? We told stories. Why not teach school children more of the wholesome proverbs and legends of our people? Tell them how we loved all that was beautiful. That we killed game only for food, not for fun. Indians think white men who kill for fun are murderers. **C**

Tell your children of the friendly acts of Indians to the white people who first settled here. Tell them of our leaders and heroes and their deeds. Tell them of Indians such as Black Partridge,[4] Shabbona,[5] and others who many times saved the people of Chicago at great danger to themselves. Put in your history books the Indian's part in the World War.[6] Tell how the Indian fought for a country of which he was not a citizen, for a flag to which he had no claim, and for a people that have treated him unjustly. **D**

The Indian has long been hurt by these unfair books. We ask only that our story be told in fairness. We do not ask you to overlook what we did, but we do ask you to understand it. A true program of America First will give a generous place to the culture and history of the American Indian.

We ask this, Chief, to keep **sacred** the memory of our people.

oratory (ôr'ə-tôr'ē) *n.* the art of making speeches

C COMPARISONS AND CONTRASTS
Reread lines 39–54. What does the Grand Council suggest schools should teach?

D HISTORICAL CONTEXT
Why does the Grand Council mention Native Americans who helped the people of Chicago?

sacred (sā'krĭd) *adj.* holy; worthy of religious veneration or respect

4. **Black Partridge:** a Potawatomi chief who befriended white settlers.
5. **Shabbona** (shä'bō-nə): a member of the Ottawa people who befriended white settlers.
6. **World War:** World War I (1914–1918), in which Great Britain, France, the United States, and their allies defeated Germany, Austria-Hungary, and their allies.

ADDITIONAL TEACHING OPPORTUNITY

Cultural and Ethnic Values Point out to students that the writer's cultural and ethnic values often have an impact on the content of a text. Note that the values and beliefs of the writers of the history textbooks cited in the letter may have had an impact on the content of their texts. Ask students to infer what the textbook writers believed about themselves and about Native Americans.

READING SKILL

C COMPARISONS AND CONTRASTS

Remind students to record their answers in the chart from page 1003. ***Possible answer:*** *The Grand Council suggests that schools should teach Native American handicrafts, songs, oratory, games, and proverbs and legends, as well as Native Americans' reverence for nature.*

ELEMENTS OF NONFICTION

D HISTORICAL CONTEXT

Possible answer: *The audience for the speech is the mayor of Chicago, so the Grand Council wants to remind him that he owes them a favor.*

SELECTION WRAP-UP

REFLECT Ask students which details in the letter they found most surprising, and why.

★ CRITIQUE Have students consider which argument they found more effective. What made the argument especially convincing?

FOR LESS-PROFICIENT READERS

Reading Skill Follow-Up: Identify Comparisons and Contrasts [paired option] Have students work in pairs to create a chart for "The First Americans" like the one shown on page 1003. Under "What Is Taught," they should list information that Native Americans consider untrue; under "What Should Be Taught," they should list what the Grand Council considers to be true about Native Americans and wants children to be taught about their culture.

"The First Americans"

What Is Taught	*What Should Be Taught*
Native Americans	*Native Americans*
• *are murderers*	• *fight to protect their property*
• *are treacherous*	• *strive for peace*
• *are always fighting each other*	• *need no locks on their homes*
• *are thieves*	• *are a civilized race skilled in handicrafts, music, oratory, games, and history*
• *are savages*	• *have helped white settlers many times and fought for the United States*

Practice and Apply

After Reading

For additional support of postreading questions, use these copy masters:

RESOURCE MANAGER—Copy Masters

Reading Check p. 118 (to check understanding of the selection)

Historical Context p. 111 (for practice of elements of nonfiction standards focus)

Question Support p. 119 (After Reading questions adapted for English learners and less-proficient readers)

Additional selection questions are provided for teachers on page 105.

ANSWERS

Comprehension

1. *The Iroquois allowed their sons to be educated in the colonists' schools in the past, and the boys did not learn anything that was useful in Iroquois society.*
2. *The textbooks refer to "Indian victories" as massacres.*
3. *The Grand Council would like textbooks to emphasize Native American weaving, pottery, music, speeches, games, and stories.*

Critical Analysis

Possible answers:

4. *Chief Canasatego's polite tone seems congenial, and his words suggest that he wants to be helpful. However, he is really meeting the condescension of the "gentlemen's" offer by extending a similarly condescending offer to educate their sons. He is also implying that the Iroquois education would make "men" of their sons in a way that European education cannot.*
5. **● STANDARDS FOCUS Historical Context** *They felt they had a voice. The letter shows Native Americans asking for respect and pointing out ways they have served their country even though the country did not treat them well.*
6. **■ STANDARDS FOCUS Identify Comparisons and Contrasts** *Students' summaries should note that Native Americans want textbooks to acknowledge their cultural accomplishments and contributions to this country. They want textbooks to stop promoting negative stereotypes of Native Americans.*
7. ***Chief Canasatego:*** *1. ability to withstand cold and hunger, 2. knowledge of how to build a cabin, 3. ability to kill a deer;* ***Grand Council:*** *1. arts and music, 2. history and legends, 3. oratory;* ***Common Values:*** *physical fitness, self-sufficiency, oratory*

Extension and Challenge

8. *Groups should identify the most important thing that the authors would consider important to learn and cite examples from the selections to support their arguments. Then, groups should decide if these things are still important today and give reasons to support their opinion.*
9. **SOCIAL STUDIES CONNECTION** *Students' research should demonstrate an understanding that in both of these battles, large numbers of people were slaughtered. Both were massacres, as the Grand Council points out in lines 8–11.*

After Reading

Comprehension

1. **Recall** Why does Chief Canasatego not want to send Iroquois sons to be educated by the colonists?
2. **Recall** According to the Grand Council Fire of American Indians, how do textbooks refer to "Indian victories"?
3. **Summarize** What cultural activities does the Grand Council Fire of American Indians think should be emphasized in textbooks?

Critical Analysis

4. **Analyze Irony** Irony occurs when what the speaker says is different from what he or she actually means. Reread lines 16–19 of "Educating Sons." What is the irony in these closing remarks? Explain your answer.
5. **Examine Historical Context** In the 1920s, Native Americans began to receive better treatment and greater rights from the federal government. In 1924, Native Americans were finally granted citizenship, which meant that for the first time, many could vote. How do you think these changes might have affected the Grand Council's decision to speak up?
6. **Identify Comparisons and Contrasts** Review the chart you completed as you read "The First Americans." Summarize the difference between what was being taught to children and what the Grand Council thought should be taught.
7. **Draw Conclusions About Values** In a Y-chart like the one shown, list three values that Chief Canasatego and the Grand Council each argue are **important** in their cultures. List the values that are common to both cultures in the stem of the Y. What conclusion can you draw about how Native American values changed over time?

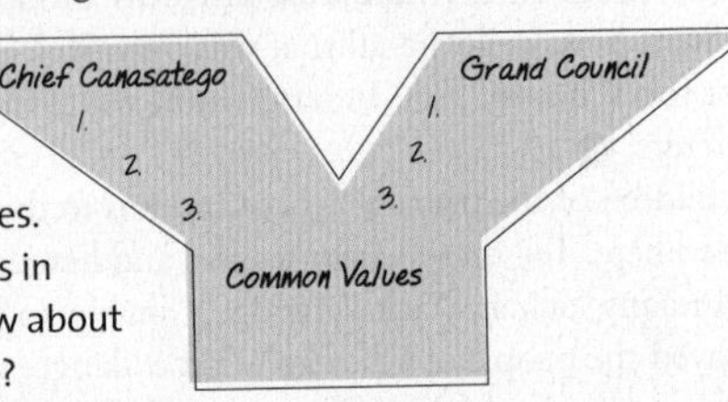

Extension and Challenge

8. **Readers' Circle** With a group, decide what each author would say is the most important thing for young people to learn. Cite lines from the speech and letter to support your views. Then discuss whether these things are still important to learn today.

George Custer, who led American forces at Little Bighorn

9.  **SOCIAL STUDIES CONNECTION** Research the Battle of Little Bighorn or the Battle of Wounded Knee. What does this information add to your understanding of the Grand Council's argument?

RESEARCH LINKS
For more on the Battle of Little Big Horn and the Battle of Wounded Knee, visit the **Research Center** at **ClassZone.com.**

Vocabulary in Context

VOCABULARY PRACTICE

For each item, choose the word that differs most in meaning from the other words. Refer to a dictionary if you need help.

1. (a) esteem, (b) revere, (c) admire, (d) scorn
2. (a) decline, (b) accept, (c) invite, (d) welcome
3. (a) loyal, (b) treacherous, (c) traitorous, (d) unreliable
4. (a) savage, (b) aristocrat, (c) scholar, (d) intellectual
5. (a) speeches, (b) oratory, (c) proclamations, (d) chitchat
6. (a) holy, (b) sacred, (c) sanctified, (d) profane

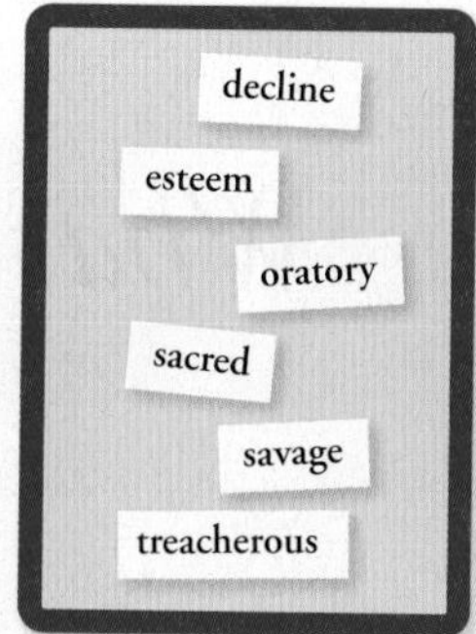

VOCABULARY IN WRITING

Imagine that a friend's family offers to teach you the traditions from their culture, which is different from yours. Using at least two vocabulary words, write a short speech in which you accept or decline the offer. You might start like this.

EXAMPLE SENTENCE

I hope you know, I hold your culture in the highest ***esteem****. I understand you have so much to teach me.*

VOCABULARY STRATEGY: ANTONYMS AND CONTEXT CLUES

You can often find **context clues** in the words and phrases that surround an unfamiliar word. **Antonyms,** or words with opposite meanings, provide one kind of context clue. For example, a passage in "The First Americans" reads: "White men call Indians savages. . . . We had [religion, philosophy, arts, music, history, and legend]. Then we were not savages, but a civilized race." The words *not* and *but* signal that *savages* is an antonym for *civilized race.*

PRACTICE In each sentence, identify an antonym for each boldfaced word. Then define the boldfaced word.

1. Although I am **ignorant** of many things, I am very knowledgeable about cats.
2. I should feel **obliged** to her for the invitation, but I'm actually feeling ungrateful.
3. He was certainly not a patriot; in fact, he was a **traitor** to his country.
4. Please stop eating unhealthy food; eat something **wholesome** for a change!
5. My parents **overlooked** my untidy bedroom but punished me for lying.

VOCABULARY PRACTICE
For more practice, go to the **Vocabulary Center** at **ClassZone.com.**

ANSWERS

Vocabulary in Context

VOCABULARY PRACTICE

1. *(d) scorn*
2. *(a) decline*
3. *(a) loyal*
4. *(a) savage*
5. *(d) chitchat*
6. *(d) profane*

 RESOURCE MANAGER—Copy Master
Vocabulary Practice p. 116

VOCABULARY IN WRITING

Suggest that students review the vocabulary words to see which ones would work best with the speech they plan to write.

VOCABULARY STRATEGY: ANTONYMS AND CONTEXT CLUES *(also an EL language objective)*

Review with students words and phrases that can signal opposite meanings, such as *but, although, in fact, however,* and *on the other hand.* Point out that the context surrounding such words can give clues to the meaning of an unfamiliar word.

Possible answers:

1. *knowledgeable; "having no information about"*
2. *ungrateful; "thankful"*
3. *patriot; "person who betrays his or her country"*
4. *unhealthy; "good for your health"*
5. *punished; "ignored"*

RESOURCE MANAGER—Copy Master
Vocabulary Strategy p. 117

Vocabulary Center at **ClassZone.com**
Additional Vocabulary Activities

DIFFERENTIATED INSTRUCTION

FOR ENGLISH LEARNERS

Vocabulary Practice Encourage students to identify the vocabulary word in each set. Ask if they can recall how the word was used in the selections. If necessary, allow them to refer back to the usage in the selections and use the knowledge of the vocabulary word to narrow down the choices in each set.

FOR ADVANCED LEARNERS/PRE-AP

Vocabulary Strategy Challenge students to create new sentences with different antonyms for the boldfaced words.

Assess and Reteach

Assess

RESOURCE MANAGER—Copy Masters
Selection Tests A, B/C pp. 121–122, 123–124

Test Generator CD

Reteach

STANDARDS LESSON FILE

Informational Texts Lesson 5: Compare-and-Contrast Order

Vocabulary Lesson 18: Synonyms and Antonyms

Focus and Motivate

OBJECTIVES

Literary Analysis
- explore the key idea of **inspiration**
- identify and analyze effectiveness of persuasive techniques, including snob appeal
- read a drama excerpt

Reading
- paraphrase

Grammar and Writing
- use parallelism to link related ideas
- use writing to analyze literature

SUMMARY

In a speech given before the Battle of Agincourt on St. Crispian's Day, King Henry V rouses his men to battle with an appeal to their desire to be special and superior to others. They will long be remembered, he tells them, for their bravery in the face of danger and their willingness to sacrifice their lives. They will be counted with him as one of a "happy few, we band of brothers."

What INSPIRES *you?*

Discuss the question and the ***KEY IDEA*** of **inspiration.** Ask students why helping a baby bird or seeing a classmate do volunteer work could be inspirational. After students complete the ***QUICKWRITE*** activity, ask them to think of ways in which they could be inspiring to others. Suggest that they create a list in their journal of ways to inpire others to become better people.

Before Reading

St. Crispian's Day Speech

Drama excerpt from *Henry V* by William Shakespeare

What INSPIRES *you?*

KEY IDEA Nursing a baby bird to health might make you want to learn more about nature. Watching a classmate work for a worthy cause could cause you to volunteer, too. **Inspiration**—a strong emotion or desire to take action—can come from many places. You might find it in songs or pictures, or in people's words or deeds. In the speech you are about to read, a king uses words to inspire courage in the face of almost certain death.

QUICKWRITE In your journal, write a paragraph about an experience, person, event, or work of art that has **inspired** you. Has the source of your inspiration caused you to change your behavior or take action in some way?

Selection Resources

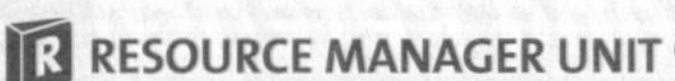

RESOURCE MANAGER UNIT 9

Plan and Teach pp. 125–132

Literary Analysis
Summary pp. 133†*, 134‡*
Persuasion in Literature pp. 135, 136†*
Question Support p. 140*

Reading
Paraphrase pp. 137, 138†*
Reading Check p. 139

Grammar and Writing
Use Correct Sentence Structure p. 141

Assessment
Selection Tests A, B/C pp. 143*, 145*
Test Generator CD

BEST PRACTICES TOOLKIT
Differentiated Instruction pp. 31–38*
Scaffolding Instruction pp. 43–46*

Graphic Organizers/Strategies
Use Video to Support Reading • Reporter's Questions

Reading Support
Audio Anthology CD*

Technology
Literature and Writing Centers at **ClassZone.com**
Write*Smart* CD

* Resources for Differentiation † Also in Spanish ‡ In Haitian Creole and Vietnamese

LITERARY ANALYSIS: PERSUASION IN LITERATURE

Playwrights often have their characters use the same persuasive techniques that nonfiction authors do. In this dramatic speech, King Henry's goal is to get his men to fight against a much stronger enemy. To do this he uses an age-old persuasive technique. This technique, now called **snob appeal,** is often used in advertising to appeal to a person's desire to be special or to think that he or she is "better than everyone else." For example, to convince you to buy designer jeans, an ad might say, "You're not ordinary, so why should you wear ordinary jeans?" As you read the speech, pay attention to how King Henry "sells" the idea of joining in the battle.

READING STRATEGY: PARAPHRASE

When you **paraphrase,** you restate something in your own words. Paraphrasing is different than summarizing. A summary covers only the work's most important points. A paraphrase covers all the content and should be about the same length as or longer than the original. If you can accurately restate the meaning of a written work in your own words, you can be certain that you understand it.

As you read "St. Crispian's Day Speech," watch for where each idea begins and ends. Paying attention to punctuation marks such as commas and dashes, as well as line breaks, will help you. Figure out the meaning of important terms by looking at footnotes, context clues, or the dictionary. Then paraphrase each idea in a chart like the one shown.

Lines	Paraphrase
1–4	*It's St. Crispian's Day. The men who survive today's battle will stand above others and feel proud every year when St. Crispian's Day comes around.*

Author Online

Writer, Actor, Businessman

William Shakespeare
1564–1616

William Shakespeare played many roles. He was the main playwright for a theater troupe called Lord Chamberlain's Men. As part owner, Shakespeare shared in the company's profits. He was also a frequent performer on stage. While he was popular during his time, with each passing century his fame has grown. His plays are still performed and adapted for the stage and screen, and his poetry is constantly quoted and taught. He is now considered one of the finest writers in the English language.

MORE ABOUT THE AUTHOR
For more on William Shakespeare, visit the **Literature Center** at **ClassZone.com.**

Background

Henry V Shakespeare's play describes the adventures of Henry V, king of England from 1413 to 1422. His reign occurred during the Hundred Years' War, in which the English and French fought for control of France. The Battle of Agincourt, a turning point in the war, is the setting for the following speech. It was 1415, and the English troops were attempting to return to England from France, where they had lost a lot of men. Their route was blocked by 20,000 to 30,000 French soldiers. King Henry had only about 6,000 men under his command. St. Crispian's Day dawned with the two armies preparing for battle. Thanks to Henry's brilliant leadership and France's poor choice of battlefields, the English were able to defeat a much larger enemy force. In 1420, Henry was recognized as the heir to the French throne.

Teach

STANDARDS FOCUS

LITERARY ANALYSIS

● PERSUASION IN LITERATURE

Read these examples aloud:

- This Super-Luxury car will make you the envy of the neighborhood.
- JOG sports drink will give you the edge you need to win the race.

Ask students: Which example uses snob appeal to sell a product? ***Answer:*** *The first example uses snob appeal by suggesting that the owner of the car will be admired by everyone else.*

CHECK UNDERSTANDING Have students share advertisements they know that use snob appeal to sell a product or service.

READING STRATEGY

■ PARAPHRASE

Have students paraphrase the information about William Shakespeare on page 1011. Remind them to cover all the facts but to use words they would use to explain the information to a friend.

CHECK UNDERSTANDING Ask students to explain how paraphrasing can help improve a reader's comprehension of a difficult text.

 **RESOURCE MANAGER—Copy Master**
Paraphrase p. 137 (for student use while reading the selection)

DIFFERENTIATED INSTRUCTION

FOR ALL STUDENTS

Expert Groups Encourage groups of students to choose one of these topics on which to become experts:

- King Henry V
- the Battle of Agincourt
- nobility and commoners in the 1400s

For general guidelines on differentiating instruction, see

 **BEST PRACTICES TOOLKIT**
Differentiated Instruction pp. 31–38

FOR LESS-PROFICIENT READERS

Vocabulary Support Tell students that Shakespeare's language, which is highly poetic and also includes idioms from the English spoken 400 years ago, is difficult for many modern readers to understand. Remind them to read slowly and to identify the beginning and ending of each complete thought, which may run over several lines. Suggest that they use context clues, the footnotes, and a dictionary to help them find the meanings of words and phrases they find difficult to understand.

FOR ENGLISH LEARNERS

Options for Reading Give students an opportunity to hear Shakespearean English before they read the speech. Find a copy of a movie version of *Henry V* and play the speech, which is in Act IV, Scene 3. Then have students listen to the *Audio Anthology CD* while they read along with the speech.

 **BEST PRACTICES TOOLKIT**
Use Video to Support Reading p. A4

Practice and Apply

ANALYZE VISUALS

Possible answer: *The men are enthusiastic and willing to follow the king.*

LITERARY ANALYSIS

Ⓐ PERSUASION

Possible answer: *The king promises that when the men are old and have forgotten many other details of their lives, they will still recall with pride their deeds in this battle.*

Lines 10–21

REINFORCE *KEY IDEA:* INSPIRATION

Discuss What aspect of the tales told by the men who survive the battle will **inspire** future generations? ***Possible answer:*** *Future generations will probably be inspired by the men's courage in the face of death.*

READING STRATEGY

Ⓑ PARAPHRASE

Have students record their answers in the chart from page 1011. ***Possible answer:*** *The elite men of England, safely at home in bed, will regret missing the battle and will feel inferior to those who did fight on St. Crispian's Day. These lines might motivate Henry's men by making them think they will be admired more than their social superiors—the "gentlemen" of England.*

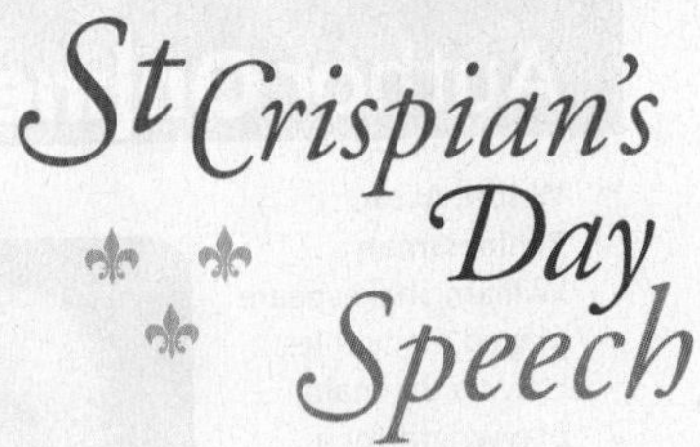

William Shakespeare

This day is call'd the feast of Crispian:[1]
He that outlives this day, and comes safe home,
Will stand a' tiptoe when this day is named,
And rouse him at the name of Crispian.
He that shall live this day, and see old age,
Will yearly on the vigil feast his neighbors,
And say, "To-morrow is Saint Crispian."
Then will he strip his sleeve and show his scars,
And say, "These wounds I had on Crispin's day."
Old men forget; yet all shall be forgot,
But he'll remember with advantages
What feats he did that day. Then shall our names,
Familiar in his mouth as household words,
Harry the King, Bedford and Exeter,
Warwick and Talbot, Salisbury and Gloucester,[2]
Be in their flowing cups freshly remember'd. Ⓐ
This story shall the good man teach his son;
And Crispin Crispian shall ne'er go by,
From this day to the ending of the world,
But we in it shall be remembered—
We few, we happy few, we band of brothers;
For he to-day that sheds his blood with me
Shall be my brother; be he ne'er so vile,[3]
This day shall gentle his condition;
And gentlemen in England, now a-bed,
Shall think themselves accurs'd they were not here;
And hold their manhoods cheap[4] whiles any speaks
That fought with us upon Saint Crispin's day. Ⓑ

ANALYZE VISUALS
In this film still from *Henry V*, what can you **infer** about the relationship between King Henry and his troops?

Ⓐ PERSUASION
What does the king promise his men in lines 10–16?

Ⓑ PARAPHRASE
Restate lines 25–28 in your own words. Why might these lines inspire Henry's men?

1. **the feast of Crispian** (krĭs′pē-ən): religious day honoring two martyred brothers (Crispian and Crispin). It falls on October 25, the day of the Battle of Agincourt.
2. **Bedford and Exeter** (ĕk′sĭ-tər), **Warwick** (wôr′ĭk) **and Talbot, Salisbury** (sôlz′bĕr′ē) **and Gloucester** (glŏs′tər): noblemen who fought with the king at the Battle of Agincourt.
3. **be he ne'er so vile:** no matter how humble or lowborn he is.
4. **hold their manhoods cheap:** not consider themselves very strong or brave.

DIFFERENTIATED INSTRUCTION

FOR LESS–PROFICIENT READERS

Comprehension Support Make sure students understand that the purpose of Henry's speech is to convince his listeners to join him in fighting a battle that may well prove fatal. Point out that the speech can be divided into two parts: lines 1–16, in which Henry describes how his men will brag about the battle on its yearly anniversary; and lines 17–28, in which he claims that these men will be his "brothers," envied by all for their bravery.

FOR ENGLISH LEARNERS

Vocabulary Support Students may have difficulty with some of the vocabulary and punctuation in the speech. Be sure to explain words and terms such as these:

- *a' tiptoe* (line 3), "tall with pride"
- *rouse him* (line 4), "become interested and alert"
- *vigil* (line 6), "eve of the holy day"
- *feats* (line 12), "brave deeds"
- *ne'er* (line 23), "never"
- *accurs'd* (line 26), "unlucky"

Lines 1–28

DISCUSSION PROMPTS

Use these prompts to help students understand the main ideas of the speech:

Connect In this speech, King Henry motivates the soldiers to join him in a battle in which they might die. Would his speech have motivated you to join him? Explain. *Responses will vary but should relate to the speech.*

Analyze Why does the king tell the men that the names in lines 14–15 will be to each soldier as "Familiar in his mouth as household words" (line 13)? In what way is this idea persuasive? ***Possible answer:*** *This is an example of snob appeal. The king is suggesting that the soldiers will be able to mention the names of famous and powerful men as if they are personal friends.*

Synthesize What does this speech reveal about the qualities a good leader needs to possess? ***Possible answer:*** *It shows that a good leader must understand what motivates his or her followers, and that he or she must make listeners believe that the leader cares about them and is an equal in times of crisis.*

SELECTION WRAP–UP

REFLECT Have students select the line or phrase from the speech that they think is most stirring or memorable. Ask them to explain what appeals to them about the line or phrase they chose.

CRITIQUE Tell students that many of Shakespeare's plays are written in rhyming verse. Point out that there is no end rhyme in the lines of this speech. Would rhyming verse have been more effective? Why or why not?

FOR LESS–PROFICIENT READERS

Reading Strategy Follow-Up: Paraphrase Have students read and paraphrase lines 17–24. Have them add this paraphrase to the chart on page 1011. Remind students to use the footnotes and context clues to help them understand the passage. ***Possible answer:*** *Each year on St. Crispian's Day, men will share their story with their children, and the soldiers will be remembered. Every soldier that fights with me today is my equal. No matter how low class he is, he will become a gentleman.*

FOR ADVANCED LEARNERS/PRE–AP

Synthesize [paired option] Have students role-play an interview between a reporter and one of Henry's men immediately after Henry delivers the speech. To plan the interview, have them use details in the speech to develop a list of Reporter's Questions.

BEST PRACTICES TOOLKIT—Transparency Reporter's Questions p. C9

Practice and Apply

After Reading

For additional support of postreading questions, use these copy masters:

RESOURCE MANAGER—Copy Masters
Reading Check p. 139 (to check understanding of the selection)
Persuasion in Literature p. 135 (for practice of literary analysis standards focus)
Question Support p. 140 (After Reading questions adapted for English learners and less-proficient readers)
Additional selection questions are provided for teachers on page 129.

ANSWERS

Comprehension

1. *They will show their scars.*
2. *He offers brotherhood.*
3. *Fighting in the battle will "gentle his condition" (line 24), or make a gentleman of him.*

Literary Analysis

Possible answers:

4. *Responses will vary. Students may mention the following: Henry's ability to motivate his men by painting a vivid picture of the rewards they will receive if they follow him; Henry fights alongside his men; he bonds with his men by calling them brothers.*
5. ● **STANDARDS FOCUS Persuasion in Literature** ***Snob Appeal/Promise:*** *"strip his sleeve and show his scars"/They will have something to brag about; "he'll remember with advantages"/They will remember firsthand; "names . . . as household words"/They will be associated with famous men; "This story shall the good man teach his son"/They will be held up as an example of goodness; "we in it shall be remembered"/They will be a part of history; "we band of brothers"/The troops are equal to the king; "This day shall gentle his condition"/They will no longer be commoners; "hold their manhoods cheap"/They will be more manly than other men.*
6. ■ **STANDARDS FOCUS Paraphrase** *Students should give reasons to support their responses.*
7. *Native American vision: remembered for their love of beauty, respect for nature, and friendly acts to the United States. King Henry's vision: remembrance for acting with bravery in a desperate situation. Similarities: pride, patriotism, bravery, loyalty, wanting to be remembered by future generations. Differences: The Native Americans have no desire to go to war, while that is King Henry's intent and purpose.*

Extension and Challenge

8. *Answers will vary, but most students will probably say that the speech continues to be powerful because it still inspires people to act in a way that will make others remember them as a part of history.*
9. **SOCIAL STUDIES CONNECTION** *Accounts of the Battle of Agincourt are readily available on the Internet and in history books about England and France during the Hundred Years' War. Students' posters should contain enough detail to show the relative advantages and disadvantages of each side in the battle.*

After Reading

Comprehension

1. **Recall** According to King Henry, on future St. Crispian's Days, how will men prove they fought at the Battle of Agincourt?
2. **Recall** What relationship does the king offer to any man who "sheds his blood" with Henry?
3. **Clarify** According to Henry, what effect will fighting in the battle have on men who are "vile"?

Literary Analysis

4. **Analyze Character** King Henry V is often cited as an example of someone who is a strong leader. What leadership qualities does Shakespeare's Henry show in the "St. Crispian's Day Speech"? Support your response with evidence from the text.
5. **Analyze Persuasion in Literature** Create a list of all the examples of **snob appeal** in the speech. Then, beside each example, tell what Henry is promising his men. Which of King Henry's appeals do you find most persuasive? Why?

Snob Appeal	*Promise*
Will stand a' tiptoe	*Will be better than others*

6. **Evaluate Paraphrase** Select one of the paraphrases you recorded in your chart. Compare it with Shakespeare's original words. Which version do you think would be more **inspirational** to people today? Why?
7. **Compare Across Texts** Members of the Grand Council Fire of American Indians clearly state how their people should be remembered in "The First Americans" (pages 1006–1007). Compare this with King Henry's vision of how his men will be remembered. What is similar and different about what the two groups want to be known for? What might help explain the differences?

Extension and Challenge

8. **Literary Criticism** The king's speech in *Henry V* is one of Shakespeare's most famous passages. What do you think gives this speech its power and continuing appeal? Support your answer.
9. **SOCIAL STUDIES CONNECTION** The skillful tactics employed by King Henry were a major factor in the English victory at Agincourt. Research how the battle was fought, and create a poster depicting the movements and strategies of Henry's troops and the French troops.

RESEARCH LINKS
For more on the Battle of Agincourt, visit the **Research Center** at **ClassZone.com.**

Reading-Writing Connection

Show your understanding of the "St. Crispian's Day Speech" by responding to these prompts. Then complete the **Grammar and Writing** exercise.

WRITING PROMPTS	SELF-CHECK
A. Short Response: Persuade Your Classmates Think of a cause that you support. Write **one paragraph** that will **inspire** your classmates to sacrifice something in order to help your cause. Use the technique of **snob appeal** in your response.	***A strong response will . . .*** • motivate readers to take action • demonstrate an understanding of snob appeal
B. Extended Response: Analyze a Speech In the "St. Crispian's Day Speech," Henry V makes an appeal to his men to follow him into battle. In **two or three paragraphs,** explain the way he convinces his men to fight a battle in which they are outnumbered.	***A well-written analysis will . . .*** • explain how Henry tries to convince his audience • use examples to illustrate your points

GRAMMAR AND WRITING

USE CORRECT SENTENCE STRUCTURE **Parallelism** is the use of similar grammatical structures to link related ideas. Parts of a sentence that have parallel meanings should have parallel structure. For example, if you're listing various activities, use the same sentence part to describe each activity—nouns with nouns, verbs with verbs, or phrases with phrases. A typical error occurs when *and* is used to join different sentence parts.

Original: Volunteering is fun, easy, and rewards you. (*The construction is not parallel because two adjectives are joined to a verb.*)

Revised: Volunteering is fun, easy, and rewarding. (*The construction is now parallel because three adjectives are joined.*)

PRACTICE Rewrite each of these sentences to make its structure parallel.

1. Volunteers are kind and sympathize with people.
2. Donating clothing, volunteering at a food bank, and work at a homeless shelter are all ways you can help others.
3. Food banks are important for people who are unemployed, disabled, or don't have a home.
4. Don't spend all your time playing video games, watching movies, and at the mall.

For more help with parallelism, see page R64 in the ***Grammar Handbook.***

Reading-Writing Connection

WRITING PROMPTS

- For **Prompt A,** have students brainstorm causes they feel strongly about. Ask them what they might be willing to sacrifice for the cause, and in what ways they might use snob appeal to promote their cause.
- For **Prompt B,** have students skim the speech to identify two examples of the way Henry convinces the men.

For writing support, see

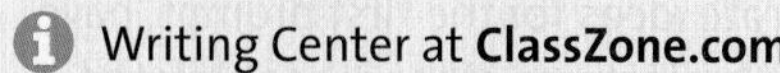
Writing Center at **ClassZone.com**

GRAMMAR AND WRITING

Review adjectives, nouns, noun clauses, verb tenses, and gerunds. Give students practice using commas and conjunctions to link words with the same part of speech and verbs with parallel tenses. To help students evaluate their writing for parallel structure, suggest that they read their sentences aloud.

Possible answers:

1. *Volunteers are kind and sympathetic toward people.*
2. *Donating clothing, volunteering at a food bank, and working at a homeless shelter are all ways you can help others.*
3. *Food banks are important for people who are unemployed, disabled, or homeless.*
4. *Don't spend all your time playing video games, watching movies, and shopping at the mall.*

RESOURCE MANAGER—*Copy Master*
Use Correct Sentence Structure p. 141

Assess and Reteach

Assess

RESOURCE MANAGER—*Copy Masters*
Selection Tests A, B/C pp. 143–144, 145–146

Test Generator CD

Reteach

STANDARDS LESSON FILE
Informational Texts Lesson 15: Persuasive Techniques
Research and Study Skills Lesson 12: Paraphrasing

DIFFERENTIATED INSTRUCTION

FOR LESS-PROFICIENT WRITERS

For Prompt A:

1. Suggest that students begin their paragraphs with a clear statement of the cause they support.
2. Have them use the technique of snob appeal as motivation.
3. Tell them to clearly state the sacrifice they hope their readers will make.

For Prompt B:

Students may organize their paragraphs in this way:

- **First paragraph:** Summarize Henry's purpose for giving the speech.
- **Second paragraph:** Explain that Henry used snob appeal in his speech and cite specific examples.
- **Third paragraph:** End with a brief statement of why the speech is effective.

Focus and Motivate

OBJECTIVES

- analyze a student model that reflects the key traits of a persuasive essay
- use the writing process to write a persuasive essay
- revise and edit, using a rubric for a strong persuasive essay
- plan and deliver a persuasive speech

WRITER'S ROAD MAP

WRITING PROMPTS 1 AND 2

To generate ideas for the first prompt, have students brainstorm other school-related issues in small groups. List ideas from each group on the board. For the second prompt, review selections in this unit together, identifying the issues and deciding whether each issue has two sides.

ADDITIONAL PROMPTS

Use these prompts for more practice writing persuasive essays:

WRITING PROMPT 3

Writing from the Media Choose an issue that is current and controversial. Express your view in a persuasive essay.

Sources to Explore

- op-ed pages in national newspapers
- lead stories on news shows
- blog topics

WRITING PROMPT 4

Writing for the Real World Complete this statement: If I were president of the United States, I would change ______. Write a persuasive essay enlisting the support of others for your proposal.

Ideas to Consider

- health care
- international affairs
- environmental policies

For additional writing prompts, see

WriteSmart CD

Writing Center at **ClassZone.com**

KEY TRAITS

Review the six ***KEY TRAITS*** with students, focusing primarily on ideas, organization, and word choice. Compare the list of traits with the rubric on page 1022.

Writing Workshop

Persuasive Essay

Which of the arguments in this unit did you find most persuasive? You can take a stand on an issue that matters to you by putting your beliefs in writing and backing them up with facts. To get started on your own persuasive essay, check out the **Writer's Road Map.**

WRITER'S ROAD MAP

Persuasive Essay

WRITING PROMPT 1

Writing for the Real World Choose an issue you feel strongly about. Write a persuasive essay in which you explain the issue and convince your readers to agree with your point of view.

Issues to Explore

- school dress codes
- locker searches
- restrictions on leaving school grounds at lunch

WRITING PROMPT 2

Writing from Literature Something you read may make you aware of an injustice. Using a selection in this unit as a springboard, write a persuasive essay about an issue that interests you.

Issues to Explore

- whether parents and teachers are overprotective ("Position on Dodgeball in Physical Education" and "The Weak Shall Inherit the Gym")
- treatment of zoo animals ("Zoos: Myth and Reality" and "Zoos Connect Us to the Natural World")

WRITING TOOLS
For prewriting, revision, and editing tools, visit the **Writing Center at ClassZone.com.**

KEY TRAITS

1. *IDEAS*
- Presents a **thesis statement** taking a position on a clearly identified issue
- Uses **convincing details** to support the position
- Answers **opposing arguments** and counterclaims

2. *ORGANIZATION*
- **Introduces** the issue in an attention-getting way
- Uses **transitions** to create a consistent organizational pattern
- **Concludes** by summarizing the position and issuing a call to action or call to agreement

3. *VOICE*
- Reflects the **writer's strong belief** in his or her opinion

4. *WORD CHOICE*
- Uses **persuasive language** effectively

5. *SENTENCE FLUENCY*
- Varies **sentence lengths and structures**

6. *CONVENTIONS*
- Uses **correct grammar, spelling, and punctuation**

Writing Workshop Resources

RESOURCE MANAGER UNIT 9

Plan and Teach pp. 147–150
Prewriting–Editing pp. 151–155
Writing Rubric p. 156
Speaking and Listening p. 157
Writing Support p. 158*

STANDARDS LESSON FILE

Writing Lessons 10, 12, 21, 22, 23, 34, 44
Speaking and Listening Lessons 1, 7

BEST PRACTICES TOOLKIT

Scaffolding Writing Instruction pp. 43–46*
Main Idea and Details • Two-Column Chart • Writing Template: Persuasive Essay • Y Chart

TECHNOLOGY

Easy Planner DVD
Writing Center at **ClassZone.com**
Write*Smart* CD

* Resources for Differentiation

Part 1: Analyze a Student Model

Michael Vickers
Arlington Middle School

Raise Your Hand for Helping Hands

Are you tired of being treated like a little kid? Do you wish you could prove to other people that you're responsible and mature and have a lot to offer to others? Well, a new program proposed by a school board member could make that wish come true. Helping Hands would give all eighth graders a chance to volunteer our services to the community. This program would benefit everyone involved, and it deserves everyone's enthusiastic support.

The Helping Hands program would require every eighth grader to do some kind of community service for four hours a month. Reading to children or senior citizens, helping out at day camps and recreation facilities, working at after-school art and sports programs, cleaning up parks and beaches—these are just some of the activities students could do. The school administrators would post a list of volunteer positions available, and each student would be able to choose a job that interested him or her. Teachers or workers at the facilities would supervise our activities and report our hours directly to the school.

The community would benefit from this program because we would provide important services at no cost. In addition, we students would gain many advantages from taking part in this program. First of all, we would be able to use skills we already have and learn new ones. Also, we would become better members of the community and get to know many different people, occupations, and work situations. This information would help us discover our interests and strengths; it might even give us ideas about future careers.

KEY TRAITS IN ACTION

Introduces the essay with a question that concerns the writer's audience of eighth graders.

Thesis statement presents the issue and the writer's position on it.

Different **sentence lengths and structures** help to make the details interesting and memorable.

Highlighted **transition** helps the reader understand the organization of the essay.

Teach

Part 1: Analyze a Student Model

Have students read the **Student Model** and **Key Traits in Action.** Then discuss the model with the class, focusing on specific examples of each trait. You may also wish to incorporate these activities:

- **Introduction** Tell students that showing readers how an issue affects them personally is an important step in winning their support. This writer uses a question to engage his readers. Ask students what other methods he might have used. ***Possible answer:*** *The writer might have started with a relevant anecdote or a hypothetical situation.*
- **Thesis Statement** Ask students what the thesis reveals about the writer's purpose in this essay. *(**Possible answer:** The writer wants to persuade readers to support the Helping Hands volunteer program.)* Ask students why knowing the writer's position at the beginning of a persuasive essay is important. ***Possible answer:*** *Knowing the writer's position enables readers to identify and evaluate all the evidence that is presented and also to see the structure of the argument.*
- **Sentence Lengths and Structures** Write this example on the board:

  One job would be reading to children or senior citizens. Volunteers could help out at day camps. They could work at recreation facilities. Another job might be working at after-school programs. Or, students could clean up parks and beaches. These are some possible activities.

  Have a student read the example aloud. Then have students read lines 9–13 and compare the two versions. Guide them to see that the sentence in the model flows more smoothly than the string of short, choppy sentences in the example.
- **Transitions** Ask students to find other transitions that the writer uses in this paragraph. ***Possible answer:*** *because, First of all, Also, even*

DIFFERENTIATED INSTRUCTION

FOR ALL STUDENTS

Student Portfolios Encourage students to save copies of their writing so they can track their progress throughout the year.

For general guidelines on differentiating writing instruction, see

BEST PRACTICES TOOLKIT
Scaffolding Writing Instruction
pp. 43–46

FOR ENGLISH LEARNERS

Language: Skill Words Review these terms:

- *argument:* writing that expresses a position on an issue or problem and supports it with reasons and evidence
- *convincing details:* facts, examples, statistics, or incidents that support the writer's argument
- *opposing argument:* argument presented by those who disagree with the writer's view
- *counterargument:* argument made by a writer to respond to an opposing argument

- **Opposing Argument** Draw students' attention to the number of details that the writer uses to develop the opposing argument. Ask: In what way does this elaboration add to the effectiveness of his argument? ***Possible answer:*** *By developing an argument that opposes his, the writer shows his grasp of the issue and his willingness to consider others' opinions. He proves that he has thought about the issue from many different angles, which increases his credibility.*
- **Persuasive Language** Remind students to consider both the denotation and the connotation of the words they choose. Point out the word *waste* in line 34. The writer might have substituted *spend* or *use,* but neither word conveys the idea of "throwing away" or misusing time. *Waste* makes readers feel that they could and should do something more productive. Ask students how the other highlighted words and phrases in this paragraph affect their reaction to what the writer is saying. ***Possible answer:*** *The word* just *in line 32 suggests that an hour is an insignificant amount of time that everyone can afford to donate to a good cause. This idea is reinforced by the phrase* few hours *in line 35. The writer eases readers' anxieties by saying in lines 35–37 that this volunteer effort won't "interfere" with their activities or prevent them from having "time to relax." Use of the word* service *in line 37 reminds readers that they would be doing a good thing.*
- **Conclusion** Ask students what tone the conclusion of the essay conveys. ***Possible answer:*** *The tone of the conclusion is one of certainty and conviction. This tone is conveyed by phrases such as "There's no question," "Support it now," and "a rousing 'Yes!'"*

For interactive student models, see

WriteSmart CD

Writing Center at **ClassZone.com**

Some students might oppose this program because they think they already spend too much time on school-related activities. Besides the actual hours spent in class, there are sports practices and games, club meetings, and homework. Most students also have chores to do at home, and many take music or other lessons. They don't want to give up what little free time they have.

Describes an **opposing argument.**

Students are very busy, of course. However, Helping Hands would require only four hours a month. That's just an hour a week. Most of us spend three or four times that much time talking on the telephone. We also waste even more time just sitting around or putting off what we're supposed to be doing. These few hours of community service wouldn't interfere with any of our other activities and would still leave us plenty of time to relax. In fact, needing to work this service into our schedules might even help us become more organized and efficient with our time.

Effectively uses **persuasive language** to answer the opposition and express the writer's **strong belief** in the program.

There's no question that this proposed program benefits the community, the school, and the students. Support it now by attending the school board meeting next week, raising your hand, and saying a rousing "Yes!" to Helping Hands.

Concludes persuasively by restating the writer's support for the program and telling readers exactly what they should do.

2

DIFFERENTIATED INSTRUCTION

FOR ENGLISH LEARNERS

Comprehension: Transitions Tell students that different types of transitions are used in persuasive essays.

- Some are used to connect supporting details. Example: It is the responsibility of voters to exercise this privilege. *First of all,* one vote might make a difference in an election. *For example,* in our city's race for mayor last year, the victorious candidate won by only four votes.
- Some show a cause-and-effect relationship. Example: *If* students prove that they can responsibly write and edit the newspaper, *then* the administration should let them.
- Some present or refute an opposing viewpoint. Example: Some people say a curfew can't be enforced, *but* they are wrong.

Have small groups identify transitions in the **Student Model** that connect details, show cause and effect, and compare or contrast.

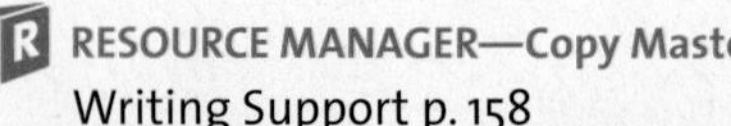
RESOURCE MANAGER—Copy Master
Writing Support p. 158

Part 2: Apply the Writing Process

PREWRITING

What Should I Do?	What Does It Look Like?
1. Analyze the prompt. Read the prompts on page 1016. Choose the one that appeals to you. Then circle the type of writing you will be doing and underline details about your purpose and audience.	**WRITING PROMPT** Choose an issue you feel strongly about. Write a (persuasive essay) in which you explain the issue and convince your readers to agree with your point of view. *This is a class assignment, so I should choose a topic that will interest other eighth graders.*
2. Find an issue that you believe deserves attention. List issues that concern you, adding your questions or comments about each. Put a star by the issue that will be the focus of your essay. **TIP Make sure the issue you choose has two sides.**	***School Issues*** • *backpack searches—are they legal?* • *Helping Hands program—a great way to prove our maturity and responsibility* * ***Community Issues*** • *violence (one-sided issue—nobody supports violence)* • *helmet law for cyclists—how can we get one passed?*
3. Create a working thesis statement. Write a sentence or two summarizing the issue and your stand on it. You can rewrite your thesis statement as you draft, so don't worry about making it perfect at this stage.	***Working thesis statement*** *Helping Hands is great because it would give all eighth graders a chance to serve the community.*
4. Collect information that supports your position. You'll need solid logic as well as specific facts, statistics, and reliable opinions to persuade your reader. Check books, local and national newspapers and magazines, and the Internet for information. **TIP Think about opposing arguments and look for details you can use to refute them.**	***Services we could provide*** • *reading to little kids or senior citizens* • *working at day camps and after-school programs* • *cleaning up litter at parks and beaches* • *others? (Check with school officials and at town hall.)*

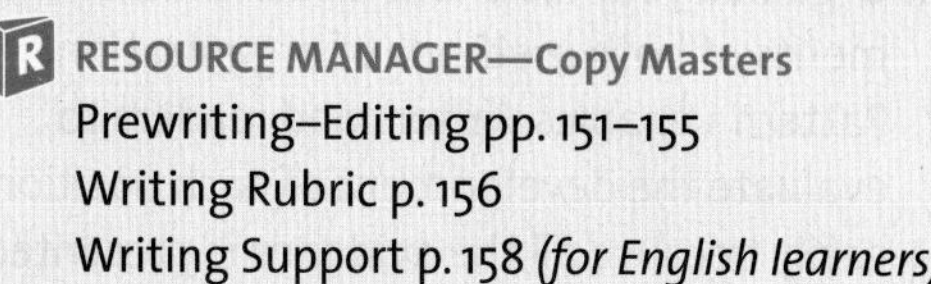

To support students during the writing process, use these copy masters:

RESOURCE MANAGER—Copy Masters
Prewriting–Editing pp. 151–155
Writing Rubric p. 156
Writing Support p. 158 *(for English learners)*

Part 2: Apply the Writing Process

PREWRITING

1. **Analyze the prompt.** Tell students that although topics and audiences vary, all persuasive writing focuses on an issue with two sides and presents an argument supported by detailed evidence, examples, and reasoning to convince others to think or act a certain way.
2. **Find an issue that you believe deserves attention.** Point out the TIP and have students work with a partner to explore the different sides of their issue. Remind them to narrow a topic that is too broad. For example, the subject of conservation is too encompassing; focusing on preservation of the Everglades would allow a writer to make a compelling argument.
3. **Create a working thesis statement.** Have partners read each other's thesis statement to see whether they can determine the issue, the writer's position, and the probable content of the essay. Have students use feedback from their partners to revise their statements.
4. **Collect information that supports your position.** Have students read the TIP and suggest that they may want to use note cards or a Main Idea and Details chart to collect and organize information on both sides of their issue.

BEST PRACTICES TOOLKIT—Transparency
Main Idea and Details p. B6

For interactive graphic organizers, see
WriteSmart CD
Writing Center at **ClassZone.com**

FOR ENGLISH LEARNERS

Task Support [mixed-readiness groups] To help students choose an issue that has two clear sides, have them work in small groups to fill out a Two-Column Chart that lists arguments for and against each of their possible topics. Discuss their ideas before students make their final decisions.

BEST PRACTICES TOOLKIT—Transparency
Two-Column Chart p. A25

FOR ADVANCED LEARNERS/PRE-AP

Synthesize [paired option] Challenge pairs of students to choose and research the same topic and then to write essays presenting opposing arguments. Ask each pair to then debate their issue in front of the class. Provide listening students with criteria for evaluating the effectiveness of each argument and ask them to vote on which side was more convincing, explaining the reasons for their choices.

DRAFTING

1. **Organize your facts and ideas.** Discuss the merits of both methods of organization. Pattern 1 enables writers and readers to evaluate the development of each position easily because all the evidence is presented at once. Pattern 2 is useful if there is an opposing argument for each major point that the writer makes.
2. **Support each key point you make.** Tell students that some or all of their key points will be opinions. Point out the statement from the **Student Model** in the right column. The writer is offering his belief that students would benefit from the program. Explain that each opinion students present must be validated with factual evidence and concrete examples. Unsubstantiated opinions will only weaken their argument.

   Before students draft the body of their essays, suggest that they organize their ideas in an outline or a graphic organizer. If they lack support for key points, encourage them to do further research.
3. **Rebut each opposing argument.** Tell students that thoroughly examining opposing arguments makes them seem knowledgeable about their topic and open to others' viewpoints. To make sure they have considered all possible objections, suggest that students take turns presenting their arguments in small groups. Ask group members to brainstorm other possible opposing positions.

   Ask a volunteer to read the TIP aloud. Then have the class turn to page 1022 and examine the rubric and peer-reader questions together.

For a persuasive essay writing template, see

- BEST PRACTICES TOOLKIT—Transparency Writing Template: Persuasive Essay pp. C16, C34
- Write*Smart* CD
- Writing Center at **ClassZone.com**

DRAFTING

What Should I Do?	*What Does It Look Like?*
1. Organize your facts and ideas. Here are two ways of organizing a persuasive essay: **Pattern 1**—Discuss all points on one side of the issue, then all points on the other side. This is the pattern the writer of the student model used. **Pattern 2**—Present the arguments for and against one key point. Then do the same for another key point, and so on.	**PATTERN 1** *Introduction and description of program* ***For Helping Hands*** • *serves community* • *helps students develop talents, learn about careers* ***Against Helping Hands*** • *students too busy* • *need free time* *Conclusion and call to action* **PATTERN 2** *Introduction and description of program* ***Opposing Argument 1:*** *students too busy* ***Counterargument 1:*** *only four hours per month* ***Opposing Argument 2:*** *need free time* ***Counterargument 2:*** *teaches organization and efficiency* *Conclusion and call to action*
2. Support each key point you make. Why do you believe what you believe? Back up your statements with strong examples and reasons.	*We students would gain many advantages from taking part in this program.* — *Key point* *We would be able to use the skills we already have and learn new ones. Also, we would get to know many different people, occupations, and work situations.* — *Support*
3. Rebut each opposing argument. Address each point on the other side of the issue and explain why it doesn't make sense. **TIP Before revising, review the key traits on page 1016 and the rubric and peer-reader questions on page 1022.**	*Some students might oppose this program because they think they already spend too much time on school-related activities. . . .* *Students are very busy, of course. However, Helping Hands would require only four hours a month. These few hours of community service wouldn't interfere with any of our other activities and would still leave us plenty of time to relax.*

DIFFERENTIATED INSTRUCTION

FOR LESS–PROFICIENT WRITERS

Organizing the Essay Provide students with this outline for organizing their information. Correlate each part to the **Student Model.**

Introduction (Paragraph 1)
- Catch readers' attention with a question, a brief story, or a startling fact.
- State your thesis.

First Major Point (Paragraph 2)
- Present first reason to support argument.
- Provide facts, examples, and other details.

Second Major Point (Paragraph 3)
- Present second reason.
- Provide facts, examples, and other details.

Opposing Arguments (Paragraph 4)
- Discuss other positions on the issue.

Counterarguments (Paragraph 5)
- Explain why each opposing argument is unconvincing.

Conclusion (Paragraph 6)
- Restate your thesis.
- Describe any action readers should take.

REVISING AND EDITING

What Should I Do?	What Does It Look Like?
1. Use emotional appeals wisely. • Reread your draft. Put a box around words or phrases that use so much flattery, pity, or fear that they may cause your reader to dismiss your entire message. • Replace these statements with appeals that include sound reasoning and evidence. **See page 1022:** Emotional Appeals	~~*Join Helping Hands to show that you are the smartest, most responsible student in this school.*~~ *Are you tired of being treated like a little kid? Do you wish you could prove to other people that you're responsible and mature and have a lot to offer to others? Well, a new program proposed by a school board member could make that wish come true.*
2. Strengthen your supporting details. • Underline details that support and explain your points. Is your support clear and relevant? • If your essay has only a few underlines, add details. If the underlined parts are confusing, replace them with clear explanations.	~~*There are all kinds of things we could do.*~~ *Reading to children or senior citizens, helping out at day camps and recreation facilities, working at after-school art and sports programs, cleaning up parks and beaches—these are just some of the activities students could do.*
3. Sharpen imprecise language. • Have a peer reader circle vague phrases like *a good idea* and *might be helpful.* • Replace these words with specific terms that persuade your reader. **See page 1022:** Ask a Peer Reader	~~*It seems like a pretty good idea, so you might want to think about joining.*~~ *This program would benefit everyone involved, and it deserves everyone's enthusiastic support.*
4. Make your conclusion complete. • End by summarizing your position on the issue and issuing a **call to action** or **call to agreement.** In other words, tell your reader what to do or what to think. • Reread your conclusion and add or revise information as needed.	~~*In conclusion, joining Helping Hands is the right thing to do.*~~ *There's no question that this proposed program benefits the community, the school, and the students. Support it now by attending the school board meeting next week, raising your hand, and saying a rousing "Yes!" to Helping Hands.*

FOR ENGLISH LEARNERS

Task Support [paired option] Review these terms with students:

- *active voice:* the subject of the sentence performs the action. *Pat caught the ball.*
- *passive voice:* the subject of the sentence is acted upon. *The ball was caught by Pat.*

Have pairs identify the verb in these sentences as either active or passive and rewrite the sentences in the other voice:

1. The show was enjoyed by the children. *(passive; The children enjoyed the show.)*
2. The art teacher designed the pamphlet. *(active; The pamphlet was designed by the art teacher.)*
3. We visited the museum. *(active; The museum was visited by us.)*
4. The test was studied for by the students. *(passive; The students studied for the test.)*

REVISING AND EDITING

1. **Use emotional appeals wisely.** Remind students to avoid appeals such as bandwagon (suggesting that readers should think or act like everyone else), exaggeration (making something seem better or worse than it really is), or loaded language (using words that evoke powerful emotions and distract readers from the facts).

   Have students rephrase each of these statements to convey the same idea without misusing an emotional appeal:

   —Participating in Helping Hands will change your life, making you a better person in every way.

   —Everyone who's anyone is into Helping Hands. Shouldn't you be, too?
2. **Strengthen your supporting details.** Remind students that in addition to providing sufficient evidence to support each main point, they may also need to include some background information to make sure readers understand the issue. Have peer readers check to be sure that someone unacquainted with the topic would still be able to follow the argument.
3. **Sharpen imprecise language.** Tell students that writers must show their firm belief in the position they are presenting. To convey a tone of conviction, they should avoid words and phrases such as *might be, could be, possibly, maybe,* and *sometimes;* unclear pronoun references; and weak, indecisive-sounding adjectives and adverbs.

   Tell students that using the active voice is another way to strengthen their writing. Point out the **Check Your Grammar** box on page 1022. Discuss the ways in which the revisions improve each statement.
4. **Make your conclusion complete.** Have partners offer feedback on each other's conclusions.

For interactive revision tools, see

WriteSmart CD

Writing Center at **ClassZone.com**

Preparing to Publish

Support for meeting the goals in the writing rubric is supplied throughout the **Writing Workshop** on pages 1016–1021.

For Rubric Bank, see

- Write*Smart* CD
- Writing Center at **ClassZone.com**

Assess and Reteach

After reading and assessing students' persuasive essays, you might use these lessons to reteach key skills:

STANDARDS LESSON FILE

- Writing Lesson 10: Using Active and Passive Voice
- Writing Lesson 12: Topic Sentence and Supporting Details
- Writing Lesson 21: Writing a Thesis Statement
- Writing Lesson 22: Writing Introductions
- Writing Lesson 23: Writing Conclusions
- Writing Lesson 34: Persuasive Writing
- Writing Lesson 44: Using Precise Words

Preparing to Publish Persuasive Essay

Apply the Rubric

A strong persuasive essay . . .

- ☑ captures the reader's attention from the first paragraph
- ☑ presents a thesis that describes the issue and the writer's opinion
- ☑ supports that opinion with convincing details
- ☑ explains opposing arguments and answers them effectively with counterclaims
- ☑ uses precise, persuasive language
- ☑ uses transitions to show how ideas are related
- ☑ varies sentence lengths and structures
- ☑ ends by restating the writer's position and calling for action or agreement

Ask a Peer Reader

- How can I make my introduction more lively?
- Which of my statements was most convincing? Why?
- Were any words or phrases weak, vague, or confusing? If so, which?

Emotional Appeals

It's fine to try to create strong feelings when you write your essay. However, make sure your appeals don't make your reader feel manipulated.

- **Overemotional appeal to pity**—How can you cruelly ignore those sad little kids who have nobody to read to them?!
- **Effective appeal to pity**—It's a chance to help the people in our community who most need and deserve our attention.

Check Your Grammar

Use the active voice whenever possible to clarify who or what is doing the action. This will help make your statements as strong and persuasive as they can be.

School administrators would post
A list of volunteer positions ~~would be posted~~.
Helping Hands would require
Only three or four hours a month ~~would be required by Helping Hands~~.

See page R57: Active and Passive Voice

Writing Online

PUBLISHING OPTIONS
For publishing options, visit the **Writing Center** at **ClassZone.com.**

ASSESSMENT PREPARATION
For writing and grammar assessment practice, go to the **Assessment Center** at **ClassZone.com.**

SPEAKING AND LISTENING

Delivering a Persuasive Speech

Turning your essay into a persuasive speech can help you reach a wider audience and get your ideas across even more effectively.

Planning the Speech

1. **Mark up your essay.** Highlight or underline the points you want to include in your speech.
2. **Write a script.** Start with a strong introduction. You can use the introduction from your essay or get your listeners' attention by telling a story, perhaps including actions or gestures.
3. **Create a visual.** Put the points you want to make on a flip chart, on transparencies, in a power presentation, or in some other visual format. Create one page for each main point and add supporting details in short bullet points. Be sure the text is large enough to be readable at the back of the room.

> ***Choose your own volunteer work.***
> - *What skills do you already have?*
> - *What skills would you like to learn?*
> - *What jobs are available?*

4. **Be clear and specific.** Use precise words that tell your listeners exactly how you feel about the issue and what you want them to do.

Delivering the Speech

1. **Read the guidelines in the Speaking and Listening Handbook (page R79).** These guidelines explain the keys to a successful persuasive speech. Learn them, and then practice your speech until you feel comfortable delivering it. Present it in front of a mirror first, and then ask your family or friends to watch.
2. **Put your visuals to work.** Make sure everyone in the audience can see the visual that you are using. Help listeners follow along by using your finger or a laser pointer to indicate which point you are talking about.

SPEAKING AND LISTENING

Have students read this page for an overview of how to prepare and present an effective persuasive speech. Encourage them to include facts to validate opinions whenever possible.

Before students begin working, review this rubric with them so that they understand their goals:

Rubric A strong persuasive speech

- begins with an effective introduction
- includes a thesis statement
- supports arguments with detailed evidence, examples, and reasoning
- reinforces important ideas in a clear visual with bullet points
- identifies and answers opposing arguments
- is logically organized
- uses precise words
- shows evidence of rehearsal

RESOURCE MANAGER—Copy Master
Speaking and Listening p. 157

STANDARDS LESSON FILE
Speaking and Listening Lesson 1: Preparing and Presenting a Speech
Speaking and Listening Lesson 7: Persuasive Speech

DIFFERENTIATED INSTRUCTION

FOR LESS–PROFICIENT WRITERS

Planning the Speech Display this example of a persuasive speech and ask a volunteer to read it aloud. Then have students compare and contrast it with lines 17–24 of the **Student Model.**

> You would benefit, too! As a volunteer, you would gain a whole new set of skills. Just think—you could learn carpentry, cooking, or lawn care. You would also meet new people and learn more about your town. This exposure to new places, people, and skills would surely help you in the future. So, by doing a good deed for others, you'd be doing one for yourself, too!

Use a Y Chart to show some of the differences between a persuasive essay and a persuasive speech. Your chart might include these points:

Speech
- less formal tone
- direct address of the audience
- repetition of key points in a visual

Essay
- formal language and tone
- first-person point of view

Both
- convincing arguments
- strong introduction, conclusion, and supporting details

BEST PRACTICES TOOLKIT—Transparency
Y Chart p. A27

Assessment Practice

CHECK READINESS

Read aloud the paragraph under **ASSESS** and stress to students that this is not the full Unit Test but a way for them to check their readiness for it. Then have students examine the skills listed under **REVIEW** and look back in the unit or in the **Student Resource Bank** for any skills they need to study.

READ THE SELECTION

Remind students to keep Unit Goals in mind as they read the passage, paying particular attention to

- argument
- persuasive techniques
- author's purpose
- fact and opinion
- comparisons and contrasts

To help students focus on the **arguments** while reading, encourage them to ask questions such as

- What is each author's position on the issue of nuclear energy? What reasons does each author offer in support of his view?
- Is the evidence that each author presents convincing? Why or why not?

ANSWER THE QUESTIONS

Direct students to pages R95–R101 of the Test-Taking Handbook to review test-taking strategies. Remind students not to choose the first alternative that seems to fit when answering a multiple-choice question. Instead, they should read through all the choices, eliminate any that are clearly wrong, and then choose the best answer—the one that is most accurate and complete.

Remind students that critical readers are constantly aware of context clues that can help them better understand what they read. Tell students to think about the gist of the sentence or paragraph to figure out what an unfamiliar word or phrase might mean. Also suggest that students look at word parts and ask themselves these questions: What parts of the word do I recognize? What is the meaning of the prefix or the suffix? Does this word remind me of any others that I know?

Assessment Practice

Reading Comprehension

ASSESS

The practice test items on the next few pages match skills listed on the Unit Goals page (page 961) and addressed throughout this unit. Taking this practice test will help you assess your knowledge of these skills and determine your readiness for the Unit Test.

REVIEW

After you take the practice test, your teacher can help you identify any skills you need to review.

- Argument
- Persuasive Techniques
- Author's Purpose
- Fact and Opinion
- Compare and Contrast
- Related Words
- Greek and Latin Words and Roots
- Capitalization of Organizations and Institutions
- Parallelism

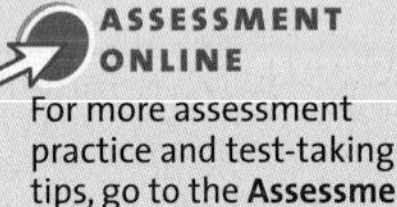

ASSESSMENT ONLINE

For more assessment practice and test-taking tips, go to the **Assessment Center** at **ClassZone.com.**

DIRECTIONS *Read this selection and answer the questions that follow.*

Nuclear Energy: Does It Make Sense for the Environment?

After decades of wariness, interest in nuclear power is picking up. Do the benefits outweigh the risks?

YES

Nuclear power is the largest source of emission-free energy generation in the United States. One of every five American homes and businesses gets its electricity from a nuclear plant.

Meeting tighter limits on air pollution is an ambitious task—one that would be virtually impossible without the clean-air benefits of nuclear power. The Department of Energy recognizes nuclear energy's essential role, identifying it as the single most effective strategy for reducing air pollution.

Nuclear power is the only expandable, large-scale energy source that avoids air pollution and can meet the electricity demands of our growing economy. Nuclear plants do not emit carbon dioxide or other greenhouse gases linked to global warming, nor do they emit pollutants that contribute to haze or smog.

Here's another way to look at nuclear energy's positive impact: Based on 1999 figures, if nuclear plants had to be replaced with oil- or coal-burning plants, the United States would have to eliminate 135 million passenger cars (about half of all cars!) just to keep our carbon dioxide emissions at current levels.

With regard to security, the nation's 103 nuclear power plants are among the best-defended industrial facilities in the United States. And today's nuclear plants have state-of-the-art safety features to prevent accidents.

Several notable environmentalists have recently endorsed nuclear energy. They believe global warming is increasingly our most pressing environmental concern, and recognize nuclear energy is a key part of the solution.

—Scott Peterson, Vice President
Nuclear Energy Institute

DIFFERENTIATED INSTRUCTION

FOR ENGLISH LEARNERS

Assessment Practice: Work Backwards

[paired option] Prepare students for the assessment by having them read the questions before reading the selection. Have pairs follow these steps to learn unfamiliar words in the test directions and questions:

1. Find words you don't recognize and write each one on an index card.
2. Look up the meaning in a dictionary.
3. Write the meaning on the back of the card.
4. Use your word cards to teach and practice the vocabulary with your partner and another pair of students.

NO

Nuclear energy is not the answer to global warming. It makes no sense to solve one set of environmental problems by creating a bigger and more serious set of problems. And nuclear energy is full of very big and very serious problems.

Although new nuclear power plants would certainly be safer than older plants, the consequences of a major accident are still the same: widespread and long-lasting radiation pollution affecting several generations. An explosion at the Chernobyl nuclear reactor in the Soviet Union in 1986 killed 31 people and caused hundreds of thousands of cases of delayed illnesses.

In addition, nuclear power plants make attractive targets for terrorists. A disaster caused by sabotage or attack would cause great harm to people and the environment. Another problem for the environment is the spent fuel from nuclear power plants, which remains toxic for thousands of years. The United States still has no operational long-term repository to store this spent fuel safely.

The process of turning uranium into fuel for nuclear reactors can be easily modified to produce uranium for nuclear bombs. Pakistan's and India's nuclear bombs were made this way. The potential use of these weapons—possibly by terrorists—would be catastrophic to our environment.

Instead of investing in nuclear power, which just trades one set of problems for another, let's invest in renewable energy sources like wind and solar energy. They may cost a little more now, but they don't cause any harm—and they don't run out.

—Kelly Kissock, Associate Professor of Engineering
University of Dayton, Ohio

ITEM ANALYSIS

COMPREHENSION AND WRITTEN RESPONSE	ITEMS	UNIT PAGES
Argument	3, 7, 9, 15	962, 969
Persuasive Techniques	4, 6, 10, 11	960, 964, 985, 1011
Author's Purpose	1, 8, 17	995
Fact and Opinion	2, 13, 14	969
Compare and Contrast	5, 12, 16	1003

VOCABULARY	ITEMS	UNIT PAGES
Related Words	1, 2, 3, 4	1001
Greek and Latin Words and Roots	5, 6, 7	978, 992

WRITING AND GRAMMAR	ITEMS	UNIT PAGES
Capitalization of Organizations and Institutions	1, 3	979
Parallelism	2, 4, 5	1015

FOR LESS–PROFICIENT READERS

Assessment Support Consider these options for completing the **Assessment Practice:**

- Have students review the questions before reading the selection.
- Select random questions in the assessment and have students demonstrate how and where to look for the answers.
- Ask students to locate unfamiliar vocabulary in the assessment. Elicit the meanings of these words from the class.
- Have students jot down useful testing words and definitions in their journals for later reference.
- Read the selection or parts of it aloud to aid in student comprehension.

McDougal Littell Assessment System

After checking student readiness with this Assessment Practice, you may administer the complete Unit 9 Test in order to more thoroughly evaluate student mastery of unit goals.

Comprehension

DIRECTIONS *Answer these questions about "Nuclear Energy: Does It Make Sense for the Environment?"*

1. The author's main purpose in writing the "Yes" response is to
   A warn people about global warming
   B report on oil- and coal-burning plants
   C prove that cars emit pollutants
   D promote the use of nuclear power

2. Which statement from the "Yes" response is an opinion?
   A "Nuclear power is the largest source of emission-free energy generation in the United States." (lines 1–2)
   B "Meeting tighter limits on air pollution is an ambitious task. . . ." (line 4)
   C "Nuclear plants do not emit carbon dioxide or other greenhouse gases linked to global warming. . . ." (lines 10–11)
   D "Several notable environmentalists have recently endorsed nuclear energy." (line 20)

3. What claim does the author of the "Yes" response make in lines 8–11?
   A Nuclear plants are a clean source of energy.
   B It is impossible to eliminate air pollution.
   C Nuclear power improves the nation's economy.
   D All types of energy have risks and benefits.

4. In line 11, the author claims that nuclear power plants do not contribute to haze or smog. This is an example of which persuasive technique?
   A appeal by association
   B ethical appeal
   C emotional appeal
   D appeal to authority

5. In lines 12–16, the author makes a comparison between
   A past and current figures on carbon dioxide emissions
   B passenger cars and other forms of transportation
   C nuclear plants and oil- and coal-burning plants
   D emissions in the United States and other parts of the world

6. What ethical issue does the author raise in the "Yes" response?
   A finding an alternative to cars
   B cutting energy costs
   C protecting the environment
   D creating convenient energy sources

7. The "Yes" response claims that "today's nuclear plants have state-of-the-art safety features to prevent accidents." Which statement in the "No" response is a counterargument to that claim?
   A "Another problem for the environment is the spent fuel from nuclear power plants, which remains toxic for thousands of years." (lines 34–35)
   B "In addition, nuclear power plants make attractive targets for terrorists. A disaster caused by sabotage or attack would cause great harm. . . ." (lines 32–34)
   C "An explosion at the Chernobyl nuclear reactor in the Soviet Union in 1986 killed 31 people and caused hundreds of thousands of cases of delayed illness." (lines 29–31)
   D "Although new nuclear power plants would certainly be safer than older plants, the consequences of a major accident are still the same: widespread and long-lasting radiation pollution. . . ." (lines 27–29)

1026

ANSWERS

Comprehension

Model a thinking process for answering multiple-choice questions.

1. **D** ***is correct.*** *The "Yes" response argues the advantages of nuclear power. Details about global warming, oil- and coal-burning plants, and pollutants are used only to illustrate positive attributes of nuclear energy, so A, B, and C can be eliminated.*
2. **B** ***is correct.*** *The measure of what is "ambitious" is subjective, or based on the author's opinion. A, C, and D could be proven true or false by consulting other sources, so they are facts rather than opinions.*
3. **A** ***is correct.*** *The details in lines 8–11 develop the idea that nuclear power is efficient and clean. B, C, and D are unsupported by the details in this part of the text.*
4. **B** ***is correct.*** *It is implied that it is important to take care of the environment. A is incorrect because the appeal does not associate nuclear power with an attractive idea or person. C is incorrect because, although the words* haze *and* smog *might stir readers' feelings of disgust, the sentence does not provide an in-depth description. No expert is cited, making D incorrect.*
5. **C** ***is correct.*** *The author compares nuclear plants, which emit no carbon dioxide, to oil- and coal-burning plants, which emit large amounts of it. A is incorrect because no actual figures on emissions are given. B and D can also be eliminated, since no other forms of transportation or rates of emission are mentioned.*
6. **C** ***is correct.*** *In lines 4–7, the author states that nuclear energy has "clean-air benefits" and has been recognized as a strategy "for reducing air pollution." The ethical issues in A, B, and D are not raised in the response.*
7. **D** ***is correct.*** *This statement addresses the claim by saying that plants may be safer but the consequences of accidents will be the same. A and B are unrelated to accidents. C relates to a past accident before the safety features existed.*
8. **D** ***is correct.*** *The author's main purpose is to argue that nuclear power remains problematic. A is incorrect because he does not explain the process of converting uranium into fuel. B is incorrect because he mentions the Chernobyl accident only as support for his main argument. In lines 32–34, the author states that nuclear plants would be attractive and deadly targets for terrorists but does not try to prove that such attacks are possible, making C incorrect.*
9. **C** ***is correct.*** *In lines 23–26 and lines 42–45, the author states his position—that nuclear energy creates more problems than it solves. A is incorrect because he concedes in lines 27–28 that new plants are safer. The statements in B and D are not included in the response.*
10. **B** ***is correct.*** *Lines 32–37 mention the threat of terrorism and the toxic waste generated by nuclear power plants, both sources of fear for people. The details in these lines do not appeal to anger, pity, or pride, making A, C, and D incorrect.*
11. **C** ***is correct.*** *The author is opposed to nuclear energy. The negative words* sabotage, catastrophic, *and* disaster *convey his disapproval and describe problems related to nuclear energy. The words in A, B, and D have no strong negative connotations and do not convey his attitude.*

8. The author's main purpose in writing the "No" response is to
   A explain how uranium is converted into fuel for nuclear reactors
   B document the consequences of the accident at Chernobyl
   C prove that terrorists can attack nuclear power plants in the United States
   D convince people that nuclear energy is not worth the risks it presents

9. What is the author's claim in the "No" response?
   A New nuclear power plants are no safer than the old ones.
   B Global warming is our most urgent environmental concern.
   C Nuclear energy creates as many problems as it solves.
   D Scientists are looking for ways to store spent nuclear fuel.

10. To which emotion does the argument in lines 32–34 appeal?
   A anger
   B fear
   C pity
   D pride

11. Which words in the "No" response convey the author's attitude toward nuclear energy?
   A widespread, nuclear, uranium
   B power, potential, operational
   C sabotage, catastrophic, disaster
   D delayed, targets, repository

12. In lines 42–45, the author contrasts forms of energy to show that
   A it makes sense to use renewable energy sources
   B nuclear energy costs more than renewable energy
   C the world has a variety of energy sources
   D it is possible to run out of nuclear resources

13. Which statement is a fact presented in both arguments?
   A Meeting tighter air pollution limits is virtually impossible without nuclear energy.
   B Uranium for fuel can easily be turned into uranium for nuclear bombs.
   C Newer nuclear power plants are safer than older nuclear power plants.
   D The nation's nuclear power plants are well defended against terrorist attacks.

14. Which opinion do the authors share?
   A Global warming is a threat to the environment.
   B Nuclear energy is a source of serious problems.
   C The uranium used for fuel can easily be processed for nuclear bombs.
   D The use of nuclear power effectively reduces air pollution.

Written Response

SHORT RESPONSE *Write two or three sentences to answer each question.*

15. Reread lines 8–11 of the "Yes" response. What evidence does the author cite to support his claim that nuclear plants are a clean source of energy?

16. Reread lines 42–45 of the "No" response. Name two of the comparisons that the author makes between nuclear energy and energy from the wind and the sun.

EXTENDED RESPONSE *Write a paragraph to answer this question.*

17. Identify the author's purpose in writing the "No" response and discuss the reasons given to support that argument.

GO ON

DIFFERENTIATED INSTRUCTION

FOR ENGLISH LEARNERS

Review Academic Vocabulary Review the definition of *argument* with students (*writing that expresses a position on an issue and supports it with reasons and evidence*). Then define these related terms and examples:

- *claim:* the writer's position on an issue or problem. Example: lines 23–26
- *reason:* a statement made to support a claim. Example: line 32
- *evidence:* facts, examples, and statistics that support a claim. Example: lines 39–40
- *counterargument:* an argument that answers an opposing viewpoint. Example: lines 44–45
- *persuasive techniques:* ways to influence others to adopt a certain opinion or belief
  —*appeal to authority:* relies on the opinions of experts. Example: lines 5–7
  —*ethical appeal:* relies on accepted moral standards. Example: lines 8–9
  —*emotional appeal:* creates strong feelings, such as fear or pity. Example: line 32

12. **A *is correct.*** *The contrast is meant to show that while wind and solar power are more expensive now, they will be better in the long run.* B *is directly contradicted by the text (line 44).* C *and* D *are implied by the comparison, but making these points is not the author's purpose.*

13. **C *is correct.*** *The first author states that nuclear plants have "state-of-the-art safety features" (line 19). The second author agrees that "new nuclear power plants would certainly be safer than older plants" (lines 27–28). Only the "Yes" response includes the details expressed in* A *(lines 4–5) and* D *(lines 17–18). Only the "No" response includes the fact stated in* B *(lines 38–39).*

14. **A *is correct.*** *Both authors indicate that global warming is an environmental problem. The first author conveys the opinion of experts on global warming in lines 20–22 and relates nuclear energy to solving this problem. The second author states in lines 23–26 that global warming is a problem that cannot be solved by nuclear energy. The authors disagree about* B *and* D*, and the first author does not bring up* C*.*

Written Response

Possible short responses:

15. *The author states that nuclear power avoids air pollution. Nuclear plants do not emit carbon dioxide, other greenhouse gases, or pollutants contributing to haze or smog.*

16. *The author states that wind and solar energy do not create problems, whereas nuclear power does. Developing wind and solar power is more expensive than nuclear energy. Wind energy and solar energy are renewable, unlike nuclear energy.*

Possible extended response:

17. *Students' paragraphs should identify the author's purpose as seeking to convince readers that the risks of nuclear energy outweigh the benefits. Students should then discuss the reasons the author gives, including the serious consequences of accidents, nuclear plants' attractiveness to terrorists, the toxicity and permanence of nuclear waste, the spent fuel cannot be safely stored, and the danger that the uranium might be modified to build nuclear bombs.*

ANSWERS

Vocabulary

1. **C** ***is correct.*** *In lines 6–7, nuclear energy is described as having an "essential role" as "the single most effective strategy for reducing air pollution," suggesting that it is very important or necessary.* Enjoyable *does not fit the context, eliminating A.* Essential *describes something that is more than merely helpful, so B can be eliminated. D is also unsupported by the context or by the meaning of* essence.
2. **B** ***is correct.*** Emission *is the noun form of* emit, *which means "to give off." Therefore,* emissions *are substances that are given off or released into the air.* A, C, *and* D *do not fit the context or the meaning of* emit.
3. **C** ***is correct.*** *A ray is a beam of light or energy. The relationship to the word* ray *eliminates A, since a ray is not a substance such as a gas. Neither B nor D fits the context of the sentence, which refers to "long-lasting radiation pollution."*
4. **A** ***is correct.*** *The terms* store *and* spent fuel *in line 36 suggest that a* repository *is a storage place, eliminating B and D. Spent fuel would need to be kept safely but not necessarily secretly, eliminating C.*
5. **A** ***is correct.*** *The text says that a "large-scale energy source" is needed to meet the needs of "our growing economy."* B *is incorrect because no human-produced energy source is needed to create natural resources.* C *is incorrect because a family would not need a "large-scale" source of electricity.* D *does not make sense in relation to the Greek word.*
6. **D** ***is correct.*** *The context phrase is "emit pollutants that contribute to haze or smog."* A, B, *and* C *can be eliminated because these items cannot be emitted or released into the air.*
7. **D** ***is correct.*** Catastrophic *is used to describe the damage nuclear weapons would cause to the environment. In this context,* A *makes sense.* A, B, *and* C *can be eliminated because* against, producing, *and* opposite direction *are unrelated to the root* kat.

Vocabulary

DIRECTIONS *Use context clues and your knowledge of related words to answer the following questions.*

1. Use what you know about the word *essence* to define the related word *essential* in line 6.
   A enjoyable
   B helpful
   C necessary
   D lasting

2. Use what you know about the word *emit* to define the related word *emissions* in line 15.
   A costs of labor and materials
   B substances released into the air
   C chances of explosion
   D dangers to the environment

3. Use what you know about the word *ray* to define the related word *radiation* in line 29.
   A a colorless, odorless gas
   B a system of pipes for heating or cooling
   C waves or particles of radioactive energy
   D a device that transmits radio signals

4. Use what you know about the word *position* to define the related word *repository* in line 36.
   A a place to put things
   B an electrical outlet for a plug
   C something hidden for safekeeping
   D one who acts on behalf of another

DIRECTIONS *Use context clues and your knowledge of Greek and Latin words and roots to answer the following questions.*

5. The word *economy* comes from the Greek word *oikonomos,* meaning "one who runs a household." What is the meaning of *economy* in line 9?
   A the system or range of financial activity in a country
   B a nation's air, water, and other natural resources
   C a family's management of its resources
   D the least expensive accommodations for travelers

6. The word *pollutants* comes from the root *per,* meaning "through," and the Latin word *lutum,* meaning "mud." What is the meaning of *pollutants* in line 11?
   A areas of low-lying, soggy ground
   B masses of rocks left by glaciers
   C tiny particles that live in swamps
   D waste material that contaminates the air

7. The word *catastrophic* comes from the root *kat,* meaning "down," and the Greek word *strephein,* meaning "to turn." What is the meaning of *catastrophic* in line 41?
   A going against the laws of nature
   B producing lower air temperatures
   C moving in an opposite direction
   D causing great suffering or damage

1028

DIFFERENTIATED INSTRUCTION

FOR ENGLISH LEARNERS

Assessment Support: Cognates Remind students to look for cognates that will help them answer the questions on this page. Spanish speakers may recognize these words:

- *essential/esencial* (item 1)
- *radiation/radiación* (item 2)
- *repository/repositorio* (item 3)
- *emissions/emisión* (item 4)
- *economy/economia* (item 5)
- *catastrophic/catastrófico* (item 7)

Assessment Support: Context Clues

1. Model this strategy for item 1: Return to the passage. Identify helpful context clues, such as "role" and "single most effective strategy." Define *essential* based on its use in the sentence and its relationship to these words. Then examine the choices to find the one most similar to that definition.
2. Assign questions to pairs of students and have them use the same strategy. Review their results.

Writing & Grammar

DIRECTIONS *Read this passage and answer the questions that follow.*

(1) In 1970, the government established the environmental protection agency to safeguard the country's land, water, and air. (2) For almost 40 years, the agency has conducted research, set standards, and enforcing activities to prevent pollution. (3) In 1975, the united nations designated the agency as an information center for environmental data. (4) Its information is reliable, complete, and offers access to everyone. (5) The agency works with organizations such as Habitat for Humanity to make land safe for housing. (6) The agency's mission has always been to give Americans an environment that is clean, healthy, and can be sustained.

1. Which words should be capitalized in sentence 1?
   A environmental, agency
   B environmental, protection, agency
   C government, protection, agency
   D land, water, air

2. How would you rewrite sentence 2 to make its structure parallel?
   A For almost 40 years, the agency has conducted research, set standards, and enforced activities to prevent pollution.
   B For almost 40 years, the agency has conducted research, set standards, and it enforces activities to prevent pollution.
   C For almost 40 years, the agency has conducted research, set standards, and to enforce activities to prevent pollution.
   D For almost 40 years, the agency has conducted research, set standards, and will enforce activities to prevent pollution.

3. Which words should be capitalized in sentence 3?
   A united, nations
   B nations, agency
   C information, environmental
   D environmental, data

4. How would you rewrite sentence 4 to make its structure parallel?
   A Its information is reliable, complete, and lacking in secrecy.
   B Its information is reliable, complete, and accessible to everyone.
   C Its information is reliable, complete, and offering everyone an opportunity to educate himself or herself.
   D Its information is reliable, complete, and without boundaries in its accessibility.

5. How would you rewrite sentence 6 to make its structure parallel?
   A The agency's mission has always been to give Americans an environment that is clean, healthy, and that has sustainability.
   B The agency's mission has always been to give Americans an environment that is clean, healthy, and that won't decay.
   C The agency's mission has always been to give Americans an environment that is clean, healthy, and wanting to be sustained.
   D The agency's mission has always been to give Americans an environment that is clean, healthy, and sustainable.

ANSWERS
Writing & Grammar

1. **B *is correct.*** Environmental Protection Agency *is the name of a government agency. Therefore, all important words in its title must be capitalized, making* A *incorrect.* C *is incorrect because* government *is a common noun.* D *is incorrect because all three words are common nouns.*
2. **A *is correct.*** *Changing* enforcing *to* enforced *creates a parallel structure with the past-tense verbs* conducted *and* set. B, C, *and* D *are incorrect because the verb forms in each do not match.*
3. **A *is correct.*** *The name of an organization such as the United Nations should be capitalized.* B *is incorrect because* agency *is a common noun in this context.* C *and* D *are incorrect because they include only common nouns that should not be capitalized.*
4. **B *is correct.*** *Changing* offers access to accessible *creates a parallel structure with the adjectives* reliable *and* complete. A *is incorrect because* lacking in secrecy *is awkward and subtly changes the original meaning of offering access.* C *is incorrect because the long phrase beginning with the verb form* offering *is not parallel with* reliable *and* complete. D *is incorrect because the prepositional phrase beginning with* without *does not create a parallel structure.*
5. **D *is correct.*** *The adjective* sustainable *creates a parallel structure with* clean *and* healthy. A, B, *and* C *are incorrect because they do not include parallel structures.*

DIFFERENTIATED INSTRUCTION

FOR ENGLISH LEARNERS
Assessment Support: Parallelism

1. Tell students that parallel structures are grammatically equal. In other words, they are the same part of speech or the same type of phrase or clause, usually connected by conjunctions (*and, but, or, yet*).
2. Display these examples and discuss why each illustrates parallel structure:
   —The horse was young, fit, and energetic.
   —We searched in the house, in the car, and in the yard.
   —What the senator says and what the senator does are often very different.
3. Have small groups write original sentences following the parallel structure of each example. Record them on the board and discuss their accuracy.
4. Read the paragraph on this page and have students pick out sentences that contain elements that are not parallel. Before students answer items 2, 4, and 5, have them think about ways they could create parallel structure in these sentences.

INTRODUCE *MORE GREAT READS*

In Unit 9, students have discussed a number of big questions. Invite students to tell which question they found most intriguing and why. Then focus attention on the three questions that appear on this page. Discuss the recommended books and their summaries, pointing out how each book connects to the related question. Encourage students to choose one or more of these "great reads" to read independently.

ClassZone.com

To find additional books that match students' interests and ability levels, visit the Literature Center at **ClassZone.com.**

Ideas for Independent Reading

Which questions from Unit 9 made an impression on you? Continue exploring them with these books.

Should wildlife stay wild?

The Exchange Student
by Kate Gilmore

One hundred years after the crash, Daria is the youngest animal breeder working with endangered animals on Earth. The last thing she needs is to host an alien exchange student named Fen who is obsessed with Daria's zoo but who won't say why.

Frightful's Mountain
by Jean Craighead George

Frightful is a peregrine falcon that has lived with Sam since she was around 10 days old. When Sam is forced to let her go, she must learn to live in the wild on her own. Will her instincts be enough to guide her?

The Wilderness Family: At Home with Africa's Wildlife
by Kobie Krüger

When Kobie moves to the African bush with her husband and three daughters, she becomes a foster mother to a lion named Leo. Can a human mother teach a young lion about life in the wild?

Are all games worth playing?

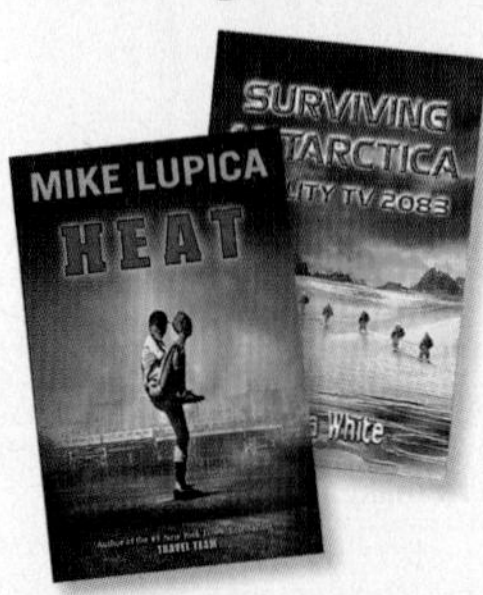

Heat
by Mike Lupica

Mike's team is sure to make it to the Little League World Series until Mike, their best pitcher, isn't allowed to play. The authorities want proof of his age, and they are asking questions about other things Mike and his brother don't want anyone to know about.

Surviving Antarctica: Reality TV 2083
by Andrea White

In 2083, five teens are chosen to reenact a historic trip to the South Pole for a television audience. They might die in the process, but they have no other way to improve their lives. Will society tolerate the way they're treated?

Game Design for Teens
by Les Pardew and Alpine Studios

How do you create a computer game? This book shows you how to take an idea for a game and make it a reality. You'll learn the skills you need and meet people who have invented successful games.

Who decides what's important?

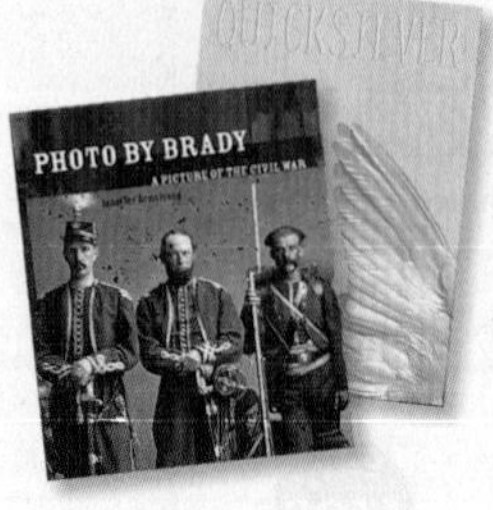

Our Eleanor
by Candace Fleming

Until Eleanor Roosevelt came along, most first ladies didn't try to affect government policy. But Eleanor was different. She persuaded her husband President Roosevelt to make the needs of poor people, women, and children a priority.

Photo by Brady: A Picture of the Civil War
by Jennifer Armstrong

The Civil War was the first war to be photographed. The images captured by the photographers who went to the battlegrounds affected the way those on the home front viewed the war.

Quicksilver
by Stephanie Spinner

Zeus, the ruler of the Greek gods, decides the fate of everyone. This book is told from the point of view of Hermes, Zeus' favorite errand boy. Hermes is quick and funny, but can he change Zeus's mind when people's lives are on the line?

The Power of Research

RESEARCH WORKSHOPS

- Research Strategies
- Writing Research Reports

1031

For help in planning this unit, see

 RESOURCE MANAGER UNIT 10
pp. 1–7

INTRODUCE THE UNIT

This unit has two parts. In the **Research Strategies Workshop,** which begins on page 1034, students are introduced to research methods that can help them locate information through a variety of print and electronic sources. Activities throughout the workshop provide students with opportunities to practice the skills they are learning and to help them understand the usefulness of research in their everyday and academic lives.

The second part of the unit, the **Writing Workshop,** begins on page 1052. This workshop provides a framework for students to apply their knowledge of research techniques to fulfill a specific academic purpose. The step-by-step instructions guide students through completing a research report.

Skills Trace

SKILLS STRAND	**Research Strategies Workshop** pp. 1034–1051
Research and Study Skills	Plan and Focus Research pp. 1035–1036 Narrow a Research Topic p. 1035 Clarify Research Goals and Develop Research Questions p. 1036 Take Notes and Organize Information p. 1036 Use the Internet to Research a Topic pp. 1037–1039, 1050 Navigate Relevant Internet Sites p. 1039 Use Library or Media Center Resources pp. 1040–1041 Choose Nonfiction Sources pp. 1042–1044 Distinguish Between Primary and Secondary Sources and Their Purposes p. 1042 Identify the Parts of a Book and Their Purposes p. 1043 Evaluate Print and Nonprint Sources for Relevancy and Reliability pp. 1045–1048, 1050 Collect Data for a Report by Conducting Interviews, Field Research, and Observations p. 1049 Become Familiar with Online Research Tools and Understand Web Addresses p. 1050 Understand Library Classification Systems (Dewey Decimal System, Library of Congress System) p. 1051
Vocabulary	Academic Vocabulary pp. 1037, 1040
Speaking, Listening, Viewing, and Media	Discuss pp. 1034, T1035–T1051

Assessment-Based Planning: Skills in red are assessed on the Unit 10 Test. **T** = Teacher's Edition page

Writing Workshop: Research Report
pp. 1052–1067

SKILLS STRAND	
Reading and Informational Texts	Analyze a Research Report pp. 1053–1055, 1066
Writing, Grammar, and Style	Write a Research Report pp. 1052–1066 Find and Narrow a Research Topic p. 1056 Locate and Evaluate Sources p. 1057 Make Source Cards p. 1058 Take Notes pp. 1059–1060 Summarize and Paraphrase Information pp. 1054, 1059 Quote Directly and Avoid Plagiarism p. 1060 Write a Thesis Statement p. 1061 Organize and Outline Information p. 1061 Document Sources pp. 1055, 1063 Prepare a Works Cited List pp. 1055, 1063, 1066 Use Transitional Words and Phrases to Create Flow pp. 1054, 1065 Support Ideas with Explanations, Details, and Facts pp. 1064 Format a Research Report p. 1053
Speaking, Listening, Viewing, and Media	Discuss pp. T1052–T1055, 1066 Creating a Multimedia Report p. 1067

Skills Assessed on the Unit 10 Test:

Reading and Informational Texts
- Analyze and evaluate a research report

Research and Study Skills
- Generate research questions
- Narrow a research topic
- Use the Internet to select and navigate relevant sites
- Use library and reference sources
- Distinguish between primary and secondary sources and their purposes
- Understand how to use the parts of a book to evaluate potential sources
- Evaluate Web sites and other sources of information for relevance and reliability
- Collect data for a report

Writing, Grammar, and Style
- Narrow a research topic
- Develop a thesis statement
- Make source cards
- Take notes and organize information
- Summarize and paraphrase information
- Avoid plagiarism
- Determine facts to include in a report
- Evaluate an introduction and a conclusion
- Support ideas with reasons and evidence
- Use transitional words and phrases to create flow
- Create a Works Cited list

For additional lesson planning help, see **Easy Planner DVD.**

OBJECTIVES

- establish prior knowledge about **research** strategies
- discuss topics of research and possible sources of information

How can RESEARCH *help me?*

Read the paragraph aloud. Ask volunteers to describe their **research** experiences in the past and what they hope to learn from this unit to help them in the future. Create a list of goals on the board and refer back to it periodically to see if students' needs are being met.

ACTIVITY Display a chart like the one on page 1032. Elicit ideas from students about what they **research** at school, at home, or in other places. For example, at school they might find out the prerequisites for taking certain classes in high school. At home, they might research the best way to conserve energy. In the shopping mall, they might investigate which store has the cheapest DVDs.

Discuss where students find accurate information. Extend the concept by having students volunteer sources that they would not trust to give them reliable data. Explore the importance of gathering valid information before making decisions. Then tell students that evaluating sources is just one of the skills they will develop in this unit.

CHECK UNDERSTANDING Ask students to list situations that might require research.

UNIT 10 **Share What You Know**

How can RESEARCH *help me?*

Doing research means locating, analyzing, and understanding information in order to answer a question. You may already be skilled at tracking down some types of information, such as movie times and sports statistics. However, there are always new resources to find and ways to improve your search. In this unit, you will learn to find, use, and evaluate sources of information. You will also learn how to improve your ability to search for sources and judge the sources you already use.

ACTIVITY What do you research at school, at home, while shopping, or while doing homework? Work with a partner to list examples.

	What I Research	Where I Find Answers
at school		
at home		
other places		

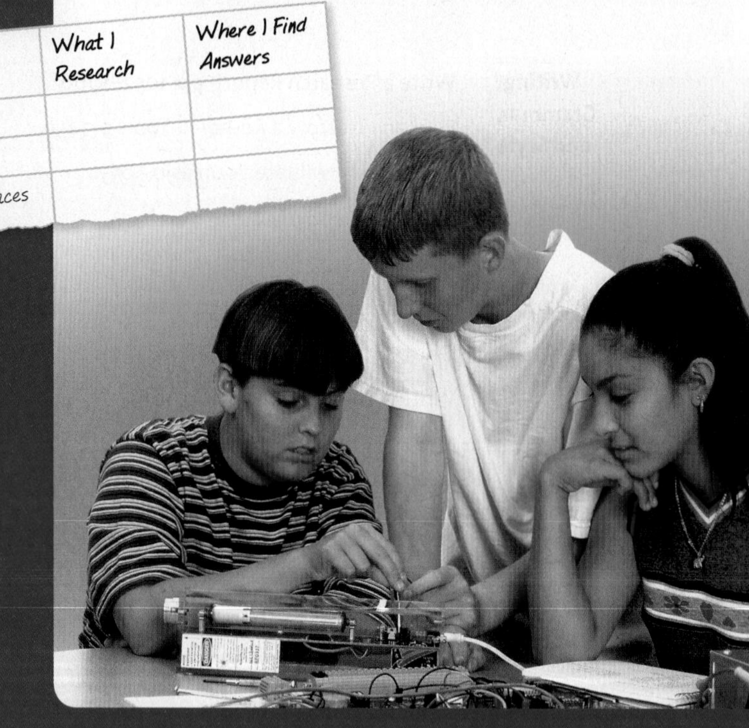

1032

Unit Resources

- RESOURCE MANAGER UNIT 10
- BEST PRACTICES TOOLKIT
- STANDARDS LESSON FILE
- Easy Planner DVD
- Write*Smart* CD
- ClassZone.com
- Audio Anthology CD
- Multi-Language Academic Vocabulary Online
- eEdition CD & Online
- McDougal Littell Assessment System

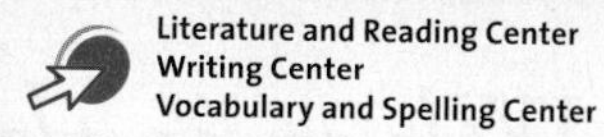

Literature and Reading Center
Writing Center
Vocabulary and Spelling Center

Preview Unit Goals

DEVELOPING RESEARCH SKILLS	• Find and narrow a topic • Search the Internet • Use library and media center resources • Choose nonfiction sources • Evaluate information and sources, including nonfiction books, periodicals, and Web sites • Conduct your own research
WRITING	• Write a research report • Narrow your research topic • Locate and evaluate sources • Take notes • Make source cards • Summarize and paraphrase • Quote directly and avoid plagiarism • Document sources • Prepare a Works Cited list • Format your paper
SPEAKING, LISTENING, AND VIEWING	• Create a Web site
ACADEMIC VOCABULARY	• research topic • research report • resources • sources • source cards • plagiarism • documentation • Works Cited

1033

Preview Unit Goals

Read the unit goals aloud as students follow along. Ask them which skills they have used in the past and which are new to them. Then suggest that they record questions about these skills and goals in their journals and look for answers as they work through the unit. Remind students about the skill strands being color coded.

Suggest that students write the Academic Vocabulary terms in their journals and add the definition of each term as they come across it in their reading. Encourage students to use the terms when they talk about their work in this unit.

ADDITIONAL UNIT GOALS

These skills will be taught in this unit but are not the major focus of the unit:

Developing Research Skills

- Clarify research goals
- Get an overview of a research topic
- Develop research questions
- Use keywords to search the Web
- Perform advanced Internet and library catalog searches
- Select relevant sites from search engine results and explore those sites
- Evaluate information based on currency, credibility of author and publisher, and relevance
- Use primary and secondary sources, reference works, databases, newspapers, and periodicals

Writing

- Write a thesis statement
- Organize and outline main ideas and supporting details

DIFFERENTIATED INSTRUCTION

FOR ENGLISH LEARNERS

Academic Vocabulary [paired option] Use the Academic Vocabulary copy master to introduce the vocabulary terms, including *research report* and *documentation.*

1. Read each word and the definition aloud.
2. Allow students to work in pairs to complete the sentences on the copy master and answer the questions in Part B.
3. Reconvene to review students' responses.

Additional Academic Vocabulary [paired option] Use the second copy master to help students study these terms from the unit: *database, hyperlink, Internet, menus, primary source, reliability, secondary source, Web site.* Read each word and sentence aloud. As a class, define the terms. Then have pairs work on Part B. Review their responses.

RESOURCE MANAGER—Copy Masters
Academic Vocabulary p. 6
Additional Academic Vocabulary p. 7

Focus and Motivate

OBJECTIVES

Developing Research Skills

- explore the key idea of **research**
- plan research
- use the Internet
- use the library or media center
- select and evaluate sources
- collect data through field research and interviews

Research Strategies Workshop

Have students skim pages 1034–1051 to preview the workshop. Remind them of the goals they identified while reviewing page 1033 and tell them that what they learn in this part of the unit will enable them to reach those goals. Explain that this workshop will help them locate, select, and use sources of information—skills that are valuable both in the classroom and in the real world.

What is the research PROCESS?

Discuss the question and the ***KEY IDEA*** with students. Direct their attention to the pairing of the words *research* and *process.* Elicit from them what *process* means (*"a series of steps that results in a finished product"*). Then ask students what this definition suggests to them about **research.** Make the point that good researchers are patient, thorough investigators who are prepared to devote time and effort to finding the best sources and the most accurate information. After students complete the ***QUICKWRITE*** activity, review their cluster diagrams as a class.

UNIT 10
Research Strategies Workshop

What is the research PROCESS?

KEY IDEA Researching a fact or two usually isn't challenging. Researching a topic, however, is a complex process that involves using several sources to find many—and sometimes conflicting—facts and opinions. Furthermore, finding the information is only the beginning of the research process. Research also requires you to evaluate the sources you find.

QUICKWRITE In this unit, you will follow a student who is interested in entering a competition for young inventors. If you were this student, how could you find information that would help you accomplish your goals? Try creating a cluster diagram like this one with questions you could ask.

Young Inventors' Competition
What inventions have teens submitted?
Who sponsors contests for young inventors?

CREATIVE THINKING ZONE

invites all teen inventors to a contest for the BEST NEW INVENTION by a teenager!

Go to our Web site for details.

1034 UNIT 10: THE POWER OF RESEARCH

Research Workshop Resources

RESOURCE MANAGER UNIT 10

Plan and Teach pp. 9–11, 14
Write Research Questions p. 15
Evaluate Search Engine Results p. 16
Explore Web Sites p. 17
Use Library Resources p. 18
Use the Parts of a Book to Find Information p. 19
Evaluate Web Sites p. 20
Evaluate Nonfiction Books p. 21
Evaluate Newspapers and Periodicals p. 22

STANDARDS LESSON FILE

Research and Study Skills Lessons 1–8
Speaking and Listening Lesson 9

BEST PRACTICES TOOLKIT

Differentiated Instruction pp. 31–38*
Graphic Organizers/Strategies
Sequence Chain • KWL: Know, Want to Know, Learned • Main Idea and Details • Three-Column Journal • Two-Column Chart • Venn Diagram

Technology

 Easy Planner DVD
WriteSmart CD

* Resources for Differentiation

inding and Narrowing Your Topic

efore you begin the research process, take a few minutes to set a research goal
nd to develop a clearer idea of your topic.

ET RESEARCH GOALS

First, write down a few goals for your research. Here is how one student listed a set of goals related to the topic of competitions for young inventors.

> ***General goal:*** *I want to enter a contest for young inventors.*
>
> ***Questions:***
>
> - ***What are the requirements?*** *Are the few simple things I've invented suitable to enter in a contest?*
> - ***What are the contests like?*** *I'd like a chance to meet other inventors and learn more about inventing in general.*
>
> ***Specific goals:*** *I want to learn more about how a young inventor like me can compete in contests, meet other inventors, and learn more about inventing.*

EARN ABOUT YOUR TOPIC

Once you have decided on some specific goals, it's time to start your search. You can use any or all of these methods.

- **Use the Internet.** Type words related to your topic, such as *teen inventors*, into a search engine. Select one or two Web pages from the search results. Then visit them to get ideas about your topic.
- **Talk with people.** Find someone who knows about your topic or shares your interest in it. Present your research goals and ask for ideas.
- **Use print resources.** Read an article on your topic or skim a nonfiction book.
- **Talk with a librarian.** Ask for suggestions for sources and ways to improve your research focus.

ARROW YOUR TOPIC

A more specific topic is easier to research than a broad topic. Here's how one student narrowed her topic after reading.

Topic	*More Specific*	*Even More Specific*
inventions	*competitions for young inventors*	*competitions for young inventors of robots*

Teach

Finding and Narrowing Your Topic

SET RESEARCH GOALS

Compare the start of the research process to planning a trip. Travelers must have a destination in mind before they decide how they will get there. Tell students that the goals they set here will guide their research journey, even if they end up changing their exact route along the way.

Review the sample goals on page 1035. Point out how the questions help the researcher define specific research goals.

LEARN ABOUT YOUR TOPIC

Tell students that like travelers who gather information about possible destinations in advance, good researchers do some preliminary research. This exploration enables them to decide if the topic is one they want to investigate further and gives them more ideas about what to look for. Review the methods that students can use to gain an overview of their topic. Tell them that, at this stage, they should not take extensive notes. Rather, in a notebook or journal, they should write down possible ideas they might want to pursue and sources that might be helpful in the future.

NARROW YOUR TOPIC

Explain that recording ideas about a possible topic in a web can help students find their focus. As they analyze different parts of their topic, they may find the one they want to concentrate on. Display a web such as this one to illustrate:

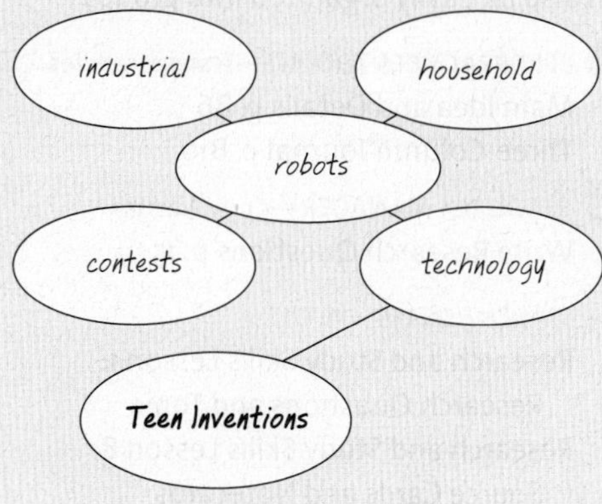

DIFFERENTIATED INSTRUCTION

FOR ALL STUDENTS

Enhance Learning Styles This workshop can be adapted to suit various learning styles.

- **Linguistic** Have groups of students develop a research handbook based on the ideas in this workshop.
- **Analytical** Have groups of students create a flow chart that shows the stages of the research process.
- **Kinesthetic** Have pairs complete the activities outlined in the text and report back to the class on the outcomes.

FOR LESS-PROFICIENT READERS

Comprehension Support [paired option] To help students understand the first stages of the research process, have them work in pairs to summarize the steps explained on pages 1035–1036, using a Sequence Chain. Review students' summaries. As a class, continue to add details to the chain to show the later stages of the process discussed on pages 1037–1044.

BEST PRACTICES TOOLKIT—Transparency
Sequence Chain pp. B21, B45

DEVELOP RESEARCH QUESTIONS

Tell students that questions such as those in the text can help direct their research efforts. Suggest that they record their questions as well as what they already know about their topic in a KWL chart. As they learn more, they can answer their original questions and add others. Explain that using the words *who, what, when, where, why,* and *how* can help them generate questions. For example, this student might also have asked *What kind of prototype or plan must be submitted to these contests? Who sponsors these contests?*

Point out the keywords indicated by the highlighting (*teen inventions, game contest, protecting ideas*). Discuss how these keywords could help the researcher obtain specific information. Clarify that keywords can include verbs as well as nouns.

BEST PRACTICES TOOLKIT—Transparency
KWL: Know, Want to Know, Learned p. A21

PREPARE TO TAKE NOTES

Tell students that whatever note-taking method they choose, they should consider organizing their information by main idea. For example, in addition to the information on contests contained in the chart, this student might have used other sections of a notebook to record details on prototypes or to make a checklist for preparing for competition.

Review some common note-taking formats, such as the Main Idea and Details chart and the Three-Column Journal. Then discuss the advantages of note cards for recording facts and ideas. This system allows the researcher to adjust the order of notes and to add more ideas during the research process. The cards can also be easily organized into groups.

BEST PRACTICES TOOLKIT—Transparencies
Main Idea and Details p. B6
Three-Column Journal p. B10

RESOURCE MANAGER—Copy Master
Write Research Questions p. 15

STANDARDS LESSON FILE
Research and Study Skills Lesson 1: Research Questions and Topic
Research and Study Skills Lesson 8: Source Cards and Notecards

DEVELOP RESEARCH QUESTIONS

After you have narrowed the focus of your topic, the next step is to ask research questions about it. Notice how these research questions can't be answered with just yes or no. Instead, they require rich, full answers.

- *Which kinds of inventions have teens submitted?*
- *How do I find a contest that will accept my new game?*
- *How can I protect my idea?*

After you write your research questions, highlight the **keywords,** or words that clearly identify your topic. You will use keywords to search library catalogs and databases and to get information from search engines.

PREPARE TO TAKE NOTES

Getting and staying organized helps you keep track of details, credit sources correctly, and do more in less time. One way to be sure you are organized is to take careful notes. If you are doing research for a report, consider using note cards. See pages 1059–1060 to learn more about this note-taking method.

For other kinds of research, try using lists and charts. Think about what kinds of information you are looking for and which format would be best for that information. Here is how one student kept track of contests she found.

Name of Competition	*Type*	*Requirements*	*Notes and Important Dates*
Creative Thinking Zone	*toys*	*fully working prototype*	*Grades 6–8 March 1 online registration*
Staples Invention Quest	*office products*	*idea described in detailed drawings and itemized specifications*	*Grades 8–12 October 15 mail-in registration form*
Craftsman NSTA Young Inventors Award	*tools*	*description and drawings—no physical prototypes*	*Grades 6–8 February 15 online registration*
Wizardkids.net	*all kinds of inventions*	*working models or drawings*	*Grades 6–12 March 15 online registration*

Many researchers start their searches online. Read on to learn how to find the best sites.

DIFFERENTIATED INSTRUCTION

FOR LESS-PROFICIENT READERS

Comprehension Support [paired option] Give students additional practice by having them identify keywords in these questions:

- What requirements must I meet to enter an inventors' contest?
- What is the date of the next inventors' contest?
- Are there prizes for winning inventors' contests?
- Where can I get ideas for new inventions?
- Do I need a sponsor for the contest?

FOR ENGLISH LEARNERS

Concept Support Tell students that keywords are main-idea words or terms that will help them find information about a specific part of a topic. Explain that when keywords are entered into the Internet or library catalog, the computer will return a list of Web sites, books, and articles that contain these words. Therefore, the more specific the keywords, the better the results will be.

Searching the Internet

The **Internet** is a system of connected computers. The World Wide Web is part of the Internet. The nickname *Web* comes from the hundreds of millions of connections, or links, from site to site. These links can lead users to billions of Web pages.

ACADEMIC VOCABULARY FOR THE INTERNET

You will use these terms when discussing online research:

- Web site
- Web page
- search engine
- keyword
- Web address
- hyperlink

SELECT SEARCH ENGINES

Search engines are Web sites that organize information based on keywords, headings, popularity among Web users, and other criteria. You can choose from many search engines. Each returns different choices because each selects and organizes information in slightly different ways. To get the best results, learn the rules for the specific search engine you are using. You might also try using the advanced search forms that most search engines offer.

USE SPECIFIC KEYWORDS AND SEARCH LIMITERS

To get the best results from a search, be specific. Try combining keywords and using search modifiers or limiters like these.

- **Use quotation marks.** Put related words together in quotation marks. A search for "young inventors" will give you results that mention both terms, in that order, right next to each other.
- **Combine terms.** Some search engines allow you to use the term AND or a plus sign to combine terms. For example, *"young inventors" AND toys* will return only pages that contain all those terms.
- **Exclude terms.** Some search engines let you exclude terms from your results by typing NOT or a minus sign. For instance, *"inventions by young people" –computers* will return all pages with the phrase "inventions by young people" except the ones that also mention computers.

TIP Identifying the best search terms is a multi-step process. Keep changing and refining your terms until you get the results you want.

This chart shows how using search limiters can give you more useful results.

YOU TYPE IN...	YOU GET...	THIS IS...
young inventors	1,090,000 results	far too many results, so you make your keywords more specific
"young inventor" competition	104 results	much better, but you can tell from the descriptions that many of the results are unrelated to your topic
+"young inventor" +toys +competition	10 results	best, because the results are closest to the research goal

Searching the Internet

ACADEMIC VOCABULARY FOR THE INTERNET

Display a three-column chart. Write the vocabulary words in the first column. Have students write their definitions in the second column. Then have them use the third column to revise the definitions with what they learn from their reading.

SELECT SEARCH ENGINES

Assess students' familiarity with the Internet by asking them to name some of their favorite search engines. *(Students may mention Google, Yahoo!, AltaVista, and Ask.)* List them on the board. Then have groups of students visit each one and evaluate their layouts and tools. Discuss their observations and draw some conclusions about when and why each search engine might be used.

USE SPECIFIC KEYWORDS AND SEARCH LIMITERS

Discuss each method that students might use to limit or focus an Internet search. Then have small groups perform their own searches, using keywords relevant to the topic in the text or their own topics. Encourage them to experiment with variations of their keywords, as the TIP suggests. For example, they might start with the keywords *teen inventors* and then place the phrase in quotes to see if there is a difference in the results. They can then add or subtract terms, such as *robots, sports equipment,* and *homework aids.*

Ask groups to keep track of their results in a Two-Column Chart. Have students share their charts. Then as a class, summarize the steps involved in planning and conducting a search for information on the Internet. ***Possible answer:*** *Choose a search engine; develop keywords from research questions or topic headings; limit and modify keywords to improve results; conduct multiple searches.*

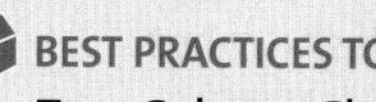

BEST PRACTICES TOOLKIT—Transparency
Two-Column Chart p. A25

STANDARDS LESSON FILE
Research and Study Skills Lesson 3: Using Reference and Search Tools

FOR ENGLISH LEARNERS

Vocabulary Support Have students list terms that they have heard in reference to the Internet. Write them on the board and help students define them.

- *cursor:* movable arrow on the screen
- *clicking:* pressing on a computer mouse to select an item on the screen
- *navigate:* find one's way through a Web site
- *users:* people who make use of a computer
- *hits:* results of an Internet search

FOR ADVANCED LEARNERS/PRE-AP

Demonstrate Search Features [small-group option] Have students form small groups, and assign each group one of the major search engines. Ask each group to investigate the search features, including the advanced search. Then have them demonstrate and explain to the class how to use each tool or feature and get the most benefit out of the search engine. Encourage students to include charts or other visual aids in their presentations.

EVALUATE SEARCH ENGINE RESULTS

Before reviewing the guidelines, point out that the keywords used for the sample search on page 1038 returned 54,300 results. Discuss what that number suggests about the focus of this particular search.

1. Tell students that search engines order their results in various ways. Some might organize them according to how closely they match the keywords. Others might list sites beginning with the most popular.
2. Review the Web addresses on the sample Google page. Explain that some *.com* or *.net* sites have useful information, but students must be aware of the underlying commercial purpose. Point out the TIP and tell students that they might also encounter sites with *.edu*. These are sponsored by educational institutions such as colleges and universities. Tell students that a tilde (~) followed by a name in a Web address usually means that an individual has been given space on the site.
3. Tell students that the more Internet searches they do, the more quickly they will be able to identify useful sites. Have volunteers read the description of each site listed on the sample page. Discuss what each reveals about the site.
4. Tell students to make sure that anything they print includes the URL (universal resource locator), which is the Web address. They will not be able to use the material if they do not know its source.

Close Read
Possible answers:

1. *The searcher used the terms* "young inventor" contest. *These terms appear in the search box at the top of the page.*
2. *Most students will say yes because the descriptions mention contests and specify that the competitions are for young inventors.*
3. *Possible new search terms include*
   - *"young inventor" contest AND robot*
   - *"young inventor" contest + robot*
   - *"teen inventor" competition + robotics*
   - *"teen inventor" AND contest AND electronics*

RESOURCE MANAGER—Copy Master
Evaluate Search Engine Results p. 16

EVALUATE SEARCH ENGINE RESULTS

Searches often return far more results, also called *hits,* than you can examine. Follow these guidelines for deciding which results to click on.

1. **Don't just click on the first result.** It may not be the right one for you.
2. **Focus first on the Web address.** Sites with *.com* and *.net* in their address are usually personal or commercial sites and may contain sales pitches or biased information. Sites with *.org* and *.gov* in their address are usually the work of government agencies or institutions such as museums and nonprofit organizations. Be aware, however, that organizations such as political parties also have *.org* addresses.
3. **Next, read the brief description the search engine provides.** If the address appears promising and the description matches your goal or keywords, click on the result. If not, you can go to the next result or the next page of results. You can also change or refine your search terms and try again.
4. **Read the page.** Print only those pages that provide information that is closely related to your topic and your research goals.

TIP In general, *.gov* and *.org* sites are more reliable than other sites because they are usually the work of large, reputable groups, and their purpose is often only to inform.

TRY IT OUT! ***Choose Search Engine Results***

This page shows the first four results from an online search.

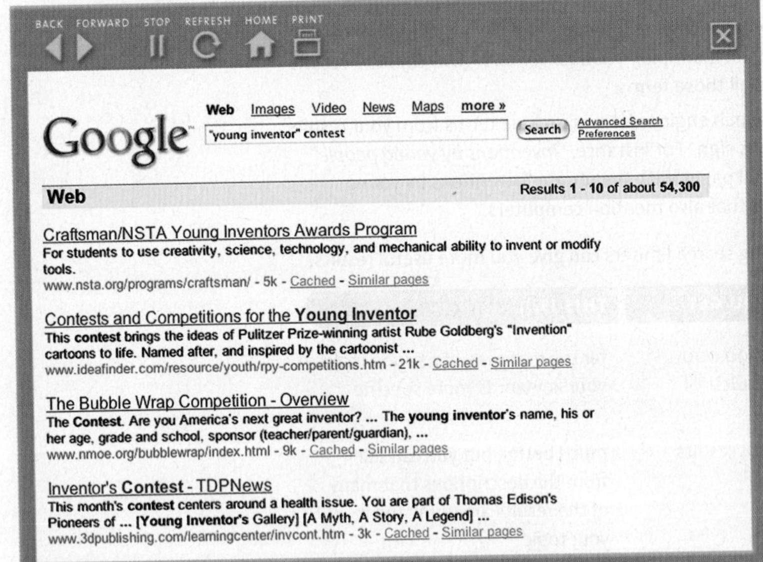

Close Read

1. What terms did the searcher use? How do you know?
2. Do you think these results would be useful to a student searching for contests for young inventors? Explain your answer.
3. How would you modify this search to find out about contests for young inventors of robots? Write your new search terms exactly as you would type them into a search box.

DIFFERENTIATED INSTRUCTION

FOR LESS–PROFICIENT READERS

Comprehension Support [small-group option] Have small groups visit a tutorial site such as *http://www.mcli.dist.maricopa.edu/webhound/index.html* or the Internet Public Library A+ Research and Writing module *http://www.ipl.org/div/aplus/skills.htm.* Encourage them to take notes on the information and use links on the site to get additional help.

FOR ENGLISH LEARNERS

Oral Language Explain to students how the various suffixes of Web addresses are pronounced in spoken English.

Suffix	Pronunciation
.com	"dot com"
.org	"dot org" or "dot o-r-g"
.edu	"dot e-d-u"
.gov	"dot guv"

EXPLORE A WEB SITE

When you click on a search result, a Web page will come up.

- **Home page**—A **home page** is the main page of a Web site. It welcomes you to the site and gives a general overview.
- **Menus and Hyperlinks**—**Menus** show the main categories of information on a Web site. Another option for finding information is **hyperlinks,** sometimes referred to simply as links. Hyperlinks and links are underlined or highlighted words, terms, URLs (Web addresses), or Web site names. Click on hyperlinks to move to another page or another site.
- **Icons**—These are small pictures or symbols that you can click on to find information. On the Web site below, clicking on the beanie icon brings up information on Jerome Lemelson's invention of a mechanical beanie.
- **Credits and Sponsor**—The **credits** tell who produced the site, when the site was created, and when it was last updated. A **sponsor** is an organization, agency, or individual that owns the site and controls its content. Knowing about the credits and sponsor helps you evaluate the site for accuracy and reliability. Look for a link that says "About This Site" or "About Us."

TRY IT OUT! ***Examine a Web Page***

This Web page contains the kinds of information shown on many home pages.

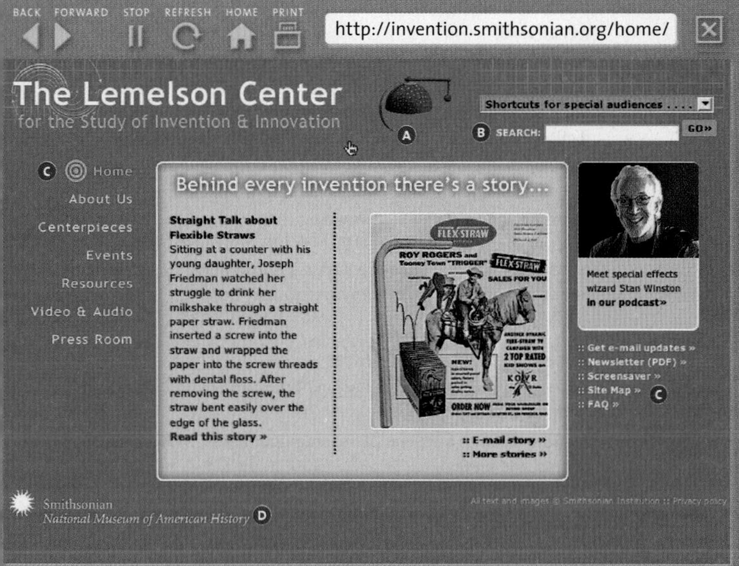

Ⓐ Icon Ⓑ Search Options Ⓒ Menus Ⓓ Sponsor

Close Read

1. Which menu item would you click on if you wanted to be notified of upcoming events at the Lemelson Center?
2. The "Search" option (item B) lets you search for a specific term or terms within the Lemelson Center site. Why is this a useful option?
3. Where would you click to find out more about who owns this site?
4. Based on what you see here, do you judge this site to be reliable? Why or why not?

EXPLORE A WEB SITE

Have students read the descriptions of Web page features on page 1039. Then discuss each feature, using the example Web page to illustrate important ideas.

- **Home Page** Explain that clicking on a search result will often take users to a page other than the home page. Tell students it is always a good idea to visit the home page, however, because it shows what other information is available at the site and often identifies the site's sponsor.
- **Menus and Hyperlinks** Explain that menus may be found across the top or bottom or down the sides of a page. Also point out that images often serve as hyperlinks.
- **Icons** Tell students that moving the cursor over an icon often displays text that explains what clicking on the icon will do.
- **Credits and Sponsor** Tell students that checking this information can save time later. Outdated sites or those sponsored by individuals who lack the proper credentials should be eliminated from a list of possible resources.

Close Read
Possible answers:

1. *The* Events *link would likely take users to a schedule of upcoming events. To be automatically notified via e-mail, users should click on* Get e-mail updates.
2. *If a user is searching for information about a specific invention, using the Search option would immediately reveal whether the site has any relevant pages; the user would not need to drill down through multiple layers of information.*
3. *To find out more about the site's creators, the user should click on* About Us.
4. *This site is sponsored by a reputable institution, the Smithsonian National Museum of American History. Also, the home page is well organized and provides a sample of well-written content. These facts suggest that the site is reliable.*

STANDARDS LESSON FILE
Research and Study Skills Lesson 4: Using a Web Site for Research

RESOURCE MANAGER—Copy Master
Explore Web Sites p. 17

FOR LESS–PROFICIENT READERS

Concept Support [paired option] Distribute print-outs of sample Web pages to pairs of students. Have them label each of these parts: *menus, icons, search options, sponsors, credits, hyperlinks.* Encourage them to identify other elements on each page as well. Review the labels and discuss the function of each feature.

FOR ADVANCED LEARNERS/PRE–AP

Demonstrate Navigation [paired option] Have students work in pairs to locate a reliable site related to young inventors or another topic of their own choosing. Then ask students to prepare a demonstration that shows the best way to navigate the site. They should include an explanation of which pages should be visited first and why. Ask them also to provide helpful visual aids.

RESEARCH STRATEGIES WORKSHOP 1039

Using Library Resources

ACADEMIC VOCABULARY FOR THE LIBRARY

Write the terms on the board. Have students work in pairs to define as many as they can. Review their definitions and have them look for the rest as they read.

LIBRARY AND MEDIA CENTER RESOURCES

Have students volunteer ideas of what resources might be found in a library. Then review the information on page 1040, discussing these additional points:

- **Books** Have students give examples of fiction and nonfiction works they have read. Then ask students which category would be helpful to them when doing research. Why?
- **Reference** Tell students that this part of the library is often a good place to begin the research process. Works such as encyclopedias give an overview of a topic that may help to narrow the focus or provide ideas for a different approach.
- **Newspapers and Periodicals** Explain the way in which the school library stores past issues. Familiarize students with any equipment they might need to use.
- **Audio and Video Resources** Ask students to brainstorm research topics for which these resources might be helpful.
- **E-Resources** Define each of these terms:
  - — *database:* a collection of information in electronic form that can be searched
  - — *e-book or e-audiobook:* a book or audiobook in electronic form
  - — *CD-ROM:* a compact disk that can store information. Some encyclopedias come in the form of CD-ROMs.
  - — *podcast:* a multimedia file downloaded from the Internet
  - — *MP3:* a file of songs or other audio data

Point out the TIP. Tell students that identifying possible resources in advance can help make their time at the library more efficient.

RESOURCE MANAGER—Copy Master
Use Library Resources p. 18

Using Library Resources

ACADEMIC VOCABULARY FOR THE LIBRARY

These terms will come in handy as you use the library or media center:

- fiction
- nonfiction
- reference work
- library catalog
- primary source
- secondary source
- table of contents
- bibliography
- glossary
- index

The Internet isn't the only place to find information. Your local public library and your school's media center are also storehouses of information. Furthermore, these places offer access to online information that you cannot get by using most search engines.

Before you start your research, learn how your library or media center is organized and what it offers. Most libraries have different sections for adults, young adults, and children. There may also be special sections devoted to business, local history, or genealogy (tracing your family tree). Many libraries and media centers offer space for quiet study. Computer terminals throughout the library allow you to find out about the library or media center's holdings, use other online sources, send e-mail, and create reports.

LIBRARY AND MEDIA CENTER RESOURCES

BOOKS

Fiction—Novels and short stories are examples of fiction. Fictional works come from the writer's imagination, but they may be based on real people, places, and events.

Nonfiction—Nonfiction works present facts and tell about real people, places, and events. Newspaper and magazine articles, scientific works, essays, speeches, history books, instructional and procedural manuals, and biographies are nonfiction.

REFERENCE

Reference desk—This is the place to ask for help with identifying and locating library materials.

Reference works—The reference section of the library includes almanacs, dictionaries, atlases, encyclopedias, and statistical abstracts. These are for use only in the library—you can't check them out and take them home.

NEWSPAPERS AND PERIODICALS

Newspapers and magazines—Most libraries and media centers carry current issues. Some also have past issues in print, on microfilm, on microfiche, or in a digitized format.

AUDIO AND VIDEO RESOURCES

DVDs—Many libraries lend documentaries, instructional films, and filmed performances.

Audio—Libraries also lend CD recordings of books, music, speeches, poems, and plays.

E-RESOURCES

Electronic collections—You can access and print out articles from databases. You can also download e-books, e-audiobooks, CD-ROMs, podcasts, and MP3s.

TIP To access e-resources from a home or other remote computer, all you need is a library card barcode, which you can get when you apply for a library card.

DIFFERENTIATED INSTRUCTION

FOR LESS–PROFICIENT READERS

Comprehension Support [small-group option] Have small groups of students arrange to take tours of the library. Design a worksheet for them to complete on their tour that asks them to identify specific examples of the resources listed on page 1040.

FOR ADVANCED LEARNERS/PRE–AP

Synthesize [small-group option] Have students work together on a floor map and guide of the school library, indicating where all of the resources discussed on page 1040 are located. Encourage them to use a computer if they wish. Have students compare maps and work on a final version that can be distributed to the class.

UNDERSTAND THE LIBRARY CATALOG

The **library catalog** is a complete index of the library's or library network's holdings. Consult the reference librarian or the online search tips for the best and fastest ways to search it.

Library catalogs provide many options for searching. The most common methods are by author, title, and keyword or subject.

- **Author**—Type the author's last name first, like this: *Twain, Mark.* If no results appear, check the spelling, or try the first name first: *Mark Twain.*
- **Title**—Type in the full title or any part of it you know. Leave out unimportant first words such as *the* and *a.*
- **Subject or Keyword**—Type in a word or phrase that names your subject, such as *inventor.* If the results are too broad, then add to your keyword, such as by typing *teen inventor.* Keep in mind that you may need to try several words and phrases before the catalog returns results you can use. For instance, you might find that the phrase *young inventor* or *patent invention* produces better results.

TRY IT OUT! ***Search a Library Catalog***

A student typed in the phrase *inventor's contests* to get to the catalog page below.

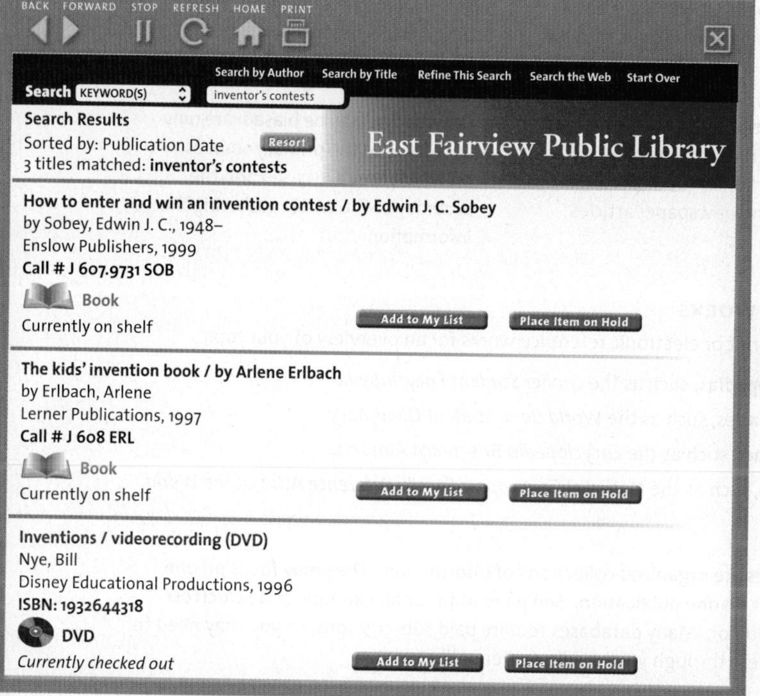

Close Read

1. How are the results on this page arranged?
2. Name five types of information the page gives for each result.
3. Name three options the user has for getting different search results.

FOR LESS–PROFICIENT READERS

Concept Support [paired option] Work with the school librarian to prepare a list of books on inventions or another relevant topic. Then have pairs of students take turns using the catalog to perform these searches:

- author (find the title of a book written by [name of specific author])
- title (find the author of [title of specific book])
- subject or keyword (find a book on a specific inventor or invention)

FOR ENGLISH LEARNERS

Vocabulary Support Point out the call numbers of the two books on the sample page. Tell students that fiction books are shelved alphabetically in the library. Nonfiction books, however, are identified by their call numbers, which indicate where in the library they are found. Point out the quick overview of the Dewey Decimal System on page 1051. Then explain that the letter *j* preceding each call number means that both books will be found in the juvenile section of the library.

UNDERSTAND THE LIBRARY CATALOG

Discuss what students know about the library catalog before they read this section.

- **Author** Explain to students that this option is useful only if they know the last name of the author. For example, a Web site might mention that a particular author is an expert in a field. In that case, the fastest search would be for the author's name.
- **Title** Tell students that this type of search can be used even if they only know a word or two in the title. The computer will locate all titles that include those words.
- **Subject or Keyword** Explain that when resources are put into a catalog system, the cataloguer assigns a subject heading. For example, a book on young inventors of robots might be given the subject heading "Robotics." Unless the words matching that subject heading are typed in, the book will not come up. Checking with the librarian to find the correct subject classification will ensure that resources are not overlooked.

  Explain that the keyword search looks for matching words in the author, title, and description of each resource. Tell students that modifying their keywords by adding terms or thinking of synonyms may produce better results, as will using both the subject and the keyword searches.

Close Read
Possible answers:

1. *The results have been sorted by date of publication.*
2. *The information includes each work's title, author, author's year of birth, publisher, publication date, call number or ISBN, and material format (such as book or DVD). Each result also tells whether the item is available or checked out.*
3. *The user might search by author or title instead of keywords, type in new keywords, sort the results differently, or refine the search, such as limiting it to certain formats. The user could also choose to search the Web for the same keywords.*

STANDARDS LESSON FILE
Research and Study Skills Lesson 2: Using Library Catalogues

Choosing Nonfiction Sources

PRIMARY AND SECONDARY SOURCES

Have volunteers take turns reading the descriptions, examples, benefits, and drawbacks of primary and secondary sources.

- **Primary Sources** Remind students that *primary* means "first." Therefore, a primary source is a firsthand account of an experience or discovery. Ask students to identify some of the primary sources they have read in this textbook.
- **Secondary Sources** Tell students that the word *secondary* means "taken from what is original or primary." Therefore, a secondary source draws from others' accounts of experiences or discoveries. Ask students to identify some of the secondary sources they have read this year.

REFERENCE WORKS

Distribute one of the reference works listed on page 1042 to small groups of students. Have them chart the organization of each resource and explain the kinds of information it provides and when it might be used.

DATABASES

Tell students that databases are gateways to sources, leading them to articles, excerpts from texts, maps, and other forms of information on a topic. Provide students with a list of the databases that they can access through the school library or media center. Discuss the purpose of each.

STANDARDS LESSON FILE
Research and Study Skills Lesson 5: Using Primary and Secondary Sources

Choosing Nonfiction Sources

Understanding different types of nonfiction sources can help you decide which ones to choose as sources.

PRIMARY AND SECONDARY SOURCES

Every nonfiction work is either a primary source or a secondary source.

TYPE OF SOURCE	BENEFITS AND DRAWBACKS
Primary sources: materials written or created by people who took part in or witnessed the events they recorded	**Benefits:** supply interesting firsthand information and details
Examples: autobiographies, public documents such as birth certificates, advertisements, speeches, letters, e-mails, diaries and journals, editorials, political cartoons, first-person newspaper and magazine articles	**Drawbacks:** may be biased because they give just one person's limited point of view; may require specialized knowledge to interpret
Secondary sources: records of events created by people who were not directly involved in or present at the events	**Benefits:** provide an overview or a broad understanding; often synthesize many points of view
Examples: textbooks, encyclopedias, reviews, documentaries, most history books, biographies, third-person magazine and newspaper articles	**Drawbacks:** may be biased; are only as reliable as the primary sources on which they are based and the accuracy of the writer gathering the information

REFERENCE WORKS

Consult print or electronic reference works for an overview of your topic.

- **Encyclopedias,** such as the *Grolier Student Encyclopedia*
- **Dictionaries,** such as the *World Book Student Dictionary*
- **Almanacs,** such as the *Encyclopedia Britannica Almanac*
- **Atlases,** such as the *National Geographic Family Reference Atlas of the World*

DATABASES

Databases are organized collections of information. They may focus on one subject or on one publication. See page 1044 for an example of a search on InfoTrac Junior. Many databases require paid subscriptions, so you may need to access them through your media center or library.

1042 UNIT 10: THE POWER OF RESEARCH

DIFFERENTIATED INSTRUCTION

FOR LESS–PROFICIENT READERS

Concept Support Have students identify each of these sources as either primary or secondary and explain their reasoning:

- diary entry of a Civil War soldier *(primary)*
- encyclopedia article about the causes of the Civil War *(secondary)*
- letter home from a passenger on the *Titanic* *(primary)*
- documentary about the *Titanic* *(secondary)*
- photograph of a 1939 high school graduating class *(primary)*

FOR ADVANCED LEARNERS/PRE–AP

Explore Resources [small-group option] Assign different groups of students one of the databases that can be accessed from the school. Ask each group to create a full description of the information the database provides and how the site might be used. Have groups collaborate on a bulletin board display that presents this information.

NONFICTION BOOKS

For in-depth information on a topic, be sure to consult nonfiction books. To decide whether a specific book is right for your research goal, follow these steps:

1. Read the **title** and **subtitle** to get a general idea of what the book is about.
2. Examine the **copyright page.** Find the latest copyright date shown. This will tell you how recent the information is.
3. Read the **table of contents.** The titles of parts and chapters will give you an overview of the book's contents. This page also often lists other useful features, such as a **bibliography** (a list of sources used), a list of suggested **further reading,** and a **glossary** (a section that lists and defines specialized terms the author uses).
4. Check the **index** for specific topics or terms that interest you. Single page numbers can signal that there is no more than a brief mention of the topic.

TRY IT OUT! *Examine the Parts of a Book*

Notice the features of the book shown below.

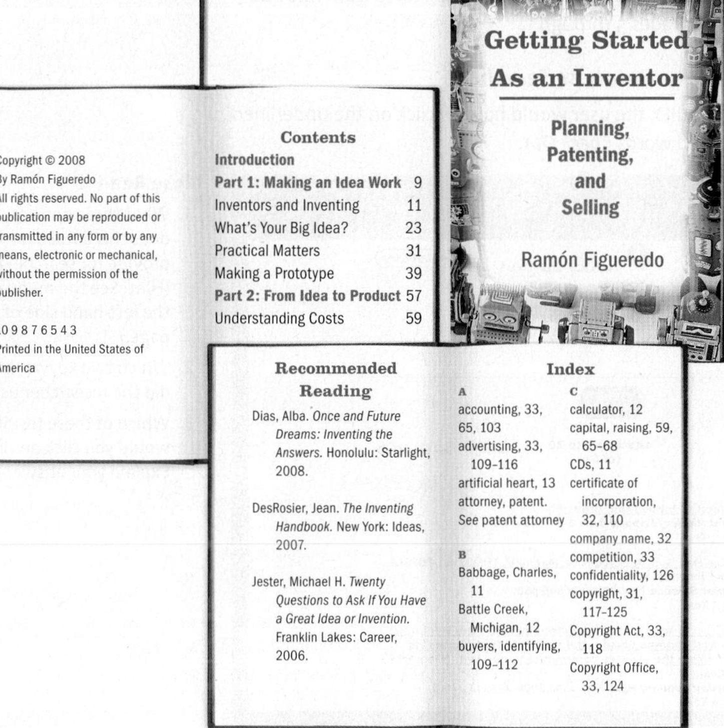

Copyright © 2008
By Ramón Figueredo
All rights reserved. No part of this publication may be reproduced or transmitted in any form or by any means, electronic or mechanical, without the permission of the publisher.
10 9 8 7 6 5 4 3
Printed in the United States of America

Contents

Introduction	
Part 1: Making an Idea Work	9
Inventors and Inventing	11
What's Your Big Idea?	23
Practical Matters	31
Making a Prototype	39
Part 2: From Idea to Product	57
Understanding Costs	59

Getting Started As an Inventor
Planning, Patenting, and Selling
Ramón Figueredo

Recommended Reading

Dias, Alba. *Once and Future Dreams: Inventing the Answers.* Honolulu: Starlight, 2008.

DesRosier, Jean. *The Inventing Handbook.* New York: Ideas, 2007.

Jester, Michael H. *Twenty Questions to Ask If You Have a Great Idea or Invention.* Franklin Lakes: Career, 2006.

Index

A
accounting, 33, 65, 103
advertising, 33, 109–116
artificial heart, 13
attorney, patent. See patent attorney

B
Babbage, Charles, 11
Battle Creek, Michigan, 12
buyers, identifying, 109–112

C
calculator, 12
capital, raising, 59, 65–68
CDs, 11
certificate of incorporation, 32, 110
company name, 32
competition, 33
confidentiality, 126
copyright, 31, 117–125
Copyright Act, 33, 118
Copyright Office, 33, 124

Close Read

1. Is this book recent enough to be helpful? How do you know?
2. Does this book give practical advice about both creating and selling an invention? Explain how you arrived at your answer.
3. Does this book contain information on making a prototype? How about on patent attorneys? Tell where you found this information.

NONFICTION BOOKS

Use the sample book pages to illustrate each point about the parts of a nonfiction book.

1. Have students identify the subtitle of the sample book. Ask them what they learn from the subtitle.
2. Point out the copyright page. Explain that if a book is reissued, it will have several copyright dates, but the most recent date is the one they should check.
3. Tell students that if their topic appears in a book's table of contents, then the book is worth examining further. Point out that both a bibliography and list of further reading can provide ideas for other books on the topic that might be useful.
4. Draw students' attention to the index page. Ask them to compare the function and organization of an index and a table of contents. Display a Venn Diagram to record students' input. ***Possible answer:***
   - ***Table of contents:*** *organized by the order in which information appears in the book*
   - ***Index:*** *organized alphabetically*
   - ***Both:*** *help readers locate information*

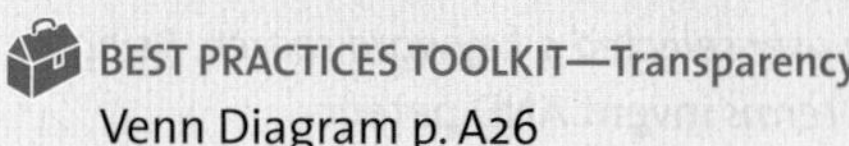

BEST PRACTICES TOOLKIT—Transparency
Venn Diagram p. A26

RESOURCE MANAGER—Copy Master
Use the Parts of a Book to Find Information p. 19

Close Read
Possible answers:

1. *Yes, the book is recent; the copyright date is 2008.*
2. *The book gives advice about both topics. The subtitle uses the words* Planning *and* Selling. *The table of contents shows that Part 1 includes chapters called "Practical Matters" and "Making a Prototype." Part 2, with its emphasis on a product, may have information about selling.*
3. *Yes. The table of contents lists a chapter called "Making a Prototype" that begins on page 39. The index has an entry for "attorney, patent." The researcher would need to look up "patent attorney" later in the index to find the exact page number(s).*

FOR LESS–PROFICIENT READERS

Comprehension Support Hand out copies of key pages of a nonfiction book (title page, copyright page, table of contents, index, bibliography). Create questions that test students' understanding of these parts of the book. For example, ask about page numbers of various topics, the copyright date, and where chapters begin and end.

FOR ENGLISH LEARNERS

Concept Support [mixed-readiness pairs] Distribute nonfiction books to pairs of students. Write these terms on the board: *title page, copyright page, table of contents, bibliography, further reading, glossary, index.* Have students copy these terms onto sticky notes and use the notes to label the appropriate parts of their nonfiction books. Then have pairs use the labeled parts to write a brief description of what their book is about.

Newspapers and Periodicals

- Have students read this section and discuss the differences and similarities between newspapers and periodicals, magazines and journals.
- Distribute copies of newspapers and news magazines to small groups of students. Ask them to summarize the main features of each publication and identify articles that might be used by someone doing research. Point out that both types of publications contain feature articles that express opinions as well as facts.
- Then explain that finding useful articles is accomplished by entering keywords into a database, such as the one on page 1044.
- Review the sample page from InfoTrac Junior, discussing the kinds of information given for each entry. Make sure students know that this database gives them access to the text of most articles.

Close Read
Possible answers:

1. *The three options are a subject search, a keyword search, and an advanced search.*
2. *The user selected a keyword search, using the terms* invent AND patent.
3. *The first result would probably be most useful. It is clearly on the topic of teen inventors. The other two articles may mention inventors or inventions and patents, but they may not mention teens or young inventors.*

Newspapers and Periodicals

Newspapers are publications that contain news and advertising. Many newspapers include other features as well, such as editorials, letters to the editor, cartoons, and puzzles. Newspapers are published daily, weekly, or very frequently. Most daily newspapers have online versions that are updated throughout the day.

Like newspapers, **periodicals** are publications issued on a regular basis. They contain news, advice, fiction, research findings, or a combination of these. Periodicals called magazines are published for the general public. Periodicals called journals are published for academic and scholarly audiences. Online versions of periodicals often include corrections, updates, and previously published articles.

Researchers often turn to recent newspaper and magazine articles for up-to-date information presented in understandable language. Older newspaper and magazine articles can offer some perspective on a particular time period.

- **Examples of Newspapers:** *Washington Post, San Francisco Chronicle, Denver Post*
- **Examples of Magazines:** *Time, Consumer Reports, Odyssey, Teen Ink, Next Step*

To find articles on your topic, use a database. The page below comes from InfoTrac Junior, a database for students in grades 5 through 12.

TRY IT OUT! *Examine an Articles Database Search*

To see each article listed in the results, the user would have to click on the underlined title of the article or the underlined words *Check Out*.

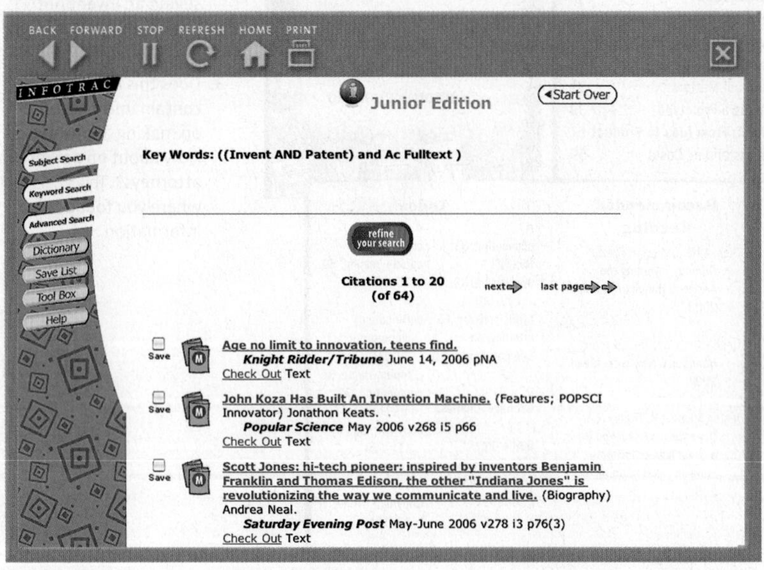

Close Read

1. What three options does this database provide for searching? (Hint: See the menu on the left-hand side of th page.)
2. Which two keywords did the researcher use?
3. Which of these results would you click on first Explain your answer.

DIFFERENTIATED INSTRUCTION

FOR LESS–PROFICIENT READERS

Concept Support [small-group option] Have students work in small groups to search a database for articles on young inventors or a topic of their own choosing. Have students find and print the text of one of the articles as well as the first page of search results. Have students summarize the process they used and what they learned.

FOR ENGLISH LEARNERS

Task Support Display a chart such as this one to summarize the steps involved in searching for Web sites, nonfiction books, or periodicals:

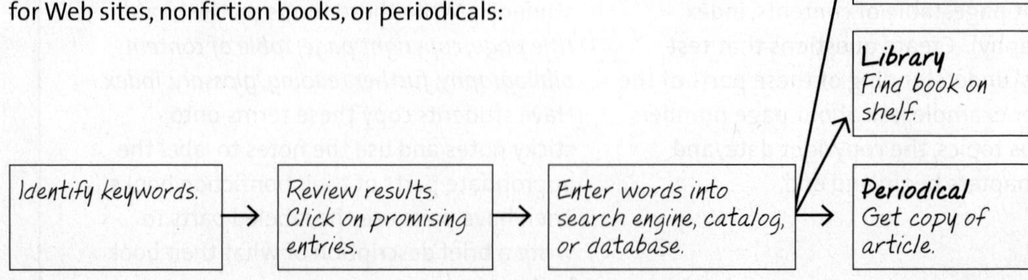

Evaluating Sources

Sources vary widely in purpose, authorship, and the care with which they were created. Therefore, always carefully evaluate the sources you use. **Evaluating** means asking and answering questions like the ones below about the trustworthiness of every book, magazine, newspaper, Web site, and other source you use. Refer to pages 1046–1048 for questions about specific types of sources.

QUESTION	REASONS TO ASK
What is the publication date?	Up-to-date information is important, especially in medicine, technology, sports, and politics. Even when you are researching an event that happened many years ago, up-to-date sources usually present the latest findings and insights.
Who is the author?	In general, look for sources of information written by people who are experts in their field. The author's profession, other publications, and awards are additional guides to his or her knowledge of the subject.
Who published the source?	Some publishers take more care to ensure accuracy than others do. Magazines and newspapers that feature articles about fads and celebrities can be unreliable. Instead, look for well-known publishers and university presses. If you're in doubt, ask a librarian for help.
What is the author's or publisher's purpose?	Many Web sites and publications have a political or commercial purpose. Some may present **biased,** or one-sided, views of topics, leaving out information that does not suit their purposes. Determine the source's intended purpose before you decide whether to use it.
Is this information useful to me?	Make sure the source is written at a level that's appropriate for you—not too childish or too scholarly. Also, study the table of contents or menus for your keywords or for other words and phrases that relate specifically to your research goals.

Evaluating Sources

Tell students that it is their responsibility to evaluate their sources. Have volunteers read the information on each question aloud. Discuss these additional ideas:

Date Discuss with students how some information does not change. For example, basic facts about a historical event, such as the invention of the steam engine, are the same whether the source is recent or several years old. Information on other topics, such as current developments in robotics, quickly becomes outdated. Explain that, in general, students should look for sources published within the last five years.

Author Tell students that sometimes authors or creators of Web sites make themselves sound like experts. Urge students to look for actual credentials, such as degrees from accredited institutions, years of experience in the field, and membership in professional organizations.

Publisher Remind students that the sponsor of a Web site is like the publisher. Ask students which Web addresses indicate a reliable publisher. ***Possible answer:*** *Addresses ending in* .gov, .org, *and* .edu *are usually reliable.*

Purpose Tell students that whether the author's or publisher's purpose is to inform or to persuade, they need to keep these guidelines in mind to help them check the accuracy and validity of the information:

- Arguments and main ideas should be supported by facts, not opinions.
- Arguments should be logical. Fallacies and appeals to emotion should be avoided.
- Conclusions drawn by the author or publisher should be based on evidence and not influenced by personal values.

Usefulness Encourage students not to waste time on sources that are only distantly related to their focus. Also tell them that checking the bibliography will help them determine the comprehensiveness of the information likely to be included in the source.

FOR LESS–PROFICIENT READERS

Concept Support Tell students that biased or one-sided sources often rely on faulty arguments. Review these terms with students and tell them to avoid sources that use one or more of these techniques:

- **Overgeneralizations** are statements too broad to be supported or proven true. Tell students to beware of words such as *all, every, none, never,* and *always*. Example: All young inventors are good students.
- **Circular reasoning** is when an argument is supported by the same idea in different words. Example: More contests should be held for young inventors because there aren't enough of these contests.
- **Either/or fallacy** is an argument that presents only two of several alternatives as if they are the only choices. Example: A person either enjoys inventing or he doesn't. This argument ignores the possibility that someone might enjoy inventing some things but not others.

EVALUATE WEB SITES

Have students read this page silently. Follow up with these additional ideas and activities:

Creator Remind students that sites sponsored by branches of the government, educational institutions, or not-for-profit organizations are more likely to have creators with bona fide credentials. In addition, a site should provide a way to obtain information about the creator.

Purpose Discuss the various purposes of Web sites. Than have small groups find and print home pages of sites that were created to persuade, to inform, or to entertain. Compare and contrast the information on each.

Accuracy Tell students to avoid Web sites with obvious errors.

Credits Remind students that a recently updated site shows evidence of careful maintenance and will also include the most current material.

Reliability Tell students that while the Internet offers a convenient way to research, they should not be satisfied with only electronic resources. Using print resources as well will help them validate their facts and discover as much as possible about their topic.

Close Read

Possible answers:

1. *The purpose of the site is to sell a service that helps inventors patent their inventions.*
2. *This site does not contain any information about the author, other than a name. The home page does not even make the services clear.*
3. *The site appears to be the work of a single individual; there is no sponsoring organization and no way to judge the accuracy of anything on the site; the site has been created for the purpose of selling; there is an unrelated ad; there is a spelling error ("Aplication").*

RESOURCE MANAGER—Copy Master
Evaluate Web Sites p. 17

STANDARDS LESSON FILE
Research and Study Skills Lesson 7: Evaluating Electronic Sources

EVALUATE WEB SITES

A book is often the result of teamwork: it has an author as well as editors and reviewers. On the other hand, a Web site may be the work of just one individual. In many cases, no one has checked or reviewed personal Web sites.

To evaluate a Web site, ask and answer these questions:

- **Who created the site?** Is the author an expert? What does the site tell you about the author(s)?
- **Why was the site created?** Consider whether the creators want to sell you something—either a product or an idea.
- **Are there problems on the site?** Watch for mistakes in facts, grammar, or spelling, which may mean that the source is unreliable.
- **Are there credits?** Look for a bibliography of the site's creator, the name of a sponsoring organization, and a "last updated" reference.
- **Could you consult a more reliable source to find coverage of the same topic?** Use a variety of sources, such as encyclopedias, almanacs, magazines, newspapers, documentaries, and interviews with experts.

TRY IT OUT! ***Examine a Personal Web Site***

What is useful about this site? What errors or problems do you see?

Close Read

1. What is the purpose of this site?
2. What is missing from this site that could help you evaluate it?
3. Name two other problems with this site.

DIFFERENTIATED INSTRUCTION

FOR LESS–PROFICIENT READERS

Concept Support Distribute copies of a reliable Web page, such as *http://www.nasa.gov/audience/forstudents/5-8/features/index.html.* Have students use the guidelines on page 1046 to help them explain why the site is reliable. Discuss their evaluations together as a group.

FOR ADVANCED LEARNERS/PRE–AP

Evaluate Web Sites Have students find two Web sites on young inventors or another topic of their choosing—one that is reliable and one that is not reliable. Have students print pages from the site and explain their evaluation of each.

EVALUATE A NONFICTION BOOK

Once you have found a book with information on your topic, how do you evaluate it? Ask and answer these questions:

- **What is the copyright date?** Look for the most recent date on the copyright page. If you see many dates, that is a good sign because it means that the book has been through many updates and printings. The book jacket may also say *revised, updated,* or *new.*
- **Is the book carefully researched?** Look for a **bibliography,** a list of works the author referred to when writing. Also, look for **footnotes** and **end notes** that help you understand where the author found specific information. Check the back of the book for an **appendix** with additional information, such as maps, charts, or tables.
- **Who is the author?** Look for an author biography on the book jacket or at the end of the book. Use the biography to learn more about the author's education, profession, and other publications.

TRY IT OUT! ***Examine a Nonfiction Book***

Decide whether this book is a reliable source for someone who is researching the topic of teen inventors who got patents. Use what you have learned about nonfiction books and about the parts of a book (page 1043).

New for 1992!
3rd Edition
About the Author
The author of ten books and numerous articles for young readers, Ilana Brodsky has written on topics that range from lasers to artificial turf to the poet Emily Dickinson. The idea for *Kids Create* was born when Brodsky stumbled into a competition for teen inventors in Omaha. "This fascinating story just screamed to be told," Brodsky explained.
Ms. Brodsky lives in Buffalo, New York, with her two cats.

Close Read

1. What is this book about?
2. Is the author an expert on this topic? What are her qualifications?
3. How up to date is this book? Is it new or revised?
4. What other parts of this book would provide information about its reliability and usefulness? (Hint: See page 1043.)

EVALUATE A NONFICTION BOOK

After volunteers have read each question and corresponding explanation, add these points and activities as desired:

Copyright Have students identify the copyright date of the sample book and discuss its significance.

Credibility Familiarize students with these parts of the book by distributing sample bibliography, footnote or end note, and appendix pages. Examine each as a class and discuss what can be learned about the book's reliability from the information contained in these parts.

Author Distribute copies of author biographies from various nonfiction books. Have students highlight the details in each biography that help them assess the author's qualifications.

Close Read

Possible answers:

1. *This book is about young people who invent in the United States.*
2. *The author is not an expert. She is a published author, but she became interested in her topic by stumbling upon it, and her short biography lists no related publications or related professional experience.*
3. *This book is not up to date. It is a revised (third) edition, but it was published in 1992.*
4. *Other parts of the book that could provide information about its reliability include a bibliography, footnotes or end notes, and an appendix. The book's table of contents, glossary, and index would reveal more about its usefulness.*

RESOURCE MANAGER—Copy Master
Evaluate Nonfiction Books p. 21

FOR LESS–PROFICIENT READERS

Concept Support [small-group option] As a class, create a checklist to evaluate a nonfiction book. For example, one question might be *Does the author have experience or academic training in the field?* Then divide students into small groups and distribute a nonfiction book to each group. Have students use the criteria to assess their source. Ask groups to present their evaluations.

EVALUATE NEWSPAPERS AND PERIODICALS

Review each of the questions that students should ask when evaluating a periodical.

Reputation Have students identify newspapers or magazines that they think would be considered well-respected or reliable. Then have them list periodicals that should not be used for serious research purposes.

Publication Distribute back issues of a periodical to groups of students. Have them discuss which articles might still have value to a researcher and why.

Author Point out that the same assumption applies if the writer of an article cannot be identified. If the publication is well-respected, then all the articles it publishes should be reliable.

Verification Tell students that a source should not be used if its facts cannot be verified or if more than one other source disagrees with it.

Close Read

Possible answers:

1. *This article is closely related to the topic; it features a teen inventor of a snow shovel.*
2. *This information is probably reliable, but a person would have to know about the publication—the* Warren Star*—to know for certain.*
3. *This information can help the reader verify information in the article; it is also an indication that the paper stands behind the information, making it likely that the information is reliable.*

If students need help . . . Read the article aloud, modeling how to use each detail to draw conclusions about its reliability.

RESOURCE MANAGER—Copy Master
Evaluate Newspapers and Periodicals p. 22

STANDARDS LESSON FILE
Research and Study Skills Lesson 6: Evaluating Print Sources

EVALUATE NEWSPAPERS AND PERIODICALS

Periodicals are a good source of recent information. Your library may offer some of them in print and many others online or on microfilm. Once you find a periodical article, you should evaluate it before you use it. Ask and answer these questions:

- **Is this magazine or newspaper well-known and respected?** Many national magazines and newspapers with large circulation numbers are reliable. If a publication prints rumors about celebrities, stories about space aliens, or miracle weight-loss cures, avoid it.
- **When was it published?** Up-to-date sources are best unless you're looking for details or insights from a particular period. For example, if you are researching a particular inventor from the past, a magazine or newspaper article from when he or she was alive and inventing could be among your best sources.
- **Who is the author?** Look for information about the writer. Assume that staff writers are as reliable as the publication in which they appear.
- **Can you verify the facts?** You should be able to verify every fact in at least one other source.

TRY IT OUT! ***Examine a Newspaper Article***

Ask questions about the periodical, the author, the facts, and other content to evaluate this article.

from the Warren Star

Warren Teen Wins Inventors' Competition

BY DERONE SANDAGE, STAFF WRITER

Judges at the Young Inventors' Convention in Buffalo have awarded first prize to a local teenager.

"Shoveling snow is nobody's favorite chore," says Warren Middle School student Alex Heisner, "so I thought I would make it a little easier."

Heisner invented the Shovel-L, a sturdy, wheeled shovel that makes snow removal less of a strain on the back and shoulders. "It works on heavy, wet snow and on the dry, powdery kind," explained the 13-year-old, who has applied for a patent. "It isn't so great with leaves, though. They mostly just blow away."

HELP FOR YOUNG INVENTORS

- The Young Inventors Convention will meet in Baltimore next October. Other area and national conventions exist.
- Try calling local colleges and universities and asking for the school of business. Professors, instructors, or business clubs may offer advice.
- The local office of the Small Business Administration can offer tips and contacts.

When Heisner demonstrated his device at the convention, judges agreed that it really did work.

See INVENTOR, page B7

Close Read

1. How well is this article related to the research topic "invention competitions for teens"?
2. Do you think the information in this article is reliable? Why or why not?
3. At the end of this article, the reporter included his e-mail address and the Web address for the Young Inventors' Convention. Why is this information important?

DIFFERENTIATED INSTRUCTION

FOR ENGLISH LEARNERS

Concept Support [mixed-readiness pairs] Hand out recent copies of the local newspaper to pairs of students. As a class, identify the major sections of the newspaper. Then have students examine the sections and list or chart the contents of each. Help students determine which parts of the paper they might use for researching academic questions and which might help them with everyday questions.

FOR ADVANCED LEARNERS/PRE–AP

Evaluate [small-group option] Ask students to work together to prepare a lesson on recognizing bias in articles from newspapers and periodicals. Suggest that they find examples that include loaded language, appeals to emotion, and unsupported opinions presented as facts, and compare them to factual, objective pieces that might be used as sources of information. Have them present guidelines to help other students distinguish between these types of writing.

Conducting Your Own Research

The Internet and the library aren't the only places you can find information on your topic. For example, you may be able to gather data by conducting a survey or doing another kind of field research or observation. You may even be able to locate experts to interview.

OBSERVATION AND FIELD RESEARCH

Doing **field research** means observing with a specific research goal in mind. For example, you might attend a young inventors' competition and collect data about the entries and the people who submitted them. Here are the field notes that one student took.

Notes on Visit to Young Inventors' Competition, Cincinnati, 4/26/2008

- *128 participants, 128 inventions*
- *participants represent 22 counties in Ohio (78 participants, or 61 percent, from Hamilton County)*
- *28 household devices; 61 devices related to computer hardware or software; 4 industrial devices; 6 transportation-related items; 4 inventions related to pets and pet care; 25 miscellaneous*
- *Youngest participant: 12 years, 7 months; oldest participant, 17 years, 8 months*
- *Sources of inspiration: 16 percent friends; 10 percent parents; 42 percent media (movies, TV, Web sites, radio, books, podcasts); 12 percent teachers or school projects; 20 percent "out of the blue"/don't know*

INTERVIEWS

Interviews can yield valuable information from primary sources. You can conduct an interview in person, by telephone, by e-mail, by instant message, or by letter. For the topic of young inventors, you might interview a successful inventor, someone who organizes inventors' competitions, or a patent attorney. Successful interviews depend on excellent preparation. See pages R83–R84 for tips and strategies.

Questions for Competition Participants

- *What does your invention do?*
- *How did you get the idea for it?*
- *What was your development process? Did you build a prototype, make sketches, or talk to experts as you made improvements to your invention?*
- *About how much did it cost to develop your invention?*
- *I would like to be an inventor. Do you have any advice for me?*

Conducting Your Own Research

Tell students that learning about their topic through print and electronic resources is a necessary and important part of their research. Depending on their topic, however, they may want to gather additional facts from interviews or field research.

OBSERVATION AND FIELD RESEARCH

Have students look over the notes that the researcher took. Ask them what major ideas the details support. ***Possible answer:*** *The notes include details on the competition participants —how many, where they are from, and what their ages are—as well as the types of inventions and the inventors' sources of inspiration.*

Discuss with students the steps a good researcher takes before a field observation, such as finding out background on the event, determining the kind of information to be obtained, and setting up a chart or other system of note taking.

INTERVIEWS

Ask students if they have ever conducted an interview to gather information. Ask them what they think a good interviewer should do to prepare besides making a list of questions. ***Possible answer:*** *Good interviewers should find out about the person they are interviewing and his or her field of expertise, decide how to record responses, and practice interviewing techniques.*

STANDARDS LESSON FILE
Speaking and Listening Lesson 9: Interview

FOR LESS–PROFICIENT READERS

Concept Support Do a field observation as a class, visiting a library exhibit or an event hosted by another class. Provide some background information to students before attending the event and encourage them to decide how they are going to take notes during their observation. Then have small groups meet to compare and contrast what they have learned. Discuss each group's results.

FOR ADVANCED LEARNERS/PRE–AP

Synthesize Have students review the field notes on this page and present them in a different format to illustrate how they might be incorporated into a report. Have students compare and contrast their revisions.

Research Tips and Strategies

Where to Search

Provide students with access to computers. Then visit one or more of the options listed under each category together. Discuss what can be found on each site and when it might be useful for research. Suggest that students list some of these addresses in their notebooks as possible resources for their own research.

Checklist for Evaluating a Source

Tell students that this checklist summarizes the ideas that have been presented on pages 1045–1048. Encourage students to copy the checklist into their notebooks.

Understanding Web Addresses

.COM Tell students that some *.com* sites can be valuable sources of information, such as *www.timeforkids.com/TFK* and *www.dke-encyc.com.*

.EDU Tell students that many *.edu* sites give useful information on specific topics, such as *www.exploratorium.edu/index.html.* However, some *.edu* sites also inform users about the institution itself, such as their own school's Web site.

.GOV Recommend that students start with *bensguide.gpo.gov* if they are seeking any information about the government.

.MIL Direct students to *www.defenselink.mil/sites/* to find the Web sites of the armed services, the Pentagon, and other branches of the defense department.

.NET These Web sites may be commercial in nature but can sometimes be useful. For example, *www.resourcelinks.net/coolkids.htm* leads students to many Web sites that might be used for research. Tell students to check out these sites if the initial description looks helpful.

.ORG These sites may cover a variety of subjects, such as *www.4kids.org* and *www.smithsonianeducation.org/students/*, or they may focus on a very specific topic.

STANDARDS LESSON FILE

Research and Study Skills Lesson 3: Using Reference and Search Tools
Research and Study Skills Lesson 6: Evaluating Print Sources
Research and Study Skills Lesson 7: Evaluating Electronic Sources

Research Tips and Strategies

Where to Search

Your options for finding information are constantly increasing. Be aware of your choices.

Search Engines

There are many search engines. Always use more than one.

- Google (www.google.com)
- Yahoo! (www.yahoo.com)
- Ask (www.ask.com)

Metasearch Tools

These tools access many search engines and combine the results.

- Dogpile (www.dogpile.com)
- Clusty (clusty.com)

Directories

Directories put Internet resources into categories.

- About (about.com)
- Google Directory (dir.google.com)
- Yahoo! Kids (kids.yahoo.com)

Virtual Libraries

Virtual libraries contain information in encyclopedias, directories, and indexes.

- Internet Public Library (www.ipl.org)
- Librarians' Internet Index (www.lii.org)

Other Web Resources

- American Memory, Library of Congress (memory.loc.gov)
- The Tech Museum of Innovation (www.thetech.org)
- U.S. Government Portal (firstgov.gov)
- Databases: ProQuest K–12, InfoTrac Junior Edition

Checklist for Evaluating a Source

- ☑ Is the information directly related to your topic?
- ☑ Is the information up to date?
- ☑ Is the author qualified to write about your topic?
- ☑ Can you determine the author's purpose?
- ☑ Is the writing at your level?
- ☑ Was the information provided by a reliable institution?
- ☑ Have experts reviewed or updated the information?
- ☑ Can you verify the facts in at least one other source?

Understanding Web Addresses

Web addresses provide clues to the site's author and purpose.

WEB ABBREVIATIONS AND MEANINGS	
.COM	commercial—businesses, products, and many personal Web sites
.EDU	education—schools, including teachers' and students' personal sites
.GOV	U.S. government—official U.S. government sites, such as whitehouse.gov, usmint.gov, nutrition.gov, and www.census.gov
.MIL	military—official U.S. armed forces and related sites
.NET	network—product information and sales
.ORG	organizations—museums, libraries, political parties, charities, and other nonprofit groups

DIFFERENTIATED INSTRUCTION

FOR LESS–PROFICIENT READERS

Concept Support [small-group option] Distribute a list of questions such as these to encourage small groups to further explore some of the sites identified on page 1050:

- Where does the "I'm Feeling Lucky" button on the Google site direct the user?
- What search tools does the Ask site provide?
- What is the Dogpile joke of the day?
- On what site do you find "Ask Earl"?

FOR ADVANCED LEARNERS/PRE–AP

Evaluate [small-group option] Have students work in small groups to develop an Internet directory that lists and annotates useful sites for student researchers. Suggest that students include the resources listed on this page and add to each category. They may wish to organize their directory by these categories or find an alternate way. Students may even wish to create their directory as a Web page, making the addresses hyperlinks that will take users directly to each site.

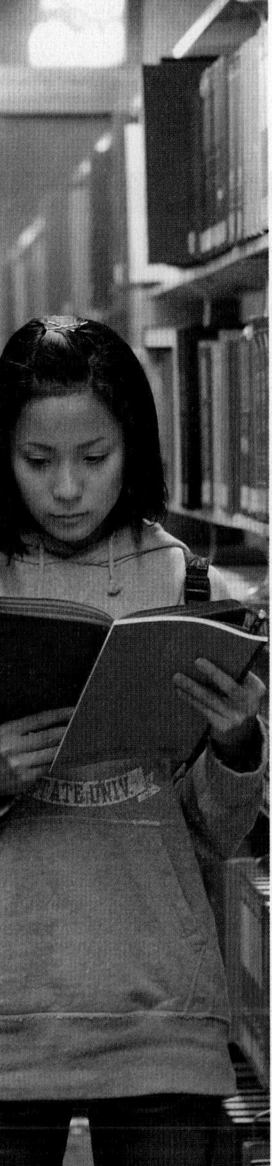

Exploring the Library or Media Center

Fiction is always arranged alphabetically according to the author's last name. Systems for classifying nonfiction vary by library. Most high school and public libraries use the Dewey decimal system. Most university and research libraries use the Library of Congress system.

DEWEY DECIMAL SYSTEM

000–099	General works
100–199	Philosophy and psychology
200–299	Religion
300–399	Social sciences
400–499	Language
500–599	Natural sciences and mathematics
600–699	Technology (applied sciences)
700–799	Art and recreation
800–899	Literature and rhetoric
900–999	Geography and history

LIBRARY OF CONGRESS SYSTEM

A	General works
B	Philosophy, psychology, religion
C–D	History
E–F	American history
G	Geography, anthropology, recreation
H	Social sciences
J	Political science
K	Law
L	Education
M	Music
N	Fine arts
P	Language and literature
Q	Science
R	Medicine
S	Agriculture
T	Technology
U	Military science
V	Naval science
Z	Bibliography and library science

Exploring the Library or Media Center

Review the Dewey decimal classifications with the class. Tell students that the groups they see on this page have ten subdivisions each, further organizing the books within them. For example, the 500–599 category includes 500 Pure science, 510 Mathematics, 520 Astronomy, 530 Physics, 540 Chemistry, 550 Earth sciences, 560 Paleontology, 570 Life sciences, 580 Botany, and 590 Zoology. Usually the call number also has numerals following a decimal point, further pinpointing the classification. For example, 578.32 and 578.91 have the same major topic but focus on different aspects.

Tell students that they will see a second number, beginning with a letter, under the call number. This refers to the author's last name and helps keep the books in order on the shelf.

STANDARDS LESSON FILE
Research and Study Skills Lesson 2: Using Library Catalogues

FOR LESS–PROFICIENT READERS

Concept Support [paired option] Have pairs of students find and list the title, author, and call number of a book in each of these categories:

- Chemistry
- Asian history
- American literature
- Mathematics
- Psychology

Review their results.

FOR ENGLISH LEARNERS

Concept Support [small-group option] Review with students the way that numbers, which include decimals, are put in order. Then write these call numbers randomly on the board and have students work in small groups to organize them as they would be found on a library shelf: 541.3 C891, 541.32 D400, 556.01 A176, 561.107 A319, 561.7 A621, 563.929 Z333.

Focus and Motivate

OBJECTIVES

- analyze a student model that reflects the key traits of a research report
- use the writing process to produce a research report
- revise and edit, using a rubric
- create a Web site

WRITER'S ROAD MAP

WRITING PROMPTS 1 AND 2

Have small groups of students brainstorm additional topics about which they are curious or find ideas by browsing encyclopedias or the Internet. For the second prompt, have students review selections that they have read this year.

ADDITIONAL PROMPTS

Use these prompts for more practice with gathering and presenting information:

WRITING PROMPT 3

Writing from Science Write a research report that answers a scientific question.

Topics to Consider

- Is there life on Mars?
- Should everyone be vaccinated against the flu?
- How accurate are weather forecasts?

WRITING PROMPT 4

Writing from History Write a research report that poses the solution to a historical mystery.

Topics to Consider

- How was Stonehenge built and why?
- What happened to Amelia Earhart?
- Where did the settlers of the Lost Colony of Roanoke go?

For additional writing prompts, see

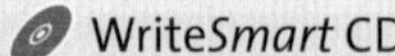

Write*Smart* CD

Writing Center at **ClassZone.com**

KEY TRAITS

Review the six ***KEY TRAITS*** with students, emphasizing ideas and organization. Compare the list of traits with the rubric on page 1066.

Writing Workshop

Research Report

Now that you have learned how to find a variety of reliable sources, you can create a research report that showcases what you know. For the best route to an informative interesting report, follow the **Writer's Road Map.**

WRITER'S ROAD MAP

Research Report

WRITING PROMPT 1

Writing from the Real World Write a research report that investigates a topic that interests you. Your report should include information from at least four sources.

Topics to Consider

- What were the achievements of the Lewis and Clark expedition?
- Do dolphins have their own language?
- Who invented baseball?

WRITING PROMPT 2

Writing from Literature Write a research report that investigates a topic you discovered in a piece of literature you read. Your report should include data from at least four sources.

Topics to Consider

- Who started the Underground Railroad? ("Harriet Tubman: Conductor on the Underground Railroad")
- Who else rode with Paul Revere? ("Paul Revere's Ride")
- What makes a person smart? (*Flowers for Algernon*)

WRITING TOOLS
For prewriting, revision, and editing tools, visit the **Writing Center** at **ClassZone.com.**

KEY TRAITS

1. *IDEAS*
- Presents a **thesis statement** that clearly identifies the topic and controlling idea of the report
- Supports the thesis with **evidence,** such as examples, facts, statistics, and expert opinions
- Synthesizes information from **multiple sources** and includes **quotations** and **paraphrases**
- Includes the **writer's own ideas**

2. *ORGANIZATION*
- Follows a clear **organizational pattern**
- Connects ideas with **transitions**
- Includes an interesting **introduction** and a thoughtful **conclusion**

3. *VOICE*
- Maintains a serious, formal **tone**

4. *WORD CHOICE*
- Uses **precise words** to explain ideas

5. *SENTENCE FLUENCY*
- Varies the **lengths of sentences**

6. *CONVENTIONS*
- Uses **correct grammar, spelling, and punctuation**
- **Credits sources**
- Uses **correct formats and style**

Writing Workshop Resources

RESOURCE MANAGER UNIT 10
Plan and Teach pp. 9, 12–14
Prewriting–Editing pp. 23–32
Publishing with Technology p. 33
Writing Support p. 34*

STANDARDS LESSON FILE
Writing Lessons 1–2, 6, 12, 19, 21–23
Research and Study Skills Lessons 8–10
Media Lesson 21

BEST PRACTICES TOOLKIT
Scaffolding Writing Instruction pp. 43–46*
Cluster Diagram • Outline • Microtheme • Writing Template: Informative Essay • Two-Column Chart

TECHNOLOGY
Easy Planner DVD
Writing Center at **ClassZone.com**

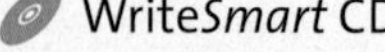

Write*Smart* CD

* Resources for Differentiation

Part 1: Analyze a Student Model

Chu 1

Jess Chu
Mr. Kinsella
English 8
6 May 2008

KEY TRAITS IN ACTION

Correct **formats and style** include the page numbers and header information that this teacher requires.

The Difficult Job of a Civil War Drummer Boy

When the Civil War broke out, many boys thought that going off to war would be an exciting adventure. When they tried to sign up, however, recruiters wouldn't let most of them become soldiers because they were too young (Murphy 8). In fact, the writer Stephen Currie says that some of these boys were under the age of eleven (3). Civil War expert Jay Hoar lists some as young as age six (227). Instead of turning these young volunteers into soldiers, the armies of the North and the South used them as musicians, especially as drummer boys (Murphy 10). Yet even those jobs had many responsibilities and dangers. For the most part, drummer boys were too young to do the difficult jobs they faced and much too young for war.

Introduction contains detailed, surprising information. Highlighted **thesis statement** makes the point that the writer will prove.

The Drummer Boy's Jobs

Drummer boys for the North and South had similar duties. One important job of every drummer was to be a kind of human clock. Drummers woke the troops up in the morning, called them to roll call and other duties, and sent them to bed (Wolfe 745; Heiser). This part of the job was not too difficult, but the day was very long for a child. It began as early as 5:45 A.M. (Wolfe 745).

A more difficult job was keeping time as the troops marched. This job was clearly challenging for many young boys. Hoar points out that at least one drummer boy was just 40 inches tall, so the drums were very big in comparison to the little boys (116). Since marches went on for miles, it's likely that carrying a big drum was exhausting.

Examples of the **writer's own ideas** are highlighted. Formal **tone** is appropriate to the topic, purpose, and audience.

Teach

Part 1: Analyze a Student Model

Have students read the **Student Model** and ***KEY TRAITS IN ACTION.*** Then discuss the model with the class, pointing out specific examples of each trait. Incorporate some or all of these activities:

- **Introduction** Explain that although the primary purpose of a research report is to inform, the facts should be presented in a lively and engaging way that shows the writer's enthusiasm about his or her subject. Ask students what facts engage the reader's attention in this introduction and why it is effective. ***Possible answer:*** *The fact that boys as young as six years old tried to enlist as soldiers is very surprising and makes the reader want to learn more.*
- **Original Ideas** Remind students that in their reports, they will use facts to support their own conclusions and judgments. They may state a conclusion first, as this writer does in the topic sentence (line 19), and then back it up with facts. Or, they may discuss the evidence first and lead up to a conclusion. Ask students what details support the writer's judgment that keeping time was a difficult task. ***Possible answer:*** *Drummer boys were often short, so the drum would have seemed large and heavy (lines 20–22). The marches were often very long, requiring the drummer boys to carry and play their instruments for prolonged periods of time (lines 22–23).*
- **Tone** Discuss with students how tone, the writer's attitude toward the subject, is conveyed by word choice and sentence structure. Point out that this writer avoids slang and colloquial expressions, using words such as *boy* and *child* instead of the more informal *kids.* Ask students to rewrite these sentences in a way that fits the tone of a research report:
  — Boy, did those kids get a shock when the reality of battle blasted them. No way did they think war was cool after that.
  — Some of those kids had to be shaking in their boots during the fighting. Talk about scary!

DIFFERENTIATED INSTRUCTION

FOR ALL STUDENTS

For general guidelines on differentiating writing instruction, see

BEST PRACTICES TOOLKIT
Scaffolding Writing Instruction pp. 43–46

FOR ENGLISH LEARNERS

Language: Skill Words Review these terms:

- *thesis statement:* a sentence that identifies the main idea of the report and suggests how the report will be organized
- *evidence:* facts, statistics, and other details taken from reliable sources
- *multiple sources:* more than one article, Web site, book, or reference work
- *paraphrase:* information from a source that is stated in the writer's own words
- *quotes:* words taken directly from a source and placed in quotation marks
- *credit sources:* identify where the writer found specific facts, examples, and ideas

- **Evidence** Read aloud lines 24–29. Point out that the writer has used two quotations as evidence in this paragraph. Direct students' attention to the citations for them. The first indicates that the phrase was simply taken from the text of the source and was written by the author, Jim Murphy. The second citation indicates that the quotation from Stephen Currie's article was in turn quoted from another, older source that was written by a different author. Ask students to skim the student model to find another quotation that first appeared in a different source from the one cited by the student writer. ***Answer:*** *The song "The Drummer Boy of Shiloh" by Will S. Hays is taken from another source and quoted in "Shiloh Inspires Writers." This documentation appears in line 47.*
- **Multiple Sources** Make sure students understand that the name and number in parentheses at the end of a sentence indicates the author of the source and the page number upon which a fact is found. Ask students to identify the sources from which the facts in lines 24–34 are taken (*Murphy, Currie, Heiser, Robertson*).
- **Organizational Pattern** Ask students to describe the order in which the writer presents facts about drummer boys in this report. ***Possible answer:*** *The writer organizes the information topically, first describing the drummer boys' jobs and then discussing drummer boys who died in battle.* Discuss other organizational patterns the writer might have chosen. For example, the writer could have followed a drummer boy through a typical day in chronological order.
- **Sentence Length** Tell students that writers use the lengths of their sentences to emphasize ideas and to create a smooth flow of details. Draw students' attention to line 49. Why does the writer state this fact in a short sentence? ***Possible answer:*** *This sentence states that many drummer boys died. The shortness of the sentence draws attention to this somber fact and reflects the shortness of the boys' lives.*

Drummers also called the men to battle, and some drummed commands during battle. They had to drum with bullets and cannon balls zooming all around them. They watched soldiers die. Sometimes, drummer boys "found themselves the target of enemy fire" (Murphy 40). When drummer boy Delavan Miller was caught in the fighting, he admitted, "I was never so scared in all my life" (quoted in Currie 6).

Well-chosen **evidence** from **multiple sources** supports the thesis.

Sometimes drummers had to help care for injured soldiers (Heiser). Drummers suffered in other ways, too. For example, hunger was constant for many Confederates, and some wore ragged clothing (Robertson 1024). Troops also faced bad weather and disease. They had to deal with being bored and homesick, too.

Transitions and subheadings help to give this report a clear **organizational pattern.**

Dying for a Cause

Many drummer boys did even more than drumming, helping with the wounded, and other chores. Although they were very young, some even gave their lives. A few were heroes.

For instance, a legend grew up about the drummer boy of Shiloh ("Shiloh"). Stories vary, but the drummer boy is said to have kept drumming even when the troops were retreating and bullets were flying (Hoar 120). In the song called "The Drummer Boy of Shiloh" by Will S. Hays, the drummer boy dies. As he dies, he says,

> "I've loved my country as my God.
> To serve them both I've tried."
> He smiled, shook hands—death seized the boy,
> Who prayed before he died (13–16, quoted in "Shiloh").

This song tells about a child who made the greatest sacrifice for his country. Many drummer boys died in the war. Some, like William Johnston at age 11, were so brave that they won the highest possible medal, the Congressional Medal of Honor (Hoar 24, 234). Others, like 12-year-old Clarence McKenzie, died from a "stray bullet" (Hoar 3).

Paraphrases most sources but **quotes** when the source is especially descriptive. Correct **formats and style** include setting off and indenting quotations of four or more lines.

Varies **lengths of sentences** and uses **precise words** to hold the reader's interest.

DIFFERENTIATED INSTRUCTION

FOR ENGLISH LEARNERS

Comprehension: Transitions [mixed-readiness groups] Remind students that transitions are used to connect ideas and show relationships between them. Have small groups fill in this chart with examples of each type of transition from the student model. Review the chart together.

For further practice with transitions, use

 **RESOURCE MANAGER—Copy Master**
Writing Support p. 34

Transition	Examples
comparison /contrast	*however (line 3), instead of (line 6), yet (line 9), but (line 17), although (line 37)*
cause and effect	*because (line 3), so (line 21), since (line 22), therefore (line 59)*
time order	*when (line 1), later (line 58)*
elaboration	*in fact (line 4), for the most part (lines 9–10), also (line 24), too (line 31), for instance (line 39)*

Chu 3

How many drummer boys died during the Civil War? Murphy says that "hundreds were killed and thousands more wounded" (43). Giving their lives was an enormous sacrifice for these children to make.

Correctly **credits sources** throughout the report.

The Last Drummer Boys

The Civil War was the last war to use drummer boys on the battlefield. Later wars were noisier, with more rifles, more soldiers, and more cannons. Therefore, no one could hear the drummer boy anymore (Murphy 41, 43). That seems like one of the few good things to come out of deadlier wars. Drummer boys of the Civil War were too young for the many challenges that they faced. Children today are lucky that this job no longer exists.

Focused, thoughtful **conclusion** sums up the writer's findings and makes a final point.

Chu 4

Works Cited

Currie, Stephen. "Drummer Boys." Cobblestone. Dec. 1999: 3-7.

Heiser, John. "Music of the Civil War." Gettysburg National Military Park Kidzpage. Dec. 2003. National Park Service. 21 Apr. 2008 <http://www.nps.gov/archive/gett/gettkidz/music.htm>.

Hoar, Jay S. Callow, Brave and True: A Gospel of Civil War Youth. Gettysburg: Thomas, 1999.

Murphy, Jim. The Boys' War. New York: Clarion, 1990.

Robertson, James I., Jr. "Soldiers." The Confederacy. New York: Simon, 1993.

"Shiloh Inspires Writers." Shiloh. 2 Dec. 2002. National Park Service. 18 Apr. 2008 <http://www.cr.nps.gov/history/online_books/hh/10/hh10h.htm>.

Wolfe, Charles K. "Music." The Confederacy. New York: Simon, 1993.

Magazine

Reliable Web site

Books

Reference book

- **Crediting Sources** Tell students that each fact or idea that is not the writer's original work must have documentation. In other words, the source from which it is taken must be identified. Review lines 36–52 to familiarize students with different formats for crediting sources. Then ask students why there is only a number in the parentheses at the end of line 54. ***Answer:*** *The author's name is already mentioned in the sentence.*
- **Conclusion** Have students reread the introduction. Then ask them why this conclusion is fitting for the report. ***Possible answer:*** *The introduction shows why young boys became involved in wars. The conclusion explains why young boys stopped being involved in wars.*
- **Works Cited** Explain that every research report must have a Works Cited list. The word *cite* means "to mention as support or evidence." So, this is a page that lists the sources from which facts or ideas were cited, or mentioned. Tell students that each source identified in the report itself, either in parentheses or within the sentences, must appear on the Works Cited list.

Point out the variety of sources the writer used and tell students that consulting a number of different resources will enrich their reports and give them a better understanding of their subjects. Then review the format of the Works Cited entries. Draw students' attention to the punctuation and order of information.

Ask students how this list is organized (*alphabetically*). Then discuss why a Works Cited list is helpful and necessary for readers of research reports. ***Possible answer:*** *Readers can check the sources for themselves if they have questions or want to find out more about the subject. They can judge the reliability of the information in the report.*

For interactive student models, see

- Write*Smart* CD
- Writing Center at **ClassZone.com**

FOR LESS–PROFICIENT WRITERS

Comprehension Support Use a graphic organizer such as this one to explore the purpose of a research report with students. Then review the format, organization, and parts of the student model. Explain to them that at the end of this workshop, their finished reports will include the same parts and will resemble the format of the model. Allow time for students to ask questions.

Purpose of Writing a Research Report

to find out new information about a subject from a variety of sources

↓

to use this information to achieve greater understanding of a subject

↓

to build on this information to offer new insights and draw conclusions

Practice and Apply

To support students during the writing process, use these copy masters:

RESOURCE MANAGER—Copy Masters
Proofreading and Editing p. 32
Writing Support p. 34 *(for English learners)*

Part 2: Apply the Writing Process

PREWRITING

1. **Select a topic and freewrite.** As a class, discuss possible topics before students freewrite independently. Remind them not to filter any thoughts but to record them all to look at later. Then have partners review each other's writing to identify directions that might be pursued.
2. **Create research questions.** Suggest that students compose questions for each of their circled words or ideas, using the words *who, what, when, where, why,* and *how.* Students might list their questions in the first column of a three-column chart.
3. **Find out more.** After students have read some general background on their subject, they should return to their charts. Suggest that they record answers to their questions in the second column and additional ideas or questions in the third.

Questions	Answers	Further Exploration
How did young kids end up in the Civil War?	They tried to enlist but were too young, so they became drummer boys.	What did drummer boys do? I'd like to know more about their activities.

4. **Make your topic more specific.** Tell students that it is better to examine a narrow topic in depth than to cover a broad topic superficially. Suggest that students review the third column of their charts to find specific ideas they might follow up on.

RESOURCE MANAGER—Copy Masters
Narrowing a Research Topic p. 23
Create Research Questions p. 24

For interactive graphic organizers, see
WriteSmart CD
Writing Center at **ClassZone.com**

Part 2: Apply the Writing Process

PREWRITING

What Should I Do? / **What Does It Look Like?**

1. Select a topic and freewrite.
Select a topic from page 1052, or focus on a topic or general subject area your teacher has assigned. Then begin freewriting about the topic. In other words, jot down ideas and associations that occur to you as you think about it. Circle ideas that you think might be interesting to research.

I liked that story we read about the Civil War. Where did Bradbury get the idea for it? What would it be like to be just a kid and in a war . . . to know that a big battle is coming and have the general admit he is scared? Were there really boys like this in the Civil War?

2. Create research questions.
Now decide what you really want to know about the idea or ideas you just circled. List questions you have. Make your questions as specific as possible.

See page 1036: Develop Research Questions

My Research Questions:
- *How did young kids end up in the Civil War?*
- *What jobs did drummer boys do?*
- *Did drummer boys ever fight, too?*

3. Find out more.
Get a better sense of your topic by visiting Web sites or by reading an encyclopedia or magazine article about your topic. As you do so, look for answers to your research questions. Make some notes.

My Answers and Other Notes:
- *Lots of boys wanted to fight in the war but were too young to be soldiers.*
- *Drummer boys kept time while the soldiers marched. They also called the men to their meals and duties.*
- *There's a lot of information about the work drummer boys did in camp and in battles. That might make a good focus.*

4. Make your topic more specific.
Think about the length of the report you have been assigned. If whole books have been written on your topic, then you probably need to find one narrow part of the topic to explore.

Narrowing My Topic:
Boys in the Civil War (too big a topic!)
↓
Drummer boys (still seems like a lot for a three-page report)
↓
The jobs drummer boys did (narrow topic)

DIFFERENTIATED INSTRUCTION

FOR LESS–PROFICIENT WRITERS

Concept Support After students have read some background on their possible topics, encourage them to complete a Cluster Diagram to help them identify a specific focus for their research.

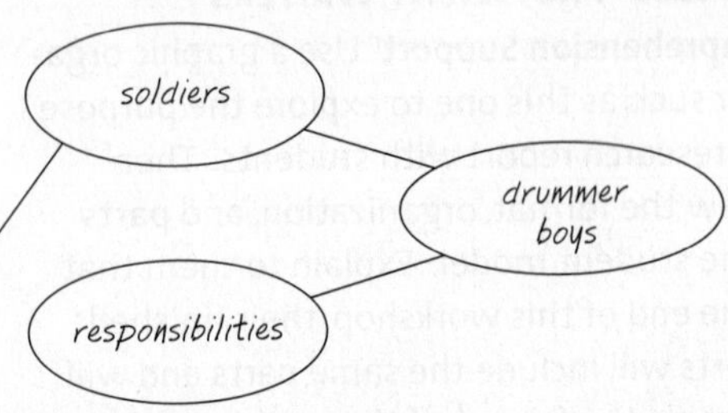

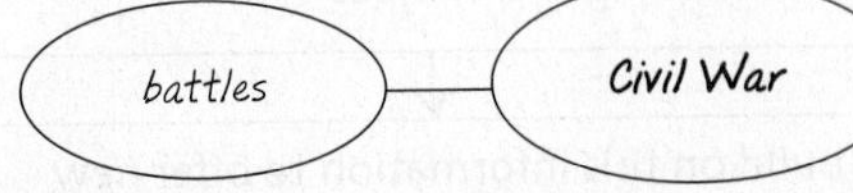

BEST PRACTICES TOOLKIT—Transparency
Cluster Diagram p. B18

RESEARCHING

What Should I Do?

1. Identify sources.
After you have narrowed your topic, you can begin the research process. The first step is to identify **keywords,** specific words or phrases that relate to your topic. You will need keywords to locate materials in the library or on the Internet. See pages 1037–1041 for help with searching for information in a library or on the Internet.

Make a chart like this one to record and analyze the sources you find.

TIP For best search results from a library catalog, read the library's online tips for searching the catalog, use the advanced search form, or ask a reference librarian for help.

What Does It Look Like?

Sources	My Comments
Library Reference Works	
"Civil War," World Book Encyclopedia	nothing about boys who went to war
Other Library Books	
The Boys' War by Jim Murphy (J973.7 M978)	full of primary source material—has a whole chapter about drummer boys
The Children's Civil War by James Marten (973.7 M377)	chapters on war and society, the war in children's literature, and children responding to the war
Web Sites	
"Young Heroes of the Civil War"	no information about the author, and no links to a home page or other sources
"Music of the Civil War" (I bookmarked this on Ted's computer)	several good facts about my topic, and the sponsor is the National Park Service

2. Evaluate what you find.
Determine whether you should actually use each source you find.

- Do not use a source if it is too difficult or too childish for you.
- Do not use a source that might not be accurate. For example, Web sites without an author, a sponsor, or working links might be the work of just one person who is not an expert.

See pages 1045–1048: Evaluating Sources

Rejected Sources

1. "Civil War," World Book Encyclopedia (no information on my narrowed topic)
2. The Children's Civil War by James Marten (not specifically about drummer boys; also too difficult for me)
3. "Young Heroes of the Civil War" (might not be an accurate source)

RESEARCHING

1. **Identify sources.** Have students list keywords related to their topics. Then review the steps they should take to locate resources, including checking reference works, library catalogs, databases of articles from periodicals and newspapers, and the Internet. Point out the TIP. Remind students also to skim bibliographies and lists of further reading for other helpful sources. Explain that keeping a chart such as the one shown on page 1057 will help them work more efficiently later.

   Tell students that during this part of the process, they may be able to narrow their focus even further as they find out more about their subject. Explain that they should not be taking notes yet. Their goal is to collect reliable resources from which they will draw information later.

2. **Evaluate what you find.** Review the criteria for assessing the reliability and usefulness of each type of source on pages 1045–1048.

   Then have students return to their chart from step 1 and cross out the sources that they will not be using. If they are left with only one or two, they need to return to their search, adjusting their keywords or broadening or narrowing their focus to help them acquire the necessary sources.

RESOURCE MANAGER—Copy Master
Sources p. 25

FOR LESS-PROFICIENT WRITERS

Concept Support To help students direct their search for sources, work with them to create a simple outline of what they hope to include in their paper. Display this example:

1. Drummer boys' jobs in the Civil War
2. Famous drummer boys in the Civil War
3. Drummer boys in other wars

Tell students to check possible sources against their outline to see if they include information on any of the major ideas.

FOR ENGLISH LEARNERS

Task Support [mixed-readiness pairs] Pair students with proficient English readers to help them locate appropriate sources on their topics. Encourage them to look for books in audio form, works in their native language, documentary films, and texts with many visuals.

FOR ADVANCED LEARNERS/PRE-AP

Synthesize Challenge students to include a primary source—such as an interview, a historical document, a letter, or a diary—among their sources. Also suggest that they locate documentary films and audio recordings related to their topic.

3. Make one index card for each source. Review with students the information recorded for each type of source. Draw their attention to these conventions:

- If there is an author, his or her name appears at the beginning of the entry. The last name appears first, followed by a comma and the first name.
- If there is no author, then the title of the article or book is the first item to appear.
- Periods separate each part of the entry.
- The source cards for Web sites include two dates. The second date tells when the user accessed, or visited, the site.

Refer students to page 1066 to review other formats they might need.

Tell students that the information they include on their source cards will help them prepare their Works Cited list. That is why they must record the details accurately. They should create a card as soon as they locate a possible source.

Allow time in class for students to create their source cards. Suggest that they have a partner check them. Remind students that they can add more sources at any time in their research process.

RESEARCHING

What Should I Do?

3. Make one index card for each source. Number each card in the top right corner. Then record the following information so you will be able to cite your source correctly later.

Online encyclopedia
- author (if given) and title of the article
- date of publication (if given)
- name of publisher
- date you accessed the article
- complete URL (Web address)

Print or CD-ROM encyclopedia
- author (if given) and title of the article
- name and year of encyclopedia
- if a CD-ROM, the term *CD-ROM*, plus the publisher and the place of publication

Web site
- author (if given) and title of page or article
- name of Web site (if given)
- date of Web site (if given)
- site sponsor or creator (if given)
- date you accessed the article
- complete URL (Web address)
- if the site comes from a print publication, the publisher, place of publication, and year of publication

Book
- author and/or editor
- title
- publisher, place of publication, and year of publication
- library call number

See page 1066: Citing Sources

What Does It Look Like?

Online encyclopedia

"American Civil War." Encyclopaedia Britannica. 2006. Encyclopaedia Britannica Online. 31 Mar. 2008 <http://searchebcom/eb/article-9006104>.

Print encyclopedia

"Civil War." The World Book Encyclopedia. 2006 ed.

Web site

Heiser, John. "Music of the Civil War." Gettysburg National Military Park Kidz-page. Dec. 2003. National Park Service. 21 Apr. 2008 <http://www.nps.gov/gett/gettkidz/music.htm>.

Book

4

Hoar, Jay S. Callow, Brave and True: A Gospel of Civil War Youth. Gettysburg, PA: Thomas, 1999.
973.7 HOAR

DIFFERENTIATED INSTRUCTION

FOR LESS–PROFICIENT WRITERS

Concept Support On the board, draw source cards as shown. Have students identify the information that is missing from each card and determine where it should be placed. ***Possible answers: Nonfiction Book:** title, publisher, call number; **Web Site:** source number, URL; **Magazine Article:** source number, title of article, date of publication, page numbers*

Nonfiction Book

1

Abercrombie, Ben. New York: 2003.

Web Site

Blake, Bella. "Drums in the 1800s." October 2007. Military Music and Choral Society. 2 May 2008.

Magazine Article

Smith, Trevor. U.S. News and World Report.

RESEARCHING

What Should I Do?	What Does It Look Like?
4. Make note cards. Now you are ready to take notes. Start with a clean index card. • Write the number of the source on it (the same number you put on the source card). • Write a specific heading for the card. Use the same heading on cards with similar information. • Write the fact or idea that interests you. • Record the page number if there is one.	*Jobs for a drummer* ③ / *Drummers woke the troops and called them to different duties, such as sick duty and work details (no page number).* *Age of boys in Civil War* ④ / *The youngest boys were just six years old (227).*
5. Take careful, responsible notes. Use these three ways to record information from a source. • **Quote** the source by copying the important phrase, sentence, or paragraph word for word. Enclose the copied words in quotation marks. • **Paraphrase** the source by using your own words to tell what the source says. Use about the same number of words as the source does. • **Summarize** the source by recording only the most important ideas in your own words. Use fewer words than the source does. **TIP Quote only when you cannot restate the idea in the source as clearly, vividly, or forcefully as the source does. Most of your notes should be summaries and paraphrases.**	**Original source** Many [boys from the North] joined because they wanted to take the defiant South and "set them straight." But most signed up for a simpler reason—to escape the boring routine of farm life and take part in an exciting adventure. Murphy, Jim, The Boys' War **Paraphrase** *Reasons boys joined up* ⑥ / *Boys from the North wanted to punish the South for being rebellious. An even more important reason for joining was that boys thought they would have a thrilling life instead of a dull one spent on a farm (Murphy 8).* **Summary** *Reasons boys joined up* ⑥ / *Northern boys wanted to beat the South and have an adventure (Murphy 8).*

4. Make note cards. Examine the sample note cards with students. Tell them that each card they make should contain just one fact or detail. This will make it easier to arrange the ideas before writing the report.

Also explain that note cards should not be kept in a particular order during the note-taking process. That is why each note should be self-explanatory. Tell students to avoid abbreviations, imprecise pronouns, or unclear references to previous notes. Display this example: *This weakened the soldiers, making them more susceptible to disease.* Point out that the note is confusing because there is no clear antecedent for *this.*

Also remind students that part of their task as researchers is to draw original conclusions from the facts they find. Suggest that while doing research, they should also write their own ideas on separate note cards and label them as such.

5. Take careful, responsible notes. Review each method of taking notes.

Quote Refer to the TIP and tell students that like the student model, their reports should have few direct quotations. Review ways that quotations can be worked into running text.

Paraphrase Suggest that when students paraphrase, they put away the original source, think about what they have read, and then write the idea in their own words on the source card.

Summarize Have students compare the summary to the paraphrase. Ask them when they might summarize and when they might choose to paraphrase. ***Possible answer:*** *Paraphrasing is used when specific facts, statistics, or examples are required to develop a main idea. A summary provides background or context for other facts.*

Set aside time for students to take notes from their own sources in class.

RESOURCE MANAGER—Copy Masters
Paraphrase and Summary 1 p. 26
Paraphrase and Summary 2 p. 27

FOR LESS–PROFICIENT WRITERS

Concept Support Choose a passage of a nonfiction work that students have previously read. Return to this part of the text and work with students to take notes on the material, using all three methods (quotation, paraphrase, and summary). Then have students take notes on a different passage independently. Compare their results to monitor their understanding of note-taking techniques.

FOR ENGLISH LEARNERS

Task Support Provide students with a note card template such as this one:

source number: ____
Heading:
Fact (in my own words):
page number: ____

6. **Avoid plagiarism.** Make sure students know that plagiarism is a serious offense that can destroy their academic credibility. Tell students that sometimes plagiarism occurs unintentionally. For example, they may copy a direct quote, intending to put the idea in their own words later, and then forget to do so. Have volunteers read each guideline aloud. Add these points in discussion:
   - **Paraphrase and summarize as you take notes.** Reinforce the idea that the majority of students' notes will be paraphrases or summaries. Also encourage them to check any notes that contain unfamiliar words or phrasing against the original source to make sure that they did not inadvertently copy the information.
   - **Don't rely heavily on a single source.** Tell students that using multiple sources helps them verify facts and make sure their information is accurate before they use it to draw conclusions.
   - **Place quotation marks around every significant word, phrase, or sentence that you copy.** Have a volunteer read the TIP aloud. Then have students decide which of these phrases from original sources should be in quotation marks:

     — *fighting appeared imminent*

     — *the North and South*

     — *drummer boy*

     — *often a mere lad*

     — *to seek adventure in the ranks*
   - **Put away your sources when you begin your draft.** Have students examine the examples on page 1060. Discuss the differences between the plagiarized and correct examples. Then have partners evaluate each other's note cards, looking for source and page numbers and language consistent with an eighth-grade writer.

RESOURCE MANAGER—Copy Masters
Avoid Plagiarism 1 p. 28
Avoid Plagiarism 2 p. 29

RESEARCHING

What Should I Do?	What Does It Look Like?
6. Avoid plagiarism. Plagiarism occurs when you use someone else's words or ideas without correctly formatting and crediting them. Follow these guidelines to avoid plagiarism. • **Paraphrase and summarize as you take notes.** Take the time to think through and understand what you are reading. Put as much of your reading as you can into your own words . • **Don't rely heavily on a single source.** Even if you find one source that is clearly superior to all others, be sure you blend the facts, ideas, and opinions from at least four sources. • **Place quotation marks around every significant word, phrase, or sentence that you copy.** Even if you copy just a few key words while paraphrasing the majority of the passage, you must put quotation marks around those words. • **Put away your sources when you begin your draft.** Don't work from an open book. Never cut and paste chunks of information from an online source. Rely on your note cards instead. **TIP When you paraphrase and summarize, you do not have to put quotation marks around common words from your source or around words that you use over and over, such as *Civil War, drummer,* and *battle*. You do have to put quotation marks around specific, descriptive words and phrases, such as in this example: *Drummer boys were often "unintended sacrifices," caught in enemy fire.***	**Original source** When fighting appeared imminent, musicians were often ordered to the rear to assist surgeons and care for the wounded. *Heiser, John, "Music of the Civil War"* **Plagiarized paraphrase** *When a battle appeared imminent, musicians were often sent to care for the wounded.* **Correctly documented paraphrase** *Drummer boys often had to help care for injured soldiers (Heiser).* **Original source** Since Shiloh was significant for the bravery of the young untrained men of the North and South alike, writers frequently wrote about the young and otherwise undistinguished soldiers rather than the . . . leaders. The drummer boy, often a mere lad who had run away from home to seek adventure in the ranks, became the subject of the most popular literature of the day. *"Shiloh Inspires Writers"* **Plagiarized summary** *The drummer boy of Shiloh became the subject of the most popular literature of the time.* **Correctly written and documented summary** *A legend grew up about the drummer boy of Shiloh ("Shiloh").*

DIFFERENTIATED INSTRUCTION

FOR LESS–PROFICIENT WRITERS

Concept Support Have students read the original passage from "Shiloh Inspires Writers" and explain why each of the following notes is an example of plagiarism. Have students rewrite the notes correctly.

Notes

1. The battle of Shiloh was significant for the bravery of men who were young and untrained and who came from both the North and the South.
2. Popular writers of the day frequently wrote about these very young soldiers, who were otherwise undistinguished.

***Possible answers:* 1.** *Shiloh was "significant for the bravery of the young untrained men" who became soldiers for both the North and the South ("Shiloh").* **2.** *Young soldiers were popular subjects for writers, who often chose to write about them instead of about great military leaders ("Shiloh").*

RESEARCHING

What Should I Do?	What Does It Look Like?
7. Write a thesis statement. A **thesis statement** is the main idea or controlling idea of your report. Everything in your report should relate to or prove your thesis statement. Be sure your thesis statement names your writing topic and says something about it. Don't worry if your thesis isn't perfect now. You can—and should—revise it after you work on your first draft.	**My topic:** Drummer boys in the Civil War ↓ **What I will say about the topic:** Drummer boys had many difficult jobs. ↓ **My working thesis statement:** Drummer boys were too young for the jobs they were given and much too young for war.
8. Organize your notes and make an outline. You can create a writing plan from your note cards by following these steps: • Separate your cards into groups with similar or related headings. • Decide on an order for the groups you created. You might organize information chronologically, in order of importance, or in any logical order that is appropriate to your thesis. • Put your cards in the most appropriate order and create an outline based on that order. **TIP The outline on this page is a formal outline, but you can also make an informal outline or create a graphic organizer such as a flow chart or sequence chain.**	**Drummer Boys in the Civil War** I. Who the drummer boys were A. Too young to be soldiers B. Had jobs that were too hard for them II. Drummer boys' duties A. Acted as human clocks B. Drummed the beat of the march C. Drummed during battle D. Sometimes helped care for wounded III. Dying for a cause A. Drummer Boy of Shiloh B. William Johnston C. Clarence McKenzie D. Number of deaths IV. Last drummer boys A. Civil War the last time drummer boys used B. Later wars too noisy to hear drums

7. Write a thesis statement. Have students read over their note cards and preliminary outline. Then have them complete this sentence: In my report I will show that ___. Explain that what they write on the line should express the purpose and the main idea of their report. In other words, it will be the first draft of their thesis statement. Have students exchange these drafts with a partner and work together on revising and polishing them.

RESOURCE MANAGER—Copy Master
Write a Thesis Statement p. 30

8. Organize your notes and make an outline. Review the sample outline on page 1061. Draw students' attention to the inclusion of specific facts in the outline. This method will help the writer put together the final report. Refer to the TIP and present other approaches students might take to organizing their material, including various graphic organizers and the Outline template. Tell students that whatever method they use, they need to keep in mind the relationships among the main ideas of the report.

As students outline their ideas, they may find that some of their notes do not seem relevant to the direction of their report. Tell students not to throw these cards away but to keep them in a separate pile until their report is completed.

Have students work on their outlines. Remind them that the order of details within each group may differ from their overall organization. For example, their report may be organized in a cause-and-effect pattern, but details within some paragraphs may be presented in sequential or spatial order.

BEST PRACTICES TOOLKIT—Transparency
Outline p. B19

FOR LESS–PROFICIENT WRITERS

Comprehension Support Tell students that each important idea they want to develop in their report should be designated as a Roman numeral section of their outline. Display this example and remind students that they may have several main ideas, each of which may become a paragraph in the report:

1. State 1st main idea
A. Identify 1st supporting detail
B. Identify 2nd supporting detail
C. Identify 3rd supporting detail

FOR ADVANCED LEARNERS/PRE–AP

Organize Report Have students use a Microtheme outline to develop and organize their reports. This outline prompts students to consider options for the introduction, formulate a thesis statement, list main ideas and supporting evidence, and develop a strong conclusion. Have students exchange their completed outlines with peer readers for discussion and comment.

BEST PRACTICES TOOLKIT—Transparency
Microtheme p. C13

DRAFTING

1. **Begin your first draft.** Encourage students to write their first draft on a computer if possible. Share these additional tips:
   - Write in complete sentences and group your ideas in paragraphs that begin with topic sentences.
   - Focus on getting all the facts you want to include in the report on paper, and worry about transitions later. However, document each idea taken from another source as you use it.
   - Include your original insights.
   - If you have trouble writing an introduction, insert your working thesis statement, work on the body paragraphs, and then return to the other parts of the introduction later.
   - If you have to work too hard to make an idea fit, it may not belong in the report.
2. **Stay focused on your thesis.** Suggest that students write their thesis statement on an index card and keep it near their keyboard or writing space so that they can easily refer to it.

   Point out the TIP. Tell students that a visual aid reinforces important ideas, summarizes information, or presents additional insights. For example, the writer of the student model might have included a timeline of wars in which drummer boys participated or a bar graph of the numbers of drummer boys on both sides during the Civil War.
3. **Weave in your sources.** Remind students that one of their goals is to capture and hold their readers' attention. Varying the ways in which they identify their sources adds fluency and interest to their writing.

For a writing template that can be adapted to a research report, see

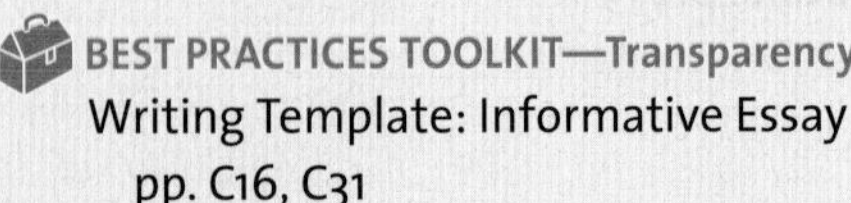

BEST PRACTICES TOOLKIT—Transparency
Writing Template: Informative Essay pp. C16, C31

Write*Smart* CD

Writing Center at **ClassZone.com**

DRAFTING

What Should I Do?	What Does It Look Like?
1. Begin your first draft. Use your outline or other organizational plan in addition to your note cards to begin creating complete sentences and paragraphs.	**Outline** *II. Drummer boys' duties* *A. Acted as human clocks* **First draft** *Drummer boys for the North and South had similar duties. One important job of every drummer was to be a kind of human clock. Drummers woke the troops up in the morning, called them to roll call and other duties, and sent them to bed.*
2. Stay focused on your thesis. Make sure each point you make relates to or proves your thesis. Sometimes it's a good idea to repeat some key words from your thesis in your topic sentences. **TIP Consider creating a chart, graph, timeline, or other visual. Be sure to give it a title that relates to your thesis. Add a source line at the bottom that tells where you found your information.**	***Thesis:*** *Drummer boys were too young to do the difficult jobs they faced.* ***Related topic sentence:*** *A more difficult job was keeping time as the troops marched.*
3. Weave in your sources. As you write, let your reader know where ideas are coming from. Try using introductory phrases like these: • "According to Murphy, . . ." • "Wolfe points out . . ." • "In 'Drummer Boys and Fifers,' Stephen Currie writes . . ."	*The writer Stephen Currie says ~~S~~ome of these boys were under the age of eleven (~~Currie~~ 3).* *Civil War expert Jay Hoar points out that ~~A~~t least one drummer was just 40 inches tall (~~Hoar~~ 116).*

DIFFERENTIATED INSTRUCTION

FOR LESS–PROFICIENT WRITERS

Concept Support [paired option] Have pairs of students determine whether each of these sentences could be a topic sentence supported by facts and details:

1. Some drummer boys were as young as six.
2. Advances in technology eliminated the need for drummer boys.
3. Drums were bigger than drummer boys.
4. Many drummer boys showed great courage.

FOR ADVANCED LEARNERS/PRE–AP

Synthesize Challenge students to incorporate a graphic organizer in their report that helps summarize, reinforce, or introduce information related to the thesis. Discuss ways of weaving this component into the body of a research report. Have students share their organizers with a partner and evaluate their effectiveness.

DRAFTING

What Should I Do?	*What Does It Look Like?*
4. Credit your sources. You have to **credit,** or document, each source you use at the end of the sentence or sentences in which it appears. Because this information appears in parentheses, it is called **parenthetical documentation.** It usually consists of the author's last name and a page number and looks like this: (Murphy 8). Here are some exceptions: • **Web site:** Because a Web site has no page numbers, use only the author's name: (Heiser). If the site does not credit an author, use a short form of the title: ("Shiloh"). • **Author named in sentence:** Use only the page number: (8). • **More than one source for a single idea:** List both sources and separate them with a semicolon: ("Shiloh"; Wolfe 745).	Drummer boys also sometimes "found themselves the target of enemy fire" (Murphy 40). — *Author and page number* Hoar points out that some drummer boys were just 40 inches tall (116). — *Author named in sentence* Drummers woke the troops up in the morning, called them to roll call and other duties, and sent them to bed (Wolfe 745; Heiser). — *Information from two sources*
5. Make a Works Cited list. Alphabetize your source cards by the author's last name. If a source does not name an author, alphabetize by title. Some common types of sources are shown here. See page 1066 of this book or the *MLA Handbook for Writers of Research Papers* for other kinds of entries.	**Works Cited** Currie, Stephen. "Drummer Boys." Cobblestone. Dec. 1999: 3-7. Heiser, John. "Music of the Civil War." Gettysburg National Military Park Kidz-page. Dec. 2003. National Park Service. 21 Apr. 2008 <http://www.nps.gov/gett/gettkidz/music.htm>. Hoar, Jay S. Callow, Brave & True: A Gospel of Civil War Youth. Gettysburg, PA: Thomas, 1999.

FOR LESS-PROFICIENT WRITERS

Concept Support [small-group option] Have several students write one of their entries on the board. After revising the format of each, have students work in small groups to create a Works Cited list with these sources. Remind students to put the entries in alphabetical order. Have groups compare their lists. Discuss and clarify discrepancies among them.

FOR ENGLISH LEARNERS

Concept Support To review the principles of alphabetizing, write these entries on the board in random order and have students alphabetize them:

Delano, Joyce. "The Youngest Civil War Soldiers."

Delany, Ramon. A Chronicle of War.

Delany, Ramon. The Tragedy of the Civil War.

"When the Drumming Stopped."

"The Young and the Brave in the Civil War."

4. Credit your sources. Review the format of the parenthetical documentation for each type of source. Draw students' attention to the examples in the right column, particularly the last one with two sources. Discuss these additional points:

- The reference is inserted before the period at the end of the sentence.
- Because every sentence that contains a fact or detail taken from another source should be documented, most sentences in a research report will include parenthetical documentation. Only those sentences that contain original conclusions, generalizations, or insights will not include documentation.

Have students highlight all of the sentences in their first drafts that lack documentation. Then have them check to be sure these sentences do not include facts, unique phrases, or ideas from any of their sources.

5. Make a Works Cited list. Remind students that all the information they need to produce this list is included on their source cards. Draw students' attention to some of the format differences: each line after the first is indented, the call numbers are not included, and each entry ends in a period.

Tell students that only those sources from which they took notes should be listed. For example, if they thought an article looked promising, but they ended up discarding all of the notes they took from it, then the article should not appear in the Works Cited list. The sources here should match exactly those cited in the student's report.

Review the Works Cited list from the student model. Point out how the title of the Web page, "Shiloh Inspires Writers," is used to place it in alphabetical order. Remind students to ignore the initial articles *a, an,* and *the* when alphabetizing.

WRITING WORKSHOP 1063

REVISING AND EDITING

1. **Take another look at your introduction.** Review the functions of the introduction as explained on page 1064. Then ask students what background information the student model provides that helps them understand the topic. ***Possible answer:*** *The introduction explains why young boys were involved in the war at all.*

   Tell students that they can also begin their reports with a relevant quotation, a vivid description, an anecdote, or an interesting fact. Suggest that they reread their note cards for ideas. Finally, point out the position of the thesis statement in the model. Explain that placing it at the end of the introductory paragraph provides a smooth transition into the body of the report.

   After students have worked on their introductions, have them discuss possible revisions with their peer readers.

2. **Improve your support.** Draw students' attention to the underlined statement in the right column and the facts that were added to support it. Tell students that they may find the additional facts they need in their discarded note pile. Or, if their support is sparse, they may have to do further research.

3. **Add your own insights and ideas.** Review the critical thinking strategies of drawing conclusions, making inferences, and generalizing. Then have students exchange papers and read each other's reports carefully, placing sticky notes where they think evidence needs to be interpreted and used to support an original insight. Ask partners also to evaluate whether the report accomplishes the purpose stated in the thesis. If not, have them suggest connections that should be made.

4. **Delete unnecessary details.** Discuss why the deleted sentence does not belong in the paragraph. Remind students that strong topic sentences will help them keep their paragraphs unified and focused. Have students return to lines 13–34 of the student model and identify the topic sentence in each paragraph.

REVISING AND EDITING

What Should I Do?	What Does It Look Like?
1. Take another look at your introduction. • Highlight the sentences that help lead up to or explain your thesis. • Do these sentences provide useful details and help to capture your reader's interest? • Add background information to help your reader understand where you are heading.	~~Armies of the North and South used drummer boys during the Civil War. These boys faced many responsibilities and dangers.~~ *When the Civil War broke out, many boys thought that going off to war would be an exciting adventure. When they tried to sign up, however, recruiters wouldn't let most of them become soldiers because they were too young (Murphy 8).*
2. Improve your support. • Ask a peer reader to underline points you made that are hard to understand or that lack support. • Add facts, explanations, reasons, or other support, as well as correct documentation. **See page 1066:** Ask a Peer Reader	*This song tells about a child who made the greatest sacrifice for his country.* ~~He wasn't the only one.~~ *Many drummer boys died in the war. For example, 12-year-old Clarence McKenzie died from a "stray bullet" (Hoar 3).*
3. Add your own insights and ideas. • Do your own ideas appear in your report, or have you merely repeated the opinions of others? • Look for places to include your own reflections and insights on the facts or opinions.	*Hoar points out that at least one drummer boy was just 40 inches tall, so the drums were very big in comparison to the little boys (116). Since marches went on for miles, it's likely that carrying a big drum was exhausting.*
4. Delete unnecessary details. • Check your report for ideas that do not relate to or prove the thesis. • Delete any words, phrases, or sentences that interfere with clarity or unity.	***Dying for a Cause*** *Many drummer boys did even more than drumming, helping with the wounded, and other chores.* ~~Some also drummed deserters out of the unit (Wolfe).~~ *Although they were young, some even gave their lives, and a few were heroes.*

DIFFERENTIATED INSTRUCTION

FOR LESS–PROFICIENT WRITERS

Concept Support Write this paragraph on the board and ask students to determine which sentences do not belong and why. *Students should identify the underlined sentences as veering from the main idea of the paragraph.*

The real issue over which the Civil War was fought is often misunderstood. Many people would say that the North fought the South to end slavery. It was a terrible war that tore families apart. The emancipation of enslaved people resulted from the war, but the real cause was states' rights. Many laborers were needed to work on the big plantations, which is why slavery began in the first place. Some states in the South felt that they had the right to secede from the Union. Can you imagine what would happen today if states just decided to secede? Their argument was that since they had voluntarily joined the Union, they could voluntarily leave it.

REVISING AND EDITING

What Should I Do?	What Does It Look Like?
5. Add transitions. • Decide whether each sentence and each paragraph flows smoothly to the next. Circle connecting words. • If you don't see many circles, add transitions to help your reader make connections between ideas.	Drummers suffered in other ways, too. For example, hunger was constant for many Confederates, and some wore ragged clothing (Robertson 1024). Troops also faced bad weather and disease.
6. Notice sentence lengths. • Reread your report. If you have many short, choppy sentences, try combining some for a more graceful flow of ideas. • If you have many long sentences, break them up with one or two short sentences to create interest and variety.	When drummer boy Delavan Miller was caught in the fighting, he admitted, "I was never so scared in all my life" (quoted in Currie 6). Many drummer boys did even more than drumming, helping with the wounded, and other chores. Although they were very young, some even gave their lives. ~~and~~ A few were heroes.
7. Make your conclusion memorable. • Decide whether your conclusion is thoughtful and interesting or just pointlessly repeats what you've already said. • Consider ending with a memorable phrase or two. • Don't overlook this opportunity to present your own thinking.	~~As my report shows, drummer boys of the Civil War faced many challenges. They had to put in long days, carry big drums, and help with the wounded.~~ The Civil War was the last war to use drummer boys on the battlefield. Later wars were noisier, with more rifles, more soldiers, and more cannons. No one could hear the drummer boys anymore (Murphy 41, 43). That seems like one of the few good things to come out of deadlier wars. Drummer boys of the Civil Wars were too young for the many challenges that they faced. Children today are lucky that this job no longer exists.

5. Add transitions. Suggest that students read their reports aloud to a partner. Ask the partners to listen for smooth transitions and connections between ideas and paragraphs.

6. Notice sentence lengths. Remind students that combining sentences can clarify the relationship between them. In the example, the first sentence becomes a subordinate clause with the addition of when, which also shows the time-order relationship between the two ideas. Have peer readers review their partner's work and suggest sentences that might be combined or shortened for greater impact.

7. Make your conclusion memorable. Remind students that the conclusion needs to reinforce the main idea. A strong conclusion might also incorporate a quotation or reflect on the significance of the ideas that have been discussed.

Display these concluding sentences that the writer of the student model might have tried. Ask students to evaluate each one.

- Although drummer boys made a valuable contribution to the war effort, the loss of their innocence and lives was too high a price to pay.
- I think being a drummer boy was hard. What do you think?

For interactive revision tools, see
WriteSmart CD
Writing Center at **ClassZone.com**
RESOURCE MANAGER—Copy Master
Proofreading and Editing p. 32

FOR ENGLISH LEARNERS

Task Support Demonstrate these methods of combining sentences:

- Create complex sentences. Make one independent clause subordinate to another.
  Young boys tried to enlist. They were patriotic. *(Young boys tried to enlist because they were patriotic.)*
- Create compound sentences by joining independent clauses.
  They woke the soldiers. They kept time on marches. *(They woke the soldiers, and they kept time on marches.)*

Have student pairs combine these sentences:

1. Many parents found out their sons had run away to war. It was too late to stop them.
2. Methods of fighting war have changed through the years. The horror of war remains the same.
3. They marched long distances. They didn't complain.

FOR ADVANCED LEARNERS/PRE–AP

Synthesize Have students find examples of memorable conclusions from essays and other nonfiction works that they have read. Have them critique the techniques used by the writers and then present their examples and analyses to the class. Discuss what methods they might incorporate in their own conclusions.

Preparing to Publish

Support for meeting the goals in the writing rubric is supplied throughout the **Writing Workshop** on pages 1052–1065.

For Rubric Bank, see

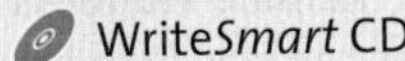
WriteSmart CD

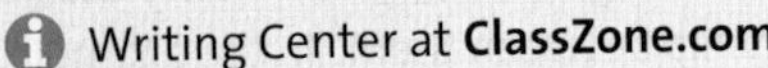
Writing Center at **ClassZone.com**

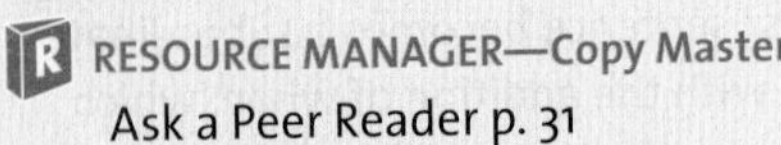
RESOURCE MANAGER—Copy Master
Ask a Peer Reader p. 31

Apply the Rubric

Review each of the qualities of a strong research report with students.

Ask a Peer Reader

Have students create a Two-Column Chart that includes the rubric points on one side and space for comments on the other. Then have students exchange their papers with peer readers and complete the checklist. Encourage them to offer specific suggestions and to identify exactly which parts of the report need improvement.

BEST PRACTICES TOOLKIT—Transparency
Two-Column Chart p. A25

Citing Sources

Review each format with students.

Formatting a Research Paper

Share these guidelines with students:

- Leave one-inch margins at the top, bottom, and sides of each page (except for page numbers).
- Follow your teacher's instructions for the kind of page headings required.
- Double-space all text, including quotations and the entries on the Works Cited page.
- Indent paragraphs one-half inch (or five spaces) from the left margin.
- Begin your Works Cited list on a separate page and indent the second and subsequent lines of entries one-half inch (or five spaces). End each entry with a period.

Have students check the *MLA Handbook for Writers of Research Papers* for additional formatting guidelines.

Preparing to Publish — Research Report

Apply the Rubric

A strong research report . . .

- ☑ has an appealing or thought-provoking introduction
- ☑ presents a clear thesis statement
- ☑ supports the thesis with evidence
- ☑ correctly summarizes, paraphrases, and quotes multiple sources
- ☑ includes the writer's own ideas and reflections
- ☑ follows a clear pattern of organization and uses transitions
- ☑ varies the lengths of sentences and uses precise words
- ☑ has a thoughtful, memorable conclusion

Ask a Peer Reader

- What is my thesis? Do I need to clarify it? If so, how?
- Where should I add more support or background information?
- Which part of my report was most interesting? Why?
- What else would you like to know about this topic?

Citing Sources

Follow these examples for citing different types of sources.

CD-ROM encyclopedia
"American Civil War." Encyclopaedia Britannica. 2004 ed. CD-ROM. Chicago: Encyclopaedia Britannica, 2006.

Newspaper or magazine article
Dolan, Sean, and Marina Hincapie. "The Real Drummer Boy of Shiloh." Pomona Herald. 6 Jan. 2008: C11+.

Interview you conducted with an expert
Shubert, William. Personal interview. 1 Apr. 2008.

Book with an editor
DeYoe, Veronica, ed. Boys Who Went to War. Chicago: Battlefield, 2008.

Film or documentary
Civil War Life. Dir. Mark Bussler. DVD. Inecom, 2003.

For more examples, see the *MLA Handbook for Writers of Research Papers*.

Writing Online

PUBLISHING OPTIONS
For publishing options, visit the **Writing Center** at **ClassZone.com**.

ASSESSMENT PREPARATION
For writing and grammar assessment practice, go to the **Assessment Center** at **ClassZone.com**.

1066 UNIT 10: THE POWER OF RESEARCH

Assess and Reteach

After reading and assessing students' reports, you might use these lessons to reteach key skills:

STANDARDS LESSON FILE

Writing Lesson 1: Finding a Writing Idea
Writing Lesson 2: Limiting or Expanding a Topic
Writing Lesson 6: Combining Sentences and Sentence Parts
Writing Lesson 12: Topic Sentence and Supporting Details
Writing Lesson 19: Transitions
Writing Lesson 21: Writing a Thesis Statement
Writing Lesson 22: Writing Introductions
Writing Lesson 23: Writing Conclusions
Research and Study Skills Lesson 8: Source Cards and Notecards
Research and Study Skills Lesson 9: Avoiding Plagiarism
Research and Study Skills Lesson 10: Documentation

Creating a Web Site

You have learned a great deal about your topic. Developing a Web site will give others an opportunity to learn about your topic, too.

Planning the Web Site

1. **Think in screens or in key ideas.** For example, two key ideas from your report about drummer boys are "Jobs Drummer Boys Did" and "Drummer Boys in Battle." Next, think of images that will help illustrate your main ideas. You might use photographs, video clips, graphic organizers, maps, charts, databases, or timelines. In addition, you could create audio narration.
2. **Create a site plan.** List your ideas for pages. Then make a map with arrows showing how your pages might link up.
3. **Sketch the pages and write the text.** Draw rough sketches of how you want each page to look. Include images, buttons, and links. Then write the text that will appear on each page. Use short, bulleted lists instead of long paragraphs.

Home page:
Drummer Boys
of the Civil War

The boys	Jobs	In Literature
Ages	In Camp	Ray Bradbury
Reasons for Joining	In Battle	Shel Silverstein

Producing the Web Site

1. **Avoid plagiarism.** Items that you find on other Web sites may be copyrighted. Some site sponsors allow students to use their elements in school projects. Be sure to credit what you use.
2. **Choose an authoring program.** This type of program helps you combine media elements into a Web document. Your school's computer specialist can help you with this step, as well as with scanning and importing your materials.
3. **Make your site clear and attractive.** Label all elements in type that is 12 points or larger. Use the same font style and size for all your headings.
4. **Revise and upload.** Ask a classmate to try out your site and give you feedback. When you have fixed any problems, make your site available on your school's internal server or on the Web.

PUBLISHING WITH TECHNOLOGY

Have students read the steps for developing a Web site. Then have students prepare for the project by familiarizing themselves with the authoring program used to put Web sites together.

Before students begin working, review this rubric with them so that they understand their goals:

Rubric A strong Web site

- is user-friendly and easily navigated with buttons and hyperlinks
- presents accurate, well-organized, and clearly displayed information
- includes text and visuals
- shows evidence of research and thought
- credits the sources of information
- has been tested and improved based on feedback

Have students use the rubric to evaluate each other's Web sites.

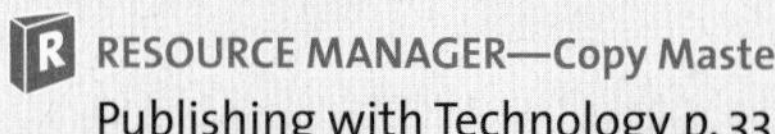

RESOURCE MANAGER—Copy Master
Publishing with Technology p. 33

STANDARDS LESSON FILE
Media Lesson 21: Creating a Web Site

DIFFERENTIATED INSTRUCTION

FOR LESS–PROFICIENT WRITERS

Planning the Web Site

1. As a class, visit two or three reliable Web sites. Discuss the way each is organized and how the pages are linked.
2. Have students review their reports and decide on two major ideas they would like to present.
3. Have students sketch their plan for three pages—a home page and two information pages that present their facts.

Producing the Web Site

1. Have students work with computer-proficient partners to collect images and create graphics for their pages.
2. Ask them to present and explain their Web sites to a small group before making final adjustments.
3. As a class, visit the operational Web sites and discuss their strengths.

WRITING WORKSHOP 1067

R1

Reading any text—whether it is a short story, poem, magazine article, newspaper, or Web page—requires the use of special strategies. For example, you might plot the events of a short story on a diagram, or use text features to spot main ideas in a magazine article. You also need to identify patterns of organization in the text. Using such strategies can help you read different texts with ease and also help you understand what you're reading.

1 Reading Literary Texts

Literary texts include short stories, novels, poems, and dramas. Literary texts can also be biographies, autobiographies, and essays. To appreciate and analyze literary texts, you will need to understand the characteristics of each type of text.

1.1 READING A SHORT STORY

Strategies for Reading

- Read the **title.** As you read the story, you may notice that the title has a special meaning.
- Keep track of **events** as they happen. Plot the events on a diagram like this one.

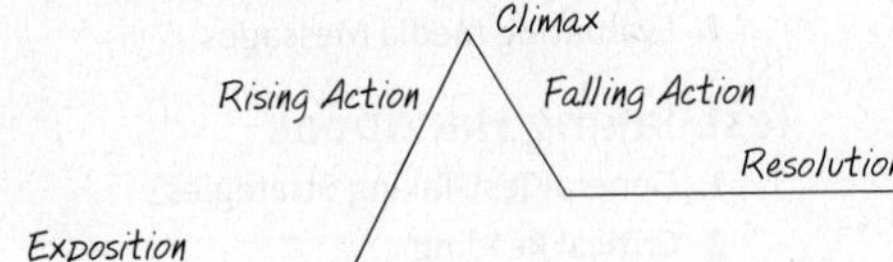

- From the details the writer provides, **visualize** the characters. **Predict** what they might do next.
- Look for specific adjectives that help you visualize the **setting**—the time and place in which events occur.

1.2 READING A POEM

Strategies for Reading

- Notice the **form** of the poem, or the number of its lines and their arrangement on the page.
- Read the poem aloud a few times. Listen for **rhyme** and **rhythm.**
- **Visualize** the images and comparisons.
- **Connect** with the poem by asking yourself what message the poet is trying to send.
- Create a word web or other **graphic organizer** to record your reactions and questions.

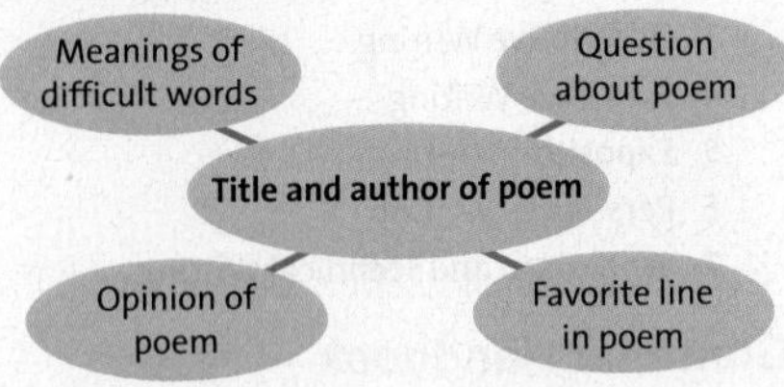

1.3 READING A PLAY

Strategies for Reading

- Read the stage directions to help you **visualize** the setting and characters.
- **Question** what the title means and why the playwright chose it.
- Identify the main conflict (struggle or problem) in the play. To **clarify** the conflict, make a chart that shows what the conflict is and how it is resolved.
- **Analyze** the characters. What do they want? How do they change during the play? You may want to make a chart that lists each character's name, appearance, and traits.

1.4 READING LITERARY NONFICTION

Strategies for Reading

- If you are reading a biography, an autobiography, or another type of biographical writing (such as a diary, a memoir, or letters), use a family tree or word web to keep track of the people mentioned.
- When reading an essay, **evaluate** the writer's ideas. Is there a clear main idea? Does the writer use appropriate details to support a main idea?

R2 READING HANDBOOK

Reading Informational Texts: Text Features

An **informational text** is writing that provides factual information. Informational materials—such as chapters in textbooks and articles in magazines, encyclopedias, and newspapers—usually contain elements that help the reader recognize their purpose, organization, and key ideas. These elements are known as **text features.**

.1 UNDERSTANDING TEXT FEATURES

Text features are design elements of a text that indicate its organizational structure or otherwise make its key ideas and information understandable. Text features include titles, headings, subheadings, boldface type, bulleted and numbered lists, and graphic aids, such as charts, graphs, illustrations, and photographs. Notice how the text features help you find key information on the textbook page shown.

- **A** The **title** identifies the topic.
- **B** A **subheading** indicates the start of a new topic or section and identifies the focus of that section.
- **C** **Questions** may be used to focus your understanding of the text.
- **D** A **bulleted list** shows items of equal importance.
- **E** **Graphic aids,** such as illustrations, photographs, charts, diagrams, maps, and timelines, often make ideas in the text clearer.
- **F** A **caption,** or the text that accompanies a graphic aid, gives information about the graphic aid that isn't necessarily obvious from the image itself.

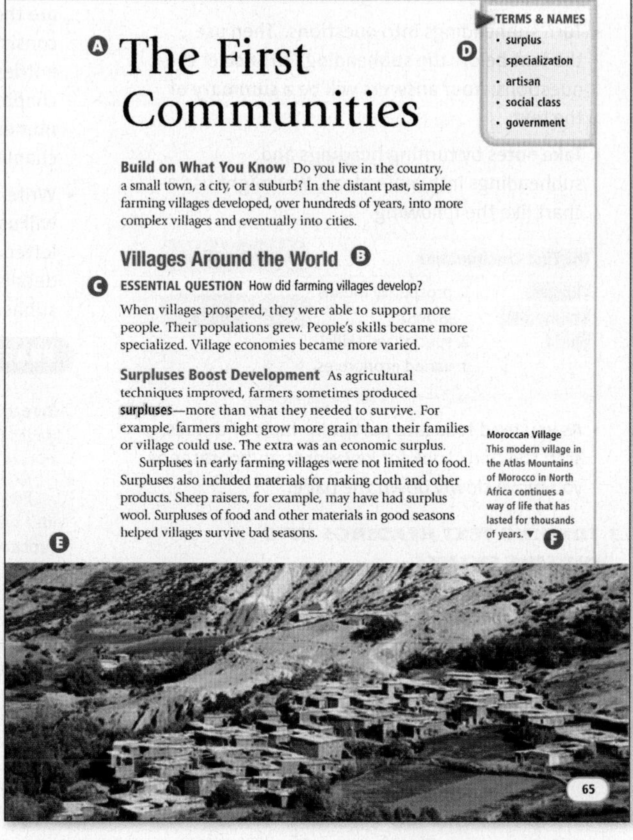

A **The First Communities**

D **TERMS & NAMES**
- surplus
- specialization
- artisan
- social class
- government

Build on What You Know Do you live in the country, a small town, a city, or a suburb? In the distant past, simple farming villages developed, over hundreds of years, into more complex villages and eventually into cities.

Villages Around the World B

C **ESSENTIAL QUESTION** How did farming villages develop?

When villages prospered, they were able to support more people. Their populations grew. People's skills became more specialized. Village economies became more varied.

Surpluses Boost Development As agricultural techniques improved, farmers sometimes produced **surpluses**—more than what they needed to survive. For example, farmers might grow more grain than their families or village could use. The extra was an economic surplus.

Surpluses in early farming villages were not limited to food. Surpluses also included materials for making cloth and other products. Sheep raisers, for example, may have had surplus wool. Surpluses of food and other materials in good seasons helped villages survive bad seasons.

Moroccan Village This modern village in the Atlas Mountains of Morocco in North Africa continues a way of life that has lasted for thousands of years. ▼ F

E

65

PRACTICE AND APPLY

1. What is a surplus?
2. What facts do the photograph and caption add to the text?
3. What informational texts do you read outside of class? Why are they informational?

READING HANDBOOK R3

PRACTICE AND APPLY

ANSWERS

1. *more than what is needed to survive*
2. *The photograph shows the reader what a modern farming village in Morocco looks like, and the caption tells you that ancient farming villages probably didn't look much different.*
3. ***Possible answers:** newspapers, magazines, user's manuals—you read them because they give factual information about current events and can teach you how to use products*

2.2 USING TEXT FEATURES

You can use text features to locate information, to help you understand it, and to take notes. Just use the following strategies when you encounter informational text.

Strategies for Reading

- **Preview** the text by looking at the title, headings, and subheadings to get an idea of the main concepts and the way the text is organized.
- Before you begin reading the text more thoroughly, **skim** it—read it quickly—to get an overview.
- Read any **questions** that appear at the end of a lesson or chapter. Doing this will help you set a purpose for your reading.
- Turn subheadings into questions. Then use the text below the subheadings to answer the questions. Your answers will be a **summary** of the text.
- **Take notes** by turning headings and subheadings into main ideas. You might use a chart like the following.

The First Communities (Main heading)	
Villages Around the World (Subheading)	1. prosperity means growth 2. specialized skills 3. varied economies

- As you read to locate particular facts or details, **scan** the text. Look for key words and phrases as you move slowly down the page.

2.3 TURNING TEXT HEADINGS INTO OUTLINE ENTRIES

After you have read a selection at least once, you can use text features to take notes in outline form. The following outline shows how one student used text headings from the sample textbook page on page R3. Study the outline and use the strategies that follow to create an outline based on text features.

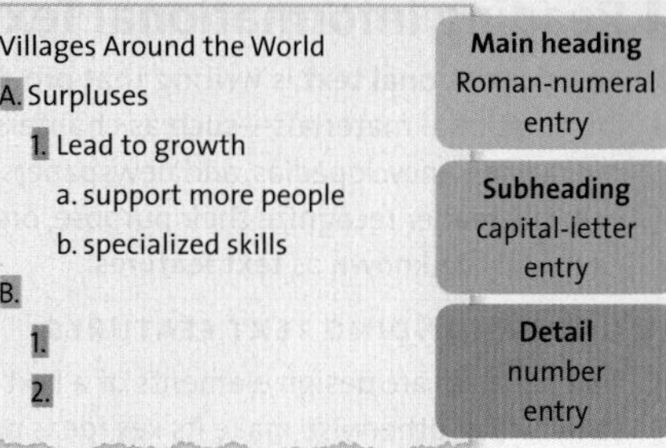

I. Villages Around the World
A. Surpluses
1. Lead to growth
a. support more people
b. specialized skills
B.
1.
2.
Main heading Roman-numeral entry
Subheading capital-letter entry
Detail number entry

Strategies for Using Text Headings

- Preview the headings and subheadings in the text to get an idea of what different kinds there are and what their positions might be in an outline.
- Be consistent. Note that subheadings that are the same size and color should be used consistently in Roman-numeral or capital-letter entries in the outline. If you decide that a chapter heading should appear with a Roman numeral, then that's the level at which all other chapter headings should appear.
- Write the headings and subheadings that you will use as your Roman-numeral and capital-letter entries first. As you read, fill in numbered details from the text under the headings and subheadings in your outline.

PRACTICE AND APPLY

Reread "So You Want to be an Entomologist?" pages 888–889. Use text features in the selection to take notes in outline form.

Preview the subheadings in the text to get an idea of the different kinds. Write the headings and subheadings you are using as your Roman numeral and capital letter entries first. Then fill in the details.

2.4 GRAPHIC AIDS

Information is communicated not only with words but also with graphic aids. **Graphic aids** are visual representations of verbal statements. They can be charts, webs, diagrams, graphs, photographs, or other visual representations of information.

R4 READING HANDBOOK

Graphic aids usually make complex information easier to understand. For that reason, graphic aids are often used to organize, simplify, and summarize information for easy reference.

Graphs

Graphs are used to illustrate statistical information. A **graph** is a drawing that shows the relative values of numerical quantities. Different kinds of graphs are used to show different numerical relationships.

Strategies for Reading

Ⓐ Read the title.

Ⓑ Find out what is being represented or measured.

Ⓒ In a circle graph, compare the sizes of the parts.

Ⓓ In a line graph, study the slant of the line. The steeper the line, the faster the rate of change.

Ⓔ In a bar graph, compare the lengths of the bars.

A **circle graph,** or **pie graph,** shows the relationships of parts to a whole. The entire circle equals 100 percent. The parts of the circle represent percentages of the whole.

MODEL: CIRCLE GRAPH

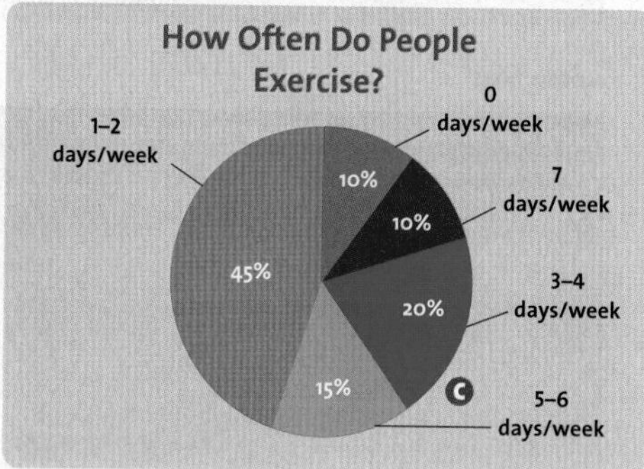

Line graphs show changes in numerical quantities over time and are effective in presenting trends such as changes in life expectancy. A line graph is made on a grid. Here, the vertical axis indicates degrees Fahrenheit, and the horizontal axis shows dates. Points on the graph indicate data. The line that connects the points highlights a trend or pattern.

MODEL: LINE GRAPH

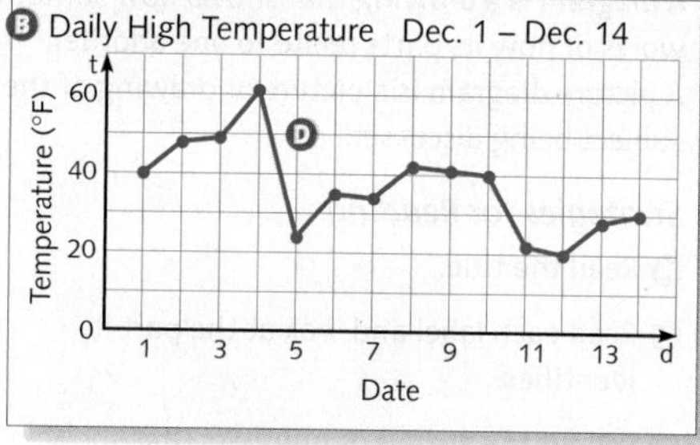

In a **bar graph,** vertical or horizontal bars are used to show or compare categories of information, such as the heights of different buildings. The lengths of the bars in this case indicate height.

MODEL: BAR GRAPH

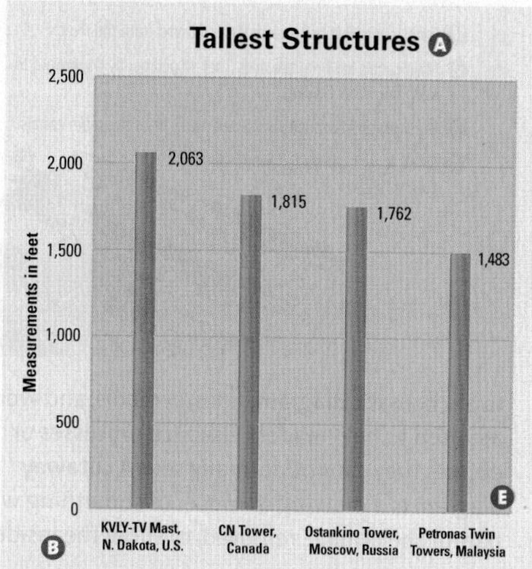

WATCH OUT! Evaluate carefully the information presented in graphs. For example, circle graphs show major factors and differences well but tend to reduce the importance of smaller factors and differences.

READING HANDBOOK R5

Diagrams

A **diagram** is a drawing that shows how something works or how its parts relate to one another.

A **picture diagram** is a picture or drawing of the subject being discussed.

Strategies for Reading

Ⓐ Read the title.

Ⓑ Read each label and look at the part it identifies.

Ⓒ Follow any arrows or numbers that show the order of steps in a process, and read any captions.

MODEL: PICTURE DIAGRAM

Ⓐ Ancient Irrigation

This model shows how an ancient irrigation system worked.

1. Gates controlled how much water flowed from the river.
2. Main canals led from the river. They sloped gently downward to keep the water flowing.
3. Medium-sized branch canals led away from the main canals.
4. Small feeder canals led water directly to the fields.

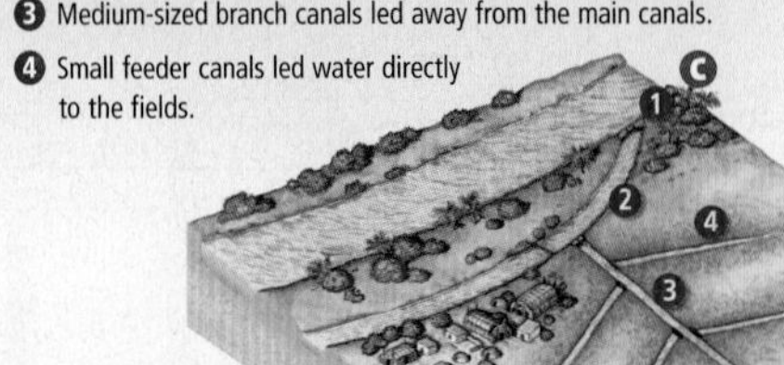

In a **schematic diagram,** lines, symbols, and words are used to help readers visualize processes or objects they cannot normally see. A **cutaway diagram** is a drawing or model of something with part of the outside removed, to show the inside.

MODEL: SCHEMATIC DIAGRAM

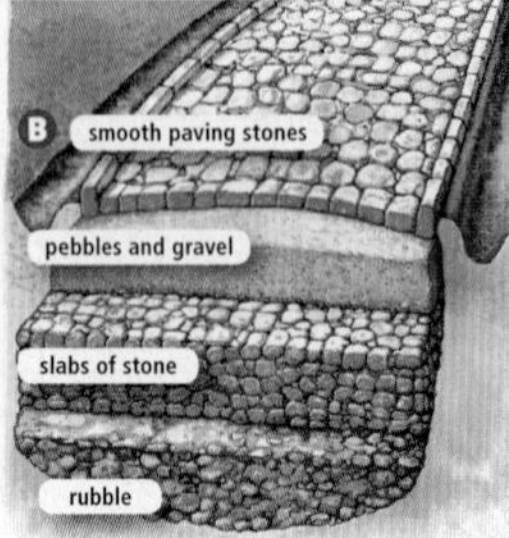

◀ **Roman Road Ⓐ Construction** Roman roads were constructed in layers. The average width of a road was 15 to 18 feet. Ⓒ

Charts and Tables

A **chart** presents information, shows a process, or makes comparisons, usually in rows or columns.

A **table** is a specific type of chart that presents a collection of facts in rows and columns and shows how the facts relate to one another.

Strategies for Reading

Ⓐ Read the title to learn what information the chart or table covers.

Ⓑ Study column headings and row labels to determine the categories of information presented.

Ⓒ Look down columns and across rows to find specific information.

MODEL: CHART

The Domestication of Animals Ⓐ

Animal	Location	Use Ⓑ
llama	South America	transport, meat
turkey	North America	meat
cattle	Europe, Asia, Africa	milk, meat
horse	Asia (southwest steppes)	transport Ⓒ
dog	Asia (possibly China)	guarding, herding, hunting

MODEL: TABLE

Ⓐ

Light Rail Meadowview Route Monday–Friday A.M.

Meadowview Ⓑ	City College	Arden/ Del Paso	Watt/I-80
6:05	6:14	6:42	6:53
7:05	7:14	7:42	7:53
7:20	7:29 Ⓒ	7:57	8:08
7:50	7:59	8:27	8:38
8:05	8:14	8:42	8:53
8:35	8:44	9:12	9:23
9:05	9:14	9:42	9:53
9:50	9:59	10:27	10:38
10:05	10:14	10:42	10:53
11:05	11:14	11:42	11:53

R6 READING HANDBOOK

Maps

A **map** visually represents a geographic region, such as a state or country. It provides information about areas through lines, colors, shapes, and symbols. There are different kinds of maps.

- **Political maps** show political features, such as national borders.
- **Physical maps** show the landforms in areas.
- **Road or travel maps** show roads and highways.
- **Thematic maps** show information on a specific topic, such as climate, weather, or natural resources.

Strategies for Reading

Ⓐ Read the title to find out what kind of map it is.

Ⓑ Read the labels to get an overall sense of what the map shows.

Ⓒ Look at the **key** or **legend** to find out what the symbols and colors on the map stand for.

MODEL: PHYSICAL MAP

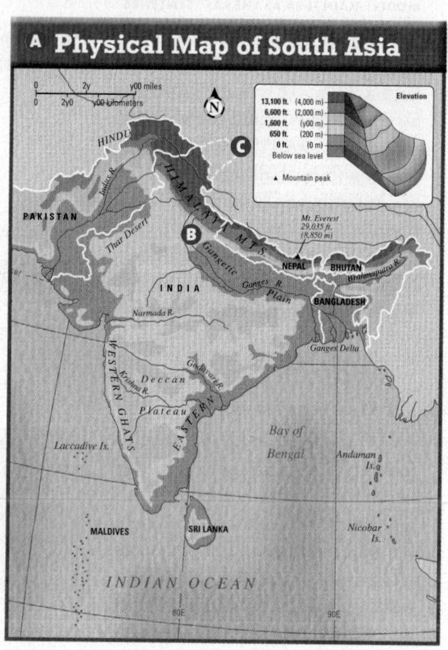

MODEL: THEMATIC MAP

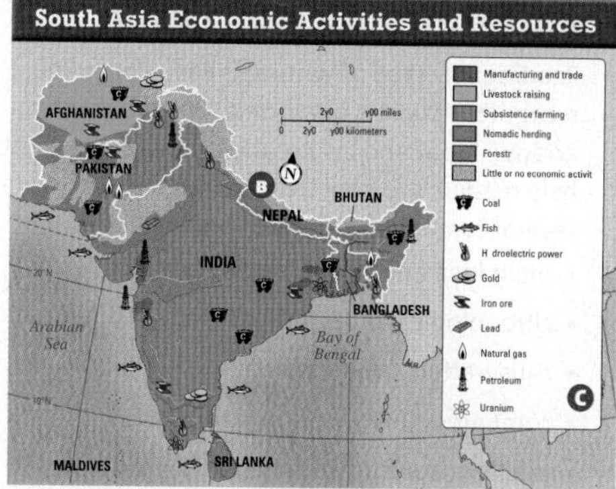

PRACTICE AND APPLY

1. According to the circle graph, how many days a week do most people exercise?
2. On which date was a temperature of 60° F recorded?
3. According to the bar graph, where is the world's tallest structure located?
4. How many kinds of canals were used in ancient irrigation?
5. What material formed the bottom layer of Roman roads?
6. According to the chart, which animal was domesticated in South America?
7. What time would you have to leave City College to get to the Watt/I-80 train station by 11:00?
8. What body of water is on the east coast of India?
9. What is the main economic activity of Afghanistan?

PRACTICE AND APPLY

ANSWERS

1. *1–2 times per week*
2. *December 4th*
3. *North Dakota, U.S.*
4. *three*
5. *rubble*
6. *llama*
7. *10:14*
8. *Bay of Bengal*
9. *raising livestock*

3 Reading Informational Texts: Patterns of Organization

Reading any type of writing is easier once you recognize how it is organized. Writers usually arrange ideas and information in ways that best help readers see how they are related. There are several common patterns of organization:

- main idea and supporting details
- chronological order
- cause-effect organization
- compare-and-contrast organization
- problem-solution organization

Writers also typically present arguments in ways that will help readers follow their reasoning.

*For more about deductive and inductive methods of organization, see **Analyzing Logic and Reasoning**, pages R22–R25.*

3.1 MAIN IDEA AND SUPPORTING DETAILS

Main idea and supporting details is a basic pattern of organization in which a central idea about a topic is supported by details. The **main idea** is the most important idea about a topic that a particular text or paragraph conveys. **Supporting details** are words, phrases, or sentences that tell more about the main idea. The main idea may be directly stated at the beginning and then followed by supporting details, or it may be merely implied by the supporting details. It may also be stated after it has been implied by supporting details.

Strategies for Reading

- To find a stated main idea in a paragraph, identify the paragraph's topic. The topic is what the paragraph is about and can usually be summed up in one or two words. The word, or synonyms of it, will usually appear throughout the paragraph. Headings and subheadings are also clues to the topics of paragraphs.
- Look for the topic sentence, or the sentence that states the most important idea the paragraph conveys. It is often the first sentence in a paragraph; however, it may appear at the end.
- To find an implied main idea, ask yourself: Whom or what did I just read about? What do the details suggest about the topic?
- Formulate a sentence stating this idea and add it to the paragraph. Does your sentence convey the main idea?

Notice how the main idea is expressed in each of the following models.

MODEL: MAIN IDEA AS THE FIRST SENTENCE

On the second day of the heat wave, the temperature soared to a sweltering 110 degrees. The sun melted the tar of the newly paved driveway. It was almost impossible to escape the fumes, which caused him to hold his nose and breathe through his mouth. The air felt like a wet blanket smothering his lungs. Each breath was a struggle.

Main idea

Supporting details

MODEL: MAIN IDEA AS THE LAST SENTENCE

His body tried to maintain a healthy temperature by producing large amounts of sweat. Because the air was so humid and there was no breeze, the sweat didn't evaporate and cool him at all. It just dripped unpleasantly, and he grew even hotter as he angrily tried to wipe it away. Despite losing all that water, he wasn't even thirsty. Though he didn't know it, he was in danger of becoming dehydrated.

Supporting details

Main idea

MODEL: IMPLIED MAIN IDEA

As he walked along the street looking for something to drink, he began to feel light-headed. He ignored the feeling for a few minutes, but then became so dizzy that he had to sit down. Soon he started to feel sick to his stomach. As he stretched out, he began to shiver. "How can I be cold when it's 110 degrees?" he wondered before he fainted.

Implied main idea: He was dehydrated, which was a serious problem.

R8 READING HANDBOOK

PRACTICE AND APPLY

Read each paragraph, and then do the following:

1. Identify the main idea in the paragraph, using one of the strategies discussed on the previous page. Tell whether it is stated or implied.
2. Evaluate the pattern of organization used in the paragraph. Does it express the main idea effectively?

The earthquake shook down in San Francisco hundreds of thousands of dollars' worth of walls and chimneys. But the conflagration that followed burned up hundreds of millions of dollars' worth of property. There is no estimating within hundreds of millions the actual damage wrought. Not in history has a modern imperial city been so completely destroyed. San Francisco is gone. Nothing remains of it but memories and a fringe of dwelling houses on its outskirts.
—Jack London, "The Story of an Eyewitness"

They never saw him. Now and then they heard whispered rumors to the effect that he was in the neighborhood. The woods were searched. The roads were watched. There was never anything to indicate his whereabouts. But a few days afterward, a goodly number of slaves would be gone from the plantation. Neither the master nor the overseer had heard or seen anything unusual in the quarter. Sometimes one or the other would vaguely remember having heard a whippoorwill call somewhere in the woods, close by, late at night. Though it was the wrong season for whippoorwills.
—Ann Petry, *Harriet Tubman: Conductor on the Underground Railroad*

3.2 CHRONOLOGICAL ORDER

Chronological order is the arrangement of events in the order in which they happen. This type of organization is used in many short stories and novels, historical writing, biographies, and autobiographies. To show the order of events, writers use order words such as *after, next,* and *later* and time words and phrases that identify specific times of day, days of the week, and dates, such as *the next morning, Tuesday,* and *March 13, 2007.*

Strategies for Reading

- Scan the text for headings and subheadings that may indicate a chronological pattern of organization.
- Look for words and phrases that identify times, such as *in a year, three hours earlier, in* A.D. *1066,* and *the next day.*
- Look for words that signal order, such as *first, afterward, then, during,* and *finally,* to see how events or steps are related.
- Note that a paragraph or passage in which ideas and information are arranged chronologically will have several words or phrases that indicate time order, not just one.
- Ask yourself: Are the events in the paragraph or passage presented in time order?

Notice the words and phrases that signal time order in the first two paragraphs of the following model.

MODEL

The Life of Jack London

Jack London was born in San Francisco, California, in 1876. His family was poor and moved frequently in search of work. In 1881, the family began working on farms. London's dislike of farming drew him to literature as a way "to get beyond the sky lines of my narrow California valley."

The Londons were unlucky in farming. When they lost their land, they moved across the bay to Oakland. To help support his family, the 10-year-old London took his first job. By the time he was 15, he had quit school and was working long hours in a factory. London became a tough teenager who knew how to fight but who never lost his burning passion for books.

Time words and phrases

Events

PRACTICE AND APPLY

ANSWERS

1. *San Francisco has been destroyed by an earthquake—stated; A person helped slaves escape without being detected—unstated*
2. *cause-and-effect order; chronological order*

READING HANDBOOK R9

PRACTICE AND APPLY

ANSWERS

1. *at the age of 17, then, the next year, in 1896, after*
2. *to take his mind off his dislike of farming and boredom with California*
3. *He didn't like being homeless.*

Living by the sea, London became fascinated by the ships that promised contact with faraway places. At the age of 17, he joined the *Sophia Sutherland* on a seal-hunting voyage to Japan. This trip provided material for his first short story, "Story of a Typhoon off the Coast of Japan," for which he won first prize in a writing contest.

London then returned to California with a passion for travel. The next year, he "hopped a train" heading east and lived as a tramp. However, homelessness persuaded him to return to high school in Oakland. In 1896, with only one year of high school behind him, he passed the entrance exam for the University of California at Berkeley.

Unfortunately, London had to give up his university studies for lack of money. After working for a while in a laundry, he joined the rush north to Canada's Klondike River in search of gold. Although London never struck it rich, his Klondike experiences inspired his later writing.

PRACTICE AND APPLY

Reread the preceding model and then do the following:

1. List three words or phrases in the last three paragraphs that indicate time or order.
2. Describe how London became interested in books.
3. Explain why he returned home after living as a tramp.

3.3 CAUSE-EFFECT ORGANIZATION

Cause-effect organization is a pattern of organization that shows causal relationships between events, ideas, and trends. Cause-effect relationships may be directly stated or merely implied by the order in which the information is presented. Writers often use the cause-effect pattern in historical and scientific writing. Cause-effect relationships may have several forms.

One cause with one effect

One cause with multiple effects

Multiple causes with a single effect

A chain of causes and effects

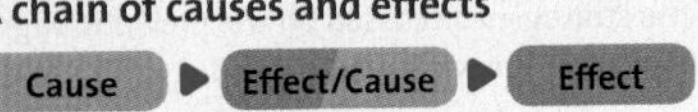

Strategies for Reading

- Look for headings and subheadings that indicate a cause-effect pattern of organization, such as "Effects of Food Allergies."
- To find the effect or effects, read to answer the question "What happened?"
- To find the cause or causes, read to answer the question "Why did it happen?"
- Look for words and phrases that help you identify specific relationships between events, such as *because, since, had the effect of, led to, as a result, resulted in, for that reason, due to, therefore, if . . . then,* and *consequently.*
- Look closely at each cause-effect relationship. Do not assume that because one event happened before another, the first event caused the second event.
- Use graphic organizers like the diagrams shown to record cause-effect relationships as you read.

Notice the words that signal causes and effects in the following model.

MODEL

We're Destroying Our Rain Forests

According to a study done by Brazilian scientists, nearly 5 million acres of rain forest are disappearing a year. That's equal to seven football fields a minute. [Effect]

The cause of this destruction is simple—cutting down trees. Every minute, around 2,000 trees are felled to create highways, railroads, and farms. Some trees, such as mahogany and teak, are harvested for their beautiful hardwood. [Signal words] [Cause]

This destruction of the rain forests has wide-ranging effects on living things. About 30,000 plant species live in the Amazon rain forest alone. These plants provide important foods such as bananas, coffee, chocolate, and nuts, as well as medicinal compounds found nowhere else. Just four square miles of a rain forest shelters more than 550 species of birds, reptiles, and amphibians. Almost 100 species worldwide face extinction every day, many due to habitat loss in rainforests.

Rain forests also act as climate regulators, balancing the exchange of oxygen and carbon dioxide in the atmosphere and helping to offset global warming. The earth's well-being will suffer as a result of the rain forests' destruction.

It is crucial that steps be taken immediately to reduce the number of trees being cut down. If this destruction is not reversed, within 50 years, thriving rain forests will be no more than a memory.

PRACTICE AND APPLY

Refer to the preceding model to do the following:

1. Use one of the graphic organizers on page R10 to show the multiple effects of cutting down trees described in the model.
2. List three words or phrases used to signal cause and effect in the last four paragraphs.

3.4 COMPARE-AND-CONTRAST ORGANIZATION

Compare-and-contrast organization is a pattern of organization that provides a way to look at similarities and differences in two or more subjects. A writer may use this pattern of organization to compare the important points or characteristics of two or more subjects. These points or characteristics are called **points of comparison.** There are two ways to develop compare-and-contrast organization:

Point-by-point organization—The writer discusses one point of comparison for both subjects, then goes on to the next point.

Subject-by-subject organization—The writer covers all points of comparison for one subject and then all points of comparison for the next subject.

Strategies for Reading

- Look in the text for headings, subheadings, and sentences that may suggest a compare-and-contrast pattern of organization, such as "Common Behaviors of Different Pets," to help you identify where similarities and differences are addressed.
- To find similarities, look for words and phrases such as *like, all, both, every,* and *in the same way.*
- To find differences, look for words and phrases such as *unlike, but, on the other hand, more, less, in contrast,* and *however.*
- Use a graphic organizer, such as a Venn diagram or a compare-and-contrast chart, to record points of comparison and similarities and differences.

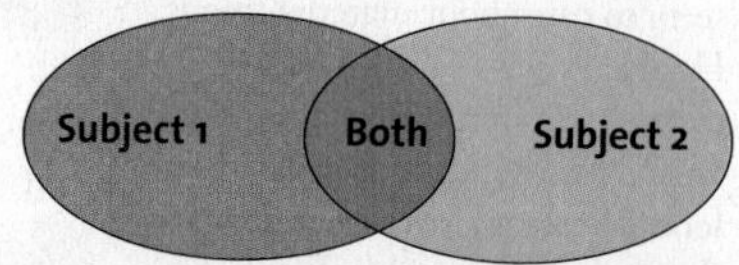

	Subject 1	Subject 2
Point 1		
Point 2		
Point 3		

As you read the following models, use the signal words and phrases to identify the similarities and differences between the subjects and how the details are organized in each text.

MODEL 1

Mr. Frank and Mr. Van Daan

Moving into a tiny apartment with people you have never met is a sure way to discover your differences. In the play *The Diary of Anne Frank,* Mr. Frank and Mr. Van Daan are in a similar situation, but have very different personalities, behaviors, and relationships with their families.

Subjects

Both men are Jews living in Nazi-occupied Amsterdam during World War II. Both have children: Mr. Frank, two daughters; and Mr. Van Daan, a son. They try to hide

Comparison words and phrases

PRACTICE AND APPLY

ANSWERS

1. *cause—cutting down trees; effect/(cause)—destruction of rain forest; effect 1—extinction of plants and animals; effect 2—endangering Earth's well-being*
2. *cause, effects, because, as a result of*

their families from the Nazis in the same apartment.

Comparison words and phrases

Despite these similarities, there are many differences between the two men. First, they have nearly opposite personalities. Mr. Van Daan is very concerned with appearances and wears expensive clothes. He can be kind, but often loses his temper. He also has strong opinions about the roles of men and women. For example, he acts embarrassed that his son Peter likes his pet cat and disapproves of Anne's outspokenness. He tells her, "A man likes a girl who'll listen to him once in a while."

Subject

Contrast words and phrases

In contrast, Mr. Frank doesn't seem to care about material things. He always stays calm and has compassion for other people. Even when Mr. Van Daan is caught stealing food, Mr. Frank tries to understand the man's behavior. Mr. Frank's attitude about women differs from Mr. Van Daan's as well. Mr. Frank never criticizes Anne for being unladylike; instead, he encourages her to be herself. He gives her a diary because he knows she loves to write, and he is proud of her creativity when she makes Hanukkah presents for everyone. As Anne says about her father, "He's the only one who's ever given me the feeling that I have any sense."

Subject

The two men also respond differently to their situation. Mr. Van Daan is self-centered and believes he suffers more from hunger than the others. He even tries to take Anne's piece of cake. Mr. Frank, on the other hand, always puts the needs of others before his own. For example, he makes the newcomer, Dr. Dussel, feel welcome and gladly offers him food. He also risks his own safety to investigate when a robber enters the downstairs warehouse.

Contrast words and phrases

Mr. Frank and Mr. Van Daan relate differently with their families. Although Mr. and Mrs. Van Daan are close, they quarrel often. Mr. Van Daan criticizes his son's slowness and threatens to get rid of his beloved cat. In contrast, Mr. Frank shows only love and respect for his wife and daughters. Even when he scolds Anne, he does it privately and gently. After Anne hurts her mother's feelings, Mr. Frank tells her that parents "can only try to set a good example. The rest you must do yourself."

The differences between Mr. Frank and Mr. Van Daan in *The Diary of Anne Frank* far outnumber their similarities. Mr. Van Daan's selfishness endangers both families, while Mr. Frank's compassion and consideration help them all make the best of a terrible situation.

MODEL 2

Two for Tea

Next to water, tea is the most popular drink worldwide. Served hot or iced, it comes in a variety of flavors to suit every taste. Yerba maté and green tea are two varieties that seem to suit the tastes of increasing numbers of people of all ages and nationalities.

Subjects

Comparison words and phrases

Yerba maté is native to South America. Made from the dried leaves of the yerba maté tree, it is traditionally brewed in hollow gourds, which are themselves called *matés.* The gourd is filled three-quarters full with leaves, and they are then covered with hot water. When the leaves have completely absorbed the moisture, more water is added. The brewed tea is then drunk through a tube with a strainer at one end called a *bombilla.* Yerba maté is sometimes served with milk, sugar, or lemon juice to cut its slight bitterness.

Yerba maté is thought to offer many health benefits. It is loaded with antioxidants that may boost

R12 READING HANDBOOK

the immune system and help prevent cancer. It also seems to aid digestion.

Green tea, on the other hand, is native to China and was exported to Japan in about A.D. 800. Unlike yerba maté, green tea usually is brewed in teapots. Only about a teaspoonful of leaves is used per pot. The leaves are steeped for only around two minutes—much less than the soaking time for yerba maté. Green tea has a very mild taste and generally is served plain in ceramic cups so the delicate taste can be savored.

Contrast words and phrases

Like yerba maté, green tea also is beneficial to health. Similarly rich in antioxidants, it has been reputed to lower cholesterol and blood sugar and also to relieve the pain of arthritis. So, the next time you have tea for two, try one of these two popular drinks—yerba maté and green tea.

Comparison words and phrases

PRACTICE AND APPLY

Refer to the preceding models to answer the following questions:

1. Which model is organized by points of comparison? Which model is organized by subject?
2. For each model, list three words or phrases that signal comparisons or contrasts.
3. Identify two points in each model that the writer compares or contrasts.
4. Make a Venn diagram or compare-and-contrast graphic to show the similarities and differences in one of the models.

3.5 PROBLEM-SOLUTION ORGANIZATION

Problem-solution organization is a pattern of organization in which a problem is stated and analyzed and then one or more solutions are proposed and examined. This pattern of organization is often used in persuasive writing, such as editorials or proposals.

Strategies for Reading

- Look for an explanation of the problem in the first or second paragraph.
- Look for words such as *problem* and *reason* that may signal an explanation of the problem.
- To find the solution, ask: What suggestion does the writer offer to solve the problem?
- Look for words such as *propose, conclude,* and *answer* that may signal a solution.

MODEL

Teachers, administrators, school board members, and parents have begun expressing concerns that the foreign language students aren't getting enough practice using their languages in conversation.

Students read dialogues from their textbooks and respond to questions. They also use the language lab to get more practice speaking the language. The facilities are limited, though, and have to be used after school, which conflicts with other activities. Also, the language lab doesn't give them real-life experience with using the new language to listen to others, either.

One solution to this problem would be to establish language tables in the lunchroom. Students taking a given language would eat lunch at a specific table one day a week. For that time, they would speak only the foreign language.

This plan has several advantages. First, it doesn't require any additional equipment, staff, or materials. Second, it wouldn't take time away from other classes or activities. Language students have to eat lunch just like everyone else, so why not make it an enjoyable learning experience?

Setting up language tables would let students supplement their language skills while nourishing their bodies. That's a recipe for success!

PRACTICE AND APPLY

Reread the model and then answer the following questions:

1. According to the model, what is the cause of the problem?
2. What solution does the writer offer? What words are a clue?

PRACTICE AND APPLY

ANSWERS

1. *point-by-point—Model 1; subject—Model 2*
2. *Model 1—both, same, similarities, differences, in contrast, on the other hand, differently; Model 2—and, on the other hand, unlike, like, also*
3. *Model 1—personalities, behavior, family relationships; Model 2—country of origin, leaves, brewing methods, how drunk, what's added*
4. *Answers will vary. Possible graphic:*

Characteristic	Yerba maté	Green tea
Country of origin	South America	China
Brewing method	Brewed in gourd, absorbs boiling water twice	Brewed in teapot for 2 minutes
Served in	bombilla	ceramic cup
What's added	milk, sugar, lemon juice	nothing
Health benefits	antioxidants, aids digestion	antioxidants, lowers cholesteral and blood sugar, relieves arthritis pain

PRACTICE AND APPLY

ANSWERS

1. *Problem: Students have no opportunity to practice the foreign language they are studying. Cause: Facilities are limited and the language lab does not offer real-life experience using the new language.*
2. *Solution: Establish language tables in the lunchroom. Clues: "one solution to this problem," "several advantages"*

4 Reading Informational Texts: Forms

Magazines, newspapers, Web pages, and consumer, public, and workplace documents are all examples of informational materials. To understand and analyze informational texts, pay attention to text features and patterns of organization.

4.1 READING A FEATURE ARTICLE

Because people often skim newspapers, newspaper publishers use devices to attract attention to articles. **Feature articles** usually address a single human-interest or lifestyle topic in-depth.

Strategies for Reading

- **A** Notice whether **text** or **graphic aids** attract your attention at first glance.
- **B** Read the **title** and other **headings** to find out more about the article's topic and organization.
- **C** Notice whether the article has a **byline,** a line naming the author.
- **D** A **caption** accompanying a graphic aid may provide information that adds to the meaning of the article.

PRACTICE AND APPLY

1. Who wrote this article?
2. What do your learn from the photograph and caption?
3. When was this birthday tribute to Poe started? By whom?

MODEL: FEATURE ARTICLE

Source: *The Washington Times*

B # Birthday Ritual a Grave Tradition

New figure brings tribute to Poe

C by Roger J. Hansen

BALTIMORE—A black-clad stranger carried on the half-century tradition here of placing three red roses and something to drink at the grave of Edgar Allan Poe in a pre-dawn visit on Jan. 19.

Because he was dressed in ordinary street clothes, the man slipped in unrecognized past two dozen people who had gathered at 3 A.M. at Westminster Church to watch the ritual.

Beginning in 1949, one man—his identity unknown—visited the grave on the poet and author's birthday. In recent years, a new man, dressed in black and wearing a hat, has sneaked into the small graveyard tucked in downtown Baltimore. . . .

Martha Womack, a high school literature teacher in Farmville, Va., was as thrilled to see the tribute this year as in her three prior visits.

"It's one of those mysteries we just don't want to lose," she said. "Every year it's a little bit different."

Ms. Womack said, "I think people are still interested in him because of the mystery surrounding his life and his death." . . .

And what would Poe make of the curious birthday tradition?

"He would love it," Ms. Womack said, her eyes lighting up. "Without a doubt, he would love it because he didn't get the attention he deserved in life. But he gets it now."

A

A raven on the top of Poe's grave recalls his famous poem. **D**

PRACTICE AND APPLY

ANSWERS

1. *Roger J. Hansen*
2. *the years Poe was born and died, and what his gravestone looks like*
3. *in 1949, an unknown man*

4.2 READING A TEXTBOOK

Each textbook that you use has its own system of organization based on the content in the book. Often an introductory unit will explain the book's organization and special features. If your textbook has such a unit, read it first.

Strategies for Reading

A Before you begin reading the lesson or chapter, read any **questions** that appear at the beginning or end of it. Then use the questions to set your purpose for reading.

B Read slowly and carefully to better understand and remember the ideas presented in the text. When you come to an unfamiliar word, first try to figure out its meaning from **context clues.** If necessary, find the meaning of the word in a **glossary** in the textbook, or in a dictionary. Avoid interrupting your reading by constantly looking up words in a dictionary.

For more information on context clues and glossaries, see the ***Vocabulary and Spelling Handbook,*** *pages R68 and R74.*

C Use the book's special features, such as sidebars, to increase your understanding of the text. A **sidebar** is a short presentation of additional information. It is usually set off in a box on the page.

D Take notes as you read. Use text features such as **subheadings** and boldfaced terms to help you organize your notes. Record your notes in graphic organizers, such as cause-effect diagrams, to help you clarify relationships among ideas.

MODEL: TEXTBOOK PAGE

Early Human Culture

A **ESSENTIAL QUESTION** What kind of culture did early humans create?

What sets humans apart from other creatures? Art, language, and religion are special to humans and help create their culture.

D **Language** Human language probably developed as a result of the need for people to work together. One theory suggests that the need for cooperation during the hunt spurred language development. Hunters needed to be able to talk to one another in order to outsmart, trap, and kill animals for food. Another theory suggests that the cooperation needed to gather and share food led to the development of language.

D **Religion** **B** **Religion** is the worship of God, gods, or spirits. Early humans probably believed that everything in nature, including rocks, trees, and animals, had a spirit. Some archaeologists believe that early cave paintings of animals were made to honor the spirits of animals killed for food.

Comparisons Across Cultures

C **Prehistoric Cave Art**

Prehistoric people in different parts of the world painted scenes on cave walls. Such rock paintings are among the oldest art in the world.

The cave art on the top was done by a Native American artist in Utah. The painting shows a holy man holding a snake. Snakes were seen as links between the human and underground worlds.

The painting at the bottom was done by an Australian Aboriginal artist. It shows a dreamtime spirit. Dreamtime is a supernatural past in which ancestor spirits shaped the natural world.

SKILLBUILDER
INTERPRETING VISUALS
Making Inferences What do these examples tell you about early human art? On the basis of their art, how important does religion seem to have been in the lives of prehistoric peoples?

54 • Chapter 2

PRACTICE AND APPLY

Reread the textbook page and answer the following questions:

1. Which subheading does the sidebar relate to?
2. What is a possible relationship between art and religion?
3. What is the answer to the Essential Question?

PRACTICE AND APPLY
ANSWERS

Possible answers:

1. *religion*
2. *Early cave paintings of animals may have been made to honor the animals' spirits.*
3. *one that included language, religion, and art*

4.3 READING A CONSUMER DOCUMENT

Consumer documents are printed materials that accompany products and services. They usually provide information about the use, care, operation, or assembly of the products they accompany. Some common consumer documents are contracts, warranties, manuals, instructions, and schedules.

Strategies for Reading

A Read the **heading** to see what information the document covers. Read the **subheadings** to learn what process each section of the instructions explains.

B Read the directions all the way through at least once.

C Look for **numbers** or **letters** that indicate the order in which the steps should be followed.

D If there is an **illustration** or **diagram,** try to match the words in the instructions to words or symbols in the graphic aid.

E Look for **verbs that describe actions** you should take, such as *turn, separate, place,* and *twist.*

MODEL: ASSEMBLY INSTRUCTIONS AND WARRANTY

A Friend Fur Good Puppy Kennel

ASSEMBLY INSTRUCTIONS A
The kennel consists of three parts:
(1) plastic top section; (2) plastic bottom section; (3) steel door.

D

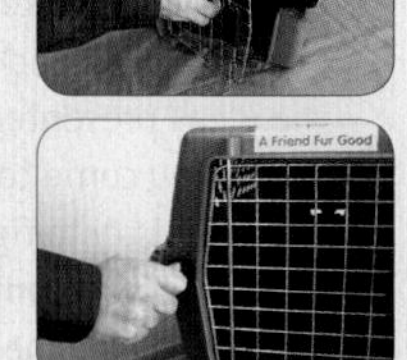

TO ASSEMBLE KENNEL A
1. Separate the two kennel halves.
2. Turn bottom half of kennel over and place flat side on floor. Place top half of kennel onto the bottom half and align pieces. C
3. Hold top section as shown and place metal door in opening so ends of hinge and latch rods fit in holes (A). Lower top section so hinge and latch rod fit into holes (B). E
4. Secure the two halves together with the 8 kennel body fasteners. Place kennel body fastener in hole and turn. Fasteners are now in the locked position. Check the locks periodically to ensure that they are tightly fastened.

LIMITED ONE-YEAR WARRANTY Warranted for one year from date of retail purchase against defects in material and workmanship.
COVERED: Replacement of defective parts and labor, and product return to consumer.
NOT COVERED: Damages caused by abuse or failure to perform normal maintenance. This warranty shall not apply to any defect or malfunction caused by damage due to unreasonable use.

MODEL: CONTRACT

PET ADOPTION CONTRACT A

The Adopter agrees to adopt the following animal (referred to here as "Animal") from A Friend Fur Good Animal Shelters:

Name/Breed____________ Age______
Color/Markings____________ Sex______

As Adopter, I agree to the following: C
1. To allow a representative of A Friend Fur Good Animal Shelters to visit my premises to ensure the terms of this agreement have been kept.
2. The Animal will be provided with adequate fresh food and water, clean, dry shelter when outside, and daily exercise.
3. To provide a safe collar with rabies and I.D. tags to be worn at all times.
4. To adopt the Animal only as a personal pet/companion and not as a guard dog.
5. If it becomes necessary to find the Animal another home, the Friend Fur Good Shelter will be contacted and the Animal shall be returned to them.

As Adopter, I accept full responsibility for the care of this animal, and I release A Friend Fur Good Animal Shelter and its representatives of any liability from this date forward.

This adoption contract is entered into this ______ day of ______, 2006, between A Friend Fur Good Animal Shelters and

Adopter's Full Name____________
Address____________
City, State, Zip____________
Home Phone____________ Work Phone____________

PRACTICE AND APPLY

Read the assembly instructions and warranty for the portable kennel and the pet adoption contract. Then answer the following questions:

1. Which text features are found in the instructions but not in the contract?
2. What action should you take if the kennel is used frequently?
3. Why would someone not request a free replacement if his or her dog destroyed the kennel door?
4. What should you do if you have to find another home for your adopted animal?

R16 READING HANDBOOK

PRACTICE AND APPLY

ANSWERS

1. *illustrations or diagrams*
2. *Check the locks that hold it together.*
3. *Damage caused by abuse of the kennel isn't covered.*
4. *Contact* A Friend Fur Good *and return the animal to them.*

4.4 READING A PUBLIC DOCUMENT

Public documents are documents that are written for the public to provide information that is of general interest or concern. These documents are often free. They can be federal, state, or local government documents. They can be speeches or historical documents. They may even be laws, posted warnings, signs, or rules and regulations.

Strategies for Reading

Ⓐ Read the **title** to find out what the notice is about.

Ⓑ Look for **subheadings** that indicate what categories of information are being discussed.

Ⓒ Pay attention to **bulleted lists.** These show individual details of equal importance.

MODEL: PUBLIC DOCUMENT

Ⓐ **Patron Code of Conduct**

A "Code of Conduct" is published to ensure that all users of the library can experience a pleasant and productive environment for study and research. Misuse of the library, whether by theft, mutilation, or vandalism of library materials or property, or by interference with the study and research of library users, shows disrespect for the institution and disregard of the rights of other patrons.

Ⓑ **Examples of Unacceptable Behavior:**

- Disruptive behavior such as rowdiness, running, noise, vandalism, or such behavior that interferes with the normal use of the library.
- Ⓒ Harassment of library staff or other patrons.
- Entering an unauthorized area, remaining in the library after closing or when requested to leave during emergency situations.
- Mutilation of library materials by marking, underlining, removal of pages, removing electronic theft detection devices or in any way defacing library property.
- Removal of library materials without authorization.
- Tampering with or intentionally damaging computer hardware, software, printer, operating systems or other associated equipment.
- Smoking, consumption of food, and the use of smokeless tobacco within the library.
- Refusal to abide by library regulations regarding return of materials and payment of fines.
- Entering the library with uncovered beverages.

In Addition:

- Children under the age of eight may not be left unattended.
- Furniture may not be rearranged.
- Cellular phone usage is limited to the first floor vestibule.
- All users must comply with library policies, federal, state and local laws.

PRACTICE AND APPLY

Refer to the public notice to answer the following questions:

1. Where are cell phones permitted in the library?
2. Can you mark or highlight interesting passages in a book you have checked out?
3. If you are entering the library and you have an open bottle of soda, what should you do?

PRACTICE AND APPLY

ANSWERS

1. *in the first floor vestibule*
2. *No. Altering the library materials is not allowed.*
3. *You should either throw away the beverage or put the cap on the bottle.*

4.5 READING A WORKPLACE DOCUMENT

Workplace documents are materials that are produced or used within a workplace, usually to aid in the functioning of a business. These may be documents generated by a business to monitor itself, such as minutes of a meeting or a sales report. These documents may also explain company policies, organizational structures, and operating procedures. Workplace documents include memos, business letters, job applications, and résumés.

Strategies for Reading

- **A** Read the **heading** in an e-mail or the **letterhead** in a business letter to determine the sender, the person who received it, and the date it was sent.
- **B** When reading an e-mail, check the **subject line** to identify what topics the e-mail will discuss.
- **C** Read the document slowly and carefully, as it may contain details that should not be overlooked.
- **D** Notice how to contact the creator of the document. You will need this information to reply or clear up anything you don't understand.
- **E** Take notes to help you remember what actions are required.

MODEL: E-MAIL

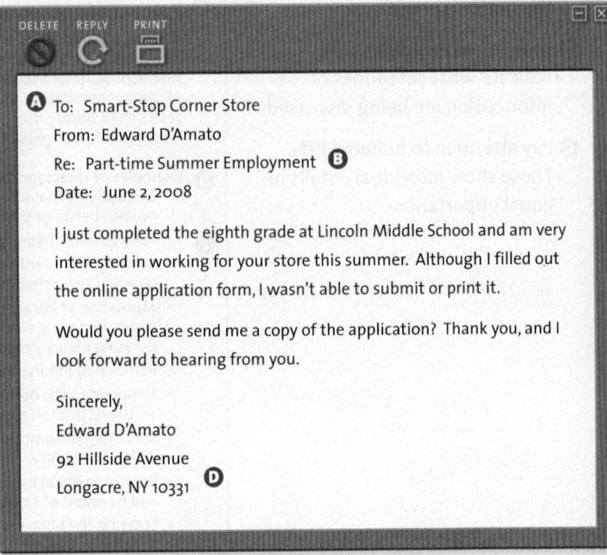

DELETE REPLY PRINT

A To: Smart-Stop Corner Store
From: Edward D'Amato
Re: Part-time Summer Employment **B**
Date: June 2, 2008

I just completed the eighth grade at Lincoln Middle School and am very interested in working for your store this summer. Although I filled out the online application form, I wasn't able to submit or print it.

Would you please send me a copy of the application? Thank you, and I look forward to hearing from you.

Sincerely,
Edward D'Amato
92 Hillside Avenue
Longacre, NY 10331 **D**

MODEL: BUSINESS LETTER

A Smart-Stop Corner Store
45 Blue Hill Avenue
Longacre, NY 10331

Edward D'Amato
92 Hillside Avenue
Longacre, NY 10331

June 3, 2008

Dear Edward:

I'm very sorry about the trouble you had using our website. Our main office will send you an application and instructions for completing and submitting it. If you don't receive these items within three working days, you can pick up the forms at the address shown above.

Yours Truly,
Darcie Grey
Darcie Grey, Manager

PRACTICE AND APPLY

Read the business e-mail and letter and answer the following questions:

1. Why did Edward D'Amato write his e-mail?
2. What action does he want the store to take?
3. According to Darcie Grey's letter, what should Edward do if he doesn't receive the application forms within three working days?

PRACTICE AND APPLY

ANSWERS

1. *He couldn't apply for a job online.*
2. *Send him the forms he needs to fill out.*
3. *He should pick up the forms at the store.*

4.6 READING ELECTRONIC TEXT

Electronic text is any text that is in a form that a computer can store and display on a screen. Electronic text can be part of Web pages, CD-ROMs, search engines, and documents that you create with your computer software. Like books, Web pages often provide aids for finding information. However, each Web page is designed differently, and information is not in the same location on each page. It is important to know the functions of different parts of a Web page so that you can easily find the information you want.

Strategies for Reading

- **A** Look at the **title** of a page to determine what topics it covers.
- **B** For an online source, such as a Web page or search engine, note the **Web address,** known as a **URL** (Universal Resource Locator). You may want to make a note of it in case you need to return to the page later.
- **C** Look for a **menu bar** along the top, bottom, or side of a Web page. Clicking on an item in a menu bar will take you to another part of the Web site.
- **D** Notice any hyperlinks to related pages. **Hyperlinks** are often underlined or highlighted in a contrasting color. You can click on a hyperlink to get to another page—one that may or may not have been created by the same person or organization.
- **E** For information that you want to keep for future reference, save documents on your computer or print them. For online sources, you can pull down the **Favorites** or **Bookmarks** menu and bookmark pages so that you can easily return to them. Printing the pages you need will allow you to highlight key ideas on a hard copy.

MODEL: WEB PAGE

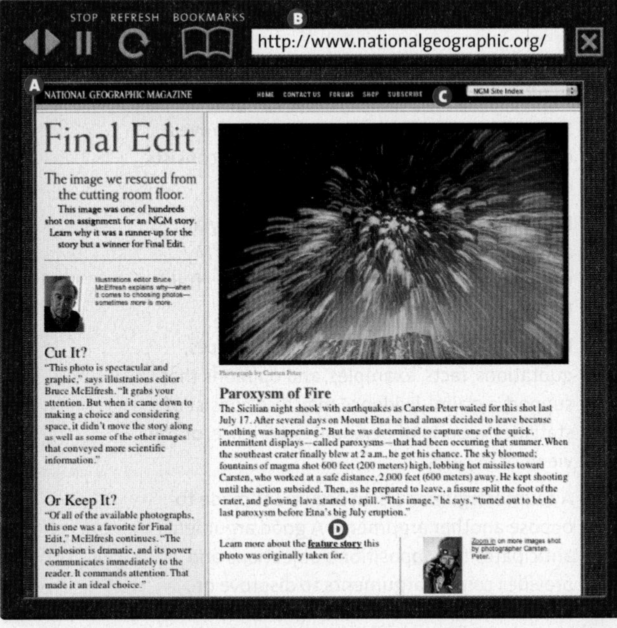

PRACTICE AND APPLY

1. What is the URL of this Web page?
2. Which hyperlinks would you click on to find further information about the photograph?
3. How could you find information about subscribing to *National Geographic* magazine?

PRACTICE AND APPLY

ANSWERS

1. *http://www.nationalgeographic.org*
2. *You can click on the hyperlink marked "feature story"*
3. *You could go to the button marked "Subscribe" in the menu bar.*

READING HANDBOOK R19

PRACTICE AND APPLY

ANSWERS

Claim: Hatchet *is a good book to read;*
Reason: *It's an entertaining adventure story, teaches important survival skills, and shows how the main character changes;*
Evidence: *Brian learns to stay safe from wild animals, find food and water, build a fire without matches, and confront the dangers of the wilderness;*
Counterargument: *People may not like that the book is about an unusual and extreme situation, but it's really about facing and learning from whatever difficulties life brings.*

5 Reading Persuasive Texts

5.1 ANALYZING AN ARGUMENT

An **argument** expresses a position on an issue or problem and supports it with reasons and evidence. Being able to analyze and evaluate arguments will help you distinguish between claims you should accept and those you should not. A sound argument should appeal strictly to reason. However, arguments are often used in texts that also contain other types of persuasive devices. An argument includes the following elements:

- A **claim** is the writer's position on an issue or problem.
- **Support** is any material that serves to prove a claim. In an argument, support usually consists of reasons and evidence.
- **Reasons** are declarations made to justify an action, decision, or belief. For example: "My reason for walking so quickly is that I'm afraid I'll be late for class."
- **Evidence** consists of the specific references, quotations, facts, examples, and opinions that support a claim. Evidence may also consist of statistics, reports of personal experience, or the views of experts.
- A **counterargument** is an argument made to oppose another argument. A good argument anticipates the opposition's objections and provides counterarguments to disprove or answer them.

Claim	I need a larger allowance.
Reason	I don't have enough money to pay for my school lunches, fees, and transportation.
Evidence	I had to borrow money from my friend two weeks in a row to buy lunch.
Counterargument	My parents say I just need to budget my allowance better, but they don't realize what my expenses are.

PRACTICE AND APPLY

Read the following book review and use a chart like the one shown to identify the claim, reason, evidence, and counterargument.

Hatchet
Reviewed by Kristen Loos

What would you do if you suddenly found yourself in the middle of a wilderness with no one else around and only a hatchet to help you survive? That's what happens to Brian Robeson, a boy about my age, in Gary Paulsen's book *Hatchet.* Even if this sounds like a situation you'll never be in, *Hatchet* is worth reading for what it says about facing your fears.

After his parents get a divorce, Brian heads up to northern Canada to spend the summer with his dad. But the pilot flying the airplane has a heart attack, and Brian is forced to crash-land it by himself. From then on, he has to take charge of the situation, or he won't live to tell about it.

From the beginning all the way to the end of the book, Brian faces big problems just to survive. He's a city kid, so he's used to opening up the refrigerator any time he wants to eat. Now, at the edge of the woods, he has to figure out things like how to be safe from wild animals and how to make a fire without matches. At first, he panics. He doesn't even know what to drink or how to find and prepare food. Even so, he doesn't give up.

One of the things I like about the book is how Brian changes. At first, he hopes he will be rescued very soon. He thinks he can hold out for a few days until his parents or a search party finds him. During this part of the book, he starts to think things out for himself. But he still gets scared easily and feels sorry for himself a lot.

Then, when a plane flies over without seeing him, he realizes that he is really on his own. He learns to make tools to fish and hunt with and to depend on himself for everything he needs. In the end, he is able to confront all kinds of dangers and still hold out hope for himself. To him, this is "tough hope."

Some readers may not like the book because they think this is an unusual situation that most people will never have to face. I don't agree, though, because I think the real message is not just about being lost in the wilderness, but about bravely dealing with whatever challenges we face in our lives.

I'm not going to spoil the book for you by saying how it ends or whether Brian gets rescued. Read it yourself for an exciting adventure and some good lessons about surviving in the wilderness. I hope you enjoy it as much as I did.

5.2 RECOGNIZING PERSUASIVE TECHNIQUES

Persuasive texts typically rely on more than just the **logical appeal** of an argument to be convincing. They also rely on ethical and emotional appeals and other **persuasive techniques**—devices that can convince you to adopt a position or take an action.

Ethical appeals establish a writer's credibility and trustworthiness with an audience. When a writer links a claim to a widely accepted value, the writer not only gains moral support for that claim but also establishes himself or herself as a reputable, moral person readers can and should trust. For example, with the following appeal, the writer reminds readers of a value they should accept and suggests that if they share this value, then they should support the writer's position: "Most of us agree that we should protect our natural resources, but we don't invest enough time or money to preserve them."

The chart shown here explains several other means by which a writer may attempt to sway you to adopt his or her position. Learn to recognize these techniques, and you are less likely to be influenced by them.

Persuasive Technique	Example
Appeals by Association	
Bandwagon appeal Suggests that a person should believe or do something because "everyone else" does	Join the millions of health-conscious people who've made Wonder Water their beverage of choice!
Testimonial Relies on endorsements from well-known people or satisfied customers	Now you can send your game over the top with Macon Ace—the racket designed and used by tennis legend Sonja Macon.
Snob appeal Taps into people's desire to be special or part of an elite group	The best deserve only the best—you deserve Beautiful Bubbles bath soap.
Appeal to loyalty Relies on people's affiliation with a particular group	Support the PTA and stand up for increased school funding.
Emotional Appeals	
Appeals to pity, fear, or vanity Use strong feelings, rather than facts, to persuade	Why go unnoticed when Pretty Face can make you the center of attention?
Word Choice	
Glittering generality A generalization that includes a word or phrase with positive connotations, to promote a product, person, or idea.	A vote for our candidate is a vote for honesty, integrity, and accountability.

READING HANDBOOK R21

PRACTICE AND APPLY

ANSWERS

Possible answers:

- ***Bandwagon appeal:*** *"Every thinking human being," "Join the aware, concerned citizens"*
- ***Testimonial/Appeal to authority:*** *"Featuring former Vice President Al Gore"*
- ***Appeal to fear:*** *"if we don't make changes soon"*
- ***Snob appeal:*** *"aware, concerned citizens"*
- ***Glittering generality:*** *"rare and important"*

PRACTICE AND APPLY

Identify the persuasive techniques used in this model.

Face the Truth

Every thinking human being should be required to see *An Inconvenient Truth.* Featuring former Vice President Al Gore, this fact-filled, frightening, yet entertaining movie critically examines global temperature changes. It highlights Mr. Gore's extensive research and lobbying about this issue and is backed up by expert testimonies, statistics, graphs, and photographs.

This is a rare and important film that tells it like it is—and it isn't pretty. For starters, if we don't make changes soon, in less than 45 years, a million species of living things could become extinct. Far from being a statement of doom, though, the movie ends with a detailed list of steps each of us can take to help save our planet. If you consider yourself an aware, concerned citizen, you must see this movie!

5.3 ANALYZING LOGIC AND REASONING

While persuasive techniques may sway you to side with a writer, they should not be enough to convince you that an argument is sound. To determine the soundness of an argument, you really need to examine the argument's claim and support and the logic or reasoning that links them. To do this, it is helpful to identify the writer's mode of reasoning.

The Inductive Mode of Reasoning

When a writer leads from specific evidence to a general principle or generalization, that writer is using **inductive reasoning.** A writer may even choose to organize all of the information in a text inductively—for example, the writer may present three paragraphs of evidence, followed by one paragraph explaining his or her conclusion. Here is an example of inductive reasoning.

SPECIFIC FACTS

Fact 1 Wind and water wear away rocks over time.

Fact 2 Earthquakes and volcanoes create immediate and drastic changes in the land.

Fact 3 The slow movement of the continents and spreading of the sea floor create new landforms.

GENERALIZATION

Natural forces continually change the surface of the earth.

Strategies for Determining the Soundness of Inductive Arguments

Ask yourself the following questions to evaluate an inductive argument:

- **Is the evidence valid and sufficient support for the conclusion?** Inaccurate facts lead to inaccurate conclusions.
- **Does the conclusion follow logically from the evidence?** From the facts listed above, the conclusion that Earth's *core* as well as its surface are constantly changing would be too broad.
- **Is the evidence drawn from a large enough sample?** These three facts are enough to support the claim. If you wanted to claim that these are the *only* forces that cause change, you would need more facts.

The Deductive Mode of Reasoning
When a writer arrives at a conclusion by applying a general principle to a specific situation, the writer is using **deductive reasoning.** If a writer wishes to organize a text deductively, he or she may begin by stating a claim and then give evidence supporting the claim. Here's an example of deductive reasoning.

Driving a car requires complete concentration.	**General principle or premise**
▼	
Talking on a cell phone divides the driver's attention.	**Specific situation**
▼	
People shouldn't talk on the phone while driving.	**Specific conclusion**

Strategies for Determining the Soundness of Deductive Arguments

Ask yourself the following questions to evaluate a deductive argument:

- **Is the general principle actually stated, or is it implied?** Note that writers often use deductive reasoning in arguments without stating the general principles. They just assume that readers will recognize and agree with the principles. So you may want to identify the general principle for yourself.
- **Is the general principle sound?** Don't just assume the general principle is sound. Ask yourself whether it is really true.
- **Is the conclusion valid?** To be valid, a conclusion in a deductive argument must follow logically from the general principle and the specific situation.

The following chart shows two conclusions drawn from the same general principle.

All spiders have eight legs.	
Accurate Deduction	**Inaccurate Deduction**
The black widow is a spider, therefore it has eight legs.	An octopus has eight legs, therefore it is a spider.

An octopus has eight legs, but it belongs to a different category of animals than the spider.

PRACTICE AND APPLY

Identify the mode of reasoning used in the following paragraph.

People do the most unexpected things. The other day when I was waiting at the stoplight on my bike, I noticed that the car in front of me was in the right lane and had its right turn signal on. Wouldn't you have assumed, just like I did, that the driver was going to turn right? Well, I was wrong, and you probably would've been, too. As soon as the light turned green, the car swerved across two lanes and turned left.

Then there was the surprise birthday party the neighborhood kids and I had for one of our friends. We'd managed to keep it a secret, so we all expected her to be really surprised and pleased. Instead, she was upset because she wasn't dressed properly for a party and was embarrassed at being caught off-guard.

I've finally learned to stop making assumptions about how other people will act. Now that seems like a logical thing to do!

PRACTICE AND APPLY

ANSWER

Deductive reasoning: *the writer presents evidence in the form of anecdotes and examples, and then draws the conclusion that he or she should stop making assumptions about how people will act.*

Identifying Faulty Reasoning

Sometimes an argument at first appears to make sense but isn't valid because it is based on a fallacy. A **fallacy** is an error in logic. Learn to recognize these common fallacies.

TYPE OF FALLACY	DEFINITION	EXAMPLE
Circular reasoning	Supporting a statement by simply repeating it in different words	My mother is always busy because **she has too much to do.**
Either/or fallacy	A statement that suggests that there are only two choices available in a situation that really offers more than two options	**Either** I grow two inches this summer **or** I'll never make any friends at my new school.
Oversimplification	An explanation of a complex situation or problem as if it were much simpler than it is	**All you have to do to get good grades** is listen carefully in class.
Overgeneralization	A generalization that is too broad. You can often recognize overgeneralizations by the use of words such as *all, everyone, every time, anything, no one,* and *none.*	**Nobody** has as many chores as I do.
Hasty generalization	A conclusion drawn from too little evidence or from evidence that is biased	I sneezed after taking a bite of the salad, so **I must be allergic to something in it.**
Stereotyping	A dangerous type of overgeneralization. Stereotypes are broad statements about people on the basis of their gender, ethnicity, race, or political, social, professional, or religious group.	**Artists are emotional** and hard to get along with.
Attacking the person or name-calling	An attempt to discredit an idea by attacking the person or group associated with it. Candidates often engage in name-calling during political campaigns.	Only **selfish** people don't do volunteer work.
Evading the issue	Responding to an objection with arguments and evidence that do not address its central point	I forgot to get the milk, **but dairy products are hard to digest anyway.**
False cause	The mistake of assuming that because one event occurred after another event, the first event caused the second one to occur	It rained this afternoon, **because I left my umbrella at home.**
Non sequitur	A conclusion that does not follow logically from the "proof" offered to support it	Mrs. Lewis will make Steve the baseball team captain. **He is already the captain of the volleyball team.**

R24 READING HANDBOOK

PRACTICE AND APPLY

Look for examples of logical fallacies in the following argument. Identify each one and explain why you identified it as such.

> Store clerks are so rude. A cashier was impatient with me in the supermarket the other day because I bought too much yogurt. They must train the employees to treat customers that way so more people will use the self-checkout lines. I need to budget more money for groceries.

5.4 EVALUATING PERSUASIVE TEXTS

Learning how to evaluate persuasive texts and identify bias will help you become more selective when doing research and also help you improve your own reasoning and arguing skills.

Strategies for Identifying Bias

Bias is an inclination for or against a particular opinion or viewpoint. A writer may reveal a strongly positive or negative bias on an issue by presenting only one way of looking at it or by heavily weighting the evidence on one side of the argument. The presence of the following is often a sign that a writer is biased:

- **unfairly weighted evidence,** which is weak or unproven evidence that a writer treats as more important or influential than it really is
- **loaded language,** which consists of words with strongly positive or negative connotations that are intended to influence a reader's attitude

EXAMPLE: *At the* Village Star, *we bring you the most relevant, up-to-the-minute news.* (Someone who works for the paper is making the claim. *Relevant* and *up-to-the-minute* have very positive connotations.)

Strategies for Identifying Propaganda

Propaganda is any form of communication that is so distorted that it conveys false or misleading information. Some politicians create and distribute propaganda. Logical fallacies such as name-calling, the either/or fallacy, and false causes are often used in propaganda. The following example shows false cause. The writer uses one fact to support a particular point of view but does not reveal another fact that does not support that viewpoint.

EXAMPLE: *Since Jack Carter was elected mayor, unemployment has decreased by 25%.* (The writer does not mention that it was the previous mayor, not Jack Carter, who was responsible for bringing in the new factory that provides the extra jobs.)

For more information on logical fallacies, see ***Identifying Faulty Reasoning,*** *page R24.*

Strategies for Evaluating Evidence

It is important to have a set of standards by which you can evaluate persuasive texts. Use the questions below to help you critically assess facts and opinions that are presented as evidence.

- **Are the presented facts verifiable?** Facts can be proved by eyewitness accounts, authoritative sources such as encyclopedias and almanacs, experts, or research.
- **Are the presented opinions well informed?** Any opinions offered should be supported by facts, be based on research or eyewitness accounts, or be the opinions of experts on the topic.
- **Is the evidence thorough?** Thorough evidence leaves no reasonable questions unanswered. If a choice is offered, background for making the choice should also be provided. If taking a side is called for, all sides of the issue should be presented.
- **Is the evidence balanced?** Be alert to evidence that is weighted unfairly and contains loaded language or other signs of bias.
- **Is the evidence authoritative?** The people, groups, or organizations that provided the evidence should have credentials that support their authority.
- **Is it important that the evidence be current?** Where timeliness is crucial, as in the areas of medicine and technology, the evidence should reflect the latest developments in the areas.

PRACTICE AND APPLY

ANSWERS

Stereotyping: *"Store clerks are so rude."*
Hasty generalization: *"A cashier was impatient with me because I bought too much yogurt."*
Unsupported inference: *"They must train their employees to treat people that way so more people will use the self-checkout lines."*
Non sequitur: *"I need to budget more money for groceries."*

PRACTICE AND APPLY

ANSWERS

Possible answers:

Elements of Bias: *Loaded language—"Ultra Bars are the tastiest and most efficient way . . ."*
Facts: *"Our bodies need a well-balanced combination of protein, carbohydrates, fats, vitamins, minerals, and trace elements to function"; "The ingredients in Ultra Bars have been chosen in the perfect proportion"*
Opinions: *"they taste terrific"; "Not only athletes should eat these—ordinary people should carry these bars with them, too . . ."*

PRACTICE AND APPLY

ANSWER

Answers will vary. Possible criticisms:

The writer's reasons make sense and are presented in logical order. The claim and reasons could be better supported (for example, he or she could provide figures on the exact costs of creating/maintaining the park, and the income from suggested activities). The argument adequately addresses and counters opposing views, but exhibits faulty logic:

- ***overgeneralization:*** *"No one who cares . . ."*
- ***either-or fallacy:*** *"Without a park, we can't ensure . . ."*
- ***circular reasoning:*** *"[Parks] are easier to supervise because it isn't as hard to police them."*

PRACTICE AND APPLY

Read the argument below. Identify the facts, opinions, and elements of bias.

Ultra Bars are the tastiest and most efficient way to get your daily requirement of important nutrients. Our bodies need a well-balanced combination of protein, carbohydrates, fats, vitamins, minerals, and trace elements to function most effectively and make us feel our best. The ingredients in Ultra Bars have been chosen in the perfect proportion to ensure you get the maximum benefit. Best of all, they taste terrific. And they aren't just for athletes—ordinary people should carry these bars with them, too, for a quick boost throughout the day!

Strategies for Determining a Strong Argument

Make sure that all or most of the following statements are true:

- The argument presents a claim or thesis.
- The claim is connected to its support by a general principle that most readers would readily agree with. Valid general principle: *Doing your best will bring you personal pride.* Invalid general principle: *Doing your best will bring you success.*
- The reasons make sense.
- The reasons are presented in a logical and effective order.
- The claim and all reasons are adequately supported by sound evidence.
- The evidence is adequate, accurate, and appropriate.
- The logic is sound. There are no instances of faulty reasoning.
- The argument adequately anticipates and addresses readers' concerns and counterclaims with counterarguments.

PRACTICE AND APPLY

Use the preceding criteria to evaluate the strength of the following proposal.

MODEL

Summary of Proposal

I propose that the city government create a park on the unused plot of land at the edge of town.

Need

We must preserve the natural beauty of the area for all to appreciate and enjoy.

Proposed Solution

The five-acre plot of land on the south side of town is now being considered for improvement.

Some people want to sell the land to a building developer. They say that doing this would be profitable for the town and also provide good housing for new residents.

It's true that the town could make money by developing the land. A park could also be a source of income, however.

The park would generate income in a number of ways. It could charge a small admission fee for summer concerts and other events. It also could lease the space to neighboring communities for their gatherings and to local food concessions and special-interest groups.

The cost of creating and maintaining a park is less than what it would bring in. Community groups already have agreed to donate plants, provide volunteers to landscape and take care of the grounds, create gazebos, and install benches, water fountains, and trashcans.

Without a park, we can't ensure the safety and health of our residents. It would have playgrounds and areas to bike, skate, picnic, and walk or jog. Unlike commercial and even residential buildings, parks do not encourage vandalism and graffiti. The chief of police has confirmed that parks are easier to supervise, too, because it isn't as hard to police them.

No one who cares about our community could fail to see how important it is to create this park.

R26 READING HANDBOOK

6 Adjusting Reading Rate to Purpose

You may need to change the way you read certain texts in order to understand what you read. To adjust the way you read, you first need to be aware of what you want to get out of the text. Then you can adjust the speed at which you read in response to your purpose and the difficulty of the material.

Determine Your Purpose for Reading

You read different types of materials for different purposes. You may read a novel for enjoyment. You may read a textbook unit to learn a new concept or to master the content for a test. When you read for enjoyment, you naturally read at a pace that is comfortable for you. When you read for information, you need to read more slowly and thoroughly. When you are being tested on material, you may think you have to read fast, especially if the test is being timed. However, you can actually increase your understanding of the material if you slow down.

Determine Your Reading Rate

The rate at which you read most comfortably is called your **independent reading level.** It is the rate that you use to read materials that you enjoy. To learn to adjust your reading rate to read materials for other purposes, you need to be aware of your independent reading level. You can figure out your reading level by following these steps:

1. Select a passage from a book or story you enjoy.
2. Have a friend or classmate time you as you begin reading the passage silently.
3. Read at the rate that is most comfortable for you.
4. Stop when your friend or classmate tells you one minute has passed.
5. Determine the number of words you read in that minute and write down the number.
6. Repeat the process at least two more times, using different passages.
7. Add the numbers and divide the sum by the number of times your friend timed you.

Reading Techniques for Informational Material

You can use the following techniques to adapt your reading for informational texts, to prepare for tests, and to better understand what you read:

- **Skimming** is reading quickly to get the general idea of a text. To skim, read only the title, headings, graphic aids, highlighted words, and first sentence of each paragraph. Also, read any introduction, conclusion, or summary. Skimming can be especially useful when taking a test. Before reading a passage, you can skim the questions that follow it in order to find out what is expected. This will help you focus on the important ideas in the text.

  When researching a topic, skimming can help you decide whether a source has information related to your topic. This will save time.
- **Scanning** is reading quickly to find a specific piece of information, such as a fact or a definition. When you scan, your eyes sweep across a page, looking for key words that may lead you to the information you want. Use scanning to review for tests and to find answers to questions.
- **Changing pace** is speeding up or slowing down the rate at which you read parts of a particular text. When you come across explanations of familiar concepts, you might be able to speed up without misunderstanding them. When you encounter unfamiliar concepts or material presented in an unpredictable way, however, you may need to slow down to understand the information.

WATCH OUT! Reading too slowly can affect your ability to understand what you read. Make sure you aren't just reading one word at a time. Practice reading phrases.

PRACTICE AND APPLY

Find an article in a magazine or textbook. Skim the article. Then answer the following questions:

1. What did you notice about the organization of the article from skimming it?
2. What is the main idea of the article?

READING HANDBOOK R27

Writing is a process through which you can explore your thoughts, experiment with ideas, and make connections. Through writing, you can record your thoughts, feelings, and ideas for yourself alone or you can choose to communicate them to an audience.

WRITING TOOLS
Go to the **Writing Center** at **ClassZone.com** for interactive models, publishing ideas, and other support.

1 The Writing Process

The writing process consists of the following stages: prewriting, drafting, revising and editing, proofreading, and publishing. These are not stages that you must complete in a set order. Rather, you may return to an earlier stage at any time to improve your writing.

1.1 PREWRITING

In the prewriting stage, you explore what you want to write about, what your purpose for writing is, whom you are writing for, and what form you will use to express your ideas. Ask yourself the following questions to get started.

Topic	• Is my topic assigned, or can I choose it? • What would I be interested in writing about?
Purpose	• Am I writing to entertain, to inform, to persuade, or for some combination of these purposes? • What effect do I want to have on my readers?
Audience	• Who is the audience? • What might the audience members already know about my topic? • What about the topic might interest them?
Format	• Which format will work best? Letter? Essay? Poem? Speech? Memoir? Short story? Article? Editorial? Review? Research paper? Instructions?

Find Ideas for Writing

- Look at magazines, newspapers, and Web sites.
- Start a log of articles you want to save for future reference.
- With a group, brainstorm as many ideas as you can. Compile your ideas into a list.
- Write down anything that comes into your head.
- Interview someone who is an expert on a particular topic.
- Use a graphic organizer, such as a cluster map, to explore secondary ideas related to a topic.

Organize Ideas

Once you've chosen a topic, you will need to compile and organize your ideas. If you are writing a description, you may need to gather sensory details. For an essay or a research paper, you may need to record information from different sources. To record notes from sources you read or view, use any or all of these methods:

- **Summarize**—Briefly retell the main ideas of a piece of writing in your own words.
- **Paraphrase**—Restate all or almost all of the information in your own words.
- **Quote**—Record the author's exact words.

Depending on what form your writing takes, you may also need to arrange your ideas in a certain pattern.

*For more information, see the **Writing Handbook**, pages R34–R41.*

1.2 DRAFTING

In the drafting stage, you put your ideas on paper and allow them to develop as you write. You don't need to worry about correct grammar and spelling at this stage. There are two ways to draft:

Discovery drafting is a good approach when you are not sure what you think about your subject. Start writing and let your feelings and ideas lead you in developing the topic.

Planned drafting may work better if you know your ideas have to be arranged in a certain way, as in a research paper. Try making a writing plan or an informal outline before you begin drafting.

R28 WRITING HANDBOOK

1.3 REVISING AND EDITING

The revising and editing stage allows you to polish your draft and make changes in its content, organization, and style. Asking questions will help you spot changes that would improve your work:

- Does my writing have a **main idea** or central focus? Is my thesis clear?
- Have I used **precise** nouns, verbs, and modifiers?
- Have I included **adequate details** and **evidence?** Have I left out any important information? Where might I add a vivid detail or example?
- Is my writing **unified?** Are all ideas and supporting details relevant to my main idea? Have I eliminated any repetitive information?
- Is my writing clear and **coherent?** Do sentences connect to one another smoothly and logically?
- Have I used a consistent **point of view?**
- Do I need to add **transitional words, phrases, or sentences** to explain relationships among ideas?
- Have I used a **variety of sentence types?** Are they well constructed? What sentences might I combine to improve the rhythm of my writing?
- Have I used a **tone** appropriate for my audience and purpose? Would informal or formal English be more appropriate?

1.4 PROOFREADING

After revising your paper, proofread it for mistakes. Ask the following questions:

- Have I corrected any errors in **subject-verb agreement** and **pronoun-antecedent agreement?**
- Have I checked for errors in **possessive forms** and in the **comparative and superlative forms** of adjectives and adverbs?
- Have I checked for errors in **confusing word pairs,** such as *it's/its, than/then,* and *too/to?*
- Have I corrected any **run-on sentences** and **sentence fragments?**
- Have I followed rules for **correct capitalization** and **punctuation marks?**
- Have I checked the dictionary for the **spellings of unfamiliar words?**

TIP If possible, don't begin proofreading right after you finish writing. Put your work away for at least a few hours. When you return to it, you will find it easier to identify and correct mistakes.

Use the proofreading symbols in the chart to mark changes on your draft.

For more information, see the ***Grammar Handbook*** *and the* ***Vocabulary and Spelling Handbook****, pages R46–R77.*

Proofreading Symbols	
∧ Add letters or words.	/ Make a capital letter lowercase.
⊙ Add a period.	¶ Begin a new paragraph.
≡ Capitalize a letter.	Delete letters or words.
⁀ Close up space.	∿ Switch the positions of letters or words.
∧ Add a comma.	

1.5 PUBLISHING AND REFLECTING

Always consider sharing your finished writing with a wider audience. Reflecting on your writing is another good way to finish a project.

Publishing Ideas

- Post your writing on a Weblog.
- Create a multimedia presentation and share it with classmates.
- Publish your writing in a school newspaper, local newspaper, or literary magazine.
- Present your work orally in a report, speech, reading, or dramatic performance.

Reflecting on Your Writing

Think about your writing process and whether you will add what you have written to your portfolio. You might ask yourself questions like these:

- Which parts of the process did I find easiest?
- What problems did I face during the writing process? How did I solve the problems?
- What changes have occurred in my writing style?
- What features in the writing of published authors or my peers can I apply to my own work?

WRITING HANDBOOK R29

1.6 PEER RESPONSE

Peer response consists of the suggestions and comments you make about the writing of your peers and also the comments and suggestions they make about your writing. You can ask a peer reader for help at any time in the writing process.

Using Peer Response as a Writer

- Indicate whether you are more interested in feedback about your ideas or about your presentation of them.
- Ask questions that require more than yes-or-no answers. These are more likely to give you specific information you can use as you revise.
- Encourage your readers to be honest, and give them plenty of time to respond thoughtfully to your writing.

Being a Peer Reader

- Respect the writer's feelings. Offer positive reactions first.
- Make sure you understand what kind of feedback the writer is looking for, and then respond accordingly.

For more information on the writing process, see the ***Introductory Unit,*** *pages 1–19.*

2 Building Blocks of Good Writing

Whatever your purpose in writing, you need to capture your reader's interest and organize your thoughts clearly.

2.1 INTRODUCTIONS

An introduction should capture your reader's attention. It may also include a thesis statement or introduce a main idea.

Kinds of Introductions

There are many different ways to write an introduction. The one you choose depends on who the audience is and on your purpose for writing.

Make a Surprising Statement Beginning with a startling statement or an interesting fact can arouse your reader's curiosity about a subject, as in this model.

MODEL

Imagine something only 15 to 20 inches long dropping out of the sky at 200 miles an hour! It would be nothing but a blur. That's exactly what makes the peregrine falcon such an effective bird of prey.

Provide a Description A vivid description sets a mood and brings a scene to life for your reader. Here, details about how a hot air balloon works set the tone for a narrative about a balloon ride.

MODEL

Whoosh! The red and yellow flame shot up into the great nylon cone. The warm air filled the balloon so that the cooler air below held the apparatus aloft. A soft breeze helped to push the balloon and basket along. The four passengers hardly noticed the noise or the heat as they stared in awe at the hilly farmland below.

Ask a Question Beginning with a question can make your reader want to read on to find out the answer. The following introduction asks about the reader's interest in exploring new places.

MODEL

Have you ever wanted to explore uncharted territory? The participants of the Lewis and Clark expedition of 1804–1806 did just that. Their purpose was to map a good water route from St. Louis and the Mississippi River to the Pacific Ocean.

R30 WRITING HANDBOOK

Relate an Anecdote Beginning with an anecdote, or brief story, can hook your reader and help you make a point in a dramatic way. The following anecdote introduces a story about a family trip.

MODEL

When I was in fifth grade, a local bank held a competition with a grand prize of a trip to the Cayman Islands. My parents entered the contest, never dreaming they would win. They also never dreamed that entering a contest would put us all smack in the middle of a hurricane.

Address the Reader Speaking directly to your reader establishes a friendly, informal tone and involves the reader in your topic.

MODEL

Show your concern for our community by supporting the campaign of Jonas Wright. Come to our next meeting at the Community Center Wednesday evening at 6:30—and bring your friends!

Begin with a Thesis Statement A thesis statement expressing a main idea may be woven into both the beginning and the end of a piece of nonfiction writing.

MODEL

There are many similarities between Mahatma Gandhi and Martin Luther King Jr. Both believed in nonviolent resistance to laws they felt were unfair. Both drew millions of people to support their causes and met tragic ends.

TIP To write the best introduction for your paper, you may want to try more than one of the methods and then decide which is the most effective for your purpose and audience.

2.2 PARAGRAPHS

A paragraph is made up of sentences that work together to develop an idea or accomplish a purpose. Whether or not it contains a topic sentence stating the main idea, a good paragraph must have unity and coherence.

Unity

A paragraph has unity when all the sentences support and develop one stated or implied idea. Use the following technique to create unity in your writing:

Write a Topic Sentence A topic sentence states the main idea of the paragraph; all other sentences in the paragraph provide supporting details. A topic sentence is often the first sentence in a paragraph, as shown in the model that follows. However, it may also appear later in a paragraph to reinforce or summarize the main idea.

MODEL

The ability to assemble complex social structures is one of the dolphins' most remarkable qualities. Dolphins live and travel in groupings called pods. These pods often show cooperative behavior and strong social bonding—separated pod-mates will still recognize one another six months later.

TIP Paying attention to topic sentences when you read literature can help you craft your own topic sentences. Notice the use of topic sentences in "Kabul's Singing Sensation" on pages 918–927. For example, the third paragraph on page 922 begins, "The soulful melancholy in Mirwais' voice is the product of hard times." The rest of the paragraph then describes some of those hard times in detail.

WRITING HANDBOOK R31

Coherence

A paragraph is coherent when all its sentences are related to one another and each flows logically to the next. The following techniques will help you achieve coherence in your writing:

- Present your ideas in the most logical order.
- Use pronouns, synonyms, and repeated words to connect ideas.
- Use transitional words to show relationships among ideas.

In the model shown here, the writer used several techniques to create a coherent paragraph.

> **MODEL**
>
> According to the English colonist John Smith, Pocahontas saved his life. A few years later, she was kidnapped by other colonists. While living with them, she fell in love with John Rolfe, and they were married. Later, Pocahontas, her husband, and their infant son traveled to England, where Pocahontas was introduced to the king.

2.3 TRANSITIONS

Transitions are words and phrases that show connections between details. Clear transitions help show how your ideas relate to one another.

Kinds of Transitions

The types of transitions you choose depend on the ideas you want to convey.

Time or Sequence Some transitions help to clarify the sequence of events over time. When you are telling a story or describing a process, you can connect ideas with such transitional words as *first, second, always, then, next, later, soon, before, finally, after, earlier, afterward,* and *tomorrow.*

> **MODEL**
>
> The first thing I did was make sure I wasn't dreaming. That was easy, because I knew my messy room wouldn't appear in anybody's dream. Before I got out of bed, though, I turned on the light and put on my glasses. Only then did I scream.

Spatial Order Transitional words and phrases such as *in front, behind, next to, along, nearest, lowest, above, below, underneath, on the left,* and *in the middle* can help your reader visualize a scene.

> **MODEL**
>
> On my mother's dresser, you can read the history of our family. On the left, a picture shows my parents' wedding. The picture in the middle is of my older brother as a baby, still toothless.

Degree of Importance Transitional words such as *mainly, strongest, weakest, first, second, most important, least important, worst,* and *best* may be used to rank ideas or to show degrees of importance.

> **MODEL**
>
> The most important quality I look for in a friend is whether he or she has interests similar to mine. Second, I want someone who can keep a secret. Least important, my new friend should get along with all my other friends.

Compare and Contrast Words and phrases such as *similarly, likewise, also, like, as, neither . . . nor,* and *either . . . or* show similarity between details. *However, by contrast, yet, but, unlike, instead, whereas,* and *while* show difference. Note how transitions show contrast in the model.

> **MODEL**
>
> Like the lawyer in "The Bet," Jerry in "A Mother in Mannville" spends much of his time alone. Both characters experience loneliness. As an orphan, however, Jerry never chooses to be alone, whereas the lawyer agrees to his solitary confinement.

TIP Both *but* and *however* can be used to join two independent clauses. When *but* is used as a coordinating conjunction, it is preceded by a comma. When *however* is used as a conjunctive adverb, it is preceded by a semicolon and followed by a comma.

EXAMPLE

Water is the best thirst quencher, but it should be cold.

Iced water can be very refreshing; however, drinking it too fast is not good for you and can cause stomach cramps.

Cause-Effect When you are writing about a cause-effect relationship, use transitional words and phrases such as *since, because, thus, therefore, so, due to, for this reason,* and *as a result* to help explain the relationship and make your writing coherent.

MODEL

My notebook might look tattered, but I treasure it because Silvio gave it to me. He was my best friend, and he moved to Texas. Since the notebook is all I have to remember him by, I will never throw it out.

.4 CONCLUSIONS

A conclusion should leave readers with a strong final impression.

Kinds of Conclusions

Good conclusions sum up ideas in a variety of ways. Here are some techniques you might try.

Restate Your Thesis A good way to conclude an essay is by restating your thesis, or main idea, in different words. The following conclusion restates the thesis introduced on page R31.

MODEL

It is ironic and tragic that the two similar leaders Mahatma Gandhi and Martin Luther King Jr. both inspired the world by preaching and practicing nonviolence, yet both died violent deaths.

Ask a Question Try asking a question that sums up what you have said and gives your reader something new to think about. This question concludes a piece of persuasive writing.

MODEL

So, if you care about your health and want to get in shape, shouldn't you talk to your doctor and begin a fitness program today?

Make a Recommendation When you are persuading your audience to take a position on an issue, you can conclude by recommending a specific course of action.

MODEL

Shawn, Maria, and Katie are real children. The next time you see a homeless person, remember these children and think about what you can do to help.

Offer an Opinion Leave your reader with something to think about by offering your personal opinion on the topic. The following model offers an opinion about homelessness.

MODEL

Any one of us could become homeless at any moment due to events we can't control. Remembering this frightening fact can help us take the problem of homelessness more seriously.

End with the Last Event If you're telling a story, you may end with the last thing that happens. Here, the ending includes the narrator's important realization.

MODEL

By the time the firefighters finally arrived, I had managed to get everyone out of the house and away from danger. Although we all were frightened and in shock, no one was badly hurt. As I watched the flames turn our home into ashes, I knew this was a night I'd never forget.

WRITING HANDBOOK R33

2.5 ELABORATION

Elaboration is the process of developing an idea by providing specific supporting details that are relevant and appropriate to the purpose and form of your writing.

Facts and Statistics A fact is a statement that can be verified, and a statistic is a fact expressed as a number. Make sure the facts and statistics you supply are from reliable, up-to-date sources.

MODEL

The heat wave this July broke all records. Temperatures rose above 100°F for 11 days in a row, and the scorching 113°F recorded at the airport on Wednesday was the highest reading ever measured here.

Sensory Details Details that show how something looks, sounds, tastes, smells, or feels can enliven a description, making readers feel they are actually experiencing what you are describing. Which senses does the writer appeal to in the following model?

MODEL

Opening the cabin door, she felt transported back to her childhood halfway across the country. The crisp air held the promise of frost, and the pine needles on the path were beginning to turn brown and curl up at the edges as if trying to stay warm.

Incidents From our earliest years, we are interested in hearing "stories." One way to illustrate a point powerfully is to relate an incident or tell a story, as shown in the example.

MODEL

Pedestrians, like drivers, should look both ways before crossing the street. I learned how dangerous it can be to break that rule when I was almost hit by a driver who was going the wrong way down a one-way street.

Examples An example can help make an abstract idea concrete or can serve to clarify a complex point for your reader.

MODEL

Narrative poetry tells a story in poetic form. "Paul Revere's Ride" by Henry Wadsworth Longfellow, for example, describes the dramatic events that took place in Massachusetts on April 18, 1775, the night before the battles of Lexington and Concord.

Quotations Choose quotations that clearly support your point, and be sure to copy each quotation word for word. Remember always to credit the source.

MODEL

In his short story "The Tell-Tale Heart," Edgar Allan Poe uses bizarre and frightening details to grip the reader with a sense of horror. "I saw it [the eye] with perfect distinctness—all a dull blue, with a hideous veil over it that chilled the very marrow in my bones . . . ."

3 Descriptive Writing

Descriptive writing allows you to paint word pictures about anything, from events of global importance to the most personal feelings. It is an essential part of almost every piece of writing.

RUBRIC: Standards for Writing

Successful descriptive writing should

- have a clear focus and sense of purpose
- use sensory details and precise words to create a vivid image, establish a mood, or express emotion
- present details in a logical order

For more information, see ***Writing Workshop: Describing a Person,*** *pages 292–299.*

3.1 KEY TECHNIQUES

Consider Your Goals What do you want to accomplish with your description? Do you want to show why something is important to you? Do you want to make a person or scene more memorable? Do you want to explain an event?

R34 WRITING HANDBOOK

Identify Your Audience Who will read your description? How familiar are they with your subject? What background information will they need? Which details will they find most interesting?

Think Figuratively What figures of speech might help make your description vivid and interesting? What simile or metaphor comes to mind? What imaginative comparisons can you make? What living thing does an inanimate object remind you of?

Gather Sensory Details Which sights, smells, tastes, sounds, and textures make your subject come alive? Which details stick in your mind when you observe or recall your subject? Which senses does your subject most strongly affect?

You might want to use a chart like the one shown here to collect sensory details about your subject.

Sights	Sounds	Textures	Smells	Tastes

Organize Your Details Details that are presented in a logical order help the reader form a mental picture of the subject. Descriptive details may be organized chronologically, spatially, by order of impression, or by order of importance.

3.2 OPTIONS FOR ORGANIZATION

Option 1: Spatial Order Choose one of these options to show the spatial order of elements in a scene you are describing.

*For more information, see **Transitions,** page R32.*

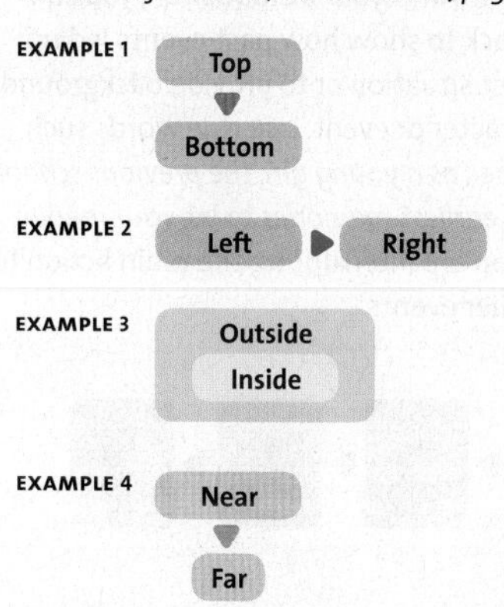

MODEL

Thunder's nostrils quivered as he was led into the barn. How would this be as a place to spend nights from now on? In the stall to the left, the straw smelled fresh. Beyond that stall, a saddle hung from the rough boards. To the right of his stall was another from which a mare looked at him curiously. So far, so good. To the far right, beyond two empty stalls, a cat lay on its side.

Option 2: Order of Impression Order of impression is the order in which you notice details.

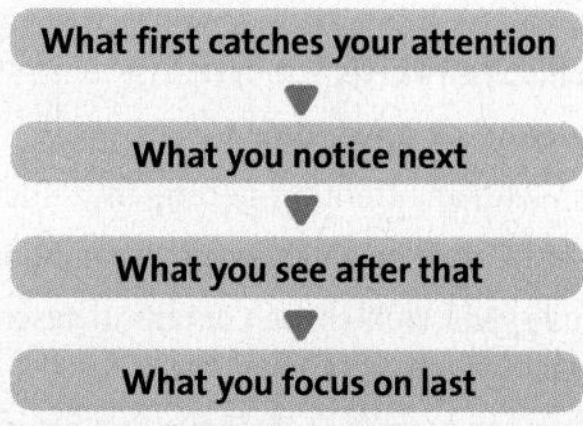

TIP Use transitions that help readers understand the order of the impressions you are describing. Some useful transitions are *after, next, during, first, before, finally,* and *then.*

MODEL

As I walked into the planetarium, I was struck by the total darkness. Gradually, my eyes adjusted, and I could see the rows of seats. Finally, daring to raise my eyes from the ground, I gasped in awe at the domed ceiling. Spangled with hundreds of glittering stars, it created the sensation of standing outside on a clear summer night.

Option 3: Order of Importance You can use order of importance as the organizing structure for a description.

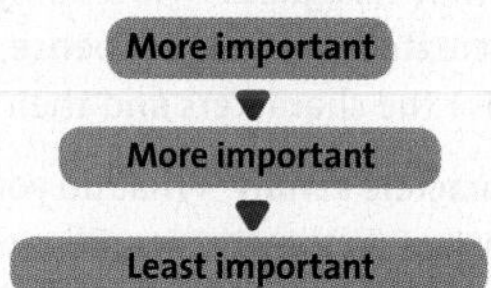

*For more information, see **Transitions,** page R32.*

WRITING HANDBOOK R35

Option 4: Chronological Order You can use chronological order as the organizing structure for a description. See section 4.2 on page R36 for an example of how this is done.

4 Narrative Writing

Narrative writing tells a story. If you write a story from your imagination, it is a fictional narrative. A true story about actual events is a nonfictional narrative. Narrative writing can be found in short stories, novels, news articles, personal narratives, and biographies.

RUBRIC: Standards for Writing

A successful narrative should

- begin with an attention-getting introduction
- present a clear incident, event, or situation
- include vivid, well-chosen details in describing characters, setting, and action
- use strategies such as dialogue and comparison/contrast to support descriptions
- explain the significance of the event for the writer
- have a logical organization with a clear beginning, middle, and end
- use language suited to the audience and purpose
- keep a consistent tone and point of view

*For more information, see **Writing Workshop: Short Story,** pages 558–565, and **Writing Workshop: Personal Narrative,** pages 144–151.*

4.1 KEY TECHNIQUES

Identify the Main Events What are the most important events in your narrative? Is each event needed to tell the story?

Describe the Setting When do the events occur? Where do they take place? How can you use setting to create mood and suspense, and to set the stage for the characters and their actions?

Depict Characters Vividly What do your characters look like? What do they think and say? How do they act? What details can show what they are like?

TIP Dialogue is an effective means of developing characters in a narrative. As you write dialogue, choose words that express your characters' personalities and that show how the characters feel about one another and about the events in the plot.

4.2 OPTIONS FOR ORGANIZATION

Option 1: Chronological Order One way to organize a narrative is to arrange the events in chronological order, as shown.

EXAMPLE

Yukiko's alarm doesn't go off, and she wakes up late on the day of an important English test.

Introduction *Characters and setting*

Panic-stricken, she leaps out of bed, throws on her clothes, and grabs her books, ignoring her mother's pleas to eat breakfast.

Event 1

She dashes into the classroom just as the final bell rings. She feels light-headed from running and not having eaten anything.

Event 2

Her mind goes blank, and she can't answer any of the questions. She takes a few minutes to calm down and tells herself she'll just do the best she can.

End *Perhaps showing the significance of the events*

Option 2: Flashback In narrative writing, it is also possible to introduce events that happened before the beginning of the story. You may want to hook your reader's interest by opening a story with an exciting event. After your introduction, you can use a flashback to show how past events led up to the present situation or to provide background about a character or event. Use clue words such as *last summer, as a young girl, the previous school year,* and *his earliest memories* to let your reader know that you are interrupting the main action to describe earlier events.

R36 WRITING HANDBOOK

Notice how the flashback interrupts the action in the model.

MODEL

As Yukiko fidgeted in her chair, she remembered a story she once read about a woman with amnesia. The woman wandered around for weeks, not remembering that she had a husband and children. The fact that the woman eventually regained her memory gave Yukiko hope that the material she'd studied so hard eventually would come back to her.

Option 3: Focus on Conflict When a fictional narrative focuses on a central conflict, the story's plot may be organized as in the following example.

EXAMPLE

Yukiko is worried about an important English test and stays up late studying. When she finally goes to bed, she forgets to set her alarm. In the morning, she wakes up in a panic, realizing that school starts in only 20 minutes.

Describe main characters and setting.

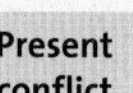

Present conflict.

She wonders whether she should try to get to class on time or pretend she is sick and take a make-up test later.

- She tells her mother the situation and asks her advice.
- She decides to race to school and take the test, since she's already studied so hard.
- She begins to feel dizzy and weak.

Relate events that make conflict complex and cause characters to change.

Yukiko gets to class just as the test is beginning. She's nervous and doesn't do as well as she could have, but she is proud of having made the right decision.

Present resolution or outcome of conflict.

5 Expository Writing

Expository writing informs and explains. You can use it to explain how to cook spaghetti, to explore the origins of the universe, or to compare two pieces of literature. There are many types of expository writing. Think about your topic and select the type that will present the information most clearly.

5.1 COMPARISON AND CONTRAST

Compare-and-contrast writing examines the similarities and differences between two or more subjects. You might, for example, compare and contrast two short stories, the main characters in a novel, or two movies.

RUBRIC: Standards for Writing

Successful compare-and-contrast writing should

- hook the reader's attention with a strong introduction
- clearly identify the subjects that are being compared
- include specific, relevant details
- follow a clear plan of organization
- use language and details appropriate to the audience
- use transitional words and phrases to clarify similarities and differences

*For more information, see **Writing Workshop: Comparison-Contrast Essay,** pages 424–431, **Writing Workshop: Personal Response to a Poem,** pages 648–655, **Writing Workshop: Literary Analysis,** pages 742–749 and **Writing Workshop: Cause-and-Effect Essay,** pages 860–867.*

Options for Organization

Compare-and-contrast writing can be organized in different ways. The examples that follow demonstrate point-by-point organization and subject-by-subject organization.

Option 1: Point-by-Point Organization

EXAMPLE

I. Similarities between older and newer childrens' books — **Point 1**

Subject A. Older books feature children as characters.

Subject B. Today's books also often include children.

II. Differences between older and newer childrens' books — **Point 2**

Subject A. Older books tend to avoid racial and social conflicts.

Subject B. Today's books are likely to describe realistic racial and social conflicts.

WRITING HANDBOOK R37

Option 2: Subject-by-Subject Organization

EXAMPLE

I. Older childrens' books — **Subject A**

Point 1. They focus on children as main characters.

Point 2. They avoid discussing racial or social conflicts.

II. Today's childrens' books — **Subject B**

Point 1. They focus on children and young people.

Point 2. They describe realistic racial and social conflicts.

*For more information, see **Writing Workshop: Comparison-Contrast Essay,** pages 424–431.*

5.2 CAUSE AND EFFECT

Cause-effect writing explains why something happened, why certain conditions exist, or what resulted from an action or a condition. You might use cause-effect writing to explain a character's actions, the progress of a disease, or the outcome of a war.

RUBRIC: Standards for Writing

Successful cause-effect writing should

- hook the reader's attention with a strong introduction
- clearly state the cause-and-effect relationship
- show clear connections between causes and effects
- present causes and effects in a logical order and use transitions effectively
- use facts, examples, and other details to illustrate each cause and effect
- use language and details appropriate to the audience

*For more information, see **Writing Workshop: Cause-and-Effect Essay,** pages 860–867.*

Options for Organization

Your organization will depend on your topic and your purpose for writing.

Option 1: Effect-to-Cause Organization If you want to explain the causes of an event, such as the risk of not having enough energy to take a test, you might first state the effect and then examine its causes.

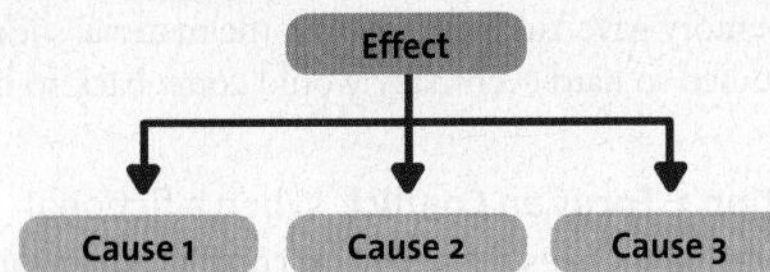

Option 2: Cause-to-Effect Organization If your focus is on explaining the effects of an event, such as the importance of eating a healthy breakfast, you might first state the cause and then explain the effects.

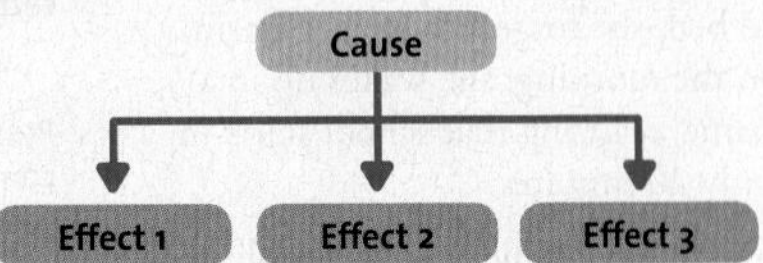

Option 3: Cause-Effect Chain Organization

Sometimes you'll want to describe a chain of cause-and-effect relationships to explore a topic such as how to do well on a test.

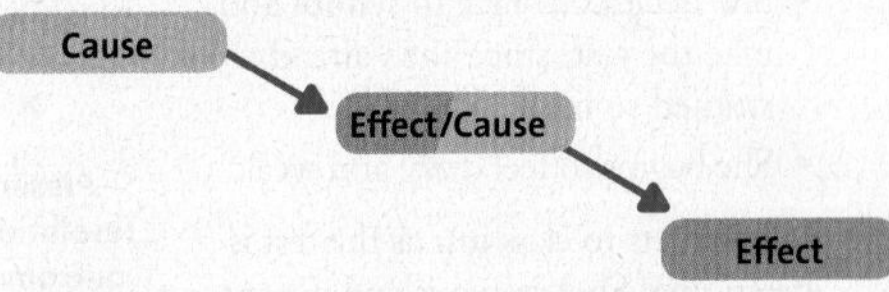

TIP Don't assume that a cause-effect relationship exists just because one event follows another. Look for evidence that the later event could not have happened if the first event had not caused it.

R38 WRITING HANDBOOK

5.3 PROBLEM-SOLUTION

Problem-solution writing clearly states a problem, analyzes the problem, and proposes a solution to the problem. It can be used to identify and solve a conflict between characters, investigate global warming, or tell why the home team keeps losing.

RUBRIC: Standards for Writing

Successful problem-solution writing should

- hook the reader's attention with a strong introduction
- identify the problem and help the reader understand the issues involved
- analyze the causes and effects of the problem
- include quotations, facts, and statistics
- explore possible solutions to the problem and recommend the best one(s)
- use language, details, and a tone appropriate to the audience

Options for Organization

Your organization will depend on the goal of your problem-solution piece, your intended audience, and the specific problem you have chosen to address. The organizational methods that follow are effective for different kinds of problem-solution writing.

Option 1: Simple Problem-Solution

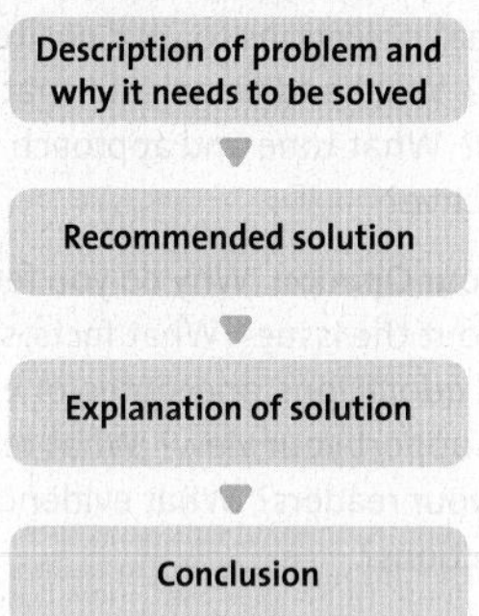

Option 2: Deciding Between Solutions

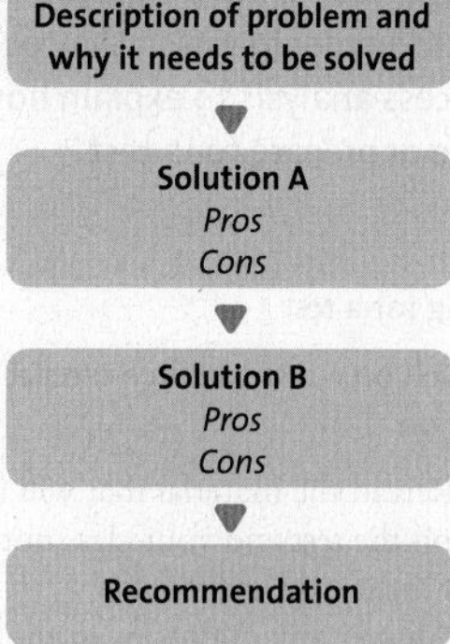

5.4 ANALYSIS

In writing an analysis, you explain how something works, how it is defined, or what its parts are.

RUBRIC: Standards for Writing

A successful analysis should

- hook the reader's attention with a strong introduction
- clearly define the subject and its parts
- use a specific organizing structure to provide a logical flow of information
- show connections among facts and ideas through transitional words and phrases
- use language and details appropriate for the audience

Options for Organization

Organize your details in a logical order appropriate to the kind of analysis you're writing. Use one of the following options: process analysis, definition analysis, or parts analysis.

WRITING HANDBOOK R39

Option 1: Process Analysis A process analysis is usually organized chronologically, with steps or stages in the order in which they occur. You might use a process analysis to explain how to program a cell phone or prepare for a test.

MODEL

Preparing for a test *(Introduce process)*

Doing well on a test requires careful preparation. *(Give background)*

Step 1: Reread the material that will be covered on the test and your class notes.
Step 2: Outline the material.
Step 3: Answer any questions in the text and make up and answer your own.
Step 4: Get plenty of sleep the night before. *(Explain steps)*

Option 2: Definition Analysis You can organize the details of a definition analysis in order of importance or impression. Use a definition analysis to explain the characteristics of a limerick, the characteristics of insects, or a quality (such as excellence).

MODEL

What is excellence?

Excellence is the quality of being first-rate, exceeding all others, and setting a standard of performance. *(Introduce term and definition)*

Feature 1: being first-rate

Feature 2: exceeding all others

Feature 3: setting a standard of performance *(Explain features)*

Option 3: Parts Analysis A parts analysis explains a subject by breaking it down into its main pieces.

MODEL

Test preparation consists of three main parts. *(Introduce subject)*

Part 1: Getting to know the material

Part 2: Practicing the material

Part 3: Resting and being healthy for the test *(Explain parts)*

6 Persuasive Writing

Persuasive writing allows you to use the power of language to inform and influence others. It includes speeches, persuasive essays, newspaper editorials, advertisements, and critical reviews.

RUBRIC: Standards for Writing

Successful persuasive writing should

- grab the reader's attention with a strong introduction
- present a well-defined thesis that states the issue and the writer's position
- support arguments with detailed evidence, examples, and reasons
- clearly distinguish between fact and opinion
- anticipate and answer counterarguments, or opposing views, with solid facts and reasons
- use sound logic and persuasive language
- conclude with a summary of points or a call to action

For more information, see ***Writing Workshop: Persuasive Essay,*** *pages 1016–1023.*

6.1 KEY TECHNIQUES

Clarify Your Position What do you believe about the issue? How can you express your opinion most clearly?

Know Your Audience Who will read your writing? What do they already know and believe about the issue? What objections to your position might they have? What additional information might they need? What tone and approach would be most effective?

Support Your Opinion Why do you feel the way you do about the issue? What facts, statistics, examples, quotations, anecdotes, or expert opinions support your view? What reasons will convince your readers? What evidence can answer their objections?

R40 WRITING HANDBOOK

Ways to Support Your Argument	
Statistics	facts that are stated in numbers
Examples	specific instances that explain points
Observations	events or situations you have seen firsthand
Anecdotes	brief stories that illustrate points
Quotations	direct statements from authorities

For more information, see ***Identifying Faulty Reasoning,*** *page R24.*

Begin and End with a Bang How can you hook your readers and make a lasting impression? What memorable quotation, anecdote, or statistic will catch their attention at the beginning or stick in their minds at the end? What strong summary or call to action can you conclude with?

MODEL

Beginning

Have you ever enjoyed the antics of the orangutans or watched the polar bears swim at Green Park Zoo? Unless we make sure that public funding for the zoo continues, those experiences will be just memories.

End

In addition to being a place for relaxation and fun, Green Park Zoo is a scientific laboratory where professionals work to create educational programs and ensure the survival of endangered species. Don't let the zoo become an endangered species itself. Support public funding today.

6.2 OPTIONS FOR ORGANIZATION

In a two-sided persuasive essay, you want to show the weaknesses of other opinions as you explain the strengths of your own.

Option 1: Reasons for Your Opinion

- Introduction states issue and your position on it
- ▼ Reason 1 with evidence and support
- ▼ Reason 2 with evidence and support
- ▼ Reason 3 with evidence and support
- ▼ Objections to whole argument
- ▼ Response to objections
- ▼ Conclusion restates your position and recommends a course of action

Option 2: Point-by-Point Basis

- Introduction states issue and your position on it
- ▼ Reason 1 with evidence and support
- ▼ Objections and responses for reason 1
- ▼ Reason 2 with evidence and support
- ▼ Objections and responses for reason 2
- ▼ Reason 3 with evidence and support
- ▼ Objections and responses for reason 3
- ▼ Conclusion restates your position and recommends a course of action

WRITING HANDBOOK R41

7 Workplace and Technical Writing

Business writing is writing done in a workplace to support the work of a company or business. You may need to do business writing to request information or complain about a product or service. Several types of formats, such as memos, letters, e-mails, and applications, have been developed to make communication easier.

RUBRIC: Standards for Writing

Successful business writing should

- clearly state the purpose of the communication in the opening paragraph
- follow a standard format
- use language that is precise and appropriate to the audience
- have a formal, respectful tone
- include only necessary information
- present information in a logical order
- conclude with a summary of important points

7.1 KEY TECHNIQUES OF WORKPLACE WRITING

Think About Your Purpose Why are you doing this writing? Do you want to order or complain about a product? If you know what you want, you're more likely to get the desired results.

Identify Your Audience Who will read your writing? What background information will they need? What tone or language is appropriate?

Use a Pattern of Organization That Is Appropriate to the Content If you have to compare and contrast two products in a letter, you can use the same compare-and-contrast organization that you would use in an essay.

Support Your Points What specific details might clarify your ideas? What reasons do you have for your statements?

Finish Strongly How can you best sum up your statements? What is your main point? What action do you want the recipients to take?

Revise and Proofread Your Writing Just as you are graded on the quality of an essay you write for a class, you will be judged on the quality of your writing in the workplace.

7.2 MATCHING THE FORMAT TO THE OCCASION

E-mail messages, memos, and letters have similar purposes but are used in different situations. The chart shows how each format can be used.

Format	Occasion
Memo	use to send correspondence **inside** the workplace only
E-mail message	use to send correspondence **inside or outside** the company
Letter	use to send correspondence **outside** the company

TIP Memos are often sent as e-mail messages in the workplace. Remember that both require formal language and standard spelling, capitalization, and punctuation.

Technical writing is used for detailed instructions or descriptions of items and processes. It is important to a variety of fields, such as science, government, and industry. Technical writing is used to present information in such a way that the reader can use it to complete a task, such as performing an experiment, assembling an object, or using a tool.

At work, at school, or in everyday life, you may have to use technical writing to leave instructions for another person.

RUBRIC: Standards for Writing

Instructions should

- present no unnecessary information
- include all essential information such as definitions of unfamiliar terms
- explain all the steps in a logical order
- use direct, precise language
- use present-tense action verbs
- use transitions and formatting, such as numbered steps, headings, and different fonts to aid understanding

R42 WRITING HANDBOOK

7.3 KEY TECHNIQUES OF TECHNICAL WRITING

Think About Your Organization As you write, make sure you are presenting your information in a sensible order. For example, you would probably list any necessary tools and materials early on. Then you would present the steps in the order in which they should be followed.

Keep Your Audience in Mind Make sure you explain what readers unfamiliar with the activity or process will need to know. Sometimes making a comparison to something the reader is familiar with can help. Graphics, such as pictures and maps, can also help make instructions easier to understand.

Use Transitions as Needed Transitions such as *first, next, after,* and *last* and numbered steps can make the order of steps clear and guide your reader from one step to the next.

Review Your Ending You can simply end with the last step, or you can end by describing the result or outcome of following the directions.

Evaluate Your Instructions Have a friend follow your instructions to make sure they are clear.

7.4 FORMATS

Business letters usually have a formal tone and a specific format as shown here. The key to writing a business letter is to get to the point as quickly as possible and to present your information clearly.

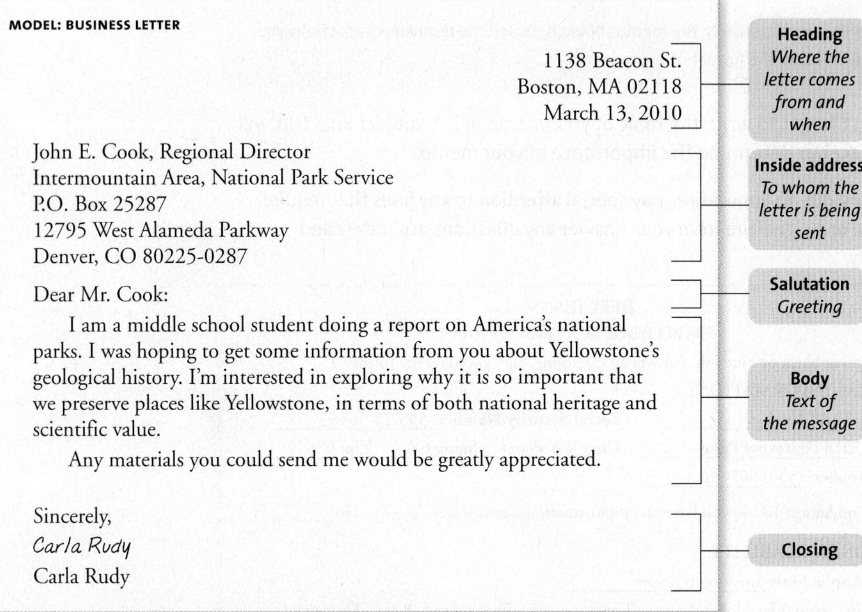

MODEL: BUSINESS LETTER

1138 Beacon St.
Boston, MA 02118
March 13, 2010

John E. Cook, Regional Director
Intermountain Area, National Park Service
P.O. Box 25287
12795 West Alameda Parkway
Denver, CO 80225-0287

Dear Mr. Cook:

I am a middle school student doing a report on America's national parks. I was hoping to get some information from you about Yellowstone's geological history. I'm interested in exploring why it is so important that we preserve places like Yellowstone, in terms of both national heritage and scientific value.

Any materials you could send me would be greatly appreciated.

Sincerely,
Carla Rudy
Carla Rudy

PRACTICE AND APPLY

1. Draft a response to the letter. Then revise your letter as necessary according to the rubric at the beginning of page R42. Make sure you have included the necessary information and have written in an appropriate tone.
2. Proofread your letter for grammatical errors and spelling mistakes. Follow the format of the model and use appropriate spacing between parts.

WRITING HANDBOOK R43

Memos are often used in the workplace as a way of sending information in a direct and concise manner. They can be used to announce or summarize meetings and to request actions or specific information.

MODEL: MEMO

To: Joellen Snipes
From: John Cook
Subject: Informational brochures
Date: March 16, 2010

Joellen, please read the attached letter and send Carla our brochure packet. It's encouraging to receive inquiries from concerned young people, so please add a personal note of thanks for her interest.

Heading
Receiver's name
Sender's name
Topic of memo
Complete date

Body

PRACTICE AND APPLY

Write a memo in response to the memo shown here. Tell the receiver what actions you have taken. Follow the format of the model.

TIP Don't forget to write the topic of your memo in the subject line. This will help the receiver determine the importance of your memo.

When filling out an application, pay special attention to any lines that require a response or a signature from you. Answer any questions accurately and completely.

JIFFY JEANS
EMPLOYMENT APPLICATION

Print clearly in black or blue ink. Answer all questions. Sign and date the form.

PERSONAL INFORMATION:

Name: Marquell Janek **Social Security Number:** 555-77-5656
Address: 7218 University Place **City:** Woodland **State:** CA **Zip:** 95659
Phone Number: (530) 667-7814

If you are under age 18, do you have an employment/age certificates? Yes X No ___

POSITION/AVAILABILITY:

Position Applied for: Stockroom helper
Days/Hours Available: Monday ____ Tuesday ____ Wednesday 6–8 PM Thursday ____
Friday ____, Saturday 8 AM–6 PM, Sunday 1 PM–6 PM
What date are you available to start work? June 19, 2010

EDUCATION:

School: Westleigh Middle School **Highest Grade Completed:** 8

I certify that information contained in this application is true and complete. I understand that false information may be grounds for not hiring me or for immediate termination of employment at any point in the future if I am hired. I authorize the verification of any or all information listed above.

Signature: Marquell Janek **Date:** 5/31/2010

R44 WRITING HANDBOOK

When writing instructions, be sure to include any materials someone would need in order to complete the task. Number or letter each step to show order.

MODEL: INSTRUCTIONS

How to Etch Glass by eHow.com

Turn a boring mirror or pane of glass into a work of art!

What you **need:**

- carbon paper
- clear contact paper
- crafts knife
- etching cream
- glass cleaner
- latex gloves
- soft, lint-free cloth
- piece of glass or mirror
- pencils
- paper towels

Steps:

1. Clean the surface you will be etching with glass cleaner and a soft cloth. Cover the surface with clear contact paper and press out all the bubbles.
2. Put the design you are using behind the glass.
3. Trace the design onto the contact paper if you are doing a mirror. Put carbon paper on top of the contact paper and then place your design on top of that. Trace the design, transferring it to the contact paper.
4. Use a crafts knife to cut the contact paper away from the areas that you want to etch. Make sure that all of the edges are stuck tight to the glass and that there are no bubbles at the edges.
5. Use a paper towel to smear a liberal layer of etching cream onto the design area.
6. Wait the amount of time required for the brand of etching cream you are using—usually 5 to 10 minutes.
7. Run cool water over the cream to rinse it off. Peel off the contact paper and rinse the glass under cool water again.

Tips:

Areas where the acid isn't thick enough will look streaked. Be sure to get a good coat of the etching cream onto the piece of glass.

Warning:

Wear latex gloves when working with etching cream. It's an acid. Apply the cream in a well-ventilated area.

Courtesy of www.ehow.com: Clear instructions on how to do (just about) anything!

PRACTICE AND APPLY

Think about something you might want someone else to do for you while you're at school, such as do your laundry or prepare dinner. Use the rubric at the bottom of page R42 to write instructions. Be sure to include the following:

- an opening statement that describes what needs to be done
- a list of tools and materials needed to perform the task
- the steps needed to perform the task, including transition words and/or numbered steps if order is important
- any special notes or warnings about a tool or step in the process

WRITING HANDBOOK R45

Writing that is full of mistakes can confuse or even annoy a reader. Punctuation errors in a letter might lead to a miscommunication and delay a reply. Sentence fragments might lower your grade on an essay. Paying attention to grammar, punctuation, and capitalization rules can make your writing clearer and easier to read.

Quick Reference: Parts of Speech

PART OF SPEECH	FUNCTION	EXAMPLES
Noun	names a person, a place, a thing, an idea, a quality, or an action	
Common	serves as a general name, or a name common to an entire group	shadow, harmonica, paw, mistake
Proper	names a specific, one-of-a-kind person, place, or thing	Chinatown, Switzerland, Jupiter, Herbert
Singular	refers to a single person, place, thing, or idea	earthquake, laboratory, medication, outcome
Plural	refers to more than one person, place, thing, or idea	chemicals, splinters, geniuses, soldiers
Concrete	names something that can be perceived by the senses	calendar, basketball, ocean, snow
Abstract	names something that cannot be perceived by the senses	democracy, authority, beauty, fame
Compound	expresses a single idea through a combination of two or more words	self-esteem, mountaintop, firefighters, light bulb
Collective	refers to a group of people or things	team, family, class, choir
Possessive	shows who or what owns something	Pandora's, Strauss's, Franks', women's
Pronoun	takes the place of a noun or another pronoun	
Personal	refers to the person making a statement, the person(s) being addressed, or the person(s) or thing(s) the statement is about	I, me, my, mine, we, us, our, ours, you, your, yours, she, he, it, her, him, hers, his, its, they, them, their, theirs
Reflexive	follows a verb or preposition and refers to a preceding noun or pronoun	myself, yourself, herself, himself, itself, ourselves, yourselves, themselves
Intensive	emphasizes a noun or another pronoun	(same as reflexives)
Demonstrative	points to one or more specific persons or things	this, that, these, those
Interrogative	signals a question	who, whom, whose, which, what
Indefinite	refers to one or more persons or things not specifically mentioned	both, all, most, many, anyone, everybody, several, none, some
Relative	introduces an adjective clause by relating it to a word in the clause	who, whom, whose, which, that

R46 GRAMMAR HANDBOOK

PART OF SPEECH	FUNCTION	EXAMPLES
Verb	Expresses an action, a condition, or a state of being	
Action	tells what the subject does or did, physically or mentally	find, know, clings, displayed, rises, crave
Linking	connects the subject to something that identifies or describes it	am, is, are, was, were, sound, taste, appear, feel, become, remain, seem
Auxiliary	precedes the main verb in a verb phrase	Be, have, can, do, could, will, would, may, might
Transitive	directs the action toward someone or something; always has an object	She opened the **door.**
Intransitive	does not direct the action toward someone or something; does not have an object	The door **opened.**
Adjective	modifies a noun or pronoun	**slight** groan, **dying** gladiators, **ancient** sea, **two** pigtails
Adverb	modifies a verb, an adjective, or another adverb	**always** closed, **very** patiently, **more** pleasant, ran **quickly**
Preposition	relates one word to another word	at, by, for, from, in, of, on, to, with
Conjunction	joins words or word groups	
Coordinating	joins words or word groups used the same way	and, but, or, for, so, yet, nor
Correlative	used as a pair to join words or word groups used the same way	both . . . and, either . . . or, neither . . . nor
Subordinating	introduces a clause that cannot stand by itself as a complete sentence	although, after, as, before, because, when, if, unless
Interjection	expresses emotion	wow, ouch, hooray

GRAMMAR HANDBOOK R47

Quick Reference: The Sentence and Its Parts

The diagrams that follow will give you a brief review of the essentials of a sentence and some of its parts.

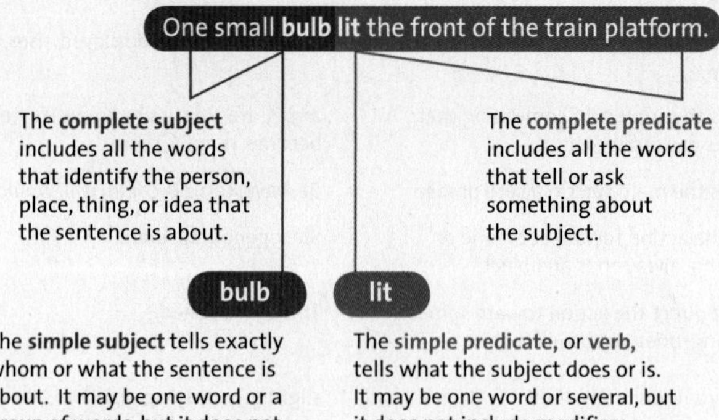

The simple subject tells exactly whom or what the sentence is about. It may be one word or a group of words, but it does not include modifiers.

Every word in a sentence is part of a complete subject or a complete predicate.

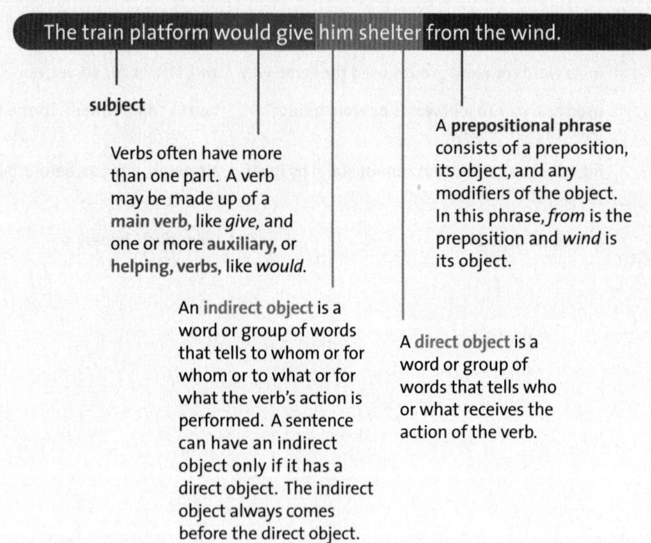

The train platform would give him shelter from the wind.
subject
Verbs often have more than one part. A verb may be made up of a main verb, like give, and one or more auxiliary, or helping, verbs, like would.
A prepositional phrase consists of a preposition, its object, and any modifiers of the object. In this phrase, from is the preposition and wind is its object.
An indirect object is a word or group of words that tells to whom or for whom or to what or for what the verb's action is performed. A sentence can have an indirect object only if it has a direct object. The indirect object always comes before the direct object.
A direct object is a word or group of words that tells who or what receives the action of the verb.

R48 GRAMMAR HANDBOOK

Quick Reference: Punctuation

MARK	FUNCTION	EXAMPLES
End Marks period, question mark, exclamation point	ends a sentence	We can start now. When would you like to leave? What a fantastic hit!
period	follows an initial or abbreviation **Exception:** postal abbreviations of states	Mrs. Dorothy Parker, McDougal Littell Inc., C. P. Cavafy, P.M., A.D., lb., oz., Blvd., Dr. NE (Nebraska), NV (Nevada)
period	follows a number or letter in an outline	I. Volcanoes A. Central-vent 1. Shield
Comma	separates part of a compound sentence	I had never disliked poetry, but now I really love it.
	separates items in a series	Her humor, grace, and kindness served her well.
	separates adjectives of equal rank that modify the same noun	The slow, easy route is best.
	sets off a term of address	Maria, how can I help you? You must do something, soldier.
	sets off a parenthetical expression	Hard workers, as you know, don't quit. I'm not a quitter, believe me.
	sets off an introductory word, phrase, or dependent clause	Yes, I forgot my key. At the beginning of the day, I feel fresh. While she was out, I was here. Having finished my chores, I went out.
	sets off a nonessential phrase or clause	Ed Pawn, the captain of the chess team, won. Ed Pawn, who is the captain, won. The two leading runners, sprinting toward the finish line, finished in a tie.
	sets off parts of dates and addresses	Mail it by May 14, 2010, to the Hauptman Company, 321 Market Street, Memphis, Tennessee.
	follows the salutation and closing of a letter	Dear Jim, Sincerely yours,
	separates words to avoid confusion	By noon, time had run out. What the minister does, does matter. While cooking, Jim burned his hand.
Semicolon	separates items in a series that contain commas	We spent the first week of summer vacation in Chicago, Illinois; the second week in St. Louis, Missouri; and the third week in Albany, New York.
	separates parts of a compound sentence that are not joined by a coordinating conjunction	The last shall be first; the first shall be last. I read the Bible; however, I have not memorized it.
	separates parts of a compound sentence when the parts contain commas	After I ran out of money, I called my parents; but only my sister was home, unfortunately.

For more help with punctuation, see

 GRAMMAR FOR WRITING
pp. 248–275

GRAMMAR HANDBOOK R49

MARK	FUNCTION	EXAMPLES
Colon	introduces a list	Those we wrote to were the following**:** Dana, John, and Will.
	introduces a long quotation	Abraham Lincoln wrote**:** "Four score and seven years ago, our fathers brought forth on this continent a new nation . . . ."
	follows the salutation of a business letter	To Whom It May Concern**:** Dear Leonard Atole**:**
	separates certain numbers	1**:**28 P.M., Genesis 2**:**5
Dash	indicates an abrupt break in thought	I was thinking of my mother**—**who is arriving tomorrow**—**just as you walked in.
Parentheses	enclose less important material	It was so unlike him **(**John is always on time**)** that I began to worry. The last World Series game **(**did you see it?**)** was fun.
Hyphen	joins parts of a compound adjective before a noun	The not**-**so**-**rich taxpayer won't stand for this!
	joins parts of a compound with *all-*, *ex-*, *self-*, or *-elect*	The ex**-**firefighter helped rescue him. Our president**-**elect is self**-**conscious.
	joins parts of a compound number (to ninety-nine)	Today is the twenty**-**fifth of November.
	joins parts of a fraction	My cup is one**-**third full.
	joins a prefix to a word beginning with a capital letter	I'm studying the U.S. presidents pre**-**1900. It snowed in mid**-**October.
	indicates that a word is divided at the end of a line	How could you have any reasonable expect**-** ations of getting a new computer?
Apostrophe	used with *s* to form the possessive of a noun or an indefinite pronoun	my friend**'**s book, my friends**'** books, anyone**'**s guess, somebody else**'**s problem
	replaces one or more omitted letters in a contraction or numbers in a date	don**'**t (omitted *o*), he**'**d (omitted *woul*), the class of **'**99 (omitted *19*)
	used with *s* to form the plural of a letter	I had two A**'**s on my report card.
Quotation Marks	set off a speaker's exact words	**"**That, I'll do,**"** Lemon said. **"**That,**"** Lemon said, **"**I'll do.**"** Did Lemon say, **"**That I'll do**"**? Lemon said, **"**That I'll do!**"**
	set off the title of a story, an article, a short poem, an essay, a song, or a chapter	I recited Alice Walker's **"**We Alone**"** at the assembly. Poe's **"**The Tell-Tale Heart**"** and Stockton's **"**The Lady or the Tiger?**"** held my interest. I enjoyed Bob Dylan's **"**Boots of Spanish Leather.**"**
Ellipses	replace material omitted from a quotation	"Her diary tells us that she **. . .** thought of ordinary things, such as going to school with other kids **. . .**"
Italics	indicate the title of a book, a play, a magazine, a long poem, an opera, a film, or a TV series, or the name of a ship	***Harriet Tubman: Conductor on the Underground Railroad, The Hitchhiker, TIME, The Magic Flute,*** the ***Iliad, Star Wars, 60 Minutes,*** the ***Mayflower***

R50 GRAMMAR HANDBOOK

Quick Reference: Capitalization

CATEGORY	EXAMPLES
People and Titles	
Names and initials of people	Jack London, T.S. Eliot
Titles used before a name	Professor Holmes, Senator Long
Deities and members of religious groups	Jesus, Allah, Buddha, Zeus, Baptists, Roman Catholics
Names of ethnic and national groups	Hispanics, Jews, African Americans
Geographical Names	
Cities, states, countries, continents	Philadelphia, Kansas, Japan, Europe
Regions, bodies of water, mountains	the South, Lake Baikal, Mount Everest
Geographic features, parks	Great Basin, Yellowstone National Park
Streets and roads, planets	318 East Sutton Drive, Charles Court, Jupiter, Mars
Organizations, Events, Etc.	
Companies, organizations, teams	Ford Motor Company, Boy Scouts of America, St. Louis Cardinals
Buildings, bridges, monuments	Empire State Building, Eads Bridge, Washington Monument
Documents, awards	Declaration of Independence, Stanley Cup
Special named events	Mardi Gras, World Series
Government bodies, historical periods and events	U.S. Senate, House of Representatives, Middle Ages, Vietnam War
Days and months, holidays	Thursday, March, Thanksgiving, Labor Day
Specific cars, boats, trains, planes	Porsche, Carpathia, Southwest Chief, Concorde
Proper Adjectives	
Adjectives formed from proper nouns	French cooking, Spanish omelet, Edwardian age, Western movie
First Words and the Pronoun I	
First word in a sentence or quotation	This is it. He said, "Let's go."
First word of sentence in parentheses that is not within another sentence	The spelling rules are covered in another section. (Consult that section for more information.)
First words in the salutation and closing of a letter	Dear Madam, Very truly yours,
First word in each line of most poetry Personal pronoun I	Then am I A happy fly If I live Or if I die.
First word, last word, and all important words in a title	"The Ransom of Red Chief," "Rules of the Game," *Roll of Thunder, Hear My Cry*

For more help with capitalization, see

GRAMMAR FOR WRITING
pp. 228–247

GRAMMAR HANDBOOK R51

1 Nouns

A **noun** is a word used to name a person, a place, a thing, an idea, a quality, or an action. Nouns can be classified in several ways.

*For more information on different types of nouns, see **Quick Reference: Parts of Speech,** page R46.*

1.1 COMMON NOUNS

Common nouns are general names, common to entire groups.

1.2 PROPER NOUNS

Proper nouns name specific, one-of-a-kind people, places, and things.

Common	Proper
legend, canyon, girl, city	Pecos Bill, Canyon de Chelly, Anne, Amsterdam

*For more information, see **Quick Reference: Capitalization,** page R51.*

1.3 SINGULAR AND PLURAL NOUNS

A noun may take a singular or a plural form, depending on whether it names a single person, place, thing, or idea or more than one. Make sure you use appropriate spellings when forming plurals.

Singular	Plural
diary, valley, revolution, calf	diaries, valleys, revolutions, calves

*For more information, see **Forming Plural Nouns,** page R74.*

1.4 POSSESSIVE NOUNS

A **possessive noun** shows who or what owns something.

*For more information, see **Forming Possessives,** page R76.*

2 Pronouns

A **pronoun** is a word that is used in place of a noun or another pronoun. The word or word group to which the pronoun refers is called its **antecedent.**

2.1 PERSONAL PRONOUNS

Personal pronouns change their form to express person, number, gender, and case. The forms of these pronouns are shown in the following chart.

	Nominative	Objective	Possessive
Singular			
First person	I	me	my, mine
Second person	you	you	your, yours
Third person	she, he, it	her, him, it	her, hers, his, its
Plural			
First person	we	us	our, ours
Second person	you	you	your, yours
Third person	they	them	their, theirs

2.2 AGREEMENT WITH ANTECEDENT

Pronouns should agree with their antecedents in number, gender, and person.

If an antecedent is singular, use a singular pronoun.

EXAMPLE: *Rachel wrote a **detective story.** It has a surprise ending.*

If an antecedent is plural, use a plural pronoun.

EXAMPLES: *The **characters** have their motives for murder.*

*Javier loves **mysteries** and reads them all the time.*

The gender of a pronoun must be the same as the gender of its antecedent.

EXAMPLE: *The **man** has to use all his wits to stay alive and solve the crime.*

The person of the pronoun must be the same as the person of its antecedent. As the chart in Section 2.1 shows, a pronoun can be in first-person, second-person, or third-person form.

EXAMPLE: ***You** want a story to grab your attention.*

For more help with pronouns, see

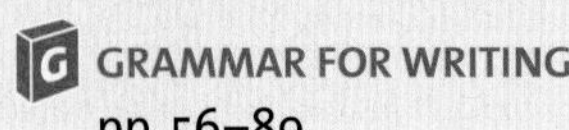

pp. 56–89

GRAMMAR PRACTICE

Rewrite each sentence so that the underlined pronoun agrees with its antecedent.

1. Lawrence Yep, author of "The Great Rat Hunt," had asthma when it was young.
2. The story's suspense keeps readers interested in them.
3. Yep and his father put out rat traps and place bait on it.
4. When the rat shows their teeth, Yep panics.
5. You and her friends should read the story sometime.

2.3 PRONOUN FORMS

Personal pronouns change form to show how they function in sentences. The three forms are the subject form, the object form, and the possessive form. For examples of these pronouns, see the chart in Section 2.1.

A **subject pronoun** is used as a subject in a sentence.

EXAMPLE: *The poem "Mi Madre" compares the desert to a mother. It was written by Pat Mora.*

Also use the subject form when the pronoun follows a linking verb.

EXAMPLE: *The person healed by the desert is she.*

An **object pronoun** is used as a direct object, an indirect object, or the object of a preposition.

SUBJECT OBJECT

We will give them to her.

OBJECT OF PREPOSITION

A **possessive pronoun** shows ownership. The pronouns *mine, yours, hers, his, its, ours,* and *theirs* can be used in place of nouns.

EXAMPLE: *The desert's gifts are hers.*

The pronouns *my, your, her, his, its, our,* and *their* are used before nouns.

EXAMPLE: *The poem changed my view of the desert.*

WATCH OUT! Many spelling errors can be avoided if you watch out for *its* and *their.* Don't confuse the possessive pronoun *its* with the contraction *it's,* meaning "it is" or "it has." The homonyms *they're* (a contraction of *they are*) and *there* ("in that place") are often mistakenly used for *their.*

TIP To decide which pronoun to use in a comparison, such as "He tells better tales than (I *or* me)," fill in the missing word(s): *He tells better tales than I tell.*

GRAMMAR PRACTICE

Write the correct pronoun form to complete each sentence.

1. The thunder and lightning frightens (her, she).
2. Has (him, he) ever eaten prickly pear?
3. The desert sings, but (its, it) songs are mysterious.
4. Raindrops in the desert would surprise (me, I).
5. The desert has lessons for all of (we, us).

2.4 REFLEXIVE AND INTENSIVE PRONOUNS

These pronouns are formed by adding *-self* or *-selves* to certain personal pronouns. Their forms are the same, and they differ only in how they are used.

A **reflexive pronoun** follows a verb or preposition and reflects back on an earlier noun or pronoun.

EXAMPLES: *He likes himself too much.*
She is now herself again.

Intensive pronouns intensify or emphasize the nouns or pronouns to which they refer.

EXAMPLES: *They themselves will educate their children.*
You did it yourself.

GRAMMAR PRACTICE ANSWERS

1. *he*
2. *it*
3. *them*
4. *its/his*
5. *your*

GRAMMAR PRACTICE ANSWERS

1. *her*
2. *he*
3. *its*
4. *me*
5. *us*

GRAMMAR HANDBOOK R53

WATCH OUT! Avoid using *hisself* or *theirselves*. Standard English does not include these forms.

NONSTANDARD: *Colorful desert flowers offer theirselves to the poem's speaker.*

STANDARD: *Colorful desert flowers offer themselves to the poem's speaker.*

2.5 DEMONSTRATIVE PRONOUNS

Demonstrative pronouns point out things and persons near and far.

	Singular	Plural
Near	this	these
Far	that	those

2.6 INDEFINITE PRONOUNS

Indefinite pronouns do not refer to specific persons or things and usually have no antecedents. The chart shows some commonly used indefinite pronouns.

Singular	Plural	Singular or Plural	
another	both	all	none
anybody	few	any	some
no one	many	more	most
neither			

TIP Indefinite pronouns that end in *one, body,* or *thing* are always singular.

INCORRECT: *Did everybody play their part well?*

If the indefinite pronoun might refer to either a male or a female, *his or her* may be used to refer to it, or the sentence may be rewritten.

CORRECT: *Did everybody play his or her part well?*

Did all the students play their parts well?

2.7 INTERROGATIVE PRONOUNS

An **interrogative pronoun** tells a reader or listener that a question is coming. The interrogative pronouns are *who, whom, whose, which,* and *what.*

EXAMPLES: *Who is going to rehearse with you?*

From whom did you receive the script?

TIP *Who* is used as a subject; *whom,* as an object. To find out which pronoun you need to use in a question, change the question to a statement.

QUESTION: *(Who/Whom) did you meet there?*

STATEMENT: *You met (?) there.*

Since the verb has a subject (*you*), the needed word must be the object form, *whom.*

EXAMPLE: *Whom did you meet there?*

WATCH OUT! A special problem arises when you use an interrupter, such as *do you think,* within a question.

EXAMPLE: *(Who/Whom) do you think will win?*

If you eliminate the interrupter, it is clear that the word you need is *who.*

2.8 RELATIVE PRONOUNS

Relative pronouns relate, or connect, adjective clauses to the words they modify in sentences. The noun or pronoun that a relative clause modifies is the antecedent of the relative pronoun. Here are the relative pronouns and their uses.

	Subject	Object	Possessive
Person	who	whom	whose
Thing	which	which	whose
Thing/Person	that	that	whose

Often, short sentences with related ideas can be combined by using a relative pronoun to create a more effective sentence.

SHORT SENTENCE: *Louisa May Alcott wrote* Hospital Sketches

RELATED SENTENCE: Hospital Sketches *describes Alcott's experiences as a volunteer nurse.*

COMBINED SENTENCE: *Louisa May Alcott wrote* Hospital Sketches, *which describes her experiences as a volunteer nurse.*

R54 GRAMMAR HANDBOOK

GRAMMAR PRACTICE

Write the correct form of each incorrect pronoun.

1. Few would have volunteered her services like Alcott did.
2. For who did she risk her own life?
3. Everyone received their care from Alcott.
4. A wounded soldier proved hisself to be respectful.
5. Whom can read her diary without being moved?

2.9 PRONOUN REFERENCE PROBLEMS

The referent of a pronoun should always be clear. Avoid problems by rewriting sentences.

An **indefinite reference** occurs when the pronoun *it*, *you*, or *they* does not clearly refer to a specific antecedent.

UNCLEAR: *People appreciate it when they learn from an author's experiences.*

CLEAR: *People appreciate learning from an author's experiences.*

A **general reference** occurs when the pronoun *it*, *this*, *that*, *which*, or *such* is used to refer to a general idea rather than a specific antecedent.

UNCLEAR: *I picture myself in the author's situation. This helps me understand her reactions.*

CLEAR: *I picture myself in the author's situation. Putting myself in her position helps me understand her reactions.*

Ambiguous means "having more than one possible meaning." An **ambiguous reference** occurs when a pronoun could refer to two or more antecedents.

UNCLEAR: *Manuel urged Simon to edit his new film review.*

CLEAR: *Manuel urged Simon to edit Manuel's new film review.*

GRAMMAR PRACTICE

Rewrite the following sentences to correct indefinite, ambiguous, and general pronoun references.

1. Adams kept seeing the hitchhiker as he walked down the road.
2. Adams didn't pick the hitchhiker up, but it made him feel like a fool.
3. The car stalled on the railroad tracks with a train coming. That almost got Adams killed.
4. When Adams tells his story, they think he's crazy.

3 Verbs

A **verb** is a word that expresses an action, a condition, or a state of being.

*For more information, see **Quick Reference: Parts of Speech,** page R47.*

3.1 ACTION VERBS

Action verbs express mental or physical activity.

EXAMPLE: *Otto Frank comforted his family.*

3.2 LINKING VERBS

Linking verbs join subjects with words or phrases that rename or describe them.

EXAMPLE: *They were in hiding during the war.*

3.3 PRINCIPAL PARTS

Action and linking verbs typically have four principal parts, which are used to form verb tenses. The principal parts are the **present,** the **present participle,** the **past,** and the **past participle.**

Action verbs and some linking verbs also fall into two categories: regular and irregular. A **regular verb** is a verb that forms its past and past participle by adding *-ed* or *-d* to the present form.

Present	Present Participle	Past	Past Participle
jump	(is) jumping	jumped	(has) jumped
solve	(is) solving	solved	(has) solved
grab	(is) grabbing	grabbed	(has) grabbed
carry	(is) carrying	carried	(has) carried

GRAMMAR PRACTICE

ANSWERS

1. *their*
2. *whom*
3. *his or her*
4. *himself*
5. *Who*

GRAMMAR PRACTICE

ANSWERS

1. *Adams kept seeing the hitchhiker as the hitchhiker walked down the road.*
2. *Adams didn't pick the hitchhiker up, which made him feel like a fool.*
3. *The car stalled on the railroad tracks with a train coming. Being stuck there almost got Adams killed.*
4. *When Adams tells his story, people think he's crazy.*

For more help with verbs, see

GRAMMAR FOR WRITING pp. 90–123

An **irregular verb** is a verb that forms its past and past participle in some other way than by adding *-ed* or *-d* to the present form.

Present	Present Participle	Past	Past Participle
begin	(is) beginning	began	(has) begun
break	(is) breaking	broke	(has) broken
go	(is) going	went	(has) gone

3.4 VERB TENSE

The **tense** of a verb indicates the time of the action or the state of being. An action or state of being can occur in the present, the past, or the future. There are six tenses, each expressing a different range of time.

The **present tense** expresses an action or state that is happening at the present time, occurs regularly, or is constant or generally true. Use the present participle.

NOW: *That snow looks deep.*

REGULAR: *It snows every day.*

GENERAL: *Snow falls.*

The **past tense** expresses an action that began and ended in the past. Use the past participle.

EXAMPLE: *The storyteller finished his tale.*

The **future tense** expresses an action or state that will occur. Use *shall* or *will* with the present participle.

EXAMPLE: *They will attend the next festival.*

The **present perfect tense** expresses an action or state that (1) was completed at an indefinite time in the past or (2) began in the past and continues into the present. Use *have* or *has* with the past participle.

EXAMPLE: *Poetry has inspired many readers.*

The **past perfect tense** expresses an action in the past that came before another action in the past. Use *had* with the past participle.

EXAMPLE: *He had built a fire before the dog ran away.*

The **future perfect tense** expresses an action in the future that will be completed before another action in the future. Use *shall have* or *will have* with the past participle.

EXAMPLE: *They will have read the novel before they see the movie version of the tale.*

TIP A past-tense form of an irregular verb is not used with an auxiliary verb, but a past-participle main irregular verb is always used with an auxiliary verb.

INCORRECT: *I have saw her somewhere before.* (*Saw* is the past-tense form of an irregular verb and shouldn't be used with *have.*)

CORRECT: *I have seen her somewhere before.*

INCORRECT: *I seen her somewhere before.* (*Seen* is the past participle of an irregular verb and shouldn't be used without an auxiliary verb.)

3.5 PROGRESSIVE FORMS

The progressive forms of the six tenses show ongoing actions. Use forms of *be* with the present participles of verbs.

PRESENT PROGRESSIVE: *Anne is arguing her case.*

PAST PROGRESSIVE: *Anne was arguing her case.*

FUTURE PROGRESSIVE: *Anne will be arguing her case.*

PRESENT PERFECT PROGRESSIVE: *Anne has been arguing her case.*

PAST PERFECT PROGRESSIVE: *Anne had been arguing her case.*

FUTURE PERFECT PROGRESSIVE: *Anne will have been arguing her case.*

WATCH OUT! Do not shift from tense to tense needlessly. Watch out for these special cases.

- In most compound sentences and in sentences with compound predicates, keep the tenses the same.

  INCORRECT: *She defied him, and he scolds her.*

  CORRECT: *She defied him, and he scolded her.*

- If one past action happens before another, do shift tenses.

  INCORRECT: *They wished they started earlier.*

  CORRECT: *They wished they had started earlier.*

R56 GRAMMAR HANDBOOK

GRAMMAR PRACTICE

Rewrite each sentence, using a form of the verb in parentheses. Identify each form that you use.

1. Frederick Douglass (write) a letter to Harriet Tubman in which he (praise) her.
2. He (say) that she (do) much to benefit enslaved people.
3. People (remember) her work with the Underground Railroad forever.
4. Both Douglass and Tubman (appear) in the history books that kids study.
5. They (inspire) seekers of justice for many years to come.

Rewrite each sentence to correct an error in tense.

1. When she went to the plantations, Tubman's signal has been the spiritual "Go Down Moses."
2. She is leading the slaves all the way from Maryland to Canada, and brought them to freedom.
3. Although she never will have been to Canada, she went bravely on.
4. They arrived safe and sound, but Tubman leaves for the South again.
5. Her life's work for the next six years had began.

3.6 ACTIVE AND PASSIVE VOICE

The voice of a verb tells whether its subject performs or receives the action expressed by the verb. When the subject performs the action, the verb is in the **active voice.** When the subject is the receiver of the action, the verb is in the **passive voice.**

Compare these two sentences:

ACTIVE: *Anton Chekhov wrote "The Bet."*

PASSIVE: *"The Bet" was written by Anton Chekhov.*

To form the passive voice, use a form of *be* with the past participle of the verb.

WATCH OUT! Use the passive voice sparingly. It can make writing awkward and less direct.

AWKWARD: *"The Bet" is a short story that was written by Anton Chekhov.*

BETTER: *Anton Chekhov wrote the short story "The Bet."*

There are occasions when you will choose to use the passive voice because

- you want to emphasize the receiver: *The king was shot.*
- the doer is unknown: *My books were stolen.*
- the doer is unimportant: *French is spoken here.*

4 Modifiers

Modifiers are words or groups of words that change or limit the meanings of other words. Adjectives and adverbs are common modifiers.

4.1 ADJECTIVES

Adjectives modify nouns and pronouns by telling which one, what kind, how many, or how much.

WHICH ONE: *this, that, these, those*

EXAMPLE: *This poem uses no capital letters.*

WHAT KIND: *electric, bright, small, open*

EXAMPLE: *An open flame would kill the moth.*

HOW MANY: *one, several, both, none, each*

EXAMPLE: *The moth wants one moment of beauty.*

HOW MUCH: *more, less, enough, as much*

EXAMPLE: *I think the cockroach has more sense than the moth.*

4.2 PREDICATE ADJECTIVES

Most adjectives come before the nouns they modify, as in the examples above. A **predicate adjective,** however, follows a linking verb and describes the subject.

EXAMPLE: *My friends are very intelligent.*

Be especially careful to use adjectives (not adverbs) after such linking verbs as *look, feel, grow, taste,* and *smell.*

EXAMPLE: *The bread smells wonderful.*

GRAMMAR PRACTICE

ANSWERS

1. *wrote—past; praised—past*
2. *said—past; had done—past perfect*
3. *will remember—future*
4. *appear—present*
5. *will inspire—future*

ANSWERS

1. *was*
2. *led*
3. *had been*
4. *left*
5. *had begun*

For more help with modifiers, see

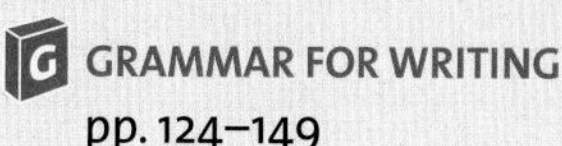

GRAMMAR FOR WRITING pp. 124–149

4.3 ADVERBS

Adverbs modify verbs, adjectives, and other adverbs by telling where, when, how, or to what extent.

WHERE: *The children played outside.*

WHEN: *The author spoke yesterday.*

HOW: *We walked slowly behind the leader.*

TO WHAT EXTENT: *He worked very hard.*

Adverbs may occur in many places in sentences, both before and after the words they modify.

EXAMPLES: *Suddenly the wind shifted.*

The wind suddenly shifted.

The wind shifted suddenly.

4.4 ADJECTIVE OR ADVERB?

Many adverbs are formed by adding *-ly* to adjectives.

EXAMPLES: *sweet, sweetly; gentle, gently*

However, *-ly* added to a noun will usually yield an adjective.

EXAMPLES: *friend, friendly; woman, womanly*

4.5 COMPARISON OF MODIFIERS

Modifiers can be used to compare two or more things. The form of a modifier shows the degree of comparison. Both adjectives and adverbs have **comparative** and **superlative** forms.

The **comparative form** is used to compare two things, groups, or actions.

EXAMPLES: *His father's hands were stronger than his own.*

My father was more courageous than I am.

The **superlative form** is used to compare more than two things, groups, or actions.

EXAMPLES: *His father's hands were the strongest in the family.*

My father was the most courageous of us all.

4.6 REGULAR COMPARISONS

Most one-syllable and some two-syllable adjectives and adverbs have comparatives and superlatives formed by adding *-er* and *-est.* All three-syllable and most two-syllable modifiers have comparatives and superlatives formed with *more* or *most.*

Modifier	Comparative	Superlative
small	smaller	smallest
thin	thinner	thinnest
sleepy	sleepier	sleepiest
useless	more useless	most useless
precisely	more precisely	most precisely

WATCH OUT! Note that spelling changes must sometimes be made to form the comparatives and superlatives of modifiers.

EXAMPLES: *friendly, friendlier* (Change *y* to *i* and add the ending.)

sad, sadder (Double the final consonant and add the ending.)

4.7 IRREGULAR COMPARISONS

Some commonly used modifiers have irregular comparative and superlative forms. They are listed in the chart. You may wish to memorize them.

Modifier	Comparative	Superlative
good	better	best
bad	worse	worst
far	farther *or* further	farthest *or* furthest
little	less *or* lesser	least
many	more	most
well	better	best
much	more	most

4.8 PROBLEMS WITH MODIFIERS

Study the tips that follow to avoid common mistakes:

Farther* and *Further Use *farther* for distances; use *further* for everything else.

Double Comparisons Make a comparison by using *-er/-est* or by using *more/most.* Using *-er* with *more* or using *-est* with *most* is incorrect.

INCORRECT: *I like her more better than she likes me.*

CORRECT: *I like her better than she likes me.*

R58 GRAMMAR HANDBOOK

Illogical Comparisons An illogical or confusing comparison results when two unrelated things are compared or when something is compared with itself. The word *other* or the word *else* should be used when comparing an individual member to the rest of a group.

ILLOGICAL: *The cockroach is smarter than any insect.* (implies that the cockroach isn't an insect)

LOGICAL: *The cockroach is smarter than any other insect.* (identifies that the cockroach is an insect)

Bad* vs. *Badly *Bad,* always an adjective, is used before a noun or after a linking verb. *Badly,* always an adverb, never modifies a noun. Be sure to use the right form after a linking verb.

INCORRECT: *Ed felt badly after his team lost.*

CORRECT: *Ed felt bad after his team lost.*

Good* vs. *Well *Good* is always an adjective. It is used before a noun or after a linking verb. *Well* is often an adverb meaning "expertly" or "properly." *Well* can also be used as an adjective after a linking verb when it means "in good health."

INCORRECT: *Helen writes very good.*

CORRECT: *Helen writes very well.*

CORRECT: *Yesterday I felt bad; today I feel well.*

Double Negatives If you add a negative word to a sentence that is already negative, the result will be an error known as a double negative. When using *not* or *-n't* with a verb, use *any-* words, such as *anybody* or *anything,* rather than *no-* words, such as *nobody* or *nothing,* later in the sentence.

INCORRECT: *We haven't seen nobody.*

CORRECT: *We haven't seen anybody.*

Using *hardly, barely,* or *scarcely* after a negative word is also incorrect.

INCORRECT: *They couldn't barely see two feet ahead.*

CORRECT: *They could barely see two feet ahead.*

Misplaced Modifiers Sometimes a modifier is placed so far away from the word it modifies that the intended meaning of the sentence is unclear. Prepositional phrases and participial phrases are often misplaced. Place modifiers as close as possible to the words they modify.

MISPLACED: *We found the child in the park who was missing.*

CLEARER: *We found the child who was missing in the park.* (The child was missing, not the park.)

Dangling Modifiers Sometimes a modifier doesn't appear to modify any word in a sentence. Most dangling modifiers are participial phrases or infinitive phrases.

DANGLING: *Looking out the window, his brother was seen driving by.*

CLEARER: *Looking out the window, Josh saw his brother driving by.*

GRAMMAR PRACTICE

Choose the correct word or words from each pair in parentheses.

1. Mark Twain's attempt at studying the law did not go (good, well).
2. That wasn't the (worse, worst) of his many occupations, however.
3. He actually wasn't a (bad, badly) riverboat pilot.
4. He didn't have (no, any) confidence as a newspaper editor.
5. Still, that turned out to be the (more, most) satisfying job he ever had.

GRAMMAR PRACTICE

Rewrite each sentence that contains a misplaced or dangling modifier. Write "correct" if the sentence is written correctly.

1. Mark Twain discovered that he was a good storyteller working as an editor.
2. Twain often added exciting details to his stories.
3. It didn't matter to Twain whether all of the details were true in his articles.
4. He wrote sixteen different articles about a single hay wagon in the paper.
5. When all else failed, he made up events.

GRAMMAR PRACTICE

ANSWERS

1. *well*
2. *worst*
3. *bad*
4. *any*
5. *most*

GRAMMAR PRACTICE

ANSWERS

1. *Working as an editor, Mark Twain discovered that he was a good storyteller.*
2. *Correct*
3. *It didn't matter to Twain whether all of the details in his articles were true.*
4. *He wrote sixteen different articles in the paper about a single hay wagon.*
5. *Correct*

For more help with the sentence and its parts, see

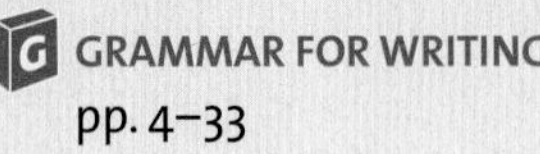

GRAMMAR FOR WRITING
pp. 4–33

For more help with phrases, see

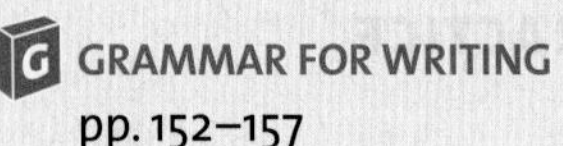

GRAMMAR FOR WRITING
pp. 152–157

5 The Sentence and Its Parts

A **sentence** is a group of words used to express a complete thought. A complete sentence has a subject and a predicate.

For more information, see ***Quick Reference: The Sentence and Its Parts,*** *page R48.*

5.1 KINDS OF SENTENCES

There are four basic types of sentences.

Type	Definition	Example
Declarative	states a fact, a wish, an intent, or a feeling	This poem is about Abraham Lincoln.
Interrogative	asks a question	Did you understand the metaphor?
Imperative	gives a command or direction	Read it more closely.
Exclamatory	expresses strong feeling or excitement	Whitman really admired Lincoln!

5.2 COMPOUND SUBJECTS AND PREDICATES

A compound subject consists of two or more subjects that share the same verb. They are typically joined by the coordinating conjunction *and* or *or.*

EXAMPLE: *A short story or novel will keep you engaged.*

A compound predicate consists of two or more predicates that share the same subject. They too are usually joined by a coordinating conjunction: *and, but,* or *or.*

EXAMPLE: *The class finished all the poetry but did not read the short stories.*

5.3 COMPLEMENTS

A **complement** is a word or group of words that completes the meaning of the sentence. Some sentences contain only a subject and a verb. Most sentences, however, require additional words placed after the verb to complete the meaning of the sentence. There are three kinds of complements: direct objects, indirect objects, and subject complements.

Direct objects are words or word groups that receive the action of action verbs. A direct object answers the question *what* or *whom.*

EXAMPLES: *Ellis recited the poem.* (Recited what?)

His performance entertained the class. (Entertained whom?)

Indirect objects tell to whom or what or for whom or what the actions of verbs are performed. Indirect objects come before direct objects. In the following examples, the indirect objects are highlighted.

EXAMPLES: *The teacher gave the speech a good grade.* (Gave to what?)

He showed his father the teacher's comments. (Showed to whom?)

Subject complements come after linking verbs and identify or describe the subjects. A subject complement that names or identifies a subject is called a **predicate nominative.** Predicate nominatives include **predicate nouns** and **predicate pronouns.**

EXAMPLES: *My friends are very hard workers.*

The best writer in the class is she.

A subject complement that describes a subject is called a **predicate adjective.**

EXAMPLE: *The pianist appeared very energetic.*

6 Phrases

A **phrase** is a group of related words that does not contain a subject and a predicate but functions in a sentence as a single part of speech.

6.1 PREPOSITIONAL PHRASES

A **prepositional phrase** is a phrase that consists of a preposition, its object, and any modifiers of the object. Prepositional phrases that modify nouns or pronouns are called **adjective phrases.** Prepositional phrases that modify verbs, adjectives, or adverbs are **adverb phrases.**

ADJECTIVE PHRASE: *The central character of the story is a villain.*

ADVERB PHRASE: *He reveals his nature in the first scene.*

R60 GRAMMAR HANDBOOK

6.2 APPOSITIVES AND APPOSITIVE PHRASES

An **appositive** is a noun or pronoun that identifies or renames another noun or pronoun. An **appositive phrase** includes an appositive and modifiers of it. An appositive usually follows the noun or pronoun it identifies.

An appositive can be either **essential** or **nonessential.** An **essential appositive** provides information that is needed to identify what is referred to by the preceding noun or pronoun.

EXAMPLE: *This Greek myth is about the gifted woman Pandora.*

A **nonessential appositive** adds extra information about a noun or pronoun whose meaning is already clear. Nonessential appositives and appositive phrases are set off with commas.

EXAMPLE: *The story, a myth, describes how evil came into the world.*

7 Verbals and Verbal Phrases

A **verbal** is a verb form that is used as a noun, an adjective, or an adverb. A **verbal phrase** consists of a verbal along with its modifiers and complements. There are three kinds of verbals: **infinitives, participles,** and **gerunds.**

7.1 INFINITIVES AND INFINITIVE PHRASES

An **infinitive** is a verb form that usually begins with *to* and functions as a noun, an adjective, or an adverb. An **infinitive phrase** consists of an infinitive plus its modifiers and complements.

NOUN: *To keep a promise is difficult.* (subject)

Pandora tried to obey the gods. (direct object)

Her chief mistake was to become too curious. (predicate nominative)

ADJECTIVE: *That was an error to regret.* (adjective modifying *error*)

ADVERB: *She opened the box to satisfy her curiosity.* (adverb modifying *opened*)

Because *to* often precedes infinitives, it is usually easy to recognize them. However, sometimes *to* may be omitted.

EXAMPLE: *Her husband helped her [to] forgive herself.*

7.2 PARTICIPLES AND PARTICIPIAL PHRASES

A **participle** is a verb form that functions as an adjective. Like adjectives, participles modify nouns and pronouns. Most participles are present-participle forms, ending in *-ing,* or past-participle forms ending in *-ed* or *-en.* In the examples below, the participles are highlighted.

MODIFYING A NOUN: *The dying man had a smile on his face.*

MODIFYING A PRONOUN: *Frustrated, everyone abandoned the cause.*

Participial phrases are participles with all their modifiers and complements.

MODIFYING A NOUN: *The dogs searching for survivors are well trained.*

MODIFYING A PRONOUN: *Having approved your proposal, we are ready to act.*

7.3 DANGLING AND MISPLACED PARTICIPLES

A participle or participial phrase should be placed as close as possible to the word that it modifies. Otherwise the meaning of the sentence may not be clear.

MISPLACED: *The boys were looking for squirrels searching the trees.*

CLEARER: *The boys searching the trees were looking for squirrels.*

A participle or participial phrase that does not clearly modify anything in a sentence is called a **dangling participle.** A dangling participle causes confusion because it appears to modify a word that it cannot sensibly modify. Correct a dangling participle by providing a word for the participle to modify.

DANGLING: *Running like the wind, my hat fell off.* (The hat wasn't running.)

CLEARER: *Running like the wind, I lost my hat.*

7.4 GERUNDS AND GERUND PHRASES

A **gerund** is a verb form ending in *-ing* that functions as a noun. Gerunds may perform any function nouns perform.

SUBJECT: *Jogging is my favorite exercise.*

DIRECT OBJECT: *My sister loves jogging.*

For more help with verbals and verbal phrases, see

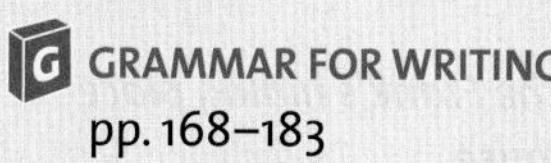

GRAMMAR HANDBOOK R61

GRAMMAR PRACTICE

ANSWERS

1. *I read an excerpt from Anne Frank's diary* ***to learn more about her experiences.***
2. ***Hiding from the Nazis,*** *Anne was able to maintain her faith in other people.*
3. *Peter Van Daan,* ***another person hiding in the Secret Annex,*** *eventually became Anne's good friend.*
4. *The Nazis found the Frank's hiding place* ***above the warehouse.***
5. ***Having read this book,*** *I know more about World War II.*

For more help with clauses, see

GRAMMAR FOR WRITING
pp. 186–188

INDIRECT OBJECT: *She gave jogging a try last year.*

SUBJECT COMPLEMENT: *Their real passion is jogging.*

OBJECT OF PREPOSITION: *The effects of jogging.*

Gerund phrases are gerunds with all their modifiers and complements.

SUBJECT: *Creating Pandora was Zeus' idea.*

OBJECT OF PREPOSITION: *She suffered greatly after defying the gods.*

APPOSITIVE: *Her husband, remembering his brother Prometheus' fate, forgave her.*

GRAMMAR PRACTICE

Rewrite each sentence, adding the type of phrase shown in parentheses.

1. I read an excerpt from Anne Frank's diary. (infinitive phrase)
2. Anne was able to maintain her faith in other people. (gerund phrase)
3. Peter Van Daan eventually became Anne's good friend. (appositive phrase)
4. The Nazis found the Franks' hiding place. (prepositional phrase)
5. I know more about World War II. (participial phrase)

8 Clauses

A **clause** is a group of words that contains a subject and a predicate. There are two kinds of clauses: independent and subordinate.

8.1 INDEPENDENT AND SUBORDINATE CLAUSES

An **independent clause** can stand alone as a sentence, as the word *independent* suggests.

INDEPENDENT CLAUSE: *I enjoyed "Pecos Bill."*

A sentence may contain more than one independent clause.

EXAMPLE: *I read it twice, and I gave it to a friend.*

In the preceding example, the coordinating conjunction *and* joins two independent clauses.

For more coordinating conjunctions, see ***Quick Reference: Parts of Speech,*** *page R47.*

A **subordinate (dependent) clause** cannot stand alone as a sentence. It is subordinate to, or dependent on, an independent clause.

EXAMPLE: *After I read it, I recommended it to my friends.*

The highlighted clause cannot stand by itself.

8.2 ADJECTIVE CLAUSES

An **adjective clause** is a subordinate clause used as an adjective. It usually follows the noun or pronoun it modifies.

EXAMPLE: *The legend that the story retells is about a cowboy.*

Adjective clauses are typically introduced by the relative pronouns *who, whom, whose, which,* and *that.*

For more information, see ***Relative Pronouns,*** *page R54.*

EXAMPLE: *Pecos Bill, who was raised by coyotes, lived with them for seventeen years.*

An adjective clause can be either essential or nonessential. An **essential adjective clause** provides information that is necessary to identify the preceding noun or pronoun.

EXAMPLE: *He needed to find people who could appreciate him.*

A **nonessential adjective clause** adds additional information about a noun or pronoun whose meaning is already clear. Nonessential clauses are set off with commas.

EXAMPLE: *He carried his horse, which had broken its ankle, around his neck.*

8.3 ADVERB CLAUSES

An **adverb clause** is a subordinate clause that is used to modify a verb, an adjective, or an adverb. It is introduced by a subordinating conjunction.

For examples of subordinating conjunctions, see ***Noun Clauses,*** *page R63.*

R62 GRAMMAR HANDBOOK

Adverb clauses typically occur at the beginning or end of sentences.

MODIFYING A VERB: *When he got bored, Nick told stories.*

MODIFYING AN ADVERB: *Most people study more than Bob does.*

MODIFYING AN ADJECTIVE: *He was excited because a cyclone was forming.*

TIP An adverb clause should be followed by a comma when it comes before an independent clause. When an adverb clause comes after an independent clause, a comma may not be needed.

8.4 NOUN CLAUSES

A **noun clause** is a subordinate clause that is used as a noun. A noun clause may be used as a subject, a direct object, an indirect object, a predicate nominative, or the object of a preposition. Noun clauses are introduced either by pronouns, such as *that, what, who, whoever, which,* and *whose,* or by subordinating conjunctions, such as *how, when, where, why,* and *whether.*

For more subordinating conjunctions, see ***Quick Reference: Parts of Speech****, page R47.*

TIP Because the same words may introduce adjective and noun clauses, you need to consider how a clause functions within its sentence. To determine if a clause is a noun clause, try substituting *something* or *someone* for the clause. If you can do it, it is probably a noun clause.

EXAMPLES: *I know whose woods these are.*

("I know *something*." The clause is a noun clause, direct object of the verb *know*.)

Give a copy to whoever wants one. ("Give a copy to *someone*." The clause is a noun clause, object of the preposition *to*.)

GRAMMAR PRACTICE

Add descriptive details to each sentence by writing the type of clause indicated in parentheses.

1. Legends delight our imaginations. (adverb clause)
2. Superheroes are exciting characters. (adjective clause)
3. Don't try to copy, though. (noun clause)
4. What would your hero be able to do? (adverb clause)
5. Superheroes can inspire us to do the best work. (adjective clause)

9 The Structure of Sentences

When classified by their structure, there are four kinds of sentences: simple, compound, complex, and compound-complex.

9.1 SIMPLE SENTENCES

A **simple sentence** is a sentence that has one independent clause and no subordinate clauses.

EXAMPLES: *Sam ran to the theater.*

Max waited in front of the theater.

A simple sentence may contain a compound subject or a compound verb.

EXAMPLES: *Sam and Max went to the movie. (compound subject)*

They clapped and cheered at their favorite parts. (compound verb)

9.2 COMPOUND SENTENCES

A **compound sentence** consists of two or more independent clauses. The clauses in compound sentences are joined with commas and coordinating conjunctions (*and, but, or, nor, yet, for, so*) or with semicolons. Like simple sentences, compound sentences do not contain any subordinate clauses.

EXAMPLES: *Sam likes action movies, but Max prefers comedies.*

The actor jumped from one building to another; he barely made the final leap.

GRAMMAR PRACTICE

ANSWERS

1. *Legends delight our imaginations* ***because they seem so impossible.***
2. *Superheroes* ***who do impossible acts*** *are exciting and entertaining.*
3. *Don't try to copy* ***what they do,*** *though.*
4. *What would your hero be able to do* ***that you couldn't?***
5. *Superhuman figures can inspire us to do the best work* ***that we can do.***

For more help with the structure of sentences, see

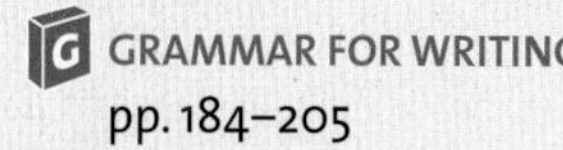
GRAMMAR FOR WRITING
pp. 184–205

GRAMMAR HANDBOOK R63

For more help with writing complete sentences, see

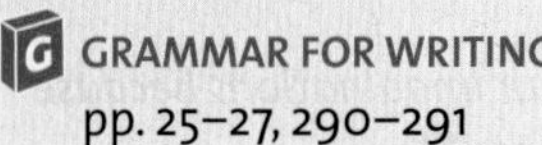

pp. 25–27, 290–291

WATCH OUT! Do not confuse compound sentences with simple sentences that have compound parts.

EXAMPLE: *The actor knew all the lines but didn't play the part well.*
(Here *but* joins parts of a compound predicate, not a compound sentence.)

9.3 COMPLEX SENTENCES

A **complex sentence** consists of one independent clause and one or more subordinate clauses.

EXAMPLES: *One should not complain unless one has a better solution.*

Mr. Neiman, who is an artist, sketched pictures until the sun went down.

9.4 COMPOUND-COMPLEX SENTENCES

A **compound-complex sentence** contains two or more independent clauses and one or more subordinate clauses. Compound-complex sentences are, simply, both compound and complex. If you start with a compound sentence, all you need to do to form a compound-complex sentence is add a subordinate clause.

COMPOUND: *All the students knew the answer, yet they were too shy to volunteer.*

COMPOUND-COMPLEX: *All the students knew the answer that their teacher expected, yet they were too shy to volunteer.*

9.5 PARALLEL STRUCTURE

When you write sentences, make sure that coordinate parts are equivalent, or **parallel,** in structure.

NOT PARALLEL: *On Saturday I practiced chess and to play the flute.* (*Practice* is a verb; *to play the flute* is a phrase.)

PARALLEL: *On Saturday I practiced chess and played the flute.* (*Practiced* and *played* are both verbs.)

NOT PARALLEL: *I want to lose weight, becoming a musician, and good grades.* (*To lose weight* is an infinitive phrase, *becoming a musician* is a gerund phrase, and *grades* is a noun.)

PARALLEL: *I want to lose weight, to become a musician, and to get good grades.* (*To lose, to become,* and *to get* are all infinitives.)

10 Writing Complete Sentences

Remember, a sentence is a group of words that expresses a complete thought. In writing that you wish to share with a reader, try to avoid both sentence fragments and run-on sentences.

10.1 CORRECTING FRAGMENTS

A **sentence fragment** is a group of words that is only part of a sentence. It does not express a complete thought and may be confusing to a reader or listener. A sentence fragment may be lacking a subject, a predicate, or both.

FRAGMENT: *Worried about not doing well.* (no subject)

CORRECTED: *Laura worried about not doing well.*

FRAGMENT: *Her mother and father.* (no predicate)

CORRECTED: *Her mother and father were both highly successful.*

FRAGMENT: *In a gentle way.* (neither subject nor predicate)

CORRECTED: *They tried to encourage her in a gentle way.*

In your writing, fragments may be a result of haste or incorrect punctuation. Sometimes fixing a fragment will be a matter of attaching it to a preceding or following sentence.

FRAGMENT: *Laura did her best. But never felt satisfied.*

CORRECTED: *Laura did her best but never felt satisfied.*

10.2 CORRECTING RUN-ON SENTENCES

A **run-on sentence** is made up of two or more sentences written as though they were one. Some run-ons have no punctuation within them. Others may have only commas where conjunctions or stronger punctuation marks are necessary.

Use your judgment in correcting run-on sentences, as you have choices. You can change a run-on to two sentences if the thoughts are not closely connected. If the thoughts are closely related, you

R64 GRAMMAR HANDBOOK

can keep the run-on as one sentence by adding a semicolon or a conjunction.

RUN-ON: *She joined more clubs her friendships suffered.*

MAKE TWO SENTENCES: *She joined more clubs. Her friendships suffered.*

RUN-ON: *She joined more clubs they took up all her time.*

USE A SEMICOLON: *She joined more clubs; they took up all her time.*

ADD A CONJUNCTION: *She joined more clubs, but they took up all her time.*

WATCH OUT! When you form compound sentences, make sure you use appropriate punctuation: a comma before a coordinating conjunction, a semicolon when there is no coordinating conjunction. A very common mistake is to use a comma alone instead of a comma and a conjunction. This error is called a **comma splice.**

INCORRECT: *He finished the job, he left the village.*

CORRECT: *He finished the job, and he left the village.*

11 Subject-Verb Agreement

The subject and verb in a clause must agree in number. Agreement means that if the subject is singular, the verb is also singular, and if the subject is plural, the verb is also plural.

11.1 BASIC AGREEMENT

Fortunately, agreement between subjects and verbs in English is simple. Most verbs show the difference between singular and plural only in the third person of the present tense. In the present tense, the third-person singular form ends in *-s.*

Present-Tense Verb Forms	
Singular	**Plural**
I sleep	we sleep
you sleep	you sleep
she he it sleeps	they sleep

11.2 AGREEMENT WITH *BE*

The verb *be* presents special problems in agreement, because this verb does not follow the usual verb patterns.

Forms of *Be*			
Present Tense		**Past Tense**	
Singular	**Plural**	**Singular**	**Plural**
I am	we are	I was	we were
you are	you are	you were	you were
she he it is	they are	she he it was	they were

11.3 WORDS BETWEEN SUBJECT AND VERB

A verb agrees only with its subject. When words come between a subject and a verb, ignore them when considering proper agreement. Identify the subject and make sure the verb agrees with it.

EXAMPLES: *Whipped cream served with berries is my favorite sweet.*

A study by scientists recommends eating berries.

11.4 AGREEMENT WITH COMPOUND SUBJECTS

Use plural verbs with most compound subjects joined by the word *and.*

EXAMPLE: *My father and his friends play chess every day.*

To confirm that you need a plural verb, you could substitute the plural pronoun *they* for *my father and his friends.*

If a compound subject is thought of as a unit, use a singular verb. Test this by substituting the singular pronoun *it.*

EXAMPLE: *Peanut butter and jelly [it] is my brother's favorite sandwich.*

Use a singular verb with a compound subject that is preceded by *each, every,* or *many a.*

EXAMPLE: *Each novel and short story seems grounded in personal experience.*

For more help with subject-verb agreement, see

GRAMMAR FOR WRITING
pp. 206–227

GRAMMAR HANDBOOK R65

When the parts of a compound subject are joined by *or, nor,* or the correlative conjunctions *either . . . or* or *neither . . . nor,* make the verb agree with the noun or pronoun nearest the verb.

EXAMPLES: *Cookies or ice cream is my favorite dessert.*

Either Cheryl or her friends are being invited.

Neither ice storms nor snow is predicted today.

11.5 PERSONAL PRONOUNS AS SUBJECTS

When using a personal pronoun as a subject, make sure to match it with the correct form of the verb *be.* (See the chart in Section 11.2.) Note especially that the pronoun *you* takes the forms *are* and *were,* regardless of whether it is singular or plural.

WATCH OUT! *You is* and *you was* are nonstandard forms and should be avoided in writing and speaking. *We was* and *they was* are also forms to be avoided.

INCORRECT: *You was a good student.*

CORRECT: *You were a good student.*

INCORRECT: *They was starting a new school.*

CORRECT: *They were starting a new school.*

11.6 INDEFINITE PRONOUNS AS SUBJECTS

Some indefinite pronouns are always singular; some are always plural.

Singular Indefinite Pronouns			
another	either	neither	one
anybody	everybody	nobody	somebody
anyone	everyone	no one	someone
anything	everything	nothing	something
each	much		

EXAMPLES: *Each of the writers was given an award.*

Somebody in the room upstairs is sleeping.

Plural Indefinite Pronouns			
both	few	many	several

EXAMPLES: *Many of the books in our library are not in circulation.*

Few have been returned recently.

Still other indefinite pronouns may be either singular or plural.

Singular or Plural Indefinite Pronouns		
all	more	none
any	most	some

The number of the indefinite pronoun *any* or *none* often depends on the intended meaning.

EXAMPLES: *Any of these topics has potential for a good article.* (any one topic)

Any of these topics have potential for good articles. (all of the many topics)

The indefinite pronouns *all, some, more, most,* and *none* are singular when they refer to quantities or parts of things. They are plural when they refer to numbers of individual things. Context will usually provide a clue.

EXAMPLES: *All of the flour is gone.* (referring to a quantity)

All of the flowers are gone. (referring to individual items)

11.7 INVERTED SENTENCES

A sentence in which the subject follows the verb is called an **inverted sentence.** A subject can follow a verb or part of a verb phrase in a question, a sentence beginning with *here* or *there,* or a sentence in which an adjective, an adverb, or a phrase is placed first.

EXAMPLES: *There clearly are far too many cooks in this kitchen.*

What is the correct ingredient for this stew?

Far from the frazzled cooks stands the master chef.

R66 GRAMMAR HANDBOOK

TIP To check subject-verb agreement in some inverted sentences, place the subject before the verb. For example, change *There are many people* to *Many people are there.*

11.8 SENTENCES WITH PREDICATE NOMINATIVES

In a sentence containing a predicate noun (nominative), the verb should agree with the subject, not the predicate noun.

EXAMPLES: *The poems of Henry Wadsworth Longfellow are a unique record of U.S. history.* (*Poems* is the subject—not *record*—and it takes the plural verb *are.*)

One unique record of U.S. history is the poems of Henry Wadsworth Longfellow. (The subject is *record*—not *poems*—and it takes the singular verb *is.*)

11.9 *DON'T* AND *DOESN'T* AS AUXILIARY VERBS

The auxiliary verb *doesn't* is used with singular subjects and with the personal pronouns *she, he,* and *it.* The auxiliary verb *don't* is used with plural subjects and with the personal pronouns *I, we, you,* and *they.*

SINGULAR: *Doesn't the poem "Paul Revere's Ride" sound almost like a news report?*

It doesn't sound like a poem, even though it rhymes.

PLURAL: *People don't know enough about history.*

Don't they think history is important?

11.10 COLLECTIVE NOUNS AS SUBJECTS

Collective nouns are singular nouns that name groups of persons or things. *Team,* for example, is the collective name of a group of individuals. A collective noun takes a singular verb when the group acts as a single unit. It takes a plural verb when the members of the group act separately.

EXAMPLES: *Our team usually wins.* (The team as a whole wins.)

The faculty vote differently on most issues. (The individual members of the faculty vote.)

11.11 RELATIVE PRONOUNS AS SUBJECTS

When the relative pronoun *who, which,* or *that* is used as a subject in an adjective clause, the verb in the clause must agree in number with the antecedent of the pronoun.

SINGULAR: *The **poem** that affects me most is "Mother to Son."*

The antecedent of the relative pronoun *that* is the singular *poem;* therefore, *that* is singular and must take the singular verb *affects.*

PLURAL: ***Langston Hughes and Gwendolyn Brooks** are African-American poets who write about overcoming life's problems.*

The antecedent of the relative pronoun *who* is the plural compound subject *Langston Hughes and Gwendolyn Brooks.* Therefore *who* is plural, and it takes the plural verb *write.*

GRAMMAR PRACTICE

Locate the subject in each sentence below. Then choose the correct verb form.

1. Daniel Keyes's story "Flowers for Algernon" (describes, describe) a mentally challenged man who takes part in a scientific experiment.
2. (Doesn't, Don't) the doctors treat him like a laboratory mouse?
3. Nobody (realizes, realize) the danger in this experiment.
4. The development of his mental abilities (become, becomes) clear in his growing language skills.
5. His perceptions, as well as his intelligence, (becomes, become) extremely sharp.
6. There (is, are) moments of joy when he falls in love with Miss Kinnian.
7. Everything (progresses, progress) well until he is fired from his job.
8. All of his insights just (makes, make) people withdraw from him.
9. Even the doctors who work with him (treat, treats) him poorly.
10. Neither Algernon's death nor Charlie's own mental failings (seems, seem) sadder than his awareness of what's happening to him.

GRAMMAR PRACTICE

ANSWERS

1. *describes*
2. *Don't*
3. *realizes*
4. *becomes*
5. *become*
6. *are*
7. *progresses*
8. *make*
9. *treat*
10. *seem*

The key to becoming an independent reader is to develop a tool kit of vocabulary strategies. By learning and practicing the strategies, you'll know what to do when you encounter unfamiliar words while reading. You'll also know how to refine the words you use for different situations—personal, school, and work.

Being a good speller is important when communicating your ideas in writing. Learning basic spelling rules and checking your spelling in a dictionary will help you spell words that you may not use frequently.

For more practice, go to the **Vocabulary Center** at **ClassZone.com.**

1 Using Context Clues

The context of a word is made up of the punctuation marks, words, sentences, and paragraphs that surround the word. A word's context can give you important clues about its meaning.

1.1 GENERAL CONTEXT

Sometimes you need to determine the meaning of an unfamiliar word by reading all the information in a passage.

Stop teasing me! Just because you are a better tennis player than I am doesn't mean you should belittle my abilities.

You can figure out from the context that *belittle* means "make something less than it is."

1.2 IDIOMS, SLANG, AND FIGURATIVE LANGUAGE

An **idiom** is an expression whose overall meaning differs from the meaning of the individual words.

A nasty case of the flu kept me under the weather. (Under the weather means "tired and sickly.")

Slang is informal language in which made-up words and ordinary words are used to mean something different from their meanings in formal English.

I'm going to jazz up this salad with some walnuts. (Jazz up means "make more interesting.")

Figurative language is language that communicates meaning beyond the literal meaning of the words.

The lone desert monument was like a sentinel standing guard. (Lone and standing guard help describe a sentinel.)

1.3 SPECIFIC CONTEXT CLUES

Sometimes writers help you understand the meanings of words by providing specific clues such as those shown in the chart.

Specific Context Clues

Type of Clue	Key Words/ Phrases	Example
Definition or restatement of the meaning of the word	or, which is, that is, in other words, also known as, also called	Olympic gymnasts are very *limber,* or **flexible.**
Example following an unfamiliar word	such as, like, as if, for example, especially, including	We collected *kindling,* such as **dry twigs and branches,** to start the fire.
Comparison with a more familiar word or concept	as, like, also, similar to, in the same way, likewise	Kari's face was *luminous,* **like the rays of the sun.**
Contrast with a familiar word or experience	unlike, but, however, although, on the other hand, on the contrary	The summer was *sultry,* but the fall was **dry and cool.**
Cause-and-effect relationship in which one term is familiar	because, since, when, consequently, as a result, therefore	When the *tree fell across the road,* it **obstructed** traffic.

*For more information, see **Vocabulary Strategy: Synonyms as Context Clues,** page 272, **Vocabulary Strategy: Idioms,** pages 325 and 726, and **Vocabulary Strategy: Antonyms and Context Clues,** page 1009.*

R68 VOCABULARY AND SPELLING HANDBOOK

2 Analyzing Word Structure

Many words can be broken into smaller parts. These word parts include base words, roots, prefixes, and suffixes.

2.1 BASE WORDS

A **base word** is a word part that by itself is also a word. Other words or word parts can be added to base words to form new words.

For more information, see ***Vocabulary Strategy: Recognizing Base Words,*** *page 892.*

2.2 ROOTS

A **root** is a word part that contains the core meaning of the word. Many English words contain roots that come from older languages such as Greek, Latin, Old English (Anglo-Saxon), and Norse. Knowing the meaning of the word's root can help you determine the word's meaning.

Root	Meaning	Example
aud (Latin)	hear	**aud**io, **aud**ition
voc (Latin)	voice	**voc**al, in**vok**e
mem, ment (Latin)	mind	**mem**ory, **ment**al, **ment**ion
chron (Greek)	time	**chron**ic, syn**chron**ize
gram (Greek)	something written	tele**gram**, **gram**mar
gen (Greek)	race, family	**gen**esis, **gen**re, **gen**ius

For more information, see ***Vocabulary Strategy: Word Roots,*** *pages 117, 372, 631, 713, 937, 978, and 992.*

2.3 PREFIXES

A **prefix** is a word part attached to the beginning of a word or word root. Most prefixes come from Greek, Latin, or Old English.

Prefix	Meaning	Example
mid-	middle, center	**mid**night
pro-	forward	**pro**ceed, **pro**cession
uni-	one	**uni**form, **uni**cycle
tele-	view	**tele**scope
multi-	many, much	**multi**media, **multi**vitamins

For more information, see ***Vocabulary Strategy: Prefixes,*** *pages 60, 236, and 414.*

2.4 SUFFIXES

A **suffix** is a word part that appears at the end of a root or base word to form a new word. Some suffixes do not change word meaning. These suffixes are

- added to nouns to change the number of persons or objects
- added to verbs to change the tense
- added to modifiers to change the degree of comparison

Suffix	Meaning	Examples
-s, -es	to change the number of a noun	lock + s = locks
-d, -ed, -ing	to change verb tense	stew + ed = stewed
-er, -est	to indicate comparison in modifiers	mild + er = milder soft + est = softest

Other suffixes can be added to the root or base to change the word's meaning. These suffixes can also determine a word's part of speech.

Suffix	Meaning	Example
-age	amount	foot**age**
-able, -ible	able, inclined to	read**able**, tang**ible**
-ant, -ent	a specific state or condition	pleas**ant**, differ**ent**

For more information, see ***Vocabulary Strategy: Suffixes that Form Nouns,*** *page 74,* ***Vocabulary Strategy: Suffixes that Form Adjectives,*** *page 926.*

VOCABULARY AND SPELLING HANDBOOK R69

Strategies for Understanding Unfamiliar Words

- Look for any prefixes or suffixes. Remove them so that you can concentrate on the base word or the root.
- See if you recognize any elements—prefix, suffix, root, or base—of the word. You may be able to guess its meaning by analyzing one or two elements.
- Think about the way the word is used in the sentence. Use the context and the word parts to make a logical guess about the word's meaning.
- Look in a dictionary to see whether you are correct.

3 Understanding Word Origins

3.1 DEVELOPMENT OF THE ENGLISH LANGUAGE

During the past 2,000 years or so, English has developed from a language spoken by a few Germanic tribes into a language that is more widely spoken and written than any other in the world. Some experts, in fact, call today's English the first truly global language. Its most valuable characteristic is its ability to change and grow, adopting new words as the need arises. The history of the English language can be divided into three main periods.

Old English About the year A.D. 449, Germanic people who lived on the European continent along the North Sea began a series of invasions into Britain. At that time, Britain was inhabited by the Celts, whose native language was Gaelic. Over a period of years, the raiders conquered and settled in Britain. The conquerors, known today as the Anglo-Saxons, prospered in Britain. In time, Britain became "Engla land," and the Anglo-Saxon languages evolved into "Englisc," or what modern scholars call Old English.

Old English was very different from the English we speak today. It was harsher in sound, had no silent letters, and was written phonetically. Few examples of Old English remain in our current English vocabulary. Those that do exist, however, are common words for people, places, things, and actions.

man *(mann)* wife *(wif)* child *(cild)*
house *(hus)* meat *(mete)* drink *(drincan)*
sleep *(slæpan)* live *(libban)* fight *(feohtan)*

In the sixth and seventh centuries, missionaries from Rome and other Christian cities arrived in England, bringing with them their knowledge of religion and ancient languages. Among the most influential figures was St. Augustine, who converted thousands of Anglo-Saxons, including a king, to Christianity. As the Anglo-Saxons accepted this faith, they also accepted words from Latin and Greek.

Latin	Greek
candle	alphabet
cup	angel
priest	box
noon	demon
scripture	school

During the late 8th century, Viking invaders from Denmark and Norway settled in northeast England. As a result, Scandinavian words became part of Old English.

sky knife are
steak leg birth
they skin seat
window them their

R70 VOCABULARY AND SPELLING HANDBOOK

Middle English The Norman Conquest brought great changes to England and its language. In 1066, England was defeated by the Normans, a people from an area in France. Their leader, William the Conqueror, staged a successful invasion of England and became the nation's new monarch. With William on the throne of England, Norman French became the language of the English court, government business, nobility, and scholars. Eventually, French words were adopted in everyday vocabulary as well.

The language that evolved is called Middle English. Middle English was not as harsh-sounding as Old English and borrowed many words from Norman French.

attorney joint mallet
baron jolly marriage
chivalry laundry merchandise
gown lodge petty

Norman French itself borrowed thousands of words from Latin and Greek, as well as from ancient Indian and Semitic languages. Consequently, Middle English also contained many of these foreign terms.

Latin	Greek	Indian	Semitic
language	circle	ginger	camel
library	hour	jungle	cinnamon
money	lantern	orange	coffee
serpent	leopard	sugar	lion
square	magnet	pepper	syrup

Modern English By the late 1400s, Middle English began to develop into Modern English. The various pronunciations, word forms, and spellings common to Middle English were becoming more uniform. One invention that aided this process was the printing press. Introduced to London around 1476, the printing press allowed printers to standardize the spellings of common English words. As a result, readers and writers of English became accustomed to following "rules" of spelling and grammar.

During this period, the English vocabulary also continued to grow as new ideas and discoveries demanded new words. As the English began to colonize and trade with other areas of the world, they borrowed foreign words. In time, the English vocabulary grew to include words from diverse languages, such as French, Dutch, Spanish, Italian, Portuguese, and Chinese. Many of these words stayed the way they were in their original languages.

French	Dutch	Spanish	Italian
ballet	boss	canyon	diva
beret	caboose	rodeo	carnival
mirage	dock	taco	spaghetti
vague	skate	tornado	studio

Portuguese	Chinese	Japanese	Native American
cashew	chow	kamikaze	caribou
mango	ginseng	karaoke	moccasin
jaguar	kung fu	sushi	papoose
yam	kow tow	tsunami	tomahawk

Today, the English language is still changing and absorbing new words. It is considered the international language of science and technology. It is also widely used in business and politics.

VOCABULARY AND SPELLING HANDBOOK R71

3.2 DICTIONARY AS A SOURCE OF WORD ORIGINS

Many dictionary entries provide information about a word's origin. This information often comes at the end of an entry, as in this example.

ge•om•e•try (jē-ŏm'ĭ-trē) *n., pl.* **-tries** **1.** The mathematics of the properties, measurement, and relationships of points, lines, angles, surfaces, and solids. **2.** Arrangement. **3.** A physical arrangement suggesting geometric forms or lines. [from Greek *geōmetriā,* from *geōmetrein,* to measure land].

3.3 WORD FAMILIES

Words that have the same root make up a word family and have related meanings. The charts below show some common Greek and Latin roots. Notice how the meanings of the example words are related to the meanings of their roots.

Latin Root	*circum,* around or about
English	**circumference** the boundary line of a circle **circumnavigation** the act of moving completely around **circumstance** a condition or fact surrounding an event
Greek Root	***monos,* single or alone**
English	**monopoly** exclusive control by one group **monologue** a speech delivered by one person **monotonous** sounded or spoken in a single unvarying tone

TIP Once you recognize a root in one English word, you will notice the same root in other words. Because these words develop from the same root, all words in the word family are similar in meaning.

For more information, see ***Vocabulary Strategy: Researching Word Origins,*** *pages 595 and 903.*

4 Synonyms and Antonyms

4.1 SYNONYMS

Positive	Negative
slender	scrawny
thrifty	cheap
young	immature

A **synonym** is a word with a meaning similar to that of another word. You can find synonyms in a thesaurus or a dictionary. In a dictionary, synonyms are often given as part of the definition of the word. The following word pairs are synonyms:

satisfy/please occasionally/sometimes

rob/steal schedule/agenda

For more information, see ***Vocabulary Strategy: Synonyms as Context Clues,*** *page 272.*

4.2 ANTONYMS

An **antonym** is a word with a meaning opposite that of another word. The following word pairs are antonyms:

accurate/incorrect similar/different

fresh/stale unusual/ordinary

For more information, see ***Vocabulary Strategy: Antonyms As Context Clues,*** *page 1009.*

5 Denotation and Connotation

5.1 DENOTATION

A word's dictionary meaning is called its **denotation.** For example, the denotation of the word *thin* is "having little flesh; spare; lean."

R72 VOCABULARY AND SPELLING HANDBOOK

5.2 CONNOTATION

The images or feelings you connect to a word add a finer shade of meaning, called **connotation.** The connation of a word goes beyond its basic dictionary definition. Writers use connotations of words to communicate positive or negative feelings.

Make sure you understand the denotation and connotation of a word when you read it or use it in your writing.

For more information, see ***Vocabulary Strategy: Denotations and Connotations,*** *pages 693, 845, and 917.*

6 Analogies

An **analogy** is a comparison between two things that are similar in some way but are otherwise not alike. Analogies are sometimes used in writing when unfamiliar subjects or ideas are explained in terms of familiar ones. Analogies often appear on tests as well. In an analogy problem, the analogy is expressed using two groups of words. The relationship between the first pair of words is the same as the relationship between the second pair of words. Some analogy problems are expressed like this:

love : hate :: war: ________________

a. soldier **b.** peace **c.** battle **d.** argument

Follow these steps to determine the correct answer:

- Read the problem as "*love* is to *hate* as ***war*** is to. . . ."
- Ask yourself how the words *love* and *hate* are related. (*Love* and *hate* are antonyms.)
- Ask yourself which answer choice is an antonym of *war*. (*Peace* is an antonym of *war,* therefore *peace* is the best answer.)

For more information, see ***Vocabulary Strategy: Analogies,*** *pages 252 and 780.*

7 Homonyms, Homographs, and Homophones

7.1 HOMONYMS

Homonyms are words that have the same spelling and sound but have different meanings.

The snake shed its skin in the shed behind the house.

Shed can mean "to lose by natural process," but an identically spelled word means "a small structure."

Sometimes only one of the meanings of a homonym may be familiar to you. Use context clues to help you figure out the meaning of an unfamiliar word.

7.2 HOMOGRAPHS

Homographs are words that are spelled the same but have different meanings and origins. Some are also pronounced differently, as in these examples.

Please close the door. (clōz)
That was a close call. (clōs)

If you see a word used in a way that is unfamiliar to you, check a dictionary to see if it is a homograph.

For more information, see ***Vocabulary Strategy: Homographs,*** *pages 356 and 798.*

7.3 HOMOPHONES

Homophones are words that sound alike but have different meanings and spellings. The following homophones are frequently misused:

it's/its	they're/their/there
to/too/two	stationary/stationery

Many misused homophones are pronouns and contractions. Whenever you are unsure whether to write *your* or *you're* and *who's* or *whose,* ask yourself if you mean *you are* and *who is/has.* If you do, write the contraction. For other homophones, such as *fair* and *fare,* use the meaning of the word to help you decide which one to use.

VOCABULARY AND SPELLING HANDBOOK R73

8 Words with Multiple Meanings

Some words have acquired additional meanings over time that are based on the original meaning.

I had to be replaced in the cast of the play because of the cast on my arm.

These two uses of *cast* have different meanings, but both of them have the same origin. You will find all the meanings of *cast* listed in one entry in the dictionary.

*For more information, see **Vocabulary Strategy: Multiple-Meaning Words,** page 281.*

9 Specialized Vocabulary

Specialized vocabulary is special terms suited to a particular field of study or work. For example, science, mathematics, and history all have their own technical or specialized vocabularies. To figure out specialized terms, you can use context clues and reference sources, such as dictionaries on specific subjects, atlases, or manuals.

*For more information, see **Vocabulary Strategy: Specialized Vocabulary,** page 220.*

10 Using Reference Sources

10.1 DICTIONARIES

A **general dictionary** will tell you not only a word's definitions but also its pronunciation, parts of speech, and history and origin, or etymology.

① **tangible** ② (tăn′jə-bəl) ③ *adj.*
④ **1a.** Discernible by the touch; palpable. **b.** Possible to touch. **c.** Possible to be treated as fact; real or concrete. **2.** Possible to understand or realize. **3.** Law that can be valued monetarily [Late Latin *tangibilis,* from Latin *tangere,* to touch] ⑤

① Entry word
② Pronunciation
③ Part of speech
④ Definitions
⑤ Etymology

A **specialized dictionary** focuses on terms related to a particular field of study or work. Use a dictionary to check the spelling of any word you are unsure of in your English class and other classes as well.

*For more information, see **Vocabulary Strategy: Using Reference Aids,** pages 85 and 461.*

10.2 THESAURI

A **thesaurus** (plural, *thesauri*) is a dictionary of synonyms. A thesaurus can be especially helpful when you find yourself using the same modifiers over and over again.

10.3 SYNONYM FINDERS

A **synonym finder** is often included in word-processing software. It enables you to highlight a word and be shown a display of its synonyms.

10.4 GLOSSARIES

A **glossary** is a list of specialized terms and their definitions. It is often found in the back of a book and sometimes includes pronunciations. Many textbooks contain glossaries. In fact, this textbook has three glossaries: the **Glossary of Literary Terms,** the **Glossary of Reading & Informational Terms,** and the **Glossary of Vocabulary in English & Spanish.** Use these glossaries to help you understand how terms are used in this textbook.

11 Spelling Rules

11.1 WORDS ENDING IN A SILENT *E*

Before adding a suffix beginning with a vowel or ***y*** to a word ending in a silent ***e,*** drop the ***e*** (with some exceptions).

amaze + -ing = amazing
love + -able = lovable
create + -ed = created
nerve + -ous = nervous

Exceptions: *change + -able = changeable; courage + -ous = courageous*

When adding a suffix beginning with a consonant to a word ending in a silent ***e,*** keep the ***e*** (with some exceptions).

late + -ly = lately
spite + -ful = spiteful
noise + -less = noiseless
state + -ment = statement

Exceptions: *truly, argument, ninth, wholly, awful,* and others

R74 VOCABULARY AND SPELLING HANDBOOK

When a suffix beginning with ***a*** or ***o*** is added to a word with a final silent ***e,*** the final ***e*** is usually retained if it is preceded by a soft ***c*** or a soft ***g.***

bridge + -able = bridgeable
peace + -able = peaceable
outrage + -ous = outrageous
advantage + -ous = advantageous

When a suffix beginning with a vowel is added to words ending in ***ee*** or ***oe,*** the final silent ***e*** is retained.

agree + -ing = agreeing **free + -ing = freeing**
hoe + -ing = hoeing **see + -ing = seeing**

11.2 WORDS ENDING IN *Y*

Before adding most suffixes to a word that ends in ***y*** preceded by a consonant, change the ***y*** to ***i.***

easy + -est = easiest
crazy + -est = craziest
silly + -ness = silliness
marry + -age = marriage

Exceptions: *dryness, shyness,* and *slyness*

However, when you add ***-ing,*** the ***y*** does not change.

empty + -ed = emptied but
empty + -ing = emptying

When adding a suffix to a word that ends in ***y*** preceded by a vowel, the ***y*** usually does not change.

play + -er = player
employ + -ed = employed
coy + -ness = coyness
pay + -able = payable

11.3 WORDS ENDING IN A CONSONANT

In one-syllable words that end in one consonant preceded by one short vowel, double the final consonant before adding a suffix beginning with a vowel, such as ***-ed*** or ***-ing.*** These are sometimes called 1+1+1 words.

dip + -ed = dipped **set + -ing = setting**
slim + -est = slimmest **fit + -er = fitter**

The rule does not apply to words of one syllable that end in a consonant preceded by two vowels.

feel + -ing = feeling **peel + -ed = peeled**
reap + -ed = reaped **loot + -ed = looted**

In words of more than one syllable, double the final consonant when (1) the word ends with one consonant preceded by one vowel and (2) when the word is accented on the last syllable.

be•gin' per•mit' re•fer'

In the following examples, note that in the new words formed with suffixes, the accent remains on the same syllable:

be•gin' + -ing = be•gin'ning = beginning
per•mit' + -ed = per•mit'ted = permitted

Exceptions: In some words with more than one syllable, though the accent remains on the same syllable when a suffix is added, the final consonant is nevertheless not doubled, as in the following examples:

tra'vel + er = tra'vel•er = traveler
mar'ket + er = mar'ket•er = marketer

In the following examples, the accent does not remain on the same syllable; thus, the final consonant is not doubled:

re•fer' + -ence = ref'er•ence = reference
con•fer' + -ence = con'fer•ence = conference

11.4 PREFIXES AND SUFFIXES

When adding a prefix to a word, do not change the spelling of the base word. When a prefix creates a double letter, keep both letters.

dis- + approve = disapprove
re- + build = rebuild
ir- + regular = irregular
mis- + spell = misspell
anti- + trust = antitrust
il- + logical = illogical

When adding ***-ly*** to a word ending in ***l,*** keep both ***l***'s. When adding ***-ness*** to a word ending in ***n,*** keep both ***n***'s.

careful + -ly = carefully
sudden + -ness = suddenness
final + -ly = finally
thin + -ness = thinness

VOCABULARY AND SPELLING HANDBOOK R75

11.5 FORMING PLURAL NOUNS

To form the plural of most nouns, just add *-s.*

prizes dreams circles stations

For most singular nouns ending in ***o,*** add *-s.*

solos halos studios photos pianos

For a few nouns ending in ***o,*** add *-es.*

heroes tomatoes potatoes echoes

When the singular noun ends in ***s, sh, ch, x,*** or ***z,*** add *-es.*

waitresses brushes ditches axes buzzes

When a singular noun ends in ***y*** with a consonant before it, change the ***y*** to ***i*** and add *-es.*

army—armies candy—candies
baby—babies diary—diaries
ferry—ferries conspiracy—conspiracies

When a vowel (***a, e, i, o, u***) comes before the ***y,*** just add *-s.*

boy—boys way—ways
array—arrays alloy—alloys
weekday—weekdays jockey—jockeys

For most nouns ending in ***f*** or ***fe,*** change the ***f*** to ***v*** and add *-es* or *-s.*

life—lives calf—calves knife—knives
thief—thieves shelf—shelves loaf—loaves

For some nouns ending in ***f,*** add *-s* to make the plural.

roofs chiefs reefs beliefs

Some nouns have the same form for both singular and plural.

deer sheep moose salmon trout

For some nouns, the plural is formed in a special way.

man—men goose—geese
ox—oxen woman—women
mouse—mice child—children

For a compound noun written as one word, form the plural by changing the last word in the compound to its plural form.

stepchild—stepchildren firefly—fireflies

If a compound noun is written as a hyphenated word or as two separate words, change the most important word to the plural form.

brother-in-law—brothers-in-law
life jacket—life jackets

11.6 FORMING POSSESSIVES

If a noun is singular, add ***'s.***

mother—my mother's car Ross—Ross's desk

Exceptions: The *s* after the apostrophe is dropped after *Jesus', Moses',* and certain names in classical mythology *(Zeus').* These possessive forms can thus be pronounced easily.

If a noun is plural and ends with ***s,*** just add an apostrophe.

parents—my parents' car
the Santinis—the Santinis' house

If a noun is plural but does not end in ***s,*** add ***'s.***

people—the people's choice
women—the women's coats

11.7 SPECIAL SPELLING PROBLEMS

Only one English word ends in ***-sede:*** *supersede.* Three words end in ***-ceed:*** *exceed, proceed,* and *succeed.* All other verbs ending in the sound "seed" are spelled with ***-cede.***

concede precede recede secede

In words with **ie** or **ei,** when the sound is long ***e*** (as in *she*), the word is spelled ***ie*** except after ***c*** (with some exceptions).

i* before *e	**thief**	**relieve**	**field**
	piece	**grieve**	**pier**
except after *c*	**conceit**	**perceive**	**ceiling**
	receive	**receipt**	
Exceptions:	**either**	**neither**	**weird**
	leisure	**seize**	

R76 VOCABULARY AND SPELLING HANDBOOK

12 Commonly Confused Words

WORDS	DEFINITIONS	EXAMPLES
accept/except	The verb ***accept*** means "to receive or believe." ***Except*** is usually a preposition meaning "excluding."	Did the teacher **accept** your report? Everyone smiled for the photographer **except** Jody.
advice/advise	***Advise*** is a verb. ***Advice*** is a noun naming that which an ***adviser*** gives.	I **advise** you to take that job. Whom should I ask for **advice**?
affect/effect	As a verb, ***affect*** means "to influence." ***Effect*** as a verb means "to cause." If you want a noun, you will almost always want ***effect***.	How deeply did the news **affect** him? The students tried to **effect** a change in school policy. What **effect** did the acidic soil produce in the plants?
all ready/already	***All ready*** is an adjective meaning "fully ready." ***Already*** is an adverb meaning "before or by this time."	He was **all ready** to go at noon. I have **already** seen that movie.
desert/dessert	***Desert*** (dĕz′ərt) means "a dry, sandy, barren region." ***Desert*** (dĭ-zûrt′) means "to abandon." ***Dessert*** (dĭ-zûrt′) is a sweet, such as cake.	The Sahara, in North Africa, is the world's largest ***desert.*** The night guard did not ***desert*** his post. Alison's favorite ***dessert*** is chocolate cake.
among/between	***Between*** is used when you are speaking of only two things. ***Among*** is used for three or more.	**Between** ice cream and sherbet, I prefer the latter. Gary Soto is **among** my favorite authors.
bring/take	***Bring*** is used to denote motion toward a speaker or place. ***Take*** is used to denote motion away from such a person or place.	**Bring** the books over here, and I will **take** them to the library.
fewer/less	***Fewer*** refers to the number of separate, countable units. ***Less*** refers to bulk quantity.	We have **less** literature and **fewer** selections in this year's curriculum.
leave/let	***Leave*** means "to allow something to remain behind." ***Let*** means "to permit."	The librarian will **leave** some books on display but will not **let** us borrow any.
lie/lay	To ***lie*** is "to rest or recline." It does not take an object. ***Lay*** always takes an object.	Rover loves to **lie** in the sun. We always **lay** some bones next to him.
loose/lose	***Loose*** (lo͞os) means "free, not restrained"; ***lose*** (lo͞oz) means "to misplace or fail to find."	Who turned the horses **loose?** I hope we won't **lose** any of them.
passed/past	***Passed*** is the past tense of pass and means "went by." ***Past*** is an adjective that means "of a former time." ***Past*** is also a noun that means "time gone by."	We **passed** through the Florida Keys during our vacation. My **past** experiences have taught me to set my alarm. Ebenezer Scrooge is a character who relives his **past.**
than/then	Use ***than*** in making comparisons. Use ***then*** on all other occasions.	Ramon is stronger **than** Mark. Cut the grass and **then** trim the hedges.
two/too/to	***Two*** is a number. ***Too*** is an adverb meaning "also" or "very." Use ***to*** before a verb or as a preposition.	Meg had **to** go **to** town, **too.** We had **too** much reading **to** do. **Two** chapters is **too** many.
their/there/they're	***Their*** means "belonging to them." ***There*** means "in that place." ***They're*** is the contraction for "they are."	**There** is a movie playing at 9 P.M. **They're** going to see it with me. Sakara and Jessica drove away in **their** car after the movie.

VOCABULARY AND SPELLING HANDBOOK R77

Effective oral communication occurs when the audience understands a speaker's message the way the speaker intends it. Good speakers and listeners do more than simply talk and hear. They use specific techniques to present their ideas effectively, and they are attentive and critical listeners.

1 Speech

In school, in business, and in community life, giving a speech can be an effective means of communicating ideas or information.

1.1 AUDIENCE, PURPOSE, AND OCCASION

Delivering a speech is an opportunity to share your ideas. Before you begin to prepare a speech, you will need to know *why* you are making the presentation and to *whom* you are presenting it. Understanding your purpose, the background and interests of your audience, and the occasion will help you select an appropriate focus and organizational structure for your speech.

- **Know Your Audience** What kind of group are you presenting to? Fellow classmates? A group of teachers? What are their interests and backgrounds? Understanding their different points of view can help you organize the information so that they understand and are interested in it.
- **Understand Your Purpose** Keep in mind your purpose for speaking. Are you trying to persuade the audience to do something? Perhaps you simply want to entertain them by sharing a story or experience. Being aware of your purpose will help you choose an appropriate tone for your speech. Decide whether you'll best accomplish your purpose by being serious or humorous.
- **Know the Occasion** Are you speaking at a special event? Is it formal? Will others besides you be giving speeches? Knowing what the occasion is will help you choose the proper language and the right length for your speech.

1.2 WRITING YOUR SPEECH

Once you understand your purpose and audience, you are ready to write your speech. Use the following guidelines to help you:

- **Create a Unified Speech** Organize your speech into paragraphs, each of which develops a single main idea. Then make sure that just as all the sentences in a paragraph support the main idea of the paragraph, all the paragraphs in your speech support the main idea of the speech.
- **Clarify Your Ideas** Make sure that you show clear relationships between ideas. Transition words can help listeners follow your ideas.

*For more information on transitions, see the **Writing Handbook,** page R32.*

- **Use Appropriate Language** The subject of your speech—and the way you choose to present it—should match your audience, your purpose, and the occasion. To share a story with your classmates, you can use informal language, such as slang. For a persuasive speech in front of a school assembly, use appropriate grammar and formal, standard American English. If you are giving an informative presentation, be sure to explain any terms that the audience may not be familiar with.
- **Provide Evidence** Include relevant facts, statistics, and incidents; quote experts to support your ideas and opinions. Include specific details and visual or media displays to clarify what you are saying.
- **Arrange Details and Evidence Effectively** In a good presentation, the main thesis statement should be supported by clearly stated evidence. The evidence can be presented as details, reasons, descriptions, or examples. Use the following chart to help you arrange your ideas.

R78 SPEAKING AND LISTENING HANDBOOK

Introduction	• Focus on one strong example or statistic. • Make sure your introduction is intense or even surprising, so that it grabs the audience's attention.
Main Body	• Try to provide at least one piece of evidence for every new idea you introduce. • Define unfamiliar terms clearly. • When possible, include well-labeled diagrams or illustrations.
Conclusion	• Leave your audience with one strong piece of evidence or a powerful detail.

- **Use Figurative Language** To help your audience follow the main ideas of your speech, be sure to draw attention to important points with similes, metaphors, and sensory images.
- **Use Precise Language** Use precise language to convey your ideas, and vary the structure and length of your sentences. You can keep the audience's attention with a word that brings out strong emotion. You can use a question or side comment to make a personal connection with the audience.
- **Start Strong, Finish Strong** As you begin your speech, consider using a "hook"—an interesting question or statement to capture the audience's attention. At the end of the speech, restate your main ideas simply and clearly. Perhaps conclude with a powerful example or anecdote to reinforce your message.
- **Revise Your Speech** After you write your speech, revise, edit, and proofread it as you would a written report. Use a variety of sentence structures to achieve a natural rhythm. Check for correct subject-verb agreement and consistent verb tense. Correct run-on sentences and sentence fragments. Use parallel structure to emphasize ideas. Make sure you use complete sentences and correct punctuation and capitalization, even if no one else will see it. Your written speech should be clear and error free. If you notice an error in your notes while you are delivering the speech, you may not remember what you actually wanted to say.

1.3 DELIVERING YOUR SPEECH

Confidence is the key to a successful presentation. Use these techniques to help you prepare and present your speech:

Prepare

- **Review Your Information** Reread your notes and review any background research. This will help you feel more confident during your speech.
- **Organize Your Notes** Some people prefer to write down only key points. Others prefer the entire script. Write each main point, or each paragraph, of your speech on a separate numbered index card. Be sure to include your most important evidence and examples.
- **Plan Your Visual Aids** If you are planning to use visual aids, such as slides, posters, charts, graphs, video clips, overhead transparencies, or computer projections, now is the time to design them and decide how to work them into your speech.

Practice

- **Rehearse** Rehearse your speech several times, possibly in front of a practice audience. Maintain good posture by standing with your shoulders back and your head up. If you are using visual aids, arrange them in the order in which you will use them. Adapt your rate of speaking, pitch, and tone of voice to your audience and setting. Glance at your notes to refresh your memory, but avoid reading them word for word. Your delivery style should express the purpose of your speech. Use the following chart to help you.

Purpose	Pace	Pitch	Tone
To persuade	fast but clear	same throughout	urgent
To inform	using plenty of pauses	same throughout	authoritative
To entertain	usually building to a "punch"	varied to create characters or drama	funny or dramatic

SPEAKING AND LISTENING HANDBOOK R79

- **Use Audience Feedback** If you had a practice audience, ask them specific questions about your delivery and the content: Did I use enough eye contact? Was my voice at the right volume? Did I stand straight, or did I slouch? Did my tone and inflection fit my purpose? Use the audience's comments to evaluate the effectiveness of your delivery.
- **Evaluate Your Performance** When you have finished each rehearsal, evaluate your performance. Did you pause to let an important point sink in or use gestures for emphasis? Make a list of the aspects of your presentation that you will try to improve for your next rehearsal.

Present

- **Begin Your Speech** Smile, and try to look relaxed.
- **Make Eye Contact** Try to make eye contact with as many audience members as possible. This will establish personal contact and help you determine whether the audience understands your speech.
- **Remember to Pause** Pausing after important points provides emphasis and gives the audience time to think about what you're saying.
- **Speak Clearly** Speak loud enough to be heard clearly, but not so loud that your voice is overwhelming. Use a conversational tone.
- **Maintain Good Posture** Stand up straight and avoid nervous movements that may distract the audience's attention from what you are saying.
- **Use Expressive Body Language** Use facial expressions to show your feelings toward your topic. Lean forward when you make an important point; move your hands and arms for emphasis. Use your body language to show your own style and reflect your personality.
- **Watch the Audience for Responses** If the audience starts fidgeting or yawning, speak a little louder or get to your conclusion a little sooner. Use what you learn to evaluate your speech and to decide what areas need improvement. Should you make changes to the organization? Do you need to rearrange any words or sentences to clarify your meaning?

Respond to Questions

Depending on the content of your speech, your audience may have questions. Follow these steps to make sure that you answer questions in an appropriate manner:

- Think about what your audience may ask and prepare answers before your speech.
- Tell your audience at the beginning of your speech that you will take questions at the end. This helps avoid audience interruptions during your speech.
- Call on audience members in the order in which they raise their hands.
- Repeat each question before you answer it to ensure that everyone has heard it. This step also gives you time to prepare your answer.

2 Different Types of Oral Presentations

2.1 INFORMATIVE SPEECH

When you deliver an informative speech, you give the audience new information, provide a better understanding of information, or enable the audience to use the information in a new way. An informative speech is presented in an objective way.

Use the following questions to evaluate the presentation of a peer or a public figure, or your own presentation.

Evaluate an Informative Speech

- Did the speaker explain the purpose of the presentation?
- Did the speaker take the audience's previous knowledge into consideration?
- Did the speaker cite a variety of sources for the information?
- Did the speaker communicate the information objectively?
- Did the speaker explain technical terms?
- Did the speaker use visual aids effectively?

R80 SPEAKING AND LISTENING HANDBOOK

2.2 RESEARCH PRESENTATION

An oral research presentation conveys information on a single researched topic. An effective research report will be organized around a clear thesis. It will support that thesis with details and evidence from a number of reliable sources.

- **Plan Your Report** Decide on a topic, and then narrow down that topic to find a focus.
- **Consider Your Purpose** Writing down your purpose in sentence or question form will help you develop your thesis.
- **Organize Your Material** Choose an order in which to present your information. Be sure that any main points are supported with details and evidence from sources you can cite.

Use the following guidelines to evaluate a research presentation.

Evaluate a Research Presentation

- Did the speaker define a clear thesis?
- Did the speaker support the thesis using specific details—such as direct quotations, general concepts, or ideas—from reliable sources?
- Did the speaker summarize or paraphrase important information on the topic, when necessary?
- Did the speaker include a variety of primary and secondary sources, and explain the value of each?
- Did the speaker use charts, maps, and graphs to organize information when appropriate?

2.3 PERSUASIVE SPEECH

When you deliver a persuasive speech, you offer a thesis or clear statement on a subject, you provide relevant evidence to support your position, and you attempt to convince the audience to accept your point of view.

*For more information, see **Speaking and Listening: Delivering a Persuasive Speech,** page 1023.*

Use the following questions to evaluate the presentation of a peer or a public figure, or your own presentation.

Evaluate a Persuasive Speech

- Did the speaker present a clear thesis or argument?
- Did the speaker anticipate and address audience concerns, biases, and counterarguments?
- Did the speaker use sound logic and reasoning in developing the argument?
- Did the speaker support the argument with convincing evidence, examples, facts, expert opinions, and quotations?
- Did the speaker balance emotional arguments with logical ones?
- Did the speaker use his or her tone, facial expressions, and gestures to hold the audience's interest?
- Is your reaction to the speech similar to other audience members'?

2.4 NARRATIVE SPEECH

When you deliver a narrative speech, you tell a story or present a subject using a story-type format. A good narrative keeps an audience informed and entertained. It also allows you to deliver a message in a creative way.

Use the following questions to evaluate a speaker or your own presentation.

Evaluate a Narrative Speech

- Did the speaker choose a setting that makes sense and contributes to a believable narrative?
- Did the speaker locate incidents in specific places?
- Does the plot flow well?
- Did the speaker make the significance of each main event clear to the audience?
- Did the speaker use words that convey the appropriate mood and tone?
- Did the speaker use sensory details that allow the audience to experience the sights, sounds, and smells of a scene and the specific actions, gestures, and thoughts of the characters?
- Did the speaker use a range of narrative devices to keep the audience interested?
- Is your reaction to the presentation similar to other audience members'?

SPEAKING AND LISTENING HANDBOOK R81

2.5 ORAL INTERPRETATION

When you read a poem, play, or story aloud, your voice can bring the literature to life.

Oral Reading

An oral reading can be a monologue, during which you assume the voice of a single character, the narrator, or the speaker in a poem. Or it may be a dialogue, during which you take the roles of two or more characters. Use the following techniques when giving an oral reading:

- **Speak Clearly** As you speak, pronounce your words carefully and clearly.
- **Control Your Volume** Make sure that you are loud enough to be heard but not shouting.
- **Pace Yourself** Read at a moderate rate, but vary your pace if it seems appropriate to the emotions of the character or to the action.
- **Vary Your Voice** Use a different voice for each character. Stress important words and phrases. Use your voice to express different emotions.

*For more information, see **Speaking and Listening: Oral Interpretation of a Poem,** page 655.*

Dramatic Reading

In a dramatic reading, several speakers participate in the reading of a play or your own original work. Use the following techniques in your dramatic reading:

- **Prepare** Rehearse your material several times. Become familiar with the humorous and serious parts of the script. Develop a special voice that fits the personality of the character you portray.
- **Project** As you read your lines, aim your voice toward the back of the room to allow everyone to hear you.
- **Perform** React to the other characters as if you were hearing their lines for the first time. Deliver your own lines with the appropriate emotion.

Use facial expressions, hand gestures, and other body movements to express your emotions.

Evaluate an Oral Interpretation

- Did the speaker speak clearly?
- Did the speaker maintain eye contact with the audience?
- Did the speaker project his or her voice at the proper volume?
- Did the speaker vary the rate of speech appropriately to express emotion, mood, and action?
- Did the speaker use a different voice for each character?
- Did the speaker stress important words or phrases?
- Did the speaker use the appropriate tone, inflections, and gestures to enhance meaning?
- Did the speaker seem aware of the interpretation's effect on listeners?

PRACTICE AND APPLY

Listen to an oral reading by a classmate or view a dramatic performance in a theater or on television. Use the preceding guidelines to evaluate it.

2.6 ORAL RESPONSE TO LITERATURE

An oral response to literature is your own personal interpretation of a piece written by someone else. It is a way to show an audience what a story, a poem, or an essay means to you. Use the following techniques to help you craft a response:

- **Select Carefully** In choosing a piece for your response, think about the assignment, your interest, and the audience.
- **Exhibit Understanding** Direct your audience to specific words, sentences, or paragraphs that are rich with meaning. Discuss why they are important to the piece. Explain the writer's techniques in developing plot, characterization, setting, or theme.
- **Organize Clearly** Construct your response around clear ideas, premises, or images. What elements of the literature are most important? How do they relate to the piece as a whole? Use examples and evidence to show how they provide insight and meaning.

R82 SPEAKING AND LISTENING HANDBOOK

Evaluate an Oral Response to Literature

- Did the speaker provide an in-depth analysis of a piece of literature?
- Did the speaker call attention to specific writing techniques and passages that helped to give the piece meaning?
- Did the speaker make inferences about the piece of literature and discuss its effect on himself or herself as a reader?
- Did the speaker support inferences and judgments with references to the piece, other pieces, or personal knowledge?
- Did the speaker present his or her ideas in a clear, well-organized manner?

PRACTICE AND APPLY

Listen as a classmate delivers an oral response to a book or an article. Use the preceding guidelines to evaluate the presentation.

3 Other Types of Communication

3.1 CONVERSATION

Conversations are informal, but they are a very important means of communicating. When two or more people exchange messages, it is important for each person to contribute and actively listen.

3.2 GROUP DISCUSSION

Successful groups assign a role to each member. These roles distribute responsibility among the members and help keep discussions focused.

Guidelines for Discussion

- Be informed about the topic.
- Participate in the discussion.
- Ask questions and give appropriate responses.
- Don't talk while someone else is talking.
- Support statements with facts and examples.
- Listen attentively; be respectful of others.
- Work toward the goal; avoid getting sidetracked by unrelated topics.

Role	Responsibilities
Chairperson	• Introduces topic • Explains goal or purpose • Participates in discussion and keeps it on track • Helps resolve conflicts • Helps group reach goal
Recorder	• Takes notes on discussion • Reports on suggestions and decisions • Organizes and writes up notes • Participates in discussion
Participants	• Contribute relevant facts or ideas to discussion • Respond constructively to one another's ideas • Reach agreement or vote on final decision

3.3 INTERVIEW

An **interview** is a formal type of conversation with a definite purpose and goal. To conduct a successful interview, use the following guidelines:

Prepare for the Interview

- Carefully select whom you will interview. Identify who has the kind of knowledge and experience you are looking for.
- Set a time, a date, and a place. Ask permission to record the interview.
- Learn all you can about the person you will interview or the topic you want information on.
- Prepare a list of questions. Create questions that encourage detailed responses instead of yes-or-no answers. Arrange your questions in order from most important to least important.
- Arrive on time with everything you need.

Conduct the Interview

- Ask your questions clearly and listen to the responses carefully. Give the person whom you are interviewing plenty of time to answer.
- Be flexible; follow up on any responses you find interesting.

SPEAKING AND LISTENING HANDBOOK R83

- Avoid arguments; be tactful and polite.
- Even if you record an interview, take notes on important points.
- Thank the person for the interview, and ask if you can call with any follow-up questions.

Follow Up on the Interview

- Summarize your notes or make a written copy of the recording as soon as possible.
- If any points are unclear or if information is missing, call and ask more questions while the person is still available.
- Select the most appropriate quotations to support your ideas.
- If possible, have the person you interviewed review your work to make sure you haven't misrepresented what he or she said.
- Send a thank-you note to the person in appreciation of his or her time and effort.

*For more information, see **Speaking and Listening: Conducting an Interview:** page 299.*

Evaluate an Interview

You can determine how effective your interview was by asking yourself these questions:

- Did you get the type of information you were looking for?
- Were your most important questions answered to your satisfaction?
- Were you able to keep the person being interviewed focused on the subject?

4 Active Listening

Active listening is the process of receiving, interpreting, evaluating, and responding to a message. When you listen to a class discussion or a formal speech, use the following strategies to get as much as you can from the message.

Listening with a Purpose

Situation	Reason for Listening	How to Listen
A guest speaker talks to your class about her career.	for information, to learn something new	Listen for ideas that interest you or add to your knowledge.
Your friend tells you about his vacation.	for enjoyment	Maintain eye contact; make comments when appropriate.

Before Listening

- Learn what the topic is beforehand. You may need to read background information about the topic or learn new terms in order to understand the speaker's message.
- Think about what you know or want to know about the topic.
- Have a pen and paper to take notes.
- Establish a purpose for listening.

While Listening

- Focus your attention on the speaker. Your facial expressions and body language should demonstrate your interest in hearing the topic. Try to ignore uncomfortable room temperature and noise.
- Listen for the speaker's purpose (usually stated at the beginning), which alerts you to main ideas.
- To help you understand the speaker's message, listen for words or phrases that signal important points, such as *to begin with, in addition, most important, finally,* and *in conclusion.*
- Listen carefully for explanations of unfamiliar terms. Use these terms to help you understand the speaker's message.
- Listen for ideas that are repeated for emphasis.
- Take notes. Write down only the most important points.
- If possible, use an outline or list format to organize main ideas and supporting points.
- Note comparisons and contrasts, causes and effects, or problems and solutions.

R84 SPEAKING AND LISTENING HANDBOOK

- As you take notes, use phrases, abbreviations, and symbols to keep up with the speaker.
- To aid your understanding, note how the speaker uses word choice, voice pitch, posture, and gestures to convey meaning.

After Listening

- Ask questions to clarify anything that was unclear or confusing.
- Review your notes right away to make sure you understand what was said.
- Summarize and paraphrase the speaker's ideas.
- You may also wish to compare your interpretation of the speech with the interpretations of others who listened to it.

4.1 CRITICAL LISTENING

Critical listening involves evaluating a spoken message to judge its accuracy and reliability. You can use the following strategies as you listen to messages from public speakers:

- **Determine the Speaker's Purpose** Think about the background, viewpoint, and possible motives of the speaker. Separate facts from opinions. Listen carefully to details and evidence used to support the message. You may want to paraphrase the speaker's purpose and point of view to help you evaluate the speech.
- **Listen for the Main Idea** Figure out the speaker's main message before allowing yourself to be distracted by seemingly convincing facts and details. To evaluate a speaker's credibility, look for anything that may indicate bias, such as material that is unfairly slanted or contains a hidden agenda.
- **Recognize the Use of Persuasive Techniques** Speakers may present information in a particular way to persuade you to buy a product or accept an idea. Persuasive devices such as glittering generalities, either/or reasoning, and bandwagon or snob appeal may represent faulty reasoning and provide misleading information.

*For more information, see **Recognizing Persuasive Techniques,** page R21.*

- **Observe Nonverbal Messages** A speaker's gestures, facial expressions, and tone of voice should reinforce the message. If they don't, you should doubt the speaker's sincerity and his or her message's reliability.
- **Give Appropriate Feedback** An effective speaker looks for verbal and nonverbal cues from you, the listener, to see how the message is being received. For example, if you understand or agree with the message, you might nod your head. If possible, during or after a presentation, ask questions to check your understanding.

4.2 VERBAL FEEDBACK

At times you will be asked to give direct feedback to a speaker. You may be asked to evaluate the way the speaker delivers the presentation as well as the content of the presentation.

Evaluate Delivery

- Did the speaker speak clearly and distinctly?
- Did the speaker pronounce words correctly?
- Did the speaker vary his or her rate of speaking?
- Did the speaker's voice sound natural and not strained?
- Was the speaker's voice loud enough?

Evaluate Content

Here's how to give constructive suggestions for improvement:

Be Specific Instead of vague statements like "Your charts need work," offer concrete suggestions, such as "Please make the type bigger so we can read the chart from the back of the room."

Discuss Only the Most Important Points Don't overload the speaker with too much feedback about too many details. Focus on important points, such as

- Is the topic too advanced for the audience?
- Are the supporting details well organized?
- Is the conclusion strong or weak?

Give Balanced Feedback Tell the speaker not only what didn't work but also what did work: "Consider dropping the last two slides, since you covered those points earlier. The first two slides really got my attention."

SPEAKING AND LISTENING HANDBOOK R85

Every day, you come into contact with some form of media. Media images and messages—from television, radio, and movies to newspapers and the Internet—are all around us. With so many options, it's more important than ever to be a smart media consumer. People who are media literate know what media products are, what they mean, and who created them. They are able to analyze and evaluate the way media messages influence the world. This section introduces some of the tools you'll need to study different forms of media.

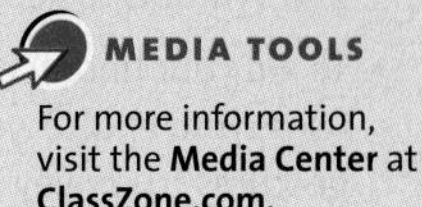

For more information, visit the **Media Center** at **ClassZone.com.**

1 Five Core Concepts in Media Literacy

from The Center for Media Literacy

The five core concepts of media literacy provide you with the basic ideas you can consider when examining media messages.

All media messages are "constructed." All media messages are made by someone. In fact, they are carefully thought out and researched and have attitudes and values built into them. Much of the information that you use to make sense of the world comes from the media. Therefore, it is important to know how a medium is put together so you can better understand the message it conveys.

Media messages are constructed using a creative language with its own rules. Each means of communication—whether it is film, television, newspapers, magazines, radio, or the Internet—has its own language and design. Therefore, the message must use the language and design of the medium that delivers the message. Thus, the medium actually shapes the message. For example, a horror film may use music to heighten suspense, or a newspaper may use a big headline to signal the importance of a story. Understanding the language of each medium can increase your enjoyment of it, as well as help you recognize any subtle attempt to persuade you.

Different people experience the same media messages differently. Personal factors such as age, education, and experience will affect the way a person responds to a media message. How many times has your interpretation of a film or book differed from that of a friend? Everyone interprets media messages differently.

Media messages have embedded values and points of view. Media messages carry underlying values, which are purposely built into them by the creators of the message. For example, a commercial's main purpose may be to persuade you to buy something, but the commercial may also aim to convince you that the product is important to a particular way of life. Understanding not only the main message but also any other points of view will help you decide whether to accept or reject the message.

Most media messages are constructed to gain profit and/or power. The creators of media messages often provide a commodity, such as information or entertainment, in order to make money. The bigger the audience, the more the media outlet can charge for advertising. Consequently, media outlets want to build large audiences in order to bring in more revenue from advertising. For example, a television network will create programming to appeal to the largest audience possible, in the hope that the viewer ratings will attract more advertising dollars.

R86 MEDIA HANDBOOK

2 Media Basics

2.1 MESSAGE

When a film or TV show is created, it becomes a media product. Each media product is created to send a **message,** or an expression of a belief or opinion, that serves a specific purpose. In order to understand the message, you will need to deconstruct it.

Deconstruction is the process of analyzing a media presentation. To analyze a media presentation you will need to ask why and how it was created, who created it, and whom it is trying to influence.

2.2 AUDIENCE

A **target audience** is the specific group of people that a product or presentation is aimed at. The members of a target audience usually share certain characteristics, such as age, gender, ethnic background, values, or lifestyle. For example, a target audience may be 11-to-14-year-olds who carry backpacks to school.

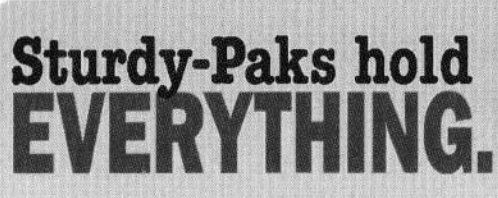
Sturdy-Paks hold
EVERYTHING.
Tough and stylish, they're
the perfect backpack for
busy, busy students

Demographics are the characteristics of a population, including age, gender, profession, income, education, ethnicity, and geographical location. Media decision makers use demographics to shape their content to suit the needs and tastes of a target audience.

2.3 PURPOSE

The **purpose,** or intent, of a media presentation is the reason it was made. All media products—from news programs to video games—are created for a specific purpose. Identifying why a media product was invented is the first step in understanding how it can influence you. The following chart shows purposes of different media products.

Purposes of Media Products	
Purpose	**Example**
Inform	news reports and articles, public service announcements, some Web sites
Persuade	advertisements, editorials, reviews, political cartoons
Entertain	most TV shows, films, recorded music; video games; most talk shows

Most media products have more than one purpose. For example, TV commercials are often entertaining, but their main purpose is to persuade you to buy something. If you aren't aware of all of a media products' purposes, you may become influenced without knowing it. This chart shows some examples.

Main and Other Purposes in Media		
Media Product	**Main Purpose**	**Other Purposes**
News broadcast	to inform	to persuade you that an issue or idea is important
Advertisement	to persuade	to entertain you; to inform you about a product
Sports coverage	to entertain	to inform you about sports or athletes

2.4 TYPES AND GENRES OF MEDIA

The term ***media*** refers to television, newspapers, magazines, radio, movies, and the Internet. Each is a **medium,** or means for carrying information, entertainment, and advertisements to a large audience.

MEDIA HANDBOOK R87

Each type of media has different characteristics, strengths, and weaknesses. The following chart shows how several types of media deliver their messages.

Type of Media	Characteristics
Newspaper article	• Provides detailed information and dramatic photographs • Uses **headlines** and **subheads** to give main ideas • Can't be updated until next edition or next day
Television news report	• Uses an **announcer,** or "anchor," to guide viewers through the news report • Uses **video footage** to bring news to life or clarify what happened • Uses **graphics** to give information at a glance • Can be updated quickly
Documentary	• Tells about historic people and places, major events, and important social, political, or environmental issues • Uses **footage,** or shots of photographs, interviews, news reports, and film clips, to help viewers understand the subject • Features **interviews** of experts or people directly involved with the subject • Uses a **voice-over narrator,** the voice of an unseen speaker, who tells viewers why the subject is important and how the information about the subject is organized
Web site	• Gives in-depth information on specialized subjects • Uses **text, still images,** and **video** • Allows users to select the information they want to receive by clicking on links • Allows users to see when the site was last updated • Can be updated quickly

*For more information, see **Types of Media**, page 10.*

2.5 PRODUCERS AND CREATORS

People who control the media are known as **gatekeepers.** Gatekeepers decide what information to share with the public and the ways it will be presented. This diagram gives some examples.

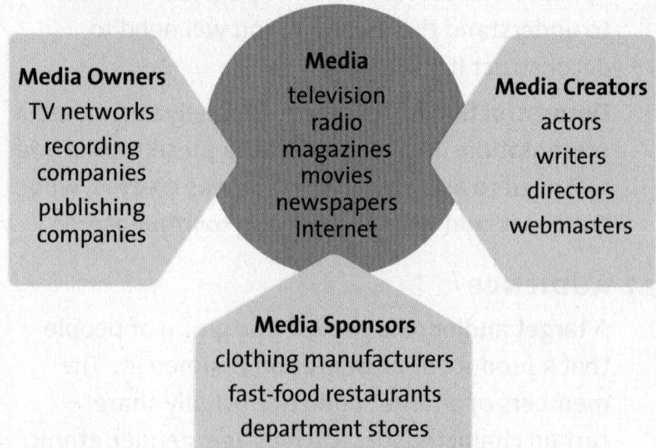

Media sponsors are companies that pay for their products to be advertised. It's important to be aware of sponsors and other gatekeepers, because they control much of what you see and hear. For example, suppose a television network executive disagrees with a particular computer company's business philosophy. As a result, she might decide not to let that company advertise on her network.

2.6 INFLUENCE OF MEDIA

Everywhere you go, you're bombarded by the media—advertisements, newspapers, magazines, radio, and television. Different kinds of media are all competing for your attention, telling you, "Buy this product. Listen to this music. Read this story. Look at this image. Think about this opinion." These media products are usually designed to sell you something. But they may also be sending subtle messages about values that they want you to believe in. Soda ads, for example, are intended to sell soda, but if you examine them closely, you will see that they often try to appeal to a set of values or a certain lifestyle. One message of the ad is that if you drink this soda, you will have as much fun as the people in the ad. The other message is that this lifestyle is good and desirable. TV shows, movies, and news programs also convey values and beliefs.

R88 MEDIA HANDBOOK

Media can also shape your opinions about the world. For example, news about crime shapes our understanding about how much and what type of crime is prevalent in the world around us. TV news items, talk show interviews, and commercials may shape what we think of a political candidate, a celebrity, an ethnic group, a country, or a region. As a result, our knowledge of someone or someplace could be completely based on the information we receive from television.

3 Film and TV

Films and television programs come in a variety of types. Films include comedies, dramas, documentaries, and animated features. Televison programs cover dramas, sitcoms, talk shows, reality shows, newscasts, and so on. Producers of films and producers of television programs rely on many of the same elements to make the action and settings seem real and to also affect the emotions of their audiences. Among these elements are scripts, visual and sound elements, special effects, and editing.

3.1 SCRIPT AND WRITTEN ELEMENTS

The writer and editor develop a story for television or film using a script and storyboard. A **script** is the text or words of a film or television show. A **storyboard** is a device used to plan the shooting of a movie or TV show. A storyboard is made up of drawings and brief descriptions of what is happening in each shot of a scene. The drawings of a storyboard help a director visualize how a finished scene might look before the scene is filmed. This storyboard shows some scenes that a student created.

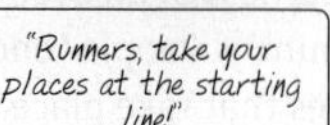

"Runners, take your places at the starting line!"

Medium shot of Squeaky getting ready

For more information, see ***Media Study: Produce Your Own Media,*** *page 257.*

3.2 VISUAL ELEMENTS

Visual elements in film and television include camera shots and angles. A **camera shot** is a single, continuous view taken by a camera. A **camera angle** is the angle at which the camera is positioned during the recording of a shot or image. Each is carefully planned to create an effect. This chart shows what different shots are used for.

Camera Shot/Angle	Effect
Establishing shot introduces viewers to the location of a scene, usually by presenting a wide view of an area	establishes the setting of a film
Close-up shot shows a close view of a person or object	helps to create emotion and make viewers feel as if they know the character
Medium shot shows a view wider than a close-up but narrower than an establishing or long shot	shows part of an object, or a character from the knees or waist up
Long shot gives a wide view of a scene, showing the full figure(s) of a person or group and the surroundings	allows the viewer to see the "big picture" and shows the relationship between characters and the environment
Reaction shot shows in some way what the subject sees	allows the viewer to see how the subject feels in order to create empathy in the viewer
Low-angle shot looks up at an object or person	makes a character, object, or scene appear more important or threatening
High-angle shot looks down on an object or person	makes a character, object, or scene seem weak or unimportant
Point-of-view (POV) shot shows a part of the story through a character's eyes	helps viewers identify with that character

3.3 SOUND ELEMENTS

Sound elements in film and television include music, voice-over, and sound effects.

MEDIA HANDBOOK R89

Music may be used to set the mood and atmosphere in a scene. Music can have a powerful effect on the way viewers feel about a story. For example, fast-paced music helps viewers feel excited during an action scene.

Voice-over is the voice of the unseen commentator or narrator of a film, TV program, or commercial.

Sound effects are the sounds added to films, TV programs, and commercials during the editing process. Sound effects, such as laugh tracks or the sounds of punches in a fight scene, can create humor, emphasize a point, or contribute to the mood.

3.4 SPECIAL EFFECTS

Special effects include computer-generated animation, manipulated video images, and fast- or slow-motion sequences in films, TV programs, and commercials.

Animation on film involves the frame-by-frame photography of a series of drawings or objects. When these frames are projected—at a rate of 24 per second—the illusion of movement is achieved.

A **split screen** is a special-effects shot in which two or more separate images are shown in the same frame. One example is when two people, actually a distance apart, are shown talking to each other.

3.5 EDITING

Editing is the process of selecting and arranging shots in a sequence. Moviemakers put shots together in ways that help you follow the action of a story. The editor decides which scenes or shots to use, as well as the length of each shot, the number of shots, and their sequence.

Cut is the transition from one shot to another. To create excitement, editors often use quick cuts, which are a series of short shots strung together.

Dissolve is a device in which one scene fades into another.

Fade-in is a device in which a white or black shot fades in to reveal the beginning of a new scene.

Fade-out is a device in which a shot fades to darkness to end a scene.

Jump cut is an abrupt and jarring change from one shot to another. A jump cut shows a break in time.

Pace is the length of time each shot stays on the screen and the rhythm that is created by the transitions between shots. Short, quick cuts create a fast pace in a story. Long cuts slow down a story.

4 News

The **news** is information on events, people, and places in your community, the region, the nation, and the world. It can be found in local newspapers, newscasts, online wire services, magazines, and documentaries. Because it's impossible to publish all the news that happens in one day in any one source, journalists have to make decisions about which stories will appear in newspapers and on newscasts. They use several factors to help them choose stories.

4.1 CHOOSING THE NEWS

Newsworthiness is the importance of an event or action that makes it worthy of media reporting. Journalists and their editors often use the following criteria in determining which stories should make the news:

Timeliness is the quality of being very current. Timely events usually take priority over previously reported events. For example, a tornado that strikes a residential area will be timely on the day it occurs. It may be on the front page of a newspaper or may be the lead story on a newscast.

Widespread impact is a characteristic of an event that could affect a large number of people. The more widespread the impact of an event, the more likely it is to be newsworthy.

Proximity measures the nearness of an event to a particular city, region, or country. People tend to be more interested in stories that take place close to where they live and that thus may affect them directly.

R90 MEDIA HANDBOOK

Human interest is a quality of stories that causes readers or listeners to feel emotions such as happiness, anger, or sadness. People are interested in reading stories about other people.

Uniqueness is the condition of being the only one of a kind. Unique or uncommon events or circumstances are likely to be interesting to an audience.

Compelling video and **photographs** grab people's attention and stay in their minds.

4.2 REPORTING THE NEWS

While developing a news story, a journalist makes a variety of decisions about how to construct the story, such as what information to include and how to organize it. The following elements are commonly used in news stories:

5 *W's* and *H* are the six questions reporters answer when writing news stories—*who, what, when, where, why,* and *how.* It is a journalist's job to answer these questions in any type of news report. These questions also provide a structure for writing and editing a story.

Inverted pyramid is the means of organizing information according to importance. In the inverted-pyramid diagram below, the most important information (the answers to the 5 *W's* and *H*) appears at the top of the pyramid. The less important details appear at the bottom. Not all stories are reported using the inverted-pyramid form. The form remains popular, however, because it helps a reader to get the important information without reading the entire story. Notice the following example.

A new study suggests that regular exercise is key to keeping cholesterol levels low.

Patients who exercised 30 minutes per day for one year decreased their cholesterol levels significantly.

Researchers also suggested easy ways for people to get 30 minutes of activity daily.

Angle or slant is the point of view from which a story is written. Even an objective report must have an angle.

Consider these two headlines that describe the same crime story.

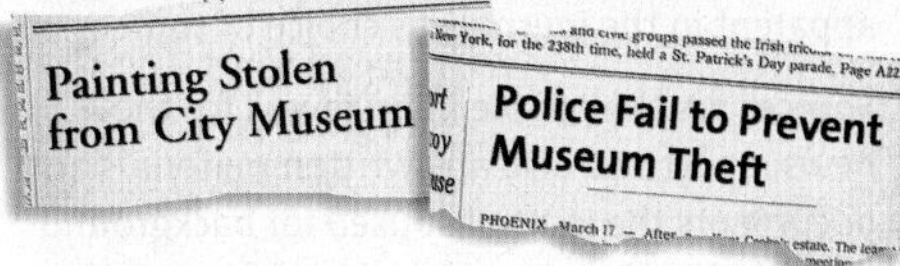

The first headline focuses on a fact. The second headline focuses on an opinion and has a negative slant.

Standards for News Reporting

The ideal of journalism is to present news in a way that is objective, accurate, and thorough. The best news stories contain the following elements:

- **Objectivity** The story takes a balanced point of view on the issues. It is not biased, nor does it reflect a specific attitude or opinion.
- **Accuracy** The story presents factual information that can be verified.
- **Thoroughness** The story presents all sides of an issue. It includes background information, telling *who, what, when, where, why,* and *how.*

Balanced Versus Biased Reporting

Objectivity in news reporting can be measured by how balanced or biased the story is.

Balanced reporting represents all sides of an issue equally and fairly. A balanced news story

- represents people and subjects in a neutral light
- treats all sides of an issue equally
- does not include inappropriate questions, such as "Why should we take pity on this thief?"
- does not show stereotypes or prejudice toward any particular race, gender, age, or religion.
- does not leave out important background information that is needed to establish a context or perspective.

MEDIA HANDBOOK R91

Biased reporting is reporting in which one side is favored over another or in which the subject is unfairly represented. Biased reporting may show an overly negative view of a subject, or it may encourage racial, gender, or other stereotypes and prejudices. Sometimes biased reporting is apparent in the journalist's choice of sources.

Sources are the people interviewed for the news report and also any written materials and documents the journalist used for background information. From each source, the journalist gets a different point of view. To decide whether news reporting is balanced or biased, you will need to pay attention to the sources. Consider a news story on a new type of diet book. If the only source given in the story is the person who wrote the book, then the report may be biased. But if the journalist also includes the perspective of someone neutral and informed, such as a nutritionist, then the report may be more balanced. This chart shows which sources are generally considered reliable, and which tend to be considered weak.

Sources for News Stories

Reliable sources	Weak sources
• experts in a field • people directly affected by the reported event (eyewitnesses) • published reports that are specifically mentioned or shown	• unnamed or anonymous sources • people who are not involved in the reported event (for example, people who heard about a story from a friend) • research, data, or reports that are not specifically named or are referred to only in vague terms (for example, "Research shows that ...")

5 Advertising

Advertising is a sponsor's paid use of various media to promote products, services, or ideas. Some common forms of advertising are shown in the chart.

Type of Ad	Description
Billboard	a large outdoor advertising sign
Print ad	typically appears in magazines and newspapers; uses eye-catching graphics and persuasive copy
Flyer	a print ad that is circulated by hand or mail
Infomercial	an extended ad on TV that usually includes detailed product information, demonstrations, and testimonials
Public service announcement	a message aired on radio or TV to promote ideas that are considered to be in the public interest
Political ad	a broadcast on radio or TV to promote political candidates
Trailer	a short film promoting an upcoming movie, TV show, or video game

Marketing is the process of transferring products and services from producer to consumer. It involves determining the packaging and pricing of a product, how it will be promoted and advertised, and where it will be sold. One way companies market their products is by becoming media sponsors.

Sponsors pay for their products to be advertised. These companies hire advertising agencies to create and produce specific campaigns for their products. They then buy television or radio airtime or magazine, newspaper, or billboard space to feature ads where the target audience is sure to see them. Because selling time and space to advertisers produces much of the income the media need to function, the media need advertisers just as much as advertisers need the media.

Product placement is the intentional and identifiable featuring of brand-name products in movies, television shows, video games, and other media. The intention is to have viewers

R92 MEDIA HANDBOOK

feel positive about a product because they see a favorite character using it. Another purpose may be to promote product recognition.

5.1 PERSUASIVE TECHNIQUES

Persuasive techniques are the methods used to convince an audience to buy a product or adopt an idea. Advertisers use a combination of visuals, sound, special effects, and words to persuade their target audience. Recognizing the following techniques can help you evaluate persuasive media messages and identify misleading information:

Emotional appeals use strong feelings, such as fear and pity, rather than facts to persuade consumers. An example of an appeal to fear might be, "Is your water safe to drink? Our filter system will help you be sure."

Bandwagon appeals use the argument that a person should believe or do something because "everyone else" does. These appeals take advantage of people's desire to be socially accepted by other people. An example of a bandwagon appeal is "Find out why everyone's talking about the hit film *A Two-Hour Story About Some Funny Characters*."

Slogans are memorable phrases used in advertising campaigns. Slogans substitute catchy phrases for facts.

Logical appeals rely on logic and facts, appealing to a consumer's reason and his or her respect for authority. Two examples of logical appeals are expert opinions and product comparison.

Celebrity ads use one of the following two categories of spokesperson:

- **Celebrity authorities** are experts in a particular field. Advertisers hope that audiences will transfer the admiration they have for the person to the product. For example, a famous athlete might endorse a particular energy drink. The company selling the drink wants people to think it must work, since an athlete wouldn't want an energy drink that didn't help her perform well.
- **Celebrity spokespeople** are famous people who endorse a product. Advertisers hope that audiences will associate the product with the celebrity.

Product comparison is comparing between a product and its competition. Often mentioned by name, the competing product is portrayed as inferior. The intended effect is for people to question the quality of the competing product and to believe the featured product is better.

6 Elements of Design

The design of a media message is just as important as the words are in conveying the message. Like words, visuals are used to persuade, inform, and entertain.

Graphics and images, such as charts, diagrams, maps, timelines, photographs, illustrations, and symbols, present information that can be quickly and easily understood. The following basic elements are used to give meaning to visuals:

Color can be used to highlight important elements such as headlines and subheads. It can also create mood, because many colors have strong emotional or psychological impacts on the reader or viewer. For example, warm colors are often associated with happiness and comfort. Cool colors are often associated with feelings of peace and contentment or sometimes with sadness.

Lines—strokes or marks—can be thick or thin, long or short, and smooth or jagged. They can focus attention and create a feeling of depth. They can frame an object. They can also direct a viewer's eye or create a sense of motion.

Texture is the surface quality or appearance of an object. For example, an object's texture can be rough, wet, or shiny. Texture can be used to create contrast. It can also be used to make an object look "real." For example, wallpaper patterns can create a sense of depth, smoothness, or roughness, even though the texture is only visual and cannot be felt.

MEDIA HANDBOOK R93

Shape is the external outline of an object. Shapes can be used to symbolize living things or geometric objects. They can emphasize visual elements and add interest. Shapes can symbolize ideas.

Notice how this movie poster uses design elements.

Lines Vertical lines guide the reader's eye upward to the lighted windows. This also helps create the visual perspective of a small person looking up at the large building.

Color Dark blues and grays suggest that the film may tell a scary story.

Shape The angular shapes and the placement of the two bright yellow windows combine to make the house look like a face with an evil grin.

7 Evaluating Media Messages

By looking closely at media products, you can see how their messages influence your opinions and your buying habits. Here are six questions to ask about any media message:

Who made—and who sponsored—this message, and for what purpose? The source of the message is a clue to its purpose. If the source of the message is a private company, that company may be trying to sell you a product. If the source is a government agency, that agency may be trying to promote a program or particular point of view. To discover the purpose, think about why its creator paid for and produced the message.

Who is the target audience and how is the message specifically tailored to it? Think about the age group, ethnic group, gender, and/or profession the message is targeting. Decide how it relates to you.

What are the different techniques used to inform, persuade, entertain, and attract attention? Analyze the elements, such as humor, music, special effects, and graphics, that have been used to create the message. Think about how visual and sound effects, such as symbols, color, photographs, words, and music, support the purpose behind the message.

What messages are communicated (and/or implied) about certain people, places, events, behaviors, lifestyles, and so forth? The media try to influence who we are, what we believe in, how we view things, and what values we hold. Look or listen closely to determine whether certain types of behavior are being depicted and if judgments or values are communicated through those behaviors. What are the biases in the message?

How current, accurate, and believable is the information in this message? Think about the reputation of the source. Note the broadcast or publication date of the message and whether the message might change quickly. If a report or account is not supported by facts, authoritative sources, or eyewitness accounts, you should question the message.

What is left out of this message that might be important to know? Think about what the message is asking you to believe. Also think about what questions come to mind as you watch, read, or listen to the message.

R94 MEDIA HANDBOOK

Strategies and Practice for State and Standardized Tests

The test items in this section are modeled after test formats that are used on many state and standardized tests. The strategies presented here will help you prepare for these tests. This section offers general test-taking strategies and tips for answering multiple-choice items, as well as short-response and extended-response questions in critical reading and writing. It also includes guidelines and samples for essay writing. For each test, read the tips in the margin. Then apply the tips to the practice items. You can also apply the tips to Assessment Practice Tests in this book.

1 General Test-Taking Strategies

- Arrive on time and be prepared. Be sure to bring either sharpened pencils with erasers or pens—whichever you are told to bring.
- If you have any questions, ask them before the test begins. Make sure you understand the test procedures, the timing, and the rules.
- Read the test directions carefully. Look at the passages and questions to get an overview of what is expected.
- Tackle the questions one at a time rather than thinking about the whole test.
- Look for main ideas as you read passages. They are often stated at the beginning or the end of a paragraph. Sometimes the main idea is implied.
- Refer back to the reading selections as needed. For example, if a question asks about an author's attitude, you might have to reread a passage for clues.
- If you are not sure of your answer, make a logical guess. You can often arrive at the correct answer by reasoning and eliminating wrong answers.
- As you fill in answers on your answer sheet, make sure you match each test item to its numbered space on the answer sheet.
- Don't look for patterns in the positions of correct choices.
- Only change an answer if you are sure your original choice is incorrect. If you do change an answer, erase your original choice neatly and thoroughly.
- Check your answers and reread your essay.

TEST—TAKING HANDBOOK R95

2 Critical Reading

As you advance into high school, you will be exposed to different types of writing, both fiction and nonfiction. You will read novels, persuasive essays, poems, historical documents, and scientific or technical information. Tests will measure your ability to read and analyze these kinds of writings. Test selections can range in length from 100 words to 500 or 600 words.

Directions: Read the selection and then answer the questions on the following page.

SELECTION

Walt has walked all the fourteen years of his life in suntanned, moose-hide moccasins, and he can go to the Indian camps and "talk big" with the men, and trade calico and beads with them for their precious furs. He can make bread without baking powder, yeast, or hops, shoot a moose at three hundred yards, and drive the wild wolf dogs fifty miles a day on the packed trail.

Last of all, he has a good heart, and is not afraid of the darkness and loneliness, of man or beast or thing. His father is a good man, strong and brave, and Walt is growing up like him.

Walt was born a thousand miles or so down the Yukon, in a trading post below the Ramparts. After his mother died, his father and he came up on the river, step by step, from camp to camp, till now they are settled down on the Mazy May Creek in the Klondike country. Last year they and several others had spent much toil and time on the Mazy May, and endured great hardships; the creek, in turn, was just beginning to show up its richness and to reward them for their heavy labor. But with the news of their discoveries, strange men began to come and go through the short days and long nights, and many unjust things they did to the men who had worked so long upon the creek.

Si Hartman had gone away on a moose hunt, to return and find new stakes driven and his claim jumped. George Lukens and his brother had lost their claims in a like manner, having delayed too long on the way to Dawson to record them. In short, it was the old story, and quite a number of the earnest, industrious prospectors had suffered similar losses.

But Walt Masters's father had recorded his claim at the start, so Walt had nothing to fear now that his father had gone on a short trip up the White River prospecting for quartz. Walt was well able to stay by himself in the cabin, cook his three meals a day, and look after things. Not only did he look after his father's claim, but he had agreed to keep an eye on the adjoining one of Loren Hall, who had started for Dawson to record it.

Loren Hall was an old man, and he had no dogs, so he had to travel very slowly. After he had been gone some time, word came up the river that he had broken through the ice at Rosebud Creek and frozen his feet so badly that he would not be able to travel for a couple of weeks. Then Walt Masters received the news that old Loren was nearly all right again, and about to move on afoot for Dawson as fast as a weakened man could.

Tips: Reading Text

1. Before reading a passage, skim the questions that follow it to help you focus your reading.
2. Look for key ideas as you read. Competition and fairness are key ideas in this passage.
3. Make predictions. The passage tells you that Walt is brave, strong, and resourceful. You can predict that he will be all right while his father and Loren Hall are gone.
4. Pay attention to the connotation of words. For example, the word *stampede* in line 37 suggests something frenzied and out of control. The word is usually applied to a herd of wild animals. Here, its connotation helps describe the ruthless newcomers to the Klondike country.

R96 TEST—TAKING HANDBOOK

Walt was worried, however; the claim was liable to be jumped at any moment because of the delay, and a fresh stampede had started in on Mazy May. He did not like the looks of the newcomers, and one day, when five of them came by with crack dog teams and the lightest of camping outfits, he could see they were prepared to make speed, and resolved to keep an eye on them. So he locked up the cabin and followed them, being at the same time careful to remain hidden. ❹

—from "The King of Mazy May" by Jack London

Directions: Answer these questions about the selection from "The King of Mazy May."

❶ stem

1. What can you infer about life in the Klondike from the description in lines 1–18?
   - **A** People need to use many skills to survive.
   - **B** The Klondike is a lonely place for most people.
   - **C** The competition for land makes people dishonest.
   - **D** Families purchase all of their supplies at trading posts.

2. The author characterizes Walt by presenting ❷
   - **A** a description of his physical appearance
   - **B** the narrator's direct comments about him
   - **C** Walt's thoughts and actions
   - **D** other characters' opinions of him.

3. The main conflict in this passage involves
   - **A** finding a place to trade rare furs
   - **B** traveling to town in dangerous weather
   - **C** protecting land from prospecting thieves
   - **D** hunting for moose along Mazy May Creek

❸ choices

4. Which is an effect of Loren Hall's accident? ❹
   - **A** Walt must stay alone in the cabin.
   - **B** Loren is delayed on his way to Dawson.
   - **C** Loren returns home instead of going to Dawson. ❺
   - **D** The Masters's claim is jumped.

Tips: Multiple Choice

A multiple-choice question consists of a stem and a set of choices. The stem is in the form of a question or an incomplete sentence. One of the choices correctly answers the question or completes the sentence. Many tests offer four answer choices, but no matter how many choices are given, you can use the same strategies to guide you to the best answer.

❶ Read the stem carefully and try to answer the question before you look at the choices.

❷ Pay attention to key words in the stem. They may direct you to the correct answer. In question 2, the word *characterizes* tells you to think about how the author develops Walt's character.

❸ Read all of the choices before deciding on an answer. In question 3, you might decide to stop at choice B, because Loren Hall falls through the ice on the way to town. The main conflict, however, is about protecting land, not about Hall's difficult trip.

❹ Some questions ask you to identify cause-and-effect relationships.

❺ After reading all of the choices, eliminate any that you know are incorrect. In question 4, you can safely reject choice C, because the passage states that Loren was going to continue on to Dawson .

Answers: **1.** C, **2.** B, **3.** C, **4.** B

TEST—TAKING HANDBOOK **R97**

3 Vocabulary

Most standardized tests include items that ask about the meanings of words. Some questions might refer to a passage you just read, while others might provide a sentence or paragraph followed by the answer choices.

1. Which of the following words from the passage on pages R96–R97 has a negative connotation? ❶

A calico (line 3)
B toil (line 13)
C industrious (line 23)
D careful (line 39)

2. Which word from the passage might include the Latin root meaning "hard"?

A endured (line 13) ❷
B earnest (line 23)
C adjoining (line 28)
D liable (line 36)

3. In line 28 of the passage, the idiom *keep an eye on* means ❸

A report to
B think about
C watch over
D measure

4. Read this dictionary entry for the word *claim*. Which definition represents the meaning of *claim* as used in the passage?

DEFINITION

v. **1.** To demand or ask for. **2.** To state to be true; assert. *n.* **1.** A demand for something as due. **2.** Something claimed in a legal manner, especially a tract of public land. **3.** A statement of something as true.

A *v.* meaning 1 ❹
B *n.* meaning 1
C *n.* meaning 2
D *n.* meaning 3

Tips: Word Meaning

❶ Connotation is the suggestion or feeling a word carries beyond its literal meaning. *Work* is a neutral word. *Effort* is a more positive word for work, but the word *toil* has a negative connotation.

❷ If you don't know the exact meaning of a word, look for clues in nearby sentences. For the word *endured* in line 13, read the description in the surrounding paragraph. Choice A is the best answer, because the passage is describing hard work and the difficult times the characters lived through.

❸ An idiom is an expression that has a meaning different from the meanings of its individual words. Since Walt is not literally keeping one of his eyes at Loren's claim, you can use context clues to help you figure out the meaning of the idiom *keep an eye on*. Some idioms can be found in the dictionary.

❹ Eliminate any answers that are not the same part of speech as the meaning of the word in the passage. *Claim* is used as a noun in the passsage, so you can rule out answer choice A.

Answers: **1.** B, **2.** A, **3.** C, **4.** C

R98 TEST–TAKING HANDBOOK

4 Writing and Grammar

You will be asked to write many essays and research papers in middle school and high school. When it comes to writing, good ideas aren't enough. You need to know how to express them. That requires knowledge of English grammar, sentence structure, and usage. To measure that skill, many standardized tests ask you to identify errors or to improve sentences and paragraphs.

Directions: Read this passage and then answer the questions.

PASSAGE

❶ (1) Jack London wrote many stories about life in the Yukon. (2) He's not the only person who loves rough terrain and cold weather. (3) Each year adventurous dog-sled racers gather in Anchorage, Alaska, for the Iditarod. (4) This race covers 1,150 miles through forests, mountains, and coastlines. (5) The racers, called mushers, steer they're teams of 12 to 16 dogs from start to finish, taking only a few breaks. (6) The dogs wear special boots <u>for paw protection from cuts and frostbite</u>. (7) The first musher to reach the Yukon River checkpoint is served a seven-course dinner. (8) I hope they feed the dogs, too!

1. The correct coordinating conjunction to join sentences 1 and 2 is

❷ **A** but
B for
C or
D so

2. What change, if any, should be made to sentence 5?

❸ **A** Change *steer* to *steers.*
B Change *they're* to *their.*
C Change *teams* to *team.*
D Make no change.

❹ **3.** What is the best way to rewrite the underlined part of sentence 6?

A for cuts and frostbite protection on paws
B to protect their paws from cuts and frostbite
C for the protection of paws from cuts and frostbite
D in order to protect from cuts and frostbite on paws

❺ **4.** What change, if any, should be made to sentence 7?

A Change *reach* to *reaches.*
B Change *is* to *are.*
C Change *served* to *serving.*
D Make no change. ❻

Tips: Grammar

1. Read the entire passage to grasp its overall meaning. Pay particular attention to any underlined parts.
2. If you are asked to combine sentences, think about how the ideas relate to each other. Use the coordinating conjunction *or* to introduce a choice. The words *for* or *so* indicate cause and effect. The word *but* expresses contrasting ideas. When you understand the connection between the two sentences, you will know which word best joins them.
3. Some items will test your knowledge of commonly confused words. Read sentences carefully to determine how each word is used before deciding which choice is best.
4. Before choosing a revision, read through all of the choices to decide which one is best. Your selection should produce a sentence that is grammatically correct.
5. Some items will test your knowledge of language conventions. Make sure that pronouns agree with antecedents and that verbs agree with subjects.
6. In test item 4, choice D says, "Make no change." Choose this answer only if the sentence is correct as it is originally written.

Answers: 1. A, **2.** B, **3.** B, **4.** D

TEST—TAKING HANDBOOK R99

5 Responding to Writing Prompts

Not all tests are multiple choice. Sometimes you have to develop your ideas into a paragraph or a short essay. You might be asked to interpret, summarize, or react to a reading selection.

Directions: Reread the selection from "The King of Mazy May" on pages R96–R97 and follow the directions for the short and extended responses.

SHORT RESPONSE

Write a well-organized paragraph comparing and contrasting the prospectors and the men of the "stampede."

SAMPLE SHORT RESPONSE

The prospectors of Mazy May, such as Walt's father and Loren Hall, couldn't be more different from the claim-jumping stampeders. (1) The prospectors "spent much toil and time" looking for gold, willing to keep working for as long as it took. The stampeders, on the other hand, seemed not to arrive until after the prospectors had worked for a year to set up their claims. (2) The stampeders plan to steal the claims and profit from the prospectors' hard work. Walt, who risks danger to protect his neighbor's claim, is the exact opposite of the "unjust" stampeders.

EXTENDED RESPONSE

Discuss in two or three paragraphs the effects of the setting in the selection from "The King of Mazy May."

SAMPLE EXTENDED RESPONSE

The setting in "The King of Mazy May"—Klondike country—affects not only the story's plot, but also its characters and conflict.

(3) Walt is a product of his setting. His whole life, he has lived and worked in the cold weather and lonely conditions of the region. As a result, he's learned to be a good hunter and dog driver. He's become self-reliant because his father must leave on prospecting trips. The skills Walt develops in the Klondike are what make him able to protect his neighbor's claim. (4)

The setting also presents specific challenges that affect the story's plot and conflict. (3) For example, the cold water of Rosebud Creek is what delays Loren Hall on his way to Dawson, and the "short days and long nights" seem to encourage the claim jumpers. Finally, the land along the creek is what brings both the prospectors and the thieves to the area in the first place.

Tips: Responding to Writing Prompts

1. Short-response prompts are often fact-based rather than interpretive. Get right to the point in your answer, and stick to the facts.
2. Make sure that you write about the assigned topic. Support your answer with details from the passage, such as a quotation, a paraphrase, or an example.
3. When you are writing an extended response, build your paragraphs around clear topic sentences that will pull your ideas together.
4. If you are asked to interpret a passage, don't just copy the author's words. Try to express the ideas in your own words. Express your ideas clearly so that the reader understands your viewpoint.
5. Proofread your response for errors in capitalization, punctuation, spelling, or grammar.

R100 TEST–TAKING HANDBOOK

6 Writing an Essay

Many tests will ask you to read a prompt and write an essay in response to it. You might be asked to write a narrative, persuasive, or expository essay. You might be asked to write a story, summarize an article, or respond to a piece of writing. It is important to read the prompt carefully and look for direction words that tell you what to write about. Because of the time constraints, an impromptu essay will not be polished. It will represent a first draft. Even so, it should be complete. Essays are scored on the following criteria:

- **Focus** Establish a point of view on your topic in the opening paragraph. Stay with that topic throughout the essay.
- **Organization** Maintain a logical progression of ideas.
- **Support for ideas** Use details and examples to develop an argument or line of thinking.
- **Style/word choice** Use words accurately and vary sentence structure.
- **Grammar** Use standard English and proofread for errors.

Writing Prompt

In 1961, the chairman of the Federal Communications Commission called television programming "a vast wasteland." Many people still feel we would be better off without television. Write a persuasive essay of four or five paragraphs supporting or rejecting this idea.

SAMPLE PERSUASIVE ESSAY

(1) I don't agree that television is "a vast wasteland." A wasteland is an ugly place where nothing grows. So, if television were only a wasteland, that would mean that it never offered people anything beautiful or exciting. It would mean that there was no information or entertainment of value that people could get from watching television programs, and that just isn't the case.

It's true that there are many low-quality programs on TV. These programs don't teach us anything. Some shows, such as soap operas, don't show people or their lives the way they actually are. They exaggerate situations and rarely offer a positive or important message.

Other programs, however, offer interesting and important information about nature, science, history, the arts, sports, or current events. These educational and exciting programs can help us grow and improve ourselves. (2)

People who don't agree with me might say that TV turns us into couch potatoes. (3) Many people do just sit in front of the television for hours, watching whatever is on, whether it's good or bad. My answer to that point of view is that we have to be responsible in choosing the programs we watch. If viewers stopped watching bad shows, those shows would eventually be canceled.

In conclusion, TV can be worthwhile if we make good decisions about its use. We just have to use our heads and take charge of the remote control. (4)

Tips: Writing an Essay

Before you begin writing, take a minute or two to gather your thoughts. You don't need to prepare a complete outline, but write the main points you want to make. In the essay here on television, program quality and personal responsibility are key issues.

1. When writing a persuasive essay, state your point of view in the introduction.
2. Facts and examples make your writing come to life. Use them in the body of your essay to clarify your points and to strengthen your arguments. The writer of this essay uses examples to illustrate some possible benefits of television.
3. Try to consider the opposing viewpoint and respond to it. In the sample essay, the student notes that some people think TV "turns us into couch potatoes." Her response is that people should be responsible about what they watch.
4. Make sure your essay has a conclusion, even if it's just a single sentence. A conclusion pulls your ideas together and lets the reader know you have finished.
5. Allow time to reread what you have written. If you have to make a correction, do so neatly and legibly.

TEST—TAKING HANDBOOK R101

Act An act is a major division within a play, similar to a chapter in a book. Each act may be further divided into smaller sections, called scenes. Plays can have as many as five acts. *The Diary of Anne Frank* has two acts.

See page 486.

Adventure Story An adventure story is a literary work in which action is the main element. An adventure novel usually focuses on a main character who is on a mission and is facing many challenges and choices.

Alliteration Alliteration is the repetition of consonant sounds at the beginning of words. Note the repetition of the *s* sound in these lines.

> **Say to them,**
> **say to the down-keepers,**
> **the sun-slappers,**
> **the self-soilers,**
> **—Gwendolyn Brooks, "Speech to the Young: Speech to the Progress-Toward"**

See page 612.
See also **Consonance.**

Allusion An allusion is a reference to a famous person, place, event, or work of literature. In "The Drummer Boy of Shiloh" by Ray Bradbury, the general makes an allusion to the poet Henry Wadsworth Longfellow.

See page 322.

Analogy An analogy is a point-by-point comparison between two things that are alike in some respect. Often, writers use analogies in nonfiction to explain unfamiliar subjects or ideas in terms of familiar ones.

See also **Extended Metaphor; Metaphor; Simile.**

Anecdote An anecdote is a brief account of an interesting incident or event that is usually intended to entertain or make a point. "O. Henry's Manuscript Found in an Attic" is an example of an anecdote.

See page 58.

Antagonist The antagonist is a force working against the protagonist, or main character, in a story, play, or novel. The antagonist is usually another character but can be a force of nature, society itself, or an internal force within the main character. In Yoshiko Uchida's retelling of "The Wise Old Woman," the cruel young lord is the antagonist.

See page 466.
See also **Protagonist.**

Assonance Assonance is the repetition of vowel sounds within nonrhyming words. An example of assonance is the repetition of the short *a* sound in the following line.

> **It's had tacks in it,**
> **—Langston Hughes, "Mother to Son"**

Author's Perspective An author's perspective is the unique combination of ideas, values, feelings, and beliefs that influences the way the writer looks at a topic. Tone, or attitude, often reveals an author's perspective. Gary Soto writes "One Last Time" from a perspective that reflects his family's history of working in the fields and his teenage desire for status and acceptance.

See page 816.
See also **Author's Purpose; Tone.**

Author's Purpose A writer usually writes for one or more of these purposes: to express thoughts or feelings, to inform or explain, to persuade, and to entertain. For example, in "The Sanctuary of School," Lynda Barry's purpose is to persuade Americans to support public schools.

See also **Author's Perspective.**

Autobiography An autobiography is a writer's account of his or her own life. In almost every case, it is told from the first-person point of view. Generally, an autobiography focuses on the most significant events and people in the writer's life over a period of time. Barack Obama's *Dreams from My Father* is an autobiography.

See page 830.
See also **Memoir.**

Ballad A ballad is a type of narrative poem that tells a story and was originally meant to be sung or recited. Because it tells a story, a ballad has a setting, a plot, and characters. Traditional ballads are written in four-line stanzas with regular rhythm and rhyme. Folk ballads were composed orally and handed down by word of mouth. These ballads usually tell about ordinary people who have unusual adventures or perform daring deeds. A literary ballad is a poem written by a poet in imitation of the form and content of a folk ballad. "Boots of Spanish Leather" is an example of a literary ballad.

Blank Verse Blank verse is unrhymed poetry written in iambic pentameter. That is, each line of blank verse has five pairs of syllables. In most pairs, an unstressed syllable is followed by a stressed syllable. The most versatile of poetic

R102 GLOSSARY OF LITERARY TERMS

forms, blank verse imitates the natural rhythms of English speech. Much of Shakespeare's drama is in blank verse.

> **This day is call'd the feast of Crispian:**
> **He that outlives this day, and comes safe home,**
> **Will stand a' tiptoe when this day is named,**
> **—William Shakespeare, "St. Crispian's Day Speech"**

Biography A biography is the true account of a person's life, written by another person. As such, biographies are usually told from a third-person point of view. The writer of a biography usually researches his or her subject in order to present accurate information. The best biographers strive for honesty and balance in their accounts of their subjects' lives. Ann Petry's *Harriet Tubman: Conductor on the Underground Railroad* is an example of a biography.
See page 258.

Cast of Characters In the script of a play, a cast of characters is a list of all the characters in the play, usually in order of appearance. It may include a brief description of each character.

Character Characters are the people, animals, or imaginary creatures who take part in the action of a work of literature. Like real people, characters display certain qualities, or character traits, that develop and change over time, and they usually have motivations, or reasons, for their behaviors.

Main character: Main characters are the most important characters in literary works. Generally, the plot of a short story focuses on one main character, but a novel may have several main characters.

Minor characters: The less important characters in a literary work are known as minor characters. The story is not centered on them, but they help carry out the action of the story and help the reader learn more about the main character.

Dynamic character: A dynamic character is one who undergoes important changes as a plot unfolds. The changes occur because of the character's actions and experiences in the story. The changes are usually internal and may be good or bad. Main characters are usually, though not always, dynamic.

Static character: A static character is one who remains the same throughout a story. The character may experience events and have interactions with other characters, but he or she is not changed because of them.

See pages 162, 179, 188, 238.
See also **Characterization; Character Traits.**

Characterization The way a writer creates and develops characters is known as characterization. There are four basic methods of characterization:

- The writer may make direct comments about a character through the voice of the narrator.
- The writer may describe the character's physical appearance.
- The writer may present the character's own thoughts, speech, and actions.
- The writer may present thoughts, speech, and actions of other characters.

See pages 258, 282.
See also **Character; Character Traits.**

Character Traits Character traits are the qualities shown by a character. Traits may be physical (brown eyes) or expressions of personality (shyness). Writers reveal the traits of their characters through methods of characterization. Sometimes writers directly state a character's traits, but more often readers need to infer traits from a character's words, actions, thoughts, appearance, and relationships. Examples of words that describe traits include *courageous, humble, generous,* and *wild.*

Climax The climax stage is the point of greatest interest in a story or play. The climax usually occurs toward the end of a story, after the reader has understood the conflict and become emotionally involved with the characters. At the climax, the conflict is resolved and the outcome of the plot usually becomes clear. For example, in Toni Cade Bambara's story "Raymond's Run," the climax occurs when Squeaky realizes that she doesn't have to win the race to prove her running skills; she can help her brother Raymond become a great runner.
See pages 24, 32.
See also **Plot.**

Comedy A comedy is a dramatic work that is light and often humorous in tone, usually ending happily with a peaceful resolution of the main conflict.

Conflict A conflict is a struggle between opposing forces. Almost every story has a main conflict—a conflict that is the story's focus. An external conflict involves a character who struggles against a force outside him- or herself, such as nature, a physical obstacle, or another character. An internal conflict is one that occurs within a character. A cultural conflict is a struggle that arises because of differing values, customs, or circumstances between groups of people.

GLOSSARY OF LITERARY TERMS R103

Examples: In O. Henry's "The Ransom of Red Chief," the kidnappers are in conflict with the boy they take captive. In Laurence Yep's memoir "The Great Rat Hunt," the young Yep is torn between wanting to prove his bravery by helping his father and wanting to avoid the rat by staying with his mother. In "Out of Bounds," Rohan's family and neighbors blame the new squatters for robberies, and Rohan's parents tell him not to make contact with the squatters.

See pages 46, 62, 118.

See also **Plot.**

Connotation A word's connotations are the ideas and feelings associated with the word, as opposed to its dictionary definition. For example, the word *mother,* in addition to its basic meaning ("a female parent"), has connotations of love, warmth, and security.

Consonance Consonance is the repetition of consonant sounds within and at the end of words, as in "lonely afternoon." Consonance is unlike rhyme in that the vowel sounds preceding or following the repeated consonant sounds differ. Consonance is often used together with alliteration, assonance, and rhyme to create a musical quality, to emphasize certain words, or to unify a poem.

See also **Alliteration.**

Couplet A couplet is a rhymed pair of lines. A couplet may be written in any rhythmic pattern.

> **Macavity, Macavity, there's no one like Macavity,**
> **He's broken every human law, he breaks the law**
> **of gravity.**
> **—T. S. Eliot, "Macavity: The Mystery Cat"**

See also **Stanza.**

Critical Essay *See* **Essay.**

Denotation A word's denotation is its dictionary definition.

See also **Connotation.**

Description Description is writing that helps a reader to picture events, objects, and characters. To create descriptions, writers often use imagery—words and phrases that appeal to the reader's senses.

Dialect A dialect is a form of a language that is spoken in a particular place or by a particular group of people. Dialects may feature unique pronunciations, vocabulary, and grammar. For example, in "The Treasure of Lemon Brown" by Walter Dean Myers, Lemon Brown speaks in a dialect that reflects his background as an African-American blues musician. His dialect includes informal grammar and nonstandard word forms.

Dialogue Dialogue is written conversation between two or more characters. Writers use dialogue to bring characters to life and to give readers insights into the characters' qualities, traits, and reactions to other characters. In fiction, dialogue is usually set off with quotation marks. In drama, stories are told primarily through dialogue.

Diary A diary is a daily record of a writer's thoughts, experiences, and feelings. As such, it is a type of autobiographical writing. The terms *diary* and *journal* are often used to mean the same thing.

See page 520.

Drama A drama, or play, is a form of literature meant to be performed by actors in front of an audience. In a drama, the characters' dialogue and actions tell the story. The written form of a play is known as a script. A script usually includes dialogue, a cast of characters, and stage directions that give instructions about performing the drama. The person who writes the drama is known as the playwright or dramatist.

Dramatic Irony *See* **Irony.**

Dynamic Character *See* **Character.**

Elegy An elegy is an extended meditative poem in which the speaker reflects on death—often in tribute to a person who has died recently—or on an equally serious subject. Most elegies are written in formal, dignified language and are serious in tone.

Epic An epic is a long narrative poem on a serious subject, presented in an elevated or formal style. It traces the adventures of a great hero whose actions reflect the ideals and values of a nation or race. Epics address universal concerns, such as good and evil, life and death, and sin and redemption. Henry Wadsworth Longfellow's *The Song of Hiawatha* is an example of an epic. The poet Homer was responsible for handing down two famous epics from ancient Greece, the *Iliad* and the *Odyssey.*

Essay An essay is a short work of nonfiction that deals with a single subject. There are many types of essays. An expository essay presents or explains information and ideas. A personal essay usually reflects the writer's experiences, feelings, and personality. A persuasive essay attempts to convince the reader to adopt a certain viewpoint. A critical essay evaluates a situation or a work of art.

See pages 718, 994.

R104 GLOSSARY OF LITERARY TERMS

Exaggeration An extreme overstatement of an idea is called an exaggeration. It is often used for purposes of emphasis or humor. In "Pecos Bill," Mary Pope Osborne exaggerates Bill's toughness and wild behavior in order to create a humorous, memorable impression of the character.

Exposition Exposition is the first stage of a typical story plot. The exposition provides important background information and introduces the setting and the important characters. The conflict the characters face may also be introduced in the exposition, or it may be introduced later, in the rising action.
See pages 24, 32.
See also **Plot.**

Expository Essay *See* **Essay.**

Extended Metaphor An extended metaphor is a figure of speech that compares two essentially unlike things at some length and in several ways. It does not contain the word *like* or *as.* For example, in "O Captain! My Captain!" Walt Whitman compares Abraham Lincoln to a ship's captain and the Civil War to a ship's journey. The comparison begins in the following lines and continues throughout the poem.

> **O Captain! my Captain! our fearful trip is done,**
> **The ship has weather'd every rack, the prize we sought is won,**
> **The port is near, the bells I hear, the people all exulting,**
> **While follow eyes the steady keel, the vessel grim and daring;**
> **—Walt Whitman, "O Captain! My Captain!"**

See also **Metaphor.**

External Conflict *See* **Conflict.**

Fable A fable is a brief tale told to illustrate a moral or teach a lesson. Often the moral of a fable appears in a distinct and memorable statement near the tale's beginning or end.
See also **Moral.**

Falling Action The falling action is the stage of the plot in which the story begins to draw to a close. The falling action comes after the climax and before the resolution. Events in the falling action show the results of the important decision or action that happened at the climax. Tension eases as the falling action begins; however, the final outcome of the story is not yet fully worked out at this stage.
See page 24, 32.
See also **Climax; Plot.**

Fantasy Fantasy is a type of fiction that is highly imaginative and portrays events, settings, or characters that are unrealistic. The setting might be a nonexistent world, the plot might involve magic or the supernatural, and the characters might have superhuman powers.

Farce Farce is a type of exaggerated comedy that features an absurd plot, ridiculous situations, and humorous dialogue. The main purpose of a farce is to keep an audience laughing. Comic devices typically used in farces include mistaken identity, wordplay (such as puns and double meanings), and exaggeration.

Fiction Fiction is prose writing that tells an imaginary story. The writer of a fictional work might invent all the events and characters or might base parts of the story on real people and events. The basic elements of fiction are plot, character, setting, and theme. Fiction includes both short stories and novels.
See also **Novel; Short Story.**

Figurative Language Figurative language is language that communicates meanings beyond the literal meanings of words. In figurative language, words are often used to symbolize ideas and concepts they would not otherwise be associated with. Writers use figurative language to create effects, to emphasize ideas, and to evoke emotions. Simile, metaphor, extended metaphor, hyperbole, and personification are examples of figurative language.
See pages 576, 582, 588.
See also **Hyperbole; Metaphor; Onomatopoeia; Personification; Simile.**

First-Person Point of View *See* **Point of View.**

Flashback In a literary work, a flashback is an interruption of the action to present events that took place at an earlier time. A flashback provides information that can help a reader better understand a character's current situation.
Example: In "Clean Sweep," Joan Bauer uses flashback to reveal what happened on the day the narrator's father died.

Foil A foil is a character who provides a striking contrast to another character. By using a foil, a writer can call attention to certain traits possessed by a main character or simply enhance a character by contrast. In Joseph Bruchac's "The Snapping Turtle" the boys at the rez provide a foil to the narrator.

Folklore The traditions, customs, and stories that are passed down within a culture are known as its folklore. Folklore includes various types of literature, such as legends, folk tales, myths, trickster tales, and fables.
See also **Fable; Folk Tale; Myth.**

GLOSSARY OF LITERARY TERMS R105

Folk Tale A folk tale is a story that has been passed from generation to generation by word of mouth. Folk tales may be set in the distant past and involve supernatural events. The characters in them may be animals, people, or superhuman beings. "The Wise Old Woman" is an example of a folk tale.

Foreshadowing Foreshadowing occurs when a writer provides hints that suggest future events in a story. Foreshadowing creates suspense and makes readers eager to find out what will happen. For example, in W. W. Jacob's story "The Monkey's Paw," the sergeant-major's warnings about the paw foreshadow the tragedy that wishing upon it brings about.

Form The structure or organization of a work of writing is often called its form. The form of a poem includes the arrangement of its words and lines on the page.

Free Verse Free verse is poetry that does not contain regular patterns of rhythm or rhyme. The lines in free verse often flow more naturally than do rhymed, metrical lines and therefore achieve a rhythm more like that of everyday speech. Although free verse lacks conventional meter, it may contain various rhythmic and sound effects, such as repetitions of syllables or words. Free verse can be used for a variety of subjects. Billy Collins's poem "Introduction to Poetry" is an example of free verse.

See pages 586, 596.

See also **Meter; Rhyme.**

Genre The term *genre* refers to a category in which a work of literature is classified. The major genres in literature are fiction, nonfiction, poetry, and drama.

Hero A hero is a main character or protagonist in a story. In older literary works, heroes tend to be better than ordinary humans. They are typically courageous, strong, honorable, and intelligent. They are protectors of society who hold back the forces of evil and fight to make the world a better place. In modern literature, a hero may simply be the most important character in a story. Such a hero is often an ordinary person with ordinary problems.

Historical Context The historical context of a literary work refers to the social conditions that inspired or influenced its creation. To understand and appreciate certain works, the reader must relate them to particular events in history.

Example: Walt Whitman wrote his poem "O Captain! My Captain!" in 1865 in response to the assassination of Abraham Lincoln.

See pages 726, 760, 854.

Historical Dramas Historical dramas are plays that take place in the past and are based on real events. In many of these plays, the characters are also based on real historical figures. The dialogue and the action, however, are mostly created by the playwright.

Historical Fiction A short story or a novel can be called historical fiction when it is set in the past and includes real places and real events of historical importance. "The Drummer Boy of Shiloh" by Ray Bradbury is an example of historical fiction.

See pages 316, 374.

Humor Humor is a quality that provokes laughter or amusement. Writers create humor through exaggeration, amusing descriptions, irony, and witty and insightful dialogue. In "Roughing It," Mark Twain uses humor to tell about his poor work habits and the job he did as a reporter.

See page 704.

Hyperbole Hyperbole is a figure of speech in which the truth is exaggerated for emphasis or humorous effect.

Idiom An idiom is an expression that has a meaning different from the meaning of its individual words. For example, "to go to the dogs" is an idiom meaning "to go to ruin."

Imagery Imagery consists of descriptive words and phrases that re-create sensory experiences for the reader. Imagery usually appeals to one or more of the five senses—sight, hearing, smell, taste, and touch—to help the reader imagine exactly what is being described. Note the appeals to sight, taste, and touch in the following lines.

> **I say feed me.**
> **She serves me red prickly pear on a spiked cactus.**
>
> **I say tease me.**
> **She sprinkles raindrops in my face on a sunny day.**
> **—Pat Mora, "Mi Madre"**

See pages 416, 576, 729.

Internal Conflict *See* **Conflict.**

Interview An interview is a conversation conducted by a writer or reporter, in which facts or statements are elicited from another person, recorded, and then broadcast or published. "Interview with a Song Catcher" is based on a conversation between Brian Handwerk and Henrietta Yurchenco.

See page 908.

R106 GLOSSARY OF LITERARY TERMS

Irony Irony is a special kind of contrast between appearance and reality—usually one in which reality is the opposite of what it seems. One type of irony is **situational irony,** a contrast between what a reader or character expects and what actually exists or happens. For example, in O. Henry's "The Ransom of Red Chief," the kidnappers pay to get rid of the boy instead of collecting a ransom for him, as they had planned. Another type of irony is **dramatic irony,** where the reader or viewer knows something that a character does not know. In the myth "Pandora's Box," the readers know that Zeus created Pandora and her box in order to punish Prometheus, but Epimetheus isn't sure. **Verbal irony** exists when someone knowingly exaggerates or says one thing and means another. David Sedaris uses verbal irony in "Us and Them" when he says, "I could make friends if I wanted to. It just wasn't the right time." He actually means that he was unpopular.

See pages 59, 718, 728.

Journal *See* **Diary.**

Legend A legend is a story handed down from the past about a specific person, usually someone of heroic accomplishments. Legends usually have some basis in historical fact.

Limerick A limerick is a short, humorous poem composed of five lines. It usually has the rhyme scheme *aabba,* created by two rhyming couplets followed by a fifth line that rhymes with the first couplet. A limerick typically has a sing-song rhythm.

Limited Point of View *See* **Point of View.**

Line The line is the core unit of a poem. In poetry, line length is an essential element of the poem's meaning and rhythm. Line breaks, where a line of poetry ends, may coincide with grammatical units. However, a line break may also occur in the middle of a grammatical unit, therefore creating a meaningful pause or emphasis. Poets use a variety of line breaks to play with sense, grammar, and syntax and thereby create a wide range of effects.

Lyric Poetry A lyric poem is a short poem in which a single speaker expresses personal thoughts and feelings. Most poems other than dramatic and narrative poems are lyric poems. In ancient Greece, lyric poetry was meant to be sung. Modern lyrics are usually not intended for singing, but they are characterized by strong melodic rhythms. Lyric poetry has a variety of forms and covers many subjects, from love and death to everyday experiences. Langston Hughes's "Mother to Son" is an example of a lyric poem.

Memoir A memoir is a form of autobiographical writing in which a writer shares his or her personal experiences and observations of significant events or people. Often informal or even intimate in tone, memoirs usually give readers insight into the impact of historical events on people's lives. *"My First Free Summer"* by Julia Alvarez is a memoir.

See page 110.

See also **Autobiography.**

Metaphor A metaphor is a comparison of two things that are basically unlike but have some qualities in common. Unlike a simile, a metaphor does not contain the word *like* or *as.* In "Identity," the speaker of the poem compares himself to a "tall, ugly weed."

See pages 576, 582.

See also **Extended Metaphor; Figurative Language; Simile.**

Meter Meter is a regular pattern of stressed and unstressed syllables in a poem. The meter of a poem emphasizes the musical quality of the language. Each unit of meter, known as a foot, consists of one stressed syllable and one or two unstressed syllables. In representations of meter, a stressed syllable is indicated by the symbol (´); an unstressed syllable by the symbol (˘). The four basic types of metrical feet are the iamb, an unstressed syllable followed by a stressed syllable (˘´); the trochee, a stressed syllable followed by an unstressed syllable (´˘); the anapest, two unstressed syllables followed by a stressed syllable (˘˘´); and the dactyl, a stressed syllable followed by two unstressed syllables (´˘˘). Note the following example of stressed and unstressed syllables.

> **By the shores of Gitche Gumee,**
> **By the shining Big-Sea-Water,**
> **Stood the wigwam of Nokomis,**
> **Daughter of the Moon, Nokomis.**
> **—Henry Wadsworth Longfellow,** ***Song of Hiawatha***

See pages 636.

See also **Rhythm.**

Minor Character *See* **Character.**

Mood Mood is the feeling or atmosphere that a writer creates for the reader. Descriptive words, imagery, and figurative language all influence the mood of a work. In "The Monkey's Paw," W. W. Jacobs creates a mood of gloom, dread, and desperation.

See pages 310, 358.

See also **Tone.**

GLOSSARY OF LITERARY TERMS R107

Moral A moral is a lesson that a story teaches. A moral is often stated at the end of a fable. Other times, the moral is implied.

See also **Fable.**

Motivation *See* **Character.**

Myth A myth is a traditional story, usually concerning some superhuman being or unlikely event, that was once widely believed to be true. Frequently, myths were attempts to explain natural phenomena, such as solar and lunar eclipses or the cycle of the seasons. For some peoples, myths were both a kind of science and a religion. In addition, myths served as literature and entertainment, just as they do for modern-day audiences. "Pandora's Box" is an example of a myth from ancient Greece.

See page 454.

Narrative Nonfiction Narrative nonfiction is writing that reads much like fiction, except that the characters, setting, and events are based on real life. *The True and Terrifying Story of the Yellow Fever Epidemic of 1793* by Jim Murphy is an example of narrative nonfiction.

See page 938.

Narrative Poetry Poetry that tells a story is called narrative poetry. Like fiction, a narrative poem contains characters, a setting, and a plot. It might also contain such elements of poetry as rhyme, rhythm, imagery, and figurative language. "Paul Revere's Ride" by Henry Wadsworth Longfellow is an example of a narrative poem.

Narrator The narrator is the voice that tells a story. Sometimes the narrator is a character in the story. At other times, the narrator is an outside voice created by the writer. The narrator is not the same as the writer. An unreliable narrator is one who tells a story or interprets events in a way that makes readers doubt what he or she is saying. An unreliable narrator is usually a character in the story. The narrator may be unreliable for a number of different reasons. For example, the narrator may not have all the facts or may be too young to understand the situation.

See also **Point of View.**

Nonfiction Nonfiction is writing that tells about real people, places, and events. Unlike fiction, nonfiction is mainly written to convey factual information. Nonfiction includes a wide range of writing—newspaper articles, letters, essays, biographies, movie reviews, speeches, true-life adventure stories, advertising, and more.

Novel A novel is a long work of fiction. Like a short story, a novel is the product of a writer's imagination. Because a novel is considerably longer than a short story, a novelist can develop the characters and story line more thoroughly.

See also **Fiction.**

Ode An ode is a type of lyric poem that deals with serious themes, such as justice, truth, or beauty. Odes appeal to both the imagination and the intellect, and many commemorate events or praise people or elements of nature. Alexander Pope's example of this poetic form is "Ode on Solitude."

Omniscient Point of View *See* **Point of View.**

Onomatopoeia Onomatopoeia is the use of words whose sounds echo their meanings, such as *buzz, whisper, gargle,* and *murmur.* As a literary technique, onomatopoeia goes beyond the use of simple echoing words. Skilled writers, especially poets, choose words whose sounds intensify images and suggest meaning. In the following lines, onomatopoeia helps the reader imagine the crying infant and the soothing mother.

> **Stilled his fretful wail by saying,**
> **"Hush! the Naked Bear will hear thee!"**
> **Lulled him into slumber, singing,**
> **"Ewa-yea! my little owlet!**
> **—Henry Wadsworth Longfellow, *Song of Hiawatha***

Oral Literature Oral literature consists of stories that have been passed down by word of mouth from generation to generation. Oral literature includes folk tales, legends, and myths. In more recent times, some examples of oral literature have been written down or recorded so that the stories can be preserved.

Parallel Episodes Parallel episodes occur when elements of a plot are repeated several times in the course of a story. Fairy tales often employ parallel episodes, as in the examples of "Goldilocks and the Three Bears" and "The Three Little Pigs." The short story "Flowers for Algernon" also contains several parallel episodes.

Personal Essay *See* **Essay.**

Personification The giving of human qualities to an animal, object, or idea is known as personification. In "the lesson of the moth," for example, the speaker, a cockroach, and the moth are personified. They have conversations with each other as if they were human.

See page 588.

See also **Figurative Language.**

R108 GLOSSARY OF LITERARY TERMS

Persuasive Essay *See* **Essay.**

Play *See* **Drama.**

Playwright *See* **Drama.**

Plot The series of events in a story is called the plot. The plot usually centers on a conflict, or struggle, faced by the main character. The action that the characters take to solve the problem builds toward a climax in the story. At this point, or shortly afterward, the problem is solved and the story ends. Most story plots have five stages: exposition, rising action, climax, falling action, and resolution.

See pages 27, 32, 46.

See also **Climax; Exposition; Falling Action; Rising Action.**

Poetry Poetry is a type of literature in which words are carefully chosen and arranged to create certain effects. Poets use a variety of sound devices, imagery, and figurative language to express emotions and ideas.

See also **Alliteration; Assonance; Ballad; Free Verse; Imagery; Meter; Narrative Poetry; Rhyme; Rhythm; Stanza.**

Point of View *Point of view* refers to the method of narration used in a short story, novel, narrative poem, or work of nonfiction. In a work told from a **first-person point of view,** the narrator is a character in the story, as in "The Tell-Tale Heart" by Edgar Allan Poe. In a work told from a **third-person point of view,** the narrative voice is outside the action, not one of the characters. If a story is told from a **third-person omniscient,** or all-knowing, point of view, as in "The Lady, or the Tiger" by Frank R. Stockton, the narrator sees into the minds of all the characters. If events are related from a **third-person limited point of view,** as in Beverly Naidoo's "Out of Bounds," the narrator tells what only one character thinks, feels, and observes.

See pages 162, 168, 222.

See also **Narrator.**

Prop The word *prop,* originally an abbreviation of the word *property,* refers to any physical object that is used in a drama. In the play *The Diary of Anne Frank,* the props include Anne's diary and Mrs. Van Daan's fur coat.

Prose The word *prose* refers to all forms of writing that are not in verse form. The term may be used to describe very different forms of writing—short stories as well as essays, for example.

Protagonist A protagonist is the main character in a story, play, or novel. The protagonist is involved in the main conflict of the story. Usually, the protagonist undergoes changes as the plot runs its course. In "Flowers for Algernon" by Daniel Keyes, Charlie is the protagonist.

Radio Play A radio play is a drama that is written specifically to be broadcast over the radio. Because the audience is not meant to see a radio play, sound effects are often used to help listeners imagine the setting and the action. The stage directions in the play's script indicate the sound effects. *The Hitchhiker* by Lucille Fletcher is an example of a radio play.

Recurring Theme *See* **Theme.**

Repetition Repetition is a technique in which a sound, word, phrase, or line is repeated for emphasis or unity. Repetition often helps to reinforce meaning and create an appealing rhythm. Note how the use of repetition in the following lines emphasizes the speaker's message about body and soul.

> **You are not your body,**
> **you are not your bones.**
> **What's essential about you**
> **Is what can't be owned.**
> **—Marilyn Nelson, "Not My Bones"**

See page 624.

See also **Alliteration; Sound Devices.**

Resolution *See* **Falling Action.**

Rhyme Rhyme is the occurrence of similar or identical sounds at the end of two or more words, such as *suite, heat,* and *complete.* Rhyme that occurs within a single line of poetry is internal rhyme. Rhyme that occurs at the ends of lines of poetry is called end rhyme. End rhyme that is not exact but approximate is called slant rhyme, or off rhyme. Notice the following example of slant rhyme involving the words *sky* and *signed.*

> **The willow is like an etching,**
> **Fine-lined against the <u>sky</u>.**
> **The ginkgo is like a crude sketch,**
> **Hardly worthy to be <u>signed</u>.**
> **—Eve Merriam, "Simile: Willow and Ginkgo"**

See pages 576, 588, 618.

GLOSSARY OF LITERARY TERMS **R109**

Rhyme Scheme A rhyme scheme is a pattern of end rhymes in a poem. A rhyme scheme is noted by assigning a letter of the alphabet, beginning with *a*, to each line. Lines that rhyme are given the same letter. Notice the rhyme scheme of the first stanza of this poem.

> **There ain't no pay beneath the sun** ***a***
> **As sweet as rest when a job's well done.** ***a***
> **I was born to work up to my grave** ***b***
> **But I was not born** ***c***
> **To be a slave.** ***b***
> **—Maya Angelou, "One More Round"**

See page 618.

Rhythm Rhythm is a pattern of stressed and unstressed syllables in a line of poetry. Poets use rhythm to bring out the musical quality of language, to emphasize ideas, and to create moods. Devices such as alliteration, rhyme, assonance, and consonance often contribute to creating rhythm.

See pages 576, 636.
See also **Meter.**

Rising Action The rising action is the stage of the plot that develops the conflict, or struggle. During this stage, events occur that make the conflict more complicated. The events in the rising action build toward a climax, or turning point.

See page 32.
See also **Plot.**

Scene In a drama, the action is often divided into acts and scenes. Each scene presents an episode of the play's plot and typically occurs at a single place and time.

See also **Act.**

Scenery Scenery is a painted backdrop or other structures used to create the setting for a play.

Science Fiction Science fiction is fiction in which a writer explores unexpected possibilities of the past or the future, using known scientific data and theories as well as his or her creative imagination. Most science fiction writers create believable worlds, although some create fantasy worlds that have familiar elements. Isaac Asimov, the author of "Hallucination," is a famous writer of science fiction.

See also **Fantasy.**

Screenplay A screenplay is a play written for film.

Script The text of a play, film, or broadcast is called a script.

Sensory Details Sensory details are words and phrases that appeal to the reader's senses of sight, hearing, touch, smell, and taste. Note the use of sensory details that appeal to sight and taste in the following example.

> **juniper, piñon, or something**
> **with hard, red berries in spring.**
> **You taste them, and they are sweet**
> **and bitter, the berries a delicacy**
> **—Simon Ortiz, "Canyon de Chelly"**

See also **Imagery.**

Setting The setting of a story, poem, or play is the time and place of the action. Sometimes the setting is clear and well-defined. At other times, it is left to the reader's imagination. Elements of setting include geographic location, historical period (past, present, or future), season, time of day, and culture.

See pages 310, 316, 332, 380.

Short Story A short story is a work of fiction that centers on a single idea and can be read in one sitting. Generally, a short story has one main conflict that involves the characters and keeps the story moving.

See also **Fiction.**

Simile A simile is a figure of speech that makes a comparison between two unlike things using the word *like* or *as*.

> **The willow is like a nymph with streaming hair;**
> **—Eve Merriam, "Simile: Willow and Ginkgo"**

See pages 576, 582.
See also **Figurative Language; Metaphor.**

Situational Irony *See* **Irony.**

Sonnet A sonnet is a poem that has a formal structure, containing 14 lines and a specific rhyme scheme and meter. A sonnet often consists of three quatrains, or four-line units, and a final couplet. The sonnet, which means "little song," can be used for a variety of subjects. John Keats's "On the Grasshopper and Cricket" is an example of a sonnet.

See also **Couplet; Rhyme Scheme.**

R110 GLOSSARY OF LITERARY TERMS

Sound Devices Sound devices, or uses of words for their connection to the sense of hearing, can convey meaning and mood or unify a work. Some common sound devices are **alliteration, assonance, consonance, meter, onomatopoeia, repetition, rhyme,** and **rhythm.** The following poem contains alliteration, repetition, assonance, consonance, rhyme, and rhythm, all of which combine to help convey both meaning and mood.

> **It's all I have to bring today—**
> **This, and my heart beside—**
> **This, and my heart, and all the fields—**
> **And all the meadows wide—**
> **Be sure you count—should I forget**
> **Some one the sum could tell—**
> **This, and my heart, and all the Bees**
> **Which in the Clover dwell.**
> **—Emily Dickinson, "It's all I have to bring today"**

See pages 282, 576, 612, 636.
See also **Alliteration; Assonance; Consonance; Meter; Onomatopoeia; Repetition; Rhyme; Rhythm.**

Speaker In poetry, the speaker is the voice that "talks" to the reader, similar to the narrator in fiction. The speaker is not necessarily the poet. For example, in Langston Hughes's poem "Mother to Son," the speaker is an older woman, not the male poet.
See pages 416, 596.

Speech A speech is a talk or public address. The purpose of a speech may be to entertain, to explain, to persuade, to inspire, or any combination of these purposes. Chief Canasatego's speech "Educating Sons" was delivered in order to explain to the European settlers why the Iroquois were rejecting the offer of a free education.
See pages 846, 1002.

Stage Directions In the script of a play, the instructions to the actors, director, and stage crew are called the stage directions. Stage directions might suggest scenery, lighting, sound effects, and ways for actors to move and speak. Stage directions often appear in parentheses and in italic type.
See pages 86, 484.

Stanza A stanza is a group of two or more lines that form a unit in a poem. Each stanza may have the same number of lines, or the number of lines may vary. Eve Merriam's poem "Simile: Willow and Ginkgo" is divided into six stanzas.
See also **Couplet; Form; Poetry.**

Static Character *See* **Character.**

Stereotype In literature, characters who are defined by a single trait are known as stereotypes. Such characters do not usually demonstrate the complexities of real people. Familiar stereotypes in popular literature include the absent-minded professor and the busybody.

Structure The structure of a work of literature is the way in which it is put together. In poetry, structure involves the arrangement of words and lines to produce a desired effect. One structural unit in poetry is the stanza. In prose, structure involves the arrangement of such elements as sentences, paragraphs, and events. "The Wise Old Woman," for example, is structured around the three challenges set forth by Lord Higa.

Style A style is a manner of writing. It involves how something is said rather than what is said. For example, "New York Day Women" by Edwidge Danticat is written in a style that makes use of sentence fragments, repetition, and unusual presentation.

Subplot A subplot is an additional, or secondary, plot in a story. The subplot contains its own conflict, which is often separate from the main conflicts of the story.
See page 521.

Surprise Ending A surprise ending is an unexpected plot twist at the end of a story. The surprise may be a sudden turn in the action or a piece of information that gives a different perspective to the entire story. The short story writer O. Henry is famous for using this device.
See page 46.

Suspense Suspense is a feeling of growing tension and excitement felt by a reader. Suspense makes a reader curious about the outcome of a story or an event within a story. A writer creates suspense by raising questions in the reader's mind. The use of foreshadowing is one way that writers create suspense.
See page 76.
See also **Foreshadowing.**

Symbol A symbol is a person, a place, an object, or an activity that stands for something beyond itself. For example, a flag is a colored piece of cloth that stands for a country. A white dove is a bird that represents peace.
Example: In "Gil's Furniture Bought and Sold" by Sandra Cisneros, the music box represents beauty.
See pages 442, 448, 476.

GLOSSARY OF LITERARY TERMS R111

Tall Tale A tall tale is a humorously exaggerated story about impossible events, often involving the supernatural abilities of the main character. Stories about folk heroes such as Pecos Bill and Paul Bunyan are typical tall tales.

Theme A theme is a message about life or human nature that the writer shares with the reader. In many cases, readers must infer what the writer's message is. One way of figuring out a theme is to apply the lessons learned by the main characters to people in real life. For example, a theme of *The Diary of Anne Frank* is that people are good at heart.

Recurring themes are themes found in a variety of works. For example, authors from different backgrounds might express similar themes having to do with the importance of family values. Universal themes are themes that are found throughout the literature of all time periods. For example, the folk tales "The Old Grandfather and His Little Grandson" and "The Wise Old Woman" both express the theme that we should treat older people with respect.

See pages 442, 454, 462, 484.
See also **Moral.**

Third-Person Point of View *See* **Point of View.**

Title The title of a piece of writing is the name that is attached to it. A title often refers to an important aspect of the work. For example, the title "Raymond's Run" refers to the climax of the story, when Squeaky realizes she can find fulfillment in helping her brother Raymond improve his skills.

Tone The tone of a literary work expresses the writer's attitude toward his or her subject. Words such as *angry, sad,* and *humorous* can be used to describe different tones. For example, the tone of Mark Twain's essay "Roughing It" is humorous.

See pages 666, 682, 734.
See also **Author's Perspective; Mood.**

Tragedy A tragedy is a dramatic work that presents the downfall of a dignified character or characters involved in historically or socially significant events. The events in a tragic plot are set in motion by a decision that is often an error in judgment on the part of the hero. Succeeding events are linked in a cause-and-effect relationship and lead inevitably to a disastrous conclusion, usually death. William Shakespeare's *Romeo and Juliet* is a famous tragedy.

Traits *See* **Character Traits.**

Turning Point *See* **Climax.**

Understatement Understatement is a technique of creating emphasis by saying less than is actually or literally true. It is the opposite of hyperbole, or exaggeration. Understatement is often used to create a humorous effect.

Universal Theme *See* **Theme.**

Unreliable Narrator *See* **Narrator.**

Verbal Irony *See* **Irony.**

Voice The term *voice* refers to a writer's unique use of language that allows a reader to "hear" a human personality in the writer's work. Elements of style that contribute to a writer's voice can reveal much about the author's personality, beliefs, and attitudes.

See page 704.

Word Choice The success of any writing depends on the writer's choice of words. Words not only communicate ideas but also help describe events, characters, settings, and so on. Word choice can make a writer's work sound formal or informal, serious or humorous. A writer must choose words carefully depending on the goal of the piece of writing. For example, a writer working on a science article would probably use technical, formal words; a writer trying to establish the setting in a short story would probably use more descriptive words.

See also **Style.**

Glossary of Reading and Informational Terms

Almanac *See* **Reference Works.**

Analogy An analogy is a comparison between two things that are alike in some way. Often, writers use analogies in nonfiction to explain an unfamiliar subject or idea by showing how it is like a familiar one.

Appeal to Authority An appeal to authority is an attempt to persuade an audience by making reference to people who are experts on a subject.

Argument An argument is speaking or writing that expresses a position on a problem and supports it with reasons and evidence. An argument often takes into account other points of view, anticipating and answering objections that opponents might raise.
See also **Claim; Counterargument; Evidence.**

Assumption An assumption is an opinion or belief that is taken for granted. It can be about a specific situation, a person, or the world in general. Assumptions are often unstated.

Author's Message An author's message is the main idea or theme of a particular work.
See also **Main Idea; Theme,** *Glossary of Literary Terms, page R112.*

Author's Perspective *See Glossary of Literary Terms, page R102.*

Author's Position An author's position is his or her opinion on an issue or topic.
See also **Claim.**

Author's Purpose *See Glossary of Literary Terms, page R102.*

Autobiography *See Glossary of Literary Terms, page R102.*

Bias In a piece of writing, the author's bias is the side of an issue that he or she favors. Words with extremely positive or negative connotations are often a signal of an author's bias.

Bibliography A bibliography is a list of related books and other materials used to write a text. Bibliographies can be good sources for further study on a subject.
See also **Works Consulted.**

Biography *See Glossary of Literary Terms, page R103.*

Business Correspondence Business correspondence is written business communications such as business letters, e-mails, and memos. In general, business correspondence is brief, to the point, clear, courteous, and professional.

Cause and Effect Two events are related by cause and effect when one event brings about, or causes, the other. The event that happens first is the **cause;** the one that follows is the **effect.** Cause and effect is also a way of organizing an entire piece of writing. It helps writers show the relationships between events or ideas.
See also **False Cause,** *Reading Handbook, page R24.*

Chronological Order Chronological order is the arrangement of events by their order of occurrence. This type of organization is used in fictional narratives and in historical writing, biography, and autobiography.

Claim In an argument, a claim is the writer's position on an issue or problem. Although an argument focuses on supporting one claim, a writer may make more than one claim in a text.

Clarify Clarifying is a strategy that helps readers understand or make clear what they are reading. Readers usually clarify by rereading, reading aloud, or discussing.

Classification Classification is a pattern of organization in which objects, ideas, and/or information are presented in groups, or classes, based on common characteristics.

Cliché A cliché is an overused expression. "Better late than never" and "hard as nails" are common examples. Good writers generally avoid clichés unless they are using them in dialogue to indicate something about a character's personality.

Compare and Contrast To compare and contrast is to identify the similarities and differences of two or more subjects. Compare and contrast is also a pattern of organizing an entire piece of writing.

Conclusion A conclusion is a statement of belief based on evidence, experience, and reasoning. A valid conclusion is one that logically follows from the facts or statements upon which it is based.

Connect Connecting is a reader's process of relating the content of a text to his or her own knowledge and experience.

Consumer Documents Consumer documents are printed materials that accompany products and services. They usually provide information about the use, care, operation, or assembly of the product or service they accompany. Some common consumer documents are applications, contracts, warranties, manuals, instructions, labels, brochures, and schedules.

GLOSSARY OF READING AND INFORMATIONAL TERMS R113

Context Clues When you encounter an unfamiliar word, you can often use context clues to understand it. Context clues are the words or phrases surrounding the word that provide hints about the word's meaning.

Counterargument A counterargument is an argument made to oppose another argument. A good argument anticipates opposing viewpoints and provides counterarguments to disprove them.

Credibility Credibility is the believability or trustworthiness of a source and the information it provides.

Critical Review A critical review is an evaluation or critique by a reviewer, or critic. Types of reviews include film reviews, book reviews, music reviews, and art show reviews.

Database A database is a collection of information that can be quickly and easily accessed and searched and from which information can be easily retrieved. It is frequently presented in an electronic format.

Debate A debate is an organized exchange of opinions on an issue. In school settings, debate is usually a formal contest in which two opposing teams defend and attack a proposition.

See also **Argument.**

Deductive Reasoning Deductive reasoning is a way of thinking that begins with a generalization, presents a specific situation, and then moves forward with facts and evidence toward a logical conclusion. The following passage has a deductive argument embedded in it: "All students in the math class must take the quiz on Friday. Since Lana is in the class, she had better show up." This deductive argument can be broken down as follows: generalization—All students in the math class must take the quiz on Friday; specific situation—Lana is a student in the math class; conclusion—Therefore, Lana must take the math quiz.

See also **Analyzing Logic and Reasoning,** *Reading Handbook, page R22.*

Diary *See Glossary of Literary Terms, page R104.*

Dictionary *See* **Reference Works.**

Draw Conclusions To draw a conclusion is to make a judgment or arrive at a belief based on evidence, experience, and reasoning.

Editorial An editorial is an opinion piece that usually appears on the editorial page of a newspaper or as part of a news broadcast. The editorial section of the newspaper presents opinions rather than objective news reports.

See also **Op/Ed Piece.**

Either/Or Fallacy An either/or fallacy is a statement that suggests that there are only two choices available in a situation when in fact there are more than two.

See also **Identifying Faulty Reasoning,** *Reading Handbook, page R24.*

Emotional Appeal An emotional appeal is a message that creates strong feelings in order to make a point. An appeal to fear is a message that taps into people's fear of losing their safety or security. An appeal to pity is a message that taps into people's sympathy and compassion for others to build support for an idea, a cause, or a proposed action. An appeal to vanity is a message that attempts to persuade by tapping into people's desire to feel good about themselves.

See also **Recognizing Persuasive Techniques,** *Reading Handbook, page R21.*

Encyclopedia *See* **Reference Works.**

Essay *See Glossary of Literary Terms, page R104.*

Ethical Appeal In an ethical appeal, a writer links a claim to a widely accepted value in order to gain moral support for the claim. The appeal also creates an image of the writer as a trustworthy, moral person.

See also **Recognizing Persuasive Techniques,** *Reading Handbook, page R102.*

Evaluate To evaluate is to examine something carefully and to judge its value or worth. Evaluating is an important skill. A reader can evaluate the actions of a particular character, for example. A reader can also form opinions about the value of an entire work.

Evidence Evidence is a specific piece of information that supports a claim. Evidence can take the form of a fact, a quotation, an example, a statistic, or a personal experience, among other things.

Expository Essay *See* **Essay,** *Glossary of Literary Terms, page R104.*

Fact Versus Opinion A **fact** is a statement that can be proved, or verified. An opinion, on the other hand, is a statement that cannot be proved because it expresses a person's beliefs, feelings, or thoughts.

See also **Generalization; Inference.**

R114 GLOSSARY OF READING AND INFORMATIONAL TERMS

Fallacy A fallacy is an error of reasoning. Typically, a fallacy is based on an incorrect inference or a misuse of evidence.

See also **Either/Or Fallacy; Logical Appeal; Overgeneralization.**

See also **Identifying Faulty Reasoning,** *Reading Handbook, page R24.*

Faulty Reasoning *See* **Fallacy.**

Feature Article A feature article is an article in a newspaper or magazine about a topic of human interest or lifestyles.

Generalization A generalization is a broad statement about a class or category of people, ideas, or things based on a study of, or a belief about, only some of its members.

See also **Overgeneralization; Stereotyping.**

Government Publications Government publications are documents produced by government organizations. Pamphlets, brochures, and reports are just some of the many forms these publications take. Government publications can be good resources for a wide variety of topics.

Graphic Aid A graphic aid is a visual tool that is printed, handwritten, or drawn. Charts, diagrams, graphs, photographs, and maps are examples of graphic aids.

See also **Graphic Aids,** *Reading Handbook, page R4.*

Graphic Organizer A graphic organizer is a "word picture"—a visual illustration of a verbal statement—that helps a reader understand a text. Charts, tables, webs, and diagrams can all be graphic organizers. Graphic organizers and graphic aids can look the same. However, graphic organizers and graphic aids do differ in how they are used. Graphic aids help deliver important information to students using a text. Graphic organizers are actually created by students themselves. They help students understand the text or organize information.

Historical Document Historical documents are writings that have played a significant role in human events. The Declaration of Independence, for example, is a historical document.

How-To Book A how-to book explains how to do something—usually an activity, a sport, or a household project.

Implied Main Idea *See* **Main Idea.**

Index The index of a book is an alphabetized list of important topics covered in the book and the page numbers on which they can be found. An index can be used to quickly find specific information about a topic.

Inductive Reasoning Inductive reasoning is the process of logical reasoning that starts with observations, examples, and facts and moves on to a general conclusion or principle.

See also **Analyzing Logic and Reasoning,** *Reading Handbook, page R22.*

Inference An inference is a logical guess that is made based on facts and one's own knowledge and experience.

Informational Text Informational text is writing that provides factual information. It often explains an idea or teaches a process. Examples include news reports, science textbooks, software instructions, and lab reports.

Internet The Internet is a global, interconnected system of computer networks that allows for communication through e-mail, listservs, and the World Wide Web. The Internet connects computers and computer users throughout the world.

Journal A journal is a periodical publication issued by a legal, medical, or other professional organization. The term may also be used to refer to a diary or daily record.

Loaded Language Loaded language consists of words with strongly positive or negative connotations, intended to influence a reader's or listener's attitude.

Logical Appeal A logical appeal is a way of writing or speaking that relies on logic and facts. It appeals to people's reasoning or intellect rather than to their values or emotions. Flawed logical appeals—that is, errors in reasoning—are called logical fallacies.

See also **Fallacy.**

Logical Argument A logical argument is an argument in which the logical relationship between the support and claim is sound.

Main Idea The main idea is the central or most important idea about a topic that a writer or speaker conveys. It can be the central idea of an entire work or of just a paragraph. Often, the main idea of a paragraph is expressed in a topic sentence. However, a main idea may just be implied, or suggested, by details. A main idea is typically supported by details.

Make Inferences *See* **Inference.**

Monitor Monitoring is the strategy of checking your comprehension as you read and modifying the strategies you are using to suit your needs. Monitoring often includes the following strategies: questioning, clarifying, visualizing, predicting, connecting, and rereading.

GLOSSARY OF READING AND INFORMATIONAL TERMS R115

Narrative Nonfiction *See Glossary of Literary Terms, page R108.*

News Article A news article is writing that reports on a recent event. In newspapers, news articles are usually brief and to the point, presenting the most important facts first, followed by more detailed information.

Nonfiction *See Glossary of Literary Terms, page R108.*

Op/Ed Piece An op/ed piece is an opinion piece that typically appears opposite ("op") the editorial page of a newspaper. Unlike editorials, op/ed pieces are written and submitted by readers.

Organization *See* **Pattern of Organization.**

Overgeneralization An overgeneralization is a generalization that is too broad. You can often recognize overgeneralizations by the appearance of words and phrases such as *all, everyone, every time, any, anything, no one,* or *none.* An example is "None of the city's workers really cares about keeping the environment clean." In all probability, there are many exceptions. The writer can't possibly know the feelings of every city worker.

See also **Identifying Faulty Reasoning,** *Reading Handbook, page R24.*

Overview An overview is a short summary of a story, a speech, or an essay.

Paraphrase Paraphrasing is the restating of information in one's own words.

See also **Summarize.**

Pattern of Organization The term *pattern of organization* refers to the way ideas and information are arranged and organized. Patterns of organization include cause and effect, chronological, compare and contrast, classification, and problem-solution, among others.

See also **Cause and Effect; Chronological Order; Classification; Compare and Contrast; Problem-Solution Order; Sequential Order.**

See also **Reading Informational Texts: Patterns of Organization,** *Reading Handbook, page R8.*

Periodical A periodical is a magazine or other publication that is issued on a regular basis.

Personal Essay *See* **Essay,** *Glossary of Literary Terms, page R104.*

Persuasion Persuasion is the art of swaying others' feelings, beliefs, or actions. Persuasion normally appeals to both the mind and the emotions of the reader.

See also **Appeal to Authority; Emotional Appeal; Ethical Appeal; Loaded Language; Logical Appeal.**

See also **Recognizing Persuasive Techniques,** *Reading Handbook, page R21.*

Predict Predicting is a reading strategy that involves using text clues to make a reasonable guess about what will happen next in a story.

Primary Source *See* **Source.**

Prior Knowledge Prior knowledge is the knowledge a reader already possesses about a topic. This information might come from personal experiences, expert accounts, books, films, or other sources.

Problem-Solution Order Problem-solution order is a pattern of organization in which a problem is stated and analyzed and then one or more solutions are proposed and examined.

Propaganda Propaganda is any form of communication that is so distorted that it conveys false or misleading information to advance a specific belief or cause.

Public Document Public documents are documents that were written for the public to provide information that is of public interest or concern. They include government documents, speeches, signs, and rules and regulations.

See also **Government Publications.**

Reference Works Reference works are sources that contain facts and background information on a wide range of subjects. Most reference works are good sources of reliable information because they have been reviewed by experts. The following are some common reference works: encyclopedias, dictionaries, thesauri, almanacs, atlases, and directories.

Review *See* **Critical Review.**

Rhetorical Question Rhetorical questions are those that have such obvious answers that they do not require a reply. Writers often use them to suggest that their claim is so obvious that everyone should agree with it.

Scanning Scanning is the process used to search through a text for a particular fact or piece of information. When you scan, you sweep your eyes across a page, looking for key words that may lead you to the information you want.

R116 GLOSSARY OF READING AND INFORMATIONAL TERMS

Scope Scope refers to a work's focus. For example, an article about Austin, Texas, that focuses on the city's history, economy, and residents has a broad scope. An article that focuses only on the restaurants in Austin has a narrower scope.

Secondary Source *See* **Source.**

Sequential Order Sequential order is a pattern of organization that shows the order of steps or stages in a process.

Setting a Purpose The process of establishing specific reasons for reading a text is called setting a purpose. Readers can look at a text's title, headings, and illustrations to guess what it might be about. They can then use these guesses to figure out what they want to learn from reading the text.

Sidebar A sidebar is additional information set in a box alongside or within a news or feature article. Popular magazines often make use of sidebars.

Signal Words In a text, signal words are words and phrases that help show how events or ideas are related. Some common examples of signal words are *and, but, however, nevertheless, therefore,* and *in addition.*

Source A source is anything that supplies information. **Primary sources** are materials created by people who witnessed or took part in the event they supply information about. Letters, diaries, autobiographies, and eyewitness accounts are primary sources. **Secondary sources** are those made by people who were not directly involved in the event or even present when it occurred. Encyclopedias, textbooks, biographies, and most news articles are examples of secondary sources.

Speech *See Glossary of Literary Terms, page R111.*

Stereotyping Stereotyping is a dangerous type of overgeneralization. It can lead to unfair judgments of people based on their ethnic background, beliefs, practices, or physical appearance.

Summarize To summarize is to briefly retell the main ideas of a piece of writing in one's own words.
See also **Paraphrase.**

Support Support is any information that helps to prove a claim.

Supporting Detail *See* **Main Idea.**

Synthesize To synthesize information means to take individual pieces of information and combine them in order to gain a better understanding of a subject.

Text Feature Text features are elements of a text, such as boldface type, headings, and subheadings, that help organize and call attention to important information. Italic type, bulleted or numbered lists, sidebars, and graphic aids such as charts, tables, timelines, illustrations, and photographs are also considered text features.
See also **Understanding Text Features,** *Reading Handbook, page R3.*

Thesaurus *See* **Reference Works.**

Thesis Statement A thesis statement is the main proposition that a writer attempts to support in a piece of writing.

Topic Sentence The topic sentence of a paragraph states the paragraph's main idea. All other sentences in the paragraph provide supporting details.

Treatment The way a topic is handled in a work is referred to as its treatment. Treatment includes the form the writing takes as well as the writer's purpose and tone.

Visualize Visualizing is the process of forming a mental picture based on written or spoken information.

Web Site A Web site is a collection of "pages" on the World Wide Web that is usually devoted to one specific subject. Pages are linked together and accessed by clicking hyperlinks or menus, which send the user from page to page within a Web site. Web sites are created by companies, organizations, educational institutions, branches of the government, the military, and individuals.

Workplace Document Workplace documents are materials that are produced or used within a work setting, usually to aid in the functioning of the workplace. They include job applications, office memos, training manuals, job descriptions, and sales reports.

Works Cited The term *works cited* refers to a list of all the works a writer has referred to in his or her text. This list often includes not only books and articles but also Internet sources.

Works Consulted The term *works consulted* refers to a list of all the works a writer consulted in order to create his or her text. It is not limited just to those works cited in the text.
See also **Bibliography.**

GLOSSARY OF READING AND INFORMATIONAL TERMS R117

Glossary of Vocabulary in English & Spanish

aberration (ăb'ə-rā'shən) *n.* an abnormal alteration
aberración *s.* alteración anormal

absurd (əb-sûrd') *adj.* ridiculously unreasonable
absurdo *adj.* que va en contra de lo razonable

accommodate (ə-kŏm'ə-dāt) *v.* to make room for
acomodar *v.* albergar; contener

acute (ə-kyo͞ot') *adj.* sharp; keen
agudo *adj.* fuerte; perspicaz

adequately (ăd'ĭ-kwĭt-lē) *adv.* enough to satisfy a requirement or meet a need
adecuadamente *adv.* de modo suficiente para cumplir un requisito o necesidad

adorn (ə-dôrn') *v.* to enhance or decorate
adornar *v.* embellecer o decorar

adversary (ăd'vər-sĕr'ē) *n.* an opponent
adversario *s.* oponente

aggression (ə-grĕsh'ən) *n.* hostile or destructive behavior or action
agresión *s.* conducta o acción hostil o destructiva

ajar (ə-jär') *adj.* partially open
entreabierto *adj.* parcialmente abierto

anguished (ăng'gwĭsht) *adj.* tormented; distressed
angustiado *adj.* atormentado; afligido

annihilate (ə-nī'ə-lāt') *v.* to completely destroy or defeat
aniquilar *v.* destruir o derrotar completamente

appendage (ə-pĕn'dĭj) *n.* a body part, such as an arm or leg, that is attached to the main part of the body
apéndice *s.* parte del cuerpo pegada al tronco, como un brazo o una pierna

apprehension (ăp'rĭ-hĕn'shən) *n.* nervousness
aprensión *s.* nerviosismo

array (ə-rā') *n.* a large number of items
conjunto *s.* gran cantidad de objetos

arrogant (ăr'ə-gənt) *adj.* displaying a sense of self-importance
arrogante *adj.* que se las da de importante

askew (ə-skyo͞o') *adj.* to one side; awry
torcido *adj.* que no es recto ni derecho

aspire (ə-spīr') *v.* to have a great ambition or an ultimate goal; to desire strongly
aspirar *v.* tener una gran ambición o una meta final; desear con fuerza

assert (ə-sûrt') *v.* to act forcefully; to take charge
afirmar *v.* dejar sentado; imponer autoridad

assurance (ə-sho͝or'əns) *n.* a guarantee or pledge
garantía *s.* compromiso

attribute (ə-trĭb'yo͞ot) *v.* to relate to a certain cause
atribuir *v.* relacionar con cierta causa

audacity (ô-dăs'ĭ-tē) *n.* shameless daring or boldness
audacia *s.* atrevimiento o descaro

authentic (ô-thĕn'tĭk) *adj.* having a verifiable origin; not counterfeit
auténtico *adj.* de origen comprobado; original

bafflement (băf'əl-mənt) *n.* confusion; puzzlement
desconcierto *s.* confusión; perplejidad

ban (băn) *v.* to prohibit
prohibir *v.* negar

barricade (băr'ĭ-kād') *n.* a structure that blocks passage
barricada *s.* estructura que bloquea el paso

basking (băsk'ĭng) *adj.* warming oneself pleasantly, as in sunlight
asoleado *adj.* expuesto al sol

beckon (bĕk'ən) *v.* to signal to come
llamar *v.* hacer señas a alguien para que se acerque

benefactor (bĕn'ə-făk'tər) *n.* a person who gives monetary or other aid
benefactor *s.* persona que da dinero o ayuda

bewilderment (bĭ-wĭl'dər-mənt) *n.* the state of being confused or astonished
perplejidad *s.* confusión o desconcierto

bound (bound) *v.* to leap forward
saltar *v.* brincar hacia adelante

brusquely (brŭsk'lē) *adv.* in an abrupt, sudden manner
bruscamente *adv.* de modo abrupto y repentino

cache (kăsh) *v.* to store in a hiding place
ocultar *v.* guardar en un escondite

R118 GLOSSARY OF VOCABULARY

cajole (kə-jōl′) *v.* to urge gently; to coax
persuadir *v.* convencer; engatusar

cavernous (kăv′ər-nəs) *adj.* as deep or vast as a cavern, or a large cave
cavernoso *adj.* profundo y oscuro como una caverna o cueva grande

circumstance (sûr′kəm-stăns′) *n.* a condition that affects or relates to an event or series of events
circunstancia *s.* situación que rodea a un suceso o serie de sucesos

clutch (klŭch) *v.* to grasp and hold tightly
agarrar *v.* estrechar y apretar firmemente

collaborate (kə-lăb′ə-rāt′) *v.* to work together on a project
colaborar *v.* trabajar en equipo en un proyecto

commence (kə-mĕns′) *v.* to begin
comenzar *v.* empezar

commend (kə-mĕnd′) *v.* to speak highly of; to praise; to recommend
elogiar *v.* ensalzar; recomendar

commotion (kə-mō′shən) *n.* a disturbance
conmoción *s.* disturbio

compel (kəm-pĕl′) *v.* to pressure by force
compeler *v.* obligar a la fuerza

compensation (kŏm′pən-sā′shən) *n.* something, such as money, received as payment
compensación *s.* dinero o cosa recibida en pago

comply (kəm-plī′) *v.* to act according to a command or request
cumplir *v.* seguir una orden o una solicitud

composer (kəm-pō′zər) *n.* one who creates musical pieces
compositor *s.* persona que crea piezas musicales

conceive (kən-sēv) *v.* to think of
concebir *v.* idear

concession (kən-sĕsh′ən) *n.* the act of yielding or conceding
concesión *s.* acción de ceder

conspicuous (kən-spĭk′yo͞o-əs) *adj.* easy to notice; obvious
conspicuo *adj.* que salta a la vista; obvio

conspiracy (kən-spîr′ə-sē) *n.* an agreement to perform together an illegal or wrongful act
conspiración *s.* alianza para preparar una acción ilegal o indebida

contaminate (kən-tăm′ə-nāt′) *v.* to make impure or unclean through contact
contaminar *v.* dañar o alterar la pureza

contemplate (kŏn′təm-plāt′) *v.* to consider carefully and at length
contemplar *v.* considerar cuidadosamente

contractor (kŏn′trăk′tər) *n.* one who agrees to provide services for a specific price
contratista *s.* persona que se compromete a realizar un servicio por determinado precio

contradiction (kŏn′trə-dĭk′shən) *n.* a denial; an expression that is opposite to
contradicción *s.* negación de algo que se da por cierto; afirmación de algo contrario a lo ya dicho

contrive (kən-trīv′) *v.* to invent or fabricate, especially by improvisation
ingeniarse *v.* inventar o idear, especialmente de modo improvisado

conventional (kən-vĕn′shə-nəl) *adj.* conforming to established practice or accepted standards; traditional
convencional *adj.* conforme a la práctica establecida o a estándares aceptados; tradicional

converge (kən-vûrj′) *v.* to come together in one place; meet
converger *v.* unirse en un punto; encontrarse

conviction (kən-vĭk′shən) *n.* a strong belief
convicción *s.* creencia fuerte

cosmic (kŏz′mik) *adj.* universal; infinitely large
cósmico *adj.* universal; infinitamente grande

counterpart (koun′tər-pärt′) *n.* one that has the same functions and traits as another
contraparte *s.* el que tiene las mismas funciones y características que otro

craftiness (krăf′tē-nĕs) *n.* deviousness or deception
picardía *s.* astucia o engaño

credulity (krĭ-do͞o′lĭ-tē) *n.* a disposition to believe too readily
credulidad *s.* tendencia a creerlo todo

GLOSSARY OF VOCABULARY R119

crevice (krĕv′ĭs) *n.* crack
grieta *s.* abertura larga y estrecha

crouch (krouch) *v.* to stoop with bent knees
acuclillarse *v.* agacharse con las rodillas dobladas

deceive (dĭ-sēv′) *v.* to cause to believe what is not true; to mislead
engañar *v.* hacer creer lo que no es cierto; descaminar

decline (dĭ-klīn′) *v.* to politely refuse
declinar *v.* rehusar cortésmente

defy (dĭ-fī′) *v.* to boldly oppose or resist
desafiar *v.* oponerse o resistirse

denounce (dĭ-nouns′) *v.* to condemn; to criticize
denunciar *v.* condenar; criticar

depravity (dĭ-prăv′ĭ-tē) *n.* moral corruption
depravación *s.* corrupción moral

deprivation (dĕp′rə-vā′shən) *n.* the condition of not having one's needs met; a lack of
privación *s.* ausencia o escasez de lo necesario para vivir

derision (dĭ-rĭzh′ən) *n.* ridicule
escarnio *s.* ridículo

descendant (dĭ-sĕn′dənt) *n.* a person whose descent can be traced to an individual or group
descendiente *s.* persona que desciende por línea directa de un individuo o grupo

devious (dē′vē-əs) *adj.* departing from the straight or direct course
tortuoso *adj.* desviado; sinuoso

diatribe (dī′ə-trīb′) *n.* bitter, abusive criticism
diatriba *s.* crítica fuerte y grosera

diminish (dĭ-mĭn′ĭsh′) *v.* to become smaller or less
disminuir *v.* hacerse más pequeño; mermar

dingy (dĭn′jē) *adj.* dirty or discolored
deslucido *adj.* sucio o manchado

disconcert (dĭs′kən-sûrt′) *v.* to ruffle; to frustrate by throwing into disorder
desconcertar *v.* alterar; contrariar

disgruntle (dĭs-grŭn′tl) *v.* to make unhappy
contrariar *v.* enfadar

disheveled (dĭ-shəv′əld) *adj.* messy; untidy
desarreglado *adj.* desordenado; desaliñado

dispel (dĭ-spĕl′) *v.* to drive away
disipar *v.* alejar

dowdy (dou′dē) *adj.* out of style; shabby
fuera de moda *adj.* sin estilo o gracia

edict (ē′dĭkt′) *n.* a command from those in power
edicto *s.* orden de una persona de autoridad

eliminate (ĭ-lĭm′ə-nāt′) *v.* to remove from consideration by defeating
eliminar *v.* quitar, separar o hacer desaparecer

eloquence (ĕl′ə-kwəns) *n.* an ability to speak powerfully and persuasively
elocuencia *s.* eficacia para persuadir o conmover con la palabra

emigrate (ĕm′ĭ-grāt′) *v.* to leave one country and settle in another
emigrar *v.* dejar el país propio y establecerse en otro

engaging (ĕn-gāj′ĭng) *adj.* charming; likeable
agradable *adj.* simpático; encantador

engross (ĕn-grōs′) *v.* to completely occupy
absorber *v.* ocupar por completo

ensnare (ĕn-snâr′) *v.* to take or catch in something
atrapar *v.* alcanzar; coger en una trampa

essential (ĭ-sĕn′shəl) *adj.* having the qualities that give something its true identity
esencial *adj.* que forma parte de la naturaleza de algo

esteem (ĭ-stēm′) *v.* to regard with respect
estimar *v.* apreciar

evoke (ĭ-vōk′) *v.* to call forth; to summon
evocar *v.* traer a la memoria

exile (ĕk′sīl′) *n.* enforced removal from one's native country
exilio *s.* abandono obligatorio de la patria

exotic (ĭg-zŏt′ĭk) *adj.* foreign; unusual; exciting
exótico *adj.* extranjero; inusual; emocionante

exploit (ĕk′sploit′) *v.* to use for selfish purposes
explotar *v.* usar con fines egoístas

R120 GLOSSARY OF VOCABULARY

fate (fāt) *n.* a power that is thought to determine the course of events
destino *s.* fuerza que se cree que determina el curso de los acontecimientos

feeble (fē'bəl) *adj.* weak or faint
débil *adj.* que tiene poca fuerza o poco vigor

fiend (fēnd) *n.* a demon; an evil spirit
demonio *s.* espíritu maligno

foreboding (fôr-bō'dĭng) *n.* a sense of impending misfortune
presentimiento *s.* sentimiento de desgracia inminente

foreman (fôr'mən) *n.* the leader of a work crew
capataz *s.* jefe de una cuadrilla de trabajo

foresight (fôr'sīt) *n.* perception of the significance of events before they have occurred
previsión *s.* percepción de la importancia de algo antes de que ocurra

fortify (fôr'tə-fī') *v.* to make strong
fortificar *v.* fortalecer

futility (fyo͞o-tĭl'ĭ-tē) *n.* uselessness
futilidad *s.* lo que no tiene ninguna importancia

glimmer (glĭm'ər) *n.* a faint sign
vislumbre *s.* señal vaga

gnarled (närld) *adj.* roughened, as from age or work
nudoso *adj.* rugoso por la edad o el trabajo

grimace (grĭm'ĭs) *n.* a facial expression of pain or disgust
mueca *s.* expresión facial de dolor o de asco

grope (grōp) *v.* to reach about with uncertainty
tantear *v.* andar a tientas

hamper (hăm'pər) *v.* to prevent the free movement of
dificultar *v.* impedir el libre movimiento

haughtily (hô'tə-lē) *adv.* proudly; scornfully
altivamente *adv.* orgullosamente; con altanería

hypocritical (hĭp'ə-krĭt'ĭ-kəl) *adj.* false or deceptive
hipócrita *adj.* falso o engañoso

immaculate (ĭ-măk'yə-lĭt) *adj.* spotless; very clean
inmaculado *adj.* sin mancha; muy limpio

immortality (ĭm'ôr-tăl'ĭ-tē) *n.* the condition of having an endless life
inmortalidad *s.* vida eterna

impair (ĭm-pâr') *v.* to weaken; damage
perjudicar *v.* debilitar; dañar

impart (ĭm-pärt') *v.* to make known; reveal
impartir *v.* dar a conocer; revelar

impartial (ĭm-pär'shəl) *adj.* not partial or biased; unprejudiced
imparcial *adj.* neutral; sin prejuicio

imply (ĭm-plī') *v.* to express indirectly
implicar *v.* expresar indirectamente

impregnable (ĭm-prĕg'nə-bəl) *adj.* impossible to enter by force
impenetrable *adj.* imposible de penetrar a la fuerza

impromptu (ĭm-prŏmp'to͞o) *adj.* unplanned
improvisado *adj.* espontáneo

impropriety (ĭm'prə-prī'ĭ-tē) *n.* an unsuitable or inappropriate act or quality
incorrección *s.* falta de decoro; falta

improvised (ĭm'prə-vīzd') *adj.* to put together with little preparation or planning **improvise** *v.*
improvisado *adj.* realizado sin plan previo **improvisar** *v.*

impudent (ĭm'pyə-dənt) *adj.* bold and disrespectful
insolente *adj.* descarado e irrespetuoso

incarnation (ĭn'-kär-nā'-shən) *n.* a bodily form
encarnación *s.* adopción de forma física

inclination (ĭn-klə-nā'shən) *n.* a tendency to prefer one thing over another
inclinación *s.* tendencia a preferir una de dos cosas

indignantly (ĭn-dĭg'nənt-lē) *adv.* angrily
con indignación *adv.* furiosamente

indiscriminately (ĭn'dĭ-skrĭm'ə-nĭt-lē) *adv.* without making careful distinctions or choices
sin discriminación *adv.* sin criterio o discernimiento

ineptitude (ĭn-ĕp'tĭ-to͞od') *n.* clumsiness; lack of competence
ineptitud *s.* torpeza; incompetencia

GLOSSARY OF VOCABULARY R121

inertia (ĭ-nûr′shə) *n.* resistance to motion, action, or change
inercia *s.* resistencia al movimiento, la acción o el cambio

inevitable (ĭn-ĕv′ĭ-tə-bəl) *n.* that which cannot be avoided or prevented
inevitable *s.* lo que no se puede evitar o prevenir

infectious (ĭn-fĕk′shəs) *adj.* capable of being transmitted by infection
infeccioso *adj.* que se puede contagiar

inflict (ĭn-flĭkt′) *v.* to deal out something unpleasant or burdensome; to impose
infligir *v.* someter a malos tratos o sufrimiento; imponer

informant (ĭn-fôr′mənt) *n.* one who gives information
informante *s.* el que da información

insolent (ĭn′sə-lənt) *adj.* insulting; arrogant
insolente *adj.* insultante; arrogante

instill (ĭn-stĭl′) *v.* to supply gradually
inculcar *v.* infundir gradualmente

interfere (ĭn′tər-fîr′) *v.* to create an obstacle
interferir *v.* crear un obstáculo

intermittently (ĭn′tər-mĭt′nt-lē) *adv.* stopping and starting at intervals
intermitentemente *adv.* que se interrumpe y prosigue a intervalos

interrogation (ĭn-tĕr′ə-gā′shən) *n.* an official or formal questioning
interrogatorio *s.* formulación oficial de preguntas

intimate (ĭn′tə-mĭt) *adj.* relating to one's deepest nature
intimo *adj.* relacionado con lo más profundo de una persona

intricate (ĭn′trĭ-kĭt) *adj.* elaborate
intrincado *adj.* elaborado

irate (ī-rāt′) *adj.* very angry
airado *adj.* furioso

irretrievably (ĭr′ĭ-trē′və-blē) *adv.* permanently; in a manner that cannot be reversed
irremediablemente *adv.* permanentemente; de modo que no se puede cambiar

junction (jŭnk′shən) *n.* a place where two roads meet
cruce *s.* punto de encuentro de dos caminos

keener (kēn′ər) *adj.* acutely sensitive
agudo *adj.* muy sensible

labyrinth (lăb′ə-rĭnth′) *n.* a maze; an intricate structure of interconnected passages
laberinto *s.* estructura formada por caminos cruzados entre sí

languish (lăng′gwĭsh) *v.* to lose strength and vitality
languidecer *v.* perder fuerza y vitalidad

lark (lärk) *n.* a carefree or spirited adventure
travesura *s.* aventura juguetona

lavishly (lăv′ĭsh-lē) *adv.* extravagantly
magníficamente *adv.* con entravagancia

legitimate (lə-jĭt′ə-mĭt) *adj.* genuine; authentic
legítimo *adj.* genuino; auténtico

legitimately (lə-jĭt′ə-mĭt-lē) *adv.* lawfully
legítimamente *adv.* legalmente

levitation (lĕv′ĭ-tā′shŭn) *n.* the act of rising into the air and floating
levitación *s.* elevación y suspensión en el aire

liable (lī′ə-bəl) *adj.* likely to
propenso *adj.* que tiene inclinación a algo

linger (lĭng′gər) *v.* to remain or stay longer
quedarse *v.* permanecer o entretenerse un rato

listless (lĭst′lĭs) *adj.* lacking energy
lánguido *adj.* sin energía

livelihood (līv′lē-hood′) *n.* a means of support; a way of making a living
sustento *s.* medio de ganarse la vida

malodorous (măl-ō′dər-əs) *adj.* having a bad odor
maloliente *adj.* que huele mal

maroon (mə-ro͞on′) *v.* to leave behind in a place from which there is little hope of escape
abandonar *v.* dejar a una persona en un lugar de donde no puede salir

meddle (mĕd′l) *v.* to intrude or interfere
entrometerse *v.* inmiscuirse o interferir

melancholy (mĕl′ən-kŏl′ē) *adj.* sad; depressed
melancólico *adj.* triste; deprimido

R122 GLOSSARY OF VOCABULARY

menace (mĕn'ĭs) *n.* a possible danger; threat
amenaza *s.* posible peligro

merit (mĕr'ĭt) *v.* to deserve
merecer *v.* ser digno de

mesmerize (mĕz'mə-rīz') *v.* to spellbind; to enthrall
cautivar *v.* fascinar; embelesar

migration (mī-grā'shən) *n.* the act of changing location seasonally
migración *s.* cambio de lugar por temporada

minuscule (mĭn'ə-skyōōl') *adj.* very small; tiny
minúsculo *adj.* muy pequeño

mobility (mō-bĭl'ĭ-tē) *n.* the capability of moving from place to place
movilidad *s.* capacidad de moverse de un lugar a otro

monotony (mə-nŏt'n-ē) *n.* tedious sameness
monotonía *s.* uniformidad o igualdad tediosa

muted (myōō'tĭd) *adj.* muffled; softened
apagado *adj.* amortiguado; suave

neglectful (nĭ-glĕkt'fəl) *adj.* characterized by a failure to properly care for someone or something
negligente *adj.* que no pone cuidado, atención o interés en lo que debe

nondescript (nŏn'dĭ-skrĭpt') *adj.* lacking unique qualities
soso *adj.* sin ninguna característica distintiva

novelty (nŏv'əl-tē) *n.* the quality of being new
novedad *s.* lo que es nuevo o reciente

offense (ə-fĕns') *n.* a violation of a moral or social code; a sin
ofensa *s.* violación de un código moral o social; pecado

ominous (ŏm'ə-nəs) *adj.* threatening
ominoso *adj.* amenazador

opaque (ō-pāk') *adj.* hidden; difficult or impossible to understand
impenetrable *adj.* difícil o imposible de entender

opportunist (ŏp'ər-tōō'nĭst) *n.* a person who takes advantage of any opportunity, without moral regard, to achieve a goal
oportunista *s.* persona que aprovecha toda oportunidad para alcanzar una meta, sin consideraciones morales

opposition (ŏp'ə-zĭsh'ən) *n.* the act of opposing or resisting
oposición *s.* acción de oponer u oponerse

oratory (ôr'ə-tôr'ē) *n.* the art of making speeches
oratoria *s.* arte de dar discursos

pandemonium (păn'də-mō'nē-əm) *n.* wild uproar or noise
pandemónium *s.* gran ruido y confusión

patronize (pā'trə-nīz') *v.* to go to as a customer
frecuentar *v.* ser cliente de

peril (pĕr'əl) *n.* danger
peligro *s.* riesgo

perpetual (pər-pĕch'ōō-əl) *adj.* continuing without interruption
perpetuo *adj.* sin interrupción

perseverance (pûr'sə-vîr'əns) *n.* steady persistence in sticking to a course of action
perseverancia *s.* firmeza y constancia en un curso de acción

pervasive (pər-vā'sĭv) *adj.* present throughout
omnipresente *adj.* que está en todas partes

philosophy (fĭ-lŏs'ə-fē) *n.* a system of values or beliefs
filosofía *s.* sistema de valores o creencias

pinnacle (pĭn'ə-kəl) *n.* a peak; a pointed top
pináculo *s.* cumbre; cima

ponder (pŏn'dər) *v.* to think or consider carefully
considerar *v.* pensar o reflexionar con atención

potential (pə-tĕn'shəl) *n.* the ability to grow or develop
potenial *s.* capacidad de crecimiento o desarrollo

predicament (prĭ-dĭk'ə-mənt) *n.* an unpleasant situation from which it is difficult to free oneself
aprieto *s.* situación incómoda de la que es difícil zafarse

primitive (prĭm'ĭ-tĭv) *adj.* of or relating to a nonindustrial, often tribal, culture
primitivo *adj.* relacionado con una cultura no industrial o tribal

prodigy (prŏd'ə-jē) *n.* a person with an exceptional talent
prodigio *s.* persona con un talento excepcional

GLOSSARY OF VOCABULARY R123

progressiveness (prə-grĕs'ĭv-nĭs) *n.* the state of advancing toward better conditions or new policies, ideas, or methods
progresismo *s.* avance hacia mejores condiciones, o nuevas medidas, ideas o métodos

propaganda (prŏp'ə-găn'də) *n.* information that supports a certain cause
propaganda *s.* información que apoya una causa

proportional (prə-pôr'shə-nəl) *adj.* having a constant relation in degree or number
proporcional *adj.* que tiene una relación constante de grado o cantidad

proposition (prŏp'ə-zĭsh'ən) *n.* a suggested plan
propuesta *s.* plan sugerido

propriety (prə-prī'ĭ-tē) *n.* the quality of being proper; appropriateness
corrección *s.* decoro; conveniencia

provisions (prə-vĭzh'ənz) *n.* necessary supplies; food
provisiones *s.* suministros necesarios; alimentos

provoke (prə-vōk') *v.* to cause; to bring up
provocar *v.* causar; suscitar

pungent (pŭn'jənt) *adj.* sharp or intense
acre *adj.* agudo o intenso

puritanical (pyo͝or-ĭ-tăn'ĭ-kəl) *adj.* strictly observant of religious practices; sternly moral
puritano *adj.* que cumple con rigor las prácticas religiosas; severamente moral

pursuit (pər-so͞ot') *n.* the act of chasing
persecución *v.* seguimiento

ramble (răm'bəl) *v.* to talk at length and aimlessly
divagar *v.* hablar sin parar y sin ton ni son

ransom (răn'səm) *n.* payment demanded for the release of a person or property
rescate *s.* dinero que se pide o se paga por la liberación de una persona o propiedad

rationalize (răsh'ə-nə-līz') *v.* to make explanations for one's behavior
justificar *v.* dar explicaciones racionales de la conducta propia

ravage (răv'ĭj) *n.* serious damage or destruction
devastación *s.* daño o destrucción grave

recuperation (rĭ-ko͞o'pə-rā'shən) *n.* a return to health or strength; recovery
recuperación *s.* regreso a la salud; mejoría

refrain (rĭ-frān') *v.* to hold oneself back; to stop
refrenar *v.* contener, dominar o hacer menos violento; parar

refuge (rĕf'yo͞oj) *n.* a source of comfort in times of trouble
refugio *v.* fuente de consuelo en momentos de dificultad

refute (rĭ-fyo͞ot') *v.* to prove as false
refutar *v.* demostrar que es falso

rehabilitation (rē'hə-bĭl'ĭ-tā'shən) *n.* the process of restoring someone to physical capability, usually through exercise and physical therapy
rehabilitación *s.* proceso de restaurar capacidades físicas con ejercicio y fisioterapia

relay (rē'lā) *n.* a race in which several team members take turns running to complete the race
carrera de relevos *s.* carrera en que los corredores de cada equipo se van relevando

remorse (rĭ-môrs') *n.* sorrow; regret
remordimiento *s.* pesar; arrepentimiento

remote (rĭ-mōt') *adj.* located far away
remoto *adj.* lejano

rendition (rĕn-dĭsh'ən) *n.* a pictorial representation; an interpretation
interpretación *s.* representación pictórica

replete (rĭ-plēt') *adj.* abundantly supplied
repleto *adj.* lleno; atiborrado

reserve (rĭ-zûrv') *n.* self-restraint in the way one looks or acts
reserva *s.* discreción o comedimiento en la forma de presentarse y de actuar

resignation (rĕz'ĭg-nā'shən) *n.* acceptance of something that is inescapable
resignación *s.* conformidad para aceptar lo que no tiene remedio

resolute (rĕz'ə-lo͞ot') *adj.* firm or determined
resuelto *adj.* firme o decidido

R124 GLOSSARY OF VOCABULARY

restrain (rĭ-strān') *v.* to hold back; to control
refrenar *v.* contener; controlar

retort (rĭ-tôrt') *n.* a quick, sharp, witty reply
réplica *s.* respuesta rápida e ingeniosa

rigid (rĭj'ĭd) *adj.* inflexible; strict
rígido *adj.* inflexible; estricto

sacred (sā'krĭd) *adj.* holy; worthy of religious veneration or respect
sagrado *adj.* santo; digno de veneración o respeto religioso

sanctuary (săngk'chōō-ĕr'ē) *n.* a place of refuge
santuario *s.* lugar de refugio

savage (săv'ĭj) *n.* a person regarded as primitive or uncivilized
salvaje *s.* persona a quien se considera primitiva o incivilizada

scale (skāl) *v.* to climb up or over; ascend
escalar *v.* subir; ascender

searing (sîr'ĭng) *adj.* hot enough to burn, char, or scorch
abrasador *adj.* que quema o chamusca

sect (sĕkt) *n.* a religious group
secta *s.* grupo religioso

secure (sĭ-kyŏŏr') *adj.* safe; protected; free from fear or anxiety
seguro *adj.* a salvo; protegido; libre de temores

sensation (sĕn-sā'shən) *n.* a state of great interest and excitement
sensación *s.* estado de gran interés y emoción; furor

sensational (sĕn-sā'shə-nəl) *adj.* intended to arouse strong curiosity or interest, especially through exaggerated details
sensacional *adj.* que llama fuertemente la atención, la curiosidad o el interés, especialmente con detalles exagerados

serendipitous (sĕr'ən-dĭp'ĭ-təs) *adj.* found by fortunate accident
fortuito *adj.* hallado por buena suerte

sheepishly (shē'pĭsh-lē) *adv.* meekly; with embarrassment
tímidamente *adv.* mansamente; con vergüenza

sidekick (sīd'kĭk') *n.* a close friend
compañero *s.* buen amigo

sinister (sĭn'ĭ-stər) *adj.* suggesting or threatening evil
siniestro *adj.* malo o con mala intención

solemn (sŏl'əm) *adj.* deeply serious
solemne *adj.* profundamente serio

specialization (spĕsh'ə-lĭ-za'shən) *n.* a focus on a particular area of study
especialización *s.* preparación en determinada área de estudio

stealthily (stĕl'thə-lē) *adv.* cautiously; secretly
furtivamente *adv.* secretamente; a hurtadillas

sterile (stĕr'əl) *adj.* barren; lacking vitality
estéril *adj.* árido; sin vitalidad

stifled (stī'fəld) *adj.* smothered **stifle** *v.*
sofocado *adj.* ahogado **sofocar** *v.*

stipulation (stĭp'yə-lā'shən) *n.* the act of laying down a condition or agreement
estipulación *s.* acción de definir condiciones o acuerdos

stoop (stōōp) *v.* to bend forward and down from the waist or the middle of the back
encorvarse *v.* doblarse por la cintura o la espalda hacia delante

straddle (străd'l) *v.* to be on both sides of
estar entre dos aguas *v.* estar por ambas partes

straggle (străg'əl) *v.* to spread out in a scattered group
dispersar *v.* separarse en un grupo extendido en distint as direcciones

strew (strōō) *v.* to spread here and there; scatter
esparcir *v.* derramar; dispersar

suavity (swä'vĭ-tē) *n.* graceful politeness
urbanidad *s.* cortesía y afabilidad

subordinate (sə-bôr'dn-ĭt) *adj.* secondary; belonging to a lower rank
subordinado *adj.* secundario; de un rango inferior

subtle (sŭt'l) *adj.* slight; difficult to detect
sutil *adj.* leve; imperceptible

GLOSSARY OF VOCABULARY R125

sullen (sŭl′ən) *adj.* showing silent resentment; sulky
hosco *adj.* resentido; huraño

summon (sŭm′ən) *v.* to send for; call
llamar *v.* mandar a traer

surrender (sə-rĕn′dər) *v.* to give up possession or control to another
rendir *v.* entregar posesiones o control

tactic (tăk′tĭk) *n.* a maneuver to achieve a goal
táctica *s.* maniobra para alcanzar una meta

tangible (tăn′jə-bəl) *adj.* able to be seen, touched, or understood
tangible *adj.* que se puede ver, tocar o entender

tentatively (tĕn′tə-tĭv-lē) *adv.* uncertainly or hesitantly
tentativamente *adv.* provisionalmente; con vacilación

tolerable (tŏl′ər-ə-bəl) *adj.* fairly good; passable
tolerable *adj.* regular; pasable

traipse (trāps) *v.* to walk or tramp around
recorrer *v.* andar de un lado para otro

transcendent (trăn-sĕn′dənt) *adj.* being above the material world
trascendente *adj.* por encima del mundo material

treacherous (trĕch′ər-əs) *adj.* not to be relied on; untrustworthy
traicionero *adj.* traidor; desleal

tremor (trĕm′ər) *n.* nervous trembling
temblor *s.* estremecimiento nervioso

turmoil (tûr′moil′) *n.* a state of extreme confusion or agitation
agitación *s.* estado de extrema confusión o caos

unabashed (ŭn′ə-băsht′) *adj.* obvious; bold
descarado *adj.* desenfadado; sin inmutarse

undaunted (ŭn-dôn′tĭd) *adj.* not discouraged; courageous
intrépido *adj.* impertérrito; sin desanimarse

unravel (ŭn-răv′əl) *v.* to undo; come apart
deshilachar *v.* deshacer; desenredar

unseemly (ŭn-sēm′lē) *adj.* inappropriate
indecoroso *adj.* impropio

valiant (văl′yənt) *adj.* brave
valiente *adj.* valeroso

vehemently (vē′ə-mənt-lē) *adv.* with intense emotion
vehementemente *adv.* con intensa emoción

vermin (vûr′mĭn) *n.*, pl. destructive and annoying insects and small animals, such as cockroaches and rats
alimañas *s.* insectos y animalitos destructivos e indeseables, como cucarachas y ratas

vex (vĕks) *v.* to disturb; to annoy
irritar *v.* molestar; sacar de quicio

vigilant (vĭj′ə-lənt) *adj.* watchful; alert
vigilante *adj.* atento; alerta

vigilantly (vĭj′ə-lənt-lē) *adv.* watchfully
vigilantemente *adv.* con atención

vigorously (vĭg′ər-əs-lē) *adv.* energetically
vigorosamente *adv.* enérgicamente

vileness (vīl′nəs) *n.* unpleasantness; disgusting quality
vileza *s.* inmundicia; asquerosidad

virtuoso (vûr′cho͞o-ō′sō) *n.* a musician with excellent abilities, techniques, and/or an attractive personal style
virtuoso *s.* músico de excelentes aptitudes, técnicas y/o estilo personal atractivo

volatile (vŏl′ə-tl) *adj.* difficult to define or pin down; unpredictable
volátil *adj.* inconstante o mudable; imprevisible

waver (wā′vər) *v.* to exhibit indecision; to hesitate
flaquear *v.* mostrar indecisión; vacilar

wince (wĭns) *v.* to flinch or shrink in pain or distress
estremecerse *v.* encogerse o contraerse por dolor o malestar

yield (yēld) *v.* to give in to another
ceder *v.* rendir

R126 GLOSSARY OF VOCABULARY

Pronunciation Key

Symbol	Examples
ă	**a**t, g**a**s
ā	**a**pe, d**ay**
ä	f**a**ther, b**a**rn
âr	f**air**, d**are**
b	**b**ell, ta**b**le
ch	**ch**in, lun**ch**
d	**d**ig, bore**d**
ĕ	**e**gg, t**e**n
ē	**e**vil, s**ee**, m**ea**l
f	**f**all, lau**gh**, **ph**rase
g	**g**old, bi**g**
h	**h**it, in**h**ale
hw	**wh**ite, every**wh**ere
ĭ	**i**nch, f**i**t
ī	**i**dle, m**y**, tr**i**ed
îr	d**ear**, h**ere**
j	**j**ar, **g**em, ba**dge**
k	**k**eep, **c**at, lu**ck**
l	**l**oad, rattl**e**
m	**m**an, see**m**
n	**n**ight, mitte**n**
ng	si**ng**, ha**ng**er
ŏ	**o**dd, n**o**t
ō	**o**pen, r**oa**d, gr**ow**
ô	**aw**ful, b**ough**t, h**o**rse
oi	c**oi**n, b**oy**
ŏŏ	l**oo**k, f**u**ll
ōō	r**oo**t, gl**ue**, thr**ough**
ou	**ou**t, c**ow**
p	**p**ig, ca**p**
r	**r**ose, sta**r**
s	**s**it, fa**c**e
sh	**sh**e, ma**sh**
t	**t**ap, hoppe**d**
th	**th**ing, wi**th**
th	**th**en, o**th**er
ŭ	**u**p, n**u**t
ûr	f**ur**, **ear**n, b**ir**d, w**or**m
v	**v**an, sa**ve**
w	**w**eb, t**w**ice
y	**y**ard, law**y**er
z	**z**oo, rea**s**on
zh	trea**s**ure, gara**ge**
ə	**a**wake, ev**e**n, penc**i**l, pil**o**t, foc**u**s
ər	perf**or**m, lett**er**

Sounds in Foreign Words

Symbol	Examples
KH	*German* **ich**, au**ch**; *Scottish* lo**ch**
N	*French* e**n**tre, bo**n**, fi**n**
œ	*French* **feu**, **cœur**; *German* sch**ö**n
ü	*French* **u**tile, **rue**; *German* gr**ü**n

Stress Marks

′ This mark indicates that the preceding syllable receives the primary stress. For example, in the word *language*, the first syllable is stressed: lăng′gwĭj.

′ This mark is used only in words in which more than one syllable is stressed. It indicates that the preceding syllable is stressed, but somewhat more weakly than the syllable receiving the primary stress. In the word *literature*, for example, the first syllable receives the primary stress, and the last syllable receives a weaker stress: lĭt′ər-ə-chŏŏr′.

GLOSSARY OF VOCABULARY **R127**

INDEX OF FINE ART

R128 INDEX OF FINE ART

Index of Skills

A

INDEX OF SKILLS **R129**

R130 INDEX OF SKILLS

INDEX OF SKILLS R131

R132 INDEX OF SKILLS

INDEX OF SKILLS R133

J

K

L

R134 INDEX OF SKILLS

INDEX OF SKILLS **R135**

N

O

R136 INDEX OF SKILLS

INDEX OF SKILLS **R137**

Q

R138 INDEX OF SKILLS

INDEX OF SKILLS **R139**

S

R140 INDEX OF SKILLS

INDEX OF SKILLS R141

R142 INDEX OF SKILLS

W

INDEX OF SKILLS **R143**

R144 INDEX OF SKILLS

INDEX OF TITLES & AUTHORS

Page numbers that appear in italics refer to biographical information.

INDEX OF TITLES & AUTHORS **R145**

R146 INDEX OF TITLES & AUTHORS

ACKNOWLEDGMENTS

UNIT 1

Houghton Mifflin: Excerpt from *Johnny Tremain* by Esther Forbes. Copyright © 1943 by Esther Forbes Hoskins. Copyright © renewed 1971 by Linwood M. Erskine, Jr., Executor of the Estate of Esther Forbes Hoskins. Reprinted by permission of Houghton Mifflin Company. All rights reserved.

Random House: "Raymond's Run," from *Gorilla, My Love* by Toni Cade Bambara. Copyright © 1971 by Toni Cade Bambara. Used by permission of Random House, Inc.

The Carol Mann Agency: "Manuscript Found in the Attic" by Marcus Rosenbaum, from *I Thought My Father Was a God: And Other True Tales from NPR's National Story Project* edited by Paul Auster. Copyright © 2001 by Paul Auster. Reprinted by permission of The Carol Mann Agency.

Sterling Lord Literistic: "Clean Sweep" by Joan Bauer, from *Shelf Life, Stories by the Book* edited by Gary Paulsen. Copyright © 2003 by Joan Bauer. Reprinted by permission of SLL/Sterling Lord Literistic, Inc.

William Morris Agency: "The Hitchhiker" by Lucille Fletcher, from *Radio's Best Plays*. Copyright © 1947, 1952, renewed 1980 by Lucille Fletcher. Reprinted by permission of William Morris Agency, LLC, on behalf of the author.

Random House: Excerpt from *Hoot* by Carl Hiassen. Copyright © 2002 by Carl Hiassen. Used by permission of Alfred A. Knopf, an imprint of Random House Children's Books, a division of Random House, Inc.

Susan Bergholz Literary Services: "My First Free Summer" by Julia Alvarez, first published in *Better Homes and Gardens*, August 2003. Copyright © 2003 by Julia Alvarez. Reprinted by permission of Susan Bergholz Literary Services, New York. All rights reserved.

Laurence Yep: "The Great Rat Hunt" by Laurence Yep, from *When I Was Your Age: Original Stories about Growing Up*, edited by Amy Ehrlich. Copyright © 1996 by Laurence Yep. Reprinted by permission of the author.

UNIT 2

Harcourt: Excerpt from "Broken Chain," from *Baseball in April and Other Stories* by Gary Soto. Copyright © 1990 by Gary Soto. Reprinted by permission of Harcourt, Inc.

Miriam Altshuler Literary Agency: "The Treasure of Lemon Brown" by Walter Dean Myers, *Boys' Life*, March 1983. Copyright © 1983 by Walter Dean Myers. Reprinted by permission of Miriam Altshuler Literary Agency, on behalf of Walter Dean Myers.

The New York Times: Excerpts from "Blues Musicians Get Help Overcoming Hard Times" by Andrew Jacobs, from the *New York Times*, March 21, 2004. Copyright © 2004 by the New York Times Co. Reprinted with permission.

Daniel Keyes: "Flowers for Algernon" by Daniel Keyes, from *The Magazine of Fantasy and Science Fiction*. Copyright © 1959, 1987 by Daniel Keyes. Reprinted by permission of the author. All rights reserved.

G.P. Putnam's Sons: "Rules of the Game," from *The Joy Luck Club* by Amy Tan. Copyright © 1989 by Amy Tan. Used by permission of G.P. Putnam's Sons, a division of Penguin Group (USA) Inc.

Virginia Driving Hawk Sneve: "The Medicine Bag" by Driving Hawk, from *Boy's Life*, March 1975. Copyright © 1975 by Virginia Driving Hawk Sneve. Used by permission of the author.

Scholastic: "Who Are You Today, Maria?" from *Call Me Maria* by Judith Ortiz Cofer. Copyright © 2004 by Judith Ortiz Cofer. Published by Scholastic Inc./Orchard Books. Reprinted by permission.

Russell & Volkening: "The Railroad Runs to Canada" and "Go On or Die," from *Harriet Tubman: Conductor of the Underground Railroad* by Ann Petry. Copyright © 1955 by Ann Petry, renewed 1983 by Ann Petry. Reprinted by permission of Russell & Volkening as agents for the author.

Houghton Mifflin: "The Mysterious Mr. Lincoln," from *Lincoln: A Photobiography* by Russell Freedman. Copyright © 1987 by Russell Freedman. Reprinted by permission of Houghton Mifflin Company. All rights reserved.

John Steventon: Excerpt from "Tribute to John Henry" by John Steventon. Used by permission of the author.

UNIT 3

Bancroft Library: Excerpt from *Journey to Topaz: A Story of the Japanese-American Evacuation* by Yoshiko Uchida. Copyright © 1971 by Yoshiko Uchida. Courtesy of the Bancroft Library, University of California, Berkeley.

Don Congdon: "The Drummer Boy of Shiloh" by Ray Bradbury. Copyright © 1960 by the Curtis Publishing Company, renewed 1988 by Ray Bradbury. Reprinted by permission of Don Congdon Associates, Inc.

Ralph M. Vicinanza: "Hallucination" by Isaac Asimov, from *Gold, The Final Science Fiction Collection*. Copyright © 1995 by Nightfall Inc./The Estate of Isaac Asimov. All rights reserved. Reprinted by permission of Ralph M. Vicinanza, Ltd.

Prometheus Books: Excerpt from "Ellis Island and I," from *The Tyrannosaurus Prescription and 100 Other Essays* by Isaac Asimov (Amherst, NY: Prometheus Books). Copyright © 1989 by Isaac Asimov. Reprinted by permission of the publisher.

Dial Books for Young Readers: Excerpt from *Roll of Thunder, Hear My Cry* by Mildred Taylor. Copyright © 1976 by Mildred D. Taylor. Used by permission of Dial Books for Young Readers, A Division of Penguin Young Readers Group, A Member of Penguin Group (USA) Inc., 345 Hudson Street, New York, NY 10014. All rights reserved.

ACKNOWLEDGMENTS **R147**

Naomi Shihab Nye: Excerpt from "Thank You in Arabic" by Naomi Shihab Nye. Copyright © 1995 by Naomi Shihab Nye. First published in *Going Where I'm Coming From* by arrangement with the author. Used by permission of the author, Naomi Shihab Nye, 2006.

Naomi Shihab Nye: "My Father and the Figtree," from *19 Varieties of Gazelle: Poems of the Middle East* by Naomi Shihab Nye. Copyright © 1994, 1995, 1998, 2002 by Naomi Shihab Nye. Reprinted with permission.

The Wylie Agency: Excerpts from "Leaving Desire, The Ninth Ward after the Hurricane" by Jon Lee Anderson, from the *New Yorker,* September 19, 2005. Copyright © 2005 by Jon Lee Anderson. Used by permission of the Wylie Agency, as agents for the author.

Arte Público Press: "Mi Madre," from *Chants* by Pat Mora. Copyright © 1986 by Arte Público Press—University of Houston. Reprinted with permission from Arte Público Press.

Simon J. Ortiz: "Canyon de Chelly" by Simon J. Ortiz, originally published in *Woven Stone*, University of Arizona Press, Tucson, AZ. Copyright © 1992 by Simon J. Ortiz. Permission granted by the author.

UNIT 4

Scholastic: "Abuela Invents the Zero," from *An Island Like You: Stories of the Barrio* by Judith Ortiz Cofer. Copyright © 2005 by Judith Ortiz Cofer. Reprinted by permission of Orchard Books/ Scholastic Inc.

Susan Bergholz Literary Services: "Gil's Furniture Bought & Sold," from *The House on Mango Street* by Sandra Cisneros. Copyright © 1984 by Sandra Cisneros. Published by Vintage Books, a division of Random House, Inc., and in hardcover by Alfred A. Knopf in 1994. Reprinted by permission of Susan Bergholz Literary Services, New York. All rights reserved.

M. Evans: "Pandora . . . The Fateful Casket," from *The Firebringer and Other Great Stories, Fifty-Five Legends That Will Live Forever* by Louis Untermeyer. Copyright © 1968 by Louis Untermeyer. Reprinted by permission of M. Evans, an imprint of Taylor Trade Publishing, Lanham, MD.

Little Simon: "The Old Grandfather and His Little Grandson," from *Twenty-Two Russian Tales for Young Children* by Leo Tolstoy, translated by Miriam Morton. Translation copyright © 1969 by Miriam Morton. Reprinted by permission of Little Simon, an imprint of Simon & Schuster Children's Publishing Division.

Bancroft Library: "The Wise Old Woman," from *The Sea of Gold and Other Tales from Japan* adapted by Yoshiko Uchida. Copyright © 1965 by Yoshiko Uchida. Courtesy of the Bancroft Library, University of California, Berkeley.

Teresa Palomo Acosta: "My Mother Pieced Quilts" by Teresa Palomo Acosta, from *Festival de Flor y Canto: An Anthology of Chicano Literature.* Copyright © by Teresa Palomo Acosta. Used by permission of the author.

BOA Editions: "quilting," from *Quilting: Poems 1987–1990* by Lucille Clifton. Copyright © 1991 by Lucille Clifton. Reprinted by permission of BOA Editions, Ltd.

Random House: *The Diary of Anne Frank* by Frances Goodrich and Albert Hackett. Copyright © 1956 by Albert Hackett, Frances Goodrich Hackett, and Otto Frank. Used by permission of Random House, Inc.

Doubleday: Excerpt from *The Diary of a Young Girl: the Definitive Edition* by Anne Frank. Edited by Otto H. Frank and Mirjam Pressler. Translated by Susan Massotty. Copyright © 1995 by Doubleday. Used by permission of Doubleday, a division of Random House, Inc.

Gerda Klein: Excerpts from "A Diary from Another World" by Gerda Weissman Klein, from *Buffalo News*. Used by permission of the author.

UNIT 5

Rosina M. Albi: Excerpt from "Street Corner Flight" by Norma Landa Flores, from *Sighs and Songs of Aztlan* edited by F. E. Albi and J. G. Nieto. Copyright © 1975 by F. E. Albi and J. G. Nieto. Reprinted by permission of Rosina M. Albi.

The Overlook Press: Excerpt from "That Day," from *I Remember Root River* by David Kherdian. Copyright © 1978 by David Kherdian. Used by permission of the Overlook Press.

Henry Holt and Company: "Stopping by Woods on a Snowy Evening," from *The Poetry of Robert Frost* edited by Edward Connery Lathem. Copyright 1923, 1969 by Henry Holt and Company. Copyright © 1951 by Robert Frost. Reprinted by permission of Henry Holt and Company, LLC.

HarperCollins: Excerpt from "Chrysalis Diary" from *Joyful Noise: Poems for Two Voices* by Paul Fleischman. Copyright © 1988 by Paul Fleischman. Used by permission of HarperCollins Publishers.

Okpaku Communications: "Sunset," from *Sounds of a Cowhide Drum* by Oswald Mbuyiseni Mtshali. Copyright © 1972 by the Third Press, Joseph Okpaku Publishing Company. Used by permission of Okpaku Communication Corporation.

Houghton Mifflin: Excerpt from "Water Picture," from *Nature: Poems Old and New* by May Swenson. Copyright © 1994 by the Literary Estate of May Swenson. Reprinted by permission of Houghton Mifflin Company. All rights reserved.

New Directions: "Aware," from *This Great Unknowing: Last Poems* by Denise Levertov. Copyright © 1999 by the Denise Levertov Literary Trust, Paul A. Lacey and Valerie Trueblood Rapport, Co-Trustees. Reprinted by permission of New Directions Publishing Corp.

The University of Georgia Press: "Lineage," from *For My People* by Margaret Walker. Copyright © 1942 by Yale University Press. Reprinted by permission of the University of Georgia Press.

Marian Reiner: "Simile: Willow and Ginkgo," from *It Doesn't Always Have to Rhyme* by Eve Merriam. Copyright © 1964 by Eve Merriam. Used by permission of Marian Reiner.

University of Arkansas Press: "Introduction to Poetry," from *The Apple That Astonished Paris* by Billy Collins. Copyright © 1988 by Billy Collins. Reprinted by permission of the University of Arkansas Press.

Harcourt: "Macavity: The Mystery Cat," from *Old Possum's Book of Practical Cats* by T. S. Eliot. Copyright © 1939 by T. S. Eliot and renewed 1967 by Esme Valerie Eliot. Reprinted by permission of Harcourt, Inc.

R148 ACKNOWLEDGMENTS

Doubleday: "The Lesson of the Moth," from *Archy and Mehitabel* by Don Marquis. Copyright © 1927 by Doubleday. Used by permission of Doubleday, a division of Random House, Inc.

Harvard University Press and the Trustees of Amherst College: "It's all I have to bring today" by Emily Dickinson, from *The Poems of Emily Dickinson*, Thomas J. Johnson, ed., Cambridge, Mass.: The Belknap Press of Harvard University Press. Copyright © 1951, 1955, 1979, 1983 by the President and Fellows of Harvard College. Reprinted by permission of the publishers and the Trustees of Amherst College.

Harcourt: "We Alone," from *Horses Make a Landscape Look More Beautiful: Poems by Alice Walker.* Copyright © 1984 by Alice Walker. Reprinted by permission of Harcourt, Inc.

Brooks Permissions: "Speech to the Young: Speech to the Progress-Toward," from *Blacks* by Gwendolyn Brooks. Copyright © by Gwendolyn Brooks. Reprinted by consent of Brooks Permissions.

Alfred A. Knopf: "Mother to Son," from *The Collected Poems of Langston Hughes* by Langston Hughes. Copyright © 1994 by the Estate of Langston Hughes. Used by permission of Alfred A. Knopf, a division of Random House, Inc.

Random House: "One More Round," from *And Still I Rise* by Maya Angelou. Copyright © 1978 by Maya Angelou. Used by permission of Random House, Inc.

Boyds Mills Press: "Not My Bones," from *Fortune's Bones, The Manumission Requiem* by Marilyn Nelson (Front Street, an imprint of Boyds Mills Press, 2003.) Poem copyright © 2003 by Marilyn Nelson. Reprinted with the permission of Boyds Mills Press, Inc.

Special Rider Music: "Boots of Spanish Leather" by Bob Dylan. Copyright © 1963 by Warner Bros. Inc. Copyright renewed 1991 by Special Rider Music. All rights reserved. International copyright secured. Reprinted by permission.

UNIT 6

The C. S. Lewis Company: Excerpt from *The Voyage of the Dawn Treader* by C. S. Lewis. Copyright © 1952 by C. S. Lewis Pte. Ltd. Extract reprinted by permission.

Brandt & Hochman: Excerpt from "The Truth About the World" by Lloyd Alexander. Copyright © 2005 by Lloyd Alexander. First published in *Guys Write for Guys Read* (Viking, 2005.) Reprinted by permission of Brandt & Hochman Literary Agents, Inc. All rights reserved.

Soho Press: Excerpt from *Krik? Krak!* by Edwidge Danticat. Copyright © 1991, 1992, 1993, 1994, and 1995 by Edwidge Danticat. Reprinted by permission of Soho Press, Inc.

The New York Times: Adaptation of "Behind Monty Hall's Doors: Puzzle, Debate and Answer?" by John Tierney, from the *New York Times*. Copyright © 1991 by the New York Times Company. Reprinted with permission.

Atheneum Books for Young Readers: Excerpt from *Kira-Kira* by Cynthia Kadohata. Copyright © 2004 by Cynthia Kadohata. Reprinted with the permission of Atheneum Books for Young Readers, an imprint of Simon & Schuster Children's Publishing Division.

Little, Brown and Co: Excerpt from *Dress Your Family in Corduroy and Denim* by David Sedaris. Copyright © 2004 by David Sedaris. By permission of Little, Brown and Co., Inc.

UNIT 7

BOA Editions: "Eating Together," from *Rose*, by Li-Young Lee. Copyright © 1986 by Li-Young Lee. Reprinted by permission of BOA Editions, Ltd.

Susan Bergholz: "Dusting," from *Homecoming: New and Collected Poems* by Julia Alvarez. Copyright © 1984, 1996 by Julia Alvarez. Used by permission of Susan Bergholz.

Barbara S. Kouts: "The Snapping Turtle" by Joseph Bruchac, from *When I Was Your Age*, Vol. Two, Candlewick Press, 1999. Copyright © 1999 by Joseph Bruchac. Reprinted by permission of Barbara S. Kouts Literary Agency.

Viking Penguin: Excerpt from *The Pearl* by John Steinbeck. Copyright © 1945 by John Steinbeck. Copyright © renewed 1973 by Elaine Steinbeck, Thom Steinbeck, and John Steinbeck IV. Used by permission of Viking Penguin, a division of Penguin Group (USA) Inc.

Gary Soto: "One Last Time," from *Living Up the Street* by Gary Soto. Copyright © 1985 by Gary Soto. Used by permission of the author.

Harcourt: "How Things Work," from *A Fire in My Hands* by Gary Soto. Copyright © 2006, 1999 by Gary Soto. Reprinted by permission of Harcourt, Inc. This material may not be reproduced in any form or by any means without the prior written permission of the publisher.

The University of Georgia Press: "Sit-ins" and "I Want to Write," from *This Is My Century, New and Collected Poems* by Margaret Walker. Copyright © 1989 by Margaret Walker Alexander. Reprinted by permission of the University of Georgia Press.

Scholastic: Excerpt from *A Dream of Freedom: The Civil Rights Movement from 1954 to 1968* by Diane McWhorter. Copyright © 2004 by Diane McWhorter. Reprinted by permission of Scholastic Inc./Nonfiction.

UNIT 8

National Geographic Society: "Female Android Debuts in S. Korea" by Victoria Gilman, from *National Geographic News*, May 15, 2006. Copyright © 2006 by National Geographic Society. Reprinted by permission of the National Geographic Society.

National Geographic Society: Excerpt from "Escape from the Blaze" by Michael Burgan, from *National Geographic World*, September 1988. Copyright © 1988 by National Geographic Society. Reprinted by permission of the National Geographic Society.

National Geographic Society: "The Spider Man Behind Spider-Man" by Bijal P. Trivedi, from *National Geographic Today*, May 2, 2002. Copyright © 2002 by National Geographic Society. Reprinted by permission of the National Geographic Society.

National Geographic Society: Excerpts from "Over the Top: The True Adventures of a Volcano Chaser" by Renee Skelton, from *National Geographic World*, June 2001. Copyright © 2001 by National Geographic Society. Reprinted by permission of the National Geographic Society.

ACKNOWLEDGMENTS **R149**

National Geographic Society: Excerpt from "Q&A: 'Songcatcher' Pioneer on Musical Heritage" by Brian Handwerk, from *National Geographic News*, June 16, 2003. Copyright © 2003 by National Geographic Society. Reprinted by permission of the National Geographic Society.

The New York Times: Excerpt from "Robo-Legs" by Michael Marriott, from the *New York Times*, June 20, 2005. Copyright © 2005 by the New York Times. Reprinted with permission.

Houghton Mifflin: Excerpt from *An American Plague: The True and Terrifying Story of the Yellow Fever Epidemic of 1793* by Jim Murphy. Copyright © 2003 by Jim Murphy. Reprinted by permission of Clarion Books, an imprint of Houghton Mifflin Company. All rights reserved.

UNIT 9

NASPE: "Position on Dodgeball in Physical Education" by NASPE. Reprinted with permission from the National Association for Sport and Physical Education (NASPE), 1900 Association Drive, Reston, VA 20191-1599.

Sports Illustrated: Excerpts from "The Weak Shall Inherit the Gym" by Rick Reilly, from *Sports Illustrated*, May 14, 2001. Copyright © 2001 by Time Inc. Reprinted courtesy of *Sports Illustrated*. All rights reserved.

The New York Times: "The Sanctuary of School" by Lynda Barry, from the *New York Times*, January 5, 1992. Copyright © 1992 by the New York Times. Reprinted with permission.

The editors have made every effort to trace the ownership of all copyrighted material found in this book and to make full acknowledgment for its use. Omissions brought to our attention will be corrected in a subsequent edition.

R150 ACKNOWLEDGMENTS

ART CREDITS

CONSULTANTS

Title page © Image 100/PunchStock; Consultants Photo © Duane McCubrey; Photo © Mark Schmidt; Photo © Bruce Forrester; Photo © McDougal Littell; Photo © Howard Gollub; Photo © Tamra Stallings; Photo © Mark Schmidt; Photo © Robert J. Marzano; Photo © McDougal Littell; Photo © Dawson & Associates Photography; Photo © Gitchell's Studio Photo © Michael Romeo; Photo © Monica Ani; Photo © William McBride; Photo © Bill Caldwell; Photo © Gabriel Pauluzzi; Photo © Steven Scheffler.

TABLE OF CONTENTS

Contents in Brief verso *top* © Edwin Wallace/Mary Evans Picture Library; *bottom, Deer Spirit Helper,* Joe Geshick. Oil. © Joe Geshick; *top* © Steve Bloom/Getty Images; *bottom* © Getty Images; **Unit 1 verso** *top left* Illustration by Howard Simpson; *top right* © er Productions/Getty Images; *bottom* Courtesy American Library Association; **recto** *left* Cover of *Kite Rider* by Geraldine McCaughrean. © 2001 by Geraldine McCaughrean. Reprinted by permission of HarperCollins Children's Books, a division of HarperCollins Publishers, New York; **Unit 2 verso** *left* From *Harlem* by Walter Dean Myers, illustrated by Christopher Myers. © 1997 by Christopher Myers. Reprinted by permission of Scholastic, Inc.; *right, Frida* (2004), Maria Sanchez. Acrylic on canvas. C. Perez Collection. © Maria Sanchez; **recto** *left* © McDougal Littell; *right* Cover of *Sir Walter Raleigh and the Quest for El Dorado* by Marc Aronson. Jacket illustration © 2000 by Kayley LeFaiver. Reprinted by permission of Clarion Books, an imprint of Houghton Mifflin Company; **Unit 3 verso** *top left, Jerusalem* (1984), Tamam Al-akhal. Palestine. Oil on canvas, 50 cm × 70 cm. Private collection; *top right* © Jupiter Images; *bottom* Courtesy American Library Association; **recto** *left* Cover of *Tofu and T. Rex* by Greg Leitich Smith. © 2005 by Greg H. Leitich. Cover photo by Michael Wang. Reprinted by permission of Little, Brown and Company; *right* Cover of *Run, Boy, Run* by Uri Orlev. Copyright © 2003 by Uri Orlev. Reprinted by permission of Houghton Mifflin Company; **Unit 4 verso** *left, Crossing Borders* (1995), Diedre Scherer. Fabric and thread. © Diedre Scherer; *right* © Joan Marcus; **recto** *left* Cover of *The Thief Lord* by Cornelia Funke. © 2000 by Cornelia Funke. Cover illustration © 2002 by Christian Birmingham. Reprinted by permission of Scholastic, Inc., New York; *right* © McDougal Littell; **Unit 5 verso** *left, Aspiration* (1936), Aaron Douglas. Oil on canvas, 60″ × 60″. © Fine Arts Museums of San Francisco purchase, the estate of Thurlow E. Tibbs, Jr., the Museum Society Auxiliary, American Art Trust Fund, Unrestricted Art Trust Fund, partial gift of Dr. Ernest A. Bates, Sharon Bell, Jo-Ann Beverly, Barbara Carleton, Dr. and Mrs. Arthur H. Coleman, Dr. and Mrs. Coyness Ennix, Jr., Nicole Y. Ennix, Mr. and Mrs. Gary Francois, Dennis L. Franklin, Mr. and Mrs. Maxwell C. Gillette, Mr. and Mrs. Richard Goodyear, Zuretti L. Goosby, Marion E. Greene, Mrs. Vivian S. W. Hambrick, Laurie Gibbs Harris, Arlene Hollis, Louis A. and Letha Jeanpierre, Daniel and Jackie Johnson, Jr., Stephen L. Johnson, Mr. and Mrs. Arthur Lathan, Lewis and Ribbs Mortuary Garden Chapel, Mr. and Mrs. Gary Love, Glenn R. Nance, Mr. and Mrs. Harry S. Parker III, Mr. and Mrs. Carr T. Preston, Fannie Preston, Pamela R. Ransom, Dr. and Mrs. Benjamin F. Reed, San Francisco Black Chamber of Commerce, San Francisco Chapter of Links, Inc., San Francisco Chapter of the N.A.A.C.P., Sigma Pi Phi Fraternity, Dr. Ella Mae Simmons, Mr. Calvin R. Swinson, Joseph B. Williams, Mr. and Mrs. Alfred S. Wilsey, and the people of the Bay Area, 1997.84; *right* © Corbis; **recto** *left* Cover of *Criss Cross* by Lynne Rae Perkins. © 2005 by Lynn Rae Perkins. Reprinted by permission of HarperCollins Children's Books, a division of HarperCollins Publishers, New York; *right* Cover of *Colibri* by Ann Cameron. Jacket design by Ana Juan. Jacket art © 2003 by Ana Juan. Reprinted by permission of Farrar, Straus and Giroux, New York; **Unit 6 verso** *top left, Lincoln 2,* Wendy Allen. Oil on canvas. © Wendy Allen; *top, right Californians Catching Wild Horses with Riata* (about 1851), Hugo Wilhelm Arthur Nahl. Oil on canvas mounted on masonite. Courtesy of the Oakland Museum of California Kahn Collection (A65.57) © Laurie Platt Winfrey/Oakland Museum/The Art Archive; *bottom* Courtesy American Library Association; **recto** *left* Cover of *Act I, Act II, Act Normal* by Martha Weston. © 2003 by Martha Weston. Jacket illustration © 2003 by Martha Weston. Reprinted by permission of Roaring Book Press, a Division of The Millbrook Press, Brookfield, Connecticut; *right* Cover of *O Pioneers* by Willa Cather. 1995, Houghton Mifflin, Boston; *right inset* © Tom Bean/Corbis; **Unit 7 verso** *top left* © Steve McCurry/Magnum Photos; *top right* Illustration by Michael McCurdy. © 1991 by Michael McCurdy, from *American Tall Tales* by Mary Pope Osborne. Used by permission of Alfred A. Knopf, an imprint of Random House Children's Books, a division of Random House, Inc.; *bottom* AP/Wide World Photos; **recto** *left* Cover from *Lizzie Bright and the Buckminster Boy* by Gary D. Schmidt. Copyright © 2004 by Gary D. Schmidt. Reprinted by permission of Clarion Books, an imprint of Houghton Mifflin Company; *right* Cover of *Gathering Blue* by Lois Lowry. © 2000 by Lois Lowry. Reprinted by permission of Random House Inc., New York; **Unit 8 verso** *left* © Science Source/Photo Researchers, Inc.; *right* © Carsten Peter/National Geographic Image Collection; **recto** *top* Courtesy American Library Association; *bottom left* From *Eragon, Inheritance, Book One* by Christopher Paolini. Text © 2003 by Christopher Paolini. Cover illustration © 2003 by John Jude Palencar. Used by permission of Alfred A. Knopf, an imprint of Random House Children's Books, a division of Random House, Inc., New York; *bottom right* Cover of *Stonecutter* by Leander Watts. Copyright © 2002 by Leander Watts. Reprinted by permission of Houghton Mifflin Company; **Unit 9 verso** *left* © Getty Images; *right* © Steve Bly/Alamy Images; **recto** *left* Cover of *The Exchange Student* by Kate Gilmore. Copyright © 1999 by Kate Gilmore. Reprinted by permission of Houghton Mifflin Company; *right* Cover of *Quicksilver* by Stephanie Spinner. Text © 2005 by Stephanie Spinner. Reprinted by permission of Alfred A. Knopf, an imprint of Random House Children's Books, a division of Random House, Inc., New York; **Unit 10** *left* Cover of *Kids Inventing!* by Susan Casey. © 2005 by Susan Mary Casey.

ART CREDITS R151

All rights reserved. Cover design by Chris Wallace. Reprinted by permission of John Wiley & Sons, Inc., Hoboken, New Jersey, Photograph by Sharon Hoogstraten; *right* © Getty Images.

INTRODUCTORY UNIT

1 *left, The Promenade, Fifth Avenue* (1986), Bill Jacklin. Oil on canvas, 243.6 cm × 182.7 cm. Private collection. © Bill Jacklin/ Bridgeman Art Library; *top right* © Bill Brooks/Masterfile; *bottom right* Detail of *Harriet Tubman* (1945), William H. Johnson. Oil on paperboard, sheet, 29⅜″ × 23⅜″. Smithsonian American Art Museum, Washington, D.C. © Smithsonian American Art Museum, Washington, D.C./Art Resource, New York; **2** *left, The Olive Tree* (2005), Ismail Shammout. Palestine. Oil on canvas, 60 cm × 80 cm. Private collection; *right* Fort Sumter National Monument/National Park Service; **3** *left* © Getty Images; *right, Communion,* Joe Geshick. © Joe Geshick; **6** © Stephen Stickler/Getty Images; **8** *top to bottom* Library of Congress; © Getty Images; © Rick Wilking/Reuters/Corbis; © Carsten Peter/National Geographic Image Collection; Commuter Rail Division of the Regional Transportation Authority, d/b/a/ Metra; **9** © Jerry Cooke/Corbis; **10** *top to bottom Whale Rider* footage provided courtesy of South Pacific Pictures Limited. © South Pacific Pictures Limited and ApolloMedia GmbH & Co 5 Filmproduktion KG 2002/© Newmarket/Courtesy The Everett Collection; © Gary Hershorn/Reuters/Corbis; Photo by Will Hart/© NBC/Courtesy of the Everett Collection/The Everett Collection; Footage courtesy of Lucasfilm Ltd. *Star Wars: Episode III-Revenge of the Sith* © 2005 Lucasfilm Ltd. & TM. All rights reserved. Used under authorization. Unauthorized duplication is a violation of applicable law; © James Leynse/Corbis; **13** © Gusto Images/Getty Images; **16** *left* © Comstock Images/Age Fotostock; *center* © SW Productions/Getty Images; *right-top background* © 2007 *The Daily Northwestern*; *right-top right* © Carsten Peter/ National Geographic Image Collection;*right: center cover background* © Bob Gelberg/Sharpshooters; *frontispiece background* The Granger Collection, New York; Amelia Earhart: © Albert L. Bresnik; Maya Lin: © 1999 Richard Howard/Black Star; Juan Seguín: Detail of *Juan Seguín* (1838), Jefferson Wright. Texas State Library and Archives Commission;Harry S. Truman: White House Collection. © White House Historical Association. Courtesy of the Harry S. Truman Library; Ida Bell Wells: The Granger Collection, New York; Abigail Adams: *Portrait traditionally said to be Abigail Adams* (about 1795), artist unknown. Oil on canvas, 30¼″ × 26½″, N-150.55. Photograph by Richard Walker. Copyright © New York State Historical Association, Cooperstown, New York; Zitkala-Sa: Negative no. Mss 299, Tom Perry Special Collections, William F. Hansen Collection, Photographic Archives, Harold B. Lee Library, Brigham Young University, Provo, Utah; Benjamin Franklin**:** © Joseph-Siffrede Duplessis/Wood River Gallery/PNI; Abraham Lincoln: Library of Congress; Martin Luther King, Jr: Photograph by Howard Sochrer/*Life* magazine © Time Inc; *right: left bottom* © Time & Life Pictures/Getty Images; *right: bottom center* © Regin Igloria; *right* Photograph by Sharon Hoogstraten; **17** *left* © Google; *right* © Ragnar Schmuck/Getty Images; **18** © Jupiter Images; **19** *left* © ImageSource/Age Fotostock; *center* © Susan Wides/ PunchStock; *right* © Corbis/Age Fotostock America, Inc.

UNIT 1

21 *left* Illustrations © 2004 by Jan Peng-Wang. From *A Song for Ba,* text © 2004 by Paul Yee. First published in Canada by Groundwood Books, Ltd. Reprinted by permission of the publisher; *right background* © StockAB/Alamy Images; *right foreground* © Michael Kelley/ Getty Images; **22** Cover of *Dragon of the Lost Sea* by Laurence Yep. © 1982 by Laurence Yep. Reprinted by permission of HarperCollins Children's Books, a division of HarperCollins Publishers, New York. Photo by Sharon Hoogstraten; **22–23** © Adam Woolfitt/Corbis; **24** *left* © Corbis; *center left* © Terje Rakke/Getty Images; *center right* © Dean Conger/Corbis; *right* © Medioimages/Getty Images; **27** © Vance Lessard/Getty Images; **31** © Photodisc/Getty Images; **32** © 2005 Getty Images; **33** © Schomburg Center for Research in Black Culture, New York Public Library/Art Resource, New York; **35** *foreground* © Michael Kelley/Getty Images; *background* © StockAB/Alamy Images; **37** © Lise Gagne/istockphoto.com; **39** © Ingram Publishing Royalty Free Photography/Fotosearch Stock Photography; **42** © er Productions/Getty Images; **46** © Warner Bros./Photofest; **47** © Bettmann/Corbis; **50** The Granger Collection, New York; **58** © Brown Brothers, Sterling, PA; **62** © Photograph by Sharon Hoogstraten; **63** © Penguin Young Readers Group; **65** © Didier Robcis/Getty Images; **66** © Andrew Syred/Photo Researchers, Inc.; **68** © Dennis Novak/Getty Images; **72** © Peter Marlow/Magnum Photos; **76** © Nick Koudis/Getty Images; **77** © Bettmann/Corbis; **86** © Louie Psihoyos/Science Faction; **87** © CBS/Landov; **89** © Gene Laughter, 2006; **90** © Ferdinando Scianna/Magnum Photos; **93** © Raymond Depardon/Magnum Photos; **96** © Andreas Feininger/Time & Life Pictures/Getty Images; **100** *top* © Les Cunliffe/Age Fotostock America, Inc.; *bottom* © Jerry Bauer; **100–101** © David R. Frazier Photolibrary, Inc./Alamy Images; **101** *top* Courtesy American Library Association; *bottom* Cover of *Hoot* by Carl Hiaasen. © 2002 by Carl Hiaasen. Cover design and illustration © 2004 by Alfred A. Knopf. Reprinted by permission of Alfred A. Knopf, an imprint of Random House Children's Books, a division of Random House, Inc.; **102–103** © Paul Harris/Getty Images; **104–105** © Junichi Kusaka/MIXA Co., Ltd./Alamy; **106**, **107** © Warner Bother/Courtesy The Everett Collection; **108** *top*, *center* © Warner Brothers Entertainment Inc. All rights reserved; *bottom* © PunchStock; **110** © Reg Charity/Corbis; **111** Photo by Bill Eichner; **113** *The Stillness of an Afternoon* (2003), Bo Bartlett. Oil on panel, 18½″ × 21″. Courtesy of the artist and P.P.O.W. Gallery, New York; **114** © GeoNova LLC; **118** © Getty Images; **119** Courtesy of Laurence Yep; **121**, **125**, **128** Illustrations © 2004 by Jan Peng-Wang. From *A Song for Ba,* text © 2004 by Paul Yee. First published in Canada by Groundwood Books, Ltd. Reprinted by permission of the publisher; **132** © AFP/Getty Images; **133** © Stock Montage; **135** Illustration © 2001 by Christopher Bing. From *The Midnight Ride of Paul Revere* by Henry Wadsworth Longfellow, graved and painted by Christopher Bing. Reprinted by permission of Handprint Books, New York; **136** © Raymond Gehman/Getty Images; **138** © Bill Brooks/Alamy Images; **141***William Dawes* (unknown), attributed to John Johnston. Oil on canvas, 35″ × 29″. © Collection of the Evanston Historical Society, Evanston, Illinois; **142** © GeoNova LLC; **144**, **150**

R152 ART CREDITS

© Craig Aurness/Corbis; **151** © Thinkstock/PunchStock; **158** *top left* Cover of *Dancing at the Odinochka* by Kirkpatrick Hill. © 2005 by Kirkpatrick Hill. Reprinted by permission of Margaret K. McElderry Books, an imprint of Simon & Schuster Children's Publishing Division, New York; Jacket design by Raquel Jaramillo; *cover bottom image* Anchorage Museum at Rasmuson Center. Library and Archives. Jasper Wyman Collection, #288; *top right* Cover of *Lord of the Deep* by Graham Salisbury. © 2001 by Graham Salisbury. Cover illustration by Joel Peter Johnson. Reprinted by permission of Dell Laurel-Leaf, an imprint of Random House Children's Books, a division of Random House, Inc., New York; *center left* Cover of *Kite Rider* by Geraldine McCaughrean. © 2001 by Geraldine McCaughrean. Reprinted by permission of HarperCollins Children's Books, a division of HarperCollins Publishers, New York; *bottom left* Cover of *Code Orange* by Caroline B. Cooney. © 2005 by Caroline B. Cooney. Reprinted by permission of Delacorte Press, an imprint of Random House Children's Books, a division of Random House, Inc., New York; *bottom right, A Girl Named Disaster* by Nancy Farmer. © 1996 by Nancy Farmer. Cover illustration © 1998 Robert Hunt. Reprinted by permission of Puffin Books, a division of the Penguin Group (USA), Inc., 375 Hudson Street, New York, New York 10014. All rights reserved.

UNIT 2

159 *left* © Mary Grace Long/Getty Images; *right* Detail of *They Moved Them* (1991), David Behrens. Oil glazing, 9¼″ × 14½″. © David Behrens, www.davidbehrens.com; **160** © BBC Films/Photofest; **160–161** *center* © DreamWorks Animation/Zuma/Corbis; **163** © Jamie Thorpe/ShutterStock; **164** © Digital Vision/PunchStock; **168** © Clarissa Leahy/Getty Images; **169** © Jerry Bauer; **171, 174** From *Harlem* by Walter Dean Myers, illustrated by Christopher Myers. © 1997 by Christopher Myers. Reprinted by permission of Scholastic, Inc.; **183** *top left* The Granger Collection, New York; *top right* © Bettmann/Corbis; *bottom left* © Getty Images; *bottom right* © Bob Adelman/Magnum Photos; **184** *left, right* AP/Wide World Photos; *center left* The Granger Collection, New York; *center right* © Bettmann/Corbis; **188** © Paul Eekhoff/Masterfile; **189** *top* © Beth Gwinn, Photographer; **189** *bottom* CBS/Landov; **191** Detail of *Mean Dog* (1998), Sylvia Chesley Smith. © Sylvia Chesley Smith/Corbis; **192** The Granger Collection, New York; **195** Corbis; **198** Todd Davidson/Illustration Works; **203** Images.com/Corbis; **205** Todd Davidson/Stock Illustration RF/Getty Images; **209** © Todd Davidson PTY Ltd/The Image Bank/Getty Images; **213** © Images.com/Corbis; **217** © Selmur/Cinema Rel. Corp./The Kobal Collection; **222** © Ariel Skelley/Corbis; **223** © Jennifer Graylock/AP/Wide World Photos; **225** © Mary Grace Long/Getty Images; **227** © Morton Beebe/Corbis; **230** © Martin Barraud/Getty Images; **234** © Corbis; **238** © Lindsay Hebberd/Corbis; **239** *top* Courtesy of Virginia Driving Hawk Sneve; *bottom* Photo of Judith Ortiz Cofer is reprinted with permission from the publisher Arte Publico Press. © 2005, University of Houston, Houston, Texas; **242** © GeoNova LLC; **245** Photo by Sharon Hoogstraten; **254** *Whale Rider* footage provided courtesy of South Pacific Pictures Limited, © South Pacific Pictures Limited and ApolloMedia GmbH & Co 5 Filmproduktion KG 2002/© Newmarket/Courtesy The Everett Collection; **255, 256** *top Whale Rider* footage provided courtesy of South Pacific Pictures Limited. © South Pacific Pictures Limited and ApolloMedia GmbH & Co 5 Filmproduktion KG 2002; **256** *bottom* © Digitalvision/PunchStock; **258** AP/Wide World Photos; **259** Courtesy of The Connecticut Women's Hall of Fame; **261** *Harriet Tubman* (1945), William H. Johnson. Oil on paperboard, sheet, 29⅜″ × 23⅜″. Smithsonian American Art Museum, Washington, D.C. © Smithsonian American Art Museum, Washington, D.C./Art Resource, New York; **262** *Through Forest, Through Rivers, Up Mountains* (1967), Jacob Lawrence. Tempera, gouache and pencil on paper, 15¹¹⁄₁₆″ × 26⅞″. The Joseph H. Hirshhorn Bequest, 1981. Smithsonian Institution, Hirshhorn Museum and Sculpture Garden. Photo by Lee Stalsworth. © 2007 The Jacob and Gwendolyn Lawrence Foundation, Seattle/Artists Rights Society (ARS), New York. Reproduction, including downloading of Lawrence works is prohibited by copyright laws and international conventions without the express written permission of Artists Rights Society (ARS), New York; **264** © GeoNova LLC; **267** *An Underground Railroad* (1967), Jacob Lawrence. Gouache and tempera on paper, 14¼″ × 13″. Collection of Marylin Bender Altschul, New York. © 2007 The Jacob and Gwendolyn Lawrence Foundation, Seattle/Artists Rights Society (ARS), New York. Reproduction, including downloading of Lawrence works is prohibited by copyright laws and international conventions without the express written permission of Artists Rights Society (ARS), New York; **269** *Harriet and the Promised Land No. 15: Canada Bound* (1967), Jacob Lawrence. Gouache and tempera over black colored pencil on very rough cream, 16½″ × 28¼″. The University of Michigan Museum of Art. Gift of Dr. James and Vivian Curtis. (1997/1.531). © 2007 The Jacob and Gwendolyn Lawrence Foundation, Seattle/Artists Rights Society (ARS), New York. Reproduction, including downloading of Lawrence works is prohibited by copyright laws and international conventions without the express written permission of Artists Rights Society (ARS), New York; **270** *top* © National Archives, Washington, D.C./The Art Archive; *frame* Library of Congress; *signature* © North Wind/North Wind Picture Archives. All rights reserved; **271** © GeoNova LLC; **274** © Grant Faint/Getty Images; **275** © Evans Chan; **277, 279** Library of Congress; **280** © William Manning/Corbis; **282** © Sean Justice/Getty Images; **283** The Granger Collection, New York; **285** Fort Sumter National Monument/National Park Service; **288** © Corbis; **290** © 2003 John Steventon; **292, 298** © Joseph Sohm; ChromoSohm Inc./Corbis; **299** © Spencer Grant/PhotoEdit; **306** *top left* Cover of *A Thief in the House of Memory* by Tim Wynne-Jones. © 2004 by Tim Wynne-Jones. Jacket design by Jay Colvin. Jacket photo by Kamil Vojar. Reprinted by permission of Melanie Kroupa Books, a division of Farrar, Straus and Giroux, New York; *top right* Cover of *Hope was There* by Joan Bauer. © 2000 by Joan Bauer. Cover photo © Stephen St. John/National Geographic/Getty Images. Reprinted by permission of Speak, an imprint of Penguin Group (USA) Inc., 345 Hudson Street, New York, NY 10014. All rights reserved; Jacket image © Stephen St. John/Getty Images; *center left* Jacket cover © 2000 by Alfred A. Knopf, a division of Random House Inc., from *Stargirl* by Jerry Spinelli. Used by permission of Alfred A. Knopf, an imprint of Random House Children's Books, a division of Random House, Inc.; *bottom left* Cover of *The Voice That Challenged a Nation Marion Anderson and the Struggle for Equal Rights* by Russell Freedman. Copyright © 2004 by Russell Freedman. Reprinted by permission of Clarion Books, an imprint of Houghton Mifflin Company, *inset bottom left* Courtesy of University of Pennsylvania Library, Marion Anderson Collection of Photographs;

ART CREDITS **R153**

bottom right Cover of *Sir Walter Raleigh and the Quest for El Dorado* by Marc Aronson. Jacket illustration © 2000 by Kayley LeFaiver. Reprinted by permission of Clarion Books, an imprint of Houghton Mifflin Company.

UNIT 3

307 *left, Letter From Home.* Mort Künstler. © 2000 Mort Künstler, Inc.; *right* © David De Lossy/Getty Images; **308** Cover of *Journey to the Center of the Earth* by Jules Verne. Cover illustration by Robin Koni. © 1965, Penguin Books. Reprinted by permission of Puffin Books, a member of Penguin Group (USA) Inc., 345 Hudson Street, New York, NY 10014. All rights reserved; **308–309** © Corbis; **310** *top* © Image Source/Alamy Images; *bottom* © Patrick Pleul/epa/Corbis; **312** *left* © AL/ShutterStock; *center* © William Gottlieb/Corbis; *right* © Piotr Przeszlo/ShutterStock; **313** © Elisabeth Perotin/ShutterStock; **316** © Aflo Foto Agency/Alamy Images; **317** © Bassouls Sophie/Corbis Sygma; **319** *The Musician,* Dale Gallon. Courtesy of Gallon Historical Art, Gettysburg, Pennsylvania; **320** *Letter From Home.* Mort Künstler. © 2000 Mort Künstler, Inc.; **322** © GeoNova LLC; **327, 328** The Granger Collection, New York; **332** © Neil Beckerman/Getty Images; **333** © Alex Gotfryd/Corbis; **335** © Bill Brooks/Masterfile; **336** © Ryan McVay/Getty Images; **338** © Photononstop/photolibrary; **343** © Awilli/zefa/Corbis; **347** © John Stuart/Mira; **350–351** © Jupiter Images; **354** *left* © Douglas Kirkland/Corbis; *top right* The Granger Collection, New York; *bottom right* Mary Evans Picture Library; **358** *bottom* © Sagel & Kranefeld/zefa/Corbis; **359** The Granger Collection, New York; **361** © Adrian Bailey/Getty Images; **362** © John Beatty/Getty Images; **365** *background* © Skye Chalmers/Getty Images; *center* © Theo Allofs/Getty Images; **369** © Barnaby Hall/Getty Images; **374** *top* © Les Cunliffe/Age Fotostock America, Inc.; *bottom* © Nancy N. Jacobs; **374–375** © Alan R. Moller/Getty Images; **375** *top* Courtesy American Library Association; *bottom* Cover of *Roll of Thunder, Hear My Cry* by Mildred D. Taylor. © 1976 by Mildred D. Taylor. Reprinted by permission of Puffin Books, a member of Penguin Group (USA) Inc., 345 Hudson Street, New York, NY 10014. All rights reserved; **376–377** © Joe Baraban/Alamy Images; **378–379** © Joe Sohm/Visions of America, LLC/Alamy Images; **380** © Ralph Lee Hopkins/Getty Images; **381** Photo by Madison Nye; **384** © GeoNova LLC; **391** © Darryl T. Branch/Photo Researchers, Inc.; **392** © Photocuisine Photography/Veer; **396** © Enigma/Alamy Images; **397** *top* © Underwood & Underwood/Corbis; *bottom* © San Francisco Chronicle; **398** © Bettmann/Corbis; **400** © Corbis; **403** © Bettmann/Corbis; **406** © Photo by Shawn Alladio; **408, 409** © Rick Wilking/Reuters/Corbis; **416** © Richard H. Johnston/Getty Images; **417** *top* Courtesy Pat Mora; *bottom* Photo by David Burkhalter. Reprinted by permission of the University of Arizona Press; **424, 430** © Daryl Benson/Masterfile; **431** *left foreground* © Michael J. Doolittle/The Image Works, Inc.; *left background* © Bill Brooks/Masterfile; *top right* © Ecliptic Blue/ShutterStock; *bottom right* © Bill Brooks/Masterfile; **438** *top left* Cover of *Full Tilt* by Neal Shusterman. © 2003 by Neal Shusterman. Cover photo © 2003 by John Madere. Reprinted by permission of Simon Pulse, an imprint of Simon & Schuster Children's Publishing Division, New York; *top right* Cover of *The Boxer* by Kathleen Karr. © 2000 by Kathleen Karr. Cover art © 2000 by Rodrigo Corral. Reprinted by permission of Farrar, Straus and Giroux; *center left* Cover of *Iqbal* by Francesco D'Adamo. © 2001 by Edizioni EL English translation © 2003 by Ann Leonori. Cover photo weaving © Robert Harding Picture Library Ltd/Alamy Images. Reprinted by permission of Aladdin Paperbacks, an imprint of Simon & Schuster Children's Publishing Division, New York; *center right* Cover of *Run, Boy, Run* by Uri Orlev. Copyright © 2003 by Uri Orlev. Reprinted by permission of Houghton Mifflin Company; *bottom left* Cover of *Tofu and T. Rex* by Greg Leitich Smith. © 2005 by Greg H. Leitich. Cover photo by Michael Wang. Reprinted by permission of Little, Brown and Company; *bottom right* Cover of *Saving the Planet* by Gail Gauthier. © 2003 by Gail Gauthier. Reprinted by permission of Penguin Putnam Books for Young Readers, 345 Hudson Street, New York 10014.

UNIT 4

439 *left, The Moon and the Abandoned Old Woman* (1891), Yoshitoshi. © Asian Art & Archaeology, Inc./Corbis; *right* © JIStock/Masterfile; **440–441** © Matthias Kulka/zefa/Corbis; **442** *left* © BananaStock/PunchStock; *center left* © Jennifer Hulshizer/Star Ledger/Corbis; *center right* © Abode/Beateworks/Corbis; *right* © Digital Vision/PunchStock; **443** © Nikolajs Strigins/ShutterStock; **448** © Atlantide Phototravel/Corbis; **449** © Gene Blevins/Corbis; **450** *top* © Image Source/PunchStock; *bottom* © Photodisc/Getty Images; **451** © ICP/Alamy Images; **454** © Pat Doyle/Corbis; **455** © Getty Images; **460** © Corbis; **462** © Hermes/Age Fotostock; **463** *top* © Time Life Pictures/Getty Images; *bottom* © June Finfer; **465** *Beggar and a Boy* (1903), Pablo Picasso. Oil on canvas, 125 cm × 92 cm. Pushkin Museum, Moscow. © Bridgeman Art Library. © 2007 Estate of Pablo Picasso/Artists Rights Society (ARS), New York. Reproduction, including downloading of Picasso works is prohibited by copyright laws and international conventions without the express written permission of Artists Rights Society (ARS), New York; **468** © GeoNova LLC; **476** © Photograph by Sharon Hoogstraten; **477** *top* © Courtesy of the author; *bottom* © Michael Glaser; **479** *American Childhood* (1995), Jan Burch Cochran. Fabric, beads, buttons, paint, baby dress, gloves. Machine pieced, hand appliquéd using beads, hand embellished. 53″ × 42″. Collection of Pam Monfort; **482** © Photo by Sharon Hoogstraten; *top left* © Getty Images; *bottom left* © Regin Igloria; *bottom right* © Getty Images; **484** © Getty Images; **485** AP/Wide World Photos; **487, 489, 494, 501, 505, 511, 514** © Joan Marcus; **520** © Getty Images; **523, 527, 533** © Joan Marcus; **541** *The Diary of Anne Frank* (2006), Oregon Shakespeare Festival. Tony De Bruno as Otto Frank. Photo © David Cooper Photography; **545, 546, 547** © Getty Images; **548** *left* Courtesy of Harry Goldsmith (Estate). © United States Holocaust Memorial Museum. The views and opinions expressed in the book and the context in which the images are used do not necessarily reflect the views or policy of, nor imply approval or endorsement by, the United States Holocaust Memorial Museum; *right* Courtesy of Hannah Kastan Weiss. © United States Holocaust Memorial Museum. The views and opinions expressed in the book and the context in which the images are used do not necessarily reflect the views or policy of, nor imply approval or endorsement by, the United States Holocaust Memorial Museum; **549** The Granger Collection, New York; **551** Courtesy of Madalae Fraser. © United States Holocaust Memorial Museum. The views and opinions expressed in the book and the context in which

R154 ART CREDITS

the images are used do not necessarily reflect the views or policy of, nor imply approval or endorsement by, the United States Holocaust Memorial Museum; **554** © Getty Images; **555** *top* Scene from *Anne Frank Remembered* appears courtesy of Sony Pictures Classics, Inc.; *center right, center left* © The Everett Collection; *bottom* © Anne Frank Stichting/Allard Bovenberg/2003 Getty Images; **556** © Getty Images; **557** *top left* © Kayte M. Deioma/PhotoEdit; *top center* © Myrleen Ferguson Cate/PhotoEdit; *top right* AP/Wide World Photos; **557** *bottom left* © Michael Newman/PhotoEdit; *bottom center* © Frank Siteman/PhotoEdit; *bottom right* © Michael Newman/PhotoEdit; **558**, **564** © Richard Sisk/Jupiter Images; **565** © James Woodson/ Getty Images; **574** *top left* Cover of *The Thief Lord* by Cornelia Funke. © 2000 by Cornelia Funke. Cover illustration © 2002 by Christian Birmingham. Reprinted by permission of Scholastic, Inc., New York; *top right* Cover of *East* by Edith Pattou. © 2003 by Edith Pattou. Jacket illustration © 2003 by Stephen T. Johnson. Reprinted by permission Harcourt, Inc., New York; *center right* Cover of *The Not-So-Star-Spangled Life of Sunita Sen* by Mitali Perkins. © 1993 by Mitali Perkins. Reprinted by permission of the publisher Little, Brown and Company, New York; *bottom left* From *The Book Thief* by Markus Zusak. © 2005 by Markus Zusak. Illustrations © 2006 by Trudy White. Jacket photo © 2006 by Colin Anderson/Brand X Pictures/ Getty Images. Reprinted by permission of Alfred A. Knopf, an imprint of Random House Children's Books, a division of Random House Inc., New York; *bottom right* Cover of *The Merlin Conspiracy* by Diana Wynne Jones. © 2003 by Diana Wynne Jones. Cover art © 2003 by Cliff Nielsen. Reprinted by permission of Harper Trophy, an imprint of HarperCollins Publishers.

UNIT 5

573 *left, La Promenade en Mer* (1988), Jean Plichart. Copper engraving. © SuperStock; *right* © Ted Mead/Getty Images; **574–575** © Photograph by Bac To Trong; **576** *foreground* © Corbis; *background* © Getty Images; **577** © Image Club Graphics; **578** © Getty Images; **579** © Laurie Barr/ShutterStock; **580** *top left* © Corbis; *bottom left* © Merryl McNaughton/ShutterStock; *right* © Robert Blomkvist/ ShutterStock; **581** *top* © Piotr Przeszlo/ShutterStock; *bottom* © Karin Lau/ShutterStock; **582** Designed by Lisa Brennan; **583** *top* © The Schlesinger Library, Radcliffe Institute, Harvard University; *bottom* © Christopher Felver/Corbis; **588** © Masterfile; **589** *top* © Bettmann/ Corbis; *bottom* © Bettmann/Corbis; **591** © G. K. Hart/Vikki Hart/ Getty Images; **593** © SuperStock; **596** © Big Cheese Photo LLC/ Alamy Images; **597** *top* © Getty Images; *bottom* Courtesy of Julio Noboa; **599** © PIER/Getty Images; **602** © David Scharf/Science Photo Library/Photo Researchers, Inc.; **604** © Lori Adamski Peek/ Getty Images; **605** *top* The Granger Collection, New York; *bottom* © Getty Images; **607** © Paul Edmondson/Getty Images; **609** © Ted Mead/Getty Images; **612** Designed by Lisa Brennan; **613** *top* © Nancy E. Crampton; *bottom* © Corbis; **618** © Just One Productions/Photofest; **619** *top* The Granger Collection, New York; *bottom, Alexander Pope* (1740), William Hoare. The Granger Collection, New York; **621** © Corbis; **624** © Mango Productions/Corbis; **625** *top* © Getty Images; *bottom* © Peter Morenus; **627** *Aspiration* (1936), Aaron Douglas. Oil on canvas, 60″ × 60″. © Fine Arts Museums of San Francisco purchase, the estate of Thurlow E. Tibbs, Jr., the Museum Society Auxiliary, American Art Trust Fund, Unrestricted Art Trust Fund, partial gift of Dr. Ernest A. Bates, Sharon Bell, Jo-Ann Beverly, Barbara Carleton, Dr. and Mrs. Arthur H. Coleman, Dr. and Mrs. Coyness Ennix, Jr., Nicole Y. Ennix, Mr. and Mrs. Gary Francois, Dennis L. Franklin, Mr. and Mrs. Maxwell C. Gillette, Mr. and Mrs. Richard Goodyear, Zuretti L. Goosby, Marion E. Greene, Mrs. Vivian S. W. Hambrick, Laurie Gibbs Harris, Arlene Hollis, Louis A. and Letha Jeanpierre, Daniel and Jackie Johnson, Jr., Stephen L. Johnson, Mr. and Mrs. Arthur Lathan, Lewis and Ribbs Mortuary Garden Chapel, Mr. and Mrs. Gary Love, Glenn R. Nance, Mr. and Mrs. Harry S. Parker III, Mr. and Mrs. Carr T. Preston, Fannie Preston, Pamela R. Ransom, Dr. and Mrs. Benjamin F. Reed, San Francisco Black Chamber of Commerce, San Francisco Chapter of Links, Inc., San Francisco Chapter of the N.A.A.C.P., Sigma Pi Phi Fraternity, Dr. Ella Mae Simmons, Mr. Calvin R. Swinson, Joseph B. Williams, Mr. and Mrs. Alfred S. Wilsey, and the people of the Bay Area, 1997.84; **629** Facial Reconstruction of Fortune by Frank Bender. © Mattatuck Museum Arts and History Center, Waterbury, Connecticut; **636** © Paul Panayiotou/Alamy Images; **637** *top* © Getty Images; *bottom* © Stock Montage; **648**, **654** © Daryl Benson/Masterfile; **655** © Larry Williams/Corbis; **662** *top left* Cover of *Uglies* by Scott Westerfeld. © 2005 by Scott Westerfeld. Cover photo © Carissa Pelleteri. Reprinted by permission of Simon Pulse, an imprint of Simon & Schuster Children's Publishing Division, New York; *top right* Cover of *Criss Cross* by Lynne Rae Perkins. © 2005 by Lynn Rae Perkins. Reprinted by permission of HarperCollins Children's Books, a division of HarperCollins Publishers, New York; *center left* Cover of *A Year Down Yonder* by Richard Peck. © 2000 by Richard Peck. Reprinted by permission of Dial Books for Young Readers, a division of Penguin Putnam, Inc., 375 Hudson Street, New York 10014. All rights reserved; *center right* Cover of *Colibri* by Ann Cameron. Jacket design by Ana Juan. Jacket art © 2003 by Ana Juan. Reprinted by permission of Farrar, Straus and Giroux, New York; *bottom left* Cover of *Let Me Play* by Karen Blumenthal. © 2005 by Karen Blumenthal. Cover photo: Bettye Lane. Reprinted by permission of Atheneum Books for Young Readers, an imprint of Simon & Schuster Children's Publishing Division; *bottom right* Cover of *The Warrior Heir* by Cinda Williams Chima. © 2006 by Cinda Williams Chima. Cover photo © Arte & Immagini srl/Corbis. Reprinted by permission of Hyperion Books for Children, New York.

UNIT 6

663 *right The Promenade, Fifth Avenue* (1986), Bill Jacklin. Oil on canvas, 243.6 cm × 182.7 cm. Private collection. © Bill Jacklin/ Bridgeman Art Library; *left* © Sherman Hines/Masterfile; **664** *top left* © Pierre Vauthey/Corbis Sygma; *top center left* © The Everett Collection; *top center* © Universal TV/The Kobal Collection; *top right* © Charles Sykes/Rex Features/Courtesy The Everett Collection; *bottom far left* © The Everett Collection; *2nd bottom left* © John Rogers/Getty Images; *bottom center* © John Springer Collection/ Corbis; *bottom center right* © The Everett Collection; *bottom right* © Roger Ressmeyer/Corbis; **665** © Bettmann/Corbis; **666** *top* © Robert Kyllo/ShutterStock; *center* © Zina Seletskaya/ShutterStock; *bottom* © ANP/ShutterStock; **668** *top left* © Jerry Bauer; *bottom left* Photo Siang Chitsa-Ard/Courtesy William Sleator; *background* © Albo/ShutterStock; **669** © Paul Maguire/ShutterStock; **670** © Aga & Miko Materne (arsat)/ShutterStock; **672** © Chad Baker/Ryan McVay/Getty Images; **673** © Getty Images; **676** © GeoNova LLC;

ART CREDITS R155

682 © Eyebyte/Alamy Images; **683** © The New York Public Library; **686** © T. Papageorgiou/age fotostock america, inc.; **695** *Let's Make a Deal,* Host Monty Hall, 1963–1976. © The Everett Collection; **698** *top* © Les Cunliffe/Age Fotostock America, Inc.; *bottom* Reed Saxon/AP/Wide World Photos; **698–699** © Reuters/Corbis; **699** *top* Courtesy American Library Association; *bottom* Cover of *Kira-Kira* by Cynthia Kadohata. © 2004 by Cynthia Kadohata. Cover photo © Julia Kuskin. Reprinted by permission of Atheneum Books for Young Readers, an imprint of Simon and Schuster Children's Publishing Division, New York; **700–701** © Bryan Mullennix/Getty Images; **702–703** © Ken Ross/Getty Images; **705** Library of Congress; **707** The Granger Collection, New York; **709** Library of Congress; **711** The Granger Collection, New York; **715** © Michael Newman/PhotoEdit; **716** © Chuck Pefley/Alamy Images; **717** © Hugh Hamrick; **720** © Christopher Stevenson/Getty Images; **723** Photograph by Sharon Hoogstraten; **728** © Kevin Fleming/Corbis; **729** National Archives; **734** © American Solar Challenge/Getty Images; **735** *top* The Granger Collection, New York; *bottom* Courtesy of Fernando R. Montemayor; **739** *Californians Catching Wild Horses with Riata* (about 1851), Hugo Wilhelm Arthur Nahl. Oil on canvas mounted on masonite. Courtesy of the Oakland Museum of California Kahn Collection (A65.57); **742**, **748** © J. David Andrews/Masterfile; **749** © Taxi/Getty Images; **756** *top left* Cover of *Cheating Lessons* by Nan Willard Cappo. © 2002 by Nan Willard Cappo. Cover photo © 2002 by Mark Tauss. Reprinted by permission of Simon Pulse, an imprint of Simon & Schuster, Children's Publishing Division, New York; *top right* Cover of *Princess Academy* by Shannon Hale. © 2005 by Shannon Hale. Jacket art © 2005 by Tim Zeltner. Reprinted by permission of Bloomsbury Publishing, New York; *center left* Cover of *Sweetgrass Basket* by Marlene Carvell. © 2005 by Marlene Carvell. Photo of Tulalip Indian School © Museum of History & Industry. Photo of girls © Larry Hirshowitz/Corbis. Reprinted by permission of Dutton Children's Books, a division of Penguin Young Readers Group, published by the Penguin Group (USA) Inc., 345 Hudson Street, New York, NY 10014. All rights reserved; *center right* Cover of *Act I, Act II, Act Normal* by Martha Weston. © 2003 by Martha Weston. Jacket illustration © 2003 by Martha Weston. Reprinted by permission of Roaring Book Press, a Division of The Millbrook Press, Brookfield, Connecticut; *bottom left* Cover of *Guinea Pig Scientists* by Leslie Dendy and Mel Boring. © 2005 by Leslie Dendy and Mel Boring. Illustration © 2005 by C. B. Mordan. Reprinted by permission of Henry Holt and Company, LLC., New York; *bottom right* Cover of *O Pioneers* by Willa Cather. 1995, Houghton Mifflin, Boston; *cover image* © Tom Bean/Corbis.

UNIT 7

757 *left Los Comaradas del Barrio* (1976), Jesse Treviño. Acrylic on canvas, 36″ × 48″. Collection of the artist; *right* © Ric Ergenbright/Corbis; **758** © PunchStock; **760** *left* © Getty Images; *right* © Margaretta Mitchell; *bottom* © Photodisc; **761** *top foreground* © Getty Images; *top background* © Artbeats; *bottom* Photo by Bill Eichner; **762** © Bettmann/Corbis; **763** © Hulton-Deutsch Collection/Corbis; Photo by Christine Lee Zilka; *center* © Ryan McVay/Getty Images; *bottom* © Corbis; **765** © Ryan McVay/Getty Images; **766** © Ariel Skelley/Corbis; **767** Courtesy Joseph Bruchac/Michael Greenlar; **771** © Betsy Cullen/Getty Images; **776** *backgound* © Skye Chalmers/Getty Images; *foreground* © Georgette Douwma/Photo Researchers, Inc.; **782** © Richard Wahlstrom/Getty Images; **783** © Colin Izod; **785** © Richard I'Anson/Lonely Planet Images; **786** Marriage necklace or Thali (1800). India (Madras). Golden pendants on black thread. (CT17149). Victoria & Albert Museum, London. © Victoria & Albert Museum, London/Art Resource, New York; **787** © Per-Anders Pettersson/Getty Images; **788** © GeoNova LLC; **793** © Robert Harding Picture Library Ltd/Alamy Images; **795** © Steve McCurry/Magnum Photos; **797** © Gideon Mendel/Corbis; **800** © Will & Deni McIntyre/Corbis; **801** © Paul Coughlin; **803**, **807** Illustration by Michael McCurdy. © 1991 by Michael McCurdy, from *American Tall Tales* by Mary Pope Osborne. Used by permission of Alfred A. Knopf, an imprint of Random House Children's Books, a division of Random House, Inc.; **810** *top* © Les Cunliffe/Age Fotostock America, Inc.; *bottom* © Bettmann/Corbis; **810–811** © Adalberto Rios Lanz/Sexto Sol/Getty Images; **811** *top* AP/Wide World Photos; *bottom* From *The Pearl* by John Steinbeck. © 2003. Reprinted with permission of Gale, a division of Thomson Learning. www.thomsonrights.com; **812–813** © Dania Delimont/Alamy Images; **814–815** © Kenny Johnson/Getty Images; **816** © Mike Powell/Getty Images; **817** Photo © Gary Soto. Courtesy of Gary Soto; **826** © Creatas/Superstock; **830** © Getty Images; **831** © Paul Mounce/Corbis; **833** © Punahou School, Hawaii; **834** © GeoNova LLC; **837** © Ric Ergenbright/Corbis; **840** © Veer; *inset right* © CBS/Photofest; **843** © Corbis; **847** © Rick Wilking/Reuters/Corbis; **850** © 2006 Larry Wright. *The Detroit News*. All rights reserved. Courtesy of Cagle Cartoons, Inc.; **852** *left* The Granger Collection, New York; *bottom* © Corbis; **853** © Jupiter Images Corporation; **854** © Paul Carstairs/Alamy Images; **855** © Tom Roster Photographer; **856** Illustration by Jerome Lagarrrigue, from *Going North* by Janice N. Harrington. Pictures © 2005 by Jerome Lagarrigue. Reprinted by permission of Farrar, Straus and Giroux; **857** From *Freedom on the Menu: The Greensboro Sit-ins* by Carole Boston Weatherford. Illustrated by Jerome La Garrigue. Painting © 2005 by Jerome La Garrigue. Used by permission of Dial Books for Young Readers, a division of Penguin Young Readers Group, a member of Penguin Group (USA) Inc., 345 Hudson Street, New York, NY 10014. All rights reserved; **859** © Jack Moebes/Corbis; **860**, **866** © Jason Ernst/Age Fotostock America, Inc.; **867** © Jeff Greenberg/Age Fotostock; **874** *top left* Cover of *Code Talker* by Joseph Bruchac. © 2005 by Joseph Bruchac. Reprinted by permission of the Penguin Group (USA) Inc., 345 Hudson Street, New York, NY 10014. All rights reserved; *top right* Cover of *Gathering Blue* by Lois Lowry. © 2000 by Lois Lowry. Reprinted by permission of Random House Inc., New York; *inset top right* © Marco Ventura; *center left* Cover of *Lizzie Bright and the Buckminster Boy* by Gary D. Schmidt. Copyright © 2004 by Gary D. Schmidt. Reprinted by permission of Clarion Books, an imprint of Houghton Mifflin Company; *center right* Cover of *Betsy and the Emperor* by Staton Rabin. © 2004 by Staton Rabin. Reprinted by permission of Margaret K. McElderry Books, an imprint of Simon & Schuster's Children's Publishing Division, New York; *bottom left* Cover of *The Outcasts of 19 Schuyler Place* by E. L. Konigsburg. © 2004 by E. L. Konigsburg. Reprinted by permission of Aladdin Books, an imprint of Simon & Schuster's Children's Publishing Division.

R156 ART CREDITS

Cover photo © Piotr Sikora/Getty Images; *bottom right* Cover of *Stop the Train!* by Geraldine McCaughrean. © 2001 by Geraldine McCaughrean. Reprinted by permission of HarperCollins Children's Books, a division of HarperCollins Publishers, Inc., New York.

UNIT 8

875 *left* © Carsten Peter/National Geographic Image Collection; *right* © Columbia/Marvel/The Kobal Collection; **876** *left* Jacket of *1000 Great Rail-Trails, A Comprehensive Directory.* Cover photos: background @ Mark Windom/Index Stock Imagery and PhotoDisc, Inc.; inset photos © PhotoDisc, Inc. Reprinted by permission of The Globe Pequot Press, Guilford, Connecticut; *center* © Tom Schierlitz/Getty Images; *right* © Corbis; **878** *top left* © Artville; *top right* © Stockfood Creative/Getty Images; *bottom* © Foodpix/Jupiter Images; **879** © Denis Scott/Corbis; **880** © Sanford/Agliolo/Corbis; **881** *top* © Yonhap–Yonhap does not obtain releases from subjects, individuals, groups, or entities contained in its photos, that no clearance is obtained from the owners of any trademarks or copyrighted materials whose marks and materials are there incidentally in photos; *bottom* © Steve Kaufman/Corbis; **883** *top* © Bettmann/Corbis; *bottom* © Blake Little/Getty Images; **884** © LWA-Dann Tardif/Corbis; **885** Courtesy of the author; **887** AP/Wide World Photos; *inset right* © Columbia/Marvel/The Kobal Collection; **890** © Peter J. Bryant/Biological Photo Service. All rights reserved; **894** © Corbis; **895**, **896–897** © Carsten Peter/National Geographic Image Collection; **898** *top* © GeoNova LLC; *bottom left* Seated man. Victim of the eruption of Mount Vesuvius. Palestra Grande, Pompeii, Italy. © Scala/Art Resource, New York; *bottom center* © Corbis; *bottom right* © Layne Kennedy/Corbis; **899** © Carsten Peter/National Geographic Image Collection; **900** *top* Illustration by Richard Bonson/Wildlife Art Ltd.; **900–901** © Carsten Peter/National Geographic Image Collection; **901** © Carsten Peter/National Geographic Image Collection; **904** NASA Kennedy Space Center (NASA-KSC); **905** *left* © Jim Ruymen/Reuters/Corbis; *right background* wood background; *right: top left* NASA/JPL/University of Maryland/AP/Wide World Photos; *top center left, top center right*; *top right* NASA Jet Propulsion Laboratory; *bottom left* NASA/AP/Wide World Photos; *bottom center, bottom right* NASA Jet Propulsion Laboratory; **906** *top left* AP/Wide World Photos; *bottom left, background* © NASA/JPL/epa/Corbis; **908** © Hugh Sitton/zefa/Corbis; **909** © Alice Handwerk; **911** © Mark Christmas/National Geographic Image Collection; **912** Courtesy Henrietta Yurchenco; **915** Photo by Joaquin A. Huerta A./Courtesy Henrietta Yurchenco; **918** © Taili Song Roth/Corbis; **919** Courtesy Jan McGirk; **920** © Robert Nickelsberg/Getty Images; **922** © GeoNova LLC; **924** © Robert Nickelsberg/Getty Images; **925** © Mark Richards/ZUMA/Corbis; **928** © Adam Gault/Getty Images; **929** © Tony Cenicola/*The New York Times*; **930**, **932** Courtesy of Hanger Prosthetics & Orthotics, Inc. www.hanger.com; **933** © Dith Pran/*New York Times*/Redux; **934** *left* © Science VU/Visuals Unlimited; *right* PBS ® and the PBS logo are registered trademarks of the Public Broadcasting Service and are used with permission. All rights reserved; **935** © Science Source/Photo Researchers, Inc.; **938** *top* © Les Cunliffe/Age Fotostock America, Inc.; *bottom* © Arthur Cohen; **938–939** The Granger Collection, New York; **939** *top* Courtesy American Library Association; *bottom* Cover of *An American Plague: The True and Terrifying Story of the Yellow Fever Epidemic of 1793* by Jim Murphy. Copyright © 2003 by Jim Murphy. Reprinted by permission of Clarion Books, an imprint of Houghton Mifflin Company; **940–941**, **942–943** The Granger Collection, New York; **944**, **950** © Alain Choisnet/Getty Images; **951** © Michael Newman/PhotoEdit; **953** *top* © Harpe/Peter Arnold, Inc.; *bottom* © Jeffrey L. Rotman/Corbis; **958** *top left* Cover of *Dare to Dream, 15 Extraordinary Lives* by Sandra McLeod Humphrey. © 2005 by Sandra McLeod Humphrey. Cover design and illustrations by Nicole Sommer. Reprinted by permission of Prometheus Books, Amherst, New York; *top right* Cover of *Stonecutter* by Leander Watts. Copyright © 2002 by Leander Watts. Reprinted by permission of Houghton Mifflin Company; *center left* From *Eragon, Inheritance, Book One* by Christopher Paolini. Text © 2003 by Christopher Paolini. Cover illustration © 2003 by John Jude Palencar. Reprinted by permission of Alfred A Knopf, an imprint of Random House Children's Books, a division of Random House, Inc., New York; *center right* Cover of *The Gadget* by Paul Zindel. © 2001 by Paul Zindel. Cover illustration by Cliff Nielsen. Used by permission of HarperCollins Children's Books, New York; *bottom left* Cover of *Mountain Solo* by Jeanette Ingold. © 2003 by Jeanette Ingold. Jacket top © Beth Dixson/Photonica/Getty Images. Jacket bottom image by Claudine Guerguerian. Cover reprinted by permission of Harcourt, Inc., New York; *bottom right* Cover of *This Land Was Made for You and Me: the Life and Songs of Woody Guthrie* by Elizabeth Partridge. © 2002 by Elizabeth Partridge. Jacket illustration © Lane Smith, 2002. Photo provided by the Library of Congress, Prints and Photographs Division. Woody Guthrie's drawings: Courtesy of the Woody Guthrie Foundation and Archives. Used by permission of the Penguin Group (USA), Inc., 375 Hudson Street, New York, New York 10014. All rights reserved.

UNIT 9

959 *left* © Peter Finger/Corbis; *right* © Getty Images; **960–961** © Louie Psihoyos/Corbis; **962** © Ronnie Kaufman/Corbis; **963** *top* © C. Fleurent/photocuisine/Corbis; *bottom* © Artville; **965** © Ken Kaminesky/Take 2 Productions/Corbis; **967** © David Woods/Corbis; **968** © Steve Bloom/Getty Images; **969** *top* Courtesy Rob Laidlaw; *bottom* © The Wildlife Society, Bethesda, Maryland; **970** © Getty Images; **975** © ALI BURAFI/AFP/Getty Images; **980** *top* © Getty Images; *bottom* Francois Mori/AP/Wide World Photos; **981** *top, bottom,* **982** *left* Footage courtesy of Lucasfilm Ltd. *Star Wars: Episode III-Revenge of the Sith* © 2005 Lucasfilm Ltd. & TM. All rights reserved. Used under authorization. Unauthorized duplication is a violation of applicable law; **982** *background* © Getty Images; **983** *center* © Stockbyte; *right* © Getty Images; **984** © Todd Gipstein/Corbis; **985** © Sports Illustrated; **986** Courtesy of the National Association for Sport and Physical Eduction; **987** © Chris Clinton/Getty Images; **988** © Sports Illustrated; **989** © Peter Finger/Corbis; **994** © 2004 Twentieth Century Fox/Photofest; **995** Courtesy of Darhansoff, Verrill, and Feldman Agency; **997** © Lynda Barry; **1002** © Corbis; **1003** © GeoNova LLC; **1005** © Steve Bly/Alamy Images; **1007** © Saulius T. Kondrotas/Alamy Images; **1008** The Granger Collection, New York; **1010** *top* Courtesy of the American Red Cross; *bottom* AP/Wide World Photos; **1011** © National Portrait Gallery, London; **1013** © Renaissance Films/BBC/Curzon Films/The Kobal Collection; **1014** © Royal Armouries Museum, Leeds, United Kingdom; **1016**, **1022** © Sam Barricklow/Workbookstock.com;

ART CREDITS **R157**

1023 © Dirk Anschutz/Getty Images; **1030** *top left* Cover of *Heat* by Mike Lupica. © 2006 by Mike Lupica. Reprinted by permission of Philomel Books, a division of Penguin Young Readers Group, 345 Hudson Street, New York, NY 10014. All rights reserved; *top right* Cover of *Surviving Antarctica: Reality TV 2083* by Andrea White. © 2005 by Andrea White. Reprinted by permission of HarperCollins Children's Books, a division of HarperCollins Publishers, New York; *center left* Cover of *Photo By Brady: A Picture of the Civil War* by Jennifer Armstrong. © 2005 by Jennifer Armstrong. Cover image National Archives. Reprinted by permission of Atheneum Books for Young Readers, an imprint of Simon & Schuster Children's Publishing Division, New York; *center right* Cover of *Quicksilver* by Stephanie Spinner. Text © 2005 by Stephanie Spinner. Reprinted by permission of Alfred A. Knopf, an imprint of Random House Children's Books, a division of Random House, Inc., New York; *bottom left* Cover of *The Exchange Student* by Kate Gilmore. Copyright © 1999 by Kate Gilmore. Reprinted by permission of Houghton Mifflin Company; *bottom right* Cover of *The Wilderness Family* by Kobie Krüger. © 2001 by Kobie Krüger. Reprinted by permission of the Ballantine Group, a division of Random House, Inc., New York.

UNIT 10 RESEARCH

1031 *left* © Getty Images; *right* Cover of *Kids Inventing!* by Susan Casey. © 2005 by Susan Mary Casey. All rights reserved. Cover design by Chris Wallace. Reprinted by permission of John Wiley & Sons, Inc., Hoboken, New Jersey; Photograph by Sharon Hoogstraten; **1032–1033** © Robin Sachs/PhotoEdit; **1034** *foreground* © CSAImages.com; *background* © Laurent Hamels/Age Fotostock America, Inc.; **1038** © Google; **1039** *inset* Lemulson Center/Smithsonian Website; Smithsonian Institution, www.SmithsonianInstitution.org **1043** © Garry Gay/Getty Images; **1046** *inset-spurs* © Bob Brown/*Richmond Times-Dispatch*/AP/Wide World Photos; **1047** *left* Marcio Jose Sanchez/AP/Wide World Photos; *right* © Rubberball Productions; **1048 1051** © Punchstock/Royalty Free; **1052, 1066** © Walter Bibikow/Jupiter Images; **1067** © David Kennedy/AgeFotostock.

STUDENT RESOURCE BANK

R03 © Ben Mangor/SuperStock Inc.; **R05** *Bar graph* © Sense Interactive Multimedia/Royalty Free; **R06** *top* © Illustration by Gary Hincks; *bottom* Cross-section of a Roman road. Illustration by Peter Bull; **R07** © GeoNova LLC; **R14** © Bill Ballenberg; **R15** *top* © 2004 Doak Heyser; *bottom* © Pam Gardner; Frank Lane Picture Agency/Corbis; **R19** © Carsten Peter/National Geographic Image Collection; **R87** *left* © Corbis; *right* © Comstock; **R94** © Sony Pictures/Courtesy Everett Collection.

BACK COVER

1502 © Image 100/PunchStock.

R158 ART CREDITS